For more than twenty years Leslie Halliwell fitted in his self-imposed task of film encyclopaedist with a full-time job as chief programme buyer for ITV (and latterly Channel Four). After his retirement he continued to influence the fourth channel's scheduling of Golden Oldies.

His publications include *Halliwell's Film Guide* (8th edition 1991 edited by John Walker); *Halliwell's Television Companion* (with Philip Purser: 3rd edition 1986); *Halliwell's Hundred*; *Halliwell's Harvest*; *Mountain of Dreams*; and *The Clapperboard Book of the Cinema* (with Graham Murray). The story of his youth at the movies, *Seats in All Parts*, evoked great enthusiasm in 1985. A series of genre studies includes *The Dead That Walk* and *Double Take and Fade Away*.

Leslie Halliwell died in January 1989.

By the same author

Halliwell's Film Guide
Halliwell's Television Companion (with Philip Purser)
The Filmgoer's Book of Quotes
Halliwell's Movie Quiz
Mountain of Dreams
The Clapperboard Book of the Cinema (with Graham Murray)
Halliwell's Hundred
Halliwell's Harvest
The Ghost of Sherlock Holmes (fiction)
Seats in All Parts: Half a Lifetime at the Movies
Return to Shangri-La (fiction)
The Dead That Walk
Double Take and Fade Away

LESLIE HALLIWELL

Halliwell's Filmgoer's and Video Viewer's Companion

Ninth Edition

Incorporating
The Filmgoer's Book of Quotes
and
Halliwell's Movie Quiz

Paladin
An Imprint of Grafton Books
A Division of HarperCollins*Publishers*

Paladin
An Imprint of HarperCollins*Publishers*
77–85 Fulham Palace Road,
Hammersmith, London W6 8JB

Published by Paladin 1989
9 8 7 6 5 4 3

First published in Great Britain by
MacGibbon & Kee Ltd 1965
Second edition 1967
Third edition 1970
Fourth edition by Granada Publishing 1974
Fifth edition (revised and reset in paperback) 1976
Sixth edition 1977
Seventh edition 1980
Eighth edition 1984
Ninth edition by Grafton Books 1988

ISBN 0 586 08877 6

Set in Times

Printed in Great Britain by
HarperCollinsManufacturing Glasgow

Contents

Foreword to the First Edition (1965) by Alfred Hitchcock

Thirty or forty years ago, when the idea of the cinema as an art form was new, people started to write highbrow treatises about it. Unfortunately, few of the books seemed to have much connection with what one saw at the local picture house. Even earlier began the still-continuing deluge of fan magazines and annuals, full of exotic photographs but short on solid information. We film-makers had our own reference books, but these were often incomprehensible to the layman and gave him more undigested facts than he needed. Nobody wrote for the sensible middlebrow picturegoer who was keenly interested in the craft of the cinema without wanting to make a religion of it.

The volume you hold in your hand aims to be the first comprehensive reference book in English for that numerous but neglected audience. I feel sure it will be welcome, for audiences are taking an increasingly serious interest in their films these days – even in the flippant ones.

A concise guide to film matters past and present is obviously a good thing to have on a handy shelf, especially when the best of the old films are constantly cropping up on TV. I hope it will prove possible to bring out revised and corrected editions on a regular basis. Not that many glaring errors will be discovered: the author has done his homework rather better than the villains in my films, who always seem to get found out sooner or later.

Speaking personally, I don't know whether it is more flattering or disturbing to find oneself pinned down like a butterfly in a book which recounts all the macabre details of one's career. But being a stickler for detail myself, I must, and do, submit; and I wish the enterprise well.

Preface to the First Edition

This book is for people who like movies. Especially it's for those who enjoyed the golden ages of the thirties and forties, now revisiting us on television, when the big studios of Hollywood turned out highly efficient and varied entertainment without being too pretentious about it. Nowadays, independent producers aim higher, which sometimes only means that they have further to fall: and most films are half as long again as they should be. But the good ones keep turning up, and Jeanne Moreau and Elvis Presley and Peter O'Toole have fans just as enthusiastic as those of Bette Davis and George Formby and Rudolph Valentino.

Everyone who watches films, whether on TV or the big screens, frequently thinks of something he'd like to check: a star's age, a director's name, what else that funny little fellow with the moustache has been in. To find out the answer to this sort of question it's sometimes been necessary to consult upwards of a dozen fairly inaccessible volumes. This book aims to bring all the available sources together while at the same time excluding inessential or dated information. A fully comprehensive work on these lines would be almost the size of the *Encyclopaedia Britannica*; but this 'potted' one should satisfy most requirements.

The arrangement is completely alphabetical, and you won't find an index at the end because the whole book is one vast index. Most of the entries refer to actors, including not only stars but several hundred familiar names from the supporting cast, people whose valiant service has seldom been recorded. Then there are directors, producers, musicians, writers and photographers – the principal ones at least. The more important the person, the longer the entry, that's a rough general rule: routine contributors get a couple of lines, Edward G. Robinson spreads over half a page. All told, however, you'll find very few of your favourites missing: if they've stuck in your memory, they're probably here. As to the list of credits, the aim has been to give the first important picture, the most recent, and a sampling of the more significant titles in between: the peak period is usually when the dates are most closely crowded. Stage work has not normally been detailed, nor has TV.

There are also notes on well-known film series, on films which have been frequently remade, on films with similar titles; on technical terms, on organizations, on general subjects like censorship and screen ratios. Finally you will find several hundred entries on individual films which seem in one way or another important, influential, or simply excellent of their kind. Unavoidably, many readers will disagree with the selection and/or the assessments: that must remain their privilege.

The emphasis is firmly on Britain and Hollywood: the book is aimed at the general filmgoer, not at the egghead student of film culture who shuns commercial entertainments in favour of middle-European or Oriental masterpieces which never get further than the National Film Theatre or a very few art houses. However, references to important foreign films and personalities are fairly numerous, and even admitting its selectiveness in this field the book still ranges more widely than anything else published in English.

No one has been omitted simply because he is dead: the entries have been selected from the whole history of the cinema. But the silent period is covered in less detail than the talkies, and probably few readers will quarrel with that.

This is a collection of facts rather than opinions; if a few of the latter *have* crept in, they are usually the ones most generally held.

L.H.

London, July 1965

Preface to the Eighth Edition

Letters and critical comments since the sixth edition have made me feel rather like an ancient monument. They will continue to be welcome, brickbats as well as bouquets, but sometimes the process of assimilation must be slow, for this is clearly one of the biggest books, in sheer number of words, between two covers, and I possess only ten fingers and one typewriter. I also produce the *Film Guide*, which seeks to complement this one. Still, the *Companion* must remain my first love, and it has become the widest ranging and more supple of the two.

One drawback in producing so many large books is lack of time in which to keep up to date by viewing the new species. My supporters will, however, know that I find little personal hardship in being so deprived: I have not seen a new film for several years which can give the perennial thrill of a midnight revival of *Casablanca* on the box, and one only has to look at a remake such as *The Lady Vanishes* to realize that today's film-makers lack even the skill to imitate satisfactorily: lines and situations are thrown away because the big studios of old no longer provide a training ground in which the apprentice can spend his first working years observing the masters.

The rosettes (❈) lightly scattered through the book were a new feature of the last edition. They admit the bearer to Halliwell's Hall of Fame, and are bestowed, as a token of respect and gratitude for significant work in a particular field over a sizeable period of film history, upon people with remarkable talents which were not easily duplicated. In each case I have given a reason for my selection, and added one film in which it seems to me that the person concerned was at his peak. These are purely personal judgements, and I reserve the right to add more in due course.

In addition to revising all entries up to the end of 1983 (and, as usual, discarding nothing) I have absorbed into this now greatly expanded tome virtually the entire contents of two other books, *Halliwell's Movie Quiz* and *The Filmgoer's Book of Quotes*. Both, I hope, provide amusement; neither was intended as a mere frivolity. The reconstituted and entirely revised *Companion* should now stand more usefully than ever as a reliable guide to ninety years of film-making, in so far as people and trends are concerned, with the *Film Guide* on hand to provide credits for individual films and the *Television Companion* to comment on matters which are its proper concern. These are the three astonishingly weighty results of a casual conversation at a 1964 cocktail party, when I airily suggested to a publisher I'd just met that he gather together a committee to compile a pocket encyclopaedia of the cinema. Needless to say, I finished up doing it myself; and that was only the beginning.

London, March 1984

Preface to the Ninth Edition

From its modest beginnings in 1965 this volume has grown, in respect of the number of words it contains, approximately sixfold, from less than two hundred thousand to getting on for a million and a half. In 1977 the complementary *Film Guide* started from scratch and has grown even larger, to the extent that it is now hard to contain within a single pair of boards. The *Companion* is more difficult to revise, but it remains my own favourite, at least as a bedtime book: even I, now that nearly a quarter of a century has passed, find many of the original entries fresh to read, and my tired eyes are led gently from one fact I had almost forgotten to a quote that makes me smile all over again.

During the passing years the nature of movies has changed, and the nature of the audience even more strikingly: the cost of a seat has gone up at least tenfold, and most people now see their movies at home on the video box. Those who venture to the cinema are well under thirty, except on rare occasions, and the old family audience has gone the way of the old family film. One scarcely sees a 'U' certificate film from one year's end to the next, whereas thirty years ago they used to constitute more than half of the titles classified. I continue to record the new films, but with less enthusiasm than I once did, for I prefer to be elevated rather than depressed, and the new film-makers remain rather too concerned to rub my nose in the gutter. Either that, or they try to tempt me with adventure fantasies which I would have found childish fifty years ago. Wit and style are what I miss, heroes who are at home in any society, and that marvellous repertory of versatile supporting actors which vanished without trace and has never been replaced.

Luckily for me, it fell to my lot in recent years to acquire and schedule several thousand 'golden oldies' for Britain's fourth television channel. What a store of riches has been revealed! An enormous postbag from delighted viewers has made the effort more than worthwhile: when you can show Conrad Veidt in *The Passing of the Third Floor Back* to an audience of five million, you really feel that you have achieved something.

Meanwhile, this new edition of the *Companion* offers more than one hundred thousand words of additions and amendments: the length, in other words, of quite a long novel. Information is up to date as at the end of 1987.

I have grown rather cynical about awards: the Hollywood ones seem more political than meaningful these days, and the British Film Academy ones so arbitrary that I have discontinued noting them. In the end it is surely the audience which notices good work, by going back to it time and again.

London, February 1988 L.H.

Acknowledgements

Again many readers have written with encouragement and suggestions. I am especially indebted to the following:

Henrik G. Melsom
Keith Burt
Michael Thornton
John Stewart
Richard Chatten
Stan Kirkby Jnr
John Horrox
Dawn Wagstaff and Jack Ullman
Russell Green
Brian Rees
Don Minifie
Virginia Yates
Jeff Hannay

There is also a gentleman who sent copious notes from a typewriter with a red and black ribbon. Alas, the notes became detached from the accompanying letter which bore his name, but if he will remind me of the latter I will certainly credit him next time.

Any further correspondence should be directed to the publisher, Grafton Books, 8 Grafton Street, London W1.

Explanatory Notes

Personal Dates The birth year of an actor or actress is often obscured beyond the powers of a crystal ball. I have chosen the earliest date in print as most likely to be accurate, though one can still be foxed by people like Groucho Marx, who eventually admitted that in their youth the brothers all took five years off their ages.

Doubtful dates are prefaced by 'c.' (circa).

(*) indicates that the person has died, but date of death is uncertain.

Film Dates I have tried to improve the dating of films, which (as many correspondents kindly pointed out) did tend to vary in some cases from entry to entry. I can only continue to plead the impossibility of cross-checking every entry in so long a book. I aim to give the year when the film was completed and first publicly shown, and most important films are well 'dated' in my memory; but sometimes, when release is held up for months over a year's end or when an American film is shown first in Britain, it is difficult to be sure what year to quote, and the guiding decision may vary according to the source consulted. In the case of TV series, the date '67' normally means that the show began in September of that year, but the season would run over into the following March or April. In the fifties such series ran for 39 episodes, but cost has dwindled them to a maximum of 24, and many are cut off at 13, with 'mid-season' replacements appearing in January for a short run.

Film Titles I have given the title by which the film is known in its country of origin. Alternative British/American titles are listed at the end of the book, after the general essay on title changes. Foreign language titles are usually translated when the original is not widely known: i.e. I use *Les Enfants du Paradis* rather than *Children of Paradise*, but *Wild Strawberries* rather than *Smultronstallet*.

Abbreviations These have been tidied up to some extent. The main ones now used are:

a	actor	oa	original author
d	director	w	screenwriter
p	producer	ph	cinematographer
orig sp	original screenplay	m	music score
		pd	production designer

The symbol '&' means that the function abbreviated is in addition to that normally expected of the subject. For instance, in an actor's list, '& pd' means that he also produced and directed.

Incomplete lists normally end with 'etc', which means that there may be up to as many films again as have been listed, or 'many others', which means that the list has only scratched the surface.

AA indicates the winning of Hollywood's Academy Award. BFA indicates the winning of the British Film Academy award, sometimes known as 'Stella' and now presented by the British Academy of Film and Television Arts.

Most significant films I have tried to show, in italics, the subject's most significant films. The reader may interpret 'significant' as meaning commercially, artistically, critically, or simply as indicating a film in which the subject gave a good typical account of himself. My aim has been to form, out of a mass of titles, the backbone of a career. Obviously I have not seen every film ever made, so I may have ignored many titles which should have been italicized. *Mea culpa*: the aim was to be helpful.

Please note that this system applies to filmographies only; in the mini-essays all titles are italicized.

Nationalities I still aim to indicate hereditary origins rather than place of birth or adopted citizenship. The fact that Joan Fontaine was born in Tokyo does not make her Japanese, and although she has lived many years in America her whole persona remains essentially British.

Complete filmographies These are indicated by the symbol '☐'. A 'complete' entry should not necessarily be taken as a sign of eminence or as the author's seal of approval: some people simply made very few films, or had compact typical careers which are worth detailing as instances of what goes on in the film business: the gradual climb, the good cameo role, the star period, the two or three 'dogs' in a row, the gradual decline, the cheap horror burlesque. On the other hand, filmographies cannot be completed for several major directors and stars because not all of their earlier films can be traced. 'Incomplete' entries still aim to indicate the beginning and end dates of a career, with the dates coming closest together over the most prolific and significant period.

Short films (less than, say, 50 minutes) are not normally accounted for unless the subject worked chiefly in this field, which deserves a book to itself.

Almost every performer and director now works in TV as well as films, but much TV production is too ephemeral to be worth recording even if one had the space to note it. I have, however, tried to show all TV *film* series (which will be more available than tape to the student of the future) in which the subject played a continuing part. I have also taken note, in the main lists, of the TV movie, which fills a 90-minute or two-hour slot, and over many years of trial and error has produced interesting features of a nostalgic kind, but even in supposedly complete filmographies the TV listings can only be partial.

Alphabetical order This is adhered to on normal dictionary lines, but fictional characters are listed under the complete name (Sherlock Holmes under S). Von Stroheim comes under V, Laura La Plante under L, Cecil B. de Mille under D. Mc and Mac are treated as one, although the spelling is of course kept distinct.

Rosettes (❁) See penultimate paragraph of the Preface to the Eighth Edition (p. viii).

Quizzes These are introduced by the symbol **?**. Most are fairly difficult, and almost all are nostalgic. Answers appear at the end of the relevant letter section. Tick the open square for each correct answer. A total score of more than 2,000 labels you a genuine film buff. More than 3,000 is little short of miraculous.

Quotations These are introduced by the symbol ¶

A Preliminary Canter

Here is an aimless romp through the classics of film history. It should be fairly simple for any keen student, and is in fact the easiest quiz in the book. Answers appear on p. 1226.

1 In what city was *Ninotchka* set?
2 Who directed *How Green Was My Valley*?
3 Name the film in which Greta Garbo played a mistress of Napoleon.
4 Name the classic silent western directed in 1923 by James Cruze.
5 What D. W. Griffith film was based on a novel called *The Chink and the Child*?
6 Whose first film as a director was *The Pleasure Garden* (1926)?
7 Who produced and directed *The Private Life of Henry VIII*?
8 Who co-wrote *Citizen Kane* with Orson Welles?
9 In *The Great Dictator*, Charles Chaplin played Hynkel, but who played Napaloni?
10 Name the Walt Disney feature cartoon in which Leopold Stokowski conducted 'a sound track concert with accompanying images'.
11 Name the film in which Gary Cooper played Lou Gehrig the baseball star.
12 Who directed *Brief Encounter*?
13 Which *Road* is missing? *Singapore*, *Zanzibar*, *Morocco*, *Rio*, *Bali*, *Hong Kong*.
14 Name the film directed by Vittorio de Sica about slum dwellers escaping into the skies on broomsticks.
15 Who wrote the screenplay of *Gone with the Wind*?
16 Famous photographer Karl Freund directed only two films, in 1932 and 1935, both in the horror field. Name them.
17 Name the director of *Strike, The General Line*, and *Alexander Nevsky*.
18 By what name is William Henry Pratt better known?
19 Name the Academy Award winning short in which Laurel and Hardy spend three reels getting a piano up a flight of steps.
20 Who played the title role (the doctor) in *The Cabinet of Dr Caligari*?
21 What comedy team first appeared in *One Night in the Tropics*?
22 The stage and film musical of the seventies. *A Little Night Music*, is based on what film by Ingmar Bergman?
23 Who played Chorus in *Henry V*?
24 Fine documentaries of World War II, *Listen to Britain* and *Fires Were Started*, were directed by whom?
25 Everyone knows Erich Maria Remarque's *All Quiet on the Western Front*; but can you name the sequel, filmed by Universal in 1937?
26 Who played Albert to Anna Neagle's Victoria in *Victoria the Great* and *Sixty Glorious Years*?
27 Who had eight credits on *In Which We Serve*, including writer and director?
28 Mickey Mouse, Goofy and Pluto are known the world over, but can you name Mickey's horsy friend who appeared in the early thirties?
29 Pola Negri appeared as Catherine the Great in what 1924 film by Ernst Lubitsch?
30 Who was the Ringo Kid in *Stagecoach*?
31 Name the two missing dwarfs: Happy, Bashful, Sneezy, Sleepy, Dopey . . .
32 Who photographed *The Magnificent Ambersons*?
33 Name the 1947 film in which Charles Chaplin played a multiple murderer.
34 What popular 1937 film (starring among others Fernandel, Raimu, Pierre Blanchar and Harry Baur) gave director Julien Duvivier his ticket to Hollywood?
35 While there he made a pretty close remake of his great success. Name it and the actress who played the title role.
36 In what film did Alec Guinness play eight parts?
37 Name the film in which Jacques Tati played a postman.
38 What was the first *Carry On*?
39 The Marx Brothers made one film which was a recognizable version of a Broadway straight comedy. Name it.
40 Name also the remake starring Frank Sinatra.
41 What star's films included *Tumbleweed*, *White Oak* and *Wild Bill Hickok*?
42 Who directed *One Flew Over the Cuckoo's Nest*?
43 What 1934 comedy won Oscars for both its stars?

44 In what film did George Raft first spin a coin, a trick that half the world imitated?
45 Who played the title role in *Baby Face Nelson* in 1957?
46 Who played Dr Watson to Peter Cushing's Sherlock Holmes in the 1957 *Hound of the Baskervilles*?
47 Who played the villainous husband in the British 1940 version of *Gaslight*?
48 Who directed, among many others, *Only Angels Have Wings*, *Bringing Up Baby* and *The Big Sleep*?
49 Who was first known as Marjorie Robertson?
50 Who wrote the music and lyrics for *Top Hat*?
51 Who were jokingly known as The Singing Capon and The Iron Butterfly?
52 In what film did Cyd Charisse take over a role from Greta Garbo?
53 What was Fritz Lang's first American film?
54 What company made *Ballet Oop*, *Willie the Kid* and *Madeleine*?
55 Who played Wilson in *Wilson*?
56 In which Marxian frolic did all the brothers impersonate Maurice Chevalier?
57 In 1939 John Grierson made what is sometimes inaccurately called the first documentary. Name it.
58 Who directed *An Italian Straw Hat*?
59 In which film did Rudolph Valentino play a Cossack lieutenant in imperial Russia?
60 On whose novel was *Whisky Galore (Tight Little Island)* based?
61 Who played Edgar Linton in William Wyler's *Wuthering Heights*?
62 Name the film by Michael Powell and Emeric Pressburger in which David Farrar played a bomb disposal expert with a drink problem.
63 With which Hitchcock film do you associate the Merry Widow waltz?
64 By what well-known studio was *The Man in the White Suit* made?
65 *The Sun Shines Bright* was a 1953 remake of a 1934 film starring what actor?
66 The title of the 1934 film was the name of the character played by that actor. Name it.
67 What film by Elia Kazan documented the unsolved New England case of the murder of a clergyman?
68 Name the short ghost story film made by Michael MacLiammoir and Hilton Edwards during one of the frequent pauses in the filming of Orson Welles' *Othello*.
69 In what Lubitsch film did the hero say, 'Waiter, you see that moon? I want to see that moon in the champagne . . .'?
70 What Busby Berkeley film contains the song 'I Only Have Eyes For You'?
71 Whose films include *A Chairy Tale*, *Pas de Deux* and *Begone Dull Care*?
72 What musical involves a search for Miss Turnstiles?
73 Who was the supervisor of the *Why We Fight* series?
74 What was historically significant about *Toot, Whistle, Plunk and Boom*?
75 Who starred in *Blossom Time*?
76 Who played a bit part as a hungry diner in the 1929 silent film *Piccadilly*?
77 Who directed *Man of Aran*?
78 Whose autobiography is called *Bulls, Balls, Bicycles and Actors*?
79 Who played Chauvelin in the 1934 *The Scarlet Pimpernel*?
80 Who played Sanders in the 1935 *Sanders of the River*?
81 In what British comedy of 1938 are the romantic leads eaten by a bear in Kent?
82 Who wrote a history of the cinema called *The Liveliest Art*?
83 Name the director of *A Propos de Nice*, *Zero de Conduite* and *L'Atalante*.
84 Name the producer of *Foreign Correspondent*, *Algiers* and the Elizabeth Taylor *Cleopatra*.
85 What affliction was suffered by Gerald McBoing Boing?
86 With what branch of cinema do you associate Bob Godfrey, Richard Williams and Ub Iwerks?
87 Who directed *Die Dreigroschenoper*?
88 Who starred in *The Black Sheep of Whitehall*, *The Goose Steps Out* and *My Learned Friend*?
89 Whose films include *Drôle de Drame*, *Quai des Brumes*, *Le Joir se Lève* and *Jenny*?
90 Name the brothers who invented a camera/projector and gave the first moving picture show to the public in 1895.
91 Whose films include *Feet First*, *Hot Water* and *The Freshman*?
92 What studio has for its trademark a mountain encircled by stars?
93 To whom was Carole Lombard married when she died?
94 Who appeared in *Twice Two*, *Helpmates* and *Men o'War*?
95 Name the all-star musical made in 1943 about sailors on leave in a big studio and

the stars putting on a show for them. (Victor Moore played Eddie Bracken's father.)

96 What was the studio?

97 What film was made in 1932 with Irene Dunne and John Boles and in 1941 with Margaret Sullavan and Charles Boyer?

98 Of what film, also starring Clark Gable, was *Mogambo* a remake?

99 For what was Georges Méliès best known?

100 Who wrote the music score for *The Adventures of Robin Hood* and *King's Row*?

101 Who starred in *Hi Nellie*, *The World Changes*, and *We Are Not Alone*?

102 Who was Valentino's leading lady in *The Sheik*?

103 Who played Doc Holliday in *My Darling Clementine*?

104 And who played Pat Garrett in *The Outlaw*?

105 As what TV series character did Adam West become famous?

106 *The Glass Key*, *The Thin Man*, *Red Harvest*, *The Maltese Falcon*. These Dashiell Hammett novels have all been filmed. Right or wrong?

107 Name the *Six Million Dollar Man*: his real name and his character name.

108 Hitler commissioned a film of the 1934 party congress at Nuremberg. As propaganda it succeeded beyond his wildest dreams. What is its title (in English) and who directed it?

109 Who directed *The Diary of Anne Frank*?

110 Who played the old man in *Wild Strawberries*?

111 In what film did the Ale and Quail Club feature?

112 What great star of the silents also starred in a 1974 TV movie called *Killer Bees*?

113 Who got his comeuppance in *The Magnificent Ambersons*?

114 Name the film about the Brontës which starred Ida Lupino, Olivia de Havilland and Nancy Coleman.

115 Who was hailed as the film industry's first centenarian?

116 Name the cinematographer of *Citizen Kane*, *The Grapes of Wrath* and *The Best Years of Our Lives*.

117 Who played *Citizen Kane* as a child? And who played his son?

118 What was the subject of *Gentleman's Agreement*?

119 Whose autobiography was *Fun in a Chinese Laundry*?

120 In what film did Laurel and Hardy deceive their wives and go to a Chicago convention?

121 What other comedian did they meet there?

122 What social and historical distinction was given to *A Matter of Life and Death (Stairway to Heaven)*?

123 Who starred in *The Green Goddess*, *The Man Who Played God*, *The Iron Duke* and *Voltaire*?

124 Who wrote the script of *My Little Chickadee*?

125 Who was the first Tarzan?

126 Who was the *second* James Bond? (Don't count *Casino Royale*.)

127 What was Ingrid Bergman's first American film?

128 Who was D. W. Griffith's chief cameraman?

129 What is the film which Griffith is said to have directed in 1939 although it is credited to Hal Roach?

130 What film was alleged at various times to have been directed by Orson Welles or Howard Hawks, though credited to Christian Nyby?

131 What film starring Rudolph Valentino was remade with Bob Hope?

132 Chaplin and others made films for the Essanay company. How was the word Essanay devised?

133 In what film did Tony Curtis play The Great Leslie?

134 Who directed *The Wages of Fear*?

135 For what film did Harold Russell win an Academy Award, and what role did he play?

136 What was Clifton Webb's character name in *Sitting Pretty*?

137 Who were the co-stars of *Mother Wore Tights*?

138 Who played the murdered Jew in *Crossfire*?

139 In what MGM film of 1940 was the song 'Mr Gallagher and Mr Shean' performed?

140 Al Shean played himself, but who played 'Mr Gallagher'?

141 In what film did Elizabeth Taylor disguise herself as a boy? (Mickey Rooney was also in it.)

142 What was the sequel to *Claudia*?

143 'The Trolley Song' comes from what movie?

144 In the same film, who played the heroine's mother and father?

145 Of whose death did Joan Fontaine think Cary Grant guilty in *Suspicion*?

146 Who played Dolittle in *Pygmalion*?
147 Who played Lennie in *Of Mice and Men*?
148 What was Charles Boyer's character name in *Algiers*?
149 Roland Young was *Topper*, but who was Mrs Topper?
150 Who played Moses in the 1923 De Mille version of *The Ten Commandments*?
151 Who played Robert Cummings' grandmother in *King's Row*?
152 The silent version of *The Phantom of the Opera* was directed by whom?
153 Who played the leading role of Jim Apperson in *The Big Parade*?
154 Who directed it?
155 Who played his first leading role in *The Winning of Barbara Worth*?
156 What actor was born in New York, made his name in Germany, was successful in American silent films but returned to Germany when sound came?
157 Who directed *The Jazz Singer*?
158 To whom did the production company Cosmopolitan belong?
159 Who made *The Old Mill*, *Flowers and Trees* and *Merbabies*?
160 What famous film runs 220 minutes?
161 For which company did music arranger Leo F. Forbstein mainly work during the thirties?
162 And with which company do you associate the musical arrangements of Joseph Gershenson?
163 In which film did Gene Kelly dance with a cartoon mouse?
164 In which film did Esther Williams swim with Tom and Jerry?
165 Who played the title role in *Laura*?
166 *Double Indemnity* was remade as a TV movie in 1973. Who played the MacMurray/Stanwyck roles?
167 In what film were Danny Kaye's leading ladies Constance Dowling and Dinah Shore?
168 In what film was Sheridan Whiteside a leading character?
169 Who played Apple Annie in *Lady for a Day*?
170 Name the 1960 remake starring Bette Davis.
171 Of what adventure film was Carl Denham the leading character?
172 Who played Humpty Dumpty in the 1933 *Alice in Wonderland*?
173 What was Mary Pickford's last film?
174 What is the title of David Niven's first volume of autobiography?
175 And the second?
176 What Bob Hope film was based on *Ruggles of Red Gap*?
177 What Hitchcock film was shot silent and hurriedly adapted for sound?
178 What famous film was adapted from Heinrich Mann's novel *Professor Unrath*?
179 What comedian starred in *The Strong Man* and *Tramp Tramp Tramp*?
180 Who directed *La Règle du Jeu*?
181 Who played the two cricket enthusiasts in *The Lady Vanishes*?
182 What Hitchcock film was based on a Francis Beeding novel, *The House of Dr Edwardes*?
183 Who starred in *The New York Hat*, and who directed it?
184 Who created the Popeye cartoons?
185 Who played Irene, Sunny, Odette and Nell Gwyn?
186 Whose first sound film was *Sous les Toits de Paris*?
187 Who directed *The Discreet Charm of the Bourgeoisie*?
188 What horror actor of the forties had fearsome features which were actually distorted by the disease acromegaly?
189 Who played Cantor Yoelson in *The Jolson Story*?
190 In what film did Sig Rumann, Alexander Granach and Felix Bressart play as a team?
191 Of what film was Trudy Kockenlocker the heroine?
192 In what film was Cecil Kellaway stoppered in a bottle?
193 In what film was he gobbled up in a bathysphere?
194 Who photographed *The Cat and the Canary* (1939)?
195 Name the Chaplin comedy in which he polluted the waters of a health spa with alcohol.
196 Who played Captain Andy in the 1936 *Showboat*?
197 And in the 1951 remake?
198 What film from a play of the same name by Marc Connelly gave a simplistic Negro version of heaven and the Bible stories?
199 Who played De Lawd?
200 Who impersonated a gorilla in *My Man Godfrey*?
201 Who starred as *Craig's Wife* in 1936?
202 *The Petrified Forest* was remade in 1946 as . . .
203 Who directed Garbo in *Camille*?
204 Though Ruby Keeler's name was not used, who played her in *The Jolson Story*?
205 What is the subject of *Champion*, *Body and Soul* and *The Set-Up*?

206 When Leslie Howard was Romeo and Norma Shearer was Juliet, who was Mercutio?
207 Who won the Academy Award, in what film, for playing Mrs O'Leary?
208 What aerial melodrama won the first Academy Award as best film, in 1928?
209 For what film in which he repeated his stage role did Paul Lukas win an Oscar?
210 When *Nothing Sacred* was remade, what was its new title, and who played Carole Lombard's role?
211 What role do Dame May Whitty and Mona Washbourne have in common?
212 Who in 1938 played the title role in *The Adventures of Tom Sawyer*?
213 Who directed *Metropolis*?
214 And who directed *The Cabinet of Dr Caligari*?
215 Who played Parris Mitchell in *King's Row*?
216 Whose films include *Thunder Below*, *The Cheat* and *My Sin*?
217 Who directed *The Sign of the Cross*?
218 What was added to the reissue during World War II?
219 The first Mickey Mouse cartoon with sound had a watery setting. Name it.
220 What director began his Hollywood career by directing *Journey's End*, which he had directed on the London stage?
221 What was Marlene Dietrich's first American film?
222 Who played Gertrude to Olivier's *Hamlet*?
223 In what film did Astaire and Rogers perform the number 'My One and Only Highland Fling'?
224 'No mean Machiavelli is smiling, cynical Sidney Kidd.' Who played him in *The Philadelphia Story*?
225 In *Bringing Up Baby* what kind of baby was it?
226 Who played the trumpet in *Genevieve*?
227 Who directed *Duck Soup*?
228 Who played Dr Armstrong in the 1945 version of *And Then There Were None*?
229 Who played Horace Femm in *The Old Dark House* and Dr Pretorious in *The Bride of Frankenstein*?
230 Who played Callahan in *Destry Rides Again*?
231 Who played the title role in *My Girl Tisa*?
232 In that film, what politician saved the day, and who played him?
233 Who or what was *Laughing Gravy*?
234 In what film was Inspector Cockrill the detective, and who played him?
235 What part did Charles Waldron play in *The Big Sleep*?
236 Who played Magwitch in David Lean's *Great Expectations*?
237 What comedian played two roles and spoofed himself in *Thank Your Lucky Stars*?
238 Who were Charles Laughton's two leading ladies in *Rembrandt*?
239 Who was Bambi's rabbit friend?
240 Who wrote the novel *Bambi* on which the film was based?
241 What segment of *Fantasia* features crocodiles, ostriches and hippopotami?
242 Who directed *All Quiet on the Western Front*?
243 Name the black acrobatic dancers who appeared mainly as speciality acts in Fox musicals of the forties.
244 Give the Christian names of the Ritz Brothers . . .
245 . . . and the Andrews Sisters.
246 Alan Ladd's last film was . . .
247 Who played Buckingham to Olivier's Richard III?
248 Who plays the title role in *Barry Lyndon*?
249 What actor subsequently knighted made his first appearance in *The Ghoul*?
250 Who played Scarlett O'Hara's mother in *Gone with the Wind*?
251 'So they call me Concentration Camp Erhardt!' Name the film in which this line becomes a running gag.
252 Name the two leading players of *Invasion of the Body Snatchers* (1956 version).

A

A Nous La Liberté (France 1931). A classic satirical comedy written and directed by René Clair, set in a factory and demonstrating the increasing mechanization of life. Photography by Georges Perinal, design by Lazare Meerson, music by Georges Auric; featuring Raymond Cordy and Henri Marchand. Chaplin's *Modern Times*, five years later, borrowed several of its ideas.

Aan (India 1952). Released internationally in abbreviated form as *Savage Princess*, this historical romantic adventure, directed by Mehboob, was the first Indian film to reach world mass markets, but its mixture of music, swashbuckling and sentiment was not to western taste.

Aaron, Sidney. Pseudonym used by Paddy Chayevsky for his last film script, *Altered States*.

Abady, Temple (–). British composer. The Woman in the Hall 47. Miranda 48. All over the Town 49. Folly to Be Wise 52. Kill Me Tomorrow 58, etc.

Abbott, Bud (1895–1974) (William Abbott). American comedian, the brusque and slightly shifty 'straight man' half of Abbott and Costello, cross-talking vaudevillians of long standing who became Universal's top stars of the early forties. Bud, seldom seen without his hat, was the bully who left the dirty work for his partner, never believed his tall but true stories of crooks and monsters, and usually avoided the pie in the face.
□*One Night in the Tropics* (their only supporting roles) 39. *Buck Privates* 40. In The Navy 41. *Hold That Ghost* 41. Keep 'Em Flying 41. Ride 'Em Cowboy 41. Rio Rita 42. Pardon My Sarong 42. Who Done It? 42. It Ain't Hay 43. Hit the Ice 43. Lost In A Harem 44. *In Society* 44. Here Come the Co-Eds 45. *The Naughty Nineties* (featuring their famous *Who's On First* routine) 45. Abbott and Costello in Hollywood 45. The Little Giant (a doomed attempt to work separately within the same film) 46. The Time of Their Lives (an interesting failure) 46. Buck Privates Come Home 47. The Wistful Widow of Wagon Gap 47. The Noose Hangs High 48. *Abbott and Costello Meet Frankenstein* 48. Mexican Hayride 48. Africa Screams 49. Abbott and Costello Meet The Killer 49. Abbott and Costello in the Foreign Legion 50. Abbott and Costello Meet the Invisible Man 51. Comin' Round the Mountain 51. Jack and the Beanstalk 52. Abbott and Costello Lost in Alaska 52. Abbott and Costello Meet Captain Kidd 52. Abbott and Costello Go to Mars 53. *Abbott and Costello Meet Dr Jekyll and Mr Hyde* 53. Abbott and Costello Meet the Keystone Kops 55. Abbott and Costello Meet the Mummy 55. Dance with Me Henry 56.

After a TV series (1953) using up all their old routines, the team split and Abbott retired. See *Costello, Lou.* In 1975 there was published *Who's On First,* a selection of frame-by-frame routines, by Richard J. Anobile. Bob Thomas's biography, *Bud and Lou,* was published in 1977, and appeared in 1978 as a TV movie, with Harvey Korman and Buddy Hackett.

† All Abbott and Costello movies depended for their effectiveness on the number of old vaudeville routines included, such as the following: 'All Because You Don't Like Mustard' and 'Jonah and the Whale' (*One Night in the Tropics*); 'Drill' (*Buck Privates*); 'Bussing the Bee' and 'Seven Times Thirteen Is Twenty-Eight' (*In the Navy*); 'The Moving Candle' (*Hold That Ghost*, *Meet Frankenstein*); 'Don't Order Anything' (*Keep 'Em Flying*, borrowed from Laurel and Hardy's *Man o' War*); 'Poker Game' (*Ride 'Em Cowboy*); 'Ten Dollars You're Not There' (*Rio Rita*); 'The Poisoned Drink' (*Pardon My Sarong*); 'The Telephone Call' (*Who Done It*); 'Bagel Street' (*In Society*); 'The Magic Act' and 'Slowly I Turned' (*Lost in a Harem*); 'The Mirror' and 'Who's on First' (*The Naughty Nineties*); 'Hole in the Wall' (*The Noose Hangs High*); 'Identification' and 'Silver Ore' (*Mexican Hayride*); 'The Gorilla' (*Africa Screams*); 'The Shovel Is My Pick' (*Meet the Mummy*).

❀ For bringing authentic vaudeville to Hollywood in a few imperishable routines; and for cheering up a generation at war. *Abbott and Costello Meet Frankenstein.*

¶ Abbott and Costello's comedy depended on caricature and contrast: the fat and the thin, the nervous and the foolhardy, the stupid and the stupider. Their work falls into well-remembered routines and reactions. There is chubby, terrified Costello calling after his partner:

Ch-ch-ch-ch-ch-i-ck!

There is his shy admission:

I'm a ba-a-a-ad boy!

There is the old pantomime gag of his seeing something alarming and running to tell his partner; by the time the latter returns the thing has naturally disappeared. There are repetitive routines such as the 'Slowly I turned' scene from *Lost in a Harem*, with its Laurel and Hardy-like inevitability. Most memorably there is skilful nightclub cross-talk, seen at its best in the 'Who's on first' sketch which first brought them to fame. Here is part of it:

A: You know, these days they give ballplayers very peculiar names. Take the St Louis team: Who's on first, What's on second, I Don't Know is on third . . .
C: That's what I want to find out. I want you to tell me the names of the fellows on the St Louis team.
I'm telling you. Who's on first, What's on second, I Don't Know is on third.
—Who's playing first?
Yes.
—I mean, the fellow's name on first base.
Who.
—The fellow playing first base.
Who.
—The guy on first base.
Who is on first.
—Well, what are you asking me for?
I'm not asking you, I'm telling you. Who is on first.
—I'm asking you—who is on first?
That's the man's name.
—That's who's name?
Yes.
—Well, go ahead, tell me.
Who!
—All I'm trying to find out is, what's the guy's name on first base.
Oh no, What is on second.
—I'm not asking you who's on second.
Who's on first.
—That's what I'm trying to find out!
What's the guy's name on first base?
What's the guy's name on second base.
—I'm not asking who's on second.
Who's on first.
—I Don't Know.
He's on third . . .

And so on, for another five minutes.

Abbott, George (1887–). American playwright and producer of lively commercial properties. He sporadically invaded Hollywood to supervise their filming, and stayed briefly to perform other services. Autobiography 1963: *Mister Abbott.*
AS ORIGINAL AUTHOR: Four Walls 28. Coquette 28. *Broadway* 29 (and 42). *Three Men On A Horse* 36. On Your Toes 39. The Boys from Syracuse 40. *The Pajama Game* (& co-d) 57. *Damn Yankees* (& co-d) 58, etc.
AS PRODUCER: *Boy Meets Girl* 38. Room Service 38. The Primrose Path 40. *The Pajama Game* 57. *Damn Yankees* 58, etc.
AS DIRECTOR: Why Bring That Up? 29. The Sea God 30. Stolen Heaven 31. Secrets of a Secretary 31. My Sin 31. Too Many Girls 40, etc.

¶ *G.A.:* I must confess that one of my main defects as a director has always been an incurable impatience.

G.A.: Many great minds have made a botch of matters because their emotions fettered their thinking.

Abbott, John (1905–). British-born character actor with staring eyes, specializing in eccentric parts; in Hollywood from 1941.
Mademoiselle Docteur 37. The Return of the Scarlet Pimpernel 37. The Saint in London 39. The Shanghai Gesture 41. Mrs Miniver 42. They Got Me Covered 42. Jane Eyre 43. The London Blackout Murders (lead) 43. The Vampire's Ghost 45. Deception 46. *The Woman in White* 48 (a memorable performance, as the grotesque invalid Frederick Fairlie). The Merry Widow 52. Public Pigeon Number One 57. Gigi 58. Who's Minding the Store 63. Gambit 66. The Store 66. 2000 Years Later 69. The Black Bird 75, others.

Abbott, Philip (1923–). American 'second lead' of the fifties.
Bachelor Party 57. *Sweet Bird of Youth* 62. The Spiral Road 62. Miracle of the White Stallions 63. Those Calloways 65. Tail Gunner Joe (TV) 77, etc.
TV series: *The F.B.I.* 65–73.

Abel, Alfred (1880–1937). German character actor of weighty personality.
Dr Mabuse 22. Phantom 22. Metropolis 26. Gold 28. Congress Dances 31. Salon Dora Greene 33. Das Hofkonzert 36. Kater Lampe 36. Frau Sylvelin 38, etc.

Abel, Walter (1898–1987). American character actor with stage experience. Made his Hollywood debut as D'Artagnan, but later settled enjoyably into variations on a single performance of harassment and nervousness, whether as father, friend of the family or professional man.
□*The Three Musketeers* 35. The Lady Consents 36. Two in the Dark 36. The Witness Chair 36. Fury 36. We Went to College 36. Second Wife 36. Portia on Trial 37. Wise Girl 37. Law of the Underworld 38. Racket Busters 38. Men with Wings 38. King of the Turf 39. Miracle on Main Street 40. Dance Girl Dance 40. *Arise My Love* (which provided him with a key line: 'I'm not happy. I'm not happy at all') 40. Michael Shayne Private Detective 40. Who Killed Aunt Maggie 40. *Hold Back the Dawn* 41. Skylark 41. Glamour Boy 41. *Beyond The Blue Horizon* 42. *Star Spangled Rhythm* 42. *Holiday Inn* 42. Wake Island 42. So Proudly We Hail 43. Fired Wife 43. Follow the Boys 44. *Mr Skeffington* 44. An American Romance 44. *The Affairs of Susan* 45. Duffy's Tavern 45. *Kiss and Tell* 45. The Kid from Brooklyn 46. 13 Rue Madeleine 46. The Fabulous Joe 47. *Dream Girl* 48. That Lady in Ermine 48. So This is Love 53. Night People 54. The Indian Fighter 55. The Steel Jungle 56. *Bernardine* 57. Raintree County 57. Handle with Care 58. Mirage 65. Quick Let's Get Married 66. Zora 71. The Man without a Country (TV) 74. Silent Night, Bloody Night 74. The Ultimate Solution of Grace Quigley 84.
Well-remembered line: 'I'm not happy. I'm not happy at all!'—*Arise My Love*

Abie's Irish Rose. Anne Nichols' long-running Broadway comedy of 1927, about a Catholic girl marrying into a Jewish family, has twice been filmed: by Victor Fleming in 1928 and by Edward Sutherland in 1946. The theme has frequently been borrowed, most recently in the 1973 TV series *Bridget Loves Bernie*.

abortion, unmentionable on the screen for many years save in continental dramas like *Carnet De Bal* 37, and officially ostracized exploitation pictures like *Amok* 34, was first permitted as a Hollywood plot point in *Detective Story* 51. Six years later, *Blue Denim* concerned an abortion that was prevented; and the later abortion scenes in *The Best of Everything* 59, *Sweet Bird of Youth* 62, *The Interns* 62, and *Love with the Proper Stranger* 64 scarcely displayed an obsession with the subject. Meanwhile however the British gave it full rein in *Saturday Night and Sunday Morning* 60, *The L-Shaped Room* 62, *Alfie* 66, and *Up the Junction* 68; by which time it had certainly lost its shock value. By 1969 Hollywood felt confident enough to use it as the plot point of a commercial thriller, *Daddy's Gone A-Hunting*, and in 1972 it became the specific subject of *To Find A Man*.

Abraham, F. Murray (1940–). American character actor.
□They Might Be Giants 71. Serpico 73. The Sunshine Boys 75. All the President's Men 76. The Ritz 76. The Big Fix 78. Scarface 83. *Amadeus* (AA) 84. The Name of the Rose 86.

Abrahams, Jim (–). American comedy screen writer, usually in association with others. Kentucky Fried Movie (also a) 77. Airplane! (also d) 80. Top Secret (also d) 84. Ruthless People (d) 86.

abstract film. One in which the images are not representational but fall into visually interesting or significant patterns: e.g. Disney's *Fantasia*, Norman McLaren's hand-drawn sound films, etc.

Academy Awards. Merit prizes given annually since 1927 by the American Academy of Motion Picture Arts and Sciences. The award is in the form of a statuette known in the trade—for reasons variously explained—as Oscar, and each April the ABC network televises the award ceremonies as an increasingly pretentious spectacular: Johnny Carson in 1979 called it 'two hours of sparkling entertainment spread out over a four-hour show'. In this volume an Academy Award is noted by the letters AA after the film title or recipient. Nominations as well as awards are noted in *Halliwell's Film Guide*.
Book 1968 by Paul Michael, *The Academy Awards*.
Book 1985 by Mason Wiley and Damien Bolo: *Inside Oscar*.

¶ *Shirley Maclaine:* The Oscar means one thing—an added million-dollar gross for the picture. It's a big publicity contest. Oh, the voting is legitimate, but there's the sentimentality. One year when I was a candidate, when Elizabeth Taylor got a hole in her throat, I cancelled my plane.

Federico Fellini: In the myth of the cinema, Oscar is the supreme prize.

Joan Crawford at first Oscar ceremony: As you danced, you saw the most important people in Hollywood whirling past you.

Frances Marion 1928: The statuette is a perfect symbol of the picture business—a powerful athletic body clutching a gleaming sword, with half of his head, the part that holds his brains, completely sliced off.

? For what films did the following actors and actresses receive Academy Awards?

1 Gale Sondergaard
2 Thomas Mitchell
3 Bing Crosby
4 Bette Davis (2)
5 Ronald Colman
6 Walter Brennan (3)
7 Helen Hayes (2)
8 Marie Dressler
9 Paul Lukas
10 Ginger Rogers
11 Joan Fontaine
12 James Cagney
13 Katharine Hepburn (4, including one shared)

And for what films did the following directors receive them?

14 Frank Lloyd (2)
15 Leo McCarey (3)
16 Norman Taurog
17 Michael Curtiz

Academy Frame. The standard film frame in a ratio of 4 to 3, more usually referred to as 1.33 to 1.

Academy Leader. Regulation length of film attached to the front of a reel about to be projected, bearing a 'countdown' and various standard images to facilitate focusing.

Accattone (Italy 1961). Written and directed by Pier Paulo Pasolini, this slum drama about the doom of a young crook seemed to mark the re-birth of Italian neo-realism, but the trend was not picked up.

accelerated motion. An effect obtained by running the camera more slowly than usual: when the resulting film is projected at normal speed, the movements seem faster because they occupy fewer frames than would normally be the case. The opposite of *slow motion* (qv).

Accent on Youth, a successful Broadway play by Samson Raphaelson, about a lazy playwright spurred to new success by his young secretary, has been filmed three times. In 1935 Herbert Marshall and Sylvia Sidney were directed by Wesley Ruggles. In 1950 it turned up as *Mr Music*, with Bing Crosby and Nancy Olson directed by Richard Haydn; and in 1959 it emerged again as *But Not For Me*, with Clark Gable and Carroll Baker, directed by Walter Lang.

Ace In The Hole (US 1951) (aka *The Big Carnival*). Produced, directed and co-written by Billy Wilder, this bleak melodrama remains one of Hollywood's bitterest attacks on the heartless commercialism of the gutter press. Based on the Floyd Collins case of the twenties, it stars Kirk Douglas as a hard-boiled reporter who deliberately delays rescue operations on a man trapped in a cave so that his story will make national headlines. Photographed by Charles Lang.

acetate. Another word for safety base, which replaced nitrate stock in the fifties and is much slower to burn.

Achard, Marcel (1899–1974). French writer.
The Merry Widow 34. Mayerling 36. Alibi (oa) 37. The Strange Monsieur Victor 38. Untel Père et Fils 40. Monsieur la Souris 43. The Paris Waltz (d only) 50. Madame De 52. La Garçonne 57. A Woman like Satan 59. A Shot in the Dark (oa) 64.

Acker, Sharon (1936–). Anglo-American leading lady.
Lucky Jim (GB) 57. Waiting For Caroline (Can.) 67. Point Blank 67. The First Time 69. Act of the Heart 70. A Clear and Present Danger (TV) 70. Hec Ramsey (TV) 72. The Stranger (TV) 73. The Hanged Man (TV) 74. Our Man Flint: Dead On Target (TV) 76. The Hostage Heart (TV) 77. The Murder That Wouldn't Die (TV) 79.
TV series: The Senator 70. Perry Mason 73. Executive Suite 76.

Ackermann, Bettye (1928–). American general purpose actress.
Face of Fire 59. Companions in Nightmare (TV) 68. Rascal 69. M*A*S*H. 70, etc.
TV series: *Ben Casey* 60–64. Bracken's World 69.

Ackland, Joss (1928–). British actor of larger-than-life personality; much on TV.
Seven Days to Noon 49. The Ghost Ship 53. Rasputin the Mad Monk 65. Crescendo 69. Mr Forbush and the Penguins 71. The House That Dripped Blood 71. Villain 71. England Made Me 72. The Happiness Cage (US) 72.

Hitler: the Last Ten Days 73. Penny Gold 73. The Three Musketeers 73. The Black Windmill 74. S.P.Y.S. 74. Great Expectations 75. Royal Flash 75. Operation Daybreak 76. Silver Bears 78. Who is Killing the Great Chefs of Europe? 78. Saint Jack 79. The Apple 80. Rough Cut 80. Dangerous Davies (TV) 81. Lady Jane 85. A Zed and Two Noughts 85. White Mischief 88, etc.

Ackland, Rodney (1908–). British writer, sporadically in films from 1930, usually in association with other scenarists.
Autobiography 1954: *The Celluloid Mistress.*
Shadows 31. Number Seventeen 32. The Case of Gabriel Perry (a only) 35. Bank Holiday 38. Young Man's Fancy 39. 49th Parallel 41. Dangerous Moonlight 41. Hatter's Castle 41. Thursday's Child (& d) 43. Wanted for Murder 46. Temptation Harbour 47. Queen of Spades 48, etc.

Acord, Art (1890–1931). American star of silent westerns: The Squaw Man 13. A Man Afraid of his Wardrobe 15. The Moon Riders 20. In the Days of Buffalo Bill 21. The Oregon Trail 23. The Call of Courage 25. Rustler's Ranch 26. Sky High Corral 26. Hard Fists 27. Loco Luck 27. Two Gun O'Brien 28. Bullets and Justice 29. Wyoming Tornado 29, etc. Sound ended his career.

Acosta, Rodolfo (1920–1974). Cold-eyed Mexican-American character actor, a frequent western villain or henchman.
The Fugitive 48. One Way Street 50. Yankee Buccaneer 52. Hondo 54. Bandido 56. The Tijuana Story (leading role) 57. Flaming Star 60. How the West Was Won 62. Rio Conchos 64. Return of the Seven 66. Flap 70. The Great White Hope 70, many others.
TV series: High Chaparral 67.

Acres, Birt (1854–1918). British cinematograph pioneer, American born, later projector manufacturer. Claimed to be the first producer of cinema films in Britain, his titles include: Haycart Crossing, Hadley 94. The Derby 95. Boxing Kangaroo 96. A Visit to the Zoo 96. Princess Maud's Wedding 96. An Unfriendly Call 97.

acting

¶ A short selection of attitudes.
George Sanders: Acting is like roller skating. Once you know how to do it, it is neither stimulating nor exciting.
Anthony Quinn: In Europe an actor is an artist. In Hollywood, if he isn't working, he's a bum.
Alfred Lunt: The secret of my success? I speak in a loud clear voice and try not to bump into the furniture.
Ethel Barrymore: We who play, who entertain for a few years, what can we leave that will last?
Alfred Hitchcock: Actors are cattle.
NB. When attacked for this remark Hitch claimed he had been misquoted: what he really said was: 'Actors should be *treated* like cattle.'
Charles Chaplin: Film acting is unquestionably a director's medium.
NB. Chaplin used to advise his silent actors: 'Don't sell it. Remember they're *peeking* at you.'
Dorothy Parker: Scratch an actor—and you'll find an actress.
Paul Newman: Acting is a question of absorbing other people's personalities and adding some of your own experience.
F. W. Marnau: Don't act—think!
Cedric Hardwicke: Actors and burglars work better at night.
Walter Matthau: I always had one ear offstage, listening for the call from the bookie.
Humphrey Bogart: The only thing you owe the public is a good performance.
Anita Loos: Joan Crawford is the only actress to read the whole script. Most actresses just read their own lines to find out what clothes they're going to wear.
Jane Fonda: You spend all your life trying to do something they put people in asylums for.
Jean-Louis Trintignant: The best actors in the world are those who feel the most and show the least.
George Raft: I'm afraid to look, because I'm probably awful.
John Barrymore: There are lots of methods. Mine involves a lot of talent, a glass, and some cracked ice.
Laurence Olivier: The main problem of the actor is not to let the audience go to sleep, then wake up and go home feeling they've wasted their money.
Shirley Booth: Acting is a way to overcome your own inhibitions and shyness. The writer creates a strong, confident personality, and that's what you become—unfortunately, only for the moment.
Will Rogers: The movies are the only business where you can go out front and applaud yourself.
Claude Rains: I learn the lines and pray to God.
John Wayne: Talk low, talk slow, and don't say too much.
Alec Guinness: First wipe your nose and check your flies.

action still. A photograph of a scene as it actually appears in the film as opposed to one specially posed for publicity purposes. Sometimes called a frame blow-up. In TV, an 'action stills' programme has come to mean one consisting of still photographs given a semblance of life by camera movement.

actor-directors were rare until around 1950 but are becoming increasingly common. Those who have dared to direct themselves include Woody Allen, Alan Arkin, Sergei Bondartchuk, Marlon Brando, Mel Brooks, Richard Burton, Richard Carlson, John Cassavetes, Charles Chaplin (always), John Clements, Jean Cocteau, William Conrad, Noel Coward, Jules Dassin, John Derek, Clint Eastwood, Pierre Etaix, Jose Ferrer, Mel Ferrer, Albert Finney, Peter Fonda, Al Freeman Jnr, Hugo Haas, Laurence Harvey, David Hemmings, Paul Henreid, Charlton Heston, Dennis Hopper, Robert Hossein, Leslie Howard, Robert Hutton, Buster Keaton, Gene Kelly, Burt Lancaster, Stan Laurel, Jerry Lewis, Peter Lorre, Ida Lupino, Burgess Meredith, Ray Milland, George Montgomery, Robert Montgomery, Anthony Newley, Paul Newman, Edmond O'Brien, Dennis O'Keefe, Laurence Olivier, Nigel Patrick, Carl Reiner, Ralph Richardson, Peter Sellers, Frank Sinatra, Mark Stevens, Jacques Tati, Peter Ustinov, Erich von Stroheim, Tom Walls, John Wayne, Orson Welles, Cornel Wilde.

Many of these gave up after one attempt, and might well have had more sustained directorial careers if, like the following, they had stuck to directing other actors: Richard Attenborough, Lionel Barrymore, James Cagney, Ricardo Cortez, Helmut Dantine, Richard Haydn, Lionel Jeffries, Alf Kjellin, Charles Laughton, Jack Lemmon, Ida Lupino, Roddy McDowall, Karl Malden, Walter Matthau, Elaine May, John Mills, Gene Nelson, Jack Nicholson, Dick Powell, Anthony Quinn, Cliff Robertson, Mickey Rooney, Don Taylor, Marshall Thompson, Mai Zetterling.

On the whole, however, perhaps the lesson of the lists is that actors should stick to acting.

? The following films were directed by people at least equally well known as actors. Can you name them?

1 *The Gangster Story* (1958)
2 *The Conqueror* (1956)
3 *Night of the Hunter* (1955)
4 *Miss Tatlock's Millions* (1948)
5 *The Amazing Mr Blunden* (1972)
6 *Sky West and Crooked* (1966) (US title: *Gypsy Girl*)
7 *Madame X* (1929)
8 *Time Limit* (1957)
9 *Short Cut to Hell* (1957)
10 *Tam Lin* (1970)
11 *Breezy* (1973)
12 *Die Verlorene* (1950)
13 *Charlie Bubbles* (1967)
14 *A Man Alone* (1955)
15 *A Guide for the Married Man* (1967)
16 *The Lady in the Lake* (1947)
17 *Running Scared* (1972)
18 *Antony and Cleopatra* (1971)
19 *On Approval* (1944)
20 *Kotch* (1971)
21 *Buck and the Preacher* (1971)
22 *My True Story* (1951)
23 *Young Winston* (1972)
24 *The Lost Moment* (1948)
25 *The Secret Fury* (1950)
26 *The Great Man* (1956)
27 *Little Murders* (1971)
28 *Rachel, Rachel* (1968)
29 *Dead Ringer* (1964)
30 *The Kentuckian* (1955)
31 *None But the Brave* (1965)
32 *Man Trap* (1961)
33 *Home at Seven* (1953) (US title: *Murder on Monday*)
34 *Beach Red* (1967)
35 *The Ceremony* (1963)

actors have seldom been the subject of biopics. Anna Neagle appeared as Peg Woffington, with Cedric Hardwicke as David Garrick, in *Peg of Old Drury* 35, and Garrick was played by Brian Aherne in *The Great Garrick* 37. Miriam Hopkins was Mrs Leslie Carter in *Lady with Red Hair* 41, Charlie Ruggles (of all people) played Otis Skinner in *Our Hearts Were Young and Gay* 44, Richard Burton was Edwin Booth in *Prince of Players* 54, and Kim Novak was *Jeanne Eagels* 56. The sixties brought Julie Andrews and Daniel Massey as Gertie Lawrence and Noel Coward in *Star!* Of the idols of its own creation, Hollywood has so far given us biographies of Valentino, Jean Harlow, Lon Chaney, Diana and John Barrymore, Lillian Roth, Buster Keaton, Pearl White, W. C. Fields and Gable and Lombard.

actors in common

? What do the following actors have in common, as far as film roles are concerned?

1 Edward Everett Horton, Bob Hope, Charles Laughton

2 Sheldon Lewis, Paul Massie, Spencer Tracy
3 Fredric March, Cedric Hardwicke, Maria Casares
4 Ilona Massey, Cedric Hardwicke, Basil Rathbone
5 Melvyn Douglas, Lew Ayres, Charles Boyer, John Gilbert, Fredric March
6 Henry Fonda, Raymond Massey, Walter Huston
7 George Montgomery, Elliott Gould, Robert Montgomery
8 Paulette Goddard, Claire Bloom, Martha Raye, Dawn Addams
9 Bette Davis, Tallulah Bankhead, Elisabeth Bergner
10 Charles Boyer, Ray Milland, Joseph Cotten, Ralph Richardson, Trevor Howard
11 Joan Fontaine, Jack Lemmon, Susan Hayward, Ray Milland
12 Bette Davis, Ronald Colman, Olivia de Havilland, Douglas Fairbanks Jnr
13 Charles Laughton, Anthony Quinn, Lon Chaney
14 Donald Cook, Eddie Quillan, Ralph Bellamy, William Gargan
15 Red Skelton, Stuart Erwin, Creighton Hale
16 Lyn Harding, George Zucco, Henry Daniell
17 Barry K. Barnes, David Niven, Leslie Howard
18 Joan Fontaine, Rosamund John, Jean Arless, Diane Baker
19 Charles Boyer, Herbert Lom, Rod Steiger
20 Herbert Lom, Lon Chaney, Claude Rains
21 Irene Dunne, Samantha Eggar, Deborah Kerr
22 Cedric Hardwicke, Peter Finch, Laurence Olivier
23 Anthony Quinn, Alec Guinness, Rex Harrison
24 Claude Rains, Louis Calhern, Warren William
25 Nick Adams, Lawrence Tierney, Warren Oates
26 Danny Kaye, Michael Redgrave, Erich von Stroheim
27 Louis Hayward, George Sanders, Jean Marais
28 Bernard Punsley, Bobby Jordan, Gabriel Dell
29 Ronald Colman, John Howard, Richard Johnson
30 Glenn Strange, Kiwi Kingston, Bela Lugosi

The Actors' Studio. Lee Strasberg's drama school in New York was well publicized during the fifties as the source of 'method' acting, which was practised by Marlon Brando among others. It corresponded closely with the Stanislavsky system: actors underwent curious mental exercises to assimilate themselves into their characters. Originally founded in 1947 by Elia Kazan and Cheryl Crawford, it now seems to have been more fashionable than influential, and after Strasberg's death in 1982 its mention was greeted by many people with a faint smile.

ACTT. The Association of Cinematograph, Television and Allied Technicians, a British trade union.

Acuff, Eddie (1902–1956). American supporting comedian, remembered as the postman in the *Blondie* series.
Shipmates Forever 35. The Petrified Forest 36. The Boys from Syracuse 40. Hellzapoppin 41. Guadalcanal Diary 43. It Happened Tomorrow 44. The Flying Serpent 46. Blondie's Big Moment 47, scores of others.

Adair, Jean (1872–1953). American stage actress best remembered by film fans as one of the sweetly murderous aunts in *Arsenic and Old Lace*.
□In the Name of the Law 22. Advice to the Lovelorn 33. *Arsenic and Old Lace* 44. Something in the Wind 46. Living in a Big Way 47.

Adam, Alfred (1909–1982). French character actor, usually of weak or villainous roles.
La Kermesse Héroique 35. Carnet de Bal 37. Boule de Suif 45. La Ferme du Pendu 48. The Witches of Salem 56. Maigret Sets a Trap 61. Le Président 61. Vivre sa Vie 62. La Vie Conjugale 63. Les Fêtes Galantes 65. Que la Fête Commence 74, etc.

Adam, Ken (1921–). British art director, in films from 1947. The sixties were for him a period of spectacular inventiveness.
Queen of Spades 48. Around the World in Eighty Days 56. The Trials of Oscar Wilde 60. *Dr Strangelove* 63. *Goldfinger* 64. The Ipcress File 65. Thunderball 65. Funeral in Berlin 66. *You Only Live Twice* 67. Chitty Chitty Bang Bang 68. Goodbye Mr Chips 69. The Owl and the Pussycat 70. Sleuth 72. Live and Let Die 73. Barry Lyndon 75. The Seven Per Cent Solution 76. The Spy Who Loved

Me 77. Moonraker 79. Pennies from Heaven 80. King David 84. Agnes of God 85. Crimes of the Heart 86, etc.

Adam, Ronald (1896–1979). British character actor specializing in well-bred but stuffy professional men.
The Drum 38. Escape to Danger 43. Green for Danger 46. Bonnie Prince Charlie 48. Angels One Five 51. Private's Progress 55. Reach for the Sky 56. Cleopatra 62. The Tomb of Ligeia 64. Who Killed the Cat? 66. Zeppelin 71, many others.
†Adam was also a busy writer, his best-remembered work being the play *An English Summer*, about the Battle of Britain.

Adams, Beverly (1945–). Canadian-born leading lady in Hollywood films.
Winter a GoGo 63. The New Interns 64. *The Silencers* 66. Birds Do It 66. Murderers' Row 66. The Torture Garden (GB) 67. The Ambushers 67, etc.

Adams, Brooke (1949–). American leading lady of the *jolie laide* type; showed more promise than performance.
Shock Waves 77. Invasion of the Body Snatchers 78. *Days of Heaven* 78. The First Great Train Robbery 79. A Man, a Woman and a Bank 79. Cuba 79. Tell Me a Riddle 80. The Dead Zone 83. Almost You 84. Key Exchange 84. The Stuff 85.

Adams, Casey (1917–). See under *Max Showalter* (his real name, which he has recently used).

Adams, Dorothy (c. 1915–). American character actress, usually of timorous or sullen ladies.
Broadway Musketeers 38. The Flame of New Orleans 41. Laura 44. The Best Years of Our Lives 46. The Foxes of Harrow 48. Carrie 52. Three for Jamie Dawn 56. The Big Country 58. From the Terrace 60. Peeper 76, etc.

Adams, Edie (1929–) (Elizabeth Edith Enke). Pert American singer-comedienne, widow of Ernie Kovacs.
□*The Apartment* 60. Lover Come Back 62. Call Me Bwana 63. It's a Mad Mad Mad Mad World 63. Under the Yum Yum Tree 63. *Love with the Proper Stranger* 64. The Best Man 64. Made in Paris 66. The Oscar 66. *The Honey Pot* 67. Box Office 82.
TV work includes: Evil Roy Slade 71. The Return of Joe Forrester 75. Word Games (Mrs Columbo) 79.

Adams, Gerald Drayson (1904–). Canadian screenwriter, former literary agent.
Dead Reckoning 47. The Big Steal 49. The Golden Horde 51. Flaming Feather 51. The Black Sleep 56. Kissing Cousins 64. Harum Scarum 65, many others.

Adams, Jane (1921–). American actress of the forties.
House of Dracula 45. Gunman's Code 46. The Brute Man 46. Batman and Robin 49.

Adams, Jill (1931–). Pert British leading lady, former model, who decorated a number of lightweight films in the fifties.
The Young Lovers 54. Doctor at Sea 55. Private's Progress 55. The Green Man 56. Brothers in Law 57. Carry On Constable 60. Doctor in Distress 63. Promise Her Anything 66, etc.

Adams, Julie (formerly Julia) (1926–) (Betty May Adams). American leading lady in Hollywood from 1947. Her essentially soft and sympathetic nature made the slight change of first name seem especially apt.
Hollywood Story 51. Bright Victory 51. Bend of the River 52. Mississippi Gambler 53. The Creature from the Black Lagoon 54. One Desire 55. Away All Boats 56. Slaughter on Tenth Avenue 57. Raymie 60. Tickle Me 65. Valley of Mystery 67. The Last Movie 71. McQ 72. The McCullochs 75. Killer Force 76. The Killer Inside Me 76, etc.
TV series: Yancey Derringer 58. The Jimmy Stewart Show 71. Code Red 81.

Adams, Maud (sometimes **Maude**) (1945–) (Maud Wikstrom). Persistently promising Swedish-American leading lady of the seventies.
The Christian Licorice Store 71. Rollerball 74. The Man with the Golden Gun 74. Killer Force 76. Tattoo 81. Octopussy 83. The Boys in the Band 70. Playing for Time (TV) 80. Nairobi Affair (TV) 85, etc.

Adams, Nick (1931–1968) (Nicholas Adamschock). American leading man who usually played neurotic or aggressive types; never quite made the big time.
Somebody Love Me (debut) 52. Mister Roberts 55. *No Time for Sergeants* 58. Pillow Talk 59. Hell is for Heroes 62. The Hook 63. Twilight of Honor 63. Monster of Terror (GB) 66. Young Dillinger 66. Frankenstein Conquers the World (Jap.) 66. Fever Heat 67, etc.
TV series: The Rebel 59–60.

Adam's Rib. 1. US 1923: Cecil B. de Mille marital drama with flashbacks to Genesis. 2. US 1949: brittle sex comedy with Spencer Tracy and Katharine Hepburn as married lawyers on opposite sides of a case. Written by Ruth Gordon and Garson Kanin, with neat direction by George Cukor, it introduced in supporting roles four striking newcomers: David Wayne, Jean Hagen, Tom Ewell and Judy Holliday.
A 1973 TV series featured Ken Howard and Blythe Danner.

Adams, Richard (1920–). British best-selling novelist who sees the world from the animals' point of view. His *Watership Down* and *The Plague Dogs* were somewhat unsatisfactorily turned into cartoon features.

Adams, Robert (1906–). West Indian Negro actor, former teacher, prominent in British films of the forties.
Sanders of the River (debut) 35. King Solomon's Mines 37. Caesar and Cleopatra 45. Men of Two Worlds (leading role) 47. Old Mother Riley's Jungle Treasure 52. Man of Africa 52. Sapphire 59, etc.

Adams, Stanley (1915–1977). American character actor.
The Atomic Kid 54. Hell on Frisco Bay 56. Breakfast at Tiffany's 61. Nevada Smith 66. The Clones 74, etc.

Adams, Tom (1938–). Burly British leading man whose career might have flourished better in the fifties.
The Great Escape 63. Licensed to Kill 65. Where the Bullets Fly 66. The Fighting Prince of Donegal 66. Fathom 67. Subterfuge 69. The Fast Kill 72. The Onedin Line (TV) 79. Mask of the Devil (TV) 84.
TV series: Spy Trap 75.

Adamson, Harold (1906–1980). American lyricist, usually with Jimmy McHugh.
Dancing Lady 33. Kid Millions 34. Suzy 36. That Certain Age 38. Nob Hill 45. If You Knew Susie 48. Gentlemen Prefer Blondes 52. An Affair to Remember 57, many others.

Adamson, Joy (1910–1980). Austrian-born wild-life expert who wrote *Born Free* and *Living Free*. A long-time resident of Kenya, she was mysteriously murdered.

adaptations. A high proportion of feature films have been adapted from other media. A poem was the basis of *The Set-Up*, but mostly the studios have raided novels and plays for their material. The cost of such rights used to be minimal, but can now run into millions of dollars, the rights to *Annie* having allegedly cost a quarter of the film's thirty-five million dollar budget. A bonus however has appeared in the form of television mini-series, which thirty or forty years after the film version, when the original material would be unfashionable with film audiences, have started the money flowing again for such items as *My Cousin Rachel*, *The Citadel* and *How Green Was My Valley*.

At one time Hollywood had the reputation of using only the title of the items it bought. Certainly the Bulldog Drummond and Sherlock Holmes series bore little relation to the stories on which they were allegedly based: it seemed to be a point of honour with screenwriters to do better (if they could). *The Grapes of Wrath* was given an upbeat ending. *Pride and Prejudice* had its period advanced fifty years to a time when the fashions were more alluring. *Wuthering Heights* lost its second half. *Rebecca* reduced its hero from a murderer to an accessory after the fact. *Foreign Correspondent* took not a single incident from its alleged basis, *Personal History* by Vincent Sheean. *Forever Amber*'s heroine became far more sinned against than sinning. *These Three* was adapted by Lillian Hellman from her own play *The Children's Hour*, but she had to change the central relationship from lesbian to heterosexual. *The Killers* wore out Hemingway's short story in the first ten minutes, and filled out the next ninety with new material. *Forbidden Planet* placed the plot of Shakespeare's *The Tempest* in outer space. Graham Greene's *The Quiet American* saw its point exactly reversed. Bernard Shaw was persuaded to add a happy ending (now the accepted one) to his anti-romantic *Pygmalion*. And Noel Coward's *Design for Living* saw the light of day in Hollywood with only one line intact, allegedly 'Kippers on toast'.

It has to be admitted that some excellent films have resulted from this tampering, and 'rearrangement' may seem in many cases preferable to the too-literal transcriptions in recent years of such properties as *Sleuth*, *The Best Whorehouse in Texas*, the Neil Simon comedies, and *Death Trap*, in which last case a new twist ending was added, but so lamely that the audience failed to grasp it.

Among the most skilled adapters from the 'golden age' are Dudley Nichols, Ben Hecht, Jules Furthman, Lamar Trotti, Philip Dunne, Casey Robinson, Samson Raphaelson, R. C. Sherriff, John Balderston and Donald Ogden Stewart.

Addams, Dawn (1930–85). Smart and glamorous British leading lady in international films. Films mainly unremarkable.
Night into Morning 51. Plymouth Adventure 52. The Robe 53. The Moon Is Blue 53. Khyber Patrol 54. A King in New York 57. The Silent Enemy 58. The Two Faces of Dr Jekyll 60. The Black Tulip 64. Ballad in Blue 65. Where the Bullets Fly 66. Vampire Lovers 70. Sappho 70. Vault of Horror 73, etc.
TV series: Star Maidens 77.

Adams, Charles (1912–). American cartoonist of ghoulish humour, much in The New Yorker from 1940. TV in 1964–65 ran *The Addams Family*, about creepy characters in a cobwebby house; with regard to films he is best remembered for his remark on attending the premiere of Cleopatra: 'I only came to see the asp.

Addinsell, Richard (1904–77). British composer.
The Amateur Gentleman 36. Fire over England 37. Goodbye Mr Chips 39. Gaslight 40. *Dangerous Moonlight* (including 'Warsaw Concerto') 40. Love on the Dole 41. Blithe Spirit 45. Scrooge 51. Beau Brummell 54. The Prince and the Showgirl 57. The Admirable Crichton 57. The Waltz of the Toreadors 62, etc.

Addison, John (1920–). British composer, in films from 1948.
The Guinea Pig 49. Seven Days to Noon 50. The Man Between 53. Private's Progress 55. *Reach for the Sky* 56. Lucky Jim 57. I Was Monty's Double 58. Look Back in Anger 59. The Entertainer 60. A Taste of Honey 61. The Loneliness of the Long Distance Runner 62. *Tom Jones* (AA) 63. Guns at Batasi 64. Moll Flanders 65. Torn Curtain 66. A Fine Madness 66. The Honey Pot 67. Smashing Time 67. Country Dance 70. Mr Forbush and the Penguins 71. Sleuth 72. Dead Cert 74. A Bridge Too Far 77. The Seven Per Cent Solution 77. Centennial (TV) 78. Pearl (TV) 80. Strange Invaders 83. The Ultimate Solution of Grace Quigley 84. Then into TV movies.

addresses which have formed film titles include *13 West Street, 13 Rue Madeleine, 13 East Street, 13 Demon Street* (TV), *Ten North Frederick, 10 Rillington Place, 15 Maiden Lane, 26 Acacia Avenue, 99 River Street* and *711 Ocean Drive*. Then there were *42nd Street, 52nd Street* and *The House on 92nd Street*, not to mention *Flamingo Road, Stallion Road, Madison Avenue, Rue de l'Estrapade, Montparnasse 19, Quai des Orfèvres, Piccadilly, Bond Street, St Martin's Lane,* etc. Nor should one forget Anna Neagle's London series: *Piccadilly Incident, The Courtneys of Curzon Street, Spring in Park Lane, I Live in Grosvenor Square* and *Maytime in Mayfair*. A clever scheme for disposing of an enemy was worked out in *Address Unknown*.

Addy, Wesley (1912–). Thin American character actor, usually of humourless or sinister appearance.
The First Legion 51. My Six Convicts 52. Kiss Me Deadly 55. The Big Knife 55. Timetable 57. The Garment Jungle 58. Ten Seconds to Hell 59. Whatever Happened to Baby Jane 62. *Seconds* 66. Mister Buddwing 66. The Grissom Gang 71. Network 76. The Europeans 79. The Verdict 82. The Bostonians 84, many others.

Adjani, Isabelle (1955–). Franco-German leading lady of international films in the late seventies.
Faustine 71. The Slap 74. *The Story of Adèle H* 75. The Tenant 76. Barocco 77. The Driver 78. Nosferatu 78. The Brontë Sisters 79. Clara et les Chics Types 80. Possession 80. Quartet 81. One Deadly Summer 83. Subway 85, etc.

Adler, Buddy (1906–1960) (Maurice Adler). American producer, with Columbia from 1948, Fox from 1954 (head of studio from 1956). *The Dark Past* 48. No Sad Songs for Me 50. Salome 53. *From Here to Eternity* (AA) 53. Violent Saturday 55. *Love is a Many Splendored Thing* 55. The Left Hand of God 55. Bus Stop 56. Anastasia 56. A Hatful of Rain 57. South Pacific 58. *The Inn of the Sixth Happiness* 58, etc.

Adler, Jay (1899–1978). American character actor, brother of Luther Adler; usually played hoboes, small-time gangsters, etc.
No Time to Marry 38. My Six Convicts 52. 99 River Street 54. The Big Combo 55. Sweet Smell of Success 57. The Brothers Karamazov 58. Seven Guns to Mesa 60. The Family Jewels 65, many others.

Adler, Larry (1914–). American harmonica virtuoso whose chief contribution to films is the score of *Genevieve* 53; also composed for *The Hellions* 61. *The Hook* 63. *King and Country* 63. *High Wind in Jamaica* 64; and appeared in *St Martin's Lane* 38. *Music for Millions* 44.

Adler, Luther (1903–84) (Lutha Adler). Heavy-featured American character actor, member of well-known theatrical family (brother Jay, sister Stella).
□Lancer Spy 37. Cornered 45. Saigon 48. The Loves of Carmen 48. *Wake of the Red Witch* 48. House of Strangers 49. D.O.A. 50. South Sea Sinner 50. Under My Skin 50. Kiss Tomorrow Goodbye 50. M 51. The Magic Face (as Hitler) 51. The Desert Fox 51. Hoodlum Empire 52. The Tall Texan 53. The Miami Story 54. Crashout 55. The Girl in the Red Velvet Swing 55. Hot Blood 56. The Last Angry Man 59. Cast a Giant Shadow 66. *The Brotherhood* 68. Crazy Joe 74. Murph the Surf 74. The Man in the Glass Booth 75. Mean Johnny Barrows 75. Voyage of the Damned 76. Absence of Malice 81.
TV series: The Psychiatrist 71. Also many guest appearances, especially in Naked City.

Adler, Renata (–). American film critic for the *New York Times* from the sixties. Book: *A Year in the Dark* 70.

Adler, Richard (1921–). American composer and lyricist who with his partner Jerry Ross (1926–55) (Jerold Rosenberg) wrote *The Pajama Game* and *Damn Yankees*.

Adler, Stella (1895–). American stage actress, sister of Luther and Jay Adler. Known at one time as Stella Ardler.
Love on Toast 38. Shadow of the Thin Man 41. My Girl Tisa 48.

The Admirable Crichton. Barrie's comedy, about master and man reversing roles after being shipwrecked on a desert island, has long fascinated film-makers. (Goldwyn is said to have lost interest after discovering that it was not what it sounded, a naval drama.) De Mille filmed it in 1919 as *Male and Female*, with Thomas Meighan and Gloria Swanson; a musical version, *We're Not Dressing*, turned up in 1934 with Bing Crosby and Carole Lombard; a further variation, *Our Girl Friday*, was filmed by Noel Langley in 1953 starring Kenneth More and Joan Collins; and in 1957 Kenneth More and Diane Cilento appeared in a more or less straight version of the play, under its original title, directed by Lewis Gilbert. More also appeared on the stage in a musical adaptation, *Our Man Crichton*.

Adolfi, John G. (1888–1933). American director at his peak in the transitional period between silent and sound. Began as an actor, but quickly turned to directing and found steady work. Three years before his death he formed an association with George Arliss and filmed the star's stage successes.
A Man and His Mate 15. The Sphinx 16. A Modern Cinderella 17. A Child of the Wild 17. Queen of the Sea 18. Who's Your Brother 19. The Darling of the Rich 22. The Little Red Schoolhouse 23. Chalk Marks 24. The Phantom Express 25. The Checkered Flag 26. Husband Hunters 27. The Little Snob 28. Fancy Baggage 29. The Show of Shows 29. Dumbbells in Ermine 30. Sinner's Holiday 30. College Lovers 30. The Millionaire 31. Alexander Hamilton 31. Compromised 31. The Man Who Played God 32. A Successful Calamity 32. Central Park 32. The King's Vacation 33. The Working Man 33. Voltaire 33, many others.

Adoree, Renee (1898–1933) (Jeanne de la Fonté). French leading lady, former circus bareback rider, who became an exotic star of Hollywood films in the twenties but could not transfer to sound and died of tuberculosis.
The Strongest 20. Made in Heaven 21. Monte Cristo 22. The Eternal Struggle 23. Women Who Give 24. The Bandolero 24. Man and Maid 25. Exchange of Wives 25. *The Big Parade* 25. La Bohème 26. The Exquisite Sinner 26. Tin Gods 26. The Flaming Forest 26. Heaven on Earth 27. Mr Wu 27. On ze Boulevard 27. Back to God's Country 27. The Cossacks 28. The Michigan Kid 28. The Mating Call 28. The Pagan 29. Tide of Empire 29. Redemption 30. Call of the Flesh 30.

Adorf, Mario (1930–). Swiss actor in European films.
The Girl Rosemarie 59. Station Six Sahara 63. Major Dundee (US) 65. Ten Little Indians 66. The Red Tent 71. Journey to Vienna 73. Fedora 78. L'Empreinte des Greantes 80. Lola 81. The Tin Drum 79. Smiley's People (TV) 80. Marco Polo (TV) 81, etc.

Adreon, Franklin (1902–). American second feature director.
Canadian Mounties vs Atomic Invaders (serial) 53. No Man's Woman 55. This Man Is Armed 56. Hell's Crossroads 57. The Steel Whip 58. The Nun and the Sergeant 62. Cyborg 2087 66. Dimension Five 66, etc.

Adrian (1903–1959) (Adrian Adolph Greenberg). American costume designer, with MGM 1927–42 and credited with the authentic images of Garbo, Shearer, Harlow, etc. Married Janet Gaynor; later opened his own fashion establishment.

Adrian, Iris (1913–) (I. A. Hostetter). American character actress, former Ziegfeld Follies dancer, familiar from the early thirties as wisecracking or tawdry blonde.
Paramount on Parade 30. Rumba 35. Our Relations 37. Professional Bride 41. The G-String Murders 42. Spotlight Scandals 44. I'm from Arkansas 45. Road to Alcatraz 46. The Paleface 48. G.I. Jane 51. Highway Dragnet 54. The Buccaneer 59. That Darn Cat 65. The Odd Couple 68. Scandalous John 71. The Shaggy D.A. 76. Murder Can Hurt You (TV) 78. Herbie Goes Bananas 80, many others.
TV series: The Ted Knight Show 78.

Adrian, Max (1902–1973) (Max Bor). Irish stage actor of high camp personality; latterly a star of mischievous revue and an impersonator of Bernard Shaw. Too richly flavoured to star in films, but made occasional character appearances.
□The Primrose Path 34. Eight Cylinder Love 34. A Touch of the Moon 36. To Catch a Thief 36. Nothing Like Publicity 36. The Happy Family 37. When the Devil Was Well 37. Why Pick on Me 37. Macushla 38. Merely Mr Hawkins 38. *Kipps* 41. Penn of Pennsylvania 41. *The Young Mr Pitt* 42. Talk About Jacqueline 42. Henry V 45. Her Favourite Husband 50. Pool of London 51. The Pickwick Papers 52. *Dr Terror's House of Horrors* 65. *The Deadly Affair* 66. Funeral in Berlin 66. Julius Caesar 70. The Music Lovers 70. The Devils 71. *The Boy Friend* 71.

advertising appears seldom as a background to movies, but when it does, satire is usually in the air, as in *Christmas in July, The Hucksters, Mr Blandings Builds His Dream House, It Should Happen To You, Lover Come Back, Good Neighbour Sam, How to Succeed in Business without Really Trying* and *Putney Swope*. It was played fairly straight in *Madison Avenue* and *The Narrowing Circle*.

Aerograd (USSR 1935). An influential propaganda piece, written and directed by Dovzhenko in the guise of a melodrama about interference by Japanese spies in the building of a Siberian airport.

aeroplanes: see *airplanes*

The Affairs of Anatol (US 1921). A famous comedy of manners from Cecil B. de Mille's early period. Starring Wallace Reid and Gloria Swanson, it was adapted from a Schnitzler play about a newly married man who spends too much time sorting out other people's affairs instead of his own.

The African Queen (GB 1951). Immensely popular film version of C. S. Forester's yarn about a hard-bitten skipper and a prim spinster who become heroes—and lovers—during a perilous escape down an African river in 1915. Directed by John Huston from James Agee's script, with rich performances from Humphrey Bogart (AA) and Katharine Hepburn. Sam Spiegel was one of the first producers to submit Hollywood stars to the rigours of real African locations; and under the circumstances Jack Cardiff's photography is a remarkable achievement.

In the mid-seventies there was a failed attempt to turn the situation into a TV series with Warren Oates; while John Wayne and Katharine Hepburn in *Rooster Cogburn* could almost be called a rip-off.

Agar, John (1921–). American leading man, once married to Shirley Temple; mainly in low-budgeters.
Fort Apache 48. Sands of Iwo Jima 49. The Magic Carpet 52. The Golden Mistress 53. Bait 54. Joe Butterfly 56. Daughter of Dr Jekyll 57. The Brain from Planet Arous 58. Journey to the Seventh Planet 61. Of Love and Desire 63. Cavalry Command 65. Waco 66. The St Valentine's Day Massacre 67. The Curse of the Swamp Creature 67. The Undefeated 69. Big Jake 71. King Kong 76, etc.

Agate, James (1877–1947). British drama critic with a passion for Sarah Bernhardt. He performed some reluctant stints of film reviewing, and the results are compiled in two volumes of *Around Cinema.* They show him as a highbrow waffler rather than a wit, and no real appreciation of the art of film comes through.

L' Age d'Or (France 1930). A surrealist film by Luis Buñuel and Salvador Dali, denigrating mankind and modern society in a succession of more or less unrelated sequences. Widely banned for alleged sacrilege and indecency, it now seems obscurely dull rather than sensational.

Agee, James (1909–1955). One of America's most respected film critics, he also wrote novels and screenplays (e.g. *The African Queen* 51). A posthumous collection

of his reviews was published under the title 'Agee on Film', and the screenplays followed. His novel *A Death in the Family* was filmed in 1963 as *All the Way Home*.
❁ For his brief, witty, incisive reviews which perfectly encapsulate hundreds of forties films.

agent. An intermediary who acts on behalf of talent and takes ten per cent (rising to fifteen) of the rewards. Agents were partly blamed for the decline of Hollywood because many were too concerned to increase their clients' income, and therefore their own, at the expense of sound economic film-making. Some also became producers, though few succeeded.
†When agent Leland Hayward married his client Margaret Sullavan, a friend cabled him: 'Congratulations on getting the other ninety per cent.'
¶ *Alva Johnston:* An agent is a guy who is sore because an actor gets ninety per cent of what he makes.

Ager, Cecelia (1898–1981). American critic for various New York magazines in the thirties. Wrote a book of essays, *Let's Go to the Pictures*.

Agfacolor. German multilayer colour process, widely used in Europe and basically the same as Russian Sovcolor and American Anscocolor (which became Metrocolor). Noted for softness and often lack of sharpness.

Agostini, Philippe (1910–). French cinematographer. Carnet de Bal (co-ph) 37. Les Anges du Pêche 43. Les Dames du Bois de Boulogne 44. Les Portes de la Nuit 46. Pattes Blanches 48. Le Plaisir (co-ph) 51. Rififi 55, etc. Directed Le Dialogue des Carmélites 59. La Soupe aux Poulets 60, etc.

Agutter, Jenny (1952–). British actress who came to leading roles as a teenager.
□East of Sudan 64. Gates to Paradise 67. Star! 68. I Start Counting 69. *The Railway Children* 70. Walkabout 70. The Snow Goose (TV) 71. A War of Children (TV) 72. Logan's Run 76. The Eagle Has Landed 77. Equus 77. Dominique 78. China Nine Liberty Thirty Seven 78. The Riddle of the Sands 79. Sweet William 79. The Survivor 80. Amy 81. An American Werewolf in London 81. Secret Places 84. Silas Marner (TV) 85.

Ah, Wilderness! Eugene O'Neill's gentle comedy of growing up in a small American town was produced on Broadway in 1933. In 1935 it was filmed by Clarence Brown, with Eric Linden, Lionel Barrymore, Wallace Beery and Mickey Rooney. In 1947 Rouben Mamoulian remade it as a semi-musical, *Summer Holiday*; in the same roles were Mickey Rooney, Walter Huston, Frank Morgan and Jackie Jenkins.

Aherne, Brian (1902–86). Gentle-mannered British leading man of stage and screen; resident from 1933 in Hollywood and New York, where he became the American ideal of the charming Britisher.
Autobiography 1969: *A Proper Job*. Also published in 1980 a memoir of George Sanders: *A Dreadful Man*.
□The Eleventh Commandment 24. King of the Castle 25. The Squire of Long Hadley 26. Safety First 26. A Woman Redeemed 27. *Shooting Stars* 28. Underground 29. The W Plan 30. Madame Guillotine 31. *I Was A Spy* 33. *Song Of Songs* 33. What Every Woman Knows 34. The Fountain 34. *The Constant Nymph* 34. Sylvia Scarlett 35. I Live My Life 35. *Beloved Enemy* 36. *The Great Garrick* 37. Merrily We Live 38. Captain Fury 39. *Juarez* (as Emperor Maximilian) 39. Vigil in the Night 40. *The Lady In Question* 40. Hired Wife 40. *My Son My Son* 40. The Man who Lost Himself 41. Skylark 41. Smilin' Through 41. My Sister Eileen 42. Forever and a Day 43. A Night to Remember 43. First Comes Courage 43. What a Woman! 43. The Locket 46. Smart Woman 48. Angel on the Amazon 48. *I Confess* 53. Titanic 53. Prince Valiant 54. A Bullet is Waiting 54. *The Swan* (first comic character role) 56. The Best of Everything 59. Susan Slade 61. *Lancelot and Guinevere* (as King Arthur) 63. The Waltz King 64. The Cavern 65. Rosie 67.

Aherne, Patrick (1901–1970). Irish light actor, brother of Brian Aherne; in America from 1936.
A Daughter in Revolt 25. Huntingtower 27. The Game Chicken 31. Trouble Ahead 36. Green Dolphin Street 47. The Paradine Case 48. Bwana Devil 52. The Court Jester 56, etc.

Ahlberg, Mac (–). Swedish director.
I a Woman 67. The Swedish Fanny Hill 68. The Voyeur 69. I a Woman Part Two 70. Nana 70, etc.

Ahn, Philip (1911–78). American actor of Korean parentage, seen in Hollywood films as an asssortment of Asiatic types.
The General Died at Dawn 36. Thank You Mr Moto 38. Charlie Chan in Honolulu 38.

They Got Me Covered 42. China Sky 45. Rogues' Regiment 48. I Was an American Spy 51. Love is a Many Splendored Thing 55. Never So Few 59. Diamond Head 63. Thoroughly Modern Millie 67. The World's Greatest Athlete 73. Voodoo Heartbeat 75, many others.
TV series: Kung Fu 71–73.

Aidman, Charles (1929–). American character actor, mostly on TV.
The Hour of the Gun 67. Countdown 67. Kotch 72. Dirty Little Billy 72. Amelia Earhart (TV) 76. Twilights Last Gleaming 77. Zoot Suit 81. Prime Suspect (TV) 81. Uncommon Valor 83, etc.

Aiello, Danny (1935–). American actor.
The Front 76. Fingers 77. Bloodbrothers 78. Fort Apache The Bronx 81. Once Upon a Time in America 84. The Purple Rose of Cairo 84. The Stuff 85.

Aimée, Anouk (1932–) (Françoise Sorya Dreyfus). Svelte French leading lady who captured many hearts in the days when she was known simply as 'Anouk'. She has subsequently lent her poise to many routine pictures.
La Maison sous la Mer 47. *Les Amants de Verone* 49. The Golden Salamander (GB) 49. Le Rideau Cramoisi 51. The Man Who Watched Trains Go By (GB) 52. Les Mauvaises Rencontres 55. Contraband Spain (GB) 55. Pot Bouille 56. Montparnasse 19 58. La Tête Contre les Murs 58. Les Dragueurs 59. The Journey (US) 59. La Dolce Vita 60. *Lola* 61. Sodom and Gomorrah 61. Eight and a Half 63. La Fuga 65. *Un Homme et une Femme* 66. Justine (US) 69. The Model Shop (US) 69. The Appointment (US) 69. Si C'Était à Refaire 76. Mon Premier Amour 78. The Tragedy of a Ridiculous Man 81. General of the Dead Army 83. Success is the Best Revenge 84. Long Live Life 84. A Man and a Woman: 20 Years Later 86, etc.

Aimos, Raymond (1889–1944). French general purpose actor of the thirties; died from war injuries.
Vingt Ans Après 22. Le Quatorze Juillet 32. Le Dernier Millardaire 34. Mayerling 36. Le Golem 36. La Belle Equipe 36. Quai des Brumes 38. De Mayerling à Sarajevo 40. Lumière d'Eté 42. Les Petites du Quai aux Fleurs 43, etc.

Ainley, Henry (1879–1945). British stage actor in occasional films.
She Stoops to Conquer 14. The Prisoner of Zenda 15. Rupert of Hentzau 15. The Great Adventure 15. The Manxman 16. Quinneys 19. The Prince and the Beggarmaid 21. Sweet Lavender 23. The Good Companions 32. The First Mrs Fraser 32. As You Like It 36, etc.

Ainley, Richard (1910–1967). British-born actor, son of Henry Ainley.
As You Like It 36. The Frog 37. A Stolen Life 39. Lady with Red Hair 40. The Smiling Ghost 41. White Cargo 42. Above Suspicion 43. Passage to Hong Kong 49, etc.

air balloons, of the spherical type with a hanging basket, have provided picturesque climaxes in films as diverse as *Trottie True, The Wizard of Oz* and *Charlie Bubbles*, while the initial part of the journey in *Around the World in Eighty Days* was accomplished in a splendidly ornate example of the species, and a dramatically styled version was used in *Five Weeks in a Balloon.* Balloons were popular for comic gags in silent films, notably Buster Keaton's *Balloonatic*. The most charming adaptation of the idea was in *The Red Balloon*, at the end of which a group of toy balloons carried the boy hero off into the sky; and the director of that film next made *Stowaway in the Sky*, which was about an air balloon over France. Balloons also featured in *Those Magnificent Men in Their Flying Machines, Mysterious Island, The Great Bank Robbery, Chitty Chitty Bang Bang, The Great Race.*

Barrage balloons, a familiar sight in the Britain of World War II, seldom featured in films apart from the Crazy Gang's *Gasbags*; but zeppelins or dirigibles were featured in *Dirigible* itself, *Hell's Angels, Madame Satan, The Assassination Bureau, The Red Tent, Zeppelin,* and of course in *The Hindenberg*.

Airplane! (US 1980). A cheap but effective spoof on airplane disaster movies, clearly written by young people who had grown up watching them on television, and especially the 1957 *Zero Hour*. Some of the jokes were sophomoric, many were sexual, but almost all got laughs. Written and directed by Jim Abrahams, David Zucker, Jerry Zucker; produced by Jon Davison; for Paramount; with Robert Hays, Robert Stack, Lloyd Bridges. A 1983 sequel, *Airplane II*, was surprisingly ineffective, or perhaps not surprisingly since it recycled much of the same material.

airplane deaths among film actors are few, considering the millions of airplane miles travelled annually since the majority of films began in the fifties to be made on location. Grace Moore was killed when a public plane crashed at Copenhagen Airport, and Leslie Howard was lost at sea on a semi-official flight in 1943. (Some say the Nazis shot down his plane in the belief that Churchill was aboard.) Deaths which have resulted from crashes of small private aircraft include those of Carole Lombard, Audie Murphy, Will Rogers and Robert Francis; while Vernon Castle and Phillips Holmes died in planes on active service.

airplanes, one of the most exciting inventions of the twentieth century, have naturally been a popular source of cinematic thrills. Films about aviation itself began with the newsreel shots of attempts by early birdmen, some of them with tragic results: these have been well preserved in a Robert Youngson one-reeler of the early fifties, *This Mechanical Age*. In the twenties began the long series of spectacular aerial dramas: *Wings, Hell's Angels, Dawn Patrol, Lucky Devils, Devil Dogs of the Air, F.P.1, Wings of the Navy, Men with Wings, Test Pilot, Only Angels Have Wings*. British films on aviation were rare, exceptions being the exciting *Q Planes* and Korda's ill-fated documentary *Conquest of the Air*; but 1939 brought a need to show the nation's strength, and this was done superbly in such films as *The Lion Has Wings, Squadron Leader X, Target for Tonight, The First of the Few, Coastal Command, Flying Fortress, Journey Together* and *The Way to the Stars*. When America entered the war we were deluged with aerial melodramas, mostly with high-sounding titles and high propagandist content: *Eagle Squadron, International Squadron, I Wanted Wings, Winged Victory, A Wing and a Prayer, The Wild Blue Yonder, Bombardier, God Is My Co-Pilot, Flying Tigers, Captains of the Clouds, Dive Bomber, Air Force, Flight Command, Thirty Seconds over Tokyo*, and many others. Even Disney weighed in with the instructional *Victory Through Air Power*.

During the forties began the still-continuing stream of biographies of aviation pioneers and air aces: *They Flew Alone* (Amy Johnson), *Gallant Journey* (John Montgomery), *Flight for Freedom* (Amelia Earhart), *Captain Eddie* (Eddie Rickenbacker), *The McConnell Story, Reach for the Sky* (Douglas Bader), *The Dam Busters* (Dr Barnes Wallis and Guy Gibson), *The Spirit of St Louis* (Lindbergh), *The One That Got Away* (Franz von Werra), *Wings of the Eagle* (Spig Wead), *Von Richthofen and Brown*, etc. Fictional additions to this cycle include *Ace Eli and Rodger of the Skies* and *The Great Waldo Pepper*.

Post-war air dramas from Hollywood showed a considerable increase in thoughtfulness. The responsibility of power was examined in *Command Decision, Twelve O'Clock High, The Beginning or the End, Strategic Air Command* and others, while the future of aviation was the subject of such films as *On the Threshold of Space, Towards the Unknown* and *X-15*. But there has also been room for spectaculars like *Lafayette Escadrille, Bombers B-52, The Longest Day* and *The Blue Max*, for such romantic dramas as *Blaze of Noon, Chain Lightning, Tarnished Angels* and *The Bridges at Toko-Ri*, and even for the more routine melodramatics of *Sky Commando, Battle Taxi, 633 Squadron, Sky Tiger, Jet Pilot, Flight from Ashiya* and *The Flight of the Phoenix*. Britain too has turned out routine recruiting thrillers like *The Red Beret* and *High Flight*, with a nod to civil aviation in *Out of the Clouds*; against these can be set the earnest probing of *The Sound Barrier* and *The Man in the Sky*, the affectionate nostalgia of *Angels One Five* and *Conflict of Wings*. *Airport* and its all-star sequels are in a category of their own, that of aerial multi-drama, inspired by *The High and the Mighty, Jet Over the Atlantic* and *Jetstorm* and continuing into the seventies with *Skyjacked*.

In films where aviation itself is not the main subject, planes can be used for a wide variety of dramatic purposes. In *Triumph of the Will* Hitler's arrival at Nuremberg was made to seem godlike by clever photography of his plane descending through the clouds. A very different effect was given in *The Best Years of Our Lives* which began with three war veterans being given a lift home in the nose of a bomber; and the same film, in the scene when Dana Andrews walks through a scrapyard full of the planes he has so recently been flying in the war, produced a ruefully moving sense of waste and futility. Godlike again was Raymond Massey's fleet of futuristic planes in *Things to Come*; and impeccable trick photography gave memorable punch to a musical, *Flying Down to Rio*, in which chorus girls apparently performed on the wings of planes in mid-air.

Any list of the most spectacular plane sequences should include Cary Grant being chased through the cornfield in *North by Northwest*; Claudette Colbert and Ray Milland escaping from Spain in *Arise My Love*; *King Kong* being cornered on the Empire State Building; the plane crashing into the sea in *Foreign Correspondent*; the climax of *Murphy's War*, and, of course, the climactic sequences of films already mentioned such as *Hell's Angels, The Blue Max, The Sound Barrier* and *Dawn Patrol.* Comedy flying sequences can be equally thrilling, as shown by George Formby in *It's in the Air*, Abbott and Costello in *Keep 'Em Flying*, the Marx Brothers in *A Night in Casablanca*, Laurel and Hardy in *The Flying Deuces*, Duggie Wakefield in *Spy for a Day*, Buddy Hackett and Mickey Rooney in *It's a Mad Mad Mad Mad World*, Jimmy Edwards in *Nearly a Nasty Accident*, Pat Boone in *Never Put It In Writing*, W. C. Fields in *Never Give a Sucker an Even Break*, Spencer Tracy in *State of the Union*, Jack Lemmon in *The Great Race*, Fred MacMurray (flying a Model T) in *The Absent-minded Professor*, James Stewart in *You Gotta Stay Happy*, and practically the whole cast of *Those Magnificent Men in Their Flying Machines*. Air hostesses were featured in *Come Fly With Me* and *Boeing-Boeing*.

Plane crashes have been the dramatic starting point of many films including *Lost Horizon, Five Came Back, Back from Eternity, Fate Is the Hunter, The Night My Number Came Up, Broken Journey, SOS Pacific, The Flight of the Phoenix, Sands of the Kalahari, Survive!, Hey I'm Alive* (TV) and *Family Flight* (TV). The *fear* that a plane will crash has also been a potent source of screen melodrama, especially in such films as *No Highway, The High and the Mighty, Julie, Zero Hour, Jet Storm, Jet over the Atlantic, The Night My Number Came Up,* the *Airport* series, and *Skyjacked*, which focus on the emotional reactions of passengers. The proximity of planes to heaven has been useful in fantasies like *Here Comes Mr Jordan, A Guy Named Joe, A Matter of Life and Death* and *The Flight That Disappeared.* Finally, plane-building was used as a symbol of power in *The Carpetbaggers*; and symbols of a more fearsome kind are the atomic bombers which figured so largely in *Dr Strangelove* and *Fail Safe.*

In 1980 the airplane crash or near-crash genre, which had been done to death in such TV movies as *SST: Disaster in the Sky* and *Murder on Flight 502*, was effectively parodied in *Airplane!*, which took its thread of plot from *Zero Hour* and hung onto it every airplane joke that anybody could think of. 1983's *Airplane II: The Sequel* was far less funny, and just to show that parody doesn't harm the chances of the jut-jawed stuff, along on TV soon after came *Starflight: The Plane That Couldn't Land*.

See also: *documentaries; helicopters.*

airships were historically shortlived, and being expensive to reconstruct appeared in few films and never very good ones. Some of the atmosphere can however be gained from *Madame Satan, Hell's Angels, The Assassination Bureau, Zeppelin* and *The Hindenburg*.

Aitken, Maria (1945–). Lanky British comedy actress, popular on TV. Film: Half Moon Street 87.

Aitken, Spottiswoode (1869–1933). American general purpose actor and character player of the silent screen, with much stage experience.
The Battle 11. The Avenging Conscience 14. The Birth of a Nation 14. Intolerance 15. Stage Struck 17. Her Kingdom of Dreams 19. Nomads of the North 20. The Unknown Wife 21. Manslaughter 22. The Young Rajah 22. Six Days 23. The Eagle 25. The Goose Woman 25. Roaring Fires 27, many others.

aka. A seventies abbreviation for 'also known as'.

? Simon Templar is a character better known as 'The Saint'. As what series characters would the following be more familiar?

1 Mrs Dagwood Bumstead
2 Michael Lanyard
3 Nick Charles
4 Robert Ordway
5 Carmelita Lindsay
6 Lawrence Talbot
7 Simon Sparrow
8 Bruce Wayne

Aked, Muriel (1887–1955). British character actress usually seen as comedy spinster or gossip.
A Sister to Assist 'Er 22 and 47. The Mayor's Nest 32. *Rome Express* 32. Friday the Thirteenth 33. Cottage to Let 41. Two Thousand Women 44. The Wicked Lady 45. *The Happiest Days of Your Life* 50. The Story of Gilbert and Sullivan 53, etc.

Akeley, Carl E. (1864–1926). American taxidermist and photographer, inventor in the early twenties of a tripod camera which first made steady panning possible.

Akins, Claude (1918–). Solidly built American character actor who was usually cast as a western villain until it was realized that he could just as well play a burly middle-aged hero, Wallace Beery style. In the late

seventies he was much in demand as a TV star.
□*From Here to Eternity* 53. Bitter Creek 54. The Caine Mutiny 54. The Raid 54. The Human Jungle 54. Down Three Dark Streets 54. Shield for Murder 54. The Sea Chase 55. Battle Stations 56. The Proud and Profane 56. Johnny Concho 56. The Burning Hills 56. The Sharkfighters 56. Hot Summer Night 57. The Kettles on Old Macdonald's Farm 57. The Lonely Man 57. Joe Dakota 57. The Defiant Ones 58. Onionhead 58. Rio Bravo 59. Don't Give Up the Ship 59. *Porgy and Bess* 59. Yellowstone Kelly 59. The Hound Dog Man 59. Comanche Station 60. Inherit the Wind 60. Claudelle Inglish 61. Merrill's Marauders 62. How the West Was Won 62. Black Gold 63. A Distant Trumpet 64. The Killers 64. Ride Beyond Vengeance 64. Return of the Seven 66. Incident at Phantom Hill 66. First to Fight 67. Waterhole Three 67. The Devil's Brigade 68. The Great Bank Robbery 69. Flap 70. A Man Called Sledge 71. The Night Stalker (TV) 71. Skyjacked 72. Battle for the Planet of the Apes 73. In Tandem (TV) 73. Timber Tramps 75. Tentacles 77.
TV series as star: *Movin' On* 74–75. B.J. and the Bear 79. The Misadventures of Sheriff Lobo 79.

Akins, Zoe (1886–1958). American playwright whose *The Greeks Had a Word for It* was filmed as *Gold Diggers* (qv); *The Old Maid* was later filmed with Bette Davis.
Screenplays include: Eve's Secret 25. Morning Glory 32. Camille 37. Desire Me 47.

Akst, Albert (c. 1890–1958). American editor, long at MGM.
The Raven 35. Johnny Eager 42. Meet Me in St Louis 44. Ziegfeld Follies 46. Easter Parade 48. Annie Get Your Gun 50. Royal Wedding 52. The Band Wagon 53. Moonfleet 55. Somebody Up There Likes Me 56, many others.

The Alamo, originally a cottonwood tree, gave its name to a Franciscan mission in San Antonio, where in 1836 180 Americans were overpowered and slaughtered by 4,000 Mexicans. As those who died included such legendary figures as Jim Bowie and Davy Crockett, the siege of the Alamo has figured in many a film, notably *Man of Conquest* 39, *The Last Command* 55 and *The Alamo* 60; while in *San Antonio* 45, Errol Flynn and Paul Kelly had a non-historic fight in the mission ruins.

Alazraki, Benito (1923–). Mexican director best known abroad for his 1955 film of Indian life, *Roots*.

Albee, Edward (1928–). American playwright whose only significant contribution to cinema was *Who's Afraid of Virginia Woolf?* 66. *A Delicate Balance* however was filmed in 1973.

¶ 'I have a fine sense of the ridiculous but no sense of humour' (quote from *Who's Afraid of Virginia Woolf?*)

Alberghetti, Anna Maria (1936–). Italian-American operatic singer who came to films as a teenager and has made occasional appearances.
Here Comes the Groom 51. The Stars Are Singing 53. The Medium 54. The Last Command 55. Ten Thousand Bedrooms 57. Cinderfella 60, etc.

Alberni, Luis (1887–1962). Spanish-American character actor who played countless small film roles.
Santa Fe Trail 30. Svengali 31. The Kid from Spain 32. Topaze 33. Roberta 35. Anthony Adverse 36. The Housekeeper's Daughter 39. That Hamilton Woman 42. Captain Carey USA 49. What Price Glory 52, etc.

Albers, Hans (1892–1960). Leading German actor with broad experience.
Irene d'Or 23. A Midsummer Night's Dream 25. Rasputin 29. The Blue Angel 30. Drei Tage Liebe 31. FP 1 32. Gold 33. Peer Gynt 35. Casanova 36. Baron Munchausen 43. The White Hell of Pitz Palu 53. Der Greifer 58. Kein Engel ist so Rein 60, etc.

Albert, Eddie (1908–) (Eddie Albert Heimberger). American character actor with radio and stage experience: for nearly forty years he has been playing honest Joes, nice guys and best friends, seldom winning the girl but allowing himself an occasional meaty role out of character.
□*Brother Rat* 38. On Your Toes 39. *Four Wives* 39. Brother Rat and a Baby 40. An Angel from Texas 40. My Love Came Back 40. A Dispatch from Reuters 40. Four Mothers 41. The Wagons Roll at Night 41. Out of the Fog 41. Thieves Fall Out 41. The Great Mr Nobody 41. Treat 'Em Rough 42. Eagle Squadron 42. Ladies' Day 43. Lady Bodyguard 43. Bombardier 43. Strange Voyage 45. Rendezvous with Annie 46. The Perfect Marriage 46. *Smash Up* 47. Time out of Mind 47. Hit Parade of 1947 47. The Dude Goes West 48. You Gotta Stay Happy 48.

The Fuller Brush Girl 50. Meet Me After the Show 51. You're in the Navy Now 51. Actors and Sin 52. *Carrie* 52. *Roman Holiday* 53. The Girl Rush 55. *Oklahoma!* 55. *I'll Cry Tomorrow* 55. *Attack!* (his most serious role) 56. *The Teahouse of the August Moon* 56. The Sun Also Rises 57. The Joker is Wild 57. The Gun Runners 58. *The Roots of Heaven* 58. *Orders to Kill* (GB) 58. Beloved Infidel 59. The Young Doctors 61. The Two Little Bears 61. Madison Avenue 62. The Longest Day 62. Who's Got the Action? 62. The Party's Over (GB) 63. Miracle of the White Stallions 65. Captain Newman MD 63. Seven Women 65. See the Man Run (TV) 71. Fireball Forward (TV) 72. McQ 72. The Take 72. The Heartbreak Kid 72. *The Longest Yard* 74. Escape to Witch Mountain 75. The Devil's Rain 75. Promise Him Anything (TV) 75. Hustle 76. Whiffs 76. Birch Interval 76. Moving Violation 76. The Word (TV) 78. Airport 80 The Concorde 79. Foolin' Around 80. How to Beat the High Cost of Living 80. Take This Job and Shove It 81. Yes Giorgio 82. Yesterday 80. This Time Forever 81. The Act 84. Dreamscape 84. Goliath Awaits (TV) 84. Head Office 85. Stitches 85.
TV series: *Leave it to Larry* 52. *Green Acres* 65–70. *Switch* 75–76.

Albert, Edward (1951–). American light actor, son of Eddie Albert; his career to date has been somewhat disappointing.
□The Fool Killer 65. Butterflies Are Free 72. Forty Carats 73. Midway 76. The Domino Principle 77. The Purple Taxi 77. The Greek Tycoon 78. The Word (TV) 78. Silent Victory (TV) 79. The Last Convertible (TV) 79. When Time Ran Out 80. Galaxy of Terror 81. Butterfly 81. The Squeeze 81. Blood Feud (TV) 81. The House where Evil Dwells 82. Ellie 84. Getting Even 85. TV Series: The Yellow Rose 83.

Albert, Marvin H. (–). American screenwriter.
Duel at Diablo 66. Rough Night in Jericho (co-w) 67. Lady in Cement (co-w) 68. Twist of Sand 68, etc.

Albertson, Frank (1909–1964). American light leading man, later character actor, in films since 1922 when he began as extra and prop boy.
Prep and Pep 28. Just Imagine 31. A Connecticut Yankee 31. Dangerous Crossroad 33. Alice Adams 35. Fury 36. The Plainsman 37. *Room Service* 38. *Bachelor Mother* 39. The Man from Headquarters 40. Man Made Monster 41. Mystery Broadcast 43. Arson Squad 45. The Hucksters 47. The Last Hurrah 58. Bye Bye Birdie 63, many others.

Albertson, Jack (1907–1981). American character actor who started as a straight man in burlesque.
Miracle on 34th Street 47. Top Banana 54. The Harder They Fall 56. Man of a Thousand Faces 57. The Shaggy Dog 59. Period of Adjustment 62. A Tiger Walks 64. How to Murder Your Wife 65. *The Subject was Roses* (AA) 68. Justine 69. Rabbit Run 70. *Willy Wonka and the Chocolate Factory* 71. The Poseidon Adventure 72. Pick Up on 101 72. Charlie's Balloon (TV) 78. Dead and Buried 81, etc.
TV series: Ensign O'Toole 62–64. Dr Simon Locke 72. *Chico and the Man* 74–77. Grandpa Goes to Washington 78.

Albertson, Mabel (1901–1982). American character comedienne, typically cast as nosey neighbour or wise and witty grandma.
Mutiny on the Blackhawk 39. She's Back on Broadway 53. Ransom 56. Forever Darling 56. *The Long Hot Summer* 58. *Home Before Dark* 58. *The Gazebo* 60. Period of Adjustment 62. *Barefoot in the Park* 67. On a Clear Day You Can See Forever 70. What's Up Doc? 72, etc.

Albicocco, Jean-Gabriel (1936–). French director with a pictorial eye.
□The Girl with the Golden Eyes 61. Le Rat d'Amérique 62. *Le Grand Meaulnes* 67. L'Amour au Feminin (part) 68. Le Coeur Fou 70. Le Petit Matin 71.

Albright, Hardie (1903–1971) (Hardy Albrecht) Underused American leading man of the thirties, of Scottish and Jewish parentage.
□ Young Sinners 31. Hush Money 31. Skyline 31. Heartbreak 31. A Successful Calamity 32. So Big 32. The Purchase Price 32. Jewel Robbery 32. The Crash 32. Three on a Match 32. Cabin in the Cotton 32. This Sporting Age 32. The Match King 32. The Working Man 32. Song of Songs 33. *Three Cornered Moon* 33. The House on 56th Street 33. Nana 34. Crimson Romance 34. The Ninth Guest 34. White Heat 34. Beggar's Holiday 34. The Scarlet Letter 34. Two Heads on a Pillow 34. The Silver Streak 34. Sing Sing Nights 34. Women Must Dress 35. Ladies Love Danger 35. Calm Yourself 35. Champagne for Breakfast 35. Red Salute 35. Granny Get Your Gun 40. Ski Patrol 40. Carolina Moon 40. Flight from Destiny 41.

Men of the Timberland 41. Bachelor Daddy 41. Marry the Boss's Daughter 41. The Loves of Edgar Allen Poe 42. Lady in a Jam 42. Pride of the Yankees 42. Army Wives 44. Captain Tugboat Annie 45. The Jade Mask 45. Sunset in Eldorado 45. Angel on My Shoulder 46. Mom and Dad 57.

Albright, Lola (1925–). Stylish, tough-talking American leading lady; roles for her Stanwyck-like personality were hard to find.
Champion 49. The Good Humour Man 50. Arctic Flight 52. The Tender Trap 56. The Monolith Monsters 57. Seven Guns to Mesa 60. *A Cold Wind in August* 61. Kid Galahad 62. The Love Cage 65. Lord Love a Duck 66. The Way West 67. Where Were You When the Lights Went Out? 68. The Impossible Years 68, etc.
TV series: *Peter Gunn* 58–60.

alcoholics have been familiar screen figures since movies began: Jack Norton and Arthur Housman made a living playing little else, and other comic inebriates include James Stewart in *Harvey*, William Powell in *The Thin Man* and its successors, Wallace Beery in *Ah Wilderness* (followed by Frank Morgan in *Summer Holiday*), Dean Martin in *Rio Bravo* (followed by Robert Mitchum in *El Dorado*) and Jackie Gleason in *Papa's Delicate Condition*.

More serious studies of alcoholism include Fredric March (followed by James Mason) in *A Star is Born*, Bing Crosby in *The Country Girl*, James Cagney and Gig Young in *Come Fill The Cup*, Spencer Tracy in *The People Against O'Hara*, Michael Redgrave in *Time Without Pity*, Claude Rains in *The White Tower*, Ingrid Bergman in *Under Capricorn*, Chester Morris in *Blind Spot*, Ray Milland in *The Lost Weekend* and *Night into Morning*, Jack Lemmon and Lee Remick in *Days of Wine and Roses*, Julie London in *The Great Man*, Van Johnson in *The Bottom of the Bottle*, Henry Fonda in *The Fugitive*, Lars Hanson in *The Atonement of Gosta Berling*, Susan Hayward in *Smash Up* and *I'll Cry Tomorrow*, Burt Lancaster in *Come Back Little Sheba*, Thomas Mitchell (followed by Bing Crosby) in *Stagecoach*, David Farrar in *The Small Back Room*, Bette Davis in *Dangerous*, Jason Robards in *Long Day's Journey Into Night*, Gregory Peck in *Beloved Infidel*, Donald O'Connor in *The Buster Keaton Story*, George Murphy in *Show Business*, Charles Laughton (followed by Robert Newton) in *Vessel of Wrath—The Beachcomber*, James Dunn in *A Tree Grows in Brooklyn*, Joan Fontaine in *Something to Live For*, Myrna Loy in *From the Terrace*, Maurice Ronet in *Le Feu Follet*, Kenneth More in *Dark Of The Sun*, Frank Sinatra in *The Joker is Wild*, Claire Bloom in *Red Sky At Morning*, Chester Morris in *Blind Spot*, and Dick Van Dyke in *The Morning After* (TV).

See also *drunk scenes*.

Alcott, John (–1986). British cinematographer.
A Clockwork Orange 71. Barry Lyndon (AA) 75. March or Die 77. Someone Is Killing the Great Chefs of Europe 78. The Shining 79. Terror Train 80. Fort Apache the Bronx 82, etc.

Alcott, Louisa M. (1832–1888). American novelist whose cosy family tales *Little Women* (qv) and *Little Men* have been frequently plundered by movie-makers.

Alda, Alan (1936–). American leading actor, son of Robert Alda.
□Gone Are the Days 63. The Extraordinary Seaman 68. Paper Lion 68. Catch 22 70. Jenny 70. The Mephisto Waltz 71. To Kill A Clown 72. The Glass House (TV) 72. The Moonshine War 74. Kill Me if You Can (as Caryl Chessman) (TV) 77. *Same Time Next Year* 78. California Suite 78. The Seduction of Joe Tynan (& w) 79. *The Four Seasons* (& w,d) 81.
TV series: *M.A.S.H.* 72–82.

¶ *A.A.:* I wouldn't live in California. All that sun makes you sterile.

Alda, Robert (1914–86) (Alphonso d'Abruzzo). American actor with radio and stage experience.
Rhapsody in Blue (as George Gershwin) 45. Cloak and Dagger 46. The Beast with Five Fingers 47. Nora Prentiss 47. April Showers 48. Tarzan and the Slave Girl 50. Two Gals and a Guy 51. Beautiful But Dangerous (Italian) 55. Imitation of Life 59. Cleopatra's Daughter 63. The Girl Who Knew Too Much 68. I Will, I Will, For Now 76. Bittersweet Love 76, etc.
TV series: Supertrain 79.

Alden, Norman (–). American character actor.
Operation Bottleneck 60. Man's Favorite Sport 63. The Devil's Brigade 68. Tora Tora Tora 70. Kansas City Bomber 72. Semi-Tough 77, etc.
TV series: Fay 75.

Alderton, John (1940–). British light leading man, a popular figure in several long-running TV series including *Emergency Ward Ten*, *Please Sir*, *Upstairs Downstairs*, *Thomas and Sarah*, *My Wife Next Door* and *Father's Day*.
The System 64. Duffy 68. Hannibal Brooks 69. Please Sir 71. Zardoz 74. It Shouldn't Happen to a Vet 76.

Aldo, G. R. (1902–1953) (Aldo Graziati). Italian cinematographer.
La Chartreuse de Parme 47. La Terra Trema 48. The Last Days of Pompeii 49. *Miracle in Milan* 51. Othello 51. Umberto D 52. Indiscretion 53. La Provinciale 53. Senso 54.

Aldon, Mari (1930–). American leading lady of the fifties; former ballet dancer.
Distant Drums 51. This Woman Is Dangerous 52. The Barefoot Contessa 54. Summertime 55, etc.

Aldrich, Robert (1918–1983). American director who declined from gritty realism to inflated melodrama. His own producer from 1962.
□Big Leaguer 53. World for Ransom 53. *Apache* 54. *Vera Cruz* 54. *Kiss Me Deadly* (& p) 55. The Big Knife (& p) 55. Autumn Leaves 56. *Attack!* (& p) 57. Ten Seconds to Hell 59. The Angry Hills 59. The Last Sunset 60. Sodom and Gomorrah (co-d) 63. *Whatever Happened to Baby Jane?* 62. Four For Texas 63. Hush Hush Sweet Charlotte 64. The Flight of the Phoenix 65. *The Dirty Dozen* 66. The Killing of Sister George 68. The Legend of Lylah Clare 69. Too Late the Hero 69. The Grissom Gang 71. Ulzana's Raid 72. Emperor of the North Pole 73. The Longest Yard 75. Hustle 76. Twilight's Last Gleaming 77. The Choirboys 77. The Frisco Kid 79. All the Marbles 81.

¶ 'His films are invariably troubled by intimations of decadence and disorder.' —*Andrew Sarris 1968*

R.A.: A director is a ringmaster, a psychiatrist and a referee.

Aleichem, Sholem (1859–1916) (Solomon Rabinovitch). Russian/Jewish storyteller whose *Tevye the Milkman* was much filmed in Yiddish and finally emerged as *Fiddler on the Roof*.

Alekan, Henri (1909–). French cinematographer.
Mademoiselle Docteur 37. Bataille du Rail 44. *La Belle et la Bête* 46. Les Maudits 47. *Une Si Jolie Petite Plage* 48. Anna Karenina 48. Juliette ou la Clef des Songes 50. Austerlitz 60. Topkapi 64. Lady L 65. Triple Cross 66. Mayerling 68. Red Sun 71. The Territory 81. La Belle Captive 83, etc.

Alexander, Ben (1911–1969) (Nicholas Benton Alexander). American boy actor of silent days; later character man.
The Little Americans 17. Little Orphan Annie 18. Hearts of the World 18. Tangled Threads 19. Family Honor 20. Boy of Mine 23. Penrod and Sam 23. Pampered Youth 25. Scotty of the Scouts 26. All Quiet on the Western Front 30. Are These Our Children 31. Tom Brown of Culver 33. Stage Mother 33. Flirtation 34. Annapolis Farewell 35. Born to Gamble 35. Splendor 35. Red Lights Ahead 37. Shall We Dance 37. Western Gold 37. The Leather Pushers 40. Criminals Within 41. Dragnet 54. Man in the Shadow 57, many others.
TV series: *Dragnet* 51–58. The Felony Squad 66–68.

Alexander, Jane (1939–) (Jane Quigley). American stage actress in occasional films.
□The Great White Hope 70. A Gunfight 71. Welcome Home Johnny Bristol (TV) 71. The New Centurions 72. Miracle on 34th Street (TV) 73. This Is the West That Was (TV) 74. Death Be Not Proud (TV) 75. *All the President's Men* 76. *Eleanor and Franklin* (TV) (as Eleanor Roosevelt) 76. The Betsy 78. Kramer versus Kramer 79. Brubaker 80. Playing for Time (TV) 80. Night Crossing 82. Testament (AAN) 83. City Heat 84. Malice in Wonderland (TV) (as Hedda Hopper) 85. Sweet Country 86, Blood and Orchids (TV) 86. Square Dance 86.

¶ *J.A.:* I never thought of myself as pretty as a child, and I have tried to bring that awareness to my roles.

J.A.: Things come up suddenly these days, but that's all right because I work better under pressure.

Alexander, Jeff (1910–). American composer.
Westward the Women 51. Escape from Fort Bravo 53. The Tender Trap 55. Gun Glory 57. Ask Any Girl 59. Kid Galahad 61. The Rounders 65. Speedway 68. Dirty Dingus Magee 70. The Sex Symbol (TV) 74. Kate Bliss and the Tickertape Kid (TV) 78, many others.

Alexander, John (1897–1982). Portly American stage actor with amiable personality.

The Petrified Forest 36. Flowing Gold 41. A Tree Grows in Brooklyn 44. *Arsenic and Old Lace* (as Uncle Teddy) 44. Mr Skeffington 45. The Jolson Story 46. Summer Holiday 48. Fancy Pants (as Theodore Roosevelt) 50. The Marrying Kind 52. The Man in the Net 59. One Foot in Hell 60, etc.

Alexander, Katherine (1901–1981). American actress specializing in sympathetic second leads.
The Barretts of Wimpole Street 34. The Painted Veil 34. The Dark Angel 36. Double Wedding 37. The Great Man Votes 39. The Hunchback of Notre Dame 39. The Vanishing Virginian 42. The Human Comedy 42. Kiss and Tell 45. John Loves Mary 49, etc.

Alexander Nevsky (USSR 1938). Sergei Eisenstein's pulsating historic spectacle has Nicolai Cherkassov as the impassive medieval warrior who conquered Teutonic Knights in a battle on the ice (photographed in summer heat by Edouard Tissé) at Nijni-Novgorod (actually shot at Lake Peipus). The splendid action sequences use music by Prokoviev in place of natural sound. Their influence was clear in Olivier's *Henry V*.

Alexander, Ross (1907–1937). Budding American leading man of the early thirties: shot himself.
□The Wiser Sex 32. Flirtation Walk 34. Gentlemen Are Born 34. Loudspeaker Lowdown 34. Social Register 34. Shipmates Forever 35. A Midsummer Night's Dream 35. Captain Blood 35. We're in the Money 35. Going Highbrow 35. Maybe It's Love 35. Brides Are Like That 36. I Married a Doctor 36. Hot Money 36. Here Comes Carter 36. Boulder Dam 36. China Clipper 36. Ready Willing and Able 37.

Alexander, Terence (1923–). British light leading man of the fifties, often in ineffectual roles; by the eighties he was a popular character support in the TV series Bergerac.
The Woman with No Name 51. The Gentle Gunman 52. The Runaway Bus 54. Portrait of Alison 55. The One That Got Away 57. Danger Within 59. The League of Gentlemen 60. The Fast Lady 62. The Long Duel 67. Waterloo 70. Vault of Horror 73. The Internecine Project 74. Ike (TV) 79, many others.

Alexander The Great (356–323 BC). A mighty warrior who became king of Macedonia at the age of twenty and quickly overran most of the Mediterranean before he died of a fever at the age of 33. He was played by Richard Burton in Robert Rossen's rather stolid 1956 biopic; William Shatner took over in a failed TV pilot of 1963; and 1980 brought forth a mini-series.

Alexandrov, Grigori (1903–1983) (G. Mormonenko). Distinguished Russian director, former assistant to Eisenstein.
Internationale 32. *Jazz Comedy* 34. *Circus* 36. *Volga-Volga* 38. The Bright Road 40. Spring 47. Glinka 52. From Man to Man 58. Lenin in Poland 61. Before October 65.

Alexieff, Alexandre (1901–1982). Franco-Russian animator who devised a method of illuminating pins stuck through a screen at various levels to produce a picture. Chief examples are *A Night on a Bare Mountain* 33, and the titles for *The Trial* 62.

Alfie (GB 1966). Bill Naughton's amusing play about a cockney Lothario, while filmed rather flatly by Lewis Gilbert, with muddy colour and no subtlety, will presumably be remembered as another stage in the cinema's progress towards complete freedom in choice of subject matter: its crude attitude to sex, expressed in raw dialogue, kept box offices busy and gave the world a new view of the British at play. Michael Caine played the long title role with relish, and even made it sympathetic.

Algar, James (1912–). American writer-director of Disney's *True Life Adventures* and associated productions.
The Living Desert 53. *The Vanishing Prairie* 54. The African Lion 55. White Wilderness 58. Jungle Cat 60. The Legend of Lobo 63. *The Incredible Journey* 63, etc.

Algiers (US 1938). The film in which Charles Boyer did *not* say 'Come with me to the Casbah'. (The line was a Hollywood legend.) The film itself, though highly successful, was a spineless remake of Julien Duvivier's *Pépé Le Moko* 36, which had Jean Gabin, in a script by Ashelbé and Henri Jeanson, as a doom-laden but romantic criminal exile who finally sacrifices himself for a woman. Tony Martin later starred in *Casbah* 48, a further Hollywood remake in semi-musical form.

Algren, Nelson (1909–1981). American novelist who writes of life's seamy side. Books include *The Man with the Golden Arm* and *A Walk on the Wild Side*.

Ali Baba. The Arabian Nights story, of a poor camel-driver who outwits forty thieves by trailing them to their magic cave which opens to a password, has been a favourite with film-makers. Edison made a version in 1902, William Fox in 1919. In 1944 Jon Hall starred in *Ali Baba and the Forty Thieves*, while in 1952 Tony Curtis was *Son of Ali Baba*. (The 1944 film was remade, with much use of footage from the original, in 1964 as *Sword of Ali Baba*, starring Peter Mann.) Meanwhile in 1954 Fernandel appeared in a French comedy version under Jacques Becker's direction. Eddie Cantor dreamed he was Ali Baba in *Ali Baba Goes to Town* 37, and the character has appeared in many other Arabian Nights films. A superior spelling was adopted for *The Adventures of Hajji Baba* 56 in which John Derek played the role.

Ali, Muhammed (1942–) (Cassius Clay). Black American heavyweight boxing champion, internationally known for his cheerfully boastful manner, for staying too long at the top, and for converting to Islam. Tried playing himself in *The Greatest* 77; also starred in a TV mini-series, *Freedom Road*.

¶ *M.A.:* When you're as great as I am, it's hard to be humble.

Alias Nick Beal (The Contact Man) (US 1949). A pleasingly successful modern version of *Faust*, with Thomas Mitchell as an honest politician almost corrupted by smooth, suave, diabolic Ray Milland. Effectively studio-set, with the magical moments under-stated and a general feeling of shape and style. Directed by John Farrow, photographed by Lionel Lindon, from Jonathan Latimer's script.

Alice in Wonderland. This Victorian nonsense classic was written by Lewis Carroll (C. L. Dodgson) and published in 1865. Most film versions—and there were several silent ones—have included material from *Through the Looking Glass*, published in 1871. Since sound there have been two American productions using actors (in 1931 with little-known players and in 1933 with Charlotte Henry and an all-star Paramount cast); a 1950 French version with Carol Marsh and Bunin's puppets; a rather stiff and unimaginative Disney cartoon of 1951; and a stolid British live-action version of 1972. In 1985 EMI brought out a curious and ineffectual piece called *Dreamchild*, in which the aged Alice Liddell, played by Coral Browne, goes to New York and is questioned about her relationship with Lewis Carroll.

Alien (GB 1979). A commercially successful horror film about astronauts who, returning to earth in their space ship, are picked off one by one by a violent extra-terrestrial with unpredictable behaviour patterns. Fashionably glossy, with dialogue hard to hear because of background computer noises, this got by on a few cunningly timed shocks and some nice design on the dead planet, but was otherwise a hasty and witless amalgam of *The Thing*, *It*, and *The Quatermass Experiment*. The alien himself, when finally glimpsed, was disappointingly conventional. Written by Dan O'Bannon; directed by Ridley Scott; with Sigourney Weaver, Tom Skerritt, John Hurt. In 1986 there appeared *Alien 2*, still with Sigourney Weaver; more or less a rehash, but longer and with more shocks.

Alison, Dorothy (1925–). Australian actress resident in Britain.
Mandy 52. Turn the Key Softly 53. The Maggie 54. Reach for the Sky 56. The Long Arm 56. The Scamp 57. Life in Emergency Ward Ten 59. Georgy Girl 66. Pretty Polly 68. Blind Terror 71. The Amazing Mr Blunden 72. A Town Like Alice (TV) 80.

All About Eve (US 1950). Writer-director Joseph L. Mankiewicz dipped his pen in venom when he wrote this story of the rise to fame of an unscrupulous actress, and won an Academy Award on both counts. Bette Davis blazed as the displaced idol, George Sanders as a waspish critic also won an Academy Award as best supporting actor, and Marilyn Monroe had a brief bit as a dumb blonde. Anne Baxter was Eve.

All Quiet on the Western Front (US 1930). Erich Maria Remarque's novel, showing World War I from the point of view of the German soldier, was turned into a landmark of cinema history by director Lewis Milestone, cinematographer Arthur Edeson and composer David Brockman. Lew Ayres, Louis Wolheim and Slim Summerville headed the cast. AA best picture, best director.
A 1979 TV remake starred Richard Thomas and cost 6 million dollars, but won favour with neither critics nor public.

all-star films. The phrase usually connotes giant musicals of the kind which started in the early days of talkies, when each studio put on an extravaganza displaying the talents of all its contract artistes, often to little effect. Titles included *Movietone Follies, Paramount on Parade, The Hollywood Revue of 1929*

(MGM), *Show of Shows* (Warner), *King of Jazz* (Universal) and *Elstree Calling*. The practice was revived during World War II: *Star Spangled Rhythm* (Paramount), *Thank Your Lucky Stars* (Warner), *Follow the Boys* (Universal), *Hollywood Canteen* (Warner) and *Stage Door Canteen* helped to cheer up the armed forces. Paramount continued into the later forties with *Variety Girl* and *Duffy's Tavern*, and Warner came up with *It's a Great Feeling* and *Starlift*. *Carnegie Hall* applied the technique to classical music.

Meanwhile dramatic films had found the value of an occasional all-star cast. *Grand Hotel, If I Had a Million, Dinner at Eight* in the early thirties were followed ten years later by *Tales of Manhattan, Forever and a Day* and *Flesh and Fantasy*, while the adoption of particular authors later in the forties produced all-star episodic films such as Somerset Maugham's *Quartet* and O'Henry's *Full House*. From the fifties, an occasional giant-screen epic would pack itself with stars: *Around the World in Eighty Days, How the West Was Won, The Greatest Story Ever Told, The Longest Day* and *A Bridge Too Far* were perhaps the most significant of these.

? All-star extravaganzas, in which the studio used to co-opt all the stars on the payroll for walk-ons, were seldom artistic successes, but they usually provided their share of memorable moments. Can you name the film in which:

1 John Barrymore recited from *Richard III*?
2 Bing Crosby sang 'Old Glory'?
3 Eddie Cantor sang 'Having a Patriotic Time'?
4 Fanny Brice appeared in her sketch 'The Sweepstake Ticket'?
5 Maurice Chevalier sang 'All I Want Is a Girl Like You' in a park in Paris?
6 Bing Crosby made his debut, as one of the Rhythm Boys?
7 Paulette Goddard, Dorothy Lamour and Veronica Lake sang 'A Sweater, a Sarong and a Peek-A-Boo Bang'?
8 Jack Benny performed a routine with Laurel and Hardy?
9 Orson Welles sawed Marlene Dietrich in half?
10 Bette Davis sang 'They're Either Too Young or Too Old'?

All That Money Can Buy (US 1941). From Stephen Vincent Benet's story 'The Devil and Daniel Webster', this delightfully American film put the Faust legend into a nineteenth-century farming setting peopled by real historical characters. Edward Arnold as lawyer Webster and James Craig as the young farmer were both outshone by Walter Huston as Mr Scratch, the amiable devil. Bernard Herrmann's vibrant music (AA) perfectly counter-pointed William Dieterle's zestful direction and production. The film has also, at various times, been known as *The Devil and Daniel Webster* and *Daniel and the Devil*.

All The King's Men (US 1949). A notable film version, written and directed by Robert Rossen, of Robert Penn Warren's exposé of American state politics, paralleling the career of the corrupt Huey Long of Louisiana. AA best picture; Broderick Crawford best actor; Mercedes McCambridge best supporting actress. John Ireland also was excellent as the jaundiced narrator. The Huey Long story was told again in a 1977 TV movie, *The Life and Assassination of the Kingfish*, with Ed Asner.

All the President's Men (US 1976). An interesting example of Hollywood's new political awareness coinciding with a good, if unresolved, true-life mystery yarn and the solid box-office appeal of Robert Redford and Dustin Hoffman, who played the 'Woodstein' team responsible for uncovering the Watergate scandal. Alan Pakula produced and directed: Jason Robards Jnr won an Academy Award as best supporting actor for playing Ben Bradlee, editor of the *Washington Post*. By the time the same subject was aired in more detail the following year in TV's *Washington: Behind Closed Doors* the public had had enough, though David Susskind followed up in 1979 with eight hours of John Dean's *Blind Ambition*.

Allan, Elizabeth (1908–). British leading lady with stage experience; adept at delicate or aristocratic heroines.
Alibi 31. Black Coffee 31. Michael and Mary 32. Nine Till Six 32. The Lodger 33. Java Head 34. *David Copperfield* (US) 34. Mark of the Vampire (US) 35. *A Tale of Two Cities* (US) 36. Camille (US) 36. Michael Strogoff (US) 37. Inquest 38. Saloon Bar 40. The Great Mr Handel 42. Went the Day Well 42. He Stoops to Conquer 44. No Highway 51. The Heart of the Matter 54. The Brain Machine 55. Grip of the Strangler 58, etc.

Alland, William (1916–). American actor, originally with Orson Welles' Mercury Theatre: played the enquiring reporter in *Citizen Kane* 41. Later became staff producer for Universal-International: *It Came from Outer Space* 53. *This Island Earth* 56. *The Lady Takes a Flyer* 58. *The Rare Breed* 65, etc. Independently produced and directed *Look in Any Window* 61.

Allbritton, Louise (1920–79). American leading lady of the forties, mainly in light comedy.
□ Danger in the Pacific 42. Parachute Nurse 42. Pittsburgh 42. Who Done It? 42. Fired Wife 43. Good Morning Judge 43. It Comes Up Love 43. *Son of Dracula* 43. Bowery to Broadway 44. Follow the Boys 44. Her Primitive Man 44. San Diego I Love You 44. This is the Life 44. Men in her Diary 45. That Night with You 45. Tangier 46. The Egg and I 47. Don't Trust your Husband 48. Sitting Pretty 48. Walk a Crooked Mile 48. The Doolins of Oklahoma 49. Felicia (Puerto Rico) 64.

Allégret, Marc (1900–73). French director of superior commercial films.
Mam'zelle Nitouche 31. Fanny 32. Lac Aux Dames 34. Les Beaux Yeux 35. Gribouille 37. Orage 38. Entrée des Artistes 38. L'Arlésienne 42. Petrus 46. Blanche Fury (GB) 47. Maria Chapdelaine 50. Blackmailed (GB) 51. Futures Vedettes 55. Lady Chatterley's Lover 55. En Effeuillant La Marguerite 56. Un Drôle de Dimanche 58. L'Abominable Homme des Douanes 63, etc.

Allégret, Yves (1907–). French director, brother of Marc Allégret.
Les Deux Timides 41. *Dédée* 47. *Une Si Jolie Petite Plage* 48. Manèges 49. Les Orgueilleux 53. Oasis 54. Germinal 63. Don't Bite, We Love You 76, etc.

Allen, Adrianne (1907–). British light actress, mostly on stage. Mother of Daniel Massey, ex-wife of Raymond.
Loose Ends 31. Black Coffee 31. The Morals of Marcus 35. The October Man 47. Vote for Huggett 49. The Final Test 53. Meet Mr Malcolm 54, etc.

Allen, Barbara Jo (1905–1974) (also known as *Vera Vague*). American comedy actress, well known on radio with Bob Hope.
Village Barn Dance 40. Ice Capades 41. Mrs Wiggs of the Cabbage Patch 42. In Rosie's Room 44. Snafu 45. Square Dance Katy 50. The Opposite Sex 56, etc.

Allen, Chesney (1894–1982). British light comedian, for many years teamed with Bud Flanagan and the Crazy Gang, from whose more violent antics he stood somewhat aloof. He retired in the forties for health reasons, but long outlived the other gang members, and in 1982 was still singing and reminiscing on TV.
□A Fire Has Been Arranged 35. Underneath the Arches 37. Okay for Sound 37. *Alf's Button Afloat* 38. *The Frozen Limits* 39. Gasbags 40. We'll Smile Again 42. Theatre Royal 43. Here Comes the Sun 44. Dreaming 44. Life is a Circus 58. Dunkirk 58.

Allen, Corey (1934–). American supporting actor specializing in depraved adolescents.
The Mad Magician 54. Night of the Hunter 55. Rebel without a Cause 55. The Shadow on the Window 57. Party Girl 58. Private Property (lead) 60. Sweet Bird of Youth 62. The Chapman Report 62. Thunder and Lightning (d only) 77. Avalanche (d, co-w) 78, etc.

Allen, Dede (1925–). American editor.
Odds Against Tomorrow 59. The Hustler 61. America America 63. *Bonnie and Clyde* 67. Little Big Man 70. Serpico 73. Dog Day Afternoon 75. The Missouri Breaks 76. Slapshot 77. The Wiz 78. Reds (& co-p) 81, many others.

Allen, Elizabeth (1934–) (Elizabeth Gillease). American leading lady with stage experience.
From the Terrace 60. Diamond Head 63. Donovan's Reef 63. Cheyenne Autumn 64. Star Spangled Girl 71. The Carey Treatment 72, etc.
TV series: Bracken's World 69. The Paul Lynde Show 72.

Allen, Fred (1894–1956) (John F. Sullivan). Baggy-eyed American radio comedian: very occasional films.
Autobiography 1954: *Treadmill to Oblivion.*
□*Thanks a Million* 35. Sally, Irene and Mary 38. Love Thy Neighbour 41. *It's in the Bag* 45. We're Not Married 52. Full House 53.

¶ *F.A.:* My eyes look as though they are peeping over two dirty ping pong balls.

F.A.: California's a great place . . . if you happen to be an orange.

'You can count on the thumb of one hand the American who is at once a comedian, a humorist, a wit and a satirist, and his name is Fred Allen.—*James Thurber*

Allen, Gracie (1902/06–1964). American comedienne who projected a scatterbrained image for thirty years on radio, TV and films, usually with her husband George Burns.
□ The Big Broadcast 32. College Humor 33. International House 33. Six of a Kind 34.

We're Not Dressing 34. The Big Broadcast of 1936 35. Here Comes Cookie 35. Love in Bloom 35. The Big Broadcast of 1937 36. College Holiday 36. *A Damsel in Distress* 37. College Swing 38. *The Gracie Allen Murder Case* 39. Honolulu 39. Mr and Mrs North 41. *Two Girls and a Sailor* 44.

Allen, Hervey (1888–1949). Popular American novelist whose mammoth *Anthony Adverse*, published in 1933, was filmed three years later.

Allen, Irving (1905–87). Polish-American producer. Hollywood experience from 1929; films include: Avalanche (d) 47. Sixteen Fathoms Deep (d) 50. New Mexico (p) 51. Slaughter Trail (d, p) 51. In Britain from early fifties as co-founder of Warwick Films (Cockleshell Heroes, Zarak, etc.). More recently: The Trials of Oscar Wilde 60. The Hellions 61. The Long Ships 64. Genghis Khan 65. The Silencers 66. The Ambushers 67. Hammerhead 68. Cromwell 70, etc. TV Series: Matt Helm 75.

Allen, Irwin (1916–). American writer-producer who began with semi-instructional entertainments and then switched to fantasy. The Sea Around Us 50. The Animal World 56. The Story of Mankind (& d) 57. The Big Circus 59. The Lost World (& d) 61. A Voyage to the Bottom of the Sea (& d) 62. Five Weeks in a Balloon (& d) 63. The Poseidon Adventure 72. The Towering Inferno (& co-d) 74. The Time Travelers (TV) 76. Swarm 78. Hanging by a Thread (TV) 79. Beyond the Poseidon Adventure 79. When Time Ran Out 80, etc.
TV series in similar vein: Voyage to the Bottom of the Sea, Lost in Space, Time Tunnel, Land of the Giants, The Swiss Family Robinson, etc.

Allen, Jay Presson (–). American screenwriter with literary aspirations.
The Prime of Miss Jean Brodie 69. Cabaret 72. Travels With My Aunt 72. Just Tell Me What You Want 79, etc.

Allen, Karen (1951–). American leading lady.
Animal House 78. Manhattan 79. The Wanderers 79. Raiders of the Lost Ark 81. Shoot the Moon 82. Split Image 82. Starman 85. Backfire 87. The Glass Menagerie 87.

Allen, Lewis (1905–86). British director in Hollywood; his career started well but spluttered out.
□Our Hearts were Young and Gay 44. *The Uninvited* 44. The Unseen 45. Those Endearing Young Charms 46. The Perfect Marriage 46. The Imperfect Lady 46. Desert Fury 47. So Evil My Love 48. Sealed Verdict 48. Chicago Deadline 49. Valentino 51. Appointment with Danger 51. At Sword's Point 52. Suddenly 54. A Bullet For Joey 55. Illegal 56. Another Time Another Place 58. Whirlpool (GB) 59. Decision at Midnight (MRA film) 63.

Allen, Lewis M. (1922–). American producer with theatrical experience.
The Connection 60. The Balcony 63. Lord of the Flies 64. Fahrenheit 451 66.

Allen, Nancy (1950–). American leading lady, wife of Brian de Palma.
The Last Detail 73. Carrie 76. 1941 79. Home Movies 79. Dressed to Kill 80. Blowout 81. Strange Invaders 83. The Buddy System 84. Not for Publication 84. The Philadelphia Experiment 84. Robocop 87. Sweet Revenge 87, etc.

Allen, Patrick (1927–). Lantern-jawed British leading man who after playing assorted villains and heroes in routine films established himself as TV's *Crane*.
1984 55. High Tide at Noon 57. The Long Haul 57–8. Dunkirk 58. Tread Softly Stranger 58. I Was Monty's Double 58. Never Take Sweets from a Stranger 60. The Traitors 62. Captain Clegg 62. The Night of the Generals 66. Night of the Big Heat 67. When Dinosaurs Ruled the Earth 69. Puppet On a Chain 71. Diamonds on Wheels 73. Persecution 74. Hard Times (TV) 78. The Wild Geese 78. The Sea Wolves 80. Who Dares Wins 82, etc.

Allen, Rex (1922–). American singing cowboy, popular on radio, in vaudeville and in second features.
Arizona Cowboy 50. Under Mexicali Stars 50. The Old Overland Trail 53. The Phantom Stallion 53, etc.
TV series: Frontier Doctor 52.

Allen, Sian Barbara (–). American actress of the seventies.
You'll Like My Mother 72. The Family Rico (TV) 72. Scream Pretty Peggy (TV) 73. Billy Two Hats 73. Eric (TV) 75. Smash-Up On Interstate 5 (TV) 76. The Lindbergh Kidnapping Case (TV) 76, etc.

Allen, Steve (1921–). American radio and TV personality, in occasional films.
□Down Memory Lane 49. I'll Get By 51. *The Benny Goodman Story* 56. The Big Circus 59. College Confidential 60. Don't Worry, We'll Think of a Title 66. A Man Called Dagger 67. Warning Shot 67. Now You See It, Now You Don't (TV) 67. Where were You when the Lights Went Out? 68. The Comic 69. The Sunshine Boys 75. Heartbeat 79. The Ratings Game (TV) 84.

¶ 'When I can't sleep, I read a book by Steve Allen.'—*Oscar Levant*
'I'm fond of Steve Allen, but not so much as he is.'—*Jack Paar*

Allen, Woody (1935–) (Allen Stewart Konigsberg). Bespectacled American night club comedian and light playwright who has made many appearances as a flustered, hypochondriacal failure but internationally remains an acquired taste.
□What's New Pussycat (& w) 65. *Casino Royale* (& co-w) 67. What's Up Tiger Lily? (& w) 67. Take the Money and Run (& w, d) 69. Don't Drink the Water (w only) 69. *Bananas* (& co-w, d) 71. Everything You Always Wanted to Know About Sex (& wpd) 72. *Play It Again Sam* (& w) 72. Sleeper (& co-w, d) 73. *Love and Death* (co-w, d) 76. The Front 76. *Annie Hall* (& co-w, d) (AA wd, best picture) 77. *Interiors* (w, d only) 78. *Manhattan* (& w, d) (BFA) 79. Stardust Memories (& w, d) 80. A Midsummer Night's Sex Comedy (& w, d) 82. Zelig (& w, d) 83. Broadway Danny Rose (& w, d) (AAw, AANd) 84, The Purple Rose of Cairo (w, d only) (AAw, BFAw) 85. *Hannah and her Sisters* (& w, d) 86. Radio Days (w, d only) 87. September (w, d only) 87.

¶ With me, it's just a genetic dissatisfaction with everything.—*W.A.*
To me, American serious pictures always have one foot in entertainment, and I like more personal drama, though there may not be a market for it.—*W.A.*
I don't want to achieve immortality through my work. I want to achieve it through not dying.—*W.A.*
Most of the time I don't have much fun. The rest of the time I don't have any fun at all.—*W.A.*
I don't believe in an after life, but I'm bringing along a change of underwear.—*W.A.*
He has a face that convinces you that God is a cartoonist.—*Jack Kroll*
It's not that I'm afraid to die. I just don't want to be there when it happens.—*W.A.*
If only God would give me a sign. Such as making a large deposit in my name in a Swiss bank.—*W.A.*
Love is the answer, but while you're waiting for the answer, sex raises some pretty good questions.—*W.A.*
Life is divided into the horrible and the miserable.—*W.A.*
Don't knock masturbation: it's sex with someone you love.—*W.A.*
I was suicidal, and would have killed myself, but I was in analysis with a strict Freudian, and if you kill yourself they make you pay for the lessons you miss.—*W.A.*

Alley, Kirstie (–). American actress.
Star Trek II 82. Blind Date 83. Champions 83. Runaway 84. North and South (TV) 85. Summer School 87.

Allgeier, Sepp (1890–1968). German cinematographer. Best-known films include: *Diary of a Lost Girl* 29. *The White Hell of Pitz Palu* 29. *William Tell* 33.

Allgood, Sara (1883–1950). Irish character actress, long with the Abbey Theatre and from 1940 in Hollywood.
□ *Blackmail* 29. *Juno and the Paycock* 30. The World the Flesh and the Devil 32. The Fortunate Fool 33. Irish Hearts 34. Lily of Killarney 34. The Passing of the Third Floor Back 35. Riders to the Sea 35. Lazybones 35. Peg of Old Drury 35. It's Love Again 36. Pot Luck 36. Southern Roses 36. *Storm in a Teacup* 37. The Sky's the Limit 37. The Londonderry Air 38. Kathleen Mavourneen 38. *That Hamilton Woman* 41. *How Green was My Valley* 41. Dr Jekyll and Mr Hyde 41. Lydia 41. The War Against Mrs Hadley 42. Roxie Hart 42. This Above All 42. It Happened in Flatbush 42. Life Begins at 8.30 42. City without Men 43. Jane Eyre 44. *The Lodger* 44. *Between Two Worlds* 44. The Keys of the Kingdom 44. The Strange Affair of Uncle Harry 45. Cluny Brown 46. Kitty 46. The Spiral Staircase 46. Mother Wore Tights 47. The Fabulous Dorseys 47. Ivy 47. Mourning Becomes Electra 47. My Wild Irish Rose 47. One Touch of Venus 48. The Man from Texas 48. The Girl from Manhattan 48. The Accused 48. Challenge to Lassie 49. Sierra 50. Cheaper by the Dozen 50.

Allied Artists Corporation. An American production company, more recently involved in TV, which flourished throughout the thirties and forties as a purveyor of routine crime and comedy second features. Its policy was to put out the poorer product under the banner of its subsidiary, *Monogram Pictures Corporation*; the 'quality' AA product was little in evidence until the fifties, when films like *Love in the Afternoon, The Friendly Persuasion* and *Al Capone* came from this stable. Meanwhile the Monogram films, boasting such attractions as Frankie Darro, the East Side Kids, the Bowery Boys, Bela Lugosi and Charlie Chan, had their faithful following, and in France attracted highbrow cinéastes to such an extent that Jean-Luc Godard dedicated his film *À Bout de Soufflé* to Monogram.

Allio, René (1924–). Thoughtful French director with sparse output.
□Les Armes Mortes 60. La Meule 62. *The Shameless Old Lady* 65. L'Une et l'Autre (& w) 65. Skin Deep 67. Pierre et Paul (& w) 68. Les Camisards 70. Rude Journée pour la Reine 74. Retour à Marseille 79.

Allister, Claud (1891–1970) (Claud Palmer). British character actor associated with monocled silly-ass roles.
Bulldog Drummond (US) 29. The Private Life of Henry VIII 32. The Private Life of Don Juan 34. Dracula's Daughter (US) 36. Captain Fury (US) 39. Charley's Aunt (US) 41. Kiss the Bride Goodbye 44. Gaiety George 46. Quartet 48. Kiss Me Kate (US) 53, etc.

Allwyn, Astrid (1909–78). Swedish-American leading lady of minor movies in the thirties.
Reputation 32. Only Yesterday 33. Follow the Fleet 36. Dimples 37. Love Affair 39. Mr Smith Goes to Washington 39. Unexpected Uncle 41. No Hands on the Clock 41. Hit Parade of 1943, etc.

Allyson, June (1917–) (Ella Geisman). Husky-voiced American leading lady who could play a tomboy or a tease, and was equally ready with a smile or a tear. Started in 1937 two-reelers, then spent five years as a Broadway chorus dancer before making her Hollywood feature debut. Her cute sexiness kept her popular for fifteen years. Married to Dick Powell 1945–63.
Autobiography 1982: *June Allyson*.
□Best Foot Forward 43. Girl Crazy 43. Thousands Cheer 43. Meet the People 44. *Two Girls and a Sailor* 44. *Music For Millions* 44. Her Highness and the Bellboy 45. The Sailor Takes a Wife 45. Two Sisters from Boston 45. Till the Clouds Roll By 46. The Secret Heart 46. High Barbaree 47. Good News 47. The Bride Goes Wild 48. The Three Musketeers 48. Words and Music (singing 'Thou Swell') 48. *Little Women* (as Jo) 49. The Stratton Story 49. The Reformer and the Redhead 50. Right Cross 50. Too Young to Kiss 51. The Girl in White 52. Battle Circus 53. Remains to be Seen 53. *The Glenn Miller Story* 54. Executive Suite 54. Woman's World 54. Strategic Air Command 55. *The Shrike* (her most dramatic role) 55. The McConnell Story 56. The Opposite Sex 56. You Can't Run Away from It 56. Interlude 57. My Man Godfrey 57. Stranger in My Arms 59. They Only Kill Their Masters 72. See the Man Run (TV) 72. Letters from Three Lovers (TV) 73. Blackout 77. Vegas (TV pilot) 78. The Kid with the Broken Halo (TV) 82.
TV series: *The June Allyson Show* 59–61.

¶ *J.A.:* MGM was my mother and father, mentor and guide, my all-powerful and benevolent crutch. When I left them, it was like walking into space.
J.A.: In real life I'm a poor dressmaker and a terrible cook—anything in fact but the perfect wife.

Almendros, Nestor (1930–). Spanish-American cinematographer.
La Collectioneuse 66. Ma Nuit chez Maud 68. Claire's Knee 70. L'Enfant Sauvage 69. Two English Girls 71. Love in the Afternoon 72. Cockfighter 74. The Story of Adèle H 75. Madame Rosa 77. *Days of Heaven* (AA) 78. Going South 78. Love on the Run 79. Kramer vs Kramer 79. The Blue Lagoon 80. The Last Metro 81. Still of the Night 82. Sophie's Choice 82. Vivement Dimanche 83. Pauline at the Beach 83. Places in the Heart 84. Heartburn 86. Nadine 87, etc.

Almond, Paul (1931–). Canadian director, from TV.
□Isabel 68. Act of the Heart 70. The Journey 72. Final Assignment 81. Up and Down 83.

Aloma of the South Seas. This sentimental romance was a silent success in 1927, with Gilda Gray and Percy Marmont. In 1941 Paramount remade it in colour, with Dorothy Lamour, Jon Hall, and lots of crocodiles and volcanoes.

Alonzo, John A. (1934–). Mexican-American cinematographer.
Bloody Mama 70. *Vanishing Point* 71. Sounder 72. Lady Sings The Blues 72. Hit!

73. The Naked Ape 73. Conrack 74. Chinatown 74. Once Is Not Enough 75. The Fortune 75. *Farewell My Lovely* 75. The Bad News Bears 76. Black Sunday 77. Close Encounters of the Third Kind (co-ph) 77. Norma Rae 79. Tom Horn 80. Black Roads 81. Zorro the Gay Blade 81. Blue Thunder 83. Cross Creek 83. Scarface 83. Runaway 84. Out of Control 85. Nothing in Common 86, etc.

Alper, Murray (1904–). American small-part character actor often seen as cab driver, soldier, etc.
The Royal Family of Broadway 30. The Girl Habit 31. Seven Keys to Baldpate 35. Winterset 36. Cocoanut Grove 38. The Roaring Twenties 39. Black Friday 40. The Maltese Falcon 41. The Big Shot 42. Mug Town 43. Wing and a Prayer 44. Angel on my Shoulder 46. Sleep my Love 48. Lost Continent 51. Devil's Canyon 53. Tanganyika 54. Calypso Joe 57. The Leech Woman 60. The Nutty Professor 63. The Outlaws is Coming 65, many others.

Alperson, Edward L. (1896–1969). American independent producer, mainly of hokum pictures; former film salesman.
Black Beauty 47. Dakota Lil 50. Invaders from Mars 53. New Faces 54. The Magnificent Matador 56. I Mobster 59. September Storm 60, many others.

Alpert, Hollis (1916–). American critic. Books include *The Dreams and the Dreamers* 62; *The Barrymores* 64.

'also known as': see *aka*.

alternative titles

? A few films over the years have been advertised with alternative secondary titles, usually connected by the word 'or'. By what main titles are these films better known?

1 *The Eighth Wonder of the World*
2 *The Shame of a Nation*
3 *The Diary of an Innocent Young Man*
4 *Love's Struggle Through the Ages*
5 *Pardon Me, but Your Teeth Are in My Neck*
6 *Where Were You the Night You Said You Shot Down Baron Von Richthofen?*
7 *How to Stop Worrying and Love the Bomb*
8 *How I Flew from London to Paris in 25 Hours 11 Minutes*
9 *How to Make a French Dish*
10 *A Story of the London Fog*
11 *Ten Weeks with a Circus*
12 *A Love Story*

Altman, Robert (1922–). American director who had a big commercial success with M*A*S*H but subsequently demonstrated an unsympathetically experimental approach.
□The Delinquents (& wp) 55. The James Dean Story (co-d & p) 57. Nightmare in Chicago 64. Countdown 68. That Cold Day in the Park 68. *M*A*S*H* 70. Brewster McCloud 71. McCabe and Mrs Miller 71. Images 72. The Long Goodbye 72. Thieves Like Us 73. California Split 74. *Nashville* 75. Buffalo Bill and the Indians 76. The Late Show (p only) 77. Welcome to L.A. (p only) 78. 3 Women (& wp) 78. *A Wedding* (& co-w, p) 78. Remember My Name (p only) 78. Quintet (& co-w, p) 78. A Perfect Couple (& co-w, p) 79. Rich Kids (p only) 79. Health (& co-w, p) 79. Popeye 80. Come Back to the Five and Dime, Jimmy Dean, Jimmy Dean 82. Streamers 83. Secret Honor 84. Fool for Love 85. Beyond Therapy 87. O.C. and Stiggs 87.

¶ *R.A.:* Film-making is a chance to live many lifetimes.

R.A.: What is a cult? It just means not enough people to make a minority.

R.A. 1986: The majors don't want to make the same pictures I do, and I'm too old to change.

Alton, John (1901–). Hungarian cinematographer, in Hollywood from 1924. Published books include *Painting with Light*.
Courageous Dr Christian 40. Atlantic City 44. T-Men 47. He Walked by Night 48. The Black Book 49. Father of the Bride 50. *An American in Paris* (AA) 51. The People Against O'Hara 51. Battle Circus 53. The Big Combo 55. Tea and Sympathy 56. The Teahouse of the August Moon 56. The Brothers Karamazov 58. Elmer Gantry 60, etc.

Alton, Robert (1897–1957) (Robert Alton Hart). American director, mainly of musical sequences: Strike Me Pink 36. Showboat 51. There's No Business Like Show Business 55, many others. Directed features: Merton of the Movies 47. Pagan Love Song 50.

Alvarado, Don (1900–1967) (José Paige). American 'latin lover' of the twenties: later appeared in character roles.
The Loves of Carmen 26. Drums of Love 27.

The Battle of the Sexes 28. The Bridge of San Luis Rey 29. Rio Rita 29. Morning Glory 33. The Devil is a Woman 35. The Big Steal 49, etc.

Alves, Joe (–). American production designer.
☐ Winning 69. Pufnstuf 70. Sugarland Express 74. Jaws 75. Close Encounters of the Third Kind 77. Jaws II 78. Escape from New York 81. Jaws 3-D 83.

Alwyn, William (1905–85). Prolific British composer who progressed from documentary scoring to fictional narrative.
Fires were Started 42. World of Plenty 43. The Way Ahead 44. *The True Glory* 45. The Rake's Progress 45. Odd Man Out 46. Captain Boycott 47. *The Fallen Idol* 48. The History of Mr Polly 49. The Magic Box 51. The Card 52. The Crimson Pirate 53. The Million Pound Note 54. The Ship That Died of Shame 55. Geordie 55. Manuela 57. Carve Her Name With Pride 58. A Night to Remember 58. The Swiss Family Robinson 60. The Running Man 63, etc.

Alyn, Kirk (1910–). American leading man, chiefly remembered for playing Superman in the 1948 serial version. Other roles in Lucky Jordan 42. Sweet Genevieve 47. Radar Patrol vs Spy King (serial) 50, etc.

Amateau, Rod (1923–). American radio writer who in the early fifties briefly became a film director and then turned his attention to half-hour comedy TV films, of which he has since made many hundreds.
The Rebel 51. Monsoon 52. Pussycat Pussycat I Love You 70. The Statue 70. Where Does It Hurt (& co-p, co-w) 72. Drive In 76. Lovelines 84. The Garbage Pail Kids Movie 87, etc.

The Amateur Gentleman. Jeffrey Farnol's Regency novel, of an inn-keeper's son who becomes involved with highwaymen and London society, was a popular subject for British movies. In 1920 Maurice Elvey directed Langhorne Burton; 1926 saw Sidney Olcott directing Richard Barthelmess in a Hollywood version; and in 1936 Douglas Fairbanks Jnr was the star of a sound version directed by Thornton Freeland.

Amato, Giuseppe (1899–1964) (Giuseppe Vasaturo). Italian producer.
Four Steps in the Clouds (& w) 42. Open City 45. Shoe Shine 46. Bicycle Thieves 49. Umberto D 52. Don Camillo 52. La Dolce Vita 59, many others.

Ambler, Eric (1909–). Popular British novelist (works filmed include *The Mask of Dimitrios, Journey Into Fear, Background to Danger, Hotel Reserve, The Light of Day*). Also screenwriter: The Way Ahead 44. The October Man 47. The Magic Box 51. The Card 52. The Cruel Sea 54. A Night to Remember 57. The Wreck of the Mary Deare 59, etc.

Ambler, Joss (1900–1959). British character actor, often seen as heavy father or police inspector.
Captain's Orders 37. Meet Mr Penny 38. Come on George 39. Contraband 40. Penn of Pennsylvania 41. The Big Blockade 42. The Next of Kin 42. The Silver Fleet 43. Candles at Nine 44. The Agitator 45. The Years Between 46. Mine Own Executioner 47. Who Goes There 52. Miss Tulip Stays the Night 55. The Long Arm 56. Soho Incident 56, many others.

Ameche, Don (1908–) (Dominic Felix Amici). American leading man with stage and radio experience. A pleasant light hero of mainly trivial films, he returned to Broadway in the sixties and became popular on TV as a circus ringmaster.
☐Sins of Man 36. *Ramona* 36. Ladies in Love 36. One in a Million 37. Love is News 37. Fifty Roads to Town 37. You Can't Have Everything 37. Love Under Fire 37. *In Old Chicago* 38. Happy Landing 38. Josette 38. *Alexander's Ragtime Band* 38. Gateway 38. *The Three Musketeers* (musical version; as D'Artagnan) 39. *Midnight* 39. *The Story of Alexander Graham Bell* (which started a long-standing joke about Ameche inventing the telephone) 39. Hollywood Cavalcade 39. *Swanee River* (as Stephen Foster) 39. Lillian Russell 40. *Four Sons* 40. Down Argentine Way 40. *That Night in Rio* (dual role) 41. Moon Over Miami 41. Kiss the Boys Goodbye 41. The Feminine Touch 41. Confirm or Deny 41. The Magnificent Dope 42. Girl Trouble 43. *Heaven Can Wait* (under Lubitsch, his best acting performance) 43. *Happy Land* 43. Something to Shout About 43. Wing and a Prayer 44. Greenwich Village 44. It's In the Bag 45. Guest Wife 45. So Goes My Love 46. That's My Man 47. Sleep My Love 48. Slightly French 49. Phantom Caravan 54. Fire One 55. A Fever in the Blood 61. Rings Around the World 66. Picture Mommy Dead 66. Shadow over Elveron (TV) 68. Suppose They Gave a War and Nobody Came 70. The Boatniks 70. Gidget Gets Married (TV) 71. Trading Places 83. *Cocoon* (AA) 84. A Masterpiece of Murder (TV) 85. Bigfoot and the Hendersons 87.

Ambrose (1896–1971). British bandleader of the thirties and later.
□ Soft Lights and Sweet Music 36. Kicking the Moon Around 38.

America, America (US 1963). A long and painstaking account, directed by Elia Kazan from his own autobiographical book, of the struggles of a poor Turk to emigrate to America. Splendidly photographed by Haskell Wexler, with a stalwart central performance from Stathis Giallelis; but needlessly uncommercial in approach.

The American Cinema, by Andrew Sarris. An influential book, first published 1968 (in paperback). Sarris lists every American director he can think of, and ranks him and his films in one of eleven categories: Pantheon Directors; The Far Side of Paradise; Expressive Esoterica; Fringe Benefits; Less Than Meets the Eye; Lightly Likable; Strained Seriousness; Oddities, One-Shots and Newcomers; Subjects for Further Research; Make Way for the Clowns; and Miscellany.

The American Civil War, despite the peaks of *The Birth of a Nation* and *Gone with the Wind*, was long thought to be an uncommerical subject for film-makers, and certainly this was confirmed by the cool reception of *The General*, *So Red the Rose*, and *The Red Badge of Courage*, among others: the cry 'Fort Sumter has been fired upon' became a guaranteed laugh with any audience. Many westerns considered the after-effects of the war, but the conflict itself was dealt with only occasionally, perhaps because of budget problems. *Drums in the Deep South*, *Alvarez Kelly*, *Prince of Players*, *Prisoner of Shark Island*, *Escape from Fort Bravo*, *The Outlaw Josey Wales* and *The Good the Bad and the Ugly* were among those to touch on the subject, while *Shenandoah* dealt thoroughly with the resulting problems for one family. In the eighties, television took up the subject with vigour but no style, in such mini-series as *Beulah Land*, *The Blue and the Gray*, and *North and South*, the story having been previously told in such longer serials as *The Americans* and *Centennial*.

American Film Institute. Government sponsored body rather belatedly founded in 1967. Based in Washington, its comprehensive catalogue will provide full detail on every American film ever made. Its first director was George Stevens Jnr.

American Graffiti (US 1973). Unexpectedly successful at the box office, this youth comedy-drama set in the early sixties started a profitable run of nostalgia culminating in the TV series *Happy Days*. It was directed by George Lucas. A 1979 sequel, *More American Graffiti*, was directed by B. W. L. Norton and sank without trace.

An American in Paris (US 1951). One of Hollywood's most pleasing musicals, a five-time Academy Award winner. Splendid MGM production values, sympathetic direction by Vincente Minnelli, Gershwin tunes and careful colour photography helped to give the excitement to which the performances of Gene Kelly, Oscar Levant and Nina Foch contributed. The final musical sequence remains unexcelled as a film ballet. AA best picture, best cinematography (Alfred Gilks, John Alton), best costume design, best scoring, best screenplay (Alan Jay Lerner).

American International Pictures. Independent production company founded in 1955 by Samuel Z. Arkoff and James H. Nicholson (both qv). After a profitable splurge of Z pictures churned out mainly by Roger Corman the company began to set its sights on the big time. In 1980 the ailing company was taken over by Filmways, which in 1982 was in its turn taken over by Orion.

American Madness (US 1932). One of the most notable early sound dramas on a social theme, in this case the American pursuit of the dollar, with Walter Huston as an honest banker driven to desperation by the corruption around him. Written by Robert Riskin and directed by Frank Capra; after its box-office failure they subsequently expressed their social comment and popular sentimental feeling in comedy vein.

The American Revolution. Because the subject means no sale in several international markets, this has not been a popular subject with film makers. D. W. Griffith's *America* in 1924 was the most thoroughgoing reconstruction. A year later, *Janice Meredith* covered some of the same ground. *Alexander Hamilton* (31) starred George Arliss and had Alan Mowbray as George Washington. Walt Disney's *Johnny Tremain* showed revolutionary figures through the eyes of an apprentice silversmith. John Paul Jones, the sailor patriot, was played in 1959 by Robert Stack in the film of the same name. In 1959 Bernard Shaw's *The Devil's Disciple* was filmed with Burt Lancaster, Kirk Douglas and

Laurence Olivier. *Lafayette* (1962) showed the war from the viewpoint of the French soldiers sent to assist. *1776* (72) is a musical version from the Broadway stage, with Howard da Silva as Ben Franklin. In the mid-seventies public broadcasting viewed the revolutionary years through a serial drama, *The Adams Chronicles*. 1984 brought an 8-hour mini-series with Barry Bostwick as George Washington.

An American Tragedy. Theodore Dreiser (qv) published his downbeat novel in 1925, about an ambitious but callow youth who is forced by the social system and his own weakness into murdering his sweetheart. Josef von Sternberg's 1931 film version though not entirely to his own liking, was a more vigorous and cinematic treatment than George Stevens' portentous 1951 remake, *A Place in the Sun*. The stars of the first version were Phillips Holmes, Sylvia Sidney and Frances Dee; of the second, Montgomery Clift, Shelley Winters and Elizabeth Taylor.

An American Werewolf in London (US/GB 1981). A significant trend in horror was introduced in this item which takes its basic strands from the old Universal standby *The Wolf Man* but adds real locations, disgusting detail of putrefaction, brilliant special effects of snouts and talons growing, and a surprising amount of semi-farcical humour. Written and directed by John Landis for producer George Folsey Jnr/Polygram; special effects by Rick Baker; with David Naughton, Jenny Agutter, Griffin Dunne.

Ames, Adrienne (1909–1947) (Adrienne Ruth McClure). American light leading lady of the thirties.
Girls About Town 31. Husband's Holiday 32. A Bedtime Story 33. You're Telling Me 34. Woman Wanted 35. City Girl 38. Panama Patrol 39, etc.

Ames, Leon (1903–) (Leon Wycoff). American character actor, a specialist in harassed or kindly fathers and suave professional men.
Murders in the Rue Morgue 32. 13 Women 32. Parachute Jumper 33. The Count of Monte Cristo 34. Reckless 35. Stowaway 36. Charlie Chan on Broadway 37. Mysterious Mr Moto 38. Code of the Streets 39. Ellery Queen and the Murder Ring 41. Crime Doctor 43. *Meet Me In St Louis* 44. Thirty Seconds over Tokyo 44. Son of Lassie 45. Weekend at the Waldorf 45. Yolanda and the Thief 45. Song of the Thin Man 47. A Date with Judy 48. *Little Women* 49. Battleground 49. Crisis 50. *On Moonlight Bay* 51. Let's Do It Again 53. Peyton Place 57. *From the Terrace* 60. The Absent-minded Professor 61. The Monkey's Uncle 65. On a Clear Day You Can See Forever 70. Hammersmith is Out 72. Just You and Me, Kid 79. Testament 83. Jake Speed 86. Peggy Sue Got Married 86, many others.
TV series: *Life With Father* 54. *Father of the Bride* 61. *Mister Ed* 60–65.

Ames, Preston (1905–1983). American production designer, who won Academy Awards for *An American in Paris* 51 and *Gigi* 58.
Brewster McCloud 70. Lost Horizon 73. Beyond the Poseidon Adventure 79. Oh God Book Two 80. The Pursuit of D. B. Cooper 81, etc.

Ames, Ramsay (1919–) (Ramsay Philips). American leading lady who started as a Universal starlet but didn't make much of a mark.
Ali Baba and the Forty Thieves 44. The Mummy's Tomb 44. Calling Dr Death 44. A Wave, a WAC and a Marine 44. Alexander the Great 56. The Running Man 63, etc.

Amfitheatrof, Daniele (1901–1983). Russian composer and arranger, in Hollywood from 1938.
I'll Be Seeing You 43. Letter from An Unknown Woman 48. The Lost Moment 48. The Desert Fox 51. The Naked Jungle 54. The Trial 55. Heller in Pink Tights 60. Major Dundee 65, many others.

Amidei, Sergei (1904–). Italian scriptwriter, associated with neo-realism.
Pietro Micca 38. Rome, Open City 45. Paisa 47. Domenica d'Agosto 50, etc.

Amis, Kingsley (1922–). British light novelist. Films of his books include Lucky Jim 57. Only Two Can Play (That Uncertain Feeling) 62. Take a Girl Like You 67.

amnesia has been a favourite theme of the movies, and the line 'Who am I?' long since became immortal. Heroes and heroines who have suffered memorably from the affliction include Ronald Colman in *Random Harvest*, John Hodiak in *Somewhere in the Night*, Greta Garbo in *As You Desire Me*, George Peppard in *The Third Day*, Cornell Borchers in *Istanbul*, Gregory Peck in *Spellbound* and *Mirage*, Phyllis Calvert in *The Woman With No Name*, Genevieve Page in *The Private*

Life of Sherlock Holmes, Jennifer Jones in *Love Letters*, Laird Cregar in *Hangover Square*, William Powell in *I Love You Again* and *Crossroads*, Joan Fontaine in *The Witches* and James Garner in *Mister Buddwing*. In *While I Live* Carol Raye was the archetypal film amnesiac, emerging out of the mist complete with theme tune. In *Portrait of Jennie* Jennifer Jones played a ghost who forgot she was dead, and the same might be said of the passengers in *Outward Bound* (remade as *Between Two Worlds*) and *Thunder Rock*. The prize for audacity was won by the scriptwriters of *The Mummy's Curse*, with its dainty modern maiden who managed to forget that she was really a 3000-year-old mummy! Perhaps the cutest twist of all was suffered by Dan Duryea in *Black Angel* and Boris Karloff in *Grip of the Strangler*: having spent the film's running time tracking down a murderer, each discovered himself to be the culprit.
See *psychology*.

Amos 'n' Andy. The original blackface double act, immensely popular for many years on American radio, consisted of Freeman F. Gosden (1899–1982) and Charles Correll (1890–1972). They made one film in 1932, *Check and Double Check*.

Amram, David (1930–). American composer.
Pull My Daisy 57. The Young Savages 60. Splendor in the Grass 61. The Manchurian Candidate 62. The Arrangement 69, etc.

Amy, George J. (1903–). American editor.
The Gorilla 30. Underworld 31. Doctor X 32. Footlight Parade 33. The Mystery of the Wax Museum 33. Dames 34. Lady Killer 34. Captain Blood 35. The Charge of the Light Brigade 36. Green Pastures 36. Dodge City 39. The Letter 40. The Sea Hawk 40. The Sea Wolf 41. Yankee Doodle Dandy 42. Air Force 43. Confidential Agent 45. Three Strangers 46. Life with Father 47. The Sound of Fury 50. Clash by Night 52. A Lion Is in the Streets 53, many others.

Amyes, Julian (1917–). British director who became a TV executive.
A Hill in Korea 56. Miracle in Soho 56, etc.

anachronisms are fun to spot, but the ones involving language are easy to defend: ancient Romans may not have used modern slang phrases such as 'nuts to you', but nor did they speak in English anyway. Rarely indeed do the studios let through such gaffes as the extra who wore a wrist watch in *The Viking Queen*, or the TV aerials in 'Victorian' London in *The Wrong Box*. Mistakes we did enjoy include the use of dynamite in *Tap Roots*, which was set in 1860 (dynamite was not invented until 1867); the British Railways signs in *Cockleshell Heroes*, set during World War II (British Railways was formed in 1948); the death of Laird Cregar by Tower Bridge in *The Lodger*, set several years before Tower Bridge was built; and the modern lounge suits sported by Colin Clive in James Whale's Frankenstein films, otherwise apparently set in nineteenth-century Europe. Even TV movies are not immune: *The Triangle Factory Fire Scandal* includes a Chaplin movie visit but is set in 1909 before Chaplin made a film. But then, even Shakespeare put a striking clock in *Julius Caesar*. See: *boo-boos*.

anaglyph. A simple system for making three-dimensional films. The two slightly differing images are printed in different colours, usually red and green, and viewed through similarly coloured lenses to sort them out into a single image. (The alternative is to use polaroid, which distinguishes the two images through lenses invisibly stripped in different directions.)

anamorphic lens. One which, in a camera, 'squeezes' a wide picture on to standard film; in a projector, 'unsqueezes' the image to fill a wide screen (usually of a 2.45:1 aspect ratio); e.g. CinemaScope, Panavision, TohoScope, HammerScope, WarnerScope, DyaliScope, which are not essentially different from each other. See: *aspect ratio*.

Anastasia (GB 1956). An interesting Hollywood investigation into a puzzle of recent history, namely the fate of the Czar's daughter alleged to have been executed during the Russian revolution. Written by Arthur Laurents from a TV play by Marcelle Maurette, and directed by Anatole Litvak, it marked Ingrid Bergman's (AA) return to the Hollywood screen after her European 'exile'. In a somewhat less fictionalized version of the story, *Is Anna Anderson Anastasia?* (Germany 1956), Lilli Palmer played the enigmatic claimant.

anatomy

? Complete the following film titles by adding in each case one word describing a portion of human or animal anatomy.

1 *Belles on Their . . . . . .*
2 *Careful Soft . . . . . .*
3 *Big Brown . . . . . .*
4 *The Screaming . . . . . .*
5 *The Hidden . . . . . .*
6 *Donovan's . . . . . .*
7 *. . . . . . at the Window*
8 *Dreaming . . . . . .*
9 *Tom . . . . . .*
10 *The . . . . . . Beach Story*
11 *The . . . . . . of Marble*
12 *Dead Man's . . . . . .*
13 *Claire's . . . . . .*
14 *Million Dollar . . . . . .*
15 *The Scarlet . . . . . .*
16 *. . . . . . to Bataan*
17 *The . . . . . . of Fu Manchu*
18 *. . . . . . in the Night*
19 *. . . . . . of the Ripper*
20 *. . . . . . of the Devil*
21 *. . . . . . of a Fugitive*
22 *. . . . . . in . . . . . .* (same word repeated)
23 *Captain Light . . . . . .*
24 *. . . . . . of the Cat*
25 *The Mummy's . . . . . .*

Anchors Aweigh (US 1945). Musical with Gene Kelly and Frank Sinatra as sailors on leave. Remarkable only as a forerunner of *On the Town* and for Kelly's delightful dance with a cartoon mouse.

ancient Egypt has not been a popular stopping place for movie-makers. Several films based on the Bible (qv), notably *The Ten Commandments*, have stayed awhile, and there were detailed reconstructions in *The Egyptian, Land of the Pharaohs,* and Kawalerowicz's *Pharaoh*. Otherwise it has been most frequently seen in flashbacks in *The Mummy* (qv) and its sequels.

Anders, Glenn (1889–1981). American stage actor who made occasional film appearances, usually sinister.
Laughter 30. By Your Leave 35. Nothing but the Truth 41. *The Lady from Shanghai* 48. M 51. Behave Yourself 51, etc.

Anders, Luana (1940–). American leading lady of minor movies of the sixties.
Life Begins at Seventeen 58. The Pit and the Pendulum 61. The Young Racers 63. Dementia 13 63. *That Cold Day in the Park* 68. B. J. Presents 71. When the Legends Die 72. Shampoo 75. The Missouri Breaks 76. Goin' South 78. Personal Best 81. Movers and Shakers 84.

Anders, Merry (c. 1932–). American light leading lady.
Les Misérables 52. Phffft 54. The Dalton Girls 57. Violent Road 58. The Hypnotic Eye 60. 20,000 Eyes 61. House of the Damned 63. Tickle Me 65. Legacy of Blood 71, etc.
TV series: The Stu Erwin Show 54. It's Always Jan 55. How to Marry a Millionaire 58.

Anders, Rudolph (1902–). American character actor.
Actors and Sin 51. Phantom from Space 52. She Demons 58. On the Double 61, etc.

Andersen, Hans Christian (1805–1875). Danish writer of fairy tales, impersonated by Danny Kaye in Goldwyn's 1952 biopic. Many of his tales were filmed by Disney as *Silly Symphonies*, and one of them was the basis of *The Red Shoes* 48.

Anderson, Barbara (–). American leading lady, chiefly remembered as Ironside's pretty assistant in the TV series.
Visions (TV) 72. Don't Be Afraid of the Dark (TV) 73. Strange Honeymoon (TV) 74. You Lie So Deep My Love (TV) 75. Doctors' Private Lives (TV) 79, etc.
TV series: A Man Called Ironside 67–75.

Anderson, Daphne (1922–) (Daphne Scrutton). British light actress chiefly associated with the stage.
Trottie True 49. The Beggar's Opera 52. Hobson's Choice 54. A Kid for Two Farthings 55. The Prince and the Showgirl 57. Snowball 60. Captain Clegg 62. The Scarlet Pimpernel (TV) 82.

Anderson, Donna (1938–). American leading lady.
On the Beach 59. Inherit the Wind 60.

Anderson, Eddie 'Rochester' (1905–1977). Black comedian long associated with Jack Benny on radio and TV. His gravel voice and rolling eyes were familiar in the thirties and forties, but his amiable stereotype became unpopular in a race-conscious age. As he said in a 1970 TV appearance, when invited to resume his old role of butler, 'Massah Benny, we don' do dat no mo' . . .'
What Price Hollywood 30. Three Men on a Horse 35. *Green Pastures* 36. Jezebel 38. *You Can't Take It With You* 38. *Gone With the Wind* 39. *Topper Returns* 41. Tales of Manhattan 42. The Meanest Man in the World 42. *Cabin In The Sky* (leading role) 43.

Broadway Rhythm 44. The Show-Off 46. It's a Mad Mad Mad Mad World 63, many others.
TV series: *The Jack Benny Show* 53–65.

Anderson, Ernest (–). Black American character actor.
In This Our Life 42. Three for Bedroom C 52. The Well 52. Whatever Happened to Baby Jane? 62, etc.

Anderson, G. M. ('Bronco Billy') (1882–1971) (Max Aronson). American silent actor, an unsuccessful vaudeville performer who drifted into films in *The Great Train Robbery* 03. Later co-founded the Essanay company and made nearly four hundred one-reel Westerns starring himself. Retired in 1920; reappeared in 1965 in *The Bounty Killer*. Special Academy Award 1957 'for his contribution to the development of motion pictures'.

Anderson, Gerry (1929–). British puppeteer who via his Century 21 productions made TV series such as *Four Feather Falls, Supercar, Fireball XL5, Captain Scarlet, Joe 90, Thunderbirds*. Less successfully he moved into gimmicky live-action with *UFO* and *Space 1999*, and into feature films with *Journey to the Far Side of the Sun*.

Anderson, Herbert (1917–). Mild-mannered American actor.
Till We Meet Again 40. The Body Disappears 41. The Male Animal 58. I Bury the Living 68. Sunrise at Campobello 60. Rascal 69, etc.
TV series: *Dennis the Menace* 59–63.

Anderson, James (1921–1969). American general purpose supporting actor.
Sergeant York 41. The Great Sinner 49. Donovan's Brain 53. I Married a Monster from Outer Space 57. The Ballad of Cable Hogue 70, many others.

Anderson, Jean (1908–). British stage and screen actress often cast as sympathetic nurse, tired mother, or spinster aunt.
The Mark of Cain 47. Elizabeth of Ladymead 49. White Corridors 51. The Franchise Affair 51. A Town Like Alice 56. Heart of a Child 57. Robbery under Arms 57. Solomon and Sheba 59. Half a Sixpence 67. The Night Digger 71. The Lady Vanishes 79, many others.
TV series: *The Brothers* 71–76.

Anderson, John (1922–). Tall, thin, pale-eyed American character actor.
The True Story of Lynn Stuart 58. Psycho 60. Ride the High Country 62. The Satan Bug 65. Welcome to Hard Times 69. Soldier Blue 70. The Hancocks (TV) 76. The Lincoln Conspiracy (as Lincoln) 78, etc.

Anderson, Dame Judith (1898–) (Frances Margaret Anderson). Australian stage actress whose splendidly icy presence made her a hit on Broadway and gave her a long career there. Her occasional movies were seldom notable, but she will be remembered for her inimitable Mrs Danvers in *Rebecca*.
□Blood Money 33. *Rebecca* 40. Forty Little Mothers 40. King's Row 41. Free and Easy 41. Lady Scarface 41. All Through the Night 42. Edge of Darkness 43. Stage Door Canteen 43. Laura 44. And Then There Were None 45. The Diary of a Chambermaid 46. The Strange Love of Martha Ivers 46. The Specter of the Rose 46. Tycoon 47. The Red House 47. Pursued 47. The Furies 50. Salome 53. The Ten Commandments 56. Cat on a Hot Tin Roof 58. Cinderfella 60. Macbeth (TV) 60. Don't Bother to Knock 61. A Man Called Horse 70. Inn of the Damned 74. Star Trek III: The Search for Spock 84.
† In 1984, at the age of 86, she made her TV soap opera debut as the grand dame in Santa Barbara (which happens to be her home town).

¶ *J.A.:* I have not myself a very serene temperament.
Famous line: 'Very stupid to kill the servants: now we don't even know where to find the marmalade.' (*And Then There Were None*)

Anderson, Lindsay (1923–). British film director and critic.
O Dreamland 53. Thursday's Children 54. Every Day Except Christmas 57. *This Sporting Life* 63. The White Bus 67. *If* 68. *O Lucky Man* 72. In Celebration 74. The Old Crowd (TV) 79. Chariots of Fire (as actor) 81. Britannia Hospital 82. The Whales of August 87, etc.

¶ 'He's a prime example of somebody who, once he has created something, tries to support it with a scaffolding of theory. But it's all rubbish: either it's worked or it hasn't.'—*Tony Richardson*
L.A.: To make a film is to create a world.
L.A.: I suppose I'm the boy who stood on the burning deck whence all but he had fled. The trouble is I don't know whether the boy was a hero or a bloody idiot.

Anderson, Loni (–). Blonde American leading lady, familiar on TV as the sexy secretary in *WKRP in Cincinnati*. The Magnificent Magical Magnet of Santa Mesa (TV) 77.

Anderson, Mary (1920–). American supporting actress.
Gone With The Wind 39. Cheers for Miss Bishop 41. Lifeboat 43. *The Song of Bernadette* 44. Wilson 44. To Each His Own 46. Underworld Story 50. I The Jury 53. Dangerous Crossing 53, etc.

Anderson, Max (1914–1959). British documentary director, with the GPO Film Unit from 1936, later Crown Film Unit. Best known for *The Harvest Shall Come* 41. *Daybreak in Udi* 48.

Anderson, Maxwell (1888–1959). American middlebrow playwright, many of whose plays were filmed.
What Price Glory 27 & 52. *All Quiet on the Western Front* (screenplay) 30. Mary of Scotland 36. Winterset 37. Elizabeth and Essex (Elizabeth the Queen) 39. The Eve of St Mark 44. Key Largo 48. Joan of Arc (Joan of Lorraine) 48. The Wrong Man (orig sp) 56. The Bad Seed 56. Anne of the Thousand Days 70.

Anderson, Michael (1920–). British director who graduated to the international scene.
□Waterfront 50. Hell Is Sold Out 51. Night Was Our Friend 52. Will Any Gentleman? 53. House of the Arrow 54. *The Dam Busters* 55. *1984* 55. *Around the World in Eighty Days* 56. Yangtse Incident 56. Chase a Crooked Shadow 57. Shake Hands with the Devil 59. The Wreck of the Mary Deare 59. All the Fine Young Cannibals 60. The Naked Edge 61. Flight from Ashiya 62. Wild and Wonderful 63. Operation Crossbow 65. *The Quiller Memorandum* 66. *The Shoes of the Fisherman* 68. Pope Joan 72. Doc Savage 75. Conduct Unbecoming 75. Logan's Run 76. Orca 77. Dominique 78. The Martian Chronicles (TV) 79. Bells 79. Murder by Phone 82. Second Time Lucky 83. Separate Vacations 86. Vegeance (TV) 86.

Anderson, Michael Jnr (1943–). British juvenile lead, former child actor, son of director Michael Anderson.
The Moonraker 57. The Sundowners 60. In Search of the Castaways 61. Play it Cool 62. The Greatest Story Ever Told 65. Major Dundee 65. The Sons of Katie Elder 65. The Glory Guys 65. WUSA 69. The Last Movie 71, etc.
TV series: The Monroes 66.

Anderson, Philip W. (1915–1980). American editor.
Sayonara 57. Cash McCall 59. The FBI Story 59. Ocean's Eleven 80. The Parent Trap 61. Gypsy 62. A Man Called Horse 70, many others.

Anderson, Richard (1926–). Thoughtful-looking American supporting actor.
The People Against O'Hara 51. The Story of Three Loves 53. Escape from Fort Bravo 54. Forbidden Planet 56. *Paths of Glory* 57. *The Long Hot Summer* 58. Compulsion 59. Seven Days in May 64. Seconds 66. Macho Callahan 70. Doctors' Wives 71. The Honkers 72, etc.
TV series: Bus Stop 61. Perry Mason 65–66. Dan August 70. Six Million Dollar Man 73–78. Bionic Woman 76–77. Cover Up 84.

Anderson, Robert (1917–). American playwright who became an occasional Hollywood scriptwriter.
Tea and Sympathy (from his play) 56. Until They Sail 57. The Nun's Story 59. The Sand Pebbles 66. I Never Sang for my Father (from his play) 70.

Anderson, Rona (1926–). Scottish actress whose film career has been desultory.
Sleeping Car to Trieste 48. Poets' Pub 49. Home to Danger 51. Black Thirteen 54. The Flaw 55. Stock Car 55. Man with a Gun 58. Devils of Darkness 65. *The Prime of Miss Jean Brodie* 69, etc.

Anderson, Warner (1911–1976). American supporting actor of solid presence but no outstanding personality.
This Is the Army 43. Destination Tokyo 43. Objective Burma 45. Abbott and Costello in Hollywood 45. Weekend at the Waldorf 45. Bad Bascomb 46. Dark Delusion 47. Song of the Thin Man 47. Command Decision 48. The Doctor and the Girl 49. *Destination Moon* (leading role) 50. The Blue Veil 51. *Detective Story* 51. Only the Valiant 51. A Lion Is in the Streets 53. The Caine Mutiny 54. Drum Beat 54. The Blackboard Jungle 55. The Line-Up 58. Armored Command 61. Rio Conchos 64, many others.
TV series: The Doctors 52. The Line-Up 59. *Peyton Place* (as the newspaper editor) 64–68.

Andersson, Bibi (1935–). Swedish actress who has ventured into international films.
Smiles of a Summer Night 55. *The Seventh Seal* 56. *Wild Strawberries* 57. The Face 58. So Close to Life 60. The Devil's Eye 61. Square of Violence 63. Now About These Women 64. My Sister My Love 66. Duel at

Diablo 66. *Persona* 66. A Question of Rape 67. The Story of a Woman 69. *The Kremlin Letter* 69. A Passion 70. The Touch 71. *Cries and Whispers* 72. My Husband, His Mistress and I 76. I Never Promised You a Rose Garden 77. An Enemy of the People 78. Quintet 79. Airport 79—the Concorde 79. Exposed 83. The Last Summer 84. Matador 85. Poor Butterfly 86, etc.

Andersson, Harriet (1932–). Swedish actress, a member of Ingmar Bergman's company.
Summer with Monika 52. *Sawdust and Tinsel* 53. A Lesson in Love 54. *Smiles of a Summer Night* 55. Through a Glass Darkly 62. To Love 64. Now About These Women 64. The Deadly Affair (GB) 66. *Cries and Whispers* 72, etc.

Andes, Keith (1920–). American light actor, usually in secondary roles.
The Farmer's Daughter 47. Clash by Night 52. Blackbeard the Pirate 52. Back from Eternity 56. The Girl Most Likely 58. Tora! Tora! Tora! 70, etc.
TV series: This Man Dawson 59. Glynis 63.

Andress, Ursula (1936–). Swiss-born glamour star, in international films.
The Loves of Casanova (It.) 54. *Dr No* 62. Four for Texas 63. Fun in Acapulco 64. *She* 64. Nightmare in the Sun 64. *What's New Pussycat?* 65. Up to his Ears 65. The Tenth Victim 65. Once Before I Die 66. The Blue Max 66. Casino Royale 67. The Southern Star 69. Perfect Friday 70. Red Sun 71. Five Against Capricorn 72. The Life and Times of Scaramouche 76. Loaded Guns 76. The Fifth Musketeer 77. The Clash of the Titans 81, etc.

Andrews, Anthony (1948–). British leading actor who graduated through TV.
QB VII (TV) 74. A War of Children (TV) 74. Take Me High 74. Percy's Progress 75. Operation Daybreak 76. Les Adolescentes 76. The Scarlet Pimpernel (title role) (TV) 82. David Copperfield (TV) 74. Ivanhoe (TV) 82. Sparkling Cyanide (TV) 83. Under the Volcano 84. The Holcroft Covenant 85. The Second Victory 86. Suspicion (TV) 87. The Lighthorsemen 87.
TV series: *Danger UXB* 78. *Brideshead Revisited* 81.

Andrews, Dana (1909–) (Carver Daniel Andrews). American leading man who showed promise in a wide variety of forties roles, but whose somewhat hard and immobile features limited him in middle age.
☐The Westerner 40. Lucky Cisco Kid 40. Sailor's Lady 40. Kit Carson 40. Tobacco Road 41. Belle Starr 41. Swamp Water 41. Ball of Fire 41. Berlin Correspondent 42. Crash Dive 43. *The Ox Bow Incident* 43. North Star 43. *The Purple Heart* 44. Wing and a Prayer 44. Up in Arms 44. *Laura* 44. State Fair 45. Fallen Angel 45. *A Walk in the Sun* 45. Canyon Passage 46. *The Best Years of Our Lives* 46. *Boomerang* 47. Night Song 47. Daisy Kenyon 47. The Iron Curtain 48. Deep Waters 48. No Minor Vices 48. Britannia Mews 48. Sword in the Desert 49. *My Foolish Heart* 50. Where the Sidewalk Ends 50. Edge of Doom 50. The Frogmen 50. Sealed Cargo 51. I Want You 51. Assignment Paris 52. Elephant Walk 53. Duel in the Jungle 54. Three Hours to Kill 54. Smoke Signal 55. Strange Lady in Town 55. Comanche 56. While the City Sleeps 56. Beyond a Reasonable Doubt 56. Night of the Demon 57. Spring Reunion 57. Zero Hour 57. The Fearmakers 58. Enchanted Island 58. The Crowded Sky 60. Madison Avenue 62. Crack in the World 65. The Satan Bug 65. In Harm's Way 65. Brainstorm 65. Town Tamer 65. The Loved One 65. Battle of the Bulge 65. Johnny Reno 66. Spy in your Eye 66. Hot Rods to Hell 67. The Frozen Dead 67. Cobra 67. Ten Million-Dollar Grab 68. The Devil's Brigade 68. The Failing of Raymond (TV) 71. Innocent Bystanders 72. The First 36 Hours of Dr Durrant (TV) 75. Airport 75 75. Take a Hard Ride 75. Shadow in the Streets (TV) 76. The Last Tycoon 76. Ike (TV) 79. Good Guys Wear Black 79. Born Again 79. The Pilot 79.
TV series: Bright Promise (daily soap opera) 71. The American Girls 78. Falcon Crest 82.

Andrews, Edward (1914–85). Beaming, bespectacled American character actor who could effortlessly become hearty, hen-pecked or sinister.
☐ *The Phenix City Story* 55. The Harder They Fall 56. Tea and Sympathy 56. These Wilder Years 56. *The Unguarded Moment* 56. Tension at Table Rock 56. Three Brave Men 57. Hot Summer Night 57. The Tattered Dress 57. Trooper Hook 57. The Fiend That Walked the West 58. Night of the Quarter Moon 59. *Elmer Gantry* 60. The Absent-Minded Professor 61. The Young Savages 61. Love in a Goldfish Bowl 61. The Young Doctors 61. Advise and Consent 62. Forty Pounds of Trouble 62. Son of Flubber 62. The Thrill of It All 63. A Tiger Walks 64. The Brass Bottle 64. Good Neighbor Sam 64. Kisses for My President 64. Youngblood Hawke 64. Send

Me No Flowers 64. The Man from Galveston 64. Fluffy 65. The Glass Bottom Boat 66. Birds Do It 66. Tora Tora Tora 70. The Trouble with Girls 70. The Million Dollar Duck 71. How to Frame a Figg 71. Now You See Him Now You Don't 72. Avanti 72. Charley and the Angel 73. The Photographer 75. Gremlins 84. Sixteen Candles 84.
TV series: Broadside 64. Supertrain 79.

Andrews, Harry (1911–). Tough-looking British stage and screen actor. Often plays sergeant-majors or other no-nonsense characters.
The Red Beret (debut) 52. The Black Knight 54. Helen of Troy 55. *A Hill in Korea* 56. Alexander the Great 56. Moby Dick 56. Saint Joan 57. *Ice Cold in Alex* 58. The Devil's Disciple 59. Solomon and Sheba 59. Circle of Deception 60. The Best of Enemies 62. Lisa 62. 55 Days at Peking 62. Barabbas 62. The Informers 63. The System 64. *The Hill* 65. Sands of the Kalahari 65. The Agony and the Ecstasy 65. Modesty Blaise 66. *The Deadly Affair* 66. The Jokers 67. Danger Route 67. The Charge of the Light Brigade 68. The Night They Raided Minsky's (US) 68. The Seagull 68. A Nice Girl Like Me 69. The Battle of Britain 69. Country Dance 70. Entertaining Mr Sloane 70. Wuthering Heights 70. Burke and Hare 71. Nicholas and Alexandra 71. I Want What I Want 71. The Ruling Class 72. Man of La Mancha 72. Theatre of Blood 73. The Mackintosh Man 74. Man at the Top 74. The Bluebird 76. Equus 77. The Four Feathers (TV) 78. Death on the Nile 78. The Big Sleep 78. Superman 78. SOS Titanic (TV) 80. The Curse of King Tut's Tomb (TV) 80. Hawk the Slayer 80. The Seven Dials Mystery (TV) 83, etc.

Andrews, Julie (1934–) (Julia Wells). British star of Hollywood films. A singing stage performer from childhood who became the original stage Eliza of *My Fair Lady* but failed to get the film role. She zoomed to international stardom the same year but her refreshingly old-fashioned image seemed to pall rather quickly.
□*Mary Poppins* (AA) 64. *The Americanization of Emily* 64. *The Sound of Music* 65. Torn Curtain 66. Hawaii 66. *Thoroughly Modern Millie* 67. *Star!* 68. Darling Lili 69. The Tamarind Seed 74. '10' 79. Little Miss Marker 80. S.O.B. 81. Victor/Victoria 82. The Man Who Loved Women 83. Duet for One 86. That's Life 86.

¶ One senses that she is realistic enough to have enjoyed the good times while they lasted, and to fall from grace gracefully. But she may fight. After *The Sound of Music*, Christopher Plummer said that:

> Working with her is like being hit over the head with a Valentine's card.

And some anonymous gentleman described her as:

> Like a nun with a switchblade.

Moss Hart said:

> She has that wonderful British strength that makes you wonder why they lost India.

Miss Andrews does seem to merit the suggestion of steel beneath the velvet. When she accepted her Oscar, which many thought went to her out of sympathy because Warners refused her the film of *My Fair Lady*, her little speech ran:

> I'd like to thank all those who made this possible—especially Jack Warner.

Having got to the top by being sweet and old-fashioned, she quickly showed signs of disliking her own image.

> I don't want to be thought of as wholesome,

she said in 1966, and promptly proved it by accepting a sexy role. She was also seen wearing a badge which read:

> Mary Poppins is a junkie.

But her serene self-confidence may be something of a sham. She once said:

> Films are much more my level. On stage I never feel quite enough . . .

One way or another, she achieved, briefly, a worldwide image best expressed by a *Time* magazine interviewer:

> She's everybody's tomboy tennis partner and their daughter, their sister, their mum . . . She is Christmas carols in the snow, a companion by the fire, a laughing clown at charades, a girl to read poetry to on a cold winter's night . . .

Andrews, Lois (1924–1968). American light leading lady.
Dixie Dugan 43. Roger Touhy Gangster 44. The Desert Hawk 50. Meet Me After the Show 51, etc.

Andrews, Robert Hardy (1903–76). American screenwriter.
If I Had a Million (oa) 32. Bataan 44. The Cross of Lorraine 44. The Hairy Ape 44. Tarzan Goes to India 62, etc.

The Andrews Sisters: Patty (1918–), Maxine (1916–) and Laverne (1913–67). American close harmony singing group, popular in light musicals of the forties.
□Argentine Nights 40. In The Navy 41. Buck

Privates 41. Hold That Ghost 41. Give Out Sisters 42. Private Buckaroo 42. What's Cookin'? 42. Always a Bridesmaid 43. How's About It? 43. Follow the Boys 44. Hollywood Canteen 44. Moonlight and Cactus 44. Swingtime Johnny 44. Her Lucky Night 45. Make Mine Music (voices) 46. Road to Rio 47. Melody Time (voices) 48.

Andrews, Stanley (1892–1969). American character actor, often seen as grizzled western veteran. He more or less ended his career as the 'old ranger' host of TV's *Death Valley Days*.
Evelyn Prentice 34. Mississippi 35. Murder Man 35. Pennies from Heaven 36. Desire 36. Madame X 37. Nancy Steele Is Missing 37. Hold That Co-Ed 38. Alexander's Ragtime Band 38. Kentucky 38. Beau Geste 39. Union Pacific 39. The Blue Bird 40. Meet John Doe 41. My Gal Sal 42. Murder My Sweet 44. Adventure 45. It's a Wonderful Life 46. Robin Hood of Texas 47. Northwest Stampede 48. The Last Bandit 49. Arizona Cowboy 50. Vengeance Valley 51. Woman of the North Country 52. Ride Vaquero 52. Dawn at Socorro 54. The Treasure of Ruby Hills 55. Frontier Gambler 56. Cry Terror 58, many others.

Andrews, Tige (c. 1923–) (Tiger Androwaous). Lebanese-American supporting actor, usually an amiable tough.
Mr Roberts 55. The Wings of Eagles 57. Imitation General 58. China Doll 58. A Private Affair 59. The Last Tycoon 76, etc.
TV series: *The Detectives, The Mod Squad.*

Andrews, Tod (1920–72). Burly American leading man of minor action films; previously known as Michael Ames.
Now Voyager 42. Action in the North Atlantic 43. From Hell It Came 60. In Harm's Way 64, etc.
TV series: The Gray Ghost 57.

Andreyev, Boris (1915–). Russian leading actor.
Tractor Drivers 39. Two Soldiers 43. The Last Hill 44. Song of Siberia 47. The Fall of Berlin 49. Ilya Muromets 56. The Gordeyev Family 59. The Cossacks 61. Aladdin 67, many others.

Andriot, Lucien (1897–1979). French-American cinematographer long in Hollywood.
Two Lives 15. Oh Boy 19. Why Trust Your Husband 21. Hell's Hole 23. Gigolo 26. White Gold 27. The Valiant 28. Hallelujah I'm a Bum 33. Anne of Green Gables 34. The Gay Desperado 36. The Lady in Question 40. The Hairy Ape 44. The Southerner 45. And Then There Were None 45. Dishonored Lady 47. Outpost in Morocco 49. Borderline 50. Home Town Story 51, many others. Later in television.

anecdotes

¶ The more scintillating luminaries of Hollywood's golden age were the subjects of many stories which may or may not have been true; most of us will wish to think they were. Here's a selection, interspersed with a few bits of pure fiction.

The waspish New York wit Dorothy Parker spent some years in Hollywood as a scriptwriter. For the first few weeks in the studio no one ever came into her office: whether from awe or from jealousy, she was ignored. She soon fixed things by taking her name off the door and putting in its place a sign reading: MEN.

The same Miss Parker had periods of indolence, and when asked for the third time why she had not delivered a script as agreed, snapped:

> Because I've been too fucking busy—and vice versa.

Miss Parker had many a battle of wits with Clare Boothe Luce, author of *The Women*. On one occasion they almost collided in a doorway. 'Age before beauty,' cooed Miss Luce, standing back. Miss Parker sailed through. 'Pearls before swine,' she remarked.

Miss Parker was asked what she thought of a certain international glamour queen. 'Remarkable', she said. 'The girl speaks eighteen languages and can't say no in any of them.'

Drink was often the downfall of the acting classes: it was certainly the reason why a film called *The Captain Hates the Sea* went way over budget on its Catalina Island location; the actors were having too much liquid fun. The producer wired from Hollywood in desperation: RETURN AT ONCE; THE COST IS STAGGERING. The answer came: SO IS THE CAST.

One famous drinker, W. C. Fields, had a guilty conscience about his success. 'During my years of poverty,' he once told an interviewer, 'I swore that if I ever got to the top I'll start a foundation to help underprivileged children. For years I could do nothing about it. Then came Hollywood and riches.' 'And did you start the foundation?' asked the interviewer, pencil poised. 'Naw,' drawled Fields. 'I didn't. I said to myself, the hell with them.'

For all their wealth, the Hollywood stars were an unhappy lot. Nick Schenk once walked round the MGM Studio, which he virtually owned, and commented: 'I've never seen so many miserable people making a hundred thousand dollars a year.'

The loss of youth's freshness concerned most of the star actresses. Marlene Dietrich once berated her photographer for unacceptable close-ups. 'What's the matter with you?' she stormed. 'Eight years ago you used to take marvellous pictures of me.' 'Ah,' he said tactfully; 'but I was much younger then.'

Cinema owners too have always bemoaned their lot. They say a couple of them once met on the street. 'How's business?' said one.

'Terrible. Two years ago I lost ten thousand dollars, last year it was twenty-five, and this year I look like being forty thousand dollars down.'

'But Ike, if things are so bad, why do you stay in show business?'

His friend shrugged. 'A fellow's got to live.'

Movies sometimes lose a lot of money; they also cost a lot to make. The famous story about Cecil B. De Mille suggests why. De Mille, they say, was preparing to shoot an elaborate and expensive scene which had to be got right the first time. Five thousand extras were on hand, not to mention camels, elephants, stunt men and a flock of birds to be released at the critical moment. Four cameras were at strategic points to accomplish the feat of recording this event, the key shot being from number four in a helicopter hovering overhead. After a day of preparation the master director called 'Action!' The many and varied performers were unleashed; fire raged; rain poured down; buildings collapsed. The master sighed and spoke to the cinematographers through his mike. 'O.K., number one?' 'Fine, chief.' 'Number two?' 'Just great, Mr De Mille.' 'Number three?' 'Perfect.' 'Number four?' No answer. 'Number four?' The intercom crackled into life: 'Ready when you are, Mr De Mille.'

De Mille was often accused of buying up books and using nothing but the title. They say that he once invited a famous author to a première and asked him afterwards what he thought of the film. 'Why, excellent,' said the distinguished guest. 'Who wrote it?' De Mille was non-plussed: 'You did. We bought it from you.' 'I would never have known,' said the author. 'In fact, I'd like to use one of your variations for a new novel.' 'That's all right,' said De Mille, 'but you'll have to give us an option on the film rights.'

Another première. Otto Preminger invited Jewish comedian Mort Sahl to be his personal guest at the first showing of the four-hour Preminger epic about the beginnings of the state of Israel, *Exodus*. After three-and-a-half hours had passed, Sahl got to his feet wearily, turned to his host, and said: 'Otto—let my people go!'

Hollywood is the place which popularized divorce. They say that when Elizabeth Taylor took her sixth husband, and the justice of the peace wanted details of her previous marriages, she said: 'What is this, a memory test?'

Then there were the two moppets playing on a Beverly Hills lawn. One said to the other: 'That man coming through the door is my daddy.' Her chum looked and sighed. 'Oh, him. We had him last year.'

And three Hollywood kids were playing games. 'Let's play marriages,' said one, 'and I'll be Mama.'

—'And I'll be Papa.'

—'And I'll be the judge.'

The much-married Zsa Zsa Gabor met a new man who offered her diamonds.

'Darling,' she said, 'I never take gifts from a perfect stranger. But who's perfect?'

Finally, the moguls. The autocratic David O. Selznick was overfond of writing memos. A member of his staff did something wrong, was fearful of the worst, and thought he might as well get it over with. So he sent Selznick a note beginning: 'In reply to your memo of tomorrow . . .'

When he was making *Gone With the Wind* Selznick was desperate for the services of Clark Gable as Rhett Butler. But Gable was under contract to Louis B. Mayer. So Selznick rang Mayer, and the conversation is reported as follows:

> 'Louis, we're both in terrible trouble about Clark Gable.'
>
> 'Why?'
>
> 'Well, you've got him and I want him.'

It was not always safe to offer even the right advice to the moguls. When Goldwyn planned to star Anna Sten in *Nana*, one of his favourite directors warned him against it. Goldwyn persisted, and the movie was a disaster. From that day forth Goldwyn never hired the director again, and when someone asked him why, he averred: 'That man was associated with one of my greatest flops.'

For obvious reasons Goldwyn's staff tended to agree with whatever the boss said. Even this nettled him, and on one occasion he burst out: 'I don't want yes-men around me. I want you to disagree once in a while—even if it costs you your job!'

Goldwyn ran rough cuts of his movies at home on a Sunday night, trying them out on the family. One such evening as soon as the end title came up he pitched into the director and editor, saying it was a lousy film and he couldn't understand it. 'Oh, come now,' said the daring director, 'surely you exaggerate. I'll bet your son here understood every word and every scene.' Goldwyn turned to the ten-year-old boy, who said: 'Why, yes, Pop: it was fine, I had no problem.' The director's triumph was short-lived, for Goldwyn turned on him with: 'What business do you think I'm in? Making pictures for children?'

Angel, Danny (Daniel M.) (1911–). British producer, in films from 1945.
Mr Drake's Duck 50. Albert R.N. 53. The Sea Shall Not Have Them 54. Reach for the Sky 56. Carve Her Name With Pride 57. The Sheriff of Fractured Jaw 58. West Eleven 63, etc.

Angel, Heather (1909–86). British born leading lady of the thirties; in Hollywood from 1933.
City of Song 30. *Berkeley Square* 33. The Informer 35. The Mystery of Edwin Drood 35. Last of the Mohicans 36. Army Girl 38. Pride and Prejudice 40. Time to Kill 42. Lifeboat 43. In the Meantime, Darling 44. The Saxon Charm 48. The Premature Burial 62. TV series: Peyton Place 64–69.

Angeli, Pier (1932–1971) (Anna Maria Pierangeli). Sensitive-looking Italian actress who after some stage experience at home moved to Hollywood but found only occasional worthy roles. Twin sister of Marisa Pavan.
□Tomorrow Is Too Late (It.) 50. Tomorrow Is Another Day (It.) 51. *Teresa* 51. The Light Touch 51. The Devil Makes Three 52. The Story of Three Loves 52. Sombrero 53. The Flame and the Flesh 54. The Silver Chalice 54. Santerella (It.) 54. Somebody Up There Likes Me 56. Port Afrique 56. The Vintage 57. Merry Andrew 58. SOS Pacific 60. The Angry Silence 60. Musketeers of the Sea (It.) 62. White Slave Ship 62. Sodom and Gomorrah 63. Battle of the Bulge 65. Spy in Your Eye 66. Missione Morte (It.) 66. Per Mille Dollari al Giorno (It.) 66. Shadow of Evil 67. Red Roses for the Fuehrer (It.) 67. One Step to Hell 68. Vive America (Sp.) 68. Les Enemoniades (Sp.) 70. Every Bastard a King 70. Adio Alexandra (It.) 71. Nelle Pieghe Della Carne 71. Octaman 72.

Angelopoulos, Theodor (–). Greek director whose *The Travelling Players* was widely praised in 1975.

angels made appearances in many silent films: *Intolerance, The Four Horsemen of the Apocalypse, The Sorrows of Satan*, and the many versions of *Uncle Tom's Cabin* and *Faust* were among them. Since sound they have remained a favourite Hollywood device, but have naturally tended to lose their wings and become more whimsical, less awesome and often of somewhat ambiguous reality, to be explained away in the last reel as a result of the hero's bump on the head. The last completely serious angels were probably those in the all-Negro *Green Pastures* 37; since then they have been played by Claude Rains in *Here Comes Mr Jordan*, Jeanette MacDonald in *I Married an Angel*, Kenneth Spencer (and others) in *Cabin in the Sky*, Jack Benny (and others) in *The Horn Blows at Midnight*, Clifton Webb and Edmund Gwenn in *For Heaven's Sake*, Henry Travers in *It's a Wonderful Life*, Leon Ames in *Yolanda and the Thief*, Kathleen Byron and a great many extras in *A Matter of Life and Death*, Robert Cummings in *Heaven Only Knows*, Cary Grant in *The Bishop's Wife*, several actors in *Angels in the Outfield*, James Mason in *Forever Darling*, Diane Cilento in *The Angel Who Pawned Her Harp*, John Philip Law in *Barbarella*, and Harry Belafonte in *The Angel Levine*. In 1978 Warren Beatty remade *Here Comes Mr Jordan* as *Heaven Can Wait* and spawned several ineffective TV imitations including Ray Bolger in *Heaven Only Knows*.

Used in a figurative sense, the word 'angel' has continued to be a favourite title component: *I'm No Angel, Angel, The Dark Angel, Angels with Dirty Faces, Angels Wash Their Faces, Angel and the Badman, Angel Face, Angel Baby, Angels in Disguise, The Angel Wore Red, Angels One Five, Angels in Exile*, etc.

See also: *fantasy*.

Angels with Dirty Faces (US 1938). A typical example of the period when Hollywood's gangster melodramas had to point a moral: the character played by James Cagney pretended to be a coward on his way to the electric chair so that he would not become an object of hero-worship for the Dead End Kids. As so often, Pat O'Brien was an Irish priest. Despite good direction by Michael Curtiz, there was precious little fun to be had from this type of social melodrama; the genre quickly declined and the Dead End Kids turned into comedians (in a so-called sequel, *Angels Wash Their Faces*).

Angelus, Muriel (1909–) (M. A. Findlay). British leading lady of the thirties who had a brief Hollywood career before retiring in 1940.
The Ringer 30. Hindle Wakes 31. The Light that Failed 39. The Great McGinty 40. The Way of All Flesh 40, etc.

Anger, Kenneth (1929–). American independent film-maker who grew up in Hollywood and also wrote *Hollywood Babylon*, a scurrilous exposé of the private lives of its stars. His films are mainly short, inscrutable and Freudian.
Fireworks 47. Eaux d'Artifice 53. Inauguration of the Pleasure Dome 54. Scorpio Rising 64. Kustom Kar Kommandos 65. Invocation of my Demon Brother 69, etc.

Angers, Avril (1922–). British character comedienne whose film appearances have been infrequent.
Skimpy in the Navy 50. Lucky Mascot 51. The Green Man 56. Devils of Darkness 65. The Family Way 66. Two a Penny 68, etc.

Anhalt, Edward (1914–). American middlebrow scriptwriter. With his wife Edna Anhalt (1914–):
Bulldog Drummond Strikes Back 48. Panic in the Streets 50. The Sniper 52. Not as a Stranger 54. The Pride and the Passion 56. The Young Lions 58, etc.
Alone: A Girl Named Tamiko 63. Becket 64. Hour of the Gun 67. The Boston Strangler 68. The Mad Woman of Chaillot 69. Jeremiah Johnson (co-w) 72. Luther 74. The Man in The Glass Booth 76. Escape to Athena 79. The Holcroft Covenant 85, etc.

Animal Farm (GB 1954). Britain's first full-length cartoon, a major achievement of the Halas and Batchelor Studios, but on the whole too conventionally animated to bring out the full satiric flavour of George Orwell's fable.

animals, as Walt Disney knew, are a sure way to success at the box office, with dogs well established as number one providers. Dog stars of the movies have included Rin Tin Tin, Strongheart (his closest rival), Ben (Mack Sennett's comedy dog), Pete (of 'Our Gang'), Asta (of the 'Thin Man' series), Daisy (so popular in the 'Blondie' films that he starred in his own movies), and of course the immortal Lassie. Less publicized canines have successfully taken on dramatic roles in such films as *The Voice of Bugle Ann, Oliver Twist, Umberto D, Greyfriars Bobby, Owd Bob, Old Yeller, Savage Sam, The Ugly Dachshund* and *The Spy with a Cold Nose*; while Dick Powell was reincarnated as a very handsome Alsatian in *You Never Can Tell.* Rhubarb has been the only 'starred' cat, though felines have played important roles in *The Cat and the Canary, The Cat Creeps, Cat Girl, Shadow of the Cat, Breakfast at Tiffany's, The Incredible Journey, A Walk on the Wild Side, The Three Lives of Thomasina, That Darn Cat, The Torture Garden* (with its diabolical pussy), *The Wrong Box, The Goldwyn Follies* (in which the Ritz Brothers were memorably assisted by hundreds of cats to sing 'Hey Pussy Pussy'), *The Bluebird* (in which a sleek black feline was humanized very satisfyingly into Gale Sondergaard), *The Tomb of Ligeia, Eye of the Cat*, and several versions of *The Black Cat.* Other animals to achieve something like stardom have included Balthasar the donkey, Flipper the dolphin, Gentle Ben the bear, Cheta the chimp (in the Tarzan films), Slicker the seal (in *Spawn of the North*), the chimp in *The Barefoot Executive*, Clarence the Cross-eyed Lion (not to mention Fluffy), the *Zebra in the Kitchen*, and a great many horses including Rex (*King of the Wild Horses*), Tarzan (with Ken Maynard), Fritz (with William S. Hart), Tony (with Tom Mix), Silver (with Buck Jones), Champion (with Gene Autry) and Trigger (with Roy Rogers). *Born Free* and its sequels made stars of lions; *Ring of Bright Water* and *Tarka the Otter* did the same for otters, and *Benji* for a little dog; then there was *The Belstone Fox*; the deer in *The Yearling*; the dolphins in *The Day of the Dolphin*; the bear in *Grizzly*; and the host of assorted animals in *Doctor Dolittle*. Perhaps one shouldn't count the anthropoids in *Planet of the Apes*.

? Movie title makers often use animal allusions because they are vivid and picturesque (though not always meaningful to the viewer). Can you supply the animals missing from the following titles?

1 *. . . . . . Seed*
2 *Cry . . . . . .*
3 *The Fallen . . . . . .*
4 *A Gathering of . . . . . .*
5 *Flying . . . . . .*
6 *After the . . . . . .*
7 *Poor . . . . . .*
8 *Brother . . . . . .*
9 *. . . . . . Feathers*
10 *The . . . . . .'s Stratagem*
11 *The . . . . . . Trap*
12 *Track of the . . . . . .*

13 *The Flight of the . . . . . .*
14 *The Sleeping . . . . . .*
15 *Dear . . . . . .*
16 *Straw . . . . . .*
17 *Madame . . . . . .*
18 *. . . . . . Squadron*
19 *The Voice of the . . . . . .*
20 *. . . . . . Woman*

animation. The filming of static drawings, puppets or other objects in sequence so that they give an illusion of movement. Sometimes called 'stop-frame animation' because only one frame of film is exposed at a time.

Leading figures in the history of animation include Winsor McKay (qv) who in 1909 introduced Gertie the Dinosaur, Emile Cohl (qv), Len Lye (qv), Max Fleischer (qv), Walt Disney (qv), the UPA Group (qv), Norman McLaren (qv), William Hanna and Joe Barbera (qv), Halas and Batchelor (qv), Ralph Bakshi (qv) and Richard Williams (qv).

Best books on the subject are *The Technique of Film Animation* by John Halas and Roger Manvell; *The Art of Walt Disney* by Christopher Finch; *The Animated Film* by Ralph Stephenson.

Anka, Paul (1941–). Canadian pop singer of the sixties, subject of the documentary *Lonely Boy* 62. Also acted the same year in *The Longest Day*, and composed the theme song.

Ankers, Evelyn (1918–85). British leading lady who did not so much act as react. She also looked decorative, and after going to Hollywood in 1940 she appeared as the well-bred heroine of innumerable co-features. Married Richard Denning.
The Villiers Diamond 33. Rembrandt 36. Knight without Armour 37. Over the Moon 39. Hold that Ghost 41. Bachelor Daddy 41. *The Wolf Man* 41. The Ghost of Frankenstein 42. The Great Impersonation 42. The Mad Ghoul 43. Hers to Hold 43. His Butler's Sister 43. Ladies Courageous 44. Weird Woman 44. The Frozen Ghost 45. The French Key 46. The Lone Wolf In London 47. The Texan Meets Calamity Jane 50. No Greater Love 60, etc.

Ankrum, Morris (1896–1964). (Morris Nussbaum.) American stage actor seen in innumerable films as lawyer, judge or Western villain.
Buck Benny Rides Again 40. Light of the Western Stars 40. Tales of Manhattan 42. *Tennessee Johnson* 42. Let's Face It 43. Barbary Coast Gent 44. The Hidden Eye 45. The Harvey Girls 46. Joan of Arc 48. Rocketship XM 50. My Favourite Spy 51. Son of Ali Baba 52. Apache 54. Earth Versus the Flying Saucers 56. Badman's Country 59. The Most Dangerous Man Alive 61, many others.

Anna and the King of Siam. Anna Leonowens' autobiography of her experiences as governess at an eastern court seemed in 1946 a strange choice for a Hollywood film, especially when Rex Harrison was cast as the King and Linda Darnell as his leading mistress. But Irene Dunne kept the strange mixture palatable, and John Cromwell's direction was smooth. The plot was immediately adapted by Rodgers and Hammerstein as a musical, filmed with great success in 1956 as *The King and I.* Walter Lang directed Deborah Kerr and Yul Brynner in the leading roles. In 1972 Brynner reprised in a TV series, *Anna and the King* (and was still playing his favourite role on stage in 1980).

Anna Christie (US 1930). Early talkie version of Eugene O'Neill's waterfront play, advertised by the famous slogan, 'Garbo Talks!' Previously filmed in 1923 with Blanche Sweet.

Anna Karenina. Tolstoy's novel has been filmed many times, twice with Garbo (as *Love* in 1927, and again in 1935). The latter version, directed by Clarence Brown with Basil Rathbone as Karenin, was not eclipsed by Alexander Korda's 1948 British remake with Vivien Leigh and Ralph Richardson, though Julien Duvivier's direction achieved some pretty effects.
A TV version in 1985 starred Jacqueline Bisset, Christopher Reeve and Paul Scofield. There had been a BBC TV serial in 1978 with Nicola Pagett, Stuart Wilson and Eric Porter.

Anna Lucasta. Philip Yordan's melodramatic play was originally (1944) set among Negroes, but on Broadway they became Polish immigrants, and it was this version which was first screened, in 1949, with Paulette Goddard as the bad girl of the family who comes back to help in a domestic crisis. In 1959 the Negro version was finally filmed with Eartha Kitt and Sammy Davis Jnr. Yordan wrote both screenplays.

Annabella (1909–) (Suzanne Charpentier). French leading lady of the thirties, in international films; once married to Tyrone Power.
Napoleon 26. Le Million 32. Le Quatorze

Juillet 33. Under the Red Robe 36. Dinner at the Ritz 37. Wings of the Morning 37. Suez 38. Hôtel du Nord 38. Bridal Suite 39. Bomber's Moon 42. Tonight We Raid Calais 43. 13 Rue Madeleine 46. Don Juan (sp) 50, etc.

Annakin, Ken (1914–). British director of very variable output. Formerly a journalist.
□ Holiday Camp 47. Broken Journey 48. Here Come the Huggetts 47. Miranda 48. Quartet (part) 48. Vote for Huggett 49. Landfall 49. Double Confession 50. Trio (part) 50. The Huggetts Abroad 51. Hotel Sahara 51. Robin Hood 52. The Planter's Wife 52. The Seekers 53. The Sword and the Rose 53. You Know What Sailors Are 53. Value for Money 55. Three Men in a Boat 56. Loser Take All 56. Across the Bridge 57. Nor the Moon by Night 58. *The Swiss Family Robinson* 60. Third Man on the Mountain 61. *Very Important Person* 61. The Longest Day 62. The Hellions 62. Crooks Anonymous 62. The Informers 63. *The Fast Lady* 63. *Those Magnificent Men in Their Flying Machines* 64. Battle of the Bulge 65. The Biggest Bundle of them All 66. The Long Duel 67. Monte Carlo or Bust 69. Call of the Wild 72. Paper Tiger 75. The Fifth Musketeer 78. The Pirate (TV) 79. Cheaper To Keep Her 80. The Pirate Movie 82. Pippi Longstocking 86.

Anne of Green Gables. L. M. Montgomery's popular novel for girls about an orphan teenager who comes to live with crusty relations and finally charms them into her way of thinking, was a great screen success for Mary Miles Minter in 1919. In 1934 Anne Shirley appeared in a sound remake, and followed it up in 1941 with a sequel, *Anne of Windy Poplars*.

Annie Hall (US 1977). This rather desultory and melancholy but extremely fashionable comedy was showered with awards and marked Woody Allen's arrival as a bankable multi-talent after years as a cult figure. He wrote it (with Marshall Brickman) and directed it as well as starring (with Diane Keaton). Basically it is no more than a fashionably trimmed anecdote about a broken romance between two city eccentrics, but it certainly hit the spot: whether it will look so good in ten years is open to doubt.

Annis, Francesca (1944–). British leading lady, former juvenile player.
The Cat Gang 58. Cleopatra 62. The Eyes of Annie Jones 63. Flipper and the Pirates (US) 64. The Pleasure Girls 65. Run with the Wind 66. The Walking Stick 69. Macbeth 71. Krull 83. Coming Out of the Ice (TV) 83. The Secret Adversary (TV) 83. Dune 86. I'll Take Manhattan (TV) 86. Under the Cherry Moon 86, etc.
TV series: *Lillie* (title role) 78. Partners in Crime 83.

Ann-Margret (1941–) (Ann-Margret Olsson). Swedish-American sex symbol and formidable cabaret performer; a hard worker who gradually became a good actress.
□Pocketful of Miracles 61. *State Fair* 62. *Bye Bye Birdie* 62. Viva Las Vegas 64. Kitten with a Whip 64. Bus Riley's Back in Town 65. The Pleasure Seekers 65. Once a Thief 65. *The Cincinnati Kid* 65. Made in Paris 66. The Swinger 66. Stagecoach 66. Murderers' Row 66. The Tiger and the Pussycat 67. Mr Kinky 68. Rebus (It.) 68. Seven Men and One Brain (It.) 69. C.C. and Co. 70. *Carnal Knowledge* 71. R.P.M. 71. The Train Robbers 73. The Outside Man 73. Tommy 75. The Twist 76. Joseph Andrews 76. The Last Remake of Beau Geste 77. The Cheap Detective 78. Magic 78. The Villain 79. Middle Age Crazy 80. I Ought to Be in Pictures 82. Lookin' to Get Out 82. The Return of the Soldier 82. Who Will Love My Children? (TV) 83. Twice in a Lifetime 85. The Two Mrs Grevilles (TV) 86. 52 Pick-Up 86. A Tiger's Tale 87.

Anouilh, Jean (1914–87). Skilful and versatile French playwright who frequently worked in the cinema.
Monsieur Vincent 47. Caroline Chérie 50. A Night with Caroline 52. Le Chevalier de la Nuit 53. The Waltz of the Toreadors 62. Becket 64, etc.

Ansara, Michael (1922–). American actor with stage experience, specializing in Indian roles.
Action in Arabia 44. Only the Valiant 51. The Robe 53. The Egyptian 54. Sign of the Pagan 54. Diane 55. Jupiter's Darling 55. Pillars of the Sky 56. The Ten Commandments 56. The Tall Stranger 57. The Lone Ranger 58. The Comancheros 62. And Now Miguel 66. Guns of the Magnificent Seven 69. Stand Up and be Counted 72. The Bears and I 74. Dear Dead Delilah 75. The Day of the Animals 76. the Manitou 77. Lethal 84. Knights of the City 86, etc.
TV series: *Broken Arrow* 56–8. Law of the Plainsman 59.

Anscocolor. American process derived from Agfacolor (qv).

Anspach, Susan (1939–). American stage actress in occasional films.
□The Landlord 70. Five Easy Pieces 70. Play It Again Sam 72. Blume in Love 72. Nashville 75. The Big Fix 78. Running 79. The Devil and Max Devlin 81. Gas 81. Montenegro 82. TV series: The Yellow Rose 83–.

Anstey, Edgar (1907–87). British documentary producer (Housing Problems 35. Enough to Eat 36, etc.). Long-time Chief Films Officer for British Transport.

Anstey, F. (1856–1934) (Thomas Anstey Guthrie). British humorous novelist.
Works filmed: *Vice Versa* 48. The Brass Bottle 64.

answer print. The first complete combined print supplied by the laboratory, usually with no very careful attempt to grade colour or contrast.

Antheil, George (1900–1959). American composer, former concert pianist.
The Plainsman 37. The Buccaneer 38. Angels over Broadway 40. Specter of the Rose 46. Knock on any Door 49. The Fighting Kentuckian 49. In a Lonely Place 50. The Sniper 51. Actors and Sin 52. The Juggler 53. Not as a Stranger 55. The Pride and the Passion 57, etc.

Anthony, Joseph (1912–) (J. A. Deuster). American director from stage and TV; former small part actor and dancer.
□The Rainmaker 56. The Matchmaker 58. Career 59. All in a Night's Work 61. The Captive City 63. Tomorrow 72.

Anthony, Tony (1937–). American leading man having some success in tough Italian Westerns.
A Stranger in Town 67. The Stranger Returns 68. Samurai on a Horse 69. Blindman 71. Comin' at Ya 81, etc.

anti-Semitism was understandably not a popular subject with film-makers when the function of movies was simply to entertain. Amiable comic Jews were permitted, in *Abie's Irish Rose, Potash and Perlmutter*, and the Cohen and Kelly series; and it was readily acknowledged that Jewry provided a flow of star talent without which show business could not continue. But thoughtful movies on the Jewish plight were almost non-existent, unless one counts such epics as *The Wandering Jew* 33 and *Jew Süss* 34. Occasionally came a cry from Europe, as in *Professor Mamlock* 36, but it was not really until *The Great Dictator* 40 that the film-going public was made aware of what was happening to the Jews in Germany. For propaganda purposes the Nazis put out a number of anti-Semitic films such as *Der Ewige Jude* and another version of *Jew Süss*; the only real reply during World War II was a gentle British movie called *Mr Emmanuel*. In *Tomorrow the World* 44, from the play about an ex-Nazi youth in America, the subject was touched on; but not till the reconstruction days of 1947 could a spade really be called a spade. In a taut murder thriller called *Crossfire*, the victim was changed from a homosexual to a Jew; then came *Gentleman's Agreement*, in which a gentile reporter posed as a Jew to expose anti-Semitism in America. Perhaps this interest was stimulated by the immense popularity of *The Jolson Story*, with its sympathetic portrait of a Jewish home; but the confusion in American minds is demonstrated by the fact that David Lean's *Oliver Twist* was banned in 1948 because of Alec Guinness' 'caricature' of Fagin! During the last decade or so there seems to have been sporadic interest in the subject. The birth of Israel generated such movies as *Sword in the Desert, Exodus, Judith* and *Cast a Giant Shadow*, and Christopher Isherwood's Berlin stories of the early thirties became first a play and film called *I Am a Camera* and later a musical and film called *Cabaret*. Poignant recollections of World War II by a girl who died in Auschwitz produced a book, play and film called *The Diary of Anne Frank*, and a little British film called *Reach for Glory*, which took a swipe at the consequences of intolerance. In 1971 the world's most successful stage musical, *Fiddler on the Roof*, was filmed; dealing with the Russian pogroms, the story has been filmed many times before in Yiddish, usually under the title 'Tevye the Milkman'. The seventies saw the pendulum swinging to the extent that we were almost swamped by films and actors proclaiming their Jewishness: Barbra Streisand, Bette Midler, Woody Allen, Elliott Gould, George Segal. The plight of the Jews under Hitler was again explored in a dozen television epics including *Inside the Third Reich, Blood and Honour, The Winds of War, The Wall* and *The House on Garibaldi Street*; while feature films on the subject of Jewishness were *The Pawnbroker* and *The Chosen*.

Antonio, Lou (–). Tough-looking American character actor who has dabbled successfully in TV direction.

America America 63. Hawaii 66. Cool Hand Luke 67. Sole Survivor (TV) 69. The Phynx 70. Partners in Crime (TV) 73.
TV series: The Snoop Sisters 73. Dog and Cat 77.

Antonioni, Michelangelo (1912–). Italian director whose reputation was boosted in the fifties by the ardent support of highbrow film magazines. Co-scripts all his own films, which largely jettison narrative in favour of vague incident and relentless character study.
Cronaca di un Amore 50. Le Amiche 55. Il Grido 57. *L'Avventura* 59. *La Notte* 60. L'Eclisse 62. *The Red Desert* 64. *Blow-Up* (GB) 67. Zabriskie Point (US) 69. The Passenger 74. The Oberwald Mystery 81. Identification of a Woman 82, etc.
¶ *M.A.:* I feel like a father towards my old films. You bring children into the world, then they grow up and go off on their own. From time to time you get together, and it's always a pleasure to see them again.

Antony, Scott (1950–). British leading juvenile of the early seventies.
Baxter 72. Savage Messiah 73. Dead Cert 73. The Mutations 74.

The Apartment (US 1960) (AA/BFA). A typically mordant comedy from director Billy Wilder, scripted by himself and I. A. L. Diamond. This one lifts the lid off New York office life, only to discover something not far removed from a Capra soft centre. Jack Lemmon finds some sympathy in the part of a clerk who advances his status by letting out his apartment to house the amorous affairs of his bosses.

Apfel, Oscar (1874–1938). American character actor.
Ten Nights in a Bar Room 22. The Social Code 23. Perils of the Coastguard 26. Code of the Cow Country 27. Not Quite Decent 29. Five Star Final 31. Wicked 31. The Maltese Falcon 31. High Pressure 32. Make Me a Star 32. Before Dawn 33. The House of Rothschild 34. Bordertown 35. The Plot Thickens 36. The Toast of New York 37, many others.

Apocalypse Now (US 1979). Moody and not all that magnificent war statement which, shot in the Philippines and vaguely patterned after Conrad's *Heart of Darkness*, took so long to come out that the press dubbed it *Apocalypse Later*. Splendid visual sequences alternated with draggy philosophy and violence, and when Marlon Brando finally turned up he was unintelligible as usual. Produced, directed, and written (with John Milius) by Francis Ford Coppola; photographed (AA) by Vittorio Storaro; with Martin Sheen, Robert Duvall.

Applause (US 1929). One of the most professionally fluent of early talkies, with director Rouben Mamoulian trying, and usually bringing off, every cinematic trick in the book as well as some of his own. On its own level the story works too: a hokey but powerful melodrama of mother love against the tawdry background of burlesque. Written by Garrett Fort from a novel by Beth Brown; photographed by George Folsey. With Helen Morgan, Joan Peers, Henry Wadsworth.

Applebaum, Louis (1918–). Canadian composer who spent time in Hollywood.
Tomorrow the World 44. The Story of GI Joe (AA) 45. Lost Boundaries 48. Teresa 51. The Whistle at Eaton Falls 51. Walk East on Beacon 52. The Mask 61, etc.

Apted, Michael (1941–). British director, from TV.
□Triple Echo 72. Stardust 74. The Squeeze 77. Agatha 79. *Coal Miner's Daughter* 80. Continental Divide 81. P'tang Yang Kipperbang (TV) 82. Gorky Park 83. First Born 84. 28 Up 84. Bring on the Night 85. Critical Condition 87.

Aquanetta (1920–) (Burnu Davenport). Exotic American leading lady of easterns and horrors in the early forties.
Arabian Nights 42. Jungle Captive 43. Jungle Woman 44. Dead Man's Eyes 44. Tarzan and the Leopard Woman 46, etc.

The Arabian Nights. This collection of ancient eastern tales, more properly called *The Arabian Nights' Entertainment*, was first collected around 1450, but Sir Richard Burton's unexpurgated Victorian translation is the one generally used. The tales, presented as told by the heroine Scheherazade, have been plundered innumerable times by film-makers. See the entries under *The Thief of Baghdad* and *Ali Baba*; note also films based on Aladdin, Sinbad the Sailor and various genies in bottles.

Arbeid, Ben (1924–). British producer.
The Barber of Stamford Hill 62. *Private Potter* 63. Children of the Damned 64.

Murder Most Foul 65. The Jokers 67. Assignment K 68. Hoffman 70. The Hireling 71. The Water Babies 76. Eagle's Wing 79.

Arbuckle, Roscoe 'Fatty' (1887–1933). Grown-up fat boy of American silent cinema. His highly successful career, mainly in two-reelers, came to grief after a sensational murder trial in 1921, and his only subsequent films were a few two-reelers in the early thirties; he also directed a few films as William Goodrich.
Biography 1976: *The Day the Laughter Stopped* by David A. Yallop.
In the Clutches of the Gang (as a Keystone Kop) 13. Fatty and Mabel's Simple Life 15. Mabel and Fatty's Married Life 16. Fatty's Flirtation 16. Fickle Fatty's Fall 17. His Wedding Night 17. Out West 17. The Bell Boy 17. The Round Up 20. The Life of the Party (feature) 20. The Travelling Salesman (feature) 21. Gasoline Gus (feature) 21, many others.

¶ 'Roscoe always said, I'll make it, darling, and you spend it.'—*Minta Durfee (wife)*

'He could throw two pies at once in different directions, but he was not precise in this feat.'—*Mack Sennett*

arc. A high-powered lamp used in projectors and studio lighting, its illumination consisting of an electrical discharge between two carbon rods.

Archaeology of the Cinema by C. W. Ceram. A well-received study of the technical development of the cinema up to 1897, published by Thames and Hudson in 1965.

Archainbaud, George (1890–1959). American director, mainly of routine westerns.
Fool's Gold 19. The Shadow of Rosalie Byrnes 20. Single Wives 24. Men of Steel 26. College Coquette 29. The Lost Squadron 32. The Return of Sophie Lang 36. Her Jungle Love 38. Thanks for the Memory 38. Untamed 40. The Kansan 43. Woman of the Town 44. King of the Wild Horses 47. Hunt the Man Down 51. Last of the Pony Riders 53, many others.

Archard, Bernard (1916–). Lean, incisive British actor with repertory experience: became famous on TV as *Spycatcher*. Village of the Damned 60. The List of Adrian Messenger 63. Face of a Stranger 66. Song of Norway 70. The Horror of Frankenstein 70. The Purple Twilight (TV) 79. The Sea Wolves 80. Krull 83. King Solomon's Mines 85, etc.

Archer, Anne (–). American leading lady.
The All-American Boy 70. The Honkers 72. Cancel My Reservation 72. Trackdown 76. Paradise Alley 78. Green Ice 80. Waltz across Texas 82. The Naked Face 84. The Check is in the Mail 85. Fatal Attraction 87, etc.
TV series: Bob and Carol and Ted and Alice 73.

Archer, John (1915–) (Ralph Bowman). American leading man of routine second features.
Flaming Frontier 38. Gangs Inc. 41. Crash Dive 43. The Last Moment 47. White Heat 49. Destination Moon 50. A Yank in Indo-China 52. Rodeo 53. The Stars Are Singing 53. No Man's Woman 55. Emergency Hospital 59. Blue Hawaii 62. Apache Rifles 64. I Saw What You Did 65. How to Frame a Figg 71, etc.

archive. A vault, usually government-sponsored, containing a selection of films to be preserved for research and for posterity.

Ardant, Fanny (1949–). French leading lady.
Les Chiens 79. Les Uns et les Autres 80. The Woman Next Door 81. *Vivement Dimanche* 82. Benvenuta 83. Sun and Night 84. Swann in Love 84.

Arden, Eve (1912–) (Eunice Quedens). American comedy actress, a tall cool lady who spent a generation as the wisecracking friend of the heroine. Originally a Ziegfeld girl.
Song of Love 29. Dancing Lady 33. Oh Doctor 37. *Stage Door* 37. Having Wonderful Time 38. At the Circus 39. Comrade X 40. Ziegfeld Girl 41. That Uncertain Feeling 41. Whistling in the Dark 41. Let's Face It 43. *Cover Girl* 44. *The Doughgirls* 44. *Mildred Pierce* 45. Night and Day 46. The Unfaithful 47. *The Voice of the Turtle* 47. The Lady Takes a Sailor 49. *Paid in Full* 50. Curtain Call at Cactus Creek 50. *Tea for Two* 50. *Three Husbands* 50. *We're Not Married* 52. The Lady Wants Mink 53. Our Miss Brooks 56. *Anatomy of a Murder* 59. *The Dark at the Top of the Stairs* 60. Sergeant Deadhead 65. A Very Missing Person (TV) 71. All My Darling Daughters (TV) 72. *Grease* 78. Under the Rainbow 81. Grease II 82, etc.
TV series: *Our Miss Brooks* 52–56.

The Eve Arden Show 59. Mothers-in-Law 67–69.
❀ For patenting the comic image of the cool, sophisticated but usually manless career woman. *Mildred Pierce.*

Arden, Robert (1921–). Anglo-American actor resident in Britain; former vocalist.
Two Thousand Women 44. No Orchids for Miss Blandish 48. *Confidential Report* 56, etc.
TV series: *Saber of London* 60.

Ardrey, Robert (1907–1980). American screenwriter, novelist and playwright.
They Knew What They Wanted 40. *Thunder Rock* (& oa) 43. The Green Years 46. The Three Musketeers 48. Madame Bovary 49. Quentin Durward 56. The Wonderful Country 58. The Four Horsemen of the Apocalypse 62. Khartoum 66, etc.

Argentina has been making films since the turn of the century, many having claim to sophistication, but the only ones to receive world distribution and acclaim were those of Leopoldo Torre-Nilsson (qv) in the fifties.

Argento, Dario (1943–). Italian thriller director.
The Bird with Crystal Plumage 70. One Night at Dinner 70. Cat O'Nine Tails 71. Four Flies on Grey Velvet 71. Le Cinque Giornate 73. Deep Red 77. Suspiria (& w) 77. Inferno 79. Unsane (Tenebrae) 82, etc.

Argyle, John F. (1911–). British director.
Paradise Alley 31. Smiling Along 31. Mutiny on the Elsinore (p only) 36. Tower of Terror (p only) 41. Send for Paul Temple (& p) 46. Once a Sinner (p only) 50, etc.

Arise My Love (US 1940). This amiable mock-heroic romantic comedy-drama is notable as Hollywood's most prompt response to the outbreak of World War II in Europe. Claudette Colbert and Ray Milland make an agreeable team as a newspaperwoman and an aviator involved in world events from the Spanish Civil War to the sinking of the *Athenia*, and Billy Wilder's slightly cynical script ends with an implicit command for America to wake up. In the circumstances, Mitchell Leisen's direction is perhaps just a little too impeccable. AA best original story: Benjamin Glazer, John Toldy.

Arkin, Alan (1934–). American leading character actor, from Broadway.
□*The Russians are Coming, The Russians are Coming* 66. Woman Times Seven 67. *Wait Until Dark* 67. Inspector Clouseau 68. *The Heart is a Lonely Hunter* 68. Popi 69. The Monitors 69. *Catch 22* 70. *Little Murders* (& d) 71. Deadhead Miles 72. Last of the Red Hot Lovers 72. Freebie and the Bean 74. Rafferty and the Gold Dust Twins 75. Hearts of the West 75. The Seven Per Cent Solution (as Freud) 76. *The Other Side of Hell* (TV) 77. Fire Sale (& d) 77. The In-Laws 79. The Magician of Lublin 79. Simon 79. Improper Channels 80. Chu Chi and the Philly Flash 81. Full Moon High 81. Deadhead Miles 82. The Return of Captain Invincible 83. Big Trouble 84. Joshua Then and Now 85. Bad Medicine 85.

Arkoff, Samuel Z. (1918–). American executive producer, co-founder with James H. Nicholson of American International Pictures.

Arlen, Harold (1905–86) (Hyman Arluck). American song composer ('Happiness Is Just a Thing Called Joe', 'That Old Black Magic', 'Blues in the Night', 'Stormy Weather', 'Accentuate the Positive', many others).
Film scores include: Strike Me Pink 36. Love Affair 39. The Wizard of Oz (AA for 'Over the Rainbow') 39. Cabin in the Sky 43. A Star Is Born 54. I Could Go On Singing 63, etc.

Arlen, Michael (1895–1956) (Dikran Kuyumjian). Armenian novelist, educated in England. In the twenties his *The Green Hat* was the basis for Garbo's *A Woman of Affairs*, and in 1948 his short story 'A Gentleman from America' became The Fatal Night.

¶ *M.A.*: My forebears were successful crooks living on the slopes of Mount Ararat.

'For all his reputation, Arlen is not a bounder. He is every other inch a gentleman.'—*Alexander Woollcott*

Arlen, Richard (1898–1976) (Cornelius van Mattemore). Rugged American leading man who rose from extra to star in the twenties, became the durable hero of scores of 'B' pictures, and later played bits.
In the Name of Love 25. Rolled Stockings 27. *Wings* 27. *The Four Feathers* 28. Thunderbolt 29. *The Virginian* 29. The Sea God 30. Touchdown 31. College Humor 33. Three Cornered Moon 33. She Made Her Bed 34. Heldorado 35. Secret Valley 36. Murder in Greenwich Village 37. Call of the Yukon 38. Mutiny on the Blackhawk 39. Legion of Lost Flyers 39. Hot Steel 40. Men of the Timberland 41. Torpedo Boat 42. Alaska Highway 43. Minesweeper 43. The Lady and

the Monster 44. Storm over Lisbon 44. The Phantom Speaks 45. Accomplice 46. Speed to Spare 48. Grand Canyon 49. Kansas Raiders 50. Flaming Feather 52. Sabre Jet 53. Devil's Harbour 54. The Mountain 56. Raymie 60. Cavalry Command 63. Law of the Lawless 64. The Human Duplicators 65. Apache Uprising 66. Red Tomahawk 67. Buckskin 68. Won Ton Ton 76, many others.

Arletty (1898–) (Leonie Bathiat). Celebrated French actress of stage and screen adept at the portrayal of world-weary, sophisticated women.
□Un Chien Qui Rapporte 31. Don't Walk About in the Nude 32. Enlevez Moi 32. Un Fil à la Patte 33. Feue la Mère de Madame 33. La Belle Aventure 33. Une Idée Folle 33. Un Soir de Réveillon 34. Je Te Confie Ma Femme 34. Le Voyage de Monsieur Perrichon 34. La Guerre des Valses 35. Pension Mimosas 35. La Fille de Madame Angot 35. L'Ecole des Cocottes 36. Amants et Voleurs 36. La Garçonne 36. Un Mari Rêve 36. Aventure à Paris 36. Faisons un Rêve 36. Messieurs des Ronds-de-Cuir 36. Les Perles de la Couronne 37. Aloha 37. Mirages 37. Desire 37. Le Petit Chose 38. La Chaleur du Sein 38. *Hôtel du Nord* 38. *Le Jour Se Lève* 39. Fric Frac 39. Circonstances Attenuantes 39. Tempête 40. Madame Sans Gêne 41. The Woman I Loved the Most 42. Bolero 42. L'Amant de Borneo 42. *Les Visiteurs du Soir* 43. *Les Enfants du Paradis* 44. Portrait d'un Assassin 49. L'Amour, Madame 52. Gibier de Potence 52. Le Père de Mademoiselle 53. Le Grand Jeu 54. L'Air de Paris 55. Huis Clos 55. Mon Curé chez les Pauvres 56. Vacances Explosives 57. Le Passager Clandestin 58. Et Ta Soeur? 59. Maxime 59. Drôle de Dimanche 60. La Gamberge 61. Les Petits Matins 61. La Loi des Hommes 61. The Longest Day 62. Tempo di Roma 63. Le Voyage à Biarritz 63. Les Volets Fermés 72.

Arling, Arthur E. (1906–). American cinematographer.
Gone with the Wind (co-ph) 39. The Yearling (AA) 46. The Homestretch 47. You're My Everything 49. Wabash Avenue 50. Red Garters 54. I'll Cry Tomorrow 55. Pay the Devil 57. The Story of Ruth 60. Notorious Landlady 62. My Six Loves 63. Straitjacket 63. The Secret Invasion 64, many others.

Arliss, Florence (1871–1950). British character actress who appeared in a few of the films of her husband George Arliss, from *The Devil* to *The House of Rothschild.*

Arliss, George (1868–1946) (George Augustus Andrews). Distinguished British stage actor of the old school who in middle age was persuaded to face the cameras and unexpectedly became a star both in Britain and America, presenting a gallery of kings, statesmen, rajahs, eccentric millionaires and rather unconvincing hoboes.
Autobiographies: *On The Stage* 26. *Up the Years from Bloomsbury* 27. *My Ten Years in the Studios* 40.
□The Devil 21. *Disraeli* 21. *The Green Goddess* 23. The Ruling Passion 23. *Disraeli* (AA) 29. *The Green Goddess* (sound) 30. Old English 30. Millionaire 31. Alexander Hamilton 31. The Man Who Played God 32. Successful Calamity 32. The King's Vacation 33. The Working Man 33. Voltaire 33. *The House of Rothschild* 34. The Tunnel 34. The Last Gentleman 34. Cardinal Richelieu 35. The Iron Duke 35. The Guvnor 35. East Meets West 36. His Lordship 37. Dr Syn 37.
❁ For the sheer autocratic determination which made him a world star despite his very limited and inflexible talent. *The House of Rothschild.*
¶ 'His small dark eyes held an ancient sadness; but his taut triangular mouth seemed always to be repressing an irrepressible mirth.'—*Bette Davis*

Arliss, Leslie (1901–). British writer who worked on Orders Is Orders 32. Jack Ahoy 34. Rhodes of Africa 36. Pastor Hall 39. The Foreman Went to France 42. Then turned director and made some of the popular Gainsborough costume melodramas of the forties.
The Night Has Eyes 42. The Man in Grey 43. Love Story 44. The Wicked Lady 45. A Man about the House 47. Idol of Paris 48. The Woman's Angle 52. Miss Tulip Stays the Night 55. See How They Run 55, etc; recently directing TV films.

Armendariz, Pedro (1912–1963). Massive Mexican actor with expansive personality; became a star in his own country, then moved on to Hollywood and Europe.
Rosario 36. Isle of Passion 41. *Maria Candelaria* 43. The Pearl 46. The Fugitive 47. Maclovia 48. Fort Apache 48. Three Godfathers 48. Tulsa 48. We Were Strangers 49. The Torch 50. *El Bruto* 52. Lucretia Borgia 52. Border River 54. The Conqueror 56. Manuela 57. The Wonderful Country 59. Francis of Assisi 61. Captain Sinbad 63. *From Russia with Love* 63, etc.

Armendariz, Pedro Jnr (1930–). Mexican–American character actor.
The Magnificent Seven Ride 72. The Deadly Trackers 73. Earthquake 74.

Armetta, Henry (1888–1945). Italian-born character actor, long in US, where he was on stage before going to Hollywood. Typecast as excitable, gesticulating foreigner.
My Cousin 18. The Silent Command 23. Street Angel 28. Romance 30. Strangers May Kiss 31. The Unholy Garden 31. Prosperity 32. What! No Beer? 33. The Man Who Reclaimed His Head 34. After Office Hours 35. Poor Little Rich Girl 36. Make a Wish 37. Everybody Sing 38. Dust be my Destiny 39. *The Big Store* 41. Anchors Aweigh 45. Colonel Effingham's Raid 46, many others.

Arms and the Man. Bernard Shaw's military comedy has only once been filmed straight: this was in 1931 (GB) with Barry Jones as Bluntschli. The stage musical comedy *The Chocolate Soldier* was based on it, but when this was filmed in 1941 Shaw's libretto was abandoned. *The Guardsman*, made in 1932 with Alfred Lunt and Lynn Fontanne, bears some resemblance to it.

Armstrong, Alun (1946–). British Shakespearean character actor, occasionally in films.
The Duellists 77. A Bridge Too Far 77. Krull 83. The French Lieutenant's Woman 83. Billy the Kid and the Green Baize Vampire 85.

Armstrong, Bess (–). American leading lady.
Jekyll and Hyde Together Again 82. High Road to China 83. Jaws 3-D 83. Nothing in Common 86.

Armstrong, Gillian (–). Australian director.
My Brilliant Career 80. Starstruck 82. Mrs Soffel (US) 84. High Tide 87.

Armstrong, Louis (1900–1971). Gravel-voiced black American jazz trumpeter and singer, affectionately known as 'Satchmo' (satchel mouth). Sporadic screen appearances, chiefly in guest spots.
□Pennies from Heaven 36. Every Day's a Holiday 37. Dr Rhythm 38. Artists and Models 38. Going Places 39. *The Birth of the Blues* 41. Cabin in the Sky 43. Jam Session 44. Atlantic City 44. Hollywood Canteen 44. *New Orleans* 47. A Song Is Born 48. The Strip 51. *Here Comes The Groom* 51. Glory Alley 51. *The Glenn Miller Story* 54. *High Society* 56. *Satchmo The Great* 57. The Beat Generation 59. *The Five Pennies* 59. *Paris Blues* 61. *Jazz On A Summer's Day* 61. When the Boys Meet the Girls 62. A Man Called Adam 66. Hello Dolly 69.

Armstrong, R. G. (c. 1920–). Tough, serious-looking American supporting actor.
Never Love a Stranger 58. *Ride The High Country* 62. Major Dundee 66. El Dorado 66. The Great White Hope 71. Stay Hungry 76. Heaven Can Wait 78. Reds 81. Hammett 82. Evilspeak 82, etc.

Armstrong, Robert (1890–1973) (Donald Robert Smith). Tough American character actor often seen as cop, sheriff, trail boss or shady investigator.
The Main Event 27. Big Money 30. The Tip-Off 31. The Most Dangerous Game 32. *King Kong* (his best role, as foolhardy film producer Carl Denham) 33. Son of Kong 33. G-Men 35. Mystery Man 37. Sky Raiders 41. Outside the Law 41. Dive Bomber 41. The Mad Ghoul 43. Gangs of the Waterfront 45. *Mighty Joe Young* (a continuation of his Kong role) 49. Las Vegas Shakedown 55. For Those Who Think Young 63, many others.
Famous line (in *King Kong*): 'Oh no, it wasn't the airplanes. It was beauty killed the beast.'

Armstrong, Todd (1939–). Stalwart American leading man of the sixties.
Walk on the Wild Side 62. Jason and the Argonauts 63. King Rat 65. A Time for Killing 68, etc.

army comedies have always been popular, and most well-known comedians have at least one to their credit. Laurel and Hardy were in *Pack Up Your Troubles* and *Blockheads and Great Guns*; Abbott and Costello in *Buck Privates*; Wheeler and Woolsey in *Half Shot at Sunrise*; Buster Keaton in *The Dough Boys*; Charlie Chaplin in *Shoulder Arms*; Harry Langdon in *A Soldier's Plaything*; Larry Semon in *Spuds*; George Jessel in *Private Izzy Murray*; Joe E. Brown in *Sons of Guns*; Jimmy Durante and Phil Silvers in *You're in the Army Now*; The Ritz Brothers in *We're in the Army Now*; Norman Wisdom in *The Square Peg*; Jerry Lewis in *The Sad Sack*; Martin and Lewis in *At War With The Army*; Bob Hope in *Caught In The Draft*; Frank Randle in *Somewhere In England*; Arthur Lucan in *Old Mother Riley Joins Up*; George K. Arthur and Karl Dane in *Rookies*; Wallace Beery and Raymond Hatton in *Behind The Front*; Alan Carney and Wally Brown in *Adventures Of A Rookie* and *Rookies In*

Burma; Joe Sawyer and William Tracy in several comedies including *Tanks a Million, About Face* and *Fall In*; Tom Wilson and Heimie Conklin in *Ham And Eggs At The Front*; George Sidney and Charlie Murray in *Lost At The Front.*

Other American successes in the genre include: *What Did You Do In The War, Daddy?*; *Two Arabian Knights*; *What Price Glory?* ; *The Cockeyed World*; *Top Sergeant Mulligan*; *The Teahouse of The August Moon*; *The Wackiest Ship In the Army*; *Operation Mad Ball*, and above all *M*A*S*H*. Britain has provided *Carry On Sergeant*; *Private's Progress*; *On The Fiddle*; *I Only Arsked*; *Idol On Parade* and *Reluctant Heroes*.
Outstanding TV series: Britain's *The Army Game* and Hollywood's *Bilko* series with Phil Silvers; *Hogan's Heroes*; *McHale's Navy*; *Gomer Pyle U.S.M.C.*; *M*A*S*H*.

Arnall, Julia (1931–). Austrian-born actress resident in Britain.
Man of the Moment 54. I Am a Camera 55. Lost 56. House of Secrets 56. Man without a Body 57. Mark of the Phoenix 59. The Quiller Memorandum 66. The Double Man 67, etc.

Arnatt, John (1917–). Solid, pipe-smoking British character actor, mostly on TV.
Only Two Can Play 62. Dr Crippen 63. Licensed to Kill 66. The Breaking of Bumbo 70. Crucible of Terror 71, many others.
TV series: Robin Hood (as the hero's perpetual adversary) 55–59.

Arnaud, Léon (1904–). French composer (and conductor) in Hollywood.
Babes in Arms 39. The Big Store 41. Dubarry Was a Lady 43. Easter Parade 48. Three Little Words 50. Sombrero 53. Seven Brides for Seven Brothers 54. Blue 68, etc.

Arnaud, Yvonne (1892–1958). French actress and pianist, long popular on the British stage.
□Desire 20. The Temptress 20. Canaries Sometimes Sing 30. Tons of Money 31. On Approval 31. *A Cuckoo in the Nest* 33. Princess Charming 34. Lady in Danger 34. Widow's Might 36. The Gay Adventure 36. The Improper Duchess 36. Stormy Weather 36. Neutral Port 40. Tomorrow We Live 42. Woman to Woman 46. The Ghosts of Berkeley Square 47. Mon Oncle 58.

Arnaz, Desi (1915–86) (Desiderio Alberto Arnaz y de Acha). Diminutive but explosive Cuban who began his career as a singer and later formed his own Latin-American band. Performed in minor film musicals during forties, then married Lucille Ball, founded Desilu Studios, and appeared in the long-running TV series *I Love Lucy* 50–61. Later films include *The Long Long Trailer* 54. *Forever Darling* 56. *The Escape Artist* 82. Produced TV series *The Mothers-in-Law* 57–58.

Arnaz, Desi Jnr (1953–). American juvenile lead of the seventies, son of Desi Arnaz and Lucille Ball. Had years of training on his mother's TV series.
Red Sky at Morning 70. Marco 73. Billy Two Hats 74. She Lives (TV) 74. Joyride 77. How to Pick Up Girls (TV) 78. A Wedding 79. The Night the Bridge Fell Down (TV) 80. The House of Long Shadows 83, etc.

Arnaz, Lucie (1951–). American leading lady, daughter of Lucille Ball and Desi Arnaz.
Who Is the Black Dahlia? (TV) 75. Billy Jack Goes to Washington 77. Death Scream (TV) 78. The Mating Season 80. Second Thoughts 83.

Arne, Peter (1920–1983) (Peter Arne Albrecht). Unsmiling Anglo-American actor in British films, usually as dastardly villain.
Time Slip 55. The Purple Plain 55. *The Moonraker* 57. Ice Cold in Alex 57. *Danger Within* 58. *The Hellfire Club* 61. The Black Torment 64. Khartoum 66. Battle Beneath the Earth 68. Murders in the Rue Morgue 71. Straw Dogs 71. Antony and Cleopatra 72. Providence 77. Victor/Victoria 82, etc.

Arnell, Richard (1917–). British composer.
The Land 40. The Third Secret 63. The Visit 64. The Man Outside 67. The Black Panther 77, etc.

Arness, James (1923–) (James Aurness). Giant-size American leading man who found his greatest fame on TV. Brother of Peter Graves.
The Farmer's Daughter 47. Battleground 49. Wagonmaster 51. The Thing (title role) 52. Big Jim McLain 53. Them 54. The Sea Chase 55. The First Travelling Saleslady 56, many others.
TV series: Gunsmoke (as Marshal Dillon) 55–75. How the West Was Won 76–79. McLain's Law 81.

¶ *J.A.:* I just wanted to see California. I wasn't thinking of acting.
J.A.: The greatest spiritual cleansing I can imagine is to dive into a big surf.

Arnheim, Rudolf (1904–). German-American critic whose published writings include *Film as Art* 32 and *Art and Visual Perception* 58.

Arno, Sig (1895–1975) (Siegfried Aron). German comedy actor in US from early thirties; latterly typecast as funny foreigner. Manon Lescaut 26. Pandora's Box 28. The Loves of Jeanne Ney 28. Diary of a Lost Girl 29. The Star Maker 38. The Great Dictator 40. The Palm Beach Story 42. Up In Arms 44. The Great Lover 48. On Moonlight Bay 51. The Great Diamond Robbery 53, many others.

Arnold, Edward (1890–1956) (Guenther Schneider). Rotund but dynamic American actor who played go-getter leading roles in the thirties. Although he later became typed as kindly father/apoplectic business man, he never lost his popularity.
Autobiography 1940, *Lorenzo Goes To Hollywood.*
□When the Man Speaks 16. The Wrong Way 17. Rasputin and the Empress 32. Okay, America 32. Afraid to Talk 32. Three on a Match 32. Whistling in the Dark 33. The White Sister 33. The Barbarian 33. Jennie Gerhardt 33. Her Bodyguard 33. The Secret of the Blue Room 33. *I'm No Angel* 33. *Roman Scandals* 33. Madame Spy 34. Sadie McKee 34. Thirty Day Princess 34. Unknown Blonde 34. Hideout 34. Million Dollar Ransom 34. The President Vanishes 34. Wednesday's Child 34. Biography of a Bachelor Girl 35. Cardinal Richelieu 35. *The Glass Key* 35. *Diamond Jim* 35. *Crime and Punishment* 35. Remember Last Night? 35. Sutter's Gold 36. *Meet Nero Wolfe* 36. *Come and Get It* 36. John Meade's Woman 37. *The Toast of New York* 37. Easy Living 37. Blossoms on Broadway 37. The Crowd Roars 38. *You Can't Take It With You* 38. Let Freedom Ring 39. Idiot's Delight 39. Man About Town 39. *Mr Smith Goes To Washington* 39. Slightly Honourable 40. The Earl of Chicago 40. Johnny Apollo 40. Lillian Russell 40. The Penalty 41. The Lady from Cheyenne 41. Meet John Doe 41. Nothing But the Truth 41. Unholy Partners 41. Design for Scandal 41. Johnny Eager 41. *All That Money Can Buy* (as Daniel Webster) 41. The War Against Mrs Hadley 42. *Eyes in The Night* 42. The Youngest Profession 42. Standing Room Only 44. Janie 44. *Kismet* 44. Mrs Parkington 44. Main Street After Dark 44. Weekend at the Waldorf 45. The Hidden Eye 45. Ziegfeld Follies 46. Janie Gets Married 46. *Three Wise Fools* 46. No Leave No Love 46. The Mighty McGurk 46. My Brother Talks to Horses 46. *Dear Ruth* 47. *The Hucksters* 47. Three Daring Daughters 48. Big City 48. Wallflower 48. Command Decision 48. John Loves Mary 49. Take Me Out to the Ball Game 49. Big Jack 49. Dear Wife 49. The Yellow Cab Man 50. Annie Get Your Gun 50. The Skipper Surprised His Wife 50. Dear Brat 51. Belles on Their Toes 52. City That Never Sleeps 53. Man of Conflict 53. Living it Up 54. The Houston Story 56. The Ambassador's Daughter 56. Miami Exposé 56.
❁ For maintaining an ebullient star personality through two decades of talkies, despite his unromantic physique. *Diamond Jim.*

Arnold, Jack (1916–). American director. It Came from Outer Space 53. The Glass Web 53. Girls in the Night 53. The Creature from the Black Lagoon 54. Tarantula 55. Red Sundown 56. The Tattered Dress 57. *The Incredible Shrinking Man* 57. Pay the Devil 57. The Lady Takes a Flyer 58. High School Confidential 58. The Mouse That Roared (GB) 59. No Name on the Bullet 59. Bachelor in Paradise 61. A Global Affair 63. Hello Down There 68. Black Eye 73. The Swiss Conspiracy 76, etc.

Arnold, Malcolm (1921–). British composer.
The Sound Barrier 52. Island in the Sun 56. *The Bridge on the River Kwai* (AA) 57. Inn of the Sixth Happiness 58. Tunes of Glory 60. The Chalk Garden 64. The Heroes of Telemark 65. The Reckoning 68, etc.

Arnoul, Françoise (1931–) (Françoise Gautsch). Sultry French leading lady of sex melodramas in the fifties.
Quai de Grenelle 50. Forbidden Fruit 52. Companions of the Night 53. La Rage au Corps 53. The Sheep Has Five Legs 54. French Can-Can 55. The Face of the Cat 57. The Devil and the Ten Commandments 61. Le Dimanche de la Vie 66, etc.

Arnt, Charles (1908–). American character actor often seen as snoop, suspicious character, or just plain ordinary fellow.
Ladies Should Listen 34. The Witness Chair 36. Remember the Night 40. Blossoms in the Dust 41. Twin Beds 42. Up in Arms 44. Cinderella Jones 46. *Dangerous Intruder* 46. That Brennan Girl 47. Wabash Avenue 50. Veils of Baghdad 53. Miracle of the Hills 59. Sweet Bird of Youth 62, many others.

Around the World in Eighty Days. Jules Verne's globe-trotting Victorian lark was first filmed by Richard Oswald in Germany in 1919. In 1956 Michael Todd made it the subject of the first of the giant-screen extravaganzas in 70mm, and the impact of location photography, much expense, and 44 stars in cameo roles was enough to gain it the year's best picture Academy Award, despite its many glaring faults. Michael Anderson directed rather uncertainly from a screenplay by S. J. Perelman, James Poe and John Farrow; David Niven as the imperturbable Phineas Fogg led the revels, with Robert Newton as Inspector Fix.

Arquette, Cliff (1906–74). American comedy actor familiar on radio and TV as hillbilly Charlie Weaver. Appeared with Abbott and Costello in *Comin' Round the Mountain.*

Arquette, Rosana (1959–). American leading lady of the eighties, usually in sultry roles. Harvest Home (TV) 78. More American Graffiti 79. Gorp 80. S.O.B. 81. *Johnny Belinda* (TV) 82. *The Executioner's Song* (TV) 83. Baby it's You 83. Off the Wall 84. Desperately Seeking Susan (BFA) 85. 8 Million Ways to Die 85. The Aviator 85. Silverado 85. After Hours 85. Nobody's Fool 86.

Arrighi, Nike (1946–). Italian-Australian leading lady.
Don't Raise the Bridge, Lower the River 67. The Devil Rides Out 68. One Plus One 68. Women in Love 69. Countess Dracula 70. Day for Night 73, etc.

Arsenal (USSR 1929). A notable propaganda piece, written and directed by Dovzhenko, contrasting trench warfare in 1918 with a worker's revolt at home.

Arsène Lupin. The gallant French jewel thief and part-time detective, created at the beginning of the century by Maurice Leblanc, has been the subject of many films, the first being a Vitagraph 1917 version starring Earle Williams. In 1932 the Barrymore brothers were in *Arsène Lupin*, John taking the title role; in 1938 Melvyn Douglas was in *Arsène Lupin Returns*; Charles Korvin took over in 1944 for *Enter Arsène Lupin*; in 1957 there was Robert Lamoureux in *The Adventures of Arsène Lupin*; and in 1962 Jean-Claude Brialy starred in *Arsène Lupin Contre Arsène Lupin.* A French TV series ran during the seventies.

Arsenic and Old Lace (US 1944). Joseph Kesselring's black farce about two dotty old ladies who poison lonely gentlemen for their own good, and proceed to have them buried in the cellar, had been a great Broadway success, presumably because it suited audiences in the war years to make fun of death. In Hollywood, however, such an attitude was a tricky innovation, and Frank Capra got it past the Hays Office by directing it at breakneck speed, with Cary Grant as the astonished nephew registering nineteen double takes to the minute. Josephine Hull and Jean Adair were the aunts, John Alexander was mad Uncle Teddy, Peter Lorre was Dr Einstein, and Raymond Massey (because Boris Karloff was regrettably unavailable) took over the gruesome Jonathan.

art director. Technician responsible for designing sets, sometimes also costumes and graphics. 'Production designer' is a more pretentious way of saying much the same thing. The importance of this work to the finished product first became noticeable in *Intolerance* and the German expressionist films of the twenties, then in such diverse talking films as *The Old Dark House, Things to Come, The Cat and the Canary* (both versions), *Citizen Kane, Trouble in Paradise, The Mystery of the Wax Museum, A Matter of Life and Death, Les Enfants du Paradis,* and *King's Row*. Important figures (all qv) include William Cameron Menzies, Anton Grot, Cedric Gibbons, Ken Adam, Vincent Korda, Hans Dreier, Alfred Junge, Carmen Dillon.

art house. American term (now displacing 'specialized hall' in GB) for cinema showing classic revivals and highbrow or off-beat new films of limited commercial appeal.

The Art of the Film, by Ernest Lindgren. A useful primer by the longtime curator of the National Film Archive; first published 1948 and revised in 1963.

Artaud, Antonin (1896–1948). French drama critic and writer who dabbled in films. Napoleon (a) 26. The Passion of Joan of Arc (a) 28. *The Seashell and the Clergyman* (w) 28.

Arthur. The legendary British king of the 5th or 6th century, central figure of the courtly love tradition and alleged creator not only of the democratic Round Table but of the idyllic city and palace of Camelot, has figured in several movies, especially in recent

years when we seem to have had need to cherish our legends. There have been three sound versions, to begin with, of *A Connecticut Yankee at King Arthur's Court* (qv); in the 1949 version Cedric Hardwicke played the King as having a perpetual cold. In 1942, Arthur Askey dreamed he was a member of the Round Table in *King Arthur Was a Gentleman*. In 1964 Disney presented in cartoon form the childhood of Arthur in *The Sword in the Stone*. In slightly more serious vein, Mel Ferrer was Arthur in *Knights of the Round Table* 54, with Robert Taylor as Lancelot and Ava Gardner as Guinevere. Anthony Bushell had the role in *The Black Knight* 54 and Mark Dignam took over in *Siege of the Saxons* 64. In the 1963 *Lancelot and Guinevere*, the three roles were taken respectively by Brian Aherne, Cornel Wilde and Jean Wallace; in the 1967 musical *Camelot* (qv), by Richard Harris, Franco Nero, and Vanessa Redgrave. In the seventies there came Bresson's *Lancelot du Lac* and Rohmer's *Perceval*. In 1980 John Boorman gave us a noisy, violent version of the legend, *Excalibur*.
TV series on the subject have included *Sir Lancelot*, an Australian cartoon series called *Arthur!*, and a Welsh serial called *Arthur of The Britons*. There is also a TV movie, *Arthur the King*.

Arthur, Beatrice (1923–) (Bernice Frankel). Dominant American comedy actress, a big TV hit 1972–76 as *Maude*.
That Kind of Woman 58. Lovers and Other Strangers 69. *Mame* 73, etc.
TV series: *Maude* 72–76 (after occasional stints as the character in All in the Family). Amanda's 83. *The Golden Girls* 85.
¶ *B.A.:* All this time I've just wanted to be blonde, beautiful, and 5 feet 2 inches tall. (She's 5 feet 11 inches.)
Famous line (from *Auntie Mame*): 'Oh my God – somebody's been sleeping in my dress!'

Arthur, George K. (1899–) (G. K. A. Brest). Small but gamy hero of the British silent screen, popular in such films as *Kipps* 21. *A Dear Fool* 22. Went to Hollywood and was popular for a while.
Madness of Youth 23. Lights of Old Broadway 25. The Salvation Hunters 25. Irene 26. The Boy Friend 26. Rookies (first of a series of comedies with Karl Dane) 27. Baby Mine 28. The Last of Mrs Cheyney 29. Chasing Rainbows 30. Oliver Twist 33. Riptide 34. Vanessa (last to date) 35. Became a financier and distributor of art shorts.

Arthur, Jean (1905–) (Gladys Greene). Petite, squeaky-voiced American leading actress who after a long and dreary apprenticeship was especially notable as the determined feminist heroine of social comedies in the thirties and forties.
□Cameo Kirby 23. The Temple of Venus 24. Fast and Fearless 24. Seven Chances 25. The Drug Store Cowboy 25. A Man of Nerve 25. Tearing Loose 25. Thundering Through 26. Born to Battle 26. The Hurricane Horseman 26. The Fighting Cheat 26. The Cowboy Cop 26. Twisted Triggers 26. The College Boob 26. The Block Signal 26. Husband Hunters 27. The Broken Gate 27. Horseshoes 27. The Poor Nut 27. Flying Luck 27. The Masked Menace 27. Wallflowers 28. Easy Come Easy Go 28. Warming Up 28. Brotherly Love 28. Sins of the Fathers 29. The Canary Murder Case 29. Stairs of Sand 29. The Mysterious Dr Fu Manchu 29. *The Greene Murder Case* 29. *The Saturday Night Kid* 29. Halfway to Heaven 29. Street of Chance 30. Young Eagles 30. Paramount on Parade 30. The Return of Dr Fu Manchu 30. Danger Lights 30. The Silver Horde 30. The Gang Buster 31. Virtuous Husband 31. The Lawyer's Secret 31. Ex-Bad Boy 31. Get That Venus 33. The Past of Mary Holmes 33. Whirlpool 34. The Defense Rests 34. The Most Precious Thing in Life 34. *The Whole Town's Talking* 35. Public Hero Number One 35. Party Wife 35. *Diamond Jim* 35. The Public Menace 35. *If You Could Only Cook* 35. *Mr Deeds Goes to Town* 36. The Ex Mrs Bradford 36. Adventure in Manhattan 36. *The Plainsman* (as Calamity Jane) 36. More Than a Secretary 36. *History is Made at Night* 37. *Easy Living* 37. *You Can't Take It With You* 38. Only Angels have Wings 39. *Mr Smith Goes to Washington* 39. Too Many Husbands 40. Arizona 40. *The Devil and Miss Jones* 41. *The Talk of the Town* 42. *The More the Merrier* 43. A Lady Takes a Chance 43. The Impatient Years 44. *A Foreign Affair* 48. *Shane* 53.
TV series: The Jean Arthur Show 66.

Arthur, Robert (1909–86) (R. A. Feder). American producer, mainly with Universal.
Buck Privates Come Home 46. Abbott and Costello Meet Frankenstein 48. The Big Heat 53. Man of a Thousand Faces 57. The Great Impostor 60. Lover Come Back 60. That Touch of Mink 62. Father Goose 64. Shenandoah 65. Blindfold 66. Hellfighters 68. Sweet Charity 69. One More Train to Rob 73, many others.

Arthur, Robert (1925–) (Robert Arthaud). American actor, former radio announcer, in general supporting roles since 1945.
Roughly Speaking 45. Twelve O'Clock High 49. Ace in the Hole 51. Young Bess 54. Top of the World 55. Hellcats 57. Young and Wild 58, others.

Arundell, Denis (1898–). British character actor (radio's Dr Morelle). Sporadic film roles include: The Show Goes On 35. The Return of Carol Deane 38. Pimpernel Smith 41. Colonel Blimp 43. Carnival 46. The History of Mr Polly 49. Something Money Can't Buy 52.

Arvidson, Linda (1884–1949). American silent actress, first wife of D. W. Griffith; she played leads in a few of his early shorts, then retired.

Arzner, Dorothy (1900–1979). A former editor who became Hollywood's only woman director of the thirties.
☐ Fashions for Women 27. Get Your Man 27. Ten Modern Commandments 27. Manhattan Cocktail 28. The Wild Party 29. Sarah and Son 30. Paramount on Parade (part) 30. Anybody's Woman 30. Honour Among Lovers 31. Working Girls 31. *Merrily We Go to Hell* 32. Christopher Strong 33. *Nana* 34. *Craig's Wife* 36. The Bride Wore Red 37. *Dance Girl Dance* 40. First Comes Courage 43.

A.S.C. Often seen on credit titles after the names of cinematographers, these initials stand for the American Society of Cinematographers, a professional association, membership of which is by invitation only. Its aims since its foundation in 1918 have been 'to advance the art and science of cinematography'.

Ashby, Hal (1936–). American director who tends to smother his undoubted talent under layers of oblique approaches, and often outstays his welcome.
AS EDITOR: The Russians Are Coming, The Russians Are Coming 66. In the Heat of the Night 67. The Thomas Crown Affair 68, etc.
AS DIRECTOR: The Landlord 70. Harold and Maude 71. The Last Detail 73. Shampoo 75. Bound for Glory 76. *Coming Home* 78. Being There 79. Second Hand Hearts 80. Lookin' to Get Out 82. Let's Spend the Night Together 83. The Slugger's Wife 85. Eight Million Ways to Die 85.

Ashcroft, Dame Peggy (1907–). Distinguished British stage actress who has appeared in films only occasionally.
The Wandering Jew 33. *The Thirty-nine Steps* 35. Rhodes of Africa 36. *Quiet Wedding* 40. The Nun's Story 58. Secret Ceremony 68. Sunday Bloody Sunday 71. Joseph Andrews 77. Hullaballoo over Bonnie and George's Pictures 78. *A Passage to India* (AA, BFA) 84, etc.
TV series: Edward and Mrs Simpson (as Queen Mary) 78. *The Jewel in the Crown* 84.

Asher, Jack (1916–). British cinematographer, brother of director Robert Asher.
Jassy 47. Lili Marlene 42. The Good Die Young 53. The Young Lovers 54. Reach for the Sky 56. Dracula 58. She'll Have to Go (& co-p) 61. The Intelligence Men 65. The Early Bird 65. That Riviera Touch 66, many others.

Asher, Jane (1946–). British leading lady, former child performer in films from 1951.
Mandy 52. The Greengage Summer 60. The Girl in the Headlines 63. The Masque of the Red Death 64. Alfie 66. *Deep End* 71. Henry VIII and His Six Wives 72. Runners 83. Success is the Best Revenge 84. Dreamchild 85, etc.

Asher, Robert (1915–). British director.
Follow a Star 59. Make Mine Mink 60. The Bulldog Breed 60. She'll Have to Go (co-p, co-w, co-d) 61. On The Beat 62. A Stitch in Time 63. The Intelligence Men 65. The Early Bird 65. Press for Time 66.

Asher, William (1919–). American 'B' director.
☐Leather Gloves (co-d) 48. The Shadow on the Window 57. The Twenty-Seventh Day 57. *Beach Party* 63. Johnny Cool 63. Muscle Beach Party 64. Bikini Beach 64. Beach Blanket Bingo 65. How to Stuff a Wild Bikini 65. Fireball 500 66. Night Warning 83. Movers and Shakers 84.

Asherson, Renée (1920–). British stage actress in occasional films.
Henry V 44. The Way Ahead 44. The Way to the Stars 44. The Small Back Room 49. The Cure for Love 50. The Day the Earth Caught Fire 62. Rasputin the Mad Monk 65. The Smashing Bird I Used to Know 68, etc.

Ashley, Edward (1904–) (E. A. Cooper). British leading man who went to Hollywood but never did better than third leads.
Men of Steel 33. Underneath the Arches 37.

Spies of the Air 39. *Pride and Prejudice* 40. Bitter Sweet 41. The Black Swan 42. Nocturne 46. The Other Love 47. Tarzan and the Mermaids 48. Macao 52. The Court Jester (as the Fox) 56. Herbie Rides Again 73. Won Ton Ton 76, etc.

Ashley, Elizabeth (1939–) (Elizabeth Cole). Cool American leading lady who makes sporadic appearances.
Autobiography 1978: *Actress: Postcards from the Road.*
□*The Carpetbaggers* 64. Ship of Fools 65. The Third Day 65. Harpy (TV) 70. Marriage of a Young Stockbroker 71. When Michael Calls (TV) 71. The Face of Fear (TV) 71. Second Chance (TV) 71. Your Money or Your Wife (TV) 72. The Heist (TV) 73. The Magician (TV) 73. Golden Needles 74. Paperback Hero 75. Rancho de Luxe 75. 92 in the Shade 75. One of my Wives is Missing 76. The Great Scout and Cathouse Thursday 76. Fire in the Sky (TV) 77. Coma 78. Windows 80. Split Image 82. Svengali (TV) 82. Dragnet 87.

Ashton, Roy (1918–). British make-up artist.
Curse of Frankenstein 57. Dracula 58. The Mummy 59. Curse of the Werewolf 61. The Reptile 66. Vault of Horror 73. The Monster Club 81, etc.

Askew, Luke (1937–). American character actor, usually in westerns.
Cool Hand Luke 67. The Green Berets 68. Easy Rider 69. The Great Northfield Minnesota Raid 72. The Culpepper Cattle Company 72. Posse 75. Rolling Thunder 77. Wanda Nevada 79, etc.

Askey, Arthur (1900–1982). Diminutive (5′ 2″) British comedian with music-hall experience; gained fame as 'Big Hearted Arthur' in radio shows.
Autobiography 1975: *Before Your Very Eyes.*
□Calling All Stars 37. Band Wagon 39. Charley's Big-Hearted Aunt 40. *The Ghost Train* 41. I Thank You 41. Back Room Boy 42. King Arthur Was a Gentleman 42. Miss London Ltd 43. Bees in Paradise 44. The Love Match 54. Ramsbottom Rides Again 56. Make Mine a Million 58. Friends and Neighbours 59. The Alf Garnett Saga 72.

Askin, Leon (c. 1920–). Rotund American supporting actor who often plays sinister or comic Russians.
Road to Bali 52. Knock on Wood 54. Son of Sinbad 55. My Gun Is Quick 58. One Two Three 61. Do Not Disturb 65. The Maltese Bippy 69. Dr Death 73, many others.

Askwith, Robin (1950–). British leading man of seventies low comedy.
If 68. Bartleby 70. Nicholas and Alexandra 71. The Four Dimensions of Greta 71. Bless this House 73. Confessions of a Window Cleaner 74. Confessions of a Pop Performer 75. Confessions of a Driving Instructor 76. Stand Up Virgin Soldiers 77. Let's Get Laid 78, etc.

Aslan, Grégoire (1908–1982) (Kridor Aslanian). Armenian character actor, usually in comic or villainous roles.
Sleeping Car to Trieste 48. Occupe-Toi D'Amélie 49. Last Holiday 50. Cage of Gold 50. Confidential Report 53. He Who Must Die 56. Roots of Heaven 56. The Criminal 60. Cleopatra 62. Paris When It Sizzles 64. The High Bright Sun 65. Moment to Moment 65. Our Man in Marrakesh 66. Lost Command 66. A Flea in Her Ear 68. You Can't Win Them All 70. Sinbad's Golden Voyage 73, many others.

Asner, Edward (1929–). Chubby American character actor who usually plays tough guys, sometimes with a heart of gold.
The Satan Bug 65. The Slender Thread 65. El Dorado 66. The Venetian Affair 67. Gunn 67. The Todd Killings 70. The Skin Game 71. Rich Man Poor Man (TV) 76. Hey I'm Alive (TV) 76. Gus 76. The Life and Assassination of the Kingfish (TV) (as Huey Long) 77. Roots (TV) 77. The Gathering (TV) 78. Fort Apache the Bronx 82. O'Hara's Wife 82. Anatomy of an Illness (TV) 83. Daniel 83. The Christmas Star (TV) 86. Bronx Zoo (TV) 87, etc.
TV series: Slattery's People 64. *The Mary Tyler Moore Show* 70–74. *Lou Grant* 77–81.
†Asner was a provocative union leader in a long-running actors' strike, and his successful series *Lou Grant* was cancelled allegedly because of his political views.

¶ *E.A.:* I really wanted to be an adventurer, to lay pipeline in South America or be a cabin boy . . . but I didn't have the guts.

'I don't know him well, but he seems an extremely angry and short-tempered man. He's enormously sensitive to criticism.'—*Charlton Heston*

aspect ratio. Relative breadth and height of screen. Before 1953 this was 4:3 or 1.33:1. 'Standard' wide screen varies from 1.66:1 to 1.85:1. Anamorphic processes are wider: SuperScope 2:1, CinemaScope and most others 2.35:1 (or 2.55:1 with magnetic stereophonic sound). Vista-Vision, a printing process, was shot in 1.33:1 but recommended for screening at up to 2:1, i.e. with top and bottom cut off and the rest magnified. The TV screen is fixed at 1.33:1, therefore all wide-screen films lose something when played on it.

The Asphalt Jungle (US 1950). W. R. Burnett's crime novel about a robbery that failed was nimbly if coldly directed by John Huston: it started the long cycle of 'caper' films which included *Rififi* and *The League of Gentlemen*, and was notable for the performances of Sam Jaffe and Louis Calhern as well as for Harold Rosson's photography. It has been remade three times: as *The Badlanders* (in western guise) in 1958, as *Cairo* in 1963, and, with a black cast, as *Cool Breeze* in 1972. It also formed the basis of a short-lived TV series.

Asquith, Anthony (1902–1968). British director, son of Lord Oxford and Asquith, nicknamed 'Puffin'. His films were always civilized and usually entertaining but both the early experiments in technique and the later upper-class comedies and dramas suffered from the same lack of warmth and humanity. Biography 1973: *'Puffin' Asquith* by R. J. Minney.
□*Shooting Stars* (co-d) 28. *Underground* 30. A Cottage on Dartmoor 30. The Runaway Princess 30. Tell England 31. Dance Pretty Lady 31. Marry Me 32. The Window Cleaner 32. Lucky Number 33. Unfinished Symphony 34. Moscow Nights 35. Forever England 35. *Pygmalion* (co-d) 37. *French Without Tears* 39. Freedom Radio 40. *Quiet Wedding* 40. Cottage to Let 41. Uncensored 42. We Dive at Dawn 43. *The Demi-Paradise* 43. Welcome to Britain (doc) 43. Two Fathers 44. *Fanny by Gaslight* 44. *The Way to the Stars* 45. While the Sun Shines 46. *The Winslow Boy* 48. The Woman in Question 50. *The Browning Version* 50. *The Importance of Being Earnest* 51. The Net 53. The Final Test 53. The Young Lovers 54. Carrington VC 55. On Such a Night (doc) 56. *Orders to Kill* 58. The Doctors' Dilemma 59. Libel 60. The Millionairess 61. Guns of Darkness 62. Two Living One Dead 62. *The VIPS* 63. The Yellow Rolls Royce 64.

Assante, Armand (1949–). American leading man.
Paradise Alley 78, Prophecy 79, Lady of the House (TV) 79. Private Benjamin 80. Love and Money 82. I the Jury 83. Unfaithfully Yours 84. Belizaire the Cajun 85.

assassination has not been a favourite film subject, though historical incidents have been examined in *Julius Caesar, Sarajevo, Nicholas and Alexandra, Nine Hours to Rama, The Assassination of Trotsky, Gandhi* and *The Parallax View*. Assassination attempts have figured in *Suddenly, The Man Who Knew Too Much, Foreign Correspondent, The Manchurian Candidate* and *The Day of the Jackal*.

assistant director. More properly 'assistant to the director', being concerned with details of administration rather than creation.

associate producer. Usually the actual producer or supervisor of the film, the title of 'executive producer' having been taken by the head of the studio.

Associated British is the only British complex of companies which has power comparable to that of the Rank Organization (qv). Its history is tied up with Elstree Studios, originally owned by British International Pictures, which after many mergers emerged as Associated British in 1933. The men involved in the story are producer Herbert Wilcox, John Maxwell, a lawyer who turned film distributor and later founded the ABC cinema chain, and J. D. Williams, a wealthy exhibitor. Distribution was arranged through Pathé Pictures, which became a powerful partner. Elstree was the first British studio to wire for sound (*Blackmail*) and the first to produce a bilingual talkie (*Atlantic*). Throughout the thirties it turned out fifteen films a year, usually unambitious but competent; and unmistakably British. In 1940 a great number of shares were sold to Warner Brothers, and in 1956 the distribution arm became known as Warner-Pathé. Other associated companies include Pathé News, Pathé Laboratories, Pathé Equipment, and ABC Television. In 1969, after several years of comparative inactivity, the complex was taken over by E.M.I.
In the eighties Cannon took over all the companies, but promptly sold the library to Jerry Weintraub.

Association of Cinematograph, Television and Allied Technicians. ACTT: the British film-makers' union. Founded 1931.

Asta. A wire-haired fox-terrier who appeared (impersonated by several dogs) in *The Thin Man* and other films between 1934 and 1947.

Astaire, Fred (1899–1987) (Frederick Austerlitz). American dancing star whose inimitable finesse and good humour delighted two generations. His half-spoken singing was almost equally delightful, and the films in which he was teamed with Ginger Rogers (*) have a magic all their own. Autobiography 1959: *Steps in Time*. Academy Award 1949 'for his unique artistry and his unique contribution to the techniques of motion pictures'.
□Dancing Lady 33. **Flying Down to Rio* 33. **The Gay Divorcee* 34. **Roberta* 35. **Top Hat* 35. **Follow the Fleet* 36. **Swing Time* 36. **Shall We Dance?* 37. A Damsel in Distress 37. **Carefree* 38. **The Story of Vernon and Irene Castle* 39. Broadway Melody 40. Second Chorus 40. *You'll Never Get Rich* 41. *Holiday Inn* 42. You Were Never Lovelier 42. The Sky's the Limit 43. Yolanda and the Thief 45. *Ziegfeld Follies* 46. *Blue Skies* 46. *Easter Parade* 48. **The Barkleys of Broadway* 48. Three Little Words 50. Let's Dance 50. Royal Wedding 51. The Belle of New York 52. *The Band Wagon* 53. Daddy Long Legs 55. *Funny Face* 57. Silk Stockings 57. *On the Beach* (dramatic role) 59. *The Pleasure of His Company* (dr) 61. Notorious Landlady (dr) 62. *Finian's Rainbow* 68. The Midas Run (dr) 69. The Over The Hill Gang Rides Again (dr: TV film) 71. That's Entertainment, Part Two 74. The Towering Inferno (dr) 75. The Amazing Dobermans (dr) 76. The Purple Taxi (dr) 77. A Family Upside Down (dr) (TV) 78. The Man in the Santa Claus Suit (dr) (TV) 80. Ghost Story (dr) 81.
TV series: It Takes a Thief 65–69.
❀ For his apparently lighter-than-air constitution, his brilliantly inventive dancing, his breezy elegance, his unlikely but effective voice, and his pleasing longevity. *Top Hat*.

¶ The most famous quote about the screen's nimblest dancer is the report of the studio talent scout on his first screen test:

> Can't act. Can't sing. Slightly bald. Can dance a little.

In later years, when he was a household name around the world, he tried to match that for humility:

> I have no desire to prove anything by dancing. I have never used it as an outlet or as a means of expressing myself. I just dance.

And:

> I just put my feet in the air and move them around.

But in another mood, he did once confess:

> I suppose I made it look easy, but gee whiz, did I work and worry.

Gene Kelly summed up his appeal:

> He can give the audience pleasure just by walking across the floor.

And Mr Kelly graciously added:

> If I'm the Marlon Brando of dancing, he's Cary Grant.

Graham Greene put it another way:

> The nearest we are ever likely to get to a human Mickey Mouse.

C. A. Lejeune produced this analysis:

> I have never met anyone who did not like Fred Astaire. Somewhere in his sad monkey-sad face, his loose legs, his shy grin, or perhaps the anxious diffidence of his manner, he has found the secret of persuading the world.

André Sennwald, in a review of *The Gay Divorcee*, was equally percipient:

> The audience meets Mr Astaire and the film at their best when he is adjusting his cravat to an elaborate dance routine or saying delicious things with his flashing feet that a lyricist would have difficulty putting into words.

While Fred Astaire said in his eighties:

> When they review my shows, they don't say whether they're good or bad—they just write about how old I am.

Asther, Nils (1897–1981). Suave, exotic Swedish leading man in Hollywood from the mid-twenties.
Topsy and Eva 27. *Sorrell and Son* 27. The Blue Danube 28. Laugh Clown Laugh 28. The Cossacks 28. Loves of an Actress 28. The Cardboard Lover 28. *Our Dancing Daughters* 28. Dream of Love 28. Wild Orchids 29. *The Single Standard* 29. The Wrath of the Seas 29. Letty Lynton 32. The Washington Masquerade 32. *The Bitter Tea of General Yen* 32. Storm at Daybreak 33. The Right to Romance 33. *By Candlelight* 34. Madame Spy 34. The Crime Doctor 34. The Love Captive 34. *Abdul the Damned* (GB) 35. Make Up (GB) 37. Dr Kildare's Wedding Day 41. The Night Before the Divorce 41. The Night of January 16th 41. Sweater Girl 42. Night Monster 42. The Hour Before Dawn 44. *The Man in Half Moon Street* 44. Son of Lassie 45. Jealousy 45. The Feathered Serpent 49. That Man from Tangier 50. Vita Frun 62. Gudrun 63.

Astin, John (1930–). American comic actor with stage experience.
West Side Story 61. That Touch of Mink 62. Candy 68. Viva Max 68. Evil Roy Slade (TV) 72. Get To Know Your Rabbit 72. The Brothers O'Toole 73. Freaky Friday 77. Body Slam 87, etc. TV series: I'm Dickens He's Fenster 63. The Addams Family 64. Operation Petticoat 77. Mary 85.

Astin, Patty Duke (1946–). American child actress who found difficulty in graceful adaptation to adult roles. Married John Astin; previously known as Patty Duke.
□I'll Cry Tomorrow 55. Somebody Up There Likes Me 56. Country Music Holiday 57. The Goddess 58. Happy Anniversary 59. 4-D Man 59. The Power and the Glory (TV) 62. *The Miracle Worker* (AA) 62. Billie 65. Valley of the Dolls 67. Me Natalie 69. My Sweet Charlie (TV) 70. Two on a Bench (TV) 71. If Tomorrow Comes (TV) 71. She Waits (TV) 71. You'll Like My Mother 72. Deadly Harvest (TV) 72. Nightmare (TV) 73. Captains and the Kings (TV) 76. A Family Upside Down (TV) 78. The Swarm 78. Hanging by a Thread (TV) 79. The Miracle Worker (TV) 79. Before and After (TV) 80. Best Kept Secrets (TV) 84.
TV series: *The Patty Duke Show* 63–65. It Takes Two 82. Hail to the Chief 85.

Astor, Gertrude (1887–1977). American silent screen actress.
Uncle Tom's Cabin 27. The Cat and the Canary 28. Camille 36. How Green Was My Valley 40. The Man Who Shot Liberty Valance 62, many others.

Astor, Mary (1906–87) (Lucille Langehanke). American leading lady who despite a stormy and well-publicized private life remained a star from the mid-twenties to the mid-forties and remained in demand for character roles. Autobiography 1959: *My Story*. 1971: *A Life on Film*. Novels include *Image of Kate* 66. *A Place Called Saturday* 69. Silent films include *The Beggar Maid* 21. The Bright Shawl 23. Puritan Passions 23. *Beau Brummell* 24. Inez from Hollywood 25. *Don Q Son of Zorro* 25. *Don Juan* 26. Rose of the Golden West 27. Two Arabian Knights 27. Heart to Heart 28. Romance of the Underworld 29.
□Sound: Ladies Love Brutes 30. The Runaway Bride 30. Holiday 30. The Lash 30. The Sin Ship 30. The Royal Bed 30. Other Men's Women 31. Behind Office Doors 31. White Shoulders 31. Smart Woman 31. Men of Chance 31. The Lost Squadron 32. A Successful Calamity 32. Those We Love 32. *Red Dust* 32. The Little Giant 33. Jennie Gerhardt 33. The Kennel Murder Case 33. Convention City 33. The World Changes 33. Easy to Love 34. The Man with Two Faces 34. Return of the Terror 34. Upper World 34. The Case of the Howling Dog 34. I am a Thief 34. Man of Iron 35. Red Hot Tires 35. Straight from the Heart 35. Dinky 35. Page Miss Glory 35. The Murder of Dr Harrigan 35. The Lady from Nowhere 36. And So They Were Married 36. *Dodsworth* 36. Trapped by Television 36. *The Prisoner of Zenda* 37. *The Hurricane* 37. Paradise for Three 38. No Time to Marry 38. There's Always a Woman 38. Woman against Woman 38. Listen Darling 39. *Midnight* 39. *Turnabout* 40. Brigham Young 40. *The Great Lie* (AA) (her most splendid bitchy performance) 41. *The Maltese Falcon* 41. *Across the Pacific* 42. *The Palm Beach Story* 42. Young Ideas 43. Thousands Cheer 43. *Meet Me in St Louis* 44. Blonde Fever 44. Claudia and David 46. Desert Fury 47. Cynthia 47. Fiesta 47. *Act of Violence* 49. Cass Timberlane 49. *Little Women* (as Marmee) 49. Any Number Can Play 49. A Kiss Before Dying 56. The Power and the Prize 56. The Devil's Hairpin 56. This Happy Feeling 58. Stranger in my Arms 59. *Return to Peyton Place* 61. *Youngblood Hawke* 64. Hush Hush Sweet Charlotte 64.
❀ For amiably sending herself up in half a dozen portraits of mature but fallible women between 1936 and 1942; and for sheer durability. *The Great Lie*.

¶ *M.A.:* I was never totally involved in movies. I was making my father's dream come true.
Famous line (from *The Great Lie*): 'If I didn't think you meant so well, I'd feel like slapping your face.'

Astruc, Alexandre (1923–). French director, former film critic.
The Crimson Curtain 51. Les Mauvaises Rencontres 54. Une Vie 56. La Proie Pour l'Ombre 61. L'Education Sentimentale 61. La Longue Marche 65.

L' Atalante (France 1934). A strange, dreamlike, influential film by Jean Vigo about a honeymoon on a barge, with Dita Parlo, Jean Daste, and Michel Simon as the skipper. Music by Maurice Jaubert, photography Boris Kaufmann.

Ates, Roscoe (1892–1962). American comic actor with inimitable nervous stutter.

South Sea Rose 29. The Big House 30. Cimarron 30. The Champ 31. Freaks 32. Alice in Wonderland 33. The People's Enemy 35. Gone with the Wind 39. Captain Caution 40. The Palm Beach Story 42. The Stranger Wore a Gun 53. The Errand Boy 61, many others.

Atherton, William (1947–). American actor of the seventies, with stage background.
□The New Centurions 72. Class of '44 73. The Sugarland Express 74. The Day of the Locust 74. The Hindenberg 76. Looking for Mr Goodbar 77. Malibu (TV) 83. Ghostbusters 84. Real Genius 85. No Mercy 86.

Atkins, Christopher (1961–). American juvenile lead of the early eighties.
The Blue Lagoon 80. Child Bride of Short Creek (TV) 81. A Night in Heaven 83, etc.

Atkins, Eileen (1934–). British character actress, highly regarded on stage.
□*Inadmissible Evidence* 68. I Don't Want to Be Born 75. Equus 77. She Fell Among Thieves (TV) 78. The Dresser 83.

Atlantic (GB 1929). Directed by E. A. Dupont, this early talkie was also the first to be made in two language versions (English and German, with different leading actors). There is now very little intrinsic interest in its melodramatics set on the sinking Titanic.

L'Atlantide (France 1921). An exotic adventure film about two wanderers who discover the lost city of Atlantis. Written and directed by Jacques Feyder, its exotic style was highly influential though its length was fatiguing. Pabst made a sound version in 1932, with Brigitte Helm. In 1948 Maria Montez was the *Siren of Atlantis*.

The Atonement of Gosta Berling (Sweden 1924). Remembered chiefly for introducing Greta Garbo to the screen, this is a strong Scandinavian brew about a clergyman, unfrocked for alcoholism, who dissipates his talents in high society. Solidly well directed by Mauritz Stiller from Selma Lagerlöf's novel; with Lars Hanson.

Attenborough, Sir Richard (1923–). British character actor who escaped from early typecasting as a young coward, revealed an ambitious range of characterizations, and went on to produce and direct.
□*In Which We Serve* 42. Schweik's New Adventures 42. The Hundred Pound Window 43. Journey Together 43. A Matter of Life and Death 46. School for Secrets 46. The Man Within 47. Dancing with Crime 47. *Brighton Rock* 47. London Belongs to Me 48. *The Guinea Pig* (as a 13-year-old) 49. The Lost People 50. Boys in Brown 50. Morning Departure 50. Hell is Sold Out 51. The Magic Box 51. The Gift Horse 52. Father's Doing Fine 53. Eight O'Clock Walk 54. The Ship that Died of Shame 54. *Private's Progress* 55. The Baby and the Battleship 56. Brothers in Law 56. The Scamp 58. Dunkirk 58. *The Man Upstairs* 58. Danger Within 58. I'm All Right Jack 58. Sea of Sand 58. Jetstorm 59. SOS Pacific 59. *The Angry Silence* (& co-p) 59. *The League of Gentlemen* (& co-p) 59. Only Two Can Play 62. *Whistle Down the Wind* (p only) 62. The Dock Brief 62. All Night Long 62. *The Great Escape* (US) 63. *Seance on a Wet Afternoon* (& p) 64. The Third Secret 64. *Guns at Batasi* (BFA) 64. The Flight of the Phoenix (US) 65. The Sand Pebbles (US) 66. Doctor Dolittle 67. The Bliss of Mrs Blossom 68. The Last Grenade 68. Only When I Larf 68. *Oh What a Lovely War* (co-p and d only) 69. David Copperfield 69. The Magic Christian 70. A Severed Head 70. *Loot* 71. 10 Rillington Place 71. Young Winston (d only) 72. Conduct Unbecoming 75. Rosebud 75. Brannigan 75. And Then There Were None 75. A Bridge Too Far (d only) 77. The Chess Players (India) 78. Magic (d only) 78. The Human Factor 79. *Gandhi* (p, d only) (AA) 82. A Chorus Line (d only) 85. Cry Freedom (d only) 87.

Atterbury, Malcolm (1907–). American character actor.
Dragnet 54. I Was a Teenage Werewolf 57. Blood of Dracula 57. Rio Bravo 59. The Birds 63. Seven Days in May 64, etc.

Atwater, Barry (1918–78). American character actor.
Nightmare 56. Pork Chop Hill 59. Sweet Bird of Youth 62. Return of the Gunfighter (TV) 66. The Night Stalker (TV) 72, etc.

Atwill, Lionel (1885–1946). Incisive but rather stolid British actor who went to Hollywood in 1932 and stayed to play teutonic villains, mad doctors and burgomasters.
□Eve's Daughter 18. For Sale 18. The Marriage Price 19. The Highest Bidder 21. Indiscretion 21. The Silent Witness 32. *Doctor X* 32. The Vampire Bat 33. The Secret of Madame Blanche 33. *The Mystery of the Wax Museum* 33. Murders in the Zoo 33. The

Sphinx 33. Song of Songs 33. The Secret of the Blue Room 33. The Solitaire Man 33. *Nana* 34. Beggars in Ermine 34. Stamboul Quest 34. One More River 34. The Age of Innocence 34. The Firebird 34. The Man Who Reclaimed His Head 35. Mark of the Vampire 35. *The Devil is a Woman* 35. The Murder Man 35. Rendezvous 35. Captain Blood 35. Lady of Secrets 36. Absolute Quiet 36. Till We Meet Again 36. *The Road Back* 37. The High Command 37. Last Train from Madrid 37. The Great Garrick 37. Lancer Spy 37. Three Comrades 38. The Great Waltz 38. *Son of Frankenstein* (memorable as the one-armed police chief) 39. *The Three Musketeers* 39. *The Hound of the Baskervilles* 39. The Gorilla 39. The Sun Never Sets 39. Mr Moto Takes a Vacation 39. The Secret of Dr Kildare 39. Balalaika 39. Charlie Chan in Panama 39. The Mad Empress 40. Johnny Apollo 40. Charlie Chan's Murder Cruise 40. The Girl in 313 40. Boom Town 40. The Great Profile 40. *Man Made Monster* 41. The Mad Doctor of Market Street 42. *To Be Or Not To Be* 42. The Strange Case of Dr RX 42. The Ghost of Frankenstein 42. Pardon My Sarong 42. Cairo 42. Night Monster 42. Junior G-Men of the Air (serial) 42. *Sherlock Holmes and the Secret Weapon* (as Moriarty) 42. Frankenstein Meets the Wolf Man 43. House of Frankenstein 44. Captain America (serial) 44. Raiders of Ghost City (serial) 44. Lady in the Death House 44. Secrets of Scotland Yard 44. Fog Island 45. Genius at Work 45. Crime Incorporated 45. *House of Dracula* 45. Lost City of the Jungle (serial) 46.

¶ See, one side of my face is gentle and kind, incapable of anything but love of my fellow man. The other profile is cruel and predatory and evil, incapable of anything but lusts and dark passions. It all depends which side of my face is turned towards you—or the camera.—*L.A.*

One doesn't easily forget, Herr Baron, an arm torn out by the roots.—*L.A. in Son of Frankenstein*

My dear, why are you so pitifully afraid? Immortality has been the dream, the inspiration of mankind through the ages. And I am going to give you immortality!—*L.A. in The Mystery of the Wax Museum*

Auberjonois, René (1940–). American character actor.
M*A*S*H 70. Brewster McCloud 71. McCabe and Mrs Miller 71. Images 72. Pete 'n Tillie 72. Panache (TV) 76. The Hindenberg 76. King Kong 76. Eyes of Laura Mars 78. Where the Buffalo Roam 80. The Christmas Star (TV) 86, etc.
TV series: Benson 80–85.

Aubert, Lenore (1913–). Yugoslavian actress in Hollywood from the late thirties, usually in sinister roles.
Bluebeard's Eighth Wife 38. They Got Me Covered 43. Action in Arabia 44. *Wife of Monte Cristo* 46. The Other Love 47. Return of the Whistler 48. *Abbott and Costello Meet Frankenstein* 48. Abbott and Costello Meet the Killer 49, etc.

Aubrey, Anne (1937–). British leading lady of a few comedies and adventures in the late fifties.
No Time To Die 58. The Man Inside 58. The Secret Man 58. The Bandit of Zhobe 59. Idol on Parade 59. Killers of Kilimanjaro 59. Jazzboat 60. In the Nick 60. Let's Get Married 60. The Hellions 61. Assignment Munich (TV) 72. The Carey Treatment 73.

Aubrey, Skye (1945–). American leading lady of a few seventies films: daughter of James Aubrey, TV executive.
Vanished (TV) 71. The Carey Treatment 72. The Longest Night (TV) 72. The Phantom of Hollywood (TV) 73, etc.

Aubry, Cecile (1929–) (Anne-José Benard). Petite French leading lady of the early fifties.
Manon 49. The Black Rose 50. Bluebeard 51. La Ironia 54, etc.

Auclair, Michel (1922–) (Vladimir Vujovic). French leading man.
La Belle et la Bête 46. Les Maudits 47. Manon 49. Justice Est Faite 50. Henriette 52. Funny Face (US) 56. The Fanatics 57. Rendezvous de Minuit 61. Symphony for a Massacre 64. The Day of the Jackal 73, etc.

Audiard, Michel (1920–85). French writer-director.
Mr Peek-a-Boo (w) 51. Gas Oil (w) 55. Les Misérables (w) 57. Babette Goes to War (w) 60. A Monkey in Winter (w) 62. Mélodie en Sous-Sol (w) 63. Tendre Voyou (w) 66. Opération Léontine (w, d) 68. Le Drapeau Noir (w, d) 71. Tendre Poulet (w, d) 78. Le Cavaleur (w, d) 79, many others.

Audley, Maxine (1923–). British stage actress who has made occasional film appearances.

The Sleeping Tiger 54. The Barretts of Wimpole Street 57. The Vikings 58. Our Man in Havana 59. The Trials of Oscar Wilde 60. Hell is a City 60. A Jolly Bad Fellow 64. Here We Go Round the Mulberry Bush 67. Frankenstein Must Be Destroyed 69, etc.

Audran, Stéphane (1939–). Cool French leading actress, in international films.
La Bonne Tisane 58. Les Cousins 59. Les Bonnes Femmes 60. Les Godelureaux 61. La Signe du Lion 62. Landru 63. Le Tigre Aime la Chair Fraiche 64. Paris vu Par 65. The Champagne Murders 67. *Les Biches* 68. La Femme Infidèle 69. The Lady in the Car with Glasses and a Gun 70. Just Before Nightfall 71. Without Apparent Motive 71. *The Discreet Charm of the Bourgeoisie* 72. Les Noces Rouges 73. Dead Pigeon on Beethoven Street 73. And Then There Were None 74. The Black Bird 75. Vincent, Paul, François and the Others 76. Folies Bourgeoises 76. Silver Bears 77. Violette Nozière 78. The Prisoner of Zenda 79. Eagle's Wing 79. Le Coeur a l'Envers 80. The Big Red One 80. Brideshead Revisted (TV) 80. Blood Relatives 81. Coup de Torchon 82. The Blood of Others 84. Cop au Vin 84. Mistral's Daughter (TV) 84. Les Plouffe 85. The Gypsy 85.

Audry, Jacqueline (1908–77). French director.
Gigi 49. L'Ingénue Libertine 50. *Olivia* 51. Huis Clos 54. In Six Easy Lessons 57. Mitsou 57. Les Petits Matins 62. Soledad 66, etc.

Auer, John H. (1909–1975). Hungarian-born American director, turning out 'B' films since the thirties.
□Frankie and Johnnie 35. The Crime of Dr Crespi 35. Rhythm in the Clouds 37. Circus Girl 37. Outside of Paradise 38. Invisible Enemy 38. I Stand Accused 38. A Desperate Adventure 38. Orphans of the Street 38. Forged Passport 39. SOS Tidal Wave 39. Smuggled Cargo 39. Calling All Marines 39. Thou Shalt Not Kill 40. Women in War 40. Hit Parade of 1941 40. A Man Betrayed 41. The Devil Pays Off 41. Pardon My Stripes 42. Moonlight Masquerade 42. Johnny Doughboy 42. Tahiti Honey 43. *Gangway for Tomorrow* 43. Seven Days Ashore 44. Moonlight in Manhattan 44. Pan Americana 45. Beat the Band 47. The Flame 48. I Jane Doe 48. Angel on the Amazon 48. The Avengers 50. Hit Parade of 1951 50. Thunderbirds 52. *City that Never Sleeps* (& p) 53. Hell's Half Acre (& p) 54. The Eternal Sea (& p) 55. Johnny Trouble (& p) 57.
Then to TV.

Auer, Mischa (1905–1967) (Mischa Ounskowsky). Lanky Russian comedy actor with prominent eyes and wild gestures. Went to Broadway after the revolution, and in 1928 arrived in Hollywood; after several false starts found himself much in demand for noble idiot roles in broken English.
□Something Always Happens 28. Marquis Preferred 28. The Benson Murder Case 30. Inside the Lines 30. Just Imagine 30. Women Love Once 30. The Unholy Garden 31. The Yellow Ticket 31. Delicious 31. The Midnight Patrol 32. No Greater Love 32. Mata Hari 32. Scarlet Dawn 32. The Monster Walks 32. Dangerously Yours 33. Sucker Money 33. Infernal Machine 33. Corruption 33. After Tonight 33. Cradle Song 33. Girl Without a Room 33. Wharf Angel 34. Bulldog Drummond Strikes Back 34. Stamboul Quest 34. I Dream too Much 34. The Crusades 35. Mystery Woman 35. Lives of a Bengal Lancer 35. Clive of India 35. Sons of Guns 36. Murder in the Fleet 36. The House of a Thousand Candles 36. One Rainy Afternoon 36. The Princess Comes Across 36. *My Man Godfrey* (in which his gorilla impersonation really put him on the map) 36. *The Gay Desperado* 36. Winterset 36. That Girl from Paris 37. Three Smart Girls 37. Top of the Town 37. We Have Our Moments 37. Pick a Star 37. Marry the Girl 37. Vogues of 1938 37. *100 Men and a Girl* 37. Merry Go Round 37. It's All Yours 38. Rage of Paris 38. *You Can't Take It With You* 38. Service de Luxe 38. Little Tough Guys in Society 38. *Sweethearts* 38. *East Side of Heaven* 39. Unexpected Father 39. *Destry Rides Again* 39. Alias the Deacon 40. Sandy is a Lady 40. Public Deb Number One 40. *Spring Parade* 40. Seven Sinners 40. Trail of the Vigilantes 40. The Flame of New Orleans 41. Hold That Ghost 41. Moonlight in Hawaii 41. *Hellzapoppin* 41. Cracked Nuts 41. *Twin Beds* 42. Around the World 43. *Lady in the Dark* 44. *Up in Mabel's Room* 44. *A Royal Scandal* 45. Brewster's Millions 45. And Then There Were None 45. Sentimental Journey 46. She Wrote the Book 46. Sofia 48. The Sky is Red 52. Song of Paris 52. *Confidential Report* 55. Futures Vedettes 55. The Monte Carlo Story 58. Mam'zelle Pigalle 58. The Foxiest Girl in Paris 58. A Dog a Mouse and a Sputnik 60. We Joined the Navy 62. Ladies First 63. The Christmas that Almost Wasn't 66. Drop Dead Darling 66.
❀ For assuring the world that Russians could be fun. *Twin Beds*.
Famous line (from *Lady in the Dark*): 'This is the end! The absolute end!'

Auger, Claudine (1942–). French leading lady, in occasional films abroad.
In the French Style 63. Thunderball 65. Triple Cross 66. Jeu de Massacre 67. The Devil in Love 67. The Bastard 68. The Crimebuster 77. Travels with Anita 79. Fantastica 80. Lovers and Liars 81. The Associate 82. Secret Places 84, etc.

August, Joseph (1890–1947). Distinguished American cinematographer.
SELECTED SILENTS: The Narrow Trail 17. Tiger Man 18. Square Deal Sanderson 19. Sand 20. O'Melley of the Mounted 21. *Travellin' On* 22. Madness of Youth 23. *Dante's Inferno* 24. *Tumbleweeds* 25. *The Road to Glory* 26. *The Beloved Rogue* 26. Fig Leaves 26. Two Arabian Knights 27. Honor Bound 28. The Black Watch 29.
□SOUND FILMS: Men Without Women 30. Double Crossroads 30. On Your Back 30. Up the River 30. Seas Beneath 31. Mr Lemon of Orange 31. Quick Millions 31. The Brat 31. Heartbreak 31. Charlie Chan's Chance 31. Silent Witness 32. Mystery Ranch 32. Vanity Street 32. No More Orchids 32. That's My Boy 32. *Man's Castle* 33. Master of Men 33. As the Devil Commands 33. Cocktail Hour 33. Circus Queen Murder 33. The Captain Hates the Sea 34. Among the Missing 34. The Defense Rests 34. Black Moon 34. Twentieth Century 34. No Greater Glory 34. Sylvia Scarlett 35. After the Dance 35. *The Informer* 35. I'll Love You Always 35. The Whole Town's Talking 35. The Plough and the Stars 36. *Mary of Scotland* 36. Every Saturday Night 36. A Damsel in Distress 37. Music for Madame 37. Super Sleuth 37. Fifty Roads to Town 37. *Michael Strogoff* 37. Sea Devils 37. Gun Law 37. This Marriage Business 38. The Saint in New York 38. *The Hunchback of Notre Dame* 39. *Gunga Din* 39. Nurse Edith Cavell 40. Man of Conquest 40. Melody Ranch 40. Primrose Path 40. *All that Money Can Buy* 41. They Were Expendable 45. *Portrait of Jennie* 48.
❁ For the imperishable visuals of his half-dozen melodramatic masterpieces. *Portrait of Jennie*.

Aulin, Ewa (1949–). Scandinavian leading lady in international films.
Candy 68. Start the Revolution without Me 69. This Kind of Love 72, etc.

Ault, Marie (1870–1951) (Mary Cragg). British character actress of stage and screen, usually in dialect comedy roles.
Woman to Woman 24. The Lodger 26. Hobson's Choice 31. *Major Barbara* 40. *Love on the Dole* 41. We Dive at Dawn 43. I See a Dark Stranger 46. Madness of the Heart 49, many others.

Aumont, Jean-Pierre (1909–) (J.-P. Salomons). French leading man, in films from 1931, Hollywood from 1941.
Autobiography 1977: *Sun and Shadow*.
Jean de la Lune 32. Maria Chapdelaine 35. Drôle de Drame 36. *Hôtel du Nord* 38. The Cross of Lorraine 42. Assignment in Brittany 43. Heartbeat 46. Song of Scheherazade 48. The First Gentleman (GB) 48. Charge of the Lancers 53. *Lili* 53. Hilda Crane 56. The Seventh Sin 57. The Devil at Four O'Clock 61. Five Miles to Midnight 63. Castle Keep 69. *La Nuit Américaine* 73. The Happy Hooker 75. Catherine and Company 75. Seven Suspects for Murder 77. Nana 83. Shadow Dance 83. The Blood of Others 84. Sweet Country 86, etc.

Aurel, Jean (1925–). French writer-director, originally of documentary shorts.
14–18 (d) 63. La Bataille de France (d) 64. De l'Amour (w, d) 65. Manon 70 (w, d) 68. Les Femmes (w, d) 69. Comme un Pot de Fraises (w, d) 74, etc.

Aurenche, Jean (1904–). French writer who with Pierre Bost (1901–1975) wrote many well-known films.
Hôtel du Nord 38. Sylvie et le Fantôme 45. La Symphonie Pastorale 46. *Le Diable au Corps* 46. Occupe-Toi d'Amélie 49. Dieu A Besoin des Hommes 50. *The Red Inn* 51. *Les Jeux Interdits* 51. Ripening Seed 53. Gervaise 56. En Cas de Malheur 57. L'Affaire d'Une Nuit 60. The Clockmaker 76, etc. Aurenche worked alone on the screenplay of *Woman in White* 65.

Auric, Georges (1899–1983). French composer.
Autobiography 1974: *Quand J'étais Là*.
Le Sang d'un Poète 30. *À Nous la Liberté* 31. Lac aux Dames 34. L'Alibi 37. Orage 38. L'Eternel Retour 43. Dead of Night 45. Caesar and Cleopatra 45. La Belle et la Bête 46. It Always Rains on Sunday 47. Corridor of Mirrors 48. Passport to Pimlico 49. *Orphée* 49. *Belles de Nuit* 52. Roman Holiday 53. The Wages of Fear 53. Father Brown 54. Rififi 55. The Witches of Salem 56. Gervaise 56. The Picasso Mystery 56. Heaven Fell That Night 58. Bonjour Tristesse 59. La Chambre Ardente 62. The Mind Benders 63. Thomas the Impostor 65. Therese and Isabelle 68. The Christmas Tree 69, many others.

Aurthur, Robert Alan (1922–78). American novelist and screenwriter.
Edge of the City 56. Warlock 59. For Love of Ivy 68. The Lost Man 70, etc.

Austen, Jane (1775–1817). The most delightful of English novelists has been oddly neglected by the screen, but the 1940 version of *Pride and Prejudice* is a distinguished and amusing one.

Austin, Charlotte (1933–). American leading lady who moved from musicals to monsters in the fifties.
Sunny Side of the Street 51. The Farmer Takes a Wife 53. How to Marry a Millionaire 53. Gorilla at Large 54. Desirée 54. Daddy Long Legs 55. How to Be Very Very Popular 55. Bride of the Beast 58, etc.

Austin, Jerry (–). Dwarf American actor.
Saratoga Trunk 43. Adventures of Don Juan 47, etc.

Austin, Ray (1932–). British director, mostly of TV episodes.
House of the Living Dead 73. Sword of Justice (TV) 79. Salvage 1 (TV) 79. Tales of the Gold Monkey (TV) 82.

Austin, Ron (–). American screenwriter.
The Happening 67. Harry in Your Pocket 73, etc.

Australia has long had a vigorous cinema movement, but it has not suited the rest of the world to take much note of it. Charles Chauvel is the continent's best-known director, but even his films have travelled remarkably little, and after World War Two, Australia leaned very heavily on American imports; though Britain, and especially Ealing Studios, offered encouragement by making a number of films there. In the early seventies Australia's traditional rough-edged action adventures gave way on the one hand to Barry Mackenzie-style smut and on the other to macabre, stylish curiosities such as *The Cars That Ate Paris* and *Picnic At Hanging Rock*; there developed from these a new, serious Australian school including such internationally well-regarded general movies as *Newsfront* and *The Chant of Jimmie Blacksmith*. Peter Weir and Fred Schepsi became OK directorial names; such films as *Breaker Morant* and *Gallipoli* were given international fanfares; *The Man from Snowy River* broke all records in Australia; Helen Morse, Mel Gibson, Bryan Brown and Judy Davis showed that Australia had skilled actors; *Mad Max* showed that Australia could dispense stylish violence with the best of them. In 1982, however, the bubble seemed about to burst. Hollywood began to steal the best talents, and the Australian unions became greedy for the kind of salaries that only Hollywood could afford to pay, while at home a valuable tax concession was withdrawn, making finance for home-grown movies more difficult. Meanwhile Australian television doggedly aped Hollywood, grinding out soap operas such as *The Sullivans*, *Cop Shop*, *Country Practice* and *Sons and Daughters*, with occasional mini-series ranging from the poverty-stricken *Sara Dane* to the more smoothly ambitious *A Town Like Alice* and *For the Term of His Natural Life*. The main problem turned out to be the lack of native subject matter, once producers had exhausted World War One, Botany Bay and sheep shearing.

Autant-Lara, Claude (1903–). French director, usually of stylish romantic dramas; former assistant to René Clair.
Ciboulette 33. L'Affaire du Courier de Lyons 37. *Fric Frac* 39. Lettres de l'Amour 42. Douce 43. Sylvie et le Fantôme 45. *Le Diable au Corps* 46. *Occupe-Toi d'Amélie* 49. *The Red Inn* 51. Ripening Seed 53. Le Rouge et le Noir 54. Marguerite de la Nuit 55. La Traversée de Paris 56. *En Cas de Malheur* 57. The Green Mare's Nest 59. Le Bois des Amants 60. The Count of Monte Cristo 61. Le Meurtrier 62. Thou Shalt Not Kill 62. The Woman in White 65. Les Patates 69. Le Rouge et le Blanc 70, etc.

auteur. A term used in the sixties and seventies by egghead critics to denote directors whom they judge to have a discernible message or attitude which runs throughout their work. Oddly enough the term is not applied to authors.

authenticator. Studio researcher responsible for establishing accuracy of all script details, ensuring use of 'clear' telephone numbers, etc.

authors as actors are few. Alexander Woolcott once had fun playing opposite Noel Coward in *The Scoundrel*; Irvin S. Cobb tried to take over the mantle of Will Rogers on the latter's death; Mickey Spillane played his own hero Mike Hammer in *The Girl Hunters* and also appeared in *Ring of Fear*. Otherwise literary lions have aspired only to bit parts, such as Compton Mackenzie in *Whisky Galore* and Hugh Walpole in *David Copperfield*. Somerset Maugham did contribute lengthy introductions to three compendiums of his short stories, but they were virtually eliminated from the release prints. Jacqueline Susann and Peter Benchley appeared as interviewers in *Valley of the Dolls* and *Jaws* respectively. Writer-director Bryan Forbes did become a popular juvenile in the fifties, and John Osborne turned villain in *Get Carter*, while Truman Capote was the sinister host of *Murder by Death*. Actors who became authors include David Niven, Dirk Bogarde, Ruth Chatterton, Mary Astor, Elissa Landi, Errol Flynn and Corinne Griffith; and many others wrote autobiographies, more or less unaided.

automobiles with personality enough to become movie titles include *Genevieve, The Fast Lady, La Belle Américaine, The Solid Gold Cadillac, The Yellow Rolls Royce, Chitty Chitty Bang Bang, The Gnome-Mobile* and *The Love Bug*. Other cars with individuality were James Bond's tricksy Aston Martin in *Goldfinger* and the one that ran on two wheels in *Diamonds are Forever*; the Flying Wombat in *The Young at Heart*; the gadget-filled limousine in *Only Two Can Play*; the airborne Model T in *The Absent-minded Professor*. The Model T was also Laurel and Hardy's favourite car, and they wrecked a great many in their time; other old cars were feaured in *The Reivers* and TV's *The Beverly Hillbillies*. Multitudes of old and strange cars were featured in *The Great Race, It's a Mad Mad Mad Mad World, Monte Carlo or Bust.* Comic car chases have been featured by Mack Sennett, Abbott and Costello, W. C. Fields and countless other comedians, and a new car was splendidly wrecked in *Tobacco Road*. Realistic chases became more and more violent in the seventies. *Bullitt* and *The French Connection* were box office hits almost for this reason alone, and imitations included *Robbery*, *Vanishing Point*, *Freebie and the Bean*, *The Car*, *The Driver*, *The Blues Brothers*, *Smokey and the Bandit*, *Every Which Way But Loose*, *The Gauntlet* and *The Hunter*. The best television film of the genre was undoubtedly *Duel*, but series from *The Dukes of Hazzard* to *T. J. Hooker* based their appeal on the number of cars crashed each week. The ultimate spoof was probably *Knight Rider*, in which the car became a secondary hero, talking back to its master and making most of his decisions. See *motor racing*.

Autry, Gene (1907–). Easy-going Texan who made innumerable minor Westerns 1934–54 as singing cowboy, usually with his horse Champion.
Boots and Saddles 37. Under Western Stars 38. Carolina Moon 40. Back in the Saddle 41. Sunset in Wyoming 42. Range War 46. Sioux City Sue 47. Guns and Saddles 49. Goldtown Ghost Riders 53, many others.
TV series: The Gene Autry Show 50.

¶ 'Autry used to ride off into the sunset. Now he owns it.'—*Anon*
G.A.: In my day, most people thought dance hall girls actually danced.

Avakian, Aram (1926–). American director,
□Lad—a Dog 62. The End of the Road 69. Cops and Robbers 73. 11 Harrowhouse 74.

Avalon, Frankie (1939–) (Francis Avallone). American light leading man and pop singer, former trumpeter.
Guns of the Timberland 60. The Alamo 60. Voyage to the Bottom of the Sea 62. Beach Blanket Bingo 65. I'll Take Sweden 65. Sergeant Deadhead 66. Fireball 500 66. Pajama Party in a Haunted House 66. How to Stuff a Wild Bikini 66. Skidoo 68. The Take 74. Grease 78. Back to the Beach 87, etc.

avant-garde. An adjective generally used to describe artists 'in advance of their time'; especially used of French surrealists in the twenties, e.g. Kirsanoff, Buñuel, Germaine Dulac.

Avedon, Doe (1928–). American leading lady who had a very short career before retiring to marry.
□*The High and the Mighty* 54. Deep in My Heart 55. The Boss 56.
TV series: Big Town 55.

Averback, Hy (1924–). American director with much TV experience, especially in comedy series.
Chamber of Horrors 66. Where Were You When the Lights Went Out? 68. *I Love You Alice B. Toklas* 68. The Great Bank Robbery 69. Suppose They Gave a War and Nobody Came 70, etc.

Avery, Margaret (–). American character actress. The Color Purple (AAN) 85.

Avery, Tex (1907–1980) (Fred Avery). American animator, best known for M.G.M. cartoons which combined savagery with hilarity. He created Droopy.

Avery, Val (–). American character actor.
King Creole 58. Too Late Blues 61. Hud 63. The Hallelujah Trail 65. The Pink Jungle 68. The Travelling Executioner 70. The Laughing Policeman 73. Let's Do It Again 75. Heroes 77. The Wanderers 79, etc.

Avildsen, John G. (1936–). American director.
□Turn on to Love 67. OK Bill 68. Guess What We Learned at School Today 69. *Joe* 70. Cry Uncle 71. Roger the Stoolie 72. Save the Tiger 73. WW and the Dixie Dance Kings 75. Foreplay (co-d) 75. *Rocky* 76. Slow Dancing in the Big City 78. The Formula 80. The President's Women 81. Neighbors 81. A Night in Heaven 83. The Karate Kid 84. The Karate Kid II 86. Happy New Year 87.

L' Avventura (Italy 1960). Here at great length we see the search for a girl lost on an island; gradually the searchers become pre-occupied with their own problems, and the girl is never found. Highbrow reaction was so favourable to this rather bewildering film by Michelangelo Antonioni that he has since been able to continue exploring life's irrationalities and enigmas, without always communicating his purpose to the audience. Photographed by Aldo Scavarda; with Gabrielle Ferzetti, Monica Vitti.

The Awful Truth (US 1937). A slender but influential and still amiable comedy, one of the first to add a touch of craziness to romantic sophistication. Leo McCarey wrote it and won an Academy Award for directing it; Cary Grant and Irene Dunne played the couple who change their minds about getting divorced, and Ralph Bellamy was a splendid foil as a bemused interloper. In 1953 the script was reshot to considerably less effect by Alexander Hall, with Ray Milland and Jane Wyman, as *Let's Do It Again*.

Axelrod, George (1922–). American comedy writer.
□Phffft 54. The Seven Year Itch (oa) 55. Bus Stop 56. Will Success Spoil Rock Hunter? (oa) 57. Breakfast at Tiffany's 61. The Manchurian Candidate 62. Paris When It Sizzles 64. Goodbye Charlie 64. How to Murder Your Wife (& p) 65. Lord Love a Duck (& p, d) 66. The Secret Life of an American Wife (& p, d) 68. The Lady Vanishes 79, etc.

Axt, Dr William (–). American composer, almost entirely for MGM in the thirties.
Don Juan 26. Ben Hur 26. White Shadows of the South Seas 28. Smilin' Through 32. Dinner at Eight 33. The Thin Man 34. David Copperfield 35. Piccadilly Jim 36. Parnell 37. Yellow Jack 38. Stand Up and Fight 39, many others.

Axton, Hoyt (–). American character actor. The Black Stallion 79. Cloud Dancer 79. Endangered Species 82. Heart like a Wheel 82. Liar's Moon 84. Gremlins 84.

Aykroyd, Dan (1950–). Canadian revue comedian who made his name on *Saturday Night Live*.
□ 1941 79. Mr Mike's Mondo Video 79. The Blues Brothers 80. Neighbours 81. Dr Detroit 82. Nothing Lasts Forever 82. Twilight Zone 83. Trading Places 83. Ghostbusters 84. Into the Night 84. Spies Like Us 85. Dragnet 87.

¶ *D.A.:* I have this kind of mild nice-guy exterior, but inside, my heart is like a steel trap. I'm really quite robotic.
D.A.: The entertainment business is not the be-all and end-all for me.

Aylmer, Sir Felix (1889–1979) (Felix Edward Aylmer Jones). Distinguished British stage character actor, a respected industry figure who from 1950 was president of Equity, the actors' trade union. In films he mainly played schoolmasters, bankers, bishops, etc. The Wandering Jew 33. The Iron Duke 35. Tudor Rose 36. As You Like It 36. *Victoria the Great* 37. The Citadel 38. Saloon Bar 40. *The Ghost of St Michael's* 41. Mr Emmanuel 44. Henry V 44. The Ghosts of Berkeley Square 47. *Hamlet* (as Polonius) 48. Edward My Son 49. Quo Vadis 51. Ivanhoe 52. The Master of Ballantrae 53. Knights of the Round Table 54. The Angel Who Pawned Her Harp 54. Saint Joan 57. *Separate Tables* 58. *Never Take Sweets from a Stranger* 60. Exodus 60. The Chalk Garden 64. Becket 64. Decline and Fall 68. Hostile Witness 68, many others.

Aylward, Gladys (1901–1970). British missionary whose exploits in China were fictionalized in *Inn of the Sixth Happiness*, in which she was played by Ingrid Bergman.

Ayres, Agnes (1896–1940) (Agnes Hinkle). American leading lady of the silent screen. Forbidden Fruit 19. The Affairs of Anatol 20. *The Sheik* 21. Racing Hearts 23. When a Girl Loves 24. Morals for Men 25. Her Market Value 26. Son of the Sheik 26. Eve's Love Letters 29, many others.

Ayres, Lew (1908–) (Lewis Ayer). Boyish American leading man of the thirties; he occasionally got a chance to prove himself a comfortable and friendly actor, but his career suffered during World War II when he declared himself a conscientious objector. □*The Kiss* 29. The Sophomore 29. Many a Slip 30. *All Quiet on the Western Front* 30. Common Clay 30. East is West 30. Doorway to Hell 30. Iron Man 31. Up for Murder 31. The Spirit of Notre Dame 31. Heaven on Earth 31. The Impatient Maiden 32. Night World 32. Okay America 32. *State Fair* 33. Don't Bet On Love 33. My Weakness 33. Cross Country Cruise 34. She Learned About Sailors 34. Servants' Entrance 34. Let's Be Ritzy 34. Lottery Lover 35. The Silk Hat Kid 35. The Leathernecks have Landed 36. Panic on the Air 36. Shakedown 36. Lady be Careful 36. Murder with Pictures 36. The Crime Nobody Saw 36. *Last Train from Madrid* 37. Hold 'Em Navy 37. Scandal Street 38. King of the Newsboys 38. *Holiday* (a key performance as Katharine Hepburn's drunken brother) 38. Rich Man Poor Girl 38. *Young Dr Kildare* 38. Spring Madness 38. Ice Follies 39. Broadway Serenade 39. Calling Dr Kildare 39. These Glamour Girls 39. The Secret of Dr Kildare 39. Remember? 39. Dr Kildare's Strange Case 40. Dr Kildare Goes Home 40. The Golden Fleecing 40. Dr Kildare's Crisis 40. Maisie Was a Lady 41. The People vs Dr Kildare 41. Dr Kildare's Wedding Day 41. Fingers at the Window 42. Dr Kildare's Victory 42. *The Dark Mirror* 46. The Unfaithful 47. *Johnny Belinda* 48. The Capture 50. New Mexico 51. No Escape 53. Donovan's Brain 54. *Advise and Consent* 61. *The Carpetbaggers* 64. Hawaii Five-O (TV pilot) 68. Marcus Welby M.D. (TV pilot) 68. Earth II (TV) 71. She Waits (TV) 72. The Man (TV) 72. The Biscuit Eater 72. The Stranger (TV) 72. The Questor Tapes (TV) 73. Battle For Planet of the Apes 73. Heatwave (TV) 74. Francis Gary Powers (TV) 76. End of the World 77. Greatest Heroes of the Bible (TV) (as Noah) 78. Damien – Omen II 78. Of Mice and Men (TV) 81. TV series: Hawkins 74. Lime Street 85.

Ayres, Robert (1914–1968). Canadian actor of strong silent types, long resident in Britain. They Were Not Divided 49. Cosh Boy 52. Contraband Spain 55. It's Never Too Late 55. A Night to Remember 57. The Sicilians 63. Battle Beneath the Earth 68, many others.

Ayrton, Randle (1869–1940). British character actor.
My Sweetheart 18. The Wonderful Year 21. Chu Chin Chow 23. Southern Love 24. Nell Gwynne 26. Passion Island 26. Glorious Youth 28. Comets 30. Dreyfus 31. Jew Süss 34. Me and Marlborough 35. Talk of the Devil 36, etc.

Aznavour, Charles (1924–) (Shahnour Aznavurjan). Armenian leading man of the small but rugged school.
Autobiography 1972: *Aznavour by Aznavour*.
La Tête contre les Murs 58. *Shoot the Pianist* 60. Passage du Rhin 61. Cloportes 65. Candy 68. The Adventurers 70. The Games 70. Un Beau Monstre 70. And Then There Were None 75. Sky Riders 76. Folies Bourgeoises 76. The Tin Drum 79, etc.

¶ *C.A.:* Live now. Tomorrow, who knows?

Answers

Academy Awards
1 *Anthony Adverse* □ 2 *Stagecoach* □ 3 *Going My Way* □ 4 *Dangerous* □ *Jezebel* □ 5 *A Double Life* □ 6 *Come and Get It* □ *In Old Kentucky* □ *The Westerner* □ 7 *The Sin of Madelon Claudet* □ *Airport* □ 8 *Min and Bill* □ 9 *Watch on the Rhine* □ 10 *Kitty Foyle* □ 11 *Suspicion* □ 12 *Yankee Doodle Dandy* □ 13 *Morning Glory* □ *Guess Who's Coming to Dinner* □ *The Lion in Winter* □ *On GoldenPond* □ 14 *The Divine Lady* □ *Cavalcade* □ 15*The Awful Truth* □ *Going My Way* □ He also received one for writing *Love Affair* □ 16 *Skippy* □ 17 *Casablanca* □

actor-directors
1 Walter Matthau □ 2 Dick Powell □ 3 Charles Laughton □ 4 Richard Haydn □ 5

Lionel Jeffries ☐ 6 John Mills ☐ 7 Lionel Barrymore ☐ 8 Karl Malden ☐ 9 James Cagney ☐ 10 Roddy McDowall ☐ 11 Clint Eastwood ☐ 12 Peter Lorre ☐ 13 Albert Finney ☐ 14 Ray Milland ☐ 15 Gene Kelly ☐ 16 Robert Montgomery ☐ 17 David Hemmings ☐ 18 Charlton Heston ☐ 19 Clive Brook ☐ 20 Jack Lemmon ☐ 21 Sidney Poitier ☐ 22 Mickey Rooney ☐ 23 Richard Attenborough ☐ 24 Martin Gabel ☐ 25 Mel Ferrer ☐ 26 Jose Ferrer ☐ 27 Alan Arkin ☐ 28 Paul Newman ☐ 29 Paul Henreid ☐ 30 Burt Lancaster ☐ 31 Frank Sinatra ☐ 32 Edmond O'Brien ☐ 33 Ralph Richardson ☐ 34 Cornel Wilde ☐ 35 Laurence Harvey ☐

actors in common

1 They all played the butler in *Ruggles of Red Gap* ☐: in 1923, 1934, and (with variations, as *Fancy Pants*) in 1950.

2 They all played *Dr Jekyll and Mr Hyde* ☐: in 1919, 1960 and 1941 respectively.

3 They all played Death ☐: in 1934 (*Death Takes a Holiday*), 1938 (*On Borrowed Time*), and 1948 (*Orphée*).

4 They all played members of the Frankenstein family ☐: in *Frankenstein Meets the Wolf Man* (1943), *Ghost of Frankenstein* (1941) and *Son of Frankenstein* (1939).

5 They all played opposite Greta Garbo ☐: in *Ninotchka* (and *Two Faced Woman*), *The Kiss*, *Conquest*, *Flesh and the Devil* (also *Love* and *Queen Christina*), and *Anna Karenina*.

6 They all played Abraham Lincoln ☐: in *Young Mr Lincoln* (1939), *Abe Lincoln in Illinois* (1940) (also *How the West Was Won*) and *Abraham Lincoln* (1930).

7 They all played Raymond Chandler's private eye Philip Marlowe ☐: in 1947 (*The Brasher Doubloon/The High Window*), 1973 (*The Long Goodbye*) and 1946 (*The Lady in the Lake*).

8 They all played opposite Charles Chaplin ☐: in 1936 (*Modern Times*) (also 1940, *The Great Dictator*), 1952 (*Limelight*), 1947 (*Monsieur Verdoux*) and 1957 (*A King in New York*).

9 They all played Catherine the Great of Russia ☐: in 1959 (*John Paul Jones*), 1945 (*A Royal Scandal*) and 1934 (*Catherine the Great*).

10 They all played the leading roles in Graham Greene adaptations ☐: *Confidential Agent*, *Ministry of Fear*, *The Third Man*, *The Fallen Idol*, *The Heart of the Matter*.

11 They all played dipsomaniacs ☐: in *Something to Live For*, *Days of Wine and Roses*, *Smash-Up*, *The Lost Weekend*.

12 They all played dual roles ☐: in *A Stolen Life* (and *Dead Ringer*), *The Masquerader* (and *The Prisoner of Zenda*), *The Dark Mirror*, *The Corsican Brothers*.

13 They all played *The Hunchback of Notre Dame* ☐: in 1939, 1956, 1923.

14 They all played *Ellery Queen* in various films of the thirties and forties ☐.

15 They all played *Merton of the Movies* ☐: in 1952, 1932 (as *Make Me a Star*) and 1923.

16 They all played Professor Moriarty in Sherlock Holmes films ☐: *The Triumph of Sherlock Holmes*, *The Adventures of Sherlock Holmes*, *The Woman in Green*.

17 They all played *The Scarlet Pimpernel* ☐: in 1934, 1939 (*The Return of the Scarlet Pimpernel*), and 1951 (*The Elusive Pimpernel*).

18 They all played murderous ladies ☐: in *Ivy*, *Green for Danger*, *Homicidal*, and *Strait Jacket* respectively.

19 They all played Napoleon Bonaparte ☐: in *Conquest*, *War and Peace* (and others), *Waterloo* respectively.

20 They all played *The Phantom of the Opera* ☐: in 1964, 1926, 1943.

21 They all played Anna Leonowens ☐: in *Anna and the King of Siam*, *Anna and the King* (TV series), and *The King and I*.

22 They all played Horatio Nelson ☐: in *Nelson*, *A Bequest to the Nation*, *Lady Hamilton*.

23 They all played Popes ☐: in *The Shoes of the Fisherman*, *Brother Sun and Sister Moon*, *The Agony and the Ecstasy*.

24 They all played Julius Caesar ☐: in *Caesar and Cleopatra*, *Julius Caesar* (1952), *Cleopatra* (1934).

25 They all played John Dillinger ☐ (public enemy number one) in *Young Dillinger*, *Dillinger* (1945), *Dillinger* (1973).

26 They all played ventriloquists ☐: in *Knock on Wood*, *Dead of Night*, *The Great Gabbo*.

27 They all played The Saint ☐: in the thirties, on TV, and in the sixties in France.

28 They are all original members of the Dead End Kids ☐.

29 They all played Bulldog Drummond ☐, the first two in the twenties and thirties, the third more recently in *Deadlier Than the Male* and *Some Girls Do*.

30 They all played the Frankenstein monster □: at Universal in the forties, at Hammer in the sixties, and in *Frankenstein Meets the Wolf Man*.

aka

1 Blondie □ 2 The Lone Wolf □ 3 The Thin Man – though the description actually applies to a character murdered in the first film of the series □ 4 The Crime Doctor □ 5 Mexican Spitfire □ 6 The Wolf Man □ 7 Doctor in the House (etc) □ 8 Batman □

all-star films

1 *Show of Shows* □ 2 *Star Spangled Rhythm* □ 3 *Thank Your Lucky Stars* □ 4 *Zeigfeld Follies* □ 5 *Paramount on Parade* □ 6 *King of Jazz* □ 7 *Star Spangled Rhythm* □ 8 *Hollywood Revue of 1929* □ 9 *Follow the Boys* □ 10 *Thank Your Lucky Stars* □

alternative titles

1 Said to be one of the few points contributed to *King Kong* □ by Edgar Wallace, who went to Hollywood in 1931 to work on the film but died before it was completed.
2 When Howard Hughes made *Scarface* □ in 1932 it was attacked as a glorification of the Al Capones of America. He therefore added this extra title to show where the film's sympathies officially lay, and even offered to make it the main title; but this never happened.
3 *Benjamin* □, the 1968 French attempt to out-dare *Tom Jones*.
4 D. W. Griffith's *Intolerance* (1915) □. The sub-title was added to make it sound more attractive to the general public, but it failed disastrously.
5 *The Fearless Vampire Killers* (1969) □, released in Britain as *Dance of the Vampires*. The sub-title indicates the kind of humour aimed at (but certainly not achieved).
6 *Darling Lili* (1969) □. Although widely mentioned during production, the alternative title was not used on release.
7 *Dr Strangelove* (1963) □. As one might have expected, the film did not provide the remedy it offered.
8 *Those Magnificent Men in their Flying Machines* (1965) □. The two titles together must form the longest billing in history.
9 *La Bonne Soupe* (1964) □. An amiable pun which did not help the film at the box office.
10 Hitchcock's *The Lodger* (1926) □.
11 Walt Disney's *Toby Tyler* (1964) □.
12 *Intermezzo* (1939) □.

anatomy

1 *Toes* □ 2 *Shoulder* □ 3 *Eyes* □ 4 *Skull* □ 5 *Hand* □ 6 *Brain* □ 7 *Fingers* □ 8 *Lips* □ 9 *Thumb* □ 10 *Palm* □ 11 *Face* □ 12 *Eyes* □ 13 *Knee* □ 14 *Legs* □ 15 *Claw* □ 16 *Back* □ 17 *Face* □ 18 *Eyes* □ 19 *Hands* □ 20 *Eye* □ 21 *Face* □ 22 *Hand* □ 23 *Foot* □ 24 *Eye* □ 25 *Hand* □

animals

1 *Dragon* □ 2 *Wolf* □ 3 *Sparrow* □ 4 *Eagles* □ 5 *Elephants* (Laurel and Hardy) or *Tigers* (John Wayne) □ 6 *Fox* □ 7 *Cow* □ 8 *Rat* □ 9 *Horse* □ 10 *Spider* □ 11 *Rabbit* □ 12 *Cat* □ 13 *Phoenix* □ 14 *Tiger* □ 15 *Octopus* □ 16 *Dogs* □ 17 *Butterfly* □ 18 *Eagle* or *Dragonfly* □ 19 *Turtle* □ 20 Women being all things to all men, a wide choice is possible: *Snake*, *Cobra*, *Spider*, *Wasp*, etc.

B

'B' picture. A low-budget production usually designed as part of a double bill or to support a more important feature. There are four excellent books on the subject: *B Movies* by Don Miller, *The Wonderful World of B Films* by Alan G. Barbour, *Kings of the Bs* by Todd McCarthy and Charles Flynn and *The Big Book of B Movies* by Robin Cross.

Babcock, Barbara (–). American character actress.
Heaven with a Gun 68. The Last Child (TV) 71. Bang the Drum Slowly 73. Chosen Survivors (TV) 74. Salem's Lot (TV) 79. The Lords of Discipline 83, etc.

Babenco, Hector (–). Mexican director. Pixote 81. Kiss of the Spider Woman (AAN) 84. Ironweed 87.

Babes in Arms (US 1939). Made immediately after *The Wizard of Oz*, this lively teenage musical directed by Busby Berkeley not only established Judy Garland as one of the brightest stars in the MGM sky but was the first of several teaming her with the irrepressible Mickey Rooney: *Strike Up the Band* 40, *Babes on Broadway* 41, *Girl Crazy* 43.

Babes in Toyland. The Victor Herbert fairy tale operetta was filmed by Hal Roach in 1934 as a vehicle for Laurel and Hardy. In 1961 Jack Donohue made a lavish but empty version for Disney, with Ray Bolger as the villain; Laurel and Hardy, curiously, were closely impersonated by Henry Calvin and Gene Sheldon.

babies who have achieved screen stardom include Baby Parsons and Baby Peggy in silent days, Baby Le Roy in the early thirties and Baby Sandy in the early forties. Shirley Temple and the Our Gang cast were scarcely weaned when they hit the big time. Other films about particular babies include *Bachelor Mother*, *Bobbikins*, and *A Diary for Timothy*.

There was a shortlived TV series about a talking baby called *Happy*; and Lucille Ball worked her own confinement into her weekly half-hour. More recently there has been a lamentable fashion for diabolical infants: *Rosemary's Baby*, *It's Alive*, *I Don't Want to be Born* and *The Devil within Her*.

Baby Doll (US 1956). Tennessee Williams wrote and Elia Kazan directed this deliberately shocking comedy about the child-wife of a 'poor white' southerner. Starring Eli Wallach, Karl Malden and Carroll Baker, it is not generally remembered with affection but did its bit towards loosening the Hollywood Production Code, which had been far too restrictive.

Baby Le Roy (1931–) (Le Roy Overacker). American toddler who appeared to general delight in comedies of the early thirties. The story goes that W. C. Fields once spiked his orange juice with gin . . .
A Bedtime Story 33. Tillie and Gus 33. Miss Fane's Baby is Stolen 33. The Old Fashioned Way 34. The Lemon Drop Kid 34. It's a Gift 35, etc.

Baby Peggy (1917–) (Peggy Montgomery). American child star of the twenties. Later appeared under her own name, and in the seventies published two books, *The Hollywood Posse* and *Hollywood Children*.
Peggy Behave 22. Captain January 23. The Law Forbids 24. The Speed Demon 25. April Fool 26. The Sonora Kid 27, etc.

Baby Sandy (1938–) (Sandra Henville). American infant performer who made money for Universal in the early forties.
□East Side of Heaven 39. Unexpected Father 39. Little Accident 39. Sandy Is a Lady 40. Sandy Gets Her Man 40. Sandy Steps Out 41. Bachelor Daddy 41. Melody Lane 41. Johnny Doughboy 42.

Bacall, Lauren (1924–) (Betty Jean Perske). Sultry American leading actress who after stage experience made her film debut opposite Humphrey Bogart ('If you want anything, just whistle . . .') and subsequently married him. Her image gradually changed to

that of an astringent and resourceful woman of the world, and in 1970 she made a triumphant return to the Broadway stage in *Applause*.
Autobiography 1978: *Lauren Bacall*.
□*To Have and Have Not* 44. Confidential Agent 45. *The Big Sleep* 46. Dark Passage 47. Key Largo 48. *Young Man with a Horn* 50. Bright Leaf 50. *How to Marry a Millionaire* 53. Woman's World 54. The Cobweb 55. Blood Alley 55. Written on the Wind 57. Designing Woman 57. The Gift of Love 58. Northwest Frontier (GB) 59. Shock Treatment 64. Sex and the Single Girl 64. *Harper* 66. Murder on the Orient Express 74. The Shootist 76. Health 79. The Fan 81.
†She made an uncredited cameo appearance in *Two Guys from Milwaukee* 46.

¶ *1944 promotion for L.B.:* Slinky! Sultry! Sensational!

L.B.: I used to tremble from nerves so badly that the only way I could hold my head steady was to lower my chin practically to my chest and look up at Bogie. That was the beginning of The Look.

L.B.: I was not a woman of the world. I'd lived with Mother all my life.

L.B.: What I learned from Mr Bogart I learned from a master, and that, God knows, has stood me in very good stead.

Baccaloni, Salvatore (1900–1969). Italian opera singer who played some comedy roles in American films.
□Full of Life 56. Merry Andrew 58. Rock a Bye Baby 59. Fanny 61. The Pigeon That Took Rome 62.

Bach, Barbara (1951–). German leading lady who played the female lead in *The Spy Who Loved Me* 77, Force Ten From Navarone 78. The Humanoid 79. Up the Academy 80. Caveman 81. The Unseen 81. Give My Regards to Broad Street 83.

Bacharach, Burt (1929–). American composer.
Lizzie (song) 57. What's New Pussycat? (score) 65. Casino Royale (score) 67. *Butch Cassidy and the Sundance Kid* (AA song, AA score) 69. The April Fools (score) 69. Lost Horizon (songs) 73.

¶ *B.B.:* The groovy thing about pop music is that it's wide open. Anything can happen.

Bachelor Mother (US 1939). A light, bright, romantic comedy showing Hollywood talents at the top of their accomplished form and introducing a new one in the shape of writer-director Garson Kanin who managed to give a fresh aspect to a collection of farcical misunderstandings over a foundling baby. Ginger Rogers, David Niven and Charles Coburn all performed nimbly. The film was reshot in 1955 as *Bundle of Joy*, but without the essential sparkle.

The Bachelor Party (US 1957). A fairly straight filming of Paddy Chayevsky's TV play, this not only showed Hollywood's willingness to learn and profit from its hated rival but was a measure of how adult it had become in a very few years. Nothing, theoretically and indeed actually, could have been more anti-box office than this study of the thwarted lives of New York office workers—a tragedy presented as comedy. With Don Murray, Jack Warden, E. G. Marshall, Carolyn Jones; directed by Delbert Mann.

Bachelor, Stephanie (1924–). American leading lady of forties B pictures.
Lady of Burlesque 43. Her Primitive Man 44. Lake Placid Serenade 44. Scotland Yard Investigator 45. I've Always Loved You 46. Blackmail 47. King of the Gamblers 48, etc.

back projection. A method of producing 'location' sequences in the studio: the players act in front of a translucent screen on which the scenic background is projected.

Back Street. Fannie Hurst's tearful novel has been filmed three times since sound: in 1932 with John Boles and Irene Dunne, directed by John M. Stahl; in 1941 with Charles Boyer and Margaret Sullavan, directed by Robert Stevenson; and in 1961 with Susan Hayward and John Gavin, directed by David Miller. The story of the married man and the woman who sacrificed all for him has worked at the box office every time.

Back To The Future. This highly successful 1985 movie was popular with all classes. With Stephen Spielberg watching over it, it was fashionable; with Michael J. Fox starring in it, it drew the teenage crowd. The story might have been found on *Twilight Zone*: Fox is a boy who goes back in time and accidentally prevents the meeting of his own mother and father, and adults liked it for the wry implications. Directed and co-written by Robert Zemeckis.

backstage is a term suggesting musicals about putting on a show. But other types of film have taken place mainly or climactically in this area. Thrillers: *The Velvet Touch, Stage Fright, The Phantom of the Opera, Charlie Chan at the Opera, Cover Girl Killer, Murder at the Vanities, the G-String Murders, Theatre of Death.* Dramas: *A Double Life, Applause, The Blue Angel, Limelight, Les Enfants du Paradis, Act One.* Comedies: *A Night at the Opera, Hellzapoppin, The Guardsman, The Royal Family of Broadway, Curtain Up*, etc. Musicals themselves got off to a pretty good start in the early thirties, best and most typical of them being *42nd Street*, which was amiably spoofed in *Movie Movie* 78.

Backus, Jim (1913–). Burly American character comedian, perhaps most famous as the voice of Mr Magoo in UPA cartoons of the fifties. Stock, vaudeville and radio experience.
Autobiography 1958: *Rocks on the Roof.*
The Great Lover 49. Hollywood Story 51. His Kind of Woman 51. I Want You 51. Pat and Mike 52. Androcles and the Lion 53. *Rebel Without a Cause* 55. The Great Man 56. Man of a Thousand Faces 57. Macabre 58. Ice Palace 60. Boys' Night Out 62. *It's A Mad Mad Mad Mad World* 63. Advance to the Rear 64. Billie 65. Where Were You When the Lights Went Out? 68. Now You See Him Now You Don't 72. Pete's Dragon 77. There Goes the Bride 80, etc.
TV series: *I Married Joan* 52–56. Hot off the Wire 60. *Gilligan's Island* 64–66. Blondie 68.

Baclanova, Olga (1899–1974). Russian actress who played leads in a few American films.
Street of Sin 27. Docks of New York 28. *Freaks* 32. Billion Dollar Scandal 33. Claudia 43, etc.

Bacon, Irving (1892–1965). American character actor in films from 1920, often as not-so-dumb country type or perplexed official.
Street of Chance 30. Million Dollar Legs 32. Private Worlds 35. Sing You Sinners 38. Meet John Doe 41. Pin Up Girl 44. Monsieur Verdoux 47. Room for One More 52. A Star is Born 54. Fort Massacre 58, many others.

Bacon, Kevin (–). American teenage actor of the late seventies.
National Lampoon's Animal House 78. Starting Over 79. Friday the 13th 80. Hero at Large 80. Only When I Laugh 81. Diner 82. Forty Deuce 82. Footloose 84. Enormous Changes at the Last Minute 85.

Bacon, Lloyd (1890–1955). American director, long under contract to Warner; former actor in Chaplin silents. Competent rather than brilliant, he nevertheless handled several memorable films among the mass of routine.
□Private Izzy Murphy 26. Fingerprints 26. Broken Hearts of Hollywood 26. The Heart of Maryland 26. White Flannels 27. A Sailor's Sweetheart 27. Brass Knuckles 27. Pay As You Enter 28. The Lion and the Mouse 28. Women They Talk About 28. *The Singing Fool* 28. Stark Mad 29. Honky Tonk 29. No Defense 29. Say it with Songs 29. So Long Lefty 30. She Couldn't Say No 30. A Notorious Affair 30. The Other Tomorrow 30. Moby Dick 30. The Office Wife 30. Kept Husbands 31. Sit Tight 31. Fifty Million Frenchmen 31. Gold Dust Gertie 31. Honor of the Family 31. Manhattan Parade 32. Fireman Save my Child 32. Alias the Doctor 32. The Famous Ferguson Case 32. *Miss Pinkerton* 32. Crooner 32. Footlight Parade 32. You Said a Mouthful 32. *42nd Street* 33. *Picture Snatcher* 33. Mary Stevens MD 33. Son of a Sailor 33. *Wonder Bar* 34. A Very Honorable Guy 34. He Was Her Man 34. Six Day Bike Rider 34. *Here Comes the Navy* 34. *Devil Dogs of the Air* 35. In Caliente 35. Broadway Gondolier 35. The Irish In Us 35. Frisco Kid 35. Sons of Guns 36. Cain and Mabel 36. Gold Diggers of 1937 36. *Marked Woman* 37. Ever Since Eve 37. *San Quentin* 37. Submarine D1 37. *A Slight Case of Murder* 38. Cowboy from Brooklyn 38. *Boy Meets Girl* 38. Racket Busters 38. Wings of the Navy 39. *The Oklahoma Kid* 39. Indianapolis Speedway 39. Espionage Agent 39. A Child Is Born 40. Invisible Stripes 40. Three Cheers for the Irish 40. *Brother Orchid* 40. Knute Rockne, All American 40. Honeymoon for Three 41. Footsteps in the Dark 41. Navy Blues 41. Affectionately Yours 41. Honeymoon for Three 41. Larceny Inc 42. Wings for the Eagle 42. Silver Queen 42. Action in the North Atlantic 43. The Sullivans 44. *Sunday Dinner for a Soldier* 44. Captain Eddie 45. Home Sweet Homicide 45. Wake Up and Dream 46. I Wonder Who's Kissing Her Now 47. You were Meant for Me 48. Give My Regards to Broadway 48. Don't Trust Your Husband 48. Mother Is a Freshman 49. It Happens Every Spring 49. Miss Grant Takes Richmond 49. Kill The Umpire 50. The Good Humor Man 50. The Fuller Brush Girl 50. Call Me Mister 51. Golden Girl 51. The Frogmen 52. The I Don't Care Girl 53. The Great Sioux Uprising 53. Walking my Baby Back Home 53. The French Line 54. She Couldn't Say No 54.

The Bad and the Beautiful (US 1952). A moderately caustic Hollywood self-exposé, this entertaining if ultimately cliché-ridden melodrama was well acted by Kirk Douglas as a talented heel, smoothly written by Charles Schnee (AA) and directed by Vincente Minelli. Gloria Grahame won an Oscar for her supporting performance as did Robert Surtees for his cinematography. Ten years later Douglas played a similar role in a not dissimilar film, *Two Weeks in Another Town*, about a Hollywood film crew in Rome: it even used clips from *The Bad and the Beautiful* to illustrate the character's previous career.

Bad Day at Black Rock (US 1955). Classic suspense melodrama turning on race hatred, with Spencer Tracy as the one-armed stranger who defies violence to prove that the townsfolk of a desert settlement were communally guilty of an old murder. Written by Millard Kaufmann, directed by John Sturges.

bad guys

? What wicked (but fascinating) characters spoke these lines, and in what films?

1 First the hunt, then the revels!
2 We'll start with a few murders. Big men. Little men. Just to show we make no distinction.
3 Some people are better off dead. Like your wife and my father, for instance.
4 A soul? A soul is nothing. Can you see it? Smell it? Touch it? No . . .
5 Listen to them: children of the night. What music they make . . .
6 Synthetic flesh! Synthetic flesh!
7 I say, marriage with Max is not exactly a bed of roses, is it?
8 Mother of mercy, is this the end of Rico?
9 In Italy for thirty years under the Borgias they had warfare, terror, murder, bloodshed – they produced Michaelangelo, Leonardo da Vinci, and the Renaissance. In Switzerland they had brotherly love, five hundred years of democracy and peace, and what did that produce? The cuckoo clock.
10 The world shall hear from me again . . .
11 I distrust a man that says when. If he's got to be careful not to drink too much it's because he's not to be trusted when he does.
12 Outdoor chess, Mr Rainsford?

And a few bad gals:

13 You have nothing to stay for. You have nothing to live for, really, have you? Look down there – it's easy, isn't it?
14 Gimme visky . . . ginger ale on the side. And don't be stingy, baby.
15 It took more than one man to change my name to Shanghai Lily.
16 If I'd been a ranch, they'd have named me the Bar Nothing.

The Bad Guys, by William K. Everson. A well-researched pictorial history of screen villains, published in 1964.

bad language. It now seems impossible that in 1938 the phrase 'not bloody likely' in Shaw's *Pygmalion* could have caused a minor sensation; or that in 1942 the seamen in *In Which We Serve* could not say 'Hell' or 'damn' in front of American audiences. But these things happened. Perhaps it was in 1953 that the rot really set in, when Otto Preminger accepted a Legion of Decency 'C' rating and the loss of a production seal for his film of *The Moon Is Blue* rather than rob it of the words 'virgin' and 'mistress'. Three years later, Mickey Shaughnessy in *Don't Go Near the Water* was allowed to mouth obscenities while the sound track amusingly bleeped them out. By the time *Pygmalion* was remade in 1964 as *My Fair Lady* the phrase originally so shocking would have had no dramatic effect; it was replaced by 'Move your bloomin' arse' In 1967–68 the floodgates really opened. *Poor Cow* and *Who's Afraid of Virginia Woolf?* were the first to allow 'bugger'. In *Here We Go Round the Mulberry Bush* Maxine Audley reproaches her husband as follows: 'Darling, you've got him pissed again'. And in *A Flea in Her Ear* Rex Harrison unchivalrously instructs Rosemary Harris to 'piss off'. That still-notorious four-letter word beginning with F was first uttered by Marianne Faithfull in *I'll Never Forget Whatshisname*, and then by Elizabeth Taylor in *Boom.* And the slang word for defecation was first uttered in *In Cold Blood, Boom, Rosemary's Baby* and *Secret Ceremony*. In general, the effect of such words on the big screen has merely been to show how meaningless, harmless and stupid they are; but over-use of them is worse than pretending they don't exist, and one wonders whether films of the mid-seventies such as *Lenny, Serpico, The Last Detail, Shampoo* and *Dog Day Afternoon* would really have been poorer without them. By the eighties it was rare to find even an 'A' or 'PG' film without bad language, and this marked another stage in the driving of better class audiences away from the cinema.

Baddeley, Angela (1904–76). British stage character actress, sister of Hermione

Baddeley. Popular on TV as Mrs Bridges in *Upstairs Downstairs* 70–75.
☐ The Speckled Band 31. Arms and the Man 32. The Ghost Train 32. Those were the Days 34. The Citadel 38. Quartet 48. Zoo Baby 57. Tom Jones 63.

Baddeley, Hermione (1906–86). British character comedienne, adept at blowsy roles; long stage experience.
☐ A Daughter in Revolt 27. The Guns of Loos 28. Caste 30. Love Life and Laughter 34. Royal Cavalcade 35. Kipps 41. It Always Rains on Sunday 47. *Brighton Rock* 47. No Room at the Inn 48. Quartet 48. *Passport to Pimlico* 49. Dear Mr Prohack 49. The Woman in Question 50. There is another Sun 51. Tom Brown's Schooldays 51. Hell is Sold Out 51. Scrooge 51. Song of Paris 52. Time Gentlemen Please 52. *The Pickwick Papers* 52. Cosh Boy 53. Counterspy 53. The Belles of St Trinian's 54. Women without Men 54. *Room at the Top* 59. Jetstorm 59. Expresso Bongo 59. Let's Get Married 60. Midnight Lace 60. Information Received 61. Rag Doll 61. Mary Poppins 64. The Unsinkable Molly Brown 64. Do Not Disturb 65. Harlow 65. Marriage on the Rocks 65. Bullwhip Griffin 67. The Happiest Millionaire 67. Up the Front 72. The Black Windmill 74. There Goes the Bride 80.
TV series: The Good Life (US) 71. Maude 74–77.

Badel, Alan (1923–1982). British stage and screen actor of considerable sensitivity, not easy to cast in leading roles.
The Stranger Left No Card 53. Salome 53. *Three Cases of Murder* 55. Magic Fire 56. This Sporting Life 63. Children of the Damned 64. *Arabesque* 66. Otley 69. Where's Jack? 69. *The Adventurers* 70. The Day of the Jackal 73. Luther 73. Telefon 77. Force Ten From Navarone 78. The Riddle of the Sands 79. Nijinsky 80, Shogun (TV) 82, etc.

Baden-Semper, Nina (1945–). West Indian leading lady, popular on British TV.
Kongi's Harvest 73. Love Thy Neighbour 74.

Badger, Clarence (1880–1964). American director at his peak in the twenties.
Jubilo 19. Doubling for Romeo 21. Miss Brewster's Millions 26. *It* 27. Hot News 28. Three Weekends 28. No No Nanette 31. The Bad Man 32. Rangle River 39, etc.

Badham, John (–). American director with a sharp visual style.
The Impatient Heart (TV) 71. Isn't It Shocking? (TV) 73. The Godchild (TV) 74. *The Law* (TV) 74. The Gun (TV) 74. Reflections of Murder (TV) 74. The Keegans (TV) 76. The Bingo Long All Stars and Travelling Motor Kings 76. *Saturday Night Fever* 77. Dracula 79. Whose Life Is It Anyway? 81. War Games 83. Blue Thunder 83. American Flyers 84. Short Circuit 85. Stakeout 87.

Badham, Mary (1952–). American teenage actress.
☐To Kill a Mockingbird 63. This Property Is Condemned 66. Let's Kill Uncle 66.

Badiyi, Reza S. (–). American director from TV, where he came to fame by devising the title sequence for Hawaii Five-O.
The Eyes of Charles Sand (TV) 72. Trader Horn 73.

Baer, Buddy (1915–) (Jacob Henry Baer). American heavyweight prizefighter, brother of Max.
Africa Screams 49. Quo Vadis 51. Jack and the Beanstalk 52. Slightly Scarlet 56. Snow White and the Three Stooges 61, etc.

Baer, Max (1909–1959). Prizewinning American boxer who made several films.
The Prizefighter and the Lady 33. Riding High 50. The Iron Road 55. The Harder They Fall 56. Over She Goes 58, etc.

Baer Max Jnr (1937–). American actor who spent nine years playing Jethro in TV's The Beverly Hillbillies, then became an independent producer.
Macon County Line 74. The McCulloughs (& a,d) 75. Ode to Billy Joe (d only) 76, etc.

Baer, Parley (–). American character actor, usually as professional type.
Comanche Territory 50. Deadline USA 52. D-Day Sixth of June 56. Cash McCall 60. Gypsy 62. Fluffy 65. Counterpoint 67. Young Billy Young 69. Punch and Jody (TV) 74. The Amazing Dobermans 66, etc.

Baggott, King (1874–1948). Tall, powerful American leading man of silent adventure dramas. Made a few early talkies, then retired.
Lady Audley's Secret 12. Ivanhoe 12. Dr Jekyll and Mr Hyde 13. The Corsican Brothers 15. Moonlight Follies 21. Going Straight 22. Tumbleweeds (d only) 25. Notorious Lady 27. The Czar of Broadway 30. Once a Gentleman 30. Scareheads 32. Romance in the Rain 34. Mississippi 35. Come Live with Me 41, many others.

Bailey, John (–). American cinematographer.
Welcome to L.A. 77. Boulevard Nights 79. American Gigolo 80. Ordinary People 80. Honky Tonk Freeway 81. Racing with the Moon 84. Silverado 85.

Bailey, Pearl (1918–). Black American entertainer and Broadway star.
Autobiography 1968: *The Raw Pearl.*
Variety Girl 47. Isn't It Romantic? 48. Carmen Jones 54. That Certain Feeling 55. St Louis Blues 57. Porgy and Bess 59. All the Fine Young Cannibals 60. The Landlord 69. Norman, Is That You? 76.

Bailey, Raymond (1904–1980). American small part actor, often a crook or lawyer.
Secret Service of the Air 39. Tidal Wave 40. I Want to Live 55. Picnic 56. The Incredible Shrinking Man 57. Al Capone 59. From the Terrace 60, many others.
TV series: My Sister Eileen 59. The Many Loves of Dobie Gillis 61–62. *The Beverly Hillbillies* (as Drysdale) 62–70.

Bailey, Robin (1919–). British comedy character actor with a penchant for dialects as well as the extremes of 'Oxford English'. A television star in such series as *I Didn't Know You Cared*, *Sorry I'm a Stranger Here Myself*, *Potter*.
The Whisperers 66. Blind Terror 70. The Four Feathers (TV) 78, etc.

Bain, Barbara (1934–). American leading lady, once married to Martin Landau. Best known on TV in series Mission Impossible (66–72). Space 1999 (75–76).
Murder Once Removed (TV) 71. Goodnight My Love 72. A Summer Without Boys (TV) 73.

Bainter, Fay (1892–1968). American character actress who came to films from the stage in 1934 and specialized in stalwart but sympathetic matrons.
□This Side of Heaven 34. *Quality Street* 37. The Soldier and the Lady 37. Make Way for Tomorrow 37. *Jezebel* (AA) 38. *White Banners* 38. Mother Carey's Chickens 38. The Arkansas Traveller 38. The Shining Hour 39. Yes My Darling Daughter 39. The Lady and the Mob 39. Daughters Courageous 39. Our Neighbours the Carters 39. Young Tom Edison 40. *Our Town* 40. A Bill of Divorcement 40. Maryland 40. Babes on Broadway 42. Woman of the Year 42. *The War Against Mrs Hadley* 42. *Mrs Wiggs of the Cabbage Patch* 42. Journey for Margaret 43. *The Human Comedy* 43. Presenting Lily Mars 43. Salute to the Marines 43. Cry Havoc 43. The Heavenly Body 43. *Dark Waters* (rare villainous role) 44. Three is a Family 44. *State Fair* 45. The Virginian 46. The Kid from Brooklyn 46. *The Secret Life of Walter Mitty* 47. Deep Valley 47. Give My Regards to Broadway 48. *June Bride* 48. Close to my Heart 51. The President's Lady 53. *The Children's Hour* 62.

Baio, Scott (1961–). American teenage actor of the early eighties.
Bugsy Malone 78. Foxes 81. The Boy Who Drank Too Much (TV) 81. Something for Joey (TV) 81. Zapped! 82. TV series: Charles in Charge 84.

Baird, Teddy (c. 1900–). British producer, in films since 1928 after journalistic experience.
The Browning Version 51. The Importance of Being Earnest 52. Carrington V.C. 56. Two Living One Dead 62, etc.

Bakaleinikoff, Constantin (1898–1966). Russian music director, long in US. With RKO 1941–52. Own scores include *Notorious* 46. *Mourning Becomes Electra* 47. *Mr Blandings Builds His Dream House* 48. *The Conqueror* 56, many others.

Bakalyan, Richard (–). American character actor, usually as villain.
The Brothers Rico 57. Up Periscope 59. Panic in Year Zero 62. Von Ryan's Express 65. The St Valentine's Day Massacre 67. Chinatown 74. Return from Witch Mountain 78, etc.

Baker, Art (1898–1966) (Arthur Shank). American general purpose actor.
Once Upon a Time 44. Spellbound 45. The Farmer's Daughter 47. *Cover Up* 48. Take One False Step 49. Cause for Alarm 51. Living It Up 54. Twelve Hours to Kill 60. Young Dillinger 65. The Wild Angels 66, etc.

Baker, Carroll (1931–). American leading lady who tried to vary her sex symbol status via roles of melodramatic intensity. After her Hollywood career fizzled she made many exploitation pictures in Italy.
Easy to Love 53. *Giant* 56. *Baby Doll* 56. The Big Country 58. The Miracle 59. But Not for Me 59. Something Wild 61. Bridge to the Sun 61. How the West was Won 63. *The Carpetbaggers* 64. Station Six Sahara 64. Cheyenne Autumn 64. The Greatest Story Ever Told 65. Sylvia 65. Mr Moses 65.

Harlow 65. Jack of Diamonds 67. The Sweet Body of Deborah 68. Paranoia 68. The Harem 68. The Spider 70. The Fourth Mrs Anderson 71. Captain Apache 71. Bloody Mary 72. Baba Yaga Devil Witch 74. Andy Warhol's Bad 77. The Devil Has Seven Faces 77. The World is Full of Married Men 79. The Watcher in the Woods 80. Star 80 83. The Secret Diary of Sigmund Freud 84. Native Son 86. Ironweed 87, etc.

¶ 'More bomb than bombshell.'—*Judith Crist*

Baker, Diane (1938–). Demure-looking American leading actress who can also handle unsympathetic roles. Many TV guest appearances.
□*The Diary of Anne Frank* 59. The Best of Everything 59. Journey to the Centre of the Earth 59. The Wizard of Baghdad 61. Tess of the Storm Country 61. Hemingway's Adventures of a Young Man 62. The 300 Spartans 62. Nine Hours to Rama 63. Stolen Hours 63. *Strait Jacket* 63. *The Prize* 63. Della (TV) 64. *Marnie* 64. *Mirage* 65. Sands of Beersheba 66. The Dangerous Days of Kiowa Jones 66. The Horse in the Grey Flannel Suit 68. Krakatoa, East of Java 68. Murder One (TV) 69. The Badge or the Cross (TV) 70. Do You Take This Stranger? (TV) 70. Wheeler and Murdoch (TV) 70. The Old Man Who Cried Wolf (TV) 70. A Little Game (TV) 71. Killer By Night (TV) 71. Congratulations, It's A Boy (TV) 71. A Tree Grows in Brooklyn (TV) 74. The Dream Makers (TV) 75. The Last Survivors (TV) 75. Baker's Hawk 76. The Summer of Sixty-Nine (TV) 77.
TV series: *Here We Go Again* 71.

Baker, George (1929–). British leading man, also on stage and TV.
The Intruder 52. The Dam Busters 55. A Hill in Korea 56. The Woman for Joe 56. *The Moonraker* 57. Tread Softly Stranger 58. No Time for Tears 59. Lancelot and Guinevere 63. Curse of the Fly 65. Mr Ten Per Cent 67. Justine 69. On Her Majesty's Secret Service 69. The Spy Who Loved Me 77. Print Out (TV) 79. Hopscotch 80. North Sea Hijack 80. The Secret Adversary (TV) 82. Goodbye Mr Chips (TV) 84. A Woman of Substance (TV) 84, etc.
TV series: I, Claudius 77.

Baker, Graham (–). Director. The Final Conflict 81. Impulse 84.

Baker, Hylda (1909–86). British Comedienne in northern music hall tradition.
□Saturday Night and Sunday Morning 60. She Knows You Know 61. Up the Junction 68. Oliver! 68. Nearest and Dearest 73.

Baker, Joe Don (1943–). Tough young American leading man of the early seventies. Cool Hand Luke 67. Guns of the Magnificent Seven 69. Adam at Six a.m. 70. Wild Rovers 71. Mongo's Back in Town (TV) 71. Welcome Home Soldier Boys 72. Junior Bonner 72. *Charley Varrick* 72. *Walking Tall* 72. The Outfit 73. Golden Needles 74. Mitchell 74. Framed 75. Crash 76. The Pack 77. To Kill a Cop (TV) 77. Power (TV) 79. Joysticks 83. The Natural 84. Fletch 84. Getting Even 85.
TV series: Eischied 79 (GB: Chief of Detectives).

Baker, Kenny (1912–85). American crooner, popular in the late thirties but subsequently little heard of.
King of Burlesque 36. The Goldwyn Follies 38. The Mikado (GB: as Nanki Poo) 39. 52nd Street 39. At the Circus 39. Hit Parade of 1941. Silver Skates 43. Doughboys in Ireland 43. The Harvey Girls 46, etc.

Baker, Phil (1896–1963). American radio personality who appeared in a few films.
Gift of Gab 34. The Goldwyn Follies 38. The Gang's All Here 43. *Take It or Leave It* 44, etc.

Baker, Rick (1950–). American make-up artist.
Octaman 71. Schlock 72. The Thing with Two Heads 72. It's Alive 74. King Kong 76. *Star Wars* 77. The Incredible Melting Man 77. *An American Werewolf in London* 81. Greystoke (AAN) 84, etc.

Baker, Robert S. (1916–). British producer: co-founder with Monty Berman of Tempean Films, which since 1948 has produced many co-features, also *The Saint* and other TV series.
□AS DIRECTOR: Blackout 50. 13 East Street 52. The Steel Key 53. Passport to Treason 56. Jack the Ripper 59. The Siege of Sidney Street 60. The Hellfire Club 60. The Treasure of Monte Cristo 61.

Baker, Roy (1916–). Notable British director whose career declined in the sixties. Served apprenticeship at Gainsborough 1934–39, then war service. Sometimes billed as Roy Ward Baker.
The October Man 47. The Weaker Sex 48. *Morning Departure* 50. I'll Never Forget You

(US) 51. *Inferno* (US) 52. Don't Bother to Knock (US) 52. Passage Home 54. Jacqueline 56. Tiger in the Smoke 56. *The One That Got Away* 57. *A Night to Remember* 58. The Singer Not the Song (& p) 60. Flame in the Streets (& p) 61. The Valiant 61. Two Left Feet 64. *Quatermass and the Pit* 67. The Anniversary 68. Moon Zero Two 69. The Vampire Lovers 70. Scars of Dracula 70. Dr Jekyll and Sister Hyde 71. Asylum 72. And Now the Screaming Starts 73. Vault of Horror 73. The Legend of the Seven Golden Vampires 74. The Monster Club 80. The Flame Trees of Thika (TV) 81, etc.

Baker, Sir Stanley (1927–1976). Virile Welsh actor who rose from character roles to stardom, projecting honesty or villainy with equal ease.
Biography 1977: *Portrait of an Actor* by Anthony Storey.
☐ Undercover 41. All over the Town 48. Obsession 49. Your Witness 50. The Rossiter Case 51. Cloudburst 51. Captain Horatio Hornblower 51. Home to Danger 51. Whispering Smith Hits London 52. Lili Marlene 52. *The Cruel Sea* 53. The Red Beret 53. *Hell Below Zero* 54. Knights of the Round Table 54. The Good Die Young 54. Beautiful Stranger 54. Helen of Troy 55. Alexander the Great 55. A Hill in Korea 56. *Richard III* (as Henry Tudor) 56. Child in the House 56. Checkpoint 57. *Campbell's Kingdom* 57. Violent Playground 57. *Hell Drivers* 57. Sea Fury 58. The Angry Hills 59. Blind Date 60. Jet Storm 60. Yesterday's enemey 60. Hell is a City 60. *The Criminal* 60. The Guns of Navarone 61. Sodom and Gomorrah 62. A Prize of Arms 62. The Man Who Finally Died 62. Eva 62. In the French Style 63. *Zulu* (& co-p) 63. Dingaka 65. Sands of the Kalahari (& co-p) 65. *Accident* 67. Robbery (& co-p) 67. Code Name: Heraclitus (TV) 67. Where's Jack? 68. Girl with Pistol 68. The Games 69. The Last Grenade 69. Perfect Friday 71. Popsy Pop 71. Schizoid 71. Who Killed Lamb? (TV) 72. Innocent Bystanders 72. Graceless Go I (TV) 74. Zorro 75.
TV series: How Green Was My Valley 76.

Baker, Tom (1935–). British character actor with a larger-than-life air. On TV from 1975 as Doctor Who.
Nicholas and Alexandra (as Rasputin) 71. Luther 73. Vault of Horror 73. The Mutations 74. Sinbad's Golden Voyage 75, etc.

Bakewell, William (1908–). American general purpose actor.
The Heart Thief 27. All Quiet on the Western Front 30. Spirit of Notre Dame 31. Three Cornered Moon 33. Cheers for Miss Bishop 41. Davy Crockett 54, many others.

Bakshi, Ralph (1939–). American animator with a message, and no holds barred.
☐*Fritz the Cat* 71. Heavy Traffic 73. The Nine Lives of Fritz the Cat 75. Coonskin 75. Wizards 77. Lord of the Rings 78. American Pop 81. Hey Good Lookin' 82.

Balaban, Barney (1888–1971). American executive, former exhibitor, president of Paramount 1936–64.

Balaban, Robert (Bob) (1945–). American character actor. Midnight Cowboy 69. Me Natalie 69. Close Encounters of the Third Kind 78. Altered States 80. Prince of the City 81. Absence of Malice 81. Whose Life Is It Anyway? 82.

Balaban, Burt (1922–1965). American director, son of Barney Balaban.
Stranger from Venus (GB) 54. Lady of Vengeance 57. High Hell 58. Murder Inc. 60. Mad Dog Coll 61. The Gentle Rain 66, etc.

Balazs, Bela (1884–1949) (Hubert Bauer). Hungarian writer. Wrote book, *Theory of the Film*.
Die Dreigroschenoper 31. *The Blue Light* 31.

Balchin, Nigel (1908–1970). British novelist: books filmed include: *Mine Own Executioner, The Small Back Room, Suspect* ('A Sort of Traitors'). Has also adapted other people's work for the screen: *The Barbarian and the Geisha, The Blue Angel* (remake), etc.

Balcon, Jill (1925–). British actress, daughter of Sir Michael Balcon.
Nicholas Nickleby 47. Good Time Girl 48. Highly Dangerous 50, etc.

Balcon, Sir Michael (1896–1977). British executive producer. During a long and distinguished career he headed Gainsborough, Gaumont-British, MGM-British, Ealing, Bryanston and independent production companies, and was directly responsible for the planning and production of many famous films.
Autobiography 1969: *A Lifetime of Films*.
His more personal projects include: Woman to Woman 23. The Pleasure Garden 25. The Lodger 26. Easy Virtue 27. Man of Aran 33.

The Man Who Knew Too Much 34. The 39 Steps 35. Sabotage 37. A Yank at Oxford 38. The Citadel 38. Goodbye Mr Chips 39. Convoy 40. The Next of Kin 41. The Bells Go Down 42. Champagne Charlie 44. Dead of Night 45. The Captive Heart 46. Hue and Cry 46. Nicholas Nickleby 47. It Always Rains on Sunday 48. Scott of the Antarctic 48. Kind Hearts and Coronets 49. Whisky Galore 49. Passport to Pimlico 49. The Blue Lamp 50. The Man in the White Suit 51. The Lavender Hill Mob 51. The Cruel Sea 53. The Ladykillers 55. Dunkirk 58. Saturday Night and Sunday Morning 60. Tom Jones 63.
❀ For steering his part of the British film industry in very much the right way, and for refusing to lower his standards. *Dead of Night.*

¶ *M.B.:* I always look for people whose ideas coincide with mine, and then I'm ready to give them a chance to make a name for themselves.

M.B.: We made films at Ealing that were good, bad and indifferent, but they were indisputably British. They were rooted in the soil of the country.

Balderston, John (1889–1954). Anglo-American screenwriter, usually in collaboration, with a penchant for romantic and fantastic themes.
Frankenstein 31. *The Mummy* 32. Smilin' Through 32 and 41. *Berkeley Square* (oa) 33. The Mystery of Edwin Drood 35. *Mad Love* 35. Lives of a Bengal Lancer 35. *Bride of Frankenstein* 35. Beloved Enemy 36. *The Prisoner of Zenda* 37. Victory 40. Tennessee Johnson 42. Gaslight 44. Red Planet Mars 52, others.

Baldi, Ferdinando (–). Italian director.
David and Goliath (co-d) 59. Duel of the Champions 71. Blindman 71, etc.

baldness has proved an attraction for a number of actors, including Yul Brynner, Telly Savalas, Edgar Kennedy, Leon Errol. Many others have been at pains to conceal it.

Baldwin, Faith (1893–1978). American novelist. Scenario credits include The Moon's Our Home 36. Men Are Such Fools 37. Apartment for Peggy 50. Queen for a Day 51.

Baldwin, Walter (1887–1977). American character actor, often in owlish or countrified roles.
Angels over Broadway 40. All that Money Can Buy 41. King's Row 42. Happy Land 43. I'll Be Seeing You 44. The Lost Weekend 45. The Best Years of our Lives 46. Mourning Becomes Electra 47. The Man from Colorado 48. Cheaper by the Dozen 50. Carrie 52. Scandal at Scourie 53. Glory 55. Cheyenne Autumn 64. Rosemary's Baby 68, many others.

Balfour, Betty (1903–). British comedienne of silent days, a popular favourite of the twenties as pert heroine of *Cinders, Love Life and Laughter* and the *Squibs* series.
The Brat 30. The Vagabond Queen 30. Paddy the Next Best Thing 33. Evergreen 35. Squibs (remake) 36. 29 Acacia Avenue 45.

Balfour, Michael (1918–). American character actor in British films who usually plays dumb gangsters, cabbies, etc.
No Orchids for Miss Blandish 48. Obsession 50. Venetian Bird 53. The Steel Key 55. Breakaway 56. Fiend without a Face 58, Make Mine Mink 60. Fahrenheit 451 66. The Fixer 68, many others.
TV series: Mark Saber 55.

Balin, Ina (1937–) (Ina Rosenberg). American leading lady, with stage experience.
Compulsion 58. The Black Orchid 59. The Comancheros 62. The Patsy 64. The Greatest Story Ever Told 65. Run like a Thief 68. Charro 69. The Projectionist 71. The Don is Dead 73, etc.

Balin, Mireille (1909–1968). French leading lady.
Don Quixote 33. Pepe le Moko 36. Gueule d'Amour 37, etc.

Ball, Lucille (1910–1989). American comedienne, a former Goldwyn girl who after a generally unrewarding youth in the movies, turned in middle age to TV and became known as one of the world's great female clowns and a highly competent production executive.
□Broadway thru a Keyhole 33. Blood Money 33. Roman Scandals 33. Moulin Rouge 33. Nana 34. Bottoms Up 34. Hold that Girl 34. Bulldog Drummond Strikes Back 34. The Affairs of Cellini 34. Kid Millions 34. Broadway Bill 34. Jealousy 34. Men of the Night 34. Fugitive Lady 34. Carnival (first billed role) 35. Roberta 35. Old Man Rhythm 35. Top Hat 35. The Three Musketeers 35. I Dream Too Much 35. Chatterbox 36. Follow the Fleet 36. The Farmer in the Dell 36. Bunker Bean 36. That Girl from Paris 36.

Don't Tell the Wife 37. *Stage Door* 37. Joy of Living 38. Go Chase Yourself 38. Having A Wonderful Time 38. *The Affairs of Annabel* 38. Room Service 38. The Next Time I Marry 38. Annabel Takes a Tour 38. Beauty for the Asking 39. Twelve Crowded Hours 39. Panama Lady 39. *Five Came Back* 39. That's Right You're Wrong 39. The Marines Fly High 40. You Can't Fool Your Wife 40. Dance Girl Dance 40. Too Many Girls 40. A Guy, a Girl and Gob 40. Look Who's Laughing 41. Valley of the Sun 42. *The Big Street* (serious role) 42. Seven Days Leave 42. *Du Barry was a Lady* 43. Best Foot Forward 43. Thousands Cheer 43. Meet the People 44. *Without Love* 45. Abbott and Costello in Hollywood 45. Ziegfeld Follies 46. The Dark Corner 46. *Easy to Wed* 46. Two Smart People 46. Lover Come Back 46. Lured 47. *Her Husband's Affairs* 47. *Sorrowful Jones* 49. Easy Living 49. Miss Grant Takes Richmond 49. *Fancy Pants* 50. The Fuller Brush Girl 50. The Magic Carpet 50. *The Long Long Trailer* 54. Forever Darling 56. *The Facts of Life* 60. Critic's Choice 63. A Guide for the Married Man 67. *Yours Mine and ours* 68. Mame 73. Stone Pillow (TV) 85.
TV series: *I Love Lucy* 51–55. *The Lucy Show* 62–68. *Here's Lucy* 68–73. Life with Lucy 86.

Ball of Fire (US 1941). A zany comedy written by Charles Brackett and Billy Wilder, directed by Howard Hawks. Its plot is cheerfully derived from 'Snow White', the seven dwarfs having become professors writing an encyclopaedia, and Snow White a strip-teaser on the run from gangsters. In view of the talent involved, the fun now seems somewhat slow and obvious despite Gary Cooper, Barbara Stanwyck and a first-rate cast. In 1948 a musical version, *A Song is Born*, became an unsuccessful vehicle for Danny Kaye.

Ball, Suzan (1933–1955). American leading lady of the early fifties.
Untamed Frontier 52. East of Sumatra 53. City Beneath the Sea 53. War Arrow 54. Chief Crazy Horse 55, etc.

Ball, Vincent (1924–). Australian actor in England.
A Town Like Alice 56. Robbery Under Arms 57. Danger Within 58. Identity Unknown 60. Where Eagles Dare 68. Oh What a Lovely War 69. Deadline (Aus) 81, etc.

Ballad of a Soldier (Russia 1959). Pleasant, sentimental, and technically very skilled, this piece of romantic hokum served to show that Soviet film-makers could beat Hollywood at its own game. The simple plot details the mishaps which prevent a soldier from spending his leave in the way he intended before returning to the front and probably death. The leading role is played by Vladimir Ivashov, but the real stars are director Grigori Chukrai and photographers Vladimir Nikolayev and Era Savaleva.

Ballard, Carroll (–). American director with a flair for wild life.
The Black Stallion 80. Never Cry Wolf 83.

Ballard, Kay(e) (1926–) (Catherine Balotta). American comedienne with stage experience.
The Girl Most Likely 56. A House is Not a Home 64. Freaky Friday 77. Falling in Love Again 80, etc.
TV series: The Mothers-in-Law 67–68.

Ballard, Lucien (1908–). Distinguished American cinematographer.
Crime and Punishment 35. The King Steps Out 36. Craig's Wife 36. The Shadow 37. Penitentiary 38. *Blind Alley* 39. The Villain Still Pursued Her 40. Wild Geese Calling 41. The Undying Monster 42. Orchestra Wives 42. Holy Matrimony 43. *The Lodger* 44. *Laura* (co-ph) 44. This Love of Ours 45. Temptation 46. Night Song 47. Berlin Express 48. The House on Telegraph Hill 51. O. Henry's Full House 52. *Inferno* (3D) 53. New Faces 54. White Feather 55. The Proud Ones 56. *The Killing* 56. Band of Angels 57. Murder by Contract 58. Al Capone 59. Pay or Die 60. The Parent Trap 61. Ride the High Country 62. *The Caretakers* 63. The New Interns 64. Boeing Boeing 65. Nevada Smith 66. *Hour of the Gun* 67. Will Penny 68. *The Wild Bunch* 69. True Grit 69. The Ballad of Cable Hogue 70. The Hawaiians 70. What's the Matter with Helen 71. Junior Bonner 72. The Getaway 72. Breakout 75. Breakheart Pass 76. St Ives 76, etc.

ballet sequences have been a boon to many indifferent films, permitting a brief glimpse into a world that is strange, alarming, but graceful and glamorous. From the time of *The Goldwyn Follies* 38, any Hollywood musical with aspirations had to have a ballet sequence, some of the most memorable being in *The Pirate, On the Town, An American in Paris, Singin' in the Rain*, and *The Band Wagon*. The custom died out in the fifties, since when there has been an over-abundance of unimaginatively presented full-length stage ballets with famous dancing stars. These, filmed at low cost, have found a market, but expensive film ballets like *Tales of Hoffman, Invitation to the Dance* and *Black Tights* had tougher going. Dramatic films set in the ballet world have included *La Mort du Cygne* (remade in Hollywood as *The Unfinished Dance*), *The Red Shoes* and *The Spectre of the Rose*; lighter stories in which the heroine is a ballerina (usually a novice) include *Waterloo Bridge, Carnival, Dance Little Lady, On Your Toes* and *St Martin's Lane*. Several comedians have found themselves pursued by plot complications on to a stage and forced to take part clumsily in the ballet in progress: Jack Buchanan in *That's a Good Girl*, Danny Kaye in *Knock on Wood*, Morecambe and Wise in *The Intelligence Men*; even Laurel and Hardy donned tutus in *The Dancing Masters*.

By the seventies ballet had lost its general popularity, but *The Turning Point* used it as a background and *Nijinsky* accentuated the homosexual element. Rudolf Nureyev, on film in several straight ballets, turned actor as *Valentino*.

?
1 Name MGM's 1948 ballet drama starring Margaret O'Brien . . .
2 . . . and the 1937 French film on which it was based, starring Mia Slavenska.
3 In 1946 Viola Essen and Ivan Kirov appeared in a weird and unsuccessful ballet melodrama scripted by Ben Hecht. Name it.
4 What studio made it in the hope of acquiring a little prestige?
5 Who played the leading role of the impresario in *The Red Shoes*?
6 In what city did Moira Shearer's suicide take place?
7 In what film did Danny Kaye find himself in the corps de ballet?
8 Name Gene Kelly's ambitious 1954 ballet film whose failure signalled not only a down trend in his own career but the end of MGM's musical heyday.
9 Name the part-cartoon segment which was released separately.
10 Which musical included the 'Girl Hunt' ballet?
11 What ballet star played a dramatic role in *Torn Curtain*? (She also danced a little.)
12 What former ballet star played dramatic roles in *The Music Lovers* and *The Boy Friend*?

balloons: See *air balloons*.

ballyhoo. An expressive term, allegedly Irish in origin, used in show business to denote the kind of publicity that has nothing to do with the merits, or indeed the actual contents, of the film in question.

Balsam, Martin (1919–). American character actor of quiet and comfortable presence: range varies from executive to stagecoach driver.
□On the Waterfront 54. *Twelve Angry Men* 57. *Time Limit* 57. Marjorie Morningstar 58. Al Capone 59. Middle of the Night 59. Everybody Go Home (It.) 60. *Psycho* (as the ill-fated private detective) 60. Ada 61. Breakfast at Tiffany's 61. The Captive City 62. Cape Fear 63. Who's Been Sleeping in My Bed? 63. *The Carpetbaggers* (as the Louis B. Mayer type studio chief) 64. Youngblood Hawke 64. *Seven Days in May* 64. Harlow 65. The Bedford Incident 65. *A Thousand Clowns* (AA) 65. After the Fox 66. Hombre 67. Me Natalie 69. Trilogy (TV) 69. *The Good Guys and the Bad Guys* 69. Tora! Tora! Tora! 70. Catch 22 70. Little Big Man 70. The Old Man Who Cried Wolf (TV) 70. Hunters Are for Killing (TV) 70. *The Anderson Tapes* 71. Confessions of a Police Commissioner (It.) 71. The Man (TV) 72. Night of Terror (TV) 72. *Summer Wishes Winter Dreams* 73. The Stone Killer 73. Six Million Dollar Man (TV) 73. Money to Burn (TV) 74. Trapped Beneath the Sea (TV) 74. The Taking of Pelham 123 74. Murder on the Orient Express 74. Miles to Go Before I Sleep (TV) 75. Corruption in the Halls of Justice (It.) 75. Mitchell 75. Death Among Friends (TV) 75. All the President's Men 76, Two Minute Warning 76. Raid on Entebbe (TV) 77. The Sentinel 77. Silver Bears 77. Rainbow (TV) 78. The Seeding of Sarah Burns (TV) 79. The House on Garibaldi Street (TV) 79. Aunt Mary (TV) 79. The Love Tapes (TV) 79. Cuba 79. There Goes the Bride 80. The Salamander 80. Little Gloria . . . Happy at Last (TV) 82. The Goodbye People 84. St Elmo's Fire 85. Death Wish 3 85. Delta Force 85. Space (TV) 87. Queenie (TV) 87. Private Investigations 87.
TV series: Archie Bunker's Place 81–82.

Balser, Ewald (1898–). Austrian character actor in German films.
Rembrandt (title role) 42. The Last Act 48. Eroica (as Beethoven) 49. William Tell 56. Jedermann 62, many others.

Bambi (US 1942). One of Disney's best-loved feature cartoons, virtually excluding the human element from its sentimentalized but charming story of the life of a forest deer, based on the book by Felix Salten.

Bancroft, Anne (1931–) (Anna Maria Italiano). Warm, ambitious and effective American leading actress who after TV experience went to Hollywood in 1952 and made inferior routine films; fled to Broadway stage and after triumph in *The Miracle Worker* returned to films as a star.
□Don't Bother to Knock 52. Tonight we Sing 53. Treasure of the Golden Condor 53. The Kid from Left Field 53. Demetrius and the Gladiators 54. The Raid 54. Gorilla at Large 54. A Life in the Balance 55. New York Confidential 55. The Naked Street 55. The Last Frontier 55. Walk the Proud Land 56. Nightfall 56. The Restless Breed 57. The Girl in Black Stockings 57. So Soon to Die (TV) 57. *The Miracle Worker* (AA, BFA) 62. *The Pumpkin Eater* (BFA) 64. *The Slender Thread* 65. Seven Women 65. *The Graduate* 68. *Young Winston* 72. The Prisoner of Second Avenue 75. The Hindenberg 76. Lipstick 76. Silent Movie 76. Jesus of Nazareth (TV) 77. *The Turning Point* 77. The Elephant Man 80. Fatso (also directed) 80. To Be or Not to Be 83. Marco Polo (TV) 81. Garbo Talks 84. Agnes of God (AAN) 85. Night Mother 86. *84 Charing Cross Road* 87.

Bancroft, George (1882–1956). Burly American actor who after a period in the Navy became popular in Broadway musicals and straight plays. Went to Hollywood in the twenties and found his strong masculine personality much in demand for tough or villainous roles, almost always in run-of-the-mill films.
The Journey's End 21. *Driven* 21. *Pony Express* 25. *Code of the West* 25. *Old Ironsides* 26. *Underworld* 27. White Gold 27. Docks of New York 28. Thunderbolt 29. Derelict 30. Ladies Love Brutes 30. Scandal Sheet 31. Lady and Gent 33. Blood Money 34. Mr Deeds Goes to Town 36. John Meade's Woman 37. Angels with Dirty Faces 38. *Stagecoach* 39. Each Dawn I Die 39. Young Tom Edison 40. Texas 41. Syncopation 41. Whistling in Dixie 42, many others.

¶ 'When words roll from his tongue, you expect them to be punctuated by lightning.'—*N.Y. Times 1929*

Band, Albert (1924–) (Alfredo Antonini). Italian-born director, in Hollywood since the forties.
The Young Guns 56. I Bury the Living (& p) 58. Face of Fire 59. I Pascali Rossi 63. The Tramplers (& p) 66. A Minute to Pray, A Second to Die (p, co-w only) 68.

The Band Wagon. 1. British farce of 1939, based on radio show, with Arthur Askey and Richard Murdoch. 2. Hollywood musical of 1953 notable for 'Girl Hunt' ballet, lively Dietz/Schwarz music and lyrics, and star performance of Jack Buchanan.

The Bandit (O Cangaceiro) (Brazil 1953). The only Brazilian film to achieve world-wide commercial success, a fact attributable less to writer-director Lima Barreto's routine outlaw story than to the theme music by G. Migliori.

Banerjee, Victor (–). Indian actor in Britain. *A Passage to India* 84. Foreign Body 87.

Bank Holiday (GB 1938). Low-budget 'slice of life' melodrama generally agreed to show the first flowering of Carol Reed's directorial talent. Still enjoyable, in its dated way, for its picture of Brighton on a pre-war summer's day.

Bankhead, Tallulah (1902–1968). Gravel-voiced, highly theatrical leading lady of American stage and screen. The daughter of an eminent politician, she titillated Broadway and London in the twenties by her extravagant performance on stage and off, and later tended to fritter away her considerable talents by living too dangerously. Films never managed to contain her. Autobiography 1952: *Tallulah*.
□When Men Betray 18. Thirty a Week 18. A Woman's Law 28. His House in Order 28. *Tarnished Lady* 31. My Sin 31. The Cheat 31. Thunder Below 32. The Devil and the Deep 32. Faithless 32. Stage Door Canteen 43. *Lifeboat* 43. *A Royal Scandal* 45. Main Street to Broadway 53. *Fanatic* (GB) 65.

¶ She said of herself:

> I'm as pure as the driven slush.

What one remembers about Miss Bankhead is not her merit as a performer, which in her heyday was considerable, but rather her well-publicized life style, which kept her in the headlines throughout the twenties and thirties. As Mrs Patrick Campbell said:

> Tallulah is always skating on thin ice. Everyone wants to be there when it breaks.

The lady herself issued such statements as:

> Cocaine isn't habit-forming. I should know—I've been using it for years.

As a result, in her later years:

> They used to photograph Shirley Temple through gauze. They should photograph me through linoleum.

But it was more sad than funny when someone asked:

Are you really the famous Tallulah?

and got the answer:

What's left of her.

She concluded:

The only thing I regret about my past is the length of it. If I had it to live over again I'd make the same mistakes, only sooner.

Sooner or later she alienated most of her friends. Howard Dietz was the one who said:

A day away from Tallulah is like a month in the country.

Banks, Don (1923–1980). Australian composer in Britain.
Captain Clegg 62. Hysteria 65. Die Monster Die 65. The Reptile 66. The Mummy's Shroud 67. The Torture Garden 68, etc.

Banks, Leslie (1890–1952). Distinguished British stage actor who after unsuccessful experiments in home-grown silent films started his film career in Hollywood. His sophistication seemed to be enhanced by his war-scarred profile.
.□*The Most Dangerous Game* 32. Strange Evidence 33. The Fire-Raisers 33. I am Suzanne 33. Night of the Party 33. The Red Ensign 34. *The Man Who Knew Too Much* 34. The Tunnel 35. *Sanders of the River* 35. Debt of Honour 36. The Three Maxims 36. Fire Over England 36. Farewell Again 37. Wings of the Morning 37. *Twenty-one Days* 39. Jamaica Inn 39. Dead Man's Shoes 39. The Arsenal Stadium 39. Sons of the Sea 40. Busman's Honeymoon 40. The Door with Seven Locks 40. Neutral Port 40. Ships with Wings 41. Cottage to Let 41. The Big Blockade 42. Went the Day Well? 42. *Henry V* (as Chorus) 44. Mrs Fitzherbert 47. The Small Back Room 48. Madeleine 49. Your Witness 50.

Banks, Monty (1897–1950) (Mario Bianchi). Italian comic dancer who appeared in many silent two-reel comedies of the twenties then moved to Britain and later turned director.
Atlantic 30. Weekend Wives 31. Almost a Honeymoon (d) 31. Tonight's the Night (d) 32. No Limit (d) 35. We're Going to be Rich (d) 38. Great Guns (US) (d) 41, etc.

Banky, Vilma (1902–) (Vilma Lonchit). Austro-Hungarian star of American silents, discovered by Sam Goldwyn during a European holiday. Popular in the twenties but could not make the transition to sound. Married Rod la Rocque.
□Im Letzen Augenblick (Hung.) 20. Galathea (Hung.) 21. Tavaszi Szerelem (Hung.) 21. Veszelyben a Pokol (Hung.) 21. Kauft Mariett-Aktien (Ger.) 22. Das Auge des Toten (Ger.) 22. Schattenkinder des Glucks (Ger.) 22. Die Letzte Stinde (Ger.) 23. The Forbidden Land (Aust.) 24. Clown aus Liebe (Aust.) 24. The Lady from Paris (Ger.) 24. Das Bildnis (Aust.) 25. Sollman Heiraten (Ger.) 25. *The Dark Angel* 25. The Eagle 25. Son of the Sheik 26. The Winning of Barbara Worth 26. The Night of Love 27. The Magic Flame 27. Two Lovers 28. The Awakening 28. This Is Heaven 29. A Lady to Love 30. De Sehnsucht Jeder Frau (Ger.) 30. The Rebel (Ger.) 33.

'She spoke no English at all: for their love scenes in *The Dark Angel*, she spoke in her own language while co-star Ronald Colman chatted away about cricket.' — *John Baxter, The Hollywood Exiles*

Bannen, Ian (1928–). British stage and TV actor who has been effective in several films.
Private's Progress 55. The Birthday Present 57. Carlton Browne of the F.O. 58. Macbeth 59. *A French Mistress* 60. *Suspect* 60. On Friday at Eleven 61. Station Six Sahara 63. Rotten to the Core 65. *The Hill* 65. The Flight of the Phoenix 65. Sailor from Gibraltar 66. Penelope 67. Lock Up Your Daughters 69. Too Late the Hero 69. Fright 71. Doomwatch 72. The Offence 72. The Mackintosh Man 73. Bite the Bullet 75. The Sweeney 77. Bastards Without Glory (It.) 78. The Watcher in the Woods 80. Eye of the Needle 81. Gandhi 82. Night Crossing 82. Gorky Park 83. Defence of the Realm 85. Lamb 85. Hope and Glory 87, etc.

Banner, John (1910–1973). American character actor of Polish origin; usually played explosive Europeans.
Once upon a Honeymoon 42. The Fallen Sparrow 44. Black Angel 47. My Girl Tisa 48. The Juggler 53. The Rains of Ranchipur 56. The Story of Ruth 60. Hitler 63. Thirty-six Hours 64, etc.
TV series: *Hogan's Heroes* 65–70. Chicago Teddy Bears 71.

Bannon, Jim (1911–86). American actor with radio experience: played second feature leads in the forties and starred in a western series as 'Red Ryder' in the fifties.
The Missing Juror 44. I Love a Mystery 45. The Thirteenth Hour 47. Daughter of the Jungle 49. The Man from Colorado 49. Rodeo 53. Chicago Confidential 58. Madame X 65, many others.
TV series: Champion 55.

Banton, Travis (1894– *). American costume designer, long at Paramount.
The Wild Party 29. Morocco 29. The Vagabond King 30. Dishonored 31. Shanghai Express 32. *The Scarlet Empress* 34. *The Devil Is a Woman* 35. The Crusades 35. Maid of Salem 37. Angel 37. Letter from an Unknown Woman 48, etc.

Bar, Jacques (1921–). French producer, often in association with American companies.
Where the Hot Wind Blows 60. Vie Privée 61. A Monkey in Winter 62. Joy House 64. Once a Thief 65. The Guns of San Sebastian 67. The Mysterious Island of Captain Nemo 73, etc.

Bara, Theda (1890–1955) (Theodosia Goodman). American actress, the first to be called a 'vamp' (because of her absurdly vampirish, man-hungry screen personality). An extra in 1915, she was whisked to stardom on some highly imaginary publicity statistics (she was the daughter of an Eastern potentate, her name was an anagram of 'Arab death', etc.). *A Fool There Was* 16 is remembered for its classic sub-title, 'Kiss Me, My Fool!'; in 1919, her popularity waning, she forsook Hollywood for the Broadway stage, and when she returned in 1925 was forced to accept parts burlesquing her former glories, e.g. *Madame Mystery* 26. Wisely, she soon retired.
□The Two Orphans 15. The Clemenceau Case 15. The Stain 15. Lady Audley's Secret 15. The Vixen 16. *A Fool There Was* 16. Sin 16. Carmen 16. Romeo and Juliet 16. The Light 16. Destruction 16. Gold and the Woman 16. The Serpent 16. Eternal Sappho 16. East Lynne 16. Her Double Life 16. *Cleopatra* 17. Madame Du Barry 17. Under Two Flags 17. Camille 17. Heart and Soul 17. The Tiger Woman 17. Salome 18. When a Woman Sins 18. The Forbidden Path 18. The She Devil 18. Rose of the Blood 18. Kathleen Mavourneen 19. La Belle Russe 19. When Men Desire 19. The Siren's Song 19. A Woman There Was 20. The Price of Silence 21. Her Greatest Love 21. The Hunchback of Notre Dame 23. The Unchastened Woman 25. Madame Mystery 26. The Dancer of Paris 26.

¶ 'She was divinely, hysterically, insanely malevolent.'—*Bette Davis*
'She made voluptuousness a common American commodity, as accessible as chewing gum.'—*Lloyd Morris*

Baratier, Jacques (1918–). French director of shorts and occasional features.
Paris la Nuit 55. Goha 57. La Poupée 62. Dragées au Poivre 63. L'Or du Duc 65, etc.

Barbeau, Adrienne (1945–). American leading lady, mostly on TV.
Red Alert (TV) 77. Someone's Watching Me (TV) 78. The Disappearance of Flight 401 (TV) 79. The Fog 80. Escape from New York 81. Swamp Thing 82. Creep Show 82, etc.
TV series: Maude 72–78.

Barber, Glynis (1955–). South African leading lady in Britain. Films include Terror and The Wicked Lady; became popular on TV in Dempsey and Makepeace.

Barbera, Joe (1910–). American animator who with William Hanna (qv) created Tom and Jerry at MGM in 1937 and controlled the output until 1957: 'the cinema's purest representation of pure energy'. Later formed an independent company which produced dozens of 'semi-animated' cartoon series for TV, including the adventures of Yogi Bear, Huckleberry Hound, the Jetsons, the Flintstones, Magilla Gorilla, Scooby Doo and Snagglepuss.

Barbier, George (1865–1945). American character actor remembered in talkies as a blustery but essentially kindly old man.
Monsieur Beaucaire 24. The Big Pond 30. The Sap from Syracuse 30. The Smiling Lieutenant 31. No Man of her Own 32. One Hour with You 32. Million Dollar Legs 32. The Big Broadcast 32. Mama Loves Papa 33. Tillie and Gus 34. Ladies Should Listen 34. *The Merry Widow* 34. The Crusades 35. The Cat's Paw 35. The Milky Way 36. The Princess Comes Across 36. *On the Avenue* 37. Hotel Haywire 37. Tarzan's Revenge 38. Little Miss Broadway 38. Sweethearts 38. News is Made at Night 39. The Return of Frank James 40. *The Man Who Came to Dinner* 41. Weekend in Havana 41. The Magnificent Dope 42. Song of the Islands 42. Hello Frisco Hello 43. Weekend Pass 44. Her Lucky Night 45, many others.

Barcroft, Roy (1902–1969) (Howard H. Ravenscroft). Beefy American character actor, usually seen as a western heavy.
In hundreds of films and serials including: Mata Hari 31. A Woman Commands 32. Night Key 37. Flaming Frontiers 38. Mexicali Rose 39. The Phantom Creeps 39. Bad Man from Red Butte 40. Flash Gordon Conquers the Universe 40. Wide Open Town 41. Riders of Death Valley 41. Romance on the Range 42. Hoppy Serves a Writ 43. Hidden Valley

Outlaws 44. The Vampire's Ghost 45. My Pal Trigger 46. Rustlers of Devil's Canyon 47. Train to Alcatraz 48. Secret Service Investigator 48. Law of the Golden West 49. Radar Patrol vs Spy King 50. Night Riders of Montana 51. Ride the Man Down 52. El Paso Stampede 53. Rogue Cop 54. Oklahoma! 55. The Last Hunt 56. Band of Angels 57. Escort West 59. When the Clock Strikes 61. Six Black Horses 62. He Rides Tall 64. Billy the Kid vs Dracula 66. Rosemary's Baby 68. The Reivers 69. Monte Walsh 70.

Bardem, Juan-Antonio (1922–). Spanish director.
Welcome Mr Marshall 52. *Death of a Cyclist* 54. Calle Mayor 56. Vengeance 57. Sonatas 59. Los Innocentes 62. Los Pianos Mecanicos 64. The Uninhibited 68. Variétés 71. Behind the Shutters 74, etc.

Bardette, Trevor (1902–1978). American character actor, usually seen as western villain.
They Won't Forget 37. The Oklahoma Kid 39. Dark Command 40. The Moon Is Down 43. The Whistler 44. The Big Sleep 46. Song of India 49. The Texas Rangers 51. Lone Star 52. The Desert Song 53. Destry 54. The Man from Bitter Ridge 55. The Hard Man 57. The Mating Game 59. Papa's Delicate Condition 63. Mackenna's Gold 69, many others.

Bardot, Brigitte (1933–) (Camille Javal). Pulchritudinous French pin-up girl who, given world publicity as a 'sex kitten', used her small but significant talents to make some routine movies very profitable.
Act of Love 54. Doctor at Sea (GB) 55. *The Light across the Street* 55. Helen of Troy 55. *And God Created Woman* 56. Heaven Fell That Night 57. Une Parisienne 57. *En Cas de Malheur* 57. Please Mr Balzac 57. The Devil is a Woman 58. Mam'zelle Pigalle 58. Babette Goes to War 59. Please Not Now 61. *The Truth* 61. *Vie Privée* 61. *Love on a Pillow* 62. *Contempt* 64. Dear Brigitte 65. *Viva Maria* 65. Two Weeks in September 67. Shalako 68. *The Novices* 70. The Legend of Frenchy King 72. Don Juan 73, etc.

¶ *B.B.:* For twenty years I was cornered and hounded like an animal. I didn't throw myself off my balcony only because I knew people would photograph me lying dead.

B.B.: I started out as a lousy actress and have remained one.

'France's most ogled export.'–*Time 1956*

'It was the first time on the screen that a woman was shown as really free on a sexual level, with none of the guilt attached to nudity or carnal pleasure.'—*Roger Vadim*

Bare, Richard (1909–). American director who moved into TV.
Smart Girls Don't Talk 48. Flaxy Martin 48. The House Across the Street 49. This Side of the Law 51. Return of the Frontiersman 51. Prisoners of the Casbah 53. Shoot-Out at Medicine Bend 57. This Rebel Breed 60. I Sailed to Tahiti with an All-Girl Crew 67, etc.

Bari, Lynn (1915–) (Marjorie Fisher; aka Marjorie Bitzer). Pert American 'second lead', often in 'other woman' roles. A chorus graduate, she was given plenty of work in the thirties and forties but almost all of it was routine.
Dancing Lady 33. Stand Up and Cheer 34. Thanks a Million 35. Sing Baby Sing 36. Wee Willie Winkie 37. Josette 38. Return of the Cisco Kid 39. Hollywood Cavalcade 39. Earthbound 40. *Sun Valley Serenade* 41. *Moon Over Her Shoulder* 41. *The Magnificent Dope* 42. *Orchestra Wives* 42. Hello Frisco Hello 43. *The Bridge of San Luis Rey* 44. Tampico 44. Captain Eddie 45. Shock 45. *Margie* 46. The Man from Texas 48. On the Loose 51. Has Anybody Seen My Gal? 52. Francis Joins the WACS 54. Women of Pitcairn Island 56. Damn Citizen 58. Trauma 64. The Young Runaways 68, many others.
TV series: Boss Lady 62.

Baring, Norah (1907–). British leading lady.
Underground 28. Cottage on Dartmoor 29. At the Villa Rose 30. Murder 30. The Lyons Mail 31. The House of Trent 33, etc.

Barker, Eric (1912–). British character comedian long popular on radio with his wife Pearl Hackney.
Autobiography 1956: *Steady Barker*.
Carry on London 37. Concert Party 37. On Velvet 38. *Brothers in Law* 57. Happy is the Bride 58. Blue Murder at St Trinian's 58. Carry On Sergeant 58. Left, Right and Centre 59. Carry On Constable 60. Heavens Above 63. The Bargee 65. The Great St Trinian's Train Robbery 66. Maroc 7 67. There's a Girl in My Soup 70.

Barker, Jess (1914–). Lightweight American leading man of minor forties films.
Cover Girl 44. Keep Your Powder Dry 44. This Love of Ours 45. Take One False Step 49. Shack Out on 101 56. The Night Walker 65, etc.

Barker, Lex (1919–1973). Blond, virile-looking American actor who in 1948 was signed to play Tarzan (qv). After five films the role passed to another actor and Barker's stock slumped, but he continued to make routine action adventures.
Battles of Chief Pontiac 52. The Price of Fear 56. Jungle Heat 57. The Girl in the Kremlin 57. Terror of the Red Mask 59. La Dolce Vita 60. Robin Hood and the Pirates 60. Winnetou I 63. Victim Five 63. Old Shatterhand 64. Winnetou II 64. Kali-Yug, Goddess of Vengeance 64. Winnetou III 65. Dynamite Morgan 67. Woman Times Seven 67. Winnetou and Shatterhand 68, etc.

Barker, Ma (1880–1935) (Kate Barker). Notorious American outlaw of the thirties, who with her four sons terrorized the central states before being shot in Florida. She was played by Jean Harvey in *Guns Don't Argue* 55, Lurene Tuttle in *Ma Barker's Killer Brood* 60, Shelley Winters in *Bloody Mama* 70, and Claire Trevor in an episode of *The Untouchables*. So-called fictional variants were played by Blanche Yurka in *Queen of the Mob* 40, Irene Dailey in *The Grissom Gang* 71 and Angie Dickinson in *Big Bad Mama* 74.

Barker, Ronnie (1929–). Portly but versatile British TV comedian, rarely seen in films; immensely popular in *The Two Ronnies* and *Porridge*.
Doctor in Distress 63. The Bargee 64. The Man Outside 67. *Futtock's End* 70. Robin and Marian 76. Porridge 79, etc.

Barker, Sir Will G. (1867–1951). Pioneer British producer of the cinema's fairground days. A former salesman and cameraman, he founded the original Ealing studio.
Henry VIII 11. Jim the Fireman 12. Sixty Years a Queen 13. Greater Love Hath No Man 13. The Fighting Parson 14. Jane Shore 15, many others.

Barkworth, Peter (1929–). Smooth British comedy actor, mostly on TV; very popular in diffident roles.
A Touch of Larceny 61. Tiara Tahiti 62. No Love for Johnnie 63. Where Eagles Dare 69. Escape from the Dark 76, etc.
TV series: *Telford's Change* 78.

Barnard, Ivor (1887–1953). British character actor of stage and screen, often of henpecked or nosey parker types.
Waltz Time 33. The Wandering Jew 34. Storm in a Teacup 37. Pygmalion 38. The Saint's Vacation 41. Hotel Reserve 44. The Wicked Lady 45. Great Expectations 46. Oliver Twist 48. *Beat the Devil* (his last and best role, as a vicious killer) 53, many others.

Barnes, Barry K. (1906–1965) (Nelson Barnes). Stylish British stage actor, in occasional films.
□*The Return of the Scarlet Pimpernel* 38. *This Man is News* 38. The Ware Case 38. Prison without Bars 39. The Midas Touch 40. Spies of the Air 40. The Girl in the News 41. Dancing with Crime 46. Bedelia 46.

Barnes, Binnie (1905–1983) (Gitelle Barnes). Self-confident British light actress who after varied experience made a few early British talkies then went to Hollywood in 1934 and played mainly smart wise-cracking ladies.
Love Lies 31. Murder at Covent Garden 31. Heads We Go 33. *The Private Life of Henry VIII* (as Katherine Howard) 33. The Private Life of Don Juan 34. Diamond Jim 35. The Last of the Mohicans 35. The Magnificent Brute 36. *Three Smart Girls* 37. The Adventures of Marco Polo 38. Three Blind Mice 38. The Divorce of Lady X 38. *The Three Musketeers* 39. Till We Meet Again 40. Tight Shoes 41. Skylark 41. *Three Girls About Town* 41. The Man from Down Under 43. Barbary Coast Gent 44. *Up in Mabel's Room* 44. *It's in the Bag* 45. The Spanish Main 45. If Winter Comes 47. My Own True Love 48. Shadow of the Eagle 50. Fugitive Lady 51. Decameron Nights 53. *The Trouble with Angels* 66. Where Angels Go, Trouble Follows 68. Forty Carats 72, many others.

Barnes, George (1893–1953). Distinguished American cinematographer.
The Haunted Bedroom 19. Silk Hosiery 21. Hairpins 22. Dusk to Dawn 24. *The Eagle* 25. *Son of the Sheik* 26. Janice Meredith 27. Sadie Thompson 28. Our Dancing Daughters 28. *Bulldog Drummond* 29. The Trespasser 29. *Condemned* 29. Raffles 30. Five and Ten 31. The Unholy Garden 31. Street Scene 31. The Wet Parade 32. Sherlock Holmes 32. Peg O' My Heart 33. *Footlight Parade* 33. Massacre 34. *Dames* 34. Flirtation Walk 34. In Caliente 35. The Singing Kid 36. Black Legion 36. *Marked Woman* 37. Hollywood Hotel 37. Gold Diggers in Paris 38. *Jesse James* 39. *Rebecca* (AA) 40. Devil's Island 40. Hudson's Bay 40. *Meet John Doe* 41. *Ladies in Retirement* 41. Rings on Her Fingers 42. Once Upon a Honeymoon 42. Mr Lucky 43. *Frenchman's Creek* 44. *Jane Eyre* 44.

None But the Lonely Heart 44. *Spellbound* 45. The Spanish Main 45. The Bells of St Mary's 45. *From This Day Forward* 46. Sinbad the Sailor 47. Mourning Becomes Electra 47. The Emperor Waltz 48. The Boy with Green Hair 48. *Force of Evil* 49. Let's Dance 50. Mr Music 50. Riding High 50. Here Comes the Groom 51. Something to Live For 52. *The War of the Worlds* 53. Little Boy Lost 53, etc.

Barnes, Joanna (1934–). American actress occasionally seen in cool supporting roles.
Home Before Dark 58. Spartacus 60. The Parent Trap 61. Goodbye Charlie 64. The War Wagon 67. B.S. I Love You 70, etc.

Barnett, Vince (1902–77). American character actor, usually of minor gangsters or downtrodden little men.
Scarface 32. I Cover the Waterfront 35. A Star is Born 37. No Leave, No Love 42. The Killers 46. Brute Force 47. The Human Jungle 54, many others.

Barney Oldfield's Race for Life. This oft-quoted film is a twenty-minute Mack Sennett short of 1912, parodying the old railroad melodramas. Mabel Normand and Ford Sterling starred.

Barnum, Phineas T. (1810–1891). American showman who is alleged to have said 'There's one born every minute' of the people who flocked to see his freak shows. He became a multi-millionaire and co-founded the famous Barnum and Bailey Circus. He was played in *A Lady's Morals* 30 and *The Mighty Barnum* 35 by Wallace Beery; in *Rocket to the Moon* 67 by Burl Ives.

Baron Münchhausen (Czechoslovakia 1962). Karel Zeman's stylish if slightly arid semi-animated fantasy is the last of a longish line of movies about the tall-story teller. Méliès made a version in 1911, Emile Cohl in 1913; Hans Albers starred in a German version in 1943. The real Münchhausen (1720–97) was a German army officer, but the collection of stories written by Rudolf Raspe (first published in English in 1785) included much material from other sources.

Barr, Patrick (1908–85). British stage, screen and TV actor who played solid dependable types from the thirties.
Norah O'Neale 34. The Return of the Scarlet Pimpernel 38. The Frightened Lady 41. The Blue Lagoon 48. Robin Hood 52. Singlehanded 53. Crest of the Wave 54. Saint Joan 57. Next to No Time 60. The Longest Day 62. Billy Liar 63. Ring of Spies 64. House of Whipcord 74, many others.

Barrat, Robert (1891–1970). American character actor in films from silent days, usually as heavy western villain.
Mayor of Hell 33. Wild Boys of the Road 33. Dark Hazard 34. Wonder Bar 34. Captain Blood 35. Dr Socrates 35. Trail of the Lonesome Pine 36. The Charge of the Light Brigade 36. The Life of Emile Zola 37. Souls at Sea 37. The Buccaneer 38. Union Pacific 39. Return of the Cisco Kid 39. Go West 40. Captain Caution 40. Riders of the Purple Sage 41. American Empire 42. They Came to Blow Up America 43. The Adventures of Mark Twain 44. Road to Utopia 45. They Were Expendable 45. The Time of Their Lives 46. Road to Rio 47. Joan of Arc 48. Canadian Pacific 49. The Baron of Arizona 50. Flight to Mars 51. Double Crossbones 51. Son of Ali Baba 52. Tall Man Riding 55, many others.
†In 1934 alone Barrat appeared in nineteen films.

Barrault, Jean-Louis (1910–). Celebrated French stage actor, in a few rewarding film roles.
Mademoiselle Docteur 36. *Drôle de Drame* 36. *La Symphonie Fantastique* 42. *Les Enfants du Paradis* 44. D'Homme à Hommes 48. La Ronde 50. Le Testament du Docteur Cordelier 59. The Longest Day 62.

Barreto, Lima (1905–1982). Brazilian director responsible for his country's best known film, *O Cangaceiro* (*The Bandit*) 53.

Barrett, Edith (1912–77). American character actress, usually in fey roles.
Ladies in Retirement 41. Jane Eyre 43. I Walked with a Zombie 43. The Song of Bernadette 43. The Swan 56, etc.

Barrett, James Lee (1929–). American screenwriter.
The D.I. 58. The Greatest Story Ever Told (co-w) 65. The Truth About Spring 65. Shenandoah 65. Bandolero 68. The Green Berets 68. The Cheyenne Social Club (& p) 70. Smokey and the Bandit (co-w) 77, etc.

Barrett, Jane (1923–1969). British leading lady.
The Captive Heart 45. Eureka Stockade 48. Time Gentlemen Please 52. The Sword and the Rose 53, etc.

Barrett, Judith (1914–) (Lucille Kelly). American leading lady of a few thirties films. Flying Hostess 36. Let Them Live 37. Armored Car 37. Illegal Traffic 38. Television Spy 39. The Great Victor Herbert 39. Road to Singapore 40. Women without Names 40, etc.

Barrett, Ray (1926–). Australian leading actor in British TV and films.
The Sundowners 60. Touch of Death 62. Jigsaw 63. The Reptile 65. Revenge 71, etc.
TV series: *The Troubleshooters* 66–71.

Barrett, Rona (1934–) (Rona Burnstein). American gossip columnist who, centred in Hollywood for the television networks, has more or less inherited the mantle of Hedda and Louella. Autobiography 1974: *Miss Rona*.

¶ I'm not friends with the stars, because if I were I couldn't tell the truth about them.—*R.B.*

I'm really a pussycat—with an iron tail.—*R.B.*

The Barretts of Wimpole Street. Rudolph Besier's play about the wooing by Robert Browning of Elizabeth Barrett against her tyrannical father's opposition was twice filmed by MGM. The 1934 version with Norma Shearer, Fredric March and Charles Laughton was a resounding success; the 1956 version with Jennifer Jones, Bill Travers and John Gielgud was a failure. Both versions were directed by Sidney Franklin. The play was later turned into a musical, *Robert and Elizabeth*, but no film has so far materialized.

Barrie, Amanda (1939–) (Amanda Broadbent). British leading lady with TV experience.
Carry On Cleo 64. I Gotta Horse 65, etc.

Barrie, Barbara (–). Pert American character actress, popular in the seventies.
One Potato Two Potato 64. Summer of My German Soldier (TV) 78. The Bell Jar 79. Breaking Away 79. Private Benjamin 80.
TV series: Breaking Away 80. Tucker's Witch 82.

Barrie, Mona (1909–) (Mona Smith). Australian 'second lead' actress, in Hollywood from early thirties.
Carolina 34. The House of Connelly 34. A Message to Garcia 36. I Met Him in Paris 37. When Ladies Meet 41. Cairo 42. Storm over Lisbon 44. I Cover Big Town 47. Strange Fascination 52. Plunder of the Sun 53, many others.

Barrie, Sir J. M. (1860–1937). British playwright whose work usually had a recognizable fey quality, which even survived the film versions.
The Admirable Crichton (qv) 17. Peter Pan 24 and 53. The Little Minister 34. What Every Woman Knows 34. Quality Street 37. Darling How Could You? ('Alice Sit by the Fire') 51. Forever Female ('Rosalind') 53, etc.

Barrie, John (1917–1980). Heavily built British character actor with long repertory experience. Played *Sergeant Cork* on TV, and in the cinema is best remembered as the police inspector in *Victim* 63.

Barrie, Wendy (1912–78) (Wendy Jenkins). Bright British leading lady who went to Hollywood in 1934 but found only mediocre roles. Had her own TV show in 1948, and was later active in local radio.
It's a Boy (GB) 32. *The Private Life of Henry VIII* (GB) 32. For Love or Money 34. A Feather in Her Hat 35. Love on a Bet 36. Dead End 37. I Am the Law 38. The Hound of the Baskervilles 39. Five Came Back 39. The Saint Takes Over 40. Who Killed Aunt Maggie? 40. The Gay Falcon 41. Eyes of the Underworld 42. Women in War 42. Forever and a Day 43. It Could Happen to You (guest appearance) 53, etc.

Barrier, Edgar (1907–1964). American character actor with stage experience.
Escape 40. Arabian Nights 42. Phantom of the Opera 43. Flesh and Fantasy 44. *A Game of Death* 45. Macbeth 48. To the Ends of the Earth 48. Cyrano de Bergerac 50. Princess of the Nile 54. On the Double 61. Irma la Douce 63, many others.

barring clause. The part of an exhibitor's contract with a renter preventing him from showing new films before other specified cinemas in the area. The showing of a film in London may thus prevent its exhibition elsewhere within a radius of fifty miles or more.

Barron, Keith (1934–). British leading actor of the angry young man type; mostly on TV.
Baby Love 69. Melody 70. The Fire Chasers 70. The Man Who Had Power over Women 70. She'll Follow You Anywhere 71. Nothing But the Night 73. The Land That Time Forgot 75. Voyage of the Damned 76. The Elephant Man 80, etc.

Barry, Don (1912–1980) (Donald Barry d'Acosta). Rugged American actor, in Hollywood from 1939 after stage experience and immediately popular as hero of second feature westerns. Sometimes known as Donald 'Red' Barry.
Night Waitress 36. The Crowd Roars 38. Calling All Marines 39. Remember Pearl Harbor 42. The Chicago Kid 45. The Dalton Gang 49. Jesse James' Women (& d) 53. I'll Cry Tomorrow 55. Walk on the Wild Side 62. Fort Utah 66. Bandolero 68. Shalako 68. Dirty Dingus Magee 70. Junior Bonner 72. Hustle 75. Orca 77. The Swarm 78, etc.
TV series: Surfside Six 60. Mr Novak 63.

Barry, Gene (1921–) (Eugene Klass). Poised and debonair American leading man who also does a song and dance act. Films routine, but TV has kept him busy.
□The Atomic City 52. The Girls of Pleasure Island 52. *The War of the Worlds* 53. Those Redheads from Seattle 53. Alaska Seas 54. *Red Garters* 54. *Naked Alibi* 54. Soldier of Fortune 55. The Purple Mask 55. The Houston Story 56. Back From Eternity 56. The 27th Day 57. China Gate 57. Ain't No Time for Glory (TV) 57. Forty Guns 57. Hong Kong Confidential 58. *Thunder Road* 58. Maroc 7 67. Prescription Murder (TV) 67. Istanbul Express (TV) 68. Subterfuge 69. Do You Take This Stranger? (TV) 70. The Devil and Miss Sarah (TV) 71. The Second Coming of Suzanne 73. Guyana, Crime of the Century 79. The Adventures of Nellie Bly (TV) 81. The Girl, The Gold Watch and Dynamite (TV) 81.
TV series: Our Miss Brooks 55. *Bat Masterson* 58–60. *Burke's Law* 63–65. *The Name of the Game* 68–70. The Adventurer 72.

Barry, Iris (1895–1969). Founder-member of the London Film Society (1925); director of New York Museum of Modern Art Film Library from 1935; president of the International Federation of Film Archives 1946; author of books on the film.

¶ *I.B.:* Film is a machine for seeing more than meets the eye.

Barry, Joan (1903–87). British leading lady of the early thirties, chiefly known for dubbing Anny Ondra's voice in *Blackmail.*
The Card 22. The Rising Generation 28. The Outsider 31. Rich and Strange 31. Ebb Tide 32. Sally Bishop 32. Rome Express 32. Mrs Dane's Defence 34, etc.

Barry, John (1933–) (J. B. Prendergast). British composer.
Beat Girl 59. Never Let Go 60. Dr No (md) 62. The Amorous Prawn 62. The L-shaped Room 62. *From Russia with Love* 63. Zulu 63. The Man in the Middle 64. Goldfinger 64. The Ipcress File 65. The Knack 65. Thunderball 65. King Rat 65. The Chase 66. *Born Free* 66. The Wrong Box 66. The Quiller Memorandum 66. Petulia 68. Boom 68. Deadfall 68. The Lion in Winter (AA) 68. Midnight Cowboy 69. Murphy's War 71. They Might Be Giants 71. Diamonds are Forever 72. The Tamarind Seed 73. The Man with the Golden Gun 74. King Kong 76. The Deep 77. The White Buffalo 77. The Betsy 78. Moonraker 79. The Black Hole 79. Raise the Titanic 80. Somewhere in Time 80. Superman 2 80. Body Heat 81. Hammett 82. Francis 82. Octopussy 83. Out of Africa (AA) 85. Jagged Edge 86. Peggy Sue got Married 86. The Living Daylights 87. Hearts of Fire 87, etc.

Barry, John (1935–1979). Anglo-American production designer.
A Clockwork Orange 73. Phase IV 73. Lucky Lady 75. Star Wars 77. Superman 78. Superman 2 80. The Empire Strikes Back 80, etc.

Barry, Philip (1896–1949). American playwright, several of whose sophisticated comedies have been filmed.
The Animal Kingdom 32 (remade as One More Tomorrow 46). Holiday 38. The Philadelphia Story 40. Without Love 45.

Barrymore, Diana (1921–1960). American actress, daughter of John Barrymore. She made a few mediocre films in the early forties but was not a successful leading lady and later succumbed to alcoholism. Her autobiography *Too Much Too Soon* was filmed in 1958 with Dorothy Malone (and Errol Flynn as John Barrymore).
□Eagle Squadron 42. *Between Us Girls* 42. Nightmare 42. Frontier Badmen 43. Fired Wife 43. *Ladies Courageous* 44.

Barrymore, Drew (1975–). American child actress of the eighties. *E.T.* 82. Firestarter 84. Irreconcilable Differences 84. Cat's Eye 84.

Barrymore, Ethel (1879–1959) (Edith Blythe). Distinguished American actress of regal presence; sister of Lionel and John, daughter of Maurice Barrymore, Made a few silents, then remained on Broadway until 1944 when she made her home in Hollywood. Autobiography 1956: *Memories*.
□The Nightingale 14. The Final Judgment 15. The Awakening of Helen Ritchie 16. Kiss of

Hate 16. The White Raven 17. The Lifted Veil 17. The Eternal Mother 17. The American Widow 17. Life's Whirlpool 17. The Call of Her People 17. Our Miss McChesney 18. The Divorcee 19. Rasputin and the Empress (only film appearance with her brothers) 32. *None but the Lonely Heart* (AA) 44. The Spiral Staircase 46. *The Farmer's Daughter* 47. Moss Rose 47. The Paradine Case 48. Night Song 48. Moonrise 49. Portrait of Jennie 49. The Great Sinner 49. That Midnight Kiss 49. Pinky 49. The Red Danube 49. The Secret of Convict Lake 51. *Kind Lady* 51. It's a Big Country 52. *Deadline* 52. Just for You 52. The Story of Three Loves 53. Main Street to Broadway 53. *Young at Heart* 54. Johnny Trouble 57.

❀ For spending her later years portraying Hollywood's idea of the indomitable old lady with a heart of gold. *The Farmer's Daughter.*

Barrymore, John (1882–1942) (John Blythe). Celebrated American stage and screen actor, brother of Ethel and Lionel Barrymore. A famous matinée idol with a 'great profile', he became a famous romantic movie star of the twenties but later squandered his talents in inferior comedies caricaturing his own alcoholism and debauchery. A great personality and a splendid if often misguided talent. Autobiography 1926: *Confessions of an Actor.* Biographies: *Good Night Sweet Prince* (1944) by Gene Fowler; *Damned in Paradise* (1977) by John Kobler. Barrymore was lampooned on film by Fredric March in *The Royal Family of Broadway*, and portrayed by Errol Flynn in *Too Much Too Soon* and Jack Cassidy in *W. C. Fields and Me.*

□Are You a Mason? 13. An American Citizen 13. The Man from Mexico 14. The Dictator 15. The Incorrigible Dukane 16. The Lost Bridegroom 16. The Red Widow 16. *Raffles* 17. On the Quiet 18. Here Comes the Bride 18. Test of Honour 19. *Dr Jekyll and Mr Hyde* 20. The Lotus Eater 21. *Sherlock Holmes* 22. *Beau Brummell* 24. *The Sea Beast* 26. *Don Juan* 26. When a Man Loves 27. *The Beloved Rogue* 27. *Tempest* 28. Eternal Love 29. *Show of Shows* (first talkie: recites Richard III) 29. General Crack 29. The Man from Blankley's 30. *Moby Dick* 30. *Svengali* 31. The Mad Genius 31. *Arsène Lupin* 32. *Grand Hotel* 32. State's Attorney 32. *A Bill of Divorcement* 32. *Rasputin and the Empress* 32. *Topaze* 33. *Reunion In Vienna* 33. *Dinner at Eight* 33. Night Flight 33. *Counsellor at Law* 33. Long Lost Father 34. *Twentieth Century* 34. *Romeo and Juliet* (as Mercutio) 36. *Maytime* 37. *Bulldog Drummond Comes Back* (as the inspector) 37. Night Club Scandal 37. Bulldog Drummond's Revenge 37. Bulldog Drummond's Peril 37. *True Confession* 38. Romance in the Dark 38. *Marie Antoinette* 38. *Spawn of the North* 38. *Hold that Co-Ed* 38. *The Great Man Votes* 39. *Midnight* 39. The Great Profile 40. Invisible Woman 41. World Premiere 41. Playmates 42.

†A colour test he made for *Hamlet* in 1933 allegedly remains in New York's Museum of Modern Art.

❀ For a few performances of fine swashbuckling, for a few more of ripe ham, and as an awful warning of what can happen to a star who becomes too sure that the world is his oyster. *Twentieth Century.*

¶ 'I like to be introduced as America's foremost actor. It saves the necessity of further effort.'—*J.B.*

'My head is buried in the sands of tomorrow, while my tail feathers are singed by the hot sun of today.'—*J.B.*

'He moved through a movie scene like an exquisite paper knife.'—*Heywood Broun*

Student to lecturer: 'Tell me, Mr Barrymore, in your view did Ophelia ever sleep with Hamlet?' J.B. to student, after much thought: 'Only in the Chicago company . . .'

'I'm fifty years old and I want to look like Jackie Cooper's grandson.'—*J.B.*

Katharine Hepburn after finishing *A Bill of Divorcement*: 'Thank goodness I don't have to act with you any more!' J.B., sweetly: 'I didn't know you ever had, darling . . .'

J.B., flinging a fish at a coughing audience: 'Busy yourselves with that, you damned walruses, while the rest of us get on with the play!'

'If you stay in front of the movie camera long enough, it will show you not only what you had for breakfast but who your ancestors were.'—*J.B.*

'I've done everything three times. The fourth time around becomes monotonous.'—*J.B.*

A producer's wife at a Hollywood party, finding J.B. relieving himself in a corner of the ladies' room: 'Mr Barrymore, this is for ladies!' J.B., turning around without buttoning up: 'So, madam, is this!'

J.B. during his last illness: 'Die? I should say not, old fellow. No Barrymore would allow such a conventional thing to happen to him.'

'The good die young—because they see no point in living if you have to be good.'—*J.B.*

(When asked why he required idiot boards

in the studio, having perfect recall elsewhere) 'My memory is full of beauty: Hamlet's soliloquies, Queen Mab's speech, the Song of Solomon. Do you expect me to clutter up all that with this horse shit?'

Famous line (from *Twentieth Century*): 'I close the iron door on you!'

Barrymore, John Jnr (1932–) (John Drew Barrymore). American actor, son of John Barrymore and Dolores Costello. Usually plays weaklings.
The Sundowners 50. The Big Night 51. Thunderbirds 52. While the City Sleeps 56. Night of the Quarter Moon 59. The Boatmen 59. The Cossacks 60. Nights of Rasputin 61. War of the Zombies 63, etc.

Barrymore, Lionel (1878–1954) (Lionel Blythe). Celebrated American character actor, brother of Ethel and John Barrymore. His career was almost entirely devoted to films, including some direction; from the early thirties he was a familiar and well-loved member of the MGM galaxy, playing sentimental crotchety grandpas and churlish millionaires. From 1938, arthritis and two falls forced him to act from a wheelchair. Autobiography 1951: *We Barrymores.*
□Friends 09. Fighting Blood 11. Judith of Bethulia 11. The New York Hat 12. The Seats of the Mighty 14. Under the Gaslight 14. Wildfire 15. A Modern Magdalen 15. The Curious Conduct 15. The Flaming Sword 15. Dora 15. A Yellow Streak 15. The Exploits of Elaine 15. Dorian's Divorce 16. The Quitter 16. The Upheaval 16. The Brand of Cowardice 16. His Father's Son 17. The End of the Tour 17. The Millionaire's Double 17. Life's Whirlpool 17. The Valley of Night 19. The Devil's Garden 20. The Copperhead 20. The Master Mind 20. Jim the Penman 21. The Great Adventure 21. Face in the Fog 22. Boomerang 22. Enemies of Women 23. Unseeing Eyes 23. The Eternal City 24. America 24. Meddling Women 24. The Iron Man 25. Children of the Whirlwind 25. The Girl Who Wouldn't Work 25. Fifty Fifty 25. I am the Man 25. The Wrongdoers 25. The Barrier 26. *The Bells* 26. The Splendid Road 26. The Temptress 26. Brooding Eyes 26. The Lucky Lady 26. Paris at Midnight 26. Women Love Diamonds 27. The Show 27. Body and Soul 27. The 13th Hour 27. Drums of Love 27. Love 27. *Sadie Thompson* 28. West of Zanzibar 28. Decameron Nights 28. The Lion and the Mouse 28. Roadhouse 28. The River Woman 28. Alias Jimmy Valentine (first talkie) 29. Mysterious Island 29. Hollywood Revue 29. Confession (d only) 29. Madame X (d only) 29. His Glorious Night (d only) 29. The Unholy Night (d only) 29. The Rogue Song (d only) 30. Free and Easy 30. Ten Cents a Dance (d only) 31. *A Free Soul* (AA) 31. The Yellow Ticket 31. Guilty Hands 31. Mata Hari 31. *The Man I Killed* 32. *Arsène Lupin* 32. *Grand Hotel* 32. Washington Masquerade 32. *Rasputin and the Empress* (as Rasputin) 32. Sweepings 33. Looking Forward 33. The Stranger's Return 33. Dinner at Eight 33. One Man's Journey 33. Night Flight 33. Christopher Bean 33. Should Ladies Behave? 33. This Side of Heaven 34. Carolina 34. The Girl from Missouri 34. Treasure Island 34. David Copperfield 34. The Little Colonel 35. Mark of the Vampire 35. Public Hero Number One 35. The Return of Peter Grimm 35. *Ah Wilderness* 35. The Voice of Bugle Ann 36. The Road to Glory 36. *The Devil Doll* 36. The Gorgeous Hussy 36. *Camille* 37. *A Family Affair* (first of Hardy Family series) 37. Captains Courageous 37. Saratoga 37. Navy Blue and Gold 37. A Yank at Oxford 38. Test Pilot 38. *You Can't Take It With You* 38. *Young Dr Kildare* (start of series, as Dr Gillespie) 38. Let Freedom Ring 39. Calling Dr Kildare 39. *On Borrowed Time* 39. The Secret of Dr Kildare 39. Dr Kildare's Strange Case 40. Dr Kildare Goes Home 40. Dr Kildare's Crisis 40. The Bad Man 41. The Penalty 41. The People vs Dr Kildare 41. Dr Kildare's Wedding Day 41. Lady Be Good 41. Dr Kildare's Victory 41. *Calling Dr Gillespie* 42. Dr Gillespie's New Assistant 42. Tennessee Johnson 43. Dr Gillespie's Criminal Case 43. Thousands Cheer 43. A Guy Named Joe 43. Three Men in White 44. Since You Went Away 44. Between Two Women 45. The Valley of Decision 45. *Three Wise Fools* 46. *It's a Wonderful Life* 46. The Secret Heart 46. *Duel in the Sun* 46. Dark Delusion 47. *Key Largo* 48. Down to the Sea in Ships 49. Malaya 50. Right Cross 50. Bannerline 51. Lone Star 52. Main Street to Broadway 53.
❀ For having a go at everything in sight, even female impersonation; and for becoming Hollywood's omnipresent crotchety grandpa. *You Can't Take It With You.*
† Lionel once wrote a novel: *Mr Cantonwine, a Moral Tale.*

Barsacq, Leon (1906–1969). Russian art director and set designer, long in France. La Marseillaise 38. Lumière d'Eté 43. *Les Enfants du Paradis* 44. L'Idiot 46. Le Silence est d'Or 47. *La Beauté du Diable* 50. Les Belles de Nuit 52. Les Diaboliques 55. Les Grandes Manoeuvres 55. The Ambassador's

Daughter (US) 56. Porte des Lilas 57. The Longest Day 62. The Visit 64. Phèdre 69, others.

Barstow, Stan (1928–). British north country novelist whose *A Kind of Loving* was successfully filmed. Some of his other material has been adapted for television.

Bart, Lionel (1930–) (Lionel Begleiter). London-born lyricist and composer who can't read music but has been phenomenally successful with West End musicals such as *Fings Ain't What They Used To Be*, *Oliver!*, *Blitz* and *Maggie May*. Has written songs and scores for films since 1957; *Oliver!* was filmed in 1968.

Bartel, Paul (c. 1940–). American actor and director.
Private Parts (d) 72. Death Race 2000 (d) 75. Eat My Dust (a) 76. Cannonball (a, d, w) 76. Grand Theft Auto (a) 77. Eating Raoul (a, d) 81. Lust in the Dust 84. Not for Publication 84. Longshot 85.

Barthelmess, Richard (1895–1963). Presentable American leading man who went straight from college into silent films. Griffith used him memorably, and in 1921 he formed his own company and was popular until the advent of talkies, which made his innocent image seem old-fashioned and condemned him to insipid character roles.
□Gloria's Romance 16. Camille 17. The Eternal Sin 17. The Moral Code 17. Rich Man Poor Man 18. The Hope Chest 19. Boots 19. The Girl Who Stayed Home 19. Three Men and a Girl 19. Peppy Polly 19. *Broken Blossoms* 19. I'll Get Him Yet 19. Scarlet Days 19. The Idol Dancer 20. The Love Flower 20. Way Down East 20. Experience 21. *Tol'able David* 21. The Seventh Day 22. Sonny 22. The Bond Boy 22. The Bright Shawl 23. The Fighting Blade 23. Twenty One 24. *The Enchanted Cottage* 24. Classmates 24. New Toys 25. Soul Fire 25. Shore Leave 25. The Beautiful City 25. Just Suppose 26. Ranson's Folly 26. The Amateur Gentleman 26. The White Black Sheep 26. *The Patent Leather Kid* 27. The Drop Kick 27. The Noose 28. Kentucky Courage 28. Wheels of Chance 28. Out of the Ruins 28. Scarlet Seas 28. Weary River 29. Drag 29. Young Nowheres 29. Show of Shows 29. Son of the Gods 30. *The Dawn Patrol* 30. The Lash 31. Way Down East 31. The Finger Points 31. The Last Flight 31. Alias the Doctor 32. *Cabin in the Cotton* 32. Central Airport 33. Heroes for Sale 33. Massacre 33. *A Modern Hero* 34. Midnight Alibi 34. Spy of Napoleon 35. Four Hours to Kill 35. *Only Angels Have Wings* 39. The Man Who Talked Too Much 40. The Mayor of 44th Street 42. *The Spoilers* 42.

¶ 'He has the most beautiful face of any man who ever went before a camera.'—*Lillian Gish*

Bartholomew, Freddie (1924–) (Frederick Llewellyn). Impeccably well-bred British child actor whose success in Hollywood films of the thirties delighted elderly aunts the world over. His somewhat toffee-nosed image fell from favour during the war and as an adult he moved out of show business into advertising.
□Fascination (GB) 30. Lily Christine (GB) 32. *David Copperfield* 35. Anna Karenina 35. Professional Soldier 35. *Little Lord Fauntleroy* 36. The Devil is a Sissy 36. Lloyds of London 36. *Captains Courageous* 37. *Kidnapped* 38. Lord Jeff 38. Listen Darling 38. Spirit of Culver 38. Two Bright Boys 39. *The Swiss Family Robinson* 40. *Tom Brown's Schooldays* 40. Naval Academy 41. Cadets on Parade 42. A Yank at Eton 42. The Town Went Wild 44. Sepia Cinderella 47. St Benny the Dip 51.

Bartlett, Hall (1922–). American independent producer whose films seldom seem quite good enough to be independent about.
□*Navajo* 52. Unchained (& wd) 55. *Drango* (& wd) 56. Zero Hour (& d) 57. All the Young Men (& d) 60. *The Caretakers* (& d) 64. A Global Affair 64. Sol Madrid 68. Changes (d) 69. The Wild Pack (d) 72. Jonathan Livingston Seagull (& d, co-w) 73.

Bartlett, Richard (–). American director.
The Lonesome Trail 55. I've Lived Before 56. Rock Pretty Baby 56. Joe Dakota 57. Slim Carter 57. Money, Women and Guns 58, etc.

Bartlett, Sy (1900–78) (Sacha Baraniev). American screenwriter, and more recently producer.
The Big Brain (w) 33. Boulder Dam (w) 35. Coconut Grove 38. Road to Zanzibar (co-w) 41. Bullet Scars 42. The Princess and the Pirate 44. 13 Rue Madeleine 46. Down to the Sea in Ships 49. *Twelve O'Clock High* (w) 49. That Lady (wp) 55. *The Big Country* (w) 57. A Gathering of Eagles (wp) 63. Che (p) 69, etc.

Bartok, Eva (1926–) (Eva Sjöke). Agreeable Hungarian leading lady in international films.

Autobiography 1959: *Worth Living For.* A Tale of Five Cities 51. Venetian Bird 52. The Crimson Pirate 52. Front Page Story 54. Ten Thousand Bedrooms 57. Operation Amsterdam 59. SOS Pacific 60. Beyond the Curtain 60. Blood and Black Lace 64, etc.

Barton, Charles (1902–1981). Routine American director, long at Universal. □Wagon Wheels 34. Car 99 35. Rocky Mountain Mystery 35. The Last Outpost (co-d) 35. Timothy's Quest 36. And Sudden Death 36. Nevada 36. Rose Bowl 36. Murder with Pictures 36. The Crime Nobody Saw 37. Forlorn River 37. Thunder Train 37. Born to the West 38. Behind Prison Gates 39. Five Little Peppers and How They Grew 39. My Son is Guilty 40. Five Little Peppers at Home 40. Island of Doomed Men 40. Babies for Sale 40. Out West with the Peppers 40. Five Little Peppers in Trouble 40. Nobody's Children 40. The Phantom Submarine 40. The Big Boss 41. The Richest Man in Town 41. Harmon of Michigan 41. Two Latins from Manhattan 41. Sing for your Supper 41. Honolulu Lu 41. Shut My Big Mouth 42. Tramp Tramp Tramp 42. Hello Anapolis 42. Parachute Nurse 42. Sweetheart of the Fleet 42. A Man's World 42. Lucky Legs 42. The Spirit of Stanford 42. Laugh Your Blues Away 42. *Reveille with Beverly* 43. Let's Have Fun 43. She Has What It Takes 43. What's Buzzin Cousin 43. Is Everybody Happy 43. What a Woman 43. Beautiful but Broke 44. Hey Rookie 44. Jam Session 44. Louisiana Hayride 44. Men in her Diary 45. White Tie and Tails 45. *The Time of Their Lives* 46. Smooth as Silk 46. The Wistful Widow of Wagon Gap 47. Buck Privates Come Home 47. Mexican Hayride 48. *Abbott and Costello Meet Frankenstein* 48. The Noose Hangs High 48. Free for All 49. Africa Screams 49. Abbott and Costello Meet the Killer 49. The Milkman 50. Double Crossbones 50. Ma and Pa Kettle at the Fair 52. Dance with Me Henry 56. The Shaggy Dog 59. Toby Tyler 60. Swinging Along 62.

Barton, Dee (–). American composer. High Plains Drifter 73. Thunderbolt and Lightfoot 74.

Barton, James (1890–1962). Grizzled, good-humoured American character actor, a veteran of burlesque and Broadway. Captain Hurricane 35. Shepherd of the Hills 41. *The Time of Your Life* 48. Yellow Sky 49. The Daughter of Rosie O'Grady 50. Wabash Avenue 50. Here Comes the Groom 51. Golden Girl 51. The Naked Hills 57. Quantez 57. *The Misfits* 61, etc.

Bartosch, Berthold (1893–1968). Austro-Hungarian animator, best known for his symbolic *L'Idée* 34.

Barty, Billy (c. 1910–). American dwarf actor who has been seen in many films from *Gold Diggers of 1933* to *Under the Rainbow* 81. Rumpelstiltskin 87.

Baryshnikov, Mikhail (1948–). Latvian ballet dancer who made his American film debut in *The Turning Point* 77 and consolidated this in *White Nights* 85, *Dancers* 87.

¶ *M.B.:* I'm not the first straight dancer or the last. Anyway, it has nothing to do with art.

Barzman, Ben (1911–). Canadian writer with Hollywood experience; in Britain from early fifties. True to Life 42. The Boy with Green Hair 48. He Who Must Die 56. Time Without Pity 57. Blind Date 59. The Ceremony 63. The Heroes of Telemark 65. The Blue Max 66, etc.

baseball has been the subject for occasional films since 1899, when *Casey at the Bat* was first made. (It turned up again in 1927 with Wallace Beery.) Biopics of famous baseball personalities include *The Stratton Story* (James Stewart), *The Babe Ruth Story* (William Bendix), *The Pride of the Yankees* (Gary Cooper as Lou Gehrig), *The Winning Team* (Ronald Reagan as G. C. Alexander), *The Pride of St Louis* (Dan Dailey as Dizzy Dean), *Fear Strikes Out* (Anthony Perkins as Jim Piersall) and *The Jackie Robinson Story.* Serious dramatic films about the sport include *The Bush Leaguer, Slide Kelly Slide* and *The Big Leaguer*. There has been a fantasy, *Angels in the Outfield*, and a who-done-it, *Death on the Diamond.* Musicals are led by *Take Me Out to the Ball Game* and *Damn Yankees*. Comedies include *Elmer the Great, Alibi Ike, Fast Company, Rhubarb, It Happens Every Spring, Speedy* (Harold Lloyd), *College* (Buster Keaton) and *Ladies' Day*. Baseball stadiums have provided memorable scenes in films on other subjects: *The FBI Story, Beau James, The Satan Bug, Experiment in Terror,* etc.

Basehart, Richard (1914–84). Thoughtful American leading actor who somehow never achieved his expected stardom; equally adept at honesty, villainy and mental disturbance. Many TV appearances.

□Cry Wolf 47. Repeat Performance 47. *He Walked by Night* 48. Roseanna McCoy 49. *The Black Book* 49. Tension 49. Outside the Wall 50. *Fourteen Hours* 51. The House on Telegraph Hill 51. Fixed Bayonets 51. Decision Before Dawn 51. The Stranger's Hand 53. Titanic 53. La Strada 54. The Good Die Young 54. La Reprise de Justice 54. La Vena d'Oro 55. Cartouche 55. Canyon Crossroads 55. Il Bidone (The Swindlers) 55. The Extra Day 56. *Moby Dick* 56. The Intimate Stranger 56. *Time Limit* 57. So Soon to Die (TV) 57. Arrivederci Dimas 57. *The Brothers Karamazov* 58. L'Ambiteuse 58. Jons und Erdme 59. Five Branded Women 60. Portrait in Black 60. For the Love of Mike 60. Passport to China 61. The Savage Guns 61. Tierra Brutal 62. *Hitler* (title role) 63. Kings of the Sun 63. The Satan Bug 65. The Sole Survivor (TV) 69. The Death of Me Yet (TV) 71. City Beneath the Sea (One Hour to Doomsday) (TV) 71. Assignment Munich (TV) 72. The Bounty Man (TV) 72. Escape of the Birdmen (TV) 72. Chato's Land 72. Rage 72. Maneater (TV) 73. And Millions Will Die 73. How the West Was Won (TV) 75. Mansion of the Doomed 76. The Island of Dr Moreau 77. WEB (TV) 78. The Bastard (TV) 78. Being There 79. The Great Georgia Bank Hoax 79. Marilyn, the Untold Story (TV) 80. Knight Rider (TV) 82.
TV series: *Voyage to the Bottom of the Sea* 64–67.

Basevi, James (c. 1890–). Anglo-American art director and special effects wizard, at Fox from the mid-twenties; notable for *The Hurricane* 38, *The Ox-Bow Incident* 43, *Jane Eyre* 44, *East of Eden* 54, *The Searchers* 56, etc.

Basinger, Kim (1954–). Sultry American leading actress, often in oversexed roles.
□ Hard Country 81. Killjoy (TV) 81. Mother Lode 82. The Man who Loved Women 83. Never Say Never Again 83. The Natural 84. Fool for Love 85. Nine and a Half Weeks 85. No Mercy 86. Blind Date 87. Nadine 87.
TV series: Dog and Cat 79. From Here to Eternity 80.

¶ *K.B.:* You have to be a little unreal to be in this business.

Baskett, James (1904–1948). Black American character actor best known for his performance as Uncle Remus in *Song of the South* 48.

Basquette, Lina (1907–). American leading lady of the twenties, former child star and dancer. Her lively private life included six husbands.
Juvenile Dancer 16. Prince for a Day 17. Penrod 22. Ranger of the North 27. Wheel of Chance 28. Show Folks 28. *The Godless Girl* 29. Dude Wrangler 30. Hard Hombre 31. Morals for Women 31. Phantom Express 32. Ebb Tide 37. Four Men and a Prayer 38, etc.

Bass, Alfie (1920–87). Pint-sized British character comedian, adept at Cockney/Jewish roles.
Johnny Frenchman 45. Holiday Camp 47. It Always Rains on Sunday 47. The Hasty Heart 49. *The Lavender Hill Mob* 51. *The Bespoke Overcoat* 55. A Kid for Two Farthings 55. A Tale of Two Cities 57. I Only Arsked 59. The Millionairess 60. Alfie 66. The Fearless Vampire Killers 67. The Magnificent Seven Deadly Sins 72. Moonraker 79, etc.
TV series: The Army Game 57–62. Bootsie and Snudge 60–63. Are You Being Served? 79.

Bass, Sam (1851–1878). American western adventurer, played by Howard Duff in *Calamity Jane and Sam Bass.*

Bass, Saul (1920–). American title designer whose ingenious credits have enlivened such films as *Carmen Jones, The Shrike, The Man with the Golden Arm, Around the World in Eighty Days, Vertigo, The Big Country, Bonjour Tristesse, North by Northwest, Psycho, Ocean's Eleven, A Walk on the Wild Side, It's a Mad Mad Mad Mad World, Bunny Lake is Missing*, many others. In 1973 he directed *Phase IV*.
† It is widely believed that Bass directed the shower sequence in *Psycho*, but this has never been confirmed.

Basserman, Albert (1867–1952). Distinguished German stage actor who came to Hollywood as refugee in 1939 and played sympathetic roles.
□Der Andere 13. Voruntersuchung 31. The Last Days Before the War 32. Kadetten 33. Ein Gewisser Herr Gran 33. Alraune 33. Letzte Liebe 38. Le Famille Lefrancois 39. Dr Ehrlich's Magic Bullet 40. *Foreign Correspondent* 40. A Dispatch from Reuters 40. Moon Over Burma 40. Knute Rockne 40. Escape 40. *The Shanghai Gesture* 41. The Great Awakening 41. New Wine 41. A Woman's Face 41. The Moon and Sixpence 42. Invisible Agent 42. Once Upon a Honeymoon 42. Fly by Night 42. Desperate Journey 42. Good Luck Mr Yates 43. Passport to Heaven 43. Reunion in France 43.

Madame Curie 44. Since You Went Away 44. *Rhapsody in Blue* 45. Strange Holiday 46. The Searching Wind 46. The Private Affairs of Bel Ami 47. Escape Me Never 47. *The Red Shoes* (GB) 48.
❁ For bringing to Hollywood a suggestion of the unique strength of the European theatre. *The Shanghai Gesture.*

Bassey, Shirley (1937–). Torrid British-born cabaret singer whose film appearances have always been as a performer.

Bassler, Robert (1903–). American producer.
My Gal Sal 42. *The Black Swan* 43. The Lodger 44. Hangover Square 45. Thunder in the Valley 47. *The Snake Pit* 48. Thieves' Highway 49. Halls of Montezuma 50. Kangaroo 52. Beneath the Twelve-mile Reef 53. Suddenly 54, etc.

Bastedo, Alexandra (1946–). Leading lady of Canadian, Italian and English ancestry.
Thirteen Frightened Girls 63. Inside Daisy Clover 66. Casino Royale 67. The Ghoul 75, etc.
TV series: *The Champions* 67.

The Bat. The spooky house melodrama by Mary Roberts Rinehart was first filmed in 1926 with Louise Fazenda and Emily Fitzroy. In 1930 came a sound variation known as *The Bat Whispers*, with Grayce Hampton and some splendid over-acting from Chester Morris. In 1959 there was a somewhat spiritless remake with Agnes Moorehead and Vincent Price.

La Bataille du Rail (France 1944–1945). A remarkable documentary, directed by René Clement, shot in occupied France during World War II to show the railwaymen's resistance to the Nazis.

Batchelor, Joy (1914–). British animator, wife of John Halas and co-founder of Halas and Batchelor Cartoon Films.

Bates, Alan (1934–). Leading British actor of stage and screen: tends to play thoughtful toughs with soft centres.
□The Entertainer 59. *A Kind of Loving* 62. *Whistle down the Wind* 62. The Caretaker 63. The Running Man 63. *Nothing But the Best* 64. *Zorba the Greek* 65. Georgy Girl 66. King of Hearts 67. *Far from the Madding Crowd* 67. The Fixer 68. *Women in Love* 69. Three Sisters 70. The Go-Between 70. *A Day in the Death of Joe Egg* 71. Impossible Object 73. Butley 73. In Celebration 74. Royal Flash 75. The Collection (TV) 76. An Unmarried Woman 77. The Shout 78. The Rose 79. Very Like a Whale (TV) 80. Nijinsky 80. Quartet 81. The Return of the Soldier 82. Britannia Hospital 82. An Englishman Abroad (TV) 83. A Voyage Around My Father (TV) 83. Dr Fischer of Geneva (TV) 83. Duet For One 86. A Prayer for the Dying 87.

Bates, Barbara (1925–1969). American leading lady, former model and ballet dancer.
This Love of Ours 45. The Fabulous Joe 48. June Bride 48. *The Inspector General* 49. Cheaper by the Dozen 49. All About Eve 50. Belles on Her Toes 52. Rhapsody 54. House of Secrets (GB) 56. Town on Trial (GB) 57. Apache Territory 58, etc.
TV series: It's a Great Life 54–55

Bates, Florence (1888–1954) (Florence Rabe). American character actress, adept at friendly or monstrous matrons. A former lawyer, she was persuaded by Alfred Hitchcock to play the role for which she is best remembered, and remained much in demand for a decade.
□The Man in Blue 37. *Rebecca* 40. Calling All Husbands 40. Son of Monte Cristo 40. Hudson's Bay 40. Kitty Foyle 40. Road Show 41. Love Crazy 41. The Chocolate Soldier 41. Strange Alibi 41. The Devil and Miss Jones 41. The Tuttles of Tahiti 42. *The Moon and Sixpence* 42. My Heart Belongs to Daddy 42. Mexican Spitfire at Sea 42. We Were Dancing 42. Slightly Dangerous 43. His Butler's Sister 43. They Got Me Covered 43. Mister Big 43. Heaven Can Wait 43. Mr Lucky 43. Since You Went Away 44. The Mask of Dimitrios 44. Kismet 44. Belle of the Yukon 44. The Racket Man 44. Saratoga Trunk 45. Tahiti Nights 45. *Tonight and Every Night* 45. Sanantonio 45. Out of This World 45. Claudia and David 46. Cluny Brown 46. The Diary of a Chambermaid 46. Whistle Stop 46. The Time the Place and the Girl 46. *The High Window* 47. Love and Learn 47. Desire Me 47. *The Secret Life of Walter Mitty* 47. Texas Brooklyn and Heaven 48. Winter Meeting 48. The Inside Story 48. River Lady 48. My Dear Secretary 48. Portrait of Jennie 48. *I Remember Mama* 48. A Letter to Three Wives 48. The Judge Steps Out 49. The Girl from Jones Beach 49. On The Town 49. Belle of Old Mexico 50. *County Fair* 50. The Second Woman 51. Lullaby of Broadway 51. The Tall Target 51. Havana Rose 51. Father Takes the Air 51. The Whistle at Eaton Falls 51. The

San Francisco Story 52. Les Miserables 52. Paris Model 53. Main Street to Broadway 53.
† In 1914, when she was 26, F.B. was the first woman lawyer in Texas.

Bates, Granville (1882–1940). American general purpose supporting actor of the thirties: storekeepers, doctors and grandpas.
Jealousy 29. The Smiling Lieutenant 31. Woman Wanted 35. 13 Hours by Air 36. They Won't Forget 37. Nancy Steele is Missing 37. Wells Fargo 37. Go Chase Yourself 38. Gold is Where You Find It 38. The Great Man Votes 39. Pride of the Blue Grass 39. Of Mice and Men 39. Jesse James 39. My Favorite Wife 40. The Mortal Storm 40. Brother Orchid 40, many others.

Bates, H. E. (1905–1974). British novelist who dabbled in the cinema. *The Purple Plain* was filmed; *The Darling Buds of May* was filmed as *The Mating Season*; *Fair Stood the Wind for France* was done on television; and he co-scripted *Summer Madness*.

Bates, Michael (1920–1978). British character actor who specialized in stupid policemen and other caricatures.
Carrington VC 55. I'm All Right Jack 59. Bedazzled 67. *Here We Go Round the Mulberry Bush* 67. Salt and Pepper 68. Don't Raise the Bridge Lower the River 68. Hammerhead 68. Patton 70. The Rise and Rise of Michael Rimmer 70. *A Clockwork Orange* 71. No Sex Please, We're British 73, etc.
TV series: It Ain't Half Hot Mum 73-77.

Bates, Ralph (1940–). Incisive British character actor who played Caligula on TV and took the natural step to Hammer horrors.
The Horror of Frankenstein 70. Lust for a Vampire 70. Dr Jekyll and Sister Hyde 71. Fear in the Night 73. Persecution 74. I Don't Want to be Born 75, etc.
TV series: Poldark, Penmarric, Dear John.

Bath, Hubert (1883–1945). British composer.
Blackmail 29. The 39 Steps 35. Rhodes of Africa 36. A Place of One's Own 44. Love Story 45, etc.

bathtubs, though especially associated with Cecil B. de Mille, have been a favourite Hollywood gimmick from early silent days. But de Mille undressed his heroines with the most showmanship, whether it was Gloria Swanson in *Male and Female*, Claudette Colbert in her asses' milk in *The Sign of the Cross* (emulated years later by Frances Day in *Fiddlers Three*) or Paulette Goddard in *Unconquered*. Other ladies who have bathed spectacularly include Joan Crawford in *The Women*, Deanna Durbin in *Can't Help Singing*, Jean Harlow in *Red Dust*, Phyllis Haver in *The Politic Flapper*, Joan Collins in *The Wayward Bus*, Elke Sommer in *The Wicked Dreams of Paula Schultz*, Gina Lollobrigida in *Belles de Nuit*, Carroll Baker in *Harlow* and Sophia Loren (who had Gregory Peck hiding in her shower) in *Arabesque*. Not that the men have had it all their own way: Roger Livesey in *Colonel Blimp* and Gary Cooper in *Love in the Afternoon* suffered in the steamroom; and all the actors who have played coal miners, including Trevor Howard in *Sons and Lovers* and Donald Crisp in *How Green Was My Valley*, know how it feels to be scrubbed all over. Marat in *Marat/Sade* spent the whole film in a tub. The most bathed male star is probably Cary Grant, who had a tub in *The Howards of Virginia*, a shower in *Mr Blandings Builds His Dream House*, another shower, fully clothed this time, in *Charade*, and a Japanese geisha bath in *Walk, Don't Run*. And Hitchcock, with *Psycho*, still takes the prize for the most memorable shower scene.

Batman. An American comic strip character created in 1939 by Bob Kane, Batman was a personable millionaire who, with his young helper Robin, donned fancy dress to fight the evil forces in society, and zoomed about in a 'batmobile' with many a pow and a splat. His chief enemies were the Riddler, the Penguin, the Joker and Catwoman. He came to the big screen in two serials, and was played in 1943 by Lewis Wilson and in 1949 by Robert Lowery. A TV series in 1965–67 starred Adam West with Burt Ward, and the villains were played by Frank Gorshin, Burgess Meredith, Cesar Romero and Lee Meriwether. A feature version emerged in 1966.

Battle, John Tucker (–). American screenwriter.
Captain Eddie 45. So Dear to My Heart 48. The Frogmen 51. A Man Alone 55. Lisbon 56, etc.

Battleship Potemkin (Russia 1925). A historical reconstruction of an incident at Odessa in the revolution of 1905. Eisenstein, directing his second film, used the theme not merely as propaganda but as a means to develop his cinematic technique. The editing of the massacre sequence on the steps is justly famous and has been frequently copied. Photographed by Edouard Tissé; assistant to Eisenstein, Grigori Alexandrov; music by Edmund Meisel. Historically, no such incident took place, but Eisenstein liked the location.

Bauchens, Anne (1882–1967). American editor, almost always for de Mille.
The Squaw Man 18. Don't Change Your Husband 19. The Affairs of Anatol 21. The Ten Commandments 23. King of Kings 27. Dynamite 29. The Sign of the Cross 32. Cleopatra 34. The Crusade 35. The Buccaneer 38. North West Mounted Police (AA) 40. Reap the Wild Wind 42. Love Letters 45. Unconquered 47. Samson and Delilah 49. The Greatest Show on Earth 52. The Ten Commandments 56, many others.

Bauer, Steven (1956–) (Steven Echevarria). Cuban character actor in Hollywood.
Scarface 83. Thief of Hearts 84.

Baum, L. Frank (1856–1919). American author who published *The Wizard of Oz* in 1900 and started an industry from it and its sequels.

Baum, Vicki (1896–1960). Austrian novelist whose chief gift to Hollywood was the much-filmed and well imitated *Grand Hotel*, which she herself revamped as *Hotel Berlin*. Autobiography 1964: *It Was All Quite Different*.

Baur, Harry (1880–1943). Celebrated French actor of stage and screen.
Shylock 10. La Voyante 23. David Golder 31. Poil de Carotte 32. Golgotha 34. Moscow Nights 35. Crime and Punishment 35. Taras Bulba 35. Un Carnet de Bal 37. The Rebel Son 38. Volpone 39. L'Assassinat du Père Noel 41. Symphonie eines Lebens 42, etc.

Bava, Mario (1914–1980). Italian director, former photographer, of period muscleman epics and pseudo-British horror stories, revered by the *cognoscenti* for his tongue-in-cheek attitude towards some of them.
Black Sunday (wphd) 60. Hercules in the Centre of the Earth (wphd) 61. Erik the Conqueror (wd) 63. The Evil Eye (wphd) 62. *Black Sabbath* (wd) 63. *Blood and Black Lace* (wphd) 64. Planet of Blood (d) 65. Dr Goldfoot and the Girl Bombs (d) 66. Curse of the Dead (wd) 67. *Diabolik* (wd) 68. The Antecedent (d) 71, etc.

Bax, Sir Arnold (1883–1953). British composer.
□Malta GC 43. Oliver Twist 48. Journey into History 48.

Baxley, Barbara (–). American character actress.
The Badlanders 58. The Savage Eye 60. All Fall Down 62. Countdown 67. No Way to Treat a Lady 68. The Impostor (TV) 74. Nashville 75. Norma Rae 79, etc.

Baxter, Alan (1908–1976). Cold-eyed American second lead of the forties; graduated to colonels and tough executives.
Mary Burns Fugitive 35. The Last Gangster 37. Gangs of New York 38. Each Dawn I Die 39. Santa Fe Trail 40. Saboteur 42. Submarine Base 43. Winged Victory 44. The Set Up 49. The Devil's Weed 49. End of the Line (in Britain) 56. The True Story of Jesse James 57. The Mountain Road 60. Judgment at Nuremburg 61. This Property is Condemned 66. Willard 71, etc.

Baxter, Anne (1923–85). American leading lady who usually played shy and innocent but proved equally at home as a schemer. Trained for the stage but was starring in Hollywood at seventeen. After 1960 found the going tough. Autobiography 1977: *Intermission*.
□Twenty Mule Team 40. The Great Profile 40. Charley's Aunt 41. Swamp Water 41. The Pied Piper 42. *The Magnificent Ambersons* 42. Crash Dive 43. *Five Graves to Cairo* 43. North Star 43. The Sullivans 44. The Eve of St Mark 44. Sunday Dinner for a Soldier 44. *Guest in the House* 45. A Royal Scandal 45. Smoky 46. Angel on My Shoulder 46. *The Razor's Edge* (AA) 46. Blaze of Noon 47. Homecoming 48. The Walls of Jericho 48. The Luck of the Irish 48. Yellow Sky 48. You're My Everything 49. A Ticket to Tomahawk 49. *All About Eve* 50. Follow the Sun 51. The Outcasts of Poker Flat 52. My Wife's Best Friend 52. Full House 52. I Confess 53. The Blue Gardenia 53. Carnival Story 54. Bedevilled 55. One Desire 55. The Spoilers 55. The Come On 56. The Ten Commandments 56. Three Violent People 57. *Chase a Crooked Shadow* 57. Summer of the Seventeenth Doll 60. Mix Me a Person 61. Cimarron 61. A Walk on the Wild Side 62. The Family Jewels 65. Frontier Woman 66. The Busy Body 67. Companions in Nightmare (TV) 67. Stranger on the Run (TV) 68. The Challengers (TV) 68. The Tall Women 68. Marcus Welby MD (TV pilot) 69. Ritual of Evil 69. The Catcher (TV) 71. Fools Parade 71. The Late Liz 71. If Tomorrow Comes

(TV) 71. Lisa Bright and Dark (TV) 72. The Moneychangers (TV) 76. Jane Austen in Manhattan 80. East of Eden (TV) 81.
TV series: Hotel 83–.

Baxter, Beryl (1926–) (Beryl Ivory). British leading lady who was groomed for stardom but starred in only one film, and that notoriously poor: *Idol of Paris* 46.
Subsequently: The Man with the Twisted Lip 51. Counterspy 53.

Baxter, Jane (1909–) (Feodora Forde). Gentle-mannered British actress of stage and screen.
The Constant Nymph 32. The Clairvoyant 34. We Live Again (US) 35. The Ware Case 39. Ships with Wings 41. The Flemish Farm 43. Death of an Angel 51, etc.

Baxter, John (1896–1975). Influential British producer-director of vigorous rough-and-ready dramas and comedies of the thirties and forties which pointed the way to fifties realism and had an amiable style of their own.
Doss House 32. *Song of the Plough* 32. Lest We Forget 34. Music Hall 35. Say It with Flowers 36. Men of Yesterday 37. Crooks Tour 39. *Love on the Dole* 40. *The Common Touch* 41. *Let the People Sing* 42. *When We are Married* 43. The Shipbuilders 45. The Second Mate 50. Judgment Deferred 51. Ramsbottom Rides Again 56, many others including Old Mother Riley and Flanagan & Allen comedies.

Baxter, Les (1922–). American composer. Hot Blood 55. The Black Sheep 56. Macabre 58. Goliath and the Barbarians 59. *House of Usher* 60. The Pit and the Pendulum 61. Panic in Year Zero 62. Tales of Terror 62. *The Raven* 63. The Comedy of Terrors 63. Muscle Beach Party 64. Dr G and the Bikini Machine 65. Wild in the Streets 58. Flare Up 69. The Dunwich Horror 70. Cry of the Banshee 70. Frogs 72. I Escaped from Devil's Island 73, many others.

Baxter, Meredith: see *Birney, Meredith Baxter*.

Baxter, Stanley (1926–). Rubber-faced Scottish comedian and impressionist of stage, screen and TV.
□Geordie 55. *Very Important Person* 61. Crooks Anonymous 62. *The Fast Lady* 63. And Father Came Too 63. Joey Boy 65.

¶ *S.B.:* I'm the best known anonymity in the business.

Baxter, Warner (1889–1951). Distinguished-looking American leading man with stage experience. Popular hero of silent melodrama; survived transition to talkies.
□Her Own Money 14. All Woman 18. Lombardi Ltd. 19. Cheated Hearts 21. First Love 21. The Love Charm 21. Sheltered Daughters 22. If I were Queen 22. The Girl in His Room 22. A Girl's Desire 22. The Ninety and Nine 22. Her Own Money (remake) 22. Blow Your Own Horn 23. In Search of a Thrill 23. St Elmo 23. Alimony 23. Christine of the Hungry Heart 24. The Female 24. The Garden of Weeds 24. His Forgotten Wife 24. Those Who Dance 24. The Golden Bed 25. Air Mail 25. The Awful Truth 25. The Best People 25. Rugged Water 25. A Son of His Father 25. Welcome Home 25. Mannequin 26. Miss Brewster's Millions 26. Mismates 26. Aloma of the South Seas 26. *The Great Gatsby* 26. The Runaway 26. The Telephone Girl 27. The Coward 27. Drums of the Desert 27. Singed 27. Danger Street 28. Three Sinners 28. *Ramona* 28. Craig's Wife 28. The Tragedy of Youth 28. A Woman's Way 28. Linda 29. Far Call 29. Thru Different Eyes 29. Behind that Curtain 29. Romance of the Rio Grande 29. *In Old Arizona* (AA) 29. West of Zanzibar 29. Happy Days 29. The Arizona Kid 30. Renegades 30. Such Men are Dangerous 30. The Cisco Kid 31. The Squaw Man 31. Doctors' Wives 31. Their Mad Moment 31. *Daddy Long Legs* 31. Surrender 31. Six Hours to Live 32. Man About Town 32. Amateur Daddy 32. Paddy the Next Best Thing 33. *42nd Street* 33. Dangerously Yours 34. I Loved You Wednesday 34. Penthouse 34. Stand Up and Cheer 34. *Broadway Bill* 34. As Husbands Go 34. Such Women are Dangerous 34. Grand Canary 35. Hell in the Heavens 35. Under the Pampas Moon 35. *One More Spring* 35. King of Burlesque 35. *Prisoner of Shark Island* 36. *The Road to Glory* 36. To Mary with Love 36. White Hunter 36. Robin Hood of El Dorado 36. Slave Ship 37. Vogues of 1938 37. Wife Doctor and Nurse 37. Kidnapped 38. I'll Give a Million 38. Wife Husband and Friend 39. Barricade 39. The Return of the Cisco Kid 39. Earthbound 40. Adam Had Four Sons 41. Crime Doctor 43. The Crime Doctor's Strangest Case 43. Lady in the Dark 44. Shadows in the Night 44. The Crime Doctor's Courage 45. The Crime Doctor's Warning 45. Just Before Dawn 46. The Crime Doctor's Man Hunt 46. The Millerson Case 47. The Crime Doctor's Gamble 47. A Gentleman from Nowhere 48. Prison Warden 49. The

Devil's Henchman 49. The Crime Doctor's Diary 49. State Penitentiary 50.

Baye, Nathalie (1948–). French leading actress.
Day for Night 73. The Green Room 78. A Girl from Lorraine 80. La Balance 82. The Return of Martin Guerre 82.

Bayes, Nora (1880–1928) (Dora Goldberg). American vaudeville singer, impersonated by Ann Sheridan in the biopic *Shine On Harvest Moon* 44.

Bayldon, Geoffrey (1924–). Lanky British character actor with a penchant for absent-minded or eccentric types.
The Stranger Left No Card 53. Dracula 58. Libel 60. The Webster Boy 62. A Jolly Bad Fellow 64. King Rat 65. *Sky West and Crooked* 65. *To Sir With Love* 66. Casino Royale 67. Otley 69. The Raging Moon 70. Scrooge 71. Asylum 72. Bullshot 83, etc.

Bayne, Beverly (1894–1982) (Pearl von Name). American silent screen star, especially when married to Francis X. Bushman.
Graustark 15. A Virginia Romance 16. Romeo and Juliet 16. The Voice of Conscience 17. The Age of Innocence 24. Eve's Loves 25, etc.

Bazin, André (1918–1958). French critic who wrote books on Welles, de Sica and Renoir: 'the spiritual father of the New Wave'. Founded 'Cahiers du Cinema'.

Bazlen, Brigid (1944–). Israeli leading lady of a few international films.
King of Kings (as Salome) 61. The Honeymoon Machine 61. How the West Was Won 62.

Beacham, Stephanie (1949–). British leading lady.
The Games 69. The Nightcomers 71. Dracula A.D. 1972 72. House of Whipcord 76. Schizo 77. Inseminoid 80, etc.
TV series: Tenko 82. Sorrell and Son 84. Connie 85. The Colbys 85. Napoleon and Josephine 87.

Beal, John (1909–) (Alexander Bliedung). American stage actor whose look of boyish innocence was useful in the thirties but tended to hamper him subsequently.
Another Language 33. Hat Coat and Glove 34. *The Little Minister* 34. Les Misérables 35. *Laddie* 35. Break of Hearts 35. The Man Who Found Himself 37. Double Wedding 37. Port of Seven Seas 38. I Am The Law 38. *The Cat and the Canary* 39. Ellery Queen and the Perfect Crime 41. The Great Commandment 42. Edge of Darkness 43. Key Witness 47. Alimony 49. My Six Convicts 52. Remains to Be Seen 53. That Night 57. The Vampire 57. Ten Who Dared 61. Amityville 3D 83, etc.
TV series: Another World 64. The Adams Chronicles 67.

Beals, Jennifer (–). American leading lady.
Flashdance (in which she did *not* do the dancing) 83. The Bride 85.

Bean, Judge Roy (1823–1902). American Western badman, a self-appointed lawmaker who kept himself in whisky from his fines. Played by Walter Brennan in *The Westerner* 40; by Edgar Buchanan in a TV series, *Judge Roy Bean* 50; and by Paul Newman in a 1972 movie *The Life and Times of Judge Roy Bean*.

The Beatles. This Liverpudlian pop group achieved astonishing popularity in the early sixties, but the pressures of success caused a split and the members went their rich but somewhat malcontented ways. They were *John Lennon* (1940–1980), *George Harrison* (1943–), *Paul McCartney* (1942–) and *Ringo Starr* (Richard Starkey) (1940–).
Films together: *A Hard Day's Night* 64. Help! 65. Let It Be 70. They also lent their music and cartoon images to *Yellow Submarine* 67 and a subsequent TV series.
Separately, Lennon was in *How I Won The War* 67; Starr in *Candy* 68, *The Magic Christian* 70, *That'll Be the Day* 73, *Caveman* 81.

¶ 'I see the Beatles have arrived from England. They were forty pounds overweight, and that was just their hair.'—*Bob Hope 1964*.

Beaton, Sir Cecil (1902–1980). British photographer and designer who advised on many films, his greatest achievements probably being *Gigi* 58 and *My Fair Lady* 64.

Beatty, Clyde (1903–1965). American animal trainer and circus owner who made a few film appearances.
□The Big Cage 33. The Lost Jungle 34. Darkest Africa 36. Africa Screams 49. Ring of Fear 54.

Beatty, Ned (1937–). Chubby American character actor.

□Deliverance 72. The Life and Times of Judge Roy Bean 72. Footsteps (TV) 72. The Thief Who Came to Dinner 73. White Lightning 73. The Marcus-Nelson Murders (TV) 73. Dying Room Only (TV) 73. The Execution of Private Slovik (TV) 74. The Last American Hero 74. Attack on Terror (TV) 75. The Deadly Tower (TV) 75. W.W. and the Dixie Dancekings 75. Nashville 75. All The President's Men 76. Network 76. Silver Streak 76. The Big Bus 76. Mikey and Nicky 76. Alambrista 77. Tail Gunner Joe (TV) 77. Lucan (TV) 77. Exorcist II 77. Shenanigans 77. Gray Lady Down 78. Superman 78. A Question of Love 78. Promises in the Dark 79. Wise Blood 79. *Friendly Fire* (TV) 79. 1941 79. Success 79. Guyana Tragedy (TV) 80. Hopscotch 80. The Incredible Shrinking Woman 81. Superman 2 81. The Toy 82. A Woman Called Golda (TV) 82. Stroker Ace 83. Touched 83. Restless Natives 84. Back to School 86. The Big Easy 86. The Fourth Protocol 87.

Beatty, Robert (1909–). Rugged, good-humoured Canadian leading man long resident in Britain.
San Demetrio, London 43. Appointment with Crime 46. *Odd Man Out* 46. *Against the Wind* 47. Counterblast 48. Another Shore 53. Captain Horatio Hornblower R.N. 51. The Square Ring 53. *Albert R.N.* 53. The Gentle Gunman 53. Tarzan and the Lost Safari 57. Something of Value 57. The Shakedown 59. The Amorous Prawn 62. 2001: A Space Odyssey 68. Where Eagles Dare 69. Man at the Top 73. Golden Rendezvous 77. The Spaceman and King Arthur 79. The Amateur 81. Superman III 83. Meeting at Reykjavik (TV) (as Ronald Reagan) 87, etc.
TV series: *Dial 999* 57–58.

Beatty, Warren (1937–) (Warren Beaty). Unruly American leading actor of the post-Brando school, with a flair for psychological maladjustment. Brother of Shirley Maclaine.
□*Splendour in the Grass* 61. The Roman Spring of Mrs Stone 61. *All Fall Down* 62. *Lilith* 65. *Mickey One* 65. Promise Her Anything 66. Kaleidoscope 66. *Bonnie and Clyde* (& p) 67. The Only Game in Town 69. McCabe and Mrs Miller 71. Dollars 72. The Parallax View 74. *Shampoo* (& p, co-w) 75. The Fortune 75. *Heaven Can Wait* (& p, w, co-d) 78. *Reds* (& p, d, co-w) (AA as director) 81. Ishtar 87.
TV series: The Many Loves of Dobie Gillis 55–59.

¶ I'm old, I'm young, I'm intelligent, I'm stupid. My tide goes in and out.—*W.B.*
Movies are fun, but they're not a cure for cancer.—*W.B.*

'Warren has an interesting psychology. He has always fallen in love with girls who have just won, or just been nominated for, an Oscar.' . . . 'Anyone who comes close to him loses a few feathers. He tends to maul you.'—*Leslie Caron*

'He was insatiable. Three, four, five times a day was not unusual for him, and he was able to accept telephone calls at the same time.'—*Joan Collins*

Beau Geste. P. C. Wren's romantic novel of a missing gem, a debt of honour, and savagery in the Foreign Legion, was filmed in 1926 with Ronald Colman as Beau and Noah Beery as the sadistic sergeant. The 1939 version had Gary Cooper and Brian Donlevy; 1966 saw Guy Stockwell and Telly Savalas in the roles (and much of the plot missing).

Le Beau Serge (France 1958). Sometimes claimed as the first 'nouvelle vague' film, this is a quiet, unsensational story about a young man who returns to his native village and tries to help an unhappy friend. Director: Claude Chabrol.

Beaudine, William (1892–1970). Prolific American director of silent family films and, later second features.
Penrod and Sam 23. Little Annie Rooney 25. *Sparrows* 26. The Life of Riley 27. The Cohens and Kellys in Paris 28. Home James 28. The Girl from Woolworth's 29. The Lady Who Dared 31. *Penrod and Sam* 31. Three Wise Girls 32. The Crime of the Century 33. The Old Fashioned Way 34. Hey Hey USA (in Britain) 36. Says O'Reilly to Macnab (in Britain) 37. Torchy Gets Her Man 38. Torchy Blane in Chinatown 39. Broadway Big Shot 42. The Mystery of the 13th Guest 53. Black Market Babies 46. Kidnapped 48. Blue Grass of Kentucky 50. Westward Ho the Wagons 56. Lassie's Greatest Adventure 63. Billy the Kid versus Dracula 66, etc.

Beaumont, Charles (1929–1967). American writer, chiefly of science fiction.
Queen of Outer Space 58. The Intruder 61. Night of the Eagle 62. The Haunted Palace 63. Seven Faces of Dr Lao 64. Mister Moses 65, etc.

Beaumont, Harry (1888–1966). American director, at his peak in the twenties.
A Man and His Money 19. Lord and Lady

Algy 19. *Main Street* 23. *Beau Brummell* 24. *Babbitt* 24. The Lover of Camille 24. *His Majesty Bunker Bean* 25. *Our Dancing Daughters* 28. *Broadway Melody* 29. Lord Byron of Broadway 30. The Florodora Girl 30. Our Blushing Brides 30. Dance Fools Dance 31. Faithless 32. *When Ladies Meet* 33. Enchanted April 35. The Girl on the Front Page 36. When's Your Birthday? 37. Maisie Goes to Reno 44. Twice Blessed 45. The Show-off 47, many others.

Beaumont, Hugh (1909–82). American second lead and second feature hero.
Flight Lieutenant 42. The Seventh Victim 43. Objective Burma 45. The Blue Dahlia 46. Bury Me Dead 47. Railroaded 49. Mr Belvedere Rings the Bell 52. Mississippi Gambler 53. The Mole People 57. The Human Duplicators 65, etc.
TV series: Leave It To Beaver 57–62.

Beaumont, Susan (1936–) (Susan Black). British leading lady of a few fifties films.
Jumping for Joy 55. High Tide at Noon 57. Innocent Sinners 58. Carry On Nurse 59. Web of Suspicion 59, etc.

Beavers, Louise (1902–1962). Black American actress who played innumerable happy housekeepers.
Coquette 29. Girls About Town 32. What Price Hollywood 32. She Done Him Wrong 33. *Imitation of Life* (her best role) 35. Rainbow on the River 36. The Last Gangster 37. Made For Each Other 39. No Time for Comedy 40. Reap the Wild Wind 42. Dubarry was a Lady 43. Delightfully Dangerous 46. *Mr Blandings Builds His Dream House* 48. My Blue Heaven 50. Teenage Rebel 56. The Goddess 58. The Facts of Life 61, many others.
TV series: *Beulah* 50.
Famous line (in *Mr Blandings*): 'If you ain't eatin' Wham, you ain't eatin' ham!'

Beck, John (1943–). American leading man of the seventies.
The Silent Gun (TV) 69. Lawman 71. The Unexpected Mrs Pollifax 72. Pat Garrett and Billy the Kid 73. Sidekicks (TV) 74. The Law (TV) 74. The Call of the Wild (TV) 76. The Big Bus 76. Sky Riders 76. Audrey Rose 77. The Other Side of Midnight 77. Wheels (TV) 78. The Time Machine (TV) 78.
TV series: Flamingo Road 80–81. Dallas 81–85.

Beck, Michael (1948–). American leading man.
Holocaust (TV) 77. Mayflower (TV) 78. The Warriors 79. Xanadu 80. Alcatraz (TV) 81. Triumphs of a Man Called Horse 84. Rear View Mirror (TV) 84. Blackout 85.

Becker, Harold (–). American director.
The Onion Field 79. The Black Marble 80. Taps 81.

Becker, Jacques (1906–1960). French director, mainly of civilized comedies.
Goupi Mains Rouges 42. Falbalas 44. *Antoine et Antoinette* 47. Rendezvous de Juillet 49. *Edouard et Caroline* 50. *Casque d'Or* 51. Rue de l'Estrapade 52. *Touchez Pas au Grisbi* 53. Ali Baba 55. The Adventures of Arsène Lupin 56. Montparnasse Nineteen 57. The Hole 60, etc.

Becker, Jean (1933–). French director, son of Jacques Becker.
Echappement Libre 62. Pas de Caviar pour Tante Olga 64. Tendre Voyou 66, etc.

Becket (GB 1964). Based on Jean Anouilh's witty if unhistorical play, this was producer Hal Wallis' first bid for prestige and led to the 'intellectual' block-busters of the later sixties. An interesting but unsatisfactory hybrid, its box office success was helped by Richard Burton and Peter O'Toole but not by Peter Glenville's stodgy direction.

Beckett, Scotty (1929–1968). Soulful-looking American child actor of the thirties and forties; one-time member of 'Our Gang'.
Whom the Gods Destroy 34. Dante's Inferno 35. The Charge of the Light Brigade 36. Marie Walewska 38. *The Bluebird* 40. *King's Row* 42. The Youngest Profession 43. *Ali Baba and the Forty Thieves* 43. Junior Miss 45. *The Jolson Story* (as young Jolson) 46. A Date with Judy 48. Battleground 49. Corky 51. Three for Jamie Dawn 56, many others.

Beckinsale, Richard (1947–1979). British comedy leading man, in several TV series.
Three for All 74. Porridge 79.

Beckley, Tony (1928–1980). British actor, often seen as young thug.
The Penthouse 67. Chimes at Midnight 67. The Long Day's Dying 68. The Lost Continent 68. Get Carter 71. Sitting Target 72. Gold 74. The Return of the Pink Panther 74. Diagnosis Murder 75. Revenge of the Pink Panther 78. When a Stranger Calls 79, etc.

Beckwith, Reginald (1908–1965). Chubby British character actor, whose high voice and impeccable timing were a constant delight. Also wrote successful plays, e.g. *Boys in Brown, A Soldier for Christmas*.
Voice in the Night 41. *Scott of the Antarctic* 48. Another Man's Poison 51. Mr Drake's Duck 52. *Genevieve* 53. *The Runaway Bus* 54. Dance Little Lady 55. *The Captain's Table* 58. The Thirty-nine Steps 59. Double Bunk 61. The Password is Courage 62. Never Put It in Writing 64. A Shot in the Dark 64. Mister Moses 65, many others.

Becky Sharp (US 1935). The first full-length feature in three-colour Technicolor, this version of *Vanity Fair* seems now only a pleasantly-photographed stage play, and director Rouben Mamoulian's experiments in colour are difficult to assess in the prints now available. Miriam Hopkins made a fair shot at the title role, and Cedric Hardwicke was excellent as the Marquis of Steyne. Ray Rennahan was cinematographer.

Beddoe, Don (1888–1979). American character actor with genial, sometimes startled, look; in hundreds of films, often as sheriff, reporter, or cop.
Golden Boy 39. *The Face behind the Mask* 41. Talk of the Town 42. Crime Inc. 45. O.S.S. 46. The Best Years of Our Lives 46. The Farmer's Daughter 47. Dancing in the Dark 49. Carrie 51. Night of the Hunter 55. *Saintly Sinners* (lead role) 61. *Jack the Giant Killer* (as a leprechaun) 62. Texas Across the River 66. The Impossible Years 68. Generation 69. How Do I Love Thee 70, many others.

Bedelia, Bonnie (1946–). American leading lady.
The Gypsy Moths 69. They Shoot Horses Don't They? 70. *Lovers and Other Strangers* 70. The Strange Vengeance of Rosalie 72. Hawkins on Murder (TV) 73. The Big Fix 78. Heart Like a Wheel 83. Between Friends (TV) 83, etc.

Bedford, Brian (1935–). British stage actor who has been in a few films.
Miracle in Soho 58. The Angry Silence 59. The Punch and Judy Man 63. The Pad 66. Grand Prix 67. Robin Hood (voice) 73, etc.
TV series: Coronet Blue 67.

Bedi, Kabir (1945–). Stalwart Indian leading man of the late seventies.
Swashbuckler 76. The Thief of Baghdad (TV) 78. Ashanti 78. Octopussy 83, etc.
TV series: Sandokan the Great 76.

Bedoya, Alfonso (1904–1957). Mexican character actor whose beaming face could provide comedy or menace.
The Treasure of the Sierra Madre (as the bandit) 47. The Pearl 48. Streets of Laredo 49. The Black Rose 50. Sombrero 52. California Conquest 52. The Stranger Wore a Gun 53. Ten Wanted Men 55. *The Big Country* 57, etc.

Beebe, Ford (1888–). American director of low-budget westerns, second features and serials . . . over 200 of them from 1916.
Laughing at Life 33. *Flash Gordon's Trip to Mars* 38. *Riders of Death Valley* 41. Night Monster 42. The Invisible Man's Revenge 44. Enter Arsène Lupin 44. Bomba the Jungle Boy 49, etc.

Beecher, Janet (1884–1955) (J. B. Meysenburg). American character actress usually seen in ladylike roles. Retired 1943.
Gallant Lady 33. The President Vanishes 34. The Mighty Barnum 34. The Dark Angel 35. Love Before Breakfast 36. The Thirteenth Chair 37. Rosalie 37. Judge Hardy's Children 38. Yellow Jack 38. Man of Conquest 39. The Mark of Zorro 40. Bitter Sweet 40. The Lady Eve 41. Silver Queen 42. Reap the Wild Wind 42. Mrs Wiggs of the Cabbage Patch 42. Henry Aldrich Gets Glamour 43, many others.

The Beegees. Three British brothers who as pop singers challenged the record of the Beatles and had an even more extravagant life style. A succession of hits culminated in their original score for *Saturday Night Fever*, which put them in the multi-millionaire category. They are Barry (born Douglas) (1947–), Maurice and Robin (both born 1949).

Beery, Noah (1884–1946). American character actor, half-brother of Wallace Beery and one of the silent screen's most celebrated villains.
The Mormon Maid 18. *The Mark of Zorro* 20. The Sea Wolf 20. Tol'able David 21. The Spoilers 22. The Coming of Amos 25. Beau Geste 26. *Don Juan* 26. Beau Sabreur 27. The Four Feathers 29. Noah's Ark 29. Tol'able David 30. The Drifter 31. Out of Singapore 32. She Done Him Wrong 33. King of the Damned (GB) 35. Our Fighting Navy (GB) 37. The Girl of the Golden West 38. Isle of Missing Men 42. This Man's Navy 45, many others.

Beery, Noah Jnr (1913–). American character actor, son of Noah Beery. Started as child actor, and later played easy-going country cousins.
The Mark of Zorro 20. Heroes of the West 26. Father and Son 29. Jungle Madness 31. The Road Back 37. Only Angels Have Wings 39. Of Mice and Men 40. Riders of Death Valley 41. Prairie Chickens 43. Gung Ho 44. Red River 48. Rocketship XM 50. White Feather 55. Inherit the Wind 60. The Seven Faces of Dr Lao 64. Incident at Phantom Hill 65. Little Fauss and Big Halsy 70. Walking Tall 73. The Best Little Whorehouse in Texas 82, many others.
TV series: Circus Boy 56–57. Custer 67. Doc Elliot 74. The Rockford Files 74–80. The Quest 83.

Beery, Wallace (1880/86–1949). American character star with circus and musical comedy experience, long under contract to MGM. Started as a grotesque female impersonator and tried every kind of part before acquiring his best remembered persona: tough, ugly, slow-thinking and easy going. Half-brother of Noah Beery.
SELECTED SILENT FILMS: Teddy at the Throttle 16. The Unpardonable Sin 19. The Virgin of Stamboul 20. The Last of the Mohicans 21. *Robin Hood* (as King Richard) 22. *Richard the Lion-Hearted* 23. The Sea Hawk 24. So Big 24. *The Lost World* (as Professor Challenger) 25. The Wanderer 25. Volcano 26. We're in the Navy Now 26. Casey at the Bat 27. Fireman Save My Child 27. Partners of Crime 28. Beggars of Life 28, many others.
□SOUND FILMS: Chinatown Nights 29. River of Romance 29. *The Big House* 30. Way for a Sailor 30. Billy the Kid 30. A Lady's Morals 30. *Min and Bill* 30. The Secret Six 31. Hell Divers 31. *The Champ* (AA) 31. *Grand Hotel* 32. Flesh 32. *Dinner at Eight* 33. *Tugboat Annie* 33. *The Bowery* 33. *Viva Villa* 34. *Treasure Island* (as Long John Silver) 34. *The Mighty Barnum* 34. West Point of the Air 35. China Seas 35. O' Shaughnessy's Boy 35. *Ah Wilderness* 35. A Message to Garcia 36. Old Hutch 36. Good Old Soak 37. *Slave Ship* 37. Bad Man of Brimstone 38. Port of Seven Seas 38. Stablemates 38. Sergeant Madden 39. *Stand Up and Fight* 39. Thunder Afloat 39. The Man from Dakota 40. Twenty Mule Team 40. Wyoming 40. Barnacle Bill 41. The Bad Man 41. The Bugle Sounds 42. Jackass Mail 42. Salute to the Marines 43. Rationing 44. *Barbary Coast Gent* 44. This Man's Navy 45. Bad Bascomb 46. The Mighty McGurk 47. A Date with Judy 48. Alias a Gentleman 48. Big Jack 49.

¶ *W.B.:* I never let anyone sucker me, not even for a nickel.
'He always made me feel uncomfortable.'—*Jackie Cooper*
W.B.: Like my dear old friend Marie Dressler, my ugly mug has been my fortune.

Beeson, Paul (1921–). British cinematographer.
Dunkirk 58. Greyfriars Bobby 61. In Search of the Castaways 62. The Moonspinners 64. To Sir with Love 66. Moon Zero Two 69. Kidnapped 70. Jane Eyre 71. A Warm December 73. The Mutations 74. One of our Dinosaurs is Missing 75. Escape from the Dark 76. Candleshoe 77. The Spaceman and King Arthur 79. Silver Dream Racer 80. Hawk the Slayer 80. Raiders of the Lost Ark 81. Never Say Never Again 83. Indiana Jones and the Temple of Doom 84. Santa Claus 85, etc.

Beethoven, Ludwig van (1770–1827). German classical composer who in view of his total deafness and unattractive physique has been surprisingly frequently portrayed in movies: by Harry Baur in *Beethoven* 36; Albert Basserman in *New Wine* 41; Rene Deltgen in *Whom the Gods Love* 41; and Karl Boehm in *The Magnificent Rebel* 60.

The Beggar's Opera. Several attempts have been made to film John Gay's 18th-century operetta of the London underworld. 1. *Die Dreigroschenoper* (Germany 1931) starred Rudolph Forster as Macheath and had music by Kurt Weill. (French version, with Albert Préjean, known as *L'Opéra de Quat' Sous.*) 2. *The Beggar's Opera* (GB 1982) was a straight version with Laurence Olivier, directed by Peter Brook. 3. *The Threepenny Opera* (Germany/US 1965) starred Curt Jurgens and Sammy Davis Jnr, directed by Wolfgang Staudte.

Begley, Ed (1901–1970). Blustery American character actor with radio and stage experience; usually seen as jovial uncle or man at the end of his tether.
□Big Town 47. Boomerang 47. Deep Waters 48. Sitting Pretty 48. The Street with No Name 48. Sorry Wrong Number 48. Tulsa 49. It Happens Every Spring 49. The Great Gatsby 49. Backfire 50. Stars in my Crown 50. Wyoming Mail 50. Convicted 50. Saddle Tramp 50. Dark City 50. Lady from Texas 51. On Dangerous Ground 51. You're In the Navy Now 51. Deadline 52. Boots Malone 52. The Turning Point 52. What Price Glory 52. Lone Star 52. *Patterns* 56. *Twelve Angry Men*

57. *Odds Against Tomorrow* 59. The Green Helmet 61. *Sweet Bird of Youth* (AA) 62. The Unsinkable Molly Brown 64. The Oscar 66. Warning Shot 66. *Billion Dollar Brain* 67. Firecreek 67. Wild in the Streets 68. Hang 'Em High 68. The Violent Enemy 69. The Silent Gun (TV) 69. The Dunwich Horror 69. The Road to Salina 71.
TV series: Leave It to Larry 52.

Begley, Ed Jnr (–). American character actor.
Now You See Him Now You Don't 72. Cockfighter 74. Stay Hungry 76. Blue Collar 78. The Concorde—Airport 79 79. This is Spinal Tap 80. The In-Laws 81. Young Doctors in Love 82. Protocol 84. Streets of Fire 85, etc.
TV series: St Elsewhere 81–

Behan, Brendan (1923–1964). Irish dramatist whose flamboyant behaviour often hit the headlines in the fifties; his only play to be filmed was *The Quare Fellow*.

Behrman, S. N. (1893–1973). American playwright and screenwriter.
He Knew Women (oa) 30. *Queen Christina* 33. Cavalcade 33. *Anna Karenina* 35. Biography of a Bachelor Girl (oa) 35. A Tale of Two Cities 35. Parnell 37. Conquest 37. *No Time for Comedy* (oa) 40. Waterloo Bridge 40. Two-faced Woman 41. The Pirate (oa) 48. Quo Vadis 51. *Me and the Colonel* (& oa) 56, etc.

Beich, Albert (1919–). American radio and film writer.
Girls in Chains 44. The Perils of Pauline 47. The Bride Goes Wild 48. Key to the City 50. The Lieutenant Wore Skirts 55. Dead Ringer 64, etc.

Being There (US 1979). An overrated parable in which Peter Sellers gave his last noteworthy performance as a simpleton whose pronouncements were thought so profound as to take him into the higher levels of politics. The message, which could also be aimed at the film itself, was caviare to the general. Written by Jerzy Kosinski, from his novel; directed by Hal Ashby; with Melvyn Douglas (AA), Shirley Maclaine, Jack Warden; for Lorimar.

Bekassy, Stephen (c.1915–). Hungarian stage actor who came to Hollywood in the forties.
A Song to Remember (as Liszt) 45. Arch of Triumph 48. Black Magic 49. Fair Wind to Java 53. Hell and High Water 54. Interrupted Melody 55. The Light in the Forest 58. Bachelor Flat 61. The Four Horsemen of the Apocalypse 62, etc.

Bel Geddes, Barbara (1922–) (Barbara Geddes Lewis). American stage actress who makes occasional films, usually as nice placid girls.
□The Gangster 47. The Long Night 47. *I Remember Mama* 48. Blood on the Moon 48. Caught 49. Panic in the Streets 50. *Fourteen Hours* 51. Vertigo 58. The Five Pennies 59. Five Branded Women 60. By Love Possessed 61. The Todd Killings 70. Summertree 71.
TV series: Dallas 78–.

Belafonte, Harry (1927–). Handsome black American ballad singer who has acted strikingly in several films.
□Bright Road 53. *Carmen Jones* 54. *Island in the Sun* 57. The World the Flesh and the Devil 59. *Odds Against Tomorrow* 59. The Angel Levine 70. Buck and the Preacher 72. Uptown Saturday Night 74.

Belasco, Leon (1902–). Wiry Russian-born small-part player of excitable balletmasters, head waiters, landlords, etc.
The Best People (debut) 26. Topper Takes a Trip 39. The Mummy's Hand 40. Nothing But the Truth 41. Pin-up Girl 44. The New Adventures of Don Juan 48. Call Me Madam 53, many others.
TV series: My Sister Eileen.

Belita (1924–) (Gladys Jepson-Turner). British ice-skating and dancing star who made a few Hollywood films.
Ice Capades 41. Silver Skates 43. Suspense 46. The Hunted 47. Never Let Me Go 53. Invitation to the Dance 56. Silk Stockings 57, etc.

Bell, Ann (–). British character actress who was always welcome but never reached the top.
Flat Two 62. Dr Terror's House of Horrors 64. To Sir with Love 66. The Witches 66. The Shuttered Room 66. The Reckoning 69. The Statue 70. Spectre (TV) 77. Very Like a Whale (TV) 80, etc.

Bell, James (1891–1973). American character actor, usually in benevolent roles.
I Am a Fugitive from a Chain Gang 32. White Woman 33. I Walked with a Zombie 42. The Spiral Staircase 45. Brute Force 47.

The Violent Hour 50. The Glenn Miller Story 54. The Lonely Man 57. Twilight of Honor 63, many others.

Bell, Marie (1900–85) (Marie-Jeanne Bellon-Downey). Distinguished French actress who appeared in a few well-remembered films. Madame Recamier 28. *Le Grand Jeu* 34. La Garçonne 35. *Carnet de Bal* 37. La Charrette Fantôme 40. Colonel Chabert 43. La Bonne Soupe 64. Hotel Paradiso 66, etc.

Bell, Monta (1891–1958). American director whose peak was in the twenties.
A Woman of Paris (co-d) 23. Broadway after Dark 24. The Snob 24. The King on Main Street 27. *Torrent* 26. After Midnight (& w) 27. Man Woman and Sin (& w) 27. The Bellamy Trial 29. East is West 30. Men in White 33. West Point of the Air 35. China's Little Devils 45, etc.

Bell, Rex (1905–1962) (George F. Beldam). American cowboy star of the thirties: left Hollywood to become Lieut.-Governor of Nevada. Married Clara Bow.
Pleasure Crazed 29. True to the Navy 30. Lightnin' 30. Tombstone 42, many others.

Bell, Tom (1933–). Gaunt British leading man of the sixties.
The Kitchen 61. *Payroll* 61. HMS Defiant 62. *The L-Shaped Room* 62. A Prize of Arms 63. Ballad in Blue 65. *He Who Rides a Tiger* 66. The Long Day's Dying 68. In Enemy Country (US) 68. Lock Up Your Daughters 69. *All the Right Noises* 69. Quest for Love 71. The Spy's Wife 71. Royal Flash 75. Holocaust (TV) 78. Wish You Were Here 87, etc.
TV series: *Out* 78.

Bellah, James Warner (1899–1976). American screenwriter, mainly on historical themes; former war correspondent.
Fort Apache 48. She Wore a Yellow Ribbon 49. Rio Grande 50. Rio Bravo 55. The Sea Chase (co-w) 55. Sergeant Rutledge 59. A Thunder of Drums 61. The Man Who Shot Liberty Valance (co-w) 62, etc.

Bellamy, Earl (1917–). Routine American director, much involved in TV series.
Blackjack Ketchum, Desperado 56. Fluffy 65. Gunpoint 65. Incident at Phantom Hill 66. Seven Alone 74. Part Two Walking Tall 75. Sidewinder One 77, etc.

Bellamy, Madge (1903–) (Margaret Philpott). American general purpose actress of the twenties.
Lorna Doone 23. Bertha the Sewing Machine Girl 27. Mother Knows Best 28, etc.

Bellamy, Ralph (1904–). Soft-voiced, serious-looking American leading man of stage and screen who in the thirties became typecast as the simple-minded rich man who never got the girl. In fact he played most kinds of parts, including detectives and villains, and later became a highly respected stage actor.
□The Secret Six 31. The Magnificent Lie 31. Surrender 31. Forbidden 32. West of Broadway 32. Disorderly Conduct 32. Young America 32. Rebecca of Sunnybrook Farm 32. The Woman in Room 13 32. Wild Girl 32. Air Mail 32. Almost Married 32. Second Hand Wife 32. Parole Girl 33. Destination Unknown 33. Picture Snatcher 33. Narrow Corner 33. Below the Sea 33. Headline Shooters 33. Flying Devils 33. Blind Adventure 33. Ace of Aces 33. Ever in My Heart 33. Spitfire 34. This Man Is Mine 34. Once to Every Woman 34. One Is Guilty 34. Before Midnight 34. The Crime of Helen Stanley 34. Girl in Danger 34. Woman in the Dark 34. Helldorado 35. The Wedding Night 35. Rendezvous at Midnight 35. Air Hawks 35. Eight Bells 35. The Healer 35. Gigolette 35. Navy Wife 35. Hands Across the Table 35. Dangerous Intrigue 36. The Final Hour 36. Roaming Lady 36. Straight from the Shoulder 36. Wild Brian Kent 36. Counterfeit Lady 37. The Man Who Lived Twice 37. *The Awful Truth* (in which his 'other man' stereotype was sealed) 37. Let's Get Married 37. The Crime of Dr Hallet 38. Fools for Scandal 38. Boy Meets Girl 38. Carefree 38. Girls' School 38. Trade Winds 38. Let Us Live 38. *Blind Alley* 39. Smashing the Spy Ring 39. Coast Guard 39. *His Girl Friday* (in which the Ralph Bellamy type was amiably mocked) 40. Flight Angels 40. Brother Orchid 40. Queen of the Mob 40. Dance Girl Dance 40. Public Deb Number One 40. Ellery Queen Master Detective (title role) 40. Meet the Wildcat 40. Ellery Queen's Penthouse Mystery 41. Footsteps in the Dark 41. Affectionately Yours 41. Ellery Queen and the Perfect Crime 41. Dive Bomber 41. Ellery Queen and the Murder Ring 41. The Wolf Man 41. The Ghost of Frankenstein 42. Lady in a Jam 42. Men of Texas 42. The Great Impersonation 42. Stage Door Canteen 43. Guest in the House 44. Delightfully Dangerous 45. Lady on a Train 45. The Court Martial of Billy Mitchell 55. *Sunrise at Campobello* (as FDR) 60. The Professionals 66. Rosemary's Baby 68. Wings of Fire (TV) 68. The Immortal (TV) 69. Doctors' Wives

71. Cancel My Reservation 72. Something Evil (TV) 72. The Log of the Black Pearl (TV) 75. Adventures of the Queen (TV) 75. Search for the Gods (TV) 75. Murder on Flight 502 (TV) 75. McNaughton's Daughter (TV) 76. Nightmare in Badham County (TV) 76. The Boy in the Plastic Bubble (TV) 76. Once an Eagle (TV) 76. The Moneychangers (TV) 76. Testimony of Two Men (TV) 77. Charlie Cobb: Nice Night for a Hanging (TV) 77. Westside Medical (TV) 77. Oh God 77. Wheels (TV) 78. The Clone Master (TV) 78. The Millionaire (TV) 78. Billion Dollar Threat (TV) 79. Condominium (TV) 79. Power (TV) 79. The Memory of Eva Ryker (TV) 83. *The Winds of War* (TV) 83. *Trading Places* 83. Space (TV) 85. Disorderlies 87.
TV series: Man Against Crime 49–53. The Eleventh Hour 64. The Survivors 69. The Most Deadly Game 69. Hunter 77.
❁ For solid service and the occasional gleam of brilliance.

Bellaver, Harry (1905–). American character actor, often seen as cop, small-time gangster or cabby.
Another Thin Man 40. The House on 92nd Street 45. No Way Out 50. The Lemon Drop Kid 51. From Here to Eternity 53. Love Me or Leave Me 55. Serenade 56. Slaughter on Tenth Avenue 57. The Old Man and the Sea 58. One Potato Two Potato 64. A Fine Madness 66. Madigan 67. God Told Me To 76. Demon 77. Blue Collar 78. Hero at Large 80, etc.
TV series: *Naked City* 58-62.

Belle de Jour (France/Italy 1967). Luis Buñuel's brilliant study of a married woman who works off her frustrations at a brothel was much more than that bald summary might make it appear: a penetrating analysis of our society and a fascinating though sometimes confusing blend of fancy and reality. With Catherine Deneuve, Jean Sorel.

La Belle et la Bête (France 1946). Jean Cocteau wrote and directed this highly imaginative film version of Perrault's eighteenth-century fairy tale. There are few plot surprises, but Christian Bérard's decor is uniquely beautiful, Henri Alekan's photography conveys exactly the right sense of mystic trickery, and the taste and charm of the whole enterprise is impeccable. Josette Day and Jean Marais play the title roles. The theme has of course been used in a wide variety of films, including *King Kong*.

Beller, Kathleen (1955–). American leading lady.
Godfather II 74. The Betsy 78. Mary White (TV) 79. Something for Joey (TV) 80. Are You in the House Alone? (TV) 82. Touched by Love 83.

Les Belles de Nuit (France/Italy 1952). A lighter-than-air confection by René Clair from a script by himself, Pierre Barillet and Jean-Paul Gredy, about a young music teacher who dreams himself back into a romantic view of history and finds his adventures becoming true when he wakes. A most agreeable, well acted, delicately pointed and civilized entertainment.

Bellocchio, Marco (1939–). Italian director.
Fists in the Pocket 65. China is Near 67. In the Name of the Father 71. Triumphal March 76. Les Yeux Fertiles 77. Salto nel Vuoto 79. Henry IV 84. Devil in the Flesh 85.

Belmondo, Jean-Paul (1933–). Interesting but unhandsome French leading actor.
Dimanche . . . Nous Volerons 56. Les Tricheurs 58. Un Drôle de Dimanche 58. Sois Belle et Tais-Toi 58. A Double Tour 59. *A Bout de Souffle* 59. Moderato Cantabile 60. La Viaccia 60. Leon Morin, Priest 61. Two Women 61. Cartouche 62. *Un Singe en Hiver* 62. Cent Milles Dollars au Soleil 63. *That Man from Rio* 64. Weekend in Dunkirk 65. Pierrot le Fou 65. Les Tribulations d'un Chinoise en Chine 65. Is Paris Burning? 66. Tendre Voyou 66. Le Voleur 67. The Brain 68. Ho! 68. The Mississippi Mermaid 69. A Man I Like 69. Le Casse 71. Scoundrel in White 72. Le Magnifique 73. Stavisky 74. The Night Caller 75. L'Alpageur 76. Le Corps de Mon Ennemi 76. L'Animal 77. Le Guignolo 80. Le Marginal 83. Vultures 83. Hold-Up 85, etc.

¶ 'New blood, new looks, new vitality, new fluidism, new eroticism, new normality for that malady-ridden strain of today's neurotic actors.'—*Marlene Dietrich*

J.P.B.: Hell, everybody knows that an ugly guy with a good line gets the chicks.

'Wrong or right I suppose he represents France.'—*Daniel Boulander*

Belmore, Bertha (1882–1953). Ample British character comedienne, a British Margaret Dumont whose dignity was inevitably shattered.

Are You a Mason? 33. Going Gay 34. Broken Blossoms 36. In the Soup 37. Over She Goes 38. Yes Madam 39, etc.

Belmore, Lionel (1867–1953). Portly British character actor in Hollywood in the thirties. The Antique Dealer 15. Madame X 20. Oliver Twist 22. Red Lights 23. The Sea Hawk 24. Never the Twain Shall Meet 25. Bardelys the Magnificent 26. Sorrell and Son 27. King of Kings 27. Rose Marie 28. The Love Parade 29. Monte Carlo 30. Alexander Hamilton 31. Frankenstein 31. Vanity Fair 32. So Big 32. The Vampire Bat 33. Cleopatra 34. Vanessa 34. The Count of Monte Cristo 34. Cardinal Richelieu 35. Clive of India 35. Little Lord Fauntleroy 36. Maid of Salem 37. The Prince and the Pauper 37. Tower of London 39. Son of Frankenstein 39. My Son My Son 40, many others.

Beloin, Edmund (1910–). American comedy writer with radio experience. Buck Benny Rides Again 40. Love Thy Neighbour 40. Because of Him 45. The Great Lover (& p) 49. A Connecticut Yankee in King Arthur's Court 49. The Sad Sack 57. G.I. Blues 60. All in a Night's Work 61, etc.

The Beloved Rogue: see *If I Were King*.

Belson, Jerry (–). American screenwriter. How Sweet It Is 68. Smile 76. Fun With Dick and Jane 77. The End 78. Smokey and the Bandit II (co-w) 80.

Belushi, John (1949–1982). Overweight American comic actor from television satire shows.
□National Lampoon's Animal House 78. Going South 78. 1941 79. Old Boyfriends 79. The Blues Brothers 80. Continental Divide 81. Neighbours 81. Salvador 86.

¶ 'A good man, but a bad boy.'—*Dan Aykroyd*

Ben Hur. There were several silent versions of Lew Wallace's semi-biblical adventure novel. Best-known is MGM's lavish spectacular of 1926, directed by Fred Niblo with Ramon Novarro and Francis X. Bushman; it was reissued with sound effects in 1931. In 1959 it was remade by MGM and William Wyler, with Charlton Heston and Stephen Boyd: the greatest praise went to the chariot race sequence directed by Andrew Marton.

Benchley, Peter (1940–). American novelist, fashionable in Hollywood for his one real hit. Grandson of Robert Benchley. Jaws 75. The Deep 77. The Island 80.

Benchley, Robert (1889–1945). American magazine humourist who exploited the small problems of twentieth-century living. He appeared in many films as a lovable bumbler, usually trying to explain something very complicated or to control a patently unmanageable situation. Benchley made many amusing shorts consisting of lectures by him on matters of science or domestic harmony. One of them, *How to Sleep* (1935), won an Academy Award.
Biography 1946: *Robert Benchley*, by his son Nathaniel.
□Feature appearances: Headline Shooter 33. Dancing Lady 33. Rafter Romance 34. Social Register 34. China Seas 35. Piccadilly Jim 36. Live Love and Learn 37. Broadway Melody of 1938 37. Hired Wife 40. *Foreign Correspondent* 40. Nice Girl 41. *The Reluctant Dragon* 41. You'll Never Get Rich 41. Three Girls about Town 41. Bedtime Story 41. Take a Letter Darling 42. The Major and the Minor 42. *I Married a Witch* 42. Flesh and Fantasy 43. Young and Willing 43. Song of Russia 43. The Sky's the Limit 43. Her Primitive Man 44. National Barn Dance 44. See Here Private Hargrove 44. Practically Yours 44. Janie 44. Pan Americana 45. *It's In the Bag* 45. Weekend at the Waldorf 45. Kiss and Tell 45. Duffy's Tavern 45. The Stork Club 45. *Road to Utopia* 45. The Bride Wore Boots 46. Snafu 46. Janie Gets Married 46. Blue Skies 46.

†In the late seventies there appeared a compilation film, *Those Wonderful Benchley Shorts*.

❀ For assuming a subtly fantasticated screen version of his own cosmopolitan personality, and delighting the world by doing so. *Road to Utopia*.

¶ 'In Milwaukee last month a man died laughing at one of his own jokes. That's what makes it so tough for us outsiders. We have to fight home competition.'—*R.B.*

'It took me fifteen years to discover that I had no talent for writing. But by then I couldn't give it up because I was too famous.'—*R.B.*

Benchley tended to spend his later years drinking in Hollywood's Garden of Allah hotel. When he finally left to go east he pointedly refrained from favouring a hated doorman. 'Sir,' said the man, 'aren't you going to remember me?' 'Sure,' said Benchley, 'I'll write you every day.'

Leaving a restaurant, Benchley approached what appeared to be a uniformed commissionaire and muttered: 'Get me a taxi.' The man bridled and said: 'Sir, I am a rear admiral in the United States Navy.' 'Really,' said Benchley. 'Then get me a battleship.'

Bendix, William (1906–1964). Familiar American character actor who usually played the tough guy with the heart of gold; his broken nose, raucous Brooklyn accent and air of amiable stupidity endeared him to a generation.
□Woman of the Year 42. The McGuerins from Brooklyn 42. Brooklyn Orchid 42. Wake Island 42. *The Glass Key* (as a murderous thug) 42. Who Done It? 42. Star Spangled Rhythm 42. The Crystal Ball 43. Taxi Mister 43. China 43. Hostages 43. Guadalcanal Diary 43. *Lifeboat* 43. *The Hairy Ape* 44. Abroad with Two Yanks 44. Greenwich Village 44. It's in the Bag 45. Don Juan Quilligan 45. A Bell for Adano 45. Sentimental Journey 45. *The Blue Dahlia* 46. The Dark Corner 46. Two Years Before the Mast 46. Whit Tie and Tails 46. I'll Be Yours 46. Blaze Noon 47. Calcutta 47. The Web 47. Where There's Life 47. Variety Girl 47. *The Time of Your Life* 48. Race Street 48. The Babe Ruth Story 48. *The Life of Riley* 49. A Connecticut Yankee in King Arthur's Court 49. *The Big Steal* 49. Streets of Laredo 49. Cover Up 49. Johnny Holiday 49. Kill the Umpire 50. Gambling House 50. Submarine Command 51. *Detective Story* 51. Macao 52. A Girl in Every Port 52. Blackbeard the Pirate 52. Dangerous Mission 54. Crashout 55. Battle Stations 56. The Deep Six 58. Idol on Parade (GB) 59. The Rough and the Smooth (GB) 59. Boy's Night Out 62. Johnny Nobody (GB) 62. The Young and the Brave 63. For Love or Money 63. Law of the Lawless 64. The Phony American 64. Young Fury 65.
TV series: *The Life of Riley* 53-58. Overland Stage 60.

¶ 'Neanderthal man reincarnated in Brooklyn.'—*David Shipman*

Benedek, Laslo (1907–). Hungarian director in Hollywood; output surprisingly meagre.
□The Kissing Bandit 48. Port of New York 49. Storm over the Tiber 52. *Death of a Salesman* 52. *The Wild One* 54. Bengal Brigade 54. Kinder Mütter und ein General (Ger.) 55. Affair in Havana 57. Moment of Danger (GB) 62. Namu the Killer Whale (& p) 66. The Daring Game 68. The Night Visitor 71. Assault on Agathon 74.

Benedict, Billy (1906–). American character actor who in his youth was one of the original 'Bowery Boys'; now plays cabbies, bartenders, etc.
Doubting Thomas 35. Way Down East 35. Ramona 36. Libeled Lady 36. That I May Live 37. King of the Newsboys 38. Little Tough Guys in Society 38. Newsboys' Home 39. Code of the Streets 39. Call a Messenger 39. The Bowery Boy 40. My Little Chickadee 40. The Mad Doctor 41. Lady in a Jam 42. Clancy Street Boys 43. Adventures of the Flying Cadets 43. Follow the Leader 44. Docks of New York 45. Hollywood and Vine 45. Spook Busters 46. The Hucksters 47. Hard Boiled Mahoney 47. Fighting Fools 49. Ghost Chasers 51. Last Train from Gun Hill 59. Lover Come Back 61. The Hallelujah Trail 65. Hello Dolly 69. The Sting 73. Farewell My Lovely 75. Won Ton Ton 76, many others.

Benedict, Dirk (1945–) (D. Niewoehner). Standard-type American leading man with mainly television experience.
Journey from Darkness (TV) 75. Cruise into Terror (TV) 78. Scavenger Hunt 79. Underground Aces 81. Body Slam 87, etc.
TV series: Chopper One 74. Battlestar Galactica 78. The A Team 83.

Benedict, Richard (1916–84) (Riccardo Benedetto). American leading man, usually in second features; sometimes played the heavy.
Till the End of Time 46. Crossfire 47. City across the River 49. State Penitentiary 50. Ace in the Hole 51. Okinawa 52. The Juggler 53. Hoodlum Empire 55. The Shrike 55. Monkey on my Back 57. Ocean's Eleven 60, etc.

Benet, Stephen Vincent (1898–1943). American poet and novelist whose *The Devil and Daniel Webster* was filmed as *All That Money Can Buy*.

Benjamin, Arthur (1893–1960). Anglo-Australian composer.
The Man Who Knew Too Much 34. The Scarlet Pimpernel 34. Turn of the Tide 35. Under the Red Robe 36. Master of Bankdam 47. An Ideal Husband 48. Above Us the Waves 55. Naked Earth 57, etc.

Benjamin, Richard (1938–). Diffident-seeming American leading man. Married Paula Prentiss.
Thunder over the Plains 53. *Goodbye Columbus* 69. Catch 22 70. *Diary of a Mad*

Housewife 70. Marriage of a Young Stockbroker 71. Portnoy's Complaint 72. The Last of Sheila 73. Westworld 73. The Sunshine Boys 76. House Calls 78. Scavenger Hunt 79. The First Family 80. How to Beat the High Cost of Living 80. The Last Married Couple in America 80. Saturday the 14th 81. My Favorite Year (d only) 82, etc. Racing with the Moon (d only) 83. City Heat (d only) 84. The Money Pit (d only) 85.
TV series: *He and She* 67. Quark 78.

¶ *R.B.*: If you are married to an actress and your wife is getting all the calls, it's very hard on the ego.

Bennet, Spencer Gordon (1893–). American silent actor and stunt man who became a famous director of serials and made fifty-two in all.
Rogue of the Rio Grande 30. Mysterious Pilot 37. Arizona Bound 42. Batman and Robin 48. Atom Man vs Superman 50. Adventures of Sir Galahad 51. Brave Warrior (feature) 52. The Atomic Submarine (feature) 60. The Bounty Killer (feature) 65, many others.

Bennett, Alma (1889–1958). American silent screen vamp.
Why Men Leave Home 14. The Silent Lover 16. The Dawn of a Tomorrow 19. Smiling Jim 22. Three Jumps Ahead 23. The Face on the Barroom Floor 23. Why Men Leave Home 24. The Lost World 25. The Light of Western Stars 25. Don Juan's Three Nights 26. Long Pants 27. Compassion 27. The Grain of Dust 28. Two Men and a Maid 29. Midnight Daddies 30, etc.

Bennett, Arnold (1867–1931). British novelist, little of whose work has been filmed. *Buried Alive* has, however, been seen in several versions, under its own title, as *The Great Adventure*, as *His Double Life*, and as *Holy Matrimony*. British studios filmed *The Card* with Alec Guinness, and less successfully *Dear Mr Prohack* with Cecil Parker.

Bennett, Barbara (1902–1958). American leading lady of a few twenties films. Sister of Constance and Joan Bennett.
Syncopation 29. Mother's Boy 29. Love among the Millionaires 30, etc.

Bennett, Belle (1891–1932). American leading lady of the silent screen.
A Soul in Trust 18. His Supreme Moment 25. If Marriage Fails 25. *Stella Dallas* 25. The Fourth Commandment 27. The Way of All Flesh 27. Mother Machree 28. The Iron Mask 29. Courage 30. Recaptured Love 31. The Big Shot 31, etc.

Bennett, Bruce (1909–) (Herman Brix). Athletic American leading man who started in films by playing Tarzan and subsequently settled down as a familiar flannel-suited second lead. Used his own name until 1940.
Student Tour 34. *The New Adventures of Tarzan* 35 (re-edited 1938 as *Tarzan and the Green Goddess*). Danger Patrol 37. Before I Hang 40. Atlantic Convoy 42. The More the Merrier 43. Sahara 43. Mildred Pierce 45. The Treasure of the Sierra Madre 47. Silver River 48. Task Force 49. The Doctor and the Girl 49. Without Honor 50. Sudden Fear 52. Dream Wife 53. Strategic Air Command 55. Three Violent People 57. The Outsider 61, many others.

Bennett, Charles (1899–). British screenwriter who worked on some of Hitchcock's thirties films and later moved to Hollywood. Usually worked in collaboration.
Blackmail 29. The Man Who Knew Too Much 34. *The Thirty-nine Steps* 35. Secret Agent 36. Sabotage 37. King Solomon's Mines 37. The Young in Heart 38. Balalaika 39. *Foreign Correspondent* 40. Joan of Paris 42. Reap the Wild Wind 42. The Story of Dr Wassell 44. Ivy 47. Madness of the Heart (& d) 48. Black Magic 49. Where Danger Lives 51. The Green Glove 52. No Escape (& d) 53. The Story of Mankind 57. The Lost World 60. Five Weeks in a Balloon 62. War Gods of the Deep 65, etc.

Bennett, Compton (1900–1974) (Robert Compton-Bennett). British director, former editor.
□*The Seventh Veil* 45. The Years Between 46. Daybreak 48. My Own True Love 49. *That Forsyte Woman* 49. *King Solomon's Mines* 50. So Little Time 52. The Gift Horse 52. It Started in Paradise 52. Desperate Moment 53. That Woman Opposite 57. After the Ball 57. The Flying Scot 57. Beyond the Curtain 60. How to Undress in Public Without Undue Embarrassment 65.

Bennett, Constance (1904–1965). Glamorous American star of the thirties, adept at worldly roles; sister of Barbara and Joan Bennett.
□Reckless Youth 22. Evidence 22. What's Wrong with the Women? 22. Cytherea 24. Into the Net 24. *The Goose Hangs High* 25. Married 25. Code of the West 25. My Son 25.

My Wife and I 25. *The Goose Woman* 25. Sally Irene and Mary 25. Wandering Fires 25. The Pinch Hitter 26. This Thing Called Love 29. Son of the Gods 30. Rich People 30. Common Clay 30. *Three Faces East* 30. Sin Takes a Holiday 30. The Easiest Way 31. Born to Love 31. The Common Law 31. Bought 31. Lady with a Past 32. *What Price Hollywood* 32. Two Against the World 32. Rockabye 32. Our Betters 33. Bed of Roses 33. After Tonight 33. *Moulin Rouge* 33. Affairs of Cellini 34. Outcast Lady 34. After Office Hours 35. Everything is Thunder (GB) 36. Ladies in Love 36. *Topper* (as a ghost) 37. *Merrily We Live* 38. Service de Luxe 38. Topper Takes a Trip 38. Tailspin 39. *Escape to Glory* 40. Law of the Tropics 41. *Two-faced Woman* 41. Wild Bill Hickok Rides 41. Sin Town 42. Madame Spy 42. Paris Underground 46. Centennial Summer 46. *The Unsuspected* 47. Smart Woman 48. Angel on the Amazon 49. As Young as You Feel 51. It Should Happen to You 53. *Madame X* 65.

¶ 'She seemed to me the quintessence of a movie star. Everything about her shone—her burnished head, her jewels, her famous smile, her lovely long legs, and the highly publicised fact that she pulled down 30,000 bucks a week.'—*David Niven*

Bennett, Enid (1895–1969). Australian leading lady in Hollywood films of the twenties.
Princess in the Dark 17. The Vamp 18. The Haunted Bedroom 19. Hairpins 20. Her Husband's Friend 21. Robin Hood 22. Scandalous Tongues 22. The Courtship of Miles Standish 23. The Sea Hawk 24. A Woman's Heart 26. The Wrong Mr Wright 27. Good Medicine 29. Skippy 31. Meet Dr Christian 39. Strike Up the Band 40, many others.

Bennett, Hywel (1944–). Welsh leading man who has usually played roles requiring a feigning of innocence.
□*The Family Way* 66. Twisted Nerve 68. *The Virgin Soldiers* 69. The Buttercup Chain 70. Loot 71. Percy 71. Endless Night 72. Alice's Adventures in Wonderland 72. The Love Ban 72. Malice Aforethought (TV) 79. Tinker Tailor Soldier Spy (TV) 79. Murder Elite (TV) 85. Deadline 87.
TV series: *Shelley* 80–85.

Bennett, Jill (1930–). Unusual-looking British actress who generally plays emancipated roles.
Moulin Rouge 53. Hell Below Zero 54. *Lust for Life* 56. The Criminal 60. The Skull 65. *The Nanny* 65. *Inadmissible Evidence* 68. *The Charge of the Light Brigade* 68. Julius Caesar 70. I Want What I Want 71. Mister Quilp 75. Full Circle 77. For Your Eyes Only 81. Britannia Hospital 82, etc.

Bennett, Joan (1910–). Popular American leading lady of the thirties and forties, one of the most attractive stars of her time. Sister of Barbara and Constance Bennett.
Autobiography 1970: *The Bennett Playbill.*
□The Valley of Decision 15. Power 28. The Divine Lady 29. Bulldog Drummond 29. Three Live Ghosts 29. Disraeli 29. Mississippi Gambler 29. Puttin' On the Ritz 30. Crazy that Way 30. Moby Dick 30. Maybe It's Love 30. Scotland Yard 30. Many a Slip 31. Doctors' Wives 31. Hush Money 31. She Wanted a Millionaire 32. Careless Lady 32. The Trial of Vivienne Ware 32. Weekends Only 32. Wild Girl 32. Me and My Gal 32. Arizona to Broadway 32. *Little Women* 33. The Pursuit of Happiness 34. The Man Who Reclaimed His Head 34. *Private Worlds* 35. Mississippi 35. Two for Tonight 35. The Man Who Broke the Bank at Monte Carlo 35. She Couldn't Take It 35. Thirteen Hours by Air 36. Big Brown Eyes 36. Two in a Crowd 36. Wedding Present 36. Vogues of 1938 37. I Met My Love Again 38. The Texans 38. Artists and Models Abroad 38. Trade Winds 39. The Man in the Iron Mask 39. *The Housekeeper's Daughter* 39. Green Hell 40. The House across the Bay 40. The Man I Married 40. Son of Monte Cristo 40. She Knew All the Answers 41. *Man Hunt* 41. Wild Geese Calling 41. Confirm or Deny 42. Twin Beds 42. The Wife Takes a Flyer 42. Girl Trouble 42. Margin for Error 43. *The Woman in the Window* 44. Nob Hill 45. *Scarlet Street* 45. Colonel Effingham's Raid 46. *The Macomber Affair* 47. The Secret Beyond the Door 47. The Woman on the Beach 47. The Scar 47. *The Reckless Moment* 49. *Father of the Bride* 50. For Heaven's Sake 50. Father's Little Dividend 51. The Guy Who Came Back 51. Highway Dragnet 54. We're No Angels 55. There's Always Tomorrow 56. Navy Wife 56. Desire in the Dust 60. House of Dark Shadows 70. Inn of the Damned 71. Gidget Gets Married (TV) 71. The Eyes of Charles Sand (TV) 72. Suspiria 77. Suddenly, Love (TV) 78. Divorce Wars (TV) 82.
TV series: Dark Shadows 66–71.

¶ *J.B. 1984:* The golden age is gone, and with it most of the people of great taste. It doesn't seem to be fun any more.

J.B.: My film career faded. A man can go on playing certain roles till he's 60. But not a woman.

Bennett, John (1928–). Swarthy British character actor.
The Challenge 59. *The Barber of Stamford Hill* 62. Kaleidoscope 66. The Forsyte Saga (TV) 68. The House that Dripped Blood 70. The House in Nightmare Park 73. Hitler, the Last Ten Days (as Goebbels) 74. The Message 77. Eye of the Needle 81, etc.

Bennett, Marjorie (1894–1982). American character actress, in films since early silent experience as a bathing beauty.
Monsieur Verdoux 47. Limelight 52. Young at Heart 55. *Whatever Happened to Baby Jane?* 62. Mary Poppins 64. Charley Varrick 73. Mother, Jugs and Speed 76, many others.

Bennett, Richard (1873–1944). Dapper American stage actor, a leading figure of his day; father of Barbara, Constance and Joan Bennett. Film appearances rare.
The Eternal City 23. The Home Towners 28. Arrowsmith 32. *If I Had a Million* (as the millionaire) 32. Nana 34. *The Magnificent Ambersons* 42. Journey into Fear 43, etc.

Bennett, Richard Rodney (1936–). British composer.
Interpol 57. Indiscreet 58. Only Two Can Play 61. Billy Liar 63. One Way Pendulum 64. The Nanny 65. Far from the Madding Crowd 67. Secret Ceremony 68. Figures in a Landscape 70. Nicholas and Alexandra 71. Lady Caroline Lamb 72. Voices 73. Murder on the Orient Express 74. Permission to Kill 75. Sherlock Holmes in New York 77. Equus 77. Yanks 79. Brinks 79. The Return of the Soldier 82. Murder with Mirrors (TV) 84. The Ebony Tower (TV) 84, etc.

Bennett, Spencer Gordon (–). American director, king of the serials: Secret Service in Darkest Africa 43. Batman and Robin 49, etc.
Films include: Brave Warrior 52. Killer Ape 53. Atomic Submarine 59. Requiem for a Gunfighter 65. The Bounty Killer 65.

Bennett, Tony (1926–) (Antonio Benedetto). Heavyweight Italian–American ballad singer, famous for leaving his heart in San Francisco. Principal film appearance in *The Oscar*.

Benny, Jack (1894–1974) (Benjamin Kubelsky). Celebrated American comedian of radio, TV and occasional films. His inimitable reproachful look, his pretence of meanness and his much maligned violin are among the trademarks which kept him popular for forty years. He graduated from burlesque, and later married his radio leading lady Mary Livingstone (Sadye Marks).
Biographies: *Jack Benny* by Irving Fein 76; *Jack Benny* by Mary Livingstone Marks and others 78.
□*Hollywood Revue of 1929* 29. Chasing Rainbows 30. Medicine Man 30. Transatlantic Merry-Go-Round 34. Broadway Melody of 1936 35. It's in the Air 35. The Big Broadcast of 1937 36. College Holiday 36. Artists and Models 37. Artists and Models Abroad 38. Man About Town 39. Buck Benny Rides Again 39. Love Thy Neighbour 40. *Charley's Aunt* 41. *To Be or Not To Be* (an outstanding performance) 42. George Washington Slept Here 42. The Meanest Man in the World 43. Hollywood Canteen 44. *It's in the Bag* 45. *The Horn Blows at Midnight* 45. A Guide for the Married Man 67.
TV series: *The Jack Benny Show* 50–65.
†Benny also made gag appearances in Without Reservations 47. Beau James 57. It's a Mad Mad Mad Mad World 63.

¶ Hold-up Man: 'Your money or your life! Come on, come on, hurry up!'
Benny: 'I'm thinking it over!'
'He couldn't ad-lib a belch after a Hungarian dinner.'—*Fred Allen* (in jest)
'He didn't just stand on the stage. He owned it.'—*Bob Hope*

Benoît-Lévy, Jean (1883–1959). French director who also wrote books on cinema.
La Maternelle 33. Hélène 37. La Mort du Cygne 38. Fire in the Straw 43, etc.

Benson, George (1911–83). British character actor of stage, screen and TV, the nervous 'little man' of countless films.
Keep Fit 37. Convoy 40. The October Man 48. Pool of London 50. The Man in the White Suit 51. The Captain's Paradise 53. Doctor in the House 54. Value for Money 56. Dracula 58. A Jolly Bad Fellow 64. A Home of Your Own 65. The Creeping Flesh 72, etc.

Benson, Martin (1918–). British character actor often seen as a smooth foreign-looking crook.
The Blind Goddess 49. West of Zanzibar 54. The King and I (US) 56. Windom's Way 58. The Three Worlds of Gulliver 60. Cleopatra 62. Behold a Pale Horse 64. Goldfinger 64.

The Secret of My Success 65. Pope Joan 72. The Omen 76. Mohammed 77. The Sea Wolves 80. Sphinx 81, many others.
TV series: Sword of Freedom 57.

Benson, Robby (1956–) (Robert Segal). American juvenile lead of the seventies.
Jory 73. *Jeremy* 73. *Death Be Not Proud* (TV) 75. Lucky Lady 76. The Death of Richie (TV) 76. One on One (& co-w) 77. The End 78. Ice Castles 78. Walk Proud 79. Die Laughing 80. Tribute 80. The Chosen 81. National Lampoon Goes to the Movies 82. City Limits 85.
TV series: Tough Cookies 86.

¶ *An anonymous critic's verdict:* Cute as Bambi and twice as smarmy.
R. B. himself: I was into show business straight from the womb.

Benson, Sally (1900–1972). American screenwriter, former film critic and novelist.
Shadow of a Doubt (co-w) 43. Meet Me in St Louis (oa) 44. Junior Miss (oa) 45. Anna and the King of Siam (co-w) 46. Come to the Stable (co-w) 49. No Man of Her Own (co-w) 50. The Farmer Takes a Wife (co-w) 53. Summer Magic (co-w) 63. Joy in the Morning (co-w) 65. The Flying Nun (co-w) 66.

Bentine, Michael (1922–). Anglo-Peruvian comedian, popular on stage and TV, who has made several unsuccessful attempts to film his goonish style of humour, for example in *The Sandwich Man* 66.

Bentley, John (1916–). British leading man who left the stage in 1946 to play in innumerable low-budget crime dramas, including series about Paul Temple and The Toff.
Hills of Donegal 47. Calling Paul Temple 48. The Happiest Days of Your Life 49. The Lost Hours 51. The Scarlet Spear 53. Golden Ivory 55. Istanbul (US) 58. Submarine Seahawk 59. The Singer Not the Song 60. Mary Had a Little 61. The Fur Collar 63, many others.
TV series: African Patrol 59.

Bentley, Thomas (c. 1880–195*). British director, former Dickensian impersonator, who began in films by making silent versions of several Dickens novels.
Young Woodley 30. *Hobson's Choice* 31. The Scotland Yard Mystery 33. *Those Were the Days* 34. The Old Curiosity Shop 35. Music Hath Charms 35. Marigold 38. The Middle Watch 39. Lucky to Me 39. Old Mother Riley's Circus 41, scores of others.

Benton, Robert (1932–). American magazine writer and art director who teamed up with David Newman to become co-screenwriter of such movies as *Bonnie and Clyde*, There Was a Crooked Man, What's Up Doc, and Superman. Turned director: Bad Company (& co-w) 70. The Late Show (& co-w) 77. *Kramer vs Kramer* (AA) 79. Still of the Night 82. Places of the Heart (AAw, AANd) 84. Nadine (w, d) 87.

¶ *R.B.:* The success of *Bonnie and Clyde* made me very miserable. It's some deep-seated neurosis I have.

Beranger, André (1895–1973). Australian Shakespearean actor who joined D. W. Griffith in Hollywood and appeared in mainly silent films.
The Birth of a Nation 15. Intolerance 16. Manhattan Madness 16. Broken Blossoms 19. The Bright Shawl 23. Beau Brummell 24. The Grand Duchess and the Waiter 26. Fig Leaves 26. Strange Cargo 29. Surrender 31. Mama Loves Papa 33. Over My Dead Body 42. Road House 48, many others.

Berenger, Tom (1950–). Brooding American leading man in the John Garfield mould.
Johnny We Hardly Knew Ye (TV) 77. Butch and Sundance 79. Flesh and Blood (TV) 80. The Dogs of War 81. The Big Chill 83. Eddie and the Cruisers 83. Platoon 86. Someone to Watch Over Me 87, etc.

Berenson, Marisa (1946–). International fashion model who has appeared in films.
□Death in Venice 72. Cabaret 72. Barry Lyndon 75. Killer Fish 78. Naked Sun 80. S.O.B. 81.

¶ *M.B.:* My ultimate goal is to become a saint.

Beresford, Bruce (1940–). Australian director.
The Adventures of Barry Mackenzie 72. Barry Mackenzie Holds His Own 74. Side by Side 75. Don's Party 76. The Getting of Wisdom 77. Money Movers 78. Breaker Morant 80. The Club 80. Puberty Blues 81. Tender Mercies (AAN) 82. King David 84. The Fringe Dwellers 85. Crimes of the Heart 86.

Beresford, Harry (1864–1944). British general purpose actor in Hollywood from silent days.
The Quarterback 26. Charles Chan Carries On 31. So Big 32. Dr X 32. The Sign of the

Cross 32. Murders in the Zoo 33. Dinner at Eight 33. Cleopatra 34. The Little Minister 34. Seven Keys To Baldpate 35. David Copperfield 35. Follow the Fleet 36. The Prince and the Pauper 37. They Won't Forget 37, many others.

Berg, Gertrude (1899–1966) (Gertrude Edelstein). Plump American character actress famous on TV and radio as Molly of the Goldberg family. She appeared in a film version, *Molly* 51, also in another TV series, *Mrs G Goes to College* 61.

Bergdahl, Victor (1878–1939). Swedish animator of the silent era.

Bergen, Candice (1946–). Stylish American leading lady, daughter of Edgar Bergen.
□*The Group* 66. The Sand Pebbles 66. The Day the Fish Came Out 67. Vivre Pour Vivre 67. The Magus 68. Getting Straight 70. Soldier Blue 70. The Adventurers 70. *Carnal Knowledge* 71. The Hunting Party 71. T R Baskin 72. 11 Harrowhouse 74. Bite the Bullet 75. The Wind and the Lion 76. The Cassandra Crossing 76. The Domino Principle 77. A Night Full of Rain 77. Oliver's Story 78. Starting Over 79. Rich and Famous 81. Gandhi 82. Stick 84. Hollywood Wives (TV) 85.

¶ *C.B.:* There are moments when I perceive us as being on the brink of another dark age, a media blitzkrieg of mindlessness.

C.B.: It takes a long time to grow up. Longer than they tell you.

Bergen, Edgar (1903–78). Mild-mannered Swedish-American ventriloquist, manipulator of Charlie McCarthy and Mortimer Snerd (special AA 1937); latterly a character actor. The Goldwyn Follies 38. Letter of Introduction 38. *You Can't Cheat an Honest Man* 39. *Charlie McCarthy Detective* 39. Look Who's Laughing 41. Here We Go Again 42. Stage Door Canteen 43. Song of the Open Road 44. *I Remember Mama* 48. The Hanged Man 64. One Way Wahine 66. Don't Make Waves 67. The Homecoming (TV) 70, etc.

Bergen, Polly (1929–) (Nellie Burgin). American singer of stage, radio and TV; also pleasing light actress in several films.
□At War with the Army 50. That's My Boy 51. Warpath 51. The Stooge 53. Cry of the Hunted 53. Arena 53. Half a Hero 54. Fast Company 54. Escape from Fort Bravo 54. *Cape Fear* 62. Belle Sommers (TV) 62. The Caretakers 63. *Move Over Darling* 63. *Kisses for My President* 64. A Guide for the Married Man 67. Death Cruise (TV) 75. Murder on Flight 502 75. Million Dollar Face (TV) 81. Born Beautiful (TV) 82. *The Winds of War* (TV) 83.

¶ *P.B.:* I'm one of those people who always needs a mountain to climb. When I get up a mountain as far as I think I'm going to get, I try to find another mountain.

Berger, Helmut (1944–) (Helmut Steinberger). Handsome Austrian actor who gives a sinister edge to his performances. *The Damned* 69. *Un Beau Monstre* 70. The Garden of the Finzi-Continis 71. Dorian Gray 72. Ash Wednesday 73. Ludwig 73. Conversation Piece 75. The Romantic Englishwoman 75. Madam Kitty 77. Roses of The Romantic Englishwoman 75. Roses of Danzig 79. Heroin 80. Victory 83. Code Name Emerald 85. Tunnel 85, etc.

Berger, Ludwig (1892–1969) (Ludwig Bamberger). German director who made some international films.
Ein Glas Wasser 22. The Waltz Dream 26. The Woman from Moscow (US) 28. Sins of the Fathers 29. Die Meistersinger 29. The Vagabond King (US) 30. Playboy of Paris 30. Waltz Time in Vienna 33. Three Waltzes 39. The Thief of Baghdad (GB/US) 40. Ballerina (Fr.) 50, etc.

Berger, Nicole (1934–1967). French leading lady.
Juliette 52. Game of Love 54. Le Premier Mai 57. Love is my Profession 58. Les Dragueurs 59. Shoot the Pianist 62, etc.

Berger, Senta (1941–). Austrian leading lady in international films.
Die Lindenwirtin vom DonausTrand (debut) 57. The Journey 59. The Secret Ways 61. The Good Soldier Schweik 62. Sherlock Holmes and the Deadly Necklace 62. The Victors 63. Major Dundee 65. The Glory Guys 65. Cast a Giant Shadow 66. The Quiller Memorandum 67. Our Man in Marrakesh 67. The Ambushers 67. Treasure of San Gennaro 68. De Sade 69. Ludwig 72. The Scarlet Letter 72. Der Reigen 73. The Swiss Conspiracy 75. Cross of Iron 77, etc.

Bergerac, Jacques (1927–). French leading man, former lawyer, in Hollywood from 1953.
Les Girls 57. Gigi 58. Thunder in the Sun 59. The Hypnotic Eye 60. Taffy and the Jungle Hunter 65, etc.

Bergere, Ouida (1885–1974). American scriptwriter of the twenties (*On with the Dance, The Cheat*, etc.) who also acted in a few films before marrying Basil Rathbone and becoming Hollywood's most lavish hostess.

Berggren, Thommy (1937–). Swedish leading actor.
Sunday in September 63. Raven's End 63. *Elvira Madigan* 67. The Adventurers 70. Joe Hill 71. Giliap 73. Kristoffers Hus 79. Broken Sky 82. The Mountain on the Other Side of the Moon 83. *Strindberg* (TV) 85. *Gosta Berlings Saga* (TV) 86, etc.

Berghof, Herbert (1909–). Austrian character actor long on American stage, also as drama teacher; films rare.
Assignment Paris 52. *Five Fingers* 52. Red Planet Mars 52. Fraulein 58. Cleopatra 62. Harry and Tonto 74. Those Lips Those Eyes 80. Times Square 83. Target 85, etc.

Berglund, Sven (1881–1937). Swedish inventor, credited in some quarters with having been the first to put sound on film.

Bergman, Henry (1868–1946). American comedy actor, the heavy villain in many a Chaplin film from *His New Job* in 1915 to *The Great Dictator* in 1940.

Bergman, Ingmar (1918–). Swedish writer-director who divides his time between stage and film. In the late fifties his films had world-wide impact because of their semi-mystic, under-explained themes and bravura presentation by a repertory of excellent actors and cameramen; more recently his work has become austere and withdrawn.
Biographical works include: *Ingmar Bergman* (1962) by Peter Cowie; *The Personal Vision of Ingmar Bergman* (1964) by Jorn Donner; *The Silence of God* (1969) by Arthur Gibson; *Ingmar Bergman* (1968) by Birgitta Steene; *Ingmar Bergman* (1969) by Robin Wood; *Cinema Borealis* (1971) by Vernon Young. Various screenplays have been published.
□Crisis 45. It Rains on Our Love 46. A Ship Bound for India 47. Night is Our Future 47. Port of Call 48. *Prison* 48. *Thirst* 49. Till Gladje 49. Summer Interlude 50. Sant Hander inte Har 50. Waiting Women 52. Summer with Monika 52. *Sawdust and Tinsel* 53. A Lesson in Love 54. Journey into Autumn 55. *Smiles of a Summer Night* 55. *The Seventh Seal* 56. *Wild Strawberries* 57. So Close to Life 58. *The Face (The Magician)* 58. *The Virgin Spring* (AA) 59. The Devil's Eye 60. *Through a Glass Darkly* (AA) 61. *Winter Light* 62. *The Silence* 63. Now About these Women 64. *Persona* 66. The Hour of the Wolf 67. The Shame 68. The Rite (TV) 69. The Touch 70. A Passion 70. *Cries and Whispers* 72. Scenes from a Marriage (TV) 74. The Magic Flute (TV) 75. Face to Face (TV) 76. The Serpent's Egg 77. Autumn Sonata 78. From the Life of the Marionettes 80. *Fanny and Alexander* 82. After the Rehearsal 84.

¶ *I.B.:* The theatre is like a faithful wife. The film is the great adventure—the costly, exacting mistress.

I.B.: I have a morbid sense of humour. I'm very open and frank, and sometimes that is a mistake.

I.B.: To shoot a film is to organise a complete universe.

I.B.: I'm not a writer. My plays and scripts are skeletons awaiting sinew.

Bergman, Ingrid (1915–1982). Gifted Swedish leading actress who went to Hollywood in 1938 and became an international star. In 1948 her romance with Roberto Rossellini (qv) caused a return to Europe where she appeared in mainly inferior films; Hollywood's door opened to her again in 1956.
Biography 1986: *As Time Goes By* by Laurence Leamer.
□Munkbrogreven 34. Branningar 35. Swedenhielms 35. Valborgsmassoafton 35. Pa Solsidan 36. *Intermezzo* 36. *En Kvinnas Ansikte* 38. En Enda Natt 38. Dollar 38. Die Vier Gesellen 38. *Intermezzo* (US remake) 39. Juninatten 40. Rage in Heaven 41. Adam Had Four Sons 41. Dr Jekyll and Mr Hyde 41. *Casablanca* 43. *For Whom the Bell Tolls* 43. *Gaslight* (AA) 44. *The Bells of St Mary's* 45. *Spellbound* 45. *Saratoga Trunk* 45. *Notorious* 46. Arch of Triumph 48. *Joan of Arc* 48. Under Capricorn 49. Stromboli 50. Europa 51. We the Women 53. Journey to Italy 54. Joan at the Stake 54. Fear 54. *Anastasia* (AA) 56. Paris Does Strange Things 57. *Indiscreet* 58. *The Inn of the Sixth Happiness* 58. Goodbye Again 61. The Visit 64. The Yellow Rolls Royce 64. Fugitive in Vienna 67. *Cactus Flower* 69. A Walk in the Spring Rain 70. From the Mixed Up Files of Mrs Basil E. Frankweiler 74. Murder on the Orient Express (AA, BFA) 74. A Matter of Time 76. Autumn Sonata 78. A Woman Called Golda (TV) 82.
❀ For the ease with which in the forties she conquered international auduences with her

presentation of innocent strength and beauty. *Spellbound.*

¶ I have no regrets. I wouldn't have lived my life the way I did if I was going to worry about what people were going to say.—*I.B.*

Sweden's greatest export since Garbo!—*publicity*

I.B.: It's not whether you really cry. It's whether the audience thinks you are crying.
Famous line (*For Whom the Bell Tolls*): 'Where do the noses go?'
Famous line (*Indiscreet*): 'How dare he make love to me and not be a married man?'

Bergner, Elisabeth (1898–1986) (Elizabeth Ettel). German leading actress who settled in Britain in the thirties and married Paul Czinner (qv). Her fey gamine character quickly dated, but she was an undoubted star.
□Der Evangelimann 24. Nju 24. Der Geiger von Florenz 26. Liebe 27. Queen Louisa 28. Dona Juana 28. Fraulein Else 29. Ariane 31. *Der Traumende Mund* 32. Ariane (GB) 33. *Catherine the Great* (GB) 34. *Escape Me Never* (GB) 35. As You Like It (GB) 36. Dreaming Lips (GB) 37. Stolen Life (GB) 39. Paris Calling (US) 41. Die Glucklichen Jahre der Thorwalds (Ger) 62. Cry of the Banshee (GB) 70. Courier to the Tsar (GB) 71. Der Fussganger (Ger) 73. Whitsun Holiday (Ger.) 79.

Berke, William (1903–1958). American director of second features.
Minesweeper 43. The Falcon in Mexico 44. Splitface 46. Jungle Jim 48. Deputy Marshal 49. Zamba the Gorilla 49. I Shot Billy the Kid (& p) 50. Four Boys and a Gun (& p) 55. Cop Hater (& p) 57, etc.

Berkeley, Ballard (1904–). British light actor of stage and screen.
The Chinese Bungalow 30. London Melody 35. The Outsider 38. In Which We Serve 42. They Made Me a Fugitive 47. The Long Dark Hall 51. Three Steps to the Gallows 56. See How They Run 57. Star! 68. The Wildcats 80, etc.

Berkeley, Busby (1895–1976) (William Berkeley Enos). American song and dance director who in the early thirties invaded Hollywood from Broadway and developed the spectacular, kaleidoscopic girlie numbers which became a feature of all musicals, quickly dated, and were joyously rediscovered in the sixties. Below, (m) signifies that Berkeley directed the musical sequences only. His occasional dramatic films were inconsiderable.
□*Whoopee* (m) 30. Kiki (m) 31. Palmy Days (m) 31. Flying High (m) 31. Night World (m) 32. Bird of Paradise (m) 32. *The Kid from Spain* (m) 32. *Forty Second Street* (m) 33. *Gold Diggers of 1933* (m) 33. She Had to Say Yes 33. *Footlight Parade* (m) 33. *Roman Scandals* (m) 33. *Wonder Bar* (m) 34. *Fashions of 1934* (m) 34. Twenty Million Sweethearts (m) 34. *Dames* (m) 34. *Gold Diggers of 1935* 35. Go into Your Dance (m) 35. Bright Lights 35. In Caliente (m) 35. I Live for Love 35. Stars Over Broadway 35. Stage Struck 36. Gold Diggers of 1937 (m) 37. The Go-Getter 37. The Singing Marine (m) 37. Varsity Show (m) 37. Hollywood Hotel 37. Men are Such Fools 38. Gold Diggers in Paris (m) 38. Garden of the Moon 38. Comet over Broadway 38. They Made me a Criminal 39. Broadway Serenade (m) 39. *Babes In Arms* 39. Fast and Furious 39. Forty Little Mothers 40. *Strike Up the Band* 40. Blonde Inspiration 41. *Ziegfeld Girl* (m) 41. *Lady Be Good* (m) 41. Babes on Broadway 41. Born to Sing (m) 41. *For Me and My Gal* 42. Girl Crazy (m) 43. *The Gang's All Here* 43. Cinderella Jones 46. Romance on the High Seas (m) 48. *Take Me Out to the Ball Game* 49. Two Weeks with Love (m) 50. Call me Mister (m) 51. Two Tickets to Broadway (m) 51. Million Dollar Mermaid (m) 52. Small Town Girl (m) 53. Easy to Love (m) 53. Rose Marie (m) 54. Jumbo (m) 62.

'His vitality and ingenuity transcended the limitations of his sensibility, and he bequeathed to posterity an entertaining record of the audacity of an escapist era.'—*Andrew Sarris, 1968*

❁ For pushing to the limit the decorative possibilities of chorus girls, grand pianos, and optical processes. *Dames.*

¶ 'If anybody wants to know what can be done with the camera, tell him to study every shot Busby Berkeley ever made.'—*Gene Kelly*

B.B.: In an era of breadlines, depression and wars, I tried to help people get away from all the misery . . . to turn their minds to something else. I wanted to make people happy, if only for an hour.

Berkeley, Sir Lennox (1903–). British composer. Only feature film score: Hotel Reserve 44.

Berkeley Square. Based on Henry James' *The Sense of the Past*, this romantic-macabre play by John Balderston concerned a man who enters his own past and falls in love with a girl of two hundred years ago. It was delicately filmed in 1933 by Frank Lloyd, with Leslie Howard in the lead. The 1951 remake with Tyrone Power, under the title *I'll Never Forget You*, seemed to lack the subtle enchantment of the original. In 1981 *Somewhere in Time*, though with different credits, was almost a remake.

Berlanga, Luis (1921–). Spanish director. Welcome Mr Marshall 52. Calabuch 56. The Executioner 63. Vivan los Novios 70. Life Size 77, etc.

Berle, Milton (1908–) (Mendel Berlinger). Brash American vaudeville and TV comedian who never quite found his niche in the movies.
Published 1974: *Milton Berle, an Autobiography*.
□New Faces of 1937 37. Radio City Revels 38. Tall Dark and Handsome 41. Sun Valley Serenade 41. Rise and Shine 41. A Gentleman at Heart 42. Whispering Ghosts 42. Over My Dead Body 42. *Margin for Error* 43. *Always Leave Them Laughing* (based on his autobiography) 49. Let's Make Love 60. *It's a Mad Mad Mad Mad World* 63. The Oscar 65. The Loved Ones 65. Don't Worry We'll Think of a Title 66. The Happening 67. Who's Minding the Mint? 67. Where Angels Go Trouble Follows 68. For Singles Only 68. Hieronymus Merkin 69. Seven in Darkness (TV) 70. Evil Roy Slade (TV) 71. Lepke 75. The Legend of Valentino (TV) 75. Won Ton Ton 76. The Muppet Movie 80. Broadway Danny Rose 84.

¶ 'The thief of bad gags.'—*Anon*
'He's been on TV for years and I finally figured out the reason for his success. He never improved.'—*Steve Allen*
† Allegedly, Berle was the child clinging to Marie Dressler's knee in *Tillie's Punctured Romance*.

Berlin has seemed to film makers a grim grey city, and history provides obvious reasons for this. Standard attitudes are shown in *The Murderers Are Amongst Us, Germany Year Zero, Four Men in a Jeep, Hotel Berlin, Berlin Express, The Man Between, Night People, The Big Lift, I Am a Camera. The Spy Who Came in from the Cold, The Man Who Finally Died, A Prize of Gold, The Quiller Memorandum, Cabaret, Escape from East Berlin, Funeral in Berlin*. But some people have found fun there, notably Billy Wilder in *People on Sunday, A Foreign Affair* and *One Two Three*; and in 1928 Walter Ruttman's stylishly kaleidoscopic documentary, *Berlin: Symphony of a Great City*, showed the place and its people to be just as sympathetic as anywhere else if they are understandingly portrayed.

Berlin, Irving (1888–) (Israel Baline). Prolific American composer and lyricist of tuneful popular songs.
The Awakening 28. The Coconuts 29. Hallelujah 29. Putting on the Ritz 30. Mammy 30. Reaching for the Moon 31. Kid Millions 34. *Top Hat* 35. *Follow the Fleet* 36. *On the Avenue* 37. *Alexander's Ragtime Band* 38. Carefree 38. Second Fiddle 39. Louisiana Purchase 42. Holiday Inn 42. *This is the Army* (in which he also appeared and sang 'Oh How I Hate to Get Up in the Morning') 43. *Blue Skies* 46. *Easter Parade* 48. *Annie Get Your Gun* 50. *Call Me Madam* 53. *There's No Business Like Show Business* 54. *White Christmas* 54. Sayonara 57, etc.
❁ For dominating three decades of musicals with an apparently endless barrage of tuneful melodies. *Alexander's Ragtime Band.*

Berlin, Jeannie (1949–). American actress, daughter of Elaine May.
□On a Clear Day You Can See Forever 70. Getting Straight 70. Move 70. The Strawberry Statement 70. The Baby Maker 70. Bone 72. Why 72. Portnoy's Complaint 71. *The Heartbreak Kid* 73. Sheila Levine 75.

Berlinger, Warren (1937–). American stage and film actor, usually seen as chubby innocent.
Teenage Rebel 56. Three Brave Men 57. Platinum High School 60. The Wackiest Ship in the Army 61. All Hands on Deck 61. Billie 65. Thunder Valley 67. The Shaggy D.A. 76. The Magician of Lublin 79. The World According to Garp 82. Free Ride 86, etc.
TV series: The Joey Bishop Show 61. The Funny Side 71. A Touch of Grace 73. Operation Petticoat 78.

Berman, Monty (1913–). British second feature producer, former cinematographer. Jack the Ripper (& d) 56. The Flesh and the Fiends 59. Sea of Sand 59. Blood of the Vampire 60. What a Carve Up 61. *The Hellfire Club* 61, many others.
TV series: *The Saint, Gideon's Way*, The Baron, The Champions, Department S, Randall and Hopkirk (Dec'd), The Adventurer, etc.

Berman, Pandro S. (1905–). Distinguished American producer who spent many years at both RKO and MGM, and maintained a high standard of product.
Morning Glory 32. *The Gay Divorcee* 34. The Little Minister 34. *Top Hat* 35. Sylvia Scarlett 36. Mary of Scotland 36. *Winterset* 36. Quality Street 37. *Stage Door* 37. Room Service 38. *The Hunchback of Notre Dame* 39. *Ziegfeld Girl* 41. Somewhere I'll Find You 42. The Seventh Cross 44. National Velvet 44. Undercurrent 46. *The Three Musketeers* 48. Madame Bovary 49. *Father of the Bride* 50. Ivanhoe 52. The Prisoner of Zenda 52. *The Blackboard Jungle* 55. Tea and Sympathy 56. Jailhouse Rock 57. The Brothers Karamazov 58. Butterfield 8 60. Sweet Bird of Youth 62. *The Prize* 63. A Patch of Blue 65, many others.
❁ For a lifetime of unobtrusive professionalism. *The Hunchback of Notre Dame.*

Berman, Shelley (1926–). American cabaret monologuist who has made a few film appearances.
□*The Best Man* 64. The Wheeler Dealers 64. Divorce American Style 67. Every Home Should have One (GB) 70.

Bern, Paul (1889–1932) (Paul Levy). American director whose suicide soon after his marriage to Jean Harlow is still a subject of controversy. (Became MGM executive.) Played in *Harlow* by Peter Lawford.
The North Wind's Malice 20. Worldly Goods 24. Tomorrow's Love 25. The Dressmaker from Paris 25. Grounds for Divorce 25, etc.
¶ *From P.B.'s suicide note:* You understand that last night was only a comedy.

Bernard, James (1925–). British composer with a predilection for horror themes. Co-authored film script, *Seven Days to Noon* 50.
The Quatermass Experiment 55. X the Unknown 56. The Curse of Frankenstein 57. Dracula 58. Windom's Way 58. The Hound of the Baskervilles 59. Kiss of the Vampire 62. The Gorgon 64. The Plague of the Zombies 65. She 65. The Torture Garden 67. Scars of Dracula 70. Frankenstein and the Monster from Hell 72. The Legend of the Seven Golden Vampires 73. Murder Elite (TV) 85, etc.

Bernard, Raymond (1891–1977). French director.
Le Petit Café 19. Le Miracle des Loups 24. The Chess Player 27. Tarkanova 30. Les Misérables 34. Le Coupable 37. J'était Une Aventurière 38. Les Otages 39. Un Ami Viendra Ce Soir 46. Maya 50. Le Jugement du Dieu 52. La Dame aux Camélias 53. Les Fruits de l'Eté 55. Le Septième Commandement 57. Le Septième Ciel 58, etc.

Bernardi, Herschel (1923–86). Balding, beaming American general purpose actor, often seen as cop or gangster.
Green Fields 37. Crime Inc. 45. Miss Susie Slagle's 46. Stakeout on Dope Street 58. The Savage Eye 60. A Cold Wind in August 61. Irma La Douce 63. The Honey Pot 67. But I Don't Want to Get Married (TV) 71. No Place to Run (TV) 72. No Deposit No Return 76. The Front 76, etc.
TV series: Peter Gunn 58–60. *Arnie* 70–71. Hail to the Chief 85.

Bernds, Edward (1905–). American second feature director, former sound mixer.
Blondie Hits the Jackpot 49. Harem Girl (& w) 52. Spy Chasers 55. World Without End (& w) 56. Quantrill's Raiders 58. Return of the Fly (& w) 59. The Three Stooges in Orbit 62. Tickle Me (w only) 65, many others.

Berners, Lord (1883–1950). British composer.
□Halfway House 44. Champagne Charlie (song arrangement only) 44. Nicholas Nickleby 47.

Bernhard, Jack (1913–). American second feature director.

Bernhardt, Curtis (or **Kurt**) (1899–1981). German director; on arrival in Hollywood in 1940, he was generally assigned to 'women's pictures' and approached them with variable style.
Three Loves 29. Thirteen Men and a Girl 31. Die Letzte Kompagnie 32. The Beloved Vagabond (GB) 36. My Love Came Back 40. Lady with Red Hair 40. Million Dollar Baby 41. Juke Girl 42. Happy Go Lucky 43. *Devotion* 44. Conflict 45. My Reputation 45. *A Stolen Life* 46. *Possessed* 47. High Wall 47. The Doctor and the Girl 49. Payment on Demand (& w) 51. Sirocco 51. The Blue Veil 51. Miss Sadie Thompson 53. *Beau Brummell* 54. Interrupted Melody 55. Gaby 56. Stefanie in Rio 60. *Kisses for My President* (& p) 64, etc.

Bernhardt, Sarah (1844–1923) (Rosalie Bernard). Famous French stage tragedienne who lent dignity if nothing else to early

silent films, and even continued working in them after her leg was amputated. After seeing herself in *Queen Elizabeth*, which in America helped found the fortunes of Paramount, she is reputed to have said: 'Mr Zukor, you have put me in pickle for all time!' She was played in *The Incredible Sarah* by Glenda Jackson.
Biography 1976: *Sarah Bernhardt* by William Emboden.
□Hamlet's Duel 00. Tosca 08. La Dame aux Camélias 11. *Queen Elizabeth* 12. Adrienne Lecouvreur 13. Jeanne Doré 14. Mères Françaises 17. La Voyante 23.

¶ 'The film audience could see her only as a figure of fun, a dumb creature jerking her sawdust heart around in a puppet world.'—*Alistair Cooke*

Bernie, Ben (1891–1943) (Benjamin Anzelvitz). American bandleader who worked up a publicity feud with Walter Winchell and consequently appeared in a film or two.
□Shoot the Works 34. Stolen Harmony 35. *Wake Up and Live* 37. Love and Hisses 37.

Bernstein, Charles (–). American composer.
Hex 73. White Lightning 73. Mr Majestyk 74.

Bernstein, Elmer (1922–). American composer-conductor.
Saturday's Hero 51. Sudden Fear 52. Cat Women of the Moon 53. *The Man with the Golden Arm* 55. The Ten Commandments 56. *The Sweet Smell of Success* 57. The Tin Star 57. God's Little Acre 58. The Buccaneer 59. *The Magnificent Seven* 60. A Walk on the Wild Side 62. To Kill a Mockingbird 62. Baby the Rain Must Fall 65. The Sons of Katie Elder 65. The Reward 65. Return of the Seven 66. *Thoroughly Modern Millie* (AA) 67. A Cannon for Cordoba 70. The Shootist 76. National Lampoon's Animal House 76. Zulu Dawn 79. Airplane 80. The Great Santini 80. Saturn Three 80. An American Werewolf in London 81. Honky Tonk Freeway 81. Going Ape 81. Five Days One Summer 82. The Chosen 82. Class 82. Trading Places 83. Ghostbusters 84, Legal Eagles 85. Spies Like Us 86. The Black Cauldron 86, etc.

Bernstein, Leonard (1918–). American concert musician, conductor and composer.
On the Town 49. On the Waterfront 54. West Side Story 61.

Bernstein, Lord (1899–) (Sidney Bernstein). British executive and producer, founder and chairman of the Granada group, including a television station and a cinema circuit. Founder member of the Film Society (1924). First to institute Saturday morning shows for children and to research audience preferences. During World War II, films adviser to the Ministry of Information and SHAEF. Produced three films with Alfred Hitchcock as director: *Rope* 48, *Under Capricorn* 49. *I Confess* 52.

Bernstein, Walter (1919–). American screenwriter.
That Kind of Woman 59. A Breath of Scandal 60. *Fail Safe* 64. The Train (co-w) 64. The Money Trap 66. The Molly Maguires 70. Semi Tough 77. The Betsy 78. Yanks 79. Little Miss Marker (d only) 80, etc.

Berri, Claude (1934–). French writer-director, usually of stories with a Jewish background. Acted in some of them.
□Les Baisers (one episode) 64. La Chance et l'Amour 64. *Le Vieil Homme et l'Enfant* 67. Mazel Tov 68. Le Pistonnée 70. Le Cinema de Papa 71. Le Sex Shop 72. Male of the Century 75. La Première Fois 76. Un Moment d'Egarement 78. Je Vous Aime 80. *Jean de Florette* 86. *Manon des Sources* 86.

Berry, John (1917–). American director with stage experience.
□Cross My Heart 45. From This Day Forward 46. Miss Susie Slagle's 46. Casbah 48. Tension 49. He Ran All the Way 51. C'est Arrivé à Paris 52. Ça Va Barder (Fr.) 55. The Great Lover (Don Juan) (Fr.) 55. Je Suis un Sentimental (Fr.) 55. Tamango 57. Oh Que Mambo (It.) 59. Maya 66. A Tout Casser 67. Claudine 74. Thieves 77. The Bad News Bears Go to Japan 78.

Berry, Jules (1883–1951) (Jules Paufichet). Saturnine French character actor.
The Crime of Monsieur Lange 34. Carrefour 39. *Le Jour Se Lève* 39. *Les Visiteurs du Soir* 42. La Symphonie Fantastique 47, etc.

Berry, Ken (1933–). American actor often seen on TV as bird-like comic hero.
Wake Me When The War Is Over (TV) 70. The Reluctant Heroes (TV) 71. Herbie Rides Again 74, etc.
TV series: F Troop 65–67. Mayberry RFD 68–71. Mama's Family 82.

Berthomieu, André (1903–1960). French director, former assistant to Julien Duvivier

and author of a book on cinema grammar.
Ces Dames aux Chapeaux Verts 29. *Le Crime de Sylvestre Bonnard* 30. Mon Ami Victor 31. L'Aristo 34. La Flamme 36. The Girl in the Taxi (GB) 37. Les Nouveaux Riches 38. L'Inconnue de Monte Carlo 39. La Neige sur le Pas 41. L'Ange de la Nuit 44. J'ai 17 Ans 45. Gringalet 46. La Femme Nue 49. Chacun son Tour 51. Scènes de Ménage 54. La Joyeuse Prison 56. Préméditation 60, many others.

Berti, Marina (1928–). Italian leading lady in occasional international films.
Prince of Foxes 49. Deported 50. Quo Vadis 51. Queen of Sheba 53. Abdullah the Great 56. Ben Hur 59. Tyrant of Syracuse 62. Cleopatra 62. Swordsman of Siena 63. Moses (TV) 76. Jesus of Nazareth (TV) 77.

Bertini, Francesca (1888–1985) (Elena Vitiello). Italian leading lady of the silent period, a model of screen beauty and fashion.
La Dea del Mare 04. Il Trovatore 09. Salome 13. Assunta Spina 15. Tosca 17. Romeo and Juliet 20. Resurrection 20. La Donna Nuda 22. Monte Carlo 28. Odette 28. Dora 43, many others.

Bertolucci, Bernardo (1940–). Italian writer-director, a former romanticist and poet who turned increasingly to censorable themes.
□The Grim Reaper 62. *Before the Revolution* 64. Love and Anger (part) 67. Partner 68. *The Spider's Stratagem* 70. The Conformist 70. *Last Tango in Paris* 72. *1900* 76. La Luna 79. Tragedy of a Ridiculous Man 81.

Bessell, Ted (–). American comic character actor.
Billie 65. Don't Drink the Water 69. Two on a Bench (TV) 71. Your Money or Your Wife (TV) 72, etc.
TV series: It's a Man's World 62. Gomer Pyle 65–66. That Girl 66–71. Hail to the Chief 85.

Besser, Joe (1916–). Rotund American burlesque comic who in the fifties became one of the Three Stooges in their declining days.

Besserer, Eugenie (1870–1934). American character actress.
The Count of Monte Cristo 12. Scarlet Days 19. The Sin of Martha Queed 21. The Rosary 22. Her Reputation 23. The Price She Paid 24. A Fool and His Money 25. The Millionaire Policeman 26. *The Jazz Singer* (as Jolson's mother) 27. Two Lovers 28. Madame X 29. Thunderbolt 29. In Gay Madrid 30. To the Last Man 33, many others.

Bessie, Alvah (1904–85). American screenwriter, blacklisted in 1949 as one of the Hollywood Ten (qv).
The Very Thought of You 44. Hotel Berlin 45. Objective Burma 45, etc.

Best, Edna (1900–1974). Soft-spoken, maternal British actress, once married to Herbert Marshall. Went to Hollywood in 1939 and stayed.
Tilly of Bloomsbury 21. A Couple of Down and Outs 23. Escape 30. *Tilly of Bloomsbury* 30. The Calendar 31. *Michael and Mary* 32. The Faithful Heart 32. *The Man Who Knew Too Much* 34. Sleeping Partners 37. *South Riding* 38. Prison without Bars 39. *Intermezzo* 39. *The Swiss Family Robinson* 40. A Dispatch from Reuters 40. The Late George Apley 46. The Ghost and Mrs Muir 47. The Iron Curtain 48, etc.

Best, James (1926–). American general purpose actor, often in westerns as sly ranch-hand.
Winchester 73 50. Kansas Raiders 51. Francis Goes to West Point 52. Seven Angry Men 55. Gaby 56. The Left Handed Gun 58. The Mountain Road 60. Shock Corridor 63. Three on a Couch 66. Firecreek 67. Ode to Billy Joe 76, etc.
TV series: The Dukes of Hazzard 79.

Best, Richard (1916–). British editor.
Desert Victory 43. Fame is the Spur 47. Mine Own Executioner 48. The Magic Box 51. The Dam Busters 54. Ice Cold in Alex 58. The Double Man 66. Otley 68. Please Sir 71. Dominique 77.

The Best Man (US 1964). About the best of the serious political films of the early sixties, this bitter comedy-drama about presidential nominations was based on Gore Vidal's play and directed by Franklin Schaffner. Lee Tracy and Henry Fonda were on top form.

The Best Remaining Seats by Ben M. Hall. A book covering the golden age of the American picture palace; published in 1961.

Best, Willie (1916–1962). Goggle-eyed black American comedian, once known as Sleep'n Eat and later the prototype frightened manservant.
Feet First 30. The Monster Walks 32. Kentucky Kernels 33. Little Miss Marker 34. Murder on a Honeymoon 35. Jalna 35. The Littlest Rebel 35. Mummy's Boys 36. Thank You Jeeves 36. Super Sleuth 37. Blondie 38.

Merrily We Live 38. Vivacious Lady 38. At the Circus 39. I Take This Woman 40. *The Ghost Breakers* 40. Road Show 41. High Sierra 41. The Body Disappears 41. The Smiling Ghost 41. Busses Roar 42. The Hidden Hand 42. Cabin in the Sky 43. Thank Your Lucky Stars 43. Home in Indiana 44. Hold That Blonde 45. The Bride Wore Boots 46. Red Stallion 47. The Shanghai Chest 48. South of Caliente 51, many others.
TV series: My Little Margie 52–54. Trouble with Father 50–55.

The Best Years of Our Lives (US 1946) (AA). On its original release, this film about the resettlement of ex-servicemen in a small American town seemed like an enduring classic. A generation later the mood of the time was impossible to recapture and much of the film seemed humdrum. But it was an important step in Hollywood's development towards maturity, presented by a highly talented group: director William Wyler (AA), cinematographer Gregg Toland, writer Robert E. Sherwood (AA), from a novel by Mackinlay Kantor. The cast included Fredric March (AA), Myrna Loy, Dana Andrews, Teresa Wright, and a handless veteran, Harold Russell (AA), whose only film this was until he popped up thirty-five years later in *Inside Moves*.

Beswick, Martine (1941–). British pin-up, decorative in occasional films.
From Russia with Love 62. Thunderball 65. One Million Years BC 66. The Penthouse 67. Dr Jekyll and Sister Hyde 71. Seizure 74. The Happy Hooker Goes to Hollywood 80, etc.

La Bête Humaine (France 1938). Based on a novel by Emile Zola, this steamy emotional melodrama with a railway setting was written and directed by Jean Renoir, with photography by Curt Courant and music by Joseph Kosma. In 1954, Fritz Lang directed a perfunctory remake called *Human Desire*, with Glenn Ford, Gloria Grahame and Broderick Crawford in the roles originally taken by Jean Gabin, Simone Simon and Michel Simon.

Bettger, Lyle (1915–). American screen actor who started in 1946 as leading man but seemed more at home in villainous roles.
No Man of Her Own 50. Union Station 50. The First Legion 51. All I Desire 53. The Greatest Show on Earth 53. The Sea Chase 55. Gunfight at the OK Corral 57. Guns of the Timberland 60. Town Tamer 65. Nevada Smith 66. The Fastest Guitar Alive 68. The Seven Minutes 71. M Station Hawaii (TV) 80, many others.
TV series: Court of Last Resort 57. Grand Jury 58–59.

Betty Boop. Doll-like cartoon creation, a wide-eyed gold-digging flapper created by Max Fleischer in 1915 and popular throughout the twenties and thirties especially after she was censored by Will H. Hays in 1935. The cartoons in which she featured were wildly imaginative and usually made comments on the social follies of their time; in the seventies they became popular through compilation features. Betty was supposedly based on 'boop-a-doop' singer Helen Kane.

Betz, Carl (1920–78). American leading man who moved from films to TV.
The President's Lady 53. Inferno 53. Vicki 53. Dangerous Crossing 53. Spinout 66, etc.
TV series: *The Donna Reed Show* 58–65. *Judd for the Defense* 67–68.

Bevan, Billy (1887–1957) (William Bevan Harris). Wide-eyed, moustachioed silent screen comedian, an Australian who moved to Hollywood and became one of Mack Sennett's troupe. Later played many small parts, often that of a bewildered policeman.
Easy Pickings 27. Riley the Cop 28. *Journey's End* 30. Sky Devils 32. *Cavalcade* 33. Alice in Wonderland 33. Limehouse Blues 34. *Dracula's Daughter* 36. Captain Fury 39. The Long Voyage Home 40. Dr Jekyll and Mr Hyde 41. The Picture of Dorian Gray 45. Cluny Brown 46. The Black Arrow 48, many others.

Bevans, Clem (1879–1963) (Clement Blevins). Long-faced and latterly white-haired American character actor who played a long succession of grandfathers, doorkeepers, oldest inhabitants and gold prospectors.
Way Down East 35. Of Human Hearts 38. Abe Lincoln in Illinois 40. *Saboteur* 42. The Human Comedy 43. Captain Eddie 45. The Yearling 46. The Paleface 48. Streets of Laredo 49. *Harvey* 50. The Stranger Wore a Gun 53. The Kentuckian 55, etc.

Bewes, Rodney (1937–). Chubby British comedy actor.
Billy Liar 63. Decline and Fall 68. Spring and Port Wine 70. Alice's Adventures in Wonderland 72. The Likely Lads 76. Jabberwocky 77. The Spaceman and King Arthur 79, etc.

TV series: *The Likely Lads* 65–69. Dear Mother Love Albert 70–72. *Whatever Happened to the Likely Lads* 73.

Bey, Turhan (1920–) (Turhan Selahattin Sahultavy Bey). Dapper Turkish leading man who had a good run in Hollywood during World War II in the absence on war service of more dynamic stars. Later became a stills photographer and moved to Vienna.
Footsteps in the Dark 41. Drums of the Congo 42. The Mummy's Tomb 42. Arabian Nights 42. White Savage 43. Background to Danger 43. The Mad Ghoul 43. Ali Baba and the Forty Thieves 43. Dragon Seed 44. Bowery to Broadway 44. The Climax 44. Frisco Sal 44. A Night in Paradise 46. Out of the Blue 47. Adventures of Casanova 48. Song of India 49. Prisoners of the Casbah 53. Stolen Identity (p only) 53, etc.

Beymer, Richard (1939–). American child actor who in the early sixties seemed about to turn into a major juvenile lead, but somehow never made it.
So Big 52. Indiscretion of an American Wife 52. Johnny Tremain 57. The Diary of Anne Frank 59. High Time 60. *West Side Story* 61. Five Finger Exercise 62. *Hemingway's Adventures of a Young Man* 62. The Longest Day 62. The Stripper 62. Cross Country 83.

Bezzerides, A. I. (1908–) (Albert Isaac Bezzerides). American screenwriter.
They Drive by Night 40. Northern Pursuit 43. *Thieves' Highway* 49. Sirocco 51. On Dangerous Ground 52. Beneath the 12 Mile Reef 53. Track of the Cat 54. *Kiss Me Deadly* 55. The Angry Hills 59, etc.

Bianchi, Daniela (1942–). Italian leading lady.
Love is My Profession 59. Sword of El Cid 62. *From Russia With Love* 63. The Balearic Caper 66. Weekend Italian Style 68. The Dirty Heroes 68, etc.

Biberman, Abner (1909–77). American character actor who spent many years playing Red Indian braves and dastardly dagoes before turning into a director.
Gunga Din 39. His Girl Friday 40. South of Pago Pago 40. South of Tahiti 41. Broadway 42. The Leopard Man 43. Salome Where She Danced 45. Captain Kidd 45. Back to Bataan 50. Elephant Walk 54. The Golden Mistress 54. The Price of Fear (d) 56. Above all Things 57. Gun for a Coward (d) 57, many others especially in TV.

Biberman, Herbert J. (1900–1971). American director whose career was harmed by his political convictions. Married Gale Sondergaard.
One Way Ticket 35. Meet Nero Wolfe 36. King of Chinatown (w only) 38. *The Master Race* (& d) 44. New Orleans (w only) 47. Abilene Town (p only) 46. Salt of the Earth (& w) 53. Slaves (& w) 69, etc.

The Bible. The extravaganza which claimed to be the 'film of the book' was conceived by Dino de Laurentiis as a nine-hour survey by several directors. It turned up in 1966 as a slow plod through Genesis by and with John Huston. Of the hundreds of films which have been inspired by the Old Testament stories, some of the most memorable are *The Private Life of Adam and Eve, Sodom and Gomorrah, Green Pastures, A Story of David, David and Bathsheba, Samson and Delilah, The Prodigal, The Ten Commandments* (two versions), *Salome, Esther and the King* and *The Story of Ruth.* For the New Testament, see under *Christ*; the immediate effects of whose life have been treated in such assorted films as *The Robe, Demetrius and the Gladiators, The Sign of the Cross, The Big Fisherman, Quo Vadis, Ben Hur, Spartacus, Fabiola, Barabbas, The Silver Chalice*, and *The Fall of the Roman Empire,* not to mention Lord Grade's six-hour *Jesus of Nazareth* for TV (a 'sequel' to his *Moses*). All this activity sparked off in 1978 a rather naive American TV series, *Greatest Heroes of the Bible.*

Bickford, Charles (1889–1967). Rugged American character actor who sometimes played stubborn or unscrupulous roles but more often projected sincerity and warmth. Autobiography 1965: *Bulls, Balls, Bicycles and Actors.*
□Dynamite 29. South Sea Rose 29. Hell's Heroes 29. *Anna Christie* 30. The Sea Bat 30. Passion Flower 30. River's End 31. The Squaw Man 31. East of Borneo 31. Pagan Lady 31. Men in Her Life 31. Panama Flo 32. *Thunder Below* 32. Scandal for Sale 32. The Last Man 32. Vanity Street 32. No Other Woman 33. Song of the Eagle 33. This Day and Age 33. White Woman 33. Little Miss Marker 34. A Wicked Woman 34. A Notorious Gentleman 35. Under Pressure 35. The Farmer Takes a Wife 35. East of Java 35. The Littlest Rebel 35. Rose of the Rancho 35. Pride of the Marines 36. The Plainsman 36. Night Club Scandal 37. Thunder Trail 37. Daughter of Shanghai 37. High Wide and

Handsome 37. Gangs of New York 38. Valley of the Giants 38. The Storm 39. Stand Up and Fight 39. Romance of the Redwoods 39. Street of Missing Men 39. Our Leading Citizen 39. One Hour to Live 39. Mutiny in the Big House 39. Thou Shalt Not Kill 39. *Of Mice and Men* 40. The Girl from God's Country 40. South to Karanga 40. Queen of the Yukon 40. *Riders of Death Valley* (serial) 41. Burma Convoy 41. Reap the Wild Wind 42. Tarzan's New York Adventure 42. Mr Lucky 43. *The Song of Bernadette* 43. Wing and a Prayer 44. Captain Eddie 45. Fallen Angel 45. *Duel in the Sun* 46. *The Farmer's Daughter* 47. The Woman on the Beach 47. *Brute Force* 47. The Babe Ruth Story 47. Four Faces West 48. *Johnny Belinda* 48. Command Decision 48. Roseanna McCoy 49. Whirlpool 49. *Treason* (as Cardinal Mindzenty) 49. Branded 50. Riding High 50. Jim Thorpe—All American 51. The Raging Tide 51. Elopement 51. The Last Posse 53. *A Star is Born* 54. Prince of Players 55. Not as a Stranger 55. The Court Martial of Billy Mitchell 55. You Can't Run Away from It 56. Mister Cory 57. So Soon to Die (TV) 57. *The Big Country* 58. The Unforgiven 60. Days of Wine and Roses 62. Della (TV) 64. *A Big Hand for the Little Lady* 66.

Bicycle Thieves (Italy 1947). Hailed throughout the world as the fount of Italian post-war realism, this simple tale of a billposter's sad quest for the stolen bicycle essential to his job was actually in a well-established Italian tradition. It was nevertheless an absorbing and brilliant film which influenced film-making in every country where it was seen. Vittorio de Sica directed from Cesare Zavattini's script, and the non-professional performances of Lamberto Maggiorani (the man) and Enzo Staiola (his son) were outstanding.

bicycling. A trade term for the sharing, usually illegally, of one print between two theatres: the manager had to make frequent bicycle trips!

The Big Broadcast (US 1932). A light-hearted entertainment which used a zany story about a radio station to bring in many radio stars of the day, and was followed by three sequels (1936, 1937, 1938). The films were smoothly made and anticipated the *Hellzapoppin* type humour of the forties.

big business was outside the range of silent movie-makers, but in the thirties, usually personified by Edward Arnold, it became a useful villain for the comedies and dramas of social conscience. A switch was made in *Dodsworth,* in which the businessman became an innocent abroad; but not until the growing affluence of the fifties did Hollywood think it worth while to probe into the personal lives of those who occupy the corridors of power. Then in quick succession we had *Executive Suite, Woman's World, Patterns of Power, The Power and the Prize* and *The Man in the Grey Flannel Suit*; while the inevitable knocking process began as early as *The Man in The White Suit* and continued with *The Solid Gold Cadillac, Cash McCall, Ice Palace, The Apartment* and *The Wheeler Dealers.*

The Big Carnival: see *Ace In The Hole.*

The Big Country (US 1958). Basically a simple, sprawling western about the family feud between two embittered old ranchers, this 165-minute spectacular was enriched by a lush score (Jerome Moross), impeccable direction (William Wyler), and a script (James R. Webb, Sy Bartlett, Robert Wilder) pretentious enough to attempt a parable of the Cold War. The acting of Charles Bickford, Burl Ives, Gregory Peck and Charlton Heston was also a help.

The Big Heat (US 1953). This competent crime film had Glenn Ford as a tough cop out to get gangsters who murdered his wife in mistake for him. It is chiefly notable because both cops and criminals were more humanized than had previously been the case, and because its use of violence (scalding coffee in the heroine's face) was something new and disturbing. Written by Sidney Boehm, photographed by Charles Lang, directed by Fritz Lang.

The Big Parade (US 1925). Though most of it now seems painfully slow and dated, King Vidor's silent film about 'the average guy who went to war' brought home to millions the realities of trench combat. It also established John Gilbert as a top star, and in two years grossed fifteen million dollars which consolidated the fortunes of MGM. Written by Laurence Stallings, photographed by John Arnold.

bigamists have been prevented by the censorship codes from achieving hero status in more than a few films; perhaps it is significant that although the Italian film called *The Bigamist* is a comedy, the American one is a solemn affair. Over the years, however, scriptwriters have achieved some sympathy and humour for the characters played by William Bendix in *Don Juan Quilligan,* Alec Guinness in *The Captain's Paradise,* Clifton Webb in *The Remarkable Mr Pennypacker,* Rex Harrison in *The Constant Husband,* Jean-Claude Drouot in *Le Bonheur* and Leo McKern in *Decline and Fall.*

Biggers, Earl Derr (1884–1933). American crime novelist, whose chief gift to the movies was Charlie Chan (qv). Also wrote original story of *The Millionaire* 31, and the much filmed play *Seven Keys to Baldpate.*

Bikel, Theodore (1924–). Heavily-built Viennese actor, guitarist and singer; can play most nationalities. International stage, TV, cabaret and film work.
The African Queen 51. The Love Lottery 54. The Pride and the Passion 57. The Defiant Ones 58. The Blue Angel 59. A Dog of Flanders 60. My Fair Lady 64. Sands of the Kalahari 65. The Russians Are Coming, The Russians Are Coming 66. My Side of the Mountain 68. Darker than Amber 70. The Little Ark 71. Victory at Entebbe (TV) 76, etc.

A Bill of Divorcement. Clemence Dane's play about the return of a deranged father from a mental institution was made into a topical film in 1932, with Katharine Hepburn in her film debut playing opposite John Barrymore. It was directed by George Cukor. By the time of John Farrow's scene-for-scene remake in 1940 the material seemed artificial and old-fashioned; Maureen O'Hara lacked Hepburn's intensity, though Adolphe Menjou was surprisingly good as the father.

Bill, Tony (1940–). American light leading man.
Come Blow Your Horn 63. None But the Brave 65. Marriage on the Rocks 66. Ice Station Zebra 68.Castle Keep 69. Flap 70, etc.
As producer: Deadhead Miles 70. Steelyard Blues 70. The Sting 73. Hearts of the West 75. Shampoo 75, etc.
As director: My Bodyguard 80.

billing. The official credits for a film, usually stating the relative sizes of type to be accorded to title, stars, character actors, etc.

Billington, Kevin (1933–). British director, from TV.
Interlude 68. The Rise and Rise of Michael Rimmer 70. The Light at the Edge of the World 71. And No One Could Save Her (TV) 72. Voices 74.

Billy the Kid, the historical, homicidal western gunslinger, has frequently been turned by the movies into some kind of hero. A favourite character of the silents, he has been seen also in numerous talkie versions. Johnny Mack Brown played him on the wide screen in *Billy the Kid* 30; pious Roy Rogers was the star of *Billy the Kid Returns* 39; in 1940 Robert Taylor was *Billy the Kid*; and in 1943 (or so) came *The Outlaw,* with a happy ending for Jack Buetel who played Billy. In 1949 Audie Murphy played Billy in *The Kid from Texas*; 1950 brought *I Shot Billy the Kid* with Don Barry; 1954 *The Law Versus Billy the Kid* with Scott Brady; 1955 *The Parson and the Outlaw* with Anthony Dexter; 1958 *The Left-handed Gun* with Paul Newman; and in 1966 we were even offered *Billy the Kid Meets Dracula*; and in 1974 Sam Peckinpah's *Pat Garrett and Billy the Kid* added new refinements of violence. There were also scores of second features in the thirties and forties, with Bob Steele or Buster Crabbe as Billy; whose real name incidentally was William Bonney and who died in 1881 at the age of 21.

Binder, Maurice (1925–). American title artist in Britain, chiefly known for designing the graphics of the James Bond films.
Indiscreet 58. The Mouse that Roared 59. The Grass is Greener 60. *Dr No* 62. Repulsion 64. The Chase 66. Bedazzled 67. The Private Life of Sherlock Holmes 71. Gold 74. Shout at the Devil 76. The Sea Wolves 80, etc.

Bing, Herman (1889–1947). Plump, explosive German comedy actor, former assistant to F. W. Murnau; in Hollywood from 1929.
Married in Hollywood 29. The Guardsman 31. Dinner at Eight 33. The Black Cat 34. Rose Marie 36. The Great Ziegfeld 36. Champagne Waltz 37. The Great Waltz 38. Sweethearts 38. The Devil with Hitler 42. Where Do We Go from Here? 45. Rendezvous 24 46, many others.

Binns, Edward (or **Ed**) (–). Solid but unremarkable American character actor.
Teresa 51. The Scarlet Hour 56. Twelve Angry Men 57. Compulsion 59. North by Northwest 59. Fail Safe 64. Chubasco 67. Patton 69. Oliver's Story 79, etc.

TV series: Brenner 59–64. The Nurses 62–64. It Takes a Thief 69–70.

Binyon, Claude (1905–78). American writer-director.
The Gilded Lily (w) 35. I Met Him in Paris (w) 37. Sing You Sinners (w) 38. Arizona (w) 40. Suddenly It's Spring (w) 44. *The Saxon Charm* (wd) 48. Family Honeymoon (wd) 49. Mother Didn't Tell Me (w) 50. Stella (wd) 50. Aaron Slick from Punkin Crick (wd) 52. *Dreamboat* (wd) 52. You Can't Run Away from It (w) 56. North to Alaska (w) 60. Satan Never Sleeps (w) 62. Kisses for My President (w) 64, etc.

biograph. 1. An old name for a cinema projector. 2. The name of Britain's first public cinema, near Victoria Station, London. Opened 1905, still operating. 3. The name of D. W. Griffith's New York studios, 1903–10.

biopic. A contraction of 'biographical picture', i.e. a film about the life of a real person. For examples see under *Composers, Courtesans, Entertainers, Explorers, Inventors, Kings and Queens, Painters, Politicians, Scientists, Soldiers, Spies, Sportsmen, Writers.*

? I
In each of the following cases, say what actor or entertainer was impersonated in what film by the person given.

1 Jill Clayburgh in 1976
2 Betty Hutton in 1945
3 Charles Ruggles in 1944
4 Brian Aherne in 1937
5 Carroll Baker in 1964
6 Miriam Hopkins in 1941
7 Keefe Brasselle in 1953
8 Richard Burton in 1954
9 Susan Hayward in 1955
10 Donald O'Connor in 1957
11 Errol Flynn in 1958
12 Danny Kaye in 1959
13 Rod Steiger in 1976
14 Kim Novak in 1957
15 James Cagney in 1957
16 Betty Hutton in 1947
17 Tony Curtis in 1953
18 Alice Faye in 1940
19 Doris Day in 1955
20 June Haver in 1949
21 June Haver and Betty Grable in 1944
22 Tommy Trinder in 1944
23 Sal Mineo in 1960
24 Ann Blyth in 1954
25 Patrice Munsel in 1950
26 Ann Sheridan in 1944
27 Betty Hutton in 1953
28 Natalie Wood in 1962
29 Diana Ross in 1974
30 Frank Sinatra in 1957

NB. The term entertainer is used in its broadest sense.

? II
The following people, all real, had films based on their lives. Name in each case the profession or calling of the person, the film, and the actor who played him or her.

1 Douglas Bader
2 Gus Kahn
3 Violette Szabo
4 Red Nichols
5 George M. Cohan
6 Alfred the Great
7 Hiram Maxim
8 Paul Ehrlich
9 Grover Cleveland Alexander
10 Alexander Graham Bell
11 Amy Johnson
12 Jenny Lind
13 Jane Froman
14 William Friese-Greene
15 Peg Woffington
16 Marjorie Laurence
17 Vesta Tilley
18 John Montgomery
19 Guy Gabaldon
20 Ernie Pyle
21 Robert Stroud
22 Sol Hurok
23 Barbara Graham
24 John Paul Jones
25 Eva Tanguay
26 Eddie Foy
27 R. J. Mitchell
28 Grace Moore
29 Thomas More
30 Gladys Aylward

Birch, Paul (c. 1900–1969). Burly American character actor.
The War of the Worlds 53. Rebel without a Cause 55. When Gangland Strikes 56. *Not of This Earth* 57. The Dark at the Top of the Stairs 60. The Man Who Shot Liberty Valance 62. It's a Mad Mad Mad Mad World 63. Welcome to Hard Times 67, etc.
TV series: Cannonball 58.

Bird, Norman (c. 1920–). British character actor, usually of underdogs.
An Inspector Calls 54. *The League of Gentlemen* 59. *Victim* 62. The Hill 65. Sky West and Crooked 65. The Wrong Box 66. A

Dandy in Aspic 68. The Virgin and the Gypsy 70. The Rise and Rise of Michael Rimmer 70. Ooh . . . You Are Awful 73. The Slipper and the Rose 76. The Medusa Touch 77. The Final Conflict 81. Queenie (TV) 87, many others.

Bird, Richard (1894–). British light actor who played genial middle-aged roles in the thirties.
Tilly of Bloomsbury 31. Mimi 35. Sensation 37. The Terror (& d) 38. The Door with Seven Locks 40. Halfway House 44. Forbidden 49, many others.

birds fit nicely into the glamorous romantic backgrounds of which Hollywood used to be so fond, but a few particular examples have been malevolent, including *The Vulture,* the owner of *The Giant Claw,* the carnivorous birds which nearly pecked *Barbarella* to death, and of course *The Birds* which turned on the human race in Hitchcock's 1963 movie. (In the various versions of Edgar Allan Poe's *The Raven,* the title character has been almost irrelevant.) Other notable birds have been seen in *Treasure Island, Birdman of Alcatraz, The Pigeon That Took Rome, Run Wild Run Free, The Bluebird, Kes, Doctor Dolittle,* and *Bill and Coo*; and in the cartoon field one must remember with affection Donald and Daffy Duck, Tweetie Pie, the Road Runner, and an assortment of other feathered friends. The heroes of *Brewster McCloud* and several other films thought they were birds; *Jonathan Livingston Seagull* was. *Mr Drake's Duck* and his Disney lookalike *The Million Dollar Duck* laid extremely valuable eggs. The pelican in *Storm Boy* stole the show from the hero; and the birds in *Tawny Pipit* and *Conflict of Wings* upset whole countrysides.

Birell, Tala (1908–1959) (Natalie Bierle). Polish-Austrian leading lady who made some international films, then settled in Hollywood.
Man in a Cage (GB) 30. Doomed Battalion 32. The Captain Hates the Sea 34. Crime and Punishment 35. Bringing Up Baby 38. Seven Miles from Alcatraz 42. The Song of Bernadette 43. Mrs Parkington 44. Song of Love 47. The House of Tao Ling 47, etc.

Birkett, Michael (1929–) (Lord Birkett). British producer, mainly of specialized entertainments.
The Caretaker 63. The Soldier's Tale 64. Modesty Blaise (associate) 66. The Marat/Sade 66. A Midsummer Night's Dream 68. King Lear 70, etc.

Birkin, Jane (1946–). English leading lady, former model, who has been seen to most advantage in continental productions.
Blow Up 66. Les Chemins de Katmandou 69. Romance of a Horsethief 71. Don Juan 73. Private Projection 73. Sept Morts sur Ordonnance 75. Catherine and Co. 75. Le Diable au Coeur 75. Death on the Nile 78, etc.

Birney, David (1944–). American leading man.
Caravan to Vaccares 74. Trial by Combat 76. Prettykill 87.
TV series: Bridget Loves Bernie 73. Serpico 76. St Elsewhere 82. Glitter 84.

Birney, Meredith Baxter (–). American leading actress, mostly on TV. Wife of David Birney; formerly known as Meredith Baxter.
Stand Up and Be Counted 71. Ben 72. The Cat Creature (TV) 73. The Stranger Who Looks Like Me (TV) 74. The Night That Panicked America (TV) 75. Target Risk (TV) 75. All the President's Men 76. The November Plan (TV) 76. Bittersweet Love 76. Beulah Land (TV) 80, etc.
TV series: *Bridget Loves Bernie* 72. Family 76. *Family Ties* 82– .

Biro, Lajos (1880–1948). Hungarian screenwriter with Hollywood experience in the twenties followed by much work for Korda in Britain.
Forbidden Paradise 24. The Last Command 27. The Way of All Flesh 28. Service for Ladies 32. *The Private Life of Henry VIII* 32. Catherine the Great 34. *The Scarlet Pimpernel* 34. Sanders of the River 35. The Divorce of Lady X 37. The Drum 38. The Four Feathers 39. *The Thief of Baghdad* 40. Five Graves to Cairo 43. A Royal Scandal 45, etc.: mostly in collaboration.

Biroc, Joseph F. (1903–). American cinematographer.
It's a Wonderful Life (co-ph) 46. Magic Town 47. Roughshod 49. Without Warning 52. The Tall Texan 53. Down Three Dark Streets 54. Nightmare 56. Run of the Arrow 56. Attack 57. The Ride Back 57. The Amazing Colossal Man 57. Home Before Dark 58. Hitler 61. The Devil at Four O'Clock 61. Bye Bye Birdie 63. Bullet for a Badman 64. Hush Hush Sweet Charlotte 64. I Saw What You Did 65. The Flight of the Phoenix 65. The Russians Are Coming, The Russians Are Coming 66. The Killing of Sister George 68.

Whatever Happened to Aunt Alice? 69. Too Late the Hero 69. The Legend of Lylah Clare 69. The Grissom Gang 71. The Organization 71. Emperor of the North Pole 73. Blazing Saddles 74. The Longest Yard 74. The Choirboys 77. Beyond the Poseidon Adventure 79. Airplane 80. All the Marbles 81. Airplane 2: the Sequel 82, etc.

Birt, Daniel (1907–1955). British director, former editor: busy in late forties.
The Three Weird Sisters 48. No Room at the Inn 49. The Interrupted Journey 49. Circumstantial Evidence 52. Background 53, etc.

The Birth of a Nation (US 1915). D. W. Griffith's monumental melodrama of the American Civil War and its aftermath, supposedly the biggest money-maker of all time (allowing for rising costs), has become something of an embarrassment to Hollywood in view of its anti-Negro bias. It remains exciting to watch, especially during the battle sequences and the final 'heroic' rescue charge of the Ku Klux Klan; and it abounds in technical innovations which became current usage. Various versions have been reissued with sound effects. Written by Griffith and Frank Woods from Thomas Dixon's novel *The Clansman*; photographed by Billy Bitzer.

Bischoff, Samuel (1890–1975). American producer, with Warners in thirties, Columbia in forties, subsequently independent.
The Charge of the Light Brigade 36. A Slight Case of Murder 37. Submarine Zone 41. You'll Never Get Rich 41. Appointment in Berlin 43. None Shall Escape 44. Mr District Attorney 47. Pitfall 48. Mrs Mike 50. The System 53. The Phenix City Story 55. Operation Eichmann 61. King of the Roaring Twenties 61. The Strangler 64, many others.

Bishop, Ed (*c* 1942–). American leading man in Great Britain. Starred in TV's *UFO* series and subsequently served as a handy transatlantic voice.
The Lords of Discipline 83.

Bishop, Joey (1918–) (Joseph Abraham Gottlieb). American TV comedian who has made few film appearances.
The Naked and the Dead 58. Sergeants Three 63. Texas across the River 66. A Guide for the Married Man 67. Who's Minding the Mint? 67, etc.
TV series: The Joey Bishop Show 61–64, 67–69.

Bishop, Julie (1914–) (Jacqueline Brown). American leading lady of routine films; also known as Jacqueline Wells.
Alice in Wonderland 33. The Bohemian Girl 36. The Nurse's Secret 41. Northern Pursuit 43. Rhapsody in Blue 45. Sands of Iwo Jima 49. Westward the Women 52. The High and the Mighty 54. The Big Land 57, many others.
TV series: My Hero 52.

Bishop, Terry (1917–1981). British director. Much TV work.
You're Only Young Twice 52. Jim Driscoll's Donkey 54. Light Fingers 57. Model for Murder 58. Cover Girl Killer 59. Danger Tomorrow 60. The Unstoppable Man 61, etc.

Bishop, William (1918–1959). American leading man, mostly in routine features.
Pillow to Post 46. The Romance of Rosy Ridge 47. Anna Lucasta 49. Lorna Doone 51. Cripple Creek 52. The Boss 56. The Oregon Trail 59, etc.
TV series: It's a Great Life 54.

Bissell, Whit (1919–). American character actor who played anything from attorneys to garage attendants.
Holy Matrimony 43. Another Part of the Forest 47. It Should Happen to You 53. The Young Stranger 57. I Was a Teenage Frankenstein 58. The Time Machine 60. Hud 63. Seven Days in May 64. Covenant with Death 67. Airport 69. The Salzburg Connection 72. Soylent Green 73. Psychic Killer 75, Casey's Shadow 68, many others.
TV series: Bachelor Father 59–61. Time Tunnel 66.

Bisset, Jacqueline (1944–). British leading lady, in American films.
□The Knack 64. Arrivederci Baby 65. Cul de Sac 66. Casino Royale 67. Two for the Road 67. The Sweet Ride 67. Capetown Affair 67. The Detective 68. Bullitt 68. The First Time 68. L'Echelle Blanche (Fr.) 69. Secret World 69. Airport 69. *The Grasshopper* 70. The Mephisto Waltz 71. Believe in Me 71. Secrets 71. Judge Roy Bean 72. Stand Up and Be Counted 72. Le Magnifique 73. La Nuit Américaine 73. The Thief Who Came to Dinner 73. Murder on the Orient Express 74. The Spiral Staircase 75. End of the Game 76. St Ives 76. The Sunday Woman 76. The Deep 77. The Greek Tycoon 78. Someone Is Killing the Great Chefs of Europe 78. When Time Ran Out 80. Rich and Famous 81. Together 81. Inchon 82. Class 83. Under the Volcano

84. Anna Karenina (TV) 84. Forbidden (TV) 85. High Season 87.

¶ *J.B.*: I'm fascinated by a man with a twinkle in his eye.

Bitter Sweet. Noel Coward's romantic operetta was twice filmed: in 1933 with Anna Neagle and Fernand Gravet, and in 1940, much altered, with Jeanette MacDonald and Nelson Eddy.

Bitzer, Billy (1874–1944) (George William Bitzer). American cameraman who worked with D. W. Griffith on his most important films and is credited with several major photographic developments.
The New York Hat 12. Judith of Bethulia 13. *Birth of a Nation* 15. *Intolerance* 16. *Hearts of the World* 18. *Broken Blossoms* 19. *Way Down East* 21. *America* 24. The Struggle 30, many others.

Bixby, Bill (1934–). Diffident American light leading man.
Lonely are the Brave 62. Irma la Douce 63. Under the Yum Yum Tree 64. Ride Beyond Vengeance 66. Spinout 67. Speedway 68. Congratulations It's a Boy (TV) 71. The Couple Takes a Wife (TV) 72. Barbary Coast (pilot) (TV) (&d) 75. The Apple Dumpling Gang 75. The Invasion of Johnson County (TV) 76, etc.
TV series: *My Favourite Martian* 63–65. The Courtship of Eddie's Father 69–70. The Magician 73. The Incredible Hulk 79–81. Goodnight Beantown 83.

Bjork, Anita (1923–). Swedish actress who made only two English-speaking appearances.
Road to Heaven 42. Woman without a Face 47. The Realm of Men 49. *Miss Julie* 51. Secrets of Women 51. Night People (US) 52. Song of the Scarlet Flower 56. Of Love and Lust 57. The Phantom Carriage 58. Good Friends and Faithful Neighbours 60. The Lady in White 62. Square of Violence 63. Loving Couples 64. Adalen 31 69, etc.

Bjornstrand, Gunnar (1909–86). Distinguished Swedish character actor.
The False Millionaire 31. Panic 39. An Adventurer 42. A Night in the Harbour 43. Frenzy 44. It Rains on Our Love 46. Night Is My Future 47. The White Cat 50. Waiting Women 52. Sawdust and Tinsel 53. *Smiles of a Summer Night* 55. Seventh Heaven 56. *The Seventh Seal* 57. Wild Strawberries 57. *The Face* 58. The Devil's Eye 60. Through a Glass Darkly 61. Winter Light 63. Loving Couples 64. Persona 66. The Sadist 66. The Red Mantle 67. The Shame 68. The Rite 69. The Pistol 74. Face to Face 76. Tabu 77. Autumn Sonata 78. The Farewell 81. Fanny and Alexander 82, etc.

Black Beauty. Anna Sewell's Victorian novel about the life of a horse has been filmed several times since sound; by Hollywood in 1933 and 1947, and in Britain in 1971. 1972 brought a TV series on the subject.

The Black Cat. Two of the best-known films under this title had nothing whatever to do with the Poe story on which they were allegedly based. They were the 1934 melodrama about devil worshippers, with Karloff and Lugosi, and the 1941 thunderstorm mystery with Basil Rathbone. The Poe story was more faithfully treated in *The Living Dead* (Ger.) 33, *Tales of Terror* (US) 62, and *The Black Cat* (US) 67.

black comedy finds humour in serious matters such as death, neurosis and sex perversion. In recent years it has become almost normal, though such films as *A Clockwork Orange* still cause controversy. We were once less sophisticated: in the early thirties, for instance, the comedy element in horror films such as James Whale's *The Bride of Frankenstein* and *The Old Dark House* was not understood, and even now is difficult to maintain on the same level, though Hammer films make sporadic attempts in this direction, and Roger Corman was rather more successful in *The Raven.* (Roman Polanski failed spectacularly in *The Fearless Vampire Killers.*) Comedies of murder date back to *The Front Page* and *Boudu Sauvé des Eaux*, with a progression through *Drôle de Drame, A Slight Case of Murder, Arsenic and Old Lace, Monsieur Verdoux, Kind Hearts and Coronets, The Red Inn, The Criminal Life of Archibaldo de la Cruz, The Naked Truth, She'll Have to Go, Candy* and *The Assassination Bureau.* Death and funerals have been the subject of jest in *Here Comes Mr Jordan, Too Many Crooks, The Loved One, The Wrong Box, Loot*, and *Harold and Maude.* On the level of social behaviour, there is black humour in *Who's Afraid of Virginia Woolf?, The Anniversary* and *The Honey Pot*, while Luis Buñuel castigates society through similar means in most of his films, notably *El, The Exterminating Angel* and *The Diary of a Chambermaid. Dr*

Strangelove managed to laugh at the destruction of the world. Finally, Laurel and Hardy understood one aspect of the genre in their many grotesque jokes involving physical distortion. Elements of black comedy are to be found in an increasing number of modern films, notably those of Billy Wilder, John Huston and Alfred Hitchcock, and in the adventures of James Bond.

Black, Isobel (–). British character actress.
Kiss of the Vampire 62. The Magnificent Two 67. David Copperfield (TV) 70. 10 Rillington Place 70. Twins of Evil 71.

Black, Karen (1942–) (Karen Zicgeler). American leading lady.
□You're a Big Boy Now 67. Hard Contract 68. Easy Rider 69. Five Easy Pieces 70. A Gunfight 71. Drive He Said 71. Born to Win 71. Cisco Pike 71. Portnoy's Complaint 72. The Pyx 73. Rhinoceros 73. The Outfit 73. Little Laura and Big John 73. The Great Gatsby 74.Airport 75 75. Law and Disorder 75. Trilogy of Terror (TV) 75. The Day of the Locust 75. Nashville 75. Family Plot 76. Ace Up My Sleeve 76. Burnt Offerings 76. Killer Fish 78. Capricorn One 78. The Last Word 79. The Rip-Off 79. In Praise of Older Women 79. The Number 79. The Naked Sun 79. Separate Ways 81. Chanel Solitaire 81. Come Back to the Five and Dime, Jimmy Dean, Jimmy Dean 82. Can She Bake a Cherry Pie 83.
Growing Pains 83. Martin's Day 84. Savage Dawn 84. Invaders from Mars 86.

¶ *K.B.:* My God, there aren't any more movie stars, which is terrific with me, it's very healthy. A lot of love now occurs in this business, people helping each other to do good work, getting high on each other's success. Isn't that great?

Black Maria. In the history of film this evocative phrase for a police van has a secondary meaning, being the nickname given to Edison's first portable studio.

Black, Noel (1937–). American director who graduated to features from shorts.
Pretty Poison 68. Cover Me Babe 70. Jennifer on my Mind 71. A Man, a Woman and a Bank 79. The Other Victim (TV) 81. Private School 83.

Black Orpheus (France 1958). The myth of Orpheus and Eurydice was given a Negro setting in this visually splendid but dramatically unsatisfactory piece written and directed by Marcel Camus. With Marpessa Dawn, Breno Mello.

The Black Pirate (US 1926). A typical Douglas Fairbanks silent swashbuckler, involving an experimental use of colour. Directed by Albert Parker, photographed by Henry Sharp.

Black, Stanley (1913–). British band-leader and composer, responsible for scoring nearly 200 films.
Rhythm Racketeers 36. Mrs Fitzherbert 47. It Always Rains on Sunday 47. Laughter in Paradise 50. The Trollenberg Terror 57. Hell is a City 60. The Young Ones 61. Summer Holiday 63. City Under the Sea 65. Crossplot 69, etc.

The Blackboard Jungle (US 1955). This classroom melodrama, written and directed by Richard Brooks, shocked filmgoers by its revelation of what teachers in big city schools have to put up with. It also introduced rock-and-roll music (over the credits), and allowed Glenn Ford to give one of his edgiest performances. Eleven years later Sidney Poitier, one of the students here, played the harassed teacher in a British imitation, *To Sir With Love.*

blackface. A vaudeville adjective for comedians or singers who found their best appeal in 'Negro' disguise, i.e. with faces entirely blacked save for thick lips. Among the singers Al Jolson was perhaps the most famous exponent of this art, with Eddie Cantor a close second; the style derived from the minstrel shows which toured America from the mid-nineteenth century and which are clearly depicted in Jolson's *Mammy* and *Swanee River*. Dockstader's minstrels are re-created in *The Jolson Story*, and Dan Emmet's in *Dixie*; while Judy Garland and Mickey Rooney created their own blackface troupe in *Babes in Arms*. Among blackface comics there were Moran and Mack, the 'two black crows'; and others who made themselves black for comic effect were Betty Grable and June Haver in *The Dolly Sisters*, Myrna Loy in *Ham and Eggs at the Front*, Gene Wilder in *Silver Streak*, Buster Keaton in *College*, Marion Davies in *Going Hollywood*, Fred Astaire in *Swing Time*, Dan Dailey in *You're My Everything*, and Chick Chandler in *The Big Shot*. In *Watermelon Man*, on the other hand, Godfrey Cambridge appeared in whiteface.

blacklisting: see *The Hollywood Ten.*

Blackmail (GB 1929). Notable as the first British sound film. Hitchcock had made it as a silent, and remade it hurriedly, with primitive dubbing for the Czech leading lady, Anny Ondra. A typical Hitchcock suspense yarn, the production has now dated badly but still manages several effective moments.

Blackman, Honor (1926–). British leading lady, a Rank 'charm school' product submerged in 'English rose' roles from 1946 until a TV series fitted her up with kinky suits and judo tactics.
Fame is the Spur 47. Quartet 48. Diamond City 49. So Long at the Fair 50. The Rainbow Jacket 53. Breakaway 55. A Night to Remember 58. The Square Peg 58. A Matter of Who 61. *Goldfinger* 64. The Secret of My Success 65. *Life at the Top* 65. Moment to Moment 65. A Twist of Sand 68. Shalako 68. The Last Grenade 69. The Virgin and the Gypsy 70. Fright 71. Something Big 71. To the Devil a Daughter 75. The Cat and the Canary 78, etc.
TV series: *The Avengers* 60–63.

Blackman, Joan (1938–). American leading lady of the sixties.
Visit to a Small Planet 61. The Great Imposter 61. Blue Hawaii 62. Twilight of Honor 63. Intimacy 66, etc.

Blackmer, Sidney (1895–1973). Suave American character actor, often seen as politician or high-class crook but also capable of sympathetic roles.
A Most Immoral Lady 29. Kismet 30. Little Caesar 30. Once a Sinner 31. Cocktail Hour 33. The Count of Monte Cristo 34. The President Vanishes 34. The Little Colonel 35. Smart Girl 35. Early to Bed 36. A Doctor's Diary 37. This is My Affair 37. Charlie Chan at Monte Carlo 37. The Last Gangster 37. Trade Winds 38. Hotel for Women 39. I Want a Divorce 40. Love Crazy 41. The Feminine Touch 41. The Panther's Claw 42. Quiet Please Murder 42. Murder in Times Square 43. Duel in the Sun 46. My Girl Tisa (as Teddy Roosevelt) 48. People will Talk 51. Johnny Dark 54. High Society 56. Tammy and the Bachelor 57. How to Murder Your Wife 65. Covenant with Death 67. Rosemary's Baby 68, many others.

blacks in films have only slowly attained equal status with whites. In early silents they were invariably depicted as slaves, a fact encouraged by the several popular versions of *Uncle Tom's Cabin.* If a film had a black role of consequence, it was usually played by a white man in blackface. But blacks began to make their own films for their own audiences, and still do, though these seldom get a general showing. The first all-black film was *Darktown Jubilee* in 1914 . . . the year that Griffith made *The Birth of a Nation*, with its strong anti-black bias. Griffith atoned for this in *The Greatest Thing in Life* 18, in which a white soldier and a black embraced, but in 1922 he again incurred the wrath of colour-sensitive critics by making *One Exciting Night*, the first film to boast the quickly stereotyped figure of the terrified black manservant. Early talkies included such all-black films as *Hearts in Dixie* and Vidor's *Hallelujah*, and in 1933 Paul Robeson appeared in a version of Eugene O'Neill's *The Emperor Jones*. Much of the interest of *Imitation of Life* 34 centred on the problems of black servant Louise Beavers and her half-white daughter. In 1936 the screen version of *Green Pastures*, depicting the simple black's idea of the Bible, was widely acclaimed but tended to perpetuate a patronizing attitude. The feeling of the South for its blacks was strongly outlined in *They Won't Forget* 37 and *Gone with the Wind* 39. *Stormy Weather* 42 and *Cabin in the Sky* 43 were all-black musicals in Hollywood's best manner, but *Tales of Manhattan* 42 was retrogressive in showing blacks as inhabitants of a vast shanty town. In *Casablanca* 42, however, Dooley Wilson was accepted on equal terms by Humphrey Bogart. Disney's *Song of the South* 46, despite an engaging performance by James Baskett, brought back the old Uncle Remus image. The post-war period generally permitted the emergence of serious black actors like James Edwards and Sidney Poitier, and films on racial themes such as *Intruder in the Dust* and *Pinky*. At last, in 1965, came films in which a black could play a straight part utterly unrelated to his colour. Poitier did so in *The Bedford Incident*, then used colour defiantly in *In the Heat of the Night* and *Guess Who's Coming to Dinner.* Remakes of well known 'white' movies were one way to bring in a wide range of coloured actors: *The Lost Man* (*Odd Man Out*), *Uptight* (*The Informer*), *Cool Breeze* (*The Asphalt Jungle*). Even *Barefoot in the Park* became a black TV series, and *Steptoe and Son* in the US became the black *Sanford and Son*. The subject was rather self-consciously aired in such films as *Change of Mind, Watermelon Man, The Landlord* and *Medium Cool.* In 1970 came *Cotton Comes to Harlem*, perhaps the first black thriller with no chip on its shoulder; in 1972 the seal of approval was set up by *Shaft*, a violent private eye thriller with an all-black cast which proved not only acceptable to all audiences but highly commercial. The floodgates opened and before 1972 was out we even had *Blacula* and *Blackenstein*. Wholly black films which followed included *Sounder, The Autobiography of Miss Jane Pittman, Uptown Saturday Night, Let's Do It Again*; and in 1977 a sensational impact was achieved by a TV serialization of Alex Haley's *Roots*, by watching which half of America sought to atone for centuries of bad white behaviour towards the blacks.

Britain, less affected by black problems, moved in parallel fashion. In the early thirties, films of *The Kentucky Minstrels*; then Paul Robeson dominating somewhat insulting material in *Sanders of the River* and subsequently earning three or four serious film vehicles of his own; the post-war attempt to understand in *Men of Two Worlds*; and problem pictures like *Simba*, about the Mau-Mau, and *Flame in the Streets*, about the prospect of a black in an East End family.

? Some questions about black actors and subjects.

1 What classic film from a novel by Thomas Dixon had its negro roles played by white actors in blackface?
2 In what film did Paul Robeson and Ethel Waters find a coat full of money?
3 In 1933 Robeson starred in a film directed by Dudley Murphy, from what Eugene O'Neill play?
4 Who played what famous story-telling character in what 1947 Disney film?
5 Who was *The Watermelon Man*?
6 What was remarkable about Sidney Poitier's role in *The Bedford Incident*?
7 Who played the old negro in danger of lynching in *Intruder in the Dust*?
8 Name Bob Hope's man-servant in *The Ghost Breakers*, and the nickname by which he was previously known.
9 Name the all-black remakes of *The Informer*, *Odd Man Out* and *The Asphalt Jungle*.
10 Fats Waller and Katherine Dunham were two of the guests in what all-star all-black musical of 1942?
11 Who played *Blacula*?
12 Name the black pianist in *Casablanca*.
13 Name the three stars of *Uptown Saturday Night*, and its sequel.
14 Who won an Academy Award for her role as Mammy in *Gone With the Wind*?
15 Who in *Mr Blandings Builds His Dream House* coined the slogan 'If you ain't eatin' WHAM you ain't eatin' ham'?
16 Who starred in *The Autobiography of Miss Jane Pittman*?
17 Give the title of King Vidor's all-black drama of 1929.
18 What black actor starred in Ealing's British coal-mining drama of 1937, and what was its title?
19 What was the title of the 1975 TV series starring Teresa Graves as a black policewoman?
20 What black actor, whose real name was Lincoln Perry, was criticized for presenting a caricature black stereotype in such films as *Steamboat Round the Bend* and *The Sun Shines Bright*?

Blackton, J. Stuart (1868–1941). British pioneer producer who spent years in America working with Edison.
Raffles 05. The Life of Moses 10. The Battle Cry of Peace 15. Womanhood 16. The Glorious Adventure (in Prizmacolour) 21. On the Banks of the Wabash 23. The Clean Heart 24. The Beloved Brute 24. Gypsy Cavalier 24. Tides of Passion 25. The Happy Warrior 25. Bride of the Storm 30, many others.

Blackwell, Carlyle (1888–1955). American stage matinée idol, in demand for romantic roles during the twenties; his declamatory style could scarcely survive the coming of sound.
Uncle Tom's Cabin 09. The Key to Yesterday 14. The Restless Sex 20. Sherlock Holmes 22. The Beloved Vagabond 23. Bulldog Drummond 23. She 25. The Wrecker 29. The Crooked Billet 30. The Calling of Dan Matthews 35, many others.

Blain, Gérard (1930–). French leading actor once thought of as a continental equivalent of James Dean. After a period of retirement he emerged again as a serious director.
Les Fruits Sauvages 54. Le Temps des Assassins 56. Crime and Punishment 56. Les Mistons 58. *Le Beau Serge* 58. *Les Cousins* 59. The Hunchback of Notre Dame 60. The Dauphins 60. Gold of Rome 61. Hatari (US) 62. La Bonne Soupe 64. Un Homme de Trop 67. Les Amis (w, d only) 71. Le Pélican (& w, d) 73. The American Friend 77. Utopia (w, d only) 78. Le Rebelle (w, d only) 80, etc.

Blaine, Vivian (1921–) (Vivienne Stapleton). Vivacious American leading lady

and personable songstress. Made comparatively few films, her greatest success being on Broadway.
□Thru Different Eyes 42. Girl Trouble 42. He Hired the Boss 43. Jitterbugs 43. Greenwich Village 44. Something for the Boys 44. Nob Hill 45. *State Fair* 45. Doll Face 45. If I'm Lucky 46. *Three Little Girls in Blue* 46. Skirts Ahoy 52. Main Street to Broadway 53. *Guys and Dolls* 55. Public Pigeon Number One 57. Katie, Portrait of a Centerfold (TV) 78. The Dark 78. The Cracker Factory (TV) 79. Sooner or Later (TV) 79. Parasite 82. I'm Going to Be Famous 83.

Blair, Betsy (1923–) (Elizabeth Boger). American character actress who often plays shy or nervous women.
□The Guilt of Janet Ames 47. A Double Life 47. *Another Part of the Forest* 48. The Snake Pit 48. Mystery Street 50. Kind Lady 51. *Marty* (BFA) 55. Calle Mayor (Sp.) 56. Il Grido (It.) 57. The Halliday Brand 57. All Night Long (GB) 61. A Delicate Balance 73.

Blair, George (1906–1970). American second feature director.
Duke of Chicago 49. Flaming Fury 49. Daughter of the Jungle 49. Insurance Investigator 51. Jaguar 55. The Hypnotic Eye 60, many others.

Blair, Janet (1921–) (Martha Lafferty). Vivacious American leading lady of co-features in the forties.
□*Three Girls About Town* 41. Blondie Goes to College 42. Two Yanks in Trinidad 42. Broadway 42. *My Sister Eileen* 42. Something to Shout About 43. Once Upon a Time 44. Tonight and Every Night 45. Tars and Spars 46. Gallant Journey 46. The Fabulous Dorseys 47. I Love Trouble 48. The Black Arrow 48. The Fuller Brush Man 48. Public Pigeon Number One 57. Boys' Night Out 62. *Night of the Eagle* (GB) 62. The One and Only Genuine Original Family Band 68.
TV series: *The Smith Family* 71–72.

Blair, Linda (1959–). American juvenile lead of the seventies who made a spectacular beginning as a possessed child.
□*The Exorcist* 74. Born Innocent (TV) 74. Sarah T, Portrait of a Teenage Alcoholic (TV) 75. Airport 75 75. Sweet Hostage (TV) 76. Victory at Entebbe (TV) 76. Exorcist II: The Heretic 78. Roller Boogie 79. Hell Night 81. Chained Heat 81. Savage Streets 82. Night Patrol 82. Red Heat 83. Savage Island 85.

Blake, Amanda (1929–) (Beverly Neill). American supporting actress.
Duchess of Idaho 50. Stars in My Crown 50. Lili 53. Sabre Jet 53. A Star is Born 54. About Mrs Leslie 54. High Society 56. Betrayal (TV) 74, etc.
TV series: *Gunsmoke* (as Kitty) 55–75.

Blake, Katherine (1928–). South African actress in Britain, mostly on TV.
Anne of the Thousand Days 70, etc.

Blake, Madge (1900–1969). American supporting actress.
Between Midnight and Dawn 50. Singin' in the Rain 52. The Long Long Trailer 54. Batman 66, etc.

Blake, Marie (1896–1978) (Blossom MacDonald). American small part actress, sister of Jeanette MacDonald. Played the receptionist in the Dr Kildare movie series of the early forties.
Mannequin 37. Young Dr Kildare 38. The Women 39. They Knew What They Wanted 39. A Child Is Born 40. I Married a Witch 42. Abbott and Costello in Hollywood 45. The Snake Pit 49. Love Nest 51. From the Terrace 60, many others.
† In *The Addams Family*, on TV in 1964, she reappeared grotesquely under the name Blossom Rock.

Blake, Robert (1933–) (Michael Gubitosi). American child actor who later attracted some unusual adult roles.
Andy Hardy's Double Life 43. The Horn Blows at Midnight 45. Treasure of Sierra Madre 47. Revolt in the Big House 58. Battle Flame 59. The Purple Gang 60. The Greatest Story Ever Told 65. *In Cold Blood* 67. *Tell Them Willie Boy Is Here* 69. Corky 72. Electra Glide in Blue 73. Coast to Coast 80. Second Hand Hearts 80. Blood Feud (TV) 83, etc.
TV series: The Richard Boone Show 64. *Baretta* 74–77. Joe Dancer 80.

Blake, Whitney (–). American character actress, mother of Meredith Baxter.
Deadline Midnight 59. The Boy Who Stole the Elephant (TV) 70. Strange Homecoming (TV) 74. The Betsy 78, etc.

Blakeley, John E. (1889–1958). British producer-director of low-budget Lancashire comedies.
□Dodging the Dole 36. Somewhere in England 40. Somewhere in Camp 42.

Somewhere on Leave 42. Demobbed 44. Under New Management 46. Home Sweet Home 46. Cup Tie Honeymoon 48. Holiday with Pay 48. Somewhere in Politics 49. What a Carry On 49. School for Randle 49. Over the Garden Wall 50. Let's Have a Murder 50. It's a Grand Life 53.

Blakeley, Tom (1918–84). British producer of second features.
Love's a Luxury 58. Tomorrow at Ten 62. Devils of Darkness 65. Island of Terror 66, etc.

Blakely, Colin (1930–87). Stocky British stage actor, in occasional films.
Saturday Night and Sunday Morning 60. This Sporting Life 62. The Informers 63. The Long ships 64. A Man for All Seasons 66. The Spy with a Cold Nose 67. *The Day the Fish Came Out* 67. Charlie Bubbles 67. The Vengeance of She 68. *Decline and Fall* 68. Alfred the Great 69. *The Private Life of Sherlock Holmes* (as Watson) 70. Something to Hide 72. Young Winston 72. Murder on the Orient Express 74. Galileo 74. Love Among the Ruins (TV) 74. It Shouldn't Happen to a Vet 76. Equus 77. The Day Christ Died (TV) 80. Loophole 80. Nijinsky 80. The Dogs of War 81. Evil Under the Sun 82. The Red Monarch (TV) 83. Paradise Postponed (TV) 86.

Blakely, Susan (1950–). American leading lady of the seventies, former model.
□Savages 72. The Lords of Flatbush 74. The Towering Inferno 74. Report to the Commissioner 75. Shampoo 75. Capone 75. *Rich Man Poor Man* (TV) 76. Secrets (TV) 77. Savages 78. Make Me an Offer (TV) 80. A Cry for Love (TV) 80. Oklahoma City Dolls (TV) 80. The Concorde – Airport 79 79. The Bunker (TV) 81. Will There Really be a Morning? (TV) 83. Over the Top 87.

Blakemore, Michael (1928–). Australian director, mostly on English stage.
A Personal History of the Australian Surf 81. Privates on Parade 82.

Blakley, Ronee (1946–). American pop singer who has made acting appearances.
□Nashville 75. Renaldo and Clara 78. The Driver 78. She Came to the Valley 79. The Baltimore Bullet 80. Lightning Over Water 81. The Private Files of J Edgar Hoover 77. Good Luck Miss Wyckoff 79. A Nightmare on Elm Street 84. I Played for You 85.

Blanc, Jean-Pierre (1942–). French director.
La Vieille Fille 71. Un Ange au Paradis 73. D'Amour et d'Eau Fraiche 75, etc.

Blanc, Mel (1908–). The voice of Warner Brothers' cartoon characters, including Bugs Bunny, Sylvester and Tweetie Pie. Makes occasional cameo appearances in films.
Neptune's Daughter 49. Kiss Me Stupid 64, etc.

Blanchar, Pierre (1892–1963). Distinguished French screen and stage actor.
Jocelyn 23. *L'Atlantide* 31. Le Diable en Bouteille 34. Crime and Punishment 35. Mademoiselle Docteur 36. L'Affaire du Courrier de Lyon 37. *Un Carnet de Bal* 37. La Symphonie Pastorale 40. Pontcarral 42. Rififi Chez les Femmes 58, etc.

Blanchard, Mari (1927–1970) (Mary Blanchard). Decorative American leading lady of fifties co-features.
Mr Music 50. Ten Tall Men 51. Veils of Baghdad 53. Black Horse Canyon 54. *Destry* 55. The Crooked Web 56. The Return of Jack Slade 56. Jungle Heat 57. No Place to Land 58. Don't Knock the Twist 62. McLintock 63. Twice Told Tales 64, etc.

Blandick, Clara (1880–1962). American character actress, often seen as sensible servant or no-nonsense aunt.
The Girl Said No 30. Huckleberry Finn 31. The Wet Parade 32. One Sunday Afternoon 33. Broadway Bill 34. The Gorgeous Hussy 36. A Star is Born 37. Huckleberry Finn 39. *The Wizard of Oz* (as Aunt Em) 39. It Started with Eve 41. Can't Help Singing 44. A Stolen Life 46. Life with Father 47. The Bride Goes Wild 48. Love That Brute 50, many others.

Blane, Ralph (1914–) (Ralph Uriah Hunsecker). American composer and lyricist who with his partner Hugh Martin (1914–) was responsible for *Best Foot Forward* and *Meet Me in St Louis*.

Blane, Sally (1910–) (Elizabeth Jung). American leading lady of the early thirties; sister of Loretta Young.
Sirens of the Sea 27. Rolled Stockings 27. The Vagabond Lover 29. Little Accident 30. Once a Sinner 31. Ten Cents a Dance 31. Disorderly Conduct 31. I am a Fugitive from a Chain Gang 32. Advice to the Lovelorn 33. The Silver Streak 35. One Mile from Heaven

37. Charlie Chan at Treasure Island 39. A Bullet for Joey 54, many others.

Blangsted, Folmar (1904–1982). American editor.
The Doughgirls 44. Rhapsody in Blue 45. Cry Wolf 47. Flamingo Road 49. Distant Drums 51. The Charge at Feather River 53. A Star is Born 54. A Cry in the Night 56. Rio Bravo 59. Taras Bulba 63. The War Lord 65. Camelot 67. The Forbin Project 70. Man of La Mancha 72. Oklahoma Crude 73, many others.

Blanke, Henry (1901–1981). German-American producer, long at Warners.
Female 33. *The Story of Louis Pasteur* 35. Satan Met a Lady 36. The Petrified Forest 36. Green Pastures 36. The Life of Emile Zola 37. Jezebel 38. *The Adventures of Robin Hood* 38. Juarez 39. The Old Maid 39. The Sea Hawk 40. *The Maltese Falcon* 41. Old Acquaintance 43.The Mask of Dimitrios 44. Deception 46. The Treasure of the Sierra Madre 47. The Fountainhead 49. Come Fill the Cup 51. King Richard and the Crusaders 54. Serenade 56. Too Much Too Soon 58. *The Nun's Story* 59. Ice Palace 60. Hell is for Heroes 62, many others.

Blankfort, Michael (1907–1982). American screenwriter, former Princeton professor.
Blind Alley 39. Adam Had Four Sons 40. Texas 41. Flight Lieutenant 42. An Act of Murder 48. Broken Arrow 50. Halls of Montezuma 51. My Six Convicts 52. The Juggler (from his novel) 53. Untamed 55. Tribute to a Bad Man 56. The Vintage 57. The Other Man (TV) 70. A Fire in the Sky (TV) 78, etc.

Blasetti, Alessandro (1900–81). Italian director mainly associated with comedy and spectaculars.
Sole 29. Nero 30. Resurrection 31. The Old Guard 33. The Countess of Parma 37. *Four Steps in the Clouds* 42. A Day of Life 46. Fabiola 48. *First Communion* 50. Altri Tempi (Infidelity) 52. Europe by Night 59. I Love You Love 61, many others.

Blatt, Edward A. (1905–). American stage director who worked briefly for Warners in the forties.
□Between Two Worlds 44. Escape in the Desert 45. Smart Woman 48.

Blatty, William Peter (1928–). American screenwriter.
The Man from the Diners' Club 63. A Shot in the Dark 64. John Goldfarb Please Come Home 65. Promise Her Anything 66. What Did You Do in the War Daddy? 66. Gunn 67. The Great Bank Robbery 69. Darling Lili 69. The Exorcist (& w, p, oa) (AA script) 73. The Ninth Configuration (& w, oa) 80, etc.

Blaustein, Julian (1913–). American producer.
Broken Arrow 50. Mister 880 50. Take Care of My Little Girl 51. Desiree 54. Storm Center 56. Bell Book and Candle 58. The Wreck of the Mary Deare 59. Two Loves 61. The Four Horsemen of the Apocalypse 62. Khartoum 66. Three into Two Won't Go 69, etc.

Blech, Hans Christian (1925–). German character actor, occasionally in international films.
L'Affaire Blum 49. Decision Before Dawn 51. The Longest Day 62. The Visit 63. The Saboteur 65. Battle of the Bulge 65. The Bridge at Remagen 69, etc.

Blessed, Brian (c. 1937–). Massive British character actor, originally 'Fancy Smith' in TV's *Z Cars*.
Brotherly Love 70. The Trojan Women 71. Man of La Mancha 72. Henry VIII and His Six Wives 73. I Claudius (TV) 76. Flash Gordon 80. High Road to China 83. War and Remembrance (TV) 88, etc.

Blier, Bernard (1916–). French actor who makes a virtue of his plumpness and baldness.
Hôtel du Nord 38. *Quai des Orfèvres* 47. *Dédée d'Anvers* 47. L'École Buissonière 48. Manèges (The Wanton) 49. Souvenirs Perdus 50. Les Misérables 57. Les Grandes Familles 58. Le Cave se Rebiffe 61. Les Saintes Nitouches 63. A Question of Honour (Italy) 66. Breakdown (& d) 67. Catch Me a Spy 71. The Tall Blond Man with One Black Shoe 74. Chez Victor 76. Le Compromis 78. Buffet Froid 80. Passione d'Amore 82, etc.

Blier, Bertrand (1939–). French director, son of Bernard Blier.
Hitler Connais Pas 62. Les Valseurs 74. Femmes Fatales 76. *Préparez Vos Mouchoirs* (AA) 78. *Buffet Froid* 80.

blimp. A soundproof cover fixed over a camera during shooting to absorb running noise.

Blind Husbands (US 1919). The start of Erich von Stroheim's brief but spectacular career as a Hollywood actor-writer-director, this bitterly ironic study of a military seducer had all the savage wit for which he is remembered as well as hints of the extravagance which caused his downfall.

blindness, a tragic affliction, has generally been treated by film-makers with discretion, though not without sentimentality. Typical is Herbert Marshall as the blind pianist in *The Enchanted Cottage*, dispensing words of wisdom with piano music in the background and the sounds of nature through the open door. Other sympathetic blind roles include Cary Grant in *Wings in the Dark*; Irene Dunne (later Jane Wyman) in *Magnificent Obsession*; Ronald Colman (later Fredric March) in *The Dark Angel*; Colman also in *The Light That Failed*; Ralph Richardson (later Laurence Harvey) in *The Four Feathers*; James Cagney in *City for Conquest*; Ida Lupino in *On Dangerous Ground*; Arthur Kennedy in *Bright Victory*; Patricia Neal in *Psyche 59* 64; John Garfield in *Pride of the Marines*; Michele Morgan in *La Symphonie Pastorale*; Virginia Cherrill in *City Lights*; Elizabeth Hartmann in *A Patch of Blue*; Michael Wilding in *Torch Song*; and Nicol Williamson in *Laughter in the Dark*. More sinister blind characters came in *Saboteur* and *Victim*; while blind detectives, not forgetting TV's *Longstreet*, include Edward Arnold in *Eyes in the Night* and *The Hidden Eye*, Van Johnson in *23 Paces to Baker Street*, Dick Powell (briefly blinded by cordite fumes) in *Murder My Sweet*; and Karl Malden in *Cat o' Nine Tails*. In thrillers, terrified blind heroines have been useful: Patricia Dainton in *Witness in the Dark*, Audrey Hepburn in *Wait Until Dark* and Mia Farrow in *Blind Terror*. Other tricks with blind characters were played in *Faces in the Dark* and *Silent Dust*, in both of which the hero's condition helped him to outwit his assailants; and *Tread Softly Stranger*, where the murderer gave himself away through fear of the only witness—who turned out to be blind. Genuinely blind actors include Esmond Knight (temporarily) playing a sighted role in *The Silver Fleet*, and Ray Charles in *Ballad in Blue*. A nice ironic point was made in *Bride of Frankenstein*, where O. P. Heggie as a blind hermit was the only human being who did not fear the monster. Other films involving blindness include *Night Song*, *Destiny*, *Man in the Dark*, and the thrice-made *Magnificent Obsession*. Finally, in *The Day of the Triffids*, almost everyone on earth was blinded.

Blinn, Holbrook (1872–1928). American silent star.
Rosita 23. Janice Meredith 24. Yolanda 25. Zander the Great 27, many others.

Bliss, Sir Arthur (1891–1975). British composer who occasionally scored films.
□*Things to Come* 36. Conquest of the Air 38. Men of Two Worlds 46. Christopher Columbus 49. The Beggar's Opera 53. Welcome the Queen 54. Seven Waves Away 56.

Blithe Spirit (GB 1945). The nearest British films have come to cocktail comedy, this smooth and glossy version of Noel Coward's ghostly farce was directed by David Lean, photographed in Technicolor by Ronald Neame, and starred Rex Harrison, Kay Hammond, Margaret Rutherford and Constance Cummings.

Blitzstein, Marc (1905–64). American composer. Film music for documentaries, including Spanish Earth 38, Native Land 42.

Bloch, Robert (1917–). American screenwriter dealing almost exclusively in horror themes with trick endings.
Psycho (oa) 60. The Cabinet of Caligari 62. Strait Jacket 63. *The Night Walker* 64. The Psychopath 66. The Deadly Bees 66. The Torture Garden 67. The House that Dripped Blood 70. Asylum 72, etc.

block booking. A system supposedly illegal but still practised, whereby a renter forces an exhibitor to book a whole group of mainly mediocre films in order to get the one or two he wants.

Blockade (US 1938). A rare indication (in its period) of Hollywood's awareness of the world outside. Walter Wanger produced this melodrama of the Spanish Civil War, but despite good intentions it wasn't easy to tell whose side the film was on. Henry Fonda and Madeleine Carroll starred.

Blocker, Dan (1928–1972). Heavyweight American character actor.
Come Blow Your Horn 63. Lady in Cement 68. The Cockeyed Cowboys of Calico County 69, etc.
TV series: Cimarron City 58. *Bonanza* (as Hoss Cartwright) 59–72.

Blomfield, Derek (1920–1964). British boy actor of the thirties.
Emil and the Detectives 35. Turn of the Tide 35. The Ghost of St Michael's 41. Alibi 42. Night and the City 50. Hobson's Choice 54.

It's Great to be Young 56. Carry On Admiral 57, etc.

Blondell, Joan (1909–1979). Amiable American comedienne who played reporters, gold-diggers or the heroine's dizzy friend in innumerable comedies and musicals of the thirties. Later graduated to occasional character roles. Autobiographical novel 1972: *Center Door Fancy*.
□Sinner's Holiday 30. The Office Wife 30. Other Men's Women 30. Illicit 31. My Past 31. Millie 31. The Reckless Hour 31. Big Business Girl 31. Night Nurse 31. Public Enemy 31. Blonde Crazy 31. Union Depot 32. The Crowd Roars 32. The Famous Ferguson Case 32. *Miss Pinkerton* 32. Big City Blues 32. Make Me a Star 32. The Greeks had a Word for Them 32. Three on a Match 32. Central Park 32. Broadway Bad 33. Lawyer Man 33. Blondie Johnson 33. *Gold Diggers of 1933* 33. Goodbye Again 33. *Footlight Parade* 33. Havana Widows 33. *Convention City* 33. Kansas City Princess 34. Smarty 34. I've Got Your Number 34. He Was Her Man 34. *Dames* 34. The Travelling Saleslady 34. Broadway Gondolier 35. We're in the Money 35. Miss Pacific Fleet 35. Colleen 36. Sons o' Guns 36. Bullets or Ballots 36. *Stage Struck* 36. *Three Men on a Horse* 36. Gold Diggers of 1937 37. The King and the Chorus Girl 37. The Perfect Specimen 37. Back in Circulation 37. *Stand-In* 37. There's Always a Woman 38. Off the Record 38. East Side of Heaven 39. The Kid from Kokomo 39. Good Girls go to Paris 39. The Amazing Mr Williams 39. Two Girls on Broadway 40. I Want a Divorce 40. *Topper Returns* 41. Model Wife 41. *Three Girls Around Town* 42. Lady for a Night 42. Cry Havoc 43. *A Tree Grows in Brooklyn* 44. Don Juan Quilligan 45. Adventure 46. The Corpse Came COD 47. Nightmare Alley 47. Christmas Eve 47. For Heaven's Sake 50. The Blue Veil 51. The Opposite Sex 56. Lizzie 57. This Could Be the Night 57. The Desk Set 58. Will Success Spoil Rock Hunter 58. Angel Baby 61. Advance to the Rear 63. The Cincinatti Kid 66. Paradise Road 66. Ride Beyond Vengeance 66. Waterhole Three 67. Stay Away Joe 68. Kona Coast 68. The Phynx 70. Support Your Local Gunfighter 71. Winner Take All 75. Death at Love House (TV) 76. Opening Night 77. Battered (TV) 78. The Rebels (TV) 78. Grease 79. The Champ 79.
TV sereies: Here Come the Brides 68–69. Banyon 72.

Blondie. Chic Young's comic strip about dumb but honest family man Dagwood Bumstead and his pretty wife was first filmed in 1938 by Columbia, with Arthur Lake and Penny Singleton, also Jonathan Hale as Mr Dithers, Larry Simms as Baby Dumpling (later Alexander) and a dog (called Daisy) with star quality. It was so successful that Columbia produced an average of one Blondie film every six months for the next ten years; most of them were directed by Frank Strayer or Abby Berlin. All had 'Blondie' in the title except *The Boss Said No* 42, *A Bundle of Trouble* 42, and *Henpecked* 46; the last of all was *Blondie's Hero* 50. Lake and Pamela Britton appeared in a TV series in the early fifties, and the project was unsuccessfully revived in 1968 with Will Hutchins and Patricia Harty.

Blood and Sand. This tragic novel of the bullring by Vicente Blasco Ibanez has twice been filmed in Hollywood. In 1922, directed by Fred Niblo, it became one of Rudolph Valentino's most popular vehicles, with Lila Lee and Nita Naldi as co-stars. In the 1941 colour version directed by Rouben Mamoulian, the leading roles were filled by Tyrone Power, Linda Darnell and Rita Hayworth.

Bloom, Claire (1931–). British leading actress who came to the screen via the Old Vic.
□The Blind Goddess 48. *Limelight* 52. Innocents in Paris 52. The Man Between 53. Richard III 56. Alexander the Great 56. The Brothers Karamazov 58. *Look Back in Anger* 59. The Buccaneer 59. Brainwashed (Ger.) 60. The Chapman Report 61. The Wonderful World of the Brothers Grimm 63. *The Haunting* 63. 80,000 Suspects 63. Il Maestro di Vigevano 64. The Outrage 64. High Infidelity 65. *The Spy Who Came in from the Cold* 66. Charly 68. Three into Two Won't Go 69. The Illustrated Man 69. A Severed Head 69. The Going Up of David Lev (TV) 71. Red Sky at Morning 71. A Doll's House 73. Islands in the Stream 77. Backstairs at the White House (TV) 79. Clash of the Titans 81. Brideshead Revisited (TV) 81. Shadowlands (TV) 85. Hold the Dream (TV) 86. Queenie (TV) 87. Sammy and Rosie Get Laid 87.

¶ *C.B.:* I think that few professions have so much to do with chance and so little to do with the calculation of will.

'She could not be more beautiful without upsetting the balance of nature.'—*Walter Kerr*

Bloom, Harold Jack (–). American screenwriter.

The Naked Spur (co-w) 53. Magnificent Obsession 54. Last of the Pharaohs (co-w) 55. A Gunfight 71. Hardcase (co-w) 72.

Bloom, Verna (–). American leading lady of the seventies.
Medium Cool 69. The Hired Hand 71. High Plains Drifter 72. Badge 373 73. Where Have All the People Gone? (TV) 74. Sarah T (TV) 75. The Blue Knight (TV) 75. Heroes 77. Contract on Cherry Street (TV) 77. National Lampoon's Animal House 78. Playing for Time (TV) 80.

bloop. To cover a splice in the sound track, usually with thick 'blooping ink'.

Blore, Eric (1887–1959). British comic actor with stage experience; went to Hollywood and played unctuous/insulting butlers and eccentric types in many films.
□A Night Out and a Day In 20. The Great Gatsby 26. Laughter 30. My Sin 31. Tarnished Lady 31. Flying Down to Rio 33. *The Gay Divorcee* 34. Limehouse Blues 34. Behold My Wife 34. Folies Bergere 34. To Beat the Band 35. The Good Fairy 35. Diamond Jim 35. The Casino Murder Case 35. I Live My Life 35. *Top Hat* 35. I Dream Too Much 35. Seven Keys to Baldpate 35. Two in the Dark 36. The Ex Mrs Bradford 36. Swing Time 36. The Smartest Girl in Town 36. Sons o' Guns 36. Piccadilly Jim 36. The Soldier and the Lady 37. Quality Street 37. Shall We Dance 37. Breakfast for Two 37. Hitting a New High 37. *It's Love I'm After* 37. Joy of Living 38. Swiss Miss 38. A Desperate Adventure 38. Island of Lost Men 39. 1000 Dollars a Touchdown 39. A Gentleman's Gentleman 39. Music in My Heart 40. The Man Who Wouldn't Talk 41. The Lone Wolf Strikes 40 (and ten other Lone Wolf adventures 40–47, all as the butler). Till We Meet Again 40. South of Suez 40. The Boys from Syracuse 40. The Earl of Puddlestone 40. *The Lady Eve* 41. Road to Zanzibar 41. Redhead 41. Lady Scarface 41. New York Town 41. The Shanghai Gesture 41. Sullivan's Travels 41. Three Girls About Town 41. *The Moon and Sixpence* 42. Confirm or Deny 42. Happy Go Lucky 43. The Sky's the Limit 43. Forever and a Day 43. Holy Matrimony 43. Submarine Base 43. San Diego I Love You 44. Penthouse Rhythm 45. Men in Her Diary 45. Easy to Look At 45. Kitty 45. Two Sisters from Boston 46. Abie's Irish Rose 46. Winter Wonderland 47. Romance on the High Seas 48. Love Happy 49. Ichabod and Mr Toad (voice of Toad) 49. *Fancy Pants* 50. Bowery to Bagdad 54.
Famous line (*Top Hat*): 'We are Jones, sir.'

blow up. To magnify an image, either a photograph for background purposes, or a piece of film (e.g. from 16mm to 35mm).

Blow-Up (GB 1966). Michelangelo Antonioni's first film in English, a fashionably decorated but empty anecdote in which, as usual, many questions are posed but none answered. David Hemmings plays a selfish photographer who thinks he has witnessed a murder but never finds out whether he imagined the whole thing; the theme is dislocated by irrelevant sex sequences. Carlos di Palma's photography is exquisite and a general sense of style prevents total boredom.

The Blue Angel (Germany 1930). This heavy melodrama, with Emil Jannings as a professor ignobly infatuated with a tawdry night club singer, was made in both German and English. The latter version made an international star of Marlene Dietrich, whose throaty rendering of 'Falling in Love Again' became a cinema landmark. Sombrely Teutonic in mood and setting, with tirelessly tricksy direction by Joseph von Sternberg, the film still packs a punch for patient audiences. It was written by Carl Zuckmayer from a novel by Heinrich Mann, with music by Frederick Hollander. Remade (unsuccessfully) in Hollywood in 1958, with Curt Jurgens and May Britt.

Blue, Ben (1901–1975) (Benjamin Bernstein). Lanky, rubber-limbed American comedian with vaudeville experience; sporadically in films, usually in cameos.
College Rhythm 33. Follow Your Heart 36. High Wide and Handsome 37. College Swing 38. Paris Honeymoon 39. For Me and My Gal 42. Thousands Cheer 43. Easy to Wed 46. One Sunday Afternoon 48. It's a Mad Mad Mad Mad World 63. *The Russians are Coming, The Russians are Coming* 66. *A Guide for the Married Man* 67. Where Were You When the Lights Went Out? 68, etc.

The Blue Lamp (GB 1950). This documentary-style crime story about the work of the London police is said to have done a great deal of good to the police image. It certainly produced many imitators, and the policeman played by Jack Warner, though killed in the film, was revived on BBC for the long-running series *Dixon of Dock Green*. Directed by Basil Dearden; BFA best British film.

Blue, Monte (1890–1963). Burly American silent hero who later appeared in innumerable bit roles.
Intolerance 16. Till I Come Back to You 18. Pettigrew's Girl 19. The Affairs of Anatol 21. Orphans of the Storm 22. Main Street 23. *The Marriage Circle* 24. The Black Swan 24. Other Women's Husbands 26. Other Men's Wives 26. So This is Paris 26. Wolf's Clothing 27. *White Shadows of the South Seas* 28. Tiger Rose 29. Isle of Escape 30. The Flood 31. The Stoker 32. Wagon Wheels 34. Lives of a Bengal Lancer 34. G Men 35. Souls at Sea 37. Dodge City 39. Geronimo 40. Across the Pacific 42. The Mask of Dimitrios 44. Life with Father 47. The Iroquois Trail 50. Apache 54, many others.

The Bluebird (US 1939). Maurice Maeterlinck's rather eerie child-fantasy, with its moral that happiness is to be found in one's own back-yard, made one of Hollywood's more successful excursions into the supernatural, moving gracefully from the land of the dead to the land of those unborn; but it appealed less widely than its brasher contemporary *The Wizard of Oz*. Filmed in soft colour, it was directed by Walter Lang with Shirley Temple, Gale Sondergaard and Eddie Collins heading the cast. There had been a silent version in 1916, with Robin MacDougall and Tula Belle. The 1976 Russian-American remake was a disaster.

Blum, Daniel (1900–1965). American writer, editor and collector; annually produced *Theatre World* and *Screen World* annuals.

Blyden, Larry (1925–1975). American comic actor, on TV and in supporting roles.
The Bachelor Party 57. Kiss Them for Me 57. On a Clear Day You Can See Forever 70, etc.
TV series: Harry's Girls 63.

Blystone, John G. (1892–1938). American director, former actor.
Dick Turpin 25. *Seven Chances* 25. Ankles Preferred 27. Mother Knows Best 28. The Sky Hawk 29. Tolable David 30. Charlie Chan's Chance 32. Shanghai Madness 33. Hell in the Heavens 34. The Magnificent Brute 36. Woman Chases Man 37. Swiss Miss 38. *Blockheads* 38, many others.

Blyth, Ann (1928–). Diminutive American songstress and leading lady who after opera training got her screen break in Donald O'Connor musicals, then graduated to dramatic roles.
□Chip off the Old Block 44. The Merry Monahans 44. Babes on Swing Street 44. Bowery to Broadway 44. *Mildred Pierce* (as the abominable daughter) 45. Swell Guy 46. Brute Force 47. Killer McCoy 47. A Woman's Vengeance 47. *Another Part of the Forest* 48. *Mr Peabody and the Mermaid* 48. Red Canyon 49. Once More My Darling 49. Top o' the Morning 49. Free For All 49. Our Very Own 50. *The Great Caruso* 51. Katie Did It 51. Thunder on the Hill 51. I'll Never Forget You 51. The Golden Horde 51. The World in his Arms 51. One Minute to Zero 52. Sally and Saint Anne 52. All the Brothers were Valiant 53. *Rose Marie* 54. The Student Prince 54. The King's Thief 55. Kismet 55. Slander 57. The Buster Keaton Story 57. *The Helen Morgan Story* 57.

Blythe, Betty (1893–1972) (Elizabeth Blythe Slaughter). American leading lady of the silent era.
Nomads of the North 20. Queen of Sheba 21. Chu Chin Chow 23. The Folly of Vanity 24. She 25. The Girl from Gay Paree 27. Glorious Betsy 28. A Daughter of Israel 28. Eager Lips 30. Tom Brown of Culver 32. Only Yesterday 33. Ever Since Eve 34. The Gorgeous Hussy 36. Gangster's Boy 38. Honky Tonk 41. Jiggs and Maggie in Society 47. My Fair Lady 64, many others.

Blythe, John (1921–). British character actor, often of spiv types.
This Happy Breed 44. Holiday Camp 48. Vote for Huggett 49. Worm's Eye View 51. The Gay Dog 54. Foxhole in Cairo 60. A Stitch in Time 64. The Bed Sitting Room 69, many others.

Boardman, Eleanor (1898–). Sympathetic American leading lady of the late silent period, who never seemed happy in sound films and retired in 1934. Was married variously to King Vidor and Harry D'Abbadie D'Arrast.
□The Stranger's Banquet 22. Gimme 23. Souls for Sale 23. Vanity Fair (as Amelia Sedley) 23. Three Wise Fools 23. Day of Faith 23. True as Steel 24. Wine of Youth 24. The Turmoil 24. Sinners in Silk 24. So This Is Marriage 24. The Silent Accuser 24. Wife of the Centaur 24. The Way of a Girl 25. Proud Flesh 25. Exchange of Wives 25. The Only Thing 25. The Circle 25. Memory Lane 26. The Auction Block 26. Bardeleys the Magnificent 26. Tell It to the Marines 26. *The Crowd* 28. Diamond Handcuffs 28. She Goes to War 29. Mamba 30. Redemption 30. *The*

Great Meadow 31. The Flood 31. Women Love Once 31. The Squaw Man 31. It Happened in Spain 34.

Bochner, Lloyd (1924–). Canadian leading man, mostly on TV but in occasional films.
Drums of Africa 63. The Night Walker 64. Sylvia 65. Harlow 65. Point Blank 67. Tony Rome 67. The Detective 68. The Young Runaways 68. The Horse in the Grey Flannel Suit 69. Ulzana's Raid 72. Mazes and Monsters (TV) 83, etc.
TV series: Hong Kong 60. The Richard Boone Show 64. Dynasty 81–.

Bock, Jerry (1928–). American song composer who with lyricist Sheldon Harnick (1924–) wrote *Fiddler on the Roof.*

Bodard, Mag (1927–). Swedish producer in France; a rare example of a woman in this job.
The Umbrellas of Cherbourg 64. The Young Girls of Rochefort 66. *Le Bonheur* 66. Mouchette 67. Benjamin 67. Le Viol 68. La Chinoise 68. *Peau d'Ane* 71, etc.

Bode, Ralph (or **Ralf D. Bode**) (–). American cinematographer.
Saturday Night Fever 77. Slow Dancing in the Big City 78. Rich Kids 79. Coal Miner's Daughter 80. Dressed to Kill 80. Raggedy Man 81. A Little Sex 82. Gorky Park 83, etc.

Bodeen, De Witt (1908–). American screenwriter.
The Seventh Victim 43. *The Curse of the Cat People* 44. The Enchanted Cottage 44. *I Remember Mama* 47. Mrs Mike 50. Twelve to the Moon 58. Billy Budd 62, etc.

The Body Snatcher (US 1945). Generally felt to be the most successful of Val Lewton's highly-regarded horror films for RKO, this version of the R. L. Stevenson story had excellent sets of old Edinburgh and a first-class performance by Henry Daniell. The subject matter has, of course, been used in several other films. Directed by Robert Wise.

Boehm, Karl or **Carl** (1928–) (Karlheinz Boehm). Blond, handsome German leading man who has appeared in a few international films.
Alraune 52. Sissi 55. Das Dreimaderhaus 58. *Peeping Tom* 59. Too Hot to Handle 60. The Magnificent Rebel (as Beethoven) 60. The Four Horsemen of the Apocalypse 62. The Wonderful World of the Brothers Grimm 63. Come Fly with Me 63. The Venetian Affair 66. Effi Briest 74, etc.

Boehm, Sydney (1908–). American screenwriter, a reliable hand at crime stories.
High Wall 48. *The Undercover Man* 49. Side Street 50. Mystery Street 50. *Union Station* 50. When Worlds Collide 52. The Savage 53. *The Big Heat* 53. The Secret of the Incas 54. Rogue Cop 54. Black Tuesday 54. Violent Saturday 55. The Tall Men 55. Hell on Frisco Bay 55. The Revolt of Mamie Stover 56. Harry Black 58. A Woman Obsessed (& p) 59. *Seven Thieves* (& p) 60. Shock Treatment 64. Sylvia 65. Rough Night in Jericho 67, etc.

Boetticher, Budd (1916–) (Oscar Boetticher). American director, former bullfighter. Has not risen above a few striking co-features, but cineastes have made him the centre of a cult.
Autobiography 1971: *When in Disgrace*.
The Missing Juror 44. Assigned to Danger 47. Sword of D'Artagnan 51. *The Bullfighter and the Lady* (& wp) 51. Red Ball Express 52. Bronco Buster 52. Horizons West 52. East of Sumatra 53. Wings of the Hawk 53. The Man from the Alamo 53. The Magnificent Matador (& w) 55. The Killer is Loose 56. Seven Men from Now 56. Decision at Sundown 57. The Tall T 57. Buchanan Rides Alone 58. Ride Lonesome 59. Westbound 59. *The Rise and Fall of Legs Diamond* 60. *Arruza* 68. A Time for Dying 69, etc.

boffins are research scientists working on hush-hush government projects. Their problems have been dramatized in such films as *The Small Back Room, School for Secrets, Suspect, The Man in the Moon, The Satan Bug, The Andromeda Strain, The Atomic City* and *The Forbin Project.*

Bogarde, Dirk (1921–) (Derek Van Den Bogaerd). British leading actor of Dutch descent. A great success in lightweight homegrown films, he later restricted his appearances and achieved international distinction as a character actor.
Autobiography 1977: *A Postillion Struck by Lightning*; 1978: *Snakes and Ladders*; 1983: *An Orderly Man.*
Biography 1974: *The Films of Dirk Bogarde* by Margaret Hinxman.
□Esther Waters 47. Once a Jolly Swagman 48. *Quartet* 48. Dear Mr Prohack 49. Boys in Brown 49. So Long at the Fair 49. The Woman in Question 50. The Blue Lamp 50. Blackmailed 51. Penny Princess 51. The Gentle Gunman 52. Hunted 52. *Doctor in the House* 53. Appointment in London 53. They Who Dare 53. Desperate Moment 53. Simba 54. The Sea Shall Not Have Them 54. *The*

Sleeping Tiger 54. For Better For Worse 54. Doctor at Sea 55. *Cast a Dark Shadow* 55. Doctor at Large 56. *The Spanish Gardener* 56. Ill Met By Moonlight 57. Campbell's Kingdom 58. The Wind Cannot Read 58. *A Tale of Two Cities* 58. The Doctor's Dilemma 59. Libel 59. Song Without End (as Liszt) (US) 60. The Angel Wore Red 60. The Singer not the Song 60. *Victim* 61. We Joined the Navy (cameo) 62. H.M.S. Defiant 62. The Password is Courage 63. I Could Go On Singing 63. The Mind Benders 63. *The Servant* (BFA) 63. Hot Enough for June 64. Doctor in Distress 64. *King and Country* 64. The High Bright Sun 65. *Darling* (BFA) 65. Modesty Blaise 66. Accident 67. Our Mother's House 67. Sebastian 67. The Fixer 68. Oh What a Lovely War 69. *The Damned* 69. Justine 69. *Death in Venice* 70. The Serpent 72. The Night Porter 74. Permission to Kill 75. Providence 77. A Bridge Too Far 77. Despair 78. The Patricia Neal Story (TV) 81.
May we Borrow Your Husband? (TV) 85.

¶ I love the camera and it loves me. Well, not very much sometimes. But we're good friends.—*D.B.*

I'll only work with new people. If you stick with your contemporaries, you're dead.—*D.B.*

'I'm still in the shell, and you're not going to crack it, ducky.'—*D.B. to Russell Harty in TV interview 1986*

Famous line (*Darling*): 'Your idea of fidelity is not having more than one man in bed at the same time.'

Bogart, Humphrey (1899–1957). American leading actor who became one of Hollywood's imperishable personalities, a cynical but amiable tough guy in a trench coat who summed up all the *films noirs* of the forties, after a long apprenticeship playing gangsters. Several biographies have been published, but none catch the full flavour of the man who influenced millions. The best are by Nathaniel Benchley, Jonah Ruddy, Clifford McCarty and Ezra Goodman.

□A Devil with Women 30. Up the River 30. Body and Soul 30. Bad Sister 30. Women of All Nations 31. A Holy Terror 31. Love Affair 32. Big City Blues 32. Three on a Match 32. Midnight 34. *The Petrified Forest* (his stage role as gangster Duke Mantee) 36. Two Against the World 36. Bullets or Ballots 36. China Clipper 36. Isle of Fury 36. The Great O'Malley 37. Black Legion 37. San Quentin 37. *Marked Woman* 37. Kid Galahad 37. *Dead End* 37. Stand In 37. Swing Your Lady 38. Men Are Such Fools 38. The Amazing Dr Clitterhouse 38. Racket Busters 38. *Angels with Dirty Faces* 38. Crime School 38. King of the Underworld 39. The Oklahoma Kid 39. Dark Victory 39. You Can't Get Away with Murder 39. *The Roaring Twenties* 39. The Return of Dr X (as a vampire) 39. Invisible Stripes 39. Virginia City 40. It All Came True 40. Brother Orchid 40. They Drive by Night 40. *High Sierra* 41. The Wagons Roll at Night 41. *The Maltese Falcon* (his archetypal performance) 41. All Through the Night 42. The Big Shot 42. *Across the Pacific* 42. *Casablanca* 42. Action in the North Atlantic 43. Thank Your Lucky Stars 43. *Sahara* 43. *To Have and Have Not* 43. Passage to Marseilles 44. Conflict 45. *The Big Sleep* 46. The Two Mrs Carrolls 47. Dead Reckoning 47. Dark Passage 47. *The Treasure of the Sierra Madre* 47. *Key Largo* 48. Knock on any Door 49. Tokyo Joe 49. Chain Lightning 50. In a Lonely Place 50. *The Enforcer* 51. Sirocco 51. *The African Queen* (AA) 52. Deadline 52. Battle Circus 53. *Beat the Devil* 54. *The Caine Mutiny* 54. Sabrina 54. *The Barefoot Contessa* 54. We're No Angels 55. The Left Hand of God 55. The Desperate Hours 55. The Harder they Fall 56.

†Bogart also appeared in a 1930 short, *Broadway's Like That*; and he made uncredited gag appearances in *Two Guys from Milwaukee* 46, *Always Together* 48, *Road to Bali* 52, *The Love Lottery* 53.

❀ For contriving to represent both Action Man and Thinking Man of the early forties; and for taking both these roles with a large pinch of salt. *Casablanca*.

¶ To some extent Bogart tended to live his film roles. As Dave Chase the Hollywood restaurateur once said:

> Bogart's a helluva nice guy till 11.30 p.m. After that he thinks he's Bogart.

So in a way his aptest quotes are from his movies. As Rick in *Casablanca*:

> I stick my neck out for nobody.

Or as Sam Spade in *The Maltese Falcon*:

> Don't be so sure I'm as crooked as I'm supposed to be.

And:

> When you're slapped, you'll take it and like it!

Stanley Kramer saw through him:

> He was playing Bogart all the time, but he was really just a big sloppy bowl of mush.

One feels that this hits the nail pretty squarely on the head: Bogie was a nice guy who enjoyed a good grouch. About, for instance, the untrained beefcake stars of the early fifties, many of them picked up for tests from sidewalks and gas stations:

Shout 'gas' around the studios today, and half the young male stars will come running.

About acting theorists:

Do I subscribe to the Olivier school of acting? Ah, nuts. I'm an actor. I just do what comes naturally.

About the industry:

I don't hurt the industry. The industry hurts itself, by making so many lousy movies—as if General Motors deliberately put out a bad car.

And:

I made more lousy pictures than any actor in history.

And about life:

The trouble with the world is that everybody in it is about three drinks behind.

Other actors, perhaps, knew him better than he knew himself.

Edward G. Robinson:

I always felt sorry for him—sorry that he had imposed upon himself the character with which he had become identified.

And Katharine Hepburn:

His yes meant yes, his no meant no. There was no bunkum about Bogart.

Famous lines:

(*The Maltese Falcon*) 'Don't be so sure I'm as crooked as I'm supposed to be.'

'Let's talk about the black bird.'

'We didn't exactly believe your story, Miss O'Shea, we believed your 200 dollars. You paid us more than if you'd been telling the truth, and enough more to make it all right.'

'Yes, angel, I'm gonna send you over.'

(*Across the Pacific*) 'When you're slapped, you're gonna take it and like it.'

(*Casablanca*) 'I came to Casablanca for the waters.' 'But we're in the middle of the desert.' 'I was misinformed.'

'Louis, I think this is the beginning of a beautiful friendship.'

(*The Big Sleep*) 'I don't mind if you don't like my manners. I don't like them myself. They're pretty bad. I grieve over them on long winter evenings.'

Bogart, Paul (1919?–). American director. □Halls of Anger 68. Marlowe 69. In Search of America (TV) 70. The Skin Game 71. Cancel My Reservation 71. Class of '44 73. Tell Me Where It Hurts (TV) 74. Winner Take All (TV) 75. Mr Ricco 75. Oh God you Devil 84.

Bogdanovich, Peter (1939–). American director with a penchant for reworking traditional themes; former film critic. □Voyage to the Planet of Prehistoric Women (as 'Derek Thomas') 68. *Targets* (& w) 68. *The Last Picture Show* (& w) 71. Directed by John Ford (doc) 71. *What's Up Doc?* (& w) 72. Paper Moon 73. Daisy Miller (& p) 74. At Long Last Love 75. Nickelodeon 77. Saint Jack 79. They All Laughed 81. Mask 84.

Bogeaus, Benedict (1904–1968). American independent producer, formerly in real estate; his films were mildly interesting though eccentric.
The Bridge of San Luis Rey 44. Captain Kidd 45. The Diary of a Chambermaid 45. Christmas Eve 47. The Macomber Affair 47. Johnny One Eye 49. Passion 54. Slightly Scarlet 56. The Most Dangerous Man Alive 61, etc.

Bohnen, Roman (1894–1949). American character actor usually seen as hard-working immigrant types.
Vogues of 1938 37. Of Mice and Men 40. So Ends our Night 41. Appointment for Love 41. Edge of Darkness 43. Mission to Moscow 43. The Song of Bernadette 43. *The Hitler Gang* 44. A Bell for Adano 45. The Strange Love of Martha Ivers 46. Mr Ace 46. The Best Years of Our Lives 46. Brute Force 47. Arch of Triumph 48. Night has a Thousand Eyes 48, etc.

Bois, Curt (1900–). Dapper German comedy actor, long in Hollywood playing head waiters and pompous clerks.
Tovarich 37. Hollywood Hotel 38. *The Great Waltz* 38. Boom Town 40. Bitter Sweet 40. Hold Back the Dawn 41. Casablanca 42. The Desert Song 43. The Spanish Main 45. *The Woman in White* 48. The Great Sinner 49. Fortunes of Captain Blood 50. *Herr Puntilla and His Servant Matti* (Ger.) 54, many others.

Boisrond, Michel (1921–). French director.
Mamzelle Pigalle 56. Une Parisienne 57. Come Dance with Me 59. Love and the Frenchwoman 60. Comment Reussir en Amour 62. Comment Epouser un Premier Ministre 64. L'Homme Qui Valait des Milliards 68. The Tender Moment 69. On Est Toujours Trop Bon avec des Femmes 71. Le Petit Poucet 72. Tell Me You Love Me 74. Catherine and Company 75, etc.

Boisset, Yves (1939–). French director.
A Cop 70. Cobra 71. L'Attentat 72. Coplan

Saves His Skin 72. Folie à Tuer 75. The Sheriff 76. The Purple Taxi 78, etc.

Bolam, James (1938–). Gritty British actor from the proletarian northeast.
The Kitchen 61. A Kind of Loving 62. Otley 69. Crucible of Terror 71. Straight on till Morning 72. O Lucky Man 73. In Celebration 74. The Likely Lads 76, etc.
TV series: *The Likely Lads* 65–69. *Whatever Happened to the Likely Lads* 73. *When the Boat Comes In* 75–77. *Only When I Laugh* 79–83. Room at the Bottom 86.

Boland, Bridget (1904–). British playwright and screenwriter.
Gaslight 39. Spies of the Air. 40. The Lost People 48. The Prisoner 54. War and Peace 56, etc.

Boland, Mary (1880–1965). American stage tragedienne who in middle age settled in Hollywood and played innumerable fluttery matrons: appeared in a series of domestic comedies with Charles Ruggles.
The Edge of the Abyss 16. His Temporary Wife 18. Personal Maid 31. *If I had a Million* 32. *Three Cornered Moon* 33. Four Frightened People 34. *Down to Their Last Yacht* 34. *Ruggles of Red Gap* 35. Early to Bed 36. Wives Never Know 36. Mama Runs Wild 37. Little Tough Guys in Society 38. *The Women* 39. New Moon 40. *Pride and Prejudice* (as Mrs Bennett) 40. In Our Time 44. Nothing But Trouble 44. Julia Misbehaves 48. Guilty Bystander 50, many others.

Boles, John (1895–1969). American operetta singer who apart from musicals proved himself useful to Hollywood as a well-behaved 'other man'.
□So This Is Marriage 24. Excuse Me 25. The Loves of Sunya 27. The Shepherd of the Hills 28. We Americans 28. The Bride of the Colorado 28. Fazil 28. The Water Hole 28. Virgin Lips 28. Man-made Woman 28. Romance of the Underworld 28. The Last Warning 29. *The Desert Song* 29. Scandal 29. *Rio Rita* 29. Song of the West 30. Captain of the Guard 30. *The King of Jazz* 30. One Heavenly Night 30. Resurrection 31. Seed 31. Frankenstein (as Victor, friend of the family) 31. Good Sport 31. Careless Lady 31. *Back Street* 32. Six Hours to Live 32. Child of Manhattan 32. My Lips Betray 33. *Only Yesterday* 33. I Believed in You 34. Music in the Air 34. Beloved 34. Bottoms Up 34. Stand Up and Cheer 34. The Life of Vergie Winters 34. Wild Gold 34. The Age of Innocence 34. The White Parade 34. Orchids to You 34. Curly Top 35. Redheads on Parade 35. The Littlest Rebel 35. Rose of the Rancho 36. A Message to Garcia 36. Craig's Wife 36. As Good as Married 37. *Stella Dallas* 37. Fight for Your Lady 37. She Married an Artist 38. Romance in the Dark 38. Sinners in Paradise 38. The Road to Happiness 42. Between Us Girls 42. Thousands Cheer 43. Babes in Bagdad 52.

Boleslawski, Richard (1889–1937) (Boleslaw Ryszart Srzednicki). Polish stage director, formerly with the Moscow Arts Theatre, who came to Hollywood in 1930 and made a few stylish movies.
□Three Meetings (USSR) 17. Treasure Girl 30. The Last of the Lone Wolf 31. Woman Pursued 31. The Gay Diplomat 31. Rasputin and the Empress 32. Storm at Daybreak 33. Beauty for Sale 33. Fugitive Lovers 33. Men in White 34. Operator 13 34. *The Painted Veil* 34. *Clive of India* 35. *Les Misérables* 35. O'Shaughnessy's Boy 35. *Metropolitan* 35. Three Godfathers 36. *Theodora Goes Wild* 36. *The Garden of Allah* 36. The Last of Mrs Cheyney 37.

Bolger, Ray (1904–87). Rubber-legged American eccentric dancer, a stage star who made too few films.
□The Great Ziegfeld 36. *Rosalie* 37. Sweethearts 38. *The Wizard of Oz* (as the scarecrow) 39. Sunny 41. Stage Door Canteen 43. Four Jacks and a Jill 44. *The Harvey Girls* 46. *Look for the Silver Lining* 49. *Where's Charley* 52. April in Paris 52. Babes in Toyland 60. The Daydreamer 66. The Entertainer (TV) 75. The Captains and the Kings (TV) 76. Heaven Only Knows (TV) 79. The Runner Stumbles 79. Just You and Me Kid 79. That's Dancing 84.
TV series: Where's Raymond 52.

Bolkan, Florinda (1941–) (Florinda Suares Bulcao). Spanish-Indian leading lady.
Candy 68. The Damned 69. Investigation of a Citizen 70. The Last Valley 70. The Anonymous Venetian 71. Detective Belli 71. Romance 71. The Island 72. A Man to Respect 72. Lizard in a Woman's Skin 72. Hearts and Minds 74. Royal Flash 75. The Right to Love 76, etc.

Bolling, Tiffany (–). American leading lady.
Kingdom of the Spiders 77.

Bologna, Joseph (1938–). American actor who with his wife Renee Taylor usually writes his own material.

Made for Each Other 71. Honor thy Father (TV) 73. Mixed Company 74. Woman of the Year (TV) 75. The Big Bus 76. Chapter Two 79. Blame It On Rio 84. The Woman in Red 84. Transylvania 6–5000 85.
TV series: Rags to Riches 87.

Bolognini, Mauro (1923–). Italian director.
Wild Love 55. Young Husbands 58. La Notte Brava 59. Il Bell'Antonio 60. La Viaccia 61. Senilita 62. Le Bambole 65. I Tre Volti 65. The Oldest Profession 67. Arabella 67. That Splendid November 68. Metello 70. Bubu 71. Down the Ancient Stairs 75. Black Journal 77, etc.

Bolt, Robert (1924–). British playwright who turned to screenwriting and direction.
Lawrence of Arabia 62. *Doctor Zhivago* 65. *A Man For All Seasons* 66. Ryan's Daughter 70. Lady Caroline Lamb (& d) 72.

Bolton, Guy (1884–1979). American playwright and screenwriter, often associated with P. G. Wodehouse.
Grounds for Divorce 25. The Love Doctor 29. The Love Parade 30. Girl Crazy (oa) 32. Ladies Should Listen (oa) 34. Anything Goes (oa) 35. Rosalie (oa) 37. Weekend at the Waldorf 45. Anastasia (oa) 56, etc.

Bomba the Jungle Boy. This second feature series was devised in 1949, from a comic strip, to use the talents of Johnny Sheffield, who had played Johnny Weissmuller's son in some Tarzan films. It never amounted to much, but twelve films were made until in 1955, after *Lord of the Jungle*, Sheffield became too old and too fat for the role.

Bonanova, Fortunio (1893–1969). Spanish opera singer and impresario who after managing his own repertory company in America in the thirties, settled in Hollywood to play excitable foreigners.
Careless Lady 32. Podoroso Caballero 36. Tropic Holiday 38. La Immaculada 39. I Was an Adventuress 40. *Citizen Kane* (as the music teacher) 41. Blood and Sand 41. The Black Swan 42. Five Graves to Cairo 43. For Whom the Bell Tolls 43. Going my Way 44. Double Indemnity 44. Monsieur Beaucaire 46. The Fugitive 47. Whirlpool 50. September Affair 51. The Moon is Blue 53. An Affair to Remember 57. Thunder in the Sun 59. The Running Man 63. Million Dollar Collar 69, many others.

Bonaparte, Napoleon: see *Napoleon Bonaparte*.

Bond, Derek (1919–). British light leading man with varied pre-film experience including the Grenadier Guards.
The Captive Heart 46. *Nicholas Nickleby* (title role) 47. *Scott of the Antarctic* 48. Broken Journey 48. The Weaker Sex 48. Christopher Columbus 49. Marry Me 49. Uncle Silas 50. The Hour of Thirteen 52. Stranger from Venus 54. Svengali 55. Trouble in Store 55. Gideon's Day 58. The Hand 60. Saturday Night Out 64. Wonderful Life 64. Press for Time 66. When Eight Bells Toll 71, etc.

Bond, Gary (1940–). British leading man.
Zulu 64. Anne of the Thousand Days 70. *Outback* 70, etc.

Bond, Julian (1930–). British writer, mainly for TV. *A Man of Our Times*, Love for Lydia, Fair Stood the Wind for France, The Far Pavilions, Strangers and Brothers.
Films: The Shooting Party, The Whistle Blower.

Bond, Lillian (1910–). British leading lady in American films of the thirties.
Just a Gigolo 31. Fireman Save My Child 32. *The Old Dark House* 32. Hot Pepper 33. Affairs of a Gentleman 34. China Seas 35. The Housekeeper's Daughter 39. The Westerner 40. The Picture of Dorian Gray 45. Man in the Attic 54. Pirates of Tripoli 55, etc.

Bond, Ward (1903–1960). Burly American actor who from the coming of sound distinguished himself in small roles, especially in John Ford films; but it took TV to make him a star.
The Big Trail 30. When Strangers Marry 33. Devil Dogs of the Air 35. You Only Live Once 37. The Oklahoma Kid 39. Young Mr Lincoln 39. Gone with the Wind 39. The Grapes of Wrath 40. *Tobacco Road* 41. The Maltese Falcon 41. Gentleman Jim 42. A Guy Named Joe 43. They Were Expendable 45. My Darling Clementine 46. Fort Apache 48. *Wagonmaster* 50. *The Quiet Man* 52. *Blowing Wild* 53. The Long Gray Line 55. *The Searchers* 56. *The Wings of Eagles* 57. *The Halliday Brand* 57. *Rio Bravo* 59, many others.
TV series: *Wagon Train* 57–60.

Bondartchuk, Sergei (1920–). Russian actor and director.
The Young Guards (a) 48. The Grasshopper

(a) 55. Othello (a) 56. *Destiny of a Man* (a, d) 59. *War and Peace* (a, d) (AA) 64. *Waterloo* (d) 70. They Fought for Their Country 75. The Steppe 78. Ten Days That Shook the World 82, etc.

Bondi, Beulah (1889–1981) (Beulah Bondy). Distinguished American character actress who from early middle age played cantankerous or kindly old ladies.
□Street Scene 31. Arrowsmith 31. Rain 32. The Stranger's Return 33. Christopher Bean 33. Finishing School 34. The Painted Veil 34. Two Alone 34. Registered Nurse 34. Ready for Love 34. Bad Boy 35. The Good Fairy 35. The Invisible Ray 36. The Trail of the Lonesome Pine 36. The Moon's Our Home 36. The Case Against Mrs Ames 36. Hearts Divided 36. The Gorgeous Hussy 37. *Maid of Salem* 37. *Make Way for Tomorrow* 37. The Buccaneer 38. Of Human Hearts 38. Vivacious Lady 38. The Sisters 38. On Borrowed Time 39. Mr Smith Goes to Washington 39. The Underpup 39. Remember the Night 40. *Our Town* 40. The Captain is a Lady 40. Penny Serenade 41. Shepherd of the Hills 41. One Foot in Heaven 41. Tonight We Raid Calais 43. Watch on the Rhine 43. I Love a Soldier 44. She's a Soldier Too 44. Our Hearts Were Young and Gay 44. And Now Tomorrow 44. The Very Thought of You 44. *The Southerner* 45. Back to Bataan 45. Breakfast in Hollywood 46. Sister Kenny 46. *It's a Wonderful Life* 46. High Conquest 47. The Sainted Sisters 48. The Snake Pit 48. So Dear to My Heart 48. The Life of Riley 49. Reign of Terror 49. Mr Soft Touch 49. The Baron of Arizona 50. The Furies 50. Lone Star 52. Latin Lovers 53. *Track of the Cat* 54. Back from Eternity 56. The Unholy Wife 57. The Big Fisherman 59. A Summer Place 59. *Tammy Tell Me True* 61. The Wonderful World of the Brothers Grimm 62. Tammy and the Doctor 63. She Waits (TV) 71.

† B.B. always said that her great regret was being passed over for the role of Ma Joad in *The Grapes of Wrath*.

Bonham Carter, Helena (*c.*1961–). British leading lady.
Lady Jane 84. A Room with a View 85.

Bonnie and Clyde (US 1967). A milestone film in its sixties-style retelling, with a blend of comedy, poetry and extreme violence, of the oft-recounted life story of two minor desperadoes of the thirties, Bonnie Parker and Clyde Barrow. Comparison with the gangster films of the thirties would be fruitful. Written by Robert Benton and David Newman, photographed by Burnett Guffey (AA), produced by Warren Beatty, directed by Arthur Penn; starring Warren Beatty and Faye Dunaway. Other variations on the story include *Gun Crazy, They Live By Night, Thieves Like Us, You Only Live Once* and *The Bonnie Parker Story*.

Bonzo was a chimpanzee who appeared in *Bedtime for Bonzo* 51 being brought up as a child under an educational experiment. A second and final film of his adventures was *Bonzo Goes to College* 52.

boo-boos occur even in the best-regulated movies; sometimes they pass the eagle eye of editor and director and find their way into the release version. Here are a few which have delighted me.
□In *Carmen Jones*, the camera tracks with Dorothy Dandridge down a shopping street, and the entire crew is reflected in the windows she passes.
□In *The Invisible Man*, when the naked but invisible hero runs from the police but is given away by his footprints in the snow, the footprints are of shoes, not feet.
□In *The Wrong Box*, the roofs of Victorian London are disfigured by TV aerials.
□In *The Viking Queen*, one character is plainly wearing a wrist watch.
□In *One Million Years B.C.,* all the girls wear false eyelashes.
□In *The Group*, set in the thirties, there are several shots of the Pan Am building in New York, built in the sixties.
□In *Stagecoach*, during the Indian chase across the salt flats one can see the tracks of rubber tyres.
□In *Decameron Nights*, Louis Jourdan as Paganino the Pirate stands on the deck of his fourteenth-century ship . . . and down a hill in the distance trundles a large white truck.
□In *Camelot*, the character played by Lionel Jeffries first meets King Arthur about an hour into the movie; yet twenty minutes earlier he is plainly visible at the king's wedding.
□In *Son of Frankenstein*, Basil Rathbone during a train journey draws attention to the weirdly stunted trees . . . one of which passes by three times during the conversation.
□In *Castle of Fu Manchu*, one of the leading characters is referred to in the film as Ingrid, in the synopsis as Anna, and in the end credits as Maria.
□In *Tea and Sympathy*, a pair of china dogs are back to back in a general view of the scene, but face to face in the close-ups.

□In *Dracula*, Bela Lugosi refers to Whitby as 'so close to London'. It is in fact 243 miles away.
□In *The Yellow Mountain* and *A Man Alone*, both westerns set in the last century, aeroplane vapour trails can be seen in the sky.
□In *The King and I*, while Yul Brynner is singing 'Puzzlement' he is wearing an ear-ring in some shots but not in others.
□In *Emma Hamilton* (1969) Big Ben is heard to strike in 1804, fifty years before it was built.
□In *The Lodger* (1944) London's Tower Bridge is shown, ten years before it was built.
□In *Hello Dolly*, set at the turn of the century, a modern car lies derelict by the side of the railway track.
□In *Anatomy of a Murder*, Lee Remick in the café scene wears a dress, but when she walks outside she is wearing slacks.
□In *Hangover Square*, the introductory title gives the date of the action as 1899, but shortly thereafter a theatre programme shows 1903.
□In *Queen Christina*, the famous final close-up apparently has the wind blowing in two directions at once, one to get the boat under way and the other to arrange Garbo's hair to the best advantage.
□In *The Desk Set*, Katharine Hepburn leaves her office carrying a bunch of white flowers. By the time she reaches the pavement they are pink.
□In *Knock on Wood*, Danny Kaye turns a corner in London's Oxford Street, and finds himself in Ludgate Hill, three miles away.
□In *23 Paces to Baker Street*, Van Johnson has an apartment in Portman Square, with a river view which seems to be that of the Savoy Hotel two miles away.
□In *Triple Cross*, a World War Two newspaper bears a headline about the cost of Concorde going up again.
□In *The Lady Vanishes*, Miss Froy writes her name in the steam on a train window, but two or three shots later the writing is quite different and in another place.
□In *The Eddie Cantor Story*, the scene is set in 1904, but Eddie sings 'Meet Me Tonight in Dreamland' which was not written till 1909.
□Similarly, in *Thoroughly Modern Millie*, clearly set in 1922 per the song title, one of the big numbers is 'Baby Face', written in 1926.
□In *Miracle on 34th Street*, a camera shadow follows Edmund Gwenn and John Payne as they walk across a square.
□ In *Broken Lance*, Katy Jurado's dress changes colour in alternate shots as she stands in a doorway talking to Spencer Tracy at the gate.
□*In North by Northwest*, Cary Grant's only suit during his stay in Chicago is a different colour out in the prairie from back at the hotel. Hitchcock said this was because of different kinds of lighting which were used.
□In *Mysterious Island*, set in 1860, an air balloon rises above a nest of TV aerials.
□In *The Alamo*, mobile trailers are clearly seen in the battle sequences, and a falling stunt man lands on a mattress.
□In *North to Alaska* during a fist fight, John Wayne loses his toupee and then regains it.
□In *The Green Berets*, the sun sets in the east during the final shot.
□In *The Scalphunters*, set in the 1800s, Ossie Davis mentions the planet Pluto, which was not discovered until 1930.
□In *Annie*, set in 1933, characters go to Radio City Music Hall and see *Camille*, which was not made until 1937.
□In *Yankee Doodle Dandy*, the *Lusitania* is sunk and there is a newspaper picture showing a ship with two funnels. The *Lusitania* had four funnels.
□In the same film a luggage label with a picture of Nelson's Column bears the legend 'Nelson Square Hotel'.
□In *Brief Encounter*, Celia Johnson runs through a downpour but remains dry.
□In *National Lampoon's Animal House*, the word Satan written on a blackboard looks totally different in adjacent slots.
□In *Quadrophenia*, clearly set in 1964, a cinema is showing Warren Beatty in *Heaven Can Wait*, made fourteen years later.
□In *Carrie*, the final dream was projected backwards to achieve the right effect. But in the background a car is also moving backwards . . .
□In *Halloween*, which is set in Illinois, all the cars have California number plates.
□In *The Birds*, the creatures which pursue the children cast no shadows.
□ In *Cain and Mabel*, a workman walks across a sound stage during a production number.
□ In *The Band Wagon*, during the train ride to Baltimore, the scenery is dark on one side and light on the other.
□ In *Knock on Wood*, a policeman rushes upstairs wearing a helmet, and into a room wearing a peaked cap.
□ In *Silk Stockings*, a typewriter shown on a table vanishes in the reverse shot taken from the balcony.

☐ In *Fire Maidens from Outer Space*, Sidney Tafler in a T-shirt glances down at his watch, and we get an insert of a watch on a fully-sleeved arm.
☐ In *Genevieve*, Kenneth More comes out of a pub carrying a pint of beer, which has become a half pint by the time he reaches his table.
☐ In *The Band Wagon*, a theatre is shown on its canopy as the Alcott; but on the programme it says the Stratton.
☐ In *Meet Me In St Louis*, during the Trolley Song, one of the extras calls 'Hi, Judy!' Judy Garland's character name is Esther.
☐ In *The Adventures of Robin Hood*, Errol Flynn takes a bite at a complete leg of mutton. In the next shot, only a bone is left.
☐ In *Round Midnight*, which is set in the fifties, there is a shot of New York's World Trade Center towers, which were built much later.
☐ In *Camelot*, Richard Harris plays one scene with a Band-Aid on his neck.
☐ In *North by Northwest*, a small boy (who has obviously been to rehearsal) puts his fingers in his ears *before* Eva Marie Saint picks up a gun to shoot Cary Grant.
☐ In *Mysterious Island*, during the air balloon sequence, it is raining *above* the clouds.
☐ In *The Smallest Show on Earth*, although the cinema is supposedly in the north of England, a taxi arriving at it stops outside Hammersmith Station.
☐ In *The Corn is Green*, the villagers are all said to be illiterate, but they cluster round to read a poster.

Booke, Sorrell (1926–). Chubby American character actor.
Gone are the Days 63. Fail Safe 64. Black Like Me 64. Lady in a Cage 64. Up the Down Staircase 67. Slaughterhouse Five 71. The Take 72. The Iceman Cometh 73. Bank Shot 74. Special Delivery 76. Freaky Friday 77. The Other Side of Midnight 77, etc.

books on the cinema: see list at end of book.

boom. A 'long arm' extending from the camera unit and carrying a microphone to be balanced over the actors so that sound can be picked up in a semi-distant shot. A 'camera boom' is a high movable platform strong enough to support the entire camera unit.

Boomerang (US 1947). This who-done-it based on the murder of a priest in a small town set a new style in semi-documentary thrillers. Written by Richard Murphy, directed by Elia Kazan.

Boone, Daniel (1734–1820). American pioneer and Indian scout who helped to open up Kentucky and Missouri. He has been frequently portrayed in films, notably by George O'Brien (*Daniel Boone*, 1936), David Bruce (*Young Daniel Boone*, 1950) and Bruce Bennett (*Daniel Boone, Trail Blazer*, 1956). In 1964 began a long-running TV series, *Daniel Boone*, starring Fess Parker.

Boone, Pat (1934–). Gentle-mannered American pop singer of the fifties; never quite made it as a straight actor, perhaps because he paraded his lack of private vices.
☐*Bernardine* 57. April Love 57. Mardi Gras 58. *Journey to the Centre of the Earth* 59. All Hands on Deck 61. State Fair 62. The Yellow Canary 63. The Main Attraction 63. The Horror of it All (GB) 63. Never Put it in Writing (GB) 64. Goodbye Charlie 64. The Greatest Story Ever Told 65. The Perils of Pauline 67. The Pigeon (TV) 69. The Cross and the Switchblade 70.

Boone, Richard (1917–1981). Craggy American character actor, often in menacing roles.
☐Halls of Montezuma 51. Call Me Mister 51. The Desert Fox 51. Return of the Texan 52. Red Skies of Montana 52. Kangaroo 52. The Way of a Gaucho 52. Man on a Tightrope 53. *Vicki* 53. *The Robe* 53. City of Bad Men 53. Beneath the Twelve-Mile Reef 53. The Siege at Red River 54. Dragnet 54. The Raid 54. Battle Stations 55. *Man Without a Star* 55. Ten Wanted Men 55. Robbers' Roost 55. Star in the Dust 56. Away all Boats 56. Lizzie 57. Garment Center 57. The Tall T 57. I Bury the Living 58. *The Alamo* 60. A Thunder of Drums 61. *Rio Conchos* 64. *The War Lord* 65. Hombre 67. Kona Coast 68. The Night of the Following Day 69. *The Arrangement* 69. Madron 70. *The Kremlin Letter* 70. Big Jake 71. In Broad Daylight (TV) 72. A Tattered Web (TV) 72. Goodnight My Love (TV) 72. Deadly Harvest (TV) 72. The Great Niagara (TV) 74. Against a Crooked Sky 75. The Shootist 76. God's Gun 77. The Big Sleep 78. Winter Kills 79. The Bushido Blade 79.
TV series: *Medic* 54–55. *Have Gun Will Travel* 57–62. *The Richard Boone Show* 63. Hec Ramsey 71–72.

Boorman, John (1933–). British director, from TV. His films tend towards the pretentious and usually fall flat on their faces.

□Catch Us if You Can 65. *Point Blank* (US) 67. *Hell in the Pacific* (US) 69. Leo the Last 70. *Deliverance* 72. Zardoz (& w) 74. Exorcist II: The Heretic 77. Long Shot (as actor, in the role of himself) 78. Excalibur 81.
Dream One (p only) 82. The Emerald Forest (& p) 85. Hope and Glory (& p) 87.

Booth, Anthony (1937–). British general purpose actor: everything from Nazis to layabouts.
Mix Me a Person 62. The L-shaped Room 62. Of Human Bondage 64. Till Death Us Do Part 68. Girl With a Pistol 69. The Garnett Saga 72, etc.
TV series: *Till Death Us Do Part* 67–71.

Booth, Edwina (1909–) (Josephine Constance Woodruff). American leading lady of the late twenties, best known for catching jungle fever while filming in Africa for *Trader Horn* 30. She retired shortly after.

Booth, Harry (–). British director, former editor.
Blitz on Britain 59. A King's Story 64. On the Buses 71. Mutiny on the Buses 72. Go for a Take 72, etc.

Booth, James (1930–) (David Geeves-Booth). British character actor who can play innocent or villainous.
The Trials of Oscar Wilde 60. The Hellions 61. In the Doghouse 62. Sparrows Can't Sing 63. French Dressing 63. *Zulu* 64. The Secret of My Success 65. Ninety Degrees in the Shade 66. *Robbery* 67. The Bliss of Mrs Blossom 68. The Man Who Had Power over Women 70. Darker than Amber 70. Macho Callahan 71. Revenge 71. That'll Be the Day 74. Brannigan 75. Airport 77 77. Wheels (TV) 78. It's Not the Size that Counts 79. The Jazz Singer 80. Zorro the Gay Blade 81. The Cowboy and the Ballerina (TV) 84. Bad Guys 85. Programmed to Kill 87, etc.

Booth, Karin (1923–). American leading lady of second features.
Big City 48. Last of the Buccaneers 50. The Texas Rangers 50. Cripple Creek 52. Let's Do It Again 53. Seminole Uprising 55. The Crooked Sky (GB) 56. Beloved Infidel 59, etc.

Booth, Margaret (c. 1902–). Distinguished American editor, long at MGM, latterly as supervisor.
Memory Lane 26. The Bridge of San Luis Rey 29. Cuban Love Song 31. New Moon 31. Susan Lenox 31. Strange Interlude 31. Bombshell 33. Dancing Lady 33. The Barretts of Wimpole Street 34. Mutiny on the Bounty 35. Camille 36. Romeo and Juliet 36. The Way We Were 73. The Sunshine Boys 76. Murder by Death 76. California Suite 78. Annie 82, many others.
†Miss Booth was given an honorary Oscar in 1977.

Booth, Shirley (1907–) (Thelma Ford Booth). Distinguished American stage actress who came to the screen for a few middle-aged roles.
□*Come Back Little Sheba* (AA) 52. About Mrs Leslie 53. Main Street to Broadway 53. Hot Spell 57. *The Matchmaker* 59. The Smugglers (TV) 68.
TV series: *Hazel* 61–65. A Touch of Grace 73.

Boothe, Powers (–). Overpowering American lead actor.
A Cry for Love (TV) 80. Cruising 81. *Guyana Tragedy* (TV) 81. Southern Comfort 81. Chandlertown (TV) 83. Red Dawn 84. The Emerald Forest 85. Extreme Prejudice 87.

Borchers, Cornell (1925–) (Cornelia Bruch). German leading actress, in a few international films.
The Big Lift 50. The Divided Heart (BFA) 55. Never Say Goodbye 56. Istanbul 57. Oasis 60, etc.

Borden, Olive (1907–1947) (Sybil Tinkle). American leading lady of the twenties.
Dressmaker from Paris 25. Three Bad Men 26. Fig Leaves 26. The Joy Girl 26. Pajamas 26. Gang War 28. Virgin Lips 28. Love in the Desert 29. Dance Hall 29. Hello Sister 30, etc.

Bordoni, Irene (1895–1953). Corsican-American revue comedienne who left Broadway to make only three films.
□Show of Shows 28. Paris 30. Louisiana Purchase 42.

Borehamwood. A British studio fourteen miles north of London, a site originally chosen by John M. East (1860–1924), a stage and silent screen actor. It opened in 1914 as Neptune Films, which folded in 1921; the stages were later taken over by Ideal, Rock, British National, and Associated Television. MGM and ABPC also had studios in nearby Elstree.

Borg, Veda Ann (1915–1973). American character actress, the archetypal hard-boiled blonde of a hundred second features.
Three Cheers for Love 36. Alcatraz Island 37. She Loved a Fireman 38. Café Hostess 39. Glamour for Sale 40. The Pittsburgh Kid 41. Duke of the Navy 42. Isle of Forgotten Sins 43. Smart Guy 44. What a Blonde 45. Mildred Pierce 45. Accomplice 46. Big Town 47. Blonde Savage 48. Forgotten Women 49. The Kangaroo Kid 50. Big Jim McLain 52. Three Sailors and a Girl 53. Bitter Creek 54. Guys and Dolls 55. Frontier Gambler 56. The Fearmakers 58. Thunder in the Sun 59. The Alamo 60, many others.

Borgia, Cesare (1476–1507) and **Lucretia** (1480–1519). The son and daughter of Pope Alexander VI were suspected of several family murders. On screen they have been played as melodramatic figures, notably by MacDonald Carey and Paulette Goddard (*Bride of Vengeance*, 1949), Orson Welles (*Prince of Foxes*, 1949), Pedro Armendariz and Martine Carol (*Lucretia Borgia*, 1952), and Franco Fabrizi and Belinda Lee (*Nights of Lucretia Borgia*, 1959). In 1981 the BBC produced a risible mini-series on the subject, with Adolfo Celi unintelligible as the founder of the clan.

Borgnine, Ernest (1915–) (Ermes Borgnino). Forceful American character actor who after stage and TV work was typecast by Hollywood as a heavy until *Marty* gave him star status.
□China Corsair 51. The Whistle at Eaton Falls 51. The Mob 51. *From Here to Eternity* 53. The Stranger Wore a Gun 53. Demetrius and the Gladiators 54. The Bounty Hunter 54. Johnny Guitar 54. Vera Cruz 54. *Bad Day at Black Rock* 54. Run for Cover 55. *Marty* (AA, BFA) 55. Violent Saturday 55. The Last Command 55. The Square Jungle 56. Jubal 56. *The Catered Affair* 56. *The Best Things in Life Are Free* 56. Three Brave Men 57. *The Vikings* 58. The Badlanders 58. Torpedo Run 58. The Rabbit Trap 58. Man on a String 60. *Pay or Die* 60. Go Naked in the World 61. Summer of the Seventeenth Doll 61. Les Guerrilleros (Sp.) 61. Il Re de Poggioreale (It.) 61. Il Giudizio Universale (It.) 61. Seduction of the South (It.) 62. Barabbas 62. McHale's Navy 64. The Flight of the Phoenix 65. The Oscar 66. *The Dirty Dozen* 67. Chuka 67. *Ice Station Zebra* 68. The Split 68. The Legend of Lylah Clare 68. The Wild Bunch 69. Suppose They Gave a War and Nobody Came 69. Vengeance is Mine (It.) 69. The Adventurers 70. Bunny O'Hare 71. Hannie Caulder 71. Rain for a Dusty Summer 71. The Trackers (TV) 71. Willard 71. Tough Guy 72. The Revengers 72. What Happened to the Mysterious Mr Foster? (TV) 72. The Poseidon Adventure 72. Emperor of the North Pole 73. The Neptune Factor 73. Law and Disorder 74. Sunday in the Country 74. Twice in a Lifetime (TV) 74. The Devil's Rain 75. Cleaver and Haven (TV) 76. Hustle 76. Shoot 76. The Prince and the Pauper 77. Jesus of Nazareth (TV) 77. The Greatest 77. Convoy 78. The Black Hole 79. The Double McGuffin 79. When Time Ran Out 80. Escape from New York 81. High Risk 81. Deadly Blessing 81. Superfuzz 81. Blood Feud (TV) 82. Young Warriors 83. Masquerade (TV) 83. Airwolf (TV) 84. The Last Days of Pompeii (TV) 84. Codename Wildgeese 84. The Dirty Dozen – The Next Mission (TV) 85.
TV series: *McHale's Navy* 62–65. Future Cop 76. Airwolf 84–86

Born Free (GB 1965). Joy Adamson's book about raising a tame lioness in Kenya was indifferently filmed by James Hill with Virginia McKenna and Bill Travers as the Adamsons. In 1971 the sequel, *Living Free*, was made with Susan Hampshire and Nigel Davenport.
A TV series followed in 1974.

Boros, Ferike (1880–1951). Hungarian actress in Hollywood.
Little Caesar 30. Svengali 31. Huddle 32. Humanity 33. The Fountain 34. Make Way for Tomorrow 37. Love Affair 39. Argentine Nights 40. Caught in the Draft 41. Once Upon a Honeymoon 42. The Doughgirls 44. The Specter of the Rose 46, etc.

Borowczyk, Walerian (1923–). Polish writer-director, formerly animator, living in France.
The Theatre of M. and Mme Kobal 67. Goto, Island of Love 68. *Blanche* 72. Immoral Tales 74. The Story of Sin 74. La Bête 75. The Streetwalker 76. Dr Jekyll and the Women 81, etc.

Borradaile, Osmond (1898–). Canadian cinematographer, in Hollywood from 1916 and later in Britain.
The Private Life of Henry VIII (2nd unit) 33. Sanders of the River (2nd unit) 35. The Scarlet Pimpernel (2nd unit) 35. Elephant Boy (2nd unit) 36. The Drum (2nd unit) 38. *The Four Feathers* (2nd unit) 39. *The Thief of Bagdad* (co-ph) 40. *The Overlanders* 46. The

Macomber Affair 47. Bonnie Prince Charlie 48. *Scott of the Antarctic* 48. I Was a Male War Bride 49. The Trap 66, etc.

Borsche, Dieter (1909–1982). German character actor.
Alles weg'n dem Hund (debut) 35. Die Nachtwache 49. Die Grosse Versuchung 52. Ali Baba (Fr.) 54. Die Barrings 55. A Time to Love and a Time to Die (US) 58. Scotland Yard vs Dr Mabuse 63. Lady Hamilton 63, etc.

Borzage, Frank (1893–1962). American director who favoured a soft, sentimental approach to romantic dramas.
SILENT FILMS INCLUDE: Humoresque 20. Get Rich Quick Wallingford 21. Children of the Dust 23. Secrets 24. The Circle 25. The Marriage Licence 26. Seventh Heaven (AA) 27. Street Angel 28. The River 29.
□SOUND FILMS: Song o' My Heart 30. *Liliom* 30. Doctors' Wives 31. Young as You Feel 31. Bad Girl (AA) 32. After Tomorrow 32. Young America 32. *A Farewell to Arms* 32. Secrets 33. *Man's Castle* 33. No Greater Glory 34. Little Man What Now? 34. Flirtation Walk 34. Living on Velvet 35. Stranded 35. Shipmates Forever 35. *Desire* 36. Hearts Divided 36. The Green Light 37. *History is Made at Night* 37. Big City 38. Mannequin 38. *Three Comrades* 38. The Shining Hour 39. Disputed Passage 39. *Strange Cargo* 40. *The Mortal Storm* 40. Flight Command 41. *Smilin' Through* 41. The Vanishing Virginian 42. Seven Sweethearts 42. Stage Door Canteen 43. His Butler's Sister 43. Till We Meet Again 44. The Spanish Main 45. I've Always Loved You 46. Magnificent Doll 46. That's My Man 47. *Moonrise* 49. China Doll 58. The Big Fisherman 59.

¶ '*History is Made at Night* is not only the most romantic tragedy in the history of the cinema but also a profound exposition of Borzage's commitment to love over probability.'—*Andrew Sarris 1968*.

Bose, Lucia (1931–). Italian leading lady, former beauty queen.
No Peace among the Olives 50. Cronaca di un Amore 51. Girls of the Spanish Steps 52. Death of a Cyclist (Sp.) 54. Le Testament d'Orphée 61, etc.

Bosley, Tom (1927–). Plump American character actor with stage and TV experience.
The Street with No Name 46. Call Northside 777 48. The World of Henry Orient 64. *Love with the Proper Stranger* 64. Divorce American Style 67. The Secret War of Harry Frigg 67. Yours Mine and Ours 68. To Find a Man 72. Gus 76. O'Hara's Wife 81. The Jesse Owens Story (TV) 84. Private Sessions (TV) 85, etc.
TV series: *Debbie* 69. Happy Days 75.

Bost, Pierre: see under *Aurenche, Jean*.

Boston Blackie was an American comic strip character, a small-time crook with a weakness for helping people. The first film about his exploits, *Boston Blackie's Little Pal*, was made in 1919. In 1923 there were two Blackie adventures with William Russell. Between 1940 and 1948 the character was revived for thirteen second features starring Chester Morris (with George E. Stone as 'the Runt'). And in 1951–53 Kent Taylor appeared in a TV series.

Bostwick, Barry (1946–). Personable, easy-going leading man of the seventies, sometimes with a startling resemblance to James Stewart.
□Jennifer on My Mind 71. Janice 72. The Chadwick Family (TV) 74. The Rocky Horror Picture Show 75. The Wrong Damn Film 75. The Quinns (TV) 77. Movie Movie 78. Murder by Natural Causes (TV) 79. Once upon a Family (TV) 80. Moviola (TV) (as John Gilbert) 80. Scruples (TV) 80. Megaforce 82. George Washington (title role) (TV) 84. A Woman of Substance (TV) 84. Deceptions (TV) 85.
TV series: Foul Play 80.

Bosustow, Stephen (1911–1981). Founder of UPA cartoons (1943) after working as artist for Disney and others. Later won Academy Awards for creation of Gerald McBoing Boing and Mr Magoo.

Boswell, Connee (1907–1976). American band singer, a polio victim who recovered sufficiently to continue her career.
Artists and Models 37. Kiss the Boys Goodbye 40. Syncopation 41, etc.

Bosworth, Hobart (1867–1943). American character actor with stage experience: films from 1909.
The Country Mouse 14. Joan the Woman 16. Oliver Twist 16. Below the Surface 20. Vanity Fair 23. Captain January 24. Zander the Great 25. The Big Parade 25. The Blood Ship 27. A Woman of Affairs 29. Mammy 30. The Miracle Man 32. Lady for a Day 33. The Crusades 35. Bullets for O'Hara 41. Sin Town 42, many others.

Boteler, Wade (1891–1943). American general purpose small part actor.
An Old Fashioned Boy 19. The Ghost Patrol 23. High School Hero 26. Top Sergeant Mulligan 28. College Lovers 30. Death Kiss 32. Belle of the Nineties 34. Whipsaw 36. You Only Live Once 37. In Old Chicago 38. Thunder Afloat 39. Castle on the Hudson 40. Kathleen 41. I Was Framed 42. Hi Buddy 43. The Last Ride 44, many others.

Botkin, Perry Jnr (–). American composer.
Bless the Beasts and Children (co-ph) 72. Skyjacked 72. Lady Ice 72. Your Three Minutes are Up 73. Tarzan the Ape Man 81.

Bottoms, Joseph (1954–). American juvenile of the seventies.
The Dove 74. Crime and Passion 76. Holocaust (TV) 78. The Black Hole 79. Cloud Dancer 80. King of the Mountain 81.
TV series: Santa Barbara 85–

Bottoms, Sam (1956–). American leading man, youngest of the Bottoms brothers.
The Last Picture Show 71. Class of '44 73. Zandy's Bride 74. Savages (TV) 74. The Outlaw Josey Wales 76. Cage without a Key (TV) 77. Apocalypse Now 79. Bronco Billy 80. Prime Risk 84, etc.

Bottoms, Timothy (1949–). Leading American juvenile actor of the early seventies.
□Johnny Got His Gun 71. *The Last Picture Show* 71. Love, Pain and the Whole Damned Thing 73. The Paper Chase 73. The White Dawn 74. The Crazy World of Julius Vrooder 74. The Moneychangers (TV) 76. Operation Daybreak 76. A Small Town in Texas 76. Rollercoaster 77. Return Engagement (TV) 78. Hurricane 79. The Other Side of the Mountain Part Two 79. *East of Eden* (TV) 80. The High Country 81. Hambone and Hillie 83. Love Leads the Way (TV) 85. Invaders from Mars 86.

Bouchet, Barbara (1943–) (Barbara Gutscher). German-American glamour girl.
In Harm's Way 65. Agent for HARM 66. Casino Royale 67. Danger Route 68. Down the Ancient Stairs 75. House of a Thousand Pleasures 76, etc.

Bouchey, Willis (1895–1977). American character actor, often seen as judge or reluctant sheriff.
Elopement 51. Suddenly 54. Johnny Concho 56. The Last Hurrah 58. Sergeant Rutledge 60. Where Love has Gone 64. Support Your Local Sheriff 69, many others.

Bouchier, Chili (1909–) (Dorothy Bouchier). British leading lady, mainly on stage.
Shooting Stars 28. Carnival 31. Get off My Foot 36. The Mind of Mr Reeder 39. The Laughing Lady 47. Old Mother Riley's New Venture 49. The Boy and the Bridge 59, others.

Boudu Sauvé des Eaux (France 1932). Written and directed by Jean Renoir, this wry little piece could qualify as the screen's first black comedy. Michel Simon appears as a pixilated tramp who proceeds to make a family very sorry they saved him from drowning.

Boule de Suif. The chief versions of Guy de Maupassant's story, about the effects of a prostitute on a band of travellers during the 1870s, were by Mikhail Romm in 1934, Robert Wise (as *Mademoiselle Fifi*, with Simone Simon) in 1944, and Christian-Jaque (with Micheline Presle) in 1945. John Ford's *Stagecoach* 39 is based on a very similar situation, as is *The Journey*.

Boulting, Ingrid (1947–). South African leading lady who made less than a dazzling impact in *The Last Tycoon* 76.

Boulting, John (1913–85) and **Roy** (1913–). Twin Britishers who after varied experience set up as writer-producer-directors of films with something to say. After World War II they became somewhat more conventional, and the early fifties were barren, but then they came up with a highly successful series of comedies pillorying national institutions. In the sixties they became directors of British Lion Films, with commercially successful but otherwise disappointing results. (Although they have produced and directed alternately, neither showed a particular style, and their films below are treated as joint efforts unless mentioned otherwise.)
□Consider Your Verdict 37. Inquest 38. Trunk Crime 38. *Pastor Hall* 39. *Thunder Rock* 42. *Desert Victory* (Roy) 44. Burma Victory (Roy) 45. *Journey Together* (John) 45. *Fame is the Spur* 46. *Brighton Rock* 46. *The Guinea Pig* 49. *Seven Days to Noon* 50. The Magic Box 51. High Treason (Roy) 52. Sailor of the King (Roy) 53. Seagulls Over Sorrento 54. Josephine and Men 54. *Private's Progress* 55. *Brothers in Law* 56. Run for the

Sun (Roy) 56. *Lucky Jim* 57. Happy is the Bride 57. Carlton Browne of the F.O. 58. *I'm All Right Jack* 59. Suspect 60. A French Mistress 61. *Heavens Above* 63. Rotten to the Core 65. The Family Way 66. Twisted Nerve 68. There's a Girl in My Soup (Roy) 70. Endless Night 72. Soft Beds and Hard Battles (Roy) 73. The Last Word (Roy) 79.
❀ For raising the sights of British films in the forties, and later for devising a strain of satirical comedy. *I'm All Right Jack*.

Boulton, David (–). British cinematographer.
The Password is Courage 62. The Haunting 63. Children of the Damned 65. The Secret of My Success 65. It 66. The Great Waltz 72, etc.

Bouquet, Michel (1926–). French general purpose actor, notably in the films of Claude Chabrol.
Monsieur Vincent 47. Manon 49. La Tour de Nesle 55. Katia 60. An Orchid for the Tiger 65. The Road to Corinth 67. The Bride Wore Black 68. The Mississippi Mermaid 69. Borsalino 70. Just Before Nightfall 71. Malpertuis 72. The Serpent 73. Les Suspects 74. Beyond Fear 75. Le Jouet 77. La Raison d'Etat 78, etc.

Bourgignon, Serge (1928–). French director of style but little substance.
Sundays and Cybele (AA) 62. The Reward 65. Two Weeks in September 67. The Picasso Summer 69.

Bourgoin, Jean (1913–). French cinematographer.
La Marseillaise 38. Goupi Mains Rouges 43. Voyage Surprise 46. Dedée d'Anvers 47. Manèges 50. Justice est Faite 50. Nous Sommes Tous des Assassins 52. Confidential Report 55. *Mon Oncle* 58. *Black Orpheus* 59. The Counterfeit Traitor 62. Gigot 62. The Longest Day 62. Germinal 63. Pas Question le Samedi 65. Qui 70. La Chambre Rouge 73, many others.

Bourneuf, Philip (1912–1979). American supporting stage actor of the older school. Films few.
Winged Victory 44. Joan of Arc 49. The Big Night 51. Beyond a Reasonable Doubt 56. Hemingway's Adventures of a Young Man 62. The Arrangement 69. The Molly Maguires 70, etc.

Bourvil (1917–1970) (André Raimbourg). Diminutive, expressive French comic actor.
La Ferme du Pendu 45. Mr Peek-a-boo 51. *La Traversée de Paris* 56. The Mirror has Two Faces 58. The Green Mare's Nest 69. Tout l'Or du Monde 62. Heaven Sent 63. The Secret Agents 65. The Big Spree 66. *The Sucker* 66. Don't Look Now 67. The Brain 68. Monte Carlo or Bust 69. The Red Circle 70, many others.

Bow, Clara (1905–1965). American leading lady, the 'It' girl of the twenties: her films depicted the gay young flapper generation and her wide-eyed vivacity was tremendously popular for a time, but she came to grief through trying to parallel her screen image in her private life.
□Beyond the Rainbow 22. Down to the Sea in Ships 22. Enemies of Women 23. Maytime 23. The Daring Years 23. Grit 24. Black Oxen 24. Poisoned Paradise 24. Daughters of Pleasure 24. Wine 24. Empty Hearts 24. This Woman 24. Black Lightning 24. Capital Punishment 25. Helen's Babies 25. The Adventurous Sex 25. My Lady's Lips 25. Parisian Love 25. Eve's Lover 25. Kiss Me Again 25. The Scarlet West 25. The Primrose Path 25. The Plastic Age 25. The Keeper of the Bees 25. Free to Love 25. The Best Bad Man 25. Lawful Cheaters 25. Two Can Play 26. The Runaway 26. *Mantrap* 26. Kid Boots 26. The Ancient Mariner 26. My Lady of Whim 26. Dancing Mothers 26. The Shadow of the Law 26. *It* 27. Children of Divorce 27. Rough House Rosie 27. *Wings* 27. Hula 27. Get Your Man 27. Red Hair 28. Ladies of the Mob 28. The Fleet's In 28. Three Weekends 28. The Wild Party 29. The Saturday Night Kid 29. Dangerous Curves 29. Paramount on Parade 30. True to the Navy 30. Love among the Millionaires 30. Her Wedding Night 30. No Limit 31. Kick In 31. Call Her Savage 32. Hoopla 33.

¶ She danced even when her feet were not moving.—*Adolph Zukor*

Being a sex symbol is a heavy load to carry, especially when one is tired, hurt and bewildered.—*Clara Bow*

'Her life and career still seem to have been dreamed up by one of her scriptwriters.'—*David Shipman*

Bowdon, Dorris (1915–). American leading lady who abruptly retired to marry Nunnally Johnson.
□Young Mr Lincoln 39. Drums Along the Mohawk 39. *The Grapes of Wrath* (as Rosasharn) 40. The Moon Is Down 42.

Bower, Dallas (1907–). British producer. Originally sound recordist, editor and writer, he became director of BBC TV 1936–1939, supervisor of Ministry of Information film production 1940–42. Associate producer *As You Like It* 36, *Henry V* 44, etc.; produced *Sir Lancelot*, TV series. As director: Alice in Wonderland (Fr.) 50. The Second Mrs Tanqueray 52. Doorway to Suspicion 57.

Bowers, William (1916–87). American screenwriter.
My Favorite Spy 42. Night and Day 46. *The Web* 47. Black Bart 48. Larceny 48. *The Gunfighter* 50. Cry Danger 51. *The Mob* 51. Split Second 53. *Five Against the House* 55. The Best Things in Life are Free 56. *The Sheepman* 58. Alias Jesse James 59. *The Last Time I Saw Archie* 61. Advance to the Rear 64. *Support Your Local Sheriff* 69, etc.

The Bowery (US 1933). Wallace Beery and George Raft are the brawling but good-natured protagonists of this rumbustious comedy-melodrama which marked Hollywood's breakaway forever from the static early talkie style. Raoul Walsh's direction abounds in vigour, the screenplay by Howard Estabrook and James Gleason is crisply funny, and the whole production brings to vivid life the teeming side-streets of New York at the turn of the century. It was the first production of Darryl Zanuck's Twentieth Century company, which the following year merged with Fox.

The Bowery Boys. From the original Dead End Kids, one splinter group became known as the Little Tough Guys, another as the East Side Kids, and yet another as the Bowery Boys (but there is overlapping). The Bowery Boys were led by Leo Gorcey and Huntz Hall; following their zany commands were Bernard Gorcey, David Gorcey, Billy Benedict, Gabriel Dell and Bobby Jordan. Between 1946 and 1958, when most of the comic young hoodlums were actually well into their forties, they made forty-eight low-budget features, at first using fairly realistic themes but later straying into fantasy. Their appeal was based on puns and slapstick, and although the films were basically quite awful they have retained a certain nostalgia. A 1976 TV scheme to revive them as the *San Pedro Bums* was a flop. See *Dead End*.

Bowie, David (1947–) (David Robert Jones). Bizarrely decorated British pop singer who makes curious forays into film acting.
□The Man Who Fell to Earth 76. Just a Gigolo 78. The Hunger 83. Merry Christmas Mr Lawrence 83. Ziggy Stardust and the Spiders from Mars 83 (recorded 73). Into the Night 84. Absolute Beginners 85. Labyrinth 86.

¶ *D.B. 1983:* I get offered so many bad movies. And they're all raging queens or transvestites or Martians.
D.B.: I'm an instant star. Just add water and stir.

Bowie, Jim (1796–1836). American folk hero who invented the Bowie knife and died at the Alamo. He was played in *The Iron Mistress* by Alan Ladd, in *The Last Command* by Sterling Hayden, in *The First Texan* by Jeff Morrow, in *Davy Crockett* by Kenneth Tobey, in *Man of Conquest* by Robert Armstrong, in *Comanche Territory* by Macdonald Carey, and in *The Alamo* by Richard Widmark. A TV series called *The Adventures of Jim Bowie* 60 starred Scott Forbes.

Bowie, Les (1913–79). British special effects technician especially noted for matte shots.
Great Expectations 46. The Red Shoes 48. Star Wars 76. Superman 78. Many Hammer films.

Bowker, Judy (1954–). British leading lady.
Brother Sun Sister Moon 73. Count Dracula (TV) 78. Clash of the Titans 81.

Bowman, Lee (1910–1979). Well-groomed American light leading man with stage experience; found a desultory career in films.
Three Men in White 36. *I Met Him in Paris* 37. Love Affair 39. Miracles for Sale 39. Florian 40. Buck Privates 41. *Kid Glove Killer* 42. Three Hearts for Julia 43. Cover Girl 44. *The Impatient Years* 44. Tonight and Every Night 45. The Walls Came Tumbling Down 46. Smash-Up 47. The House by the River 50. Double Barrel Miracle 55. Youngblood Hawke 64, etc.
TV series: Ellery Queen 50.

Box, Betty E. (1920–). British producer, sister of Sydney Box and once assistant to him. For many years she turned out comedies and dramas with box office appeal but little cinematic flavour, usually in association with director Ralph Thomas.
Miranda 48. Here Come the Huggetts 49. *Doctor in the House* 53. The Iron Petticoat 56. A Tale of Two Cities 58. The Thirty-nine Steps 59. No Love for Johnnie 61. A Pair of Briefs 63. No My Darling Daughters 63. The

High Bright Sun 65. Deadlier than the Male 66. The High Commissioner 68. Percy 70. The Love Ban 72. Percy's Progress 74, many others.

Box, John (1920–). British production designer.
Lawrence of Arabia (AA) 62. *Doctor Zhivago* (AA) 65. *A Man For All Seasons* 66. *Oliver* (AA) 68. The Looking Glass War (p only) 69. *Nicholas and Alexandra* (AA) 71. Travels with my Aunt 73. Rollerball 74. *The Great Gatsby* 74. Sorcerer 76. A Passage to India 84, etc.

Box, Muriel (1905–). British writer-producer-director, wife of Sydney Box. Autobiography 1974: *Odd Woman Out*.
The Seventh Veil (w) 46. The Years Between (w) 47. The Man Within (wp) 47. *The Brothers* (w) 48. Dear Murderer (wp) 48. A Girl in a Million (wp) 50. The Happy Family (wd) 52. The Beachcomber (wd) 54. To Dorothy a Son (d) 54. The Truth about Women (pd) 57. Rattle of a Simple Man (d) 64, etc.

Box, Sydney (1907–1983). British writer-producer who had considerable success in the decade after World War II.
The Seventh Veil 46. The Years Between 47. *Holiday Camp* 47. Jassy 47. *The Brothers* 48. Dear Murderer 48. *Quartet* 48. Don't Take it to Heart (p only) 48. Broken Journey 48. Daybreak 49. A Girl in a Million 50. So Long at the Fair (p only) 51. *The Prisoner* 55, etc.

boxing. Actual prizefighters whose lives have been fictionalized on film include Jim Corbett (Errol Flynn in *Gentleman Jim*), John L. Sullivan (Greg McClure in *The Great John L*), Joe Louis (Coley Wallace in *The Joe Louis Story*), Rocky Graziano (Paul Newman in *Somebody Up There Likes Me*), and Jack Johnson (James Earl Jones in *The Great White Hope*). Purely fictional boxing films have tended to emphasize the corruption of the fight game: *The Ring, The Square Ring, The Square Jungle, Iron Man, Kid Galahad, Kid Nightingale, The Champ, The Crowd Roars, Body and Soul, The Set Up, Champion, Golden Boy, No Way Back, The Good Die Young, Run With the Wind, The Harder They Fall*, and from Europe *Walkover* and *Boxer*. Boxing comedy is rare once one discounts the Joe Palooka series, but most comedians have taken part in boxing sequences: Abbott and Costello in *Meet the Invisible Man*, Harold Lloyd in *The Milky Way*, Danny Kaye in *The Kid from Brooklyn*, Chaplin in *The Champion*, etc. The only boxing fantasy was *Here Comes Mr Jordan*, in which Robert Montgomery's soul was transferred into that of a prizefighter. The most violent boxing film was undoubtedly *Raging Bull*, in which Robert de Niro put on fifty pounds to play the ageing Jake La Motta.

Boxleitner, Bruce (1950–). American leading man, mostly on TV.
Six Pack Annie 75. Kiss Me Kill Me (TV) 76. Tron 82, etc.
TV series: How the West Was Won 76. Bring 'Em Back Alive 82. Scarecrow and Mrs King 83.

Boyd, Stephen (1928–77) (William Millar). Irish leading man in international films; fairly popular during the sixties.
☐ Born for Trouble 55. An Alligator Named Daisy 55. A Hill in Korea 56. *The Man Who Never Was* (as the German spy) 56. Seven Waves Away 57. Island in the Sun 57. Seven Thunders 57. Heaven Fell that Night 57. The Bravados 58. *Ben Hur* (as Messala) 59. Woman Obsessed 59. The Best of Everything 59. The Big Gamble 61. The Inspector 62. Jumbo 62. Imperial Venus 63. *The Fall of the Roman Empire* 64. The Third Secret 64. Genghis Khan 64. The Oscar 66. Fantastic Voyage 66. The Bible 66. The Caper of the Golden Bulls 67. Assignment K 68. Shalako 68. Slaves 69. Carter's Army (TV) 71. The Hands of Cormac Joyce (TV) 71. Key West (TV) 72. Hannie Caulder 72. The Man Called Noon 73. Marta 74. Kill, Kill, Kill 74. Those Dirty Dogs 74. Evil in the Deep 75. The Lives of Jenny Dolan (TV) 75. Left Hand of the Law 76. The Squeeze 77. The Devil Has Seven Faces 77. Impossible Love 77.

Boyd, William (1895–1972). Unassuming American leading man, in films from 1919, internationally famous from 1934 as cowboy hero Hopalong Cassidy, in which guise he made scores of second features and TV episodes.
Why Change your Wife? 19. The Temple of Venus 23. Changing Husbands 24. The Volga Boatmen 26. King of Kings 27. *Two Arabian Knights* 27. Skyscraper 28. The Leatherneck 29. The Benson Murder Case 30. The Spoilers 30. The Painted Desert 31. Murder by the Clock 31. Lucky Devils 33. Port of Lost Dreams 34. *Hopalong Cassidy* 35, many others but all subsequent films as Cassidy; last in 1948.

Boyd, William 'Stage' (1890–1935). American stage actor, so known to distinguish

him from his Hopalong Cassidy namesake.
Sky Devils 32. Painted Woman 32. *Oliver Twist* (as Sikes) 33, etc.

Boyer, Charles (1899–1978). Gentlemanly French romantic actor in international films: went to Hollywood first in 1929, and later gained a reputation as the screen's 'great lover'.
Biography 1964: *Charles Boyer* by Larry Swindell.
□L'Homme du Large 20. Chantelouve 21. Le Grillon du Foyer 22. L'Esclave 23. La Ronde Infernale 27. Le Capitain Fracasse 27. *La Barcarolle d'Amour* 28. Le Procès de Mary Dugan 28. The Big House (French version) 30. The Magnificent Lie 31. Tumultes 31. *Red-headed Woman* 32. The Man from Yesterday 32. F.P.I. (French version) 32. The Only Girl 33. L'Impervier 33. The Battle (as a Japanese) 34. *Caravan* 34. Liliom 35. Private Worlds 35. Break of Hearts 35. Shanghai 35. Le Bonheur 36. *The Garden of Allah* 36. *Mayerling* 37. *Tovarich* 37. *Conquest* (as Napoleon) 37. *History is Made at Night* 37. *Algiers* 38. Orage 38. *Love Affair* 39. When Tomorrow Comes 39. Le Corsaire 39. *All This and Heaven Too* 40. Les Amoureux 40. Back Street 41. *Hold Back the Dawn* 41. Appointment for Love 41. Tales of Manhattan 42. The Constant Nymph 43. Flesh and Fantasy (& p) 43. *Gaslight* 44. Confidential Agent 45. Together Again 45. Cluny Brown 46. Arch of Triumph 48. A Woman's Vengeance 48. The Thirteenth Letter 51. The First Legion 52. *The Happy Time* 52. Thunder in the East 53. *Madame de . . .* 53. The Cobweb 55. Lucky to Be a Woman 55. Paris Palace Hotel 56. Nana 56. Around the World in Eighty Days 56. La Parisienne 58. The Buccaneer 58. Maxime 58. *Fanny* 62. The Four Horsemen of the Apocalypse 62. Les Démons de Minuit 62. Love is a Ball 63. Adorable Julia 64. *A Very Special Favour* 64. How to Steal a Million 66. Is Paris Burning? 66. Casino Royale 67. *Barefoot in the Park* 68. The April Fools 69. The Madwoman of Chaillot 69. The Day the Hot Line got Hot 69. Lost Horizon 73. Stavisky 74. A Matter of Time 76.
TV series: *Four Star Theatre* 56. *The Rogues* 64.
❁ For capitalizing on the accepted image of the romantic Frenchman and proving that he could also act. *Love Affair.*

¶ 'We got a French actor here on a 6-month option, but I'm letting him go home because nobody can understand the guy's accent.'—*Irving Thalberg* 1932.

Famous line (which he never actually said in *Algiers*): *'Come with me to the Casbah.'*

Boyer, François (1920–). French screenwriter, also novelist.
Le Point du Jour 49. *Jeux Interdits* (& oa) 52. Chiens Perdus sans Collier 55. Le Joueur 58. Les Magiciennes 60. Un Singe en Hiver 62. War of the Buttons 62. Weekend in Dunkirk 64. The 25th Hour 67. Mords Pas On t'Aime 76, etc.

Boyer, Jean (1901–1965). French director.
Monsieur, Madame et Bibi 32. Un Mauvais Garçon 36. Circonstances Attenuantes 39. Serenade 40. Romance de Paris 41. Bolero 42. La Bonne Etoile 43. La Femme Fatale 45. Les Aventures de Casanova 47. All Roads Lead to Rome 49. Le Rosier de Madame Husson 50. Le Passe-Muraille 51. Coiffeur pour Dames 52. Femmes de Paris 53. J'avais Sept Filles 54. Fernandel the Dressmaker 56. Sénéchal le Magnifique 57. Nina 58. Coup de Bamboo 62. Relaxe-toi Chérie 64, many others.

Boyle, Catherine (1929–) (Caterina di Francavilla). Winsome Italian-English TV personality who has made a few film appearances.
Not Wanted on Voyage 52. Intent to Kill 56. The Truth About Women 57, etc.

Boyle, Peter (1933–). Rotund, balding American character actor of the seventies, a former monk who became a key performer in fashionable films of his time.
□The Virgin President 68. Medium Cool 69. *Joe* 70. Diary of a Mad Housewife 70. T. R. Baskin 71. *The Candidate* 72. Steelyard Blues 73. Slither 73. Kid Blue 73. The Friends of Eddie Coyle 72. The Man Who Could Talk to Kids (TV) 73. Crazy Joe 74. *Young Frankenstein* (as the monster) 74. Taxi Driver 76. Swashbuckler 76. *Tail Gunner Joe* (TV) (as Senator Joe McCarthy) 77. FIST 78. Superman 78. Beyond the Poseidon Adventure 79. Brink's 79. From Here to Eternity (TV) 79. Hardcore 79. In God We Trust 80. Where the Buffalo Roam 80. Outland 81. Hammett 82. Yellowbeard 83. Johnny Dangerously 84. Morons from Outer Space 85. Turk 182 85.

Boyle, Robert (1910–). American production designer.
The Thrill of it All 63. The Birds 63. Marnie 64. The Russians are Coming, The Russians are Coming 66. How to Succeed in Business

67. In Cold Blood 67. The Thomas Crown Affair 68. Gaily Gaily 69. The Landlord 70. Fiddler on the Roof 71. Portnoy's Complaint 72. Mame 74. The Shootist 76. The Big Fox 78. Winter Kills 79. Private Benjamin 80, etc.

Boys' Town (US 1938). MGM's highly successful sentimentalized biography of Father Flanagan and his work among juvenile semi-delinquents. Set the Hollywood fashion in boys and priests for year. Spencer Tracy (AA) and Mickey Rooney starred; Norman Taurog directed. The sequel, *Men of Boys' Town*, was less interesting.

Bozzuffi, Marcel (1929–). Balding French character actor.
Z 69. The American 69. The Lady in the Car 70. The French Connection 71. Images 72. Nightmare for a Killer 72. Caravan to Vaccares 76. La Grande Bourgeoise 77. *La Cage aux Folles* 79. La Cage au Folles II 81, etc.

Brabin, Charles (1883–1957). British film director who made a career in Hollywood but retired early.
Stella Maris 18. *So Big* 23. Twinkletoes 26. Hard Boiled Haggerty 27. The Bridge of San Luis Rey 29. Call of the Flesh 30. Sporting Blood 31. Beast of the City 32. *The Mask of Fu Manchu* 32. Stage Mother 33. A Wicked Woman 34, many others.

Brabourne, John (1924–) (Lord Brabourne). British producer, in films from 1950.
Harry Black 58. Sink the Bismarck 60. HMS Defiant 62. The Mikado 66. Tales of Beatrix Potter 71. *Murder on the Orient Express* 74. Death on the Nile 78. The Mirror Crack'd 80. Evil Under the Sun 82. A Passage to India 84. Little Dorrit 87, etc.

Bracken, Eddie (1920–). American comic actor, popular in the forties as the nervous hayseed type; made his best films for Preston Sturges. Later found stage success.
□Too Many Girls 40. Life with Henry 41. Reaching for the Sun 41. Caught in the Draft 41. Sweater Girl 42. The Fleet's In 42. Star Spangled Rhythm 42. Happy Go Lucky 43. Young and Willing 43. *The Miracle of Morgan's Creek* 43. *Hail the Conquering Hero* 44. Rainbow Island 44. Out of This World 45. Bring on the Girls 45. Duffy's Tavern 45. Hold That Blonde 45. Ladies' Man 47. Fun on a Weekend 47. The Girl from Jones Beach 49. Summer Stock 50. Two Tickets to Broadway 51. We're Not Married 52. About Face 52. A Slight Case of Larceny 53. National Lampoon's Vacation 83

Brackett, Charles (1892–1969). American writer-producer, of generally sophisticated material; enjoyed long association with Billy Wilder.
Tomorrow's Love (oa) 25. Pointed Heels (oa) 29. Secrets of a Secretary (oa) 31. Enter Madame (w) 35. Piccadilly Jim (w) 36. Bluebeard's Eighth Wife (w) 38. Midnight (w) 39. Ninotchka (w) 39. Arise My Love (w) 40. Hold Back the Dawn (w) 41. The Major and the Minor (w) 42. *Five Graves to Cairo* (wp) 43. *The Uninvited* (p) 43. *The Lost Weekend* (wp) (AA) 45. To Each His Own (wp) 46. *A Foreign Affair* (wp) 48. *Sunset Boulevard* (wp) (AA) 50. Niagara (wp) 52. Titanic (wp) 52. Woman's World (p) 54. The King and I (p) 56. Ten North Frederick (p) 58. Journey to the Centre of the Earth (wp) 59. State Fair (p) 61, many others.

Brackett, Leigh (1915–1978). American lady screenwriter.
The Big Sleep 46. Rio Bravo 59. 13 West Street 62. Hatari 62. El Dorado 67. Rio Lobo 70. The Long Goodbye 73. The Empire Strikes Back 80, etc.

Brackman, Jacob (–). American screenwriter.
The King of Marvin Gardens 72. Times Square 80, etc.

Bradbury, Ray (1920–). American science fiction writer who has dabbled in films.
It Came from Outer Space (oa) 53. The Beast from 20,000 Fathoms (oa) 54. Moby Dick (w) 56. Fahrenheit 451 (oa) 66. The Illustrated Man (oa) 69. Something Wicked This Way Comes 83, etc.

Braden, Bernard (1916–). Canadian TV personality, in Britain since 1938. Occasional film appearances. Long married to Barbara Kelly.
Love in Pawn 52. The Full Treatment 61. The Day the Earth Caught Fire 62. The War Lover 63, etc.

Bradford, Richard (–). Thickset American character actor.
The Chase 66. The Missouri Breaks 76. Goin' South 78. More American Graffiti 79. Panic on Page One (TV) 79.
TV series: Man in a Suitcase 66.

Bradley, David (1919–). American director who showed promise as an amateur but never seemed to make it professionally. □Peer Gynt 41. Julius Caesar 50. Talk About a Stranger 52. Dragstrip Riot 58. Twelve to the Moon 60. Madmen of Mandoras 64.

Bradna, Olympe (1920–). Slightly built French circus performer who had a brief Hollywood career following a stage tour, and retired on marriage to an American.
□Three Cheers for Love 36. College Holiday 36. Last Train from Madrid 37. *Souls at Sea* 37. Stolen Heaven 38. Say It in French 38. The Night of Nights 39. South of Pago Pago 40. Highway West 41. Knockout 41. International Squadron 41.

Brady, Alice (1892–1939). American stage actress who in her last few years made many films, either as a fluttery society matron or as a drab housewife.
□La Bohème 16. Bought and Paid for 16. Betsy Ross 17. Woman and Wife 18. A Dark Lantern 19. The Fear Market 19. The Snow Bride 23. *When Ladies Meet* 33. Broadway to Hollywood 33. Beauty for Sale 33. Stage Mother 33. Should Ladies Behave? 33. Miss Fane's Baby is Stolen 34. *The Gay Divorcee* 34. Let 'Em Have It 34. Gold Diggers of 1935 35. Lady Tubbs 35. Metropolitan 35. The Harvester 35. *My Man Godfrey* 36. Go West Young Man 36. Mind Your Own Business 36. *Three Smart Girls* 37. Call It a Day 37. Mama Steps Out 37. Mr Dodd Takes the Air 37. One Hundred Men and a Girl 37. Merry Go Round of 1938. *In Old Chicago* (AA) 38. Joy of Living 38. Goodbye Broadway 38. Zenobia 39. *Young Mr Lincoln* 39.

Brady, Scott (1924–85) (Gerald Tierney). Tough-looking American leading man of the fifties, brother of Lawrence Tierney.
Canon City 48. He Walked by Night 48. Port of New York 49. Undercover Girl 50. Kansas Raiders 51. *The Model and the Marriage Broker* 52. Perilous Journey 53. Johnny Guitar 54. Gentlemen Marry Brunettes 55. Mohawk 56. The Maverick Queen 56. They Were So Young 58. Battle Flame 59. Black Spurs 65. Castle of Evil 66. Red Tomahawk 67. Doctors' Wives 70. Nightmare in Wax 70. Dollars 71. The China Syndrome 79. The Winds of War (TV) 83, many others.
TV series: Shotgun Slade 59–60.

Braeden, Eric (–) (Hans Gudegast). German general purpose actor in international films.
Colossus of Rhodes 57. The Law and Jake Wade 59. Escape from the Planet of the Apes 70, etc.

Brahm, John (1893–1982) (Hans Brahm). German director who in the thirties moved first to Britain, then to Hollywood. Films generally competent, but routine.
□ENGLISH-SPEAKING FILMS: Scrooge 35. The Last Journey 35. *Broken Blossoms* (British remake) 36. Counsel for Crime 37. Penitentiary 38. Girls' School 38. Let Us Live 39. Rio 39. *Escape to Glory* 40. Wild Geese Calling 41. *The Undying Monster* 42. Tonight We Raid Calais 42. Wintertime 43. The Lodger 44. *Hangover Square* 44. Guest in the House 44. *The Locket* 46. *The Brasher Doubloon* 47. Singapore 47. The Thief of Venice 49. Face to Face 52. The Miracle of Fatima 52. The Diamond Queen 53. The Mad Magican 54. Special Delivery 55. Bengazi 55. So Soon to Die (TV) 57. A Death of Princes (TV) 61. Hot Rods to Hell 67.
'His quiet virtues of visual tastefulness and dramatic balance were unable to sustain his career.' *—Andrew Sarris, 1968*

Braithwaite, Dame Lilian (1873–1948). Distinguished British stage actress in occasional films.
□The World's Desire 15. The Climax 15. Masks and Faces 15. The Woman Who Was Nothing 16. Justice 16. The Gay Lord Quex 16. Dombey and Son 16. Because 18. The Chinese Puzzle 19. General Post 20. Castles in Spain 20. Downhill 27. Carnival 31. Man of Mayfair 31. The Chinese Puzzle 32. *A Man About the House* 47.

Brakhage, Stan (1933–). American underground film-maker.
Interim 51. Desistfilm 54. Nightcats 56. Flesh of Morning 57. An Intercourse 59. The Dead 60. Mothlight 63. Black Vision 65. Lovemaking 68. Sexual Meditations 70. Fox Fire Child Watch 71, many others.

Brambell, Wilfrid (1912–85). British character actor, specializing in grotesques. Celebrated on TV as old Steptoe in *Steptoe and Son* (64–73); film appearances usually cameos.
Autobiography 1976: *All Above Board.*
Another Shore 48. Dry Rot 56. Serious Charge 58. What a Whopper 61. *In Search of the Castaways* 62. The Three Lives of Thomasina 63. *A Hard Day's Night* 64. Crooks in Cloisters 64. Where the Bullets Fly 66. Witchfinder General 68, etc.

Bramble, A. V. (c. 1880–1963). British director, former actor.
Fatal Fingers 16. Wuthering Heights 18. The

Will 21. The Card 22. Chick 28. Shooting Stars (p & co-d) 28. The Man Who Changed his Name 29. Mrs Dane's Defence 33. An Outcast of the Islands (a only) 51, etc.

Branagh, Kenneth(–). British leading actor.
Fortunes of War (TV 87). A Month in the Country 87.

Branch, Sarah (1938–). British leading lady of the early sixties.
Sands of the Desert 60. Hell is a City 61. Sword of Sherwood Forest 61, etc.

Brand, Max (1892–1944) (Frederick Faust). American popular novelist whose major bequests to Hollywood were *Destry Rides Again* and the Dr Kildare books. Killed in action as a war correspondent.

Brand, Neville (1921–). Thickset American actor with stage and TV experience; often seen as Red Indian or gangster. In films from 1948 after ten years in the US Army: he was the fourth most decorated soldier.
D.O.A. 49. Halls of Montezuma 51. Stalag 17 53. *Riot in Cell Block Eleven* 54. Mohawk 55. The Tin Star 57. Cry Terror 58. Five Gates to Hell 59. *The Scarface Mob* (as Al Capone) 60. Huckleberry Finn 60. Birdman of Alcatraz 62. That Darn Cat 65. The Desperados 69. The Train Robbers 73. Scalawag 74. The Mad Bomber 75. Eaten Alive 76. The Quest (TV) 76. Captains Courageous (TV) 77. The Ninth Configuration 80. Without Warning 80, many others.
TV series: The Untouchables 59–62 (as Al Capone). Laredo 66–67.

Brandauer, Klaus Maria (*c.*1950–). Austrian leading actor who has made his mark in occasional English-speaking films. *Mephisto* 82. Never Say Never Again 83. *Colonel Redl* 85. *Out of Africa* (AAN) 85.

Brando, Jocelyn (1919–). American character actress, sister of Marlon Brando; film appearances rare.
The Big Heat 53. China Venture 53. Nightfall 56. The Explosive Generation 61. The Ugly American 63. Bus Riley's Back in Town 65. The Chase 66. A Question of Love (TV) 78, etc.

Brando, Marlon (1924–). Unsmiling American leading actor whose prototype is the primitive modern male; he has however attempted a wide range of parts which have not always suited his 'method' technique and mumbling accent.
Biography 1974: *Brando* by René Jordan.
□*The Men* 50. *A Streetcar Named Desire* 51. *Viva Zapata* (BFA) 52. *Julius Caesar* (as Mark Antony) (BFA) 53. *The Wild One* 53. *On the Waterfront* (AA, BFA) 54. Desirée (as Napoleon) 54. Guys and Dolls 55. *The Teahouse of the August Moon* 56. Sayonara 57. *The Young Lions* 58. The Fugitive Kind 60. One Eyed Jacks (also directed) 60. Mutiny on the Bounty (as Fletcher Christian) 62. The Ugly American 63. Bedtime Story 64. The Saboteur 65. *The Chase* 66. The Appaloosa 66. A Countess from Hong Kong 67. Reflections in a Golden Eye 67. Candy 68. The Night of the Following Day 68. Queimada 70. The Nightcomers 71. *The Godfather* (AA) 72. *Last Tango in Paris* 72. The Missouri Breaks 76. Superman 78. Roots: the New Generations (TV) 79. Apocalypse Now 79. The Formula 80.

¶ Acting is an empty and useless profession.—*M.B.*

Most of the time he sounds like he has a mouth full of wet toilet paper.—*Rex Reed*

I have eyes like those of a dead pig.—*M.B.*

Acting is the expression of a neurotic impulse. It's a bum's life. Quitting acting, that's the sign of maturity.—*M.B.*

Once you're a star actor, people start asking you questions about politics, astronomy, archaeology, and birth control.—*M.B.*

An actor's a guy who, if you ain't talking about him, ain't listening.—*M.B.*

He was deeply rebellious against the bourgeois spirit, the over-ordering of life.—*Elia Kazan*

Democracy is a fine way to run a country, but it's a hell of a way to make pictures.—*Lillian Hellman after working with Brando on The Chase*

'An angel as a man, a monster as an actor.'—*Bernardo Bertolucci*

'He was in a unique position. He could have done anything. But he didn't choose to.'—*Rod Steiger*

'I'm not interested in making an assessment of myself and stripping myself for the general public to view.'—*M.B.*

Famous line (*On The Waterfront*): 'I coulda had class. I coulda been a contender.'

Brandon, Henry (1912–) (Henry Kleinbach). American character actor, a reliable menace for thirty years.
Babes in Toyland (as Barnaby) 34. The Garden of Allah 36. I Promise to Pay 37. Son

of Monte Cristo 40. Edge of Darkness 43. Canon City 48. Scarlet Angel 52. Scared Stiff 53. Vera Cruz 54. The Searchers 56. The Buccaneer 58. Two Rode Together 61. *Where the North Wind Blows* 75, many others.

Brandon, Michael (–). American leading man.
Lovers and Other Strangers 70. Four Flies on Grey Velvet 73. FM 78. A Vacation in Hell 79. Between Two Brothers (TV) 81. Deadly Messages (TV) 83, etc.
TV series: Emerald Point 83. Dempsey and Makepeace 84–86.

Brasselle, Keefe (1923–1981). American light leading man who made little headway in movies but later, with the help of James Aubrey of CBS, became a television producer with several unsuccessful shows such as *The Baileys of Balboa* and *Mr Broadway*. He wrote a bitter novel about his experiences and called it *The CanniBalS*.
□Janie 44. River Gang 45. Railroaded 47. Not Wanted 48. Dial 1119 50. A Place in the Sun 51. Bannerline 51. It's a Big Country 52. Skirts Ahoy 52. *The Eddie Cantor Story* (title role) 53. Three Young Texans 54. Mad at the World 55. Battle Stations 56. West of Suez 57. If You Don't Stop It You'll Go Blind 77.

Brasseur, Claude (1936–). French actor, son of Pierre Brasseur.
Eyes without a Face 60. Les Menteurs 61. The Vanishing Corporal 62. Germinal 63. Bande à Part 64. Un Homme de Trop 67. Portrait of Marianne 70. Such a Gorgeous Kid Like Me 72. Seins de Glace 74. Aggression 75. Pardon Mon Affaire 76. Une Histoire Simple 78. Ils Sont Grands ces Petits 79, many others.

Brasseur, Pierre (1903–1972) (P. Espinasse). Distinguished French stage actor in occasional films from 1925.
Claudine à l'École 28. Café de Paris 33. *Quai des Brumes* 38. Lumière d'Été 42. *Les Enfants du Paradis* 44. Les Portes de la Nuit 46. Julie de Carneilhan 50. Bluebeard 51. Porte des Lilas 55. Eyes without a Face 59. Il Bell' Antonio 60. Deux Heures à Tuer 65. A New World 66. King of Hearts 67. Birds in Peru 68, etc.

Bray, Robert (1917–1983). American actor of the strong silent type.
Blood on the Moon 48. Warpath 52. Bus Stop 56. The Wayward Bus 57. My Gun is Quick (as Mike Hammer) 58. Never So Few 60, etc.
TV series: Man from Blackhawk 54. Stagecoach West 60. Lassie 67–68.

Brazil has had a very patchy production history. One of its best directors, Alberto Cavalcanti, spent most of his career abroad, and failed in the fifties to spark local production. Despite subsequent attempts, the best-known Brazilian film is still 1953's *O'Cangaceiro* (*The Bandit*).

Brazzi, Rossano (1916–). Handsome Italian romantic lead who apart from local work appeared in some successful international films.
Volcano 48. *Little Women* 49. *Three Coins in the Fountain* 54. The Barefoot Contessa 54. *Summertime* 55. The Story of Esther Costello 57. Legend of the Lost 57. Interlude 57. *South Pacific* 58. A Certain Smile 58. Count Your Blessings 59. The Light in the Piazza 62. Rome Adventure 62. Dark Purpose 64. The Battle of the Villa Fiorita 65. The Christmas that Almost Wasn't (& d) 66. The Bobo 67. Woman Times Seven 67. Krakatoa 68. The Italian Job 69. Honeymoon with a Stranger (TV) 69. The Survivors (TV) 69. The Adventurers 70. Psychout for Murder 70. The Great Waltz 72. Master of Love 74. The White Telephone 76. The Final Conflict 81. The Voice 82. Fear City 84. Final Justice 85. Formula for a Murder 86, etc.

break figure. A specified amount of takings after which an exhibitor pays a greater percentage to the renter. For the protection of both parties many contracts are on a sliding scale, with the exhibitor paying anything from 25% to 50% of the gross according to the business he does.

breakaway furniture is specially constructed from balsa wood for those spectacular saloon brawls in which so much damage is apparently done to stars and stunt men.

Breakston, George (1922–1973). American who, born in France, went to Hollywood as a child and acted for several years; later went to Africa and produced many routine adventure films and TV series, usually with British backing.
AS ACTOR: Great Expectations 34. Mrs Wiggs of the Cabbage Patch 34. The Dark Angel 35. Love Finds Andy Hardy 38. Jesse James 35. The Courtship of Andy Hardy 42, etc.
AS PRODUCER: Urubu 48. Tokyo File 212 51. The Scarlet Spear (& d) 54. Golden Ivory 55. Escape in the Sun 56. Woman and the Hunter 57. Shadow of Treason (& d) 63. The Boy Cried Murder (& d) 66, etc.

Breathless (À Bout de Souffle) (France 1959). The first film of Jean-Luc Godard, with François Truffaut's story providing a somewhat less anarchic narrative than one finds in Godard's later solo efforts. In the vanguard of the 'new wave', it had an improvised plot apparently dedicated to the proposition that life is just one damned thing after another with death as the end; superficially it was about a small-time gangster's busy life with pauses for sex. Dedicated to Monogram Pictures. With Jean-Paul Belmondo, Jean Seberg. A US remake in 1983 starred Richard Gere.

Brecher, Irving (1914–). American radio writer who moved on to Hollywood and received solo credit for two Marx Brothers scripts.
New Faces of 1937 37. *At the Circus* 39. Go West 40. Shadow of the Thin Man 41. Dubarry was a Lady 53. *Meet Me in St Louis* 44. Yolanda and the Thief 45. Summer Holiday 47. The Life of Riley (& pd) 49. Somebody Loves Me (& d) 52. Cry for Happy 61. Sail a Crooked Ship (& d) 61. Bye Bye Birdie 63, etc.
TV series: The People's Choice.

Brecht, Bertolt (1898–1956). German poet and playwright whose 'alienation method' (by which audiences are forced by various theatrical devices to remember that they are watching a play) has been influential on films from *Citizen Kane* to *Alfie*. His *Dreigroschenoper*, based on *The Beggar's Opera*, has been filmed twice; films have also been made of *Mother Courage*, *Herr Puntila* and *Galileo*. His sole Hollywood credit is for the script of *Hangmen Also Die*.

Breck, Peter (1930–). American general purpose actor.
A Man for Hanging 72. Benji 74, etc.
TV series: Black Saddle 58–59. The Big Valley 65–68. Also episodes of Maverick (as Bat Masterson).

Breen, Bobby (1927–). American boy singer of the thirties; later gave up films for night club work.
Let's Sing Again 36. Rainbow on the River 36. Make a Wish 37. Hawaii Calls 37. Breaking the Ice 38. Fisherman's Wharf 39. Way Down South 39. Johnny Doughboy 43, etc.

Breen, Joseph (1890–1965). American executive, for many years administrator of the Production Code. (See *censorship*.)

Breen, Richard L. (1919–1967). American scenarist. Former president of Screenwriters' Guild.
A Foreign Affair (co-author) 48. Miss Tatlock's Millions 49. The Model and the Marriage Broker 51. Niagara 53. Titanic (AA) 53. Dragnet 54. Pete Kelly's Blues 55. Stopover Tokyo (& d) 57. Wake Me When It's Over 60. Captain Newman 63. Do Not Disturb 65. Tony Rome 67, many others.

Bremer, Lucille (1922–). American dancer. MGM groomed her for stardom in the forties, but her career was brief.
□Meet Me in St Louis 44. *Yolanda and the Thief* 45. *Ziegfeld Follies* 45. Till the Clouds Roll By 46. Dark Delusion 47. Adventures of Casanova 48. Ruthless 48. Behind Locked Doors 48.

Brendel, El (1890–1964). Mild-mannered American comic actor, a fake Swede from vaudeville with an attractive way of fracturing the English language.
The Campus Flirt 26. Wings 27. *Sunny Side Up* 29. The Big Trail 30. *Just Imagine* 30. Mr Lemon of Orange 30. Delicious 31. Hot Pepper 32. My Lips Betray 33. God's Country and the Woman 37. Little Miss Broadway 38. *If I Had My Way* 40. Captain Caution 40. Machine Gun Mama 44. The Beautiful Blonde from Bashful Bend 49. The She Creature 56, many others.

Brennan, Eileen (1935–). Brassy American character actress.
□Divorce American Style 67. The Last Picture Show 71. Playmates (TV) 72. The Blue Knight (TV) 73. Scarecrow 73. The Sting 73. Daisy Miller 74. My Father's House (TV) 75. The Night That Panicked America (TV) 75. At Long Last Love 75. Hustle 75. Murder by Death 76. The Death of Richie (TV) 77. All that Glitters (TV) 77. Last of the Cowboys 77. The Great Smokey Roadblock 78. FM 78. The Cheap Detective 78. My Old Man (TV). 79. Black Beauty (TV) 79. *Private Benjamin* 80. When the Circus came to Town (TV) 80. The Funny Farm 82. Pandemonium 82. Clue 85.
TV series: Private Benjamin 81–82 (cancelled because of her car accident). Off the Rack 85.

Brennan, Michael (1912–). 'Tough guy' British supporting actor, in films from 1932.
The Clouded Yellow 50. Ivanhoe 52. Trouble in Store 56. The Day They Robbed the Bank of England 60. Thunderball 65. Lust for a Vampire 70, many others.

Brennan, Walter (1894–1974). Popular American character actor who played toothless old men in his thirties, and was still a star in his seventies. Best remembered as a countrified wit, he also played villains and city slickers.
□The Long Long Trail 29. The Shannons of Broadway 29. Smiling Guns 29. King of Jazz 30. One Hysterical Night 30. Dancing Dynamite 31. Neck and Neck 31. Law and Order 32. Texas Cyclone 32. Two Fisted Law 32. All American 32. Parachute Jumper 32. Man of Action 33. Fighting for Justice 33. Sing Sinner Sing 33. Strange People 33. Silent Men 33. One Year Later 33. Good Dame 34. Half a Sinner 34. Northern Frontier 35. The Wedding Night 35. Bride of Frankenstein 35. Lady Tubbs 35. Man on the Flying Trapeze 35. Metropolitan 35. Barbary Coast 35. Seven Keys to Baldpate 35. These Three 36. Three Godfathers 36. The Moon's Our Home 36. Fury 36. The Prescott Kid 36. *Come and Get It* (AA) 36. Banjo on my Knee 36. She's Dangerous 36. When Love is Young 37. The Affair of Cappy Ricks 37. Wild and Woolly 37. *The Adventures of Tom Sawyer* 38. The Buccaneer 38. The Texans 38. Mother Carey's Chickens 38. *Kentucky* (AA) 38. The Cowboy and the Lady 38. The Story of Vernon and Irene Castle 38. They Shall Have Music 39. *Stanley and Livingstone* 39. Joe and Ethel Turp Call on the President 39. Northwest Passage 40. Maryland 40. *The Westerner* (AA: as Judge Roy Bean) 40. This Woman is Mine 41. Nice Girl 41. *Meet John Doe* 41. *Sergeant York* 41. *Swamp Water* 41. Rise and Shine 41. Pride of the Yankees 42. Stand By for Action 42. Slightly Dangerous 43. Hangmen also Die 43. North Star 43. Home in Indiana 43. *To Have and Have Not* 44. The Princess and the Pirate 44. Dakota 45. A Stolen Life 46. Centennial Summer 46. Nobody Lives Forever 46. *My Darling Clementine* (as old Clanton) 46. Driftwood 47. Scudda Hoo Scudda Hay 48. Red River 48. Blood on the Moon 48. The Green Promise 49. The Great Dan Patch 49. Brimstone 49. Task Force 49. Singing Guns 50. A Ticket to Tomahawk 50. Curtain Call at Cactus Crick 50. The Showdown 50. Surrender 50. Best of the Bad Men 51. Along the Great Divide 51. The Wild Blue Yonder 51. Return of the Texan 52. Lure of the Wilderness 52. Sea of Lost Ships 53. The Far Country 54. Drums Across the River 54. Four Guns to the Border 54. At Gunpoint 55. Bad Day at Black Rock 55. *Come Next Spring* 56. Glory 56. Goodbye My Lady 56. The Proud Ones 56. Tammy and the Bachelor 57. The Way to the Gold 57. God is my Partner 57. *Rio Bravo* 59. How the West was Won 62. Those Calloways 64. The Oscar 66. *Who's Minding the Mint?* 67. The Gnome-mobile 67. The One and Only Genuine Original Family Band 67. Support Your Local Sheriff 69. The Over the Hill Gang (TV) 70. The Young Country (TV) 70. Two for the Money (TV) 71. The Over the Hill Gang Rides Again (TV) 71. Smoke in the Wind 71. Home for the Holidays (TV) 72.
TV series: *The Real McCoys* 57–63. Tycoon 64. *The Guns of Will Sonnett* 67–68. To Rome with Love 69.
❀ For long and spirited service, with and without his teeth. *The Westerner.*

Brenner, Jules (–). American cinematographer.
Johnny Got His Gun 71. The Glass House (TV) 72. Dillinger 73. Posse 75. Outlaw Blues 77. When You Comin' Back Red Ryder? 79, etc.

Brenon, Herbert (1880–1958). Irish director, in Hollywood after stage experience: a big name of the twenties.
Ivanhoe 13. The Kreuzer Sonata 15. War Brides 16. The Passing of the Third Floor Back 18. The Sign on the Door 21. The Spanish Dancer 23. *Peter Pan* 24. A Kiss for Cinderella 24. *Beau Geste* 26. *Sorrell and Son* (GB) 27. The Great Gatsby 27. Laugh Clown Laugh 28. The Rescue 29. Beau Ideal 29. Oliver Twist 33. Wine Women and Song 34. The Housemaster (GB) 38. At the Villa Rose (GB) 38. Yellow Sands (GB) 38. The Flying Squadron (GB) 40, etc.

Brent, Eve (1930–). American leading lady who played Jane in *Tarzan's Fight for Life* 55. *Tarzan and the Trappers* 57.

Brent, Evelyn (1899–1975) (Mary Elizabeth Riggs). American leading lady of the silent era; made a few talkies, then retired apart from some bit parts in the forties.
The Other Man's Wife 19. The Shuttle of Life (GB) 20. Sybil (GB) 21. Married to a Mormon (GB) 22. Silk Stocking Sal 24. Smooth as Satin 25. Love 'Em and Leave 'Em 26. Queen of Diamonds 26. *Underworld* 27. Beau Sabreur 28. A Night of Mystery 28. The Mating Call 28. *Broadway* 29. *Slightly Scarlet* 30. Madonna of the Streets 30. The Pagan Lady 31. The World Gone Mad 33. Home on the Range 35. Night Club Scandal 37. Mr Wong Detective 38. The Mad Empress 40. The Seventh Victim 43. Bowery Champs 44. The Golden Eye 48, many others.

Brent, George (1904–1979) (George Brent Nolan). Irishman who went to Hollywood and after years as a tough hero developed into a light leading man very effective against strong actresses such as Bette Davis and Myrna Loy. □SOUND FILMS: Under Suspicion 30. Lightning Warrior 31. Homicide Squad 31. Once a Sinner 31. Fair Warning 31. Charlie Chan Carries On 31. Ex Bad Boy 31. So Big 32. The Rich Are Always With Us 32. Weekend Marriage 32. Miss Pinkerton 32. Purchase Price 32. The Crash 32. They Call It Sin 32. Luxury Liner 33. *Forty Second Street* 33. The Keyhole 33. Lilly Turner 33. Baby Face 33. Female 33. Stamboul Quest 34. Housewife 34. Desirable 34. *The Painted Veil* 34. Living on Velvet 35. Stranded 35. *Front Page Woman* 35. The Goose and the Gander 35. Special Agent 35. In Person 35. The Right to Live 35. Snowed Under 36. The Golden Arrow 36. The Case Against Mrs Ames 36. Give Me Your Heart 36. More than a Secretary 36. God's Country and the Woman 37. The Go-getter 37. Mountain Justice 37. Gold Is Where you Find It 37. Submarine D-1 37. *Jezebel* 38. Racket Busters 38. Secrets of an Actress 38. Wings of the Navy 39. *Dark Victory* 39. The Old Maid 39. *The Rains Came* 39. The Man who Talked Too Much 40. Till We Meet Again 40. The Fighting 69th 40. South of Suez 40. Adventure in Diamonds 40. Honeymoon for Three 41. *The Great Lie* 41.They Dare Not Love 41. International Lady 41. Twin Beds 42. The Gay Sisters 42. In This Our Life 42. You Can't Escape Forever 42. Silver Queen 42. Experiment Perilous 44. *The Affairs of Susan* 45. My Reputation 45. *The Spiral Staircase* 45. Tomorrow Is Forever 46. Lover Come Back 46. Temptation 46. Slave Girl 47. Out of the Blue 47. The Corpse Came COD 47. Christmas Eve 47. Luxury Liner 48. Angel on the Amazon 48. Red Canyon 49. Illegal Entry 49. Kid from Cleveland 49. Bride for Sale 49. FBI Girl 51. The Dark Page (GB) 51. Montana Belle 52. Tangier Incident 53. Born Again 78.
TV series: Wire Service 56.
❀ For behaving like the perfect gentleman in company with some extremely difficult ladies. *The Rains Came*.

Brent, Romney (1902–1976) (Romulo Larralde). Dapper Mexican actor in British films in the thirties, later elsewhere.
East Meets West 36. Dreaming Lips 37. School for Husbands 37. Under the Red Robe 37. Dinner at the Ritz (& w) 37. Let George Do It 40. The Adventures of Don Juan 48. The Virgin Queen 55. Don't Go Near the Water 57. The Sign of Zorro 58, etc.

Breon, Edmund (1882–1951) (Edmund McLaverty). Beaming, monocled British stage actor, often seen as amiable bumbler. In Hollywood from late twenties, Britain 1933–42.
The Dawn Patrol 30. I Like your Nerve 31. *Three Men in a Boat* 33. No Funny Business 33. The Scarlet Pimpernel 35. Keep Fit 37. A Yank at Oxford 38. Goodbye Mr Chips 39. The Outsider 39. She Shall Have Music 42. Gaslight 44. Casanova Brown 44. *The Woman in the Window* 45. *Dressed To Kill* 46. Forever Amber 47. Enchantment 48. Challenge to Lassie 50. At Sword's Point 51, etc.

Bresler, Jerry (1912–77). American independent producer.
Main Street after Dark 44. Bewitched 45. The Web 47. *Another Part of the Forest* 48. The Flying Missile 50. The Mob 51. Assignment Paris 52. Lizzie 57. *The Vikings* 58. Gidget Goes Hawaiian 61. Diamond Head 63. Major Dundee 65. Pussycat Pussycat I Love You 70, etc.

Bressart, Felix (1890–1949). German character actor in Hollywood from late thirties, usually in downtrodden comic roles; a genuine original.
□Drei von der Tankstelle 31. Der Wahre Jakob 31. Das Alte Lied 31. Nie Wieder Liebe 31. Eine Freundin so Goldig wie Du 31. Der Schrecken der Garnison 32. Hirsekorn Greift Ein 32. Der Herr Buerovorsteher 32. Holzapfel Weiss Alles 33. Drei Tage Mittelarrest 33. Der Sohn der Weissen Berge 33. Der Glueckszylinger 34. Und Wer Kuesst Mich? 35. Three Smart Girls Grow Up 39. Bridal Suite 39. Swanee River 39. *Ninotchka* 39. The Shop Around the Corner 40. It All Came True 40. Edison the Man 40. Third Finger Left Hand 40. Bitter Sweet 40. Comrade X 40. Escape 40. Ziegfeld Girl 40. Blossoms in the Dust 41. Married Bachelor 41. Kathleen 41. Mr and Mrs North 41. *To Be or Not to Be* 42. Crossroads 42. Iceland 42. Three Hearts for Julia 43. Song of Russia 43. Above Suspicion 43. Greenwich Village 44. The Seventh Cross 44. Blonde Fever 44. Dangerous Partners 44. Without Love 45. Ding Dong Williams 46. I've Always Loved You 46. The Thrill of Brazil 46. Her Sister's Secret 46. A Song Is Born 48. Portrait of Jennie 48. Take One False Step 49.

Bresslaw, Bernard (1933–). British comic actor who sprang to fame as giant-sized dope in TV series *The Army Game* 57–62 but proved lacking in big screen star quality.
I Only Arsked 57. Too Many Crooks 58. The Ugly Duckling 59. Morgan 66. Carry on Screaming 66. Up Pompeii 70. Vampira 74. One of our Dinosaurs is Missing 76. Hawk the Slayer 80. Krull 83, many others in small roles.

Bresson, Robert (1907–). Elusive French writer-director of austere, introspective, low-budget films.
□Les Anges du Péché 43. *Les Dames du Bois de Boulogne* 44. *Le Journal d'un Curé de Campagne* 50. Un Condamné à Mort s'est Echappé 56. Pickpocket 59. The Trial of Joan of Arc 62. Au Hasard Balthazar 66. Mouchette 67. Une Femme Douce 69. Quatre Nuits d'un Rêveur 71. Lancelot du Lac 74. Le Diable Probablement 77. L'Argent 83.

¶ *R.B.:* A film is not a spectacle: it is pre-eminently a style.

Brest, Martin (–). American director.
Hot Tomorrows 78. Going in Style 79. Beverly Hills Cop 84.

Bretherton, David (–). American editor.
The Bottom of the Bottle 56. Peyton Place 57. The Diary of Anne Frank 59. The Facts of Life 60. State Fair 62. The Train 64. The Honey Pot 67. Lovers and Other Strangers 70. Cabaret 72. Westworld 74. Harry and Walter Go to New York 76. Winter Kills 79. The First Great Train Robbery 79. The Big Red One 80. Cannery Row 82, many others.

Bretherton, Howard (1896–1969). American director of second features.
Hills of Kentucky 27. The Redeeming Sin 29. Isle of Escape 30. The Match King 32. Ladies They Talk About 33. The Return of the Terror 34. The Leathernecks have Landed 36. It Happened out West 37. The Girl Who Dared 44. Prince of Thieves 48. Whip Law 50, many others.

Brett, Jeremy (1935–) (Jeremy Huggins). British light leading man.
War and Peace 56. The Wild and the Willing 61. The Very Edge 63. *My Fair Lady* 64. The Medusa Touch 77. Florence Nightingale (TV) 84. Deceptions (TV) 84, etc.
TV series: The Adventures of Sherlock Holmes 84– .

Brewster's Millions. This much-filmed comedy, about a man who inherits a vast legacy providing he can spend his first million in secret within twenty-four hours, began as a novel by George McCutcheon which was turned into a play by Winchell Smith and Byron Ongley. It was filmed in 1921 with Fatty Arbuckle, in 1935 with Jack Buchanan, in 1945 with Dennis O'Keefe, and in 1961 (as *Three on a Spree*) with Jack Watling.

Brialy, Jean-Claude (1933–). French leading man.
Éléna et les Hommes 56. Lift to the Scaffold 57. Le Beau Serge 58. The Four Hundred Blows 59. Tiré au Flanc 61. La Chambre Ardente 62. The Devil and Ten Commandments 62. La Ronde 64. Un Homme de Trop 67. King of Hearts 67. Le Rouge et le Noir 70. Claire's Knee 71. The Phantom of Liberty 74. Catherine and Company 75. Le Point de Mire 77. Robert et Robert 78. La Banquière 80. The Judge and the Assassin 81. The Demon of the Isle 83, etc.
Also directed: Eglantine 72. Closed Shutters 73. Un Amour de Pluie 74, etc.

Brian, David (1914–). Stalwart American second lead, a former song-and-dance man who came to Hollywood in 1949 and sank into a groove of toughness and reliability, with a streak of villainy when required.
Flamingo Road 49. Beyond the Forest 49. *Intruder in the Dust* 49. The Damned Don't Cry 50. Breakthrough 50. Inside Straight 51. This Woman is Dangerous 52. Million Dollar Mermaid 52. The High and the Mighty 54. Timberjack 55. The First Travelling Saleslady 56. The Rabbit Trap 59. A Pocketful of Miracles 61. How the West was Won 62. The Rare Breed 68. The Destructors 69. The Seven Minutes 71, many others.
TV series: *Mr District Attorney* 54–55. The Immortal 70.

Brian, Mary (1908–) (Louise Dantzler). Charming American leading lady of the twenties; her roles diminished with sound and finally petered out.
Peter Pan (as Wendy) 24. The Little French Girl 25. Brown of Harvard 26. Beau Geste 26. Running Wild 27. Shanghai Bound 27. Harold Teen 28. Varsity 28. The Man I Love 29. *The Virginian* 29. The Light of Western Stars 30. *The Royal Family of Broadway* 30. *The Front Page* 31. Blessed Event 32. Girl Missing 33. College Rhythm 34. Charlie Chan in Paris 35. Killer at Large 36. The Amazing

Quest of Ernest Bliss (GB) 36. Navy Bound 37. Calaboose 43. The Dragnet 48, many others.

Briant, Shane (1946–). British general purpose actor.
Demons of the Mind 70. Straight on till Morning 71. Captain Kronos 72. Frankenstein and the Monster from Hell 72, etc.

Brice, Fanny (1891–1951) (Fanny Borach). American Jewish entertainer who made a virtue of her plainness. Screen appearances rare, but four films were based on her life: *Broadway Thro' a Keyhole* 33, *Rose of Washington Square* 38, *Funny Girl* 68, *Funny Lady* 75.
□*My Man* 28. Night Club 29. Be Yourself 30. The Great Ziegfeld 36. Everybody Sing 38. Ziegfeld Follies 45.

Bricusse, Leslie (1931–). British lyricist and composer.
Charley Moon 56. Stop the World I Want to Get Off 65. Doctor Dolittle (AA) 67. Goodbye Mr Chips 69. Scrooge 70. Revenge of the Pink Panther 78. Superman 78. The Sea Wolves 80. Victor/Victoria 82, etc.

The Bride of Frankenstein (US 1935). At once the best of the horror films and a gentle mockery of them, this elegant Gothic piece with its eighteenth-century prologue is full of wry humour and pictorial delights. Its reputation rests on James Whale's direction and the script by John Balderston and Anthony Veiller; but Karloff as the monster, Elsa Lanchester as Mary Shelley and Ernest Thesiger as Dr Praetorius are gloriously grotesque.

Bridge, Al (1891–1957). Gravel-voiced American character actor chiefly memorable in Preston Sturges comedies.
Christmas in July 40. The Palm Beach Story 42. *Hail the Conquering Hero* 44, etc.

The Bridge of San Luis Rey. Thornton Wilder's fatalistic twenties novel, tracing the lives of five people who happened to be on a Peruvian rope bridge when it collapsed, was filmed rather unsatisfactorily in 1929 by Charles Brabin and in 1944 by Rowland V. Lee. The many films which have copied its theme and structure include *Friday the Thirteenth* and *Phone Call from a Stranger*.

The Bridge on the River Kwai (GB 1957). Literally adapted by Carl Foreman and Michael Wilson from Pierre Boulle's novel, this anti-heroic war film about the absurdity of behaviour in a Burmese prison camp during World War II is carefully directed by David Lean (AA) and has fascinating performances from Alec Guinness (AA) and Sessue Hayakawa. Despite these assets and its great visual beauty, its plot development is clumsy and its climax confusing, so that its various messages take second place to its spectacular highlights.

A Bridge Too Far (US 1977). This war spectacular is chiefly interesting as a belated attempt to make an all-star blockbuster on an unlikely theme: the tragic defeat of the British paratroops at Arnhem in 1944. In view of the subject, the hiring of fourteen stars to play cameo roles at up to two million dollars a go was rather unseemly, and despite good moments, mainly provided by Laurence Olivier, this was a solemn, overlong, undistinguished effort by producer Joseph Levine, writer William Goldman and director Richard Attenborough.

Bridges, Alan (1927–). British director, from TV.
□*An Act of Murder* 65. *Invasion* 66. The Lie (TV) 70. The Hireling 73. Brief Encounter (TV) 75. Out of Season 75. Summer Rain (Can.) 76. The Return of the Soldier 82. The Shooting Party 84.

Bridges, Beau (1941–). American leading man, son of Lloyd Bridges.
Force of Evil 48. The Red Pony 49. The Incident 67. For Love of Ivy 68. *Gaily Gaily* 69. *The Landlord* 70. Adam's Woman 70. The Christian Licorice Store 71. Hammersmith is Out 72. Child's Play 72. Loving Molly 73. The Other Side of the Mountain 75. Medical Story (TV) 75. One Summer Love 76. Swashbuckler 76. Two Minute Warning 76. Greased Lightning 77. The Fifth Musketeer 77. The Four Feathers (TV) 78. The President's Mistress (TV) 78. Norma Rae 79. The Child Stealer (TV) 79. The Runner Stumbles (TV) 79. Honky Tonk Freeway (TV) 81. Love Child 82. Night Crossing 82. Dangerous Company (TV) 82. Heart Like a Wheel 83. Witness for the Prosecution (TV) 84. Space (TV) 85. The Red Light Sting (TV) 86. The Wild Pair (& d) 87.
TV series: Ensign O'Toole 62–64. United States 80.

Bridges, James (c. 1928–). American writer-director.

□The Appaloosa (co-w only) 66. The Forbin Project (w only) 70. The Baby Maker 70. The Paper Chase 73. September 30, 1955 77. The China Syndrome 79. Urban Cowboy 80. Mike's Murder 82. Perfect 84.

Bridges, Jeff (1949–). American leading man of the early seventies, son of Lloyd Bridges.
□Halls of Anger 70. In Search of America (TV) 70. The Last Picture Show 71. Fat City 71. Bad Company 72. The Last American Hero 73. Lolly Madonna XXX 73. The Iceman Cometh 73. Thunderbolt and Lightfoot 74. Rancho de Luxe 75. *Hearts of the West* 75. Stay Hungry 76. King Kong 76. Somebody Killed Her Husband 79. Winter Kills 79. Success 79. Heaven's Gate 80. Cutter's Way 81. Tron 82. Kiss Me Goodbye 82. Against All Odds 83. Starman (AAN) 84. Jagged Edge 85. 8 Million Ways to Die 85. The Morning After 86. Nadine 87.

Bridges, Lloyd (1913–). American general purpose actor and sometimes leading man, who over thirty years has brought a sense of integrity to many westerns and melodramas.
Here Comes Mr Jordan 41. The Lone Wolf Takes a Chance 41. Atlantic Convoy 42. The Heat's On 43. The Master Race 44. Strange Confession 45. Miss Susie Slagle's 46. Canyon Passage 46. Ramrod 47. Sixteen Fathoms Deep 48. Moonrise 49. *Home of the Brave* 49. Trapped 49. Rocketship XM 50. The White Tower 50. *Try and Get Me* 51. Little Big Horn 51. The Whistle at Eaton Falls 51. High Noon 52. Plymouth Adventure 52. City of Bad Men 53. The Tall Texan 53. The Limping Man (GB) 54. Apache Woman 55. Wetbacks 56. The Rainmaker 56. *The Goddess* 58. Around the World Under the Sea 66. Attack on the Iron Coast 68. *The Love War* (TV) 70. The Silent Gun (TV) 70. To Find a Man 72. Haunts of the Very Rich (TV) 72. Trouble Comes to Town (TV) 73. Running Wild 73. Crime Club (TV) 73. Death Race (TV) 73. Stowaway to the Moon (TV) 75. The Return of Joe Forrester (TV) 75. Roots (TV) 77. Telethon (TV) 77. The Great Wallendas (TV) 78. The Critical List (TV) 78. Airplane 80. Grace Kelly (TV) 82. Weekend Warriors 86. The Wild Pair 87, etc.
TV series: *Sea Hunt* 57–60. The Lloyd Bridges Show 62. *The Loner* 65. San Francisco International 70. Joe Forrester 75. Paper Dolls 85.

Bridie, James (1888–1951) (Osborne Henry Mavor). Pawky Scottish dramatist whose works were more suited to stage than screen. Two films which did result were *Flesh and Blood* (from *A Sleeping Clergyman)* and *Folly to Be Wise* (from *It Depends What You Mean)*.

Brief Encounter (GB 1946). One of the great post-war British films, this low-key, French-influenced romance between middle-aged people both comfortably married to other partners boasted a discerning script by Noel Coward, impeccable direction by David Lean, gleaming photography by Robert Krasker and poignant performances by Celia Johnson and Trevor Howard. Its stiff-upper-lip Britishness has caused it to be unfairly revalued, but it will certainly be cherished in a more tender age. The 1975 TV remake with Richard Burton and Sophia Loren was abysmal.

Briers, Richard (1933–). British comic character actor, a farceur who inherited the mantle of Ralph Lynn and was popular on TV in *The Marriage Lines* and *The Good Life*.
Girls at Sea 58. The Girl on the Boat 62. Fathom 67. Rentadick 72.

Briggs, Harlan (1880–1952). American small part actor.
Dodsworth 36. A Family Affair 37. One Wild Night 38. Calling Dr Kildare 39. Abe Lincoln in Illinois 40. One Foot in Heaven 41. Tennessee Johnson 43. State Fair 45. A Double Life 48. Carrie 52, many others.

Briggs, Johnny (1935–). British character actor, often a cockney on the wrong side of the law.
Diplomatic Corpse 58. Light up the Sky 60. 633 Squadron 64. Perfect Friday 70. Carry on Behind 75, many others.

Brighton Rock (GB 1947). Graham Greene worked on the screen play of his tough 'entertainment' about a racetrack gang run by a vicious adolescent. The Boulting Brothers produced it in bravura fashion, with a softened ending which was criticized; the film was acclaimed for its new realism and attacked for its new viciousness. Both it and Richard Attenborough's performance now seem rather tame.

Briley, John (–). American-born screenwriter in Britain.
Postman's Knock 61. Children of the Damned 64. Pope Joan 72. That Lucky Touch 75.

Eagle's Wing 79. *Gandhi* (AA) 82.
Cry Freedom 87.

Brimley, Wilford (1935–). American character actor who plays wise, rough-edged old gents and hovers just below the star level.
The Electric Horseman 79. Brubaker 79. Borderline 80. The China Syndrome 80. Heaven's Gate 80. Death Valley 82. Absence of Malice 82. Tender Mercies 83. Ten to Midnight 83. Country 84. Hotel New Hampshire 84. The Natural 84. American Justice 85. Cocoon 85. Thompson's Last Run (TV) 85. Remo Williams 85.
TV series: *Our House* 86– .

Brinegar, Paul (*c.*1908–86). American character actor who played the trail cook in TV's *Rawhide* and twenty years later was in the *Matt Houston* series. Films very occasional, from *The Gal Who Took the West* 49 to *High Plains Drifter* 73.

Bringing Up Baby (US 1938). This classic example of thirties crazy comedy was full of upper-bracket people behaving in a ridiculous and even anti-social manner in pursuit of a dog, a dinosaur bone, and an escaped pet leopard. Katharine Hepburn was the zany rich girl and Cary Grant the staid archaeologist, with May Robson and Charles Ruggles strong in support. Howard Hawks directed from a script by Hagar Wilde and Dudley Nichols. Hawks re-used portions of the script in *Man's Favourite Sport* 64 and Peter Bogdanovich virtually remade the film as *What's Up Doc?* 72.

Brissac, Virginia (1894–1979). American supporting actress, a familiar face in mother and neighbour roles.
A Tree Grows in Brooklyn 44. Monsieur Verdoux 47. The Snake Pit 48. Cheaper by the Dozen 50. Rebel Without a Cause 55, many others.

Brisson, Carl (1895–1958) (Carl Pedersen). Danish leading man who made films in Britain.
The Ring 28. The Manxman 29. The American Prisoner 29. Song of Soho 30. Murder at the Vanities 34. All the King's Horses 35, etc.

Brisson, Frederick (1912–84). Danish producer with long experience in Britain (pre-39) and Hollywood. Married Rosalind Russell and subsequently masterminded her appearances.
□The Velvet Touch 48. Never Wave at a WAC 53. The Girl Rush 55. The Pajama Game 57. Damn Yankees 58. Five Finger Exercise 62. Under the Yum Yum Tree 63. Generation 69. Mrs Pollifax—Spy 71.

The British Empire has provided a useful background for innumerable movies: some comic, some tragic, but most of them plain adventurous. The Elizabethan adventurers roistered through films like *The Sea Hawk, The Virgin Queen* and *Seven Seas to Calais*; the westward voyage occupied *Plymouth Adventure*; Australia provided the canvas for *Under Capricorn, Robbery Under Arms,* and *Botany Bay*; *Mutiny on the Bounty* showed the British in the South Seas; Africa was the subject of *Zulu, The Four Feathers, Khartoum, Sundown, Rhodes of Africa, The Sun Never Sets* and (for the anti-British view) *Ohm Krüger*; and favourite of all far-flung outposts, India provided splendid terrain for such adventures as *The Drum, Northwest Frontier, Gunga Din, King of the Khyber Rifles, The Rains Came, Charge of the Light Brigade* and *Lives of a Bengal Lancer.* When the Empire was at its height, one could view the British influence as benevolent (*Pacific Destiny*), maiden-auntish (*Sanders of the River*), or merely acquisitive (*Victoria the Great*).

The inevitable break-up was rather less well covered. Even American independence has been played down by Hollywood producers with an eye on the British market, though of course it comes into such films as *Last of the Mohicans, Lafayette, Daniel Boone,* and even Disney's *Ben and Me.* Emergent Africa was the theme of *Men of Two Worlds* as long ago as 1946, but between that and the independent state depicted in *Guns at Batasi* came the Mau Mau period shown in *Simba, Safari* and *Something of Value. The High Bright Sun* dealt with Cyprus; *The Planter's Wife* and *The Seventh Dawn* with Malaya; *Exodus, Judith* and *Cast a Giant Shadow* with Israel; scores of films with the Irish troubles; *Bhowani Junction* and *Nine Hours to Rama* with India. But the emergence of new states is a painful business as a rule, and most of these films give the impression of so much tasteless picking at sore points. The unexpected 1982 success of *Gandhi* may however begin a more serious process of revaluing imperial history.
See also: *Ireland.*

British Film Academy. Organization founded 1946 'for the advancement of the film'. Since 1959 amalgamated with the Society of Film and Television Arts. Its award statuette is known as Stella, and is noted in this book by the letters BFA.

British Film Institute. Partly government-subsidized organization founded 1933 'to encourage the use and development of cinema as a means of entertainment and instruction'. Includes the National Film Archive (founded 1935) and the National Film Theatre (founded after the 1951 Festival of Britain). Also library, information section, stills collection, film distribution agency, lecture courses, etc. Chief publications: *Monthly Film Bulletin, Sight and Sound.*

British Lion Film Corporation. A film production company of the twenties which, in the thirties, became mainly a distributor of cheap American product but was revived after World War II by the control of Alexander Korda, then by Michael Balcon, the Boulting Brothers and Frank Launder and Sidney Gilliat. It merged in 1976 with EMI.

British title changes

? Here are titles of British films as they were released in America. Name the original British titles.

1 *Immortal Battalion* (1944)
2 *The Rape of Malaya* (1956)
3 *The Creeping Unknown* (1955)
4 *The Golden Virgin* (1957)
5 *Stairway to Heaven* (1945)
6 *African Fury* (1952)
7 *Haunted Honeymoon* (1940)
8 *The Promoter* (1952)
9 *Die Die My Darling* (1965)
10 *Spitfire* (1942)
11 *Mister V* (1941)
12 *Johnny in the Clouds* (1945)
13 *The Conqueror Worm* (1968)
14 *The Girl Was Young* (1938)
15 *A Woman Alone* (1937)
16 *Tight Little Island* (1949)
17 *Desert Attack* (1958)
18 *Man of Evil* (1944)
19 *The Detective* (1954)
20 *Pursuit of the Graf Spee* (1956)

Britt, May (1933–) (Maybritt Wilkens). Swedish leading lady, in a few Hollywood films.
Affairs of a Model 52. La Lupa 54. *The Young Lions* 58. The Hunters 58. The Blue Angel 59. Murder Inc. 60. Secrets of Woman 61. Haunts 77, etc.

Brittany, Morgan (1953–) (Suzanne Caputo). American child actress, later leading lady.
Gypsy 62. The Birds 63. Marnie 64. Yours, Mine and Ours 68. The Day of the Locust 75. Gable and Lombard 76. Samurai (TV) 79. Death Car on the Freeway (TV) 79. Stunt Seven (TV) 80, etc.
TV series: Dallas, Glitter.

Britton, Barbara (1920–1980) (Barbara Brantingham Czukor). American leading lady of the forties who went straight from college to Hollywood.
Secret of the Wastelands 40. Louisiana Purchase 41. Wake Island 42. Reap the Wild Wind 42. So Proudly We Hail 43. *Till We Meet Again* 44. The Story of Dr Wassell 44. The Great John L. 45. Captain Kidd 45. The Virginian 46. The Fabulous Suzanne 47. Gunfighters 47. Albuquerque 48. I Shot Jesse James 49. Champagne for Caesar 50. Bandit Queen 50. The Raiders 52. Bwana Devil 53. The Spoilers 55, etc.
TV series: Mr and Mrs North 53–54.

Britton, Pamela (1923–1974). Lightweight American actress, mainly familiar as TV's *Blondie* and in the *My Favorite Martian* series.
Anchors Aweigh 45. Key to the City 50. If It's Tuesday This Must Be Belgium 74, etc.

Britton, Tony (1925–). British stage, screen and TV actor of quiet and polished style.
Salute the Toff 52. Loser Take All 57. The Birthday Present 57. Operation Amsterdam 58. The Rough and the Smooth 59. Suspect 60. Stork Talk 61. The Break 63. There's a Girl in My Soup 70. Sunday Bloody Sunday 71. The Day of the Jackal 73. Night Watch 74. The People That Time Forgot 76, etc.
TV Series: Father Dear Father, Robin's Nest, Don't Wait Up.

Broadway

? Superstardom on New York's Great White Way is not always appreciated by Hollywood producers, who when buying a hit for transfer to the screen often prefer to do their own casting. Here are some Hollywood films with their stars; but can you say who played the roles on Broadway?

1 *Mame*: Lucille Ball
2 *Sweet Charity*: Shirley Maclaine
3 *Man of La Mancha*: Peter O'Toole
4 *On a Clear Day You Can See Forever*: Barbra Streisand

5 *Fiddler on the Roof*: Topol
6 *A Little Night Music*: Elizabeth Taylor
7 *West Side Story*: Natalie Wood
8 *My Fair Lady*: Audrey Hepburn
9 *The Sound of Music*: Julie Andrews
10 *Oklahoma*: Gordon Macrae
11 *Guys and Dolls*: Marlon Brando
12 *Cabaret*: Liza Minnelli

Broadway Bill (US 1934). A hard-boiled but soft-centred racetrack comedy directed by Frank Capra in the ebullient style which was to become his trademark. From a script by Robert Riskin and a story by Mark Hellinger, it starred Warner Baxter and Myrna Loy. In 1951 Capra remade it as *Riding High*, a semi-musical with Bing Crosby and Coleen Gray.

Broadway Melody (US 1929) (AA). Early sound musical which, imitated, improved and expanded, set the style for all backstage yarns of the thirties. Harry Beaumont directed; Anita Page, Bessie Love and Charles King starred. MGM later used the title but not the plot for *Broadway Melody of 1936* and followed with *Broadway Melody of 1938* and *Broadway Melody of 1940*; there was to have been one for 1944 but the title was changed to *Broadway Rhythm*.

Broccoli, Albert R. ('Cubby') (1909–). American independent producer resident in London since 1951; successful as co-chief of Warwick Productions and later the James Bond films.
Hell Below Zero 54. The Black Knight 54. Cockleshell Heroes 55. Zarak 56. Fire Down Below 57. The Man Inside 59. *Dr No* 62. Call Me Bwana 63. From Russia With Love 63 (and subsequent Bond films). Chitty Chitty Bang Bang 68, many others.

Broderick, Helen (1890–1959). Wry-faced American stage comedienne whose wisecracks enlivened many thirties comedies. Mother of Broderick Crawford.
□Fifty Million Frenchmen 31. *Top Hat* 35. To Beat the Band 35. Love on a Bet 36. Murder on the Bridle Path 36. Swing Time 36. The Bride Walks Out 36. Smartest Girl in Town 36. We're on the Jury 37. Meet the Missus 37. Life of the Party 37. Radio City Revels 38. She's Got Everything 38. The Rage of Paris 38. The Road to Reno 38. Service de Luxe 38. Stand Up and Fight 39. Naughty but Nice 39. Honeymoon in Bali 39. The Captain Is a Lady 40. No No Nanette 40. Virginia 41. Nice Girl 41. Father Takes a Wife 41. Are Husbands Necessary 42. Stage Door Canteen 43. Chip Off the Old Block 44. Her Primitive Man 44. Three Is a Family 44. Love Honor and Goodbye 45. Because of Him 46.

Broderick, James (1927–1982). Worried-looking American character actor.
The Group 66. Alice's Restaurant 69. The Taking of Pelham One Two Three 74. Dog Day Afternoon 75. The Shadow Box (TV) 80, etc.
TV series: Brenner 59. *Family* 76–80.

Broderick, Matthew (1961–).
American juvenile lead of the early eighties; son of James Broderick.
Max Dugan Returns 83. *War Games* 83. Ladyhawke 84. On Valentine's Day 85. Ferris Bueller's Day Off 86. Project X 87.

Brodie, Steve (1919–) (John Stevens). Tough-looking American leading man and character actor, mainly in second features. This Man's Navy 45. Young Wife 46. Trail Street 47. Home of the Brave 49. Winchester 73 50. Only the Valiant 51. Lady in the Iron Mask 52. The Beast from Twenty Thousand Fathoms 53. The Caine Mutiny 54. Gun Duel in Durango 57. Three Came to Kill 60. Of Love and Desire 63, etc.

Brodine, Norbert (1893–1970).
Distinguished American cinematographer.
SELECTED SILENT FILMS: Almost a Husband 19. The Invisible Power 21. A Blind Bargain 22. Brass 23. *The Sea Hawk* 24. The Eagle of the Sea 25. Paris at Midnight 26. The Clown 27. Beware of Bachelors 28. Her Private Affair 29.
□SOUND FILMS: Rich People 29. This Thing Called Love 29. The Divorcee 30. Holiday 30. Let Us Be Gay 30. Beyond Victory 31. The Guardsman 31. Pagan Lady 31. The Passionate Plumber 32. Beast of the City 32. Night Court 32. Bachelor's Affairs 32. Unashamed 32. Wild Girl 32. Uptown New York 32. The Death Kiss 32. Whistling in the Dark 33. Clear all Wires 33. Made on Broadway 33. Broadway to Hollywood 33. Deluge 33. Counsellor at Law 33. The Crosby Case 34. Love Birds 34. *Little Man What Now* 34. The Human Side 34. There's Always Tomorrow 34. Cheating Cheaters 34. The Good Fairy 35. Princess O'Hara 35. She Gets Her Man 35. Lady Tubbs 35. The Affair of Susan 36. Don't Get Personal 36. Nobody's Fool 36. *Libeled Lady* 36. Nobody's Baby 37. Pick a Star 37. *Topper* 37. *Merrily We Live* 37. Swiss Miss 38. There Goes My Heart 38.

Topper Takes a Trip 39. Captain Fury 39. The Housekeeper's Daughter 39. Of Mice and Men 39. *One Million Years B.C.* 40. Turnabout 40. Captain Caution 40. Model Wife 41. Road Show 41. Lady for a Night 41. Dr Gillespie's Criminal Case 43. The Dancing Masters 43. The Bullfighters 45. Don Juan Quilligan 45. *The House on 92nd Street* 45. Sentimental Journey 46. Somewhere in the Night 46. *Thirteen Rue Madeleine* 46. *Kiss of Death* 47. *Boomerang* 47. Sitting Pretty 48. I Was a Male War Bride 49. *Thieves' Highway* 49. *The Frogmen* 51. The Desert Fox 51. Five Fingers 52.

Brodney, Oscar (1905–). American comedy writer, former lawyer. With Universal from the forties, working mainly on routine series and light costume dramas.
When Johnny Comes Marching Home 43. Are You With It? 48. Yes Sir That's My Baby 49. Francis 50. Little Egypt 53. The Glenn Miller Story 54. Lady Godiva 55. Tammy and the Bachelor 57. Bobbikins (GB) (& p) 59. Tammy and the Doctor 63. The Brass Bottle 64. I'd Rather Be Rich 64, etc.

Brodszky, Nicholas (1905–1958). Russian-born composer, long in America and Britain.
French Without Tears 39. Quiet Wedding 40. The Way to the Stars 45. A Man About the House 47. The Toast of New Orleans 50. Latin Lovers 53. The Opposite Sex 56, etc.

Broken Arrow (US 1950). A James Stewart western which does not wear particularly well as entertainment but is significant for its renewal of a sympathetic attitude towards the Indians and its depiction of their chief, Cochise, played by Jeff Chandler, as an honourable man. Directed by Delmer Daves from a script by Michael Blankfort. A TV series starring John Lupton and Michael Ansara appeared in 1975.

Broken Blossoms. It suited D. W. Griffith's rather Victorian outlook to film Thomas Burke's *The Chink and the Child*, a sentimental tale of a gentle Chinaman and an innocent waif in a highly imaginary Limehouse, and his 1919 version, being played for every last tear by Richard Barthelmess and Lillian Gish, was a great success. In 1936 Griffith was assigned to do a British remake with Emlyn Williams and Dolly Haas, but he resigned during preparation and Hans (John) Brahm took over. By now the tale was too outmoded for popular success, but it was interestingly done in the arty manner.

Brolin, James (1940–). American leading man.
Take Her She's Mine 63. Goodbye Charlie 64. Von Ryan's Express 65. Morituri 65. Our Man Flint 67. The Boston Strangler 68. Short Walk to Daylight (TV) 72. Skyjacked 72. Westworld 73. Trapped (TV) 73. Class of 63 (TV) 73. *Gable and Lombard* (as Gable) 76. The Car 77. Steel Cowboy (TV) 78. The Amityville Horror 79. High Risk 81, Peewee's Big Adventure 85, etc.
TV series: *Marcus Welby M.D.* 69–75. Hotel 83–.

Bromberg, J. Edward (1903–1951). Plump, wide-eyed Hungarian actor, in America from infancy; usually in gentle roles.
□Under Two Flags 36. Sins of Man 36. The Crime of Dr Forbes 36. Girls' Dormitory 36. Star for a Night 36. Ladies in Love 36. Reunion 36. Stowaway 36. Fair Warning 37. That I May Live 37. Seventh Heaven 37. Charlie Chan on Broadway 37. Second Honeymoon 37. Mr Moto Takes a Chance 37. The Baroness and the Butler 38. One Wild Night 38. Four Men and a Prayer 38. Sally, Irene and Mary 38. Rebecca of Sunnybrook Farm 38. I'll Give a Million 38. *Suez* 38. Jesse James 39. Wife, Husband and Friend 39. *Hollywood Cavalcade* 39. Three Sons 39. Strange Cargo 40. The Return of Frank James 40. *The Mark of Zorro* 40. Hurricane Smith 41. Dance Hall 41. The Devil Pays Off 41. Pacific Blackout 42. Invisible Agent 42. Life Begins at 8.30 42. Tennessee Johnson 42. Reunion in France 42. Halfway to Shanghai 42. Lady of Burlesque 43. Phantom of the Opera 43. Son of Dracula 43. Chip Off the Old Block 44. Voice in the Wind 44. Easy to Look At 45. The Missing Corpse 45. Pillow of Death 45. Salome Where She Danced 45. The Walls Came Tumbling Down 46. Tangier 46. Cloak and Dagger 46. Queen of the Amazons 47. Arch of Triumph 48. *A Song Is Born* 48. I Shot Jesse James 49. Guilty Bystander 50.

Bromberger, Hervé (1918–). French director.
Identité Judiciaire 51. Les Fruits Sauvages 54. Les Loups dans la Bergerie 60. Mort Où Est Ta Victoire? 64, etc.

Bromfield, John (1922–) (Farron Bromfield). American second lead; leading man of second features.
Harpoon 48. Rope of Sand 49. Paid in Full 50. The Furies 50. Flat Top 52. Easy to Love 53. Ring of Fear 53. Crime Against Joe 55. Manfish 56. Hot Cars 57, etc.

TV series: Sheriff of Cochise 56–57. U.S. Marshal 58–59.

Bromfield, Louis (1896–1956). American popular novelist. *The Rains Came* was twice filmed; *Mrs Parkington* once. *It All Came True* and *Johnny Vagabond* were both taken from Bromfield stories.

Bromiley, Dorothy (1935–). British leading lady of very few films.
The Girls of Pleasure Island (US) 53. It's Great to be Young 55. A Touch of the Sun 56. The Criminal 60, etc.

Bron, Eleanor (1934–). Bloomsburyish British TV revue actress.
Help 65. Alfie 66. Two for the Road 67. Women in Love 69, etc.

Bronson, Betty (1906–1971) (Elizabeth Bronson). Lively American leading lady of the twenties; did not succeed in talkies.
Peter Pan (title role) 24. The Golden Princess 25. Are Parents People? 25. A Kiss for Cinderella 26. *Ben Hur* 26. The Cat's Pajamas 26. Everybody's Acting 27. Brass Knuckles 27. *The Singing Fool* 28. Companionate Marriage 28. Sonny Boy 29. The Locked Door 29. Medicine Man 30. The Yodelling Kid from Pine Ridge 37. Who's Got the Action? 62. Blackbeard's Ghost 67. Evel Knievel 71, etc.

Bronson, Charles (1922–) (Charles Buchinski). Sombre-looking, deep-featured American character actor who can deal with a variety of types from Russian to Red Indian, from villainous to sturdily heroic. At the age of fifty he suddenly became a star.
You're In the Navy Now 51. Pat and Mike 52. House of Wax 53. Apache 54. *Drumbeat* 54. Vera Cruz 54. Target Zero 55. Jubal 56. Run of the Arrow 57. Machine Gun Kelly 57. When Hell Broke Loose 58. Never so Few 59. *The Magnificent Seven* 60. A Thunder of Drums 61. Lonely are the Brave 62. The Great Escape 63. The Sandpiper 65. Battle of the Bulge 65. This Property is Condemned 66. *The Dirty Dozen* 67. Guns for San Sebastian 68. Adieu l'Ami 68. Once Upon a Time in the West 69. Rider in the Rain 69. Twinky 69. Violent City (It.) 70. You Can't Win Them All 70. Cold Sweat 71. *Chato's Land* 72. The Mechanic 72. *The Valachi Papers* 72. Wild Horses 73. The Stone Killer 73. Mr Majestyk 74. *Death Wish* 74. Breakout 75. *Hard Times* 75. Breakheart Pass 76. From Noon Till Three 76. St Ives 76. Raid on Entebbe (TV) 76. Telefon 77. The White Buffalo 77. Love and Bullets 79. Cabo Blanco 80. Borderline 80. Death Hunt 81. Death Wish II 82. Ten to Midnight 83. The Evil that Men Do 84. Death Wish III 85. Assassination 86. Death Wish IV 87, many others.
TV series: Man with a Camera 58–59. Redigo 63. The Travels of Jamie McPheeters 64.

¶ *C.B.:* Someday I'd like a part where I can lean my elbow against a mantelpiece and have a cocktail.

C.B.: I guess I look like a rock quarry that someone has dynamited.

C.B.: Acting is the easiest thing I've ever done. I guess that's why I'm stuck with it.

Bronson, Lillian (1902–). American character actress.
Happy Land 43. A Tree Grows in Brooklyn 44. The Hucksters 47. The Next Voice You Hear 51. Walk on the Wild Side 62. The Americanization of Emily 64, many others.

Bronston, Samuel (1910–). American independent producer who in 1959 set up a studio in Madrid and made several international epics but ran into financial difficulty.
Jack London 43. A Walk in the Sun 46. John Paul Jones 59. King of Kings 60. El Cid 61. Fifty Five Days at Peking 62. The Fall of the Roman Empire 64. Circus World 64. Savage Pampas (co-p) 66, etc.

Brontë, Charlotte (1816–1855). British novelist whose *Jane Eyre* has been frequently filmed, most recently in 1934 with Virginia Bruce and Colin Clive, in 1944 with Joan Fontaine and Orson Welles, and in 1971 with Susannah York and George C. Scott. Its central situation, of a governess in the house of a mysterious but romantic tyrant, has also been frequently plagiarized.

Brontë, Emily (1818–1848). British novelist, sister of Charlotte Brontë, and author of *Wuthering Heights* (qv), much filmed in Britain before the definitive 1939 version. A somewhat romantic film about the sisters was filmed in 1943 under the title *Devotion*, with Olivia de Havilland as Charlotte and Ida Lupino as Emily.

Brook, Clive (1887–1974) (Clifford Brook). Distinguished British leading man of stage and screen, for forty years the perfect gentleman (with very occasional caddish lapses). Popular in Hollywood in the twenties and early thirties.

□ A Debt of Honour 19. Trent's Last Case 20. Kissing Cup's Race 20. Her Penalty 20. The Loudwater Mystery 21. Daniel Deronda 21. A Sportsman's Wife 21. Sonia 21. Christie Johnstone 21. Woman to Woman 21. Through Fire and Water 22. This Freedom 22. Out to Win 22. The Reverse of the Medal 23. The Royal Oak 23. The Money Habit 24. The White Sheik 24. Recoil 24. The Wine of Life 24. The Passionate Adventure 24. Human Desires 24. Christine of the Hungry Heart 24. The Mirage 24. When Love Grows Cold 25. Enticement 25. The Social Exile 25. Playing With Souls 25. If Marriage Fails 25. The Woman Hater 25. Compromise 25. Seven Sinners 25. The Home Maker 25. The Pleasure Buyers 25. Three Faces East 26. Why Girls Go Back Home 26. For Alimony Only 26. You Never Know Women 26. The Popular Sin 26. Afraid to Love 27. Barbed Wire 27. *Underworld* 27. Hula 27. The Devil Dancer 27. French Dressing 27. Midnight Madness 28. The Yellow Lily 28. The Perfect Crime 28. Forgotten Faces 28. Interference 29. A Dangerous Woman 29. *The Four Feathers* 29. Charming Sinners 29. The Return of Sherlock Holmes 29. The Laughing Lady 29. Slightly Scarlet 30. Paramount on Parade 30. Sweethearts and Wives 30. Anybody's Woman 30. Scandal Sheet 31. East Lynne 31. Tarnished Lady 31. The Lawyer's Secret 31. Silence 31. Twenty Four Hours 31. Husband's Holiday 31. *Shanghai Express* 32. The Man from Yesterday 32. The Night of June 13th 32. *Sherlock Holmes* 32. Make Me a Star 32. *Cavalcade* 33. Midnight Club 33. Gallant Lady 33. If I Were Free 34. Where Sinners Meet 34. Let's Try Again 34. The Love Affair of the Dictator 35. Dressed to Thrill 35. The Lonely Road 36. Love in Exile 36. *Action for Slander* 37. The Ware Case 38. *Return to Yesterday* 40. Convoy 40. Freedom Radio 41. Breach of Promise 41. The Flemish Farm 43. Shipbuilders 43. *On Approval* 44 (also d). The List of Adrian Messenger 63.

¶ *C.B. 1933:* Hollywood is a chain gang and we lose the will to escape. The links of the chain are forged not with cruelties but with luxuries.

Brook, Faith (1922–). British actress of stage, screen and TV; daughter of Clive Brook.
Jungle Book 42. Uneasy Terms 48. Wicked as They Come 56. Chase a Crooked Shadow 57. The Thirty-nine Steps 59. To Sir With Love 66. North Sea Hijack 80. The Sea Wolves 80. The Razor's Edge 83. Sins (TV) 86. The Two Mrs Grenvilles (TV) 86, etc.

Brook, Lesley (1916–). British leading lady of a few sentimental dramas of the forties.
The Vulture 37. Dead Men Tell No Tales 39. Rose of Tralee 41. Variety Jubilee 42. I'll Walk Beside You 43. The Trojan Brothers 46. House of Darkness 48, etc.

Brook, Lyndon (1926–). British actor of stage, screen and TV; son of Clive Brook.
Train of Events 49. The Purple Plain 54. Reach for the Sky 56. Innocent Sinners 58. Song Without End (US) 60. Invasion 66. Pope Joan 72, etc.

Brook, Sir Peter (1925–). British stage director whose film experiments have been largely unsuccessful.
□The Beggar's Opera 52. Moderato Cantabile 60. Lord of the Flies 63. The Marat-Sade 66. Tell Me Lies 67. King Lear 70. Meetings with Remarkable Men 77. Carmen 83.

¶ *P.B.:* We've had an enormous amount of trips into people's private visions. They're played out: it's exactly what's true of nudity, when you've seen one you've seen them all.

Brook-Jones, Elwyn (1911–1962). Thick-set British character actor usually seen in villainous roles.
Dangerous Moonlight 40. Tomorrow We Live 42. Odd Man Out 46. The Three Weird Sisters 48. I'll Get You For This 50. Beau Brummell 54. The Pure Hell of St Trinian's 61, etc.

Brooke, Hillary (1914–) (Beatrice Peterson). Statuesque, blonde American leading lady of forties co-features; on TV in the fifties in the much revived Abbott and Costello series.
New Faces of 1937. Eternally Yours 39. Unfinished Business 41. Sherlock Holmes and the Voice of Terror 42. Lady in the Dark 44. Practically Yours 44. Ministry of Fear 44. *The Woman in Green* 45. Road to Utopia 45. Strange Journey 46. Big Town 47. Big Town After Dark 47. Let's Live Again 48. Africa Screams 49. The Admiral was a Lady 50. Insurance Investigator 51. Confidence Girl 52. Abbott and Costello Meet Captain Kidd 52. Mexican Manhunt 53. Dragon's Gold 54. The House across the Lake (GB) 54. Bengazi 55. Spoilers of the Forest 57, many others.
TV series: My Little Margie 52–55. The Abbott and Costello Show 53–54.

Brooke-Taylor, Tim (1940–). British light comedian, one of the Goodies. Mostly on radio and TV.

Twelve Plus One 70. The Statue 70. Willy Wonka and the Chocolate Factory 70.

Brooks, Geraldine (1925–77) (Geraldine Stroock). Intense young American actress of the forties; never fulfilled her promise.
Possessed 47. *Cry Wolf* 47. The Younger Brothers 49. *The Reckless Moment* 49. Challenge for Lassie 50. Volcano 50. The Green Glove 52. Street of Sinners 56. Johnny Tiger 66, etc.
TV series: Faraday and Co. 73. The Dumplings 76.

Brooks, Hazel (1924–). American second lead of the mid-forties.
Body and Soul 47. Sleep My Love 48.

Brooks, James L. (–). American writer-director.
Terms of Endearment (AAw, AAd) 83. Broadcast News (w, d) 87.

Brooks, Jean (1921–). Stylish-looking American leading lady who worked briefly for RKO in the forties.
The Seventh Victim 43. The Leopard Man 43. The Falcon and the Co-Eds 44. Two O'Clock Courage 46. The Falcon's Alibi 46, etc.

Brooks, Leslie (1922–) (Leslie Gettman). American leading lady of the forties.
Undercover Agent 42. Nine Girls 44. Tonight and Every Night 45. The Cobra Strikes 48. Romance on the High Seas 48, etc.

Brooks, Louise (1906–85). American leading lady of the twenties who made her best films in Germany and remained an attractive critical enigma.
Autobiography 1982 (with Hollis Alpert): *Lulu in Hollywood.*
□The Street of Forgotten Men 25. The American Venus 26. A Social Celebrity 26. It's the Old Army Game 26. The Show Off 26. Just Another Blonde 26. Love 'em and Leave 'em 27. Evening Clothes 27. Rolled Stockings 27. The City Gone Wild 27. Now We're in the Air 27. *A Girl in Every Port* 28. *Beggars of Life* 28. *Pandora's Box* (Ger.) 29. The Canary Murder Case 29. *Diary of a Lost Girl* (Ger.) 30. Prix de Beauté (Fr.) 30. It Pays to Advertise 31. God's Gift to Women 31. Empty Saddles 36. When You're in Love 36. King of Gamblers 37. Overland Stage Raiders 38.

¶ 'Not one woman exerted more magic, not one had her genius of interpretation.'—*Ado Kyrou, 1957*

'Her favourite form of exercise was walking off a movie set, which she did with the insouciance of a little girl playing hopscotch.'—*Anita Loos*

Brooks, Mel (1926–) (Melvin Kaminsky). American writer-producer-director of offbeat comedies.
□The Producers 68. Putney Swope (a only) 69. The Twelve Chairs (also acted) 70. *Blazing Saddles* (also acted) 74. *Young Frankenstein* 74. Silent Movie (also acted) 76. High Anxiety (also acted) 78. The Muppet Movie (a only) 79. History of the World Part One (also acted) 81. To Be or Not to Be (p, a) 83. Spaceballs 87.

¶ If you got it, flaunt it.—*M.B.*

'When I write, I keep Tolstoy around because I want great limits. I want big thinking.'—*M.B.*

'The death of Hollywood is Mel Brooks and special effects. If Mel Brooks had come up in my time he wouldn't have qualified to be a busboy.'—*Joseph L. Mankiewicz*

Brooks, Phyllis (1914–) (Phyllis Weiler). Blonde American leading lady of co-features in the thirties and forties.
I've Been Around 34. McFadden's Flats 35. You Can't Have Everything 37. Rebecca of Sunnybrook Farm 38. Charlie Chan in Reno 39. Slightly Honourable 40. *The Shanghai Gesture* 41. Hi Ya Sailor 43. The Unseen 45. High Powered 45, etc.

Brooks, Rand (1918–). American leading man, usually in minor films.
Gone with the Wind 39. Florian 40. Son of Monte Cristo 41. Joan of Arc 47. The Steel Fist 52. Man from the Black Hills 56. Comanche Station 60. The Sex Symbol (TV) 74, etc.
TV series: Rin Tin Tin 54–56.

Brooks, Ray (1939–). British leading man with repertory experience.
HMS Defiant 62. Play it Cool 62. Some People 63. *The Knack* 65. Daleks Invasion Earth 2150 AD 66. Alice's Adventures in Wonderland 72. Tiffany Jones 73. House of Whipcord 74, etc.

Brooks, Richard (1912–). American writer-director whose reputation is somewhat higher than his films seem to justify. He wrote however one of the best novels about Hollywood, *The Producer.*
□White Savage (w only) 42. Cobra Woman (w only) 44. Swell Guy (w only) 46. The

Killers (co-w only) 46. Brute Force (w only) 47. Crossfire (oa only) 47. To the Victor (w only) 48. Key Largo (w only) 48. Any Number Can Play (w only) 49. *Crisis* 50. Mystery Street (w only) 50. Storm Warning (co-w only) 50. The Light Touch 51. Deadline 52. Battle Circus 52. The Last Time I Saw Paris (d only) 54. Take the High Ground (d only) 54. The Flame and the Flesh (d only) 54. *The Blackboard Jungle* 55. *The Last Hunt* 56. The Catered Affair (d only) 56. Something of Value 57. The Brothers Karamazov 58. Cat on a Hot Tin Roof 58. *Elmer Gantry* (AA w) 60. Sweet Bird of Youth 62. Lord Jim (& p) 65. The Professionals (& p) 66. *In Cold Blood* (& p) 67. The Happy Ending (& p) 70. Dollars (& p) 72. Bite The Bullet (& p) 75. Looking for Mr Goodbar 77. Wrong Is Right 82. Fever Pitch 85.

¶ 'Although most of his films display something of value on first viewing, none can take the high ground in retrospect.'—*Andrew Sarris,* 1968.

Brophy, Edward S. (1895–1960). American character actor, often a gangster or a very odd kind of valet: a rotund, cigar-chewing little man in a bowler hat, oddly likeable despite his pretence of toughness.
Those Three French Girls 30. *The Champ* 31. Freaks 32. What, No Beer? 33. *The Thin Man* 34. Death on the Diamond 34. Mad Love (miscast as a murderer) 35. Remember Last Night 35. Strike Me Pink 36. Kelly the Second 36. *A Slight Case of Murder* 37. You Can't Cheat an Honest Man 39. Calling Philo Vance 40. Buy Me That Town 41. All Through the Night 42. Broadway 42. Cover Girl 44. The Thin Man Goes Home 44. The Falcon in San Francisco (and series) 45. *Wonder Man* 45. It Happened on Fifth Avenue 47. *The Last Hurrah* 58, many others.

Brosnan, Pierce (1952–). Irish leading man of the matinée-idol type.
The Long Good Friday 80. The Manions of America (TV) 81. Nancy Astor (TV) 81. Nomads 85. The Fourth Protocol 86. Noble House (TV) 87. The Deceivers 88.
TV series: Remington Steele 82–.

¶ *P.B.:* I don't see myself as a hunk of the month.
'A new Cary Grant, sexy but suave, manly though mannered, with subtlety instead of slapstick.'—*People*

brothels were reasonably prominent in silent films, but the Hays Code banished them and for many years one had to look to the French for such revelations as were to be found in *Le Plaisir* and *Adua et sa Compagnie.* In the sixties, however, the doors opened. Comic Victorian brothels were shown in *The Assassination Bureau* and *The Best House in London*, and a French version in *Lady L. Ulysses* showed the Dublin version. *A House is not a Home* told the 'true' story of Polly Adler. The brothel in *The Balcony* was symbolic, in *House of a Thousand Dolls* fantastic, in *How Sweet It Is* charming, in *Games that Lovers Play* whimsical, in *The Last Detail* grimly realistic. *Walk on the Wild Side* concentrated on the depressing aspects and even sported a lesbian madam. Nowadays every western has one, notably *Waterhole Three, Five Card Stud, Hang 'em High, McCabe and Mrs Miller, Dirty Dingus Magee, The Cheyenne Social Club* and *The Ballad of Cable Hogue*; nor are police thrillers such as *Badge 343* complete without them.

Brother Orchid (US 1939). The virtual end of the thirties gangster cycle was marked by this warm comedy in which Edward G. Robinson plays a gangster who, left for dead after being 'taken for a ride', is cared for by monks and literally sees the light. Directed by Lloyd Bacon.

Brother Rat, a 1936 Broadway success by Fred Finklehoffe and John Monks Jnr, about fun and games at a military institute, was filmed in 1938 by William Keighley, with Ronald Reagan, Wayne Morris and Eddie Albert in the leads. A thin sequel, *Brother Rat and a Baby*, followed in 1940. The original play was remade in 1952 as *About Face*, with Gordon Macrae and Eddie Bracken.

The Brothers Karamazov. Dostoevsky's nineteenth-century novel of Russian family life was filmed by Dmitri Buchowetzki in Germany in 1921, with Emil Jannings; the same country produced the next version, *The Murder of Dmitri Karamazov,* in 1930, with Fritz Kortner under the direction of Fedor Ozep. In 1958 Richard Brooks made a Hollywood version with Yul Brynner, and the Russian director Pyriev completed a Russian film of the book in 1967.

Brough, Mary (1863–1934). British character comedienne usually seen as battleaxe or suspicious landlady, especially in the Aldwych farces. In films from 1914. The Amazing Quest of Ernest Bliss 20. Squibs Wins the Calcutta Sweep 22. A Sister to Assist 'Er 22 and 27. Dawn 28. *Rookery Nook* 30. On Approval 30. Tons of Money 31. Plunder 31. A Night Like This 32. Thark 32. *A Cuckoo in the Nest* 33. Up to the Neck 33. Turkey Time 33, etc.

Brown, Barry (1951–1978). American leading man who shot himself.
Flesh 68. Halls of Anger 70. Escape of the Birdmen (TV) 71. The Great Northfield Minnesota Raid 71. Bad Company 72. Daisy Miller 74. The Disappearance of Aimee (TV) 76. Piranha 78, etc.

Brown, Blair (1948–). American leading lady.
The Choirboys 77. Wheels (TV) 78. And I Alone Survived (TV) 78. The Child Stealer (TV) 79. Altered States 80. One Trick Pony 80. Continental Divide 81. Kennedy (TV) (as Jackie) 83. A Flash of Green 84.

Brown, Bryan (1947–). Australian leading actor.
Newsfront 79. Breaker Morant 79. The Chant of Jimmie Blacksmith 80. Winter of Our Dreams 81. A Town Like Alice (TV) 81. Far East 82. The Thorn Birds (TV) 83. Kim (TV) 83. Give my Regards to Broad Street 84. Parker 85. Eureka Stockade (TV) 85. The Empty Beach 85. F/X 85. Rebel 85. The Good Wife 86, Taipan 86. The Shiralee (TV) 87.

Brown, Charles D. (1887–1948). Bland-faced American character actor who played scores of detectives, officials and executives.
The Dance of Life 29. Murder by the Clock 31. The Woman I Stole 33. It Happened One Night 34. Thoroughbreds Don't Cry 37. Charlie Chan in Reno 39. The Grapes of Wrath 39. Fingers at the Window 42. Jam Session 44. The Killers 46. Merton of the Movies 47, many others.

Brown, Clarence (1890–). American director, with MGM and Garbo for many years; most at home with sentimental themes and busy pictorial values.
□The Great Redeemer 20. The Last of the Mohicans 20. The Light in the Dark 22. Don't Marry for Money 23. The Acquittal 23. The Signal Tower 24. Butterfly 24. Smouldering Fires 25. *The Eagle* 25. *The Goose Woman* 25. Kiki 26. *Flesh and the Devil* 26. Trail of 98 28. A Woman of Affairs 29. Wonder of Women 29. Navy Blues 29. *Anna Christie* 30. Romance 30. Inspiration 31. A Free Soul 31. Possessed 31. Emma 32. Letty Lynton 32. The Son Daughter 32. Looking Forward 33. Night Flight 33. Sadie McKee 34. Chained 34. *Anna Karenina* 35. *Ah Wilderness* 35. Wife versus Secretary 36. The Gorgeous Hussy 36. *Conquest* 37. Of Human Hearts 38. Idiot's Delight 38. *The Rains Came* 39. *Edison the Man* 40. Come Live with Me (& p) 41. They Met in Bombay 41. *The Human Comedy* (& p) 43. The White Cliffs of Dover 44. National Velvet 44. *The Yearling* 46. Song of Love (& p) 47. *Intruder in the Dust* (& p) 49. To Please a Lady (& p) 50. Angels in the Outfield (& p) 51. It's a Big Country (part) 51. When in Rome (& p) 51. Plymouth Adventure 52. Never Let Me Go (p only) 53.

'His career is not without a certain amiability in its evolution from German Expressionism to American Gothic.'—*Andrew Sarris, 1968*

❀ For persuading a commercially minded studio to let his films represent its cultural pretensions. *Intruder in the Dust.*

Brown, David (1916–). American producer, a New York journalist who became story editor at Fox and later joined Richard Zanuck in Zanuck-Brown, which made *The Sting* and *Jaws*.

Brown, Ed (–). American cinematographer.
The Hot Rock 72. Lovin' Molly 74. The Education of Sonny Carson 74, etc.

Brown, George H. (1913–). British producer, former production manager.
Sleeping Car to Trieste 48. The Chiltern Hundreds 50. The Seekers 54. Jacqueline 56. Dangerous Exile 57. Tommy the Toreador 60. Murder at the Gallop 63. Guns at Batasi 64. The Trap 66. Finders Keepers 66. Assault 70. Revenge 71. Innocent Bystanders 72. Open Season 74, etc.

Brown, George Sanford (1943–). Black American character actor.
The Comedians 67. Dayton's Devils 68. Bullitt 68. The Forbin Project 70. The Man 72. Wild in the Sky 72. Roots (TV) 77, The Night the City Screamed (TV) 80. In Defense of Kids (TV) 83. The Jesse Owens Story (TV) 84, etc.
TV series: The Rookies 72–74.

Brown, Georgia (1933–) (Georgia Klot). British cabaret songstress in occasional films.

The Fixer 67. Lock Up Your Daughters 69. The Raging Moon 71. Nothing but the Night 73. The Bawdy Adventures of Tom Jones 76. The Seven Per Cent Solution 77.

Brown, Harry (1917–86). American novelist and screenwriter, mainly on war themes.
The True Glory (co-w) 45. A Walk in the Sun (oa) 46. Arch of Triumph 48. Sands of Iwo Jima 49. A Place in the Sun (co-w) 51. Bugles in the Afternoon 52. The Sniper (co-w) 52. Eight Iron Men 52. All the Brothers Were Valiant (co-w) 53. D-Day Sixth of June (co-w) 56. Between Heaven and Hell (co-w) 57. El Dorado (oa) 66, etc.

Brown, Harry Joe (1892–1972). American producer with long experience in all branches of show business; latterly concentrated on Randolph Scott westerns.
Parade of the West (d only) 30. Madison Square Garden (d only) 32. Sitting Pretty (d only) 33. Captain Blood 35. Alexander's Ragtime Band 38. The Rains Came 39. Young People 40. Western Union 41. *Knickerbocker Holiday* (& d) 44. Gunfighters 47. Fortunes of Captain Blood 50. Hangman's Knot 52. Three Hours to Kill 54. Screaming Mimi 58. Ride Lonesome 59, many others.

Brown, James (1920–). Stalwart American supporting actor, in many westerns of the forties and fifties.
The Forest Rangers 42. Corvette K225 44. Objective Burma 45. The Fabulous Texan 47. Sands of Iwo Jima 50. Springfield Rifle 52. The Woman They Almost Lynched 53. A Star Is Born 54. The Police Dog Story 61. Irma La Douce 63. Town Tamer 65. Whiffs 75. Mean Johnny Barrows 76, etc.
TV series: Rin Tin Tin 54–56.

Brown, Jim (1936–). Black American leading man, former athlete.
□Rio Conchos 64. The Dirty Dozen 67. Dark of the Sun 68. The Split 68. Ice Station Zebra 68. Riot 68. *100 Rifles* 69. Tick Tick Tick 70. The Grasshopper 70. El Condor 70. Kenner 71. Black Gunn 72. Slaughter 72. Slaughter's Big Rip-off 73. I Escaped from Devil's Island 73. The Slams 74. Three the Hard Way 74. Take a Hard Ride 75. Kid Vengeance 77. Fingers 78. One Down Two to Go 81. Pacific Inferno 84.

Brown, Joe (1941–). Amiable British pop singer, in occasional films.
What a Crazy World 63. Three Hats for Lisa 65, etc.

Brown, Joe E. (1892–1973). Wide-mouthed American star comedian of the thirties, with background in circus, vaudeville and basketball.
Autobiography 1956: *Laughter is a Wonderful Thing*.
□ Crooks Can't Wait 28. Me, Gangster 28. Road House 28. Dressed to Kill 28. The Circus Kid 28. Hit of the Show 28. Take Me Home 28. Burlesque 28. Don't Be Jealous 28. In Old Arizona 29. Sunny Side Up 29. Molly and Me 29. *Sally* 29. My Lady's Past 29. On with the Show 29. Painted Faces 29. The Cockeyed World 29. The Ghost Talks 29. Protection 29. Up the River 30. Maybe It's Love 30. Song of the West 30. Born Reckless 30. City Girl 30. Hold Everything 30. The Lottery Bride 30. Top Speed 30. Going Wild 31. Local Boy Makes Good 31. Broadminded 31. Sit Tight 31. *The Tenderfoot* 32. Fireman Save My Child 32. *You Said a Mouthful* 32. Elmer the Great 32. Son of a Sailor 32. The Circus Clown 34. Six Day Bike Rider 34. A Very Honourable Guy 34. *A Midsummer Night's Dream* 35. Alibi Ike 35. *Bright Lights* 36. Polo Joe 36. Sons of Guns 36. Earthworm Tractors 36. Fit for a King 37. When's Your Birthday 37. Flirting with Fate 38. The Gladiator 38. Wide Open Faces 38. Beware Spooks 39. One Thousand Dollars a Touchdown 39. So you won't Talk 40. Shut my Big Mouth 42. The Daring Young Man 42. Joan of Ozark 42. Chatterbox 43. Pin Up Girl 44. Hollywood Canteen 44. Casanova in Burlesque 44. *The Tender Years* 49. *Showboat* 51. Around the World in 80 Days 56. *Some Like It Hot* 59. A Comedy of Terrors 63. It's a Mad Mad Mad Mad World 63.

Brown, John (or **Johnny**) **Mack** (1904–1974). American leading man of the thirties, former football star.
The Bugle Call 26. The Divine Woman 27. *Our Dancing Daughters* 28. Coquette 29. Jazz Heaven 29. *Billy the Kid* 30. The Secret Six 31. *The Last Flight* 31. Saturday's Millions 33. Female 33. Belle of the Nineties 34. Riding the Apache Trail 36. Wells Fargo 37. Bad Man from Red Butte 40. Ride 'Em Cowboy 41. The Right to Live 45. Stampede 49. Short Grass 50. The Bounty Killer 65. Apache Uprising 65, many others.

Brown, John Moulder: see *Moulder Brown, John*

Brown, Karl (1897–). American cinematographer of the twenties; retired early.
Autobiography 1976: *Adventures with D. W. Griffith*.

The Birth of a Nation (2nd unit) 15. The Fourteenth Man 20. Gasoline Gus 21. The Dictator 22. *The Covered Wagon* 23. Ruggles of Red Gap 23. Merton of the Movies 24. Beggar on Horseback 25. *Pony Express* 25. Mannequin 26, etc.

Brown, Nacio Herb (1896–1964). American light composer who usually supplied the music for Arthur Freed's lyrics: 'Broadway Melody', 'Singin' in the Rain', 'Good Morning', 'You Are My Lucky Star', many others.

Brown, Pamela (1917–1975). British stage actress in occasional films, usually in haughty or eccentric roles.
One of Our Aircraft is Missing 42. *I Know Where I'm Going* 45. Tales of Hoffman 51. The Second Mrs Tanqueray 52. Personal Affair 53. Richard III 56. The Scapegoat 59. Becket 64. Secret Ceremony 68. Wuthering Heights 70. On a Clear Day You Can See Forever 70. Lady Caroline Lamb 72. Dracula (TV) 73, etc.

Brown, Phil (1916–). American second lead, usually in diffident roles; moved to Europe in 1950.
I Wanted Wings 41. Calling Dr Gillespie 42. The Impatient Years 44. Without Reservations 46. The Killers 46. If You Knew Susie 48. Moonrise 49. *Obsession* 50. The Green Scarf 54. Camp on Blood Island 58. The Bedford Incident 65. Tropic of Cancer 69, etc.

Brown, Robert (c. 1918–). Burly British actor of stage, TV and film.
Helen of Troy 55. A Hill in Korea 56. Campbell's Kingdom 57. Ben Hur 59. Sink the Bismarck 60. The Masque of the Red Death 64. One Million Years BC 66. Private Road 71.
TV series: Ivanhoe 57.

Brown, Rowland (1901–1963). American director whose career waned curiously after a promising start.
□*Quick Millions* 31. Hell's Highway 32. Blood Money 33. The Devil is a Sissy (co-w only) 37.

Brown, Tom (1913–). American juvenile lead of the thirties; the 'boy next door' type. Re-emerged in the sixties as one of the villagers in the long-running TV series *Gunsmoke*.
The Hoosier Schoolmaster 24. The Lady Lies 29. Queen High 30. *Tom Brown of Culver* 32. Three Cornered Moon 33. Judge Priest 34. Anne of Green Gables 34. *Freckles* 35. I'd Give My Life 36. Maytime 37. In Old Chicago 38. Duke of West Point 38. Sergeant Madden 39. Sandy is a Lady 40. The Pay Off 43. The House on 92nd Street 45. Buck Privates Come Home 47. Duke of Chicago 49. The Quiet Gun 57, many others.

Brown, Vanessa (1928–) (Smylla Brind). American juvenile leading lady of a few late forties films; usually demure.
Margie 46. *The Late George Apley* 47. Mother Wore Tights 47. The Foxes of Harrow 47. The Heiress 49. Tarzan and the Slave Girl 50. The Bad and the Beautiful 52. Rosie 68. Bless the Beasts and Children 71. The Witch Who Came from the Sea 76, etc.
TV series: My Favourite Husband 54.

Brown, Wally (1898–1961). American comedian, a fast-talking vaudevillian who teamed with Alan Carney (qv) in a few comedy second features of the forties.
Adventures of a Rookie 44. Rookies in Burma 44. Step Lively 44. Zombies on Broadway 45. Genius at Work 45. As Young As You Feel 51. The High and the Mighty 54. The Absent-minded Professor 61, etc.
TV series: Cimarron City 58.

Browne, Coral (1913–). Australian stage actress long in Britain, usually in worldly comedy roles; films few.
The Amateur Gentleman 36. Black Limelight 38. Let George Do It 40. Piccadilly Incident 46. *Auntie Mame* (US) 58. The Roman Spring of Mrs Stone 61. Dr Crippen 64. *The Killing of Sister George* 68. Theatre of Blood 73. The Drowning Pool 75. An Englishman Abroad (TV) 83. American Dreamer 84. Dreamchild 85, etc.
TV series: Time Express 79.

Browne, Irene (1891–1965). British stage actress, usually in dignified roles; films few.
The Letter 29. Cavalcade 33. Berkeley Square 33. The Amateur Gentleman 36. Pygmalion 38. The Prime Minister 40. *Quartet* 48. Madeleine 50. All at Sea 57. Rooney 58, etc.

Browne, Roscoe Lee (1925–). Black American character actor.
Topaz 69. *The Liberation of L. B. Jones* 70. The Cowboys 72. Cisco Pike 72. Superfly Two 73. Logan's Run 76. Twilight's Last Gleaming 77. Nothing Personal 80. Jumpin' Jack Flash 86, etc.

Browning, Ricou (1930–). American diver and stunt man who became a specialist in underwater direction for Ivan Tors.
The Creature from the Black Lagoon (also played title role) 54. Flipper 63. Around the World Under the Sea 66. Lady in Cement 68, etc.

Browning, Tod (1882–1962). American director remembered chiefly for his horror films of the twenties and early thirties; revaluation has made them less striking than once was thought.
The Brazen Beauty 18. The Virgin of Stamboul 20. Under Two Flags 22. The White Tiger 23. The Unholy Three 25. The Mystic (& w) 25. The Unknown 27. *London After Midnight* 27. West of Zanzibar 28. Where East is East 29. The Thirteenth Chair 29. The Unholy Three (sound remake) 30. *Dracula* 30. Iron Man 31. *Freaks* 32. Fast Workers 33. Mark of the Vampire 35. *The Devil Doll* 36. Miracles for Sale 39, etc.

Brownlow, Kevin (1938–). British producer-director who made his first film, *It Happened Here*, on a shoestring budget over seven years. It was released in 1966. Published 1969 *The Parade's Gone By*, a collection of interviews with silent movie stars. His 1975 film *Winstanley* was a clever but cheerless historical reconstruction; his 1979 book *The War, The West and The Wilderness* was another classic tome of research into silent filming.
TV series: *Hollywood* 79.

Bruce, Brenda (1918–). British stage, TV and occasionally screen actress.
Millions Like Us 43. They Came to a City 45. Piccadilly Incident 46. My Brother's Keeper 48. Marry Me 52. The Final Test 53. Law and Disorder 57. Nightmare 63. The Uncle 65, etc.

Bruce, David (1914–1976) (Marden McBroom). American light leading man familiar in Universal films during World War II.
The Sea Hawk 40. Singapore Woman 42. The Mad Ghoul 43. Ladies Courageous 44. Christmas Holiday 44. Can't Help Singing 44. Salome Where She Danced 45. Lady on a Train 45. Prejudice 48. Masterson of Kansas 55, etc.
TV series: Beulah 52.

Bruce, George (1898–). American screenwriter.
Navy Blue and Gold 37. The Crowd Roars 38. The Duke of West Point 38. The Man in the Iron Mask 39. Son of Monte Cristo 40. South of Pago Pago 40. The Corsican Brothers 41. Miss Annie Rooney 42. Stand By for Action 43. Salute to the Marines 43. Two Years Before the Mast 46. Killer McCoy 47. Walk a Crooked Mile 48. Rogues of Sherwood Forest 50. Lorna Doone 51. Valentino 51. Kansas City Confidential 53. Solomon and Sheba 59, many others.

Bruce, Lenny (1926–66) (Leonard Alfred Schneider). Dirty-talking American nightclub comedian, a nine-day wonder who was impersonated on film by Dustin Hoffman in *Lenny*.

¶ 'Lenny, despite what his cultists and the Hoffman movie said, was dirty and sick. He had no redeeming social values.'—*James Bacon*

Bruce, Nigel (1895–1953). Tubby British comedy actor, mainly in Hollywood from 1934; usually played well-meaning upper class buffoons, and was the screen's most memorable Dr Watson.
□ Red Aces 29. Birds of Prey 30. The Squeaker 31. Escape 31. The Calendar 31. Lord Camber's Ladies 32. The Midshipmaid 32. Channel Crossing 32. I Was a Spy 33. Springtime for Henry 34. Stand Up and Cheer 34. Coming Out Party 34. Murder in Trinidad 34. The Lady is Willing 34. Treasure Island 34. The Scarlet Pimpernel 35. *Becky Sharp* 35. Jalna 35. *She* 35. The Man Who Broke the Bank at Monte Carlo 35. The Trail of the Lonesome Pine 36. Under Two Flags 36. The White Angel 36. The Charge of the Light Brigade 36. Follow your Heart 36. Make Way for a Lady 36. The Man I Married 36. Thunder in the City 37. The Last of Mrs Cheyney 37. The Baroness and the Butler 38. Kidnapped 38. Suez 38. *The Hound of the Baskervilles* 39. The Adventures of Sherlock Holmes 39. The Rains Came 39. *Rebecca* 40. Adventure in Diamonds 40. *The Bluebird* 40. Susan and God 40. Lillian Russell 40. A Dispatch from Reuters 40. Hudson's Bay 40. Playgirl 41. Free and Easy 41. The Chocolate Soldier 41. This Woman is Mine 41. Suspicion 41. Roxie Hart 42. This Above All 42. Eagle Squadron 42. Sherlock Holmes and the Voice of Terror 42. Sherlock Holmes and the Secret Weapon 42. Journey for Margaret 42. Sherlock Holmes in Washington 43. Crazy House (cameo) 43. Forever and a Day 43. Lassie Come Home 43. Sherlock Holmes Faces Death 43. Follow the Boys 44. The

Pearl of Death 44. Spider Woman 44. Gypsy Wildcat 44. *The Scarlet Claw* 44. *Frenchman's Creek* 44. Son of Lassie 45. *House of Fear* 45. The Corn is Green 45. The Woman in Green 45. Pursuit to Algiers 45. Terror by Night 46. Dressed to Kill 46. The Two Mrs Carrolls 47. The Exile 47. Julia Misbehaves 48. Vendetta 50. Savage Drums 51. Hong Kong 51. Bwana Devil 53. *Limelight* 53. World for Ransom 53.
❁For regrettably but amusingly fixing the image of the upper class English dodderer. *Rebecca*.

Bruce, Virginia (1910–1982) (Helen Virginia Briggs). American light leading lady of the thirties.
Woman Trap 29. The Love Parade 29. Safety in Numbers 30. Hell Divers 31. The Wet Parade 32. Kongo 32. *Jane Eyre* (title role) 34. Dangerous Corner 34. Escapade 35. Metropolitan 35. The Great Ziegfeld 36. Born to Dance 36. Between Two Women 37. Arsène Lupin Returns 38. Yellow Jack 38. Society Lawyer 39. Flight Angels 40. Invisible Woman 41. Pardon My Sarong 42. Careful Soft Shoulders 42. Action in Arabia 44. Love Honour and Goodbye 45. Night has a Thousand Eyes 48. The Reluctant Bride (GB) 52. Strangers When We Meet 60, many others.

Bruckman, Clyde (1895–1955). American writer-director of many silent comedies; especially associated with Keaton, Lloyd and Fields.
Sherlock Jnr (w) 24. *The Navigator* (w) 24. *The General* (wd) 27. *Feet First* (wd) 30. *Movie Crazy* (d) 32. The Man on the Flying Trapeze (d) 35, many others.

Brummell, Beau (1778–1840). A famous British dandy and politician who has been the subject of two biopics: in 1924 with John Barrymore (directed by Harry Beaumont) and in 1954 with Stewart Granger (directed by Curtis Bernhardt).

Brunel, Adrian (1892–1958). British director with pleasant reputation in the twenties as an intellectual at large. Autobiography 1952: *Nice Work*.
Bookworms (short) 21. The Bump (short) 23. *The Man Without Desire* 23. Crossing the Great Sagrada (short) 24. *Blighty* 27. *The Constant Nymph* 27. The Vortex 28. While Parents Sleep 35. The City of Beautiful Nonsense 26. Prison Breaker 36. The Lion Has Wings 39. The Girl Who Forgot 40, etc.

Brunius, Jacques (1906–1967). French actor, once critic and assistant to Clair and Renoir; later resident in Britain.
L'Age d'Or 30. Partie de Campagne 37. Sea Devils 53. To Paris with Love 55. Orders to Kill 58, etc.

Bruns, George (1913–1983). American composer whose film scores were almost all for Disney.

Brute Force (US 1947). A confected, violent but harrowingly exciting prison melodrama which marked Jules Dassin's debut as a notable director. Photographed by William Daniels, written by Richard Brooks, with powerful performances by Burt Lancaster, Charles Bickford and Hume Cronyn.

Bryan, Dora (1923–) (Dora Broadbent). British stage and film comedienne, specializing in warm-hearted tarts of the cockney or northern variety.
Odd Man Out 46. The Fallen Idol 48. The Cure for Love 48. The Blue Lamp 50. High Treason 51. Lady Godiva Rides Again 51. Mother Riley Meets the Vampire 52. Time Gentlemen Please 53. Fast and Loose 54. See How They Run 55. Cockleshell Heroes 56. The Green Man 57. Desert Mice 59. The Night We Got the Bird 60. *A Taste of Honey* (BFA: leading role) 61. The Great St Trinian's Train Robbery 66. The Sandwich Man 66. Two a Penny 68. Hands of the Ripper 71. Up the Front 72, etc.

Bryan, Jane (1918–) (Jane O'Brien). Sympathetic American leading lady of the later thirties.
□The Case of the Black Cat 36. Marked Woman 37. Kid Galahad 37. Confession 37. A Slight Case of Murder 38. *The Sisters* 38. Girls on Probation 38. Brother Rat 38. Each Dawn I Die 39. The Old Maid 39. These Glamour Girls 39. *We are not Alone* 39. Invisible Stripes 40. Brother Rat and a Baby 40.

Bryan, John (1911–1969). British producer and production designer.
Great Expectations (des) (AA) 46. Pandora and the Flying Dutchman (des) 51. *The Card* 52. The Purple Plain 54. The Spanish Gardener (& w) 56. Windom's Way 57. The Horse's Mouth 58. There Was a Crooked Man 60. Tamahine 62. After the Fox 66. The Touchables 68, etc.

Bryant, Michael (1928–). Serious-looking British character actor of stage and TV; films occasional.
Life for Ruth 62. The Mindbenders 63. Goodbye Mr Chips 69. Nicholas and Alexandra (as Lenin) 71. Gandhi 81, etc.

Bryant, Nana (1888–1955). Dignified but friendly American character actress who usually played middle-class mums or rich patrons.
A Feather in Her Hat 35. Theodora Goes Wild 36. Mad About Music 38. Espionage Agent 39. Nice Girl 41. Calling Dr Gillespie 42. The Song of Bernadette 43. Brewster's Millions 45. The Unsuspected 47. Harvey 50. Bright Victory 51. About Mrs Leslie 54. The Private War of Major Benson 55, many others.

Brynner, Yul (1915–85) (Youl Bryner). Bald-headed international star of somewhat mysterious background: variously alleged to have originated in Switzerland and Russia, but assuredly American by adoption. A Broadway stage success, especially as the king in *The King and I*: long dominant in films though not easy to cast.
□Port of New York 49. *The King and I* (AA) 56. The Ten Commandments 56. *Anastasia* 56. *The Brothers Karamazov* 58. The Buccaneer 58. The Journey 58. The Sound and the Fury 59. Solomon and Sheba 59. Once More with Feeling 60. Surprise Package 60. *The Magnificent Seven* 60. The Testament of Orpheus 60. Escape from Zahrain 62. *Taras Bulba* 62. Kings of the Sun 63. Flight from Ashiya 64. *Invitation to a Gunfighter* 64. The Saboteur 65. Cast a Giant Shadow 66. Return of the Seven 66. The Poppy is also a Flower 66. Triple Cross 66. The Double Man 67. The Long Duel 67. Villa Rides 68. The Madwoman of Chaillot 69. The File of the Golden Goose 69. The Battle of Neretva 70. Indio Sabata 70. The Magic Christian 70. The Light at the Edge of the World 71. Romance of a Horsethief 71. Adios Sabata 71. Catlow 72. Fuzz 72. The Serpent 72. Westworld 73. The Ultimate Warrior 74. Futureworld 76. Anger in his Eyes (Italian) 76.
TV series: *Anna and the King* 72.
❁ For proving that bald is beautiful at the box-office. *The Magnificent Seven.*
¶ *Y.B.:* People don't know my real self and they're not about to find out.

B.S.C. British Society of Cinematographers, a professional society founded in the fifties, similar in aims to the A.S.C. (qv).

Buchan, John (1875–1940). British adventure novelist oddly neglected by the cinema apart from *The Thirty-nine Steps*, no version of which bears much resemblance to the original; and a 1927 version of *Huntingtower*.

Buchanan, Edgar (1902–79). Jovial American character actor, in innumerable westerns and rustic dramas as hayseed, crooked judge, comic side-kick or straight villain.
My Son is Guilty 39. Arizona 40. The Richest Man in Town 41. The Desperados 42. Destroyer 43. Buffalo Bill 44. The Fighting Guardsman 45. Abilene Town 46. Framed 47. The Black Arrow 48. The Best Man Wins 48. Red Canyon 49. Devil's Doorway 50. The Great Missouri Raid 51. The Big Trees 52. Shane 53. Human Desire 54. Day of the Badman 57. The Sheepman 58. Edge of Eternity 60. Cimarron 61. Ride the High Country 62. McLintock 63. The Rounders 65. Welcome to Hard Times 67. Benji 75, many others.
TV series: Hopalong Cassidy 51–52. Judge Roy Bean 53. Petticoat Junction 63–69. Cade's County 71.

Buchanan, Jack (1891–1957). Debonair British entertainer, a memorable song-and-dance man of stage and screen in the twenties and thirties: good-looking, long-legged, nasal of voice and debonair in appearance.
Biography 1978: *Top Hat and Tails* by Michael Marshall.
□Bulldog Drummond's Third Round 25. Happy Landing 25. Toni 27. Confetti 28. Paris 29. Show of Shows 29. *Monte Carlo* 30. Goodnight Vienna 32. A Man of Mayfair 32. *Yes Mr Brown* 32. Magic Night 32. *Brewster's Millions* 33. That's a Good Girl 33. That Girl 34. Come out of the Pantry 35. Sons o'Guns 35. When Knights were Bold 36. Limelight 36. Smash and Grab 37. Break the News 37. This'll Make You Whistle 37. The Sky's the Limit 38. *The Gang's All Here* 39. Alias the Bulldog 39. The Middle Watch 39. Bulldog Sees it Through 40. *The Band Wagon* 53. As Long as They're Happy 53. Josephine and Men 55. The Diary of Major Thompson 56.

Buchholz, Horst (1933–). German leading man, in occasional international films.
Marianne de Ma Jeunesse (debut) 54. Himmel Ohne Sterne 55. King in Shadow 56. The Confessions of Felix Krull 57. Resurrection 58. *Tiger Bay* 59. *The Magnificent Seven* 60. Fanny 61. *One Two*

Three 61. Nine Hours to Rama 63. The Empty Canvas 64. Marco the Magnificent 65. That Man in Istanbul 66. Cervantes 66. L'Astragale 68. The Great Waltz 72. The Catamount Killing 75. Raid on Entebbe (TV) 77. Avalanche Express 79, etc.

Buchman, Sidney (1902–1975). American writer-producer of good commercial films.
Matinée Ladies (oa) 27. *The Sign of the Cross* (co-w) 32. I'll Love You Always (w) 35. The King Steps Out (w) 36. *Theodora Goes Wild* (w) 36. *Mr Smith Goes to Washington* (w) 39. The Howards of Virginia (w) 40. *Here Comes Mr Jordan* (w) (AA) 41. *The Talk of the Town* (w) 42. *A Song to Remember* (wp) 45. Over 21 (p) 45. Jolson Sings Again (wp) 49. Saturday's Hero (w) 51. Cleopatra (w) 63. *The Group* (wp) 66, many others.

Buck, Frank (1888–1950). American explorer who made several animal films. Appeared in *Africa Screams* 50.
Bring 'Em Back Alive 32. Fang and Claw 36. Jungle Menace 37. Jacare, Killer of the Amazon 42, etc.
† In 1982 Buck was impersonated by Bruce Boxleitner in a short-lived TV series called *Bring 'Em Back Alive*, based in 1939 Singapore and involving Buck with spies as well as animals.

Buck, Jules (1917–). American producer who in the late fifties came to Britain and founded Keep Films with Peter O'Toole.
Fixed Bayonets 51. Treasure of the Golden Condor 53. The Day they Robbed the Bank of England 60. *Becket* 64. Great Catherine 66. The Ruling Class 71, etc.

Buck, Pearl (1892–1973). American novelist and missionary to the Far East. Works filmed include *The Good Earth, Dragon Seed, Satan Never Sleeps*.

Buck Rogers. An American comic strip which first appeared in 1929, adapted by Phil Nowlan from his novel *Armageddon 2419*. By the early thirties the title had become *Buck Rogers in the 25th Century*: the hero was an air force lieutenant who woke up after a five-century sleep to find America overrun by Mongols, followed by pirates from outer space. Buster Crabbe starred in a Universal serial of 1939, and in 1950 television made its first series with Ken Dibbs. In 1978 there followed 37 colour episodes starring Gil Gerard.

Buckner, Robert (1906–). American screenwriter, later producer.
Gold is Where You Find It 38. Jezebel 38. The Oklahoma Kid 39. *Dodge City* 39. Virginia City 39. *Santa Fe Trail* 40. Dive Bomber 41. Yankee Doodle Dandy 42. Gentleman Jim (p) 42. Mission to Moscow (p) 43. Confidential Agent (& p) 45. Rogues' Regiment (& p) 48. Sword in the Desert (& p) 49. Bright Victory (& p) 51. Love Me Tender 56. From Hell to Texas (& p) 58. Return of the Gunfighter 68, etc.

Bucquet, Harold S. (1891–1946). English director in Hollywood.
Young Dr Kildare 39. *On Borrowed Time* 39. The Secret of Dr Kildare 39. We Who Are Young 40. Dr Kildare Goes Home 40. The Penalty 41. Kathleen 41. Calling Dr Gillespie 42. The War Against Mrs Hadley 42. The Adventures of Tartu (GB) 43. Dragon Seed 44. Without Love 45, etc.

Budd, Roy (1949–). British composer and jazz pianist.
Soldier Blue 70. Zeppelin 71. Get Carter 71. Flight of the Doves 71. Pulp 72. The Stone Killer 73. The Internecine Project 74. Paper Tiger 75. Sinbad and the Eye of the Tiger 77. The Wild Geese 78. The Sea Wolves 80. Who Dares Wins 82. etc.

Buetel, Jack (1917–). American western leading man who was little seen after a highly publicized debut.
The Outlaw (as Billy the Kid) 43. Best of the Badmen 51. The Half Breed 52. Jesse James' Women 54. Mustang 59, etc.
TV series: Judge Roy Bean 53.

Bugs Bunny. Warners' famous cartoon character, the wise-cracking Brooklynesque rabbit who maintained his aplomb in all situations. Voiced by Mel Blanc. Catchphrase: 'What's up Doc?' First appearance in *Porky's Hare Hunt* 1937; 'retired' 1963; reappeared in seventies as 'compere' of TV specials grouping his old cartoons.
AA 1958: *Knighty Knight Bugs*.
† One of Bugs' creators claimed that the character was inspired by the sight of Clark Gable eating a carrot in *It Happened One Night*.

Bujold, Geneviève (1942–). French-Canadian leading lady.
French Can Can 56. La Guerre est Finie 63. King of Hearts 67. Isabel 67. Act of the

Heart 70. *Anne of the Thousand Days* (as Anne Boleyn) 70. Earthquake 74. Obsession 76. Swashbuckler 76. Alex and the Gypsy 76. Another Man, Another Chance 77. Murder by Decree 78. Coma 78. Final Assignment 80. Monsignor 81. Tightrope 84. Choose Me 85. Trouble in Mind 85, etc.

Bull, Peter (1912–84). Portly British character actor often in haughty, aggressive or explosively foreign roles.
Autobiography 1959: *I Know The Face But . . .*
Sabotage 37. The Ware Case 39. The Turners of Prospect Road 47. Oliver Twist 48. Saraband for Dead Lovers 48. The African Queen 51. The Malta Story 53. Footsteps in the Fog 55. Tom Jones 63. Dr Strangelove 63. The Old Dark House 63. Dr Dolittle 67. Lock Up Your Daughters 69. The Executioner 70. Up the Front 72. Alice's Adventures in Wonderland 72. Joseph Andrews 77. The Brute 78. Yellowbeard 83, many others.

Bulldog Drummond. 'Sapper' (Herman Cyril McNeile) created this famous character, an amateur James Bond of the twenties with old-fashioned manners and an army background. First portrayed on screen by Carlyle Blackwell in 1922; later by Jack Buchanan (1925 and 1940), Ronald Colman (1928 and 1934), Kenneth McKenna (1930), Ralph Richardson (1934), Atholl Fleming in Jack Hulbert's *Bulldog Jack* (1935), John Lodge (1937), Ray Milland (1937), John Howard, in eight films (1937–39), Ron Randell, in two films (1947), Tom Conway, in two films (1948), Walter Pidgeon in *Calling Bulldog Drummond* (1951) and Richard Johnson in *Deadlier than the Male* (1966) and *Some Girls Do* (1968).

bullfights have understandably not been a popular ingredient of English-speaking films, apart from the romanticism of the two versions of *Blood and Sand* and the cynicism of *The Last Flight* 31 and *The Sun Also Rises*. Several continental films, including *The Moment of Truth*, have tried to convey the mystique of bullfighting, but it has more often been seen as a background for suspense films (*The Caper of the Golden Bulls*) and comedy (*The Kid from Spain*, Laurel and Hardy in *The Bullfighters* and *Tommy the Toreador*, Abbott and Costello in *Mexican Hayride*, Peter Sellers in *The Bobo*, etc.). The three more recent American attempts to make a serious drama on the subject (*The Bullfighter and the Lady, The Brave Bulls* and *The Magnificent Matador*) were notably unpopular, while *Arruza* by Budd Boetticher (himself an ex-bullfighter) was never properly finished.

Bunny, John (1863–1915). British actor who became the funny fat man of early American silent comedy; made more than 150 shorts, usually with Flora Finch.

Buñuel, Luis (1900–1983). Spanish writer-director who worked in France in the twenties and thirties, made many films in Mexico 1945–60, then returned to Europe. A once-notorious surrealist, his later films mocked hypocrisy and the shows of religion.
Biographies were published by Adonis Kyrou in 1963 and by Raymond Durgnat in 1967.
□Un Chien Andalou 28. *L'Age d'Or* 30. Land Without Bread 32. Grand Casino 46. El Gran Calavera 49. *Los Olvidados* 50. Suzana la Perverse 50. La Hija del Engaño 51. Una Mujer Sin Amor 51. Subida al Cielo 51. The Brute 52. Wuthering Heights 52. *Robinson Crusoe* 52. *El* 53. La Ilusión Viaja en Tranvia 53. El Rio y la Muerte 54. The Criminal Life of Archibaldo de la Cruz 55. La Mort en ce Jardin 56. Cela S'Appelle L'Aurore 58. La Fièvre Monte à El Pao 59. Nazarin 59. The Young One 60. *Viridiana* 61. *The Exterminating Angel* 62. Diary of a Chambermaid 64. *Belle de Jour* 66. Simon of the Desert 66. The Milky Way 69. Tristana 70. *The Discreet Charm of the Bourgeoisie* 72. *The Phantom of Liberty* 74. *That Obscure Object of Desire* 77.
❀ For making surrealism irresistible by mixing it with deft film-making techniques and suave direction of actors. *The Discreet Charm of the Bourgeoisie.*

¶ *L.B.:* I've always found insects exciting.

Buono, Victor (1938–1982). Massively bulky American character actor who moved to films via the amateur theatre.
□*Whatever Happened to Baby Jane?* 62. Four for Texas 63. *The Strangler* 64. Robin and the Seven Hoods 64. The Greatest Story Ever Told 65. Hush Hush Sweet Charlotte 65. Young Dillinger 65. The Silencers 66. Who's Minding the Mint? 67. Beneath the Planet of the Apes 69. In the Name of our Father (It.) 69. The Wrath of God 72. The Mad Butcher 72. Crime Club (TV) 72. Goodnight My Love (TV) 72. Northeast of Seoul 74. Arnold 75. Brenda Starr (TV) 75. High Risk (TV) 76. Man from Atlantis (TV) 77. The Evil 78. Return of the Mod Squad (TV) 79. Backstairs

at the White House (TV) 79. The Man with Bogart's Face 80.

Burden, Hugh (1913–85). British character actor.
One of Our Aircraft is Missing 41. The Way Ahead 44. Fame is the Spur 46. Sleeping Car to Trieste 48. The Malta Story 53. No Love for Johnnie 61. Funeral in Berlin 66. The Statue 71. Blood from the Mummy's Tomb 71. The House in Nightmare Park 73, etc.

Burge, Stuart (1918–). British director, from TV.
□There Was a Crooked Man 60. Uncle Vanya 63. Othello 65. The Mikado 67. Julius Caesar 70.

Burgess, Anthony (1917–) (John Burgess Wilson). British novelist whose chief contribution to the cinema is *A Clockwork Orange*.

Burke, Alfred (1918–). British stage, screen and TV actor usually in cold, unsympathetic or other-worldly roles.
Touch and Go 56. The Man Upstairs 58. The Angry Silence 59. Children of the Damned 64. The Nanny 65. One Day in the Life of Ivan Denisovitch 71, etc.
TV series: Public Eye 69–73.

Burke, Billie (1885–1970) (Mary William Ethelbert Appleton Burke). American stage star who married Florenz Ziegfeld; Myrna Loy played her in *The Great Ziegfeld*. After a few early silents she settled in Hollywood in the thirties and played variations on the dithery matron role she made her own.
Autobiographies: *With A Feather On My Nose* (1949), *With Powder on My Nose* (1959).
□Gloria's Romance 16. Peggy 16. The Land of Promise 17. The Mysterious Miss Terry 17. Arms and the Girl 18. Eve's Daughter 18. Let's Get a Divorce 18. In Pursuit of Polly 18. The Make Believe Wife 18. Good Gracious Annabelle 19. The Misleading Widow 19. Sadie Love 19. Wanted, a Husband 19. Away Goes Prudence 20. The Frisky Mrs Johnson 21. The Education of Elizabeth 21. *A Bill of Divorcement* 32. Christopher Strong 33. *Dinner at Eight* 33. Only Yesterday 33. Finishing School 34. Where Sinners Meet 34. We're Rich Again 34. Forsaking all Others 34. Society Doctor 35. After Office Hours 35. Becky Sharp 35. Doubting Thomas 35. *A Feather in Her Hat* 35. She Couldn't Take It 35. Splendour 35. My American Wife 36. Piccadilly Jim 36. Craig's Wife 36. Parnell 36. *Topper* 37. The Bride Wore Red 37. Navy Blue and Gold 37. Everybody Sing 38. *Merrily We Live* 38. *The Young in Heart* 38. Topper Takes a Trip 38. Zenobia 39. Bridal Suite 39. The Wizard of Oz 39. Eternally Yours 39. Remember 39. And One Was Beautiful 40. Irene 40. Dulcy 40. Hullaballoo 40. The Captain is a Lady 40. The Ghost Comes Home 40. The Wild Man of Borneo 41. Topper Returns 41. One Night in Lisbon 42. *The Man Who Came to Dinner* 41. What's Cookin'? 42. In This Our Life 42. They All Kissed the Bride 42. Girl Trouble 42. Hi Diddle Diddle 42. Gildersleeve on Broadway 43. You're a Lucky Fellow Mr Smith 43. So's Your Uncle 44. *The Cheaters* 45. Swing Out Sister 45. Breakfast in Hollywood 46. The Bachelor's Daughters 46. The Barkleys of Broadway 49. And Baby Makes Three 49. Father of the Bride 50. The Boy from Indiana 50. Three Husbands 51. Father's Little Dividend 51. Small Town Girl 53. The Young Philadelphians 59. Sergeant Rutledge 60. Pepe 60.
TV series: Doc Corkle 52.
Famous line (*The Wizard of Oz*): 'Close your eyes and tap your heels together three times. And think to yourself, there's no place like home.'

Burke, James (1886–1968). Irish-American character actor who played more New York cops than he could count.
A Lady's Profession 33. Little Miss Marker 34. Ruggles of Red Gap 35. Song and Dance Man 36. Dead End 37. Dawn Patrol 38. At the Circus 39. Ellery Queen Master Detective 40. The Maltese Falcon 41. Army Surgeon 42. A Night to Remember 43. The Horn Blows at Midnight 45. Two Years Before the Mast 46. Nightmare Alley 47. June Bride 48. Copper Canyon 50. Lone Star 52. Lucky Me 54, many others.

Burke, Johnny (1908–1964). American songwriter who often supplied lyrics for Jimmy Van Heusen's music. 'Pennies from Heaven', 'Moonlight Becomes You', 'Swinging on a Star' (AA 44), many others.

Burke, Kathleen (1913–1980). American leading lady who made a few thirties appearances after being dubbed 'the panther woman' in 1932's *Island of Lost Souls*.

Burke, Marie (1894–) (Marie Holt). British actress, mostly on stage.
After the Ball 33. Odette 50. The Constant

Husband 55. The Snorkel 58. Rattle of a Simple Man 64, etc.

Burke, Martin (–). Canadian director. The Clown Murders 76. Power Play 78. The Last Chase 81.

Burke, Patricia (1917–). British actress, daughter of Marie Burke.
The Lisbon Story 45. The Trojan Brothers 45. Love Story 46. While I Live 47. Forbidden 49. The Happiness of Three Women 54. Spider's Web 60. The Day the Fish Came Out 67, etc.

Burke, Paul (1926–). American leading man, who on TV projected integrity with great success but has done few movies.
South Sea Woman 53. Screaming Eagles 56. *Valley of the Dolls* 67. The Thomas Crown Affair 68. Daddy's Gone A-Hunting 69. Lt. Schuster's Wife (TV) 72. Psychic Killer 75. Little Ladies of the Night (TV) 77. Wild and Wooly (TV) 78. Beach Patrol (TV) 79, etc.
TV series: Harbormaster 57. Five Fingers 59. Noah's Ark 60. Naked City 60–63. Twelve O'Clock High 67. Dynasty 83.

Burks, Robert (1910–1968). American cinematographer.
□Make Your Own Bed 44. Escape in the Desert 45. To the Victor 48. A Kiss in the Dark 49. *The Fountainhead* 49. Beyond the Forest 49. Task Force 49. The Glass Menagerie 50. Close to My Heart 51. *Strangers on a Train* 51. Tomorrow is Another Day 51. *Come Fill The Cup* 51. *The Enforcer* 51. The Miracle of our Lady of Fatima 52. Room for One More 52. Mara Maru 52. The Desert Song 53. So This is Love 53. Hondo 53. *I Confess* 53. The Boy from Oklahoma 54. Dial M for Murder 54. *Rear Window* 54. *To Catch a Thief* 55. The Trouble with Harry 56. The Man Who Knew Too Much 56. The Vagabond King 56. The Wrong Man 57. The Spirit of St Louis (co-ph) 58. *Vertigo* 58. The Black Orchid 59. *North By Northwest* 59. But Not for Me 59. The Rat Race 60. The Great Imposter 61. The Pleasure of His Company 61. *The Music Man* 62. *The Birds* 63. Marnie 64. Once a Thief 65. A Patch of Blue 66. A Covenant with Death 67. Waterhole Three 67.

burlesque. A word of Italian origin which came to mean an acted 'spoof' of a serious subject. In America it was applied to what the British would call music hall or variety, and eventually connoted striptease and low comedians. It died out as an institution in the thirties: Mamoulian's film *Applause* 29 gives a vivid picture of its latter days. George Watters and Arthur Hopkins' play *Burlesque*, popular in the twenties, concerns a comedian who leaves his long-suffering wife for other women and the demon rum. It was filmed three times, most recently as *When My Baby Smiles at Me* 48, with Betty Grable and Dan Dailey. The heyday of burlesque was also evoked in *The Night They Raided Minsky's* 68, in *Lady of Burlesque* and in *Gypsy*.

The Burmese Harp (Japan 1956). Kon Ichikawa's long, savage epic of the Burmese campaign of 1943–44 centres on a soldier who after horrifying adventures sees that his vocation is to bury the unknown dead. Lead played by Shoji Yasui; written by Natto Wada.

Burnaby, Davy (1881–1949). Heavyweight, monocled British entertainer.
The Co-optimists 29. Three Men in a Boat 33. Are You a Mason? 34. Boys Will Be Boys 35. Feather Your Nest 37. Many Tanks Mr Atkins 39. etc.

burned out. Cinematographer's jargon for 'over-exposed'.

Burness, Pete (1910–). American animator who worked his way through *The Little King* and *Tom and Jerry* to U.P.A. and *Bullwinkle*.

Burnett, Carol (1933–). Lanky, long-faced American revue and television star who despite being a household word at home hasn't made much of an impression in the overseas market.
□Who's Been Sleeping in My Bed? 63. Pete 'n' Tillie 72. The Front Page 74. A Wedding 78. The Grass Is Always Greener Over the Septic Tank (TV) 78. *Green Fire* (TV) 79. Health 80. The Four Seasons 81. Chu Chu and the Philly Flash 81. Annie 82.
TV series: Stanley 56. The Garry Moore Show 60s. *The Carol Burnett Show* 70s.

¶ *C.B.:* How many people do you know who can make a lot of money by crossing their eyes and doing pratfalls?

C.B.: Celebrity was a long time in coming; it will go away. Everything goes away.

Burnett, Frances Hodgson (1849–1924). English novelist whose screen contributions include the much-filmed children's stories *Little Lord Fauntleroy* and *The Secret Garden*.

A Little Princess made a solid vehicle for Shirley Temple.

Burnett, W. R. (1899–1982). American writer of gangster novels and screenplays which have been influential.
Little Caesar (oa) 30. *Scarface* (oa) 32. Dr Socrates (oa) 35. *High Sierra* (oa) 40. Crash Dive (w) 43. Nobody Lives Forever (w) 46. The Asphalt Jungle (oa) 50. Captain Lightfoot (w) 54. Sergeants Three (w) 62, many others.

Burnette, Smiley (1911–1967) (Lester Alvin Burnette). Tubby American character comedian who for many years made low-budget westerns as the side-kick of Charles Starrett or Gene Autry.
TV series: Petticoat Junction 63–67.

Burns, Bob ('Bazooka') (1893–1956). Folksy American comedian and humorist who after radio success appeared in several light films.
The Big Broadcast of 1937 37. Waikiki Wedding 37. Wells Fargo 37. Your Arkansas Traveller 38. Tropic Holiday 38. Our Leading Citizen 39. Alias the Deacon 40. Belle of the Yukon 44, etc.

Burns, Catherine (1945–). American young character actress of the seventies.
□Me Natalie 69. *Last Summer* 69. Red Sky at Morning 71. The Catcher (TV) 71. Night of Terror (TV) 72. Two for the Money (TV) 72. Amelia Earhart (TV) 76. The Word (TV) 78.

Burns, David (1902–1971). American character actor who often played the hero's buddy, the villain's henchman, or a fast-talking agent.
The Queen's Affair (GB) 34. The Sky's the Limit (GB) 38. A Girl Must Live (GB) 38. Knock On Wood 54. Deep in My Heart 55. Let's Make Love 60. The Tiger Makes Out 67. Who is Harry Kellerman? 71, etc.

Burns, George (1896–) (Nathan Birnbaum). American vaudeville comedian who married his partner Gracie Allen (qv) and spent many successful years on radio and TV, puffing philosophically at his cigar as he suffered her harebrained schemes. At the age of eighty he again became a big star and a national institution.
Autobiography 1955: *I Love Her, That's Why.* 1976: *Living It Up.*
□The Big Broadcast 32. College Humor 33. International House 33. Six of a Kind 34. We're Not Dressing 34. Many Happy Returns 34. Love in Bloom 35. The Big Broadcast of 1936 35. Here Comes Cookie 35. College Holiday 36. A Damsel in Distress 37. College Swing 38. Honolulu 39. *The Sunshine Boys* (AA) 75. *Oh God* 77. Sergeant Pepper's Lonely Hearts Club Band 78. Just You and Me Kid 79. Two of a Kind 79. Oh God Book Two 80. Going in Style 80. Oh God Book Three 83. Oh God! You Devil 84.
TV series: The Burns and Allen Show 50–57. The George Burns Show 59–60. Wendy and Me 64.

¶ 'My husband will never chase another woman. He's too fine, too decent, too old.'—*Gracie Allen 1960*

Acting is all about honesty. If you can fake that, you've got it made.—*G.B.*

Burns, Mark (1936–). British leading man.
The Charge of the Light Brigade 67. The Adventures of Gerard 70. A Day on the Beach 70. Death in Venice 70. A Time for Loving 72. Juggernaut 74. The Maids 75. The Stud 78. The Bitch 79. The Wicked Lady 83, etc.

Burns, Michael (–). American leading man of the sixties.
The Wizard of Baghdad 60. Mr Hobbs Takes a Vacation 62. The Raiders 64. Forty Guns to Apache Pass 66. The Mad Room 68. Thumb Tripping 72. The Magnificent Magical Magnet of Santa Mesa (TV) 77, etc.
TV series: Wagon Train 63–65.

Burns, Wilfred (1917–). British composer.
Fools Rush In 49. Thunder over Tangier 57. Till Death Us Do Part 68. Dad's Army 71, etc.

Burr, Raymond (1917–). Heavily-built Canadian leading man who for years played Hollywood heavies and then achieved TV stardom as Perry Mason.
□Without Reservations 46. San Quentin 46. Code of the West 47. Desperate 47. Pitfall 48. Raw Deal 48. Fighting Father Dunne 48. Ruthless 48. Sleep My Love 48. The Adventures of Don Juan 48. Walk a Crooked Mile 48. Station West 48. I Love Trouble 48. Criss Cross 49. Bride of Vengeance 49. Black Magic 49. Abandoned 49. The Red Light 49. Love Happy 49. Unmasked 50. Borderline 50. Key to the City 50. *A Place in the Sun* 51. His Kind of Woman 51. Bride of the Gorilla 51. New Mexico 51. M 51. FBI Girl 51. The Whip Hand 51. Meet Danny Wilson 52. Mara Maru 52. Horizons West 52. The Blue Gardenia 53. Fort Algiers 53. Bandits of

Corsica 53. Tarzan and the She Devil 53. Serpent of the Nile 54. Casanova's Big Night 54. Gorilla at Large 54. Khyber Patrol 54. *Rear Window* 54. Passion 54. Thunder Pass 54. They Were So Young 55. You're Never Too Young 55. Count Three and Pray 55. A Man Alone 55. The Brass Legend 56. Please Murder Me 56. Godzilla 56. Great Day in the Morning 56. The Secret of Treasure Mountain 56. A Cry in the Night 56. Ride the High Iron 56. Crime of Passion 57. Affair in Havana 57. Desire in the Dust 60. P.J. 68. 77 Park Avenue (TV) 77. The Jordan Chance (TV) 78. Tomorrow Never Comes 78. Love's Savage Fury (TV) 79. Out of the Blue 80. The Curse of King Tut's Tomb (TV) 80. The Return 80. The Night the City Screamed (TV) 80. Peter and Paul (TV) 81. Airplane II: the Sequel 82. Perry Mason Returns (TV) 85 (and several subsequent TV movies).

TV series: *Perry Mason* 57–65. *Ironside* 67–74. Kingston: Confidential 77. Centennial 78.

Burroughs, Edgar Rice (1875–1950). American novelist, the creator (in 1914) of *Tarzan of the Apes* (qv).

¶ *E.R.B.:* I am one of those fellows who have few adventures. I always get to the fire after it's out.

Burrows, Abe (1910–85) (Abram Borowitz). American librettist: *Guys and Dolls*, *Can Can*, *Silk Stockings*, *How to Succeed in Business*, etc.

Burstyn, Ellen (1932–) (Edna Gilhooley). Leading American actress of the seventies.
□Goodbye Charlie 64. For Those who Think Young 65. Pit Stop 69. Tropic of Cancer 69. Alex in Wonderland 70. The Last Picture Show 71. The King of Marvin Gardens 72. Thursday's Game (TV) 73. *The Exorcist* 73. Harry and Tonto 74. *Alice Doesn't Live Here Anymore* (AA) 75. Providence 77. Same Time Next Year 78. A Dream of Passion 78. Resurrection 80. Silence of the North 82. The Ambassador 84.
The People vs Jean Harris (TV) 83. The Ambassador 84. Surviving (TV) 85. Twice in a Lifetime 85.
† In the 1964 series *The Doctors* E.B. appeared as Ellen McRae.

¶ *E.B.:* Acting feels like a congenital condition to me—it's in my genes.

Burton, LeVar (1958–). Black American character actor who played the young Kunta Kinte in TV's *Roots*.
Billy: Portrait of a Street Kid (TV) 77. Looking for Mr Goodbar 77. Guyana Tragedy (TV) 80. The Hunter 80. The Supernaturals 86.

Burton, Richard (1925–1984) (Richard Jenkins). Welsh leading actor whose dark brooding good looks did not bring him immediate film success either in Britain or in Hollywood. His 1963 marriage to Elizabeth Taylor, however, helped him climb to the crest of what these days passes for stardom, as did their subsequent divorces and reunions. High living and a kind of contempt for his work kept him from the heights of both serious achievement and popular acclaim.

Biography 1986: *Burton, the Man Behind the Myth*, by Penny Junor
□The Last Days of Dolwyn 48. Now Barabbas was a Robber 49. Waterfront 50. The Woman with No Name 50. Green Grow the Rushes 51. *My Cousin Rachel* 52. The Robe 53. The Desert Rats 53. Prince of Players 54. The Rains of Ranchipur 55. *Alexander the Great* 56. Seawife 57. Bitter Victory 58. *Look Back in Anger* 59. The Bramble Bush 59. Ice Palace 60. The Longest Day 62. *Cleopatra* 62. *The V.I.P.s* 63. *Becket* 64. *The Night of the Iguana* 64. The Sandpiper 65. *The Spy Who Came in from the Cold* 65. *Who's Afraid of Virginia Woolf?* 66. *The Taming of the Shrew* 67. Dr Faustus (& co-d) 67. The Comedians 67. Boom 68. Where Eagles Dare 68. Candy 68. *Staircase* 69. *Anne of the Thousand Days* (as Henry VIII) 70. Raid on Rommel 71. Villain 71. Under Milk Wood 71. The Assassination of Trotsky 72. Hammersmith is Out 72. Bluebeard 72. Divorce His, Divorce Hers (TV) 73. Sutjeska (Yug.) 73. Massacre in Rome 74. The Klansman 74. The Voyage 74. Brief Encounter (TV) 75. Exorcist II: The Heretic 77. Equus 77. The Medusa Touch 77. The Wild Geese 78. Sergeant Steiner 79. Absolution 79. Tristan and Isolt 80. Wagner 83. Circle of Two 80. 1984 84. Ellis Island (TV) 84.

¶ I've done the most awful rubbish in order to have somewhere to go in the morning.—*R.B.*

When I played drunks I had to remain sober because I didn't know how to play them when I was drunk.—*R.B.*

An actor is something less than a man, while an actress is something more than a woman.—*R.B.*

Certainly most movie executives were making love to the starlets. But then, so were most of us actors.—*R.B. of Hollywood in the fifties*

The Burtons offered me a drink and rolled in a liquor cart from the bedroom which was its permanent abode, and the conversation afterwards was limited to a discussion of twentieth-century poetry.—*William Fadiman*

Cable from Laurence Olivier to Burton at the height of the *Cleopatra* scandal: 'Make up your mind, dear heart. Do you want to be a great actor or a household word?'

Burton, replying: 'Both.'

'There is no longer any novelty in watching the sad disintegration of his acting career.'—*Roger Ebert*

'Who could take that scruffy arrogant buffoon seriously?'—*Eddie Fisher*

Burton, Robert (1895–1964). American character actor who played many executives, sheriffs and detectives.
Inferno 53. The Big Heat 54. Riot in Cell Block Eleven 56. Spirit of St Louis 57. Birdman of Alcatraz 62, many others.

Burton, Wendell (–). American character actor.
The Sterile Cuckoo 69. Fortune and Men's Eyes 70. Being There 79. East of Eden (TV) 81, etc.

Busch, Mae (1897–1946). Cynical-looking Australian-born leading lady of Hollywood silents who later became an excellent foil for Laurel and Hardy in some of their best two-reelers.
The Grim Game 19. The Devil's Pass-key 20. *Foolish Wives* 21. The Christian (GB) 23. Nellie the Beautiful Cloak Model 24. Married Flirts 24. The Unholy Three 25. San Francisco Nights 27. While the City Sleeps 28. A Man's Man 29. Wicked 31. *Come Clean* 31. Scarlet Dawn 32. Their First Mistake 32. Sucker Money 33. Sons of the Desert 33. The Private Life of Oliver the Eighth 34. The Bohemian Girl 36. Daughter of Shanghai 37. Prison Farm 38. Women without Names 40. Ziegfeld Girl 40, many others.

Busch, Niven (1903–). American novelist and screenwriter.
Babbitt (w) 34. In Old Chicago (w) 38. The Westerner (w) 40. Duel in the Sun (oa) 46. Pursued (w) 47. The Furies (oa) 50. The Moonlighter (oa & w) 52. Treasure of Pancho Villa (w) 56, etc.

buses have often provided a dramatic background for film plots. *Man-Made Monster* and *The October Man* began with bus accidents, and one of the stories in *Dead of Night* ended with one. Strangers met on a bus in *Friday the Thirteenth, It Happened One Night, San Diego I Love You* (in which Buster Keaton defied regulations by driving his bus along the seashore), *Bus Stop* and *The Wayward Bus*. Parting at the bus station was featured in *Orchestra Wives, Dark Passage, Two Tickets to Broadway*, and *Rattle of a Simple Man*; romances were conducted on a bus in *Violent Playground* and *Underground*; a trap was set for a criminal in a bus station in *Down Three Dark Streets*. Passengers on buses broke into song in *Keep Your Seats Please, Ride 'Em Cowboy* and *Summer Holiday*. As for comedy effects using buses, there was the little boy whose head stuck in the bus wheel in *Monsieur Hulot's Holiday*, Will Hay driving a bus round a race-track in *Ask a Policeman*, Bob Hope wrecking an Irish bus outing in *My Favourite Blonde*, Frankie Howerd losing his way in the fog in *The Runaway Bus*, Richard Burton escorting his matrons on a bus tour in *The Night of the Iguana*, and Laurel and Hardy driving a bus on to a roller coaster in *The Dancing Masters* . . . among others. The only comedies about bus crews were the spinoffs from the British TV series *On the Buses*. *The Big Bus* was a spoof on disaster movies.

Busey, Gary (1944–). American light actor.
Dirty Little Billy 72. Lolly Madonna XXX 73. The Last American Hero 73. The Execution of Private Slovik (TV) 74. Thunderbolt and Lightfoot 74. The Law (TV) 74. The Gumball Rally 76. A Star Is Born 76. Straight Time 77. Big Wednesday 78. The Buddy Holly Story 78. Carny 80. D.C. Cab 83. The Bear 84. Insignificance 85. Silver Bullet 85. Eye of the Tiger 86. Lethal Weapon 87. Let's Get Harry 87. Bulletproof 87, etc.
TV series: The Texas Wheelers 74.

Bush, Billy 'Green' (–). American character actor of the seventies.
40 Carats 73. Electra Glide in Blue 74. Alice Doesn't Live Here Anymore 74. Mackintosh and T. J. 75. Tom Horn 80, etc.

Bush, Dick (1931–). British cinematographer.
Savage Messiah 73. Mahler 74. Tommy 74. In Celebration 74. The Legacy 78. Yanks 79. One Trick Pony 80. Little Gloria . . . Happy At Last (TV) 82. Victor Victoria 83. Crimes of Passion 85. The Journey of Natty Gann 85. Nazi Hunter (TV) 86, etc.

Bushell, Anthony (1904–). Bland-faced British leading man of the thirties who started his career in Hollywood; later turned to playing occasional brigadiers and concentrated his efforts on production.
Disraeli 29. *Journey's End* 30. Three Faces East 30. Five Star Final 31. A Woman Commands 32. I Was a Spy 33. The Ghoul 33. Soldiers of the King 33. The Scarlet Pimpernel 34. Dark Journey 37. Farewell Again 37. The Return of the Scarlet Pimpernel 38. The Lion Has Wings 39. Hamlet (co-p only) 48. The Angel with the Trumpet (& d) 49. The Miniver Story 50. The Long Dark Hall (& pd) 51. High Treason 51. Who Goes There? 52. The Red Beret 53. The Purple Plain 54. The Battle of the River Plate 56. Richard III (co-p only) 56. The Wind Cannot Read 57. The Terror of the Tongs 61. The Queen's Guards 63, etc.

Bushman, Francis X. (1883–1966). Heavily built American leading actor of the silent era, once known as the handsomest man in the world. After a return to the stage, made a brief comeback in 1926 and later played bit parts in unsuitable films of the sixties.
The Magic Wand 12. The Spy's Defeat 13. One Wonderful Night. 14. Under Royal Patronage 14. Graustark 15. The Return of Richard Neal 15. Romeo and Juliet 15. The Great Secret 16. Red White and Blue Blood 17. Social Quicksands 18. The Masked Bride 25. *Ben Hur* (as Messala) 26. The Lady in Ermine 27. The Thirteenth Juror 27. The Grip of the Yukon 29. Once a Gentleman 30. Hollywood Boulevard 36. David and Bathsheba 51. Sabrina 54. The Story of Mankind 57. The Ghost in the Invisible Bikini 66, many others.

¶ 'All the people love you, but I can't even have the love of half the people.'—*President Taft*

'His is the best known name and face in the world.'—*Arthur Brisbane*

business is just as essential as art or entertainment to the continuance of movies: and the greatest moguls are those who have had an eye to all three.

¶ *J. B. Priestley, 1937:* Hollywood's trade, which is dreams at so many dollars per thousand feet, is managed by businessmen pretending to be artists and by artists pretending to be businessmen. In this queer atmosphere, nobody stays as he was; the artist begins to lose his art, and the businessman becomes temperamental and overbalanced.

Irving Thalberg, 1933: No picture can be considered a success unless it appeals to the matinee trade. When you've got a picture women want to see, the men will have to go along. But a woman can always keep a man away from a picture that only attracts him.

Alfred Hitchcock: That wasn't the ending I wanted for *Blackmail*, but I had to change it for commercial reasons.

Darryl F. Zanuck: We are in this business primarily to provide entertainment, but in doing so we do not dodge the issue if we can also provide enlightenment.

Billy Wilder: In certain pictures I do hope they will leave the cinema a little enriched, but I don't make them pay a buck and a half and then ram a lecture down their throats.

Joseph E. Levine: You can fool all the people all the time if the advertising is right and the budget is big enough.

Cliff Robertson: This isn't exactly a stable business. It's like trying to stand up in a canoe with your pants down.

Bob Hope: Business has been bad lately. The other night I rang up a local theatre and asked, what time does the main feature start? The manager replied: 'What time can you get here?'

Bussières, Raymond (1907–1982). Long-faced, mournful-looking French character actor.
Nous les Gosses 41. Les Portes de la Nuit 46. Quai des Orfèvres 47. Alice au Pays des Merveilles 51. Ma Pomme 51. Casque d'Or 52. Justice est Faite 52. Belles de Nuit 54. Porte des Lilas 55. Paris Palace Hotel 58. Fanny 61. Paris When It Sizzles 64. Up from the Beach 65. Drôles de Zèbres 77. Les Sous-Doues 80, many others.

Butch Cassidy and the Sundance Kid (US 1969). An easy-going, self-parodying western which happened to succeed in all departments and so started a hail of imitations, especially as its amiability formed a necessary contrast to the harshness and violence of most westerns in the late sixties. Directed by George Roy Hill from a script by William Goldman; photographed by Conrad Hall; with Paul Newman and Robert Redford. Its theme song, 'Raindrops Keep Falling on my Head', was an enormous popular success. A less successful 'prequel' appeared in 1979 under the title *Butch and Sundance: The Early Years.*

Butcher, Ernest (1885–1965). British character actor who spent a lifetime playing mild little men.

Variety Jubilee 42. Tawny Pipit 43. My Brother Jonathan 48, many others.

Butler, Artie (–). American composer.
The Harrad Experiment 73. For Pete's Sake 74.

Butler, Bill (–). American cinematographer.
The Rain People 69. Drive He Said 71. The Conversation 74. Jaws 75. One Flew Over the Cuckoo's Nest 75. Alex and the Gypsy 76. Demon Seed 77. Damien: Omen II 78. Capricorn One 78. Grease 78. Rocky II 78. Can't Stop the Music 80. Stripes 81. A Little Sex 82. Rocky III 82.

Butler, David (1894–1979). American director of light entertainments: occasional promise but little fulfilment. Former actor.
High School Hero 27. Win That Girl 28. *Sunny Side Up* 29. *Just Imagine* 30. *A Connecticut Yankee* 31. Business and Pleasure 32. Hold Me Tight 33. Bottoms Up 34. Bright Eyes 34. The Little Colonel 35. The Littlest Rebel 35. Captain January 36. White Fang 36. Ali Baba Goes to Town 37. Kentucky 38. East Side of Heaven 39. That's Right You're Wrong (& p) 39. If I Had My Way (& p) 40. You'll find Out (& p) 40. *Caught in the Draft* 41. *Road to Morocco* 42. They Got Me Covered 43. *Thank Your Lucky Stars* 43. Shine on Harvest Moon 44. The Princess and the Pirate 44. San Antonio 45. Two Guys from Milwaukee 46. My Wild Irish Rose 47. Two Guys from Texas 48. Look for the Silver Lining 49. The Daughter of Rosie O'Grady 50. Tea for Two 50. Lullaby of Broadway 51. Painting the Clouds with Sunshine 51. Where's Charley? 52. By the Light of the Silvery Moon 53. *Calamity Jane* 53. King Richard and the Crusaders 54. Glory (& p) 56. The Right Approach 61. C'mon Let's Live a Little 67, etc.

Butler, Frank (1890–1967). British-born writer, long in Hollywood.
College Humor 33. Babes in Toyland 34. Strike Me Pink 36. Road to Singapore 40. Road to Morocco 42. Going My Way (AA) 44. Incendiary Blonde 45. The Perils of Pauline 47. Whispering Smith 49. Strange Lady in Town 55, many others.

Butler, Michael (1944–). American cinematographer.
Charley Varrick 74. Harry and Tonto 74. The Car 77. The Gauntlet 77. Telefon 77. Wanda Nevada 79. A Small Circle of Friends 80. The Cannonball Run 81, etc.

Butler, Robert (–). American director, from TV.
Guns in the Heather 69. The Computer Wore Tennis Shoes 69. The Barefoot Executive 71. Scandalous John 71. Death Takes a Holiday (TV) 71. Now You See Him Now You Don't 71, etc.

butlers. Hollywood has always been fascinated by butlers, especially those who give an impression of British imperturbability. Actors notably benefiting from this penchant include Arthur Treacher (who played Jeeves on film in the thirties), Robert Greig, Charles Coleman, Aubrey Mather, Melville Cooper, Halliwell Hobbes, Barnett Parker, Alan Mowbray and Eric Blore (whose butlers usually had a kind of suppressed malevolence). The catch-phrase 'the butler did it' was however seldom true of murder mysteries, though Bela Lugosi played some very sinister servants in the forties, Richard Haydn was guilty of at least one murder in *And Then There Were None*; the butler in *The Hound of the Baskervilles* certainly had something to hide. Another villainous 'man's man' was Philip Latham in *Dracula Prince of Darkness*: he lured the count's victims. Comedy butlers are led by Charles Laughton as *Ruggles of Red Gap* and by Edward Brophy, who often played an American imitation of the real thing, Richard Hearne in *The Butler's Dilemma*, Edward Rigby in *Don't Take It to Heart*, and Laurel and Hardy, who in *A Chump at Oxford* took literally an instruction to 'serve the salad undressed'. Jack Buchanan pretended to be his own butler in *Lord Richard in the Pantry*, and William Powell and Divid Niven, who both played *My Man Godfrey*, had their own reasons for going into service. Other butlers with something to hide were found in *White Tie and Tails* and *The Baroness and the Butler*, and in *Spring in Park Lane* Michael Wilding was a mysterious footman. In *The Fallen Idol* Ralph Richardson's butler was almost arrested for a murder he didn't commit. Perhaps television gave us the most famous butler of all: Gordon Jackson as Hudson in *Upstairs Downstairs*.

Butterworth, Charles (1896–1946). Balding American comic actor who through the thirties played his own style of shy upper-class bachelor, never getting the girl and sometimes drowning his sorrows in drink.
□The Life of the Party 30. Illicit 30. The Bargain 31. Side Show 31. The Mad Genius 31. Beauty and the Boss 32. *Love Me Tonight*

32. Manhattan Parade 32. The Nuisance 33. Penthouse 33. My Weakness 33. The Cat and the Fiddle 34. Student Tour 34. Forsaking All Others 34. *Bulldog Drummond Strikes Back* (as Algy) 34. Hollywood Party 34. *Ruggles of Red Gap* 34. The Night Is Young 35. Baby Face Harrington 35. Orchids to You 35. Magnificent Obsession 35. The Moon's Our Home 36. Half Angel 36. We Went to College 36. Rainbow on the River 36. Swing High Swing Low 37. Every Day's a Holiday 37. Thanks for the Memory 38. Let Freedom Ring 39. The Boys from Syracuse 40. Second Chorus 40. Road Show 41. Blonde Inspiration 41. Sis Hopkins 41. What's Cookin' 42. A Night in New Orleans 42. Give Out Sisters 42. Always a Bridesmaid 43. The Sultan's Daughter 43. This Is the Army 43. The Bermuda Mystery 44. Dixie Jamboree 44. Follow the Boys 44.

¶ *C.B. in Love Me Tonight:* I fell flat on my flute.

Butterworth, Donna (1956–). American child actress.
The Family Jewels 65. Paradise Hawaiian Style 66.

Butterworth, Peter (1919–1979). British comedian usually seen as well-meaning bumbler.
William Comes to Town 49. Penny Princess 51. Mr Drake's Duck 52. Carry On series 58–77. The Ritz 76. Carry On Emmanuelle 78, many others.

Buttolph, David (1902–). American composer.
Show Them no Mercy 35. Nancy Steele is Missing 37. Four Sons 40. *The Mark of Zorro* 40. *Tobacco Road* 41. Moontide 42. My Favorite Blonde 42. Crash Dive 43. The Hitler Gang 44. The House on 92nd Street 45. Somewhere in the Night 46. Kiss of Death 47. Rope 48. Roseanna McCoy 49. Three Secrets 50. The Enforcer 51. My Man and I 52. *House of Wax* 53. Secret of the Incas 54. The Lone Ranger 56. The Big Land 57. The Horse Soldiers 59. Guns of the Timberland 60. The Man from Galveston 64, many others.

Buttons, Red (1918–) (Aaron Chwatt). American vaudeville and TV comic who graduated to strong supporting roles in occasional movies.
□Winged Victory 44. *Sayonara* (AA) 57. Imitation General 58. The Big Circus 59. One, Two, Three 61. Hatari 62. Five Weeks in a Balloon 62. The Longest Day 62. A Ticklish Affair 63. Your Cheating Heart 65. Up from the Beach 65. Harlow 65. Stagecoach 66. Breakout (TV) 67. *They Shoot Horses Don't They?* 69. Who Killed Mary What's Her Name? 71. The Poseidon Adventure 72. Louis Armstrong, Chicago Style 75. The New Original Wonder Woman (TV) 75. Gable and Lombard 76. Viva Knievel 77. Pete's Dragon 77. Telethon (TV) 78. Vegas (TV pilot) 78. Movie Movie 78. The Users (TV) 78. C.H.O.M.P.S. 79. When Time Ran Out 80. The Dream Merchants (TV) 80. Reunion at Fairborough (TV) 85.
TV series: *The Red Buttons Show* 52. The Double Life of Henry Phyfe 66.

Buttram, Pat (–). American comic character actor who usually plays hayseeds.
National Barn Dance 44. Beyond the Purple Hills 50. Twilight of Honor 63. The Sweet Ride 67, etc.
TV series: Green Acres 65–71.

Butts, Dale (1910–). American composer, almost entirely for Republic.
Flame of the Barbary Coast 45. Catman of Paris 46. The Plunderers 48. Sea of Lost Ships 53. Santa Fe Passage 55. Affair in Reno 57, many others.

Buzzell, Edward (1897–1985). American director of competent but not very individual output; former musical comedy actor.
Virtue 32. Ann Carver's Profession 33. Cross Country Cruise 34. Transient Lady 35. The Luckiest Girl in the World 36. As Good as Married 37. Fast Company 38. Honolulu 39. *At the Circus* 39. Go West 40. Married Bachelor 41. Ship Ahoy 42. The Youngest Profession 43. Keep Your Powder Dry 45. *Easy to Wed* 46. Three Wise Fools 46. Song of the Thin Man 47. Neptune's Daughter 49. A Woman of Distinction 50. Confidentially Connie 53. Ain't Misbehavin' (& w) 55. Mary Had a Little (GB) 61, etc.

Buzzi, Ruth (1936–). American comedienne who came to the fore as the frustrated spinster in TV's *Laugh-In*.
Freaky Friday 77. The Villain 79.

Bwana Devil (US 1953). A poor jungle adventure which has some historical interest as the first feature film to be produced in 3-D. As written, produced and directed by Arch Oboler, it had little else to offer; Robert Stack and Nigel Bruce led the struggling cast.

Bygraves, Max (1922–). British entertainer who has played in several films. Autobiography 1976: *I Wanna Tell You a Story*.
Skimpy in the Navy 49. Tom Brown's Schooldays 50. Charley Moon 56. A Cry from the Streets 57. Bobbikins 59. Spare the Rod 61, etc.

Byington, Spring (1893–1971). American stage actress who settled in Hollywood in the thirties and played a long succession of birdbrained wives, scatty matrons, gossip columnists, and loving mums.
Little Women (as Marmee) 33. Werewolf of London 35. Way Down East 35. Mutiny on the Bounty 35. Ah Wilderness 35. Every Saturday Night (and ensuing Jones Family series; qv) 36. Dodsworth 36. Theodora Goes Wild 36. It's Love I'm After 37. The Adventures of Tom Sawyer 38. Jezebel 38. *You Can't Take It with You* 38. The Story of Alexander Graham Bell 39. A Child is Born 40. The Bluebird 40. Meet John Doe 41. The Devil and Miss Jones 41. When Ladies Meet 41. Roxie Hart 42. *Rings on Her Fingers* 42. Presenting Lily Mars 43. Heaven Can Wait 43. The Heavenly Body 44. I'll Be Seeing You 45. The Enchanted Cottage 45. Dragonwyck 46. Singapore 47. BF's Daughter 48. In the Good Old Summertime 49. Louisa 50. Walk Softly Stranger 50. According to Mrs Hoyle 51. Angels in the Outfield 51. Because You're Mine 52. The Rocket Man 54. Please Don't Eat the Daisies 60, many others.
TV series: *December Bride* 54–58. Laramie 59–62.

¶ *S.B. 1959:* TV keeps me young because it keeps me busy, keeps my mind alert, my senses sharp and my interest up.

Byrd, Ralph (1909–1952). Tough-looking American leading man, mainly in second features.
Hell Ship Morgan 31. Dick Tracy 38. Desperate Cargo 41. Guadalcanal Diary 43. Mark of the Claw 47. The Redhead and the Cowboy 51, etc.
TV series: Dick Tracy 51.

Byrne, Eddie (1911–1981). Irish character actor, in British films.
Odd Man Out 46. The Gentle Gunman 52. *Time Gentlemen Please* (leading role) 53. A Kid for Two Farthings 55. The Admirable Crichton 57. The Mummy 59. The Bulldog Breed 60. Mutiny on the Bounty 62. Devils of Darkness 65. Island of Terror 66. Stardust 74, many others.

Byrne, Gabriel (1950–). Irish leading man.
The Outsider 79. Excalibur 81. The Keep 83. Hannah K 83. Reflections 83. Christopher Columbus (TV) 83. Defence of the Realm 85. Gothic 86. Lionheart 87.

Byrnes, Edd (1933–) (Edward Breitenberger). American TV juvenile of the fifties; never quite made it in movies.
Darby's Rangers 58. Up Periscope 59. Yellowstone Kelly 59. The Secret Invasion 64. Payment in Blood 69, etc.
TV series: *77 Sunset Strip* 58–63. Sweepstakes 79.

Byrum, John (–). American director.
Heartbeat 79. The Razor's Edge 84. The Whoopee Boys 86.

Byron, Arthur (1872–1943). American character actor.
The Mummy 32. Mayor of Hell 33. Marie Galante 34. Fog Over Frisco 34. Oil for the Lamps of China 35. Prisoner of Shark Island 36, many others.

Byron, Lord (1788–1824) (George Gordon). English poet who has been played on the screen by Dennis Price in *The Bad Lord Byron*, by Richard Chamberlain in *Lady Caroline Lamb*, by Gavin Gordon in *The Bride of Frankenstein*, and by Noel Willman in *Beau Brummell*.

Byron, Kathleen (1922–). British leading actress of the forties; on stage and screen.
The Young Mr Pitt 41. The Silver Fleet 43. A Matter of Life and Death 46. *Black Narcissus* (as a mad nun) 46. The Small Back Room 48. Madness of the Heart 49. The Reluctant Widow 50. Four Days 51. The Gambler and the Lady 54. Hand in Hand 60. Night of the Eagle 62. Private Road 71. Twins of Evil 71. One of Our Dinosaurs is Missing 76, etc.

Byron, Walter (1899–1972) (Walter Butler). British leading man who had success in America.
White Heat 26. Passion Island 27. The Awakening 28. The Sacred Flame 29. Queen Kelly 29. Not Damaged 30. The Dancers 30. The Last Flight 31. Roar of the Dragon 32. Society Girl 32. British Agent 34. Folies Bergere 35. Mary of Scotland 36. Trade Winds 38, many others.

Byrum, John (1947–). American writer-director.
☐Inserts 75. Mahogany (w only) 75. Harry and Walter Go to New York (w only) 76. Heartbeat 79. Sphinx (w only) 81.

Answers

bad guys

1 Count Zaroff (Leslie Banks) in *The Most Dangerous Game* (1932), sometimes known as *The Hounds of Zaroff* □. Zaroff is a rich villain who lures men to his island in order to hunt them, and keeps a trophy room of human heads. Needless to say, Joel McCrea outwits him.

2 Claude Rains as *The Invisible Man* (1933) □. Griffin has been turned by the power of his invisibility drugs into a raving megalomaniac.

3 Robert Walker as Bruno Anthony explaining to Guy Haines (Farley Granger) his plan for swapping murders at the outset of Hitchcock's *Strangers on a Train* (1951) □.

4 One can almost hear Walter Huston relishing these lines from *All That Money Can Buy* (1941) □. In this New Hampshire version of *Faust* he played the devil, or Mr Scratch as he was locally known. James Craig was the easily persuaded victim.

5 The voice has been imitated a million times, but only Bela Lugosi, as *Dracula* (1930) □, could extract the chilling essence from these simple lines.

6 Very difficult! Preston Foster as the mad doctor in the preposterous finale of *Doctor X* (1932) □. Having appeared to be the only character who cannot be the strangler, because he has only one arm, he is seen in his laboratory rapidly growing another by the application of the compound to which he refers.

7 Inimitably spoken by George Sanders as the caddish cousin Jack Favell in *Rebecca* (1940) □.

8 One of the most famous lines in movies: Edward G. Robinson expiring at the end of *Little Caesar* (1930) □.

9 And one of the most famous speeches, written by Orson Welles to extend his tiny role as Harry Lime in *The Third Man* (1949) □. It ends the famous ferris wheel scene in which he defends his black market activities.

10 The yellow peril, Fu Manchu, played by Christopher Lee in *The Face of Fu Manchu* (1965) □.

11 Sidney Greenstreet as 'the fat man', Gutman, in *The Maltese Falcon* (1941) □: a rich and memorable portrayal of an oily but estimable villain.

12 Count Zaroff again, in *The Most Dangerous Game* □.

13 *Rebecca* □ again, but this time the dark housekeeper Mrs Danvers, played by Judith Anderson; here she tries to persuade the second Mrs de Winter to commit suicide.

14 A well-remembered line because it was the first to be spoken on the screen by Greta Garbo, as the waterfront tramp in *Anna Christie* (1931) □.

15 An unspeakable line, one would think, but at the beginning of *Shanghai Express* (1932) □ Marlene Dietrich still gets away with it.

16 Rita Hayworth as *Gilda* □, in a self-knocking mood.

ballet

1 *The Unfinished Dance* □ 2 *La Mort du Cygne* □ 3 *The Spectre of the Rose* □ 4 Republic □ 5 Anton Walbrook □ 6 Monte Carlo □ 7 *Knock on Wood* □ 8 *Invitation to the Dance* □ 9 *The Magic Lamp* □ 10 *The Band Wagon* □ 11 Tamara Toumanova □ 12 Christopher Gable □

biopics I

1 Carole Lombard □ *Gable and Lombard* □ 2 Texas Guinan □ *Incendiary Blonde* □ 3 Otis Skinner □ *Our Hearts Were Young and Gay* □ 4 David Garrick □ *The Great Garrick* □ 5 Jean Harlow □ *Harlow* □ 6 Mrs Leslie Carter □ *Lady With Red Hair* □ 7 Eddie Cantor □ *The Eddie Cantor Story* □ 8 Edwin Booth □ *Prince of Players* □ 9 Lillian Roth □ *I'll Cry Tomorrow* □ 10 Buster Keaton □ *The Buster Keaton Story* □ 11 John Barrymore □ *Too Much Too Soon* □ 12 Red Nichols □ *The Five Pennies* □ 13 W. C. Fields □ *W. C. Fields and Me* □ 14 Jeanne Eagels □ *Jeanne Eagels* □ 15 Lon Chaney □ *Man of a Thousand Faces* □ 16 Pearl White □ *The Perils of Pauline* □ 17 Houdini □ *Houdini* □ 18 Lillian Russell □ *Lillian Russell* □ 19 Ruth Etting □ *Love Me or Leave Me* □ 20 Marilyn Miller □ *Look for the Silver Lining* □ 21 The Dolly Sisters □ *The Dolly Sisters* □ 22 George Leybourne □ *Champagne Charlie* □ 23 Gene Krupa □ *The Gene Krupa Story* (GB: *Drum Crazy*) □ 24 Helen Morgan □ *The Helen Morgan Story* (GB: *Both Ends of the Candle*) □ 25 Nellie Melba □ *Melba* □ 26 Nora Bayes □ *Shine on Harvest Moon* □ 27 Blossom Seeley □ *Somebody Loves Me* □ 28 Gypsy Rose Lee

☐ *Gypsy* ☐ 29 Billie Holiday ☐ *Lady Sings the Blues* ☐ 30 Joe E. Lewis ☐ *The Joker Is Wild* ☐

biopics II

1 Aviator ☐ *Reach for the Sky* ☐ Kenneth More ☐ 2 Songwriter ☐ *I'll See You in My Dreams* ☐ Danny Thomas ☐ 3 Spy ☐ *Carve Her Name With Pride* ☐ Virginia McKenna ☐ 4 Bandleader and trumpeter ☐ *The Five Pennies* ☐ Danny Kaye ☐ 5 Entertainer, playwright and songwriter ☐ *Yankee Doodle Dandy* ☐ James Cagney ☐ 6 King ☐ *Alfred the Great* ☐ David Hemmings ☐ 7 Inventor ☐ *So Goes My Love* (GB: *A Genius in the Family*) ☐ Don Ameche ☐ 8 Research scientist ☐ *The Story of Dr Ehrlich's Magic Bullet* ☐ Edward G. Robinson ☐ 9 Baseball player ☐ *The Winning Team* ☐ Ronald Reagan ☐ 10 Inventor ☐ *The Story of Alexander Graham Bell* ☐ (GB: *The Modern Miracle*) Don Ameche ☐ 11 Aviatrix ☐ *They Flew Alone* (US: *Wings and the Woman*) ☐ Anna Neagle ☐ 12 Singer ☐ *A Lady's Morals* ☐ Grace Moore ☐ 13 Singer ☐ *With a Song in My Heart* ☐ Susan Hayward ☐ 14 Inventor ☐ *The Magic Box* ☐ Robert Donat ☐ 15 Actress ☐ *Peg of Old Drury* ☐ Anna Neagle ☐ 16 Singer ☐ *The Interrupted Melody* ☐ Eleanor Parker ☐ 17 Music hall performer ☐ *After the Ball* ☐ Pat Kirkwood ☐ 18 Aviation pioneer ☐ *Gallant Journey* ☐ Glenn Ford ☐ 19 War veteran ☐ *Hell to Eternity* ☐ Jeffrey Hunter ☐ 20 War correspondent ☐ *The Story of GI Joe* ☐ Burgess Meredith ☐ 21 Convict ☐ *Birdman of Alcatraz* ☐ Burt Lancaster ☐ 22 Impresario ☐ *Tonight We Sing* ☐ David Wayne ☐ 23 Convicted murderess ☐ *I Want to Live* ☐ Susan Hayward ☐ 24 Sailor ☐ *John Paul Jones* ☐ Robert Stack ☐ 25 Entertainer ☐ *The I Don't Care Girl* ☐ Mitzi Gaynor ☐ 26 Comedian ☐ *The Seven Little Foys* ☐ Bob Hope ☐ 27 Aircraft inventor ☐ *The First of the Few* ☐ Leslie Howard ☐ 28 Singer ☐ *So This Is Love* ☐ Kathryn Grayson ☐ 29 Statesman ☐ *A Man for All Seasons* ☐ Paul Scofield ☐ 30 Missionary ☐ *The Inn of the Sixth Happiness* ☐ Ingrid Bergman ☐

blacks in films

1 *The Birth of a Nation* ☐ 2 *Tales of Manhattan* ☐ 3 *The Emperor Jones* ☐ 4 James Baskett ☐ played Uncle Remus ☐ in *Song of the South* ☐ 5 Godfrey Cambridge ☐ 6 His colour was not mentioned ☐ 7 Juano Hernandez ☐ 8 Willie Best ☐ Sleep 'n Eat ☐ 9 *Uptight* ☐ *The Lost Man* ☐ *Cool Breeze* ☐ 10 *Stormy Weather* ☐ 11 William Marshall ☐ 12 Dooley Wilson ☐ 13 Sidney Poitier ☐ Harry Belafonte ☐ Bill Cosby ☐ *Let's Do It Again* ☐ 14 Hattie McDaniel ☐ 15 Louise Beavers ☐ 16 Cicely Tyson ☐ 17 *Hallelujah* ☐ 18 Paul Robeson ☐ *The Proud Valley* ☐ 19 *Get Christie Love* ☐ 20 Stepin Fetchit ☐

British title changes

1 *The Way Ahead* ☐ 2 *A Town Like Alice* ☐ 3 *The Quatermass Experiment* ☐ 4 *The Story of Esther Costello* ☐ 5 *A Matter of Life and Death* ☐ 6 *Cry the Beloved Country* ☐ 7 *Busman's Honeymoon* ☐ 8 *The Card* ☐ 9 *Fanatic* ☐ 10 *The First of the Few* ☐ 11 *Pimpernel Smith* ☐ 12 *The Way to the Stars* ☐ 13 *Witchfinder General* ☐ 14 *Young and Innocent* ☐ 15 *Sabotage* ☐ 16 *Whisky Galore* ☐ 17 *Ice Cold in Alex* ☐ 18 *Fanny by Gaslight* ☐ 19 *Father Brown* ☐ 20 *The Battle of the River Plate* ☐

Broadway

1 *Angela Lansbury* ☐ 2 *Gwen Verdon* ☐ 3 *Richard Kiley* ☐ 4 *Barbara Harris* ☐ 5 *Zero Mostel* ☐ 6 *Glynis Johns* ☐ 7 *Carol Lawrence* ☐ 8 *Julie Andrews* ☐ 9 *Mary Martin* ☐ 10 *Howard Keel* ☐ 11 *Robert Alda* ☐ 12 *Jill Haworth* ☐

C

Caan, James (1938–). American leading man who has not quite made the front rank, but continues promising.
□Irma La Douce 63. Lady in a Cage 64. The Glory Guys 65. Red Line 7000 65. El Dorado 67. Games 67. Journey to Shiloh 68. Countdown 68. Submarine XI 68. The Rain People 69. Rabbit Run 70. Man Without Mercy 70. *Brian's Song* (TV) 71. T. R. Baskin 72. *The Godfather* 72. Slither 73. Cinderella Liberty 75. Freebie and the Bean 75. The Gambler 75. Funny Lady 75. Godfather Two (cameo) 75. Rollerball 75. The Killer Elite 76. Harry and Walter Go to New York 76. A Bridge Too Far 77. Another Man, Another Chance 77. Comes a Horseman 78. Chapter Two 79. Hide in Plain Sight (& d) 80. Les Uns et les Autres 81. Thief 81. Bolero 81. Kiss Me Goodbye 82. Gardens of Stone 87.

¶ *J.C.:* My acting technique is to look up at God just before the camera rolls and say, 'Give me a break.'

Cabanne, Christy (1888–1950). American silent film director for Griffith and Fairbanks; declined to second features when talkies came.
Enoch Arden 15. Flirting with Fate 16. Reckless Youth 22. Youth for Sale 24. The Masked Bride 27. Altars of Desire 27. Hotel Continental 32. Daring Daughters 33. A Girl of the Limberlost 34. Keeper of the Bees 35. The Last Outlaw 36. Criminal Lawyer 37. Mutiny on the Blackhawk 39. The Mummy's Hand 40. Scattergood Baines 41. Drums of the Congo 42. Keep 'Em Slugging 43. Scared to Death 46. Robin Hood of Monterey 47. Back Trail 48, many others.

Cabaret (US 1972). A striking musical in its own right, this further variation of *I am a Camera* (qv) by way of a stage musical unwisely tried to be shocking and jettisoned all the middle-aged characters who gave it dramatic strength, but contrived to present a vivid picture of Berlin in the early thirties. Liza Minnelli (AA) and Joel Grey (AA) dealt vibrantly with the musical numbers, but the real star was choreographer/director Robert Fosse (AA). The film won five other Academy Awards.

Cabin in the Sky (US 1943). This all-black musical drama, a variation on the Faust theme, marked an important step forward in Hollywood's humanizing of coloured people, though they still seemed to live in a never-never all-black ghetto. Directed by Vincent Minnelli from the stage play by Lynn Root, John Latouche and Vernon Duke; photographed by Sidney Wagner; with Eddie Anderson, Ethel Waters and Lena Horne.

The Cabinet of Dr Caligari (Germany 1919). Classic horror film, valued not only for its expressionist sets and clever story finally revealed to have been told by a madman, but for its unmistakable influence on German film-making of the twenties. Werner Krauss, Conrad Veidt and Lil Dagover starred, Robert Weine directed from a script by Carl Mayer and Hans Janowitz; Willi Hameister was photographer. Allowing for certain primitive aspects, it still has power to thrill; certainly more so than the inferior American remake of 1962, which used the gimmicks but little else.

Cabiria (Italy 1913). A famous silent spectacle set in Caesarean Rome and concerning the romantic adventures of a lively lady saved as an infant from sacrifice to Baal. Her strong-man servant is one Maciste, who has reappeared as hero of scores of Italian adventure films since. Directed by Pastrone from a scenario by himself and Gabriele d'Annunzio; starring Lidia Quaranta, Bartolomeo Pagano. The original film ran over four hours: a condensed sound version was issued in 1930 and in 1950 came a rather poor remake. Fellini's *Nights of Cabiria* (Italy 1957) is something else again, a wry modern comedy about the ill-luck of a cheerful prostitute, starring Giulietta Masina. This emerged again in 1969 as the Hollywood musical *Sweet Charity*, with Shirley Maclaine.

cable. A method of disseminating television programmes by underground cable whose fibres can accommodate a great many channels, none of them subject to interference from the others. From the mid-seventies it became highly popular in America because of poor airwave reception in many areas; as a subscription service it also screened fewer commercials and most of its movies were uncut. These advantages however did not apply in most other countries, where it had a slower start.

cable cars have added excitement to the climax of many a film adventure, notably *Night Train to Munich, The Trollenberg Terror, Edge of Eternity, Second Chance, Where Eagles Dare, Hannibal Brooks* and *The Double Man.* In 1979 Irwin Allen made a four-hour TV suspenser, *Hanging by a Thread*, entirely about a cable car accident; but it failed to thrill.

Cabot, Bruce (1904–1972) (Etienne Pelissier de Bujac). Square-jawed American hero of many a thirties action adventure; later turned up as a western villain.
Roadhouse Murder 32. *King Kong* 33. Murder on the Blackboard 34. Let 'Em Have It 35. Show Them No Mercy 35. Fury 36. Legion of Terror 37. Love Takes Flight 37. Smashing the Rackets 38. Homicide Bureau 39. Dodge City 39. Captain Caution 40. The Flame of New Orleans 41. Wild Bill Hickok Rides 42. The Desert Song 43. Salty O'Rourke 45. Fallen Angel 46. Angel and the Badman 47. Sorrowful Jones 49. Fancy Pants 50. Best of the Badmen 51. Kid Monk Baroni 52. The Quiet American 58. John Paul Jones 59. The Comancheros 61. Hatari 62. Law of the Lawless 64. Cat Ballou 65. The War Wagon 67. The Green Berets 68. Big Jake 71. Diamonds are Forever 71, many others.

Cabot, Sebastian (1918–77). Weighty British character actor who became popular on American TV as the incarnation of the pompous but amiable Englishman.
Secret Agent 36. Love on the Dole 41. The Agitator 45. They Made Me a Fugitive 47. Dick Barton Strikes Back 48. Old Mother Riley's Jungle Treasure 50. Ivanhoe 52. Babes in Baghdad 52. Romeo and Juliet 54. *Kismet* 55. Dragoon Wells Massacre 57. Terror in a Texas Town 58. The Time Machine 60. Twice Told Tales 63. The Family Jewels 65, etc.
TV series: *Checkmate* 59–61. *A Family Affair* 66–70. Ghost Story 73.

Cabot, Susan (1927–86) (Harriet Shapiro). American leading lady of the fifties.
The Enforcer 50. Flame of Araby 51. Battle at Apache Pass 52. Duel at Silver Creek 52. Ride Clear of Diablo 54. Fort Massacre 58. The Wasp Woman 60, etc.

Cacavas, John (1930–). American composer.
Redneck 72. Horror Express 72. The Satanic Rites of Dracula 74. Airport 75 75. Airport 77 77. Murder at the World Series (TV) 77. Superdome (TV) 78. Hangar 18 80.

Cacoyannis, Michael (1922–). Greek director, trained in England.
Windfall in Athens 53. Stella 54. A Girl in Black 55. A Matter of Dignity 57. One Last Spring 59. The Wastrel 61. Electra 62. *Zorba the Greek* 65. The Day the Fish Came Out 67. The Trojan Women 71. Iphigenia 76. Sweet Country (b&w) 86.

Cadell, Jean (1884–1967). Sharp-faced Scottish character actress, typically cast as acidulous spinster and latterly dowager.
The Loves of Robert Burns 30. Fires of Fate 33. *David Copperfield* (as Mrs Micawber) 34. Love from a Stranger 37. *Pygmalion* 38. Quiet Wedding 40. The Young Mr Pitt 42. Dear Octopus 43. I Know Where I'm Going 45. Jassy 47. *Whisky Galore* 48. Madeleine 50. The Late Edwina Black 51. Marry Me 52. Rockets Galore 56. *A Taste of Money* (leading role) 62, many others.

Caesar, Adolph (*c.*1932–86). Black American actor who made an impression in *A Soldier's Story* 85, and received an Academy Award nomination.
The Color Purple 85.

Caesar and Cleopatra (GB 1945). Notorious as Britain's most expensive picture, this entertaining version of Shaw's comedy was produced with unnecessary elaboration and recklessness by Gabriel Pascal. It did not do particularly well at the box office but has strong entertainment value mainly deriving from Shaw and the performances of Claude Rains and Vivien Leigh.

Caesar, Irving (1895–). American song composer and lyricist. Among others: *No No Nanette, Hit the Deck, Wonder Bar.*

Caesar, Sid (1922–). American comedian, seldom in films but a big TV hit of the fifties, especially in *Your Show of Shows.*
□Tars and Spars 45. The Guilt of Janet Ames

47. It's a Mad Mad Mad Mad World 63. A Guide for the Married Man 67. The Busy Body 67. Ten from Your Show of Shows 74. Airport 75 75. Silent Movie 76. The Cheap Detective 78. Grease 78. The Fiendish Plot of Fu Manchu 80. History of the World Part One 81. Grease 2 82. Cannonball Run 2 83. Over the Brooklyn Bridge 83. Stoogemania 86. The Emperor's New Clothes 87.

La Cage aux Folles (France/Italy 1978). A frantic farce about a homosexual night club owner who pretends to be straight, this normally competent product achieved an amazing international success and in 1983 became a Broadway musical. Directed by Edouard Molinaro from a play by Jean Poiret; with Ugo Tognazzi, Michel Serrault. *La Cage aux Folles II*, which followed in 1981, was a disaster shunned by all.

Cage, Nicholas (1964–) (N. Coppola). American leading actor. Rumblefish 83. Racing with the Moon 83. The Cotton Club 84. Birdy 85. Raising Arizona 87, etc.

Cagney, James (1899–86). American leading actor whose cocky walk and punchy personality took him out of the vaudeville chorus to become one of the most memorable stars of the thirties and forties.
Autobiography 1976: *Cagney by Cagney*.
□Sinners' Holiday 30. Doorway to Hell 30. The Steel Highway 30. The Millionaire 31. Other Men's Women 31. *The Public Enemy* 31. Smart Money 31. Blonde Crazy 31. Taxi 32. The Crowd Roars 32. Winner Take All 32. Hard to Handle 33. The Picture Snatcher 33. Mayor of Hell 33. *Footlight Parade* 33. *Lady Killer* 33. Jimmy the Gent 34. He was her Man 34. Here Comes the Navy 34. The St Louis Kid 34. *Devil Dogs of the Air* 35. *G-Men* 35. The Irish in Us 35. *A Midsummer Night's Dream* (as Bottom) 35. The Frisco Kid 35. Ceiling Zero 35. Great Guy 36. Something to Sing About 37. *Boy Meets Girl* 38. *Angels with Dirty Faces* 38. The Oklahoma Kid 39. Each Dawn I Die 39. *The Roaring Twenties* 39. The Fighting 69th 40. Torrid Zone 40. City for Conquest 40. *Strawberry Blonde* 41. The Bride Came C.O.D. 41. Captains of the Clouds 42. *Yankee Doodle Dandy* (AA; as George M. Cohan) 42. Johnny Come Lately 43. Blood on the Sun 45. 13 Rue Madeleine 46. *The Time of Your Life* 48. *White Heat* 49. West Point Story 50. Kiss Tomorrow Goodbye 50. Come Fill the Cup 51. Starlift 51. What Price Glory? 52. A Lion is in the Streets 53. Run for Cover 55. Love Me or Leave Me 55. The Seven Little Foys (guest) 55. *Mister Roberts* 55. Tribute to a Bad Man 56. These Wilder Years 56. *Man of a Thousand Faces* (as Lon Chaney) 57. Short Cut to Hell (d only) 58. Never Steal Anything Small 59. Shake Hands with the Devil 59. The Gallant Hours 60. *One Two Three* 61. Arizona Bushwhackers (narrator only) 68. Ragtime 81. Terrible Joe Moran (TV) 84.

❀ For refining the image of the irrepressible Irishman; for inventing a unique form of dancing; and, whether as gangster or cop, for providing work for a thousand imitators. *Yankee Doodle Dandy*.

¶ He can't even put a telephone receiver back on the hook without giving the action some special spark of life.—*Time*

There's not much to say about acting but this. Never settle back on your heels. Never relax. If you relax, the audience relaxes. And always mean everything you say.—*J.C.*

Cagney has an inspired sense of timing, an arrogant style, a pride in the control of his body and a conviction and lack of self-consciousness that is unique in the deserts of the American cinema.—*Lincoln Kirstein, 1932*

He can do nothing which is not worth watching.—*Graham Greene*

I'm sick of carrying guns and beating up women.—*J.C.* 1931.

I admire him for quitting when he was at the top.—*Robert Redford*

Famous line (*White Heat*): 'Made it, ma—top of the world!'

Famous line (*Yankee Doodle Dandy*): 'My mother thanks you, my father thanks you, my sister thanks you—and I thank you.'

? In which film did James Cagney:

1 Constantly hitch his shoulders?
2 Join the Canadian Air Corps?
3 Bring in a banana crop?
4 Stage live prologues for movie theatres?
5 Promote a grapefruit diet?
6 Philosophize in a bar?
7 Become president of a longshoremen's union?
8 Train OSS undercover agents?
9 Get himself jailed for vagrancy?
10 Extract his co-star from a cactus patch?
11 Play a dentist?
12 Become a coward in the front line during World War I?
13 Play a Hollywood scriptwriter?
14 Co-star with Edward G. Robinson?
15 Play a movie theatre usher?

Cagney, Jeanne (?1908–84) (Jean Cagney). American actress, in occasional films: sister of James Cagney.
Golden Gloves 40. Yankee Doodle Dandy 42. The Time of Your Life 48. Don't Bother to Knock 52. A Lion is in the Streets 53. Man of a Thousand Faces 57. Town Tamer 65, etc.

Cagney, William (1902–). American producer, brother of James Cagney.
Johnny Come Lately 43. Blood on the Sun 45. The Time of Your Life 48. Kiss Tomorrow Goodbye 50. A Lion is in the Streets 53, etc.

Cahn, Edward L. (1899–1963). American director of second features.
Homicide Squad 31. *Law and Order* 32 (his best film, with Walter Huston as Wyatt Earp). Confidential 35. Main Street After Dark 44. The Checkered Coat 48. Prejudice 48. Experiment Alcatraz (& p) 51. The Creature with the Atom Brain 55. Girls in Prison 56. Curse of the Faceless Man 58. Guns, Girls and Gangsters 58. It, The Terror from Beyond Space 58. Riot in a Juvenile Prison 61. Beauty and the Beast 62. Incident in an Alley 63, many others.

Cahn, Sammy (1913–) (Samuel Cohen). American lyricist who has written many film songs, usually with James Van Heusen. Won Academy Awards for four songs: 'Three Coins in the Fountain', 'High Hopes', 'All the Way' and 'Call Me Irresponsible'.
Autobiography 1974: *I Should Care.*
Tonight and Every Night 44. Anchors Aweigh 45. Wonder Man 45. West Point Story 50. April in Paris 53. The Court Jester 55, etc.

Cain, James M. (1892–1977). American novelist of the hard-boiled school; also worked in Hollywood.
She Made Her Bed (oa) 34. Stand Up and Fight (w) 38. When Tomorrow Comes (oa) 39. *Double Indemnity* (oa) 44. Gypsy Wildcat (w) 44. *Mildred Pierce* (oa) 45. *The Postman Always Rings Twice* (oa) 46. Serenade (oa) 56, etc.

Caine, Michael (1933–) (Maurice Micklewhite). British light leading man with effective mild manner and deliberately unconcealed cockney origin. Played for years in second features before his international appeal was discovered.
How to Murder a Rich Uncle 56. A Hill in Korea 56. Blind Spot 58. The Key 58. Passport to Shame 58. The Wrong Arm of the Law 62. Solo for Sparrow 62, etc.

□COMPLETE FROM 1963: *Zulu* 63. *The Ipcress File* 65. *Alfie* 66. The Wrong Box 66. Gambit 66. Funeral in Berlin 66. Woman Times Seven 67. Hurry Sundown 67. Billion Dollar Brain 67. Deadfall 68. The Magus 68. Play Dirty 68. The Italian Job 69. The Battle of Britain 69. Too Late the Hero 69. The Last Valley 70. *Get Carter* 71. Zee and Co 71. Kidnapped 72. Pulp 72. *Sleuth* 73. The Black Windmill 73. The Marseilles Contract 74. The Wilby Conspiracy 75. Peeper 75. The Romantic Englishwoman 75. The Man Who Would Be King 76. Harry and Walter Go To New York 76. The Eagle Has Landed 76. A Bridge Too Far 77. Silver Bears 77. Swarm 78. Ashanti 78. *California Suite* 78. Beyond the Poseidon Adventure 79. Dressed to Kill 80. The Island 80. The Hand 81. Victory 81. Deathtrap 82. *Educating Rita* (AAN) 83. The Honorary Consul 83. The Jigsaw Man 83. Blame It On Rio 84. Water 84. The Holcroft Covenant 84. *Hannah and Her Sisters* 85. Sweet Liberty 86. Half Moon Street 86. The Whistle Blower 86. Mona Lisa 86. The Fourth Protocol 86. Jaws—The Revenge 87.

¶ *M.C.:* I'll always be there because I'm a skilled professional actor. Whether or not I've any talent is beside the point.
M.C.: John Wayne once advised me, talk low, talk slow and don't talk too much. And then I went and made *Sleuth*.
M.C.: I'm a sort of boy next door. If that boy has a good scriptwriter.

The Caine Mutiny (US 1954). Humphrey Bogart gave his last notable performance as the paranoiac Captain Queeg in this solid film version by Edward Dmytryk of Herman Wouk's bestseller about the courtroom drama following a modern naval mutiny. The film is otherwise significant as an example of the adult but not difficult themes being pursued by Hollywood at this time: long-time idols like the US Navy could be questioned but not yet toppled.

Calamity Jane (c. 1848–1903) (Martha Jane Canary). This rootin' tootin' shootin' woman of the old west has been glamorized many times for the movies, notably by Jean Arthur in *The Plainsman* 36, Frances Farmer in *Badlands of Dakota* 41, Jane Russell in *The Paleface* 48, Yvonne de Carlo in *Calamity Jane and Sam Bass* 49, Evelyn Ankers in *The Texan Meets Calamity Jane* 50, Doris Day in *Calamity Jane* 53, Judi Meredith in *The Raiders* 64, and Abby Dalton in *The Plainsman* 66.

Calder-Marshall, Anna (1949–). British leading actress.
Pussycat Pussycat I Love You 70. *Wuthering Heights* 70. Zulu Dawn 79.

Caldwell, Erskine (1903–). American novelist who attacked social injustice in several novels which by their sensationalism earned him a fortune. *Tobacco Road* was filmed as a farce; *God's Little Acre* had to be taken straight.

Calhern, Louis (1895–1956) (Carl Vogt). Distinguished American stage actor who was in films occasionally from silent days and later became one of MGM's elder statesmen.
□What's Worth While? 21. The Blot 21. Too Wise Wives 21. Women, Wake Up 22. The Last Moment 23. Stolen Heaven 31. Road to Singapore 31. Blonde Crazy 31 The Call It Sin 32. Night After Night 32. Okay America 32. Afraid to Talk 32. The Woman Accused 33. Twenty Thousand Years in Sing Sing 33. Frisco Jenny 33. Strictly Personal 33. World Gone Mad 33. Diplomaniacs 33. Duck Soup 33. Affairs of Cellini 34. Man with Two Faces 34. The Count of Monte Cristo 34. Sweet Adeline 34. The Arizonian 34. Woman Wanted 35. The Last Days of Pompeii 35. The Gorgeous Hussy 36. Her Husband Lies 36. The Life of Emile Zola 37. Fast Company 38. Juarez 39. Fifth Avenue Girl 39. Charlie McCarthy Detective 39. I Take this Woman 40. Dr Ehrlich's Magic Bullet 40. Heaven Can Wait 43. Nobody's Darling 43. Up in Arms 44. The Bridge of San Luis Rey 44. Notorious 46. Arch of Triumph 48. The Red Pony 49. The Red Danube 49. *Annie Get Your Gun* (as Buffalo Bill) 50. Nancy Goes to Rio 50. *The Asphalt Jungle* 50. Devil's Doorway 50. A Life of Her Own 50. *The Magnificent Yankee* 50. Two Weeks with Love 50. Man with a Cloak 51. It's a Big Country 51. Invitation 52. We're Not Married 52. Washington Story 52. *The Prisoner of Zenda* 52. Confidentially Connie 53. Remains To Be Seen 53. Julius Caesar (title role) 53. Latin Lovers 53. Main Street to Broadway 53. Rhapsody 54. Executive Suite 54. The Student Prince 54. Men of the Fighting Lady 54. Betrayed 54. Athena 54. The Blackboard Jungle 55. The Prodigal 55. Forever Darling 56. High Society 56.

Calhoun, Rory (1922–) (Francis Timothy Durgin). Amiable American leading man of fifties action films; did not make the first rank.
Something for the Boys 44. The Red House 47. Miraculous Journey 48. Massacre River 49. Rogue River 50. I'd Climb the Highest Mountain 51. *With a Song in My Heart* 52. Powder River 53. *How to Marry a Millionaire* 53. Four Guns to the Border 54. Dawn at Socorro 54. Treasure of Pancho Villa 55. The Spoilers 55. Raw Edge 56. The Big Caper 57. The Hired Gun 57. The Colossus of Rhodes 60. Marco Polo 61. A Face in the Rain 62. The Gun Hawk 64. Apache Uprising 65. Finger on the Trigger 67. Dayton's Devils 68. Night of the Lepus 72. Avenging Angel 84, many others.
TV series: The Texan 58–59. Capitol 82–

Callahan, Gene (–). American production designer.
The Friends of Eddie Coyle 73. Bloodbrothers 78. King of the Gypsies 78. Chapter Two 79. Seems Like Old Times 80. Whose Life Is It Anyway? 81, etc.

Callan, Michael (1935–) (Martin Caliniff). American leading man, former dancer.
They Came to Cordura 58. The Flying Fontaines 59. Mysterious Island 61. Bon Voyage 62. The Interns 63. The Victors 63. Cat Ballou 65. You Must Be Joking 65. Lepke 75, etc.
TV series: Occasional Wife 66.

Callard, Kay (–). Canadian leading lady in Britain in the fifties.
They Who Dare 54. Find the Lady 56. Intent to Kill 58. Freedom to Die 62, etc.
TV series: Knight Errant 58–60.

Callas, Maria (1923–1977) (Maria Kalogeropolos). Celebrated Greek-American opera singer who in 1971 played the non-singing role of *Medea*.

Calleia, Joseph (1897–1975) (Joseph Spurin-Calleja). Humorous but often sinister Maltese character actor who after world tours as an opera singer settled in Hollywood in the thirties and played several distinguished roles.
His Woman 31. Public Hero Number One 35. After the Thin Man 36. Winner Take All 37. *Algiers* 38. Juarez 39. *Five Came Back* 39. *Golden Boy* 39. My Little Chickadee 40. The Monster and the Girl 41. Jungle Book 42. *The Glass Key* 42. For Whom the Bell Tolls 43. The Conspirators 44. *Gilda* 46. Lured 47. Four Faces West 48. Noose (GB) 48. Vendetta 50. Branded 51. Valentino 51. When in Rome 52. Treasure of Pancho Villa 55. Hot Blood 56. Serenade 56. Wild is the Wind 57. Touch of Evil 58. Cry Tough 59. The Alamo 60. Johnny Cool 63, many others.

Callow, Simon (1949–). British stage actor, in occasional films.
☐ Amadeus 84. A Room with a View 86. Maurice 87.

Calloway, Cab (1907–) (Cabell Calloway). High-spirited black American band leader and entertainer, in occasional films.
Autobiography 1976: *Of Minnie the Moocher and Me.*
The Big Broadcast 32. International House 33. The Singing Kid 36. Manhattan Merry Go Round 37. *Stormy Weather* 43. Sensations of 1945 44. St Louis Blues 58. The Cincinnati Kid 65. A Man Called Adam 66. The Blues Brothers 80, etc.

Calthrop, Donald (1888–1940). Slightly-built British stage actor whose film appearances were usually as nervy villains.
The Gay Lord Quex 18. Nelson 19. *Shooting Stars* 27. *Blackmail* 29. Atlantic 30. Murder 30. The Bells 31. Number Seventeen 32. The Ghost Train 32. Rome Express 32. I Was a Spy 33. Friday the Thirteenth 33. Sorrell and Son 34. The Clairvoyant 34. Scrooge 35. Broken Blossoms 36. Fire Over England 36. Dreaming Lips 37. Let George Do It 40. Major Barbara 40, etc.

Calvert, E. H. (1873–1941). American silent screen director who later had a second career as an actor, usually in military roles.
AS DIRECTOR: One Wonderful Night 14. The Slim Princess 15. The Man Trail 15. The Outer Edge 15. A Daughter of the City 15, etc.
AS ACTOR: The House of Pride 12. Vultures of Society 16. The Silent Partner 23. Inez from Hollywood 24. Sally 25. Ella Cinders 26. Rookies 27. The Wizard 27. Legion of the Condemned 28. The Canary Murder Case 29. The Virginian 29. The Love Parade 30. The Benson Murder Case 30. Beyond Victory 31. The Mysterious Rider 33. Here Comes the Groom 34. The Oregon Trail 36, many others.

Calvert, Phyllis (1915–) (Phyllis Bickle). British leading lady of the forties, former child actress; usually played good girls.
Two Days to Live 39. They Came by Night 39. Charley's Big Hearted Aunt 40. Let George Do It 40. *Kipps* 41. The Young Mr Pitt 42. Uncensored 42. *The Man in Grey* 43. *Fanny by Gaslight* 44. Two Thousand Women 44. *Madonna of the Seven Moons* 44. They Were Sisters 45. Men of Two Worlds 46. The Magic Bow 46. The Root of All Evil 47. Time Out of Mind (US) 47. *My Own True Love* (US) 48. Broken Journey 48. Appointment with Danger (US) 49. The Golden Madonna 49. The Woman with No Name 50. Mr Denning Drives North 51. *Mandy* 52. The Net 53. It's Never Too Late 55. Child in the House 56. Indiscreet 58. Oscar Wilde 60. The Battle of the Villa Fiorita 65. Twisted Nerve 68. Oh What a Lovely War 69. The Walking Stick 69, etc.
TV series: *Kate* 70–71.

Calvet, Corinne (1925–) (Corinne Dibos). French leading lady, a statuesque blonde who had some success in Hollywood in the early fifties.
Autobiography 1983: *Has Corinne Been a Good Girl?*
La Part de l'Ombre 45. Rope of Sand 49. When Willie Comes Marching Home 50. On the Riviera 51. What Price Glory? 52. Powder River 53. Flight to Tangier 53. The Far Country 54. So This Is Paris 55. The Plunderers of Painted Flats 58. Bluebeard's Ten Honeymoons 60. Hemingway's Adventures of a Young Man 62. Apache Uprising 65. Dr Heckle and Mr Hype 80, etc.

Calvin, Henry (1918–1975) (Wimberly Calvin Goodman Jnr). Rotund American comedy actor who for a while appeared in Disney films imitating Oliver Hardy.
Babes in Toyland 60. Toby Tyler 63.
TV series: Zorro.

Cambern, Donn (–). American editor.
Easy Rider 69. The Last Picture Show 71. Steelyard Blues 72. Blume in Love 73. Cinderella Liberty 74. The Hindenburg 75. The Other Side of Midnight 77. Time after Time 80. Willie and Phil 80. The Cannonball Run 81. Paternity 81, etc.

Cambridge, Godfrey (1929–1976). Black American comic actor.
The Last Angry Man 59. Gone are the Days 63. The Busy Body 67. The President's Analyst 67. Bye Bye Braverman 68. The Biggest Bundle of Them All 68. *Watermelon Man* 70. *Cotton Comes to Harlem* 70. The Biscuit Eater 72. Come Back Charleston Blue 72, etc.

Camelot (US 1967). This overlong film version by Joshua Logan of the Lerner and Loewe stage musical proved to be a deliberately sober retelling of the Arthurian myth, with too few successful flights of fancy and too little of the wit of T. H. White's *The*

Once and Future King on which it was based. The music however was splendid, and intelligence was evident though misapplied. Richard Harris and Vanessa Redgrave were perhaps the last non-singers to be entrusted with major singing roles; they were in any case upstaged by John Truscott's set designs. See also: *Arthur*.

cameo. A word coined (in its cinematic sense) by Mike Todd when persuading famous stars to accept walk-on parts for *Around the World in Eighty Days*.

Camerini, Mario (1895–1981). Italian director of the old commercial school.
The House of Pulcini 24. Kiff Tebbi 27. Rotaie 29. Giallo 33. Il Grande Appello 36. Il Signor Max 37. Il Documento Fatale 39. Una Romantica Avventura 40. I Promessi Sposi 41. Due Lettere Anonime 45. The Captain's Daughter 47. Molti Sogni per le Strade 48. Il Brigante Musolino 50. Wife for a Night 51. Ulysses 54. The Miller's Wife 55. Primo Amore 58. Via Margutta 60. And Suddenly It's Murder 60. Kali-Yug Goddess of Vengeance 63. Don Camillo and Modern Youth 72, many others.

Cameron, Earl (1925–). Jamaican actor seen in many British films.
Pool of London 50. Emergency Call 51. The Heart of the Matter 53. Simba 55. Safari 56. Sapphire 59. Flame in the Streets 61. Guns at Batasi 64. Thunderball 65. Battle Beneath the Earth 68. Mohammed 77, etc.

Cameron, John (1944–). British composer.
Poor Cow 67. The Ruling Class 68. Kes 70. Every Home Should Have One 70. All the Right Noises 71. A Touch of Class (AAN) 73. Scalawag 73. Night Watch 73. Out of Season 75. Great Scout and Cathouse Thursday 76. Nasty Habits 77. The Thief of Baghdad 78. Sunburn 79. Lost and Found 79. The Mirror Crack'd 80, etc.

Cameron, Rod (1910–1983) (Nathan Cox). Rugged Canadian star of many a Hollywood second feature; originally labourer, engineer, and stand-in for Fred MacMurray.
Christmas in July 40. Northwest Mounted Police 40. The Monster and the Girl 41. The Remarkable Andrew 42. Wake Island 42. Gung Ho 43. Boss of Boom Town 44. Salome Where She Danced 45. The Runaround 46. The Bride Wasn't Willing 46. The Plunderers 48. Panhandle 49. The Sea Hornet 51. Ride the Man Down 53. Escapement (GB) 57. The Gun Hawk 63. The Bounty Killer 65. Old Firehand (Ger.) 66. The Last Movie 71. Evel Knievel 71. Jessie's Girls 76, many others.
TV series: City Detective 53–54. Coronado 9 59. State Trooper 57–59.

Camille. The Dumas *fils* tear-jerker about a courtesan dying of tuberculosis has been a favourite vehicle for many actresses. On screen, Bernhardt did it in 1912, Clara Kimball Young in 1915, Theda Bara in 1917, Nazimova (with Rudolph Valentino) in 1920, Pola Negri in 1920, Norma Talmadge (with Gilbert Roland) in 1927 and Garbo (with Robert Taylor) in 1936. In post-war years many producers must have eyed it longingly before deciding that it belonged to a bygone age: but in 1969 *Camille 2000* arrived, decked out with drugs and heavy sex.
In 1982 *La Traviata* (the opera version) was filmed, and in 1985 came a straight TV movie version.

Camp, Joe (–). American director of independent family films: *Benji*, *For the Love of Benji*, etc.

Campanella, Joseph (1927–). American stage and TV actor who makes occasional film appearances.
Murder Inc. 61. The Young Lovers 64. The St Valentine's Day Massacre 67. Ben 72, etc.
TV series: *Mannix* 67–69. The Bold Ones 70.

Campanile, Pasquale Festa (–1986). Italian director.
The Chastity Belt 67. The Girl and the General 68. The Libertine 69. La Calandria 73, etc.

Campbell, Beatrice (1923–1980). British leading lady.
Wanted for Murder 46. Things Happen at Night 48. Silent Dust 48. Last Holiday 50. The Mudlark 50. Laughter in Paradise 51. Grand National Night 53. Cockleshell Heroes 55, etc.

Campbell, Colin (1883–1966). Diminutive Scottish character actor, long in Hollywood.
Tillie's Tomato Surprise 15. Where Lights are Low 21. The Grail 23. The White Monkey 25. Big Boy 30. Alice in Wonderland 33. San Francisco Docks 41. Mrs Miniver 42. The Lodger 44. Moss Rose 47. The Fan 49. Abbott and Costello Meet the Keystone Kops 55. The Lost World 60.

Campbell, Colin (1937–). Young British proletarian actor of the sixties.
Saturday Night Out 63. The Leather Boys 63. The High Bright Sun 65.

Campbell, Eric (1878–1917). Scottish actor who played the bearded heavy in some of Chaplin's most famous two-reelers 1916–17: *Easy Street, The Cure, The Adventurer,* etc.

Campbell, Glen (1935–). American pop singer, venturing into films.
True Grit 69. Norwood 69.

Campbell, Judy (1916–) (Judy Gamble). British leading lady of stage and TV; film appearances infrequent.
Saloon Bar 40. Breach of Promise 41. The World Owes Me a Living 44. Green for Danger 46. Bonnie Prince Charlie 48. There's a Girl in My Soup 70. Forbush and the Penguins 71, etc.

Campbell, Mrs Patrick (1865–1940) (Beatrice Tanner). Leading British stage actress, the original Eliza in *Pygmalion,* who spent her last years playing supporting roles in Hollywood. Marie Dressler caricatured her as Carlotta Vance in *Dinner at Eight.*
□The Dancers 30. Riptide 34. One More River 34. Outcast Lady 34. Crime and Punishment 35.

'She has an ego like a raging tooth.'—*W. B. Yeats*

(Reported conversation) 'You are handsome enough to be in pictures.' —'But Mrs Campbell, my name is Joseph Schildkraut.' —'Never mind, you can change it.'

(When offered the role of the pawnbroker in *Crime and Punishment*) 'I could not possibly become a tradesperson.'

Campbell, Patrick (1913–1980). British humorist and screenplay writer, the latter usually with Vivienne Knight.
Captain Boycott 47. Helter Skelter 50. The Oracle 54. Lucky Jim 57. Go to Blazes 62. Girl in the Headlines 63, etc.

Campbell, William (1926–). American actor, often seen as personable villain or friend of the hero.
The Breaking Point 50. The People Against O'Hara 52. Escape from Fort Bravo 53. The High and the Mighty 54. Man without a Star 55. Cell 2455 Death Row (as Caryl Chessman) 55. Backlash 56. Eighteen and Anxious 57. The Naked and the Dead 58. The Young Racers 63. The Secret Invasion 64. Hush Hush Sweet Charlotte 64. Dementia 13 65. Blood Bath 66. Black Gunn 72. Dirty Mary Crazy Larry 74, etc.
TV series: Cannonball 58.

Campos, Rafael (1936–85). Dominican actor best remembered for The Blackboard Jungle 55.

Camus, Marcel (1912–1982). French director, chiefly known for *Black Orpheus* 58.

Canada has made strenuous efforts through the years to promote a native film industry, but the trouble has been that its best talents are easily siphoned off to Hollywood or Britain, and few genuinely Canadian films have earned world acclaim; among those to raise interest have been *Mon Oncle Antoine* and *The Apprenticeship of Duddy Kravitz*. The National Film Board of Canada, however, has had a stimulating effect on world documentary, especially when under the leadership of John Grierson: and Norman McLaren's experimental cartoons are enjoyed the world over.

Films wholly or largely set in Canada have included *Saskatchewan, Quebec, Northwest Mounted Police, The Canadians, River's End, The Naked Heart, Northern Pursuit, Island in the Sky, Hudson's Bay, Rose Marie* and *Jalna.* Until the end of the seventies the best of them was probably the wartime *49th Parallel*, but the eighties brought new efforts in the direction of international co-production, and although the first fruits seemed heavily influenced by current Hollywood fashion, signs of a new vitality have undoubtedly emerged.

Canale, Gianna Maria (1927–). Italian leading lady, occasionally seen in international films.
Rigoletto 49. Go For Broke 51. The Man from Cairo 53. Theodora Slave Empress 54. The Silent Enemy 58. The Whole Truth 58. Queen of the Pirates 60. Scaramouche 63, etc.

Canary, David (–). American western actor who played for a while in both *Wagon Train* and *Bonanza*.
Hombre 67. Sharks' Treasure 64. Posse 75. The Dain Curse (TV) 78, etc.

Candy, John (–). American supporting actor. The Silent Partner 78. Lost and Found 79. Stripes 81. Brewster's Millions 84. Splash! 84. Summer Rental 84. Volunteers 85. Little Shop of Horrors 87.

Cannes. A Riviera watering place which since the late forties has housed a film festival having more to do with commerce than with art. Rex Reed described it as a place 'where you lie on the beach and look at the stars—or vice versa'.

cannibalism has been featured in such documentaries as *The Sky Above, The Mud Below,* but it is rare in fiction films. Apart from the Swedish short *Midvinterblot,* the main examples are from the seventies: *Welcome to Arrow Beach* and *Survive!*

Canning, Victor (1911–). British detective novelist whose works have often been filmed.
Spy Hunt 50. The Golden Salamander 51. Venetian Bird 53. The House of the Seven Hawks 59. Masquerade 63.

Cannon and Ball (Tommy Derbyshire, 1938– ; Robert Harper, 1944–). British comedians from the working-men's club circuit. First film, *The Boys in Blue* 83.

Cannon, Dyan (1938–) (Samile Diane Friesen). American leading actress who tends to play floosies.
The Rise and Fall of Legs Diamond 59. *Bob and Carol and Ted and Alice* 69. Doctors' Wives 70. The Anderson Tapes 71. The Love Machine 71. *Such Good Friends* 72. Shamus 72. The Last of Sheila 73. Child Under a Leaf 75. Revenge of the Pink Panther 77. *Heaven Can Wait* 78. Lady of the House (TV) 79. Coast to Coast 80. Honeysuckle Rose 80. Deathtrap 82. Author! Author! 82, etc. Master of the Game (TV) 83. Jenny's War (TV) 84, etc.

Cannon, Esma (1896–1972). Diminutive British character actress often seen in bit parts. Notable in *Sailor Beware* 56.

Cannon, J. D. (1922–). Cold-eyed American character actor.
An American Dream 66. Cool Hand Luke 67. Cotton Comes to Harlem 70. Lawman 71. Testimony of Two Men (TV) 77. Killing Stone (TV) 78. Ike (TV) 79. Raise the Titanic 80. Walking through the Fire (TV) 80. Death Wish 2 81.
TV series: McCloud 71–76.

Cannon, Robert (1901–1964). American animator, a leading figure at UPA during the formative period and the designer of simplified, witty cartoons like *Gerald McBoing Boing* and *Christopher Crumpet*.

Canova, Diana (1953–). American light actress, daughter of Judy Canova.
The First Nudie Musical 76. Love Boat II (TV) 77. With This Ring (TV) 78.
TV series: Soap 77–80. But I'm a Big Girl Now 81. Foot in the Door 83. Throb 86.

Canova, Judy (1916–1983) (Juliet Canova). American hillbilly comedienne whose strident yodelling and cornfed humour enlivened a number of forties programmers.
□In Caliente 35. Broadway Gondolier 35. Going Highbrow 35. Artists and Models 37. Thrill of a Lifetime 37. Scatterbrain 40. Sis Hopkins 41. Puddin'head 41. Sleepytime Gal 42. True to the Army 42. Joan of Ozark 42. Chatterbox 43. Sleepy Lagoon 43. Louisiana Hayride 44. Hit the Hay 45. Singin' in the Corn 45. Honeychile 51. Oklahoma Annie 52. The WAC from Walla Walla 52. Untamed Heiress 54. Carolina Cannonball 55. Lay That Rifle Down 55. The Adventures of Huckleberry Finn 60.

Cantinflas (1911–) (Mario Moreno). Mexican clown, acrobat and bullfighter who made unambitious local comedies for years and was briefly beckoned by Hollywood in the fifties. Immensely popular in Spanish-speaking countries.
Neither Blood Nor Sand 41. Romeo and Juliet 44. *Around the World in Eighty Days* 56. *Pepe* 59, many others.

Cantor, Eddie (1892–1964) (Edward Israel Itskowitz). Rolling-eyed American vaudeville entertainer whose inimitable high-toned voice and sprightly movement made him a big Hollywood star of the thirties. He later made a huge hit in radio, and wrote several autobiographical books including *Take My Life* (57), *The Way I See It* (59) and *As I Remember Them* (62). He appeared briefly in a 1953 biopic, *The Eddie Cantor Story,* in which he was played by Keefe Brasselle, and in 1956 received an Academy Award 'for distinguished service to the film industry'.
□Kid Boots 26. Special Delivery 27. Glorifying the American Girl 29. *Whoopee* 30. Palmy Days 31. *The Kid from Spain* 32. *Roman Scandals* 33. Kid Millions 34. Strike Me Pink 35. Ali Baba Goes to Town 37. Forty Little Mothers 40. *Thank Your Lucky Stars* 43. *Show Business* 44. If You Knew Susie 48. The Story of Will Rogers (guest) 52.

¶ Another bride; another groom;
Another sunny honeymoon;
Another season; another reason
For makin' whoopee . . .
—*Cantor's most famous song*

Canty, Marietta (–1986). Black American character actress.
The Searching Wind 46. Home Sweet Homicide 47. Father of the Bride 50. The I Don't Care Girl 53. My Foolish Heart 50, etc.

Canutt, Yakima (1895–1986) (Enos Edward Canutt). Famous half-Indian stunt man of American westerns for half a century. Later graduated to second unit direction on epics of the sixties.
† Canutt was the world's champion rodeo rider 1917–23.

Capellani, Albert (1870–1931). French director of silent films, in Hollywood from 1915.
Camille 15. La Vie de Bohème 16. Daybreak 17. The Red Lantern 19. The Fortune Teller 20. The Young Diana 22. Sisters 22, etc.

Capone, Al (1899–1947). Italian-American gangster, the king of Chicago during the roaring twenties. Has been impersonated many times on screen, notably by Paul Muni (*Scarface*), Edward G. Robinson (*Little Caesar*), Rod Steiger (*Al Capone*), Neville Brand (*The Scarface Mob*), Jason Robards (*The St Valentine's Day Massacre*).
¶ 'It was ironic that he, who was guilty of committing countless murders, had to be punished merely for failing to pay taxes on the money he had made by murder.'—*Herbert Hoover*

Capote, Truman (1925–84) (Truman Persons). American novelist. Works filmed include *Breakfast at Tiffany's, In Cold Blood.* Contributed to scripts of *Beat the Devil, The Innocents.* Appeared as actor in *Murder by Death* 76.

Capra, Frank (1897–). Italian-American director who is justly celebrated for a stylish handful of thirties and forties comedies demonstrating a whimsical attachment to the common man and to the belief that even the nastiest of us can be human if given a chance. His best films are masterpieces of timing and organization, but his career ended with sentimental and flabby remakes of his own successes.
Autobiography 1971: *The Name Above the Title.*
□The Strong Man 26. Tramp Tramp Tramp 26. Long Pants 27. For the Love of Mike 27. That Certain Feeling 28. So This is Love 28. The Matinée Idol 28. The Way of the Strong 28. Say it with Sables 28. Submarine 28. Power of the Press 28. The Younger Generation 29. The Donovan Affair 29. Flight 29. Ladies of Leisure 30. Rain or Shine 30. Dirigible 31. The Miracle Woman 31. Forbidden 31. *Platinum Blonde* 32. *American Madness* 32. The Bitter Tea of General Yen 32. *Lady for a Day* 33. *It Happened One Night* (AA) 34. *Mr Deeds Goes to Town* (AA) 36. *Lost Horizon* 37. *You Can't Take It With You* (AA) 38. *Mr Smith Goes to Washington* 39. *Meet John Doe* 41. *Why We Fight* (war documentaries) 42–44. Arsenic and Old Lace 44. *It's A Wonderful Life* 46. State of the Union 48. Riding High 50. Here Comes the Groom 51. A Hole in the Head 59. Pocketful of Miracles 61.
❀ For presenting an amiable if mythical picture of Mr Joe Smith American, and for doing so with great style. *It's a Wonderful Life.*
¶ 'He has achieved his effects mainly through a brilliantly fluid editing style, a command of masses of people, and a constantly moving camera.'—*Charles Higham*
F.C.: I made some mistakes in drama. I thought drama was when the actors cried. But drama is when the audience cries.
'The obligatory scene in most Capra films is the confession of folly in the most public manner possible.'—*Andrew Sarris*

Captain Blood. Swashbuckling melodrama from Rafael Sabatini's novel, filmed in 1925 with J. Warren Kerrigan, in 1935 with Errol Flynn. In 1962 Flynn's son Sean starred in an Italian-made *Son of Captain Blood*; and, during the early fifties, Louis Hayward starred in *The Fortunes of Captain Blood* and *Captain Blood Fugitive* (*Captain Pirate*).

Capucine (1933–) (Germaine Lefebvre). Lean and beautiful French model who has been leading lady of a number of international films.
Song Without End 60. North to Alaska 60. A Walk on the Wild Side 62. *The Pink Panther* 63. The Seventh Dawn 64. What's New Pussycat? 65. The Honey Pot 67. The Queens 67. Fraulein Doktor 68. Satyricon 69. Red Sun 72. Jaguar Lives 78. Arabian Adventure 79. Martin Eden (TV) 79. Trail of the Pink Panther 82. Curse of the Pink Panther 83.

car crashes have been responsible for the deaths of several film actors including James Dean, Charles Butterworth, Ernie Kovacs,

Cardiff, Jack (1914–). Superb British colour cinematographer who became an indifferent director of routine films.
AS CINEMATOGRAPHER: *Wings of the Morning* 37. *The Four Feathers* 39. *Western Approaches* 44. Caesar and Cleopatra 45. *A Matter of Life and Death* 46. *Black Narcissus* (AA) 46. *The Red Shoes* 48. Pandora and the Flying Dutchman 51. The Barefoot Contessa 54. *War and Peace* 56. The Vikings 58. The Prince and the Pauper 77. The Fifth Musketeer 78. Death on the Nile 78. Avalanche Express 79. The Awakening 80. Ghost Story 81. The Dogs of War 81. The Far Pavilions (TV) 83. Conan the Destroyer 84. The Last Days of Pompeii (TV). Taipan 86, etc.
□AS DIRECTOR: Intent to Kill 58. Beyond this Place 59. Scent of Mystery 60. *Sons and Lovers* 60. My Geisha 62. The Lion 62. The Long Ships 64. Young Cassidy 65. The Liquidator 65. Dark of the Sun 67. Girl on a Motorcycle (& p, & ph) 69. The Mutations 74. Penny Gold 74. Ride a Wild Pony 76.

Cardinale, Claudia (1939–). Italian leading lady who was given the international star build-up but did not quite manage the front rank.
Persons Unknown 58. Upstairs and Downstairs (GB) 58. Il Bell'Antonio 59. Rocco and his Brothers 60. Cartouche 61. The Leopard 62. Eight and a Half 63. *The Pink Panther* 63. Circus World 64. Vaghe Stella dell'Orsa 65. Blindfold 65. Lost Command 66. The Professionals 66. Don't Make Waves 67. The Queens 67. Day of the Owl 68. The Hell with Heroes 68. Once Upon a Time in the West 69. A Fine Pair 69. Adventures of Brigadier Gerard 70. Popsy Pop 70. The Red Tent 71. Papal Audience 71. Days of Fury 73. Conversation Piece 76. Midnight Pleasures 76. Escape to Athena 78. The Salamander 80. Burden of Dreams 82. Princess Daisy (TV) 83. Henry IV 84. Woman of Wonders 85. History 86, etc.

Carere, Christine (1930–) (Christine de Borde). French leading lady who had a brief Hollywood career.
Olivia 50. Les Collégiennes 57. *A Certain Smile* 57. Mardi Gras 58. A Private's Affair 59. I Deal in Danger 66, etc.

Carette (1897–1966) (Julien Carette). Dapper French character actor.
L'Affaire est dans le Sac 32. La Grande Illusion 37. La Bête Humaine 38. La Marseillaise 38. *La Règle du Jeu* 39. Adieu Léonard 43. Sylvie et le Fantôme 45. Les Portes de la Nuit 46. *Occupe-Toi d'Amélie* 49. *The Red Inn* 51. Éléna et les Hommes 55. Archimède le Clochard 59. The Green Mare's Nest 61, many others.

Carew, Arthur Edmund (1894–1937). American character actor.
Rio Grande 20. The Ghost Breaker 22. Trilby 23. The Phantom of the Opera 25. The Torrent 26. Uncle Tom's Cabin 27. The Cat and the Canary 27. Sweet Kitty Bellairs 30. Doctor X 32. The Mystery of the Wax Museum 33. Charlie Chan's Secret 36, many others.

Carewe, Edwin (1883–1940) (Jay Fox). American director of silent films noted for their pictorial beauty.
The Final Judgment 15. The Trail to Yesterday 18. Shadow of Suspicion 19. Rio Grande 20. Son of the Sahara 24. Resurrection 27. Ramona 28. Evangeline 29. The Spoilers 30. Are We Civilized? 34, etc.

Carey, Harry (1878–1947). American leading man of silent westerns who later became a character actor in quiet dependable roles.
Riding the Trail 11. Travellin' On 14. Two Guns 17. The Outcasts of Poker Flat 19. Desperate Trails 20. Man to Man 22. Roaring Rails 24. The Texas Trail 25. Trail of 98 27. *Trader Horn* 30. Law and Order 32. Barbary Coast 35. Sutter's Gold 36. Kid Galahad 37. King of Alcatraz 38. *Mr Smith Goes to Washington* 39. They Knew What They Wanted 40. The Spoilers 42. Happy Land 43. The Great Moment 44. Duel in the Sun 46, many others.

Carey, Harry, Jnr (1921–). American light actor, son of Harry Carey; followed his father's example and was seen mostly in westerns.
Pursued 47. Red River 48. So Dear to My Heart 49. Wagonmaster 50. Rio Grande 50. Island in the Sky 53. The Long Gray Line 55. The Searchers 56. The River's Edge 57. Rio Bravo 59. The Great Imposter 61. Alvarez Kelly 66. Bandolero 68. One More Time 71. A Man from the East 74. Nickelodeon 76. The Long Riders 80. Endangered Species 82. Princess Daisy (TV) 83. The Whales of August 87, many others.

Carey, Joyce (1898–) (Joyce Lawrence). British stage actress, daughter of Lilian Braithwaite; made a few silent films then appeared more regularly as upper-class ladies in the forties and fifties.
God and the Man 21. The Newcomes 25. *In Which We Serve* 42. Blithe Spirit 45. *The Way to the Stars* 45. *Brief Encounter* 47. The October Man 48. London Belongs to Me 48. The Chiltern Hundreds 49. The Astonished Heart 50. Happy Go Lovely 51. Cry the Beloved Country 52. The End of the Affair 55. The Eyes of Annie Jones 63. A Nice Girl Like Me 69. The Black Windmill 74, etc.

Carey, Leonard (1893–1977). British character actor in Hollywood in the forties, best remembered as old Ben in *Rebecca* 40.

Carey, Macdonald (1913–). American leading man, usually the sympathetic good guy in routine romantic comedy-dramas.
Dr Broadway 42. Wake Island 42. Shadow of a Doubt 43. Suddenly It's Spring 46. Dream Girl 47. East of Java 49. Streets of Laredo 49. The Lawless 50. Copper Canyon 50. Let's Make It Legal 51. My Wife's Best Friend 52. Stranger at My Door 56. Blue Denim 59. The Damned (GB) 62. Tammy and the Doctor 63. Broken Sabre 65. End of the World 77, etc.
TV series: Dr Christian 56. Lock Up 59–60. Days of our Lives 73– .

Carey, Phil or **Philip** (1925–). American leading man of the rugged but good-humoured type, in routine films of the fifties and sixties; latterly in senior officer roles.
Operation Pacific 51. *Pushover* 54. Mister Roberts 55. Port Afrique 56. *Wicked As They Come* 56. Screaming Mimi 58. Tonka 59. The Time Travellers 64. The Great Sioux Massacre (as Custer) 65. The Seven Minutes 71. Fighting Mad 76, many others.
TV series: 77th Bengal Lancers 56. Philip Marlowe 59. Laredo 66–67.

Carey, Timothy (c. 1925–). Heavy-eyed American character actor, often a loathsome villain.
Hellgate 52. Alaska Seas 54. The Killing 56. Paths of Glory 57. One-Eyed Jacks 61. Reprieve 62. Bikini Beach 64. Waterhole Three 67. Head 68. Minnie and Moskowitz 71. The Conversation 73. The Killing of a Chinese Bookie 75. Speedtrap 77. Fast Walking 82. D.C. Cab 85. Echo Park 86, etc.

Carfagno, Edward C. (–). American art director.
Best Foot Forward 43. The Secret Heart 46. Neptune's Daughter 49. Quo Vadis 51. The Story of Three Loves 52. The Bad and the Beautiful (AA) 53. Julius Caesar (AA) 53. Ben Hur (AA) 59. Ada 61. The Cincinnati Kid 65. The Shoes of the Fisherman 69. Skyjacked 73. The Man Who Loved Cat Dancing 73. Hindenburg 75. The Last Hard Men 76. Gable and Lombard 76. Demon Seed 77. Looking for Mr Goodbar 77. Meteor 79. Time after Time 79. Little Miss Marker 80. Beulah Land (TV) 81. Wrong is Right 83. Sudden Impact 83, etc.

Cargill, Patrick (1918–). Impeccable British farce actor with long stage experience.
The Cracksman 63. This is my Street 63. A Stitch in Time 64. *A Countess from Hong Kong* 66. Inspector Clouseau 68. Every Home Should Have One 70. Up Pompeii 71. Father Dear Father 73. The Picture Show Man (Austr.) 77, etc.
TV series: *Father Dear Father* 68–73, 77. The Many Wives of Patrick 77–78.

Carle, Gilles (1929–). Canadian director.
Red 69. Bernadette 72. La Tête de Normande St Onge 75. Fantastica 80. Les Plouffe 81. Maria Chapdelaine 83.

Carle, Richard (1871–1941) (Charles Carleton). American character actor.
Zander The Great 25. Eve's Leaves 26. The Understanding Heart 27. Madame X 28. Brothers 30. One Hour With You 32. Morning Glory 33. Caravan 34. The Ghost Walks 35. Anything Goes 36. One Rainy Afternoon 36. True Confession 37. Persons in Hiding 39. The Great McGinty 40. The Uncertain Feeling 41, many others.

Carlin, Lynn (1930–). American character actress.
Faces 68. Tick Tick Tick 70. *Taking Off* 71. Wild Rovers 71. Battle Beyond the Stars 80, etc.

Carlino, Lewis John (1932–). American screenwriter.
The Brotherhood 68. Reflection of Fear 71. The Mechanic 72. Crazy Joe 74. The Sailor Who Fell from Grace with the Sea (& d, p) 76. I Never Promised You a Rose Garden 77. Resurrection 80. The Great Santini (& d) 80. Class (d only) 83, etc.

Carlisle, Kitty (1915–) (Catherine Holzman). American operatic singer, briefly with MGM in the thirties.
□Murder at the Vanities 34. She Loves Me Not 34. Here is my Heart 34. *A Night at the Opera* 35. Hollywood Canteen 43.

Carlisle, Mary (1912–). American leading lady of the thirties.
Justice for Sale 32. College Humor 33. One Frightened Night 35. Love in Exile 36. Dr Rhythm 38. Call a Messenger 40. Baby Face Morgan 42, etc.

Carlo-Rim (1905–) (Jean-Marius Richard). French writer-director, mainly of Fernandel comedies.
L'Armoire Volante 47. Les Truands (Lock Up the Spoons) 56. Le Petit Prof 59, etc.

Carlson, Richard (1912–77). American leading man of the forties, mainly in routine films; played the diffident juvenile so long that he had nothing to give to mature roles.
The Young in Heart 38. Winter Carnival 39. The Ghost Breakers 40. No No Nanette 40. Back Street 41. Hold that Ghost 41. *The Little Foxes* 41. White Cargo 42. Presenting Lily Mars 43. So Well Remembered 47. Behind Closed Doors 48. King Solomon's Mines 50. The Blue Veil 51. Valentino 51. Whispering Smith Hits London 52. The Magnetic Monster 53. It Came from Outer Space 53. All I Desire 53. Riders to the Stars (& d) 54. The Creature from the Black Lagoon 54. Four Guns to the Border (d only) 54. Three for Jamie Dawn 56. The Helen Morgan Story 57. Appointment with a Shadow (d only) 59. Kid Rodelo (& d) 66. The Power 68. The Valley of Gwangi 69, many others.
TV series: I Led Three Lives 52. Mackenzie's Raiders 58.

Carlson, Veronica (1944–). British leading lady, mainly in screamies.
Dracula has Risen from the Grave 68. Frankenstein must be Destroyed 69. The Horror of Frankenstein 70. Pussycat Pussycat I Love You 70, etc.

Carmel, Roger C. (1929–86). Rotund American character actor.
Goodbye Charlie 64. The Silencers 66. Gambit 66. The Venetian Affair 66. Skullduggery 69. Thunder and Lightning 77.
TV series: Fitz and Bones 81.

Carmen. Prosper Mérimée's high-romantic tale of a fatal gypsy whose worthless attractions wreck men's lives was promptly turned by Bizet into an opera which has been filmed many times, notably as *Carmen Jones* 54. The straight dramatic story, however, probably holds the record for the number of film versions it has spawned:

France	1909	with Victoria Lepanto
Spain	1910	actress unknown
US	1913	Marguerite Snow
US	1913	Marion Leonard
Spain	1914	actress unknown
US	1915	Geraldine Farrar
US	1915	Edna Purviance (*Burlesque on Carmen*)
US	1916	Theda Bara
US	1918	Pola Negri
US	1921	Raquel Miller
US	1927	Dolores del Rio
France	1942	Vivianne Romance
US	1948	Rita Hayworth
US/WG	1966	Uta Levke

Carmichael, Hoagy (1899–1981) (Hoaglund Howard Carmichael). American song composer and lyricist, best known for 'Stardust' and 'In the Cool, Cool, Cool of the Evening' (AA 1951). Also a slow-speaking actor of light supporting roles, usually involving his singing at the piano.
Autobiographies: *The Stardust Road* 46. *Sometimes I Wonder* 65.
As actor/performer: To Have and Have Not 44. Canyon Passage 46. *The Best Years of Our Lives* 46. Young Man with a Horn 50. Belles on Their Toes 52. Timberjack 55, etc.
TV series: Laramie 59–62.

Carmichael, Ian (1920–). British light leading man, adept at nervous novices; long experience in revue.
Meet Mr Lucifer 54. The Colditz Story 54. Storm over the Nile 55. *Simon and Laura* 55. *Private's Progress* 55. *Brothers in Law* 57. *Lucky Jim* 57. Happy is the Bride 57. The Big Money 57. Left, Right and Centre 59. *I'm All Right, Jack* 59. School for Scoundrels 60. Light Up the Sky 60. Double Bunk 61. The Amorous Prawn 62. Hide and Seek 63. Heavens Above 63. Smashing Time 67. The Magnificent Seven Deadly Sins 71. From Beyond the Grave 75. The Lady Vanishes 79, etc.

Carminati, Tullio (1894–1971) (Count Tullio Carminati de Brambilla). Italian romantic actor who had a modest career in British and American as well as European films.

The Bat 26. Three Sinners 28. Moulin Rouge 33. *One Night of Love* 34. *The Three Maxims* 35. Safari 40. The Golden Madonna 49. La Beauté du Diable 51. Roman Holiday 53. Saint Joan 57. El Cid 61. The Cardinal 63, many others.

Carne, Judy (1939–). Pert British actress who found fame as the 'sock it to me' girl in Hollywood's *Laugh-In* TV series.
A Pair of Briefs 63. The Americanization of Emily 64. All the Right Noises 69, etc.
TV series: Fair Exchange 62. The Baileys of Balboa 64. Love on a Rooftop 66. Laugh-In 67–72.

Carné, Marcel (1903–). Certainly the most brilliant of French directors 1937–45; his career later suffered a semi-eclipse.
□Jenny 36. *Drôle de Drame* 37. *Quai des Brumes* 38. Hôtel du Nord 38. *Le Jour Se Lève* 39. *Les Visiteurs du Soir* 42. *Les Enfants du Paradis* 44. Les Portes de la Nuit 46. La Marie du Port 48. Juliette Ou La Clef des Songes 51. Thérèse Racquin 53. L'Air de Paris 54. Le Pays d'Où Je Viens 56. Les Tricheurs 58. Terrain Vague 60. Du Mouron pour les Petits Oiseaux 62. Three Rooms in Manhattan 65. The Young Wolves 68. Les Assassins de l'Ordre 71. La Vie a Belles Dents (w only) 80.
❀ For creating, almost single-handedly, the images of French *film noir* in the thirties. *Les Enfants du Paradis.*

¶ 'The precise mood of the period—a sense of fatalism enveloping a pair of doomed lovers, drably poetic urban settings—is to be found in his work.'—*Roy Armes*

Un Carnet de Bal (France 1937). A romantic trifle which found director Julien Duvivier at the top of his cinematic form and was influential because of its linking of several stories through an inanimate object (a dance programme remembered by the heroine). As an entertainment it now seems thin despite its star cast, but it sent Duvivier off to Hollywood where he directed a partial remake (*Lydia*) and some variations (*Tales of Manhattan, Flesh and Fantasy*).

Carney, Alan (1911–1973). American comedy supporting actor who in the mid-forties made some second features with Wally Brown (qv). His solo appearances were sparse.
Mr Lucky 43. The Pretender 47. Lil Abner 59. It's a Mad Mad Mad Mad World 63. The Love Bug Rides Again 73, etc.

Carney, Art (1918–). American comedy actor, popular on TV, especially from 1955 in *The Honeymooners*.
Pot O'Gold 41. The Yellow Rolls Royce 64. A Guide for the Married Man 67. *Harry and Tonto* (AA) 74. Won Ton Ton 76. Lanigan's Rabbi (TV) 76. *The Late Show* 77. Movie Movie 78. Sunburn 79. Roadie 80. Steel 80. St Helens 81. Take This Job and Shove It 81. Firestarter 84. The Naked Face 84. Izzy and Moe (TV) 85, etc.

Carney, George (1887–1947). British character actor of stage and screen.
Say It With Flowers 34. Father Steps Out (title role) 37. The Stars Look Down 39. Convoy 40. *Love on the Dole* 41. The Common Touch 41. Tawny Pipit 44. I Know Where I'm Going 45. Good Time Girl 47, etc.

carnivals: see *funfairs*.

Carnovsky, Morris (1897–). Distinguished American stage actor, with long experience in Jewish theatre. Films regrettably few.
□The Life of Emile Zola 37. Tovarich 37. Edge of Darkness 43. Address Unknown 44. The Master Race 44. Our Vines Have Tender Grapes 45. *Rhapsody in Blue* 45. Cornered 45. Miss Susie Slagle's 45. *Dead Reckoning* 47. Dishonored Lady 47. Joe Palooka in The Knockout 47. Saigon 48. Maneater of Kumaon 48. Siren of Atlantis 48. Gun Crazy 49. Thieves' Highway 49. Western Pacific Agent 50. Cyrano de Bergerac 50. The Second Woman 51. A View from the Bridge 62. The Gambler 74.

Carol, Martine (1922–1967) (Maryse Mourer). French leading lady popular in undressed roles in the early fifties.
Voyage Surprise 48. *Caroline Chérie* 50. A Night with Caroline 52. *Lucrezia Borgia* 52. The Bed 53. The Beach 54. Nana 55. *Lola Montes* 55. Action of the Tiger 57. Ten Seconds to Hell 59. Le Cave Se Rebiffe 61. Hell is Empty 66, etc.

Carol, Sue (1906–1982) (Evelyn Lederer). American leading lady of the early thirties. Widow of Alan Ladd.
Is Zat So? 27. Girls Gone Wild 29. Dancing Sweeties 30. Her Golden Calf 30. Graft 31. Secret Sinners 34. A Doctor's Diary 37, etc.

Caron, Leslie (1931–). French leading lady and dancer who after being discovered by Gene Kelly followed a successful English-speaking career in light drama and comedy. □*An American In Paris* 51. Man with a Cloak 51. Glory Alley 52. The Story of Three Loves 53. *Lili* (BFA) 53. The Glass Slipper 54. Daddy Longlegs 55. Gaby 56. *Gigi* 58. The Doctor's Dilemma 58. The Man Who Understood Women 59. The Subterraneans 60. Austerlitz 60. *Fanny* 61. Guns of Darkness 63. *The L-Shaped Room* (BFA) 62. Three Fables of Love 63. Father Goose 64. A Very Special Favour 65. Promise Her Anything 66. Is Paris Burning? 66. Head of the Family 68. Madron 69. Purple Night 71. Chandler 72. QB VII (TV) 74. The Man Who Loved Women 77. Valentino 77. Sérail 77. Goldengirl 79, Tous Vedettes 80. The Contract 80. Imperatives 82. Master of the Game (TV) 84. Dangerous Moves 85. The Genius 85.

Carpenter, Carleton (1926–). American light leading man groomed by MGM in the early fifties.
Lost Boundaries 48. Father of the Bride 50. Summer Stock 51. Fearless Fagan 53. Sky Full of Moon 53. Take the High Ground 53. Up Periscope 59. Some of My Best Friends Are 71.

Carpenter, John (1948–). American director who in the late seventies swiftly carved a niche for himself with scary but derivative horror thrillers.
The Resurrection of Broncho Billy (short) (AA) 70. *Dark Star* 74. *Assault on Precinct 13* 76. Someone's Watching Me (TV) 77. Halloween 78. Eyes of Laura Mars (w only) 78. Elvis (TV) 79. The Fog 79. Escape from New York (& co-w) 81. Halloween II (co-w, co-p only) 81. The Thing 82. Halloween III (co-p only) 83. Christine 83. Starman 84. Big Trouble in Little China 86. Something Wild (a only) 86.

¶ *J.C.:* Movies are pieces of film stuck together in a certain rhythm, an absolute beat, like a musical composition. The rhythm you create affects the audience.

Carpenter, Paul (1921–1964). Canadian leading man long in Britain as hero of scores of second features.
School for Secrets 46. Albert RN 53. Night People 54. The Sea Shall Not Have Them 55. Fire Maidens from Outer Space 56. The Iron Petticoat 56. Jet Storm 59. Murder Reported 60. Call Me Bwana 63, etc.

The Carpetbaggers (US 1963). The film of Harold Robbins' salacious novel was a watered-down affair but still helped to break the Production Code, and stands also as an example of how Joe Levine's publicity machine could make a mountain out of a molehill. Set in Hollywood in the thirties, the film had George Peppard as a Howard Hughes-type mogul and Carroll Baker as a Jean Harlow-type star, with a remarkably effective last performance from Alan Ladd as the hero's sidekick Nevada Smith, whose unlikely early life in the west was promptly turned into another movie starring Steve McQueen.

Carr, Allan (1941–). Chubby American impresario associated with *Grease, La Cage aux Folles* and the unsuccessful *Can't Stop the Music*.

Carr, Darleen (–). American leading lady mainly familiar in TV series: *The John Forsythe Show*, *The Smith Family*, *The Oregon Trail*, etc.
Monkeys Go Home 66. The Impossible Years 68. The Beguiled 70. Runaway (TV) 73. Young Joe the Forgotten Kennedy (TV) 77, etc.

Carr, Jane (1909–1957) (Rita Brunstrom). British leading lady, in occasional films.
Taxi to Paradise 33. Lord Edgware Dies 37. Lilac Domino 37. The Lady from Lisbon 37. It's Not Cricket 48. 36 Hours 54, etc.

Carr, John Dickson (1905–1977). American detective story writer, curiously few of whose many novels have been adapted for the screen.
Man with a Cloak 51. That Woman Upstairs 52. Dangerous Crossing 52, etc.

Carr, Mary (1874–1973). Leading American character actress of the twenties; the archetypal white-haired old mother.
Mrs Wiggs of the Cabbage Patch 19. *Over the Hill to the Poorhouse* 20. Silver Wings 22. Why Men Leave Home 24. The Wizard of Oz 25. Jesse James 27. Lights of New York 28. Beyond Victory 31. Change of Heart 34. East Side of Heaven 36. Friendly Persuasion 56, many others.

Carr, Thomas (1907–). American director, mainly of second feature westerns. Went into TV.
Bandits of the Badlands 45. Red River Renegades 46. Code of the Saddle 47. Colorado Ranger 50. Wyoming Roundup 52. Captain Scarlett 53. The Bowery Boys Meet the Monsters 54. Bobby Ware Is Missing 55.

Three for Jamie Dawn 56. The Tall Stranger 57. Gunsmoke in Tucson 58. Cast a Long Shadow 59. Sullivan's Empire 67, many others.

Carradine, David (1936–) (John Arthur Carradine). Lanky sad-eyed American character actor, son of John Carradine.
The Violent Ones 67. Young Billy Young 69. The McMasters 70. Macho Callahan 71. Boxcar Bertha 72. You and Me (& d) 73. Mean Streets 73. Death Race 2000 75. Cannonball 76. *Bound for Glory* 76. Carquake 77. Thunder and Lightning 77. The Silent Flute 78. Cloud Dancer 80. The Long Riders 80. Safari 3000 82. The Winged Serpent 82. Mr Horn 82. Lone Wolf McQuade 82. Safari 3000 84. Armed Response 86. North and South (TV) 86. Wheels of Terror 87.
TV series: *Shane* 66. *Kung Fu* 72–74.

Carradine, John (1906–) (Richmond Reed Carradine). Gaunt American actor who scored a fine run of character roles in the thirties and forties but later sank to mad doctors in cheap horror movies, touring meanwhile with one-man Shakespeare readings. Played 1930–35 under the name John Peter Richmond.
Tol'able David 30. The Sign of the Cross 32. Cleopatra 34. Bride of Frankenstein 35. Dimples 36. The Prisoner of Shark Island 36. The Garden of Allah 36. Winterset 36. Captains Courageous 36. The Last Gangster 37. The Hurricane 37. Alexander's Ragtime Band 38. Jesse James 39. Drums along the Mohawk 39. *Five Came Back* 39. *Stagecoach* 39. Brigham Young 40. *The Grapes of Wrath* 40. Blood and Sand 41. Man Hunt 41. Son of Fury 42. Hitler's Madman (as Heydrich) 43. Gangway for Tomorrow 43. *Bluebeard* (title role) 44. The Invisible Man's Revenge 44. It's In the Bag 45. *House of Frankenstein* (as Dracula) 45. Fallen Angel 45. House of Dracula 45. The Face of Marble 46. The Private Affairs of Bel Ami 47. C-Man 49. Casanova's Big Night 54. The Egyptian 54. The Kentuckian 55. The Black Sleep 56. The Ten Commandments 56. Hell Ship Mutiny 57. The Last Hurrah 58. The Cosmic Man 59. Sex Kittens go to College 60. Invasion of the Animal People 62. *The Man Who Shot Liberty Valance* 62. Cheyenne Autumn 64. Billy the Kid vs Dracula 66. Hillbillies in a Haunted House 67. The Fiend with the Electronic Brain 67. The Astro-Zombies 68. The Good Guys and the Bad Guys 69. Bigfoot 69. The McMasters 70. The Seven Minutes 71. Boxcar Bertha 72. The House of the Seven Corpses 73. Silent Night Bloody Night 74. The Shootist 76. The Sentinel 77. The Bees 78. The Boogey Man 80. The Scarecrow 82. The House of Long Shadows 83. Evils of the Night 85. Peggy Sue Got Married 86. The Tomb 87, many others.

Carradine, Keith (1950–). American leading man of the seventies, half brother of David Carradine.
□A Gunfight 71. McCabe and Mrs Miller 71. Hex 73. Emperor of the North 73. The Godchild (TV) 74. Thieves Like Us 74. Nashville 75. Lumiere 76. Welcome to L.A. 77. Pretty Baby 78. An Almost Perfect Affair 79. Old Boyfriends 79. The Long Riders 80. Southern Comfort 81. Maria's Lovers 83. Choose Me 85. Chiefs (TV) 85. Scorned and Swindled (TV) 85. Blackout 86. Half a Lifetime 86. Backfire 87.

Carradine, Robert (1954–). American leading man, youngest son of John Carradine (brother of Keith, half-brother of David).
The Cowboys 72. Mean Streets 73. Aloha Bobby and Rose 75. You and Me 75. Jackson County Jail 76. Cannonball 76. Orca 77. Coming Home 78. The Big Red One 80. Heartaches 82. Wavelength 83. Revenge of the Nerds 84. Number One with a Bullet 87. Revenge of the Nerds II 87, etc.

Carré, Ben (1883–1978). American art director.
The Blue Bird 18. *Phantom of the Opera* 25. Mare Nostrum 25. *Don Juan* 26. The Jazz Singer 27. *Dante's Inferno* 35, many others.

Carrera, Barbara (–). Nicaraguan leading lady of smouldering personality.
Puzzle of a Downfall Child 70. The Master Gunfighter 75. Embryo 76. The Island of Dr Moreau 78. Never Say Never Again 83, Wild Geese II 84, etc.
TV Series: Dallas 84–

Carreras, James (1900–). British production executive, former exhibitor; chairman of Hammer Films.

Carreras, Michael (1927–). British producer-director for Hammer Films of which he has been managing director since 1971; son of James Carreras.
Blackout (p) 54. The Snorkel (p) 57. Ten Seconds to Hell (p) 58. Passport to China (pd) 61. The Two Faces of Dr Jekyll (d) 61. Maniac (d) 62. What a Crazy World (d) 63.

The Curse of the Mummy's Tomb (d) 64. She (p) 65. One Million Years B.C. (p) 67. The Lost Continent (pd) 68, etc.

Carrick, Edward (1905–) (Edward Anthony Craig). British art director, son of Edward Gordon Craig.
Autumn Crocus 34. Jump for Glory 36. Captain Boycott 47. The Divided Heart 54. Tiger Bay 59. What a Crazy World 63. The Nanny 65, many others.

Carrie (US 1976). A repressed teenage girl with a religious fanatic mother discovers she has telekinetic powers and uses them homicidally in this unpleasant but commercially sensational thriller which established Brian de Palma as a big-time director. Written by Lawrence D. Cohen; with Sissy Spacek, Piper Laurie, William Katt, John Travolta.

Carrière, Jean-Claude (1931–). French screen writer who began by collaborating with Tati and Etaix.
Viva Maria 65. Le Voleur 67. Borsalino 67. Taking Off 71. The Discreet Charm of the Bourgeoisie 72, etc. (usually in collaboration).

Carrillo, Leo (1880–1961). American light character actor. A Spanish Californian from a wealthy landowning family, he enjoyed many years in Hollywood as an assortment of amiably talkative fellows, usually in fractured English.
Mr Antonio 29. Hell Bound 31. Girl of the Rio 31. The Broken Wing 32. Moonlight and Pretzels 33. Manhattan Melodrama 34. In Caliente 32. *The Gay Desperado* 36. *History Is Made at Night* 37. Blockade 38. Rio 39. Lillian Russell 40. Horror Island 41. Riders of Death Valley 41. Sin Town 42. Top Sergeant 43. Ghost Catchers 44. Mexicana 45. The Fugitive 47. The Gay Amigo 48. Pancho Villa Returns 50, many others.
TV series: The Cisco Kid 51–55.

¶ Ze female of ze species she is a-deadlier zan ze male.—*L. C. in History Is Made at Night*

Carroll, Diahann (1935–) (Carol Diahann Johnson). Black American entertainer and actress. Carmen Jones 54. Porgy and Bess 59. Goodbye Again 60. Paris Blues 61. Hurry Sundown 67. The Split 68. Claudine 74, etc.
TV series *Julia* 68–70. Dynasty 85– .

Carroll, Joan (1932–) (Joan Felt). American child star of the forties.
Primrose Path 40. Laddie 41. Petticoat Larceny 43. Meet Me in St Louis 44. Tomorrow the World 45. The Bells of St Mary's 46, etc.

Carroll, John (1906–1979) (Julian La Faye). Latin-American leading man with a decent singing voice but not much personality.
□Marianne 29. Devil May Care 29. Hearts in Exile 29. Rogue Song 30. Dough Boys 30. Monte Carlo 30. New Moon 30. Reaching for the Moon 30. Go into Your Dance 35. Hi Gaucho 35. The Accusing Finger 36. Murder on the Bridle Path 36. Muss 'Em Up 36. We Who Are About to Die 37. Zorro (serial) 37. Death in the Air 37. Rose of the Rio Grande 38. I am a Criminal 38. Only Angels Have Wings 39. Wolf Call 39. Congo Maisie 40. Phantom Raiders 40. Susan and God 40. Hired Wife 40. Go West 40. Sunny 41. This Woman is Mine 41. Lady be Good 41. *Rio Rita* 42. Pierre of the Plains 42. Fying Tigers 42. Hit Parade of 1943 42. The Youngest Profession 43. Bedside Manner 45. A Letter for Evie 45. Fiesta 47. Wyoming 47. The Fabulous Texan 47. The Flame 47. Old Los Angeles 48. I Jane Doe 48. Angel in Exile 48. The Avengers 50. Surrender 50. Hit Parade of 1951 50. Belle Le Grande 52. The Farmer Takes a Wife 53. Geraldine 53. The Reluctant Bride 55. Decision at Showdown 57. Plunderers of Painted Flats 59.

Carroll, Leo G. (1892–1972). Distinguished, dry-faced British character actor long based in Hollywood; usually played doctors, judges or academics.
□What Every Woman Knows 34. Sadie McKee 34. Outcast Lady 34. Stamboul Quest 34. The Barretts of Wimpole Street 34. Murder on a Honeymoon 35. The Right to Live 35. Clive of India 35. The Casino Murder Case 35. London by Night 37. Captains Courageous 37. A Christmas Carol 38. The Private Lives of Elizabeth and Essex 39. *Wuthering Heights* 39. Bulldog Drummond's Secret Police 39. Charlie Chan in the City of Darkness 39. Tower of London 39. *Rebecca* 40. Charlie Chan's Murder Cruise 40. Waterloo Bridge 40. Scotland Yard 41. Bahama Passage 41. This Woman is Mine 41. Suspicion 41. *The House on 92nd Street* 45. *Spellbound* 45. Forever Amber 47. Time Out of Mind 47. Song of Love 47. The Paradine Case 48. So Evil My Love 48. Enchantment 48. The Happy Years 50. Father of the Bride 50. The First Legion 51. Strangers on a Train

51. The Desert Fox 51. The Snows of Kilimanjaro 52. The Bad and the Beautiful 52. Rogues' March 52. Treasure of the Golden Condor 52. Young Bess 53. We're No Angels 55. Tarantula 55. The Swan 56. *North by Northwest* 59. The Parent Trap 61. One Plus One 61. *The Prize* 63. That Funny Feeling 65. The Spy with My Face 66. One of Our Spies Is Missing 66. One Spy Too Many 66.
TV series: *Topper* 53–54, *Going My Way* 62. *The Man from U.N.C.L.E.* (as Mr Waverly) 64–67.

Carroll, Lewis (1832–1898) (Charles Lutwidge Dodgson). British writer, an Oxford lecturer in mathematics who wrote *Alice in Wonderland* (qv).

Carroll, Madeleine (1906–87) (Marie Madeleine Bernadette O'Carroll). British leading lady of the thirties and forties; her gentle, well-bred air made her popular in Hollywood for a while.
□*The Guns of Loos* 28. The First Born 28. What Money Can't Buy 29. The American Prisoner 29. Atlantic 30. *Young Woodley* 30. Escape 30. The W Plan 30. Madame Guillotine 31. Kissing Cup's Race 31. French Leave 31. The Written Law 31. Fascination 32. School for Scandal 33. Sleeping Car 33. *I Was a Spy* 33. The World Moves On 34. Loves of a Dictator 35. *The Thirty-nine Steps* 35. The Case Against Mrs Ames 36. Secret Agent 36. *The General Died at Dawn* 36. Lloyds of London 36. *On the Avenue* 37. *The Prisoner of Zenda* 37. It's All Yours 38. Blockade 38. Honeymoon in Bali 39. Café Society 39. My Son My Son 40. Safari 40. Northwest Mounted Police 40. Virginia 41. One Night in Lisbon 41. Bahama Passage 42. *My Favourite Blonde* 42. White Cradle Inn 46. Don't Trust Your Husband 48. *The Fan* 49.

Carroll, Nancy (1905–1965) (Ann La Hiff). Warmly-remembered American leading lady of early talkie musicals and light dramas. Biography 1969: *The Films of Nancy Carroll* by Paul L. Nemcek.
□Ladies Must Dress 27. Abie's Irish Rose 28. Easy Come Easy Go 28. Chicken à la King 28. The Water Hole 28. Manhattan Cocktail 28. *The Shopworn Angel* 29. The Wolf of Wall Street 29. Sin Sister 29. Close Harmony 29. The Dance of Life 29. Illusion 29. Sweetie 29. Dangerous Paradise 30. Honey 30. Paramount on Parade 30. The Devil's Holiday 30. Follow Through 30. *Laughter* 30. Stolen Heaven 31. The Night Angel 31. Personal Maid 31. Broken Lullaby 32. Wayward 32. Scarlet Dawn 32. Hot Saturday 32. Undercover Man 32. Child of Manhattan 33. The Woman Accused 33. The Kiss Before the Mirror 33. I Love that Man 33. Springtime for Henry 34. Transatlantic Merry-go-round 34. Jealousy 34. I'll Love You Always 35. After the Dance 35. Atlantic Adventure 35. There Goes My Heart 38. That Certain Age 38.

Carry On. This astonishingly successful series of low-budget British farces, with their thin production values and witless emphasis on the physical, began in 1958 with an army comedy called *Carry On Sergeant,* and since then roughly two a year have rolled off the assembly lines of producer Peter Rogers and director Gerald Thomas. The Carry On sequence to date is Nurse, Teacher, Constable, Regardless, Cruising, Cabby, Jack, Spying, Cleo, Cowboy, Screaming, Follow That Camel, Don't Lose Your Head, Doctor, Up the Khyber, Camping, Again Doctor, Loving, Up the Jungle, Henry, At Your Convenience, Matron, Abroad, Girls, Dick, Behind, England, Emmanuelle. (*Carry On Admiral* and *What A Carry On* are horses of a different colour.) The struggling comedians most likely to be involved are Sid James, Kenneth Williams, Hattie Jacques, Kenneth Connor, Jim Dale, Charles Hawtrey and Joan Sims.

¶ *Peter Rogers:* We're vulgar but we're never crude.

Carson, Charles (c. 1898–1977). British character actor of stage and screen, seen latterly as distinguished old gentlemen.
Leap Year 32. Sanders of the River 35. Victoria the Great 37. Dark Journey 37. Quiet Wedding 40. Pink String and Sealing Wax 45. Cry the Beloved Country 52. Reach for the Sky 56. The Trials of Oscar Wilde 60, many others.

Carson, Jack (1910–1963). Beefy Canadian comedy actor; a former vaudevillian, he usually played 'smart guys' who were really dumber than the suckers they tried to take.
□You Only Live Once 37. Stage Door 37. Stand In 37. Too Many Wives 37. It Could Happen To You 37. Music for Madame 37. The Toast of New York 37. Reported Missing 37. The Saint in New York 37. Vivacious Lady 37. Mr Doodle Kicks Off 38. Crashing Hollywood 38. She's Got Everything 38. Night Spot 38. Law of the Underworld 38. This Marriage Business 38. Having Wonderful Time 38. Maids Night Out 38. Everybody's Doing It 38. Quick Money 38. Bringing Up Baby 38. Go Chase Yourself 38. Carefree 38.

Destry Rides Again 39. The Kid from Texas 39. Mr Smith Goes to Washington 39. Legion of Lost Flyers 39. The Escape 39. The Honeymoon's Over 39. The Girl in 313 40. Shooting High 40. Young As You Feel 40. Enemy Agent 40. Parole Fixer 40. Alias the Deacon 40. Queen of the Mob 40. Sandy Gets His Man 40. Love Thy Neighbour 40. Lucky Partners 40. I Take this Woman 40. Typhoon 40. *The Strawberry Blonde* 41. Mr and Mrs Smith 41. Love Crazy 41. The Bride Came COD 41. Navy Blues 41. Blues in the Night 41. The Male Animal 42. Gentleman Jim 42. Larceny Inc. 42. Wings for the Eagle 42. The Hard Way 42. Princess O'Rourke 43. Thank Your Lucky Stars 43. Shine On Harvest Moon 44. Arsenic and Old Lace 44. The Doughgirls 44. *Make Your Own Bed* (leading role) 44. *Roughly Speaking* 45. *Mildred Pierce* 45. One More Tomorrow 46. The Time The Place and The Girl 46. Two Guys from Milwaukee 46. Love and Learn 47. April Showers 48. Romance on the High Seas 48. Two Guys from Texas 48. John Loves Mary 49. My Dream is Yours 49. It's a Great Feeling 49. Bright Leaf 50. Mr Universe 51. The Groom Wore Spurs 51. The Good Humor Man 51. Dangerous When Wet 53. Phffft! 54. *Red Garters* 54. *A Star is Born* 54. Ain't Misbehavin' 54. The Bottom of the Bottle 56. The Magnificent Roughnecks 56. The Tattered Dress 57. *Cat on a Hot Tin Roof* 58. Rally Round the Flag Boys 58. The Tarnished Angels 58. The Bramble Bush 60. King of the Roaring Twenties 61. Sammy the Way Out Seal (TV) 62.
Famous Line (*Mildred Pierce*): 'Oh boy! I'm so smart it's a disease!'

Carson, Jeannie (1928–) (Jean Shufflebottom). Vivacious British entertainer who became popular in America and then surprisingly retired.
Love in Pawn 51. As Long as They're Happy 54. An Alligator Named Daisy 56. Rockets Galore 57. Seven Keys 62, etc.
TV series: *Hey Jeannie!* 56.

Carson, John (1927–). British character actor with a James Mason-like voice. Much on TV, especially heard on commercials.
The Plague of the Zombies 67. The Man Who Haunted Himself 70. Taste the Blood of Dracula 70. Captain Kronos Vampire Hunter 72, etc.

Carson, Johnny (1925–). American comedian and late night talk show host.
¶ 'He's an anaesthetist. Prince Valium.'—*Mort Sahl*

Carson, Kit (1809–1868). American western frontiersman and guide who became a legendary figure and has been portrayed in several films, notably *Kit Carson* 39 in which he was played by Jon Hall (also on TV by Bill Williams).

Carstairs, John Paddy (1912–1970) (John Keys). British director, usually of light-hearted subjects; also comic novelist and painter.
Autobiographies: *Honest Injun* 1942. *Hadn't We the Gaiety* 1945. *Kaleidoscope and a Jaundiced Eye* 1946.
The Saint in London 39. Spare a Copper 40. He Found a Star 40. Dancing with Crime 46. *Sleeping Car to Trieste* 48. *The Chiltern Hundreds* 49. Made in Heaven 52. Trouble in Store 53. Up to His Neck 54. Up in the World 56. Just My Luck 57. The Square Peg 58. Tommy the Toreador 59. Sands of the Desert 60. Weekend with Lulu 61, many others.

Carsten, Peter (1929–) (Pieter Ransenthaler). German character actor in America.
Mr Superinvisible 73, etc.

Carter, Ann (1936–). American child star of the forties.
I Married a Witch 42. North Star 43. *Curse of the Cat People* 44. The Two Mrs Carrolls 46. Song of Love 47. A Connecticut Yankee in King Arthur's Court 49, etc.

Carter, Ben (1911–1947). Black American character actor.
Gone with the Wind 39. *Maryland* 40. Tin Pan Alley 40. Chad Hanna 40. Reap the Wild Wind 42. The Harvey Girls 46, etc.

Carter, Helena (1923–) (Helen Rickerts). American leading lady of second features in the forties: former model.
Time Out of Mind 46. River Lady 48. Double Crossbones 51. The Golden Hawk 52. Invaders from Mars 53, etc.

Carter, Jack (1922–) (John Chakrin). American night club and TV comic of the fifties.
The Horizontal Lieutenant 62. Viva Las Vegas 63. The Extraordinary Seaman 64, etc.

Carter, Janis (1921–) (J. Dremann). American leading lady of minor films in the forties; former radio experience.
Cadet Girl 41. Notorious Lone Wolf 43. Paula 44. The Fighting Guardsmen 45. I Love

Trouble 47. The Woman on Pier 13 49. My Forbidden Past 51. Flying Leathernecks 51. The Half-Breed 52, etc.

Carter, Mrs Leslie (1862–1937) (Caroline Louise Dudley). American stage actress, a protégée of David Belasco; a 1940 biopic, *Lady with Red Hair,* starred Miriam Hopkins. Film appearances rare.
□Du Barry 15. The Heart of Maryland 15. The Vanishing Pioneer 34. Rocky Mountain Mystery 34.

Carter, Nell (–). Black American comedy actress.

cartoon: a film composed of animated drawings, carefully varied to give the appearance of motion. Gertie the Dinosaur, who appeared in 1909, is thought to be the first cartoon character; Mutt and Jeff followed soon after. In the twenties, Pat Sullivan's Felix the Cat and Max Fleischer's Out of the Inkwell series vied for popularity until both were ousted by Walt Disney, who with Ub Iwerks created Mickey Mouse and his familiar friends. In the thirties, Disney went on to Silly Symphonies, Fleischer to Popeye. Other creations were Woody Woodpecker (Walter Lantz), Mighty Mouse, Heckle and Jeckle, Tom and Jerry (Hanna-Barbera for MGM) and Bugs Bunny. Disney's Donald Duck became more popular than Mickey. In the forties, David Hand made British cartoons for the Rank Organisation, but they were not commercially successful. The fifties brought U.P.A. with their new refined lines, intellectual conceptions and sophisticated jokes; Mr Magoo and Gerald McBoing Boing led the new characters but quickly palled. Then the needs of television led to innumerable cartoon series which for the sake of economy had to be only semi-animated and had little vitality; the best of them were The Flintstones and Yogi Bear. These series proliferated into hundreds and not until 1972 did anyone try an adult cartoon series, Hanna-Barbera's *Wait Till Your Father Gets Home*.

Feature-length cartoons were started by Disney in 1937 with *Snow White and the Seven Dwarfs*; Fleischer responded in 1939 with *Gulliver's Travels.* Disney's outstanding serious cartoon was *Fantasia* 40, an interpretation of classical music. Later, French and Japanese cartoons flooded the market, but inspiration was lacking in most of them. Halas and Batchelor's British *Animal Farm* was a fair summation of Orwell's fable, but their later attempts to interpret Gilbert and Sullivan failed. In recent years the cartoon has been put to every kind of serious and comic purpose, including propaganda and advertising, and many prizewinners have come from Europe. Ralph Bakshi's ruderies of Fritz the Cat were startling, but he atoned with his careful rendering of *Lord of the Rings*.

Cartwright, Veronica (1949–). American leading lady.
The Children's Hour 62. The Birds 63. Inserts 77. Going South 78. Invasion of the Body Snatchers 78. Alien 79. Guyana Tragedy (TV) 80. Prime Suspect (TV) 81.
TV series: Daniel Boone 64–70.

Caruso, Anthony (c. 1913–). American character actor, usually seen as menace.
Johnny Apollo 40. Sunday Punch 42. Objective Burma 45. Wild Harvest 47. Bride of Vengeance 49. Tarzan and the Slave Girl 50. The Iron Mistress 52. Phantom of the Rue Morgue 54. Hell on Frisco Bay 56. The Badlanders 58. The Most Dangerous Man Alive 61. Young Dillinger 65. Flap 70, many others.

Caruso, Enrico (1873–1921). Celebrated Italian operatic tenor who appeared in a few silent films and was played by Mario Lanza in *The Great Caruso* 51.

Carver, Louise (1898–1956) (Louise Spilger Murray). American character actress, a famous silent comedienne.
The Extra Girl 23. Shameful Behaviour 26. The Fortune Hunter 27. The Man from Blankley's 30. The Big Trail 30. Side Show 31. Hallelujah I'm a Bum 33. Every Night at Eight 35, etc.

Carver, Lynne (1909–1955) (Virginia Reid Sampson). American general purpose actress.
Roberta 35. Maytime 37. A Christmas Carol 38. Calling Dr Kildare 39. Charley's Aunt 41. Tennessee Johnson 42. Law of the Valley 44. Crossed Trails 48, etc.

Cary, Tristam (1925–). British composer.
The Ladykillers 55. Town on Trial 57. Tread Softly Stranger 58. Sammy Going South 63. Quatermass and the Pit 67. Blood from the Mummy's Tomb 71, etc.

Casablanca (US 1942: AA). This archetypal Hollywood melodrama of the forties was lucky on several counts. It nearly starred Ronald Reagan and Ann Sheridan instead of Humphrey Bogart and Ingrid Bergman; it happened to provide good parts for Warner regulars such as Greenstreet, Lorre, Sakall and especially Claude Rains; its mood anticipated the *films noirs* which came full flood at war's end; it hit the news accidentally by being released shortly before the Casablanca conference; and almost as an afterthought it had Dooley Wilson singing 'As Time Goes By'. Its intentional merits included a tense and witty script by the Epstein twins and Howard Koch (AA), skilled direction by Michael Curtiz (AA), and the usual A-film Warner lustre. Bogart gave one of his best-remembered good-bad guy performances and set the seal on a comparatively modest professional spy thriller which just happened to wrap up a whole era in an entertaining package.

†In 1955 a TV series was made starring Charles McGraw and Marcel Dalio in the Bogart and Rains roles. It ran to eight episodes. In 1983 a second effort was doomed to failure, this time with David Soul and Hector Elizondo.

Casanova, Giovanni (1725–1798). The celebrated Italian lover, whose career was much romanticized during his lifetime and afterwards, was a popular cinema figure although until the seventies his exploits had to be bowdlerized. Principal films are as follows:

France 1946:	*Les Aventures de Casanova*, Georges Guetary
US 1948:	*The Adventures of Casanova*, Arturo de Cordova
Italy 1955:	*Casanova*, Gabriele Ferzetti
Italy 1965:	*Casanova 70*, Marcello Mastroianni
Italy 1969:	*Casanova the Venetian*, Leonard Whiting
Italy/West Germany/ France 1977:	*The Rise and Rise of Casanova*, Tony Curtis
UK 1971:	*Casanova* (TV serial by Dennis Potter), Frank Finlay
Italy 1977:	*Fellini's Casanova*, Donald Sutherland
Italy 1978:	*The Return of Casanova*, Giulio Boseti

And in 1954 Vincent Price played Casanova in a Bob Hope spoof, *Casanova's Big Night*.

Casares, Maria (1922–) (Maria Casares Quiroga). Dark-eyed, solemn-looking French-Spanish character actress.
Les Enfants du Paradis 43. Les Dames du Bois de Boulogne 44. La Chartreuse de Parme 47. Bagarres 48. *Orphée* (as Death) 49. Le Testament d'Orphée 59. The Rebel Nun 74. Flavia 76, etc.

case histories from medical files, which would once have been considered pretty dull plot material, have recently been presented quite starkly to paying audiences who appear to have relished them. In the forties, *Lady in the Dark* was a richly decorated trifle, and even *The Snake Pit* and *Mandy* had subsidiary love interest, but in recent years we have had such unvarnished studies as *El* (paranoiac jealousy), *Pressure Point* (fascist tendencies), *A Child is Waiting* (mentally handicapped children), *Life Upside Down* (withdrawal), *The Collector* (sex fantasies), *Repulsion, In Cold Blood, 10 Rillington Place* and *The Boston Strangler* (homicidal mania), *Bigger Than Life* (danger from drugs), *The Three Faces of Eve* and *Lizzie* (split personality), *Marnie* (frigidity), *Morgan* (infantile regression), and *Family Life*. At least the pretence of studying a case history relieves writers of the responsibility of providing a dramatic ending.
See also: *dreams*; *fantasy*; *amnesia*.

Casey, Bernie (–). Black American character actor.
Tick Tick Tick 69. Black Gunn 72. Cornbread Earl and Me 75. Brothers 77, etc.

Cash, Johnny (1932–). American folk singer.
Five Minutes to Live 62. *A Gunfight* 70. The Pride of Jesse Hallam (TV) 80. Murder in Coweta County 83. The Baron and the Kid 84.

Cash, Rosalind (1945–). Black American leading lady.
□Klute 71. The Omega Man 71. The All-American Boy 71. The New Centurions 72. Hickey and Boggs 72. Melinda 72. Uptown Saturday Night 74. Amazing Grace 74. Hit the Open Man 75. Dr Black, Mr Hyde 76. The Monkey Hustle 76. The Class of Miss McMichael 78. Flashpoint (TV) 79. Guyana Tragedy (TV) 80. Wrong is Right 82.

Casino Royale (GB 1966). At once the ultimate in spy kaleidoscopes and the folly that killed off the fashion, this huge shapeless romp is living proof that all the money and talent in the world won't necessarily make a good movie . . . not, at least, when the script seems to have been put together with paste at a late-night party. If the distinguished directors and actors who made it had fun, they failed to communicate it to the audience.

Caspary, Vera (1899–1987). American romantic crime novelist.
The Night of June 13th (oa) 32. I'll Love You Always (w) 35. Scandal Street (oa) 38. Lady from Louisiana (w) 41. *Laura* (oa) 44. Claudia and David (w) 46. Bedelia (oa, w) 46. A Letter to Three Wives (w) 48. Three Husbands (oa, w) 51. The Blue Gardenia (oa) 53. Bachelor in Paradise (oa) 61, etc.

Casper the Friendly Ghost. A genial spirit from the Paramount cartoon factory of the forties. The idea of a baby ghost seemed at the time to be in poorish taste.

Casque d'Or (Golden Marie) (France 1952). The flavour and detail of French low-life in the nineties are subtly caught by director Jacques Becker in this much-admired melodrama starring Simone Signoret and Serge Reggiani.

Cass, Henry (1902–). British director with stage experience as actor and producer.
Lancashire Luck 37. 29 Acacia Avenue 45. The Glass Mountain 48. No Place for Jennifer 49. Last Holiday 50. Young Wives' Tale 51. Windfall 55. Blood of the Vampire 59. The Hand 60. Give a Dog a Bone 66, etc.

Cass, Maurice (1884–1954). American character actor of Russian origin; often played old men.
Two for Tonight 35. Charlie Chan at the Opera 37. Son of Monte Cristo 40. Blood and Sand 41. Charley's Aunt 41. Up in Arms 44. Angel on My Shoulder 46. Spoilers of the North 47. We're Not Married 52, many others.

Cass, Peggy (1924–). American comedy actress, mainly on Broadway: films few.
□The Marrying Kind 52. *Auntie Mame* 58. Gidget Goes Hawaiian 62. If It's Tuesday This Must Be Belgium 69. Age of Consent 69. Paddy 70.

Cassavetes, John (1929–). Slight, intense, American actor who played a variety of parts and later became an experimental director.
□Taxi 54. The Night Holds Terror 55. Crime in the Streets 56. Edge of the City 57. Saddle the Wind 58. Virgin Island 58. The Webster Boy 61. *Shadows* (d only) 61. Too Late Blues (d only) 62. A Child is Waiting (d only) 62. The Killers 64. The Dirty Dozen 67. Affair in Havana 67. The Devil's Angels 67. Rosemary's Baby 68. *Faces* (w, d only) 68. Bandits in Rome (It.) 69. If It's Tuesday This Must be Belgium 69. Husbands (& w, d) 70. Machine Gun McCain 70. *Minnie and Moskowitz* (& w, d) 71. A Woman Under the Influence (w, d only) 74. Capone 75. Two Minute Warning 76. Mikey and Nicky 76. Opening Night (& w, d) 78. The Killing of a Chinese Bookie (w, d only) 78. Brass Target 78. The Fury 78. Flesh and Blood (TV) 80. Gloria (w, p, d only) 80. Whose Life is it Anyway? 81. Tempest 82. The Incubus 82. Love Streams (w, p, d) 83. Marvin and Tige 83. Big Trouble 84.
TV series: *Johnny Staccato* 59.

¶ 'As a director, too much of the time he is groping when he should be gripping.'—*Andrew Sarris*, 1968

'One of the most garrulous noncomformists in show business.—*Anon*

J.C.: People have forgotten how to relate or respond . . . what I'm trying to do with my movies is build something audiences can respond to.

J.C.: When I started making films, I wanted to make Frank Capra pictures. But I've never been able to make anything but these crazy, tough pictures. You are what you are.

Cassel, Jean-Pierre (1932–) (Jean-Pierre Crochon). French leading man.
Les Jeux de l'Amour 60. L'Amant de Cinq Jours 61. The Vanishing Corporal 62. La Ronde 64. Those Magnificent Men in Their Flying Machines 65. Les Fêtes Galantes 65. Is Paris Burning? 66. Jeu de Massacre 67. Baxter 71. The Discreet Charm of the Bourgeoisie 72. The Three Musketeers 74. Murder on the Orient Express 74. That Lucky Touch 75, etc.

Cassel, Seymour (1935–). American character actor.
Too Late Blues 61. The Killers 64. The Sweet Ride 68. Faces 68. The Revolutionary 70. *Minnie and Moskowitz* 71. The Last Tycoon 76. The Killing of a Chinese Bookie 78. Convoy 78. California Dreaming 79, etc.

cassettes. In 1970–71 the show business world awaited a revolution which despite enormous expense and drum-beating failed to happen at the time. The idea was to make available one's favourite film, or any other kind of entertainment, in miniaturized cartridge form which could be played back whenever one wished through new equipment. Unfortunately international agreement on the type of hardware could not be achieved, and none of the prototype gadgets were compatible. Moreover the trade was still busy selling colour TV, so by general consensus the new miracle was deferred until the eighties, when under the name 'video', and with fewer competing systems, it was a success beyond the industry's wildest dreams or fears. By 1984 one in every five homes had the equipment, and films new and old were cheaply available on hire from a myriad of local shops. The British success with the system caused more cinema closures, but was not equalled in other countries.

Cassidy, Jack (1926–1976). American light actor, mostly on TV; husband of Shirley Jones and father of David Cassidy.
Look in any Window 62. FBI Code 98 64. Guide for the Married Man 67. Your Money or Your Wife (TV) 72. Phantom of Hollywood (TV) 74. The Eiger Sanction 75.W. C. Fields and Me (as John Barrymore) 76, etc.
TV series: He and She 67.

Cassidy, Joanna (1944–). American leading lady of the seventies.
The Laughing Policeman 73. The Outfit 73. Bank Shot 74. Stunts 77. Blade Runner 82. Under Fire 83. Hollywood Wives (TV) 85. Club Paradise 86. The Fourth Protocol 87.

Cassidy, Ted (1932–79). Giant-size American character actor who became popular in 1964 as Lurch the butler in TV's *The Addams Family*.
Mackenna's Gold 68. Harry and Walter Go to New York 76. The Last Remake of Beau Geste 77, etc.

cast. The actors in a movie.

Castellani, Renato (1913–85). Italian director.
Un Colpo di Pistola 41. My Son the Professor 46. E Primavera 50. Due Soldi di Speranza 51. Romeo and Juliet (GB) 54. Nella Città l'Inferno 59. Il Brigante 61. Mare Matto 62. Three Nights of Love 64. Sotto il Cielo Stellato 66. Ghosts Italian Style 67. Una Breva Stagione 69. Leonardo da Vinci (TV) 72, etc.

Castellano, Richard (1931–). Fat Italian-American character actor who came to fame in *Lovers and Other Strangers* 69 and in 1972 had his own TV series, *The Super,* as well as appearing in *The Godfather* 72.

Castelnuovo, Nino (1937–). Italian leading man.
La Garçonnière 60. Escapade in Florence 62. Les Parapluies de Cherbourg 64. Camille 2000 69, etc.

Castelnuovo-Tedesco, Mario (1895–1968). Italian composer in America.
The Return of the Vampire 44. The Black Parachute 44. *And Then There Were None* 45. Night Editor 46. Time out of Mind 47. Mark of the Avenger 51, etc.

casting. To the old Hollywood, casting usually meant type-casting, or bending the character to suit the star. In the seventies, stars became less important, and leading actors became more chameleon-like. Even so, many best-remembered performances have been given by actors who were second or third choice. The original requirement for *Dracula* was Paul Muni, not Bela Lugosi. Clark Gable was thought of for Tarzan. Greta Garbo was asked to play Dorian Gray as a woman. Gloria Swanson's role in *Sunset Boulevard* was first offered to Mae West. Humphrey Bogart got *High Sierra* and *The Maltese Falcon* only because George Raft turned them down. Robert Montgomery, Fredric March, Carole Lombard and Myrna Loy all turned down *It Happened One Night* before Gable and Colbert accepted. Carole Lombard however benefited when Miriam Hopkins turned down *Twentieth Century*. Olivier's role as Maxim de Winter in *Rebecca* was first offered to William Powell and Ronald Colman. Doris Day was offered Mrs Robinson in *The Graduate*. Lana Turner gave way to Lee Remick on *Anatomy of a Murder*. Bette Davis would have been Scarlett O'Hara if she hadn't thought Errol Flynn was to play Rhett. George Jessel would have starred in *The Jazz Singer* if his demands had been less outrageous. Danny Thomas would have starred in *The Jolson Story* if he had agreed to have his nose shortened. Marlon Brando, Montgomery Clift and Paul Newman were all sought for *East of Eden* before James Dean got the role. Bette Davis played Margo in *All About Eve* only because Claudette Colbert gave it up. Ingrid Bergman was second choice to Vera Zorina for *For Whom the Bell Tolls*. Jack Nicholson took over from Rip Torn in *Easy Rider*, Marlon Brando from Montgomery Clift in *On The Waterfront*. Bette Davis turned down *Mildred Pierce* and Joan Crawford grabbed it. Olivia de Havilland, not Vivien Leigh, was first choice for *A Streetcar named Desire*. Ingrid Bergman won Oscars for *Gaslight*, first offered to Hedy

Lamarr, and *Anastasia*, intended for Jennifer Jones; but she turned down *The Farmer's Daughter* and *To Each His Own*, which won Oscars for Loretta Young and Olivia de Havilland. If Grace Kelly hadn't become Princess of Monaco, she would have played in *Cat on a Hot Tin Roof* and *Designing Woman*, not Elizabeth Taylor or Lauren Bacall. William Holden got *Sunset Boulevard* after Montgomery Clift said no. Frank Sinatra walked out of *Carousel*: Gordon MacRae took over. Ginger Rogers replaced the ailing Judy Garland in *The Barkleys of Broadway*. Deborah Kerr got *From Here to Eternity* when Joan Crawford withdrew. Vivien Leigh thought herself too young to play the role in *Suddenly Last Summer* which went to Katharine Hepburn. Shirley Temple was wanted for Judy Garland's role in *The Wizard of Oz*; W. C. Fields was to have been the wizard, but argued over money. Fields himself only got Micawber in *David Copperfield* because Charles Laughton walked out after two days of filming.

¶ Casting: deciding which of two faces the public is least tired of.—*anonymous definition*

I couldn't go on forever being Little Miss Fixit who burst into song.—*Deanna Durbin*

No matter what roles I play, I can't get Caligari out of my system.—*Conrad Veidt*

I was a thirteen-year-old boy for thirty years.—*Mickey Rooney*

After *The Wizard of Oz* I was typecast as a lion, and there aren't all that many parts for lions.—*Bert Lahr*

If I made *Cinderella*, the audience would be looking for the body in the coach.—*Alfred Hitchcock*

They get to know your face too well out there in Hollywood, and you're finished.—*Ethel Griffies*

Aren't you tired, Spence, of always playing Spencer Tracy?

—What am I supposed to do, play Bogart?

Castle, Don (1919–1966). American leading man of forties second features.
Love Finds Andy Hardy 38. I Take this Woman 40. Power Dive 41. Tombstone 42. The Guilty 47. The Invisible Wall 47, etc.

Castle, Irene and **Vernon** (Irene Foote, Vernon Blythe). A dancing team who were highly popular in American cabaret 1912–17. Irene (1893–1969) was American, Vernon (1893–1918) was British. Apart from some 1914 shorts, their only feature together was *The Whirl of Life* 15; but Irene alone made a number of dramatic films, especially after Vernon's death in an air crash: *Patria* 17, *The Hillcrest Mystery* 18, *The Invisible Bond* 19, *The Broadway Bride* 21, *No Trespassing* 22, etc. In 1939 Fred Astaire and Ginger Rogers appeared in *The Story of Vernon and Irene Castle*; in 1958 Irene published an autobiography, *Castles in the Air*.

Castle, John (1940–). British character actor.
The Lion in Winter 68. The Promise 69. Antony and Cleopatra 71. Man of La Mancha 72. The Incredible Sarah 77. The Three Hostages (TV) 78. Eagle's Wing 79. Night Shift 80. Second Star to the Right 80.

Castle, Mary (1931–). American leading lady.
Criminal Lawyer 51. Eight Iron Men 52. The Lawless Breed 53. The Jailbreakers 61, etc.

Castle, Nick (1910–1968). American dance director.
Swanee River 39. Hellzapoppin 42. Royal Wedding 47. Red Garters 54, others.

Castle, Peggie (1927–1973). American leading lady of fifties second features.
Mr Belvedere Goes to College 49. Buccaneer's Girl 50. Air Cadet 51. I the Jury 53. The Long Wait 54. Jesse James' Women 54. Target Zero 55. Bury Me Dead 57. Seven Hills of Rome 58, etc.
TV series: Lawman 58–61.

Castle, Roy (1933–). British light entertainer, in occasional films.
Dr Terror's House of Horrors 66. Dr Who and the Daleks 66. Carry on Up the Khyber 71. Legend of the Werewolf 75, etc.

Castle, William (1914–77) (William Schloss). American director of second features (1941–57) who became a cheerful purveyor of gimmicky horror films involving give-away insurance policies, mobile skeletons, tingling seats, etc; these he not only produced and directed but introduced in the Hitchcock manner.
Autobiography 1976: *Step Right Up! . . . I'm Gonna Scare The Pants off America.*
□The Chance of a Lifetime 43. Klondyke Kate 43. *The Whistler* 44. *When Strangers Marry* 44. She's a Soldier Too 44. The Mark of the Whistler 44. Voice of the Whistler 46. Just Before Dawn 46. Mysterious Intruder 46. The Return of Rusty 46. The Crime Doctor's Manhunt 46. The Crime Doctor's Gamble 47.

Texas Brooklyn and Heaven 48. The Gentleman from Nowhere 48. Johnny Stool Pigeon 49. Undertow 49. It's a Small World 50. The Fat Man 51. Hollywood Story 51. Cave of Outlaws 51. Serpent of the Nile 53. Fort Ti 53. Conquest of Cochise 53. Slaves of Babylon 53. Charge of the Lancers 54. Drums of Tahiti 54. Jesse James vs the Daltons 54. Battle of Rogue River 54. The Iron Glove 54. The Saracen Blade 54. The Law vs Billy the Kid 54. Masterson of Kansas 54. The Americano 55. New Orleans Uncensored 55. The Gun that Won the West 55. Duel on the Mississippi 55. The Houston Story 56. Uranium Boom 56. *Macabre* 58. *House on Haunted Hill* 59. The Tingler 59. Thirteen Ghosts 60. *Homicidal* 61. Sardonicus 61. Zotz! 62. Thirteen Frightened Girls 63. The Old Dark House 63. Strait Jacket 64. *The Night Walker* 64. I Saw What You Did 65. Let's Kill Uncle 66. The Busy Body 67. The Spirit is Willing 67. Rosemary's Baby (p only) 68. Project X 68. The Sex Symbol (TV) (as actor) 74. Shanks (& p) 74. Shampoo (as actor) 75. Bug (p only) 75. Day of the Locust (as actor) 75.
TV series: Ghost Story 72.

? casts

Can you name the films which featured these groups of actors? They are not necessarily in order of billing, and the nominal star is not always included.

1 Lee Marvin, Anne Bancroft, Raymond Burr, Lee J. Cobb
2 Lee Marvin, Ernest Borgnine, Dean Jagger, Spencer Tracy
3 Lee J. Cobb, George Voskovec, Jack Warden, Ed Begley
4 Onslow Stevens, Lionel Atwill, Lon Chaney Jnr, John Carradine
5 Ernest Thesiger, Eva Moore, Gloria Stuart, Charles Laughton
6 Thomas Mitchell, Jane Darwell, Harry Davenport, Leslie Howard
7 Gladys Cooper, Nigel Bruce, Reginald Denny, Joan Fontaine
8 Everett Sloane, Joseph Cotten, Gus Schilling, George Coulouris
9 George Zucco, Gale Sondergaard, John Beal, Bob Hope
10 Josephine Hull, Jean Adair, Peter Lorre, Cary Grant
11 Frank Morgan, Billie Burke, Bert Lahr, Jack Haley
12 Melvyn Douglas, Ina Claire, Felix Bressart, Sig Ruman
13 Frank Sinatra, Gene Kelly, Jules Munshin, Esther Williams
14 Peter Lorre, Boris Karloff, Bela Lugosi, Kay Kyser
15 Frank Reicher, Fay Wray, Robert Armstrong, Bruce Cabot
16 John Wayne, Frank Sinatra, Yul Brynner, Senta Berger
17 Richard Conte, James Caan, Diane Keaton, Sterling Hayden
18 Robert Shaw, Wendy Hiller, Susannah York, Orson Welles
19 George Kennedy, Barbara Hale, Dean Martin, Jean Seberg
20 James Stewart, Ruth Hussey, Roland Young, Virginia Weidler
21 Barry Fitzgerald, Victor McLaglen, Maureen O'Hara, John Wayne
22 Dame May Whitty, Paul Lukas, Michael Redgrave, Cecil Parker
23 Eve Arden, Arthur O'Connell, Ben Gazzara, Lee Remick
24 Ava Gardner, Martin Balsam, Burt Lancaster, Fredric March
25 Carroll Baker, Mercedes McCambridge, Elizabeth Taylor
26 Marilyn Monroe, Hugh Marlowe, Gregory Ratoff, George Sanders
27 John McIntyre, Vera Miles, Martin Balsam, John Gavin
28 Myrna Loy, Teresa Wright, Hoagy Carmichael, Dana Andrews
29 Martha Raye, Jane Frazee, Hugh Herbert, Mischa Auer
30 Bette Davis, Claude Rains, Brian Aherne, John Garfield
31 Thomas Mitchell, Jean Arthur, Guy Kibbee, Claude Rains
32 Myrna Loy, George Brent, Maria Ouspenskaya, Nigel Bruce
33 Bela Lugosi, Maria Ouspenskaya, Warren William, Claude Rains
34 Maria Ouspenskaya, Claude Rains, Charles Coburn, Nancy Coleman
35 John Howard, Jane Wyatt, Edward Everett Horton, H. B. Warner
36 Claude Rains, Basil Rathbone, Ian Hunter, Olivia de Havilland
37 Claude Rains, Henry Daniell, Flora Robson, Brenda Marshall
38 Lee J. Cobb, Vincent Price, William Eythe, Charles Bickford
39 Vincent Price, Cedric Hardwicke, Nan Grey, John Sutton
40 Vincent Price, Basil Rathbone, Boris Karloff, Barbara O'Neil
41 Vincent Price, Peter Lorre, Boris Karloff, Jack Nicholson
42 Vincent Price, Cedric Hardwicke, William Eythe, Alexander Knox
43 Gene Tierney, Don Ameche, Laird Cregar, Eugene Pallette

44 Claude Rains, Edward Everett Horton, Evelyn Keyes, Halliwell Hobbes
45 David Frost, Maggie Smith, Rod Taylor, Louis Jourdan
46 Al Jolson, Hobart Cavanagh, Tyrone Power, Alice Faye
47 Bette Davis, Claude Rains, Paul Henreid, Gladys Cooper
48 Bette Davis, Claude Rains, Walter Abel, Jerome Cowan
49 Humphrey Bogart, Mary Astor, Sidney Greenstreet, Sen Yung
50 Humphrey Bogart, Sidney Greenstreet, Peter Lorre, S. Z. Sakall

The Cat and the Canary. An eccentric will read at midnight in a spooky house, with secret panels behind which a maniac lurks, are the ingredients of John Willard's stage thriller of 1922, which prompted a host of Hollywood imitations as well as being itself filmed three times. Paul Leni's 1927 version was a semi-surrealist send-up, with Creighton Hale and Laura la Plante. Rupert Julian's sound remake of 1930 was retitled *The Cat Creeps,* and featured Helen Twelvetrees and Raymond Hackett. In 1939 came Elliott Nugent's very satisfactory comedy vehicle for Bob Hope and Paulette Goddard, with Gale Sondergaard as the sinister housekeeper and some elegant photography by Charles Lang. A British remake followed in 1967.

Cat Ballou (US 1965). A spoof western directed with some but not quite enough flair by Eliot Silverstein from a joky script by Walter Newman and Frank Pierson. An amusing ballad by Nat King Cole and Stubby Kaye effectively linked disparate threads of story, and Lee Marvin collected an Oscar for guying a dual role.

Cat People (US 1942). Allegedly the first monster film to refrain from showing its monster, this was the first of the much praised low-budget thrillers produced by Val Lewton at RKO. Directed by Jacques Tourneur from a script by De Witt Bodeen, and atmospherically photographed by Nicholas Musuraca, it begins slowly but builds up to suspenseful set-pieces on a lonely street and in a darkened swimming bath. A 1981 remake added sex, gore and what passed for style, but it is not likely to be remembered.

catchphrases

¶ Although Garbo got into the act with 'I want to be alone' and Boyer impersonators have had a ball with a line Boyer never spoke, 'Come with me to the Casbah', it is comedians who devise and need readily identifiable catchphrases, so that audiences have something to laugh at without even being warmed up. Here are a few which should be immediately recognized.

Diminutive Arthur Askey came up with

I thank you (pronounced Ay Theng Yow)

and was annoyed when Cyril Fletcher used the slight variation

Thanking you . . .

as well as:

Dreaming oh my darling love of thee.

Sandy Powell had

Can you hear me, mother?

George Formby contracted this, in moments of stress, to

Ohh, muvver!

when he wasn't telling everyone that it had

Turned out nice again!

Flanagan and Allen's most notable trade mark was simply

Oi!

while Will Hay perfected a sniff. Max Miller however told his audiences:

There'll never be another!

and when they laughed at his floral suit, asked:

Well, what if I am?

When Old Mother Riley needed help, she screamed:

Mrs Ginocchi, S O S !

and of her errant daughter she inevitably demanded:

Where've you been, who've you been with, what've you been doing, and why?

Robb Wilton reminisced about

The day war broke out

and Tommy Trinder called his audience

You lucky people!

Bruce Forsyth also gets on chummily with his audience, asking for applause with

Didn't he do well?

Jack Warner was worried for his property:

Mind my bike . . .

and Robertson Hare always anticipated disaster:

Oh, calamity!

Schoolmasterish Jimmy Edwards told his audience to

Wake up at the back, there!

While Ben Lyon was constantly afraid that his mother-in-law in the audience might take umbrage at any insulting lines from the stage:

Not you, momma, sit down!

The famous radio series *It's That Man Again* practically consisted of catchphrases, including

Can I do you now, sir?
Don't forget the diver . . .
After you, Claude . . . no, after you, Cecil . . .
I go, I come back.
Good morning, nice day.
I don't mind if I do.
Boss, boss, sumpn terrible's happened . . .
This is Funf speaking . . .

After *ITMA*'s demise, other radio shows caught on to the idea, Arthur Askey producing

Hello, playmates!
Before your very eyes.
Don't be filthy.

and

These jokes are free for pantomime!

Sam Costa was recognized by:

Good morning, sir, was there something?

While *Take It from Here* also added its share of phrases to the language:

Gently, Bentley.
A *mauve* one.
Clumsy clot.
Oh Eth . . . oh, Ron . . .

More recently, Frankie Howerd has wished his audiences:

And the best of luck!

Max Bygraves has asserted himself:

I've arrived, and to prove it, I'm here.

Cates, Gilbert (1934–) (Gilbert Katz). American director with Broadway and TV experience.
□*I Never Sang for My Father* 69. To All My Friends on Shore (TV) 71. Summer Wishes, Winter Dreams 73. The Affair (TV) 73. Johnny We Hardly Knew Ye (TV) 77. The Promise 79. Oh God Book Two 80. The Last Married Couple in America 80. Backfire 87.

Cates, Phoebe (1963–). American leading lady who after modelling experience became an instant star in 1984 as the heroine of the TV mini-series *Lace*. Fast Times at Ridgmont High 82. Paradise 82. Private School 83. Gremlins 84.

Catherine the Great (1729–1798), 'mother of all the Russias', has appeared in the following screen personifications:

Pola Negri	*Forbidden Paradise* 24
Marlene Dietrich	*The Scarlet Empress* 34
Elisabeth Bergner	*Catherine the Great* 34
Tallulah Bankhead	*A Royal Scandal* 45
Viveca Lindfors	*Tempest* 58
Bette Davis	*John Paul Jones* 59
Hildegarde Neff	*Catherine of Russia* 62
Jeanne Moreau	*Great Catherine* 68

What a pity that Mae West's play *Catherine Was Great* never reached the screen . . .

Catlett, Walter (1889–1960). Bespectacled American comedian with long vaudeville experience; his flustered gestures often characterized inept crooks, commercial travellers or justices of the peace.
Second Youth 24. Summer Bachelors 29. Why Leave Home? 29. Palmy Days 31. Rain 32. Mama Loves Papa 33. The Captain Hates the Sea 34. Mr Deeds Goes to Town 36. On the Avenue 37. *Bringing Up Baby* 38. Pop Always Pays 40. Horror Island 41. Yankee Doodle Dandy 42. They Got Me Covered 43. Ghost Catchers 44. I'll Be Yours 47. *Look for the Silver Lining* 49. Here Comes the Groom 51. Father Takes the Air 51. Friendly Persuasion 56, many others.

Catto, Max (1907–). Popular British adventure novelist.
Daughter of Darkness (oa) 48. A Prize of Gold (oa) 54. West of Zanzibar (w) 54. Seven Thieves (oa) 60. The Devil at Four O'Clock (oa) 61. Mister Moses (oa) 65, etc.

Caulfield, Joan (1922–). Demure American leading lady of the forties.
□Miss Susie Slagle's 46. *Monsieur Beaucaire* 46. *Blue Skies* 46. *Dear Ruth* 47. Welcome Stranger 47. The Unsuspected 47. The Sainted Sisters 48. Larceny 48. Dear Wife 50. The Petty Girl 50. The Lady Says No 51. The Rains of Ranchipur 55. Cattle King 63. Red Tomahawk 66. Buckskin 68.
TV series: My Favorite Husband 53. Sally 57.

Cavalcade (US 1933) (AA). Noel Coward's patriotic twentieth-century pageant was brought to the screen by Frank Lloyd (AA) in a spectacular if rather lifeless Hollywood version, with a mainly British cast led by Clive Brook and Diana Wynyard. Art direction by William Darling (AA).

Cavalcanti, Alberto (1897–1982). Brazilian director who made interesting films in several countries but never quite achieved a masterpiece.
Rien que les Heures 26. En Rade 27. Sea Fever 29. North Sea 38. Men of the Lightship 41. *Went the Day Well* 42. Champagne Charlie 45. Dead of Night (part) 45. *Nicholas Nickleby* 47. They Made Me A Fugitive 47. The First Gentleman 48. For Them That Trespass 49. O Canto do Mar (Braz.) 53. Herr Puntila (Ger.) 55. La Prima Notte (It.) 58. Yerma (It.) 62, etc.

Cavanagh, Paul (1895–1964). Suave British actor who went to Hollywood in the twenties and spent the rest of his career playing elegant villains, understanding husbands, and murder victims.
The Runaway Princess 29. Grumpy 30. The Devil to Pay 30. The Squaw Man 31. The Devil's Lottery 32. A Bill of Divorcement 32. The Kennel Murder Case 33. Tarzan and his Mate 34. *The Notorious Sophie Lang* 34. *Goin' to Town* (opposite Mae West) 35. Champagne Charlie 36. Romance in Flanders 37. Crime over London 38. Reno 39. The Case of the Black Parrot 40. Maisie was a Lady 41. The Strange Case of Dr RX 42. The Hard Way 43. The Scarlet Claw 44. The Man in Half Moon Street 44. House of Fear 45. The Verdict 46. Humoresque 46. Ivy 47. You Gotta Stay Happy 48. The Iroquois Trail 50. House of Wax 53. Casanova's Big Night 54. The Purple Mask 55. Francis in the Haunted House 56. Diane 57. The Four Skulls of Jonathan Drake 59, many others.

Cavanaugh, Hobart (1886–1950). Mild-mannered, bald and bespectacled American character actor usually seen as clerk, nervous husband or frightened caretaker.
San Francisco Nights 27. I Cover the Waterfront 33. Convention City 33. Housewife 34. I Sell Anything 34. Don't Bet on Blondes 35. A Midsummer Night's Dream 35. Stage Struck 36. Cain and Mabel 36. Reported Missing 37. *Rose of Washington Square* (as a double act with Al Jolson) 39. An Angel from Texas 40. Meet the Chump 41. Horror Island (as the villain) 41. The Magnificent Dope 42. Sweet Rosie O'Grady 43. Kismet 44. Black Angel 46. You Gotta Stay Happy 48. Stella 50, many others.

Cavani, Liliana (1937–). Italian director.
□Night Encounter 61. Philip Pétain 64. Francis of Assisi 66. Galileo 68. The Cannibals 69. The Hospital 71. The Night Porter 74. Beyond Evil 77. The Berlin Affair 85.

Cawthorn, Joseph (1868–1949). American character actor of the thirties.
Very Confidential 27. Silk Legs 28. Jazz Heaven 29. The Taming of the Shrew 29. Dixiana 30. Kiki 31. White Zombie 32. Love me Tonight 32. Whistling in the Dark 33. Housewife 34. The Last Gentleman 34. Go into Your Dance 35. Naughty Marietta 35. The Great Ziegfeld 36. Lillian Russell 40. The Postman Didn't Ring 42, many others.

Cayatte, André (1909–). French lawyer who became writer-director of films with something to say.
Justice est Faite 50. *Nous Sommes Tous les Assassins* 52. An Eye for an Eye 56. The Mirror Has Two Faces 57. The Crossing of the Rhine 60. La Vie Conjugale 63. A Trap for Cinderella 65. Die of Loving 70, etc.

Cazale, John (1936–78). American character actor.
The Godfather 72. The Conversation 74. The Godfather Part Two 74. *Dog Day Afternoon* 75. *The Deer Hunter* 78, etc.

Cazenove, Christopher (1945–). British leading man, mostly on TV.
Royal Flash 74. East of Elephant Rock 75. Zulu Dawn 79. Eye of the Needle 80. From a Far Country 80. The Letter (TV) 81. Heat and Dust 82. Mata Hari 83. Jenny's War (TV) 84. Lace II (TV) 85. The Fantasist 86.
TV series: Dynasty 86–

Cecchi D'Amico, Suso (1914–) (Giovanna Cecchi D'Amico). Italian screenwriter.
Vivere in Pace 46. Bicycle Thieves 49. Miracle in Milan 51. Bellissima 51. Le Amiche 55. Rocco and his Brothers 60, many others.

Cecil, Henry (1902–1976). British novelist, a county court judge who poked fun at the vagaries of the British legal system in a series of amusing but rather overstretched books, of which *Brothers in Law* was successfully filmed.

Cecil, Jonathan (1939–). British light comic actor usually seen as gangling ineffective types.
The Yellow Rolls Royce 64. Otley 68. The Private Life of Sherlock Holmes 71. Barry Lyndon 75. Rising Damp 80. History of the World Part One 81. Dead Man's Folly (TV) 85. Second Victory 86. Murder in Three Acts (TV) 86. Little Dorrit 87, etc.

cel. The sheet of celluloid on which cartoon animators draw their foreground actions, one cel per film frame.

Celi, Adolfo (1922–86). Solidly-built Italian character actor who followed a Brazilian stage career by playing villains in international films.
Escape into Dreams 50. *That Man from Rio* 64. Von Ryan's Express 65. *Thunderball* 65.

El Greco 66. Grand Prix 67. The Honey Pot 67. The Bobo 67. Grand Slam 68. Fragment of Fear 70. Murders in the Rue Morgue 71. Hitler—The Last Ten Days 73. And Then There Were None 75. The Next Man 76. Sandokan 77. Cafe Express 79. The Borgias (TV) 82, etc.

Cellier, Frank (1884–1948). British stage actor who seemed to frown a lot and usually played unsympathetic types.
Soldiers of the King 33. The Thirty-nine Steps 35. Rhodes of Africa 36. Tudor Rose 36. Non Stop New York 37. Sixty Glorious Years 38. The Ware Case 39. Quiet Wedding 40. Love on the Dole 41. Give Us the Moon 44. Quiet Weekend 46. The Blind Goddess 48, etc.

censorship. Each country has found it necessary to apply its own rules for film producers; in Britain and America at least these rules were drawn up and enforced at the request of the industry itself. The British Board of Film Censors was founded in 1912. For many years films were classified as 'U' (for universal exhibition), 'A' (adults and accompanied children only) or (from 1933) 'H' (horrific; prohibited for persons under 16). In 1951, with the growing emphasis on sex, 'H' was replaced by 'X', which includes sex *and* horror. In the sixties X came to mean over eighteen, AA no one under 14, and A was simply a warning to parents (children could still get in unaccompanied). In America, the Arbuckle scandal of 1921 precipitated the founding of the 'Hays Office' (named after its first paid president) by the Motion Picture Producers and Distributors of America. The first Production Code was issued in 1930 and has undergone constant amendment especially since *The Moon is Blue* 53, and very rapidly indeed since *Room at the Top* 59; in 1966 *Who's Afraid of Virginia Woolf?* almost swamped it completely and a revised, broadened code was issued. In 1968 this was replaced by a new rating system: 'X', 'R' (restricted), 'PG' (parental guidance advised) and 'G' (general audience). The independent and very strict Catholic Legion of Decency was founded in 1934 and issues its own classifications; it recently changed its name to the National Catholic Office for Motion Pictures.
Best books: Murray Schumach's *The Face on the Cutting Room Floor* and Doug McClelland's *The Unkindest Cuts.*

¶ We are paid to have dirty minds.—*John Trevelyan, British censor, 1968*

Any film that isn't fit to be shown to my youngest child isn't fit to be shown to anybody.—*Chicago Chief of Police, 1936*

The Seashell and the Clergyman is apparently meaningless. If it has any meaning, it is doubtless objectionable.—*British Board of Film Censors, 1929*

Travesties of religious rites . . . references to royalty . . . hangings or executions either serious or comic . . . political propaganda . . . too much shooting . . . intoxication . . . cruelty . . . companionate marriage . . . free love . . . immodesty . . . vamping . . . vulgar noises . . . harsh screams . . . the divinity . . . life after death . . . British officers shown in an unflattering light . . .—*themes banned by the British censor, 1930*

The cinema needs continual repression of controversy if it is to stave off disaster.—*Lord Tyrrell, Chairman of British Board of Film Censors, 1936*

They can't censor the gleam in my eye.—*Charles Laughton, told that incest had been removed from his role in The Barretts of Wimpole Street*

The inanities blessed by the Hays Office are more genuinely corrupting than any pornography.—*Joseph Wood Krutch*

It is in the interest of producers to maintain a certain moral standard since, if they don't do this, the immoral films won't sell.—*Jean Renoir*

Hollywood buys a good story about a bad girl and changes it to a bad story about a good girl.—*Anon, 1930s*

The Hays Office warned us that we couldn't show the heroine as a prostitute. We had to put a sewing machine in her apartment, so in that way she was not a whore but a seamstress.—*Fritz Lang on Man Hunt*

The industry must have towards that sacred thing, the mind of a child, towards that clean virgin thing, that unmarked slate, the same responsibility, the same care about the impressions made on it, that the best clergyman or the most inspired teacher of youth would have.—*Will Hays, 1930s*

Will Hays is my shepherd, I shall not want, He maketh me to lie down in clean postures.—*Gene Fowler*

Hollywood must never permit censorship to collapse. It's far too good for the box office.—*Claude Binyon*

What critics call dirty in our movies, they call lusty in foreign films.—*Billy Wilder*

In a novel a hero can lay ten girls and marry a virgin for the finish. In a movie, this is not allowed. The hero, as well as the heroine, has to be a virgin. The villain can lay anyone he wants, have as much fun as he wants cheating and stealing, getting rich and whipping the servants. But you have to shoot him in the end. When he falls with a bullet in his forehead, it is advisable that he clutch at the Gobelin tapestry on the library wall and bring it down over his head like a symbolic shroud. Also, covered by such a tapestry, the actor does not have to hold his breath while being photographed as a dead man.—*Herman J. Mankiewicz, 1930s*

I don't like censorship, but nor do I like the absence of it.—*Robert Rossen, 1950s*

The trouble with censors is they worry if a girl has cleavage. They ought to worry if she hasn't any.—*Marilyn Monroe, 1950s*

Nowadays when a film is awarded the production seal the producer cries: Where have we failed?—*Bob Hope, 1962*

They are doing things on the screen now that I wouldn't do in bed. If I could.—*Bob Hope, 1965*

They are doing things on the screen now that the French don't even put on postcards.—*Bob Hope, 1970*

The Americans are nice people, but right now they're behaving like small boys who've just discovered what sex is.—*John Trevelyan, British Board of Film Censors, 1970*

The only censor is the audience, which will decide whether it wants it and how soon it gets fed up with it.—*Lord Eccles, Minister for the Arts, 1972*

? Some questions about films which in their time extended the bounds of permissiveness.

1 Who starred in *Our Dancing Daughters*, *Our Modern Maidens* and *Our Blushing Brides*?
2 What Otto Preminger comedy was issued in defiance of the Production Code ban?
3 Clark Gable as Rhett Butler in *Gone with the Wind* was finally allowed to speak a line which offended the Hays Office. What was it?
4 Who rewrote Noël Coward's *Design for Living* for the screen, leaving, he believed, just one of the Master's lines?
5 What much-banned novel, by whom, was filmed in 1933 as *The Story of Temple Drake*?
6 Who sang, in what film, 'I Like a Man Who Takes His Time'?
7 Who wrote the play *Who's Afraid of Virginia Woolf*?
8 What was missing from the version of *The Bachelor Party* released in Great Britain?
9 Name the three leading actresses in *The Killing of Sister George*.
10 In what film did Hedy Lamarr swim in the nude, and who directed it?
11 By the time *My Fair Lady* was made, the phrase 'not bloody likely' which had caused such a commotion in the original *Pygmalion*, was felt to be too tame. What phrase – applied to a horse at Ascot – replaced it?
12 What 1945 British film had to be reshot because the ladies' decolletage was too revealing for American audiences?
13 And why did the Americans reject David Lean's *Oliver Twist*?
14 In what film did Mickey Shaughnessy mouth obscenities which the sound track obligingly bleeped out?
15 In what film did Rex Harrison instruct a lady to 'piss off'?

Central Casting. The talent agency through whose doors passed many unknowns who stayed that way. In the thirties the Hollywood office had a sign above the door: DON'T TRY TO BECOME AN ACTOR. FOR EVERY ONE WE EMPLOY, WE TURN AWAY THOUSANDS.

Cervantes, Miguel de (1547–1616). Spanish novelist whose *Don Quixote* (qv) has been much filmed.

Cervi, Gino (1901–74). Stocky Italian character actor.
Frontier 34. An Ideal Marriage 39. Four Steps in the Clouds 42. Fabiola 47. Furia 48. *The Little World of Don Camillo* (as the mayor) 51. OK Nero 52. Three Forbidden Stories 53. Indiscretion 53. Maddalena 53. The Return of Don Camillo 54. Wife for a Night 55. The Naked Maja 59. Wild Love 60. The Revolt of the Slaves 61. Becket 64, many others.

Chabrol, Claude (1930–). Variable but generally distinguished French director, credited with starting the *nouvelle vague*.
□*Le Beau Serge* 58. Les Cousins 59. A Double Tour 59. Les Bonnes Femmes 60. Les Godelureaux 60. The Third Lover 61. The Seven Deadly Sins (part) 61. Les Plus Belles Escroqueries du Monde (part) 61. Ophelia 62. Landru 62. Paris vu Par (part) 64. Le Tigre se Parfume à la Dynamite 64. Le Tigre Aime la Chair Fraîche 65. Marie Chantal 65. Line of Demarcation 66. The Champagne Murders 67. The Road to Corinth 68. *Les Biches* 68. La Femme Infidèle 69. *The Beast Must Die* 69. La Rupture 70. *The Butcher* 70. Just Before Nightfall 71. La Decade Prodigieuse 71. Blood Wedding 71. Ten Days' Wonder 72. The Wolf Trap 72. Scoundrel in White 72.

Ophelia 73. Nada 73. Innocents with Dirty Hands 73. Une Partie de Plain 73. Les Magiciens 73. Le Banc de la Desolation 74. Folies Bourgeoise 77. Alice 77. Violette Nozière 78. Il Etait Un Musicien 78. Fantomas I (TV) 78. Fantomas IV (TV) 78. Monsieur Prokoviev (TV) 78. La Bouche à l'Oreille 78. Les Menteurs 79. Blood Relatives 79. Le Cheval d'Orgeuil 80. Les Fantômes du Chapelier 81. Le Sang des Autres 83. Cop au Vin 84. Inspector Lavardin 86.

Chaffey, Don (1917–). British director; started in art department at Gainsborough in the early forties.
Time is My Enemy 53. The Girl in the Picture 56. The Flesh is Weak 57. A Question of Adultery 58. *The Man Upstairs* 59. Danger Within 59. Dentist in the Chair 60. Greyfriars Bobby 60. Nearly a Nasty Accident 60. A Matter of Who 61. The Prince and the Pauper 62. *Jason and the Argonauts* 63. A Jolly Bad Fellow 64. One Million Years B.C. 66. The Viking Queen 67. A Twist of Sand 68. Creatures the World Forgot 71. Persecution 73. Pete's Dragon 77. The Gift of Love (TV) 78. The Magic of Lassie 78. C.H.O.M.P.S. 79. Lassie: the New Beginning (TV) 79. Strike Force (TV) 79. Hollywood Beat (TV) 84. International Airport (TV) 85, etc.

Chagrin, Francis (1905–1972). Russian-born composer in films (mostly British) from 1934; has composed over 200 scores.
Last Holiday 50. An Inspector Calls 54. The Colditz Story 55. The Snorkel 58. Danger Within 59. Greyfriars Bobby 60. In the Cool of the Day 63, etc.

Chakiris, George (1933–). American dancer (from the chorus) and leading man; his star blazed for a while in the early sixties.
Brigadoon 54. Two and Two Make Six (GB) 60. *West Side Story* (AA) 61. Diamond Head 63. Kings of the Sun 63. Flight from Ashiya 64. 633 Squadron 64. The High Bright Sun (GB) 65. Is Paris Burning? 66. The Young Girls of Rochefort 67. The Big Cube 69. Return to Fantasy Island (TV) 78. Why Not Stay for Breakfast (GB) 80, etc.

Chaliapin, Feodor (1873–1938). Russian opera singer who appeared in two films and was played by Ezio Pinza in *Tonight We Sing*.
□Pskovityanka 15. *Don Quixote* 33.

Challis, Christopher (1919–). Distinguished British cinematographer.
□Theirs is the Glory 46. End of the River 47. *The Small Back Room* 48. Tales of Hoffman 50. Gone to Earth 50. The Elusive Pimpernel 52. *Genevieve* 53. Angels One Five 53. 24 Hours in a Woman's Life 53. Saadia 54. The Story of Gilbert and Sullivan 54. Twice Upon a Time 54. Malaga 54. The Flame and the Flesh 54. Oh Rosalinda 55. Quentin Durward 55. Raising a Riot 55. The Battle of the River Plate 56. Footsteps in the Fog 56. Ill Met By Moonlight 56. The Spanish Gardener 56. Miracle in Soho 56. Windom's Way 56. Floods of Fear 57. Rooney 57. Sink the Bismarck 60. The Grass is Greener 61. Surprise Package 61. The Captain's Table 62. Never Let Go 62. Blind Date 62. Flame in the Streets 63. HMS Defiant 64. Five Golden Hours 64. The Long Ships 64. Those Magnificent Men in Their Flying Machines 64. *The Victors* 65. A Shot in the Dark 65. The Americanization of Emily 65. Return from the Ashes 65. *Arabesque* 66. Two for the Road 67. Kaleidoscope 67. A Dandy in Aspic 68. Chitty Chitty Bang Bang 69. Staircase 69. The Private Life of Sherlock Holmes 71. Villain 71. Catch Me a Spy 71. Mary Queen of Scots 72. Follow Me 72. The Boy Who Turned Yellow 72. The Little Prince 74. Mister Quilp 75. The Incredible Sarah 76. The Deep 77. Force Ten From Navarone 78. The Riddle of the Sands 79. The Mirror Crack'd 80. Evil Under the Sun 81. Top Secret 84.

Chamberlain, Cyril (1909–). British small-part player often seen as average man, policeman or dull husband.
This Man in Paris 39, London Belongs to Me 48. Trouble in Store 53. Blue Murder at St Trinian's 58. Carry On Constable 60, many others.

Chamberlain, Richard (1935–). Boyish-looking American leading man who used his success in a TV series to establish himself as a serious international actor.
□The Secret of the Purple Reef 60. A Thunder of Drums 62. Twilight of Honor 63. Joy in the Morning 65. Petulia 68. The Madwoman of Chaillot 69. Julius Caesar 70. *The Music Lovers* (as Tchaikovsky) 70. *Lady Caroline Lamb* (as Byron) 72. The Last of the Belles (TV) 74. The Three Musketeers 74. The Four Musketeers 75. The Towering Inferno 75. *The Slipper and the Rose* 76. The Count of Monte Cristo (TV) 76. The Man in the Iron Mask (TV) 77. The Last Wave 78. Swarm 78. Shogun (TV) 80. Murder by Phone 82. *The Thorn Birds* (TV) 83.

King Solomon's Mines 85. Raoul Wallenberg, Lost Hero (TV) 85. Allan Quatermain and the Lost City of Gold 86. The Bourne Identity 88.
TV series: *Dr Kildare* 61–66.

The Champ (US 1931). A mawkish tale about a boozy boxer and his small long-suffering son, this now-dated movie won an Academy Award for Wallace Beery and for scriptwriter Francis Marion. It also confirmed the stardom of boy actor Jackie Cooper. It was remade in 1952 as *The Clown,* a vehicle for Red Skelton, and in 1979 by Zeffirelli, with Jon Voight.

Champion (US 1949). One of the first anti-boxing films, and Stanley Kramer's first big success as producer. Written by Carl Foreman, starring Kirk Douglas, Arthur Kennedy, Lola Albright.

Champion, Gower (1919–1981). American dancer who appeared with his then wife Marge in several musicals of the early fifties; later turned director.
Till the Clouds Roll By (solo) 46. Mr Music 50. *Show Boat* 51. Lovely to Look At 52. Give a Girl a Break 53. Jupiter's Darling 55. Three for the Show 55. My Six Loves (d) 63. Bank Shot (d) 74, etc.

Champion, Marge (1923–) (Marjorie Belcher). American dancer who teamed with her then husband Gower (qv). Solo appearances include *The Story of Vernon and Irene Castle* 39; later appeared as character actress.
The Swimmer 67. The Party 68.

Chance, Naomi (1930–). Stylish British leading lady who appeared sporadically in the fifties.
Dangerous Voyage 53. The Saint's Return 54. Operation Bullshine 59. The Trials of Oscar Wilde 60, etc.

Chandler, Chick (1905–). Wiry American hero or second lead of many a second feature in the thirties and forties.
Melody Cruise 33. Murder on a Honeymoon 35. Woman Wise 36. Born Reckless 37. Alexander's Ragtime Band 38. Time Out for Murder 38. Hotel for Women 39. Hollywood Cavalcade 39. Honeymoon Deferred 40. Cadet Girl 41. Hot Spot 41. The Big Shot 42. He Hired the Boss 43. Irish Eyes are Smiling 44. Seven Doors to Death 44. The Chicago Kid 45. Do You Love Me? 46. Lost Continent 47. Family Honeymoon 49. The Great Rupert 50. Aaron Slick from Punkin Crick 52. Battle Cry 55. The Naked Gun 58. It's a Mad Mad Mad Mad World 63, many others.
TV series: Soldiers of Fortune 55.

Chandler, George (1899–1985). American character actor, an ex-vaudevillian who specialized in sly or comically nervous roles.
The Light of Western Stars 30. Blessed Event 32. Hi Nellie 34. Fury 36. Three Men on a Horse 36. Nothing Sacred 37. Jesse James 39. Arizona 41. *Roxie Hart* 42. It Happened Tomorrow 44. This Man's Navy 45. Dead Reckoning 47. Kansas Raiders 50. Hans Christian Andersen 52. The High and the Mighty 54. Spring Reunion 57. Dead Ringer 64. One More Time 71, many others.

Chandler, Helen (1909–1965). American leading lady of the thirties: her early retirement through personal problems robbed Hollywood of an interesting personality.
□The Music Master 27. Joy Girl 27. Mother's Boy 29. Salute 29. The Sky Hawk 29. A Rough Romance 30. Outward Bound 30. Mother's Cry 30. *Dracula* 31. Daybreak 31. *The Last Flight* 31. Salvation Nell 31. Fanny Foley Herself 31. A House Divided 32. Vanity Street 32. Behind Jury Doors 32. Christopher Strong 33. Alimony Madness 33. Dance Hall Hostess 33. Goodbye Again 33. The Worst Woman in Paris 33. Long Lost Father 34. Midnight Alibi 34. Unfinished Symphony (GB) 35. It's a Bet (GB) 35. Radio Parade (GB) 35. Mr Boggs Steps Out (GB) 37.

Chandler, Jeff (1918–1961) (Ira Grossel). American leading man with the unusual attraction of prematurely grey hair; carved a solid niche for himself by playing an Indian, but his films seldom rose above co-feature level.
□Johnny O'Clock 47. Invisible Wall 47. Roses are Red 47. Mr Belvedere Goes to College 49. Sword in the Desert 49. Abandoned 49. *Broken Arrow* (as Cochise) 50. Two Flags West 50. Deported 50. Bird of Paradise 51. Smuggler's Island 51. Iron Man 51. Flame of Araby 51. The Battle at Apache Pass 52. Yankee Buccaneer 52. Red Ball Express 52. Because of You 52. The Great Sioux Uprising 53. East of Sumatra 53. Yankee Pasha 54. War Arrow 54. Sign of the Pagan 54. Foxfire 55. The Female on the Beach 55. The Spoilers 55. Toy Tiger 55. Away all Boats 56. Pillars of the Sky 56. Drango 57. The Tattered Dress 57. *Jeanne*

Eagels 57. Man in the Shadow 57. The Lady Takes a Flyer 58. Raw Wind in Eden 58. Stranger in my Arms 59. Thunder in the Sun 59. Ten Seconds to Hell 59. The Jayhawkers 59. The Plunderers 60. A Story of David (TV) 60. Return to Peyton Place 61. Merrill's Marauders 61.

Chandler, Joan (1923–1979). American leading lady, briefly featured in the forties.
Humoresque 47. The Street with No Name 48. Rope 49, etc.

Chandler, John Davis (1937–). American character player usually seen as neurotic, twitching villain.
The Young Savages 61. Mad Dog Coll (title role) 61. Major Dundee 65. Once a Thief 65. The Good Guys and the Bad Guys 69. Barquero 70. Shootout 71. Capone 75. Jaws of Death 76. Whiskey Mountain 77, etc.

Chandler, Lane (1899–1972) (Robert Oakes). American western character actor.
Open Range 27. Texas Tornado 34. Two Gun Justice 38. Sundown Jim 42. Northwest Stampede 48. Montana 50. Requiem for a Gunfighter 65, many others.

Chandler, Raymond (1888–1959). American crime novelist to whom literary acclaim came late in life. Several films and a TV series were based on the exploits of his cynical but incorruptible private eye Philip Marlowe.
The Falcon Takes Over (oa) 42. Time to Kill (oa) 42. *Double Indemnity* (w) 44. And Now Tomorrow 44. The Unseen 45. *Murder My Sweet* (oa) 45. *The Big Sleep* (oa) 46. *The Lady in the Lake* (oa) 46. The Blue Dahlia (w) 45. The Brasher Doubloon (oa) 47. *Strangers on a Train* (w) 51. Marlowe (oa) 69. The Long Goodbye (oa) 72. Farewell my Lovely (oa) 76. The Big Sleep (oa) 79.
TV series: Philip Marlowe 59.

¶ He looked as inconspicuous as a tarantula on a slice of angel food.—*Farewell my Lovely*

The edges of the folded handkerchief in her breast pocket looked sharp enough to slice bread.—*The Lady in the Lake*

She had a lot of face and chin. She had pewter-coloured hair set in a ruthless permanent, a hard beak and large moist eyes with the sympathetic expression of wet stones. There was lace at her throat, but it was the kind of throat that would have looked better in a football sweater.—*The High Window*

R.C.: The making of a motion picture is an endless contention of tawdry egos, almost none of them capable of anything more creative than credit stealing and self promotion.

Chaney, Lon (1883–1930) (Alonzo Chaney). American star character actor, known as 'the man of a thousand faces' because of his elaborate disguises in macabre roles; hence the joke, 'Don't step on that spider, it might be Lon Chaney.' A 1957 biopic, *Man of a Thousand Faces,* starred James Cagney.
□Where the Forest Ends 14. The Chimney Sweep 15. The Oyster Dredger 15. The Stool Pigeon 15. Fires of Rebellion 17. Triumph 17. That Devil Bateese 18. Riddle Gawne 18. The Kaiser, Beast of Berlin 18. Paid in Advance 19. The Rap 19. The Unholy Three 19. *The Miracle Man* 19. False Faces 19. Victory 19. The Wolf Breed 19. The Wicked Darling 19. Nomads of the North 19. Treasure Island 20. Daredevil Jack 20. *The Penalty* 21. Outside the Law 21. The Ace of Hearts 21. Bit o' Life 21. For Those We Love 21. The Night Rose 21. The Trap 22. Quincy Adams Sawyer 22. Shadows 22. *A Blind Bargain* 22. Flesh and Blood 22. Voices of the City 22. The Light in the Dark 22. Oliver Twist 22. *The Hunchback of Notre Dame* 23. The Shock 23. All the Brothers were Valiant 23. While Paris Sleeps 23. He Who Gets Slapped 24. The Next Corner 24. *The Phantom of the Opera* 25. The Tower of Lies 25. The Monster 25. *The Unholy Three* 25. The Black Bird 26. The Road to Mandalay 26. Tell it to the Marines 26. Mr Wu 27. The Unknown 27. Mockery 27. *London After Midnight* 27. The Big City 28. Laugh Clown Laugh 28. While the City Sleeps 28. West of Zanzibar 28. The Thunder 29. Where East is East 29. The Unholy Three 30.
❀ For becoming an international household word through his ability to distort his own body and hide it under layers of disguise. *The Phantom of the Opera.*

¶ *L.C.:* My whole career has been devoted to keeping people from knowing me.

Chaney, Lon, Jnr (1906–1973) (Creighton Chaney). Massive American character actor, who largely followed his father's type of role in progressively inferior films, with many bit parts. In *Man of a Thousand Faces* he was played by Roger Smith.
Bird of Paradise 32. Lucky Devils 33. Sixteen Fathoms Deep 34. The Life of Vergie Winters 35. Accent on Youth 35. Wife, Doctor and Nurse 37. Love and Hisses 37. Charlie Chan

on Broadway 37. Road Demon 38. Mr Moto's Gamble 38. Jesse James 39. Frontier Marshal 39. *Of Mice and Men* (his best performance, as Lennie) 39. One Million BC 40. Northwest Mounted Police 40. Man Made Monster 41. *The Wolf Man* 41. North to the Klondike 42. *The Ghost of Frankenstein* (as the monster) 42. The Mummy's Tomb 42. Frankenstein Meets the Wolf Man 43. Son of Dracula 43. Ghost Catchers 44. Weird Woman 44. Dead Man's Eyes 44. House of Frankenstein 45. Strange Confession 45. My Favourite Brunette 47. Sixteen Fathoms Deep 48. *Abbott and Costello Meet Frankenstein* 48. Captain China 49. Once a Thief 50. Behave Yourself 51. High Noon 52. A Lion is in the Streets 53. Casanova's Big Night 54. Not as a Stranger 55. Manfish 56. The Black Sleep 56. Cyclops 57. The Defiant Ones 58. The Alligator People 59. The Haunted Palace 63. Witchcraft 64. Apache Uprising 66. Hillbillies in a Haunted House 67. Buckskin 68, many others.
TV series: *The Last of the Mohicans* (as Chingachgook) 56.

Chang (US 1927). Famous documentary by Merian Cooper and Ernest Schoedsack telling how a tribesman of Siam guards his family against the terrors of the encroaching jungle. Originally ended with a stampede of elephants on the 'Magnascope', an early form of giant screen.

change-over. Transition from one reel of film to another during projection. A reel originally lasted ten minutes but most 35mm projectors now take 20 or 30 minutes. Change-over cues are given in the form of dots which appear on the top right-hand corner of the screen a standard number of seconds before the end of the reel.

Channing, Carol (1921–). Vivacious American cabaret comedienne whose films have been few.
□Paid in Full 50. The First Travelling Saleslady 56. *Thoroughly Modern Millie* 67. Skidoo 69.

¶ *C.C.:* I am terribly shy, but of course no one believes me. Come to think of it, neither would I.

'She never just enters a room. Even when she comes out of the bathroom, her husband applauds.'—*George Burns*

Channing, Stockard (1944–) (Susan Stockard). Tomboy-type American leading lady, mainly on television.
□The Girl Most Likely To (TV) 73. The Fortune 75. Sweet Revenge 76. The Big Bus 76. Lucan 77. The Cheap Detective 78. Grease 78. Silent Victory (TV) 79. The Fish That Saved Pittsburgh 79. Safari 3000 82. Without a Trace 83. Heartburn 86. The Men's Club 86.

Chapin, Billy (1943–). American child actor of the fifties.
Cluny Brown 48. Tobor the Great 53. Naked Alibi 54. There's No Business Like Show Business 54. A Man Called Peter 55. Violent Saturday 55. *Night of the Hunter* 55, etc.

Chaplin, Sir Charles (1889–1977). A legendary figure in his own lifetime despite a comparatively limited output, this British pantomimist went to the US in 1910 with Fred Karno's troupe and was invited to join the Keystone company; later also worked for Essanay and Mutual, and these early two-reelers are held by many to be superior to the later, more pretentious features which he produced himself. Honorary AA 1971.
Autobiographical books: *My Trip Abroad* 1922. *My Wonderful Visit* 1930. *My Autobiography* 1964. *My Life in Pictures* 1974.
Other books: *The Little Fellow* by Peter Cotes and Thelma Nicklaus; *Charlie Chaplin* by Theodore Huff; *My Life with Chaplin* by Lita Grey Chaplin; *The Great Charlie* by Robert Payne; *Charlie Chaplin. His Life and Art* by William Dodgson Bowman; *Sir Charlie* by Edwin P. Hoyt.
□SHORTS: Making a Living 14. Kid Auto Races at Venice (in which he first wore the improvised tramp costume in which he later became famous) 14. Mabel's Strange Predicament 14. Between Showers 14. A Film Johnnie 14. Tango Tangle 14. His Favorite Pastime 14. Cruel Cruel Love 14. The Star Boarder 14. Mabel at the Wheel 14. Twenty Minutes of Love 14. The Knockout 14. Tillie's Punctured Romance 14. Caught in a Cabaret 14. Caught in the Rain 14. A Busy Day 14. The Fatal Mallet 14. Her Friend the Bandit 14. Mabel's Busy Day 14. Mabel's Married Life 14. Laughing Gas 14. The Property Man 14. The Face on the Barroom Floor 14. Recreation 14. The Masquerader 14. His New Profession 14. The Rounders 14. The New Janitor 14. These Love Pangs 14. Dough and Dynamite 14. Gentlemen of Nerve 14. His Musical Career 14. His Trysting Place 14. Getting Acquainted 14. His Prehistoric Past 14. His New Job 15. A Night Out 15. The Champion

15. In the Park 15. A Jitney Elopment 15. *The Tramp* 15. By the Sea 15. Work 15. A Woman 15. The Bank 15. Shanghaied 15. A Night in the Show 15. Carmen 16. Police 16. The Floorwalker 16. The Fireman 16. The Vagabond 16. One a.m. 16. The Count 16. *The Pawnshop* 16. Behind the Screen 16. *The Rink* 16. *Easy Street* 17. *The Cure* 17. *The Immigrant* 17. *The Adventurer* 17. Triple Trouble 18. *A Dog's Life* 18. The Bond 18. *Shoulder Arms* 18. Sunnyside 19. A Day's Pleasure 19. *The Idle Class* 21. Pay Day 22. □FEATURES: *The Kid* 20. The Pilgrim 23. A Woman of Paris (directed only) 23. *The Gold Rush* 24. *The Circus* (AA) 28. *City Lights* 31. *Modern Times* 36. *The Great Dictator* 40. *Monsieur Verdoux* 47. *Limelight* 52. A King in New York (GB) 57. A Countess from Hong Kong (GB) 66.

For combining precision of comedy technique with a sentimental view of the common man which pleased the millions of oppressed and disarmed sophisticated criticism. *Easy Street.*

¶ The son of a bitch is a ballet dancer!

So pronounced W. C. Fields, having been urged to sit through and enjoy a Chaplin movie. Fields promptly realized that the Chaplin brand of comic art was not only more popular than his own, but one which it was impossible for him to emulate. He continued:

> He's the best ballet dancer that ever lived, and if I get a good chance I'll strangle him with my bare hands . . .

Many people have been jealous of Chaplin's success, partly because he was never modest about it. His poverty-stricken childhood made him mercenary, and once at the top he displayed a private personality it was difficult to like. Even his friend Mary Pickford called him:

> That obstinate, suspicious, egocentric, maddening and lovable genius of a problem child.

And Chaplin had never found a way of making friends with his public. Even in his autobiography he seemed at pains to present himself unsympathetically, as when he recalled telling Mack Sennett:

> The public doesn't line up outside the box office when your name appears as they do for mine.

His memories of his manifold romantic activities are tastelessly presented:

> Like everyone else's, my sex-life went in cycles. Sometimes I was potent, other times disappointing.

In the more intimate details his phrasing is curious to say the least:

> [She was] a big handsome woman of twenty-two, well built, with upper regional domes immensely expansive and made alluring by an extremely low décolleté summer dress which, on the drive home, evoked my libidinous curiosity . . .

His willingness to prognosticate on matters of which he plainly knows little, such as the true authorship of the Shakespeare plays, is often foolhardy:

> I can hardly think it was the Stratford boy. Whoever wrote them had an aristocratic personality.

His philosophy is usually naïve, as in his much-attacked defence of murder in *Monsieur Verdoux*:

> Wars, conflict, it's all business. One murder makes a villain. Millions, a hero. Numbers sanctify . . .

Determined to make his clown a tragic hero, he is frequently guilty of relentless sentimentality. The opening title of *The Kid* runs:

> A picture with a smile and perhaps a tear.

As Hannen Swaffer once said:

> His gospel is like Mary Pickford's: the hope of a little child.

Billy Wilder was more caustic:

> When he found a voice to say what was on his mind, he was like a child of eight writing lyrics for Beethoven's Ninth.

He frequently over-estimated himself. Of *The Great Dictator* he declared:

> I made this picture for the Jews of the world.

He was a poor loser. Having been forced to leave the United States, which made him rich and to which he owed a large amount in back taxes, he stated:

> I have no further use for America. I wouldn't go back there if Jesus Christ was President.

Over the years he had alternately denied and proclaimed his Jewishness. This was a typical announcement of the late forties:

> I am not a Jew! I am a citizen of the world! I am not a communist! I am a peacemonger!

A rather limited attitude is struck in his remark about Negroes:

> They have suffered too much ever to be funny to me.

(Yet Chaplin's own comedy derives from poverty and deprivation.) He took credit for every aspect of his films, and frequently denied it to those who helped him most. Yet he was not an inventive director:

I am the unusual and do not need camera angles.

Cinematographer Karl Struss said of him:

He has no knowledge of camera direction. His films are completely theatre.

Yet there is no denying that Chaplin managed very well by feeding his own self-importance. He used to say:

You have to believe in yourself, that's the secret.

And as late as 1960:

I remain one thing and one thing only, and that is a clown. It places me on a far higher plane than any politician.

In a sense he was right. Despite all Chaplin's failings, his tramp is an archetypal creation which strikes a chord in everybody and will live as long as films can be preserved. Chaplin always knew the virtue of simplicity:

All I need to make a comedy is a park, a policeman and a pretty girl.

That was in 1916, and ambition soon overtook him. Colleen Moore in her autobiography *Silent Star* tells that in 1922 a producer was contemplating a life of Christ, and Chaplin demanded audience and became very excited:

I want to play the role of Jesus. I'm a logical choice. I look the part. I'm a Jew. And I'm a comedian . . . And I'm an atheist, so I'd be able to look at the character objectively . . .

The funny thing is, he was very likely right. But Andrew Sarris saw the other side of his psyche:

He will die as he has lived, an unregenerate classicist who believes in making movies he can feel in his frayed lace valentine heart.

While nobody denied his business acumen, least of all Sam Goldwyn:

Chaplin is no business man—all he knows is that he can't take anything less.

And Douglas Fairbanks in 1925 saw the emotional force of his screen personality:

He shows one inadequate man struggling against all the forces of nature.

Chaplin's essential trouble was that he could never take advice. That he needed it was shown by his remark during pre-production of the truly awful *A Countess from Hong Kong*:

A millionaire falling in love with a prostitute. What better story could they want than that?

Chaplin, Geraldine (1944–). Actress daughter of Charles Chaplin.
□Doctor Zhivago 65. A Countess from Hong Kong 66. Stranger in the House 67. Peppermint Frappé (Sp.) 67. I Killed Rasputin 68. Honeycomb (Sp.) 69. The Hawaiians 70. Zero Population Growth 72. Innocent Bystanders 72. The Three Musketeers 74. *Nashville* 75. Buffalo Bill and the Indians 76. Roseland 77. Welcome to L.A. 77. Cria! 77. The Word (TV) 78. Remember My Name 78. The Mirror Crack'd 80. Les Uns et les Autres 80. Voyage en Douce 81. Life is a Novel 81. Bolero 82. Love on the Ground 83.

Chaplin, Saul (1912–) (Saul Kaplan). American song-writer, arranger and producer.
Rookies on Parade (c) 41. Time Out for Rhythm (c) 41. *An American in Paris* (arr) (AA) 51. *Seven Brides for Seven Brothers* (arr) (AA) 54. Can Can (p) 59. *West Side Story* (p) 61. *The Sound of Music* (p) 65. Star! (p) 68. That's Entertainment, Part Two (p) 76, etc.

Chaplin, Syd (1885–1965). British comedian, elder brother of Charles Chaplin; popular internationally in the twenties.
A Submarine Pirate 15. ShoulderArms 18. King Queen Joker 21. Her Temporary Husband 23. The Perfect Flapper 24. Charley's Aunt 25. Oh What a Nurse 26. The Better 'Ole 27. The Missing Link 27. A Little Bit of Fluff 28, etc.

Chaplin, Sydney (1926–). Actor son of Charles Chaplin; has not achieved the distinction of which he seems capable.
Limelight 52. Confession 55. Land of the Pharaohs 55. Four Girls in Town 56. Quantez 57. Follow that Man 61. A Countess from Hong Kong 66. The Sicilian Clan 70, etc.

Chapman, Edward (1901–77). British character actor of solid dependable types, corrupt aldermen and northern millowners.
Juno and the Paycock 29. Murder 30. The Skin Game 31. *Things to Come* 35. Rembrandt 36. The Man Who Could Work Miracles 37. The Citadel 38. The Proud Valley 39. The Briggs Family 40. They Flew Alone 42. Ships with Wings 42. *The October Man* 47. *It Always Rains on Sunday* 47. Mr Perrin and Mr Traill 49. *The Card* 52. Folly to be Wise 53. A Day to Remember 54. His Excellency 55. School for Scoundrels 60. Oscar Wilde (as Queensberry) 60. A Stitch in Time 63. Joey Boy 64, many others.

Chapman, Graham (1941–). British character comedian, a member of the Monty Python group (qv) who also has a go on his own.
The Odd Job 78. Yellowbeard 83.

Chapman, Lonny (–). American character actor.
Young at Heart 54. Baby Doll 57. The Birds 63. The Reivers 69. The Cowboys 71. Where the Red Fern Grows 74. Moving Violation 76. Norma Rae 79, etc.

Chapman, Marguerite (1916–). Dependable American heroine of many forties co-features.
Charlie Chan at the Wax Museum 40. The Body Disappears 41. Parachute Nurse 42. Destroyer 43. My Kingdom for a Cook 43. Pardon My Past 45. The Walls Came Tumbling Down 46. Mr District Attorney 47. Coroner Creek 48. Kansas Raiders 50. Man Bait 51. Flight to Mars 51. The Seven Year Itch 55. The Amazing Transparent Man 61, etc.

Chapman, Michael (–). American cinematographer.
The Last Detail 73. The White Dawn 73. Taxi Driver 76. The Front 76. Fingers 78. Invasion of the Body Snatchers 78. The Last Waltz 78. Hardcore 79. The Wanderers 79. Raging Bull 80, etc.

character actor. Usually thought of as one who does not play romantic leads.

characters

? With what films do you associate the following characters?

1 Robert E. Lee Prewitt
2 Miss Froy
3 Macaulay Connor
4 Gaylord Ravenal
5 Boss Jim Gettys
6 John J. McCreedy
7 Maximilian de Winter
8 Lady Catherine de Burgh
9 Max Corkle
10 Ashley Wilkes
11 Louis Renault
12 Joel Cairo
13 Horace Femm
14 Theo Kretschmar-Schuldorff
15 Eva Lovelace
16 Huntley Haverstock
17 Charlie Allnut
18 Trudy Kockenlocker
19 Kaspar Gutman
20 Larson E. Whipsnade

The Charge of the Light Brigade. The American film of this name was directed by Michael Curtiz for Warners in 1936 and had a completely fictitious story taking place mainly in India, with the Balaclava events as an afterthought. As a piece of Hollywood stunting, however, the charge has scarcely been surpassed, and Errol Flynn in the lead consolidated his stardom. Tony Richardson's British film of 1968 attempts, and fails, to tell the true story of what happened; the rewards here are a few moments of Victoriana and some splendid bridging animation by Richard Williams.

Chariots of Fire (GB 1981). An account of racial and other tensions behind the 1924 Olympics and in particular its effect on the careers of two British athletes. On its premiere this unlikely film for the eighties was generally thought to be slow and without box office potential, but it clearly filled a void, became a talking point, and went on to win Academy Awards for best picture, best screenplay, best score and best costume design. Written by Colin Welland; directed by Hugh Hudson; produced by David Puttnam; with Ian Charleson, Ben Cross, Ian Holm.

Charisse, Cyd (1921–) (Tula Ellice Finklea). Stylish, long-legged American dancer and heroine of MGM musical dramas of the fifties.
Autobiography 1976: *The Two of Us* (with Tony Martin)
□Mission to Moscow 43. Something to Shout About 43. Ziegfeld Follies 45. The Harvey Girls 46. Three Wise Fools 46. Till the Clouds Roll By 46. Fiesta 47. *The Unfinished Dance* 47. On an Island with You 48. Words and Music 48. The Kissing Bandit 49. East Side West Side 49. Tension 49. Mark of the Renegade 51. The Wild North 52. *Singin' in the Rain* 52. Sombrero 53. Easy to Love 53. *The Band Wagon* 53. Brigadoon 54. Deep in My Heart 54. *It's Always Fair Weather* 55. Meet Me in Las Vegas 56. *Invitation to the Dance* 57. Silk Stockings 57. Twilight for the Gods 58. Party Girl 58. Five Golden Hours 61. Black Tights 61. *Two Weeks in Another Town* 62. The Silencers 67. Maroc 7 67. Assassination in Rome 67. Call Her Mom (TV) 72. Warlords of Atlantis 78. Portrait of an Escort (TV) 80.
† She missed the lead in *Easter Parade* when she broke a leg, and in *An American in Paris* when she was pregnant.

Charles I of England (1600–1649) (reigned 1625–1649) has not been a popular screen figure. Alec Guinness in *Cromwell* provided the nearest to a full-length portrait; cameos were given by Hugh Miller in *The Vicar of Bray* and Robert Rietty in *The Scarlet Blade*.

Charles II of England (1630–1685) (reigned 1660–1685) has been a popular screen figure, attracting the talents of Cedric Hardwicke in *Nell Gwyn*, Vincent Price in *Hudson's Bay*, George Sanders in *Forever Amber*, and Douglas Fairbanks Jnr in *The Exile*.

Charles, Maria (1929–) (Maria Zena Schneider). Diminutive British redhead, familiar as Jewish matron in TV's *Agony*. □Folly to Be Wise 52. The Deadly Affair 66. Eye of the Devil 67. The Return of the Pink Panther 74. Great Expectations (TV) 75. Cuba 79. Victor Victoria 82.

Charleson, Ian (1954–). British leading actor.
Chariots of Fire 81. Gandhi 82. Greystoke 84. The Sun Also Rises (TV) 84. Car Trouble 85.

Charlesworth, John (1935–1960). British teenage actor of the fifties.
Tom Brown's Schooldays 51. Scrooge 51. John of the Fair 54. Yangtse Incident 57. The Angry Silence 59, etc.

Charley's Aunt. Brandon Thomas' 1896 farce has been filmed many times, notably in 1925 with Syd Chaplin, in 1931 with Charles Ruggles, in 1940 with Arthur Askey, in 1941 with Jack Benny, in 1952 (as *Where's Charley*) with Ray Bolger, in Germany 1954 with Heinz Ruhmann and in Austria 1963 with Peter Alexander.

Charlie Bubbles (GB 1967). A small but pleasing bitter comedy about the horrors of being a very rich author with a working-class background. Albert Finney, director, extracts a perfect performance from Albert Finney, actor; he also handles comic set-piece scenes with great bravura and accuracy of mood. Billie Whitelaw (BFA) is a splendidly shrewish ex-wife, and the whole adds up to a fine sardonic comment on the affluent society.

Charlie Chan. Earl Derr Biggers' polite oriental detective with the large family and an even more plentiful supply of wise and witty sayings was first featured by Hollywood in a 1926 serial; George Kuwa played him. Kamiyama Sojin played him once in 1928, E. L. Park once in 1929, Warner Oland sixteen times (1931–37), Sidney Toler twenty-two times (1938–47) and Roland Winters six times (1948–52). J. Carrol Naish then took over for thirty-nine TV films (1957), and in 1971 Ross Martin appeared as Chan in a TV feature. 1972 brought an animated TV cartoon series, *Charlie Chan and the Chan Clan*: Chan was voiced by Keye Luke, who had played Chan's number two son so often in the thirties. A veil is best drawn over the so-called spoof of 1981's *Charlie Chan and the Curse of the Dragon Queen*, in which Peter Ustinov took over the role of the famous detective.

The 'classic' Chan films were as follows:

1929: *Behind That Curtain*
1931: *Charlie Chan Carries On*, *The Black Camel*
1932: *Charlie Chan's Chance*, *Charlie Chan's Greatest Case*
1934: *Charlie Chan's Courage*, *Charlie Chan in London*
1935: *Charlie Chan in Paris*, *Charlie Chan in Egypt*, *Charlie Chan in Shanghai*
1936: *Charlie Chan's Secret*, *Charlie Chan at the Circus*, *Charlie Chan at the Racetrack*, *Charlie Chan at the Opera*
1937: *Charlie Chan at the Olympics*, *Charlie Chan on Broadway*
1938: *Charlie Chan at Monte Carlo* (last Oland), *Charlie Chan in Honolulu*
1939: *Charlie Chan in Reno*, *Charlie Chan at Treasure Island*, *Charlie Chan in the City of Darkness*
1940: *Charlie Chan in Panama*, *Charlie Chan's Murder Cruise*, *Charlie Chan in the Wax Museum*, *Murder over New York*
1941: *Dead Men Tell*, *Charlie Chan in Rio*
1942: *Castle in the Desert* (after which the series moved from Fox to Monogram and consequently lower budgets)

Charlot, André (1882–1956). French producer of intimate star revues in London and New York in the twenties. Later played small parts in Hollywood films.

Charrel, Erik (1894–1974). German producer best known abroad for *Congress Dances* 31, which he also directed.

Charteris, Leslie (1907–) (Leslie Charles Bowyer Yin). Chinese-English crime novelist, creator of 'the Saint' (qv).

Charters, Spencer (1878–1943). American character actor; usually played rural fellows who may have been deaf but not too dumb to outsmart the city slicker.
Little Old New York 23. Janice Meredith 24. Whoopee 30. The Bat Whispers 30. The Front Page 31. The Match King 32. Female 33. Wake up and Dream 34. It's a Gift 34. The Ghost Walks 34. The Raven 35. Colleen 36. Banjo on my Knee 36. Mountain Music 37. In Old Chicago 38. Professor Beware 38.

Topper Takes a Trip 38. Jesse James 39. Drums Along the Mohawk 39. Alias the Deacon 40. Our Town 40. Tobacco Road 41. The Remarkable Andrew 42. Juke Girl 42, many others.

Chartoff, Robert (–). American producer, usually with Irwin Winkler.
The Split 68. Leo the Last 69. They Shoot Horses Don't They? 69. The Mechanic 72. Up the Sandbox 72. The Gambler 74. Nickelodeon 76. Rocky 76. New York New York 77. Comes a Horseman 78. Rocky II 79. Raging Bull 80, etc.

the chase has always been a standard ingredient of film-making, providing a foolproof way of rounding off a comedy or thriller in good style. In silent days it was necessary to every comedian, from the Keystone Kops to Buster Keaton, while westerns inevitably concluded with the goodies chasing the baddies, and even *Intolerance* has a four-stranded chase finale. Sound comedies began by using the chase more sparingly, but René Clair's *Le Million* 32 was a superbly sustained example of the fuller orchestration now possible, and later sophisticated comedies like *It Happened One Night, Sullivan's Travels, The Runaround, Sex and the Single Girl, Good Neighbour Sam* and *What's Up Doc?* have not disdained using the chase as a basic theme; nor of course have broader comedians such as Harold Lloyd, W. C. Fields, Laurel and Hardy and Abbott and Costello, and Stanley Kramer devised a super chase in the marathon *It's a Mad Mad Mad Mad World* 63, to be rivalled in 1965 by *The Great Race*. Most of the old chase gags were crammed into the finale of *A Funny Thing Happened on the Way to the Forum* 67. Ealing comedies of the late forties and early fifties (*The Lavender Hill Mob, Whisky Galore, The Man in the White Suit, A Run For Your Money*) also used chases brilliantly to broaden their shafts of satire.

More serious films using the chase theme include: *You Only Live Once, Stagecoach, Out of the Past, High Sierra, They Live By Night, Odd Man Out, The Capture, The Chase, Tell Them Willie Boy Is Here, Figures in a Landscape*, and the innumerable versions of *Les Misérables*, which also sparked off five television series: *The Fugitive, Run For Your Life, Branded, Run Buddy Run*, and *Kung Fu*. Thrillers which have featured exciting chases include the Bond adventures, many Hitchcocks including *The Thirty-nine Steps* and *North by Northwest, The Naked City, Robbery, Bullitt, Vanishing Point, The French Connection, Puppet on a Chain, Dirty Mary Crazy Larry, Race with the Devil, Escape from Zahrain* and *The Seven-Ups*.

Chase, Borden (c. 1899–1971). American screenwriter.
Under Pressure 35. Blue White and Perfect 41. Destroyer 43. Flame of the Barbary Coast 45. Tycoon 47. Montana 48. Red River 48. The Great Jewel Robber 50. Lone Star 51. Bend of the River 52. The World in his Arms 52. Man without a Star 55. Backlash 56. Night Passage 57. Gunfighters of Casa Grande 65, many others.

Chase, Charlie (1893–1940) (Charles Parrott). Toothbrush-moustached American comedian who made many two-reel comedies from 1924, usually as henpecked husband.
☐COMPLETE TALKIE SHORTS: The Big Squawk 29. Leaping Love 29. Snappy Sneezer 29. Crazy Feet 29. Stepping Out 29. Great Gobs 29. The Real McCoy 30. Whispering Whoopee 30. All Teed Up 30. Fifty Million Husbands 30. Fast Work 30. Girl Shock 30. Dollar Dizzy 30. Looser than Loose 30. High Cs 30. Thundering Tenors 31. *The Pip from Pittsburgh* 31. Rough Seas 31. One of the Smiths 31. The Panic Is On 31. Skip the Maloo 31. What a Bozo 31. The Hasty Marriage 31. The Tabasco Kid 32. The Nickel Nurser 32. In Walked Charley 32. First in War 32. Young Ironsides 32. Good Grief 32. Now We'll Tell One 32. Mr Bride 32. *Fallen Arches* 32. Nature in the Wrong 33. His Silent Racket 33. Arabian Tights 33. Sherman Said It 33. Midsummer Mush 33. *Luncheon at Twelve* 33. The Cracked Iceman 34. Four Parts 34. I'll Take Vanilla 34. Another Wild Idea 34. It Happened One Day 34. Something Simple 34. You Said a Hatful 34. Fate's Fathead 34. *The Chases of Pimple Street* 34. Okay Toots 35. Poker at Eight 35. Southern Exposure 35. The Four Star Boarder 35. Nurse to You 35. Manhattan Monkey Business 35. Public Ghost Number One 35. Life Hesitates at 40 36. The Count Takes the Count 36. Vamp Till Ready 36. *On the Wrong Trek* 36. *Neighborhood House* 36. The Grand Hooter 37. From Bad to Worse 37. The Wrong Miss Wright 37. Calling All Doctors 37. The Big Squirt 37. Man Bites Lovebug 37. Time Out for Trouble 38. The Mind Needer 38. Many Sappy Returns 38. The Nightshirt Bandit 38. Pie à la Maid 38. The Sap Takes a Rap 39. The Chump Takes a Bump 39. *Rattling Romeo* 39. Skinny the Moocher 39. Teacher's Pest 39. The Awful Good 39. *The Heckler* 40. South of the Boudoir 40.
†Feature appearance: *Sons of the Desert* 33.

Chase, Chevy (1943–) (Cornelius Crane Chase). American light leading man.
Tunnelvision 76. *Foul Play* 78. O Heavenly Dog 80. Seems Like Old Times 80. Under the Rainbow 81. Modern Problems 81. National Lampoon's Vacation 83. Deal of the Century 83. Fletch 85. National Lampoon's European Vacation 85. Spies Like Us 85. Three Amigos 86.

¶ *C.C.:* I guess I look so straight and normal nobody expects me to pick my nose and fall.

Chase, Ilka (1900–1978). American columnist who occasionally brightened films.
Autobiographies: *Past Imperfect* 1945. *Free Admission* 1948.
Why Leave Home? 29. South Sea Rose 29. Free Love 30. The Animal Kingdom 32. Soak the Rich 36. Stronger than Desire 39. *Now Voyager* 42. No Time for Love 43. Miss Tatlock's Millions 48. Johnny Dark 54. The Big Knife 55. Ocean's Eleven 60, etc.
TV series: The Trials of O'Brien 65.

Chase, James Hadley (1906–85) (René Raymond). British author of violent crime stories, set in the United States via a slang dictionary and a vivid imagination. His most famous, *No Orchids for Miss Blandish*, was filmed in 1948 and again, as *The Grissom Gang*, in 1971. Other films: *I'll Get You for This* 49, *The Man in the Raincoat* 56, *Young Girls Beware* 58, *What Price Murder* 58.

Chase, Mary (1907–1981). American playwright best known for her whimsical comedy *Harvey*, filmed with James Stewart.

Chatterton, Ruth (1893–1961). Dignified American leading lady, popular in twenties and thirties after stage success; later had success as novelist.
□Sins of the Fathers 28. The Doctor's Secret 29. The Dummy 29. *Madame X* 29. Charming Sinners 29. The Laughing Lady 29. Sarah and Son 30. Paramount on Parade 30. The Lady of Scandal 30. Anybody's Woman 30. The Right to Love 30. Unfaithful 31. The Magnificent Lie 31. Once a Lady 31. Tomorrow and Tomorrow 32. The Rich are Always with Us 32. The Crash 32. Frisco Jenny 33. Lilly Turner 33. Female 33. Journal of a Crime 33. Lady of Secrets 36. Girls' Dormitory 36. *Dodsworth* 36. The Rat (GB) 38. A Royal Divorce (GB) 38.

Chauvel, Charles (1897–1959). Australian writer-producer-director.
In the Wake of the Bounty 33. Forty Thousand Horsemen 42. The Rats of Tobruk 48. The Rugged O'Riordans 48. Jedda 53, many others.

Chayevsky, Paddy (1923–1981) (Sidney Stuchevsky). Distinguished but latterly somewhat hysterical American writer whose greatest success was in TV.
Autobiography 1978: *Altered States.*
□As Young as You Feel (oa) 51. *Marty* (AA) 55. The Catered Affair (oa) 56. *The Bachelor Party* 57. The Goddess (w) 58. Middle of the Night (oa) 59. The Americanization of Emily (w) 64. *The Hospital* (w) (AA) 71. Network 76. Altered States 80 (as Sidney Aaron).
† His non-Jewish first name is said to originate from his pretending in the army to be Catholic so as to go to mass rather than do fatigues.

Cheaper by the Dozen (US 1950). Based on the life of Frank Gilbreth, a slightly eccentric efficiency expert and father of twelve children, this very popular film spawned a sequel (*Belles on Their Toes* 52) and caused a resurgence of family movies as well as comedies starring Clifton Webb as an irascible but affectionate father.

The Cheat (US 1915). This melodrama by Hector Turnbull was a huge commercial success in its day, with Sessue Hayakawa as the wily Japanese who loans money to a foolish society dame, ill-treats her when she will not succumb to his lascivious desires, and is killed by her husband. Cecil B. de Mille directed; the film was remade by George Fitzmaurice in 1923, George Abbott in 1931, and in 1937 (in France) by Marcel L'Herbier.

Checker, Chubby (1941–) (Ernest Evans). Endlessly gyrating American pop singer-dancer, briefly popular in the early sixties.
Twist Around the Clock 62. Don't Knock the Twist 62, etc.

Cheech and Chong. An American comedy team of the seventies to whom nothing is sacred, and amateurism is rampant. Their words and deeds are fouler even than those of Scotland's Billy Connolly.
Cheech and Chong's Next Movie 80. Cheech and Chong's Nice Dreams 81. It Came from Hollywood 82.

¶ 'You go to our movies for four reasons: to laugh, cry, get scared, get a hard-on.

If you can do all four at the same time, hey, it's the ultimate pizza combo, man.'—*Cheech*

Chekhov, Anton (1860–1904). Introspective Russian writer whose plays about the melancholies of the upper classes have been frequently filmed, though never very commercially. Sidney Lumet's version of *The Seagull*, with Simone Signoret and James Mason, was perhaps the gamest try.

Chekhov, Michael (1891–1955). Russian character actor who set up drama schools in London and New York; films sparse.
□Song of Russia 44. In Our Time 44. *Spellbound* 45. *Spectre of the Rose* 46. Cross My Heart 46. Abie's Irish Rose 46. Arch of Triumph 47. Invitation 51. Holiday for Sinners 52. Rhapsody 54.

Chenal, Pierre (1903–) (Pierre Cohen). French director. Crime and Punishment 35. The Late Mathias Pascal 36. *Alibi* 37. Le Dernier Tournant 39. Sirocco 45. Clochemerle 48. Native Son (US) 51. Sinners of Paris 59, etc.

Cher (1946–) (Cher Bono, formerly Cherilyn Sarkisian). American pop singer, once of Sonny and Cher, now turned actress. Good Times 68. Come Back to the Five and Dime, Jimmy Dean, Jimmy Dean 83. Silkwood (AAN) 83. Mask 85. The Witches of Eastwick 87. Moonstruck 87.

¶ 'When you take away those wild wings, there's an honest, complex screen presence underneath.'—*New York Times*

Cherkassov, Nicolai (1903–1966). Russian leading actor of epic hero stature. Autobiography 1957: *Notes of a Soviet Actor*.
□Baltic Deputy 37. *Peter the Great* 37. Ski Battalion 38. Friends 39. Captain Grant's Children 39. The Man with the Gun 38. *Alexander Nevsky* 38. Lenin in October 39. General Suvorov 41. *Ivan the Terrible Part One* 42. In the Name of Life 42. Ivan the Terrible Part Two 44. Spring 48. The First Front 49. Ivan Pavlov 50. Mussorgsky 51. Rimsky Korsakov 54. *Don Quixote* 53.

Cherrill, Virginia (1908–). American leading lady, a society girl who had a brief film career in the early thirties.
□*City Lights* (as the blind girl) 31. Girls Demand Excitement 31. The Brat 31. Delicious 31. Fast Workers 33. The Nuisance 33. Charlie Chan's Greatest Case 33. White Heat 34. What Price Crime 35. Troubled Waters 35.

Cherry, Helen (1915–). Cool and gracious British actress, mostly on stage; wife of Trevor Howard.
The Courtneys of Curzon Street 48. Adam and Evelyn 49. Morning Departure 50. Young Wives' Tale 51. Castle in the Air 53. Three Cases of Murder 55. High Flight 57. The Naked Edge 61. Flipper's New Adventure 64. Hard Contract 69. 11 Harrowhouse 74, etc.

Chester, Hal E. (1921–). American teenage actor who, as Hally Chester, was one of the 'Little Tough Guys' in 1938–40. Later became producer and settled in Europe.
Joe Palooka Champ 46. The Underworld Story 50. The Highwayman 53. Crashout 55. The Bold and the Brave 56. Night of the Demon 57. School for Scoundrels 60. Hide and Seek 64. The Secret War of Harry Frigg 67. The Double Man 67, etc.

Chesterton, G. K. (1874–1936). English novelist and journalist, an irrepressible wit whose chief bequest to the cinema is the clerical detective Father Brown, played in movies by Walter Connolly and Alec Guinness and on TV by Heinz Roemheld and Kenneth More.

Chevalier, Maurice (1888–1972). Inimitable French singing entertainer, known throughout the world for his accent, his straw hat and his jutting lower lip. Became famous in Paris revues of the twenties, went to Hollywood in the thirties, remained in Europe in the forties, then re-emerged as an international star. Special Academy Award 1958 'for his contributions to the world of entertainment for more than half a century'. Autobiographies: 1949 *The Man in the Straw Hat*. 1960 *With Love*; 1972 *I Remember It Well*.
□SOUND FILMS: Innocents in Paris 29. *The Love Parade* 30. Paramount on Parade 30. The Big Pond 30. Playboy of Paris 30. The Smiling Lieutenant 31. *One Hour With You* 32. *Love Me Tonight* 32. Bedtime Story 33. The Way to Love 33. The Merry Widow 34. *Folies Bergère* 35. L'Homme du Jour 36. Avec Le Sourire 36. Break the News 36. The Beloved Vagabond 37. Pièges 39. *Le Silence est d'Or* 47. Le Roi 49. Ma Pomme 50. J'Avais Sept Filles 55. Love in the Afternoon 57. *Gigi* 58. Count Your Blessings 59. Can Can 59. Black Tights 60. A Breath of Scandal 60. Pepe 60. *Fanny* 61. Jessica 62. *In Search of the Castaways* 62. A New Kind of Love 63. Panic Button 64. I'd Rather be Rich 64. Monkeys Go Home 67.
❀ For his incomparable technique as a singing entertainer; and for cheering up two

widely separate generations of the international audience. *Love Me Tonight.*

¶ *M.C.:* Love the public the way you love your mother.

'The 70-odd years young Maurice Chevalier takes his place beside children and animals as one of the great scene stealers of all times.'—*Mike Connelly*

Chevallier, Gabriel (1895–1969). French novelist whose chief gift to the film world was *Clochemerle*, about the furore caused by the building of a public lavatory in a French village.

Cheyney, Peter (1896–1951). British mystery writer who created Lemmy Caution and Slim Callaghan, some of whose adventures were filmed.
Deputy Drummer (w) 32. Uneasy Terms (w) 48. Meet Mr Callaghan (w) 50. Diplomatic Courier 52. Alphaville 65.

Chiari, Mario (1909–). Italian production designer.
Miracle in Milan 51. The Golden Coach 54. Neapolitan Fantasy 54. I Vitelloni 54. The Sea Wall 56, etc.

Chiari, Walter (1924–) (Walter Annichiarico). Italian comic actor, occasionally in international films.
Bellissima 51. OK Nero 51. The Moment of Truth 53. Nana 56. The Little Hut 57. Bonjour Tristesse 58. Pepote 58. Chimes at Midnight 66. *They're a Weird Mob* 66. Squeeze a Flower 69. The Valachi Papers 72, etc.

Chief Thundercloud (1899–1955) (Victor Daniels). American Indian actor who began in films as a stuntman.
Ramona 36. Union Pacific 38. Western Union 41. The Falcon Out West 44. Unconquered 47. The Half Breed 51, many others.

Chief Thundercloud (1901–1967) (Scott Williams). American actor of Indian descent who appeared in many second feature westerns and played Tonto on radio.

La Chienne (France 1931). Written and directed by Jean Renoir from a novel by La Fouchardière, this bitter melodrama had Michel Simon as an unhappy man who takes up with a prostitute (Janie Mareze), kills her, and allows another man to be condemned in his place. It was remade by Fritz Lang in Hollywood in 1945, as *Scarlet Street*, with Edward G. Robinson and Joan Bennett. Heavy and unconvincing, this version was important as the first American film in which justice was not seen to be done after a crime . . . though Robinson was shown years later, tortured by remorse.

A Child is Waiting (US 1963). From Abby Mann's script, Stanley Kramer produced and John Cassavetes directed this most delicate of problem pictures, exploring the world of mentally handicapped children. Over-tactfulness rendered it rather obvious as a motion picture, but its sincerity is as obvious as its professional polish, and that such a film should have come from Hollywood at all is encouraging. Burt Lancaster, Judy Garland, and Bruce Ritchey as a withdrawn child, give excellent performances.

child stars have been popular with every generation of filmgoers. Throughout the twenties Mary Pickford stayed at the top by remaining a child as long as, and after, she could; with only slight competition from Baby Peggy, Madge Evans, Dawn O'Day (later Anne Shirley) and Wesley Barry. Stronger competititors, perhaps, were Junior Coghlan and, around 1930, Junior Durkin; strongest of all was Jackie Coogan, immortalized by Chaplin as *The Kid* in 1920 and subsequently cast in all the standard juvenile roles. The child comedians who composed *Our Gang* for Hal Roach started in the twenties and went on, with cast changes, into the forties: best remembered of them are Joe Cobb, Jean Darling, Johnny Downs, Mickey Daniels, Farina, Spanky Macfarland, Alfalfa Switzer, Darla Hood and Buckwheat Thomas.

Jackie Cooper also started in *Our Gang* but became a star in his own right after playing in *The Champ* and *Skippy*. In the early thirties his main rival was Dickie Moore, a lad of somewhat gentler disposition. Soon both were displaced in popular favour by Freddie Bartholemew in *David Copperfield*; but no boy could hold a candle to the multi-talented prodigy Shirley Temple, a star in 1933 at the age of five. She captivated a generation in a dozen or more hurriedly-produced sentimental comedies, and neither the angelic British Binkie Stuart nor the mischievous Jane Withers could cast the same spell.

Noting a splendid performance by twelve-year-old Robert Lynen in the French *Poil de Carotte*, we next encounter the still irrepressible Mickey Rooney, who popped up variously as Puck, Andy Hardy or a one-man-band. Then in 1937, the year that the Mauch twins appeared in *The Prince and the Pauper*, an MGM short called *Every Sunday* introduced two singing teenage girls, Deanna Durbin and Judy Garland, who went on to achieve enormous popularity in maturing roles until both were overtaken by personal difficulties. Another child who went on to musical stardom was vaudeville-bred Donald O'Connor, first seen in *Sing You Sinners*. But little more was seen of Tommy Kelly, who played *Tom Sawyer*, or Ann Gillis, or Terry Kilburn, or even Roddy McDowall until he re-emerged as a character actor twenty-five years later.

The early forties saw Edith Fellows as a good girl and Virginia Weidler, so marvellous in *The Philadelphia Story*, as a bad one. Baby Sandy appeared in a few comedies, as had Baby Le Roy ten years earlier; neither was seen on screen after the toddler stage. Two infant Dead-End Kids, Butch and Buddy, roamed mischievously through several Universal comedies. Margaret O'Brien and Peggy Ann Garner were two truly remarkable child actresses who never quite managed the transition to adult stardom. Teenagers Ann Blyth and Peggy Ryan partnered Donald O'Connor in many a light musical. Other child actors of the period were Ted Donaldson, Diana Lynn, Darryl Hickman and Sharyn Moffett, while Skippy Homeier gave an electrifying performance as the young Nazi in *Tomorrow the World*. In the post-war years Europe contributed Ivan Jandl in *The Search*; Britain had George Cole and Harry Fowler for cockney roles, Jeremy Spenser for well-bred ones, Anthony Wagner and Jean Simmons in *Great Expectations*, and very memorable performances from Bobby Henrey in *The Fallen Idol* and John Howard Davies in *Oliver Twist*. Hollywood responded with thoughtful Claude Jarman, tearful Bobs Watson, spunky Bobby Driscoll and Tommy Rettig, and pretty little misses Gigi Perreau and Natalie Wood.

The fifties brought William (now James) Fox in *The Magnet*, Brigitte Fossey and Georges Poujouly in *Les Jeux Interdits*, Mandy Miller in *Mandy,* Vincent Winter and Jon Whiteley in *The Kidnappers*, Brandon de Wilde in *Shane*, and Patty McCormack as the evil child in *The Bad Seed*. In 1959 Hayley Mills embarked on a six-year reign (somewhat outshone in *Whistle down the Wind* by Alan Barnes); the similar and equally capable American actress Patty Duke confined herself principally to stage and TV apart from *The Miracle Worker*. Then there have been Disney's over-wholesome Tommy Kirk and Annette Funicello, Fergus McClelland in *Sammy Going South*, Jean-Pierre Léaud in *The Four Hundred Blows*, William Dix in *The Nanny*, Matthew Garber and Karen Dotrice in *Mary Poppins*, Deborah Baxter in *A High Wind in Jamaica*, Mark Lester and Jack Wild in *Oliver*, Tatum O'Neal in *Paper Moon*, Linda Blair in *The Exorcist*, Ando in *Paper Tiger*, Kim Richards and Ike Eisenmann in *Escape to Witch Mountain*, Ricky Schroder in *The Champ*, . . . and more moppets are inevitably waiting in the wings, though the recent tendency has been for them to make one appearance and disappear from the boards.

The Childhood of Maxim Gorki (Russia 1938). Mark Donskoi's trilogy—the later sections are *Out in the World* and *My Universities*—subordinate propaganda to a highly pictorial evocation of old Russia. They are perhaps the most humane and personal of Soviet films.

childhood portrayed by grown-ups was instanced by Joan Fontaine in *Letter from an Unknown Woman*; by Ginger Rogers in *The Major and the Minor*; by Ginger Rogers and Alan Marshal in *Tom Dick and Harry*; by Ginger Rogers and Cary Grant in *Monkey Business*; and by Jack Buchanan, Fred Astaire and Nanette Fabray in the 'Triplets' number in *Band Wagon*. One might also add Judy Garland in *The Wizard of Oz*: she was seventeen when she played Dorothy.

Children of Hiroshima (Japan 1953). Written and directed by Kaneto Shindo, this strikingly stylish semi-documentary begins with an unforgettable impressionistic montage of the dropping of the first A-bomb, then continues on a more soberly journalistic note as it follows a young schoolmistress round the stricken city seven years later.

Children's Film Foundation. British company formed in 1951 to produce and distribute specially-devised entertainment films for children's Saturday matinées. Sponsored by trade organizations.

Chiles, Linden (–). American character actor who usually plays well-educated types.
Sanctuary 61. A Rage to Live 64. Texas across the River 67. Death Be Not Proud (TV) 75. James at 15 (TV) 77, etc.

Chiles, Lois (1950–). American leading lady of the late seventies.

The Way We Were 73. The Great Gatsby 74. Death on the Nile 78. Coma 78. Moonraker 79. Courage 84. Sweet Liberty 85. Creepshow 2 87, etc.

Chin, Tsai (c. 1938–). Chinese leading lady in international films.
The Face of Fu Manchu 65. Invasion 66. The Brides of Fu Manchu 66. You Only Live Twice 67. Rentadick 72, etc.

China was making films of a kind early in the century, but development of the industry was sporadic until the fifties, when the communists churned out many propaganda dramas.

The China Syndrome (US 1980). Topical suspense melodrama illustrating the dangers of atomic stockpiles. Written by Mike Gray, T. S. Cook and James Bridges; directed by James Bridges; for Bruce Gilbert and Columbia; with Jane Fonda, Michael Douglas, Jack Lemmon. There was a prompt TV rip-off under the title *The Plutonium Incident*.

The Chinese Bungalow. A popular British stage melodrama of the twenties, by Marian Osmond and James Corbett, this was first filmed in 1925 by Sinclair Hill, with Matheson Lang repeating his stage performance as the sinister oriental who covets an English rose. He also appeared in the 1930 sound version, with Anna Neagle as his victim: J. B. Williams directed. In 1940 the tale was remade with Paul Lukas and Kay Walsh, directed by George King.

Ching, William (1912–). American general purpose actor of the forties.
Something in the Wind 47. D.O.A. 50. Belle le Grand 51. Pat and Mike 52. Scared Stiff 53, etc.

Chitty, Eric (1906–77). British character actor who spent many years playing crotchety little men, notably in the TV series *Please Sir*.
Contraband 40. Raising a Riot 55. Doctor Zhivago 65. The Railway Children 70. Great Expectations 75. A Bridge Too Far 77, many others.

Chodorov, Edward (1904–). American screenwriter.
The World Changes 33. Kind Lady 35. The Story of Louis Pasteur (co-w) 35. Yellow Jack 38. Undercurrent 46. The Hucksters 47. Roadhouse 48, etc.

Chodorov, Jerome (1911–). American writer, usually with Joseph Fields.
Louisiana Purchase 41. My Sister Eileen 42. Junior Miss 45. Happy Anniversary 59 (all from their plays), etc.

Chomsky, Marvin (1929–). American director of efficient but nondescript style.
□Assault on the Wayne (TV) 70. *Family Flight* (TV) 71. Evel Knievel 71. Mongo's Back in Town (TV) 71. Fireball Forward (TV) 72. Female Artillery (TV) 73. The FBI vs Alvin Karpis (TV) 74. Mrs Sundance (TV) 74. Attack on Terror (TV) 74. Kate McShane (TV) 75. A Matter of Wife and Death (TV) 75. Murph the Surf 75. Brinks: the Great Robbery (TV) 76. Law and Order (TV) 76. *Roots* (co-d) (TV) 76. Danger in Paradise (TV) 77. Little Ladies of the Night (TV) 77. MacKintosh and TJ 77. Good Luck Miss Wyckoff 78. *Holocaust* 78. Hollow Image 79. King Crab. Dr Franken 80. Attica (TV) 80. Evita Peron (TV) 81. My Body My Child (TV) 82. Inside the Third Reich (TV) 82. Nairobi Affair (TV) 84. Tank 84. Robert Kennedy and his Times (TV) 85.

Chong, Rae Dawn (1962–). Canadian-born actress. Quest for Fire 79. Commando 85. The Color Purple 85. Choose Me 86. Soul Man 86.

Chopin, Frederic (1810–1849). Polish pianist and composer most famous in film circles for his love affair with the eccentric Georges Sand. ('Frederic, stop composing that Polonaise jangle!' said Merle Oberon to Cornel Wilde in *A Song to Remember*.) His chief cinematic interpreters have been as follows:

1935	*Un Amour de Frederic Chopin*	Jean Servais
1945	*A Song to Remember*	Cornel Wilde
1951	*The Young Chopin*	Czeslaw Wollejko
1960	*Song Without End*	Alex Davion
1975	*Lisztomania*	Ken Colley

Choureau, Etchika (1923–). French leading lady.
Children of Love 53. The Fruits of Summer 55. Lafayette Escadrille (US) 57. Darby's Rangers (US) 58, etc.

Chow, Raymond (1929–). Chinese producer who in the early eighties expanded his interests from kung fu action films, through his Golden Harvest group, to international star vehicles such as *The Cannonball Run* and *The Return of the Soldier*.

Chrétien, Henri (1879–1956). French inventor of the anamorphic lens subsequently used in CinemaScope and allied processes.

Christ on the screen was for many years a controversial subject: film-makers have usually preferred to imply his presence by a hand, a cloak, or simply reactions of onlookers. However, even in the first ten years of cinephotography there were several versions of his life, and in 1912 Robert Henderson played the role in a 'super' production of *From the Manger to the Cross*. In 1916 came *Civilisation*, with George Fisher as Christ on the battlefields, and in the same year *Intolerance*, in which Howard Gaye was Jesus. In 1927 Cecil B. de Mille's *King of Kings* had H. B. Warner in the role; any offence was minimized by having his first appearance a misty fade-in as the blind girl regains her sight. In 1932 Duvivier made *Golgotha*, with Robert le Vigan; twenty years then went by before Christ's next appearance on the screen, played by a non-professional, Robert Wilson, in a sponsored movie called *Day of Triumph*. In 1961 Jeffrey Hunter appeared as Christ in *King of Kings*, which was unfortunately tagged by the trade *I Was a Teenage Jesus*. George Stevens' disappointing 1965 colossus, *The Greatest Story Ever Told*, cleverly cast Swedish Max von Sydow in the part; in the same year came Pasolini's *The Gospel According to St Matthew*, with Enrique Irazoqui; and in 1969 Buṇuel cast Bernard Verley as Christ in *The Milky Way*. Christ-like figures of various kinds have been found in such films as *The Passing of the Third Floor Back, The Fugitive, Strange Cargo* and *The Face*; while films about the direct influence of Christ's life include *Quo Vadis, The Last Days of Pompeii, Ben Hur, Barabbas, The Wandering Jew* and *The Robe*, in which the voice of Christ was provided by Cameron Mitchell. The most recent Christs have been in the modernized pop-operas *Godspell* and *Jesus Christ Superstar*; a TV series, *Jesus of Nazareth*; and a TV movie with a literal slant, *The Day Christ Died*.

Christensen, Benjamin (1879–1959). Danish director whose career faded after a sojourn in Hollywood.
The Mysterious X 13. The Night of Revenge 15. Häxan (Witchcraft through the Ages) 21. Seine Frau Die Unbekannte 23. The Devil's Circus 25. Mockery 27. The Hawk's Nest 28. Seven Footprints to Satan 29, others.

Christian, Linda (1923–) (Blanca Rosa Welter). Mexican-born leading lady who appeared in a few international films, then married into European nobility.
Holiday in Mexico 46. Green Dolphin Street 47. Tarzan and the Mermaids 48. The Happy Time 52. Athena 54. Thunderstorm 56. The House of Seven Hawks 59. The VIPs 63. How to Seduce a Playboy 66, etc.

Christian, Paul: see *Hubschmid, Paul.*

Christian-Jaque (1904–) (Christian Maudet). French writer-director, former journalist.
Les Disparus de Saint-Agil 38. La Symphonie Fantastique 42. Sortilèges 44. *Un Revenant* 46. D'Homme à Hommes 48. Souvenirs Perdus 50. Bluebeard 51. *Fanfan la Tulipe* 51. Lucrezia Borgia 52. Adorables Creatures 52. Nana 54. Si Tous les Gars du Monde (Race for Life) 55. Babette Goes to War 59. Madame Sans Gêne 61. The Black Tulip 63. The Secret Agents (The Dirty Game) (co-director) 66. The Saint Versus . . . 66. Two Tickets to Mexico (Dead Run) 67. La Ville a Belles Dents 80, etc.

Christians, Mady (1900–1951) (Margarethe Marie Christians). Austrian-born stage actress in occasional Hollywood films.
The Waltz Dream (GB) 26. Slums of Berlin 27. The Runaway Princess (GB) 29. A Wicked Woman 35. Escapade 36. Seventh Heaven 37. Heidi 37. Address Unknown 44. All My Sons 48. Letter from an Unknown Woman 48, etc.

Christie, Dame Agatha (1891–1976) (Mary Clarissa Miller). Best-selling British mystery novelist and playwright whose innumerable puzzle plots have been strangely neglected by film-makers.
Lord Edgware Dies (and other films starring Austin Trevor as Hercule Poirot) 36. And Then There Were None 45. Witness for the Prosecution 58. Spider's Web 60. Murder She Said 62. Murder at the Gallop 63. The Alphabet Murders 66. Murder on the Orient Express 74. Death on the Nile 78. The Mirror Crack'd 80. Why Didn't They Ask Evans? (TV) 80. The Seven Dials Mystery (TV) 81. Evil Under the Sun 82. Murder Is Easy (TV) 82. A Caribbean Mystery (TV) 82. Sparkling Cyanide (TV) 82. A 1982 TV series, *The Agatha Christie Hour*, was derived from her lighter stories of the twenties, only some of them hinging on detection.

† A mysterious episode in her own life was fictitiously cleared up in *Agatha* 79.

¶ *A.C.:* I'm a sausage machine, a perfect sausage machine.
A.C.: An archaeologist is the best husband a woman can have. The older she gets, the more interested he is in her.

Christie, Al (1886–1951). American comedy producer, mainly of two-reelers, in Hollywood from 1914 and a rival of Mack Sennett. Features include *Tillie's Punctured Romance* 17, *Up in Mabel's Room* 26; produced and directed *Charley's Aunt* 25.

Christie, Audrey (1912–). American supporting actress of the fifties.
Deadline 52. Carousel 56. Splendor in the Grass 61. The Unsinkable Molly Brown 64. The Ballad of Josie 68. Mame 73, etc.

Christie, Howard (1912–). American producer.
Lady on a Train 44. Abbott and Costello Meet the Invisible Man 50. The Purple Mask 55. Away All Boats 56. Gunfight at Abilene 60. Nobody's Perfect 68, other routine films.

Christie, Julie (1940–). Striking British leading actress whose choice of roles has not always been fortunate.
□Crooks Anonymous 62. The Fast Lady 63. *Billy Liar* 63. Young Cassidy 64. *Darling* (AA, BFA) 65. *Doctor Zhivago* 65. Fahrenheit 451 66. Far From the Madding Crowd 67. Petulia 68. In Search of Gregory 69. The Go-Between 71. McCabe and Mrs Miller 71. *Don't Look Now* 74. Shampoo 75. Nashville 75. Demon Seed 77. Heaven Can Wait 78. Memoirs of a Survivor 82. The Return of the Soldier 82. The Gold Diggers 83. Heat and Dust 83. Power 86. Miss Mary 86.

Christine, Virginia (1917–). American character actress.
Edge of Darkness 42. The Mummy's Curse 45. The Killers 46. Cyrano de Bergerac 50. Never Wave at a WAC 53. Not as a Stranger 55. Nightmare 56. Invasion of the Body Snatchers 56. The Careless Years 58. Judgment at Nuremberg 61. The Prize 63. Guess Who's Coming to Dinner 67, etc.

Christmas has provided a favourite sentimental climax for many a film. Films wholly based on it include *The Holly and the Ivy, Tenth Avenue Angel, Miracle on 34th Street, White Christmas, Christmas Eve, Christmas in Connecticut, The Bishop's Wife, I'll Be Seeing You,* and the many versions of *Scrooge.* There were happy Christmas scenes in *The Bells of St Mary, The Inn of the Sixth Happiness, The Man Who Came to Dinner, Holiday Inn, Since You Went Away, Three Godfathers, It's A Wonderful Life, Young at Heart, Meet Me in St Louis, On Moonlight Bay, Little Women, The Cheaters, Desk Set* and *Young at Heart* among others; while unhappy Christmases were spent in *Things to Come, Full House* ('The Gifts of the Magi'), *The Apartment, Meet John Doe, The Glenn Miller Story, The Christmas Tree, Christmas Holiday,* and *The Victors.* (Nor was there much for the characters in *The Lion in Winter* to celebrate at the Christmas court of 1189.)
Santa Claus himself put in an appearance in *Miracle on 34th Street* (played by Edmund Gwenn), *The Lemon Drop Kid* (played by Bob Hope), *The Light at Heart* (played by Monty Woolley), and *Robin and the Seven Hoods* (played by the Sinatra clan). Disney features him in *Babes in Toyland* and a short cartoon, *The Night Before Christmas*; and in their 1934 version of *Babes in Toyland* Laurel and Hardy found him an irate employer.
Christmas was celebrated in unlikely settings in *Knights of the Round Table, Conquest of Space, Scott of the Antarctic, Encore* ('Winter Cruise'), *Destination Tokyo* (in a submarine), *The Nun's Story* (in a Congo Mission), and *Black Narcissus* (in an Indian nunnery).

? 1 In what film did Bing Crosby first sing 'White Christmas'?
2 Who played the Ghost of Christmas Past to Albert Finney's Scrooge?
3 Who played Scrooge in MGM's 1938 *A Christmas Carol*?
4 Name the film in which Ralph Richardson played an East Anglian parson whose family came home for Christmas.
5 Name the 'angels' in *We're No Angels.*
6 In what film were Kenneth More and James Robertson Justice among those who spent Christmas in a snowy waste?
7 In what film did Lee Marvin play one of the three wise men?
8 What prophetic film began with Christmas shopping in 1940?
9 What famous American Christmas comedy, more recently remade for TV, was retitled *The Big Heart* in Britain in 1947?

Christopher, Dennis (1955–). American leading man of the eighties.

The Boys in Company C 77. A Wedding 78. Breaking Away 79. California Dreaming 80. Fade to Black 80. Chariots of Fire 81. Don't Cry It's Only Thunder 82. Flight of the Spruce Goose 86. Jake Speed 86.

Chrystall, Belle (1911–). British leading lady of the thirties.
Hindle Wakes 31. Friday the Thirteenth 33. Edge of the World 38, etc.

Chukrai, Grigori (1920–). Russian director.
The Forty First 56. Ballad of a Soldier 59. Clear Sky 61. There Was an Old Man and an Old Woman 65, etc.

Churches have provided a setting for many pretty secular-minded films, from the various versions of *The Hunchback of Notre Dame* to the use of a church as a refuge during a flood in *When Tomorrow Comes*. Other memorable moments include Bogart confessing the plot of *Dead Reckoning* to a priest; Robert Donat's sermon in *Lease of Life* and Orson Welles' in *Moby Dick*; the scandalous confessions in *Les Jeux Interdits* and the dramatic one in *I Confess*; the murder of Becket; the bombed but well-used churches in *Mrs Miniver* and *Sundown*; the thing in the rafters of Westminster Abbey in *The Quatermass Experiment*; the attempted murder in Westminster Cathedral in *Foreign Correspondent* and the fall from the church tower in *Vertigo*; the spies in the mission chapel in *The Man Who Knew Too Much*; the arrest of *Pastor Hall*; Arturo de Cordova going mad during a service in *El*; the church-tower climax of *The Stranger*; the Russian services in *Ivan the Terrible* and *We Live Again*; Cagney dying on the church steps in *The Roaring Twenties*; the church used as refuge against the Martians in *The War of the Worlds*; the church used for a town meeting in *High Noon*; the Turkish mosque and espionage rendezvous in *From Russia with Love*; the comic rifling of offertory boxes in *Heaven Sent*; the finale of *Miracle in the Rain* in the church porch; the meeting in church of the protagonists of *The Appaloosa*; the characters finally trapped in a church in *The Exterminating Angel*; the churches swept away by the elements in *The Hurricane* and *Hawaii*; the church rendezvous in *Alice's Restaurant*; the church with the moving statue in *The Miracle of the Bells*; and all the many films in which the protagonists are *priests*, *monks* and *nuns* (qv).

Churchill, Berton (1876–1940). Forceful Canadian stage actor who in later years settled in Hollywood and played stern bosses and fathers.
Tongues of Flame 24. Nothing but the Truth 29. Secrets of a Secretary 31. The Rich are Always with Us 32. American Madness 32. Master of Men 33. Hi Nellie 34. Dames 34. Babbitt 34. Page Miss Glory 35. Parole 36. Parnell 37. The Singing Marine 37. Sweethearts 38. *Stagecoach* (as the absconding banker) 39. The Way of All Flesh 40. Turnabout 40, many others.

Churchill, Diana (1913–). British leading lady, mostly on stage.
School for Husbands 36. Housemaster 38. House of the Arrow 40. Eagle Squadron (US) 44. Scott of the Antarctic 48. The History of Mr Polly 49, etc.

Churchill, Donald (1930–). British light actor who developed from callow young men to eccentric middle-aged creations. Also wrote many TV scripts.
Victim 60. The Wild Affair 63, etc.
TV series (a, w) include Bulldog Breed 62. Never a Cross Word 68. Moody and Pegg 63. Spooner's Patch 80.

Churchill, Frank (1901–1942). American composer, always with Disney and the author of several hit songs.
Three Little Pigs ('Who's Afraid of the Big Bad Wolf?') 33. *Snow White and the Seven Dwarfs* 37. *Dumbo* 41. *Bambi* 42, etc.

Churchill, Marguerite (1910–). Pert American leading lady of the thirties.
The Valiant 29. Seven Faces 29. Born Reckless 30. The Big Trail 30. Charlie Chan Carries On 31. Quick Millions 31. Forgotten Commandments 32. Girl without a Room 33. The Walking Dead 36. Dracula's Daughter 36. Legion of Terror 36, etc.

Churchill, Sarah (1914–1982). British actress, daughter of Sir Winston Churchill.
He Found a Star 40. All Over the Town 47. *Royal Wedding* (US) 51. Serious Charge 58, etc.

Churchill, Sir Winston (1874–1965). British statesman and author who has been the subject of a major documentary, *The Finest Hours* 64, and a TV series, *The Valiant Years* 60. He was impersonated by Dudley

Field Malone in *Mission to Moscow* 43, by Patrick Wymark in *Operation Crossbow* 65, by a number of Russian actors in various propaganda pieces, by Simon Ward in *Young Winston* 72, by Nigel Stock in *A Man Called Intrepid* 79 and by Wensley Pithey in *Ike* 79.

¶ 'He would rather make love to a word than to a woman.—*Ingrid Bergman*

Ciampi, Yves (1921–1982). French director. Suzanne et ses Brigands 50. Un Grand Patron 51. L'Esclave 53. Les Héros sont Fatigués 55. Typhoon over Nagasaki 57. Qui êtes-vous Monsieur Sorge 60. Le Ciel sur la Tête 62. A Quelques Jours 69, etc.

Ciannelli, Eduardo (1887–1969). Italian character actor, long in Hollywood; his finely-etched features and incisive speech were usually employed in villainous roles, but he could also strike sympathetic chords.
Reunion in Vienna 33. The Scoundrel 35. *Winterset* 36. Marked Woman 37. Law of the Underworld 38. Gunga Din 39. Foreign Correspondent 40. The Mummy's Hand 40. They Met in Bombay 41. Cairo 42. They Got Me Covered 43. *The Mask of Dimitrios* 44. The Conspirators 44. Dillinger 45. Wife of Monte Cristo 46. Perilous Holiday 47. The Creeper 48. Rapture 50. The People Against O'Hara 51. Volcano 53. Mambo 55. Helen of Troy 55. Houseboat 58. The Visit 64. Mackenna's Gold 68. The Brotherhood 68. The Secret of Santa Vittoria 69, many others. TV series: *Johnny Staccato* 59.

Cicognini, Alessandro (1906–). Italian composer.
Four Steps in the Clouds 42. Shoeshine 46. Bicycle Thieves 48. I Miserabili 48. Tomorrow is Too Late 50. Miracle in Milan 51. Don Camillo 52. Umberto D 52. Due Soldi di Speranza 52. Gold of Naples 54. Ulysses 54. Summer Madness 55. The Black Orchid 58, etc.

Cilento, Diane (1933–). Versatile Australian leading actress whose talent has not been fully tested in movies.
Wings of Danger 52. The Angel who Pawned Her Harp 54. The Passing Stranger 54. Passage Home 55. The Woman for Joe 56. *The Admirable Crichton* 57. Jet Storm 59. The Full Treatment 60. The Naked Edge 61. I Thank a Fool 62. *Tom Jones* 63. The Third Secret 64. *Rattle of a Simple Man* 64. The Agony and the Ecstasy 65. *Hombre* 67. Negatives 68. Zero Population Growth 72. The Wicker Man 73. Hitler: the Last Ten Days 74. For the Term of His Natural Life TV 82. The Boy Who Had Everything 84, etc.

Cimarron (US 1931) (AA). This famous western was directed by Wesley Ruggles from a script by Howard Estabrook based on Edna Ferber's novel about Yancey Cravat and the opening of the Cimarron Strip. Richard Dix and Irene Dunne starred. In 1961 Anthony Mann, to little effect, directed a remake with Glenn Ford and Maria Schell.

Cimino, Michael (1940–). American screenwriter/director.
□Silent Running (co-w) 72. Magnum Force (co-w) 73. Thunderbolt and Lightfoot (wd) 74. *The Deer Hunter* (wd) (AA) 78. Heaven's Gate (w, d) 80. The Year of the Dragon 85.

¶ *M.C.:* Films are home movies of your past.

the cinema

¶ A few fragments of thought:

C. G. Jung: The cinema, like the detective story, makes it possible to experience without danger all the excitement, passion and desirousness which must be suppressed in a humanitarian ordering of society.
Orson Welles: It has no boundary . . . it is a ribbon of dream.
Dore Schary: The most collaborative of the arts.
Jean-Luc Godard: Truth twenty-four times a second.
V. I. Lenin: Of all the arts, the cinema is the most important for us.
Jean Cocteau: That temple of sex, with its goddesses, its guardians and its victims . . .
Sheila Black: An uncomfortable way of watching television.
Howard Collins (manager in 1953 of Roxy Theatre, NY): The film is not an art but a super tabloid for young and old, moron and genius. Her sister muses are the comic strips, the pulp magazines, the radio and all other forms of entertainment based on democratic rather than aesthetic principles.
Jean-Luc Godard: Of course a film should have a beginning, a middle and an end. But not necessarily in that order.
John Boorman: I always think that watching films is very like dreaming.
John Russell Taylor: Whoever it was who first thought the cinema was an art, he should have kept his mouth shut. Not that it isn't, but there are so many terrible instances of films made specifically to be art which come perilously close to making us doubt the whole proposition.

Budd Schulberg: The film does best when it concentrates on a single character. It does *The Informer* superbly. It tends to lose itself in the ramifications of *War and Peace.*
Josef von Sternberg: The finished product is not finished when the actor is. The work is completed by a pair of shears.
Pudovkin: Editing is the foundation of the film art.
William Wellman: Get a director and a writer and leave them alone. That's how the best pictures get made.
John Simon: Any attempt in America to make a film a work of art must be hailed. Usually, in the same breath, it must be farewelled.
James Agate: The American film mind, though it can deal competently enough with the stupendous, cannot help vulgarizing any scene which approaches the intimate.
James Agate again, in 1921: Collectively the audience is, in the matter of aesthetic, totally uneducated. They gape before the screen today as the thirteenth-century play-goer gaped at the morality play.
Wolcott Gibbs: Most Hollywood comedies are so vulgar, witless and dull that it is preposterous to write about them in any publication not meant to be read while chewing gum.
François Truffaut: Cinema is an improvement on life.
Michael Winner: If you want art, don't mess about with movies. Buy a Picasso.
H. L. Mencken in 1927 knew the score: The movies languish as a fine art because the men who determine what is to get into them haven't the slightest visible notion that such a thing as a fine art exists. And *Penelope Gilliatt* in the eighties brought matters up to date: Filmmaking has now reached the same stage as sex—it's all technique and no feeling.

cinema vérité. A fashionable term of the sixties for what used to be called candid camera. A TV-style technique of recording life and people as they are, in the raw, using handheld cameras, natural sound and the minimum of rehearsal and editing. Chiefly applied to *Chronique d'une Eté* 61, *Le Joli Mai* 62, and the documentaries of Richard Leacock and the Maysles brothers.

cinemas have only rarely provided a background for film situations. A Hollywood première and a sneak preview were shown in *Singin' in the Rain,* and *The Oscar* revealed all about the Academy Awards ceremony. Characters in *Sherlock Junior, Borderlines* and *Merton of the Movies* (Red Skelton version) clambered on to the stage while a film was showing. Projectionists were featured in *Clash by Night, The Blob, The Great Morgan,* and *Hellzapoppin*; also in *The Smallest Show on Earth,* the only film concerned with the running of a cinema as its main plot unless one counts *The Last Picture Show* in which the small town cinema is an essential background to the character development. Fred Allen in *It's in the Bag* had a terrible time trying to find a seat in a full house; Dillinger was killed coming out of a cinema in *The F.B.I. Story*; Bogart was nearly shot in a Chinese cinema in *Across the Pacific,* and Anthony Perkins met Valli in a Siamese one in *This Angry Age* (*The Sea Wall*). A cinema was used as a rendezvous for spies in *The Traitors* and *Sabotage*; a church was used as a cinema in *Sullivan's Travels* when chain-gang convicts watched Mickey Mouse. Mark Stevens and Joan Fontaine in *From This Day Forward* visited a news cinema but were too much in love to heed the warnings of impending war. Louis Jourdan and Linda Christian watched Valentino at the local in *The Happy Time,* and astronauts watched Bob Hope in a space station in *Conquest of Space.* Deanna Durbin got a murder clue in a cinema in *Lady on a Train*; and in *Bullets or Ballots* Humphrey Bogart took Barton MacLane to see a documentary about his nefarious career. Ray Danton in *The Rise and Fall of Legs Diamond* excused himself during a performance to rob the shop next door. The monster in *The Tingler* escapes into a silent cinema. Linda Hayden in *Baby Love* was accosted in a cinema. Robert Cummings in *Saboteur* started a riot in Radio City Music Hall, on the stairs of which Danny Kaye sang in *Up in Arms.* Fredric March watched a Thomas Ince silent at the local nickelodeon in *One Foot in Heaven.* In *Brief Encounter,* Celia Johnson and Trevor Howard thought the organist was the best part of the programme. Polly Bergen in *The Caretakers* went crazy and climbed up in front of the screen. *Bonnie and Clyde* found time between robberies to see a *Gold Diggers* movie. In *Eye Witness* a cinema manager was killed during the Saturday night performance; and in *Targets* a killer was apprehended by Boris Karloff at a drive-in. A drive-in was used as a rendezvous in *White Heat* and a 42nd Street cinema was a homosexual rendezvous in *Midnight Cowboy.* Home movies figured most notably in *Rebecca* and *Adam's Rib.* See *excerpts, theatres.*

CinemaScope. Wide-screen process copyrighted by Fox in 1953 and first used in *The Robe*; invented many years earlier by Henri Chrétien. Other companies either adopted it or produced their own trade name: WarnerScope, SuperScope, etc. Basically, the camera contains an anamorphic lens which 'squeezes' a wide picture on to a standard 35mm frame (which has a breadth/height ratio of 4:3 or 1.33:1). This, when projected through a complementary lens, gives a picture ratio on screen of 2.55:1 with stereophonic magnetic sound, or 2.35:1 with optical sound. Directors found the new shape awkward to compose for, the easiest way of handling it being to park the camera and let the actors move, a reversion to early silent methods. Although wide screens are said to have helped the box office, they have effectively prevented the full use of cinematic techniques. Oddly enough Fox in the mid-sixties quietly dropped their own system and moved over to Panavision.

¶ The wide, wide screen may have saved the industry, but it came close to killing the art. Hear these justified cries of woe.
Rouben Mamoulian: The worst shape ever devised.
George Stevens: It's fine if you want a system that shows a boa constrictor to better advantage than a man.
Samuel Goldwyn: A wide screen makes a bad film twice as bad.
Fritz Lang: It is a formula for a funeral, or for snakes, but not for human beings.
Leon Shamroy: It wrecked the art of film for a decade.
Irving Brecher: Why not keep the screen the same size and reduce the size of the audience?
Fritz Lang: There was a time when all I looked for was a good story, but nowadays everything has to look the size of Mount Rushmore, and the actors in close-up look as though they belong there.
James Mason: Processed by De Luxe, it made all films look like very cheap colour advertisements in magazines.
Charles Higham: It resulted in a collapse of visual quality even more disastrous than that which accompanied the dawn of sound.

Cinematograph Exhibitors' Association. The British theatre-owners' protective association, founded in 1912 with 10 members. In 1922 there were 2000, in 1950, 4000.

cinematographer. Lighting cameraman or chief photographer.

Cinemobile. A massive truck into which everything necessary for location shooting, including dressing rooms and toilets, can be packed.

Cinerama. Extra-wide-screen system, invented by Fred Waller. Three projectors, electronically synchronized, were used to put the picture on the screen in three sections: this gave a disturbing wobble at the joins, though the range of vision was sometimes magnificently wide, as in the aerial shots and roller coaster sequence in *This is Cinerama* 52. After ten years of scenic but cinematically unremarkable travelogues (*Cinerama Holiday, Seven Wonders of the World, Search for Paradise,* etc.), the first story film in the process, *How the West Was Won,* was made in 1962. Shortly afterwards the three-camera system was abandoned in favour of 'single-lens Cinerama' which is virtually indistinguishable from CinemaScope except for the higher definition resulting from using wider film. 'Cinemiracle', a similar process, was short-lived.
The released Cinerama features were:
This is Cinerama 52
Cinerama Holiday 55
Seven Wonders of the World 56
Search for Paradise 57
South Seas Adventure 58
The Wonderful World of the Brothers Grimm 62
How the West was Won 62
It's a Mad Mad Mad Mad World (single lens) 63
Circus World 64
The Best of Cinerama 64
Battle of the Bulge 65
Grand Prix 66
Cinerama's Russian Adventure 66
Ice Station Zebra 68
Custer of the West 68
2001: A Space Odyssey 68
Krakatoa–East of Java 69

Cioffi, Charles (1935–). American character actor of the seventies.
Klute 71. The Don is Dead 73. The Thief who Came to Dinner 73. Crazy Joe 74. The Next Man 76. The Other Side of Midnight 77. Dog and Cat (TV) 77. Time after Time 79. Missing 82.
TV series: Assignment Vienna 72. Get Christy Love 74.

circuit. A chain of cinemas under the same ownership, often playing the same release programme.

circuses, according to the cinema, are full of drama and passion behind the scenes. So you would think if you judged from *Variety, Freaks, The Wagons Roll at Night, The Greatest Show on Earth, The Big Show, The Big Circus, Sawdust and Tinsel, Circus of Horrors, Tromba, Four Devils, The Three Maxims, Trapeze, Captive Wild Woman, Ring of Fear, Charlie Chan at the Circus, A Tiger Walks, Circus World, The Trojan Brothers, Circus of Fear, Berserk, The Dark Tower, He Who Gets Slapped, Flesh and Fantasy, Man on a Tightrope, Chad Hanna, Pagliacci, Far From the Madding Crowd*, and *Vampire Circus*. But there is a lighter side, as evidenced by *Doctor Dolittle, Yo Yo, Jumbo, High Wide and Handsome, Lady in the Dark, Life is a Circus, The Marx Brothers at the Circus, Three Rings Circus*, Chaplin's *The Circus, The Great Profile, You Can't Cheat an Honest Man, Road Show, Merry Andrew*, and *Toby Tyler*. TV series have included *Circus Boy, Frontier Circus* and *The Greatest Show on Earth*.

The Cisco Kid. This ingratiating Latin rogue was first played by Warner Baxter in Irving Cummings' 1931 film. In 1937 Cesar Romero played him in the first of a series; Gilbert Roland appeared in *The Gay Cavalier* and others; the role was taken over in 1945 by Duncan Renaldo, who has also been in TV series. The Kid's side-kicks have included Leo Carrillo and Chris-Pin Martin.

The Citadel (GB 1938). Masterly film version of Cronin's novel about a doctor's rise from Welsh slums to Harley Street, directed by King Vidor for MGM-British, with Robert Donat and Ralph Richardson. In 1983 BBC TV produced a slightly soggy but earnest ten-hour version starring Ben Cross.

Citizen Kane (US 1941). Often acclaimed as the best film of all time: certainly none has used the medium with more vigour and enthusiasm. Herman J. Mankiewicz' script paralleled the career of newspaper magnate William Randolph Hearst, making the point that money isn't everything. Orson Welles, the boy wonder of American radio, produced and directed it as a cinematic box of tricks, often somewhat obscuring the story of a journalist's quest for the truth after Kane's death; nevertheless there isn't a dull scene in the film's 119 minutes. Cameraman Gregg Toland and composer Bernard Herrmann contributed massively to the general effect of a new joyous era in film-making, and many of Welles' Mercury Company of theatre actors launched new careers for themselves: Joseph Cotten, Everett Sloane, Agnes Moorehead, George Coulouris, Ray Collins, Paul Stewart, and Welles himself as Kane. After thirty years the film seems scarcely to have faded at all. See *The Citizen Kane Book* 1971, edited by Pauline Kael.

¶ There is a man
A certain man
And for the poor you may be sure
That he'll do all he can.
Who is this one—
This fav'rite son—
Who by his action
Has the Traction magnates on the run?
Who loves to smoke?
Enjoys a joke?
Who wouldn't get a bit upset
If he were really broke?
With wealth and fame
He's still the same—
I'll bet you five you're not alive
If you don't know his name!
What is his name?
It's Mister Kane!
He doesn't like that Mister, he likes
Good old Charlie Kane!—*song from film*

City Lights (US 1931). Chaplin's depression-period comedy in which the tramp meets a drunken millionaire and a blind flower girl. Comedy over-flooded with sentiment, but some brilliant moments.

Civilisation (US 1916). One of the few films of its time which can stand beside the work of Griffith, Thomas Ince's film is a painstaking anti-war allegory intended to keep America neutral in World War I: Christ returns to earth in human form to work for peace. A very fluent piece of film-making.

Clair, René (1898–1981) (René Chomette). Distinguished French director of light comedy; he brought to the screen a nimble command of technique, an optimistic outlook, and a total lack of malice or message.
Novel 1925: *Star Turn*.
□Paris Qui Dort 23. Entr'acte 24. La Fantôme du Moulin Rouge 24. Le Voyage Imaginaire 25. La Proie du Vent 26. Les Deux Timides 28. *An Italian Straw Hat* 28. *Sous Les Toits de Paris* 29. *Le Million* 31. *A Nous la Liberté* 31. Le Quatorze Juillet 33. Le Dernier Milliardaire 34. The Ghost Goes

West 35. Break the News 36. The Flame of New Orleans 41. *I Married a Witch* 42. Forever and a Day (part) 43. *It Happened Tomorrow* 44. *And Then There Were None* 45. Le Silence est d'Or 46. La Beauté du Diable 49. *Les Belles de Nuit* 52. Les Grandes Manoeuvres 55. Porte des Lilas 56. Tout l'Or du Monde 60. Love and the Frenchwoman (part) 60. Les Quatres Vérités (part) 62. Les Fêtes Galantes 65.

'Once too good to be called even the French Lubitsch, he now seems more like the French Mamoulian.'—*Andrew Sarris, 1968*

'A film-maker who would sooner raise a soufflé than roast an ox.'—*Alexander Walker*

❀ For creating films in which, by a dextrous combination of sound and picture, the feet of the characters appeared never to touch the ground. *Le Million.*

Claire, Ina (1892–1985) (Ina Fagan). American stage actress who made occasional films.
The Puppet Crown 15. Wild Goose Chase 15. Polly with a Past 20. The Awful Truth 29. The Royal Family of Broadway 31. Rebound 31. The Greeks Had a Word for Them 32. Ninotchka 39. Claudia 43, etc.

clairvoyance on the screen seems to have caused a remarkable amount of suffering to Edward G. Robinson: he was haunted by the effects of a prophecy in *Flesh and Fantasy, Nightmare* and *Night Has a Thousand Eyes.* Other frightened men for similar reasons were Claude Rains in *The Clairvoyant,* Dick Powell in *It Happened Tomorrow,* George Macready in *I Love a Mystery,* Mervyn Johns in *Dead of Night,* and Michael Hordern in *The Night My Number Came Up.*

Clampett, Bob (*c.*1914–84). American animator, in at or near the birth of Bugs Bunny, Porky Pig, Daffy Duck and Tweety.

clapperboard. A hinged board recording film details. At the beginning of each 'take' it is held before the camera for identification and then 'clapped' to make a starting point in the sound track. This point is then sychronized with the image of the closed board.

Clare, Mary (1894–1970). British character actress, latterly in formidable matron roles.
Becket 24. Hindle Wakes 31. The Constant Nymph 33. The Clairvoyant 34. The Passing of the Third Floor Back 35. Young and Innocent 37. The Lady Vanishes 38. A Girl Must Live 39. Old Bill and Son 40. *Mrs Pym of Scotland Yard* (title role) 40. Next of Kin 42. *The Night Has Eyes* 42. The Hundred-Pound Window 44. The Three Weird Sisters 48. *Oliver Twist* 48. Moulin Rouge 53. Mambo 55. The Price of Silence 59, many others.

Clarence, O. B. (1870–1955). British stage actor who played benevolent doddering roles in a number of films.
Liberty Hall 14. Perfect Understanding 32. Friday the Thirteenth 33. The Scarlet Pimpernel 34. Seven Sinners 36. Pygmalion 38. Inspector Hornleigh Goes To It 41. Penn of Pennsylvania 42. On Approval 43. A Place of One's Own 44. Great Expectations (as the Aged P) 46. Uncle Silas 47, many others.

Clark, Bob (–). Canadian director.
□Children Shouldn't Play with Dead Things 72. Black Christmas 72. Breaking Point 76. Murder by Decree 79. Tribute 80. Porky's 82. Porky's II 83. A Christmas Story 83. Rhinestone 84. Turk 182 85.

Clark, Bobby (1888–1960). Bouncy American vaudeville comedian who with Paul McCullough made thirty-six two-reel comedies for RKO between 1928 and 1936, when McCullough died. Clark made only one solo film appearance, in *The Goldwyn Follies* 38.

Clark, Candy (1949–). American leading lady of the seventies.
American Graffiti 73. The Man Who Fell to Fat City 72. American Graffiti 73. The Man Who Fell to Earth 76. I Will, I Will, For Now 76. Citizen's Band 77. When You Comin' Back, Red Ryder? 79. More American Graffiti 79. Blue Thunder 83. Amityville 3D 83.

Clark, Cliff (1893–1953). Short, stocky American character actor who played tough sheriffs and police inspectors in forties co-features.
Mr Moto's Gamble 38. Kentucky 39. Honolulu 39. The Grapes of Wrath 40. Double Alibi 40. Manpower 41. Kid Glove Killer 42. The Falcon's Brother 42. The Falcon in Danger 43. The Falcon out West 44. Bury Me Dead 47. Deep Waters 48. The Men 50. Cavalry Scout 51. The Sniper 52, many others.

Clark, Dane (1913–) (Bernard Zanville). Pint-sized American tough guy of the forties, a poor man's Garfield.

Tennessee Johnson 43. Destination Tokyo 43. The Very Thought of You 44. God is My Co-Pilot 45. A Stolen Life 46. Her Kind of Man 46. That Way with Women 47. Deep Valley 47. Whiplash 48. *Moonrise* 49. Barricade 50. Without Honour 50. Highly Dangerous (GB) 50. Go Man Go (& co-p) 53. Port of Hell 54. The Toughest Man Alive 55. Murder by Proxy (GB) 55. This Man is Armed 56. The Outlaw's Son 57. The McMasters 70, etc.
TV series: Justice 52. Bold Venture 54. Wire Service 56. The New Perry Mason 73.

Clark, Ernest (1912–). British character actor of all media, usually in cold, tight-lipped roles.
Private Angelo 49. Doctor in the House 53. Beau Brummell 54. The Dam Busters 55. Time without Pity 57. A Tale of Two Cities 58. Sink the Bismarck 60. Nothing but the Best 64. Arabesque 66. Salt and Pepper 68, many others.

Clark, Fred (1914–1968). Bald-domed American character comedian, usually in explosive roles.
□The Unsuspected 47. Ride the Pink Horse 47. Hazard 48. Cry of the City 48. Two Guys from Texas 48. Fury at Furnace Creek 48. Mr Peabody and the Mermaid 49. Alias Nick Beal 49. Flamingo Road 49. The Younger Brothers 49. Task Force 49. White Heat 49. The Lady Takes a Sailor 49. *Sunset Boulevard* 50. The Eagle and the Hawk 50. Return of the Frontiersman 50. The Jackpot 50. Mrs O'Malley and Mr Malone 50. The Lemon Drop Kid 51. Hollywood Story 51. A Place in the Sun 51. Meet Me After the Show 51. Three for Bedroom C 52. Dreamboat 52. The Stars are Singing 53. The Caddy 53. How to Marry a Millionaire 53. Here Come the Girls 53. Living It Up 54. Abbott and Costello Meet the Keystone Kops 54. Daddy Longlegs 55. How to be Very Very Popular 55. The Court Martial of Billy Mitchell 55. Miracle in the Rain 56. The Birds and the Bees 56. *The Solid Gold Cadillac* 56. Back from Eternity 56. Joe Butterfly 57. The Fuzzy Pink Nightgown 57. *Don't Go Near the Water* 57. Mardi Gras 58. Auntie Mame 58. The Mating Game 59. It Started with a Kiss 59. Visit to a Small Planet 60. Bells are Ringing 60. Zotz 62. Boys' Night Out 62. Hemingway's Adventures of a Young Man 62. Move Over Darling 63. John Goldfarb Please Come Home 64. The Curse of the Mummy's Tomb (GB) 65. Sergeant Deadhead 65. Dr Goldfoot and the Bikini Machine 65. When the Boys meet the Girls 65. War Italian Style 67. The Horse in the Grey Flannel Suit 68. Skidoo 68. I Sailed to Tahiti with an All-Girl Crew 68.
TV series: *The Double Life of Henry Phyfe* 65. Also with Burns and Allen for several seasons.

Clark, James B. (1908–). American director, former editor.
Under Fire 57. Sierra Baron 58. The Sad Horse 59. A Dog of Flanders 60. One Foot in Hell 60. The Big Show 60. Misty 61. Flipper 63. Island of the Blue Dolphins 64. And Now Miguel 66. My Side of the Mountain 68. The Little Ark 71, etc.

Clark, Jim (1931–). British editor.
The Grass is Greener 61. The Innocents 61. Charade 63. The Pumpkin Eater 64. Darling 65. Zee and Co. 72. The Day of the Locust 75. Marathon Man 76. Yanks 79. Agatha 79. Honky Tonk Freeway 81. The Killing Fields (AA) 84. The Frog Prince 84. The Mission 86, etc.
Also director: □The Christmas Tree 68. Every Home Should Have One 70. Rentadick 72. Madhouse 74.

Clark, Ken (–). American supporting actor, usually in tough roles.
The Proud Ones 56. Between Heaven and Hell 56. Attack of the Giant Leeches 58. Hercules Against the Barbarians 64. From the Orient with Fury 65, many others.

Clark, Marguerite (1883–1940). American heroine of the silent screen, a rival for Mary Pickford in waif-like and innocent roles. Retired 1921.
Wildflower 14. The Goose Girl 15. Molly Make-Believe 16. Snow White 17. Prunella 18. Mrs Wiggs of the Cabbage Patch 18. Girls 19. All-of-a-Sudden Peggy 20. Scrambled Wives 21.

Clark, Matt (–). American character actor, mostly as western villain.
Will Penny 67. Monte Walsh 70. Emperor of the North 73. Hearts of the West 75. Kid Vengeance 77. Brubaker 80. The Legend of the Lone Ranger 81. Honkytonk Man 82. Love Letters 82. Country 84. Return to Oz 84. Tuff Turf 84, etc.

Clark, Petula (1932–). British child actress who later made it big as a singer and settled in France.
□Medal for the General 44. Murder in Reverse 45. London Town 46. Strawberry Roan 47. *Here Come the Huggetts* 48. Vice Versa 48. Easy Money 48. Don't Ever Leave

Me 49. Vote for Huggett 49. The Huggetts Abroad 50. Dance Hall 50. The Romantic Age 50. White Corridors 51. Madame Louise 51. Made in Heaven 52. *The Card* 52. The Runaway Bus 54. The Gay Dog 54. The Happiness of Three Women 55. Track the Man Down 56. That Woman Opposite 57. Daggers Drawn 64. Finian's Rainbow 68. *Goodbye Mr Chips* 69. Never Never Land 81.

Clark, Robert (1905–). British executive, longtime director (resigned 1969) of Associated British Picture Corporation. Former lawyer; producer of many ABPC films including *The Hasty Heart, The Dam Busters*, etc.

Clark, Susan (1940–). Canadian leading lady in Hollywood.
□Banning 67. Madigan 68. Coogan's Bluff 68. Something for a Lonely Man (TV) 68. The Challengers (TV) 68. The Forbin Project 69. Tell Them Willie Boy is Here 69. Skullduggery 69. Valdez is Coming 70. The Skin Game 71. The Astronaut (TV) 71. Showdown 73. Trapped (TV) 73. Airport 75 74. The Midnight Man 74. The Apple Dumpling Gang 75. *Babe* (TV) 75. Night Moves 75. *Amelia Earhart* (TV) 76. Murder by Decree 78. Promises in the Dark 79. City on Fire 79. The North Avenue Irregulars 80. Double Negative 80. Nobody's Perfekt 81. Porky's 81. Maid in America (TV) 82. TV series: Webster 83–

Clarke, Arthur C. (1917–). British science fiction writer who provided the basis for *2001: A Space Odyssey*. Non-fiction interests include the popular science TV series of 1981, *Arthur C. Clarke's Mysterious World.*

Clarke, Charles G. (1899–1983). American cinematographer.
The Light That Failed 23. Friendly Enemies 25. Whispering Smith 26. Upstream 27. The Exalted Flapper 29. So This Is London 30. The Cat and the Fiddle 34. Tarzan and His Mate 34. The Return of the Cisco Kid 39. *Moontide* 42. Guadalcanal Diary 43. *Margie* 46. Miracle on 34th Street 47. The Iron Curtain 48. Sand 49. The Big Lift 50. Destination Gobi 53. Prince of Players 55. Carousel 56. The Barbarian and the Geisha 58. The Sound and the Fury 59. Return to Peyton Place 59. Madison Avenue 62, many others.

Clarke, Mae (1910–). Pert American leading lady at her peak in the early thirties; from musical comedy.
Big Time 29. Fall Guy 30. *The Front Page* 31. *Public Enemy* 31. *Waterloo Bridge* 31. Frankenstein 31. Night World 32. The Penguin Pool Murder 32. Parole Girl 33. Penthouse 33. Lady Killer 33. Nana 34. The Silk Hat Kid 35. Wild Brian Kent 36. Trouble in Morocco 37. Women in War 40. Sailors on Leave 41. Flying Tigers 42. Here Come the Waves 44. Kitty 45. Daredevils of the Clouds 48. Annie Get Your Gun 50. The Great Caruso 51. Because of You 52. Women's Prison 55. Mohawk 56. Ask Any Girl 59. Big Hand for a Little Lady 66. Thoroughly Modern Millie 67, many others.
†Miss Clarke probably regrets that her chief claim to fame arises from having a grapefruit pushed into her face by James Cagney in *Public Enemy*.

Clarke, Shirley (1925–). American director of the New York *cinema vérité* school.
The Connection 60. Cool World 63. Portrait of Jason 67, etc.

Clarke, T. E. B. (1907–). British screenwriter, former journalist; associated with the heyday of Ealing comedy. Autobiography 1974: *This is where I Came In.*
Johnny Frenchman 45. Against the Wind 46. Hue and Cry 46. *Passport to Pimlico* 48. The Blue Lamp 50. *The Lavender Hill Mob* 51. *The Titfield Thunderbolt* 53. Barnacle Bill 57. Law and Disorder 58. Gideon's Day 58. Sons and Lovers 60. The Horse Without a Head 63. A Man Could Get Killed 66, etc.

Clarke-Smith, D. A. (1888–1959). British character actor, mainly on stage.
Atlantic 30. The Ghoul 33. Warn London 34. Sabotage 36. The Flying Fifty-Five 39. Frieda 47. Quo Vadis 51. The Baby and the Battleship 56, etc.

Claudia (US 1943). Rose Franken's whimsical book about a child-wife who matures when she hears that her mother is dying was filmed in 1943 with Dorothy McGuire (who played the role on Broadway) and Robert Young. Three years later came a sequel, *Claudia and David*, with the same stars.

Clavell, James (1922–). Australian writer of Anglo-Irish descent.
The Fly 58. Five Gates to Hell (& pd) 58. Walk Like a Dragon (& pd) 60. The Sweet and the Bitter (wpd) (Can.) 62. The Great Escape 63. The Satan Bug 65. King Rat (oa) 65. To Sir With Love (& pd) 66. Where's Jack? (& pd) 69. Shogun (TV) 80.

¶ *J.C.:* I'm not a novelist, but a storyteller. I'm not a literary figure at all:

Claxton, William F. (–). American director.
Fangs of the Wild 55. The Quiet Gun 57. Desire in the Dust 60. Law of the Lawless 64. Night of the Lepus 72, etc.

Clay, Nicholas (1946–). British leading man.
The Night Digger 71. The Darwin Adventure 75. Tristan and Isolde 76. Zulu Dawn 78. Excalibur 81. Lady Chatterley's Lover 81. Evil Under the Sun 82.

Clayburgh, Jill (1945–). American leading lady of the seventies.
□The Wedding Party 69. The Telephone Book 71. Portnoy's Complaint 72. The Thief Who Came to Dinner 73. The Terminal Man 74. The Art of Crime (TV) 74. *Hustling* (TV) 74. Griffin and Phoenix (TV) 76. *Gable and Lombard* (as Lombard) 76. Silver Streak 76. Semi-Tough 77. *An Unmarried Woman* 78. La Luna 79. Starting Over 79. It's My Turn 80. First Monday in October 81. I'm Dancing as Fast as I Can 82. Hannah K 83. Where Are The Children? 85. Shy People 87.

Clayton, Ethel (1884–1966). American silent star actress.
Her Own Money 12. The College Widow 15. Pettigrew's Girl 19. Sham 21. If I Were Queen 22. The Remittance Woman 23. Wings of Youth 25. Mother Machree 28. Hit the Deck 30. Continental 32. Secrets 33. Artists and Models 37. The Buccaneer 38. Ambush 39, many others.

Clayton, Jack (1921–). British producer-director who worked his way up through the industry.
□The Bespoke Overcoat (pd) 55. Three Men in a Boat (p) 56. *Room at the Top* (d) 58. *The Innocents* (d) 61. *The Pumpkin Eater* (d) 64. Our Mother's House (d) 67. The Great Gatsby (d) 74. Something Wicked This Way Comes 83. The Lonely Passion of Judith Hearne 87.

¶ *J.C.:* I don't believe in being fashionable. Try to be, and you're usually out of date before you start.

Cleese, John (1939–). Tall British comic actor, often on TV satirizing familiar types.
Interlude 68. The Best House in London 68. The Rise and Rise of Michael Rimmer 70. And Now for Something Completely Different 71. The Love Ban 72. Monty Python and the Holy Grail 74. The Life of Brian 79. The Secret Policeman's Ball 80. Time Bandits 82. Privates on Parade 82. Monty Python and the Meaning of Life 83. Yellowbeard 83. *Clockwise* 85, etc.
TV series: *Fawlty Towers* 75, 79.

¶ *J.C.:* Filming is like a long air journey: there's so much hanging around and boredom that they keep giving you food.

Clemens, Brian (1931–). British screenwriter especially associated with *The Avengers*; author of many TV thrillers.
□Station Six Sahara 64. The Corrupt Ones 64. And Soon the Darkness 70. See No Evil 71. Dr Jekyll and Sister Hyde 71. Captain Kronos Vampire Hunter (&d) 72. The Golden Voyage of Sinbad 73.

Clemens, William (1905–). American director of second features.
□Man Hunt 36. The Law in Her Hands 36. The Case of the Velvet Claws 36. Down the Stretch 36. Here Comes Carter 36. Once a Doctor 37. The Case of the Stuttering Bishop 37. Talent Scout 37. The Footloose Heiress 37. Missing Witnesses 37. Torchy Blane in Panama 38. Accidents will Happen 38. Mr Chump 38. Nancy Drew Detective 38. Nancy Drew Reporter 39. Nancy Drew Trouble Shooter 39. Nancy Drew and the Hidden Staircase 39. The Dead End Kids on Dress Parade 39. Calling Philo Vance 40. King of the Lumberjacks 40. Devil's Island 40. She Couldn't Say No 41. Knockout 41. The Night of January 16th 41. A Night in New Orleans 42. Sweater Girl 42. Lady Bodyguard 43. The Falcon in Danger 43. The Falcon and the Co-Eds 43. The Falcon Out West 44. Crime by Night 44. The Thirteenth Hour 47.

Clement, Dick (1937–). British writer-director.
The Jokers (co-w) 67. *Otley* (co-w, d) 69. A Severed Head (d) 70. Villain (w) 71. Catch Me a Spy (co-w, d) 71. The Likely Lads 76. The Prisoner of Zenda (w) 79. Porridge (wd) 79. Bullshot (d) 83. Water (d) 84, etc.

Clément, René (1913–). Distinguished French director whose later films have disappointed.
□*Bataille du Rail* 43. Les Maudits 46. Le Père Tranquille 46. Au Dela des Grilles 49. Le Château de Verre 50. *Les Jeux Interdits* 51. Knave of Hearts (GB) 53. *Gervaise* 55. The Sea Wall 56. Plein Soleil 59. Quelle Joie de Vivre 61. The Day and the Hour 63. The

Love Cage 65. Is Paris Burning? 66. Rider on the Rain 69. The House under the Trees 71. And Hope to Die 72. Wanted: Babysitter 75.

Clementi, Pierre (1941–). French leading actor.
The Leopard 63. *Belle de Jour* 67. Benjamin 68. The Milky Way 70. Pigsty 70. The Conformist 71. Steppenwolf 74. Les Apprentis Sorciers 77. La Chanson de Roland 78, etc.

Clements, Sir John (1910–).
Distinguished British actor-manager, on stage from 1930.
Ticket of Leave 35. Things to Come 36. Rembrandt 36. Knight Without Armour 36. South Riding 38. The Housemaster 39. *The Four Feathers* 39. Convoy 40. This England 41. Ships with Wings 41. Tomorrow We Live 42. Undercover 42. They Came to a City 45. Call of the Blood (& wpd) 47. The Silent Enemy 57. *The Mind Benders* 63. Oh What a Lovely War 69, etc.

Clements, Stanley (1926–1981). American actor familiar in the forties as tough teenager.
Tall Dark and Handsome 41. Going My Way 44. Salty O'Rourke 45. Bad Boy 49. Jet Job 52. Robbers' Roost 55. Up in Smoke 59. Saintly Sinners 61. Tammy and the Doctor 63, many others.

Cléo de 5 à 7 (France 1961). A highly personal film by Agnes Varda about a young woman who thinks she is dying and sees the world around her with heightened perception. With Corinne Marchand; photographed by Jean Rabier.

Cleopatra (69–30 B.C.). The sultry Egyptian queen has been portrayed in many films, notably in a Méliès trick film of 1899; by unspecified American actresses in 1908 and 1909; by Helen Gardner in 1911; by Theda Bara in 1917; by Claudette Colbert in the de Mille version of 1934; by Vivien Leigh in Pascal's 1945 *Caesar and Cleopatra*; by Rhonda Fleming in *Serpent of the Nile* 1953; by Hedy Lamarr in *The Story of Mankind* 1957; by Elizabeth Taylor in the well-publicized 1962 version; and by Amanda Barrie in a spoof, *Carry On Cleo*, in 1963. There seems to be something about the lady that encourages waste, for the Leigh version was Britain's most expensive film and the Taylor version the world's; in neither case did the money show on the screen.

Cleveland, George (1886–1957). American character actor, typically cast as grizzled old prospector.
Keeper of the Bees 35. Revolt of the Zombies 36. Goldtown Ghost Riders 38. Port of Missing Girls 38. Mutiny in the Big House 39. Call Out the Marines 41. The Spoilers 42. Woman of the Town 44. Can't Help Singing 44. Dakota 45. The Runaround 46. The Wistful Widow of Wagon Gap 47. Please Believe Me 50. Trigger Jnr 52. Untamed Heiress 54, many others.
TV series: *Lassie* 55–57.

? clichés
The following lines have come to seem more risible than was the author's original intention. Can you say in what films they originated, and who spoke them?

1 The calla lilies are in bloom again . . .
2 Nothing like this has come to Rome since Romulus and Remus!
3 When you say that, smile!
4 It seemed like a good idea at the time.
5 Cast adrift in an open boat . . .
6 I don't need that spear. It's only a young lion.
7 We have ways of making men talk.
8 You're going out a youngster – but you've got to come back a star!
9 You ain't heard nothing yet!
10 These are modern times . . . 1804 . . .
11 Yes, I killed him. And I'm glad, I tell you. Glad, glad, glad!
12 Excuse me while I slip into something more comfortable . . .
13 If you want anything, just whistle . . .
14 Café Mozart, eight o'clock.

Cliff, Laddie (1891–1937) (Clifford Perry). British light comedian and composer.
The Co-Optimists 30. Sleeping Car 33. Happy 33, etc.

cliffhanger. Trade name for a serial, especially an episode ending in an unresolved situation which keeps one in suspense till next time.

Clift, Montgomery (1920–1966). Romantic American leading actor of stage and screen, usually in introspective roles; his career was jeopardized in 1956 by a car accident which somewhat disfigured him.
Biographies: *Monty* by Robert La Guardia, 1977; *Montgomery Clift* by Patricia Bosworth, 1978.

□*The Search* 48. *Red River* 48. The Heiress 49. The Big Lift 50. *A Place in the Sun* 51. I Confess 53. *From Here to Eternity* 53. Indiscretion of an American Wife 54. Raintree County 57. The Young Lions 58. Lonelyhearts 59. Suddenly Last Summer 59. Wild River 60. The Misfits 60. Judgment at Nuremberg 61. *Freud* 63. The Defector 66.

Clifton, Elmer (1890–1949). American director, mainly of second features; started as an actor with Griffith.
Boots 19. Nugget Nell 19. Mary Ellen Comes to Town 21. Down to the Sea in Ships 22. The Wreck of the Hesperus 27. Virgin Lips 28. Six Cylinder Love 31. Crusade against Rackets 37. Isle of Destiny 40. Swamp Woman 41. Seven Doors to Death 44. Not Wanted 49, many others.

Cline, Edward (1892–1961). American comedy director who began with the Sennett bathing beauties.
Summer Girls 18. Three Ages 23. Captain January 24. Old Clothes 25. *Sherlock Junior* 26. Let it Rain 27. Soft Cushions 27. Ladies Night in a Turkish Bath 27, etc.
□SOUND FILMS COMPLETE: Broadway Fever 29. His Lucky Day 29. The Forward Pass 29. In the Next Room 30. Sweet Mama 30. Leathernecking 30. Hook Line and Sinker 30. The Widow from Chicago 30. Cracked Nuts 31. The Naughty Flirt 31. The Girl Habit 31. *Million Dollar Legs* 32. Parole Girl 33. So This is Africa 33. Peck's Bad Boy 34. The Dude Ranger 34. When a Man's a Man 35. The Cowboy Millionaire 35. It's a Great Life 36. F Man 36. On Again Off Again 37. Forty Naughty Girls 37. High Flyers 37. Hawaii Calls 38. Go Chase Yourself 38. Breaking the Ice 38. Peck's Bad Boy with the Circus 38. *My Little Chickadee* 40. The Villain Still Pursued Her 40. *The Bank Dick* 40. Meet the Chump 41. Cracked Nuts 41. Hello Sucker 41. *Never Give a Sucker an Even Break* 41. Snuffy Smith 32. What's Cookin' 42. Private Buckaroo 42. Give Out Sisters 42. Behind the Eight Ball 42. He's My Guy 43. Crazy House 43. Swingtime Johnny 44. Ghost Catchers 44. Slightly Terrific 44. Moonlight and Cactus 44. Night Club Girl 44. See My Lawyer 45. Penthouse Rhythm 45. Bringing Up Father 46. Jiggs and Maggie in Society 48. Jiggs and Maggie in Court 48.

Clive, Colin (1898–1937) (Clive Greig). British leading man who looked older than his years; in Hollywood from 1930, playing fraught, serious roles.
□*Journey's End* 30. *Frankenstein* (title role) 31. The Stronger Sex (GB) 31. Lily Christine (GB) 32. Christopher Strong 33. Looking Forward 33. The Key 34. *Jane Eyre* (as Rochester) 34. One More River 34. Clive of India 35. The Right to Live 35. *The Bride of Frankenstein* 35. The Girl from Tenth Avenue 35. *Mad Love* 35. The Man who Broke the Bank at Monte Carlo 35. *History is Made at Night* 37. The Woman I Love 37.

Clive, E. E. (1879–1940). British character actor who came late in life to Hollywood and played a succession of sour-faced but often amiable butlers, burgomasters and statesmen, with a sprinkling of lower orders.
□The Invisible Man 33. The Poor Rich 34. The Gay Divorcee 34. Long Lost Father 34. One More River 34. Riptide 34. Bulldog Drummond Strikes Back 34. Charlie Chan in London 34. The Mystery of Edwin Drood 35. *The Bride of Frankenstein* 35. Remember Last Night 35. We're in the Money 35. Gold Diggers of 1935 35. Stars Over Broadway 35. A Tale of Two Cities 35. Captain Blood 35. Atlantic Adventure 35. Father Brown Detective 35. Sylvia Scarlett 35. The Widow from Monte Carlo 35. The King Steps Out 36. Little Lord Fauntleroy 36. Love Before Breakfast 36. Dracula's Daughter 36. The Unguarded Hour 36. Trouble for Two 36. Piccadilly Jim 36. All American Champ 36. Libeled Lady 36. Tarzan Escapes 36. Isle of Fury 36. *The Charge of the Light Brigade* 36. Cain and Mabel 36. Palm Springs 36. Ticket to Paradise 36. Lloyds of London 36. The Dark Hour 36. Live Love and Learn 36. They Wanted to Marry 37. Maid of Salem 37. Bulldog Drummond Escapes 37. *Bulldog Drummond Comes Back* 37. Bulldog Drummond's Revenge 37. Ready Willing and Able 37. It's Love I'm After 37. On the Avenue 37. Love Under Fire 37. Danger Love at Work 37. *Personal Property* 37. Night Must Fall 37. The Emperor's Candlesticks 37. Beg Borrow or Steal 37. Arsène Lupin Returns 38. The First Hundred Years 38. The Last Warning 38. Kidnapped 38. Gateway 38. Submarine Patrol 38. Bulldog Drummond's Peril 38. Bulldog Drummond in Africa 38. Arrest Bulldog Drummond 39. I'm from Missouri 39. The Little Princess 39. Bulldog Drummond's Secret Police 39. Man About Town 39. Bulldog Drummond's Bride 39. The Hound of the Baskervilles 39. Rose of Washington Square 39. The Adventures of Sherlock Holmes 39. The Honeymoon's Over 39. Raffles 39. Bachelor Mother 39. The Earl of Chicago 40. Congo Maisie 40. Pride and Prejudice 40. Foreign Correspondent 40.

Cloche, Maurice (1907–). French director, in films (as documentarist) from 1933.
La Vie est Magnifique 38. Monsieur Vincent 47. Cage aux Filles 48. Né de Père Inconnu 50. Les Filles de la Nuit 57. Coplan, Secret Agent 64, etc.

Cloerec, René (1911–). French composer. Douce 43. Le Diable au Corps 46. The Red Inn 51. Occupe-Toi d'Amélie 51. La Blé en Herbe 53. En Cas de Malheur 57, many others.

Clooney, Rosemary (1928–). Breezy American cabaret singer who made a few film appearances. A TV movie, *Rosie*, was filmed in 1982.
Autobiography 1977: *This for Remembrance*.
□The Stars are Singing 53. Here Come the Girls 53. *Red Garters* 54. *White Christmas* 54. Deep in My Heart 54.

Cloquet, Ghislain (–1982). Belgian cinematographer. Mickey One 65. Love and Death 75. *Tess* (AA) 79.

Close Encounters of the Third Kind (US 1977). An extremely thin and pretentious piece of science fiction, made on an unnecessarily massive budget to accommodate elaborate and fairly convincing space craft which visit earth for no particular purpose. *It Came from Outer Space* in 1955 was more suspenseful, at least as meaningful, and had a better plot; but the audiences of the seventies were out for what seemed like novelty, and obediently trooped along. Written and directed by Steven Spielberg, with a battery of photographers and not much dialogue one could hear; with Richard Dreyfuss in an unplayable part. Eighteen months after its release. Spielberg had second thoughts and issued a so-called 'Special Edition' which rang the box office bell only in Great Britain. It wisely eliminated the mud-building in the kitchen, but unwisely added some scenes inside the space ship, which made it look rather like the Empire Exhibition of 1924.

Close, Glenn (1945–). American leading actress of the eighties. The World According to Garp 82. The Big Chill (AAN) 84. Something about Amelia (TV) 84. The Natural (AAN) 84. Maxie 85. *Jagged Edge* 85. *Fatal Attraction* 87.

Closely Observed Trains (Czechoslovakia 1966). Jiri Menzel's oddly likeable little tragi-comedy won the 1968 Academy Award for the best foreign film. Apart from a strangely downbeat ending, it consists of a number of amusing scenes and characters set in a country railway station during World War II.

close-up. Generally applied to a head-and-shoulders shot of a person or any close shot of an object. The first close-up is said to be that of Fred Ott sneezing in an Edison experimental film of 1900. See *long shot.*

Clothier, William H. (1903–). American cinematographer.
Sofia 48. Confidence Girl 52. Track of the Cat 54. Blood Alley 55. The Man in the Vault 56. The Horse Soldiers 59. The Alamo 60. The Deadly Companions 61. The Man Who Shot Liberty Valance 62. A Distant Trumpet 64. Cheyenne Autumn 64. Shenandoah 65. The Way West 67. The War Wagon 67. Firecreek 67. The Devil's Brigade 68. Hellfighters 68. The Cheyenne Social Club 70. Big Jake 71. The Train Robbers 73, etc.

Clouse, Robert (–). American director.
Happy Mothers Day, Love George (w only) 73. Enter the Dragon 73. Golden Needles 74. Black Belt Jones 74. The Ultimate Warrior (wd) 74.

Cloutier, Suzanne (1927–). French-Canadian leading lady.
Temptation (US) 46. Au Royaume des Cieux 47. Juliette ou la Clef des Songes 50. Othello 51. Derby Day (GB) 51. Moulin Rouge 53. Romanoff and Juliet (US) 61, etc.

Clouzot, Henri-Georges (1907–1977). French writer-director, noted for suspense melodramas.
Un Soir de Rafle (w) 31. Le Dernier des Six (w) 41. Les Inconnus dans la Maison (w) 42. L'Assassin Habite au 21 (wd) 42. *Le Corbeau* (wd) 43. *Quai des Orfèvres* (wd) 47. Manon (wd) 49. Retour à la Vie (wd) 49. *The Wages of Fear* (wd) 53. *Les Diaboliques* (wd) 54. The Picasso Mystery (wd) 56. Les Espions (wd) 57. The Truth (wd) (AA) 60. La Prisonnière (wd) 70, etc.

Clouzot, Vera (1921–1960). Portuguese actress, wife of H. G. Clouzot.
The Wages of Fear 53. Les Diaboliques 54. Les Espions 57, etc.

Clunes, Alec (1912–1970). British stage actor who made occasional film appearances. Convoy 40. Saloon Bar 40. Melba 53.

Quentin Durward 56. *Richard III* 56. Tomorrow at Ten 62, etc.

Clurman, Harold (1901–1980). American stage director chiefly associated with New York's Group Theatre of the thirties. Directed one very pretentious film: *Deadline at Dawn* 46. Autobiography 1974: *All People Are Famous.*

Clute, Chester (1891–1956). American character comedian. His startled look, small stature, tiny moustache and bald pate made him an inimitable henpecked husband or harassed clerk in scores of films.
Dance Charlie Dance 37. Rascals 38. Annabel Takes a Tour 38. Dancing Co-Ed 39. Hired Wife 40. She Couldn't Say No 41. Yankee Doodle Dandy 43. Chatterbox 43. Arsenic and Old Lace 44. Guest Wife 45. Angel on my Shoulder 46. Something in the Wind 47. Mary Ryan Detective 46, many others.

Clyde, Andy (1892–1967). Scottish acrobatic comedian, long in Hollywood as western side-kick and hero of innumerable two-reelers, often as grizzled, toothless old fool.
The Goodbye Kiss 28. Million Dollar Legs 32. The Little Minister 34. McFadden's Flats 35. Two in a Crowd 36. Abe Lincoln in Illinois 39. The Green Years 46, many others.
TV series: The Real McCoys 57–60. Lassie 63. No Time for Sergeants 64–65.

coal mines and the bravery of the men who work in them formed a theme which commanded the respect of cinema audiences for many years. Apart from *Kameradschaft* (the French-German border), *Black Fury* (US), and *The Molly Maguires* (US) all the major films on this subject have been about Britain: *The Proud Valley, The Stars Look Down, How Green Was My Valley, The Citadel, The Corn is Green, The Brave Don't Cry, Sons and Lovers, Women in Love.*

Coates, Anne V. (1925–). British editor.
Grand National Night 53. Lost 56. The Horse's Mouth 59. Tunes of Glory 60. Lawrence of Arabia (AA) 63. Becket 64. The Bofors Gun 68. The Adventurers 70. Bequest to the Nation 73. Murder on the Orient Express 74. The Eagle Has Landed 77. The Legacy 79. The Elephant Man 80. Ragtime 81. The Bushido Blade 81, many others.

Coates, Eric (1886–1957). British composer.
□The Old Curiosity Shop 35. Nine Men 43. The Dam Busters 55. High Flight 57.

Cobb, Irvin S. (1876–1944). American humorous writer who appeared in a few films and was touted as another Will Rogers after that actor's death.
□Pardon My French 21. Peck's Bad Boy 21. The Five Dollar Baby 22. The Great White Way 24. Turkish Delight 27. *Steamboat Round the Bend* 34. Everybody's Old Man 36. Pepper 36. Hawaii Calls 38. The Arkansas Traveller 38. The Young in Heart 38.

Cobb, Lee J. (1911–1976) (Leo Jacoby). Powerful American character actor who forsook stage for screen.
□North of the Rio Grande 37. Ali Baba Goes to Town 37. Rustler's Valley 37. Danger on the Air 38. The Phantom Creeps 39. *Golden Boy* 39. Men of Boys' Town 41. This Thing Called Love 41. Paris Calling 42. Tonight We Raid Calais 43. Buckskin Frontier 43. *The Moon is Down* 43. The Song of Bernadette 43. Winged Victory 44. *Anna and the King of Siam* 46. Boomerang 47. Johnny O'Clock 47. Captain from Castile 47. Call Northside 777 48. The Miracle of the Bells 48. The Luck of the Irish 48. *The Dark Past* 48. Thieves' Highway 49. The Man Who Cheated Himself 50. Sirocco 51. The Family Secret 51. The Fighter 52. The Tall Texan 53. Yankee Pasha 54. Gorilla at Large 54. *On the Waterfront* 54. Day of Triumph 54. The Racers 55. The Road to Denver 55. The Left Hand of God 55. *The Man in the Grey Flannel Suit* 56. Miami Exposé 56. *Twelve Angry Men* 57. The Garment Jungle 57. The Three Faces of Eve 57. The Brothers Karamazov 58. Man of the West 58. Party Girl 58. The Trap 59. Green Mansions 59. But Not for Me 59. Exodus 60. The Four Horsemen of the Apocalypse 62. How the West Was Won 62. *Come Blow Your Horn* 63. Our Man Flint 66. In Like Flint 67. Il Giorno della Guetta (It.) 67. Mackenna's Gold 68. Coogan's Bluff 68. They Came to Rob Las Vegas 68. The Liberation of L. B. Jones 70. Macho Callahan 70. Lawman 70. Heat of Anger (TV) 71. Double Indemnity (TV) 73. The Exorcist 73. The Man Who Loved Cat Dancing 73. Dr Max (TV) 74. The Great Ice Rip-Off (TV) 74. Trapped Beneath the Sea (TV) 74. That Lucky Touch 75.
TV series: *The Virginian* 62–66. The Young Lawyers 70.

Coborn, Charles (1852–1945) (Colin McCallum). British music hall artiste famous for his longevity and his rendering of 'The Man Who Broke the Bank at Monte Carlo'.
Say it with Flowers 34. Music Hall 35. Variety Jubilee 41, etc.

Coburn, Charles (1877–1961). Distinguished American actor. A stage star for many years, he came late in life to Hollywood and delighted audiences for another twenty years in roles of crusty benevolence.
□Boss Tweed 33. The People's Enemy 35. Of Human Hearts 38. Vivacious Lady 38. Yellow Jack 38. Lord Jeff 38. Idiot's Delight 39. The Story of Alexander Graham Bell 39. Made for Each Other 39. *Bachelor Mother* 39. Stanley and Livingstone 39. In Name Only 39. Road to Singapore 40. Florian 40. Edison the Man 40. Three Faces West 40. The Captain is a Lady 40. *The Lady Eve* 41. *The Devil and Miss Jones* 41. Our Wife 41. Unexpected Uncle 41. H. M. Pulham Esq. 41. King's Row 41. In This Our Life 42. George Washington Slept Here 42. *The More the Merrier* (AA) 43. The Constant Nymph 43. *Heaven Can Wait* 43. Princess O'Rourke 43. My Kingdom for a Cook 43. *Knickerbocker Holiday* 44. Wilson 44. The Impatient Years 44. Together Again 44. A Royal Scandal 45. Rhapsody in Blue 45. Over 21 45. Colonel Effingham's Raid 45. Shady Lady 45. *The Green Years* 46. Lured 47. BF's Daughter 48. The Paradine Case 48. Green Grass of Wyoming 48. Impact 49. Yes Sir That's My Baby 49. Everybody Does It 49. The Doctor and the Girl 49. The Gal who Took the West 49. Louisa 50. Peggy 50. Mr Music 50. The Highwayman 51. *Monkey Business* 52. *Has Anybody Seen My Gal?* 52. Gentlemen Prefer Blondes 53. Trouble along the Way 53. The Long Wait 54. The Rocket Man 54. How to Be Very Very Popular 55. The Power and the Prize 56. Around the World in Eighty Days 56. Town on Trial 57. The Story of Mankind 57. How to Murder a Rich Uncle 57. Stranger in My Arms 59. The Remarkable Mr Pennypacker 59. John Paul Jones (as Benjamin Franklin) 59. Pepe 60.
❀ For becoming a beloved international star after the age of sixty. *The More the Merrier*.
Famous line (to Marilyn Monroe, playing his secretary in *Monkey Business*): 'Find someone to type this.'
Famous line (to Barbara Stanwyck in *The Lady Eve*): 'We must be crooked but never common.'

Coburn, James (1928–). American leading man of lithe movement and easy grin; career has been patchy.
□Ride Lonesome 59. Face of a Fugitive 59. *The Magnificent Seven* 60. Hell is for Heroes 62. The Great Escape 63. *Charade* 63. The Man from Galveston 64. The Americanization of Emily 64. Major Dundee 65. A High Wind in Jamaica 65. The Loved One 65. *Our Man Flint* 66. What Did You Do in the War, Daddy? 66. Dead Heat on a Merry Go Round 66. In Like Flint 67. Waterhole Three 67. The President's Analyst 67. Duffy 68. Candy 68. Hard Contract 68. Blood Kin 69. *A Fistful of Dynamite* 71. The Carey Treatment 72. The Honkers 72. A Reason to Live, A Reason to Die 72. Pat Garrett and Billy the Kid 73. The Last of Sheila 73. Harry in Your Pocket 73. The Internecine Project (GB) 74. Bite the Bullet 75. Hard Times 75. The Last Hard Men 75. Midway 76. Sky Riders 76. Cross of Iron 77. The Dain Curse (TV) 78. California Suite 78. Firepower 79. The Muppet Movie 79. Goldengirl (TV) 79. Loving Couples 80. The Baltimore Bullet 80. Mr Patman 80. Looker 81. High Risk 81. Malibu (TV) 83. Digital Dreams 83. Draw! 84. Sins of the Father (TV) 85. Martin's Day 85. The Lions Roar 85. The Leonski Incident 85. Death of a Soldier 86.
TV series: Klondyke 60. Acapulco 60.

Coca, Imogene (1908–). American TV appearances.
Under the Yum Yum Tree 64. Rabbit Test 78. The Return of the Beverly Hillbillies (TV) 81 National Lampoon's Vacation 83.
TV series: *Grindl* 63. It's About Time 66.

Cochise (c. 1818–1874). Peace-loving Apache Indian chief who became a prominent cinema character after Jeff Chandler played him in *Broken Arrow* 50, and later in *Battle at Apache Pass* 52 and *Taza Son of Cochise* 53. John Hodiak took over for *Conquest of Cochise* 53. Previously, Antonio Moreno had played him in *Valley of the Sun* and Miguel Inclan in *Fort Apache*. Michael Ansara took over in the TV series *Broken Arrow*.

Cochran, Steve (1917–1965) (Robert Cochran). American leading man, usually a good-looking heavy, in mainly poor films.
Wonder Man 45. The Best Years of Our Lives 46. The Chase 46. The Kid from Brooklyn 47. A Song is Born 48. White Heat 49. The Damned Don't Cry 50. *Storm Warning* 50. The Tanks are Coming 51. Operation Secret 52. The Desert Song 53. Carnival Story 54. *Come Next Spring* 56. The Weapon (GB) 56. I, Mobster 58. The Beat Generation 59. The Deadly Companions 61. Of Love and Desire 63. Mozambique 65, etc.

Coco, James (1928–87). Chubby American comic actor.

□Ensign Pulver 64. Generation 69. End of the Road 70. The Strawberry Statement 70. Tell Me That You Love Me Junie Moon 70. A New Leaf 71. Such Good Friends 71. Man of La Mancha 72. *The Wild Party* 75. Murder by Death 76. Bye Bye Monkey 78. The Cheap Detective 78. Charleston 78. Scavenger Hunt 79. Wholly Moses 80. Only When I Laugh 81. The Muppets Take Manhattan 84.
TV series: Calucci's Department 73. The Dumplings 76.

Cocteau, Jean (1889–1963). Fanciful French poet and writer who occasionally dabbled in cinema with effective if slightly obscure results.
□*Le Sang d'un Poète* (wd) 30. La Comédie du Bonheur (w) 40. Le Baron Fantôme (w) 43. L'Eternel Retour (w) 43. Les Dames du Bois de Boulogne (co-w) 44. *La Belle et la Bête* (w, co-d) 46. Ruy Blas (w) 47. L'Aigle a Deux Têtes (d) 48. Les Parents Terribles (wd) 48. Les Enfants Terribles (w) 50. *Orphée* (wd) 50 *Le Testament d'Orphée* (wd) 59. La Princesse de Clèves (w) 60. Thomas l'Imposteur (w) 65.
❀ For bringing a unique visual imagination to the cinema. *Orphée*.
¶ *J.C.:* A film is a petrified fountain of thought.

Codee, Ann (1890–1961). American character actress who played a variety of middle-aged roles for many years.
Hi Gaucho 35. Captain Caution 40. Old Acquaintance 44. The Other Love 47. On the Riviera 51. Kiss Me Kate 53. Daddy Long Legs 55. Can Can 59, etc.

Cody, Iron Eyes (–). American Indian actor.
The Iron Horse 24. Ride 'Em Cowboy 42. The Paleface 48. Broken Arrow 50. Sitting Bull 54. The Great Sioux Massacre 67. El Condor 70, many others.

Cody, Lew (1884–1934) (Louis Coté). Smartly-dressed American leading man of the silent screen; his French accent affected his sound career.
Comrade John 15. The Demon 18. *Don't Change Your Husband* 19. The Sign on the Door 21. Secrets of Paris 22. Within the Law 23. *Rupert of Hentzau* (title role) 23. The Shooting of Dan McGrew 24. Exchange of Wives 25. Adam and Evil 27. On Ze Boulevard 27. Beau Broadway 28. What a Widow 30. Dishonoured 31. Sporting Blood 31. The Tenderfoot 32. Sitting Pretty 33. Shoot the Works 34, many others.

Cody, William Frederick (Buffalo Bill) (1846–1917). American guide, Indian scout, bison hunter and carnival showman. He has been played in movies by James Ellison in *The Plainsman* 36, Joel McCrea in *Buffalo Bill* 42, Louis Calhern in *Annie Get Your Gun* 50, Charlton Heston in *Pony Express* 52, Clayton Moore in *Buffalo Bill in Tomahawk Territory* 53, Gordon Scott in *Buffalo Bill* (Ger.) 64, Guy Stockwell in *The Plainsman* 66 and Paul Newman in *Buffalo Bill and the Indians* 76. He was a favourite hero of silent movies.

Coe, Barry (1934–). American juvenile actor of the fifties.
On The Threshold of Space 56. Peyton Place 57. The Bravados 58. One Foot in Hell 60. The 300 Spartans 62, etc.
TV series: Follow the Sun 61.

Coe, Fred (1914–79). American producer-director from stage and TV.
The Left-handed Gun (p) 58. The Miracle Worker (p) 62. A Thousand Clowns (pd) 65. Me Natalie (d) 69, etc.

Coe, Peter (1929–). British director with stage experience. First film: *Lock Up Your Daughters* 69.

Coen, Franklin (–). American screenwriter.
This Island Earth (co-w) 55. The Train (co-w) 64. Alvarez Kelly 66, etc.

co-feature. A moderate-budget production designed (or fated) to form equal half of a double bill.

Coffee, Lenore (–1984). American screenwriter.

Coffin, Tristam (–). American actor.
No Greater Sin 41. Blackmail 47. Outrage 50. Undercover Girl 50, etc.
TV series: 26 Men 56.

Coghlan, Junior (1916–) (Frank Coghlan). American boy star of the twenties; previously played baby roles.
Slide, Kelly, Slide 26. The Country Doctor 27. River's End 31. Penrod and Sam 32. Boys' Reformatory 39. The Adventures of Captain Marvel (serial) 40. Henry Aldrich for President 41. The Sand Pebbles 66.

Cohan, George M. (1878–1942). Dapper American actor-dancer-author-composer of the Broadway stage. Songs include: 'Mary's a Grand Old Name', 'Give My Regards to Broadway', 'Over There', 'Yankee Doodle Dandy'; plays include the much-filmed *Seven Keys to Baldpate* (qv). Film appearances: *Broadway Jones* 16. *Hit-the-Trail Holiday* 18. *The Phantom President* 32. *Gambling* 34, etc. Was impersonated by James Cagney in a biopic, *Yankee Doodle Dandy* 42, and in *The Seven Little Foys* 55.

¶ *G.M.C.:* (to Spencer Tracy): Whatever you do, kid, always serve it with a little dressing.

G.M.C.: I don't care what you say about me so long as you spell my name right.

Cohen, Herman (c. 1928–85). American producer and director of low-budget horror films.
I Was a Teenage Werewolf 57. Konga 61. Black Zoo 63. Berserk 68. Crooks and Coronets 69. Trog 70. Craze 73, etc.

Cohen, Larry (1938–). American creator of 'realist' horror films.
Bone 72. It's Alive (wpd) 76. Demon (wpd) 77. The Private Files of J. Edgar Hoover 77. Dial Rat for Terror (Housewife) (wpd) 80. It Lives Again (wpd) 80. The Winged Serpent 81, etc.

Cohen, Norman (1936–1983). Irish director.
□Brendan Behan's Dublin 67. The London Nobody Knows 68. Till Death Us Do Part 68. Dad's Army 70. Adolf Hitler, My Part in His Downfall 72. Stand Up Virgin Soldiers 77.

The Cohens and the Kellys. This series of domestic farces about a Jew and an Irishman played by George Sidney and Charlie Murray began in 1926 (title as shown). Subsequent adventures were: (*The Cohens and Kellys*) *in Paris* 28, *in Scotland* 30, *in Africa* 31, *in Hollywood* 33, *in Trouble* 33, etc.

Cohl, Emile (1857–1938) (Emile Courte). Pioneer French cartoonist of the 1908–18 period.
Fantasmagorie 08. Les Allumettes Animées 09. Don Quichotte 09. Aventures d'une Bout de Papier 11. Monsieur Stop 13. Snookums (series) (US) 13–15. Les Pieds Nickelés 18, many others.

Cohn, Arthur (1928–). Swiss producer.
The Sky Above the Mud Below 63. Woman Times Seven 67. Sunflower 70. *The Garden of the Finzi-Continis* (AA) 71. Wolf of the Seven Seas 74. Black and White in Colour (co-p) 76. Dangerous Moves (AA) 84, etc.

Cohn, Harry (1891–1958). American executive, chief of Columbia Pictures (qv) for many years; a former song-plugger and vaudevillian who built the company in 1924, reputedly from his sales of a film called *Traffic in Souls*.
Biography 1967: *King Cohn*, by Bob Thomas.
❁ For enjoying his career as an ogre and for bringing a Poverty Row studio up to the big time. *Gilda*.

¶ When the big boss of Columbia Studios died in 1958, you could take your pick of brickbats and bouquets. The most famous tasteless comment came from Red Skelton on hearing of the huge crowds at Cohn's funeral:

> It proves what they always say: give the public what they want to see, and they'll come out for it.

Then there was Hedda Hooper:

> You had to stand in line to hate him.

And George Jessel:

> Hed was a great showman, and he was a son of a bitch.

And Elia Kazan:

> He liked to be the biggest bug in the manure pile.

And Samuel Goldwyn:

> He never learned how to live.

And Budd Schulberg:

> He was the meanest man I ever knew—an unreconstructed dinosaur.

But Cohn had a few defenders. There was Artie Shaw:

> He was a lovable old pirate.

And, surprisingly, Ethel Barrymore:

> He knew the score.

One thing was sure, Cohn thoroughly enjoyed his long tyranny. He said once:

> Gower Street is paved with the bones of my executive producers.

And again:

> I don't have ulcers: I give them.

Despite his frequent ill-treatment of actors and other creative people, he always averred:

> I kiss the feet of talent.

He was disappointed in the treatment he got back from the stars he had created:

> I have never met a grateful performer in the movies.

He maintained his confidence in his own ability:

> Great pictures make great stars. This girl (Novak) has had five hit pictures. Send me your mother or your aunt and we will do the same for them.

He certainly knew what he wanted, and he had a long record of success. One of his mottoes was:

Let Rembrandt make character studies, not Columbia.

He once said to Daniel Taradash:

Promise me you'll never make a picture where the characters walk out of the room backward.

He claimed:

All I need to make pictures is an office.

In a more self-knowing mood, he admitted:

If I wasn't head of a studio, who would talk to me?

But he concluded:

It's better than being a pimp.

He once expounded his entire philosophy to Robert Parrish, who had asked to be allowed to direct good pictures:

I make fifty-two pictures a year here. Every Friday the front door opens on Gower Street and I spit a picture out. A truck picks it up and takes it away to the theatres, and that's the ball game. Now, if that door opens and I spit and nothing comes out, you and everybody else around here is out of work. So let's cut this crap about only good pictures . . . I run this place on the basis of making *one* good picture a year. I'll lay everything on the line for that one. I don't care if it's Capra, or Ford, or Riskin; or Milestone—that's the good one. The rest of the time I just have to keep spitting out.

As Frank Sinatra said:

He had a sense of humour like an open grave.

† Columbia was once known as the Pine Tree Studio (because it has so many Cohns).

cokuloris. A palette with random irregular holes, placed between lights and camera to prevent glare and give a better illusion of real-life light and shadow.

Colbert, Claudette (1905–) (Lily Claudette Chauchoin). French leading lady who went to America as a child and became one of Hollywood's most durable and versatile light actresses of the golden age, most typically cast in smart emancipated roles.

☐For the Love of Mike 28. The Hole in the Wall 29. The Lady Lies 29. The Big Pond 30. Young Man of Manhattan 30. Manslaughter 30. Honour among Lovers 31. The Smiling Lieutenant 31. Secrets of a Secretary 31. His Woman 31. The Wiser Sex 32. Misleading Lady 32. The Man from Yesterday 32. The Phantom President 32. *The Sign of the Cross* (as Poppaea) 32. Tonight is Ours 33. I Cover the Waterfront 33. *Three Cornered Moon* 33. The Torch Singer 33. Four Frightened People 34. *It Happened One Night* (AA) 34. Cleopatra 34. *Imitation of Life* 34. The Gilded Lily 35. Private Worlds 35. She Married Her Boss 35. The Bride Comes Home 35. Under Two Flags 36. Maid of Salem 37. *I Met Him in Paris* 37. Tovarich 37. Bluebeard's Eighth Wife 38. Zaza 39. *Midnight* 39. It's a Wonderful World 39. Drums along the Mohawk 39. Boom Town 40. *Arise My Love* 40. Skylark 41. Remember the Day 41. *The Palm Beach Story* 42. So Proudly We Hail 43. No Time for Love 43. *Since You Went Away* 44. Practically Yours 45. Guest Wife 45. Tomorrow is Forever 46. Without Reservations 46. The Secret Heart 46. *The Egg and I* 47. Sleep My Love 48. Family Honeymoon 49. Bride for Sale 49. *Three Came Home* 50. The Secret Fury 50. Thunder on the Hill 51. Let's Make it Legal 51. The Planter's Wife (GB) 52. Love and the Frenchwoman 54. Si Versailles M'était Conte 55. Texas Lady 55. Parrish 60. The Two Mrs Grenvilles (TV) 86.

❀ For being more than a match for her male stars through twenty years of romantic comedy. *Midnight.*

¶ *C.C. in Midnight:* The moment I saw you, I had an idea you had an idea.

the cold war has occupied the cinema right from Churchill's Fulton speech in 1948. For three years diehard Nazis had been the international villains par excellence, but a change was required, and Russians have been fair game ever since, in films like *The Iron Curtain, Diplomatic Courier, I Was a Communist for the FBI, I Married a Communist, The Big Lift, Red Snow, The Red Danube, Red Menace, Red Planet Mars, The Journey, From Russia With Love* and innumerable pulp spy thrillers, as well as such classier productions as *The Third Man, The Man Between* and *The Spy Who Came in from the Cold.* Rather surprisingly none of these caused much escalation of tension between the nations, and cooler feelings have permitted comedies like *One Two Three, Dr Strangelove* and *The Russians are Coming, The Russians are Coming*; while such terrifying panic-button melodramas as *Fail Safe* and *The Bedford Incident* are probably our best guarantee that the dangers are realized on both sides.

Cole, Dennis (1940–). American general purpose actor who plays almost entirely on television.
Powderkeg (TV) 70. The Connection (TV) 73. Barbary Coast (TV) 74. Cave-In (TV) 79.
TV series: *The Felony Squad* 66–68. Lancer 68–69. Bearcats 71.

Cole, George (1925–). British comedy actor who made his film debut as a cockney child evacuee; usually plays the befuddled innocent.
Cottage to Let 41. Henry V 44. *Quartet* 48. Morning Departure 50. Laughter in Paradise 50. Lady Godiva Rides Again 51. Scrooge 51. *Top Secret* 51. Will Any Gentleman? 52. Happy Ever After 53. Our Girl Friday 53. The Belles of St Trinian's 54. A Prize of Gold 55. The Weapon 56. It's a Wonderful World 56. The Green Man 57. Blue Murder at St Trinian's 58. Too Many Crooks 58. The Bridal Path 59. The Pure Hell of St Trinian's 60. Cleopatra 62. Dr Syn 63. One-Way Pendulum 64. The Legend of Young Dick Turpin 65. The Great St Trinian's Train Robbery 66. The Vampire Lovers 70. Fright 71. Take Me High 73. The Bluebird 76, etc.
TV series: *A Man of Our Times* 68. *Minder* 79–81, 84. The Bounder 81.

Cole, Jack (1914–1974). American dancer and choreographer.
Moon Over Miami (d) 41. Kismet (d) 44. Tonight and Every Night (ch) 45. The Jolson Story (ch) 46. On the Riviera (ch) 51. Designing Woman (dch) 55. Let's Make Love (ch) 61, etc.

Cole, Lester (1904–85). American screenwriter. If I Had a Million 32. The President's Mystery 34. The Crime of Dr Hallet 36. The Invisible Man Returns 39. Hostages 42. None Shall Escape 44. Objective Burma 45. Blood on the Sun 45. The Romance of Rosy Ridge 47. High Wall 48. Operation Eichmann (as Lewis Copley) 61, etc. One of the blacklisted Hollywood Ten.

Cole, Michael (–). American leading man, mostly on television.
The Last Child (TV) 71. Beg Borrow or Steal (TV) 73. Evening in Byzantium (TV) 78, etc.
TV series: *The Mod Squad* 68–72.

Cole, Nat King (1919–65) (Nathaniel Coles). American Negro pianist and singer who made occasional film appearances.
The Blue Gardenia 53. St Louis Blues (as W. C. Handy) 58. The Night of the Quarter Moon 59. *Cat Ballou* 65, etc.

Cole, Sidney (1908–). British producer, a former editor who worked at Ealing through its finest hours. Subsequently produced Black Beauty (72) and Dick Turpin (78) for TV.

Coleman, Charles (1885–1951). Australian character actor in Hollywood; almost always played the perfect portly butler.
That's my Daddy 28. Bachelor Apartment 31 Gallant Lady 33. Down to Their Last Yacht 34. Poor Little Rich Girl 36. That Certain Age 38. Mexican Spitfire 39. It Started with Eve 41. Twin Beds 42. The Whistler 44. The Runaround 46. The Imperfect Lady 47, many others.

Coleman, Cy (1929–). American song composer, usually with lyricist **Carolyn Leigh** (1926–). *Sweet Charity* is his only score to be filmed.

Coleman, Dabney (1932–). American comic actor, usually the heavy.
This Property Is Condemned 66. I Love My Wife 70. The Brotherhood of the Bell (TV) 70. Bad Ronald (TV) 74. Returning Home (TV) 75. Maneaters Are Loose (TV) 78. North Dallas Forty 79. How to Beat the High Cost of Living 80. Melvin and Howard 80. *Nine to Five* 80. Nothing Personal 80. On Golden Pond 81. Young Doctors in Love 82. Tootsie 82. War Games 83. The Muppets Take Manhattan 84. Cloak and Dagger 85. The Man with One Red Shoe 85, Dragnet 87, etc.
TV series: That Girl 66–70. Mary Hartman, Mary Hartman 76. Forever Fernwood 77. Buffalo Bill 83.

Coleman, Gary (1968–). Black American juvenile actor, star of TV's *Diff'rent Strokes*.
On the Right Track 81. Jimmy the Kid 82. The Kid with the Broken Halo (TV) 82. The Kid with the 200 IQ (TV) 82. Jimmy the Kid 82. The Fantastic World of D. C. Collins (TV) 83. Playing with Fire (TV) 84.

Coleman, Nancy (1917–). American leading lady of the forties, usually in timid roles.
King's Row 42. Dangerously They Live 42. The Gay Sisters 42. Desperate Journey 42. Edge of Darkness 43. In Our Time 44. *Devotion* (as Anne Brontë) 45. Her Sister's Secret 46. Mourning Becomes Electra 47. That Man from Tangier 53. Slaves 68, etc.

Colette (Sidonie-Gabrielle Colette) (1873–1954). French writer, usually on sex themes.

Claudine à l'Ecole 38. Gigi 48 and 58. Julie de Carnelihan 50. L'Ingénue Libertine 51. Ripening Seed 54.

Colicos, John (1928–). Canadian character actor in occasional films.
Anne of the Thousand Days 70. Raid on Rommel 71. Red Sky at Morning 71. Doctors' Wives 71. The Wrath of God 72. Scorpio 73. Drum 76. Breaking Point 76. Phobia 80. The Changeling 80. The Postman Always Rings Twice 81, etc.
TV series: Battlestar Galactica 78.

Colin, Jean (1905–). British leading lady of the thirties; appearances sporadic.
The Hate Ship 30. Compromising Daphne 30. *The Mikado* 39. Bob's Your Uncle 41. Laxdale Hall 54, etc.

Colin, Sid (1920–). British TV comedy scriptwriter.
I Only Arsked 58. The Ugly Duckling 59. Up Pompeii 70. Up the Chastity Belt 71. Up the Front 72. Percy's Progress 74, etc.

Colla, Richard A. (–). American director.
Zigzag 70. *Fuzz* 72. Live Again, Die Again (TV) 74. The Tribe (TV) 74. The UFO Incident (TV) 75.

Colleano, Bonar (1924–1958) (Bonar Sullivan). Wise-cracking American actor, from family of acrobats; worked chiefly in Britain.
The Way to the Stars 45. A Matter of Life and Death 46. While the Sun Shines 46. Good Time Girl 47. One Night With You 48. Sleeping Car to Trieste 48. Pool of London 50. A Tale of Five Cities 52. Eight Iron Men (US) 52. The Sea Shall Not Have Them 55. Interpol 57. No Time To Die 58, etc.

colleges: see *universities.*

Collier, Constance (1878–1955) (Laura Constance Hardie). Distinguished British stage actress who spent her later years in Hollywood playing great ladies with caustic tongues and eccentric habits.
Autobiography 1929: *Harlequinade.*
□Intolerance 16. The Code of Marcia Gray 16. Macbeth 16. Bleak House 20. The Bohemian Girl 22. *Our Betters* 33. Dinner at Eight 33. Peter Ibbetson 34. Shadow of Doubt 35. Anna Karenina 35. Girls' Dormitory 36. Professional Soldier 36. Little Lord Fauntleroy 36. Thunder in the City 37. Wee Willie Winkie 37. *Stage Door* 37. She Got What She Wanted 37. A Damsel in Distress 37. Zaza 39. Susan and God 40. Half a Sinner 40. Weekend at the Waldorf 45. *Kitty* 45. Monsieur Beaucaire 46. The Dark Corner 46. The Perils of Pauline 47. *An Ideal Husband* 48. Rope 48. The Girl from Manhattan 48. Whirlpool 50.

Collier, John (1901–1980). British writer of polished macabre stories; his screen work was sporadic.
Sylvia Scarlett 35. Her Cardboard Lover 42. Deception 46. Roseanna McCoy 49. The Story of Three Loves 53. I Am a Camera 55. The War Lord 65, etc.

Collier, Lois (1919–) (Madelyn Jones). American leading lady of forties B pictures.
A Desperate Adventure 38. The Phantom Plainsman 42. Cobra Woman 44. Weird Woman 44. Ladies Courageous 44. The Naughty Nineties 45. The Crimson Canary 45. The Cat Creeps 46. A Night in Casblanca 46. Slave Girl 47. Out of the Storm 48. Miss Mink of 1949 49. Flying Disc Man from Mars 51. Missile Monsters 58, etc.

Collier, William (1866–1944) (William Senior). American stage actor, usually of comedy character roles; moved to Hollywood in 1929.
Six Cylinder Love 31. The Cheater 34. Josette 38. Thanks for the Memory 38. Invitation to Happiness 39. There's Magic in Music 41, many others.

Collin, John (1931–). British character actor.
Star! 68. Before Winter Comes 69. Innocent Bystanders 72, etc.

Collinge, Patricia (1892–1974). Irish-American stage actress who made occasional film appearances.
The Little Foxes 41. Shadow of a Doubt 43. Casanova Brown 44. Teresa 51. The Nun's Story 58, etc.

Collings, David (1940–). British character actor, much on TV.
Scrooge (as Bob Cratchit) 70. Elizabeth R (TV) 71. Mahler 74. Hennessy 75. The 39 Steps 78.

Collins, Anthony (1893–1964). British composer.
The Rat 37. Victoria the Great 37. Sixty Glorious Years 38. Nurse Edith Cavell 40.

The Courtneys of Curzon Street 47. Odette 50. Derby Day 52. Laughing Anne 53, etc.

Collins, Cora Sue (1927–). American child star of the thirties.
They Just Had to Get Married 33. Queen Christina 33. Torch Singer 34. The Scarlet Letter 35. Anna Karenina 35. Magnificent Obsession 36. The Adventures of Tom Sawyer 38, etc.

Collins, Eddie (1884–1940). American character comedian from Vaudeville; crowded a few films into his last years.
In Old Chicago 38. Kentucky Moonshine 38. Charlie Chan in Honolulu 38. Young Mr Lincoln 39. Hollywood Cavalcade 39. *The Bluebird* 39. The Return of Frank James 40.

Collins, Gary (1938–). Easy-going American leading man, familiar on television in the seventies: the lead in *Born Free* (series).
The Pigeon That Took Rome 62. Airport 69. Killer Fish 77, etc.
Other TV series: The Wackiest Ship in the Army 65. The Iron Horse 66. The Sixth Sense 72.

Collins, Jackie (1939–). British light novelist, sister of Joan Collins. Works filmed include *The World Is Full of Married Men*, *The Stud*, *The Bitch*.

Collins, Joan (1933–). British leading lady whose sultry charms won her parts in an assortment of international films.
Autobiography 1978: *Past Imperfect*.
I Believe in You 52. Cosh Boy 53. Our Girl Friday 53. Turn the Key Softly 53. The Good Die Young 54. Land of the Pharaohs 55. The Virgin Queen 55. The Girl in the Red Velvet Swing 55. The Opposite Sex 56. The Wayward Bus 57. Island in the Sun 57. Sea Wife 57. The Bravados 58. Rally Round the Flag Boys 58. Seven Thieves 60. Road to Hong Kong 62. Warning Shot 66. Heironymus Merkin 69. The Executioner 69. Subterfuge 69. Up in the Cellar 70. Drive Hard, Drive Fast (TV) 70. Quest for Love 71. Revenge 71. Tales That Witness Madness 73. Alfie Darling 74. I Don't Want to Be Born 75. The Moneychangers (TV) 76. Empire of the Ants 77. The Stud 78. The Bitch 79. Game for Vultures 79. Sunburn 79. Nutcracker 82. The Wild Women of Chastity Gulch (TV) 82. The Making of a Male Model (TV) 83. Her Life as a Man (TV) 84. The Cartier Affair (TV) 85. Sins (TV) 85. Monte Carlo (TV) 86, etc.
TV series: *Dynasty* 81– .

¶ *J.C.:* Dynasty was the opportunity to take charge of my career rather than walking around like a library book waiting to be loaned out.

J.C.: (of her character in *The Bitch*): She appears to have the world by the balls, but underneath she's trying to solve the problem of loneliness, which I think is the universal problem of all rich people.

J.C.: Even when you win the rat race, you're still a rat.

J.C.: The secret of having a personal life is not answering too many questions about it.

Collins, Lewis (1946–). British leading man familiar from TV's *The Professionals* 78–80.
Who Dares Wins 82.

Collins, Ray (1890–1965). American stage actor who came to Hollywood with Orson Welles, stayed to play kindly uncles and political bosses.
□The Grapes of Wrath 40. *Citizen Kane* (as Boss Jim Geddes) 41. The Big Street 42. Highways by Night 42. The Navy Comes Through 42. The Commandos Strike at Dawn 42. *The Magnificent Ambersons* 42. The Human Comedy 43. Slightly Dangerous 43. Crime Doctor 43. Salute to the Marines 43. Whistling in Brooklyn 43. See Here Private Hargrove 43. The Hitler Gang 44. The Eve of St Mark 44. The Seventh Cross 44. Barbary Coast Gent 44. Can't Help Singing 44. Roughly Speaking 45. The Hidden Eye 45. Miss Susie Slagle's 45. Leave Her to Heaven 45. Up Goes Maisie 46. A Night in Paradise 46. Badman's Territory 46. Boys' Ranch 46. Crack-Up 46. Three Wise Fools 46. Two Years Before the Mast 46. The Return of Monte Cristo 46. The Best Years of Our Lives 46. *The Bachelor and the Bobbysoxer* 47. Red Stallion 47. The Swordsman 47. The Senator Was Indiscreet 47. Homecoming 48. A Double Life 48. Good Sam 48. For the Love of Mary 48. The Man from Colorado 48. Command Decision 48. Red Stallion in the Rockies 48. Hideout 49. It Happens Every Spring 49. The Fountainhead 49. The Heiress 49. Free for All 49. Francis 49. Paid in Full 50. Kill the Umpire 50. The Reformer and the Redhead 50. Summer Stock 50. You're in the Navy Now 51. Ma and Pa Kettle Back on the Farm 51. Vengeance Valley 51. Reunion in Reno 51. I Want You 51. The Racket 51. Invitation 52. Dreamboat

52. Young Man with Ideas 52. The Desert Song 53. Ma and Pa Kettle at the Fair 53. Column South 53. Ma and Pa Kettle on Vacation 53. The Kid from Left Field 53. Bad for Each Other 53. Rose Marie 54. Athena 54. The Desperate Hours 55. Texas Lady 55. Never Say Goodbye 56. The Solid Gold Cadillac 56. Spoilers of the Forest 57. Touch of Evil 58. I'll Give My Life 61.
TV series: Halls of Ivy 54. Perry Mason 57–65.

Collins, Russell (1897–1965). Hardened-looking American character actor.
Shockproof 49. Niagara 53. Miss Sadie Thompson 53. Bad Day at Black Rock 55. Soldier of Fortune 56. The Enemy Below 57. The Matchmaker 58. Fail Safe 64, etc.
TV series: The Detectives 59–61. Many Happy Returns 64.

Collins, Wilkie (1824–89). British novelist, credited with being the inventor of the detective story via *The Moonstone,* whose complications have resisted filming. *The Woman in White* however was filmed with some fidelity in 1947.

Collinson, Peter (1938–1980). British director who quickly slumped from arty pretentiousness to routine thrillers.
□The Penthouse 67. Up the Junction 68. The Long Day's Dying 68. *The Italian Job* 69. You Can't Win 'em All 70. Fright 71. Straight on till Morning 72. Innocent Bystanders 72. The Man Called Noon 73. Open Season 74. And Then There Were None 74. The Spiral Staircase 75. The Sell Out 75. Tomorrow Never Comes 77. Tigers Don't Cry 77. The House on Garibaldi Street (TV) 79. The Earthling 80.

Collyer, June (1907–1968) (Dorothy Heermance). American leading lady in a few light films of the early thirties; married Stuart Erwin.
Woman Wise 27. East Side West Side 28. Charley's Aunt 31. Alexander Hamilton 31. The Ghost Walks 35, etc.
TV series: The Stuart Erwin Show 53.

Colman, Ronald (1891–1958).
Distinguished British romantic actor whose gentle manners, intelligence and good looks thrilled two generations. Turned to acting after World War I wounds, and went to Hollywood in 1920.
Biography 1975: *A Very Private Person* by Juliet Benita Colman.
□The Toilers 19. A Son of David 19. The Snow in the Desert 19. The Black Spider 20. Anna The Adventuress 20. Handcuffs or Kisses 21. The Eternal City 23. *The White Sister* 23. Twenty Dollars a Week 24. Tarnish 24. Romola 24. Her Night of Romance 24. A Thief in Paradise 24. His Supreme Moment 25. The Sporting Venus 25. Her Sister from Paris 25. *The Dark Angel* 25. Stella Dallas 25. Lady Windermere's Fan 25. Kiki 26. *Beau Geste* 26. The Winning of Barbara Worth 26. The Night of Love 27. The Magic Flame 27. The Lovers 28. The Rescue 29. *Bulldog Drummond* 29. Condemned 29. *Raffles* 30. The Devil to Pay 30. The Unholy Garden 31. *Arrowsmith* 31. Cynara 32. The Masquerader 33. Bulldog Drummond Strikes Back 34. Clive of India 35. The Man who Broke the Bank at Monte Carlo 35. *A Tale of Two Cities* 35. Under Two Flags 36. *Lost Horizon* 37. *The Prisoner of Zenda* 37. If I were King 38. The Light that Failed 39. Lucky Partners 40. My Life with Caroline 41. *The Talk of the Town* 42. *Random Harvest* 42. Kismet 44. The Late George Apley 47. *A Double Life* (AA) 48. Champagne for Caesar 50. Around the World in Eighty Days 56. The Story of Mankind 57.
TV series: *Halls of Ivy* 54.
❁ For conquering world audiences by steadfastly playing the old-fashioned British gentleman adventurer in a number of elegant guises. *The Prisoner of Zenda.*

¶ 'He is as ingratiating when he talks as when he was silent.'—*New York Times 1929*

'He led the perfect colonial life in Hollywood. The longer he stayed there the more English he got—but he never wanted to go home.'—*Douglas Fairbanks Jnr*

R.C. (to his agent): Before God I'm worth 35 dollars a week. Before the motion picture industry I'm worth anything you can get.

'He is an excellent director's dummy. He has no personality of his own, only an appearance.'—*alleged screen test report.*

'When Colman looks at the camera, the whole world knows what he is thinking.'—*New Yorker 1937*

Colonna, Jerry (1903–86). American comic actor with strong, high-pitched voice, walrus moustache and bulging eyes.
College Swing 38. Little Miss Broadway 38. Road to Singapore 39. Sis Hopkins 41. True to the Army 42. Star-Spangled Rhythm 42. Ice Capades 42. Atlantic City 44. It's in the Bag 45. Road to Rio 47. Kentucky Jubilee 51. Meet Me in Las Vegas 56. Andy Hardy Comes Home 58, etc.

colour prints of a primitive kind were made

as long ago as 1898. During the next few years many films were hand-coloured by stencil, and two unsatisfactory processes, KinemaColor and Gaumont colour, were tried out. D. W. Griffith in *The Birth of a Nation* 14 developed the French practice of tinting scenes for dramatic effect: blue for night, orange for sunshine, etc. In 1918 red-and-green Technicolor was tried out along with half a dozen other processes. 1921: Prizmacolour was used for the British historical film *The Great Adventure*. 1923: de Mille used a colour sequence in *The Ten Commandments*. 1926: *The Black Pirate* was shot in two-colour Technicolor. 1932: first three-colour Technicolor film, Disney cartoon *Flowers and Trees* (AA). 1934: colour used in dramatic sequences of *La Cucaracha* and *The House of Rothschild*. 1935: first feature film entirely in three-strip colour, *Becky Sharp*. 1937: first British Technicolor feature, *Wings of the Morning*. 1939: two-colour Cinecolor, very cheap, became popular for low-budget westerns. 1942: Technicolor introduced monopack process, using one negative instead of three and making equipment less cumbersome and more flexible. 1948: Republic adopted Trucolor. 1949: Anscocolor, later to become Metrocolor, used on *The Man on the Eiffel Tower*. 1951: Supercinecolor (3 colours) adopted by Columbia in *Sword of Monte Cristo*. 1952: Eastmancolor used in *Royal Journey*; Warners adopted it as Warnercolor. 1954: Fox adopted De Luxe Color.

Today, with new colours springing up all the time, effectiveness seems to depend not on the trademark but on how well the film is shot, processed and printed.

colour sequences in otherwise black-and-white movies were used at first experimentally (see above) but have also been employed for dramatic effect. Early examples include *The Ten Commandments* 23, *Ben Hur* 26, *The Wedding March* 28, *Chasing Rainbows* 30; many of the early sound musicals went into colour for their final number, and this went on as late as *Kid Millions* 35. *Victoria the Great* 37 had colour for the final 'Empress of India' scenes. *The Wizard of Oz* 39 had the Oz scenes in colour and the Kansas scenes in sepia. *Irene* 40 went into colour for the 'Alice Blue Gown' number—which made the second half of the film anti-climactic. *The Moon and Sixpence* 42 blazed into colour for the fire at the end . . . and the same director, Albert Lewin, used a similar trick whenever the picture was shown in *The Picture of Dorian Gray* 44. *A Matter of Life and Death* 45 had earth in colour, heaven in a rather metallic monochrome. *Task Force* 49 went into colour for its final battle reels, most of which consisted of blown-up 16mm war footage. *The Secret Garden* 49 played the same trick as *The Wizard of Oz*. *The Solid Gold Cadillac* 56 had a few final feet of colour to show off the irrelevant car of the title. In 1958 *I Was a Teenage Frankenstein* revived the old dodge of colour for the final conflagration. In *Cleo de 5 à 7* only the ominous Tarot cards were in colour. In *Irene* only the Alice Blue Gown sequence. In *The House of Rothschild* only the court finale. In *If*, nobody was ever able to work out why black and white alternated with colour until someone guessed that the producers kept on running out of money as shooting progressed. And *Is Paris Burning?* 66 used colour for the climactic victory sequence, having been forced into black-and-white for the rest of the movie by the necessity of using old newsreel footage. In few of the above cases has reissue printing maintained the original intention: printing short sequences in colour is time-consuming. See also: *tinting*.

? colours of the rainbow

Films often have colourful titles. For the following fifteen films, supply the colour.

1 *The Fuzzy . . . . . . Nightgown*
2 *The . . . . . . Danube* (1949)
3 *The Man in the . . . . . . Suit*
4 *. . . . . . Planet Mars*
5 *The . . . . . . Gardenia*
6 *. . . . . . Sky*
7 *The . . . . . . Mask*
8 *The . . . . . . Jungle*
9 *. . . . . . Tuesday*
10 *. . . . . . Banners*
11 *The . . . . . . House*
12 *. . . . . . Fire*
13 *The . . . . . . Kimono*
14 *. . . . . . Angel* (1952)
15 *Big . . . . . .*

Now for fifteen in which the colour is given; but supply the missing word.

16 *. . . . . . Scarlet*
17 *The . . . . . . Wore Black*
18 *The . . . . . . Wore Red*
19 *. . . . . . in a Golden Eye*
20 *. . . . . . with Red Hair*
21 *The . . . . . . in Green*
22 *The . . . . . . in Grey*
23 *Navy Blue and . . . . . .*
24 *The . . . . . . in White*
25 *Red . . . . . . and Blue*

26 . . . . . . *Amber*
27 *Blue, White and . . . . . .*
28 *Black Market . . . . . .*
29 . . . . . . *Over the White House*
30 *Blue . . . . . ., White . . . . . .*

Colpi, Henri (1921–). French editor.
Night and Fog 55. The Picasso Mystery 56. Hiroshima Mon Amour 59. Last Year in Marienbad 61, many others.
Also director: □Une Aussi Longue Absence 61. Codine 63. Mona 66. Heureux Qui Comme Ulysse 70. Mysterious Island 73.

Columbia Pictures. American production and distribution company long considered one of the 'little two' (the other being Universal) against the 'big five' (MGM, RKO, Fox, Warner and Paramount). Columbia originated with one man, Harry Cohn, who founded it in 1924 after a career as a salesman and shorts producer. Throughout the thirties and forties he turned out competent co-features and second features, apart from prestige pictures such as the Capra comedies and an ill-fated Kramer deal; he was also prepared to spend big money on certainties such as Rita Hayworth and *The Jolson Story*. From the late forties, with films like *All the King's Men, Born Yesterday* and *From Here to Eternity*, the company began to pull itself into the big-time, and when Cohn died in 1958 it was one of the leaders of international co-production, with such major films to its credit as *On the Waterfront* and *The Bridge on the River Kwai,* with *Lawrence of Arabia* and *A Man For All Seasons* to come. It also produces and distributes TV films through its subsidiary Screen Gems (Columbia Television).
Books: *King Cohn* by Bob Thomas; *Hail Columbia* by Rochelle Larkin.

Columbo, Russ (1908–1934) (Ruggerio de Rudolpho Columbo). American violinist, vocalist, songwriter and bandleader who appeared in a few films.
Wolf Song 29. The Street Girl 29. Hellbound 31. Broadway through a Keyhole 33. Wake Up and Dream 34, etc.

Colvig, Vance (1892–1967). American actor who spent most of his career at the Disney studio and became the voice for Pluto and Goofy. He was also co-author of the song 'Who's Afraid of the Big Bad Wolf?'

combined print. One on which both sound and picture (always produced separately) have been 'married', i.e. a standard print as shown in cinemas. See *double-headed print.*

Comden, Betty (1918–) (Elizabeth Cohen). American screenwriter who has collaborated with Adolph Green on books and lyrics of many Broadway shows and films.
Good News 47. The Barkleys of Broadway 49. On the Town 49. Singin' in the Rain 52. Band Wagon 54. Auntie Mame 58. What a Way to Go 64, etc.

? comebacks
Each of the following films featured the reappearance of a former star who had not been seen on the big screen for at least five years. Name the stars concerned.

1 *The Prime of Miss Jean Brodie* (1969)
2 *Hi Diddle Diddle* (1943)
3 *Bernardine* (1957)
4 *None But the Lonely Heart* (1944)
5 *The Great Man* (1956)
6 *State Fair* (1962)
7 *Madame X* (1966)
8 *Some Like It Hot* (1959)
9 *We Were Strangers* (1948)
10 *Sunset Boulevard* (1950)
11 *Mad Wednesday* (1947)
12 *Mister Roberts* (1955)
13 *Hud* (1963)

? comedians
Here are some of the less successful films of well-known comedians. Which comedians?

1 *Welcome Danger*
2 *Dance with Me Henry*
3 *The Rogue Song*
4 *Just My Luck*
5 *A Dog's Life*
6 *Battling Butler*
7 *Man About Town*
8 *On the Double*
9 *Dandy Dick*
10 *The Old Fashioned Way*
11 *We're Going to Be Rich*
12 *Oh Sailor Behave*
13 *Hoots, Mon*
14 *The Farmer's Daughter* (1940)
15 *Some Like It Hot* (1939)
16 *Forty Little Mothers*
17 *The Big Mouth*
18 *Get Cracking*
19 *Earthworm Tractors*
20 *Straight, Place and Show*

comedy: see *comedy teams; crazy comedy; light comedians; satire; sex; social comedy; slapstick.*

? **comedy**
Film buffs should have no difficulty in tracking down the classic comedies from which these memorable moments emanate . . .

1 You shouldn't eat chocolates in your condition, Mr . . . . . . It's very bad for you.
– I had an aunt who ate a box of chocolates every day of her life. She lived to be a hundred and two, and when she had been dead three days, she looked healthier than you do now.

2 If I find a forgotten man first, I win. Is that clear?

3 If we bring a little joy into your humdrum lives, it makes us feel our work ain't been in vain for nothin'.

4 This is the screwiest picture I was ever in.

5 I understand we understand each other.
– Quite.

6 No beds. They can't have beds!

7 If we had known, we would have greeted you with flowers.
– Don't make an issue of my womanhood.

8 Behold the walls of Jericho! Maybe not as thick as the ones Joshua blew down with his trumpet, but a lot safer. You see, I have no trumpet.

9 Why, was I so unattractive, so distant, so forbidding?
– You were extremely attractive, and as for distant and forbidding, quite the reverse, but you were also a little the worse, or better, for wine, and there are rules about that.

10 Remember, men, we're fighting for this woman's honour . . . which is probably more than she ever did!

comedy teams in the accepted sense began in vaudeville, but, depending so much on the spoken word, could make little headway in films until the advent of the talkies. Then they all tried, and many (Amos 'n' Andy, Gallagher and Shean, Olsen and Johnson) didn't quite make it, at least not immediately. Laurel and Hardy, who had been successful in silents by the use of mime, adapted their methods very little and remained popular; during the thirties they were really only challenged by Wheeler and Woolsey, whose style was more frenetic, and briefly by Burns and Allen. From 1940 the cross-talking Abbott and Costello reigned supreme, with an occasional challenge from Hope and Crosby and the splendid *Hellzapoppin* from Olsen and Johnson. Then came Martin and Lewis, who didn't appeal to everybody, Rowan and Martin, who in 1957 didn't appeal to anybody, and sporadic attempts to popularize such teams as Brown and Carney and Allen and Rossi. In Britain, comedy teams were popular even in poor films: the best of them were Jack Hulbert and Cicely Courtneidge, Tom Walls and Ralph Lynn, Lucan and MacShane ('Old Mother Riley'), Arthur Askey and Richard Murdoch, and the Crazy Gang, a bumper fun bundle composed of Flanagan and Allen, Naughton and Gold, and Nervo and Knox. One should also mention Basil Radford and Naunton Wayne, not cross-talkers but inimitable caricaturists of the Englishman abroad; and others, not strictly comedians, who raised a lot of laughs together: Edmund Lowe and Victor McLaglen, Slim Summerville and Zasu Pitts, Joan Blondell and Glenda Farrell, George Sidney and Charlie Murray, Marie Dressler and Polly Moran, Wallace Beery and Raymond Hatton, James Cagney and Pat O'Brien. Recent teams include Morecambe and Wise and Cannon and Ball. See *Movie Comedy Teams* by Leonard Maltin.

Of larger groups, among the most outstanding are Our Gang, the Keystone Kops, the Marx Brothers, the Three Stooges, the Ritz Brothers, Will Hay with Moore Marriott and Graham Moffat, the 'Carry On' team, the Beatles and the Monty Python team.

See also: *romantic teams*.

¶ Nobody should try to play comedy unless they have a circus going on inside.—*Ernst Lubitsch*

Comencini, Luigi (1916–). Italian director.
Bambini in Città 46. Proibito Rubare 48. The Mill on the Po (co-writer only) 49. La Città Si Difende (co-writer only) 51. Persiane Chiuse 51. Bread, Love and Dreams (& w) 53. Bread, Love and Jealousy 54. Mariti in Città 58. Bebo's Girl 63. Le Bambole (part) 65. Misunderstood 67. Casanova 69, etc.

Comer, Anjanette (1942–). American leading lady.
Quick Before It Melts 65. The Loved One 65. The Appaloosa 66. Banning 66. Guns for San Sebastian 68. Rabbit, Run 70. The Firechasers (TV) 70. The Baby 73. Lepke 74. Fire Sale 77, etc.

Comfort, Lance (1908–1966). British director, formerly cameraman.

Penn of Pennsylvania 41. Hatter's Castle 41. When We Are Married 42. Old Mother Riley, Detective 42. Daughter of Darkness (& p) 45. Great Day 45. Silent Dust 48. Portrait of Clare 50. Eight o'Clock Walk 54. At the Stroke of Nine 57. Make Mine a Million 58. The Ugly Duckling 59. Touch of Death 62. Tomorrow at Ten 62. Devils of Darkness 65, others.

Directed many episodes of TV series, especially *Douglas Fairbanks Presents* which he also co-produced.

comic strips in newspapers have always been avidly watched by film producers with an eye on the popular market. Among films and series so deriving are the following:

Gertie the Dinosaur (cartoon series) 19; The Gumps (two-reelers) 23–28; *Bringing Up Father* 16 (drawn), 20 (two-reeler), 28 (feature with J. Farrell MacDonald and Marie Dressler), 45 (series of 'Jiggs and Maggie' features with Joe Yule and Renee Riano); *The Katzenjammer Kids* (cartoon series) 17 and 38, *Krazy Kat* (various cartoons 16–38); *Ella Cinders* (with Colleen Moore) 22; *Tillie the Toiler* (with Marion Davies) 27; *Skippy* (with Jackie Cooper) 30; *Little Orphan Annie* 32 (with Mitzi Green) and 38 (with Ann Gillis); *Joe Palooka* 34 (with Stu Erwin) and 47–51 (with Joe Kirkwood); *Blondie* (with Penny Singleton) 38–48; *Gasoline Alley* (with James Lydon) 51; *Lil Abner* (qv); *Popeye* (qv); *Jungle Jim* 49–54; *Prince Valiant* 54; *Up Front* 51–53; *Felix the Cat* (qv); *Old Bill* (GB) 40; *Dick Barton* (GB) in various personifications; *Jane* (GB) in an abysmal 1949 second feature; and, of course, *Modesty Blaise* 66, *Batman* 66, *Barbarella* 68, and *Fritz the Cat* 71.

Strip characters whose adventures were turned into Hollywood serials during the thirties and forties include *Tailspin Tommy, Mandrake the Magician, Don Winslow of the Navy, Jet Jackson Flying Commando, Flash Gordon, Batman, Buck Rogers in the 25th century, Brick Bradford* ('in the centre of the earth'), *Chandu, Superman, Dick Tracy* (also in forties features), *The Lone Ranger* and *Red Ryder*.

In the late seventies comic strip characters became popular TV action heroes, and until the balloon burst audiences were overwhelmed by the antics of *The Incredible Hulk, Wonder Woman, Buck Rogers in the 25th Century*, etc., following on the success of TV's own creations in this vein, *The Six Million Dollar Man, Bionic Woman* and *The Man from Atlantis*.

Comin' thro the Rye (GB 1924). A sentimental Victorian love story directed by Cecil Hepworth. Slow-moving but pleasantly photographed, it is valued as an example of the 'superior' British silent film of its time. Starred Alma Taylor and James Carew. (Miss Taylor had also starred with Stewart Rome in an earlier 1916 version, also directed by Hepworth.)

Comingore, Dorothy (1913–1971). American actress who made few films but will always be remembered as the second Mrs Kane. Formerly known as Kay Winters and Linda Winters.

□Campus Cinderella 38. Comet over Broadway 38. Prison Train 38. Trade Winds 38. Blondie Meets the Boss 39. North of the Yukon 39. Scandal Sheet 39. Mr Smith Goes to Washington 39. Café Hostess 39. Pioneers of the Frontier 40. *Citizen Kane* 41. The Hairy Ape 44. Any Number Can Play 49. The Big Night 51.

? common words

Supply the one word which is missing from the following groups of titles. All the films are first features: no age limit.

1 *Paris . . . . . .: Family . . . . . .: . . . . . . for Three*
2 *It's . . . . . . I'm After: Appointment for . . . . . .: . . . . . . Crazy*
3 *They Came to a . . . . . .: . . . . . . for Conquest: . . . . . . Streets*
4 *Escape in the . . . . . .: . . . . . . Fury: The Painted . . . . . .*
5 *Hired . . . . . .: Fired . . . . . .: Behold My . . . . . .*
6 *. . . . . . Girl: The . . . . . .: The Wild . . . . . .*
7 *Mr . . . . . .: . . . . . . for Millions: The . . . . . . Lovers*
8 *The . . . . . . Changes: . . . . . .'s End: Up the . . . . . .*
9 *. . . . . . of Events: The . . . . . .: Night . . . . . .*
10 *. . . . . . on Trial: Our . . . . . .: . . . . . . without Pity*
11 *A Stolen . . . . . .: A Double . . . . . .: . . . . . . Returns*
12 *The . . . . . . People: . . . . . . Command: . . . . . . Patrol*
13 *No Time for . . . . . .: The . . . . . . Man: The Human . . . . . .*
14 *. . . . . . of Strangers: . . . . . . of Bamboo: . . . . . . of Numbers*
15 *. . . . . . the Sun: . . . . . . That Dream: . . . . . . the Boys*
16 *The . . . . . .'s Our Home: New . . . . . .: Over the . . . . . .*
17 *The . . . . . . Dawn: . . . . . . Alibi: . . . . . . City*

18 *Thrill of a . . . . . : . . . . . . on the High Seas: An American . . . . . .*
19 *. . . . . . Happy: Party . . . . . . :*
The . . . . . . Hunters
20 *. . . . . . of Surrender: . . . . . . without End: The Desert . . . . . .*
21 *Love . . . . . . : The Deadly . . . . . . : Top Secret . . . . . .*
22 *The . . . . . . Below: Beloved . . . . . . : Public . . . . . .*
23 *The . . . . . . Years: . . . . . . Fire: The . . . . . . Glove*
24 *Star Spangled . . . . . . : Broadway . . . . . : . . . . . . on the River*
25 *Pick a . . . . . . : . . . . . . of Midnight: Make Me a . . . . . .*

communism has always been treated by Hollywood as a menace. In the thirties one could laugh at it, in *Ninotchka* and *He Stayed for Breakfast*. Then in World War II there was a respite during which the virtues of the Russian peasantry were extolled in such films as *Song of Russia* and *North Star*. But with the Cold War, every international villain became a commie instead of a Nazi, and our screens were suddenly full of dour dramas about the deadliness of 'red' infiltration: *I Married a Communist, I Was a Communist for the FBI, The Red Menace, The Iron Curtain, Trial, My Son John, Walk East on Beacon, The Red Danube, Red Snow, Red Planet Mars, Blood Alley, Big Jim McLain, The Manchurian Candidate*. In the early sixties a documentary compilation of red aggression was released under the title *We'll Bury You*. The British never seemed to take the peril seriously, though the agitator in *The Angry Silence* was clearly labelled red.
† 'Communism,' said the butler in *Soak the Rich*, 'is the growing pains of the young.'

Como, Perry (1912–) (Pierino Como; also known as Nick Perido). American popular singer of Italian ancestry and barber apprenticeship. His deceptively relaxed manner made him immensely popular on television in the sixties and seventies.
□Something for the Boys 44. Doll Face 45. If I'm Lucky 46. Words and Music 48.

¶ *P.C.:* The audience knows I'm not going to do anything after all these years to upset them.

'I'm convinced that his voice comes out of his eyelids.'—*Oscar Levant*

compilation films have become commonplace on TV through such series as *Twentieth Century, Men of Our Time* and *The Valiant Years*, all using library material to evoke a pattern of the past. Thanks to the careful preservation of original documentary material, film-makers have been able, over the last thirty years or so, to give us such films on a wide variety of subjects and to develop an exciting extra dimension of film entertainment which also serves a historical need.

The first outstanding efforts in this direction were made by H. Bruce Woolfe in his twenties documentaries of World War I, mixing newsreel footage with reconstructed scenes. In 1940 Cavalcanti assembled his study of Mussolini, *Yellow Caesar*; and in 1942 Frank Capra, working for the US Signal Corps, gave a tremendous fillip to the art of the compilation film with his 'Why We Fight' series. Paul Rotha's *World of Plenty* 43 was a clever study of world food shortages using all kinds of film material including animated diagrams and acted sequences. In 1945 Carol Reed and Garson Kanin, in *The True Glory*, gave the story of D-Day to Berlin an unexpected poetry, and in 1946 Don Siegel in his short *Hitler Lives* showed all too clearly what a frightening potential the compilation form had as propaganda. Nicole Védrès in 1947 turned to the more distant past and in *Paris 1900* produced an affectionate portrait of a bygone age; Peter Baylis followed this with *The Peaceful Years*, covering the period between the two wars. In 1950 Stuart Legg's *Powered Flight* traced the history of aviation.

The Thorndikes, working in East Germany, started in 1956 their powerful series *The Archives Testify*, attributing war crimes to West German officials; this aggressive mood was followed in their *Du und Mancher Kamerad* ('The German Story') and *The Russian Miracle*, though in the latter case they seemed somewhat less happy in praising than in blaming. In 1959 George Morrison's *Mise Eire* graphically presented the truth of the much-fictionalized Irish troubles; and in 1960 came the first of the films about Hitler, Erwin Leiser's *Mein Kampf*, to be sharply followed by Rotha's *The Life of Adolf Hitler* and Louis Clyde Stoumen's rather fanciful *Black Fox*. Jack Le Vien, producer of the last-named, went on to make successful films about Churchill (*The Finest Hours*) and the Duke of Windsor (*A King's Story*). Now every year the compilations come thick and fast. From France, *Fourteen-Eighteen*; from BBC TV, twenty-six half-hours of *The Great War*; from Granada TV, *The Fanatics* (suffragettes), *The World of Mr Wells* (H.G., that is) and a long-running weekly series, *All Our Yesterdays*, which consisted entirely of old newsreels; from Associated-British, *Time to Remember*, a series devoting half an hour to each year of the century; from Italy, *Allarmi Siam' Fascisti*, a history of the fascist movement; from Japan, *Kamikaze*, about the suicide pilots; from France, Rossif's *Mourir à Madrid* and *The Fall of Berlin*. The list will be endless, because even though every foot of old newsreel were used up, one could begin again, using different editing, juxtapositions and commentary to achieve different effects. Best book on the subject: Jay Leyda's *Films Beget Films*.

In the late fifties there began a pleasing fashion for compilations of scenes from fictional films on a theme. This began with Robert Youngson's masterly evocations of silent slapstick: *The Golden Age of Comedy*, *When Comedy Was King*, etc. TV series such as *Silents Please* and *Hollywood and the Stars* followed suit. In the seventies MGM had an immense success with *That's Entertainment*, compiled from its past successes, and also brought out *The Big Parade of Comedy*. Twentieth Century Fox turned its backlog into a television series, *That's Hollywood*; and for a while wherever one looked in Hollywood there was at least one studio cutting room devoted to turning over and reassembling highlights of the past.

See also: *documentary*.

composers have frequently been lauded on cinema screens, usually in story lines which bore little relation to their real lives, and the films were not often box office successes. Here are some of the subjects of musical biopics:

George Frederick Handel (1685–1759): Wilfred Lawson, *The Great Mr Handel* 42.

Wolfgang Amadeus Mozart (1756–91): Stephen Haggard, *Whom the Gods Love* 36; Hannes Steltzer, *Die Kleine Nachtmusik* 39; Gino Cervi, *Eternal Melody* 39; Oskar Werner, *The Life of Mozart* 56; Tom Hulce, *Amadeus* (84).

Ludwig van Beethoven (1770–1827): Albert Basserman, *New Wine* 41; Ewald Balser, *Eroica* 49; Karl Boehm, *The Magnificent Rebel* 60.

Niccolò Paganini (1782–1840): Stewart Granger, *The Magic Bow* 47.

Franz Schubert (1797–1828): Nils Asther, *Love Time* 34; Richard Tauber, *Blossom Time* 34; Hans Jaray, *Unfinished Symphony* 35; Alan Curtis *New Wine* 41; Tino Rossi, *La Belle Meunière* 47; Claude Laydu, *Symphony of Love* 54; Karl Boehm, *Das Dreimaederlhaus* 58.

Vincenzo Bellini (1801–35); Phillips Holmes, *The Divine Spark* 35.

Hector Berlioz (1803–69): Jean-Louis Barrault, *La Symphonie Fantastique* 40.

Frederic Chopin (1810–49): Jean Servais, *Adieu* 35; Cornel Wilde, *A Song to Remember* 44; Czeslaw Wollejko, *The Young Chopin* 52; Alexander Davion, *Song Without End* 60.

Robert Schumann (1810–56): Paul Henreid, *Song of Love* 47.

Franz Liszt (1811–86): Stephen Bekassy, *A Song to Remember* 44; Henry Daniell, *Song of Love* 47; Will Quadflieg, *Lola Montez* 55; Dirk Bogarde, *Song Without End* 60; Henry Gilbert, *Song of Norway* 70; Roger Daltrey, *Lisztomania* 75.

Richard Wagner (1813–83): Alan Badel, *Magic Fire* 56; Trevor Howard, *Ludwig* 73.

Johann Strauss Jnr (1825–99): Esmond Knight, *Waltzes from Vienna* 33; Anton Walbrook, *Vienna Waltzes* 34. Fernand Gravet, *The Great Waltz* 38; Kerwin Matthews, *The Waltz King* 60; Horst Buchholz, *The Great Waltz* 72.

Stephen Foster (1826–64): Don Ameche, *Swanee River* 39; Bill Shirley, *I Dream of Jeannie* 52.

Johannes Brahms (1833–97): Robert Walker, *Song of Love* 47.

W. S. Gilbert (1836–1911) and Arthur Sullivan (1842–1900): Nigel Bruce and Claud Allister, *Lillian Russell* 41; Robert Morley and Maurice Evans, *The Story of Gilbert and Sullivan* 53.

Peter Ilich Tchaikovsky (1840–93): Frank Sundstrom, *Song of My Heart* 47; Innokenti Smoktunovsky, *Tchaikovsky* 69; Richard Chamberlain, *The Music Lovers* 70.

Nikolai Rimsky-Korsakov (1844–1908): Jean-Pierre Aumont, *Song of Scheherezade* 47.

Edvard Grieg (1843–1907): Toralv Maurstad, *Song of Norway* 70.

John Philip Sousa (1854–1932): Clifton Webb, *Stars and Stripes Forever* 52.

Victor Herbert (1859–1924): Walter Connolly, *The Great Victor Herbert* 39; Paul Maxey, *Till the Clouds Roll By* 46.

Gustav Mahler (1860–1911): Robert Powell, *Mahler* 74.

Leslie Stuart (1866–1928): Robert Morley, *You Will Remember* 40.

W. C. Handy (1873–1948): Nat King Cole, *St Louis Blues* 57.

Jerome Kern (1885–1945): Robert Walker, *Till the Clouds Roll By* 47.

Sigmund Romberg (1887–1951): Jose Ferrer, *Deep in My Heart* 54.

Irving Berlin (1888–): Tyrone Power, *Alexander's Ragtime Band* 38.

Cole Porter (1892–1964): Cary Grant, *Night and Day* 45.
George Gershwin (1898–1937): Robert Alda, *Rhapsody in Blue* 45.
The list of biopics of lesser modern composers would be long indeed.

composite print: see *combined print* for which it is an alternative term.

Compson, Betty (1896–1974). American leading lady of the twenties, in Christie comedies from 1915.
The Miracle Man 19. Kick In 22. Woman to Woman (GB) 23 and 29. The Enemy Sex 24. The Fast Set 26. The Barker 28. Docks of New York 28. The Great Gabbo 29. On with the Show 30. The Gay Diplomat 31. Destination Unknown 33. Laughing Irish Eyes (GB) 36. A Slight Case of Murder 38. Strange Cargo 40. Mr and Mrs Smith 41. Claudia and David 46. Hard-Boiled Mahoney 48, many others.

Compton, Fay (1894–1978). British stage actress who made occasional film appearances.
She Stoops to Conquer 14. One Summer's Day 17. The Labour Leader 17. A Woman of No Importance 21. The Old Wives' Tale 21. Mary Queen of Scots 22. This Freedom 23. Robinson Crusoe 27. Fashions in Love (US) 29. Tell England 31. Autumn Crocus 34. The Mill on the Floss 35. The Prime Minister 41. Odd Man Out 46. London Belongs to Me 48. Laughter in Paradise 50. Othello 52. Aunt Clara 54. The Story of Esther Costello 57. The Haunting 63. The Virgin and the Gypsy 70, others.

Compton, Joyce (1907–) (Eleanor Hunt). American light second lead of the thirties.
Syncopating Sue 26. Dangerous Curves 29. Three Rogues 31. Only Yesterday 33. Magnificent Obsession 35. The Toast of New York 37. Balalaika 39. City for Conquest 40. Blues in the Night 42. Pillow to Post 45. Grand Canyon 51, etc.

computers in the mid-seventies became so commonplace as barely to rate a mention, forming the basis of such films as *Rollover* and *War Games* and TV series such as *Knight Rider* and *Whiz Kids*. Some of their earlier uses in film, however, were in Disney's *The Computer Wore Tennis Shoes*; in the unpleasant *Demon Seed*; in space fiction such as *The Forbin Project*, *2001* and *Dark Star*; in *Billion Dollar Brain*; and in a rather advanced TV movie of 1971 called *Paper Man*.

Conaway, Jeff (1950–). American general purpose actor.
Jennifer on My Mind 71. The Eagle Has Landed 76. Grease 78, etc.
TV series: Taxi 78–82.

concentration camps, until long after World War II, were thought too harrowing a subject for film treatment; but a few serious reconstructions have emerged, notably *The Last Stage* (Poland) 48, *Kapo* (Italy) 60, *Passenger* (Poland) 61, and *One Day in the Life of Ivan Denisovitch* 71, while the shadow of Auschwitz hangs over *The Diary of Anne Frank* 59 and *The Pawnbroker* 64. An alleged British concentration camp in South Africa was depicted in the Nazi film *Ohm Krüger* 42. The best documentary on the subject was probably Resnais' *Night and Fog*. In 1978 TV included much footage on the subject in *Holocaust*, which was quickly followed by *Playing for Time*. *Shoah* (1986) used no archive footage at all, but spent its nine hours in long interviews with survivors.

concerts of serious music naturally figure largely in films about the lives of composers (qv), and also in those concerned to show off living musicians: *They Shall Have Music, Music for Millions, Battle for Music, Tonight We Sing, Carnegie Hall, A Hundred Men and a Girl, Rhapsody in Blue.* In the forties a string of romantic films were centred on classical musicians and had concert climaxes: *Dangerous Moonlight, Love Story, The Seventh Veil, Intermezzo, The Great Lie*; this style later returned in *Interlude*. Other dramatic and comic concerts were featured in *Unfaithfully Yours, Tales of Manhattan, The Man Who Knew Too Much, The World of Henry Orient, The Bride Wore Black, Counterpoint* and *Deadfall*. The most influential film concert was certainly *Fantasia*, and the most poignant probably Myra Hess' recital in the blitz-beset National Gallery in *Listen to Britain*.

Confessions of a Nazi Spy (US 1939). First of the anti-Hitler films made in Hollywood before World War II began. This Warner melodrama, blending fact with fiction, toned in well with the company's social and biographical output and was often exciting in its own right. While its innovations of technique have since become standard, and its propaganda content now seems naïve, it remains an important landmark pointing the way to *The House on 92nd Street*, *Boomerang*, etc. Anatole Litvak directed a cast including Edward G. Robinson as the

G-man and Francis Lederer and Paul Lukas as spies.

confidence tricksters have figured as minor characters in hundreds of films, but full-length portraits of the breed are few and choice. Harry Baur in *Volpone* and Rex Harrison in *The Honey Pot*; Roland Young, Billie Burke, Janet Gaynor and Douglas Fairbanks Jnr in *The Young in Heart*; Gene Tierney, Laird Cregar and Spring Byington in *Rings on Her Fingers*; Tyrone Power in *Nightmare Alley* and *Mississippi Gambler*; Mai Zetterling in *Quartet*; Paul Newman in *The Hustler*; Charles Coburn and Barbara Stanwyck in *The Lady Eve*; David Niven and Marlon Brando in *Bedtime Story*; George C. Scott in *The Flim Flam Man*; Richard Attenborough and David Hemmings in *Only When I Larf*; James Garner in *The Skin Game*; Newman and Robert Redford in *The Sting*; Ryan and Tatum O'Neal in *Paper Moon*; James Coburn in *Dead Heat on a Merry-go-Round*; Robert Wagner and Eddie Albert in *Switch*.

Congress Dances (Germany 1931). This handsome historical romance, shot in three languages, showed a new face of German film-making and made world stars of Lilian Harvey and Conrad Veidt. Directed by Erik Charell, with music by Werner Heymann.

Conklin, Chester (1888–1971) (Jules Cowles). American silent slapstick comedian, in innumerable short comedies for Keystone and Sennett; features rarer.
Greed 24. Rubber Heels 27. Gentlemen Prefer Blondes 28. Her Majesty Love 31. Hallelujah I'm a Bum 33. *Modern Times* 36. Hollywood Cavalcade 39. The Great Dictator 40. Hail the Conquering Hero 44. The Perils of Pauline 47. Big Hand for a Little Lady 66, etc.

Conklin, Heinie (1880–1959) (Charles Conklin). American character comedian, one of the original Keystone Kops.

Conlin, Jimmy (1884–1962). Bird-like little American character comedian, in many films, notably those of Preston Sturges.
College Rhythm 33. And Sudden Death 36. Sullivan's Travels 41. The Palm Beach Story 42. Ali Baba and the Forty Thieves 44. Mad Wednesday 47. The Great Rupert 50. Anatomy of a Murder 59, many others.

A Connecticut Yankee at the Court of King Arthur. Three American versions have been made of this Mark Twain fantasy: 1920 with Harry Myers, 1931 with Will Rogers, and 1949 with Bing Crosby.

? connections
Can you find a connection – it could be an actor, a writer, a theme, anything – between each of the following pairs?

1 *The Power and the Glory*, *Citizen Kane*
2 Olivier in *Rebecca*, Aherne in *Juarez*
3 Lionel Stander, Jack Carson
4 Dan O'Herlihy, Paul Mantee
5 *The Spiral Staircase*, *Mad Wednesday*
6 *The Lady Vanishes*, *So Long at the Fair*
7 *The Lady Vanishes*, *The Spiral Staircase*
8 *The Invisible Man*, *Journey's End* (two links)
9 *Passage to Marseilles*, *The Life of Emile Zola*
10 *The Bishop's Wife*, *It's a Wonderful Life*
11 James Stewart, Stewart Granger
12 *The Little Foxes*, *The Grapes of Wrath*
13 *The Merry Widow*, *Shadow of a Doubt*
14 *Saboteur*, *Dark Passage*
15 *Dr Jekyll and Mr Hyde* (1931), *Dark Passage*
16 Wallace Beery, Claude Rains
17 *The Last Days of Pompeii*, *Journey to the Center of the Earth*
18 *Sylvia Scarlett*, *Wings of the Morning*
19 *Un Carnet de Bal*, *Tales of Manhattan*
20 Herbert Marshall in *Foreign Correspondent*. Leo G. Carroll in *Spellbound*
21 *Bwana Devil*, *The Robe*
22 *King Kong* (1933), *The French Connection*
23 Robert Morley, Peter Finch
24 *My Last Duchess*, *You Just Kill Me*
25 *Hellzapoppin*, *Citizen Kane*
26 *The Scarlet Empress*, *Lost Horizon*
27 *Foreign Correspondent*, *Fate Is the Hunter*
28 Errol Flynn, Robert Shaw
29 *The Wizard of Oz*, *Charlie Bubbles*
30 John Howard, Ron Randell
31 *Footsteps in the Dark*, *Lady on a Train*
32 *All That Money Can Buy*, *Alias Nick Beal*
33 *Rebecca*, *Duel in the Sun*
34 *Rebecca*, *Edward My Son*
35 *The Man Who Knew Too Much* (1934), *The Secret Partner*
36 *Tobacco Road*, *God's Little Acre*
37 *Harvey*, *Night of the Lepus*

38 *The Tall Target, Mrs O'Malley and Mr Malone*
39 Barry Fitzgerald, Richard Attenborough
40 W. C. Fields, Ralph Richardson

Connell, Richard (1893–1949). American writer whose chief bequest to Hollywood was his short story 'The Most Dangerous Game', filmed in 1932 (aka *The Hounds of Zaroff*) and remade several times. He also provided the original story for other films: *Seven Faces* 29. *F Man* 36. *Brother Orchid* 40.

Connelly, Christopher (–). American light leading man, mostly on television.
Corky 72. Benji 74. Hawmps 76. The Norsemen 78, etc.
TV series: Peyton Place 64–69. Paper Moon 74.

Connelly, Marc (1890–1980). American playwright whose *The Green Pastures* was influentially filmed in 1936. He occasionally contributed to screenplays, e.g. *I Married a Witch*; and other movies based on his work are *Merton of the Movies*, *Make Me a Star*, *Dulcy* and *Beggar on Horseback*, all from the late twenties and early thirties.

Connery, Neil (1938–). British leading man who made a brief appearance; Sean Connery's brother.
Operation Kid Brother 66. The Body Stealers 70, etc.

Connery, Sean (1929–) (Thomas Connery). Virile Scots leading man who shot to fame as James Bond and has been unable to escape the image.
□No Road Back 55. Time Lock 56. Hell Drivers 57. Action of the Tiger 57. Another Time Another Place 58. Darby O'Gill and the Little People 59. Tarzan's Greatest Adventure 59. Frightened City 60. On the Fiddle 61. The Longest Day 62. *Doctor No* 62. *From Russia With Love* 63. Woman of Straw 64. Marnie 64. *Goldfinger* 64. *The Hill* 65. Thunderball 65. A Fine Madness 66. You Only Live Twice 67. Shalako 68. The Molly Maguires 69. The Red Tent 69. The Anderson Tapes 71. Diamonds are Forever 71. The Offence 72. Zardoz 74. Ransom 74. Murder on the Orient Express 74. The Wind and the Lion 75. The Man Who Would Be King 76. Robin and Marian 76. The Next Man 76. A Bridge Too Far 77. The First Great Train Robbery 78. Meteor 79. Cuba 79. Outland 81. Time Bandits 81. Five Days One Summer 82. Wrong is Right 82. Never Say Never Again 83. Sword of the Valiant 83. Highlander 85. The Name of the Rose 86. The Untouchables 87. The Adventures of Baron Munchhausen 88.

¶ *S.C.:* I have always hated that damn James Bond. I'd like to kill him.
'With the exception of Lassie, he's the only person I know who's never been spoiled by success.'—*Terence Young*

Connolly, Billy (1942–). Scatological Scottish comedian, often hard to understand for Sassenachs. Big Banana Feet 77. Absolution 78. Water 84.

¶ *B.C.:* I set out to be a cross between Lenny Bruce and Robert the Bruce—my main thrust was the body and its functions and malfunctions—the absurdity of the thing.

Connolly, Walter (1887–1940). Chubby American character actor who spent his last years in films playing rasping millionaires and choleric editors.
□No More Orchids 32. Washington Merry Go Round 32. Man Against Woman 32. Lady for a Day 33. East of Fifth Avenue 33. The Bitter Tea of General Yen 33. Paddy the Next Best Thing 33. Master of Men 33. Man's Castle 33. *It Happened One Night* 34. Once to Every Woman 34. Eight Girls in a Boat 34. Twentieth Century 34. Whom the Gods Destroy 34. Servants Entrance 34. Lady by Choice 34. Broadway Bill 34. The Captain Hates the Sea 34. White Lies 34. *Father Brown Detective* 35. She Couldn't Take It 35. So Red the Rose 35. One Way Ticket 35. The Music Goes Round 36. *Soak the Rich* 36. The King Steps Out 36. Libelled Lady 36. The Good Earth 37. Nancy Steele is Missing 37. Let's Get Married 37. The League of Frightened Men 37. First Lady 37. *Nothing Sacred* 37. Penitentiary 38. Start Cheering 38. Four's a Crowd 38. Too Hot to Handle 38. The Girl Downstairs 39. The Adventures of Huckleberry Finn 39. Bridal Suite 39. Good Girls Go to Paris 39. Coast Guard 39. Those High Gray Walls 39. *Fifth Avenue Girl* 39. *The Great Victor Herbert* 39.

¶ I am sitting here, Mr Cook, toying with the idea of cutting out your heart and stuffing it—like an olive!—*W.C. in Nothing Sacred*

Connor, Edric (1915–1968). British West Indian actor and singer.
Cry the Beloved Country 52. Moby Dick 56. Fire Down Below 57. Four for Texas 63. Nobody Runs Forever 68, many others.

Connor, Kenneth (1918–). British radio and TV comedian adept at nervous or shy roles. A mainstay of the 'Carry On' film series.
There Was a Young Lady 53. The Black Rider 55. Davy 57. Carry On Sergeant 58. Carry On Nurse 59. Dentist in the Chair 60. Carry On Constable 60. What a Carve-up 61. Gonks Go Beat 65. Carry On England 76. Carry On Emmanuelle 78, etc.

Connor, Kevin (1937–). British director, former editor.
□The Land That Time Forgot 75. From Beyond the Grave 75. At the Earth's Core 76. Dirty Knights' Work 76. The People That Time Forgot 77. Warlords of Atlantis 78. Arabian Adventure 79. Motel Hell 80. The House Where Evil Dwells 82.

Connors, Chuck (1921–) (Kevin Connors). Tough guy American hero/villain, his thin smile being adaptable to friendship or menace.
Pat and Mike 52. South Sea Woman 53. Naked Alibi 54. Target Zero 55. Three Stripes in the Sun 55. Designing Woman 57. Geronimo 62. Move Over Darling 63. Synanon 65. Broken Sabre 65. Ride Beyond Vengeance 66. Captain Nemo and the Underwater City 69. Kill 'Em All and Come Back Alone 70. The Deserter 70. Pancho Villa 71. Embassy 72. Soylent Green 72. The Mad Bomber 72. 99 44/100% Dead 74. Banjo Hackett (TV) 76. Nightmare in Badham County (TV) 76. Roots (TV) 77. The Night They Took Miss Beautiful (TV) 77. Standing Tall (TV) 78. The Tourist Trap 79. Airplane 2: the Sequel 82. Summer Camp Nightmare 85, etc.
TV series: *Rifleman* 57–61. Arrest and Trial 63. Branded 64–65. Cowboy in Africa 67. The Thrillseekers 72. The Yellow Rose 83.

Connors, Michael (1925–) (Kreker Ohanian). American action hero of films and TV. Formerly known as Touch Connors.
Sudden Fear 52. The Ten Commandments 56. Where Love has Gone 64. Good Neighbour Sam 64. Situation Hopeless but not Serious 65. Harlow 65. *Stagecoach* 66. Kiss the Girls and Make them Die 67. The Killer who Wouldn't Die (TV) 76. S.S. Casino (TV) 79. Avalanche Express 79, etc.
TV series: *Tightrope* 57. *Mannix* 67–74. Today's FBI 81.

Conrad, Con (1891–1938) (Conrad K. Dober). American song composer whose 'The Continental' in 1934 won the first song Oscar.
Broadway 29. Happy Days 30. Palmy Days 31. *The Gay Divorcee* 34. Reckless 35. The Great Ziegfeld 36. The Story of Vernon and Irene Castle 39, etc.

Conrad, Jess (1940–). British pop singer and lightweight actor.
Too Young to Love 59. Konga 61. The Boys 62. The Golden Head 65. Hell is Empty 67. The Assassination Bureau 69, etc.

Conrad, Joseph (1857–1924) (Teodor Josef Konrad Korzeniowski). Polish-Ukrainian novelist, former seaman, who settled in Britain.
Lord Jim 26 and 65. Sabotage 37. Victory 30 and 40. An Outcast of the Islands 52. Laughing Anne 53.

Conrad, Michael (1925–1983). Giant-sized American character actor.
The War Lord 65. Sol Madrid 67. The Todd Killings 70. The Longest Yard 74. Baby Blue Marine 76, etc.
TV series: Delvecchio 76. *Hill Street Blues* 81.

Conrad, Robert (1935–) (Conrad Robert Falk). Short but personable American leading man who never carried his TV popularity over to the big screen.
□Palm Springs Weekend 63. Young Dillinger 65. The DA: Murder One (TV) 69. Weekend of Terror (TV) 70. The DA: Conspiracy to Kill (TV) 71. Five Desperate Women (TV) 71. The Adventures of Nick Carter (TV) 72. The Last Day (TV) 75. Live a Little Steal a Lot 75. Smash-up on Interstate Five (TV) 77. Sudden Death 77. Centennial (TV) 78. The Wild Wild West Revisited (TV) 79. Breaking Up Is Hard to Do (TV) 80. Wrong Is Right 82.
Will (TV) 82. Confessions of a Married Man (TV) 84. Two Fathers' Justice (TV) 86.
TV series: Hawaiian Eye 59–62. *The Wild Wild West* 65–68. Assignment Vienna 72. Hard Knox 83. Ba Ba Black Sheep 76–77. A Man Called Sloan 79.
Assignment Vienna 72. Hard Knox 83.

Conrad, William (1920–). Heavily-built American radio writer and actor who came to Hollywood to play unpleasant villains, but later became a producer-director.
The Killers (a) 46. Arch of Triumph (a) 48. One Way Street (a) 50. Cry Danger (a) 51. Lone Star (a) 52. The Naked Jungle (a) 54.

Johnny Concho (a) 56. The Ride Back (a) 57. Two on a Guillotine (pd) 64. Brainstorm (pd) 65. Chamber of Horrors (p) 66. An American Dream (p) 67. Covenant with Death (p) 67. Countdown (p) 68. The Brotherhood of the Bell (a) (TV) 70. O'Hara US Treasury (a) (TV) 71. Night Cries (a) (TV) 78. Keefer (a) (TV) 79. The Mikado (a) (TV) 82.
TV series (as actor): *Cannon* 71–75. Nero Wolfe 77.

Conried, Hans (1917–1982). Tall, weedy American comic actor with precise diction and a richly variable voice.
Dramatic School 37. Crazy House 43. Mrs Parkington 44. The Senator Was Indiscreet 47. My Friend Irma 49. The Twonky 53. *The Five Thousand Fingers of Doctor T* 53. Bus Stop 56. Rockabye Baby 58. The Patsy 64. The Brothers O'Toole 73. Oh God Book Two 80, many others.

Conroy, Frank (1890–1964). British stage actor who went to Hollywood in the early thirties, generally played domestic tyrants.
The Royal Family of Broadway 30. Grand Hotel 32. Call of the Wild 35. Wells Fargo 37. *The Ox-Bow Incident* 42. Naked City 48. Lightning Strikes Twice 51. The Last Mile 59, etc.

The Constant Nymph. Margaret Kennedy's popular sentimental novel about the Sanger family and the handsome tutor has been filmed three times: in 1927 with Ivor Novello and Mabel Poulton, directed by Adrian Brunel; in 1933 with Brian Aherne and Victoria Hopper, directed by Basil Dean (co-author of the play version); and in 1944 with Charles Boyer and Joan Fontaine, directed by Edmund Goulding.

Constantine, Eddie (1917–). Tough American actor popular in France where he plays Peter Cheyney heroes in crime films.
SOS Pacific 59. Treasure of San Teresa 60. Riff Raff Girls 62. Alphaville 65. Beware of a Holy Whore 77. The Long Good Friday 80. Box Office 83. Soap Bubbles 85. Macaroni Blues 86, many others.

Constantine, Michael (1927–) (Constantine Joanides). Greek-American character actor, mostly on TV.
The Last Mile 59. The Hustler 61. Island of Love 63. Beau Geste 66. Hawaii 66. Skidoo 68. If it's Tuesday This Must Be Belgium 69. The Reivers 69. Peeper 74. Voyage of the Damned 76. Raid on Entebbe (TV) 77. The North Avenue Irregulars 79, etc.
TV series: Hey Landlord. *Room 222*. Sirota's Court. Amanda's 83.

Conte, Richard (1911–1975) (Nicholas Conte). Amiable Italian-American action hero in films of varying merit; often seen as oppressed hero or sympathetic gangster.
☐ Heaven with a Barbed Wire Fence 39. *Guadalcanal Diary* 43. The Purple Heart 44. *A Walk in the Sun* 45. A Bell for Adano 45. Captain Eddie 45. The Spider 45. Somewhere in the Night 46. 13 Rue Madeleine 46. The Other Love 47. Call Northside 777 48. Cry of the City 48. Appointment with Murder 48. Thieves' Highway 49. Big Jack 49. *House of Strangers* 49. Whirlpool 49. The Sleeping City 50. Under the Gun 50. Hollywood Story 51. The Raging Tide 51. Thief of Damascus 52. The Fighter 52. The Raiders 52. Desert Legion 53. The Blue Gardenia 53. Slaves of Babylon 53. Highway Dragnet 54. A Race for Life 54. Target Zero 55. The Big Combo 55. Bengazi 55. New York Confidential 55. The Big Tip-Off 55. I'll Cry Tomorrow 55. Full of Life 56. The Brothers Rico 57. Little Red Monkey 57. This Angry Age 58. They Came to Cordura 59. Ocean's Eleven 60. Pepe 60. Who's Been Sleeping in My Bed? 63. The Eyes of Annie Jones 64. Circus World 64. Synanon 65. Stay Tuned for Terror 65. The Greatest Story Ever Told 65. Assault on a Queen 65. Tony Rome 66. Hotel 67. Lady in Cement 68. Operation Cross Eagle 69. Explosion 70. The Godfather 72.
TV series: The Four Just Men 59. The Jean Arthur Show 66.

Conti, Bill (–). American composer.
Blume in Love 73. Harry and Tonto 74. Next Stop Greenwich Village 76. *Rocky* 76. Citizens' Band 77. F.I.S.T. 78. An Unmarried Woman 78. Paradise Alley 78. The Big Fix 78. Hurricane 79. Rocky II 79. Gloria 80. Private Benjamin 80. For Your Eyes Only 81. Victory 81. I the Jury 82. Rocky III 82. Split Image 82. The Right Stuff (AA) 83. Unfaithfully Yours 84. The Karate Kid 84. Mass Appeal 85. Nomads 85.

Conti, Tom (c. 1945–). Saturnine British actor, mostly on stage and TV.
Flame 74. Galileo 74. Eclipse 76. Full Circle 76. The Glittering Prizes (TV) 76. The Duellists 77. Blade on the Feather (TV) 80. The Wall (TV) 80. Merry Christmas Mr Lawrence 83. *Reuben Reuben* (AAN) 83.

American Dreamer 84. Saving Grace 84. Miracles 85. Heavenly Pursuits 85. Nazi Hunter (TV) 86. Beyond Therapy 87.

continuity. The development of cinematic narrative from beginning to end of a film. If continuity is good the audience will be carried smoothly from one scene to another without disturbing breaks or lapses of detail.

contrast. The tone range in a print. Heavy contrast results in 'soot and whitewash', i.e. blurry blacks and burnt-out whites.

Converse, Frank (1938–). American general purpose actor.
Hurry Sundown 67. Hour of the Gun 67. A Tattered Web (TV) 70. Dr Cook's Garden (TV) 73. The Rowdyman 73. Cruise into Terror (TV) 78.
TV series: Coronet Blue 67. NYPD 67–68. *Movin' On* 74–75. The Second Family Tree 83.

Conway, Gary (1938–) (Gareth Carmody). American light leading man.
I was a Teenage Frankenstein (as the monster) 57. Young Guns of Texas 59. Black Gunn 72. Once is not Enough 75. The Farmer (& p) 77, etc.
TV series: *Burke's Law* 63–65. Land of the Giants 68–69.

Conway, Jack (1887–1952). American action director, launched as acting member of D. W. Griffith's stock company; long with MGM.
□The Old Armchair 12. Bond of Fear 18. Because of a Woman 18. Little Red Decides 18. Her Decision 18. You Can't Believe Everything 18. Diplomatic Mission 19. Desert Law 19. Riders of the Dawn 20. Lombardi Limited 20. Dwelling Place of Light 21. The Money Changers 21. The Spenders 21. The Kiss 21. A Daughter of the Law 21. Step On It 22. A Parisian Scandal 22. The Millionaire 22. Across the Deadline 22. Another Man's Shoes 22. Don't Shoot 22. The Long Chance 22. The Prisoner 23. Sawdust 23. Quicksands 23. What Wives Want 23. Trimmed in Scarlet 23. Lucretia Lombard 23. The Trouble Shooter 24. The Heart Buster 24. The Roughneck 25. The Hunted Woman 25. The Only Thing 25. Brown of Harvard 26. Soul Mates 26. The Understanding Heart 27. Twelve Miles Out 27. Quicksands 27. The Smart Set 28. Bringing Up Father 28. While the City Sleeps 28. Alias Jimmy Valentine 29. *Our Modern Maidens* 29. Untamed 29. They Learned about Women 30. *The Unholy Three* 30. New Moon 30. The Easiest Way 31. Just a Gigolo 31. *Arsène Lupin* 32. But the Flesh is Weak 32. Red-headed Woman 32. Hell Below 33. The Nuisance 33. The Solitaire Man 33. *Viva Villa* 34. The Girl from Missouri 34. The Gay Bride 34. One New York Night 35. *A Tale of Two Cities* 35. *Libelled Lady* 36. Saratoga 37. *A Yank at Oxford* 38. Too Hot to Handle 38. Let Freedom Ring 39. Lady of the Tropics 39. *Boom Town* 40. Love Crazy 40. Honky Tonk 40. Crossroads 42. Assignment in Brittany 43. Dragon Seed 44. High Barbaree 47. *The Hucksters* 47. Julia Misbehaves 48.

Conway, Morgan (1900–81). Tough-guy American actor of forties B pictures, chiefly notable as the screen's first Dick Tracy.
Looking for Trouble 34. Crime Ring 38. Blackwell's Island 39. Brother Orchid 40. Sing Your Worries Away 42. Jack London 44. *Dick Tracy* 45. Badman's Territory 46. Dick Tracy vs Cueball 46, others.

Conway, Tim (1933–). American television comic who found a niche in Disney films.
McHale's Navy 64. The World's Greatest Athlete 73. The Apple Dumpling Gang 75. Gus 76. The Billion Dollar Hobo 77. The Apple Dumpling Gang Rides Again 79. The Prize Fighter 79. The Private Eyes 80. The Long Shot 85, etc.
TV series: McHale's Navy 62–65. The Tim Conway Show 70. Later with Carol Burnett. Ace Crawford 83.

Conway, Tom (1904–1967) (Thomas Sanders). British light leading man, brother of George Sanders; well-liked as 'the Falcon' in the forties, but his career declined very suddenly.
Sky Murder 40. The Trail of Mary Dugan 41. Grand Central Murder 42. *The Falcon's Brother* 42. *Cat People* 42. I Walked with a Zombie 43. The Falcon Strikes Back 43. The Seventh Victim 43. The Falcon Out West 44 (and five other Falcon adventures ending in 1946). Criminal Court 46. Repeat Performance 47. One Touch of Venus 48. Confidence Girl 52. Park Plaza 505 (GB) 53. Barbados Quest (GB) 55. The Last Man to Hang (GB) 56. The She-Creature 56. Twelve to the Moon 60. What a Way to Go (unbilled) 64, many others.
TV series: Mark Saber 52–54. The Betty Hutton Show 59.

Conyers, Darcy (1919–1973). British director, former actor.
Ha'penny Breeze (& p) 52. The Devil's Pass (& wp) 56. The Night We Dropped a Clanger 60. Nothing Barred 61. In the Doghouse 62, etc.

Coogan, Jackie (1914–84). American child actor of the twenties who achieved outstanding star status but later reappeared as a less appealing adult in minor roles.
The Kid 20. *Peck's Bad Boy* 21. *Oliver Twist* 21. My Boy 22. Trouble 22. Daddy 23. Circus Days 23. Long Live the King 24. A Boy of Flanders 24. The Rag Man 24. Little Robinson Crusoe 25. Johnny Get Your Gun 25. Old Clothes 25. Johnny Get Your Hair Cut 26. The Bugle Call 27. Buttons 27. Tom Sawyer 30. Huckleberry Finn 31. Home on the Range 35. College Swing 38. Kilroy was Here 47. Outlaw Women 52. Lost Women 56. High School Confidential 58. A Fine Madness 66. The Shakiest Gun in the West 68. Marlowe 69. Cahill 73. The Escape Artist 82, many others.
TV series: Cowboy G-Men 52. McKeever and the Colonel 62. *The Addams Family* 64 (as Uncle Fester).

Cook, Clyde (1891–1984). Australian clown and dancer who played in many Mack Sennett comedies and settled in California. Subsequently played character roles.
Soldiers of Fortune 19. Skirts 21. The Eskimo 22. He Who Gets Slapped 24. The Winning of Barbara Worth 26. Good Time Charley 27. The Spieler 28. The Taming of the Shrew 29. Sunny 30. Blondie of the Follies 32. Oliver Twist 33. Barbary Coast 35. Kidnapped 38. The Little Princess 39. The Sea Hawk 40. White Cargo 42. To Each His Own 46. Pride of Maryland 51, many others.

Cook, Donald (1900–1961). American stage leading man who never quite made it in Hollywood.
The Public 31. The Mad Genius 31. The Man Who Played God 32. Frisco Jenny 33. Long Lost Father 34. Gigolette 35. Show Boat 36. Two Wise Maids 37. Bowery to Broadway 44. Patrick the Great 45. Our Very Own 50, etc.

Cook, Elisha, Jnr (1902–). American character actor adept at cowards and neurotics.
□Her Unborn Child 30. Two in a Crowd 36. Pigskin Parade 36. Love Is News 37. Breezing Home 37. Wife, Doctor and Nurse 37. Danger Love at Work 37. Life Begins in College 37. They Won't Forget 37. The Devil Is Driving 37. My Lucky Star 38. Submarine Patrol 38. Three Blind Mice 38. Grand Jury Secrets 39. Newsboys' Home 39. He Married His Wife 40. Stranger on the Third Floor 40. Public Deb Number One 40. Love Crazy 40. Tin Pan Alley 40. Man at Large 41. Sergeant York 41. Ball of Fire 41. *The Maltese Falcon* (as Wilmer the gunsel) 41. *I Wake Up Screaming* 41. A Gentleman at Heart 42. In This Our Life 42. Sleepytime Gal 42. A-Haunting We Will Go 42. Manila Calling 42. Hellzapoppin 42. Wildcat 42. Casanova Brown 44. *Phantom Lady* 44. Up in Arms 44. Dark Mountain 44. *Dark Waters* 44. Dillinger 44. Why Girls Leave Home 44. *The Big Sleep* 46. Blonde Alibi 46. Cinderella Jones 46. The Falcon's Alibi 46. Joe Palooka Champ 46. Two Smart People 46. Born to Kill 47. The Fall Guy 47. The Long Night 47. The Gangster 47. Flaxy Martin 49. The Great Gatsby 49. Behave Yourself 51. Don't Bother to Knock 51. I the Jury 53. Thunder over the Plains 53. *Shane* 53. The Outlaw's Daughter 54. Drum Beat 54. Timberjack 55. The Indian Fighter 55. Trial 55. *The Killing* 56. Accused of Murder 56. The Lonely Man 57. Voodoo Island 57. Baby Face Nelson 57. Plunder Road 57. Chicago Confidential 57. House on Haunted Hill 58. Day of the Outlaw 59. Platinum High School 60. College Confidential 60. One Eyed Jacks 61. Papa's Delicate Condition 63. The Haunted Palace 63. Black Zoo 63. Johnny Cool 63. Blood on the Arrow 64. The Glass Cage 64. Welcome to Hard Times 67. Rosemary's Baby 68. The Great Bank Robbery 69. El Condor 70. The Movie Murderer (TV) 70. Night Chase (TV) 70. The Great Northfield Minnesota Raid 72. Blacula 72. The Night Stalker (TV) 72. Emperor of the North Pole 73. Electra Glide in Blue 73. The Outfit 73. The Black Bird 75. Messiah of Evil 75. Winterhawk 75. St Ives 76. Mad Bull (TV) 77. 1941 79. The Champ 79. Leave 'Em Laughing (TV) 80. Carny 80. Tom Horn 80. Harry's War 80. Salem's Lot 80. Hammett 82. This Girl for Hire 84. National Lampoon Goes to the Movies 84.

¶ 'As he has grown older, the vulnerable look has congealed in his face so that his very presence has become an open invitation to destroy him.'—*Ian Cameron*

Cook, Fielder (1923–). American TV director who makes occasional films.
□*Patterns of Power* 56. Home is the Hero (Eire) 59. *Big Hand for a Little Lady* 66. How to Save a Marriage 67. Prudence and

the Pill 68. Teacher Teacher (TV) 69. Who Killed the Mysterious Mr Foster? (TV) 70. Goodbye Raggedy Ann (TV) 71. Eagle in a Cage 71. The Hands of Cormac Joyce (TV) 72. Miracle on 34th Street (TV) 73. From the Mixed Up Files of Mrs Basil E. Frankenweiler 73. This Is the West that Was (TV) 74. Judge Horton and the Scottsboro Boys (TV) 76. Beauty and the Beast (TV) 77.

Cook, Peter (1937–). British cabaret comedian and writer.
□The Wrong Box 66. Bedazzled 68. A Dandy in Aspic 68. Monte Carlo or Bust 69. The Bed Sitting Room 69. The Rise and Rise of Michael Rimmer 70. The Adventures of Barry Mackenzie 72. The Hound of the Baskervilles 77. Yellowbeard 83. Supergirl 84.
TV series: The Two of Us 81.

Coop, Denys (1920–1981). British cameraman.
A Kind of Loving 61. Billy Liar 63. This Sporting Life 63. One Way Pendulum 64. King and Country 65. Bunny Lake is Missing 65. The Double Man 67. My Side of the Mountain 68. 10 Rillington Place 70, etc.

Cooper, Ben (1930–). American light juvenile lead, mainly in westerns.
The Woman They almost Lynched 52. Perilous Journey 53. Johnny Guitar 54. Jubilee Trail 54. The Eternal Sea 55. The Last Command 56. *The Rose Tattoo* 57. Chartroose Caboose 60. Gunfight at Comanche Creek 64. Arizona Raiders 65. Red Tomahawk 67, many others.

Cooper, Frederick (1890–1945). Ferrety-looking British character actor who managed a few choice roles.
Thunder Rock 42. The Great Mr Handel 42. Henry V (as Nym) 44, etc.

Cooper, Gary (1901–1961) (Frank J. Cooper). Slow-speaking, deep-thinking American leading man, a long-enduring Hollywood star who always projected honest determination. Was cowboy and cartoonist before becoming a film extra; progressed to two-reelers and became a star in his first feature, *The Winning of Barbara Worth* 26. Special Academy Award 1960 'for his many memorable screen performances and for the international recognition he, as an individual, has gained for the film industry'.
□The Thundering Herd 25. Wild Horse Mesa 25. The Lucky Horseshoe 25. The Vanishing American 25. The Eagle 25. The Enchanted Hill 26. Watch Your Wife 26. It 27. Children of Divorce 27. Arizona Bound 27. Wings 27. Nevada 27. The Last Outlaw 27. Beau Sabreur 28. Legion of the Condemned 28. Doomsday 28. Half a Bride 28. *Lilac Time* 28. The First Kiss 28. Shopworn Angel 28. Wolf Song 29. The Betrayal 29. The Virginian 29. Only the Brave 29. The Texan 29. Seven Days' Leave 30. A Man from Wyoming 30. The Spoilers 30. Morocco 30. Fighting Caravans 31. I Take This Woman 31. His Woman 31. The Devil and the Deep 32. *A Farewell to Arms* 32. *City Streets* 32. If I Had a Million 32. One Sunday Afternoon 33. Alice in Wonderland (as the White Knight) 33. Today We Live 33. Design for Living 34. Peter Ibbetson 34. Operator Thirteen 34. The Wedding Night 35. *Lives of a Bengal Lancer* 35. Now and Forever 35. Desire 36. *Mr Deeds Goes to Town* 36. The General Died at Dawn 36. *The Plainsman* 37. Souls at Sea 37. The Adventures of Marco Polo 38. Bluebeard's Eighth Wife 38. The Cowboy and the Lady 39. *Beau Geste* 39. The Real Glory 39. *The Westerner* 40. Northwest Mounted Police 40. *Meet John Doe* 41. *Sergeant York* (AA) 41. Ball of Fire 41. Pride of the Yankees 42. *For Whom the Bell Tolls* 43. The Story of Dr Wassell 44. Saratoga Trunk 44. Casanova Brown 44. Along Came Jones (& p) 45. Cloak and Dagger 46. Unconquered 47. Good Sam 48. The Fountainhead 49. Task Force 49. Bright Leaf 50. Dallas 50. You're in the Navy Now 51. Distant Drums 51. Springfield Rifle 52. *High Noon* (AA) 52. Return to Paradise 52. Blowing Wild 53. Garden of Evil 54. *Vera Cruz* 54. The Court Martial of Billy Mitchell 55. Friendly Persuasion 56. Love in the Afternoon 56. *Ten North Frederick* 58. Man of the West 58. They Came to Cordura 59. The Hanging Tree 59. The Wreck of the Mary Deare 59. The Naked Edge (GB) 61.
Cameo appearances: Variety Girl 47. It's a Great Feeling 49. Alias Jesse James 55.
❀ For his sheer domination of the Hollywood scene for the first twenty years of the talkies. *Mr Deeds Goes to Town.*

¶ The most underrated actor I ever worked with

said Henry Hathaway.

> He was a poet of the real

said Clifford Odets. Whatever that means, it would have embarrassed Cooper. Perhaps Carl Sandburg put it another way:

> One of the most beloved illiterates this country has ever known.

Cooper had no very high estimate of his own talent:

People ask me how come you been around so long. Well, it's through playing the part of Mr Average Joe American.

He had Mr Average Joe's reputed insularity:

From what I hear about communism, I don't like it because it isn't on the level.

He distrusted the socialism of plays like *Death of a Salesman*:

Sure there are fellows like Willy Loman, but you don't have to write plays about them.

He enjoyed his niche:

Until I came along, all the leading men were handsome, but luckily they wrote a lot of stories about the fellow next door.

For a man without acting training, he managed very well. King Vidor thought that:

He got a reputation as a great actor just by thinking hard about the next line.

Coop's own explanation was simpler:

To get folks to like you, I figured you sort of had to be their ideal. I don't mean a handsome knight riding a white horse, but a fellow who answered the description of a right guy.

Richard Arlen summed up:

Coop just likes people, it's as simple as that.

But Richard Zanuck latched on to another Cooper essential: he was part of the great outdoors:

You could never put Coop in a small hat and get your money back.

Famous line (*Sergeant York*): 'Folks back home used to say I could shoot a rifle before I was weaned.They was exaggerating some.'
Famous line (*The Virginian*): 'If you want to call me that, smile.'
Famous line (*For Whom the Bell Tolls*): 'A man fights for what he believes in, Fernando.'

Cooper, George A. (1916–). British character actor of vengeful types.
Miracle in Soho 56. Violent Playground 58. Tom Jones 63. Nightmare 64. Life at the Top 65. The Strange Affair 68, etc.

Cooper, Dame Gladys (1888–1971). Distinguished, gracious British stage actress who essentially began her film career in Hollywood at the age of 52, subsequently airing her warm aristocratic personality in many unworthy roles and a few good ones.
Autobiography: *Gladys Cooper* 31; biography by Sewell Stokes: *Without Veils* 53.
□Masks and Faces 17. The Sorrows of Satan 17. My Lady's Dress 18. The Bohemian Girl 22. Bonnie Prince Charles 23. Dandy Donovan 31. The Iron Duke 35. *Rebecca* 40. Kitty Foyle 40. That Hamilton Woman 41. The Black Cat 41. The Gay Falcon 41. This Above All 42. Eagle Squadron 42. *Now Voyager* 42. Forever and a Day 43. Mr Lucky 43. Princess O'Rourke 43. The Song of Bernadette 43. The White Cliffs of Dover 44. Mrs Parkington 44. The Valley of Decision 45. Love Letters 45. The Green Years 46. The Cockeyed Miracle 46. Green Dolphin Street 47. Beware of Pity 47. The Bishop's Wife 47. Homecoming 48. The Pirate 48. The Secret Garden 49. Madame Bovary 49. Thunder on the Hill 51. At Sword's Point 52. The Man Who Loved Redheads 54. *Separate Tables* 58. The List of Adrian Messenger 63. *My Fair Lady* 64. The Happiest Millionaire 67. A Nice Girl Like Me 69.
TV series: *The Rogues* 64.

Cooper, Jackie (1921–). 'Little tough guy' American child actor who in adult life found roles getting rarer and became a powerful TV executive.
□*Our Gang* shorts 27–28. Movietone Follies 28. Sunny Side Up 29. *Skippy* 31. Young Donovan's Kid 31. *The Champ* 31. Sooky 31. When a Feller Needs a Friend 32. Divorce in the Family 32. Broadway to Hollywood 33. *The Bowery* 33. *Treasure Island* 34. Peck's Bad Boy 34. Lone Cowboy 34. Dinky 35. O'Shaughnessy's Boy 35. Tough Guy 36. The Devil is a Sissy 36. Boy of the Streets 37. White Banners 38. That Certain Age 38. Gangster's Boy. 38. Newsboys' Home 39. Scouts to the Rescue 39. Spirit of Culver 39. Streets of New York 39. Two Bright Boys 39. What a Life 39. The Big Guy 39. Seventeen 40. The Return of Frank James 40. Gallant Sons 40. Life with Henry 41. Ziegfeld Girl 41. Her First Beau 41. Glamour Boy 41. Syncopation 42. Men of Texas 42. The Navy Comes Through 42. Where are your Children? 44. Stork Bites Man 47. Kilroy Was Here 47. French Leave 48. Everything's Ducky 61. Shadow on the Land (TV) 68. The Astronaut (TV) 71. The Love Machine 71. Maybe I'll Come Home in the Spring (TV) 71. Stand Up and Be Counted (d only) 72. Chosen Survivors 74. The Day the Earth Moved (TV) 74. The Invisible Man (TV) 75. Mobile Two (TV) 75. Superman 78. Superman II 80. Superman III 83. Superman IV 87.
TV series: The People's Choice 56– 58. Hennessey 59–71. Mobile One 75.

Cooper, James Fenimore (1789–1851). American adventure novelist whose 'westerns' include *The Last of the Mohicans*, *The*

Pathfinder and *The Deerslayer*, all frequently filmed.

Cooper, Melville (1896–1973). British comedy character actor, long in Hollywood playing pompous upper-class idiots.
☐ The Calendar 31. Black Coffee 31. Two White Arms 32. Forgin' Ahead 33. Leave It to Me 33. To Brighton with Gladys 33. The Private Life of Don Juan 34. The Scarlet Pimpernel 34. The Bishop Misbehaves (US from now on) 35. The Gorgeous Hussy 36. The Last of Mrs Cheyney 37. Thin Ice 37. The Great Garrick 37. Tovarich 37. Women Are Like That 37. *The Adventures of Robin Hood* (as Sheriff of Nottingham) 38. Gold Diggers in Paris 38. Four's a Crowd 38. Hard to Get 38. The Dawn Patrol 38. Comet over Broadway 38. Dramatic School 38. Garden of the Moon 38. I'm from Missouri 39. Blind Alley 39. The Sun Never Sets 39. Two Bright Boys 39. Rebecca 40. Too Many Husbands 40. *Pride and Prejudice* (his best role, as the pompous Mr Collins) 40. Murder over New York 40. Submarine Zone 40. The Flame of New Orleans 41. The Lady Eve 41. Scotland Yard 41. You Belong to Me 41.This Above All 42. The Affairs of Martha 42. Random Harvest 42. Life Begins at 8.30 42. The Immortal Sergeant 43. Hit Parade of 1943 43. Holy Matrimony 43. My Kingdom for a Cook 43. Heartbeat 46. 13 Rue Madeleine 46. The Imperfect Lady 47. Enchantment 48. The Red Danube 49. Love Happy 49. And Baby Makes Three 49. The Underworld Story 50. Father of the Bride 50. Let's Dance 50. The Petty Girl 50. It Should Happen to You 53. Moonfleet 55. The King's Thief 55. Diane 55. Bundle of Joy 56. Around the World in 80 Days 56. The Story of Mankind 57. From the Earth to the Moon 58.

Cooper, Merian C. (1893–1973). American executive producer associated with many adventurous films. Special Academy Award 1952 'for his many innovations and contributions to the art of the motion picture'.
Grass 25. *Chang* 27. The Four Feathers 29. *King Kong* 33. The Last Days of Pompeii 35. The Toy Wife 38. Fort Apache 48. Mighty Joe Young 49. Rio Grande 50. The Quiet Man 52. *This is Cinerama* 52. The Searchers 56, etc.

Cooper, Miriam (1892–1976). American silent screen actress who married Raoul Walsh.
Autobiography 1978: *Dark Lady of the Silents*.
A Blot on the Scutcheon 11. When Fate Frowned 14. His Return 15. The Woman and the Law 18. Kindred of the Dust 22. Her Accidental Husband 23, many others.

Cooper, Stuart (1942–). American director who got his first breaks in Britain.
Little Malcolm and his Struggle against the Eunuchs 74. Overlord 75. The Disappearance 77. A.D. (TV) 84. The Long Hot Summer (TV) 85.

Cooper, Violet Kemble (1886–1961). British stage actress who appeared in a few Hollywood films in the thirties.
Our Betters 33. Vanessa 34. David Copperfield (as Miss Murdstone) 35. The Invisible Ray 36. Romeo and Juliet 36, etc.

Cooper, Wilkie (1911–). British cinematographer, once a child actor.
The Rake's Progress 45. Green for Danger 46. Captain Boycott 47. London Belongs to Me 48. Stage Fright 50. The Admirable Crichton 57. Jason and the Argonauts 63. One Million Years BC 66, etc.

Coote, Robert (1909–1982). British stage character actor who filmed mainly in Hollywood; familiar in amiable silly-ass roles.
Sally in Our Alley 31. *A Yank at Oxford* 38. Gunga Din (US) 39. You Can't Fool Your Wife 40. The Commandos Strike at Dawn 43. A Matter of Life and Death 46. The Ghost and Mrs Muir 47. Forever Amber 47. Bonnie Prince Charlie 48. The Three Musketeers 48. The Elusive Pimpernel 50. Rommel, Desert Fox 51. *The Prisoner of Zenda* 52. The Constant Husband 55. Othello (as Roderigo) 55. The Swan 56. Merry Andrew 58. The League of Gentlemen 59. The Golden Head 65. A Man Could Get Killed 66. The Swinger 66. Prudence and the Pill 68. Up the Front 72. Theatre of Blood 73. Institute for Revenge (TV) 79, etc.
TV series: *The Rogues* 64.

Cope, Kenneth (1931–). British TV actor, usually of Liverpudlian types.
The Criminal 60. The Damned 62. Genghis Khan 65. Dateline Diamonds 65. She'll Follow You Anywhere 71, etc.
TV series: Coronation Street. Randall and Hopkirk (Deceased).

Copland, Aaron (1900–). American composer.
☐*The City* 39. *Of Mice and Men* 39. *Our Town* 40. North Star 43. Fiesta 47. *The Red Pony* 49. The Heiress 49, Something Wild 61.

Copley, Peter (1915–). British stage actor who makes occasional film appearances, usually in quiet, downtrodden or slightly sinister roles.
The Golden Salamander 49. The Card 52. The Sword and the Rose 53. Foreign Intrigue 56. Victim 61. King and Country 64, etc.

Coppel, Alec (1910–1972). Australian playwright and screenwriter.
Over the Moon (w) 39. Obsession (oa) 46. Mr Denning Drives North (w) 51. The Captain's Paradise (w) 53. The Gazebo (oa) 59. Moment to Moment (w) 66. The Bliss of Mrs Blossom (w) 69.

Coppola, Francis Ford (1939–). American writer-director who graduated from nudie movies.
□Dementia 63. This Property is Condemned (w) 65. Is Paris Burning? (w) 66. *You're a Big Boy Now* (wd) 67. Finian's Rainbow (d) 68. The Rain People (wd) 69. Patton (w only) (AA) 71. *The Godfather* (AA) (co-w) 72. American Graffiti (p only) 73. The Great Gatsby (w only) 74. The Conversation (w, p, d) 74. The Godfather Part Two (AA) (w, d, p) 74. Apocalypse Now (BFA) 79. One from the Heart (w, p, d) 82. Hammett (p) 82. The Escape Artist (p) 82. The Outsiders 83. Rumblefish 83. Peggy Sue Got Married 86. Gardens of Stone 87.

¶ *F.F.C.:* I bring to my life a certain amount of mess.
'He is his own worst enemy. If he directs a little romance, it had to be the biggest, most overdone little romance in movie history.'—*Kenneth Turan*
F.F.C.: If you don't bet, you don't have a chance to win.
F.F.C.: Basically, both the Mafia and America feel they are benevolent organizations. And both the Mafia and America have their hands stained with blood from what it is necessary to do to protect their power and interests.

? **copycats I**
What, in terms of roles they have played, do the following actors have in common? Name the films concerned.

1 Cary Grant, Clifton Webb, Claude Rains
2 Cary Grant, Jack Lemmon, Jimmy Durante
3 Ronald Colman, Jack Benny, Richard Burton
4 Barry K. Barnes, Leslie Howard, David Niven
5 Keefe Brasselle, Larry Parks, Barbra Streisand
6 John Barrymore, Fredric March, Spencer Tracy
7 Irene Dunne, Anna Neagle, Fay Compton
8 Clifton Webb, Richard Chamberlain, Maurice Evans, Wilfred Lawson
9 Anna Neagle, Burt Lancaster, Betty Hutton, Groucho Marx
10 John Gielgud, George Arliss, Alec Guinness
11 Cecil Kellaway, Jimmy O'Dea, Tommy Steele, Don Beddoe
12 Michael Rennie, Jeff Morrow, James Arness, Paul Birch
13 Arthur Franz, Jon Hall, Vincent Price
14 Phyllis Calvert, Joanne Woodward, Eleanor Parker
15 Henry Fonda, Lew Ayres, Fredric March, Peter Sellers
16 Humphrey Bogart, Ronald Colman, Steve McQueen, Joseph Schildkraut
17 Allison Hayes, Buddy Baer, Glenn Langan
18 Ray Milland, Walter Huston, Laird Cregar
19 Judy Garland, Albert Finney, David Niven
20 Cedric Hardwicke, Maria Casares, Fredric March
21 Yul Brynner, Jean Peters, Robert Newton
22 Yvonne de Carlo, Doris Day, Jean Arthur
23 Erich von Stroheim, Danny Kaye, Michael Redgrave
24 Montagu Love, Charles Laughton, Sid James
25 Nancy Coleman, Ida Lupino, Olivia de Havilland
26 James Garner, Burt Lancaster, Henry Fonda
27 Bobby Watson, Luther Adler, Richard Basehart
28 Boris Karloff, Warner Oland, Peter Lorre
29 Kay Hammond, Robert Donat, Rex Harrison
30 Lee Remick, Gig Young, Ray Milland

? **copycats II**
Give the common link between the following, in terms of roles played, themes used, etc. Name the films concerned.

1 Paul Muni, Ann Dvorak, Cary Grant, Frank Lovejoy
2 H. G. Wells, Mary Shelley, Bram Stoker, R. L. Stevenson
3 Agnes Moorehead, Dustin Hoffman, Sam Jaffe, Charles Boyer
4 John Carradine, Berton Churchill,

Donald Meek, Thomas Mitchell
5 Vincent Price, Laurence Olivier, Basil Rathbone
6 Gene Kelly, George Sanders, Tyrone Power, Laurence Harvey
7 John Fraser, Laird Cregar, Jack Palance, Ewen Solon
8 Peter Lorre, Charles Laughton, Peter Ustinov
9 James Garner, John Hodiak, Ronald Colman, Gregory Peck
10 Charlie Ruggles, Jack Benny, Arthur Askey, Ray Bolger
11 Rod Steiger, Herbert Lom, Marlon Brando, Kenneth Haigh
12 *Scarface*, *The Outlaw*, *Vendetta*, *The Front Page*
13 John Gilbert, Charles Boyer, Melvyn Douglas, Robert Taylor
14 *Stormy Weather*, *Hallelujah*, *Cabin in The Sky*
15 Walter Abel, Don Ameche, Gene Kelly, Michael York
16 *Storm Warning*, *The FBI Story*, *The Cardinal*
17 Susan Hayward, Ray Milland, James Cagney, Jack Lemmon
18 *The Big Trail*, *The Bat Whispers*, *Billy the Kid*
19 *Mr Music*, *Copacabana*, *Skidoo*
20 Otis Skinner, Ronald Colman, Howard Keel
21 Melvyn Douglas, Warren William, Gerald Mohr
22 Cedric Hardwicke, Laurence Olivier, Richard Johnson, Peter Finch
23 Rosemary Lane, Loretta Young, Joan Bennett
24 Edmond O'Brien, Clifton Webb, Alec Guinness, Rex Harrison
25 *The Flying Deuces*, *Beau Geste*, *Rogue's Regiment*
26 *The Lady from Shanghai*, *Strangers on a Train*, *The Dancing Masters*
27 Jeffrey Hunter, Max Von Sydow, H. B. Warner
28 Fredric March, Jean Gabin, Michael Rennie
29 *Kind Hearts and Coronets*, *Drop Dead Darling (Arrivederci Baby)*, *Get Carter*
30 *Liliom*, *The Matchmaker*, *I Am a Camera*, *Tom Dick and Harry*
31 Seymour Hicks, Alastair Sim, Reginald Owen, Albert Finney
32 *West of Zanzibar*, *Tell It to the Marines*, *The Penalty*
33 Ronald Reagan, George Murphy, Shirley Temple
34 *Psycho*, *It Happened One Night*, *A Guide for the Married Man*
35 *Bullitt*, *Petulia*, *The Maltese Falcon*
36 *Les Misérables*, *The Third Man*, *He Walked by Night*
37 *The Fiend Who Walked the West*, *Barricade* (1950), *The Unfaithful*
38 *A Fistful of Dollars*, *The Magnificent Seven*, *The Outrage*
39 *The Black Room*, *The Masquerader*, *The Prisoner of Zenda*, *Wonder Man*
40 *Hog Wild*, *Me and My Pal*, *Night Owls*, *Helpmates*

copyright. British law relating to film copyright is notably vague, but in practice the owner of a film is protected against piracy for fifty years. In America copyright must be renewed in the 28th year, which has resulted in some fatal errors: e.g. MGM now have no control over *Till the Clouds Roll By* because they forgot to renew it, and Chaplin renewed only the version of *The Gold Rush* including his specially composed forties music track.

Coquillon, John (–). British cinematographer.
Witchfinder General 68. Scream and Scream Again 69. The Oblong Box 69. Triple Echo 72. Cross of Iron 77. The Four Feathers (TV) 78. The 39 Steps 78. Final Assignment 80. The Changeling 80. The Amateur 82. The Osterman Weekend 83. Master of the Game (TV) 83. The Last Place on Earth (TV) 84. Clockwise 85, etc.

Corbett, Glenn (1929–). American second lead.
The Fireball 50. Man on a String 60. The Mountain Road 60. All the Young Men 60. Homicidal 61. Pirates of Blood River (GB) 61. Shenandoah 65. Big Jake 71. Dead Pigeon on Beethoven Street (WG) 72, etc.
TV series: It's a Man's World 63. Route 66 63. The Road West 64.

Corbett, Gretchen (1947–). American character actress, mostly on TV.
Out of It 70. Let's Scare Jessica to Death 71. The Savage Bees (TV) 76. The Other Side of the Mountain Part Two 78. Secrets of Three Hungry Wives (TV) 78, etc.
TV series: The Rockford Files 74–80.

Corbett, Harry H. (1925–1982). British stage actor who played tough guys, regional types and maniacs in an assortment of films before gaining great TV popularity in *Steptoe and Son*; subsequently starred in a number of unsatisfactory comedy vehicles.
Floods of Fear 57. Nowhere to Go 58. Cover Girl Killer 60. Sammy Going South 62. What

a Crazy World 63. Ladies Who Do 63. The Bargee 64. Rattle of a Simple Man 64. Joey Boy 65. The Sandwich Man 66. Carry On Screaming 66. Crooks and Coronets 69. The Magnificent Seven Deadly Sins 71. Steptoe and Son 72, etc.

Corbett, Leonora (1907–1960). British stage actress who made few films.
Heart's Delight 32. The Constant Nymph 33. Friday the Thirteenth 33. Farewell Again 36, etc.

Corbett, Ronnie (1930–). Pint-sized British TV comedian, one of the Two Ronnies.
Rockets Galore 58. Casino Royale 67. Some Will Some Won't 70. The Rise and Rise of Michael Rimmer 70. No Sex Please We're British 73, etc.

Corbucci, Sergio (1927–). Italian director.
Duel of the Titans 61. Son of Spartacus 62. The Slave 63. Minnesota Clay 64. Django 65. The Hellbenders 66. The Campanieros 71, etc.

Corby, Ellen (1913–) (Ellen Hansen). American character actress specializing in nosey neighbours and prim spinsters.
The Dark Corner 46. The Spiral Staircase 46. *I Remember Mama* 48. Fighting Father Dunne 48. Madame Bovary 49. On Moonlight Bay 51. About Mrs Leslie 54. The Seventh Sin 57. Macabre 58. Visit to a Small Planet 60. The Strangler 64. The Gnome-Mobile 67, many others.
TV series: Please Don't Eat the Daisies 65. *The Waltons* 72–81.

Corcoran, Donna (1943–). American child actress of the fifties.
Angels in the Outfield 51. Don't Bother to Knock 52. Scandal at Scourie 53. Dangerous when Wet 53. Gypsy Colt 54. Violent Saturday 55, etc.

Corcoran, Kevin (1949–). American child actor of the fifties and sixties.
Untamed 55. Old Yeller 59. The Shaggy Dog 59. Toby Tyler 60. The Swiss Family Robinson 61. Babes in Toyland 62. Bon Voyage 63. Savage Sam 64. A Tiger Walks 65, etc.

Cord, Alex (1931–) (Alexander Viespi). Italian-American leading man.
Synanon 65. Stagecoach 66. The Brotherhood 68. Stiletto 69. Dead or Alive 69. The Last Grenade 69. The Dead Are Alive 72. Genesis II (TV) 73. Chosen Survivors 74. Sidewinder One 77. Greyeagle 77. Beggarman, Thief (TV) 79. Goliath Awaits (TV) 81, etc.
TV series: Airwolf 84–86.

Corday, Mara (1932–) (Marilyn Watts). American leading lady of the fifties.
Sea Tiger 52. So This Is Paris 54. Man Without a Star 55. The Quiet Gun 57. The Black Scorpion 57. The Gauntlet 77, etc.

Corday, Paula (1924–) (also known as Paule Croset and Rita Corday). Anglo-Swiss leading lady who went to Hollywood in the forties.
The Falcon Strikes Back 43. The Body Snatcher 45. The Exile 47. Sword of Monte Cristo 51. Because You're Mine 52. The French Line 54, etc.

Cordell, Frank (1918–1980). British composer.
The Voice of Merrill 52. The Rebel 60. Khartoum 66. Ring of Bright Water 69. Cromwell 71. A Choice of Weapons 76, etc.

Cording, Harry (1891–1954). British supporting actor in Hollywood, usually as tough, blunt types.
The Knockout 25. Captain of the Guard 30. Forgotten Commandments 33. The Crusades 35. Mutiny on the Bounty 35. Sutter's Gold 36. The Prince and the Pauper 37. The Adventures of Robin Hood 38. The Hound of the Baskervilles 39. The Wolf Man 41. Arabian Nights 42. Lost in a Harem 44. The House of Fear 45. Terror by Night 46. A Woman's Vengeance 48. Samson and Delilah 49. Mask of the Avenger 51. Road to Bali 52. Titanic 53. Demetrius and the Gladiators 54. East of Eden 55, many others.

Cordy, Raymond (1898–1956) (R. Cordiaux). French comedy actor, especially seen in René Clair's films.
Le Million 31. À Nous la Liberté 31. Le Quatorze Juillet 33. Le Dernier Milliardaire 34. Ignace 37. Les Inconnus dans la Maison 42. Le Silence est d'Or 46. La Beauté du Diable 49. Les Belles de Nuit 52. Les Grandes Manoeuvres 55, etc.

Corey, Jeff (1914–). Gaunt American supporting actor seen as farmer, gangster, junkie, wino, convict, cop, and even Wild Bill Hickok.
All that Money Can Buy 41. My Friend Flicka 43. The Killers 46. Brute Force 47. Home of the Brave 49. Bright Leaf 50.

Rawhide 51. Red Mountain 52. The Balcony 63. Lady in a Cage 64. Mickey One 65. The Cincinnati Kid 65. *Seconds* 66. In Cold Blood 67. True Grit 69. *Little Big Man* 71. Catlow 72. Paper Tiger 75. Oh God 77. Butch and Sundance: The Early Days 79. Battle Beyond the Stars 80. The Sword and the Sorcerer 82. Conan the Destroyer 84, many others.

Corey, Wendell (1914–1968). American leading actor who usually played solid dependable types.
□Desert Fury 47. I Walk Alone 47. The Search 48. Maneater of Kumaon 48. Sorry Wrong Number 48. The Accused 48. Any Number Can Play 49. The File on Thelma Jordon 49. Holiday Affair 49. No Sad Songs for Me 50. The Furies 50. Harriet Craig 50. The Great Missouri Raid 50. Rich Young and Pretty 51. The Wild Blue Yonder 51. The Wild North 52. Carbine Williams 52. My Man and I 52. Laughing Anne (GB) 53. Jamaica Run 53. Hell's Half Acre 54. Rear Window 54. The Big Knife 55. The Bold and the Brave 56. The Killer is Loose 56. The Rack 56. The Rainmaker 56. Loving You 57. The Light in the Forest 58. Alias Jesse James 59. Blood on the Arrow 64. Agent for Harm 65. Waco 66. Women of the Prehistoric Planet 66. Picture Mommy Dead 66. Red Tomahawk 67. Cyborg 2087 67. The Astro Zombies 68. Buckskin 68.
TV series: Harbor Command 57. Peck's Bad Girl 59. The Eleventh Hour 62.

Corfield, John (1893–). British producer in films from 1929; co-founder of British National Films with Lady Yule and J. Arthur Rank.
Turn of the Tide 35. Laugh It Off 40. Gaslight 40. Headline 42. Bedelia 46. The White Unicorn 47. My Sister and I 48, etc.

Corman, Gene (–). American producer, brother of Roger Corman.
Tower of London 62. The Secret Invasion 64. Tobruk 66. You Can't Win 'Em All 70, etc.

Corman, Roger (1926–). American director who during the fifties made a record number of grade Z horror films, then presented an interesting series of Poe adaptations; when he seemed poised for better things his career slowed almost to a halt. Has normally produced his own films.
□Five Guns West 55. Apache Woman 55. The Day the World Ended 56. Swamp Woman 56. The Gunslinger 56. Oklahoma Woman 56. It Conquered the World 56. Naked Paradise 57. Attack of the Crab Monsters 57. *Not of this Earth* 57. The Undead 57. Rock all Night 57. Carnival Rock 57. Teenage Doll 57. Sorority Girl 57. The Viking Women and the Sea Serpent 57. War of the Satellites 57. Machine Gun Kelly 58. Teenage Caveman 58. She-Gods of Shark Reef 58. I Mobster 59. Wasp Woman 59. *A Bucket of Blood* 59. Ski Troop Attack 60. *House of Usher* 60. The Little Shop of Horrors 60. The Last Woman on Earth 60. Creature from the Haunted Sea 60. Atlas 60. The Pit and the Pendulum 61. The Premature Burial 62. *The Intruder* 62. Tales of Terror 62. Tower of London 62. *The Raven* 63. The Young Racers 63. The Haunted Palace 63. The Terror 63. X—The Man with X-ray Eyes 63. *The Masque of the Red Death* 64. Secret Invasion 64. *The Tomb of Ligeia* 65. The Wild Angels 66. The St Valentine's Day Massacre 67. The Trip 67. Bloody Mama 70. Gas-s-s! 70. Von Richthofen and Brown 71. Boxcar Bertha (p only) 72. I Escaped from Devil's Island (co-p only) 73. Big Bad Mama (p only) 74. Cockfighter (p only) 74. Grand Theft Auto (p only) 77. Thunder and Lightning (p only) 77. Piranha (p only) 78. St Jack (p only) 78. Battle Beyond the Stars (p only) 80. Humanoids from the Deep (p only) 80. Smokey Bites the Dust (p only) 81. Forbidden World (p only) 82.
†In the seventies Corman became a distributor (New World Pictures) and specialized in foreign films.

¶ I've never made the film I wanted to make. No matter what happens, it never turns out exactly as I hoped.—*R.C.*

Poe writes the first reel or the last reel. Roger does the rest.—*James H. Nicholson*

All my films have been concerned simply with man as a social animal.—*R.C., 1970*

I think there is always a political undercurrent in my films. With the exception of *The Intruder*, I tried not to put it on the surface.—*R.C.*

Cornelius, Henry (1913–1958). British director with a subtle comedy touch.
□It Always Rains on Sunday (co-w only) 47. *Passport to Pimlico* 48. The Galloping Major (& w) 51. *Genevieve* 53. I am a Camera 55. Next to No Time 57. Law and Disorder 58.

Cornfield, Hubert (1929–). American director.
□Sudden Danger 56. Lure of the Swamp 57. Plunder Road 59. *The Third Voice* 59. Angel Baby (co-d) 61. Pressure Point 62. Night of the Following Day 68.

Corri, Adrienne (1930–) (Adrienne Riccoboni). Tempestuous red-headed British leading lady of Italian descent.
The River 51. The Kidnappers 53. Devil Girl from Mars 54. *Lease of Life* 54. Make Me an Offer 54. The Feminine Touch 55. Three Men in a Boat 56. Corridors of Blood 58. The Rough and the Smooth 59. The Hellfire Club 61. The Tell-Tale Heart 61. A Study in Terror 65. Bunny Lake is Missing 65. The Viking Queen 67. Moon Zero Two 69. A Clockwork Orange 71. Vampire Circus 72. Madhouse 74, etc.

Corrigan, Douglas 'Wrong Way' (1907–). American aviator who in 1939 left New York for Los Angeles and landed in Ireland, thus deserving the title Wrong Way Corrigan. In the same year he played himself in the film *The Flying Irishman*.

Corrigan, Lloyd (1900–1969). Chubby American character actor, usually in jovial roles; also directed some films in the thirties.
The Splendid Crime 25. Daughter of the Dragon (d) 31. The Broken Wing (d) 32. Murder on a Honeymoon (d) 35. The Dancing Pirate (d) 36. Night Key (d) 37. Young Tom Edison 40. *The Ghost Breakers* 40. The Great Man's Lady 42. Since You Went Away 44. The Bandit of Sherwood Forest 45. Stallion Road 47. Cyrano de Bergerac 50. Son of Paleface 52. The Bowery Boys Meet the Monsters 54. Hidden Guns 57. The Manchurian Candidate 62, many others.

Corrigan, Ray 'Crash' (1903–1976) (Ray Benard). American leading man, hero of innumerable second feature westerns.
The Three Mesquiteers 36. Wild Horse Rodeo 38. The Purple Vigilantes 38. Three Texas Steers 39. West of the Pinto Basin 40. Wrangler's Roost 41. Rock River Renegades 42.

The Corsican Brothers. The romantic adventure novel by Dumas *père* presents a splendid dual role for an actor. King Baggott starred in the first film version in 1915, followed by Dustin Farnum in 1919 and Douglas Fairbanks Jnr in 1940. *The Return of the Corsican Brothers* (or *Bandits of Corsica*), starring Richard Greene, followed in 1953; and the original was remade in France in 1960, with Geoffrey Toone.

Cort, Bud (1950–) (Walter Edward Cox). American actor with a tendency to play demented youths.
M*A*S*H 70. The Travelling Executioner 70. Brewster McCloud 70. *Harold and Maude* 72.Why Shoot the Teacher 77. Hitler's Son 78. Die Laughing 80. She Dances Alone 82. Love Letters 83. Electric Dreams 84. Maria's Lovers 84. Invaders from Mars 86, etc.

Cortesa, Valentina (1924–). Italian leading lady in international films.
The Glass Mountain 48. Thieves' Highway 49. Malaya 50. The House on Telegraph Hill 51. Les Misérables 52. The Barefoot Contessa 54. Le Amiche 55. Magic Fire 56. Calabuch 58. Barabbas 62. The Visit 64. Juliet of the Spirits 65. The Legend of Lylah Clare 68. La Nuit Américaine 73. When Time Ran Out 80; The Adventures of Baron Munchhausen 88, etc.

Cortez, Ricardo (1899–1977) (Jake Kranz). American leading man, groomed in the twenties as a Latin lover in the Valentino mould. Later developed outside interests and quit movies after a sojourn in routine roles.
Sixty Cents an Hour 23. Pony Express 24. *The Torrent* 26. *The Sorrows of Satan* 27. The Private Life of Helen of Troy 27. Behind Office Doors 28. Ten Cents a Dance 31. Melody of Life 32. The Phantom of Crestwood 33. *Wonder Bar* 34. Special Agent 35. The Walking Dead 36. Talk of the Devil (GB) 36. Mr Moto's Last Warning 38. City Girl (d only) 38. Free, Blonde and Twenty One (d only) 40. World Première 40. I Killed That Man 42. Make Your Own Bed 44. The Locket 46. Blackmail 47. The Last Hurrah 58, many others.

Cortez, Stanley (1908–) (Stanley Kranz). American cinematographer, brother of Ricardo Cortez; in Hollywood from silent days.
□Four Days Wonder 37. The Wildcatter 37. Armored Car 37. The Black Doll 38. Lady in the Morgue 38. Danger on the Air 38. Personal Secretary 38. The Last Express 38. For Love or Money 38. The Forgotten Woman 39. They Asked for It 39. Hawaiian Nights 39. Risky Business 39. Laugh It Off 39. Alias the Deacon 39. The Leatherpushers 40. Meet the Wildcat 40. Love Honor and Oh Baby 40. The Black Cat 40. A Dangerous Game 41. San Antonio Rose 41. Moonlight in Hawaii 41. Badlands of Dakota 41. Bombay Clipper 42. Eagle Squadron 42. *The Magnificent Ambersons* 42. Flesh and Fantasy 43. The Powers Girl 43. Since You Went Away (co-ph) 44. Smash Up 47. The Secret Beyond the Door 48. Smart Woman 48. The Man on the Eiffel Tower 49. Underworld

Story 50. The Admiral was a Lady 50. The Basketball Fix 51. Fort Defiance 51. Models Inc 52. Abbott and Costello Meet Captain Kidd 52. The Diamond Queen 53. Dragon's Gold 53. Shark River 53. Riders to the Stars 54. Black Tuesday 54. *The Night of the Hunter* 55. Man from Del Rio 56. Top Secret Affair 57. The Three Faces of Eve 57. Thunder in the Sun 59. Vice Raid 60. The Angry Red Planet 60. Dinosaurus 60. Back Street 61. Shock Corridor 63. The Candidate 64. Nightmare in the Sun 64. The Naked Kiss 65. The Navy vs the Night Monsters 66. The Ghost in the Invisible Bikini 66. Blue 68. The Bridge at Remagen 69. The Date 71. Do Not Fold, Spindle or Mutilate (TV) 72. Another Man, Another Chance (co-ph) 77.

Cosby, Bill (1938–). Black American leading man and TV personality.
□To All My Friends on Shore (TV) (& p) 71. Hickey and Boggs 72. Uptown Saturday Night 74. Let's Do It Again 76. Mother, Jugs and Speed 76. A Piece of the Action 77. Top Secret (TV) 78. California Suite 79. Leonard Part 6 87. The Adventures of Baron Munchhausen 88, etc.
TV series: *I Spy* 66–68. The Bill Cosby Show 69. Fat Albert and the Cosby Kids 72. Cos 76. The Bill Cosby Show 85– .

Cosmatos, George Pan (1941–). Greek director of international adventures.
Massacre in Rome 74. The Cassandra Crossing 77. Escape to Athena 79. Rambo: First Blood II 84. Cobra 85.

¶ *G.P.C.:* My pictures appeal all round the world. I do slick American pictures with a European sensitivity.

Cossart, Ernest (1876–1951). Portly British actor, inevitably cast by Hollywood in butler roles.
The Scoundrel 35. Desire 36. The Great Ziegfeld 36. Angel 37. Zaza 39. The Light That Failed 39. Tom Brown's Schooldays 40. *Charley's Aunt* 41. Casanova Brown 44. Cluny Brown 46. John Loves Mary 49, many others.

Cossins, James (1933–). British character actor, usually of pompous, flustered type.
The Anniversary 68. Lost Continent 68. Melody 70. Villain 71, etc.

Costa-Gavras (1933–) (Constantin Costa-Gavras). Russo-Greek director, in France from childhood.
□The Sleeping Car Murders 65. Un Homme de Trop 67. 'Z' (AA) 68. L'Aveu 70. State of Siege 72. Special Section 75. Missing (AA co-w) 82. Hannah K 83.

Costello, Dolores (1905–79). Gentle American silent screen heroine; married John Barrymore.
Lawful Larceny 23. *The Sea Beast* 25. Bride of the Storm 26. When a Man Loves 27. Old San Francisco 27. Glorious Betsy 28. The Redeeming Sin 29. *Noah's Ark* 29. Show of Shows 29. Second Choice 30. Expensive Women 31. Little Lord Fauntleroy 36. King of the Turf 39. *The Magnificent Ambersons* 42. This is the Army 43, many others.

Costello, Helene (1904–1957). American silent screen leading lady.
The Man on the Box 25. Bobbed Hair 25. Don Juan 26. In Old Kentucky 27. *Lights of New York* 28. Midnight Taxi 28. The Circus Kid 28, etc.

Costello, Lou (1906–1959) (Louis Cristillo). Dumpy American comedian, the zanier half of Abbott and Costello. For films, see *Bud Abbott*. Costello finally made one on his own, *The Thirty-Foot Bride of Candy Rock* 59.

Costello, Maurice (1877–1950). American matinée idol, in films from 1907.
A Tale of Two Cities 11. The Night Before Christmas 12. Human Collateral 20. Conceit 21. Glimpses of the Moon 23. The Mad Marriage 25. Camille 27. Hollywood Boulevard 36. Lady from Louisiana 41, others.

Costner, Kevin (–). American leading actor.
Night Shift 82. Table For Five 83. Testament 83. American Flyers 84. Fandango 84. Silverado 85. Sizzle Beach 86. The Untouchables 87. No Way Out 87. The Winning Streak 88.

Cottafavi, Vittorio (1914–). Italian director, mainly of cut-rate spectaculars. Has won critical approval for stylish handling of some of them.
Revolt of the Gladiators 58. The Legions of Cleopatra 59. The Vengeance of Hercules 60. Hercules Conquers Atlantis 61.

Cotten, Joseph (1905–). Tall, quiet American leading man, former drama critic and Broadway stage star.

Autobiography 1987: *Vanity will get you Somewhere*
□*Citizen Kane* 41. *The Magnificent Ambersons* 42. *Journey into Fear* 42. Lydia 41. *Shadow of a Doubt* 43. Hers to Hold 43. Gaslight 44. Since You Went Away 44. Love Letters 45. *I'll Be Seeing You* 45. Duel in the Sun 46. The Farmer's Daughter 47. *Portrait of Jennie* 48. Under Capricorn 49. Beyond the Forest 49. *The Third Man* 49. Two Flags West 50. Walk Softly Stranger 50. September Affair 50. Half Angel 51. Man with a Cloak 51. Peking Express 52. Untamed Frontier 52. The Steel Trap 52. Niagara 52. Blueprint for Murder 53. Special Delivery 54. The Bottom of the Bottle 55. The Killer is Loose 56. The Halliday Brand 56. From the Earth to the Moon 58. The Angel Wore Red 60. The Last Sunset 61. Hush Hush Sweet Charlotte 64. The Money Trap 65. The Great Sioux Massacre 65. The Tramplers 66. The Oscar 66. The Hell-benders 67. Jack of Diamonds 67. Brighty 67. Some May Live (TV) 67. Petulia 68. Days of Fire (It.) 68. Keene 69. Cutter's Trail (TV) 69. The Lonely Profession (TV) 69. Latitude Zero 69. The Grasshopper 70. Do You Take This Stranger (TV) 70. The Abominable Dr Phibes 71. City Beneath the Sea (TV) 71. Doomsday Voyage 71. Tora! Tora! Tora! 71. White Comanche 71. Lady Frankenstein 71. Baron Blood 72. Assault on the Wayne (TV) 72. The Screaming Woman (TV) 72. The Devil's Daughter (TV) 72. The Scientific Cardplayer 72. Soylent Green 73. A Delicate Balance 73. The Lindbergh Kidnapping Case (TV) 76. Twilight's Last Gleaming 76. Airport 77 77. Caravans 78. Churchill and the Generals (TV) 79. Island of Mutations 79. Guyana, Crime of the Century 79. The Survivor 80. Heaven's Gate 80. The Hearse 80. Delusion 81. The House Where Evil Dwells 82.
TV series: On Trial. Hollywood and the Stars.
† Cotten made an unbilled gag appearance as a doctor in *Touch of Evil*.

Couffer, Jack (1922–). American director with a penchant for natural history.
□Ring of Bright Water 69. The Darwin Adventure 72. Jonathan Livingston Seagull 73.

Coulouris, George (1903–). British character actor, in America 1930–50; usually in explosive roles.
Christopher Bean 33. All This and Heaven Too 40. The Lady in Question 40. *Citizen Kane* 41. This Land is Mine 43. *Watch on the Rhine* 43. Between Two Worlds 44. The Master Race 44. Hotel Berlin 45. Confidential Agent 45. The Verdict 46. Sleep My Love 47. A Southern Yankee 48. *An Outcast of the Islands* 51. Doctor in the House 53. The Runaway Bus 54. I Accuse 57. Womaneater 59. Conspiracy of Hearts 60. King of Kings 61. The Skull 65. Arabesque 66. The Assassination Bureau 69. Blood from the Mummy's Tomb 71. Papillon 73. Mahler 74. Murder on the Orient Express 74. The Antichrist 75. The Ritz 76. The Long Good Friday 80, many others.

The Count of Monte Cristo. This popular adventure yarn by Alexandre Dumas was filmed in 1912 with Hobart Bosworth, and again in the same year with James O'Neill. John Gilbert starred in the 1923 silent film, but the best-remembered version is the 1934 talkie remake with Robert Donat, directed by Rowland V. Lee. Oddly enough it has never since been remade in English, though French versions were made in 1942, 1953 and 1961 starring respectively Pierre Richard Willm, Jean Marais and Louis Jourdan; a TV version starring Richard Chamberlain followed in 1976; and there have been over a dozen films using the name Monte Cristo to cover a multitude of plots, some of them present-day: *Sword of Monte Cristo, Wife of Monte Cristo, Monte Cristo's Revenge*, etc. A TV series of 1956 starred George Dolenz.

? couples
Who played the following couples, and in what films?

1 Norman Maine and Vicki Lester in 1937?
2 C. K. Dexter Haven and Tracy Lord in 1940?
3 Charles and Ruth Condomine in 1945?
4 Dr Frederick Steele and Judith Traherne in 1939?
5 Don Birnam and Helen St James in 1945?
6 Joseph and Maria Tura in 1942?
7 Al and Milly Stephenson in 1946?
8 'J.B.' and Dr Constance Peterson in 1945?
9 Immanuel Rath and Lola Frohlich in 1930?
10 Rudolf Rassendyll and Princess Flavia in 1937?
11 Mr and Mrs Maximilian de Winter in 1940?
12 The Ringo Kid and Dallas in 1939?
13 The Duc de Praslin and Henriette Deluzy-Desportes in 1940?
14 Dr Alec Harvey and Laura Jesson in 1946?

15 Yancey and Sabra Cravat in 1930?
16 Walter Neff and Phyllis Dietrichson in 1944?
17 Henry Van Cleve and Martha Strabel in 1943?
18 George Gibbs and Emily Webb in 1940?
19 Major Rama Safti and Lady Edwina Esketh in 1939?
20 Peter Warne and Ellie Andrews in 1934?

Courant, Curt (c. 1895–). German cinematographer who did his best work elsewhere.
Quo Vadis 24. Woman in the Moon 29. Perfect Understanding (GB) 33. Amok 34. The Man Who Knew Too Much (GB) 34. The Iron Duke (GB) 35. Broken Blossoms (GB) 36. La Bête Humaine 38. Louise 39. Le Jour Se Lève 39. De Mayerling à Sarajevo 40. Monsieur Verdoux (US) 47. It Happened in Athens 61, etc.

Courcel, Nicole (1930–) (Nicole Andrieux). French leading lady of warm personality.
La Marie du Port 49. Versailles 53. La Sorcière 55. The Case of Dr Laurent 56. Sundays and Cybele 62, etc.

Court, Hazel (1926–). Red-headed British leading lady; moved into horror films and went to live in Hollywood.
Champagne Charlie 44. Dear Murderer 46. My Sister and I 48. It's Not Cricket 48. Bond Street 50. The Curse of Frankenstein 56. The Man Who Could Cheat Death 59. Doctor Blood's Coffin 60. The Premature Burial 62. The Masque of the Red Death 64, etc.
TV series: Dick and the Duchess 57.

Courtenay, Tom (1937–). Lean British actor specializing in under-privileged roles.
Billy Liar 63. *The Loneliness of the Long Distance Runner* 63. Private Potter 62. King and Country 64. Operation Crossbow 65. King Rat 65. Doctor Zhivago 65. The Night of the Generals 66. The Day the Fish Came Out 67. A Dandy in Aspic 68. *Otley* 69. One Day in the Life of Ivan Denisovitch 71. Catch Me a Spy 71. *The Dresser* (AAN) 83. Happy New Year 87. Leonard Part 6 87, etc.

¶ *T.C.:* There just doesn't seem to be a market for something with aspiration anymore.

courtesans have always been viewed by the cinema through rose-coloured glasses. There have been innumerable films about Madame du Barry, Madame Sans Gêne and Nell Gwynne; Garbo played Camille and Marie Walewska as well as Anna Christie; even Jean Simmons had a shot at Napoleon's *Désirée*, and Vivien Leigh was a decorative Lady Hamilton. Martine Carol played Lola Montes in the Max Ophüls film, Yvonne de Carlo in *Black Bart* (in which she became involved in western villainy during an American tour).
See also: *prostitutes*.

Courtland, Jerome (1926–). Gangling young American lead of forties comedies.
Kiss and Tell 45. Man from Colorado 48. Battleground 49. The Barefoot Mailman 52. The Bamboo Prison 55. Tonka 59. O Sole Mio (It.) 60. Mary Read, Pirate (It.) 61. Thanis, Son of Attila (It.) 61. Black Spurs 65. Diamonds on Wheels (d only) 73. Pete's Dragon (co-p only) 77, etc.
TV series: Tales of the Vikings 60.

Courtneidge, Dame Cicely (1893–1980). British comedienne; wife of Jack Hulbert. On stage from 1901; her great vitality made her a musical comedy favourite.
Autobiography 1953: *Cicely*.
☐ Elstree Calling 30. *The Ghost Train* 31. *Jack's the Boy* 32. Happy Ever After 32. Aunt Sally 33. *Soldiers of the King* 33. Falling for You 33. Things are Looking Up 34. Me and Marlborough 35. Everybody Dance 36. Take my Tip 37. *Under Your Hat* 40. Miss Tulip Stays the Night 56. The Spider's Web 60. *The L-Shaped Room* 62. Those Magnificent Men in their Flying Machines 65. The Wrong Box 66. Not Now Darling 72.

¶ When I was in Delhi,
I lay on my—hm, hm,
In a flat-bottomed canoe.
They all called me barmy,
But I know the army!
The nation depends on you!
—*sung by C.C. in Under Your Hat*

courtroom scenes have been the suspenseful saving grace of more films than can be counted; and they also figure in some of the best films ever made.

British courts best preserve the ancient aura of the law; among the films they have figured in are *London Belongs to Me, The Paradine Case, Eight O'Clock Walk, Life for Ruth, Twenty-one Days, Brothers in Law, The Winslow Boy, Witness for the Prosecution, The Blind Goddess* and *The Dock Brief*. The last four are based on stage plays, as are the American *Madame X, Counsellor at Law*, and *The Trial of Mary Dugan*. Other American films depending heavily on courtroom denouements include *They Won't Believe Me, The Unholy Three, The Mouthpiece,*

Boomerang, They Won't Forget, The Missing Juror, Trial, the Young Savages, The Criminal Code, To Kill a Mockingbird, Criminal Lawyer, Fury, The Lawyer, A Free Soul, The Seven Minutes, The People Against O'Hara, The Lady from Shanghai, Twilight of Honour, An American Tragedy (and its remake *A Place in the Sun*), the several Perry Mason films, and *Young Mr Lincoln*. These, even the last-named, were fictional: genuine cases were reconstructed in *I Want to Live, Cell 2455 Death Row, Compulsion, Inherit the Wind, Dr Ehrlich's Magic Bullet, The Witches of Salem, The Trials of Oscar Wilde, Judgment at Nuremberg, The Life of Emile Zola, Dr Crippen, Captain Kidd, Landru* and *The Case of Charles Peace*. Comedy courtroom scenes have appeared in *I'm No Angel, Mr Deeds Goes to Town, You Can't Take It With You, Roxie Hart, My Learned Friend, Adam's Rib, Pickwick Papers, Brothers in Law, What's Up Doc?, Star!* and *A Pair of Briefs*.

Films in which special interest has centred on the jury include *Twelve Angry Men, Murder* (*Enter Sir John*), *Perfect Strangers* (*Too Dangerous to Love*), *Justice est Faite* and *The Monster and the Girl* (in which the criminal brain inside the gorilla murders the jurors at his trial one by one). Ghostly juries figured in *All That Money Can Buy* and *The Remarkable Andrew*. The judge has been the key figure in *The Judge Steps Out, Talk of the Town, The Bachelor and the Bobbysoxer*, and *Destry Rides Again*; and we are constantly being promised a film of Henry Cecil's *No Bail for the Judge. Anatomy of a Murder* remains the only film in which a real judge (Joseph E. Welch) has played a fictional one. A lady barrister (Anna Neagle) had the leading role in *The Man Who Wouldn't Talk*.

Specialized courts were seen in *M* (convened by criminals), *Saint Joan* and *The Hunchback of Notre Dame* (church courts), *Black Legion* (Ku Klux Klan), *The Devil's Disciple* (18th-century military court), *Kind Hearts and Coronets* (a court of the House of Lords), *The Wreck of the Mary Deare* (mercantile), *Cone of Silence* (civil aviation), *A Tale of Two Cities* and *The Scarlet Pimpernel* (French Revolutionary courts). Courts in other countries were shown in *The Lady in Question, The Count of Monte Cristo, Crack in the Mirror, A Flea in Her Ear, La Vérité, and Can Can* (French); *The Purple Heart* (Japanese); *The Fall of the Roman Empire* (ancient Roman); *The Spy Who Came in from the Cold* (East German); and *Shoeshine* (Italian). Coroners' courts were featured in *Inquest, My Learned Friend* and *Rebecca*.

Courts martial figured largely in *The Caine Mutiny, Time Limit, The Man in the Middle, Across the Pacific, The Rack, Carrington VC* and *The Court Martial of Billy Mitchell*. There was also a TV series called *Court Martial* (*Counsellors at War* in the US).

Heavenly courts were convened in *A Matter of Life and Death, Outward Bound* and *The Flight That Disappeared*; while other fantasy courts appeared in *Rashomon, Morgan, One Way Pendulum, Alice in Wonderland, The Balcony, The Wonderful World of the Brothers Grimm, The Trial, All That Money Can Buy*, and *The Remarkable Andrew*. The court in *Planet of the Apes* is perhaps best classed as prophetic, along with that in *1984*.

TV series based on trials and lawyers include *The Law and Mr Jones, Harrigan and Son, Sam Benedict, The Trials of O'Brien, Perry Mason, Arrest and Trial, The Defenders, The D.A., The Verdict is Yours, Judd for the Defense, Owen Marshall, Petrocelli* and *Adam's Rib*.

Cousteau, Jacques-Yves (1910–). French underwater explorer and documentarist.
The Silent World 56. World Without Sun 64, etc.

Coutard, Raoul (1924–). French cinematographer.
Ranuntcho 50. A Bout de Souffle 59. Shoot the Pianist 60. *Lola* 60. *Jules et Jim* 61. Vivre Sa Vie 61. Bay of Angels 62. Les Carabiniers 63. Silken Skin 63. Pierrot le Fou 65. Made in USA 66. Sailor from Gibraltar 66. The Bride Wore Black 67. 'Z' 68. L'Aveu 70. L'Explosion 70. Embassy 72. The Jerusalem File 72. A Pain in the A . . . 73. Le Crabe-Tambour 77. Le Legion saute sur Kolwezi (d only) 80, etc.

The Covered Wagon (US 1923). A big-scale pioneer western which, though it now seems tame, did much to establish the form. Directed by James Cruze, photographed by Karl Brown, edited by Dorothy Arzner, written by Jack Cunningham from a novel by Emerson Hough.

Cowan, Jerome (1897–1972). American character actor with an easy manner. In films from 1936 (*Beloved Enemy*: out of character as a fanatical Irishman). He played hundreds of supporting roles, typically in *The Maltese*

Falcon 41 as the detective killed while searching for the mysterious Floyd Thursby; played the lead in *Crime by Night* 43, *Find The Blackmailer* 44. Latterly graduated from jealous rivals to executives, from lawyers to judges.
Claudia and David 46. The Unfaithful 47. Miracle on 34th Street 48. June Bride 48. The Fountainhead 49. Young Man with a Horn 50. Dallas 51. The System 53. Visit to a Small Planet 60. Frankie and Johnny 65. The Gnome-Mobile 67. The Comic 69, many others.
TV series: The Tab Hunter Show 60. Tycoon 64.

Cowan, Lester (c. 1905–). American producer from 1934.
My Little Chickadee 39. Ladies in Retirement 41. The Story of G.I. Joe 45. Love Happy 50. Main Street to Broadway 52, etc.

Cowan, Maurice (1891–1974). British producer of mainly routine films.
Derby Day 52. Turn the Key Softly 55. The Gypsy and the Gentleman 57, etc.

Coward, Sir Noel (1899–1973). British actor-writer-composer-director, the bright young man of international show business in the twenties and thirties.
Autobiographies: *Present Indicative* 1933, *Future Indefinite* 1949. Biographies: *A Talent to Amuse* by Sheridan Morley, 1969; *The Life of Noel Coward* by Cole Lesley, 1976.
Coward was portrayed in *Star!* 68 by Dan Massey. *The Noel Coward Diaries* were published in 1982.
□Hearts of the World (a) 18. Private Lives (oa) 31. Cavalcade (oa) 33. Tonight is Ours (oa) 33. Bitter Sweet (oa) 33 and 40. Design for Living (oa) 34. *The Scoundrel* (a) 35. *In Which We Serve* (awpd) (AA) 41. We Were Dancing (oa) 42. *Blithe Spirit* (oa) 45. This Happy Breed (oa) 45. *Brief Encounter* (oa) 46. The Astonished Heart (a) 49. Meet Me Tonight (oa) 50. Around the World in Eighty Days (a) 56. *Our Man in Havana* (a) 59. Surprise Package (a) 60. Paris When it Sizzles (a) 64. Bunny Lake is Missing (a) 65. Boom (a) 66. The Italian Job (a) 69.
❀ For displaying, if only intermittently, a wholly professional talent to amuse. *In Which We Serve.*

¶ 'Destiny's tot.'—*Alexander Woollcott*

Cowen, William J. (1883–1964). American director.
□Kongo 32. Oliver Twist 33. Woman Unafraid 34.

Cowl, Jane (1884–1950). American leading stage actress who made very few film appearances.
□The Garden of Lies 15. The Spreading Dawn 17. Once More My Darling 49. No Man of Her Own 49. The Secret Fury 50. Payment on Demand 50.

Cox, Alex (–). American director.
Repo Man 84. Sid and Nancy 86. Straight to Hell 87.

Cox, Ronny (1938–). American character actor with stage background.
The Happiness Cage 72. *Deliverance* 72. Bound for Glory 76. The Car 77. The Onion Field 79. Taps 81. The Beast Within 82. Robocop 87
TV series: Apple's Way 74.

Cox, Vivian (1915–). British producer.
Father Brown 54. The Prisoner 55. Bachelor of Hearts 58, etc.

Cox, Wally (1924–1973). American comic actor, usually seen as the bespectacled, weedy character he played in the TV series *Mr Peepers* 52–54 and *Hiram Holliday* 58.
□ State Fair 62. Spencer's Mountain 63. Fate is the Hunter 64. The Bedford Incident 65. Morituri 65. The Yellow Rolls Royce 65. A Guide for the Married Man 67. The One and Only Genuine Original Family Band 68. The Boatniks 70. The Cockeyed Cowboys of Calico County 70. Up Your Teddy Bear 70.

Crabbe, Buster (1907–1983) (Clarence Linden Crabbe). American athlete who became leading man of 'B' pictures.
King of the Jungle 33. Tarzan the Fearless 33. Nevada 36. *Flash Gordon's Trip to Mars* 38. Buck Rogers 39. Queen of Broadway 43. Caged Fury 48. Gunfighters of Abilene 59. Arizona Raiders 65, many others.
TV series: Captain Gallant 55.

Crabe, James (–). American cinematographer.
Zigzag 70. Save the Tiger 72. W.W. and the Dixie Dancekings 72. Rocky 76. Players 79. The China Syndrome 79. How to Beat the High Cost of Living 80. The Baltimore Bullet 80. The Formula 80.

Crabtree, Arthur (1900–1975). British director, former cameraman.

Madonna of the Seven Moons 44. They Were Sisters 45. Dear Murderer 46. Caravan 46. The Calendar 48. Lili Marlene 50. Hindle Wakes 52. The Wedding of Lili Marlene 53. West of Suez 57. Morning Call 58. Horrors of the Black Museum 59, etc.

Craig, Alec (1878–1945). Scottish character actor in Hollywood; often played misers, moneylenders and downtrodden roles.
Mutiny on the Bounty 35. Mary of Scotland 36. Winterset 36. Vivacious Lady 38. Tom Brown's Schooldays 40. Cat People 42. Holy Matrimony 43. Lassie Come Home 43. Spider Woman 44. Kitty 46, many others.

Craig, Edward Gordon (1872–1966) (Henry Edward Wardell). British stage designer, father of Edward Carrick (qv). Though not directly employed in films, his stage designs were influential to people like William Cameron Menzies and Anton Grot.

Craig, H. A. L. (Harold) (1925–1978). British screenwriter.
Anzio 68. Waterloo 70. Mohammed 77, etc.

Craig, James (1912–86) (John Meador). American leading man, usually the good-natured but tough outdoor type.
Thunder Trail 37. The Buccaneer 38. The Man They Could Not Hang 39. Zanzibar 40. Kitty Foyle 40. *All That Money Can Buy* (the 'Faust' role, and his best) 41. Valley of the Sun 41. The Omaha Trail 42. The Human Comedy 43. Lost Angel 43. Kismet 44. Our Vines Have Tender Grapes 45. Boys Ranch 45. Little Mister Jim 46. Northwest Stampede 48. Side Street 50. Drums in the Deep South 51. Hurricane Smith 52. Fort Vengeance 53. While the City Sleeps 56. Four Fast Guns 59. The Hired Gun 67, many others.

¶ *J.C.:* I was out there in Hollywood on vacation, and I saw a lot of people making movies. If they could do it, why couldn't I?

Craig, Michael (1928–) (Michael Gregson). British light leading man, a former crowd artist groomed by the Rank Organization; later attempted more ambitious roles before settling in Australia.
Malta Story 53. The Love Lottery 54. Yield to the Night 55. House of Secrets 56. High Tide at Noon 57. Campbell's Kingdom 58. The Silent Enemy 58. Nor the Moon by Night 58. Sea of Sand 59. Sapphire 59. Upstairs and Downstairs 59. *The Angry Silence* (& w) 59. Cone of Silence 60. Doctor in Love 60. Mysterious Island 61. *Payroll* 61. A Pair of Briefs 62. Life for Ruth 62. The Iron Maiden 62. Stolen Hours 63. Of a Thousand Delights (Vaghe Stella dell'Orsa) 65. Life at the Top 65. Modesty Blaise 66. Sandra (It.) 66. *Star!* 68. The Royal Hunt of the Sun 69. Twinky 69. Brotherly Love 70. A Town Called Bastard 71. Vault of Horror 73. The Emigrants (TV) 77. The Timeless Land (TV) 77. Turkey Shoot 82. Stanley 83, etc.

Craig, Wendy (1934–). British comedy actress, especially on TV in *Not in Front of the Children, And Mother Makes Three, Nanny*, etc.
The Mind Benders 63. The Servant 63. The Nanny 65. Just Like a Woman 66. I'll Never Forget Whatshisname 67. Joseph Andrews, 77, etc.

Craig, Yvonne (1941–). American leading lady.
The Young Land 60. By Love Possessed 61. Seven Women from Hell 62. Kissin' Cousins 64. One Spy Too Many 66. In Like Flint 67, etc.

Craigie, Jill (1914–). British documentary director.
The Way We Live 46. Blue Scar 48. The Million Pound Note (w only) 51. Windom's Way (w only) 57, etc.

Crain, Jeanne (1925–). American leading lady of the forties; usually the personification of sweetness and light.
□The Gang's All Here 43. Home in Indiana 44. In the Meantime Darling 44. Winged Victory 44. *State Fair* 45. Leave Her to Heaven 45. Centennial Summer 46. *Margie* 46. Apartment for Peggy 48. You Were Meant for Me 48. A Letter to Three Wives 49. The Fan 49. *Pinky* 49. Cheaper by the Dozen 50. Take Care of My Little Girl 51. People Will Talk 51. The Model and the Marriage Broker 52. Belles on Their Toes 52. Full House 52. Dangerous Crossing 53. City of Bad Men 53. Vicki 53. Duel in the Jungle (GB) 54. Man Without a Star 55. Gentlemen Marry Brunettes 55. The Second Greatest Sex 55. The Fastest Gun Alive 56. The Tattered Dress 57. The Joker is Wild 58. Guns of the Timberland 60. Twenty Plus Two 61. Queen of the Nile (It.) 61. With Fire and Sword (It.) 61. Pontius Pilate (It.) 61. Madison Avenue 62. 52 Miles to Terror 64. The Night God Screamed 71. Skyjacked 72.

Cramer, Rychard (1889–1960). Malevolent-looking American character actor, a memorable foil for Laurel and Hardy in *Scram, Saps at Sea*, etc.

Crane, Bob (1929–78). American light comic actor, popular in TV series *Hogan's Heroes*.
□Return to Peyton Place 61. Mantrap 61. The Wicked Dreams of Paula Schultz 68. Superdad 74. Gus 76.

Crane, Richard (1919–69). American juvenile lead of the forties.
Susan and God 40. This Time for Keeps 42. Happy Land 43. None Shall Escape 44. Captain Eddie 45. Behind Green Lights 46. Triple Threat 48. Dynamite 49. The Last Outpost 51. The Neanderthal Man 53. The Eternal Sea 55. The Deep Six 58. The Alligator People 59. House of the Damned 63. Surf Party 64, etc.
TV series: Hawaiian Eye 60–62.

crane shot. A high-angle shot in which the camera travels up, down or laterally while mounted on a travelling crane.

Crane, Stephen (1871–1900). American novelist who crystallized aspects of the Civil War in *The Red Badge of Courage*.

The Cranes are Flying (Russia 1957). The simple but moving story of a wartime Moscow romance, distinguished by Mikhail Kalatozov's direction, Urusevsky's mobile camerawork, and the performance of Tatiana Samoilova.

Cravat, Nick (1911–). Small, agile American actor, once Burt Lancaster's circus partner.
The Flame and the Arrow 51. The Crimson Pirate 52. King Richard and the Crusaders 54. Three-Ring Circus 55. Kiss Me Deadly 55. Davy Crockett 56. Run Silent, Run Deep 59. The Scalphunters 68. Ulzana's Raid 72. The Island of Dr Moreau 77, etc.

Craven, Frank (1875–1945). American stage character actor who spent his later years in Hollywood; typically cast as kindly pipe-smoking philosopher.
□We Americans 28. The Very Idea 29. State Fair 33. That's Gratitude 34. He Was Her Man 34. Let's Talk It Over 34. City Limits 34. Funny Thing Called Love 34. *Barbary Coast* 35. Car 99 35. Vagabond Lady 35. Small Town Girl 36. The Harvester 36. Penrod and Sam 37. Blossoms on Broadway 37. You're Only Young Once 37. Penrod and his Twin Brother 38. Our Neighbours the Carters 39. Miracles for Sale 39. Dreaming Out Loud 40. City for Conquest 40. *Our Town* (his stage role) 40. The Lady from Cheyenne 41. The Richest Man in Town 41. In This Our Life 41. *Thru Different Eyes* 42. Pittsburgh 42. Girl Trouble 42. Son of Dracula 43. Harrigan's Kid 43. Jack London 43. The Human Comedy 43. Keeper of the Flame 43. Destiny 44. My Best Gal 44. They Shall Have Faith 44. The Right to Live 45. Colonel Effingham's Raid 45.

Craven, Gemma (1950–). Irish-born leading lady of the seventies.
□*The Slipper and the Rose* 76. Why Not Stay for Breakfast 79. Wagner 83.
TV series: Pennies from Heaven 77.

Craven, Wes (–). American director of horror nasties.
Summer of Fear 78. The Hills Have Eyes 79. Deadly Blessing 81. A Nightmare on Elm Street 84. Deadly Friend 86.

Crawford, Andrew (1917–). Scottish character actor.
The Brothers 46. Dear Murderer 47. London Belongs to Me 48. Morning Departure 50. Shadow of the Cat 61, etc.

Crawford, Anne (1920–1956) (Imelda Crawford). British leading lady with gentle, humorous personality.
They Flew Alone (debut) 42. The Peterville Diamond 42. The Dark Tower 42. The Hundred-Pound Window 43. Millions Like Us 43. Two Thousand Women 44. They Were Sisters 45. Caravan 46. Bedelia 46. Master of Bankdam 47. Daughter of Darkness 48. The Blind Goddess 48. It's Hard To Be Good 49. Tony Draws a Horse 49. Thunder on the Hill (US) 50. Street Corner 52. Knights of the Round Table 53. Mad about Men 55, etc.

Crawford, Broderick (1910–). Beefy American character actor, son of Helen Broderick; began by playing comic stooges and gangsters, with acting performances coming later; after a long spell in TV his popularity waned.
Woman Chases Man 37. The Real Glory 39. Eternally Yours 39. Beau Geste 39. Slightly Honorable 40. When the Daltons Rode 40. The Black Cat 41. Butch Minds the Baby 42. Broadway 42. Sin Town 42. *The Runaround* 46. Slave Girl 47. The Flame 47. The Time of Your Life 48. Anna Lucasta 49. *All the King's Men* (AA) 50. *Born Yesterday* 51. The Mob 51. Lone Star 52. Scandal Sheet 52. Last of the Comanches 52. Stop You're Killing Me

52. Night People 54. Human Desire 54. Down Three Dark Streets 54. New York Confidential 55. Il Bidone (The Swindlers) 55. Not as a Stranger 55. The Fastest Gun Alive 56. The Decks Ran Red 58. Up from the Beach 65. The Oscar 66. The Texican 66. Red Tomahawk 66. The Vulture 67. Embassy 72. Terror in the Wax Museum 73. Smashing the Crime Syndicate 73. Mayday at 40,000 Feet (TV) 77. *The Private Files of J. Edgar Hoover* 78. A Little Romance 79. There Goes the Bride 80. Liar's Moon 82, etc.
TV series: *Highway Patrol* 55–58. King of Diamonds 61. The Interns 70.

¶ *B.C.:* My trademarks are a hoarse, grating voice and the face of a retired pugilist: small narrowed eyes set in puffy features which look as though they might, years ago, have lost on points.

Crawford, Howard Marion: see *Marion-Crawford, Howard.*

Crawford, Joan (1906–77) (Lucille le Sueur; known for a time as Billie Cassin). American leading lady; one of Hollywood's most durable stars, first as a flapper of the jazz age and later as the personification of the career girl and the repressed older woman. Few of her films have been momentous, but she has always been 'box office', especially with women fans, who liked to watch her suffering in mink.
Autobiography 1962: *A Portrait of Joan*. In 1978 her adopted daughter Christine Crawford published *Mommie Dearest*, which painted her as a monster and caused a sensation. A film version of the book was released in 1981, with Faye Dunaway playing J.C.
□Pretty Ladies 25. The Only Thing 25. Old Clothes 25. Sally, Irene and Mary 25. The Boob 25. Paris 25. Tramp Tramp Tramp 26. The Taxi Dancer 27. Winners of the Wilderness 27. The Understanding Heart 27. The Unknown 27. Twelve Miles Out 27. Spring Fever 27. West Point 28. Rose Marie 28. Across to Singapore 28. The Law of the Range 28. Four Walls 28. *Our Dancing Daughters* 28. Dream of Love 28. The Duke Steps Out 29. Our Modern Maidens 29. Hollywood Revue 29. Untamed 29. Montana Moon 30. Our Blushing Brides 30. Paid 30. Dance Fools Dance 31. Laughing Sinners 31. This Modern Age 31. Possessed 31. Letty Lynton 32. *Grand Hotel* 32. *Rain* 32. Today We Live 33. *Dancing Lady* 33. Sadie McKee 34. Chained 34. Forsaking All Others 34. No More Ladies 35. I Live My Life 35. *The Gorgeous Hussy* 36. Love on the Run 36. The Last of Mrs Cheyney 37. The Bride Wore Red 37. Mannequin 38. The Shining Hour 38. Ice Follies 39. *The Women* 39. Strange Cargo 40. Susan and God 40. *A Woman's Face* 41. When Ladies Meet 41. They All Kissed the Bride 42. Reunion in France 42. Above Suspicion 43. Hollywood Canteen 44. *Mildred Pierce* (AA) 45. *Humoresque* 46. *Possessed* 47. Daisy Kenyon 47. Flamingo Road 49. The Damned Don't Cry 50. Harriet Craig 50. Goodbye My Fancy 51. This Woman is Dangerous 52. *Sudden Fear* 52. Torch Song 53. Johnny Guitar 54. The Female on the Beach 55. Queen Bee 55. Autumn Leaves 56. The Story of Esther Costello (GB) 57. The Best of Everything 59. *Whatever Happened to Baby Jane?* 62. The Caretakers 63. Strait Jacket 64. Della (TV) 64. I Saw What You Did 65. The Karate Killers (TV) 67. Berserk (GB) 67. Night Gallery (TV pilot) 69. Trog 70.
❀ For sheer determination. *Mildred Pierce.*

¶ *J.C.:* Everybody imitated my fuller mouth, my darker eyebrows. But I wouldn't copy anybody. If I can't be me, I don't want to be anybody. I was born that way.

'Whenever she came to the realisation that the men she loved simply didn't come back, she compensated by adopting children.'—*Hedda Hopper*

Famous line (*The Female on the Beach*): 'I wouldn't have you if you were hung with diamonds—upside down!'

J.C.: The most mportant thing a woman can have, next to her talent of course, is her hairdresser.

'The best time I ever had with her was when I pushed her downstairs in *Baby Jane*.'—*Bette Davis*

'With her emergence as a film star she dieted off her excess weight, lowered her voice range by several tones, was taught how to dress by Adrian and how to enter a room by Douglas Fairbanks Jnr. And she never let up in her quest for self-improvement.'—*Radie Harris*

J.C.: Inactivity is one of the great indignities of life. The need to work is always there, bugging me.

J.C.: I never go out unless I look like Joan Crawford the movie star. If you want to see the girl next door, go next door.

'She was a mean, tipsy, powerful, rotten-egg lady.'—*Mercedes McCambridge*

'She's like that old joke about Philadelphia. First prize 4 years with Joan. Second, eight.'—*Franchot Tone*

'I tried to be a good listener. I decided that was what she wanted all along—not so much a friend as an audience.'—*June Allyson*

Crawford, John (1926–). Forgettable American leading man.
Cyrano de Bergerac 50. Actors and Sin 52. Slaves of Babylon 53. Battle of Royne River 54. Orders to Kill 58. John Paul Jones 59. Floods of Fear 59. Hell is a City 60. The 300 Spartans 62. Captain Sinbad 63. The Americanization of Emily 64, etc.
TV series: The Waltons 72–81.

Crawford, Michael (1942–) (Michael Dumble-Smith). Lively British comedy lead, former child actor.
Soap Box Derby 50. Blow Your Own Trumpet 54. Two Living One Dead 62. The War Lover 63. Two Left Feet 63. *The Knack* 65. A Funny Thing Happened on the Way to the Forum 66. *The Jokers* 66. How I Won the War 67. *Hello Dolly* 69. The Games 69. Hello Goodbye 70. Alice's Adventures in Wonderland 72, etc.
TV series: Sir Francis Drake 62. *Some Mothers Do 'Ave 'Em* 74–79. Chalk and Cheese 79.

crazy comedy has two distinct meanings in the cinema. On one hand it encompasses the Marx Brothers, *Hellzapoppin* and custard pies; for this see *Slapstick*. On the other it means the new kind of comedy which came in during the thirties, with seemingly adult people behaving in what society at the time thought was a completely irresponsible way. The Capra comedies, for instance, are vaguely 'agin' the government', upholding Mr Deeds' right to give away his money and play the tuba, the Vanderhofs' right not to work, and Mr Smith's right to be utterly honest. This endearing eccentricity permeated many of the funniest and most modern comedies of the period. William Powell and Myrna Loy in *The Thin Man* were a married couple who upheld none of the domestic virtues. In *Libelled Lady* four top stars behaved like low comedians. In *My Man Godfrey* a rich man pretended to be a tramp and so reformed a party of the idle rich who found him during a 'scavenger hunt'. *Theodora Goes Wild, I Met Him in Paris* and *Easy Living* had what we would now call 'kooky' heroines. In *True Confession* Carole Lombard confessed to a murder she hadn't done, and was told by John Barrymore that she would 'fry'; in *Nothing Sacred* she pretended to be dying of an obscure disease and was socked on the jaw by Fredric March. Hal Roach introduced comedy ghosts, played by two of Hollywood's most sophisticated stars, in *Topper,* and followed it up with two sequels as well as three individual and endearingly lunatic comedies called *The Housekeeper's Daughter* (a battle of fireworks), *Turnabout* (a husband and wife exchange bodies) and *Road Show* (an asylum escapee runs a travelling circus). *The Awful Truth* had no respect for marriage; *You Can't Take It With You* had no respect for law, business, or the American way of life. A film called *Bringing Up Baby* turned out to be about a leopard and a brontosaurus bone; *Boy Meets Girl* was a farcical send-up of Hollywood; and *A Slight Case of Murder* had more corpses than characters. *The Women* had its all-female cast fighting like tiger-cats. *Road to Singapore* began as a romantic comedy but degenerated into snippets from Joe Miller's gag-book; and any Preston Sturges film was likely to have pauses while the smart and witty hero and heroine fell into a pool. In *Here Comes Mr Jordan* the hero was dead after five minutes or so and spent the rest of the film trying to get his body back.

The genre was by this time well established, and although America's entry into the war modified it somewhat it has remained fashionable and popular ever since. A 1966 film like *Morgan* may seem rather startling, but in fact it goes little further in its genial anarchy than *You Can't Take It With You*; only the method of expression is different. What modern crazy comedies lack is the clear pattern which produced so many little masterpieces within a few years: even direct imitations like *What's Up Doc?* fail to produce the same results.

The Crazy Gang. Three pairs of British music hall comedians made up this famous group which was enormously popular on stage from 1935 till 1962. Bud Flanagan (qv) and Chesney Allen (qv); Jimmy Nervo (James Holloway) (1890–1975) and Teddy Knox (1896–1974); Charlie Naughton (1887–1976) and Jimmy Gold (1886–1967).
□OK for Sound 37. Alf's Button Afloat 38. The Frozen Limits 39. Gasbags 40. Life is a Circus 54.

Creasey, John (1908–1973). British thriller writer, author under various pseudonyms of more than six hundred books. Creator of the Toff, the Baron and Gideon of Scotland Yard.

The Creature from the Black Lagoon (US 1954). A poor horror film which spawned one of Universal's more inept monsters, an amphibious chap in a rubber suit who was called the gill man but remained singularly unimpressive and restricted in two sequels:

Revenge of the Creature 55 and *The Creature Walks Among Us* 56. Ricou Browning played the part, and the underwater photography was the best thing in the film.
†Very unusually, this Universal movie was visited and discussed by the leading players in *The Seven Year Itch*, a Twentieth Century Fox film.
† David Frye once described President Gerald Ford as follows:
'He looks like the guy in the movie who is the first to see the Creature.'

credits. Titles at beginning or end of film (nowadays very often five minutes *after* the beginning) listing the names of the creative talents concerned.

? What films had among their screen credits the following somewhat unusual lines?

1 By William Shakespeare. Additional dialogue by Sam Taylor.
2 Based on an idea by William Shakespeare.
3 After a play by William Shakespeare. Long, long after.
4 This picture is dedicated to the fifty.
5 To the memory of Irving Grant Thalberg we dedicate this, his last great achievement.
6 Co-starring the city of Paris . . .
7 A film by Otto Preminger [first time].
8 With Mr Joseph Young as himself.
9 Fangs by Dr Ludwig von Krankheit.
10 Introducing James Best.
11 A serio-comic phantasy.
12 A bedpanorama of hospital life.
13 Introducing Alistair Cooke, distinguished journalist and commentator.
14 Academy Award statuettes are used in this picture by permission of the Academy of Motion Picture Arts and Sciences.
15 As presented for 666 performances in its triumphal run at the Ethel Barrymore Theatre, New York.

creeping title. One which moves up (or sometimes across) the screen at reading pace. Also known as *roller title*.

Cregar, Laird (1916–1944). Heavyweight American character actor who had a tragically brief but impressive career in a rich variety of roles.
□Granny Get Your Gun 40. Oh Johnny How You Can Love 40. Hudson's Bay 40. Blood and Sand 41. *Charley's Aunt* 41. *I Wake Up Screaming* 41. Joan of Paris 42. Rings on Her Fingers 42. This Gun for Hire 42. *Ten Gentlemen from West Point* 42. *The Black Swan* 42. Hello Frisco Hello 43. *Heaven Can Wait* 43. Holy Matrimony 43. *The Lodger* 44. Hangover Square 44.
❀ For providing such a memorable gallery of middle-aged characters while still in his early twenties. *The Black Swan*.

Crehan, Joseph (1884–1966) (Charles Wilson). American character actor, often as sheriff or cop.
Stolen Heaven 31. Before Midnight 33. Identity Parade 34. Boulder Dam 36. Happy Landing 38. Stanley and Livingstone 39. The Roaring Twenties 39. Brother Orchid 40. Texas 42. Phantom Lady 44. Deadline at Dawn 46. The Foxes of Harrow 48. Red Desert 54, many others.

Crenna, Richard (1926–). American leading man, formerly boy actor on radio and TV.
Red Skies of Montana 52. It Grows on Trees 52. Over Exposed 56. John Goldfarb Please Come Home 65. Made in Paris 65. The Sand Pebbles 66. Wait Until Dark 67. Star! 68. Marooned 69. The Deserter 70. Thief (TV) 71. Doctors' Wives 71. Red Sky at Morning 71. Catlow 72. The Man Called Noon 73. Double Indemnity (TV) 73. Nightmare (TV) 75. Breakheart Pass 76. Dirty Money (Fr.) 77. Body Heat 81. *Table for Five* 83, etc.
TV series: Our Miss Brooks 52–56. The Real McCoys 57–62. Slattery's People 64–65. All's Fair 76. It Takes Two 83. Rambo: First Blood 2 86. The Flamingo Kid 86.

Crews, Laura Hope (1880–1942). American stage actress who played character parts in many films, usually as fluttery matron.
Charming Sinners 29. New Morals for Old 32. Escapade 35. *Camille* 36. Thanks for the Memory 38. *Gone with the Wind* (as Aunt Pittypat) 39. The Bluebird 40. The Flame of New Orleans 41. One Foot in Heaven 41, many others.

Cribbins, Bernard (1928–). British comedy character actor and recording star. Played light support roles in several films.
Two Way Stretch 60. The Girl on the Boat 62. The Wrong Arm of the Law 62. Carry On Jack 63. Crooks in Cloisters 64. She 65. The Sandwich Man 66. Daleks Invasion Earth 2150 A.D. 66. The Railway Children 70. Frenzy 72. The Water Babies 78, etc.
Dangerous Davies (TV) 81, etc.

Crichton, Charles (1910–). British director, former editor. Latterly directing TV episodes.
For Those in Peril 44. Dead of Night (part) 45. Painted Boats 45. *Hue and Cry* 46. Against the Wind 47. Another Shore 48. Train of Events 49. Dance Hall 50. *The Lavender Hill Mob* 51. Hunted 52. *The Titfield Thunderbolt* 53. The Love Lottery 54. The Divided Heart 54. The Man in the Sky 56. Law and Disorder 57. Floods of Fear (& w) 58. The Battle of the Sexes 59. The Boy Who Stole a Million 60. The Third Secret 63. He Who Rides a Tiger 65, etc.
TV series: Dick Turpin 78.

Crichton, Michael (1942–). American novelist and screenwriter.
The Andromeda Strain (oa) 71. The Carey Treatment (oa) 72. The Terminal Man (oa) 72. *Pursuit* (oa, d) (TV) 72. *Westworld* (wd) 73. Coma (d) 77. The Great Train Robbery (w, d) 78. Looker (w, d) 80. Runaway 84.

The Crime Doctor. The hero of this Hollywood-concocted series was a criminal restored by a brain operation to the sober pursuance of his former profession as a doctor. That was in 1943: once the series got under way the premise was forgotten and Warner Baxter was simply a psychiatrist whose involvement in and solution of various complicated crimes was both unlikely and (usually) accidental. The series died with Baxter in 1951.

Crime Does Not Pay. A series of 48 two-reelers, made by MGM between 1935 and 1948 in a very imitable but entertaining hard-hitting style. The first, called *Buried Loot,* introduced Robert Taylor; other budding stars were featured later, and the series proved a valuable training ground for directors, including Jules Dassin and Fred Zinnemann.

The Crime of Monsieur Lange (France 1935). An influential satirical fantasy, written by Jacques Prévert and others, directed by Jean Renoir; about workers who take over a factory when the boss absconds.

Crime Without Passion (US 1934). A melodrama made in New York by writer-directors Ben Hecht and Charles Macarthur, who had hopes of founding a new school of film-making; but the result, despite Claude Rains, was a plain and uncommercial though well-made account of an advocate who murders a young girl and suffers the consequences.

criminals—real-life ones—whose careers have been featured in films include Burke and Hare (*The Flesh and the Fiends, Burke and Hare*), Cagliostro (*Black Magic*), Al Capone (*Little Caesar, The Scarface Mob, Al Capone*), Caryl Chessman (*Cell 2455 Death Row*), Crippen (*Dr Crippen*), John Wilkes Booth (*Prince of Players*), Jack the Ripper (*The Lodger, A Study in Terror, Jack the Ripper,* many others), Landru (*Landru, Bluebeard, Monsieur Verdoux, Bluebeard's Ten Honeymoons*), Leopold and Loeb (*Rope* and *Compulsion*), Christie (*10 Rillington Place*), Charles Peace (*The Case of Charles Peace*), Dick Turpin (qv), Jesse James (qv), Vidocq (*A Scandal in Paris*), Robert Stroud (*Birdman of Alcatraz*), Barbara Graham (*I Want to Live*), Rasputin (qv), Eddie Chapman (*Triple Cross*), and the various American public enemies of the thirties: *Bonnie and Clyde, Dillinger, Baby Face Nelson, Bloody Mama* (Barker), *A Bullet for Pretty Boy* (Floyd), etc. The clinical sixties also brought accounts of the motiveless murderers of *In Cold Blood* and of *The Boston Strangler.* Criminal movements have been very well explored in fictional films, especially the Mafia, the Thugs, Murder Inc. and the racketeers and bootleggers of the twenties.

Crisp, Donald (1880–1974). Distinguished British screen actor, in Hollywood from 1906; worked with D. W. Griffith and directed some silents, but from 1930 settled on acting and played mainly stern character roles.
Home Sweet Home 14. The Birth of a Nation 15. Broken Blossoms 19. Why Smith Left Home (d) 19. The Bonnie Brier Bush (d) 21. The Mark of Zorro (d) 22. Ponjola (d) 23. *Don Q Son of Zorro* (ad) 25. The Black Pirate 26. Man Bait (d) 27. Stand and Deliver (d) 28. The Return of Sherlock Holmes 29. Runaway Bride (d) 30. Svengali 31. Red Dust 32. Crime Doctor 34. The Little Minister 34. Mutiny on the Bounty 35. Mary of Scotland 36. Beloved Enemy 36. Parnell 37. Jezebel 38. The Sisters 38. *The Dawn Patrol* 38. Wuthering Heights 39. The Old Maid 39. *Brother Orchid* 40. The Sea Hawk 40. Dr Jekyll and Mr Hyde 41. *How Green Was My Valley* (AA) 41. The Gay Sisters 42. Lassie Come Home 43. *The Uninvited* 44. National Velvet 44. Valley of Decision 45. Ramrod 47. Whispering Smith 49. Bright Leaf 50. Prince

Valiant 54. The Man from Laramie 55. Saddle the Wind 58. The Last Hurrah 58. Pollyanna 60. Greyfriars Bobby 61. Spencer's Mountain 63, many others.

Cristal, Linda (1936–) (Victoria Maya). Argentinian leading lady, in Hollywood from 1956.
Comanche 56. The Fiend Who Walked the West 58. The Perfect Furlough 58. Cry Tough 59. The Alamo 60. Panic in the City 68. Mr Majestyk 74, etc.
TV series: The High Chaparral 67–71.

Cristaldi, Franco (1924–). Italian producer of good reputation.
La Pattuglia Sperduta 53. La Sfida 59. L'Assassino 60. Salvatori Giuliano 61. Divorce Italian Style 63. The Red Tent 69, etc.

critics

¶ Very little film criticism is quotable: at its best it is an expression of personality rather than wit. The reviews one remembers tend to be the scathing ones, especially those dismissive one-liners which are really unforgivable but linger over the arch of years:

> *No Leave, No Love.* No comment.
> *I Am a Camera.* Me no Leica.
> *Lost in a Harem.* But with Abbott and Costello.
> *Aimez-vous Brahms?* Brahms, oui.
> *Ben Hur.* Loved Ben, hated Hur.
> *Samson and Delilah.* A movie for de Millions.
> *Bill and Coo.* By conservative estimate, one of the God-damnedest things ever seen.

The authors of these pearls are now, by me, forgotten, with the exception of the last, which came from the pen of James Agee, a lamented American writer whose economical, literate reviews delighted all film enthusiasts in the forties and established a few Hollywood reputations. His collected reviews should all be read with affection; here we can spare room for five of his more waspish put-downs:

> *Random Harvest.* I would like to recommend this film to those who can stay interested in Ronald Colman's amnesia for two hours and who could with pleasure eat a bowl of Yardley's shaving soap for breakfast.
> During the making of *Pin Up Girl* Betty Grable was in an early stage of pregnancy—and everyone else was evidently in a late stage of paresis.
> *Tycoon.* Several tons of dynamite are set off in this picture—none of it under the right people.
> *You Were Meant For Me.* That's what you think.
> *Star Spangled Rhythm.* A variety show including everyone at Paramount who was not overseas, in hiding or out to lunch.

A few more moments of invective. First, *Variety* on Hedy Lamarr's independent production *The Strange Woman*:

> Hedy bit off more than she could chew, so the chewing was done by the rest of the cast, and what was chewed was the scenery.

And Pamela Kellino on *The Egyptian*:

> One of those great big rotten pictures Hollywood keeps on turning out.

And Stanley Kauffmann on *Isadora*:

> This long but tiny film . . .

And the *New Statesman* (Frank Hauser) on *Another Man's Poison*:

> Like reading Ethel M. Dell by flashes of lightning.

And the *Saturday Evening Post* on *Macabre*:

> It plods along from its opening scene in a funeral parlor to its dénouement in a graveyard, unimpeded by the faintest intrusion of good taste, literacy, or sense.

And Don Herold on *The Bride Walks Out*:

> You've seen this a million times on the screen, but they keep on making it, and folks keep asking me why I am so dyspeptic regarding the cinema. Because I have judgment, is the answer.

And John Simon on *Camelot*:

> This film is the Platonic idea of boredom, roughly comparable to reading a three-volume novel in a language of which one knows only the alphabet.

And David Lardner on *Panama Hattie*:

> This film needs a certain something. Possibly burial.

And Judith Crist on *Five Card Stud*:

> So mediocre that you can't get mad at it.

And Charles Champlin on *The Missouri Breaks*:

> A pair of million dollar babies in a five and ten cent flick.

Now for some self-criticism. Joseph L. Mankiewicz on his own movie *Cleopatra*:

> This picture was conceived in a state of emergency, shot in confusion, and wound up in blind panic.

He also called it:

> The toughest three pictures I ever made.

Ethel Barrymore, when asked her opinion of *Rasputin and the Empress*, in which she co-starred with her brothers Lionel and John, replied:

I thought I was pretty good, but what those two boys were up to I'll never know.

Erich Von Stroheim, reminiscing on his own much-mutilated picture *Greed*:

When ten years later I saw the film myself, it was like seeing a corpse in a graveyard.

Otto Preminger on *Saint Joan*:

My most distinguished flop. I've had much less distinguished ones.

And Victor Fleming, director of *Gone with the Wind*, refusing David O. Selznick's offer of a percentage of the profits instead of salary:

Don't be a damn fool, David. This picture is going to be one of the biggest white elephants of all time.

Philip French on *Carry on Emmanuelle*:

Put together with an almost palpable contempt for its audience, this relentless sequence of badly written, badly timed dirty jokes is surely one of the most morally and aesthetically offensive pictures to emerge from a British studio.

Similarly misguided was Adolph Zukor when he first read the script of *Broken Blossoms*:

You bring me a picture like this and want money for it? You may as well put your hand in my pocket and steal it. It isn't commercial. Everyone in it dies.

I can recall only three memorable items of praise. Cecilia Ager on *Citizen Kane*:

It's as though you had never seen a movie before.

Terry Ramsaye on *Intolerance*:

The only film fugue.

And Woodrow Wilson on *The Birth of a Nation*:

Like writing history with lightning. And it's all true.

My own favourite critiques also include Sarah Bernhardt's enthusiastic remark when she saw her 1912 version of *Queen Elizabeth*:

Mr Zukor, you have put the best of me in pickle for all time.

And the comment of macabre New Yorker cartoonist Charles Addams, when asked his opinion after the première of *Cleopatra*:

I only came to see the asp.

And the anonymous reviewer of a Jack Benny violin concert:

Jack Benny played Mendelssohn last night. Mendelssohn lost.

Come to that, another anonymous gentleman had a pretty good definition of critics:

Yawning as a profession.

Channing Pollock defined a critic as:

A legless man who teaches running.

To Whitney Balkett he was:

A bundle of biases held together by a sense of taste.

And to Ken Tynan:

A man who knows the way but can't drive a car.

Mel Brooks was scathing:

Critics can't even make music by rubbing their back legs together.

R.W. Emerson was dismissive:

Taking to pieces is the trade of those who cannot construct.

Perhaps the wisest reflection on the critics was made by Rouben Mamoulian:

The most important critic is Time.

Crocker, Barry (–). Australian leading man.
Squeeze a Flower 69. The Adventures of Barry Mackenzie 72. Barry Mackenzie Holds His Own 74.

Crockett, Davy (1786–1836). American trapper and Indian scout who became a legendary hero and a politician before dying at the Alamo (qv). He has been portrayed on film by George Montgomery (*Indian Scout*), Fess Parker (*Davy Crockett, Davy Crockett and the River Pirates*), Arthur Hunnicutt (*The Last Command*) and John Wayne (*The Alamo*), among others.

Crompton, Richmal (1890–1969). British writer for children, author of the 'William' books which have been filmed from time to time.

Cromwell, John (1888–1979). Distinguished American director with stage background.
□The Dummy (acted only) 29. The Mighty 29. The Dance of Life 29. Close Harmony 29. Street of Chance 30. Tom Sawyer 31. The Texan 30. For the Defense 30. Scandal Street 31. Rich Man's Folly 31. Vice Squad 31. Unfaithful 31. The World and the Flesh 31. Sweepings 33. The Silver Cord 33. Double Harness 33. Ann Vickers 33. Spitfire 34. This Man is Mine 34. *Of Human Bondage* 34. The Fountain 34. Jalna 35. Village Tale 35. I Dream Too Much 35. Little Lord Fauntleroy 36. To Mary With Love 36. Banjo on My Knee 36. *The Prisoner of Zenda* 37. *Algiers* 38. Made for Each Other 38. In Name Only 39. Abe Lincoln in Illinois 39. Victory 40. So Ends Our Night 41. Son of Fury 42. *Since You Went Away* 44. The Enchanted Cottage 45. *Anna and the King of Siam* 46. Dead Reckoning 47. Night Song 47. Caged 50. The Company She Keeps 51. The Racket 51. Top Secret Affair (a only) 57. The Goddess 58.

The Scavengers 60. A Matter of Morals 61. *Three Women* (a only) 77. *A Wedding* (a only) 78.

Cromwell, Oliver (1599–1658). The Puritan Protector of England during the Civil War has been shown on screen as a repressed rather than a heroic figure, as follows:

1937	*The Vicar of Bray*	George Merritt
1949	*Cardboard Cavalier*	Edmund Willard
1958	*The Moonraker*	John Le Mesurier
1968	*Witchfinder General*	Patrick Wymark
1970	*Cromwell*	Richard Harris

Cromwell, Richard (1910–1960) (Roy Radebaugh). American leading man, gentle hero of early sound films.
☐*Tol'able David* 30. Fifty Fathoms Deep 31. Shanghaied Love 31. Maker of Men 31. That's My Boy 32. Emma 32. The Strange Love of Molly Louvain 32. Age of Consent 32. Tom Brown of Culver 32. This Day and Age 33. Hoopla 33. Above the Clouds 34. Carolina 34. Among the Missing 34. Name the Woman 34. When Strangers Meet 34. Most Precious Thing in Life 34. *Lives of a Bengal Lancer* 35. McFadden's Flats 35. Life Begins at Forty 35. Men of the Hour 35. Unknown Woman 35. Annapolis Farewell 35. Poppy 36. Our Fighting Navy (GB) 37. The Road Back 37. The Wrong Road 37. Jezebel 38. Come On Leathernecks 38. Storm Over Bengal 38. Young Mr Lincoln 39. Enemy Agent 40. The Villain Still Pursued Her 40. Village Barn Dance 40. Parachute Battalion 41. Riot Squad 42. Baby Face Morgan 42. Bungalow 13 48.

Cronenberg, David (1948–). Canadian director of outlandish and generally over-the-top horror films.
Crimes of the Future 70. Squirm 74. Shivers 75. Rabid 77. The Brood 80. Scanners 81. Videodrome 83. The Dead Zone 83.
The Fly 86

¶ *D.C.:* My dentist said to me the other day, I've enough problems in my life, so why should I see your films?

D.C.: A friend of mine saw *Videodrome*, said he really liked it, and added, you know someday they're going to lock you up.

D.C.: I don't have a moral plan. I'm a Canadian.

'He works from his dreams. If he'd just dream a little more normally, I'd love to work with him again.'—*James Woods*

Cronenweth, Jordan (–). American cinematographer.
Brewster McCloud 70. Play it as it Lays 72. Zandy's Bride 74. The Front Page 74. Handle With Care 77. Rolling Thunder 77. Altered States 80. Cutter's Way 81. Blade Runner 82. Best Friends 82. Gardens of Stone 87, etc.

Cronin, A. J. (1896–1981). British novelist, former doctor.
Grand Canary 34. The Citadel 38. The Stars Look Down 39. Shining Victory 41. Hatter's Castle 41. The Keys of the Kingdom 44. The Green Years 46. The Spanish Gardener 56. TV series: Dr Finlay's Casebook 59–66.

Cronjager, Edward (1904–1960). American cinematographer.
The Quarterback 26. The Virginian 30. Cimarron 31. Roberta 35. The Gorilla 39. *Hot Spot* 41. *Heaven Can Wait* 43. Canyon Passage 46. The House by the River 50. Treasure of the Golden Condor 53. Beneath the Twelve-Mile Reef 53, many others.

Cronyn, Hume (1911–) (Hume Blake). Canadian character actor of stage and screen; married Jessica Tandy.
☐*Shadow of a Doubt* 43. Phantom of the Opera 43. The Cross of Lorraine 43. *The Seventh Cross* 44. Main Street After Dark 44. *Lifeboat* 44. A Letter for Evie 45. The Sailor Takes a Wife 45. The Green Years 46. The Postman Always Rings Twice 46. Ziegfeld Follies 46. The Beginning or the End 47. *Brute Force* 47. The Bride Goes Wild 48. Top o' the Morning 49. People Will Talk 51. Crowded Paradise 56. *Sunrise at Campobello* 60. Cleopatra 63. Hamlet 64. Gaily Gaily 69. The Arrangement 70. There Was a Crooked Man 70. The Parallax View 74. Conrack 74. Rollover 80. Honky Tonk Freeway 81.
The World According to Garp 82. Brewster's Millions 84. Impulse 84. Cocoon 85. The Thrill of Genius 85.

¶ *H.C.:* To act you must have a sense of truth and some degree of dedication.

Crosbie, Annette (1934–). British character actress, popular on TV as Catherine of Aragon and Queen Victoria.
The Public Eye 72. The Slipper and the Rose 76, etc.

Crosby, Bing (1901–1977) (Harry Lillis Crosby). Star American crooner of the thirties and forties; former band singer, later an agreeable comedian, romantic lead and straight actor.
Autobiography 1953: *Call Me Lucky*.

Biography 1982: *The Hollow Man* by Robert F. Slatzer

□ King of Jazz 30. Check and Double Check 31. Reaching for the Moon 31. Confessions of a Co-Ed 31. The Big Broadcast 32. College Humor 33. Too Much Harmony 33. Going Hollywood 33. We're Not Dressing 34. She Loves Me Not 34. Here is My Heart 34. *Mississippi* 35. Two for Tonight 35. The Big Broadcast of 1936 36. *Anything Goes* 36. Rhythm on the Range 36. Pennies from Heaven 36. Waikiki Wedding 37. Double or Nothing 37. Dr Rhythm 38. *Sing You Sinners* 38. Paris Honeymoon 39. East Side of Heaven 39. The Star Maker 39. *Road to Singapore* 40. If I Had My Way 40. Rhythm on the River 40. Road to Zanzibar 41. Birth of the Blues 41. *Holiday Inn* 42. Road to Morocco 42. Star Spangled Rhythm 43. Dixie 43. *Going My Way* (AA) 44. Here Come The Waves 45. Duffy's Tavern 45. Road to Utopia 45. The Bells of St Mary's 45. Blue Skies 46. Variety Girl 47. Welcome Stranger 47. Road to Rio 47. The Emperor Waltz 48. A Connecticut Yankee in King Arthur's Court 49. Top o' the Morning 49. Riding High 50. Mr Music 50. Here Comes the Groom 51. Just for You 52. Road to Bali 52. Little Boy Lost 53. White Christmas 54. *The Country Girl* 54. Anything Goes 56. High Society 56. Man on Fire 57. Say One for Me 59. High Time 60. Pepe 60. Road to Hong Kong 62. Robin and the Seven Hoods 64. Stagecoach 66. Dr Cook's Garden (TV) 70.
TV series: The Bing Crosby Show 64.
†Crosby made gag appearances in a number of films, including *My Favorite Blonde*, *The Princess and the Pirate*, *My Favorite Brunette*, *Scared Stiff* and *Let's Make Love*.

❀ For his songs; and for his acceptance as a member of everybody's family over a fifty-year career. *Holiday Inn*.

¶ Honestly, I think I've stretched a talent which is so thin it's almost transparent over a quite unbelievable term of years.—*B.C.*

He was an average guy who could carry a tune.—*B.C.'s own epitaph*

Once or twice I've been described as a light comedian. I consider this the most accurate description of my abilities I've ever seen.—*B.C.*

† Crosby also apeared in 6 Mack Sennett two-reelers of the early thirties; and his voice was heard in *Out of this World* 45 and *Ichabod and Mr Toad* 49.

Crosby, Bob (1913–). American bandleader, brother of Bing.
Let's Make Music 40. Reveille with Beverly 43. See Here Private Hargrove 44. Two Tickets to Broadway 51. The Five Pennies 59, etc.

Crosby, Floyd (1899–1986). American cinematographer who worked on everything from documentary to horror thrillers.
□*Tabu* (AA) 31. *The River* (co-ph) 37. The Fight for Life 40. My Father's House 47. Of Men and Music 50. The Brave Bulls 51. *High Noon* 52. Man in the Dark 53. The Steel Lady 53. Man Crazy 53. Stormy 54. The Snow Creature 54. The Monster from the Ocean Floor 54. The Fast and the Furious 54. Five Guns West 55. The Naked Street 55. Shack Out on 101 55. Hell's Horizon 55. Apache Woman 55. Naked Paradise 56. She Gods of Shark Reef 56. Attack of the Crab Monsters 56. Rock all Night 56. Reform School 57. Teenage Doll 57. Ride Out for Revenge 57. Hell Canyon Outlaws 57. Carnival Rock 57. War of the Satellites 57. Suicide Battalion 58. Cry Baby Killer 58. Machine Gun Kelly 58. The Old Man and the Sea (co-ph) 58. Wolf Larsen 58. Hot Rod Gang 58. Teenage Caveman 58. I Mobster 59. Crime and Punishment USA 59. The Miracle of the Hills 59. The Wonderful Country 59. Blood and Steel 59. The Rookie 60. Twelve Hours to Kill 60. *House of Usher* 60. The High Powered Rifle 60. Walk Tall 60. Freckles 60. Operation Bottleneck 61. The Pit and the Pendulum 61. A Cold Wind in August 61. The Purple Hills 61. The Little Shepherd of Kingdom Come 61. The Gambler Wore a Gun 61. Seven Women from Hell 62. The Explosive Generation 62. Woman Hunt 62. The Premature Burial 62. The Two Little Bears 62. Tales of Terror 62. The Firebrand 62. The Broken Land 62. Terror at Black Falls 62. *The Raven* 63. Black Zoo 63. Yellow Canary 63. The Young Racers 63. X—The Man with X-Ray Eyes 63. The Comedy of Terrors 64. Bikini Beach 64. Pajama Party 64. The Haunted Palace 64. Raiders from Beneath the Sea 65. Beach Blanket Bingo 65. How to Stuff a Wild Bikini 65. Sergeant Deadhead 65. Sallah 65. Fireball 500 66. The Cool Ones 67.

Croset, Paule: see *Corday, Paula*.

Crosland, Alan (1894–1936). Routine American director who happened to handle two innovative films.
Enemies of Women 23. Under the Red Robe 23. Three Weeks 24. Bobbed Hair 25. *Don Juan* (first film with synchronized music) 26. The Beloved Rogue 27. Old San Francisco 27. *The Jazz Singer* (first film with talking

sequences) 27. Glorious Betsy 28. General Crack 29. Song of the Flame 30. Captain Thunder 31. Weekends Only 32. The Case of the Howling Dog 34. Lady Tubbs 35. The Great Impersonation 35, many others.

Crosman, Henrietta (1861–1944). American stage actress, a grande dame who made a few films.
□The Unwelcome Mrs Hatch 14. How Molly Made Good 15. Broadway Broke 23. Wandering Fires 25. *The Royal Family of Broadway* 30. Pilgrimage 33. Three on a Honeymoon 34. Carolina 34. Such Women Are Dangerous 34. Among the Missing 34. The Curtain Falls 34. Menace 34. Elinor Norton 35. The Right to Live 35. *The Dark Angel* 35. Hitch Hike to Heaven 36. Charlie Chan's Secret 36. The Moon's Our Home 36. Girl of the Ozarks 36. Follow Your Heart 37. Personal Property 37.

Cross, Ben (1948–). British leading man of somewhat lugubrious countenance.
Chariots of Fire 81. The Citadel (TV) 83. The Far Pavilions (TV) 83. The Assisi Underground 85.

cross cutting. Interlinking fragments of two or more separate sequences so that they appear to be taking place at the same time. One of the most famous examples is the climax of *Intolerance* which intertwines four stories; and in more modern times *The Godfather* crosscut a murder with a baptism.

Cross, Eric (1902–). British cinematographer.
Make Up 37. Song of Freedom 38. The First of the Few 42. Don't Take It To Heart 44. The Chance of a Lifetime 49. Hunted 52. The Kidnappers 53. Private's Progress 55. The One That Got Away 57. Behind the Curtain 60, many others.

Crosse, Rupert (1927–1973). Black American actor best remembered for *The Reivers* 68, and for the TV series *Partners*.

Crossfire (US 1947). First of the American racialist dramas, a tough adult thriller about the murder of a Jew. (In Richard Brooks' original novel it was a homosexual.) Adapted by John Paxton, directed by Edward Dmytryk, with Robert Ryan as the anti-Semite and Robert Young as the patient cop.

Crossley, Syd (1885–1960). British music hall comedian who played comic supporting roles in many films. In US in twenties.
Keep Smiling 25. Fangs of the Wild 28. Atlantic 29. Tonight's the Night 31. Those were the Days 34. Dandy Dick 35. Music Hath Charms 36. The Ghost Goes West 36. Silver Blaze 37. Penny Paradise 38, many others.

Crothers, Rachel (1878–1958). American playwright; works much filmed.
When Ladies Meet 33 and 41. As Husbands Go 34. Splendour 35. Mother Carey's Chickens 38. Susan and God 40, etc.

Crothers, Scatman (1910–86) (Sherman Crothers). American black actor with a penchant for comedy.
Between Heaven and Hell 56. Lady in a Cage 64. Hello Dolly 69. The Great White Hope 70. Lady Sing the Blues 72. The Fortune 74. One Flew Over the Cuckoo's Nest 75. The Shootist 76. Silver Streak 77. Scavenger Hunt 79. Bronco Billy 80. The Shining 80. Twilight Zone 83. The Journey of Natty Gann 85, etc.
TV series: Chico and the Man 74–77. One of these Days 82. Casablanca 83. Morning Star, Evening Star 86.

Crouse, Lindsay (–). American leading lady, daughter of Russel Crouse.
All the President's Men 76. Between the Lines 77. Slapshot 77. The Verdict 82. Iceman 82. Places in the Heart (AAN) 85.

Crouse, Russel (1893–1966). American librettist, usually with **Howard Lindsay** (1888–1968). Their musicals to have been filmed include *Anything Goes, Call Me Madam* and *The Sound of Music*. Non-musicals: *Life with Father, State of the Union*, etc.

The Crowd (US 1928). King Vidor directed and co-wrote this early experiment in social realism, an account of the drab life of a city clerk. James Murray and Eleanor Boardman starred. In 1933 Vidor made a sequel, *Our Daily Bread*, showing his couple leaving the town for a farming community: Tom Keene and Karen Morley were the stars.

The Crowd Roars. There are two films under this title. Howard Hawks made the first in 1932, with James Cagney as a racing driver; Richard Thorpe made the second with Robert Taylor as a boxer. The plots are dissimilar.

Crowley, Pat (1929–). American leading lady of the fifties.

Forever Female 53. Money from Home 54. Red Garters 54. There's Always Tomorrow 55. Hollywood or Bust 56. Key Witness 60. To Trap a Spy 64. A Family Upside Down (TV) 78, etc.
TV series: Please Don't Eat the Daisies 65–66. Joe Forrester 75.

Crowther, Bosley (–1981). American film critic. Long with the *New York Times*.

Cruickshank, Andrew (1907–1988). Scottish stage actor who has appeared in a number of films, usually as doctor or judge. A national figure on TV as Dr Cameron in *Dr Finlay's Casebook* 59–66.
Auld Lang Syne 37. The Mark of Cain 47. Paper Orchid 49. Your Witness 50. The Cruel Sea 53. Richard III 56. Innocent Sinners 58. Kidnapped 60. *There Was a Crooked Man* 60. El Cid 61. Murder Most Foul 64, etc.

Cruise, Tom (1962–). American leading juvenile of the eighties.
Endless Love 81. Taps 81. Losin' It 83. All the Right Moves 83. The Outsiders 83. Risky Business 84. Legend 84. *Top Gun* 85. *The Color of Money* 86.

Crutchley, Rosalie (1921–). Striking, lean-featured British stage actress who makes occasional film appearances.
Take My Life 47. Give Us This Day 49. Quo Vadis 51. Make Me an Offer 55. The Spanish Gardener 56. *A Tale of Two Cities* (as Madame Lafarge) 58. Beyond This Place 59. Sons and Lovers 60. Freud 62. The Girl in the Headlines 63. Behold a Pale Horse 64. Jane Eyre (TV) 70. Blood from the Mummy's Tomb 71. Who Slew Auntie Roo? 71. Man of La Mancha 72. Mahler 74. Smiley's People (TV) 82, etc.

Cruz, Brandon (–). American child actor of the seventies.
But I Don't Want to Get Married (TV) 70. The Going Up of David Lev (TV) 72. The Bad News Bears 76. The One and Only 78.
TV series: *The Courtship of Eddie's Father* 69–71.

Cruze, James (1884–1942) (Jens Cruz Bosen). Danish-American silent screen actor who broke his leg and turned to direction.
AS ACTOR: A Boy of Revolution 11. She 11. The Star of Bethlehem 12. Joseph in the Land of Egypt 14. *The Million Dollar Mystery* (serial) 14. The Twenty Million Dollar Mystery (serial) 15. Nan of Music Mountain 17. Too Many Millions 18, etc.
AS DIRECTOR: Too Many Millions 18. The Dollar a Year Man 21. One Glorious Day 22. The Dictator 22. *The Covered Wagon* 23. *Hollywood* 23. Ruggles of Red Gap 23. To the Ladies 23. Merton of the Movies 24. The Goose Hangs High 25. *Beggar on Horseback* 25. Pony Express 25. *Old Ironsides* 26. The Mating Call 27. The Great Gabbo 29. Salvation Nell 31. *Washington Merry Go Round* 32. I Cover the Waterfront 33. David Harum 34. Helldorado 34. *Sutter's Gold* 36. Prison Nurse 38. Gangs of New York 38, many others.

Cuba produced its first film in 1897, but native film-making was swamped by American imports until the Communist revolution of 1959, when a politically conscious programme was begun. Tomas Alea is the best known Cuban director.

Cucciolla, Ricardo (1932–). Italian leading actor.
Italia Brava Gente 65. Grand Slam 67. Sacco and Vanzetti 71, etc.

Cugat, Xavier (1900–). Chubby, beaming Spanish-American bandleader and caricaturist, a feature of many MGM musicals of the forties.
Autobiography 1948: *Rumba is my Life*.
You Were Never Lovelier 42. Two Girls and a Sailor 44. Holiday in Mexico 46. This Time for Keeps 47. A Date with Judy 48. Neptune's Daughter 49. Chicago Syndicate 55, etc.

Cukor, George (1899–1983). American director, from the Broadway stage; proved to be one of Hollywood's most reliable handlers of high comedy and other literate material.
□Grumpy (co-d) 30. Virtuous Sin (co-d) 30. The Royal Family of Broadway 30. Tarnished Lady 30. Girls About Town 31. *One Hour with You* (with Lubitsch) 32. *What Price Hollywood?* 32. A Bill of Divorcement 32. Rockabye 32. Our Betters 33. *Dinner at Eight* 33. *Little Women* 33. *David Copperfield* 34. Sylvia Scarlett 35. Romeo and Juliet 36. *Camille* 36. *Holiday* 38. Zaza 39. *The Women* 39. Susan and God 40. *The Philadelphia Story* 40. A Woman's Face 41. Two-faced Woman 41. Her Cardboard Lover 42. *Keeper of the Flame* 43. Gaslight 44. Winged Victory 44. Desire Me (co-d) 47. A Double Life 47. *Adam's Rib* 49. Edward My Son (GB) 49. A Life of Her Own 50. Born Yesterday 50. The

Model and the Marriage Broker 52. The Marrying Kind 52. Pat and Mike 52. The Actress 53. It Should Happen to You 53. *A Star is Born* 54. Bhowani Junction 56. Les Girls 57. Wild is The Wind 57. Heller in Pink Tights 59. Song Without End (part) 60. Let's Make Love 61. The Chapman Report 62. *My Fair Lady* (AA) 64. Justine 69. Travels with My Aunt 73. Love Among the Ruins (TV) 75. The Bluebird 76. The Corn Is Green (TV) 79. Rich and Famous 81.

'When a director has provided polished tasteful entertainments of a high order consistently over a period of thirty years, it is clear that said director is much more than a mere entertainer.'—*Andrew Sarris*

❀ For adding to Hollywood a sense of light culture; and for his discretion in handling a score of the film colony's more temperamental ladies. *The Philadelphia Story*.

¶ 'His films vary drastically in their visual texture, their style reposing mainly in the theatrically accomplished handling of the actors.'—*Charles Higham*

Culp, Robert (1930–). American leading man.
P. T. 109 62. The Raiders 63. Sunday in New York 64. Rhino! 64. *Bob and Carol and Ted and Alice* 69. Hannie Caulder 71. Hickey and Boggs (& d) 72. See The Man Run (TV) 72. The Castaway Cowboy 74. A Cry for Help (TV) 75. Inside Out 75. Sky Riders 76. The Great Scout and Cathouse Thursday 76. Breaking Point 76. Word Games (TV) 79. Goldengirl 79. Turk 182 84, etc.
TV series: Trackdown 57. *I Spy* 65–67. *The Greatest American Hero* 81–82.

Culver, Roland (1900–84). British stage actor of impeccable English types, usually comic.
77 Park Lane 32. Nell Gwynn 34. Paradise for Two 37. *French Without Tears* (his stage role) 39. *Quiet Wedding* 40. Night Train to Munich 40. Talk about Jacqueline 42. *On Approval* 43. Dear Octopus 43. *Dead of Night* 45. Wanted for Murder 46. To Each His Own (US) 47. Down to Earth (US) 47. The Emperor Waltz (US) 48. Isn't It Romantic? 48. *Trio* (as Somerset Maugham) 50. The Holly and the Ivy 54. The Man Who Loved Redheads 55. Touch and Go 57. Bonjour Tristesse 58. The Yellow Rolls-Royce 64. A Man Could Get Killed 65. Fragment of Fear 70. Bequest to the Nation 73. The Word (TV) 78, others.

Cummings, Constance (1910–) (Constance Halverstadt). American stage actress, long resident in England.
The Criminal Code (US) 31. The Guilty Generation (US) 31. Movie Crazy (US) 32. Channel Crossing 32. Broadway thro' a Keyhole (US) 33. Glamour 34. Looking for Trouble 34. Remember Last Night? (US) 35. Seven Sinners 36. *Busman's Honeymoon* 40. This England 41. The Foreman Went to France 42. *Blithe Spirit* 45. John and Julie 55. The Intimate Stranger 56. The Battle of the Sexes 59. Sammy Going South 62. In the Cool of the Day 63, etc.

Cummings, Irving (1888–1959). American director, former actor; in films from 1909.
SELECTED SILENT FILMS: As Man Desires 25. The Johnstown Flood 26. The Brute 27, etc.
□ In Old Arizona (co-d) 29. Behind That Curtain 29. Cameo Kirby 30. On the Level 30. A Devil with Women 30. A Holy Terror 31. *The Cisco Kid* 31. Attorney for the Defense 32. Night Club Lady 32. Man Against Woman 32. Man Hunt 33. The Woman I Stole 33. The Mad Game 33. I Believed in You 34. Grand Canary 34. The White Parade 34. It's a Small World 35. Curly Top 35. Nobody's Fool 36. Poor Little Rich Girl 36. Girls Dormitory 36. White Hunter 36. Vogues of 1938 37. Merry go Round of 1938 37. Little Miss Broadway 38. Just Around the Corner 38. *The Story of Alexander Graham Bell* 38. *Hollywood Cavalcade* 39. Everything Happens at Night 39. *Lillian Russell* 40. Down Argentine Way 40. *That Night in Rio* 41. Belle Starr 41. Louisiana Purchase 41. My Gal Sal 42. Springtime in the Rockies 42. Sweet Rosie O'Grady 43. What a Woman 44. The Impatient Years 44. *The Dolly Sisters* 45. Double Dynamite 51.

Cummings, Jack (1900–). American producer, especially of musicals; long with MGM.
The Winning Ticket 35. Born to Dance 36. Go West 40. Ship Ahoy 42. Bathing Beauty 44. Neptune's Daughter 49. Three Little Words 50. Lovely to Look At 52. Kiss Me Kate 53. Seven Brides for Seven Brothers 54. Many Rivers to Cross 55. The Teahouse of the August Moon 56. The Blue Angel 59. Can Can 60. Bachelor Flat 62. Viva Las Vegas 64, many others.

Cummings, Robert (1908–). American light leading man of the forties.

The Virginia Judge 35. Forgotten Faces 36. Last Train from Madrid 37. Souls at Sea 37. Three Smart Girls Grow Up 38. Rio 39. Spring Parade 40. The Devil and Miss Jones 41. Moon over Miami 41. *It Started with Eve* 41. *King's Row* 41. *Saboteur* 42. Princess O'Rourke 43. You Came Along 45. The Bride Wore Boots 46. The Chase 46. Heaven Only Knows 47. The Lost Moment 47. Sleep My Love 48. The Accused 48. Paid in Full 50. For Heaven's Sake 50. The Barefoot Mailman 51. Marry Me Again 53. Lucky Me 54. Dial M for Murder 54. How to be Very Very Popular 55. My Geisha 62. Beach Party 63. What a Way to Go 64. *The Carpetbaggers* 64. Promise Her Anything 66. Stagecoach 66. 5 Golden Dragons 67. Partners in Crime (TV) 73, many others.
TV series: My Hero 52. *The Bob Cummings Show* 54–61. My Living Doll 64.

Cummins, Peggy (1925–). British leading lady, former teenage star.
Dr O'Dowd 39. The Late George Apley (US) 47. Moss Rose (US) 47. Green Grass of Wyoming (US) 48. Escape (US) 48. My Daughter Joy 50. Who Goes There? 52. To Dorothy a Son 54. The March Hare 55. Night of the Demon 57. Dentist in the Chair 60. In the Doghouse 62, etc.

Cunard, Grace (1893–1967) (Harriet Jeffries). American silent serial queen.
The Broken Coin 13. The Purple Mask 15. Peg o' the Ring 18. The Last Man on Earth 24. Untamed 29. Resurrection 31. Ladies They Talk About 33, many others.

Cunningham, Cecil (1888–1959). American character actress, usually in hard or wisecracking roles.
Their Own Desire 29. Monkey Business 31. Mata Hari 31. The Impatient Maiden 32. Blonde Venus 32. Baby Face 33. The Life of Vergie Winters 34. Come and Get It 36. Artists and Models 37. College Swing 38. Lady of the Tropics 39. Lillian Russell 40. New Moon 40. Back Street 41. Blossoms in the Dust 41. I Married an Angel 42. Twin Beds 42. The Hidden Hand 42. Du Barry was a Lady 43. Wonder Man 45. Saratoga Trunk 45. My Reputation 46. The Bride Goes Wild 48, many others.

Cuny, Alain (1908–). Tall, imposing French actor, in occasional films.
Les Visiteurs du Soir 42. Il Cristo Proibito 50. The Hunchback of Notre Dame 56. Les Amants 58. The Milky Way 68. Satyricon 69. Valparaiso Valparaiso 70. Emmanuelle 74. Il Contesto 75. Cadaveri Eccelenti 76. Christ Stopped at Eboli 79. Les Jeux de la Comtesse 80, etc.

Cupito, Suzanne: See *Brittany, Morgan*

Currie, Finlay (1878–1968) (Finlay Jefferson). Veteran Scottish actor with stage and music-hall experience.
The Case of the Frightened Lady 32. Rome Express 32. Edge of the World 38. The Bells Go Down 42. *Great Expectations* (as Magwitch) 46. *Sleeping Car to Trieste* 48. *The History of Mr Polly* 49. Trio 50. Treasure Island 50. *The Mudlark* (as John Brown) 51. Quo Vadis 51. Kangaroo 51. *People Will Talk* (US) 52. Ivanhoe 52. Rob Roy 53. Treasure of the Golden Condor 53. Captain Lightfoot 54. Beau Brummell 54. The End of the Road (leading role) 54. Make Me an Offer 55. King's Rhapsody 56. Around the World in 80 Days 56. Saint Joan 57. Zarak 57. The Little Hut 57. Naked Earth 57. Dangerous Exile 57. Ben Hur (US) 59. Tempest 59. Solomon and Sheba 59. The Angel Wore Red 60. Huckleberry Finn 60. Kidnapped 60. Five Golden Hours 61. Francis of Assisi 61. The Inspector 62. Hand in Hand 62. The Amorous Prawn 62. Corridors of Blood 63. The Cracksman 63. West Eleven 63. The Three Lives of Thomasina 63. Billy Liar 63. The Fall of the Roman Empire 64. Who Was Maddox? (leading role) 64. The Battle of the Villa Fiorita 65. Bunny Lake is Missing 65, etc.

Curry, Tim (1946–). British actor, hard to cast but with a wide range.
The Rocky Horror Picture Show 74. Will Shakespeare (TV) (title role) 76. The Shout 77. Times Square 80. Oliver Twist (TV) 81. Annie 82. The Ploughman's Lunch 83. Baby 83. Legend 85. Clue 86.

Curtis, Alan (1909–1953) (Harold Neberroth). American leading man, and sometimes villain, of many 'B' pictures of the forties.
Walking on Air 36. Winterset 36. Mannequin 38. Hollywood Cavalcade 39. Buck Privates 40. The Great Awakening 41. Two Tickets to London 43. Hitler's Madman 43. *Phantom Lady* 44. Destiny 44. The Invisible Man's Revenge 44. The Naughty Nineties 45. Philo Vance's Gamble 48. The Masked Pirate 50, etc.

Curtis, Dan (1928–). American producer specializing in horror themes for TV.

Dark Shadows (serial) 66. The Night Strangler (TV) 72. *The Norliss Tapes* (TV) 73. Dracula (TV) (& d) 73. Kolchak, the Night Stalker (TV series) 74. Supertrain (TV) 79, etc.
As director: House of Dark Shadows 70. Burnt Offerings 76. Melvin Purvis G-Man (TV) 77. The Raid on Coffeyville (TV) 79. *The Winds of War* (& p) 83.

Curtis, Jamie Lee (1958–). American leading lady who seemed to get stuck in horrors. Daughter of Tony Curtis and Janet Leigh.
Operation Petticoat (TV) 78. Halloween 79. Prom Night 80. Terror Train 80. The Fog 80. Halloween II 81. Road Games 81. Love Letters 83. Trading Places 83. Grandview USA 84. Perfect 85. Amazing Grace and Chuck 87, etc.
TV series: Operation Petticoat 78.

Curtis, Ken (1916–) (Curtis Gates). American character actor, seldom seen outside westerns.
Song of the Prairie 45. Lone Star Moonlight 46. Call of the Forest 49. Rio Grande 50. Mr Roberts 55. The Searchers 56. The Last Hurrah 58. Escort West 59. Two Rode Together 61. Cheyenne Autumn 64. Pony Express Rider 76, many others.
TV series: *Gunsmoke* (as Festus) 63–76.

Curtis, Tony (1925–) (Bernard Schwarz). Bouncy American leading man of fifties actioners who constantly sought a wider range.
Published novel 1977: *Kid Andrew Cody and Julie Sparrow*.
□Criss Cross 49. City Across the River 49. The Lady Gambles 49. Johnny Stool Pigeon 49. Francis 49. I was a Shoplifter 50. Sierra 50. Kansas Raiders 50. Winchester 73 50. *The Prince Who Was a Thief* 51. Flesh and Fury 52. No Room for the Groom 52. Son of Ali Baba 52. *Houdini* 53. The All American 53. Forbidden 53. Beachhead 54. The Black Shield of Falworth 54. Johnny Dark 54. So This is Paris 54. The Purple Mask 54. Six Bridges to Cross 55. The Square Jungle 55. *Trapeze* 56. The Rawhide Years 56. Mister Cory 57. The Midnight Story 57. *Sweet Smell of Success* 57. *The Vikings* 58. Kings go Forth 58. *The Defiant Ones* 58. The Perfect Furlough 58. *Some Like It Hot* 59. Operation Petticoat 59. Pepe 60. Who Was That Lady? 60. The Rat Race 60. *Spartacus* 60. The Great Imposter 60. The Outsider 61. Forty Pounds of Trouble 62. Taras Bulba 62. The List of Adrian Messenger 63. Captain Newman MD 63. Wild and Wonderful 64. Goodbye Charlie 64. Sex and the Single Girl 64. *The Great Race* 65. Boeing Boeing 65. Not With My Wife You Don't 66. Drop Dead Darling 67. Don't Make Waves 67. The Chastity Belt 68. *The Boston Strangler* 68. Those Daring Young Men in their Jaunty Jalopies 69. You Can't Win Them All 70. Suppose They Gave a War and Nobody Came 71. Third Girl from the Left (TV) 73. Lepke 75. Casanova 76. The Count of Monte Cristo (TV) 76. The Last Tycoon 76. The Manitou 78. Scarlett 78. The Bad News Bears Go to Japan 78. Little Miss Marker 80. The Mirror Crack'd 80. The Scarlett O'Hara Wars (TV) 81. Inmates (TV) 81. Portrait of a Showgirl (TV) 82. Brain Waves 83. Insignificance (TV) 85. King of the City 85. The Last of Philip Banter 86.
TV series: *The Persuaders* 71. McCoy 75. Vegas 78.

Curtiz, Michael (1888–1962) (Mihaly Kertesz). Hungarian director of more than sixty films in Europe before settling in Hollywood, where he made some of the smoothest spectacles and melodramas of the thirties and forties and also became famous for his fractured English.
□ENGLISH-SPEAKING FILMS: The Third Degree 26. A Million Bid 27. The Desired Woman 27. Good Time Charley 27. Tenderloin 28. *Noah's Ark* 28. Hearts in Exile 29. Glad Rag Doll 29. The Madonna of Avenue A 29. The Gamblers 29. *Mammy* 30. Under a Texas Moon 30. The Matrimonial Bed 30. Bright Lights 30. A Soldier's Plaything 30. River's End 30. God's Gift to Women 31. The Mad Genius 31. The Woman from Monte Carlo 32. Alias the Doctor 32. The Strange Love of Molly Louvain 32. *Doctor X* 32. Cabin in the Cotton 32. Twenty Thousand Years in Sing Sing 33. *The Mystery of the Wax Museum* 33. The Keyhole 33. Private Detective 33. Goodbye Again 33. The Kennel Murder Case 33. Female 33. Mandalay 34. *British Agent* 34. Jimmy the Gent 34. The Key 34. *Black Fury* 35. The Case of the Curious Bride 35. *Front Page Woman* 35. Little Big Shot 35. *Captain Blood* 35. The Walking Dead 36. *The Charge of the Light Brigade* 36. Mountain Justice 37. Stolen Holiday 36. Kid Galahad 37. The Perfect Specimen 37. Gold is Where You Find It 38. *The Adventures of Robin Hood* 38. *Four Daughters* 38. Four's a Crowd 38. *Angels with Dirty Faces* 38. Dodge City 39. Daughters Courageous 39. Four Wives 39. Elizabeth and Essex 39. Virginia City 40. *The Sea Hawk* 40. Santa Fe Trail 41. Dive Bomber 41. *The Sea*

Wolf 41. Captains of the Clouds 42. *Yankee Doodle Dandy* 42. *Casablanca* (AA) 42. Mission to Moscow 43. This is the Army 43. Passage to Marseilles 44. Janie 44. Roughly Speaking 45. *Mildred Pierce* 45. Night and Day 46. Life with Father 47. The Unsuspected 47. Romance on the High Seas 48. My Dream is Yours 49. Flamingo Road 49. The Lady Takes a Sailor 49. Young Man with a Horn 50. Bright Leaf 50. The Breaking Point 51. Jim Thorpe—All American 51. Force of Arms 51. I'll See You in My Dreams 52. The Story of Will Rogers 52. The Jazz Singer 53. Trouble Along the Way 53. The Boy from Oklahoma 54. The Egyptian 54. White Christmas 54. We're No Angels 55. The Scarlet Hour 56. The Vagabond King 56. The Best Things in Life are Free 56. The Helen Morgan Story 57. The Proud Rebel 58. King Creole 58. The Hangman 59. The Man in the Net 59. The Adventures of Huckleberry Finn 60. A Breath of Scandal 60. Francis of Assisi 61. The Comancheros 62.

'When one speaks of a typical Warners film in the thirties and forties, one is generally speaking of a typical Curtiz film of those periods.'—*Andrew Sarris, 1968*

❀ For the striking Teutonic influence which he brought to a score of thirties melodramas; and for the apparent ease with which he handled top action films in a language which did not come easily to him. *Casablanca.*

¶ Bring on the empty horses!—*instruction attributed to M.C.*

This man Cole Porter, he sticked to purpose of making good music, come hell or hayride.—*M.C. of his film Night and Day*

Curzon, George (1896–1976). British stage actor, in occasional films from early thirties, usually in aristocratic or sinister roles.
The Impassive Footman 32. Lorna Doone 35. *Young and Innocent* 37. Sexton Blake and the Hooded Terror 38. Uncle Silas 47. Harry Black 58, etc.

Cusack, Cyril (1910–). Diminutive Irish actor with fourteen years' Abbey Theatre experience. Film debut as child in 1917.
Odd Man Out 47. The Blue Lagoon 48. The Elusive Pimpernel 50. The Blue Veil (US) 51. Soldiers Three (US) 51. The Man Who Never Was 56. *Jacqueline* 56. The Spanish Gardener 56. Ill Met by Moonlight 57. Floods of Fear 58. Shake Hands with the Devil 59. A Terrible Beauty 59. The Waltz of the Toreadors 62. Eighty Thousand Suspects 63. The Spy Who Came in from the Cold 65. I Was Happy Here 66. *Fahrenheit 451* 66. The Taming of the Shrew 67. Oedipus the King 67. Galileo (It.) 68. David Copperfield 69. King Lear 70. Harold and Maude (US) 71. The Day of the Jackal 73. The Homecoming 73. The Abdication 74. Execution Squad 76. An Eye for an Eye 78. Strumpet City (TV) 80. Tristam and Isolt 81. True Confessions 81. Menace Unseen (TV) 88, many others.

Cusack, Sinead (1948–). Irish leading lady, daughter of Cyril Cusack.
□David Copperfield 69. Alfred the Great 69. Hoffman 70. Revenge 71. Tam Ling 71. The Last Remake of Beau Geste 77.

Cushing, Peter (1913–). British character actor of stage, TV and screen. His slightly fussy manner at first confined him to mild roles, but since allying himself with the Hammer horror school he has dealt firmly with monsters of all kinds.
□The Man in the Iron Mask (US) 39. A Chump at Oxford (US) 39. Vigil in the Night (US) 40. Laddie (US) 40. They Dare Not Love (US) 41. Women in War (US) 42. *Hamlet* (as Osric) 47. Moulin Rouge 53. The Black Night 54. The End of the Affair 55. Magic Fire (US) 56. Time Without Pity 56. Alexander the Great 56. *The Curse of Frankenstein* 57. Violent Playground 57. The Abominable Snowman 57. *Dracula* 58. The Revenge of Frankenstein 58. Suspect 59. The Hound of the Baskervilles 59. John Paul Jones (US) 59. The Mummy 59. Cone of Silence 60. Brides of Dracula 60. The Hellfire Club 61. Fury at Smugglers Bay 61. The Flesh and the Fiends 61. Sword of Sherwood Forest 61. The Naked Edge 61. Captain Clegg 62. *Cash on Demand* 63. The Man Who Finally Died 63. The Gorgon 64. The Evil of Frankenstein 64. Dr Terror's House of Horrors 65. She 65. Dr Who and the Daleks 65. Island of Terror 66. Daleks Invasion Earth 66. The Skull 66. Frankenstein Created Woman 67. The Blood Beast Terror 67. Some May Live (TV) 67. Night of the Big Heat 67. The Torture Garden 67. Corruption 68. Frankenstein Must Be Destroyed 69. Scream and Scream Again 69. The House that Dripped Blood 70. The Vampire Lovers 70. One More Time 70. I Monster 70. Twins of Evil 71. Incense for the Damned 71. Dracula AD 1972 72. Dr Phibes Rises Again 72. Nothing But the Night 72. *Tales from the Crypt* 72. The Creeping Flesh 73. Asylum 73. Fear in the Night 73. The Satanic Rites of Dracula 73. Frankenstein and the Monster from Hell 73. From Beyond the Grave 74. The Beast Must Die 74. Horror Express 74. Shatter 74. The Legend of the Seven Golden

Vampires 74. And Now the Screaming Starts 74. Madhouse 74. The Ghoul 75. Legend of the Werewolf 75. La Grande Trouille 75. Shock Waves 75. Trial by Combat 76. The Uncanny 76. The Devil's Men 76. At the Earth's Core 76. Battle Flag 77. Star Wars 77. The Great Houdinis (TV) 77. Hitler's Son 78. Arabian Adventure 79. A Touch of the Sun 79. The House of Long Shadows 83. Monster Island 81. The Masks of Death (V) (as Sherlock Holmes) 85. Biggles 86.

custard pies as a comic weapon were evolved at the Keystone studio around 1915, and most silent comedians relied heavily on them. In the thirties Mack Sennett staged a splendid one for a nostalgic farce called *Keystone Hotel*. Other notable pie fighters have included Laurel and Hardy in *The Battle of the Century* 28; the whole cast of *Beach Party* 63; and most of the cast of *The Great Race* 64 and *Smashing Time* 65.

Custer, George Armstrong (1839–1876). American major-general whose romantic eccentricities and foolish death at Little Big Horn have been favourite screen fodder. The screen Custers include Dustin Farnum in *Flaming Frontier* 26, Frank McGlynn in *Custer's Last Stand* 36, Ronald Reagan in *Santa Fe Trail* 40, Addison Richards in *Badlands of Dakota* 41, Errol Flynn in the large-scale Custer biopic *They Died with Their Boots On* 41, James Millican in *Warpath* 51, Sheb Wooley in *Bugles in the Afternoon* 52, Britt Lomond in *Tonka* 58, Phil Carey in *The Great Sioux Massacre* 65, Robert Shaw in *Custer of the West* 67, Leslie Nielsen in *The Plainsman* (TV) and Richard Mulligan in *Little Big Man* 70. There has also been a TV series, *The Legend of Custer*, with Wayne Maunder.

cut. Noun: abrupt transition from one shot to another, the first being instantaneously replaced by the second (as opposed to a wipe or a dissolve). Verb: to edit a film, or (during production) to stop the camera running on a scene.

cutaway. An intervening shot allowing an editor to change the focus of action, e.g. clouds or a clock face.

Cuthbertson, Allan (1920–). Australian actor in Britain, adept at supercilious roles. Carrington VC 55. Law and Disorder 57. *Room at the Top* 59. Tunes of Glory 60. Term of Trial 62. The Informers 63. The Seventh Dawn 64. Life at the Top 65. Press for Time 66. The Winds of War (TV) 83, many others.

cutting copy. The first print assembled from the 'rushes'. When this is deemed satisfactory, the negative will be cut to match it, and release prints made.

Cutts, Graham (1885–1958). British director, eminent in silent days.
Flames of Passion 24. Woman to Woman 26. The Rat 27. The Sign of Four 32. Aren't Men Beasts? 37. Just William 39, etc.

Cutts, Patricia (1926–74). British child actress and leading lady. Daughter of Graham Cutts.
Self Made Lady 31. Just William's Luck 49. Your Witness 50. The Man Who Loved Redheads 55. Merry Andrew 58. The Tingler (US) 58. Private Road 71, etc.

Cybulski, Zbigniew (1927–67). Polish leading actor.
□ *A Generation* 54. *Ashes and Diamonds* 58. The Eighth Day of the Week 59. Pociag 59. He, She or It 62. Love at Twenty 62. Silence 63. How to be Loved 63. To Love 64. Salto 65. *The Saragossa Manuscript* 65. Jowita 67.
†Wajda's *Everything for Sale* was inspired by his accidental death.

cyclorama. A smooth, curved giant screen at the back of the set, cunningly lit to give the impression of daylight.

Cyrano de Bergerac. Edmond Rostand's nineteenth-century play about the mock-heroic cavalier with the romantic yearnings and the unfortunately long nose was filmed in Italy in 1909 and 1922, and in France in 1946. In 1950 came Stanley Kramer's American version, directed by Michael Gordon, starring Jose Ferrer (AA); a fair exam crib of the play, it was not much of a motion picture. In 1964 Abel Gance directed a French pastiche, *Cyrano et D'Artagnan*. Charles Laughton, incidentally, played a famous actor in *Because of Him* 45, and at one point was seen as Cyrano. The original Cyrano lived 1619–55 and was a French writer of comedies: whether he had a long nose is uncertain.

Czechoslovakian films were almost unknown in Western countries until recently, when the gentle realistic comedies of Milos Forman (*Peter and Pavla, A Blond in Love*) began winning festival prizes. Other notable Czech films of the last few years include Pavel

Juráček's *Josef Kilian,* Jan Kádar and Elmar Klos's *The Shop on the High Street,* and Jan Nemec's *Diamonds of the Night* and Jiři Menzel's *Capricious Summer.*

Czinner, Paul (1890–1972). Hungarian producer-director, long in Britain: husband of Elisabeth Bergner. From 1955 he concentrated on films of opera and ballet, using multiple cameras.
Der Traumende Mund 32. Catherine the Great 33. Escape Me Never 35. As You Like It 36. Dreaming Lips 37. Stolen Life 39. The Bolshoi Ballet 55. The Royal Ballet 59. Der Rosenkavalier 61. Romeo and Juliet 66, etc.

Answers

James Cagney

1 *Angels with Dirty Faces* ☐ 2 *Captains of the Clouds* ☐ 3 *Torrid Zone* ☐ 4 *Footlight Parade* ☐ 5 *Hard to Handle* ☐ 6 *The Time of Your Life* ☐ 7 *Never Steal Anything Small* ☐ 8 *13 Rue Madeleine* ☐ 9 *Johnny Come Lately* ☐ 10 *The Bride Came COD* ☐ 11 *The Strawberry Blonde* ☐ 12 *The Fighting 69th* ☐ 13 *Boy Meets Girl* ☐ 14 *Smart Money* ☐ 15 *Lady Killer* ☐

casts

1 *Gorilla at Large* ☐ 2 *Bad Day at Black Rock* ☐ 3 *Twelve Angry Men* ☐ 4 *House of Dracula* ☐ 5 *The Old Dark House* (1932) ☐ 6 *Gone with the Wind* ☐ 7 *Rebecca* ☐ 8 *Citizen Kane* ☐ 9 *The Cat and the Canary* ☐ 10 *Arsenic and Old Lace* ☐ 11 *The Wizard of Oz* ☐ 12 *Ninotchka* ☐ 13 *Take Me Out to the Ball Game* ☐ 14 *You'll Find Out* ☐ 15 *King Kong* ☐ 16 *Cast a Giant Shadow* ☐ 17 *The Godfather* ☐ 18 *A Man for All Seasons* ☐ 19 *Airport* ☐ 20 *The Philadelphia Story* ☐ 21 *The Quiet Man* ☐ 22 *The Lady Vanishes* ☐ 23 *Anatomy of a Murder* ☐ 24 *Seven Days in May* ☐ 25 *Giant* ☐ 26 *All About Eve* ☐ 27 *Psycho* ☐ 28 *The Best Years of Our Lives* ☐ 29 *Hellzapoppin* ☐ 30 *Juarez* ☐ 31 *Mr Smith Goes to Washington* ☐ 32 *The Rains Came* ☐ 33 *The Wolf Man* ☐ 34 *King's Row* ☐ 35 *Lost Horizon* (1937) ☐ 36 *The Adventures of Robin Hood* ☐ 37 *The Sea Hawk* ☐ 38 *The Invisible Man Returns* ☐ 39 *Tower of London* (1962) ☐ 40 *Tower of London* (1939) ☐ 41 *The Raven* (1963) ☐ 42 *Wilson* ☐ 43 *Heaven Can Wait* ☐ 44 *Here Comes Mr Jordan* ☐ 45 *The VIPs* ☐ 46 *Rose of Washington Square* ☐ 47 *Now Voyager* ☐ 48 *Mr Skeffington* ☐ 49 *Across the Pacific* ☐ 50 *Casablanca* ☐

censorship

1 Joan Crawford ☐ 2 *The Moon Is Blue* ☐ 3 'Frankly, my dear, I don't give a damn' ☐ 4 Ben Hecht ☐ 5 *Sanctuary* ☐ William Faulkner ☐ 6 Mae West ☐ *She Done Him Wrong* ☐ 7 Edward Albee ☐ 8 The scene in which the bachelors watch blue movies ☐ 9 Beryl Reid ☐ Susannah York ☐ Coral Browne ☐ 10 *Extase* or *Ecstasy* ☐ Gustav Machaty ☐ 11 'Move your bloomin' arse' ☐ 12 *The Wicked Lady* ☐ 13 Alec Guinness's Fagin was held to be anti-Semitic ☐ 14 *Don't Go Near the Water* ☐ 15 *A Flea in Her Ear* ☐

characters

1 The bugler in *From Here to Eternity*, played by Montgomery Clift. ☐
2 *The Lady Vanishes*: Dame May Whitty was the lady who vanished. ☐
3 James Stewart in *The Philadelphia Story* played this socially conscious reporter; ditto Frank Sinatra in the musical remake *High Society*. ☐
4 The hero of *Showboat*, as played at various times by Joseph Schildkraut, Allan Jones and Howard Keel. ☐
5 *Citizen Kane*'s political grafter, played by Ray Collins. ☐
6 Spencer Tracy's one-armed avenger in *Bad Day at Black Rock*. ☐
7 Of course: Laurence Olivier in *Rebecca*. ☐
8 Jane Austen fans will recognise the dowager noblewoman in *Pride and Prejudice*, played in the 1940 film by Edna May Oliver. ☐
9 Robert Montgomery's naturally bewildered fight manager in *Here Comes Mr Jordan*; James Gleason played him. ☐
10 In *Gone with the Wind*, as played by Leslie Howard, the original love in the life of Scarlett O'Hara. ☐
11 Claude Rains's 'poor corrupt official' in *Casablanca*. ☐
12 The thief with the scented stationery in *The Maltese Falcon*: played by Peter Lorre. ☐
13 Ernest Thesiger's gin addict in *The Old Dark House* (1932). ☐

14 The real hero of *The Life and Death of Colonel Blimp*: the good German played by Anton Walbrook. ☐
15 The actress heroine of *Morning Glory* and its remake *Stage Struck*, as played by Katharine Hepburn and Susan Strasberg. ☐
16 He changed his name from Johnny Jones at the beginning of *Foreign Correspondent*: it's Joel McCrea. ☐
17 Would you believe Humphrey Bogart? That's his character name in *The African Queen*. ☐
18 Preston Sturges always gave his people crazy names: this is Betty Hutton in *The Miracle of Morgans Creek*. ☐
19 Back to *The Maltese Falcon*: we couldn't leave out Sydney Greenstreet. ☐
20 One of W. C. Fields's expansive noms-de-plume: this one befitting the owner of a circus, is from *You Can't Cheat an Honest Man*. ☐

Christmas

1 *Holiday Inn* ☐ 2 Alec Guinness ☐ 3 Reginald Owen ☐ 4 *The Holly and the Ivy* ☐ 5 Humphrey Bogart ☐ Peter Ustinov ☐ Aldo Ray ☐ 6 *Scott of the Antarctic* ☐ 7 *Donovan's Reef* ☐ 8 *Things to Come* ☐ 9 *Miracle on 34th Street* ☐

clichés

1 For years this was included in impersonations of Katharine Hepburn. In fact she did not even speak it in her own character, but in the play within the play in *Stage Door* (1937). ☐
2 A curious lapse on the part of writer-director Joseph L. Mankiewicz, this immortal line was spoken by one member of the crowd to another at the entry into Rome of *Cleopatra* (1962). ☐
3 The ultimate riposte in the nose-to-nose confrontation between Gary Cooper and Walter Huston in *The Virginian* (1930). ☐
4 The earliest use of this I know—and a very effective one—is in a 1931 movie called *The Last Flight*, about a group of American servicemen who hang around Europe after World War I, for want of anything better to do. Slightly shell-shocked, they mostly come to tragic ends, and one of them is gored to death after leaping into the arena during a bullfight. When the journalists outside the hospital ask his friend why the man should have done such a thing, the friend (Richard Barthelmess) says thoughtfully: 'Because it seemed like a good idea at the time.' In this context, the phrase is almost a comment on the futility of war. ☐
5 Who but Charles Laughton as Captain Bligh in the 1935 version of *Mutiny on the Bounty*? ☐
6 Victor Mature in *Samson and Delilah* (1949). ☐
7 Again the earliest use I have come across—and I stand to be corrected—is by Douglass Dumbrille as the evil Mohammed Khan in *Lives of a Bengal Lancer* (1935). ☐
8 Warner Baxter (producer) to Ruby Keeler (chorus girl) as she takes the stage for the ailing star in *42nd Street* (1933). ☐
9 Al Jolson, of course. They are in fact the first words ever spoken on the screen, in the second reel of *The Jazz Singer* (1927). ☐
10 Many costume pictures use this gag, which is usually followed by a joke about income tax having risen to fourpence in the pound. I am unable to date it earlier than *Forever and a Day* (1943) in which it is spoken by Ray Milland. ☐
11 Bette Davis at her most melodramatic, in *The Letter* (1941). They used the line as catch-phrase on the posters, though it does not appear in this form in the film as edited. ☐
12 Jean Harlow to Ben Lyon in *Hell's Angels* (1930). ☐
13 Lauren Bacall to Humphrey Bogart in *To Have and Have Not* (1944). ☐
14 This was the time and place of Harry Lime's fatal appointment in *The Third Man* (1949), though the line is not spoken in the film. It was later used as a joke, notably in *Carry on Spying*. ☐

colours of the rainbow

1 pink ☐ 2 red ☐ 3 white ☐ 4 red ☐ 5 blue ☐ 6 yellow ☐ 7 purple ☐ 8 pink ☐ 9 black ☐ 10 white ☐ 11 red ☐ 12 green ☐ 13 crimson ☐ 14 scarlet ☐ 15 red ☐ 16 slightly ☐ 17 bride ☐ 18 bride ☐ 19 reflections ☐ 20 lady ☐ 21 woman ☐ 22 man ☐ 23 gold ☐ 24 woman ☐ 25 hot ☐ 26 forever ☐ 27 perfect ☐ 28 babies ☐ 29 Gabriel ☐ 30 water ☐ death ☐

comebacks

1 Celia Johnson ☐ 2 Pola Negri ☐ 3 Janet Gaynor ☐ 4 Ethel Barrymore ☐ 5 Ed Wynn ☐ 6 Alice Faye ☐ 7 Constance Bennett ☐ 8 Joe E. Brown ☐ 9 Ramon Novarro ☐ 10 Gloria Swanson ☐ 11 Harold Lloyd ☐ 12 Henry Fonda ☐ 13 Melvyn Douglas ☐

comedians

1 Harold Lloyd □ 2 Abbott and Costello □ 3 Laurel and Hardy □ 4 Norman Wisdom □ 5 Charlie Chaplin □ 6 Buster Keaton □ 7 Jack Benny □ 8 Danny Kaye □ 9 Will Hay □ 10 W. C. Fields □ 11 Gracie Fields □ 12 Olsen and Johnson □ 13 Max Miller □ 14 Martha Raye □ 15 Bob Hope □ 16 Eddie Cantor □ 17 Jerry Lewis □ 18 George Formby □ 19 Joe E. Brown □ 20 The Ritz Brothers □

comedy

1 Monty Woolley as the unbearable Sheridan Whiteside in *The Man Who Came to Dinner* (1941), retorting to Mary Wickes as Miss Treen, the nurse. □

2 Gail Patrick as Cornelia in *My Man Godfrey* (1936), a comedy of the depression years in which the idle rich went on a 'scavenger hunt' with human derelicts as trophies. Naturally, the one she finds is only in disguise. □

3 Jean Hagen as the intolerable silent movie queen in *Singin' in the Rain* (1952), risking her reputation by opening her mouth at a première. □

4 Spoken by a camel, straight to camera, in *Road to Morocco* (1942). □

5 Understatement can go no further. Henry Daniell and Cary Grant in *The Philadelphia Story* (1940). □

6 The redoubtable, diminutive Eva Moore, annoyed at the incursion of strangers into *The Old Dark House* (1932). (Yes, a comedy it really is.) □

7 Greta Garbo as the lady comrade in *Ninotchka* (1939), responding to the gallantry of Alexander Granach. □

8 Clark Gable in *It Happened One Night* (1934). Claudette Colbert has been forced to spend a night with him in a motel room, but he hangs a blanket on a line between the beds. In the end of course, the walls come down. □

9 *The Philadelphia Story* (1940) again. Katharine Hepburn thinks she misbehaved with James Stewart, but he tells her she simply got a little drunk and he put her to bed. Then she gets mad . . . □

10 Who but Groucho Marx? And to whom would he be referring but Margaret Dumont? The movie is *Duck Soup* (1933). □

common words

1 *Honeymoon* □ 2 *Love* □ 3 *City* □ 4 *Desert* □ 5 *Wife* □ 6 *Party* □ 7 *Music* □ 8 *River* □ 9 *Train* □ 10 *Town* □ 11 *Life* □ 12 *Lost* □ 13 *Comedy* □ 14 *House* □ 15 *Follow* □ 16 *Moon* □ 17 *Naked* □ 18 *Romance* □ 19 *Girl* □ 20 *Song* □ 21 *Affair* □ 22 *Enemy* □ 23 *Green* □ 24 *Rhythm* □ 25 *Star* □

connections

1 Both concerned a search for the truth about a man recently deceased □ 2 Both characters were named Maximilian □ 3 Both played the obnoxious publicist in different versions of *A Star Is Born* □ 4 O'Herlihy played *Robinson Crusoe*, Mantee *Robinson Crusoe on Mars* □ 5 Both included excerpts from silent movies □ 6 Both were based on the old story of the lady who vanished and her companion who was assured she never existed □ 7 Both were based on novels by Ethel Lina White □ 8 R. C. Sheriff wrote them □ James Whale directed them □ 9 Both involved Devil's Island □ 10 Both involved angels helping people in trouble □ 11 James Stewart is the real name of both □ 12 Both were photographed by Gregg Toland □ 13 The Merry Widow Waltz is central to both □ 14 The villain of both films finally falls from a high place □ 15 The first scenes of each use subjective camera □ 16 Both played Professor Challenger in versions of *The Lost World* □ 17 A volcanic eruption is the climax of each □ 18 The heroine disguises herself as a boy in each case □ 19 Both were directed by Julien Duvivier or, if you like, both are composed of episodes □ 20 Each plays a villain who commits suicide at the end □ 21 The first 3–D film and the first CinemaScope film □ 22 Both had elevated railway sequences □ 23 Both played Oscar Wilde in rival films of 1960 □ 24 Both were tentative titles for the film finally released in the US as *Arrivederci Baby* and in GB as *Drop Dead Darling* □ 25 The first contained a joke about the sledge in the second □ 26 Sam Jaffe played an eccentric character part in each □ 27 Each involved an airplane crash □ 28 Both played Custer □ 29 The leading character escapes by air balloon at the end □ 30 Both played Bulldog Drummond □ 31 Ralph Bellamy is the villain of each □ 32 The Devil is a leading figure in each □ 33 Both were David O. Selznick productions □ 34 In both, the title character was never seen □ 35 Both had scenes involving a dentist □ 36 Both were from novels by Erskine Caldwell □ 37 Both concern oversize rabbits □ 38 Both take place mainly on a train □ 39 Both played the murderer in versions of *And Then There Were None* □ 40 Both played Micawber in versions of *David Copperfield* □

copycats I

1 They all played angels ☐: *The Bishop's Wife* ☐ *Heaven Only Knows* ☐ *Here Comes Mr Jordan* ☐

2 They all dressed as women ☐: *I Was a Male War Bride* ☐ *Some Like It Hot* ☐ *You're in the Army Now* ☐

3 They all played Shakespearean actors ☐: *A Double Life* ☐ *To Be or Not to Be* ☐ *Prince of Players* ☐

4 They all played the Scarlet Pimpernel ☐: *Return of the Scarlet Pimpernel* ☐ *The Scarlet Pimpernel* ☐ *The Elusive Pimpernel* ☐

5 They all impersonated great entertainers ☐: *The Eddie Cantor Story* ☐ *The Jolson Story* ☐ *Funny Girl/Funny Lady* ☐

6 They all played *Dr Jekyll and Mr Hyde* ☐

7 They all played Queen Victoria ☐: *The Mudlark* ☐ *Victoria the Great* or *Sixty Glorious Years* ☐ *The Prime Minister* ☐

8 They all played famous composers ☐: Sousa in *Stars and Stripes Forever* (GB: *Marching Along*) ☐ Tchaikovsky in *The Music Lovers* ☐ Sullivan in *The Story of Gilbert and Sullivan* ☐ Handel in *The Great Mr Handel* ☐

9 They all performed (or appeared to) on the flying trapeze ☐: *The Three Maxims* ☐ *Trapeze* ☐ *The Greatest Show on Earth* ☐ *At the Circus* ☐

10 They all played Disraeli ☐: *The Prime Minister* ☐ *Disraeli* ☐ *The Mudlark* ☐

11 They all played leprechauns ☐: *The Luck of the Irish* ☐ *Darby O'Gill and the Little People* ☐ *Finian's Rainbow* ☐ *Jack the Giant Killer* ☐

12 They all played visitors from outer space ☐: *The Day the Earth Stood Still* ☐ *This Island Earth* ☐ *The Thing from Another World* ☐ *Not of This Earth* ☐

13 They all played the invisible man ☐: *Abbott and Costello Meet the Invisible Man* ☐ *Invisible Agent* or *The Invisible Man's Revenge* ☐ *The Invisible Man Returns* ☐

14 They all had split personalities ☐: *Madonna of the Seven Moons* ☐ *The Three Faces of Eve* ☐ *Lizzie* ☐

15 They all played US Presidents ☐: *Fail Safe* (and others) ☐ *Advise and Consent* ☐ *Seven Days in May* ☐ *Dr Strangelove* ☐

16 They all served time on Devil's Island ☐: *Passage to Marseilles* ☐ *Condemned* ☐ *Papillon* ☐ *The Life of Emile Zola* ☐

17 They all played giants ☐: *Attack of the Fifty Foot Woman* ☐ *Jack and the Beanstalk* ☐ *The Amazing Colossal Man* ☐

18 They all played the Devil ☐: *Alias Nick Beal* ☐ *All That Money Can Buy* ☐ *Heaven Can Wait* ☐

19 They all made journeys by air balloon ☐: *The Wizard of Oz* ☐ *Charlie Bubbles* ☐ *Around the World in Eighty Days* ☐

20 They all played Death ☐: *On Borrowed Time* ☐ *Orphée* ☐ *Death Takes a Holiday* ☐

21 They all played famous pirates ☐: *The Buccaneer* ☐ *Anne of the Indies* ☐ *Blackbeard the Pirate* ☐

22 They all played Calamity Jane ☐: *Calamity Jane and Sam Bass* ☐ *Calamity Jane* ☐ *The Plainsman* ☐

23 They all played ventriloquists ☐: *The Great Gabbo* ☐ *Knock on Wood* ☐ *Dead of Night* ☐

24 They all played Henry VIII ☐: *The Prince and the Pauper* ☐ *The Private Life of Henry VIII* ☐ *Carry on Henry* ☐

25 They all played the Brontë sisters ☐ in *Devotion* ☐

26 They all played Wyatt Earp ☐: *Hour of the Gun* ☐ *Gunfight at the OK Corral* ☐ *My Darling Clementine* ☐

27 They all played Hitler ☐: Watson innumerable times but principally in *The Hitler Gang* ☐ *The Magic Face* ☐ *Hitler* ☐

28 They all played oriental detectives who had series to themselves ☐: Mr Wong ☐ Charlie Chan ☐ Mr Moto ☐

29 They all played ghosts ☐: *Blithe Spirit* ☐ *The Ghost Goes West* ☐ *The Ghost and Mrs Muir* ☐

30 They all played alcoholics ☐: *Days of Wine and Roses* ☐ *Come Fill the Cup* ☐ *The Lost Weekend* ☐

copycats II

1 All played the title characters in films beginning with 'I' ☐: *I Was a Fugitive from a Chain Gang* ☐ *I Was an American Spy* ☐ *I Was a Male War Bride* ☐ *I Was a Communist for the FBI* ☐ 2 All wrote stories which became Hollywood monster classics ☐: *The Invisible Man* ☐ *Frankenstein* ☐ *Dracula* ☐ *Dr Jekyll and Mr Hyde* ☐ 3 All played centenarians ☐: *The Lost Moment* ☐ *Little Big Man* ☐ *Lost Horizon* ☐ *Lost Horizon* ☐ 4 All appeared together in *Stagecoach* ☐ 5 All played Richard III ☐ *Tower of London 62* ☐ *Richard III* ☐ *Tower of London 39* ☐ 6 All played leads in films from novels by Somerset Maugham ☐ *Christmas Holiday* ☐ *The Moon and Sixpence* ☐ *The Razor's Edge*

□ *Of Human Bondage* □ 7 All played Jack the Ripper □ *A Study in Terror* □ *The Lodger* □ *Man in the Attic* □ *Jack the Ripper* □ 8 All played Nero □ *The Story of Mankind* □ *The Sign of the Cross* □ *Quo Vadis* □ 9 All played amnesiacs □ *Mister Buddwing* □ *Somewhere in the Night* □ *Random Harvest* □ *Mirage* □ 10 All played the lead in *Charley's Aunt* □ 11 All played Napoleon □ *Waterloo* □ *War and Peace* or *The Young Mr Pitt* □ *Desiree* □ *Eagle in a Cage* □ 12 All were produced by Howard Hughes □ 13 All played opposite Greta Garbo □ *Queen Christina* and several silents □ *Conquest/Marie Walewska* □ *Ninotchka* or *Two-Faced Woman* □ *Camille* □ 14 All were played by all-black casts □ 15 All played D'Artagnan in various versions of *The Three Musketeers* □ 16 All concerned the Ku Klux Klan □ 17 All played dipsomaniacs □ *Smash-up* □ *The Lost Weekend* □ *Come Fill the Cup* □ *Days of Wine and Roses* □ 18 All were made around 1930 in early wide screen systems □ 19 All featured Groucho Marx □ 20 All played the lead in versions of *Kismet* □ 21 All at various times played The Lone Wolf □ 22 All played Lord Nelson □ *Nelson* □ *Lady Hamilton* □ *Emma Hamilton* □ *A Bequest to the Nation* □ 23 Each had two sisters who were also actresses □ 24 All played bigamists □ *The Bigamist* □ *The Remarkable Mr Pennypacker* □ *The Captain's Paradise* □ *The Constant Husband* □ 25 All concerned the Foreign Legion □ 26 All had climaxes in funfairs □ 27 All played Christ □ *King of Kings* 60 □ *The Greatest Story Ever Told* □ *King of Kings* 27 □ 28 All played Jean Valjean in *Les Misérables* □ 29 The hero of each was a multi-murderer □ 30 Each was remade as a musical □ *Carousel* □ *Hello Dolly* □ *Cabaret* □ *The Girl Most Likely* □ 31 All have played Scrooge □ 32 All starred Lon Chaney □ 33 All went into politics □ 34 All had scenes in motels □ 35 All were set in San Francisco □ 36 All had scenes in sewers □ 37 All were uncredited remakes □ *Kiss of Death* □ *The Sea Wolf* □ *The Letter* □ 38 All were remade from Japanese originals □ *Yojimbo* □ *Seven Samurai* □ *Rashomon* □ 39 In each case a dual role was involved □ 40 All are Laurel and Hardy shorts □

couples

1 Fredric March and Janet Gaynor in *A Star Is Born.* □
2 Cary Grant and Katharine Hepburn in *The Philadelphia Story.* □
3 Rex Harrison and Constance Cummings in *Blithe Spirit.* □
4 George Brent and Bette Davis in *Dark Victory.* □
5 Ray Milland and Jane Wyman in *The Lost Weekend.* □
6 Jack Benny and Carole Lombard in *To Be or Not to Be.* □
7 Fredric March and Myrna Loy in *The Best Years of Our Lives.* □
8 Gregory Peck and Ingrid Bergman in *Spellbound.* □
9 Emil Jannings and Marlene Dietrich in *The Blue Angel.* □
10 Ronald Colman and Madeleine Carroll in *The Prisoner of Zenda.* □
11 Laurence Olivier and Joan Fontaine in *Rebecca.* □
12 John Wayne and Claire Trevor in *Stagecoach.* □
13 Charles Boyer and Bette Davis in *All This and Heaven Too.* □
14 Trevor Howard and Celia Johnson in *Brief Encounter.* □
15 Richard Dix and Irene Dunne in *Cimarron.* □
16 Fred MacMurray and Barbara Stanwyck in *Double Indemnity.* □
17 Don Ameche and Gene Tierney in *Heaven Can Wait.* □
18 William Holden and Martha Scott in *Our Town.* □
19 Tyrone Power and Myrna Loy in *The Rains Came.* □
20 Clark Gable and Claudette Colbert in *It Happened One Night.* □

credits

1 The 1929 talkie version of *The Taming of the Shrew*, tailored for Mary Pickford and Douglas Fairbanks. □
2 *Carry on Cleo* (1964). □
3 *The Boys from Syracuse* (1940), derived from *A Comedy of Errors.* □
4 *The Great Escape* (1963). In this prisoner-of-war drama, based on fact, the fifty were escaped allied prisoners who were shot by the Gestapo. □
5 *The Good Earth* (1938), the film upon which Thalberg was working at the time of his death. This posthumous credit was the only one he ever took. □
6 *The Man on the Eiffel Tower*, a curious American thriller made in 1950 and starring Charles Laughton as Inspector Maigret. □
7 *The Man with the Golden Arm* (1956). The credit caused a great deal of comment in Hollywood, not least from Nelson Algren, author of the original novel; it was the first time a producer or

director had claimed authorship of a movie. ☐

8 *Mighty Joe Young* (1949), the comedy successor to *King Kong*. ☐

9 *The Fearless Vampire Killers* (1967). Fortunately or not, this kind of humour was not carried through into the film. ☐

10 *Three on a Couch*, a 1967 Jerry Lewis comedy. The strange thing was that Mr Best scarcely needed introducing, having been a familiar face in movies and TV for the previous ten years. ☐

11 *Son of Kong* (1933), the hurried sequel to *King Kong*. Compared to its original it was so weak that its makers decided to present it, rather tentatively, as a comedy. ☐

12 *Carry on Doctor* (1968). ☐

13 *The Three Faces of Eve* (1957). ☐

14 *A Star Is Born* (1954). ☐

15 *The Women* (1939). ☐

D

DEFA (Deutsche Film Aktiengesellschaft). The East German party line film production company which absorbed UFA in 1946.

Da Costa, Morton (1914–) (Morton Tecosky). American director of stage musicals and three films.
□Auntie Mame 58. *The Music Man* 62. Island of Love 64.

Da Silva, Howard (1909–86) (Harold Silverblatt). Tough, suspicious-looking American character actor with stage experience. Graduated from bit parts to a peak in the late forties, then had McCarthy trouble.
Abe Lincoln in Illinois 39. The Sea Wolf 41. The Big Shot 43. *The Lost Weekend* 45. The Blue Dahlia 46. Blaze of Noon 47. Unconquered 47. They Live by Night 48. The Great Gatsby 49. Three Husbands 50. Fourteen Hours 51. M 51. David and Lisa 62. The Outrage 65. Nevada Smith 66. '1776' 72. The Great Gatsby 74. Mommie Dearest (as Louis B. Mayer) 81, etc.

Dade, Stephen (1909–). British cinematographer, in films from 1927.
We'll Meet Again 42. Caravan 46. The Brothers 47. Snowbound 49. A Question of Adultery 57. Bluebeard's Ten Honeymoons 60. Zulu 64. City under the Sea 65. The Viking Queen 66, many others.

Daddy Longlegs. Jean Webster's sentimental novel about a January–May romance against an orphanage setting was filmed in 1919 with Mary Pickford and Mahlon Hamilton; in 1930 with Janet Gaynor and Warner Baxter; in 1935, disguised as *Curly Top*, with Shirley Temple; and in 1955, as a musical, with Leslie Caron and Fred Astaire.

Daffy Duck. The talkative game bird of a hundred Warner cartoons was allegedly modelled on Harpo Marx.

D'Agostino, Albert S. (1893–1970). American art director, in Hollywood from early silent days; with RKO 1936–58.
The Raven 35. Mr and Mrs Smith 41. The Enchanted Cottage 44. Notorious 46. The Woman on the Beach 47. Mourning Becomes Electra 48. Clash by Night 51. Androcles and the Lion 53. Back from Eternity 56, many others.

Dagover, Lil (1897–1980) (Marta Maria Liletts). Distinguished German actress.
The Cabinet of Dr Caligari 19. Destiny 21. Dr Mabuse Der Spieler 22. Chronicles of the Grey House 24. Tartuffe 26. Hungarian Rhapsody 27. The White Devil 30. Congress Dances 31. Kreuzer Sonata 35. Fredericus 39. Die Fussganger 73. Karl May 74, etc.

Daguerre, Louis (1787–1851). French pioneer of photography; his original copper-plated prints were known as *daguerrotypes*.

Dahl, Arlene (1924–). Red-haired American leading lady, former model; also beauty columnist.
□Life with Father 47. *My Wild Irish Rose* 47. The Bride Goes Wild 48. A Southern Yankee 48. Reign of Terror 49. Scene of the Crime 49. Ambush 49. The Outriders 50. Three Little Words 50. Watch the Birdie 50. Inside Straight 51. No Questions Asked 51. Caribbean 52. Jamaica Run 53. Desert Legion 53. Sangaree 53. The Diamond Queen 53. Here Come the Girls 54. Woman's World 54. Bengal Brigade 54. Slightly Scarlet 56. Wicked as They Come (GB) 56. Fortune is a Woman (GB) 57. *Journey to the Centre of the Earth* 59. Kisses for My President 64. The Land Raiders 69. The Road to Khatmandu 69. TV series: One Life to Live 82

¶ *A.D.:* With enthusiasm anything is possible.
A.D.: I considered the years in Hollywood nothing but an interim. What I always wanted was to be a musical comedy star.

Dahl, Roald (1916–). Norwegian writer of British adoption; switches from children's books to macabre short stories.

Chitty Chitty Bang Bang 69. You Only Live Twice 69. Willy Wonka and the Chocolate Factory 70, etc.
TV series (which he also introduced): *Roald Dahl's Tales of the Unexpected* 79.

Dahlbeck, Eva (1920–). Swedish actress, often in Ingmar Bergman's films.
Waiting Women 52. The Village (GB) 53. Smiles of a Summer Night 55. So Close to Life 61. Now About These Women 64. Loving Couples 64. Les Creatures 65. The Red Mantle 67. People Meet 69, etc.

Dailey, Dan (1914–78). Lanky American actor-dancer with wide experience in vaudeville and cabaret.
The Mortal Storm 40. Dulcy 40. Ziegfeld Girl 41. Moon over Her Shoulder 41. Lady Be Good 41. Panama Hattie 42. Give Out Sisters 42. *Mother Wore Tights* 47. *Give My Regards to Broadway* 48. You Were Meant for Me 48. When My Baby Smiles at Me 48. Chicken Every Sunday 49. My Blue Heaven 50. *When Willie Comes Marching Home* 50. A Ticket to Tomahawk 50. I Can Get It for You Wholesale 51. Call Me Mister 51. Pride of St Louis 51. What Price Glory? 52. Meet Me at The Fair 53. There's No Business Like Show Business 54. *It's Always Fair Weather* 55. Meet Me in Las Vegas 56. *The Best Things in Life are Free* 56. The Wings of Eagles 56. Oh Men, Oh Women 57. The Wayward Bus 57. Pepe 60. Hemingway's Adventures of a Young Man 62. The Private Files of J. Edgar Hoover 77, others.
TV series: The Four Just Men 59. The Governor and J.J. 69. Faraday and Company 73.

dailies: see *rushes*.

Dainton, Patricia (1930–). British leading lady who started as a teenager.
Don't Ever Leave Me 49. The Dancing Years 50. Castle in the Air 52. Operation Diplomat 54. The Passing Stranger 57. Witness in the Dark 60, etc.

Dalby, Amy (c. 1888–1969). British character actress who normally on screen played ageing spinsters.
The Wicked Lady 45. The Man Upstairs 57. The Lamp in Assassin Mews 62. *The Secret of My Success* 65. Who Killed the Cat? 66. The Spy with a Cold Nose 67, etc.

Dale, Charles (1881–1971) (Charles Marks). American vaudevillian who, with Joe Smith (qv), made up Smith and Dale, the inspiration for *The Sunshine Boys*.
□Manhattan Parade 31. The Heart of New York 32. Two Tickets to Broadway 51.

Dale, Esther (1885–1961). American character actress usually a motherly soul, nurse or grandma.
Crime without Passion 34. Curly Top 35. Fury 36. Dead End 37. Prison Farm 38. Tell No Tales 39. The Mortal Storm 40. Back Street 41. North Star 43. Margie 44. Stolen Life 46. The Egg and I 47. Ma and Pa Kettle 49. No Man of Her Own 50. Ma and Pa Kettle at the Fair 52. The Oklahoman 57, many others.

Dale, Jim (1935–) (James Smith). British pop singer turned light comedian and member of the 'Carry On' team.
Raising the Wind 62. Carry On Spying 64. Carry On Cleo 65. The Big Job 65. Carry On Cowboy 66. Carry On Screaming 66. Lock Up Your Daughters 69. *The National Health* 73. Digby 73. Joseph Andrews 77. *Pete's Dragon* 77. Bloodshy 79. The Spaceman and King Arthur 79, etc.

Dalen, Zale (–). Canadian director.
Skip Tracer 77. Hounds of Notre Dame 80.

Daley, Cass (1915–1975) (Catherine Dailey). American comedienne whose shouted songs and acrobatic contortions were a feature of several light musicals of the forties.
The Fleet's In 41. Star Spangled Rhythm 42. Crazy House 43. Out of This World 45. Ladies' Man 46. Here Comes the Groom 51. Red Garters 54. The Spirit Is Willing 67, etc.

Dali, Salvador (1904–84). Spanish surrealist painter who collaborated with Luis Buñuel in making two controversial films: *Un Chien Andalou* 29 and *L'Age D'Or* 30. Later designed the dream sequence for *Spellbound* 45.

Dalio, Marcel (1900–83) (Israel Mosche Blauschild). Dapper French comedy actor, frequently in Hollywood.
La Grande Illusion 37. Pepe le Moko 37. *La Règle du Jeu* 39. Unholy Partners 41. Casablanca 42. The Song of Bernadette 43. Temptation Harbour (GB) 46. On the Riviera 51. *The Happy Time* 52. The Snows of Kilimanjaro 52. Lucky Me 54. Sabrina Fair 54. Miracle in the Rain 56. Pillow Talk 59. Can Can 59. Jessica 62. Wild and Wonderful 63. Lady L 65. The 25th Hour 67. How Sweet It Is 68. Catch 22 70. The Mad Adventures of Rabbi Jacob 73. L'Ombre de Château 76. Brigade Mondaine 80, many others.

Dall, Evelyn (c. 1914–). American nightclub singer who appeared in some British film extravaganzas of the forties.
He Found a Star 41. King Arthur Was a Gentleman 42. Miss London Ltd 43. Time Flies 44, etc.

Dall, John (1918–1971). American stage leading man; played in occasional films.
□For the Love of Mary 45. *The Corn is Green* 46. Something in the Wind 47. *Rope* 48. Another Part of the Forest 48. Gun Crazy 49. The Man Who Cheated Himself 50. Spartacus 60. Atlantis the Lost Continent 61.

Dallesandro, Joe (1948–). American actor associated with 'underground' films.
Heat 72. Warhol's Frankenstein 74. Warhol's Dracula 74.

Dalrymple, Ian (1903–). British writer-producer.
South Riding (w only) 38. The Citadel (w only) 38. The Lion Has Wings 39. Once a Jolly Swagman 46. The Woman in the Hall 48. The Wooden Horse 50. The Heart of the Matter 52. Three Cases of Murder 55. The Admirable Crichton 57. A Cry from the Streets 58, etc.

Dalton, Audrey (1934–). British leading lady in Hollywood.
My Cousin Rachel 52. The Girls of Pleasure Island 53. Titanic 53. Casanova's Big Night 54. The Prodigal 55. Separate Tables 58. Mr Sardonicus 62. The Bounty Killer 65, etc.

Dalton, Dorothy (1894–1972). American silent screen leading lady with stage experience.
The Disciple 14. Black is White 20. Moran of the Lady Letty 22. The Crimson Challenge 22. Fogbound 23. The Moral Sinner 24. The Lone Wolf 24, etc.

Dalton, Timothy (1944–). Saturnine British stage actor in occasional films.
The Lion in Winter 68. *Wuthering Heights* 70. Mary Queen of Scots 71. Lady Caroline Lamb 72. Sextette 78. Agatha 79. Flash Gordon 80. Chanel Solitaire 81. Mistral's Daughter (TV) 84. Florence Nightingale (TV) 84. The Doctor and the Devils 85. Sins (TV) 85. *The Living Daylights* (as James Bond) 87, etc.

Daltrey, Roger (1944–). British pop singer given dramatic roles by Ken Russell.
□Tommy 74. Lisztomania 75. The Legacy 79. McVicar 80.

¶ *R.D.:* Of course, chicks keep popping up. When you're in a hotel, a pretty young lady makes life bearable.

Daly, James (1918–78). American stage actor; film appearances rare.
□The Court Martial of Billy Mitchell 55. The Young Stranger 57. I Aim at the Stars 60. Planet of the Apes 68. The Big Bounce 68. The Five Man Army 69. Wild in the Sky 72. The Resurrection of Zachary Wheeler 73.
TV series: Foreign Intrigue 55. *Medical Center* 69–75.

Daly, Mark (1887–1957). British character actor, on stage from 1906, screen from 1930 often as cheerful tramp.
The Private Life of Henry VIII 32. A Cuckoo in the Nest 33. The Ghost Goes West 36. Wings of the Morning 37. Next of Kin 42. Bonnie Prince Charlie 49. Lease of Life 54. The Shiralee 57, many others.

Daly, Tyne (1947–). American leading lady.
John and Mary 69. Angel Unchained 70. Heat of Anger (TV) 71. Play It As It Lays 72. The Entertainer (TV) 75. The Enforcer 76. Telefon 77. Speedtrap 77. The Women's Room (TV) 80. Zoot Suit 82.
TV series: Cagney and Lacey 82.

Damaged Goods. Eugene Brieux's propaganda play about venereal disease has been popular 'under the counter' fare since it was written in 1903. The chief film versions were in 1919 (British), 1937 (American) and 1961 (American).

Les Dames du Bois de Boulogne (France 1944). Robert Bresson's cold, talky film has over the years become something of a cult. It updates a story by Diderot about a jealous woman's revenge on her lover; but its style is so refined and thin as to be almost the antithesis of cinema. Maria Casares has a splendid stab at the leading role.

Damiani, Damiano (1922–). Italian director.
The Empty Canvas 64. A Bullet for the General 66. Confessions of a Police Captain 71. The Tempter 74. The Genius 75. I Am Afraid 77. Goodbye and Amen 78. L'Ultimo Nome 79, etc.

Damiano, Gerald (–). American director of hard core porn movies.
Deep Throat 73. The Devil in Miss Jones 73, etc.

Damita, Lili (1901–) (Lilliane Carré). French leading lady who made a few American films and married Errol Flynn.
The Rescue 28. The Bridge of San Luis Rey 29. The Cockeyed World 29. The Match King 31. This Is the Night 32. Goldie Gets Along 33. The Frisco Kid 35. L'Escadrille de la Chance (Fr.) 36, etc.

The Damned. Films under this title include: 1. René Clément's 1949 melodrama of submarines in the Atlantic during World War II. 2. Joseph Losey's 1964 science-fiction extravaganza about other-worldly children kept in a scientific dug-out in the Dorset cliffs. 3. Luchino Visconti's 1969 account of a German armaments family under the Nazis.

Damon, Cathryn (1933–87). American comedy actress who played the slightly more sensible sister in TV's *Soap*.
Friendships, Secrets and Lies (TV) 80. How to Beat The High Cost of Living 80.

Damon, Mark (1935–). American leading man in routine films.
Between Heaven and Hell 56. The Fall of the House of Usher 60. The Young Racers 63. Anzio 68. There Is No Thirteen 77. The Choirboys (co-p only) 77, etc.

Damone, Vic (1929–) (Vito Farinola). American light leading man and singer.
Rich, Young and Pretty 51. The Strip 51. Athena 53. Deep in My Heart 55. Kismet 55. Hell to Eternity 60, etc.

Dampier, Claude (1879–1955) (Claude Cowan). British comedian noted for nasal drawl and country yokel characterization. Long on stage and music hall.
Boys Will Be Boys 35. Mr Stringfellow Says No 37. Riding High 39. Don't Take It to Heart 44. Meet Mr Malcolm 53, etc.

Dana, Bill (–). American television comedian who used to play Mexicans.
Rossetti and Ryan (TV) 77. A Guide for the Married Woman 78. The Hungry i Reunion 81.
TV series: The Bill Dana Show 62–65. No Soap Radio 82. Zorro and Son 83.

Dana, Leora (1923–1983). American general purpose actress.
Three-Ten to Yuma 57. Kings Go Forth 58. Some Came Running 58. Pollyanna 60. A Gathering of Eagles 63. Shoot the Moon 82, etc.

Dana, Viola (1897–1987) (Violet Flugrath). American silent screen actress, usually in light comedy and fashionable drama.
Molly the Drummer Boy 14. Rosie O'Grady 17. A Chorus Girl's Romance 20. The Willow Tree 20. Open All Night 24. Merton of the Movies 24. Winds of Chance 25. Kosher Kitty Kelly 26. The Sisters 29, etc.

dance bands in the thirties and forties were so popular as to be stars in their own films: Henry Hall's in *Music Hath Charms*, Kay Kyser's in half a dozen films including *That's Right You're Wrong*, Paul Whiteman's in *King of Jazz*, Tommy and Jimmy Dorsey's in *The Fabulous Dorseys*. Also frequently on hand to assist the stars were the bands of Glenn Miller, Xavier Cugat, Woody Herman and Harry James, to name but a few. In the fifties bands became too expensive to maintain, but *The Glenn Miller Story* and *The Benny Goodman Story* reawakened interest, and Louis Armstrong kept the flag flying till the day he died. The Seventies brought signs of a revival of interest in the big bands, in such movies as *W. W. and the Dixie Dancekings* and *The Buddy Holly Story*.

Dance, Charles (1946–). British leading actor.
Saigon (TV) 83. *The Jewel in the Crown* (TV) 84. For Your Eyes Only 84. Plenty 86. Good Morning Babylon 86. Out on a Limb (TV) 87. The Golden Child 87.

Dandridge, Dorothy (1923–1965). Black American leading lady, former child actress.
A Day at the Races 37. Lady from Louisiana 41. Drums of the Congo 42. Bright Road 52. *Carmen Jones* 54. Island in the Sun 57. The Decks Ran Red 58. Porgy and Bess 59. Tamango 59. Moment of Danger 60, etc.

Dane, Karl (1886–1934) (Karl Daen). Lanky Danish character actor who almost accidentally became a popular comedian at the end of the silent period, but could not survive sound.
Lights of Old Broadway 25. *The Big Parade* 25. The Scarlet Letter 26. The Red Mill 27. *Rookies* 27. Baby Mine 28. Circus Rookies 28. Alias Jimmy Valentine 28. Speedway 29. Montana Moon 30. The Big House 30. Billy the Kid 30, etc.

Daneman, Paul (1925–). British light leading man, mainly on stage.
The Clue of the New Pin 61. Zulu 63. How I Won the War 67. Oh What a Lovely War 69, etc.
TV series: Spy Trap.

D'Angelo, Beverly (1954–). American leading lady.
Every Which Way But Loose 78. Hair 79. Coal Miner's Daughter 80. Paternity 81. Honky Tonk Freeway 81. The Woo Woo Kid 87.

Dangerous Moonlight (GB 1940). The film which featured Richard Adinsell's 'Warsaw Concerto' and by its success started the crop of concerto movies which finally proved so tiresome in the forties. Basically a romantic melodrama of the Polish Air Force, with Anton Walbrook and Sally Gray; directed by Brian Desmond Hurst.

Daniell, Henry (1894–1963). Incisive, cold-eyed British stage actor, a popular Hollywood villain of the thirties and forties.
□Jealousy 29. The Awful Truth 29. The Last of the Lone Wolf 30. Path of Glory 34. The Unguarded Hour 36. *Camille* 36. Under Cover of Night 37. The Thirteenth Chair 37. The Firefly 37. Madame X 37. Holiday 38. Marie Antoinette 38. The Private Lives of Elizabeth and Essex 39. We Are Not Alone 39. All This and Heaven Too 40. *The Sea Hawk* 40. The Great Dictator 40. *The Philadelphia Story* 40. A Woman's Face 41. Dressed to Kill 41. Four Jacks and a Jill 41. The Feminine Touch 41. Castle in the Desert 42. Random Harvest 42. Sherlock Holmes and the Voice of Terror 42. Reunion in France 42. The Great Impersonation 42. Nightmare 42. Mission to Moscow 43. *Sherlock Holmes in Washington* 43. Watch on the Rhine 43. Jane Eyre 43. *The Suspect* 44. The Chicago Kid 45. Hotel Berlin 45. The Woman in Green 45. *The Body Snatcher* 45. Captain Kidd 45. The Bandit of Sherwood Forest 46. Song of Love 47. The Exile 47. Siren of Atlantis 48. Wake of the Red Witch 48. The Secret of St Ives 49. Buccaneer's Girl 50. The Egyptian 54. The Prodigal 55. Diane 55. The Man in the Grey Flannel Suit 56. Lust for Life 56. Les Girls 57. The Story of Mankind 57. The Sun Also Rises 57. Witness for the Prosecution 57. Mr Cory 57. From the Earth to the Moon 58. The Four Skulls of Jonathan Drake 59. Voyage to the Bottom of the Sea 61. The Comancheros 61. Madison Avenue 62. The Notorious Landlady 62. Five Weeks in a Balloon 62. The Chapman Report 62. My Fair Lady 64.
Famous Line (*The Philadelphia Story*): 'I understand we understand each other.'

Daniels, Bebe (1901–1971) (Virginia Daniels). American leading lady of the silent screen. Film debut at seven; played opposite Harold Lloyd and became a popular star; later married Ben Lyon, moved to Britain and appeared with their family on radio and TV.
Male and Female 19. Why Change Your Wife? 20. The Affairs of Anatol 21. Pink Gods 22. Unguarded Women 24. Monsieur Beaucaire 24. Campus Flirt 26. She's a Sheik 27. Rio Rita 29. Alias French Gertie 30. Reaching for the Moon 30. The Maltese Falcon 31. Forty-Second Street 33. Counsellor at Law 33. The Return of Carol Deane 35. Hi Gang (GB) 40. Life with the Lyons (GB) 53. The Lyons in Paris (GB) 55, etc.

Daniels, William (1895–1970). Distinguished American cinematographer.
□Foolish Wives 21. Merry Go Round (co-ph) 23. Helen's Babies (co-ph) 24. *Greed* (co-ph) 25. Women and Gold 25. The Merry Widow (co-ph) 25. Bardelys the Magnificent 26. The Boob 26. Dance Madness (co-ph) 26. *Flesh and the Devil* 26. Money Talks 26. Monte Carlo 26. The Temptress (co-ph) 26. The Torrent 26. Altars of Desire 27. Captain Salvation 27. Love 27. On Ze Boulevard 27. Tillie the Toiler 27. The Actress 28. Bringing Up Father 28. Dream of Love 28. Lady of Chance 28. The Latest from Paris 28. The Mysterious Lady 28. Sally's Shoulders 28. A Woman of Affairs 28. *The Kiss* 29. The Last of Mrs Cheyney 29. Their Own Desire 29. The Trial of Mary Dugan 29. Wild Orchids 29. Wise Girls 29. Anna Christie 30. Montana Moon 30. Romance 30. Strictly Unconventional 30. Strangers May Kiss 31. The Great Meadow 31. Inspiration 31. A Free Soul 31. Susan Lenox 31. *Mata Hari* 32. Lovers Courageous 32. Grand Hotel 32. As You Desire Me 32. Skyscraper Souls 32. Rasputin and the Empress 33. The White Sister 33. Dinner at Eight 33. The Stranger's Return 33. Broadway to Hollywood 33. Christopher Bean 33. *Queen Christina* 33. The Barretts of Wimpole Street 34. The Painted Veil 34. Naughty Marietta 35. *Anna Karenina* 35. Rendezvous 35. Rose Marie 36. Romeo and Juliet 36. *Camille* 36. Personal Property 37. Broadway Melody of 1938 37. Double Wedding 37. The Last Gangster 37. Beg Borrow or Steal 37. Marie Antoinette 38. Three Loves Has Nancy 38. Dramatic School 38. Idiot's Delight 39. Stronger Than Desire 39. Ninotchka 39. Another Thin Man 39. The Shop Around the Corner 40. The Mortal Storm 40. New Moon 40. So Ends Our Night 41. Back Street 41. They Met in Bombay 41. Shadow of the Thin Man 41. Dr Kildare's Victory 41. *Keeper of the Flame* 42. Girl

Crazy 42. Brute Force 47. Lured 47. *The Naked City* (AA) 48. For the Love of Mary 48. Family Honeymoon 48. The Life of Riley 49. Illegal Entry 49. Abandoned 49. The Gal who Took the West 49. Woman in Hiding 49. Winchester 73 50. Harvey 50. Deported 50. Thunder on the Hill 51. Bright Victory 51. The Lady Pays Off 51. When in Rome 52. Pat and Mike 52. Glory Alley 52. Plymouth Adventure 52. Never Wave at a WAC 53. Forbidden 53. Thunder Bay 53. *The Glenn Miller Story* 53. War Arrow 54. The Far Country 54. Six Bridges to Cross 55. Foxfire 55. The Shrike 55. Strategic Air Command 55. The Girl Rush 55. The Benny Goodman Story 55. Away All Boats (co-ph) 56. The Unguarded Moment 56. Istanbul 56. Night Passage 57. Interlude 57. My Man Godfrey 57. Voice in the Mirror 57. Cat on a Hot Tin Roof 58. Some Came Running 59. Stranger in My Arms 59. A Hole in the Head 60. Never So Few 60. Can Can 60. Ocean's Eleven 60. All the Fine Young Cannibals 60. Come September 61. Jumbo 62. How the West was Won (co-ph) 63. Come Blow Your Horn 63. The Prize 63. Robin and the Seven Hoods (& p) 64. Von Ryan's Express 65. Marriage on the Rocks 65. Assault on a Queen (& p) 66. In Like Flint 67. Valley of the Dolls 67. The Impossible Years 68. Marlowe 68. The Maltese Bippy 69. Move 70.

¶ *W.D.:* We try to tell the story with light, and the director tells it with action.

Daniels, William (1927–). Dapper American stage actor who came to films and TV in mid-career.
Family Honeymoon 49. A Thousand Clowns 65. The President's Analyst 67. *The Graduate* 67. Two for the Road 67. Marlowe 69. *1776* (as John Adams) 72. The Parallax View 74. Black Sunday 77. The One and Only 78. Sunburn 79. The Blue Lagoon 80. All Night Long 81. Reds 81, many others.
TV series: *Captain Nice* 66. The Nancy Walker Show 76. Freebie and the Bean 80. *St Elsewhere* 82.

Daniely, Lisa (1930–). Anglo-French leading lady.
Lili Marlene 50. Hindle Wakes 51. The Wedding of Lili Marlene 53. Tiger by the Tail 55. The Vicious Circle 57. An Honourable Murder 60. The Lamp in Assassin Mews 62, etc.

Danischewsky, Monja (1911–). Russian writer-producer, in Britain since twenties. Publicist and writer for Ealing 1938–48. Produced *Whisky Galore* 48. *The Galloping Major* 50. *The Battle of the Sexes* 61, etc. Screenplays, *Topkapi* 64. *Mister Moses* 65. Autobiography 1966: *White Russian, Red Face*. 1972: *Out of my Mind*.

Danish cinema was one of the first to start production. Nordisk studios were founded in 1906 and from 1910 to 1915 Danish films were as internationally popular as those of any country in the world. But the talent was all drained away, first by the merger with Germany's UFA studios in 1917 and later by a steady trek to Hollywood. Carl Dreyer, one of the wanderers, later returned to Denmark and made there such major films as *Day of Wrath* and *Ordet*; but no Danish school ever emerged again.

Dankworth, Johnny (1927–). British bandleader who has written scores.
The Criminal 60. Saturday Night and Sunday Morning 60. The Servant 64. Return from the Ashes 65. Accident 67. The Last Grenade 69. Ten Rillington Place 70.

Danner, Blythe (1944–). American young actress of the seventies.
□Dr Cook's Garden (TV) 70.1776 72. To Kill a Clown 72. Lovin' Molly 74. The Last of the Belles (TV) 74. Sidekicks (TV) 74. Hearts of the West 75. Futureworld 76. A Love Affair: The Eleanor and Lou Gehrig Story (TV) 78. Are You in the House Alone? (TV) 78. *Too Far to Go* (TV) 79. The Great Santini 80. Man, Woman and Child 83. Brighton Beach Memoirs 86.
TV series: Adam's Rib.

Dano, Royal (1922–). American general purpose supporting actor.
□Undercover Girl 49. Under the Gun 50. *The Red Badge of Courage* (as The Tattered Man) 51. Flame of Araby 51. Bend of the River 52. Johnny Guitar 54. The Far Country 55. The Trouble with Harry 55. Tribute to a Bad Man 55. Santiago 56. Moby Dick 56. Tension at Table Rock 56. Crime of Passion 57. Trooper Hook 57. All Mine to Give 57. Man in the Shadow 57. Saddle the Wind 57. Handle with Care 58. Man of the West 58. Never Steal Anything Small 59. These Thousand Hills 59. Hound Dog Man 59. Face of Fire 59. Huckleberry Finn 60. Cimarron 60. Posse from Hell 61. King of Kings 61. Savage Sam 61. Seven Faces of Dr Lao 64. Gunpoint 66. The Dangerous Days of Kiowa Jones (TV) 66. Welcome to Hard Times 67. The Last Challenge 67. Day of the Evil Gun

68. If He Hollers Let Him Go 68. The Undefeated 69. Backtrack (TV) 69. Run Simon Run (TV) 70. Moon of the Wolf (TV) 72. The Great Northfield Minnesota Raid 72. The Culpepper Cattle Company 72. Howzer 72. Ace Eli and Rodger of the Skies 73. Cahill 73. Electra Glide in Blue 73. Big Bad Mama 74. The Wild Party 75. Huckleberry Finn (TV) 75. Capone 75. Manhunter (TV) 76. Drum 76. Messiah of Evil 76. The Outlaw Josey Wales 76. The Killer Inside Me 76. Murder in Peyton Place (TV) 77. Donner Pass (TV) 78. Strangers (TV) 79. Take This Job and Shove It 81. Hammett 82. Something Wicked This Way Comes 83. The Right Stuff 83. Teachers 84.

Danova, Cesare (1926–). Italian leading man, often in Hollywood.
The Captain's Son 47. The Three Corsairs 52. Don Juan 55. The Man Who Understood Women 59. Cleopatra 63. Viva Las Vegas 64. Chamber of Horrors 66. Che 69. Tentacles 77, etc.
TV series: Garrison's Gorillas 67.

Danson, Ted (1947–). Tall, craggy American leading man.
The Onion Field 79. Body Heat 81. Creepshow 82. Something About Amelia (TV) 84. Little Treasure 85. Just Between Friends 85. A Fine Mess 86.
TV series: *Cheers* 82– .

Dante, Michael (1931–) (Ralph Vitti). American 'second lead' with a screen tendency to villainy.
Fort Dobbs 58. Westbound 59. Seven Thieves 60. Kid Galahad 62. The Naked Kiss 64. Harlow 65. The Farmer 77, etc.

Dantine, Helmut (1917–1982). Lean good-looking Austrian actor, in US from 1938. Latterly an executive with the Joseph M. Schenk organization.
International Squadron 41. *Mrs Miniver* 41. Passage to Marseilles 44. Hotel Berlin 45. Escape in the Desert 45. Northern Pursuit 45. Shadow of a Woman 46. Whispering City 48. Call Me Madam 53. Stranger from Venus (GB) 54. War and Peace 56. Fraulein 57. Thundering Jets (d only) 58. Operation Crossbow 65. Garcia 74, etc.

Danton, Ray (1931–). Tall, dark American leading man with radio experience.
Chief Crazy Horse 52. The Spoilers 55. I'll Cry Tomorrow 55. *Too Much Too Soon* 58. *The Rise and Fall of Legs Diamond* 59. Ice Palace 60. A Fever in the Blood 61. *The George Raft Story* 61. The Chapman Report 62. The Longest Day 62. Sandokan the Great (It.) 63. Tiger of Terror (It.) 64. The Spy Who Went into Hell (Ger.) 65. The Deathmaster (d only) 72. The Centrefold Girls 74, etc.
TV series: The Alaskans 59.

D'Antoni, Philip (1929–). American producer for cinema and TV.
The French Connection 71. The Connection (TV) 73. Mr Inside Mr Outside (TV) 73. The Seven-Ups (& d) 74.

The Danziger Brothers (Edward and Harry). American producers who after making *Jigsaw* 46, and two or three other films came to England, set up New Elstree Studios and spent fifteen years producing hundreds of second features and TV episodes, hardly any worth recalling.

Darby, Ken (1909–). American composer and arranger.
Song of the South 46. So Dear to My Heart 48. Rancho Notorious 52. The Robe 53. The Egyptian 54. Bus Stop 56. Hound Dog Man 59. How the West Was Won 62. The Greatest Story Ever Told 65, many others.

Darby, Kim (1947–) (Deborah Zenby). American leading lady.
Bus Riley's Back in Town 65. A Time for Giving 69. *True Grit* 69. Norwood 69. The Grissom Gang 71. Rich Man Poor Man (TV) 76. The One and Only 78. The Pink Telephone 78. The Last Convertible (TV) 79. Better Off Dead 85, etc.

Darc, Mireille (1938–) (M. Aigroz). French leading lady
Tonton Flingeurs 64. Galia 65. Du Rififi à Paname 66. Weekend 67. Jeff 68. Blonde from Peking 68. There was Once a Cop 72. The Tall Blond Man With One Black Shoe 74.

Darcel, Denise (1925–) (Denise Billecard). French leading lady, in Hollywood from 1947.
To the Victor 48. Battleground 49. Tarzan and the Slave Girl 50. Westward the Women 51. Dangerous When Wet 53. Flame of Calcutta 53. Vera Cruz 54. Seven Women from Hell 62, etc.

D'Arcy, Alex (1908–) (Alexander Sarruf). Egyptian light actor who has appeared in films of many nations.

Champagne 28. A Nous la Liberté 31. La Kermesse Héroique 35. The Prisoner of Zenda 37. Fifth Avenue Girl 39. Marriage Is a Private Affair 44. How to Marry a Millionaire 53. Soldier of Fortune 56. Way Way Out 66. The St Valentine's Day Massacre 67. Blood of Dracula's Castle (as Dracula) 69. The Seven Minutes 71, etc.

Darden, Severn (1937–). American comedy character actor.
Dead Heat on a Merry Go Round 67. The President's Analyst 67. Luv 68. Pussycat Pussycat I Love You 70. Vanishing Point 71. The Hired Hand 71. Cisco Pike 71. The War Between Men and Women 72. Who Fears the Devil 74. In God We Trust 79. Why Would I Lie 80. Saturday the 14th 81, etc.

Darien, Frank (*c.* 1878–1955). American character actor often seen as meek or downtrodden little man.
Five Star Final 31. The Miracle Man 32. Professional Sweetheart 33. Marie Galante 34. Brides are Like That 36. Love Finds Andy Hardy 38. At the Circus 39. *The Grapes of Wrath* 40. Hellzapoppin 42. Tales of Manhattan 42. The Outlaw 43. Bowery to Broadway 44. Kiss and Tell 45. Claudia and David 46. You Gotta Stay Happy 46. Merton of the Movies 47. The Flying Saucer 50, many others.

Darin, Bobby (1936–1973) (Walden Robert Cassotto). American pop singer who alternated lightweight appearances with more serious roles.
Come September 60. Pepe 60. Too Late Blues 61. *Pressure Point* 62. Captain Newman MD 63. That Funny Feeling 65. Gunfight at Abilene 67. Stranger in the House 67. The Happy Ending 69, etc.

The Dark Angel. Guy Bolton's melodramatic play about a romantic triangle and war blindness was filmed by George Fitzmaurice in 1925, with Ronald Colman, Vilma Banky and Wyndham Standing; Sidney Franklin remade it in 1935 with Fredric March, Merle Oberon and Herbert Marshall.

Dark Victory (US 1939). Romantic drama which began a trend towards unhappy endings: Bette Davis played a socialite dying of a brain tumour. Directed by Edmund Goulding. Remade 1963 as *Stolen Hours*, with Susan Hayward; but the time was past and it did not appeal.

Darling (GB 1965). A scathing but ultimately pointless attack on some worthless members of the affluent society, in particular a selfish girl who gets through men at a rate of knots and leaves despair in her wake. John Schlesinger's direction kept it interesting in a repellent way, but it has already dated alarmingly. With Julie Christie (AA, BFA), Dirk Bogarde (BFA); from a script by Frederic Raphael (AA, BFA); art direction by Ray Simm (BFA).

Darling, William (1882–*) (Wilhelm Sandorhazi). Hungarian-American art director, long with Twentieth Century Fox.
A Question of Honor 22. Seven Faces 29. Renegades 30. *Cavalcade* (AA) 33. In Old Kentucky 35. The Littlest Rebel 35. Under Two Flags 36. Lloyds of London 36. On the Avenue 37. *The Rains Came* 39. The Song of Bernadette (AA) 33. The Keys of the Kingdom 44. Anna and the King of Siam (AA) 46, etc.

Darnborough, Anthony (1913–). British producer.
The Calendar 47. Quartet 48. The Astonished Heart 50. The Net 52. To Paris with Love 55. The Baby and the Battleship 56, etc.

Darnell, Linda (1921–1965) (Monetta Eloisa Darnell). Wide-eyed American leading lady of the forties.
□Hotel for Women 39. Daytime Wife 39. Stardust 40. Brigham Young 40. The Mark of Zorro 40. Chad Hanna 40. Blood and Sand 41. Rise and Shine 41. The Loves of Edgar Allan Poe 42. The Song of Bernadette (as the Virgin Mary) 43. City Without Men 43. Buffalo Bill 44. *It Happened Tomorrow* 44. Summer Storm 44. Sweet and Lowdown 44. The Great John L 45. Fallen Angel 45. Hangover Square 45. Anna and the King of Siam 46. Centennial Summer 46. My Darling Clementine 46. Forever Amber 47. The Walls of Jericho 48. Unfaithfully Yours 48. A Letter to Three Wives 48. Slattery's Hurricane 49. Everybody Does It 49. No Way Out 50. Two Flags West 50. The Thirteenth Letter 51. The Lady Pays Off 51. The Guy who Came Back 51. Saturday Island 52. Night Without Sleep 52. Blackbeard the Pirate 52. Second Chance 53. This Is My Love 54. Forbidden Women (It.) 55. The Last Five Minutes (It.) 56. Dakota Incident 56. Zero Hour 57. Homeward Borne (TV) 57. Black Spurs 65.

D'Arrast, Harry D'Abbabie (1893–1968). American director of the twenties, with a reputation for style.

□Service for Ladies 27. A Gentleman of Paris 27. Serenade 27. The Magnificent Flirt 28. Dry Martini 28. Raffles (part) 30. *Laughter* 30. Topaze 33. It Happened in Spain 34.

Darren, James (1936–) (James Ercolani). American leading man whose appeal seems to have waned with maturity although he is still seen occasionally on TV.
Rumble on the Docks 56. Operation Mad Ball 57. Gidget 59. Let No Man Write My Epitaph 60. *The Guns of Navarone* 61. Diamondhead 63. For Those Who Think Young 64, etc.
TV series: Time Tunnel 66. T. J. Hooker 83.

Darrieux, Danielle (1917–). Vivacious French leading lady, in films since 1931.
Le Bal 32. *Mayerling* 36. *The Rage of Paris* (US) 38. *Battement de Coeur* 39. Premier Rendezvous 44. *Occupe-Toi d'Amélie* 49. La Ronde 50. Le Plaisir 51. Rich, Young and Pretty (US) 51. Five Fingers (US) 52. Adorables Créatures 52. *Madame De* 53. Alexander the Great (US) 55. Le Rouge et le Noir 57. Marie Octobre 58. Lady Chatterley's Lover 59. Murder at 45 RPM 61. The Greengage Summer (GB) 61. Landru 63. L'Or du Duc 65. Le Dimanche de la Vie 66. The Young Girls of Rochefort 67. L'Homme à la Buick 67. Birds in Peru 68. The Lonely Woman 75. L'Année Sainte 76. La Cavaleur 79. At the Top of the Stairs 83. The Scene of the Crime 86, many others.

Darro, Frankie (1917–1976) (Frank Johnson). Tough-looking little American actor, former child and teenage player; star of many second features.
So Big 24. The Cowboy Cop 26. Long Pants 27. The Circus Kid 28. The Mad Genius 31. Wild Boys of the Road 33. Broadway Bill 34. Charlie Chan at the Race Track 36. Racing Blood 37. Chasing Trouble 39. Laughing at Danger 40. Freddie Steps Out 45. Heart of Virginia 48. Across the Wide Missouri 51. Operation Petticoat 59, many others.

Darrow, Clarence (1857–1938). Celebrated American defence lawyer, impersonated by Orson Welles in *Compulsion* 58, and by Spencer Tracy in *Inherit the Wind* 60. In the seventies Henry Fonda played him in a one-man stage and TV show.

Darvi, Bella (1927–1971) (Bayla Wegier). Polish-French leading lady, in a few Hollywood films after being discovered by Darryl Zanuck.
□Hell and High Water 54. The Egyptian 54. The Racers 55. Je Suis Un Sentimental 55. Sinners of Paris 59. Lipstick 65.

Darwell, Jane (1880–1967) (Patti Woodward). American character actress, usually in warm-hearted motherly roles.
Rose of the Rancho 14. Brewster's Millions 20. Tom Sawyer 30. Back Street 32. Design for Living 34. Life Begins at Forty 35. Captain January 36. Slave Ship 37. Three Blind Mice 38. Jesse James 39. The Rains Came 39. Gone with the Wind 39. *The Grapes of Wrath* (AA: as the indomitable Ma Joad) 40. *All That Money Can Buy* 41. Private Nurse 41. The Ox Bow Incident 43. The Impatient Years 44. *Captain Tugboat Annie* (title role) 46. My Darling Clementine 46. Three Godfathers 48. Wagonmaster 50. Caged 50. The Lemon Drop Kid 51. Fourteen Hours 51. We're Not Married 52. The Sun Shines Bright 52. Hit the Deck 55. The Last Hurrah 58. Mary Poppins 64, many others.
❀ For the sheer maternal strength of her characterizations. *The Grapes of Wrath.*

Famous line (*The Grapes of Wrath*): 'Can't nobody lick us, pa. We're the people.'

Dassin, Jules (1911–). American director, former radio writer and actor. Joined MGM 1941 to direct shorts (including a two-reel version of *The Tell-Tale Heart*); moved to features; left for Europe during the McCarthy witch hunt of the late forties.
□Nazi Agent 42. The Affairs of Martha 42. Reunion in France 42. Young Ideas 43. The Canterville Ghost 44. A Letter for Evie 44. Two Smart People 46. *Brute Force* 47. *Naked City* 48. *Thieves' Highway* (& a) 49. Night and the City (GB) 50. *Rififi* (also acted, as Perlo Vita) 54. He Who Must Die 56. Where the Hot Wind Blows 58. *Never on Sunday* (also acted) 60. Phaedra 62. Topkapi 64. 10.30 p.m. Summer 66. Survival 68. Uptight 68. Promise at Dawn 70. Dream of Passion 78. Circle of Two 80.

Daugherty, Herschel (–). American director, from TV.
The Light in the Forest 58. The Raiders 63, etc.

Dauphin, Claude (1903–1978) (Claude Franc-Nohain). Dapper French actor of stage and screen: in films from 1930.
Entrée des Artistes 38. Battement de Coeur 39. Les Deux Timides 42. English Without Tears (GB) 44. Deported (US) 50. Le Plaisir 51. Casque d'Or 52. Little Boy Lost (US) 53.

Innocents in Paris (GB) 54. Phantom of the Rue Morgue (US) 54. The Quiet American (US) 58. The Full Treatment 60. Lady L 65. Two for the Road 67. Hard Contract 69. Rosebud 75. The Tenant 76, many others. TV series: Paris Precinct.

Davenport, Doris (1915–1980). American leading lady, formerly a Goldwyn Girl. Played several bit parts, but was prominent only in *Kid Millions* 35, *The Westerner* 40, *Behind the News* 40.

Davenport, Dorothy (1895–1977). American director of silent days; married Wallace Reid.

Davenport, Harry (1866–1949). American character actor; long stage career, then in Hollywood as chucklesome, benevolent old man.

□Her Unborn Child 30. My Sin 31. His Woman 32. Get That Venus 33. Three Cheers for Love 34. The Scoundrel 35. Three Men on a Horse 36. The Case of the Black Cat 36. King of Hockey 36. Fly Away Baby 36. The Life of Emile Zola 37. Under Cover of Night 37. Her Husband's Secretary 37. White Bondage 37. They Won't Forget 37. Mr Dodd Takes the Air 37. First Lady 37. The Perfect Specimen 37. Paradise Express 37. As Good as Married 37. Armored Car 37. Wells Fargo 37. Fit for a King 37. Gold is Where You Find It 38. Saleslady 38. The Sisters 38. The Long Shot 38. The First Hundred Years 38. Marie Antoinette 38. The Cowboy and the Lady 38. Reckless Living 38. The Rage of Paris 38. Tailspin 38. Young Fugitives 38. *You Can't Take It With You* 38. The Higgins Family 38. Orphans of the Street 38. Made for Each Other 39. My Wife's Relatives 39. Should Husbands Work 39. The Covered Trailer 39. Money to Burn 39. Exile Express 39. Death of a Champion 39. The Story of Alexander Graham Bell 39. Juarez 39. Gone with the Wind 39. *The Hunchback of Notre Dame* 39. Dr Ehrlich's Magic Bullet 40. Granny Get Your Gun 40. Too Many Husbands 40. Grandpa Goes to Town 40. Lucky Partners 40. I Want a Divorce 40. All This and Heaven Too 40. Foreign Correspondent 40. That Uncertain Feeling 41. I Wanted Wings 41. Hurricane Smith 41. The Bride Came COD 41. One Foot in Heaven 41. King's Row 41. *Son of Fury* 42. Larceny Inc 42. Ten Gentlemen from West Point 42. Tales of Manhattan 42. Heading for God's Country 43. We've Never Been Licked 42. Riding High 43. *The Ox Bow Incident* 43. The Amazing Mrs Holliday 43. Gangway for Tomorrow 43. Government Girl 43. Jack London 43. Princess O'Rourke 43. *Meet Me In St Louis* 44. The Impatient Years 44. The Thin Man Goes Home 44. Kismet 44. Music for Millions 45. *The Enchanted Forest* 45. Too Young to Know 45. This Love of Ours 45. She Wouldn't Say Yes 45. Courage of Lassie 46. Blue Sierra 46. A Boy a Girl and a Dog 46. Faithful in My Fashion 46. Three Wise Fools 46. War Brides 46. Lady Luck 46. Claudia and David 46. Pardon My Past 46. Adventure 46. The Farmer's Daughter 47. That Hagen Girl 47. Stallion Road 47. Keeper of the Bees 47. Sport of Kings 47. The Fabulous Texan 47. *The Bachelor and the Bobbysoxer* 47. Three Daring Daughters 48. The Man from Texas 48. For the Love of Mary 48. That Lady in Ermine 48. The Decision of Christopher Blake 48. Down to the Sea in Ships 49. Little Women 49. Tell It To the Judge 49. *That Forsyte Woman* 49. Riding High 50.

❄ For being everybody's cheerful grandpa. *The Hunchback of Notre Dame.*

Davenport, Nigel (1928–). Breezy, virile British actor, much on TV.

Peeping Tom 59. In the Cool of the Day 63. A High Wind in Jamaica 65. Sands of the Kalahari 65. Where the Spies Are 66. *A Man for All Seasons* 67. Red and Blue 67. Play Dirty 68. Sinful Davey 69. *The Virgin Soldiers* 69. The Royal Hunt of the Sun 69. No Blade of Grass 71. Villain 71. *Living Free* 72. Mary Queen of Scots 72. Dracula (TV) (as Van Helsing) 73. Phase IV 73. The Island of Dr Moreau 77. An Eye for an Eye 78. Zulu Dawn 79. Nighthawks 81, etc.

TV series: *Prince Regent* (as George III) 79.

Daves, Delmer (1904–1977). American writer-producer-director with highly miscellaneous experience. Writer with MGM from 1933, writer-director with Warners from 1943.

Destination Tokyo (wd) 43. The Red House (wd) 47. *Dark Passage* (wd) 47. Broken Arrow (d) 50. Bird of Paradise (wd) 51. Never Let Me Go (d) 53. Demetrius and the Gladiators (d) 54. Jubal (wd) 56. The Last Wagon (wd) 56. *3.10 to Yuma* (d) 57. Cowboy (wd) 58. The Hanging Tree (d) 59. Parrish (wd) 61. Spencer's Mountain (wpd) 62. Youngblood Hawke (wd) 64. The Battle of the Villa Fiorita (wpd) 65, many others.

'He remains the property of those who can enjoy stylistic conviction in an intellectual vacuum.'—*Andrew Sarris, 1968*

Daviau, Allen (–). American cinematographer.
The Color Purple (AAN) 85. Empire of the Sun 87.

David Copperfield (US 1934). Probably the most successful and satisfactory 'Hollywood classic', an impeccable costume narrative, richly acted, with the true Dickens flavour. George Cukor directed; Hugh Walpole worked on the screenplay (and played the vicar). Cast included W. C. Fields (Micawber), Freddie Bartholomew (young David), Frank Lawton (David as a man), Edna May Oliver (Aunt Betsy), Basil Rathbone (Mr Murdstone), Roland Young (Uriah Heep), Lionel Barrymore (Dan Peggotty), Jessie Ralph (Nurse Peggotty), etc. The 1969 all-star remake was intended for TV in the States, theatres elsewhere; despite interesting performances, it lacked narrative grip.

David, Saul (1921–). American producer.
Von Ryan's Express 65. Our Man Flint 67. Fantastic Voyage 67. Skullduggery 69. The Black Bird 75. Logan's Run 76.

David, Thayer (1926–1978) (David Thayer Hersey). American character actor.
A Time to Love and a Time to Die 58. *Journey to the Centre of the Earth* 59. The Story of Ruth 60. The Eiger Sanction 74. The Duchess and the Dirtwater Fox 76. Meet Nero Wolfe (TV) 77. House Calls 78, etc.

Davidson, John (1886–1969). American character actor, a piercing-eyed, white-haired villain of the twenties and thirties.
The Green Cloak 15. The Spurs of Sybil 18. The Bronze Bell 21. Under Two Flags 22. Monsieur Beaucaire 24. Kid Gloves 29. Arsène Lupin 32. Dinner at Eight 33. Hold That Girl 34. The Last Days of Pompeii 35. Mr Moto Takes a Vacation 38. Arrest Bulldog Drummond 30. Miracles for Sale 39. Captain Marvel 41. Captain America 44. The Purple Monster Strikes 45. Shock 46. Daisy Kenyon 47. A Letter to Three Wives 48. Oh You Beautiful Doll 49. A Gathering of Eagles 63, many others.

Davidson, John (1941–). American light singer and leading man, mostly on television.
The Happiest Millionaire 67. The One and Only Genuine Original Family Band 68. Coffee, Tea or Me (TV) 73. The Mitera Targets (TV) 78. Shell Game (TV) 78.
TV series: The Entertainers. Kraft Music Hall. The Girl with Something Extra. That's Incredible.

Davidson, Max (1875–1950). American slapstick comedian of twenties two-reelers, spotlighted in *Laurel and Hardy's Laughing Twenties.*

Davidson, William B. (1888–1947). American character actor, in hundreds of small roles, usually as pompous, lecherous or overbearing businessman.
A Modern Cinderella 17. The Capitol 19. Partners of the Night 20. Adam and Eva 23. Women and Gold 25. The Gaucho 28. For the Defense 30. Sky Devils 32. Fog over Frisco 34. Dangerous 35. Earthworm Tractors 36. Easy Living 37. Love on Toast 38. Indianapolis Speedway 39. Maryland 40. My Little Chickadee 40. Juke Girl 42. Up in Arms 44. See My Lawyer 45. My Darling Clementine 46. The Farmer's Daughter 47, many others.

Davies, Betty Ann (1910–1955). British stage actress, usually in tense roles; occasional films from early thirties.
Chick 34. Kipps 41. It Always Rains on Sunday 47. The History of Mr Polly 49. *Trio* 50. Cosh Boy 52. Grand National Night 53. The Belles of St Trinian's 54, etc.

Davies, Jack (1913–). British comedy scriptwriter, busy since 1932 on Will Hay and Norman Wisdom comedies, 'Doctor' series, etc.
Laughter in Paradise 51. Top Secret 52. An Alligator Named Daisy 56. *Very Important Person* 61. *The Fast Lady* 62. Those Magnificent Men in Their Flying Machines 65. Gambit 66. Monte Carlo 68. Doctor in Trouble 70. Paper Tiger 75, many others.

Davies, John Howard (1939–). British child actor, who became a BBC TV director.
Oliver Twist 48. The Rocking-Horse Winner 50. Tom Brown's Schooldays 51, etc.

Davies, John Rhys (1944–). Heavyweight British character actor, a good roisterer.
Shogun (TV) 80. Sphinx 81. Raiders of the Lost Ark 81. Victor/Victoria 81. Ivanhoe (TV) 82, etc.

Davies, Marion (1897–1961) (Marion Douras). American leading lady famous less for her rather mediocre films than for being the protégée of William Randolph Hearst the newspaper magnate, who was determined to

make a star out of her. She enjoyed moderate success 1917–36, then retired. Biography 1973 by Fred Lawrence Guiles. Pictorial autobiography collated 1975 by Pamela Pfau: *The Times We Had.*
□Runaway Romany 17. Cecilia of the Pink Roses 18. The Burden of Proof 18. Getting Mary Married 19. The Cinema Murder 19. The Dark Star 19. The Belle of New York 19. The Restless Sex 20. April Folly 20. Enchantment 21. Buried Treasure 21. The Bride's Play 22. Beauty Worth 22. When Knighthood was in Flower 22. The Young Diana 22. Daughter of Luxury 22. Little Old New York 22. Adam and Eva 23. Janice Meredith 24. Yolanda 24. Lights of Old Broadway 25. Zander the Great 25. Beverly of Graustark 26. Quality Street 27. The Fair Co-ed 27. The Red Mill 27. Tillie the Toiler 27. The Cardboard Lover 28. The Patsy 28. *Show People* 28. Hollywood Revue 29. Marianne 29. The Gay Nineties 29. Not so Dumb 30. The Floradora Girl 30. It's a Wise Child 31. Five and Ten 31. Bachelor Father 31. Polly of the Circus 32. Blondie of the Follies 32. The Dark Horse 32. Peg O' My Heart 33. Operator 13 34. Going Hollywood 34. *Page Miss Glory* 35. Hearts Divided 36. Cain and Mabel 36. Ever Since Eve 37.

¶ Upon my honour
I saw a madonna
Sitting alone in a niche
Above the door
Of the glamorous whore
Of a prominent son-of-a-bitch.
—*attributed to Dorothy Parker on seeing the elaborate dressing room built by W. R. Hearst for M.D. at MGM*

M.D.: With me it was 5 percent talent and 95 percent publicity.

'She was quite a comedian, and would have been a star in her own right without the cyclonic Hearst publicity.'—*Charles Chaplin*

Davies, Rupert (1916–1976). British character actor, formerly in small roles, then famous as TV's *Maigret.*
The Key 58. Sapphire 59. The Uncle 65. The Spy Who Came in from the Cold 65. Brides of Fu Manchu 66. House of a Thousand Dolls 67. Witchfinder General 68. Waterloo 70. Zeppelin 71, etc.
TV series: Sailor of Fortune 56.

Davies, Valentine (1905–). American screenwriter.
Three Little Girls in Blue 46. *Miracle on 34th Street* (AA original story) 47. You Were Meant for Me 48. Chicken Every Sunday 48. It Happens Every Spring 49. On the Riviera 51. The Glenn Miller Story 54. *The Benny Goodman Story* (& d) 55. The Bridges at Toko-Ri 55. Strategic Air Command 55. Bachelor in Paradise 61, etc.

Davies, Windsor (1930–). British comedy character actor who rather overdoes the blustering sergeant-major act.
The Alphabet Murders 65. Hammerhead 67. Sex Clinic 71. Mister Quilp 74. Carry on Behind 74. Not Now Comrade 76, etc.
TV series: It Ain't Half Hot, Mum 73–77.

Davion, Alexander (1929–). Anglo-French leading man, mostly on stage and American TV.
Song Without End (as Chopin) 60. Paranoiac 63. Valley of the Dolls 67. The Royal Hunt of the Sun 69. Incense for the Damned 71, etc.
TV series: Gideon's Way 64. The Man Who Never Was 66. Custer 67.

Davis, Bette (1908–) (Ruth Elizabeth Davis). Inimitably intense American dramatic actress; a box-office queen for ten years from 1937, she later played eccentric roles.
Autobiographies: 1962 *The Lonely Life.* 1975 *Mother Goddam* (with Whitney Stone).
□Bad Sister 31. Seed 31. Waterloo Bridge 31. Way Back Home 31. The Menace 31. *The Man Who Played God* 32. Hell's House 32. So Big 32. The Rich are Always with Us 32. The Dark Horse 32. *Cabin in the Cotton* 32. Three on a Match 32. Twenty Thousand Years in Sing Sing 32. Parachute Jumper 32. The Working Man 33. Ex Lady 33. Bureau of Missing Persons 33. Fashions of 1934 34. The Big Shakedown 34. Jimmy the Gent 34. Fog over Frisco 34. *Of Human Bondage* 34. Housewife 34. Bordertown 34. The Girl from Tenth Avenue 35. *Front Page Woman* 35. Special Agent 35. *Dangerous* (AA) 35. The Petrified Forest 36. The Golden Arrow 36. Satan Met a Lady 36. Marked Woman 37. Kid Galahad 37. That Certain Woman 37. It's Love I'm After 37. *Jezebel* (AA) 38. The Sisters 38. *Dark Victory* 39. Juarez 39. *The Old Maid* 39. *The Private Lives of Elizabeth and Essex* 39. All This and Heaven Too 40. *The Letter* 40. *The Great Lie* 41. The Bride Came COD 41. *The Little Foxes* 41. *The Man Who Came to Dinner* 41. In This Our Life 42. *Now Voyager* 42. Watch on the Rhine 43. Thank Your Lucky Stars 43. Old Acquaintance 43. *Mr Skeffington* 44. Hollywood Canteen 44. *The Corn is Green* 45. A Stolen Life 46. Deception 46. Winter

Meeting 48. June Bride 48. Beyond the Forest 49. *All About Eve* 50. Payment on Demand 51. Another Man's Poison 51. Phone Call from a Stranger 52. The Star 52. The Virgin Queen 55. The Catered Affair 56. Storm Center 56. John Paul Jones 59. The Scapegoat 59. A Pocketful of Miracles 61. *Whatever Happened to Baby Jane?* 62. Dead Ringer 64. The Empty Canvas 64. Where Love Has Gone 64. *Hush Hush Sweet Charlotte* 64. *The Nanny* 65. *The Anniversary* 67. Connecting Rooms 69. Bunny O'Hare 71. Madame Sin (TV) 71. The Scientific Cardplayer 72. The Judge and Jake Wyler (TV) 73. Scream Pretty Peggy (TV) 74. Burnt Offerings 76. The Disappearance of Aimée (TV) 76. The Dark Secret of Harvest Home (TV) 78. Return from Witch Mountain 78. Death on the Nile 78. Strangers (TV) 79. White Mama (TV) 79. The Watcher in the Woods 80. Skyward (TV) 81. Family Reunion (TV) 81. *Little Gloria . . . Happy at Last* (TV) 82. *A Piano for Mrs Cimino* (TV) 82. Hotel (TV) 83. Right of Way (TV) 83. *The Whales of August* 87.

❀ For her ten-year domination of the woman's picture'. *The Great Lie.*

¶ For a girl with no looks, Bette Davis rose fast to the top and stayed there a long time. When she first arrived in Hollywood the official greeter missed her at the station, and his later excuse was:

> No one faintly like an actress got off the train.

Carl Laemmle is credited with two waspish remarks about her:

> I can't imagine any guy giving her a tumble.

And:

> She has as much sex appeal as Slim Summerville.

She herself confesses:

> When I saw my first film test I ran from the projection room screaming.

She finally settled for a career without glamour:

> I was the first star who ever came out of the water looking wet.
>
> Nobody knew what I looked like because I never looked the same way twice.

Determination carried her through. As her later husband Gary Merrill said:

> Whatever Bette had chosen to do in life, she would have had to be the top or she couldn't have endured it.

She admitted this herself:

> If Hollywood didn't work out I was all prepared to be the best secretary in the world.

As David Zinman summarizes:

> All she had going for her was her talent.

But by 1937 she was at the top of the tree, dishing out hell to those who had dished it out to her. Said her once co-star Brian Aherne:

> Surely no one but a mother could have loved Bette Davis at the height of her career.

E. Arnot Robertson in 1935 had expressed a similar feeling in a different way:

> She would probably have been burned as a witch if she had lived two or three hundred years ago. She gives the curious feeling of being charged with power which can find no ordinary outlet.

By the early fifties she was no longer a bankable star, and work was suddenly in short supply. She inserted a full-page ad in the Hollywood trade papers:

> MOTHER OF THREE: divorcee; American. Twenty years experience as an actress in motion pictures. Mobile still and more affable than rumour would have it. Wants steady employment in Hollywood. (Has had Broadway.) References upon request.

She reflected bitterly on her career at the top:

> I was the only star they allowed to come out of the water looking wet.

Jack L. Warner however remembered her with affection:

> An explosive little broad with a straight left.

But despite all difficulties she persevered, and was still acting as she neared eighty. Vincent Canby said:

> Her career has been recycled more often than the average rubber tire.

Famous line (*Cabin in the Cotton*): I'd like to kiss yuh, but I just washed my hair.
Famous line (*All About Eve*): Fasten your seat belts, it's going to be a bumpy night.
Famous line (*Old Acquaintance*): There comes a time in every woman's life when the only thing that helps is a glass of champagne.
Famous line (*Now Voyager*): Oh, Jerry, don't let's ask for the moon: we have the stars.
† One story has it that she named the awards statuette Oscar because its backside resembled that of her first husband, Ham Oscar Nelson.

? In what film did Bette Davis:

1 Wear jodhpurs and drink poison?
2 Play Billie Burke's daughter?
3 Play Queen Elizabeth I for the second time?
4 Scandalize her family by wearing a red dress?
5 Watch an execution with George Brent?
6 Go mad in court?

7 Get murdered? (Two answers)
8 Play a bedridden invalid?
9 Cover a small-town wedding?
10 Play twins? (Two answers)
11 Console Claude Rains?
12 Murder Claude Rains?
13 Wear only the top half of her pyjamas?
14 Kill her lover?
15 Allow her husband to die?
16 Go mad and run away into the darkness?

Davis, Brad (1950–). American leading actor.
Midnight Express 77. A Small Circle of Friends 80. Chariots of Fire 81. Querelle 84. Chiefs (TV) 84. Robert Kennedy and his Times (TV) 84. Blood Ties 86. Cold Steel 87, etc.

Davis, Carl (1936–). American composer in Britain, best known for his silent film scores: *Napoleon*, *The Crowd*, Hollywood TV series, etc.
The Bofors Gun 68. Up Pompeii 71. Rentadick 72. Man Friday 75. The Sailor's Return 77. The French Lieutenant's Woman (BFA) 81, etc.

Davis, Desmond (1927–). British director, former cameraman.
□*Girl with Green Eyes* 64. The Uncle 65. *I Was Happy Here* 66. Smashing Time 67. A Nice Girl like Me 69. Clash of the Titans 81. The Sign of Four (TV) 83. The Country Girls (TV) 83.

Davis, James (or **Jim**) (1915–1981). Burly American actor who despite star billing opposite Bette Davis subsided quickly into second feature westerns.
White Cargo 42. Swing Shift Maisie 43. Gallant Bess 46. The Fabulous Texan 47. *Winter Meeting* 48. Brimstone 49. Cavalry Scout 52. Woman of the North Country 52. The Fighting 7th 52. The Last Command 54. Timberjack 55. The Maverick Queen 56. Alias Jesse James 59. Fort Utah 66. Rio Lobo 70. Big Jake 71. The Honkers 72. Bad Company 72. Monte Walsh 72. The Deputies (TV) 76. The Choirboys 77. Comes a Horseman 78. The Day Time Ended 80, many others.
TV series: Stories of the Century. *Rescue 8. The Cowboys.* Dallas 78–80.

Davis, Joan (1907–1961). Rubber-faced American comedienne, in show business from infancy, who enlivened many routine musicals of the thirties and forties.
□Millions in the Air 35. Bunker Bean 35. The Holy Terror 67. On the Avenue 37. Time Out for Romance 37. Wake Up and Live 37. Angel's Holiday 37. You Can't Have Everything 37. The Great Hospital Mystery 37. Sing and Be Happy 37. *Thin Ice* 37. Life Begins in College 37. Love and Kisses 37. Sally, Irene and Mary 38. Josette 38. My Lucky Star 38. *Hold that Coed* 38. Just Around the Corner 38. Tailspin 39. Daytime Wife 39. Too Busy to Work 39. Free, Blonde and Twenty One 40. Manhattan Heartbeat 40. Sailor's Lady 40. For Beauty's Sake 41. Sun Valley Serenade 41. *Hold that Ghost* 41. Two Latins from Manhattan 42. Yokel Boy 42. Sweetheart of the Fleet 42. He's My Guy 43. Two Senoritas from Chicago 43. Around the World 43. *Show Business* 44. Beautiful but Broke 44. Kansas City Kitty 44. She Gets Her Man 45. *George White's Scandals* 45. She Wrote the Book 46. If You Knew Susie 48. The Traveling Saleswoman 50. Love that Brute 50. The Groom Wore Spurs 51. Harem Girl 53.TV series: I Married Joan 52–56.

Davis, Sir John (1906–). British executive, a former accountant who became chairman of the Rank Organization. After the artistic extravagance of the mid-forties, he imposed financial stability; but subsequent film production was comparatively routine and in the late sixties dwindled to nothing as the group was diversified into other fields.

Davis, Judy (1956–). Round-faced Australian leading lady.
My Brilliant Career (BFA) 79. Winter of Our Dreams 81. Hoodwink 81. Heatwave 82. Who Dares Wins 82. A Woman Called Golda (TV) 82. A Passage to India (AAN) 84. Kangaroo 86. High Tide 87.

Davis, Nancy (1921–) (Anne Frances Robbins). American leading lady of a few fifties films: married Ronald Reagan.
Shadow on the Wall 50. The Doctor and the Girl 50. Night into Morning 51. It's a Big Country 53. Donovan's Brain 53. Crash Landing 57. Hellcats of the Navy 59, etc.

Davis, Ossie (1917–). Black American actor of massive presence.
No Way Out 50. The Joe Louis Story 53. Gone are the Days (& w) 63. *The Hill* 65. *The Scalphunters* 68. Sam Whiskey 69. Slaves 69. Cotton Comes to Harlem (d only) 70. Kongi's Harvest (d only) 71. Black Girl (d only) 72. Malcolm X 72. Gordon's War (d

only) 73. Let's Do It Again 75. Hot Stuff 79. Harry and Son 83. Avenging Angel 84, etc.

Davis, Sammy Jnr (1925–). Black American singer and entertainer, a bundle of vitality who describes himself as 'a one-eyed Jewish Negro'.
Autobiography 1966: *Yes I Can.*
□*Anna Lucasta* 58. *Porgy and Bess* 59. *Ocean's Eleven* 60. Pepe 60. A Raisin in the Sun 61. Sergeants Three 62. Convicts Four 62. Nightmare in the Sun 63. Johnny Cool 63. Robin and the Seven Hoods 64. The Threepenny Opera 65. A Man Called Adam 66. Salt and Pepper 68. Sweet Charity 68. Man without Mercy 69. Gone with the West 69. The Pigeon (TV) 71. One More Time 70. The Trackers (TV) 71. Poor Devil (TV) 73. Cinderella at the Palace (TV) 78. Stop the World I Want to Get Off 78. The Cannonball Run 81. Heidi's Song 82.

Davis, Stringer (1896–1973). Gentle-mannered British character actor who was usually to be found playing small roles in the films of his wife Margaret Rutherford.
The Happiest Days of Your Life 50. Curtain Up 53. Murder Most Foul 62. Murder Ahoy 64, etc.

Davison, Bruce (1948–). Slightly-built young American character actor.
Last Summer 69. The Strawberry Statement 70. *Willard* 71. The Jerusalem File 71. Ulzana's Raid 72. Mame 73. The Affair (TV) 73. Mother, Jugs and Speed 76. Short Eyes 77. Brass Target 78. High Risk 81. Crimes of Passion 84. Spies Like Us 85, etc.

Daw, Evelyn (1912–1970). American leading lady of the thirties.
Something to Sing About 37. Panamint's Bad Man 38, etc.

The Dawn Patrol (US 1930). Famous melodrama of World War I flyers, directed by Howard Hawks, starring Richard Barthelmess and Douglas Fairbanks Jnr. Retailored 1938 for Errol Flynn, using much of the same footage and exactly the same script (by John Monk Saunders).

Dawson, Anthony (1916–). Lean-faced British character actor.
The Way to the Stars 45. The Queen of Spades 48. The Long Dark Hall 51. Dial M for Murder (US) 54. Midnight Lace (US) 60. Seven Seas to Calais (US) 63, etc.
The 'Anthony Dawson' who directs Italian costume epics is in fact the nom-de-film of Antonio Margheriti.

Dawson, Ralph (1897–). American editor.
Lady of the Night 25. The Singing Fool 28. Outward Bound 30. Girl Missing 33. The Story of Louis Pasteur 35. A Midsummer Night's Dream 35. Anthony Adverse 36. The Adventures of Robin Hood 38. Ivy 47. All My Sons 48. Undertow 49. Harvey 51. Island in the Sky 53. The High and the Mighty 54, many others.

Day, Clarence (1874–1935). American humorist whose light pieces about his family were the basis for the apparently immortal play *Life with Father*, which was successfully filmed in 1947.

Day, Dennis (1921–) (Eugene Patrick McNulty). American singer and light actor of the forties and fifties, most familiar from Jack Benny's radio and TV show.
Buck Benny Rides Again 40. Music in Manhattan 44. One Sunday Afternoon 48. I'll Get By 50. Golden Girl 51. The Girl Next Door 53, etc.

Day, Doris (1924–) (Doris Kappelhoff). Vivacious American dance band singer who achieved instant star status in 1948 and preserved her eminence by transferring to a brand of innocent sex comedy which was all her own and pleased the sixties.
Biography 1976: *Doris Day, Her Own Story* by A. E. Hotcher.
□*Romance on the High Seas* 48. My Dream is Yours 49. It's a Great Feeling 49. Young Man with a Horn 50. Tea for Two 50. West Point Story 50. *Storm Warning* 50. Lullaby of Broadway 51. *On Moonlight Bay* 51. I'll See You in My Dreams 51. Starlift 51. The Winning Team 52. April in Paris 52. By the Light of the Silvery Moon 53. *Calamity Jane* 53. Lucky Me 54. *Young at Heart* 55. Love Me or Leave Me 55. The Man Who Knew Too Much 56. Julie 56. *The Pajama Game* 57. Teacher's Pet 58. The Tunnel of Love 58. It Happened to Jane 59. *Pillow Talk* 59. Please Don't Eat the Daisies 60. Midnight Lace 60. Lover Come Back 62. *That Touch of Mink* 62. Jumbo 62. The Thrill of It All 63. Move Over Darling 63. Send Me No Flowers 64. Do Not Disturb 65. The Glass Bottom Boat 66. Caprice 67. The Ballad of Josie 68. Where Were You When the Lights Went Out? 68. With Six You Get Egg Roll 68.
TV series: *The Doris Day Show* 68–72. Doris Day's Best Friends 85.

❀ For her box-office domination of sixties comedies by playing the perennial virgin. *That Touch of Mink.*

¶ I've been around so long I can remember Doris Day before she was a virgin.—*Groucho Marx*

She thinks she doesn't get old. She told me once it was her cameraman who was getting older. She was going to fire him.—*Joe Pasternak*

'Just about the remotest person I know.'—*Kirk Douglas*

'No one guessed that under all those dirndls lurked one of the wildest asses in Hollywood.'—*Ross Hunter*

'My doctor won't let me watch Doris Day. I have a family history of diabetes.'—*Marvin Kitman*

Day for Night (La Nuit Américaine) (France 1973). An amusing, affectionate and unobtrusively skilful look behind the scenes while a movie is being made with a lot of very temperamental actors. Certainly the best of its kind, and purely for entertainment. Written and directed by Francois Truffaut, with Jean-Pierre Aumont, Valentina Cortesa.

Day, Frances (1907–84) (Frances Victoria Schenk). American revue star, in London from 1925.
□ The Price of Divorce 27. OK Chief 30. Big Business 30. The First Mrs Frazer 32. Two Hearts in Waltztime 34. The Girl from Maxim's 34. Temptation 34. Oh Daddy 34. Public Nuisance No. 1 36. You Must Get Married 36. Dreams Come True 36. Who's Your Lady Friend? 37. The Girl in the Taxi 37. Kicking the Moon Around 38. Room for Two 40. *Fiddlers Three* (as Poppea) 44. Tread Softly 52. There's Always a Thursday 57. Climb up the Wall 60.

¶ Little Day, you've had a busy man.—*Bud Flanagan, when F.D. turned up for rehearsals looking decidedly shaggy.*

Day, Jill (1932–). British pop singer and leading lady.
Always a Bride 54. All for Mary 56.

Day, Josette (1914–1978) (J. Dagory). French leading lady.
Allo Berlin, Ici Paris 32. La Fille du Puisatier 40. *La Belle et la Bête* 45. Les Parents Terribles 48. Four Days' Leave 50, etc.

Day, Laraine (1917–) (Laraine Johnson). American leading lady of the forties, with stage experience.
Autobiographical book 1952: *Day With The Giants.*
Stella Dallas 37. Scandal Sheet 38. Border G-Men 38. *Young Dr Kildare* (and others in the series) 39. My Son, My Son 40. *Foreign Correspondent* 40. *The Trial of Mary Dugan* 41. Unholy Partners 41. Fingers at the Window 41. Journey for Margaret 42. Mr Lucky 43. The Story of Dr Wassell 43. Bride by Mistake 44. Those Endearing Young Charms 45. Keep Your Powder Dry 45. *The Locket* 46. Tycoon 47. My Dear Secretary 48. I Married a Communist 49. Without Honour 49. The High and the Mighty 54. Toy Tiger 56. Three for Jamie Dawn 57. The Third Voice 59. Murder on Flight 502 (TV) 75. Return to Fantasy Island (TV) 78, etc.

Day of Wrath (Denmark 1943). Carl Dreyer's horrifying drama of a medieval witch-hunt, uncannily photographed by Karl Andersson so that every scene looks like a Rembrandt painting. A sombre classic, written by Dreyer and others from a novel by Wiers Jenssons; music by Paul Schierbeck; cast headed by Lisbeth Movin, Thorkild Roose.

Day, Richard (1894–1972). American production designer.
We Live Again 35. *The Dark Angel* (AA) 35. Dodsworth (AA) 36. *The Little Foxes* 41. *How Green Was My Valley* (AA) 41. This Above All (AA) 42. My Gal Sal (AA) 43. *A Streetcar Named Desire* (AA) 51. On the Waterfront 54. Exodus 60. The Greatest Story Ever Told 65. The Chase 66. Valley of the Dolls 67. Tora! Tora! Tora! 70, etc.

Day, Robert (1922–). British director, former cameraman.
The Green Man 57. Grip of the Strangler 58. First Man into Space 58. Corridors of Blood 59. Bobbikins 59. Two-Way Stretch 60. The Rebel 61. Operation Snatch 62. Tarzan's Three Challenges 64. She 65. Tarzan and the Valley of Gold 66. Tarzan and the Great River 67. Ritual of Evil (TV) 69. The House on Greenapple Road (TV) 70. Banyon (TV) 70. In Broad Daylight (TV) 71. Mr and Mrs Bo Jo Jones (TV) 71. Death Stalk (TV) 75. Switch (TV) 75. Having Babies (TV) 76. Logan's Run (TV) 77. The Initiation of Sarah (TV) 77. The Grass Is Always Greener Over the Septic Tank (TV) 78. *Murder by Natural Causes* (TV) 79. Walking Through the Fire (TV) 79. The Man with Bogart's Face 80, etc.

Day Lewis, Daniel (1958–). British actor.
Gandhi 83. The Bounty 84. My Beautiful Laundrette 85. A Room with a View 85.

De Anda, Peter (1940–). Black American leading man of the seventies.
Cutter (TV) 72. Come Back Charleston Blue 72. The New Centurions 72, etc.

De Antonio, Emile (1920–). American experimental documentarist with pink tendencies.
Point of Order 64. Rush to Judgment 67. America Is Hard to See 68. In the Year of the Pig 69. Milhouse 71. Painters Painting 73, etc.

De Banzie, Brenda (1915–1981). British character actress who got her big chance on the edge of middle age; later played flouncy matrons.
The Long Dark Hall 51. I Believe in You 52. *Hobson's Choice* 54. The Purple Plain 54. What Every Woman Wants 54. A Kid for Two Farthings 55. The Man Who Knew Too Much 56. The Thirty-nine Steps 59. *The Entertainer* 60. Flame in the Streets 61. The Mark 61. The Pink Panther 63. Pretty Polly 67, etc.

De Benning, Burr (–). American character actor.
Beach Red 67. Sweet November 69. City Beneath the Sea (TV) 71. St Ives 76. The Incredible Melting Man 77. Hanging by a Thread (TV) 79, etc.

De Bray, Yvonne (1889–1954). French character actress, in films from 1943.
Gigi 48. *Les Parents Terribles* 49. Olivia 50. Caroline Cherie 50. Nous Sommes Tous des Assassins 52, etc.

De Broca, Philippe (1933–). French director.
□*Les Jeux de l'Amour* 60. Le Farceur 60. The Seven Deadly Sins (part) 61. L'Amant de Cinq Jours 61. Cartouche 62. *Les Veinards* (part) 63. *That Man from Rio* 63. Un Monsieur de Compagnie 64. Tribulations Chinoise en Chine 65. The Oldest Profession 67. King of Hearts 67. Devil by the Tail 68. Give Her the Moon 70. Le Poudre d'Escampette 71. Chère Louise 72. Le Magnifique 73. Dear Inspector 77. Psy 80. On a Volé la Cuisse de Jupiter 80. Louisiana 84. The Gypsy 85.

De Brulier, Nigel (1878–1948). British actor in Hollywood: career waned with sound.
Intolerance 16. The Four Horsemen of the Apocalypse 21. The Three Musketeers (as Richelieu) 21. Salome 23. The Hunchback of Notre Dame 23. Ben Hur 26. Wings 27. Noah's Ark 29. The Iron Mask 29. Moby Dick 31. Rasputin and the Empress 32. Mary of Scotland 36. The Garden of Allah 36. The Hound of the Baskervilles 39. One Million B.C. 40. The Adventures of Captain Marvel 48, many others.

De Camp, Rosemary (1913–). American character actress specializing in active motherly types.
Cheers for Miss Bishop 41. Jungle Book 42. This is the Army 43. *The Merry Monahans* 44. *Rhapsody in Blue* 45. From this Day Forward 46. Nora Prentiss 47. Night unto Night 49. The Big Hangover 50. *On Moonlight Bay* 51. By the Light of the Silvery Moon 53. Many Rivers to Cross 55. Thirteen Ghosts 60. Blind Ambition (TV) 79. Saturday the 14th 81, etc.
TV series: The Life of Riley. *The Bob Cummings Show*. That Girl.
† Miss De Camp was thirteen years James Cagney's junior—but in *Yankee Doodle Dandy* she played his mother.

De Carlo, Yvonne (1922–) (Peggy Middleton). Canadian leading lady, a star in the forties of Hollywood's most outrageous easterns and westerns.
Salome Where She Danced 45. Frontier Gal 45. Song of Scheherezade 47. Brute Force 47. Slave Girl 47. Black Bart (as Lola Montez) 48. Casbah 48. River Lady 48. *Criss Cross* 49. Calamity Jane and Sam Bass 49. The Desert Hawk 50. Tomahawk 51. Hotel Sahara 51. Scarlet Angel 52. Sombrero 53. Sea Devils 52. The Captain's Paradise 53. Passion 54. Magic Fire 56. The Ten Commandments 56. Death of a Scoundrel 56. Band of Angels 57. McLintock 63. Law of the Lawless 64. Munster Go Home 66. The Power 68. The Seven Minutes 71. Guyana Cult of the Damned 80. The Man with Bogart's Face 80. Liar's Moon 82. Flesh and Bullets 85. A Masterpiece of Murder (TV) 86, etc.
TV series: *The Munsters* 64–65.

De Casalis, Jeanne (1896–1966). British revue comedienne and character actress, best known as radio's 'Mrs Feather' in dithery telephone monologues. Autobiography 1953: *Things I Don't Remember*.
Nell Gwyn 34. Cottage to Let 41. Charley's Big Hearted Aunt 41. Those Kids from Town 42. Medal for the General 44. This Man Is Mine 46. Woman Hater 48, etc.

De Cordoba, Pedro (1881–1950). American stage actor, lean and often sinister, in many silent and sound films.
Carmen 15. Maria Rosa 16. Runaway Romany 20. Young Diana 22. The Crusades 35. Anthony Adverse 36. The Light That Failed 39. The Ghost Breakers 40. The Mark of Zorro 40. Son of Fury 42. For Whom the Bell Tolls 43. The Beast with Five Fingers 47. When the Redskins Rode 50, etc.

De Cordova, Arturo (1908–1973) (Arturo Garcia). Mexican leading man with flashing grin and impudent eyes. Popular in Mexico since 1935; made a few Hollywood films in the forties.
For Whom the Bell Tolls 43. Hostages 43. *Frenchman's Creek* 44. Incendiary Blonde 44. A Medal for Benny 45. Masquerade in Mexico 45. The Flame 47. New Orleans 47. The Adventures of Casanova 48. *El* (Mex.) 51. Kill Him for Me 53, etc.

De Cordova, Frederick (1910–). American director with stage and TV experience.
□Too Young to Know 45. Her Kind of Man 46. That Way with Women 47. Love and Learn 47. Always Together 47. Wallflower 48. For the Love of Mary 48. The Countess of Monte Cristo 48. Illegal Entry 49. The Gal who Took the West 49. Buccaneer's Girl 50. Peggy 50. The Desert Hawk 50. Bedtime for Bonzo 51. Katie Did It 51. Little Egypt 51. Finders Keepers 51. Here Come the Nelsons 52. Bonzo Goes to College 52. Yankee Buccaneer 53. Column South 53. I'll Take Sweden 65. Frankie and Johnny 66.

De Corsia, Ted (1904–1973). American character actor with long vaudeville experience; usually played surly villains.
The Lady from Shanghai 47. *Naked City* 48. The Enforcer 51. Vengeance Valley 51. Man In the Dark 53. Twenty Thousand Leagues Under The Sea 54. The Big Combo 55. Slightly Scarlet 56. The Killing 56. Baby Face Nelson 57. Gunfight at the O.K. Corral 57. Blood on the Arrow 61. The Quick Gun 64. Nevada Smith 66. Five Card Stud 68, many others.
TV series: Steve Canyon 57-60.

De Courville, Albert (1887–1960). British stage director who directed a few film comedies.
Wolves 30. The Midshipmaid 32. This is the Life 33. Things Are Looking Up 34. The Case of Gabriel Perry 35. Seven Sinners 36. Crackerjack 38. The Lambeth Walk 38. An Englishman's Home 39, etc.

De Cuir, John (1918–). American production designer.
Naked City 48. The Snows of Kilimanjaro 51. Call Me Mister 52. The King and I 56. South Pacific 57. Cleopatra 62. The Agony and the Ecstasy 65. Hello Dolly 69. The Great White Hope 70. Once is not Enough 75. Raise the Titanic 80. Dead Men Don't Wear Plaid 82, etc.

De Filippo, Eduardo (1900–84) (Eduardo Passarelli). Italian actor and director of many and varied talents.
Tre Uomini in Frac (a) 32. Il Cappello a Tre Punte (a) 40. In Campagna e Caduta una Stella (w, d, a) 40. Il Sogno di Tutti (a) 40. La Vita Ricomincia (a) 45. Assunta Spina (w, a) 47. Napoli Milionaria (w, d, a) 50. Altri Tempi (a) 51. Filumena Marturano (w, d, a) 51. The Girls of the Spanish Steps (a) 52. Villa Borghese (a) 53. Napoletani a Milano (w, d, a) 53. Questi Fantasmi (w, d, a) 54. Fortunella (d, a) 58. Raw Wind in Eden (a) 58. Ghosts of Rome (a) 60. Shoot Loud, Louder, I Don't Understand (w, d, a) 66, others.

De Forest, Lee (1873–1961). American inventor, pioneer of many developments in wireless telegraphy, also the De Forest Phonofilm of the twenties, an early experiment in synchronized sound.

De Funes, Louis (1908–1983). French character comedian.
Lock up the Spoons 56. Femmes de Paris 58. Taxi 59. A Pied a Cheval et en Spoutnik 61. The Sucker 65. Fantomas 66. Don't Look Now 67. Jo 71. The Mad Adventures of Rabbi Jacob 73. Up a Tree 75. What's Cooking in Paris 77. Les Charlots 79. L'Avare 80, many others.

De Govia, Jackson (–). American production designer.
Boulevard Nights 79. Butch and Sundance, the Early Years 79. It's My Turn 80. My Bodyguard 80, etc.

De Grasse, Robert (1900–1971). American cinematographer, with RKO from 1934.
Three Pals 26. Fury of the Wild 29. Break of Hearts 35. *Stage Door* 37. The Story of Vernon and Irene Castle 39. Bachelor Mother 39. Kitty Foyle 40. Forever and a Day 43. Step Lively 44. *The Body Snatcher* 45. The

Miracle of the Bells 48. Home of the Brave 49. The Men 50. Chicago Calling 52, many others.

De Grunwald, Anatole (1910–1967). British producer, in films since 1939.
French Without Tears (w) 39. Quiet Wedding (w) 40. The First of the Few (w) 41. The Demi-Paradise 42. The Way to the Stars 45. The Winslow Boy (& w) 48. The Holly and the Ivy (& w) 54. The Doctor's Dilemma 58. Libel (& w) 61. Come Fly with Me 62. The VIPs 63. The Yellow Rolls-Royce 64. Stranger in the House 67, others.

De Grunwald, Dmitri (c. 1913–). British producer, brother of Anatole de Grunwald.
The Dock Brief 62. Perfect Friday 67. Connecting Rooms 69. The Last Grenade 69. Murphy's War 71. That Lucky Touch 75, etc.

De Haven, Carter (1887–1977). American stage star who appeared in a few silent films. His son **Carter de Haven Jnr** (1910–1979) was a production manager, especially for Chaplin.

De Haven, Gloria (1924–). American soubrette, films mostly light musicals of no enduring quality.
□Modern Times 36. The Great Dictator 40. Susan and God 40. Keeping Company 41. Two Faced Woman 41. The Penalty 41. *Best Foot Forward* 43. Thousands Cheer 43. Broadway Rhythm 44. *Two Girls and a Sailor* 44. Step Lively 44. The Thin Man Goes Home 44. Between Two Women 45. Summer Holiday 48. Scene of the Crime 49. The Doctor and the Girl 49. Yes Sir That's My Baby 49. The Yellow Cab Man 50. Three Little Words 50. Summer Stock 50. I'll Get By 50. Two Tickets to Broadway 51. Down among the Sheltering Palms 53. So This Is Paris 55. The Girl Rush 55. Call Her Mom 72. Who Is the Black Dahlia? 75. Banjo Hackett 76. Sharon, Portrait of a Mistress 77. Evening in Byzantium 78.
TV series: Ryan's Hope 75. Nakia 79.

De Havilland, Olivia (1916–). British-born leading lady, sister of Joan Fontaine. In Hollywood from teenage as leading lady of comedy, romance and costume drama; later proved herself an actress.
Semi-autobiography 1960: *Every Frenchman Has One.*
□*A Midsummer Night's Dream* 35. The Irish in Us 35. Alibi Ike 35. Captain Blood 35. Anthony Adverse 36. The Charge of the Light Brigade 36. Call It a Day 36. The Great Garrick 36. It's Love I'm After 37. Gold Is Where You Find It 37. Four's a Crowd 38. *The Adventures of Robin Hood* 38. Hard To Get 38. Wings of the Navy 39. Dodge City 39. *Gone with the Wind* 39. Elizabeth and Essex 39. Raffles 40. My Love Came Back 40. Santa Fe Trail 40. Strawberry Blonde 41. Hold Back the Dawn 41. They Died with Their Boots On 41. The Male Animal 42. In This Our Life 42. Government Girl 43. Thank Your Lucky Stars 43. Princess O'Rourke 43. The Well-Groomed Bride 45. *Devotion* (as Charlotte Brontë) 46. *The Dark Mirror* 46. *To Each His Own* (AA) 46. *The Snake Pit* 47. *The Heiress* (AA) 49. My Cousin Rachel 52. That Lady 55. Not as a Stranger 55. The Ambassador's Daughter 56. The Proud Rebel 58. Libel (GB) 60. The Light in the Piazza 62. Lady in a Cage 64. *Hush Hush Sweet Charlotte* 64. The Adventurers 69. Pope Joan 72. The Screaming Woman (TV) 72. The Fifth Musketeer 77. Airport 77 77. The Swarm 78. Roots: The Next Generation (TV) 79. Murder Is Easy (TV) 82. Charles and Diana: A Royal Romance (TV) (as the Queen Mother) 82.
❁ For her development from a charming leading lady to a star actress of some distinction. *The Dark Mirror.*
Famous line (*The Heiress*): 'Yes, I can be very cruel. I have been taught by masters.'

De La Motte, Marguerite (1903–1950). American leading lady of silent films.
The Mark of Zorro 20. The Three Musketeers 21. When a Man's a Man 24. The Beloved Brute 24. Red Dice 26. The Unknown Soldier 26. The Iron Mask 28. Woman's Man 34. Reg'lar Fellers 42, etc.

De La Patelliere, Denys (1921–). French director.
Le Défroque (w only) 52. Les Aristocrates 56. Retour de Manivelle 57. Les Grandes Familles 59. Marco the Magnificent 65. Du Rififi à Paname 66. Black Sun 66, etc.

De La Tour, Frances (1944–). Angular British character actress who plays both comedy and drama.
Country Dance 69. Every Home Should Have One 70. Our Miss Fred 72. To the Devil a Daughter 76. Wombling Free 77, etc.
TV series: Rising Damp 74–78, Flickers 81. Murder with Mirrors (TV) 84.

De Lane Lea, William (1900–1964). British executive, pioneer of sound dubbing processes.

De Laurentiis, Dino (1919–). Italian producer who made a stab at Hollywood in the seventies.
Bitter Rice 48. Ulysses 52. La Strada 54. Barabbas 62. The Bible 65. Kiss the Girls and Make Them Die 67. Anzio 68. Barbarella 68. Waterloo 69. Wild Horses 73. Death Wish 74. King Kong 76. The White Buffalo 77. King of The Gypsies 78. Hurricane 79. The Brinks Job 79. Flash Gordon 80. Ragtime 81. Conan the Barbarian 82. Fighting Back 82.
The Bounty 84. Dune 85. Cat's Eye 85. Manhunter 86, etc.

De Luise, Dom (1933–). Rotund American comedy star who became one of the Mel Brooks repertory company.
The Glass Bottom Boat 65. The Twelve Chairs 70. Blazing Saddles 73. Sherlock Holmes' Smarter Brother 75. Silent Movie 76. The World's Greatest Lover 78. The End 78. Hot Stuff (& d) 79. The Muppet Movie 79. Fatso 80. Smokey and the Bandit II 80. The Last Married Couple in America 80. Wholly Moses 80. The Cannonball Run 81. History of the World Part One 81. The Best Little Whorehouse in Texas 82. Happy (TV) 83.
Johnny Dangerously 84. Haunted Honeymoon 86.
TV series: Lotsa Luck 73.

¶ *D. De L.:* I'm actually a thin serious person but I play fat and funny, but only for the movies.

De Luxe Color is the Twentieth Century-Fox version of Eastmancolor but usually comes out decidedly blue.

De Marney, Derrick (1906–1978). Good-looking British actor with stage experience.
Music Hall 35. Things to Come 36. *Young and Innocent* 37. Victoria the Great (as Disraeli) 37. Blonde Cheat (US) 38. The Spider 39. The Lion Has Wings 40. Dangerous Moonlight 40. The First of the Few 42. Latin Quarter (& co-p) 46. Uncle Silas 47. Sleeping Car to Trieste 48. She Shall Have Murder (& p) 50. Meet Mr Callaghan (& p) 54. Private's Progress 55. Doomsday at Eleven 62. The Projected Man 66, etc.

De Marney, Terence (1909–1971). British actor with stage experience, brother of Derrick de Marney.
The Mystery of the Marie Celeste 36. I Killed the Count 38. Dual Alibi 46. No Way Back 49. Uneasy Terms 49. The Silver Chalice (US) 55. Death Is a Woman 66. All Neat in Black Stockings 69.

De Maupassant, Guy (1850–1893). French short storywriter. Work filmed includes *Diary of a Madman, Une Vie, Le Rosier de Madame Husson,* and many versions of *Boule de Suif.*

De Mille, Cecil B. (1881–1959). American producer-director, one of Hollywood's pioneers and autocrats. Notable in the twenties for sex comedies, in the thirties and forties for action adventures, then for biblical epics; all now seem very stolid, but were enormously successful in their day.
Autobiography 1959.
□*The Squaw Man* 13. The Virginian 14. The Call of the North 14. What's His Name 14. The Man from Home 14. Rose of the Rancho 14. The Girl of the Golden West 15. The Warrens of Virginia 15. The Unafraid 15. The Captive 15. Wild Goose Chase 15. The Arab 15. Chimmie Fadden 15. Kindling 15. Maria Rosa 15. Carmen 15. Temptation 15. Chimmie Fadden Out West 15. *The Cheat* 15. The Golden Chance 16. The Trail of the Lonesome Pine 16. Joan the Woman 16. The Heart of Nora Flynn 16. The Dream Girl 16. A Romance of the Redwoods 17. The Little American 17. The Woman God Forgot 17. The Devil Stone 17. The Whispering Chorus 18. Old Wives for New 18. We Can't Have Everything 18. Till I Come Back to You 18. The Squaw Man 18. Don't Change Your Husband 19. For Better for Worse 19. Male and Female 19. Why Change your Wife? 20. Something to Think About 20. Forbidden Fruit 21. *The Affairs of Anatol* 21. Fool's Paradise 22. Saturday Night 22. Manslaughter 22. Adam's Rib 23. *The Ten Commandments* 23. Triumph 24. Feet of Clay 24. The Golden Bed 25. The Road to Yesterday 25. The Volga Boatmen 26. *King of Kings* 27. The Godless Girl 28. Dynamite 29. Madame Satan 30. The Squaw Man 31. *The Sign of the Cross* 32. This Day and Age 33. Four Frightened People 34. Cleopatra 34. *The Crusades* 35. *The Plainsman* 36. The Buccaneer 38. *Union Pacific* 39. Northwest Mounted Police 40. *Reap The Wild Wind* 42. The Story of Dr Wassell 44. Unconquered 47. Variety Girl (actor) 47. Samson and Delilah 49. Sunset Boulevard (as actor) 50. The Greatest Show on Earth 52. The Ten Commandments 56. The Buccaneer (p only) 59.

'He remained true to the literary tradition of Cooper's Leatherstocking Tales and to the dramatic conventions of David Belasco.'—*Andrew Sarris, 1968*

❀ For making himself an unseen star by imposing the personality of an autocratic schoolmaster on a variety of somewhat dubious material. *The Sign of the Cross.*

¶ Ready when you are, Mr de Mille. It's the tag line of a long shaggy dog story, the purpose of which is to establish de Mille as the producer of enormous, stagey biblical epics. Towards the end of his life he did submerge himself in this role, but his career embraced almost every kind of movie. Whatever the show, he made a success of it, and he was respected throughout Hollywood as a disciplinarian who always got his films out under budget. There was a joke during World War II:

> Anyone who leaves de Mille for the armed forces is a slacker.

He is credited with sending back a writer's script and attaching a terrifying cover note:

> What I have crossed out I didn't like. What I haven't crossed out I am dissatisfied with.

He exercised supreme control over his stars, and once said to Paulette Goddard:

> Remember you are a star. Never go across the alley even to dump garbage unless you are dressed to the teeth.

He told his staff:

> You are here to please me. Nothing else on earth matters.

He went to extreme lengths to prove his authority. Arthur Miller thought:

> I never met such an egotist in my life. Even if he was wrong and knew it, once he said it it had to be.

His brother William was awed by his ambition and achievement:

> The trouble with Cecil is that he always bites off more than he can chew—and then chews it.

The same William cast a wry eye on Cecil's first Bible picture in the twenties:

> Having attended to the underclothes, bathrooms and matrimonial irregularities of his fellow citizens, he now began to consider their salvation.

Even when Cecil dealt with heavenly themes, he kept his feet on earth. He said to a scriptwriter:

> It's just a damn good hot tale, so don't get a lot of thees, thous and thums on your mind.

His comparative ignorance of his favourite subject provoked a much-repeated clerihew:

> Cecil B. de Mille
> Much against his will
> Was persuaded to keep Moses
> Out of the Wars of the Roses.

He saw the Bible as a ready-made script factory:

> Give me any couple of pages of the Bible and I'll give you a picture.

He took neither credit nor blame for his themes:

> I didn't write the Bible and didn't invent sin.

He was also quite clear where his support lay:

> I make my pictures for people, not for critics.

His approach to actresses was on similarly direct lines. In 1934, when he thought of Claudette Colbert as Cleopatra, he said to her:

> How would you like to be the wickedest woman in history?

But he knew that what really mattered to a movie is not the star but the producer:

> A picture is made a success not on a set but over the drawing board.

Action was another essential ingredient:

> I will trade you forty gorgeously beautiful Hawaiian sunsets for one good sock in the jaw.

He chuckled at the result of his labours:

> Every time I make a picture the critics' estimate of American public taste goes down ten per cent.

Typical reaction was Pauline Kael's:

> He made small-minded pictures on a big scale.

But Graham Greene had a soft spot for him:

> There has always been a touch of genius as well as absurdity in this warm-hearted sentimental salvationist.

I learned an awful lot from him by doing the opposite.—*Howard Hawks*

'He wore baldness like an expensive hat, as though it were out of the question for him to have hair like other men.'—*Gloria Swanson*

'He didn't make pictures for himself or for the critics. He made them for the public.'—*Adolph Zukor*

De Mille, Katherine (1911–) (Katherine Lester). American leading lady of the thirties.
Viva Villa 34. Call of the Wild 35. Ramona 36. Banjo on My Knee 37. Blockade 38. Reap the Wild Wind 42. The Story of Dr Wassell 44. Unconquered 47. The Gamblers 50, etc.

De Mille, William (1878–1955). American director. Elder brother of Cecil B. de Mille, with theatrical background.
Nice People 22. Craig's Wife 28. Captain Fury (p only) 39, etc.

De Mornay, Rebecca (1962–). American actress.
Testament 83. Risky Business 84. The Trip to Bountiful 85. Runaway Train 85.

De Niro, Robert (1943–). Leading American actor of the seventies, usually in downbeat roles and somewhat handicapped by possessing the kind of face you don't remember.
□ Greetings 68. Sam's Song 69. The Wedding Party 69. Hi Mom 70. Bloody Mama 70. Born to Win 71. The Gang that couldn't Shoot Straight 71. Jennifer on my Mind 71. *Bang the Drum Slowly* 73. *Mean Streets* 73. The Godfather Part Two (AA) 74. Taxi Driver 76. The Last Tycoon 76. 1900 76. New York New York 77. *The Deer Hunter* 78. *Raging Bull* (for which he became fifty pounds overweight) (AA) 80. True Confessions 81. King of Comedy 83. Once Upon a Time in America 84. Falling in Love 85. Brazil 85. The Mission 86. Angel Heart 87. The Untouchables 87.
¶ There is a mixture of anarchy and discipline in the way I work.—*R. de N.*
After my first movies, I gave interviews. Then I thought, what's so important about where I went to school, and hobbies . . . what does any of that have to do with acting, with my own head?—*R. de N.*

De Palma, Brian (1940–). American director who began in the satirical underground school, then graduated to glossy shock/horrors, usually in clever imitation of somebody else's style.
□Murder à la Mod (& w) 68. *Greetings* 68. The Wedding Party 69. Dionysus 70. Hi Mom 70. Get to Know Your Rabbit 72. Sisters 73. Phantom of the Paradise (& w) 74. Obsession 76. *Carrie* 76. The Fury 78. Home Movies 79. Dressed to Kill 80. Blow Out 81. Scarface 83. Kennedy 78. Body Double 84. Wise Guys 85. The Untouchables 87.
¶ A superb cinematic talent unable to do more than play doctor with his toy implements.—*Sunday Times, 1981*
B. de P.: My films deal with a stylised, expressionistic world that has a kind of grotesque beauty about it.

De Putti, Lya (1901–1932). Hungarian leading lady of the twenties.
The Phantom (Ger.) 25. *Variety* (Ger.) 25. The Sorrows of Satan (US) 26. The Heart Thief (US) 27. Buck Privates 28. The Informer (GB) 29, etc.

De Rochemont, Louis (1899–1978) American producer, from the world of newsreel. Devised *The March of Time* 34; later produced semi-documentaries like *The House on 92nd Street* 46 and *Boomerang* 47; and was involved in many ventures including Cinerama and Cinemiracle.

De Santis, Giuseppe (1917–). Italian director.
Caccia Tragica 47. *Bitter Rice* 49. *No Peace among the Olives* 50. Rome Eleven O'Clock 51. A Husband for Anna 53. Men and Wolves 56. La Garconnière 60, etc.

De Santis, Joe (1909–). American character actor who often plays Italianate gangsters.
Slattery's Hurricane 49. Man with a Cloak 51. The Last Hunt 56. Tension at Table Rock 57. And Now Miguel 66. The Professionals 66. Blue 68, etc.

De Sarigny, Peter (1911–). South African-born producer, in Britain from 1936.
The Malta Story 53. Simba 55. True as a Turtle 56. Never Let Go 61, etc.

De Seta, Vittorio (1923–). Italian director, mainly of shorts until *Bandits at Orgosolo* 62.

De Sica, Vittorio (1901–1974). Italian actor and director, in the latter respect an important and skilful realist. Well known in Italy in the thirties, but not elsewhere until after World War II.
Teresa Venerdi (d) 41. I Bambini ci Guardino (d) 42. *Shoeshine* (AA) (d) 46. *Bicycle Thieves* (AA) (d) 48. *Miracle in Milan* (d) 50. *Umberto D* (d) 52. *Madame De* (a) 52. Stazione Termini (Indiscretion) (d) 52. Bread, Love and Dreams (a) 53. Gold of Naples (d) 54. A Farewell to Arms (a) 57. Il Generale della Rovere (a) 59. Two Women (d) 61. The Condemned of Altona (d) 63. Yesterday, Today and Tomorrow (d) (AA) 64. Marriage Italian Style (d) 64. A New World (d) 66. The Biggest Bundle of Them All (a) 66. After the Fox (d) 66. Woman Times Seven (d) 67. The Shoes of the Fisherman (a) 68. A Place for Lovers (d) 69. Sunflower (d) 70. *The Garden of the Finzi-Continis* (d) 71. The Voyage (d) 73, etc.
TV series as actor: *The Four Just Men* (GB) 59.
❀ For a half-dozen splendid films dotting a very variable career. *Miracle in Milan.*
¶ 'A fine actor, a polished hack, and a flabby whore—not necessarily in that order.'—*Stanley Kauffmann*

De Souza, Edward (1933–). British leading man, mostly on stage.
The Roman Spring of Mrs Stone 61. The Phantom of the Opera 62. Kiss of the Vampire 63, etc.

De Sylva, Buddy (1895–1950). American lyricist, one-third of songwriting team Brown, Henderson and De Sylva, whose story was told in *The Best Things in Life Are Free*. Shows filmed include *Big Boy, Good News*. As B. G. De Sylva, he later became head of production for Paramount Studios, and in *Star Spangled Rhythm* was spoofed by Walter Abel (as G. B de Soto).

De Toth, André (1912–). Hungarian-American director, mainly of routine actioners. Oddly enough, directed one of the first 3-D films; having only one eye, he could not see the effect.
□Ot Ora 40 (Hung.) 38. Ketlany Azultean (Hung.) 38. Har Het Bologsag (Hung.) 38. Semmelweis (Hung.) 38. Balalaika (Hung.) 39. Toprini Nasz (Hung.) 39. Passport to Suez 43. None Shall Escape 44. *Dark Waters* 44. Ramrod 47. The Other Love 47. Pitfall 48. Slattery's Hurricane 49. Man in the Saddle 51. Carson City 52. Springfield Rifle 52. Last of the Comanches 52. *House of Wax* 53. The Stranger Wore a Gun 53. Thunder Over the Plains 53. Crime Wave 54. Riding Shotgun 54. Tanganyika 54. The Bounty Hunter 54. The Indian Fighter 55. Monkey on My Back 57. Hidden Fear 57. The Two Headed Spy (GB) 59. Day of the Outlaw 59. Man on a String 60. Morgan the Pirate 61. The Mongols 62. Gold for the Caesars 64. Play Dirty (GB) 69.

De Vinna, Clyde (1892–1953). American cinematographer.
SELECTED SILENTS: The Raiders 16. Madam Who 18. Leave it to Me 20. Yellow Men and Gold 22. The Victor 23. Ben Hur (co-ph) 26. California 27. White Shadows in the South Seas (cò-ph) (AA) 28. The Pagan 29.
□SOUND FILMS: *Trader Horn* 31. The Great Meadow (co-ph) 31. Shipmates 31. Politics 31. Tarzan the Ape Man (co-ph) 32. Bird of Paradise (co-ph) 32. Eskimo 33. Tarzan and His Mate (co-ph) 34. *Treasure Island* 34. West Point of the Air 35.The Last of the Pagans 35. Ah Wilderness 35. Old Hutch 36. Good Old Soak 36. Bad Man of Brimstone 38. Of Human Hearts 38. Fast Company 38. The Girl Downstairs 39. Bridal Suite 39. Blackmail 39. They All Come Out 39. Twenty Mule Team 40. Phantom Raiders 40. Wyoming 40. The Bad Man 41. The People vs Dr Kildare 41. Barnacle Bill 41. Tarzan's Secret Treasure 41. The Bugle Sounds 41. Jackass Mail 41. Whistling in Dixie 42. The Immortal Sergeant 43. Within these Walls 45. The Caribbean Mystery 45. It's a Joke Son 47. Sword of the Avenger 48. The Jungle 52.

De Vito, Danny (–). American comedy character actor.
One Flew Over the Cuckoo's Nest 75. The World's Greatest Lover 77. Going Ape 80. Romancing the Stone 83. Terms of Endearment 83. Johnny Dangerously 84. The Jewel of the Nile 85. Ruthless People 86. Wise Guys 87. Tin Men 87. Throw Momma from the Train (& d) 87.

De Vol, Frank (–). American composer of background scores.
The Big Knife 55. Kiss Me Deadly 55. Attack 56. Pillow Talk 59. Whatever Happened to Baby Jane? 62. McLintock 63. Hush Hush Sweet Charlotte 64. Send Me No Flowers 64. Cat Ballou 65. The Flight of the Phoenix 65. Guess Who's Coming to Dinner 67. The Dirty Dozen 67. Krakatoa East of Java 68. Ulzana's Raid 71. The Longest Yard 74. Doc Savage 75. The Choirboys 77. The Frisco Kid 79. Herbie Goes Bananas 80.

De Vorzon, Barry (–). American composer.
The Warriors 79. The Ninth Configuration 80. Xanadu 80.

De Wilde, Brandon (1942–1972). American child actor, later juvenile lead.
□ *The Member of the Wedding* 52. *Shane* 53. Goodbye My Lady 56. Night Passage 57. The Missouri Traveller 58. Blue Denim 59. All Fall Down 62. *Hud* 63. In Harm's Way 65. Those Calloways 65. The Deserter 70. Wild in the Sky 72.
TV series: Jamie 54.

De Wolfe, Billy (1907–1974) (William Andrew Jones). Toothy, moustachioed American comedy actor, formerly dancer, with vaudeville and night club experience. (Famous act: a lady taking a bath.)
Dixie 43. Blue Skies 46. *Dear Ruth* 47. Dear Wife 50. Tea for Two 50. Lullaby of Broadway 51. *Call Me Madam* 53. Billie 65. The World's Greatest Athlete 73, etc.
TV series: That Girl 66–71. The Pruitts of Southampton 67. Good Morning World 67. The Queen and I 69. The Debbie Reynolds Show 69. The Doris Day Show 70–71.

De Wolff, Francis (1913–). Bearded, burly, British character actor.
Adam and Evelyne 48. Under Capricorn 49. Treasure Island 50. Scrooge 51. Ivanhoe 53. The Master of Ballantrae 55. Geordie 55, many others.

De Young, Cliff (1945–). American general purpose actor.
Sunshine (TV) 73. Harry and Tonto 74. The Night that Panicked America (TV) 75. The Lindbergh Kidnapping Case (TV) (title role) 76. Blue Collar 78. King (TV) (as Bobby Kennedy 78. Shock Treatment 81. The Hunger 83. Protocol 84. F/X 85. Flight of the Navigator 87, etc.

Deacon, Brian (1949–). British general purpose actor.
Triple Echo 73. Vampire 74. Lillie (TV) 78. A Zed and Two Noughts 86.

Deacon, Richard (1921–84). Bald, bespectacled American character actor who usually played comic snoops.
Abbott and Costello Meet the Mummy 55. The Power and the Prize 56. The Remarkable Mr Pennypacker 58. Blackbeard's Ghost 68. Piranha 78, many others.
TV series: Leave It to Beaver 57–63. *Dick Van Dyke* 61–66. Mothers-in-Law 67–68.

Dead End (US 1937). Set-bound but powerful melodrama from Sidney Kingsley's play about a New York slum. Its success led Hollywood to produce more social dramas; it provided an important part for Humphrey Bogart as the returning gangster; and it introduced the Dead End Kids. As entertainment it has dated, despite Gregg Toland's photography and William Wyler's direction.

Dead of Night (GB 1945). An Ealing omnibus of ghost stories, almost the first serious British treatment of the supernatural. Quality varies, but the Michael Redgrave sequence about a deranged ventriloquist has lost none of its power, and the linking story about an architect caught up in an endless series of recurring dreams is neatly underplayed until its phantasmagoric climax and brilliant trick ending. Directors: Cavalcanti ('Christmas Party' and 'Ventriloquist'), Basil Dearden ('Hearse Driver' and linking story), Charles Crichton ('Golf') and Robert Hamer ('Haunted Mirror'). The format was borrowed in the late sixties for the series of Robert Bloch/Amicus portmanteaux, and the ventriloquist situation was used in 1978 in *Magic*.

deaf mutes have been movingly portrayed by Jane Wyman in *Johnny Belinda*, Mandy Miller in *Mandy*, Harry Bellaver in *No Way Out*, and Alan Arkin *The Heart Is a Lonely Hunter*. Dorothy McGuire in *The Spiral Staircase* was mute but not deaf; Patty Duke in *The Miracle Worker* was deaf but could make sounds.

Dean, Basil (1888–1978). British stage producer who also directed several important films for Associated Talking Pictures, which he founded. He was also responsible for the formation in wartime of the organization of travelling entertainers, ENSA, often known disrespectfully as Every Night Something Awful but standing in fact for Entertainments National Service Association.
Autobiography 1973: *Mind's Eye*.
The Impassive Footman 32. The Constant Nymph (& co-w) 33. Java Head 34. Sing As We Go 34. Lorna Doone 35. Twenty-one Days 39, etc.

Dean, Eddie (c. 1908–) (Edgar D. Glossup). American star of western second features in the thirties and fifties.
Renegade Trail 39. Sierra Sue 41. Romance of the West 47. Hawk of Powder River 50, many others.

Dean, Isabel (1918–) (Isabel Hodgkinson). British stage actress, usually in upper-class roles: very occasional film appearances.
The Passionate Friends 47. Twenty-four Hours of a Woman's Life 52. The Story of Gilbert and Sullivan 53. Out of the Clouds 55. Virgin Island 58. The Light in the Piazza 62. A High Wind in Jamaica 65. Inadmissible Evidence 68. Catch Me a Spy 71. Five Days One Summer 82, etc.

Dean, James (1931–1955). Moody young American actor who after a brief build-up in small roles was acclaimed as the image of the mid-fifties; his tragic death in a car crash caused an astonishing world-wide outburst of emotional necrophilia. A biopic, *The James Dean Story*, was patched together in 1957.
□Has Anybody Seen My Gal? 51. Sailor Beware 51. Fixed Bayonets 52. Trouble Along the Way 53. *East of Eden* 55. *Rebel Without A Cause* 55. *Giant* 56.

¶ 'Another dirty shirt-tail actor from New York.'—*Hedda Hopper*
'He was sad and sulky. You kept expecting him to cry.'—*Elia Kazan*

Dean, Julia (1878–1952). American stage actress who made a few movies after she retired to California.
How Molly Made Good 15. Curse of the Cat People 44. O.S.S. 46. Nightmare Alley 48. People Will Talk 51. Elopement 51, etc.

Dean, Man Mountain (1899–1963). American wrestler who played comedy roles in a few films.
Reckless 35. The Gladiator 36. Surprise Package 60, etc.

Dear Ruth (US 1947). Norman Krasna's play, about a teenager who writes love letters to a service man using her elder sister's name and photograph, was pleasantly if unremarkably filmed by William D. Russell with a cast including William Holden, Joan Caulfield, Mona Freeman, Edward Arnold and Billy de Wolfe. So successful was it that two sequels were called for: *Dear Wife* 49. *Dear Brat* 51.

Dearden, Basil (1911–1971). British director, former editor. Began by co-directing Will Hay's last films for Ealing, then formed a writer-producer-director partnership with Michael Relph.
□The Black Sheep of Whitehall (co-d) 41. The Goose Steps Out (co-d) 42. The Bells Go Down 43. My Learned Friend (co-d) 43. The Halfway House 44. They Came to a City 44. Dead of Night (part) 45. *The Captive Heart* 46. Frieda 47. Saraband for Dead Lovers 48. Train of Events (co-d) 49. *The Blue Lamp* 50. Cage of Gold 50. Pool of London 51. I Believe in You (co-d) 52. The Gentle Gunman 52. The Square Ring 53. The Rainbow Jacket 54. Out of the Clouds (co-d) 55. The Ship That Died of Shame (co-d) 55. Who Done It (co-d) 56. The Smallest Show on Earth 57. Violent Playground 58. *Sapphire* 59. *The League of Gentlemen* 60. Man in the Moon 60. The Secret Partner 61. *Victim* 61. All Night Long (co-d) 62. Life for Ruth 62. The Mind Benders 63. A Place to Go 63. Woman of Straw 64. Masquerade 65. Khartoum 66. Only When I Larf 68. The Assassination Bureau 69. The Man Who Haunted Himself 70.

Dearing, Edgar (1893–1974). American character actor, often seen as tough cop.
Thanks for Everything 35. Swing Time 37. Miss Annie Rooney 42, many others.

death has always fascinated film-makers, though the results have often appeared undergraduatish, as fantasy tends to look when brought down to a mass-appeal level. Death has been personified in *Death Takes a Holiday* by Fredric March and in the 1971 TV remake by Monte Markham, in *On Borrowed Time* by Cedric Hardwicke, in *Here Comes Mr Jordan* by Claude Rains, in *Orphée* by Maria Casares, in *The Seventh Seal* by Bengt Ekerot, by Richard Burton in *Boom*, by George Jessel in *Heironymous Merkin* and by several actors in *The Masque of the Red Death*. In *Devotion*, Ida Lupino as Emily Brontë dreamed of death on horseback coming to sweep her away; in *The Bluebird* Shirley Temple ventured into the land of the dead to see her grandparents. Most of the characters in *Thunder Rock*, and all in *Outward Bound* (remade as *Between Two Worlds* and later varied for TV as *Haunts of the Very Rich*) were already dead at the start of the story. Other films to involve serious thought about death include *Dark Victory, Jeux Interdits, All the Way Home, Sentimental Journey, No Sad Songs for Me, One Way Passage, Paths of Glory, Wild Strawberries,* and *Ikuru*.

Comedies taking death lightly included *A Slight Case of Murder, Kind Hearts and Coronets, The Trouble with Harry, Too Many Crooks, The Criminal Life of Archibaldo de la Cruz, Send Me No Flowers, The Assassination Bureau, The Loved One, The Wrong Box, Arrivederci Baby, Kiss the Girls and Make Them Die, Arsenic and Old Lace* and *Une Journée Bien Rempliée*.

Death of a Salesman (US 1952). Produced by Stanley Kramer and directed by Laslo Benedek, this screen adaptation of Arthur Miller's play about the tragedy of an American 'good guy' for whom life turns sour had an air of being done on the cheap; but Fredric March's performance was peerless and the time-transitions were effected with skill and simplicity.

Death Wish (US 1974). Controversial, unpalatable suspenser about a widower who avenges his wife's death at the hands of New York muggers by becoming an armed back street vigilante. After an unpleasant start it develops almost into a comedy but the handling is not skilful enough to avoid a sour taste. Directed by Michael Winner from a novel by Brian Garfield; Charles Bronson was in typically quizzical form and in 1982 continued his performance in a sequel, *Death Wish II*, which certainly overstepped the boundaries of good taste.

Debucourt, Jean (1894–1958) (J. Pelisse). French character actor with long stage experience.
Le Petit Chose 22. La Chute de la Maison Usher 28. Douce 43. Le Diable au Corps 46. Occupe-Toi d'Amélie 49, etc.

? debuts
What stars made their first feature film appearances in the following movies?

1 *Red Haired Alibi* (1932)
2 *The Painted Desert* (1931)
3 *Grand Old Girl* (1935)
4 *Fighter Squadron* (1948)
5 *Late Extra* (1935)
6 *Tall Story* (1960)
7 *Up the River* (1930)
8 *Tammy and the Doctor* (1963)
9 *Golden Boy* (1939)
10 *Las Vegas Nights* (1941)
11 *The Strange Love of Martha Ivers* (1946)
12 *Claudia* (1943)
13 *The Maltese Falcon* (1941)
14 *Night after Night* (1932)
15 *Heaven with a Barbed Wire Fence* (1939)
16 *The Trouble with Harry* (1955)
17 *Four Daughters* (1938)
18 *Port of New York* (1949)
19 *For Me and My Gal* (1942)
20 *Dark City* (1950)
21 *The Invisible Man* (1933)
22 *No Way Out* (1950)
23 *A Devil with Women* (1930)
24 *The Killers* (1945)
25 *Esther Waters* (1947)
26 *This Is the Night* (1932)
27 *The Speckled Band* (1931)
28 *The Queen of Spades* (1948)
29 *Lassie Come Home* (1943)
30 *Bad Sister* (1931)

Decae, Henri (1915–). Distinguished French cinematographer.
Le Silence de la Mer 49. Les Enfants Terribles 49. Crève-Coeur 52. Bob le Flambeur 55. Lift to the Scaffold 57. Le Beau Serge 58. A Double Tour 59. Les Quatre Cents Coups 59. Les Cousins 59. Plein Soleil 59. Les Bonnes Femmes 60. Léon Morin, Priest 61. Sundays and Cybele 62. Dragées au Poivre 63. Viva Maria 65. Weekend at Dunkirk 65. Night of the Generals 66. Le Voleur 67. The Comedians 67. Castle Keep 69. The Sicilian Clan 70. The Light at the Edge of the World 71. Bobby Deerfield 77. The Island 80. Exposed 83.

Decker, Diana (1926–). Bright, blonde, American leading lady, in Britain from 1939; became known through toothpaste commercials ('Irium, Miriam?').
Fiddlers Three 44. Meet Me at Dawn 48. Murder at the Windmill 49. Is Your Honeymoon Really Necessary? 53. Lolita 62. Devils of Darkness 65, etc.
TV series: Mark Saber 54

Deckers, Eugene (1917–1977). French character actor who played continental types in British films after 1946.
Sleeping Car to Trieste 48. The Elusive Pimpernel 50. The Lavender Hill Mob 51. Father Brown 54. Port Afrique 56. Northwest Frontier 59. Lady L 66. The Limbo Line 68, many others.

Decoin, Henri (1896–1969). French director, in films since 1929.
Abus de Confiance 37. Les Inconnus dans la Maison 42. La Fille du Diable 46. Three Telegrams 50. The Truth about Bebe Donge 52. The Lovers of Toledo 53. Razzia sur la Chnouf 55. Charmants Garçons 57. The Face of the Cat 58. Outcasts of Glory 64, many others.

Dee, Frances (1908–) (Jean Dee). American leading lady of the thirties, long married to Joel McCrea; a former extra, she was chosen by Chevalier to play opposite him in her first speaking role.
Playboy of Paris 31. An American Tragedy 31. Rich Man's Folly 32. King of the Jungle 33. Becky Sharp 35. If I Were King 38. So Ends Our Night 41. Meet the Stewarts 42. I Walked with a Zombie 43. Happy Land 43. Bel Ami 48. Four Faces West 48. They Passed This Way 48. Payment on Demand 51. Because of You 53. Mr Scoutmaster 53. Gypsy Colt 54, etc.

Dee, Ruby (1923–). (Ruby Ann Wallace). Black American actress.
No Way Out 50. Tall Target 51. Go Man Go 53. Edge of the City 57. Take a Giant Step 59. *A Raisin in the Sun* 61. The Balcony 62. Buck and the Preacher 72. Black Girl 72. Cat People 82.

Dee, Sandra (1942–) (Alexandra Zuck). Petite American leading lady, former model.
Until They Sail 57. The Reluctant Debutante 58. Gidget 59. *Imitation of Life* 59. A Summer Place 59. Portrait in Black 60. Romanoff and Juliet 61. Come September 62. Tammy and the Doctor 63. Take Her She's Mine 64. That Funny Feeling 65. A Man Could Get Killed 66. Doctor, You've Got to be Kidding 67. Rosie 68. The Daughters of Joshua Cabe (TV) 72. Houston We've Got a Problem (TV) 74. Manhunter (TV) 76. Fantasy Island (TV) 77, etc.

Deeley, Michael (1931–). British producer, latterly EMI executive.
The Case of the Mukkinese Battlehorn 61.

One Way Pendulum 64. Robbery 67. The Italian Job 69. Murphy's War 70. The Man Who Fell to Earth 75. Nickelodeon 76. The Deer Hunter 78, etc.

deep focus. Dramatic camera technique which brings both foreground and background objects into equal focus and clarity; notably used in *Citizen Kane* and *Hamlet.*

The Deer Hunter (US 1978). Marathon piece of American self-flagellation over the Vietnam war; a clear award winner at home, but not easy to sit through for many less directly involved. Its point could certainly have been made in half the time, with more conventional use of film grammar. Written and directed by Michael Cimino (AA); with Robert de Niro, John Cazale, Christopher Walker (AA), John Savage; edited by Peter Zinner (AA). AA best picture.

definitions

¶ A selection, chosen for entertainment rather than instruction.
Agent: A guy who is sore because an actor gets ninety per cent of what he makes.
Casting: Deciding which of two faces the public is least tired of.
Disneyland: The biggest people trap ever built by a mouse.
Double feature: A show that enables you to sit through a picture you don't care to see, so you can see one you don't like.—Henry Morgan
Epic: The easiest kind of picture to make badly.—Charlton Heston
It: The indefinable something.—Elinor Glyn, creator of 'It'
Musicals: A series of catastrophes ending with a floor show.—Oscar Levant
Oomph: The sound a fat man makes when he bends over to tie his laces in a phone booth.—Ann Sheridan
Romanoff's Restaurant: A place where a man can take his wife and family and have a lovely seven-course meal for $3,400.—George Jessel
Starlet: Any woman under thirty not actively employed in a brothel.
Television: A medium, so called because it is neither rare nor well done.—Ernie Kovacs

Defoe, Daniel (1659–1731). English writer whose work included the oft-filmed *Robinson Crusoe* (qv); also *Moll Flanders,* which the 1965 film resembled but slightly.

Defore, Don (1917–). American second lead, the good guy or dumb hearty westerner of dozens of forgettable films in the forties and fifties.
You Can't Escape Forever 42. A Guy Named Joe 43. Thirty Seconds Over Tokyo 44. The Affairs of Susan 45. You Came Along 45. Ramrod 47. Romance on the High Seas 48. Too Late for Tears 48. My Friend Irma 49. Dark City 50. The Guy Who Came Back 51. She's Working Her Way Through College 52. Battle Hymn 57. The Facts of Life 61. A Rare Breed (TV) 81, etc.
TV series: Ozzie and Harriet 52–65. Hazel 61–65.

Degermark, Pia (1949–). Swedish leading lady in international films.
Elvira Madigan 67. The Looking Glass War 71.

Dehn, Paul (1912–1976). British screenwriter, former film critic.
Seven Days to Noon 51. Orders to Kill 58. *Goldfinger* 64. The Spy Who Came in from the Cold 65. The Deadly Affair 66. The Taming of the Shrew 67. Beneath the Planet of the Apes (and two sequels) 67. Fragment of Fear (& p) 69. Murder on the Orient Express 74, etc.

Dehner, John (1915–) (John Forkum). American character actor, usually as sympathetic smart alec or dastardly villain.
Captain Eddie 45. The Secret of St Ives 49. Last of the Buccaneers 50. Lorna Doone 51. Scaramouche 52. Apache 54. Carousel 56. The Left-handed Gun (as Pat Garrett) 58. Timbuktu 59. The Chapman Report 62. Critic's Choice 63. Youngblood Hawke 63. Stiletto 69. Support Your Local Gunfighter 71. Fun with Dick and Jane 77. The Boys from Brazil 78, etc.
TV series: The Roaring Twenties 61. The Baileys of Balboa 64. The Virginian 67. The Doris Day Show 71. Temperatures Rising 73. Big Hawaii 77. The Boys from Brazil 78. Enos 80. The Right Stuff 83. Creator 84. Jagged Edge 85.

Deighton, Len (1929–). British writer of convoluted spy thrillers.
The Ipcress File (oa) 63. Funeral in Berlin (oa) 66. Billion Dollar Brain (oa) 67. Only When I Larf (w) 68, etc.

Dekker, Albert (1905–1968). Dutch-American stage actor of long experience; film career disappointing.
□The Great Garrick 37. Marie Antoinette 38. The Last Warning 38. She Married an Artist

38. The Lone Wolf in Paris 38. Extortion 38. Paris Honeymoon 39. Never Say Die 39. Hotel Imperial 39. Beau Geste 39. The Man in the Iron Mask 39. The Great Commandment 39. *Dr Cyclops* 40. Strange Cargo 40. Rangers of Fortune 40. Seven Sinners 40. You're the One 41. Blonde Inspiration 41. Reaching for the Sun 41. Buy Me That Town 41. Honky Tonk 41. *Among the Living* 41. Night in New Orleans 42. Wake Island 42. Once Upon a Honeymoon 42. Star Spangled Rhythm 42. The Lady Has Plans 42. In Old California 42. Yokel Boy 42. The Forest Rangers 42. Woman of the Town 43. War of the Wildcats 43. Buckskin Frontier 43. The Kansan 43. Experiment Perilous 44. Incendiary Blonde 45. Hold that Blonde 45. Salome Where She Danced 45. The French Key 46. *The Killers* 46. California 46. Suspense 46. The Pretender 47. Gentleman's Agreement 47. Wyoming 47. Cass Timberland 47. Slave Girl 47. The Fabulous Texan 47. Fury at Furnace Creek 48. Lulu Belle 48. Search for Danger 49. Bride of Vengeance 49. Tarzan's Magic Fountain 49. The Kid from Texas 50. Destination Murder 50. The Furies 50. As Young as You Feel 51. Wait til the Sun Shines Nellie 52. The Silver Chalice 54. East of Eden 55. Kiss Me Deadly 55. Illegal 55. She Devil 57. These Thousand Hills 59. Middle of the Night 59. The Wonderful Country 59. Suddenly Last Summer 59. The Sound and the Fury 59. Come Spy with Me 67. The Wild Bunch 69.

Del Giudice, Filippo (1892–1961). Italian producer who settled in England and became managing director of Two Cities Films.
French without Tears 39. In Which We Serve 42. Henry V 44. The Way Ahead 44. Blithe Spirit 45. Odd Man Out 47. The Guinea Pig 48, many others.

Del Rio, Dolores (1905–1983) (Dolores Asunsolo). Mexican leading lady with aristocratic background; beautiful and popular star of the twenties and thirties.
Joanna (debut) 25. High Stepper 26. What Price Glory? 27. *The Loves of Carmen* 27. Resurrection 28. Evangeline 29. The Bad One 30. The Dove 31. Bird of Paradise 32. Flying Down to Rio 33. Wonder Bar 34. Madame Du Barry 34. Lancer Spy 37. *Journey into Fear* 42. Portrait of Maria 45. The Fugitive 47. *Cheyenne Autumn* 64. Once upon a Time 67, many others.

Del Ruth, Roy (1895–1961). Very competent American director, former gag writer for Mack Sennett.
□SOUND FILMS: Conquest 29. The Desert Song 29. The Hottentot 29. Gold Diggers of Broadway 29. The Aviator 29. Hold Everything 30. The Second Floor Mystery 30. Three Faces East 30. The Life of the Party 30. My Past 31. Divorce Among Friends 31. *The Maltese Falcon* 31. Side Show 31. Blonde Crazy 31. Taxi 32. Beauty and the Boss 32. Winner Take All 32. *Blessed Event* 32. Employees Entrance 33. The Mind Reader 33. The Little Giant 33. Captured 33. Bureau of Missing Persons 33. *Lady Killer* 33. Bulldog Drummond Strikes Back 34. Upperworld 34. Kid Millions 34. *Folies Bergere* 35. Broadway Melody of 1936 35. *Thanks a Million* 35. It Had to Happen 36. Private Number 36. Born to Dance 36. *On the Avenue* 37. Broadway Melody of 1938 37. Happy Landing 38. My Lucky Star 38. Tail Spin 39. The Star Maker 39. Here I Am A Stranger 39. He Married His Wife 40. *Topper Returns* 41. The Chocolate Soldier 41. Maisie Gets Her Man 42. Dubarry was a Lady 43. Broadway Rhythm 44. Barbary Coast Gent 44. It Happened on Fifth Avenue 47. The Babe Ruth Story 48. The Red Light 49. Always Leave Them Laughing 49. West Point Story 50. On Moonlight Bay 51. Starlift 51. About Face 52. Stop You're Killing Me 52. Three Sailors and a Girl 53. Phantom of the Rue Morgue 54. The Alligator People 59. Why Must I Die 60.

Delair, Suzy (1916–). Vivacious French entertainer, in several films.
Quai des Orfèvres 47. Lady Paname 49. Robinson Crusoe Land 50. Gervaise 55. Rocco and his Brothers 60. Is Paris Burning? 66, etc.

Delaney, Shelagh (1939–). British playwright whose chief contributions to the screen are *A Taste of Honey* and *Charlie Bubbles*.

Delannoy, Jean (1908–). French director, formerly journalist and cutter.
La Symphonie Pastorale 40. *L'Eternel Retour* 43. Les Jeux Sont Faits 47. *Dieu a Besoin des Hommes* 49. Le Garçon Sauvage 51. The Moment of Truth 52. Marie Antoinette 56. Notre Dame de Paris 56. Maigret Sets a Trap 57. Le Soleil des Voyous 67, many others.

Delerue, Georges (1924–). French composer.
Hiroshima Mon Amour 58. Les Jeux de L'Amour 60. Une Aussi Longue Absence 61. Shoot the Pianist 61. Jules et Jim 61. Silken

Skin 63. The Pumpkin Eater 64. Viva Maria 65. A Man for All Seasons 66. The 25th Hour 67. Interlude 68. Women in Love 69. The Conformist 70. The Horseman 70. The Day of the Dolphin 73. The Slap 74. Julia 77. Tendre Poulet 77. Get Out Your Handkerchiefs 78. A Little Romance (AA) 79. Love on the Run 79. True Confessions 81. Partners 82. The Escape Artist 82. Exposed 83. Agnes of God 85, many others.

Delevanti, Cyril (1887–1975). British-born stage actor who played aged gentlemen for many years.
Mary Poppins 64. *Night of the Iguana* 64. The Greatest Story Ever Told 65. Counterpoint 67. The Killing of Sister George 68. Bedknobs and Broomsticks 71. Black Eye 73, many others.

Delfont, Bernard (Lord Delfont, formerly Barnet Winogradsky) (1910–). British show business entrepreneur, brother of Lord Grade; mainly involved in live entertainment until the seventies when he came to head the EMI entertainment complex.

Deliverance (US 1972). A curiously harsh, violent fable about four men who go out to challenge the elements and end up humbled or injured by nature's strength and their own weaknesses. Directed by John Boorman from a novel by James Dickey; with Burt Reynolds, Jon Voight, Ronny Cox, Ned Beatty.

Dell, Dorothy (1915–1934) (Dorothy Goff). American beauty queen whose film career was cut short by a car crash.
□Wharf Angel 34. Little Miss Marker 34. Shoot the Works 34.

Dell, Gabriel (1920–). (Gabriel del Vecchio) American actor, one of the original Dead End Kids (qv) who in the sixties emerged as a TV character actor.

Dell, Jeffrey (1904–85). British comedy writer, author in the thirties of *Nobody Ordered Wolves*, a satirical novel of the film industry.
Sanders of the River (co-w) 35. The Saint's Vacation 41. Thunder Rock (co-w) 42. *Don't Take it to Heart* (& d) 44. It's Hard to Be Good (& d) 48. The Dark Man (& d) 50. Brothers-in-Law (co-w) 56. Lucky Jim (co-w) 58. Carlton-Browne of the F.O. (& co-d) 59. A French Mistress (co-w) 61. Rotten to the Core (co-w) 65. The Family Way (co-w) 66, etc.

Delluc, Louis (1892–1924). Pioneer French director of the twenties, associated with the impressionist school.
□Fièvre 21. La Femme de Nulle Part 22. L'Innondation 24.

Delon, Alain (1935–). Romantic-looking French leading man.
Plein Soleil 59. Rocco and his Brothers 60. The Eclipse 61. The Leopard 62. The Big Snatch 63. The Black Tulip 64. The Yellow Rolls Royce 64. The Love Cage 65. Once a Thief 65. Lost Command 66. Is Paris Burning? 66. Texas Across the River 66. Les Aventuriers 66. Histoires Extraordinaires 67. Diabolically Yours 67. Samurai 67. Girl on a Motorcycle 67. La Piscine 67. Jeff 68. *Borsalino* 70. The Sicilian Clan 70. The Red Circle 70. Red Sun 71. The Assassination of Trotsky 72. Scorpio 72. Dirty Money 72. Borsalino and Co. 73. Shock 74. The Investigator 74. The Gypsy 75. Zorro 75. Mr Klein 76. Farewell Friend 77. The Concorde – Airport 79 79. Harmonie 79. Trois Hommes à Abattre 80. *Swann in Love* 84. Cop's Honour 85. The Passage 86, etc.

Delon, Nathalie (1938–) (Francine Canovas). French leading actress.
Le Samourai 67. La Sorelle 69. When Eight Bells Toll 71. Bluebeard 72. The Romantic Englishwoman 75, etc.

Delorme, Daniele (1926–) (Gabrielle Girard). French leading lady.
Gigi 48. La Cage aux Filles 49. Sans Laisser d'Adresse 51. Tempi Nostri 54. Prisons de Femmes 58. La Guerre des Boutons (p only) 62. Pardon Mon Affaire 77.

Delvaux, André (1926–). Belgian director.
The Man Who Had His Hair Cut Short 67. Un Soir Un Train 68. *Rendezvous at Bray* 73, etc.

Demarest, William (1892–1983). American character actor, an 'old pro' with vast vaudeville experience before film debut in 1927.
The Jazz Singer 27. Fingerprints 27. The Murder Man 35. Wedding Present 36. Rosalie 38. Mr Smith Goes to Washington 39. Tin Pan Alley 40. The Great McGinty 40. *Sullivan's Travels* 41. The Palm Beach Story 42. *Hail the Conquering Hero* 43. *The Miracle of Morgan's Creek* (as Officer Kockenlocker) 43. Once upon a Time 44. Pardon My Past 45. Along Came Jones 45. *The Jolson Story* 46. The Perils of Pauline 47. On Our Merry Way 49. Jolson Sings Again 50. *The First*

Legion 51. Riding High 51. Dangerous When Wet 52. Escape from Fort Bravo 53. Jupiter's Darling 54. The Rawhide Years 56. Son of Flubber 63. It's a Mad Mad Mad Mad World 63. That Darn Cat 65. The McCullochs 75. Won Ton Ton 76, over a hundred others.
TV series: Wells Fargo 56–58. Love and Marriage 59. My Three Sons 67–71.
❀ For his reliability in a wide variety of roles, and for his ability to be instantly recognized and welcomed by people who didn't know his name. *Hail the Conquering Hero*.

Demick, Irina (1937–). Franco-Russian leading lady in international films.
The Longest Day 62. Those Magnificent Men in Their Flying Machines 65. Up From The Beach 65. Cloportes 65. Prudence and the Pill 68, etc.

Demme, Jonathan (1944–). American director.
Caged Heat 74. Crazy Mama 75. Fighting Mad 77. Citizens' Band 78. Last Embrace 78. *Melvin and Howard* 80. Something Wild 87.

Demongeot, Mylene (1936–). Blonde French leading lady, briefly flaunted as sex symbol.
Les Enfants de L'Amour 54. It's a Wonderful World (GB) 56. *The Witches of Salem* 56. Bonjour Tristesse 57. Upstairs and Downstairs (GB) 59. The Giant of Marathon 60. Gold for the Caesars 62. Uncle Tom's Cabin (Ger.) 65. Fantomas 66. The Vengeance of Fantomas 67. The Private Navy of Sgt O'Farrell 68. By the Blood of Others 77, etc.

Dempster, Austin (–). British cinematographer.
Bedazzled 67. Otley 69. The Looking Glass War 69, etc.

Dempster, Carol (1901–). American leading lady of the silent screen, especially for D. W. Griffith.
Scarlet Days 19. The Love Flower 20. Dream Street 21. *One Exciting Night* 22. America 24. Isn't Life Wonderful? 24. That Royle Girl 26. The Sorrows of Satan 26, etc.

Demy, Jacques (1931–). French director.
□*Lola* 60. The Seven Deadly Sins (part) 61. La Baie des Anges 62. *Les Parapluies de Cherbourg* 64. The Young Girls of Rochefort 67. The Model Shop (US) 70. Peau d'Ane 71. The Pied Piper 72. The Slightly Pregnant Man 73. Lady Oscar 79.

Dench, Dame Judi (1934–). British stage actress.
□The Third Secret 64. A Study in Terror 65. He Who Rides a Tiger 66. Four in the Morning (BFA) 66. A Midsummer Night's Dream 68. Luther 73. Dead Cert 74. Saigon – Year of the Cat (TV) 83. Wetherby 84. 84 Charing Cross Road 87. A Handful of Dust 88.
TV series: A Fine Romance 81–84.

Deneuve, Catherine (1943–) (Catherine Dorleac). French leading lady, sister of Françoise Dorleac.
Vice and Virtue 62. *Les Parapluies de Cherbourg* 64. *Repulsion* (GB) 65. Das Liebeskarussell (Who Wants to Sleep?) 65. Les Créatures 66. The Young Girls of Rochefort 67. *Belle de Jour* 67. Benjamin 68. Manon 70 68. Mayerling 68. The April Fools (US) 69. The Mississippi Mermaid 69. *Tristana* 70. Peau d'Ane 71. The Lady in Red Boots 74. Hustle 76. Le Sauvage 76. L'Argent des Autres 78. Ils Sont Grands ces Petits 79. Le Dernier Metro 80. The Hunger 83. Abattre 80. The African 84. Fort Saganne 85. The Scene of the Crime 86, etc.

Denham. An English village north of London where in 1936 Korda opened a huge film studio which was later taken over by the Rank Organisation but closed in the fifties so that production could be concentrated at Pinewood a few miles away.

Denham, Maurice (1909–). British character actor with stage experience from 1934.
It's Not Cricket 48. London Belongs to Me 48. The Spider and the Fly 50. The Million Pound Note 54. Simon and Laura 55. Checkpoint 56. Night of the Demon 57. Our Man in Havana 59. Sink the Bismarck 60. HMS Defiant 62. The Seventh Dawn 64. Hysteria 65. The Alphabet Murders 65. After the Fox 66. The Midas Run 69. The Virgin and the Gypsy 70. Countess Dracula 70. Nicholas and Alexandra 71. Luther 73. Shout at the Devil 75. Julia 77. 84 Charing Cross Road, and many others.

Denham, Reginald (1894–1983). British playwright (usually with Edward Percy) who also directed several films.
Borrow a Million 34. Death at Broadcasting House 34. The Price of Wisdom 35. Lucky Days 35. The House of the Spaniard 36. Kate Plus Ten 38. Anna of Brooklyn 59, etc.

Denison, Michael (1915–). British leading man with firm but gentle manner; married to Dulcie Gray.
Autobiography 1973: *Overture and Beginners.*
Tilly of Bloomsbury 40. Hungry Hill 46. *My Brother Jonathan* 47. *The Glass Mountain* 47. The Blind Goddess 48. The Importance of Being Earnest 51. Angels One Five 51. The Franchise Affair 52. Landfall 53. The Tall Headlines 52. The Truth about Women 56. Faces in the Dark 61, etc.

Denmark: see *Danish cinema.*

Dennehy, Brian (1940–). Heavily built American character actor, mostly on television.
□Johnny We Hardly Knew Ye (TV) 77. It Happened at Lakewood Manor (TV) 77. Semi Tough 77. Foul Play 78. Ruby and Oswald (TV) 78. A Death in Canaan (TV) 78. A Real American Hero (as Buford Pusser) (TV) 78. Pearl (TV) 79. Silent Victor (TV) 79. '10' 79. Butch and Sundance 79. Little Miss Marker 80. A Rumour of War (TV) 80. Split Image 82. First Blood 82. Gorky Park 83. Never Cry Wolf 83. Cocoon 85. Silverado 85. Twice in a Lifetime 85. Legal Eagles 86. The Belly of an Architect 87. Best Seller 87.
TV series: *Big Shamus Little Shamus* 79. Star of the Family 82.

Denner, Charles (1926–). French leading actor.
Landru 62. *Life Upside Down* 63. The Sleeping Car Murder 66. The Two of Us 68. The Bride Wore Black 68. A Gorgeous Bird Like Me 72. And Now My Love 75. The Man Who Loved Women 77. Le Coeur a L'Envers 80, etc.

Denning, Richard (1914–) (Louis A. Denninger). American leading man who from 1937 played light romantic roles and manly athletes.
Hold 'Em Navy 37. Persons in Hiding 38. Union Pacific 39. Golden Gloves 40. Adam Had Four Sons 41. Beyond the Blue Horizon 42. The Glass Key 42. Seven Were Saved 46. Black Beauty 46. Caged Fury 48. No Man of Her Own 48. Weekend with Father 50. Scarlet Angel 51. Hangman's Knot 53. The Creature from the Black Lagoon 54. Assignment Redhead (GB) 56. The Black Scorpion 57. Twice Told Tales 63, many others, mainly second features.
TV series: Mr and Mrs North 53–54. The Flying Doctor 59. Michael Shayue 60. Karen 64. Hawaii Five-O (occasionally) 68–79.

Dennis, Sandy (1937–) (Sandra Dale Dennis). American leading actress.
□Splendour in the Grass 61. *Who's Afraid of Virginia Woolf?* (AA) 66. Up the Down Staircase 67. The Fox 68. Sweet November 68. That Cold Day in the Park 69. A Touch of Love 69. The Out-of-Towners 69. The Only Way Out is Dead 70. Something Evil (TV) 71. Mr Sycamore 75. Nasty Habits 76. God Told Me To 76. Three Sisters 77. Perfect Gentlemen (TV) 78. The Four Seasons 81. Come Back to the Five and Dime, Jimmy Dean, Jimmy Dean 82. The Execution (TV) 84.

¶ *Pauline Kael on S.D.:* She has made an acting style out of post-nasal drip.
S.D.: When you finish an acting stint, there's nothing except money. You have to keep going, giving the best you've got, to get something intangible.

Denny, Reginald (1891–1967) (Reginald Leigh Daymore). British actor, on stage from childhood. From 1919 starred in many Hollywood action comedies and when sound came in began to play amiable stiff-upper-lip Britishers. More or less retired after 1950 to devote time to his aircraft company.
49 East 20. Footlights 21. *The Leather Pushers* 22. The Abysmal Brute 23. *Skinner's Dress Suit* 25. Oh Doctor 26. California Straight Ahead 27. Embarrassing Moments 29. Madame Satan 30. Private Lives 32. Of Human Bondage 34. Anna Karenina 35. Romeo and Juliet 36. Several Bulldog Drummond films 37–38 (as Algy). *Rebecca* (as Frank Crawley) 40. Sherlock Holmes and the Voice of Terror 42. Love Letters 45. The Macomber Affair 47. The Secret Life of Walter Mitty 47. *Mr Blandings Builds His Dream House* (as Mr Simms) 48. Abbott and Costello Meet Dr Jekyll and Mr Hyde 53. Around the World in Eighty Days 56. Fort Vengeance 59. Cat Ballou 65. Batman 66, many others.

Dent, Vernon (1894–1963). American character actor, a pompous butt for the Three Stooges in many of their two-reelers.

dentists are seldom popular chaps, but Preston Sturges made a film about one of them, the inventor of laughing gas: *The Great Moment. The Counterfeit Traitor* had a spy dentist. Sinister dentists were found in *The Man Who Knew Too Much* (original version), *The Secret Partner,* and *Footsteps in the Dark,* and a comic one, in the person of Bob Hope, in *The Paleface.* Dentistry is the subject of two British farces: *Dentist in the Chair* and *Dentist on the Job*. W. C. Fields once made a film of his sketch *The Dentist*; and Laurel and Hardy in *Leave 'Em Laughing* were overcome by laughing gas. The most notable dentist hero was in the twice remade *One Sunday Afternoon*; and the most villainous dentist is certainly Laurence Olivier in *Marathon Man*. The dentist with the most hectic private life was Walter Matthau in *Cactus Flower*.

Denver, Bob (1935–). American TV comedian.
Take Her She's Mine 63. For Those Who Think Young 64. Who's Minding the Mint? 67. The Sweet Ride 67. Do You Know The One About the Travelling Saleslady 68, etc.
TV series: Dobie Gillis 59–62. Gilligan's Island 64–66. The Good Guys 68. Dusty's Trail 73.

Denver, John (1943–) (Henry John Deutschendorf Jnr). American guitarist, singer and songwriter whose first film was *Oh God* 77.

Depardieu, Gérard (1948–). French leading actor.
Le Tueur 71. L'Affaire Dominici 72. Deux Hommes dans la Ville 73. Les Valseuses 74. Stavisky 74. Vincent François Paul et les Autres 75. La Dernière Femme 76. 1900 76. Le Camion 77. Get Out Your Handkerchiefs 78. Le Sucre 78. Le Dernier Metro 80. Mon Oncle d'Amérique 80. The Woman Next Door 81. Danton 82. The Moon in the Gutter 83. Fort Saganne 85. Jean de Florette 85. Street of Departures 86. Under the Sun of Satan 87.

¶ 'There appears to be nothing he cannot do well on the screen.'—*New York Times*

department stores have usually been a background for comedy. New York store backgrounds have often shown the native superiority of the working girl to snobbish shopwalkers and obtuse management, as in *Bachelor Mother* and its remake *Bundle of Joy, The Devil and Miss Jones* and the 1924 *Manhandled*. Broader comedy elements were to the fore in *Miracle on 34th Street, Modern Times, The Big Store, Who's Minding the Store?, Fitzwilly* and *How to Save a Marriage*. British comedies with store settings include *Kipps, The Crowded Day, Laughter in Paradise, Keep Fit,* and *Trouble in Store*.

Deray, Jacques (1927–). French director.
Le Gigolo 60. Rififi in Tokyo 61. Symphony for a Massacre 63. Our Man in Marrakesh 66. The Swimming Pool 69. Borsalino 70. The Outside Man 72. Flic Story 75. Le Gang 77. A Butterfly on the Shoulder 78. Trois Hommes à Abattre 80. Le Marginal 83, etc.

Derek, Bo (1957–) (Mary Cathleen Collins). American pin-up who rather curiously caused a press sensation in her first starring film. Wife of John Derek.
□Orca Killer Whale 77. '10' 79. A Change of Seasons 80. Tarzan the Ape Man 81. Fantasies 81. Bolero 84.

Derek, John (1926–) (Derek Harris). American light-leading man.
I'll Be Seeing You 45. *Knock on any Door* 49. *All The King's Men* 49. *Rogues of Sherwood Forest* 50. Mask of the Avenger 51. Scandal Sheet 51. Mission Over Korea 53. The Adventures of Hajji Baba 54. *Prince of Players* 55. Run for Cover 55. The Leather Saint 56. The Ten Commandments 56. Omar Khayyam 57. Prisoner of the Volga 60. Exodus 60. Nightmare in the Sun 64. Once Before I Die (& d) 66. Childish Things (& d) 69. Tarzan the Ape Man (& ph) 81. Fantasies (& ph) 81. Bolero 84, etc.
TV series: Frontier Circus 61.

Dern, Bruce (1936–). American general purpose actor, usually seen as tough guy or psychotic.
Wild River 60. Marnie 64. The Wild Angels 66. The Trip 67. The War Wagon 67. Will Penny 68. Castle Keep 69. Number One 69. They Shoot Horses Don't They? 69. Bloody Mama 70. The Incredible Two-headed Transplant 70. Drive He Said 71. The Cowboys 72. *Silent Running* 72. The King of Marvin Gardens 72. The Laughing Policeman 73. The Great Gatsby 74. Posse 75. *Family Plot* 75. *Smile* 75. Black Sunday 76. Won Ton Ton 77. *Coming Home* 78. The Driver 78. Middle Age Crazy 80. Tattoo 81. Harry Tracy 81. That Championship Season 82. On the Edge 84. The Big Town 87, etc.
TV series: Stony Burke 62.

¶ *B.D.:* I've played more psychotics and freaks and dopers than anyone.

Dern, Laura (1966–). American actress of the eighties, daughter of Bruce Dern.
Teachers 84. Mask 85. Smooth Talk 86.

Derr, Richard (1917–). American leading man, usually in minor films.

Ten Gentlemen from West Point 42. Tonight We Raid Calais 43. The Secret Heart 47. Joan of Arc 48. When Worlds Collide 51. Something To Live For 52. Terror is a Man 59. Three in the Attic 68. The Drowning Pool 75, etc.

Desailly, Jean (1920–). French leading man.
Le Voyageur de la Toussaint 42. Sylvie et la Fantôme 45. *Occupe-Toi d'Amélie* 49. Les Grandes Manoeuvres 55. Maigret Sets a Trap 59. Le Doulos 62. *Le Peau Douce* 64. The Twenty-Fifth Hour 66. Un Flic 72. The Assassination of Trotsky 72. Le Cavaleur 74. Pile ou Face 80. Le Professionel 81. Le Fou du Roi 84, etc.

Deschanel, Caleb (1944–). American cinematographer.
The Black Stallion 79. More American Graffiti 79. Being There 79. The Escape Artist (d) 82. The Right Stuff (AAN) 83. The Natural (AAN) 84.

desert islands have provided the locale of many a film adventure. *Robinson Crusoe* has been filmed several times, with two recent variations in *Robinson Crusoe on Mars* and *Lt. Robin Crusoe USN*. *Treasure Island* too has survived three or four versions, to say nothing of imitations like *Blackbeard the Pirate* and parodies such as *Abbott and Costello Meet Captain Kidd* and *Old Mother Riley's Jungle Treasure*. *The Admirable Crichton* (qv) is perhaps the next most overworked desert island story, with *The Swiss Family Robinson* following on. Dorothy Lamour found a few desert islands in films like *Typhoon* and *Aloma of the South Seas*; the inhabitants of *The Little Hut* had one nearly to themselves; Joan Greenwood and co. were marooned on a rather special one in *Mysterious Island*. *Our Girl Friday* played the theme for sex; *Dr Dolittle* found educated natives on one; Cary Grant lived on one as a reluctant spy in *Father Goose*. *Sea Wife*, *Lord of the Flies* and *The Day the Fish Came Out* were three recent but not very successful attempts to take the theme seriously: *Hell in the Pacific* was one that did work. *The Blue Lagoon* was treated decorously in the fifties and sexily in the eighties.

A comic TV series on the subject was *Gilligan's Island* 64–66; a serious one, *The New People* 69.

The Desert Song. The popular operetta by Sigmund Romberg, Otto Harbach and Oscar Hammerstein was filmed in 1929, with John Boles and Carlotta King; in 1943, with Dennis Morgan and Irene Manning, and in 1952, with Gordon Macrae and Kathryn Grayson.

deserts have figured in many a western, from *Tumbleweed* to *Mackenna's Gold*. Other films which have paid particularly respectful attention to the dangers that too much sand can provide include *The Sheik* and *Son of the Sheik*, *Greed*, *The Lost Patrol*, *The Garden of Allah*, *Sahara*, *Five Graves to Cairo*, *Ice Cold in Alex*, *Sea of Sand*, *Desert Rats*, *Play Dirty*, *An Eye for an Eye*, *Inferno*, *Zabriskie Point*, *The Sabre and the Arrow*, *Legend of the Lost*, *The Ten Commandments*, *She*, *Lawrence of Arabia*, *The Black Tent*, *Oasis*, *Sands of The Kalahari*, *The Flight of the Phoenix*, *Garden of Evil* and *The Professionals*.

Desmond, Florence (1905–) (Florence Dawson). British dancer and impersonator, seen in many stage revues but few films.
Sally in Our Alley 31. No Limit 35. *Keep Your Seats Please* 37. Hoots Mon 40. Three Came Home (US) 50. Charley Moon 56. Some Girls Do 68, etc.

Desmond, William (1878–1949) (William Mannion). Irish leading man of the American silent screen, mostly in westerns.
The Sunset Trail 24. Blood and Steel 26. Tongues of Scandal 29. Hell Bent for Frisco 31. Flying Fury 33. Arizona Days 36, etc.

Desmonde, Jerry (1908–1967). British character actor with long music-hall experience, a perfect foil for comedians from Sid Field to Norman Wisdom.
London Town 46. Cardboard Cavalier 48. Follow a Star 59. A Stitch in Time 63. The Early Bird 65, many others.

Desni, Tamara (1913–). Russian-born, British-resident leading lady.
Jack Ahoy 34. Fire over England 36. The Squeaker 37. Traitor Spy 40. Send for Paul Temple 46. Dick Barton at Bay 50, etc.

Desny, Ivan (1922–). Continental leading man, in films from 1948.
Madeleine (GB) 50. La Putain Respectueuse 52. Lola Montes 55. Anastasia 56. The Mirror Has Two Faces 58. The Magnificent Rebel 60. Das Liebeskarussel (Who Wants to Sleep?) 65. The Mystery of Thug Island 66. I Killed Rasputin 68. Mayerling 68. The Adventures of Gerard 70. Paper Tiger 75. The Marriage of Maria Braun 78. Bloodline 79. The Lady without Camelias 80, etc.

Destry Rides Again (US 1939). Tragi-comic western based on Max Brand's story of the diffident hero who finally buckles on his guns. (Filmed several times, the latest being the 1955 *Destry* with Audie Murphy, it also in 1964 became a TV series with John Gavin.) This version has become a classic for several reasons: Marlene Dietrich's brilliant comeback performance as Frenchy, with songs like 'See What the Boys in the Back Room Will Have'; George Marshall's crisply professional direction; and near-perfect cast including James Stewart, Mischa Auer, Charles Winninger, Samuel S. Hinds, Brian Donlevy and Una Merkel (whose on-screen fight with Dietrich caused a mild censorship problem at the time).

Deutsch, Adolph (1897–1980). American composer associated with Warner and MGM.
The Smiling Lieutenant 31. The Great Garrick 37. Indianapolis Speedway 39. The Fighting 69th 40. They Drive By Night 40. *The Maltese Falcon* 41. High Sierra 41. Across the Pacific 42. The Mask of Dimitros 43. Uncertain Glory 44. Intruder in the Dust 49. Father of the Bride 50. The Long Long Trailer 53. The Rack 56. Tea and Sympathy 56. The Matchmaker 57. Les Girls 57. Some Like It Hot 59. The Apartment 60, many others.

Deutsch, David (1926–). British producer, in films from 1949. Son of Oscar Deutsch who founded the Odeon circuit.
Blind Date 59. Nothing But the Best 64. Catch Us If You Can 65. Lock Up Your Daughters 69, etc.

Deutsch, Ernst (1890–1969). German character actor.
Die Rache der Toten (debut) 16. The Golem 20. Lady Godiva 21. The Marriage of Corbal (GB) 35. Nurse Edith Cavell (US) 39. The Man I Married (US) 40. So Ends Our Night (US) 41. The Third Man (GB) 49. Der Wasserdoktor 58.

Devane, William (1939–). Craggy, toothy American leading actor who rode the crest for a while in the late seventies.
□The Pursuit of Happiness 71. My Old Man's Place 71. McCabe and Mrs Miller 71. Mortadella 71. Irish Whiskey Rebellion 73. The Bait (TV) 73. Crime Club (TV) 73. *Missiles of October* (TV) (as John F. Kennedy) 73. Report to the Commissioner 75. *Fear on Trial* (TV) (as John Henry Faulk) 75. *Family Plot* 76. Marathon Man 76. Red Alert (TV) 77. Black Beauty (TV) 77. The Bad News Bears in Breaking Training 77. Rolling Thunder 77. *From Here to Eternity* (TV) 79. Yanks 79. The Dark 79. Honky Tonk Freeway 81. Testament 83.
Jane Doe (TV) 84.
TV series: Knots Landing 84– .

Devereaux, Ed (–). Australian character actor who in addition to starring in the *Skippy* TV series appeared in some international films.
Floods of Fear 58. Carry on Regardless 61. The Wrong Arm of the Law 63. They're a Weird Mob 66. The Nickel Queen 71. Barry Mackenzie Holds His Own 74. Pressure 75, etc.

the devil has made frequent appearances in movies. There were versions of *Faust* in 1900, 1903, 1904, 1907, 1909, 1911, 1921 and 1925, the last of these featuring Emil Jannings as Mephistopheles. Later variations on this theme include *The Sorrows of Satan* 27, with Adolphe Menjou; *All That Money Can Buy* 41, with Walter Huston as Mr Scratch; *Alias Nick Beal* 49, with Ray Milland; *La Beauté du Diable* 50 with Gérard Philippe; *Damn Yankees* 58 with Ray Walston; *Bedazzled* 67 with Peter Cook; and *Doctor Faustus* 68 with Andreas Teuber. In other stories, Satan was played by Helge Nissen in *Leaves From Satan's Book* 20, Jules Berry in *Les Visiteurs du Soir* 42, Alan Mowbray in *The Devil with Hitler* 42, Rex Ingram in *Cabin in the Sky* 43, Laird Cregar in *Heaven Can Wait* 43, Claude Rains in *Angel on My Shoulder* 46, Stanley Holloway in *Meet Mr Lucifer* 53, Richard Devon in *The Undead* 57, Vincent Price in *The Story of Mankind* 57, Cedric Hardwicke in *Bait* 54, Vittorio Gassman in *The Devil in Love* 67, Stig Järrel in *The Devil's Eye* 60, Donald Pleasence in *The Greatest Story Ever Told* 65, Burgess Meredith in *Torture Garden* 68, Pierre Clement in *The Milky Way* 68, Ralph Richardson in *Tales From the Crypt* 71. In the Swedish *Witchcraft through the Ages* 21 the devil was played by the director, Benjamin Christensen. Devil worship has been the subject of *The Black Cat* 34, *The Seventh Victim* 43, *Night of the Demon* 57, *Back from the Dead* 57, *The Witches* 66, *Eye of the Devil* 66, *The Devil Rides Out* 68, *Rosemary's Baby* 68; while the last-named presaged a rash of diabolically-inspired children in *The Exorcist, I Don't Want to be Born, It's Alive, Devil Within Her* and *The Omen*.

? Who played the devil—or his emissary in the following?

1 *The Devil with Hitler*
2 *Les Visiteurs du Soir*
3 *Cabin in the Sky*
4 *Heaven Can Wait*
5 *Angel on My Shoulder*
6 *The Story of Mankind*
7 *Damn Yankees*
8 *Tales from the Crypt*
9 *All That Money Can Buy*
10 *Meet Mr Lucifer*
11 *The Sorrows of Satan*
12 *Alias Nick Beal*

Deville, Michel (1931–). French director.
Ce Soir ou Jamais 60. L'Appartement de Filles 63. Benjamin 67. Bye Bye Barbara 69. The Bear and the Doll 71. La Femme en Bleu 73. Love at the Top 74. L'Apprenti Salaud 77. Le Dossier 51 79. Le Voyage en douce 80. Eaux Profondes 81. La Petite Bande 83. Peril en la Demeure 84, etc.

Devil's Island, the French Guianan penal colony, has intermittently fascinated film-makers. Apart from the versions of the Dreyfus case (*Dreyfus, The Life of Emile Zola, I Accuse*), there have been Ronald Colman in *Condemned to Devil's Island,* Donald Woods in *I Was a Prisoner on Devil's Island*, Boris Karloff in *Devil's Island*, Clark Gable in *Strange Cargo*, Humphrey Bogart in *Passage to Marseilles*, Bogart and company in *We're No Angels*, Eartha Kitt in *Saint of Devil's Island*, Steve McQueen in *Papillon*, and Jim Brown in *I Escaped From Devil's Island*. The prison colony opened in 1852 and closed in 1946.

Devine, Andy (1905–1977). Fat, husky-voiced American character comedian, seen in innumerable westerns.
We Americans 28. Hot Stuff 29. Law and Order 32. Midnight Mary 33. Stingaree 34. Way Down East 35. Romeo and Juliet 36. A Star is Born 37. In Old Chicago 28. *Stagecoach* 39. When the Daltons Rode 40. Badlands of Dakota 41. Sin Town 42. Crazy House 43. Ghost Catchers 44. Frisco Sal 45. Canyon Passage 46. The Vigilantes Return 47. Old Los Angeles 48. *The Red Badge of Courage* 51. New Mexico 51. Montana Belle 52. Island in the Sky 53. Pete Kelly's Blues 55. The Adventures of Huckleberry Finn 60. Two Rode Together 61. The Man who Shot Liberty Valance 62. It's a Mad Mad Mad Mad World 63. Zebra in the Kitchen 65. The Ballad of Josie 68. A Whale of a Tale 77, many others.
TV series: *Wild Bill Hickok* 51-54. Andy's Gang 57. Flipper 64.

Devon, Laura (1940–). American leading lady from TV.
Goodbye Charlie 65. Red Line 7000 66. Gunn 67, etc.

Devry, Elaine (1935–). American leading lady.
Mantrap 61. Diary of a Madman 63. Guide for the Married Man 67. The Boy Who Cried Werewolf 73, etc.

Dewaere, Patrick (1946–1982). French leading man.
Les Mariés de l'An II 70. Going Places 73. Get Out Your Handkerchiefs 78. Coup de Tête 78. Psy 80. Hotel of the Americas 81. Plein Sud 81. Paradise for All 83, etc.

Dewhurst, Colleen (1926–). American general purpose actress.
□The Nun's Story 59. Man on a String 60. A Fine Madness 63. The Last Run 71. The Cowboys 72. McQ 74. The Story of Jacob and Joseph (TV) 74. Annie Hall 77. Ice Castles 78. Silent Victory (TV) 79. Studs Lonigan (TV) 79. When a Stranger Calls 79. Final Assignment 80. Tribute 80. Guyana Tragedy (TV) 80. A Perfect Match (TV) 81. The Dead Zone 83.

Dexter, Anthony (1919–) (Walter Fleischmann). American leading man with stage experience. Cast as Rudolph Valentino, he never lived down the tag, and his subsequent roles have been in small-scale action dramas and science-fiction quickies.
Valentino 51. The Brigand 52. Captain John Smith and Pocahontas 53. Captain Kidd and the Slave Girl 54. Fire Maidens from Outer Space (GB) 54. He Laughed Last 56. The Parson and the Outlaw (as Billy the Kid) 57. Twelve to the Moon 59. Thoroughly Modern Millie 67, etc.

Dexter, Brad (1922–). American character actor often seen as a tough hoodlum.
The Asphalt Jungle 50. Macao 52. Untamed 55. The Oklahoman 57. The Magnificent Seven 60. Taras Bulba 62. Bus Riley's Back in Town 64. Von Ryan's Express 65. Blindfold 66. The Naked Runner (p only) 67. The Lawyer (p only) 69, etc.

Dexter, John (1935–). British director.
□The Virgin Soldiers 69. Sidelong Glances of a Pigeon Kicker 70. I Want What I Want 71.

Dexter, Maury (1927–). American producer-director of second features.
The Third Voice (p) 60. Harbour Lights (pd) 63. The Day Mars Invaded Earth (pd) 63. House of the Damned (pd) 63. The Naked Brigade (d) 65. The Outlaw of Red River (pd) 65. Maryjane (pd) 68. Hell's Belles (pd) 70, etc.

Dey, Susan (1952–). American juvenile. actress of the seventies.
Skyjacked 72. Terror on the Beach (TV) 73. Cage without a Key (TV) 75. Mary Jane Harper Cried Last Night (TV) 77. First Love 77.
TV series: The Partridge Family 70–74. Emerald Point 83. L.A. Law 86.

Dheigh, Khigh (1910–). Oriental American character actor familiar on TV as the evil villain of *Hawaii Five-O*.
The Manchurian Candidate 62. Judge Dee (TV) 77.

Dhery, Robert (1921–) (Robert Foullcy). Dapper French cabaret comedian and pantomimist.
Les Enfants du Paradis 44. Sylvie et la Fantôme 45. La Patronne (d only) 49. *Ah, Les Belles Bacchantes* (Femmes de Paris) (& wp) 54. *La Belle Américaine* (& wp) 61. Allez France (& wp) 64. Le Petit Baigneur (& wp) 67. A Time for Loving 71. Malevil 80, etc.

Di Venanzo, Gianni (1920–1966). Italian cinematographer, in films from 1941.
Amore in Città 53. L'Amiche 55. Il Grido 57. I Soliti Ignoti 58. Salvatore Giuliano 61. La Notte 61. L'Éclisse 62. Eva 62. *Eight and a Half* 63. *Juliet of the Spirits* 65, etc.

Le Diable Au Corps (France 1946). A tragic love story of World War I, written by Aurenche and Bost, directed by Claude Autant-Lara, with Gérard Philipe and Micheline Presle. Its international success was a boost for the post-war French cinema. The original novel was by Raymond Radiguet, who died in 1923 at the age of twenty.

Les Diaboliques (The Fiends) (France 1954). Suspense thriller which has become a minor classic partly because of the twists of its Boileau-Narcejac plot (frequently copied since), partly because of the acting of Simone Signoret and Vera Clouzot, but chiefly because of Henri-Georges Clouzot's spell-binding direction. In 1976 it was redone as a TV movie, *Reflections of Murder*.

? dialogue
From internal evidence, elephantine memory, or plain guesswork, please name the actors who spoke the following lines, and also name the films.

1 Most girls would give their eyes to see Monte.
—Wouldn't that rather defeat the purpose?

2 I've never been so insulted in all my life.
—Well, it's early yet.

3 You're the most beautiful plank in your husband's platform.
—That's a heck of a thing to call a woman!

4 I have a confession to make to you. Baron, you are a crook. You robbed the gentleman in room 253, 5, 7 and 9.
—Countess, believe me, before you left this room I would have told you everything. And let me say this with love in my heart—Countess, you are a thief . . .

5 You don't understand . . . every night when the moon is full, I turn into a wolf.
—You and fifty million other guys!

6 You used to be in pictures. You used to be big.
—I am big. It's the pictures that got small.

7 Do you know I read somewhere that machinery is going to take the place of every profession?
—Oh, my dear, that's something *you'll never* have to worry about.

8 You don't love me any more, do you?
—That is an ungallant question which women always want answered gallantly.

9 How's you little flowers making out?
—We's okay, Lawd.

10 In these days, old man, nobody thinks in terms of human beings. Governments don't, so why should we? They talk of the people and the proletariat, and I talk of the mugs. It's the same thing. They have their five year plans and so have I.
—You used to believe in a God.
Oh, I still *believe*, old man. In God and Mercy and all that. The dead are happier dead. They don't miss much here, poor devils.

11 Pity he had no children.
—Oh, but I have. Thousands of them. And all boys.

12 . . . Shows what I say is true. No difference between the sexes. None. Men, women. The same.
—They are, huh?
Well, maybe there *is* a difference. But it's a little difference.

—Yuh. Well, as the French say.
How do they say?
—*Vive la différence!*
Which means?
—Which means: hurray for that little difference!

13 Oh, I wish I were a woman of thirty-six, dressed in black satin, with a string of pearls.
—You would not be here with me if you were.

14 Boss, you're in danger. Your life is hanging on a thread.
—So are my pants.
You're gonna get killed
—I wish they'd tell me these things. I don't mind being killed, but I resent hearing it from a character whose head comes to a point.

15 I really can't go on accepting these gifts, though you're awfully kind.
—I'm not kind. I never give anything without expecting something in return. I always get paid.

16 Must you flirt?
—I don't have to, but I find it natural.
Suppress it.
—I'll try.
For my own information would you call your approach towards me typical of the local morale?
—Madame, it is that kind of approach which has made Paris what it is.

17 Is your husband working on a case?
—Yes, a case of Scotch.

18 I cannot get used to fighting with furniture. Where did you learn it?
—That all goes with the old school tie.

19 Do you believe people come back from the dead?
—You mean like Republicans?

20 Can't you speak Arabic?
—No sir, we're just a couple of Singapore Eskimos.

21 Your arrival, my good Giacomo, shows imagination and brilliance.
—Did you expect less?

22 Don't these big empty houses scare you?
—Not me, I was in vaudeville.

23 This place is getting like an asylum.
—All you need to start an asylum is an empty room and the right kind of people.

24 Shall we drink to a blitzkrieg?
—I prefer a slow encirclement.

25 I love you.
—Gee, that's swell, honey.

26 I came to Casablanca for the waters.
—But we're in the middle of the desert!
I was misinformed.

Diamond, I. A. L. (1915–) (Itek Dommnici, later Isadore Diamond). Romanian-American screenwriter, his best work being in collaboration with Billy Wilder. Murder in the Blue Room 44. Never Say Goodbye 46. Always Together 47. The Girl from Jones Beach 49. Something for the Birds 52. That Certain Feeling 56. Love in the Afternoon 57. Merry Andrew 58. *Some Like It Hot* 59. *The Apartment* 60. *One Two Three* 61. Irma la Douce 63. Kiss Me Stupid 64. The Fortune Cookie 66. Cactus Flower 69. *The Private Life of Sherlock Holmes* 70. Avanti 72. The Front Page 74. Fedora 78, etc.

Diamond, Neil (1941–). American pop singer who failed to break into the movies in 1981 with *The Jazz Singer*.

¶ *N.D.:* I'm not there to entertain people. We're there to do something together.

A Diary for Timothy (GB 1945). One of World War II's most brilliantly-assembled documentaries, a picture of Britain in the war's last months, looking to the future through the eyes of four men and a baby. Written by E. M. Forster, produced by Basil Wright, directed by Humphrey Jennings, with commentary by Michael Redgrave. Fifteen years later Granada TV mounted a programme to trace what had happened to the characters in the film.

Diary of a Chambermaid. Octave Mirabeau's eccentric novel of the decadent French squirearchy was filmed rather unsatisfactorily by Jean Renoir in America in 1945, with Paulette Goddard, Francis Lederer and Burgess Meredith. Luis Buñuel directed a French remake in 1964, with Jeanne Moreau and a more sympathetic cast.

Dick, Douglas (1920–). Innocent-looking American 'second lead'.
The Searching Wind 46. Saigon 47. The Accused 48. Home of the Brave 49. The Red Badge of Courage 51. The Gambler from Natchez 55. The Oklahoman 57. North to Alaska 60, etc.

Dick Tracy. The lantern-jawed detective of the comic strips made sporadic film appearances, notably when impersonated by Ralph Byrd or Morgan Conway in a number of forties second features and serials. In 1951 Byrd starred in a TV series. Tracy also appeared in a TV cartoon series in the fifties, and in *TV Funnies* in 1971.

Dickens, Charles (1812–1870). Prolific British novelist whose gusto in characterization and plot-weaving made his books ideal cinema material until the last decade when producers seem to have thought them old-fashioned. Most filmed has perhaps been *A Christmas Carol*, usually personified as *Scrooge* (qv); but *Oliver Twist* (qv) runs it a close second. There had been several early silent versions of *David Copperfield* before Cukor's splendid 1934 version (qv), and *The Old Curiosity Shop* was popular as the basis of one-reelers before the talkie versions with Hay Petrie (1935) and Anthony Newley (1975). *A Tale of Two Cities* had been a popular stage play under the title *The Only Way*; after many early versions it was directed as a spectacular by Frank Lloyd in 1917, with William Farnum; as a British silent in 1926, with Martin Harvey; as a vehicle for Ronald Colman in 1935; and in a rather uninspired British version of 1958 starring Dirk Bogarde. A 1969 all-star version of *David Copperfield* was primarily intended for American TV.

Other Dickens novels less frequently filmed include *The Mystery of Edwin Drood*, once as an early British silent and again in Hollywood in 1935, with Claude Rains as John Jasper; *Great Expectations*, which had two silent versions, a rather dull Hollywood remake of 1934 and the magnificent David Lean version of 1946 (qv); *Dombey and Son*, under the title *Rich Man's Folly*, starring George Bancroft in 1931; *Nicholas Nickleby*, the only picturization of which was the patchy Ealing version of 1947; and *The Pickwick Papers*, seen in various potted versions in silent days and in Noel Langley's superficial version of 1952.

Dickens' novels which were filmed in the silent period but not since sound include *The Cricket on the Hearth, Martin Chuzzlewit, Our Mutual Friend* and *Barnaby Rudge*. *Little Dorrit* was made in Germany in 1933 with Anny Ondra, and in 1987 by the Richard Brabourne group at a 6½-hour length with a cast headed by Alec Guinness.

Dickinson, Angie (1931–) (Angeline Brown). Capable American leading lady, former beauty contest winner, in films from 1954.
□Lucky Me 54. Man with the Gun 55. Tennessee's Partner 55. The Return of Jack Slade 55. Gun the Man Down 56. Hidden Guns 56. The Black Whip 56. Tension at Table Rock 56. Shootout at Medicine Bend 57. Calypso Joe 57. China Gate 57. I Married a Woman 58. Cry Terror 58. Rio Bravo 59. The Bramble Bush 60. Ocean's Eleven 60. A Fever in the Blood 61. The Sins of Rachel Cade 62. Rome Adventure 62. Jessica 62. Captain Newman MD 63. The Killers (TV) 64. The Art of Love 65. The Chase 66. Cast a Giant Shadow 66. Point Blank 67. The Last Challenge 67. Sam Whiskey 69. Young Billy Young 69. Some Kind of a Nut 69. The Love War (TV) 70. Thief (TV) 71. Pretty Maids All in a Row 71. The Resurrection of Zachary Wheeler 71. See the Man Run (TV) 71. The Norliss Tapes (TV) 73. The Outside Man 73. Pray for the Wildcats (TV) 74. Big Bad Mama 74. Labyrinth 79. Pearl (TV) 79. Dressed to Kill 80. Death Hunt 80. Klondike Fever 80. Charlie Chan and the Curse of the Dragon Queen 81.
TV series: Police Woman 75–78. Cassie and Co. 81.

¶ *A.D.:* I dress for women, and undress for men.

Dickinson, Desmond (1902–). British cinematographer. Detective Lloyd (serial) 31. Men of Two Worlds 45. Fame is the Spur 46. *Hamlet* 47. The History of Mr Polly 49. Morning Departure 50. The Browning Version 52. The Importance of Being Earnest 52. Carrington VC 55. Orders to Kill 58. City of the Dead 60. Sparrows Can't Sing 63. A Study in Terror 65. Circus of Blood 67. Decline and Fall 68. Who Slew Auntie Roo? 71. The Fiend 71, etc.

Dickinson, Thorold (1903–84). British director, in films from 1925. Retired to teach film theory at Slade School, London.
Book 1971: *A Discovery of Cinema.*
□The High Command 36. The Arsenal Stadium Mystery 39. *Gaslight* 39. The Prime Minister 41. *Next of Kin* 41. Men of Two Worlds 45. *The Queen of Spades* 48. The Secret People 52. Hill 24 Doesn't Answer 55.

Dickson, Dorothy (1894–). American musical comedy star who spent most of her career in Britain.
Money Mad 17. Channel Crossing 32. Danny Boy 34. Sword of Honour 39, etc.

Dickson, Gloria (1916–45) (Thais Dickerson). American leading lady of the thirties.
They Won't Forget 37. Racket Busters 38. No Place to Go 39. They Made Me a Criminal 39. I Want a Divorce 40. The Big Boss 41. Affairs of Jimmy Valentine 42. Lady of Burlesque 43, etc.

Dickson, Paul (1920–). British director, hailed for documentaries. *The Undefeated* 49, *David* 51. His feature films have been less distinguished: *Satellite in the Sky* 56. *The Depraved* 57, many second features and TV episodes.

Dierkes, John (1905–1975). Gaunt American supporting actor.
Macbeth 48. *The Red Badge of Courage* 51. Shane 53. The Naked Jungle 54. Jubal 56. The Alamo 60. The Comancheros 61. The Haunted Palace 63, many others.

Dieterle, William (1893–1972) (Wilhelm Dieterle). Distinguished German director, long in Hollywood; at his best, an incomparable master of crowd scenes and pictorial composition. Formerly an actor in Germany, e.g. in Leni's *Waxworks*.
□Die Heilige und ihr Narr 26. The Weavers 29. Behind the Altar 29. The Dance Goes On 31. *The Last Flight* 31. Her Majesty Love 31. Man Wanted 32. Jewel Robbery 32. The Crash 32. Six Hours to Live 32. Scarlet Dawn 32. Lawyer Man 32. Grand Slam 33. Adorable 33. Devils in Love 33. Female 33. From Headquarters 33. Fashions of 1934 34. Fog Over Frisco 34. Madame du Barry 34. The Firebird 34. The Secret Bride 35. Dr Socrates 35. *A Midsummer Night's Dream* 35. *The Story of Louis Pasteur* 35. Concealment 35. Men on Her Mind 36. The White Angel 36. Satan Met a Lady 36. The Great O'Malley 37. Another Dawn 37. *The Life of Emile Zola* 37. Blockade 38. *Juarez* 39. *The Hunchback of Notre Dame* 39. *Dr Ehrlich's Magic Bullet* 40. A Dispatch from Reuters 40. *All That Money Can Buy* 41. Syncopation 42. Tennessee Johnson 42. Kismet 44. *I'll Be Seeing You* 44. Love Letters 45. This Love of Ours 45. The Searching Wind 47. The Accused 48. *Portrait of Jennie* 48. Rope of Sand 49. Paid in Full 50. Dark City 50. September Affair 50. Volcano 50. Peking Express 51. Red Mountain 51. Boots Malone 52. The Turning Point 52. Salome 53. Elephant Walk 54. Magic Fire 56. Omar Khayyam 57. Dubrowsky (Yug.) 58. Mistress of the World (Ger.) 60. The Confession 66.
❁ For marshalling the tricks of his trade with spectacular professionalism. *Portrait of Jennie*.

Dietrich, Marlene (1901–) (Maria Magdalena von Losch). German singer-actress long in America, a legend of glamour despite many poor films and her domination in the thirties by the heavy style of Josef Von Sternberg.
□Der Mensch am Wege 23. The Tragedy of Love 24. Der Sprung ins Leben 24. Joyless Street 25. Manon Lescaut 26. Cafe Electric 26. A Modern Dubarry 27. Sein Groesster Bluff 27. Der Jux Baron 27. Princess Olala 28. I Kiss Your Hand Madame 28. Die Frau nach der Man Sich Sehnt 28. Das Schiff der Verlorenen Menschen 29. Gefahren der Brautzeit 30. *The Blue Angel* 30. Morocco 30. Dishonoured 31. *Shanghai Express* 32. Blonde Venus 32. Song of Songs 33. *The Scarlet Empress* 34. The Devil Is a Woman 35. *Desire* 36. The Garden of Allah 36. Knight Without Armour (GB) 37. Angel 37. *Destry Rides Again* 39. Seven Sinners 40. The Flame of New Orleans 41. Manpower 41. The Lady Is Willing 42. The Spoilers 42. Pittsburgh 42. Follow the Boys 44. Kismet 44. Martin Roumagnac (Fr.) 46. Golden Earrings 47. *A Foreign Affair* 48. Stage Fright (GB) 50. No Highway (GB) 51. Rancho Notorious 52. The Monte Carlo Story 53. Around the World in Eighty Days 56. Witness for the Prosecution 57. Touch of Evil 58. Judgment at Nuremberg 61. Paris When It Sizzles 64. Just a Gigolo 78.
❁ For enjoying being a legend. *Destry Rides Again*.

¶ If she had nothing but her voice, she could break your heart with it. But she also has that beautiful body and the timeless loveliness of her face.—*Ernest Hemingway*

Age cannot wither her, nor custom stale her infinite sameness—*David Shipman*

I have a child and I have made a few people happy. That is all.—*M.D.*

The relationship between the make-up man and the film actor is that of accomplices in crime—*M.D.*

There is a lack of dignity to film stardom.—*M.D.*

She has sex but no positive gender. Her masculinity appeals to women and her sexuality to men.—*Ken Tynan*

The legs aren't so beautiful, I just know what to do with them.—*M.D.*

I never ever took my career seriously.—*M.D.*

It took more than one man to change my name to Shanghai Lily.—*M.D. in Shanghai Express*

See what the boys in the back room will
have
And tell them I'm having the same.
See what the boys in the back room will
have
And give me the poison they name.
And if I die, don't bring a preacher
To witness all my follies and my shame;

Just see what the boys in the back room will have
And tell them I sighed—
And tell them I cried—
And tell them I died of the same!—*M.D. in Destry Rides Again*

Dietz, Howard (1896–1983). American librettist and writer, with MGM from its inception. Best film score: *The Band Wagon* 53.
Autobiography 1974: *Dancing in the Dark.*

Diffring, Anton (1918–). German actor, in British films from 1951; often the villainous Nazi or the protagonist of a horror film.
State Secret 50. *Albert RN* 53. The Sea Shall Not Have Them 55. The Colditz Story 55. *I Am a Camera* 56. *The Man Who Could Cheat Death* 59. Circus of Horrors 60. Incident at Midnight 63. The Heroes of Telemark 65. Fahrenheit 451 66. The Double Man 67. Counterpoint (US) 67. Where Eagles Dare 68. Zeppelin 71. The Swiss Conspiracy 75. Operation Daybreak 76. Vanessa 76. Valentino 77, etc.

Digges, Dudley (1879–1947). Versatile Irish character actor, with Abbey Theatre experience; played a variety of good roles in Hollywood in the thirties.
□*Condemned* 29. Outward Bound 30. Upper Underworld 30. *The Maltese Falcon* 31. The Ruling Voice 31. Alexander Hamilton 31. Devotion 31. The Hatchet Man 32. The Strange Case of Clara Deane 32. Roar of the Dragon 32. The First Year 32. Tess of the Storm Country 32. The King's Vacation 33. Mayor of Hell 33. Silk Express 33. The Narrow Corner 33. The Invisible Man 33. The Emperor Jones 33. Before Dawn 33. Fury of the Jungle 34. Caravan 34. The World Moves On 34. Massacre 34. What Every Woman Knows 34. I am a Thief 34. Notorious Gentleman 35. Kind Lady 35. *Mutiny on the Bounty* 35. China Seas 35. The Bishop Misbehaves 35. Three Live Ghosts 36. The Voice of Bugle Ann 36. The Unguarded Hour 36. *The General Died at Dawn* 36. Valiant is the Word for Carrie 36. Love is News 37. *The Light that Failed* 39. The Fight for Life 40. *Raffles* 40. Son of Fury 42. The Searching Wind 46.

Dighton, John (1909–). British writer, in films from 1935.
Let George Do It 40. Nicholas Nickleby 47. Saraband for Dead Lovers 48. *Kind Hearts and Coronets* 49. *The Happiest Days of Your Life* (from his own play) 49. The Man in the White Suit 51. Roman Holiday 53. Summer of the Seventeenth Doll 60, many others.

Dignam, Basil (1905–1979). British character actor, in innumerable small parts, often as barrister or other professional man.
His Excellency 53. Brothers in Law 57. Room at the Top 59. The Silent Partner 61. Life for Ruth 63. Victim 62, etc.

Dignam, Mark (1909–). British character actor, brother of Basil Dignam. Also plays professional men.
Murder in the Cathedral 52. The Maggie 54. The Prisoner 55. Sink the Bismarck 60. No Love for Johnnie 62. Hamlet 69, etc.

Diller, Phyllis (1917–). Zany, grotesque American comedienne who has had trouble adapting her TV style to movies.
□Splendor in the Grass 60. Boy Did I Get a Wrong Number 66. Eight on the Lam 67. The Private Navy of Sergeant O'Farrell 68. Did You Hear the One about the Travelling Saleslady? 68. The Adding Machine (GB) 69. Pink Motel 82.
TV series: The Pruitts of Southampton 66. The Beautiful Phyllis Diller Show 68.

¶ *P.D.:* It's a good thing that beauty is only skin deep, or I'd be rotten to the core.

P.D.: I have an agreement with Bob Hope. I don't make fun of his nose and he doesn't ridicule my body.

P.D.: My house used to be haunted, but the ghosts haven't been back since the night I tried on all my wigs.

Dillinger, John (1903–1934). American gangster of the thirties, public enemy number one; he was shot after leaving a cinema (where he had seen *Manhattan Melodrama*). He has been played in *Dillinger* 45 by Lawrence Tierney, in *Young Dillinger* 64 by Nick Adams, and in *Dillinger* 73 by Warren Oates.

Dillman, Bradford (1930–). Lean American actor, a staple of TV movies and series.
A Certain Smile 58. *Compulsion* 59. Circle of Deception 61. Francis of Assisi 61. A Rage to Live 65. The Helicopter Spies 67. The Bridge at Remagen 69. Suppose They Gave a War and Nobody Came 71. Brother John 71. Escape from the Planet of the Apes 71. The Way We Were 73. The Iceman Cometh 73.

Mastermind 77. The Lincoln Conspiracy (as John Wilkes Booth) 77. The Swarm 78. Piranha 78. Guyana Cult of the Damned 80. Sudden Impact 83. The Treasure of the Amazon 85, etc.
TV series: Court Martial (GB) 65, many guest appearances; King's Crossing 81.

Dillon, Carmen (1908–). British art designer.
The Five Pound Man 37. Quiet Wedding 41. The Demi Paradise 43. *Henry V* 44. The Way to the Stars 45. *Hamlet* 48. Cardboard Cavalier 49. The Importance of Being Earnest 52. *Richard III* 56. A Tale of Two Cities 58. Carry on Constable 60. The Chalk Garden 64. Accident 67. The Go Between 71. Bequest to the Nation 73, many others.

Dillon, John Francis (1887–1934). American director.
Children of the Ritz 29. Sally 29. Kismet 30. The Finger Points 31. The Cohens and Kellys in Hollywood 32. Call Her Savage 32. Humanity 33. The Big Shakedown 34, etc.

Dillon, Matt (1964–). American teenage actor of the early eighties.
Liar's Moon 82. Tex 82. The Outsiders 84. Rumble Fish 84. The Flamingo Kid 85. Target 85. Rebel 85. Native Son 86. The Big Town (The Arm) 87.

Dillon, Melinda (1939–). American leading actress.
The April Fools 69. Slapshot 77. Close Encounters of the Third Kind 77. Bound for Glory 78. The Critical List (TV) 78. F.I.S.T. 78. Reunion (TV) 80. Absence of Malice 81. Bigfoot and the Hendersons 87.

¶ *Steven Spielberg:* She gives off a lovely light.

Dillon, Robert (–). American screenwriter.
Prime Cut 72. 99 and 44/100 per cent Dead 74. French Connection II 75.

Dinehart, Alan (1886–1944). American supporting actor who played many bluff-businessman roles.
The Brat 31. Street of Women 32. Rackety Rax 32. Supernatural 33. Cross Country Cruise 34. Jimmy the Gent 34. The Cat's Paw 34. Dante's Inferno 35. Your Uncle Dudley 35. Thanks a Million 35. Charlie Chan at the Race Track 36. Step Lively Jeeves 37. Ali Baba Goes to Town 37. Rebecca of Sunnybrook Farm 38. Second Fiddle 39. Slightly Honorable 39. Girl Trouble 42. Fired Wife 43. Moon over Las Vegas 44. The Whistler 44. Oh What a Night 44, many others.

Dinelli, Mel (–). American screenwriter.
Beware My Lovely 52. Jeopardy 53. Lizzie 57, etc.

Dingle, Charles (1887–1956). American stage actor who made occasional screen appearances, usually in cheerfully wicked roles.
□One Third of a Nation 33. *The Little Foxes* 41. Unholy Partners 41. Johnny Eager 42. Calling Dr Gillespie 42. Are Husbands Necessary 42. The Talk of the Town 42. George Washington Slept Here 42. Tennessee Johnson 42. Somewhere I'll Find You 42. Edge of Darkness 43. Someone to Remember 43. She's for Me 43. The Song of Bernadette 43. Home in Indiana 44. National Barn Dance 44. Together Again 44. A Medal for Benny 45. Here Come the Co-eds 45. Guest Wife 45. Cinderella Jones 46. Wife of Monte Cristo 46. Centennial Summer 46. Three Wise Fools 46. Sister Kenny 46. The Beast with Five Fingers 46. Duel in the Sun 46. My Favorite Brunette 47. Welcome Stranger 47. The Romance of Rosy Ridge 47. *State of the Union* 48. If You Knew Susie 48. A Southern Yankee 48. Big Jack 49. Never Wave at a WAC 52. Call Me Madam 53. The President's Lady 53. Half a Hero 53. The Court Martial of Billy Mitchell 55.

dinosaurs: see *monster animals*.

The Dionne Quins (1934–) appeared in two films, *Reunion* 36 and *The Country Doctor* 36. They were Cecile, Annette, Emilie (d 1954), Marie (d 1970), Yvonne.

director. Normally the most influential creator of a film, who may not only shoot scenes on the studio floor but also supervise script, casting, editing, etc., according to his standing. In more routine films these functions are separately controlled.

¶ A selection of directorial attitudes:
Charlton Heston: I feel very strongly that the director is supposed to be the boss. Art was never created by democracy.
Victor Fleming: Don't get excited. Obstacles make a better picture.
Rouben Mamoulian: You can have all the philosophy you like: if a film doesn't come across in graphic terms, it falls short.
D. W. Griffith: There is no suspense like the suspense of a delayed coition.

John Huston: I don't try to guess what a million people will like. It's hard enough to know what I like.
David Lean: Always cast against the part and it won't be boring.
Richard Lester: Film-making has become a kind of hysterical pregnancy.
Joseph L. Mankiewicz: I am never quite sure whether I am one of the cinema's elder statesmen or just the oldest whore on the beat.
Roman Polanski: The best films are best because of nobody but the director.
François Truffaut: I renew myself at the fountain of the past.
Josef von Sternberg: I regard actors as marionettes, as pieces of colour in my canvas.
Henry Blanke: You should think of each shot you make as the most important one in the film.
Ross Hunter; I have never made a picture to please me. Do you imagine I'd make a film like *Tammy* for me?
King Vidor: The director is the channel through which a motion picture reaches the screen.
Betty Blythe: The director is the only man besides your husband who can tell you how many of your clothes to take off.
Orson Welles: No one can pretend to be a film director unless he also does his own editing.
François Truffaut: Shooting a film is like taking a stagecoach ride in the old west. At first you look forward to a nice trip. Later you just hope to reach your destination.
Burt Lancaster: It's the best job in picture business because when you're a director, you're God. And you know, that's the best job in town.
Mike Nichols: It's not a film maker's job to explain his technique, but to tell his story the best way he can.
Fritz Lang: Each picture has some sort of rhythm which only the director can give it. He has to be like the captain of a ship.
Samuel Fuller: Am I a cult director? Yeah, I love all of that. I want to join the cult of the 100 to 200 million grossers and still make an artistic picture.
Brian de Palma: I like stylization. I try to get away with as much as possible until people start laughing at it.

directors' appearances in films are comparatively few. Hitchcock remains the unchallengeable winner, with moments in over thirty of his fifty-odd films, including the confined *Rope* (in which his outline appears on a neon sign) and *Lifeboat* (in which he can be seen in a reducing ad. in a newspaper). Preston Sturges can be glimpsed in *Sullivan's Travels*, and in *Paris Holiday*, as a French resident, gets a whole scene to himself. John Huston, uncredited, plays a tourist in *The Treasure of the Sierra Madre* and a master of foxhounds in *The List of Adrian Messenger*; he has more recently begun to take sizeable credited roles, e.g. in *The Cardinal* and *The Bible*. The Paramount lot became a familiar scene in many forties pictures, with notable guest appearances by Mitchell Leisen in *Hold Back the Dawn* and Cecil B. de Mille in *Sunset Boulevard, The Buster Keaton Story, Star-Spangled Rhythm, Variety Girl, Son of Paleface* and others. Jean Cocteau played an old woman in *Orphée* and appeared throughout *The Testament of Orphée*. Nicholas Ray was the American ambassador in *55 Days in Peking*. Jules Dassin played major roles in *Rififi* (as Perlo Vita) and *Never on Sunday*, as did Jean Renoir in *La Règle du Jeu*. Hugo Fregonese was a messenger in *Decameron Nights*, Samuel Fuller a Japanese cop in *House of Bamboo*. Others who can be glimpsed in their own work include Tony Richardson in *Tom Jones*, Michael Winner in *You Must Be Joking*, George Marshall in *The Crime of Dr Forbes*, Frank Borzage in *Jeanne Eagels*, Robert Aldrich in *The Big Knife*, Ingmar Bergman in *Waiting Women*, King Vidor in *Our Daily Bread*, William Castle (producer) in *Rosemary's Baby*, Claude Chabrol in *Les Biches* and *The Road to Corinth*, and Joseph Losey in *The Intimate Stranger* (which he made under the name of Joseph Walton). Huston, Polanski, Truffaut and Bondartchuk are among those who have played major roles in their own and other films.

disaster films have always been popular. In the thirties large crowds flocked to see *Tidal Wave, San Francisco, The Last Days of Pompeii, In Old Chicago* and *The Rains Came*. World War II was disaster enough for the forties, but the fifties brought *Titanic, A Night to Remember*, and *Invasion USA*, and the sixties *The Devil at Four O'Clock* and *Krakatoa East of Java*. It was the seventies, however, that found the killing of large numbers of people to be really top box office. *Earthquake* and *The Towering Inferno* were giants of their kind, and even though *The Hindenberg* was not clever enough to attract, there were plenty of successful imitators: *The Swarm, Avalanche, Meteor*, etc. TV contributions include *Smash-up on Interstate*

Five, Hanging by a Thread, The Death of Ocean View Park and *Disaster on the Coastliner.*

? 1 Name the star who played Lady Edwina Esketh in *The Rains Came*, the name of the actress in the remake, the title of that remake, and the author of the original novel.

2 Who played the Iron Jaw Woman in what Cecil B. de Mille epic which climaxed in a train wreck?

3 What athletic hero began his career in 1938 in *The Hurricane*, and what 'monster' did he later portray?

4 In what silent epic was the fall of Babylon depicted, and who directed it?

5 Disaster was narrowly averted in a film in which Helen Hayes played a stowaway. Name the film and the author of the original novel.

6 A British film about a famous disaster featured Kenneth More, Honor Blackman, Michael Goodliffe and David McCallum. Name the film and the year of the disaster.

7 What kind of disaster is common to *The Blue Bird* (1940) and *Bambi*? Name the original author in each case.

8 What disaster movie had a geographically incorrect title?

9 Which historical character, allegedly responsible for starting a celebrated disaster, has been played by Peter Lorre, Peter Ustinov, and Charles Laughton; and in what films?

10 What disaster film of the seventies was directed by Ronald Neame from a novel by Paul Gallico?

11 In what film was Bette Davis caught up in the San Francisco earthquake of 1906? Who wrote the original novel?

12 In what film did Rod Taylor play a pilot whose apparent error caused a disaster on take-off which was investigated by Glenn Ford? Who wrote the original novel?

13 Name the film in which Linda Darnell fled from the London fire of 1666. Name the author of the original novel.

14 In *The Good Earth*, Chinese life and livelihood were threatened by a plague of . . . what? Who wrote the original novel?

15 What kind of disaster was common to *The Brave Don't Cry, The Proud Valley* and *Black Fury*?

16 In which film were John Mills and Richard Attenborough trapped in a submarine at the bottom of the sea?

17 What natural phenomenon threatened the cast of *The Devil at Four O'Clock*? Who wrote the original novel?

18 Name the science fiction producer responsible for, among others, *The War of the Worlds, Conquest of Space* and *When Worlds Collide*.

19 Who was the author of *Things to Come*? What did he prophesy for 1940? What followed it?

20 What natural disaster was common to *The Last Days of Pompeii* and *Her Jungle Love*?

The Discreet Charm of the Bourgeoisie (France 1972). This hilarious surrealist comedy about a group of friends who just can't seem to get together for dinner is almost certainly director Luis Buñuel's most typical and most likeable film, though it does slightly overstay its welcome.

disguise has featured in many hundreds of films, and was in the twenties the perquisite of Lon Chaney, all of whose later films featured it. Lon Chaney Jnr has also had a tendency to it, as had John Barrymore; while most of the Sherlock Holmes films involved it. Other notable examples include Henry Hull in *Miracles for Sale*; Donald Wolfit in *The Ringer*; Marlene Dietrich in *Witness for the Prosecution*; Jack Lemmon and Tony Curtis in *Some Like It Hot*; Alec Guinness in *Kind Hearts and Coronets*; Peter Sellers in *The Naked Truth* and *After the Fox*; Rod Steiger in *No Way to Treat a Lady*; Tony Randall in *Seven Faces of Dr Lao*; John Barrymore in *Bulldog Drummond Comes Back*; Michael Caine in *Sleuth*; Dustin Hoffman in *Tootsie*; and practically the entire cast of *The List of Adrian Messenger*. Extensions of disguise are the split personality films: *Dr Jekyll and Mr Hyde, Lizzie, The Three Faces of Eve, Sybil.*

See also: *transvestism*; *multiple roles.*

Dishy, Bob (–). American character actor.
The Tiger Makes Out 67. Lovers and Other Strangers 70. The Big Bus 76. The First Family 80. The Last Married Couple in America 80. Author! Author! 82.

Diskant, George E. (1907–1965). American cinematographer.
Riff Raff 47. The Narrow Margin 50. On Dangerous Ground 51. The Bigamist 53, others.

Disney, Walt (1901–1966). American animator and executive whose name is a household word all over the world. Formerly a commercial artist, he produced his first Mickey Mouse cartoon in 1928, using his own voice; also Silly Symphonies, one of which (*Flowers and Trees* 33) was the first film in full Technicolor. Donald Duck first appeared in 1936. First full-length cartoon: *Snow White and the Seven Dwarfs* 37, followed by *Pinocchio* 39, *Fantasia* 40, *Dumbo* 41, *Bambi* 43, *The Three Caballeros* (combining cartoon and live action) 44, *Cinderella* 50, *Alice in Wonderland* 51, *Peter Pan* 53, *Lady and the Tramp* 56, *The Sleeping Beauty* 59, *One Hundred and One Dalmatians* 61, *The Sword in the Stone* 63, *Winnie the Pooh and the Honey Tree* 66, *The Jungle Book* 67, *The Aristocats* 70, *Robin Hood* 73, *The Rescuers* 76. First live-action feature *Treasure Island* 50, followed by a plentiful supply including westerns (*Westward Ho the Wagons, The Nine Lives of Elfego Baca*), adventure classics (*Kidnapped, Dr Syn*), animal yarns (*Greyfriars Bobby, Old Yeller, The Incredible Journey*), cosy fantasies with music (*In Search of the Castaways, Mary Poppins*), trick comedies (*The Absent-Minded Professor, Son of Flubber*) and plain old-fashioned family fun (*Bon Voyage, The Ugly Dachshund*). The patchiness of these films has meant that although the Disney label is still a sure sign of suitability for children, it no longer necessarily indicates quality of any other kind. In 1948 began the irresistible series of 'True-Life Adventures' (cleverly jazzed-up animal documentaries containing much rare footage) and in 1953 came the first feature of this kind, *The Living Desert*; the series has unfortunately died out.

Disney's long list of Academy Awards are all for shorts, apart from 'special awards' for *Snow White, Fantasia, The Living Desert* and *The Vanishing Prairie*. They include a special award for creating *Mickey Mouse* 32. *Three Little Pigs* 33. *The Tortoise and the Hare* 34. *Three Orphan Kittens* 35. *The Old Mill* 37. *Ferdinand the Bull* 38. *The Ugly Duckling* 39. *Lend a Paw* 41. *Der Fuhrer's Face* 42. *Seal Island* 48. *Beaver Valley* 50. *Nature's Half Acre* 51. *Water Birds* 52. *Toot Whistle Plunk and Boom* 53. *Bear Country* 53. *The Alaskan Eskimo* 53. *Men against the Arctic* 55. *The Wetback Hound* 57. *White Wilderness* 58. *Ama Girls* 58. *The Horse with the Flying Tail* 60. *Winnie the Pooh and the Blustery Day* 68, etc.

A biography, *Walt Disney*, was published in 1958 by his daughter Diane, and in 1968 came Richard Schickel's iconoclastic *The Disney Version*. A massive informational tome is Christopher's Finch's *The Art of Walt Disney* 73. Further information was contained in 1973 in *Disney Animation: The Illusion of Life*, by Frank Thomas and Ollie Johnston.

❀ For creating a whole new world of magic as a corrective to the real one. *Pinocchio*.

¶ 'Disney has the best casting. If he doesn't like an actor, he just tears him up.'—*Alfred Hitchcock*

W.D.: I love Mickey Mouse more than any woman I've ever known.

'At the bottom line he was a down-to-earth farmer's son who happened to be a genius.'—*Ward Kimball*

Disraeli, Benjamin (1804–1881), novelist and prime minister, has been notably portrayed on screen by George Arliss in 1921 and 1930 (in each case his wife Florence Arliss played Mrs Disraeli), by Derrick de Marney in *Victoria the Great* 37 and *Sixty Glorious Years* 38, by John Gielgud in *The Prime Minister* 40; and by Alec Guinness in *The Mudlark* 50. In a rather dismal 1978 TV series he was played by Ian McShane.

dissolve (or mix). A change of scene accomplished by gradually exposing a second image over the first while fading the first away.

distributor (or renter). A company which, for a percentage of the profits or a flat fee, undertakes to rent a film to exhibitors on the producing company's behalf. Originally major producers like MGM, Warner and Paramount distributed their own films exclusively, but with the rise of independent producers the situation has become much more fluid, with distributors bidding for the films they consider most likely to succeed at the box office and tying up successful producers to long-term contracts.

¶ *Arthur Mayer:* It's easy enough to make fun of a distributor today, but how can you help but feel sorry for the poor bastard? He's faced with the daily decision whether or not to commit large sums of capital to producers who want to make pictures for release a year from now. Now, we all realize that exhibitors haven't a clue about what the kids want to see today. How can anyone possibly know what kids will want to see a year from now?

Divine (1945–1988) (Glenn Divine). American transvestite performer whose chief claim to screen fame was *Lust in the Dust* 83.

¶ *D.:* Of course, the last thing my parents wanted was a son who wears a cocktail dress that glitters, but they've come around to it.

Dix, Richard (1894–1949) (Ernest Brimmer). Stalwart American leading man of the twenties and thirties, after which his vehicles declined.
Dangerous Curve Ahead 21. Fools First 22. The Sin Flood 22. The Christian (GB) 23. Souls for Sale 23. Icebound 24. Unguarded Women 24. Too Many Kisses 25. The Lady who Lied 25. *The Vanishing American* 25. The Quarterback 26. Shanghai Bound 27. Sporting Goods 28. Moran of the Marines 28. Nothing but the Truth 29. *Seven Keys to Baldpate* 29. Shooting Straight 30. *Cimarron* 31. The Public Defender 31. The Lost Squadron 32. Roar of the Dragon 32. The Great Jasper 33. Ace of Aces 33. Stingaree 34. West of the Pecos 34. The Arizonian 35. The Tunnel (GB) 35. Special Investigator 36. The Devil's Playgound 37. The Devil is Driving 37. Sky Giant 38. Man of Conquest 39. Here I am a Stranger 39. Cherokee Strip 40. Badlands of Dakota 41. Tombstone 42. Eyes of the Underworld 42. The Kansan 43. Top Man 43. The Ghost Ship 43. The Whistler 44. Mark of the Whistler 44, many others.

Dix, William (1956–). British child actor of the sixties.
The Nanny 65. Doctor Dolittle 67.

Dixon, Adele (1908–). British musical comedy actress and singer, rarely in films.
Uneasy Virtue 31. The Happy Husband 32. Calling the Tune 36. Banana Ridge 41. Woman to Woman 47, etc.

Dixon, Jean (1896–1981). American stage actress, in a few films.
The Lady Lies 29. The Kiss Before the Mirror 33. Sadie McKee 34. She Married Her Boss 35. My Man Godfrey 36. You Only Live Once 37. Joy of Living 38. *Holiday* 38, etc.

Dixon, Thomas (1864–1946). American Baptist minister who wrote the anti-Negro novel *The Clansman,* on which Griffith's *The Birth of a Nation* was based.

Dmytryk, Edward (1908–). American director, in films from 1923. After years of second features he gained a reputation as a stylist with some tough adult thrillers of the forties; but after years of exile due to the McCarthy witch-hunt his more ambitious recent films have seemed impersonal.
Autobiography 1979: *It's a Hell of a Life but Not a Bad Living.*
□The Hawk 35. Television Spy 39. Emergency Squad 40. Golden Gloves 40. Mystery Sea Raider 40. Her First Romance 40. The Devil Commands 41. Under Age 41. Sweetheart of the Campus 41. Blonde from Singapore 41. Confessions of Boston Blackie 41. Secrets of the Lone Wolf 41. Counter Espionage 42. Seven Miles from Alcatraz 42. Hitler's Children 43. The Falcon Strikes Back 43. Behind the Rising Sun 43. Captive Wild Woman 43. Tender Comrade 44. *Murder My Sweet* 44. Back to Bataan 45. Cornered 46. Till the End of Time 46. *Crossfire* 47. So Well Remembered (GB) 47. Obsession (GB) 48. Give Us This Day (GB) 49. Mutiny (Fr.) 52. The Sniper 52. Eight Iron Men 52. The Juggler 53. *The Caine Mutiny* 54. Broken Lance 54. The End of the Affair (GB) 54. Soldier of Fortune 55. The Left Hand of God 55. The Mountain (& p) 56. Raintree County 57. The Young Lions 58. Warlock 59. The Blue Angel 59. The Reluctant Saint (It.) 61. A Walk on the Wild Side 62. The Carpetbaggers 63. Where Love Has Gone 64. *Mirage* 65. Alvarez Kelly 66. Anzio 68. Shalako 68. Bluebeard 72. The Human Factor 75. He is My Brother 76.

¶ *E.D.:* My lifelong ambition has been to spend my money as soon as I can get it.

Dobie, Alan (1932–). British leading actor, usually in astringent roles on stage or TV.
Seven Keys 62. The Comedy Man 64. The Long Day's Dying 68. Alfred the Great 69. The Chairman 69, etc.

Dobson, Tamara (1947–). Black American leading lady.
Cleopatra Jones 73. Cleopatra Jones and the Casino of Gold 75. Norman Is That You? 76. Murder at the World Series (TV) 77.

Docks of New York (US 1928). A late silent melodrama directed by Josef Von Sternberg in a manner realistic for twenties Hollywood, pretentious in retrospect; from a script by Jules Furthman about a coal stoker who rescues and marries a would-be suicide. With George Bancroft, Betty Compson, Olga Baclanova.

Dr Christian was the kindly country doctor hero, played by Jean Hersholt, of a number of unambitious little films which came out between 1938 and 1940, based on a radio series and inspired by the publicity surrounding Dr Dafoe, who delivered the Dionne Quins in 1934. In 1956 Macdonald Carey featured in a TV series of the same name, but he played the nephew of the original Dr Christian.

Dr Cyclops (US 1939). Horror film making a notable advance in colour trick photography but a disappointing film to come from Ernest Schoedsack. Albert Dekker was the mad scientist who reduced the rest of the cast to midgets.

Dr Ehrlich's Magic Bullet (US 1940). One of the Warner biographical series which also included Pasteur, Zola, Juarez and Reuter, this engrossing production has Edward G. Robinson bearded and unrecognizable as the German research chemist who discovered a cure for syphilis. Directed with great accomplishment by William Dieterle, and splendidly produced and acted. The subject made it a Hollywood milestone.

Doctor in The House (GB 1953). First in a long and increasingly bawdy series of comedies adapted from Richard Gordon's collections of anecdotes about a doctor's life. All have been lucrative but only the first had genuine vitality: the TV series which began in 1970 was better.

Dr Jekyll and Mr Hyde. Robert Louis Stevenson's classic thriller of split personality has become one of the screen's most popular and oft-borrowed themes. There was a Selig version in 1908 and a Danish one in 1909. James Cruze appeared in a Universal version in 1912, and in 1913 King Baggott appeared in a rival production. A British version came out in the same year. 1919 brought Sheldon Lewis as the doctor (copies still exist) and in 1921 John Barrymore gave a brilliant portrayal in the role, with very little use of trick photography or make-up. Meanwhile in Germany in 1920 Conrad Veidt, directed by Murnau, had had an equally splendid shot at the character. In 1932 Fredric March won an Academy Award for his performance in Rouben Mamoulian's version, which was remade in 1941 with Spencer Tracy. Louis Hayward suffered the fatal dose in *Son of Dr Jekyll* 51; Boris Karloff (as well as Lou Costello and Reginald Denny) underwent the transformation in *Abbott and Costello Meet Dr Jekyll and Mr Hyde* 53; Gloria Talbot was *Daughter of Dr Jekyll* 57; and in 1958 Sylvester the cartoon cat was 'translated' in *Dr Jekyll's Hyde*. In 1959 Bernard Bresslaw was in a funny version, *The Ugly Duckling,* and in 1960 the same studio, Hammer, had Paul Massie in a serious version called *The Two Faces of Dr Jekyll,* in which for the first time the evil side of the character was handsomer than the good. Another comic version was Jerry Lewis' *The Nutty Professor* 63. In 1970 Hammer produced a transvestite version, *Doctor Jekyll and Sister Hyde,* in which Ralph Bates changed into Martine Beswick. *I, Monster* 71 turned out to be another stab at the original story. Television's first version was Renoir's 1958 *The Testament of Dr Cordelier*; 1973 brought a musical version for TV, with Kirk Douglas, following an excellent straight Canadian TV adaptation in 1968 with Jack Palance. A TV series of the late seventies, *The Incredible Hulk*, is a variation on the theme.

Dr Kildare. Max Brand's novels about a young intern were first filmed in 1938 with Joel McCrea in the leading role of a film called *Interns Can't Take Money*. In the same year MGM made *Young Dr Kildare* starring Lew Ayres, the first of a popular series of nine films, with Lionel Barrymore as crusty old Dr Gillespie. In 1943 Ayres gave up his role and six films were made starring Barrymore only, with various interns including Van Johnson and Philip Dorn. No movies about Blair Hospital have been made since 1947, but in 1961 MGM revived the characters in a TV series starring Richard Chamberlain and Raymond Massey: it ran five years. In 1972 a half-hour soap opera version began with Mark Jenkins and Gary Merrill.

Dr Mabuse. The master criminal hero-villain of two films directed in Germany by Fritz Lang: *Dr Mabuse the Gambler* 22 and *The Testament of Dr Mabuse* 32. The latter was blatant anti-Nazi propaganda and caused Lang to hurry to Hollywood. In the late fifties the character was revived by Lang and others, but to less effect.

Dr Strangelove (GB/US 1963). The first nuclear comedy, full of black laughter about what might happen if a madman pressed *that* button. Directed by Stanley Kubrick (from Peter George's novel *Red Alert*) to great critical acclaim; but cinematically and dramatically somewhat tortuous and even dull once one knew what it was about. Full credit, however, to the sets of Ken Adam and to

Peter Sellers in his three roles. Won three BFA awards: best film, best British film, and United Nations Award.

Dr Syn. Russell Thorndyke's novel about the smuggling vicar of Dymchurch was filmed in 1938 with George Arliss, in 1961 with Peter Cushing, (as *Captain Clegg*) and in 1963 with Patrick McGoohan.

Doctor Zhivago (US 1965). MGM insist on 'Doctor' being spelt out, and this may serve as a key to the pretentiousness of this would-be epic from Boris Pasternak's novel of modern Russia. The story has been simplified until there is almost nothing of it and Zhivago is a nonentity; what's left plays like a thin variant on *Gone with the Wind*. The chief demerit is Robert Bolt's tortuous screenplay, which has characters making inexplicable appearances and disappearances; but David Lean's direction is self-indulgent, wasting time on inessentials, and only Frederick Young's cinematography (AA) emerges with full credit. Maurice Jarre (AA) wrote the score.

Doctorow, E. L. (1931–). American novelist whose *Ragtime* created an original, almost cinematic, method of prose storytelling which simply could not be afforded in the disappointing film version. There was an earlier film of his *Welcome to Hard Times*.

doctors (in the medical sense) have been crusading heroes of many movies: fictional epics that come readily to mind include *Arrowsmith, The Citadel, Magnificent Obsession, Private Worlds, Men in White, The Green Light, Disputed Passage, Yellow Jack, The Last Angry Man, Not as a Stranger, Johnny Belinda, The Girl in White, The Doctor and the Girl, Green Fingers, The Outsider, The Crime of Dr Forbes, The Interns, The New Interns, The Young Doctors, Behind the Mask, Doctor Zhivago,* and *White Corridors*. A few have even commanded whole series to themselves: *Dr Kildare, Dr Christian, Dr Gillespie, The Crime Doctor*. Once-living doctors have received the accolade of a Hollywood biopic: *The Story of Louis Pasteur, Dr Ehrlich's Magic Bullet, Prisoner of Shark Island* (Dr Mudd), *L'Enfant Sauvage* (Dr Jean Retard), *The Story of Dr Wassell, Il Est Minuit Dr Schweizer*. Many less single-minded films have had a background of medicine and doctors as leading figures: *The Nun's Story, King's Row, No Way Out, People Will Talk, The Hospital*. More or less villainous doctors were found in *The Flesh and the Fiends, Frankenstein, Dr Socrates, Dr Jekyll and Mr Hyde, Green for Danger, Dr Cyclops, The Hands of Orlac, Dr Goldfoot,* and *The Amazing Dr Clitterhouse*. TV series on medical subjects have included *Medic* 54–55. *Ben Casey* 60–65. *Dr Kildare* 61–66. *Dr Christian* 56. *Dr Hudson's Secret Journal* 55–56. *The Nurses* 62–63. *The Doctors and the Nurses* 64. *Marcus Welby M.D.* 69. *The Bold Ones* 68–72. *Police Surgeon* 72. *St Elsewhere* 82. *Ryan's Four* 83.
See also: *hospitals*.

documentary was not coined as a word until 1929, but several famous films, including Ponting's *With Scott to the Antarctic,* Lowell Thomas' *With Allenby in Palestine,* and Flaherty's *Nanook of the North,* had before 1921 brought an attitude to their reportage which made them more than mere travel films. In Britain during the twenties, H. Bruce Woolfe made a series of painstaking and still evocative reconstructions of the battles of World War I; while Cooper and Schoedsack went even further afield for the exciting material in *Grass* and *Chang*. 1928 brought Eisenstein's *The General Line,* a brilliant piece of farming propaganda, and Turin's *Turksib,* a showy account of the building of the Turko-Siberian railway. John Grierson, who invented the term 'documentary', made in 1929 a quiet little two-reeler about Britain's herring fleet, and called it *Drifters*; for the next ten years Britain's official and sponsored film units produced such brilliant results as *Shipyard, Coalface, Housing Problems, Song of Ceylon, North Sea* and *Night Mail*. In 1931 Vigo made his satirical documentary *A Propos de Nice,* and shortly afterwards Eisenstein was at work on his never-finished *Thunder over Mexico,* brilliant fragments of which survive as *Time in the Sun*. Travel films by explorers like the Martin Johnsons proliferated during the thirties; Flaherty spent two uncomfortable years off the Irish coast to make his *Man of Aran,* and later produced in India the semi-fictional *Elephant Boy*. Pare Lorenz produced cinematic poetry out of America's geographical problems in *The Plow that Broke the Plains* and *The River*.

World War II stimulated documentarists to new urgency and new techniques, brilliantly exemplified by Frank Capra's *Why We Fight* series for the US Signal Corps, turning unpleasant facts into breathtaking entertainment. With a predictably understated approach the British units produced a more sober but equally stirring series of reports on the war (*Western Approaches, Desert Victory, Target for Tonight*) and the home front (*Listen to Britain, Fires Were Started, A Diary for Timothy*), many of them directed by Britain's first documentary poet, Humphrey Jennings. The two countries combined resources to present a brilliant, high-flying compilation film about the last year of war, *The True Glory*.

Since 1945 the use of documentary for advertising (often very subtly) and teaching has so proliferated that no simple line of development can be shown. Television has relentlessly explored and elaborated every technique of the pioneers, with special attention to 'action stills', compilation films, and hard-hitting popular journalist approaches such as NBC's White Paper series and Granada's *World in Action*. Entertainment films devised a popular blend of fact and fiction in such neo-classics as *Boomerang, The House on 92nd Street* and *Naked City*. At last documentary was accepted as an agreeable blend of instruction and pleasure; and in the changed environment Flaherty's lyrical *Louisiana Story* seemed slow and solemn.

Book: *Documentary, a History of the Non-fiction film*, by E. Barnouw, was published by OUP in 1974.

¶ 'The story of the documentary movement is the story of how, not without a scar or two, we got by.'—*John Grierson*

Dodd, Claire (1908–1973). Pert supporting actress or second lead of the thirties.
Our Blushing Brides 30. An American Tragedy 31. The Match King 32. *Hard to Handle* 33. Footlight Parade 33. Babbitt 34. *The Case of the Curious Bride* 35. The Glass Key 35. The Case of the Velvet Claws 36. Three Loves Has Nancy 38. Charlie Chan in Honolulu 39. The Black Cat 41. The Mad Doctor of Market Streeet 42, many others.

Dodsworth (US 1936). William Wyler made, for its time, a remarkably adult and intelligent film of Sinclair Lewis' novel about a dull but sincere businessman who tries to preserve his marriage to a selfish woman. With Walter Huston and Ruth Chatterton, as the Americans abroad, Mary Astor as the other woman.

Dolan, Robert Emmett (1906–1972). American composer, in Hollywood from 1941.
Scores include: Birth of the Blues 41. Going My Way 44. The Bells of St Mary's 45. My Son John 51, etc. Produced White Christmas 54. Anything Goes 56, etc.

La Dolce Vita (Italy 1959). Federico Fellini's 'exposé' of 'the sweet life', a sprawling persuasive, orgiastic movie assumed by many to have contributed to a decline in standards because it reported without condemning.

Doleman, Guy (1923–). Australian character actor, in British films.
Phantom Stockade 53. The Shiralee 57. The Ipcress File 65. Thunderball 65. The Idol 66, etc.

Dolenz, George (1908–1963). Dullish Trieste-born leading man who played leads in some Hollywood films from 1941.
Unexpected Uncle 41. Enter Arsène Lupin 45. Vendetta 50. My Cousin Rachel 53. The Purple Mask 55. The Four Horsemen of the Apocalypse 62, others.
TV series: The Count of Monte Cristo 55.

dolly. A trolley on which a camera unit can be soundlessly moved about during shooting: can usually be mounted on rails. A 'crab dolly' will move in any direction.

Dolly, Jenny (1893–1941) and **Dolly, Rosie** (1893–1970) (Janszieka and Roszika Deutsch). European-American twins who became a world famous singing act and in 1918 starred in *The Million Dollar Dollies*. In 1946 Betty Grable and June Haver portrayed them in *The Dolly Sisters*.

Domergue, Faith (1925–). American leading lady, launched in 1950 with a publicity campaign which misfired. However, she played competently in a number of films.
Vendetta 50. Where Danger Lives 50. This Island Earth 55. California 63. Prehistoric Planet Women 66. One on Top of the Other 70. Legacy of Blood 71. The House of the Seven Corpses 73, etc.

Domingo, Placido (1941–). Spanish operatic tenor, who makes occasional films.
Autobiography 1984: *My First Forty Years*.
La Traviata 82. Carmen 84. Otello 86.

Don Juan. The amorous adventures of this legendary rascal, a heartless seducer created in stories by Gabriel Tellez (1571–1641), have been filmed several times, notably with John

Barrymore in 1927, Douglas Fairbanks Snr in 1934, Errol Flynn in 1948 and (of all people) Fernandel in 1955. Versions of the opera, *Don Giovanni,* are legion: the most elaborate was directed by Joseph Losey in 1979.

Don Quixote. There have been many screen versions of Cervantes' picaresque novel about the adventures of the addled knight and his slow but faithful lieutenant Sancho Panza . . . but none have been entirely successful because the genius of the book is a purely literary one. There was a French production in 1909; an American one in 1916 directed by Edward Dillon; a British one in 1923 directed by Maurice Elvey and starring Jerrold Robertshaw with George Robey. In 1933 Pabst made a British film of the story with Chaliapin and (again) George Robey; meanwhile a Danish director, Lau Lauritzen, had done one in 1926. The next batch of Quixotes began in 1947 with Rafael Gil's Spanish version; but the Russian production of 1957, directed by Kozintsev with Cherkassov in the title role, was probably the best of all. Since 1958 Orson Welles has been filming sections of his own version, which it looks as though we may never see; a Jugoslavian cartoon version appeared in 1961; in 1962 Finland, of all nations, contributed its own Quixote, directed by Eino Ruutsalo; and in 1972 the BBC and Universal made a TV film with Rex Harrison. The popular stage musical *Man of la Mancha,* filmed in 1972, is based on the life of author Miguel de Cervantes (1547–1616) and its correlation with that of his hero. There followed in 1973 a ballet version with Rudolph Nureyev.

Donahue, Troy (1936–) (Merle Johnson). American beefcake hero of the sixties.
Tarnished Angels 57. This Happy Feeling 58. The Perfect Furlough 59. Imitation of Life 59. A Summer Place 59. The Crowded Sky 61. *Parrish* 61. Susan Slade 61. Rome Adventure 62. Palm Springs Weekend 63. A Distant Trumpet 64. My Blood Runs Cold 65. Rocket to the Moon 67. Sweet Saviour 71. Godfather Two 75. The Legend of Frank Woods 77. Malibu (TV) 83, etc.
TV series: Hawaiian Eye 59–60. Surfside Six 60–62.

Donald Duck. Belligerent Disney cartoon character who was introduced in 1934 in *The Wise Little Hen,* was quickly streamlined and became more popular than Mickey Mouse. Still going strong.

Donald, James (1917–). British stage actor who has been in occasional films since 1941; usually plays a man of conscience rather than action.
The Missing Million 41. In Which We Serve 42. The Way Ahead 44. Broken Journey 47. *The Small Voice* 47. Trottie True 49. *White Corridors* 51. Brandy for the Parson 51. The Gift Horse 52. The Pickwick Papers 52. The Net 53. Beau Brummell 54. Lust for Life 56. *The Bridge on the River Kwai* 57. The Vikings 58. The Great Escape 63. King Rat 65. Cast a Giant Shadow 66. *The Jokers* 67. Hannibal Brooks 69. David Copperfield 69. The Royal Hunt of the Sun 69. The Big Sleep 78, etc.

Donaldson, Ted (1933–). American child star of the forties.
Once Upon a Time 44. *A Tree Grows in Brooklyn* 45. For the Love of Rusty 47 (and others in this series). The Decision of Christopher Blake 48. Phone Call from a Stranger 52, etc.

Donat, Peter (1928–). Canadian character actor.
My Old Man's Place 71. The Godfather Part Two 74. Russian Roulette 75. The Hindenburg 75. F.I.S.T. 78. A Different Story 78. The China Syndrome 79, etc.

Donat, Robert (1905–1958). Distinguished British stage actor (of Polish descent) with an inimitably melodious voice; he made some impressive films despite asthma which blighted his career. Biography 1968: *Robert Donat* by J. C. Trewin.
□Men of Tomorrow 32. That Night in London 32. Cash 32. The Private Life of Henry VIII 33. *The Count of Monte Cristo* 34. *The Thirty-Nine Steps* 35. *The Ghost Goes West* 36. Knight without Armour 37. *The Citadel* 38. *Goodbye Mr Chips* (AA) 39. *The Young Mr Pitt* 42. The Adventures of Tartu 43. Perfect Strangers 45. Captain Boycott (guest appearance) 47. *The Winslow Boy* 48. The Cure for Love (& d) 50. The Magic Box 50. Lease of Life 55. Inn of the Sixth Happiness 58.
❀ For the ethereal quality, partly caused by illness, of a few of his greatest performances. *Goodbye Mr Chips.*

Donath, Ludwig (1900–1967). Austrian character actor busy in America from the thirties.
The Strange Death of Adolf Hitler 43. *The Jolson Story* 46. Cigarette Girl 47. Jolson Sings Again 50. The Great Caruso 51. Sins of Jezebel 53. Torn Curtain 66, many others.

Donehue, Vincent J. (1916–1966). American stage director who came to Hollywood to make *Lonelyhearts* 59. *Sunrise at Campobello* 60.

Donen, Stanley (1924–). American director, former dancer; later branched out from musicals to sophisticated comedies and thrillers.
□*On The Town* (co-d) 49. Royal Wedding 51. Fearless Fagan 51. Give a Girl a Break 51. Love is Better than Ever 52. *Singin' in the Rain* (co-d) 52. *Seven Brides for Seven Brothers* 54. Deep in My Heart 54. It's Always Fair Weather (co-d) 55. *Funny Face* 57. *The Pajama Game* (& co-p) 57. Kiss Them for Me 57. *Indiscreet* (& p) 58. Damn Yankees (& co-p) 58. Once More with Feeling (& p) 60. Surprise Package (& p) 60. The Grass is Greener (& p) 61. *Charade* (& p) 63. Arabesque (& p) 66. Two for the Road (& p) 67. Bedazzled (& p) 67. Staircase (& p) 69. The Little Prince (& p) 73. Lucky Lady (& p) 76. Movie Movie 78. Saturn Three 80. Blame It on Rio 85.

Doniger, Walter (1917–). American writer.
Mob Town 41. Red Sundown 49. Cease Fire 52. The Steel Jungle (& d) 56. Madonna Red 78, etc.

Donlan, Yolande (1920–). American leading lady who had great success on the British stage as the dumb blonde in *Born Yesterday*; settled in England and married Val Guest.
Autobiography 1976: *Shake the Stars Down.*
Turnabout 41. Miss Pilgrim's Progress 50. *Mr Drake's Duck* 50. Penny Princess 51. They Can't Hang Me 55. *Expresso Bongo* 59. Jigsaw 62. Eighty Thousand Suspects 63. Seven Nights in Japan 76, etc.

Donlevy, Brian (1899–1972). Irish-American leading man, later character actor, in Hollywood after stage experience; characteristically in fast-talking tough roles with soft centres.
Mother's Boy 28. Barbary Coast 35. In Old Chicago 38. We're Going To Be Rich (GB) 38. Jesse James 39. *Beau Geste* (as the evil sergeant) 39. *Destry Rides Again* 39. *The Great McGinty* (leading role) 40. Brigham Young 40. The Great Man's Lady 40. A Gentleman after Dark 41. Billy the Kid 41. The Remarkable Andrew 41. Wake Island 42. *The Glass Key* 42. Nightmare 42. Hangmen Also Die 43. The Miracle of Morgan's Creek 43. *An American Romance* 44. Two Years Before the Mast 44. The Virginian 45. The Trouble with Women 46. The Beginning or the End 47. Kiss of Death 47. The Lucky Stiff 48. Shakedown 50. Hoodlum Empire 52. The Woman They Almost Lynched 53. The Big Combo 55. The Quatermass Experiment (GB) 55. A Cry in the Night 56. Quatermass II (GB) 56. Cowboy 58. Never So Few 59. The Errand Boy 61. Curse of the Fly (GB) 65. How to Stuff a Wild Bikini 65. The Fat Spy 66. Waco 66. Rogues' Gallery 67, etc.
TV series: Dangerous Assignment 52.

Donnagio, Pino (–). American composer.
Don't Look Now 73. Carrie 76. Piranha 78. Dressed to Kill 80. The Howling 81. Blow Out 82.

Donnell, Jeff (1921–). Pert American actress who played the heroine's friend in many routine comedies of the forties, now plays mothers.
A Night to Remember 43. He's My Guy 45. In a Lonely Place 50. Thief of Damascus 52. Sweet Smell of Success 57. Gidget Goes Hawaiian 61. The Iron Maiden (GB) 62. Stand Up and Be Counted 72. The Amazing Spiderman (TV) 77, etc.
TV series: The George Gobel Show 56. Matt Helm 75.

Donnelly, Donal (1932–). Irish stage actor, in occasional films.
The Rising of the Moon 57. Shake Hands with the Devil 59. Young Cassidy 65. The Knack 65. Up Jumped a Swagman 65, etc.

Donnelly, Dorothy (1880–1928). American stage actress who became lyricist and librettist for Sigmund Romberg, and was played by Merle Oberon in *Deep in My Heart* 54.

Donnelly, Ruth (1896–1982). American character actress, a wisecracking girl friend in the thirties, latterly in maternal roles.
Rubber Heels 27. Transatlantic 31. Ladies They Talk About 33. Footlight Parade 33. Convention City 33. Wonder Bar 34. Alibi Ike 35. Mr Deeds Goes to Town 36. More than a Secretary 36. *A Slight Case of Murder* 38. *Holiday* 38. Mr Smith Goes to Washington 39. My Little Chickadee 39. Rise and Shine 41. Pillow to Post 45. Cinderella Jones 46. *The Snake Pit* 48. I'd Climb the Highest Mountain 51. The Spoilers 55. Autumn Leaves 56. The Way to the Gold 57, many others.

Donner, Clive (1926–). British director, former editor, in films since 1942, directing since the mid-fifties.
□The Secret Place 56. Heart of a Child 57. A Marriage of Convenience 59. The Sinister Man 60. Some People 62. The Caretaker 63. *Nothing But the Best* 63. What's New Pussycat? 65. Luv 67. *Here We Go Round the Mulberry Bush* 67. Alfred the Great 69. Vampira 74. Spectre (TV) 76. Rogue Male (TV) 76. The Three Hostages (TV) 77. She Fell Among Thieves (TV) 78. The Thief of Baghdad (TV) 78. The Nude Bomb 80. Charlie Chan and the Curse of the Dragon Queen 81. Oliver Twist (TV) 82. The Scarlet Pimpernel (TV) 82. Arthur the King (TV) 83.

Donner, Jörn (1933–). Finnish writer-director.
Sunday in September 63. *To Love* 65. Black on White 67. Portraits of Women 69, etc.

Donner, Richard (c. 1939–). American director.
X-15 62. Salt and Pepper (GB) 68. Twinky (GB) 69. *The Omen* 76. Superman 78. Superman II (uncredited) 80. Inside Moves 80. The Final Conflict 81. The Toy 82. Ladyhawke 84. Lethal Weapon 87, etc.

Donohue, Jack (1910–84). American director, former Ziegfeld Follies dancer. Worked on many MGM musicals.
The Yellow Cab Man 50. Watch the Birdie 51. Calamity Jane (dances only) 53. Lucky Me 54. Babes in Toyland 61. Marriage on the Rocks 65. Assault on a Queen 66, etc.

Donovan, King (1919–87). American general purpose actor, usually in support roles; a frequent TV guest star.
Cargo to Capetown 50. The Beast from Twenty Thousand Fathoms 53. *Invasion of the Body Snatchers* 56. The Hanging Tree 59, many others.
TV series: The Bob Cummings Show 54. Please Don't Eat the Daisies 66.

Donskoi, Mark (1897–1980). Russian director celebrated for his 'Maxim Gorki trilogy'.
The Pigeon 29. Alien Shore 30. Fire 31. *The Childhood of Maxim Gorki* 38. *My Apprenticeship* 39. *My Universities* 40. How the Steel Was Tempered 42. The Rainbow 44. The Village Teacher 47. Mother 56. The Gordeyev Family 59. A Mother's Heart 66. A Mother's Devotion 67. Nadyezhda 73, others.

Dooley, Paul (1928–). American character actor associated chiefly with the films of Robert Altman.
Slapshot 77. A Wedding 78. A Perfect Couple 79. Breaking Away 79. Rich Kids 79. Health 80. Popeye 80. Paternity 81. Endangered Species 82. Kiss Me Goodbye 82. Going Berserk 83. Big Trouble 84. Sixteen Candles 85. O.C. and Stiggs 87, etc.

Doonan, Patric (1925–1958). British stage and screen actor, usually in honest, put-upon roles. Son of comedian George Doonan.
Once a Jolly Swagman 48. The Blue Lamp 50. The Gentle Gunman 52. The Net 53. Seagulls over Sorrento 54. Cockleshell Heroes 55, many second features.

dope sheet. A list of the contents of a piece of film, usually applied to newsreel libraries.

Dor, Karin (1938–). German leading lady.
Treasure of Silver Lake 62. Winnetou II 64. The Face of Fu Manchu 65. You Only Live Twice 67. Topaz 69. Live and Let Die 73, etc.

Doran, Ann (1914–). American character actress, often a friend of the heroine.
Penitentiary 38. Blondie 38. Blue, White and Perfect 42. The More the Merrier 43. Fear in the Night 46. The Snake Pit 48. Rebel without a Cause 55. The Man Who Turned to Stone 58. The Rawhide Trail 60. Rosie 67. First Monday in October 81, many others.
TV series: *Longstreet* 71. Shirley 79.

Dorfmann, Robert (1912–). French producer.
Jeux Interdits 52. Road to Salina 69. The Red Circle 70. Red Sun 71. Papillon 73, etc.

Dorleac, Françoise (1941–1967). French leading lady, killed in car crash. Sister of Catherine Deneuve.
That Man from Rio 64. Genghis Khan 65. Where the Spies Are 65. Cul de Sac (GB) 66. The Young Girls of Rochefort 67. Billion Dollar Brain 67, etc.

Dorn, Dolores (1935–) (D. Dorn-Heft). American stage actress briefly in Hollywood.
Phantom of the Rue Morgue 54. Uncle Vanya 58. Underworld USA 60. 13 West Street 62. Tell Me a Riddle 80, etc.

Dorn, Philip (1905–1975) (Frits van Dongen). Dutch stage actor who went to Hollywood in 1940 and was used mainly in sincere refugee or thoughtfully professional

roles: returned to Holland in the fifties, later settled in California.
Ski Patrol 40. *Escape* 40. Ziegfeld Girl 41. Tarzan's Secret Treasure 41. Calling Dr Gillespie 41. *Random Harvest* 42. Reunion in France 42. Chetniks 43. *Passage to Marseilles* 44. Blonde Fever 44. Escape in the Desert 45. I've Always Loved You 46. *I Remember Mama* 48. Panther's Moon 49. Sealed Cargo 51, etc.

Dorne, Sandra (1925–). British 'platinum blonde', often in tawdry roles.
Eyes That Kill 45. Once a Jolly Swagman 48. The Beggars' Opera 51. Roadhouse Girl 54. The Gelignite Gang 56. The Iron Petticoat 57. Orders to Kill 58. The Devil Doll 64. All Coppers Are . . . 72, etc.

Doro, Marie (1882–1956) (Marie Steward). American leading lady of the silent screen, one of Zukor's 'Famous Players'.
The Morals of Marcus 15. The White Pearl 15. Oliver Twist (title role) 16. The Heart of Nora Flynn 16. The Wood Nymph 16. The Mysterious Princess 19. Twelve Ten 19. Maid of Mystery 20, etc.

Dors, Diana (1931–84) (Diana Fluck). British 'blonde bombshell' who played good-time girls from the mid-forties. Wrote several catchpenny memoirs.
The Shop at Sly Corner 46. Holiday Camp 47. Dancing with Crime 47. My Sister and I 48. Peggy and the Pownall Case 48. *Oliver Twist* 48. Good Time Girl 48. The Calendar 49. Here Come the Huggetts 49. Vote for Huggett 49. It's Not Cricket 49. A Boy a Girl and a Bike 49. Diamond Lily 49. Dance Hall 50. Lady Godiva Rides Again 51. Worm's Eye View 51. The Last Page 52. My Wife's Lodger 52.The Weak and the Wicked 52. Is Your Honeymoon Really Necessary? 52. It's a Grand Life 53. The Great Game 53. The Saint's Return 54. Value for Money 55. A Kid for Two Farthings 55. Miss Tulip Stays the Night 55. As Long as They're Happy 55. *Yield to the Night* 56. I Married a Woman (US) 56. The Unholy Wife (US) 56. The Long Haul 57. The Love Specialist (It.) 57.Tread Softly, Stranger 58. Passport to Shame 59. On the Double (US) 60. Scent of Mystery (US) 60. The Big Bankroll (US) 61. Mrs Gibbons' Boys 62. West Eleven 63. Allez France 64. The Sandwich Man 66. Berserk 67. Danger Route 67. Hammerhead 68. Baby Love 69. There's a Girl in My Soup 70. Deep End 71. Hannie Caulder 71. The Pied Piper 71. Every Afternoon 72. Nothing But the Night 73. The Amazing Mr Blunden 72. The Amorous Milkman 72. Theatre of Blood 73. Steptoe and Son Ride Again 73. Craze 73. Rosie 74, etc.

D'Orsay, Fifi (1904–1983) (Yvonne Lussier). Vivacious Canadian leading lady of Hollywood films in the early thirties.
Hot for Paris 30. *Just Imagine* 31. Silk Stockings 32. Wonder Bar 34. Accent on Youth 45. Wild and Wonderful 63. The Art of Love 65, others.

Dorsey, Jimmy (1904–1957) and **Tommy** (1905–1956). American bandleaders and brothers; individually they decorated many musicals of the forties, and came together in a biopic, *The Fabulous Dorseys* 46.

Dorziat, Gabrielle (1880–1979) (G. Sigrist). French character actress.
Mayerling 36. La Fin du Jour 39. Premier Rendezvous 41. *Les Parents Terribles* 48. Manon 49. Little Boy Lost 53. Act of Love 54. Les Espions 57. Germinal 63, etc.

Dostoievsky, Fyodor (1821–1881). Russian writer, chiefly of doom-laden novels, of which the most frequently-filmed is *Crime and Punishment*; there have also been attempts at *The Idiot, The Brothers Karamazov, White Nights, The Great Sinner, Pyriev* and others.

Dotrice, Karen (1955–). British child actress who matured gracefully.
The Three Lives of Thomasina 63. Mary Poppins 64. The Gnome-Mobile 67. Joseph Andrews 77. The 39 Steps 79, etc.

Dotrice, Michele (1947–). British leading actress, mostly on TV.
And Soon the Darkness 70. Jane Eyre (TV) 73. Not Now Comrade 76, etc.

Dotrice, Roy (1923–). British stage actor with a strong line in senile impersonation.
The Heroes of Telemark 65. A Twist of Sand 68. Lock Up Your Daughters 69. One of Those Things 71. Nicholas and Alexandra 71. Family Reunion (TV) 82. Amadeus 84. Eliminators 85. Young Harry Houdini (TV) 87, etc.

double exposure. This occurs when two or more images are recorded on the same piece of film. Used for trick shots when two characters played by the same actor have to meet; also for dissolves, dream sequences, etc.

double-headed print. One in which sound and picture are recorded on separate pieces of film, usually at cutting copy stage or before OK is received to make combined negative.

Double Indemnity (US 1944). The forties now seem a pretty 'dated' era, but this tawdry crime story, about a man who murders his mistress's husband for his insurance money, still packs a punch by virtue of Billy Wilder's direction and a witty script in which Wilder and Raymond Chandler had a hand. Fred MacMurray and Edward G. Robinson are in good form: Barbara Stanwyck's *femme fatale* has worn less well. From a novel by James Cain; photographed by John Seitz with music by Miklos Rozsa. An undistinguished TV copy was made in 1973, with Richard Crenna and Samantha Eggar.

A Double Life (US 1947). The film for which Ronald Colman belatedly won an Oscar was an arrant piece of nonsense about an actor who got his Othello mixed up with his private life. Neither Garson Kanin's script not George Cukor's direction could give it the quality it aimed for.

double take. A form of comic reaction to a piece of news or situation. The subject at first fails to take it in, and after a few moments the penny drops with a start. Cary Grant and Oliver Hardy were among the prime exponents of the device, but the comedian who really brought it to the point of art was James Finlayson, who not only had the most pronounced reactions but added a slow withdrawal of the head, calling the entire effect a 'double take and fade away'.

Doucet, Catherine (1875–1958) (Catherine Green). American stage actress of imposing presence; played dowagers in a few films.
As Husbands Go 33. Little Man What Now 34. Accent on Youth 35. Millions in the Air 35. *These Three* 36. Poppy 36. When You're in Love 37. It Started with Eve 41. Nothing But the Truth 41. Family Honeymoon 49, etc.

Douglas, Angela (1940–). British general purpose actress.
Shakedown 59. Some People 61. The Comedy Man 63. Carry On Cowboy 64. Carry On Follow That Camel 66. Carry On Up the Khyber 67. Maroc 7 68. Digby 74.

Douglas, Donald (1905–1945) (Douglas Kinleyside). Quiet-spoken American actor, usually seen as smooth villain or 'good loser'.
Men in White 34. Alexander's Ragtime Band 38. Whistling in the Dark 41. The Crystal Ball 43. Show Business 44. Farewell My Lovely 44. Club Havana 45. Gilda 46, etc.

Douglas, Donna (1933–) (Doris Smith). Chirpy American blonde supporting player who found fame and fortune 1962–70 as Ellie Mae in TV's *The Beverly Hillbillies*.
Career 62. Lover Come Back 62. Frankie and Johnny 66, etc.

Douglas, Gordon (1909–). American director, former comedy writer for Hal Roach. Jobs have grown in importance but talent remains routine.
Saps at Sea 40. Broadway Limited 41. The Devil with Hitler 43. Zombies on Broadway 45. If You Knew Susie 48. The Doolins of Oklahoma 49. Kiss Tomorrow Goodbye 50. Only the Valiant 51. I Was a Communist for the FBI 51. Come Fill the Cup 51. Mara Maru 52. The Iron Mistress 53. So This is Love 53. The Charge at Feather River 53. *Them* 54. Young at Heart 54. Sincerely Yours 55. The Big Land 56. Bombers B-52 58. Yellowstone Kelly 59. The Sins of Rachel Cade 60. Gold of the Seven Saints 61. Follow That Dream 62. Call Me Bwana 63. Robin and the Seven Hoods 64. Rio Conchos 64. Sylvia 65. Harlow 65. Stagecoach 66. Way Way Out 66. In Like Flint 67. Chuka 67. Tony Rome 67. *The Detective* 68. Lady in Cement 68. Skullduggery 69. Viva Knievel 77, etc.

Douglas, Jack (1927–). British comedian who has appeared exclusively in *Carry Ons*. Much on TV.

Douglas, Kirk (1916–). (Issur Danielovitch Demsky). American leading actor with stage experience; started playing weaklings and gangsters but graduated to tense, virile, intelligent heroes in films of many kinds.
□*The Strange Love of Martha Ivers* 46. *Out of the Past* 47. I Walk Alone 47. My Dear Secretary 47. Mourning Becomes Electra 47. The Walls of Jericho 48. A Letter to Three Wives 48. *Champion* 49. Young Man with a Horn 50. The Glass Menagerie 51. *Ace in the Hole* 51. Along the Great Divide 51. *Detective Story* 51. The Big Trees 52. The Big Sky 52. The Bad and the Beautiful 52. The Story of Three Loves 53. The Juggler 53. Act of Love 54. Ulysses (It.) 54. Twenty Thousand Leagues under the Sea 54. Man without a Star 55. The Racers 55. The Indian

Fighter 55. *Lust for Life* (as Van Gogh) 56. Top Secret Affair 57. *Gunfight at the OK Corral* (as Doc Holliday) 57. *Paths of Glory* 57. The Vikings 58. Last Train from Gun Hill 58. The Devil's Disciple 59. *Spartacus* 60. Town Without Pity 61. The Last Sunset 61. Strangers When We Meet 61. *Lonely Are the Brave* 62. Two Weeks in Another Town 62. *The List of Adrian Messenger* 63. For Love or Money 63. The Hook 63. *Seven Days in May* 64. In Harm's Way 65. The Heroes of Telemark 65. *Cast a Giant Shadow* 66. Is Paris Burning? 66. The Way West 67. The War Wagon 67. A Lovely Way to Die 68. The Brotherhood 68. The Arrangement 69. There Was a Crooked Man 70. A Gunfight 71. The Light at the Edge of the World 71. Catch Me a Spy 71. A Man to Respect 72. Scalawag (& d) 73. Mousey (TV) 73. Posse (& d) 75. Once is not Enough 75. The Moneychangers (TV) 76. Victory at Entebbe (TV) 76. Holocaust 2000 77. The Fury 78. Saturn Three 79. Home Movies 79. The Villain 79. The Final Countdown 80. The Man from Snowy River 82. Remembrance of Love (TV) 82. Eddie Macon's Run 83. Tough Guys 86.

❀ For determination and intelligence above the call of duty. *Ace in the Hole.*

¶ He's wanted to be Burt Lancaster all his life.—*John Frankenheimer*

My kids never had the advantage I had. I was born poor.—*K.D.*

I want my sons to surpass me, because that's a form of immortality.—*K.D.*

Champion established the essential Kirk Douglas persona—a ruthless, selfish, fiercely driven upstart.—*Stephen Farb and Marc Green, Hollywood Royalties*

I've made a career of playing sons of bitches—*K.D.*

Kirk never makes an effort towards people. He's pretty much wrapped up in himself.—*Doris Day*

Famous line (*Ace in the Hole*): 'I'm a thousand a day man, Mr Boot. You can have me for nothing.'

† The name of Douglas's company is Bryna. It was his mother's forename.

Douglas, Lloyd C. (1877–1951). American best-selling novelist: a doctor who did not begin writing till in his fifties. Films of his books include *The Green Light, Magnificent Obsession, The Robe, White Banners, Disputed Passage, The Big Fisherman.*

Douglas, Melvyn (1901–1981) (Melvyn Hesselberg). Suave, polished American leading man of the thirties and forties, most at home in a dinner jacket with an elegant lady on his arm; later spent some years on Broadway and emerged as a fine character actor.

□Tonight or Never 31. Prestige 32. The Wiser Sex 32. Broken Wing 32. As You Desire Me 32. *The Old Dark House* 32. Nagana 33. The Vampire Bat 33. Counsellor at Law 33. Woman in the Dark 34. *Dangerous Corner* 34. People's Enemy 35. She Married Her Boss 35. Mary Burns Fugitive 35. Annie Oakley 35. *The Lone Wolf Returns* 35. And So They Were Married 36. The Gorgeous Hussy 36. Theodora Goes Wild 36. Women of Glamour 37. Captains Courageous 37. *I Met Him In Paris* 37. Angel 37. I'll Take Romance 37. There's Always a Woman 38. Arsène Lupin Returns 38. The Toy Wife 38. Fast Company 38. *That Certain Age* 38. The Shining Hour 38. There's That Woman Again 38. Tell No Tales 38. Good Girls Go to Paris 39. The Amazing Mr Williams 39. *Ninotchka* 39. Too Many Husbands 40. He Stayed for Breakfast 40. Third Finger Left Hand 40. This Thing Called Love 41. That Uncertain Feeling 41. A Woman's Face 41. Our Wife 41. Two Faced Woman 41. They All Kissed the Bride 42. Three Hearts for Julia 43. Sea of Grass 47. The Guilt of Janet Ames 47. *Mr Blandings Builds His Dream House* 48. My Own True Love 48. A Woman's Secret 49. The Great Sinner 49. My Forbidden Past 51. On the Loose 51. Billy Budd 62. *Hud* (AA) 63. Advance to the Rear 64. The Americanization of Emily 64. Rapture 65. Hotel 67. Companions in Nightmare (TV) 72. *I Never Sang for My Father* 69. Hunters are for Killing (TV) 70. Death Takes a Holiday (TV) 71. The Going Up of David Lev (TV) 71. One is a Lonely Number 72. The Candidate 72. Death Squad (TV) 73. Murder or Mercy? (TV) 74. The Tenant 76. Twilight's Last Gleaming 76. The Seduction of Joe Tynan 79. Tell Me a Riddle 79. Being There (AA) 79. The Changeling 81. Ghost Story 81. TV series: Steve Randall 52. Hollywood Confidential 54.

❀ For perfecting the image of the smart-spoken thirties playboy. *Ninotchka.*

¶ *M.D.:* The Hollywood roles I did were boring: I was soon fed up with them. It's true they gave me a world-wide reputation I could trade on, but they also typed me as a one-dimensional non-serious actor.

Douglas, Michael (1945–). American leading man of the seventies, son of Kirk Douglas.

Hail Hero 70. Adam at 6 a.m. 70. Summertree 71. When Michael Calls (TV) 72. Napoleon and Samantha 72. One Flew Over the Cuckoo's Nest (co-p only) 75. Coma 78. Running 79. The China Syndrome 80. It's My Turn 80. The Star Chamber 83. Romancing the Stone 84. A Chorus Line 85. Jewel of the Nile 86. Fatal Attraction 87. Wall Street 87, etc.
TV series: *The Streets of San Francisco* 72–75.

¶ *M.D. (1980):* The exciting thing about making movies today is that everything is up for grabs. And you had better grab.

Douglas, Paul (1907–1959). Burly American actor with unexpected comedy sense.
□*A Letter to Three Wives* 48. It Happens Every Spring 49. Everybody Does It 49. The Big Lift 50. Love that Brute 50. Panic in the Streets 50. *Fourteen Hours* 51. The Guy who Came Back 51. Angels in the Outfield 51. When in Rome 52. Clash by Night 52. We're Not Married 52. Never Wave at a WAC 52. Forever Female 53. *Executive Suite* 54. The Maggie 54. Green Fire 54. *Joe Macbeth* 55. The Leather Saint 56. *The Solid Gold Cadillac* 56. The Gamma People 56. This Could Be the Night 57. Beau James 57. Fortunella (It.) 58. The Mating Game 59.

Douglas, Robert (1909–) (Robert Douglas Finlayson). British stage leading man who made some home-grown films during the thirties; moved to Hollywood after the war and played mainly suave villains in routine melodramas, then went into TV direction.
P.C. Josser 31. The Blarney Stone 34. The Street Singer 36. The Challenge 38. Over the Moon 39, etc; war service; The End of the River 47. The Decision of Christopher Blake 48. The New Adventures of Don Juan 48. Sons of the Musketeers 51. Ivanhoe 52. The Prisoner of Zenda 52. Fair Wind to Java 53. King Richard and the Crusaders 54. The Virgin Queen 55. The Scarlet Coat (as Benedict Arnold) 55. Night Train to Paris (GB) (d only) 64, etc.

Dourif, Brad (1950–). American character actor.
One Flew Over the Cuckoo's Nest 76. Gruppenbild mit Dame 77. The Eyes of Laura Mars 78. Wise Blood 79. Studs Lonigan 79. Guyana Tragedy (TV) 80. Heaven's Gate 80. Ragtime 81. Dune 84. Blue Velvet 86. Impure Thoughts 86.

Dove, Billie (1904–) (Lilian Bohny). American leading lady of the twenties; could not adapt to sound.
Beyond the Rainbow 22. Polly of the Follies 22. Wanderer of the Wasteland 24. The Black Pirate 26. One Night at Susie's 28. Painted Angel 30. Blondie of the Follies 32. Diamond Head 62, etc.

Dovzhenko, Alexander (1894–1956). Russian writer-director, former teacher; in films since 1925.
Arsenal 29. *Earth* 30. Ivan 32. *Aerograd* 35. Life in Blossom 47, etc.

Dow, Peggy (1928–) (Peggy Varnadow). American leading lady who before retiring to marry made a strong impression in several films of the early fifties.
□Undertow 49. Woman in Hiding 50. Showdown 50. The Sleeping City 50. *Harvey* 50. Reunion in Reno 51. You Never Can Tell 51. *Bright Victory* 51. I Want You 51.

Dowd, Nancy (1944–). American screenwriter.
Slapshot 77. Coming Home 78.

Dowling, Constance (1923–1969). American leading lady who flowered briefly in the forties.
Knickerbocker Holiday 44. Up in Arms 44. The Flame 47. Gog 54, etc.

Dowling, Doris (1921–). American leading lady, sister of Constance Dowling. Briefly in Hollywood character roles, then moved to Italy.
The Lost Weekend 45. The Blue Dahlia 46. Bitter Rice 48. Othello 51. Running Target 58, etc.
TV series: My Living Doll 64.

Dowling, Eddie (1894–1976) (Joseph Nelson Goucher). American singer, comedian and director of the Broadway stage; appeared only in silent films.

Dowling, Joan (1929–1954). British teenage actress who failed to get mature roles.
Hue and Cry 46. *No Room at the Inn* 48. Landfall 49. Pool of London 51. Woman of Twilight 52, etc.

Down, Lesley-Anne (1954–). British leading lady of the late seventies; made her name on TV in *Upstairs, Downstairs.*
All The Right Noises 69. Assault 70.

Scalawag 74. The Pink Panther Strikes Again 76. A Little Night Music 77. The Betsy 78. *The One and Only Original Phyllis Dixey* (TV) 78. The Great Train Robbery 79. Hanover Street 79. Rough Cut 80. Sphinx 81. The Hunchback of Notre Dame (TV) 82. Murder is Easy (TV) 81. Nomads 84. The Last Days of Pompeii (TV) 84. Arch of Triumph (TV) 85. *North and South* (TV) 86.

Downs, Cathy (1924–78). American leading lady of a few forties films.
Diamond Horseshoe 45. My Darling Clementine 46. The Noose Hangs High 48. Short Grass 50. Gobs and Gals 52, etc.
TV series: Joe Palooka 54.

Downs, Johnny (1913–). American light leading man and dancer, former member of 'Our Gang'.
The Clock Strikes Eight 35. Melody Girl 40. All-American Co-Ed 41. Harvest Melody 44. The Right to Love 45. Cruising Down the River 53, many others.

Doyle, Sir Arthur Conan (1859–1930). British novelist and creator of Sherlock Holmes (qv). His other chief bequest to the screen is the twice-filmed *The Lost World*.

Doyle, David (1925–). American character actor.
Parades 72. Lady Liberty 72. The Comeback 77, etc.
TV series: Bridget Loves Bernie 73. Charlie's Angels 76–80.

Doyle, Laird (1907–1936). American screenwriter.
Oil for the Lamps of China 35. The Prince and the Pauper 36. Another Dawn 37. Strangers on Honeymoon (GB) 37, etc.

Dozier, William (1908–). American producer, former talent agent. With RKO, Columbia and Goldwyn in forties; independently made *Two of a Kind* 51. *Harriet Craig* 53; then into TV.

Drach, Michel (1930–). French director.
Amélie ou le Temps d'Aimer 60. Diamond Safari 65. Elise ou la Vraie Vie 69. Les Violons du Bal 73. Parlez-moi d'Amour 75. Le Passé Simple 77, etc.

Dracula. The Transylvanian vampire count created by Bram Stoker in his novel published 1897 has been on the screen in many manifestations. Max Schreck played him in Murnau's German silent *Nosferatu* 23. Bela Lugosi first donned the cloak for Universal's *Dracula* 31, was not in *Dracula's Daughter* 36 but reappeared as one of Dracula's relations in *Return of the Vampire* 44 and played the Count in *Abbott and Costello Meet Frankenstein* 48. Lon Chaney starred in *Son of Dracula* 43; John Carradine took over in *House of Frankenstein* 45 and *House of Dracula* 46; Francis Lederer had a go in *The Return of Dracula* 58. Also in 1958 came the British remake of the original *Dracula* (*Horror of Dracula*) with Christopher Lee; David Peel was one of the Count's disciples in *Brides of Dracula* 60 and Noel Willman another in *Kiss of the Vampire* 63; while Lee ingeniously reappeared in 1965 as *Dracula Prince of Darkness,* in 1968 in *Dracula Has Risen from the Grave*, in 1969 in *Taste the Blood of Dracula,* and in 1970 in *Scars of Dracula.* In the same year Ingrid Pitt was *Countess Dracula* and 1972 brought *Vampire Circus.* Meanwhile the Count had American rivals in Count Yorga, in *The House of Dark Shadows* and in *Blacula.* (Hollywood in 1957 had produced a lady vampire in *Blood of Dracula,* and in 1965 *Billy the Kid Meets Dracula.* Polanski's failed satire of 1967, *The Fearless Vampire Killers,* had Ferdy Mayne as Von Krolock, who was Dracula in all but name.) *Dracula AD 1972* and *The Satanic Rites of Dracula* were further variations on the main theme, both with Mr Lee; while Jack Palance in 1973 did a TV film version of the original story for Dan Curtis. It seemed that the Count, though officially dead, was unlikely ever to lie down for long; but no one could have been prepared for the profusion of Dracula variations of the late seventies, by which time Hammer had given up participating. Klaus Kinski aped Schreck in a remake of *Nosferatu.* George Hamilton appeared in a sexy spoof, *Love at First Bite.* Laurence Olivier played Van Helsing to Frank Langella's *Dracula.* Would it never end?

Drag: see Female Impersonation.

Dragoti, Stan (–). American director.
Dirty Little Billy 73. Love at First Bite 78. Mr Mom 83.

Drake, Alfred (1914–) (Alfredo Capurro). Italian-American singer-dancer popular in Broadway shows; his only film has been *Tars and Spars* 44.

Drake, Betsy (1923–). American leading lady, formerly on stage; married for a time to Cary Grant.

Every Girl Should Be Married 48. Pretty Baby 50. The Second Woman 51. Room for One More 52. Clarence the Cross-Eyed Lion 65. Players 79, etc.

Drake, Charles (1914–) (Charles Ruppert). American actor usually found in dullish, good-natured 'second leads'.
Dive Bomber 41. The Man Who Came to Dinner 41. Yankee Doodle Dandy 42. Air Force 43. You Came Along 44. Conflict 45. A Night in Casablanca 45. Whistle Stop 46. Tarzan's Magic Fountain 49. Harvey 50. Gunsmoke 52. It Came from Outer Space 53. The Glenn Miller Story 53. All That Heaven Allows 55. The Price of Fear 56. The Third Day 65. Valley of the Dolls 67. The Swimmer 68. The Arrangement 69. The Seven Minutes 71, others.
TV series: Rendezvous (GB) 61.

Drake, Charlie (1925–) (Charles Springall). Diminutive British TV comedian with high-pitched voice and tendency to acrobatic slapstick.
Sands of the Desert 60. Petticoat Pirates 61. The Cracksman 63. Mister Ten Per Cent 66, etc.

Drake, Dona (1920–) (Rita Novella). Mexican singer, dancer and general livewire, former band vocalist as Rita Rio.
Aloma of the South Seas 41. Road to Morocco 42. Salute for Three 43. The House of Tao Ling 47. So This Is New York 48. Beyond the Forest 49. Valentino 51. Princess of the Nile 54, etc.

Drake, Fabia (1904–) (F. D. McGlinchy). British stage and screen character actress: usually plays battleaxes.
Meet Mr Penny 38. All over the Town 48. Young Wives' Tales 51. Fast and Loose 54. The Good Companions 57, many others.

Drake, Frances (1908–). American leading lady of the thirties.
The Jewel 33. Bolero 34. Ladies Should Listen 34. Forsaking All Others 34. *Les Misérables* 35. Mad Love 35. The Invisible Ray 36. And Sudden Death 36. Love Under Fire 37. There's Always a Woman 38. It's a Wonderful World 39. I Take This Woman 40, etc.

Drake, Tom (1918–1982) (Alfred Alderdyce). American actor, the 'boy next door' of many a forties film.
Two Girls and a Sailor 44. Meet Me in St Louis 44. *The Green Years* 46. I'll Be Yours 47. Master of Lassie 48. Never Trust a Gambler 51. Sudden Danger 55. The Sandpiper 65. Red Tomahawk 67. The Spectre of Edgar Allan Poe 72. The Return of Joe Forrester (TV) 75, etc.

Draper, Peter (1925–). British playwright and screenwriter.
The System 64. I'll Never Forget Whatshisname 67. The Buttercup Chain 70, etc.

Drayton, Alfred (1881–1949) (Alfred Varick). Bald British actor who in later life often played comedy villains in stage farces co-starring Robertson Hare.
Iron Justice 15. A Little Bit of Fluff 19. Honeypot 20. A Scandal in Bohemia 25. The Squeaker 30. The W Plan 31. The Calendar 31. Friday the Thirteenth 33. Jack Ahoy 34. The Crimson Circle 36. So This Is London 38. A Spot of Bother 40. The Big Blockade 42. They Knew Mr Knight 44. The Halfway House 44. *Nicholas Nickleby* (as Squeers) 47. Things Happen at Night 48, etc.

dreams, with their opportunities for camera magic and mystery, are dear to Hollywood's heart. The first film with dream sequences followed by a psychological explanation was probably Pabst's *Secrets of a Soul*; the trick caught on very firmly in such later pictures as *Lady in the Dark, A Matter of Life and Death, Spellbound, Dead of Night, Fear in the Night, Farewell My Lovely, The Secret Life of Walter Mitty, Possessed, Dream Girl, Three Cases of Murder* and *The Night Walker*. In *Vampyr* and *Wild Strawberries* the hero dreamed of his own funeral; and in *Devotion* Ida Lupino dreamed of death as a man on horseback coming across the moor to sweep her away. Recently, flashbacks have become less fashionable than a story told as in a series of daydreams by the main character, the past mingling with the present, as in *Death of a Salesman* and *I Was Happy Here. Roman Scandals, A Connecticut Yankee at the Court of King Arthur, Ali Baba Goes to Town, Fiddlers Three* and *Dreaming* are but five examples of the many comedies in which a character has been knocked on the head and dreams himself back in some distant time.

In the mid-forties such films as *The Woman in the Window, The Strange Affair of Uncle Harry* and *The Horn Blows at Midnight* set the fashion for getting the hero out of some impossible situation by having him wake up and find he'd been dreaming. This was scarcely fair in adult films, though it had honourable origins in *Alice in Wonderland* and *The Wizard of Oz*. Nor is there much excuse for the other favourite script trick of having one's cake and eating it, as in *Portrait of Jennie* and *Miracle in the Rain*, when some ghostly occurrence to the hero is passed off as dream until he finds some tangible evidence—a scarf, a coin or some other memento—that it was real.

The closest a film dream came to coming true was in *The Night My Number Came Up*, when the foreseen air crash was narrowly averted. In the brilliantly clever frame story of *Dead of Night*, the hero dreams he will commit a murder, and does, only to wake up and find the whole sequence of events beginning again: he is caught in an endless series of recurring nightmares.

See also: *fantasy*.

Dreier, Alex (1916–). Rotund American character actor, former news presenter.
Chandler 72. The Carey Treatment 72. Murdock's Gang (TV) 74.

Dreier, Hans (1884–1966). German art director, primarily associated with Lubitsch and, like him, long in Hollywood.
The Hunchback of Notre Dame 23. *Forbidden Paradise* 24. The Love Parade 29. *Dr Jekyll and Mr Hyde* 31. *Trouble in Paradise* 32. *Cleopatra* 34. Desire 36. Bluebeard's Eighth Wife 38. Dr Cyclops 39. Reap the Wild Wind 42. For Whom the Bell Tolls 43. *Lady in the Dark* 43. Incendiary Blonde 45. The Emperor Waltz 48. Samson and Delilah 49. *Sunset Boulevard* 50. A Place in the Sun 51, many others.
❀ For ingeniously influencing fashions for interior decoration in the early thirties. *Trouble in Paradise*.

Dreifuss, Arthur (1908–). German-born American director of second features, former child conductor and choreographer.
□Mystery in Swing 40. Reg'lar Fellers 41. Baby Face Morgan 42. Boss of Big Town 42. The Payoff 42. Sarong Girl 43. Melody Parade 43. Campus Rhythm 43. Nearly Eighteen 43. The Sultan's Daughter 43. Ever Since Venus 44. Eadie was a Lady 45. Booked on Suspicion 45. Boston Blackie's Rendezvous 45. The Gay Senorita 45. Prison Ship 45. Junior Prom 46. Freddie Steps Out 46. High School Hero 46. Vacation Days 47. Betty Co-Ed 47. Little Miss Broadway 47. Two Blondes and a Redhead 47. Sweet Genevieve 47. Glamor Girl 48. Mary Lou 48. I Surrender Dear 48. An Old Fashioned Girl 49. Manhattan Angel 49. Shamrock Hill 49. There's a Girl in My Heart 49. Life Begins at 17 58. The Last Blitzkrieg 58. Juke Box Rhythm 58. *The Quare Fellow* 62. Riot on Sunset Strip 67. The Love Ins 67. For Singles Only 68. A Time to Sing 68. The Young Runaways 68.

Dreiser, Theodore (1871–1945). Serious American novelist, a social realist who was popular in the early part of the century. Films of his books include *An AmericanTragedy* (remade as *A Place in the Sun*), *Jennie Gerhardt* and *Carrie*.

Dresdel, Sonia (1909–1976) (Lois Obee). British stage actress usually cast in masterful roles.
The World Owes Me a Living 42. While I Live 47. This Was a Woman 47. The Fallen Idol 48. The Clouded Yellow 50. The Third Visitor 51. Now and Forever 54. The Trials of Oscar Wilde 60. Lady Caroline Lamb 72, etc.

Dresser, Louise (1881–1965) (Louise Kerlin). American character actress of the thirties, former vaudevillian.
Prodigal Daughters 23. The Eagle 25. Not Quite Decent 27. Mammy 30. State Fair 33. The Scarlet Empress 34. Maid of Salem 37, etc.

Dressler, Marie (1869–1934) (Leila Von Koerber). American comedy character actress, the heavyweight heroine of silent comedy and star of MGM comedy-dramas of the early thirties.
Autobiographical books: *The Life Story of an Ugly Duckling* 1924, *My Own Story* 1934.
□*Tillie's Punctured Romance* 14. Tillie's Tomato Surprise 15. Tillie's Nightmare 15. The Scrublady 17. The Agonies of Agnes 18. The Red Cross Nurse 18. The Callahans and the Murphys 27. Breakfast at Sunrise 27. The Joy Girl 27. Bringing Up Father 28. The Patsy 28. The Divine Lady 29. The Vagabond Lovers 29. Hollywood Revue of 1929. Road Show 29. Chasing Rainbows 30. One Romantic Night 30. Let Us Be Gay 30. Derelict 30. *Anna Christie* 30. Caught Short 30. The Swan 30. The March of Time 30. Call of the Flesh 30. The Girl Said No 30. *Min and Bill* (AA) 30. Reducing 31. Politics 31. *Emma* 32. *Prosperity* 32. *Tugboat Annie* 33. *Dinner at Eight* 33. Christopher Bean 33.
❀ For turning her unlikely personality into true star quality at an advanced age. *Dinner at Eight*.

¶ I'm too homely for a prima donna and too ugly for a soubrette.—*M.D.*
You're only as good as your last picture.—*M.D.*
I have been known to grande dame it, at times.—*M.D.*

Dreville, Jean (1906–). French director.
Cage aux Rossignols 43. La Ferme du Pendu 46. Le Visiteur 47. Operation Swallow (The Battle for Heavy Water) 47. Les Casse-Pieds 48. Horizons Sans Fin 53. A Pied a Cheval et en Spoutnik 58. Normandie-Niemen 60. Lafayette 61. The Sleeping Sentry 66, etc.

Drew, Ellen (1915–) (Terry Ray). American light leading lady of the forties.
College Holiday 36. Hollywood Boulevard 36. Night of Mystery 37. Murder Goes to College 37. The Buccaneer 38. You and Me 38. Sing you Sinners 38. If I Were King 38. Geronimo 39. French Without Tears 39. *Christmas In July* 40. The Mad Doctor 41. Our Wife 41. The Remarkable Andrew 42. The Impostor 44. China Sky 45. Isle of the Dead 46. Johnny O'Clock 47. The Swordsman 47. The Crooked Way 49. Davy Crockett Indian Scout 50. The Great Missouri Raid 50. The Outlaw's Son 57, many others.

Drew, Mr and Mrs Sidney (1864–1919 and 1868–1925) (Sidney White and Lucille McVey). American stage actors who appeared in a number of very popular middle-class domestic film comedies.
Duplicity 16. Hypochondriacs 17. Henry's Ancestors 17. Her First Love 17. His Deadly Calm 17. His First Love 18. A Youthful Affair 18. Romance and Rings 19. Once a Mason 19. Harold the Last of the Saxons 19. The Charming Mrs Chase 20, etc.

Dreyer, Carl (1889–1968). Celebrated Danish director whose later works were few but notable.
□Praesidenten 20. *Leaves from Satan's Book* 20. Praesteenken 21. Elsker Hverandre 22. Once Upon a Time 22. Michael 24. Du Skal Aere Din Hustru 25. Glomsdal Bruden 26. *The Passion of Joan of Arc* 28. *Vampyr* 32. *Day of Wrath* 43. Tva Manniskor 45. Ordet 55. Gertrud 64.

Dreyfus, Alfred (1859–1935). The French officer unjustly sentenced to Devil's Island in 1885 for selling secrets, but reprieved by Zola's advocacy, has been played on screen by Cedric Hardwicke in *Dreyfus* (GB 1930) (Fritz Kortner in the German version), by Joseph Schildkraut in *The Life of Emile Zola* (US 1937) and by Jose Ferrer in *I Accuse* (GB 1957).

Dreyfuss, Richard (1947–). American leading man in Hollywood.
□Hello Down There 68. The Young Runaways 69. The Graduate 67. Dillinger 73. The Second Coming of Suzanne 73. *American Graffiti* 73. *The Apprenticeship of Duddy Kravitz* 74. *Jaws* 75. Inserts 75. Victory at Entebbe (TV) 76. Close Encounters of the Third Kind 77. The Goodbye Girl (AA, BFA) 77. The Big Fix 78. The Competition 80. Whose Life is It Anyway? 81.
Down and Out in Beverly Hills 85. Stand By Me 86. Stakeout 87. Tin Men 87. Nuts 87.

¶ *R.D.:* Behind all art is ego, and I am an artist and I am unique.
R.D.: I enjoyed the journey to the top but then found myself disappointed.
R.D.: The motion picture business is run by corporate thieves.

Drifters (GB 1929). John Grierson's first documentary, a study of North Sea herring fishers which now seems dull but on its first screening was a new departure and a revelation.

Driscoll, Bobby (1937–1968). American boy actor of the forties and fifties; AA 1949 as best child actor.
Lost Angel 43. The Sullivans 44. From This Day Forward 46. So Goes My Love 46. Song of the South 46. If You Knew Susie 48. So Dear to My Heart 48. *The Window* 49. *Treasure Island* 50. *The Happy Time* 52. Peter Pan (voice) 53. The Scarlet Coat 55, etc.

¶ *B.D.:* I was carried on a satin cushion and then dropped in a garbage can.

Drivas, Robert (1938–86). American leading man, mainly on TV.
Where It's At 69. Janice 73. Road Movie 74. God Told Me To 76. Demon 77, etc.

drive-in. A cinema in the open air, with loudspeakers relaying the sound track into your car. There are 6–7,000 in the USA alone.

Drôle de Drame (France 1937). Intellectual crazy comedy written by Jacques Prévert (from J. Storer Clouston's *The Lunatic at Large*) and directed by Marcel Carné, with a star cast headed by Françoise Rosay, Jean-Louis Barrault, Michel Simon and Louis Jouvet. Made with great vigour, but considerably ahead of its time.

Dru, Joanne (1923–) (Joanne la Coque). American leading lady of the forties, formerly model.
Abie's Irish Rose 46. *Red River* 48. *All the King's Men* 49. She Wore a Yellow Ribbon 49. Wagonmaster 50. Vengeance Valley 51. Return of the Texan 52. Thunder Bay 53. Three Ring Circus 54. Sincerely Yours 55. The Light in the Forest 58. September Storm 60. Sylvia 65. Supersnooper 80, etc.
TV series: Guestward Ho 61.

drug addiction, long forbidden by the Hays Code, even in Sherlock Holmes films (though it featured in Chaplin's *Easy Street* in 1916), has recently been the subject of many intense reforming movies such as *The Man with the Golden Arm, A Hatful of Rain, Bigger than Life, Monkey on My Back* and *Synanon. Confessions of an Opium Eater*, on the other hand, is a throwback to the Hollywood films of the twenties, when almost every adventure involved a chase through a Chinatown opium den. The addiction has provided plots for many thrillers about the tireless efforts of agents of the US Narcotics Bureau: *Johnny Stool Pigeon, To the Ends of the Earth, Sol Madrid, The Poppy is Also a Flower, The French Connection*, etc. In the late sixties drugs began to be advocated as a permissible opting out, or to be freely and seriously discussed, in such films as *The Trip, Chappaqua* and *Beyond the Valley of the Dolls*; *Panic in Needle Park*; *Born to Win*; *Believe in Me*; *Jennifer on my Mind*; and *Lenny*.

drunk scenes have been the delight of many actors as well as audiences. Who can judge between the charms of the following? Greta Garbo in *Ninotchka*; Robert Montgomery in *June Bride*; Jean Arthur in *Mr Smith Goes to Washington*; Laurel and Hardy in *The Bohemian Girl* and *Scram*; Lionel Barrymore in *A Free Soul*; Eva Marie Saint in *That Certain Feeling*; Errol Flynn in *The Sun Also Rises*; Katharine Hepburn in *The Desk Set*; Leslie Caron in *Father Goose*; Fredric March in *There Goes My Heart*; Lee Marvin in *Cat Ballou* (accompanied by a drunken horse); Albert Finney in *Saturday Night and Sunday Morning*; Alan Bates in *A Kind of Loving*; Bette Davis in *Dark Victory*; Claudia Cardinale in *The Pink Panther*; Charles Laughton in *Hobson's Choice*; Katharine Hepburn in *The Philadelphia Story* and *State of the Union*; Lucille Ball in *Yours Mine and Ours*; Arthur Askey in *The Love Match*; Dan Dailey in *It's Always Fair Weather*; Vanessa Redgrave in *Isadora*; Julie Andrews in *Star!*; Dean Martin and Tony Curtis in *Who Was That Lady?* Martin indeed has deliberately built himself an off-screen alcoholic reputation, as did W. C. Fields.
See also: *alcoholics*.

Drury, Allen (1918–). American novelist, whose *Advise and Consent* became one of the better film exposés of Washington.

Drury, James (1934–). American second lead and TV western star.
Forbidden Planet 56. Love Me Tender 56. Bernardine 57. Pollyanna 60. Ride the High Country 62. The Young Warriors 65, etc.
TV series: *The Virginian* 62–69, Firehouse 74.

dry ice. A chemical substance which in water produces carbon dioxide gas and gives the effect of a low-hanging white ground mist, very effective in fantasy sequences.

Dryhurst, Edward (1904–) (Edward Roberts). British producer, former writer, in films from 1920.
So Well Remembered 47. Master of Bankdam 48. Noose 48. While I Live 49. Castle in the Air 52, etc.

Du Maurier, Daphne (1907–1989). Best-selling British novelist of whose works *Rebecca, Jamaica Inn, Frenchman's Creek, The Years Between, Hungry Hill, My Cousin Rachel, The Scapegoat, The Birds* and *Don't Look Now* have been filmed.

Du Maurier, Sir Gerald (1873–1934). British stage actor who appeared in occasional films.
☐ Masks and Faces 16. Escape 30. Lord Camber's Ladies 32. I Was a Spy 33. Catherine the Great 34. The Scotland Yard Mystery 34. Jew Suss 34.

dubbing has several shades of meaning, within the general one of adding sound (effects, music, song, dialogue) to pictures already shot. It can mean re-recording; or replacing original language dialogue by a translation; or having someone else provide top notes for a star who can't sing. Here is an incomplete list of singers who provided uncredited voice-overs for actors who couldn't quite measure up.
Band Wagon India Adams for Cyd Charisse, *The Belle of New York* Anita Ellis for Vera-Ellen, *Brigadoon* Carole Richards for Cyd

Charisse, *Call Me Madam* Carole Richards for Vera-Ellen, *Cover Girl* Nan Wynn for Rita Hayworth, *Down to Earth* Anita Ellis for Rita Hayworth, *Gigi* Betty Wand for Leslie Caron, *Gilda* Nan Wynn for Rita Hayworth, *The Great Ziegfeld* Allan Jones for Dennis Morgan, *Gypsy* Lisa Kirk for Rosalind Russell, *Happy Go Lovely* Eve Boswell for Vera-Ellen, *The Helen Morgan Story* Gogi Grant for Ann Blyth, *Interrupted Melody* Eileen Farrell for Eleanor Parker, *The Jolson Story* Al Jolson for Larry Parks, *The King and I* Marni Nixon for Deborah Kerr, *Meet Me in St Louis* Arthur Freed for Leon Ames, *The Merry Widow* Trudy Erwin for Lana Turner, *My Fair Lady* Marni Nixon for Audrey Hepburn, *Orchestra Wives* Pat Friday for Lynn Bari, *Pal Joey* Jo Ann Greer for Rita Hayworth, *South Pacific* Muriel Smith for Juanita Hall, *South Pacific* Giorgio Tozzi for Rosanno Brazzi, *Showboat* Annette Warren for Ava Gardner, *A Song is Born* Jeri Sullivan for Virginia Mayo, *The Sound of Music* Bill Lee for Christopher Plummer, *State Fair* (1945) Lorraine Hogan for Jeanne Crain, *To Have and Have Not* (believe it nor not) Andy Williams for Lauren Bacall, *Torch Song* India Adams for Joan Crawford, *West Side Story* Marni Nixon for Natalie Wood, *West Side Story* Jim Bryant for Richard Beymer, *West Side Story* Betty Wand for Rita Moreno, *White Christmas* Trudy Stevens for Vera-Ellen, *With a Song in My Heart* Jane Froman for Susan Hayward.

Dubbing of speaking parts is comparatively rare, but note Joan Barry for Anny Ondra in *Blackmail* and Angela Lansbury for Ingrid Thulin in *The Four Horsemen of the Apocalypse*.

Dubbins, Don (1929–). American second lead of the fifties.
From Here to Eternity 53. Tribute to a Bad Man 56. These Wilder Years 57. From the Earth to the Moon 58. The Enchanted Island 58. The Prize 63, etc.

Duchin, Eddy (1909–51). American pianist and bandleader, best remembered for being impersonated by Tyrone Power in *The Eddy Duchin Story*.
□ Mr Broadway 32. Coronado 35. Hit Parade 37.

Duck Soup (US 1933). Probably the most perfect, zany and absolute of the vintage Marx Brothers romps, a Ruritanian spy send-up with Margaret Dumont and Louis Calhern as butts. Gags by various hands including Nat Perrin and Arthur Sheekman; music by Bert Kalmar and Harry Ruby.

Dudgeon, Elspeth (1871–1955). British stage actress who made her first appearance on screen disguised as an old man.
The Old Dark House (as John Dudgeon) 32. The Moonstone 34. Becky Sharp 35. Camille 36. The Great Garrick 37. Mystery House 38. Pride and Prejudice 40. Random Harvest 42. The Canterville Ghost 44. If Winter Comes 47. The Paradine Case 48. The Great Sinner 49, etc.

Dudley-Ward, Penelope (1919–1982). British leading lady of the forties.
The Case of the Frightened Lady 39. The Demi-Paradise 43. The Way Ahead 44, etc.

Duel in the Sun (US 1946). When first released this was the longest film since *Gone with the Wind*; it became notorious for its emphasis on violence and for casting Gregory Peck and Jennifer Jones as no-good villains who finally shot each other to death. The screenplay, by David Busch and producer David O. Selznick, was tasteless and King Vidor's direction, despite some good western action sequences, unremarkable.

Duel, Pete (1940–1971) (Peter Deuel). American leading man.
A Time for Giving 69. Cannon for Cordoba 70. The Young Country (TV) 71, etc.
TV series: Love on a Rooftop 66. *Alias Smith and Jones* 70.

duels are fought in hundreds of low-budget action dramas, but the well-staged ones are rare enough to be recounted. Basil Rathbone fought Errol Flynn in *The Adventures of Robin Hood* (and later spoofed the occasion in *The Court Jester*). He also lost to Tyrone Power in *The Mark of Zorro*; Flynn also encountered Rathbone in *Captain Blood* and Henry Daniell in *The Sea Hawk*. Douglas Fairbanks Snr fought duels in *The Mark of Zorro, The Black Pirate* and others; Douglas Fairbanks Jnr was a memorable opponent for Ronald Colman in *The Prisoner of Zenda* (later restaged for James Mason and Stewart Granger and mimicked by Tony Curtis and Ross Martin in *The Great Race*) and duelled again in *The Corsican Brothers*. Granger also duelled with Mason in *Fanny by Gaslight*, but used pistols this time; it was back to foils again for *Scaramouche* and *Swordsman of Siena*. John Barrymore fought splendid duels in his silent films, notably *Don Juan* and

General Crack, later opposing Rathbone in *Romeo and Juliet.* In the forties Cornel Wilde became fencer in chief, in such films as *Bandit of Sherwood Forest, Forever Amber* and *Sons of the Musketeers.* All the versions of *The Three Musketeers* involved duelling, but Gene Kelly turned it into a splendid series of acrobatic feats. Paul Henreid duelled in *The Spanish Main*, Larry Parks in *The Swordsman*, Fredric March in *The Buccaneer*, Charlton Heston in *El Cid*, Louis Hayward in half a dozen low-budgeters. In more serious films Ferrer duelled in *Cyrano de Bergerac* and Olivier in *Hamlet*, and there was a pistol duel in the Russian *War and Peace* and the Italian *Colpi di Pistola.* The most recent major films to feature duels are *Barry Lyndon* and *Royal Flash.*

Duff, Howard (1917–). American actor with stage experience; usually plays good-looking but shifty types.
Brute Force 47. *Naked City* 48. All My Sons 48. Calamity Jane and Sam Bass 50. Woman in Hiding 50. Shakedown 50. Steel Town 52. Women's Prison 54. While the City Sleeps 56. Boys' Night Out 62. Sardanapalus the Great (It.) 63. The Late Show 77. In the Glitter Palace (TV) 78. A Wedding 78. Kramer vs Kramer 79. Double Negative 80. Oh God Book Two 80. No Way Out 87, etc.
TV series: Mr Adams and Eve 56–57. Dante 60. The Felony Squad 66–68. Flamingo Road 80–81.

Duffell, Peter (1924–). British director.
The House that Dripped Blood 71. England Made Me 72. Inside Out 75. The Far Pavilions (TV) 84.

Dugan, Dennis (1948–). American leading man, usually in rather clumsy comic roles; much on TV.
Harry and Walter Go to New York 76. The Spaceman and King Arthur 79.
Empire Inc 84. Shadow Chasers 85.
TV series: Richie Brockelman 77.

Dugan, Tom (1889–1955). American supporting comic actor, often seen as Irish cop or minor criminal.
Sharp Shooters 27. Lights of New York 28. Sonny Boy 29. Bright Lights 31. Doctor X 32.Grand Slam 33. Palooka 34. Princess O'Hara 35. Pick a Star 37. Four Daughters 38. The Housekeeper's Daughter 39. The Ghost Breakers 40. The Monster and the Girl 41. *To Be Or Not To Be* 42. Bataan 43. Up in Arms 44. Bringing Up Father 46. Good News 47. Take Me Out to the Ball Game 49. The Lemon Drop Kid 51, many others.

Duggan, Andrew (1923–). American character actor of stalwart types.
Patterns 56. The Bravados 58. The Chapman Report 62. FBI Code 98 66. The Secret War of Harry Frigg 67. The Skin Game 71. Jigsaw (TV) 72. The Bears and I 74. It's Alive 77. The Private Files of J. Edgar Hoover 78, etc.
TV series: Bourbon Street Beat 59. Room for One More 61. Twelve O'Clock High 65–67. Lancer 68–69.

Duggan, Pat (1910–). American producer, former performer and writer.
Red Garters 54. The Vagabond King 56. The Search for Bridey Murphy 57. The Young Savages 61, etc.

Duke, Daryl (–). Canadian director in Hollywood.
The Psychiatrist (TV) 70. Happiness Is a Warm Clue (TV) 73. The President's Plane Is Missing (TV) 73. I Heard the Owl Call My Name (TV) 73. Payday 73. A Cry for Help (TV) 75. *Griffin and Phoenix* (TV) 76. The Silent Partner 78. Hard Feelings 82. *The Thorn Birds* (TV) 83. Florence Nightingale (TV) 84. Tai-pan 86.

Duke, Ivy (1895–). Star of British silent screen; married to Guy Newall.
The Garden of Resurrection 18. The Lure of Crooning Water 20. The Persistent Lover 22. The Starlit Garden 23. The Great Prince Shan 24. A Knight in London 29, etc.

Duke, Patty: see *Astin, Patty Duke.*

Duke, Vernon (1903–1969) (Vladimir Dubelsky). Russian-American song composer. Shows filmed include *Cabin in the Sky,* but he wrote mostly for revue.

Dukes, David (–). American leading man.
A Fire in the Sky (TV) 77. A Little Romance 79. The First Deadly Sin 80. Only when I Laugh 81. Without a Trace 83. The Winds of War (TV) 83. Space (TV) 85.

Dulac, Germaine (1882–1942) (G. Saisset-Schneider). French woman director.
Ames de Fous 18. Le Diable dans la Ville 24. The Seashell and the Clergyman 26. Theme and Variations 30, etc.

Dullea, Keir (1936–). American leading man, usually in roles of nervous tension.

The Hoodlum Priest 61. *David and Lisa* 62. Mail Order Bride 64. The Thin Red Line 64. Bunny Lake is Missing 65. Madame X 66. The Fox 68. De Sade 69. 2001: A Space Odyssey 69. Last of the Big Guns 73. Paperback Hero 73. Paul and Michelle 74. Black Christmas 75. Full Circle 77. Leopard in the Snow 78. Brave New World (TV) 79. Brain Waves 83. 2010 84. The Next One 85, etc.

Dumas, Alexandre, père (1802–1870). Highly industrious French novelist, mainly of swashbuckling adventures. Films resulting include several versions of *The Count of Monte Cristo* and *The Three Musketeers, The Man in the Iron Mask, The Fighting Guardsman* and *The Black Tulip*.

Dumas, Alexandre, fils (1824–1895). French novelist best known for *Camille*, which has been filmed several times.

Dumbrille, Douglass (1890–1974). Canadian character actor, long in Hollywood and typecast as smooth, suave villain of many a 'B' picture and an admirable foil for many great comedians.
His Woman 31. That's My Boy 32. Elmer the Great 33. Voltaire 33. Lady Killer 34. Broadway Bill 34. Naughty Marietta 35. Crime and Punishment 35. Lives of a Bengal Lancer 35. *Mr Deeds Goes to Town* 36. *A Day at the Races* 37. The Firefly 37. Ali Baba Goes to Town 37. Mr Moto on Danger Island 38. The Three Musketeers 39. Charlie Chan at Treasure Island 39. *The Big Store* 41. Ride 'Em Cowboy 42. Lost in a Harem 44. The Frozen Ghost 45. *Road to Utopia* 46. The Cat Creeps 46. Christmas Eve 47. Alimony 49. Riding High 50. Son of Paleface 52. Jupiter's Darling 55. The Ten Commandments 56. The Buccaneer 58. Shock Treatment 63, many others.
TV series: The Life of Riley 53–58. The Phil Silvers Show 63. Petticoat Junction 64–65.

Dumke, Ralph (1900–1964). Heavily-built American supporting actor.
All the King's Men 49. Mystery Street 50. The Mob 51. Lili 53. Rails into Laramie 54. The Solid Gold Cadillac 56. The Buster Keaton Story 57, etc.

Dumont, Margaret (1889–1965) (Margaret Baker). American character comedienne, the stately butt of many a comedian, notably Groucho Marx ('Ah, Mrs Rittenhouse, won't you . . . lie down?').
□*The Coconuts* 29. *Animal Crackers* 30. The Girl Habit 30. *Duck Soup* 33. The Gridiron Flash 34. Fifteen Wives 34. Kentucky Kernels 34. *A Night at the Opera* 35. Orchids to You 35. Rendezvous 35. The Song and Dance Man 36. Anything Goes 36. *A Day at the Races* 37. The Life of the Party 37. High Flyers 37. Youth on Parole 37. Wise Girl 37. Dramatic School 39. *At The Circus* 39. *The Big Store* 41. Never Give a Sucker an Even Break 41. For Beauty's Sake 41. Born to Sing 41. Sing Your Worries Away 42. Rhythm Parade 42. About Face 42. The Dancing Masters 43. Bathing Beauty 44. Seven Days Ashore 44. Up in Arms 44. The Horn Blows at Midnight 45. Diamond Horseshoe 45. Sunset in El Dorado 45. The Little Giant 46. Susie Steps Out 46. Three for Bedroom C 52. Stop You're Killing Me 53. Shake Rattle and Rock 56. Auntie Mame 58. Zotz! 62. What a Way to Go 64.
TV series: My Friend Irma 52–54.
❀ For suffering beyond the call of comic duty. *A Day at the Races.*

Duna, Steffi (1913–) (Stephanie Berindey). Hungarian dancer who appeared in some dramatic roles in the thirties.
The Indiscretions of Eve 31. La Cucaracha 35. The Dancing Pirate 36. Anthony Adverse 36. Pagliacci 37. Waterloo Bridge 40. River's End 41, etc.

Dunaway, Faye (1941–). American leading lady.
□Hurry Sundown 67. The Happening 67. *Bonnie and Clyde* 67. The Thomas Crown Affair 68. The Extraordinary Seaman 69. A Place for Lovers 69. The Arrangement 69. Little Big Man 70. Puzzle of a Downfall Child 71. Doc 71. The Deadly Trap 71. Oklahoma Crude 73. The Three Musketeers 73. Chinatown 74. The Four Musketeers 74. The Towering Inferno 74. 3 Days of the Condor 75. Voyage of the Dammed 76. *Network* (AA) 76. The Disappearance of Aimée (TV) 76. The Eyes of Laura Mars 78. The Champ 79. The First Deadly Sin 80. Mommie Dearest 81. Evita Peron (TV) 82. The Wicked Lady 83. Duet for One 84. Christopher Columbus (TV) 84. Supergirl 84. Ordeal by Innocence 85. Barfly 87.

¶ *F.D.:* A star today has to take charge of every aspect of her career. There are no studios left to do it for you.

Dunbar, Dixie (1915–) (Christina Dunbar). American dancer and light lead, in films of the thirties.

George White's Scandals 34. King of Burlesque 36. Sing Baby Sing 36. Rebecca of Sunnybrook Farm 38. Alexander's Ragtime Band 38, etc.

Duncan, Archie (1914–1979). Burly Scottish actor, the 'Little John' of TV's Robin Hood series.
Operation Diamond 47. The Bad Lord Byron 48. The Gorbals Story 51. Robin Hood 53. The Maggie 53. Laxdale Hall 54. Johnny on the Run 56. Harry Black 58. Lancelot and Guinevere 63. Ring of Bright Water 69, etc.

Duncan, David (1913–). American screenwriter.
Sangaree 53. The Black Scorpion 57. The Thing that Couldn't Die 58. Monster on the Campus 58. The Leech Woman 60. The Time Machine 60.

Duncan, Sandy (1946–). Tomboyish American leading lady.
□Million Dollar Duck 71. *Star Spangled Girl* 71. Roots (TV) 77. The Cat from Outer Space 78.
TV series: *Funny Face* 71.

Duning, George (1908–). American music director and composer.
The Corpse Came COD 46. To the Ends of the Earth 48. The Dark Past 49. No Sad Songs for Me 50. The Mob 51. Paula 52. Salome 53 The Man from Laramie 55. Picnic 56. Cowboy 57. 3.10 to Yuma 57. Bell Book and Candle 58. Houseboat 58. The Last Angry Man 59. The World of Suzie Wong 61. Toys in the Attic 63. Dear Brigitte 65. Any Wednesday 66. Terror in the Wax Museum 73. The Man with Bogart's Face 80, many others.

Dunn, Emma (1875–1966). British character actress, long in Hollywood, typically as housekeeper.
Old Lady 31 20. Pied Piper Malone 23. Side Street 29. Bad Sister 31. Hard to Handle 33. The Glass Key 35. Mr Deeds Goes to Town 36. Thanks for the Memory 38. Son of Frankenstein 39. The Great Dictator 40. Ladies in Retirement 41. I Married a Witch 42. It Happened Tomorrow 44. Life with Father 47. The Woman in White 48, many others.

Dunn, James (1905–1967). Genial American leading man of the thirties; later seized one good acting chance but slipped into low-budget westerns.
Bad Girl 31. Over the Hill 31. Sailor's Luck 33. Hold Me Tight 33. Stand Up and Cheer 34. Baby Take a Bow 34. Bright Eyes 34. The Daring Young Man 35. Don't Get Personal 36. Mysterious Crossing 37. Shadows over Shanghai 38. Government Girl 43. *A Tree Grows in Brooklyn* (AA) 45. That Brennan Girl 46. Killer McCoy 48. The Golden Gloves Story 50. The Bramble Bush 60. The Nine Lives of Elfego Baca 62. Hemingway's Adventures of a Young Man 62. The Oscar 66, etc.
TV series: It's A Great Life 54.

Dunn, Michael (1935–1973) (Gary Neil Miller). American dwarf actor.
Ship of Fools 65. You're a Big Boy Now 67. No Way to Treat a Lady 68. Madigan 68. Boom 68. Justine 69. Murders in the Rue Morgue 71. Goodnight My Love (TV) 72. The Mutations 74, etc.

Dunne, Griffin (–). American leading man of the eighties.
□ Head over Heels 79. The Fan 81. An American Werewolf in London 81. Cold Feet 83. Almost You 84. Johnny Dangerously 84. After Hours 85. Who's That Girl? 87.

Dunne, Irene (1901–). Gracious American leading lady of the thirties and forties, usually in sensible well-bred roles.
□Leathernecking 30. *Cimarron* 31. The Great Lover 31. Consolation Marriage 31. Bachelor Apartment 31. *Back Street* 32. *Symphony of Six Million* 32. Thirteen Women 32. No Other Women 33. The Secret of Madame Blanche 33. The Silver Cord 33. *Ann Vickers* 33. If I Were Free 34. This Man is Mine 34. Stingaree 34. The Age of Innocence 34. Sweet Adeline 35. *Roberta* 35. *Magnificent Obsession* 35. *Show Boat* 36. *Theodora Goes Wild* 36. *The Awful Truth* 37. High Wide and Handsome 37. Joy of Living 38. *Love Affair* 39. Invitation to Happiness 39. When Tomorrow Comes 39. *My Favourite Wife* 40. Penny Serenade 41. Unfinished Business 41. Lady in a Jam 42. A Guy Named Joe 43. The White Cliffs of Dover 44. Together Again 45. Over Twenty One 45. *Anna and the King of Siam* 46. *Life with Father* 47. *I Remember Mama* 48. Never a Dull Moment 50. *The Mudlark* (as Queen Victoria) 51. It Grows on Trees 52.
❀ For epitomizing the American lady of a gentler, more romantic age than ours. *Love Affair.*

Dunne, Philip (1908–). American screenwriter.

Student Tour 34. The Last of the Mohicans 36. Lancer Spy 37. Suez 38. Stanley and Livingstone 39. The Rains Came 39. Swanee River 39. How Green was My Valley 41. The Late George Apley 47. Forever Amber 47. The Luck of the Irish 48. Pinky 49. David and Bathsheba 51. The Robe 53. Prince of Players (& pd) 55. Hilda Crane (& d) 56. Ten North Frederick (& d) 58. Blue Denim (& d) 59. Lisa (d only) 62. The Agony and the Ecstasy 65. Blindfold (& d) 66, many others.

Dunning, George (1920–79). Canadian animator whose main feature work was *The Yellow Submarine*.

Dunning, Ruth (1911–1983). British character actress, mainly on TV.

Dunnock, Mildred (1904–). American character actress specializing in motherly types.
The Corn is Green 45. Kiss of Death 47. *Death of a Salesman* 51. Viva Zapata 52. The Jazz Singer 53. Love Me Tender 56. Baby Doll 56. Peyton Place 57. The Nun's Story 57. Cat on a Hot Tin Roof 58. Butterfield 8 60. Something Wild 61. Sweet Bird of Youth 62. Behold a Pale Horse 64. Seven Women 66. Whatever Happened to Aunt Alice? 69. Murder or Mercy (TV) 74. The Spiral Staircase (GB) 75, etc.

dupe negative. One made from the original negative (via a lavender print) to protect it from wear by producing too many copies.

duping print (or **lavender print**). A high quality print made from the original negative. From it dupe negatives can be made.

Dupont, E. A. (Ewald André) (1891–1956). German director who moved with unhappy results to Britain and Hollywood.
Baruh 23. *Variety* 26. Love Me and the World Is Mine 27. Moulin Rouge 28. *Piccadilly* 28. Atlantic 30. Ladies Must Love 33. The Bishop Misbehaves 35. Forgotten Faces 36. Hell's Kitchen 39. The Scarf (& w) 50. The Neanderthal Man 53. Return to Treasure Island 54. Magic Fire (co-w only) 56, etc.

Dupree, Minnie (1873–1947). American character actress seen infrequently as sweet old lady.
Night Club 29. *The Young in Heart* 38. Anne of Windy Poplars 40, etc.

Duprez, June (1918–84). British leading lady.
The Crimson Circle 36. The Spy in Black 38. The Four Feathers 39. The Thief of Baghdad 41. None But the Lonely Heart (US) 44. *And Then There Were None* (US) 45. Calcutta (US) 46. That Brennan Girl (US) 47. The Kinsey Report (US) 61, etc.

Dupuis, Paul (1916–76). French-Canadian leading man popular in British films in the late forties.
Johnny Frenchman 45. The White Unicorn 47. Sleeping Car to Trieste 48. Passport to Pimlico 49. The Reluctant Widow 50, etc.

Durante, Jimmy 'Schnozzle' (1893–1980). Long-nosed, well-loved American comedian with long career in vaudeville and night clubs. Film appearances spasmodic, and most successful when involving his old routines: 'Umbriago', 'Ink-a-dink', etc.
Biographies: *Schnozzola* 1951 by Gene Fowler; *Goodnight Mrs Calabash* 1963 by William Cahn.
□Roadhouse Nights 30. The New Adventures of Get-Rich-Quick Wallingford 31. Cuban Love Song 31. The Passionate Plumber 32. The Wet Parade 32. Speak Easily 32. The Phantom President 33. Blondie of the Follies 33. Meet the Baron 33. What No Beer 33. Hell Below 33. Broadway to Hollywood 33. George White's Scandals 34. Hollywood Party 34. Joe Palooka 34. She Learned About Sailors 34. Strictly Dynamite 34. Student Tour 34. Carnival 35. Land without Music (GB) 34. Sally, Irene and Mary 38. Start Cheering 38. Little Miss Broadway 38. Melody Ranch 40. *You're in the Army Now* 40. *The Man who Came to Dinner* 41. Two Girls and a Sailor 44. Music for Millions 45. *Two Sisters from Boston* 46. It Happened in Brooklyn 47. This Time for Keeps 47. On an Island with You 48. The Great Rupert 50. The Milkman 50. Beau James 57. Pepe 60. The Last Judgment 61. *Jumbo* 62. It's a Mad Mad Mad Mad World (cameo) 63.

¶ Everybody wants to get into de act!—*J.D., catchphrase*

Dere's a million good-looking guys in the world, but I'm a novelty.—*J.D.*

Goodnight, Mrs Calabash, wherever you are.—*J.D., closing words of music hall act.* (Mrs Calabash was his pet name for his late wife.)

I don't split infinitives. When I go to work on 'em, I break 'em up into little pieces.—*J.D.*

Duras, Marguerite (1914–). French novelist. Works filmed: *The Sea Wall,*

Hiroshima Mon Amour, Moderato Cantabile and *Sailor from Gibraltar.*

Durbin, Deanna (1921–) (Edna Mae Durbin). Canadian girl singer who won instant world-wide success as a teenage star; her career faltered after ten years when weight problems added to a change in musical fashion brought about her premature retirement. Special Academy Award 1938 'for bringing to the screen the spirit and personification of youth'.
□Every Sunday 36. *Three Smart Girls* 36. *One Hundred Men and a Girl* 37. *Mad about Music* 38. *That Certain Age* 38. Three Smart Girls Grow Up 38. First Love 39. It's a Date 39. Spring Parade 40. Nice Girl 40. *It Started with Eve* 41. The Amazing Mrs Holliday 42. Hers to Hold 43. His Butler's Sister 43. Christmas Holiday 44. *Can't Help Singing* 44. Lady on a Train 45. Because of Him 45. I'll Be Yours 46. Something in the Wind 47. Up in Central Park 47. For the Love of Mary 48.
❀ For pleasing world audiences by being the character she despised: 'Little Miss Fixit who bursts into song.' *That Certain Age.*

¶ *D.D. in 1959:* Just as a Hollywood pin-up represents sex to dissatisfied erotics, so I represented the ideal daughter millions of fathers and mothers wished they had.
Joe Pasternak, her producer: She is one of those personalities whom the world will insist on regarding as its private property.

Durfee, Minta (1897–1975). American leading lady of knockabout comedies 1914–16, including some with Chaplin. Married Roscoe Arbuckle and retired, but much later played bit parts.

Durkin, Junior (1915–1935) (Trent Durkin). American juvenile player who was Huck Finn in *Tom Sawyer* 30 and *Huckleberry Finn* 31.

Durning, Charles (1933–). Burly American TV actor who slowly gained a star footing in movies.
□ Harvey Middleman Fireman 65. I Walk the Line 70. Hi Mom 70. Deadhead Miles 72. Dealing 72. Sisters 72. The Connection (TV) 73. The Sting 73. The Front Page 74. Dog Day Afternoon 75. The Hindenburg 75. The Trial of Chaplain Jensen (TV) 75. Queen of the Stardust Ballroom (TV) 75. Switch (TV) 75. Captains and the Kings (TV) 76. Breakheart Pass 76. Harry and Walter Go to New York 76. Twilight's Last Gleaming 77. Special Olympics (TV) 78. *The Choirboys* 78. The Greek Tycoon 78. An Enemy of the People 78. The Fury 78. F.I.S.T. 79. Studs Lonigan (TV) 79. The Muppet Movie 79. North Dallas Forty 79. Tilt 79. Starting Over 79. When a Stranger Calls 79. Die Laughing 80. The Final Countdown 80. True Confessions 81. Sharkey's Machine 81. *The Best Little Whorehouse in Texas* 82. Tootsie 82. To Be or Not to Be (AAN) 83. Two of a Kind 83. Side by Side 83. Mass Appeal 84. Stick 85. The Man with One Red Shoe 85. Stand Alone 85. Private Conversations 85. Tough Guys 86. Happy New Year 87. A Tiger's Tale 87.

Duryea, Dan (1907–1968). Laconic, long-faced American character actor often typecast as whining villain.
□*The Little Foxes* 41. Ball of Fire 41. Pride of the Yankees 42. That Other Woman 42. Sahara 43. Man from Frisco 44. Ministry of Fear 44. None but the Lonely Heart 44. *The Woman in the Window* 44. Mrs Parkington 45. Main Street After Dark 44. The Great Flamarion 45. Lady on a Train 45. Scarlet Street 45. Along Came Jones 45. The Valley of Decision 45. *Black Angel* 46. White Tie and Tails 46. Black Bart 48. River Lady 48. *Another Part of the Forest* 48. Larceny 48. *Criss Cross* 49. Manhandled 49. Too Late for Tears 49. Johnny Stoolpigeon 50. One Way Street 50. The Underworld Story 50. Winchester 73 50. Al Jennings of Oklahoma 50. *Chicago Calling* 51. Sky Commando 53. Thunder Bay 53. 36 Hours 53. World for Ransom 54. Ride Clear of Diablo 54. Silver Lode 54. This is My Love 54. Rails in to Laramie 54. The Marauders 55. Foxfire 55. Storm Fear 56. Battle Hymn 57. The Burglar 57. Night Passage 57. Slaughter on Tenth Avenue 57. Kathy O 58. Platinum High School 60. Six Black Horses 62. He Rides Tall 64. Taggart 64. Walk a Tightrope 64. Do You Know This Voice? 64. The Bounty Killer 65. Incident at Phantom Hill 65. *The Flight of the Phoenix* 65. The Hills Run Red 67. Stranger on the Run (TV) 67. Five Golden Dragons 67. The Bamboo Saucer 68.
TV series: China Smith 58. Peyton Place 68.

¶ 'The crime movie equivalent of an absolute bounder.'—*Ian Cameron*

Duse, Elèonora (1858–1924). Eminent Italian tragedienne whose one film appearance was in *Cenere* 16.

Duvall, Robert (1931–). American character actor, often seen as nervous villain. Captain Newman MD 63. To Kill a

Mockingbird 63. The Chase 65. Bullitt 68. The Rain People 69. True Grit 69. M*A*S*H 70. Lawman 71. *The Godfather* 72. The Great Northfield Minnesota Raid 72. Joe Kidd 72. The Godfather Part Two 74. The Outfit 74. Breakout 75. Killer Elite 76. Network 76. The Seven Per Cent Solution (as Dr Watson) 76. The Greatest 77. The Eagle Has Landed 77. The Betsy 78. Ike (TV) 79. Apocalypse Now (BFA) 79. The Great Santini 80. True Confessions 81. The Pursuit of D. B. Cooper 81. Tender Mercies (AA) 83. The Stone Boy 84. The Natural 84. The Lightship 85. Hotel Colonial 87. Let's Get Harry 87, etc.

Duvall, Shelley (1949–). American actress.
Brewster McCloud 70. McCabe and Mrs Miller 71. Thieves Like Us 74. Nashville 75. Three Women 77. Annie Hall 77. The Shining 80. Popeye 80. Time Bandits 81, Roxanne 87, etc.

Duvivier, Julien (1896–1967). Celebrated French director of the thirties whose touch seemed to falter after a wartime sojourn in Hollywood.
Hacadelma 19. Poil de Carotte 25 and 32. David Golder 30. Maria Chapdelaine 33. Le Golem 35. La Belle Equipe 36. *Pépé Le Moko* 37. *Un Carnet de Bal* 37. The Great Waltz (US) 38. *La Fin du Jour* 39. La Charrette Fantôme 39. Lydia (US) 41. Tales of Manhattan (US) 42. Flesh and Fantasy (US) 43. The Imposter (US) 44. *Panique* 46. Anna Karenina (GB) 48. Au Royaume des Cieux 49. Sous le Ciel de Paris 51. *Don Camillo* 52. La Fête à Henriette 54. L'Affaire Maurizius 54. Voici le Temps des Assassins 55. The Man in the Raincoat 57. Pot-Bouille 57. Marie Octobre 59. La Femme et le Pantin 59. La Grande Vie 61. La Chambre Ardente 62. Chair de Poule 63, etc.

Dvorak, Ann (1912–1979) (Ann McKim). Smart but sensitive American leading lady of the thirties.
Hollywood Revue 29. Way out West 30. The Guardsman 31. This Modern Age 31. The Crowd Roars 32. *Scarface* 32. The Strange Love of Molly Louvain 32. Three on a Match 32. The Way to Love 33. Heat Lightning 34. Housewife 34. I Sell Anything 34. G Men 35. Folies Bergère 35. *Dr Socrates* 35. We Who Are About to Die 36. Racing Lady 37. The Case of the Stuttering Bishop 37. Merrily We Live 38. Blind Alley 39. Café Hostess 40. Girls of the Road 40. Squadron Leader X (GB) 41. This Was Paris (GB) 42. Escape to Danger 44. Flame of the Barbary Coast 45. Abilene Town 46. The Long Night 47. The Walls of Jericho 48. A Life of Her Own 50. I Was an American Spy 51. The Secret of Convict Lake 51, etc.

Dwan, Allan (1885–1981). Veteran American director, former writer; he competently handled commercial movies of every type.
Wildflower 14. The Good Bad Man 15. Manhattan Madness 16. A Modern Musketeer 18. Luck of the Irish 20. *Robin Hood* 22. Big Brother 23. Zaza 23. Manhandled 24. Stage Struck 25. *The Iron Mask* 29. Man to Man 31. Mayor of Hell 33. Human Cargo 36. Heidi 37. Suez 38. The Three Musketeers (Ritz Brothers version) 39. Trail of the Vigilantes 40. Rise and Shine 41. Abroad with Two Yanks 44. Up in Mabel's Room 44. Brewster's Millions 45. Getting Gertie's Garter 46. Angel in Exile 48. *Sands of Iwo Jima* 49. The Wild Blue Yonder 51. Montana Belle 52. The Woman They Almost Lynched 53. Silver Lode 54. Tennessee's Partner 55. Hold Back the Night 56. Slightly Scarlet 56. The River's Edge 57. The Most Dangerous Man Alive 61, scores of others.

¶ *A.D.:* If you get your head up above the mob, they try to knock it off. If you stay down, you last forever.

Dwyer, Leslie (1906–86). Plump cockney character actor, in films from childhood.
The Fifth Form at St Dominic's 21. The Flag Lieutenant 31. The Goose Steps Out 41. The Way Ahead 44. Night Boat to Dublin 46. When the Bough Breaks 48. The Calendar 48. Midnight Episode 50. Laughter in Paradise 51. Hindle Wakes 52. Where There's a Will 53. Act of Love 54. Left, Right and Centre 59. I've Gotta Horse 64, many others.

Dyall, Franklin (1874–1950). British stage actor.
Atlantic 30. The Ringer 32. The Private Life of Henry VIII 33. The Iron Duke 35. Fire Over England 36. Bonnie Prince Charlie 49, etc.

Dyall, Valentine (1908–85). Gaunt British actor with resounding voice, famous as radio's wartime 'Man in Black'. Son of stage actor Franklin Dyall. Film debut *The Life and Death of Colonel Blimp* 43; later in many supporting roles, notably Henry V 44. Caesar and Cleopatra 45. Brief Encounter 46. Vengeance Is Mine 48. City of the Dead 60. The Haunting 63. The Horror of It All 65, etc.

Dyer, Anson (1876–*). Pioneer British cartoonist: many entertainment shorts, also work for government departments.

Dylan, Bob (1941–) (Robert Allen Zimmerman). American singer in occasional films.
Don't Look Back 66. Renaldo and Clara 78. Hearts of Fire 87.

dynamic frame. A concept invented in 1955 by an American, Glenn Alvey: the screen was maximum size, i.e. CinemaScope, but individual scenes were to be masked down to whatever ratio suited them best, e.g. rather narrow for a corridor. Only one experimental British film, a version of H. G. Wells' *The Hole in the Wall,* was made in dynamic frame, which proved distracting and has in any case been overtaken by multiscreen experiments of the sixties.

Dyneley, Peter (1921–1977). British character actor.
Beau Brummel 54. The Young Lovers 55. The Split 60. Call Me Bwana 63. Chato's Land 72, etc.

Answers

Bette Davis

1 *Another Man's Poison* ☐ 2 *In This Our Life* ☐ 3 *The Virgin Queen* ☐ 4 *Jezebel* ☐ 5 *Front Page Woman* ☐ 6 *Bordertown* ☐ 7 *Fog Over Frisco* ☐ *Dead Ringer* ☐ 8 *Phone Call from a Stranger* ☐ 9 *June Bride* ☐ 10 *A Stolen Life* ☐ *Dead Ringer* ☐ 11 *Mr Skeffington* ☐ 12 *Deception* ☐ 13 *Old Acquaintance* ☐ 14 *The Letter* ☐ 15 *The Little Foxes* ☐ 16 *Juarez* ☐

debuts

1 Shirley Temple ☐ 2 Clark Gable ☐ 3 Fred MacMurray ☐ (*The Gilded Lily* was released first.) ☐ 4 Rock Hudson ☐ 5 James Mason ☐ 6 Jane Fonda ☐ 7 Spencer Tracy ☐ 8 Peter Fonda ☐ 9 William Holden ☐ 10 Frank Sinatra ☐ 11 Kirk Douglas ☐ 12 Dorothy McQuire ☐ 13 Sydney Greenstreet ☐ 14 Mae West ☐ 15 Glenn Ford ☐ 16 Shirley MacLaine ☐ 17 John Garfield ☐ 18 Yul Brynner ☐ 19 Gene Kelly ☐ 20 Charlton Heston ☐ 21 Claude Rains ☐ 22 Sidney Poitier ☐ 23 Humphrey Bogart ☐ 24 Burt Lancaster ☐ 25 Dirk Bogarde ☐ 26 Cary Grant ☐ 27 Raymond Massey ☐ 28 Edith Evans ☐ 29 Elizabeth Taylor ☐ 30 Bette Davis ☐

the devil

1 Alan Mowbray ☐ 2 Jules Berry ☐ 3 Rex Ingram ☐ 4 Laird Cregar ☐ 5 Claude Rains ☐ 6 Vincent Price ☐ 7 Ray Walston ☐ 8 Ralph Richardson ☐ 9 Walter Huston ☐ 10 Stanley Holloway ☐ 11 Adolphe Menjou ☐ 12 Ray Milland ☐

dialogue

1 A silly remark and a smooth answer: Florence Bates and Laurence Olivier in *Rebecca* (1940) ☐
2 Groucho Marx gets in everywhere. The insulted lady is Esther Muir, and the film is *A Day at the Races* (1937) ☐
3 A political comedy, *State of the Union* (1948). The speakers are Adolphe Menjou and Katharine Hepburn ☐
4 This has the delightful smell of high comedy from a gentler era. It has in fact the Lubitsch touch, being from *Trouble in Paradise* (1932), written by Samson Raphaelson. The speakers are Miriam Hopkins and Herbert Marshall ☐
5 When did Lon Chaney as the Wolf Man meet with wisecracks? In *Abbott and Costello Meet Frankenstein* (1948), when he tried out his familiar routine on Lou Costello ☐
6 William Holden and Gloria Swanson in *Sunset Boulevard* (1950) ☐
7 The famous conclusion to *Dinner at Eight* (1933). Good timer Jean Harlow exchanges small talk with Marie Dressler, and gets more than she bargained for ☐

8 It has to be Noël Coward, and it is, in *The Scoundrel* (1935); the lady is Julie Haydon □
9 Rex Ingram as De Lawd inspecting his universe in *Green Pastures* (1936) □
10 The clue here is the phrase 'old man'. In fact this is the summit of Orson Welles's argument to Joseph Cotten in the Ferris wheel sequence of *The Third Man* (1949) □
11 *Goodbye Mr Chips* (1939), with Robert Donat rallying briefly from his deathbed □
12 Katharine Hepburn and Spencer Tracy in *Adam's Rib* (1949) □
13 *Rebecca* again: Joan Fontaine and Laurence Olivier □
14 Easy: Chico and Groucho Marx in *A Night in Casablanca* (1945) □
15 Vivien Leigh and Clark Gable in *Gone with the Wind* (1939) □
16 Greta Garbo and Melvyn Douglas in *Ninotchka* (1939) □
17 Yes, the first thought is the right one: Myrna Loy speaking of her tipsy spouse William Powell in *The Thin Man* □
18 Splendidly tooled dialogue to match its source, *The Prisoner of Zenda.* We mean the 1937 version with Douglas Fairbanks Jnr and Ronald Colman □
19 The snappy wisecrack par excellence comes from Bob Hope in *The Cat and the Canary*. Nydia Westman was the questioner □
20 A choice moment from *Our Relations.* For plot purposes Ollie has listened to a wild scheme of Stan's involving dressing up in turbans and oriental bedspreads, and they have both landed in the clink, where they are questioned by one of the genuine faith □
21 You can almost hear Basil Rathbone speak the line, and Danny Kaye give the response, in *The Court Jester* □
22 This is Nydia Westman and Bob Hope again, in the same sequence from *The Cat and the Canary* □
23 The film is *My Man Godfrey*; the first speaker has not been identified, but the second is Eugene Pallette □
24 The comical courtship of Carole Lombard by Stanley Ridges in *To Be or Not to Be* □
25 Ruby Keeler and Dick Powell in *Gold Diggers of 1943* □
26 Humphrey Bogart and Claude Rains in *Casablanca* □

disaster films

1 Myrna Loy □ Lana Turner □ *The Rains of Ranchipur* □ Louis Bromfield □ 2 Dorothy Lamour □ *The Greatest Show on Earth* □ 3 Jon Hall □ the invisible man □ 4 *Intolerance* □ D. W. Griffith □ 5 *Airport* □ Arthur Hailey □ 6 *A Night to Remember* □ 1912 □ 7 A forest fire □ Maurice Maeterlinck □ Felix Salten □ 8 *Krakatoa: East of Java* □ (Krakatoa is west of Java.) 9 Nero □ *The Story of Mankind* □ *Quo Vadis* □ *The Sign of the Cross* □ 10 *The Poseidon Adventure* □ 11 *The Sisters* □ Myron Brinig □ 12 *Fate Is the Hunter* □ Ernest K. Gann □ 13 *Forever Amber* □ Kathleen Winsor □ 14 Locusts □ Pearl Buck □ 15 A coal mine cave-in □ 16 *Morning Departure* (US: *Operation Disaster*) □ 17 A volcano □ Max Catto □ 18 George Pal □ 19 H. G. Wells □ War □ Plague □ 20 A volcanic eruption □

E

E.T.—The Extra-Terrestrial (US 1982). Modest fantasy about a curious timid being who is left behind from a flying saucer and befriended by suburban children. Overlong for its purpose, it touched a chord, and the commercial response was nothing short of terrific, showing that even in the cynical eighties we all need a dream world to retire to. Written by Melissa Mathison; directed by Steven Spielberg; for Universal; with Henry Thomas, Dee Wallace. Academy Awards: best score (John Williams), best sound, best visual effects (E.T. was created by Carlo Rimbaldi).

Eady, David (1924–). British director. The Bridge of Time (documentary) 52. Three Cases of Murder (one story) 55. In the Wake of a Stranger 58. Faces in the Dark 60, etc.

Eagels, Jeanne (1894–1929). American leading lady of the twenties; her private life was highly publicized and Kim Novak played her in a 1957 biopic. Biography 1930: *The Rain Girl* by Edward Doherty.
□ The World and the Woman 16. Fires of Youth 17. Under False Colours 17. The Cross Bearer 18. Man, Woman and Sin 27. The Letter 29. Jealousy 29.

Ealing Studios. This famous little studio in suburban west London now houses the BBC. In its heyday in the forties and fifties it was the independent home of scores of well-paced comedies featuring the likes of Will Hay and George Formby, and from 1948 on aspired a little higher, to quiet comedies of the English character, usually featuring a downtrodden group who rebelled against authority. The resulting films, including *The Lavender Hill Mob, Whisky Galore* and *The Titfield Thunderbolt,* became known the world over. The credit for these films is largely due to Michael Balcon as impresario and often to T.E.B. Clarke as writer; but results were less happy when the studio tackled epic themes such as *Scott of the Antarctic* and *The Cruel Sea,* though it certainly brought off non-comic subjects like *Dead of Night* and *Mandy*. See Charles Barr's 1977 book, *Ealing Studios;* also Michael Balcon's *A Lifetime of Films* and George Perry's *Forever Ealing*.
A collection of Ealing posters, edited by David Wilson, was published in 1983 under the title *Projecting Britain*.

Earles, Harry (1902–85). German–American midget who appeared in *The Unholy Three* 25 and 30, *Freaks* 32, *The Wizard of Oz* 39.

Earp, Wyatt (1848–1928). American frontier marshal, the most famous lawman of the wild west. Screen impersonations of him include Walter Huston in *Law and Order* 31, George O'Brien in *Frontier Marshal* 35, Randolph Scott in *Frontier Marshal* 39, Richard Dix in *Tombstone* 42, Henry Fonda in *My Darling Clementine* 46, Joel McCrea in *Wichita* 55, Burt Lancaster in *Gunfight at the OK Corral* 57, James Stewart in *Cheyenne Autumn* 64, James Garner in *Hour of the Gun* 67, Harris Yulin in *Doc* 70. There was also a long-running TV series starring Hugh O'Brian.

Earth (Russia 1930). Dovzhenko's epic drama on the relation of man to the soil. Written by the director, photographed by Daniel Demutski.

Earthquake (US 1973). Predictable all-star disaster melodrama with boring personal stories backing the razing to the ground of the city of Los Angeles via very variable trick effects. Notable for the first use of 'Sensurround', a stereophonic sound device which created a frightening rumble and for most people a pain in the chest.

Easdale, Brian (1909–). British composer: GPO Film Unit shorts 34–38. Ferry Pilot 42. Black Narcissus 46. The Red Shoes (AA) 48. An Outcast of the Islands 51. The Battle of the River Plate 56. Peeping Tom 60, etc.

Eason, B. Reeves (1886–1956). American action director, mostly of second features.
SELECTED SILENT FILMS: Moon Rider 20. *Ben Hur* (chariot race) 26.
□SOUND FILMS: The Lariat Kid 29. Winged Horseman 29. Troopers Three 30. The

Roaring Ranch 30. Trigger Tricks 30. Spurs 30. The Galloping Ghost 31. The Sunset Trail 32. Honor of the Press 32. The Heart Punch 32. Cornered 33. Behind Jury Doors 33. Alimony Madness 33. Revenge at Monte Carlo 33. Her Resale Value 33. Dance Hall Hostess 33. Red River Valley 36. Land Beyond the Law 37. Empty Holsters 37. Prairie Thunder 37. Sergeant Murphy 38. The Kid Comes Back 38. Daredevil Drivers 38. Call of the Yukon 38. Blue Montana Skies 39. Mountain Rhythm 39. Men with Steel Faces 40. Murder in the Big House 42. Spy Ship 42. Truck Busters 43. Rimfire 49.

Also directed action scenes in major films, notably *The Charge of the Light Brigade* 36.

East Lynne. Mrs Henry Wood's heavy-going Victorian novel, in which mother and baby are literally cast out into the cold, cold snow, was a favourite silent film subject. There were British versions in 1912 and 1921, and an American one in 1925; but the 1931 sound remake, with Ann Harding, was not a success.

East of Eden (US 1955). Notable for introducing the young James Dean as a teenage rebel of yesteryear, this version by Elia Kazan of John Steinbeck's novel about father-son relationships in agricultural California before World War I had emotional power to make up for its rather sluggish pace and inflated biblical parallels. Raymond Massey and Jo Van Fleet (AA) were the mainstays of a film which at least treated its audience as adults. A 1981 television version ran eight hours and more or less reverted to the plot structure of the original book, of which the film used only the last third. Centre of attention now was Jane Seymour as the evil madam-to-be.

The East Side Kids. Set up in 1939 by Monogram as a Poverty Row challenge to the Dead End Kids, the original team consisted of Hally Chester, Harris Berger, Frankie Burke, Donald Hines, Eddie Brian and Sam Edwards. They were later joined by Bobby Jordan and Leo Gorcey from Dead End, and within a few years elements of both rival gangs were absorbed into the Bowery Boys.

Eastman, George (1854–1932). American pioneer of cinematography: invented the roll film, which made him a millionaire.

Eastwood, Clint (1930–). American leading man who after TV success made his big screen name in Italian westerns, then returned to Hollywood and became one of the big action stars of the late sixties.

Biography 1977: *Clint Eastwood, the Man Behind the Myth* by Patrick Agan.

□Revenge of the Creature 55. Francis in the Navy 55. Lady Godiva 55. Tarantula 55. Never Say Goodbye 56. The First Travelling Saleslady 56. Star in the Dust 56. Escapade in Japan 57. Ambush at Cimarron Pass 58. Lafayette Escadrille 58. *A Fistful of Dollars* 64. *For a Few Dollars More* 65. *The Good The Bad and The Ugly* 66. The Witches 67. Hang 'Em High 68. *Coogan's Bluff* 68. Where Eagles Dare 69. Paint Your Wagon 69. Kelly's Heroes 70. Two Mules for Sister Sara 70. The Beguiled 71. *Play Misty for Me* (& d) 71. *Dirty Harry* 71. Joe Kidd 72. Breezy (d only) 73. High Plains Drifter (& d) 73. Magnum Force 73. Thunderbolt and Lightfoot 74. The Eiger Sanction (& d) 75. The Outlaw Josey Wales (& d) 76. The Enforcer 76. The Gauntlet (& d) 77. Every Which Way But Loose 78. Escape From Alcatraz 79. Any Which Way You Can 80. Bronco Billy (& d) 80. Firefox 82. Honky Tonk Man 82. Sudden Impact 83. Tightrope 84. City Heat 84. Pale Rider 85. Heartbreak Ridge (& d) 86.

TV series: *Rawhide* 58–65.

❀ For being the cynical tough guy the seventies seemed to want. *Dirty Harry*.

¶ I like to play the line and not wander too far to either side. If a guy has just had a bad day in the mines and wants to see a good shoot-'em-up, that's great.—*C.E.*

I've never worked with a guy who was less conscious of his good image.—*Don Siegel of C.E.*

My involvement goes deeper than acting or directing. I love every aspect of the creation of motion pictures and I guess I'm committed to it for life.—*C.E.*

Whatever success I've had is due to a lot of instinct and a little luck.—*C.E.*

I've always had the ability to say to the audience, watch this if you like, and if you don't, take a hike.—*C.E.*

I try to approach film intellectually—how it moves me. If you start below the intellectual level, I think you're starting without the nucleus.—*C.E.*

Easy Rider (US 1969). A highly influential, cheaply made film which typified a section of America's aimlessly rebellious, death-wishing youth in its casual tale of two motor cyclists trekking across the country and finding nothing to respect, only a meaningless death. By and with Peter Fonda and Dennis Hopper.

Easy Street (US 1917). Perhaps Chaplin's most notable two-reeler, a deft combination of farce and social documentary, with jokes about the Salvation Army, overcrowded slums and drug addiction. Still poignant and funny.

Eaton, Mary (1901–1948). American leading lady whose brief teaming with Ziegfeld and the Marx Brothers makes her career a footnote at least to film history.
□His Children's Children 23. Broadway after Dark 24. *Glorifying the American Girl* 29. *The Coconuts* 29.

Eaton, Shirley (1936–). Pneumatic blonde British leading lady.
Doctor at Large 56. Sailor Beware 57. Carry on Sergeant 58. Carry on Nurse 59. What a Carve Up 62. The Girl Hunters 63. Goldfinger 64. Rhino 65. Ten Little Indians 65. Around the World Under the Sea 66. Eight on the Lam 67. Sumuru 68, many others.

Eberhardt, Mignon C. (1899–). American detective novelist, several of whose works were filmed.
While the Patient Slept 30. The Murder of Dr Harrigan 36. Murder by an Aristocrat 36. The Great Hospital Mystery 37. Mystery House 38, etc.

Ebsen, Buddy (1908–) (Christian Rudolf Ebsen). American actor-dancer of the thirties, usually in 'countrified' parts; later emerged as a character actor and achieved his greatest success in a long-running TV series.
Broadway Melody of 1936. Captain January 36. Born to Dance 36. Banjo on My Knee 36. The Girl of the Golden West 38. Four Girls in White 39. Parachute Battalion 41. Sing Your Worries Away 42. Thunder in God's Country 51. Night People 54. Red Garters 54. Davy Crockett 55. Attack 56. Breakfast at Tiffany's 61. The Interns 62. Mail Order Bride 64. The One and Only Genuine Original Family Band 68. The Daughters of Joshua Cabe (TV) 72. Horror at 37,000 Feet (TV) 72. The President's Plane is Missing (TV) 74. Smash-up on Interstate Five (TV) 77. Leave Yesterday Behind (TV) 78. *The Critical List* (TV) 81. The Bastard (TV) 78. The Return of the Beverly Hillbillies (TV) 81, etc.
TV series: Northwest Passage 57. *The Beverly Hillbillies* 62–70. Barnaby Jones 72–80. Matt Houston 85.
† Ebsen was to have played the Tin Man in *The Wizard of Oz*, but was badly affected by the aluminium dust in the make-up.

Eburne, Maude (1875–1960). Diminutive American character actress who usually played frowning matrons and nosey neighbours.
The Bat Whispers 30. The Guardsman 31. The Vampire Bat 33. Lazy River 34. *Ruggles of Red Gap* 35. Champagne Waltz 37. Meet Doctor Christian 39. West Point Widow 41. Bowery to Broadway 44. The Suspect 45. Mother Wore Tights 47. Arson Inc. 50, many others.

Ecstasy: see *Extase*.

Eddy, Helen Jerome (1897–). American character actress who retired early. Always in high class films.
Rebecca of Sunnybrook Farm 16. The March Hare 21. The Country Kid 23. The Dark Angel 25. Camille 27. The Divine Lady 29. Skippy 31. Mata Hari 31. Madame Butterfly 32. The Bitter Tea of General Yen 33. Riptide 34. Keeper of the Bees 35. Stowaway 36. Winterset 36. The Garden of Allah 36. Outside the Law 38. Strike Up the Band 40, many others.

Eddy, Nelson (1901–1967). Romantic American actor-singer with opera background; famous on screen for series of operettas with Jeanette MacDonald.
□Broadway to Hollywood 31. Dancing Lady 33. Student Tour 34. *Naughty Marietta* 35. *Rose Marie* 36. *Maytime* 37. Rosalie 37. The Girl of the Golden West 38. *Sweethearts* 38. Let Freedom Ring 39. Balalaika 39. *New Moon* 40. Bitter Sweet 40. The Chocolate Soldier 41. I Married an Angel 43. Phantom of the Opera 43. Knickerbocker Holiday 44. Make Mine Music (voice only) 46. Northwest Outpost 47.
†Eddy and MacDonald were rudely known in some quarters as The Singing Capon and The Iron Butterfly.

Edelman, Louis F. (1901–1976). American producer.
Once Upon a Time 44. White Heat 48. I'll See You in My Dreams 52, etc.
TV series include *Wyatt Earp* and *The Big Valley*.

Edelmann, Herb (1930–). Bald, lanky American character actor, usually in comic roles.

In Like Flint 67. Barefoot in the Park 67. The Odd Couple 68. The Front Page 74. The Yakuza 75. Charge of the Model-Ts 77. Smorgasbord 83, etc.
TV series: The Good Guys 68. Strike Force 81. Nine to Five 82. St Elsewhere 83– .

Eden, Barbara (1934–) (Barbara Huffman). American leading lady, former chorine.
Back from Eternity 56. Twelve Hours to Kill 60. Flaming Star 60. Voyage to the Bottom of the Sea 61. Five Weeks in a Balloon 62. The Wonderful World of the Brothers Grimm 63. The Brass Bottle 64. Seven Faces of Dr Lao 64. The Feminist and the Fuzz (TV) 71. The Woman Hunter (TV) 72. A Howling in the Woods (TV) 72. The Amazing Dobermans 76. Harper Valley PTA 78, etc.
TV series: How to Marry a Millionaire 58. I Dream of Jeannie 65–70. Harper Valley PTA 81.

Edens, Roger (1905–1970). American musical supervisor who moulded many MGM musicals, often as associate to producer Arthur Freed. Academy Awards for Easter Parade 48. On the Town 49. Annie Get Your Gun 50. Produced Deep in My Heart 55. Funny Face 56. Hello Dolly 69, etc.

Edeson, Arthur (1891–1970). American cinematographer.
Wild and Woolly 17. *Robin Hood* 23. *The Thief of Baghdad* 24. *The Lost World* 25. The Bat 26. The Patent Leather Kid 27. In Old Arizona 28. *All Quiet on the Western Front* 30. *Frankenstein* 31. The Old Dark House 32. *The Invisible Man* 33. Mutiny on the Bounty 35. They Won't Forget 37. Each Dawn I Die 39. They Drive by Night 40. Sergeant York 41. *The Maltese Falcon* 41. *Casablanca* 42. Thank Your Lucky Stars 43. The Mask of Dimitrios 44. The Fighting O'Flynn 48, many others.

Edgar, Marriott (1880–1951). British comedy scenarist, in films from 1935. Worked on many of the best vehicles of Will Hay and the Crazy Gang.
Good Morning Boys 36. Oh Mr Porter 38. Alf's Button Afloat 38. The Frozen Limits 39. The Ghost Train 41, many others; later on children's films. Also author of the 'Sam Small' and 'Albert' monologues made famous by Stanley Holloway.

edge numbers. Serial numbers printed along the edge of all film material to assist identification when re-ordering sections.

Edison, Thomas Alva (1847–1931). American inventor of the phonograph and the incandescent lamp, among over a thousand other devices including the kinetoscope (a combined movie camera and projector), edge perforations and the 35 mm gauge. Biopics: *Young Tom Edison* 39 with Mickey Rooney; *Edison the Man* 40 with Spencer Tracy.

editor. Technician who assembles final print of film from various scenes and tracks available; works closely under director's control except in routine pictures.

¶ *Alfred Hitchcock:* Editing is crucial. Imagine James Stewart looking at a mother nursing her child. You see the child, then cut back to him. He smiles. Now Mr Stewart is a benign old gentleman. Take away the middle piece of film and substitute a girl in a bikini. Now he's a dirty old man.

Edouard et Caroline (France 1950). Jacques Becker's slight but charming comedy of a tiff between a young married couple was highly influential on later style. Anne Vernon and Daniel Gelin starred.

Edouart, Farciot (–1980). American special effects man, with Paramount for many years.
Alice in Wonderland 33. Lives of a Bengal Lancer 35. Sullivan's Travels 41. Reap the Wild Wind 42. Unconquered 47. Ace in the Hole 51. The Mountain 56, many others.

Edwards, Blake (1922–) (William Blake McEdwards). American writer-producer-director with a leaning for all kinds of comedy. Married to Julie Andrews, who now appears mainly in his films, not always to her own advantage.
□Panhandle (aw) 47. All Ashore (w) 53. Cruising down the River (w) 53. Drive a Crooked Road (w) 54. Sound Off (w) 54. Bring Your Smile Along (wd) 55. My Sister Eileen (w) 55. He Laughed Last (wd) 55. Mr Cory (wd) 56. Operation Mad Ball (w) 57. This Happy Feeling (wd) 58. The Perfect Furlough (wd) 58. Operation Petticoat (d) 59. High Time (d) 60. Breakfast at Tiffany's (d) 61. Experiment in Terror (d) 62. Notorious Landlady (w) 62. *Days of Wine and Roses* (d) 62. The Pink Panther (wd) 63. A Shot in the Dark (wpd) 64. *The Great Race* (wpd) 64. Soldier in the Rain (w) 64. What Did You Do in the War, Daddy? (wpd) 66. Waterhole Three (p) 67. Gunn (pd) 67. The Party (wpd) 68. Darling Lili (wpd) 69. Wild Rovers (wpd) 71. The Carey Treatment (wpd) 72. The

Tamarind Seed (wd) 74. The Return of the Pink Panther (wpd) 74. The Pink Panther Strikes Again (wpd) 76. Revenge of the Pink Panther (wpd) 78. '10' (wpd) 79. S.O.B. (wpd) 81. Trail of the Pink Panther (wpd) 82. Curse of the Pink Panther (wpd) 83. The Man Who Loved Women (w, d) 83. Micki and Maude (d) 84. Blind Date (d) 86. A Fine Mess (d) 86. That's Life! (d) 87.
TV series: Richard Diamond, Dante, Peter Gunn (all as creator).

¶ *B.E.:* Make 'em redecorate your office. That's primary, to let them know where you stand. Then, when you're shooting interior sequences, use your own interior decorator and set dresser. That way, everything on the set will fit your house when you're finished.

Edwards, Cliff (1895–1971). Diminutive American entertainer known as 'Ukelele Ike'.
Hollywood Revue 29. Parlour Bedroom and Bath 31. Hell Divers 31. Flying Devils 33. Red Salute 35. Bad Guy 39. Pinocchio (voice of Jiminy Cricket) 40. The Monster and the Girl 41. The Falcon Strikes Back 43. She Couldn't Say No 45. The Avenging Rider 53, many others.

Edwards, Henry (1882–1952). Gentlemanly British romantic lead of the twenties; later directed some films and came back to acting as amiable elderly man.
Broken Threads 18. The Amazing Quest of Ernest Bliss 22. A Lunatic at Large 23. *The Flag Lieutenant* 26. Fear 27. Three Kings 28. Call of the Sea 31. The Flag Lieutenant (talkie) 31. The Barton Mystery (d) 32. General John Regan 33.Discord Driven (d) 33. Scrooge (d) 35. Juggernaut (d) 37. Spring Meeting (d) 41. Green for Danger 46. Oliver Twist 48. London Belongs to Me 48. Madeleine 50. The Long Memory 52, many others.

Edwards, Hilton (1903–82). Irish producer and impresario, long with the Abbey Theatre. In 1953 made *Return to Glennascaul* and in 1961 appeared in *Victim*. Also on TV in Orson Welles' *Filming Othello*.

Edwards, J. Gordon (1867–1925). American director of silent epics, especially for Theda Bara.
Anna Karenina 15. Under Two Flags 16. Cleopatra 17. Salome 18. The Queen of Sheba 21. Nero 22. The Shepherd King 23, many others.

Edwards, James (1922–1970). Black American actor, on stage from 1945.
The Set-Up 49. *Home of the Brave* 49. The Member of the Wedding 52. The Caine Mutiny 54. The Phoenix City Story 55. Men in War 57. The Sandpiper 65, etc.

Edwards, Jimmy (1920–). Moustachioed British comedian of stage, radio and TV. Autobiography 1953: *Take It From Me.*
Murder at the Windmill 48. Treasure Hunt 52. Three Men in a Boat 55. Bottoms Up 60. Nearly a Nasty Accident 61. Rhubarb 70, etc.

Edwards, Meredith (1917–). Balding Welsh character actor with stage experience.
A Run for Your Money 50. The Blue Lamp 50. Girdle of Gold 53. The Cruel Sea 53. The Long Arm 56. The Trials of Oscar Wilde 60. Only Two Can Play 61. This Is My Street 64, etc.

Edwards, Penny (1919–). American light leading lady of the forties.
Let's Face It 43. That Hagen Girl 47. Two Guys from Texas 48. The Wild Blue Yonder 51. Street Bandits 52. Powder River 53, etc.

Edwards, Vince (1928–) (Vincento Eduardo Zoine). American leading man of the tough/sincere kind.
Mr Universe 51. Hiawatha 52. The Killing 56. City of Fear 58. *Murder by Contract* 59. The Victors 63. The Devil's Brigade 68. Hammerhead 68. The Desperadoes 69. The Mad Bomber 72. The Power and the Passion (TV) 79. Space Raiders 83, etc.
TV series: *Ben Casey* 60–65. Matt Lincoln 70.

Egan, Eddie (1924–). Burly American policeman whose exploits were the basis of *The French Connection* (qv). He subsequently left the force and played small parts in films.
TV series: Joe Forrester 75. Eischied 79.

Egan, Peter (1945–). British TV leading man who has sporadically appeared on stage and in films.
The Hireling 73. Callan 74. Hennessy 75. A Woman of Substance (TV) 84. The Perfect Spy (TV) 87.
TV series: Lillie (as Oscar Wilde) 78. Prince Regent 79. Ever Decreasing Circles 85– .

Egan, Richard (1921–87). Virile American leading man once thought likely successor to Clark Gable but who was mainly confined to westerns and action dramas.

The Damned Don't Cry 49. Undercover Girl 50. Split Second 52. Demetrius and the Gladiators 54. Wicked Woman 54. Gog 54. Underwater 55. Untamed 55. Violent Saturday 55. The View from Pompey's Head 55. Seven Cities of Gold 55. Love Me Tender 56. Tension at Table Rock 56. These Thousand Hills 58. A Summer Place 59. Pollyanna 60. Esther and the King 60. The 300 Spartans 62. The Destructors 66. Chubasco 68. The Big Cube 69. The Day of the Wolves (TV) 72. The Sweet Creek County War 79, etc.
TV series: Empire 62. Redigo 64.

Ege, Julie (1943–). Decorative Norwegian leading lady in British films of the seventies.
Every Home Should Have One 70. Up Pompeii 70. Creatures the World Forgot 71. The Magnificent Seven Deadly Sins 71. Rentadick 72. The Garnett Saga 72. Not Now Darling 73. Craze 73. The Mutations 74, etc.

Eggar, Samantha (1939–). British leading lady, in international films.
□The Wild and the Willing 62. Dr Crippen 63. Doctor in Distress 63. Psyche 59 63. *The Collector* 65. Return from the Ashes 65. Walk Don't Run 66. Doctor Dolittle 67. The Molly Maguires 69. The Walking Stick 69. The Lady in the Car 70. The Light at the Edge of the World 72. The Dead are Alive 72. A Name for Evil 72. Double Indemnity (TV) 73. All the Kind Strangers (TV) 74. The Seven Per Cent Solution 76. The Killer Who Wouldn't Die (TV) 76. Why Shoot the Teacher? 77. The Uncanny 77. Welcome to Blood City 77. Ziegfeld: the Man and His Women (TV) 78. Hagen (TV pilot) 79. The Brood 79. The Exterminator 80. Demonoid 81.
TV series: *Anna and the King* 72.

? ego
'Ego' is Latin for 'I'. Name the actor or actress playing the 'I' of the following films.

1 *I Was an American Spy*
2 *I Remember Mama*
3 *I Was a Male War Bride*
4 *I Know Where I'm Going*
5 *I Was a Teenage Werewolf*
6 *I Want to Live*
7 *I Met Him in Paris*
8 *I Married a Monster from Outer Space*
9 *I Married a Witch*
10 *I Am the Law*
11 *If I Were King*
12 *I Am a Camera*
13 *I'll Cry Tomorrow*
14 *I Loved a Woman*
15 *I Am Suzanne*

Eichhorn, Lisa (1952–). American leading lady.
The Europeans 79. Yanks 79. Why Would I Lie 80. Cutter's Way 81. Opposing Force 87.

Eight and a Half (Italy 1963). Fellini's beautiful, irresponsible, sometimes incomprehensible but highly cinematic extravaganza for our times, about a film director with doubts. Superbly photographed by Gianni de Venanzo, with a fine central part for Marcello Mastroianni. AA 1963: best foreign film.

8mm. A substandard gauge used mostly by amateurs. Sound used to require 9.5mm, but recently 'super 8' was introduced.

Eikenberry, Jill (–). American leading lady of the early eighties.
The Deadliest Season (TV) 77. A Night Full of Rain 77. Butch and Sundance 79. Hide in Plain Sight 80. Arthur 81, etc.
TV series: Nurse 82.

Eilbacher, Lisa (–). American leading lady.
The War Between Men and Women 72. Wheels (TV) 78. The Winds of War (TV) 83. Beverly Hills Cop 84.

Eilers, Sally (1908–1978). Quiet-spoken American leading lady of the thirties.
The Goodbye Kiss 28. She Couldn't Say No 30. Quick Millions 31. The Black Camel 31. Over the Hill 31. State Fair 33. She Made Her Bed 34. Alias Mary Dow 34. Strike Me Pink 35. Talk of the Devil 36. Danger Patrol 37. Nurse from Brooklyn 38. They Made Her a Spy 39. Full Confession 39. I Was a Prisoner on Devil's Island 41. A Wave a WAC and a Marine 44. Coroner Creek 48. Stage to Tucson 50, many others.

Eisenmann, Ike (–). American child actor of the seventies.
Escape to Witch Mountain 74. Banjo Hackett (TV) 76. Return from Witch Mountain 78. The Hound of Hell (TV) 79, etc.
TV series: Fantastic Journey 77.

Eisenstein, Sergei (1898–1948). Russian director, one of the cinema giants.
Biographies: *Sergei Eisenstein* by Marie Seton, 1952; *Eisenstein* by Yon Barna, 1966.
□*Strike* 24. *The Battleship Potemkin* 25. *October* (Ten Days That Shook the World) 27. *The General Line* 28. *Que Viva Mexico* (unfinished: sections later released under this title and as *Time in the Sun*) 32. *Alexander Nevsky* 38. *Ivan the Terrible* 42–46.

Books published include *Film Form, The Film Sense, Notes of a Film Director.*
❀ For virtually inventing montage, and for using the grammar of film-making more vividly and purposefully than almost anyone else. *Alexander Nevsky.*

Eisinger, Jo (–). American screenwriter.
The Spider 45. Gilda 46. The Sleeping City 50. Night and the City 51. The System 53. Bedevilled 55. The Poppy is Also a Flower (Danger Grows Wild) 66, many others.

Eisler, Hanns (1898–1962). German composer who in the forties scored some Hollywood films (*None But the Lonely Heart, The Woman on the Beach,* etc.). In Germany, *Aktion J* 61, many others.

Eisley, Anthony (–). American general purpose actor.
The Naked Kiss 64. Frankie and Johnny 65. Journey to the Centre of Time 67. Star! 68. Blood of Frankenstein 70. The Doll Squad 73. Secrets (TV) 77, etc.
TV series: Hawaiian Eye 59–73. Capitol 82–84.

Eisner, Lotte H. (1896–1983). German film historian. Most noted book: *The Haunted Screen.*

Ekberg, Anita (1931–). Statuesque Swedish blonde who decorated a number of films in various countries.
The Golden Blade 53. Blood Alley 55. Artists and Models 55. Back from Eternity 56. War and Peace 56. Zarak 56. Interpol 57. Sign of the Gladiator 58. La Dolce Vita 59. The Mongols 60. Boccaccio 70 61. Summer is Short (Sw.) 62. Il Comandante (It.) 63. Call Me Bwana 63. Four for Texas 63. The Alphabet Murders 65. Who Wants to Sleep (Das Liebeskarussel) 65. Way Way Out 66. The Glass Sphinx 67. If It's Tuesday, This Must Be Belgium 69. The Divorcee 70. The Clowns 70, etc.

Ekk, Nikolai (1902–). Russian director.
The Road to Life 31. The Nightingale 36, etc.

Ekland, Britt (1942–) (Britt-Marie Eklund). Swedish leading lady in international films.
□Too Many Thieves (TV) 66. After the Fox 66. The Bobo 67. The Double Man 68. The Night They Raided Minsky's 68. Stiletto 69. Percy 71. Get Carter 71. A Time for Loving 71. Night Hair Child 71. Baxter 72. Endless Night 72. Asylum 72. The Wicker Man 73. The Man with the Golden Gun 73. Royal Flash 74. The Ultimate Thrill 74. Casanova 77. High Velocity 77. King Solomon's Treasure 77. The Great Wallendas (TV) 77. Ring of Passion (TV) 79. Satan's Mistress 82.

¶ *B.E.:* The ideal man doesn't exist. A husband is easier to find.
B.E.: I said I don't sleep with married men, but what I meant was I don't sleep with happily married men.

Ekman, Gosta (1890–1948). Swedish leading actor.
Charles XII 24. Faust 26. Intermezzo 36, etc.

El (Mexico 1953). A haunting psychological melodrama written and directed by Luis Buñuel, with Arturo de Cordova as a happily married man who unaccountably goes mad with jealousy.

Elam, Jack (1916–). Laconic, swarthy American character actor, often seen as western villain or sinister comic relief.
Rawhide 50. Kansas City Confidential 52. The Moonlighter 53. Vera Cruz 54. Moonfleet 55. Kiss Me Deadly 55. *Gunfight at the OK Corral* 57. Baby Face Nelson 57. Edge of Eternity 59. The Comancheros 62. The Rare Breed 66. The Way West 67. Firecreek 67. Once Upon a Time in the West 69. Support Your Local Sheriff 69. Rio Lobo 70. Support Your Local Gunfighter 71. A Knife for the Ladies 74. Creature from Black Lake 76. Grayeagle 77. Lacy and the Mississippi Queen (TV) 78. The Villain 79. The Sacketts (TV) 79. Soggy Bottom USA 82. Jinxed 82, etc.
TV series: *The Dakotas* 62. Temple Houston 63. The Texas Wheelers 77. Struck By Lightning (as the Frankenstein monster) 79.

Eldredge, John (1917–1960). Mild-looking American actor usually cast as weakling brother or bland schemer.
The Man with Two Faces 34. Persons in Hiding 38. Blossoms in the Dust 41. The French Key 47. Champagne for Caesar 50. Lonely Hearts Bandits 52. The First Travelling Saleslady 56, many others.

Eldridge, Florence (1901–) (Florence McKechnie). Distinguished American stage actress, wife of Fredric March. Film appearances occasional.
Six Cylinder Love 23. The Studio Murder Mystery 29. The Matrimonial Bed 30. The Story of Temple Drake 33. Les Misérables 35. Mary of Scotland (as Elizabeth I) 36. *An Act of Murder* 48. *Another Part of the Forest*

48. Christopher Columbus 49. Inherit the Wind 60, etc.

Eldridge, John (1904–61). British documentary and feature director.
Waverley Steps 47. Three Dawns to Sydney 49. Brandy for the Parson 51. Laxdale Hall 53. Conflict of Wings 54, etc.

the electric chair has figured prominently in innumerable gangster and prison movies, notably *Two Seconds, Twenty Thousand Years in Sing Sing, Angels with Dirty Faces* and *The Last Mile. Front Page Woman* concentrated on the reporters ushered in to watch. The death cell scenes in *Double Indemnity* were deleted before the film's release. The most horrific sequence of this kind was the gas chamber climax of *I Want To Live.*

electronovision. A much-touted form of transfer from videotape to film, thought likely to save money in putting great stage performances onto the big screen. Unfortunately it proved technically and aesthetically unacceptable, and the two features shot in it in 1965 are only interesting if one can ignore the technical shortcomings. They are *Harlow* with Carol Lynley and *Hamlet* with Richard Burton.

Elephant Boy (GB 1937). Directed by Robert Flaherty and Zoltan Korda, this adaptation of Kipling's 'Toomai of the Elephants' had the air of a fictionalized travel film but was a great commercial success because of the popularity of the boy Sabu, who became a star and went to Hollywood. Its Indian backgrounds were charming and authentic. A TV series followed in 1974.

elephants have come closest to starring roles in *Zenobia, Elephant Boy* and *Hannibal Brooks*; but they were the subject of concern in *Chang, Where No Vultures Fly, Elephant Walk, Maya,* and *Roots of Heaven,* and Tarzan and Dorothy Lamour (in her jungle days) usually had one around as a pet. (*Tarzan Goes to India* had a splendid elephant stampede.) Circus elephants were stars of *Jumbo,* and above all of *Dumbo.*

Eles, Sandor (1936–). Hungarian leading man in Britain.
The Naked Edge 61. The Evil of Frankenstein 64. And Soon the Darkness 70. Countess Dracula 70. The Greek Tycoon 78, etc.

elevators: see *lifts*.

Elfand, Martin (–). American producer.
Serpico 73. Dog Day Afternoon 75. It's My Turn 80.

Elg, Taina (1931–). Finnish leading lady in international films.
The Prodigal 55. Diane 56. Gaby 56. Les Girls 57. Imitation General 57. Watusi 58. The Thirty-Nine Steps 59, etc.

Eliot, T. S. (1888–1965). American poet who lived mainly in England. His play *Murder in the Cathedral* was his only work adapted for the cinema.

Elizabeth I, Queen of England (1533–1603), has been notably played by Flora Robson in *Fire Over England* 36 and *The Sea Hawk* 40; by Florence Eldridge in *Mary of Scotland* 36; by Bette Davis in *Elizabeth and Essex* 39 and *The Virgin Queen* 55; by Sarah Bernhardt in *Queen Elizabeth* 12; by Agnes Moorehead in *The Story of Mankind* 57; by Irene Worth in *Seven Seas to Calais* 63; by Catherine Lacey in *The Fighting Prince of Donegal* 65, and by Glenda Jackson in a 1971 TV series followed by *Mary Queen of Scots* 72; Jean Simmons played the young queen in *Young Bess* 53; Jean Kent had the role in the TV series *Sir Francis Drake.*

Elizondo, Hector (1936–). American character actor, mainly on stage.
Pocket Money 71. Stand Up and Be Counted 72. The Taking of Pelham One Two Three 74. Report to the Commissioner 75. Thieves 77. Cuba 79. American Gigolo 80. The Fan 81. Young Doctors in Love 82, etc.
TV series: Freebie and the Bean 80.
Casablanca 83. The Flamingo Kid 84. Private Resort 85. Nothing in Common 86.

Ellenshaw, Peter (c. 1914–). British special effects artist and production designer, with Disney since 1950.
Things to Come 36. Victoria the Great 37. The Drum 38. A Matter of Life and Death 45. The Red Shoes 48. Treasure Island 50. *20,000 Leagues Under the Sea* 54. Johnny Tremain 57. Darby O'Gill and the Little People 59. In Search of the Castaways 61. *Mary Poppins* 64. The Island at the Top of the World 74. *The Black Hole* 79, etc.

Ellery Queen. The fictional American detective was played by four actors between 1935 and 1943: Donald Cook, Eddie Quillan,

Ralph Bellamy and William Gargan. The name is a pseudonym for two authors: *Frederick Dannay* (1905–71) and *Manfred Lee* (1905–). In 1971 Peter Lawford turned up in a TV movie, *Don't Look Behind You*, and in 1975 there was a TV series with Jim Hutton, following a 1954 one with George Nader.

Ellington, Duke (1899–1974) (Edward Kennedy Ellington). Celebrated black American bandleader and pianist.
Hit Parade 37. New Faces 37. Reveille with Beverly 43. Anatomy of a Murder 59. Paris Blues 61. Change of Mind (m only) 69, etc.

Elliot, Laura (1929–). American supporting actress.
Special Agent 49. Paid in Full 50. *Strangers on a Train* 51. When Worlds Collide 52. Jamaica Run 53. About Mrs Leslie 54, etc.

Elliott, Denholm (1922–). British stage and screen actor, often of well-mannered ineffectual types, latterly in more sophisticated roles.
Dear Mr Prohack 49. The Sound Barrier 52. The Cruel Sea 53. The Heart of the Matter 53. They Who Dare 54. The Night My Number Came Up 55. Pacific Destiny 56. Scent of Mystery (Holiday in Spain) 59. Station Six Sahara 63. *Nothing But the Best* 64. The High Bright Sun 65. You Must Be Joking 65. King Rat 65. Alfie 66. The Spy with a Cold Nose 67. Maroc 7 67. *Here We Go Round the Mulberry Bush* 67. The Night They Raided Minsky's 68. Too Late the Hero 69. The Rise and Rise of Michael Rimmer 70. Percy 70. Quest for Love 71. A Doll's House 73. Madame Sin 73. The Apprenticeship of Duddy Kravitz 75. Robin and Marian 75. Russian Roulette 76. A Bridge Too Far 77. The Boys from Brazil 78. Saint Jack 79. Cuba 79. Bad Timing 80. Sunday Lovers 80. Raiders of the Lost Ark 81. The Missionary 82. Brimstone and Treacle 82. Trading Places 83. The Razor's Edge 84. A Private Function (BFA) 84. A Room With a View 85. Defence of the Realm (BFA) 85. Maurice 87. The Happy Valley (TV) 87. September 87. The Bourne Identity 88, etc.

Elliott, Robert (1879–1951). Irish leading man of American silents.
Spirit of Lafayette 17. Resurrection 18. A Woman There Was 19. A Virgin Paradise 21. Man and Wife 23. Romance of the Underworld 28. Thunderbolt 29. The Divorcee 30. Five Star Final 31. Phantom of Crestwood 32. Crime of the Century 33. Girl of the Limberlost 34. Circumstantial Evidence 35. Trade Winds 38. Gone with the Wind 39. Captain Tugboat Annie 45, many others.

Elliott, Sam (1944–). American leading man of the seventies.
□The Games 70. Frogs 72. Molly and Lawless John 72. The Blue Knight (TV) 73. I Will Fight No More Forever (TV) 75. Evel Knievel (TV) 75. Lifeguard 76. Once an Eagle (TV) 77. The Last Convertible (TV) 79. Aspen (TV) 79. The Sacketts (TV) 79. The Legacy 79. Wild Times (TV) 80. Murder in Texas (TV) 81. The Shadow Riders (TV) 82. Travis McGee (TV) 82.

Elliott, 'Wild Bill' (1904–1965) (Gordon Elliott). Burly American leading man of the twenties who later appeared in many second feature westerns and mysteries.
The Private Life of Helen of Troy 27. Broadway Scandals 28. The Great Divide 31. Wonder Bar 34. False Evidence 40. Blue Clay 42. The Plainsman and the Lady 46. The Fabulous Texan 48. Hellfire 49. The Longhorn 51. Dial Red O 55. Chain of Evidence 57, etc.

Ellis, Don (1933–1978). American composer, former jazz trumpeter.
Moon Zero Two 69. The French Connection 71. The Seven Ups 73. French Connection II 75. Ruby 77, etc.

Ellis, Edward (1872–1952). American stage character actor who made a number of films in the thirties, usually as stern father or judge.
I Am a Fugitive from a Chain Gang 32. From Headquarters 33. The President Vanishes 34. The Return of Peter Grimm 35. Fury 36. Maid of Salem 37. *A Man to Remember* 38. Three Sons 39. A Man Betrayed 41. The Omaha Trail 42, etc.

Ellis, Mary (1900–) (Mary Elsas). American leading lady and singer famous in British stage musicals, especially those of Ivor Novello.
Bella Donna 34. Paris Love Song 35. All the King's Horses 35. Glamorous Night 36. The Three Worlds of Gulliver 61, etc.

Ellis, Patricia (1916–1970) (Patricia Gene O'Brien). American leading lady of the thirties.
Three on a Match 32. 42nd Street 33. Picture Snatcher 33. The St Louis Kid 34. The Case of the Lucky Legs 34. Boulder Dam 36. Melody for Two 37. Blockheads 38. Back

Door to Heaven 39. Fugitive at Large 39, etc.

Ellis, Vivian (1904–). British song composer and lyricist. Shows filmed include *Mr Cinders* and *Under Your Hat,* but most of his tinkly tunes aired only on the London stage.

Ellison, James (1910–) (James Ellison Smith). Genial American leading man, mainly seen in routine westerns.
The Play Girl 32. Hopalong Cassidy 35. The Plainsman (as Buffalo Bill) 36. Vivacious Lady 38. Fifth Avenue Girl 39. Ice Capades 41. Charley's Aunt 41. The Undying Monster 42. I Walked with a Zombie 43. The Ghost Goes Wild 46. Calendar Girl 47. Last of the Wild Horses 48. Lone Star Lawman 50. Dead Man's Trail 52, etc.

Elmer Gantry (US 1960). In this lengthy version written (AA) and directed by Richard Brooks, Sinclair Lewis's novel about old-time revivalist religion has its emotions compromised and its satire blunted; but the flavour of the book often filters through, and the film benefits from John Alton's colour photography and the broad, beaming, zestful performance of Burt Lancaster (AA) as the hymn and hellfire salesman.

Elmes, Guy (1920–). British writer.
The Planter's Wife (co-w) 51. The Stranger's Hand 53. Across the Bridge (co-w) 57. Swordsman of Siena 62. A Face in the Rain 63. El Greco 66. The Night Visitor 71, etc.

Elphick, Michael (1946–). Heavy-set British character actor of all media.
Fraulein Doktor 67. Cry of the Banshee 69. Blind Terror 70. O Lucky Man 73. The Elephant Man 80. Privates on Parade 83. Gorky Park 83. Masada (TV) 83. Hitler's S.S. (TV) 84. Ordeal by Innocence 85. Supergrass 85. Little Dorrit 87.
TV series: Boon 85– . Three Up Two Down 85– .

Elsom, Isobel (1893–1981) (Isobel Reed). British stage actress who starred in over 60 early British romantic films; went to Hollywood in the late thirties and played innumerable great ladies.
A Debt of Honour 19. Dick Turpin's Ride to York 22. The Sign of Four 23. The Wandering Jew 23. The Love Story of Aliette Brunon 24. Stranglehold 30. Illegal 31. *Ladies in Retirement* 41. You Were Never Lovelier 42. Between Two Worlds 44. The Unseen 45. Of Human Bondage 46. Ivy 47. Love from a Stranger 47. Monsieur Verdoux 47. Desiree 54. 23 Paces to Baker Street 57. The Miracle 59. Who's Minding the Store? 63. My Fair Lady 64, others.

Elstree Studios. Production complex at Borehamwood, north of London, started in the twenties by British International, which later became Associated British (qv). After many vicissitudes the facilities and library passed into the hands of Thorn–EMI, who sold out in the eighties to Cannon, who sold off the library to Weintraub. In 1982 Patricia Warren wrote a useful book: *Elstree, the British Hollywood.*

Eltinge, Julian (1882–1941) (William J. Dalton). American female impersonator who appeared in a few silent films.
The Countess Charming 17. Over the Rhine 18. Madame Behave 24, etc.

Elton, Sir Arthur (1906–1973). British producer especially associated with documentary; GPO Film Unit 34–37, Ministry of Information 37–45, Shell Film Unit 45 on. Founder Film Centre, governor BFI, etc.

Elvey, Maurice (1887–1967) (William Folkard). Veteran British director of over three hundred features.
Maria Marten 12. Comradeship 18. Nelson 19. At the Villa Rose 20. The Elusive Pimpernel 20. The Hound of the Baskervilles 21. Dick Turpin's Ride to York 22. The Love Story of Aliette Brunon 24. The Flag Lieutenant 26. Hindle Wakes 27. Balaclava 28. High Treason 30. The School for Scandal 30. Sally in Our Alley 31. In a Monastery Garden 31. The Water Gypsies 32. The Lodger 32. The Wandering Jew 33. The Clairvoyant 34. *The Tunnel* 34. Heat Wave 35. The Return of the Frog 37. For Freedom 39. Room for Two 39. Under Your Hat 40. The Lamp Still Burns 43. The Gentle Sex (co-d) 43. Medal for the General 44. Salute John Citizen 44. *Beware of Pity* 46. The Third Visitor 51. My Wife's Lodger 52. Fun at St Fanny's 55. Dry Rot 56, many others.

Elvira Madigan (Sweden 1967). Bo Widerberg's ravishingly beautiful film about lovers who would rather starve than live apart caused a small resurgence in romance. Photographed by Jorgen Persson.

Ely, Ron (1938–) (Ronald Pierce). American athlete who was television's Tarzan and starred in one other movie, *Doc Savage* 75.

Emerson, Faye (1917–1983). American socialite leading lady popular for a time in the forties.
Between Two Worlds 44. The Mask of Dimitrios 44. Hotel Berlin 45. Danger Signal 45. Nobody Lives Forever 46. Guilty Bystander 50. A Face in the Crowd 57, etc.

Emerson, Hope (1897–1960). Brawny 6′ 2″ American character actress, in films from early thirties.
Smiling Faces 32. Cry of the City 48. Adam's Rib 49. Caged 50. Casanova's Big Night 54. The Day They Gave Babies Away 56. Rock a Bye Baby 58, many others.
TV series: Doc Corkle 52. Peter Gunn 58–60.

Emerton, Roy (1892–1944). Long-nosed British character actor: an eminently hissable villain.
The Sign of Four 32. Java Head 34. Lorna Doone (as Carver) 35. Doctor Syn 38. The Drum 38. Busman's Honeymoon 40. The Thief of Baghdad 40. The Man in Grey 43. Henry V 44, etc.

Emery, Dick (1918–1983). Chubby British TV comedian with a flair for disguise.
Light Up the Sky 60. A Taste of Money 62. The Wrong Arm of the Law 63. Baby Love 69. *Ooh You Are Awful* 72, etc.

Emery, Gilbert (1875–1945) (Gilbert Emery Bensley Pottle). British character actor long in Hollywood as police commissioners, lords of the manor, etc.
Behind that Curtain 29. The Royal Bed 30. A Farewell to Arms 32. The House of Rothschild 34. One More River 34. Clive of India 35. Magnificent Obsession 35. Dracula's Daughter 36. A Man to Remember 38. Nurse Edith Cavell 39. Raffles 39. Rage in Heaven 41. That Hamilton Woman 41. The Loves of Edgar Allan Poe 42. Between Two Worlds 44. The Brighton Strangler 45, many others.

Emery, John (1905–1964). American stage and screen actor of suave and sometimes Mephistophelean types.
Here Comes Mr Jordan 41. Spellbound 45. Blood on the Sun 45. The Woman in White 48. The Gay Intruders 48. Let's Live Again 49. The Mad Magician 54. Ten North Frederick 57. Youngblood Hawke 64, many others.

Emhardt, Robert (1901–). American character actor, short and tubby; once understudied Sydney Greenstreet.
The Iron Mistress 52. 3.10 to Yuma 57. Underworld USA 60. The Stranger 61. Kid Galahad 62. *The Group* 66. Where Were You When the Lights Went Out? 68. Lawman 71. Alex and the Gypsy 76, etc.

Emil and the Detectives. Erich Kastner's German novel of schoolboys who track down a thief has been filmed five times: in 1932 (Germany) by Gerhardt Lamprecht; in 1935 (GB) by Milton Rosmer; in 1954 (Germany) by R. A. Stemmle; in 1956 in Japan; and in 1963 (US) by Peter Tewkesbury for Walt Disney.

Emmer, Luciano (1918–). Italian director.
Domenica d'Agosto 50. The Girls of the Spanish Steps 52. The Bigamist 56, etc.

Emmett, E. V. H. (1902–1971). British commentator, for many years the voice of Gaumont-British and Universal News. Producer of occasional documentaries, also features at Ealing 1946–50.

Emney, Fred (1900–1980). Heavyweight British comedian, characterized by a growl, a cigar, and a top hat.
Brewster's Millions 35. Yes Madam 39. Just William 40. Let the People Sing 42. Fun at St Fanny's 56. San Ferry Ann 65. The Sandwich Man 66. Lock Up Your Daughters 69, etc.

the end of the world has been fairly frequently considered in movies, and not only in the recent crop of panic button dramas like *Dr Strangelove, The Bedford Incident* and *Fail Safe*. Movement of the earth was threatened in *The Day the Earth Stood Still* and stopped (by Roland Young) in *The Man Who Could Work Miracles*. Plague very nearly ended everything in *Things to Come*. Danger from other planets looming perilously close was only narrowly averted in *Red Planet Mars*, while in *When Worlds Collide* and *The Day the Earth Caught Fire* the worst happened. Another kind of danger was met in *Crack in the World*. The Martians nearly got us in *The War of the Worlds*. In *Five* there were only five people left alive, in *The World, the Flesh and the Devil* only three, and in *On the Beach* none at all. See also *Planet of the Apes*, *Damnation Alley*, *Panic in Year Zero* and *The Omega Man*.

Endfield, Cy (1914–83). American director, in films since 1942. Made second features until 1951; thereafter resident in Britain.
Gentleman Joe Palooka 47. Stork Bites Man (& w) 47. The Argyle Secrets (& w) 48.

Underworld Story 50. *The Sound of Fury* 51. Tarzan's Savage Fury 52. The Search 55. Child in the House 56. *Hell Drivers* 57. Sea Fury 58. Jet Storm 59. Mysterious Island 61. *Zulu* 63. Sands of the Kalahari 65. De Sade 69. Universal Soldier 71, etc.

Endore, Guy (1900–1970). American screenwriter and novelist.
Mark of the Vampire 35. Mad Love 35. The Raven 35. The Devil Doll 36. The League of Frightened Men 37. Carefree 38. The Story of G.I. Joe 45. Whirlpool (oa) 49. He Ran All the Way 51. Curse of the Werewolf (oa) 61, etc.

Les Enfants du Paradis (France 1944). A superbly evocative and pictorial romance of Paris's 'theatre street' in the 1840s. Jacques Prévert's script mingles fact and fiction, farce and tragedy; Marcel Carné directs with superb control of the rich detail. The fine cast includes Arletty, Jean-Louis Barrault, Pierre Brasseur and Marcel Herrand, photography by Roger Hubert and Marc Fossard, music by Joseph Kosma and Maurice Thiriet.

Engel, Morris (1918–86). American producer-director of off-beat semi-professional features.
The Little Fugitive 53. Lovers and Lollipops 55. Weddings and Babies 58.

Engel, Samuel G. (1904–84). American producer.
My Darling Clementine 46. Sitting Pretty 48. Rawhide 50. Belles on Their Toes 52. Daddy Long Legs 55. Boy on a Dolphin 57. The Story of Ruth 60. The Lion 62, others.

English, John (1903–1969). British director of second features, long in America; a specialist in serials.
Arizona Days 37. Drums of Fu Manchu 40. Captain Marvel 41. King of the Texas Rangers 41. Captain America 44. Don't Fence Me In 45. The Phantom Speaks 45. Murder in the Music Hall 46. Loaded Pistols 48. Riders in the Sky 49. Valley of Fire 51, many others.

? English versions
Foreign language films have sometimes been so successful in their own countries that Hollywood or British studios have bought up the rights and made English-language versions, usually poorer than the originals, and often at the cost of the loss of those originals to the public. Can you name the English language remakes of the following? Also the star who replaced the one shown below?

1. *Le Jour Se Lève* (France, 1939, Jean Gabin)
2. *Pièges* (France, 1939, Maurice Chevalier)
3. *Rashomon* (Japan, 1950, Toshiro Mifune)
4. *La Bête Humaine* (France, 1938, Jean Gabin)
5. *Monsieur La Souris* (France, 1942, Raimu)
6. *La Mort du Cygne* (France, 1937, Mia Slavenska (adult role))
7. *The Hands of Orlac* (Germany, 1926, Conrad Veidt)
8. *Pépé Le Moko* (France, 1937, Jean Gabin)
9. *Les Inconnus dans la Maison* (France, 1942, Raimu)
10. *Yojimbo* (Japan, 1961, Toshiro Mifune) (actually remade in Italy)
11. *Le Corbeau* (France, 1943, Pierre Fresnay)
12. *Seven Samurai* (Japan, 1954, Toshiro Mifune)

Englund, George H. (1926–). American producer-director.
The World, the Flesh and the Devil (p) 59. The Ugly American (pd) 62. Signpost to Murder (d) 64. Dark of the Sun (p) 67. Zachariah (d) 70. Snowjob (d) 71, etc.

Englund, Ken (1914–). American writer, in films from 1938.
Good Sam 47. The Secret Life of Walter Mitty 48. The Caddy 53. The Vagabond King 56, etc.

Englund, Robert (1948–). American character actor who became a mild cult after playing the demoniacal Freddie in *Nightmare on Elm Street* and its sequels.

Ennis, Skinnay (1907–1963). American bandleader and vocalist who appeared in such thirties films as *College Swing*, *Sleepytime Gal* and *Follow the Band*.

Enoch Arden was a character in a Tennyson poem who came back to his family after having been long supposed dead. Films with an 'Enoch Arden' theme include *Tomorrow Is Forever* (with Orson Welles), *The Years Between* (with Michael Redgrave), *My Two Husbands* (with Fred MacMurray) and its remake *Three for the Show* (with Jack

Lemmon), *My Favourite Wife* (with Irene Dunne) and its remake *Move Over Darling* (with Doris Day), *Piccadilly Incident* (with Anna Neagle), *Return from the Ashes* (with Ingrid Thulin), *Desire Me* (with Robert Mitchum), *Laura* (with Gene Tierney), *Man Alive* (with Pat O'Brien), and *The Man from Yesterday* (with Clive Brook). D. W. Griffith in 1910 and 1911 made short versions of the original story.

Enrico, Robert (1931–). French director.
Incident at Owl Creek 64. Au Coeur de la Vie 65. La Belle Vie 65. Les Aventuriers 67. Zita 67. Ho! 68. Rum Runner 76. The Old Gun 76. L'Empreinte des Géants 80, etc.

Enright, Ray (1896–1965). American director, former editor and Sennett gagman. Films mostly routine.
Tracked by the Police 27. Dancing Sweeties 30. Havana Widows 33. Twenty Million Sweethearts 34. Dames 34. Alibi Ike 35. Miss Pacific Fleet 35. Earthworm Tractors 36. Slim 37. *Swing Your Lady* 37. Gold Diggers in Paris 38. Angels Wash Their Faces 39. On Your Toes 39.

entertainers, including actors and impresarios, have frequently been the subject of biopics, and if all their stories have seemed much the same, that is Hollywood's fault rather than theirs. Here is a reasonably comprehensive list:
Always Leave Them Laughing Milton Berle, *After the Ball* Pat Kirkwood as Vesta Tilley, *The Buster Keaton Story* Donald O'Connor, *Champagne Charlie* Tommy Trinder as George Leybourne and Stanley Holloway as the Great Vance, *The Dolly Sisters* Betty Grable & June Haver, *The Eddie Cantor Story* Keefe Brasselle, *The Fabulous Dorseys* Tommy and Jimmy Dorsey, *The Five Pennies* Danny Kaye as Red Nichols, *Funny Girl* Barbra Streisand as Fanny Brice, *The Gene Krupa Story* Sal Mineo, *The Glenn Miller Story* James Stewart, *The Great Caruso* Mario Lanza, *The Great Ziegfeld* William Powell, *Gypsy* Natalie Wood as Gypsy Rose Lee, *Harlow* Carroll Baker/Carol Lynley, *The Helen Morgan Story* Ann Blyth, *Houdini* Tony Curtis, *The I Don't Care Girl* Mitzi Gaynor as Eva Tanguay, *Incendiary Blonde* Betty Hutton as Texas Guinan, *Interrupted Melody* Eleanor Parker as Marjorie Laurence, *Jeanne Eagels* Kim Novak, *The Joker is Wild* Frank Sinatra as Joe E. Lewis, *The Jolson Story* Larry Parks, *A Lady's Morals* Grace Moore as Jenny Lind, *Lady Sings the Blues* Diana Ross as Billie Holliday. *Lady With Red Hair* Miriam Hopkins as Mrs Leslie Carter and Claude Rains as David Belasco, *Lillian Russell* Alice Faye, *Look for the Silver Lining* June Haver as Marilyn Miller, *Love Me or Leave Me* Doris Day as Ruth Etting, *Man of a Thousand Faces* James Cagney as Lon Chaney, *Melba* Patrice Munsel, *Peg of Old Drury* Anna Neagle as Peg Woffington, *Prince of Players* Richard Burton as Edwin Booth, *The Seven Little Foys* Bob Hope as Eddie Foy, *Shine on Harvest Moon* Ann Sheridan as Nora Bayes, *Somebody Loves Me* Betty Hutton as Blossom Seeley, *So This Is Love* Kathryn Grayson as Grace Moore, *Star!* Julie Andrews as Gertrude Lawrence and Daniel Massey as Noel Coward, *The Story of Vernon and Irene Castle* Fred Astaire and Ginger Rogers, *The Story of Will Rogers* Will Rogers Jnr, *Tonight We Sing* David Wayne as Sol Hurok, *Too Much Too Soon* Dorothy Malone as Diana Barrymore and Errol Flynn as John Barrymore, *With a Song in My Heart* Susan Hayward as Jane Froman, *Yankee Doodle Dandy* James Cagney as George M. Cohan, *Young Man With a Horn* Kirk Douglas as Bix Beiderbecke, *Your Cheatin' Heart* George Hamilton as Hank Williams, *Lenny* Dustin Hoffman as Lenny Bruce, *W.C. Fields and Me* Rod Steiger as W. C. Fields, *Gable and Lombard* James Brolin and Jill Clayburgh.

Ephron, Henry (1912–). American screenwriter who invariably worked as a team with his wife Phoebe Ephron (1914–71). He also produced a few films.
Bride by Mistake 44. Always Together 46. John Loves Mary 49. *The Jackpot* 50. On the Riviera 51. Belles on Their Toes 52. There's No Business Like Show Business 54. Daddy Long Legs 55. Carousel (& p) 56. The Best Things in Life are Free (p only) 56. *Desk Set* 57. Take Her She's Mine 63. Captain Newman MD 64, etc.

epidemics featured memorably in *Jezebel, Yellow Jack, Arrowsmith, The Rains Came, Forever Amber, Panic in the Streets, The Killer That Stalked New York, Elephant Walk No Blade of Grass, The Andromeda Strain, Eighty Thousand Suspects, The Omega Man, Things to Come, Isle of the Dead, The Satan Bug* and *The Seventh Seal.*

episodic films in a sense have always been with us—*If I Had a Million*, after all, came out in 1932, and *Intolerance* in 1915—but it was in the forties, possibly spurred by the all-star variety films intended to help the war effort, that they achieved their greatest popularity. Julien Duvivier, who had made *Un Carnet du Bal* in Paris, remade it in Hollywood as *Lydia* and followed it with *Tales of Manhattan* which was linked by a tail coat and *Flesh and Fantasy* which was linked by the ramblings of a club bore. The stories in *Forever and a Day* were held together by a house, *Easy Money* by football pools, *Train of Events* by a railway accident, *Meet Mr Lucifer* by television. Then came the author complex: *Quartet* (Somerset Maugham), *Le Plaisir* (Maupassant), *Meet Me Tonight* (Noël Coward). The French took over with films like *The Seven Deadly Sins, The Devil and Ten Commandments, Life Together*; and the Italians were at it with *Four Kinds of Love, Made in Italy* and *The Queens*. For English-speaking markets the form was killed in the mid-fifties by the advent of the half-hour TV play, but the sixties saw a brief revival with *How the West Was Won* and *The Yellow Rolls Royce*. The eighties are showing signs: the Italians are at it again with *Sunday Lovers* and Hollywood assigned four directors to one story each for *Twilight Zone*.

epitaphs

¶ Over the years, a few stars have been nudged by the press into composing their own epitaphs. Herewith a selection of this grave humour.
W. C. Fields: On the whole, I'd rather be in Philadelphia.
Cary Grant: He was lucky—and he knew it.
Edward Everett Horton: A nice part—only four 'sides', but good company and in for a long run.
Lionel Barrymore: Well, I've played everything but a harp.
Hedy Lamarr: This is too deep for me.
Dorothy Parker: Excuse my dust.
Warner Baxter: Did you hear about my operation?
William Haines: Here's something I want to get off my chest.
Lewis Stone: A gentleman farmer goes back to the soil.
Constance Bennett: Do not disturb.
Wallace Ford: At last I get top billing.
Preston Sturges:

Now I've laid me down to die
I pray my neighbours not to pry
Too deeply into sins that I
Not only cannot here deny
But much enjoyed as time flew by . . .

Epstein, Jean (1897–1953). French director since 1922; also wrote books on film theory.
Coeur Fidèle 23. The Fall of the House of Usher 28. Finis Terrae 28. Mor Vran 30. His sister **Marie Epstein** (1899–) often worked with him, and herself directed La Maternelle 33. La Mort du Cygne 38, etc.

Epstein, Julius J. (1909–) and **Philip G.** (1909–52). American twin screenwriters.
Four Daughters 38. Four Wives 39. No Time for Comedy 40. Strawberry Blonde 41. The Man Who Came to Dinner 41. *Casablanca* (AA) 42, Mr Skeffington (& p) 44. Romance on the High Seas 48. My Foolish Heart 49. Forever Female 53. The Last Time I Saw Paris 54. Then Julius alone: The Tender Trap 55. Tall Story 60. Take a Giant Step (& p) 61. Fanny 61. Send Me No Flowers 64. Any Wednesday (& p) 66, Pete 'n Tillie (& p) 72. Reuben Reuben (AAN) 83, etc.

L'Equipage. Directed by Maurice Tourneur in 1927, this was a popular silent drama of a triangular love affair in which the male participants were airmen during World War I. Anatole Litvak remade it in 1935 (with Charles Vanel, Annabella and Jean Pierre Aumont); then went to Hollywood and in 1937 made an English version, *The Woman I Love* (with Paul Muni, Miriam Hopkins and Louis Hayward).

Erdman, Richard (1925–). American actor who began playing callow youths and now takes rather crustier roles.
Thunder across the Pacific 44. Objective Burma 45. The Men 50. The Happy Time 52. Benghazi 55. Bernardine 57. Saddle the Wind 58. Namu the Killer Whale 66. The Brothers O'Toole (d only) 73. Heidi's Song 82, others.
TV series: The Tab Hunter Show 60.

Erice, Victor (1940–). Spanish director.
Los Desafios 69. Spirit of the Beehive 73. El Sur 83.

Erickson, Leif (1911–86) (William Anderson). American 'second lead', former singer. In unspectacular roles from 1935.
Wanderer of the Wasteland 35. College Holiday 36. Ride a Crooked Mile 38. Nothing But the Truth 41. Eagle Squadron 42. Sorry, Wrong Number 48. Fort Algiers 50. Carbine Williams 52. On the Waterfront 54. The Fastest Gun Alive 56. Tea and Sympathy 57. Straitjacket 63. Mirage 65. Twilight's Last Gleaming 76, many others.
TV series: High Chaparral 67–71.

Ericson, John (1927–) (Joseph Meibes). German-born leading man, long in America.
Teresa (debut) 51. Rhapsody 54. Green Fire 54. Bad Day at Black Rock 54. The Return

of Jack Slade 55. Forty Guns 57. Pretty Boy Floyd 59. Under Ten Flags 60. The Seven Faces of Dr Lao 64. The Destructors 66. Operation Bluebook 67. Bedknobs and Broomsticks 71. Hustler Squad 76. Crash 77, etc.
TV series: Honey West 65.

Erotikon. There are two films of this title, both dealing with sexual experience and adultery. 1. Sweden 1920, written and directed by Mauritz Stiller, about a scientist who takes up with his niece when his wife proves unfaithful. 2. Czechoslovakia 1929, written and directed by Gustav Machaty, about a poor girl who takes a rich lover.

Errol, Leon (1881–1951). Australian comedian who in 1910 left medicine for Broadway musical comedy and vaudeville, lately becoming familiar to filmgoers as twitchy, bald-pated, henpecked little man in innumerable thirties two-reelers and a number of features, mainly unworthy of his talents.
Paramount on Parade 30. Only Saps Work 30. One Heavenly Night 30. Alice in Wonderland 33. *We're Not Dressing* 34. Princess O'Hara 35. Make a Wish 37. *Mexican Spitfire* (first of a series with Lupe Velez in which Errol appeared as the drunken Lord Epping) 39. Pop Always Pays 40. Six Lessons from Madame la Zonga 41. Never Give a Sucker an Even Break 41. Higher and Higher 43. Hat Check Honey 44. The Invisible Man's Revenge 44. What a Blonde 45. Mama Loves Papa 45. Joe Palooka Champ (first of another series) 46. The Noose Hangs High 48, etc.
❁ For bringing a breath of inspired vaudeville to some pretty tired Hollywood formats, and for inventing Lord Epping. *Mexican Spitfire.*

Erskine, Chester (1905–86). American writer-producer-director.
Call it Murder (pd) 34. The Egg and I (wpd) 47. All My Sons (wp) 48. Take One False Step (co-wpd) 49. Androcles and the Lion (wd) 53. Witness to Murder (wp) 57. The Wonderful Country (p) 59, etc.

Erwin, Stuart (1903–1967). American character comedian, who usually played Mr Average or the hero's faithful but slow-thinking friend. Mother Knows Best 28. The Trespasser 29. Sweetie 29. Men Without Women 30. Dude Ranch 31. Misleading Lady 32. International House 33. Palooka 34. After Office Hours 35. All American Chump 36. Slim 37. Three Blind Mice 38. Hollywood Cavalcade 39. Our Town 40. Cracked Nuts 41. Blondie for Victory 42. He Hired the Boss 43. The Great Mike 44. Pillow to Post 45. Killer Dill 47. Strike it Rich 48. Father is a Bachelor 50. For the Love of Mike 60. Son of Flubber 64. The Misadventures of Merlin Jones 64, many others.
TV series: *The Trouble with Father* 53. The Greatest Show on Earth 63. The Bing Crosby Show 65.

Escape. There are several films under this title. 1. D. W. Griffith 1914; from a play by Paul Armstrong about sex problems in the slums; with Blanche Sweet. Remade 1928 with Virginia Valli. 2. The play by John Galsworthy, about a man on the run from Dartmoor, was filmed by Basil Dean in 1930, with Gerald du Maurier, and by Joseph L. Mankiewicz in 1948, with Rex Harrison. 3. Ethel Vance's novel about an ingenious extrication of the hero's mother from a concentration camp was filmed by Mervyn le Roy in 1940, with Robert Taylor, Nazimova, Norma Shearer and Conrad Veidt. 4. A 1971 TV movie with Christopher George as an escapologist.

Escape Me Never. The two films under this title have no connection. In 1935 Paul Czinner directed Elisabeth Bergner in a tale of an unwed mother and a struggling musician; in 1947 Peter Godfrey had Errol Flynn as a composer torn between two women.

Eskimos have seldom been seriously tackled by the cinema. Documentaries abound, from *Nanook of the North* to *Eskimo,* and *Ukaliq* is a charming cartoon of Eskimo folklore, but the fictional stuff such as *Savage Innocents* and *The White Dawn* has been dull and unsympathetic.

Esmond, Carl (1905–) (Willy Eichberger). Good-looking Austrian actor usually in haughty or arrogant roles, first in Britain and later in Hollywood.
Evensong 33. Invitation to the Waltz 37. Dawn Patrol 38. Thunder Afloat 39. Pacific Rendezvous 42. The Story of Dr Wassell 43. *Ministry of Fear* 44. *Address Unknown* 44. Without Love 45. This Love of Ours 45. Catman of Paris 46. Smash-Up 47. Walk a Crooked Mile 48. The Desert Hawk 50. Mystery Submarine 51. The World in His Arms 52. From the Earth to the Moon 58. Thunder in the Sun 59. Agent for Harm 66. Morituri 66, etc.

Esmond, Jill (1908–). British leading lady of the thirties, later in Hollywood.
The Skin Game 31. Ladies of the Jury 32. No Funny Business 32. This Above All 42. Random Harvest 42. The White Cliffs of Dover 44. The Bandit of Sherwood Forest 46. Escape 48. Night People 54. A Man Called Peter 55, etc.

Essanay. A production company formed in 1907 by G. K. Spoor and G. M. Anderson (S and A). Mainly remembered for enormous output of early westerns and for Chaplin's first comedies.

Essex, David (1947–). British pop singer.
□Assault 70. Carry on Henry 71. All Coppers Are... 71. That'll Be the Day 73. Stardust 74. Silver Dream Racer 80.

Essex, Harry (1910–). American writer.
Boston Blackie and the Law 43. He Walked by Night 48. The Killer That Stalked New York 50. Kansas City Confidential 52. It Came from Outer Space 53. I The Jury (& d) 55. Mad at the World (& d) 56. The Lonely Man 57. The Sons of Katie Elder (co-w) 64, others; also many TV episodes.

establishing shot. Opening shot of sequence, showing location of scene or juxtaposition of characters in action to follow.

Estabrook, Howard (1884–1978). American screenwriter.
The Four Feathers 28. Hell's Angels 30. *Cimarron* (AA) 31. A Bill of Divorcement 32. The Masquerader 33. David Copperfield 34. International Lady 39. The Bridge of San Luis Rey 44. The Human Comedy 45. The Girl from Manhattan 48. Lone Star 51. The Big Fisherman 59, others.

Estevez, Emilio (1962–). American leading man, son of Martin Sheen.
Tex 82. Repo Man 84. The Breakfast Club 84. St Elmo's Fire 84. That was Then . . . This is Now 85. Maximum Overdrive 86. Wisdom 86. Stakeout 87.

Estrada, Erik (1948–). American leading man of Puerto Rican descent.
The New Centurions 74. Trackdown 76. Fire! (TV) 77. Hour of the Assassin 87.
TV series: *Chips* 77–82.

Estridge, Robin (1920–). British screenwriter.
Above Us the Waves 54. The Young Lovers 54. Campbell's Kingdom 57. Northwest Frontier 59. Escape from Zahrain 62. Eye of the Devil 67, etc.

Etaix, Pierre (1928–). French mime comedian, former circus clown and assistant to Tati.
Rupture (short) 61. Happy Anniversary (short) 61. The Suitor 62. Yo Yo 65. As Long As You Have Your Health 67. Le Grand Amour 69, etc.

L'Eternel Retour (France 1943). Jean Cocteau wrote and co-directed (with Jean Delannoy) this modernized, freewheeling but sombre version of the Tristan and Isolde legend. The Nazi occupiers approved its Teutonic appearance, but the French saw in it a message of hope. With Jean Marais, Madeleine Sologne.

Etting, Ruth (1896–1978). American popular singer of the twenties, a version of whose life was told in 1955 in *Love Me or Leave Me.* Very briefly on screen.
□Roman Scandals 33. Hips Hips Hooray 33. Gift of Gab 34.

Eustrel, Anthony (1903–1979). British character actor.
The Silver Fleet 43. Caesar and Cleopatra 45. The Robe 53, etc.

Evans, Barry (1945–). British light leading man.
Here We Go Round the Mulberry Bush 67. Die Screaming Marianne 71, etc.
TV series: Mind Your Language 77–81.

Evans, Clifford (1912–85). Welsh actor with stage experience. In films from 1936, at first as leading man and latterly as character actor.
Ourselves Alone 36. The Mutiny on the Elsinore 37. The Luck of the Navy 39. The Proud Valley 39. His Brother's Keeper 39. The Saint Meets the Tiger 40. *Love on the Dole* 41. Penn of Pennsylvania 41. Suspected Person 42. *The Foreman Went to France* 42; war service; The Silver Darlings 47. While I Live 48. Valley of Song 52. The Gilded Cage 55. Passport to Treason 56. Violent Playground 58. SOS Pacific 60. Curse of the Werewolf 62. Kiss of the Vampire 63. The Long Ships 64. Twist of Sand 69. One Brief Summer 70, etc.
TV series: Stryker of the Yard, The Power Game, etc.

Evans, Dale (1912–) (Frances Octavia Smith). American leading lady of the forties, former band singer; appeared frequently with

Roy Rogers, and in 1947 married him.
Orchestra Wives 42. Swing Your Partner 43. Casanova in Burlesque 44. The Yellow Rose of Texas 44. Utah 45. Belles of Rosarita 45. My Pal Trigger 46. Apache Rose 47. Slippy McGee 48. Susanna Pass 49. Twilight in the Sierras 50. Trigger Jnr 51. Pals of the Golden West 51, many others.
TV series: The Roy Rogers Show 51–56.

Evans, Dame Edith (1888–1976). Distinguished British stage actress who made occasional films.
Biographies 1977: *Ned's Girl* by Bryan Forbes. *Edith Evans: A Personal Memoir* by Jean Batters.
□A Welsh Singer 15. East is East 15. *The Queen of Spades* 48. *The Last Days of Dolwyn* 48. *The Importance of Being Earnest* 51. Look Back in Anger 59. The Nun's Story 59. Tom Jones 63. The Chalk Garden 64. Young Cassidy 65. *The Whisperers* (BFA) 67. Fitzwilly (US) 68. Prudence and the Pill 68. Crooks and Coronets 69. The Madwoman of Chaillot 69. David Copperfield 69. Scrooge 70. A Doll's House 73. Craze 73. QB VII (TV) 74. The Slipper and the Rose 76. Nasty Habits 76.

¶ *E.E.:* As a young actress I always had a rule. If I didn't understand a line I always said it as though it were improper.

Evans, Gene (1922–). Stocky American actor in demand for heavy roles since 1947.
Berlin Express 48. Park Row 52. Donovan's Brain 53. The Golden Blade 53. Hell and High Water 54. The Sad Sack 57. Operation Petticoat 59. Apache Uprising 65. Support Your Local Sheriff 69. The Ballad of Cable Hogue 70. Walking Tall 73. Devil Times Five 77, etc.
TV series: My Friend Flicka 57. Matt Helm 75. Spencer's Pilots 76.

Evans, Joan (1934–) (Joan Eunson). American actress who played teenage roles in the early fifties.
Our Very Own 50. On the Loose 51. Roseanna McCoy 51. Skirts Ahoy 52. Edge of Doom 54. The Fortune Hunter 54. No Name on the Bullet 59. The Flying Fontaines 60, etc.

Evans, Linda (1943–). Blonde American leading lady.
Twilight of Honor 63. Those Calloways 64. Female Artillery (TV) 73. The Klansman 74. Mitchell 75. Nowhere to Run (TV) 78. Avalanche Express 79. The Gambler Part Two (TV) 83. *The Last Frontier* (TV) 86.
TV series: The Big Valley 65–69. Hunter 77. *Dynasty* 81–.

Evans, Madge (1909–1981). American actress, a child star of silent days, pretty heroine of mainly unremarkable films in the thirties.
The Sign of the Cross 14. The Burglar 16. Classmates 24. Son of India 29. Lovers Courageous 30. The Greeks Had a Word for Them 32. Hallelujah I'm a Bum 33. Dinner at Eight 33. Grand Canary 34. David Copperfield 34. The Tunnel (GB) 35. Piccadilly Jim 37. The Thirteenth Chair 37, etc.

Evans, Maurice (1901–). Eloquent Welsh actor who, long in America, distinguished himself on the Broadway stage.
White Cargo 30. Raise the Roof 30. Wedding Rehearsal 32. Scrooge (GB) 35. Kind Lady 51. The Story of Gilbert and Sullivan (as Sullivan) 53. Androcles and the Lion (as Caesar) 53. Macbeth (title role) 59. The War Lord 65. Jack of Diamonds 67. Planet of the Apes 67. Rosemary's Baby 68. Terror in the Wax Museum 73, etc.
TV series: Bewitched 68–71.

Evans, Norman (1901–1962). British north-country music hall comedian famous for toothless characterisation and female impersonation.
Demobbed 45. Under New Management 46. Over the Garden Wall 50, etc.

Evans, Ray (1915–). American song-writer: 'Buttons and Bows' (AA 48), 'Que Sera Sera' (AA 56), many others.

Evans, Rex (1903–1969). British character actor in Hollywood. Often played stately butlers, as in *The Philadelphia Story* 40. Other appearances include *Camille* 36, *It Should Happen to You* 53, *The Matchmaker* 58. Ran an art gallery in his spare time.

Evans, Robert (1930–). Bland-faced American juvenile of the fifties; gave up acting to become a Paramount production executive, then went independent.
Lydia Bailey 52. *The Man of a Thousand Faces* (as Irving Thalberg) 57. The Sun Also Rises 57. The Fiend Who Walked the West (title role) 58. The Best of Everything 59, etc.
AS PRODUCER: Chinatown 74. The Great Gatsby 74. Marathon Man 76. Black Sunday 77. Players 79. Popeye 80. Urban Cowboy 80, etc.

Eve, Trevor (*c.* 1950–). Slightly-built British leading man who became popular from 1979 as TV's radio station detective *Shoestring*, but made little headway subsequently.

Dracula 79. Jamaica Inn (TV) 82. Lace (TV) 84. The Corsican Brothers (TV) 84. Shadow Chasers (TV) 85.

Evein, Bernard (1929–). French art director.
Les Amants 57. Les Jeux de L'Amour 60. Zazie dans le Métro 61. Lola 61. Cléo de 5 à 7 62. La Baie des Anges 62. Le Feu Follet 63. The Umbrellas of Cherbourg 64. Do You Like Women? 64. Viva Maria 65. The Young Girls of Rochefort 67. Woman Times Seven 67, etc.

Evelyn, Judith (1913–1967) (J. E. Allen). American stage actress; often played neurotic woman.
The Egyptian 54. Rear Window 54. Hilda Crane 56. The Tingler 59, etc.

Everest, Barbara (1890–1968). British stage actress who appeared in many films, latterly in motherly roles.
Lily Christine 31. The Wandering Jew 33. The Passing of the Third Floor Back 35. He Found a Star 40. Mission to Moscow (US) 43. Jane Eyre (US) 43. The Uninvited (US) 44. The Valley of Decision (US) 45. Wanted for Murder 46. Frieda 47. Madeleine 49. Tony Draws a Horse 51. The Man Who Finally Died 62, etc.

Everett, Chad (1937–) (Raymond Cramton). Handsome American leading man of the sixties; films unremarkable.
Claudelle Inglish 61. The Chapman Report 62. Get Yourself a College Girl 65. The Singing Nun 66. First to Fight 67. The Last Challenge 67. The Firechasers (TV) 70. The French Atlantic Affair (TV) 79. Airplane 2: the sequel 82, etc.
TV series: *Medical Center* 69–75. Hagen 79. The Rousters 83.

Everett, Rupert (1961–). British semi-juvenile player of the eighties.
Princess Daisy (TV) 83. *Another Country* 84. Dance with a Stranger 85. The Right Hand Man 86. Duet for One 86. Hearts of Fire 87.

Evergreen (GB 1935). Nostalgic Jessie Matthews vehicle often quoted as Britain's best musical. Victor Saville directed, with script contribution by Emlyn Williams.

Evers, Jason (1922–) (Herbert Evers). American general purpose actor.
A Piece of the Action 77.
TV series: The Young Lawyers 70.

Ewell, Tom (1909–) (S. Yewell Tompkins). American comic actor with wide stage experience.
□*Adam's Rib* 49. A Life of Her Own 50. An American Guerilla in the Philippines 50. Mr Music 50. Finders Keepers 51. Up Front 51. Back at the Front 52. Abbott and Costello Lost in Alaska 52. *The Seven Year Itch* 55. The Lieutenant Wore Skirts 55. The Great American Pastime 56. The Girl Can't Help It 57. A Nice Little Bank that Should be Robbed 58. Tender is the Night 61. State Fair 62. Suppose They Gave a War and Nobody Came 70. To Find A Man 72. They Only Kill Their Masters 72. The Great Gatsby 74. Promise Him Anything (TV) 75.
TV series: *The Tom Ewell Show* 60. Baretta 75–77. Best of the West 81.

excerpts from films are sometimes incorporated into other films in which characters go to a cinema or watch television. So in *Hollywood Cavalcade* Don Ameche watched a rough-cut of *The Jazz Singer,* just as ten years later Larry Parks in *Jolson Sings Again* watched a rough cut of himself in *The Jolson Story*; an unidentified silent comedy was being played in the room below when the first murder took place in *The Spiral Staircase*; Linda Christian and Louis Jourdan saw *Son of the Sheik* at their local in *The Happy Time,* and Fredric March and his son watched a William S. Hart film in *One Foot in Heaven.* Prisoners watched *Wings of the Navy* during *Each Dawn I Die* and *The Egg and I* during *Brute Force*; and the chain gang in *Sullivan's Travels* roared with laughter at a Mickey Mouse cartoon. Footage from *Phantom of the Opera* was shown in *Hollywood Story,* from *Comin' thru' the Rye* in *The Smallest Show on Earth,* from *Tol'able David* in *The Tingler,* from *Queen Kelly* in *Sunset Boulevard,* from *Camille* in *Bridge to the Sun,* from *Destination Tokyo* in *Operation Pacific,* and from *Boom Town* in *Watch the Birdie.* Other movies shown in 'cinemas' in later films include: *Uncle Tom's Cabin* in *Abbott and Costello Meet the Keystone Kops*; *Gold Diggers of 1933* in *Bonnie and Clyde*; *Crossroads* in *The Youngest Profession*; *Casablanca* in *First to Fight*; *Red River* in *The Last Picture Show*; *Hell Divers* in *The Wings of Eagles*; *Task Force* in *White Heat*; *The Walking Dead* in *Ensign Pulver*; *Tin Pan Alley* in *Wing and a Prayer*; *Now Voyager* in *Summer of '42*; *Red Dust* in *Heavy Traffic*; various Bogart films in *Play It Again Sam; Caprice* in *Caprice* (Doris Day went to the movies, saw herself on the screen, and didn't like it). In *Two Weeks in Another Town,* which had a plot pretty close to that of *The Bad and the Beautiful,* Kirk Douglas watched himself in–*The Bad and the Beautiful*! The Bette Davis character in *Whatever Happened to Baby Jane?* was criticized as a bad actress on the strength of clips from early Bette Davis movies, *Ex-Lady* and *Parachute Jumper.* In the same film Joan Crawford watched herself on TV in *Sadie McKee*; and in *Walk Don't Run* there was a flash of James Stewart dubbed in Japanese in *Two Rode Together.* Finally the cosmonauts on their space station in *Conquest of Space* were entertained by a showing of *Here Come the Girls* . . . thus showing, as one critic remarked, that in 50 years' time TV will still be relying on old movies!

Other uses for old footage in new films include such gags as Bob Hope in *Road to Bali* meeting up with Humphrey Bogart in *The African Queen*; and economy dictates such measures as the ten-minute chunk of *The Mummy* at the beginning of *The Mummy's Hand* and the use in *Singin' in the Rain,* as part of a 'new' picture in production, of sequences from Gene Kelly's version of *The Three Musketeers.* Similarly bits of *The Sheik* were in *Son of the Sheik,* and *Topper* in *Topper Takes a Trip.* Great chunks of the *Joan of Arc* battles turned up in *Thief of Damascus,* as did *The Black Knight* in *Siege of the Saxons* and *The Four Feathers* in *Storm Over the Nile* and *East of Sudan.* Universal's *Sword of Ali Baba* used so much footage from their *Ali Baba and the Forty Thieves* that one actor had to be engaged to replay his original part! It was however wit rather than economy that persuaded Preston Sturges to open *Mad Wednesday* with the last reel of *The Freshman* and the Boris Karloff clips were central to the concept of *Targets.* As for *Dead Men Don't Wear Plaid*, the new footage was constructed entirely to fit in with clips from old movies, so that the hero appeared to be taking part in forties scenes with the likes of Dorothy Lamour and Alan Ladd.

exchange. An American enterprise: a middleman business which for a commission deals with the small exhibitors of an area on behalf of major renters.

Executive Suite (US 1954). In the fifties, Hollywood took a sudden interest in big business, notably in this all-star adaptation of Cameron Hawley's novel about a boardroom struggle for power. Script by Robert Wise; with Barbara Stanwyck and Fredric March heading an all-star cast. The film's success provoked a rash of boardroom melodramas including *Patterns of Power, The Power and the Prize* and *Cash McCall.* A TV version followed in 1976.

Exodus (US 1961). Otto Preminger's marathon film of the birth of Israel, from the book by Leon Uris. Seldom exciting, it was a good solid plod, with Paul Newman and Ralph Richardson leading a good cast. Irresistible is the story that Mort Sahl at a Hollywood preview stood up after three hours, turned to the director, and said: 'Otto: let my people go.'

exploitation. A trade word covering all phases of publicity, public relations and promotion, especially in the case of 'exploitation pictures' which have no discernible merit apart from the capability of being sensationalized.

The Exorcist (US 1974). Sensational supernatural horror piece about a young girl possessed by the devil. Apparent seriousness covered slipshod scripting, but the shocks of bad language, loud noises and vomit appealed mightily to an audience in search of new and greater sensations yet wanting to believe in God. Written by William Peter Blatty, directed by William Friedkin; with Ellen Burstyn, Linda Blair, Jason Miller, Max Von Sydow. A poor sequel, Exorcist II: The Heretic, followed in 1977.

explorers have inspired many documentaries but surprisingly few features except wholly fictitious ones like *Trader Horn, She* and *The Lost World. Marco Polo* has thrice been dealt with, and *Christopher Columbus* got the full Rank treatment as well as featuring in the satirical *Where Do We Go From Here?* The Pilgrim Fathers were the heroes of *Plymouth Adventure,* and Drake of *Seven Seas to Calais.* Lewis and Clark in *The Far Horizons,* were played by Fred MacMurray and Charlton Heston. *Scott of the Antarctic* was played by John Mills, and Amundsen in *The Red Tent* by Sean Connery; Pierre Radisson in *Hudson's Bay* by Paul Muni; Cortez in *Captain from Castile* by Cesar Romero; Pizarro in *The Royal Hunt of the Sun* by Robert Shaw; Junipero Serra in *Seven Cities of Gold* by Michael Rennie. *Penn of Pennsylvania* and *Stanley and Livingstone* were in the practical sense explorers, though driven by other motives; *Aguirre Wrath of God* seemed to be driven chiefly by greed.

expressionism. A term indicating the fullest utilization of cinematic resources to give dramatic larger-than-life effect, as in

Citizen Kane or, in a different way, *The Cabinet of Dr Caligari.* In a secondary sense it also allows the fullest expression to be given, by the above means, to states of emotion.

Extase (Czechoslovakia 1933) (aka *Ecstasy*). Gustav Machaty directed this mildly experimental, symbol-crammed erotic drama, widely publicized on account of Hedy Lamarr's nude swimming sequence.

exterior. A shot taken in normal lighting outside the studio.

The Exterminating Angel (Mexico 1962). An enigmatic but fascinating film exercise, written and directed by Luis Buñuel, in which a group of dinner guests find themselves psychologically incapable of going home despite attacks of sickness and violent death. Though it is packed with apparent clues, Buñuel himself said there is 'no rational explanation'.

extra. A crowd player with no lines to speak.

Eythe, William (1918–1957). American leading man of the forties.
The Ox-Bow Incident 42. The Song of Bernadette 43. The Eve of St Mark 44. A Royal Scandal 45. The House on 92nd Street 45. Meet Me at Dawn 47. Customs Agent 50, etc.

Answers

ego
1 Ann Dvorak ☐ 2 Barbara Bel Geddes ☐ 3 Cary Grant ☐ 4 Wendy Hiller ☐ 5 Michael Landon ☐ 6 Susan Hayward ☐ 7 Claudette Colbert ☐ 8 Gloria Talbot ☐ 9 Fredric March ☐ 10 Edward G. Robinson ☐ 11 Ronald Colman ☐ 12 Laurence Harvey ☐ 13 Susan Hayward ☐ 14 Edward G. Robinson ☐ 15 Lilian Harvey ☐

English versions
1 *The Long Night* ☐ Henry Fonda ☐ 2 *Lured/Personal Column* ☐ George Sanders ☐ 3 *The Outrage* ☐ Paul Newman ☐ 4 *Human Desire* ☐ Glenn Ford ☐ 5 *Midnight Episode* ☐ Stanley Holloway ☐ 6 *The Unfinished Dance* ☐ Cyd Charisse ☐ 7 *Mad Love* ☐ Colin Clive ☐ 8 *Algiers* ☐ Charles Boyer ☐ or *Casbah* ☐ Tony Martin ☐ 9 *Stranger in the House* (US: *Cop Out*) ☐ James Mason ☐ 10 *A Fistful of Dollars* ☐ Clint Eastwood ☐ 11 *The Thirteenth Letter* ☐ Charles Boyer ☐ 12 *The Magnificent Seven* ☐ Yul Brynner ☐

F

Fabares, Shelley (1942–). American juvenile leading lady of the early sixties. Daughter of Nanette Fabray.
Never Say Goodbye 56. Summer Love 58. Ride the Wild Surf 64. Girl Happy 65. Hold On 66. Spinout 66. Clambake 67, etc.
TV series: One Day at a Time 81–.

Fabian (1942–) (Fabian Forte Bonaparte). American teenage idol, singer and guitarist.
The Hound Dog Man (debut) 59. North to Alaska 60. Mr Hobbs Takes a Vacation 62. Dear Brigitte 65. Ten Little Indians 65. Fireball 500 66. The Devil's Eight 68. A Bullet for Pretty Boy 70. Lovin' Man 72, etc.

Fabian, Françoise (1932–) (Michele Cortes de Leone y Fabianera). Spanish leading actress who has made several forays into international films.
Mamzelle Pigalle 56. Fernandel the Dressmaker 56. The Fanatics 57. Maigret Sees Red 63. Le Voleur 67. *Belle de Jour* 67. *Ma Nuit Chez Maud* 70. La Bonne Année 73. Down the Ancient Stairs 75. Salut l'Artiste 76. Madame Claude 77, etc.

Fabray, Nanette (1920–) (Nanette Fabares). American comedy actress and singer, former child star of 'Our Gang' comedies.
Adult films: Elizabeth and Essex 39. Band Wagon 53. The Happy Ending 69. Amy 81, etc.
TV series: Peck's Bad Girl 59. Caesar's Hour 64.

Fabre, Saturnin (1884–1961). French character actor.
Pépé le Moko 37. Il Etait Neuf Celibataires 42. Un Ami Viendra Ce Soir 46. Les Portes de la Nuit 46. Clochemerle 52. La Fête à Henriette 54, etc.

Fabri, Zoltan (1917–). Hungarian director.
Professor Hannibal 56. The Last Goal 61. Twenty Hours 65, etc.

Fabrizi, Aldo (1905–). Italian character actor, known abroad.
Open City 45. Vivere in Pace 47. First Communion 50. Cops and Robbers 54. Altri Tempi 55. The Angel Wore Red 60. The Birds the Bees and the Italians 65. Made in Italy 68.

A Face in the Crowd (US 1957). Directed by Elia Kazan from a Budd Schulberg story, this was a potent attack on the cult of personality in TV. Andy Griffith made a strong impression as the brash hick intoxicated by his own success; so did Patricia Neal as his mentor who finally destroys him.

fade in. Gradual emergence of a scene from blackness to full definition; opposite of *fade out.*

? fade outs I
The last line of a movie is likely to be the most memorable. Can you name the actors who spoke the following lines, and say what movies they ended?

1 I guess Rosebud is just a piece in a jigsaw puzzle . . . a missing piece.
2 Hello. Clara?
3 O'Lan, you are the earth.
4 Every word that boy said is the truth. I'm not fit for office!
5 Look, Ma—top of the world! (Not quite the last.)
6 The lobsters are back!
7 I steal . . .
8 Madness! Madness!
9 It was beauty killed the beast.
10 All right, Mr de Mille, I'm ready for my close-up now.
11 Now for Australia and a crack at those Japs!
12 After all, tomorrow is another day . . .
13 Darling, you're crying. I believe you're really sentimental after all.
14 This is the people's war! It is our war! We are the fighters! Fight it, then! Fight it with all that is in us! And God defend the right!
15 She was beautiful when she died . . . a hundred years ago.
16 Always the same. People come, people go. Nothing ever happens.

17 That's the dumbest thing I ever heard . . .
18 Well, Tillie, when the hell are we going to get some dinner?
19 Come and see a fat old man sometime.
20 Think of it—three of them married and the other two tottering on the brink!
21 Thank you, sir—I'm glad it's off my mind at last . . .
22 Where the devil are my slippers, Eliza?

? fade outs II

Of what films were these the last scenes?

1 A reporter, stabbed some while ago, falls into the camera, dead.
2 Two men walk away from the camera across a darkened airport tarmac.
3 A tramp and a girl walk away from the camera up an empty road towards the hills.
4 An amiable fellow leaves a large gated house and strolls into the sunset while chatting with an apparently invisible friend.
5 A taxi driver claims to be a coffee pot.
6 In a lane near a cemetery, a man and a woman approach each other but pass without speaking.
7 A woman sings in a pot, and four men throw things at her.
8 After a visit to a tobacconist, a man remembers his past life and returns to the woman and the home he most loved.
9 A murderer is crushed under a fairground carousel.
10 In a house on fire, a monogrammed pillow is consumed by the flames.
11 In a studio representation of Venice, two people dance over a bridge.
12 A theatrical producer looks out of a window and in the lonely night street sees a woman catch up with a man who is walking slowly away.
13 A boatman, munching a sandwich, walks into an island house as two people leave.
14 A small boat is being towed into port but the two people in it prefer to be left alone; they let the rope go and sink from sight.
15 A neon sign for Cook's Tours flashes on and off.
16 A soldier is shot dead while reaching for a butterfly.
17 A man sits on a fence, finishes a peach pie, gets out a notebook, studies it carefully, looks up in thought, spots someone in the audience, smiles and points . . .
18 A lone man battling a snowstorm in a mountain land rounds a corner and sees ahead the destination he has long been seeking. Bells begin to ring.
19 An elderly gentleman is ushered to an elevator in which he expects to descend. But his saturnine host assures him that his direction is 'up'.
20 A wedding car carrying bride and bridegroom drives up a hill away from the camera.
21 A woman changes her mind about joining her lover on a train to Paris and sets off to comfort the wounded admirer she has previously rejected.
22 The hero and heroine joyfully enter a room in which an old lady sits playing a piano.
23 After being threatened with hanging, hero and heroine find themselves unexpectedly waterbound and swimming for shore.
24 The heroine runs happily towards the camera calling: 'Stephen!'
25 An ex-schoolmaster staggers back to his former classroom and dies there.
26 An architect finds himself caught up in an endless cycle of recurring dreams about a professional visit to a stranger named Eliot Foley at his home, Pilgrims Farm.
27 An old man calls on a married couple to see their young son, who looks suspiciously like himself. The father looks at the audience and says: 'We adopted him . . .'
28 Police take the heroine to an elevator, which begins to descend as the hero walks away.
29 A murderer released from prison suddenly realizes he has left his incriminating memoirs inside.
30 A young girl wakes up in bed to find that well-wishers present include her aunt and uncle, three farm-hands and a travelling showman.

Fahrenheit 451 (GB 1966). A pale but oddly haunting version by François Truffaut of Ray Bradbury's cynically prophetic vision of a society where books are outlawed and firemen start fires (of literature) rather than putting them out. Ultimately quite moving, it could have been more cinematically paced. Nicolas Roeg's photography gleams; Oskar Werner's performance is a major asset. (The title gives the temperature at which book paper spontaneously combusts.)

Fairbanks, Douglas (1883–1939) (Douglas Ullman). Swashbuckling American star of the

silent screen, the acrobatic, zestful, ever-smiling hero of many comedies and costume adventures, almost all of which he produced himself. Despite long stage experience, sound did not suit him, and his thirties films showed a marked decline. He had a famous marriage with Mary Pickford, and in 1919, with Chaplin and Griffith, they were co-founders of United Artists Film Corporation.
Posthumous AA 1939 'for his unique and outstanding contribution to the international development of the motion picture'.
Biographies: *The Fourth Musketeer* by Elton Thomas, 1953; *The Fairbanks Album* by Richard Schickel, 1976; *His Majesty the American* by John C. Tibbetts and James M. Welsh, 1977.
□The Lamb 15. Double Trouble 15. His Picture in the Papers 16. The Habit of Happiness 16. The Good Bad Man 16. Reggie Mixes In 16. Flirting with Fate 16. The Mystery of the Leaping Fish 16. The Half Breed 16. Manhattan Madness 16. American Aristocracy 16. The Matrimaniac 16. The Americano 16. In Again Out Again 17. Wild and Woolly 17. Down to Earth 17. The Man from Painted Post 17. Reaching for the Moon 17. A Modern Musketeer 18. Headin' South 18. Mr Fix-It 18. Say Young Fellow 18. Bound in Morocco 18. He Comes Up Smiling 18. Arizona (& wd) 18. Knickerbocker Buckaroo 19. His Majesty the American 19. When the Clouds Roll By 20. The Mollycoddle 20. *The Mark of Zorro* (& w) 20. The Nut (& w) 21. *The Three Musketeers* 21. *Robin Hood* (& w) 21. *The Thief of Baghdad* (&w) 23. *Don Q Son of Zorro* 25. *The Black Pirate* 26. The Gaucho (& w) 27. The Iron Mask (& w) 29. The Taming of the Shrew 29. Reaching for the Moon 30. Around the World in Eighty Minutes (& w) 31. Mr Robinson Crusoe 32. The Private Life of Don Juan 34.
❀ For giving his high spirits to a world which needed them. *The Black Pirate.*

¶ Quotes about the elder Fairbanks all point the same way: despite his comparatively short stature, he was much larger than life.

He has such verve. We can use his body, said D. W. Griffith. From that day Fairbanks kept himself in rigorous training, believing that:

> The man that's out to do something has to keep in high gear all the time.

He managed. An anonymous critic in 1920 put his finger on the Fairbanks magic:

> He smiles, and you feel relieved.

Alistair Cooke called him:

> A sort of Ariel,

and added:

> At a difficult period in American history, Douglas Fairbanks appeared to know all the answers.

Director Allan Dwan commented:

> Stunt men have had to imitate him and it always looked like a stunt when they did it. With him it always looked right.

But Mary Pickford, who should know, had a minority view:

> In his private life Douglas always faced a situation in the only way he knew, by running away from it.

Fairbanks, Douglas Jnr (1909–).
American leading man who has spent much time in Britain; of more conventional debonair mould than his father, he spent as much time in drawing rooms as on castle battlements, but was at home in any surroundings. During the early fifties, produced and sometimes played in innumerable TV half hours under the title *Douglas Fairbanks Presents.*
Biography 1955: *Knight Errant* by Brian Connell.
□Party Girl 20. Stephen Steps Out 23. Air Mail 25. Wild Horse Mesa 25. Stella Dallas 25. The American Venus 25. Padlocked 26. Manbait 26. Is Zat So? 27. A Texas Steer 27. The Barker 28. A Woman of Affairs 28. *The Jazz Age* 29. Fast Life 29. Our Modern Maidens 29. The Careless Age 29. The Forward Pass 29. Show of Shows 29. Loose Ankles 30. *The Dawn Patrol* 30. Little Accident 30. The Way of All Men 30. *Outward Bound* 30. Little Caesar 30. One Night at Susie's 30. Chances 31. I Like Your Nerve 31. Union Depot 32. It's Tough to be Famous 32. Love is a Racket 32. Parachute Jumper 32. The Narrow Corner 33. *Morning Glory* 33. Captured 33. The Life of Jimmy Dolan 33. *Catherine the Great* 34. Success at any Price 34. Mimi 35. The Amateur Gentleman 35. Accused 36. Jump for Glory 36. *The Prisoner of Zenda* (as Rupert of Hentzau) 37. Joy of Living 38. The Rage of Paris 38. Having Wonderful Time 38. *The Young in Heart* 38. *Gunga Din* 39. The Sun Never Sets 39. Rulers of the Sea 39. Green Hell 40. Safari 40. Angels over Broadway 40. The Corsican Brothers 41. *Sinbad the Sailor* 47. The Exile 47. That Lady in Ermine 48. The Fighting O'Flynn 49. *State Secret* 50. Mr Drake's Duck 51. The Crooked Hearts (TV) 72. Ghost Story 81. The Hostage Tower (TV) 81.

Fairbrother, Sydney (1873–1941) (S. Tapping). British character actress, in films occasionally from 1916.
Iron Justice 16. The Third String 31. Chu Chin Chow 33. The Crucifix 34. The Last Journey 36. King Solomon's Mines (as Gagool) 37. Little Dolly Daydream 38, etc.

Fairchild, Morgan (1950–) (Patsy McClenny). American leading lady.
The Initiation of Sarah (TV) 78. Murder in Music City (TV) 79. The Dream Merchants (TV) 80. The Seduction 82.
TV series: Flamingo Road 80–81.

Fairchild, William (1918–). British screenwriter.
Morning Departure 50. An Outcast of the Islands 51. The Gift Horse 52. The Net 53. The Malta Story 53. Front Page Story 54. John and Julie (& d) 54. Value for Money 57. The Silent Enemy (& d) 58. Star! 68. Embassy 72. Invitation to the Wedding 85, etc.

Fairhurst, Lyn (1920–). British writer.
Band of Thieves 62. Touch of Death 63. Be My Guest 64. Devils of Darkness 65, etc.

fairy tales: see *fantasy*.

Faith, Adam (1940–) (Terence Nelhams). British pop singer turned actor.
Never Let Go 60. Beat Girl 61. Mix Me a Person 62. Stardust 74, etc.

Faith, Percy (1908–76). American orchestral conductor and composer. Scores include *Love Me or Leave Me* 55, *I'd Rather Be Rich* 64, *The Oscar* 66.

Faithfull, Geoffrey (1894–1979). British cinematographer, with Hepworth from 1908.
The Lavender Hill Mob 51. Corridors of Blood 59. Village of the Damned 60. On the Beat 62, etc.

Faithfull, Marianne (1947–). British leading lady.
I'll Never Forget Whatshisname 67. Girl on a Motorcycle 68. Hamlet 69.

The Falcon was a Robin Hood of crime who appeared in many second features of the forties, originally inspired by a Michael Arlen character. At RKO, George Sanders appeared in *A Date with the Falcon, The Falcon Takes Over* and *The Falcon's Brother,* in which he was 'killed' and his role assumed by his real-life brother, Tom Conway, who proceeded to make nine more Falcon features of declining merit. In nearly all these films Edward Brophy appeared as Goldie, the bumbling valet. Around 1950 John Calvert made a couple of very inferior Falcon movies for a small independent company.

Falconetti (1901–1946) (Marie Falconetti). French stage actress, unforgettable in her only film, *The Passion of Joan of Arc* 28.

Falk, Peter (1927–). Fast-talking, cast-eyed American actor from the off-Broadway stage.
□Wind Across the Everglades 58. The Bloody Brood 59. Pretty Boy Floyd 59. The Secret of the Purple Reef 60. Murder Inc. 60. Pocketful of Miracles 61. Pressure Point 62. The Balcony 63. It's a Mad Mad Mad Mad World 63. Robin and the Seven Hoods 64. *The Great Race* 65. Italiano Brava Gente 65. Too Many Thieves (TV) 66. Penelope 66. Luv 67. Prescription Murder (TV) (his first appearance as Columbo) 67. Anzio 68. Castle Keep 69. Machine Gun McCain 70. A Step Out of Line (TV) 70. Husbands 70. Operation Snafu 70. Ransom for a Dead Man (start of Columbo series) (TV) 71. A Woman Under the Influence 76. Murder by Death 76. Griffin and Phoenix (TV) 76. Mikey and Nicky 76. The Brinks Job 78. The Cheap Detective 78. The In-Laws 79. All the Marbles 81. Big Trouble 84. Happy New Year 87. The Princess Bride 87.
TV series: *The Trials of O'Brien* 65. *Columbo* 71–78.

Falkenburg, Jinx (1919–) (Eugenia Falkenburg). Tall, good-looking American model who made a few light comedies and musicals in the forties.
Biography 1951: *Jinx*.
Two Latins from Manhattan 42. Sing for Your Supper 42. Lucky Legs 43. Tahiti Nights 44. Talk about a Lady 46, etc.

The Fallen Idol (GB 1948). One of Carol Reed's most subtle and successful films, from Graham Greene's story about a boy who sees what he thinks is a murder and tries to cover up for his friend. With Ralph Richardson, Michele Morgan, Bobby Henrey; music by William Alwyn. BFA (best British film).

The Fall of the House of Usher. This grisly tale by Edgar Allan Poe was filmed by Jean Epstein in 1928, by Americans Melville Webber and James Watson in the same year, by British semi-professionals in 1950, and by Roger Corman in 1960.

falling is, of all man's inherited fears, the one most spectacularly played on by Hollywood, where the shot of the villain's hand slipping away from the hero's frenzied grasp, followed by a quick-fading scream, has become a screen stereotype. Harold Lloyd's skyscraper comedies played on this fear, as have the films of many comedians since; in *The Horn Blows at Midnight,* for instance, Jack Benny is only one of six people hanging on to each other's coat-tails from the top of a high building. All circus films, and that includes *The Marx Brothers at the Circus,* base one or two of their thrills on trapeze acts that might go wrong. And whenever a villain starts climbing upwards, as Ted de Corsia did in *Naked City,* or along a ledge, as the same accident-prone Ted de Corsia did in *The Enforcer,* the audience grits its teeth and waits for the inevitable. The whole action of *Fourteen Hours* was based on the question whether a potential suicide would or would not jump from a ledge.

Some of the screen's most spectacular falls include Walter Abel's in *Mirage,* the key to the whole action; Agnes Moorehead's (through a window) in *Dark Passage*; Charlotte Henry's in *Alice in Wonderland*; Cedric Hardwicke's in *Hunchback of Notre Dame*; W. C. Fields' (from an aeroplane) in *Never Give a Sucker an Even Break*; Alan Ladd's (through a roof) in *The Glass Key*; Slim Pickens' (on the bomb) in *Dr Strangelove*; Eleanor Parker's in *An American Dream*; *King Kong*'s (from the top of the Empire State Building); William Bendix's from a skyscraper in *The Dark Corner*. To Alfred Hitchcock falls are a speciality: Edmund Gwenn fell from Westminster Cathedral in *Foreign Correspondent,* Norman Lloyd from the torch of the Statue of Liberty in *Saboteur,* while *Vertigo* not only boasted three falls but based its entire plot on the hero's fear of heights. Falls under trains and buses are legion, but in *The Well* a little girl fell down an old wellshaft, in *The List of Adrian Messenger* a victim fell to his death in a lift (as did characters in *Hotel* and *House of Wax,* while in *Ivy* Joan Fontaine fell down a lift shaft), in Somerset Maugham's *Encore* an acrobat hoped to fall safely into a water tank; and an unnamed gentleman was pushed out of *The High Window* by Florence Bates.

the family is the centre of most people's lives, so naturally there have been many memorable film families. Those popular enough to have warranted a series include the Joneses, the Hardys, the Huggetts, the Wilkinses of *Dear Ruth, The Cohens and the Kellys,* the Bumsteads of *Blondie* and the *Four Daughters* saga. World War II brought a sentimental attachment to the family which in Hollywood expressed itself in *Happy Land, The Human Comedy, Our Town, The Happy Time, Since You Went Away, Meet Me in St Louis, A Genius in the Family, The Sullivans* and *The Best Years of Our Lives*; in Britain, *Salute John Citizen, The Holly and the Ivy, Dear Octopus, Quiet Wedding, This Man is Mine*. Semi-classical treatments of the theme include *Cavalcade, The Swiss Family Robinson, Pride and Prejudice, Little Women, Scrooge* and *Whiteoaks*. Odd families, ranging from the merely sophisticated to the downright bizarre, were seen in *Three Cornered Moon, The Old Dark House, The Royal Family of Broadway, My Man Godfrey, You Can't Take It With You, The Young in Heart, The Little Foxes, Tobacco Road, The Bank Dick, House of Strangers, An Inspector Calls, Sweethearts, Treasure Hunt, Holiday, The Philadelphia Story, The Anniversary,* and *The Lion in Winter*. Vaudeville families were seen in *Yankee Doodle Dandy, The Merry Monahans, The Seven Little Foys, The Buster Keaton Story* and *There's No Business Like Show Business*. There has recently been a fashion for the large family, started by *Cheaper by the Dozen* and *Chicken Every Sunday* in 1949 and reprised by *With Six You Get Egg Roll* and *Yours Mine and Ours* in 1968 and a TV series *The Brady Bunch* in 1969. Other charming families have included those in *Our Vines Have Tender Grapes, Background, The Happy Family, Four Sons, The Holly and the Ivy, Made in Heaven, 29 Acacia Avenue, Little Murders, Never Too Late, This Happy Breed* and *My Wife's Family*; but the most memorable family of all is likely to remain the Joads in *The Grapes of Wrath,* unless it is one of the real families put under the microscope by American and British TV.

? Who played:

1 Ryan O'Neal's father in *Love Story*?
2 Bette Davis' mother in *Now Voyager*?
3 Vivien Leigh's father in *Gone with the Wind*?
4 Janet Gaynor's grandmother in *A Star Is Born*?
5 Freddie Bartholomew's aunt in *David Copperfield*?
6 Juanita Moore's daughter in *Imitation of Life*?

7 Elizabeth Taylor's husband in *Ash Wednesday*?
8 Rosalind Russell's sister in *My Sister Eileen*?
9 Eugene Pallette's wife in *Heaven Can Wait*?
10 Greer Garson's husband in *Madame Curie*?
11 Dana Andrews' wife in *The Best Years of Our Lives*?
12 Anne Bancroft's husband in *The Graduate*?
13 Deanna Durbin's father in *One Hundred Men and a Girl*?
14 Katharine Hepburn's father in *The Philadelphia Story*?
15 Greer Garson's mother in *Pride and Prejudice*?
16 Joan Crawford's daughter in *Mildred Pierce*?
17 Richard Haydn's mother in *Cluny Brown*?
18 Paul Muni's sister in *Scarface*?
19 Robert Taylor's wife in *Conspirator*?
20 Walter Huston's wife in *Dodsworth*?
21 Gladys Cooper's husband in *Rebecca*?
22 Lionel Barrymore's grandson in *On Borrowed Time*?
23 Paul Muni's wife in *The Good Earth*?
24 Bette Davis' husband in *Juarez*?
25 Ronald Colman's brother in *Lost Horizon*?
26 Katharine Hepburn's sister in *Holiday*?
27 Raymond Massey's wife in *The Old Dark House*?
28 Betty Hutton's sister in *The Miracle of Morgan's Creek*?
29 Celia Johnson's husband in *Brief Encounter*?
30 Orson Welles' father in *Citizen Kane*?
31 James Stewart's sister in *Harvey*?
32 Ernest Thesiger's sister, brother and father in *The Old Dark House*?
33 Al Jolson's father in *The Jazz Singer*?
34 Oliver Hardy's wife in *Sons of the Desert*?
35 Laurence Olivier's wife in *Wuthering Heights*?
36 Edward Everett Horton's wife in *Top Hat*?
37 Genevieve Tobin's husband in *One Hour with You*?
38 James Cagney's father in *The Strawberry Blonde*?
39 Claude Rains' daughter in *King's Row*?
40 Susan Hayward's father in *I Married a Witch*?
41 Henry Fonda's mother in *The Grapes of Wrath*?
42 Albert Finney's wife in *Charlie Bubbles*?
43 Errol Flynn's father in *That Forsyte Woman*?
44 Rosalind Russell's brother in *Mourning Becomes Electra*?
45 Jean Arthur's mother in *You Can't Take It with You*?
46 Mickey Rooney's aunt in *A Family Affair*?
47 Agnes Moorehead's nephew in *The Magnificent Ambersons*?
48 Colin Clive's father in *Frankenstein*?
49 Carole Lombard's mother in *My Man Godfrey*?
50 Dean Stockwell's grandfather in *The Green Years*?
51 Joseph Cotten's niece in *Shadow of a Doubt*?
52 David Niven's wife in *Murder by Death*?

Famous Players. A production company founded by Adolph Zukor in New York in 1912, following his success in distributing Sarah Bernhardt in *Queen Elizabeth*. The motif was 'famous players in famous plays', which could not work too well as the films were silent; but the tag caught on and the company did well enough. It was later absorbed into Paramount.

? famous roles

Say who, in what films:

1 Played Regina Giddens, Catherine the Great . . . and said 'Fasten your seat belts, it's going to be a bumpy night.'
2 Played Alfred Kralik, Elwood P. Dowd . . . and said 'The prettiest sight in this fine pretty world is the sight of the privileged class enjoying its privileges.'
3 Played Sam Spade, Roy Earle . . . and said 'A press agent is many things, most of them punishable by law.'
4 Played Catherine Earnshaw, Lady Blakeney . . . and said 'Frederic, you must stop this Polonaise jangle!'
5 Played Louis Renault, Job Skeffington . . . and said 'Any more objections to the new tax, from our Saxon friends?'
6 Played Martin Snyder, Rocky Sullivan . . . and said 'My mother thanks you, my father thanks you, my sister thanks you and I thank you.'
7 Played Tony Camonte, Professor Joseph Elsner . . . and said 'Not only is an innocent man crying out for justice; but more, much more—a great nation is in desperate danger of forfeiting her honour!'
8 Played Dona St Columb, Tessa Sanger . . . and said 'You didn't love her! You didn't love her!'

9 Played Mike Conovan, Major Robert Rogers . . . and said 'They're murderers. I know the law says they're not because I'm still alive, but that's not their fault.'
10 Played Sam Grunion, Gordon Miller . . . and said 'Oh, no, not for me, three men on a horse.'
11 Played Dan Roman, Sergeant John M. Stryker . . . and said 'I watched you with that baby—that other woman's baby. You looked—well, nice.'
12 Played James Corbett, Captain Geoffrey Vickers . . . and said 'It's injustice I hate, not Normandy.'

Fanck, Arnold (1889–1974). German director, renowned for mountaineering films. □Wunder des Schneeschuhs 19. Kampf mit dem Berge 21. Der Heilige Berg 25. Der Grosse Sprung 27. The White Hell of Pitz Palu (co-d) 29. Storm over Mont Blanc 30. Der Weisse Rausch 31. SOS Iceberg 33. Der Ewige Traum 34. Die Tochter des Samurai 37. Ein Robinson 40.

Fanny. Originally one of Marcel Pagnol's 1932–34 trilogy (the others: *Marius* and *César*) about the Marseilles waterfront, this tale of a girl left pregnant by a sailor was almost unrecognizable in the MGM version *Port of Seven Seas* 38. The film was subsequently turned into a stage musical, and in 1960 Joshua Logan filmed this—but deleted the songs! The stars were Leslie Caron, Maurice Chevalier and Charles Boyer.

fans have been with us as long as the star system. One way of describing them is as people who adore an actor whatever he's doing and whether he's good or not. Another definition is: 'People who tell an actor he's not alone in the way he feels about himself.' Judy Garland once played a fan when she sang 'Dear Mr Gable'; and MGM made a whole movie about them, called *The Youngest Profession. The Fan* who pursued Lauren Bacall was quite another matter, a homicidal lunatic; and Eve in *All About Eve* was another fan who didn't do her star any good.

Fantasia (US 1940). Disney's ambitious concert sequence of cartoons caused dissension at first but seems to have established its reputation and its popularity after forty years. Despite lapses of inventiveness and taste, three of its eight pieces are extremely well done: the Bach Toccata and Fugue, Stravinsky's Rite of Spring and Mussorgsky's Night on the Bare Mountain. Leopold Stokowski conducted the Philadelphia Symphony Orchestra.

fantasy has always been a popular form of cinema entertainment because the camera can lie so well, and trick work is most easily used in an unrealistic or fanciful story. The early films of Méliès and his innumerable imitators set a high standard and were still popular when the sombre German classics of the twenties—*The Golem, Nosferatu, Faust, Warning Shadows, The Niebelungen Saga, Metropolis*—awakened filmgoers to the possibilities of the medium for sustaining impossible situations throughout a whole serious feature.

Although Ince's *Civilisation* showed Christ on the battlefields, and the twenties brought such films as *The Four Horsemen of the Apocalypse, The Lost World* and *The Sorrows of Satan,* Hollywood did not fully explore the possibilities of fantasy until sound. Then in quick succession picturegoers were startled by *Outward Bound, Dracula, Frankenstein, Berkeley Square, King Kong* and *The Invisible Man. The Scoundrel,* with Noel Coward, was the forerunner of the few serious ghost films: *The Uninvited, The Return of Peter Grimm, Earthbound, The Ghost and Mrs Muir, Portrait of Jennie, The Haunting,* etc. Comic ghosts have, of course, been legion, notably in the *Topper* films, *The Ghost Breakers, I Married a Witch, The Canterville Ghost, The Man in the Trunk, The Remarkable Andrew, Thirteen Ghosts, The Spirit Is Willing, Blackbeard's Ghost, Wonder Man,* and so on. There were even singing ghosts in *Maytime, Bitter Sweet* and *Carousel.* Britain's contributions to the genre were few but choice: *The Ghost Goes West, Blithe Spirit, Things to Come, The Man Who Could Work Miracles, A Matter of Life and Death, Dead of Night.*

In 1936 *Green Pastures* showed the Negro view of heaven, and *On Borrowed Time* three years later paved the way for the heavenly comedies of the forties: *Here Comes Mr Jordan, That's the Spirit, A Guy Named Joe, Heaven Can Wait, Down to Earth, The Horn Blows at Midnight, You Never Can Tell,* even *Ziegfeld Follies* (in which Ziegfeld's shade wrote in his diary 'Another *heavenly* day . . .'). For many years the last in this vein was *Carousel* 56; but 1968 brought *Barbarella* with its slightly tarnished angel, and *The Adding Machine* had its own perverse view of the hereafter. Meanwhile objects with magical properties were well served in *Alf's Button Afloat, A Thousand*

and One Nights, The Thief of Baghdad, Turnabout and *The Picture of Dorian Gray.*

Among the many fairy tales filmed are *The Bluebird, The Wizard of Oz, Alice in Wonderland, The Glass Slipper, Tom Thumb, Mary Poppins* and a selection in *Hans Christian Andersen* and *The Wonderful World of the Brothers Grimm.* Disney's cartoon versions included *Pinocchio, Dumbo, The Sleeping Beauty, Cinderella, Peter Pan,* and, of course, *Snow White and the Seven Dwarfs,* which was cannily adapted for grown-ups by Billy Wilder as *Ball of Fire. Lost Horizon* was a kind of grown-up fairy tale too; and *The Red Shoes* as shown was certainly not for children. Original fairy tales for both categories were *The Luck of the Irish,* with Cecil Kellaway as a leprechaun, and *Miracle on 34th Street,* with Edmund Gwenn as Santa Claus. Modern fairy tales adapted for the screen include: *Chitty Chitty Bang Bang, Mary Poppins, Bedknobs and Broomsticks* and *Willy Wonka and the Chocolate Factory.*

In France during the occupation Marcel Carné made *Les Visiteurs du Soir,* a medieval fantasy with allegorical overtones, and after the war poet Jean Cocteau once again turned his attention to the cinema with such results as *La Belle et la Bête, Love Eternal, Orphée,* and *The Testament of Orphée.* More recently Albert Lamorisse has produced fantasies like *Crin Blanc* and *The Red Balloon.* Japan electrified the world with *Rashomon* and other strange, fanciful, stylized entertainments; Russia contributed many solidly-staged versions of old legends like *Sadko* and *Epic Hero and the Beast* (*Ilya Muromets*).

Since 1950, when in Hollywood Dick Powell played an Alsatian dog in *You Never Can Tell* and James Stewart in *Harvey* had a white rabbit six feet high which the script could never quite categorize as fact or hallucination, fantastic elements have been infiltrating into supposedly realistic films to such an extent that it is now difficult to separate them, especially in the films of Fellini, Antonioni, Tony Richardson, Richard Lester and Robert Altman.

See also: *dreams; horror; prophecy; space exploration.*

? In what films did the following unlikely events take place?

1 Irene Dunne found a natural supply of money in the garden. (1952)
2 A caterpillar danced to the strains of 'Yes, Sir, That's My Baby'. (1944)
3 An angel gave a downtrodden, despairing hero a review of his past life. (1945)
4 A murdered girl came back as a ghost to trap her killer. (1941)
5 A baby was able to talk like an adult. (1960)
6 A man discovered he could fly. (1966)
7 A cat avenged her mistress' murder. (1962)
8 The voice of God spoke on the radio. (1950)
9 A Model T Ford was driven through the air over Washington. (1961)
10 Baseballs were made of a special material enabling them to curve away from the batsmen. (1950)
11 A dog was reincarnated as Dick Powell and solved his own murder. (1950)
12 Scientists were miniaturized and injected into the blood stream of a scientist to save his life. (1967)
13 A pixillated toucan spread good feelings through New York City. (1968)
14 A timid soul found his true metier when he turned into a dolphin. (1964)
15 An atomic cloud made a man become smaller and smaller until he was invisible to the naked eye. (1957)
16 A cat became the owner of a baseball team. (1950)

Fantomas (France 1913–14). Famous thriller serial in five parts, about the exploits of a character reminiscent of Robin Hood, Raffles and the Ringer. Directed by Louis Feuillade (qv). Subsequent versions were made in 1932 by Paul Fejos, 1947 by Jean Sacha, 1949 by Robert Vernay, and 1964-65-66 by André Hunebelle.

Fantoni, Sergio (1930–). Italian leading man in international films.
Esther and the King 60. The Prize 63. Kali-Yug Goddess of Vengeance 63. Von Ryan's Express 65. Do Not Disturb 65. What Did You Do in the War, Daddy? 66. Hornet's Nest 70. Bad Man's River 71, etc.

Fapp, Daniel (1901–). American cinematographer.
Kitty 45. Golden Earrings 47. Bride of Vengeance 49. Union Station 50. Knock on Wood 54. Living It Up 54. Desire under the Elms 58. One, Two, Three 61. West Side Story (AA) 61. I'll Take Sweden 65. Our Man Flint 66. Lord Love a Duck 66. Sweet November 67. Ice Station Zebra 68. Marooned 69, many others.

Faragoh, Francis Edward (1898–). American screenwriter, often in collaboration.

Her Private Affair 29. *Little Caesar* 31. *Frankenstein* 31. The Last Man 32. Becky Sharp 35. The Return of Peter Grimm 35. The Dancing Pirate 36. My Friend Flicka 43. Renegades 46. Easy Come Easy Go 47, etc.

farce was once called 'tragedy with its trousers down'. Like melodrama, it presents exaggerated accounts of things that might happen in life. Comedy is more plausible than farce, but farce is often more enjoyable, involving more happenings, more chases, more doors slamming, more misunderstandings and mistaken identities. Good farce must be played with great style, and no lapses are permitted until the curtain comes down. Major exponents in Britain have been The Aldwych team of Tom Walls, Ralph Lynn and Robertson Hare and the Whitehall team headed by Brian Rix. In Hollywood good farce has been more occasional, but one might highlight *Nothing Sacred*, *To Be or Not to Be*, *Topper Returns*, *Love Crazy* and *The Palm Beach Story* (or almost anything else by Preston Sturges, who so delighted in controlled disorder). France gave us Fernandel and Pierre Etaix. The real trouble with farce on film is that it needs an audience: watched cold, it can often seem merely silly, and great stage farces such as Feydeau's *Hotel Paradiso* don't really translate.

Farentino, James (1938–). American leading man, mostly on TV.
Psychomania 64. Ensign Pulver 64. The War Lord 65. The Pad 66. Banning 67. Rosie 68. Me Natalie 69. The Story of a Woman 70. Jesus of Nazareth (TV) 77. Son-Rise (TV) 79. The Final Countdown 80. Dead and Buried 81. Evita Peron (TV) 81.
TV series: The Bold Ones 69–71. *Cool Million* 71. Dynasty 81–.

A Farewell to Arms. Hemingway's tough-romantic anti-war novel has twice been filmed: in 1933 by Frank Borzage, with Gary Cooper and Helen Hayes, and in 1958 by Charles Vidor, with Rock Hudson and Jennifer Jones. Neither version was a triumph artistically, but the first proved more popular than the second, which was badly inflated by David O. Selznick into a pseudo-epic.

Fargas, Antonio (–). Puerto Rican actor who became popular as Huggy Bear in TV's *Starsky and Hutch*.
Putney Swope 69. Shaft 71. Cleopatra Jones 73. The Gambler 74. Car Wash 76. Next Stop Greenwich Village 76. Pretty Baby 78, etc.

Fargo, James (–). American director.
Caravans 78. Every Which Way But Loose 78. Forced Vengeance 82, etc.

Farmer, Frances (1914–1970). American leading lady of the thirties who trained in New York's Group Theatre, found Hollywood distasteful and retired prematurely through ill-health and family pressures. In 1972 was published a posthumous autobiography, *Will There Ever Be a Morning*, which was also the title of a TV movie in 1983, in which she was portrayed by Susan Blakely. In the same year Jessica Lange played her in a theatrical film, *Frances*.
□Too Many Parents 36. Border flight 36. Rhythm on the Range 36. *Come and Get It* 36. The Toast of New York 37. Exclusive 37. Ebb Tide 37. Ride a Crooked Mile 38. South of Pago Pago 40. Flowing Gold 40. World Première 41. Badlands of Dakota 41. Among the Living 41. Son of Fury 42. The Party Crashers 58.

¶ The nicest thing I can say about Frances Farmer is that she is unbearable.—*William Wyler*

Cinderella goes back to the ashes on a liquor-slicked highway.—*Louella Parsons*

Farmer, Mimsy (1945–). American leading lady of the sixties.
Spencer's Mountain 63. Bus Riley's Back in Town 65. Hot Roads to Hell 67. The Devil's Angels 67. Move 69. Road to Salina 69. Four Flies on Gray Velvet 71. La Legion saute sur Kolwesi 80.

The Farmer's Daughter (US 1947). A lightweight political comedy from a screenplay by Allen Rivkin and Laura Kerr, directed by H. C. Potter, photographed by Milton Krasner, this romantic fable gained an Academy Award for Loretta Young as the Swedish maid who influences her congressman employer. Joseph Cotten, Ethel Barrymore and Charles Bickford were strong in support. In 1963–65 there followed a popular TV series on the subject, with Inger Stevens, William Windom and Cathleen Nesbitt.

Farnon, Robert (1917–). Canadian composer.
Spring in Park Lane 48. Captain Horatio Hornblower 51. Gentlemen Marry Brunettes 55. All for Mary 56. The Little Hut 57. Road to Hong Kong 62. The Truth About Spring 65. Shalako 68. Bear Island 79, etc.

Farnsworth, Richard (*c.* 1922–). American character actor.
The Duchess and the Dirtwater Fox 76. Comes a Horseman 78. Tom Horn 80. Resurrection 80. *The Grey Fox* 82. Waltz Across Texas 83. The Natural 84. Rhinestone 84. Sylvester 85. Space Rage 87.

Farnum, Dustin (1870–1929). American cowboy star of silent days. Brother of William Farnum.
The Squaw Man 13. The Virginian 14. The Scarlet Pimpernel 17. The Corsican Brothers 19. Flaming Frontier 26, etc.

Farnum, Franklyn (1876–1961). American leading man of the silent screen, especially westerns; appeared in more than a thousand films.

Farnum, William (1876–1953). American leading man of the silent screen.
The Spoilers 14. Les Misérables 17. The Lone Star Ranger 19. If I Were King 20. A Stage Romance 22. The Man Who Fights Alone 24. The Painted Desert 31. Supernatural 33. The Crusades 35. The Spoilers 42. Captain Kidd 45. Samson and Delilah 49. Jack and the Beanstalk 52, many others.

Farr, Derek (1912–86). British leading man of stage and screen, married to Muriel Pavlow; former schoolmaster.
The Outsider 40. Spellbound 40. Quiet Wedding 40. Quiet Weekend 46. Wanted for Murder 46. Teheran 47. Bond Street 48. Noose 48. Silent Dust 49. Man on the Run 49. Young Wives' Tale 51. Reluctant Heroes 52. The Dam Busters 55. Town on Trial 56. Doctor at Large 57. The Truth About Women 58. Attempt to Kill 61. The Projected Man 66. Thirty is a Dangerous Age Cynthia 68, etc.

Farr, Jamie (1936–) (Jamiel Farah). Long-nosed American character actor who reached his greatest comic heights in TV's *M*A*S*H* and *Aftermash*.
Ride Beyond Vengeance 65. Who's Minding the Mint? 67. With Six You Get Egg Roll 68. The Blue Knight (TV) 73, etc.

Farr, Felicia (1932–). American leading lady.
Timetable 56. Jubal 56. 3.10 to Yuma 57. The Last Wagon 57. Hell Bent for Leather 60. Kiss Me Stupid 64. The Venetian Affair 67. Charley Varrick 73, etc.

Farrar, David (1908–). Tall, virile-looking British leading man whose career faltered when he went to Hollywood and played villains.
Autobiography 1948: *No Royal Road*.
Return of a Stranger 38. The Sheepdog of the Hills 41. Suspected Person 41. Danny Boy 42. The Night Invader 42. The Dark Tower 43. They Met in the Dark 44. The World Owes Me a Living 44. Meet Sexton Blake (title role) 44. The Echo Murders 45. The Lisbon Story 46. The Trojan Brothers 46. *Black Narcissus* 46. Frieda 47. *Mr Perrin and Mr Traill* 48. *The Small Back Room* 48. Diamond City 49. Night Without Stars 51. The Golden Horde (US) 51. Gone to Earth 52. Duel in the Jungle 54. The Black Shield of Falworth (US) 54. Lilacs in the Spring 55. The Sea Chase (US) 55. Lost 56. I Accuse 57. Solomon and Sheba (US) 59. John Paul Jones (US) 59. Beat Girl 60. The 300 Spartans 62, etc.

Farrar, Geraldine (1882–1967). American operatic star who, unexpectedly, appeared for Samuel Goldwyn as heroine of silent films.
Carmen 15. Maria Rosa 16. The Devil Stone 17. Joan the Woman 17. Flame of the Desert 19. The Riddle Woman 20, etc.

Farrebique (France 1947). A drama-documentary of primitive farm life in Aveyron, marked by a tremendous feeling for the land and for life. Written and directed by Georges Rouquier, photographed (with much use of time-lapse) by André Danton, with music by Henri Sanguet.

Farrell, Charles (1901–). Gentle-mannered American leading man of the twenties; formed a well-liked romantic team with Janet Gaynor. Retired in middle age to become Mayor of Palm Springs.
The Ten Commandments 23. Wings of Youth 25. Old Ironsides 26. *Seventh Heaven* 27. Street Angel 28. Lucky Star 29. Sunny Side Up 29. High Society Blues 30. Liliom 30. Merely Mary Ann 31. Tess of the Storm Country 32. Aggie Appleby, Maker of Men 33. Change of Heart 34. Fighting Youth 35. Moonlight Sonata (GB) 37. Tailspin 39. The Deadly Game 42, etc.
TV series: My Little Margie 52–54. The Charlie Farrell Show 56, 60.

Farrell, Charles (1901–). Irish character actor who has been playing bit parts in British films since childhood.
Creeping Shadows 31. Meet Mr Penny 38. Meet Sexton Blake 44. Night and the City 50. The Sheriff of Fractured Jaw 58, etc.

Farrell, Glenda (1904–1971). American leading lady and comedienne of the thirties, often seen as wisecracking reporter; made a comeback in the fifties as character actress. Little Caesar (debut) 30. Three on a Match 31. I Am a Fugitive from a Chain Gang 32. *The Mystery of the Wax Museum* 32. Hi Nellie 33. Gold Diggers of 1935 35. In Caliente 36. *Torchy Blane in Chinatown* (and ensuing series) 39. Johnny Eager 41. A Night for Crime 42. Heading for Heaven 47. I Love Trouble 48. Apache War Smoke 52. Girls in the Night 52. Susan Slept Here 54. The Girl in the Red Velvet Swing 55. The Middle of the Night 59. Kissing Cousins 64. The Disorderly Orderly 64. Tiger by the Tail 68, many others.

Farrell, James T. (1904–1979). Irish-American novelist best known for his twice-filmed Studs Lonigan trilogy.

Farrell, Sharon (–). American general purpose actress.
Kiss Her Goodbye 59. Forty Pounds of Trouble 63. A Lovely Way to Die 68. Marlowe 69. The Reivers 69. Quarantined (TV) 70. The Love Machine 71. The Eyes of Charles Sand (TV) 72. It's Alive 76. The Last Ride of the Dalton Gang (TV) 79, etc.

Farrow, John (1904–1963). Stylish Australian director, former research scientist; in Hollywood from the mid-thirties. Also wrote many of his own scripts.
□Men in Exile 37. West of Shanghai 37. She Loved a Fireman 38. Little Miss Thoroughbred 38. My Bill 38. Broadway Musketeers 38. Women in the Wind 39. The Saint Strikes Back 39. Sorority House 39. *Five Came Back* 39. Full Confession 39. Reno 39. Married and in Love 40. A Bill of Divorcement 40. Wake Island 42. The Commandos Strike at Dawn (& w) 43. China 43. *The Hitler Gang* (& w) 44. You Came Along 45. Two Years Before the Mast (& w) 46. California 46. Easy Come Easy Go 47. Blaze of Noon 47. Calcutta 47. *The Big Clock* 48. Night Has a Thousand Eyes 48. Beyond Glory 48. *Alias Nick Beal* 49. Red Hot and Blue 49. Where Danger Lives 50. Copper Canyon 50. *His Kind of Woman* (& w) 51. Submarine Command 51. Ride Vaquero 53. *Plunder of the Sun* 53. Botany Bay 53. Hondo 54. A Bullet is Waiting 54. The Sea Chase (& w) 55. Back from Eternity 56. The Unholy Wife 57. John Paul Jones (& w) 59.

Farrow, Mia (1945–) (Maria Farrow). American leading lady, daughter of John Farrow and Maureen O'Sullivan.
□Guns at Batasi 64. A Dandy in Aspic 67. Rosemary's Baby 68. Secret Ceremony 68. John and Mary 69. See No Evil 71. Follow Me 72. Goodbye Raggedy Ann (TV) 72. Scoundrel in White 72. The Great Gatsby 73. Full Circle 77. *Death on the Nile* 78. A Wedding 78. Avalanche 78. The Hurricane 79. A Midsummer Night's Sex Comedy 82. Zelig 83. Broadway Danny Rose 84. Supergirl 84. The Purple Rose of Cairo 85. Hannah and Her Sisters 86. Radio Days 87. September 87. TV series: Peyton Place 64–67.

¶ *M.F.:* If I seem to be running, it's because I'm pursued.

fashions were the basis of many a woman's film of the thirties: *Roberta, Fashions of 1934, Vogues of 1938*. Later attempts to recapture this interest had an air of *déjà vu*: *Maytime in Mayfair, It Started in Paradise, Lucy Gallant, Designing Woman*. But the wheel turns, and the seventies brought *Mahogany* and the eighties *Chanel Solitaire*.

Fassbinder, Rainer Werner (1946–1982). Fashionable German director of the seventies, usually with something despairing to say about the current state of society.
Gods of the Plague 69. Katzelmacher 69. The Pedlar of Four Seasons 71. The Bitter Tears of Petra Von Kant 72. Wild Game 73. Martha 73. Effi Briest 74. Fear Eats the Soul 74. Fox 75. Fear 75. Mother Kusters Goes to Heaven 75. Tenderness of the Wolves 75. Chinese Roulette 76. Satan's Brew 76. Despair 77. The Marriage of Maria Braun 78. In a Year with 13 Moons 78. Berlin Alexanderplatz 79, etc.

¶ *R.W.F.:* I hope to build a house with my films. Some of them are the cellar, some are the walls, and some are the windows. But I hope in time there will be a house.

Fast, Howard (1914–). American historical novelist. Works filmed include *Freedom Road*, *The Last Frontier*, *Spartacus*, *The Immigrants*.

fast motion: see *accelerated motion*.

Father Brown (GB 1954). The only British attempt to film the adventures of G. K. Chesterton's tubby detective-priest was a civilized comedy with all concerned on the same wavelength. A quietly witty script by Thelma Schnee, polished direction by Robert Hamer, and high comedy acting by Alec Guinness, Peter Finch, Joan Greenwood and Ernest Thesiger made it a film with a rare flavour. On television, Kenneth More played the role in a 1974 series. In 1934 Walter Connolly played the role in a Hollywood second feature, *Father Brown Detective*. In West Germany, Heinz Ruhmann played the role in two sixties films, and Josef Meinrad in a 1969 TV series. In 1980 Barnard Hughes played the priest on TV in *The Girl in the Park*.

Father of the Bride (US 1950). The American domestic comedy *par excellence*, taken from Edward Streeter's book and starring Spencer Tracy as the harassed pa. A sequel, *Father's Little Dividend* 51, was somewhat less effective. Leon Ames later played the role in a TV series.

Faulds, Andrew (1923–). British character actor and M.P.
The Card 52. The One That Got Away 56. Payroll 61. Jason and the Argonauts 64. The Prince and the Pauper 65. The Devils 70. The Music Lovers 71. Mahler 74. Lisztomania 76, etc.

Faulkner, William (1897–1962). Distinguished American novelist. Works filmed include *Sanctuary, Intruder in the Dust, The Sound and the Fury*. Also collaborated on screenplays:
Road to Glory 36. To Have and Have Not 44. The Big Sleep 46. Land of the Pharaohs 55, etc.

¶ *W.F.:* It's not Hollywood's fault. The writer is not accustomed to money. It goes to his head and destroys him.

Faust, Johann (1488–1541). These at least are the approximate dates of a German conjurer, the scanty details of whose wandering life were the basis of plays by Marlowe (1593) and later Goethe (1808) which turned into classics. The theme of the man who sells his soul to the devil in exchange for a rich full life has been seen in innumerable film versions, including many musical ones based on Gounod's opera, and a puppet one from Czechoslovakia. The first straight version was made in France in 1905; the most famous silent version is Murnau's of 1926, with Emil Jannings and Gosta Ekman. 1941 brought Dieterle's *All That Money Can Buy*, from Stephen Vincent Benet's *The Devil and Daniel Webster*; René Clair's version, *La Beauté du Diable*, followed in 1949, *Alias Nick Beal* in the same year, Autant-Lara's *Marguerite de la Nuit* in 1955, *Damn Yankees* in 1958 and Richard Burton's *Dr Faustus* in 1967. There were modernized versions in France 63, USA 64 and Rumania 66, and a Spanish version of 1957, *Faustina*, in which the hero becomes a heroine. The latest variations on the theme are *Bedazzled* 67, a comic extravaganza with Peter Cook as the tempter and Dudley Moore as the tempted and *Hammersmith Is Out* 72 with Richard Burton and Peter Ustinov.

Fawcett, Farrah (formerly Farrah Fawcett-Majors) (1947–).
American pin-up who enjoyed brief success as one of the original 1976 *Charlie's Angels*.
□ A Man I Like 67. Myra Breckinridge 70. The Feminist and the Fuzz (TV) 71. The Great American Beauty Contest (TV) 73. Murder on Flight 502 (TV) 75. Logan's Run Somebody Killed Her Husband 78. Sunburn 78. Strictly Business 79. The Helper 79. Saturn Three 79. The Cannonball Run 80. Extremities 86.

¶ *F.F.:* Marriages that last are with people who do not live in Los Angeles.
'She is uniquely suited to play a woman of limited intelligence.'—*Harry and Michael Medved*

Fay, Frank (1894–1961). American light actor and vaudeville star who made a few undistinguished films.
Show of Shows 29. God's Gift to Women 31. Stars over Broadway 35. They Knew What They Wanted 40. Spotlight Scandals 43. Love Nest 51, etc.

Faye, Alice (1912–) (Ann Leppert). American leading lady of the thirties and forties, once a singer with Rudy Vallee's band. Her wry expression tended to limit her roles, but she was a key star of her time and commanded a loyal following.
□George White's Scandals 34. Now I'll Tell 34. She Learned About Sailors 34. 365 Nights in Hollywood 34. George White's 1935 Scandals 35. Every Night at Eight 35. Music is Magic 35. King of Burlesque 36. Poor Little Rich Girl 36. Sing Baby Sing 36. Stowaway 36. On the Avenue 37. Wake Up and Live 37. You Can't Have Everything 37. You're a Sweetheart 37. Sally Irene and Mary 38. *In Old Chicago* 38. *Alexander's Ragtime Band* 38. Tailspin 39. *Rose of Washington Square* 39. *Hollywood Cavalcade* 39. Barricade 39. Little Old New York 40. *Lillian Russell* 40. Tin Pan Alley 40. That Night in Rio 41. The Great American Broadcast 41. Weekend in Havana 41. *Hello Frisco Hello* 43. The Gang's

All Here 43. Fallen Angel 45. State Fair 62. The Magic of Lassie 78.

Faylen, Frank (1907–85) (Frank Ruf). American character actor with stage experience. Played scores of bartenders, gangsters, sheriffs, cops, etc., from 1936.
Bullets or Ballots 36. The Grapes of Wrath 40. Top Sergeant Mulligan 42. *The Lost Weekend* (his best role, as the male nurse) 45. Blue Skies 46. Road to Rio 47. Detective Story 51. Riot in Cell Block Eleven 54. Killer Dino 58. The Monkey's Uncle 65. Funny Girl 68, many others.
TV series: Dobie Gillis 59–62.

Fazan, Adrienne (–). American editor.
The Bride Wore Red 37. Barbary Coast Gent 44. The Kissing Bandit 48. *An American in Paris* 51. *Singin' in the Rain* 52. Deep in My Heart 54. Invitation to the Dance 56. *Gigi* (AA) 58. The Gazebo 59. Two Weeks in Another Town 62. This Property is Condemned 66. The Comic 69, many others.

Fazenda, Louise (1895–1962). American leading lady of the Mack Sennett era: bathing beauty, slapstick comedienne, later a character actress.
The Beautiful and Damned 22. Main Street 23. Cheaper to Marry 25. Bobbed Hair 25. The Bat 26. The Red Mill 27. The Terror 28. Riley the Cop 28. Noah's Ark 29. The Desert Song 29. No No Nanette 30. Leathernecking 30. Cuban Love Song 31. Alice in Wonderland 33. Wonder Bar 34. Colleen 36. The Road Back 37. Swing Your Lady 38. The Old Maid 39, many others.

FBI. The US governmental crime fighting agency was set up in 1924 by J. Edgar Hoover and became famous for its heroic stand against the public enemies of the thirties, when its agents became known as G-Men. Surface glamour concealed an immensely painstaking organisation relying heavily on science, but only the glamour was shown in such films as *Show 'Em No Mercy, G-Men, Persons in Hiding, Let 'Em Have It, The FBI Story, FBI Girl, Parole Fixer, Confessions of a Nazi Spy, FBI Code 98, Walk East on Beacon* and *Queen of the Mob. The House on 92nd Street* in 1945 gave the best impression of the FBI at work, but its sequel *The Street with No Name* reverted to stereotype, which was maintained by Quinn Martin's nine-year TV series. In 1978, *The Private Files of J. Edgar Hoover* provided a rather superficial exposé.

Fearing, Kenneth (1902–1961). American novelist of urban cynicism: *The Big Clock* is his chief contribution to the screen.

feature film. Normally accepted to mean a (fictional) entertainment film of more than 3000 feet in length (approx. 34 minutes). Anything less than this is technically a 'short'. NB. In journalism and television a 'feature' usually means a *non*-fiction article or documentary.

featured players. Those next in importance to the stars: usually billed after the title.

Federation of Film Societies. British organization which issues information and arranges screening for film societies; also publishes magazine *Film*.

Fegté, Ernst (1900–1976). German production designer, in Hollywood from the early thirties.
The General Died at Dawn 36. The Palm Beach Story 42. I Married a Witch 42. Five Graves to Cairo 43. Frenchman's Creek (AA) 44. Concerto 47. Angel and the Badman 47, etc.

Fehmiu, Bekim (1932–). Stalwart Slav leading man in international films.
The Happy Gypsies 66. *The Adventurers* 70. The Deserter 71. Permission to Kill 75. Black Sunday 76. Madam Kitty 77, etc.

Fehr, Rudi (1911–). German-American editor.
Invisible Enemies (GB) 35. Honeymoon for Three 41. Desperate Journey 42. Watch on the Rhine 43. The Conspirators 44. Humoresque 46. Possessed 47. Key Largo 48. The Inspector General 49. House of Wax 53. Dial M for Murder 54, many others.

Feiffer, Jules (1929–). American satirical strip cartoonist, venturing into screenwriting.
Little Murders 71. Carnal Knowledge 71, etc.

Feist, Felix E. (1906–1965). American director, at first of short subjects including Pete Smith Specialities; in Hollywood from 1928.
□Stepping Sisters 32. The Deluge 33. All By Myself 43. You're a Lucky Fellow Mr Smith 43. This is the Life 44. Pardon My Rhythm 44. Reckless Age 44. George White's Scandals 45. The Devil Thumbs a Ride (& w) 47. The Winner's Circle 47. The Threat 49.

Treason 49. The Golden Gloves Story 50. The Man Who Cheated Himself 50. Tomorrow is Another Day 51. The Basketball Fix 51. This Woman is Dangerous 52. The Big Trees 52. The Man Behind the Gun 52. Donovan's Brain 53. Pirates of Tripoli 55.

Fejos, Paul (1893–1963). Hungarian director, in America from 1923.
The Last Moment 27. Lonesome 28. Erik the Great 29. Broadway 29. The Big House (co-d) 30. Maria (Hung.) 32. The Golden Smile (Dan.) 35. A Handful of Rice (Swedish) 38.

Feld, Fritz (1900–). Dapper German character comedian, once stage director for Max Reinhardt; long in Hollywood playing temperamental head waiters and clerks.
Broadway 29. I Met Him in Paris 37. Bringing Up Baby 38. Idiot's Delight 39. *At the Circus* (as Jardinet) 39. Sandy is a Lady 40. *World Première* 41. Iceland 42. Phantom of the Opera 43. The Great John L 45. Catman of Paris 46. The Secret Life of Walter Mitty 47. My Girl Tisa 48. Mexican Hayride 49. The Jackpot 50. Full House 52. The Patsy 64. Barefoot in the Park 67. Hello Dolly 69. The Love Bug Rides Again 73. Silent Movie 76. The World's Greatest Lover 77. History of the World Part One 81, many others.

Feldman, Charles K. (1904–1968) (Charles Gould). American producer, former lawyer and talent agent.
Pittsburgh 42. Follow the Boys 44. To Have and Have Not 44. The Big Sleep 46. Red River 48. The Red Pony 49. A Streetcar Named Desire 51. The Seven Year Itch 54. A Walk on the Wild Side 62. The Seventh Dawn 64. What's New Pussycat? 65. The Group 66. Casino Royale 67, etc.

Feldman, Marty (1933–1983). Pop-eyed British TV comic who from writing TV comedy scripts became a limited but well-known international star in his own right.
Every Home Should Have One 69. Young Frankenstein 73. The Adventures of Sherlock Holmes' Smarter Brother 75. Silent Movie 76. The Last Remake of Beau Geste 77. High Anxiety 78. Sex with a Smile 79. In God We Trust 80. Yellowbeard 83, etc.

Feldon, Barbara (1939–). American leading lady of the seventies who came to notice on TV.
Fitzwilly 67. Playmates (TV) 72. Smile 74. Let's Switch (TV) 75. No Deposit No Return 76. A Vacation in Hell (TV) 79, etc.
TV series: *Get Smart* 65–69.

Feldshuh, Tovah (1952–). American leading lady who came to the fore in *Holocaust* (TV) 78 but then failed to justify her promise.
Scream Pretty Peggy (TV) 73. The Amazing Howard Hughes (TV) 77. Terror out of the Sky (TV) 78. The Triangle Factory Fire Scandal (TV) 79. Cheaper to Keep Her 80. The Women's Room (TV) 80. The Idolmaker 80. Daniel 83, etc.

Felix (The Cat). Cartoon creation of Pat Sullivan, a perky and indestructible character highly popular in the twenties; in the fifties revived for TV by other hands in more streamlined style.

Felix, Maria (1915–). Mexican actress of strong personality.
The Kneeling Goddess 47. Dona Diabla 49. Mare Nostrum 50. Messalina 52. The Kidnapping 52. French Can Can 53. Les Héros Sont Fatigués 55, many Mexican films.

Felix, Seymour (1892–1961). American dance director, in films since 1929.
The Great Ziegfeld (AA) 36. Alexander's Ragtime Band 38. Cover Girl 44. The I Don't Care Girl 52, many others.

Fell, Norman (1924–). Sad-looking American character actor.
Ocean's Eleven 61. Pork Chop Hill 59. Bullitt 68. If It's Tuesday This Must Be Belgium 69. The Stone Killer 73. Guardian of the Wilderness 76. On the Right Track 81. Paternity 81, etc.
TV series: 87th Precinct 61–64. The Man from UNCLE 68. Dan August 71. Needles and Pins 74. *Three's Company* 77–78. The Ropers 79–80, etc.

Fellini, Federico (1920–). Fashionable and influential Italian director, formerly cartoonist. Film actor and writer from 1941. Biography 1977: *Fellini the Artist* by Edward Murray.
□AS DIRECTOR: Lights of Variety 50. The White Sheik 50. I Vitelloni 53. *La Strada* 54. Il Bidone 55. Notti di Cabiria 57. *La Dolce Vita* 59. Boccaccio 70 (part) 62. *Eight and a Half* 63. Juliet of the Spirits 65. Histoires Extraordinaires (part) 68. *Satyricon* 69. The Clowns 70. Fellini Roma 72. Amarcord 74. Casanova 77. City of Women 81. And the Ship Sails On 83. *Ginger and Fred* 85.

¶ *F.F.:* I always direct the same film. I can't distinguish one from another.

F.F.: Our dreams are our real life.

Fellowes, Rockliffe (1885–1950). Canadian general purpose actor in Hollywood films of silent days.
The Easiest Way 17. In Search of a Sinner 20. The Spoilers 23. The Garden of Weeds 24. East of Suez 25. Syncopating Sue 26. The Taxi Dancer 27. The Third Degree 27. The Charlatan 29. Outside the Law 30. Monkey Business 31. Lawyer Man 32. The Phantom Broadcast 33. The Black Page 34, many others.

Fellows, Edith (1923–). American teenage star of the thirties.
Riders of Death Valley 32. Jane Eyre 34. Pennies from Heaven 36. Five Little Peppers 38. Five Little Peppers in Trouble 41. Girls' Town 42. Her First Romance 47, etc.

Fellows, Robert (1903–1969). American producer.
Virginia City 39. They Died with Their Boots On 41. The Spanish Main 45. A Yankee in King Arthur's Court 49. Hondo 54. The High and the Mighty 54, etc.

Felmy, Hansjoerg (1931–). German leading man.
Der Stem von Afrika (debut) 56. Wir Wunderkinder 58. Buddenbrooks 59. Station Six Sahara 63. Torn Curtain 66.

Felton, Verna (1890–1966). American character actress, often seen as neighbour or busybody.
The Gunfighter 50. New Mexico 52. Picnic 55. Little Egypt 55. The Oklahoman 57, etc.
TV series: December Bride 54–59. Pete and Gladys 60.

female impersonation: see *transvestism.*

La Femme du Boulanger (*The Baker's Wife*) (France 1938). Like all Marcel Pagnol's films, this peasant comedy about a baker whose bread suffers when his wife leaves him has little cinematic merit but survives by virtue of Pagnol's warm script, Raimu's acting and the affectionate regard for village life.

Fennell, Albert (1920–). British producer best known for TV's *The Avengers* and *The Professionals.*
The Green Scarf 54. Next to No Time 57. Tunes of Glory 59. The Innocents 61. Night of the Eagle 62. And Soon The Darkness 71. Dr Jekyll and Sister Hyde 71. The Legend of Hell House 73, etc.

Fenton, Frank (1906–1957). American general purpose supporting actor.
Lady of Burlesque 42. Buffalo Bill 44. Magic Town 46. Red River 48. Island in the Sky 53. Emergency Hospital 56. Hellbound 58, many others.

Fenton, George (–). British composer.
Company of Wolves 84. 84 Charing Cross Road 87. Cry Freedom 87.

Fenton, Leslie (1902–1978). British-born director of Hollywood 'B' pictures. (Former actor in many silent films and early talkies including *What Price Glory?, The Man I Love, Broadway, Public Enemy, F.P.1*, etc.)
□*Tell No Tales* 39. Stronger than Desire 39. The Man from Dakota 40. The Golden Fleecing 40. The Saint's Vacation 41. Tomorrow the World 46. Pardon my Past 46. On Our Merry Way (co-d) 48. Saigon 48. Lulu Belle 48. Whispering Smith 48. Streets of Laredo 49. The Redhead and the Cowboy 50.

Ferber, Edna (1887–1968). American novelist, some of whose works were filmed.
Biography 1978: *Ferber* by Julia Goldsmith Gilbert.
Our Mrs McChesney 18. Mother Knows Best 28. Showboat 29, 35 and 51. The Royal Family of Broadway 31. Cimarron 31 and 61. So Big 32 and 53. Dinner at Eight 33. Come and Get It 36. Stage Door (with George S. Kaufman) 38. Saratoga Trunk 43. Giant 56. Ice Palace 59.

Ferguson, Elsie (1883–1961). American leading lady of silent melodramas about the upper classes. Popular 1918–27, then retired.
Barbary Sheep 17. The Lie 18. Song of Songs 18. A Society Exile 19. His House in Order 20. Sacred and Profane Love 21. Outcast 22, etc.

Ferguson, Frank (1899–1978). Toothy American character actor, often in comic bit parts.
This Gun For Hire 42. The Miracle of the Bells 48. Abbott and Costello Meet Frankenstein 49. Elopement 51. Johnny Guitar 54. Andy Hardy Comes Home 58. Raymie 60, many others.
TV series: My Friend Flicka 56. Peyton Place 64–68.

Ferman, James (1930–). British executive, former television director; since 1975 secretary of the British Board of Film Censors.

¶ *J.F.:* The instinctive good taste of the artist usually prevents him from indulging in unnecessarily explicit detail. But we are faced too rarely with the work of first-class artists.

Fernandel (1903–1971) (Fernand Contandin). Rubber-faced French comedian with toothy grin and music-hall background. Films usually 'naughty but nice'.
Regain (Harvest) 37. Un Carnet de Bal 37. *Fric Frac* 39. *La Fille du Puisatier* 40. *The Red Inn* 51. Forbidden Fruit 52. The *Don Camillo* series from 1952. *The Sheep Has Five Legs* 54. Paris Holiday 57. The Cow and I 59. Croesus 60. La Cuisine au Beurre 63. Le Voyage du Père 66. L'Homme a la Buick 67, Heureux qui comme Ulysse 69, etc.

Fernandez, Emilio (1904–). Prolific Mexican director, few of whose films have been seen abroad.
Isle of Passion 41. Maria Candelaria 44. The Pearl 45. Rio Escondido 47. Maclovia 48. The Torch 50. Garcia 74. Breakout 75, etc.

Ferrara, Adel (–). American director.
Torch 50. Garcia 74. Breakout 75. Driller Killer 79. Fear City 84. The Gladiator (TV) 86. China Girl 87, etc.

Ferrell, Conchata (1943–). American character actress.
A Death in Canaan (TV) 78. *Heartland* 80. The Girl Called Hatter Fox (TV) 80. The Seduction of Miss Leona (TV) 81. Rape and Marriage (TV) 81, etc.

Ferrer, Jose (1909–) (Jose Vincente Ferrer y Centron). Distinguished American stage actor of Puerto Rican origin; film career spotty but interesting.
□*Joan of Arc* (as the dauphin) 48. Whirlpool 49. Crisis 50. *Cyrano de Bergerac* (AA) 50. Anything Can Happen 52. *Moulin Rouge* (as Toulouse Lautrec) 53. Miss Sadie Thompson 53. The Caine Mutiny 54. Deep in My Heart 54. The Shrike (& d) 55. Cockleshell Heroes (& d) (GB) 56. The Great Man (& wd) 56. I Accuse (& d) 58. The High Cost of Loving (d) 58. Return to Peyton Place (d only) 61. State Fair (d only) 62. Lawrence of Arabia 62. Nine Hours to Rama 63. Stop Train 349 64. Cyrano contre d'Artagnan (Fr.) 64. The Greatest Story Ever Told 65. *Ship of Fools* 65. Enter Laughing 67. Cervantes 67. The Aquarians (TV) 70. Banyon (TV) 71. Cross Current (TV) 71. The Missing Are Deadly (TV) 73. The Marcus Nelson Murders (TV) 73. Order to Kill 75. Medical Story (TV) 75. Roman Grey (TV) 75. E Lollipop 75. The Big Bus 76. Voyage of the Damned 76. The Sentinel 77. Crash 77. The Private Files of J. Edgar Hoover 78. Dracula's Dog 78. The Swarm 78. Natural Enemies 79. The Big Brawl 80. The French Atlantic Affair (TV) 79. Gideon's Trumpet (TV) 80. The Dream Merchants (TV) 80. Evita Peron (TV) 81. Blood Feud (TV) 82. A Midsummer Night's Sex Comedy 82. Blood Tide 82. To Be or Not to Be 83. Dune 84. The Evil That Men Do 84. Ingrid 85. Blood and Orchids (TV) 85.

Ferrer, Mel (1917–). Sensitive-looking American leading man, former radio producer and writer.
Girl of the Limberlost (d only) 45. *Lost Boundaries* 49. The Secret Fury (d only) 50. Vendetta (d only) 50. Born to Be Bad 50. The Brave Bulls 51. *Scaramouche* 52. Rancho Notorious 52. Lili 53. Knights of the Round Table (GB) 54. Saadia 54. Oh! Rosalinda (GB) 55. War and Peace 56. The Vintage 57. The Sun Also Rises 57. Fraulein 58. The World the Flesh and the Devil 59. Green Mansions (d only) 59. Blood and Roses 61. The Fall of the Roman Empire 64. Sex and the Single Girl 64. El Greco 65. Wait Until Dark (p only) 67. Every Day's a Holiday (& wdp) (Sp.) 67. A Time for Loving (& p) 71. Embassy (p only) 72. W (p only) 73. Brannigan 75. Eaten Alive 77. The Norseman 78. The Fifth Floor 80. The Top of the Hill (TV) 80. The Memory of Eva Ryker (TV) 81. Fugitive Family (TV) 81, etc.

Ferreri, Marco (1928–). Italian director.
El Pisito (Sp.) 56. The Wheelchair (Sp.) 60. Queen Bee 63. The Bearded Lady 64. Wedding March 65. Dillinger Is Dead 68. Liza 72. Blowout 73. The Last Woman 76, The Future is Woman 84. I Love You 86, etc.
'The master of bad taste.'—*Sunday Times*

Ferris, Barbara (1940–). British leading lady.
Catch Us If You Can 66. Interlude 68. A Nice Girl Like Me 69.

Ferzetti, Gabriele (1925–) (Pasquale Ferzetti). Italian leading man.
William Tell 48. Cuore Ingrato 51. Three Forbidden Stories 52. Puccini 54. Le Amiche 55. Donatello 56. L'Avventura 59. Torpedo Bay 64. Once Upon a Time in the West 69. On Her Majesty's Secret Service 69. Hitler—The Last Ten Days 73. The Night Porter 74. A Matter of Time 76. End of the Game 76, etc.

festivals. Since World War II a great many cities round the world have derived excellent publicity from annual film festivals. Producers, distributors and actors in search of accolades now diligently trek each year to Cannes, Venice, Berlin, Mar del Plata, Cork, Edinburgh, Karlovy Vary, San Sebastian, Moscow, etc., while London and New York offer résumés in October.

Fetchit, Stepin (1892–1985) (Lincoln Perry). Gangly, slow-moving American Negro comedian, popular in films of the thirties.
In Old Kentucky 29. Stand Up and Cheer 33. Steamboat Round the Bend 35. Charlie Chan in Egypt 35. Dimples 36. On the Avenue 37. Zenobia 39. Bend of the River 52. The Sun Shines Bright 53, many others.

Feuillade, Louis (1873–1925). Newly-rediscovered and fêted French director who made marathon silent serials about master criminals.
Fantomas 13. Les Vampires 15. Judex (remade by Franju 63) 16–17. Tih Minh 18. Parisette 21, etc.

Feuillere, Edwige (1907–) (Edwige Cunati). Distinguished French actress, a leading member of the Comédie Française.
Le Cordon Bleu 30. Topaze 32. I Was An Adventuress 38. Sans Lendemain 40. La Duchesse de Langeais 42. *L'Idiot* 46. L'Aigle a Deux Têtes 47. Woman Hater (GB) 48. *Olivia* 50. Adorable Creatures 52. *Le Blé en Herbe* 53. The Fruits of Summer 54. En Cas de Malheur (Love Is My Profession) 57. Crime Doesn't Pay 62. Do You Like Women? 64, etc.

Feydeau, Georges (1862–1921). French writer of stage farces, many of which have become classics and are often filmed, the best cinematic examples being *Occupe Toi d'Amelie* 49 and *Hotel Paradiso* 66.

Feyder, Jacques (1888–1948) (Jacques Frederix). French director, former actor; married Françoise Rosay.
L'Atlantide 21. Crainquebille 22. Thérèse Raquin 28. *Les Nouveaux Messieurs* 29. The Kiss (US) 29. Le Grand Jeu 34. *La Kermesse Héroique* 35. Knight without Armour (GB) 37. Les Gens du Voyage 38. La Loi du Nord 39. Une Femme Disparait 41, Macadam (supervised only) 45, etc.

Fiander, Lewis (1938–). Australian-born stage and TV actor in Britain.
Dr Jekyll and Sister Hyde 71. The Abdication 73. Death is Child's Play 75. Sweeney 2 78. The Doctor and the Devils 86, etc.

Fiedel, Brad (–). American composer.
The Calendar Girl Murders (TV) 83. The Terminator 85. Compromising Positions 85. Fright Night 85. Desert Bloom 86. Popeye Doyle 87, etc.

F.I.D.O. The Film Industry Defence Organization, a body formed by British renters and exhibitors to prevent old feature films being sold to television. It collapsed in 1964 after five years during which no renter dared sell his product for fear of reprisals.

Fiedler, John (1925–). Mild, bespectacled American character actor.
Twelve Angry Men 57. Stage Struck 58. That Touch of Mink 62. The World of Henry Orient 64. Kiss Me Stupid 64. Fitzwilly 67. The Odd Couple 68. True Grit 69. Making It 71. The Shaggy D.A. 76. The Cannonball Run 81. Savannah Smiles 82, etc.
TV series: Newhart 73–78.

Field, Betty (1918–1973). American character actress who played a variety of roles from neurotic girls to slatternly mums.
□What a Life 39. *Of Mice and Men* 39. Seventeen 40. Victory 40. The Shepherd of the Hills 41. Blues in the Night 41. *King's Row* 42. Are Husbands Necessary? 42. Flesh and Fantasy 43. The Great Moment 44. Tomorrow the World 44. *The Southerner* 45. The Great Gatsby 49. Picnic 55. Bus Stop 56. Peyton Place 57. The Hound Dog Man 59. Butterfield 8 60. Bird Man of Alcatraz 62. Seven Women 65. How to Save a Marriage 68. Coogan's Bluff 68.

Field, Mary (1896–1968). British executive long associated with films specially made for children. From 1926 worked as continuity girl, editor, etc., also directed some instructional films, including the *Secrets of Nature* series. Well-known writer and lecturer on social aspects of film.

Field, Mary (c. 1905–). American character comedienne, usually as prissy spinster.
Wild Geese Calling 41. *Ball of Fire* 41. The Affairs of Susan 45. A Song Is Born 48. Sitting Pretty 48, etc.

Field, Rachel (1894–1942). American novelist.
□All This and Heaven Too 40. And Now Tomorrow 44. Time Out of Mind 47.

Field, Sally (1946–) (S. F. Mahoney). Diminutive American actress who played the lead in TV series *Gidget* 65, *The Flying Nun* 67–69. The Girl with Something Extra 73.
The Way West 67. Home for the Holidays (TV) 72. Maybe I'll Come Home in the Spring (TV) 72. Marriage Year One (TV) 72. Stay Hungry 76. Sybil (TV: Emmy) 76. Smokey and the Bandit 77. Heroes 77. Hooper 78. The End 78. *Norma Rae* (AA) 79. Smokey and the Bandit II 80. Back Roads 81. Absence of Malice 81. Kiss Me Goodbye 82. *Places in the Heart* (AA) 84. Murphy's Romance 85, etc.

Field, Shirley Ann (1938–). British leading lady with stage experience; career waned after a promising start.
Dry Rot 56. Once More with Feeling 59. The Entertainer 59. *Saturday Night and Sunday Morning* 60. The Man in the Moon 60. The Damned 61. The War Lover 62. Lunch Hour 63. Kings of the Sun (US) 63. Doctor in Clover 66. *Alfie* 66. My Beautiful Laundrette 84, etc.

Field, Sid (1904–1950). British comedian who after years in music hall became West End star in 1943. First film, *London Town* 46, valuable as record of his sketches; second and last, *Cardboard Cavalier* 48, a patchy historical farce.

¶ *S.F.:* It took me thirty years to become an overnight star.
† Catchphrase: What a per*for*mance!

Field, Virginia (1917–) (Margaret Cynthia Field). British-born second lead of Hollywood films in the forties.
The Primrose Path (GB) 35. Lloyds of London 37. Lancer Spy 38. Waterloo Bridge 40. Hudson's Bay 41. The Perfect Marriage 46. Dial 1119 50. The Big Story 58. The Earth Dies Screaming 65, others.

Fielding, Fenella (c. 1930–). Anglo-Rumanian leading lady, usually in outrageously exaggerated roles on stage and TV.
In the Doghouse 62. The Old Dark House 63. Doctor in Clover 66. Carry on Screaming 66. Arrivederci Baby 66. Lock Up Your Daughters 69, etc.

Fielding, Jerry (1922–1980). American composer.
Advise and Consent 62. The Wild Bunch 69. Johnny Got His Gun 71. Lawman 71. The Nightcomers 71. Straw Dogs 71. Chato's Land 72. Bring Me the Head of Alfredo Garcia 74. The Outlaw Josey Wales 76. Demon Seed 77. Semi-Tough 77. The Big Sleep 78. Beyond the Poseidon Adventure 79. Escape from Alcatraz 80. High Midnight (TV) 80, etc.
Much TV, including *Hogan's Heroes, McMillan and Wife,* The Bionic Woman.

Fielding, Henry (1707–54). Influential English novelist whose chief bequests to films have been *Tom Jones, Lock Up Your Daughters* (indirectly) and *Joseph Andrews*.

Fielding, Marjorie (1892–1956). British stage actress who usually played strict but kindly gentlewomen. Repeated her stage role in *Quiet Wedding* 40 and was subsequently in many films.
The Demi-Paradise 43. Quiet Weekend 46. Spring in Park Lane 47. The Conspirator 49. The Chiltern Hundreds 49. The Franchise Affair 50. The Lavender Hill Mob 51. Mandy 52. Rob Roy 53, etc.

Fields, Benny (1894–1959) (Benjamin Geisenfeld). American vaudevillian whose career was linked with Blossom Seeley. Their story was told (more or less) in *Somebody Loves Me*.
□Mr Broadway 33. The Big Broadcast of 1937 36. Minstrel Man 44.

Fields, Freddie (1923–). American agent and producer.
Lipstick 76. Looking for Mr Goodbar 77. American Gigolo 80. Wholly Moses 80. Victory 81, etc.

Fields, Dame Gracie (1898–1979) (Grace Stansfield). British singer and comedienne whose Lancashire humour and high spirits helped working-class audiences through the thirties depression. An inimitable voice and personality.
Autobiography 1960: *Sing As We Go*.
□*Sally in our Alley* 31. Looking on the Bright Side 32. This Week of Grace 33. Love Life and Laughter 33. *Sing As We Go* 34. Look Up and Laugh 35. Queen of Hearts 36. The Show Goes On 37. We're Going to Be Rich 38. Keep Smiling 38. Shipyard Sally 39. Stage Door Canteen 43. *Holy Matrimony* 43. Molly and Me 45. Paris Underground 45.
❀ For keeping a nation cheerful. *Sing As We Go*.

Fields, Stanley (1884–1941) (Walter L. Agnew). American character actor, former prizefighter and vaudevillian.

Mammy 30. Little Caesar 30. Island of Lost Souls 32. Kid Millions 35. Way Out West 37. Algiers 38. New Moon 40, many others.

Fields, Verna (–1982). American editor. The Savage Eye 60. Studs Lonigan 60. Medium Cool 69. What's Up Doc? 72. American Graffiti 73. Paper Moon 73. *Jaws* (AA) 75, etc.

Fields, W. C. (1879–1946) (William Claude Dukinfield). Red-nosed, gravel-voiced, bottle-hitting, misogynist American comedian around whose intolerance and eccentric habits many legends have been built. After a hard life as a tramp juggler, his off-beat personality found a niche in silent films, though sound was necessary to his full flowering as a screen personality. Many of his routines were made up as he went along; once he sold for $25,000 a story line written on the back of an envelope. Books on him include *W. C. Fields, His Follies and Fortunes* (Robert Lewis Taylor 1949), *The Films of W. C. Fields* (Donald Deschner 1960). Rod Steiger impersonated him in an inaccurate 1976 film of his life, *W. C. Fields and Me*, from a book by his mistress Carlotta Monti.
□*Pool Sharks* 15. Janice Meredith 24. Sally of the Sawdust 25. That Royle Girl 26. It's the Old Army Game 26. So's Your Old Man 26. The Potters 27. Running Wild 27. Two Flaming Youths 27. Tillie's Punctured Romance 27. Fools for Luck 28. The Golf Specialist 30. Her Majesty Love 31. Million Dollar Legs 32. If I Had a Million 32. The Dentist 32. The Fatal Glass of Beer 32. The Pharmacist 33. The Barber Shop 33. International House 33. Tillie and Gus 33. Alice in Wonderland (as Humpty Dumpty) 33. Six of a Kind 34. You're Telling Me 34. The Old Fashioned Way 34. Mrs Wiggs of the Cabbage Patch 34. *It's a Gift* 34. *David Copperfield* (as Micawber) 34. Mississippi 35. The Man on the Flying Trapeze 35. Poppy 36. The Big Broadcast of 1938 37. You Can't Cheat an Honest Man 39. *My Little Chickadee* 40. *The Bank Dick* 40. *Never Give a Sucker an Even Break* 41. Follow the Boys 44. Song of the Open Road 44. Sensations of 1945 44.
❀ For making a disreputable character almost entirely sympathetic; and for moments of inspired surrealism. *It's a Gift*.

¶ Today the centre of a cult which would have astonished him, W. C. Fields was one of life's genuine oddballs, able to see the funny side of his own misanthropy and to turn it to commercial use. In most of his films he was strait-jacketed, but the few he controlled personally are uniquely Fieldsian, anarchic and paceless, fantasticated versions of his unyielding private life with a few in-jokes for good measure. They feature such characters as

J. Frothingham Waterbury
Ogg Ogilvie
Filthy McNasty
Ouliotta Haemoglobin
F. Snoopington Pinkerton
Elmer Prettywillie
T. Frothingwell Bellows
A. Pismo Clam
Ambrose Wolfinger
Egbert Souse
Cuthbert J. Twillie
Larson E. Whipsnade

Fields' own pseudonyms, either for professional use on his screenplays or merely to conceal a new bank account, include

Primrose Magoo
Mahatma Kane Jeeves
Otis Criblecoblis
Ampico J. Steinway
Charles Bogle
Felton J. Satchelstern

He had a splendid command of the English language which effectively silenced criticisms when he was cast as Micawber in *David Copperfield*. His nasal delivery and orotund phrasing were imitated the world over, and they are essential to the effectiveness of such oft-quoted lines as:

> I must have a drink of breakfast.

or:

> Somebody left the cork out of my lunch.

or (of an elderly lady dressed to kill):

> She's all done up like a well kept grave.

or:

> I exercise extreme self control. I never drink anything stronger than gin before breakfast.

or:

> If at first you don't succeed, try again. Then quit. No use being a damn fool about it.

or:

> There's an Ethiopian in the fuel supply.

or:

> I never vote for anyone. I always vote against.

His oaths were splendid, consisting of such watered-down versions of profanity as 'Godfrey Daniel!' or 'Great Mother of Pearl!' He was indeed a profane and outlandish man. When his lady neighbour in Beverly Hills came out to remonstrate with him for standing in the middle of his new green lawn and shooting the singing birds with a rifle, he is alleged to have growled:

> I'll go on shooting the bastards till they learn to shit green . . .

When another lady, an inquiring journalist this time, asked why he never drank water, he gave the simple reason:

> Fish fuck in it.

He occasionally mentioned to acquaintances that he was involved in charity work, and when asked what charity he would murmur: 'The F.E.B.F.' When an explanation of the initials was requested, it was given as:

> Fuck Everyone but Fields.

As his biographer Robert Lewis Taylor said:

> His main purpose seemed to be to break as many rules as possible and cause the maximum amount of trouble for everybody.

He hated children and animals, and once said of a churlish friend:

> Anyone who hates small dogs and children can't be all bad.

It is of course alleged that when co-starring with Baby Le Roy he spiked the infant's milk with gin, and when Le Roy proved unfit for further work that day stalked around yelling:

> The kid's no trouper!

He hated women too:

> Women are like elephants. I like to look at them but I wouldn't want to own one.

and:

> A woman drove me to drink. I never had the courtesy to thank her for it.

But he was essentially impartial:

> I am free of all prejudices. I hate everybody equally.

fights provide the climax to many a film, but only the outstandingly staged ones remain in the mind. The slugging match between the two heroes of *The Spoilers* (qv) became a tradition, as each of the five versions tried to outdo the previous one. John Wayne had many fighting triumphs, notably against Victor McLaglen in *The Quiet Man*; *McLintock* and *North to Alaska* seemed at times to have more brawling than dialogue. Spoof fights were probably topped by the saloon brawl in *The Great Race*; serious ones by the solemn allegorical punch-up in *The Big Country*. Other good western fights are found in *Shane, The Sheepman,* and (between Dietrich and Una Merkel) in *Destry Rides Again*. For viciousness within a serious picture the waterfront fights in *Edge of the City* and *On the Waterfront* take some beating.

Figueroa, Gabriel (1907–). Mexican cinematographer who worked in Hollywood with Gregg Toland and on Luis Buñuel's Mexican films.
The Fugitive 47. Maclovia 50. Night of the Iguana 64. Kelly's Heroes 70, etc.

? the film and the face
Name the film in which each of the following characters played a leading role, and say what actor played the part.

1 Cody Jarrett
2 Wallace Wooley
3 Adrienne Fromsett
4 Enrique Claudin
5 Holly Martins
6 Walter Neff
7 Yancey Cravat (1930)
8 Sydney Fairfield (1932)
9 Percy Blakeney (1934)
10 Henriette Deluzy-Desportes
11 Tony Camonte
12 Brigid O'Shaughnessy (1940)
13 Enrico Bandello
14 Mortimer Brewster
15 Charles Condomine
16 Elizabeth Bennet
17 Jefferson Smith
18 Geoffrey T. Spaulding
19 Jedediah Leland
20 Marcus Superbus
21 Regina Giddens
22 Tom Joad
23 Arthur Seaton
24 Violet Venable
25 Harold Bissonette

film making is not too frequently used as a background for movies, as movies about movies are thought to be bad box office. Certainly not too many of the following were big hits: *OK for Sound, The Best Pair of Legs in the Business, Go for a Take, The Comedy Man, The Bad and the Beautiful, Two Weeks in Another Town, It's a Great Feeling, Shooting Stars, Pick a Star, A Star is Born, The Carpetbaggers, Eight and a Half, Hellzapoppin, Day for Night, Stand In, Singin' In The Rain, Abbott and Costello Meet the Keystone Kops, Gable and Lombard, Harlow, W. C. Fields and Me, The Big Knife, Once in a Lifetime, Wonderful Life, Hollywood Cavalcade, Hollywood Boulevard, Hollywood Story, Nickelodeon, The Last Tycoon, Everything for Sale, The Stunt Man*.

film noir. A French phrase meaning *dark film*. It was probably first applied to the moody, downbeat character melodramas of the late thirties, such as *Quai des Brumes* and *Le Jour se Lève*, but it soon came to be thought of as applying chiefly to the American urban crime film of the forties, for instance *Double Indemnity*, *Laura*, *Scarlet Street* (based on a French original) and the versions of Raymond Chandler novels.

? film of the book
Many films are retitled and rewritten from less famous books. Can you name the films made from the following?

1 *The Wheel Spins* by Ethel Lina White
2 *The Midwich Cuckoos* by John Wyndham
3 *The Gun* by C. S. Forester
4 *Killing a Mouse on Sunday* by Emeric Pressburger
5 *The Brick Foxhole* by Richard Brooks
6 *Benighted* by J. B. Priestley
7 *The Curse of Capistrano* by Johnston McCulley
8 *Mute Witness* by Robert L. Pike
9 *Glory for Me* by Mackinlay Kantor
10 *Sobbin' Women* by Stephen Vincent Benet
11 *The Light of Day* by Eric Ambler
12 *Stage to Lordsburg* by Ernest Haycox
13 *A Mule for the Marquesa* by Frank O'Rourke
14 *Seven and a Half Cents* by Richard Bissell
15 *Night Bus* by Samuel Hopkins Adams
16 *The Small Woman* by Alan Burgess
17 *Washington Square* by Henry James
18 *Personal History* by Vincent Sheean
19 *The Secret Agent* by Joseph Conrad
20 *Red Alert* by Peter George
21 *The House of Dr Edwardes* by Francis Beeding
22 *Hell's Playground* by Vera Simonton
23 *A Shilling for Candles* by Josephine Tey
24 *Man Running* by Selwyn Jepson
25 *Bad Time at Hondo* by Don Maguire
26 *The Basement Room* by Graham Greene

film society. A club formed to show high quality revivals and new films not normally found in public cinemas.

films à clef are those which appear to be fiction but are really based on factual cases with the names changed. The obvious example is *Citizen Kane*, which parallels the career of William Randolph Hearst. Others are *The Great Dictator*, in which Hynkel is obviously Hitler; *Compulsion*, based on the Leopold and Loeb murder; *Inherit the Wind*, about the Scopes monkey trial; *The Moon and Sixpence*, in which Charles Strickland stands in for Paul Gaugin; *The Man Who Came to Dinner*, in which Sheridan Whiteside is Alexander Woolcott, Banjo is Harpo Marx, and Beverly Carlton is Noel Coward; *Young Cassidy*, drawn from the early life of Sean O'Casey; *All About Eve*, in which Margo Channing was said to be Tallulah Bankhead and Addison de Witt George Jean Nathan; *Twentieth Century*, in which Oscar Jaffe is an amalgam of Jed Harris and David Belasco; *All the King's Men* and *A Lion is in the Streets*, both essentially about Huey Long; *The Lost Moment*, in which the old lady is allegedly Claire Clairemont, the aged mistress of Byron; *The Adventurers*, in which the characters are supposedly based on Porfirio Rubirosa, Barbara Hutton, Aristotle Onassis and Maria Callas; *The Carpetbaggers*, plainly about Howard Hughes; *Little Caesar*, who was plainly Al Capone; *Major Barbara*, in which Adolphus Cusins was Gilbert Murray; *Call Me Madam*, based on the exploits of Perle Mesta; *The Winslow Boy*, based on the Archer-Shee case, with Sir Robert Morton standing in for Sir Edward Carson; *An American Tragedy*, from the real life Chester Gillette murder case; Monsieur Verdoux, who was Landru; *Death of a Scoundrel*, from the career of Charles Rubenstein; *The Prisoner*, inspired by the sufferings of Cardinal Mindzenty; *Fame is the Spur*, in which Homer Radshaw was Ramsay MacDonald; and if you like *Dr Jekyll and Mr Hyde*, whose story was inspired by the burglarious second life of Deacon William Brodie; or even any Sherlock Holmes story, as Holmes was modelled on Dr Joseph Bell.

Where Love Has Gone was modelled on the Lana Turner case in which her daughter murdered her lover; and *Imitation of Life* also reflected the Turner career, as *Dancing Lady* and *Torch Song* reflected Joan Crawford's. *The Barefoot Contessa* was vaguely drawn from Rita Hayworth's international goings-on, though the star who played her, Ava Gardner, was also no slouch in the fun department. *Bombshell* was an obvious echo of Jean Harlow's own troubles with hangers-on. *I Could Go on Singing* featured Judy Garland clearly playing herself; *The Devil Is a Woman* can be seen as Sternberg's farewell to Dietrich (with Lionel Atwill playing himself), just as Orson Welles cast himself as bedevilled by his then wife Rita Hayworth in *The Lady from Shanghai*. The leading roles in *Will Success Spoil Rock Hunter*, *After the Fox*, *The Band Wagon*, *Blondie of the Follies* and *Kiss Me Stupid* were clearly based on those who played them: Jayne Mansfield,

Victor Mature, Fred Astaire, Marion Davis and Dean Martin. The same can be said of Gloria Swanson in *Sunset Boulevard*, Bette Davis in *The Star*, Errol Flynn in *The Sun Also Rises*, Hedy Lamarr in *The Female Animal*, Marlene Dietrich in *No Highway*, John Wayne in *The Shootist*, John Barrymore in *The Great Profile* and Zero Mostel in *The Front*. *The Goddess* reflected Marilyn Monroe's marriage with Joe Di Maggio. *Flight for Freedom*, though not using Amelia Earhart's name, gave a fictional solution to the aviatrix's real-life disappearance. *Funny Girl* was the official biography of Fanny Brice, but *Rose of Washington Square* also had lots of similarities. *All About Eve*'s leading character, Margo Channing, according to its creator, was based on Elisabeth Bergner. *New York New York* seemed to be taken from Doris Day's autobiography. *Smash-Up* was allegedly based on the drinking problems of Bing Crosby's first wife Dixie Lee, just as *Written on the Wind* had connections with the suicide of Libby Holman's first husband. Evangelist Aimee Semple McPherson was clearly impersonated by Barbara Stanwyck in *The Miracle Woman* and by Jean Simmons in *Elmer Gantry*. Columnist Walter Winchell was parodied in several Lee Tracy vehicles—Tracy even looked like him—and also by Burt Lancaster in *Sweet Smell of Success*. The Robert Ryan character in *Caught* was allegedly based on Howard Hughes. Bette Midler in *The Rose* is clearly Janis Joplin. *The Greek Tycoon* is clearly inspired by Aristotle Onassis and Jackie Kennedy. In *It's Tough to Be Famous*, Douglas Fairbanks Jnr could only be Charles Lindbergh. James Cagney and Pat O'Brien in *Boy Meets Girl* were inspired by Charles McArthur and Ben Hecht. In *The Last Tycoon*, Robert de Niro was Irving Thalberg. Anne Baxter in *You're My Everything* was Clara Bow. The sliding marriage in *A Star Is Born* could have been based on Al Jolson and Ruby Keeler, or on John Gilbert and Greta Garbo. Patty Duke in *Valley of the Dolls* was Judy Garland. And so on.

La Fin du Jour (France 1939). A delightful comedy-drama set in a home for old actors, with subtle direction by Julien Duvivier and effortlessly effective performances from Michel Simon, Louis Jouvet and Victor Francen.

Finch, Flora (1869–1940). British-born actress, formerly on stage; famous as John Bunny's partner in early film comedies. After his death in 1915 she formed her own production company and was in many silent films of the twenties.

Finch, Jon (1941–). British leading man.
□The Vampire Lovers 70. Horror of Frankenstein 71. Macbeth 71. Sunday Bloody Sunday 71. Frenzy 72. Lady Caroline Lamb 72. The Final Programme 73. Diagnosis: Murder 74. A Faithful Wife (Fr.) 75. The Man with the Green Cross (Sp.) 76. Battleflag (Sp.) 76. Death on the Nile 78. El Barracho (Sp.) 78. Breaking Glass 80. Peter and Paul (TV) 81. Riviera (TV) 82. Giro City (TV) 85.

Finch, Peter (1916–1977) (William Mitchell). Thoughtful-looking British leading actor who spent many years in Australia before returning to become an international star.
□Dad and Dave Come to Town 37. Red Sky at Morning 37. Mr Chedworth Steps Out 38. Rats of Tobruk 44. The Power and the Glory 45. Eureka Stockade 47. Train of Events 49. The Wooden Horse 50. The Miniver Story 50. *Robin Hood* (as Sheriff) 51. The Heart of the Matter 53. The Story of Gilbert and Sullivan 53. Elephant Walk 54. *Father Brown* (as Flambeau) 54. Make Me an Offer 54. The Dark Avenger 55. Passage Home 55. Josephine and Men 55. *Simon and Laura* 55. *The Battle of the River Plate* (as Langsdorff) 56. *A Town Like Alice* (BFA) 56. The Shiralee 56. Robbery Under Arms 57. Windom's Way 57. Operation Amsterdam 58. Kidnapped 59. *The Nun's Story* 59. The Sins of Rachel Cade 60. *The Trials of Oscar Wilde* (BFA) 60. *No Love for Johnnie* (BFA) 61. I Thank a Fool 62. In the Cool of the Day 63. Girl with Green Eyes 64. The Pumpkin Eater 64. Judith 65. The Flight of the Phoenix 65. 10.30 pm Summer 67. *Far from the Madding Crowd* 67. The Legend of Lylah Clare 68. The Red Tent 69. *Sunday Bloody Sunday* (BFA) 71. Something to Hide 72. England Made Me 72. *Lost Horizon* 73. A Bequest to the Nation 73. The Abdication 73. *Network* (AA, BFA) 76. Raid on Entebbe (TV) 86.

fine grain print. One of high quality stock (avoiding the coarseness of silver salt deposit); used for making dupe negatives.

Fine, Larry (1911–1975) (Laurence Feinberg). American comedian, one of the Three Stooges (qv).

Finklehoffe, Fred F. (1911–1977). American writer-producer.

Brother Rat (co-w & co-w original stage play) 39. For Me and My Gal (co-w) 42. Meet Me in St Louis (w) 44. The Egg and I (co-wp) 47. At War with the Army (co-wp) 50, etc.

Finland has produced many films for internal consumption, but language and subject barriers have made them unsuitable for international sale. Probably the best known Finnish film is Edvin Laine's *The Unknown Soldier* 55.

Finlay, Frank (1926–86). British stage and TV actor who made tentative screen appearances.
Life for Ruth 62. The Informers 63. Othello (as Iago) 65. Robbery 67. Inspector Clouseau 68. Twisted Nerve 68. Cromwell 69. Assault 71. Gumshoe 71. Danny Jones 71. Sitting Target 72. Shaft in Africa 73. The Three Musketeers 74. The Four Musketeers 75. Murder by Decree 79. Enigma 82. The Ploughman's Lunch 83. Arch of Triumph (TV) 84. The Key 85. Sakharov 85. Life Force 85. In the Secret State (TV) 86, etc.
TV successes include The Last Days of Hitler (title role), Casanova (title role) and Bouquet of Barbed Wire.

Finlayson, James (1877–1953). Scottish comic actor who went to Hollywood in early silent days and became an indispensable comic villain, known for the exaggerated reaction known as a 'double take and fade away'. A memorable opponent for Laurel and Hardy.
Small Town Idol 21. Ladies Night in a Turkish Bath 28. Lady Be Good 28. The Dawn Patrol 30. *Big Business* 30. Pardon Us 31. Fra Diavolo 33. Our Relations 36. *Way Out West* 37. Blockheads 38. The Flying Deuces 39. The Perils of Pauline 47. Grand Canyon Trail 48. Royal Wedding 51, many others.

Finnerman, Gerald Perry (1931–). American photographer, mostly in television.
Night Gallery (TV) 69. The Lost Man 69. Brother John 70. They Call Me Mr Tibbs 70. Joe Forrester (TV) 76. Salvage (TV) 78. Ziegfeld the Man and His Women (TV) 78. That Man Bolt 78. The Dream Merchants (TV) 80. Smorgasbord 83, etc.

Finney, Albert (1936–). Leading British actor whose comparatively few films have tended to be controversial.
□The Entertainer 59. *Saturday Night and Sunday Morning* 60. *Tom Jones* 63. The Victors 63. Night Must Fall (& p) 63. Two for the Road 67. *Charlie Bubbles* (& pd) 68. The Picasso Summer 69. Scrooge 70. Gumshoe (& p) 71. Alpha Beta 73. Murder on the Orient Express (as Hercule Poirot) 74. The Duellists 77. Wolfen 80. Looker 80. Loophole 80. Annie 82. Shoot the Moon 82. The Dresser (AAN) 83. Under the Volcano (AAN) 84. The Biko Inquest (TV) 85. Orphans 87.

Firbank, Ann (–). British actress, usually in refined roles.
Behind the Mask 58. Nothing Barred 61. The Servant 65. Darling 65. Accident 67. A Severed Head 70. Sunday Bloody Sunday 71. Asylum 74. Stories from a Flying Trunk 79, etc.

fire is a standard part of the melodramatist's equipment, whether it be used for disposing of country houses with too many memories (*Dragonwyck, Rebecca, The Lost Moment, The Fall of the House of Usher, The Tomb of Ligeia, Gone with the Wind*) or whole cities (*Forever Amber, In Old Chicago, Quo Vadis*). Sometimes, as in *House of Wax*, it makes a splendid starting point; though to judge from *She* one can't rely on its life-prolonging qualities. Its use in realistic films is rare, though cases of arson were seriously studied in *On the Night of the Fire* and *Violent Playground*. The fires of hell were most spectacularly re-created in the 1935 version of *Dante's Inferno*. Comedies about firemen include *Where's That Fire?* (Will Hay), *Fireman Save My Child, Harvey Middleman Fireman*, and *Go to Blazes* (Dave King); and firemen who start fires instead of putting them out are prophesied in *Fahrenheit 451*. Oil fires were spectacularly depicted in *Tulsa, Wildcat*, and *Hellfighters*. The classic study of conventional firemen remains *Fires Were Started*; TV series which took up the theme include *Emergency* and *Firehouse*. For many, the greatest screen fire will be the burning of Atlanta in *Gone with the Wind*, but *The Towering Inferno* was probably the most spectacular. Finally fire was always a splendid aid for serial producers, as the oft-used title 'Next Week: Through the Flames' may suggest.
See also: *forest fires*.

Fire Over England (GB 1936). A charade of the Spanish Armada, produced by Alexander Korda with an eye to repeating his 'Henry VIII' success. Directed by William K. Howard. Now chiefly remembered for its gallery of star talents: Flora Robson, Leslie Banks, Laurence Olivier, Vivien Leigh, Raymond Massey, etc.

Fires Were Started (GB 1943). Humphrey Jennings' documentary about the Auxiliary Fire Service during the London blitz is slower and slighter than one might expect from an official tribute, but the treatment gives it an almost poetic quality, and all its people—real firemen—live in the memory.

firing squads have figured chiefly in films about World War I (*Paths of Glory*, *King and Country*) or those telling the lives of spies (*Mata Hari*, *Nurse Edith Cavell*, *Carve Her Name With Pride*). Other uses have been in *Dishonoured*, *The Fugitive*, *Custer of the West*, *The Victors*, *The Long Ride Home*, *Reach for Glory*, *The Counterfeit Traitor* and *The Ceremony*; and firing squads were given a comic effect in *The Captain's Paradise*, *Casino Royale*, *Morgan* and *The Ambushers*.

? first lines
What films began with the following narration? The first group are spoken by an unseen storyteller.

1 Deep among the lonely sunbaked hills of Texas the great and weatherbeaten stone still stands . . .
2 I never knew the old Vienna before the war, with its Strauss music, its glamour and easy charm . . . Constantinople suited me better.
3 Come closer! [There's a catch here!]
4 Call me Ishmael . . .
5 Last night I dreamed I went to Manderley again . . .
6 Our story takes us down this shadowed path to a dark and guarded building in the British midlands . . .

The following are put up on the screen to be read:

7 This is a Hallowe'en tale of Brooklyn, where anything can happen, and usually does . . .
8 This picture is dedicated to all the beautiful women in the world who have shot their husbands full of holes out of pique . . .
9 The first law of every being is to preserve itself and live. You sow hemlock, and you live to see ears of corn ripen.—*Machiavelli*
10 New York, skyscraper champion of the world, where the slickers and know-it-alls peddle gold bricks to each other and truth, crushed to earth, rises more phoney than a glass eye . . .
11 This story takes place in Paris, in those wonderful days when a siren was a brunette and not an alarm . . . and when a Frenchman turned out the lights, it wasn't because of an air raid . . .
12 This is a story of the period between two world wars—an interim during which insanity cut loose, liberty took a nose dive, and humanity was kicked around somewhat . . .
13 This concerns the destruction of an empire, brought about by the mad ambition of one man. A few of the characters are still alive. The rest met death by violence.
14 In the seventeenth century Holland was a world power, her ships carried treasure to Amsterdam from all over the world, but her proudest glory was the son of a miller from Leyden . . .
15 This is the story of that unconquerable fortress—the American home, 1943.
16 This is a story of passion, bloodshed, desire and death—everything, in fact, that makes life worth living.
17 To the Commandos and Airborne Troops of Great Britain—the spirit of whose actions it has been humbly attempted to recapture in some ensuing scenes—this film is dedicated.
18 For those who believe in God, no explanation is necessary. For those who do not, no explanation is possible.
19 This is the story of two men who met in a banana republic. One of them was honest all his life—except for one crazy minute. The other was dishonest all his life—except for one crazy minute. They both had to leave the country.
20 And so they lived happily ever after—or did they?
21 During that happy yesterday of entertainment which was called vaudeville, its pulsating heart was the Palace Theatre . . .
22 Most of what follows is true.

First National was a Hollywood company founded in 1917. During the next twelve years it was very active, with films featuring Chaplin, Pickford, Milton Sills and Richard Barthelmess. In 1929 it was taken over by Warner Brothers, who however kept the name going for certain product until the mid-thirties.

The First of the Few (GB 1942). Leslie Howard wrote and directed this gentle, cinematically unremarkable but moving film about R. J. Mitchell, inventor of the Spitfire plane. It proved to be one of World War II's most inspirational films, typifying the idealist attitude. It is notable also for William Walton's background music, including the 'Spitfire' prelude and fugue.

Firth, Colin (1960–). British leading man. Camille (TV) 84. Dutch Girls (TV) 85. Lost Empires (TV) 86.

Firth, Peter (1953–). British juvenile character lead of the late seventies.
□Brother Sun, Sister Moon 71. Diamonds on Wheels 73. Aces High 76. Equus 77. Joseph Andrews 77. When You Coming Home, Red Ryder? 79. Tess 80. The Aerodrome (TV) 83. Life Force 85. Letter to Brezhnev 85.

Fischbeck, Harry (–). American cinematographer.
Wives of Men 18. The Devil 21. The Green Goddess 23. Monsieur Beaucaire 24. A Sainted Devil 24. Cobra 25. Sally of the Sawdust 25. That Royle Girl 25. The Sorrows of Satan 26. Serenade 27. Manhattan Cocktail 28. The Canary Murder Case 29. The Mysterious Dr Fu Manchu 29. Ladies Love Brutes 30. The Spoilers 30. Working Girls 31. Lady and Gent 32. Terror Aboard 33. Search for Beauty 34. Double Door 34. Millions in the Air 35. The Jungle Princess 36. John Meade's Woman 37. Bulldog Drummond's Revenge 37. Prison Farm 38. Persons in Hiding 39. Parole Fixer 40, many others.

Fischer, Gunnar (1911–). Swedish cinematographer who has worked on most of Ingmar Bergman's films.
Smiles of a Summer Night 55. The Seventh Seal 56. Wild Strawberries 57. The Face 58. The Devil's Eye 60, etc.

Fischer, O. W. (1915–1973). Leading Austrian actor, in films since 1936 but hardly known outside Germany.
Sommerliebe 42. Seven Letters 44. Heidelberger Romanze 51. Der Traumende Mund 52. The Heart Plays False 53. Ludwig II (title role) 54. El Hakim 57. Arms and the Man 58. Uncle Tom's Cabin 65, many others.

Fischinger, Oskar (1900–1967). German animator who pre-dated *Fantasia* in his attempt to illustrate music with abstract forms.
Composition in Blue 33. Allegretto 36. Motion Painting Number One 47, etc.

Fisher, Carrie (1956–). American leading lady of routine talent, daughter of Debbie Reynolds and Eddie Fisher.
□Shampoo 75. Star Wars 77. Mr Mike's Mondo Video 78. The Empire Strikes Back 80. The Blues Brothers 80. Under the Rainbow 81. Return of the Jedi 83. Hannah and her Sisters 86.

¶ *C.F.:* I always wanted to do what my mother did—get all dressed up, shoot people, fall in the mud. I never considered anything else.

Fisher, Eddie (1928–). American nightclub singer and actor.
Bundle of Joy 56. Butterfield 8 60, etc.

Fisher, Gerry (1926–). British cinematographer.
AS OPERATOR: The Devil's Disciple 59. Suddenly Last Summer 60. Night Must Fall 63. Guns at Batasi 64. Modesty Blaise 66.
AS CINEMATOGRAPHER: Accident 67. Sebastian 68. Interlude 68. The Go-Between 70. Macho Callahan 71. See No Evil 71. The Amazing Mr Blunden 72. A Bequest to the Nation 73. S.P.Y.S. 74. Juggernaut 74. The Romantic Englishwoman 74. Aces High 76. Mr Klein 77. The Last Remake of Beau Geste 77. The Island of Dr Moreau 77. Fedora 78. Don Giovanni 79. Wise Blood 79. The Ninth Configuration 80. Wolfen 81. Victory 81. Yellowbeard 82. The Holcroft Covenant 84. Highlander 85, etc.

Fisher, Terence (1904–1980). British director, former editor, in films from 1933. Work mainly routine; latterly associated with Hammer horror. Also worked for TV, especially *Douglas Fairbanks Presents.*
To the Public Danger 47. Portrait from Life 48. Marry Me 49. The Astonished Heart 49. So Long at the Fair 50. Home to Danger 51. Kill Me Tomorrow 55. The Curse of Frankenstein 56. Dracula 57. The Hound of the Baskervilles 58. Brides of Dracula 59. The Two Faces of Dr Jekyll 60. The Phantom of the Opera 62. The Gorgon 64. Dracula, Prince of Darkness 65. Island of Terror 66. The Devil Rides Out 68. Frankenstein and the Monster from Hell 73, etc.

Fiske, Minnie Maddern (1866–1932). American stage actress who made two silent films.
□Tess of the D'Urbervilles 13. Vanity Fair 15.

A Fistful of Dollars. The first internationally successful 'spaghetti western', made in Italy in 1964 by Sergio Leone. With a ludicrous plot borrowed from a Japanese

Samurai saga, it made a star of Clint Eastwood as the death-dealing 'man with no name', and was rapidly followed by *For a Few Dollars More, The Good the Bad and the Ugly*, and numerous imitations.

Fisz, Benjamin (1922–). Polish-born independent producer, long in England.
Hell Drivers 57. Sea Fury 58. On the Fiddle 61. Heroes of Telemark (co-p) 65. The Battle of Britain (co-p) 69. A Town Called Bastard 71, etc.

Fitzgerald, Barry (1888–1961) (William Shields). Diminutive Irish character actor who found his way to Hollywood and eventually achieved star status, usually in irascible or whimsical 'Oirish' roles.
□Juno and the Paycock 30. When Knights were Bold 36. *The Plough and the Stars* 36. *Ebb Tide* 37. Bringing Up Baby 38. Marie Antoinette 38. Four Men and a Prayer 38. The Dawn Patrol 38. The Saint Strikes Back 39. Pacific Liner 39. Full Confession 39. *The Long Voyage Home* 40. San Francisco Docks 41. The Sea Wolf 41. How Green Was My Valley 41. Tarzan's Secret Treasure 41. The Amazing Mrs Holliday 43. Two Tickets to London 43. Corvette K225 43. *Going My Way* (AA) 44. I Love a Soldier 44. None but the Lonely Heart 44. Incendiary Blonde 45. *And Then There Were None* 45. Duffy's Tavern 45. The Stork Club 45. Two Years Before the Mast 46. California 46. Easy Come Easy Go 47. Welcome Stranger 47. Variety Girl 47. The Sainted Sisters 48. *The Naked City* 48. Miss Tatlock's Millions 48. Top o' the Morning 49, The Story of Seabiscuit 49. *Union Station* 50. Silver City 51. *The Quiet Man* 52. Happy Ever After 54. The Catered Affair 56. *Rooney* 57. Broth of a Boy 59.

Fitzgerald, Ella (1918–). Black American singer and entertainer.
Ride Em Cowboy 41. Pete Kelly's Blues 55. St Louis Blues 56. Let No Man Write My Epitaph 60, etc.

Fitzgerald, F. Scott (1896–1940). American novelist and chronicler of 'the jazz age'; was played by Gregory Peck in a biopic, *Beloved Infidel*, in 1959. Films of his work include *The Great Gatsby, The Last Tycoon, Tender is the Night*; his one complete screenplay is *Three Comrades*.
In the seventies Fitzgerald was played on TV by Richard Chamberlain and Jason Miller.

Fitzgerald, Geraldine (1912–). Irish leading lady who played in British films from 1935; went to Hollywood in 1939 but had rather disappointing roles. In her sixties made a stage comeback as a folk singer.
Turn of the Tide 35. The Mill on the Floss 36. Dark Victory 39. *Wuthering Heights* 39. Till We Meet Again 40. Flight from Destiny 41. The Gay Sisters 42. Watch on the Rhine 43. Ladies Courageous 44. *Wilson* 44. Uncle Harry 45. Three Strangers 46. O.S.S. 46. Nobody Lives Forever 47. So Evil My Love (GB) 48. Ten North Frederick 58. The Fiercest Heart 61. The Pawnbroker 65. Rachel Rachel 69. The Last American Hero 73. Harry and Tonto 74. Echoes of a Summer 76. Yesterday's Child (TV) 77. The Quinns (TV) 77. Arthur 81. The Mango Tree 82. Easy Money 83. Kennedy (TV) 83, etc.

Fitzgerald, Walter (1896–1976) (Walter Bond). British character actor, on stage from 1922, films from 1930.
Murder at Covent Garden 30. This England 40. Squadron Leader X 41. Strawberry Roan 45. Mine Own Executioner 47. Treasure Island 50. Pickwick Papers 52. Personal Affair 53. Lease of Life 54. Cockleshell Heroes 55. Something of Value 57. Third Man on the Mountain 59. HMS Defiant 62, others.

Fitzmaurice, George (1885–1941). American director of French origin, noted in the twenties for visual style.
A Society Exile 19. On with the Dance 20. Experience 21. *Belladonna* 23. Cytherea 24. *The Dark Angel* 25. *Son of the Sheik* 26. Rose of the Golden West 27. *Lilac Time* 28. His Captive Woman 29. Tiger Rose 29. The Devil to Pay 30. One Heavenly Night 30. The Unholy Garden 31. Mata Hari 32. As You Desire Me 32. Petticoat Fever 36. The Emperor's Candlesticks 37. Arsène Lupin Returns 38. Adventure in Diamonds 40, many others.

Fitzpatrick, James A. (1902–1980). American documentarist, who from 1925 produced and narrated innumerable travel shorts ('Fitzpatrick Traveltalks'), invariably concluding 'And so we leave . . .' Wrote, produced and directed one feature, *Song of Mexico* 45.

Five Fingers (US 1952). L. C. Moyzich's book *Operation Cicero*, about the British Ambassador in Ankara's valet, who during World War II sold secrets to the Germans, can be credited with the post-war reawakening of interest in spying which led eventually to the Bond spoofs. In Joseph L. Mankiewicz's film, Cicero was played by James Mason. There was a TV series of the same name in 1959 with David Hedison.

Five Graves to Cairo (US 1943). Spy story set in the African desert in 1943 and using Rommel as a chief character; a remarkable illustration of writer-director Billy Wilder's penchant for turning headlines into entertainment. Also boasts an ingenious plot and a fascinating performance by Erich von Stroheim.

Five Star Final (US 1932). A famous melodrama of the hardboiled newspaperman school, about a ruthless editor whose probing of a long-dead scandal drives two people to suicide. Directed by Mervyn le Roy, from a play by Louis Weitzenkorn; with Edward G. Robinson.

Fix, Paul (1901–1983) (Paul Fix Morrison). American general purpose actor who played hundreds of sheriffs, ranchers, doctors, etc., from the twenties.
The First Kiss 28. Ladies Love Brutes 30. The Last Mile 32. Zoo in Budapest 33. Little Man What Now? 34. Prisoner of Shark Island 36. Souls at Sea 37. News is Made at Night 39. The Ghost Breakers 40. In Old Oklahoma 43. Dakota 45. Tycoon 47. California Passage 50. Hondo 53. The High and the Mighty 54. Blood Alley 55. Giant 56. To Kill a Mockingbird 63. Shenandoah 65. Nevada Smith 66. El Dorado 67. The Day of the Evil Gun 68. Something Big 71. Grayeagle 77. Wanda Nevada 80, many others.
TV series: The Rifleman 57–61.

The Flag Lieutenant. The stiff-upper-lip stage melodrama by W. P. Drury and Lee Trevor, about the intrepid exploits of a naval officer in an outpost of empire, was filmed as a silent in 1919 with George Wynn, and in 1926 with Henry Edwards. In 1932 Edwards appeared in a sound remake, his leading lady being Anna Neagle.

Flagg, Fannie (–). American TV comedienne, notably in *The New Dick Van Dyke Show.*
Five Easy Pieces 70. Some of My Best Friends Are 71. Stay Hungry 76. Sex and the Married Woman (TV) 77. Rabbit Test 78. Grease 78, etc.

Flagstad, Kirsten (1895–1962). Norwegian operatic soprano whose only film appearance was, surprisingly, in *The Big Broadcast of 1938.*

Flaherty, Robert (1884–1951). Very influential American documentary pioneer, originally an explorer; noted for superb visual sense.
Biography 1963: *The Innocent Eye* by Arthur Calder-Marshall.
□*Nanook of the North* 20. The Pottery Maker 25. Moana (co-d) 26. 24-Dollar Island 27. *White Shadows in the South Seas* (co-d) 28. Tabu (co-d) 31. Industrial Britain (co-d) 33. *Man of Aran* 34. *Elephant Boy* (co-d) 37. The Land 42. Louisiana Story 48.

¶ His films slip so easily into the stream of fictional cinema that they hardly seem like documentaries at all.—*Andrew Sarris*

Flanagan, Bud (1896–1968) (Robert Winthrop). Genial British comedian, long teamed with Chesney Allen (qv for list of films); they formed part of the Crazy Gang. Wrote and sang catchy, sentimental songs: 'Hometown', 'Underneath the Arches', 'Umbrella Man', 'Strolling'.

Flanagan, Fionnula (or **Fionnuala**) (–). Irish-American character actress, mostly in TV.
Ulysses 67. *Rich Man Poor Man* (TV) 76. Nightmare in Badham County (TV) 76. Mary White (TV) 77. Young Love First Love (TV) 79. Mr Patman 80. Through Naked Eyes (TV) 83. Scorned and Swindled (TV) 84, etc.
TV series: How the West Was Won 79.

Flanders, Ed (1934–). American character actor and Truman impersonator.
Goodbye Raggedy Ann (TV) 71. Indict and Convict (TV) 74. The Legend of Lizzie Borden (TV) 75. Eleanor and Franklin (TV) 76. *The Amazing Howard Hughes* (TV) 77. MacArthur 77. Collision Course (TV) 77. Backstairs at the White House (TV) 79. The Ninth Configuration 80. Salem's Lot (TV) 80. True Confessions 81. The Pursuit of D. B. Cooper 81, many others.

Flannery, Susan (1943–). American general purpose actress, from TV soap opera *Days of Our Lives.*
The Towering Inferno 74. The Moneychangers (TV) 76. The Gumball Rally 76. Anatomy of a Seduction (TV) 79. Women in White (TV) 79, etc.

Flash Gordon. American newspaper strip hero whose exploits were featured in three famous Hollywood serials starring Buster Crabbe. In the original *Flash Gordon* 36 our hero and his friends saved the Earth from collision with another planet at the cost of being stranded there at the mercy of the wicked Emperor Ming. *Flash Gordon's Trip to Mars* 38 and *Flash Gordon Conquers the Universe* 40 were compounded of similar elements. The directors respectively were Frederick Stephani; Ford Beebe and Robert Hill; and Ray Taylor. A softcore spoof, *Flesh Gordon*, appeared in 1974. In 1980 Dino de Laurentiis presented a lavish but empty remake of the original, and in the following year came a cartoon remake from Filmation.

flashback: a break in chronological narrative during which we are shown events of past time which bear on the present situation. The device is as old as the cinema: you could say that *Intolerance* was composed of four flashbacks. As applied to more commonplace yarns, however, with the flashback narrated by one of the story's leading characters, the convention soared into popularity in the thirties until by 1945 or so a film looked very dated indeed if it was not told in retrospect. In the fifties flashbacks fell into absolute disuse, but are now creeping back into fashion again. Some notable uses are:

The Power and the Glory 33, which was advertised as being in 'Narratage' because Ralph Morgan spoke a commentary over the action. *Bride of Frankenstein* 35, which was narrated by Elsa Lanchester as Mary Shelley; the gag was that she also played the monster's mate. *The Great McGinty* 40, in which the flashback construction revealed the somewhat corrupt leading figures finally as penniless, thus mollifying the Hays Office. *Rebecca* 40, in which the introductory narrative, while revealing that Manderley was to go up in flames, also comforted in the knowledge that the hero and heroine would be saved. *Citizen Kane* 41, the complex structure of which was so influential that a whole host of pictures followed in which we tried to get at the truth about a character already dead, by questioning those who knew him: cf. *The Killers, The Rake's Progress, The Moon and Sixpence, The Bridge of San Luis Rey, The Woman in Question, Letter from an Unknown Woman, Rashomon, The Great Man*, even *Doctor Zhivago*. *Hold Back the Dawn* 41, in which Charles Boyer as a penniless refugee visited Paramount Studios and sold his story to Mitchell Leisen. *The Mummy's Hand* 41, in which the ten-minute chunk telling how the mummy came to be buried alive was lifted straight from the 1932 film *The Mummy*. (Such economies have become commonplace.) *Roxie Hart* 42, in which George Montgomery told a twenty-year-old tale about a notorious lady who at the end of the film was revealed as the mother of his large family. *Ruthless* 48, a tortuous Zachary Scott melodrama, reviewed as follows by the British critic C. A. Lejeune:

Beginning pictures at the end
Is, I'm afraid, a modern trend;
But I'd find *Ruthless* much more winning
If it could end at the beginning.

Road to Utopia 45, in which Hope and Lamour appeared as old folks telling the story; as a pay-off their 'son' appeared, looking just like Crosby, and Hope told the audience: 'We adopted him.' *Passage to Marseilles* 44, a complex melodrama ranging from Devil's Island to war-torn Britain; it has flashbacks within flashbacks *within flashbacks*. In *Dead of Night* 45, all the characters told supernatural experiences to a psychiatrist, who was then murdered by one of them; the murderer then woke up with no recollection of his nightmare, and proceeded to meet all the other characters again as though for the first time, being caught in an endless series of recurring dreams. *Enchantment* 47, and later *Death of a Salesman* 52, and many films up to *I Was Happy Here* 66, in which characters walk straight out of the present into the past, dispensing with the boring 'I remember' bit. *Edward My Son* 49 and *Teahouse of the August Moon* 56, in which characters step out of the play to tell the story to the audience. *Dead Reckoning* 47, in which Humphrey Bogart confesses the entire plot to a priest. *Kind Hearts and Coronets* 49, in which the story springs from the memoirs of a murderer being written on the night before his execution. *Sunset Boulevard* 50, in which the story is told by the dead hero. *An Inspector Calls* 54, in which a supernatural figure visits a family to make them remember their harsh treatment of a girl who has committed suicide. *Repeat Performance* 47, in which a desperate husband relives the events of the year, leading up to his predicament, and gets a chance to change the outcome. *A Woman's Face* 41, in which the story was based on the recollections of eight courtroom witnesses. *The Locket* and *Lust for Gold*, in which complex flashbacks framed and divided the action.

If the format is to catch on again it will have to be more deftly used than in two sixties films: *Ride Beyond Vengeance*, with its completely irrelevant framing story about a census-taking, and *Lady L*, in which the framing story with the characters as old folks is only marginally less inept than the basic one. Two big-scale musicals, *Star!* and *Funny Girl,* have flashbacks with style but little purpose, and *Little Big Man* barely used its framework except to show that Dustin Hoffman can play a 121-year-old.

? It used to be fashionable to tell stories in retrospect. Name the films which had their stories narrated by:

1 A dead man floating in a pool.
2 Humphrey Bogart, to a priest.
3 Brian Donlevy, while tending bar.
4 Charles Boyer, to Mitchell Leisen.
5 Joan Fontaine, as a character with no first name.
6 Herbert Marshall, as a famous author.
7 A house.
8 Alec Guinness, in South America.
9 George Montgomery, to a barman.
10 Robert Benchley, mostly in insets.
11 Spencer Tracy, straight to camera.
12 Marlon Brando, straight to camera.
13 Dennis Price, via his character's memoirs.
14 Flora Robson, to Miles Mander.

Flavin, James (1906–1976). Irish-American supporting actor, usually as genial or bewildered cop.
King Kong 33. The Grapes of Wrath 40. Cloak and Dagger 46. Desert Fury 47. Mighty Joe Young 50. Fighter Attack 53. Mister Roberts 55. The Last Hurrah 58. It's a Mad Mad Mad Mad World 63. Cheyenne Autumn 64. Bullwhip Griffin 67, many others.

fleapit. An affectionate British term for the kind of tatty little cinema in which, it was sometimes alleged, the management loaned a hammer with each ticket.

Fleischer, Max (1889–1972). Austrian-born cartoonist and producer, long in Hollywood. Created Betty Boop, Koko, Out of the Inkwell series, Popeye the Sailor, etc. His brother **Dave Fleischer** (1894–1979) worked as his administrative head.
Gulliver's Travels 39. Mr Bug Goes to Town 41.

Fleischer, Richard (1916–). American director, son of Max Fleischer; former shorts producer. His films usually sound more interesting than they prove to be.
□Child of Divorce 46. Banjo 47. Bodyguard 48. So This Is New York 49. Make Mine Laughs 49. Trapped 49. Follow Me Quietly 49. The Clay Pigeon 49. The Armored Car Robbery 50. *The Narrow Margin* 51. *The Happy Time* 52. Arena 53. *Twenty Thousand Leagues under the Sea* 54. Violent Saturday 55. The Girl in the Red Velvet Swing 55. Bandido 56. Between Heaven and Hell 56. *The Vikings* 57. These Thousand Hills 58. Compulsion 59. Crack in the Mirror 60. The Big Gamble 61. Barabbas 62. *Fantastic Voyage* 66. Doctor Dolittle 67. *The Boston Strangler* 68. Che! 69. Tora! Tora! Tora! 70. The Last Run 70. Blind Terror 70. The New Centurions 71. 10 Rillington Place 71. Soylent Green 72. The Don is Dead 73. Mr Majestyk 74. The Spikes Gang 74. Mandingo 75. The Incredible Sarah 76. The Prince and the Pauper 77. Ashanti 78. The Jazz Singer 80. Tough Enough 82. Amityville 3D 83. Conan, King of Thieves 84. Conan the Destroyer 85. Red Sonja 86. Million Dollar Mystery 87.

Fleming, Eric (1924–1966). Taciturn American general purpose actor.
Conquest of Space 55. Fright 57. Curse of the Undead 59. The Glass Bottom Boat 66, etc.
TV series: *Rawhide* (as Gil Favor, trail boss) 58–65.

Fleming, Ian (1888–1969). Australian-born character actor, long in British films as doctors, civil servants, solicitors, etc. A memorable Dr Watson in the thirties series with Arthur Wontner as Sherlock Holmes.
Second to None 26. The School for Scandal 30. The Sleeping Cardinal 31. The Missing Rembrandt 32. The Triumph of Sherlock Holmes 35. The Crouching Beast 35. Jump for Glory 37. The Nursemaid who Disappeared 39. The Butler's Dilemma 43. George in Civvy Street 45. Quartet 48. The Woman in Question 50. The Voice of Merrill 52. The Seekers 54. High Flight 57. Bluebeard's Ten Honeymoons 60. No My Darling Daughter 61. The Boys 63. The Return of Mr Moto 65, many others.

Fleming, Ian (1906–1964). Creator of James Bond, whose exploits have been so successfully filmed from the novels.

Fleming, Rhonda (1922–) (Marilyn Louis). Red-haired American leading lady of the forties and fifties.
When Strangers Marry 43. Spellbound 45. The Spiral Staircase 45. Adventure Island 46. Out of the Past (Build My Gallows High) 47. A Yankee in King Arthur's Court 49. Cry Danger 50. The Redhead and the Cowboy 51.

The Great Lover 51. Little Egypt 52. The Golden Hawk 52. Serpent of the Nile 53. Inferno 53. Yankee Pasha 54. The Killer Is Loose 56. Slightly Scarlet 56. Gunfight at the OK Corral 57. Gun Glory 57. Home Before Dark 58. Alias Jesse James 59. The Big Circus 59. Run For Your Wife 66. The Nude Bomb 80, etc.

Fleming, Victor (1883–1949). American director, long with MGM: he was in charge of a few outstanding films, but they seemed to succeed for other reasons.
□When the Clouds Roll By 20. The Mollycoddle 20. Mamma's Affair 21. Woman's Place 22. Red Hot Romance 22. The Lane That Had No Turning 22. Anna Ascends 22. Dark Secrets 23. Law of the Lawless 23. To the Last Man 23. Call of th. Canyon 23. Empty Hands 24. The Code of the Sea 24. A Son of His Father 25. Adventure 25. The Devil's Cargo 25. Lord Jim 25. The Blind Goddess 26. *Mantrap* 26. Rough Riders 27. The Way of all Flesh 27. Hula 27. Abie's Irish Rose 28. The Awakening 28. Wolf Song 29. *The Virginian* 29. Common Clay 30. Renegades 30. Around the World in Eighty Minutes 31. *The Wet Parade* 32. *Red Dust* 32. The White Sister 33. Bombshell 33. *Treasure Island* 34. Reckless 35. The Farmer Takes a Wife 35. Captains Courageous 37. *Test Pilot* 38. *The Wizard of Oz* 39. *Gone with the Wind* (AA) (with assistance) 39. *Dr Jekyll and Mr Hyde* 41. Tortilla Flat 42. A Guy Named Joe 43. Adventure 45. Joan of Arc 48.

Flemyng, Gordon (1934–). British director, from TV.
Solo for Sparrow 62. Five to One 63. Dr Who and the Daleks 65. Great Catherine 68. The Split 68. The Last Grenade 69, etc.

Flemyng, Robert (1912–). British actor who usually plays attractive professional men. On stage from 1931, films from 1936 (*Head Over Heels*).
The Guinea Pig 49. The Blue Lamp 50. The Holly and the Ivy 52. The Man Who Never Was 55. Funny Face (US) 56. Windom's Way 57. A Touch of Larceny 59. The Terror of Dr Hitchcock (It.) 63. The Deadly Affair 66. The Spy with a Cold Nose 67. The Blood Beast Terror 67. Young Winston 72. Travels with my Aunt 73. The Medusa Touch 77. The 39 Steps 78, etc.

Flesh and Fantasy (US 1943). One of the earliest compendiums of short stories, linked only by the ramblings of a club bore. In this case, unfortunately; the stories were poorly chosen, and Julien Duvivier's direction somewhat flavourless. The form did not achieve any popularity until 1948 with Somerset Maugham's *Quartet*, and then after three or four years of all-star casts in tenuously linked anecdotes, the advent of television playlets killed the idea stone dead. See also: *Tales of Manhattan*.

Fletcher, Bramwell (1904–). British light leading man of the thirties.
Chick 30. To What Red Hell 30. Raffles (US) 31. Svengali (US) 31. The Mummy (US) 32. The Scarlet Pimpernel 34. Random Harvest (US) 42. White Cargo (US) 42. The Immortal Sergeant (US) 42, etc.

Fletcher, Cyril (1913–). British comedian and entertainer who has made appearances in a few films: *Yellow Canary* 43. *Nicholas Nickleby* 47. *A Piece of Cake* 48, etc.

Fletcher, Louise (1936–). American character actress.
Thieves Like Us 74. Russian Roulette 75. *One Flew Over the Cuckoo's Nest* (AA) 75. Exorcist II: The Heretic 77. *The Cheap Detective* 78. Thou Shalt Not Commit Adultery (TV) 78. The Lady in Red 79 Natural Enemies 79. The Magician of Lublin 79. The Lucky Star 80. Mama Dracula (Fr.) 80. Strange Behaviour 81. *Brainstorm* 83. Firestarter 84. The Boy Who Could Fly 85. Invaders from Mars 86, etc.

Flicker, Theodore J. (c. 1929–). American director, former Greenwich Village satirist.
The Troublemaker 64. The President's Analyst 68. Up in the Cellar (& w) 70. Playmates (TV) 72. Guess Who's Sleeping in My Bed (TV) 73. Just a Little Inconvenience (TV) 77. Last of the Good Guys (& w) 78. Where the Ladies Go (TV) 80. Soggy Bottom USA 82, etc.

Flippen, Jay C. (1898–1971). Bulky American character actor with vaudeville background; often seen as cop, sergeant or sheriff.
Marie Galante 34. Intrigue 48. Love that Brute 50. Flying Leathernecks 51. Bend of the River 52. The Wild One 53. The Far Country 55. Oklahoma 55. *The Killing* 56. Night Passage 57. From Hell to Texas 58.

Studs Lonigan 60. Cat Ballou 65. Firecreek 67. Hellfighters 68. The Seven Minutes 71, many others.
TV series: Ensign O'Toole 62.

Flon, Suzanne (1923–). French leading actress.
La Cage aux Filles 49. La Belle Image 51. Moulin Rouge 53. Mr Arkadin 55. *Thou Shalt Not Kill* 61. A Monkey in Winter 62. The Trial 62. The Train 64. Le Soleil des Voyous 67. Le Silencieux 73. Mr Klein 76. Blackout 77. Comme un Boomerang 77. L'Eté meurtrier 83, etc.

Florey, Robert (1900–79) French-born director, in Hollywood since 1921.
The Romantic Age 27. The Coconuts 29. *The Murders in the Rue Morgue* 32. Ex Lady 33. The Woman in Red 34. Hollywood Boulevard 36. Hotel Imperial 38. The Face Behind the Mask 40. Lady Gangster 42. Dangerously They Live 43. God Is My Co-Pilot 44. *The Beast with Five Fingers* 46. Monsieur Verdoux (co-d) 47. Rogues' Regiment 48. Outpost in Morocco 48. Johnny One Eye 49. The Gangster We Made 50, many second features; latterly directed hundreds of TV films. Also wrote several scripts, including work on *Frankenstein* 31.

Flowers, Bess (1900–87). American bit part player, 'queen of the Hollywood extras', who appeared in literally hundreds of films between 1922 and 1962.

Fluellen, Joel (–). Black American character actor.
Two Guys from Milwaukee 46. The Burning Cross 47. You're in the Navy Now 51. Affair in Trinidad 52. The Decks Ran Red 59. A Raisin in the Sun 61. The Chase 66. The Skin Game 71. The Bingo Long Travelling All Stars and Motor Kings 76, many others.

The Fly (US 1958). An unpleasant horror film given big studio treatment in lieu of taste and style, based on an unfortunate mix-up during transmission through space of human and insect atoms. David (then Al) Hedison was the unfortunate victim. There were two sequels: *Return of the Fly* 60 and *Curse of the Fly* 64.

Flying Down to Rio (US 1933). The musical that started the Astaire-Rogers cycle; also notable for a brilliantly-photographed finale with chorus girls on the wings of flying aeroplanes. Nominal stars Dolores del Rio and Gene Raymond; directed by Thornton Freeland.

Flynn, Errol (1909–1959). Tasmanian leading man who led an adventurous life on and off screen and by his handsome impudence maintained a world-wide following for nearly twenty years before hard living got the better of him. Wrote two autobiographical books, *Beam Ends* (1934) and *My Wicked Wicked Ways* (1959), and a novel, *Showdown* (1952); one of several biographies was *The Life and Crimes of Errol Flynn* (1977) by Lionel Godfrey.
□In the Wake of the Bounty (as Fletcher Christian) 33. Murder at Monte Carlo (GB) 34. The Case of the Curious Bride 34. Don't Bet on Blondes 35. *Captain Blood* 35. *The Charge of the Light Brigade* 36. The Green Light 36. The Prince and the Pauper 37. Another Dawn 37. The Perfect Specimen 37. *The Adventures of Robin Hood* 38. Four's a Crowd 38. The Sisters 38. *The Dawn Patrol* 38. Dodge City 39. Elizabeth and Essex 39. Virginia City 39. *The Sea Hawk* 40. Santa Fe Trail 40. Footsteps in the Dark 41. Dive Bomber 41. *They Died with Their Boots On* 41. Desperate Journey 42. *Gentleman Jim* 42. Edge of Darkness 43. Northern Pursuit 43. Thank Your Lucky Stars 43. Uncertain Glory 44. Objective Burma 45. San Antonio 45. Never Say Goodbye 45. Cry Wolf 46. Escape Me Never 47. Silver River 47. The New Adventures of Don Juan 48. *That Forsyte Woman* (as Soames) 49. Montana 50. Rocky Mountain 50. Kim 51. The Adventures of Captain Fabian (& w) 51. Mara Maru 52. Against All Flags 52. The Master of Ballantrae (GB) 53. Crossed Swords (It.) 53. Lilacs in the Spring (GB) 55. The Dark Avenger (GB) 55. King's Rhapsody (GB) 56. The Big Boodle 56. Istanbul 57. The Sun Also Rises 57. *Too Much Too Soon* (as John Barrymore) 58. Roots of Heaven 58. Cuban Rebel Girls 59.
TV series: Errol Flynn Theatre 57.
†He made an uncredited cameo appearance in Always Together 47.
❁ For living several lives in half of one, and almost getting away with it. *The Adventures of Robin Hood.*

¶ He was one of the wild characters of the world

said Ann Sheridan. His wicked wicked ways were well known, but nobody ever admitted to disliking him for them; perhaps because, as Jack L. Warner said:

> To the Walter Mittys of the world he was all the heroes in one magnificent, sexy, animal package.

Henry King's view was that

He loved to talk about how much he could drink and the women he'd made love to, but most of it was just the rationalizations of a disappointed moralist.

Old drinking cronies like David Niven (who shared with him a house called Cirrhosis-by-the-sea) and Peter Finch later talked of him with affection. Lewis Milestone perhaps exaggerated slightly when he said:

His faults harmed no one but himself.

But even the people he did jar against seem to have borne him little ill-will, with the possible exception of the Australian creditors from whom he escaped before going to Hollywood. In a later broadcast to the people down under, he said jovially:

If there's anyone listening to whom I owe money, I'm prepared to forget it if you are.

Gene Autry said:

He spent more time on a bar stool, or in court, or in the headlines, or in bed, than anyone I knew.

And David Niven summed up his own experience:

The great thing about Errol was that you knew precisely where you were with him—because he *always* let you down.

Famous line (*The Adventures of Robin Hood*): It's injustice I hate, not the Normans.

Famous line (*Desperate Journey*): Now for Australia and a crack at those Japs!

A lot of people certainly looked at him and tut-tutted. Herbert Wilcox thought that:

His love of life defeated his ability as an artist.

And Leslie Mallory described his life as:

A fifty-year trespass against good taste.

There were other ways of looking at his behaviour. One of his wives, Nora Eddington, said rather proudly:

He wasn't afraid of anything, particularly if there was a challenge to it.

Some of the things he did were a reaction against being under-employed:

I felt like an impostor, taking all that money for reciting ten or twelve lines of nonsense a day.

He defended himself blithely:

The public has always expected me to be a playboy, and a decent chap never lets his public down.

And:

Women won't let me stay single, and I won't let myself stay married.

He exaggerated cheerfully in the cause of publicity:

I allow myself to be understood as a colourful fragment in a drab world.

But he was determined to have a good time:

I'll live this half of my life, I don't care about the other half.

He gleefully acknowledged his troubles:

My difficulty is trying to reconcile my gross habits with my net income.

And at the end he could say:

I've had a hell of a lot of fun, and I've enjoyed every minute of it.

At his passing, Tony Britton cabled Trevor Howard:

Old Errol died laughing. Can you beat that?

? In which film did Errol Flynn:

1 Play a role subsequently played by Doug McClure?
2 Play an Indian?
3 Wear hornrimmed glasses?
4 Dress up as Santa Claus?
5 Take part in a gunfight in the Alamo?
6 Play a French criminal condemned to the guillotine?
7 Capture Nazis in the Canadian Arctic?
8 Play a Norwegian patriot?
9 Play a medical researcher into aviation hazards?
10 Expose a murderous dentist?
11 Duel with Henry Daniell (and his double)?
12 Defeat Humphrey Bogart, who was playing a half-breed outlaw?
13 Take a role originally played by Richard Barthelmess?
14 Kill Alan Hale in a duel?
15 Get murdered?

Flynn, Joe (1925–74). American character comedian, much on TV.
Did You Hear the One about the Travelling Saleslady? 68. Million Dollar Duck 71. Superdad 74, etc.
TV series: McHale's Navy 62–65.

Flynn, John (–). American director.
□The Sergeant 68. The Jerusalem File 72. The Outfit 73. Rolling Thunder 77. Defiance 80. Marilyn, the Untold Story (TV) 80. Touched 83.

Flynn, Sean (1941–70). Athletic American leading man, son of Errol Flynn.
Son of Captain Blood 62. Duel at Rio Grande 62. Five Ashore in Singapore, etc.

Foch, Nina (1924–). Cool, blonde, Dutch-born actress, long in America. Also associate

director of George Stevens' *The Diary of Anne Frank*.
□The Return of the Vampire 43. Nine Girls 43. Cry of the Werewolf 44. Shadows in the Night 44. A Song to Remember 44. I Love a Mystery 44. Escape in the Fog 45. Prison Ship 45. *My Name Is Julia Ross* 45. Johnny o'Clock 46. The Guilt of Janet Ames 48. The Dark Past 49. Undercover Man 50. *An American in Paris* 51. Young Man with Ideas 51. Scaramouche 52. Fast Company 53. Sombrero 53. *Executive Suite* 54. Four Guns to the Border 54. You're Never Too Young 55. Illegal 55. The Ten Commandments 56. Three Brave Men 57. Spartacus 60. Cash McCall 60. Prescription Murder (TV) 67. Gidget Grows Up (TV) 69. Such Good Friends 71. Female Artillery (TV) 73. Salty 73. The Great Houdinis (TV) 76. Mahogany 76. Jennifer 78.

fog has been a godsend to many a cinematic entertainment, whether it's the genuine pea-souper inseparable from Hollywood's idea of London, or the ankle-high white mist which used to distinguish heaven and dream sequences. Fog can provide a splendid dramatic background, especially in horror-thrillers like *Dracula, The Wolf Man* and *The Cat and the Canary*; but too often it is simply imposed on a film to force a particular atmosphere, as in *Footsteps in the Fog, Fog over Frisco, Fog Island, Winterset, Out of the Fog* and *The Notorious Landlady. Barbary Coast* seemed to be permanently enveloped in fog, as did the village in *Sherlock Holmes and the Scarlet Claw*: while in *The Adventures of Sherlock Holmes* London had fog in May! Fog was dramatically used in *The VIPs* and *The Divorce of Lady X* (for bringing people together in a hotel); in *The Runaway Bus* (for bringing people together in an abandoned village); in *Midnight Lace* (for masking the identity of the voice threatening Doris Day); in *Twenty-Three Paces to Baker Street* (for hampering the villain but not the blind hero); in *Alias Nick Beal* (as a background for the devil's materialization); in *The Lost Continent* (as a nauseous yellow background for the weird community); in *Random Harvest* (as a means for the hero's escape); and in the various versions of *The Sea Wolf* (for causing the accident that brings hero and heroine together on Wolf Larsen's boat). Even comedies find it useful: the chase through fog in *After the Fox* results in happy confusion. Oddly enough John Carpenter's film *Fog* made insufficient use of its titular commodity.

Folies Bergère. This innocuous 1935 musical comedy was written by Bess Meredith and Hal Long as a vehicle for Maurice Chevalier, who played a dual role; at the climax his double had to masquerade to his wife as himself. It was too good an idea not to be used again. In 1941 came *That Night in Rio* with Don Ameche; in 1951 *On the Riviera* with Danny Kaye. Kaye apparently liked it so much that he had it altered a little and it served for *On The Double* 61, as well.

Folsey, George J. (1898–). American cinematographer.
The Fear Market 20. Born Rich 24. *Applause* 29. The Smiling Lieutenant 31. Reckless 35. *The Great Ziegfeld* 36. The Shining Hour 38. Lady Be Good 41. Meet Me in St Louis 44. A Guy Named Joe 44. Under the Clock 45. The Green Years 46. Green Dolphin Street 47. State of the Union 48. Take Me Out to the Ball Game 48. The Great Sinner 49. *Adam's Rib* 49. Man with a Cloak 51. Million Dollar Mermaid 53. Executive Suite 54. Seven Brides for Seven Brothers 55. The Fastest Gun Alive 56. Imitation General 58. I Passed for White 60. The Balcony 63, etc.

Fonda, Henry (1905–1982). American leading actor who used to play gauche young fellows and graduated to roles of amiable wisdom. Long stage experience; father of Jane and Peter Fonda.
□The Farmer Takes a Wife 35. Way Down East 35. I Dream Too Much 36. The Trail of the Lonesome Pine 36. *The Moon's Our Home* 36. Spendthrift 36. Wings of the Morning (GB) 37. You Only Live Once 37. Slim 37. That Certain Woman 37. I Met My Love Again 37. Jezebel 38. Blockade 38. Spawn of the North 38. The Mad Miss Manton 38. Jesse James 39. Let Us Live 39. The Story of Alexander Graham Bell 39. *Young Mr Lincoln* 39. Drums Along the Mohawk 39. *The Grapes of Wrath* 40. Lilian Russell 40. The Return of Frank James 40. Chad Hanna 40. *The Lady Eve* 41. Wild Geese Calling 41. You Belong to Me 41. The Male Animal 42. Rings on Her Fingers 42. *The Ox Bow Incident* 43. The Big Street 42. Tales of Manhattan 42. The Magnificent Dope 42. The Immortal Sergeant 42; war service; *My Darling Clementine* (as Wyatt Earp) 46. The Long Night 47. The Fugitive 47. Daisy Kenyon 47. On Our Merry Way 48. Fort Apache 48; long absence on stage; Mister Roberts 55. The Wrong Man 56. War and Peace 56. *Twelve Angry Men* (BFA) (& p) 57. *Stage Struck* 57. The Tin Star 57.

Warlock 59. The Man Who Understood Women 59. Advise and Consent 61. The Longest Day 62. How the West Was Won 62. Spencer's Mountain 63. The Best Man 64. *Fail Safe* 64. The Dirty Game 64. Sex and the Single Girl 64. The Battle of the Bulge 65. The Rounders 65. In Harm's Way 65. Big Hand for a Little Lady 66. Welcome to Hard Times 67. Firecreek 67. Stranger on the Run (TV) 67. Madigan 68. Yours, Mine and Ours 68. The Boston Strangler 68. Once upon a Time in the West 69. Too Late the Hero 69. There Was a Crooked Man 70. The Cheyenne Social Club 70. Sometimes a Great Notion 71. The Red Pony (TV) 72. The Serpent 72. The Alpha Caper (TV) 73. Ash Wednesday 73. My Name is Nobody (It.) 73. Inside Job 75. Midway 76. Captains and the Kings (TV) 76. Tentacles 77. Rollercoaster 77. The Great Smokey Roadblock 78. The Swarm 78. Home to Stay (TV) 78. Fedora 78. Roots: The Next Generations (TV) 79. Wanda Nevada 79. Gideon's Trumpet (TV) 79. City on Fire 79. Meteor 79. *On Golden Pond* (AA) 81.
TV series: The Deputy 59–60. The Smith Family 70–71.

† In 1980 Fonda was given an honorary Oscar 'in recognition of his brilliant accomplishments'.

❁ For being a forty-year paradox: a self-effacing star. *Twelve Angry Men*.

¶ *H.F.:* I ain't really Henry Fonda. Nobody could have that much integrity.
A lean, stringy, dark-faced piece of electricity walked out on the screen and he had me. I believed my own story again.—*John Steinbeck on watching The Grapes of Wrath*

Fonda, Jane (1937–). American leading lady, daughter of Henry Fonda. Stage and modelling experience.
□Tall Story (debut) 60. Walk on the Wild Side 61. The Chapman Report 62. Period of Adjustment 62. In the Cool of the Day 63. Sunday in New York 63. La Ronde 64. Joy House 65. Cat Ballou 65. The Chase 66. Any Wednesday 66. The Game is Over (Fr.) 66. Hurry Sundown 67. Barefoot in the Park 67. Histoires Extraordinaires 67. Barbarella 68. They Shoot Horses Don't They? 69. *Klute* (AA) 71. F.T.A. (& p) 72. Tout va Bien 72. Steelyard Blues 72. A Doll's House 74. The Bluebird 76. Fun with Dick and Jane 77. Julia (BFA) 77. Coming Home (AA) 78. California Suite 78. Comes a Horseman 79. The China Syndrome (BFA) 80. The Electric Horseman 80. Nine to Five 81. On Golden Pond 81. Rollover 81. The Dollmaker (TV) 84. Agnes of God 85. The Morning After 86.

¶ *J.F.:* Being a movie star is not a purpose.
J.F.: I'm hard-working. Honest.

Fonda, Peter (1939–). American actor, son of Henry Fonda.
Tammy and the Doctor 63. The Victors 63. Lilith 64. The Wild Angels 66. The Trip 67. *Easy Rider* (& p) 69. The Last Movie 71. The Hired Hand (& d) 71. Two People 73. Dirty Mary Crazy Larry 74. Open Season 74. Race with the Devil 75. Killer Force 75. Fighting Mad 76. 92 in the Shade 76. Futureworld 76. Outlaw Blues 77. High Ballin' 78. Wanda Nevada (& d) 79. The Hostage Tower (TV) 80. Cannonball Run 81. Split Image 82.

¶ *P.F.:* Civilization has always been a bust.

Fontaine, Joan (1917–) (Joan de Havilland; sister of Olivia). British-born leading actress, in America from childhood. Became typed as a shy English rose; later made efforts to play sophisticated roles. Autobiography 1978: *No Bed of Roses*.
□No More Ladies 35. Quality Street 37. You Can't Beat Love 37. Music for Madame 37. Maid's Night Out 38. A Damsel in Distress 38. Blonde Cheat 38. The Man Who Found Himself 38. The Duke of West Point 38. Sky Giant 38. Gunga Din 39. Man of Conquest 39. The Women 39. *Rebecca* 40. *Suspicion* (AA) 41. This Above All 42. The Constant Nymph 43. *Jane Eyre* 43. *Frenchman's Creek* 44. The Affairs of Susan 45. *From This Day Forward* 46. Ivy 47. The Emperor Waltz 48. Kiss the Blood off My Hands 48. *Letter from an Unknown Woman* 48. You Gotta Stay Happy 48. Born To Be Bad 50. September Affair 50. Darling How Could You? 51. Something To Live For 52. Ivanhoe 52. Decameron Nights (GB) 53. Flight to Tangier 53. The Bigamist 53. Casanova's Big Night 54. Serenade 56. Beyond a Reasonable Doubt 56. Island in the Sun 56. Until They Sail 57. A Certain Smile 58. Tender Is the Night 61. Voyage to the Bottom of the Sea 61. The Devil's Own (The Witches) (GB) 66. The Users (TV) 79.

❁ For successfully playing several variations on what was clearly a limited theme. *Rebecca*.

¶ *J.F.:* If you keep marrying as I do, you learn everybody's hobby.
Famous line (*Rebecca*): Last night I dreamed I went to Manderley again.

Fontanne, Lynn (1887–1983). Celebrated British-born stage actress, long in America and the wife of Alfred Lunt. Never really took to the screen.

□The Man Who Found Himself 25. Second Youth 26. The Guardsman 32. Stage Door Canteen 43.

Foolish Wives (US 1921). Most typical of Erich Von Stroheim's extravagant, overcharged sex dramas, this tragi-farce is set on the Riviera where a family of swindlers prey on rich women. Stroheim wrote, directed, and gives a rapacious performance. Photographer William Daniels.

footage. Length of a film expressed in feet.

For Whom the Bell Tolls (US 1943). Ernest Hemingway's novel about an American living with guerrillas during the Spanish Civil War, and sacrificing his life for their cause, was made by Sam Wood into a disappointingly tedious and self-satisfied film in which the whole cast struck unconvincing attitudes, mostly in broken English. Katina Paxinou won an Oscar for her performance; Gary Cooper and Ingrid Bergman seemed to wish they were elsewhere. The basic situation, incidentally, was borrowed ten years later by a Sterling Hayden second feature called *Fighter Attack*.

Foran, Dick (1910–1979) (Nicholas Foran). Burly American leading man of light comedies and westerns in the early forties; often played the good guy who didn't get the girl.
Stand Up and Cheer 34. Shipmates Forever 35. The Petrified Forest 36. The Perfect Specimen 37. Four Daughters 38. Daughters Courageous 39. The Mummy's Hand 40. Horror Island 41. Butch Minds the Baby 42. He's My Guy 43. Guest Wife 45. Fort Apache 48. El Paso 49. Al Jennings of Oklahoma 51. Chicago Confidential 57. Atomic Submarine 60. Taggart 64, many others.
TV series: OK Crackerby 65.

Forbes, Bryan (1926–) (John Clarke). Lively British small-part actor who became a useful scriptwriter, director and production executive.
Autobiography 1976: *Notes for a Life*.
□AS ACTOR: The Small Back Room 48. All Over the Town 48. Dear Mr Prohack 49. The Wooden Horse 50. Green Grow the Rushes 51. Appointment in London 52. Sea Devils 53. Wheel of Fate 53. The Million Pound Note 54. *An Inspector Calls* 54. Up to his Neck 54. The Colditz Story 54. Passage Home 55. Now and Forever 55. The Quatermass Experiment 55. The Last Man to Hang 55. The Extra Day 56. It's Great to be Young 56. The Baby and the Battleship 56. Satellite in the Sky 56. Quatermass II 57. The Key 58. I Was Monty's Double 58. Yesterday's Enemy 59. *The League of Gentlemen* 59. The Guns of Navarone 61. A Shot in the Dark 64.
□AS WRITER/PRODUCER/DIRECTOR: Cockleshell Heroes (w) 56. The Baby and the Battleship (w) 56. The Black Tent (w) 56. House of Secrets (w) 56. *I Was Monty's Double* (w) 58. The Captain's Table (w) 59. The Angry Silence (w) 59. *The League of Gentlemen* (w) 60. Man in the Moon (w) 60. *Whistle down the Wind* (d) 61. *Only Two Can Play* (w) 62. Station Six Sahara (w) 62. *The L-Shaped Room* (wd) 62. Of Human Bondage (w) 64. The High Bright Sun (w) 64. Seance on a Wet Afternoon (wd) 64. King Rat (wd) 65. The Wrong Box (pd) 66. *The Whisperers* (wd) 67. Deadfall (wd) 67. The Madwoman of Chaillot (d) 69. The Raging Moon (wd) 70. The Stepford Wives (d) 74. The Slipper and the Rose (wd) 76. International Velvet (wd) 78. Sunday Lovers (d part) 80. Jessie (TV) (d) 80. Better Late Than Never 82.

¶ He perpetually pursues the anticliché only to arrive at anticlimax.—*Andrew Sarris, 1968*

I may not have come up the hard way, but I have come up the whole way.—*B.F.*

An actor must have arrogance, conceit . . . I would never have made it as an actor, but I still have that conceit.—*B.F.*

If you treat the production of films like the production of shoes, you end up with Hush Puppies.—*B.F.*

(Of his period as production controller at EMI): I wish Bernie Delfont had had the courage of my convictions more often.—*B.F.*

I knew I was there at Elstree to be shot at, but I never found time to be fitted for a bullet-proof vest.—*B.F.*

Forbes, Mary (1882–1974). British character actress in Hollywood, usually as haughty society lady.
Sunny Side Up 29. A Farewell to Arms 32. Blonde Bombshell 33. Les Misérables 35. Wee Willie Winkie 37. The Awful Truth 37. Always Goodbye 38. You Can't Take It With You 38. The Adventures of Sherlock Holmes 40. This Above All 42. The Picture of Dorian Gray 44. Ivy 47. You Gotta Stay Happy 48. The Ten Commandments 56, many others.

Forbes, Meriel (1913–) (M. Forbes-Robertson). British stage actress, wife of Sir Ralph Richardson.

Borrow a Million 35. Young Man's Fancy 39. Come on George 39. The Gentle Sex 43. The Captive Heart 46. Home at Seven 52. Oh What a Lovely War 69.

Forbes, Ralph (1902–1951) (Ralph Taylor). British leading man who became a Hollywood star in the late twenties.
The Fifth Form at St Dominics (GB) 21. Beau Geste 26. Mr Wu 29. The Trail of '98 30. Bachelor Father 31. Smilin' Through 32. The Barretts of Wimpole Street 33. The Three Musketeers 36. Romeo and Juliet 36. If I Were King 39. Elizabeth and Essex 39. Frenchman's Creek 44, etc.

Forbes, Scott (1921–). Minor American leading man of the fifties.
Rocky Mountain 50. Raton Pass 51. Operation Pacific 51. Subterfuge 68. The Mind of Mr Soames, many others.

Forbidden Paradise (US 1924). Ernst Lubitsch's famous touch was here applied to the love life of Catherine the Great of Russia, as personified by Pola Negri. A milestone in satire, it was not well served by Lubitsch's own sound remake, *A Royal Scandal* (1945).

Forbidden Planet (US 1956). One of the few science-fiction romps to win critical acclaim, this lively futuristic comic strip, directed by Fred M. Wilcox, was actually a reworking of *The Tempest,* with Walter Pidgeon as Morbius/Prospero fighting monsters from his own *id.* His tame robot Robby also appeared in *The Invisible Boy* 57, and reappeared in a 60s TV series, *Lost in Space.*

Forbstein, Leo F. (–1948). American musical director, credited on all Warner sound films up to 1948.

Force of Evil (US 1949). A fascinating and influential little thriller about the numbers racket, written and directed by Abraham Polonsky, who was then lost to Hollywood because of the red witch hunt. Photographed by George Barnes; starring John Garfield.

Ford, Alexander (1908–80). Polish director who made films from 1930. Best known abroad: *The Young Chopin* 51. *Five Boys from Barska Street* 53. *Knights of the Teutonic Order* 60.

Ford, Cecil (1911–1980). Former Irish actor who turned production manager on some notable films: *Moby Dick* 56. *Around the World in Eighty Days* 56. *The Bridge on the River Kwai* 57. *The Inn of the Sixth Happiness* 58. Produced: *The Guns of Navarone* 61. *633 Squadron* 64, others.

Ford, Constance (1929–). American general purpose actress of the fifties.
The Last Hunt 56. A Summer Place 59. Home from the Hill 60. Claudelle Inglish 61. All Fall Down 62. The Cabinet of Caligari 62. The Caretaker 63, etc.

Ford, Dorothy (1923–). Tall American leading lady of the forties and fifties.
An American Romance 44. Here Come the Coeds 45. Love Laughs at Andy Hardy 47. Three Godfathers 49. One Sunday Afternoon 49. Jack and the Beanstalk 52. The High and the Mighty 54, etc.

Ford, Francis (1883–1953) (Francis O'Fearna). American character actor, often seen as grizzled, cheery westerner; formerly star of early silents and serials. Brother of John Ford.
The Deserter 12. The Invader 13. The Broken Coin 15. Charlie Chan's Greatest Case 33. The Informer 35. Prisoner of Shark Island 36. In Old Chicago 38. Drums across the Mohawk 39. Lucky Cisco Kid 40. The Ox-Bow Incident 42. The Big Noise 44. My Darling Clementine 46. Wagonmaster 50. The Sun Shines Bright 52, many others.

Ford, Glenn (1916–) (Gwyllyn Ford). Stocky Canadian-born star of Hollywood dramas; from the early forties he radiated integrity and determination, and continued his stardom into tortured middle-aged roles.
□Heaven with a Barbed Wire Fence 39. My Son is Guilty 39. Convicted Woman 40. Men Without Souls 40. Babies for Sale 40. Blondie Plays Cupid 40. The Lady in Question 40. So Ends Our Night 41. Texas 41. Go West Young Lady 41. The Adventures of Martin Eden 42. Flight Lieutenant 42. The Desperadoes 43. Destroyer 43. *Gilda* 46. A Stolen Life 46. Framed 47. The Mating of Millie 48. The Loves of Carmen 48. The Return of October 48. The Man from Colorado 48. The Undercover Man 49. Mr Soft Touch 49. Lust for Gold 49. The Doctor and the Girl 49. The White Tower 50. Convicted 50. The Redhead and the Cowboy 50. The Flying Missile 50. Follow the Sun 51. The Secret of Convict Lake 51. The Green Glove 52. Affair in Trinidad 52. Young Man with Ideas 52. Time Bomb 53. The Man from the Alamo 53. Plunder of the Sun 53. *The Big*

Heat 53. Appointment in Honduras 53. Human Desire 54. The Americano 55. The Violent Men 55. *The Blackboard Jungle* 55. Interrupted Melody 55. Trial 55. Ransom 56. Jubal 56. *The Fastest Gun Alive* 56. The Teahouse of the August Moon 56. *3.10 to Yuma* 57. Don't Go Near the Water 57. Cowboy 58. *The Sheepman* 58. Imitation General 58. Torpedo Run 58. It Started with a Kiss 59. The Gazebo 59. Cimarron 60. Cry for Happy 61. Pocketful of Miracles 61. The Four Horsemen of the Apocalypse 62. Experiment in Terror 62. Love is a Ball 63. The Courtship of Eddie's Father 63. Advance to the Rear 64. Fate is the Hunter 64. Dear Heart 64. The Rounders 65. The Money Trap 66. Is Paris Burning 66. Rage 67. The Last Challenge 67. A Time for Killing 67. Day of the Evil Gun 68. Heaven with a Gun 69. Smith! 69. Brotherhood of the Bell (TV) 70. Santee 73. Jarrett (TV) 73. The Disappearance of Flight 412 (TV) 74. Punch and Jody (TV) 74. The Greatest Gift (TV) 75. Midway 76. Once an Eagle (TV) 76. Evening in Byzantium (TV) 78. Superman 78. The Sacketts (TV) 79. Beggarman Thief (TV) 80. Happy Birthday to Me 81. Virus 82.
TV series: *Cade's County* 71. Holvak 75.

¶ *G.F.:* If they tried to rush me, I'd always say I've only got one other speed, and it's slower.

Ford, Harrison (1892–1957). American leading man of the silent screen.
The Mysterious Mrs M. 17. Food for Scandal 20. Foolish Wives 22. Janice Meredith 24. That Royle Girl 25. Up in Mabel's Room 26. The Girl in the Pullman 27. Three Weekends 28. Love in High Gear 32, many others.

Ford, Harrison (1942–). American action lead who became a star of major movies in the late seventies.
□Dead Heat on a Merry Go Round 66. A Time for Killing 67. Luv 67. Journey to Shiloh 68. Getting Straight 70. The Intruders (TV) 70. Zabriskie Point 70. American Graffiti 73. The Conversation 74. Dynasty (TV) 76. The Possessed (TV) 77. Heroes 77. *Star Wars* 77. Force Ten from Navarone 78. Apocalypse Now (bit) 79. Hanover Street 79. The Frisco Kid 79. The Empire Strikes Back 80. *Raiders of the Lost Ark* 81. Blade Runner 82. Return of the Jedi 83. Indiana Jones and the Temple of Doom 84. Witness (AAN) 85. The Mosquito Coast 87.

¶ *H.F.:* Before, I was grateful for a job, almost any job. Now, I'm apprehensive, but I know I have other options, and when I ask for the money, they pay it. It's that simple.

H.F.: I don't use any particular method. I'm from the let's pretend school of acting.

Ford, John (1895–1973) (Sean O'Fearna). Distinguished Irish-American director who from 1917 made over 125 features, many of them silent westerns. In the thirties he built up to a handful of incomparable human dramas; in the forties he turned towards roving, brawling, good-natured outdoor action films using a repertory of his favourite actors. His best films are milestones, but he disclaimed any artistic pretensions.
Biography, 1982: *The Unquiet Man* by Dan Ford (grandson).
SELECTED SILENT FILMS: The Tornado 17. A Woman's Fool 18. Bare Fists 19. The Wallop 21. Silver Wings 22. The Face on the Bar Room Floor 23. *The Iron Horse* 24. Lightnin' 25. Three Bad Men 26. Four Sons 28. Mother Machree 28. Riley the Cop 28. Strong Boy 29.
□SOUND FILMS: Black Watch 29. Salute 29. *Men Without Women* 30. Born Reckless 30. Up the River 30. The Seas Beneath 30. The Brat 31. *Arrowsmith* 31. Air Mail 32. Flesh 32. Pilgrimage 33. Doctor Bull 33. *The Lost Patrol* 34. The World Moves On 34. *Judge Priest* 34. *The Whole Town's Talking* 35. *The Informer* (AA) 35. *Steamboat Round the Bend* 35. Prisoner of Shark Island 36. Mary of Scotland 36. The Plough and the Stars 36. Wee Willie Winkie 37. *The Hurricane* 37. Four Men and a Prayer 38. Submarine Patrol 38. *Stagecoach* 39. *Young Mr Lincoln* 39. *Drums Along the Mohawk* 39. *The Grapes of Wrath* 40. The Long Voyage Home 40. *Tobacco Road* 41. *How Green Was My Valley* (AA) 41. Why We Fight and other war documentaries 42–45. They Were Expendable 45. *My Darling Clementine* 46. The Fugitive 47. Fort Apache 48. Three Godfathers 48. *She Wore A Yellow Ribbon* 49. When Willie Comes Marching Home 50. Wagonmaster 50. Rio Grande 50. This is Korea 51. *The Quiet Man* (AA) 52. What Price Glory? 52. Mogambo 53. *The Sun Shines Bright* 54. The Long Gray Line 55. Mister Roberts (co-d) 55. *The Searchers* 56. The Wings of Eagles 57. The Rising of the Moon 57. *The Last Hurrah* 58. Gideon's Day 59. The Horse Soldiers 59. Sergeant Rutledge 60. Two Rode Together 61. The Man Who Shot Liberty Valance 62. How the West Was Won (part) 63. Donovan's Reef 63. Cheyenne Autumn 64. Young Cassidy (part) 64. Seven Women 66.

'He developed his craft in the twenties, achieved dramatic force in the thirties, epic sweep in the forties, and symbolic evocation in the fifties.'—*Andrew Sarris, 1968*

❀ For half-a-dozen simply marvellous films. *The Grapes of Wrath.*

¶ *J.F.:* Anybody can direct a picture once they know the fundamentals. Directing is not a mystery, it's not an art. The main thing about directing is: photograph the people's eyes.

J.F.: It's no good asking me to talk about art.

Arthur Miller, photographer: He never once looked in the camera when we worked together. You see, the man had bad eyes, as long as I knew him, but he was a man whose veins ran with the business.

John M. Smith: Knockabout comedy and tragedy co-exist with perfect ease in his work, which throughout a long career shows a clear development and progression.

Henry Fonda: He had instinctively a beautiful eye for the camera. But he was also an egomaniac.

Charles Higham: His films look entirely different one from another, the style emerging rather from a personal response to people: affectionate, warm, with a rural decency and intimacy.

Ford, Paul (1901–1976) (Paul Ford Weaver). American character actor best known on TV as the harassed colonel in the Bilko series and star of *The Baileys of Balboa.*
The House on 92nd Street 45. Lust for Gold 49. Perfect Strangers 50. *The Teahouse of the August Moon* 56. The Matchmaker 58. Advise and Consent 61. *The Music Man* 62. *Never Too Late* 65. Big Hand for a Little Lady 66. The Russians Are Coming, The Russians Are Coming 66. The Spy with a Cold Nose (GB) 67. The Comedians 67, etc.

Ford, Wallace (1897–1966) (Sam Grundy). British general purpose actor who went to Hollywood in the early thirties and after a few semi-leads settled into character roles.
Freaks 32. Lost Patrol 34. *The Informer* 35. OHMS (GB) 36. The Mummy's Hand 40. Inside the Law 42. Shadow of a Doubt 43. The Green Years 46. Embraceable You 48. *Harvey* 50. The Nebraskan 53. Destry 55. Johnny Concho 56. The Last Hurrah 58. A Patch of Blue 66, etc.
TV series: The Deputy 59.

Forde, Eugene (1898–). American director of second features, former silent screen actor.
Charlie Chan in London 33. Buy Me That Town 41. Berlin Correspondent 42. Jewels of Brandenberg 46. Invisible Wall 47, many others.

Forde, Walter (1896–) (Thomas Seymour). British director, formerly a popular slapstick comedian of the silents: *Wait and See, Would You Believe It*, many shorts, one of which was featured in *Helter Skelter* 49. Directed some high-speed farces and several thrillers and melodramas.
The Silent House 28. Lord Richard in the Pantry 30. *The Ghost Train* 31. Jack's the Boy 32. *Rome Express* 32. Orders Is Orders 33. Jack Ahoy 34. Chu Chin Chow 34. *Bulldog Jack* 35. King of the Damned 35. Land Without Music 36. The Gaunt Stranger 38. The Four Just Men 39. Inspector Hornleigh on Holiday 39. *Saloon Bar* 40. Sailors Three 40. The Ghost Train 41. Atlantic Ferry 41. Charley's Big-Hearted Aunt 41. *It's That Man Again* 42. Time Flies 44. Master of Bankdam 47. Cardboard Cavalier 48, many others.

Foreign Correspondent (US 1940). Hitchcock's first American thriller, a welcome return to his best form apart from the final message: 'Don't let the lights go out all over Europe!' Splendid moments in a Dutch windmill, a crashing aeroplane, and Westminster Cathedral.

the foreign legion has been taken reasonably seriously in the three versions of *Beau Geste*, the two versions of *Le Grand Jeu, Beau Sabreur, China Gate, Rogue's Regiment, Ten Tall Men*, and *The Legion's Last Patrol.* It was sent up something wicked by Laurel and Hardy in *Beau Hunks* and *The Flying Deuces*; by Abbott and Costello *In the Foreign Legion*; and by the Carry On gang in *Follow That Camel.*

Foreman, Carl (1914–84). American writer-producer-director, latterly resident in Britain.
So This Is New York (w) 48. The Clay Pigeon (w) 49. Home of the Brave (w) 49. *Champion* (w) 49. The Men (w) 50. Cyrano de Bergerac (w) 50. *High Noon* (w) 52. *The Bridge on the River Kwai* (w) 57. The Key (wp) 58. *The Guns of Navarone* (wp) 61. The Victors (wpd) 63. Born Free (p) 65. Mackenna's Gold (p) 68. The Virgin Soldiers (p) 69. Young Winston (wp) 72. Force Ten from Navarone (p) 78. When Time Ran Out (co-w) 80.

Foreman, John (–). American producer, former agent.
WUSA 70. They Might Be Giants 71. The

Effect of Gamma Rays on Man in the Moon Marigolds 72. The Life and Times of Judge Roy Bean 72. The Man Who Would Be King 75. The First Great Train Robbery 78, etc.

Forest, Mark (1933–) (Lou Degni). American athlete and gymnast who appeared in many Italian muscle-man epics.
□Goliath and the Dragon 60. Maciste the Mighty (Son of Samson) 60. The Strongest Man in the World 61. Death in the Arena 62. Goliath and the Sins of Babylon 63. The Terror of Rome Against the Son of Hercules 63. Hercules Against the Sons of the Sun 64. The Lion of Thebes 64. Hercules Against the Barbarians 64. Hercules Against the Mongols 64. Kindar the Invulnerable 64.

forest fires have made a roaring climax for many films including *The Blazing Forest, Red Skies of Montana, Guns of the Timberland, The Bluebird, The Big Trees* and *Ring of Fire*. None was more dramatic than the cartoon version in *Bambi*.

Forester, C. S. (1899–1966). British adventure novelist. Works filmed include *Captain Horatio Hornblower, The African Queen, Payment Deferred, The Pride and the Passion* ('The Gun').

Forever and a Day (US 1943). Originally conceived as a World War II charity appeals film called *Let the Rafters Ring*, this all-star production finally consisted of episodes in the life of an English family (and their house) from 1804 to 1942. Many hands were involved in the script, and there was a different director for each episode: René Clair, Edmund Goulding, Cedric Hardwicke, Frank Lloyd, Victor Saville, Robert Stevenson, Herbert Wilcox. Almost every Hollywood-based actor with English connections took part.

Forman, Milos (1932–). Czech director of realistic comedies.
□Peter and Pavla 64. *A Blonde in Love* 65. The Fireman's Ball 68. *Taking Off* (US) 71. *One Flew Over the Cuckoo's Nest* (AA) 75. *Hair* 79. Ragtime 81. Amadeus (AA) 83.

¶ *M.F.:* On *One Flew Over the Cuckoo's Nest*: One of the criteria of casting was that we couldn't afford to have a prick in the company.

Formby, George (1905–1961) (George Booth). British north country comedian with a toothy grin and a ukelele, long popular in music halls.
Biography 1974: *George Formby* by Alan Randal and Ray Seaton.
□Boots Boots (debut) 33. Off the Dole 34. *No Limit* 35. *Keep Your Seats Please* 36. Feather Your Nest 37. *Keep Fit* 37. I See Ice 38. *It's in the Air* 38. Trouble Brewing 39. Come On, George 39. *Let George Do It* 40. Spare a Copper 41. Turned Out Nice Again 41. South American George (dual role) 42. Much Too Shy 42. Get Cracking 43. Bell-Bottom George 43. He Snoops To Conquer 44. I Didn't Do It 45. George in Civvy Street 46.

Forrest, Frederic (–). American leading man of the seventies.
□Where the Legends Die 72. The Don is Dead 74. The Conversation 74. The Gravy Train 74. Larry (TV) 74. Promise Him Anything (TV) 75. Permission to Kill 75. The Missouri Breaks 77. It Lives Again 79. Apocalypse Now 79. The Rose 79. One from the Heart 82. Hammett 82. Saigon—Year of the Cat (TV) 83. Valley Girl 83. The Stone Boy 84. Best Kept Secrets (TV) 84. Return 85. Where are the Children? 85. Season of Dreams 87.

Forrest, Sally (1928–) (Katharine Scully Feeney). American leading lady of the early fifties.
Not Wanted 49. Mystery Street 50. Never Fear 50. Hard Fast and Beautiful 51. Excuse My Dust 51. The Strange Door 51. The Strip 51. Son of Sinbad 55. Ride the High Iron 57, etc.

Forrest, Steve (1924–) (William Forrest Andrews). American leading man, brother of Dana Andrews.
The Bad and the Beautiful 52. Phantom of the Rue Morgue 54. Prisoner of War 54. Bedevilled 55. The Living Idol 57. Heller in Pink Tights 60. The Yellow Canary 63. Rascal 69. The Wild Country 71. Wanted the Sundance Woman (TV) 76. North Dallas Forty 79. The Manions of America (TV) 81. Malibu (TV) 83. Hollywood Wives (TV) 84. Spies Like Us 85, etc.
TV series: The Baron 65. S.W.A.T. 75–76. Dallas 86.

Forst, Willi (1903–1980) (Wilhelm Frohs). Austrian director and actor.
Maskerade (wd) 34. Bel Ami (awd) 39. Operette (awd) 40. Wiener Maedelin (aw) 45. The Sinner (wd) 50. Vienna, City of My Dreams (d) 57, etc.

Forster, Robert (1942–). Sardonic-looking American leading man with echoes of John Garfield.
□*Reflections in a Golden Eye* 67. The Stalking Moon 68. Justine 69. Medium Cool 69. Pieces of Dreams 70. Cover Me Babe 72. Death Squad (TV) 73. The Don Is Dead 73. Nakia (TV) 74. Stunts 77. Avalanche 78. Standing Tall 78. The Black Hole 79. Alligator 80. Vigilante 83. Goliath Awaits (TV) 84.
TV series: *Banyon* 71.

Forster, Rudolph (1884–1968). German leading actor of heavy personality, seen abroad chiefly in *Die Dreigroschenoper* (*The Threepenny Opera*; as Macheath) 32.

Forsyth, Bill (1947–). Scottish writer-director who met with instant success for his small local comedies.
□That Sinking Feeling 80. *Gregory's Girl* 81. Local Hero 83. Housekeeping 87.

Forsyth, Bruce (1927–). Bouncy, beaming, British TV comedian whose film appearances have been scant.
□Star! 68. Hieronymus Merkin 69. The Magnificent Seven Deadly Sins 71. Bedknobs and Broomsticks 71.

Forsyth, Frederick (1938–). British writer of adventure thrillers, most of which have been picked up as screen material: *The Day of the Jackal*, *The Odessa File*, *The Dogs of War*, *The Fourth Protocol*.

¶ *F.F.:* I've yet to be convinced that the film business is a profession for adults.

Forsyth, Rosemary (1944–). American leading actress.
Shenandoah (debut) 65. The War Lord 65. Texas Across the River 66. Where It's At 69. Whatever Happened to Aunt Alice? 69. How Do I Love Thee? 70. City Beneath the Sea (TV) 71. One Little Indian 73. Black Eye 74. Gray Lady Down 78, etc.

Forsythe, John (1918–) (John Freund). Smooth American leading man with Broadway experience.
Destination Tokyo 43. Captive City 52. Escape from Fort Bravo 53. The Trouble with Harry 56. *The Ambassador's Daughter* 56. See How They Run (TV) 64. Kitten with a Whip 65. Madame X 66. In Cold Blood 67. Topaz 69. The Happy Ending 69. Murder Once Removed (TV) 71. The Healers (TV) 75. The Feather and Father Gang (TV) 77. The Users (TV) 79. And Justice For All 79, etc.
TV series: Bachelor Father 57–61. The John Forsythe Show 65. To Rome with Love 69–70. Charlie's Angels (voice only) 76–80. *Dynasty* 81–.

¶ *J.F.:* I can't afford to bulge. Being a 64-year-old sex symbol is a hell of a weight to carry.

Forty-Ninth Parallel (GB 1941). Producer-director team Michael Powell and Emeric Pressburger made this impressive all-star propaganda piece about a stranded submarine-load of Nazis on the run through Canada. Laurence Olivier, Leslie Howard and Anton Walbrook starred as assorted democrats; Eric Portman leapt to stardom as the chief Nazi.

Forty-Second Street (US 1933). Classic 'putting-on-a-show' musical from Hollywood's 'golden age', with a genuine backstage atmosphere and a fairly caustic script. Music by Al Dubin and Harry Warren; directed by Lloyd Bacon with a cast including Warner Baxter, Ruby Keeler, Dick Powell, Ginger Rogers and Bebe Daniels; climaxing in three superb Busby Berkeley production numbers.

Fosse, Bob (1927–87). American dancer who became a Broadway director.
□Give a Girl a Break 52. The Affairs of Dobie Gillis 52. Kiss Me Kate 53. My Sister Eileen (& ch) 55. *The Pajama Game* (ch only) 57. Damn Yankees (ch only) 58. *Sweet Charity* (directed and choreographed) 68. *Cabaret* (d, ch) (AA) 72. Lenny (d) 74. The Little Prince (a only) 75. *All That Jazz* (allegedly based on his life) (d, ch) 79. Star 80 (w, d) 83.

Fossey, Brigitte (1945–). French juvenile actress of the fifties.
Jeux Interdits 52. Le Grand Meaulnes 67. Adieu l'Ami 68. M Comme Mathieu 71. Un Mauvais Fils 80. Enigma 82, etc.

Foster, Barry (1931–). British light actor, usually figuring as comic relief, but popular on TV as the Dutch detective Van der Valk.
Sea of Sand 56. Yesterday's Enemy 59. King and Country 64. The Family Way 66. Robbery 67. Twisted Nerve 68. Ryan's Daughter 70. Frenzy 72. Divorce His Divorce Hers (TV) 73. The Sweeney 77. The Three Hostages (TV) 78. The Wild Geese 78. Smiley's People (TV) 81. A Woman Called Golda (TV) 82. Heat and Dust 83, To Kill a King 84. The Whistle Blower 86, etc.

Foster, Dianne (1928–) (D. Laruska). Canadian leading lady who has made British and American films.
The Quiet Woman (GB) 51. Isn't Life Wonderful? (GB) 53. Drive a Crooked Road (US) 54. The Kentuckian (US) 55. The Brothers Rico (US) 57. Gideon's Day (GB) 58. The Last Hurrah (US) 58. King of the Roaring Twenties (US) 61. Who's Been Sleeping in My Bed (US) 63, etc.

Foster, Jodie (1962–). American child actress who has been precociously cast.
Tom Sawyer 73. One Little Indian 73. *Alice Doesn't Live Here Any More* 74. *Bugsy Malone* 76. *Taxi Driver* 76. The Little Girl Who Lives Down the Lane 76. Candleshoe 77. Freaky Friday 77. Carny 80. Foxes 80. O'Hara's Wife 81. Svengali (TV) 82. The Blood of Others 84. Hotel New Hampshire 84. Five Corners 87, etc.
TV series: Bob and Carol and Ted and Alice 73. Paper Moon 74.

Foster, Julia (1941–). British leading lady.
The Small World of Sammy Lee 63. Two Left Feet 63. The System 64. The Bargee 64. One-Way Pendulum 64. Alfie 66. Half a Sixpence 67. All Coppers Are 72, etc.

Foster, Lewis (1899–1974). American director, former Hal Roach gag writer; won an Oscar in 1939 for the original story of *Mr Smith Goes to Washington.*
The Lucky Stiff (& w) 48. Manhandled (& w) 49. Captain China 49. The Eagle and the Hawk (& w) 40. Crosswinds 51. Those Redheads from Seattle (& w) 53. Top of the World 55. The Bold and the Brave 56. Tonka (& w) 58, etc.

Foster, Meg (–). American leading lady with striking blue eyes, mostly on TV.
The Death of Me Yet (TV) 71. Sunshine (TV) 73. Things in Their Season (TV) 74. James Dean (TV) 76. A Different Story 79. The Legend of Sleepy Hollow 79. Carny 80. Guyana Tragedy (TV) 81. Ticket to Heaven 81. The Osterman Weekend 83, etc.
TV series: Sunshine 73. Cagney and Lacey 82–84.

Foster, Norman (1900–1976). American leading man of the early thirties; became a director and had a rather patchy career.
Gentlemen of the Press 29. It Pays to Advertise 31. Reckless Living 31. Alias the Doctor 32. Skyscraper Souls 32. State Fair 33. Professional Sweetheart 33. Orient Express 34. Behind the Green Lights 35. High Tension 36. I Cover Chinatown (& d) 36. ☐DIRECTED ONLY: Fair Warning 37. Think Fast Mr Moto 37. Thank You Mr Moto 37. Walking Down Broadway 38. Mysterious Mr Moto 38. Mr Moto Takes a Chance 38. Mr Moto's Last Warning 39. Charlie Chan in Reno 39. Mr Moto Takes a Vacation 39. *Charlie Chan at Treasure Island* 39. Charlie Chan in Panama 40. Viva Cisco Kid 40. Ride Kelly Ride 41. Scotland Yard 41. *Journey Into Fear* 42. Rachel and the Stranger 48. Kiss the Blood off My Hands 48. Tell It to the Judge 49. Father is a Bachelor 50. Woman on the Run 50. Navajo 52. Sky Full of Moon 52. Sombrero 53. Davy Crockett 55. Davy Crockett and the River Pirates 56. The Nine Lives of Elfego Baga 58. The Sign of Zorro 60. Indian Paint 66. Brighty 67.

Foster, Preston (1901–1970). Handsome American leading man of the thirties, former clerk and singer.
Nothing But the Truth (debut) 30. Life Begins 31. *The Last Mile* 31. Wharf Angel 34. The Informer 35. The Last Days of Pompeii 35. Annie Oakley 36. The Plough and the Stars 37. First Lady 38. News Is Made at Night 38. Geronimo 39. Moon over Burma 40. Northwest Mounted Police 40. Unfinished Business 41. Secret Agent of Japan 42. My Friend Flicka 43. The Bermuda Mystery 44. The Valley of Decision 45. The Last Gangster 45. The Harvey Girls 46. Ramrod 47. Green Grass of Wyoming 48. Tomahawk 49. The Tougher They Come 51. The Big Night 52. Kansas City Confidential 53. I the Jury 55. Destination 60,000 58. Advance to the Rear 64. The Time Travellers 65. Chubasco 68, many others.
TV series: Waterfront 54–55. Gunslinger 60.

Foster, Stephen (1826–1864). American songwriter of popular sentimental ballads: 'Old Folks at Home', 'Beautiful Dreamer', etc. Impersonated on screen by Douglass Montgomery in *Harmony Lane* 35, Don Ameche in *Swanee River* 39, and Bill Shirley in *I Dream of Jeannie* 52.

Foster, Susanna (1924–) (Suzan Larsen). American operatic singer and heroine of several forties films.
The Great Victor Herbert 40. *There's Magic in Music* 41. The Hard Boiled Canary 42. Top Man 43. *Phantom of the Opera* 43. The Climax 44. Bowery to Broadway 44. This Is the Life 44. Frisco Sal 45. That Night with You 45, etc.

Foulger, Byron (1900–1970). American small-part actor, the prototype of the worried, bespectacled clerk.
The Prisoner of Zenda 37. Edison the Man 40. Sullivan's Travels 41. Since You Went Away 44. Champagne for Caesar 49. The Magnetic Monster 53. The Long Hot Summer 59. The Gnome-Mobile 67, innumerable others.
TV series: Petticoat Junction 69.

Four Daughters. The three Lane sisters and Gale Page appeared as Claude Rains' musical daughters in this dollop of sweetness and light which despite its computerized script was a big hit in 1938. It can be credited with introducing the angry-young-man hero, and at the same time a new actor, John Garfield. All these components were reproduced the following year in a film called *Daughters Courageous* which however dealt with different people in a different milieu; the original characters then reappeared in *Four Wives* 39 and *Four Mothers* 40. *Four Sons* 40 was something else again, an anti-Nazi propaganda piece about the break-up of a German family. In 1955 the original *Four Daughters* was remade as a semi-musical, *Young at Heart*, with Doris Day and Frank Sinatra.

The Four Feathers. A. E. W. Mason's novel of the old Empire, with heroism and cowardice in the Sudan after General Gordon's death, was magnificently filmed by Alexander Korda in 1939, with John Clements and Ralph Richardson. Much of the same footage reappeared in Zoltan Korda's 1955 remake *Storm over the Nile*, stretched into CinemaScope and not improved thereby. (The action scenes have also been used in several other films, e.g. *Zarak* 57, *Master of the World* 61, *East of Sudan* 64.) There was a British silent version in 1921 starring Harry Ham and Cyril Perceval, and a Hollywood one in 1928 starring Richard Arlen and Clive Brook; either would be preferable to the 1978 TV movie with Beau Bridges.

The Four Horsemen of the Apocalypse. In 1921 Rex Ingram directed a spectacular version of Ibanez' novel about love, war and death, notable for introducing Rudolph Valentino as a star. Vincente Minnelli remade it in 1962 with Glenn Ford and an updated script by Robert Ardrey and John Gay, but by now the entire conception seemed to belong to a Victorian novelette.

The Four Hundred Blows (France 1958). This influential 'new wave' film, written and directed by François Truffaut, was basically a moving account of a small boy's adventures in the big city while on the run from an unhappy home and school life. Henri Decae's location photography was masterly.

Four Steps in the Clouds (Italy 1942). A still enjoyable and historically significant step forward in Italian light realist comedy; a film full of sunshine and *joie de vivre* with little relation to the war then raging. Gino Cervi plays a young commuter who by a series of mischances spends twenty-four hours in complicated excitements before returning to his wife and family. Written by Giuseppe Amato, directed by Alessandro Blasetti.

Fourteen Hours (US 1951). This suspenser, based on the real case of a man who stood on a ledge threatening suicide and defied police to come and get him, was well written (John Paxton from an article by Joel Sayre) and directed (Henry Hathaway); it seemed at the time to point to new profitable combinations of actuality and entertainment, though there was some over-dramatization and a happy outcome was substituted for the real tragic one. Richard Basehart was in his element as the unfortunate central figure.

Fowlds, Derek (1937–). British comedy character actor, usually in unassuming roles.
The Smashing Bird I Used to Know 69. Hotel Paradiso 66. Tower of Evil 71.
TV series: *Yes Minister* 81–.

Fowler, Gene (1890–1960). American writer, close friend of John Barrymore and author of his biography *Good Night Sweet Prince*.

Fowler, Gene Jnr (–). American director.
□I Was a Teenage Werewolf 56. Gang War 58. Showdown at Boot Hill 58. I Married a Monster from Outer Space 59. Here Come the Jets 59. The Rebel Set 59. The Oregon Trail 59.

Fowler, Harry (1926–). British cockney actor on screen since the early forties, often in cameo roles.
Those Kids from Town 42. Champagne Charlie 44. Hue and Cry 46. For Them That Trespass 48. I Believe in You 52. Pickwick Papers 53. Home and Away 56. Idol on Parade 59. Ladies Who Do 63. Doctor in Clover 66. The Prince and the Pauper 77, many others.

TV series: The Army Game, Our Man at St Mark's.

Fowler, Hugh (c. 1904–75). American editor.
Les Misérables 52. Gentlemen Prefer Blondes 53. The Last Wagon 56. Say One for Me 59. The Lost World 60. The List of Adrian Messenger 63. Stagecoach 66. Planet of the Apes 67. Patton (AA) 70. The Life and Times of Judge Roy Bean 72, many others.

Fowles, John (1926–). British novelist whose slightly mystic themes have generally attracted film-makers, though not always with satisfactory results: *The Collector*, *The Magus*, *The French Lieutenant's Woman*.

Fowley, Douglas (1911–). American character actor often seen as nervous or comic gangster.
Let's Talk it Over 34. Crash Donovan 36. Charlie Chan on Broadway 37. Mr Moto's Gamble 38. Dodge City 39. Ellery Queen Master Detective 40. Tanks a Million 41. Jitterbugs 42. The Kansan 43. One Body Too Many 44. The Hucksters 47. If You Knew Susie 48. Battleground 49. Edge of Doom 50. Criminal Lawyer 51. *Singin' in The Rain* (as the hysterical director) 52. The High and the Mighty 54. Macumba Love (p and d only) 59. Desire in the Dust 60. Barabbas 62. From Noon till Three 76. The White Buffalo 77, many others.
TV series: The Life and Legend of Wyatt Earp (as Doc Holliday) 56–61. Pistols and Petticoats 66. Gunsmoke 68–74.

Fox, Bernard (–). British character actor in Hollywood: plays a rather stiff gent of the old school.
Soho Incident 56. The Safecracker 58. Honeymoon Hotel 64. Star 68. Big Jake 71. The Hound of the Baskervilles (TV) (as Dr Watson) 72. Herbie Goes to Monte Carlo 77, etc.

Fox, Charles (1940–). American composer.
Barbarella (co-m) 67. Goodbye Columbus 69. Star Spangled Girl 71. The Laughing Policeman 73. The Other Side of the Mountain 75. Foul Play 78. Nine to Five 80. Why Would I Lie 80. Zapped! 82, etc.
Much TV including Happy Days, The Love Boat.

Fox, Edward (1937–). Diffident British leading man of the seventies.
The Naked Runner 67. The Long Duel 67. Oh What a Lovely War 69. Skullduggery 69. The Breaking of Bumbo 70. The Go-Between 71. *The Day of the Jackal* 73. Doll's House 73. Galileo 74. The Squeeze 77. A Bridge Too Far 77. The Cat and the Canary 78. Force Ten From Navarone 78. *Edward and Mrs Simpson* (TV) 78. The Mirror Crack'd 80. Gandhi 82. Never Say Never Again 83. The Dresser 83. The Shooting Party 84. The Bounty 84. Wild Geese 2 85, etc.

Fox, James (1939–). British leading man, who usually plays a weakling. Once a child actor, notable in *The Magnet* 50 (as William Fox). Returned to acting 1982 after a ten-year break in good works. Brother of Edward Fox, and very similar in style.
Autobiography 1983: *Comeback*.
The Loneliness of the Long Distance Runner The Servant 63. Tamahine 64. Those Magnificent Men in Their Flying Machines 65. King Rat 65. The Chase 65. Thoroughly Modern Millie 67. Duffy 68. Isadora 68. Arabella 69. Performance 70. Runners 83. A Passage to India 84. Greystoke 84. Absolute Beginners 85. The Whistle Blower 86. High Season 87, etc.

Fox, Michael J. (1961–). American leading man who plays younger than his years.
Midnight Madness 82. Class of 84 83. *Back to the Future* 85. Teen Wolf 85. Poison Ivy (TV) 85. The Secret of my Success 87. Light of Day 87.
TV series: *Family Ties* 83–

Fox, Sidney (1910–1942). American leading lady of the early thirties.
Bad Sister 31. The Mouthpiece 32. Once In a Lifetime 32. Murders in the Rue Morgue 32. Midnight 34, etc.

Fox, Wallace (1898–1958). American director.
The Amazing Vagabond 29. Cannonball Express 32. Powdersmoke Range 35. The Last of the Mohicans (co-d) 36. Racing Lady 37. Pride of the Plains 40. Bowery Blitzkrieg 41. Kid Dynamite 43. Riders of the Santa Fe 44. Mr Muggs Rides Again 45. Gunman's Code 46. Docks of New York 48. Six Gun Mesa 50. Montana Desperado 51, many others.

Fox, William (1879–1952) (Wilhelm Fried). Hungarian-American pioneer and executive, the Fox of 20th Century Fox. Moved from the garment industry into exhibition, production and distribution. *Upton Sinclair Presents*

William Fox, a biography, was published in 1933.

¶ *W.F.:* I always bragged of the fact that no second of those contained in the twenty-four hours ever passed but that the name of William Fox was on the screen, being exhibited in some theatre in some part of the world.

Foxwell, Ivan (1914–). British producer, in films since 1933.
No Room at the Inn 47. The Intruder 51. The Colditz Story 54. Manuela 56. A Touch of Larceny 59. Tiara Tahiti 62. The Quiller Memorandum 66. Decline and Fall (also wrote) 68, etc.

Foxworth, Robert (1941–). American general purpose actor.
The New Healers (TV) 72. Frankenstein (TV) 73. The Devil's Daughter (TV) 73. The Questor Tapes (TV) 74. Mrs Sundance (TV) 74. James Dean (TV) 76. Treasure of Matecumbe 76. It Happened at Lake Wood Manor (TV) 77. Death Moon (TV) 78. Damien: Omen II 78. Prophecy 79. The Black Marble 80.
TV series: Falcon Crest 81–.

Foxx, Redd (1922–) (John Elroy Sanford). Black American vaudevillian who became a seventies star in the long-running *Sanford and Son*.
Norman, Is That You? 76.

Foy, Bryan (1895–1977). American producer, mostly of low budgeters at Warner. Wrote song, 'Mr Gallagher & Mr Shean'; and was the oldest of the 'seven little Foys'.
The Home Towners (d) 28. Little Old New York (d) 28. The Gorilla (d) 31. Berlin Correspondent 42. Guadalcanal Diary 43. Doll Face 46. Trapped 49. Breakthrough 50. Inside the Walls of Folsom Prison 51. The Miracle of Fatima 52. *House of Wax* 53. The Mad Magician 54. Women's Prison 55. Blueprint for Robbery 61. PT 109 63, many others.

Foy, Eddie Snr (1854–1928) (Edward Fitzgerald). Famous American vaudeville comedian who made few film appearances but was several times impersonated by Eddie Foy Jnr: in *Yankee Doodle Dandy, Wilson, Bowery to Broadway*, etc. Bob Hope played him in *The Seven Little Foys*.
Films include A Favourite Fool 15.

Foy, Eddie Jnr (1905–1983). American vaudeville entertainer, son of another and one of the 'seven little Foys'.
Fugitive from Justice 40. The Farmer Takes a Wife 53. Lucky Me 54. *The Pajama Game* 57. Bells Are Ringing 60. Thirty Is a Dangerous Age, Cynthia 67, etc.
TV series: Fair Exchange 63.

Foyer Cards. Elaborate, oversized stills with coloured borders bearing credits, all designed for lobby display. A collection of them by John Kobal was published in 1983: it bore the wince-making title *Foyer Pleasure*.

Fraker, William A. (1923–). American cinematographer.
Games 67. The Fox 67. The President's Analyst 67. *Bullitt* 68. Rosemary's Baby 68. Paint Your Wagon 69. *Monte Walsh* (& d) 70. Day of the Dolphin 73. Lipstick 76. Exorcist II: The Heretic 77. Looking for Mr Goodbar 77. American Hot Wax 78. Hard Contract 78. 1941 79. Old Boyfriends 79. Hollywood Knights 80. Sharkey's Machine 81. The Legend of the Lone Ranger (d only) 81. The Best Little Whorehouse in Texas 82. War Games 83. Protocol 84. Murphy's Romance (AAN) 85. Burglar 87, etc.

frame. A single picture on a strip of film. At normal sound projection speed, 24 frames are shown each second.

France's national film history falls into a pattern of clearly-defined styles. First of note was that of Louis Feuillade, whose early serials had tremendous panache. In the twenties came René Clair, with his inimitable touch for fantastic comedy, and a little later Jean Renoir, whose view of the human comedy was wider but equally sympathetic. Sacha Guitry contributed a series of rather stagey but amusing high comedies; Jean Vigo in his brief career introduced surrealism. Marcel Pagnol made a number of self-indulgent regional comedies which were hugely enjoyable but had little to do with cinema. Then beginning in the thirties came an unsurpassed group of adult entertainments from the writer-director team of Jacques Prévert and Marcel Carné; these were widely copied by less talented hands and the resulting stream of sex dramas, seldom less than competent, preserved the legend of the naughty French. Other notable directors were Julien Duvivier, the romantic; Jacques Becker, at his happiest in comedy; and Jacques Feyder, who generally made melodramas with flashes of insight. Henri-Georges Clouzot developed into the French Hitchcock, and Cocteau's art films reached a wide public. In the forties Robert Bresson, René Clément and Jacques Tati all began to make themselves felt. The fifties were in danger of becoming a dull period, with no new talent of note, when the 'new wave' (qv) changed the whole direction of French film-making and made some of the older hands look suddenly and undeservedly old-fashioned. Directors well-regarded in the sixties include Jacques Demy, François Truffaut, Jean-Luc Godard, Louis Malle, Jean-Pierre Melville, Claude Lelouch and Georges Franju. In the seventies, Eric Rohmer, Jacques Deray, Yves Boisset and Costa-Gavras.

Among French male stars of note are Raimu, Michel Simon, Harry Baur, Fernandel, Louis Jouvet, Jean Gabin, Pierre Fresnay, Jean-Louis Barrault, Gérard Philippe, Pierre Brasseur, Maurice Chevalier, Charles Boyer and Jean-Paul Belmondo. Of the women, the most influential have been Ginette Leclerc, Michele Morgan, Danielle Darrieux, Arletty, Simone Signoret, Brigitte Bardot, Jeanne Moreau, Françoise Dorleac and Catherine Deneuve.

France, C. V. (1868–1949). British stage character actor, most typically seen in films as dry lawyer or ageing head of household.
Lord Edgware Dies 35. Scrooge 35. Victoria the Great 37. A Yank at Oxford 38. If I Were King (US) 39. Night Train to Munich 40. Breach of Promise 41. The Halfway House 44, etc.

Francen, Victor (1888–1977). Belgian stage actor, occasionally in French films from 1921, but most familiar in Hollywood spy dramas during World War II.
Crépuscule d'Epouvante 21. Après l'Amour 31. Nuits de Feu 36. Le Roi 36. J'Accuse 38. Sacrifice d'Honneur 38. La Fin du Jour 39. Tales of Manhattan 42. Mission to Moscow 43. Devotion 43. The Mask of Dimitrios 44. The Conspirators 44. Passage to Marseilles 44. Confidential Agent 45. The Beast with Five Fingers 46. La Nuit s'achève 49. The Adventures of Captain Fabian 51. Hell and High Water 54. Bedevilled 55. A Farewell to Arms 58. Fanny 61. Top-Crack 66, many others.

Franciosa, Anthony or **Tony** (1928–) (Anthony Papaleo). Italian-American leading actor with lithe movement and ready grin.
A Face in the Crowd (debut) 57. This Could Be the Night 57. *A Hatful of Rain* (his stage role) 57. Wild Is the Wind 58. *The Long Hot Summer* 58. The Naked Maja 59. Career 59. The Story on Page One 59. Go Naked in the World 60. Period of Adjustment 62. Rio Conchos 64. The Pleasure Seekers 65. A Man Could Get Killed 65. Assault on a Queen 66. The Swinger 66. Fathom (GB) 67. The Sweet Ride 68. In Enemy Country 68. A Man Called Gannon 68. Across 110th Street 72. The Drowning Pool 75. The World is Full of Married Men (GB) 79. Firepower 79. Death Wish II 82. Unsane (Tenebrae) 82, etc.
TV series: Valentine's Day 64. *The Name of the Game* 68–70. Search 72. Matt Helm 75.

Francis. The talking mule of several Universal comedies (1950–56) was the direct ancestor of TV's talking palomino *Mister Ed*, also produced by Arthur Lubin. Francis' first master was Donald O'Connor, but later Mickey Rooney took over the reins. Francis was 'voiced' by Chill Wills, Ed by Allan Lane.

Francis, Alec B. (1869–1934). British-born character actor in Hollywood films as elderly gentleman.
Flame of the Desert 19. Smiling Through 22. Three Wise Fools 23. Charley's Aunt 25. Tramp Tramp Tramp 26. The Terror 28. Outward Bound 30. Arrowsmith 31. The Last Mile 32. Oliver Twist 33. Outcast Lady 34, many others.

Francis, Anne (1930–). American leading lady of several fifties films: formerly model, with radio and TV experience.
Summer Holiday (debut) 48. So Young So Bad 50. Elopement 52. Lydia Bailey 52. Susan Slept Here 54. Bad Day at Black Rock 54. The Blackboard Jungle 55. Forbidden Planet 56. Don't Go Near the Water 57. Girl of the Night 60. The Satan Bug 65. Funny Girl 68. The Love God 69. More Dead than Alive 70. Pancho Villa 71. Haunts of the Very Rich (TV) 72. A Masterpiece of Murder (TV) 86, etc.
TV series: Honey West 65. My Three Sons 71.

Francis, Arlene (1908–) (Arlene Kazanjian). American TV personality who has appeared in a few films.
Stage Door Canteen 43. All My Sons 48. One Two Three 61. The Thrill of it All 63, etc.

Francis, Connie (1938–) (Concetta Franconero). American pop singer who has had some light films built around her.

Where the Boys Are 63. Follow the Boys 64. Looking for Love 65, etc.

Francis, Derek (1923–84). Portly British character actor, often in self-important roles. Bitter Harvest 63. Ring of Spies 64. The Comedy Man 64. Carry on Camping 69. To the Devil a Daughter 75. Jabberwocky 77, etc.

Francis, Freddie (1917–). British cinematographer who turned to direction with less distinguished results.
Mine Own Executioner 47. Time without Pity 57. Room at the Top 59. *Sons and Lovers* (AA) 60. The Innocents 61.The French Lieutenant's Woman 80. The Elephant Man 81. Dune 85, etc.
AS DIRECTOR ONLY: Two and Two make Six 61. Vengeance 62. Paranoiac 63. Nightmare 63. The Evil of Frankenstein 64. Traitor's Gate 65. The Skull 65. The Deadly Bees 66. They Came from Beyond Space 66. The Torture Garden 67. Dracula has Risen from the Grave 68. Mumsy Nanny Sonny and Girlie 69. Tales from the Crypt 71. Asylum 72. Tales that Witness Madness 73. Legend of the Werewolf 74. The Doctor and the Devils 86, etc.

Francis, Ivor (*c.* 1911–86). American character actor who played self-important or bumbling types.
I Love My Wife 70. The Late Liz 71. The World's Greatest Athlete 73. Superdad 74. The Prisoner of Second Avenue 75. The North Avenue Irregulars 78, etc.
TV series: Gilligan's Island 64–67. Dusty's Trail 73.

Francis, Kay (1899–1968) (Katherine Gibbs). Lady-like, serious-faced American star of women's films in the thirties.
□Gentlemen of the Press 29. The Coconuts 29. Dangerous Curves 29. Illusion 29. The Marriage Playground 29. Behind the Makeup 30. *Street of Chance* 30. Paramount on Parade 30. A Notorious Affair 30. Raffles 30. For the Defence 30. Let's Go Native 30. The Virtuous Sin 30. Passion Flower 30. Scandal Sheet 31. Ladies' Man 31. The Vice Squad 31. Transgression 31. Guilty Hands 31. Twenty-Four Hours 31. Girls about Town 31. The False Madonna 32. Strangers in Love 32. Man Wanted 32. Street of Women 32. Jewel Robbery 32. *One Way Passage* 32. *Trouble in Paradise* 32. *Cynara* 32. The Keyhole 33. Storm at Daybreak 33. Mary Stevens MD 33. I Loved a Woman 33. The House on 56th Street 33. Mandalay 34. Wonder Bar 34. Doctor Monica 34. British Agent 34. Stranded 34. The Goose and the Gander 35. Living on Velvet 35. I Found Stella Parish 35. *The White Angel* (as Florence Nightingale) 36. Give Me Your Heart 36. Stolen Holiday 37. Confession 37. Another Dawn 37. *First Lady* 37. Women are Like That 38. My Bill 38. Secrets of an Actress 38. Comet over Broadway 38. King of the Underworld 39. Women in the Wind 39. In Name Only 39. It's a Date 40. Little Men 40. When the Daltons Rode 40. Play Girl 40. The Man Who Lost Himself 40. *Charley's Aunt* 41. The Feminine Touch 41. Always in My Heart 42. Between Us Girls 42. Four Jills in a Jeep 44. Divorce 45. Allotment Wives 45. Wife Wanted 46.

Francis, Robert (1930–1955). American leading man whose budding career was cut short by an air crash.
The Caine Mutiny 54. The Long Gray Line 55, etc.

Franciscus, James (1934–). American leading man.
Four Boys and a Gun 56. I Passed for White 60. The Outsider 61. The Miracle of the White Stallions 63. Youngblood Hawke 64. The Valley of Gwangi 69. Marooned 69. Beneath the Planet of the Apes 69. Cat O'Nine Tails 71. The Dream Makers (TV) 75. The Amazing Dobermans 76. The Greek Tycoon 78. When Time Ran Out 80. Jacqueline Bouvier Kennedy (TV) 81. Butterfly 82. The Great White 82, etc.
TV series: Naked City 58. Mr Novak 63–64. Longstreet 71. Hunter 77.

Francks, Don (1932–). Canadian singer whose first notable film role was in *Finian's Rainbow* 68.

Franju, Georges (1912–87). French director, former set designer. Co-founder of Cinémathèque Française. Best-known documentaries: *Le Sang des Bêtes* 49. *Hôtel des Invalides* 51. *Le Grand Melies* 51. Features: *La Tête contre les Murs* (*The Keepers*) 58. *Eyes without a Face* 59. Spotlight on a Murderer 61. Thérèse Desqueyroux 62. Judex 63. Thomas the Impostor 64. Les Rideaux Blancs 65.

Frank, Charles (1910–). British director, former dubbing expert.
Uncle Silas 47. Intimate Relations 53, etc.

Frank, Fredric M. (1911–77). American scriptwriter.
The Greatest Show on Earth (co-w) 52. The Ten Commandments (co-w) 56. El Cid (co-w) 61, etc.

Frank, Gerold (1907–). American 'ghost writer' who co-authored the autobiographies of such luminaries as Sheilah Graham, Lillian Roth and Diana Barrymore.

Frank, Harriet: see *Ravetch, Irving.*

Frank, Melvin (1917–). American comedy scriptwriter and latterly producer/director.
WITH NORMAN PANAMA: *My Favourite Blonde* 42. Thank Your Lucky Stars 43. Road to Utopia 45. Monsieur Beaucaire 46. *Mr Blanding Builds His Dream House* 48. The Reformer and the Redhead 50. Above and Beyond 52. White Christmas 56. That Certain Feeling 56. Lil Abner 59. *The Facts of Life* 61. Road to Hong Kong 62. Strange Bedfellows 65, etc.
SOLO: A Funny Thing Happened on the Way to the Forum (wp) 66. Buona Sera Mrs Campbell (wpd) 68. A Touch of Class (wpd) 72. The Duchess and the Dirtwater Fox (wpd) 76. The Prisoner of Second Avenue (pd) 75. Lost and Found (wpd) 79.

Frankau, Ronald (1894–1951). British stage and radio comedian with an 'idle rich' characterization.
The Calendar 31. His Brother's Keeper 39. Double Alibi 46. The Ghosts of Berkeley Square 47, etc.

Frankel, Benjamin (1906–1973). British composer. Scores include The Years Between 46. The Seventh Veil 46. Mine Own Executioner 47. Sleeping Car to Trieste 48. Appointment with Venus 51. The Importance of Being Earnest 52. A Kid For Two Farthings 55. Simon and Laura 55. Happy is the Bride 58. Libel 59. Guns of Darkness 62. Night of the Iguana 64. Battle of the Bulge 65, etc.

Frankel, Cyril (1921-). British director, former documentarist with Crown Film Unit.
Devil on Horseback 54. Make Me an Offer 55. It's Great To Be Young 56. No Time for Tears 57. She Didn't Say No 58. Alive and Kicking 58. Never Take Sweets from a Stranger 61. Don't Bother To Knock 61. On the Fiddle 61. The Very Edge 63. The Witches (The Devil's Own) 66. The Trygon Factor 67. Permission to Kill 75, etc.

Frankenheimer, John (1930–). Ebullient American director, formerly in TV.
□*The Young Stranger* 57. The Young Savages 61. All Fall Down 61. *The Manchurian Candidate* 62. *Birdman of Alcatraz* 62. *Seven Days in May* 64. The Train 64. *Seconds* 66. Grand Prix 67. The Extraordinary Seaman 68. The Fixer 68. The Gypsy Moths 69. I Walk the Line 70. The Horsemen 71. Impossible Object 73. The Iceman Cometh 73. 99 44/100 Dead 74. French Connection II 75. Black Sunday 76. Prophecy 79. The Challenge 82. The Holcroft Covenant 85. 52 Pick-Up 86.

Frankenstein. The man/monster theme was explored in American movies of 1908 (with Charles Ogle) and 1916 (*Life Without Soul*), also in Italy in 1920 (*Master of Frankenstein*). The 1931 Hollywood film, written by Robert Florey and directed by James Whale, borrowed as much from Wegener's *The Golem* 22 as from Mary Shelley's early 19th-century novel; but despite censorship problems the elements jelled, with Boris Karloff a great success as the monster composed from dead bits and pieces, and a legend was born. Sequels included *Bride of Frankenstein* (qv) 35. *Son of Frankenstein* 39. *Ghost of Frankenstein* 41. *Frankenstein Meets the Wolf Man* 43. *House of Frankenstein* 45. *House of Dracula* 45. *Abbott and Costello Meet Frankenstein* 48; among those who took over from Karloff were Lon Chaney, Bela Lugosi and Glenn Strange. In 1956 the original story was remade in Britain's Hammer Studios under the title *The Curse of Frankenstein*; colour and gore were added, and sequels, with various monsters, came thick and fast: *The Revenge of Frankenstein* 58. *The Evil of Frankenstein* 63. *Frankenstein Created Woman* 67. *Frankenstein Must Be Destroyed* 69. *Horror of Frankenstein* 70. *Frankenstein and the Monster from Hell* 73. A variation on the original monster make-up was used by Fred Gwynne in the TV comedy series, *The Munsters* 64–65. There have also been several recent American, Japanese and Italian attempts to cash in on the name of Frankenstein in cheap exploitation pictures: *I Was a Teenage Frankenstein* 57. *Frankenstein 1970* 58. *Frankenstein Versus the Space Monsters* 65. *Frankenstein Conquers the World* 68. *Lady Frankenstein* 70, etc.
In 1973 a four-hour TV version called *Frankenstein: The True Story* (which it could scarcely be) was co-authored by Christopher Isherwood but proved merely a laborious reworking of the earlier films, with occasional references back to the book, but no humour.

Franklin, Pamela (1949–). British juvenile actress of the sixties.
The Innocents 61. The Lion 62. The Third Secret 64. The Nanny 65. Our Mother's House 67. The Night of the Following Day 68. *The Prime of Miss Jean Brodie* 69. Sinful Davey 69. David Copperfield 69. And Soon the Darkness 70. Necromancy 72. The Legend of Hell House 73. Food for the Gods 76, etc.

Franklin, Richard (–). Australian director.
Patrick 78. Road Games 81. *Psycho II* 83. Cloak and Dagger 84. Link 86.

Franklin, Sidney (1893–1972). American producer-director, in Hollywood since leaving school. Academy Award 1942 'for consistent high achievement'.
Martha's Vindication (d) 16. Heart o' the Hills (d) 19. Dulcy (d) 23. Beverly of Graustark (d) 26. The Last of Mrs Cheyney (d) 29. Private Lives (d) 31. The Guardsman (d) 32. Smiling Through (d) 32. Reunion in Vienna (d) 33. The Barretts of Wimpole Street (d) 33. The Dark Angel (d) 35. The Good Earth (d) 37. On Borrowed Time (p) 39. Waterloo Bridge (p) 40. Mrs Miniver (p) 42. Random Harvest (p) 42. The White Cliffs of Dover (p) 44. The Yearling (p) 46. The Miniver Story (p) 50. Young Bess (p) 54. The Barretts of Wimpole Street (d) 57, many others.

Franklyn, William (1926–). Smooth British character actor, popular on TV.
Quatermass II 57. Fury at Smugglers' Bay 58. Pit of Darkness 62. The Legend of Young Dick Turpin 64. The Intelligence Men 65. The Satanic Rites of Dracula 73, etc.

Frankovich, Mike (1910–). American producer, a former sports commentator and screenwriter. During the fifties he ran Columbia's British organization, and in the sixties became their head of world production, then turned independent again.
Fugitive Lady 51. Decameron Nights 53. Footsteps in the Fog 55. Joe Macbeth 56. Marooned 69. Bob and Carol and Ted and Alice 69. Cactus Flower 69. Butterflies are Free 72. Forty Carats 73. The Shootist 76, etc.

Franz, Arthur (1920–). American leading man, latterly character actor; radio, stage and TV experience.
Jungle Patrol (debut) 48. Sands of Iwo Jima 49. Abbott and Costello Meet the Invisible Man 51. The Sniper 52. Eight Iron Men 52. The Caine Mutiny 54. The Unholy Wife 57. Running Target 58. Hellcats of the Navy 59. Alvarez Kelly 66. Anzio 68. Sisters of Death 77. That Championship Season 82, etc.

Franz, Eduard (1902–1983). American character actor, often seen as foreign dignitary, Jewish elder, or psychiatrist.
The Iron Curtain 48. Francis 50. The Thing 51. The Jazz Singer 52. Dream Wife 53. Broken Lance 54. The Ten Commandments 56. Man Afraid 57. A Certain Smile 58. The Story of Ruth 60. Hatarı 62. The President's Analyst 67, many others.
TV series: The Breaking Point 63. Zorro 78.

Fraser, Bill (1907–87). British comic character actor, TV's 'Snudge'. Wide stage experience; film parts since 1938 usually bits till latterly.
Meet Me Tonight 52. The Americanization of Emily 65. Joey Boy 65. Masquerade 65. I've Gotta Horse 65. Up the Chastity Belt 71. That's Your Funeral 72, etc.

Fraser, John (1931–). British leading man with stage experience, sporadically in films.
The Good Beginning 53. Touch and Go 55. The Good Companions 57. Tunes of Glory 59. *The Trials of Oscar Wilde* (as Lord Alfred Douglas) 60. El Cid 61. Fury at Smugglers Bay 61. The Waltz of the Toreadors 62. Repulsion 65. Operation Crossbow 65. Isadora 68. Schizo 77, etc.

Fraser, Liz (1933–). British character actress, specializing in dumb cockney blondes.
Wonderful Things 58. I'm All Right, Jack 59. Two-Way Stretch 60. The Rebel 61. Double Bunk 61. Carry On Regardless 61. The Painted Smile (leading role) 61. Raising the Wind 62. Live Now Pay Later 63. The Americanization of Emily 64. The Family Way 66. Up the Junction 68. Dad's Army 70. Confessions of a Driving Instructor 76. Confessions from a Holiday Camp 77, etc.

Fraser, Moyra (1923–). Australian comedienne in British stage and TV.
Here We Go Round the Mulberry Bush 67. Prudence and the Pill 68. The Boy Friend 71, etc.

Fraser, Richard (1913–1971). Scottish-born leading man of some American second features in the forties.

How Green Was My Valley 41. The Picture of Dorian Gray 44. Fatal Witness 46. The Cobra Strikes 48. Alaska Patrol 51, etc.

Fraser, Ronald (1930–). Stocky British character actor, in films and TV since 1954.
The Sundowners 59. The Pot Carriers 62. The Punch and Judy Man 63. Crooks in Cloisters 64. The Beauty Jungle 64. The Flight of the Phoenix 65. The Whisperers 67. The Killing of Sister George 68. Sinful Davey 69. Too Late the Hero 69. The Rise and Rise of Michael Rimmer 70. The Magnificent Seven Deadly Sins 71. Rentadick 72. Ooh You Are Awful 72. Swallows and Amazons 74. Paper Tiger 75. The Wild Geese 78. Trail of the Pink Panther 82.

Frawley, James (1937–). American director.
The Christian Licorice Store 70. Kid Blue 73. Delancey Street (TV) 75. The Eddie Capra Mysteries (pilot) (TV) 76. The Big Bus 76. The Muppet Movie 79. The Great American Traffic Jam (TV) 80.

Frawley, William (1887–1966). Stocky, cigar-chewing American comedy character actor from vaudeville, in innumerable films as taxi driver, comic gangster, private detective or incompetent cop.
Moonlight and Pretzels 33. Crime Doctor 34. Alibi Ike 35. Desire 36. High Wide and Handsome 37. Professor Beware 38. Persons in Hiding 39. One Night in the Tropics 40. Footsteps in the Dark 42. *Roxie Hart* 42. Whistling in Brooklyn 43. Going My Way 44. Lady on a Train 45. The Crime Doctor's Manhunt 46. Miracle on 34th Street 47. The Babe Ruth Story 48. East Side West Side 49. Kill the Umpire 50. The Lemon Drop Kid 51. Rancho Notorious 52. Safe at Home 62, etc.
TV series: *I Love Lucy* 51–60. My Three Sons 60–63.

Frazee, Jane (1918–85) (Mary Jane Frehse). Vivacious American singer and leading lady of minor musicals in the forties.
Buck Privates 41. Moonlight in Havana 42. When Johnny Comes Marching Home 42. Practically Yours 44. Swing and Sway 44. Kansas City Kitty 45. Incident 48. Rhythm Inn (last appearance), etc.
TV series: Beulah 52.

Freaks (US 1932). Tod Browning's macabre drama set in a circus and with real freaks in the cast enjoyed a greater reputation than it deserved because it was unseen for thirty years owing to a censor's ban. Now it seems interesting but unsatisfactory, a curious aberration of the Irving Thalberg regime at MGM.

Frears, Stephen (1931–). British director.
Gumshoe 71. Saigon—Year of the Cat (TV) 83. The Hit 84. My Beautiful Laundrette 85. Prick Up Your Ears 87. Sammy and Rosie Get Laid 87.

Frechette, Mark (1947–75). American leading man of *Zabriskie Point*; subsequently died in prison.

Freda, Riccardo (1909–). Egyptian-Italian director who brings some style to exploitation pictures; former art critic.
Les Misérables 46. Theodora, Slave Express 54. I Vampiri 57. The Giant of Thessaly 61. The Terror of Dr Hitchcock 62. The Spectre 63. Coplan FX 18 Casse Tout (The Exterminators) 65, etc.

Frederick, Lynne (–). British leading lady, widow of Peter Sellers.
No Blade of Grass 70. Vampire Circus 71. Henry VIII and His Six Wives 72. Schizo 76. Voyage of the Damned 76. The Prisoner of Zenda 79, etc.

Frederick, Pauline (1883–1938) (Pauline Libbey). American leading lady of silent days.
Bella Donna 15. The Slave Island 16. Sleeping Fires 17. Her Final Reckoning 18. The Peace of Roaring River 19. *Madame X* 20. La Tosca 21. Married Flirts 24. Her Honour the Governor 26. On Trial 28. The Sacred Flame 29. This Modern Age 31. The Phantom of Crestwood 32. My Marriage 36. Thank You Mr Moto 38, etc.

Fredericks, Ellsworth (–). American cinematographer.
Invasion of the Body Snatchers 56. The Friendly Persuasion 56. Sayonara 57. High Time 60. Seven Days in May 64. Pistolero 66. The Power 67. Mister Buddwing 67, etc.

free cinema. A term applied to their own output by a group of British documentarists of the fifties, e.g. Lindsay Anderson, Karel Reisz. Their aim was to make 'committed' films which cared about the individual and the significance of the everyday. The resulting films were not always better than those produced by professional units with more commercial intent. The most notable were *O Dreamland, Momma Don't Allow, The March* *to Aldermaston, Every Day Except Christmas* and *We Are the Lambeth Boys*, the two latter films being sponsored by commercial firms.

Freed, Arthur (1894–1973) (Arthur Grossman). American producer, mainly of musicals for MGM, many of them featuring his own lyrics.
Hold Your Man (ly only) 33. Hollywood Party (ly only) 34. Broadway Melody of 1936 (ly only). Broadway Melody of 1938 (ly only). *Babes In Arms* (& ly) 39. Strike Up the Band 40. Lady Be Good (& ly) 41. Cabin in the Sky 43. Meet Me in St Louis 44. Ziegfeld Follies 46. The Pirate 48. *On the Town* 49. Annie Get Your Gun 50. Showboat 51. *An American in Paris* 51. *Singin' in The Rain* (& ly) 52. *Band Wagon* 53. Kismet 55. Invitation to the Dance 56. *Gigi* 58. Bells are Ringing 60. The Light in the Piazza 62, many others.

Freed, Bert (1919–). Burly American character actor.
Why Must I Die? 60. Fate Is the Hunter 64. P.J. 67. Billy Jack 71. Till Death 77. Barracuda 79, etc.

Freedman, Jerrold (1919–). American director.
Kansas City Bomber 72. Borderline 80.

Freeland, Thornton (1898–). American director, former cameraman.
Three Live Ghosts 29. Whoopee 30. *Flying Down to Rio* 33. Brewster's Millions (GB) 35. The Amateur Gentleman (GB) 36. Jericho (GB) 37. The Gang's All Here (GB) 39. Over the Moon (GB) 39. Too Many Blondes 41. Meet Me at Dawn 47. The Brass Monkey (Lucky Mascot) (GB) 48. Dear Mr Prohack (GB) 49, etc.

Freeman, Al Jnr (1934–). Black American leading man.
Black Like Me 64. Dutchman 67. The Detective 68. Finian's Rainbow 68. Castle Keep 69. The Lost Man 70. A Fable (& d) 71, etc.

Freeman, Everett (1911–). American writer, usually in collaboration.
Larceny Inc. 42. Thank Your Lucky Stars 43. The Secret Life of Walter Mitty 47. Million Dollar Mermaid 52. My Man Godfrey 57. The Glass Bottom Boat 66. Where Were You When the Lights Went Out? (& co-p) 68, many others.

Freeman, Frank Y. (1890–). American executive, vice president of Paramount in charge of the studio from 1938 until his retirement.

Freeman, Howard (1899–1967). American character actor, usually in comic roles as businessman on the make.
Pilot Number Five 43. Once Upon a Time 44. Take One False Step 49. Scaramouche 52. Remains To Be Seen 53. Dear Brigitte 65, many others.

Freeman, Joan (–). American general purpose actress.
The Remarkable Mr Pennypacker 58. Come September 61. The Rounders 65. The Fastest Guitar Alive 66. The Reluctant Astronaut 67, etc.

Freeman, Kathleen (c. 1919–). American character actress.
Naked City 47. Lonely Heart Bandits 52. Bonzo Goes To College 52. Full House 52. Athena 54. The Fly 58. The Ladies' Man 61. The Disorderly Orderly 65. Three on a Couch 66. Support Your Local Gunfighter 71. Stand Up and Be Counted 72, etc.
TV series: Topper 53. Funny Face 71. Lotsa Luck 74.

Freeman, Leonard (1921–1974). American TV producer best known for *Hawaii Five-O*.

Freeman, Mona (1926–) (Monica Freeman). American leading lady, at her peak as a troublesome teenager in the forties.
□National Velvet 44. Our Hearts were Young and Gay 44. Till We Meet Again 44. Here Come the Waves 44. Together Again 44. Roughly Speaking 45. Junior Miss 45. Danger Signal 45. Black Beauty 46. That Brennan Girl 46. Our Hearts Were Growing Up 46. Variety Girl 47. *Dear Ruth* 47. Mother Wore Tights 47. Isn't It Romantic? 48. Streets of Laredo 49. The Heiress 49. Dear Wife 49. Branded 50. Copper Canyon 50. I Was a Shoplifter 50. Dear Brat 51. Darling How Could You? 51. The Lady from Texas 51. Flesh and Fury 52. Jumping Jacks 52. Angel Face 52. Thunderbirds 52. Battle Cry 55. The Road to Denver 55. The Way Out (GB) 56. Before I Wake (GB) 56. Hold Back the Night 56. Huk 56. Dragoon Wells Massacre 57. The World was his Jury 58.

Freeman, Robert (c. 1935–). British director, former fashion director and title artist (*A Hard Day's Night, Help*).

The Touchables 68. World of Fashion (short) 68. L'Echelle Blanche 69.

freeze frame. A printing device whereby the action appears to 'freeze' into a still, this being accomplished by printing one frame many times.

Fregonese, Hugo (1908–87). Argentine-born director, former journalist, in Hollywood from 1945.
One-Way Street 50. Saddle Tramp 51. Apache Drums 51. Mark of the Renegade 52. My Six Convicts 52. Decameron Nights 53. Blowing Wild 54. The Man in the Attic 54. The Raid 53. Black Tuesday 54. Seven Thunders (GB) 57. Harry Black 58. Marco Polo 61. Apaches Last Battle (Old Shatterhand) (Ger.) 64. Savage Pampas (Sp.) 66, etc.

The French Connection (US 1971) (AA). Moderate police yarn about New York cops tracking down heroin smugglers. Its success was due to a splendid car chase, a strong performance by Gene Hackman as a brutish cop, and a fashionable use of bad language and wild sound (which often rendered the dialogue unintelligible). Directed by William Friedkin from a script by Ernest Tidyman. A 1975 sequel, *French Connection II*, continued the chase to Marseilles, but the storyline was pointless and repetitive.

French, Harold (1897–). British stage actor and producer, in films since 1931. Biography 1970: *I Swore I Never Would*. 1972: *I Thought I Never Could*.
AS DIRECTOR: The House of the Arrow 39. Jeannie 41. Unpublished Story 42. The Day Will Dawn 42. Secret Mission 42. *Dear Octopus* 43. English Without Tears 44. Mr Emmanuel 44. Quiet Weekend 46. My Brother Jonathan 47. The Blind Goddess 48. Quartet (part) 48. The Dancing Years 49. Trio (part) 50. Encore (part) 51. The Hour of 13 52. Isn't Life Wonderful 53. Rob Roy 53. Forbidden Cargo 54. The Man Who Loved Redheads 55, etc.

French, Leslie (1899–). Diminutive British character player.
This England 41. *Orders to Kill* 58. The Leopard 63. More than a Miracle 67. Death in Venice 70, etc.

French, Valerie (1931–). British actress, in occasional Hollywood films.
Jubal 56. Garment Center 57. Decision at Sundown 57. The Four Skulls of Jonathan Drake 59. Shalako 68, etc.

Frend, Charles (1909–1977). British director.
AS EDITOR: Waltzes from Vienna 33. Secret Agent 36. Sabotage 37. Young and Innocent 37. The Citadel 38. Goodbye Mr Chips 39. Major Barbara 40, etc.
□AS DIRECTOR: The Big Blockade 42. The Foreman Went to France 42. *San Demetrio London* (& w) 43. Johnny Frenchman 45. Return of the Vikings 45. The Loves of Joanna Godden 47. Scott of the Antarctic 48. A Run for Your Money 49. The Magnet 49. *The Cruel Sea* 53. Lease of Life 54. The Long Arm 56. Barnacle Bill 58. Cone of Silence 60. Girl on Approval 62. Torpedo Bay 62. The Shy Bike 67.

Fresnay, Pierre (1897–1975) (Pierre Laudenbach). Distinguished French stage actor who made many films.
Marius (debut) 31. Fanny 32. César 34. The Man Who Knew Too Much (GB) 34. *La Grande Illusion* 37. Le Corbeau 43. *Monsieur Vincent* 47. *God Needs Men* 50. The Fanatics 57, others.

Freud (US 1962). A biographical film written by Charles Kaufman and Wolfgang Reinhardt, directed by John Huston in the actual Viennese locations, with a cast including Montgomery Clift, Susannah York and Larry Parks; but to little avail in terms of public response despite the sensational incidents depicted. Significant as a contrast to the Warner biographical films of the late thirties, which were very similar but hugely successful.

Freud, Sigmund (1856–1939). Viennese physician who became the virtual inventor of psychoanalysis and the discoverer of sexual inhibition as a mainspring of human behaviour; a gentleman, therefore, to whom Hollywood has every reason to be grateful.

Freund, Karl (1890–1969). Czech-born cinematographer, famous for his work in German silents like The Last Laugh 24. Metropolis 26. Variety 26. Berlin 27, etc.
SINCE IN USA: *The Mummy* (& d) 33. Moonlight and Pretzels (d only) 33. Madame Spy (d only) 33. Mad Love (d only) 35. Camille 36. *The Good Earth* (AA) 37. Marie Walewska 38. Pride and Prejudice 40. The Seventh Cross 44. Key Largo 48. Bright Leaf 50, many others.

Frey, Leonard (1938–). American character actor.
The Magic Christian 70. Tell Me That You Love Me Junie Moon 70. *The Boys in the Band* 70. Fiddler on the Roof 71. Shirts/Skins (TV) 73. Where the Buffalo Roam 80.
TV series: Best of the West 81.

Friderici, Blanche (1870/78–1933). American character actress of stark, dour presence.
Trespassing 22. Sadie Thompson 28. Jazz Heaven 29. Billy the Kid 30. Kismet 30. Night Nurse 31. Murder by the Clock 32. Mata Hari 31. Love Me Tonight 32. A Farewell to Arms 32. If I Had a Million 32. Flying Down to Rio 33. It Happened One Night 34, many others.

Fried, Gerald (1926–). American composer.
Killer's Kiss 55. Terror in a Texas Town 58. A Cold Wind in August 60. The Cabinet of Caligari 62. One Potato Two Potato 64. The Killing of Sister George 68. Too Late the Hero 69. The Grissom Gang 71. Soylent Green 73. Roots (TV) 76. Testimony of Two Men (TV) 77. Foul Play 78. Little Darlings 80. Nine to Five 80, many others.

Friedhofer, Hugo (1902–1981). American composer.
The Adventures of Marco Polo 38. China Girl 42. The Lodger 44. The Woman in the Window 45. *The Best Years of Our Lives* (AA) 46. The Bishop's Wife 47. Joan of Arc 48. Broken Arrow 50. Ace in the Hole 51. Above and Beyond 52. Vera Cruz 54. The Rains of Ranchipur 55. The Harder They Fall 56. One-Eyed Jacks 59. The Secret Invasion 64. The Red Baron 71. Die Sister Die 78, etc.

Friedkin, William (1939–). American director, from TV.
Good Times 67. The Birthday Party 68. The Night They Raided Minsky's 68. The Boys in the Band 70. *The French Connection* (AA) 71. *The Exorcist* 73. Sorcerer 77. The Brinks Job 79. Cruising 80. Deal of the Century 84. To Live and Die in L.A. 85.

¶ *W.F.:* By the time a film of mine makes it into the theatres, I have a love-hate relationship with it. There is always something I could have done to make it better.

Friedman, Seymour (–). American second feature director.
Trapped by Boston Blackie 48. Prison Warden 49. Customs Agent 50. Criminal Lawyer 51. Son of Dr Jekyll 51. Escape Route (co-d) (GB) 53. Secret of Treasure Mountain 56, etc.

Friedman, Stephen (–). American producer.
Loving Molly (& w) 73. Little Darlings 80. Hero at Large 80, etc.

Friels, Colin (–). Australian leading man.
High Tide 87. Ground Zero 87. Warm Nights on a Slow Moving Train 87.

Friend, Philip (1915–). British leading man with stage experience.
Pimpernel Smith 41. Next of Kin 42. The Flemish Farm 43. Great Day 45. My Own True Love (US) 48. Panthers' Moon (US) 50 The Highwayman (US) 51. Background 53. Son of Robin Hood 59. Stranglehold 62, etc.

Friese-Greene, William (1855–1921). Pioneer British inventor who built the first practical movie camera in 1889. Died penniless; his life was the subject of *The Magic Box* 51.
Biography 1948: *Friese-Greene, Close-Up of an Inventor* by Ray Allister.

Friml, Rudolf (1879–1972). Czech-American composer of operettas which were frequently filmed: *The Firefly, Rose Marie, The Vagabond King,* etc.

Frings, Ketti (1909–1981) (Catherine Frings). American scenarist.
Hold Back the Dawn (& original novel) 41. Guest in the House 44. The Accused 48. Dark City 50. Because of You 52. Come Back Little Sheba 53. Foxfire 55, etc.

Fritsch, Willy (1901–73). Popular German leading man, in films since 1921.
The Spy 28. Congress Dances 31. Drei Von Der Tankstelle 31 (and 55). Amphitryon 35. Film Ohne Titel 47, many others.

Fritz the Cat (US 1971). Satirical animated feature by Ralph Bakshi from his comic strip for adults only; the feline hero gets into some pretty repellent adventures in the urban underground. The contrast between the subject and the old-fashioned Tom and Jerry style was striking, but a sequel was less effective.

Frobe, Gert (1913–). German character actor first seen abroad as the downtrodden little man of *Berliner Ballade* 48; later put on weight and emerged in the sixties as an international semi-star, usually as villain.
Ewiger Walzer 54. Double Destin 54.The Heroes Are Tired 55. He Who Must Die 56. The Girl Rosemarie 58. Menschen im Hotel 59. The Thousand Eyes of Dr Mabuse 60. The Longest Day 62. Die Dreigroschenoper 63. The Testament of Dr Mabuse 64. *Goldfinger* 64. Those Magnificent Men in Their Flying Machines 65. Is Paris Burning? 66. Du Rififi à Paname 67. I Killed Rasputin 67. Rocket to the Moon 67. Monte Carlo or Bust 69. Dollars 71. Ludwig 72. And Then There Were None 75. The Serpent's Egg 77. Bloodline 79. Le Coup de Parapluie 80, etc.

Froeschel, George (1891–1979). Viennese-American scriptwriter, long in Hollywood; often one of a team.
Waterloo Bridge 40. The Mortal Storm 40. Mrs Miniver 42. Random Harvest 42. The White Cliffs of Dover 44. Command Decision 48. The Miniver Story 50. Scaramouche 52. Never Let Me Go 53. Betrayed 54. Quentin Durward 55. Me and the Colonel 58, many others.

Frohlich, Gustav (1902–). German actor (from *Metropolis* 26) and director (*The Sinner* 51, etc.). Few of his films have been exported.
Asphalt 29. Stadt Anatol 36. Der Grosse König 41, etc.

From Caligari to Hitler. This 'psychological history of the German film' by Siegfried Kracauer was first published in 1946 and quickly became the standard work on its subject. It embraces Nazi propaganda films as well as the silent classics of the twenties.

From Here to Eternity (US 1953) (AA). A seething melodramatic attack on the US Army, this over-sexed, over sentimentalized and thoroughly unattractive picture, from James Jones' 'realistic' novel, was extremely well directed by Fred Zinnemann (AA) from a scenario by Daniel Taradash (AA). Photographed by Burnett Guffey (AA), with solid performances from Burt Lancaster, Frank Sinatra (AA), Deborah Kerr, Montgomery Clift, Donna Reed (AA) and Ernest Borgnine. A six-hour TV version appeared in 1979, directed by Buzz Kulik, with William Devane and Natalie Wood, and a subsequent one-hour series followed the further adventures of the surviving characters.

From This Day Forward (US 1945). An early example of American romantic realism, a simple love story shot on the streets of New York. Written by Hugo Butler; photographed by George Barnes; directed by John Berry; with Joan Fontaine and Mark Stevens.

Froman, Jane (1907–1980). American band singer, whose heroic resumption of her career following an air crash was portrayed in *With a Song in My Heart*, in which she was played by Susan Hayward.

Frome, Milton (–). American comedy character actor, often in bad-tempered bits.
You're Never Too Young 55. Short Cut to Hell 59. I'd Rather Be Rich 64. The St Valentine's Day Massacre 67. The Strongest Man in the World 75, etc.

The Front Page. Ben Hecht and Charles MacArthur's tough, hard-boiled Broadway comedy was first filmed in 1930 by Lewis Milestone, with Pat O'Brien as the fast-talking reporter who shields an escaped murderer, and Adolphe Menjou as his scheming editor. In 1940 Howard Hawks remade it as *His Girl Friday*, with a sex switch: Rosalind Russell played the reporter and Cary Grant her boss. 1974 brought Billy Wilder's freewheeling version with Jack Lemmon and Walter Matthau.

Frontière, Dominic (1931–). American composer.
The Marriage Go Round 60. Hero's Island 62. The Outer Limits (TV) 63. Billie 65. The Invaders (TV) 67. Hang 'Em High 68. Popi 69. Chisum 70. Cancel My Reservation 72. Hammersmith is Out 72. Freebie and the Bean 74. Brannigan 75. The Gumball Rally 76. Washington Behind Closed Doors (TV) 77. The Stunt Man 80. Modern Problems 81, etc.

frost on movie windows is usually produced from a mixture of epsom salts and stale beer.

Frost, David (1939–). Britain's Mr Television of the sixties, later exported to America; mixes entertainment shows with hard-hitting political interviews, and latterly financed a number of rather indifferent movies.
The Rise and Rise of Michael Rimmer 70. The Slipper and the Rose 76.

¶ He has risen without trace.—*Kitty Muggeridge*
Hello, good evening, and welcome. —*catchphrase*

Fruet, Bill (–). Canadian director.
Death Weekend 76. Search and Destroy 79. Funeral Home 81. Death Bite 83, etc.

Frye, Dwight (1899–1943). American character actor who made a corner in crazed hunchbacks.
□ The Night Bird 27. Doorway to Hell 30. Man to Man 31. The Maltese Falcon 31. *Dracula* 31. The Black Camel 31. *Frankenstein* 31. By Whose Hand 32. Attorney for the Defense 32. The Invisible Man 33. Strange Adventure 33. Western Code 33. The Vampire Bat 33. The Circus Queen Murder 33. King Solomon of Broadway 33. The Crime of Dr Crespi 33. The Great Impersonation 35. Atlantic Adventure 35. Bride of Frankenstein 35. Florida Special 36. Alibi for Murder 36. The Man who Found Himself 36. Something to Sing About 36. Beware of Ladies 37. The Shadow 37. Great Guy 37. Sea Devils 37. Renfrew of the Royal Mounted 37. Invisible Enemy 38. Fast Company 38. Adventure in Sahara 38. Who Killed Gail Preston 38. Sinners in Paradise 38. Conspiracy 39. Son of Frankenstein 39. The Man in the Iron Mask 39. I Take This Woman 39. Gangs of Chicago 40. Phantom Raiders 40. Drums of Fu Manchu 40. Sky Bandits 40. Mystery Ship 41. Son of Monte Cristo 41. The People vs Dr Kildare 41. Blonde from Singapore 41. The Devil Pays Off 41. Prisoner of Japan 42. The Ghost of Frankenstein 42. Sleepytime Gal 42. Danger in the Pacific 42. Frankenstein meets the Wolf Man 43. Dead Men Walk 43. Submarine Alert 43. Hangmen Also Die 43. Dangerous Blondes 43.

Fryer, Robert (1920–). American producer, former casting director.
The Boston Strangler 68. The Prime of Miss Jean Brodie 69. Myra Breckinridge 69. The Salzburg Connection 71. Travels with My Aunt 73. Mame 73. The Abdication 73. Voyage of the Damned 76.

Fu Manchu. Sax Rohmer's oriental master-criminal was played by Harry Agar Lyons in a series of British two-reelers in the twenties. Warner Oland played him in *The Mysterious Fu Manchu* 29, *The Return of Fu Manchu* 30 and *Daughter of the Dragon* 31; Boris Karloff in *Mask of Fu Manchu* 32, and Henry Brandon in *Drums of Fu Manchu* 41. Otherwise he was oddly neglected until the sixties series starring Christopher Lee, beginning with *The Face of Fu Manchu* 65 and *Brides of Fu Manchu* 66: it degenerated into shambling nonsense.

Fuest, Robert (1927–). British director, from TV.
□Just Like a Woman 66. And Soon the Darkness 70. *Wuthering Heights* 70. The Abominable Dr Phibes 71. Dr Phibes Rises Again 72. The Final Programme (& w) 73. The Devil's Rain (US) 76. The Revenge of the Stepford Wives (TV) 80.

The Fugitive. Under this title there have been at least two silent adventures, two second feature westerns, one Polish and one Indian film. John Ford's *The Fugitive* 47 is deservedly the best known of all, a pictorially beautiful if depressing account of the last struggles of a 'whisky priest' in Mexico, from Graham Greene's book *The Power and the Glory*. There was also a successful modern TV series of the same title.

Fujimoto, Tak (–). Japanese-American cinematographer.
Remember My Name 78. Last Embrace 79. Borderline 80. Melvin and Howard 80. Where the Buffalo Roam 80. Heart Like a Wheel 83, etc.

Fuller, Leslie (1889–1948). Beefy British concert-party comedian who was popular in broad comedy films of the thirties.
□ Not so Quiet on the Western Front 30. Kiss Me Sergeant 30. Why Sailors Leave Home 30. Old Soldiers Never Die 31. Poor Old Bill 31. What a Night 31. The Last Coupon 32. Old Spanish Customers 32. Tonight's the Night 32. Hawleys of the High Street 33. The Pride of the Force 33. A Political Party 34. The Outcast 34. Lost in the Legion 34. Doctor's Orders 34. Strictly Illegal 35. Captain Bill 35. The Stoker 35. One Good Turn 36. Boys will be Girls 37. The Middle Watch 39. Two Smart Men 40. My Wife's Family 41. Front Line Kids 42. What do we do Now 45.

Fuller, Robert (1934–). American leading man, mostly on TV.
Return of the Seven 66. Incident at Phantom Hill 67. The Hard Ride 70. The Gatling Gun 72. Mustang Country 76, etc.
TV series: *Laramie* 59–62. Wagon Train 62–63. Emergency 72–77.

Fuller, Samuel (1912–). American writer-director who has also produced most of his own pictures; which have normally been violent melodramas on topical subjects.
□I Shot Jesse James 49. The Baron of Arizona 50. Fixed Bayonets 51. The Steel Helmet 51. Park Row 52. Pickup on South Street 52. Hell and High Water 54. House of Bamboo 55. Run of the Arrow 55. China Gate 56. Forty Guns 57. Verboten 58. The Crimson Kimono 59. Underworld USA 60. Merrill's Marauders 62. Shock Corridor 64. The Naked Kiss 66. Shark 67. Dead Pigeon on Beethoven Street 72 (West Ger.). The American Friend (acted only) 77. The Big Red One 80. White Dog 82.

Fullerton, Fiona (1955–). British juvenile actress of the seventies.
Run Wild Run Free 69. Nicholas and Alexandra 71. Alice's Adventures in Wonderland 72. Gauguin the Savage (TV) 80. A View to a Kill 85. Shaka Zulu (TV) 87. Hold the Dream (TV) 87, etc.

Fulton, John P. (1902–1965). American special effects photographer, responsible for the tricks in most of the *Invisible Man* series and other fantasy movies.

funerals provided a starting point for *The Third Man, Frankenstein, The Great Man, Death of a Salesman, The Bad and the Beautiful, Citizen Kane,* and *Keeper of the Flame*; figured largely in *The Premature Burial, The Mummy, The Egyptian, The Fall of the House of Usher, The Counterfeit Traitor, Funeral in Berlin, The Godfather, The Glass Key, I Bury the Living, Miracle in Milan, Doctor Zhivago* and *Hamlet*; and formed a climax for *Our Town*. In *Vampyr* and *Wild Strawberries* the hero dreamed of his own funeral; and in *Holy Matrimony* Monty Woolley attended his own funeral, having arranged to have his valet's body mistaken for his. Funerals were taken lightly in *I See a Dark Stranger, Little Caesar, Kind Hearts and Coronets, Too Many Crooks, A Comedy of Terrors, Charade, The Wrong Box, I Love You Alice B. Toklas, Robin and the Seven Hoods, Monsieur Hulot's Holiday, Entr'acte, Ocean's Eleven, Comrade X, What a Way to Go, The Private Life of Sherlock Holmes,* and above all *The Loved One.*

funfairs have provided fascinating settings for many a bravura film sequence. *The Wagons Roll at Night, Nightmare Alley, Dante's Inferno, Rollercoaster* and *The Ring* were set almost entirely on fairgrounds. Tawdry or 'realistic' funfairs were shown in *Jeanne Eagels, Saturday Night and Sunday Morning, East of Eden, Picnic,* and *Inside Daisy Clover;* glamorized or sentimentalized ones cropped up in *The Wolf Man, My Girl Tisa, State Fair, Roseanna McCoy, The Great Ziegfeld* and *Mr and Mrs Smith.* Musicals like *On the Town, On the Avenue, Coney Island, Centennial Summer, State Fair* and *Down to Earth* had funfair sequences and they are also used to excellent advantage in thrillers: *Brighton Rock, Spider Woman, Horrors of the Black Museum, Gorilla at Large, The Third Man, Lady from Shanghai, Strangers on a Train.* Naturally funfairs are also marvellous places for fun: though not for Eddie Cantor in *Strike Me Pink,* Tony Curtis in *Forty Pounds of Trouble,* Laurel and Hardy in *The Dancing Masters,* or Bob Hope (fired from a cannon) in *Road to Zanzibar. The Beast from 20,000 Fathoms* was finally cornered in a funfair; *Dr Caligari* kept his cabinet in one. The star who made the most of a funfair sequence was undoubtedly Mae West as the carnival dancer in *I'm No Angel,* in which she delivered her famous line: 'Suckers!'

Funicello, Annette (1942–). American leading lady, former juvenile actress; was host of Disney's TV Mickey Mouse Club, and in his films is known simply as 'Annette'.
Johnny Tremain 57. The Shaggy Dog 61. Babes in Toyland 61. The Misadventures of Merlin Jones 63. Bikini Beach 64. The Monkey's Uncle 65. Fireball 500 66. Back to the Beach 87, etc.

? funny men

Comedians are often accused of stealing each other's gags, but in fact a good comic is inseparable from his own material. The following lines are all typical of their proprietors, a formidable array of leading laughtermakers. Which? And in which films?

1 Lemonade . . . in a dirty glass!
2 I brought you some hard boiled eggs and some nuts.
3 I got that note from Bing Crosby—and boy was he glad to get rid of it!
4 Get your tuttsi-fruttsi ice cream . . .
5 So they call me Concentration Camp Erhardt?
6 Either this guy's dead or my watch has stopped.
7 I'm a ba-a-a-a-ad boy!
8 Yes, indubitably . . .
9 Who will be the next to outwit me? This is a game of chance . . .

10 I'm a controversial figure. My friends either dislike me or hate me.

Funt, Allen (1914–). American TV trickster who appeared for years on *Candid Camera* and in 1970 produced and starred in a film version, *What Do You Say to a Naked Lady?*

Furie, Sidney J. (1933–). Canadian director with a restless camera; came to Britain 1959, Hollywood 1966.
□A Dangerous Age 57. A Cool Sound from Hell 58. The Snake Woman 60. Doctor Blood's Coffin 61. During One Night 61. Three on a Spree 61. The Young Ones 61. The Boys 62. The Leather Boys 63. Wonderful Life 64. *The Ipcress File* 65. Day of the Arrow 65. The Appaloosa 66. The Naked Runner 67. The Lawyer 69. Little Fauss and Big Halsy 70. Lady Sings the Blues 72. Hit 73. Sheila Levine Is Dead and Living in New York 75. Gable and Lombard 76. The Boys in Company C 77. The Entity 82. Purple Hearts 84. Iron Eagle 85. Superman IV 87.
TV series: Hudson's Bay 59.

Furneaux, Yvonne (1928–). French leading lady in British films.
Meet Me Tonight 52. The Dark Avenger 55. Lisbon 56. The Mummy 59. La Dolce Vita 59. Enough Rope (Fr.) 63. *Repulsion* 64. The Scandal (Fr.) 66, etc.

Furrer, Urs (1934–1975). Swiss-born American cinematographer.
Pigeons 70. Desperate Characters 71. Shaft 71. Shaft's Big Score 72. Dr Cook's Garden (TV) 72. The Seven Ups 73, etc.

Furse, Judith (1912–). British character actress who often plays district nurses, matrons, heavy schoolmistresses, etc.
Goodbye Mr Chips 39. English Without Tears 44. Black Narcissus 46. The Man in the White Suit 51. Doctor at Large 57. Serious Charge 59, etc.

Furse, Margaret (1911–1974). British costume designer.
Oliver Twist 48. The Mudlark 50. The Inn of the Sixth Happiness 58. Sons and Lovers 60. Young Cassidy 64. Anne of the Thousand Days 70. Mary Queen of Scots 72. Love Among the Ruins (TV) 75, etc.

Furse, Roger (1903–1972). British stage designer.
Henry V (costumes only) 44. The True Glory 45. Odd Man Out 47. Hamlet 47. Ivanhoe 52. Richard III 56. The Prince and the Showgirl 57. Saint Joan 57. Bonjour Tristesse 58. The Roman Spring of Mrs Stone 61. Road to Hong Kong 62, etc.

Furthman, Jules (1888–1966). Seminal American writer, usually in collaboration.
Treasure Island 20. The Way of All Flesh 27. *Shanghai Express* 32. *Mutiny on the Bounty* 35. Spawn of the North 38. Only Angels Have Wings 39. The Outlaw 43. To Have and Have Not 44. The Big Sleep 46. Nightmare Alley 48. Jet Pilot 50 (released 57). Peking Express 51, many others.

Fury (US 1936). Fritz Lang's first and best indictment of lynch law, but with a happy ending. Important and influential, coming two years before *They Won't Forget,* it was also highly commercial, with a suspenseful plot and a star performance from Spencer Tracy as the man unjustly accused. Written by Lang and Bartlett Cormack from a novel by Norman Krasna; photographed by Joseph Ruttenberg, with music by Franz Waxman.

Fury, Billy (1941–1983) (Ronald Wycherly). British pop singer.
□Play it Cool 62. I've Gotta Horse 65. That'll Be the Day 73.

Fusco, Giovanni (1906–1968). Italian composer, especially associated with Antonioni.
Cronaca di un Amore 50. Le Amiche 51. Il Grido 57. Hiroshima Mon Amour 59. L'Avventura 59. The Eclipse 62. The Red Desert 64. The War is Over 66, etc.

Fyffe, Will (1884–1947). Pawky Scots comedian, famous in the halls for his song 'I Belong to Glasgow'.
Happy 34. Annie Laurie 36. Cotton Queen 37. Owd Bob 38. The Mind of Mr Reeder 39. Rulers of the Sea (US) 39. For Freedom 40. Neutral Port 40. Heaven Is Round the Corner 44. The Brothers 47, etc.

Answers

fade outs I

1 No prizes for naming the film: Rosebud points only to *Citizen Kane* (1941). But the speaker? The reporter, Thompson, played by William Alland who later became a producer at Universal □

2 Obviously a phone call . . . the one made by Ernest Borgnine at the end of *Marty* (1955) when he has decided that he means to continue his friendship with the plain girl played by Betsy Blair □

3 Paul Muni's final speech to the stars in *The Good Earth* (1937). His wife O'Lan, played by Luise Rainer, has just died □

4 Difficult because, although these are the last clear lines of dialogue in the movie, they are followed by two or three minutes of shouting and general hubbub. The speaker is Claude Rains, playing corrupt Senator Paine in *Mr Smith Goes to Washington* (1939). □ His admission, in full Senate, brings wild rejoicing from all concerned, and the film ends with a shot of Harry Carey, as president of the assembly, giving up his attempt to restore order and relaxing in his chair with a smile. The published script has subsequent wind-up scenes, but they were either deleted before the première or never filmed.

5 James Cagney as the psychopathic mother-fixated gangster Cody Jarrett in *White Heat* (1949), as he blows himself up by firing a bullet into the giant gas cylinder on top of which he has been cornered by police.

6 Practically impossible, but irresistible. It comes from a 1956 Rank British film *High Tide at Noon*, set in the lobster fishing communities of Nova Scotia. □ The young lovers are separated by various complications including the disappearance of lobsters from the locality. The heroine returns years later, to be greeted with this ecstatic news by her boyfriend Michael Craig, and the scene fades out on a seaside clinch and track-back which should figure in any collector's compendium of clichés.

7 Paul Muni in *I Am a Fugitive from a Chain Gang* (1932). □ At the end of the film, a victim of circumstance, he has been on the run for years, when one night he meets again his old girlfriend. 'What do you do now?' she asks helplessly. 'I steal . . .' is his chilling reply as he fades into the darkness.

8 James Donald at the end of *The Bridge on the River Kwai* (1958) by which time the intentions of the leading characters are vague enough to give his remark a double meaning □

9 Robert Armstrong as Carl Denham speaking the epitaph on *King Kong* (1933) as the monster ape lies dead at the foot of the Empire State Building □

10 Gloria Swanson as Norma Desmond in *Sunset Boulevard* (1950). The ageing film star has killed her lover and become quite mad, so that as she descends the stairs to the waiting police cars she imagines that the newspaper photographers are studio cameramen waiting to capture her beauty □

11 This has to be Errol Flynn, and it is. The film is *Desperate Journey* (1942), the scene an aeroplane as he speeds back to England after apparently decimating the Nazi strength in Germany □

12 Vivien Leigh as Scarlett O'Hara in *Gone with the Wind* (1939). □ Of course.

13 Heather Sears in *Room at the Top* (1959). □ Her bridegroom Joe Lampton has made her pregnant and got what he always wanted, money and prestige; but as they drive away in the wedding car and she sees a tear in his eye, she does not realize that he is thinking of his dead mistress, the only woman he has really loved.

14 I doubt whether anyone would guess the source of this quote as *Mrs Miniver* (1942). The film ends on a service in the bombed village church, and these are the last words of the sermon preached by Henry Wilcoxon □

15 Edward Van Sloan as he stands by the body of *Dracula's Daughter* (1936) and agrees with Otto Kruger's comment about her beauty □

16 Irony, of course. A great deal did happen to the people in *Grand Hotel* (1933), but doorman Jean Hersholt didn't know about it □

17 *What's Up, Doc?* (1972). This is Ryan O'Neal's reaction to the use by Barbra Streisand of his own famous line from *Love Story*, 'Love means never having to say you're sorry' □

18 Spencer Tracy's last screen line in his last picture, *Guess Who's Coming to Dinner* □
19 John Wayne in the film which brought him an Oscar for letting it all hang out: *True Grit* □
20 Mary Boland as the dithery Mrs Bennet in *Pride and Prejudice* □
21 Not easy. Wylie Watson as the doomed Mr Memory in Hitchcock's *The 39 Steps* □
22 Not difficult. Leslie Howard, back to camera, slouching in his chair, hat tipped back over his head, in *Pygmalion*. (Or Rex Harrison in *My Fair Lady*.) □

fade outs II

1 *Ace in the Hole* □ 2 *Casablanca* □ 3 *Modern Times* □ 4 *Harvey* □ 5 *Arsenic and Old Lace* □ (He is replying to Cary Grant's assertion that *he* is the son of a sea cook.) 6 *The Third Man* □ 7 *Duck Soup* □ 8 *Random Harvest* □ 9 *Strangers on a Train* □ 10 *Rebecca* □ 11 *Top Hat* □ 12 *The Country Girl* □ 13 *And Then There Were None* □ 14 *Dr No* □ 15 *Scarface* □ 16 *All Quiet on the Western Front* □ 17 *All That Money Can Buy* □ 18 *Lost Horizon* (1937) □ 19 *Heaven Can Wait* □ 20 *Room at the Top* □ 21 *The Devil Is a Woman* (1935) □ 22 *The Lady Vanishes* □ 23 *African Queen* □ 24 *The Women* □ 25 *The Blue Angel* □ 26 *Dead of Night* □ 27 *Road to Utopia* □ 28 *The Maltese Falcon* □ 29 *Kind Hearts and Coronets* □ 30 *The Wizard of Oz* □

families

1 Ray Milland □ 2 Gladys Cooper □ 3 Thomas Mitchell □ 4 May Robson □ 5 Edna May Oliver □ 6 Susan Kohner □ 7 Henry Fonda □ 8 Janet Blair □ 9 Marjorie Main □ 10 Walter Pidgeon □ 11 Virginia Mayo □ 12 Murray Hamilton □ 13 Adolphe Menjou □ 14 John Halliday □ 15 Mary Boland □ 16 Ann Blyth □ 17 Una O'Connor □ 18 Ann Dvorak □ 19 Elizabeth Taylor □ 20 Ruth Chatterton □ 21 Nigel Bruce □ 22 Bobs Watson □ 23 Luise Rainer □ 24 Brian Aherne □ 25 John Howard □ 26 Doris Nolan □ 27 Gloria Stuart □ 28 Diana Lynn □ 29 Cyril Raymond □ 30 Harry Shannon □ 31 Josephine Hull □ 32 Eva Moore □ Brember Wills □ John Dudgeon (actually Elspeth Dudgeon) □ 33 Warner Oland □ 34 Mae Busch □ 35 Geraldine Fitzgerald □ 36 Helen Broderick □ 37 Roland Young □ 38 Alan Hale □ 39 Betty Field □ 40 Robert Warwick □ 41 Jane Darwell □ 42 Billie Whitelaw □ 43 Harry Davenport □ 44 Michael Redgrave □ 45 Spring Byington □ 46 Sara Haden □ 47 Tim Holt □ 48 Frederick Kerr □ 49 Alice Brady □ 50 Charles Coburn □ 51 Teresa Wright □ 52 Maggie Smith □

famous roles

1 Bette Davis: *The Little Foxes*, *John Paul Jones*, *All About Eve* □
2 James Stewart: *The Shop Around the Corner*, *Harvey*, *The Philadelphia Story* □
3 Humphrey Bogart: *The Maltese Falcon*, *High Sierra*, *The Barefoot Contessa* □
4 Merle Oberon: *Wuthering Heights*, *The Scarlet Pimpernel*, *A Song to Remember* □
5 Claude Rains: *Casablanca*, *Mr Skeffington*, *The Adventures of Robin Hood* □
6 James Cagney: *Love Me Me or Leave Me*, *Angels with Dirty Faces*, *Yankee Doodle Dandy* □
7 Paul Muni: *Scarface*, *A Song to Remember*, *The Life of Emile Zola* □
8 Joan Fontaine: *Frenchman's Creek*, *The Constant Nymph*, *Rebecca* □
9 Spencer Tracy: *Pat and Mike*, *Northwest Passage*, *Fury* □
10 Groucho Marx: *Love Happy*, *Room Service*, *A Day at the Races* □
11 John Wayne: *The High and the Mighty*, *Sands of Iwo Jima*, *Stagecoach* □
12 Errol Flynn: *Gentleman Jim*, *The Charge of the Light Brigade*, *The Adventures of Robin Hood* □

fantasy

1 *It Grows on Trees* □ 2 *Once Upon a Time* □ 3 *It's a Wonderful Life* □ 4 *Topper Returns* □ 5 *Bobbikins* □ 6 *Birds Do It* □ 7 *Shadow of the Cat* □ 8 *The Next Voice You Hear* □ 9 *The Absent-Minded Professor* □ 10 *It Happens Every Spring* □ 11 *You Never Can Tell* (GB: *You Never Know*) □ 12 *Fantastic Voyage* □ 13 *What's So Bad About Feeling Good?* □ 14 *The Incredible Mr Limpet* □ 15 *The Incredible Shrinking Man* □ 16 *Rhubarb* □

the film and the face

1 *White Heat* □ James Cagney □ 2 *I Married a Witch* □ Fredric March □ 3 *The Lady in the Lake* □ Audrey Totter □ 4 *Phantom of the Opera* □ Claude Rains □ 5 *The Third Man* □ Joseph Cotten □ 6 *Double Indemnity* □ Fred MacMurray □ 7 *Cimarron* □ Richard Dix □ 8 *A Bill of Divorcement* □ Katharine Hepburn □ 9 *The Scarlet*

Pimpernel ☐ Leslie Howard ☐ 10 *All This and Heaven Too* ☐ Bette Davis ☐ 11 *Scarface* ☐ Paul Muni ☐ 12 *The Maltese Falcon* ☐ Mary Astor ☐ 13 *Little Caesar* ☐ Edward G. Robinson ☐ 14 *Arsenic and Old Lace* ☐ Cary Grant ☐ 15 *Blithe Spirit* ☐ Rex Harrison ☐ 16 *Pride and Prejudice* ☐ Greer Garson ☐ 17 *Mr Smith Goes to Washington* ☐ James Stewart ☐ 18 *Animal Crackers* ☐ Groucho Marx ☐ 19 *Citizen Kane* ☐ Joseph Cotten ☐ 20 *The Sign of the Cross* ☐ Fredric March ☐ 21 *The Little Foxes* ☐ Bette Davis ☐ 22 The Grapes of Wrath ☐ Henry Fonda ☐ 23 *Saturday Night and Sunday Morning* ☐ Albert Finney ☐ 24 *Suddenly Last Summer* ☐ Katharine Hepburn ☐ 25 *It's a Gift* ☐ W. C. Fields ☐

film of the book

1 Hitchcock's *The Lady Vanishes* (1938) ☐ 2 *Village of the Damned* ☐ 3 *The Pride and the Passion* ☐ 4 *Behold a Pale Horse* ☐ 5 *Crossfire* ☐ 6 *The Old Dark House* ☐ 7 *The Mark of Zorro* ☐ 8 *Bullitt* ☐ 9 *The Best Years of Our Lives* ☐ 10 *Seven Brides for Seven Brothers* ☐ 11 *Topkapi* ☐ 12 *Stagecoach* ☐ 13 *The Professionals* ☐ 14 *The Pajama Game* ☐ 15 *It Happened One Night* ☐ 16 *The Inn of the Sixth Happiness* ☐ 17 *The Heiress* ☐ 18 *Foreign Correspondent* ☐ 19 *Sabotage* (US title *A Woman Alone*). ☐ When he made this film in 1937, Hitchcock was unable to use the original title, as only the previous year he had made a quite different film called *Secret Agent.* 20 *Dr Strangelove* ☐ 21 Hitchcock's *Spellbound* ☐ 22 *White Cargo* ☐ 23 Hitchcock's *Young and Innocent* (*The Girl Was Young*) ☐ 24 Hitchcock's *Stage Fright* ☐ 25 *Bad Day at Black Rock* ☐ 26 *The Fallen Idol* ☐

first lines

1 *Duel in the Sun*. Narrator, Orson Welles ☐
2 *The Third Man*. Narrator—no, not Joseph Cotten, but allegedly Carol Reed ☐
3 Very difficult. Film buffs over fifty will remember that Warners used to make trailers for all their thrillers starting with Sydney Greenstreet in a far-off spotlight. 'Come closer,' he said, 'I have a tale to unfold . . .' Needless to say the trailer was usually better than the film. ☐
4 *Moby Dick*. Narrator, in the 1956 version, Richard Basehart ☐
5 The most famous line in film history: *Rebecca*, of course. Narrator, Joan Fontaine ☐
6 *Random Harvest*. The dark and guarded house is a military mental asylum. Narrator said to be James Hilton ☐
7 *Arsenic and Old Lace* ☐
8 *Roxie Hart* ☐
9 *Little Caesar* ☐
10 *Nothing Sacred*. Ben Hecht's style is inimitable ☐
11 *Ninotchka* ☐
12 Another unmistakable style—Chaplin's. The film, *The Great Dictator* ☐
13 *Rasputin and the Empress* ☐
14 *Rembrandt* ☐
15 *Since You Went Away* ☐
16 *Irma la Douce* ☐
17 Olivier's *Henry V* ☐
18 *The Song of Bernadette* ☐
19 *The Great McGinty* ☐
20 *The Palm Beach Story*: only Preston Sturges could begin a film with the end title ☐
21 *Babes in Arms* ☐
22 *Butch Cassidy and the Sundance Kid* ☐

flashbacks

1 *Sunset Boulevard* ☐ 2 *Dead Reckoning* ☐ 3 *The Great McGinty* ☐ 4 *Hold Back the Dawn* ☐ 5 *Rebecca* ☐ 6 *The Moon and Sixpence* or *The Razor's Edge* ☐ (In both of which he played Somerset Maugham) 7 *Enchantment* ☐ 8 *The Lavender Hill Mob* ☐ 9 *Roxie Hart* ☐ 10 *Road to Utopia* ☐ 11 *Edward My Son* ☐ 12 *The Teahouse of the August Moon* ☐ 13 *Kind Hearts and Coronets* ☐ 14 *Wuthering Heights* ☐

Errol Flynn

1 *Against All Flags* ☐ 2 *Kim* ☐ 3 *Cry Wolf* ☐ 4 *Never Say Goodbye* ☐ 5 *San Antonio* ☐ 6 *Uncertain Glory* ☐ 7 *Northern Pursuit* ☐ 8 *Edge of Darkness* ☐ 9 *Dive Bomber* ☐ 10 *Footsteps in the Dark* ☐ 11 *The Sea Hawk* ☐ 12 *Virginia City* ☐ 13 *The Dawn Patrol* ☐ 14 *The Prince and the Pauper* ☐ 15 *The Case of the Curious Bride* ☐

funny men

1 Bob Hope in a crowded bar in *Road to Utopia*, trying not to be thought a sissy ☐
2 Stan Laurel visiting Oliver Hardy in *County Hospital*, obviously about to be no comfort at all ☐
3 Jimmy Durante in almost every film he made ☐

4 Chico Marx, Hollywood's only Jewish Italian, in *A Day at the Races* ☐
5 Jack Benny playing for time in *To Be or Not to Be* ☐
6 Groucho Marx, also in *A Day at the Races*, pretending to be a doctor but unable to resist a crack ☐
7 Lou Costello's inevitable cry of self-reproach ☐
8 A line delivered in Robertson Hare's plummiest tones at each impending disaster ☐
9 W. C. Fields issuing sucker bait in *It's a Gift* ☐
10 Oscar Levant, self-styled 'the world's oldest child prodigy'. He also said, of his role in *Humoresque*, 'I played an unsympathetic part—myself.' ☐

G

G Men (US 1935). Following public outcry about glamorized gangster films, James Cagney went over to the law in this competent semi-documentary about J. Edgar Hoover's men. Directed by William Keighley, with a shoot-'em-up climax which is still rousing.

Gaal, Franceska (1904–72) (Fanny Zilveritch). Hungarian leading lady who made three American films: The Buccaneer 38. Paris Honeymoon 39. The Girl Downstairs 39.

Gabel, Martin (1912–86). Balding, rotund American character actor, mostly on stage. The Lost Moment (d only) 47. Fourteen Hours 51. M 51. The Thief 52. Tip on a Dead Jockey 57. Marnie 64. Lord Love a Duck 66. Divorce American Style 67. Lady in Cement 68. There was a Crooked Man 70. The Front Page 75. The First Deadly Sin 80, etc.

Gabel, Scilla (1937–). Buxom Italian leading lady in international films.
Queen of the Pirates 60. Village of Daughters 62. Sodom and Gomorrah 62. Revenge of the Gladiators 65. Modesty Blaise 66, etc.

Gabin, Jean (1904–1976) (Alexis Moncourgé). Distinguished French actor, former Folies Bergère extra, cabaret entertainer, etc. His stocky virility and world-weary features kept him a star from the early thirties.
□Chacun sa Chance 30. Mephisto 31. Paris Beguin 31. Gloria 31. Tout Ca ne vaut pas l'Amour 31. Coeur de Lilas 32. La Belle Marinère 32. Les Gaités de l'Escadron 32. La Foule Hurle 33. L'Etoile de Valencia 33. Adieu les Beaux Jours 33. Le Tunnel 33. De Haut en Bas 33. Au Bout du Monde 34. Zouzou 34. *Maria Chapdelaine* 34. Passage Interdit 35. Varietés 35. Golgotha 35. La Bandera 36. *La Belle Equipe* 36. Les Bas-Fonds 36. *Pépé le Moko* 37. *La Grande Illusion* 37. Le Messager 37. Gueule d'Amour 37. *Quai des Brumes* 38. *La Bête Humaine* 38. Le Recif de Corail 38. *Le Jour se Lève* 39. Remorques 41. Moontide (US) 42. The Imposter (US) 42. Martin Roumagnac 46. Miroir 47. Au Dela des Grilles 49. La Marie du Port 50. It's Easier for a Camel (It.) 51. Victor 51. Night is my Kingdom 51. Le Plaisir 52. The Truth about Bébé Donge 52. Bufere 53. La Vierge du Rhin 53. Leur Dernière Nuit 53. *Touchez Pas au Grisbi* 54. L'Air de Paris 54. Napoleon 55. French Can Can 55. Razzia sur la Chnouff 55. Port of Desire 55. Lost Dogs 56. Important People 56. Gas-Oil 56. Voici le Temps des Assassins 56. Pig Across Paris 56. Le Sang à la Tête 56. Crime and Punishment 56. Le Rouge est Mis 57. Les Misérables 57. The Case of Dr Laurent 58. Le Désordre et la Nuit 58. *Maigret Sets a Trap* 58. En Cas de Malheur 58. Les Grandes Familles 58. The Tramp 59. Maigret et l'Affaire Saint-Fiacre 59. Rue des Prairies 59. Le Baron de l'Ecluse 60. Les Vieux de la Vieille 61. Le President 61. Le Cave se Rebiffe 61. *A Monkey in Winter* 62. Le Gentleman d'Epsom 62. Mélodie en Sous-sol 63. Maigret Sees Red 63. Monsieur 64. The Ungrateful Age 65. God's Thunder 65. Rififi in Panama 66. Le Jardinier d'Argenteuil 67. Le Soleil des Voyous 67. Le Pacha 67. The Tattooed Man 68. Fin de Journée 69. The Sign of the Bull 69. The Sicilian Clan 70. La Horse 70. Le Drapeau Noir Flotte sur la Marmite 71. Le Tueur 72. *Le Chat* 72. L'affaire Dominici 73. Deux Hommes dans la Ville 74. Verdict 74. L'Année Sainte 76.
❀ For forcing such a wide range of roles, without ever losing sympathy, to fit his own dominant personality. *Quai des Brumes*.

Gable, Christopher (1940–). British actor, ex-ballet dancer.
Women in Love 69. The Music Lovers 70. The Boy Friend 71. The Slipper and the Rose 76.

Gable, Clark (1901–1960). American leading man who kept his popularity for nearly thirty years, and was known as the 'king' of Hollywood. His big ears were popular with caricaturists; his impudent grin won most female hearts.
□Forbidden Paradise 24. The Merry Widow 25. The Pacemakers 25. The Plastic Age 25. North Star 26. The Painted Desert 30. The

Easiest Way 31. Dance Fools Dance 31. A Free Soul 31. The Finger Points 31. The Secret Six 31. Laughing Sinners 31. Night Nurse 31. Sporting Blood 31. Susan Lenox 32. Possessed 32. Hell's Divers 32. Polly of the Circus 32. *Red Dust* 32. Strange Interlude 32. No Man of Her Own 32. The White Sister 32. Dancing Lady 33. Hold Your Man 33. Night Flight 33. *It Happened One Night* (AA) 34. Men in White 34. Manhattan Melodrama 34. Chained 34. After Office Hours 35. Forsaking All Others 35. *Mutiny on the Bounty* 35. China Seas 35. Call of the Wild 35. Wife Versus Secretary 36. *San Francisco* 36. Cain and Mabel 36. Love on the Run 37. Parnell 37. Saratoga 37. Test Pilot 38. Too Hot to Handle 38. Idiot's Delight 39. *Gone with the Wind* 39. Strange Cargo 40. Boom Town 40. Comrade X 40. They Met in Bombay 41. Honky Tonk 41. Somewhere I'll Find You 41; war service; Adventure 45. *The Hucksters* 47. Homecoming 48. Command Decision 48. Any Number Can Play 49. Key to the City 50. To Please a Lady 50. Across the Wide Missouri 51. Lone Star 52. Never Let Me Go (GB) 53. Mogambo 53. Betrayed 54. The Tall Men 55. Soldier of Fortune 55. The King and Four Queens 56. Band of Angels 57. Teacher's Pet 58. Run Silent Run Deep 58. But Not for Me 59. It Started in Naples 59. *The Misfits* 61.

❀ For effortlessly maintaining a Hollywood legend, and for doing so with cheerful impudence. *Gone with the Wind.*

¶ The King of Hollywood? He modestly disclaimed the title, but there was sense to it: he always seemed to be in charge. As the *New York Times* said:

> Gable was as certain as the sunrise. He was consistently and stubbornly all man.

He said himself:

> The only reason they come to see me is that I know life is great—and they know I know it.

And again:

> I'm no actor and I never have been. What people see on the screen is me.

What they saw, they liked. Publicity man Ralph Wainwright said:

> All of his life people turned around to stare at him.

This was remarkable considering his famous physical drawback, well phrased by Howard Hughes:

> His ears made him look like a taxicab with both doors open.

Milton Berle called him:

> The best ears of our lives.

It didn't stop him from influencing the world, and not only the female half of it. Historian Frederick Lewis Allen recalled that:

> When Clark Gable in *It Happened One Night* disclosed that he wore no undershirt, the knitwear manufacturers rocked from the shock to their sales.

But Gable disclaimed his sexual reputation:

> Hell, if I'd jumped on all the dames I'm supposed to have jumped on—I'd have had no time to go fishing.

Eve Arden remembered:

> He used to claim that he was very dull in bed.

Carole Lombard confirmed this:

> Listen, he's no Clark Gable at home.

And her husband nodded ruefully:

> I can't emote worth a damn.

David Selznick knew the secret:

> Gable has enemies all right, but they all like him.

Gable himself summed up:

> This King stuff is pure bull. I eat and drink and go to the bathroom just like anybody else. I'm just a lucky slob from Ohio who happened to be in the right place at the right time.

And seven years after his death, Joan Crawford could say:

> He was king of an empire called Hollywood. The empire is not what it was—but the king has not been dethroned, even after death.

Famous line (*It Happened One Night*): Behold the walls of Jericho!

Famous line (*Gone with the Wind*): Frankly, my dear, I don't give a damn.

? In what film did Clark Gable:

1 Romance Carole Lombard?
2 Play a boxer in love with a musical comedy star?
3 Escape from a New Guinea penal colony?
4 Befriend an Indian chief played by Jack Holt?
5 Fall for a girl named Snapshot?
6 Help a friend search for his soul and pray for a baby's life?
7 Contend with William Boyd for the hand of Helen Twelvetrees?
8 Catch a night bus from Miami towards New York?
9 Captain a ship heading for Hong Kong?
10 Play Blackie Norton?
11 Perform a song-and-dance act with a troupe of six girls?
12 Play an Irish patriot?

13 Smuggle a girl out of Russia? (Two possible answers)
14 Play a newsreel photographer?
15 Play an advertising executive?
16 Play a mayor?
17 Defend Texas against the Mexicans?
18 Play a role previously taken by Herbert Marshall and Bing Crosby?
19 Play a jewel thief?
20 Die in the arms of Helen Hayes?

Gabor, Eva (1921–). Hungarian leading lady, sister of Zsa Zsa Gabor.
Autobiography 1954: *Orchids and Salami.*
Pacific Blackout 41. Forced Landing 41. A Royal Scandal 45. Wife of Monte Cristo 46. Song of Surrender 49. The Mad Magician 54. Tarzan and the Slave Girl 54. The Truth about Women 56. Gigi 58. A New Kind of Love 63. Youngblood Hawke 63.
The Princess Academy 87, etc.
TV series: *Green Acres* 65–70.

Gabor, Zsa Zsa (1919–) (Sari Gabor). Exotic international leading lady, Miss Hungary of 1936, who has decorated films of many nations.
Autobiography 1961: *My Story.*
Lovely To Look At (US) 52. Lili (US) 53. Moulin Rouge (GB) 53. Public Enemy Number One (Fr.) 54. Diary of a Scoundrel (US) 56. The Man Who Wouldn't Talk (GB) 57. Touch of Evil (US) 58. Queen of Outer Space (US) 59. Arrivederci Baby 66. Picture Mommy Dead (US) 66. Up the Front (GB) 72, etc.

¶ *Z.Z.G.:* I believe in large families: every woman should have at least three husbands.

Z.Z.G.: I never hated a man enough to give him his diamonds back.

Z.Z.G.: Husbands are like fires: they go out if unattended.

She's an expert housekeeper. Every time she gets divorced, she keeps the house.—*Henny Youngman*

Her face is inscrutable, but I can't vouch for the rest of her.—*Oscar Levant*

Gahagan, Helen (1900–1980). American actress who limited herself to just one film: the title role in the 1935 version of *She*. Married Melvyn Douglas.

Gainsborough. A British film company of the thirties, associated with costume drama and Aldwych farces. Subsequently merged with Rank.

Galeen, Henrik (1881–1949). Dutch writer-director, a leading figure of German silent cinema.
The Student of Prague (wd) 12. *The Golem* (wd) 14. *The Golem* (w) 20. Nosferatu (w) 22. Waxworks (w) 25. The Student of Prague 26. Alraune 27. After the Verdict 30. Salon Dora Greene 36, many others.

Gallagher, Skeets (1891–1955) (Richard). Cheerful American vaudevillian, in some films of the early talkie period.
The Racket 28. It Pays to Advertise 31. Merrily We Go to Hell 32. Riptide 34. Polo Joe 37. Idiot's Delight 39. Zis Boom Bah 42. The Duke of Chicago 50, etc.

Gallian, Ketti (1913–59). French leading lady in America; films few.
⊡Marie Galante 34. Under the Pampas Moon 35. Espionage 37. Shall We Dance 37.

Gallico, Paul (1897–1976). American novelist, whose work has been much adapted.
Wedding Present 36. Joe Smith American 42. Pride of the Yankees 42. The Cock 45. Never Take No for an Answer 52. Lili 53. Merry Andrew 58. Next to No Time 58. The Three Lives of Thomasina 63. The Snow Goose (TV) 71. The Poseidon Adventure 72, etc.

Gallone, Carmine (1886–1973). Veteran Italian director who ranged from opera to action epics.
Pawns of Passion 28. Un Soir de Rafle 30. My Heart is Calling 34. Madame Butterfly 39. Manon Lescaut 40. La Traviata 47. Faust and the Devil 49. La Forza del Destino 51. Tosca 56. Michael Strogoff 59. Carthage in Flames 59, many others.

Galloway, Don (1937–). American TV leading man, familiar in *Ironside*.
The Rare Breed 66. Rough Night in Jericho 67. The Ride to Hangman's Tree 67. Lt Schuster's Wife (TV) 72, etc.

Gallu, Samuel (1918–). American director, former opera singer.
Theatre of Death 66. The Man Outside 67. The Limbo Line 68.

Galsworthy, John (1867–1933). British novelist who wrote about the upper middle class. Works filmed include *Escape* 30 and 48. *The Skin Game* 31. *Loyalties* 34. *Twenty-one Days* 39. *That Forsyte Woman* 49, etc.

Galton, Ray (1930–). British comedy writer; with Alan Simpson, co-author of successful TV series, e.g. *Hancock's Half-Hour, Steptoe and Son*; films include *The Rebel* 61. *The Wrong Arm of the Law* 62. *The Bargee* 64. *The Spy with a Cold Nose* 67, etc.

Galvani, Dino (1890–1960). Distinguished-looking Italian actor, in films (mainly British) from 1908.
Atalantic 30. In a Monastery Garden 32. Midnight Menace 35. Mr Satan 38. It's That Man Again (as Signor So-So) 42. Sleeping Car to Trieste 49. Father Brown 54. Checkpoint 57. Bluebeard's Ten Honeymoons 60, many others.

Gam, Rita (1928–). American stage leading lady in occasional films.
The Thief 52. Sign of the Pagan 54. Night People 54. Magic Fire 55. Mohawk 56. King of Kings 61. Klute 71. Such Good Friends 71, etc.

gambling, in the indoor sport sense, is quite a preoccupation of film-makers. Gregory Peck in *The Great Sinner* played a man who made a great career of it, as did James Caan in *The Gambler* and George Segal in *California Split*; while in *The Queen of Spades* Edith Evans learnt the secret of winning at cards from the devil himself. Other suspenseful card games were played in *The Cincinnati Kid, Lucky Jordan, The Lady Eve, Hazard,* and *Big Hand for a Little Lady*; snooker pool was the game in *The Hustler*; old-time Mississippi river-boats were the setting for *Mississippi Gambler, The Naughty Nineties, Frankie and Johnny* and a sequence in *The Secret Life of Walter Mitty*. Roulette, however, is the most spectacular and oft-used film gambling game, seen in *The Shanghai Gesture, Robin and the Seven Hoods, Ocean's Eleven, The Big Snatch, Doctor No, La Baie des Anges, Quartet* (the 'Facts of Life' sequence), *Seven Thieves, The Las Vegas Story, The Only Game in Town, The Big Sleep, Gilda, Kaleidoscope*, and many others. Second features with such titles as *Gambling House, Gambling Ship* and *Gambling on the High Seas* were especially popular in the forties. Musically, the filmic high-point was undoubtedly the 'oldest established permanent floating crap game in New York' number in *Guys and Dolls*. This stemmed from the writings of Damon Runyon, also adapted in such films as *Sorrowful Jones* and *The Lemon Drop Kid*. The most comic game on film was perhaps the hand of poker played between Judy Holliday and Broderick Crawford in *Born Yesterday*.

Gambon, Michael (1940–). British stage actor, in occasional films.
The Beast Must Die 75. Turtle Diary 85.

Gamley, Douglas (1924–). Australian composer in Britain.
The Admirable Crichton 57. Gideon's Day 59. Watch It Sailor 61. The Horror of It All 64. Spring and Port Wine 70.

Gance, Abel (1889–1981). French producer-director, in films since 1910. Pioneer of wide-screen techniques.
Baberousse 16. *J'Accuse* 19 and 37. La Roue 21. *Napoleon* 27. La Fin du Monde 31. Lucrezia Borgia 35. Une Grande Amour de Beethoven 36. Paradis Perdu 39. La Tour de Nesle 54. The Battle of Austerlitz 60, etc.
†Gance's *Napoleon* had sterling qualities which were never properly noted because of its length, its wide-screeen reels, and the fact that silents were overwhelmed by sound soon after its release. In the late seventies, however, film scholar Kevin Brownlow assembled a five-hour version to which Thames TV added a newly commissioned musical score; in this version it was shown again triumphantly in the early eighties, in all the capitals of the world.

Gandhi (GB 1982). It was a fourteen-year dream for producer-director Richard Attenborough (AA on both counts) to make this rather heavy-going 200-minute biopic. Even with his cast of thousands, and considerable financial assistance from the Indian government, he cannot have imagined that it would be such a critical and commercial success, coming as it did at a time of inspirational dearth in the cinema. A splendid star performance by a perfectly cast leading actor cannot stop *Gandhi* from being not much more than textbook history, but the fact is that many years had passed since this type of film had been attempted, and there were enough filmgoers who saw it as something new to make it pay. Written by John Briley (AA); music by Ravi Shankar; photographed by Billy Williams and Ronnie Taylor (AA); with Ben Kingsley (AA).

gangsters, a real-life American menace of the twenties, provided a new kind of excitement for early talkies like *Little Caesar* and *Public Enemy*, which told how their heroes got into criminal activities but didn't rub in the moral very hard. The pace of the action, however, made them excellent

movies, and critics defended them against religious pressure groups. *Quick Millions, Scarface, Lady Killer, The Little Giant* and *Public Enemy's Wife* were among the titles which followed; then Warner Brothers cleverly devised a way of keeping their thrills while mollifying the protesters: they made the policeman into the hero, in films like *G-Men, I Am the Law, Bullets or Ballots.* By 1938 it seemed time to send up the whole genre in *A Slight Case of Murder*, with its cast of corpses, and in the later *Brother Orchid* the gangster-in-chief became a monk; yet in 1940 the heat had cooled off sufficiently to allow production of *The Roaring Twenties*, one of the most violent gangster movies of them all. The war made gangsters old-fashioned, but in the late forties Cagney starred in two real psychopathic toughies, *White Heat* and *Kiss Tomorrow Goodbye.* After that the fashion was to parody gangsterism, in *Party Girl, Some Like It Hot*, and a couple of Runyon movies; but the success of a French film called *Rififi* and a TV series called *The Untouchables* left the field wide open for redevelopment. Successes in the sixties included *Bonnie and Clyde, The St Valentine's Day Massacre, Pay or Die, The Rise and Fall of Legs Diamond, King of the Roaring Twenties*, and from the French *Borsalino* and various *Rififi* sequels. The seventies brought British gang violence in *Get Carter, Villain, The Squeeze* and *Sweeney*, and in 1972 the gigantic success of *The Godfather* spawned sequels, rivals (*The Valachi Papers*) and parodies (*The Gang That Couldn't Shoot Straight*).
In 1987 *The Untouchables* was remade with great success for the cinema screen.

Gann, Ernest K. (1910–). American adventure novelist. Films of his work include *The High and the Mighty, Blaze of Noon, Fate Is the Hunter.*

Ganz, Bruno (1941–). German leading actor.
The Marquise von O 73. Lumière 76. The American Friend 77. Nosferatu 78. The Boys from Brazil 78. Camille 80. Circle of Deceit 81.

Ganzer, Alvin (–). American second feature director.
The Girls of Pleasure Island (co-d) 53. The Leather Saint 56. When the Boys Meet the Girls 65. Three Bites of the Apple 67, etc.

Garas, Kaz (–). American leading man.
The Last Safari 68. Ben 72, etc.

Garber, Matthew (1956–77). British child actor.
The Three Lives of Thomasina 63. Mary Poppins 64. The Gnome-Mobile 67.

Garbo, Greta (1905–) (Greta Gustafson). Swedish leading actress who was taken to Hollywood by her director Mauritz Stiller and became a goddess of the screen, her aloof beauty carefully nurtured by MGM through the late twenties and early thirties. Her early retirement enhanced the air of mystery which has always surrounded her. Special Academy Award 1954 'for her unforgettable screen performances'.
Biographies: 1954, *Garbo* by John Bainbridge. 1970, *Garbo* by Norman Zierold.
□Peter the Tramp 22. The Atonement of Gösta Berling 24. Joyless Street 25. The Torrent 26. The Temptress 26. *Flesh and the Devil* 27. Love 27. The Mysterious Lady 27. The Divine Woman 28. The Kiss 29. A Woman of Affairs 29. Wild Orchids 29. The Single Standard 29. *Anna Christie* 30. Romance 30. Inspiration 31. Susan Lennox 31. Mata Hari 31. *Grand Hotel* 32. As You Desire Me 32. *Queen Christina* 33. The Painted Veil 34. *Anna Karenina* 35. *Camille* 36. Conquest 37. *Ninotchka* 39. Two Faced Woman 41.

❀ For stretching a mystery over twelve splendid years and for knowing when to quit. *Queen Christina.*

¶ Boiled down to essentials, she is a plain mortal girl with large feet.

So wrote Herbert Kretzmer, sick of the 'sphinx' image, which in the early thirties was overpowering. Alistair Cooke called her:

> Every man's harmless fantasy mistress. She gave you the impression that, if your imagination had to sin, it could at least congratulate itself on its impeccable taste.

Life in 1928 hailed her thus:

> She is the dream princess of eternity, the knockout of the ages.

Richard Watts Jnr called her:

> That fascinating, inscrutable, almost legendary personage . . .

The *New York Mirror* said:

> Her alluring mouth and volcanic, slumbrous eyes stimulate men to such passion that friendships collapse.

Graham Greene in his review of *Conquest* defined her:

> A great actress? Oh, undoubtedly, one wearily assents, but what dull pompous films they make for her, hardly movies at all so retarded are they by her haggard equine renunciations, the slow consummation of her noble adulteries!

To Clare Boothe Luce she was:

A deer in the body of a woman, living resentfully in the Hollywood zoo.

A 1929 critic said:

She is a woman who marches to some unstruck music, unheard by the rest of us.

Rouben Mamoulian thought her:

A wonderful instrument.

Even the sensible Lillian Gish considered that:

Garbo's temperament reflected the rain and gloom of the long dark Swedish winters.

More recently Ken Tynan remarked:

What when drunk one sees in other women, one sees in Garbo sober.

Remoteness was part of her charm. To Fredric March:

Co-starring with Garbo hardly constituted an introduction.

To James Wong Howe, the famous cameraman:

She was like a horse on the track. Nothing, and then the bell goes, and something happens.

But the image always had its knockers, including the lady herself:

I never said, I want to be alone. I only said I want to be let alone.

(She did say it actually, but in *Grand Hotel*.) She added:

My talent falls within definite limits. I'm not a versatile actress.

She also said with a smile:

I'm a woman who's unfaithful to a million men.

But the fact is, men were not her fans. It was women who queued to see her suffer. J. Robert Rubin of MGM noted in wonder:

Garbo was the only one we could kill off. The Shearer and Crawford pictures had to end in a church, but the public seemed to enjoy watching Garbo die.

George Cukor, who directed her several times, thought:

She is a fascinating actress but she is limited. She must never create situations. She must be thrust into them. The drama comes in how she rides them out.

When she suddenly retired in 1941, her reason, given much later, was:

I had made enough faces.

And:

Being in the newspapers is awfully silly to me. I have nothing to contribute.

David Niven commented:

The longer she stayed away, the stronger and stranger the Garbo myth grew.

In the seventies, thirty years after her retirement, her movies were still making money all over the world and the lady herself was front-page news. You can't kill a legend. And it wasn't the movies that kept the interest; as Richard Whitehall remarked:

Subtract Garbo from most of her films, and you are left with nothing.

Isobel Quigley remained undecided:

I can't make up my mind whether Garbo was a remarkable actress or simply a person so extraordinary that she made everything she did, including acting, seem remarkable.

C. Aubrey Smith's appraisal was the oddest of all:

She's a rippin' gel.

Famous line (*Ninotchka*): Don't make an issue of my womanhood.

Famous line (*Anna Christie*): Gimme visky, ginger ale on the side. And don't be stingy, baby.

Famous line (*Queen Christina*): I have been memorising this room. In the future, in my memory, I shall live a great deal in this room.

The Garden of Allah. Robert Hichens' novel about a sophisticated woman whose husband turns out to be an escaped Trappist monk was filmed as a silent in 1917, with Tom Santschi and Helen Ware, and again in 1927 with Ivan Petrovitch and Alice Terry. The 1936 sound remake had excellent early colour, elegant direction by Richard Boleslawski, and exotic performances from Charles Boyer and Marlene Dietrich.

†The Garden of Allah was also a lush hotel on Sunset Boulevard, where during the twenties and thirties many stars enjoyed riotous visits. Sheilah Graham wrote about it in a book of the same title.

Gardenia, Vincent (1922–) (Vincent Scognamiglio). American comic character actor.

Mad Dog Coll 61. A View from the Bridge 61. The Pursuit of Happiness 71. Cold Turkey 71. Hickey and Boggs 72. Bang the Drum Slowly 73. *Death Wish* 74. The Front Page 74. Greased Lightning 77. Fire Sale 77. Heaven Can Wait 78. Home Movies 79. The Dream Merchants (TV) 80. Death Wish II 81. *Kennedy* (as J. Edgar Hoover) (TV) 83. Little Shop of Horrors 86. Moonstruck 87, etc.

Gardiner, Reginald (1903–1980). British actor who perfected the amiable silly ass type, in Hollywood from 1936.

The Lovelorn Lady 32. Borrow a Million 34. *Born to Dance* 36. Everybody Sing 37. Marie Antoinette 38. Sweethearts 39. *The Great Dictator* 40. My Life with Caroline 41. *The Man Who Came to Dinner* 41. Captains of the Clouds 42. The Immortal Sergeant 43. Molly and Me 44. Christmas in Connecticut 45. Cluny Brown 46. Fury at Furnace Creek 48. Wabash Avenue 50. Halls of Montezuma 51. The Black Widow 54. Ain't Misbehaving 55. The Birds and the Bees 56. Mr Hobbs Takes a Vacation 62. Do Not Disturb 65. Sergeant Deadhead 66, many others.
TV series: The Pruitts of Southampton 66.
Famous line (*The Man Who Came to Dinner*): I've very little time, and so the conversation will be entirely about me, and I shall love it.

Gardner, Arthur (–). American independent producer, of Levy-Gardner-Laven.
Without Warning 52. Down Three Dark Streets 54. Geronimo 62. The Glory Guys 65. The Scalphunters 68. The McKenzie Break 70. The Hunting Party 71. Kansas City Bomber 72. Brannigan 75. Gator 76, etc.
TV series include: Rifleman, The Detectives, Law of the Plainsman, The Big Valley.

Gardner, Ava (1922–). American leading lady of the forties and fifties, once voted the world's most beautiful woman.
Biographies: *Ava* 1960 by David Hanna; *Ava Gardner* 1984 by John Daniell.
□We Were Dancing 42. Joe Smith American 42. Sunday Punch 42. This Time for Keeps 42. Calling Dr Gillespie 42. Kid Glove Killer 42. Pilot No. 5 43. Hitler's Madman 43. Ghosts on the Loose 43. Reunion in France 43. Dubarry was a Lady 43. Young Ideas 43. Lost Angel 43. Swing Fever 44. Music for Millions 44. Three Men in White 44. Blonde Fever 44. Maisie Goes to Reno 44. Two Girls and a Sailor 44. She Went to the Races 45. Whistle Stop 46. *The Killers* 46. *The Hucksters* 47. Singapore 47. One Touch of Venus 48. The Great Sinner 49. East Side West Side 49. The Bribe 49. My Forbidden Past 52. *Show Boat* 51. *Pandora and the Flying Dutchman* 51. Lone Star 52. The Snows of Kilimanjaro 52. Ride Vaquero 53. *Mogambo* 53. Knights of the Round Table 53. *The Barefoot Contessa* 54. Bhowani Junction 56. The Little Hut 57. *The Sun Also Rises* 57. The Naked Maja 59. On the Beach 59. The Angel Wore Red 60. 55 Days at Peking 63. Seven Days in May 64. *The Night of the Iguana* 64. The Bible 66. Mayerling 68. Tam Lin 70. Judge Roy Bean 72. Earthquake 74. Permission to Kill 75. The Bluebird 76. The Cassandra Crossing 77. The Sentinel 77. City on Fire 79. The Kidnapping of the President 80. Priest of Love 81.

¶ 'A lady of strong passions, one of them rage.'—*Mickey Rooney (former husband)*

A.G.: Although no one believes me, I have always been a country girl, and still have a country girl's values.

Gardner, Ed (1901–63). American radio comic who starred in the 1945 film version of his series *Duffy's Tavern.*

Gardner, Erle Stanley (1889–1970). American best-selling crime novelist, the creator of Perry Mason (qv).

Gardner, Joan (1914–). British leading lady of the thirties who married Zoltan Korda.
Men of Tomorrow 32. Catherine the Great 34. The Scarlet Pimpernel 35. The Man Who Could Work Miracles 36. Dark Journey 39. The Rebel Son (last to date) 39, etc.

Garfein, Jack (1930–). American stage and screen director, married to Carroll Baker.
The Strange One 57. Something Wild 62.

Garfield, Allen (1939–). Heavy-set American character actor who reverted in 1979 to his real name of **Allen Goorwitz.**
Get to Know Your Rabbit 72. Slither 73. Busting 74. The Long Goodbye 74. The Conversation 74. The Front Page 74. Nashville 76. Mother Jugs and Speed 76. Gable and Lombard (as Louis B. Mayer) 76. Brinks 79. One Trick Pony 80. The Stunt Man 80. Continental Divide 81. One from the Heart 82. The Black Stallion Returns 83. Get Crazy 83, etc.

Garfield, John (1913–1952) (Julius Garfinkle). American leading actor, usually in aggressive or embittered roles; formerly a star of New York's leftish Group Theatre.
Biography 1978: *John Garfield* by James Beaver.
□*Four Daughters* 38. Blackwell's Island 38. *They Made Me a Criminal* 39. Juarez 39. Daughters Courageous 39. Dust Be My Destiny 39. Saturday's Children 40. East of the River 40. Castle on the Hudson 40. Flowing Gold 40. *The Sea Wolf* 41. Out of the Fog 41. Tortilla Flat 42. Dangerously They Live 42. Air Force 43. The Fallen

Sparrow 43. Thank Your Lucky Stars 43. Between Two Worlds 44. Hollywood Canteen 44. Destination Tokyo 44. Pride of the Marines 45. Nobody Lives Forever 46. *The Postman Always Rings Twice* 46. *Humoresque* 46. *Body and Soul* 47. *Gentleman's Agreement* 47. We Were Strangers 48. *Force of Evil* 49. Under My Skin 50. The Breaking Point 50. He Ran All the Way 51.
†Cameo roles: Four Wives 39. Hollywood Canteen 44. Jigsaw 49.

¶ Projected on the screens of the world, he was the Eternal Outsider, obliged to glimpse Paradise but not to dwell there.—*Larry Swindell*
• His feeling never changed that he was mandated by the American public to go in there and keep punching for them.—*Clifford Odets*
† Garfield is alleged to have turned down the role of Kowalski in *A Streetcar Named Desire*.

Garfunkel, Arthur (1941–). American pop singer, half of Simon and Garfunkel; occasional actor.
□Catch 22 70. Carnal Knowledge 71. Bad Timing 79. Good to Go 86.

Gargan, Ed (1902–1964). American character actor, brother of William Gargan; often seen as comedy cop or prizefighter's manager.
Gambling Ship 33. Belle of the Nineties 34. Miss Pacific Fleet 35. My Man Godfrey 36. Big City 37. Gateway 38. Another Thin Man 39. Road to Singapore 40. A Date with the Falcon 41. Over My Dead Body 42. Hit the Ice 43. The Falcon Out West 44. The Bullfighters 45. Wonder Man 45. Gallant Bess 46. Little Miss Broadway 47. You Gotta Stay Happy 48. Red Light 49. Belle of Old Mexico 50. Bedtime for Bonzo 51, hundreds of others, often in one-line or one-shot roles.

Gargan, William (1905–79). American light leading man of the thirties and forties, usually in 'good guy' roles; retired when left voiceless after operation. Brother of Ed Gargan. Autobiography 1969: *Why Me?*
The Misleading Lady 32. *Rain* 32. The Story of Temple Drake 33. Four Frightened People 34. Black Fury 35. The Milky Way 36. You Only Live Once 37. The Crowd Roars 38. *The Housekeeper's Daughter* 39. Turnabout 40. *They Knew What They Wanted* 40. Bombay Clipper 41. Miss Annie Rooney 42. The Canterville Ghost 44. The Bells of St Mary's 45. Till the End of Time 46. Night Editor 46. The Argyle Secrets 48. Miracle in the Rain 56, many others.
TV series: *Martin Kane* 57.

Garland, Beverly (1926–) (Beverly Fessenden). Pert and pretty leading lady of some fifties Hollywood films; more successful on TV.
DOA 49. The Glass Web 53. The Miami Story 54. The Desperate Hours 55. It Conquered the World 56. Not of this Earth 56. The Joker is Wild 57. The Alligator People 59. Twice Told Tales 63. Pretty Poison 68. The Mad Room 69. Airport 75 74. Roller Boogie 79. It's My Turn 80, etc.
TV series: *Decoy* 57. The Bing Crosby Show 64. My Three Sons 66–69.

Garland, Judy (1922–1969) (Frances Gumm). American entertainer and leading lady who for many years radiated the soul of show business. The child of vaudeville performers, on stage from five years old, she later seemed unable to stand the pace of her own success; but her resultant personal difficulties only accentuated the loyalty of her admirers. Special Academy Award 1939 'for her outstanding performance as a screen juvenile'. Biographical books include *The Other Side of the Rainbow* 1971 by Mel Torme.
□Every Sunday (short) 36. Pigskin Parade 36. Broadway Melody of 1938 37. Thoroughbreds Don't Cry 38. Everybody Sing 38. Listen Darling 38. Love Finds Andy Hardy 38. *The Wizard of Oz* 39. *Babes in Arms* 39. Andy Hardy Meets a Debutante 39. Strike Up the Band 40. Little Nellie Kelly 40. Ziegfeld Girl 41. Life Begins for Andy Hardy 41. Babes on Broadway 41. *For Me and My Gal* 42. Presenting Lily Mars 42. Girl Crazy 42. Thousands Cheer (guest) 43. *Meet Me in St Louis* 44. Ziegfeld Follies 45. *The Clock* 45. The Harvey Girls 46. Till the Clouds Roll By (guest) 46. The Pirate 47. *Easter Parade* 48. Words and Music (guest) 48. In the Good Old Summertime 49. Summer Stock 50. *A Star Is Born* 54. Judgment at Nuremberg 60. A Child Is Waiting 62. I Could Go On Singing (GB) 63.
❀ For her incredible voice; and for drawing cathartic tears as much by her own life as by her performances. *The Wizard of Oz*.

¶ *J.G.:* If I'm such a legend, why am I so lonely?
I didn't know her well, but after watching her in action I didn't want to know her well.—*Joan Crawford*

An angel with spurs.—*Joe Pasternak, producer*

J.G.: I had the stage mother of all time. If I wasn't well, and didn't want to go on, she'd yell 'Get out on that stage or I'll tie you to the bedpost.'

You see that girl? She used to be a hunchback. You see what I've made her into?—*Louis B. Mayer*

Her mental attitude may have been pathetic but it turned her into a great bore.—*Anita Loos*

Famous line (*The Wizard of Oz*): If I ever go looking for my heart's desire again, I won't look any further than my own backyard, because if it isn't there, I never really lost it to begin with.

Garmes, Lee (1897–1978). Distinguished American cinematographer, in Hollywood from 1916.
The Grand Duchess and the Waiter 26. The Private Life of Helen of Troy 27. Disraeli 29. Lilies of the Field 30. Whoopee 30. Morocco 30. Dishonoured 31. City Streets 31. An American Tragedy 31. *Shanghai Express* (AA) 32. *Scarface* 32. Smilin' Through 32. *Zoo in Budapest* 33. Crime without Passion 34. The Scoundrel 34. Dreaming Lips (GB) 37. Gone with the Wind (co-ph) (uncredited) 39. Angels over Broadway 40. *Lydia* 41. Jungle Book 42. Guest in the House 44. Since You Went Away 44. *Love Letters* 45. *Duel in the Sun* 46. The Spectre of the Rose (& co-p) 46. The Secret Life of Walter Mitty 47. The Paradine Case 48. Our Very Own 50. Detective Story 51. Actors and Sin (& co-d) 52. The Desperate Hours 55. Land of the Pharaohs 55. The Big Fisherman 59. Hemingway's Adventures of a Young Man 62. Lady in a Cage 64. Big Hand for a Little Lady 66. How to Save a Marriage 68, etc.
❀ For his contributions to black-and-white photography, and especially for the effects he created with 'north light'. *Zoo in Budapest.*

¶ *L.G.:* A cameraman is often the saviour of a film. His lighting can be the main factor in its success.

Garner, James (1928–) (James Baumgarner). Amiable, good-looking American leading man of the sixties; showed a sense of humour among the action and romance, but did not quite measure up as a substitute for Clark Gable.
□Toward the Unknown 56. The Girl He Left Behind 56. Shoot out at Medicine Bend 57. Sayonara 57. Darby's Rangers 58. Up Periscope 59. Cash McCall 59. The Children's Hour 62. Boys' Night Out 62. *The Great Escape* 63. *The Thrill of It All* 63. The Wheeler Dealers 63. Move Over Darling 63. *The Americanization of Emily* 64. *Thirty Six Hours* 64. The Art of Love 65. Duel at Diablo 66. A Man Could Get Killed 66. Mister Buddwing 66. Grand Prix 66. Hour of the Gun (as Wyatt Earp) 67. The Pink Jungle 68. How Sweet It Is 68. *Support Your Local Sheriff* 69. Marlowe 69. A Man Called Sledge 70. *The Skin Game* 71. Support Your Local Gunfighter 71. They Only Kill Their Masters 72. One Little Indian 73. The Castaway Cowboy 74. The New Maverick (TV) 78. Health 80. The Fan 81. Victor/Victoria 82. The Long Summer of George Adams (TV) 82. Tank 84. Murphy's Romance (AAN) 85. Space (TV) 85.
TV series: *Maverick* 57–61. Nichols 71. The Rockford Files 74–80. Bret Maverick 81.

¶ He is a master at playing dumb while maintaining a sense of shrewdness and dignity. He always throws us off guard. He is the macho stud who makes fun of himself; he is the scaredy-cat we know will not let us down in the end.—*Esquire*

J.G.: I became an actor by accident; I'm a businessman by design.

J.G.: I am an actor. I hire out. I am not afraid of hurting my image.

Garner, Peggy Ann (1931–84). American child star of the forties; Academy Award 1944 as 'outstanding child actress'. Did not make it as adult star.
□Little Miss Thoroughbred 38. Blondie Brings Up Baby 39. In Name Only 39. Abe Lincoln in Illinois 40. The Pied Piper 42. Eagle Squadron 42. *Jane Eyre* 44. *A Tree Grows in Brooklyn* 45. The Keys of the Kingdom 45. Nob Hill 45. Junior Miss 45. Home Sweet Homicide 46. Daisy Kenyon 47. Thunder in the Valley 47. The Sign of the Ram 48. The Lovable Cheat 49. Bomba the Jungle Boy 49. The Big Cat 49. Teresa 51. The Black Widow 54. Eight Witnesses 54. The Black Forest 54. The Cat 67. A Wedding 78.

Garnett, Tay (1895–1977). American director, a light professional talent. Autobiography 1974: *Light Up Your Torches and Pull on Your Tights.*
□Celebrity 28. The Spieler 28. Flying Fools 29. Oh Yeah 29. Officer O'Brien 30. *Her Man* (& w) 30. Bad Company 31. *One Way Passage* (& w) 32. Prestige 32. Okay America 32. Destination Unknown 33. SOS Iceberg 33. China Seas (& w) 35. She Couldn't Take

It 35. Professional Soldier 35. Love is News (& w) 37. *Slave Ship* (& w) 37. Stand In 37. Joy of Living 38. Trade Winds (& w) 38. Eternally Yours (& p) 39. Slightly Honorable (& wp) 40. Seven Sinners 40. Cheers for Miss Bishop (& w) 41. My Favorite Spy 42. Bataan 43. The Cross of Lorraine 43. Mrs Parkington 44. The Valley of Decision 45. The Postman Always Rings Twice 46. Wild Harvest 47. A Connecticut Yankee in King Arthur's Court 49. The Fireball (& w) 50. Soldiers Three 51. Cause for Alarm 51. One Minute to Zero 52. Main Street to Broadway 53. The Black Knight 54. Seven Wonders of the World 56. A Terrible Beauty 60. Cattle King 63. The Delta Factor 70. The Temper Tramp 73.

Garnett, Tony (1936–). British producer.
□*Kes* 69. The Body 70. *Family Life* 71. Prostitute 80. Handgun (& d) 82.

Garr, Teri (1952–). American leading lady of the late seventies.
Oh God 77. Close Encounters of the Third Kind 77. Mr Mike's Mondo Video 78. The Black Stallion 79. Honky Tonk Freeway 81. Wrong Is Right 82. One from the Heart 82. Tootsie 82. The Sting II 82. The Black Stallion Returns 83. Mr Mom 83. Firstborn 84. After Hours 85.

Garrett, Betty (1919–). Peppy American singer and actress with musical comedy experience.
□Big City (debut) 46. Words and Music 48. Take Me Out to the Ball Game 48. Neptune's Daughter 49. *On the Town* 49. My Sister Eileen 55. The Shadow on the Window 57.
TV series: All in the Family 73–75. Laverne and Shirley 76.

Garrett, Oliver H. P. (1897–1952). American screenwriter.
Forgotten Faces 28. *Street of Chance* 30. She Couldn't Take It 35. One Third of a Nation 39. The Man I Married 40. Flight for Freedom 43. Duel in the Sun 46. Dead Reckoning 47. Sealed Cargo 51, etc.

Garrett, Otis (c. 1895–1941). American director.
□The Black Doll 37. The Last Express 38. Personal Secretary 38. Danger on the Air 38. *Lady in the Morgue* 38. The Witness Vanishes 39. The Mystery of the White Room 39. Exile Express 39. Margie 40. Sandy Gets Her Man 41.

Garrett, Pat (1850–1908). American western adventurer who allegedly, as sheriff, shot Billy the Kid (qv). Actors who have played him include Wallace Beery in *Billy the Kid* 30, Thomas Mitchell in *The Outlaw*, Charles Bickford in *Four Faces West*, Frank Wilcox in *The Kid from Texas*, John Dehner in *The Left-Handed Gun*, Glenn Corbett in *Chisum*, James Coburn in *Pat Garrett and Billy the Kid*.
On TV, Barry Sullivan was Garratt in *The Tall Men*.

Garrick, David (1717–1779). Famous English actor who has been impersonated on screen by Cedric Hardwicke in *Peg of Old Drury* 34 and Brian Aherne in *The Great Garrick* 37.

Garrick, John (1902–) (Reginald Doudy). British stage actor of the twenties and thirties; made some film appearances, usually as 'the other man'.
The Lottery Bride (US) 31. Chu Chin Chow 33. Rocks of Valpre 35. Sunset in Vienna 37. The Great Victor Herbert (US) 39, etc.

Garrison, Sean (1937–). American leading man of the sixties.
Moment to Moment 66. Banning 67, etc.
TV series: Dundee and the Culhane 67.

Garson, Greer (1908–). Red-haired Anglo-Irish leading lady who after stage experience was cast as Mrs Chipping in *Goodbye Mr Chips* 39 and promptly went to Hollywood, where her gentle aristocratic good looks enabled her to reign as a star for ten years.
□Remember 39. *Pride and Prejudice* 40. *Blossoms in the Dust* 41. When Ladies Meet 41. *Mrs Miniver* (AA) 42. *Random Harvest* 42. *Madame Curie* 43. Mrs Parkington 44. The Valley of Decision 45. Adventure 45. Desire Me 47. Julia Misbehaves 48. *That Forsyte Woman* 49. The Miniver Story 50. The Law and the Lady 51. Scandal at Scourie 52. Julius Caesar 53. Her Twelve Men 53. Strange Lady in Town 54. Sunrise at Campobello (as Eleanor Roosevelt) 60. Pepe 60. The Singing Nun 66. The Happiest Millionaire 67. Little Women (TV) 78.

¶ *Pauline Kael:* One of the most richly syllabled queenly horrors of Hollywood.
Metro's Glorified Mother.—*Anon*
The mixture of Irish charm, natural red-haired beauty and her unceasing capacity to project the shopgirl's vision of the great lady made her an incontestable star in a decade that required a staunch, wholesome ideal.—*New Yorker*

G.G.: If you're going to be typed, there are worse moulds in which you can be cast.

After Greer Garson they stopped trying to make English stars out here.—*Anna Lee 1983*

Gary, Lorraine (–). American general purpose actress.
Jaws 75. I Never Promised You a Rose Garden 77. Jaws II 78. 1941 79. Just You and Me Kid 79. Jaws – The Revenge 87.

Gary, Romain (1914–1980). French novelist. Chief films from his work are *The Roots of Heaven* and *Lady L*; his autobiography, *Promise at Dawn*, was also filmed.

Gaslight. Patrick Hamilton's stage suspense thriller, about a Victorian wife deliberately being driven insane by her murderous husband, was perfectly filmed in Britain in 1939 by Thorold Dickinson with Anton Walbrook, Diana Wynyard and Frank Pettingell. MGM promptly bought and destroyed the negative, and in 1943 produced an opulent and inferior remake with Charles Boyer, Ingrid Bergman (AA) and Joseph Cotten, directed by George Cukor. In Britain this version was known as *The Murder in Thornton Square*; prints of the original version did survive and have been shown in America as *Angel Street.*

Gasnier, Louis J. (1882–1963). American director: mostly of foreign language versions.
Darkened Rooms 29. The Lawyer's Secret 31. Forgotten Commandments 32. Gambling Ship 33. The Last Outpost 35. Bank Alarm 37. Murder on the Yukon 40. Fight On Marines 42, etc.

Gassman, Vittorio (1922–). Italian actor and matinée idol, in occasional films since 1946.
Bitter Rice 48. Sombrero (US) 53. Rhapsody (US) 54. War and Peace 56. Tempest 57. The Love Specialist 60. Barabbas 62. The Devil in Love 66. Woman Times Seven 67. Lucky Thirteen 70. We All Loved Each Other So Much 73. Scent of a Woman 75. The Prophet 76. A Wedding 78. Quintet 79. The Nude Bomb 80. La Terrazzo 80. Il Turno 81. Sharkey's Machine 81. Tempest 82. La Vie est un Roman 83.

Gastoni, Lisa (1935–). Italian leading lady in British films of the fifties.
The Runaway Bus 54. Man of the Moment 55. The Baby and the Battleship 56. Intent to Kill 58. Hello London 59. Passport to China 64. Maddalena 72. The Last Days of Mussolini 74, etc.

Gate of Hell (Jigokumon) (Japan 1953). Known principally for its outstanding use of Eastmancolor, this medieval legend was directed by Teinosuke Kinugasa and photographed by Kohei Suziyama. Academy Award 1954: 'best foreign film'.

Gates, Larry (1915–). American character actor, often seen as small town merchant or middle-aged good guy.
Has Anybody Seen My Gal? 52. The Girl Rush 54. Invasion of the Body Snatchers 56. Jeanne Eagels 57. Cat on a Hot Tin Roof 58. One Foot in Hell 60. The Hoodlum Priest 62. Toys in the Attic 63. The Sand Pebbles 67. Airport 69, etc.

Gates, Nancy (1926–). American leading lady of the forties and fifties.
The Great Gildersleeve 42. The Spanish Main 45. The Atomic City 52. The Member of the Wedding 53. Suddenly 54. The Search for Bridey Murphy 56. The Brass Legend 56. Death of a Scoundrel 56. Some Came Running 59. Comanche Station 60, etc.

Gateson, Marjorie (1891–1977). American character actress of dignified mien.
The Beloved Bachelor 31. Silver Dollar 32. Cocktail Hour 33. Lady Killer 33. Big Hearted Herbert 34. Your Uncle Dudley 35. The Milky Way 36. Wife versus Secretary 36. First Lady 37. Stablemates 38. Geronimo 39. Pop Always Pays 40. Submarine Zone 41. Rings on Her Fingers 42. The Youngest Profession 43. Ever Since Venus 44. One More Tomorrow 46. Passage West 51. The Caddy 53, many others.

Gaudio, Tony (1885–1951) (Gaetono Gaudio). Italian cinematographer, long in Hollywood.
The Mark of Zorro 20. Secrets 24. The Temptress 25. Two Arabian Knights 27. *Hell's Angels* 30. Sky Devils 32. Bordertown 35. The Story of Louis Pasteur 35. *Anthony Adverse* (AA) 36. *The Life of Emile Zola* 37. *The Adventures of Robin Hood* 38. Juarez 39. *The Letter* 40. The Great Lie 41. The Constant Nymph 43. A Song to Remember 45. Love From a Stranger 47. The Red Pony 49, many others.

Gauge, Alexander (1914–1960). Heavyweight British actor, Friar Tuck in TV's *Robin Hood* series.

The Interrupted Journey (debut) 49. Murder in the Cathedral 51. Pickwick Papers 52. Fast and Loose 54. Martin Luther 55. The Iron Petticoat 56. The Passing Stranger 57, etc.

Gaumont, Leon (1863–1946). Pioneer French inventor, producer and exhibitor. Founder of Gaumont Studios at Shepherds Bush, also Gaumont circuit, both later sold to Rank. Invented sound on disc in 1902.

Gautier, Dick (1939–). American leading man of the seventies.
Wild in the Sky 72. Fun with Dick and Jane 77. Billy Jack Goes to Washington 78, etc.
TV series: *Here We Go Again* 71.

Gavin, John (1928–). American leading man.
A Time To Live and a Time To Die 58. Imitation of Life 59. Spartacus 60. Psycho 60. A Breath of Scandal 61. Back Street 61. Romanoff and Juliet 61. Thoroughly Modern Millie 67. The Madwoman of Chaillot 69. Pussycat Pussycat I Love You 70. Rich Man Poor Man (TV) 76. Jennifer 78, etc.
TV series: Destry 64. Convoy 65.

Gawthorne, Peter (1884–1962). Splendidly pompous-looking British stage actor, often seen as general, admiral or chief constable in comedies of the thirties.
Sunny Side Up (US) 29. Charlie Chan Carries On (US) 31. Jack's the Boy 32. The Iron Duke 35. Wolf's Clothing 36. Alf's Button Afloat 38. *Ask a Policeman* 40. Much Too Shy 42. The Case of Charles Peace 49. Five Days 54, many others.

Gaxton, William (1893–1963) (Arturo Gaxiola). American entertainer who made a few film appearances.
Fifty Million Frenchmen 31. Something to Shout About 42. Best Foot Forward 43. Tropicana 44. Diamond Horseshoe 45, etc.

Gay, John (–). American writer.
Run Silent Run Deep 58. The Four Horsemen of the Apocalypse (co-w) 62. The Hallelujah Trail 65. No Way to Treat a Lady 68.

Gaye, Gregory (c. 1900–). American character actor.
Dodsworth 36. Hollywood Boulevard 36. Ninotchka 39. Cash 42. The Bachelor and the Bobbysoxer 47. The Eddy Duchin Story 56. Auntie Mame 58, etc.

Gaynor, Janet (1906–84) (Laura Gainer). American leading lady of the twenties and thirties, immensely popular in simple sentimental films, especially when teamed with Charles Farrell. Played in many short comedies and westerns before achieving star status.
□The Johnstown Flood 26. The Shamrock Handicap 26. The Midnight Kiss 26. The Blue Eagle 26. The Return of Peter Grimm 26. *Seventh Heaven* (AA) 27. *Sunrise* 27. Two Girls Wanted 27. Street Angel 28. Four Devils 29. Christina 29. Lucky Star 29. Sunny Side Up 29. Happy Days 30. High Society Blues 30. The Man Who Came Back 30. *Daddy Longlegs* 31. Merely Mary Ann 31. Delicious 31. The First Year 32. Tess of the Storm Country 32. *State Fair* 33. Adorable 33. Paddy the Next Best Thing 33. Carolina 34. Change of Heart 34. Servants' Entrance 34. One More Spring 35. The Farmer Takes a Wife 35. Small Town Girl 36. Ladies in Love 36. *A Star is Born* 37. Three Loves Has Nancy 38. *The Young in Heart* 38. Bernardine 57.
Famous line (*A Star is Born*): Hello, everybody. This is Mrs Norman Maine.

Gaynor, Mitzi (1930–) (Francesca Mitzi von Gerber). American light leading lady with singing and dancing talents.
□My Blue Heaven 50. Take Care of My Little Girl 51. *Golden Girl* 51. We're Not Married 51. Bloodhounds of Broadway 51. The I Don't Care Girl 53. Down Among the Sheltering Palms 53. Three Young Texans 54. There's No Business Like Show Business 54. Anything Goes 56. The Birds and the Bees 56. The Joker is Wild 57. Les Girls 57. *South Pacific* 58. Happy Anniversary 59. Surprise Package 60. For Love or Money 63.

Gayson, Eunice (1931–). British leading lady, also on stage.
Dance Hall 50. Street Corner 53. Out of the Clouds 54. Zarak 57. The Revenge of Frankenstein 58. Dr No 62. From Russia with Love 63.

? gazetteer
Name the countries, states or cities omitted from the following film titles.

1 *A High Wind in* . . . . . .
2 *Action in* . . . . . .
3 *They Came to Blow Up* . . . . . .
4 *Candlelight in* . . . . . .
5 *The* . . . . . . *Gesture*
6 *Joan of* . . . . . .
7 . . . . . . *Canteen*

8 *Tonight We Raid . . . . . .*
9 *Masquerade in . . . . . .*
10 *Hotel . . . . . .*
11 *Mission to . . . . . .*
12 *Ten Gentlemen from . . . . . .*
13 *The Tuttles of . . . . . .*
14 *The . . . . . . Strangler*
15 *Miss V from . . . . . .*
16 *Night Train to . . . . . .*
17 *The Last Train from . . . . . .*
18 *Little Old . . . . . .*
19 *I Met Him in . . . . . .*
20 *Doughboys in . . . . . .*
21 *Fog over . . . . . .*
22 *Back to . . . . . .*
23 *. . . . . . I Love You*
24 *Hello . . . . . . Hello*
25 *Two Yanks in . . . . . .*

NB. All these films were made before 1950.

Gazzara, Ben (1930–) (Biago Gazzara). American actor, usually of rebellious types.
□The Strange One 57. *Anatomy of a Murder* 59. The Young Doctors 61. Convicts Four 62. The Captured City 62. A Rage to Live 65. If It's Tuesday This Must Be Belgium 69. The Bridge at Remagen 69. Husbands 70. When Michael Calls (TV) 71. The Passionate Thief 71. Pursuit (TV) 72. Fireball Forward (TV) 72. The Family Rico (TV) 72. Indict and Convict (TV) 73. The Neptune Factor 73. Maneater (TV) 73. *QB VII* (TV) 74. Capone 75. High Velocity 76. The Sicilian Connection 76. Voyage of the Damned 76. The Killing of a Chinese Bookie 76. The Death of Richie (TV) 77. The Trial of Lee Harvey Oswald (TV) 77. Opening Night 77. Saint Jack 79. Bloodline 79. They all Laughed 81. Inchon 81. Tales of Ordinary Madness 83. The Girl From Trieste 83. An Early Frost (TV) 85. The Professor 86.
TV series: *Arrest and Trial* 63. *Run for Your Life* 65–67.

Geer, Will (1902–78) (William Ghere). American character actor with a penchant for sinister old men.
The Misleading Lady 32. Deep Waters 48. Intruder in the Dust 49. Broken Arrow 50. The Tall Target 51. Salt of the Earth 53. Advise and Consent 61. *Seconds* 66. In Cold Blood 67. Bandolero 68. The Reivers 70. Brother John 70. Napoleon and Samantha 72. Executive Action 73. Jeremiah Johnson 73. Moving Violation 76. Billion Dollar Hobo 78, etc.
TV series: *The Waltons* 72–78.

Geesink, Joop (1913–84). Dutch puppeteer who in the late thirties made several shorts under the general heading of 'Dollywood'.

Geeson, Judy (1948–). British leading lady who started with sexy teenage roles.
Berserk 67. To Sir With Love 67. Here We Go Round the Mulberry Bush 67. Prudence and the Pill 68. Hammerhead 68. Three into Two Won't Go 69. The Executioner 69. 10 Rillington Place 70. One of Those Things 71. Who Killed the Mysterious Mr Foster? (TV) 71. Doomwatch 72. Fear in the Night 72. Brannigan 75. The Eagle Has Landed 76, etc.
TV series: Danger UXB 79.

Geeson, Sally (1950–). British juvenile actress of the sixties, sister of Judy Geeson.
□What's Good for the Goose 68. Cry of the Banshee 70. The Oblong Box 70. Forbush and the Penguins 71. Carry on Abroad 72. Bless This House 73 (and TV series). Carry on Girls 74.

Gelin, Daniel (1921–). French leading man with stage experience. In films since 1941.
Rendezvous de Juillet 49. *Edouard et Caroline* 50. *La Ronde* 50. Les Mains Sales 51. Rue de l'Estrapade 53. Les Amants du Tage (The Lovers of Lisbon) 54. The Man Who Knew Too Much (US) 55. Charmants Garçons 57. There's Always a Price Tag 58. Carthage in Flames 60. The Season for Love 65. Black Sun 66. Le Souffle au Coeur 71, Far from Dallas 72. Trop c'est Trop 74. Nous irons Vous au Paradis 77.

Gemma, Giuliano (1940–). Italian leading man of spaghetti westerns.
The Titans 62. Goliath and the Sins of Babylon 63. Adios Gringo 65. A Pistol for Ringo 65. Day of Anger 67. A Man to Respect 72, etc.

Gemora, Charlie (1903–61). American character actor with an unusual speciality: playing gorillas, notably in *The Gorilla* and *At the Circus*. They say he even appeared in a few shots of *King Kong*.

The General (US 1926). Famous Buster Keaton silent comedy-adventure with a Civil War setting and a train as co-hero. Basically a succession of impeccably-timed gags devised by Keaton himself. The story was used by Walt Disney in somewhat more serious vein for *The Great Locomotive Chase* 56.

The General Died at Dawn (US 1936). A rather pretentious melodrama which gave the impression of being backed by political thought, concerning an idealistic American's fight against a Chinese warlord. It paved the way for Hollywood involvement in the Spanish Civil War. Directed by Lewis Milestone, with Gary Cooper, Madeleine Carroll and Akim Tamiroff.

The General Line (The Old and the New) (Russia 1928). A brilliant semi-documentary, photographed by Tissé and directed by Eisenstein, intended as propaganda to introduce the newest and most productive methods to Soviet peasant farmers.

A Generation (Poland 1954). Andrzej Wajda's famous trilogy (the other two titles being *Kanal* 56, *Ashes and Diamonds* 58) gave a vivid picture of life in wartime Poland. Its impact is largely responsible for the resurgence of that country's film industry during the sixties.

Genevieve (GB 1953). A sophisticated comedy, written by William Rose and directed by Henry Cornelius, which marked a turn away from Ealing's polished innocence towards a more realistic Chelsea-based robustness. Despite many imitations its freshness and *joie de vivre* have not been equalled. Larry Adler's harmonica score immensely assisted the frolicsome story of a vintage car race from London to Brighton, and there were made to measure parts for Kenneth More, Kay Kendall, Dinah Sheridan and John Gregson.

Genina, Augusto (1892–1957). Italian pioneer director.
La Gloria 13. Prix de Beauté 30. The White Squadron 35. Bengasi 42. Heaven Over the Marshes 49. Three Forbidden Stories 52. Maddalena 54. Frou Frou 55, many others.

Genn, Leo (1905–78). Bland British character actor, formerly a practising barrister.
Immortal Gentleman 35. Dream Doctor 36. Jump for Glory 37. Kate Plus Ten 38. Contraband 40. The Way Ahead 44. *Henry V* 44. Caesar and Cleopatra 45. *Green for Danger* 46. Mourning Becomes Electra (US) 48. The Velvet Touch (US) 48. *The Snake Pit* (US) 48. The Wooden Horse 50. The Miniver Story 50. *Quo Vadis* 51. Plymouth Adventure (US) 52. Personal Affair 53. The Green Scarf 55. Beyond Mombasa 56. Lady Chatterley's Lover (Fr.) 56. Moby Dick 56. I Accuse 57. No Time To Die 58. Too Hot To Handle 60. The Longest Day 62. Fifty-Five Days at Peking 62. Ten Little Indians 65. Circus of Fear 67. Connecting Rooms 69. Die Screaming Marianne 70, etc.

Gentleman's Agreement (US 1947) (AA). An earnest indictment of anti-Semitism, written by Moss Hart from Laura Hobson's novel, and directed by Elia Kazan, with Gregory Peck and John Garfield. Not very lively as a film, but immensely significant to Hollywood as the first of a series of anti-racialist pictures.

Gentlemen Prefer Blondes. Anita Loos' comic novel about a gold-digging twenties chorus girl on the make in the millionaire set was filmed in 1928 by Mal St Clair, with Ruth Taylor and Alice White, then in 1953 by Howard Hawks with Marilyn Monroe and Jane Russell.

George, Chief Dan (1899–1982). Canadian Indian actor.
□Smith! 69. *Little Big Man* 70. Alien Thunder 73. Harry and Tonto 74. The Bears and I 74. The Outlaw Josey Wales 76. Shadow of the Hawk 76. Americathon 79.

George, Christopher (1929–1983). American TV leading man.
El Dorado 68. Tiger by the Tail 69. Escape (TV) 69. The Immortal (TV) 69. Man on a String (TV) 72. I Escaped from Devil's Island 73. Grizzly 76. Day of the Animals 77. Whiskey Mountain 77. Mortuary 83, etc.
TV series: The Rat Patrol 66. The Immortal 69, etc.

George, Gladys (1900–1954) (Gladys Clare). American leading actress with stage experience.
□Red Hot Dollars 20. Home Spun Folks 20. The Easy Road 21. Chickens 21. The House that Jazz Built 21. Straight is the Way 34. *Valiant is the World for Carrie* 36. They Gave Him a Gun 37. *Madame X* 37. Love is a Headache 38. Marie Antoinette 38. *The Roaring Twenties* 39. Here I Am a Stranger 39. I'm from Missouri 39. A Child is Born 40. The Way of all Flesh 40. The House Across the Bay 40. *The Maltese Falcon* 41. The Lady from Cheyenne 41. Hit the Road 41. The Hard Way 42. Nobody's Darling 43. The Crystal Ball 43. Minstrel Man 44. Christmas Holiday 44. Steppin In Society 45. The Best Years of Our Lives 46. Millie's Daughter 47.

Alias a Gentleman 48. Flamingo Road 49. Undercover Girl 50. Bright Leaf 50. He Ran all the Way 51. Detective Story 51. Lullaby of Broadway 51. Dark City 51. Silver City 53. It Happens Every Thursday 54.

George, Grace (1879–1961). American stage actress whose one film, in 1943, was *Johnny Come Lately*.

George, Heinrich (1893–1946). German leading man of the twenties.
Kean 21. Lady Hamilton 21. Lucretia Borgia 22. Metropolis 26. Dreyfus 30. Jew Suss 40. The Postmaster 40. Kolberg 45.

George, Linda Day (1944–) (formerly **Linda Day**). American leading lady of the seventies. Started in TV's *Petticoat Junction*; wife of Christopher George.
The Sound of Anger (TV) 68. The House on Greenapple Road (TV) 70. Chisum 71. Set This Town on Fire (TV) 71. She Cried Murder (TV) 73. The Trial of Chaplain Jensen (TV) 75. Murder at the World Series (TV) 77. Cruise into Terror (TV) 78. Casino (TV) 80. The Junkman 82. Mortuary 83, many others.

George, Muriel (1883–1965). Plump, motherly British character actress who often played charladies or landladies. Music-hall background.
His Lordship (debut) 32. Yes Mr Brown 33. Dr Syn 37. A Sister to Assist 'Er (leading role) 38. Quiet Wedding 40. Dear Octopus 43. The Dancing Years 49. Simon and Laura 55, many others.

George, Susan (1950–). British leading lady, former child actress; usually typed as sexpot.
Billion Dollar Brain 67. The Strange Affair 68. Twinky 68. All Neat in Black Stockings 69. Spring and Port Wine 69. The Looking Glass War 69. Die Screaming Marianne 70. Eye Witness 70. Fright 71. The Straw Dogs 71. Dirty Mary Crazy Larry 73. Sonny and Jed 74. Mandingo 75. Out of Season 75. A Small Town in Texas 76. Tintorea 77. Tomorrow Never Comes 78. Enter the Ninja 81. Venom 82. The Jigsaw Man 84. Lightning 86, etc.

Georgy Girl (GB 1966). The dying fall of Britain's 'new wave', this eccentric comedy cast Lynn Redgrave as a plain Jane who envies her glamorous but selfish girl friend; she finally settles for adopting the friend's unwanted baby and marriage to a lecherous businessman. Touches of zany black comedy did not give the wanted illusion of freshness. With James Mason and Charlotte Rampling; directed by Silvio Narizzano from Peter Nichols' rather desperate screenplay.

Gerald, Jim (1889–1958) (Jacques Guenod). French actor, in occasional films from 1911. An Italian Straw Hat 27. La Chant au Marin 31. French Without Tears (as le professeur) 39. Boule de Suif 45. The Crimson Curtain 52. Father Brown 54. Fric Frac en Dentelles 57, etc.

Gerald McBoing Boing (US 1951). The first Stephen Bosustow cartoon for UPA, whose spareness of line and sharpness of wit contrasted happily with Disney's chocolate-box period. It concerned a little boy who could speak only sounds. There were a couple of less successful sequels.

Gerard, Gil (1943–). American leading man who generates a little wisdom amid the derring-do.
Airport 77 76. Ransom for Alice (TV) 77. Killing Stone (TV) 78. Buck Rogers in the Twentieth Century (TV) 79. Hear No Evil (TV) 83, etc.
TV series: Buck Rogers 80–81.

Gerasimov, Sergei (1906–85). Russian director, best known abroad for *And Quietly Flows the Don* 57. Formerly an actor.

Geray, Steve (1904–1973) (Stefan Gyergyay). Hungarian character actor of stage and screen, usually seen as mild-mannered little fellow. In London from 1934, Hollywood from 1941.
Dance Band 34. Inspector Hornleigh 39. Man at Large 41. *The Moon and Sixpence* (as Dirk Stroeve) 42. Night Train from Chungking 43. The Mask of Dimitrios 44. *So Dark the Night* (leading role) 46. *Gilda* 46. I Love Trouble 48. The Big Sky 52. Call Me Madam 53. The Birds and the Bees 56. Count Your Blessings 59. Dime with a Halo 63, many others.

Gere, Richard (1949–). American leading man of the late seventies.
□Report to the Commissioner 75. Strike Force (TV) 75. Baby Blue Marine 76. Looking for Mr Goodbar 77. Days of Heaven 78. Bloodbrothers 78. *Yanks* 79. American Gigolo 79. An Officer and a Gentleman 82. The Honorary Consul 83. Breathless 83. The Cotton Club 84. King David 85. Power 85. No Mercy 86.

Gering, Marion (1901–77). Polish-Russian director with long stage experience; in America from 1925.
The Devil and the Deep 32. Madame Butterfly 33. Jennie Gerhardt 33. Thirty Day Princess 34. Rumba 35. Lady of Secrets 36. Thunder in the City (GB) 37. She Married an Artist 38. Sarumba (& co-p) 50, etc.

Germaine, Mary (1933–). British leading lady of the fifties.
Laughter in Paradise 51. Where's Charley? 52. Women of Twilight 53. The Green Buddha (last to date) 54, etc.

German cinema had its most influential period in the years following World War I, when depression and despair drove directors into a macabre fantasy world and produced films like *The Golem, The Cabinet of Dr Caligari, Nosferatu, Warning Shadows* and *Waxworks*; it is also notable that many of the makers of these films later went to Hollywood and exerted a strong influence there. G. W. Pabst was somewhat more anchored to reality, apart from the stylish *Die Dreigroschenoper*; Fritz Lang seemed primarily interested in the criminal mentality, though he produced masterworks of prophecy and Teutonic legend. With the advent of Hitler most of Germany's genuine creative talent was forced abroad; the main achievements of the thirties were Leni Riefenstahl's colossal propaganda pieces *Triumph of the Will* and *Olympische Spiele*. The anti-British war-time films have their interest, but the post-war German cinema was not producing competent thrillers and comedies for the home market. In the seventies however a new realistic school developed in the hands of Rainer Fassbinder, Werner Herzog, etc. Notable German players include Werner Krauss, Conrad Veidt, Emil Jannings, Marlene Dietrich, Anton Walbrook and Gert Frobe.

Germi, Pietro (1914–1974). Italian director, in films since 1945.
In the Name of the Law 49. The Road to Hope 50. Man of Iron 56. Maledetto Imbroglio (A Sordid Affair) 59. Divorce Italian Style 61. Seduced and Abandoned 63. The Birds the Bees and the Italians 65. Alfredo Alfredo 73, many others.

Geronimo (1829–1909). Apache Indian chief who dealt destruction to the whites. Memorably impersonated by Chief Thundercloud in *Geronimo* 38, Jay Silverheels in *The Battle at Apache Pass* 52, Chuck Connors in *Geronimo* 62.

Gerrard, Gene (1892–1971) (Eugene O'Sullivan). British music hall comedian with engaging light style: starred in several comedy musicals of the thirties.
Let's Love and Laugh 31. *My Wife's Family* 31. *Out of the Blue* (& d) 31. Let Me Explain Dear (& d) 32. The Love Nest 33. It's a Bet 35. No Monkey Business 35. Where's Sally? 36. Glamour Girl 37, etc.

Gershenson, Joseph (1904–). Russian musician, long in US. In films from 1920; head of Universal music department from 1941. Not himself a composer.

Gershwin, George (1898–1937) (Jacob Gershowitz). American popular composer of scores of songs and concert pieces. Contributed to many films. His biography was told in *Rhapsody in Blue* 45, and his music was used exclusively in *An American in Paris* 51. Three hitherto unpublished songs were even used in *Kiss Me Stupid* 64.

¶ His was a modernity that reflected the civilisation we live in as excitingly as the headline in today's newspaper.—*Ira Gershwin*

He was a child of his age who never became old enough to outlive his usefulness.—*Charles Schwartz*

Gershwin, Ira (1896–1983) (Israel Gershowitz). American lyricist, brother of George Gershwin. He wrote for stage from 1918, films from 1931.
Delicious 31. Goldwyn Follies 39. Cover Girl 44. An American in Paris 51. Kiss Me Stupid 64, many others.

Gertie the Dinosaur. Early American cartoon character created by Winsor McKay in 1909.

Gertsman, Maury (c. 1910–). American cinematographer.
Strange Confession 45. Terror by Night 46. Singapore 47. Rachel and the Stranger 48. One Way Street 50. Meet Danny Wilson 52. The World in My Corner 55. Kelly and Me 57. Gunfight in Abilene 66, many others.

Gervaise (France 1956). Written by Jean Aurenche and Pierre Bost from Zola's novel, directed by René Clement, this seamy story presented a vivid picture of 19th-century Paris, comparable with David Lean's Dickens films. Delightfully acted by Maria Schell, François Perier and Suzy Delair.

Getchell, Robert (–). American screenwriter.

Alice Doesn't Live Here Any More 74. Bound for Glory 76. Mommie Dearest (co-w) 81, etc.

The Ghost Breaker. This American stage thriller by Paul Dickey and Charles W. Goddard, about an heiress's voodoo-haunted castle, was filmed in 1915 with H. B. Warner and in 1922 (directed by Alfred E. Green) with Wallace Reid. In 1940 George Marshall directed a talkie version as a vehicle for Bob Hope, and the result was an oddly successful combination of laughs and horror, with contributions from Willie Best, Paulette Goddard and Paul Lukas. (The title, incidentally, was made plural.) In 1953 Marshall remade it, with remarkable fidelity to the 1940 script, as a vehicle for Martin and Lewis under the title *Scared Stiff*, with Lizabeth Scott and Carmen Miranda; the results were hardly stimulating.

The Ghost Goes West (GB 1936). René Clair showed British films a lighter touch than they had known before in this fantasy of a gay Scottish ghost who follows his castle when it is moved stone by stone to America. Robert Donat shone in a dual role.

The Ghost Train. This hugely successful British stage comedy-thriller by Arnold Ridley, about stranded passengers at a lonely Cornish station being used by gun-runners, was first filmed in 1928, directed by C. Bolvary, with Guy Newall as the silly-ass hero who turns out to be a policeman. A talkie version followed in 1931 with Jack Hulbert, directed by Walter Forde, who also directed the 1941 remake in which the leading role was split between Arthur Askey and Richard Murdoch.

ghosting. Another word for dubbing, especially when a star apparently singing is actually miming to the voice of the real artist. See *dubbing*.

Ghostley, Alice (1926–). American revue comedienne and character actress.
New Faces 54. To Kill a Mockingbird 62. My Six Loves 63. The Flim Flam Man 67. Viva Max 68. Ace Eli and Rodger of the Skies 72, etc.

ghosts: see *fantasy*.

Giallelis, Stathis (1939–). Greek actor who went to Hollywood.
America America 63. Cast a Giant Shadow 66. The Eavesdropper 67, etc.

Giannini, Giancarlo (1942–). Italian leading actor of the seventies.
Rita the Mosquito 66. Anzio 68. The Secret of Santa Vittoria 69. The Pizza Triangle 70. The Seduction of Mimi 72. The Sensual Man 73. Swept Away 74. *Seven Beauties* 76. The Innocent 76. A Night Full of Rain 77. Travels with Anita 79. Suffer or Die 79. American Dreamer 84. Fever Pitch 85. Saving Grace 86, etc.

giants are infrequently encountered in films, but Harold Lloyd met one in *Why Worry?*, as did Abbott and Costello in *Lost in a Harem*. Costello also met *The Thirty Foot Bride of Candy Rock*, not to be confused with *The Attack of the Fifty Foot Woman*. Then there was *The Giant of Marathon*, and Glenn Langan played *The Amazing Colossal Man* in two films. Back to Abbott and Costello again: it was they who appeared with Buddy Baer in *Jack and The Beanstalk*.

Gibbons, Cedric (1893–1960). American art director; worked for Edison 1915–17, Goldwyn 1918–24, MGM 1924 on. Co-directed one film, *Tarzan and His Mate* 34. Designed the 'Oscar' statuette.
The Bridge of San Luis Rey (AA) 29. The Merry Widow (AA) 34. Pride and Prejudice (AA) 40. Blossoms in the Dust (AA) 41. Gaslight (AA) 44. The Yearling (AA) 46. Little Women (AA) 49. An American in Paris (AA) 51, hundreds of others.

Gibbs, Anthony (1925–). British editor.
Oscar Wilde 60. A Taste of Honey 61. Tom Jones 63. The Knack 64. Petulia 68. Performance 70. Fiddler on the Roof 71. Jesus Christ Superstar 74. Juggernaut 75. Rollerball 75. A Bridge Too Far 77, many others.

Gibbs, Gerald (c. 1910–). British cinematographer.
Whisky Galore 49. Fortune Is a Woman 57. The Man Upstairs 58. The Leather Boys 63. A Jolly Bad Fellow 64. Mister Ten Per Cent 67, etc.

Gibney, Sheridan (1903–). American screenwriter.
I Am a Fugitive from a Chain Gang 32. The World Changes 33. The Story of Louis Pasteur (AA) 36. Green Pastures 36. Letter of Introduction 38. Disputed Passage 39. Cheers for Miss Bishop 41. Once Upon a Honeymoon 42. Our Hearts Were Young and Gay 44. The Locket 47, etc.

Gibson, Alan (1938–). Canadian director in Britain.
□Crescendo 69. Goodbye Gemini 70. Dracula AD 1972 72. The Satanic Rites of Dracula 73. Crash 77. Churchill and the Generals (TV) 79. A Woman Called Golda (TV) 82. Witness for the Prosecution (TV) 82. Martin's Day 84.

Gibson, Helen (1892–1977) (Rose August Wenger). American leading lady of the silent screen; of Swiss descent; married to Hoot Gibson. Former stunt girl. Appeared in *Hollywood Story* 51.
The Hazards of Helen (serial) 15. No Man's Woman 20. The Wolverine 21, etc.

Gibson, Henry (1935–). Diminutive American comedy character actor who came to the fore in TV's *Laugh-In*.
Kiss Me Stupid 64. Evil Roy Slade (TV) 72. Nashville 75. The Last Remake of Beau Geste 78. Amateur Night at the Dixie Bar and Grill (TV) 79. A Perfect Couple 79. Health 80. The Blues Brothers 80. The Incredible Shrinking Woman 81, etc.

Gibson, Hoot (1892–1962) (Edward Richard). American cowboy hero of silent films; in Hollywood from 1911 after real cowpunching experience. Films good-humoured but not memorable.
The Hazards of Helen 15. The Cactus Kid 19. The Denver Dude 22. Surefire 24. Galloping Fury 27. Points West 29. Spirit of the West 32. Powdersmoke Range 33. Sunset Range 35. The Marshal's Daughter 53. The Horse Soldiers 59. Ocean's Eleven 61, hundreds of others.
† Allegedly, his name became Hoot because he loved to go owl-hunting.

Gibson, Mel (1956–). Australian leading actor.
□ Summer City 77. Tim 78. Attack Force 2 80. The Year of Living Dangerously 83. The Bounty 84. The River 84. Mrs Soffel 84. Mad Max Beyond Thunderdome 85. Lethal Weapon 87.

Gibson, Wynne (1899–1987). American leading lady, from the chorus.
Nothing But the Truth 30. Ladies of the Big House 32. I Give My Love 34. The Captain Hates the Sea 34. Gangs of New York 38. Café Hostess 40. The Falcon Strikes Back 43, many others.

Gidding, Nelson (c. 1915–). American screenwriter.
I Want To Live 58. Odds against Tomorrow 59. Nine Hours to Rama 61. The Inspector 62. The Haunting 64. Lost Command 66. The Andromeda Strain 70. The Hindenberg 75, etc.

Gidget: an American teenager of the early sixties, a kind of female Andy Hardy. The first film was released in 1959 and starred Sandra Dee. Then in 1961 came *Gidget Goes Hawaiian* with Deborah Walley, and in 1963 *Gidget Goes to Rome* with Cindy Carol. In 1969 and 1971 there were TV movies called *Gidget Grows Up* with Karen Valentine, and *Gidget Gets Married* with Monie Ellis; in 1972 came a cartoon version, *Gidget Makes the Wrong Connection.* In 1965 there was also a TV series with Sally Field.

Giehse, Therese (1898–1975). German stage actress whose occasional films included *Kinder, Mutter und Ein General* 58 and *Black Moon* 75.

Gielgud, Sir John (1904–). Distinguished British stage actor who has made occasional films.
Autobiographies: *Early Stages* 1953; *Distinguished Company* 1972. *An Actor and his Times* 1979.
□Who Is the Man? 24. The Clue of the New Pin 29. Insult 32. The Good Companions 32. Secret Agent 36. The Prime Minister (as Disraeli) 40. *Julius Caesar* (as Cassius) 53. Richard III 56. The Barretts of Wimpole Street 57. Saint Joan 57. Becket 64. The Loved One 65. Chimes at Midnight 66. Around the World In Eighty Days 66. Sebastian 67. *The Charge of the Light Brigade* 68. Assignment to Kill 68. The Shoes of the Fisherman 68. Oh What a Lovely War 69. Julius Caesar 70. Eagle in a Cage 71. Probe (TV) 72. Lost Horizon 73. Frankenstein, the True Story (TV) 73. QB VII (TV) 74. 11 Harrowhouse 74. Luther 74. Gold 74. *Murder on the Orient Express* 74. Galileo 75. Aces High 76. Joseph Andrews 77. *Providence* 77. Murder by Decree 79. Les Misérables (TV) 79. A Portrait of the Artist as a Young Man 79. Caligula 79. The Human Factor 79. The Elephant Man 80. The Formula 80. The Seven Dials Mystery (TV) 80. Marco Polo (TV) 80. *Arthur* (AA) 81. Sphinx 81. Lion of the Desert 81. Chariots of Fire 81. Priest of Love 81. *Brideshead Revisited* (TV) 81. Gandhi 82. Wagner (TV) 82. The Conductor 82. The Wicked Lady 83. Invitation to a Wedding 83. Wagner 83. The Shooting Party 84. Scandalous 84. The Scarlet and the Black (TV) 82. Inside the Third Reich (TV) 82. The

Far Pavilions (TV) 84. The Master of Ballantrae (TV) 84. Camille (TV) 85. Romance on the Orient Express (TV) 86. The Whistle Blower 86. Plenty 86. War and Remembrance (TV) 88.

Gifford, Alan (1905–). American character actor in British films.
It Started in Paradise 52. Lilacs in the Spring 54. The Iron Petticoat 56. A King in New York 57. Too Young to Love 60. Carry On Cowboy 66, Arrivederci Baby 66. Phase IV 73, etc.

Gifford, Frances (1922–). American leading lady of the forties, trained as lawyer. Career subsequently halted by ill-health.
Hold That Woman 40. Jungle Girl 41. My Son Alone 42. Tarzan Triumphs 43. She Went to the Races 45. Little Mister Jim 46. Luxury Liner 48. Riding High 49. Sky Commando 53, etc.

Gigi (US 1958) (AA). Colette's novel of a *fin-de-siècle* Parisian cocotte was filmed straight in the forties with Daniele Delorme, but is now best known in the form of the American musical, directed by Vincente Minnelli (AA) with a Lerner and Loewe score (AA). Cecil Beaton's designs (AA) shared honours with Leslie Caron, Maurice Chevalier and Louis Jourdan. The film won nine Academy Awards.

Gigli, Beniamino (1890–1957). Famous Italian tenor who starred in several films.
Forget Me Not 35. Ave Maria 37. Pagliacci 42. Night Taxi 50, etc.

Gigolos are figures from another age, when women could be imposed on, but they were memorably played by David Niven in *Dodsworth,* Montgomery Clift in *The Heiress,* Fred MacMurray in *The Lady is Willing,* Burt Lancaster in *Sorry Wrong Number,* William Holden in *Sunset Boulevard,* Van Johnson in *Invitation,* Bekim Fehmiu in *The Adventurers,* Jon Voight in *Midnight Cowboy,* Charles Grodin in *The Heartbreak Kid,* Helmut Berger in *Ash Wednesday,* and David Bowie in *Just a Gigolo.*

Gilbert, Billy (1893–1971). American character comedian usually seen as a fat, excitable Italian. In films since 1929, after vaudeville experience: a memorable stooge for Laurel and Hardy, the Three Stooges and the Marx Brothers.
Noisy Neighbours (debut) 29. The Music Box 32. Sutter's Gold 37. Snow White and the Seven Dwarfs (as the voice of Sneezy) 37. Blockheads 38. Destry Rides Again 39. *The Great Dictator* (as Goering) 40. *His Girl Friday* 40. Tin Pan Alley 41. Anchors Aweigh 45. Down Among the Sheltering Palms 52. Five Weeks in a Balloon 62, many others.

Gilbert, John (1895–1936) (John Pringle). American leading man of the twenties. From a theatrical family, he worked his way from bit parts to romantic leads, but sound revealed his voice to be less dashing than his looks.
□Hell's Hinges 16. Bullets and Brown Eyes 16. The Apostle of Vengeance 16. The Phantom 16. The Eye of the Night 16. Shell 43 16. The Princess of the Dark 16. Happiness 16. The Millionaire Vagrant 16. Hater of Men 17. Golden Rule Kate 16. The Devil Dodger 17. Nancy Comes Home 18. More Trouble 18. Shackled 18. Three X Gordon 18. Wedlock 18. The Mask 18. The Dawn of Understanding 18. White Heather 19. The Busher 19. Heart o' the Hills 19. The Red Viper 19. Should Women Tell? 19. Widow By Proxy 19. The Servant in the House 20. The Great Redeemer 20. The White Circle 20. Deep Waters 21. Ladies Must Live 21. Gleam o' Dawn 22. Monte Cristo 22. Arabian Love 22. The Yellow Stain 22. Honor First 22. Calvert's Valley 22. The Love Gambler 22. While Paris Sleeps 22. Truxten King 23. The Madness of Youth 23. Saint Elmo 23. *Cameo Kirby* 23. A California Romance 23. Just Off Broadway 24. The Wolf Man 24. A Man's Mate 24. The Lone Ranch 24. Romance Ranch 24. His Hour 24. He Who Gets Slapped 24. The Snob 24. The Wife of the Centaur 25. *The Merry Widow* 25. *The Big Parade* 25. La Boheme 26. Bardelys the Magnificent 26. *Flesh and the Devil* 27. The Show 27. Twelve Miles Out 27. *Love* 27. Man, Woman and Sin 28. The Cossacks 28. Four Walls 28. Marks of the Devil 28. A Woman of Affairs 29. Desert Nights 29. Hollywood Revue 29. His Glorious Night (the talkie which killed his romantic image) 29. Redemption 30. Way for a Sailor 30. Gentleman's Fate 31. The Phantom of Paris 31. West of Broadway 32. Downstairs 32. Fast Workers 33. Queen Christina 33. The Captain Hates the Sea 35.

Gilbert, Lewis (1920–). British director, former actor and documentarist.
□The Little Ballerina 47. Marry Me (w only) 49. Once a Sinner 50. There Is another Sun 50. The Scarlet Thread 51. Emergency Call

52. Time Gentlemen Please 52. Cosh Boy 53. Johnny on the Run 53. *Albert RN* 53. The Sea Shall Not Have Them 54. *The Good Die Young* 54. Cast a Dark Shadow 55. *Reach for the Sky* 56. The Admirable Crichton 57. Carve Her Name with Pride 57. A Cry from the Streets 58. Ferry to Hong Kong 59. *Sink The Bismarck* 60. Light Up the Sky 60. The Greengage Summer 61. HMS Defiant 62. The Seventh Dawn 64. Alfie 66. You Only Live Twice 67. The Adventurers 70. Friends (& w) 71. Paul and Michelle 73. Operation Daybreak 75. Seven Nights in Japan 76. The Spy Who Loved Me 77. Moonraker 79. Educating Rita 83. Not Quite Jerusalem 84.

¶ *L.G.:* Paramount backed *Alfie* because it was going to be made for £500,000, normally the sort of money spent on executives' cigar bills.

Gilbert, Olive (1898–1981). Welsh contralto, in opera and musical comedy.
□ Glamorous Night 37. The Dancing Years 50. King's Rhapsody (voice only) 55.

Gilbert, Paul (1917–) (Paul MacMahon). American comedy dancer, former trapezist.
So This Is Paris 55. The Second Greatest Sex 55. You Can't Run Away from It 56. Women of the Prehistoric Planet 66, etc.
TV series: The Duke 54.

Gilbert, W. S. (1836–1911) (William Schwenck) and **Sullivan, Sir Arthur** (1842–1900). Celebrated British composers (words and music respectively) of the Savoy operas of the eighties, most cherished for their comic aspects and still performed all over the world by the D'Oyly Carte Company. Many film versions have been made, notably of *The Mikado*. In 1954 came a moderate biopic, *The Story of Gilbert and Sullivan*, with Robert Morley and Maurice Evans.

Gilbreth, Elizabeth (1908–). American author of *Cheaper by the Dozen* and *Belles on Their Toes*, two books of reminiscences which centre on her father, who tried to apply his time-and-motion-study techniques to bringing up his large family.

Gilchrist, Connie (1901–85) (Rose Gilchrist). American character actress of stage and screen.
Billy the Kid 41. The Hucksters 47. A Letter to Three Wives 49. The Man in the Grey Flannel Suit 56. Some Came Running 58. Auntie Mame 59. Say One For Me 59. A House Is Not a Home 64. Sylvia 65. Tickle Me 65. Fuzz 70, etc.
TV series: Long John Silver 55.

Gilda (US 1946). A highly professional example of the glossy *film noir* coming out of Hollywood in the somewhat dejected period following World War II, when victory had turned to ashes. Everyone in this tale is cynical and at least partly corrupt: George Macready as the nominal villain evokes more sympathy than hero (Glenn Ford) or heroine (Rita Hayworth). Charles Vidor's direction is showy but controlled, and Hayworth's song numbers (including 'Put the Blame on Mame') show her at her most torrid. Other films of this time and genre include *Till the End of Time, The Blue Dahlia, Johnny O'Clock, Build My Gallows High* and *The Strange Love of Martha Ivers*.

Giler, David (–). American screenwriter with many TV credits.
Myra Breckinridge (co-w) 70. The Parallax View (co-w) 74. The Black Bird (& d) 75. Fun with Dick and Jane (co-w) 77. Alien (co-w) 79. Southern Comfort (co-w) 81.

Gilford, Jack (1907–) (Jacob Gellman). American comic actor with long stage career.
Hey Rookie 53. Main Street to Broadway 53. A Funny Thing Happened on the Way to the Forum 66. Mister Buddwing 66. Enter Laughing 67. The Happening 67. Who's Minding the Mint? 67. They Might Be Giants 71. Catch 22 71. *Save the Tiger* 73. Harry and Walter Go to New York 76. Wholly Moses 80. Caveman 81. Hotel (TV) 82. Cocoon 85, etc.

Gilles, Genevieve (1946–) (Genevieve Gillaizeau). French leading lady, protégée of Darryl Zanuck.
□World of Fashion (short) 67. Hello-Goodbye 69.

Gillette, William (1855–1937). American stage actor famous for his personification of *Sherlock Holmes*, which he played on film in 1916.

Gilliam, Terry (1940–). American director/animator, one of the Monty Python team (qv).
AS DIRECTOR: Jabberwocky 76. Time Bandits 81. Brazil 85. The Adventures of Baron Munchhausen 88.

Gilliat, Leslie (1917–). British producer, brother of Sidney Gilliat, with whom he usually works.

Gilliat, Sidney (1908–). British comedy screenwriter usually in collaboration with Frank Launder (qv); they have also produced most of their films since the forties.
Rome Express 33. *Friday the Thirteenth* 33. Jack Ahoy 34. Chu Chin Chow 34. Bulldog Jack 35. Where There's a Will 36. Seven Sinners 36. Take My Tip 37. *A Yank at Oxford* 38. *The Lady Vanishes* 38. The Gaunt Stranger 38. Jamaica Inn 39. *Ask a Policeman* 39. They Came by Night 40. *Night Train to Munich* 40. *Kipps* 41. *The Young Mr Pitt* 42. Millions Like Us (& d) 43. *Waterloo Road* (& d) 44. *The Rake's Progress* (& d) 45. *Green for Danger* (& d) 46. London Belongs to Me (& d) 48. *State Secret* (& d) 50. The Story of Gilbert and Sullivan (& d) 53. The Constant Husband (& d) 55. Fortune is a Woman (& d) 57. Left Right and Centre (& d) 59. *Only Two Can Play* (& d) 62. The Great St Trinian's Train Robbery (& d) 65, etc.

Gilliatt, Penelope (1933–). British critic and screenwriter: Sunday Bloody Sunday 72.

Gillie, Jean (1915–1949). British leading lady, former chorine.
School for Stars 35. Brewster's Millions 35. While Parents Sleep 36. Sweet Devil 38. Tilly of Bloomsbury 40. Sailors Don't Care 40. The Gentle Sex 43. *Tawny Pipit* 44. Decoy (US) 47. The Macomber Affair (US) 47, etc.

Gilling, John (1910–85). British writer-director who turned out dozens of crime and adventure pot-boilers after the war.
The Greed of William Hart (w) 48. The Man from Yesterday (wd) 49. No Trace (wd) 50. Mother Riley Meets the Vampire (wd) 52. The Voice of Merrill (d) 52. The Gamma People (wd) 55. Odongo (wd) 56. Interpol (wd) 57. High Flight (d) 57. The Man Inside (wd) 58. Idol on Parade (d) 59. The Flesh and the Fiends (wd) 59. The Challenge (wd) 60. Fury at Smuggler's Bay (wd) 61. Shadow of the Cat (wd) 62. Pirates of Blood River (wd) 62. The Scarlet Blade (wd) 63. The Brigand of Kandahar (wd) 64. The Plague of the Zombies (wd) 65. The Mummy's Shroud (wd) 67, many others.

Gillingwater, Claude (1870–1939). American stage actor who came to films to play irascible old men.
Little Lord Fauntleroy 21. Dulcy 23. Daddies 24. Daddy Long Legs 31. The Captain Hates the Sea 34. A Tale of Two Cities 36. Prisoner of Shark Island 36. Conquest 37. Café Society 39, etc.

Gillis, Ann (1927–) (Alma O'Connor). American child star of the thirties; adult roles routine.
The Garden of Allah 37. Off to the Races 37. *The Adventures of Tom Sawyer* 38. The Underpup 39. Little Men 40. Nice Girl 41. In Society 44. Since You Went Away 44. Janie Gets Married 46, etc.

Gillmore, Margalo (1897–1986). American stage actress in occasional films.
Wayward 32. Perfect Strangers 50. The Law and the Lady 51. Skirts Ahoy 52. Woman's World 54. Gaby 56. High Society 56, etc.

Gilmore, Lowell (1907–1960). British general purpose actor.
The Picture of Dorian Gray 44. Calcutta 47. Dream Girl 48. Tripoli 50. Lone Star 52. Plymouth Adventure 52. Saskatchewan 54, etc.

Gilmore, Peter (–). British light actor, familiar on TV as the hero of *The Onedin Line*.
Bomb in the High Street 61. Carry on Jack 64. Doctor in Clover 66. My Lover My Son 69. The Abominable Dr Phibes 71. Warlords of Atlantis 78, etc.

Gilmore, Stuart (1913–71). American editor.
Arrest Bulldog Drummond 38. The Lady Eve 41. Sullivan's Travels 41. The Palm Beach Story 42. The Miracle of Morgan's Creek 43. Hail the Conquering Hero 44. Road to Utopia 45. Vendetta 50. The French Line 54. Underwater 55. Journey to the Center of the Earth 59. The Alamo 60. Hatari 62. A Rage To Live 65. Hawaii 66. Thoroughly Modern Millie 67. Sweet Charity 69. Airport 70. The Andromeda Strain 71, many others.
□AS DIRECTOR: The Virginian 46. Hot Lead 51. Captive Women 52. The Half Breed 52. Target 52.

Gilmore, Virginia (1919–86) (Sherman Poole). American leading lady of the forties; films routine.
Winter Carnival 39. Laddie 40. Swamp Water 41. The Loves of Edgar Allan Poe 42. Orchestra Wives 42. Chetniks 43. Wonder Man 45. Close Up 48. Walk East on Beacon 52, etc.

Gilroy, Frank D. (1925–). American playwright and screenwriter.
The Fastest Gun Alive 56. The Gallant Hours 60. The Subject Was Roses 68. The Only

Game in Town 69. Desperate Characters (& d) 71. From Noon till Three (& d) 74. Once in Paris (& d) 78, etc.

Gilson, René (1931–). French director.
□L'Escadron Volapuk 70. On n'Arrête pas le Printemps 71. La Brigade 73. Juliette et l'Air du Temps 76. Ma Blonde Entends-tu dans la Ville 80.

gimmicks. There are those who would classify such developments as 3-D, CinemaScope and even talkies under this heading. The genuine gimmick however is a more fleeting affair, a momentary method for getting audiences into cinemas for reasons that have little to do with the quality of the film. William Castle is the established master. For *Macabre* he offered free insurance if one died of heart failure. For *Homicidal*, a fright break before the climax when cowards could leave—and even get their money back if they could stand to go home without learning the awful secret. For *The House on Haunted Hill*, 'Emergo', in which a skeleton on wires shot above the audience's head at a suitable point in the film. For *The Tingler*, a device which wired up certain seats to give people a small electric shock. In competition, the producers of *Chamber of Horrors* thought up the fear flasher and the horror horn to warn weak spirits when a nasty moment was coming.

Gingold, Hermione (1897–1987). British revue comedienne who delighted in grotesque characters.
Autobiography 1958: *The World is Square*.
Someone at the Door 36. Meet Mr Penny 39. The Butler's Dilemma 43. Cosh Boy 52. *Pickwick Papers* 52. Our Girl Friday 53. Around the World in Eighty Days 56. *Bell, Book and Candle* (US) 58. *Gigi* (US) 58. *The Music Man* (US) 61. I'd Rather Be Rich (US) 64. Harvey Middlemann, Fireman (US) 65. Munster Go Home (US) 66. Banyon (TV) 71. *A Little Night Music* 76. Garbo Talks 84, etc.

¶ *H.G.:* I had all the schooling any actress needs. I learned enough to sign contracts.

Girard, Bernard (c. 1929–). American director.
□Ride Out for Revenge 57. Green Eyed Blonde 57. The Party Crashers 58. As Young as we Are 58. A Public Affair 62. Dead Heat on a Merry Go Round 68. The Mad Room 69. Gone with the West 69. The Happiness Cage 72.

Girardot, Annie (1931–). French leading lady.
Thirteen at Table 56. Maigret Sets a Trap 58. Vice and Virtue 63. Vivre pour Vivre 67. Les Gauloises Bleues 68. Dillinger Is Dead 69. A Man I Like 69. The Novices 70. Traitement de Choc 73. The Slap 76. Une Robe Noire pour un Tueur 80. Le Coeur a l'Envers 80. La Vie Continue 81, All Night Long 81. Memories, Memories 84. Departure, Return 85, etc.

Girardot, Etienne (1856–1939). Dapper Anglo-French character actor, in many American plays and films.
The Violin of Monsieur 12. The Kennel Murder Case 33. *Twentieth Century* 34. Clive of India 35. Metropolitan 35. Go West Young Man 36. *The Great Garrick* 37. Professor Beware 38. The Hunchback of Notre Dame 39. Isle of Destiny 40, many others.

Girotti, Massimo (1918–). Italian leading man.
Obsession 42. Caccia Tragica 47. Fabiola 47. Bellissima 51. Aphrodite 57. Theorem 68. Mr Klein 76. Cagliostro 76, etc.

Gish, Dorothy (1898–1968) (Dorothy de Guiche). Famous American silent star, in films for D. W. Griffith from 1912: *Hearts of the World, Orphans of the Storm*, etc. On stage between 1928 and 1944.
Our Hearts Were Young and Gay 44. The Whistle at Eaton Falls 51. The Cardinal 63, etc.

Gish, Lillian (1896–) (Lillian de Guiche). Famous American silent star, sister of Dorothy Gish, and also a D. W. Griffith discovery. From mid-twenties spent much time on stage, but filmed occasionally. Directed one film, Remodelling her Husband 21.
Autobiography 1969: *The Movies, Mr Griffith, and Me*.
Birth of a Nation 14. *Intolerance* 16. *Broken Blossoms* 18. *Way Down East* 20. Orphans of the Storm 22. The Scarlet Letter 26. Annie Laurie 27. His Double Life 34. The Commandos Strike at Dawn 43. Miss Susie Slagle's 46. *Duel in the Sun* 46. Portrait of Jennie 48. *Night of the Hunter* 55. Orders to Kill 58. The Unforgiven 59. Follow Me Boys 66. Warning Shot 66. The Comedians 67. Twin Detectives (TV) 76. Poltergeist 82. Psycho II 83. Hambone and Hillie 85. Sweet Liberty 85. The Whales of August 87, etc. Special AA 1970.

❀ For her early stardom and her later graciousness; and for achieving the longest acting career in show business. *Way Down East.*

¶ *L.G.:* You know, when I first went into the movies Lionel Barrymore played my grandfather. Later he played my father and finally he played my husband. If he had lived, I'm sure I would have played his mother. That's the way it is in Hollywood. The men get younger and the women get older.
L.G.: Fans always write asking why I didn't smile more in films. I did in *Annie Laurie*, but I can't recall that it helped much.
L.G.: I can't remember a time when I wasn't acting, so I can't imagine what I would do if I stopped now.
L.G.: I don't care for modern films—all crashing cars and close-ups of people's feet.
L.G.: I've never been in style, so I can't go out of style.

Gist, Robert (1924–). American general purpose actor; turned director once, then went into TV.
Jigsaw 49. I Was a Shoplifter 50. The Band Wagon 53. D Day Sixth of June 56. Operation Petticoat 59. Blueprint for Robbery 61. An American Dream (d only) 66, etc.

Givney, Kathryn (1897–1978). American general purpose character actress.
Isn't It Romantic? 48. Operation Pacific 51. Three Coins in the Fountain 54. Guys and Dolls 55. The Wayward Bus 57. The Man in the Net 59, etc.

Givot, George (1903–84). American character actor, usually in hearty roles.
When's Your Birthday 37. Marie Walewska 38. Dubarry Was a Lady 43. Riff Raff 46. Captain Blood Fugitive 52. Miracle in the Rain 56, etc.

Glaser, Paul Michael (1943–). American leading man who leaped to fame as Starsky in TV's *Starsky and Hutch*, but subsequently found roles scarce.
□Fiddler on the Roof 71. Butterflies Are Free 72. Trapped Beneath the Sea (TV) 74. The Great Houdinis (TV) 77. Phobia 80. Wait till Your Mother Gets Home (TV) 81. Princess Daisy (TV) 82. The Running Man (d) 87.

Glass, Ned (1905–84). Crusty American character actor.
Storm Warning 50. Back from the Dead 57. Experiment in Terror 62. Blackbeard's Ghost 68. Save the Tiger 72, etc.
TV series: Bridget Loves Bernie 73.

glass shot. Usually a scenic shot in which part of the background is actually painted on a glass slide held in front of the camera and carefully blended with the action. In this way castles, towns, etc., may be shown on a location where none exist, without the expense of building them.

Gleason, Jackie (1916–87). Heavyweight American TV comedian who as a young man played small movie roles, then returned as a star but never found his niche.
Biography 1956: *The Golden Ham* by Jim Bishop.
Navy Blues 41. Orchestra Wives 42. Springtime in the Rockies 42. The Desert Hawk 50. *The Hustler* (as Minnesota Fats) 61. Gigot (& w) 62. Requiem for a Heavyweight 62. Papa's Delicate Condition 63. Soldier in the Rain 63. Skidoo 68. How to Commit Marriage 69. Don't Drink the Water 69. How Do I Love Thee? 70. Mr Billion 77. Smokey and the Bandit 77. Smokey and the Bandit II 80. The Sting II 82. Smokey and the Bandit III 83. The Toy 83. Izzy and Moe (TV) 85, etc.
TV series: The Life of Riley 49. *The Honeymooners* 49–54. The Jackie Gleason Show 64–70.

¶ *J.G.:* I'm no alcoholic, I'm a drunkard. The difference is, drunkards don't go to meetings.
Jackie's consistent: he's got a fat mouth and a fat belly.—*Joe Namath*
J.G.: I have no use for humility, I am a fellow with an exceptional talent.

Gleason, James (1886–1959). American character actor noted for hard-boiled comedy roles, usually in Brooklynese. On stage from infancy; also wrote several plays.
A Free Soul 30. Her Man 30. Oh Yeah (& oa) 30. Orders Is Orders (GB) 33. Murder on the Bridle Path 36. The Higgins Family 38. On Your Toes 39. Meet John Doe 41. *Here Comes Mr Jordan* 41. A Guy Named Joe 43. Arsenic and Old Lace 44. *Once Upon a Time* 44. A Tree Grows in Brooklyn 44. This Man's Navy 45. Captain Eddie 45. Down to Earth 47. The Bishop's Wife 48. The Life of Riley 49. Come Fill the Cup 51. *Suddenly* 54. The Last Hurrah 58, many others.
TV series: The Life of Riley 54–57 (as postman).

❁ For adding a little comic acid to any number of routine comedies. *Here Comes Mr Jordan.*

Gleason, Lucille (1886–1947). American character actress, wife of James Gleason, with whom she often appeared.
The Shannons of Broadway 29. Nice Women 32. Beloved 33. Klondike Annie 36. First Lady 37. *The Higgins Family* (& four subsequent episodes) 38. Lucky Partners 40. The Clock 45, etc.

Gleason, Russell (1908–1945). American juvenile actor, son of James and Lucille Gleason.
Strange Cargo 29. All Quiet on the Western Front 30. Nice Women 32. Private Jones 33. Off to the Races 37. Big Business (as Jones Family member) 37. *The Higgins Family* (& four subsequent episodes) 38. News is Made at Night 39. Unexpected Uncle 41. Salute to the Marines 43. The Adventures of Mark Twain 44, etc.

Glen, John (1932–). British director.
For Your Eyes Only 81. Octopussy 83. A View to a Kill 85. The Living Daylights 87.

The Glenn Miller Story (US 1953). Influential in giving a strong nostalgic twist to the aimless pop music of the fifties, this sentimental biography of the well-liked bandleader was otherwise a routine production, with a characteristic performance from James Stewart.

Glenn, Roy Snr (1905–71). Black American character actor.
Bomba and the Jungle Girl 52. The Golden Idol 54. Written on the Wind 56. A Raisin in the Sun 61. Dead Heat on a Merry-go-round 66. *Guess Who's Coming to Dinner?* 67. Escape from the Planet of the Apes 71, many others.

Glenn, Scott (1942–). American leading man.
Hex 73. Fighting Mad 76. Apocalypse Now 79. Urban Cowboy 80. Personal Best 82. The Challenge 82. The Right Stuff 83. Wild Geese 84. The River 84. Silverado 85.

Glennon, Bert (1893–1967). Distinguished American cinematographer.
Ramona 16. The Torrent 20. *The Ten Commandments* 23. Woman of the World 26. The Patriot 28. Java Head 34. *The Hurricane* 37. *Drums along the Mohawk* 39. *Stagecoach* 39. They Died with Their Boots On 41. Dive Bomber 42. Destination Tokyo 44. The Red House 47. *Wagonmaster* 50. Operation Pacific 50. The Big Trees 52. *House of Wax* 53. The Mad Magician 54. Sergeant Rutledge 60, many others.

Glenville, Peter (1913–). British stage director who has made occasional films, usually of theatrical successes.
□The Prisoner 54. Me and the Colonel 58. Summer and Smoke 60. Term of Trial 61. *Becket* 64. Hotel Paradiso 66. The Comedians 67.

The Glorious Adventure (GB 1921). A restoration drama directed by J. Stuart Blackton, notable as the first British feature in a colour process (Prizmacolour). Not an artistic success.

Glover, Brian (1934–). British character actor (also occasional writer).
Kes 69. Mister Quilp 75. Jabberwocky 75. Trial by Combat 76. The First Great Train Robbery 78. An American Werewolf in London 81. Britannia Hospital 82. Laughterhouse (w) 84.

Glover, Julian (1935–). British general purpose actor chiefly on stage and TV.
Tom Jones 63. Girl with Green Eyes 64. I Was Happy Here 66. Alfred the Great 69. The Adding Machine 69. Wuthering Heights 70. Nicholas and Alexandra 71. Dead Cert 74. Juggernaut 75. The Brute 77. For Your Eyes Only 81, etc.

Glyn, Elinor (1864–1943). Extravagant British romantic novelist whose 'daring' *Three Weeks* was filmed in Hollywood in 1924 and proved both sensational and influential. Her grandson Anthony Glyn wrote her biography in 1968. She invented the catchword 'It' for sex appeal, and this in 1926 was made the basis of a movie which brought fame to Clara Bow and in which Miss Glyn consented to appear.

Glynne, Mary (1898–1954). British stage actress of the well-bred school.
The Cry of Justice 19. The Hundredth Chance 20. The Good Companions (as Miss Trant) 32. Emil and the Detectives 34. Scrooge 35. The Heirloom Mystery (last film) 37, etc.

Gobel, George (1919–). American TV comedian of 'little man' appeal.

□The Birds and the Bees 56. I Married a Woman 57. The Invisible Woman (TV) 83. The Fantastic World of D. C. Collins (TV) 84. TV series: Harper Valley PTA 80.

Godard, Jean-Luc (1930–). Semi-surrealist French writer-director of the 'new wave', his talent often muffled by incoherent narrative.
À Bout de Souffle (Breathless) (d only) 60. Une Femme Est Une Femme 61. Vivre Sa Vie 62. Le Petit Soldat 63. Les Carabiniers 63. Bande à Part 64. Une Femme Mariée 64. Alphaville 65. Pierrot Le Fou 66.
Made in USA 66. Weekend 67. One Plus One 69. Numero Deux 75.
One Plus One 69. Numero Deux 75.
Comment Ça Va 76. Ici et Ailleurs 77. Sauve Qui Peut 80, etc.

¶ *J.L.G.:* My aesthetic is that of the sniper on the roof.
J.L.G.: The cinema is truth 24 times a second.
J.L.G.: You don't make a movie, the movie makes you.
Since Godard's films have nothing to say, perhaps we could have 90 minutes' silence instead of each of them.—*John Simon*

Goddard, Paulette (1911–) (Marion Levy). Pert, pretty American leading lady of the early forties; started as a Goldwyn girl, married Charlie Chaplin and Burgess Meredith, and when her not inconsiderable career petered out married Erich Maria Remarque.
Biography 1986: *Paulette* by Joe Morella and Edward Epstein.
□The Girl Habit 31. The Mouthpiece 32. The Kid from Spain 32. *Modern Times* 36. The Young in Heart 38. Dramatic School 38. The Women 39. *The Cat and the Canary* 39. *The Ghost Breakers* 40. The Great Dictator 40. Northwest Mounted Police 40. Second Chorus 40. Pot o' Gold 41. Nothing But the Truth 41. Hold Back the Dawn 41. The Lady Has Plans 42. *Reap The Wild Wind* 42. The Forest Rangers 42. Star Spangled Rhythm 43. The Crystal Ball 43. So Proudly We Hail 43. Standing Room Only 44. I Love a Soldier 44. Duffy's Tavern 45. *Kitty* 45. *The Diary of a Chambermaid* 46. Suddenly It's Spring 47. Variety Girl 47. Unconquered 47. An Ideal Husband (GB) 47. On Our Merry Way 48. Hazard 48. Bride of Vengeance 49. Anna Lucasta 49. The Torch 50. Babes in Baghdad 52. Vice Squad 53. Paris Model 53. Sins of Jezebel 53. Charge of the Lancers 54. The Stranger Came Home (GB) 54. Time of Indifference 66. The Snoop Sisters (TV) 72.

Goddard, Willoughby (1932–). Heavyweight British character actor, mostly on TV.
In the Wake of a Stranger 59.
TV series: *William Tell* 57.

Godden, Rumer (1907–). Much-filmed British novelist.
Black Narcissus 46. Enchantment 48. The River 51. The Greengage Summer 61. Battle of the Villa Fiorita 65, etc.

The Godfather (US 1972) (AA). An enormously commercial picturization of a violent Mafia-whitewashing gangster novel by Mario Puzo. Francis Ford Coppola's movie worked in sequences rather than as a whole, but was marked by some distinguished photography (Gordon Willis) and a notable star debut by Al Pacino. Marlon Brando's much-touted performance in the rather small title role seemed more a triumph of make-up and facial wiring than of acting. *The Godfather Part Two* was released in 1974, but proved too complex for general audiences.

Godfrey, Bob (1921–). British animator: shorts include *Polygamous Polonius, The Do-It-Yourself Cartoon Kit, The Plain Man's Guide to Advertising, Great,* etc.

Godfrey, Peter (1899–1970). British stage actor and producer who in the thirties directed two quickies, subsequently went to Hollywood and remained to direct routine films.
□The Lone Wolf Spy Hunt 39. Unexpected Uncle 41. Highways by Night 42. Make Your Own Bed 44. Hotel Berlin 45. Christmas in Connecticut 45. One More Tomorrow 46. The Two Mrs Carrolls 47. Cry Wolf 47. That Hagen Girl 47. Escape Me Never 47. *The Woman in White* 48. The Decision of Christopher Blake 48. The Girl from Jones Beach 49. One Last Fling 49. Barricade 50. The Great Jewel Robber 50. He's a Cockeyed Wonder 50. One Big Affair 52. Please Murder Me 56.

Godsell, Vanda (c. 1919–). British character actress, usually in blowsy roles.
The Large Rope 54. Hour of Decision 57. Hell Is a City 60. This Sporting Life 63. The Earth Dies Screaming 64. Who Killed the Cat? 66, etc.

Godzilla. A Japanese monster creation first seen in the film of that name in 1955. Apparently closely related to *Tyrannosaurus rex*, he has since suffered at the hands of King Kong and the Thing in inferior sequels. He remained rather plainly a man in a rubber suit.

Godzilla's screen appearances:
Godzilla 54
Gigantis the Fire Monster 55
King Kong vs Godzilla 62
Godzilla vs the Thing 64
Ghidrah the Three Headed Monster 65
Monster Zero 65
Godzilla vs the Sea Monster 66
Son of Godzilla 68
Destroy all Monsters 69
Godzilla's Revenge 69
Godzilla vs the Smog Monster 71
Godzilla vs Gigan 71
Godzilla vs Megalon 76
Godzilla vs the Cosmic Monster 77
Godzilla on Monster Island 78
Space Godzilla 79

Goetz, Ben (1891–1979). American executive, long with MGM and in charge of their British studios in the forties.

Goetz, William (1903–1969). American producer, in films since 1923, chiefly with Fox and Universal. As independent, he latterly produced the following.
The Man from Laramie 55. Sayonara 57. They Came to Cordura 58. Me and the Colonel 58. Song Without End 60, etc.

Goff, Ivan (1910–). Australian-born screenwriter; usually in collaboration with Ben Roberts (qv).
My Love Came Back 40. *White Heat* 49. Captain Horatio Hornblower 51. Come Fill the Cup 51. Full House 52. King of the Khyber Rifles 53. Green Fire 54. Serenade 56. Man of a Thousand Faces 57. Shake Hands with the Devil 59. Portrait in Black 60, etc.
TV series: The Rogues 64. Charlie's Angels 75. Time Express 79.

Going My Way (US 1944) (AA). Produced and directed by Leo McCarey (AA) from his own story, this chunk of sweetness and light about a singing priest in a poor district was immensely popular and had several imitators. Bing Crosby (AA) and Barry Fitzgerald (AA) each won new laurels. A TV series of the same name, made in 1962, starred Gene Kelly, but he neither sang nor danced in it. *The Bells of St Mary's* 45 also starred Crosby as Father O'Malley and was a kind of sequel.

Golan, Gila (c. 1940–). Hollywood leading lady of indeterminate background, being a European war orphan of probably Polish-Jewish parentage.
Ship of Fools 65. Our Man Flint 66. Three on a Couch 66. The Valley of Gwangi 69, etc.

Golan, Menahem (1931–). Israeli director.
Biography 1986: *Hollywood a Go-go* by Andrew Yule.
Sallah 66. Tevye and His Seven Daughters 68. What's Good for the Goose? (GB) 69. Lepke 74. Diamonds 76. The Passover Plot (p only) 77. The Magician of Lublin 79, etc.
† In the seventies Golan with his cousin Yoram Globus formed the Golan–Globus production company. The next step was the Cannon international film empire, but the 'go-go boys' soon faced a dozen film flops and inevitable retrenchment.

¶ *M.G.:* If you make an American film with a beginning, a middle and an end, with a budget of less than five million dollars, you must be an idiot to lose money.
M.G. (Cannes 1986): We have some good news. We didn't buy anything today.

The Gold Diggers. This Broadway play by Avery Hopwood, about a group of girls in search of millionaire husbands, was filmed in 1923 under its original title, in 1929 as *Gold Diggers of Broadway* and in 1951 as *Painting the Clouds with Sunshine*. It also figured largely in the plot of *The Greeks Had a Word for Them* (1932), which was the basis of *How to Marry a Millionaire* 53 and the resulting TV series of the latter title. *Gold Diggers of 1933* was the first of five annual Warner musicals loosely based on the theme, their lethargic plots being more or less compensated for by Busby Berkeley's kaleidoscopic dance ensembles.

Gold, Ernest (1921–). Viennese-American composer.
Girl of the Limberlost 45. The Falcon's Alibi 46. Unknown World 51. Jennifer 53. The Naked Street 55. Too Much Too Soon 57. On the Beach 59. Exodus (AA) 60. Inherit the Wind 60. Judgment at Nuremberg 60. A Child Is Waiting 62. Pressure Point 62. It's a Mad Mad Mad Mad World 63. Ship of Fools 65. The Secret of Santa Vittoria 69. Small Miracle (TV) 73. Betrayal (TV) 74. Cross of Iron 77. Fun with Dick and Jane 77. The Runner Stumbles 79. Tom Horn 80. Safari 3000 82, etc.

Gold, Jack (1930–). British TV director who moved into films.
□*The Bofors Gun* 68. The Reckoning 69. The National Health 73. *Catholics* (TV) 73. Who? 74. Man Friday 75. *The Naked Civil Servant* (TV) 75. Aces High 76. The Medusa Touch

77. Charlie Muffin (TV) 79. The Sailor's Return (TV) 79. Praying Mantis (TV) 82. Sakharov 84. The Chain 85. Escape from Sobibor (TV) 86.

Gold, Jimmy: see *The Crazy Gang.*

The Gold Rush (US 1924). Often accepted as Chaplin's greatest comedy, this sentimental farce played against a background of snow and ice has wonderfully-timed moments, though most of the fun is near the beginning and pathos takes over too firmly later on. Photographed by Rollie Totheroh.

Goldbeck, Willis (1899–1979). American director, former writer (co-author of *Freaks*). Dr Gillespie's New Assistant 42. Between Two Women 44. She Went to the Races 45. Love Laughs at Andy Hardy 46. Johnny Holiday 50. Ten Tall Men 51, etc.

Goldberg, Whoopi (1949–) (Caryn Johnson). Black American actress. The Color Purple (AAN) 85. Jumpin' Jack Flash 87. Fatal Beauty 87. Burglar 88.

Goldblum, Jeff (1952–). Lanky American leading man, rather difficult to cast. California Split 74. Death Wish 74. Nashville 75. Next Stop Greenwich Village 76. Between the Lines 77. Invasion of the Body Snatchers 78. Remember My Name 78. Thank God It's Friday 78. Escape from Athena 79. The Big Chill 83. Buckaroo Banzai 84. Silverado 85. Into the Night 85. Transylvania 6-5000 85. *The Fly* 86. Beyond Therapy 87. Life Story (TV) 87, etc.
TV series: Tenspeed and Brown Shoe 81.

Golden, Michael (1913–). British character actor.
Send for Paul Temple 46. Hungry Hill 47. Escape 48. The Blue Lamp 50. The Green Scarf 55, etc.

Goldenberg, Billy (1936–). American composer.
The Grasshopper 69. Red Sky at Morning 70. Duel (TV) 71. The Marcus Nelson Murders (TV) 72. The Last of Sheila 73. Reflections of Murder (TV) 73. The Domino Principle 76. Scavenger Hunt 78. King (TV) 78. Haywire (TV) 81. The Diary of Anne Frank (TV) 82. Reuben Reuben 83, etc.
Several TV series include Kojak, Columbo, McCloud, Harry O, Executive Suite.

¶ *W.G.:* Movies are a group endeavour, and people don't want to know that. They want to know that Clint Eastwood is really Superman and Richard Attenborough is Plato reincarnated.

Goldman, James (1927–). American playwright and screenwriter.
The Lion in Winter (oa & w) 68. *They Might Be Giants* 71. Nicholas and Alexandra 72. Robin and Marian 75.

Goldman, William (1931–). American screenwriter.
Soldier in the Rain (oa) 63. Masquerade 65. Harper 66. No Way to Treat a Lady (oa) 67. *Butch Cassidy and the Sundance Kid* (AA) 69. The Hot Rock 71. The Great Waldo Pepper 75. All the President's Men 76. Marathon Man (& oa) 77. A Bridge Too Far 77. Magic (& oa) 78. Butch and Sundance: The Early Days 79, etc.

Goldner, Charles (1900–1955). Austrian character actor, in Britain from the thirties. Room for Two 40. Brighton Rock 47. One Night With You 48. Third Time Lucky 48. Give Us This Day 49. Black Magic 49. Shadow of the Eagle 50. *The Captain's Paradise* 54, etc.

Goldoni, Lelia (c. 1938–). American actress.
Shadows 59. Hysteria 64. The Italian Job 69. Alice Doesn't Live Here Any More 74. The Day of the Locust 75. Baby Blue Marine 76. Bloodbrothers 78. Invasion of the Body Snatchers 78. The Disappearance of Sister Aimee (TV) 79. Scruples (TV) 81, etc.

Goldsmith, Jerry (1929–) (Jerrald Goldsmith). American composer.
Black Patch 57. City of Fear 59. Lonely Are the Brave 62. The Prize 63. Seven Days in May 64. Lilies of the Field 64. In Harm's Way 65. The Trouble with Angels 66. Stagecoach 66. The Blue Max 66. Seconds 66. The Sand Pebbles 66. In Like Flint 67. Planet of the Apes 68. Patton 70. Tora! Tora! Tora! 71. The Mephisto Waltz 71. Papillon 73. The Reincarnation of Peter Proud 75. Chinatown 75. The Omen (AA) 76. Islands in the Stream 77. MacArthur 77. Capricorn One 78. The Boys from Brazil 78. Coma 78. Magic 78. Alien 79. Star Trek: the Motion Picture 79. The First Great Train Robbery 80. The Final Conflict 81. Outland 81. Raggedy Man 81. Poltergeist 82. Psycho II 83.
Under Fire (AAN) 83. Gremlins 84. King

Solomon's Mines 85. Poltergeist 2 85. Hoosiers 86. Extreme Prejudice 86. Innerspace 87, etc.
TV series: Twilight Zone. Dr Kildare. The Man from UNCLE. The Waltons, etc.

Goldstein, Robert (1903–1974). American producer, with Twentieth Century-Fox for many years.

Goldstone, James (1931–). American director, from TV.
□The Inheritors (TV) 64. Scalplock (TV) 66. Ironside (TV pilot) 67. Jigsaw (TV) 68. Shadow Over Elveron (TV) 68. A Clear and Present Danger (TV) 69. A Man Called Gannon 69. Winning 69. Brother John 70. Red Sky at Morning 71. The Gang that Couldn't Shoot Straight 72. They Only Kill Their Masters 72. Cry Panic (TV) 74. Dr Max (TV) 74. Things in Their Season (TV) 74. Eric (TV) 75. Journey fromDarkness (TV) 75. Swashbuckler 76. Rollercoaster 77. When Time Ran Out 80.

Goldstone, Richard (1912–). American producer.
The Outriders 50. Inside Straight 51. The Tall Target 51. The Devil Makes Three 52. Cinerama's South Seas Adventure 58. No Man is an Island (& wd) 62. The Sergeant 68, etc.

Goldwyn, Samuel (1882–1974) (Samuel Goldfish). Polish-American producer, in Hollywood from 1910. Co-produced *The Squaw Man* (1913); a top producer ever after, with a high reputation for star-making; he always refused to make any but family films. Books on Goldwyn: *The Great Goldwyn* by Alva Johnston (1937); *Samuel Goldwyn Presents* by Alvin H. Marill (1976); *Goldwyn* by Arthur Marx (1976).
□FILMS SINCE SOUND: *Bulldog Drummond* 29. Condemned 29. Raffles 30. Whoopee 30. One Heavenly Night 30. The Devil To Pay 30. Street Scene 31. The Unholy Garden 31. Tonight or Never 31. *Arrowsmith* 31. The Greeks Had a Word for Them 32. Cynara 32. The Kid from Spain 32. The Masquerader 33. *Roman Scandals* 33. Nana 34. We Live Again 34. Kid Millions 34. The Wedding Night 35. The Dark Angel 35. Barbary Coast 35. Splendor 35. Strike Me Pink 36. These Three 36. *Dodsworth* 36. Come and Get It 36. Beloved Enemy 36. Woman Chases Man 37. *Hurricane* 37. Stella Dallas 37. *Dead End* 37. The Adventures of Marco Polo 38. The Goldwyn Follies 38. The Cowboy and the Lady 38. The Real Glory 39. *Wuthering Heights* 39. They Shall Have Music 39. Ra—es 40. *The Westerner* 40. *The Little Foxes* 41. Ball of Fire 41. The Pride of the Yankees 41. They Got Me Covered 43. North Star 43. Up in Arms 44. The Princess and the Pirate 44. Wonder Man 45. The Kid from Brooklyn 46. *The Best Years of Our Lives* 46. The Secret Life of Walter Mitty 47. The Bishop's Wife 47. A Song is Born 48. Enchantment 48. Roseanna McCoy 49. My Foolish Heart 49. Our Very Own 50. Edge of Doom 50. I Want You 51. Hans Christian Andersen 52. Guys and Dolls 55. Porgy and Bess 59.
❀ For giving the appearance of culture and refinement while keeping his standards modest though irreproachable. *Wuthering Heights.*

¶ He was the archetypal movie mogul: the glove salesman from Minsk who became more American than apple pie and founded his credo on the family audience. His maxims included:

> Motion pictures should never embarrass a man when he brings his wife to the theatre.

and:

> I seriously object to seeing on the screen what belongs in the bedroom.

He was proud of his art:

> The picture makers will inherit the earth.

As an executive, he certainly knew his own mind:

> A producer shouldn't get ulcers: he should give them.

and:

> I was always an independent, even when I had partners.

and:

> In this business it's dog eat dog, and nobody's going to eat me.

He was a great showman:

> What we want is a story that starts with an earthquake and works its way up to a climax . . .

But his logic was all his own:

> I don't care if it doesn't make a nickel. I just want every man, woman and child in America to see it!

That was about *The Best Years of Our Lives.* He disdained subtlety. When a harassed publicist devised a campaign that began:

> The directing skill of Rouben Mamoulian, the radiance of Anna Sten and the genius of Samuel Goldwyn have combined to bring you the world's greatest entertainment . . .

Goldwyn nodded approval:

> That's the kind of advertising I like. Just the facts. No exaggeration . . .

He is said to have telegraphed Eisenstein as follows:

Have seen your picture (*The Battleship Potemkin*) and enjoyed it very much. Should like you to do something of the same kind, but cheaper, for Ronald Colman.

With this kind of gall, it is not surprising that intellectuals like Robert Sherwood continued to relish his company:

I find I can live with Sam just as one lives with high blood pressure.

Did he really coin all the famous Goldwynisms which have filled so many books? Not all of them, perhaps. One doubts the authenticity of:

Directors are always biting the hand that lays the golden egg.

and:

In two words: im-possible,

and:

Tell me, how did you love the picture?

and:

We have all passed a lot of water since then.

But I imagine Goldwyn probably did say, rather wittily:

Gentlemen, kindly include me out.

and:

Let's bring it up to date with some snappy nineteenth century dialogue.

and:

Anyone who goes to a psychiatrist should have his head examined.

and:

I had a great idea this morning, but I didn't like it.

and:

A verbal contract isn't worth the paper it's written on.

His film appreciation was untutored but vivid, like his speaking style:

When everybody's happy with the rushes, the picture's always a stinker,

he once said; and he can't have been alone among Hollywood producers in vowing:

I'd hire the devil himself if he'd write me a good story.

Lindsay Anderson summed him up in 1974:

There are lucky ones whose great hearts, shallow and commonplace as bedpans, beat in instinctive tune with the great heart of the public, who laugh as it likes to laugh, weep the sweet and easy tears it likes to weep . . . Goldwyn is blessed with that divine confidence in the rightness (moral, aesthetic, commercial) of his own intuition—and that I suppose is the chief reason for his success.

Goldwyn had in fact summed up himself rather nicely:

I am a rebel. I make a picture to please me. If it pleases me, there is a chance it will please others. But it has to please me first.

And his son Samuel Goldwyn Jnr was taught the value of his legacy:

With every picture he made, my father raised the money, paid back the bank, and kept control of the negative. He said, you be careful of these films: some people will tell you they're not worth anything, but don't you believe it.

Goldwyn, Samuel Jnr (1926–). American producer, son of Samuel Goldwyn. The Man with the Gun 55. Sharkfighters 56. The Proud Rebel 58. Huckleberry Finn 60. The Young Lovers (& d) 65. Cotton Comes to Harlem 70. Come Back Charleston Blue 72. The Golden Seal 83. A Prayer for the Dying 87, etc.

The Golem (Germany 1920). This classic legend, previously filmed in 1914, was written and directed by Henrik Galeen and Paul Wegener; the latter also played the clay monster brought to life by a rabbi to save the persecuted Jews. Brilliant Grimm-like medieval sets, photographed by Karl Freund, make the second part of the film still fresh, and both in detail and general development it was closely copied in *Frankenstein* 31. The story was remade in France in 1936 (with Harry Baur) and in Czechoslovakia in 1953, and in 1922 a British film called *It* borrowed the idea.

Golitzen, Alexander (1907–). American production designer.

Gombell, Minna (1900–1973) (also known as Winifred Lee and Nancy Carter). American character actress of the thirties and forties, usually in hard-boiled roles.
Doctors' Wives (debut) 31. The Thin Man 34. Babbitt 35. Banjo on My Knee 37. The Great Waltz 38. The Hunchback of Notre Dame 39. Boom Town 40. A Chip Off the Old Block 44. Man Alive 46. Pagan Love Song 51. I'll See You in My Dreams 52, etc.

Gomez, Thomas (1905–1971). Bulky American stage character actor who became a familiar villain or detective in Hollywood films.
□Sherlock Holmes and the Voice of Terror 42. Arabian Nights 42. Pittsburgh 42. Who

Done It 42. White Savage 43. Corvette K 225 43. Frontier Badmen 43. Crazy House 43. The Climax 44. Phantom Lady 44. Dead Man's Eyes 44. Follow the Boys 44. In Society 44. Bowery to Broadway 44. Can't Help Singing 45. Patrick the Great 45. I'll Tell the World 45. The Daltons Ride Again 45. Frisco Sal 45. A Night in Paradise 45. Swell Guy 46. *The Dark Mirror* 46. Singapore 47. *Ride the Pink Horse* 47. Captain from Castile 47. Johnny O'Clock 47. Casbah 48. Angel in Exile 48. Key Largo 48. *Force of Evil* 48. Come to the Stable 49. Sorrowful Jones 49. That Midnight Kiss 49. The Woman on Pier 13 49. Kim 50. The Toast of New Orleans 50. The Eagle and the Hawk 50. The Furies 50. Anne of the Indies 51. The Harlem Globetrotters 53. The Sellout 51. The Merry Widow 52. Macao 52. Pony Soldier 52. Sombrero 53. The Gambler from Natchez 54. The Adventures of Haiiji Baba 54. The Looters 55. The Magnificent Matador 55. Las Vegas Shakedown 55. Night Freight 55. Trapeze 56. The Conqueror 56. John Paul Jones 59. But Not for Me 59. Summer and Smoke 61. Stay Away Joe 68. Beneath the Planet of the Apes 70.
TV series: Life with Luigi 52.

Gone with the Wind (US 1939) (AA). For many years the longest film (220 minutes) ever to be released in the western hemisphere, this enormously successful romance of the American Civil War, from Margaret Mitchell's novel, was a splendidly professional job. It starred Vivien Leigh (AA), Clark Gable, Leslie Howard and Olivia de Havilland; Victor Fleming (AA) directed most of it, with contributions from George Cukor and Sam Wood. Ernest Haller (AA) and Ray Rennahan (AA) were cinematographers, and the production was designed by William Cameron Menzies. The Technicolor which was so splendid at the time now seems less impressive. Producer David O. Selznick had to release through MGM in order to get Gable's services, and that company has reissued it many times with immense profit. In 1968 an 'adapted' negative was made for showing in 70 mm: it was successful financially if not aesthetically.

The Good Companions (GB 1932). J. B. Priestley's sprawling comic novel of English life was filmed by Victor Saville in rather primitive style, but its very *naiveté* remains infectious, and there are attractive performances by Edmund Gwenn, Jessie Matthews, Max Miller and others. Remade by J. Lee-Thompson in 1957, with Eric Portman and Janette Scott, with only fair success. In 1980 Yorkshire TV mounted a nine-hour TV version with music, but it missed the bus at every stop.

Goodbye Mr Chips (GB 1939). A highly successful product of MGM's short-lived British studio under Michael Balcon (1937–39), this sentimental biography of a schoolmaster, from James Hilton's novel, was impeccably produced, with a brilliant performance from Robert Donat (AA). Directed by Sam Wood. Remade in 1969 as an overlong and lifeless semi-musical with Peter O'Toole, directed by Herbert Ross; and in 1983 as a six-part BBC serial, with Roy Marsden.

Goodliffe, Michael (1914–1976). British stage actor often cast as officer, professional man or diplomat.
The Small Back Room (debut) 48. The Wooden Horse 50. Rob Roy 53. The Adventures of Quentin Durward 55. The Battle of the River Plate 56. A Night To Remember 58. Sink the Bismarck 60. The Trials of Oscar Wilde 60. Jigsaw 62. The Seventh Dawn 64. The Man with the Golden Gun 73, many others.
TV series: *Sam* 73–75.

Goodman, Benny (1909–86). American clarinettist and bandleader, the 'King of Swing'.
Hollywood Hotel 38. Hello Beautiful 42. The Gang's All Here 44. Sweet and Lowdown 44. A Song Is Born 48, etc.
Provided the music for The Benny Goodman Story 55, in which he was portrayed by Steve Allen.

Goodman, David Zelag (–). American screenwriter.
Lovers and Other Strangers 69. Monte Walsh 70. Straw Dogs 71. Man on a Swing 73. Farewell My Lovely 74. Logan's Run 76. March or Die 77. The Eyes of Laura Mars 78. Freedom Road (TV) 79.

Goodrich, Frances (1891–1984). American screenwriter, almost always in collaboration with her husband Albert Hackett.
The Secret of Madame Blanche 33. *The Thin Man* 34. Ah Wilderness 35. Naughty Marietta 35. Another Thin Man 39. The Hitler Gang 44. Lady in the Dark 44. *It's a Wonderful Life* 46. The Pirate 48. Summer Holiday 48. Easter Parade 49. *Father of the Bride* 50.

Father's Little Dividend 51. The Long Long Trailer 54. Seven Brides for Seven Brothers 55. The Diary of Anne Frank 60. Five Finger Exercise 62, etc.

Goodwin, Bill (1910–1958). American character actor, usually of genial type in routine films.
Wake Island 42. So Proudly We Hail 43. Bathing Beauty 44. Spellbound 45. House of Horrors 46. *The Jolson Story* 46. Heaven Only Knows 47. Jolson Sings Again 49. Tea for Two 50. The Atomic Kid 54. The Big Heat 54. The Opposite Sex 56, etc.

Goodwin, Harold (1917–). British character actor usually seen as cockney serviceman or small-time crook.
Dance Hall 50. The Card 52. The Cruel Sea 53. The Dam Busters 55. Sea of Sand 58. The Mummy 59. The Bulldog Breed 61. The Comedy Man 63. The Curse of the Mummy's Tomb 64. Frankenstein Must Be Destroyed 69, many others.

Goodwin, Ron (1930–). British composer.
I'm All Right Jack 59. The Trials of Oscar Wilde 60. Postman's Knock 62. Murder She Said 62. Lancelot and Guinevere 63. 633 Squadron 64. Operation Crossbow 65. Those Magnificent Men in Their Flying Machines 65. The Alphabet Murders 65. Where Eagles Dare 68. Battle of Britain 70. Frenzy 72. The Happy Prince 74. One of Our Dinosaurs is Missing 75. Candleshoe 77. Force Ten From Navarone 78, etc.

Goodwins, Leslie (1899–1969). British-born director, in Hollywood for many years. Films mainly routine second features.
'Mexican Spitfire' series 39–44. Glamour Boy 39. Pop Always Pays 40. Silver Skates 43. Murder in the Blue Room 44. What a Blonde 45. The Mummy's Curse 46. Gold Fever 52. Fireman Save My Child 54. Paris Follies of 1956 56.

Goolden, Richard (1895–1981). British character actor, on stage and screen for many years, usually in henpecked or bewildered roles; created the radio character of Old Ebenezer the night watchman.
Whom the Gods Love 38. Meet Mr Penny 38. Mistaken Identity 43, etc.

Goorwitz, Allen: see *Garfield, Allen*.

Gorcey, Bernard (1888–1955). American character actor and ex-vaudevillian, father of Leo Gorcey, with whom he often appeared in the Bowery Boys series.
Abie's Irish Rose 28. The Great Dictator 40. Out of the Fog 41. No Minor Vices 49. Pick-Up 51, many others.

Gorcey, Leo (1915–1969). Pint-sized American second feature star, one of the original Dead End Kids; his screen personality was that of a tough, fast-talking, basically kindly Brooklyn layabout, and he developed this in scores of routine films, mostly under the Bowery Boys banner.
Dead End 37. Mannequin 38. Crime School 38. *Angels With Dirty Faces* 38. Hell's Kitchen 39. Angels Wash Their Faces 39. Invisible Stripes 40. Pride of the Bowery 40. Spooks Run Wild 41. Mr Wise Guy 42. Destroyer 43. Midnight Manhunt 45. Bowery Bombshell 46. Spook Busters 46. Hard Boiled Mahoney 47. Jinx Money 48. Angels in Disguise 49. Lucky Losers 50. Crazy over Horses 51. No Holds Barred 52. Loose in London 52. The Bowery Boys Meet the Monsters 54. Bowery to Bagdad 55. Crashing Las Vegas 56. The Phynx 69, many others.

Gordon, Bert (1898–1974). American radio comedian. Known as The Mad Russian, he made a few films in the forties.

Gordon, Bert I. (1922–). American producer-director of small independent horror exploitation films.
The Beginning of the End 57. The Amazing Colossal Man 57. Cyclops 57. The Boy and the Pirates 60. The Magic Sword 62. Picture Mommy Dead 66. How to Succeed with Sex (wd only) 69. Necromancy (pd) 73. The Mad Bomber 75. Food of the Gods 76. Empire of the Ants 77, etc.

Gordon, Bruce (1919–). American character actor, invariably a heavy.
Love Happy 50. The Buccaneer 58. Rider on a Dead Horse 61. Slow Run 68, etc.
TV series: *The Untouchables* (as Frank Nitti) 59–62. Run Buddy Run 66.

Gordon, C. Henry (1882–1940). American character actor, often seen as maniacally evil villain or Indian rajah.
Charlie Chan Carries On 31. Rasputin and the Empress 32. Mata Hari 32. Lives of a Bengal Lancer 35. *The Charge of the Light Brigade* 36. The Return of the Cisco Kid 38. Kit Carson 40. Charlie Chan at the Wax Museum 40, etc.

Gordon, Colin (1911–1972). British light comedy actor, on stage from 1931; often seen as mildly cynical civil servant or schoolmaster.
Bond Street 47. The Winslow Boy 48. The Man in the White Suit 51. *Folly To Be Wise* 52. Escapade 55. The Safecracker 58. Please Turn Over 59. Night of the Eagle 62. The Pink Panther 63. The Family Way 66. Casino Royale 67, many others.

Gordon, Gale (1905–) (Gaylord Aldrich). Plump, fussy American comedy actor, best known on TV.
Here We Go Again 42. A Woman of Distinction 50. Don't Give Up the Ship 59. Visit to a Small Planet 60. Sergeant Deadhead 65. Speedway 68, etc.
TV series: My Favorite Husband 53–54. Our Miss Brooks 52–56. The Brothers 57. Dennis the Menace 59–63. *The Lucy Show* 62–68. Life with Lucy 86.

Gordon, Gavin (1901–70). American general purpose actor.
Romance (lead) 30. The Bitter Tea of General Yen 32. The Scarlet Empress 34. Bride of Frankenstein 35. Windjammer 38. Paper Bullets 41. Centennial Summer 46. Knock on Wood 54. The Bat 59, etc.

Gordon, Hal (1894–1946). Hearty British comedy actor, often seen as good-natured foil to star comedian.
Adam's Apple 31. Happy 34. Captain Bill 36. Keep Fit 37. It's in the Air 38. Old Mother Riley, Detective 43. Give Me the Stars 45 (last appearance), etc.

Gordon, Lawrence (1934–). American producer who veers between films and television (where he was the original producer of *Burke's Law*).
Dillinger 73. Hard Times 75. Rolling Thunder 77. Hooper 78. The Driver 78. The End 78. The Warriors 79. Xanadu 80. Paternity 81. 48 Hours 82.

Gordon, Leo (1922–). Thick-set American character actor, usually in tough guy roles.
China Venture 53. Riot in Cell Block 11 53. Seven Angry Men 55. The Conqueror 55. The Man Who Knew Too Much 56. Cry Baby Killer (& w) 57. The Big Operator 59. The Stranger 62. The Terror (& w) 63. The Haunted Palace 64. Beau Geste 66. Tobruk (& w) 66. The St Valentine's Day Massacre 67. You Can't Win 'Em All 71, etc.
TV series: Enos 81.

Gordon, Mack (1904–1959). American lyricist.
Tin Pan Alley 40. Lillian Russell 40. Sun Valley Serenade ('Chattanooga Choo Choo') 41. Orchestra Wives ('Kalamazoo') 42. Mother Wore Tights 47. Wabash Avenue 50, etc.

Gordon, Mary (1882–1963). Tiny Scottish character actress in Hollywood; best remembered as the perfect Mrs Hudson in many a Sherlock Holmes film.
The Home Maker 25. The Black Camel 31. The Little Minister 34. The Bride of Frankenstein 35. The Plough and the Stars 36. Kidnapped 38. The Hound of the Baskervilles 39. Tear Gas Squad 40. Appointment for Love 41. The Mummy's Tomb 42. Sherlock Holmes Faces Death 43. The Woman in Green 45. Little Giant 46. The Invisible Wall 47, many others.

Gordon, Michael (1909–). American director with stage experience.
□Boston Blackie Goes to Hollywood 42. Underground Agent 42. One Dangerous Night 43. Crime Doctor 43. *The Web* 47. Another Part of the Forest 48. An Act of Murder 48. The Lady Gambles 49. Woman in Hiding 49. Cyrano de Bergerac 50. I Can Get It for You Wholesale 51. The Secret of Convict Lake 51. Wherever She Goes 53. *Pillow Talk* 59. Portrait in Black 60. Boys' Night Out 62. For Love of Money 63. Move Over Darling 63. A Very Special Favor 65. Texas Across the River 66. The Impossible Years 68. How Do I Love Thee 70.

Gordon, Ruth (1896–1985) (Ruth Gordon Jones). Distinguished American stage actress who wrote several screenplays with her husband Garson Kanin, saw two of her own plays filmed, and had a long sporadic career as film actress.
□AS WRITER: Over 21 (oa/solo) 45. *A Double Life* 48. *Adam's Rib* 49. The Marrying Kind 52. Pat and Mike 52. The Actress (oa/solo) 53. Rosie (oa/solo) 58.
□AS ACTRESS: Camille 15. The Wheel of Life 16. Abe Lincoln in Illinois 40. Dr Ehrlich's Magic Bullet 40. Two Faced Woman 41. Edge of Darkness 43. Action in the North Atlantic 43. Inside Daisy Clover 66. Lord Love a Duck 66. *Rosemary's Baby* (AA) 68. Whatever Happened to Aunt Alice? 69. Where's Poppa? 70. *Harold and Maude* 72. Isn't It Shocking? (TV) 73. Panic 75. The Big Bus 76. The Great Houdinis (TV) 76. Look What Happened to Rosemary's Baby (TV)

76. Prince of Central Park (TV) 77. Boardwalk 78. Perfect Gentlemen (TV) 78. *Every Which Way But Loose* 78. My Bodyguard 80. Any Which Way You Can 80. Don't Go to Sleep (TV) 83. Jimmy the Kid 83. Maxie 85. Delta Pi 85.

Gordon, Steve (1938–1982). American writer-director.
The One and Only (co-p, w) 78. Arthur (w, d) 80.

Goretta, Claude (1929–). French director.
The Invitation 73. *The Lacemaker* 77. La Provenciale (A Girl from Lorraine) 80. La Morte de Mario Ricci 82, etc.

Goring, Marius (1912–). British stage and screen actor adept at neurotic or fey roles.
Consider Your Verdict (debut) 36. Rembrandt 37. *The Case of the Frightened Lady* 38. *A Matter of Life and Death* 45. The Red Shoes 48. Mr Perrin and Mr Traill 49. So Little Time 52. *Ill Met by Moonlight* 57. Exodus 60. The Inspector (Lisa) 62. Up From the Beach 65. Girl on a Motorcycle 68. Subterfuge 69. First Love 70. Zeppelin 71. Holocaust (TV) 78, etc.
TV series: The Scarlet Pimpernel 54. The Expert 70–75.

Gorky, Maxim (1868–1936) (Alexei Maximovitch Peshkov). Russian writer whose autobiography was filmed by Donskoi as *The Childhood of Maxim Gorky* (qv), *Out in the World* and *My Universities*. Other filmed works include *The Lower Depths* (many times) and *The Mother*.

Gorman, Cliff (1936–). American leading man of the seventies.
Justine 69. The Boys in the Band 70. Cops and Robbers 73. Rosebud 75. An Unmarried Woman 78. All That Jazz 79. Night of the Juggler 80, etc.

Gorney, Karen Lynn (–). American leading lady who was top-billed with Travolta in *Saturday Night Fever* 77.

Gorshin, Frank (1935–). Wiry American impressionist and character actor, popular as 'The Riddler' in TV's Batman series.
The True Story of Jesse James 57. Warlock 59. Studs Lonigan 60. Ring of Fire 61. The George Raft Story 61. Batman 65. Sky Heist (TV) 75. Underground Aces 81, etc.

Gortner, Marjoe (1941–). American evangelist turned actor (following a 1972 documentary on his life called *Marjoe*).
□The Marcus Nelson Murders (TV) 73. Earthquake 74. The Gun and the Pulpit (TV) 74. Food of the Gods 76. Bobbie Joe and the Outlaw 76. Sidewinder One 77. Viva Knievel 77. Acapulco Gold 78. Starcrash 79. When You Comin' Back Red Ryder 79. Hellhole 85.

Gosho, Heinosuke (1901–1981). Japanese director, best known for *Four Chimneys* 52. *Adolescence* 55. *When a Woman Loves* 59.

Gossett, Lou (aka Louis Gossett Jnr) (1936–). Black American character actor of striking presence.
Companions in Nightmare (TV) 68. The Landlord 70. The River Niger 72. It's Good to Be Alive (TV) 74. Sidekicks (TV) 74. Delancey Street (TV) 75. Roots (TV) 77. The Choirboys (TV) 77. The Deep (TV) 77. Little Ladies of the Night (TV) 78. To Kill a Cop (TV) 78. *The Lazarus Syndrome* (TV) (and series) 79. The Critical List (TV) 78. Backstairs at the White House (TV) 79. This Man Stands Alone (TV) 79. Don't Look Back (TV) 81. *An Officer and a Gentleman* (AA) 82. Sadat (TV) 83. Jaws 3D 83. Finders Keepers 84. Enemy Mine 85. Iron Eagle 85. Firewalker 86.
TV series: The Powers of Matthew Starr 82.

Gotell, Walter (–). British character actor, often as Nazi or KGB menace.
Treasure of San Teresa 59. The Guns of Navarone 61. The Damned 61. Our Miss Fred 72. The Spy Who Loved Me 77. The Boys from Brazil 78. For Your Eyes Only 80, etc.

Gottlieb, Carl (1938–). American screenwriter, with TV comedy experience.
Jaws 75. Which Way Is Up 77. Jaws 2 78. The Jerk 79. Caveman (& d) 81, etc.

Gottschalk, Ferdinand (1869–1944). Bald-domed English character actor in Hollywood.
Zaza 26. Grand Hotel 32. The Sign of the Cross 32. Les Misérables 35. The Garden of Allah 36, many others.

Goudal, Jetta (1898–1985). French leading lady of American silent films.
The Bright Shawl 24. Open All Night 24. Spanish Love 25. Road to Yesterday 25. The Coming of Amos 25. 3 Faces East 26. White Gold 27. Forbidden Woman 28. Her Cardboard Lover 28. Lady of the Pavements 30. Business and Pleasure 32, etc.

Gough, Michael (1917–). Tall British stage (since 1936) and screen (since 1946) actor; has recently gone in for homicidal roles.
Blanche Fury (debut) 46. The Small Back Room 48. The Man in the White Suit 51. Richard III 56. Dracula 57. Horrors of the Black Museum 58. The Horse's Mouth 59. Konga 61. Black Zoo 63. Dr Terror's House of Horrors 65. Circus of Blood 67. Trog 70. The Corpse 70. The Go-Between 70. Henry VIII and His Six Wives 72. Horror Hospital 73. The Boys from Brazil 78. Suez 1956 (TV) (as Anthony Eden) 79. The Dresser 83. Memed My Hawk 83. Out of Africa 85, many others.

Gould, Elliott (1938–) (Elliot Goldstein). American actor whose very unhandsomeness made him the man for the early seventies.
□The Confession 66. The Night They Raided Minsky's 68. *Bob and Carol and Ted and Alice* 69. M*A*S*H 70. Getting Straight 70. Move 70. I Love My Wife 70. The Touch 70. Little Murders 71. The Long Goodbye 72. Busting 73. S.P.Y.S. 74. California Split 74. Who? 74. Nashville 74. Whiffs 76. I Will . . . I Will . . . for Now 76. Harry and Walter Go to New York 76. Mean Johnny Barrows 76. A Bridge Too Far 77. Matilda 78. The Silent Partner 78. Capricorn One 78. Escape to Athena 79. The Lady Vanishes 79. The Muppet Movie 79. Falling in Love Again 80. The Last Flight of Noah's Ark 80. Dirty Tricks 81. The Devil and Max Devlin 81. Rites of Marriage (TV) 82. The Muppets Take Manhattan 84. The Naked Face 84. Inside Out 86.
TV series: E. R. 84. Together We Stand 86.

¶ *E.G.:* Success didn't change me. I was distorted *before* I became a star.

Gould, Harold (1923–). American light character actor.
He and She 69. Where Does It Hurt? 71. Love and Death 75. Silent Movie 76. The Big Bus 76. Feather and Father (TV) 77. *Washington: Behind Closed Doors* (TV) 77. The Feather and Father Gang 77. Seems Like Old Times 80. The Man in the Santa Claus Suit (TV) 80. Moviola (TV) 80.

Gould, Morton (1913–). American composer (and conductor).
Delightfully Dangerous 42. Cinerama Holiday 55. Holocaust (TV) 77.

Goulding, Alfred J. (1896–1972). American director; active with Harold Lloyd in the twenties and later with Laurel and Hardy (*A Chump at Oxford*).

Goulding, Edmund (1891–1959). British director in Hollywood; a safe handler of the big female stars of the thirties and forties.
□Sun Up 25. Sally Irene and Mary 25. Paris 26. Women Love Diamonds 26. Love 27. *The Trespasser* (& w) 29. The Devil's Holiday (& w) 30. Paramount on Parade (part) 30. Reaching for the Moon (& w) 30. The Night Angel (& w) 31. *Grand Hotel* 32. Blondie of the Follies 32. Riptide 34. The Flame Within (& wp) 35. That Certain Woman (& w) 37. White Banners 38. The Dawn Patrol 38. *Dark Victory* 39. *The Old Maid* 39. We Are Not Alone 39. Till We Meet Again 40. *The Great Lie* 41. Forever and a Day (co-d) 43. The Constant Nymph 43. *Claudia* 43. Of Human Bondage 46. *The Razor's Edge* 46. *Nightmare Alley* 47. Everybody Does It 49. Mister 880 50. We're Not Married 52. Down Among the Sheltering Palms 53. Teenage Rebel 56. Mardi Gras 58.

Goulet, Robert (1933–) (Stanley Applebaum). Canadian singer and leading man, with experience mainly on TV.
Honeymoon Hotel 63. I'd Rather Be Rich 64. Underground 70. Atlantic City USA 80.
TV series: The Blue Light 64.

governesses have most frequently been personified by Deborah Kerr: in *The King and I, The Innocents*, and *The Chalk Garden*: Julie Andrews runs a close second with *Mary Poppins* and *The Sound of Music*; as does Bette Davis with *All This and Heaven Too* and *The Nanny*. Joan Fontaine's contribution to the gallery was *Jane Eyre*, and Susannah York later followed in her footsteps.

Gowland, Gibson (1872–1951). English character actor in mainly American films.
The Promise 17. Blind Husbands 19. Ladies Must Love 21. Shifting Sands 23. *Greed* 24. The Phantom of the Opera 25. Don Juan 26. Topsy and Eva 27. Rose Marie 28. The Mysterious Island 29. The Sea Bat 30. Doomed Battalion 32. SOS Iceberg 33. The Secret of the Loch 34. The Mystery of the Marie Celeste 36. Cotton Queen 37, many others.

Gozzi, Patricia (1950–). French juvenile actress of the sixties.
Sundays and Cybele 62. Rapture 65, etc.

Grable, Betty (1916–1973). American leading lady who personified the peaches-and-

cream appeal which was required in the forties but which later seemed excessively bland. She performed efficiently in a series of light musicals and dramas, and was the most famous pin-up of World War II.
☐Let's Go Places 30. New Movietone Follies of 1930 30. Whoopee 30. Kiki 31. Palmy Days 31. The Greeks had a Word for Them 32. The Kid from Spain 32. Child of Manhattan 32. Probation 32. Hold 'Em Jail 32. Cavalcade 33. What Price Innocence 33. Student Tour 34. *The Gay Divorcee* 34. The Nitwits 35. Old Man Rhythm 35. Collegiate 35. Follow the Fleet 36. Pigskin Parade 36. Don't Turn 'Em Loose 36. This Way Please 37. Thrill of a Lifetime 37. College Swing 38. Give Me a Sailor 38. Campus Confessions 38. Man About Town 39. Million Dollar Legs 39. The Day the Bookies Wept 39. *Down Argentine Way* 40. *Tin Pan Alley* 40. *Moon Over Miami* 41. A Yank in the RAF 41. *I Wake Up Screaming* 41. Footlight Serenade 42. Song of the Islands 42. Springtime in the Rockies 42. *Coney Island* 43. Sweet Rosie O'Grady 43. Four Jills in a Jeep 44. Pin Up Girl 44. Diamond Horseshoe 45. The Dolly Sisters 45 The Shocking Miss Pilgrim 47. *Mother Wore Tights* 47. That Lady in Ermine 48. When My Baby Smiles at Me 48. The Beautiful Blonde from Bashful Bend 49. Wabash Avenue 50. My Blue Heaven 50. Call Me Mister 51. Meet Me After the Show 51. The Farmer Takes a Wife 53. *How To Marry A Millionaire* 53. Three for the Show 54. How to be Very Very Popular 55.

¶ *B.G.:* There are two reasons why I'm in show business, and I'm standing on both of them.

B.G.: I'm strictly an enlisted man's girl.

B.G.: There's nothing mysterious about me.

I don't think Betty would want an Oscar on her mantelpeice. She has every Tom, Dick and Harry at her feet.—*Nunnally Johnson*

Grade, Lew (Lord Grade) (c. 1906–) (Lewis Winogradsky). British impresario, brother of Lord Delfont, long in charge of Associated Television, latterly producing feature films for family audiences.
Biography 1982: *My Fabulous Brothers* by Rita Grade Freeman. 1984: *The Grades* by Hunter Davies. Autobiography 1987: *Still Dancing*.
Voyage of the Damned 76. March or Die 77. The Cassandra Crossing 77. The Boys from Brazil 78. Movie Movie 78. Firepower 79. The Legend of the Lone Ranger 80. Raise the Titanic 80. *On Golden Pond* 81, etc.

¶ *L.G.:* All my shows are great. Some of them are bad, but they're all great.

L.G.: I intend to produce more feature films than any major studio in the world. I am only 68 and just beginning. By the time I am 70 British films will rule the world.

grading: the laboratory process of matching the density and brightness of each shot to the next.

The Graduate (US 1967). Set in the well-to-do suburbs of Los Angeles, and concerning an aimless young man whose protest at society takes the form of being seduced by one of his father's friends and then falling in love with her daughter, this beautifully photographed film (Robert Surtees) from a book by Charles Webb was filled with bitter hilarity and showed that a wide-screen film can still look good. Its enormous commercial success was presumably due to its comparative frankness on sexual matters; its direction (Mike Nichols: AA) and acting (Dustin Hoffman, Anne Bancroft) were impeccable.

Graetz, Paul (1901–1966). Franco-Austrian independent producer.
Le Diable au Corps 46. Monsieur Ripois (Knave of Hearts) 53. Is Paris Burning? 66, etc.

Graham, Morland (1891–1949). Stocky Scottish character actor, on stage and screen from twenties.
The Scarlet Pimpernel 35. Jamaica Inn 39. Old Bill and Son (as Old Bill) 40. The Ghost Train 41. The Shipbuilders 44. The Brothers 47. Bonnie Prince Charlie 48. Whisky Galore 48, etc.

Graham, Sheilah (c. 1912–). British gossip columnist in America, companion of F. Scott Fitzgerald. Author of *Beloved Infidel*, *The Garden of Allah*, etc.

Graham, William (c. 1930–). American director, from TV. (Sometimes billed as William A. Graham.)
The Doomsday Flight (TV) 66. Waterhole Three 67. Then Came Bronson (TV) 68. Submarine X1 68. Change of Habit 69. Thief (TV) 71. *Birds of Prey* (TV) 73. Get Christie Love (TV) 74. Trapped Beneath the Sea (TV) 74. 21 Hours at Munich (TV) 76. *Minstrel Man* (TV) 77. *The Amazing Howard Hughes* (TV) 77. Contract on Cherry Street

(TV) 77. And I Alone Survived (TV) 78. Transplant (TV) 79. Guyana Tragedy (TV) 81. Harry Tracy 81. Mothers Against Drunk Drivers (TV) 82, etc.

Grahame, Gloria (1924–81) (Gloria Hallward). Blonde American leading lady, usually in offbeat roles.
□Blonde Fever (debut) 44. Without Love 45. It's a Wonderful Life 46. It Happened in Brooklyn 47. Merton of the Movies 47. Song of the Thin Man 47. *Crossfire* 47. Roughshod 48. A Woman's Secret 48. *In a Lonely Place* 50. *The Bad and the Beautiful* (AA) 52. Macao 52. Sudden Fear 52. The Glass Wall 53. Man on a Tightrope 53. Prisoners of the Casbah 53. The Greatest Show on Earth 53. Naked Alibi 54. *The Big Heat* 54. The Good Die Young (GB) 54. Human Desire 55. The Man Who Never Was (GB) 55. Not as a Stranger 55. The Cobweb 55. Oklahoma 56. Ride Out for Revenge 57. Odds Against Tomorrow 59. Ride Beyond Vengeance 66. The Todd Killings 70. Black Noon (TV) 71. Chandler 72. The Loners 72. Blood and Lace 72. Tarot 73. Mama's Dirty Girls 74. The Girl on the Late Late Show (TV) 75. Rich Man Poor Man (TV) 76. Mansion of the Doomed 76. Seventh Avenue (TV) 77. Head Over Heels 79. Melvin and Howard 80. A Nightingale Sang in Berkeley Square 80.

Grahame, Margot (1911–82). British leading lady of the thirties, with stage experience.
The Love Habit 30. Rookery Nook 30. Sorrell and Son 34. The Informer (US) 35. The Three Musketeers (US) 36. Michael Strogoff (US) 37. The Shipbuilders 44. Broken Journey 48. The Romantic Age 49. Venetian Bird 52. Orders Are Orders 55. Saint Joan 57, etc.

Grainer, Ron (1922–1981). Australian composer in Britain.
A Kind of Loving 62. Nothing But the Best 64. To Sir with Love 67. Lock Up Your Daughters 68. In Search of Oregon 70. The Omega Man 71. Yellow Dog 73. I Don't Want to Be Born 75, many others.

Grainger, Edmund (1906–1981). American producer and executive, long with RKO. Specialized in quality action pictures.
Diamond Jim 35. Sutter's Gold 36. International Squadron 41. Wake of the Red Witch 48. Sands of Iwo Jima 49. Flying Leathernecks 50. One Minute to Zero 52. Treasure of Pancho Villa 55. Green Mansions 59. Home from the Hill 60. Cimarron 61, many others.

A Grammar of the Film, by Raymond Spottiswoode. First published in 1935, this book remains an essential theoretical study of film technique.

Granach, Alexander (1890–1945). Polish character actor who went to Hollywood in the late thirties.
Biography 1945: *There Goes An Actor*.
Warning Shadows 23. Kameradschaft 31. *Ninotchka* 39. Hangmen Also Die 43. For Whom the Bell Tolls 43. The Hitler Gang 44. A Voice in the Wind 44. The Seventh Cross 44, etc.

Grand Hotel (US 1932). The Hollywood all-star film *par excellence,* from Vicki Baum's novel; it allowed effective parts for Garbo, the Barrymore brothers, Joan Crawford and Wallace Beery. Not very cinematic, as directed by Edmund Goulding, but immensely popular. AA best picture of its year. More or less remade in 1945 as *Weekend at the Waldorf,* but with no impact whatever. A 1959 West German remake, *Menschen im Hotel,* had Michele Morgan in Garbo's role and O. W. Fischer in John Barrymore's.

Le Grand Jeu (France 1933). This melodrama by Charles Spaak and Jacques Feyder about the off-duty problems of Foreign Legionnaires was filmed by Feyder in 1933 and had memorable performances by Françoise Rosay and Marie Bell. Robert Siodmak's 1953 remake was flavourless despite the presence of Arletty and Gina Lollobrigida.

Grand Prix (US 1966). An absurdly cliché-ridden and poorly scripted motor-racing spectacular decorated by half a dozen brilliantly exciting race sequences directed by John Frankenheimer and photographed by Lionel Lindon with all the showmanship—and showing off—they could muster. (These sequences were also notable for experimental use of multiscreen effects.) The actors paled into complete insignificance.

La Grande Illusion (France 1937). Jean Renoir's great anti-war film, set in a German prison camp for officers in 1917, commanded by Erich Von Stroheim. A subtler piece than most of the recent variations on this theme, it was written by Charles Spaak and Renoir, with music by Joseph Kosma and photography by Christian Matras and Claude Renoir.

Granger, Farley (1925–). American leading man who began his film career straight from school.
North Star (debut) 43. They Live By Night 47. *Rope* 48. *Strangers on a Train* 51. Hans Christian Andersen 52. Senso (Italian) 53. The Girl in the Red Velvet Swing 55. Rogues' Gallery 68. Something Creeping in the Dark (It.) 71. The Serpent 72. Confessions of a Sex Maniac (It.) 72. They Call Me Trinity (It.) 72. The Man Called Noon 73. Arnold 75. Black Beauty (TV) 78. The Imagemaker 85. The Whoopee Boys 86, etc.

Granger, Stewart (1913–) (James Lablanche Stewart). British leading man, on stage from 1935.
Autobiography 1981: *Sparks Fly Upward.*
□A Southern Maid 33. Give Her a Ring 34. So This Is London 38. Convoy 40. Secret Mission 42. Thursday's Child 43. *The Man in Grey* 43. The Lamp Still Burns 43. Fanny by Gaslight 43. *Waterloo Road* 44. *Love Story* 44. Madonna of the Seven Moons 44. *Caesar and Cleopatra* 45. Caravan 46. The Magic Bow (as Paganini) 46. *Captain Boycott* 47. Blanche Fury 48. Saraband for Dead Lovers (as Koenigsmark) 48. Woman Hater 49. Adam and Evelyne 49. *King Solomon's Mines* (US) 50. The Light Touch (US) 51. Soldiers Three 51. The Wild North 52. *Scaramouche* (US) 52. The Prisoner of Zenda (US) 52. Young Bess (US) 53. Salome (US) 53. All the Brothers Were Valiant (US) 54. *Beau Brummell* (US) 54. Green Fire (US) 55. Moonfleet (US) 55. Footsteps in the Fog 55. Bhowani Junction 56. The Last Hunt (US) 56. Gun Glory 57. The Little Hut 57. The Whole Truth 58. Harry Black and the Tiger 58. North to Alaska (US) 60. The Secret Partner 61. Sodom and Gomorrah 62. Swordsman of Siena (It.) 62. The Legion's Last Patrol (It.) 63. Among Vultures (Ger.) 64. The Secret Invasion 64. The Crooked Road 65. Der Oelprinz (Ger.) 65. Mission Hong Kong 65. Requiem for a Secret Agent 66. Glory City 66. Where Are You Taking that Woman? 66. The Trygon Factor 67. The Last Safari 67. The Flaming Frontier 68. The Hound of the Baskervilles (TV) (as Holmes) 71. The Wild Geese 77. The Royal Romance of Charles & Diana (TV) 82.
TV series: The Men from Shiloh 70.

¶ *S.G.:* I've never done a film I'm proud of.

Grangier, Gilles (1911–). French director.
Le Cavalier Noir 44. L'Amour Madame 52. Archimède le Clochard 58. Le Cave Se Rebiffe 61. La Cuisine au Beurre 63. Train d'Enfer 65. L'Homme à la Buick 67. Fin de Journée 69, etc.

Grant, Arthur (1915–1972). British cinematographer.
Hell Is a City 60. Jigsaw 62. Eighty Thousand Suspects 63. The Tomb of Ligeia 64. Blood from the Mummy's Tomb 71, etc.

Grant, Cary (1904–86) (Archibald Leach). Debonair British-born leading man with a personality and accent all his own; varied theatrical experience before settling in Hollywood. Special AA 1969.
□This Is the Night 32. Sinners in the Sun 32. Hot Saturday 32. Merrily We Go to Hell 32. The Devil and the Deep 32. Madame Butterfly 33. Blonde Venus 33. *She Done Him Wrong* 33. Alice in Wonderland (as the Mock Turtle) 33. The Eagle and the Hawk 33. Woman Accused 33. Gambling Ship 33. I'm No Angel 33. Thirty Day Princess 34. Born To Be Bad 34. Kiss and Make Up 34. Enter Madame 34. Ladies Should Listen 34. Wings in the Dark 35. The Last Outpost 35. Sylvia Scarlett 35. Big Brown Eyes 35. Suzy 36. Wedding Present 36. The Amazing Quest of Mr Ernest Bliss (GB) 36. When You're in Love 36. *The Awful Truth* 37. The Toast of New York 37. *Topper* 37. *Bringing Up Baby* 38. Holiday 38. *Gunga Din* 39. Only Angels Have Wings 39. In Name Only 39. *My Favorite Wife* 40. The Howards of Virginia 40. *His Girl Friday* 40. *The Philadelphia Story* 40. Penny Serenade 41. Suspicion 41. Talk of the Town 42. Once upon a Honeymoon 42. Destination Tokyo 43. Mr Lucky 43. Once upon a Time 44. None But the Lonely Heart 44. *Arsenic and Old Lace* 44. Night and Day (as Cole Porter) 45. Notorious 46. *The Bachelor and the Bobbysoxer* 47. The Bishop's Wife (as an angel) 48. Every Girl Should Be Married 48. *Mr Blandings Builds His Dream House* 48. I Was a Male War Bride 49. Crisis 50. People Will Talk 51. Room for One More 52. Monkey Business 52. Dream Wife 53. To Catch a Thief 55. The Pride and the Passion 57. *An Affair to Remember* 57. Kiss Them for Me 57. *Indiscreet* (GB) 58. Houseboat 58. *North by Northwest* 59. Operation Petticoat 59. The Grass Is Greener 60. That Touch of Mink 62. Charade 63. Father Goose 64. Walk Don't Run 66.
❀ For being the world's most admired sophisticated man for twenty-five years. *Mr Blandings Builds His Dream House.*

¶ *C.G.:* Everyone tells me I've had such an interesting life, but sometimes I think its been nothing but stomach disturbances and self-concern.

When a journalist wired his agent 'How old Cary Grant?', Grant himself replied: 'Old Cary Grant fine. How you?'

The drama in a Cary Grant movie is always seeing whether the star can be made to lose his wry, elegant and habitual aplomb.—*Richard Schickel*

A completely private person, totally reserved, and there is no way into him.—*Doris Day*

Cary's enthusiasm made him search for perfection in all things, particularly the three that meant most to him—film making, physical fitness and women.—*David Niven*

C.G.: I improve on misquotation.

C.G.: I think making love is the best form of exercise.

C.G.: I'd like to have made one of those big splashy Technicolor musicals with Rita Hayworth.

Grant, James Edward (1902–66). American writer.
Whipsaw 35. We're Going to Be Rich 38. Belle of the Yukon 44. The Great John L. 45. Angel and the Bad Man (& d) 46. Sands of Iwo Jima 49. Big Jim McLain 52. Hondo 54. Ring of Fear (co-w and d) 54. The Alamo 60. McLintock 63, etc.

Grant, Kathryn (1933–) (Olive Grandstaff). American leading lady who retired to marry Bing Crosby.
Arrowhead 53. Living it Up 54. The Phoenix City Story 55. Mister Cory 56. Gunman's Walk 58. Operation Mad Ball 58. The Seventh Voyage of Sinbad 58. The Big Circus 60, etc.

Grant, Kirby (1914–85) (K. G. Horn). Dutch-Scottish-American leading man, former bandleader.
Red River Range 39. Ghost Catchers 44. The Lawless Breed 47. Trail of the Yukon 50. Snow Dog 51. Yukon Gold 52. The Court Martial of Billy Mitchell 55. Yukon Vengeance 55, etc.
TV series: Sky King 53–54.

Grant, Lawrence (1870–1952). British character actor in American films.
The Great Impersonation 21. His Hour 24. The Grand Duchess and the Waiter 26. Doomsday 28. The Canary Murder Case 29. *Bulldog Drummond* 29. The Cat Creeps 30. Daughter of the Dragon 31. The Unholy Garden 31. Jewel Robbery 32. The Mask of Fu Manchu 32. Grand Hotel 32. Shanghai Express 32. Queen Christina 33. By Candlelight 34. Nana 34. Werewolf of London 34. The Devil is a Woman 35. Little Lord Fauntleroy 36. The Prisoner of Zenda 37. Bluebeard's Eighth Wife 38. Son of Frankenstein 39. Women in War 40. Dr Jekyll and Mr Hyde 41. Confidential Agent 45, many others.

Grant, Lee (1929–) (Lyova Rosenthal). Dynamic American stage actress, sporadically seen in films.
□*Detective Story* 51. Storm Fear 55. Middle of the Night 59. The Balcony 63. An Affair of the Skin 63. Terror in the City 66. Divorce American Style 67. In the Heat of the Night 67. Valley of the Dolls 67. Buona Sera Mrs Campbell 68. The Big Bounce 69. Perilous Voyage (TV) 69. Marooned 69. There Was a Crooked Man 70. *The Landlord* 70. Night Slaves (TV) 70. Plaza Suite 71. The Neon Ceiling (TV) 71. Ransom for a Dead Man (TV) 71. Lt Schuster's Wife (TV) 72. Portnoy's Complaint 72. Partners in Crime (TV) 73. What Are Best Friends For (TV) 73. The Internecine Project 74. *Shampoo* (AA) 75. Voyage of the Damned 76. Airport 77 77. The Spell (TV) 77. The Mafu Cage 77. The Swarm 78. Damien: Omen II 78. Backstairs at the White House (TV) 79. When You Comin' Back Red Ryder 79. You Can't Go Home Again (TV) 79. Tell Me a Riddle (d only) 80. Little Miss Marker 80. Charlie Chan and the Curse of the Dragon Queen 81. Visiting Hours 82. Will There Really Be a Morning? (TV) 83. Teachers 84. The Big Town 87.

Granville, Bonita (1923–). American child actress of the thirties; adult career gradually petered out but she became a producer.
Westward Passage 32. Cradle Song 33. Ah Wilderness 35. *These Three* 36. Maid of Salem 37. Call it a Day 37. Merrily We Live 38. Nancy Drew Detective (and subsequent series) 38. Angels Wash Their Faces 39. Escape 40. H.M. Pulham Esq 41. The Glass Key 42. Now Voyager 42. *Hitler's Children* 43. Youth Runs Wild 44. Love Laughs at Andy Hardy 46. The Guilty 47. Treason 50. The Lone Ranger 56. Lassie's Greatest Adventure (p) 63, etc.
TV series: Lassie (p) 55–67.

The Grapes of Wrath (US 1940). John Ford's (AA) film of John Steinbeck's novel about the migration of poor workers from the mid-western dustbowl to the Californian fruit valleys is not only one of the earliest Hollywood exposés of social injustice but one of the most moving and beautiful films to come out of America. Gregg Toland's soft, warm photography, Alfred Newman's music and Nunnally Johnson's screenplay provide a perfect background for the performances of Henry Fonda, Jane Darwell (AA) and a fine cast.

Grapewin, Charley (1869–1956). American character actor best remembered in movies for his range of grizzled old gentlemen.
Only Saps Work 30. The Night of June 13th 32. Heroes for Sale 33. Judge Priest 34. Ah Wilderness 35. Alice Adams 35. Libelled Lady 36. The Good Earth 37. Captains Courageous 37. Big City 37. Three Comrades 38. The Wizard of Oz 39. *The Grapes of Wrath* 40. Ellery Queen Master Detective 40. *Tobacco Road* (as Jeeter Lester) 41. They Died With Their Boots On 41. Crash Dive 42. The Impatient Years 44. Gunfighters 47. Sand 49. When I Grow Up 51, many others.

Grass (US 1925). Cooper and Schoedsack's feature-length documentary was shot among the Baktyari tribe of north-west Persia during their twice-yearly migration in search of grass. Though an impressive achievement at the time, it was less stirring than the same team's *Chang*, which followed in 1927.

Grauman, Sid (1879–1950). Showbiz-loving American impresario, he of the Chinese Theatre on Hollywood Boulevard.

Grauman, Walter (1922–). American director, from TV.
Lady in a Cage 63. 633 Squadron 64. A Rage to Live 65. I Deal in Danger 66. The Last Escape 69.
TV series include The Untouchables, Naked City, Route 66, The Felony Squad.

Graves, Peter (1925–) (Peter Aurness). American leading man, usually in 'B' action pictures: brother of James Arness.
Rogue River (debut) 50. Fort Defiance 52. Red Planet Mars 52. Stalag 17 53. Beneath the Twelve-Mile Reef 53. Black Tuesday 55. It Conquered the World 56. Wolf Larsen 59. A Rage to Live 65. The Ballad of Josie 67. The Five Man Army 68. Call to Danger (TV) 73. The President's Plane Is Missing (TV) 73. Scream of the Wolf (TV) 74. The Underground Man (TV) 74. Where Have All the People Gone (TV) 74. Dead Man on the Run (TV) 75. Disaster in the Sky (TV) 77. The Rebels (TV) 79. Airplane 80. Death Car on the Freeway (TV) 80. The Memory of Eva Ryker (TV) 81. Airplane 2: the Sequel 82. Savannah Smiles 82. The Winds of War (TV) 83. Number One with a Bullet 87, etc.
TV series: Fury 55–59. Whiplash 60. Court Martial (Counsellors at War) 66. Mission Impossible 66–72.

Graves, Peter (1911–). British light leading man, tall and suave, usually in musical comedy.
Kipps (debut) 41. King Arthur Was a Gentleman 42. Bees in Paradise 44. I'll Be Your Sweetheart 44. Waltz Time 45. The Laughing Lady 46. Spring Song 47. Mrs Fitzherbert (as the Prince Regent) 47. Spring in Park Lane 48. Maytime in Mayfair 49. Derby Day 52. Lilacs in the Spring 54, etc.: latterly in cameo roles, e.g. The Wrong Box 66, The Slipper and the Rose 76.

Graves, Ralph (1901–1977). American silent star of heroic roles.
Talkies include: Submarine 28. Dirigible 30. Ladies of Leisure 30.
Later became writer and producer of minor films.

Graves, Teresa (c. 1947–). Black American leading lady.
Black Eye 73. Get Christie Love (TV) (and series) 74. Vampira 74.

Gravet, Fernand (1904–1970) (Fernand Martens). Debonair French leading man with some Hollywood experience.
Bitter Sweet 33. The Great Waltz 38. Fools for Scandal 38. Le Dernier Tournant 38. La Ronde 50. Short Head 53. How to Steal a Million 66. The Madwoman of Chaillot 69, etc.

Gray, Allan (1904–). Polish-born composer in Britain.
Emil and the Detectives (Ger.) 36. The Life and Death of Colonel Blimp 43. *A Matter of Life and Death* 45. Mr Perrin and Mr Traill 48. *The African Queen* 51. The Planter's Wife 52, etc.

Gray, Billy (c. 1940–). American juvenile actor of the fifties.
Specter of the Rose 46. Fighting Father Dunne 49. *On Moonlight Bay* 52. The Day the Earth Stood Still 52. The Seven Little Foys 55. Two for the Seesaw 62, etc.

Gray, Carole (1940–). South African leading lady in British films of the sixties.

The Young Ones 61. Curse of the Fly 64. Rattle of a Simple Man 64. Island of Terror 66, etc.

Gray, Charles (1928–) (Donald M. Gray). British stage and TV actor usually seen in smooth unsympathetic roles.
The Entertainer 60. The Man in the Moon 61. Masquerade 65. The Night of the Generals 66. The Secret War of Harry Frigg (US) 67. *The Devil Rides Out* 68. The File of the Golden Goose 69. Cromwell 69. *Diamonds are Forever* 71. The Beast Must Die 74. Seven Nights in Japan 76. The Seven Per Cent Solution (as Mycroft Holmes) 76. Silver Bears 77. The Legacy 78.
The Mirror Crack'd 80. The Jigsaw Man 84. An Englishman Abroad (TV) 84.

Gray, Colleen (1922–) (Doris Jensen). American leading lady of the forties.
Kiss of Death 47. Nightmare Alley 47. Fury at Furnace Creek 48. *Red River* 48. Sand 49. Riding High 50. The Sleeping City 51. Kansas City Confidential 52. Sabre Jet 53. Arrow in the Dust 54. The Killing 56. Hell's Five Hours 57. The Leech Woman 60. Town Tamer 65. PJ 68, etc.
TV series: Window on Main Street 61.

Gray, Dolores (1924–). Statuesque American singer-dancer, on stage in musical comedy (played *Annie Get Your Gun* in London).
□It's Always Fair Weather 54. Kismet 55. The Opposite Sex 56. Designing Woman 57.

Gray, Donald (1914–1978) (Eldred Tidbury). One-armed British leading man, former radio actor and announcer; best known as TV's Mark Saber. Films include Strange Experiment 37. The Four Feathers 39. Idol of Paris 48. Saturday Island (Island of Desire) 52. Timeslip 55. Satellite in the Sky 56, etc.

Gray, Dulcie (1919–) (Dulcie Bailey). Gentle-mannered British leading lady, married to Michael Denison.
A Place of One's Own 44. They Were Sisters 45. Mine Own Executioner 47. The Glass Mountain 48. Angels One Five 51. A Man Could Get Killed 65, etc.

Gray, Gary (1936–). American boy actor of the forties.
A Woman's Face 41. Address Unknown 44. The Great Lover 47. Rachel and the Stranger 48. Father Is a Bachelor 49. The Next Voice You Hear 50. The Painted Hills 51. The Party Crashers 58, others.

Gray, Gilda (1901–1959) (Marianna Michalska). Polish dancer who went to America and is credited with inventing the shimmy.
Aloma of the South Seas 26. The Devil Dancer 28. Rose Marie 36, etc.

Gray, Nadia (1923–) (Nadia Kujnir-Herescu). Russian-Roumanian leading lady, in European and British films.
The Spider and the Fly 49. Night Without Stars 51. Valley of Eagles 51. Neapolitan Fantasy 54. Folies Bergère 56. The Captain's Table 58. Parisienne 59. La Dolce Vita 59. Maniac 63. Two for the Road 67. The Naked Runner 67, etc.

Gray, Sally (1916–) (Constance Stevens). Popular British screen heroine of thirties and forties, with stage experience from 1925.
School for Scandal 30. Radio Pirates 35. Cheer Up 35. The Saint in London 38. The Lambeth Walk 38. Dangerous Moonlight 40. Carnival 46. *Green for Danger* 46. They Made Me a Fugitive 47. The Mark of Cain 48. Silent Dust 49. Obsession 49. Escape Route 52, etc.

Grayson, Godfrey (–). British second feature director, especially for the Danzigers.
Room to Let 50. To Have and to Hold 51. The Fake 53. Black Ice 57. High Jump 59. Spider's Web 60. So Evil So Young 61. She Always Gets Their Man 62, etc.

Grayson, Kathryn (1922–) (Zelma Hedrick). American singing star in Hollywood from 1941 (as one of Andy Hardy's dates).
□Andy Hardy's Private Secretary 40. Andy Hardy's Spring Fever 41. The Vanishing Virginian 41. Rio Rita 42. Seven Sweethearts 42. Thousands Cheer 43. Anchors Aweigh 45. Two Sisters from Boston 46. Ziegfeld Follies 46. Till the Clouds Roll By 46. It Happened in Brooklyn 47. The Kissing Bandit 48. The Midnight Kiss 49. The Toast of New Orleans 50. Grounds for Marriage 50. *Show Boat* 51. Lovely to Look At 52. The Desert Song 53. So This is Love (as Grace Moore) 53. *Kiss Me Kate* 53. The Vagabond King 55. That's Entertainment Two 76.

Great Britain had been making films for more than fifty years when finally a 'British school' emerged capable of influencing world production. Hollywood films had invaded British cinemas during World War I, and British audiences liked them; so the battle for power was won with only faint stirrings of resistance. British films were tepid, shoddy, stilted, old-fashioned in acting and production; and for many years they were kept that way by short-sighted government legislation, intended to help the industry, ensuring that at least a proportion (usually a third) of local product must be shown in every British cinema. Thus began the long list of 'quota quickies', deplorable B pictures whose producers knew they could not fail to get their money back. In the mid-thirties, Britain was producing 200 films a year, but they reflected nothing of life and offered little in the way of entertainment.

Exceptions to this general rule were the suspense thrillers of Alfred Hitchcock; a couple of promising dramas from Anthony Asquith; some well-produced entertainments from Victor Saville, such as *The Good Companions* and *South Riding*; Herbert Wilcox's popular view of such historical figures as Nell Gwyn and Queen Victoria; and the ambitious and often masterly, but not particularly British, productions of Alexander Korda, whose *Rembrandt* and *Things to Come* could still justify their inclusion in any list of the world's ten best. The British music-hall tradition also survived remarkably well in skilful low-budget productions with such stars as Gracie Fields, George Formby, Will Hay and the Crazy Gang; the two directors most concerned, Marcel Varnel and Walter Forde, had much to tell anyone who cared to listen about the art of screen comedy, as had writers Val Guest, Frank Launder and Sidney Gilliat.

In 1939 MGM had achieved three notable British productions—*A Yank at Oxford, Goodbye Mr Chips* and *The Citadel*—but the war swept away all plans and British studios started anew. Their renaissance began through the splendid documentaries of Humphrey Jennings, Harry Watt and Basil Wright, graduates of the GPO Film Unit which had been turning out excellent short films in the thirties but failing to secure cinema bookings for them. The strong feelings of national pride and urgency percolated to the fiction film, first in stories of social comment (*The Proud Valley, The Stars Look Down, Love on the Dole*), then in topical entertainments like Carol Reed's *Night Train to Munich* and Thorold Dickinson's *Next of Kin.* Noel Coward's *In Which We Serve* came as a revelation of style and substance, and what it did for the navy was done for the army by Reed's *The Way Ahead* and for the air force by Asquith's *The Way to the Stars.* The home front was covered with equal sensitivity by Launder and Gilliat's *Millions Like Us,* Leslie Howard's *The Gentle Sex,* and Coward's *This Happy Breed.*

Even non-war films had a fresh impetus. Gabriel Pascal made an excellent *Major Barbara* to follow the success of his 1938 *Pygmalion.* Dickinson's *Gaslight,* Reed's *Kipps,* and Asquith's *Quiet Wedding* were all excellent of their kind. The new team of Michael Powell and Emeric Pressburger brought a fresh command and insight to some unlikely but ambitious themes in *The Life and Death of Colonel Blimp* and *A Matter of Life and Death.* Korda supplied *The Thief of Baghdad, Lady Hamilton* and *Perfect Strangers.* The Boulting Brothers followed up *Pastor Hall* with the thoughtful *Thunder Rock.* Launder and Gilliat followed the realistic *Waterloo Road* with sparkling comedy-dramas (*The Rake's Progress, I See a Dark Stranger*), and a classic who-done-it (*Green for Danger*). Gainsborough Studios turned out several competent costume dramas on the Hollywood model. In 1945 the future of British films seemed bright indeed with Olivier's *Henry V,* Coward and Lean's *Blithe Spirit,* and Ealing Studios' supernatural omnibus *Dead of Night* earning popular approval, and such films as *Brief Encounter* and *Odd Man Out* in the works.

In the next few years the industry was beset by financial problems and diminishing audiences. Then Britain's leading film magnate, J. Arthur Rank, set out to conquer by means which proved regrettable. Originally attracted to the cinema as a means for spreading the Methodist religion, he now determined to impress world markets by a series of enormously expensive and generally arty productions, few of which recovered their costs: *Caesar and Cleopatra* is the most notorious. The more modestly-budgeted pictures proved to have little to say now that the end of the war had removed their main subject; and with exceptions like *Mine Own Executioner, The Red Shoes,* and *The Third Man* the field was thin until the celebrated Ealing comedies (*Passport to Pimlico, Whisky Galore, The Man in the White Suit, Kind Hearts and Coronets*) began to attract world audiences. But these too had their day, and all through the fifties British studios were trying in vain to find subjects to replace them. During this period many stars found their way to Hollywood, and then gradually began to drift back as kingpins of international co-productions, ventures which seldom turned out very happily. It was not till the relaxed hand of censorship permitted *Room at the Top, Saturday Night and Sunday Morning, The Leather Boys, Tom Jones, Georgy Girl, Blow Up,* James Bond and *Alfie* that British films at last set the world afire by showing just what you could get away with if you did it with sufficient skill and truth. Unfortunately even sex and violence must pall . . . so what next? The stopgap answer of the late sixties and early seventies was low comedy, much of it borrowed from TV; but that couldn't last, and didn't. By 1980 so many cinemas had closed that it was impossible to make ends meet on films for English consumption alone, and British studios and unions had priced themselves out of the international market. It remained for enterprising financiers such as Goldcrest to stimulate international palates with what would once have seemed very unlikely themes (*Chariots of Fire, Gandhi*); between these occasional highspots good reviews were achieved for a number of outspoken low-budget realistic dramas, most of them partly financed by the new television Channel Four, which aired them after a usually brief run in cinemas. Cinema was no longer a mass entertainment, but a means of attracting specific minorities.

The Great Caruso (US 1951). The film which confirmed Mario Lanza on his brief but triumphant career as a top singing star and also proved to a surprised Hollywood that opera can be big business if given the right sugar coating.

The Great Dictator (US 1940). Chaplin's satire on Hitler has many moments of bitter hilarity but is marred by the sentimentality of the ghetto scenes. The first film in which Chaplin spoke coherently, and the last in which he used his famous tramp character.

Great Expectations (GB 1946). Dickens' novel has been filmed several times, but never with such definition, pace and attention to detail as in the *de luxe* version directed by David Lean and produced by Ronald Neame. Most outstanding in an excellent cast were John Mills, Jean Simmons, Alec Guinness, Finlay Currie and Martita Hunt; Guy Green (AA) was cinematographer and John Bryan (AA) was production designer. The best previous version was made in Hollywood in 1934, with Phillips Holmes and Jane Wyatt.

The Great Gatsby. F. Scott Fitzgerald's mordant story of an ex-gangster who meets his death among the Long Island high livers was filmed in 1926 with Warner Baxter, in 1949 with Alan Ladd, and in 1974 with Robert Redford. The first was by all accounts the most successful, the second being merely surprising for biting off more than it could chew and the third swamped by decoration and overlength.

The Great Impersonation. E. Phillips Oppenheim's cunningly-constructed spy thriller was filmed in 1921 with James Kirkwood; in 1935 with Edmund Lowe; and in 1942 with Ralph Bellamy.

The Great Movie Stars, by David Shipman. These two volumes (the first subtitled *The Golden Years*, the second *The International Years*) first appeared in the early seventies, and comprise nearly four hundred witty though capsuled accounts of star careers, with every film given an appropriate if passing mention.

The Great Race (US 1965). A lavish and often splendid period comedy about a 1908 auto race from New York to Paris, this engaging Blake Edwards film was written by Arthur Ross with nods to Valentino, Laurel and Hardy and *The Prisoner of Zenda.* Some of the gags are prolonged, but the film is always good to look at, and the zany leading roles are comfortably filled by Tony Curtis, Jack Lemmon, Natalie Wood, Peter Falk and Ross Martin.

The Great Train Robbery (US 1903). An eleven-minute western sometimes inaccurately hailed as the first story film; but it was the longest of its time, and it did have all the elements of its modern descendants, with careful editing and a sense of cinema showmanship. Directed by Edwin S. Porter.

The Great Ziegfeld (US 1936). A mammoth musical drama of its time, running three hours and recounting the life story of Broadway's great showman. William Powell played the part, and Robert Z. Leonard directed. Academy Awards went to the film (best picture), to Luise Rainer, and to Seymour Felix for the dance direction of the central number with its enormous revolving set.

The Greatest Story Ever Told (US 1965). George Stevens' immensely long life of Christ (in Cinerama) was plainly a labour of love: he was quoted as hoping that it would still be showing 'at the end of the century and after'. But despite beautiful moments it was fatally compromised by the casting of stars in bit parts and by the heavy-handedness evident in all Stevens' later films. The publicity about deciding to shoot it in Utah (because Utah was 'more like Palestine than Palestine') didn't help; but Max Von Sydow was an excellent Christ. At the box office, the picture died.

Greco, Juliette (1927–). French singer who acted in several films both at home and abroad.
Au Royaume des Cieux 49. The Green Glove 52. *The Sun Also Rises* 57. Naked Earth 58. Roots of Heaven 59. Whirlpool 59. Crack in the Mirror 60, etc.

Greece has had a film industry since 1912, but its development has been affected by political upheavals, and the results have had little international appeal, the best known directors being Michael Cacoyannis and Greg Tallas. The personality of Melina Mercouri and the music of Mikis Theodorakis were however more successfully exported.

Greed (US 1923). Originally an estimated nine hours long, cut by June Mathis to two, this realistic study of money as the root of all evil, set in contemporary American settings, was both Erich Von Stroheim's triumph and his downfall; for it made his extravagance a talking-point in Hollywood and a few years later he was forced to retire from directing. Here he also wrote the scenario, from Frank Norris' novel *McTeague*; his cinematographers were Ben Reynolds, William Daniels and Ernest Schoedsack and his leading actors Zasu Pitts, Gibson Gowland and Jean Hersholt.

Green, Adolph (1915–). American writer of books and lyrics for many Broadway shows and musical films, usually with Betty Comden (qv).

Green, Alfred E. (1889–1960). American director of mainly routine but generally competent films; in Hollywood from 1912.
Little Lord Fauntleroy 20. Ella Cinders 23. Through the Back Door 26. The Green Goddess 30. Old English 31. Smart Money 31. Disraeli 31. The Rich Are Always with Us 32. Parachute 33. Dangerous 35. Duke of West Point 38. South of Pago Pago 40. Badlands of Dakota 41. Meet the Stewarts 42. A Thousand and One Nights 44. *The Jolson Story* 46. The Fabulous Dorseys 47. They Passed This Way 48. Four Faces West 48. Cover Up 49. Invasion USA 52. The Eddie Cantor Story 53, many others.

Green, Danny (1903–). Heavyweight British character actor usually in cheerful—or sometimes menacing—cockney roles. Appeared in some American silents.
Crime over London 37. Fiddlers Three 44. The Man Within 47. No Orchids for Miss Blandish 48. Little Big Shot 52. A Kid for Two Farthings 55. The Lady Killers 55. Beyond This Place 59, many others.

Green, Guy (1913–). British cinematographer who became a useful director.
AS CINEMATOGRAPHER: In Which We Serve 42. The Way Ahead 44. *Great Expectations* (AA) 46. Take my Life 47. *Oliver Twist* 48. Captain Horatio Hornblower 51. The Beggar's Opera 52. Rob Roy 53, etc.
□AS DIRECTOR: River Beat 54. Portrait of Alison 55. Lost 56. House of Secrets 56. The Snorkel 58. Sea of Sand 58. SOS Pacific 59. *The Mark* 60. *The Angry Silence* 60. The Light in the Piazza 62. Diamond Head 63. A Patch of Blue 65. Pretty Polly 67. The Magus 68. A Walk in the Spring Rain 70. Luther 73. Once is Not Enough 75. The Devil's Advocate 77. Strong Medicine (TV) 85.

Green, Harry (1892–1958). American comedian, primarily on stage; former lawyer.
Close Harmony 31. Bottoms Up 34. The Cisco Kid and the Lady 37. Star Dust 40. Joe MacBeth (GB) 55. A King in New York (GB) 57, etc.

Green, Hughie (1920–). Canadian actor in Britain, former juvenile, then popular TV quizmaster and talent scout.
Little Friend 34. Midshipman Easy 36. Tom Brown's Schooldays (US) 39. If Winter Comes (US) 48. Paper Orchid 49, etc.

Green, Janet (1914–). British screenwriter.
The Clouded Yellow 49. Cast a Dark Shadow (oa) 54. Lost 55. The Long Arm 56. *Sapphire* (BFA) 59. Midnight Lace (oa) 60. Life for Ruth 62. *Victim* 62. Seven Women 66, etc.

Green, Johnny (1908–). American composer, band leader, songwriter; in Hollywood from 1933. Scored Easter Parade (AA) 47. An American in Paris (AA) 51. Oliver (AA) 68, many others.

Green, Martyn (1899–1975). British light opera singer, with the D'Oyly Carte Company for many years; settled in America.
Autobiography 1952: *Here's A How De Do.*
□*The Mikado* 39. The Story of Gilbert and Sullivan 53. A Lovely Way to Die 68.

Green, Mitzi (1920–1969) (Elizabeth Keno). American child performer of the thirties.
Honey 30. Tom Sawyer 30. Little Orphan Annie 32. Transatlantic Merry-Go-Round 34, etc.: later appeared in Lost in Alaska 52. Bloodhounds of Broadway 52.
TV series: So This is Hollywood 54.

Green, Nigel (1924–1972). Dominant British character actor with stage experience.
Reach for the Sky 56. Bitter Victory 58. The Criminal 60. Jason and the Argonauts 63. *Zulu* 64. *The Ipcress File* 65. *The Face of Fu Manchu* 65. The Skull 66. Let's Kill Uncle (US) 66. *Deadlier than the Male* 66. *Tobruk* (US) 67. Africa Texas Style 67. Play Dirty 68. Wrecking Crew (US) 69. The Kremlin Letter 69. Countess Dracula 70. The Ruling Class 71, etc.
TV series: William Tell 57.

Green Pastures (US 1936). A fairly lavish and sympathetic film version, directed by William Keighley, of the Marc Connelly play from Roark Bradford's stories showing the simple Negro interpretation of the Bible, with Heaven as a gigantic 'fish fry' and 'De Lawd' played by Rex Ingram as a dignified old Negro. The first film since *Hallelujah* 29 to give a fairly serious account of Negro thought, it did not entirely avoid a patronizing air.

Green, Philip (1917–). British composer.
The March Hare 54. John and Julie 55. Rooney 57. Innocent Sinners 58. Operation Amsterdam 59. Sapphire 59. The Bulldog Breed 61. Victim 62. It's All Happening (& co-p) 63. The Intelligence Men 65. Masquerade 65, etc.

Greenberg, Gerald (1936–). American editor.
Bye Bye Braverman 68. The Boys in the Band 70. The French Connection (AA) 71. The Seven Ups 73. The Taking of Pelham One Two Three 75. The Missouri Breaks 76. Apocalypse Now 79.

Greenberg, Stanley R. (–). American screenwriter.
Welcome Home Johnny Bristol (TV) 72. Skyjacked 72. Soylent Green 73. The Missiles of October (TV) 73. The Silence (TV) 76. Blind Ambition (TV) 79. FDR, the Last Years (TV) 81, etc.

Greene, Clarence (c. 1918–). American writer-producer, usually in collaboration with Russel Rouse.
The Town Went Wild 45. D.O.A. 48. The Well 51. New York Confidential 55. A House Is Not a Home 64. The Oscar 66. Caper of the Golden Bulls 67, etc.
TV series: Tightrope 57.

Greene, David (1924–). British director, former small-part actor; became a TV director in Canada and the U.S.
□The Shuttered Room 66. Sebastian 68. The Strange Affair 68. I Start Counting (& p) 69. The People Next Door 70. Madame Sin (TV) 72. *Godspell* 73. Ellery Queen (TV) 75. Rich Man Poor Man (TV) (co-d) 76. Roots (co-d) TV 77. Lucan (TV pilot) 77. The Man in the Iron Mask (TV) 77. Gray Lady Down 78. The Trial of Lee Harvey Oswald (TV) 78. Friendly Fire (TV) 79. A Vacation in Hell (TV) 80. Hard Country 81. World War III (TV) 81. Ghost Dancing (TV) 81.

Greene, Graham (1904–). Distinguished British novelist who has provided material for many interesting films.
Stamboul Train (Orient Express) 34. This Gun for Hire 42. The Ministry of Fear 43. Confidential Agent 45. The Man Within 46. Brighton Rock 47. The Fugitive 48. The Fallen Idol 48. The Third Man 49. The Heart of the Matter 53. The Stranger's Hand 54. The End of the Affair 55. The Quiet American 58. Our Man in Havana 59. The Comedians 67. Travels with My Aunt 73, etc.

Greene, Lorne (1915–87). solidly-built supporting actor, former opera singer.
A Funny Thing Happened on the Way to the Forum 67. The Ritz 76. The Seven Per Cent Solution 76.

Greene, Lorne (1915–87). Solidly-built Canadian character actor.
The Silver Chalice 54. Tight Spot 55. Autumn Leaves 56. Peyton Place 57. The Gift of Love 58. The Trap 58. Legacy of a Spy (TV) 68. The Harness (TV) 71. Earthquake 74, etc.
TV series: Sailor of Fortune 56. *Bonanza* (as Ben Cartwright) 59–71. Griff 74. Battlestar Galactica 78. Code Red 81.

Greene, Max (1896–1968) (Mutz Greenbaum). German cinematographer, long in Britain.

The Stars Look Down 39. Hatter's Castle 41. Spring in Park Lane 48. Maytime in Mayfair 49. Night and the City 50, etc.

Greene, Richard (1914–85). Good-looking, lightweight British leading man with brief stage experience before 1938 film debut resulted in Hollywood contract.
□*Four Men and a Prayer* 38. My Lucky Star 38. Submarine Patrol 38. Kentucky 38. The Little Princess 38. *The Hound of the Baskervilles* 39. Stanley and Livingstone 39. Here I Am a Stranger 39. Little Old New York 40. I Was an Adventuress 40. Unpublished Story 42. Flying Fortress 42. Yellow Canary 43. Don't Take It to Heart 45. Gaiety George 46. Forever Amber 47. The Fighting O'Flynn 48. The Fan 48. That Dangerous Age 49. Now Barabbas 49. The Desert Hawk 50. My Daughter Joy 50. Shadow of the Eagle 50. Lorna Doone 51. Black Castle 51. Rogue's March 53. Captain Scarlet 53. Bandits of Corsica 54. Contraband Spain 55. Beyond the Curtain 60. Sword of Sherwood Forest 61. Dangerous Island 67. Blood of Fu Manchu 68. Kiss and Kill 69. Tales from the Crypt 72.
TV series: *Robin Hood* 55–59.

Greene, W. Howard (–1956). American colour cinematographer.
Trail of the Lonesome Pine 36. *The Garden of Allah* 36. *A Star is Born* 37. Nothing Sacred 37. *The Adventures of Robin Hood* 38. Jesse James 39. Elizabeth and Essex 39. Northwest Mounted Police 40. Blossoms in the Dust 41. The Jungle Book 42. Arabian Nights 42. *Phantom of the Opera* (AA) 43. Ali Baba and the Forty Thieves 44. Can't Help Singing 44. Salome Where she Danced 45. A Night in Paradise 46. Tycoon 47. High Lonesome 50. Quebec 51. The Brigand 52. Gun Belt 53, etc.

Greenleaf, Raymond (1892–1963). American character actor, usually seen as benevolent elderly man.
Storm Warning 51. Angel Face 53. Violent Saturday 54. *When Gangland Strikes* (leading role) 56. The Story on Page One 60, many others.

Greenstreet, Sydney (1879–1954). Immense British stage actor long in America; a sensation in his first film, made at the age of 61, he became a major star of the forties.
□*The Maltese Falcon* 41. They Died with Their Boots On 41. *Across the Pacific* 42. Casablanca 42. Background to Danger 42. Passage to Marseilles 44. *Between Two Worlds* 44. *The Mask of Dimitrios* 44. The Conspirators 44. Hollywood Canteen 44. Pillow to Post 45. Conflict 45. Christmas in Connecticut 45. *Three Strangers* 46. Devotion (as Thackeray) 46. The Verdict 46. That Way with Women 47. *The Hucksters* 47. *The Woman in White* 48. The Velvet Touch 48. Ruthless 48. Flamingo Road 49. It's a Great Feeling 49. Malaya 50.
❀ For his inimitable chuckle; and for the sheer improbability of his success. *The Maltese Falcon*.

¶ By gad, sir, you're a fellow worth knowing, a character. No telling what you'll say next, except that it'll be something astonishing.—*S.G. in The Maltese Falcon.*

I distrust a man who says when. He's got to be careful not to drink too much, because he's not to be trusted when he does. Well, sir, here's to plain speaking and clear understanding. You're a close-mouthed man?

—No, I like to talk.

—Better and better. I distrust a close-mouthed man. He generally picks the wrong time to talk, and says the wrong things. Talking's something you can't do judiciously, unless you keep in practice.—*ibid.*

Greenwood, Charlotte (1890–1978). Tall American comedienne and eccentric dancer, on stage from 1905.
Autobiography 1947: *Never Too Tall.*
Jane 18. Baby Mine 27. So Long Letty 30. Palmy Days 32. Down Argentine Way 40. Springtime in the Rockies 43. Up in Mabel's Room 44. Home in Indiana 47. Peggy 50. Dangerous When Wet 52. Glory 55. Oklahoma 56. The Opposite Sex 56, etc.

Greenwood, Jack (1919–). British producer, responsible for second-feature crime series: Edgar Wallace, Scales of Justice, Scotland Yard, etc.

Greenwood, Joan (1921–87). Plummy-voiced British leading lady of the forties.
□John Smith Wakes Up 40. My Wife's Family 40. He Found a Star 41. *The Gentle Sex* 42. They Knew Mr Knight 44. Latin Quarter 44. A Girl in a Million 45. The Man Within 46. *The October Man* 47. The White Unicorn 47. *Saraband for Dead Lovers* 48. The Bad Lord Byron 48. Whisky Galore 49. *Kind Hearts and Coronets* 49. Flesh and Blood 50. The Man in the White Suit 50. Young Wives' Tale 51. Mr Peek-a-Boo 51. *The Importance of Being Earnest* 52. Knave of Hearts 54. *Father Brown* 54. Moonfleet (US) 55. Stage Struck (US) 57. Mysterious

Island 62. The Amorous Prawn 62. Tom Jones 63. The Moon Spinners 64. Girl Stroke Boy 71. The Uncanny 77. The Hound of the Baskervilles 78. The Water Babies 78.

¶ *Karel Reisz:* She speaks her lines as though suspecting in them some hidden menace that she can't quite identify.

Greenwood, John (1889–1975). British composer.
To What Red Hell? 30. The Constant Nymph 33. Elephant Boy 37. Pimpernel Smith 41. San Demetrio, London 44. Frieda 47. Quartet 48. The Last Days of Dolwyn 48. Trio 50. The Gentle Gunman 52, others.

Greenwood, Walter (1903–1974). British writer who chronicled industrial life, notably in *Love On the Dole*.

Greer, Jane (1924–) (Bettyjane Greer). Cool American leading lady of the forties; could play good-humoured dames, well-bred ladies or *femmes fatales*.
□Pan Americana 45. Two O'Clock Courage 45. George White's Scandals 45. Dick Tracy 45. The Falcon's Alibi 46. Bamboo Blonde 46. Sunset Pass 46. Sinbad the Sailor 46. *They Won't Believe Me* 47. *Out of the Past* 47. Station West 48. *The Big Steal* 49. You're in the Navy Now 51. The Company She Keeps 51. The Prisoner of Zenda 52. Desperate Search 52. You for Me 52. The Clown 53. Down Among the Sheltering Palms 53. *Run for the Sun* 56. *Man of a Thousand Faces* 57. Where Love Has Gone 64. Billie 65. The Outfit 74. The Shadow Riders (TV) 82. Against All Odds 84.

Gregg, Everley (1898–1959). British character actress.
The Private Life of Henry VIII 32. The Ghost Goes West 36. Pygmalion 38. Brief Encounter 45, etc.

Gregg, Hubert (1914–). British songwriter, screenwriter, and light actor, married to Pat Kirkwood. On stage from 1933, films from 1942.
In Which We Serve 42. 29 Acacia Avenue 45. Vote for Huggett 49. Robin Hood 52. The Maggie 54. Simon and Laura 55. Stars in My Eyes 57, etc.

Gregor, Nora (c. 1890–1949). Austrian leading lady.
The Trial of Mary Dugan (US) 29. His Glorious Night (US) 30. *La Règle du Jeu* (Fr.) 39, etc.

Gregory, James (1911–). American character actor with stage experience, a familiar Hollywood 'heavy' or senior cop.
Naked City 48. The Frogmen 51. The Scarlet Hour 56. The Young Stranger 57. Al Capone 59. Two Weeks in Another Town 62. *The Manchurian Candidate* 62. P.T.109 63. A Distant Trumpet 64. The Sons of Katie Elder 65. A Rage To Live 65. *The Silencers* 66. Clambake 68. The Hawaiians 70. Million Dollar Duck 71. Shootout 71. The Main Event 79, etc.
TV series: The Lawless Years 59. Barney Miller 81.

Gregory, Paul (c. 1905–) (Jason Lenhart). American impresario who teamed with Charles Laughton in the forties to present dramatized readings: also produced *Night of the Hunter* 55, which Laughton directed, and *The Naked and the Dead* 58.

Gregory's Girl (GB 1981). A modest romantic comedy about teenage problems, generally thought delightful, and despite the handicap of broad Scottish accents enough to give producer-director Bill Forsyth an international reputation. He went on to make *Local Hero*, with American star Burt Lancaster, but it was less successful.

Gregson, John (1919–1975). Scottish leading man, a likeable and dependable star of British comedies and action dramas in the fifties.
□Saraband for Dead Lovers 48. Scott of the Antarctic 48. Whisky Galore 49. The Hasty Heart 49. Train of Events 49. Treasure Island 50. Cairo Road 50. *The Lavender Hill Mob* 51. Angels One Five 51. *The Brave Don't Cry* 51. Venetian Bird 52. The Holly and the Ivy 52. The Titfield Thunderbolt 53. *Genevieve* 53. The Weak and the Wicked 53. Conflict of Wings 54. To Dorothy a Son 54. The Crowded Day 54. Above Us the Waves 55. Value for Money 55. Three Cases of Murder 55. *Jacqueline* 56. The Battle of the River Plate 56. True as a Turtle 56. Miracle in Soho 57. *Rooney* 57. Sea of Sand 58. *The Captain's Table* 58. SOS Pacific 59. Faces in the Dark 60. Hand in Hand 60. Treasure of Monte Cristo 61. Frightened City 61. *Live Now Pay Later* 62. Tomorrow at Ten 62. The Longest Day 62. The Night of the Generals 66. Fright 71.
TV series: Gideon's Way 64. Shirley's World 71.

Greig, Robert (1880–1958). Australian character actor, long in Hollywood; the doyen of portly pompous butlers.

Animal Crackers 30. Tonight or Never 31. Love Me Tonight 32. Trouble in Paradise 32. Horse Feathers 32. Merrily We Go to Hell 33. Pleasure Cruise 33. Clive of India 35. Lloyds of London 36. Easy Living 37. Algiers 38. No Time for Comedy 40. The Lady Eve 41. Sullivan's Travels 42. *The Moon and Sixpence* 42. I Married a Witch 42. The Palm Beach Story 42. The Great Moment 44. The Picture of Dorian Gray 45. The Cheaters 45. Unfaithfully Yours 48, many others.

Grémillon, Jean (1901–59). French director with limited but interesting output since 1929. Remorques 39. Lumière d'Eté 42. Pattes Blanches 48, etc.

Grenfell, Joyce (1910–79) (Joyce Phipps). Angular British comedienne adept at refined gaucherie; a revue star and solo performer, on stage from 1939.
The Demi-Paradise 42. The Lamp Still Burns 43. While the Sun Shines 46. *The Happiest Days of Your Life* 49. Stage Fright 50. *Laughter in Paradise* 51. Genevieve 53. The Million Pound Note 54. The Belles of St Trinian's 54. Happy Is the Bride 57. Blue Murder at St Trinian's 58. The Pure Hell of St Trinian's 60. The Old Dark House 63. The Americanization of Emily 64. The Yellow Rolls Royce 64, etc.

Greville, Edmond (1906–1966). French director; assistant to Dupont on *Piccadilly* 30, to Clair on *Sous les Toits de Paris* 32. Remous 34. Mademoiselle Docteur 37. L'Ile du Pêché 39. Passionelle 46. Noose (GB) 48. The Romantic Age (GB) 49. But Not In Vain (also wrote and produced) (GB) 49. Port du Désir 56. Guilty (GB) 56. Beat Girl (GB) 60. The Hands of Orlac (GB) 61. Les Menteurs 61, etc.

Grey, Joel (1932–) (Joe Katz). American singing entertainer who took a long time to hit stardom, managed it on the New York stage in *Cabaret*, but proved difficult to cast. □About Face 52. Come September 63. Man on a String (TV) 71. *Cabaret* .(AA) 72. Man on a Swing 74. Buffalo Bill and the Indians 76. The Seven Per Cent Solution 76. Remo Williams . . . the Adventure Begins 85.

Grey, Lita (1908–) (Lillita MacMurray). American juvenile actress of the twenties who appeared with Chaplin, became his child bride, and is the mother of Sydney Chaplin. In the late sixties, wrote *My Life with Chaplin.*

Grey, Nan (1918–) (Eschal Miller). American leading lady of the late thirties. Dracula's Daughter 36. Three Smart Girls 36. Three Smart Girls Grow Up 38. Tower of London 39. The Invisible Man Returns 40. Sandy Is a Lady 41, etc.

Grey, Virginia (1917–). American leading lady of minor films in the thirties and forties. Uncle Tom's Cabin (debut) 27. Misbehaving Ladies 31. Secrets 33. Dames 34. The Firebird 34. The Great Ziegfeld 36. Rosalie 37. Test Pilot 38. The Hardys Ride High 39. Hullaballoo 40. Blonde Inspiration 41. The Big Store 41. Grand Central Murder 42. Idaho 43. Strangers in the Night 44. Blonde Ransom 45. House of Horrors 46. Unconquered 47. Who Killed Doc Robbin? 48. Jungle Jim 49. Slaughter Trail 51. Desert Pursuit 52. Target Earth 54. The Last Command 55. Crime of Passion 56. The Restless Years 58. Portrait in Black 60. Back Street 61. Black Zoo 63. Love Has Many Faces 65. Madame X 66. Rosie 68. Airport 69, many others.

Grey, Zane (1875–1939). American novelist whose western yarns provided the basis of hundreds of silent and sound movies. He lacked sophistication, but as late as 1960 TV had its *Zane Grey Theatre*.

Greyfriars Bobby (US 1960). Elinor Atkinson's sentimental novel of old Edinburgh, about a dog who lies on his master's grave, was filmed agreeably enough by Disney. It had also been used as the plot of *Challenge to Lassie* 49.

Griem, Helmut (1940–). German leading man in international films.
The Damned 69. The Mackenzie Break 70. *Cabaret* 72. Ludwig 73. Voyage of the Damned 76. Sergeant Steiner 79, etc.

Grier, Pam (1949–). Black American leading lady.
Beyond the Valley of the Dolls 70. Twilight People 72. Blacula 72. Hit Man 72. Coffy 74. Black Mama White Mama 74. The Arena 74. Sheba Baby 75. Friday Foster 75. Drum 76. Greased Lightning 77. Fort Apache the Bronx 81. Something Wicked This Way Comes 83, etc.

Grier, Roosevelt (1932–). Black American footballer, cousin of Pam Grier; makes occasional showbiz appearances.
The Thing with Two Heads 72. Skyjacked 72. Evil in the Deep 76.

Grierson, John (1898–1972). Distinguished British documentarist. Founded Empire Marketing Board Film Unit 30. GPO Film Unit 33; Canadian Film Commissioner 39–45, etc. Produced *Drifters* 29. *Industrial Britain* 33. *Song of Ceylon* 34. *Night Mail* 36, etc. In 1957–63 he had his own weekly TV show *This Wonderful World* showing excerpts from the world's best non-fiction films.

Gries, Tom (1922–1977). American director (also producer and co-writer) with varied Hollywood experience from 1946 and much TV.
☐Hell's Horizon 55. The Girl in the Woods 58. *Will Penny* (& w) 68. 100 Rifles 69. Number One 69. The Hawaiians 70. Fools 71. Earth II (TV) 71. Call to Danger (TV) 72. The Glass House (TV) 72. Journey through Rosebud 72. Migrants (TV) 73. Lady Ice 73. QB VII (TV) 74. Breakout 75. Breakheart Pass 76. Helter Skelter (TV) 76. The Greatest 77.

Griffies, Ethel (1878–1975) (Ethel Woods). Angular British character actress, in Hollywood for many years.
Waterloo Bridge 31. Love Me Tonight 32. The Mystery of Edwin Drood 35. Kathleen 37. We are Not Alone 39. Irene 40. Great Guns 41. *Time to Kill* 42. Jane Eyre 44. The Horn Blows at Midnight 45. Devotion 46. The Homestretch 47. The Birds 63. *Billy Liar* (GB) 63, many others.

Griffin, Josephine (1928–). British leading lady.
The Weak and the Wicked 54. The Purple Plain 54. The Man Who Never Was 56. The Spanish Gardener (last to date) 56, etc.

Griffith, Andy (1926–). Tall, slow-speaking American comic actor, adept at wily country-boy roles.
A Face in the Crowd (debut) 57. No Time for Sergeants 58. Onionhead 58. Winter Kill (TV) 73. Hearts of the West 75. *Washington: Behind Closed Doors* (TV) 76. The Girl in the Empty Grave (TV) 77. Deadly Game (TV) 77. Centennial (TV) 78.
Next Generations (TV) 79. Fatal Vision (TV) 85, etc.
From Here to Eternity (TV) 79. Roots: The Next Generations (TV) 79, etc.
TV series: The Andy Griffith Show 60–68. The Headmaster 70. Salvage 78.

Griffith, Corinne (1898–1979). American leading lady of the twenties.
The Yellow Girl 22. Six Days 23. Lilies of the Field 24. Love's Wilderness 24. The Marriage Whirl 25. Infatuation 25. Syncopating Sue 26. Three Hours 27. The Garden of Eden 28. The Divine Lady 29. Saturday's Children 29. Back Pay 30. Lily Christine 30. Papa's Delicate Condition (oa only) 52, etc.

Griffith, D. W. (David Wark) (1874–1948). American film pioneer, the industry's first major producer-director; he improved the cinema's prestige, developed many aspects of technique, created a score of stars, and was only flawed by his sentimental Victorian outlook, which in the materialistic twenties put him prematurely out of vogue and in the thirties out of business. Best book about him: *The Movies, Mr Griffith, and Me*, by Lillian Gish.
SELECTED EARLY FILMS: For the Love of Gold 08. The Song of the Shirt 08. Edgar Allan Poe 09. The Medicine Bottle 09. The Drunkard's Reformation 09. The Cricket on the Hearth 09. What Drink Did 09. The Violin Maker of Cremona 09. Pippa Passes 09. In the Watches of the Night 09. Lines of White on a Sullen Sea 09. Nursing a Viper 09. The Red Man's View 09. In Old California 10. Ramona 10. In the Season of Buds 10. The Face at the Window 10. The House with Closed Shutters 10. The Usurer 10. The Chink at Golden Gulch 10. Muggsy's First Sweetheart 10. The Italian Barber 10. The Manicure Lady 11. What Shall We Do with Our Old? 11. *The Lonedale Operator* 11. The Spanish Gypsy 11. Paradise Lost 11. Enoch Arden 11. Through Darkened Vales 11. The Revenue Man and the Girl 11. A Mender of Nets 12. The Goddess of Sagebrush Gulch 12. The Old Actor 12. *Man's Genesis* 12. The Sands of Dee 12. *The Musketeers of Pig Alley* 12. My Baby 12. *The New York Hat* 12. The God Within 12. The One She Loved 12. The Mothering Heart 13. The Sheriff's Baby 13. The Battle at Elderbrush Gulch 13. *Judith of Bethulia* 13. The Escape 14. The Avenging Conscience 14. The Mother and the Law 14. Home Sweet Home 14, many others.
☐FROM 1915: *The Birth of a Nation* 15. *Intolerance* 16. *Hearts of the World* 18. The Great Love 18. The Greatest Thing in Life 18. A Romance of Happy Valley 19. *Broken Blossoms* 19. The Girl Who Stayed at Home 19. True Heart Susie 19. Scarlet Days 19. The Greatest Question 19. The Idol Dancer 20. The Love Flower 20. *Way Down East* 20. Dream Street 21. *One Exciting Night* 22. *Orphans of the Storm* 22. The White Rose 23.

America 24. Isn't Life Wonderful 25. Sally of the Sawdust 26. That Royle Girl 26. *The Sorrows of Satan* 26. Drums of Love 28. The Battle of the Sexes 28. Lady of the Pavements 29. Abraham Lincoln 30. The Struggle 31. One Million Years B.C. (reputed contribution) 39.

'It is time D. W. Griffith was rescued from the pedestal of an outmoded pioneer. The cinema of Griffith, after all, is no more outmoded than the drama of Aeschylus.'—*Andrew Sarris, 1968*

❁ For enduring the fate of most monuments, and for deserving the tribute in the first place, despite being a personality with clearly unlikeable aspects. *Intolerance*.

¶ He was the first to photograph thought, said Cecil B. De Mille. It was quite a compliment. But Griffith was full of contradictions. His brain was progressive, his emotions Victorian. For a few years the two aspects were able to join in public favour, but he could not adapt himself to the brisker pace of the twenties, when he made many such blinkered and stubborn pronouncements as:

> We do not want now and we never shall want the human voice with our films.

When the inevitable happened in 1928 he declared:

> We have taken beauty and exchanged it for stilted voices.

He could be tactless too, as when in 1918 he commented:

> Viewed as drama, the war is somewhat disappointing.

Yet this was the man of whom Gene Fowler could say:

> He articulated the mechanics of cinema and bent them to his flair.

Lillian Gish, a great admirer of Griffith, said:

> He inspired in us his belief that we were working in a medium that was powerful enough to influence the whole world.

To Mack Sennett:

> He was my day school, my adult education program, my university . . . (but) he was an extremely difficult man to know.

He said himself:

> The task I'm trying to achieve above all is to make you see . . .

He knew his own value, as many an actor found when asking for a rise:

> It's worth a lot more than money to be working for me!

This was true enough up to the time of *The Birth of a Nation*, which President Wilson described as:

> Like writing history with lightning.

But it became less so after the box-office flop of *Intolerance*, which Gene Fowler called:

> The greatest commercial anticlimax in film history.

He became an embarrassment to Hollywood because his ideas seemed outmoded; in the thirties he scarcely worked at all. When he died in 1948 Hedda Hopper, recalling the marks made by stars in the wet cement at Hollywood's Chinese Theatre, said:

> Griffith's footprints were never asked for, yet no one has ever filled his shoes . . .

And James Agee added:

> There is not a man working in movies, nor a man who cares for them, who does not owe Griffith more than he owes anyone else.

Ezra Goodman commented:

> At Griffith's funeral, the sacred cows of Hollywood gathered to pay him homage. A week before, he probably could not have gotten any of them on the telephone.

It is sad indeed that death had to come before such tributes as Frank Capra's:

> Since Griffith there has been no major improvement in the art of film direction.

And Carmel Myers':

> He was the umbrella that shaded us all.

And John Simon's:

> Griffith did for film what Sackville and Norton, the authors of *Goborduc*, did for drama.

He did what he did genuinely, and straight from the heart. His best films are passionate and tender, terrifying and pregnant, works of art certainly, and products too of an imagination far ahead of its time.—*Paul O'Dell*

It's about time that DWG was rescued from the pedestal of an outmoded pioneer. The cinema of Griffith is no more outmoded, after all, than the drama of Aeschylus.—*Andrew Sarris*

D.W.G.: Remember how small the world was before I came along. I brought it all to life: I moved the whole world onto a 20-foot screen.

Griffith, Edward H. (1894–). American director. Scrambled Wives 21. Unseeing Eyes 23. Bad Company 25. Afraid to Love 27. Paris Bound 29. Holiday 30. Rebound 31. The Animal Kingdom 32. Another Language 33. Biography of a Bachelor Girl 35. No More Ladies 35. Ladies in Love 36. Café Metropole 37. Café Society 39. Safari 40. Virginia 40. One Night in Lisbon 41. Bahama Passage 42. The Sky's the Limit 43. Perilous Holiday 46, etc.

Griffith, Hugh (1912–1980). Flamboyant Welsh actor, former bank clerk.
Neutral Port (debut) 40; war service; The Three Weird Sisters 48. London Belongs to Me 48. The Last Days of Dolwyn 48. A Run for Your Money 49. Laughter in Paradise 51. The Galloping Major 51. The Beggar's Opera 52. *The Titfield Thunderbolt* 53. The Sleeping Tiger 54. Passage Home 55. *Lucky Jim* 57. *Ben Hur* (AA) 59. The Day They Robbed the Bank of England 60. Exodus 61. The Counterfeit Traitor 62. *Tom Jones* 63. The Bargee 64. Moll Flanders 65. Oh Dad, Poor Dad 66. Sailor from Gibraltar 66. How to Steal a Million 66. The Chastity Belt 67. Oliver 68. The Fixer 68. Start the Revolution Without Me 69. Cry of the Banshee 70. Wuthering Heights 70. The Abominable Dr Phibes 71. Who Slew Auntie Roo? 72. What 72. Craze 73. Take Me High 73. Luther 75. Loving Cousins 76. Joseph Andrews 77. The Last Remake of Beau Geste 77. The Passover Plot 77, others.

Griffith, James (1919–). American general purpose actor.
Bright Leaf 50. Rhubarb 51. The Law vs Billy the Kid (as Pat Garrett) 54. Anything Goes 56. The Big Fisherman 59. The Amazing Transparent Man 61, etc.

Griffith, Kenneth (1921–). Sharp-eyed Welsh actor of stage and screen, often the envious 'little man'.
Love on the Dole 41. The Shop at Sly Corner 45. Bond Street 48. High Treason 50. Lucky Jim 57. I'm All Right, Jack 59. Circus of Horrors 59. *Only Two Can Play* 61. Rotten to the Core 65. The Bobo 67. The Whisperers 67. Revenge 71. The House in Nightmare Park 73, many others.

Griffith, Raymond (1894–1937). Dapper American comedian of the twenties.
Fools First 22. The Eternal Three 23. Changing Husbands 24. Poisoned Paradise 24. Open All Night 24. Miss Bluebeard 24. A Regular Fellow 25. *Fine Clothes* 25. *Hands Up* 25. *Wet Paint* 26. You'd Be Surprised 27. Time to Love 27. Wedding Bills 27. *All Quiet on the Western Front* (as the dying soldier) 30, etc.

Griffith, Richard (1912–1969). American film critic and curator of New York's Museum of Modern Art.

Griffiths, Jane (1929–1975). British leading lady of the fifties.
The Million Pound Note 54. The Green Scarf 54. Dead Man's Evidence 62. The Traitors 63, etc.

Griffiths, Richard (1947–). Sizeable British actor of the eighties.
Greystoke 84. Gorky Park 84. A Private Function 85.
TV series: Bird of Prey 84.

Griggs, Loyal (1906–1978). American cinematographer.
Shane (AA) 53. Elephant Walk 54. We're No Angels 55. The Ten Commandments 56. The Hangman 59. Walk Like a Dragon 60. The Slender Thread 66. Hurry Sundown 67. P.J. 68, others.

Grimault, Paul (1905–). French animator.
Le Petit Soldat 47, many shorts.

Grimes, Gary (1955–). American juvenile lead of the seventies.
□*Summer of 42* 71. The Culpeper Cattle Co. 72. Class of 44 73. Cahill 73. The Spikes Gang 74. Once an Eagle (TV) 76. Gus 76.

Grimes, Stephen (–). American production designer.
Reflections in a Golden Eye 67. Ryan's Daughter 71. Murder by Death 76. The Electric Horseman 79. Urban Cowboy 80. Out of Africa 85, etc.

Grimes, Tammy (1934–). American comedy actress who never really made it in the movies.
□Three Bites of the Apple 67. Arthur Arthur 69. The Other Man (TV) 70. Play It As It Lays 72. The Borrowers (TV) 73. Horror at 37,000 Feet (TV) 73. Somebody Killed Her Husband 78. You Can't Go Home Again (TV) 79. The Runner Stumbles 79. Can't Stop the Music 80.

Grimm, Jakob (1785–1863) and **Wilhelm** (1786–1859). German writers of philology and—especially—fairy tales. The latter are familiar throughout the world and have been the basis of many children's films by Walt Disney and others. A thin biopic, *The Wonderful World of the Brothers Grimm*, was made in 1962.

Grimm, Oliver (1948–). German child actor of the fifties.
My Name is Nicki 52. Father Needs a Wife 52. My Father the Actor 56. Kleiner Mann – ganz gross 57, etc.

Grinde, Nick (1891–1979). American director.
Excuse Me 25. Upstage 26. Beyond the Sierra 28. *The Bishop Murder Case* 30. Good News 30. This Modern Age 31. Vanity Street 32. Ladies Crave Excitement 35. Public Enemy's Wife 36. White Bondage 37. King of Chinatown 39. The Man They Could Not Hang 39. Behind the Door 40. Hitler Dead or Alive 43. Road to Alcatraz 45, etc.

grip. A technician who builds or arranges the film set; a specialized labourer. The chief grip on a picture is usually credited as 'Key Grip'.

Grizzard, George (1925–). American stage actor, usually in sneaky roles in films.
From the Terrace 60. *Advise and Consent* 62. Warning Shot 66. Happy Birthday Wanda June 71. Travis Logan DA (TV) 71. Indict and Convict (TV) 74. The Stranger Within (TV) 74. Attack on Terror (TV) 75. The Lives of Jenny Dolan (TV) 75. Comes a Horseman 78. The Night Rider (TV) 79. Firepower 79. Seems Like Old Times 80.

Grock (1880–1959) (Adrien Wettach). Swiss clown who made a few silent films in Britain, and later in Germany. A biopic, *Farewell Mr Grock*, was made in 1954.

Grodin, Charles (1935–). American leading man.
□Rosemary's Baby 68. Sex and the College Girl 70. Catch 22 70. *The Heartbreak Kid* 72. 11 Harrowhouse 74. King Kong 76. Thieves 77. Heaven Can Wait 78. Just You and Me (TV) 78. The Grass Is Always Greener Over the Septic Tank (TV) 78. Sunburn 79. Real Life 79. It's My Turn 80. Seems Like Old Times 80. The Great Muppet Caper 81. The Incredible Shrinking Woman 81. The Lonely Guy 83. Movers and Shakers 84. The Woman in Red 84. The Last Resort 86.

¶ *Pauline Kael:* He keeps threatening to be funny but he rarely makes it.

Grosbard, Ulu (1929–). Belgian-American director, former diamond-cutter and Broadway director.
□The Subject Was Roses 68. Who Is Harry Kellerman and Why Is He Saying Those Terrible Things About Me? 71. Straight Time 78. True Confessions 81. Falling in Love 84.

Grossmith, George (1874–1935). British musical comedy star who appeared in a few films.
□ Women Everywhere 30. Service for Ladies 32. Wedding Rehearsal 32. The Girl from Maxim's 33. Princess Charming 34.

Grot, Anton (1884–1974) (Antocz Franziszek Groszewski). Polish art director, in Hollywood from the twenties: the driving force of Warner's thirties dream machine.
Robin Hood 20. The Thief of Bagdad 24. Don Q Son of Zorro 25. The Volga Boatmen 26. White Gold 27. Show Girl 28. Her Private Life 30. *Svengali* 31. *Little Caesar* 31. The Mad Genius 32. *Doctor X* 32. Gold Diggers of 1933 33. *The Mystery of the Wax Museum* 33. Captain Blood 35. Anthony Adverse 35. *A Midsummer Night's Dream* 35. The Life of Emile Zola 37. *Juarez* 39. *The Sea Hawk* 40. *The Sea Wolf* 41. The Conspirators 44. *Mildred Pierce* 45. *Possessed* 47. *The Unsuspected* 47. Backfire 50, many others.
❁ For putting his unmistakable stamp on so many films whose visuals linger in the memory. *The Mystery of the Wax Museum.*

The Group (US 1966). A faithful and entertaining film version of Mary McCarthy's immensely detailed novel about the lives of some young women graduates in the thirties. Sidney Buchman's script and Sidney Lumet's direction keep the stories nicely contrasted. Of a cast of near-unknowns, impressive performances come from Joan Hackett, Jessica Walter, Elizabeth Hartman, Kathleen Widdoes and others.

Group 3. A British production company set up in 1951 by the National Film Finance Corporation. In charge were John Baxter, John Grierson and Michael Balcon, and their aim was to make low-budget films employing young talent. The venture was regarded with suspicion by the trade, and the results were not encouraging—a string of mildly eccentric comedies and thrillers lucky to get second feature circuit bookings. Some of the titles: *Judgement Deferred, Brandy for the Parson, The Brave Don't Cry, You're Only Young Twice, The Oracle, Laxdale Hall, Time Gentlemen Please.*

Gruber, Frank (1904–1969). American screenwriter.
Death of a Champion (oa) 39. The Kansan (oa) 43. *The Mask of Dimitrios* 44. Terror by Night 47. Fighting Man of the Plains 49. The Great Missouri Raid 51. Denver and Rio Grande 52. Hurricane Smith 52. Backlash (oa) 56. The Big Land (oa) 57. Town Tamer 65. Arizona Raiders (oa) 67, etc.
TV: created *Tales of Wells Fargo.*

Gruenberg, Louis (1884–1964). Russian-American composer.
Stagecoach (co-w) 39.

Gruendgens, Gustav (1899–1963). German stage actor and director; films occasional.
M (a) 31. Pygmalion (a) 35. Capriolen (d) 37. Friedemann Bach (a) 41. Faust (ad) 61.

Grune, Karl (1890–1962). Czech-Austrian director in German films.
The Street 23. At the Edge of the World 27. Waterloo 28. Abdul the Damned (GB) 35. Pagliacci (GB) 37, etc.

Grusin, Dave (1934–). American composer.
Divorce American Style 67. The Graduate 67. Candy 68. The Mad Room 69. Tell them Willie Boy is Here 69. The Pursuit of Happiness 71. The Great Northfield Minnesota Raid 72. Bobby Deerfield 77. The Goodbye Girl 77. The Cheap Detective 78. And Justice for All 79. The Electric Horseman 79. My Bodyguard 80. On Golden Pond 81. Absence of Malice 81. Reds 81. The Little Drummer Girl 84. Falling in Love 84. The Goonies 85.

Guard, Dominic (1956–). British juvenile actor of the seventies.
The Go-Between 70. The Hands of Cormac Joyce (TV) 72. Bequest to the Nation 73. The Count of Monte Cristo (TV) 74. Picnic at Hanging Rock 75. Gandhi 82. A Woman of Substance (TV) 84.

Guardino, Harry (1925–). Leading American TV actor, in occasional films.
Houseboat 58. Pork Chop Hill 59. The Five Pennies 59. King of Kings 61. Hell is for Heroes 62. Rhino 64. Bullwhip Griffin 67. Madigan 68. Lovers and Other Strangers 69. Red Sky at Morning 71. Dirty Harry 71. Capone 75. St. Ives 76. The Enforcer 76. Street Killing (TV) 76. Rollercoaster 77. Goldengirl (TV) 79. Any Which Way You Can 80, etc.
TV series: The Reporter 64. Monty Nash 71.

Guareschi, Giovanni (1908–68). Italian author of the 'Don Camillo' stories about a parish priest's comic struggles with a communist mayor. Several were filmed with Fernandel and Gino Cervi.

Guess Who's Coming to Dinner (US 1967). A commercially successful sugar-coated race relations pill, showing the genteel and sympathetic reactions of an enlightened and wealthy couple to the news that their daughter is going to marry a distinguished black man. All bets are hedged, and the characters do little more than sit around and chat on a single set, but so much talent is involved that the effect is strangely enjoyable if traumatic. Spencer Tracy, whose last film this was, and Katharine Hepburn, who won an Academy Award for her performance, played the parents, with Sidney Poitier (who else?) as the bone of contention. William Rose (AA) wrote the screenplay; Stanley Kramer produced and directed with his usual bloodless competence.

Guest, Val (1911–) (Valmond Guest). British writer-producer-director, former journalist. Worked on screenplays of thirties comedies for Will Hay, Arthur Askey, the Crazy Gang, etc. Married to Yolande Donlan.
Screenplays mostly in collaboration, include: The Maid of the Mountains 32. Good Morning Boys 36. Okay for Sound 37. *Oh Mr Porter* 38. Convict 99 38. *Alf's Button Afloat* 38. Band Waggon 39. The Frozen Limits 39. Old Bones of the River 39. *Ask a Policeman* 40. Charley's Aunt 40. Gasbags 40. Inspector Hornleigh Goes to It 41. *The Ghost Train* 41. Back Room Boy 42. London Town 46. Paper Orchid 49.
□AS DIRECTOR (usually writer also): Miss London Ltd. 43. Bees in Paradise 44. Give Us the Moon 44. I'll Be Your Sweetheart 45. Just William's Luck 47. William Comes to Town 48. Murder at the Windmill 49. Miss Pilgrim's Progress 50. The Body Said No 50. *Mr Drake's Duck* 51. Penny Princess 52. *The Runaway Bus* 54. Life with the Lyons 54. Men of Sherwood Forest 54. Dance Little Lady 54. They Can't Hang Me 54. The Lyons in Paris 55. Break in the Circle 55. *The Quatermass Experiment* 55. It's A Wonderful World 55. The Weapon 56. Carry On Admiral 57. *Quatermass II* 57. The Abominable Snowman 57. Camp on Blood Island 58. Up the Creek 58. Life is a Circus 59. Yesterday's Enemy 59. *Expresso Bongo* 60. Further Up the Creek 60. Hell is a City 60. The Full Treatment 60. The Day the Earth Caught Fire 62. *Jigsaw* 63. 80,000 Suspects 63. The Beauty Jungle 64. Where the Spies are 65. Casino Royale (wd) 67. Assignment K 67. When Dinosaurs Ruled the World 68. Toomorrow 70. Au Pair Girls 72. Confessions of a Window Cleaner 74. The Diamond Mercenaries 76. Dangerous Davies (TV) 80. The Boys in Blue 83.

Guetary, Georges (1915–) (Lambros Worloou). Greek/Egyptian singer who became popular in French cabaret and musical comedy. Only American film: An American in Paris 51.

Guffey, Burnett (1905–1983). Distinguished American cinematographer.
Cover Girl 44. Johnny O'Clock 46. Gallant Journey 46. The Reckless Moment 48. *All the King's Men* 49. In a Lonely Place 50. The Sniper 52. *From Here to Eternity* (AA) 53. Human Desire 55. The Harder They Fall 56. Edge of Eternity 59. Birdman of Alcatraz 62. King Rat 65. *Bonnie and Clyde* (AA) 67. The Split 68. The Madwoman of Chaillot 69. The Great White Hope 70, etc.

Guilaroff, Sydney (1910–). American star hairdresser, long at MGM.

Guild, Nancy (1925–). American leading lady.
Somewhere in the Night 46. The High Window 47. Give My Regards to Broadway 49. Abbott and Costello Meet the Invisible Man 51. Francis Covers the Big Town 54. Such Good Friends 71, etc.

Guilfoyle, Paul (1902–1961). American character actor usually in sly or sinister roles.
Special Agent 36. Blind Alibi 38. Time to Kill 42. Sweetheart of Sigma Chi 46. Miss Mink of 1949. Mighty Joe Young 50. Torch Song 52. Julius Caesar 53. Valley of Fury 55, many others.
AS DIRECTOR: Captain Scarface 53. A Life at Stake 54. Tess of the Storm Country 60.

Guillaume, Robert (1930–). Handsome black American leading man and comedian, former opera singer.
Seems Like Old Times 80.
TV series: *Soap* 77–80. *Benson* 79–.

Guillermin, John (1925–). British director who started in second features and graduated to international spectaculars.
□Torment 49. Smart Alec 50. Two on the Tiles 51. Four Days 51. Song of Paris 52. Miss Robin Hood 52. Operation Diplomat 53. Adventure in the Hopfields 54. The Crowded Day 54. Thunderstorm 55. Double Jeopardy 55. *Town on Trial* 56. The Whole Truth 57. *I Was Monty's Double* 58. Tarzan's Greatest Adventure 59. The Day They Robbed The Bank of England 60. Never Let Go (& w) 60. Waltz of the Toreadors 62. Tarzan Goes to India 62. Guns at Batasi 64. Rapture 65. *The Blue Max* 66. P.J. 68. House of Cards 68. The Bridge at Remagen 69. El Condor 70. Skyjacked 72. Shaft in Africa 74. The Towering Inferno (co-d) 74. King Kong 76. Death on the Nile 78. Mr Patman 80. Crossover 83. Sheena Queen of the Jungle 84. King Kong Lives 86.

the guillotine, that French instrument of execution, cast its shadow over a variety of films including *Marie Antoinette, A Tale of Two Cities, Uncertain Glory, The Scarlet Pimpernel*, and *Mad Love*. The Carry On gang managed to make fun with it in *Don't Lose Your Head*. Private guillotines were employed for diabolical purposes in *The Mystery of the Wax Museum, House of Wax, Chamber of Horrors* and *Two on a Guillotine*.

Guinan, Texas (188*–1934) (Mary Louise Guinan). Canadian star entertainer of twenties speakeasies: her catchphrase was 'Hello, sucker!', and she was one of Broadway's most prominent attractions. Betty Hutton played her in *Incendiary Blonde* 45.
□The Gun Woman 18. Little Miss Deputy 19. I am the Woman 21. The Stampede 21. Queen of the Night Clubs 29. Glorifying the American Girl 29. Broadway through a Keyhole 33.

Guinness, Sir Alec (1914–). Distinguished British stage actor, who in the late forties started a spectacular film career, first as a master of disguise, then as a young hero and later as any character from an Arab king to Hitler. Special AA 1980.
Autobiography 1985: *Blessings in Disguise*.
□Evensong 33. Great Expectations (as Herbert Pocket) 46. *Oliver Twist* (as Fagin) 48. *Kind Hearts and Coronets* (playing eight roles) 49. A Run for Your Money 49. Last Holiday 50. *The Mudlark* (as Disraeli) 50. *The Lavender Hill Mob* 51. *The Man in the White Suit* 51. *The Card* 52. The Captain's Paradise 52. The Malta Story 53. *Father Brown* 54. To Paris with Love 54. The Prisoner 55. The Ladykillers 55. The Swan 56. Barnacle Bill 57. *The Bridge on the River Kwai* (AA, BFA) 57. The Scapegoat 58. The Horse's Mouth (& w) 58. Our Man in Havana 59. *Tunes of Glory* 60. A Majority of One 61. HMS Defiant 62. Lawrence of Arabia 62. The Fall of the Roman Empire 64. Situation Hopeless but Not Serious 64. Doctor Zhivago 66. Hotel Paradiso 66. The Quiller Memorandum 66. The Comedians 67. Cromwell (as Charles I) 69. Scrooge 70. Hitler: The Last Ten Days (as Hitler) 73.

Brother Sun and Sister Moon 73. Murder by Death 76. Star Wars 77. Tinker Tailor Soldier Spy (TV) 79. The Empire Strikes Back 80. Raise the Titanic 80. Little Lord Fauntleroy (TV) 80. Smiley's People (TV) 82. Lovesick 83. A Passage to India 84. Monsignor Quixote (TV) 85. Little Dorrit 87. A Handful of Dust 88.

❁ For a multitude of disguises in which he never allowed humanity to be swamped by dexterity. *Father Brown.*

† Honorary Oscar 1979 'for advancing the art of screen acting'.

¶ *A.G.:* I gave my best performances, perhaps, during the war—trying to be an officer and a gentleman.

A.G.: I don't know what else I could do but pretend to be an actor.

A.G.: Once I've done a film, it's finished. I never look at it again.

Guiol, Fred (1898–1964). American director, mainly of second features; also worked as assistant on many of George Stevens' pictures.
Live and Learn 30. The Cohens and Kellys in Trouble 33. The Nitwits 35. Hayfoot 41. Here Comes Trouble 48, many others.

Guitry, Sacha (1885–1957). Distinguished French writer-director, in films occasionally over a long period. Autobiography 1956: *If Memory Serves.* Biography 1968: *The Last Boulevardier* by James Harding.
Ceux de Chez Nous 15. Les Deux Couverts 32. Bonne Chance 35. Le Roman d'un Tricheur 36. Quadrille 38. Ils Etaient Neuf Célibataires 39. Donne-moi tes yeux 43. Le Comedien 49. Deburau 51. Versailles 54. Napoleon 55. La Vie à Deux 57, etc.

Gulager, Clu (c. 1929–). American leading man, mostly on TV.
The Killers (TV) 64. Winning 69. San Francisco International (TV) 70. The Last Picture Show 71. The Glass House (TV) 72. Footsteps (TV) 72. Call to Danger (TV) 73. McQ 74. The Killer Who Wouldn't Die (TV) 76. The Other Side of Midnight 77. A Force of One 79. Touched by Love 80. The Return of the Living Dead 85. Hunter's Blood 86, etc.
TV series: The Tall Man 60–61. The Virginian 64–68. The Survivors 69. San Francisco International 70.

Gulliver's Travels. Jonathan Swift's savage allegory was naturally seen by Hollywood as merely a child's fantasy. Max Fleischer's 1939 feature cartoon seemed at the time to have as much charm and skill as a Disney production, but it has worn disappointingly. Jack Sher's 1960 live action version, *The Three Worlds of Gulliver*, had neat trick work but a less than absorbing screenplay.

Gunfight at the OK Corral (US 1957). A somewhat psychologically-motivated version of the celebrated if semi-legendary confrontation between Wyatt Earp and the Clanton gang in 1881 at Tombstone, Arizona. Here Burt Lancaster was Earp, with Kirk Douglas as Doc Holliday, roles played in *My Darling Clementine* 46 by Henry Fonda and Victor Mature. Randolph Scott also played Earp in an earlier version, *Frontier Marshal* 39, and the TV series *Wyatt Earp* starred Hugh O'Brian.

Gunga Din. Rudyard Kipling's narrative poem of the northwest frontier was re-written in 1939 by Joel Sayre and Fred Guiol as a rousing combination of high adventure and barrack room comedy, directed by George Stevens and starring Douglas Fairbanks Jnr, Cary Grant and Victor McLaglen. In 1951 *Soldiers Three*, directed by Tay Garnett with Stewart Granger, David Niven and Walter Pidgeon, amounted almost to a remake; while in 1961 John Sturges directed Frank Sinatra, Dean Martin and Peter Lawford in a pastiche called *Sergeants Three*, set in the American west.

Gunn, Gilbert (c. 1912–). British director, former documentarist.
The Elstree Story 51. The Strange World of Planet X 57. Girls at Sea 58. Operation Bullshine 59. What a Whopper 62, etc.

Gunn, Moses (1929–). Black American actor.
The Great White Hope 70. Carter's Army (TV) 70. The Wild Rovers 71. Shaft 72. The Hot Rock 72. Haunts of the Very Rich (TV) 73. Rollerball 75. Remember My Name 78. The Ninth Configuration 80. Ragtime 81. Amityville II 82. Firestarter 84. Heartbreak Ridge 86.
TV series: Father Murphy 81.

The Guns of Navarone (GB 1961). Typical of the expensive multi-star action adventures of the early sixties, this entertaining yarn of World War II was reasonably suspenseful and certainly typical of the international co-productions of this time. A botched-up semi-sequel, *Force Ten from Navarone*, appeared in 1978.

Gurie, Sigrid (1911–1969) (S. G. Haukelid). American/Norwegian leading lady of the late thirties.
The Adventures of Marco Polo 38. Algiers 38. Rio 40. Three Faces West 40. Dark Streets of Cairo 41. A Voice in the Wind 44. Sword of the Avenger 48, etc.

Guthrie, A. B. (1901–). American adventure novelist. *These Thousand Hills* and *The Big Sky* became films.

Guthrie, Arlo (1947–). American ballad singer, son of another (Woody Guthrie, whose story was told in *Bound for Glory*). Major film appearance in *Alice's Restaurant*.

Gutowski, Gene (1925–). Polish producer with US TV experience.
Four Boys and a Gun 56. Station Six Sahara (GB) 63. Repulsion (GB) 65. Cul-de-Sac (GB) 66. The Fearless Vampire Killers (GB) 66, etc.

Guttenberg, Steve (1958–). American juvenile of the early eighties.
The Chicken Chronicles 77. Players 79. Diner 81. Police Academy 84. Police Academy II 85. Cocoon 85. Bad Medicine 85. Short Circuit 86. The Bedroom Window 86.

Guy-Blache, Alice (1873–1968). The first French woman director, at work in the early 1900s.
La Fée aux Choux 00. Le Voleur Sacrilège 03. Paris La Nuit 04. La Vie du Christ 06, etc.

Guzman, Pato (–). American production designer.
I Love You Alice B. Toklas 68. Bob and Carol and Ted and Alice 69. Alex in Wonderland 70. Blume in Love 73. An Unmarried Woman 78. The In-Laws 79. Hide in Plain Sight 80. Willie and Phil 80. Tempest 82.

Gwenn, Edmund (1875–1959). Stocky English stage actor who in middle age became a Hollywood film star and gave memorable comedy portrayals into his eighties.
□SILENT FILMS: The Real Thing at Last 16. Unmarried 20. The Skin Game 20.
□SOUND FILMS: How He Lied to Her Husband 31. Money for Nothing 31. Condemned to Death 31. Frail Women 31. Hindle Wakes 31. Tell Me Tonight 32. The Admiral's Secret 32. Love on Wheels 32. *The Skin Game* 32. *The Good Companions* 33. I Was a Spy 33. Early to Bed 33. Cash 33. Smithy 33. *Friday the Thirteenth* 33. Marooned 33. Java Head 34. Spring in the Air 34. Channel Crossing 34. Passing Shadows 34. Waltzes from Vienna 34. Father and Son 34. Warn London 34. The Bishop Misbehaves 35. Sylvia Scarlett 35. The Walking Dead 36. Anthony Adverse 36. All American Chump 36. Mad Holiday 36. *Laburnum Grove* 36. Parnell 37. A Yank at Oxford 38. *South Riding* 38. Penny Paradise 38. An Englishman's Home 38. Cheer Boys Cheer 39. The Earl of Chicago 40. Madmen of Europe 40. The Doctor Takes a Wife 40. *Pride and Prejudice* 40. *Foreign Correspondent* (rare villainous role) 40. Scotland Yard 41. Cheers for Miss Bishop 41. The Devil and Miss Jones 41. *Charley's Aunt* 41. One Night in Lisbon 41. A Yank at Eton 42. The Meanest Man in the World 43. Forever and a Day 43. *Lassie Come Home* 43. *Between Two Worlds* (his original 'Outward Bound' stage role) 44. The Keys of the Kingdom 45. Bewitched 45. Dangerous Partners 45. She Went to the Races 45. Of Human Bondage 46. Undercurrent 46. *Miracle on 34th Street* (AA) 47. Thunder in the Valley 47. Life with Father 47. Green Dolphin Street 47. Apartment for Peggy 48. Hills of Home 48. Challenge to Lassie 49. A Woman of Distinction 50. Louisa 50. *Pretty Baby* 50. *Mister 880* 50. For Heaven's Sake 50. Peking Express 51. Sally and St Anne 52. Bonzo Goes to College 52. Les Misérables 52. Something for the Birds 52. Mister Scoutmaster 52. The Bigamist 53. *Them* 54. The Student Prince 54. *The Trouble with Harry* 55. It's a Dog's Life 55. Calabuch 57.
❄ For having the talent for remaining a star into his eighties, and the discretion not always to insist on star billing. *Pride and Prejudice*.

Gwynn, Michael (1916–1976). British stage actor in occasional films.
The Runaway Bus 54. The Secret Place 57. The Revenge of Frankenstein (as the monster) 58. Village of the Damned 60. The Virgin Soldiers 69, etc.

Gwynne, Anne (1918–) (Marguerite Gwynne Trice). American leading lady of the forties, former model.
Sandy Takes a Bow 39. Jailhouse Blues 41. The Strange Case of Doctor RX 42. Weird Woman 44. House of Frankenstein 45. Fear 46. The Ghost Goes Wild 46. Dick Tracy Meets Gruesome 48. Call of the Klondike 51. Breakdown 52. The Meteor Monster 57, etc.

Gwynne, Fred (1926–). Lanky, lugubrious American comic actor who appeared in TV series Car 54 Where Are You? 61–62, and The Munsters 64–65.
On the Waterfront 54. Munster Go Home 66. Captains Courageous (TV) 77. La Luna 78. Simon 80. The Cotton Club 84. Fatal Attraction 87, etc.

Gynt, Greta (1916–) (Greta Woxholt). Norwegian leading lady, popular in British films of the forties.
The Arsenal Stadium Mystery 39. Dark Eyes of London 39. The Common Touch 41. Tomorrow We Live 42. It's That Man Again 42. Mr Emmanuel 44. London Town 46. Dear Murderer 47. Take My Life 47. The Calendar 48. Mr Perrin and Mr Traill 48. Shadow of the Eagle 50. Soldiers Three (US) 51. Forbidden Cargo 54. Bluebeard's Ten Honeymoons 60. The Runaway 66, others.

gypsies have not been a favourite subject for movies but glamorized versions have turned up in *Gypsy Wildcat, Golden Earrings, Caravan, Hot Blood*, and *The Man in Grey*. Something closer to the real thing, perhaps, was on view in *Sky West and Crooked, The Gypsy and the Gentleman,* and *Alex and the Gypsy,* while TV failed to get going a gypsy detective series called *Roman Grey*. The screen's most memorable gypsy was probably Maria Ouspenskaya as Maleva in *The Wolf Man* and *Frankenstein Meets the Wolf Man.* The most authentic were probably in Hungary's *I Even Met Happy Gypsies.*

Answers

Clark Gable
1 *No Man of Her Own* ☐ 2 *Cain and Mabel* ☐ 3 *Strange Cargo* ☐ 4 *Across the Wide Missouri* ☐ 5 *Homecoming* ☐ 6 *Adventure* ☐ 7 *The Painted Desert* ☐ 8 *It Happened One Night* ☐ 9 *China Seas* ☐ 10 *San Francisco* ☐ 11 *Idiot's Delight* ☐ 12 *Parnell* ☐ 13 *Comrade X* ☐ *Never Let Me Go* ☐ 14 *Too Hot to Handle* ☐ 15 *The Hucksters* ☐ 16 *Key to the City* ☐ 17 *Lone Star* ☐ 18 *But Not for Me* ☐ (a remake of *Accent on Youth* and *Mr Music*) 19 *They Met in Bombay* ☐ 20 *The White Sister* ☐

gazetteer
1 *Jamaica* ☐ 2 *Arabia* ☐ 3 *America* ☐ 4 *Algeria* ☐ 5 *Shanghai* ☐ 6 *Paris* ☐ 7 *Hollywood* ☐ 8 *Calais* ☐ 9 *Mexico* ☐ 10 *Berlin* ☐ 11 *Moscow* ☐ 12 *West Point* ☐ 13 *Tahiti* ☐ 14 *Brighton* ☐ 15 *Moscow* ☐ 16 *Munich* ☐ 17 *Madrid* ☐ 18 *New York* ☐ 19 *Paris* ☐ 20 *Ireland* ☐ 21 *Frisco* ☐ 22 *Bataan* ☐ 23 *San Diego* ☐ 24 *Frisco* ☐ 25 *Trinidad* ☐

Haanstra, Bert (1916–). Dutch documentarist.
Mirror of Holland 50. The Rival World 55. Rembrandt Painter of Man 56. Glass 58. Fanfare (feature) 58. Zoo 62. The Human Dutch 64. The Voice of the Water 66, etc.

Haas, Charles (1918–). American director.
□Star in the Dust 56. Screaming Eagles 56. Showdown at Abilene 56. Summer Love 58. Wild Heritage 58. The Beat Generation 59. The Big Operator 59. Girls' Town 59. Platinum High School 60.

Haas, Dolly (1910–). German leading lady of the thirties, in a few international films.
Dolly's Way to Stardom 30. Liebes-commando 32. Der Page vom Dalmasse Hotel 34. *Broken Blossoms* (GB) 36. Spy of Napoleon (GB) 37. I Confess (US) 53, etc.

Haas, Hugo (1901–1968). Czech character actor, in Hollywood from the late thirties; later took to writing and directing low-budget melodramas as vehicles for himself.
Skeleton on Horseback 39. Summer Storm 44. A Bell for Adano 45. Dakota 45. Holiday in Mexico 46. The Foxes of Harrow 47. My Girl Tisa 48. King Solomon's Mines 50. Vendetta 50. The Girl on the Bridge (& wd) 51. Pickup (& wd) 51. Strange Fascination (& wd) 52. Thy Neighbour's Wife (& wd) 53. Hold Back Tomorrow (& wd) 55. The Other Woman (& wd) 55. Edge of Hell (& wd) 56. *Lizzie* (& wd) 57. Born to be Loved (& wd) 59. Night of the Quarter Moon (& wd) 59. Paradise Alley (& wd) 61, etc.

Hackathorne, George (1895–1940). American light actor of the later silents.
The Little Minister 21. The Last of the Mohicans 20. Merry Go Round 23. Magnificent Obsession 35. Gone with the Wind 39, many others.

Hackett, Albert (1900–). American writer, usually with his wife Frances Goodrich (qv).

Hackett, Buddy (1924–) (Leonard Hacker). Tubby American comedian with vaudeville experience.
Walking My Baby Back Home 53. God's Little Acre 58. *The Music Man* 62. *It's a Mad Mad Mad Mad World* 63. The Golden Head 65. The Love Bug 69. The Good Guys and the Bad Guys 69. Bud and Lou (TV) 78, etc.
TV series: Stanley 56.

Hackett, Joan (1934–1983). American leading lady usually seen in unglamorous roles.
□*The Group* 66. Will Penny 67. Support Your Local Sheriff 69. Assignment to Kill 69. The Other Man (TV) 70. How Awful About Allan (TV) 70. The Young Country (TV) 71. Five Desperate Women (TV) 71. The Rivals 73. The Last of Sheila 73. Class of 63 (TV) 73. Reflections of Murder (TV) 74. The Terminal Man 74. Mackintosh and T. J. 75. Treasure of Matecumbe 76. Stonestreet (TV) 77. The Possessed (TV) 77. Pleasure Cove (TV) 79. Mr Mike's Mondo Video 79. The North Avenue Irregulars 79. One Trick Pony 80. The Long Days of Summer (TV) 80. Only When I Laugh 81. The Long Summer of George Adams (TV) 82. The Escape Artist 82.

Hackett, Raymond (1902–1958). American leading man who had brief popularity during the changeover from silent to sound.
The Loves of Sunya 28. Madame X 29. Our Blushing Brides 29. The Trial of Mary Dugan 30. The Sea Wolf 30. The Cat Creeps 31. Seed 31, etc.

Hackford, Taylor
An Officer and a Gentleman 83. Against All Odds 84. White Nights 86.

Hackman, Gene (1930–). Virile American character actor who unexpectedly became a star of the early seventies.
□Mad Dog Coll 61. Lilith 64. Hawaii 66. First to Fight 67. A Covenant with Death 67. Banning 67. *Bonnie and Clyde* 67. The Split 68. Shadow on the Land (TV) 68. Riot 69. Downhill Racer 69. *I Never Sang For My Father* 69. The Gypsy Moths 69. Marooned 70. Doctors' Wives 71. The Hunting Party 71. *The French Connection* (AA) 71. Cisco Pike 72. Prime Cut 72. The Poseidon Adventure 72. The Conversation 73. Scarecrow 73.

Zandy's Bride 74. Young Frankenstein 74. Bite the Bullet 75. French Connection II 75. Lucky Lady 75. Night Moves 76. The Domino Principle 77. A Bridge Too Far 77. March or Die 77. Superman 78. Superman II 80. All Night Long 81. Reds 81. Eureka 83.

Two of a Kind 83. Uncommon Valor 83. Under Fire 83. Misunderstood 84. Target 85. Twice in a Lifetime 85. Hoosiers 86. No Way Out 87. Superman IV 87.

¶ *G.H.*: People in the street still call me Popeye, and *The French Connection* was 15 years ago. I wish I could have another hit and a new nickname.

Hackney, Alan (1924–). British comedy writer.
Private's Progress 55. I'm All Right, Jack 59. Two-way Stretch (c-w) 60. Swordsman of Siena 62. You Must Be Joking 65, etc.

Haddon, Peter (1898–1962) (Peter Tildsley). British light actor, usually in silly-ass roles.
Death at Broadcasting House 34. The Silent Passenger (as Lord Peter Wimsey) 35. Kate Plus Ten 38. Helter Skelter 49. The Second Mrs Tanqueray 54, etc.

Haden, Sara (1897–1981). American actress of quiet, well-spoken parts, best remembered as the spinster aunt of the Hardy family.
Spitfire (debut) 34. Magnificent Obsession 35. First Lady 38. H. M. Pulham Esquire 41. Lost Angel 43. Mr Ace 45. Our Vines Have Tender Grapes 45. She-Wolf of London (as villainess) 46. The Bishop's Wife 48. A Life of her Own 50. A Lion is in the Streets 53. Andy Hardy Comes Home 58, many others.

Hadjidakis, Manos (1925–). Greek composer.
Stella 55. A Matter of Dignity 57. *Never On Sunday* (AA) 59. America America 63. Blue 68, etc.

Hadley, Reed (1911–1974) (Reed Herring). American 'second lead'.
Fugitive Lady 38. The Bank Dick 41. Guadalcanal Diary 43. Leave Her to Heaven 46. The Iron Curtain 48. Captain from Castile 49. Dallas 51. Big House USA 55. The St Valentine's Day Massacre 68, etc.
TV series: Racket Squad 51–53. Public Defender 53–54.

Hageman, Richard (1882–1966). Dutch-American composer.
Stagecoach 39. Paris Calling 40. The Fugitive 47. Fort Apache 48. She Wore a Yellow Ribbon 48. Three Godfathers 49. Wagonmaster 50, etc.

Hagen, Jean (1924–77) (Jean Verhagen). American comedy character actress, usually of Brooklynesque dames; also minor leading lady.
□Side Street 49. *Adam's Rib* 49. Ambush 50. The Asphalt Jungle 50. A Life of Her Own 50. Night into Morning 50. No Questions Asked 51. *Singin' In the Rain* (a splendid performance as the silent star with the ghastly voice) 52. Shadow in the Sky 52. Carbine Williams 52. Latin Lovers 53. Arena 53. Half a Hero 53. The Big Knife 55. Spring Reunion 57. The Shaggy Dog 59. Sunrise at Campobello 60. Panic in Year Zero 62. Dead Ringer 64.
TV series: Make Room for Daddy 53–55.
Famous line (*Singin' in the Rain*): If we bring a little joy into your humdrum lives, we feel all out hard work ain't been in vain for nothin'.

Haggar, William (1851–1924). British pioneer producer, a former fairground showman who made short sensational films featuring himself and his family.
The Maniac's Guillotine 02. The Wild Man of Borneo 02. Mirthful Mary 03. A Dash for Liberty 03. The Sign of the Cross 04. The Life of Charles Peace 05. Desperate Footpads 07. Maria Marten 08. The Dumb Man of Manchester 08, etc.

Haggard, Sir H. Rider (1856–1925). British adventure novelist, whose most famous novel, *She*, has been filmed at least nine times. There have also been two versions of *King Solomon's Mines*, and two lightly disguised variants, *Watusi* and *King Solomon's Treasure*.

Haggard, Piers (1939–). British director.
Wedding Night 69. Satan's Skin 70. Pennies from Heaven (TV) 78. The Fiendish Plot of Dr Fu Manchu 80. Venom 82, etc.

Haggerty, Dan (1941–). Hefty American leading man, notably on TV in *The Legend of Grizzly Adams*.
The Tender Warrior 70. Hex 73. When the North Wind Blows 74. Starbird and Sweet William 75. Frontier Freemont 76. Desperate Women (TV) 79. Condominium (TV) 80, etc.

Hagman, Larry (1930–). American comedy leading man, much on TV; son of Mary Martin.
Ensign Pulver 64. Fail Safe 64. In Harm's

Way 65. The Group 65. Vanished (TV) 70. Up in the Cellar 70. Beware the Blob (TV) 71. A Howling in the Woods (TV) 72. The Alpha Caper (TV) 73. Stardust 74. Harry and Tonto 74. Mother Jugs and Speed 76. The Eagle Has Landed 76. Crash 77, etc.
TV series: *I Dream of Jeannie* 65–70. The Good Life 71. Here We Go Again 71. *Dallas* 78– .

¶ *L.H.:* People I meet really want me to be J.R., so it's hard to disappoint them.
L.H.: I was born with success. Lucky for me. I am able to handle it. Also, I damn well deserve it!

Hagmann, Stuart (1939–). American director.
The Strawberry Statement 70. Believe in Me 71, etc.

Haigh, Kenneth (1929–). British stage actor, the original lead of *Look Back in Anger*, has tended to remain in angry young man roles.
My Teenage Daughter 56. High Flight 56. Saint Joan 57. Cleopatra 63. A Hard Day's Night 64. The Deadly Affair 66. A Lovely Way to Die (US) 68. Eagle in a Cage 71. Man at the Top 73. The Bitch 79, etc.
TV series: *Man at the Top* 71–73.

Hailey, Arthur (1920–). American novelist who rigorously researches specific milieux and weaves a plot through them. Films of his work include *Hotel*, *Airport*, *The Moneychangers*, *Wheels*, *Flight into Danger* (which became *Zero Hour* and was parodied as *Airplane*).

Haines, William (1900–1973). American leading man of the silents.
Three Wise Fools 23. Tower of Lies 24. Brown of Harvard 25. Tell It to the Marines 27. Alias Jimmy Valentine 28. Navy Blues 30. The Adventures of Get-Rich-Quick Wallingford 31. The Fast Life 33. The Marines Are Coming 35, etc.

Hakim, André (1915–). Egyptian-born producer, long in US.
Mr Belvedere Rings the Bell 52. The Man Who Never Was 56, etc.

Hakim, Robert (1907–) and **Raymond** (1909–1980). Egyptian-born brothers who were in and out of film production from 1927.
Pepe Le Moko 36. La Bête Humaine 38. Le Jour Se Lève 39. The Southerner 44. Her Husband's Affairs 47. The Long Night 47. The Blue Veil 52. Belle de Jour 67. Isadora 68, many others.

Halas, John (1912–). Hungarian-born animator, long in Britain producing in association with his wife Joy Batchelor (1914–) a stream of efficient short cartoons, many sponsored by official organizations.
FEATURES: *Animal Farm* 54. Ruddigore 67.

Hale, Alan (1892–1950) (Rufus Alan McKahan). Jovial American actor, a hero of silent action films from 1911 and a familiar cheerful figure in scores of talkies.
The Cowboy and the Lady (debut) 11. The Four Horsemen of the Apocalypse 21. Robin Hood (as Little John) 22. The Covered Wagon 23. Main Street 24. She Got What She Wanted 27. The Rise of Helga 30. So Big 32. It Happened One Night 34. The Last Days of Pompeii 35. Jump for Glory (GB) 36. Stella Dallas 37. *The Adventures of Robin Hood* (as Little John) 38. Dodge City 39. The Man in the Iron Mask 40. The Sea Hawk 40. Tugboat Annie Sails Again 41. *Strawberry Blonde* 41. Manpower 41. *Desperate Journey* 42. Action in the North Atlantic 43. Destination Tokyo 44. Hotel Berlin 45. Escape in the Desert 45. Night and Day 45. My Wild Irish Rose 47. Pursued 48. The New Adventures of Don Juan 48. *My Girl Tisa* 49. Rogues of Sherwood Forest (as Little John) 50, many others.
❀ For innumerable stalwart performances, including three as Little John. *The Adventures of Robin Hood*.

Hale, Alan, Jnr (1918–). American character actor who bids fair to be his father's double.
To the Shores of Tripoli 42. One Sunday Afternoon 48. The Gunfighter 50. The Big Trees 52. Rogue Cop 54. Young at Heart 54. The Indian Fighter 55. The Killer is Loose 56, many others.
TV series: *Casey Jones* 57. *Gilligan's Island* 64–66.

Hale, Barbara (1922–). Pleasant American leading lady of the forties.
Higher and Higher 43. The Falcon in Hollywood 44. First Yank into Tokyo 45. Lady Luck 46. The Boy with Green Hair 48. The Window 48. *Jolson Sings Again* 49. The Jackpot 50. Lorna Doone 51. A Lion is in the Streets 53. Unchained 54. The Far Horizons 55. The Oklahoman 57. Airport 69, many others.
TV series: *Perry Mason* (as Della Street) 57–65.

Hale, Binnie (1899–1984) (Beatrice Mary Hale-Monro). British revue comedienne of the thirties, sister of Sonnie Hale. Films rare.
This is the Life 34. The Phantom Light 35. Hyde Park Corner 36. Love from a Stranger 37. Take a Chance 37.

Hale, Creighton (1882–1965) (Patrick Fitzgerald). American leading man of the twenties, sometimes in meek-and-mild comedy roles.
The Exploits of Elaine 15. The Thirteenth Chair 19. Way Down East 20. Trilby (as Little Billee) 23. *The Marriage Circle* 24. The Circle 25. Beverly of Graustark 26. Annie Laurie 27. *The Cat and the Canary* 27. Rose Marie 28. Holiday 30. The Masquerader 33. Hollywood Boulevard 36. The Return of Dr X 39. The Gorilla Man 42. Bullet Scars 45. The Perils of Pauline 47, many others.

Hale, Georgia (1903–). American leading lady of the twenties.
The Gold Rush 24. The Salvation Hunters 25. The Great Gatsby 26. The Last Moment 48, etc.

Hale, Georgina (1943–). Generally strident British actress.
Eagle in a Cage 70. The Devils 71. Mahler 74. Sweeney 2 78. The World Is Full of Married Men 78. McVicar 80. The Watcher in the Woods 80. Castaway 86, etc.

Hale, Jonathan (1892–1966) (J. Hatley). American character actor, former consular attaché, in films from 1934, usually as mildly exasperated business man or hero's boss.
Lightning Strikes Twice 34. Alice Adams 35. Fury 36. The Blondie series (as Mr Dithers) 38–50. Her Jungle Love 39. Johnny Apollo 40. Call Northside 777 48. The Steel Trap 52. The Night Holds Terror 56. Jaguar 58, many others.

Hale, Louise Closser (1872–1933). American character actress with long stage experience.
The Hole in the Wall 29. Dangerous Nan McGrew 30. Platinum Blonde 31. Rasputin and the Empress 33. Shanghai Express 32. Today We Live 33. Dinner at Eight 33, etc.

Hale, Monte (1919–). American western star of the forties. Mostly with Republic.
Home on the Range 47. South of Rio 48. Rainbow Valley 49. The Missourians 50. Giant 56. The Chase 66, many others.

Hale, Richard (1893–1981). American supporting actor.
The Other Love 47. All the King's Men 50. Scaramouche 52. Julius Caesar 53. Moonfleet 55. Pillars of the Sky 56. Ben Hur 59. Sergeants Three 62, etc.

Hale, Sonnie (1902–1959) (John Robert Hale-Monro). British light comedian of the thirties, mostly on stage.
□ On with the Dance 27. The Parting of the Ways 27. Tell me Tonight 32. Happy Ever After 32. Friday the Thirteenth 33. Early to Bed 33. Evergreen 34. Wild Boy 34. My Song for You 34. My Heart is Calling 34. Are You a Mason? 34. Marry the Girl 35. First a Girl 35. It's Love Again 36. Head over Heels (d only) 37. Gangway (d only) 37. Sailing Along (d only) 38. The Gaunt Stranger 38. Let's Be Famous 39. Fiddlers Three 44. London Town 46.
† *A French Mistress* 60 was based on his play.

Hale, William (1928–). American director, from TV.
The Naked Hunt 58. Gunfight in Abilene 66. Journey to Shiloh 67, etc.

Hale's Tours. In 1902 at the St Louis Exposition, George C. Hale, ex-chief of the Kansas City Fire Department, had the bright idea of shooting a film from the back of a moving train and screening the result in a small theatre decorated like an observation car. During the screening bells clanged, train whistles sounded and the 'coach' rocked slightly. The idea was so successful that it toured for several years in the United States.

Haley, Bill (1926–1981). American rock-and-roll musician and bandleader; Bill Haley and his Comets provided the title music for *The Blackboard Jungle* and starred in *Rock around the Clock*, which caused cinema riots in 1956.

Haley, Jack (1899–1979). Diffident American light comedian, popular in the thirties and forties.
Follow Thru 30. Sitting Pretty 33. The Girl Friend 35. *Poor Little Rich Girl* 36. Wake Up and Live 37. Pick a Star 37. Rebecca of Sunnybrook Farm 38. *Alexander's Ragtime Band* 38. Hold that Co-Ed 38. *The Wizard of Oz* (as the Tin Man) 39. Moon over Miami 41. Beyond the Blue Horizon 42. F Man 42. Higher and Higher 43. Scared Stiff 44. George White's Scandals 45. People are Funny 45. Vacation in Reno 47. Norwood 69, etc.

Haley, Jack Jnr (1934–). American executive, best known for marrying Liza Minnelli and assembling *That's Entertainment*. Directed *Norwood* 69 and *The Love Machine* 71.

Haley, Jackie Earle (1961–). American juvenile of the seventies.
The Day of the Locust 74. Damnation Alley 75. The Bad News Bears 76. The Bad News Bears in Breaking Training 77. Breaking Away 79, etc.

Hall, Alexander (1894–1968). American director from 1932, previously on Broadway.
□Sinners in the Sun 32. Madame Racketeer 32. The Girl in 419 33. Midnight Club 33. Torch Singer 33. Miss Fane's Baby is Stolen 34. Little Miss Marker 34. The Pursuit of Happiness 34. Limehouse Blues 34. Going to Town 35. Annapolis Farewell 35. Give Us This Night 36. Yours for the Asking 36. Exclusive 37. There's Always a Woman 38. I am the Law 38. There's That Woman Again 38. The Lady's From Kentucky 39. Good Girls Go to Paris 39. The Amazing Mr Williams 39. The Doctor Takes a Wife 40. He Stayed for Breakfast 40. This Thing Called Love 40. *Here Comes Mr Jordan* 41. Bedtime Story 41. They All Kissed the Bride 42. My Sister Eileen 42. The Heavenly Body 43. Once Upon a Time 44. She Wouldn't Say Yes 45. Down to Earth 47. The Great Lover 49. Love that Brute 50. Louisa 50. Up Front 51. Because You're Mine 52. Let's Do it Again 53. Forever Darling 56.

Hall, Anthony Michael (1968–). American juvenile of the mid-eighties.
Sixteen Candles 84. The Breakfast Club 85. Weird Science 85. Out of Bounds 86.

Hall, Charles (1899–1959). American character actor, often in comedy two-reelers; memorable as the victim of many a Laurel and Hardy mishap culminating in a tit-for-tat disaster.

Hall, Charles, D. (1899–1968). British-born production designer, long in Hollywood; a a key craftsman of his time.
The Gold Rush 24. *The Phantom of the Opera* 25. The Cohens and the Kellys 26. *The Cat and the Canary* 27. The Man Who Laughs 28. The Circus 28. The Last Warning 29. *Broadway* 29. *All Quiet on the Western Front* 30. *Dracula* 30. *Frankenstein* 31. City Lights 32. *The Old Dark House* 32. *The Invisible Man* 33. By Candlelight 33. *The Bride of Frankenstein* 35. The Good Fairy 35. Showboat 36. *Modern Times* 36. My Man Godfrey 36. Captain Fury 39. Big House USA 55, etc.
❁ For bringing to Hollywood Gothic a mixture of English and German artistic sensibilities.

Hall, Conrad L. (1926–). American cinematographer.
Morituri 65. Harper 66. The Professionals 66. *Cool Hand Luke* 67. In Cold Blood 67. Hell in the Pacific 69. *Butch Cassidy and the Sundance Kid* 69. Tell Them Willie Boy is Here 69. The Happy Ending 70. Fat City 72. Marathon Man 76. Black Widow 87, etc.

Hall, Grayson (–1985). American stage actress remembered for one film performance, in *Night of the Iguana* 64.

Hall, Henry (1898–). British bandleader of the thirties, popular on radio. Appeared in a few films including *Music Hath Charms* 36. Autobiography 1955: *Here's to the Next Time*.

Hall, Huntz (1920–) (Henry Hall). Long-faced American character actor, the 'dumb-bell' second lead of the original Dead End Kids and later of the Bowery Boys.
Dead End 37. Crime School 38. Angels with Dirty Faces 38. The Return of Doctor X 39. Give Us Wings 40. Spooks Run Wild 41. Private Buckaroo 42. Wonder Man 45. Bowery Bombshell 46. Bowery Buckaroos 47. Jinx Money 48. Angels in Disguise 49. Lucky Losers 50. Ghost Chasers 51. No Holds Barred 52. Loose in London 53. Paris Playboys 54. High Society 55. Dig That Uranium 56. Spook Chasers 57. In the Money 58. The Gentle Giant 67. The Love Bug Rides Again 73. The Escape Artist 82, many others.
TV series: Chicago Teddy Bears 71.

Hall, James (1900–1940) (James Brown). American leading man of the early talkie period.
The Campus Flirt 26. Stranded in Paris 27. Rolled Stockings 27. Four Sons 28. Smiling Irish Eyes 29. The Canary Murder Case 29. The Saturday Night Kid 29. Dangerous Nan McGrew 30. *Hells Angels* 30. Millie 31. The Good Bad Girl 31. Divorce Among Friends 31. Manhattan Tower 33, etc.

Hall, Jon (1913–1979) (Charles Locher). Athletic American leading man who became a star in his first year as an actor but whose roles gradually diminished in stature; he retired to a photography business.

Charlie Chan in Shanghai 36. Mind Your Own Business 36. The Girl from Scotland Yard 37. *The Hurricane* 37. Kit Carson 40. South of Pago Pago 40. Aloma of the South Seas 41. Eagle Squadron 42. Invisible Agent 42. Arabian Nights 42. White Savage 43. Ali Baba and the Forty Thieves 44. Cobra Woman 44. The Invisible Man's Revenge 44. San Diego I Love You 45. Sudan 45. The Michigan Kid 47. Last of the Redmen 47. Prince of Thieves 48. Deputy Marshal 49. Hurricane Island 50. When the Redskins Rode 51. Last Train from Bombay 52. The Beachgirls and the Monster (& d) 65. Five the Hard Way (co-p & ph only) 69, etc.
TV series: Ramar of the Jungle 52–53.

Hall, Juanita (1901–1968). American black character actress and singer, best remembered in the stage and screen versions of *South Pacific* (as Bloody Mary) and *Flower Drum Song*.

Hall, Sir Peter (1930–). British theatrical producer who ventured into films.
Published 1983: *Peter Hall's Diaries*.
□Work is a Four-Letter Word 68. A Midsummer Night's Dream 68. Three Into Two Won't Go 69. Perfect Friday 70. The Homecoming 73. Akenfield 74.

Hall, Porter (1888–1953). Wry-faced American character actor with stage experience before settling in Hollywood.
□*The Thin Man* 34. Murder in the Private Car 34. The Case of the Lucky Legs 35. The Story of Louis Pasteur 35. The Petrified Forest 36. Too Many Parents 36. The Princess Comes Across 36. And Sudden Death 36. *The General Died at Dawn* 36. Satan Met a Lady 36. The Plainsman 36. Snowed Under 36. Let's Make a Million 37. Bulldog Drummond Escapes 37. Souls at Sea 37. Make Way for Tomorrow 37. King of Gamblers 37. Hotel Haywire 37. This Way Please 37. True Confession 37. Wild Money 37. Wells Fargo 37. Scandal Street 38. Stolen Heaven 38. Dangerous to Know 38. Bulldog Drummond's Peril 38. Prison Farm 38. King of Alcatraz 38. The Arkansas Traveller 38. Men with Wings 38. Tom Sawyer Detective 38. Mr Smith Goes to Washington 39. Grand Jury Secrets 39. They Shall Have Music 39. His Girl Friday 40. Dark Command 40. Arizona 40. Trail of the Vigilantes 40. Sullivan's Travels 41. The Parson of Panamint 41. Mr and Mrs North 41. The Remarkable Andrew 42. Butch Minds the Baby 42. A Stranger in Town 43. The Desperadoes 43. Woman of the Town 43. Standing Room Only 44. The Miracle of Morgan's Creek 44. Going My Way 44. Double Indemnity 44. The Great Moment 44. Mark of the Whistler 44. Blood on the Sun 45. Bring on the Girls 45. Kiss and Tell 45. *Murder He Says* 45. Weekend at the Waldorf 45. Unconquered 47. Miracle on 34th Street 47. Singapore 47. You Gotta Stay Happy 48. That Wonderful Urge 48. The Beautiful Blonde from Bashful Bend 49. *Intruder in the Dust* 49. Chicken Every Sunday 49. *Ace in the Hole* 51. The Half Breed 52. Carbine Williams 52. Holiday for Sinners 52. Pony Express 53. Vice Squad 53. Return to Treasure Island 54.

Hall, Thurston (1883–1958). American character actor adept at choleric executives. Long stage experience; ran his own touring companies.
Cleopatra (as Mark Antony) 18. Theodora Goes Wild 36. Professor Beware 38. The Great McGinty 40. He Hired the Boss 43. Brewster's Millions 45. The Secret Life of Walter Mitty 47. Affair in Reno 56, scores of others.
TV series: Topper 53–54.

Hall, Willis (1929–). British playwright and screenwriter (in collaboration with Keith Waterhouse).
The Long and the Short and the Tall 61. Whistle Down the Wind 61. A Kind of Loving 62. Billy Liar 63, etc.

Hallatt, May (1882–*). British character actress, mainly on stage.
No Funny Business 33. The Lambeth Walk 39. Painted Boats 45. *Black Narcissus* 46. The Pickwick Papers 52. *Separate Tables* 58. Make Mine Mink 60, etc.

Hallelujah (US 1929). This famous film, directed by King Vidor, was probably the first serious screen treatment of Negro life, but despite an all-coloured cast it now seems exaggerated, patronizing and sentimental. The story concerns a Negro murderer who becomes a priest.

Haller, Daniel (1928–). American director, former art director on Roger Corman's Poe films, etc.
□Die Monster Die 67. The Devil's Angels 68. The Wild Racers 68. Paddy 70. The Dunwich Horror 70. Pieces of Dreams 70. The Desperate Miles (TV) 75. Sword of Justice (TV pilot) 78. Little Women (TV) 78. Little Mo (TV) 78.

Haller, Ernest (1896–1970). Distinguished American cinematographer.

Neglected Wives 20. Outcast 22. Stella Dallas 25. Weary River 29. The Dawn Patrol 31. The Emperor Jones 33. Dangerous 35. Jezebel 38. *Gone with the Wind* (AA) 39. Dark Victory 39. All This and Heaven Too 40. Saratoga Trunk 43. Mr Skeffington 44. *Mildred Pierce* 45. Humoresque 46. *My Girl Tisa* 47. The Flame and the Arrow 50. Rebel without a Cause 55. Back from the Dead 57. God's Little Acre 58. Man of the West 58. The Third Voice 59. Whatever Happened to Baby Jane? 62. Lilies of the Field 64. Dead Ringer 64, many others.

Halliday, John (1880–1947). Suave and dapper Scottish actor, long in Hollywood. □The Woman Gives 20. East Side Sadie 29. Father's Sons 30. Recaptured Love 30. Scarlet Pages 30. Smart Women 31. Consolation Marriage 31. The Ruling Voice 31. Millie 31. Once a Sinner 31. Captain Applejack 31. Fifty Million Frenchmen 31. The Spy 31. Transatlantic 31. Men of Chance 32. The Impatient Maiden 32. The Age of Consent 32. Weekends Only 32. Bird of Paradise 32. Perfect Understanding 33. Terror Aboard 33. Bed of Roses 33. The House on 56th Street 33. Woman Accused 33. Return of the Terror 34. Housewife 34. A Woman's Man 34. Happiness Ahead 34. Registered Nurse 34. The Witching Hour 34. Desirable 34. Finishing School 34. Mystery Woman 35. The Dark Angel 35. The Melody Lingers On 35. Peter Ibbetson 35. *Desire* 36. Fatal Lady 36. Three Cheers for Love 36. *Hollywood Boulevard* 36. Arsene Lupin Returns 38. Blockade 38. That Certain Age 39. The Light that Failed 39. Hotel for Women 39. Intermezzo 39. *The Philadelphia Story* 40. Lydia 41. Escape to Glory 41.
Famous line (*The Philadelphia Story*): 'What most wives fail to realise is that their husbands' philandering has nothing to do with *them*.'

Halop, Billy (1920–1976). American actor, the erstwhile leader of the Dead End Kids: stardom failed to materialize, and he descended to bit parts.
Dead End 37. Crime School 38. Little Tough Guy 38. Angels with Dirty Faces 38. You Can't Get Away with Murder 39. Angels Wash Their Faces 39. Call a Messenger 39. Tom Brown's Schooldays 40. Hit the Road 41. Mob Town 41. Junior Army 43. Dangerous Years 47. Mister Buddwing 66. Fitzwilly 66, many others.
TV series; All in the Family 72–76.

Halperin, Victor (1895–*). American director.
Party Girl 29. Ex Flame 30. *White Zombie* 32. Supernatural 33. I Conquer the Sea 36. Revolt of the Zombies 36. Nation Aflame 37. Torture Ship 39. Buried Alive 40. Girls' Town 42.

Halsey, Brett (–). American leading man.
The Glass Web 53. Ma and Pa Kettle at Home 54. Cry Baby Killer 58. The Best of Everything 59. Desire in the Dust 60. Return to Peyton Place 61. Twice Told Tales 63. Spy in Your Eye 65. Where Does It Hurt? 72, etc.

Halton, Charles (1876–1959). American character actor, inimitable as a sour-faced bank clerk, professor or lawyer.
Come and Get It 36. Penrod and Sam 37. Dead End 37. The Prisoner of Zenda 37. The Saint in New York 38. Room Service 38. Jesse James 39. Swanee River 39. Dodge City 39. Juarez 39. The Shop around the Corner 40. *Dr Cyclops* 40. Foreign Correspondent 40. Stranger on the Third Floor 40. The Westerner 40. Tobacco Road 41. The Smiling Ghost 41. *To Be or Not to Be* 42. Across the Pacific 42. Jitterbugs 43. Wilson 44. Rhapsody in Blue 45. The Best Years of Our Lives 46. Three Godfathers 48. The Nevadan 50. Here Comes the Groom 51. Carrie 52. Friendly Persuasion 56, many others.

Hamer, Gerald (1886–1973). British character actor in Hollywood.
Swing Time 36. Bulldog Drummond's Bride 39. Sherlock Holmes Faces Death 43. The Scarlet Claw 44. The Sign of the Ram 48, etc.

Hamer, Robert (1911–1963). British director, erratic but at his best impeccably stylish.
□San Demetrio London (w only) 43. Dead of Night (mirror sequence & w) 45. Pink String and Sealing Wax 45. *It Always Rains on Sunday* (& w) 47. *Kind Hearts and Coronets* (& w) 49. The Spider and the Fly 49. His Excellency (& w) 52. The Long Memory (& w) 52. *Father Brown* 54. To Paris With Love 54. The Scapegoat 59. *School for Scoundrels* 60. A Jolly Bad Fellow (w only) 63.

Hamill, Mark (1952–). American leading man.
□Sarah T (TV) 75. Delancey Street (TV) 75. Eric (TV) 75. Mallory (TV) 76. The City (TV) 77. *Star Wars* 77. Corvette Summer 78. The Big Red One 79. The Empire Strikes Back 80. The Night the Lights Went Out in Georgia 81. Return of the Jedi 83.

¶ *M.H.:* I'm waiting for my body to catch up with my age.
M.H.: Acting in *Star Wars* I felt like a raisin in a giant fruit salad, and I didn't even know who the cantaloupes were.

Hamilton, Bernie (–). Burly black American actor.
Let No Man Write My Epitaph 60. 13 West Street 62. Captain Sinbad 63. The Swimmer 67. The Lost Man 69. The Organization 71. Scream Blacula Scream 73. Bucktown 75, etc.
TV series: *Starsky and Hutch* 75–79.

Hamilton, Donald (1913–). American thriller writer, creator of Matt Helm. The resulting films and TV series were undistinguished to say the least.

Hamilton, George (1939–). American leading man, usually in serious roles.
Crime and Punishment USA (debut) 58. Home from the Hill 60. All the Fine Young Cannibals 60. Angel Baby 61. By Love Possessed 61. A Thunder of Drums 61. The Light in the Piazza 62. The Victors 63. *Act One* (as Moss Hart) 63. Viva Maria 65. Your Cheating Heart 65. Doctor, You've Got To Be Kidding 67. The Long Ride Home 67. Jack of Diamonds 67. The Power 67. Evel Knievel 72. The Man Who Loved Cat Dancing 73. Once Is Not Enough 75. The Dead Don't Die (TV) 75.
Roots (TV) 77. The Strange Possession of Mrs Oliver (TV) 77. Killer on Board (TV) 77. The Users (TV) 78. Institute for Revenge (TV) 79. *Love at First Bite* (as Dracula) 79. Zorro the Gay Blade 81, etc.
TV series: The Survivors 69. Paris 7000 70. Dynasty 85. Spies 86.

Hamilton, Guy (1922–). British director, former assistant to Carol Reed.
□The Ringer 52. The Intruder 53. *An Inspector Calls* 54. The Colditz Story 54. Charley Moon 56. Manuela 57. The Devil's Disciple 58. A Touch of Larceny 59. The Best of Enemies 62. The Party's Over 63. The Man in the Middle 64. *Goldfinger* 64. Funeral in Berlin 66. The Battle of Britain 70. Diamonds are Forever 71. Live and Let Die 72. The Man with the Golden Gun 73. Force Ten from Navarone (also p) 78. The Mirror Crack'd 80. Evil under the Sun 82. Remo Williams . . . the Adventure Begins 85.

Hamilton, John (1886–1958). Chubby American character actor, in hundreds of small parts as judge, cop, lawyer.
Rainbow Riley 26. White Cargo 30. Legion of Terror 37. Rose of Washington Square 39. The Maltese Falcon (as district attorney) 41. Meet Miss Bobby Socks 44. Law of the Golden West 49. The Pace that Thrills 52. On the Waterfront 54, many others.
TV series: Superman 51–57.

Hamilton, Lloyd (1891–1935). American silent slapstick comedian, in many two-reelers from 1914.

Hamilton, Margaret (1902–85). American character actress, a former kindergarten teacher who came to films via Broadway and usually played hatchet-faced spinsters or maids.
Another Language 33. These Three 36. Nothing Sacred 37. *The Wizard of Oz* 39. Invisible Woman 41. *Guest in the House* 44. Mad Wednesday 47. State of the Union 48. The Great Plane Robbery 50. Thirteen Ghosts 60. The Daydreamer 66. Rosie 67. The Anderson Tapes 71. Brewster McCloud 71, etc.

Hamilton, Murray (1923–86). American general purpose actor.
Bright Victory 50. No Time for Sergeants 58. The FBI Story 59. Seconds 66. The Graduate 67. No Way to Treat a Lady 68. The Boston Strangler 68. If It's Tuesday This Must Be Belgium 69. The Way We Were 73. Jaws 75. Jaws 2 78. 1941 79. The Amityville Horror 79. Brubaker 80, etc.

Hamilton, Neil (1899–1984). Stalwart American leading man of silent days.
White Rose 23. America 24. Isn't Life Wonderful? 25. Beau Geste 26. The Great Gatsby 27. Why Be Good? 28. Keeper of the Bees 29. The Dawn Patrol 30. The Wet Parade 31. The Animal Kingdom 32. Tarzan the Ape Man 32. One Sunday Afternoon 33. Tarzan and His Mate 34. Federal Fugitives 41. The Little Shepherd of Kingdom Come 61. Madame X 66, many others.
TV series: Batman 65–67.

Hamilton, Patrick (1904–62). British novelist and playwright whose work inspired a small but significant group of films.
□*Gaslight* 39 and 44. Hangover Square 44. Rope 49.

Hamlet (GB 1948). This, the most celebrated of the screen Hamlets (for others, see under Shakespeare), won Academy Awards as the best picture of its year, for Laurence Olivier's performance, for Roger

Furse's art direction and costume design, and for Carmen Dillon's set decoration. Those critics not overwhelmed by its prestige value, however, have often found it cold and empty, marred by injudicious text-cutting and a tendency to rove pointlessly and endlessly down corridors at the expense of action. Notable in the cast were Basil Sydney as Claudius, Eileen Herlie as Gertrude, Jean Simmons as Ophelia, Felix Aylmer as Polonius and Stanley Holloway as the gravedigger. Olivier produced and directed but the real star was Desmond Dickinson for his deep focus photography.
†A Russian version of the play appeared in 1964, starring Innokenti Smoktunovsky, directed by Grigori Kozintsev, and with music by Shostakovich.

Hamlin, Harry (1952–). American light leading man.
Movie Movie 78. Studs Lonigan (TV) 79. Clash of the Titans 81. King of the Mountain 81. Dragonslayer 81. Making Love 82. Blue Skies Again 83. Maxie 85. Space (TV) 85.

Hamlisch, Marvin (1945–). American composer (and pianist).
The Swimmer 68. The April Fools 69. Flap 70. The Sting (AA) 73. The Way We Were (AA song and score) 73. The Prisoner of Second Avenue 75. The Spy Who Loved Me 77. Same Time Next Year 78. Ice Castles 79. Chapter Two 79. Starting Over 79. Ordinary People 80. Seems Like Old Times 80. Pennies from Heaven 81. The Fan 81. I Ought to Be in Pictures 82. Sophie's Choice 82.

¶ *M.H.:* My whole life revolves around dessert.
M.H.: To put something on the earth that wasn't there yesterday, that's what I like.

Hammer, Will (1887–*). British producer, the original founder of Hammer films.

Hammerstein II, Oscar (1895–1960). Immensely successful American lyricist who wrote many stage musicals, usually with Richard Rodgers (qv). *The King and I, South Pacific, The Sound of Music,* etc.

Hammett, Dashiell (1894–1961). American writer of detective novels and occasional screenplays.
City Streets (& w) 31. The Maltese Falcon 31. The Thin Man 34. The Glass Key 35. The Maltese Falcon 41. The Glass Key 42. Watch on the Rhine (w) 43, etc.
†Wim Wenders' film *Hammett*, which appeared in 1982, was a pastiche in which the real Hammett became one of his own detective creations. In the vein of the Chandler movies, but less entertaining, it had minority appeal.

Hammid, Alexander (c. 1910–) (Alexander Hackenschmied). Czech documentarist in America.
Hymn of the Nations 46. Of Men and Music 51. To the Fair 65, etc.

Hammond, Kay (1909–1980) (Dorothy Standing). Plummy-voiced British leading lady, mostly on stage; married to John Clements.
Children of Chance 30. A Night in Montmartre 31. Almost a Divorce 32. Out of the Blue 32. A Night Like This 32. Sally Bishop 32. Yes Madam 33. Sleeping Car 33. Bitter Sweet 33. Two on a Doorstep 36. Jeannie 41. *Blithe Spirit* (as Elvira) 45. Call of the Blood 48. Five Golden Hours 61, etc.

Hammond, Peter (1923–). British juvenile player of the forties; became a TV and film director.
They Knew Mr Knight 46. Holiday Camp 47. Fly Away Peter 48. Morning Departure 50. Vote for Huggett 50. The Adventurers 51. Spring and Port Wine (d only) 69, etc.

Hampden, Walter (1879–1955) (Walter Hampden Dougherty). American stage actor with a long career behind him when he came to Hollywood.
□Warfare of the Flesh 17. The Hunchback of Notre Dame 39. All This and Heaven Too 40. North West Mounted Police 40. They Died with Their Boots On 41. Reap the Wild Wind 42. The Adventures of Mark Twain 44. All About Eve 50. The First Legion 51. Five Fingers 52. Sombrero 53. Treasure of the Golden Condor 53. The Silver Chalice 54. Sabrina 54. Strange Lady in Town 55. The Prodigal 55. The Vagabond King 56.

Hampshire, Susan (1938–). Talented British leading lady, somewhat handicapped by her own demureness.
□ Upstairs and Downstairs 59. Expresso Bongo 59. During One Night 61. The Long Shadow 61. The Three Lives of Thomasina 63. Night Must Fall 64. Wonderful Life 64. The Fighting Prince of Donegal 66. The Trygon Factor 67. Paris in August 67. Violent Enemy 69. Monte Carlo or Bust 69. David Copperfield (TV) 69. A Time for Loving 72.

Living Free 72. Neither the Sea Nor the Sand 72. Baffled (TV) 72. Malpertius 72. The Lonely Woman 76.
TV series: *The Forsyte Saga* (as Fleur) 68. *The Pallisers* 75.

Hampton, Hope (1899–1982). American leading lady of the silents.
The Bait 21. The Gold Diggers 23. Hollywood 23. The Truth About Women 24. Lover's Island 25. The Unfair Sex 26, etc.

Hampton, Louise (1881–1954). British character actress.
Goodbye Mr Chips 39. Busman's Honeymoon 40. Bedelia 46, etc.

Hancock, John (1939–). American director.
□Let's Scare Jessica to Death 73. Bang the Drum Slowly 74. Baby Blue Marine 76. California Dreaming 78.

Hancock, Sheila (1933–). British comic actress of stage and TV.
Light Up the Sky 58. The Girl on the Boat 61. Night Must Fall 63. The Anniversary 67. Take a Girl Like You 70, etc.

Hancock, Tony (1924–1968). Popular British radio and TV comedian.
Biography 1969: *Hancock* by Freddie Hancock and David Nathan.
□ Orders are Orders 61. The Rebel 61. The Punch and Judy Man 62. Those Magnificent Men in their Flying Machines 65. The Wrong Box 66.

¶ A comedian with a touch of genius who had no enemy except himself.—*J. B. Priestley*

Hand, David (1900–86). American animator, formerly with Disney; came to Britain 1945 to found cartoon unit for Rank. Some pleasing results (*Musical Paintbox* series, etc); but it was a financial failure and Hand returned to America in 1950.

Handl, Irene (1902–). Dumpy British character comedienne, frequently seen as maid or charlady; became a star in her later years.
The Girl in the News 41. Pimpernel Smith 41. Temptation Harbour 46. Silent Dust 48. One Wild Oat 51. The Belles of St Trinian's 54. A Kid for Two Farthings 56. Brothers in Law 57. *I'm All Right Jack* 59. Make Mine Mink 60. The Rebel 61. Heavens Above 63. Morgan 66. Smashing Time 67. On a Clear Day You Can See Forever 70. The Private Life of Sherlock Holmes 71. For the Love of Ada 72. Adventures of a Private Eye 76. Stand Up Virgin Soldiers 77, etc.
TV series: *For the Love of Ada* 70–72. Maggie and Her 78–79.

Handley, Tommy (1894–1949). British radio comedian most famous for his long-running, morale-building *Itma* series during World War II.
Elstree Calling 30. Two Men in a Box 38. *It's That Man Again* 42. Time Flies 43. Tom Tom Topia (short) 46.

hands. The clutching hand was long a staple of melodrama; usually hairy, with long fingernails, it came out of shadowed panelling and menaced the heroine in hundreds of thrillers such as *The Cat and the Canary*. Severed hands were also a favourite: passing fancies in most of the mummy films, they received more detailed attention in *The Beast with Five Fingers, Chamber of Horrors, The Hand*, and the various versions of *The Hands of Orlac*.

The Hands of Orlac. This improbable thriller by Maurice Renard, about a pianist who loses his hands in an accident and has the hands of a murderer grafted on, has been the basis of three film versions: 1. Directed by Robert Wiene in 1924 (Ger.), with Conrad Veidt and Werner Krauss. 2. Directed by Karl Freund in 1934 (US), as *Mad Love*, with Colin Clive and Peter Lorre. 3. Directed by Edmond Greville in 1961 (GB), with Mel Ferrer and Donald Wolfit.

Handy, W. C. (1873–1958) (William Christopher Handy). Blind, black, American blues pioneer; was impersonated by Nat King Cole in *St Louis Blues*.

Haney, Carol (1928–1964). American dancer, former assistant to Gene Kelly.
□Kiss Me Kate 53. Invitation to the Dance 54. *The Pajama Game* 57.

Hanks, Tom (1957–). American leading man of the eighties.
□ He Knows You're Alone 80. Bachelor Party 83. Splash! 84. The Man with One Red Shoe 85. Volunteers 85. The Money Pit 85. Nothing in Common 86. Every Time We Say Goodbye 86. Dragnet 87.

Hanley, Jenny (1947–). British light leading lady and television personality, daughter of Dinah Sheridan and Jimmy Hanley.

Joanna 68. On Her Majesty's Secret Service 69. Tam Lin 70. Scars of Dracula 72. The Private Life of Sherlock Holmes 73. Soft Beds Hard Battles 74. Alfie Darling 75, etc.

Hanley, Jimmy (1918–1970). Former British child actor developed as 'the boy next door' type by Rank in the forties.
Little Friend 34. Boys Will Be Boys 35. Night Ride 37. There Ain't No Justice 39. Salute John Citizen 42. For You Alone 44. The Way Ahead 44. Henry V 44. 29 Acacia Avenue 45. The Captive Heart 46. Master of Bankdam 47. It Always Rains on Sunday 48. It's Hard To Be Good 49. Here Come the Huggetts (and ensuing series) 49–52. The Blue Lamp 50. The Black Rider 54. The Deep Blue Sea 56. Lost Continent 68, etc.

Hanna, William (1910–). American animator who with his partner **Joe Barbera** created Tom and Jerry for MGM, later founding their own successful company creating innumerable semi-animated series for TV: Huckleberry Hound, Yogi Bear, The Flintstones, The Jetsons, Wait Till Your Father Gets Home, etc.

Hannah, Daryl (1960–). American leading lady of the eighties.
The Fury 78. Hard Country 81. Blade Runner 82. The Pope of Greenwich Village 84. *Splash!* 84. Clan of the Cave Bear 86. Legal Eagles 86. Roxanne 87. Wall Street 87.

Hannam, Ken (–). Australian director.
Sunday Too Far Away 74. Break of Day 76. Summerfield 77. Dawn! 78.

Hanray, Lawrence (1874–1947). British stage character actor of great dignity.
The Private Life of Henry VIII 32. The Scarlet Pimpernel 34. The Man Who Could Work Miracles 36. Hatter's Castle 41, etc.

Hansberry, Lorraine (1930–1965). Black American playwright, whose *A Raisin in the Sun* was filmed.

Hansen, Juanita (1895–1961). American leading lady of the silents, especially in serials.
His Pride and Shame 16. Secret of the Submarine 16. Dangers of a Bride 17. The Brass Bullet 18. The Lost City 20. The Yellow Arm 21. Broadway Madonna 22. The Jungle Princess 23, etc.

Hanson, Lars (1887–1965). Swedish stage actor who made silent films abroad but after the coming of sound remained in Sweden.
Ingeborg Holm (debut) 13. Dolken 16. Erotikon 19. The Atonement of Gosta Berling 24. The Scarlet Letter (US) 26. The Divine Woman (US) 27. The Wind (US) 28. The Informer (GB) 28, etc.

Hansson, Peter (1922–) (Peter Hansen). American general purpose actor.
Branded 50. When Worlds Collide 51. Darling How Could You 53. Three Violent People 56. The Deep Six 58. Harlow 65, etc.

Harareet, Haya (1931–) (Haya Hararit). Israeli leading lady.
Hill 24 Does Not Answer 55. Ben Hur 59. The Secret Partner 61. The Lost Kingdom 61. The Interns 62. Our Mother's House (co-w only) 67, etc.

Harburg, E. Y. (1896–1981) (Edgar 'Yip' Harburg). American lyricist chiefly noted for the songs in *The Wizard of Oz*; also wrote 'Brother Can You Spare a Dime', 'Happiness Is a Thing Called Joe', 'Can't Help Singing', 'Lydia the Tattooed Lady', 'Last Night When We Were Young', 'April in Paris', 'How Are Things in Glocca Morra', etc.

hard ticket. A phrase used in the sixties to describe film exhibition of the type once called 'road show': separate performances, reserved seats, long runs and high prices.

Hardin, Ty (1930–) (Orton Hungerford). Muscular leading man of the sixties, mostly on TV.
I Married a Monster from Outer Space 58. The Chapman Report 62. PT 109 63. Battle of the Bulge 65. Berserk (GB) 67. Custer of the West 68. The Last Rebel 71, etc.
TV series: *Bronco* 58–61. Riptide 69.

¶ *T.H.:* I'm really a very humble man. Not a day passes that I don't thank God for my looks and my talent.

Harding, Ann (1902–1981) (Dorothy Gatley). Gentlewomanly American leading lady of thirties romances.
□Paris Bound 29. Her Private Affair 29. Condemned 29. *Holiday* 30. Girl of the Golden West 30. East Lynne 31. Devotion 31. Prestige 31. Westward Passage 32. The Conquerors 32. *The Animal Kingdom* 32. When Ladies Meet 33. Double Harness 33. Right to Romance 33. Gallant Lady 33. The Life of Vergie Winters 34. The Fountain 34. *Biography of a Bachelor Girl* 35. Enchanted April 35. The Flame Within 35. Peter

Ibbetson 35. The Lady Consents 36. The Witness Chair 36. *Love from a Stranger* (GB) 37. Eyes in the Night 42. Mission to Moscow 43. North Star 43. Janie 44. Nine Girls 44. Those Endearing Young Charms 45. Janie Gets Married 46. It Happened on Fifth Avenue 47. Christmas Eve 47. The Magnificent Yankee 50. Two Weeks with Love 50. The Unknown Man 51. The Man in the Grey Flannel Suit 56. I've Lived Before 56. Strange Intruder 56.

Harding, Gilbert (1907–60). Explosive British TV personality who appeared in a few films.
The Gentle Gunman 52. Meet Mr Lucifer 53. As Long as They're Happy 55. An Alligator Named Daisy 55. Expresso Bongo 60, etc.

Harding, Lyn (1867–1952) (David Llewellyn Harding). British stage actor who made a splendid 'heavy' in some films of the twenties and thirties.
The Barton Mystery 20. When Knighthood Was in Flower (as Henry VIII) 21. The Speckled Band (as Moriarty) 31. *The Triumph of Sherlock Holmes* (as Moriarty) 35. Spy of Napoleon 36. Fire Over England 36. Knight without Armour 37. *Goodbye Mr Chips* (as Chips' first headmaster) 39. The Prime Minister 40, etc.

Hardwicke, Sir Cedric (1893–1964). Distinguished British stage actor who settled in Hollywood and too frequently allowed his talents to be squandered on inferior material. Autobiography 1961: *A Victorian in Orbit.*
□Nelson 26. Dreyfus 31. Rome Express 32. Orders is Orders 32. The Ghoul 33. *Nell Gwyn* (as Charles II) 34. The Lady is Willing 34. Jew Süss 34. King of Paris 34. Bella Donna 34. Peg of Old Drury 35. Les Misérables 35. *Becky Sharp* 35. Things to Come 36. Tudor Rose 36. Laburnum Grove 36. The Green Light 37. *King Solomon's Mines* (as Allan Quartermain) 37. *On Borrowed Time* (as Death) 39. *Stanley and Livingstone* (as Livingstone) 39. The Hunchback of Notre Dame (as Frollo) 39. The Invisible Man Returns 40. *Tom Brown's Schooldays* (as Dr Arnold) 40. The Howards of Virginia 40. *Victory* 40. Suspicion 41. Sundown 41. The Ghost of Frankenstein 42. Valley of the Sun 42. Invisible Agent 42. The Commandos Strike at Dawn 42. Forever and a Day 43. *The Moon is Down* 43. The Cross of Lorraine 43. The Lodger 44. Wing and a Prayer 44. Wilson 44. The Keys of the Kingdom 45. Sentimental Journey 46. The Imperfect Lady 47. Ivy 47. Lured 47. Song of My Heart 47. A Woman's Vengeance 47. Beware of Pity 47. *Nicholas Nickleby* 47. Tycoon 47. *I Remember Mama* 48. *The Winslow Boy* 48. Rope 48. A Connecticut Yankee in King Arthur's Court 49. Now Barabbas 49. The White Tower 50. Mr Imperium 51. The Desert Fox 51. The Green Glove 52. Caribbean 52. Salome 53. Botany Bay 53. Bait 54. *Richard III* 55. Helen of Troy 55. Diane 56. Gaby 56. The Vagabond King 56. The Power and the Prize 56. The Ten Commandments 56. Around the World in Eighty Days 56. The Story of Mankind 57. Baby Face Nelson 57. Five Weeks in a Balloon 62. The Pumpkin Eater 64.
TV series: Mrs G Goes to College 61.

The Hardy Family. Between 1937 and 1947 fifteen highly successful modest-budget films were made by MGM about the vicissitudes of a 'typical family' in a small midwestern town: father just happened to be a judge who enjoyed man-to-man talks with his teenage son, the wildly untypical Mickey Rooney. Everyone was insufferably nice in these films: father Lewis Stone (Lionel Barrymore did the first episode), mother Fay Holden, daughter Cecilia Parker, aunt Sara Haden. Perhaps because of this they did not last into the post-war period, and an attempt to revive them in 1958 (*Andy Hardy Comes Home*) failed rather miserably. The series was given a special Academy Award in 1942 for 'furthering the American way of life'.

The films were as follows:

1936: A Family Affair
1938: You're Only Young Once; Judge Hardy's Children; Love Finds Andy Hardy; Out West with the Hardys
1939: The Hardys Ride High; Andy Hardy Gets Spring Fever; Judge Hardy and Son
1940: Andy Hardy Meets Debutante
1941: Andy Hardy's Private Secretary; Life Begins for Andy Hardy
1942: The Courtship of Andy Hardy; Andy Hardy's Double Life
1944: Andy Hardy's Blonde Trouble
1946: Love Laughs at Andy Hardy
1958: Andy Hardy Comes Home

Hardy, Oliver (1892–1957). Ample-figured American comedian, the fat half of the screen's finest comedy team, noted for his genteel pomposity, tie twiddle and long-suffering look at the camera.
Biography 1961: *Mr Laurel and Mr Hardy* by John McCabe.

SELECTED SOLO APPEARANCES: Outwitting Dad 13. Playmates 15. Lucky Dog 17. He Winked and Won 17. The Chief Cook 18. The Three Ages 23. Rex, King of the Wild Horses 24. The Wizard of Oz (as the Tin Man) 24. The Nicklehopper 25. Zenobia 39. The Fighting Kentuckian 49. Riding High 50, many others.
☐LAUREL AND HARDY FILMS: Slipping Wives 26. With Love and Hisses 27. Sailors Beware 27. Do Detectives Think? 27. Flying Elephants 27. Sugar Daddies 27. Call of the Cuckoo 27. The Rap 27. Duck Soup 27. Eve's Love Letters 27. Love 'Em and Weep 27. Why Girls Love Sailors 27. Should Tall Men Marry? 27. Hats Off 27. Putting Pants on Philip 27. *The Battle of the Century* 27. Leave 'Em Laughing 28. From Soup to Nuts 28. *The Finishing Touch* 28. *You're Darn Tootin'* 28. Their Purple Moment 28. Should Married Men Go Home? 28. Early to Bed 28. *Two Tars* 28. Habeas Corpus 28. We Faw Down 28. Liberty 28. Wrong Again 29. That's My Wife 29. *Big Business* 29. *Double Whoopee* 29. *Berth Marks* 29. *Men O'War* 29. *The Perfect Day* 29. They Go Boom 29. Bacon Grabbers 29. Angora Love 29. Unaccustomed as We Are 29. Hollywood Revue of 1929. The Hoosegow 29. Night Owls 30. Blotto 30. The Rogue Song (feature) 30. Brats 30. Be Big 30. Below Zero 30. The Laurel and Hardy Murder Case 30. *Hog Wild* 30. Another Fine Mess 30. Chickens Come Home 30. *Laughing Gravy* 31. Our Wife 31. *Come Clean* 31. Pardon Us (f) 31. One Good Turn 31. Beau Hunks 31. *Helpmates* 31. Any Old Port 31. *The Music Box* (AA) 32. The Chimp 32. *County Hospital* 32. *Scram* 32 Pack Up Your Troubles (f) 32. Their First Mistake 32. *Towed in a Hole* 33. Twice Two 33. Me and My Pal 33. *Fra Diavolo* (f) 33. *The Midnight Patrol* 33. *Busy Bodies* 33. *Dirty Work* 33. *Sons of the Desert* (f) 33. Oliver the Eighth 33. Hollywood Party (f) 34. *Going Bye Bye* 34. *Them Thar Hills* 34. *Babes in Toyland* (f) 34. The Live Ghost 34. *Tit for Tat* 35. The Fixer Uppers 35. Thicker than Water 35. Bonnie Scotland (f) 35. The Bohemian Girl (f) 36. *Our Relations* (f) 36. *Way out West* (f) 36. Pick a Star (f) 37. Swiss Miss (f) 38. *Blockheads* (f) 38. *The Flying Deuces* (f) 39. *A Chump at Oxford* (f) 40. Saps at Sea (f) 40. Great Guns (f) 41. A Haunting We Will Go (f) 42. Air Raid Wardens (f) 43. Jitterbugs (f) 43. The Dancing Masters (f) 43. The Big Noise (f) 44. Nothing but Trouble (f) 44. The Bullfighters (f) 45. Robinson Crusoeland (Atoll K) (f) 52.
☐COMPILATION FEATURES: The Golden Age of Comedy 58. When Comedy was King 60. Days of Thrills and Laughter 61. Thirty Years of Fun 62. MGM's Big Parade of Comedy 65. Laurel and Hardy's Laughing Twenties 65. The Crazy World of Laurel and Hardy 66. The Further Perils of Laurel and Hardy 69. Four Clowns 69. The Best of Laurel and Hardy 74.
❁ For his many unique qualities, seen to best advantage in his partnership with Stan Laurel. *Blockheads*.

Hardy, Robert (1925–). British character actor, mostly on TV.
The Spy Who Came in from the Cold 65. How I Won the War 67. 10 Rillington Place 70. The Far Pavilions (TV) 84. The Shooting Party (TV) 84. Jenny's War (TV) 84, etc.
TV series: *Elizabeth R* 71. All Creatures Great and Small 77–79. *Churchill: the Wilderness Years* 81.

Hardy, Thomas (1840–1928). British novelist of dour country stories. Works principally filmed, neither satisfactorily, are *Tess of the D'Urbervilles* and *Far From the Madding Crowd*.

Hare, Lumsden (1875–1964). Irish character actor, long in Hollywood.
Charlie Chan Carries On 31. Clive of India 35. She 35. Gunga Din 39. Rebecca 40. The Lodger 44. Challenge to Lassie 49. Julius Caesar 53. The Four Skulls of Jonathan Drake 59, many others.

Hare, Robertson (1891–1979). Bald-headed British comedian, the put-upon little man of the Aldwych farces of the twenties and thirties, transferred intact from stage to screen.
Autobiography 1958: *Yours Indubitably*.
Rookery Nook 30. A Cuckoo in the Nest 33. Thark 33. Fishing Stock 35. Aren't Men Beasts? 38. Banana Ridge 41. He Snoops To Conquer 45. Things Happen at Night 48. *One Wild Oat* 51. Our Girl Friday 53. Three Men in a Boat 56. The Young Ones 61, etc.

Harewood, Dorian (–). Black American actor.
Sparkle 75. Gray Lady Down 77. Looker 81. Against All Odds 83. The Falcon and the Snowman 84. Full Metal Jacket 87.

Harker, Gordon (1885–1967). British comic actor, the jutting-lipped Cockney of many a thirties comedy.
The Ring (debut) 27. The Calendar 31. *Rome Express* 33. Friday the Thirteenth 33. Boys Will Be Boys 35. Millions 37. The Return of

the Frog 38. *Inspector Hornleigh* 40. *Saloon Bar* 41. Warn That Man 43. 29 Acacia Avenue 45. Things Happen at Night 48. Her Favourite Husband 50. The Second Mate 50. Derby Day 52. Small Hotel 58. Left, Right and Centre 59, etc.

Harlan, Kenneth (1895–1967). American leading man of the silent screen.
Cheerful Givers 17. The Hoodlum 19. The Beautiful and the Damned 22. The Broken Wing 23. Bobbed Hair 24. Twinkletoes 26. San Francisco 36. Paper Bullets 41. The Underdog 44, many others.

Harlan, Otis (1865–1940). Tubby American character actor with long stage experience.
What Happened to Jones? 25. Lightnin' 26. Man to Man 31. The Hawk 32. Married in Haste 34. Diamond Jim 35. A Midsummer Night's Dream 35. Mr Boggs Steps Out 38, many others.

Harlan, Russell (1903–1974). American cinematographer, former stunt man.
Hopalong Rides Again 37. Stagecoach War 40. The Kansan 43. *A Walk in the Sun* 45. *Red River* 48. The Big Sky 52. *Riot in Cell Block Eleven* 54. The Blackboard Jungle 55. This Could Be the Night 57. Witness for the Prosecution 57. Run Silent Run Deep 58. King Creole 58. The Spiral Road 62. Hatari 62. To Kill a Mockingbird 62. Quick Before It Melts 65. Tobruk 66. Darling Lili 70, etc.

Harlan, Veit (1899–1964). German director.
Kreutzer Sonata 36. Jew Süss 40. Der Grosse Konig 41. Opfergang 43. Die Blaue Stunde 52. The Third Sex 57, etc.

Harline, Leigh (1907–1969). American screen composer.
Snow White and the Seven Dwarfs (songs) 37. Pinocchio (songs) (AA) 39. His Girl Friday 40. The More the Merrier 43. Road to Utopia 45. The Farmer's Daughter 47. The Big Steal 49. Monkey Business 52. Broken Lance 54. The Wayward Bus 57. Ten North Frederick 58. Warlock 60. Seven Faces of Dr Lao 63. Strange Bedfellows 64, etc.

Harling, W. Franke (1887–1958). American composer.
One Hour with You 32. So Big 32. The Scarlet Empress 34. So Red the Rose 35. Souls at Sea 37. Stagecoach (co-w) 39. Penny Serenade 41. The Lady Is Willing 42, etc.

Harlow, Jean (1911–1937) (Harlean Carpentier). American leading lady and most sensational star of the early thirties, a wisecracking 'platinum blonde' with a private life to suit her public image.
Biographies: 1937, *Hollywood Comet* by Dentner Davies. 1964, *Harlow* by Irving Shulman.
□Moran of the Marines 28. Double Whoopee (short) 29. The Unkissed Man 29. The Fugitive 29. Close Harmony 29. New York Nights 29. The Love Parade 29. Weak but Willing 29. Bacon Grabbers (short) 29. The Saturday Night Kid 29. The Love Parade 30. *Hell's Angels* 30. City Lights 31. The Secret Six 31. Iron Man 31. *Public Enemy* 31. Goldie 31. Platinum Blonde 31. Three Wise Girls 32. Beast of the City 32. *Red Headed Woman* 32. *Red Dust* 32. *Dinner at Eight* 33. Hold Your Man 33. *Bombshell* 33. The Girl from Missouri 34. Reckless 35. *China Seas* 35. Riffraff 35. Wife vs Secretary 35. Suzy 36. *Libelled Lady* 36. Personal Property 37. Saratoga 37.
❀ For combining a sophistication which she acted with an innocence which was her own. *Red Dust*.

¶ *Clark Gable:* She didn't want to be famous. She wanted to be happy.
Spencer Tracy: A square shooter if ever there was one.
Excuse me while I slip into something more comfortable.—*Jean Harlow in Hell's Angels*
Last lines of *Dinner at Eight*:
Jean Harlow: 'You know, the other day I read a book. It said that machinery is going to take the place of every profession.'
Marie Dressler: 'Oh, my dear: that's something you'll *never* have to worry about!'

Harlow, John (1896–). British writer-director, former music-hall performer.
Spellbound (d) 40. Candles at Nine (d) 43. Meet Sexton Blake (d) 44. The Agitator (d) 45. Appointment with Crime (wd) 46. Green Fingers (wd) 47. *While I Live* (Dream of Olwen) (wd) 48. Old Mother Riley's New Venture (d) 49. Those People Next Door (d) 52, etc.

Harman, Hugh (1903–1982). American animator who in the early thirties, with Rudolph Ising, formed Harman-Ising and made some brilliantly inventive cartoons for MGM. Later originated Merrie Melodies and Looney Tunes, and was cited by the Nobel Peace jury for *Peace on Earth* (1940).

Harmon, Mark (1951–). Competent American leading man, difficult to distinguish from several others.
Eleanor and Franklin: the White House Years (TV) 77. Centennial 78. Comes a Horseman 78. Beyond the Poseidon Adventure 79. *The Dream Merchants* (TV) 80. Summer School 87.
TV series: Flamingo Road 81–82.

Harolde, Ralf (1899–1974) (R. H. Wigger). American supporting actor often seen as thin-lipped crook.
Night Nurse 32. A Tale of Two Cities 35. Horror Island 41. Baby Face Morgan 42. Farewell My Lovely (as the doctor) 44. Alaska Patrol (last film) 51, many others.

Harper, Gerald (1929–). Aristocratic-looking British actor familiar on TV as *Adam Adamant* and *Hadleigh*.
The Admirable Crichton 57. A Night to Remember 58. The League of Gentlemen 59. The Punch and Judy Man 64. The Lady Vanishes 79, etc.

Harper, Jessica (c. 1955–). American leading lady.
Inserts 76. Suspiria 77. The Evictors 79. Shock Treatment 81. Pennies from Heaven 81. My Favorite Year 82, etc.

Harper, Valerie (1940–). American leading comedy actress, a star of TV.
The Ones in Between 72. Freebie and the Bean 74. Thursday's Game (TV) 74. Night Terror (TV) 77. The Last Married Couple in America 79.
TV series: *The Mary Tyler Moore Show* 70–73. *Rhoda* 74–78.

Harrigan, William (1894–1966). American general purpose actor of the thirties and forties.
On the Level 17. Cabaret 27. Nix on Dames 27. Born Reckless 30. Pick Up 33. The Invisible Man 33. G Men 35. The Silk Hat Kid 35. Federal Bullets 37. Hawaii Calls 38. Back Door to Heaven 39. The Farmer's Daughter 47. Flying Leathernecks 51. Street of Sinners 55, etc.

Harrington, Curtis (1928–). American director who made experimental shorts before graduating to features.
□Night Tide 63. Voyage to a Prehistoric Planet 64. Queen of Blood 66. Games 67. How Awful About Allan (TV) 70. What's the Matter with Helen? 71. Who Slew Auntie Roo? 73. The Cat Creature (TV) 73. Killer Bees (TV) 74. The Dead Don't Die (TV) 74. The Killing Kind 76. Ruby 77. Devil Dog (TV) 78.

Harris, Barbara (1936–). American leading lady.
A Thousand Clowns 65. Oh Dad . . . 66. Plaza Suite 71. Who is Harry Kellerman . . .? 71. The War Between Men and Women 72. Family Plot 76. Freaky Friday 77. Movie Movie 78. The Seduction of Joe Tynan 79. Second Hand Hearts 80. Night Magic 85. Peggy Sue Got Married 86, etc.

Harris, Jack (1905–71). British editor.
The Sleeping Cardinal 31. The Wandering Jew 33. The Face at the Window 39. Let the People Sing 42. This Happy Breed 44. Blithe Spirit 45. Brief Encounter 45. Great Expectations 46. Oliver Twist 48. Where No Vultures Fly 51. The Crimson Pirate 53. Indiscreet 58. The Sundowners 60. Billy Budd 62. The Chalk Garden 64. Three Sisters 70, many others.

Harris, James B. (1924–). American producer, associated with director Stanley Kubrick.
The Killing 56. Paths of Glory 57. Lolita 62. The Bedford Incident (& d) 65. Some Call It Loving 71. Telefon 77, etc.

Harris, Jed (1906–1979) (Jacob Horowitz). American theatrical impresario of the thirties and forties, notorious for toughness and rudeness; lampooned in films *Twentieth Century* and *The Saxon Charm*.

Harris, Joel Chandler (1848–1908). American journalist and story writer who created the characters of Uncle Remus and Brer Rabbit, filmed by Disney in *Song of the South*.

Harris, Jonathan (1914–). American character actor, popular in prissy roles in TV series *The Third Man* 59–61, *The Bill Dana Show* 63–64, *Lost in Space* 65–68.
Botany Bay 54. The Big Fisherman 59, etc.

Harris, Julie (1925–). American stage actress, adept at fey roles. Films occasional.
□*The Member of the Wedding* 53. East of Eden 55. I am a Camera 56. The Truth about Women 56. Sally's Irish Rogue 60. Requiem for a Heavyweight 62. *The Haunting* 63. Harper 66. You're a Big Boy Now 66. *Reflections in a Golden Eye* 67. The Split 68.

The House on Greenapple Road (TV) 69. How Awful About Allan (TV) 70. The People Next Door 70. Home for the Holidays (TV) 72. The Greatest Gift (TV) 74. The Hiding Place 75. Voyage of the Damned 76. The Bell Jar 79. Backstairs at the White House (TV) 79.
TV series: The Family Holvak 76. Thicker Than Water 77. Knots Landing 81.

Harris, Julie (–). British costume designer.
The Naked Edge 61. The Fast Lady 62. The Chalk Garden 64. Darling 65. The Wrong Box 65. Casino Royale 67. Goodbye Mr Chips 69. Live and Let Die 73. Rollerball 74. The Slipper and the Rose 76, many others.

Harris, Julius (–). Black American character actor.
Slaves 69. Incident in San Francisco (TV) 71. Shaft's Big Score 73. A Cry for Help (TV) 75. King Kong 76. Rich Man Poor Man (TV) 76. Victory at Entebbe (as Idi Amin) (TV) 76. Islands in the Stream 77. Looking for Mr Goodbar 77. Ring of Passion (TV) 78. The First Family 80, etc.

Harris, Mildred (1901–1944). American leading lady of the silent era, first wife of Charles Chaplin.
Intolerance 15. Borrowed Clothes 18. Fool's Paradise 21. Fog 23. Unmarried Wives 24. My Neighbour's Wife 25. The Mystery Club 26. The Show Girl 27. Sea Fury 29. No No Nanette 30. Lady Tubbs 35. Reap the Wild Wind 42. The Story of Dr Wassell 44, etc.

Harris, Phil (1904–). American bandleader and comic singer; in occasional films.
Melody Cruise 33. Man about Town 39. Buck Benny Rides Again 40. Here Comes the Groom 51. The Glenn Miller Story 54. The High and the Mighty 54. Anything Goes 56. The Wheeler Dealers 63. The Cool Ones 67, etc.

Harris, Richard (1932–). Gaunt Irish leading actor. Usually cast as a rebel, he tries to match the part in real life.
□Alive and Kicking 58. Shake Hands with the Devil 59. The Wreck of the Mary Deare 59. A Terrible Beauty 60. All Night Long 61. The Long the Short and the Tall 61. The Guns of Navarone 61. *Mutiny on the Bounty* 62. *This Sporting Life* 63. The Red Desert 64. I Tre Volti 64. Major Dundee 65. The Heroes of Telemark 65. The Bible 66. Hawaii 66. Caprice 66. *Camelot* (as King Arthur) 67. The Molly Maguires 69. A Man Called Horse 69. Bloomfield (& d) 70. *Cromwell* (title role) 70. The Snow Goose (TV) 71. Man in the Wilderness 71. The Deadly Trackers 73. 99 44/100 Dead 74. Juggernaut 75. Robin and Marian 75. The Return of a Man Called Horse 76. Echoes of a Summer 76. Gulliver's Travels 76. The Cassandra Crossing 77. Orca—Killer Whale 77. Golden Rendezvous 77. The Wild Geese 78. Game for Vultures 79. The Last Word 79. The Revengers 79. Your Ticket Is No Longer Valid 79. Highpoint 80. Tarzan the Ape Man 81.

¶ He's something of a fuck-up, no question.—*Charlton Heston*
He hauls his surly carcass from movie to movie, being dismembered. I'd just as soon wait till he's finished.—*Pauline Kael*

Harris, Robert (1900–). British classical actor who has played occasional film roles.
How He Lied to Her Husband 31. The Life and Death of Colonel Blimp 43. The Bad Lord Byron 48. That Lady 55. Oscar Wilde 60. Decline and Fall 68, etc.

Harris, Robert H. (1911–1981). American character actor, usually beaky, officious and unsympathetic.
Bundle of Joy 56. How to Make a Monster 58. America America 63. Mirage 65. Valley of the Dolls 67, etc.
TV series: The Goldbergs 56. Court of Last Resort 57–60.

Harris, Rosemary (1930–). British leading lady, chiefly on stage.
Beau Brummel 54. The Shiralee 55. A Flea in Her Ear 68. Holocaust (TV) 77. The Boys from Brazil 78. The Chisholms (TV) 78.

Harris, Theresa (–). Black American actress.
Morocco 30. Blood Money 33. Morning Glory 33. Jezebel 38. Santa Fe Trail 40. Blossoms in the Dust 40. I Walked with a Zombie 43. Three Little Girls in Blue 46. Neptune's Daughter 49. And Baby Makes Three 50. The Company She Keeps 51, many others.

Harris, Vernon (c. 1910–). British screenwriter.
Albert RN (co-w) 53. The Sea Shall Not Have Them (co-w) 55. Reach for the Sky 56. Ferry to Hong Kong 57. The Admirable Crichton 57. Light up the Sky 61. Oliver 68. Paul and Michelle (co-w) 75, etc.

Harrison, Doane (–1968). American editor.

Youth and Adventure 25. Celebrity 28. The Spieler 29. Her Man 30. 13 Hours by Air 36. Midnight 39. Hold Back the Dawn 41. The Major and the Minor 42. Five Graves to Cairo 43. The Uninvited 44. The Lost Weekend 45. A Foreign Affair 48. Branded 50, etc. Later associate producer for Billy Wilder.

Harrison, Joan (1911–). British writer-producer, assistant for many years to Alfred Hitchcock.
Jamaica Inn (w) 39. Rebecca (w) 40. Foreign Correspondent (w) 40. Suspicion (w) 41. Saboteur (w) 42. Dark Waters (w) 44. Phantom Lady (p) 44. Uncle Harry (p) 45. Ride the Pink Horse (p) 47. Circle of Danger (p) 51, etc.
TV series: *Alfred Hitchcock Presents* (p) 55–63.

Harrison, Kathleen (1898–). British character actress, usually seen as a cockney but born in Lancashire. On stage from 1926; films made her an amiable, slightly dithery but warm-hearted national figure.
Hobson's Choice (debut) 31. The Ghoul 33. Broken Blossoms 36. Night Must Fall (US) 37. *Bank Holiday* 38. The Outsider 39. *The Ghost Train* 41. Kipps 41. *In Which We Serve* 42. Dear Octopus 43. Great Day 45. *Holiday Camp* 47. *The Winslow Boy* 48. Bond Street 48. Oliver Twist 48. *Here Come the Huggetts* (and ensuing series) 49–52. Waterfront 50. Scrooge 51. Pickwick Papers 52. *Turn the Key Softly* 53. Cast a Dark Shadow 54. Where There's a Will 54. Lilacs in the Spring 54. *All for Mary* 55. Home and Away 56. A Cry from the Streets 58. Alive and Kicking 58. Mrs Gibbons' Boys 62. West Eleven 63. Lock Up Your Daughters 69, many others.

Harrison, Linda (1945–). American leading lady, briefly evident at 20th Century Fox: married Richard Zanuck.
Way Way Out 66. A Guide for the Married Man 67. Planet of the Apes 67. Airport 75 75.
TV series: Bracken's World 69–70.

Harrison, Rex (1908–) (Reginald Carey). Debonair British leading actor of pleasant if limited range, on stage since 1924; films have only occasionally given him the right material. Autobiography 1974: *Rex*.
□The Great Game 30. The School for Scandal 30. All at Sea 34. Get Your Man 34. Leave It to Blanche 35. Men Are Not Gods 36. *Storm in a Teacup* 37. School for Husbands 37. St Martin's Lane 38. The Citadel 38. Over the Moon 39. The Silent Battle 39. Ten Days in Paris 39. *Night Train to Munich* 40. *Major Barbara* 40. I Live in Grosvenor Square 45. *Blithe Spirit* 45. *The Rake's Progress* 46. Anna and the King of Siam (US) 46. The Ghost and Mrs Muir (US) 47. The Foxes of Harrow (US) 47. Unfaithfully Yours (US) 48. Escape 48. The Long Dark Hall 51. The Fourposter (US) 52. King Richard and the Crusaders (as Saladin) (US) 54. The Constant Husband 55. The Reluctant Debutante (US) 58. Midnight Lace (US) 60. The Happy Thieves (US) 62. Cleopatra (US) 62. *My Fair Lady* (AA) (US) 64. The Yellow Rolls-Royce 64. The Agony and the Ecstasy (US) (as a medieval pope) 65. The Honey Pot (US) 67. Doctor Dolittle (US) 67. A Flea in Her Ear (US/Fr.) 68. Staircase 69. Don Quixote (TV) 72. The Prince and the Pauper 77. The Fifth Musketeer 77. Ashanti 78. Shalimar 78. Crossed Swords 78. A Time to Die 79.

¶ *R.H. (1980):* I'm now at the age where I've got to prove that I'm just as good as I never was.
Famous line (*Blithe Spirit*): If you're trying to compile an inventory of my sex life, I feel it only fair to warn you that you've omitted several episodes. I shall consult my diary and give you a complete list after lunch.

Harrison, Richard (–). American strongman in Italian spectaculars.
Executioner on the High Seas 61. Invincible Gladiator 61. Perseus among the Monsters 63. Spy Killers 65. Adventures of the Bengal Lancers 65. Vengeance 68. Commando Attack 70. The Way of the Godfather 73.

Harrold, Kathryn (1950–). American leading lady.
Yes Giorgio 82. The Sender 82. Into the Night 84. McGruder and Loud (TV) 84. Raw Deal 86.

Harron, Robert (Bobby) (1894–1920). American juvenile lead who joined D. W. Griffith's company almost from school; died in shooting accident.
Man's Genesis 12. The Birth of a Nation 14. Intolerance 16. Hearts of the World 18. True Heart Susie 19, many others.

Harryhausen, Ray (1920–). American trick film specialist and model maker; invented 'Superdynamation'. 1972: published *Film Fantasy Scrapbook*.
Mighty Joe Young 50. It Came from Beneath the Sea 52. Twenty Million Miles to Earth 57.

The Three Worlds of Gulliver 60. *Jason and the Argonauts* 63. The First Men in the Moon 64. One Million Years B.C. 66. The Valley of Gwangi 69. The Golden Voyage of Sinbad 73. Sinbad and the Eye of the Tiger 77, etc.

Hart, Dolores (1938–) (D. Hicks). American lady of a few films in the late fifties. Retired to become a nun.
Loving You 56. Wild is the Wind 57. Lonelyhearts 59. Sail a Crooked Ship 60. Lisa 62, etc.

Hart, Dorothy (1923–). American second lead of the fifties.
Naked City 47. Take One False Step 49. Undertow 49. I Was a Communist for the FBI 51. Tarzan's Savage Fury 52, etc.

Hart, Harvey (1928–). Canadian director, from TV, now in Hollywood.
□Dark Intruder 65. Bus Riley's Back in Town 65. Sullivan's Empire 67. The Sweet Ride 68. The Young Lawyers (TV) 69. Fortune and Men's Eyes 71. The Pyx 73. Panic on the 5.22 (TV) 74. Can Ellen Be Saved? (TV) 74. Murder or Mercy? (TV) 74. Shoot 77. Goldenrod (TV) 77. Prince of Central Park (TV) 77. W.E.B. (TV) 78. Captains Courageous (TV) 78. Standing Tall (TV) 78. Like Normal People (TV) 79. The Aliens Are Coming (TV) 79. High Coast 81. Utilities 83.

Hart, Lorenz (1895–1943). American lyricist, mostly with Richard Rodgers as composer. Shows filmed include *On Your Toes*, *Pal Joey*, *The Boys from Syracuse*. Played by Mickey Rooney in *Words and Music*.

Hart, Moss (1904–1961). American playwright (usually in collaboration with George S. Kaufman) and theatrical producer. Wrote occasional screenplays.
Autobiography 1958: *Act One* (filmed 1963).
Once in a Lifetime (oa) 32. You Can't Take It With You (oa) 38. *The Man Who Came to Dinner* (oa) 41. George Washington Slept Here (oa) 42. Lady in the Dark (oa) 44. Winged Victory (w) 44. *Gentleman's Agreement* (w) 47. Hans Christian Andersen (w) 52. A Star Is Born (w) 54. Prince of Players (w) 55, etc.

Hart, Richard (1915–1951). American leading man with a very brief Hollywood career.
□Green Dolphin Street 47. Desire Me 47. B.F.'s Daughter 48. The Black Book 49.

Hart, William S. (1870–1946). Mature, solemn-faced hero of innumerable silent westerns; one of the key performers of the twenties. The initial 'S' is variously reputed to have stood for 'Shakespeare' and 'Surrey'.
Autobiography 1929: *My Life East and West.*
The Disciple 15. The Captive God 16. The Return of Draw Egan 16. Hell's Hinges 17. Truthful Tolliver 17. Blue Blazes Rawden 18. Selfish Yates 18. Riddle Gawne 18. The Border Wireless 18. Wagon Tracks 18. The Poppy Girl's Husband 19. The Toll Gate 20. Sand 20. Cradle of Courage 20. O'Malley of the Mounted 21. White Oak 21. Travellin' On 22. Hollywood 23. Wild Bill Hickok 23. Singer Jim McKee 24. *Tumbleweeds* 25, many others.

¶ His frequently austere look breathed dedication to the west as a subject suited for all the artistic possibilities of cinema.—*Allen Eyles*

Harte, Bret (1836–1902) (Francis Brett Harte). American short-story writer who wandered the old west. Works filmed include *The Outcasts of Poker Flat*, *Tennessee's Partner*.

Hartford-Davis, Robert (1923–77). British producer-director, in films since 1939.
That Kind of Girl 62. The Yellow Teddybears 63. Saturday Night Out 63. Black Torment 64. Gonks Go Beat 65. The Sandwich Man 66. Corruption 68. The Smashing Bird I Used to Know 69. The Fiend 71. Black Gunn (US) 72. The Take (US) 74, etc.

Hartl, Karl (1899–). Austrian director.
The Doomed Battalion 31. F.P.1. Doesn't Answer 32. Gold 34. The Gypsy Baron 35. The Man Who Was Sherlock Holmes 37. Whom the Gods Love 42. The Angel with the Trumpet 48. The Wonder Kid 51. Journey into the Past 54. Mozart 55. Love is Red 57, others. Also scenarist for many of the above.

Hartley, Mariette (1940–). Underused leading lady who makes an occasional impression.
Ride the High Country 62. Drums of Africa 63. Marooned 67. Barquero 70. The Return of Count Yorga 71. Earth II (TV) 71. Sandcastles (TV) 72. Genesis II (TV) 73. The Killer Who Wouldn't Die (TV) 76. The Last Hurrah (TV) 77. Improper Channels 81. No Place to Hide (TV) 82.

Hartman, David (1937–). Tall, gangling American leading man who after a few years mostly in television gained a permanent niche as anchor man for ABC's *Good Morning America*.
The Ballad of Josie 68. Nobody's Perfect 69. Ice Station Zebra 69. San Francisco International (TV) 70. The Feminist and the Fuzz (TV) 71. I Love a Mystery (TV) 73. You'll Never See Me Again (TV) 73. Miracle on 34th Street (TV) 74. The Island at the Top of the World 75, etc.
TV series: The Bold Ones 69–71. Lucas Tanner 76.

Hartman, Don (1901–1958) (Samuel Hartman). American comedy screenwriter.
The Gay Deception 35. The Princess Comes Across 35. Waikiki Wedding 37. Tropic Holiday 38. Paris Honeymoon 39. The Star Maker 39. *Road to Singapore* 40. Life with Henry 41. *Road to Zanzibar* 41. Nothing but the Truth 41. *Road to Morocco* 42. True to Life 42. Up in Arms 44. The Princess and the Pirate 44. Down to Earth (& p) 47. It Had to be You (& d) 47. Every Girl Should Be Married (& pd) 48. Mr Imperium (& d) 51. Desire Under the Elms (p) 57. The Matchmaker (p) 58, many others.

Hartman, Elizabeth (1941–87). American leading actress.
A Patch of Blue 66. The Group 66. You're a Big Boy Now 67. The Fixer 68. The Beguiled 71. Walking Tall 73.

Hartnell, William (1908–1975). Thin-lipped British character actor who rose briefly to star status in the forties after playing many small-time crooks and tough sergeants.
Follow the Lady 33. While Parents Sleep 35. Midnight at Madame Tussaud's 36. Farewell Again 37. They Drive by Night 39. Flying Fortress 40. Suspected Person 41. The Peterville Diamond 42. The Bells Go Down 43. Headline 43. *The Way Ahead* 44. The Agitator 44. Murder in Reverse 45. Strawberry Roan 46. Appointment with Crime 46. Odd Man Out 46. Temptation Harbour 47. *Brighton Rock* 47. Now Barabbas 49. The Lost People 49. The Dark Man 50. The Magic Box 51. The Holly and the Ivy 52. The Ringer 52. Will any Gentleman? 53. Footsteps in the Fog 54. Private's Progress 55. Hell Drivers 57. Carry on Sergeant 58. Piccadilly Third Stop 60. This Sporting Life 62. Heaven's Above 63, many others.
Popular on TV in the sixties as the first Dr Who.

Harvey (US 1950). It was fashionable at the time to despise this as inferior to the stage play about a genial alcoholic who is accompanied by an invisible white rabbit six feet high. But James Stewart coped admirably with most of the googly lines; Josephine Hull was a positive delight as his much-abused sister; the supporting cast included gems from Cecil Kellaway, Wallace Ford, and Jesse White; and Henry Koster's direction, while not exciting, gave Mary Chase's script its full head.

Harvey, Anthony (1931–). British editor, later director.
AS EDITOR: Private's Progress 56. Happy is the Bride 58. The Angry Silence 60. Lolita 62. Dr Strangelove 63. The Whisperers 67, etc.
□AS DIRECTOR: Dutchman (& e) 66. The Lion in Winter 68. They Might Be Giants 71. The Glass Menagerie (TV) 73. The Abdication 74. The Disappearance of Aimee (TV) 76. Players 79. Eagle's Wing 79. Richard's Things (TV) 81. Svengali (TV) 83. The Ultimate Solution of Grace Quigley 85.

Harvey, Forrester (1880–1945). Irish character actor, long in Hollywood.
The Lilac Sunbonnet 22. The Flag Lieutenant 26. The Ring 27. The White Sheik 28. Sky Devils 32. Tarzan the Ape Man 32. Red Dust 33. The Invisible Man 33. The Painted Veil 34. The Mystery of Edwin Drood 35. Jalna 35. Lloyds of London 36. Personal Property 37. Kidnapped 38. Mysterious Mr Moto 38. Let Us Live 39. Rebecca 40. A Chump at Oxford 40. Little Nellie Kelly 40. The Wolf Man 41. Random Harvest 42. Scotland Yard Investigator 45, many others.

Harvey, Frank (1912–1981). British playwright and screenwriter.
Saloon Bar (oa) 40. Things Happen at Night (oa) 48. Seven Days to Noon (w) 50. High Treason (w) 52. Private's Progress (w) 55. I'm All Right Jack (w) 59. Heaven's Above (w) 63. No My Darling Daughter (pa/w) 63, etc.

Harvey, Laurence (1928–1973) (Larushka Mischa Skikne). Lithuanian-born leading man who worked his way slowly from British second features to top Hollywood productions, but was only briefly in fashion.
Biographies: 1973, *The Prince* by Emmett and Des Hickey. 1974, *The Laurence Harvey Story* by Hans Borgett. 1976, *One Tear is Enough* by Paulene Stone.
□House of Darkness 48. Man on the Run 48.

The Dancing Years 48. The Man from Yesterday 49. Cairo Road 49. The Scarlet Thread 50. Landfall 50. The Black Rose 50. There is Another Sun 51. A Killer Walks 51. I Believe in You 52. Women of Twilight 52. Innocents in Paris 53. Knights of the Round Table 53. Romeo and Juliet 54. King Richard and the Crusaders 54. The Good Die Young 55. I Am a Camera 55. Storm over the Nile 56. Three Men in a Boat 57. After the Ball 57. The Truth About Women 58. The Silent Enemy 58. *Room at the Top* 59. Expresso Bongo 59. The Alamo 60. Butterfield Eight 60. The Long and the Short and the Tall 61. Two Loves 61. Summer and Smoke 61. A Walk on the Wild Side 62. The Wonderful World of the Brothers Grimm 63. A Girl Named Tamiko 63. The Manchurian Candidate 63. The Running Man 63. The Ceremony (& pd) 64. Of Human Bondage 64. The Outrage 64. Darling 65. Life at the Top 65. The Spy with the Cold Nose 66. A Dandy in Aspic 67. The Winter's Tale 68. Rebus 68. Kampf um Rom 69. He and She 69. The Magic Christian 70. WUSA 71. Flight into the Sun 72. Night Watch 73. Welcome to Arrow Beach 73.

'He demonstrated conclusively that it is possible to succeed without managing to evoke the least audience interest or sympathy and to go on succeeding despite unanimous critical antipathy and overwhelming public apathy.'—*David Shipman*

Harvey, Lilian (1906–1968). British leading lady who in the thirties became star of German films.
Leidenschaft 25. Die Tolle Lola 227. Drei von der Tankstelle 30. *Congress Dances* 31. Happy Ever After 32. My Weakness (US) 33. I Am Suzanne (US) 34. Invitation to the Waltz (GB) 35. Capriccio 38. Serenade (Fr.) (last film) 39, etc.

Harvey, Paul (1884–1955). American character actor who often played the choleric executive or kindly father.
Advice to the Lovelorn 34. Rebecca of Sunnybrook Farm 38. Algiers 38. Stanley and Livingstone 39. Maryland 40. Pillow to Post 45. The Late George Apley 47. Father of the Bride 50. The First Time 52. Three for the Show 55, hundreds of others.

Haskell, Peter (–). American leading man.
The Ballad of Andy Crocker (TV) 69. The Eyes of Charles Sand (TV) 72. Phantom of Hollywood (TV) 73. Christina 74. The Night They Took Miss Beautiful (TV) 77. The Cracker Factory (TV) 79, etc.
TV series: Bracken's World 69.

Haskin, Byron (1899–1984). American director with a penchant for science fiction; some interesting films among the routine. Cameraman and special effects expert through the thirties.
□Matinée Ladies 27. Ginsberg the Great 27. Irish Hearts 27. The Siren 28. *I Walk Alone* 47. Maneater of Kumaon 48. Too Late for Tears 49. Treasure Island 50. Tarzan's Peril 51. Warpath 51. Silver City 51. Denver and Rio Grande 52. *The War of the Worlds* 53. His Majesty O'Keefe 53. The Naked Jungle 54. Long John Silver 55. Conquest of Space 55. The First Texan 56. The Boss 56. From the Earth to the Moon 58. The Little Savage 59. Jet over the Atlantic 59. September Storm 60. Armored Command 61. *Captain Sinbad* 63. *Robinson Crusoe on Mars* 64. The Power 67.

Hasse, O. E. (1903–1978). German character actor: dubbed the voices of Spencer Tracy and Paul Muni.
Peer Gynt 34. Rembrandt 42. Berliner Ballade 48. Epilog 50. Decision Before Dawn (US) 51. I Confess (US) 53. Canaris 54. Mrs Warren's Profession 59. State of Siege 72. Ice Age 75, etc.

Hassett, Marilyn (1947–). American leading lady.
Quarantined (TV) 70. They Shoot Horses Don't They? 72. *The Other Side of the Mountain* 76. Two Minute Warning 76. The Other Side of the Mountain: Part Two 77. The Bell Jar 79.

Hasso, Signe (1910–). Swedish leading lady of the forties, in Hollywood.
Assignment in Brittany 43. The Seventh Cross 44. *The House on 92nd Street* 45. Johnny Angel 45. A Scandal in Paris 46. Where There's Life 47. *To the Ends of the Earth* 48. A Double Life 48. Outside the Wall 50. Crisis 50. Picture Mommy Dead 66. Reflection of Fear 71. The Black Bird 75. I Never Promised You a Rose Garden 77, etc.

Hatfield, Hurd (1918–). American leading man whose coldly handsome face proved to be his misfortune.
□Dragon Seed 44. *The Picture of Dorian Gray* 45. The Diary of a Chambermaid 46. The Beginning or the End 47. The Unsuspected 47. The Checkered Coat 48.

Joan of Arc 48. Chinatown at Midnight 48. Tarzan and the Slave Girl 50. Destination Murder 51. The Left Handed Gun 58. King of Kings 61. El Cid 61. Mickey One 65. The Boston Strangler 68. Thief (TV) 70. Von Richthofen and Brown 71. The Norliss Tapes (TV) 73. The Word (TV) 78. You Can't Go Home Again (TV) 79. Crimes of the Heart 86.

Hathaway, Henry (1898–1985). American director, in films (as child actor) from 1907. Acted till 1932, then directed westerns. Later became known as a capable handler of big action adventures and thrillers.
□Wild Horse Mesa 32. Heritage of the Desert 33. Under the Tonto Rim 33. Sunset Pass 33. Man of the Forest 33. To the Last Man 33. Come On Marines 34. The Last Round-Up 34. Thundering Herds 34. The Witching Hour 34. Now and Forever 34. *Lives of a Bengal Lancer* 35. Peter Ibbetson 35. Trail of the Lonesome Pine 36. Go West Young Man 36. Souls at Sea 37. Spawn of the North 38. The Real Glory 39. Johnny Apollo 40. Brigham Young 40. Shepherd of the Hills 41. Sundown 41. Ten Gentlemen from West Point 42. China Girl 43. Home in Indiana 44. A Wing and a Prayer 44. Nob Hill 45. *The House on 92nd Street* 45. The Dark Corner 46. 13 Rue Madeleine 46. *Kiss of Death* 47. Call Northside 777 48. Down to the Sea in Ships 49. The Black Rose 50. You're in the Navy Now 51. Rawhide 51. Fourteen Hours 51. *Rommel, Desert Fox* 51. Diplomatic Courier 52. *Niagara* 52. White Witch Doctor 53. Prince Valiant 54. Garden of Evil 54. The Racers 54. The Bottom of the Bottle 55. Twenty-three Paces to Baker Street 56. Legend of the Lost 57. From Hell to Texas 58. A Woman Obsessed 59. Seven Thieves 60. *North to Alaska* 60. How the West Was Won (part) 62. Circus World 64. The Sons of Katie Elder 65. Nevada Smith 66. The Last Safari 67. Five Card Stud 68. True Grit 69. Raid on Rommel 71. Shootout 72.
❀ For long-standing professionalism in handling all types of subject. *The House on 92nd Street.*

¶ *H.H.:* Being educated is making the pictures themselves, if you make it your business to pay attention.

H.H.: To be a good director you've got to be a bastard. I'm a bastard and I know it.

His charm consists of minor virtues uncorrupted by major pretensions.
—*Andrew Sarris*

Hattie, Hilo (1901–1979). Hawaiian entertainer who in 1942 made her only Hollywood musical: *Song of the Islands*.

Hatton, Raymond (1887–1971). American character actor, the comic side-kick of a hundred minor westerns; in Hollywood from 1911. Formed a comedy team with Wallace Beery 1926–29.
Oliver Twist 16. Whispering Chorus 18. Male and Female 19. Jes' Call Me Jim 20. The Affairs of Anatol 21. Ebb Tide 22. The Hunchback of Notre Dame 23. The Fighting American 24. In the Name of Love 25. Born to the West 26. *Behind the Front* 26. *We're In the Navy Now* 26. Fireman Save My Child 27. The Woman God Forgot 27. We're in the Air Now 27. Partners in Crime 28. Hell's Heroes 29. Midnight Mistery 30. Woman Hungry 31. The Squaw Man 31. Polly of the Circus 32. Terror Trail 33. Wagon Wheels 34. Laughing Irish Eyes 36. Roaring Timber 37. Love Finds Andy Hardy 38. Kit Carson 40. Tall in the Saddle 44. Black Gold 47. Operation Haylift 50. Shake Rattle and Rock 56. In Cold Blood 67, many others.

Hatton, Rondo (1894–1946). American actor who suffered from facial and bodily deformity as a result of acromegaly; he was rather tastelessly cast as a monstrous killer in several low-budget mysteries of the early forties.
□ Hell Harbor 30. In Old Chicago 38. Alexander's Ragtime Band 38. The Hunchback of Notre Dame 39. Captain Fury 39. Chad Hanna 40. Moon over Burma 40. The Big Guy 40. The Cyclone Kid 42. The Moon and Sixpence 42. Sleep Lagoon 43. The Ox Bow Incident 43. *The Pearl of Death* 44. Raiders of Ghost City 44. The Princess and the Pirate 44. Johnny Doesn't Live Here Any More 44. The Royal Mounted Rides Again 45. Jungle Captive 45. Spider Woman Strikes Back 46. House of Horrors 46. The Brute Man 46.

Hauer, Rutger (1944–). Dutch leading actor.
Soldier of Orange 77. Blade Runner 82. Eureka 83. The Osterman Weekend 83. A Breed Apart 84. Ladyhawke 85. Flesh and Blood 85. The Hitcher 86. Wanted Dead or Alive 86.

The Haunted Screen, by Lotte Eisner. First published in the thirties, this is a significant study of German cinema between 1913 and 1933, concentrating (according to its sub-title) on 'expressionism and the influence of Max Reinhardt'.

Havelock-Allan, Sir Anthony (1905–). British producer.
This Man Is News 38. In Which We Serve (associate) 42. Blithe Spirit 45. Brief Encounter 46. Great Expectations 46. Oliver Twist 48. The Small Voice 49. Never Take No for an Answer 51. The Young Lovers 54. Orders to Kill 58. The Quare Fellow 61. An Evening with the Royal Ballet 64. Othello 65. The Mikado 67, etc.

Haver, June (1926–) (June Stovenour). American leading lady of the forties, mostly in musicals; married Fred McMurray. Retired.
□The Gang's All Here 43. Home in Indiana 44. Irish Eyes Are Smiling 44. Where Do We Go from Here? 45. *The Dolly Sisters* 45. Three Little Girls in Blue 46. Wake Up and Dream 46. I Wonder Who's Kissing Her Now 47. Scudda Hoo Scudda Hay 48. Oh You Beautiful Doll 49. *Look for the Silver Lining* (as Marilyn Miller) 49. The Daughter of Rosie O'Grady 50. I'll Get By 50. Love Nest 51. The Girl Next Door 53.

Haver, Phyllis (1899–1960) (Phyllis O'Haver). American leading lady of the silent screen, a former Sennett bathing beauty.
Small Town Idol 20. Temple of Venus 23. Fig Leaves 25. Up in Mabel's Room 26. The Way of All Flesh 28. Hard Boiled 29. Hell's Kitchen 29, many others.

Havers, Nigel (1952–). Elegant British actor.
Chariots of Fire 79. A Passage to India 84. Burke and Wills 86. The Whistle Blower 86. Empire of the Sun 87.
TV series: Don't Wait Up 83– . The Charmer 87.

Havlick, Gene (c. 1895–1959). American editor.
Beauty and Bullets 28. Madonna of the Streets 30. Shopworn 32. Broadway Bill 34. Mr Deeds Goes to Town 36. *Lost Horizon* (AA) 37. You Can't Take It with You 38. Mr Smith Goes to Washington 39. His Girl Friday 40. The Wife takes a Flyer 42. A Song to Remember 45. Relentless 48. Son of Dr Jekyll 51. Jungle Maneaters 54. Screaming Mimi 58, many others.

Havoc, June (1916–) (June Hovick). American leading lady, former child actress; sister of Gypsy Rose Lee.
Autobiography 1960: *Early Havoc.*
Four Jacks and a Jill 42. Brewster's Millions 45. The Story of Molly X 49. Once a Thief 50. A Lady Possessed 51. Three for Jamie Dawn 57. The Private Files of J. Edgar Hoover 78. Can't Stop the Music 80, etc.
TV series: Willy 54.

Hawkins, Jack (1910–1973). Dominant British actor; after long apprenticeship, became an international star in middle age, but in 1966 lost his voice after an operation; his subsequent minor appearances were dubbed.
Autobiography 1974: *Anything For a Quiet Life.*
Birds of Prey 30. The Lodger 32. The Good Companions 32. The Lost Chord 33. I Lived with You 33. The Jewel 33. A Shot in the Dark 33. Autumn Crocus 34. Death at Broadcasting House 34. *Peg of Old Drury* 35. Beauty and the Barge 37. The Frog 37. Who Goes Next 38. A Royal Divorce 38. Murder Will Out 39. The Flying Squad 40. Next of Kin 42. *The Fallen Idol* 48. Bonnie Prince Charlie 48. The Small Back Room 48. *State Secret* 50. The Black Rose 50. The Elusive Pimpernel 50. The Adventurers 51. No Highway 51. Home at Seven 51. *Angels One Five* 52. The Planter's Wife 52. Mandy 52. *The Cruel Sea* 53. Twice Upon a Time 53. The Malta Story 53. The Intruder 53. Front Page Story 54. The Seekers 54. The Prisoner 55. Touch and Go 55. Land of the Pharaohs 55. The Long Arm 56. The Man in the Sky 56. Fortune is a Woman 57. *The Bridge on the River Kwai* 57. Gideon's Day 58. The Two Headed Spy 58. *The League of Gentlemen* 59. *Ben Hur* (US) 59. Two Loves (US) 61. Five Finger Exercise (US) 62. *Lawrence of Arabia* 62. Lafayette 63. *Rampage* (US) 63. Zulu 63. The Third Secret 64. Guns at Batasi 64. Masquerade 65. Lord Jim 65. Judith 65. Great Catherine 67. Shalako 68. Oh What a Lovely War 69. Monte Carlo or Bust 69. Waterloo 70. The Adventures of Gerard 70. Nicholas and Alexandra 71. Kidnapped 72. Young Winston 72. Theatre of Blood 73. Tales that Witness Madness 73, etc.
TV series: *The Four Just Men* 59.
❁ For humorously perpetuating the image of the friendly World War II officer. *The League of Gentlemen.*

Hawks, Howard (1896–1977). American director, at his best an incomparable provider of professional comedies and action dramas. In films from 1918, at first as writer and editor.
Books include *Howard Hawks* by Robin Wood; *The Cinema of Howard Hawks* by

Peter Bogdanovich; *Hawks on Hawks* (devised by Joe McBride).
□Tiger Love (w only) 24. The Road to Glory (& w) 26. Fig Leaves (& w) 26. The Cradle Snatchers 27. Paid to Love 27. A Girl in Every Port (& w) 28. Fazil 28. The Air Circus 28. Trent's Last Case (& w) 29. *The Dawn Patrol* 30. The Criminal Code 31. The Crowd Roars 32. *Scarface* 32. Tiger Shark 32. Today We Live 33. *Twentieth Century* 34. Viva Villa (part) 34. *Barbary Coast* 35. Ceiling Zero 36. Road to Glory 36. Come and Get It (co-d) 36. *Bringing Up Baby* 38. Only Angels Have Wings 39. *His Girl Friday* 40. Sergeant York 41. Ball of Fire 41. Air Force 42. Corvette K 225 (p only) 44. *To Have and Have Not* 44. *The Big Sleep* 46. A Song Is Born 48. *Red River* 48. I Was a Male War Bride 49. The Thing from Another World (p only) 52. The Big Sky 52. Monkey Business 52. Full House (one episode) 52. Gentlemen Prefer Blondes 53. Land of the Pharaohs 55. *Rio Bravo* 58. Hatari 62. Man's Favourite Sport 64. Red Line 7000 65. El Dorado 66. Rio Lobo 70.

'He stamped his remarkably bitter view of life on adventure, gangster and private eye melodramas, the kind of thing Americans do best and appreciate least.'—*Andrew Sarris, 1968*

❀ For the remarkably consistent vigour with which he presented a man's world invaded by a woman. *His Girl Friday.*

¶ *H.H.:* For me the best drama is one that deals with a man in danger.

Hawn, Goldie (1945–). American leading lady who scored as blonde dimwit on TV's *Laugh-In.*
□The One and Only Genuine Original Family Band 68. *Cactus Flower* (AA) 69. *There's a Girl in My Soup* 70. Butterflies are Free 72. Dollars 72. The Sugarland Express 73. The Girl from Petrovka 74. Shampoo 75. The Duchess and the Dirtwater Fox 76. Foul Play 78. Travels with Anita 79. Private Benjamin 80. Seems Like Old Times 80. Best Friends 82. Protocol 84. Swing Shift 84. Wildcats 85. Overboard 87.
TV series: Good Morning World 67.

Haworth, Jill (1945–). British leading lady in Hollywood.
Exodus 60. In Harm's Way 65. It 66. Home for the Holidays (TV) 72. The Mutations 74.

Haworth, Ted (1917–). American production designer.
Villa Rides 68. The Kremlin Letter 70. The Beguiled 71. Harry and Tonto 74. Telefon 77. Bloodline 79. Rough Cut 80. Death Hunt 81. Jinxed 82, etc.

Hawthorne, Nathaniel (1804–1864). American novelist whose books *The Scarlet Letter, Twice-Told Tales* and *The House of Seven Gables* have been much adapted for the screen.

Hawthorne, Nigel (1929–). British star character actor.
A Tale of Two Cities (TV) 80. The Hunchback of Notre Dame (TV) 81. Firefox 82. Gandhi 82. Dream Child 84. Turtle Diary 84. Jenny's War (TV) 84. The Chain 86.
TV series: *Yes Minister* (as Sir Humphrey) 81–.

Hawtrey, Charles (1914–). Spindle-shanked British comic actor, long cast as ageing schoolboy in Will Hay and other comedies; in the sixties, a familiar member of the 'Carry On' team.
Good Morning Boys 37. Where's That Fire 40. The Goose Steps Out 42. A Canterbury Tale 48. The Galloping Major 50. Brandy for the Parson 52. *You're Only Young Twice* 53. Carry on Sergeant 58. Carry on Nurse 59. Carry on Jack 54. Carry on Cowboy 67. Carry on at Your Convenience 71. Carry on Abroad 72, many others.

Hay, Alexandra (c. 1944–). American leading lady.
Skidoo 68. The Model Shop 69. The Love Machine 71. 1000 Convicts and a Woman 71, etc.

Hay, Will (1888–1949). British character comedian, one of the screen's greats; after many years in the music halls, starred in several incomparable farces playing variations on his favourite role of an incompetent, seedy schoolmaster.
Biography 1978: *Good Morning Boys* by Ray Seaton.
□Those Were the Days 34. Dandy Dick 34. Radio Parade 35. Boys will be Boys 35. Where There's a Will 36. Windbag the Sailor 36. *Good Morning Boys* 37. Convict 99 38. Hey Hey USA 38. *Old Bones of the River* 38. *Oh Mr Porter* 38. *Ask a Policeman* 39. Where's that Fire? 39. *The Ghost of St Michael's* 41. The Black Sheep of Whitehall 41. The Big Blockade 42. The Goose Steps Out 42. *My Learned Friend* 44.
❀ For developing an unforgettable comic persona which lives in the memory independently of his films; and for persuading

us to root for that character despite its basically unsympathetic nature. *Oh Mr Porter.*

¶ *W.H.:* A good comedy scenario is very near pathos. The character I play is really a very pathetic fellow.

W.H.: I've always found something funny in the idea of a hopelessly inefficient man blundering through a job he knows nothing about.

Hayakawa, Sessue (1889–1973). Japanese actor, a popular star of American silents; more recently in occasional character roles.
The Typhoon 14. *The Cheat* 15. Forbidden Paths 17. The Tong Man 19. Daughter of the Dragon 29. Tokyo Joe 49. Three Came Home 50. *The Bridge on the River Kwai* 57. The Geisha Boy 59. The Swiss Family Robinson 60. Hell to Eternity 61, etc.

Hayden, Harry (1884–1955). Tubby American character actor who played scores of bankers, clergymen and unassuming family chaps.
I Married a Doctor 36. Black Legion 36. Ever Since Eve 37. Kentucky 38. Angels with Dirty Faces 38. Swanee River 39. Christmas in July 40. The Palm Beach Story 42. Up in Mabel's Room 44. The Killers 46. The Unfinished Dance 47. Intruder in the Dust 49. Double Dynamite 51. Army Bound 52, many others.

Hayden, Linda (1951–). British leading lady; started by playing teenage sexpots.
Baby Love 69. Taste the Blood of Dracula 69. Satan's Skin 70. Something to Hide 72. Confessions of a Window Cleaner 74. Let's Get Laid 77, etc.

Hayden, Russell (1912–1981) (Pate Lucid). American 'second string' leading man, for many years Hopalong Cassidy's faithful sidekick. Later produced TV westerns.
Hills of Old Wyoming (debut) 37. Range War 39. Lucky Legs 42. 'Neath Canadian Skies 46. Seven Were Saved 47. Silver City 49. Valley of Fire 51, many others.
TV series: Cowboy G-Men 52. Judge Roy Bean 55.

Hayden, Sterling (1916–86) (Sterling Walter Relyea). Rangy American leading man and part-time explorer.
Autobiography 1963: *Wanderer*. 1978: *Voyage.*
Virginia 40. Bahama Passage 41. Blaze of Noon 47. El Paso 49. Manhandled 49. *The Asphalt Jungle* 50. Denver and Rio Grande 52. The Golden Hawk 52. The Star 52. So Big 53. Prince Valiant 54. Arrow in the Dust 54. Johnny Guitar 54. Suddenly 54. Timberjack 55. The Eternal Sea 55. The Last Command 55. *The Killing* 56. Crime of Passion 56. Five Steps to Danger 56. Zero Hour 57. Terror in a Texas Town 58. Dr Strangelove 63. Hard Contract 69. Loving 70. The Godfather 72. The Long Goodbye 73. Cobra 73. Deadly Strangers 74. Is It Any Wonder 75. 1900 77. King of the Gypsies 78. The Outsider 79. Winter Kills 79. Nine to Five 80. Venom 82. Lighthouse of Chaos 83. Voyager 84, etc.

¶ *S.H.:* If I had the dough, I'd buy up the negative of every film I ever made . . . and start one hell of a fire.

S.H.: I don't think there are many other businesses where you can be paid good money and not know what you're doing.

S.H.: I started at the top and worked my way down.

Haydn, Richard (1905–85). British revue star of the thirties, in Hollywood from 1941, usually in adenoidal character cameos.
Ball of Fire (debut) 41. Charley's Aunt 41. Forever and a Day 43. And Then There Were None 45. *Cluny Brown* 46. *Sitting Pretty* 47. Miss Tatlock's Millions (& d) 48. Mr Music (& d) 50. Dear Wife (d only) 50. Jupiter's Darling 54. Please Don't Eat the Daisies 60. *The Lost World* 60. Mutiny on the Bounty 62. Five Weeks in a Balloon 62. The Sound of Music 65. Clarence the Cross-Eyed Lion 65. Bullwhip Griffin 66. Young Frankenstein 74, many others.

Haye, Helen (1874–1957) (Helen Hay). Distinguished British stage actress (debut 1898), in occasional films, usually as kindly dowager.
Tilly of Bloomsbury 21. Atlantic 30. Congress Dances 31. *The Spy in Black* 39. Kipps 41. *Dear Octopus* 43. Anna Karenina 48. Richard III 56, many others.

Hayers, Sidney (1921–). British director, in films since 1942. Former editor and second unit director.
□Violent Moment 58. The White Trap 59. Circus of Horrors 59. Echo of Barbara 60. The Malpas Mystery 60. *Payroll* 61. *Night of the Eagle* 62. This Is My Street 63. Three Hats for Lisa 65. The Trap 66. Finders Keepers 66. The Southern Star 69. Mr Jerico 69. The Firechasers 70. Assault 71. Revenge 71. All Coppers Are . . . 72. Deadly Strangers 74. What Changed Charley Farthing 74. Diagnosis Murder (TV) 74.

Hayes, Alfred (–1985). American screenwriter.
Paisa 46. Clash by Night 51. Act of Love 54. The Left Hand of God 55. The Double Man 67, etc.

Hayes, Allison (1930–1977) (Mary Jane Hayes). American leading lady of a few films in the fifties.
Francis Joins the WACs 54. The Purple Mask 55. The Blackboard Jungle 55. Mohawk 56. The Zombies of Mora Tau 57. Attack of the Fifty-Foot Woman (title role) 58. Who's Been Sleeping in My Bed? 63. Tickle Me 65.
TV series: Acapulco 60.

Hayes, George 'Gabby' (1885–1969). Bewhiskered American character comedian, in minor westerns from silent days.
The Rainbow Man 29. Beggars in Ermine 34. The Lost City 35. Three on the Trail 36. Mountain Music 37. Hopalong Rides Again 38. Gold is Where You Find It 38. Man of Conquest 39. Wagons Westward 40. Melody Ranch 41. In Old Oklahoma 43. Tall in the Saddle 44. Utah 45. My Pal Trigger 46. Wyoming 47. Return of the Badmen 48. El Paso 49. The Cariboo Trail 50, many others.
TV series: The Gabby Hayes Show 50.

Hayes, Helen (1900–) (Helen Hayes Brown). Distinguished American stage actress who made a number of film appearances.
Autobiographies: *A Gift of Joy* 1965; *On Reflection* 1969; *Twice Over Lightly* 1981.
□The Weavers of Life 17. Babs 20. *The Sin of Madelon Claudet* (AA) 31. Arrowsmith 31. *A Farewell to Arms* 32. The Son Daughter 33. The White Sister 33. Another Language 33. Night Flight 33. What Every Woman Knows 34. Crime without Passion (unbilled) 34. Vanessa 35. Stage Door Canteen 43. My Son John 51. Main Street to Broadway 53. *Anastasia* 56. Third Man on the Mountain (unbilled) 59. *Airport* (AA) 69. Do Not Fold Spindle or Mutilate (TV) 71. Herbie Rides Again 73. The Snoop Sisters (TV) 73 (and series). One of Our Dinosaurs is Missing 75. Victory at Entebbe (TV) 76. Candleshoe 77. A Family Upside Down (TV) 78. The Moneychangers (TV) 79. Murder Is Easy (TV) 82. A Caribbean Mystery (TV) 83. Murder With Mirrors (TV) 84.

¶ *H.H. (on having a theatre named after her):* An actor's life is so transitory. Suddenly you're a building.

Hayes, John Michael (1919–). American screenwriter.
Rear Window 54. To Catch a Thief 55. The Trouble with Harry 56. Peyton Place 57. *The Carpetbaggers* 63. Where Love Has Gone 64. Harlow 65. Judith 66. Nevada Smith 66, etc.

Hayes, Margaret (1915–1977). American character actress, also in TV and public relations.
The Blackboard Jungle 55. Violent Saturday 55. Omar Khayyam 57. Fraulein 57. Damn Citizen 58, etc.

Hayes, Melvyn (1935–). British comedy character actor, a former child star who was part of Cliff Richard's support in *The Young Ones*, *Summer Holiday*, etc; later became familiar on TV in *It Ain't Half Hot Mum*.
The Curse of Frankenstein 56. No Trees in the Street 58. The Young Ones 61. Summer Holiday 62. Wonderful Life 64. A Walk with Love and Death 69. Love Thy Neighbour 73. Carry on England 76, etc.

Hayes, Patricia (1910–). British character actress, mainly in low-life comedy roles. Much on TV.
Candles at Nine 44. Nicholas Nickleby 46. The Love Match 54. The Battle of the Sexes 59. Goodbye Mr Chips 69. Love Thy Neighbour 73. The Corn Is Green (TV) 79. The Never Ending Story 84. Little Dorrit 87, etc.

Hayles, Brian (1930–78). British scriptwriter, from TV.
Warlords of Atlantis 78. Arabian Adventure 79.

Haymes, Dick (1918–80). Argentine-born crooner, former radio announcer.
Irish Eyes Are Smiling (debut) 44. Diamond Horseshoe 45. *State Fair* 45. Do You Love Me? 46. The Shocking Miss Pilgrim 47. Up in Central Park 48. One Touch of Venus 48. St Benny the Dip 51. All Ashore 53. Betrayal (TV) 74, etc.

Hays, Robert (1948–). American leading man of the early eighties.
The Young Pioneers (TV) 76. Delta County USA (TV) 78. The Initiation of Sarah (TV) 78. The Fall of the House of Usher (TV) 79. Airplane 80. Take This Job and Shove It 81. Airplane 2: the Sequel 82. Touched 83. Trenchcoat 82. Cat's Eye 85.

Hays, Will H. (1879–1954). American executive, for many years (1922–45) president of the Motion Picture Producers and

Distributors Association of America, and author of its high-toned Production Code (1930), which for many years put producers in fear of 'the Hays office'. *The Memoirs of Will H. Hays* was published in 1955.

¶ *W.H. (1930):* Good taste is good business.

Hayter, James (1907–1983). Portly, jovial British character actor, on stage from 1925, films from 1936.
Sensation 36. Sailors Three 41. School for Secrets 46. *Nicholas Nickleby* (as the Cheeryble twins) 47. The Blue Lagoon 48. *Trio* 50. Tom Brown's Schooldays 51. Robin Hood (as Friar Tuck) 52. *Pickwick Papers* (title role) 53. The Great Game 53. A Day to Remember 54. Touch and Go 56. Port Afrique 58. The Thirty-Nine Steps 59. Stranger in the House 67. Oliver 68. David Copperfield 69. Song of Norway 70, many others.
TV series: Are You Being Served? 78.

Haythorne, Joan (1915–) (Joan Haythornthwaite). British stage actress, usually in aristocratic roles.
School for Secrets 46. Jassy 47. Highly Dangerous 50. Svengali 54. The Weak and the Wicked 54. The Feminine Touch 56. Three Men in a Boat 56. Shakedown 59. So Evil So Young 61, etc.

Hayton, Lennie (1908–1971). American composer.
The Bugle Sounds 41. Meet the People 43. Salute to the Marines 43. The Harvey Girls 45. Summer Holiday 46. The Hucksters 47. The Pirate 48. Battleground 49. On the Town (co-w) (AA) 49. Inside Straight 51. Singin' in the Rain 52. Battle Circus 53. Star! 68. Hello Dolly (co-w) (AA) 69, etc.

Hayward, Leland (1902–1971). American talent agent and stage producer. Recently produced films.
Mister Roberts 55. The Spirit of St Louis 57. The Old Man and the Sea 58, etc.

Hayward, Louis (1909–85) (Seafield Grant). Mild-mannered, South African-born leading man with stage experience; in Hollywood from 1935.
□ Chelsea Life (GB) 33. The Man Outside (GB) 33. I'll Stick to You (GB) 33. The Thirteenth Candle (GB) 33. The Love Test (GB) 34. *Sorrell and Son* (GB) 34. The Flame Within 35. Anthony Adverse 36. The Luckiest Girl in the World 36. Midnight Intruder 37. The Rage of Paris 38. *The Saint in New York* 38. *Duke of West Point* 39. *The Man in the Iron Mask* 39. *My Son, My Son* 40. Son of Monte Cristo 40. Ladies in Retirement 41. And Then There Were None 45. Monte Cristo's Revenge 47. Young Widow 47. Repeat Performance 47. The Black Arrow 48. Walk a Crooked Mile 48. Pirates of Capri 49. The Fortunes of Captain Blood 50. Son of Dr Jekyll 51. The Lady and the Bandit 51. Lady in the Iron Mask 52. Captain Pirate 52. Royal African Rifles 53. The Saint's Return (GB) 53. Duffy of San Quentin 54. *The Search for Bridey Murphy* 56. Chuka 67. Terror in the Wax Museum 73.
TV series: The Lone Wolf 53. The Pursuers 63. The Survivors 69.

Hayward, Susan (1918–1975) (Edythe Marrener). Vivacious American leading lady, in films from 1938 after modelling experience: often in aggressive roles.
Biography 1974: *Divine Bitch* by Doug McLelland.
□Girls on Probation 38. Our Leading Citizen 39. $1000 A Touchdown 39. Beau Geste 39. Adam Had Four Sons 41. Sis Hopkins 41. Among the Living 41. Reap the Wild Wind 42. The Forest Rangers 42. I Married a Witch 42. Star Spangled Rhythm 42. Change of Heart 43. Jack London 43. Young and Willing 43. The Fighting Seabees 44. And Now Tomorrow 44. The Hairy Ape 44. Canyon Passage 45. Deadline at Dawn 46. Smash-Up 47. They Won't Believe Me 47. The Lost Moment 47. Tap Roots 48. The Saxon Charm 48. *Tulsa* 49. *My Foolish Heart* 49. House of Strangers 49. I'd Climb the Highest Mountain 50. *I Can Get It For You Wholesale* 51. Rawhide 51. David and Bathsheba 51. *With a Song in My Heart* 52. The Lusty Men 52. The Snows of Kilimanjaro 52. The President's Lady 53. White Witch Doctor 53. Demetrius and the Gladiators 54. Garden of Evil 54. Untamed 55. Soldier of Fortune 55. The Conqueror 55. *I'll Cry Tomorrow* (as Lilian Roth) 55. Top Secret Affair 57. *I Want To Live* (as Barbara Graham) (AA) 58. A Woman Obsessed 59. Thunder in the Sun 59. The Marriage-Go Round 60. Ada 61. Back Street 61. Stolen Hours (GB) 63. I Thank a Fool (GB) 63. Where Love Has Gone 64. The Honey Pot 67. Valley of the Dolls 67. Fitzgerald and Pride (TV) 71. Heat of Anger (TV) 71. The Revengers 72. Say Goodbye Maggie Cole (TV) 72.

Hayworth, Rita (1918–87) (Margarita Carmen Cansino). Star American leading lady and dancer of the forties, often in tempestuous roles; on stage from six years old; of Latin and Irish ancestry. From 1980 her decline from Alzheimer's disease was well known. Lynda Carter played her in a 1983 TV movie, *Rita Hayworth: the Love Goddess*. Biography 1977: *Rita Hayworth, The Time, The Place and The Woman* by John Kobal.
□Dante's Inferno 35. Under the Pampas Moon 35. Charlie Chan in Egypt 35. Paddy O'Day 35. Human Cargo 36. A Message to Garcia 36. Meet Nero Wolfe 36. Rebellion 36. Old Louisiana 37. Hit the Saddle 37. Trouble in Texas 37. Criminals of the Air 37. Girls Can Play 37. The Game that Kills 37. Paid to Dance 37. The Shadow 37. Who Killed Gail Preston? 38. There's Always a Woman 38. Convicted 38. Juvenile Court 38. Homicide Bureau 38. The Lone Wolf's Spy Hunt 39. Renegade Ranger 39. *Only Angels Have Wings* 39. Special Inspector 39. Music in My Heart 40. Blondie on a Budget 40. Susan and God 40. *The Lady in Question* 40. Angels over Broadway 40. *The Strawberry Blonde* 41. Affectionately Yours 41. Blood and Sand 41. *You'll Never Get Rich* 41. My Gal Sal 42. Tales of Manhattan 42. You Were Never Lovelier 42. *Cover Girl* 44. Tonight and Every Night 45. *Gilda* 46. Down to Earth 47. *The Lady from Shanghai* 48. The Loves of Carmen 48. Affair in Trinidad 52. Salome 53. *Miss Sadie Thompson* 53. Fire Down Below 57. *Pal Joey* 57. *Separate Tables* 58. They Came to Cordura 59. The Story on Page One 59. The Happy Thieves 62. Circus World 64. The Money Trap 66. The Poppy is also a Flower 67. The Rover 68. Sons of Satan 68. The Road to Salina 70. The Naked Zoo 71. The Wrath of God 72.

❀ For supplying the kind of glamour the forties needed, and for doing it with the saving grace of humour. *Gilda*.

¶ *R.H.:* Every man I knew had fallen in love with Gilda and wakened with me.

R.H.: A girl is . . . a girl. It's nice to be told you're successful at it.

R.H.: I haven't had everything from life. I've had too much.

R.H.: I never really thought of myself as a sex symbol—more as a comedienne who could dance.

Hazell, Hy (1920–1970) (Hyacinth Hazel O'Higgins). British revue and musical comedy artist.
Meet Me at Dawn 46. Paper Orchid 49. Celia 49. The Lady Craved Excitement 50. The Night Won't Talk 52. Up in the World 56. The Whole Truth 58, etc.

Head, Edith (1907–1981). American dress designer, in Hollywood from the twenties. First solo credit *She Done Him Wrong* 33; later won Academy Awards for The Heiress 49. Samson and Delilah 51. A Place in the Sun 52, etc; worked on Olly Olly Oxen Free 78. Appeared in *The Oscar* 66. Autobiography 1940: *The Dress Doctor*.

Head, Murray (1946–). Young British actor of the seventies.
Sunday Bloody Sunday 71. Gawain and the Green Knight 73.

Healey, Myron (1922–). American general purpose actor; Doc Holliday in the *Wyatt Earp* TV series.
I Dood It 43. The Man from Colorado 48. Salt Lake Raiders 50. Fort Osage 52. Rage at Dawn 55. Hell's Crossroads 57. Escape from Red Rock 58. Gunfight at Dodge City 59. Harlow 65. Mirage 65. True Grit 69. Which Way to the Front? 70, many others.

Healy, Ted (1886–1937). Tough-looking, cigar-chewing American vaudevillian who originated the Three Stooges and took them to Hollywood.
Soup to Nuts 30. Dancing Lady 33. The Band Plays On 34. Mad Love 35. San Francisco 36. Hollywood Hotel 37, etc.

Heard, John (1946–). American general purpose actor.
First Love 77. Between the Lines 79. Head over Heels 80. Heartbeat 80. Cutter's Way 81. Cat People 82, etc.

Hearne, Richard (1908–1979). British acrobatic comedian, in music hall and circus practically from the cradle. Made occasional films, often in his character of 'Mr Pastry'.
Dance Band 35. Millions 37. Miss London Ltd 42. The Butler's Dilemma 43. One Night with You 48. Helter Skelter 49. Captain Horatio Hornblower 50. Madame Louise 51. Miss Robin Hood 52. Something in the City 53. Tons of Trouble 56, etc.

Hearst, William Randolph (1863–1951). American newspaper magnate thought to have been the original of *Citizen Kane*. Also noted for pushing his protégée Marion Davies (qv) to film stardom by buying a production company solely for her vehicles.
Biography 1961: *Citizen Hearst* by W. A. Swanberg.

Heatherton, Joey (1944–). American leading lady, former child stage performer.
Twilight of Honor 64. Where Love Has Gone 64. My Blood Runs Cold 64. Bluebeard 72. The Happy Hooker Goes to Washington 77, etc.

Heaven: see *fantasy*.

Heaven Can Wait (US 1943). One of the most charming, polished and unexpected comedies of Ernst Lubitsch, this half-forgotten film drew surprisingly warm performances from Don Ameche and Gene Tierney, the former as a lately deceased gentleman describing his youthful follies to a suave and sympathetic Satan in a very luxurious version of Hell. Script by Samson Raphaelson from Laslo Bus-Fekete's play *Birthday*. The period settings and fantasy endpapers, all in colour, made it a great success in the middle of World War II.

Heavens Above (GB 1963). The Boulting Brothers' long-awaited satire on the church turned out to be a long-drawn-out sentimental comedy which pulled its punches and drifted too often into tedious irrelevance. Peter Sellers made a dull fellow of the proletarian parson, but there were compensations in the contributions of Cecil Parker, Miles Malleson and Ian Carmichael as church dignitaries.

Hecht, Ben (1894–1964). American writer and critic with screenplay credits going back to silent days. Often worked in collaboration with Charles MacArthur.
Autobiographies: *A Child of the Century, Gaily Gaily*.
Biography 1978: *The Five Lives of Ben Hecht* by Doug Fetherling.
Underworld (w) (AA) 28. The Great Gabbo (oa) 29. *The Front Page* (oa) 31. Topaze (w) 33. Twentieth Century (oa) 34. *Crime Without Passion* (wd) 34. *The Scoundrel* (wd) (AA) 35. *Soak the Rich* (wpd) 36. *Nothing Sacred* (w) 37. The Goldwyn Follies (w) 38. *Wuthering Heights* (w) 39. *Angels Over Broadway* (wpd) 40. Lydia (w) 41. Tales of Manhattan (w) 42. The Black Swan (w) 42. *Spellbound* (w) 45. *Notorious* (w) 46. The Specter of the Rose (wpd) 46. Her Husband's Affairs (w) 47. The Miracle of the Bells (w) 48. Whirlpool (w) 49. Actors and Sin (wpd) 52. Monkey Business (w) 52. Miracle in the Rain (w) 56. Legend of the Lost (w) 58. Circus World (w) 64, etc.
❀ For being connected in some way with most of the enjoyable hard-boiled comedies and melodramas with which one associates Hollywood in the thirties and forties. *Nothing Sacred*.

¶ *B.H.:* Hollywood held the lure . . . tremendous sums of money for work that required no more effort than a game of pinochle.

B.H.: Movies are one of the bad habits that have corrupted our century. They have slipped into the American mind more misinformation in one evening than the Dark Ages could muster in a decade.

B.H.: A movie is never any better than the stupidest man connected with it.

B.H.: The movies are an eruption of trash that has lamed the American mind and retarded Americans from becoming cultured people.

Hecht, Harold (1903–75). American producer, formerly dance director and literary agent. From 1947 produced jointly with Burt Lancaster and later James Hill.
Vera Cruz 54. Marty 55. Trapeze 56. Separate Tables 58. Taras Bulba 63. Cat Ballou 65. The Way West 67, etc.

Heckart, Eileen (1919–). American character actress, mainly on stage.
Miracle in the Rain 56. The Bad Seed 56. Somebody Up There Likes Me 57. Hot Spell 57. Heller in Pink Tights 60. Up the Down Staircase 68. No Way to Treat a Lady 68. Butterflies Are Free (AA) 72. Zandy's Bride 74. The Hiding Place 75. Burnt Offerings 77. Sunshine Christmas (TV) 77. Suddenly Love (TV) 78. Backstairs at the White House (TV) 79. White Mama (TV) 81. FDR: The Last Year (TV) 81. Heartbreak Ridge 86.

Heckerling, Amy (–). American director.
Fast Times at Ridgmont High 82. Johnny Dangerously 84. National Lampoon's European Vacation 85.

Heckroth, Hein (1901–1970). German art director who did work in Britain, mainly for Powell and Pressburger.
Caesar and Cleopatra 45. *A Matter of Life and Death* 46. *The Red Shoes* (AA) 48. Tales of Hoffman 51. The Story of Gilbert and Sullivan 53. The Battle of the River Plate 56. Torn Curtain (US) 66, etc.

Hedison, David (formerly **Al Hedison**) (1926–) (Ara Heditsian). American leading man, mostly on TV.
The Enemy Below 57. *The Fly* 58. Son of

Robin Hood 59. The Lost World 60. Marines Let's Go 61. The Greatest Story Ever Told 65. Live and Let Die 73. The Cat Creature (TV) 73. Adventures of the Queen (TV) 75. The Lives of Jenny Dolan (TV) 75. Murder in Peyton Place (TV) 77. The Power Within (TV) 79. North Sea Hijack 80. The Naked Face 84. Smart Alec 85.

TV series: *Five Fingers* 59. *Voyage to the Bottom of the Sea* 64–67.

Hedley, Jack (1930–). Amiable British leading man best remembered as TV's 'Tim Frazer'.
Room at the Top (debut) 59. Make Mine Mink 60. Lawrence of Arabia 62. In the French Style 63. The Scarlet Blade 63. *Of Human Bondage* 64. Witchcraft 65. The Anniversary 67. Goodbye Mr Chips 69. Brief Encounter (TV) 74. For Your Eyes Only 81. Sophia Loren (TV) 81, etc.

Hedren, Tippi (1935–) (Nathalie Hedren). American leading lady, former TV model.
□*The Birds* 63. Marnie 64. A Countess from Hong Kong 66. The Man with the Albatross 69. Tiger by the Tail 69. Satan's Harvest 69. Mr Kingstreet's War 73. The Harrad Experiment 73. Roar 82. The Thrill of Genius 85.

Heerman, Victor (1892–). Anglo-American director, in US from boyhood.
□Don't Ever Marry 20. The Poor Simp 20. A Divorce of Convenience 21. The Chicken in the Case 21. My Boy 22. John Smith 22. Love Is an Awful Thing 22. Rupert of Hentzau 23. Modern Matrimony 23. The Dangerous Maid 23. The Confidence Man 24. Old Home Week 25. Irish Luck 25. For Wives Only 26. Rubber Heels 26. Ladies Must Dress 27. Love Hungry 28. Personality 30. Paramount on Parade 30. *Animal Crackers* 30. Sea Legs 30. Also screenwriter, usually in collaboration.

Heffron, Richard T. (1930–). American director, from TV.
Newman's Law 73. Toma (TV pilot) 73. Outrage (TV) 73. The Rockford Files (TV pilot) 74. The Morning After (TV) 74. The California Kid (TV) 74. Locusts (TV) 74. I Will Fight No More Forever (TV) 75. Death Scream (TV) 75. Trackdown 76. Futureworld 76. Young Joe the Forgotten Kennedy (TV) 77. Outlaw Blues 77. See How She Runs (TV) 78. True Grit (TV) 78. A Rumor of War (TV) 80. Foolin' Around 80. I the Jury 82. Anatomy of an Illness (TV) 82.

Heflin, Van (1910–1971) (Emmett Evan Heflin). Purposeful American leading man of the forties, craggy character actor of the fifties and sixties.
□A Woman Rebels 36. The Outcasts of Poker Flat 37. Flight from Glory 37. Saturday's Heroes 37. Annapolis Salute 37. Back Door to Heaven 39. *Santa Fe Trail* 40. The Feminine Touch 41. H. M. Pulham Esq 41. *Johnny Eager* (AA) 41. *Kid Glove Killer* 42. Seven Sweethearts 42. Grand Central Murder 42. Tennessee Johnson 42. Presenting Lily Mars 43. *The Strange Love of Martha Ivers* 46. Till the Clouds Roll By 46. Possessed 47. Green Dolphin Street 47. Tap Roots 48. B.F.'s Daughter 48. The Three Musketeers 48. Act of Violence 48. Madame Bovary 48. East Side 48. East Side West Side 49. Tomahawk 51. *The Prowler* 51. Weekend with Father 51. My Son John 52. Wings of the Hawk 53. *Shane* 53. Tanganyika 54. South of Algiers (GB) 54. The Raid 54. Woman's World 54. The Black Widow 54. Count Three and Pray 55. Battle Cry 55. *Patterns* 56. *3.10 to Yuma* 57. Gunman's Walk 58. They Came to Cordura 59. Tempest 59. Five Branded Women 60. Under Ten Flags 60. Cry of Battle 63. The Wastrel 64. To Be a Man 64. The Greatest Story Ever Told 65. Once a Thief 65. Stagecoach 66. The Man Outside (GB) 67. Each Man for Himself 68. *Airport* 69. The Big Bounce 69. The Last Child (TV) 71.

Heggie, O. P. (1879–1936). Australian character actor of stage and, latterly, Hollywood screen.
The Mysterious Dr Fu Manchu 29. East Lynne 31. Smiling Through 32. Midnight 3. The Count of Monte Cristo 34. Bride of Frankenstein (as the blind hermit) 35. Prisoner of Shark Island 36, etc.

Heifits, Joseph (1904–). Russian director, from 1928. Known in thirties for *Baltic Deputy*, but did not come to western notice again until *The Lady with the Little Dog* 59. In the Town of S 65. Salute Marya 70.

Heindorf, Ray (1908–1980). American musical director.
Hard to Get 38. Strawberry Blonde 41. Yankee Doodle Dandy (AA) 42. This is the Army (AA) 43. Calamity Jane 53. A Star is Born 54. The Music Man (AA) 62. Finian's Rainbow 68, many others.

Heinz, Gerard (1903–1972). German character actor, mainly in British movies.

Thunder Rock 42. Went the Day Well? 42. Caravan 46. His Excellency 51. The Man Inside 57. House of the Seven Hawks 59. The Guns of Navarone 61. The Cardinal 63. The Dirty Dozen 67, many others.

The Heiress (US 1949). Oscars for best actress (Olivia de Havilland) and best art direction and costume design were won by this adaptation of the play by Ruth and Augustus Goetz from Henry James' novel *Washington Square*, about an unattractive spinster who finally turns the tables on her money-seeking suitor. With Montgomery Clift, Ralph Richardson; directed by William Wyler.

Heisler, Stuart (1894–1979). Competent American director.
□Straight from the Shoulder 36. Poppy 37. The Hurricane (co-d) 38. The Biscuit Eater 40. *The Monster and The Girl* 41. Among the Living 41. The Remarkable Andrew 42. *The Glass Key* 42. Along Came Jones 45. *Blue Skies* 46. Vendetta (co-d) 46. *Smash Up* 47. Tulsa 49. Tokyo Joe 49. Chain Lightning 50. Dallas 50. Storm Warning 50. Journey into Light 51. Saturday Island 52. *The Star* 53. Beachhead 54. This is My Love 54. I Died a Thousand Times 55. The Lone Ranger 56. The Burning Hills 56. Hitler 62.

Heiss, Carol (1940–). German-Swiss skating star: she came to Hollywood for one movie, *Snow White and the Three Stooges* 61.

Held, Anna (1873–1918). German singer-dancer who married Ziegfeld and starred in his early Follies. Luise Rainer portrayed her in *The Great Ziegfeld* and Barbara Parkins in *Ziegfeld, the Man and His Women*. She made one film appearance in 1916: *Madame La Présidente*.

Held, Edward (1894–1985). American set designer.
Lost Horizon 37. The Hurricane 38. The Goldwyn Follies 38. Wuthering Heights 39. Kings Row 41. Across the Pacific 42. Them 54, etc.

Held, Martin (1908–). German leading actor.
Black Eyes 51. Captain from Kopenick 56. Roses for the Prosecutor 59. The Oldest Profession 67. The Serpent 72.

helicopters, restricted in scope, have been put to sound dramatic use in two films about helicopter services, *Battle Taxi* and *Flight from Ashiya*; while their potential for thrill sequences was well explored in *The Bridges at Toko-Ri, Experiment in Terror, From Russia with Love, Arabesque, Caprice, You Only Live Twice, The Satan Bug, Fathom, The Las Vegas Story, Where Eagles Dare, Masquerade, Tarzan in the Valley of Gold, That Riviera Touch, The Wrecking Crew, Figures in a Landscape, Birds of Prey, Breakout* and *Russian Roulette*. TV series on the subject include *Chopper One*, *Chopper Squad*, *Riptide*, *Blue Thunder* and *Air Wolf*. See also *airplanes*.

hell has been used more figuratively than realistically in movies; but what passed for the real thing did appear in *Dante's Inferno*, *Heaven Can Wait*, *Hellzapoppin* and *Angel on My Shoulder*, not to mention a Sylvester cartoon called *Satan's Waitin'*.

Heller, Joseph (1923–). American satirical novelist, whose *Catch 22* was rather unsatisfactorily filmed.

Heller, Lukas (1930–). German-born screenwriter, associated chiefly with Robert Aldrich.
Whatever Happened to Baby Jane? 62. Hush Hush Sweet Charlotte (co-w) 64. The Dirty Dozen (co-w) 67. The Killing of Sister George 68. The Deadly Trackers 73. Damnation Alley (co-w) 77, etc.

Heller, Otto (1896–1970). Czech-born cinematographer, in Britain since early thirties. Had more than 300 features to his credit.
The High Command 36. Tomorrow We Live 42. Mr Emmanuel 44. I Live in Grosvenor Square 45. *The Queen of Spades* 48. The Winslow Boy 48. Never Take No for an Answer 51. The Divided Heart 54. Manuela 57. The Light in the Piazza 62. West Eleven 63. The Ipcress File 65. Alfie 66. Funeral in Berlin 66. Duffy 68. Bloomfield 70, etc.

Hellinger, Mark (1903–1947). American journalist who scripted some films and later turned producer.
Biography 1952: *The Mark Hellinger Story* by Jim Bishop.
The Killers 46. Brute Force 47. Naked City (also narrated) 48.

Hellman, Jerome (1928–). American producer, former agent.
The World of Henry Orient 64. A Fine

Madness 66. *Midnight Cowboy* 69. The Day of the Locust 75. *Coming Home* 78. Promises in the Dark 79.

Hellman, Lillian (1905–84). American playwright who adapted much of her own work for the screen and also wrote other screenplays.
Autobiographies: 1969, *An Unfinished Woman*. 1974, *Pentimento*, which was filmed as *Julia*, 1977.
These Three 36. *The Little Foxes* 41. Watch on the Rhine 43. North Star 43. The Searching Wind 46. *Another Part of the Forest* 48. *The Children's Hour* 62. Toys in the Attic 63. The Chase 66. Julia 77, etc.

¶ *L.H.:* I cannot and will not cut my conscience to fit this year's fashions.

Hellman, Marcel (1898–1985). Rumanian producer, long in Britain.
The Amateur Gentleman 36. Jeannie 41. Happy Go Lucky 51. Northwest Frontier 59. Moll Flanders 65, many others.

Hellman, Monte (1931–). American director of cheapies.
□The Beast from Haunted Cave 59. Flight to Fury 65. Back Door to Hell 65. The Shooting 65. Ride the Whirlwind 71. Two Lane Blacktop 71. Cockfighter 74. China 9, Liberty 37 78.

Hello, Hollywood, by Allen Rivkin and Laura Kerr. Published in 1962, this is a 600-page collection of essays and journalistic pieces about the movies, 'by the people who make them'. Required reading for addicts.

Hell's Angels (US 1927–1930). Started as a silent and re-shot for sound, this aerial spectacular of World War I, produced and directed by Howard Hughes, still survives by virtue of its highly dramatic combat scenes, including a zeppelin raid over London. The personal story is badly dated, though the scene in which Jean Harlow allures Ben Lyon by changing into 'something more comfortable' is not to be missed.

Hellzapoppin (US 1942). Directed by H. C. Potter from the stage show starring Ole Olsen and Chic Johnson, this crazy farce now seems insufficiently daring: there's actually a plot and a love interest! Many of the gags, however, still work, and as a whole it was more successful in popularizing this kind of entertainment than the Marx Brothers had been.

Helm, Brigitte (1906–) (Gisele Eve Schittenhelm). German star actress of the twenties.
Metropolis 26. *The Loves of Jeanne Ney* 27. Alraune 28. Countess of Monte Cristo 31. L'Atlantide 31. Gold 33. The Blue Danube 34, etc.

Helm, Fay (c. 1910–). American actress.
Racket Busters 38. Dark Victory 39. A Child Is Born 40. Night Monster 42. Phantom Lady (title role) 44. Sister Kenny 46. The Locket 47, etc.

Helmond, Katherine (1933–). Saucer-eyed American comedy actress.
Baby Blue Marine 74. Dr Max (TV) 74. Locusts (TV) 74. The Legend of Lizzie Borden (TV) 75. Family Plot 76. Little Ladies of the Night (TV) 77. Getting Married (TV) 79. Pearl (TV) 79. Time Bandits 81. Brazil 84. Shadey 85, etc.
TV series: *Soap* 77–80.

Helpmann, Sir Robert (1909–86). Australian ballet dancer and actor of stage and screen, in Britain from 1930.
One of Our Aircraft Is Missing 42. Henry V 44. The Red Shoes 48. Tales of Hoffman 50. 55 Days in Peking 62. The Quiller Memorandum 66. Chitty Chitty Bang Bang 68. Alice's Adventures in Wonderland 72. Don Quixote (& co-d) 73, others.

Helton, Percy (1894–1971). Chubby little American comedy actor; his round face expressed surprise and dismay in innumerable small roles.
Silver Wings 22. Miracle on 34th Street 47. The Set Up 49. My Friend Irma 49. Call Me Madam 52. A Star is Born 54. Butch Cassidy and the Sundance Kid 69, many others.

Hemingway, Ernest (1899–1961). Distinguished American novelist. Works filmed include *A Farewell to Arms* 32 and 57. *Spanish Earth* (original screenplay and production) 37. *For Whom the Bell Tolls* 43. *The Killers* 46 and 64. *The Macomber Affair* 47. *The Snows of Kilimanjaro* 53. *The Sun Also Rises* 57. *The Old Man and the Sea* 58. *Adventures of a Young Man* 62. *To Have and Have Not* was filmed three times (inaccurately); in 1944, 1951 (as *The Breaking Point*) and 1956 (as *The Gun Runner*).

Hemingway, Margaux (1955–). American fashion model and occasional leading lady, granddaughter of Ernest Hemingway.

□Lipstick 76. Killer Fish 80. They Call Me Bruce 82. Over the Brooklyn Bridge 83. The Killing Machine 85.

Hemingway, Mariel (1961–). American actress, sister of Margaux Hemingway.
Lipstick 76. I Want to Keep My Baby (TV) 76. Manhattan 79. Personal Best 82. Star 80 83. Creator 84. The Mean Season 84. Superman IV 87. The Suicide Club 87.

Hemmings, David (1941–). Slightly-built British leading man who after appearing in many second features suddenly seemed to have the acceptable image for the late sixties.
No Trees in the Street 59. The Wind of Change 60. Some People 62. Live It Up 63. Dateline Diamonds 65. Eye of the Devil 66. *Blow Up* 66. Camelot 67. *The Charge of the Light Brigade* 68. A Long Day's Dying 68. Only When I Larf 68. Barbarella 68. Alfred the Great 69. The Walking Stick 69. Fragment of Fear 69. Unman Wittering and Zigo 70. The Love Machine 71. Running Scared (d only) 72. Mister Quilp 75. The Squeeze 77. Islands in the Stream 77. The Prince and the Pauper 77. Just a Gigolo (&d) 78. Murder by Decree 79. Charlie Muffin (TV) 79. Race for the Yankee Zephyr (d only) 81. The Survivor (d only) 81. Man, Woman and Child 82, etc.

Hempel, Anouska (–). British leading lady, much on TV.
On Her Majesty's Secret Service 69. Scars of Dracula 70. The Magnificent Seven Deadly Sins 71. Go for a Take 72. Slaves 73. Double Exposure 76, etc.

Henabery, Joseph (1886–1976). American silent actor who played Lincoln in *The Birth of a Nation* and later directed Gish and Fairbanks.
His Majesty the American 19. A Sainted Devil 24, etc.

Henderson, Florence (1934–). American singer and actress with theatrical experience.
Song of Norway 70.
TV series: The Brady Bunch 69–73.

Henderson, Marcia (1930–). American leading lady of the fifties.
Thunder Bay 53. The Glass Web 53. Naked Alibi 54. Back to God's Country 54, etc.

Henderson, Ray (1896–1970) (Raymond Brost). American composer, mainly with collaborators B. G. De Sylva and Lew Brown; the late twenties constituted their most successful period.

Hendrix, Wanda (1928–1981). American leading lady.
Confidential Agent 45. Ride the Pink Horse 47. Miss Tatlock's Millions 48. Prince of Foxes 49. Captain Carey USA 50. The Highwayman 52. The Last Posse 53. The Black Dakotas 54. Johnny Cool 63. Stage to Thunder Rock 65, etc.

Hendry, Ian (1931–85). Virile, aggressive British leading actor, mostly on TV.
In the Nick 60. *Live Now Pay Later* 62. The Girl in the Headlines 53. Children of the Damned 63. This is My Street 63. *The Beauty Jungle* 64. Repulsion 65. The Hill 65. The Sandwich Man 66. Casino Royale 67. Doppelganger 69. The Southern Star 69. The Mackenzie Break 70. Get Carter 71. The Jerusalem File 72. All Coppers Are . . . 72. Tales from the Crypt 72. Theatre of Blood 73. Assassin 73. The Internecine Project 74. The Bitch 79, etc.

Henie, Sonja (1910–1969). Norwegian skating star who appeared in light Hollywood musicals of the thirties and forties.
Autobiography 1940: *Wings on My Feet*.
□*One in a Million* 36. Thin Ice 37. Happy Landing 38. My Lucky Star 38. Second Fiddle 39. Everything Happens at Night 39. Sun Valley Serenade 41. Iceland 42. Wintertime 43. It's a Pleasure 45. The Countess of Monte Cristo 48. Hello London (GB) 58.

¶ Sonja, you'll never go broke. All you have to do is hock your trophies.—*Radie Harris*

Hennesy, Dale (–). American production designer.
Everything You Always Wanted to Know About Sex 72. Sleeper 73. Young Frankenstein 74. Logan's Run 76. Norma Rae 79. The Competition 80. Wholly Moses 80. Annie 82, etc.

Henning-Jensen, Astrid (1914–). Danish woman director.

Henreid, Paul (1907–) (Paul von Henreid). Austrian leading man of the thirties; fled to Britain, then to Hollywood, where his immobile good looks made him a suitable leading man, in the absence at war of home-grown talent, for a number of strong-willed leading ladies.
Goodbye Mr Chips 39. *Night Train to Munich*

40. Joan of Paris 41. *Now Voyager* 42. Casablanca 42. In Our Time 44. Between Two Worlds 44. The Conspirators 44. The Spanish Main 45. Devotion 46. Of Human Bondage 46. Deception 46. Song of Love 47. The Scar 48. Rope of Sand 49. So Young So Bad 50. Last of the Buccaneers 50. For Men Only (& pd) 51. Thief of Damascus 52. Siren of Baghdad 53. Deep in My Heart (as Ziegfeld) 54. Pirates of Tripoli 55. A Woman's Devotion (& d) 57. Holiday for Lovers 59. The Four Horsemen of the Apocalypse 62. Dead Ringer (d only) 64. Operation Crossbow 65. The Madwoman of Chaillot 69. The Failing of Raymond (TV) 71. Mrs R (TV) 75. Exorcist II: The Heretic 77, etc.

¶ He looks as though his idea of fun would be to find a nice cold damp grave and sit in it.—*Richard Winnington, 1946, of Henreid's performance in Of Human Bondage*

Henrey, Bobby (1939–). British child actor, notable in *The Fallen Idol* 48. Retired after *The Wonder Kid* 50.

Henry Aldrich, the accident-prone American teenager of the forties, created on radio by Ezra Stone, was played by Jimmy Lydon in a number of small-town comedies of the forties, with Charles Smith as his friend Dizzy.

Henry, Buck (1930–) (B. Zuckerman). Mild-looking American actor-writer of abrasive comedy.
The Troublemaker (w) 64. The Graduate (w) 67. Candy (w) 68. *Catch 22* (w) 70. The Owl and the Pussycat (w) 70. *Taking Off* (a) 71. The Day of the Dolphin (w) 73. The Man Who Fell to Earth (w) 76. Old Boyfriends (a) 79. The First Family (wd) 80. Gloria (a) 80, etc.

Henry, Charlotte (1913–1980). American juvenile actress of the early thirties.
Rebecca of Sunnybrook Farm 32. Alice in Wonderland 33. Babes in Toyland 34. Charlie Chan at the Opera 37. Stand and Deliver 41, etc.

Henry, Justin (1971–). American child star. *Kramer vs Kramer* 79. Martin's Day 84. Tiger Town 84. Sixteen Candles 84.

Henry, Mike (1939–). American ex-athlete who came to the screen briefly as Tarzan. *Tarzan and the Valley of Gold* 65. Tarzan and the Great River 67. Tarzan and the Jungle Boy 68. Skyjacked 72, etc.

Henry, O. (1862–1910) (William Sydney Porter). American story writer who for the last ten years of his life wrote a weekly story for the *New York World*. A compendium of them was used in *O. Henry's Full House* 52, and there followed a TV series, *The O. Henry Playhouse* 56.

Henry V (GB 1944). Laurence Olivier directed this Shakespearean spectacular, timed for victory, and also starred in it. The method of starting in the Globe Theatre, moving gradually into reality for the battle and then returning was controversial, but in general the production could not have been more splendid. Leslie Banks, Robert Newton and Leo Genn stood out in a remarkable cast, and the Agincourt charge sequence is justly famous. Photographed in Technicolor by Robert Krasker, with music by William Walton.

Henry VIII (1491–1547). This most recognizable of British royal figures was most memorably played by Charles Laughton in 1933 in *The Private Life of Henry VIII*. He reprised not too successfully, twenty years later, in *Young Bess*. Other major interpreters were Keith Michell (*Henry VIII and His Six Wives*), Richard Burton (*Anne of the Thousand Days*) and Robert Shaw (*A Man for All Seasons*). Impersonators in supporting roles include Frank Cellier (*Tudor Rose*), Montagu Love (*The Prince and the Pauper*, 1937), Lyn Harding (*Les Perles de la Couronne*, 1937), James Robertson Justice (*The Sword and the Rose*, 1953), Paul Rogers (*The Prince and the Pauper*, 1962), Charlton Heston (*The Prince and the Pauper*, 1977), and Sid James in *Carry On Henry*.

Henry, William (1918–). American leading man, former child actor, later in callow roles.
Lord Jim 26. The Thin Man 34. Tarzan Escapes 36. Four Men and a Prayer 38. Blossoms in the Dust 41. Women in Bondage 44. Federal Man 49. Jungle Moonmen 54. Mister Roberts 55. The Lone Ranger and the Lost City of Gold 58. How the West Was Won 62, etc.

Henson, Gladys (1897–1983) (Gladys Gunn). Irish character actress often seen as plump, homely mum, or latterly grand-mum. On stage from 1910.
The Captive Heart 45. It Always Rains on Sunday 47. *London Belongs to Me* 48. *The Blue Lamp* 50. Lady Godiva Rides Again 51. Those People Next Door 52. Cockleshell Heroes 55. The Leather Boys 63, etc.

Henson, Jim (1936–). American puppeteer, creator of TV's *Sesame Street* and *The Muppet Show*; also movies: The Dark Crystal 82. Labyrinth 86.

Henson, Leslie (1891–1957). British stage comedian with bulging eyes; often in musical farces.
Autobiography 1948: *Yours Faithfully*.
The Sport of Kings 30. It's a Boy 33. A Warm Corner 34. Oh Daddy 35. The Demi-Paradise 43. Home and Away 56, etc.

Henson, Nicky (1945–). British general purpose actor.
Witchfinder General 68. There's a Girl in My Soup 70. All Coppers Are 71. Penny Gold 72. Vampira 74. The Bawdy Adventures of Tom Jones 76.

Hepburn, Audrey (1929–) (Audrey Hepburn-Ruston). Belgian-born star actress of Irish-Dutch parentage; after small parts in English films, rose rapidly to Hollywood stardom as elegant gamine.
□One Wild Oat 51. Young Wives' Tale 51. Laughter in Paradise 51. The Lavender Hill Mob 51. Monte Carlo Baby 52. The Secret People 52. *Roman Holiday* (AA, BFA) 53. Sabrina 54. *War and Peace* 56. *Funny Face* 57. Love in the Afternoon 57. *The Nun's Story* (BFA) 59. Green Mansions 59. The Unforgiven 60. Breakfast at Tiffany's 61. The Children's Hour 62. Charade 63. Paris When it Sizzles 64. My Fair Lady 64. How to Steal a Million 66. Two for the Road 66. *Wait Until Dark* 67. Robin and Marian 76. Bloodline 79. They All Laughed 81.
❀ For providing the fifties with a fashionable image between a tomboy and a lady (and oddly failing to combine the two in *My Fair Lady*). *Roman Holiday*.

Hepburn, Katharine (1907–). Dominant American star actress with Bryn Mawr personality; one of the most durable, talented and likeable interpreters of emancipated feminine roles.
Biographies: 1973, *Tracy and Hepburn* by Garson Kanin. 1976, *Kate* by Charles Higham.
□*A Bill of Divorcement* 32. Christopher Strong 33. *Morning Glory* (AA) 33. *Little Women* 33. Spitfire 34. Break of Hearts 34. The Little Minister 34. Alice Adams 35. Sylvia Scarlett 35. Mary of Scotland 36. A Woman Rebels 36. Quality Street 37. *Stage Door* 37. *Bringing Up Baby* 38. *Holiday* 38. *The Philadelphia Story* 40. *Woman of the Year* 42. Keeper of the Flame 42. Stage Door Canteen 43. Dragon Seed 44. Without Love 45. Undercurrent 46. Sea of Grass 47. Song of Love 47. State of the Union 48. *Adam's Rib* 49. *The African Queen* 51. *Pat and Mike* 52. *Summer Madness* 55. The Rainmaker 56. The Iron Petticoat (GB) 56. *Desk Set* 57. *Suddenly Last Summer* 59. *Long Day's Journey Into Night* 62. *Guess Who's Coming to Dinner* (AA) 67. *The Lion in Winter* (AA, BFA) 68. The Madwoman of Chaillot 69. The Trojan Women 71. The Glass Menagerie (TV) 73. A Delicate Balance 73. Love Among the Ruins (TV) 74. Rooster Cogburn 75. Olly Olly Oxen Free 78. The Corn Is Green (TV) 79. On Golden Pond (AA, BFA) 81. The Ultimate Solution of Grace Quigley 84.
❀ For her unique qualities of understanding, diction and movement; and for winning two Oscars thirty years after being declared box-office poison. *The Philadelphia Story*.

¶ The screen's first lady has never had a lot to say for herself. Her most thoughtful piece of self-analysis was:

> I was fortunate to be born with a set of characteristics that were in the public vogue.

Cecil Beaton was more poetic than kind in his description:

> She has a face that belongs to the sea and the wind, with large rocking-horse nostrils and teeth that you just know bite an apple every day.

Robert Hopkins said of her physical angularity:

> You could throw a hat at her, and wherever it hit, it would stick.

Tennessee Williams thought her a dream actress:

> She makes dialogue sound better than it is by a matchless clarity and beauty of diction, and by a fineness of intelligence and sensibility that illuminates every shade of meaning in every line she speaks.

One feels too that she brings similar high standards to every corner of her life. She said of herself:

> When I started out, I didn't have any desire to be an actress or to learn how to act. I just wanted to be famous.

Perhaps only chance kept her from being the first woman president. She obviously has the charm, as Garson Kanin says:

> As the years go by she does not lose her old admirers, she goes on gaining new ones.

Other self-musings:

> I've had a fascinating life. I don't think I'm the least bit peculiar, but people tell me I am.

And:

> Acting is the most minor of gifts. After all, Shirley Temple could do it when she was four.

And:

> We used to laugh so much then. Now everything is so solemn, so joyless. One must laugh. One cannot moan everlastingly.

And:

> My privacy is my own. I am the one to decide whether it will be invaded.

And:

> I am revered rather like an old building. Yet I still seem to be master of my fate. The boat may be only a canoe, but I'm paddling it.

Three final opinions from other people: first, Humphrey Bogart:

> She talks at you as though you were a microphone . . . she lectured the hell out of me on temperance and the evils of drink. She doesn't give a damn how she looks. I don't think she tries to be a character. I think she *is* one.

And James Agate:

> She has a cheekbone like a death's head attached to a manner as sinister and aggressive as crossbones.

And our old friend anon.:

> A cross between Donald Duck and a Stradivarius.

Famous line (*Stage Door*): The calla lilies are in bloom again . . .
Famous line (*The Philadelphia Story*): I'm going crazy. I'm standing here, on my own two hands, and going crazy.
Famous line (*The African Queen*): Nature, Mr Allnut, is what we are put into this world to rise above.

Hepton, Bernard (1925–). Tall, serious-looking British character actor, mostly on TV (*Colditz*, *The Squirrels*, *Secret Army*).
Get Carter 71. Henry VIII and His Six Wives 71. Voyage of the Damned 76. Tinker Tailor Soldier Spy (TV) 79. Gandhi 82. Smiley's People (TV) 82, etc.

Hepworth, Cecil (1874–1953). Pioneer British film producer-director. For many years had his own stock company of stars and was financially successful, though his films were old-fashioned and sentimental. Wrote first book on cinema 1897: *Animated Photography*. Autobiography 1951: *Came the Dawn*.
The Quarrelsome Anglers 98. Two Cockneys in a Canoe 99. Wiping Something off the Slate 00. How it Feels to be Run Over 00. The Glutton's Nightmare 01. Alice in Wonderland 03. Firemen to the Rescue 03. Rescued by Rover 05. Blind Fate 12. His Country's Bidding 14. The Canker of Jealousy 14. The Man Who Stayed at Home 15. Trelawney of the Wells 16. Annie Laurie 16. Comin' Through the Rye 16. Nearer My God to Thee 17. The Touch of a Child 18. The Forest on the Hill 19. Alf's Button 20. Wild Heather 21. The Pipes of Pan 22. Strangling Threads 22. *Comin' Through the Rye* (remake) 24. The House of Marney 27, many others.

Herbert, F. Hugh (1897–1957). American comedy screenwriter.
Adam and Evil 27. Hotel Continental 32. If You Could Only Cook (oa) 35. That Certain Age (oa) 38. Melody Ranch 40. West Point Widow 41. Together Again 44. *Kiss and Tell* (& oa) 45. Home Sweet Homicide 46. *Margie* 46. Scudda Hoo Scudda Hay (& d) 48. *Sitting Pretty* 48. Our Very Own 50. The Girls of Pleasure Island (& d) 53. *The Moon is Blue* (& oa) 53. The Little Hut 57, many others.

Herbert, Holmes (1882–1956) (Edward Sanger). British stage actor, on the Hollywood screen from 1917, usually in quiet British roles—butler, lawyer or clerk.
Gentlemen Prefer Blondes 27. The Terror 28. Dr Jekyll and Mr Hyde 32. The Mystery of the Wax Museum 33. Mark of the Vampire 35. Lloyds of London 37. Stanley and Livingstone 39. This Above All 42. The Uninvited 44. Sherlock Holmes and the Secret Code (Dressed to Kill) 46. David and Bathsheba 51. The Brigand 52, etc.

Herbert, Hugh (1887–1952). American eccentric comedian, remembered for nervous 'woo woo' exclamation.
Caught in the Fog 28. Laugh and Get Rich 31. The Lost Squadron 32. Strictly Personal 33. Convention City 33. Wonder Bar 34. Dames 34. A Midsummer Night's Dream 35. One Rainy Afternoon 36. Top of the Town 37. Gold Diggers in Paris 38. The Great Waltz 38. Eternally Yours 39. La Conga Nights 40. The Black Cat 41. *Hellzapoppin* 41. Cracked Nuts 42. Mrs Wiggs of the Cabbage Patch 42. There's One Born Every Minute 43. Kismet 44. Men in Her Diary 45. Carnegie Hall 46. A Song is Born 48. The Beautiful Blonde from Bashful Bend 49. Havana Rose 51, many others.

Herbert, Percy (1925–). British character actor, usually seen as cockney rating or private.
The Baby and the Battleship 56. The Bridge on the River Kwai 57. *Tunes of Glory* 61. Mysterious Island 62. Mutiny on the Bounty 63. One Million Years BC 66. Tobruk (US) 66. The Viking Queen 67. The Royal Hunt of the Sun 69. Man in the Wilderness 71. Captain Apache 71. Doomwatch 72. Craze 73.
TV series: Cimarron Strip 67.

Herbert, Victor (1859–1924). Irish popular composer long dominant in New York; played by Walter Connolly in *The Great Victor Herbert* 39. Scores filmed include *The Red Mill* and *Naughty Marietta*.

Hercule Poirot was the creation of best-selling detective novelist Agatha Christie. Belgian, not French, he had already retired to grow vegetable marrows when first introduced in *The Mysterious Affair At Styles* (1920); his last case, *Curtain*, was published after the author's death in 1976. For at least part of his career he had a devoted Watson figure in the shape of Captain Hastings. Three lost British films of the early thirties had Austin Trevor in the role. Tony Randall more or less parodied him in *The Alphabet Murders* (1966). In 1974 Albert Finney played him over-emphatically in *Murder on the Orient Express*; Peter Ustinov took over for *Death on the Nile* (1978) and *Evil Under the Sun* (1981). On the whole he is better read about than watched.

Here Comes Mr Jordan (US 1941). This 'heavenly' comedy, from Harry Segal's play about a boxer who dies too early and is sent back to earth only to find that his body has been cremated, was a great success in wartime America and had several imitators. Directed by Alexander Hall, with Robert Montgomery, Claude Rains, Edward Everett Horton, James Gleason. Remade fairly literally in 1978 as *Heaven Can Wait*; *Down to Earth* was a 1947 sequel with music.

Herlie, Eileen (1919–) (Eileen Herlihy). Scottish stage actress who has made occasional films.
Hungry Hill (debut) 47. Hamlet 48. The Angel with the Trumpet 49. The Story of Gilbert and Sullivan 53. Isn't Life Wonderful? 53. For Better For Worse 54. She Didn't Say No 58. Freud 62. The Seagull 68.

Herlihy, James Leo (1927–). American novelist, whose *All Fall Down* and *Midnight Cowboy* were fairly memorably filmed.

Herman, Jerry (1932–). American composer of popular shows: those filmed include *Hello Dolly* and *Mame*.

Hernandez, Juano (1896–1970). Black American character actor with powerful presence.
Intruder in the Dust 48. The Breaking Point 50. *Young Man with a Horn* 50. Kiss Me Deadly 55. Trial 55. Ransom 56. Something of Value 57. The Pawnbroker 64. The Extraordinary Seaman 68, etc.

? heroines and heroes
In what well-known films were the leading romantic characters named as follows? And who played them?

1 Lady Edwina Esketh and Major Rama Safti
2 Snapshot and Ulysses
3 Henriette Deluzy-Desportes and the Duc de Praslin
4 Laura Jesson and Dr Alec Harvey
5 Judith Traherne and Dr Frederick Steele
6 Maggie Cutler and Bert Jefferson
7 Helen St James and Don Birnam
8 Barbara Undershaft and Adolphus Cusins
9 Klara Novak and Alfred Kralik
10 Clara Snyder and Marty Pilletti
11 Ilsa Lund Laszlo and Rick Blaine
12 Elaine Harper and Mortimer Brewster
13 Fran Kubelik and C. C. Baxter
14 Trudy Kockenlocker and Norval Jones
15 Eddie Doyle and Terry Malloy
16 Madge Owens and Hal Carter
17 Mary Kate Danaher and Sean Thornton
18 Kathy Selden and Don Lockwood
19 Brigid O'Shaughnessy and Sam Spade (1940)
20 Marie Browning and Harry Morgan
21 Vicki Lester and Norman Maine (1954)
22 Dr Constance Petersen and J.B.
23 Joey Drayton and John Prentice
24 Sarah Brown and Sky Masterson
25 Elaine Robinson and Ben Braddock
26 Pearl Chavez and Lewt McCanles
27 Phyllis Dietrichson and Walter Neff
28 Irena Dubrovna and Oliver Reed
29 Holly Golightly and Paul Varjak
30 Lise Bourvier and Jerry Mulligan

Herrmann, Bernard (1911–1975). American composer and orchestral conductor.
□*Citizen Kane* 41. *All that Money Can Buy*

(AA) 41. *The Magnificent Ambersons* 42. Jane Eyre 43. Hangover Square 45. Anna and the King of Siam 46. The Ghost and Mrs Muir 47. The Day the Earth Stood Still 51. On Dangerous Ground 51. Five Fingers 52. The Snows of Kilimanjaro 52. White Witch Doctor 53. Beneath the 12-mile Reef 53. King of the Khyber Rifles 53. Garden of Evil 54. The Egyptian 54. Prince of Players 55. The Kentuckian 55. *The Trouble with Harry* 56. The Man in the Grey Flannel Suit 56. The Man who Knew Too Much 56. The Wrong Man 57. A Hatful of Rain 57. Vertigo 58. The Naked and the Dead 58. The Seventh Voyage of Sinbad 58. *North by Northwest* 59. Blue Denim 59. Journey to the Centre of the Earth 59. *Psycho* 60. The Three Worlds of Gulliver 60. Mysterious Island 61. Cape Fear 61. Tender is the Night 62. Jason and the Argonauts 63. Marnie 64. Joy in the Morning 65. Fahrenheit 451 66. The Bride wore Black 67. Twisted Nerve 69. Obsessions 69. The Battle of Neretva 70. The Night Diggers 71. Endless Night 72. Sisters 73. It's Alive 74. *Taxi Driver* 76. Obsession 76.
❀ For musical backing second to none. *All that Money Can Buy.*

Herrmann, Edward (1943–). American character actor.
Lady Liberty 71. The Paper Chase 72. The Day of the Dolphin 73. The Great Gatsby 74. The Great Waldo Pepper 75. *Eleanor and Franklin* (as Franklin Roosevelt) (TV) 76. Eleanor and Franklin: The White House Years (TV) 77. The Betsy 78. A Love Affair: The Eleanor and Lou Gehrig Story (TV) 79. Freedom Road (TV) 79. The North Avenue Irregulars 79. Reds 81. Harry's War 81. A Little Sex 82. Annie (as FDR) 82. Mrs Soffel 84. Compromising Positions 84. The Man with One Red Shoe 85. The Lost Boys 87, etc.

Hersey, John (1914–). American novelist, most famous for his pamphlet reportage, *Hiroshima.* One novel was filmed: *A Bell for Adano.*

Hershey, Barbara: see *Seagull, Barbara Hershey.*

Hersholt, Jean (1886–1956). Phlegmatic Danish character actor in Hollywood, in sub-Jannings roles.
Princess Virtue 16. The Four Horsemen of the Apocalypse 21. *Greed* 23. Stella Dallas 25. The Secret Hour 28. Abie's Irish Rose 28. The Rise of Helga 30. Transatlantic 31. *Grand Hotel* 32. The Mask of Fu Manchu 32. Christopher Bean 35. Mark of the Vampire 35. Seventh Heaven 35. The Country Doctor (as Dr Dafoe) 35. Crime of the Century 36. Heidi 37. Alexander's Ragtime Band 38. Meet Doctor Christian (and ensuing series) 38–40. They Meet Again 41. Stage Door Canteen 43. Dancing in the Dark 49. Run for Cover 55, others.
†A much respected industry figure, he was largely responsible for the foundation of the Motion Picture Country Home and Hospital in Calabasas.

¶ *J.H., 1954:* Dr Christian is such a sweet sentimental fellow, I'd hate to be stuck with playing him for the rest of my life.

Hervey, Irene (1910–) (Irene Herwick). American leading lady of light films in the forties.
Three on a Honeymoon 34. East Side of Heaven 39. Destry Rides Again 39. Unseen Enemy 42. Half Way to Shanghai 43. My Guy 44. Mr Peabody and the Mermaid 49. Teenage Rebel 56. Going Steady 59. Cactus Flower 69, etc.
TV series: Honey West 65.

Herzog, Werner (1942–). German director.
□Signs of Life 67. Even Dwarfs Started Small 70. Fata Morgana 71. Land of Silence and Darkness 72. *Aguirre*
Land of Silence and Darkness 72. *Aguirre Wrath of God* 73. The Enigma of Kaspar Hauser 74. Heart of Glass 76. Stroszek 77. Nosferatu 79. Wozzeck 79. *Fitzcarraldo* 82. Ballad of the Little Soldier 84. The Dark Glow of the Mountains 84. Where the Green Ants Dream 85.

¶ *W.H.:* I'm not out to win prizes—that's for dogs and horses.

Heslop, Charles (1883–1966). British comic actor, longtime star of stage farces.
Waltzes from Vienna 33. The Lambeth Walk 39. Flying Fortress 42. The Late Edwina Black 51. Follow a Star 59.

Hessler, Gordon (1930–). American director in Britain.
The Last Shot You Hear 64. The Oblong Box (& p) 69. Scream and Scream Again 70. Cry of the Banshee (& p) 70. Murders in the Rue Morgue (& p) 71. Embassy 72. Sinbad's Golden Voyage 73. Scream Pretty Peggy (TV) 73. Skyway to Death (TV) 74. A Cry in the Wilderness (TV) 74. The Strange Possession of Mrs Oliver (TV) 77. The Secrets of Three Hungry Wives (TV) 78. Wheels of Terror 87, etc.

Heston, Charlton (1924–) (John Charlton Carter). Stalwart American leading actor with stage experience; seemed likely for a time to become typed in biblical and medieval epics. Autobiography 1978: *An Actor's Life*.
□Dark City 50. The Greatest Show on Earth 52. The Savage 52. Ruby Gentry 52. The President's Lady (as Andrew Jackson) 52. Pony Express 53. Arrowhead 53. Bad for Each Other 54. The Naked Jungle 54. The Secret of the Incas 54. The Far Horizons 55. The Private War of Major Benson 55. Lucy Gallant 55. *The Ten Commandments* (as Moses) 56. Three Violent People 56. Touch of Evil 58. The Big Country 58. The Buccaneer 58. The Wreck of the Mary Deare 59. Ben Hur (AA) 59. El Cid 61. The Pigeon that Took Rome 62. Diamond Head 62. 55 Days at Peking 63. The Greatest Story Ever Told 65. Major Dundee 65. The Agony and the Ecstasy (as Michelangelo) 65. *The War Lord* 65. *Khartoum* (as General Gordon) 66. Counterpoint 67. *Planet of the Apes* 67. *Will Penny* 68. Number One 69. Beneath the Planet of the Apes 69. Julius Caesar 70. The Hawaiians 70. The Omega Man 71. Antony and Cleopatra (& d) 71. Skyjacked 72. Call of the Wild 72. Soylent Green 73. Earthquake 73. The Three Musketeers 73. The Four Musketeers 74. Airport 75 74. The Last Hard Men 76. Two Minute Warning 76. Midway 76. Gray Lady Down 77. The Prince and the Pauper 77. The Awakening 80. The Mountain Men 80. Mother Lode 82. Chiefs (TV) 83.
TV series: The Colbys 85–86.

¶ A careful and successful actor, Heston has been blessed with the kind of impressive face and physique that inevitably got him cast as a succession of epic heroes. This was a mixed blessing to his career. On the one hand, as he said:

> There's a special excitement in playing a man who made a hole in history large enough to be remembered centuries after he died.

Commercially, furthermore:

> If you can't make a career out of two de Milles, you'll never do it.

On the other hand:

> After spending all of last winter in armour it's a great relief to wear costume that bends.

Heston has continued to explore, without having to resort to character parts. He knows however that:

> The minute you feel you have given a faultless performance is the time to get out.

And

> I have played three presidents, three saints and two geniuses. If that doesn't create an ego problem, nothing does.

Heydt, Louis Jean (1905–1960). American character actor, often seen as a man with something to hide.
Test Pilot 38. Each Dawn I Die 39. Gone with the Wind 39. Dive Bomber 41. Our Vines Have Tender Grapes 45. The Furies 50. The Eternal Sea 55, many others.

Heyer, John (1916–). Australian documentarist, former cameraman; with the Shell Film Unit 1948–56.
The Back of Beyond 54. Playing with Water 54. The Forerunner 57. Tumult Pond 62, etc.

Heyes, Douglas (1923–). American director, from TV.
Kitten with a Whip 65. Beau Geste 67, etc.

Heyman, John (1933–). British agent and producer.
Privilege 66. Boom! 68. Secret Ceremony 69. Twinky 70. Bloomfield 71. The Go-Between 71, etc.

Heymann, Werner (1896–). German composer who went to Hollywood.
Spione 28. Congress Dances 31. Bluebeard's Eighth Wife 38. Ninotchka 39. One Million B.C. 39. The Shop Around the Corner 40. That Uncertain Feeling 41. To Be or Not to Be 42. Hail the Conquering Hero 44. Knickerbocker Holiday 44. Kiss and Tell 45. Mad Wednesday 47. Tell It to the Judge 49. Congress Dances (Ger.) 55, etc.

Heyward, Louis M. (Deke) (1920–). American producer, especially associated with horror films made in Europe for AIP.
De Sade 69. Wuthering Heights 70. The Abominable Dr Phibes 71. Murders in the Rue Morgue 71, etc.

Heywood, Anne (1931–) (Violet Pretty). British leading lady, former beauty contestant.
Find the Lady 55. Checkpoint 56. Dangerous Exile 56. The Depraved 57. Violent Playground 58. Floods of Fear 58. Upstairs and Downstairs 59. A Terrible Beauty 60. Petticoat Pirates 61. Stork Talk 62. Vengeance 62. The Very Edge 62. Ninety Degrees in the Shade 66. *The Fox* 68. The Chairman 69. The Awful Story of the Nun of Monza (It) 69. The Midas Run 69. I Want

What I Want 71. Trader Horn 73. The Nun and the Devil (It) 73. Good Luck Miss Wyckoff 79, etc.

Heywood, Pat (1927–). British character actress.
Romeo and Juliet 68. All the Way Up 69. 10 Rillington Place 71. Who Slew Auntie Roo? 72, etc.

Hibbert, Geoffrey (1922–1969). British actor who played callow youths around 1940 but turned rather quickly into a character man.
Love on the Dole 41. The Common Touch 42. Next of Kin 42. Orders to Kill 58. Crash Drive 59, etc.

Hibbs, Jesse (1906–85). American director, mainly of routine 'B' features.
□The All American 53. Ride Clear of Diablo 54. Black Horse Canyon 54. Rails into Laramie 54. The Yellow Mountain 54. To Hell and Back 55. The Spoilers 55. World in My Corner 56. Walk the Proud Land 56. Joe Butterfly 57. Ride a Crooked Trail 58.

Hibler, Winston (1911–1976). American producer, almost entirely of wild life material for Disney.

Hickey, William (–). American character actor.
Prizzi's Honor (AAN) 85.

Hickman, Darryl (1931–). American juvenile actor who was later seen in heavy roles.
The Grapes of Wrath 40. Hearts in Springtime 41. Boys' Ranch 45. Dangerous Years 46. Prisoner of War 53. Tea and Sympathy 54, etc.
TV series: The Blue and the Gold 58.

Hickman, Dwayne (1934–). American juvenile, former child actor.
Captain Eddie 45. The Return of Rusty 46. The Sun Comes Up 49. Rally Round the Flag Boys 59. Beach Party 64, others.
TV series: The Affairs of Dobie Gillis 59.

Hickman, Howard (1880–1949). Chubby American supporting actor, often seen as conventioneer, suburban husband or judge.

Hickok, Wild Bill (1837–1876). American frontier gunfighter of wild west days, frequently personified on screen.
Wild Bill Hickok 21: William S. Hart. *The Plainsman* 36: Gary Cooper. *Badlands of Dakota* 41: Richard Dix. *Wild Bill Hickok Rides* 41: Bruce Cabot. *Dallas* 50: Reed Hadley. *Pony Express* 52: Forrest Tucker. *Calamity Jane* 53: Howard Keel. *The Raiders* 55: Robert Culp. *The Plainsman* 66: Don Murray. *Little Big Man* 70: Jeff Corey. Guy Madison starred as Hickok in a TV series (51–54).

Hickox, Douglas (1929–). British director.
□The Giant Behemoth (co-d) 58. Four Hits and a Mister 62. It's All Over Town 64. Just for You 64. Les Bicyclettes de Belsize 69. Entertaining Mr Sloane 70. Sitting Target 72. Theatre of Blood 73. Brannigan 75. Sky Riders 76. Zulu Dawn 79. The Hound of the Baskervilles (TV) 83. Mistral's Daughter (TV) 84. Blackout 85. Sins (TV) 86. I'll Take Manhattan (TV) 87.

Hickox, Sid (1895–). American cinematographer, long with Warners.
The Little Giant 26. The Private Life of Helen of Troy 27. Lilac Time 28. The Gorilla 31. A Bill of Divorcement 32. Frisco Jenny 33. Dames 34. Special Agent 35. San Quentin 37. A Slight Case of Murder 38. Flowing Gold 40. The Big Shot 42. Edge of Darkness 43. To Have and Have Not 44. The Horn Blows at Midnight 45. The Big Sleep 46. Dark Passage 47. White Heat 49. Along the Great Divide 51. Them 54. Battle Cry 55, many others.

Hicks, Russell (1895–1957). American character actor who almost always played executive types. Actor and director from silent days; in hundreds of films.
Laughing Irish Eyes 36. In Old Chicago 38. The Three Musketeers 39. The Big Store 41. His Butler's Sister 43. Bandit of Sherwood Forest 46. Bowery Battalion 51. Seventh Cavalry 56, many others.

Hicks, Sir Seymour (1871–1949). British stage farceur, also writer and producer. Occasional film appearances.
Autobiographies: *Between Ourselves* 1930; *Me and My Missus* 1939.
Always Tell Your Wife 22. Sleeping Partners 26. The Secret of the Loch 34. Vintage Wine 35. *Scrooge* 35. Pastor Hall 39. *Busman's Honeymoon* 40. Silent Dust 48, etc.

Hickson, Joan (1906–). British character actress, in innumerable films as understanding mum or slightly dotty aunt.
Widow's Might 34. Love from a Stranger 37.

I See a Dark Stranger 45. The Guinea Pig 48. Seven Days to Noon 50. The Card 52. The Man Who Never Was 56. Happy is the Bride 57. The 39 Steps 59. Murder She Said 61. A Day in the Death of Joe Egg 70. Theatre of Blood 73, many others.
† At the age of nearly 80, J.H. made a big hit on TV in adaptations of Agatha Christie's Miss Marple stories.

Higgins, Colin (–). American screenwriter.
Harold and Maude 71. Silver Streak 77. Foul Play (& d) 78. Nine to Five (& d) 80. The Best Little Whorehouse in Texas (co-w, d) 82.

Higgins, Jack (1929–). British adventure novelist. Chief film of his work: *The Eagle Has Landed.*

Higgins, Ken (1919–). British cinematographer.
French Dressing 63. Darling 65. The Virgin Soldiers 69. You Can't Win 'Em All 70.

High Noon (US 1952). An influential western of classic economy and some symbolism, the action ranging over a few hours during which one man searches desperately for support against a gang of revengeful outlaws. Written by Carl Foreman, directed by Fred Zinnemann, with Gary Cooper and a first-rate cast. The ballad was written by Dmitri Tiomkin.

High Sierra (US 1941). Modish melodrama with Humphrey Bogart as a gangster on the run and Ida Lupino as the girl who befriends him too late. Gloomily directed by Raoul Walsh, from a script by W. R. Burnett and John Huston; chiefly notable for its early example of an anti-hero. Remade 1955 by Stuart Heisler as *I Died a Thousand Times*, with Jack Palance, Shelley Winters, and no flair.

Highsmith, Patricia (1921–). American detective novelist. Works filmed include *Strangers on a Train*, *Purple Noon* (*The Talented Mr Ripley*) and *Enough Rope* (*The Blunderer*).

Hildyard, Jack (1908–). British cinematographer.
School for Secrets 46. While the Sun Shines 46. Vice Versa 48. The Sound Barrier 52. Hobson's Choice 54. The Deep Blue Sea 55. Summertime 55. *The Bridge on the River Kwai* (AA) 57. The Journey 59. Suddenly Last Summer 59. The Millionairess 60. 55 Days at Peking 62. The VIPs 63. The Yellow Rolls Royce 64. Battle of the Bulge 66. Casino Royale 67. The Long Duel 67. Villa Rides 68. Topaz 70. Puppet on a Chain 71. The Beast Must Die 74. The Message 76. The Wild Geese 78. Lion of the Desert 80, etc.

The Hill (GB 1965). An engagingly arrant melodrama, played mostly for laughs, about brutalities in a North African prison camp during World War II. This raucous but stylish film unfortunately has pretensions which, coupled with poor sound recording, finally make it seem overblown and empty. But there are compensations in Sidney Lumet's direction, Oswald Morris' harsh photography, and the performances of Harry Andrews, Ian Hendry and Ossie Davis.

Hill, Arthur (1922–). Canadian actor, on British and American stage and screen.
Miss Pilgrim's Progress 49. I Was a Male War Bride 49. Salute the Toff 52. Life with the Lyons 54. The Deep Blue Sea 55. The Ugly American 63. In the Cool of the Day 63. Moment to Moment 65. *Harper* 66. Petulia 68. The Chairman 69. *The Andromeda Strain* 70. The Pursuit of Happiness 70. Futureworld 76. A Bridge Too Far 77. Hagen (TV) 79. Butch and Sundance 79. The Champ 79. A Little Romance 79. Dirty Tricks 81. Making Love 82. The Amateur 82. One Magic Christmas, etc.
TV series: *Owen Marshall Counsellor at Law* 71–73. Hagen 80.

Hill, Benny (1925–) (Alfred Hawthorne Hill). British vaudeville comedian and mimic, star of an occasional TV variety show with the emphasis on smut. An astonishing success on late night American TV in 1979 and thereafter.
□Who Done It? 56. Light Up the Sky 59. Those Magnificent Men in Their Flying Machines 65. Chitty Chitty Bang Bang 68. The Italian Job 69. The Best of Benny Hill 74.

Hill, George (1888–1934). American director.
Through the Dark 23. The Midnight Express 24. Zander the Great 25. Tell It to the Marines 26. The Cossacks 28. The Flying Fleet 29. *The Big House* 30. *Min and Bill* 30. The Secret Six 31. Hell Divers 31. Clear all Wires 33, etc.

Hill, George Roy (1922–). American director with New York stage background.

□Period of Adjustment 63. Toys in the Attic 63. *The World of Henry Orient* 64. Hawaii 66. Thoroughly Modern Millie 67. *Butch Cassidy and the Sundance Kid* 69. *Slaughterhouse Five* 72. The Sting (AA) 73. The Great Waldo Pepper 75. Slap Shot 77. A Little Romance 79. The World According to Garp 82. The Little Drummer Girl 84.

Hill, Howard (1898–1975). American archer who, besides making sports shorts in the forties, 'doubled' for Errol Flynn in several films.

Hill, James (1919–). British director, former documentarist.
Journey for Jeremy 47. The Stolen Plans (& w) 52. The Clue of the Missing Ape (& w) 53. *Giuseppina* (& w) (AA) 61. The Kitchen 62. The Dock Brief 62. Every Day's a Holiday 64. A Study in Terror 65. Born Free 66. Captain Nemo and the Underwater City 69. Black Beauty 71. The Belstone Fox 73, etc.

Hill, James (1916–). American producer.
Vera Cruz 54. The Kentuckian 55. Trapeze 56, etc.

Hill, Sinclair (1894–1945). British director most eminent in the twenties.
The Tidal Wave 20. Don Quixote 23. Indian Love Lyrics 23. Boadicaea 25. Beyond the Veil 25. The Chinese Bungalow 26. The King's Highway 27. A Woman Redeemed 27. *The Guns of Loos* 28. *The Price of Divorce* 28. The First Mrs Fraser 30. The Man from Toronto 33. My Old Dutch 34. Follow Your Star 38, etc.

Hill, Steven (1924–) (Solomon Berg). American stage actor.
A Lady without Passport 50. The Goddess 58. A Child is Waiting 62. The Slender Thread 67. It's My Turn 80. Yentl 83, etc.
TV series: Mission Impossible 67.

Hill, Terence (1941–) (Mario Girotti). Italian leading man of spaghetti westerns.
The Leopard 63. Seven Seas to Calais 63. Blood River 67. Boot Hill 69. They Call Me Trinity 70. Man of the East 72. My Name is Nobody 73. Watch Out, We're Mad 74. Mr Billion 77. March or Die 77. Deux Super Flics 78. Super Fuzz 80, etc.

Hill, Walter (1942–). American screenwriter.
□Hickey and Boggs 72. The Thief Who Came to Dinner 72. The Getaway 72. The Mackintosh Man 73. The Drowning Pool 74. Hard Times (& d) 75. The Driver (& d) 78. The Warriors (& d) 78. The Long Riders (& d) 80. Southern Comfort (& co-w) 81. 48 Hours (co-w, d) 82. Brewster's Millions 84. Streets of Fire 85. Crossroads 85. Extreme Prejudice 87.

hillbillies became a stereotype of the thirties cinema, and subsequently made infrequent appearances before the enormous success of the TV series *The Real McCoys* 57–62 and *The Beverly Hillbillies* 62–70. Notable hillbillies through the years include the Kettles, Lum and Abner, the Weaver Brothers and Elviry; the Ritz Brothers in *Kentucky Moonshine*; Annie in *Annie Get Your Gun*; and the characters in *Roseanna McCoy*, *Thunder Road*, *Lil Abner*, *Guns in the Afternoon*, *Feudin' Fussin' and A-Fightin'*, *The Moonshine War*, *I Walk the Line*, and *Coming Round the Mountain*; while the denizens of *Tobacco Road*, geographically not hillbillies, splendidly personified the image. Cartoon-wise, Elmer Fudd in the Bugs Bunny series is an old-fashioned hillbilly, and Disney produced a twenty-minute version of *The Martins and the Coys,* followed in 1975 by a TV movie, *The Hatfields and the McCoys.* In 1980 *Coal Miner's Daughter* brought to general notice the rags-to-riches story of singer Loretta Lynn, and in 1983 Cheryl Ladd plumbed a similar milieu in a TV movie, *Kentucky Woman.*

Hiller, Arthur (1923–). Canadian-American director, from TV.
□Massacre at Sand Creek (TV) 56. Homeward Borne (TV) 57. The Careless Years 57. Miracle of the White Stallions 63. The Wheeler Dealers 63. The Americanization of Emily 64. Promise Her Anything 66. Penelope 66. Tobruk 67. The Tiger Makes Out 67. Popi 69. The Out-of-Towners 70. *Love Story* 70. Plaza Suite 70. The Hospital 71. Man of La Mancha 72. The Crazy World of Julius Vrooder 74. The Man in the Glass Booth 75. W. C. Fields and Me 76. Silver Streak 76. Nightwing 79. The In-Laws 79. Making Love 82. Author! Author! 82. Romantic Comedy 83. The Lonely Guy 84. Teachers 84. Outrageous Fortune 87.

Hiller, Wendy (1912–). Distinguished British stage actress with inimitable voice and clarity of diction; her films have been fewer than one would like.
□Lancashire Luck 37. *Pygmalion* 38. *Major Barbara* 40. *I Know Where I'm Going* 45. An

Outcast of the Islands 51. Single Handed 52. Something of Value 57. How to Murder a Rich Uncle 57. *Separate Tables* (AA) 58. *Sons and Lovers* 60. Toys in the Attic 63. *A Man for All Seasons* 66. David Copperfield 69. Murder on the Orient Express 74. Voyage of the Damned 76. The Cat and the Canary 77. The Elephant Man 80. The Curse of King Tut's Tomb (TV) 80. Making Love 82. The Death of the Heart 86. The Lonely Passion of Judith Hearne 87.
Famous line (*Pygmalion*): Walk? Not bloody likely. I'm going to take a taxi.
Famous line (*Pygmalion*): I washed me face and hands before I came, I did.

Hillerman, John (c. 1931–). Dapper American actor, mainly of comedy roles.
Paper Moon 73. At Long Last Love 76. The Day of the Locust 76. Lucky Lady 77. Sunburn 79. History of the World Part One 81, etc.
TV series: The Betty White Show 77. Magnum 80–.

Hilliard, Harriet (1914–) (Peggy Lou Snyder). American leading lady of thirties romantic comedies and musicals, e.g. *Follow the Fleet* 36. *She's My Everything* 38. *Sweetheart of the Campus* 41. *Canal Zone* 42, etc. Married Ozzie Nelson and for fourteen years from 1952 appeared with him in their weekly TV show *Ozzie and Harriet*; they also appeared with their family in the film *Here Come the Nelsons* 51. TV series: *Ozzie's Girls* 73.
TV movie 1976: *Smash-up on Interstate Five*. 73.

Hillier, Erwin (1911–). British cinematographer.
The Lady from Lisbon 41. The Silver Fleet 43. Great Day 45. *I Know Where I'm Going* 45. London Town 47. *The October Man* 48. Mr Perrin and Mr Traill 49. Where's Charley? 52. *The Dam Busters* 55. Shake Hands with the Devil 59. A Matter of Who 62. Sammy Going South 63. Operation Crossbow 65. Sands of the Kalahari 65. Eye of the Devil 66. The Quiller Memorandum 66. The Shoes of the Fisherman 68, etc.

Hillyer, Lambert (1889–). American director of westerns which declined in stature after his days of writing and directing for William S. Hart.
The Toll Gate 20. *Travellin' On* 22. *White Oak* 23. *The Spoilers* 23. The Branded Sombrero 28. Beau Bandit 30. Master of Men 33. *Dracula's Daughter* 36. The Invisible Ray 37. Batman (serial) 41. Blue Clay 42. The Case of the Baby Sitter 47. Sunset Pass 49, many others.

Hilton, James (1900–1954). British novelist whose work was turned by himself and others into several highly successful films. Also worked as scenarist on other films, including *Mrs Miniver* 42.
Knight Without Armour 37. *Lost Horizon* 37. *Goodbye Mr Chips* 39. We Are Not Alone 39. *Random Harvest* 42. The Story of Dr Wassell 43. So Well Remembered 47, etc.

¶ *J.H.:* Tempted by Hollywood, a writer must decide whether he would rather say a little less exactly what he wants, to millions, or a little more exactly, to thousands.

Hindle, Art (1948–). Canadian leading man.
Black Christmas 75. A Small Town in Texas 76. Invasion of the Body Snatchers 78. The Clone Master (TV) 78. The Power Within (TV) 79. The Brood 79.

Hindle Wakes. This now dated Lancashire drama by Stanley Houghton, about the mill-girl who gets pregnant by the boss's son, has been a staple of British films. There were silent versions in 1918 with Ada King and in 1926 with Estelle Brody; in 1931 Belle Chrystall starred in a sound remake, and as late as 1951 it was popular again with Lisa Daniely.

Hinds, Anthony (1922–). British producer, in films since 1946, latterly associated with Hammer's horror films. Also writes screenplays under the name 'John Elder'.

Hinds, Samuel S. (1875–1948). Dignified American character actor, formerly a lawyer for thirty-five years; specialized in kindly fathers and crooked lawyers.
Gabriel over the White House 33. She 35. Trail of the Lonesome Pine 36. Test Pilot 38. *You Can't Take It with You* 38. *Destry Rides Again* 39. The Strange Case of Doctor RX 41. The Spoilers 42. A Chip off the Old Block 44. The Boy with Green Hair 48, many others.

Hines, Gregory (–). Black American actor/dancer.
Wolfen 81. The Cotton Club 84. White Nights 85. Running Scared 86.

Hines, Johnny (1895–1970). American star comedian of the twenties; roles declined as sound came in.
Little Johnny Jones 23. The Speed Spook 24. The Crackerjack 25. The Brown Derby 26. Home Made 27. The Runaround 31. Whistling in the Dark 32. Her Bodyguard 33. Society Doctor 35. Too Hot to Handle 38, etc.

Hingle, Pat (1923–). Burly American character actor with stage and TV experience.
On the Waterfront 54. The Strange One 57. No Down Payment 57. Splendor in the Grass 61. The Ugly American 63. Invitation to a Gunfighter 64. Nevada Smith 66. Hang 'Em High 68. Bloody Mama 69. Norwood 69. W.U.S.A. 70. The Carey Treatment 72. One Little Indian 73. Running Wild 73. The Gauntlet 77. Norma Rae 79. Sudden Impact 83. Brewster's Millions 84. Maximum Overdrive 86, etc.
TV series: Stone 79.

Hird, Thora (1913–). British north-country character comedienne, mother of Janette Scott; often plays acidulous landladies, etc. Autobiography 1976: *Seen and Hird*.
The Black Sheep of Whitehall 41. Corridor of Mirrors 46. The Blind Goddess 48. Conspirator 50. The Long Memory 53. Simon and Laura 55. The Entertainer 60. *A Kind of Loving* 62. Rattle of a Simple Man 64. The Nightcomers 71, many others.
TV series include: Meet the Wife. First Lady. Flesh and Blood. In Loving Memory. Hallelujah.

Hiroshima Mon Amour (France/Japan 1959). Alain Resnais' cinematically explorative study of the effect of our war-torn past on the love affair of a Frenchwoman and a Japanese businessman. Original, influential, generally rewarding. Written by Marguerite Duras, with Emmanuele Riva, Eiji Okada.

Hirsch, Judd (1936–). American character actor who nearly became a star.
The Law (TV) 74. Fear on Trial (TV) 75. The Legend of Valentino (TV) 75. The Keegans (TV) 78. King of the Gypsies 78. Sooner or Later (TV) 79. Ordinary People 80. Without a Trace 83.
TV series: Delvecchio 75. *Taxi* 78–82. Detective in the House 85.

Hirsch, Robert (1926–). French character actor of the Comédie Française.
No Questions on Saturday 64. Kiss Me General 66, etc.

Hirschfeld, Gerald (1921–). American cinematographer.
Goodbye Columbus 69. Last Summer 69. Diary of a Mad Housewife 71. Doc 71. Summer Wishes Winter Dreams 73. *Young Frankenstein* 74. The Car 77. The World's Greatest Lover 77. Americathon 79. The Bell Jar 79. Sunday Lovers 80. Neighbors 81. My Favorite Year 82. To Be or Not to Be 83, etc.

Hiscott, Leslie (1894–1968). British director, in films from 1919.
The Passing of Mr Quinn 28. Black Coffee 32. While London Sleeps 33. The Triumph of Sherlock Holmes 35. She Shall Have Music 35. Tilly of Bloomsbury 40. The Seventh Survivor 41. Welcome Mr Washington 44. The Time of His Life 52. Tons of Trouble 56, etc.

histories of the cinema have generally been unrewarding. Shortest and best may be Arthur Knight's *The Liveliest Art* (1957 but later revised). In 1938 Bardeche and Brasillach wrote *The History of Motion Pictures* in French, but it didn't translate easily. Paul Rotha's *The Film Till Now* (first published in 1930 but revised in 1967 with a later section by Richard Griffith) is heavy with thought and strongest on documentary and the European schools. The American cinema is dealt with in Lewis Jacobs' *The Rise of the American Film* (1939/68) and the silent years were well covered, mainly from a business viewpoint, in *A Million and One Nights* (1926) by Terry Ramsaye. A more light-hearted account is Ezra Goodman's *The Fifty Year Decline and Fall of Hollywood* (1961). Of more recent efforts, the best is probably David Shipman's *The Story of Cinema* (first of two volumes, 1982). Peter Cowie in 1971 produced a two-volume anthology called *A Concise History of the Cinema*. Silent cinema has not been specially well documented, though Kevin Brownlow's *The Parade's Gone By* (1968) is a brilliant collection of interviews with its survivors, and *The Real Tinsel* (1970) by Bernard Rosenberg and Harry Silverstein does almost as good a job.

Of picture histories, the grand-daddy is Paul Rotha's *Movie Parade*, first published in 1936 and revised in 1950 with the help of Roger Manvell. Ernest Lindgren's *A Picture History of the Cinema* (1960) is excellent if somewhat highbrow. Daniel Blum's *A Pictorial History of the Silent Screen* and *A Pictorial History of the Talkies*, both much reprinted, are useful reminders but contain no comment. Idiosyncratic but certainly liveliest is *The Movies* by Arthur Mayer and Richard Griffith, which has never been out of print since it first appeared in 1957.

The History of the British Film is the title of a multi-volume work of detailed research undertaken in the forties by Rachael Low. By the end of the seventies six volumes had been published, bringing the story up to the thirties. Meanwhile Denis Gifford did a valiant job with his *The British Film Catalogue*, which currently covers 1895–1970 but is due for revision. George Perry and Roy Armes have both produced concise histories, while Charles Oakley's *Where We Came In* is more on the business side.

Hitchcock, Sir Alfred (1899–1980). British director, in Hollywood more or less since 1940. His name, his profile, and his lugubrious voice are a trademark around the world for suspense thrillers with a touch of impudence, using techniques which are purely cinematic; though of course he frequently fell below his own high standards. Of innumerable books written about him, the most detailed and typical is probably *Le Cinema Selon Hitchcock* by François Truffaut (1966, translated into English). Others include *Hitch* by John Russell Taylor (the 'official' biography); *Alfred Hitchcock* by George Perry; and a Freudian analysis, *The Secret Life of Alfred Hitchcock* by Donald Spoto.

□The Pleasure Garden 25. The Mountain Eagle 25. *The Lodger* 26. Downhill 27. Easy Virtue 27. *The Ring* 27. The Farmer's Wife 28. Champagne 28. The Manxman 29. *Blackmail* 29. Elstree Calling (sketches) 30. Juno and the Paycock 30. *Murder* 30. The Skin Game 31. Rich and Strange 31. *Number Seventeen* 32. Waltzes from Vienna 33. *The Man Who Knew Too Much* 34. *The Thirty-Nine Steps* 35. Secret Agent 36. Sabotage 37. Young and Innocent 37. *The Lady Vanishes* 38. Jamaica Inn 39. *Rebecca* 40. *Foreign Correspondent* 40. Mr and Mrs Smith 41. Suspicion 41. Saboteur 42. *Shadow of a Doubt* 43. Lifeboat 43. *Spellbound* 45. *Notorious* 46. The Paradine Case 47. Rope 48. Under Capricorn 49. Stage Fright 50. *Strangers on a Train* 51. I Confess 53. Dial M For Murder 54. *Rear Window* 54. To Catch a Thief 55. *The Trouble with Harry* 55. The Man Who Knew Too Much 56. The Wrong Man 57. Vertigo 58. *North by Northwest* 59. *Psycho* 60. *The Birds* 63. Marnie 64. Torn Curtain 66. Topaz 69. Frenzy 72. Family Plot 76.

TV series: *Alfred Hitchcock Presents* 55–61.

†In 1944 Hitch also directed two war documentaries for the Ministry of Information: *Bon Voyage* and *Aventure Malagache*.

'His reputation has suffered from the fact that he has given audiences more pleasure than is permissible for serious cinema. No one who is so entertaining could possibly seem profound to the intellectual puritans.'—*Andrew Sarris, 1968*

'He gets most fun out of making pictures at the blueprint stage: shooting is boring. He turns his back on the scene while they're shooting to prove this is something that happens automatically.'—*James Mason*

❁ For his understanding of the craft of the cinema; and for his virtuosity in expressing it. *Foreign Correspondent.*

¶ Hitch did not even have to build up his own legend: eager critics like Truffaut did it for him. The suspense master did, however, oblige the press with a varietv of *bon mots* about himself and his work. Personally I like best his story of how he caused consternation in a crowded elevator by muttering very audibly to a friend:

> I didn't think the old man would bleed so much.

His little epigrams include:

> Drama is life with the dull bits left out.

and:

> Always make the audience suffer as much as possible.

and:

> There is no terror in a bang, only in the anticipation of it.

and:

> Terror is a matter of surprise; suspense, of forewarning.

and

> I've become a body of films, not a man. I *am* all those films.

and:

> A good film is when the price of the admission, the dinner and the babysitter was well worth it.

and:

> The cinema is not a slice of life, it's a piece of cake.

and:

> Sometimes you find that a film is liked only for its content, without any regard to the style or the manner in which the story is told. But that, after all, is the art of the cinema.

And his defence if the tricks don't work:

> All things considered, I think I'm doing well if I get the sixty per cent of my original conception on the screen.

He despised long dialogue sequences:

A film maker isn't supposed to say things. He's supposed to show them.

He despised actors too. One of his most widely publicized remarks was:

Actors are cattle.

His current star, Carole Lombard, promptly led a troop of oxen onto the shooting stage and herself headed for home. Hitch thought it discreet to tell the press:

I didn't say actors are cattle. What I said was, actors should be *treated* like cattle.

He clearly knew himself to be typecast as a mystery man:

If I made *Cinderella*, the audience would be looking out for a body in the coach.

Perhaps his most quoted admission is:

That was the ending I wanted for *Blackmail*, but I had to change it for commercial reasons.

Many tributes have been paid to him, but John Frankheimer's is all-embracing:

Any American director who says he hasn't been influenced by him is out of his mind.

Cary Grant was happy with Hitch:

He couldn't have been a nicer fellow. I whistled coming to work on his films.

Andrew Sarris saw Hitch's problem:

His reputation has suffered from the fact that he has given audiences more pleasure than is permissible in serious cinema.

Doggedly into his seventies he continued to invent mayhem:

When people say I'm seventy I say that's a confounded lie. I'm twice 35, that's all. Twice 35.

He had little reason for complaint:

Even my failures make money and become classics a year after I make them.

And he continued to be a realist:

The length of the film should be directly related to the endurance of the human bladder.

? What Hitchcock film:

1 Was based on the true case of Manny Balestrero?
2 Was written by Raymond Chandler and Czenzi Ormonde?
3 Had a famous single shot which began by taking in an entire dance hall and ended up focusing on the twitching eye of the drummer?
4 Featured Wylie Watson as Mr Memory?
5 Was shot in Munich, San Remo and Lake Como?
6 Had a shot up through the ceiling showing pacing feet in the room above?
7 Was a whodunit starring Herbert Marshall?
8 Had John Gavin as hero?
9 Was photographed entirely in one set? (Two answers.)
10 Had Albert Bassermann as Van Meer?
11 Was based on a book by Somerset Maugham?
12 Was based on a book by Joseph Conrad?
13 Concerned a fisherman and a lawyer in love with the same girl?
14 Included a sequence in Radio City Music Hall?
15 Climaxed with a chase through the British Museum?
16 Had a scene in which the hero outwitted a villainous dentist and forced him to inhale his own chloroform?
17 Featured Jessie Royce Landis as the hero's mother?
18 Allowed the director to make his usual quick appearance only as a reducing ad in a newspaper?
19 Had the villain, by use of subjective camera, shoot himself and the audience at the same time?
20 Had a scene in which the heroine found a shrunken head in her bed?

Hitler, Adolf (1889–1945) (Adolf Schickelgruber). German fascist dictator, subject of many screen documentaries, notably *Mein Kampf* 63 and *The Life of Adolf Hitler* 65. Actors who have impersonated him include Chaplin in *The Great Dictator* 40; Luther Adler in *The Magic Face* 51 and *The Desert Fox* 52; Ludwig Donath in *The Strange Death of Adolf Hitler* 43: Tom Dugan in *To Be or Not To Be* 42 and *Star Spangled Rhythm* 42; Albin Skoda in *The Last Act* 55; Richard Basehart in *Hitler* 61; Billy Frick in *Is Paris Burning?* 66; Kenneth Griffith in *The Two Headed Spy* 59; and Sidney Miller in *Which Way to the Front?* 69 and Alec Guinness in *Hitler: The Last Ten Days* 73. Most frequent Hitler-player, however, is Robert Watson, who in the forties seemed to do little else: apart from an excellent serious portrayal in *The Hitler Gang* 44, he supplied Hitler walk-ons in *The Devil with Hitler* 42, *That Nazty Nuisance* 43, *Hitler Dead or Alive* 43, *The Miracle of Morgan's Creek* 44, *The Story of Mankind* 57, and many others.

In the eighties television began to show renewed interest in fanciful presentations of Hitler. Anthony Hopkins played him in *The Bunker*; Derek Jacobi in *Inside the Third Reich*; and Gunther Riesner in *The Winds of War*.

¶ A psychopath who somehow found his way from a padded cell to Potsdam.—*Malcolm Muggeridge*

Hively, Jack (c. 1907–). American director.
□They Made Her a Spy 39. Panama Lady 39. The Spellbinder 39. Three Sons 39. Two Thoroughbreds 39. The Saint's Double Trouble 40. The Saint Takes Over 40. Anne of Windy Poplars 40. Laddie 40. The Saint in Palm Springs 41. They Met in Argentina 41. Father Takes a Wife 41. Four Jacks and a Jill 41. Street of Chance 42. Are You With It? 48. Starbird and Sweet William 76.

Hobart, Rose (1906–) (Rose Keefer). American actress, usually in character roles.
Liliom 30. Dr Jekyll and Mr Hyde 32. Tower of London 39. Nothing but the Truth 41. Ziegfeld Girl 41. The Soul of a Monster 44. The Farmer's Daughter 46. Mickey 48, etc.

Hobbes, Halliwell (1877–1962). British character actor, long the impeccable butler, on stage from 1898, films from 1929 (after which he lived in Hollywood).
Charley's Aunt 30. Dr Jekyll and Mr Hyde 32. *The Masquerader* 33. Bulldog Drummond Strikes Back 35. Dracula's Daughter 36. *You Can't Take It with You* 38. Lady Hamilton 41. *Sherlock Holmes Faces Death* 43. If Winter Comes 47. That Forsyte Woman 49. Miracle in the Rain 56, scores of others.

Hobbs, Jack (1893–1968). British actor on screen from silent days, usually in genial roles.
The Sin Game 30. Trouble in Store 34. No Limit 35. Millions 37. *It's in the Air* 38. Behind These Walls 48. *Worm's Eye View* 51, etc.

Hobson, Valerie (1917–). British leading lady with 'upper-class' personality.
□Eyes of Fate 33. Two Hearts in Waltztime 34. The Path of Glory 34. Badger's Green 34. Strange Wives (US) 34. Rendezvous at Midnight (US) 35. Werewolf of London (US) 35. Bride of Frankenstein (US) (arguably in title role) 35. The Mystery of Edwin Drood (US) 35. Chinatown Squad (US) 35. The Great Impersonation (US) 35. Oh What a Night 35. August Weekend (US) 36. Tugboat Princess (US) 36. The Secret of Stamboul 36. No Escape 36. Jump for Glory 37. The Drum 38. Q Planes 38. *This Man is News* 38. This Man in Paris 39. *The Spy in Black* 39. The Silent Battle 39. *Contraband* 40. Atlantic Ferry 41. Unpublished Story 42. The Adventures of Tartu 43. The Years Between 46. *Great Expectations* 46. Blanche Fury 47. The Small Voice 48. *Kind Hearts and Coronets* 49. Train of Events 49. The Interrupted Journey 49. The Rocking Horse Winner 49. *The Card* 51. Who Goes There 52. Meet Me Tonight 52. The Voice of Merrill 53. Background 53. Knave of Hearts 54.

Hobson's Choice. This famous stage comedy by Harold Brighouse, set in industrial Salford at the turn of the century and showing how a heavy father gets his come-uppance, has been filmed three times in Britain. The 1920 version, directed by Percy Nash, with Joe Nightingale and Joan Ritz, was much improved on by the 1931 sound remake directed by Thomas Bentley, with Frank Pettingell and Viola Lyel. This was eclipsed, however, by David Lean's brilliant 1954 production, with Charles Laughton as the tyrant shoeseller, Brenda de Banzie as his stubborn daughter, and John Mills as her intended.

Hoch, Winton C. (1905–1979). American cinema tographer, former research physicist.
Dr Cyclops 40. Captains of the Clouds 42. So Dear to My Heart 48. Joan of Arc (co-ph) (AA) 48. *She Wore a Yellow Ribbon* (AA) 49. Tulsa 49. Halls of Montezuma 51. *The Quiet Man* (co-ph) (AA) 52. Mr Roberts 55. *The Searchers* 56. Darby O'Gill and the Little People 59. The Lost World 60. Five Weeks in a Balloon 62. *Robinson Crusoe on Mars* 64. The Green Berets 68, etc.

Hodge, Patricia (1946–). British TV actress (*Jemima Shore Investigates*, etc), who in 1983 had her first major film role in *Betrayal*.

Hodges, Ken (1922–). British cinematographer.
Faces in the Dark 60. The Comedy Man 63. The Jokers 67. Negatives 68. Every Home Should Have One 70. A Day in the Death of Joe Egg 70. The Ruling Class 72. Bedevilled 73. Flash Gordon 80, etc.

Hodges, Mike (1932–). British director, from TV.
□Suspect (TV) 69. Rumour (TV) 70. Get Carter 71. Pulp 72. The Terminal Man (US) (& p) 73. Flash Gordon 79. Morons from Outer Space 84. A Prayer for the Dying 87.

Hodiak, John (1914–1955). Serious-looking American leading man of the forties, of Ukrainian descent.

□ A Stranger in Town 43. I Dood It 43. Song of Russia 43. Swing Shift Maisie 43. *Lifeboat* 44. Marriage is a Private Affair 44. Maisie Goes to Reno 44. Sunday Dinner for a Soldier 44. You Can't Do That to Me 44. *A Bell for Adano* 45. Ziegfeld Follies 46. The Harvey Girls 46. Somewhere in the Night 46. Two Smart People 46. The Arnelo Affair 47. Love from a Stranger 47. Desert Fury 47. Homecoming 48. Command Decision 48. Ambush 49. The Bribe 49. A Lady Without Passport 50. Battleground 50. The Miniver Story 50. Night into Morning 51. The People Against O'Hara 51. Across the Wide Missouri 51. Battle Zone 52. The Sellout 52. Conquest of Cochise 53. Ambush at Tomahawk Gap 53. Mission over Korea 53. Dragonfly Squadron 54. Trial 55. On the Threshold of Space 56.

Hoellering, George (c. 1899–1980). producer of *Hortobagy*, long in Britain as specialized distributor and exhibitor; also producer of *Murder in the Cathedral* 51.

Hoey, Dennis (1893–1960) (Samuel David Hyams). British character actor, mostly in Hollywood; a memorably obtuse Lestrade to Basil Rathbone's Sherlock Holmes.
Tell England 30. The Good Companions 32. Chu Chin Chow 34. The Wandering Jew 34. Brewster's Millions 35. Maria Marten 36. This Above All 42. Sherlock Holmes and the Secret Weapon 42. Spider Woman 44. Pearl of Death 44. House of Fear 45. Kitty 46. Where There's Life 47. If Winter Comes 47. Wake of the Red Witch 48. David and Bathsheba 51, many others.

Hoffenstein, Samuel (1890–1947). Lithuanian-American screenwriter, always in collaboration.
An American Tragedy 31. *Dr Jekyll and Mr Hyde* 31. *Love Me Tonight* 32. Song of Songs 33. Marie Galante 34. Desire 36. Conquest 38. The Great Waltz 39. Lydia 41. Flesh and Fantasy 43. Phantom of the Opera 43. Laura 44. Cluny Brown 46. Give My Regards to Broadway 48.

Hoffman, Basil (1941–). American character actor.
Lady Liberty 72. At Long Last Love 75. All the President's Men 76. Close Encounters of the Third Kind 77. The Electric Horseman 79. Ordinary People 80. My Favorite Year 82, etc.

Hoffman, Dustin (1937–). Diffident American leading actor who suited the mood of the late sixties and made a big comeback in the early eighties.
□Madigan's Millions 66. The Tiger Makes Out 67. *The Graduate* 67. *Midnight Cowboy* 69. John and Mary 69. Little Big Man 70. Who is Harry Kellerman . . . ? 71. Alfredo Alfredo 72. Straw Dogs 72. Papillon 73. Lenny 74. *All the President's Men* 76. Marathon Man 76. Straight Time 78. Agatha 79. *Kramer vs Kramer* (AA) 80. *Tootsie* 83.

¶ *D.H.:* A good review from a critic is just another stay of execution.
D.H.: I don't like the fact that I have to get older so fast, but I like the fact that I'm ageing so well.
Famous line (*The Graduate*): Mrs Robinson, if you don't mind my saying so, this conversation is getting a little strange.

Hoffmann, Kurt (1912–). German director, mainly of comedies.
Quax der Bruch pilot 41. I Think Often of Piroschka 55. The Confessions of Felix Krull 57. Wir Wunderkinder 58, etc.

Hogan, James P. (1891–1943). American director.
Last Train from Madrid 37. Ebb Tide 38. The Texans 39. Power Dive 41. The Mad Ghoul 43. The Strange Death of Adolf Hitler 44, etc.

Hohl, Arthur (1889–1964). Staring-eyed American character actor who often played rustic types.
The Cheat 31. Island of Lost Souls 32. Man's Castle 33. Cleopatra 34. Show Boat 36. The Road Back 37. Kidnapped 38. Blackmail 39. Moontide 42. The Scarlet Claw 44. The Yearling 46. The Vigilantes Return 47, many others.

hokum. A word allegedly derived from an Indian word for a stodgy food, it came to mean pure entertainment of a routine kind, usually involving fast action. From it came the adjective 'hokey'. It was not always applied in the pejorative sense: many of most people's favourite films are basically hokum, in that they do not advance the art, but they may show it at its professional best.

¶ *Robert Sherwood:* Who invented hokum? Think how much money he'd have made from the film producers if he'd sold his invention on a royalty basis.

Holbrook, Hal (1925–). American general purpose stage and TV actor, also Mark Twain impersonator.
The Group 66. Wild in the Streets 68. A Clear and Present Danger (TV) 69. The

People Next Door 70. Suddenly Single (TV) 71. *That Certain Summer* (TV) 72. Magnum Force 73. All the President's Men 76. Midway 76. Julia 77. Murder by Natural Causes (TV) 79. Natural Enemies 79. Capricorn One 79. The Legend of the Golden Gun (TV) 79. Fog 80. The Killing of the President 80. Creepshow 82. The Star Chamber 82, etc.
TV series: *The Bold Ones* 70–71.

Holden, Fay (1894–1973) (Fay Hammerton). British stage actress who went to Hollywood in the thirties and found a niche as the mother of the Hardy family. Once known as Dorothy Clyde.
Wives Never Know 36. Exclusive 37. Judge Hardy's Children 38. Sweethearts 38. The Hardys Ride High 39. Bitter Sweet 40. Andy Hardy's Private Secretary 41. Ziegfeld Girl 41. Blossoms in the Dust 41. Andy Hardy's Double Life 43. Andy Hardy's Blonde Trouble 44. Canyon Passage 46. Love Laughs at Andy Hardy 46. Samson and Delilah 49. The Big Hangover 50. Andy Hardy Comes Home 58, many others.

Holden, Gloria (1908–). London-born leading lady, long in Hollywood.
Dracula's Daughter (title role) 36. The Life of Émile Zola 37. Test Pilot 38. A Child Is Born 40. The Corsican Brothers 41. Behind the Rising Sun 43. The Hucksters 47. Dream Wife 53. The Eddy Duchin Story 57. This Happy Feeling 68, etc.

Holden, William (1872–1932). American general purpose actor of the late silent period, usually in small roles; no relation to the later William Holden.
The First Kiss 28. Dynamite 30, etc.

Holden, William (1918–1981) (William Beedle). Good-looking American leading man who hit his greatest popularity in the fifties.
□*Golden Boy* 39. Invisible Stripes 40. Our Town 40. Those were the Days 40. Arizona 40. I Wanted Wings 41. Texas 41. The Fleet's In 42. The Remarkable Andrew 42. Meet the Stewarts 42. Young and Willing 43. Blaze of Noon 47. Dear Ruth 47. Variety Girl 47. *Rachel and the Stranger* 48. Apartment for Peggy 48. The Man from Colorado 48. The Dark Past 49. The Streets of Laredo 49. Miss Grant Takes Richmond 49. Dear Wife 49. Father is a Bachelor 50. *Sunset Boulevard* 50. Union Station 50. *Born Yesterday* 50. Force of Arms 51. Submarine Command 51. Boots Malone 52. The Turning Point 52. *Stalag 17* (AA) 53. The Moon is Blue 53. Forever Female 53. Escape from Fort Bravo 53. Executive Suite 54. Sabrina 54. The Country Girl 54. The Bridges at Toko-Ri 54. *Love is a Many-Splendored Thing* 55. *Picnic* 55. The Proud and Profane 56. Toward the Unknown 56. *The Bridge on the River Kwai* 57. The Key 58. The Horse Soldiers 59. The World of Suzie Wong 60. Satan Never Sleeps 62. The Counterfeit Traitor 62. The Lion 62. Paris When it Sizzles 64. The Seventh Dawn 64. Alvarez Kelly 66. Casino Royale 67. The Devil's Brigade 68. The Christmas Tree 69. *The Wild Bunch* 69. Wild Rovers 71. The Revengers 72. The Blue Knight (TV) 72. Breezy 73. Open Season 74. The Towering Inferno 74. *Network* 76. 21 Hours at Munich (TV) 77. Ashanti 78. Damien: Omen II 78. Fedora 78. Escape to Athena 79. The Earthling 80. When Time Ran Out 80. S.O.B. 81.

¶ *Pete Martin:* When you look at him, the map of the U.S. is right there on his face.

W.H.: I'm a whore, all actors are whores. We sell our bodies to the highest bidder.

W.H.: Take any picture you can. One out of four will be good, one out of ten will be very good, and one out of fifteen will get you an Academy Award.

Famous line (*Picnic*): I gotta get somewhere in this world. I just gotta.

Holender, Adam (–). American cinematographer.
Midnight Cowboy 69. Puzzle of a Downfall Child 70. Panic in Needle Park 71. Promises in the Dark 79. The Seduction of Joe Tynan 79. Simon 80.

Holiday (US 1938). A slightly bitter comedy of manners, more refined than the well-known crazy comedies of the thirties but in a similar mood, about a thinking man who marries into the idle rich, but at the last minute swaps his conventional intended for her eccentric sister. Directed by George Cukor from Philip Barry's play, with typically graceful performances from Katharine Hepburn and Cary Grant, and almost equally memorable contributions from Edward Everett Horton, Lew Ayres and Henry Kolker. Edward H. Griffith had directed a previous version in 1930, with Ann Harding, Mary Astor, Robert Ames and Edward Everett Horton in the same role as in 1938.

Holiday, Billie (1915–1959) (Eleonora Fagan). Black American blues singer whose only film appearance was *New Orleans* 47.

Diana Ross played her in *Lady Sings the Blues* 75.

Holland has produced two major documentarists: Joris Ivens and Bert Haanstra. Fiction films have not been the country's forte, though Fons Rademakers has his adherents.

Hollander, Frederick (1892–1976). German song composer, long in America. *The Blue Angel* 30. Desire 36. *Destry Rides Again* 39. The Man Who Came to Dinner 42. A Foreign Affair 48. The Five Thousand Fingers of Dr T 53, etc.

Holles, Antony (1901–1950). British actor who often played excitable foreigners.
The Lodger 32. Brewster's Millions 35. Dark Journey 37. Neutral Port 41. Warn That Man 43. Carnival 46. Bonnie Prince Charlie 49. The Rocking-Horse Winner 50, others.

Holliday, Doc (1849–1885). American wild west character; a tubercular dentist and poker-player who oddly changed to the right side of the law when he teamed up with Wyatt Earp in *Tombstone*. Played inaccurately but picturesquely on screen by Cesar Romero in *Frontier Marshal* 39; Walter Huston in *The Outlaw* 41; Kent Taylor in *Tombstone* 42; Victor Mature in *My Darling Clementine* 46; James Griffith in *Masterson of Kansas* 55; Kirk Douglas in *Gunfight at the OK Corral* 56; Arthur Kennedy in *Cheyenne Autumn* 64; Jason Robards in *Hour of the Gun* 67; Stacy Keach in *Doc* 70; and Douglas Fowley in the TV series *Wyatt Earp*.

Holliday, Judy (1922–1965) (Judith Tuvim). American revue star who shot to fame in the fifties as a slightly daffy blonde in a handful of well-scripted comedies.
Biography 1982: *Judy Holliday* by Gary Casey.
□Greenwich Village 44. Something for the Boys 44. Winged Victory 44. Adam's Rib 49. *Born Yesterday* (AA) 50. The Marrying Kind 52. *It Should Happen to You* 53. Phffft 54. *The Solid Gold Cadillac* 56. Full of Life 56. Bells are Ringing 60.

Holliman, Earl (1928–). American general purpose actor who can play innocent or villainous.
Destination Gobi 53. The Bridges at Toko-Ri 54. Broken Lance 54. The Big Combo 55. Forbidden Planet 56. Giant 56. The Rainmaker 56. Gunfight at OK Corral 57. Trooper Hook 57. Hot Spell 58. The Trap 59. Last Train from Gun Hill 59. Visit to a Small Planet 60. Summer and Smoke 61. Armored Command 61. The Sons of Katie Elder 65. Covenant with Death 67. Anzio 68. Smoke 69. Trapped (TV) 73. I Love You, Goodbye (TV) 74. Alexander: The Other Side of Dawn (TV) 77. Sharkey's Machine 81. The Thorn Birds (TV) 82.
TV series: Hotel de Paree 59. The Wide Country 62. Police Woman 75–77.

Hollingsworth, John (1916–1963). British conductor for many film scores of the forties.

Holloway, Stanley (1890–1982). British north-country comedian, entertainer, singer and character actor with a long list of international credits in revue, musical comedy and variety as well as films.
Autobiography 1969: *Wiv a Little Bit of Luck*.
□The Rotters 21. *The Co-Optimists* 30. Sleeping Car 33. The Girl from Maxim's 33. Lily of Killarney 34. Love at Second Sight 34. Sing as We Go 34. Road House 34. D'Ye Ken John Peel? 35. In Town Tonight 35. *Squibs* 35. Play Up the Band 35. Song of the Forge 36. *The Vicar of Bray* 36. Cotton Queen 37. Sam Small Leaves Town 37. Our Island Nation 37. Major Barbara 41. *Salute John Citizen* 42. *The Way Ahead* 44. *Champagne Charlie* 44. *This Happy Breed* 44. *The Way to the Stars* 45. *Brief Encounter* 45. Caesar and Cleopatra 45. Wanted for Murder 46. Carnival 46. Meet Me at Dawn 46. *Nicholas Nickleby* (as Mr Crummles) 47. Snowbound 48. Saraband for Dead Lovers 48. One Night With You 48. Noose 48. The Winslow Boy 48. *Hamlet* (as the gravedigger) 48. Another Shore 48. Passport to Pimlico 49. The Perfect Woman 49. Midnight Episode 50. One Wild Oat 50. *The Lavender Hill Mob* 51. Lady Godiva Rides Again 51. The Magic Box 51. The Happy Family 52. Meet Me Tonight 52. *The Titfield Thunderbolt* 52. *The Beggar's Opera* 53. A Day to Remember 53. *Meet Mr Lucifer* 53. Fast and Loose 53. An Alligator Named Daisy 55. Jumping for Joy 55. Alive and Kicking 58. No Trees in the Street 58. Hello London 58. *No Love for Johnnie* 61. On the Fiddle 61. *My Fair Lady* (as Doolittle) 64. In Harm's Way 64. Ten Little Indians 64. The Sandwich Man 66. Mrs Brown You've Got a Lovely Daughter 68. Run a Crooked Mile (TV) 69. The Private Life of Sherlock Holmes 70. The Flight of the Doves 71. Up the Front 72. Journey into Fear 76.
TV series: *Our Man Higgins* 62.

Holloway, Sterling (1905–). Slow-speaking American comic actor, usually of

yokels or hillbillies. Busiest in the thirties; latterly the voice of many Disney characters. Casey at the Bat 27. Alice in Wonderland 33. Life Begins at Forty 35. Professor Beware 38. The Bluebird 40. A Walk in the Sun 46. The Beautiful Blonde from Bashful Bend 49. Shake, Rattle and Rock 56. Live a Little Love a Little 68, many others.
TV series: The Life of Riley 53–58. The Baileys of Balboa 64.

Hollywood. The American film city, nominally a suburb of Los Angeles, was founded in 1912 when a number of independent producers headed west from New York to avoid the effects of a patents trust. The site was chosen because of its nearness to the Mexican border in case of trouble, and because the weather and location possibilities were excellent. By 1913 Hollywood was established as the film-maker's Mecca, and continued so for forty years. Several factors combined in the late forties to affect its unique concentration. Actors transformed themselves into independent producers and reduced the power of the 'front office'; stars now made the films they liked instead of the ones to which they were assigned. The consequent break-up of many big studios, which now simply sold production space to independent outfits, weakened continuity of product. Each production now had to start from scratch; there was no longer a training ground for new talent, nor was the old production gloss always in evidence. The communist witch-hunt unfortunately drove many leading talents to Europe, and some found they preferred Shepperton or Cinecitta to California. The coming of CinemaScope, a device to halt the fall in box office returns which resulted from the beginning of commercial TV, meant that real locations were now necessary, as studio sets would show up on the screen. So began the world-wide trekking now evident in American production: generally speaking only routine product and TV episodes are made in the film city itself, but each distribution set-up will have up to a dozen films being made in various parts of the globe.

Books about Hollywood include *Hello Hollywood* (1962) by Allen Rivkin and Laura Kerr; *Hollywood* (1974) by Garson Kanin: *The Hollywood Exiles* (1976) by John Baxter; *Hollywood and the Great Fan Magazines* (1970) by Martin Levin; *Hollywood the Haunted House* (1969) by Paul Mayersberg; *Flesh and Fantasy* (1978) by Penny Stallings; *This Was Hollywood* (1960) by Beth Day; *Gone Hollywood* (1979) by Christopher Finch and Linda Rosenkrantz; *The Pink Palace* (1978) by Sandra Lee Stuart; *The Garden of Allah* (1971) by Sheilah Graham; *The Shattered Silents* (1978) by Alexander Walker; *Some Time in the Sun* (1976) by Tom Dardis; *Hollywood the Dream Factory* (1951) by Hortense Powdermaker; *The Hollywood Studios* (1978) by Roy Pickard; *Hollywood Babylon* (1975) by Kenneth Anger. And some classics: *Hollywood, The Movie Colony, The Movie Makers* (1939) by Leo Rosten; *America at the Movies* (1945) by Margaret Farrand Thorp; *Picture* (1951) by Lillian Ross; *The Studio* (1968) by John Gregory Dunne; *Hollywood, the Pioneers* (1979) by Kevin Brownlow and John Kobal; *The Parade's Gone By* (1968) by Kevin Brownlow; *The Real Tinsel* (1970) by Bernard Rosenberg and Harry Silverstein; *The Fifty Year Decline and Fall of Hollywood* (1961) by Ezra Goodman. Plus all the books about individual stars, directors, studios and producers, especially: *King Cohn* (1967) by Tony Thomas; *Memo from David O, Selznick* (1972) by Rudy Behlmer; and *David O. Selznick's Hollywood* (1980) by Richard Haver.

¶ The legendary film city—sometimes referred to as Sodom-by-the-Sea—seems far from glamorous to the casual visitor. Geographically, it is not a city at all but a mere suburban segment of a forty-mile-square jigsaw puzzle of dormitory areas which all run into each other. James Gleason, Dorothy Parker, and several other people are credited with calling Los Angeles:

> Seventy-two suburbs in search of a city.

No matter who said it, it's still true. L.A. also remains a supreme example of man's inhumanity to man, the promised land that only humans have polluted. Even before the glorious climate was filtered through several layers of smog, the values were all wrong. The residents were almost all on the run from somewhere else, and tended to idle their lives away under the sun, pursuing the buck when they could and taking the biggest for the best. Ethel Barrymore's first impressions, in 1932, were vivid:

> The people are unreal. The flowers are unreal, they don't smell. The fruit is unreal, it doesn't taste of anything. The whole place is a glaring, gaudy, nightmarish set, built up in the desert.

The heat, the richness and the sweet smells are certainly enervating. Shirley Maclaine, hot from Broadway, saw the difference at once:

> The most important deals in the movie industry are finalized on the sun-

drenched turf of golf courses or around turquoise swimming pools, where the smell of barbecue sauce is borne on gentle breezes and wafts over the stereo system of houses that people seldom leave.

Cedric Hardwicke felt the danger:

God felt sorry for actors, so he gave them a place in the sun and a swimming pool. The price they had to pay was to surrender their talent.

There's always a price tag. Fred Allen knew it when he said:

California is a great place . . . if you happen to be an orange.

Someone else called it 'Siberia with palms'. Raymond Chandler aptly summed up L.A. as:

A city with all the personality of a paper cup.

Joe Frisco thought of it as:

The only town in the world where you can wake up in the morning and listen to the birds coughing in the trees.

Stephen Vincent Benet was even more picturesque:

Of all the Christbitten places in the two hemispheres, this is the last curly kink in the pig's tail.

Hollywood is superior to other parts of L.A. only by virtue of the dusty hills into which it nestles on its northern side. The fact that most comments on it are cynical seems inevitable in an industrial area where the product is an intangible dream. Human beings must get injured in the process, their souls bruised by the struggle for fame, their bodies tossed onto the junkheap the minute they pass their prime. Hollywood has always sought, and then misused, the services of great talent. In the early thirties so many New York actors and writers made the four-day train journey and shortly returned in dejection that a saying sprang up on Broadway:

Never buy anything in Hollywood that you can't put on the Chief.

Billie Burke, a longtime resident, declared that:

To survive there, you need the ambition of a Latin-American revolutionary, the ego of a grand opera tenor, and the physical stamina of a cow pony.

Moss Hart called Beverly Hills:

The most beautiful slave quarters in the world.

Nelson Algren had a brief but unhappy experience:

I went out there for a thousand a week, and I worked Monday and I got fired Wednesday. The fellow who hired me was out of town Tuesday.

Walter Pidgeon liked the system:

It was like an expensive, beautifully-run fan club. You didn't need to carry money. Your face was your credit card—all over the world.

But Dorothy Parker saw its dangers:

Hollywood money isn't money. It's congealed snow.

Hedda Hopper put it another way:

Our town worships success, the bitch goddess whose smile hides a taste for blood.

John Huston saw through the illusion:

Hollywood has always been a cage . . . a cage to catch our dreams.

George Jean Nathan gave the most all-embracing description:

Ten million dollars worth of intricate and ingenious machinery functioning elaborately to put skin on baloney.

Oscar Levant was bitter:

Strip the phony tinsel off Hollywood and you'll find the real tinsel underneath.

Wilson Mizner thought it:

A trip through a sewer in a glass-bottomed boat,

and varied this thought as:

A sewer with service from the Ritz Carlton.

Dudley Field Malone found it:

A town where inferior people have a way of making superior people feel inferior.

Elinor Glyn in 1927 wondered:

Where else in the world will you find a coloured cook bursting into the dining room to say 'You folks better hustle to dinner if you don't want the stuff to get cold'?

H. L. Mencken marvelled at its reputation:

Immorality? Oh, my God, Hollywood seemed to me to be one of the most respectable towns in America. Even Baltimore can't beat it.

Leo Rosten saw its lotus-land attraction:

Fortunes were made overnight, and along with the speculators, the oil men and the real estate promoters, another group came to the promised land—the old, the sick and the middle-aged, who came not to woo Mammon but to sit out their savings in the sun and die in the shadow of an annuity and an orange tree.

Herman Weinberg saw the dangers:

Whatever goes into the Hollywood grist mill, it comes out the same way. It is a meat-grinder that will take beef and suet, pheasant and turnips, attar of roses and limburger and turn it all into the same kind of hash that has served so many so well for so long.

To Ginger Rogers,

Hollywood is like an empty wastebasket.

To John Schlesinger,

An extraordinary kind of temporary place.

To Carrie Fisher,

You can't find true affection in Hollywood because everyone does the fake affection so well.

To Sylvester Stallone,

The only way to be a success in Hollywood is to be as obnoxious as the next guy.

To Rod Steiger,

A community of lonely people searching for even the most basic kind of stimulation in their otherwise mundane lives.

To Groucho Marx,

It provided the kind of luxury that exists today only for the sons of Latin-American dictators.

To Marilyn Monroe,

A place where they pay you 50,000 dollars for a kiss and 50 cents for your soul.

To Rex Reed,

A place where, if you don't have happiness, you send out for it.

Elinor Glyn was waspish about it:

When I arrived, spittoons were still being placed in rows down the centre of a set which was supposed to be the baronial hall of an old English castle.

Lana Turner survived the dream:

It was all beauty and it was all talent, and if you had it they protected you.

Josef Von Sternberg was downright cynical:

You can seduce a man's wife there, rape his daughter and wipe your hands on his canary, but if you don't like his movie, you're dead.

Lauren Bacall spoke from other people's experience:

The only place in the world where an amicable divorce means that each gets fifty per cent of the publicity.

Evelyn Keyes recalled:

The big studios were each headed by a Big Daddy who reigned supreme.

Louis Sherwin remembered:

They knew only one word of more than one syllable, and that was FILLUM.

Wilson Mizner, in similar vein:

What I like about Hollywood is that you can get along knowing only two words of English: swell and lousy.

He added:

I spent several years there, and I think all the heroes are in the audience.

An anonymous wag called it:

Paradise with a lobotomy.

But for Joseph L. Mankiewicz it had saving graces, in the thirties at least:

The old moguls were really impressed to know that Lion Feuchtwanger and Aldous Huxley and Thomas Mann were living in Pacific Palisades. They reached for things in those days. Even Bernard Shaw came out to look around. I don't think he'd come today.

Ernst Lubitsch saw another danger, that the dream might be dangerously more attractive than reality:

I've been to Paris France and I've been to Paris Paramount. Paris Paramount is better.

Some failed to relish the easy life. After a short stay in 1932 Sergei Eisenstein packed his bags. When asked at the station 'Are you coming back?' he replied:

No, I'm *going* back.

And an anonymous wag complained:

In Hollywood you can be forgotten while you're out of the room going to the toilet.

F. Scott Fitzgerald was whimsical about it:

I accepted the assignment with the resignation of a ghost assigned to a haunted house.

A character in Gavin Lambert's *The Slide Area* had a different slant:

The past is out of place here, mister. You don't feel it, you only feel the future.

To Grover Jones it was:

The only asylum run by the inmates.

Walter Winchell called it:

A town that has to be seen to be disbelieved.

And Marlon Brando dismissed it as:

A cultural boneyard.

Ken Murray loved it, but admitted it to be:

A place where you spend more than you make, on things you don't need, to impress people you don't like.

Ethel Barrymore was finally repelled:

It looks, it feels, as though it had been invented by a Sixth Avenue peepshow man.

And Sonny Fox summed it all up:

Hollywood is like a world's fair that's been up a year too long.

All such remarks spring mainly from the system. But perhaps the people were partly to blame.

I'll miss Hollywood. Of the twenty friends I thought I had, I'll miss the six I really had, remarked Lauren Bacall wryly on her way to Broadway. And Errol Flynn once said:

> They've great respect for the dead in Hollywood, but none for the living.

Richard Burton responded frankly to a question about Hollywood morals:

> Certainly most movie executives were making love to starlets. But then, so were most of us actors.

Alfred Hitchcock, on the other hand, maintained:

> We lead a very suburban life here. We're in bed by nine o'clock every night.

And that reminds one of the anonymous thirties complaint about Hollywood's fabled social life:

> No matter how hot it gets during the day, there's nothing to do at night.

Anonymous too was the mogul-hater who averred:

> There's nothing wrong with the place, that six first-class funerals wouldn't cure.

Nepotism was of course rife. When Louis B. Mayer appointed his daughter's husband William Goetz to a key position at MGM, someone cracked:

> The son-in-law also rises.

And Ogden Nash devised a famous couplet about the head of Universal:

> Uncle Carl Laemmle
> Has a very large faemmle.

Ethics were out, as Dorothy Parker knew:

> The only -ism Hollywood believes in is plagiarism.

Glamour and insincerity gave it the atmosphere of a luxury liner, as someone said in the thirties:

> I have this terrible apprehension that suddenly the boat is going to dock and I shall never see any of you again.

Phyllis Batelli called it:

> A place where great-grandmothers dread to grow old.

And there's an old saying:

> In Hollywood the eternal triangle consists of an actor, his wife and himself.

(There is another version which runs 'an actor, his wife and his agent'. Take your choice.) Walter Winchell thought:

> They shoot too many pictures and not enough actors.

One can hardly be surprised that people are false when the movies themselves were sham for so many years. Arthur Freed produced the Scottish fantasy *Brigadoon* on the MGM lot and defended himself by saying:

> I went to Scotland and found nothing there that looks like Scotland.

A wise saying of Hollywood's heyday, by David O. Selznick:

> Nothing here is permanent. Once photographed, life here is ended.

But the system had its rueful supporters. Orson Welles:

> Hollywood's all right: it's the pictures that are bad.

Raymond Chandler:

> If my books had been any worse I should not have been invited to Hollywood, and if they had been any better I should not have come.

An anonymous writer:

> They ruin your stories. They trample on your pride. They massacre your ideas. And what do you get for it? A fortune.

Typically, Hollywood was often ignorant of the talent it had bought. Bert Lahr didn't make it until his third trip, and said wryly:

> If you want to be a success in Hollywood, be sure and go to New York.

Richard Dyer McCann wrote truthfully:

> The most familiar, solid, bedrock certainty in Hollywood is sudden change.

Certainly, the town depended on fashion, and its well-set ways were in themselves a mere fashion. By 1956, David Selznick found the place to be:

> Like Egypt, full of crumbled pyramids.

Fred Allen had said in 1941 that:

> Hollywood is a place where people from Iowa mistake each other for stars.

In the fifties the mistake became pardonable: male leads were required to look less like matinee idols and more like the slob next door, or the fellow at the gas station. Humphrey Bogart was heard to remark:

> I came out here with one suit and everybody said I looked like a bum. Twenty years later Marlon Brando comes out with only a sweat shirt and the town drools over him. That shows you how much Hollywood has progressed.

Hollywood was desperate in the face of TV and better living standards. One trend followed another: in the sixties, for instance, English actors became more fashionable than ever before, and Bob Hope quipped:

> There'll always be an England, even if it's in Hollywood.

By the end of the sixties the old complaints were being repeated with a new veneer of resigned cynicism. Paul Mayersburg:

> The desert of Southern California cannot be said to have created a religion, but it has contributed greatly to the development of a way of life that operates at the extremity of our civilization. When you reach Los Angeles you are as far West as you can go.

An anonymous agent:

> You fail upwards here. A guy makes a ten million dollar picture, the thing is not that he's made a bomb [i.e. disaster] but that he's made a ten million dollar picture. So next time out, they give him a twelve million dollar picture.

Whether Hollywood finally succeeds or goes under, it has had a fair run, long enough to confound two doubting remarks of 1915, by Carl Laemmle:

> I hope I didn't make a mistake coming out here.

And D. W. Griffith:

> It's a shame to take this country away from the rattlesnakes.

Perhaps the rattlesnakes are just biding their time.

Hollywood on film has generally been shown as the brassy, gold-digging, power-conscious society which, in the nature of things, it can hardly fail to be. There was a somewhat sentimental period in the twenties and thirties, with *Ella Cinders, Hollywood, Going Hollywood, Hollywood Cavalcade*, and *Hollywood Boulevard*; but satire had already struck in such films as *The Last Command, Merton of the Movies, Show People, The Lost Squadron, What Price Hollywood, Lady Killer, Something to Sing About, Once in a Lifetime, Stardust, Hollywood Hotel, Stand In, A Star Is Born* and *Boy Meets Girl*. The moguls didn't seem to mind the film city being shown as somewhat zany, as in *The Goldwyn Follies*, Disney's *Mother Goose Goes Hollywood, The Cohens and Kellys in Hollywood, Abbott and Costello in Hollywood, The Jones Family in Hollywood, Movie Crazy, Never Give a Sucker an Even Break*, and *Hellzapoppin*; but they preferred the adulatory attitude best expressed in *The Youngest Profession*, which concerned the autograph hunters who lay in wait at the studio exits.

During the forties Paramount was the studio most addicted to showing itself off, though the front office can't have relished watching Preston Sturges bite the hand that fed him in *Sullivan's Travels*. The story of *Hold Back the Dawn* was supposedly told to sentimental Mitchell Leisen during a lunch break on the studio floor; Crosby and Hope based a score of gags on Paramount; and the studio was the setting for *Star Spangled Rhythm*, an all-star musical which encouraged other studios to emulate it, with Warner's *Thank Your Lucky Stars* and *It's a Great Feeling*, Universal's *Follow the Boys*, the independent *Stage Door Canteen*, and later Paramount's less successful reprise, *Variety Girl*.

In 1950 *Sunset Boulevard* took a really sardonic look at the film city, and set a fashion for scathing movies like *The Star, The Bad and the Beautiful, The Barefoot Contessa* and *The Big Knife*. As though to atone, almost every studio threw in a light-hearted, nostalgic look at Hollywood's golden era: *Singin' in the Rain, The Perils of Pauline, Jolson Sings Again, The Eddie Cantor Story*. But in the last few years the only really affectionate review of Hollywood's past has been in the Cliff Richard musical *Wonderful Life*, though Jerry Lewis continued to paint zany pictures of studio life in *The Errand Boy, The Ladies' Man* and *The Patsy*. The rest was all denunciation and bitterness: *Hollywood Boulevard, Hollywood Story, The Wild Party, The Day of the Locust, Inserts, The Big Knife, The Goddess, Two Weeks in Another Town, The Carpetbaggers, Harlow, Inside Daisy Clover, The Loved One, Whatever Happened to Baby Jane, The Legend of Lylah Clare, Myra Breckinridge*, and *The Oscar*. A 1969 TV series, *Bracken's World*, was set in a film studio (20th Century Fox) and saw it as a kind of valley of the dolls—and the studio scenes in *that* movie were none too convincing.

See 1975 book by Rudy Behlmer and Tony Thomas: *Hollywood's Hollywood, the Movies about the Movies*.

The Hollywood Ten. Alvah Bessie, Herbert Biberman, Lester Cole, Edward Dmytryk, Ring Lardner Jnr, John Howard Lawson, Albert Maltz, Sam Ornitz, Adrian Scott and Dalton Trumbo were the famous band of writers, producers and directors who in 1947 refused to tell the Unamerican Activities Committee whether or not they were communists. All served short prison sentences and had difficulty getting work in Hollywood for several years.

Holm, Celeste (1919–). Cool, calm, American stage actress whose films have usually provided her with wisecracking roles. □Three Little Girls in Blue 46. Carnival in Costa Rica 47. *Gentleman's Agreement* (AA) 47. Road House 48. *The Snake Pit* 48. Chicken Every Sunday 48. Come to the Stable 49. Everybody Does It 49. A Letter to Three Wives (narrator only) 49. *All About Eve* 50. Champagne for Caesar 50. The Tender Trap 55. *High Society* 56. Bachelor Flat 61. Cosa Nostra, Arch Enemy of the FBI

(TV) 66. Doctor You've Got to be Kidding 67. The Delphi Bureau (TV) 72. Tom Sawyer 73. The Underground Man (TV) 74. Death Cruise (TV) 74. Captains and the Kings (TV) 76. Bittersweet Love 76. Love Boat II (TV) 78. The Private Files of J. Edgar Hoover 78. Backstairs at the White House (TV) 79. Midnight Lace (TV) 80.
TV series: Nancy 70.

Holm, Ian (1932–) (Ian Holm Cuthbert). British stage actor recently emerging in films. □The Bofors Gun (BFA) 68. A Midsummer Night's Dream 68. The Fixer 68. Oh What a Lovely War 69. A Severed Head 70. Nicholas and Alexandra 71. Mary Queen of Scots 72. Young Winston 72. The Homecoming 73. Juggernaut 75. Shout at the Devil 76. Robin and Marian 76. Jesus of Nazareth (TV) 77. The Man in the Iron Mask (TV) 77. March or Die 77. Holocaust (TV) 77. Alien 79. The Lost Boys (TV) 79. SOS Titanic (TV) 79. All Quiet on the Western Front (TV) 80. Time Bandits (TV) 81. Chariots of Fire (BFA) 81. Return of the Soldier 82. Greystoke 84. Dance with a Stranger 85. Wetherby 85. Brazil 85. Laughterhouse 85. Dreamchild 86.

Holmes, Phillips (1907–1942). American juvenile lead who went straight from college to Hollywood; son of Taylor Holmes. His rather stiff personality soon lost its appeal. □Varsity 28. His Private Life 28. Illusion 29. The Wild Party 29. Stairs of Sand 29. The Return of Sherlock Holmes 29. Pointed Heels 29. Only the Brave 30. Paramount on Parade 30. The Devil's Holiday 30. Grumpy 30. Her Man 30. Man to Man 30. The Dancers 30. The Criminal Code 31. Stolen Heaven 31. Confessions of a Co-Ed 31. *An American Tragedy* 31. The Man I Killed 32. Two Kinds of Women 32. Make Me a Star 32. 70,000 Witnesses 32. Night Court 33. The Secret of Madame Blanche 33. Men Must Fight 33. Looking Forward 33. Storm at Daybreak 33. The Big Brain 33. Dinner at Eight 33. Penthouse 33. Beauty for Sale 33. Stage Mother 33. Private Scandal 34. Nana 34. Caravan 34. Great Expectations 34. Million Dollar Ransom 34. The Divine Spark 34. No Ransom 35. Ten Minute Alibi (GB) 35. Chatterbox 36. House of a Thousand Candles 36. General Spanky 36. The Dominant Sex (GB) 37. The Housemaster (GB) 38.

Holmes, Taylor (1872–1959). Veteran American character actor with long stage experience; latterly seen as amiably crooked politician or confidence trickster.
Efficiency Edgar's Courtship 17. Ruggles of Red Gap (title role) 18. One Hour of Love 28. The First Baby 36. Boomerang 47. Nightmare Alley 47. Father of the Bride 50. The First Legion 51. Beware My Lovely 52. The Maverick Queen 56, many others.

Holt, Charlene (1939–). American leading lady, former star of TV commercials (and *The Tom Ewell Show*).
Man's Favourite Sport? 64. Red Line 7000 66. El Dorado 67, etc.

Holt, Jack (1888–1951) (Charles John Holt II). Tough-looking American leading man of silent and sound action films.
A Cigarette—That's All 15. The Little American 16. The Woman Thou Gavest Me 18. Held by the Enemy 20. Bought and Paid For 22. Empty Hands 24. Wanderer of the Wasteland 25. Vengeance 28. Hell's Island 30. *Dirigible* 31. War Correspondent 32. Whirlpool 33. The Littlest Rebel 35. *San Francisco* 36. Passport to Alcatraz 40. Holt of the Secret Service 43. They Were Expendable 45. Flight to Nowhere 46. Brimstone 49. Task Force 49. Across the Wide Missouri 51, many others.

Holt, Jennifer (1920–) (Elizabeth Holt). American leading lady of 'B' westerns; daughter of Jack Holt.
Stick to Your Guns 42. Cheyenne Round up 43. Oklahoma Raiders 44. Buffalo Bill Rides Again 47, etc.

Holt, Nat (1892–1971). American independent producer.
Badman's Territory 46. Trail Street 47. Return of the Badmen 48. Fighting Man of the Plains 49. The Great Missouri Raid 51. Denver and Rio Grande 52. Pony Express 53. Flight to Tangier 53, etc.
TV series: Tales of Wells Fargo 57–61. Overland Trail 60.

Holt, Patrick (1912–) (Patrick Parsons). Bland British leading man of the forties, later in character roles.
The Return of the Frog 38. Sword of Honour 39. Convoy 41. Hungry Hill 47. Master of Bankdam 47. The Mark of Cain 48. Portrait from Life 49. Marry Me 49. Guilt is My Shadow 50. The Dark Avenger 55. Miss Tulip Stays the Night 56. Thunderball 65. Murderers' Row 66. Hammerhead 68. No Blade of Grass 71. Lillie (TV) 78. Playing Away 86, many others.

Holt, Seth (1923–1971). British director, formerly editor and associate producer for Ealing.
□Nowhere to Go 58. Taste of Fear 61. Station Six Sahara 63. *The Nanny* 65. Danger Route 67. Monsieur Lecoq 68. Blood from the Mummy's Tomb 71.

Holt, Tim (1919–1973) (Charles John Holt III). American leading man, son of Jack Holt. In films from 1937, and was hero of many low-budget westerns.
History Is Made at Night 37. The Law West of Tombstone 38. Stagecoach 39. The Swiss Family Robinson 40. *The Magnificent Ambersons* 42. Hitler's Children 42. My Darling Clementine 46. *The Treasure of the Sierra Madre* 47. The Mysterious Desperado 49. His Kind of Woman 51. The Monster That Challenged the World 57, etc.

Homans, Robert E. (1874–1947). Round-faced American character actor, in hundreds of movies, usually as country cop.
Legally Dead 23. The Bandit Buster 26. Princess from Hoboken 27. Obey Your Husband 28. Isle of Lost Ships 29. Trigger Tricks 30. The Black Camel 31. Young America 32. She Done Him Wrong 33. The Woman in Red 35. Black Legion 36. Easy Living 37. The Amazing Dr Clitterhouse 38. The Grapes of Wrath 40. Honky Tonk 41. Night Monster 42. It Ain't Hay 43. Pin Up Girl 44. Captain Eddie 45. Girl on the Spot 46, many others.

Homeier, Skip (1929–). American child actor of the forties, later in a variety of supporting roles.
Tomorrow the World 44. Boys' Ranch 46. Mickey 48. The Gunfighter 50. Fixed Bayonets 51. Sailor Beware 52. Beachhead 54. At Gunpoint 56. Comanche Station 60. The Ghost and Mr Chicken 66. Starbird and Sweet William 76. The Greatest 77, etc.
TV series: *Dan Raven* 60.

Un Homme et une Femme (France 1966). A slight, sophisticated modern love story which achieved international box-office success because audiences were waiting for a reversion from the kitchen sink school and found it in this glossy accumulation of television commercial tricks. Critics busied themselves with theories as to why certain scenes were shot in colour and others in black and white, until director Claude Lelouch admitted that he ran out of funds and simply couldn't afford any more colour stock. Anouk Aimée and Jean-Louis Trintignant were the protagonists; Francis Lai's music helped immeasurably.

Homoki-Nagy, Istvan (1914–). Hungarian naturalist who has made many films of wild life including *From Blossom Time Till Autumn Frost.*

Homolka, Oscar (1899–1978). Viennese-born character actor, a fine 'heavy'. On stage from 1918, international films from mid-thirties.
□Dreyfus (Ger.) 30. Hokuspokus (Ger.) 30. Der Weg Nach Rio (Ger.) 31. Im Geheimdienst (Ger.) 31. Nachtkolonne (Ger.) 31. 1914 (Ger.) 31. Zwischen Nacht und Morgen (Ger.) 31. Die Nachte von Port Said (Ger.) 32. Moral und Liebe (Ger.) 33. Spione am Werk (Ger.) 33. Unsichbara Gegner (Austria) 33. *Rhodes of Africa* 35. *Sabotage* 36. Everything Is Thunder 36. Ebb Tide 37. Hidden Power 37. Seven Sinners 40. Comrade X 40. The Invisible Woman 41. Rage in Heaven 41. Ball of Fire 41. Mission to Moscow 43. Hostages 43. Code of Scotland Yard 47. *The Shop at Sly Corner* 47. *I Remember Mama* 48. Anna Lucasta 49. The White Tower 50. Top Secret 52. The House of the Arrow 53. Prisoner of War 54. The Seven Year Itch 55. War and Peace 56. A Farewell to Arms 57. The Key 58. Tempest 58. Mr Sardonicus 61. Boy's Night Out 62. The Wonderful World of the Brothers Grimm 63. The Long Ships 64. Joy in the Morning 65. *Funeral in Berlin* 66. The Happening 67. Billion Dollar Brain 67. The Madwoman of Chaillot 69. Assignment to Kill 69. The Executioner 70. Song of Norway 70. The Tamarind Seed 74.

homosexuality can be said to have arrived during the late sixties as a fit subject for the western cinema, producers having toyed gingerly with it for the previous three decades. During the forties, there were clear intimations of it in *The Maltese Falcon, Victory,* and *Rope*. The fifties brought *Strangers on a Train, I Vitelloni, Serious Charge,* Germany's *The Third Sex,* and *Suddenly Last Summer,* and the decade was rounded off with two productions of the life of Oscar Wilde. *Cat on a Hot Tin Roof* 58 and *Spartacus* 60 were probably the last Hollywood movies to have homosexual inferences deliberately removed from the original. In 1962 the subject came right out into the open with Victim, a well-intentioned thriller about the blackmail of homosexuals;

A Taste of Honey featured a sympathetic homosexual; and both *Advise and Consent* and *The Best Man* concerned allegations of homosexuality against American politicians. On the other hand *Lawrence of Arabia* was so reticent about its hero's sexual make-up that it was difficult to know what estimate was being made; but for good measure Peter O'Toole was raped a second time in *Lord Jim*. Universal romantic comedies now began to make fun of the subject: in *That Touch of Mink* Gig Young's psychiatrist thought he was in love with Cary Grant, and in *A Very Special Favour* Rock Hudson deliberately made Leslie Caron think him effeminate so that she would 'rescue him'. The floodgates were now open: in rapid succession we had *A View From the Bridge,* with its male kiss; *The Servant,* with its odd relationship between master and man; *The Leather Boys*; *Stranger in the House*; *The Fearless Vampire Killers*, with its young homosexual bloodsucker; the miscast and unhappy *Staircase*; *The Detective*, which made New York appear to be a very gay city; *The Gay Deceivers*, in which two young men avoided the draft by pretending to be queer; *Reflections in a Golden Eye*; *Midnight Cowboy*; *The Boys in the Band*, the first sympathetic homosexual comedy; *The Boston Strangler* and *Funeral in Berlin*, with scenes in transvestite bars; *If, Young Woodley, Tea and Sympathy, Riot, The Sergeant* and *Villain*, which revealed camp goings-on in school, prison, the army and gangland. *Girl Stroke Boy* revealed the plight of parents who could not tell whether their son was engaged to a girl or a boy. In *Myra Breckinridge* homosexuality was almost lost in a welter of more spectacular perversions. Historical figures such as Richard the Lionheart and Tchaikovsky had their sexual pecadilloes explored in *The Lion in Winter* and *The Music Lovers*, and Billy Wilder jokingly investigated *The Private Life of Sherlock Holmes*. It seems likely that, having secured public sympathy for their plight, homosexuals will now overstep the mark in merely sordid productions such as *Fortune and Men's Eyes, The Queens, Some of My Best Friends Are*, and the semi-underground ramblings of Andy Warhol and his clan. TV movies invaded the territory in 1973 with *That Certain Summer*. There wasn't much further to go, especially as 'gays' had their own porno films. 1978 brought the last curiosity: *A Different Story,* the love affair of a homosexual and a lesbian.
See also: *Lesbianism*.

Honegger, Arthur (1892–1955). Swiss composer who worked on French and British pictures.
La Roue 22. Napoleon 27. Les Miserables 34. L'Idée 34. Mayerling 36. *Pygmalion* 38. *Pacific 231* 46.

Hood, Darla (1931–1979). American child actress noted for appearances in Our Gang between 1935 and 1942.

Hooks, Robert (1937–). Black American leading man.
Sweet Love Bitter 66. Hurry Sundown 67. Crosscurrent (TV) 71. Trapped (TV) 73. Aaron Loves Angela 75. The Killer Who Wouldn't Die (TV) 76. Just an Old Sweet Song (TV) 76. Airport 77 77. To Kill a Cop (TV) 78. A Women Called Moses (TV) 78. Backstairs at the White House (TV) 79. Hollow Image (TV) 79. Fast Walking 82.
TV series: N.Y.P.D. 67.

Hooper, Tobe (–). American horror director.
The Texas Chainsaw Massacre 74. Eaten Alive 76. Salem's Lot (TV) 79. The Funhouse 81. Poltergeist 82. Lifeforce 85. Invaders from Mars 86. Texas Chainsaw Massacre II 86.

Hoover, J. Edgar (1895–1972). American executive, director of the Federal Bureau of Investigation from 1935. In 1939 Paramount made several low-budgeters drawn from his book *Persons in Hiding*; in 1959 he appeared briefly in *The FBI Story*. Subsequently he was impersonated by Erwin Fuller in *Lepke*, by Broderick Crawford in *The Private Files of J. Edgar Hoover*, and by Sheldon Leonard in *The Brinks Job*, by Vincent Gardenia in *Kennedy* (TV) and by Ernest Borgnine in *Blood Feud* (TV).

Hopalong Cassidy, the genial black-garbed hero of scores of western second features since 1935, was created by novelist Clarence E. Mulford. William Boyd (qv) was his only screen and TV personification.

Hope, Anthony (1863–1933) (Sir Anthony Hope Hawkins). British adventure novelist whose *The Prisoner of Zenda* and its sequel *Rupert of Hentzau* have frequently been filmed.

Hope, Bob (1903–) (Leslie Townes Hope). Wisecracking American star comedian, a major name in entertainment for nearly forty years. Born in Britain, he spent years in American vaudeville and musical comedy before establishing himself as a big star of the forties, usually as a comic coward who makes

good. Special Academy Awards in 1940, 1944 and 1952, mainly in appreciation of his troop shows and charitable ventures.
Autobiographical books: 1958, *Have Tux Will Travel*. 1963, *I Owe Russia $2000*. 1976, *The Last Christmas Show*. 1977, *The Road to Hollywood*.
□The Big Broadcast of 1938. College Swing 38. Give Me a Sailor 38. *Thanks for the Memory* 38. Never Say Die 39. Some Like It Hot 39. *The Cat and the Canary* 39. *Road to Singapore* 40. *The Ghost Breakers* 40. *Road to Zanzibar* 41. Caught in the Draft 41. Nothing But the Truth 41. Louisiana Purchase 41. *My Favorite Blonde* 42. *Road to Morocco* 42. Star Spangled Rhythm 42. They Got Me Covered 42. Let's Face It 43. The Princess and the Pirate 44. Road to Utopia 45. Monsieur Beaucaire 46. My Favorite Brunette 47. Where There's Life 47. Variety Girl 47. Road to Rio 48. *The Paleface* 48. Sorrowful Jones 48. The Great Lover 49. *Fancy Pants* 50. The Lemon Drop Kid 51. My Favorite Spy 51. Son of Paleface 52. Road to Bali 52. Off Limits 53. Here Come the Girls 53. Casanova's Big Night 54. The Seven Little Foys 54. That Certain Feeling 56. The Iron Petticoat 56. Beau James 57. Paris Holiday 58. Alias Jesse James 59. *The Facts of Life* 60. Bachelor in Paradise 61. Road to Hong Kong 62. Critics Choice 63. Call Me Bwana 63. A Global Affair 64. I'll Take Sweden 65. Boy Did I Get a Wrong Number 66. The Oscar 66. Eight on the Lam 67. The Private Navy of Sgt O'Farrell 68. How to Commit Marriage 69. Cancel My Reservation 72. The Muppet Movie (guest) 79. Masterpiece of Murder (TV) 85.
❄ For a string of bright comedies which perfectly suited the forties. *The Cat and the Canary*.

¶ *B.H.:* I was lucky, you know, I always had a beautiful girl and the money was good. Although I would have done the whole thing over for, oh, perhaps half.

Chevy Chase (1980s): Bob Hope is still about as funny as he ever was. I just never thought he was that funny in the first place.
B.H.: My wife raised the kids and I was the guest of honour. For years, they thought I was the meter man.
Famous line (*The Cat and the Canary*): I get goose pimples. Even my goose pimples get goose pimples.
Famous line (*The Ghost Breakers*): The girls call me Pilgrim, because every time I dance with one I make a little progress.

Hope, Vida (1918–1963). British character actress, usually in comic proletarian roles; also stage director.
English Without Tears 44. Nicholas Nickleby 47. It Always Rains on Sunday 48. *The Man in the White Suit* 51. Lease of Life 54. Family Doctor 58, etc.

Hopkins, Anthony (1921–). British composer.
Vice Versa 48. Decameron Nights 53. The Pickwick Papers 53. Cast a Dark Shadow 55. Billy Budd 62, etc.

Hopkins, Anthony (1941–). British character actor.
The Lion in Winter 68. The Looking Glass War 70. *When Eight Bells Toll* 71. Young Winston (as Lloyd George) 72. A Doll's House 73. All Creatures Great and Small 74. QB VII (TV) 74. The Girl from Petrovka 74. Juggernaut 74. The Lindbergh Kidnapping Case (TV) 76. Dark Victory (TV) 76. Victory at Entebbe (TV) 76. Audrey Rose 77. A Bridge Too Far 77. International Velvet 78. *Magic* 78. Mayflower (TV) 80. A Change of Seasons 80. The Elephant Man 83. The Bunker (as Hitler) (TV) 81. Peter and Paul (TV) 81. The Hunchback of Notre Dame (TV) 82. A Married Man (TV) 82. The Bounty 83. Mussolini and I (TV) 84. Hollywood Wives (TV) 85. Guilty Conscience (TV) 85. 84 Charing Cross Road 87.

Hopkins, Bo (1942–). American action hero.
The Wild Bunch 69. Monte Walsh 70. The Culpeper Cattle Company 72. The Getaway 72. American Graffiti 73. White Lightning 73. The Nickel Ride 74. The Day of the Locust 75. Tentacles 77. Aspen (TV) 77. Thaddeus Rose and Eddie (TV) 78. Midnight Express 78. More American Graffiti 79. The Fifth Floor 80.
TV series: Doc Elliott 73. Dynasty 80–81.

Hopkins, John (1931–). British writer, mostly for TV.
The Virgin Soldiers (w) 69. The Offence (w) 72. Murder by Decree 78, etc.

Hopkins, Miriam (1902–1972). American leading lady of the thirties; her rather brittle style has dated.
□Fast and Loose 30. The Smiling Lieutenant 31. Twenty Four Hours 31. *Dr Jekyll and Mr Hyde* 32. Two Kinds of Women 32. Dancers in the Dark 32. The World and the Flesh 32. *Trouble in Paradise* 32. *The Story of Temple Drake* 33. Design for Living 33. The Stranger's Return 33. All of Me 34. She

Loves Me Not 34. The Richest Girl in the World 34. *Becky Sharp* 35. Barbary Coast 35. Splendor 35. *These Three* 36. Men Are Not Gods (GB) 37. The Woman I Love 37. Woman Chases Man 37. Wise Girl 37. The Old Maid 39. Virginia City 40. *Lady With Red Hair* 41. A Gentleman After Dark 42. *Old Acquaintance* 43. The Heiress 49. The Mating Season 51. Carrie 52. The Outcasts of Poker Flat 52. The Children's Hour 62. Fanny Hill 65. The Chase 66.

Hopkins, Shirley Knight: see *Knight, Shirley*.

Hopper, Dennis (1935–). American juvenile of the fifties who later blossomed into a fashionable actor and director.
I Died a Thousand Times 55. Rebel Without a Cause 55. Giant 56. The Story of Mankind 57. Key Witness 60. Night Tide 63. The Sons of Katie Elder 65. The Trip 67. Cool Hand Luke 67. *Easy Rider* (& d) 69. The Last Movie (& wd) 71. Kid Blue (& d) 72. Mad Dog Morgan 76. The American Friend 77. Tracks 77. Apocalypse Now 79. Out of the Blue (& d) 80. The Osterman Weekend 83. The Inside Man 84. My Science Project 85. Blue Velvet 86. Hoosiers 86.
TV series: Medic 54–55.

Hopper, Hedda (1890–1966) (Elda Furry). American general purpose actress, mainly in silent days; in later life became a powerful Hollywood columnist.
Autobiographies: 1952, *From Under My Hat*. 1963, *The Whole Truth and Nothing But*.
Biography 1972: *Hedda and Louella* by George Eels.
Virtuous Wives 19. Heedless Moths 21. Sherlock Holmes 22. Has the World Gone Mad? 23. Reno 24. The Teaser 25. Don Juan 26. Wings 27. Harold Teen 28. His Glorious Night 29. Holiday 30. The Common Law 31. Speak Easily 32. Beauty For Sale 33. Little Man What Now? 34. Alice Adams 35. Dracula's Daughter 36. Topper 37. Thanks for the Memory 38. The Women 39. Queen of the Mob 40. Reap the Wild Wind 42. Sunset Boulevard 50. Pepe 60. The Oscar 66, many others.

¶ *H.H.:* Nobody's interested in sweetness and light.

Hopper, Jerry (1907–). American director of routine action films and TV series.
□The Atomic City 52. Hurricane Smith 52. Pony Express 53. Alaska Seas 54. The Secret of the Incas 54. Naked Alibi 54. Smoke Signal 55. The Private War of Major Benson 55. One Desire 55. The Square Jungle 55. Never Say Goodbye 56. Toy Tiger 56. The Sharkfighters 56. Everything but the Truth 56. The Missouri Traveller 58. Blueprint for Robbery 61. Madron 70.

Hopper, Victoria (1909–). Canadian leading lady of a few British films of the thirties.
□*The Constant Nymph* 33. *Lorna Doone* 34. Whom the Gods Love 36. Laburnum Grove 36. The Lonely Road 36. The Mill on the Floss 37. Escape from Broadmoor 38.

Hopper, William (1915–1969) (William Furry). American general purpose supporting actor, son of Hedda Hopper.
Footloose Heiress 37. Torchy Blane 38. Track of the Cat 54. Rebel Without a Cause 55. The Bad Seed 56. Twenty Million Miles to Earth (lead) 57, etc.
TV series: *Perry Mason* (as Paul Drake) 57–65.

Hopton, Russell (1900–1945). American light leading man.
Ella Cinders 26. Street Scene 31. Night World 32. Lady Killer 33. He Was Her Man 34. Death from a Distance 35. High Wide and Handsome 37. The Saint Strikes Back 39. A Night of Adventure 44. Zombies on Broadway 45, etc.

Hordern, Sir Michael (1911–). British character actor, on stage from 1937; film appearances usually as careworn official.
The Girl in the News (debut) 39: war service: School for Secrets 46. Mine Own Executioner 47. Good Time Girl 48. Passport to Pimlico 48. The Hour of Thirteen 51. The Heart of the Matter 53. The Baby and the Battleship 55. *The Spanish Gardener* 56. Sink the Bismarck 60. El Cid 61. The VIPs 63. Dr Syn 63. Genghis Khan 65. The Spy Who Came In from the Cold 66. Khartoum 66. *A Funny Thing Happened on the Way to the Forum* 66. The Taming of the Shrew 67. Where Eagles Dare 68. *The Bed-Sitting Room* 69. Anne of the Thousand Days 70. Futtock's End 70. Girl Stroke Boy 71. England Made Me 72. Alice's Adventures in Wonderland (as the Mock Turtle) 72. Theatre of Blood 73. The Mackintosh Man 73. Mister Quilp 74. Royal Flash 74. Lucky Lady 75. *The Slipper and the Rose* 76. Joseph Andrews 76. The Medusa Touch 77. Shogun (TV) 80. Ivanhoe (TV) 81. Oliver Twist (TV) 81. Gandhi 82. *The Missionary* 82. Yellowbeard 83. Lady Jane 84. Paradise Postponed (TV) 85. Scoop (TV) 87.

Horn, Camilla (1906–). German actress who had brief careers in Hollywood and Britain before retiring.
Faust 26. Tempest 28. The Return of Raffles 32. Luck of a Sailor (GB) 34, etc.

Horn, Leonard (1926–1975). American director, from TV.
Rogues' Gallery 68. The Magic Garden of Stanley Sweetheart 70. Going All Out 71, etc.

Hornbeck, William W. (1901–1983). American editor, with Mack Sennett until 1929, working mainly on two-reel comedies.
The Extra Girl 23. Roman Scandals 33. The Scarlet Pimpernel 34. *Things To Come* 36. The Four Feathers 39. Lady Hamilton 42. *Why We Fight* series 43-45. *It's a Wonderful Life* 46. State of the Union 48. *A Place in the Sun* (AA) 51. Shane 53. Giant 56. The Quiet American 58, many others.

Hornblow, Arthur Jnr (1893–1976). American producer, in Hollywood from 1926.
Bulldog Drummond 29. Ruggles of Red Gap 34. The Cat and the Canary 39. Gaslight 44. Weekend at the Waldorf 45. The Hucksters 47. The Asphalt Jungle 50. Oklahoma 56. Witness for the Prosecution 57. The War Lover 63, many others.

Horne, David (1898–1970). Portly British character actor, mainly on stage; almost always in pompous roles.
General John Regan 33. The Mill on the Floss 36. The First of the Few 42. The Seventh Veil 45. The Rake's Progress 45. The Man Within 46. It's Hard To Be Good 49. Madeleine 50. Lust for Life 56. The Devil's Disciple 59, many others.

Horne, Geoffrey (c. 1926–). British general purpose actor.
The Bridge on the River Kwai 57. Tempest 58. Bonjour Tristesse 58, etc.

Horne, James V. (1880–1942). American director, in Hollywood from 1911. Made some of Laurel and Hardy's best two-reelers, and appeared as the villain in *Beau Hunks*.
The Third Eye 20. American Manner 24. *College* 27. Bonnie Scotland 35. The Bohemian Girl 36. *Way Out West* 37. Holt of the Secret Service 42, many others.

Horne, Lena (1917–). Lithe and sultry black American singer whose best appearances were in forties musicals.
Autobiographies: 1950, *In Person*. 1966 (with Richard Schickel): *Lena*.
□The Duke is Tops 38. Panama Hattie 42. *Cabin in the Sky* 43. *Stormy Weather* 43. Thousands Cheer 43. I Dood It 43. Swing Fever 43. Broadway Rhythm 44. Two Girls and a Sailor 44. Ziegfeld Follies 46. Till the Clouds Roll By 46. Words and Music 48. Duchess of Idaho 50. Meet Me In Las Vegas 56. *Death of a Gunfighter* (dramatic role) 69.

¶ *L.H.:* In my early days I was a sepia Hedy Lamarr. Now I'm black and a woman, singing my own way.

Horne, Victoria (c. 1920–). American comedienne.
The Scarlet Claw 44. The Ghost and Mrs Muir 47. The Snake Pit 48. Abbott and Costello Meet the Killer 49. *Harvey* 50. Affair with a Stranger 53, etc.

Horner, Harry (1910–). Czech-born production designer with stage experience in Vienna and New York.
Our Town 40. *The Little Foxes* 41. A Double Life 47. *The Heiress* (AA) 49. Born Yesterday 50. *The Hustler* (AA) 61. They Shoot Horses, Don't They? 69. Harry and Walter Go to New York 76. Audrey Rose 77. Moment to Moment 78. The Driver 78, etc.
AS DIRECTOR: Beware My Lovely 52. Red Planet Mars 52. New Facs 54. A Life in the Balance 55. The Wild Party 56. Man from Del Rio 56, etc.

Horner, James (–). American composer.
Battle Beyond the Stars 80. Humanoids from the Deep 80. Star Trek II: The Wrath of Khan 82. 48 Hours 82. Krull 83. Gorky Park 83. The Dresser 83.

Hornung, E. W. (1866–1921). British novelist, creator of the gentleman burglar A. J. Raffles, who was impersonated on screen by Ronald Colman and David Niven, and on television by Anthony Valentine.

horror as a staple of screen entertainment really emanates from Germany (although Edison shot a picture of *Frankenstein* as early as 1908). Before World War I Wegener had made a version of *The Golem,* which he improved on in 1920: it was this second version which directly influenced the Hollywood horror school stimulated by James Whale. What is surprising is that Hollywood took so long to catch on to a good idea, especially as the Germans, in depressed post-war mood, relentlessly turned out such macabre films as *The Cabinet of Dr Caligari* (with Veidt as a hypnotically-controlled monster), *Nosferatu* (Murnau's brilliantly personal account of Bram Stoker's 'Dracula'), *Waxworks* (Leni's three-part thriller about Ivan the Terrible, Haroun-al-Raschid and Jack the Ripper); *The Hands of Orlac* and *The Student of Prague*. Most of the talents involved were exported to Hollywood by 1927; but the only horror film directly resulting was Leni's *The Cat and the Canary*, which was a spoof. California did encourage Lon Chaney, but his films were grotesque rather than gruesome; and John Barrymore had already been allowed in 1921 to impersonate *Dr Jekyll and Mr Hyde* (a role to be played even more for horror by Fredric March in 1932). By the end of the twenties, the European horror film was played out except for Dreyer's highly individual *Vampyr*; the ball was in Hollywood's court.

In 1930 Tod Browning filmed the stage version of *Dracula*, using a Hungarian actor named Bela Lugosi; shortly after, Robert Florey wrote and James Whale directed a version of *Frankenstein* that borrowed freely from *The Golem*. Both films (see individual entries) were wildfire successes, and the studio involved, Universal, set out on a steady and profitable progress through a series of sequels. In 1932 Karloff appeared in *The Mummy*, and in 1933 Claude Rains was *The Invisible Man*; these characters were added to the grisly band. In 1935 the studio made *Werewolf of London*, which led five years later to *The Wolf Man* giving Lon Chaney Jnr a useful sideline. By 1945, despite the upsurge in supernatural interest during the war, these characters were thought to be played out, and in the last two 'serious' episodes they appeared *en masse*. In 1948 they began to meet Abbott and Costello, which one would have thought might ensure their final demise; but more of that later.

Meanwhile other landmarks had been established. Browning made the outlandish *Freaks*, and in 1935 the spoof *Mark of the Vampire*. James Whale in 1932 made *The Old Dark House*, an inimitably entertaining mixture of disagreeable ingredients. Warners in 1932 came up with *Doctor X* and *The Mystery of the Wax Museum* (remade as *House of Wax*) and later got some mileage out of *The Walking Dead*. Paramount went in for mad doctors, from *The Island of Dr Moreau* (*Island of Lost Souls*) to *Doctor Cyclops*, and at the beginning of World War II produced scary remakes of *The Cat and the Canary* and *The Ghost Breakers*. RKO were busy with *King Kong* and *She*, MGM with *The Devil Doll*. In the early forties Universal began a listless anthology series under the title *Inner Sanctum*, and later failed in *The Creature from the Black Lagoon* to add another intriguing monster to their gallery. By far the most significant extension of the genre was the small group of depressive but atmospheric thrillers produced by Val Lewton at RKO in 1942–45, the best of them being *The Body Snatcher, The Cat People* and *I Walked with a Zombie*.

After the war, little was heard of horror until the advent of science fiction in 1950. After this we heard a very great deal of nasty visitors from other planets (*The Thing*, *Invasion of the Body Snatchers*), mutations (*The Fly, This Island Earth*), robots (*The Day the Earth Stood Still, Forbidden Planet*) and giant insects (*Them, Tarantula*). To please the teenage audience, fly-by-night producers thought up fantastic horror-comic variations and came up with titles like *The Blob, I Married a Monster from Outer Space* and *I Was a Teenage Werewolf*; such crude and shoddy productions cheapened the genre considerably. The Japanese got into the act with rubber-suited monsters like *Godzilla* and *Rodan*; then, surprisingly, it was the turn of the British. Hammer Films, a small independent outfit with an old Thames-side house for a studio, impudently remade the sagas of Frankenstein, Dracula *et alia*, and the results have been flooding the world's screens for more than twenty years now, marked by a certain bold style, lack of imagination, and such excess of blood-letting that several versions have to be made for each film (the bloodiest for Japan, the most restrained for the home market). Britain also produced commendable screen versions of *The Quatermass Experiment* and other TV serials.

Since 1955 horror has been consistently in fashion, at least in the world's mass markets, and film-makers have been busy capping each other by extending the bounds of how much explicit physical shock and horror is permissible. (This, of course, does not make for good films.) If Franju was revolting in the detail of *Eyes Without a Face*, Hitchcock certainly topped him in *Psycho* and was himself outdone by William Castle in *Homicidal*, and by the perpetration in the seventies of films like *Blood Feast* and *Death Line*. (*Psycho* also gave the screen an inventive horror-writing talent in Robert

Bloch, who has since been kept as busy as he could wish.) And the cheapjack American nasties at least provided a training ground for producer-director Roger Corman, who between 1960 and 1964 made a series of Poe adaptations much admired for style and enthusiasm if not for production detail. The trend in the early seventies was towards the compendiums of graveyard horror typified by *Tales from the Crypt* and *The House that Dripped Blood*, and towards such combinations of spoof and nastiness as *Theatre of Blood, Shivers* and *Squirm*.

The video craze of the early eighties revealed a significant and rather worrying minority of people who doted on excesses of horror, not only on the recent wave of teenage assassination thrillers like *Friday the Thirteenth*, *Hell Night* and *Terror Train*, but on 'nasties' such as *Driller Killer* and *I Spit on Your Grave*, which seemed to have been made explicitly for the new medium. This cheap rubbish, with neither style nor imagination, had nothing at all to do with the great achievements of the genre, though indications of talent were found by some in the work of John Carpenter (*Halloween*) and David Cronenberg (*The Brood*).

Best books: *An Illustrated History of Horror Films* (1968) by Carlos Clarens; *A Pictorial History of Horror Films* (1973) by Dennis Gifford.

? In which horror films were the following lines heard?

1 Listen to them . . . creatures of the night. What music they make!
2 An intellectual carrot—the mind boggles!
3 To new worlds of Gods and Monsters!
4 What we need is young blood . . . and brains . . .
5 I'm going to tear the skin from your body—bit by bit!
6 Hoi, have you got the wrong vampire!
7 There just isn't room for two doctors and two vampires in one small town . . .
8 Have a potato . . .
9 Get away from that lever—you'll blow us all to atoms!
10 I have here a collection of the world's most astounding horrors . . .
11 I never drink . . . wine . . .
12 It went for a little walk . . .
13 Just room for one inside, sir!
14 I know you have a civil tongue in your head—I sewed it there myself!
15 (Complete the following verse:)
Even the man who is pure in heart
And says his prayers by night
....
And the moon is pure and bright!
16 Kill, then love! When you have known that, you have known everything . . .

horses have in several cases risen to the rank of star. All the great cowboy heroes had their familiar steed: Trigger for Roy Rogers, Topper for Hopalong Cassidy, Fritz for William S. Hart, Tarzan for Ken Maynard, Tony for Tom Mix, Silver for Buck Jones, Blackjack for Allan Rocky Lane, Koko for Rex Allen, White Flash for Tex Ritter, Champion for Gene Autry. Other movies strongly featuring horses have included *National Velvet*, *The Red Pony*, *Red Stallion*, *The Black Stallion*, *Crin Blanc*, *King of the Wild Horses*, *My Friend Flicka*, *Green Grass of Wyoming*, *Thunderhead Son of Flicka*, *Sand*, *Fury*.

Horsfall, Bernard (1930–). British character actor.
On Her Majesty's Secret Service 69. Gold 74. Shout at the Devil 76, etc.

Horsley, John (–). British character actor, often seen as plain clothes man or executive.
Highly Dangerous 48. The Long Memory 51. The Runaway Bus 54. Father Brown 54. Above Us the Waves 55. Bond of Fear 56, etc.

Horton, Edward Everett (1886–1970). American star comic actor with inimitable crooked smile and diffident manner; a favourite throughout the twenties, thirties and forties.
Too Much Business 22. Ruggles of Red Gap (title role) 23. Marry Me 25. The Nutcracker 26. The Terror 28. Sonny Boy 29. The Hottentot 29. The Sap 29. Take the Heir 30. *Holiday* 30. Once a Gentleman 30. Kiss Me Again 31. The Front Page 31. Six Cylinder Love 31. *Trouble in Paradise* 32. A Bedtime Story 33. Soldiers of the King (GB) 33. *Alice in Wonderland* (as the Mad Hatter) 33. It's a Boy (GB) 34. The Merry Widow 34. *The Gay Divorcee* 35. The Devil is a Woman 35. In Caliente 35. *Top Hat* 35. Your Uncle Dudley 35. The Private Secretary (GB) 35. The Man in the Mirror (GB) 36. *Lost Horizon* 37. Shall We Dance? 37. Angel 37. The Great Garrick 37. Bluebeard's Eighth Wife 38. *Holiday* (repeat of 1930 role) 38. That's Right You're Wrong 39. Ziegfeld Girl 41. Sunny 41. *Here Comes Mr Jordan* 41. The Body Disappears 41. The Magnificent Dope 42. Forever and a Day 43. *Thank Your Lucky Stars* 43. The Gang's All Here 43. Her Primitive Man 44.

Summer Storm 44. *San Diego I Love You* 44. Arsenic and Old Lace 44. Lady on a Train 45. Cinderella Jones 46. Down to Earth 47. Her Husband's Affairs 47. The Story of Mankind 57. *Pocketful of Miracles* 61. Sex and the Single Girl 64. The Perils of Pauline 67. 2000 Years Later 69. Cold Turkey 70, many others.
TV series: *F Troop* (as a Red Indian chief) 65.
❁ For redeeming many a dull comedy by his superior twittering and double takes. *Trouble in Paradise*.

Horton, Robert (1924–) (Mead Howard Horton). Good looking American leading man who made it big on TV in the late fifties but could not manage the transfer to the big screen.
The Tanks are Coming 51. Bright Road 53. Prisoner of War 54. This Man is Armed 56. The Dangerous Days of Kiowa Jones 66. The Green Slime 69, etc.
TV series: *Wagon Train* 57–61. *A Man Called Shenandoah* 65.

Hoskins, Bob (1942–). Stocky, untutored British character actor who made a big critical hit in TV's *Pennies from Heaven*.
Zulu Dawn 79. The Long Good Friday 80. Pink Floyd: The Wall 82. The Honorary Consul 83. Mussolini and I (TV) 84. The Dunera Boys (TV) 84. Lassiter 84. The Cotton Club 84. Brazil 85. Sweet Liberty 85. Mona Lisa 85. A Prayer for the Dying 87. The Lonely Passion of Judith Hearne 87.

hospitals have been the setting of many films. *Life Begins* and its remake *A Child is Born* were set in the maternity wards, *No Time for Tears* in the children's wards. *Young Dr Kildare* started a whole series about a general hospital, and soon they were *Calling Dr Gillespie*. Other general hospital dramas include *White Corridors, The Lamp Still Burns, Behind the Mask, Life in Emergency Ward Ten, Emergency Hospital*; thrillers set among the wards include *Intent to Kill, The Sleeping City, Green for Danger* (the best of all), *Eye Witness* and *The Carey Treatment*, which last is in the vein of savage black humour evidenced in the early seventies by such films as *The Hospital* and *Where Does It Hurt?* Gentler hospital comedy has been found in *Doctor in the House, Twice Round the Daffodils, Trio*, and several episodes of the 'Carry On' series which have specialized in bedpan humour. TV series on the subject include *Medic, The Nurses, The Doctors and the Nurses, Doctor Kildare, Ben Casey, Dr Hudson's Secret Journal, Dr Christian, General Hospital, West Side Medical, Trapper John, Quincy, St Elsewhere*.

Hossein, Robert (1927–). French actor.
Rififi 55. The Wicked Go to Hell (& d) 55. Girls Disappear 58. La Musica 60. Enough Rope 63. Marco the Magnificent 65. I Killed Rasputin (& d) 68. The Burglars (& d) 71. Les Uns et les Autres 80. Les Misérables (d only) 82, etc.

hotels have frequently formed a useful setting for films wanting to use the 'slice of life' technique. Thus *Grand Hotel, Hotel for Women, Stage Door, Hotel Berlin, Weekend at the Waldorf, Separate Tables* and *Hotel* itself; while *Ship of Fools* is a variation on the same theme. The hotel background was a valuable dramatic asset to films as varied as *The Last Laugh, The October Man, Don't Bother to Knock, Hotel du Nord, Pushover, Honeymoon Hotel, Room Service* (and its remake *Step Lively*), *Hotel Reserve, Hotel Sahara, The Horn Blows at Midnight, Hotel for Women, Hollywood Hotel, Paris Palace Hotel, Bedtime Story, The Best Man, The Greengage Summer, A Hole in the Head*, and *The Silence*. Hotel security did not prevent attempts on the hero's life in *Journey into Fear* and *Foreign Correspondent*. The most bewildering hotel was certainly that in *So Long at the Fair*; the most amusing hotel sequences may have been in *Ninotchka, The Bellboy, Hotel Paradiso, A Flea in Her Ear* or *The Perfect Woman*. And hotels which had no accommodation to offer sparked off quite a few comedies during World War II, including *Government Girl, Standing Room Only* and *The More the Merrier* (later remade as *Walk Don't Run*). The hotel format endeared itself to television, which brought forth such variations as *Love Boat, Fantasy Island* and *Paradise Cove*; 1983 brought back *Hotel* itself, with shooting in San Francisco's Fairmont. The hotels no one would wish to revisit are those which sheltered Janet Leigh in *Psycho* and Jack Nicholson in *The Shining*.

Houdini, Harry (1873–1926) (Ehrich Weiss). American escapologist and magician extraordinary, in films from 1918. A biopic in 1953 starred Tony Curtis, and a 1976 TV movie, *The Great Houdinis*, Paul Michael Glaser.
Biography 1969: *Houdini, the Unknown Story* by Christopher Milbourne.

The Master Mystery (serial) 18. The Grim Game 19. Terror Island 20. The Man from Beyond 21. Haldane of the Secret Service 23, etc.

Hough, John (1941–). British director in international films.
□Wolfshead 69. Eye Witness 70. Twins of Evil 71. Treasure Island 72. The Legend of Hell House 73. Dirty Mary Crazy Larry 74. Escape to Witch Mountain 75. Brass Target 78. The Watcher in the Woods 80. Triumphs of a Man Called Horse 82. The Incubus 82. Biggles 85. American Gothic 87.

Houghton, Katharine (1945–). American leading lady of *Guess Who's Coming to Dinner* 67; niece of Katharine Hepburn.

The Hounds of Zaroff: see *The Most Dangerous Game.*

House, Billy (1890–1961). Rotund American character actor, formerly trumpet player.
Smart Money 32. Merry Go Round 37. Bedlam 44. The Stranger 45. Trail Street 46. The Egg and I 47. Where Danger Lives 50. People Will Talk 51, etc.

House of Wax (US 1953). The film which seemed to gain public approval for 3-D (until CinemaScope proved the stronger card) was actually a simplified remake of the old horror film *The Mystery of the Wax Museum* 32, with Vincent Price in Lionel Atwill's old part as the disfigured madman who creates a new wax face for himself.

The House on 92nd Street (US 1946). Producer Louis de Rochemont here brought his March of Time technique to bear on a semi-fictional spy story with a clever mystery plot and a myriad of new documentary tricks. The brisk journalistic method was highly influential, and Henry Hathaway's direction neared his best.

Houseman, John (1902–) (Jacques Haussmann). American producer. After varied experience, helped Orson Welles to found his Mercury Theatre in New York in 1937, later followed him to Hollywood; unexpectedly became a star actor in his seventies.
Autobiographies: *Runthrough* 1972; *Front and Center* 1980.
The Blue Dahlia 46. Letter from an Unknown Woman 48. They Live by Night 48. The Bad and the Beautiful 52. Julius Caesar 53. Executive Suite 54. Lust for Life 56. Two Weeks in Another Town 62. This Property is Condemned 66, etc.
AS ACTOR: Seven Days in May 64. *Paper Chase* (AA) 74. Three Days of the Condor 75. Rollerball 75. Meeting at Potsdam (TV) (as Churchill) 76. Fear on Trial (TV) 76. St Ives 76. Captains and the Kings (TV) 76. Washington Behind Closed Doors (TV) 77. Aspen (TV) 77. Tentacles 77. The Cheap Detective 78. Old Boyfriends 79. My Bodyguard 80. The Fog 80. Wholly Moses 80. Ghost Story 81. Murder by Phone 82.
TV series: *The Paper Chase* 78 and 83. Silver Spoons 82.

houses have been the dramatic centre of many films: there was even one, *Enchantment*, in which the house itself told the story. The films of Daphne du Maurier's novels usually have a mysterious old house at the crux of their plots, as in *Rebecca, Frenchman's Creek, Jamaica Inn, My Cousin Rachel.* So in *Dragonwyck*; so in *House of Fear*; so, of course, in *Jane Eyre* and *Wuthering Heights*. Both *Citizen Kane* and *The Magnificent Ambersons* are dominated by unhappy houses, as is *Gaslight*. Thrillers set in lonely houses full of secret panels and hidden menace are exemplified by *The Spiral Staircase, The Black Cat, Night Monster, The House on Haunted Hill, The Cat and the Canary, The Ghost Breakers, The House that Dripped Blood, Whatever Happened to Baby Jane?, The Beast with Five Fingers, Ladies in Retirement* and *And Then There Were None*. Haunted houses are rarer, but those in *The Uninvited, The Unseen, The Innocents, The Enchanted Cottage* and *The Haunting* linger vividly in the memory. So for a different reason does the Bates' house in *Psycho*. Happier houses of note include the rose-covered cottage in *Random Harvest,* the family mansions of *Forever and a Day* and *Enchantment,* the red-decorated Denver house in *The Unsinkable Molly Brown,* the laboriously built country seat of *Mr Blandings Builds His Dream House,* the labour-saving modern house of *Mon Oncle*, the broken-down houses of *George Washington Slept Here* and *Father Came Too*, and dear old *Rookery Nook.* And filmgoers have various reasons to remember *The House on 92nd Street, The House on Telegraph Hill, House of Strangers, House of Horrors, House of Bamboo, House of Numbers, House of the Damned, House of the Seven Hawks, House of Women, House by the River, House of Seven Gables, House of Dracula, House of*

Frankenstein, House of Wax, Sinister House, The Red House, Crazy House, The Old Dark House, The House of Usher, The House of the Seven Gables and the house in *House* and *House II*. The house in *Malpertius* brought little comfort; come to that, nor did the noble pile in *Brideshead Revisited*.

? The answers are films with the word *House* in the title. Name the house:

1 In which Lon Chaney Jnr was cured of lycanthropy.
2 In which Shelley Winters played a famous madam.
3 Which changed insects to birds and starred Robert Taylor.
4 Introduced Emergo and included in its cast Carol Ohmart and Elisha Cook Jnr.
5 Which, as a TV pilot film, starred Christopher George, but led to a series starring Burt Reynolds.
6 In which Vincent Price played a role first essayed by Lionel Atwill.
7 Which used the March of Time technique to uncover communist spies.
8 Which had its plot reused by *Broken Lance* and *The Big Show*.
9 In which Robert Ryan ran rackets in Tokyo.
10 In which Orson Welles was cornered on the Colosseum in Rome.

Housman, Arthur (1888–1942). American character actor, usually seen as incoherent but gentlemanly drunk in comedies of the early thirties.
Under the Red Robe 23. Manhandled 24. The Bat 26. Sunrise 27. Fools for Luck 28. The Singing Fool 28. Broadway 29. The Squealer 30. Five and Ten 31. *Scram* (Laurel and Hardy two-reeler) 32. She Done Him Wrong 33. Mrs Wiggs of the Cabbage Patch 34. Our Relations 36. Step Lively Jeeves 37, etc.

Houston, Donald (1923–). Burly, capable Welsh leading man of the early fifties. Later a useful character actor.
□*The Blue Lagoon* 48. A Run for Your Money 49. Dance Hall 50. My Death is a Mockery 51. Crow Hollow 52. The Red Beret 53. Small Town Story 53. The Large Rope 53. Devil's Point 54. The Happiness of Three Women 54. Doctor in the House 54. The Flaw 55. Double Cross 55. The Girl in the Picture 56. Find the Lady 56. Yangtse Incident 57. The Surgeon's Knife 57. A Question of Adultery 58. The Man Upstairs 58. Danger Within 58. *Room at the Top* 58. The Mark 61. Twice Round the Daffodils 62. The Prince and the Pauper 62. Maniac 62. The Longest Day 62. The 300 Spartans 63. Doctor in Distress 63. Carry on Jack 63. 633 Squadron 64. A Study in Terror 65.The Viking Queen 66. Where Eagles Dare 68. My Lover My Son 70. Tales that Witness Madness 73. Voyage of the Damned 76. The Sea Wolves 80. Clash of the Titans 81. The Secret Adversary (TV) 82.

Houston, Glyn (1926–). Welsh character actor, brother of Donald Houston; much on TV.
The Blue Lamp 50. Payroll 60. Solo for Sparrow (lead role) 62. The Secret of Blood Island 65. Invasion 66. Are You Being Served? 77. The Sea Wolves 80, etc.

Houston, Renée (1902–1980) (Katherina Houston Gribbin). British vaudeville and revue artiste, once teamed with her sister Billie, later with Donald Stewart; more recently character actress of screen and TV. Autobiography 1974: *Don't Fence Me In*.
Mr Cinders 34. A Girl Must Live 38. Old Bill and Son 40. Two Thousand Women 44. The Belles of St Trinians 54. *A Town Like Alice* 56. *Time Without Pity* 57. The Horse's Mouth 59. The Flesh and the Fiends 60. Three on a Spree 61. Repulsion 64. Carry On at Your Convenience 71, etc.

Houston, Sam (1793–1863). An American hero of the early days of Texas, played on film by Richard Boone in *The Alamo*, William Farnum in *The Conqueror*, Richard Dix in *Man of Conquest*, Moroni Olsen in *Lone Star*, Hugh Sanders in *The Last Command* and Joel McCrea in *The First Texan*.

Hovey, Tim (1945–). American child actor of the mid-fifties.
The Private War of Major Benson 55. Toy Tiger 56. Man Afraid 57, etc. Later on TV.

How Green Was My Valley (US 1941) (AA best picture). A stagey but oddly moving film version of Richard Llewellyn's novel about a Welsh mining family several decades ago. The elaborate village set was used again in other movies including *The Moon Is Down*. Directed by John Ford (AA); with Walter Pidgeon, Donald Crisp (AA) and Maureen O'Hara; photographed by Arthur Miller (AA).

How the West Was Won (US 1962). Historically important as the first all-star continuous story film—and almost the last—

in three-lens Cinerama. (*The Wonderful World of the Brothers Grimm* was contemporaneous, but the single-lens system,
almost indistinguishable from other wide-screen methods, was introduced in 1963.) A patchy western directed by George Marshall, Henry Hathaway and John Ford, it has spectacular action sequences which dwarf the chatter of an all-star cast. Photographers: Charles Lang Jnr, William Daniels, Milton Krasner, Joseph la Shelle, Harold A. Wellman.
NB: the TV series which began in 1977 was not related except by title.

How to Marry a Millionaire (US 1953). The second released film, and the first comedy, in CinemaScope. Showed no mastery of the technique but provided Marilyn Monroe with a good comedy part. Written by Nunnally Johnson, directed by Jean Negulesco.

Howard, Arthur (1910–). British character actor, brother of Leslie Howard, often seen as schoolmaster, clerk, etc.
Passport to Pimlico 48. *The Happiest Days of Your Life* 49. The Intruder 53. The Shoes of the Fisherman 68. Zeppelin 70. Steptoe and Son 72. One of Our Dinosaurs Is Missing 75, etc.

Howard, Curly (1906–1952) (Jerome Horowitz). American comedy actor: the fat, bald member of The Three Stooges (qv).

Howard, Cy (1915–). American director.
Lovers and Other Strangers 69. Every Little Crook and Nanny 75. Won Ton Ton (co-w only) 76.

Howard, Esther (1893–1965). American character actress, usually in blowsy roles.
Ladies of the Big House 31. Ready for Love 35. Serenade 39. Sullivan's Travels 41. Farewell My Lovely 44. The Lady Gambles 49, etc.

Howard, John (1913–) (John Cox). Good-looking, useful American leading man of the thirties and forties, mainly in routine films.
Annapolis Farewell 35. Soak the Rich 36. *Lost Horizon* 37. *Bulldog Drummond Comes Back* (and ensuing series) 37. Penitentiary 38. Prison Farm 38. Disputed Passage 39. Green Hell 40. *The Philadelphia Story* 40. The Invisible Woman 40. The Mad Doctor 41. Tight Shoes 41. The Undying Monster 42. Isle of Missing Men 43. Love from a Stranger 47. I Jane Doe 48. The Fighting Kentuckian 49. Experiment Alcatraz 51. The High and the Mighty 54. Unknown Terror 58, etc.
TV series: *Dr Hudson's Secret Journal* 55–56. Adventures of Seahawk 58.

Howard, Joyce (1922–). British leading lady of the forties.
Freedom Radio 40. Love on the Dole 41. The Gentle Sex 43. They Met in the Dark 43. Woman to Woman 46. Mrs Fitzherbert 47. Shadow of the Past 50, etc.

Howard, Kathleen (1879–1956). Canadian character actress, former opera singer; memorable as W. C. Fields' frequent screen wife.
Death Takes a Holiday 34. You're Telling Me 34. The Man on the Flying Trapeze 35. It's a Gift 35. Laura 44. The Late George Apley 47, etc.

Howard, Ken (1944–). Hulking American leading man who came to the fore on TV.
□Tell Me That You Love Me Junie Moon 70. Such Good Friends 71. The Strange Vengeance of Rosalie 72. *1776* 72. Superdome (TV) 78. The Critical List (TV) 78. A Great American Hero (TV) 80. The Victims (TV) 81. Second Thoughts 83.
TV series: Adam's Rib 73. Manhunter 74. The White Shadow 78.

Howard, Leslie (1890–1943) (Leslie Stainer). Distinguished British actor of Hungarian origin; his image was that of the romantic intellectual who had only to ignore women to be idolized. He was equally successful in American films.
Biography 1959: *A Very Remarkable Father*, by his daughter Ruth Howard.
□*Outward Bound* 30. Never the Twain Shall Meet 31. A Free Soul 31. Five and Ten 31. Devotion 31. Service for Ladies 32. Smilin' Through 32. The Animal Kingdom 32. Secrets 33. Captured 33. *Berkeley Square* 33. The Lady is Willing 34. *Of Human Bondage* 34. British Agent 34. *The Scarlet Pimpernel* 35. *The Petrified Forest* 36. Romeo and Juliet 36. It's Love I'm After 36. Stand-In 37. *Pygmalion* (& co-d) 38. *Gone with the Wind* 39. *Intermezzo* 39. Pimpernel Smith (& pd) 41. 49th Parallel 41. *The First of the Few* (& oa, d) 42. The Gentle Sex (pd only) 43. The Lamp Still Burns (p only) 43.
❁ For having more Englishness than any pure Englishman, and for conquering world audiences with it. *Pygmalion.*

¶ He had a passion for England and the English ideal that was almost Shakespearean.—*C. A. Lejeune.*
Famous line (*The Petrified Forest*): Let there be killing. All the evening I've had a feeling of destiny closing in.
Famous line (*Pygmalion*): Where the devil are my slippers, Eliza?

Howard, Moe (1895–1975) (Moses Horowitz). American comedy actor, the fringed and violent member of The Three Stooges (qv).

Howard, Ron: see *Howard, Ronny*.

Howard, Ronald (1918–). British actor, son of Leslie Howard; formerly reporter.
While the Sun Shines (debut) 46. The Queen of Spades 48. Tom Brown's Schooldays 51. Drango (US) 56. Babette Goes to War 59. Spider's Web 60. The Curse of the Mummy's Tomb 64. Africa Texas Style 67. The Hunting Party 71, many others.
TV series: *Sherlock Holmes* 55. Cowboy in Africa 67.

Howard, Ron (1953–). American child actor of the sixties.
The Journey 59. The Music Man 62. The Courtship of Eddie's Father 63. Smoke 69. The Wild Country 71. American Graffiti 73. The Spikes Gang 75. The Shootist 76. Grand Theft Auto (& d) 77. More American Graffiti 79. Night Shift (d only) 82. Splash! (d only) 84. Cocoon (d only) 85. Gung Ho (d only) 85.
TV series: The Andy Griffith Show 60–68. The Smith Family 71–2. Happy Days 74–.

Howard, Shemp (1891–1955) (Samuel Horowitz). American character comedian, brother of Moe Howard of the Three Stooges and occasional substitute for him; usually played tramps and bartenders.
Soup to Nuts 30. Headin' East 37. *The Bank Dick* 40. Buck Privates 41. *Hellzapoppin* 41. Pittsburgh 42. Crazy House 43. Blondie Knows Best 46. Africa Screams 49, many others.

Howard, Sidney (1891–1939). American playwright whose chief contributions to Hollywood were *The Late Christopher Bean, They Knew What They Wanted, Yellow Jack*, and most of the script of *Gone with the Wind* (for which he won a posthumous Oscar).

Howard, Sydney (1884–1946). Plump British comedian famous for fluttering gestures. On stage from 1912, films from 1930.
□ Splinters 29. French Leave 30. Tilly of Bloomsbury 31. Almost a Divorce 31. *Up for the Cup* 31. Splinters in the Navy 31. The Mayor's Nest 32. It's a King 32. Up for the Derby 32. *Night of the Garter* 33. Trouble 33. It's a Cop 34. Transatlantic Merry Go Round (US) 34. Where's George? 35. *Fame* 36. Chick 36. Splinters in the Air 37. What a Man 37. Shipyard Sally 39. Tilly of Bloomsbury 40. Once a Crook 41. Mr Proudfoot Shows a Light 32. *When we are Married* 43. Flight from Folly 45.

Howard, Trevor (1916–88). Distinguished British leading man, on stage from 1934; later concentrated on films.
□The Way Ahead (debut) 44. The Way to the Stars 45. *Brief Encounter* 46. I See a Dark Stranger 46. *Green for Danger* 46. So Well Remembered 47. They Made Me a Fugitive 47. The Passionate Friends 48. *The Third Man* 49. The Golden Salamander 49. Odette 50. The Clouded Yellow 51. An Outcast of the Islands 52. The Gift Horse 52. *The Heart of the Matter* 53. The Lovers of Lisbon (Fr.) 54. The Stranger's Hand 54. Cockleshell Heroes 55. Around the World in Eighty Days 56. Run for the Sun (US) 56. Interpol 57. Manuela 57. *The Key* (BFA) 58. Roots of Heaven 59. Moment of Danger 60. *Sons and Lovers* 60. *Mutiny on the Bounty* (as Captain Bligh) 62. The Lion 62. The Man in the Middle 64. Father Goose 64. Von Ryan's Express 65. Operation Crossbow 65. Morituri 65. The Liquidator 65. The Poppy is Also a Flower 66. Triple Cross 66. The Long Duel 67. Pretty Polly 68. *The Charge of the Light Brigade* 68. The Battle of Britain 69. Twinky 69. *Ryan's Daughter* 70. *The Night Visitor* 71. Catch Me a Spy 71. Mary Queen of Scots 72. Kidnapped 72. Pope Joan 72. Ludwig 72. The Offence 72. *Catholics* (TV) 73. Craze 73. A Doll's House 73. Persecution 74. 11 Harrowhouse 74. Who? 74. Death in the Sun 75. Conduct Unbecoming 75. Hennessy 75. The Bawdy Adventures of Tom Jones 76. Eliza Fraser 76. Aces High 76. Slaves 77. The Last Remake of Beau Geste 77. Stevie 77. Superman 78. Night Flight (TV) 78. Hurricane 79. Meteor 79. The Sea Wolves 80. Windwalker 80. Staying On (TV) 80. Light Years Away 81. Inside the Third Reich (TV) 82. The Deadly Game (TV) 82. Gandhi 82. The Missionary 82. Sir Henry at Rawlinson End 82. Sword of the Valiant 84. Foreign Body 85.

¶ *T.H.:* I've been number two in films for donkey's years.

Howard, William K. (1899–1954). American director who made some interesting films in the thirties.
East of Broadway 24. Code of the West 25. Gigolo 26. The Main Event 27. The River Pirate 28. Live Love and Laugh 29. Scotland Yard 30. Don't Bet on Women 31. Transatlantic 31. *Sherlock Holmes* 32. *The Power and the Glory* 33. The Cat and the Fiddle 34. Evelyn Prentice 34. Vanessa 35. *Mary Burns Fugitive* 35. The Princess Comes Across 36. *Fire Over England* (GB) 36. Back Door to Heaven 39. Bullets for O'Hara 41. Johnny Come Lately 43, etc.

Howe, James Wong (1899–1976) (Wong Tung Jim). Distinguished Chinese cinematographer, in Hollywood from 1917.
□Drums of Fate 23. The Woman with Four Faces 23. Call of the Canyon 23. The Spanish Dancer 23. To the Last Man 23. The Trail of the Lonesome Pine 23. The Alaskan 24. The Breaking Point 24. The Side Show of Life 24. The Best People 25. The Charmer 25. The King on Main Street 25. Not So Long Ago 25. Mantrap 26. Padlocked 26. Sea Horses 26. The Song and Dance Man 26. The Rough Riders 27. Sorrell and Son 27. Four Walls 28. The Perfect Crime 28. Laugh Clown Laugh 28. Desert Nights 29. Today 30. The Criminal Code 31. Transatlantic 31. The Spider 31. The Yellow Ticket 31. Surrender 31. Dance Team 32. After Tomorrow 32. Amateur Daddy 32. Man about Town 32. Chandu the Magician 32. Hello Sister 33. Beauty for Sale 33. The Power and the Glory 33. The Show Off 34. *The Thin Man* 34. Hollywood Party 34. Stamboul Quest 34. Have a Heart 34. Biography of a Bachelor Girl 34. The Night is Young 35. Mark of the Vampire 35. The Flame Within 35. O'Shaughnessy's Boy 35. Three Live Ghosts 35. Whipsaw 36. Fire Over England 36. Farewell Again 36. Under the Red Robe 37. *The Prisoner of Zenda* 37. The Adventures of Tom Sawyer 37. Algiers 38. Comet Over Broadway 38. They Made Me a Criminal 39. The Oklahoma Kid 39. Daughters Courageous 39. Dust Be My Destiny 39. On Your Toes 39. Abe Lincoln in Illinois 39. *Dr Ehrlich's Magic Bullet* 40. Saturday's Children 40. Torrid Zone 40. City for Conquest 40. A Dispatch from Reuter's 40. The Strawberry Blonde 41. Shining Victory 41. Navy Blues 41. Out of the Fog 41. *King's Row* 41. Yankee Doodle Dandy 42. The Hard Way 42. Hangmen also Die 43. Air Force 43. North Star 43. Passage to Marseille 44. Objective Burma 45. Counterattack 45. Confidential Agent 45. Danger Signal 45. My Reputation 46. Nora Prentiss 47. Pursued 47. Body and Soul 47. Mr Blandings Builds His Dream House 48. The Time of Your Life 48. The Eagle and the Hawk 49. The Baron of Arizona 50. Tripoli 50. The Brave Bulls 51. He Ran All the Way 51. Behave Yourself 51. The Lady Says No 52. Main Street to Broadway 53. Come Back Little Sheba 54. The Rose Tattoo (AA) 55. *Picnic* 56. Death of a Scoundrel 56. Drango 56. *Sweet Smell of Success* 57. The Old Man and the Sea 58. Bell Book and Candle 58. The Last Angry Man 59. The Story on Page One 60. Song Without End 60. Tess of the Storm Country 61. *Hud* (AA) 63. The Outrage 64. The Glory Guys 65. This Property is Condemned 66. *Seconds* 67. Hombre 67. The Heart is a Lonely Hunter 69. The Molly Maguires 70. Last of the Mobile Hotshots 70. Funny Lady 75.
Directed *Go Man Go* 52.
❀ For the visual sensitivity which is evident in every shot of every one of his films. *King's Row*.

Howell, C. Thomas (–). American juvenile lead of the eighties.
□ The Outsiders 83. Grandview USA 84. Red Dawn 84. Tank 84. Secret Admirer 85. The Hitcher 86. Soul Man 86. A Tiger's Tale 87.

Howells, Ursula (1922–). British actress, mainly on stage and TV. Film roles infrequent.
Flesh and Blood 51. The Constant Husband 55. They Can't Hang Me 55. The Long Arm 56. Dr Terror's House of Horrors 65. Mumsy Nanny Sonny and Girly 68. Crossplot 69, etc.

Howerd, Frankie (1921–) (Francis Howard). British eccentric comedian of stage and TV.
Autobiography 1977: *On My Way I Lost It.*
□*The Runaway Bus* 54. An Alligator Named Daisy 55. Jumping for Joy 55. The Ladykillers 55. A Touch of the Sun 56. Further Up the Creek 59. Watch It Sailor 61. The Cool Mikado 63. Mouse on the Moon 63. The Great St Trinian's Train Robbery 66. Carry On Doctor 68. Carry On Up the Jungle 69. *Up Pompeii* 70. Up the Chastity Belt 71. Up the Front 72. *The House in Nightmare Park* 73. Sergeant Pepper's Lonely Hearts Club Band 78.

Howes, Bobby (1895–1972). Diffident, diminutive British leading man of stage musical comedies in the thirties.

□The Guns of Loos 28. Third Time Lucky 31. Lord Babs 32. For the Love of Mike 32. Over the Garden Wall 34. Please Teacher 37. Sweet Devil 38. *Yes Madam* 38. Bob's Your Uncle 41. The Trojan Brothers 45. Happy Go Lovely 51. The Good Companions 57. Watch It Sailor 61.

Howes, Sally Ann (1930–). British child actress of the forties, later an occasional leading lady. Daughter of Bobby Howes.
□*Thursday's Child* 43. Halfway House 44. *Dead of Night* 45. Pink String and Sealing Wax 45. Nicholas Nickleby 47. My Sister and I 48. Anna Karenina 48. *The History of Mr Polly* 48. Fools Rush In 49. Stop Press Girl 50. Honeymoon Deferred 51. The Admirable Crichton 57. Chitty Chitty Bang Bang 68. The Hound of the Baskervilles (TV) 72. Female Artillery (TV) 72. Death Ship 80.

Howlett, Noel (1901–84). British stage actor who appeared in small film roles from 1936, often as solicitor, auctioneer or civil servant.
A Yank at Oxford 46. Corridor of Mirrors 47. The Blind Goddess 49. Father Brown 54. The Scapegoat 59. Some Will Some Won't 70, etc.

Howlin, Olin (1896–1959) (formerly known as **Olin Howland**). American character actor, in innumerable small film roles since the early talkies.
So Big 32. Nothing Sacred 37. This Gun for Hire 42. The Wistful Widow 47. Them 54. The Blob 58, etc.

Hoyt, Arthur (1873–1953). American character actor who played mild or henpecked in hundreds of silent and sound movies.
Love Never Dies 16. The Grim Game 19. Camille 21. Kissed 22. Souls for Sale 23. Sundown 24. The Lost World 25. Shanghai Bound 27. The Criminal Code 31. Call Her Savage 32. Only Yesterday 33. Wake Up and Dream 34. The Raven 35. Mr Deeds Goes to Town 36. A Star Is Born 37. The Black Doll 38. East Side of Heaven 39. The Great McGinty 40. The Lady Eve 41. The Palm Beach Story 42. The Miracle of Morgan's Creek 44. Hail the Conquering Hero 44. Mad Wednesday 47. Brute Force 47, many others.

Hoyt, John (1905–) (John Hoysradt). Incisive American character actor, sometimes cast as German officer or stylish crook.
O.S.S. 46. *Rommel, Desert Fox* 51. New Mexico 52. When Worlds Collide 52. Androcles and the Lion 53. Julius Caesar 53. The Blackboard Jungle 55. Trial 55. The Conqueror 56. Six Inches Tall 58. Never So Few 60. Duel at Diablo 66. Flesh Gordon 74, many others.

Hubbard, John (1914–). American light leading man who starred in several Hal Roach comedies.
The Housekeeper's Daughter 39. *Turnabout* 40. Road Show 41. Gunfight at Comanche Creek 63. Fate Is the Hunter 64. Duel at Diablo 66. Herbie Rides Again 73, etc.
TV series: The Mickey Rooney Show 54. Don't Call Me Charlie 62.

Hubbard, Lucien (1888–1971). American screenwriter.
The Perils of Pauline 14. Wild Honey 22. The Vanishing American 25. Wings 27. Five Star Final 22. 42nd Street 33. The Casino Murder Case (& p) 35. A Family Affair (& p) 37. Ebb Tide (p) 37. Nick Carter Master Detective (p) 39, etc.

Huber, Harold (1904–1959). American character actor, former lawyer; often seen as sly crook or dumb detective.
The Bowery 33. The Thin Man 34. G-Men 35. San Francisco 36. A Slight Case of Murder 38. Kit Carson 40. The Lady from Chungking 43. Let's Dance 50, many others.
TV series: I Cover Times Square 50.

Hubley, John (1914–1977). American animator, associated with the early days of UPA; a co-creator of Mr Magoo. Latterly worked on experimental documentary cartoons: *Of Stars and Men*, etc.

Hubley, Season (–). American leading lady of the seventies.
Lolly Madonna XXX 73. Catch My Soul 74. She Lives (TV) 74. Death Flight (TV) 77. Loose Change (TV) 78. Elvis (TV) 79. Hardcore 79. Escape from New York 81. Prettykill 87.

Hubschmid, Paul (1917–) (known in US as **Paul Christian**). German-Swiss leading man, in international films; also on stage, especially as Higgins in *My Fair Lady*.
Maria Ilona 40. Baghdad 49. The Thief of Venice 52. The Beast from 20,000 Fathoms 53. Der Tiger von Eschnapur 59. Journey to the Lost City 60. Mozambique 66. *Funeral in Berlin* 66. Skullduggery 69, many others.

Huckleberry Finn. Mark Twain's lively Mississippi boy had film adventures in 1919, when he was played by Lewis Sargent; in 1931, by Junior Durkin; in 1939, by Mickey Rooney; and in 1960, by Eddie Hodges. He also turned up in several of the films about Tom Sawyer (qv).

Hud (US 1962). This realistic, ambling melodrama of a modern western ne'er-do-well was refreshingly off-beat for Hollywood. Written by Irving Ravetch and Harriet Frank Jnr; directed by Martin Ritt; photographed by James Wong Howe (AA); with Paul Newman, Patricia Neal (AA), Melvyn Douglas (AA).

Hudd, Walter (1898–1963). British character actor of stage and screen; usually played aloof characters and in 1936 was cast as T. E. Lawrence but the production was abandoned.
Rembrandt 36. Black Limelight 37. Elephant Boy 37. The Housemaster 38. Major Barbara 40. I Know Where I'm Going 45. Paper Orchid 49. Life For Ruth 62, etc.

Huddleston, David (1930–). Oversized American actor often found in westerns.
All the Way Home 63. A Lovely Way to Die 66. Slaves 69. Rio Lobo 70. Bad Company 72. Fools Parade 72. Brock's Last Case (TV) 73. The Gun and the Pulpit (TV) 74. The Oregon Trail (TV) 76. Blazing Saddles 76. Capricorn One 78. Kate Bliss and the Tickertape Kid (TV) 78. Smokey and the Bandit II 80. Santa Claus, the Movie 85, etc.

Hudson, Hugh (–). British director.
□ *Chariots of Fire* 81. Greystoke 84. Revolution 86.

Hudson, Rochelle (1914–1972). American leading lady who played *ingénue* roles in the thirties.
Laugh and Get Rich 30. She Done Him Wrong 33. Les Misérables 35. Way Down East 36. Smuggled Cargo 39. Island of Doomed Men 40. Meet Boston Blackie 41. Rubber Racketeers 42. Queen of Broadway 43. Skyliner 49. Rebel without a Cause 55. The Night Walker 65. Broken Sabre 65, etc.

Hudson, Rock (1925–85) (Roy Scherer). Giant-sized American leading man who did very well in Hollywood despite lack of acting training, moving from westerns to sob stories to sophisticated comedies.
□Fighter Squadron 48. Double Crossbones 48. Undertow 49. I Was a Shoplifter 50. One Way Street 50. Winchester 73 50. Peggy 50. The Desert Hawk 50. Shakedown 50. The Fat Man 50. Air Cadet 51. Tomahawk 51. Iron Man 51. Bright Victory 51. Bend of the River 52. Here Come the Nelsons 52. Scarlet Angel 52. Has Anybody Seen My Gal? 52. Horizons West 52. The Lawless Breed 52. Gun Fury 53. Seminole 53. Sea Devils (GB) 53. The Golden Blade 53. Back to God's Country 53. Taza Son of Cochise 53. *Magnificent Obsession* 54. Bengal Brigade 54. Captain Lightfoot 55. One Desire 55. All That Heaven Allows 55. Never Say Goodbye 56. *Giant* 56. Battle Hymn 56. *Written on the Wind* 56. Four Girls in Town 56. Something of Value 57. *The Tarnished Angels* 57. A Farewell to Arms 57. Twilight for the Gods 58. This Earth is Mine 59. *Pillow Talk* 59. The Last Sunset 61. Come September 61. Lover Come Back 61. The Spiral Road 62. A Gathering of Eagles 63. Marilyn (narrator) 63. Man's Favourite Sport? 64. Send Me No Flowers 64. Strange Bedfellows 64. A Very Special Favor 65. Blindfold 66. *Seconds* 66. Tobruk 67. Ice Station Zebra 68. A Fine Pair 69. The Undefeated 69. Darling Lili 69. Hornet's Nest 70. Pretty Maids all in a Row 71. Showdown 73. Embryo 76. Avalanche 78. Wheels (TV) 78. The Mirror Crack'd 80. The Martian Chronicles (TV) 80. The Ambassador 84. The Vegas Strip War (TV) 84.
TV series: *McMillan and Wife* 71–75. McMillan 76. The Devlin Connection 82. Dynasty 85.

¶ That big, lumpy Rock Hudson.—*James Dean*

R.H.: I can't play a loser: I don't look like one.

I call him Ernie because he's certainly no Rock.—*Doris Day*

Hue and Cry (GB 1946). One of the first post-war Ealing comedies, typical in its use of London bomb-site locations and its exhilarating spoof of authority; basically a lively 'tuppenny blood' boys' adventure about crooks in Covent Garden. Written by T. E. B. Clarke, directed by Charles Crichton; with Alastair Sim and Jack Warner; music George Auric; photography Douglas Slocombe.

Huffaker, Clair (1927–). American screenwriter.
Flaming Star 60. Seven Ways from Sundown 60. Rio Conchos 64. Tarzan and the Valley of Gold 47. The War Wagon 67, etc.

Huffman, David (1945–85). American general purpose actor.

F.I.S.T. 78. Ice Castles 78. The Onion Field 79. Blood Beach 81. Firefox 82.

Huggins, Roy (1914–). American screenwriter, later TV producer.
I Love Trouble 48. The Lady Gambles 49. Sealed Cargo 51. Hangman's Knot (& d) 52. *Pushover* 54. A Fever in the Blood (& p) 61, etc.
TV series: *The Fugitive* (p) 63–66. Run for Your Life (p) 65–67, etc.

Hughes, Barnard (1915–). American character actor familiar on TV as *Doc*.
Midnight Cowboy 69. Where's Poppa 71. The Hospital 72. Rage 72. Sisters 73. Oh God 77. Best Friends 82. Tron 82. Maxie 85. The Lost Boys 87, etc.
TV series: Mr Merlin 81.

Hughes, Howard (1905–1976). American businessman and celebrated recluse of eccentric habits; once an enthusiastic film-maker. A character based on him was played by George Peppard in *The Carpetbaggers* 64. Biographies: 1967, *The Bashful Billionaire* by Albert Gerber. 1967, *Howard Hughes* by John Keats. Tommy Lee Jones played him in a 1977 TV movie, *The Amazing Howard Hughes*, and Jason Robards Jnr in Melvin and Howard in 1981. Other Hughes-like figures were seen in *Caught* (Robert Ryan), *The Barefoot Contessa* (Warren Stevens), *Harlow* (Leslie Nielsen) and *Diamonds are Forever* (Jimmy Dean).
Two Arabian Knights (p) 27. *Hell's Angels* (pd) 30. The Front Page (p) 31. *Scarface* (p) 32. Sky Devils 32. *The Outlaw* (pd) 43. Jet Pilot (p) 56. The Conqueror (p) 56, etc.

¶ Hughes never fired anybody. If he wanted to get rid of somebody, he'd merely put somebody in over the guy.—*Sam Bischoff*

There are two good reasons why men go to see her. Those are enough.—*H.H. on Jane Russell*

This is a very simple engineering problem.—*H.H., designing a bra for Jane Russell*

In his heyday he boasted of deflowering 200 virgins in Hollywood. He must have got them all.—*Jimmy the Greek*

Hughes, Kathleen (1929–) (Betty von Gerlean). Blonde American leading lady of the fifties.
Mother is a Freshman 49. For Men Only 51. The Golden Blade 53. It Came from Outer Space 53. The Glass Web 53. Dawn at Socorro 54. Cult of the Cobra 55. Promise Her Anything 66. The President's Analyst 67, etc.

Hughes, Ken (1922–). British director who has tackled a great variety of projects with variable success.
□Wide Boy 52. Black Thirteen 53. The Brain Machine 53. Little Red Monkey (& w) 53. Confession (& w) 53. Timeslip (& w) 53. The House Across the Lake (& w) 54. *Joe Macbeth* (& w) 55. Wicked as They Come (& w) 56. The Long Haul 57. Jazzboat 60. In the Nick 60. *The Trials of Oscar Wilde* (& w) 60. The Small World of Sammy Lee (& w) 63. Of Human Bondage 64. Drop Dead Darling (& w) 66. Casino Royale (co-d) 67. Chitty Chitty Bang Bang (& w) 69. *Cromwell* (& w) 70. The Internecine Project 74. Alfie Darling 74. Sextette 77. Night School 80.

Hughes, Lloyd (1896–1958). American leading man of the twenties.
The Turn in the Road 19. Hail the Woman 21. Tess of the Storm Country 22. *The Sea Hawk* 24. *The Lost World* 24. The Desert Flower 25. Ella Cinders 26. Loose Ankles 26. The Stolen Bride 27. The Mysterious Island 29. Moby Dick 30. Hell Bound 31. The Miracle Man 32. Harmony Lane 35. Romance of the Redwoods 39, many others.

Hughes, Mary Beth (1919–). American leading lady of the forties, mainly in second features.
These Glamour Girls 39. Lucky Cisco Kid 40. Orchestra Wives 42. *The Ox-Bow Incident* 43. I Accuse My Parents 44. Caged Fury 47. Gun Battle at Monterey 57. How's Your Love Life? 77, etc.

Hughes, Roddy (1891–*). Welsh character actor in films from 1934, often in roly-poly comedy roles.
The Stars Look Down 39. The Ghost of St Michael's 41. Hatter's Castle 41. Nicholas Nickleby 47. Scrooge 51. Sea Wife 57, etc.

Hughes, Wendy (–). Australian leading actress.
□ Sidecar Racers 75. High Rolling 77. Newsfront 78. Kostas 78. *My Brilliant Career* 79. Touch and Go 80. Partners 81. A Dangerous Summer 81. Lonely Hearts 82. Careful, He Might Hear You 83. My First Wife 84. An Indecent Obsession 85. I Can't Get Started 85. Promises to Keep 86. Warm Nights on a Slow Moving Train 87.

Hulbert, Claude (1900–1963). British 'silly ass' comedian, brother of Jack Hulbert.
Champagne 28. Naughty Husbands 30. A Night Like This 32. The Mayor's Nest 32. *Thark* 32. Radio Parade 33. A Cup of Kindness 34. *Bulldog Jack* 34. Wolf's Clothing 36. The Vulture 37. His Lordship Regrets 38. *Sailors Three* 40. *The Ghost of St Michael's* 41. The Dummy Talks 43. *My Learned Friend* 44. London Town 46. The Ghosts of Berkeley Square 47. Cardboard Cavalier 48. Fun at St Fanny's 55. Not a Hope in Hell 60, etc.

Hulbert, Jack (1892–1978). Jaunty, long-chinned British light comedian, popular in films of the thirties.
Autobiography 1976: *The Little Woman's Always Right.*
□Elstree Calling 30. *The Ghost Train* 31. Sunshine Susie 31. *Jack's the Boy* 32. Love on Wheels 32. Happy Ever After 32. Falling for You 33. Jack Ahoy 34. The Camels are Coming 34. *Bulldog Jack* 34. Jack of all Trades 36. Take My Tip 37. Paradise for Two 37. Kate Plus Ten 38. Under Your Hat 40. Into the Blue 51. The Magic Box 51. Miss Tulip Stays the Night 55. Spider's Web 60. The Cherry Picker 72. Not Now Darling 73.

Hulce, Tom (1953–). Young American character actor of the eighties.
□ '9/30/55' 77. National Lampoon's Animal House 78. Those Lips, Those Eyes 80. Amadeus (AAN, as Mozart) 84. Echo Park 85. Slam Dance 87.

Hull, Henry (1890–1977). Versatile American character actor.
The Volunteer 17. One Exciting Night 22. The Hoosier Schoolmaster 24. For Woman's Favour 24. Midnight 34. Great Expectations 34. *Werewolf of London* (leading role) 35. Yellow Jack 38. Boys' Town 38. The Great Waltz 38. Jesse James 39. Miracles for Sale 39. Judge Hardy and Son 39. My Son My Son 40. High Sierra 40. Lifeboat 43. Woman of the Town 44. Objective Burma 45. Mourning Becomes Electra 47. The Walls of Jericho 48. The Great Gatsby 49. Hollywood Story 51. Inferno 53. The Man with the Gun 55. The Proud Rebel 58. The Sheriff of Fractured Jaw 58. Master of the World 61. The Chase 66. Covenant with Death 67, many others.

Hull, Josephine (1884–1957) (Josephine Sherwood). Bubbly little American stage actress who gave two memorable film performances.
□ After Tomorrow 32. Careless Lady 32. *Arsenic and Old Lace* 44. *Harvey* (AA) 50. The Lady from Texas 51.
Famous line (*Harvey*): Myrtle Mae, you have a lot to learn, and I hope you never learn it.

Hull, Warren (1903–1974). American leading man of many second features: also radio hero of such serials as Mandrake the Magician and The Spider.
Miss Pacific Fleet 35. The Walking Dead 36. Night Key 37. Wagons Westward 40. Bowery Blitzkrieg 41, etc.

Hulme, Kathryn C. (1900–81). Author of *The Nun's Story*, which was filmed with Audrey Hepburn playing her.

Humberstone, H. Bruce (1903–). American director, a competent craftsman of action films and musicals.
If I Had a Million (part) 32. The Crooked Circle 32. Charlie Chan in Honolulu 37. Pack Up Your Troubles 39. Lucky Cisco Kid 40. Tall, Dark and Handsome 41. *Sun Valley Serenade* 41. Hot Spot 41. To the Shores of Tripoli 42. *Hello, Frisco Hello* 43. *Wonder Man* 45. Three Little Girls in Blue 46. *Fury at Furnace Creek* 48. East of Java 49. Happy Go Lovely (GB) 51. She's Working Her Way Through College 52. The Desert Song 53. The Purple Mask 55. Tarzan and the Lost Safari 57. Madison Avenue 61, etc.

Hume, Benita (1906–1967). British leading lady of the thirties; in Hollywood from 1935; retired to marry Ronald Colman.
The Constant Nymph 28. High Treason 29. Service for Ladies 32. The Flying Fool 32. Lord Camber's Ladies 33. Jew Süss 34. The Garden Murder Case 36. Tarzan Escapes 36. The Last of Mrs Cheyney 37. Peck's Bad Boy with the Circus 39, etc.
TV series: Halls of Ivy 55.

Hume, Alan (1924–). British cinematographer.
The Legend of Hell House 72. Carry on Girls 73. The Land that Time Forgot 74. Trial by Combat 76. Bear Island 80. The Eye of the Needle 81. For Your Eyes Only 81. Return of the Jedi 83. Octopussy 83.

Hume, Kenneth (1926–1967). British producer, former editor.
Cheer the Brave (wpd) 50. Hot Ice (wd) 51. Sail into Danger (wd) 57. Mods and Rockers (pd) 64. I've Gotta Horse (pd) 65, etc.

Humphries, Barry (1931–). Australian entertainer.
Les Patterson Saves the World 87.

The Hunchback of Notre Dame. Victor Hugo's novel *Notre Dame de Paris* has been filmed three times under this title; in 1923 with Lon Chaney, in 1939 with Charles Laughton, and in 1956 with Anthony Quinn. The last of these was disappointing; the earlier two are considerable cinematic achievements, William Dieterle's 1939 version in particular standing out as a masterpiece of studio technique. The 1982 TV movie with Anthony Hopkins never seized the imagination.

Hungary has had one of the most flourishing film histories in Europe, and many of its talents found their way to Hollywood, including Michael Curtiz, Alexander Korda and Bela Lugosi. The native films were seldom exported, oddly enough, until after a strong Soviet influence made itself felt: Zoltan Fabri and Miklos Jancso are now respected names.

Hunnicutt, Arthur (1911–1979). American actor of slow-speaking country characters.
Wildcat 42. Lust for Gold 49. Broken Arrow 50. The Red Badge of Courage 51. The Big Sky 52. The French Line 54. The Last Command 56. The Kettles in the Ozarks 56. Apache Uprising 65. Cat Ballou 65. El Dorado 66. Million Dollar Duck 71. The Revengers 72. Harry and Tonto 74. The Spikes Gang 74. Moonrunners 75, etc.

Hunnicutt, Gayle (1942–). American leading lady of the sixties.
□The Wild Angels 66. P. J. 68. Marlowe 69. Eye of the Cat 69. Fragment of Fear 70. Freelance 70. Scorpio 72. The Legend of Hell House 72. Running Scared 72. Voices 73. Nuits Rouges 73. The Spiral Staircase 75. Blazing Magnum 76. The Sellout 76. Once In Paris 78. A Man Called Intrepid (TV) 79. The Martian Chronicles (TV) 79. Kiss of Gold (TV) 80. The Return of the Man from UNCLE (TV) 83. The First Modern Olympics (TV) 84. A Woman of Substance (TV) 85. Target 85. Strong Medicine (TV) 86. Dream West (TV) 86. Turnaround 87.

Hunt, Linda (1945–). Diminutive American character actress.
The Year of Living Dangerously (AA) (as a man) 83. The Bostonians 84. Silverado 85. Eleni 85. Dune 85. Waiting for the Moon (as Alice B. Toklas) 87.

Hunt, Marsha (1917–) (Marcia Hunt). American leading lady who usually plays gentle characters.
Virginia Judge (debut) 35. Hollywood Boulevard 36. The Hardys Ride High 38. These Glamour Girls 39. *Pride and Prejudice* 40. Blossoms in the Dust 41. Kid Glove Killer 42. Seven Sweethearts 42. The Human Comedy 43. *Lost Angel* 43. None Shall Escape 43. Cry Havoc 44. The Valley of Decision 45. A Letter for Evie 45. Carnegie Hall 46. Take One False Step 49. Mary Ryan, Detective 50. The Happy Time 52. No Place to Hide 56. Blue Denim 59. The Plunderers 60. Johnny Got His Gun 71, etc.
TV series: Peck's Bad Girl 59.

Hunt, Martita (1900–1969). British stage and screen actress who graduated from nosy spinsters to *grandes dames*.
I Was a Spy (debut) 33. Spare a Copper 39. The Man in Grey 43. The Wicked Lady 45. *Great Expectations* (as Miss Havisham) 46. The Ghosts of Berkeley Square 47. My Sister and I 48. The Fan 49. *Treasure Hunt* 52. Melba 53. Three Men in a Boat 56. Anastasia 56. *Brides of Dracula* 60. The Unsinkable Molly Brown 64. Bunny Lake Is Missing 65, others.

Hunt, Peter (1928–). British director, former editor.
□On Her Majesty's Secret Service 69. Gulliver's Travels 73. Gold 74. Shout at the Devil 76. The Beasts are on the Streets (TV) 78. Flying High (TV) 79. Death Hunt 80. Rendezvous Hotel (TV) 81. The Last Days of Pompeii (TV) 83.

Hunter, Evan (1926–) (Salvadore Lombino). American novelist and screenwriter who also writes as Ed McBain.
The Blackboard Jungle (oa) 55. Strangers When We Meet (w) 60. The Young Savages (w) 61. The Birds (w) 63. Mister Buddwing (oa) 66, etc.
TV series: 87th Precinct 61. The Chisholms 78.

Hunter, Glenn (1897–1945). American leading man of the twenties.
The Case of Becky 21. The Country Flapper 22. Smilin' Through 22. Puritan Passions 23. *Merton of the Movies* 24. West of the Water Tower 24. The Pinch Hitter 25. For Beauty's Sake 41, etc.

Hunter, Ian (1900–1975). British actor of dependable characters: on stage from 1919, films soon after.
Mr Oddy 22. Not for Sale 24. Confessions 25. The Ring 27. Something Always Happens 31. The Sign of Four (as Dr Watson) 32. Death at Broadcasting House 34. A Midsummer Night's Dream (US) 35. The White Angel (US) 36. Call It a Day (US) 37. *52nd Street* (US) 38. The Adventures of Robin Hood (as King Richard) (US) 38. Tower of London (US) 39. Strange Cargo (US) 40. Bitter Sweet (US) 40. Billy the Kid (US) 41. *Dr Jekyll and Mr Hyde* (as Lanyon) (US) 41. A Yank at Eton (US) 42. Bedelia 46. White Cradle Inn 47. The White Unicorn 48. *Edward My Son* 49. Appointment in London 52. Don't Blame the Stork 53. The Battle of the River Plate 56. Fortune Is a Woman 57. Northwest Frontier 59. The Bulldog Breed 60. Dr Blood's Coffin 61. Guns of Darkness 63, many others.

Hunter, Jeffrey (1925–1969) (Henry H. McKinnies). American leading man, in films from 1951 after radio experience.
Fourteen Hours (debut) 51. Red Skies of Montana 52. Singlehanded 53. White Feather 55. The Searchers 56. A Kiss Before Dying 56. The True Story of Jesse James 57. No Down Payment 57. The Last Hurrah 57. Hell to Eternity 60. *King of Kings* (as Jesus) 61. The Longest Day 62. Vendetta 65. Brainstorm 65. Custer of the West 66. The Private Navy of Sgt O'Farrell 68, many others.
TV series: Temple Houston 63.

Hunter, Kim (1922–) (Janet Cole). Pert, dependable American leading lady who after brief stage experience started a rather desultory film career.
□The Seventh Victim 43. Tender Comrade 43. When Strangers Marry 44. You Came Along 45. *A Matter of Life and Death* (GB) 45. A Canterbury Tale (GB) 46. *A Streetcar Named Desire* (AA) 51. *Deadline U.S.A.* 52. Anything Can Happen 52. Storm Center 56. The Young Stranger 57. Bermuda Affair 58. Money Women and Guns 58. Lilith 64. Planet of the Apes 67. The Swimmer 68. Beneath the Planet of the Apes 70. Dial Hot Line (TV) 70. In Search of America Dial Hot Line (TV) 70. In Search of America (TV) 71. Escape from the Planet of the Apes 71. The Magician (TV) 73. Unwed Father (TV) 74. Born Innocent (TV) 74. Bad Ronald (TV) 74. Ellery Queen (TV) 75. The Dark Side of Innocence (TV) 76. Once an Eagle (TV) 76. Backstairs at the White House (TV) 79.

Hunter, Ross (1921–) (Martin Fuss). American producer; a former actor, he has specialized in remakes of glossy dramas from Hollywood's golden age, and has seldom failed to make hot commercial properties of them.
AS ACTOR: A Guy a Gal and a Pal 45. Sweetheart of Sigma Chi 47, The Bandit of Sherwood Forest 47. The Groom Wore Spurs 51, etc.
AS PRODUCER: Take Me to Town 53. *Magnificent Obsession* 54. One Desire 55. The Spoilers 55. All that Heaven Allows 56. Battle Hymn 57. My Man Godfrey 57. *Pillow Talk* 58. *Imitation of Life* 59. Portrait in Black 60. Tammy Tell Me True 61. Back Street 61. Flower Drum Song 61. The Thrill of it All 63. The Chalk Garden 64. Madame X 66. The Pad 66. *Thoroughly Modern Millie* 67. *Airport* 69. Lost Horizon 73.The Lives of Jenny Dolan (TV) 76. A Family Upside Down (TV) 78. The Best Place to Be (TV) 78. Suddenly Love (TV) 79, etc.

¶ *R.H.:* The way life looks in my pictures is the way I want life to be. I don't want to hold a mirror up to life as it is. I just want to show the part which is attractive.

Hunter, T. Hayes (1881–1944). American director, in Britain in the thirties.
Desert Gold 19. Earthbound 20. The Triumph of the Scarlet Pimpernel 29. The Silver King 29. The Frightened Lady 31. Sally Bishop 33. *The Ghoul* 33, etc.

Hunter, Tab (1931–) (Andrew Arthur Kelm). Athletic American leading man, a teenage rave of the fifties.
The Lawless (debut) 48. Saturday Island 52. Gun Belt 53. Return to Treasure Island 53. *Track of the Cat* 54. Battle Cry 55. The Sea Chase 55. The Burning Hills 56. The Girl He Left Behind 57. Gunman's Walk 57. *Damn Yankees* 58. That Kind of Woman 59. The Pleasure of His Company 60. The Golden Arrow (It.) 62. City under the Sea 65. Birds Do It 66. Hostile Guns 67. Judge Roy Bean 72. The Timber Tramps 73. Grease II 82. Pandemonium 82. Polyester 82. Lust in the Dust 85, etc.
TV series: The Tab Hunter Show 60.

Huntington, Lawrence (1900–1968). British director, mainly of routine thrillers.
Suspected Person (& w) 41. Night Boat to Dublin 41. *Wanted for Murder* 46. *The Upturned Glass* 47. When the Bough Breaks 48. *Mr Perrin and Mr Traill* 48. Man on the Run (& w) 49. The Franchise Affair (& w)

51. There Was a Young Lady (& w) 53. Contraband Spain (& w) 55. Stranglehold 62. The Fur Collar (& wp) 63, etc.

Huntley, Raymond (1904–). British character actor, often of supercilious types or self-satisfied businessmen: on stage from 1922, screen from 1934.
Rembrandt 37. *Night Train to Munich* 40. *The Ghost of St Michael's* 41. School for Secrets 45. Mr Perrin and Mr Traill 48. *Trio* 50. Room at the Top 59. Only Two Can Play 62. Rotten to the Core 65. Hostile Witness 67. Destiny of a Spy (TV) 69. *That's Your Funeral* 73, many others.

Huppert, Isabelle (1955–). French leading lady in international films.
Faustine 71. Cesar and Rosalie 72. Les Valseuses 74. Rosebud 75. The Judge and the Assassin 76. *The Lacemaker* 77. *Violette Nozière* 78. Heaven's Gate 80. Sauve Qui Peut 80. Camp de Torchon 81. The Trout 82, etc.

Hurndall, Richard (1910–84). Incisive British character actor.
Joanna 67. I Monster 71. Royal Flash 75. The Prince and the Pauper 77, etc.

Hurok, Sol (1889–1974). Distinguished American impresario whose life in classical music was recounted in *Tonight we Sing* 53.

Hurst, Brandon (1866–1947). British character actor in Hollywood; better roles in silents than sound films.
Legally Dead 23. *The Hunchback of Notre Dame* 23. He Who Gets Slapped 24. *The Thief of Baghdad* 24. The Grand Duchess and the Waiter 26. Love 27. Interference 29. A Connecticut Yankee 31. White Zombie 32. The Lost Patrol 34. The Charge of the Light Brigade 36. Mary of Scotland 36. If I Were King 38. Stanley and Livingstone 39. If I Had My Way 40. Dixie 43. Jane Eyre 44. House of Frankenstein 44. Devotion 46. Road to Rio 47, many others.

Hurst, Brian Desmond (1900–86). Irish director who made many kinds of film.
Sensation 36. Glamorous Night 37. Prison Without Bars 39. On the Night of the Fire 40. *Dangerous Moonlight* 41. Alibi 42. The Hundred Pound Window 43. Theirs Is the Glory 45. Hungry Hill 47. The Mark of Cain 48. Tom Brown's Schooldays (p only) 51. *Scrooge* 51. The Malta Story 53. Simba 55. The Black Tent 56. Dangerous Exile 57. Behind the Mask 58. His and Hers 60. The Playboy of the Western World 62, etc.

Hurst, David (1925–). Austrian actor who played some comedy roles in British films.
The Perfect Woman 49. So Little Time 52. Mother Riley Meets the Vampire 52. As Long As They're Happy 53. The Intimate Stranger 56. After the Ball 57. Hello Dolly (US) 69, etc.

Hurst, Fannie (1889–1968). American popular novelist, several of whose romantic novels, usually with a tragic finale, have been filmed more than once: *Humoresque, Imitation of Life, Back Street,* etc.

Hurst, Paul (1889–1953). American character actor in hundreds of cameo roles from 1912, usually as gangster, bartender, outlaw or cop.
The Red Raiders 27. Tugboat Annie 32. Riff Raff 34. Gone with the Wind 39. Caught in the Draft 41. Jack London 44. Yellow Sky 49. The Sun Shines Bright 53, many others.

Hurst, Veronica (1931–). British light leading lady of the fifties.
Laughter in Paradise 51. Angels One Five 51. The Maze (US) 53. Will Any Gentleman? 53. The Yellow Balloon 54. Peeping Tom 58. Dead Man's Evidence 62. Licensed to Kill 64. The Boy Cried Murder 66, etc.

Hurt, John (1940–). Offbeat British stage and film leading man.
□ The Wild and the Willing 62. This is my Street 63. *A Man for all Seasons* 66. The Sailor from Gibraltar 67. Before Winter Comes 69. Sinful Davey 69. In Search of Gregory 70. *10 Rillington Place* 71. Forbush and the Penguins 71. The Pied Piper 72. The Ghoul 74. Little Malcolm and His Struggle against the Eunuchs 74. *The Naked Civil Servant* (TV) 75. I Claudius (TV) 76. East of Elephant Rock 78. The Disappearance 78. The Shout 78. *Midnight Express* 78. Spectre (TV) 78. Alien 79. Heaven's Gate 80. *The Elephant Man* (BFA) 80. Night Crossing 81. History of the World Part One 81. Partners 82. The Osterman Weekend 83. Champions 84. 1984 84. The Hit 84. Success is the Best Revenge 84. Sunset People 84. Jake Speed 86. Rocinante 86. From the Hip 87. Aria 87.

Hurt, Mary Beth (1948–) (Mary Supinger). American leading lady.
Head over Heels 82. The World According to Garp 82.

Hurt, William (1950–). American leading actor.
Altered States 80. Eyewitness 81. Body Heat 81. The Big Chill 83. Gorky Park 83. *Kiss of the Spider Woman* (AA, BFA) 85. Children of a Lesser God 86. Broadcast News 87.

Hussein, Waris (1938–). Anglo–Indian director, mostly for TV.
□A Touch of Love 68. Quackser Fortune 69. Melody 71. The Possession of Joel Delaney 72. The Six Wives of Henry VIII 72. Divorce His, Divorce Hers (TV) 73. *The Glittering Prizes* (TV) 75. *Edward and Mrs Simpson* (TV) 78. *Little Gloria . . . Happy at Last* (TV) 82. Winter of our Discontent (TV) 83. Arch of Triumph (TV) 84. Surviving (TV) 85. Copacabana (TV) 86. When the Bough Breaks (TV) 86.

Hussey, Olivia (1951–). British leading lady, born in Argentina.
□The Battle of the Villa Fiorita 65. Cup Fever 65. *Romeo and Juliet* 68. All the Right Noises 69. Summertime Killer 72. *Lost Horizon* 73. Black Christmas 75. Jesus of Nazareth (TV) 77. The Cat and the Canary 77. Death on the Nile 78. The Pirate (TV) 79. The Man with Bogart's Face 80. Turkey Shoot 81. Escape 2000 81. Virus 82.

Hussey, Ruth (1914–) (Ruth Carol O'Rourke). Smart, competent, sometimes wisecracking American leading lady of the early forties.
□Madame X 37. Big City 37. Judge Hardy's Children 38. Man Proof 38. Marie Antoinette 38. Hold that Kiss 38. Rich Man Poor Girl 38. Time Out for Murder 38. Spring Madness 38. Honolulu 39. Within the Law 39. Maisie 39. The Women 39. Another Thin Man 39. Blackmail 39. *Fast and Furious* 39. Northwest Passage 40. Susan and God 40. *The Philadelphia Story* 40. Flight Command 40. Free and Easy 41. Our Wife 41. Married Bachelor 41. *H. M. Pulham Esq* 41. Pierre of the Plains 42. Tennessee Johnson 42. Tender Comrade 43. *The Uninvited* 44. Marine Raiders 44. Bedside Manner 45. I Jane Doe 48. The Great Gatsby 49. Louisa 50. Mr Music 50. That's My Boy 51. Woman of the North Country 52. Stars and Stripes Forever 52. The Lady Wants Mink 53. The Facts of Life 60. My Darling Daughters' Anniversary (TV) 72.

The Hustler (US 1961) (BFA best film). Robert Rossen wrote, produced and directed this unusual film from Walter Tevis' novel, with Paul Newman as a professional pool player who meets his match in Minnesota Fats, played by Jackie Gleason. Other key roles are cleverly played by George C. Scott and Myron McCormick, and the the CinemaScope photography by Eugene Shuftan (AA), together with Harry Horner's (AA) art direction, adds immeasurably to the total effect. A tragic subplot involving Piper Laurie is less successful. In 1986 Paul Newman starred in a kind of sequel, *The Color of Money*, which caught up with his character a quarter of a century later.

Huston, Anjelica (1952–). American leading lady, daughter of John Huston.
Sinful Davey 69. A Walk With Love and Death 69. The Last Tycoon 76. Swashbuckler 76. The Last Tycoon 76. Frances 82. The Ice Pirates 83. *Prizzi's Honor* 85. Good to Go 86. The Dead 87. Gardens of Stone 87. A Handful of Dust 88.

Huston, John (1906–87). Unpredictable but occasionally splendid American director, son of Walter Huston.
Biography 1965: *King Rebel*, by W. F. Nolan. Autobiography 1981: *An Open Book*.
AS SCREENWRITER ONLY: Murders in the Rue Morgue 32. The Amazing Dr Clitterhouse 38. Jezebel 38. High Sierra 40. Sergeant York 41. Three Strangers 46, etc.
□AS DIRECTOR: *The Maltese Falcon* (& w) 41. In This Our Life 42. Across the Pacific 42. Report from the Aleutians 43. Battle of San Pietro 45. Let There Be Light 45 (four other official war documentaries 44–45). *The Treasure of the Sierra Madre* (& w) (AA) 47. *Key Largo* (& w) 48. We Were Strangers 49. *The Asphalt Jungle* (& w) 50. The Red Badge of Courage (& w) 51. *The African Queen* (& w) 52. Moulin Rouge (& w) 53. Beat the Devil (& w) 54. Moby Dick (& w) 56. Heaven Knows Mr Allison (& w) 57. The Barbarian and the Geisha 58. The Roots of Heaven (& w) 58. The Unforgiven 60. The Misfits 60. *Freud* 62. The List of Adrian Messenger 63. *The Night of the Iguana* (& w) 64. The Bible 66. Casino Royale (part) 67. Reflections in a Golden Eye 67. Sinful Davey 69. A Walk with Love and Death 69. The Kremlin Letter 70. *Fat City* 72. Judge Roy Bean 72. The Mackintosh Man 73. The Man Who Would Be King 75. Wise Blood 79. Phobia 80. Victory 81. Annie 82. Under the Volcano 84. *Prizzi's Honor* (AAN) 85. The Dead 87.
□AS ACTOR: The Treasure of the Sierra Madre (uncredited) 47. The List of Adrian

Messenger (uncredited) 63. *The Cardinal* 63. *The Bible* (as Noah) 66. Casino Royale 67. Candy 68. A Walk with Love and Death 68. De Sade 69. The Kremlin Letter 70. The Bridge and the Jungle 70. Myra Breckinridge 70. The Deserter 70. Man in the Wilderness 71. Judge Roy Bean 72. Battle for the Planet of the Apes 73. Chinatown 74. Breakout 75. The Wind and the Lion 75. Tentacles 77. Sherlock Holmes in New York (TV) 77. The Word (TV) 78. Winter Kills 79. The Visitor 79. Jaguar Lives 79. Head On 80. Love Sick 83. Young Giants 83.

¶ *J.H.:* I don't try to guess what a million people will like. It's hard enough to know what I like.

J.H.: I fail to see any continuity in my work from picture to picture.

J.H.: I completely storyboarded *The Maltese Falcon* because I didn't want to lose face with the crew: I wanted to give the impression that I knew what I was doing.

J.H. (1984): There is nothing more fascinating—and more fun—than making movies. Besides, I think I'm finally getting the hang of it.

Huston, Walter (1884–1950) (W. Houghston). Distinguished American character actor of stage and screen: latterly projected roguery and eccentricity with great vigour. He also played bit parts in his son John's first two films, as Captain Jacoby in *The Maltese Falcon* 41, and a bartender in *In This Our Life* 42. After his death his stage recording of 'September Song', played in *September Affair* 50, became a big hit.

□Gentlemen of the Press 28. The Lady Lies 29. *The Virginian* 30. The Bad Man 30. The Virtuous Sin 30. *Abraham Lincoln* 30. The Criminal Code 31. Star Witness 31. The Ruling Voice 31. A Woman from Monte Carlo 31. A House Divided 32. *Law and Order* (as Wyatt Earp) 32. Beast of the City 32. The Wet Parade 32. Night Court 32. *American Madness* 32. Kongo 32. *Rain* 32. Hell Below 32. Gabriel over the White House 33. The Prizefighter and the Lady 33. Storm at Daybreak 33. Ann Vickers 33. Keep 'Em Rolling 33. The Tunnel (GB) 34. Rhodes of Africa (GB) 36. *Dodsworth* 36. Of Human Hearts 38. The Light That Failed 39. *All That Money Can Buy* (as the devil) 41. Swamp Water 41. The Shanghai Gesture 42. Always in My Heart 42. Yankee Doodle Dandy 42. Mission to Moscow 42. Edge of Darkness 42. North Star 43. *The Outlaw* (as Doc Holliday) 43. Dragon Seed 44. *And Then There Were None* 45. Dragonwyck 46. Duel in the Sun 46. *The Treasure of the Sierra Madre* (AA) 47. Summer Holiday 47. The Great Sinner 49. The Furies 50.

❆ For star quality combined with acting ability; whatever the proportions, no audience could look away when he was on screen. *Dodsworth.*

¶ *W.H.:* Son, give 'em a good show, and always travel first class.

W.H.: Hell, I ain't paid to make good lines sound good. I'm paid to make bad lines sound good.

Famous line (*All That Money Can Buy*): A soul—a soul is nothing. Can you see it, smell it, touch it, no.

Hutcheson, David (1905–1976). British light comedian who often played monocled silly-asses, mainly on stage.

This'll Make You Whistle 35. Sabotage at Sea 41. Convoy 42. School for Secrets 46. *Vice Versa* 48. Sleeping Car to Trieste 48. The Elusive Pimpernel 50. The Evil of Frankenstein 64. The National Health 73, etc.

Hutchins, Will (1932–). Bland-faced American leading man who came to fame in 57–60 as TV's *Sugarfoot.*

No Time for Sergeants 58. Merrill's Marauders 62. The Shooting 66. Clambake 67, etc.

Hutchinson, Josephine (1898–*). American actress who usually played sweet or maternal types.

Happiness Ahead 34. The Story of Louis Pasteur 36. Son of Frankenstein 39. Somewhere in the Night 46. Ruby Gentry 52. Miracle in the Rain 56. North By Northwest 59. Huckleberry Finn 60. Baby the Rain Must Fall 64. Nevada Smith 66. Rabbit Run 70, etc.

Huth, Harold (1892–1967). British light leading man of silent days; later became producer-director.

One of the Best 27. Balaclava 28. The Silver King 29. Leave it to Me 30. The Outsider 31. Sally Bishop 32. Rome Express 32. The Ghoul 33. The Camels are Coming 34. Take My Tip 37. Hell's Cargo (d) 39. East of Piccadilly (d) 40. Busman's Honeymoon (p) 40. Breach of Promise (d) 42. Love Story (p) 44. They Were Sisters (p) 45. Caravan (p) 46. Night Beat (pd) 47. My Sister and I (pd) 48. Look Before You Love (pd) 48. One Wild Oat (p) 51. Police Dog (p) 55. The Hostage (d) 56. Idol on Parade (p) 59. The Trials of Oscar Wilde (p) 60. The Hellions (p) 61, etc.

Hutton, Betty (1921–) (Betty Thornberg). Blonde and bouncy American leading lady of many singing/dancing light entertainments of the forties.
□*The Fleet's In* 42. *Star Spangled Rhythm* 42. Happy Go Lucky 43. Let's Face It 43. *The Miracle of Morgan's Creek* 44. And the Angels Sing 44. Here Come the Waves 44. *Incendiary Blonde* (as Texas Guinan) 45. Duffy's Tavern 45. The Stork Club 45. Cross My Heart 46. *The Perils of Pauline* 47. Dream Girl 48. Red Hot and Blue 49. *Annie Get Your Gun* 50. Let's Dance 50. Somebody Loves Me 52. The Greatest Show on Earth 52. Spring Reunion 57.

Hutton, Brian G. (1935–). American director.
□Fargo 65. The Pad 66. Sol Madrid 67. *Where Eagles Dare* 68. Kelly's Heroes 70. Zee and Co 71. Night Watch 73. The First Deadly Sin 80. High Road to China 83.

Hutton, Jim (1934–79). American leading man who usually played gangly types.
A Time to Love and a Time to Die 58. Bachelor in Paradise 61. The Horizontal Lieutenant 62. The Honeymoon Machine 62. Period of Adjustment 63. The Hallelujah Trail 65. Never Too Late 65. *Walk Don't Run* 66. Who's Minding the Mint 67. The Green Berets 68. Hellfighters 69, etc.
TV series: Ellery Queen 74.

Hutton, Lauren (1943–) (Mary Hutton). American leading lady.
Little Fauss and Big Halsy 71. The Gambler 74. Welcome to L.A. 77. Viva Knievel 77. Someone's Watching Me! (TV) 78. A Wedding 78. American Gigolo 80. Zorro the Gay Blade 81. Paternity 81. Lassiter 83. Once Bitten 85.

Hutton, Marion (1920–87) (Marion Thornburg). American singer, with the Glenn Miller band; appeared in a few forties musicals. Sister of Betty Hutton.
Orchestra Wives 42. Crazy House 44. In Society 44. Babes on Swing Street 45. Love Happy 50, etc.

Hutton, Robert (1920–) (Robert Bruce Winne). American leading man of the forties.
Destination Tokyo 44. Janie 44. Too Young To Know 45. Time Out of Mind 47. Always Together 48. The Steel Helmet 51. Casanova's Big Night 54. Invisible Invaders 58. Cinderfella 60. The Slime People (& pd) 62. The Secret Man (GB) 64. Finders Keepers (GB) 66. They Came from Beyond Space (GB) 68, etc.

Hutton, Timothy (1960–). Leading young American actor of the early eighties, son of Jim Hutton.
Ordinary People 80. Taps 81. Daniel 83. Iceman 84. The Falcon and the Snowman 85 Turk 182 85. Made in Heaven 87.

Huxley, Aldous (1894–1963). Distinguished British novelist who spent some time in Hollywood and worked on the screenplays of *Pride and Prejudice* 40 and *Jane Eyre* 43.

¶ His erudition was staggering. I never discovered how many languages he knew, but one day I found him in his office at MGM reading Persian.—*Anita Loos*

Hyams, Leila (1905–77). Vivacious, blonde American leading lady of the twenties.
Sandra 24. Summer Bachelors 26. The Brute 27. The Wizard 27. Alias Jimmy Valentine 28. Spite Marriage 29. The Idle Rich 29. The Bishop Murder Case 30. The Big House 30. The Flirting Widow 30. Men Call it Love 31. The Phantom of Paris 31. Red Headed Woman 32. Freaks 32. Island of Lost Souls 32. Sing Sinner Sing 33. Affairs of a Gentleman 34. Ruggles of Red Gap 35. Yellow Dust 36, many others.

Hyams, Peter (1943–). American director.
T. R. Baskin (w, p only) 71. The Rolling Man (TV) 72. *Goodnight My Love* (TV) 73. Busting (& w) 74. Our Time (& w) 74. Peeper 76. Telefon (co-w only) 77. Capricorn One (& w) 78. Hanover Street (& w) 79. The Hunter (& w) 80. Outland (& w) 81. The Star Chamber 83. 2010 84. Running Scared 86.

Hyde-White, Wilfrid (1903–). Impeccably British character actor of stage and screen, mainly in comedy roles.
Murder by Rope 37. *The Third Man* 49. The Story of Gilbert and Sullivan 54. See How They Run 55. The Adventures of Quentin Durward 56. *North-West Frontier* 59. Carry On Nurse 59. Two-Way Stretch 61. *My Fair Lady* 64. John Goldfarb Please Come Home 64. You Must Be Joking 65. Ten Little Indians 65. The Liquidator 65. Our Man in Marrakesh 66. Chamber of Horrors 66. Skullduggery 69. Gaily Gaily 69. Fragment of Fear 70. A Brand New Life (TV) 73. The Great Houdinis (TV) 76. The Cat and the Canary 78. The Rebels (TV) 79. In God We Trust 80. Oh God Book Two 80. Damien: Leper Priest (TV) 80. The Toy 82, etc.
TV series: *The Associates* 79.

Hyer, Martha (1929–). American light leading lady of the fifties, in mainly routine films.

The Locket 46. The Woman on the Beach 47. The Velvet Touch 48. The Clay Pigeon 49. The Lawless 50. Salt Lake Raiders 50. Abbott and Costello Go to Mars 52. So Big 53. Riders to the Stars 54. Sabrina 54. Francis in the Navy 55. Red Sundown 56. Battle Hymn 57. Mister Cory 57. My Man Godfrey 57. Paris Holiday 58. Houseboat 58. Some Came Running 59. The Best of Everything 59. Ice Palace 60. The Last Time I Saw Archie 61. A Girl Named Tamiko 62. Wives and Lovers 63. The Carpetbaggers 64. The First Men in the Moon 64. The Sons of Katie Elder 65. The Chase 66. The Happening 67. Massacre at Fort Grant 68. Crossplot 69. Once You Kiss a Stranger 70, many others.

Hyland, Diana (1936–1977) (Diana Gentner). American stage and TV actress. At her death she had just begun to star in the TV series *Eight is Enough*.
One Man's Way 64. The Chase 66. The Boy in the Plastic Bubble (TV) 76.

Hylands, Scott (–). American leading man.
Daddy's Gone A Hunting 68. Fools 70. Earth II (TV) 71. Earthquake 74. Bittersweet Love 76. The Boys in Company C 77. With This Ring (TV) 78.

Hylton, Jack (1892–1965). British bandleader who appeared in two films: *She Shall Have Music* 35 and *Band Wagon* 40. Later impresario.

Hylton, Jane (1926–1979). British actress, in films after 1945.
When the Bough Breaks 47. Here Come the Huggetts 49. *It Started in Paradise* 52. The Weak and the Wicked 53. House of Mystery 59, many others.

Hylton, Richard (1921–1962). American actor with stage experience.
Lost Boundaries 48. The Secret of Convict Lake 51. Fixed Bayonets 51. The Pride of St Louis 52, etc.

Hyman, Eliot (1905–1980). American entrepreneur who made a fortune from buying up Hollywood libraries for sale to television, notably Monogram and Warner. Formed Seven Arts, film financers and distributors.

Hyman, Kenneth (1928–). American executive producer; formerly with Allied Artists and Seven Arts in Britain, now independent. Son of Eliot Hyman.
The Hound of the Baskervilles 59. The Roman Spring of Mrs Stone 61. Gigot 62. The Small World of Sammy Lee 63. The Hill 65. The Dirty Dozen 66, etc.

Hymer, Warren (1906–1948). American character actor with stage experience; usually seen as dim-witted gangster.
Up the River 30. Charlie Chan Carries On 31. Twenty Thousand Years in Sing Sing 32. Kid Millions 35. San Francisco 36. Tainted Money 37. Destry Rides Again 39. Meet John Doe 41. Baby Face Morgan 42. Joe Palooka Champ 46, many others.

hypnosis on the screen has mainly been a basis for melodrama. *Svengali* was its most demonic exponent, but others who followed in his footsteps were Jacques Bergerac in *The Hypnotic Eye*, Boris Karloff in *The Climax*, Bela Lugosi in *Dracula*, Charles Gray in *The Devil Rides Out*, Erich Von Stroheim in *The Mask of Diljon*, Christopher Lee in *The Face of Fu Manchu*, Orson Welles in *Black Magic*, and Jose Ferrer in *Whirlpool* (in which, immediately after major surgery, he hypnotized himself into leaving his bed and committing a murder). In *Fear in the Night* and its remake *Nightmare*, De Forrest Kelley and Kevin McCarthy were hypnotized into becoming murderers. Comic uses are legion, the perpetrators including Lugosi in *Abbott and Costello Meet Frankenstein*, Karloff in *The Secret Life of Walter Mitty*, Gale Sondergaard in *Road to Rio*, the cast of *How to be Very Very Popular*, Yves Montand in *On a Clear Day You Can See Forever*, Alan Badel in *Will Any Gentleman*, Mildred Natwick in *The Court Jester*, and Pat Collins in *Divorce American Style*. The chief serious study of the subject has been *Freud*, though one might also count *The Search for Bridey Murphy*.

Hyson, Dorothy (1915–). British leading lady of the thirties, with stage experience (mainly in Aldwych farces).
Soldiers of the King 33. The Ghoul 33. Turkey Time 33. Sing As We Go 34. A Cup of Kindness 34. Spare a Copper 40, etc.

Hytten, Olaf (1888–1955). Scottish character actor in American films.
It Is The Law 24. The Salvation Hunters 27. Daughter of The Dragon 31. Berkeley Square 33. Becky Sharp 35. The Good Earth 37. The Adventures of Robin Hood 38. Our Neighbours The Carters 40. The Black Swan 42. The Lodger 44. Three Strangers 46. Perils of The Jungle 53, etc.

Answers

heroines and heroes

1 *The Rains Came* □ Myrna Loy □ Tyrone Power □ 2 *Homecoming* □ Lana Turner □ Clark Gable □ 3 *All This and Heaven Too* □ Bette Davis □ Charles Boyer □ 4 *Brief Encounter* □ Celia Johnson □ Trevor Howard □ 5 *Dark Victory* □ Bette Davis □ George Brent □ 6 *The Man Who Came to Dinner* □ Bette Davis □ Richard Travis □ 7 *The Lost Weekend* □ Jane Wyman □ Ray Milland □ 8 *Major Barbara* □ Wendy Hiller □ Rex Harrison □ 9 *The Shop Around the Corner* □ Margaret Sullavan □ James Stewart □ 10 *Marty* □ Betsy Blair □ Ernest Borgnine □ 11 *Casablanca* □ Ingrid Bergman □ Humphrey Bogart □ 12 *Arsenic and Old Lace* □ Priscilla Lane □ Cary Grant □ 13 *The Apartment* □ Shirley MacLaine □ Jack Lemmon □ 14 *The Miracle of Morgan's Creek* □ Betty Hutton □ Eddie Bracken □ 15 *On the Waterfront* □ Eva Marie Saint □ Marlon Brando □ 16 *Picnic* □ Kim Novak □ William Holden □ 17 *The Quiet Man* □ Maureen O'Hara □ John Wayne □ 18 *Singin' in the Rain* □ Debbie Reynolds □ Gene Kelly □ 19 *The Maltese Falcon* □ Mary Astor □ Humphrey Bogart □ 20 *To Have and Have Not* □ Lauren Bacall □ Humphrey Bogart □ 21 *A Star Is Born* □ Judy Garland □ James Mason □ 22 *Spellbound* □ Ingrid Bergman □ Gregory Peck □ 23 *Guess Who's Coming to Dinner* □ Katharine Houghton □ Sidney Poitier □ 24 *Guys and Dolls* □ Jean Simmons □ Marlon Brando □ 25 *The Graduate* □ Katharine Ross □ Dustin Hoffman □ 26 *Duel in the Sun* □ Jennifer Jones □ Gregory Peck □ 27 *Double Indemnity* □ Barbara Stanwyck □ Fred MacMurray □ 28 *Cat People* □ Simone Simon □ Kent Smith □ 29 *Breakfast at Tiffany's* □ Audrey Hepburn □ George Peppard □ 30 *An American in Paris* □ Leslie Caron □ Gene Kelly □

Alfred Hitchcock

1 *The Wrong Man* □ 2 *Strangers on a Train* □ 3 *Young and Innocent* (US: *The Girl Was Young*) □ 4 *The 39 Steps* □ 5 *The Pleasure Garden* □ 6 *The Lodger* □ 7 *Murder* □ 8 *Psycho* □ 9 *Rope* □ *Lifeboat* □ 10 *Foreign Correspondent* □ 11 *The Secret Agent* □ 12 *Sabotage* (US: *A Woman Alone*) □ 13 *The Manxman* □ 14 *Saboteur* □ 15 *Blackmail* □ 16 *The Man Who Knew Too Much* (1934) □ 17 *North by Northwest* □ 18 *Lifeboat* □ 19 *Spellbound* □ 20 *Under Capricorn* □

horror

1 The line is inseparable from the actor: Bela Lugosi in the 1930 version of *Dracula* □
2 Spoken by the reporter in *The Thing from Another World* (1952), when the scientists have explained what kind of 'thing' they are dealing with □
3 A lively toast by Ernest Thesiger as Dr Praetorius, the evil genius of *Bride of Frankenstein* (1935) □
4 Mr Lugosi again, this time spoofing himself in *Abbott and Costello meet Frankenstein* (1948). □ As he speaks he is benignly patting the head of Costello, for whom he sees a use in the reactivation of the Frankenstein monster.
5 The trouble with this climax to *The Black Cat* (1934) is that one can hardly depict the realization of the threat. The speaker is Lugosi, the victim Boris Karloff. □ As usual in films called *The Black Cat*, the cat has nothing to do with the story.
6 The funniest line in that otherwise disappointing spoof *The Fearless Vampire Killers* (or *Dance of the Vampires*) (1968). □ Alfie Bass is a Jewish vampire, so naturally scoffs at the crucifix held out to ward him off.
7 Max Adrian as the impeccable bloodsucker in *Dr Terror's House of Horrors* (1967), expressing regret for despatching his young rival □
8 Ernest Thesiger in *The Old Dark House* (1932) presiding over a very miserable supper party. □ His other characteristic line in the same film was 'Have some gin: it's my only weakness', and this was carried over intact into *Bride of Frankenstein* three years later.
9 Why such a lever should exist in the laboratory of *Bride of Frankenstein* (1935) was never explained, but it made a fine dramatic climax. The speaker was Ernest Thesiger, but fans will recall that he was insufficiently persuasive □
10 Not *House of Wax* but *House of Frankenstein* (1944) which was originally

due to be called *Chamber of Horrors*. The owner of the travelling freak show was George Zucco, despatched in the first reel by J. Carrol Naish □

11 Bela 'Dracula' Lugosi again. □ At the time he was more interested in the blood oozing from a prick in his victim's finger.

12 Another line carried over from one film to another. In *The Mummy* (1932) Bramwell Fletcher stammers it out when asked what has happened to the mummy, which has just driven him half-mad by coming to life. □ The same director, Karl Freund, later used it in *Mad Love* (1935), applied by a passer-by to a wax figure which apparently becomes mobile but has actually been replaced by the heroine.

13 In the first story in *Dead of Night* (1945), a convalescent sees from a window a hearse, the driver of which (Miles Malleson) makes this chilling observation. Leaving hospital, he is about to board a bus when the conductor makes the same remark. He waves it on, and sees it crash over an embankment □

14 From the sadder days of the horror film: Whit Bissell speaks to his creation in *Teenage Frankenstein* (1957) □

15 'May become a wolf when the wolf bane blooms' declaimed with perfect emphasis by Maria Ouspenskaya in *The Wolf Man* (1941) □

16 Pretty strong stuff for 1932: Leslie Banks in *The Most Dangerous Game* □

houses

1 *House of Dracula* □ 2 *A House Is Not a Home* □ 3 *The House of Seven Hawks* □ (the original novel was called *The House of Seven Flies*) 4 *House on Haunted Hill* □ 5 *The House on Greenapple Road* (pilot series for *Dan August*) □ 6 *House of Wax* □ 7 *The House on 92nd Street* □ 8 *House of Strangers* □ 9 *House of Bamboo* □ 10 *House of Cards* □

I

I Am a Camera: see *Cabaret.*

I Am a Fugitive from a Chain Gang (US 1932). Arguably the first American social melodrama to urge actual reforms; also the first of Warner's 'prestige' films of the thirties. Paul Muni played the man forced against his will into a life of crime. Written by Sheridan Gibney and Brown Holmes; directed by Mervyn Le Roy.

I, Claudius (GB 1937). Alexander Korda's ambitious epic of ancient Rome, based on Robert Graves' highly readable book, was never finished: star Merle Oberon was injured in a car crash and the production, which had presented Korda with many problems, was abandoned after two or three reels were in the can. Nearly thirty years later, in 1965, a television film, *The Epic That Never Was*, pieced the story together and made one wish that more had been shot, if only for the sake of Georges Perinal's photography and the performances of Charles Laughton and Emlyn Williams. Director Josef Von Sternberg seemed less at home with the material. A TV serial starring Derek Jacobi followed in 1976.

I Love a Mystery. This American radio programme began in 1939; its title referred to the creator (Carleton Morse), the audience, and the three adventurers who form a detective agency. During the forties the title was used to headline a series of second features from Columbia, weird mysteries in a similar vein to Universal's *Inner Sanctum*. They now had only two heroes (Jim Bannon, Barton Yarborough) and were *I Love a Mystery* 45, *The Devil's Mask* 46, *The Unknown* 46. In 1968 Universal made a very dim TV pilot starring Les Crane, David Hartman and Hagen Beggs.

I Married a Witch (US 1942). Generally considered René Clair's best American film, this gay fantasy starred Fredric March and Veronica Lake, with Cecil Kellaway as a most delightful old sorcerer. It directly inspired the more recent TV series *Bewitched*, *I Dream of Jeannie* and *The Girl With Something Extra*.

Ibbetson, Arthur (1922–). British cinematographer.
The Horse's Mouth 58. The Angry Silence 59. The League of Gentlemen 60. *Tunes of Glory* 61. Whistle Down the Wind 61. The Inspector 62. Nine Hours to Rama 63. I Could Go On Singing 63. The Chalk Garden 64. Sky West and Crooked 65. A Countess from Hong Kong 66. Inspector Clouseau 68. Where Eagles Dare 68. The Walking Stick 69. Anne of the Thousand Days 70. The Railway Children 70. Willie Wonka and the Chocolate Factory 71. A Doll's House 73. Frankenstein: the True Story (TV) 73. 11 Harrowhouse 74. It Shouldn't Happen to a Vet 76. A Little Night Music 77. The Medusa Touch 77. The Prisoner of Zenda 79. Hopscotch 80. Little Lord Fauntleroy (TV) 80. Witness for the Prosecution 83. Master of the Game (TV) 83. The Bounty 84. Santa Claus 84.

Ibert, Jacques (1890–1962). French composer.
The Italian Straw Hat 28. Don Quixote 34. Golgotha 35. La Charrette Fantôme 38. Panique 47. Macbeth 48. Invitation to the Dance 56, etc.

Ibsen, Henrik (1828–1906). Norwegian dramatist who against great opposition brought social problems to the stage. Works filmed include *A Doll's House*, *An Enemy of the People*.

Ichikawa, Kon (1915–). Distinguished Japanese director.
The Heart 54. The Punishment Room 55. *The Burmese Harp* 55. Odd Obsessions 58. *Fires on the Plain* 59. The Sin 61. An Actor's Revenge 63. *Alone on the Pacific* 66.
To Love Again 71. The Wanderers 73. I Am a Cat 75. The Inugami Family 76. Matababi 77. Queen Bee 78. The Devil's Island 78. The Phoenix 79. Actress 87, etc.

Idiot's Delight (US 1939). Robert Sherwood's play marked Broadway's earliest reaction to the war clouds looming over Europe. This hasty film version, with Clark Gable as the eager hoofer and Norma Shearer as the fake duchess, managed to be as false as its continental backcloths, despite Clarence Brown's direction, and probably made the danger seem remote instead of imminent to many Americans. In the early sixties a short lived TV series called *Harry's Girls* borrowed the central character if little else.

If . . . (GB 1967). An agreeably anarchic though overlong and formless attack on the British public school system, written by David Sherwin and directed by Lindsay Anderson. Much of it seemed as meaningless as its random alternation between colour and monochrome, but its box office success (partly due to some full frontal nudity) was undoubted and led to a flurry of surrealist movies with much less in the way of observation to commend them.

If I Had a Million (US 1933). Probably the first short story compendium; this one had the connecting link of a sudden windfall to a variety of people. The most quoted episode (each had a different director) is that in which Charles Laughton, as a down-trodden clerk, blows a raspberry to his boss.

If I Were King. Justin McCarthy's play, a historical adventure about François Villon, was filmed in 1920 with William Farnum and in 1938 with Ronald Colman. On it was based Rudolf Friml's operetta *The Vagabond King*, filmed in 1930 with Dennis King and Jeanette Macdonald, and in 1955 with Oreste Kirkop and Kathryn Grayson.

If Winter Comes. A. S. M. Hutchinson's sentimental romance about the effect of malicious gossip in a village community was first filmed in 1923 with Percy Marmont and Ann Forrest, directed by Harry Millarde. In 1947 MGM unconvincingly up-dated it for Walter Pidgeon and Deborah Kerr, with direction by Victor Saville.

Ifield, Frank (1936–). British-born ballad singer who grew up in Australia.
Only film: *Up Jumped a Swagman* 65.

Ihnat, Steve (1934–1972). Czech-born general purpose actor in Hollywood, mostly in TV.
□The Chase 66. Countdown 67. The Hour of the Gun 67. Kona Coast 68. Madigan 69. Fuzz 72. *The Honkers* (wd only) 72, etc.

Ihnen, Wiard (1897–1979). American production designer.
Blonde Venus 32. Madam Butterfly 32. Duck Soup 33. Cradle Song 33. The Trumpet Blows 34. Becky Sharp 35. Go West Young Man 36. Hollywood Cavalcade 39. Jane Eyre 44. Wilson 44. Along Came Jones 45. Blood on the Sun 45. The Time of Your Life 48. I the Jury 53, etc.

Iles, Francis (1893–1970). British crime novelist who also wrote as Anthony Berkeley. *Before the Fact* formed the basis for Hitchcock's *Suspicion*; *Malice Aforethought* was filmed for television with Hywel Bennett.

Illing, Peter (1899–1966). German-born character actor, in British films since the forties.
The End of the River 46. Eureka Stockade 48. I'll Get You for This 51. The Young Lovers 54. Zarak 56. Whirlpool 59. Sands of the Desert 60. The Twenty-fifth Hour 66, many others.

I'm All Right Jack (GB 1959). An ironic comedy on the serious subject of labour relations, with Peter Sellers as the communist shop steward and Ian Carmichael as the innocent who precipitates a strike. The Boulting Brothers produced and directed from an enjoyable if uneven script by themselves and Frank Harvey based on Alan Hackney's novel *Private Life*.

Image, Jean (1911–). French animator, best known abroad for his cartoon feature *Johnny Lionheart (Jeannot L'Intrépide)* 50.

Imi, Tony (1937–). British cinematographer.
The Raging Moon 69. Dulcima 70. The Slipper and the Rose 76. International Velvet 78. Brass Target 78. The Sea Wolves 80. Inside the Third Reich (TV) 82. Little Gloria . . . Happy at Last (TV) 82. Night Crossing 82. Princess Daisy (TV) 83. Sakharov (TV) 84. A Christmas Carol (TV) 84. Reunion at Fairborough (TV) 85. Oceans of Fire 85. Queenie (TV) 87.

Imitation of Life. Fannie Hurst's romantic novel, with its naïve but moving early depiction of a race problem (a black girl tries to pass for white), was filmed in 1934 with Claudette Colbert, Warren William and Louise Beavers; director John M. Stahl. In 1959 it was glossily refashioned for Lana Turner, John Gavin and Juanita Moore; directed by Douglas Sirk, photography by Russell Metty.

? **impersonations**
The following people all existed. For what work were they best known, and who portrayed them in what films?

1 Violette Szabo
2 Tom Gaddis
3 Paris Singer
4 Lady Gregory
5 Mrs Leslie Carter
6 W. C. Handy
7 Frank B. Gilbreth
8 Pierre Curie
9 Alvin York
10 Morey Bernstein
11 Mary Shelley
12 James Doolittle
13 Odette Churchill
14 Barnes Wallis
15 Ernie Pyle
16 Polly Adler
17 Sol Hurok
18 William Friese-Greene
19 Paul Ehrlich
20 Marjorie Laurence

impresarios presented on film include Sol Hurok, by David Wayne in *Tonight We Sing*; Rupert D'Oyly Carte, by Peter Finch in *The Story of Gilbert and Sullivan*; Walter de Frece, by Laurence Harvey in *After the Ball*; David Belasco, by Claude Rains in *Lady With Red Hair*; Lew Dockstatter, by John Alexander in *The Jolson Story*; Noel Coward by Daniel Massey, and André Charlot by Alan Oppenheimer, in *Star!*; and Florenz Ziegfeld, by William Powell in *The Great Ziegfeld* and by Walter Pidgeon in *Funny Girl*. Of fictional impresarios, the most memorable were those played by John Barrymore in *Maytime* and Anton Walbrook in *The Red Shoes*.

impressionism. Generally understood to mean contriving an effect or making a point by building up a sequence from short disconnected shots or scenes.

in-jokes were especially frequent when Hollywood was a parochial society, and many must have been so private as to escape the general eye. The following, however, seem reasonably typical. *The Black Cat* (34): Boris Karloff as a devil worshipper has to be heard reciting an invocation to Satan, which to please the Hays Code is made up of such Latin phrases as 'cave canem' (beware of the dog), 'cum grano salis' (with a grain of salt), 'in vino veritas' (in wine is truth) and 'reductio ad absurdum est' (it is shown to be impossible). *Bride of Frankenstein*: Ernest Thesiger repeats a line ('It's my only weakness') from his previous role for the same director in *The Old Dark House*. *Mad Love*: a statue apparently comes to life, and a frightened onlooker says 'It went for a little walk', which is a line used of the monster in *The Mummy*, the same director's previous film. *His Girl Friday*: Cary Grant refers to the execution of a fellow named Archie Leach, which is Grant's own real name. *Hellzapoppin*: Olsen and Johnson see a sledge on a film set and remark 'I thought they burned that', a reference to Rosebud in *Citizen Kane*. *Song of the Thin Man*: William Powell finds a razor blade and remarks 'Somerset Maugham has been here', a reference to the author's current best-seller *The Razor's Edge*. *The Maltese Falcon* and *In This Our Life*: Walter Huston plays uncredited bit parts under his son John's direction. (One of innumerable similar instances.) *On the Town*: Frank Sinatra is subjected to good-natured joshing about his real-life marriage to Ava Gardner. *Arise My Love*: Ray Milland, asked whether he was a test pilot, replies 'No, that was Clark Gable', referring to the recently released *Test Pilot*. *Northern Pursuit*: Errol Flynn, then in the middle of a real-life rape case, tells the heroine she is the only girl he has ever loved, then looks at the audience and says: 'What am I saying?' *How to Marry a Millionaire*: Lauren Bacall, then married to Humphrey Bogart, says in conversation 'That old man in *The African Queen*, I'm crazy about him'. *The Big Store*: Groucho tells the audience: 'This scene should have been in Technicolor but Mr Mayer said it was too expensive'. (Again, many similar instances exist, notably in the *Road* films, which are full of studio gags such as 'Paramount will protect us 'cause we're signed for five more years'.) *Another Dawn*: in the thirties, whenever a cinema canopy was shown, it usually advertised a non-existent film under this title; but in 1938 Warners were stuck for a title for their new Errol Flynn film, so they irrelevantly and cynically called it *Another Dawn*. *Some Like It Hot*: Tony Curtis has to impersonate a millionaire and as part of the disguise gives a devastatingly accurate impression of Cary Grant's voice, only to be told scathingly by Jack Lemmon 'Nobody talks like that!' In the same movie, and also in *Singin' in the Rain*, a gangster tosses a coin in imitation of George Raft in *Scarface*. *The VIPs*: asked for her home phone number, Elizabeth Taylor gives 'Grosvenor 7060', which is the number of

MGM's London office. *Star Spangled Rhythm*: the harassed and excitable producer played by Walter Abel is named G. B. de Soto, in imitation of B. G. de Sylva, then a Paramount producer. *The Wings of Eagles*: the film director, John Dodge, is played by Ward Bond as an imitation of John Ford, who directed *The Wings of Eagles*. *Irma La Douce*: the pimps' union is called the Mecs' Paris Protective Association, or MPPA, which also stands for Motion Picture Producers Association, an organization which gave director Billy Wilder some trouble. *Caprice*: heroine Doris Day goes to the movies and sees a Doris Day movie. *One Two Three*: James Cagney threatens a girl with a grapefruit, mimicking his own action thirty years before in *Public Enemy*: he also steals from *Little Caesar* the line 'Mother of mercy, is this the end of Rico?' *The Entertainer*: reference is made to Sergeant Ossie Morris; the film was photographed by Ossie Morris. *Finian's Rainbow*: Fred Astaire has a short speech which consists, with different emphasis, of the words of one of his old songs. *The House that Dripped Blood*: Geoffrey Bayldon as a mad scientist is made up to look like Ernest Thesiger in *Bride of Frankenstein*. *How to Marry a Millionaire*: Betty Grable fails to recognize a Harry James recording (she was married to him at the time). *For The First Time*: there is reference to a convict named Cocozza, which happens to be star Mario Lanza's real name. *Connecting Rooms*: Bette Davis passes a poster mentioning stage star Margo(t) Channing, the name of the character she played in *All About Eve*. (The name is also used for one of the unseen characters in *Sleuth*.) *Pete 'n' Tillie*: Walter Matthau takes his girl to a cinema showing *Lonely Are the Brave*, one of his own earlier films. *Aaron Slick From Punkin Crick*: a waiter in a café scene calls 'Give that Perlberg-Seaton order special attention'. (Perlberg and Seaton produced and directed the film.) *Road to Utopia*: Bob Hope says Bing Crosby's voice is 'just right for selling cheese', a reference to Bing's then-current radio show, *Kraft Music Hall*. *Godfather II*: Troy Donahue plays a character called Merle Johnson, which is his own real name. *Dames*: Dick Powell is told 'Miss Warren, Miss Dubin and Miss Kelly are outside', a reference to song writers Al Dubin and Harry Warren and dress designer Orry-Kelly. *Strange Boarders*: Tom Walls sees a picture of Disraeli and says 'Good old George, what a make-up', a reference to George Arliss' penchant for playing historical characters. *What's New Pussycat*: a stranger who bumps into Peter O'Toole in a night club turns out to be Richard Burton, who asks 'Don't you know me from someplace?' *West of the Divide*: in this 1934 quickie western John Wayne assumes the identity of a bandit whose image (i.e. his own) he sees on a wanted poster. The poster appeared in two other Wayne films that year. *A Chump at Oxford*: Laurel and Hardy foil a raid on the Finlayson National Bank, a clear reference to their favourite supporting player, James of that ilk. *The Lady in the Lake*: Crystal Kingsley, the character who never appears because she is dead, is listed as being played by Ellay Mort ('elle est morte'). *Gold Diggers of 1933*: a songwriter is told, 'Dubin and Warren are out! You're writing the score!' (Dubin and Warren wrote the score.) *Weekend at the Waldorf*: Walter Pidgeon imitates John Barrymore and Ginger Rogers says, 'Why, that's right out of *Grand Hotel*!' (from which *Weekend at the Waldorf* was adapted). *Trent's Last Case*: Orson Welles, who had played Othello in London a year previously, says: 'I saw *Othello* in London last year, but the fellow was not very good.' *The Howling*: most of the characters bear the names of horror film directors. *Quo Vadis*: Peter Ustinov as Nero says as he dies 'Is this the end of Nero?', echoing Edward G. Robinson's line at the end of *Little Caesar*, 'Is this the end of Rico?'

In the Heat of the Night (US 1967; AA). Basically a rather unconvincing murder mystery set in a sweltering small town in the deep south, this screenplay by Sterling Silliphant (AA) benefited from fine colour photography by Haskell Wexler and splendid acting from Rod Steiger (AA) and Sidney Poitier, whose conflict (as lazy sheriff and arrogant Philadelphia detective) was intensified by race bitterness. Norman Jewison produced and directed. Two 'sequels' starring Poitier, *They Call Me Mister Tibbs* and *The Organization*, were disappointing.

In Which We Serve (GB 1942). The first really important film about naval aspects of World War II, this was very much a Noel Coward enterprise. He surprised everyone at the time not only by producing, co-directing, and writing the script and music, but by his serious and effective performance as the captain of a doomed destroyer. Highly effective propaganda in Britain, the film was given a special Academy Award. Cast included Bernard Miles, John Mills, Richard Attenborough and Celia Johnson.

Ince, Ralph (1882–1937). American leading man of the twenties who rather oddly ended his career in Britain directing quota quickies.
AS ACTOR: The Land of Opportunity 20. The Sea Wolf 25. Bigger than Barnum's 26. Wall Street 29. Little Caesar 30. The Big Gamble 31. The Hatchet Man 32. The Tenderfoot 32. Havana Widows 33, etc.
AS DIRECTOR: A Man's Home 21. Homeward Bound 23. A Moral Sinner 24. Smooth as Satin 25. Bigger than Barnum's 26. South Sea Love 28. Lucky Devils 33. What's in a Name? 34. Murder at Monte Carlo 34. Blue Smoke 35. It's You I Want 35. Hail and Farewell 36. The Vulture 36. The Man Who Made Diamonds 37, many others.

Ince, Thomas (1882–1924). American director, a contemporary of D. W. Griffith and some say an equal innovator; he certainly systematized production methods. Best remembered now for *Custer's Last Fight* 12. *Civilization* 15. *Human Wreckage* 23.

incest has scarcely been fashionable film fare, though the theatrical acceptance of it goes back to *Oedipus Rex* (filmed in 1969) and one supposes *The Bible* (filmed in 1966) which fails to explain how else Adam and Eve's two sons propagated the species. It has been implied in a handful of American films from *Scarface* to *Toys in the Attic*, and more or less clearly stated in *Mourning Becomes Electra, A View from the Bridge* and *Chinatown.* Its full flowering came with the British *Country Dance*, but as expected the French had beaten us to it with *Souffle au Coeur*, though it became more explicit in *La Luna. My Lover My Son* is another recent example.

Indecent Exposure, by David McClintick. This 1982 book ironically recapitulated the events leading up to the indictment of David Begelman, head of Columbia Pictures, for fraud and misappropriation. The book was chiefly an indictment of Hollywood, for Cliff Robertson, the actor who revealed the affair, seemed to be prevented from working, while those most culpable went from strength to strength within the industry.

independent producer. One not employed by a studio or distributor, who raises his own finance and makes his own deals. For many years independent productions tended to lack big studio expertise, and Tallulah Bankhead is said to have remarked, after viewing one of them, 'I don't see what that producer has got to be so independent about.' Since the breakup of the big studios in the fifties, however, most productions have been 'independent', and as Billy Wilder remarked, 'You now spend eighty per cent of your time making deals and only twenty per cent making pictures.'

India has provided the setting for English-speaking films mainly of the military kind: *King of the Khyber Rifles, The Drum, Lives of a Bengal Lancer, Gunga Din, Soldiers Three, The Charge of the Light Brigade* (1936 version), *Bengal Brigade*, and *Conduct Unbecoming.* Civilian interests were the concern of *They Met in Bombay, The Rains Came, Elephant Boy, Bhowani Junction, Monsoon, The River Song of India, Calcutta, Thunder in the East, Northwest Frontier, Nine Hours to Rama* and *The Guru.* Of native Indian films only a few have percolated to western cinemas, mostly directed by Mehboob, Satyajit Ray, or James Ivory.
In the eighties there was a sudden flowering of interest in the last days of the Raj, especially on television: thus *The Jewel in the Crown, The Far Pavilions, Mountbatten the Last Viceroy*, and in the cinema *Heat and Dust* and *A Passage to India.*

Indians: *see Red Indians.*

the industry

¶ Some moments of horse sense:

Every time you pick up the trades you seem to find there's some new man sitting in the chair at one of the studios. This game of musical chairs that the majors play with studio heads is ridiculous.—*Mike Frankovich*

I am frequently told that my films don't make money. Since I have averaged one film a year for thirty years—some of them expensive ones—I can only conclude that somebody is making money.—*Joseph Losey*

Isn't it funny
That films never seem to make money
When everyone in the racket
Obviously makes a packet?—*Basil Boothroyd*

The infant industry has taken the ribbons from her hair. She has put away some of her bright toys—she is growing up. She may have a child one day, and the child's name may be Television, but that's another story.—*Edmund Goulding (1929)*

Inescort, Frieda (1900–1976) (Frieda Wightman). Scottish-born actress of well bred roles, once secretary to Lady Astor; on stage from 1922. Went to Hollywood to begin film career.
If You Could Only Cook 35. Call it a Day 37. Beauty for the Asking 38. Woman Doctor 39. Pride and Prejudice 40. The Amazing Mrs Holliday 43. The Return of the Vampire 43. The Judge Steps Out 47. Foxfire 55. The Crowded Sky 60, etc.

The Informer (US 1935). Despite, or perhaps because of, its murky expressionist studio look, this film of Liam O'Flaherty's novel about Dublin during the troubles was able to turn melodrama into something approaching a tragedy. It won Academy Awards for director John Ford, Max Steiner's music, Dudley Nichols' script, and Victor McLaglen's performance as the half-witted brute who betrays his friend for a handful of silver. Joseph H. August's photography was also notable. There was a previous British silent version in 1928, starring Lars Hanson; and in 1968 Jules Dassin made a black variation called *Uptight.*

Inge, William (1913–1973). American playwright, most of whose work has been translated to the screen.
Come Back Little Sheba 52. Picnic 56. Bus Stop 56. The Dark at the Top of the Stairs 60. Splendor in the Grass (w) 61. The Stripper 63. Good Luck Miss Wyckoff 79, etc.

Ingels, Marty (1936–). American character comedian.
Ladies' Man 60. Armored Command 61. The Horizontal Lieutenant 62. Wild and Wonderful 64. The Busy Body 67. For Singles Only 68, etc.
TV series: *I'm Dickens He's Fenster* 62.

Ingham, Barrie (1934–). British light leading man and general purpose actor.
Tiara Tahiti 62. Invasion 66. Dr Who and the Daleks 66. A Challenge for Robin Hood (title role) 68, etc.

Ingram, Rex (1892–1950) (Reginald Hitchcock). Irishman who went to Hollywood and became first an actor and screenwriter, then a noted director of silent spectaculars.
Biography 1980: *Rex Ingram* by Liam O'Leary.
AS ACTOR: The Great Problem 16. Reward of the Faithless 17. Under Crimson Skies 19. Trifling Women 22, etc.
AS DIRECTOR: *The Four Horsemen of the Apocalypse* 21. The Conquering Power 21. *The Prisoner of Zenda* 22. Where the Pavement Ends 23. *Scaramouche* 23. The Arab 24. *Mare Nostrum* 26. The Magician 26. The Garden of Allah 27. Baroud 31. Love in Morocco 33, etc.

Ingram, Rex (1895–1969). Impressive black actor, in films from 1929: former doctor.
□Hearts in Dixie 29. The Sign of the Cross 32. King Kong 33. The Emperor Jones 33. Harlem After Midnight 34. Captain Blood 35. *The Green Pastures* (as De Lawd) 36. *Huckleberry Finn* 39. *The Thief of Baghdad* 40. The Talk of the Town 42. Sahara 43. Cabin in the Sky 43. Fired Wife 43. Dark Waters 44. A Thousand and One Nights 45. Moonrise 48. King Solomon's Mines 50. Tarzan's Hidden Jungle 55. The Ten Commandments 56. Congo Crossing 56. Hell on Devil's Island 57. God's Little Acre 58. Anna Lucasta 59. Escort West 59. Watusi 59. Desire in the Dust 60. Elmer Gantry 60. Your Cheating Heart 64. Hurry Sundown 67. Journey to Shiloh 67.

Ingster, Boris (c. 1913–). American writer-director.
The Last Days of Pompeii (co-w) 35. Happy Landing (w) 38. Stranger on the Third Floor (d) 40. Paris Underground (w) 45. The Judge Steps Out (wd) 49. Forgery (d) 50. Something for the Birds (co-w) 52, etc.

Inherit the Wind (US 1960). Although essentially a filmed play, this is probably the most satisfactory cinematic example of Stanley Kramer's work as a producer-director. Based on Jerome Laurence and Robert E. Lee's dramatization of the Scopes' 'monkey trial' of the twenties, when a schoolmaster in a God-fearing community was put in the dock for teaching evolution, the film benefits enormously from the performances of Spencer Tracy and Fredric March as defence and prosecution counsels (in real life Clarence Darrow and William Jennings Bryan). An absorbing entertainment, cleanly photographed by Ernest Laszlo.

The Inn of the Sixth Happiness (GB 1958). A glamorized but generally successful version of the life of Gladys Aylward, an indomitable British missionary to China in the thirties. Ingrid Bergman, theoretically miscast, gave a commanding star performance; Robert Donat in his last film was most moving as a mandarin converted to Christianity. Directed by Mark Robson, photographed by Frederick Young, this was hailed as a reversion to 'family entertainment' after what seemed at the time a period of over-sophistication.

Inner Sanctum. A series of second features made by Universal in the early forties, starring Lon Chaney Jnr and offering apparently supernatural phenomena which are explained away in the last reel. Based on a radio series; introduced for no very clear reason by a spiel from a misshapen head within a crystal ball on a boardroom table! Titles were *Calling Dr Death, Weird Woman, Pillow of Death, Dead Man's Eyes, The Frozen Ghost, Strange Confession.* A 1953 TV series starred Paul McGrath.

insanity in the cinema has usually been of the criminal kind: Robert Montgomery (and Albert Finney) in *Night Must Fall*, Keir Dullea in *Bunny Lake Is Missing*, Bette Davis in *Whatever Happened to Baby Jane?* and *The Nanny*, Franchot Tone in *Phantom Lady*, George Brent in *The Spiral Staircase*, Joseph Cotten in *Shadow of a Doubt*, Edward G. Robinson in *The Sea Wolf*, Robert Ryan in *Beware My Lovely*, Ivan Kirov in *Spectre of the Rose*, Robert Mitchum in *Night of the Hunter*, Douglass Montgomery in *The Cat and the Canary*, Anthony Perkins in *Psycho*, Hywel Bennett in *Twisted Nerve*, Oliver Reed in *Paranoiac*, Brember Wills in *The Old Dark House* and hundreds of others. Indeed, most screen villains have been, if not psychopathic, at least subject to an *idée fixé*: and many a tortured hero has had a mad wife in the attic. Insanity has however been played quite frequently for comedy, notably in *Harvey, Miss Tatlock's Millions, The Criminal Life of Archibaldo de la Cruz* and *Drôle de Drame.* Serious studies of insanity and its effects are on the increase, not only through fictitious situations as shown in *A Bill of Divorcement, The Shrike, Suddenly Last Summer, Of Mice and Men, David and Lisa, Shock Corridor, Shock Treatment, Diary of a Madman, One Flew over the Cuckoo's Nest* and *Cul de Sac*, but also in more clinical investigations such as *The Snake Pit, El, Labyrinth, La Tête contre les Murs, Morgan, Pressure Point, A Child Is Waiting, Lilith* and *Repulsion*. A mixture of attitudes is found in the scientific fantasy of *Charly*; while *Bedlam* was a curious attempt at a horror film set entirely in an asylum, a setting later used by *The Marat/Sade.* In *King of Hearts* the insane are shown to be wiser than the rest, like Mr Dick in *David Copperfield.*

insects on the screen have generally been of the monstrous kind: *Tarantula, The Black Scorpion, The Wasp Woman, The Fly, Them*, and *The Monster That Challenged the World* come to mind. Of course, normal-sized ants can be monstrous enough if seen in quantity, as in *The Naked Jungle*, or if you are as small as *The Incredible Shrinking Man.* Giant spiders are perhaps the most popular breed: there was a particularly loathsome one in *The Thief of Baghdad.* Friendly insects have included those who went to the 'ugly bug ball' in *Summer Magic*; and the dancing caterpillar of *Once upon a Time.* The most symbolic insect was certainly the butterfly in *All Quiet on the Western Front*; the most abundant, the locust in *The Good Earth.* A documentary feature about insects of the most dramatic kind was *The Hellstrom Chronicle.*

insert shot. One inserted into a dramatic scene, usually for the purpose of giving the audience a closer look at what the character on screen is seeing, e.g. a letter or a newspaper headline.

insults

¶ A choice selection, from scripts and from life.

Tony Curtis, about having to make love to Marilyn Monroe:

> It's like kissing Hitler.

George Sanders to Anne Baxter in *All About Eve*:

> That I should want you at all suddenly seems to me the height of improbability.

Louis B. Mayer to Greta Garbo's agent:

> Tell her that in America men don't like fat women.

Monty Woolley to Mary Wickes in *The Man Who Came to Dinner*:

> You have the touch of a sex-starved cobra.

Charles Winninger to Fredric March in *Nothing Sacred*:

> The hand of God reaching down into the mire couldn't elevate you to the depths of degradation.

And in the same movie, Walter Connolly to Fredric March:

> I am sitting here, Mr Cook, toying with the idea of removing your heart and stuffing it—like an olive!

Billy Wilder, after listening to Cliff Osmond singing for a part:

> You have Van Gogh's ear for music.

Jan Sterling to Kirk Douglas in *Ace in the Hole*:

> I've met a lot of hard-boiled eggs in my time, but you—you're twenty minutes!

Walter Matthau to Barbra Streisand on the set of *Hello Dolly*:

> I have more talent in my smallest fart than you have in your entire body.

And later:

> I have no disagreement with Barbra Streisand. I was merely exasperated by her tendency towards megalomania.

Mae West of W. C. Fields during the filming of *My Little Chickadee*:

> There's no one in the world quite like Bill—thank God.

Intermezzo. A simple romantic tale, larded with classical music, this was originally filmed in Sweden in 1936 by Gustav Molander, with Gosta Ekman and Ingrid Bergman. In 1939 Bergman recreated the role in Hollywood opposite Leslie Howard; the film, known in Britain as *Escape to Happiness*, was directed by Gregory Ratoff.

Intolerance (US 1916). D. W. Griffith's epic film, sub-titled 'Love's Struggle Through the Ages', is a sentimentally-conceived examination of intolerance in four periods of history. The narrative moves constantly from one story to another, with frenzied cross-cutting at the climax. The spectacle of the Babylon sequence is on a massive scale, but the public were confused and the film was long considered a commercial failure. Written by Griffith, photographed by Billy Bitzer.

Invasion of the Body Snatchers (US 1956). A catch-penny title obscures the most subtle film in the science-fiction cycle, with no visual horror whatever; about a small town whose population is taken over by 'duplicates' from outer space. Directed by Don Siegel; from Jack Finney's novel; with Kevin McCarthy and Dana Wynter. An expensive but ill-advised remake appeared in 1978.

inventors have been the subject of many screen biographies; indeed, Don Ameche had to live down his invention of the telephone in *The Story of Alexander Graham Bell* and of the sub-machine gun in *A Genius in the Family*. Mickey Rooney appeared as *Young Tom Edison* and Spencer Tracy as *Edison the Man*; James Stewart was *Carbine Williams*; Robert Donat played William Friese-Greene, inventor of the movie camera, in *The Magic Box*. Joel McCrea in *The Great Moment* invented laughing gas; *The Sound Barrier* covered Sir Frank Whittle's invention of the jet engine, and *The Dam Busters* has Michael Redgrave as the inventor of the bouncing bomb, Dr Barnes Wallis. That prolific inventor Galileo was played in an Italian film by Cyril Cusack and more recently by Topol. In *I Aim At the Stars* Curt Jurgens was Wernher von Braun. Benjamin Franklin was portrayed not by an actor but by Disney's cartoonists in *Ben and Me*. Charles Coburn later took over in *John Paul Jones* and Howard da Silva in *1776*.

The Invisible Man. The rights to H. G. Wells' tragi-comic fantasy novel were bought by Universal in 1933; the resulting film, directed by James Whale with splendid trick effects by Arthur Edeson, made a star of Claude Rains although his face was seen only briefly, in death. Universal later made a sporadic low-budget series alternating between farce and melodrama: *The Invisible Man Returns* (Vincent Price) 40, *The Invisible Woman* (Virginia Bruce) 40, *Invisible Agent* (Jon Hall) 42, *The Invisible Man's Revenge* (Jon Hall) 44, *Abbott and Costello Meet the Invisible Man* (Arthur Franz) 51. Meanwhile invisibility had been put to excellent comic effect in the *Topper* series (qv) and many other movies. *Invisible Boy* 57 was something else again, a sequel to *Forbidden Planet*; but in the early sixties a new series of 'invisible man' movies emanated from Argentina and Mexico: there was a TV series in 1958 and another in 1975; and in 1972 the Disney studios had fun with invisibility in *Now You See Him, Now You Don't*.

Invitation to the Dance (US/GB 1956). This ambitious ballet film in three parts was devised and directed by Gene Kelly, who also starred. Its lack of commercial success harmed his career, especially as it was not quite the masterpiece which had been anticipated. The cartoon sequence has been shown separately as *The Magic Lamp*.

The Ipcress File (GB 1965). A 'realistic' espionage picture which offered a useful corrective to the adventures of James Bond, this astringent movie was more coherent than the Len Deighton novel from which it sprang, but suffered from director Sidney Furie's apparent determination to smother it in weird camera angles. However, it clearly marked out Michael Caine for stardom; and it won

BFA awards as the best British picture, also for Ken Adam's art direction and Otto Heller's photography. Subsequent adventures of 'Harry Palmer' were *Billion Dollar Brain* and *Funeral in Berlin*.

Ireland to film-makers has rather too often meant 'the troubles', which were celebrated in *Beloved Enemy, The Informer, The Gentle Gunman, Shake Hands with the Devil*, and the films of Sean O'Casey's plays, including *Juno and the Paycock* and *The Plough and the Stars*. (Rod Taylor played O'Casey, lightly disguised, in *Young Cassidy*.) More romantic or whimsical views of Eire were expressed in *The Luck of the Irish, The Rising of the Moon, Top of the Morning, Broth of a Boy, Home is the Hero, The Quiet Man, I See a Dark Stranger, Happy Ever After, Hungry Hill, The Search for Bridey Murphy, Jacqueline, Rooney, Never Put It In Writing* and *Ulysses*; realism was sought in *Odd Man Out, Parnell, Captain Boycott, No Resting Place, A Terrible Beauty*, and *Ryan's Daughter*. The number of Irish characters on the screen is of course legion, the most numerous and memorable varieties being priests, drunks, New York cops, and Old Mother Riley. The new 'troubles' of the early seventies and eighties have been, at the time of writing, too horrifying to provoke much response from makers of fiction films, apart from a TV movie called *War of Children* and a low-budget American exploiter called *The Outsider*.

Ireland, Jill (1936–). British leading lady of the fifties, later married to Charles Bronson.
Oh Rosalinda 55. Three Men in a Boat 55. Hell Drivers 57. Robbery under Arms 57. Carry On Nurse 59. Raising the Wind 61. Twice Round the Daffodils 62. Villa Rides (US) 68. Rider on the Rain (US) 70. The Mechanic (US) 72. Wild Horses (US) 73. The Valachi Papers (It.) 73. The Streetfighter 75. Breakheart Pass (US) 76. From Noon Till Three (US) 76. Death Wish II 82. Assassination 86, etc.
TV series: Shane 66.

¶ *J.I.:* I'm in so many Charles Bronson films because no other actress will work with him.

Ireland, John (1879–1962). British composer whose only film score was *The Overlanders* (47).

Ireland, John (1914–). Canadian leading man in Hollywood; a popular tough-cynical hero of the early fifties, he declined with unaccountable rapidity to bit parts and second features.
A Walk in the Sun 45. Behind Green Lights 46. The Gangster 47. Raw Deal 48. Red River 48. I Shot Jesse James 49. Anna Lucasta 49. The Doolins of Oklahoma 49. *All the King's Men* 49. Cargo to Capetown 50. The Scarf 51. Red Mountain 51. Hurricane Smith 52. Outlaw Territory 53. Security Risk 54. *The Good Die Young* (GB) 54. Queen Bee 55. Gunfight at the OK Corral 57. Party Girl 58. No Place to Land 59. Spartacus 60. Brushfire 62. The Ceremony 63. The Fall of the Roman Empire 64. I Saw what you Did 65. Fort Utah 67. Caxambu 67. Arizona Bushwackers 68. One on Top of the Other 70. The House of the Seven Corpses 73. Welcome to Arrow Beach 75. The Swiss Conspiracy 76. Love and the Midnight Auto Supply 77. Madam Kitty 77. The Shape of Things to Come 79. Guyana 80. The Incubus 82, many others.
TV series: The Protectors 61.

Irene (1901–1962). Long-standing MGM costume designer.

iris. An adjustable diaphragm in the camera which opens or closes from black like an expanding or contracting circle, giving a similar effect on the screen. So called because it resembles the iris of the human eye.

Irons, Jeremy (1948–). British leading man of the introspective type.
Nijinsky 80. *The French Lieutenant's Woman* 81. *Brideshead Revisited* (TV) 81. Moonlighting 82. The Captain's Doll (TV) 82. Betrayal 82. The Wild Duck 83. Swann in Love 84. The Mission 85, etc.

¶ *J.I.:* Actors often behave like children and so we're taken for children. I want to be grown-up.

Irvin, John (–). British director, from TV.
Tinker Tailor Soldier Spy (TV) 80. The Dogs of War 80. Ghost Story 81. Champions 84. Raw Deal 86. Hamburger Hill 87.

Irving, Amy (1953–). American leading lady of the early eighties.
Carrie 78. The Fury 79. Voices 79. Honeysuckle Rose 80. The Competition 81. Yentl (AAN) 83. Micki and Maude 84. Rumpelstiltskin 87, etc.

Irving, George (1874–1961). American character actor, long on the Broadway stage, for some while a film director, and most memorable in middle-aged businessman roles. The Jungle 14. Madonna of the Streets 24. Wild Horse Mesa 25. Craig's Wife 28. Thunderbolt 29. The Spoilers 30. Island of Lost Souls 32. Dangerous 35. Sutter's Gold 36. The Toast of New York 37. Bringing Up Baby 38. New Moon 40. Son of Dracula 43. Christmas Holiday 44. Magic Town 47, many others.

Irving, John (1942–). American novelist whose *The World According to Garp* was filmed in 1982.

Irving, Washington (1783–1859). American humorist and storyteller whose *Rip Van Winkle* and *The Legend of Sleepy Hollow* have been filmed at various times and in various ways.

Irwin, May (1863–1958). American actress who appeared in one of the very first short films, 1896's *The Kiss*; her only other film, in 1914, was *Mrs Black is Back*.

Isherwood, Christopher (1904–86). English novelist of the thirties who wrote the stories on which *I Am a Camera* and *Cabaret* were based. He later settled in California and co-wrote a few screenplays: Rage in Heaven 42. Forever and a Day 43. Diane 55. The Loved One 65. Sailor from Gibraltar 67. Frankenstein: the True Story (TV) 73.

¶ *C.I.:* It's no good explaining to people why one lives in Hollywood. They either understand or they don't.

Israel's native films have been few owing to problems of finance and language: *Hill 24 Does Not Answer* 55 is still the most notable, though a few comedies have been exported. The country's problems however have been fully aired in *Exodus*, *Judith*, *Cast a Giant Shadow*, *QB VII* and *Raid on Entebbe*, while Ingrid Bergman appeared as *Golda Meir* in a mini series.

It Always Rains on Sunday (GB 1947). A once-praised example of early English realism which cannot now stand comparison with the *Saturday Night and Sunday Morning* school. Basically a cliché-ridden slice of hokum about an escaped convict in London's East End, its often effective low-life atmosphere was chiefly attributable to Douglas Slocombe's photography and to the cosy familiarity of its long list of British players led by Jack Warner and Googie Withers.

It Happened Here (GB 1957–1963). A remarkable first film by two semi-professionals, Kevin Brownlow and Andrew Mollo, shot on a tiny budget over a period of seven years. In dramatically unwieldly but frequently vivid fashion it paints a grim picture of what might have happened if the Nazis had invaded London in 1942, and although sometimes let down by its dialogue sequences, the fake newsreel montages alone make it an achievement of more than mere cleverness.

It Happened One Night (US 1934). This enormously successful romantic comedy was written by Robert Riskin (AA), directed by Frank Capra (AA), starred Claudette Colbert (AA) as a runaway heiress and Clark Gable (AA) as a wandering journalist. (It also won the Award for the best picture.) Its lively good humour and piquant dialogue endeared it to all comers; if today it seems on the slow side, it is infinitely preferable to the 1956 remake, *You Can't Run Away From It*, with June Allyson and Jack Lemmon.

Italian cinema was an international force in the early years of the century with spectaculars like *Cabiria* and *Quo Vadis*. It later succumbed to the power of Hollywood and was little heard from until the post-war realist movement brought de Sica to world eminence. *Bicycle Thieves* was the high water mark of achievement; afterwards came a slow slide into the commercialism of the fifties, which however re-established Rome—and Cinecitta Studios—as a world force in film making, together with the idiosyncratic fancies of Fellini and Antonioni. Many big Hollywood films were made on Italian locations, the familiar cut-rate spectaculars peopled by mythical strong-men along with the 'spaghetti westerns' which aped Hollywood traditions but added an extra helping of violence.

An Italian Straw Hat (Un Chapeau de Paille d'Italie) (France 1928). Probably René Clair's most famous silent comedy, this account of a hilariously impeded marriage, though now occasionally ponderous, set a new style in fast-paced yet stylish visual fun. Written by Clair from a play by Eugene Labiche.

It's a Mad Mad Mad Mad World (US 1963). A marathon attempt to revive silent slapstick comedy and combine it with the modern taste for violence, all in colour and single-lens Cinerama. A large star cast played second fiddle to the stunt men; Stanley Kramer produced and directed from a script by William and Tania Rose.

It's a Wonderful Life (US 1946). Frank Capra's own favourite among his films, this frantic but sentimental comedy concerns a would be suicide (James Stewart) saved by an elderly angel (Henry Travers) who points out in vivid form how his small town friends would have missed him had he not lived. A splendid piece of film pyrotechnics, with a host of familiar actors in full throttle; written by Frances Goodrich, Albert Hackett, and Capra, whose last film in this vein it proved to be. It was remade for television in 1977 under the title *It Happened One Christmas*.

Iturbi, Jose (1895–1980). Spanish pianist and conductor who made his American concert debut in 1929; in the forties appeared in a number of MGM musicals and helped to popularise classical music.
□Thousands Cheer 43. Two Girls and a Sailor 44. Music for Millions 44. A Song to Remember (dubbed piano for Cornel Wilde; his recording of a Chopin Polonaise sold over one million copies) 44. Anchors Aweigh 45. Holiday in Mexico 46. Three Daring Daughters 48. That Midnight Kiss 49.

Ivan, Rosalind (1884–1959). American character actress, mainly on stage.
The Suspect 44. Three Strangers 46. The Corn Is Green 46. Ivy 47. The Robe 53. Elephant Walk 54, etc.

Ivan the Terrible (USSR 1942–1946). Eisenstein's two-part historical film is full of splendidly grotesque imagery. Part One was released in 1942; Part Two was banned temporarily for political reasons and when eventually released proved somewhat disappointing because its colour experiments compared unfavourably with the brilliant black and white of Part One.

Ivano, Paul (1900–84). American cinematographer.
The Dancers 25. No Other Woman 28. Atlantic Flight 37. *The Shanghai Gesture* 41. See My Lawyer 44. Spider Woman Strikes Back 46. Champagne for Caesar 50. For Men Only 52. Hold Back Tomorrow 55. Lizzie 57. Chubasco 68, many others, especially second unit shooting.

Ivens, Joris (1898–). Dutch writer-director best known for documentaries.
Autobiography 1969: *The Camera and I*.
Rain 29. Zuidersee 30. New Earth 34. Spanish Earth 37. The 400 Millions 39. The Power and the Land 40. Song of the Rivers 53. The Threatening Sky 66, etc.

Ives, Burl (1909–) (Burl Icle Ivanhoe). American actor and ballad-singer, once itinerant worker and professional footballer. His paunchy figure, beard and ready smile are equally adaptable to villainous or sympathetic parts.
Smoky (debut) 46. East of Eden 54. *Cat on a Hot Tin Roof* 57. Wind Across the Everglades 58. *The Big Country* (AA) 58. Our Man in Havana 59. The Brass Bottle 64. Rocket to the Moon 67. The McMasters 70. The Only Way Out is Dead 70. Baker's Hawk 76. Just You and Me, Kid 79. Earthbound (TV) 81, Uphill all the Way 84, etc.
TV series: O.K. Crackerby 65. The Bold Ones 69.

Ivory, James (1928–). American director who makes films in India.
□The Householder 62. *Shakespeare Wallah* 64. The Guru 69. Bombay Talkie 70. Savages (US) 72. The Wild Party (US) 75. Autobiography of a Princess 75. Roseland 77. Hullaballoo over Bonnie and George's Pictures 78. The Europeans 79. Jane Austen in Manhattan 79. Quartet 81. *Heat and Dust* 83. The Bostonians 84. *A Room with a View* 86. *Maurice* 87.

Iwerks, Ub (1900–71). American animator, long associated with Disney (he drew the first Mickey Mouse cartoon, *Plane Crazy*). Formed own company in 1930 to create Flip the Frog; went back to Disney 1940 as director of technical research. AA 1959 for improvements in optical printing, 1965 for advancing techniques of travelling matte. Iwerks did much of the complex trick work for Hitchcock's *The Birds*.

Answers

impersonations

1 Spy; Virginia McKenna; *Carve Her Name with Pride* □
2 Writer; Edmond O'Brien; *Bird Man of Alcatraz* □
3 Industrialist; Jason Robards; *Isadora* □
4 Writer and patron of the arts; Edith Evans; *Young Cassidy* □
5 Actress; Miriam Hopkins; *Lady With Red Hair* □
6 Composer; Nat King Cole; *St Louis Blues* □
7 Efficiency expert; Clifton Webb; *Cheaper by the Dozen* □
8 Research scientist; Walter Pidgeon; *Madame Curie* □
9 War hero; Gary Cooper; *Sergeant York* □
10 Psychic experimenter; Louis Hayward; *The Search for Bridey Murphy* □
11 Writer; Elsa Lanchester; *The Bride of Frankenstein* □
12 Colonel; Spencer Tracy; *Thirty Seconds Over Tokyo* □
13 Spy; Anna Neagle; *Odette* □
14 Research scientist; Michael Redgrave; *The Dam Busters* □
15 War correspondent; Burgess Meredith; *The Story of G.I. Joe* □
16 Madam; Shelley Winters; *A House Is Not a Home* □
17 Impresario; David Wayne; *Tonight We Sing* □
18 Inventor; Robert Donat; *The Magic Box* □
19 Research scientist; Edward G. Robinson; *Dr Ehrlich's Magic Bullet* □
20 Opera singer; Eleanor Parker; *Interrupted Melody* □

J

Jack the Ripper. The unknown murderer of London prostitutes in 1888–89 has stimulated several flights of film fancy. Pabst brought him in to carry off the heroine of *Pandora's Box* 28. Two years earlier Alfred Hitchcock had directed the first film adaptation of Mrs Belloc Lowndes' novel *The Lodger*, but in this version Ivor Novello was found not to be the Ripper after all. Further versions were offered by Maurice Elvey in 1932 (Ivor Novello), John Brahm in 1944 (Laird Cregar) and Hugo Fregonese in 1953 (Jack Palance as *The Man in the Attic*). Further slight variations were posed in *The Phantom Fiend* 35 and *The Strangler* 64, while the long-standing puzzle was 'solved' in *Jack the Ripper* 58, *A Study in Terror* 65 and a TV 'Thriller' episode called *Yours Truly Jack the Ripper*. The Ripper was used as an alibi by *Dr Jekyll and Sister Hyde* 71, and the sins of the fathers were passed on in *Hands of the Ripper* 72, with Angharad Rees as the Ripper's daughter. In the seventies there was a German variation with Klaus Kinski, and in *Time after Time* the Ripper landed in modern San Francisco via H. G. Wells' time machine.

Jacks, Robert L. (1922–). American producer, long with Fox.
Man on a Tightrope 53. White Feather 55. A Kiss Before Dying 56. Bandido 57. Roots of Heaven 59. Man in the Middle 64. Zorba the Greek 65. Bandolero 68, many others.

Jackson, Anne (1925–). American actress, wife of Eli Wallach; films rare.
□So Young So Bad 50. The Journey 58. Tall Story 60. The Tiger Makes Out 67. How to Save a Marriage 67. *The Secret Life of an American Wife* 68. Lovers and Other Strangers 70. Zigzag 70. Dirty Dingus Magee 70. The Angel Levine 70. Nasty Habits 76. The Bell Jar 79. The Shining 80. A Woman Called Golda (TV) 82.

Jackson, Freda (1909–). British character actress with a penchant for melodrama; on stage from 1934, films from 1942.
A Canterbury Tale 42. Henry V 44. Beware of Pity 46. Great Expectations 46. *No Room at the Inn* 47. Women of Twilight 49. The Crowded Day 53. Brides of Dracula 60. The Third Secret 64. Monster of Terror 65, etc.

Jackson, Glenda (1937–). British star actress.
□ This Sporting Life 63. The Marat/Sade 66. Tell Me Lies 67. Negatives 68. *Women in Love* (AA) 69. The Music Lovers 70. *Sunday Bloody Sunday* 71. The Boy Friend (uncredited) 71. Mary Queen of Scots (as Queen Elizabeth) 71. A Touch of Class (AA) 72. The Triple Echo 72. A Bequest to the Nation 73. The Maids 73. The Tempter 74. The Romantic Englishwoman 75. Hedda 76. The Incredible Sarah 76. Nasty Habits 76. House Calls 77. The Class of Miss MacMichael 78. Stevie 78. Lost and Found 79. Health 80. Hopscotch 80. The Patricia Neal Story (TV) 81. Return of the Soldier 82. Giro City (TV) 83. Sakharov (TV) 84. Turtle Diary 85. Sakharov (TV) 84. Turtle Diary 85. Business as Usual 87.
TV series: *Elizabeth R* 71.

¶ *G.J.:* I had no real ambition about acting, but I knew there had to be something better than the bloody chemist's shop.

Walter Matthau: She's an absolute dreamboat, the epitome of professionalism, a splendid actress, and she has all the make-up of a fully rounded person.

Jackson, Gordon (1923–). Scottish actor whose rueful expression got him typecast as a weakling; maturity brought more interesting roles.
The Foreman Went to France (debut) 42. Millions Like Us 43. Nine Men 43. San Demetrio, London 44. Pink String and Sealing Wax 45. The Captive Heart 46. Against the Wind 47. Eureka Stockade 48. *Whisky Galore* 48. The Lady with a Lamp 51. Meet Mr Lucifer 54. Pacific Destiny 56. *Tunes of Glory* 60. The Great Escape (US) 62. *The Ipcress File* 65. Cast a Giant Shadow (US) 66. The Fighting Prince of Donegal 66. The Prime of Miss Jean Brodie 69. Run Wild Run Free 69. Kidnapped 72. Russian Roulette 75. Spectre (TV) 77. The Medusa Touch 77. The Last Giraffe (TV) 79. A Town Like Alice

TV (80). The Shooting Party 84. The Masks of Death 85. The Whistle Blower 86. My Brother Tom (TV) 86. Beyond Therapy 87, others.
TV series: *Upstairs Downstairs* 70–75. The Professionals 77–81.

Jackson, Kate (1948–). Stunningly attractive American leading lady.
☐Limbo 70. The Seven Minutes 70. Night of Dark Shadows 71. Satan's School for Girls (TV) 73. Killer Bees (TV) 74. Death Cruise (TV) 74. Death Scream (TV) 75. Death at Love House (TV) 76. James at 15 (TV) 77 Thunder and Lightning 77. Topper (TV) 79. *Jacqueline Bouvier Kennedy* (TV) 81. *Making Love* 81. Rage of Angels (TV) 83.
TV series: Dark Shadows 67–71. The Rookies 71–74. *Charlie's Angels* 76–80.

Jackson, Pat (1916–). British director, a war documentarist whose later output has been disappointing.
Ferry Pilot 41. *Western Approaches* 44. The Shadow on the Wall (US) 48. *White Corridors* 50. Something Money Can't Buy 52. The Feminine Touch 55. Virgin Island 58. Snowball 60. What a Carve Up 62. Seven Keys 62. Don't Talk to Strange Men 62. Seventy Deadly Pills 64, etc.

Jackson, Selmer (1888–1971). American character actor who played hundreds of unobtrusive fathers, doctors, scientists and executives.
Dirigible 31. Doctor X 32. The Witching Hour 34. Front Page Woman 35. The Westland Case 37. Stand Up and Fight 39. The Grapes of Wrath 40. It Started with Eve 41. It Ain't Hay 43. The Sullivans 44. The French Key 46. Mighty Joe Young 49. Elopement 51. Autumn Leaves 56. The Gallant Hours 60, many others.
†In 1940 alone Jackson appeared in twenty films.

Jackson, Thomas E. (1886–1967). American character actor often seen as police officer.
Little Caesar 30. Doctor X 32. Terror Aboard 33. The Mystery of the Wax Museum 33. Call of the Wild 35. Hollywood Boulevard 36. The Westland Case 37. Torchy Gets Her Man 38. Golden Gloves 40. Law of the Tropics 41. The Woman in the Window 44. The Big Sleep 46. Dead Reckoning 47. Stars and Stripes Forever 52. Attack of the Fifty Foot Woman 58. Synanon 65, many others.

Jacobi, Derek (1938–). British actor who played the lead in *I Claudius* on TV.
The Day of the Jackal 73. Blue Blood 74. The Odessa File 74. Philby, Burgess and Maclean (TV) 77. The Medusa Touch 77. The Human Factor 79. The Hunchback of Notre Dame (TV) (as Frollo) 82. Inside the Third Reich (TV) (as Hitler) 82. Enigma 82. Mr Pye (TV) 86. Little Dorrit 87.

Jacobi, Lou (1913–). Chubby American character actor.
Song Without End 60. Irma la Douce 62. Everything you Always Wanted to Know about Sex 72. Roseland 77. Arthur 81. The Lucky Star 81. My Favorite Year 82.

Jacobs, Arthur P. (1918–1973). American independent producer, former publicist.
☐What a Way to Go 64. Dr Dolittle 67. Planet of the Apes 68. The Chairman 69. Goodbye Mr Chips 69. Beneath the Planet of the Apes 69. Escape from the Planet of the Apes 71. Conquest of the Planet of the Apes 72. Tom Sawyer 73. Huckleberry Finn 73.

Jacobs, W. W. (1863–1943). British short story writer: *The Monkey's Paw* has been filmed many times.

Jacobsson, Ulla (1929–1982). Leading Swedish actress.
One Summer of Happiness 51. Smiles of a Summer Night 55. Love is a Ball 63. Zulu 64. The Heroes of Telemark 65, etc.

Jacoby, Scott (1956–). American juvenile lead.
Baxter 72. Rivals 73. Love and the Midnight Auto Supply 77. The Little Girl Who Lives Down the Lane 77, etc.

Jacoves, Felix (1907–). American director.
Homicide 48. Embraceable You 49, etc.

Jacques, Hattie (1924–1980). Oversized British comedienne, well known at the Players' Theatre and on TV. In most of the 'Carry On' films.
Nicholas Nickleby 47. Oliver Twist 48. Trottie True 49. The Pickwick Papers 52. Make Mine Mink 61. In the Doghouse 62. The Bobo 67. Crooks and Coronets 69, etc.

Jaeckel, Richard (1926–). American actor, former Fox mail boy, who made a name playing frightened youths in war films.
Guadalcanal Diary 43. Jungle Patrol 48. Sands of Iwo Jima 49. The Gunfighter 50. Come Back Little Sheba 52. The Violent Men 55. Attack! 55. 3.10 to Yuma 57. The Gallant

Hours 60. Town Without Pity 61. Four for Texas 63. Town Tamer 65. The Dirty Dozen 67. The Devil's Brigade 68. The Green Slime 69. Chisum 70. Sometimes a Great Notion 71. Chosen Survivors 74. Grizzly 76. Day of the Animals 77. *The Dark* 79. Herbie Goes Bananas 80. All the Marbles 81, etc.
TV series: Frontier Circus 61. Banyon 70. Firehouse 74. Salvage 77.

Jaeger, Frederick (–). Anglo-German general purpose actor.
The Black Tent 56. I Was Monty's Double 59. The Looking Glass War 69. Scorpio 72. The Seven Per Cent Solution 76. The Passage 78, etc.

Jaffe, Carl (1902–74). Aristocratic-looking German actor, long in England.
Over the Moon 39. The Lion Has Wings 40. The Life and Death of Colonel Blimp 43. Gaiety George 46. Appointment in London 53. Operation Crossbow 65. The Double Man 67, many others.

Jaffe, Sam (1893–1984). American character actor of eccentric appearance and sharp talent. On stage from 1916, films from 1933.
□We Live Again 34. *The Scarlet Empress* 34. *Lost Horizon* (as the High Lama) 37. Gunga Din 39. Stage Door Canteen 43. 13 Rue Madeleine 46. Gentleman's Agreement 47. The Accused 48. Rope of Sand 49. *The Asphalt Jungle* 50. Under the Gun 50. I Can Get It for You Wholesale 51. The Day the Earth Stood Still 51. All Mine to Give 57. Les Espions 57. The Barbarian and the Geisha 58. Ben Hur 59. A Guide for the Married Man 67. Guns for San Sebastian 68. The Great Bank Robbery 69. Night Gallery (TV) 69. Quarantined (TV) 70. The Kremlin Letter 70. The Old Man Who Cried Wolf (TV) 70. The Dunwich Horror 70. Who Killed the Mysterious Mr Foster? (TV) 71. Bedknobs and Broomsticks 71. QB VII (TV) 74. Battle Beyond the Stars 80. The End 81. Nothing Lasts Forever 82. On the Line 83.
TV series: Ben Casey 60–64.

Jaffe, Stanley (1940–). American producer.
Goodbye Columbus 69. Bad Company 72. The Bad News Bears 76. *Kramer vs Kramer* 78, etc.

Jagger, Dean (1903–?82) (Dean Jeffries). American star character actor of the forties, usually in sympathetic roles; later seen as colonels, fathers, town elders, etc.
Women from Hell 29. College Rhythm 34. Home on the Range 34. Men without Names 35. Revolt of the Zombies 36. Exiled to Shanghai 37. *Brigham Young* (title role) 40. Western Union 41. The Men in Her Life 41. The Omaha Trail 42. North Star 43. When Strangers Marry 44. I Live in Grosvenor Square (GB) 45. Sister Kenny 46. Pursued 47. *Twelve O'Clock High* (AA) 49. Dark City 50. Denver and Rio Grande 52. It Grows on Trees 52. The Robe 53. *Executive Suite* 54. Bad Day at Black Rock 55. The Great Man 56. X the Unknown (GB) 57. The Proud Rebel 58. The Nun's Story 59. Elmer Gantry 60. Parrish 61. The Honeymoon Machine 62. First to Fight 67. Firecreek 68. The Kremlin Letter 70. The Brotherhood of the Bell (TV) 70. Vanishing Point 71. The Glass House (TV) 72. God Bless Dr. Shagetz 77. End of the World 77. Alligator 80, many others.
TV series: Mr Novak 63–64.

Jagger, Mick (1939–). Heavy-faced British pop idol whose film career didn't get off the ground.
□Ned Kelly 69. Performance 70. Gimme Shelter 70.

¶ He sees all women as tarts.—*Bianca Jagger*

Jaglom, Henry (1941–). American writer-director of eccentric films.
□A Safe Place 71. Tracks 72. Other People 79. Sitting Ducks (& a) 80. Can She Bake a Cherry Pie 83. Someone to Love 87.

Jakubowska, Wanda (1907–). Polish woman director.
The Last Stop 48. Soldier of Victory 43. An Atlantic Story 54. Farewell to the Devil 56. Encounters in the Dark 60. The Hot Line 65, etc.

James Bond, the over-sexed one man spy machine created by Ian Fleming, first came to the screen in the guise of Sean Connery in *Dr No* 62. Connery continued in *From Russia with Love* 63, *Goldfinger* 64, *Thunderball* 65, *You Only Live Twice* 67; David Niven appeared as 'Sir James' in *Casino Royale* 67. George Lazenby took over for *On Her Majesty's Secret Service* 69; Connery came back for *Diamonds Are Forever* 71; Roger Moore signed on for *Live and Let Die, The Man with the Golden Gun, The Spy who Loved Me, Moonraker, For Your Eyes Only* and *Octopussy*. In 1983 Connery returned as Bond in *Never Say Never Again*.
Moore's last outing, in 1985, was *A View to a Kill*. Timothy Dalton took over for 1987's *The Living Daylights*.

James, Clifton (1893–1963). British character actor who so resembled Field Marshal Montgomery that during World War II he was hired to impersonate him and hoodwink the Germans, as told in the subsequent book and film, *I Was Monty's Double*.

James, Clifton (1921–). Corpulent American character actor.
David and Lisa 64. Cool Hand Luke 67. Tick Tick Tick 70. Live and Let Die 72. The Man with the Golden Gun 73. The Bank Shot 74. Silver Streak 76. The Bad News Bears in Breaking Training 77. Superman II 80, etc.
TV series: City of Angels 76.

James, Harry (1916–83). American band-leader and trumpeter who appeared in occasional films.
Springtime in the Rockies 42. Best Foot Forward 43. Bathing Beauty 44. Do You Love Me 46. Carnegie Hall 47. I'll Get By 50. The Benny Goodman Story 56, etc.

James, Henry (1843–1916). American novelist who lived in Europe. Film versions include *Berkeley Square*, *The Lost Moment*, *The Heiress*, *The Innocents*, *Daisy Miller*.

¶ *H.J.:* I've always been interested in people, but I've never liked them.
Poor Henry James! He's spending eternity walking round and round a stately park and the fence is just too high for him to peep over and he's just too far away to hear what the countess is saying.—*Somerset Maugham*

James, Jesse (1847–1882). American wild west outlaw who has acquired the legend of a Robin Hood but in fact plundered ruthlessly as head of a gang which also included his sanctimonious elder brother **Frank James** (1843–1915). Among the many screen personifications of Jesse are Tyrone Power in *Jesse James* 39; Lawrence Tierney in *Badman's Territory* 46; Macdonald Carey in *The Great Missouri Raid* 52; Audie Murphy in *Kansas Raiders* 53; Willard Parker in *The Great Jesse James Raid* 53; Robert Wagner in *The True Story of Jesse James* 56; Dale Robertson in *Fighting Man of the Plains* 59; Ray Stricklyn in *Young Jesse James* 60; Chris Jones in a TV series *The Legend of Jesse James* 65; Robert Duvall in *The Great Northfield Minnesota Raid* 72; James Keach in *The Long Riders* 80 (brother Stacy was brother Frank); and Clayton Moore in several Republic serials. Henry Fonda was in *The Return of Frank James* 40.

James, M. R. (1862–1936). English ghost story writer, an academic with a splendid command of language. *The Night of the Demon* is a fairly satisfactory film version of *Casting the Runes*.

James, Sid (or **Sidney**) (1913–1976). Crumple-faced South African comedy actor, in Britain from 1946. A familiar face on TV and in scores of movies, including most of the 'Carry On' series from 1958.
Black Memory 46. Once a Jolly Swagman 48. The Man in Black 49. The Lavender Hill Mob 51. The Titfield Thunderbolt 53. Joe Macbeth 55. The Silent Enemy 57. Too Many Crooks 58. Tommy the Toreador 59. Double Bunk 60. What a Carve Up 62. The Big Job 65. Don't Lose Your Head 67. Bless This House 73, many others.
TV series: *Taxi*, *Hancock*, *Citizen James*, *Bless This House*.

Jameson, Jerry (–). American director.
The Dirt Gang 72. The Bat People 74. The Elevator (TV) 74. The Secret Night Caller (TV) 74. *Heatwave* (TV) 74. Hurricane (TV) 74. Terror on the 40th Floor (TV) 75. The Deadly Tower (TV) 75. The Invasion of Johnson County (TV) 76. Airport 77 77. A Fire in the Sky (TV) 77. High Noon Part Two (TV) 78. Raise the Titanic 80.

Jamison, Bud (1894–1944). American character actor, a stock Columbia player who played the heavy in most of the Three Stooges two-reelers.

Jancso, Miklos (1921–). Hungarian director.
Cantata 63. My Way Home 64. The Round Up 65. The Red and the White 67. Silence and Cry 68. Winter Wind 70. The Pacifist 71. Agnus Dei 71. Red Psalm 72. Electra 74. Private Vice and Public Virtue 76. Masterwork 77. Hungarian Rhapsody 79, etc.

Jane Eyre. Charlotte Brontë's romantic melodrama ('Reader, I married him') was screened in various silent versions, including one in 1913 with Ethel Grandin as Jane and Irving Cummings as the gloomy Mr Rochester; another in 1915 with Louise Vale and Alan Hale; and in 1921 with Mabel Ballin and Norman Trevor. There have been three sound versions: in 1934 with Virginia Bruce and Colin Clive, in 1943 with Joan Fontaine and Orson Welles, and in 1972 with Susannah York and George C. Scott.

Janis, Conrad (1926–). American teenage player of the forties.
Snafu 45. Margie 46. The High Window 46. Beyond Glory 48. Keep it Cool 58. The Duchess and the Dirtwater Fox 76. Roseland 77. Oh God Book Two 80. Brewster's Millions 84. Nothing in Common 86, etc.
TV series: Quark 76. Mork and Mindy 78–80.

Janis, Elsie (1889–1956) (Elsie Bierbauer). American musical comedy star who made a few silent movies such as *Betty in Search of a Thrill* and *A Regular Girl*; only talkie, *Women in War* 42.

Janney, Leon (1917–1980). American child actor, a member of the original Our Gang.
Doorway to Hell 30. Penrod and Sam 31. Should Ladies Behave 32, etc.

Janni, Joseph (1916–). Italian producer, in England from 1939.
The Glass Mountain 48. Romeo and Juliet 53. *A Town Like Alice* 56. *A Kind of Loving* 62. Darling 65. Modesty Blaise 66. Far From the Madding Crowd 67. *Poor Cow* 68. *Sunday Bloody Sunday* 71. Made 72. Yanks 79, etc.

Jannings, Emil (1882–1950) (Theodor Emil Janenz). Distinguished German actor, on stage from ten years old. Entered films through his friend Ernst Lubitsch.
☐Im Banne der Leidenschaft 14. Passionels Tagebuch 14. Frau Eva 15. Vendetta 16. Wenn Vier Dasselbe Tun 17. Life is a Dream 18. The Eyes of the Mummy 18. The Brothers Karamazov 18. Der Stier von Oliviera 18. Rose Bernd 18. *Madame Dubarry* 19. Anne Boleyn 20. Kohlhiesel's Daughter 21. Danton 21. The Wife of the Pharaoh 21. Tragedy of Love 22. Ratten 22. *Othello* 23. Peter the Great 24. All for Gold 24. *Quo Vadis* 24. Nju 24. *The Last Laugh* 24. Waxworks 24. Tartuffe 25. *Faust* 26. *Variety* 26. *The Way of All Flesh* (AA) (US) 27. *The Last Command* (AA) (US) 28. The Street of Sin (US) 28. The Patriot (US) 28. The Sins of the Fathers (US) 29. The Betrayal (US) 29. *The Blue Angel* 30. Darling of the Gods 31. The Tempest 31. Le Roi Pausaole 32. Der Schwarze Walfisch 34. *The Old and the Young King* 35. Traumulus 35. Der Herrscher 37. The Broken Jug 37. Robert Koch 39. Ohm Kruger 40. Die Entlassing 42. An Old Heart Becomes Young Again 42. Where is Herr Belling 45.

'Nine people out of ten, if asked to say who is the greatest actor on the screen, would unhesitatingly reply Emil Jannings.'—*Lionel Collier, Picturegoer, 1929*

❁ For being the last ham of the old school to become an international star. *The Blue Angel.*

Janssen, David (1930–1980) (David Meyer). American leading man, very successful on TV; film roles routine, persona doggedly glum.
Yankee Buccaneer 52. Chief Crazy Horse 54. The Square Jungle 55. Toy Tiger 56. The Girl He Left Behind 56. *Hell to Eternity* 60. Ring of Fire 60. Mantrap 61. *King of the Roaring Twenties* (as Arnold Rothstein) 61. My Six Loves 63. Warning Shot 67. The Green Berets 68. The Shoes of the Fisherman 68. Where It's At 69. A Time for Giving 69. Macho Callahan 70. Birds of Prey (TV) 73. Fer de Lance (TV) 74. Once is not Enough 75. Stalk the Wild Child (TV) 76. The Swiss Conspiracy 76. Two Minute Warning 76. Mayday at 40,000 Feet 77. Warhead 77. The Word (TV) 78. The Golden Gate Murders (TV) 79. High Ice (TV) 79. City in Fear (TV) 79, etc.
TV series: *Richard Diamond* 59. *The Fugitive* 63–66. O'Hara U.S. Treasury 71. Harry O 73–75.

Janssen, Eileen (1937–). American child actress of the forties.
The Green Years 46. About Mrs Leslie 54. The Search for Bridie Murphy 56, etc.

Janssen, Werner (1899–). American composer.
The General Died at Dawn 36. Blockade 38. Eternally Yours 39. Slightly Honorable 40. Guest in the House 44. The Southerner 45. A Night in Casablanca 46. Ruthless 48, etc.

Japan has a cinema tradition all of its own, based on No plays and samurai epics, both with a style quite alien to the west. The first breakthrough was made in the fifties by the vivid films of Kurosawa, such as *Rashomon* and *Seven Samurai*; other directors who came to be respected if not entirely understood are Gosho, Ozu, Mizoguchi, Ichikawa, Kinugasa and Kobayashi.

Jarman, Claude, Jnr (1934–). American boy actor of the forties.
The Yearling (special AA) 46. High Barbaree 47. Intruder in the Dust 49. Rio Grande 51.

Fair Wind to Java 53. The Great Locomotive Chase 56, etc.

Jarman, Derek (1942–). Controversial British director.
Autobiography 1983: *Dancing Ledge*.
Sebastiane (& co-w) 76. Jubilee (& co-w) 77. The Tempest (& w) 79. Caravaggio (& w) 86.

Jarre, Maurice (1924–). French composer.
Hôtel des Invalides 52. La Têtre contre les Murs 59. Eyes Without a Face 59. Crack in the Mirror 60. *The Longest Day* 62. *Lawrence of Arabia* (AA) 62. Weekend at Dunkirk 65. *Dr Zhivago* (AA) 65. Is Paris Burning? 66. The Professionals 66. The 25th Hour 67. Five Card Stud 68. Isadora 68. The Damned 69. *Ryan's Daughter* 70. Ash Wednesday 74. Great Expectations (TV) 76. The Last Tycoon 76. Jesus of Nazareth (TV) 76. Mohammed 76. March or Die 77. Winter Kills 79. Resurrection 80. The Black Marble 80. Taps 81. Lion of the Desert 81. Young Doctors in Love 82. Firefox 82. The Year of Living Dangerously 83. A Passage to India (AA) 84. The Bride 84. Mistress (AAN, BFA) 84. Enemy Mine 85. The Mosquito Coast 86.

Jarrott, Charles (1927–). British director, from TV.
□Time to Remember 62. *Anne of the Thousand Days* 70. Mary Queen of Scots 72. Lost Horizon 73. The Dove 74. Escape from the Dark 76. The Other Side of Midnight 77. The Last Flight of Noah's Ark 79.
Condorman 81. The Amateur 82. The Boy in Blue 85.

Jarvis, Martin (*c.*1944–). British leading man in all media.
The Last Escape 70. Taste the Blood of Dracula 70. Ike (TV) 79. The Bunker (TV) 81.
TV series: Rings on their Fingers 78–80.

Jason, David (1940–). British comedy character actor, mostly on radio and TV.
Under Milk Wood 73. Royal Flash 75. The Water Babies 78. The Odd Job 78. Porterhouse Blue (TV) 87.
TV series: A Sharp Intake of Breath, Open All Hours, Only Fools and Horses.

Jason, Leigh (1904–79). American director, mainly of second features.
The Price of Fear 28. Wolves of the City 29. High Gear 33. The Mad Miss Manton 38. Lady for a Night 39. Model Wife 41. Three Girls About Town 41. Nine Girls 44. Lost Honeymoon 46. Out of the Blue 48. Okinawa 52, etc.

Jason, Rick (1929–). American leading man of the fifties.
Sombrero 53. The Saracen Blade 54. The Lieutenant Wore Skirts 55. The Wayward Bus 57. The Witch Who Came from the Sea 76, etc.
TV series: The Case of the Dangerous Robin 60. *Combat* 62–67.

Jason, Sybil (1929–). South African child actress of the thirties.
Barnacle Bill (GB) 35. Little Big Shot (GB) 36. The Singing Kid (US) 36. The Little Princess (US) 39. The Bluebird (US) 40, etc.

Jason, Will (1899–1970). American second feature director.
The Soul of a Monster 44. Thief of Damascus 52, many others.

Jaubert, Maurice (1900–1940). French composer.
L'Affaire Est dans le Sac 32. Le Quatorze Juillet 33. Zéro de Conduite 33. L'Atalante 34. Drôle de Drame 37. *Un Carnet de Bal* 37. *Quai des Brumes* 38. *Le Jour Se Lève* 39. La Fin du Jour 39, etc.

Jaws. A 1975 box-office sensation about a killer shark lurking near a seaside resort, this modest shocker proved slow-moving and only moderately well-made, but hit the big time simply because of the barrage of publicity with which it was launched and because sharks were a new fad. *Jaws 2*, a spiritless rehash for teenagers, followed in 1978, *Jaws 3D* in 1983 and *Jaws: the Revenge* in 1987.

Jay, Ernest (1894–1957). British stage character actor.
Tiger Bay 34. Broken Blossoms 36. Don't Take It to Heart 44. Vice Versa 47. The History of Mr Polly 49. Edward My Son 49. I Believe in You 52. Who Done It? 55. The Curse of Frankenstein 56.

Jayne, Jennifer (1932–). British leading lady.
Once a Jolly Swagman 48. The Blue Lamp 50. It's a Grand Life 53. The Man Who Wouldn't Talk 57. The Trollenberg Terror 58. Raising the Wind 61. On the Beat 63. The Liquidator 65. The Medusa Touch 78. The Jigsaw Man 83, etc.

Jayston, Michael (1936–) (Michael James). British stage actor commanding reputable film roles.
□Cromwell 70. *Nicholas and Alexandra* 71. Follow Me 72. Alice's Adventures in Wonderland 72. A Bequest to the Nation 73. Tales that Witness Madness 73. The Homecoming 73. Craze 73. The Internecine Project 74. She Fell Among Thieves (TV) 78. Tinker Tailor Soldier Spy (TV) 80. Dominique 78. Zulu Dawn 79.

jazz has been featured in American movies since they began to talk; Al Jolson always acknowledged its influence on his style. Jazz bands featured as specialties through the thirties, but in the forties began a line of films purporting to investigate the origins of jazz: *Birth of the Blues, New Orleans, Syncopation* and *St Louis Blues*. Fictional stories relying on a jazz background include *Young Man with a Horn, Paris Blues, Pete Kelly's Blues, Blues in the Night* and *Cabin in the Sky*; while most of the famous dance bands of the forties were to some extent indebted to the inspiration of jazz, the American Negro's musical idiom.

The Jazz Singer (US 1927). The 'first talking film' has only a few patches of dialogue and some songs; but Al Jolson's personality is so vibrant that one can imagine the sensation he originally caused. The well-worn sentimental story is efficiently directed by Alan Crosland. There was a 1953 remake starring Danny Thomas and a 1980 one with Neil Diamond.

Jean, Gloria (1928–) (Gloria Jean Schoonover). Former American child singer, on screen from 1939 as second-feature rival to Deanna Durbin.
□The Underpup 39. If I Had My Way 40. A Little Bit of Heaven 40. Never Give a Sucker an Even Break 41. What's Cookin'? 42. Get Hep to Love 42. It Comes Up Love 42. When Johnny Comes Marching Home 42. Mister Big 43. Moonlight in Vermont 43. Follow the Boys 44. Pardon My Rhythm 44. The Ghost Catchers 44. Reckless Age 44. Destiny 44. I'll Remember April 44. Easy to Look At 45. River Gang 45. Copacabana 47. I Surrender Dear 48. An Old Fashioned Girl 49. Manhattan Angel 49. There's a Girl in My Heart 50. Air Strike 55. The Ladies' Man 61.

Jeanmaire, Zizi (Renee) (1924–). French leading lady and ballet dancer, in occasional films.
Hans Christian Andersen 52. Anything Goes 56. Folies Bergère 56. Charmants Garçons 57. Black Tights 60, etc.

Jeans, Isabel (1891–1985). British stage actress, invariably in aristocratic roles.
Tilly of Bloomsbury 21. The Rat 25. Downhill 27. Easy Virtue 28. Sally Bishop 33. *Tovarich* (US) 38. Suspicion (US) 41. Banana Ridge 41. Great Day 45. It Happened in Rome 57. *Gigi* 58. A Breath of Scandal 60. *Heavens Above* 63, etc.

Jeans, Ursula (1906–1973) (Ursula McMinn). British stage actress, long married to Roger Livesey; in occasional films.
The Gypsy Cavalier (debut) 31. Cavalcade 33. Dark Journey 37. Mr Emmanuel 44. The Woman in the Hall 46. The Weaker Sex 48. The Dam Busters 55. Northwest Frontier 59. The Queen's Guards 61. The Battle of the Villa Fiorita 65, etc.

Jeanson, Henri (1900–70). French writer.
Pepe le Moko 37. Un Carnet de Bal 37. Prison Without Bars 38. Carmen 42. Nana 55. L'Affaire d'une Nuit 60, etc.

Jeayes, Allan.(1885–1963). British stage actor of dignified heavy presence; played supporting roles in many films.
The Impassive Footman 32. The Scarlet Pimpernel 34. Rembrandt 37. Elephant Boy 37. The Four Feathers 39. The Thief of Baghdad 40. The Man Within 46. Saraband for Dead Lovers 48. Waterfront 50, many others.

Jefford, Barbara (1930–). British stage actress, more recently in films.
Ulysses 67. The Bofors Gun 68. A Midsummer Night's Dream 68. The Shoes of the Fisherman 68. Lust for a Vampire 70, etc.

Jeffrey, Peter (1929–). British general purpose actor.
Becket 64. If 67. The Abominable Dr Phibes 71. The Horsemen 71. Dr Phibes Rises Again 72. The Odessa File 74. Midnight Express 78, etc.

Jeffreys, Anne (1923–) (Anne Carmichael). American leading lady of the forties, formerly in opera.
I Married an Angel 42. Step Lively 44. Dillinger 45. Riff Raff 47. Return of the Badmen 49. Boys Night Out 62, etc.
TV series: Topper 53. Love That Jill 58.

Jeffries, Lionel (1926–). Bald British character comedian, who rose to co-star status, then turned to direction.
Stage Fright 50. Windfall 54. The Baby and the Battleship 55. Law and Disorder 57. The Nun's Story 58. Idol on Parade 59. *Two-Way Stretch* 60. *The Trials of Oscar Wilde* 60. The Hellions 61. The Notorious Landlady 61. The Wrong Arm of the Law 63. Call Me Bwana 63. The Long Ships 64. *The First Men in the Moon* 64. The Truth about Spring 65. The Secret of My Success 65. You Must Be Joking 65. Arrivederci Baby 66. *The Spy with a Cold Nose* 67. Rocket to the Moon 67. *Camelot* 67. Chitty Chitty Bang Bang 68. Eyewitness 70. Who Slew Auntie Roo 71. Royal Flash 75. The Prisoner of Zenda 79. Cream in My Coffee (TV) 80. Better Late Than Never 81, etc.
□AS DIRECTOR: *The Railway Children* 70. The Amazing Mr Blunden 72. Baxter 72. The Water Babies 78. Wombling Free 78.

Jenkins, Allen (1900–1974) (Alfred McGonegal). 'Tough guy' American comic actor, a staple of Warners' repertory in the thirties.
The Girl Habit 31. Rackety Rax 32. I am a Fugitive from a Chain Gang 32. 42nd Streat 33. Professional Sweetheart 33. Jimmy the Gent 34. The St Louis Kid 34. Page Miss Glory 35. Miss Pacific Fleet 35. The Singing Kid 36. Three Men on a Horse 36. The Perfect Specimen 37. Dead End 37. Swing Your Lady 37. *A Slight Case of Murder* 38. The Amazing Dr Clitterhouse 38. Five Came Back 39. *Destry Rides Again* 39. Tin Pan Alley 40. Footsteps in the Dark 41. Maisie Gets Her Man 42. *Wonder Man* 45. Wild Harvest 47. Bodyhold 49. Behave Yourself 51. Pillow Talk 59. Robin and the Seven Hoods 64. Doctor You've Got to be Kidding 67. The Front Page 74, many others.
TV series: *Hey Jeannie* 56.

Jenkins, George (1914–). American production designer.
The Best Years of Our Lives 46. The Secret Life of Walter Mitty 47. Roseanna McCoy 49. The Miracle Worker 62. Mickey One 65. Wait Until Dark 67. Me Natalie 69. The Angel Levine 70. The Paper Chase 73. Night Moves 75. *All the President's Men* (AA) 76. Comes a Horseman 78. The China Syndrome 79, etc.

Jenkins, Jackie 'Butch' (1937–). Buck-toothed American child star of the forties, son of Doris Dudley; retired because he developed a stutter.
□*The Human Comedy* 43. National Velvet 44. An American Romance 44. Abbott and Costello in Hollywood 45. Our Vines Have Tender Grapes 45. Boys' Ranch 46. Little Mister Jim 46. My Brother Talks to Horses 46. Big City 48. The Bride Goes Wild 48. Summer Holiday 48.

Jenkins, Megs (1917–). Plump British actress of kindly or motherly roles, on stage from 1933.
The Silent Battle 39. *Green for Danger* 46. The Brothers 47. The Monkey's Paw 48. *The History of Mr Polly* 49. White Corridors 51. Ivanhoe 52. The Cruel Sea 53. The Gay Dog 54. John and Julie 55. The Man in the Sky 56. Conspiracy of Hearts 59. *The Innocents* 61. The Barber of Stamford Hill 62. Bunny Lake Is Missing 65. Stranger in the House 67. Oliver 68. David Copperfield 69, etc.

Jenks, Frank (1902–1962). American character comedian, usually seen as Runyonesque stooge, cop or valet.
When's Your Birthday? 37. You Can't Cheat an Honest Man 39. Dancing on a Dime 40. Rogues' Gallery 45. Loonies on Broadway 46. The She-Creature 56, many others.
TV series: Colonel Flack 53.

Jennings, Al (1864–1961). American outlaw of the old west who among other pursuits became a silent screen actor.
The Lady of the Dugout 18. Fighting Fury 24. The Sea Hawk 24. The Demon 26. Loco Luck 27. Land of Missing Men 30, etc.

Jennings, De Witt (1879–1937). American character actor, stern and bulky.
The Warrens of Virginia 15. Three Sevens 21. The Enemy Sex 24. Exit Smiling 26. Alibi 29. The Big Trail 30. Min and Bill 30. Caught Plastered 31. Movie Crazy 32. Mystery of the Wax Museum 33. Little Man What Now 34. Mutiny on the Bounty 35. Sins of Man 36. Slave Ship 37, many others.

Jennings, Humphrey (1907–1950). Distinguished British documentarist, with the GPO Film Unit from 1934. Responsible for a fine World War II series of sensitive film records of the moods of the time.
The First Days (co-d) 39. *London Can Take It* (co-d) 40. *Listen to Britain* 41. The Silent Village 43. *Fires Were Started* 43. *A Diary for Timothy* 45, etc. Also: The Cumberland Story 47. *Dim Little Island* 49. Family Portrait 50, etc.
❀ For his unbroken series of poetic and cinematic images of Britain at war. *Listen to Britain.*

Jens, Salome (1935–). American leading lady, in very occasional films.
☐*Angel Baby* 61. The Fool Killer 65. Seconds 66. Me Natalie 69. In the Glitter Palace (TV) 77. Sharon: Portrait of a Mistress (TV) 77. From Here to Eternity (TV) 79. Cloud Dancer 80. Harry's War 81. Clan of the Cave Bear 85. Just Between Friends 85.

Jergens, Adele (1922–). American leading lady, mainly in second features.
A Thousand and One Nights 44. Ladies of the Chorus 48. Blonde Dynamite 50. Somebody Loves Me 52. The Cobweb 55. Girls in Prison 56. The Lonesome Trail 58, etc.

Jerome, Jerome K. (1859–1927). British humorist and essayist. His *Three Men in a Boat* and *The Passing of the Third Floor Back* were filmed several times.

Jerrold, Mary (1877–1955) (Mary Allen). British character actress, mainly on stage; in films, played mainly sweet old ladies.
Alibi 31. Friday the Thirteenth 33. The Man at the Gate 41. *The Way Ahead* 44. *The Queen of Spades* 48. Mr Perrin and Mr Traill 49. Top of the Form 52, etc.

Jessel, George (1898–1981). American entertainer, in vaudeville from childhood. After making the mistake of turning down *The Jazz Singer*, he had a very spasmodic film career, but in the fifties he produced a number of musicals for Fox.
Autobiographies: 1946, *So Help Me*. 1955, *This Way Miss*. 1975, *The World I Live In*.
AS ACTOR: The Other Man's Wife 19. Private Izzy Murphy 26. Lucky Boy (My Mother's Eyes) 29. Love Live and Laugh 29. Stage Door Canteen 43. Four Jills in a Jeep 44. The I Don't Care Girl 53. The Busy Body 57. Heironymus Merkin 69, etc.
AS PRODUCER: Do You Love Me 46. When My Baby Smiles at Me 48. Dancing in the Dark 49. Meet Me After the Show 51. Golden Girl 51. Wait Till the Sun Shines Nellie 52. The I Don't Care Girl 53. Tonight We Sing 53, etc.

¶ *Eddie Cantor:* Did you ever catch him at a funeral? It's wonderful. All through the years he makes notes on his friends. He wants to be ready.
That son of a bitch started his reminiscences when he was eight years old.—*Walter Winchell*

Jessel, Patricia (1920–1968). British character actress, mostly on stage.
Quo Vadis 51. *City of the Dead* 61. A Jolly Bad Fellow 64. A Funny Thing Happened on the Way to the Forum 66, etc.

Jessua, Alain (1932–). French writer-director of off-beat films.
Life Upside Down 63. Jeu de Massacre 67. Traitement de Choc 73. Armageddon 77. Les Chiens 79, etc.

Jeux Interdits (France 1952). A powerful anti-war film and a plea for innocence with a fresh angle: two children whose parents have been killed in an air raid are sheltered by peasants and invent their own game of death. Their world is shown as the only innocent one, all adults being in some way corrupt; but the world does not understand. Directed by René Clement from a novel by Françoise Boyer; with Brigitte Fossey and Georges Poujouly.

Jew Süss (Germany 1940). This remake of the legend of a Jew who, inspired by a demoniacal rabbi, takes over Wurtemberg but is finally toppled from power, was a natural theme for Nazi Germany, and Veit Harlan's film is said to have been dictated and supervised by Goebbels. There were earlier, more temperate versions, including a British one in 1934.

jewel thieves were fashionable with Hollywood film-makers in the thirties, the heyday of Raffles, the Lone Wolf, and Arsène Lupin; they were the subject of Lubitsch's best comedy, *Trouble in Paradise*. In the sixties they seemed to come into their own again, with *To Catch a Thief, The Greengage Summer, Topkapi, The Pink Panther* and *Jack of Diamonds*.

Jewell, Isabel (1913–1972). Diminutive American leading lady of the thirties, a minor 'platinum blonde' who graduated to character parts.
Blessed Event 33. Counsellor at Law 33. Manhattan Melodrama 34. A Tale of Two Cities 35. The Man Who Lived Twice 37. Marked Woman 37. *Lost Horizon* 37. Gone with the Wind 39. The Leopard Man 43. The Bishop's Wife 48. The Story of Molly X 48. Bernardine 57, many others.

Jewison, Norman (1926–). Canadian director, from TV.
☐Forty Pounds of Trouble 63. The Thrill of It All 63. Send Me No Flowers 64. The Art of Love 65. *The Cincinnati Kid* 65. *The Russians Are Coming, The Russians Are Coming* (& p)

66. *In the Heat of the Night* (pd) 67. The Thomas Crown Affair (pd) 68. The Landlord (p) 69. Gaily, Gaily (pd) 69. Fiddler on the Roof (pd) 71. Jesus Christ Superstar (pd) 73. Rollerball 75. And Justice for All (& co-p) 79. The Dogs of War (co-p only) 81. Best Friends (& p) 82. A Soldier's Story 84. Agnes of God 85. Moonstruck 87.

Jews and their plight in Europe under the Nazis were the subject of *So Ends Our Night, The Great Dictator, Professor Mamlock, Mr Emmanuel* and *The Diary of Anne Frank.* The problems of the new state of Israel were treated in *Sword in the Desert, Exodus, The Juggler, Judith* and *Cast a Giant Shadow*; while looking further back in history we find many versions of *Jew Süss* and *The Wandering Jew*, also *The Fixer* and the *Fiddler on the Roof.* American films about Jews used to show them as warm-hearted comic figures: *Kosher Kitty Kelly, Abie's Irish Rose, The Cohens and the Kellys.* Gertrude Berg continued this tradition on TV in the fifties. Recently films set in Jewish milieux have treated their characters more naturally, if with a touch of asperity: *No Way to Treat a Lady, I Love You Alice B. Toklas, Bye Bye Braverman, Funny Girl, The Night They Raided Minsky's, Goodbye Columbus, Portnoy's Complaint, Hester Street, Lies My Father Told Me, The Apprenticeship of Duddy Kravitz, The Chosen*; while TV revived for the world the plight of Jews under Hitler in *Holocaust* and *Playing for Time*, and Woody Allen has found a vein of internationally appreciated mordant humour in the foibles and follies of Jewishness. See also: *anti-semitism.*

Jhabvala, Ruth Prawer (–). Screenwriter, originally Polish, inseparable from the directorial works of James Ivory (qv).

Joan of Arc has had her story told several times on film. In 1916 Geraldine Farrar played her in *Joan the Woman.* Dreyer's classic *The Passion of Joan of Arc*, with Falconetti, came in 1928; and in 1930 Marco de Gastyne directed *Saint Joan the Maid* with Simone Genevois. In Germany, Angela Salloker had the role in 1935. The next two were Hollywood failures: Victor Fleming's *Joan of Arc* 48, with Ingrid Bergman, and Otto Preminger's *Saint Joan* 57, with Jean Seberg. Hedy Lamarr also made a brief appearance as Joan in *The Story of Mankind* 57. In 1962 Robert Bresson made his highly specialized *The Trial of Joan of Arc* with Florence Carrez.

Jobert, Marlène (1943–). French leading lady.
Masculin Feminin 66. Le Voleur 66. L'Astragale 68. Rider on the Rain 69. Last Known Address 70. Catch Me a Spy 72. Ten Days' Wonder 72.

Joe Palooka. The dumb boxer hero of the famous American comic strip was first on screen in 1934, played by Stuart Erwin. Ten years later Joe Kirkwood, an amateur golfer, played him in a Monogram series, with Leon Errol (later James Gleason) as his manager Knobby Walsh.

Joffe, Charles H. (–). American producer almost exclusively associated with the films of Woody Allen.
Take the Money and Run 69. Bananas 70. Everything You Always Wanted to Know about Sex 72. Sleeper 73. Love and Death 73. The Front 76. Annie Hall 77. Stardust Memories 80, A Midsummer Night's Sex Comedy 82. Zelig 83.

Joffe, Roland (1945–). British director with TV experience.
The Killing Fields (AAN) 84. The Mission 85.

Johann, Zita (1904–). American leading lady of the early thirties.
The Struggle 31. Tiger Shark 32. *The Mummy* 32. Luxury Liner 33. Grand Canary 34, etc.

John, Elton (1947–) (Reginald Dwight). British pop singer.
Tommy 75.

John, Rosamund (1913–) (Nora Jones). Gentle-mannered British leading lady who turned in several pleasing performances in the forties.
□The Secret of the Loch 34. The First of the Few 42. *The Gentle Sex* 43. The Lamp Still Burns 43. Tawny Pipit 44. *The Way to the Stars* 45. Green for Danger 46. The Upturned Glass 47. Fame is the Spur 47. When the Bough Breaks 47. No Place for Jennifer 49. She Shall Have Murder 50. Never Look Back 52. Street Corner 53. Operation Murder 56.

Johnny Who?

? In the following films, who played Johnny?

1 *Johnny Cool*
2 *Johnny Guitar*
3 *Johnny O'Clock*
4 *Johnny Concho*
5 *Johnny Dark*
6 *Johnny Come Lately*
7 *Johnny Allegro*

8 *Johnny Eager*
9 *Johnny Tremain*
10 *No Love for Johnnie*

Johns, Glynis (1923–). Husky-voiced British actress, daughter of Mervyn Johns; on stage (as child) from 1935.
South Riding (debut) 36. Prison Without Bars 38. 49th Parallel 41. Halfway House 44. *Perfect Strangers* 45. This Man Is Mine 46. Frieda 47. *Miranda* (as a mermaid) 47. An Ideal Husband 47. State Secret 50. Appointment with Venus 51. *The Card* 52. The Sword and the Rose 53. Personal Affair 53. Rob Roy 53. The Weak and the Wicked 54. The Beachcomber 55. Mad About Men 55. *The Court Jester* (US) 56. The Day They Gave Babies Away (US) 56. Shake Hands with the Devil 59. The Sundowners 60. The Spider's Web 61. *The Chapman Report* (US) 62. Mary Poppins (US) 64. Dear Brigitte (US) 65. Don't Just Stand There (US) 68. Lock Up Your Daughters 69. Under Milk Wood 71. Vault of Horror 73. Little Gloria, Happy at Last (TV) 83, etc.
TV series: Glynis 63.

Johns, Mervyn (1899–). Welsh character actor, on stage from 1923; usually plays mild-mannered roles.
Lady in Danger (debut) 34. Jamaica Inn 39. *Saloon Bar* 40. *Next of Kin* 41. Went the Day Well? 42. My Learned Friend 44. *Dead of Night* 45. *Pink String and Sealing Wax* 45. Scrooge 51. The Intimate Stranger 56. No Love for Johnnie 61. 80,000 Suspects 63. The Heroes of Telemark 65. Who Killed the Cat? 66. The House of Mortal Sin 77, many others.

Johnson, Arch (–). Burly American character actor.
Somebody Up There Likes Me 56. G.I. Blues 58. Twilight of Honor 63. Sullivan's Empire 67. Walking Tall 73. The Buddy Holly Story 77, many others.

Johnson, Arte (1934–). Small-scale American comic actor.
Miracle in the Rain 56. The Subterraneans 60. The President's Analyst 67. Charge of the Model Ts 77. Love at First Bite 79, etc.
TV series: Soap, Glitter.

Johnson, Ben (1919–). American character actor, a staple of John Ford and other westerns for years. Former stunt rider.
Three Godfathers 49. Mighty Joe Young 49. She Wore a Yellow Ribbon 49. *Wagonmaster* 50. Rio Grande 50. Fort Defiance 51. Shane 53. Slim Carter 57. Fort Bowie 60. One Eyed Jacks 61. Major Dundee 65. The Rare Breed 66. Will Penny 67. The Wild Bunch 69. The Undefeated 69. *The Last Picture Show* (AA) 71. Corky 72. Junior Bonner 72. Dillinger 73. The Sugarland Express 73. Bite the Bullet 75. Hustle 76. Breakheart Pass 76. The Greatest 77. The Town That Dreaded Sundown 77. The Swarm 78. Terror Train 80. The Hunter 80. Red Dawn 84, many others.

Johnson, Dame Celia (1908–82). Distinguished British actress, on stage from 1928, usually in well-bred roles: films rare.
□*In Which We Serve* (debut) 42. *Dear Octopus* 42. This Happy Breed 44. *Brief Encounter* 46. The Astonished Heart 49. I Believe In You 52. The Captain's Paradise 53. The Holly and the Ivy 54. A Kid for Two Farthings 56. The Good Companions 57. The Prime of Miss Jean Brodie 69. Les Misérables (TV) 78. Staying On (TV) 79. The Hostage Tower (TV) 80. Les Miserables (TV) 80.

Johnson, Chic (1891–1962). Portly American vaudeville comedian (with partner Ole Olsen).
□Oh Sailor Behave 30. Fifty Million Frenchmen 31. Gold Dust Gertie 31. Country Gentlemen 36. All over Town 37. Hellzapoppin 41. Crazy House 43. Ghost Catchers 44. See My Lawyer 45, etc.

Johnson, Don (–). American leading man of the seventies.
Zachariah 70. The Harrad Experiment 73. Return to Macon County 75. Law of the Land (TV) 76. The City (TV) 77. Ski Lift to Death (TV) 78. Beulah Land (TV) 79. The Long Hot Summer (TV) 85, many others.
TV series: From Here to Eternity 79. *Miami Vice* 85– .

Johnson, Katie (1878–1957). British character actress who became a star in her old age.
Jeannie 41. The Years Between 46. I Believe in You 52. *The Ladykillers* 55. How to Murder a Rich Uncle 56, many others.

Johnson, Kay (1904–75) (Catherine Townsend). American leading lady of the thirties.
□*Dynamite* 29. The Ship from Shanghai 30. This Mad World 30. Billy the Kid 30. The Spoilers 30. Madam Satan 30. Passion Flower 30. The Single Sin 31. The Spy 31. American Madness 32. Thirteen Women 32. Eight Girls in a Boat 34. This Man Is Mine 34. Of Human Bondage 34. Their Big Moment 34.

Village Tale 35. Jalna 35. White Banners 38. The Real Glory 39. Son of Fury 42. Mr Lucky 43. The Adventures of Mark Twain 44.

Johnson, Lamont (1920–). American director, from TV.
□Covenant with Death 67. Kona Coast (TV) 68. Deadlock (TV) 69. My Sweet Charlie (TV) 70. The Mackenzie Break 70. A Gunfight 71. That Certain Summer (TV) 72. The Groundstar Conspiracy 72. You'll Like My Mother 72. The Last American Hero 73. The Execution of Private Slovik (TV) 74. Fear on Trial (TV) 75. Lipstick 76. One On One 77. Somebody Killed Her Husband 78. Sunny Side 79. Foxes 80. Crisis at Central High (TV) 80. Off the Minnesota Strip 80. Escape from Iran (TV) 81. Cattle Annie and Little Britches 81. Spacehunter 83.

Johnson, Laurie (1927–). British composer, mainly notable for themes of television's *The Avengers* and *The Professionals*.
The Good Companions 57. Tiger Bay 59. I Aim at the Stars 60. Dr Strangelove 63. First Men in the Moon 63. The Beauty Jungle 64. And Soon the Darkness 70. The Belstone Fox 74, etc.

Johnson, Lynn-Holly (1960–). American leading lady.
Ice Castles 78. For Your Eyes Only 81. The Watcher in the Woods 81.

Johnson, Martin (1884–1937) and **Osa** (1894–1953). American explorers who made several feature-length films.
Jungle Adventure 21. Simba 28. Congorilla 32. Wings over Africa 34. Baboona 35. Borneo 38. I Married Adventure 40, etc.
A Johnson Safari Museum is situated in Chanute, Kansas (Mrs Johnson's birthplace).

Johnson, Noble (1897–198?). Black American actor who played a multitude of fearsome native chiefs.
Robinson Crusoe (as Friday) 22. The Ten Commandments 23. The Navigator 24. Hands Up 26. Vanity 27. Redskin 28. The Four Feathers 29. Moby Dick 30. The Mummy 32. *King Kong* 33. She 35. Conquest 37. The Ghost Breakers 40. Jungle Book 42. A Game of Death 45. She Wore a Yellow Ribbon 49. North of the Great Divide 50, many others.

Johnson, Nunnally (1897–1977). American screenwriter, producer and director.
□AS WRITER: Rough House Rosie 27. A Bedtime Story (co-w) 33. Mama Loves Papa (co-w) 33. Moulin Rouge (co-w) 34. *The House of Rothschild* 34. *Bulldog Drummond Strikes Back* 34. Kid Millions (co-w) 35. Cardinal Richelieu (co-w) 35. Thanks a Million 35. The Man Who Broke the Bank at Monte Carlo (co-w) 35. *The Prisoner of Shark Island* (& p) 36. The Country Doctor (p only) 36. The Road to Glory (p only) 36. Dimples (p and original idea) 36. Banjo on My Knee (& p) 36. Nancy Steele Is Missing (p only) 37. Cafe Metropole (p only) 37. Slave Ship (p only) 37. Love under Fire (p only) 37. *Jesse James* (& p) 39. Wife, Husband and Friend (& p) 39. *Rose of Washington Square* (& p) 39. *The Grapes of Wrath* (& p) 40. I Was an Adventuress (p only) 40. Chad Hanna (& p) 40. *Tobacco Road* 41. *Roxie Hart* (& p) 42. The Pied Piper (& p) 42. Life Begins at 8.30 (& p) 42. The Moon Is Down (& p) 43. Holy Matrimony (& p) 43. Casanova Brown (& p) 44. *The Woman in the Window* (& p) 45. The Keys of the Kingdom (co-w) 44. Along Came Jones 45. *The Dark Mirror* (& p) 46. The Senator Was Indiscreet (p only) 47. Mr Peabody and the Mermaid (& p) 48. Everybody Does It (& p) 49. Three Came Home (& p) 49. The Gunfighter (co-w, p) 50. *The Mudlark* (& p) 50. The Long Dark Hall 51. *The Desert Fox* (& p) 51. Phone Call from a Stranger (& p) 52. We're Not Married (& p) 52. My Cousin Rachel (& p) 52. How to Marry a Millionaire (& p) 53. Night People (& p, d) 53. Black Widow (& p, d) 54. How to Be Very Very Popular (& p, d) 55. The Man in the Grey Flannel Suit (& d) 56. Oh Men Oh Women (& p, d) 56. *The Three Faces of Eve* (& p, d) 57. The Man Who Understood Women (& p, d) 57. The Angel Wore Red (& d) 60. Flaming Star (co-d) 60. Mr Hobbs Takes a Vacation 62. Take Her She's Mine 63. The World of Henry Orient (co-d) 64. Dear Brigitte 65. The Dirty Dozen (co-w) 67.

❀For being involved in so many of Hollywood's most intelligent pictures. *The Grapes of Wrath*.

Johnson, Rafer (1935–). American black actor, formerly Olympic athlete.
The Fiercest Heart 61. The Sins of Rachel Cade 61. Wild in the Country 61. The Lion 63, etc.

Johnson, Richard (1927–). British leading man of stage and screen.
Captain Horatio Hornblower 51. Never So Few (US) 59. Cairo (US) 62. *The Haunting*

63. Eighty Thousand Suspects 63. The Pumpkin Eater 64. Operation Crossbow 65. Moll Flanders 65. Khartoum 66. *Deadlier Than the Male* (as Bulldog Drummond) 66. Danger Route 67. La Strega in Amore (It.) 67. Oedipus The King 68. A Twist of Sand 68. Lady Hamilton (as Nelson) (German) 68. Some Girls Do 68. Julius Caesar 70. Hennessy 75. Aces High 76. The Four Feathers (TV) 78. Haywire (TV) 81. The Aerodrome (TV) 83. Turtle Diary (also p) 85. Lady Jane 86, etc.

Johnson, Rita (1912–1965). American actress who usually played 'the other woman'.
Serenade 39. Edison the Man 40. Here Comes Mr Jordan 41. Thunderhead, Son of Flicka 44. They Won't Believe Me 47. Family Honeymoon 49. Susan Slept Here 54. Emergency Hospital 56. The Day They Gave Babies Away 57, etc.

Johnson, Tor (1916–1971). Bald, menacing American character actor.
Ghost Catchers 44. Road to Rio 47. The Lemon Drop Kid 51. Bride of the Monster 55. Carousel 56. Plan 9 from Outer Space 56. Night of the Ghouls 59, etc.

Johnson, Van (1916–) (Charles Van Johnson). American light leading man, in films since 1941 after stage experience.
Murder in the Big House (debut) 41. *Dr Gillespie's New Assistant* 42. The Human Comedy 43. A Guy Named Joe 43. The White Cliffs of Dover 44. Two Girls and a Sailor 44. Thirty Seconds over Tokyo 44. Thrill of a Romance 45. Weekend at the Waldorf 45. Easy to Wed 45. No Leave, No Love 45. High Barbaree 46. The Romance of Rosy Ridge 47. State of the Union 48. The Bride Goes Wild 48. In the Good Old Summertime 49. *Battleground* 50. Go for Broke 51. When in Rome 52. Plymouth Adventure 52. *The Caine Mutiny* 54. Brigadoon 55. The Last Time I Saw Paris 55. The End of the Affair (GB) 55. *Miracle in the Rain* 56. Twenty-Three Paces to Baker Street 57. Kelly and Me 57. Beyond This Place (GB) 59. Subway in the Sky (GB) 60. Wives and Lovers 63. Divorce American Style 67. Where Angels Go Trouble Follows 68. Battle Squadron (It.) 69. Company of Killers (TV) 70. Rich Man Poor Man (TV) 76, others.
TV series: Glitter 84.

Johnston, Eric A. (1895–1963). American executive, successor to Will H. Hays as President of the M.P.A.A. (Motion Picture Association of America) (1945–63).

Johnston, Margaret (1917–). Australian actress who has made occasional British films, notably in mid-forties.
The Prime Minister (debut) 40. *The Rake's Progress* 45. A Man About the House 47. Portrait of Clare 50. The Magic Box 51. Knave of Hearts 53. Touch and Go 55. *Night of the Eagle* 62. Life at the Top 65. The Psychopath 66. Sebastian 67, etc.

Johnston, Oliver (1888–1966). British character actor.
Room in the House 55. *A King in New York* 57. A Touch of Larceny 60. Dr Crippen 62. Cleopatra 63. A Countess from Hong Kong 67, etc.

Jolley, I. Stanford (1900–1978). American western character actor.
The Sombrero Kid 42. Frontier Fury 43. Lightning Raiders 45. Prairie Express 47. Waco 52. The Young Guns 56. 13 Fighting Men 60, many others.

Jolson, Al (1886–1950) (Asa Yoelson). Celebrated Jewish-American singer and entertainer, of inimitable voice and electric presence. After years as a big Broadway attraction, he starred in the first talking picture and although his fortunes subsequently declined, a biopic using his voice made him a world celebrity again in his sixties.
Biographies: *The Immortal Jolson* (1962) by Pearl Sieben; *Al Jolson* (1972) by Michael Friedland; *Sonny Boy* (1975) by Barrie Anderton.
□*The Jazz Singer* 27. *The Singing Fool* 28. Sonny Boy 29. Say It with Songs 29. Mammy 30. Big Boy 30. Hallelujah I'm a Bum 33. Wonder Bar 34. Go into Your Dance 35. The Singing Kid 36. *Rose of Washington Square* 39. Hollywood Cavalcade 39. Swanee River 39. Rhapsody in Blue 45. *The Jolson Story* (voice only) 46. *Jolson Sings Again* (voice only) 49.
❋ For heralding an era, and for being a star again twenty years later without even being seen. *Rose of Washington Square.*

¶ It was easy enough to make Jolson happy at home. You just had to cheer him for breakfast, applaud wildly for lunch, and give him a standing ovation for dinner.—*George Burns*

He was more than just a singer or an actor. He was an experience.—*Eddie Cantor*

A.J.: I'll tell you when I'm going to play the Palace. That's when Eddie Cantor and George Burns and Groucho Marx and Jack Benny are on the bill. I'm going to buy out the whole

house, and sit in the middle of the orchestra and say: Slaves, entertain the king!
Famous line (*The Jazz Singer*): You ain't heard nothin' yet!

Jones, Allan (1907–). American (originally Welsh) singing star of the thirties.
□Reckless 35. *A Night at the Opera* 35. Rose Marie 36. The Great Ziegfeld (voice only, dubbing for Dennis Morgan) 36. Showboat 36. A Day at the Races 37. *The Firefly* 37. Everybody Sing 38. Honeymoon in Bali 39. The Great Victor Herbert 39. The Boys from Syracuse 40. One Night in the Tropics 40. There's Magic in Music 42. True to the Army 42. Moonlight in Havana 42. Rhythm of the Islands 43. Larceny with Music 43. Crazy House 43. You're a Lucky Fellow Mr Smith 43. When Johnny Comes Marching Home 43. Sing a Jingle 44. The Singing Sheriff 44. Senorita from the West 45. Honeymoon Ahead 45. A Swinging Summer 65. Stage to Thunder Rock 67.

Jones, Barry (1893–1981). British character actor, usually in diffident roles; a well-known stage actor from 1921.
Arms and the Man (as Bluntschli) 31. Squadron Leader X 42. Dancing with Crime 46. Frieda 47. The Calendar 48. *Seven Days to Noon* (leading role) 50. White Corridors 51. *The Clouded Yellow* 51. Appointment with Venus 52. Plymouth Adventure (US) 52. Return to Paradise 53. Demetrius and the Gladiators 54. Prince Valiant (US) 54. *Brigadoon* (US) 55. The Glass Slipper 55. Alexander the Great 56. War and Peace 56. Saint Joan 57. *The Safecracker* 58. The Thirty Nine Steps 59. The Heroes of Telemark 65. A Study in Terror 65, etc.

Jones, Buck (1889–1942) (Charles Gebhardt). Popular American western star of the twenties and thirties, mainly in second features.
Straight from the Shoulder 20. Skid Proof 23. Hearts and Spurs 25. Riders of the Purple Sage 26. The Flying Horseman 27. The Lone Rider 30. Border Law 32. The California Trail 33. When a Man Sees Red 34. Boss Rider of Gun Creek 36. Unmarried 39. Riders of Death Valley 41, many others.

Jones, Carolyn (1929–1983). Dark-eyed American leading lady, usually in off-beat roles.
Road to Bali 52. House of Wax 52. The Big Heat 53. Invasion of the Body Snatchers 55. The Opposite Sex 56. *The Bachelor Party* 57. Marjorie Morningstar 58. Last Train from Gun Hill 58. A Hole in the Head 59. Ice Palace 60. A Ticklish Affair 63. Heaven with a Gun 68. Color Me Dead 70. Eaten Alive 77. Good Luck Miss Wyckoff 79. The French Atlantic Affair (TV) 80. The Dream Merchants (TV) 80, etc.
TV series: *The Addams Family* (as Morticia) 64–65. Capitol 82–83.

Jones, Christopher (1941–). American leading man.
Chubasco 67. Wild in the Streets 68. The Looking Glass War 69. Three in the Attic 69. *Ryan's Daughter* 70, etc.
TV series: *The Legend of Jesse James* 65.

Jones, Chuck (1915–) (Charles M. Jones). American animator, long with Warners directing Daffy Duck, Bugs Bunny and Sylvester. Features include *Gay Purree* 62. *The Phantom Tollbooth* 69.

Jones, David (1934–). British director.
Betrayal 84. 84 Charing Cross Road 87.

Jones, Dean (1933–). American leading man who usually plays well-behaved fellows.
Tea and Sympathy 56. Handle with Care 58. Never So Few 60. *Under the Yum Yum Tree* 64. The New Interns 64. Two on a Guillotine 64. That Darn Cat 65. The Ugly Dachshund 66. Any Wednesday 66. Monkeys Go Home 67. Blackbeard's Ghost 67. The Love Bug 69. Million Dollar Duck 71. Snowball Express 73. Mr Superinvisible 76. The Shaggy D.A. 76. Herbie Goes to Monte Carlo 77. Born Again 78, etc.
TV series: Ensign O'Toole 62. Chicago Teddy Bears 71.

Jones, Emrys (1915–1972). British stage actor.
One of Our Aircraft is Missing 42. The Rake's Progress 45. The Wicked Lady 46. Nicholas Nickleby 47. The Small Back Room 48. Three Cases of Murder 55. Oscar Wilde 60, etc.

The Jones Family. A 1936 second feature called *Every Saturday Night* started off a series of seventeen about a comicalized small town American family in which Pa was Jed Prouty and Ma was Spring Byington. They had four years of popularity without ever quite equalling MGM's Hardy family, which had more sentimentality.

Jones, Freddie (1927–). Clever British character actor who has yet to control a tendency towards twitchy caricatures.
The Bliss of Mrs Blossom 68. Otley 69. Frankenstein Must be Destroyed 70. Goodbye Gemini 70. Antony and Cleopatra 72. Sitting Target 72. The Satanic Rites of Dracula 73. The Elephant Man 80. Firefox 82. Krull 83. Dune 85. Firestarter 85, etc.

Jones, Gordon (1911–1963). American second lead of the football player type.
They All Kissed the Bride 42. My Sister Eileen 43. Flying Tigers 44. The Secret Life of Walter Mitty 47, etc.
TV series: The Abbott and Costello Show.

Jones, Grace (–). Black American performer.
Conan the Destroyer 84. A View to a Kill 85. Vamp 86.

Jones, Griffith (1910–). British light leading man, on stage from 1930.
The Faithful Heart (debut) 32. Catherine the Great 34. The Mill on the Floss 36. A Yank at Oxford 38. *The Four Just Men* 39. Young Man's Fancy 39. Atlantic Ferry 40. This Was Paris 41. Henry V 44. The Wicked Lady 45. *The Rake's Progress* 45. *They Made Me a Fugitive* 47. Good Time Girl 48. Miranda 48. Look Before You Love 49. Honeymoon Deferred 51. Star of My Night 53. The Sea Shall Not Have Them 55. Face in the Night 57. Kill Her Gently 59. Strangler's Web 63. Decline and Fall 68, many others.

Jones, Harmon (1911–1972). Canadian director in Hollywood.
□As Young As You Feel 51. The Pride of St Louis 52. Bloodhounds of Broadway 52. The Silver Whip 53. City of Bad Men 53. The Kid from Left Field 53. Gorilla at Large 54. Princess of the Nile 54. Target Zero 55. A Day of Fury 56. Canyon River 56. The Beast of Budapest 58. Bullwhip 58. Wolf Larsen 58. Don't Worry We'll Think of a Title 66.

Jones, Henry (1912–). American character actor of stage, TV, and occasional films; usually plays the guy next door or the worm who turns.
The Lady Says No 51. *The Bad Seed* 56. The Girl Can't Help It 57. Vertigo 58. The Bramble Bush 60. Angel Baby 60. Never Too Late 65. Project X 67. Stay Away Joe 68. Support Your Local Sheriff 69. The Skin Game 71. Pete 'n' Tillie 72. The Outfit 74. Nine to Five 80, etc.
TV series: Channing 63. Phyllis 75–76.

Jones, James (1921–1977). American novelist famous for *From Here to Eternity*, which was filmed, as was *Some Came Running*.

Jones, James Cellan (1930–). British director, in several senior TV posts.
Bequest to the Nation 72. *Jennie* (TV) 74. The Day Christ Died (TV) 80. Oxbridge Blues (TV) 84. Fortunes of War (TV) 87.

Jones, James Earl (1931–). Black American leading actor.
The Great White Hope 70. The Man (TV) 73. Claudine 74. The Bingo Long Travelling All Stars 76. Deadly Hero 76. Swashbuckler 76. The River Niger 76. The Last Remake of Beau Geste 77. Jesus of Nazareth (TV) 77. The Greatest 77. Exorcist II: The Heretic 77. Star Wars (voice of Darth Vader) 77. A Piece of the Action 77. The Greatest Thing That Almost Happened (TV) 77. Roots II (TV) (as Alex Haley) 79. The Bushido Blade 80. Conan the Barbarian 82. Allan Quatermain and the Lost City of Gold 86. Gardens of Stone 87, etc.
TV series: Paris 79.

Jones, Jennifer (1919–) (Phyllis Isley). Intense, variable American leading actress, in small film roles from 1939.
□Dick Tracy's G Men 39. The New Frontier 39. *The Song of Bernadette* (AA) 43. Since You Went Away 44. Love Letters 45. Cluny Brown 46. Duel in the Sun 46. *Portrait of Jennie* 48. We Were Strangers 49. Madame Bovary 49. *Carrie* 51. Gone to Earth (GB) 51. Ruby Gentry 52. Indiscretion 54. Beat the Devil 54. *Love Is a Many-Splendored Thing* 55. Good Morning, Miss Dove 55. The Man in the Grey Flannel Suit 56. The Barretts of Wimpole Street 57. A Farewell to Arms 58. Tender Is the Night 61. The Idol (GB) 66. Angel Angel Down We Go 69. The Towering Inferno 74.

Jones, Kenneth V. (1924–). British composer.
Sea Wife 56. The Horse's Mouth 58. The Trials of Oscar Wilde 60. The Tomb of Ligeia 64. Who Slew Auntie Roo? 71. The Brute 77. Leopard in the Snow 78, many others.

Jones, L. Q. (1936–) (J. E. McQueen). American character actor.
The Wild Bunch 69. The Ballad of Cable

Hogue 70. The Hunting Party 71. The Brotherhood of Satan (& p) 71. Mother, Jugs and Speed 76.

Jones, Marcia Mae (1924–). American child actress of the thirties.
King of Jazz 31. These Three 36. Heidi 37. The Little Princess 39. Tomboy 40. Nice Girl 41. Nine Girls 44. Arson Inc. 50. Chicago Calling (under the name of Marsha Jones) 52. Rogue's Gallery 68, etc.

Jones, Paul (1901–1968). American producer, long with Paramount.
The Great McGinty 40. Sullivan's Travels 41. Road to Morocco 42. The Virginian 46. Dear Ruth 47. Here Come the Girls 53. Living It Up 54. Pardners 56. The Disorderly Orderly 64, many others.

Jones, Paul (1942–) (Paul Pond). British leading man, former pop singer.
Privilege 66. Demons of the Mind 71, etc.

Jones, Peter (1920–). British character comedian.
Fanny by Gaslight 44. The Yellow Balloon 53. Albert R.N. 53. Danger Within 58. Never Let Go 61. Romanoff and Juliet 61. Press for Time 66. Just Like a Woman 66. The Return of the Pink Panther 75. Carry On England 76, etc.

Jones, Quincy (1935–). Black American composer.
The Pawnbroker 65. The Deadly Affair 66. In Cold Blood 67. MacKenna's Gold 69. Bob and Carol and Ted and Alice 70. Cactus Flower 71. The Anderson Tapes 72. The Getaway 72. The Hot Rock 72. The New Centurions 72. *Roots* (TV) 77. The Wiz 78, etc.

Jones, Shirley (1934–). American singer and leading lady who blossomed into a substantial actress.
□Oklahoma 55. Carousel 56. April Love 57. Never Steal Anything Small 58. Bobbikins (GB) 59. Pepe 60. *Elmer Gantry* (AA) 60. Two Rode Together 61. *The Music Man* 62. A Ticklish Affair 63. Bedtime Story 64. Dark Purpose 64. Fluffy 65. The Secret of My Success 65. Silent Night Lonely Night (TV) 69. But I Don't Want to Get Married (TV) 70. The Cheyenne Social Club 70. The Happy Ending 70. The Girls of Huntington House (TV) 73. The Family Nobody Wanted (TV) 75. Winner Take All (TV) 75. The Lives of Jenny Doland (TV) 75. Yesterday's Child (TV) 77. Evening in Byzantium (TV) 78. Who'll Save Our Children? (TV) 78. A Last Cry for Help (TV) 79. Beyond the Poseidon Adventure 79. The Children of An Lac (TV) 80. Inmates (TV) 81.
TV series: *The Partridge Family* 70–73. Shirley 79.

Jones, Spike (1911–1965) (Lindley Armstrong Jones). Pint-sized American bandleader ('Spike Jones and his City Slickers'), popular in the forties for crazy variations on well-known songs.
Thank Your Lucky Stars 43. Bring on the Girls 45. Variety Girl 47. Fireman Save My Child 55, etc.

Jones, Terry (1942–). British performer/director, one of the Monty Python group.

Jones, Tommy Lee (1946–). American leading man of the late seventies.
Love Story 70. Jackson County Jail 75. Charlie's Angels (pilot) (TV) 76. Smash Up on Interstate Five (TV) 76. *The Amazing Howard Hughes* (TV) 77. Rolling Thunder 77. Eyes of Laura Mars 78. The Betsy 78. Coal Miner's Daughter 80. Back Roads 81. The Executioner's Song (TV) 82. Nate and Hayes 83. The Big Town 87.

Jordan, Bobby (1923–1965). American actor, one of the original Dead End Kids.
Dead End 37. Angels with Dirty Faces 38. They Made Me a Criminal 39. That Gang of Mine 40. Pride of the Bowery 41. Let's Get Tough 42. Clancy Street Boys 43. Bowery Champs 44. Bowery Bombshell 46. Hard Boiled Mahoney 47. Treasure of Monte Cristo 49. This Man is Armed 56, many others.

Jordan, Neil (–). British director.
Angel (Ireland) 82. Company of Wolves 84. Mona Lisa 85.

Jordan, Richard (1938–). American leading actor.
Lawman 70. Valdez is Coming 71. The Friends of Eddie Coyle 73. The Yakuza 75. Kamouraska 75. Rooster Cogburn 75. *Captains and the Kings* (TV) 76. Logan's Run 76. Les Misérables (TV) 78. Interiors 78. The Defection of Simas Kurdika (TV) 78. Old Boyfriends 79. Raise the Titanic 80. The French Atlantic Affair (TV) 80. Dune 84. The Mean Season 84. The Men's Club 86, etc.

Jory, Victor (1902–1982). Saturnine Canadian actor, on stage from mid-twenties. Usually a villain on screen.
Sailor's Luck (debut) 32. A Midsummer Night's Dream (as Oberon) 35. *The Adventures of Tom Sawyer* (as Injun Joe) 38. Gone with the Wind 39. Unknown Guest 44. The Gallant Blade 48. Canadian Pacific 49. Cat Women of the Moon 53. Valley of the Kings 54. Diary of a Scoundrel 56. The Man Who Turned to Stone 58. The Fugitive Kind 60. *The Miracle Worker* 63. Cheyenne Autumn 64. Mackenna's Gold (narration only) 69. A Time for Dying 69. Flap 70. Papillon 73. Devil Dog, Hound of Hell (TV) 78. The Mountain Men 80, many others.
TV series: Manhunt 59–60.

Joseph, Robert (1913–1969). American producer.
The Third Secret (& w) 63, etc.

Josephson, Erland (1923–). Swedish character actor.
So Close to Life 58. Hour of the Wolf 68. A Passion 69. Cries and Whispers 72. Scenes from a Marriage 73. Face to Face 75. Beyond Evil 77. Autumn Sonata 78. Marmalade Revolution (& w, co-d) 79. Montenegro 80, etc.

Joslyn, Allyn (1905–1981). American character comedian whose crumpled features admirably portrayed bewilderment.
They Won't Forget (debut) 37. Bedtime Story 41. A Yank in Dutch 42. *Heaven Can Wait* 43. Bride by Mistake 44. Junior Miss 45. *It Shouldn't Happen to a Dog* 47. If You Knew Susie 48. As Young As You Feel 51. Titanic 53. The Fastest Gun Alive 56. The Brothers O'Toole 73, many others.
TV series: The Ray Bolger Show 53. The Eve Arden Show 57. McKeever and the Colonel 62. Don't Call Me Charlie 62. The Addams Family 64.

Jour de Fête (France 1949). The first full-length comedy written and directed by Jacques Tati, who stars as the rural postman with a sudden ambition to be efficient. The climactic sequence of visual gags is hilarious, but as in his later films Tati needs stronger control. In the seventies a curious but quite effective colour version was issued, the whole film being printed in sepia with hand-tinting of significant objects.

Le Jour Se Lève (France 1939). This memorable melodrama may have been over-praised because it was subsequently bought up and threatened with destruction to make way for an inferior American remake (*The Long Night* 47). Nevertheless it drew great tension from Jacques Prevert's tragic story of a man who kills a girl's persecutor and, cornered by the police, commits suicide. Directed by Marcel Carne, with music by Maurice Jaubert and photography by Curt Courant; also first-rate performances by Jean Gabin, Arletty and Jules Berry.

Jourdan, Louis (1919–) (Louis Gendre). Smooth French leading man who has made films also in Britain and Hollywood.
Le Corsaire (debut) 39. The Paradine Case 48. *Letter from an Unknown Woman* 48. Madame Bovary 49. Bird of Paradise 50. Anne of the Indies 51. *The Happy Time* 52. *Rue de l'Estrapade* 52. Decameron Nights 53. *Three Coins in the Fountain* 54. The Swan 56. Julie 56. *Gigi* 58. The Best of Everything 59. Can-Can 60. The Count of Monte Cristo 61. *The VIPs* 62. Made in Paris 65. Peau d'Espion 67. A Flea in Her Ear 68. Run a Crooked Mile (TV) 71. The Count of Monte Cristo (TV) 76. The Silver Bears 77. The Man in the Iron Mask (TV) 77. Swamp Thing 82. Octopussy 83, etc.
TV series: Paris Precinct 53.

Journal d'Un Curé de Campagne (France 1950). Written and directed by Robert Bresson from Georges Bernanos' novel, this spare, ascetic film tells of a young priest's difficulties and early death in his first parish. Claude Laydu's withdrawn performance is exactly in keeping.

Journey into Fear (US 1942). Set up by Orson Welles before he fell out of favour with RKO, this tight little thriller from Eric Ambler's book bears unmistakable signs of his influence though technically directed by Norman Foster. Brilliantly atmospheric in its Constantinople settings, it provides excellent roles for Joseph Cotten, Dolores del Rio and Welles himself as Colonel Haki of the Turkish Secret Police. Its influence can be seen in *The Third Man*. The 1974 remake went sadly awry.

Journey to the Center of the Earth (US 1959). Jules Verne's fantastic novel was here adapted by Charles Brackett and Walter Reisch, directed by Henry Levin and photographed by Leo Tover. Despite some cardboard sets, it successfully set a light whimsical trend in science fiction, with James Mason as an earnest professor and Arlene

Dahl as a Victorian lady who makes tea several miles down.

Journey's End (GB/US 1930). This film version of R. C. Sheriff's play set in the World War I trenches was an early example of Anglo-American co-production. It was also the last major film of producer George Pearson, and it took to Hollywood two interesting talents: actor Colin Clive and director James Whale, both of whom were involved in these capacities in the London stage production. In 1976 came an 'aerial version', *Aces High*.

Jouvet, Louis (1887–1951). Distinguished French actor of stage and screen.
☐Topaze 33. Doctor Knock 33. *La Kermesse Héroïque* 35. Mister Flow 36. Les Bas-Fonds 36. Mademoiselle Docteur 36. Un Carnet de Bal 37. *Drôle de Drame* 37. Alibi 37. Forfaiture 37. La Marseillaise 38. Ramuntcho 38. La Maison du Maltais 38. Entrée des Artistes 38. L'Education du Prince 38. Le Drame de Shanghai 38. *Hôtel du Nord* 38. La Fin du Jour 39. La Charrette Fantôme 39. Serenade 40. *Volpone* 40. Untel Père et Fils 40. Un Revenant 46. Copie Conforme 46. *Quai des Orfèvres* 47. Les Amoureux Sont Seuls au Monde 48. Entre Onze Heures et Minuit 49. Retour à la Vie 49. Miquette et Sa Mère 49. Doctor Knock (remake) 50. Une Histoire d'Amour 50.

Joy, Leatrice (1894–1985) (Leatrice Joy Zeidler). Vivacious, self-confident American leading lady of the twenties.
Bunty Pulls the Strings 20. The Marriage Cheat 21. Manslaughter 22. You Can't Fool Your Wife 23. The Ten Commandments 23. Triumph 24. The Dressmaker from Paris 25. For Alimony Only 26. Angel of Broadway 27. The Blue Danube 28. A Most Immoral Lady 29. First Love 39. Red Stallion in the Rockies 49. Love Nest 52, etc.

Joy, Nicholas (1894–1964). American small part actor often seen as beaming toff or benevolent father.
Daisy Kenyon 47. If Winter Comes 47. The Great Gatsby 49. And Baby Makes Three 50. Man with a Cloak 51. Affair with a Stranger 53. Desk Set 57, etc.

Joyce, Alice (1889–1955). American leading lady of the silent screen.
Womanhood 17. The Lion and the Mouse 19. Cousin Kate 21. The Green Goddess 23. Daddy's Gone a-Hunting 25. The Squall 29. Song o' My Heart 38, etc.

Joyce, Brenda (1918–) (Betty Leabo). American leading lady, former model. Played innocent types in the forties, then retired.
The Rains Came (debut) 39. Little Old New York 40. Maryland 40. Marry the Boss's Daughter 41. Whispering Ghosts 42. The Postman Didn't Ring 42. Little Tokyo USA 43. Strange Confession 45. The Enchanted Forest 46. Tarzan and the Huntress 47. Shaggy 48. Tarzan's Magic Fountain 49, etc.

Joyce, Yootha (1927–1980). Angular British character actress, popular in TV comedy series *A Man About the House* and *George and Mildred*.
Sparrows Can't Sing 62. The Pumpkin Eater 64. Stranger in the House 67. Burke and Hare 71. George and Mildred 80.

Joyless Street (Germany 1925). Much-censored study of prostitution and other vices, a rare German film of the period to centre on squalid fact rather than romantic fantasy. Directed by G. W. Pabst, with a cast including Greta Garbo, Asta Nielsen and Werner Krauss.

Judd, Edward (1932–). British general purpose actor.
The Day the Earth Caught Fire 61. Stolen Hours 63. The Long Ships 63. *The First Men in the Moon* 64. Strange Bedfellows 65. Island of Terror 66. Invasion 66. The Vengeance of She 68. Living Free 71. Universal Soldier 71. Vault of Horror 73. Assassin 73, The Incredible Sarah 76, etc.

Judex (France 1916). A super-serial by Louis Feuillade, enjoying belated recognition (in a six-hour version) as a primitive precursor of James Bond. A remake was directed by Georges Franju in 1963.

Judge, Arline (1912–1974). American general purpose leading lady.
Bachelor Apartment 31. Girl Crazy 32. Name This Woman 35. King of Burlesque 36. Valiant Is the Word for Carrie 37. The Lady Is Willing 42. From This Day Forward 45. Two Knights in Brooklyn 49, etc.

Judge Priest (US 1934). Directed by John Ford, this southern-state comedy-drama fairly oozed with local colour and provided a fat part for Will Rogers as a kindly old local judge. (Irvin S. Cobb, from whose writings it was taken, took over a couple of Will Rogers' roles after the actor died in an air crash in 1935.) In 1952 Ford remade the film as *The Sun Shines Bright*, with Charles Winninger.

Juillard, Robert (1906–). French cinematographer.
Germany Year Zero 48. Jeux Interdits 52. Les Belles de Nuit 52. Les Grandes Manoeuvres 55. Austerlitz 60, etc.

Jules et Jim (France 1961). François Truffaut's affectionate recreation of a period (pre-1914) and a curious triangular love affair has been enthusiastically adopted as a credo by sophisticated young people in many countries. Jeanne Moreau's performance transcends the lumpiness of the script, which ends in uneasy gloom. *Willie and Phil* was an uneasy 1980 American remake, written and directed by Paul Mazursky.

Julia, Raul (1940–). Puerto Rican character actor in Hollywood.
Eyes of Laura Mars 78. One from the Heart 82. The Escape Artist 82. Tempest 82. Compromising Positions 85. Kiss of the Spider Woman 85. The Morning After 86, etc.

Julian, Rupert (1886–1943). American director of the twenties.
Merry Go Round 23. Love and Glory 24. Hell's Highroad 25. *The Phantom of the Opera* 25. Three Faces West 26. Yankee Clipper 27. The Leopard Lady 28. Love Comes Along 30. The Cat Creeps 30, etc.

Julius Caesar (102–44 B.C.). The Roman emperor has been memorably portrayed by Claude Rains in *Caesar and Cleopatra*, Warren William in the 1934 *Cleopatra* and Rex Harrison in the 1962 remake. The Shakespeare play was filmed many times in silent days, but the only notable sound versions in English have been Joseph L. Mankiewicz's 1953 production with Louis Calhern as Caesar, James Mason as Brutus, and John Gielgud as Cassius, and the 1970 version with Gielgud as Caesar, Richard Johnson as Cassius, and Charlton Heston as Mark Antony. A British second feature of 1959, *An Honourable Murder*, brought the story up to date as a melodrama of boardroom intrigue. In *Carry On Cleo* Kenneth Williams played Caesar, and may have started the decline and fall of the Roman empire.

Jump, Gordon (–). Plump Canadian character actor, familiar as the boss in TV series *WKRP in Cincinnati*.
Conquest of the Planet of the Apes 72. House Calls 78. Four Days in Dallas (TV) 78. The Fury 78, etc.

jump-cutting. Moving abruptly from one scene to another to make a dramatic point, e.g. from cause to effect.

June (1901–85) (June Howard Tripp). British musical comedy star of the 20s and 30s. Married Lord Inverclyde; divorced. Films few. Autobiography 1960: *The Glass Ladder*.
□ Auld Lang Syne 17. Tom Jones 17. *The Lodger* 26. Forever and a Day 43. The River (voice only) 51.

June, Ray (1898–1958). American cinematographer.
Wandering Husbands 24. The Silent Avenger 27. Alibi 29. Arrowsmith 31. Horse Feathers 32. Riptide 34. I Cover the Waterfront 35. Night Must Fall 37. Test Pilot 38. The Hoodlum Saint 46. A Southern Yankee 48. Crisis 50. The Reformer and the Redhead 51. Sombrero 53. The Court Jester 55. Funny Face 56. Houseboat 58, many others.

Junge, Alfred (1886–1964). German art director with long experience at UFA; in Britain from the twenties.
Piccadilly 28. The Good Companions 32. *The Man Who Knew Too Much* 34. Bulldog Jack 35. *King Solomon's Mines* 37. The Citadel 38. *Goodbye Mr Chips* 39. The Silver Fleet 42. *The Life and Death of Colonel Blimp* 43. I Know Where I'm Going 45. *A Matter of Life and Death* 45. *Black Narcissus* (AA) 46. Edward My Son 49. The Miniver Story 50. Ivanhoe 52. Mogambo 53. *Invitation to the Dance* 56. The Barretts of Wimpole Street 57. A Farewell to Arms 58, many others.

Junge, Winfried (1936–). German woman director.

Jungle Jim. This sub-Tarzan character began as a comic strip, and in 1937 Forde Beebe directed a serial on his exploits. In 1948 began the rather tired series tossed off for Columbia with a paunchy Johnny Weissmuller in the title role: it started ineptly and quickly became ridiculous.

The Jungle Princess (US 1936). This Paramount programmer about a beautiful female Tarzan, directed by William Thiele, put Dorothy Lamour in a sarong for the first time and started her off on a series of similar exploits: *Her Jungle Love, Aloma of the South Seas, Typhoon, Beyond the Blue Horizon, Rainbow Island*, etc.

Junkin, John (1930–). Tall, balding British character comic actor, a TV familiar.

The Break 63. Kaleidoscope 66. Simon Simon 70, etc.

Jurado, Katy (1927–) (Maria Jurado Garcia). Spirited Mexican actress who has made Hollywood films.
The Bullfighter and the Lady 51. High Noon 52. Arrowhead 53. Broken Lance 54. Trial 55. Trapeze 56. One-Eyed Jacks 59. Barabbas 61. One Eyed Jacks 61. Pat Garrett and Billy the Kid 63. Smoky 66. Covenant with Death 67. Stay Away Joe 68. Pat Garrett and Billy the Kid 72. Evita Peron (TV) 82. Under the Volcano 84, etc.

Juran, Nathan (1907–). Austrian art director, long in the US. Won Academy Award for *How Green Was My Valley* 41. Later became a director of action films.
□The Black Castle 52. Gunsmoke 53. Law and Order 53. The Golden Blade 53. Tumbleweed 53. Highway Dragnet 54. Drums along the River 54. The Crooked Web 55. The Deadly Mantis 57. Hellcats of the Navy 57. Twenty Million Miles to Earth 57. The Seventh Voyage of Sinbad 58. Good Day for a Hanging 58. Flight of the Lost Balloon 61. *Jack the Giant Killer* 62. Siege of the Saxons 63. First Men in the Moon 64. East of Sudan 65. The Land Raiders 70. The Boy Who Cried Werewolf 73.

Jurgens, Curt (1912–1982). German stage leading man, in films from 1935; after the war he played internationally.
Koenigswalzer (debut) 35. Der Engel mit der Posanne 48. Orientexpress 54. The Devil's General 54. Les Héros Sont Fatigués 55. *An Eye for an Eye* 56. Without You It Is Night (& d) 56. And Woman Was Created 57. *Me and the Colonel* 57. The Enemy Below 57. Inn of the Sixth Happiness 58. The Blue Angel 58. Ferry to Hong Kong 58. *I Aim at the Stars* (as Wernher von Braun) 59. Tamango 60. Chess Novel 60. The Threepenny Opera 63. Lord Jim 64. Das Liebeskarussel (Who Wants to Sleep) 65. The Assassination Bureau 68. The Battle of Neretva 70. Nicholas and Alexandra 71. Vault of Horror 73. Soft Beds and Hard Battles 74. The Spy Who Loved Me 77. I, Cagliostro 77. Sergeant Steiner 79. Goldengirl (TV) 79. Just a Gigolo 80, etc.

Jurow, Martin (1914–). American producer.
The Hanging Tree 58. The Fugitive Kind 60. Breakfast at Tiffany's 61. Soldier in the Rain 63. The Great Race 65, etc.
Retired to practise law.

Justice est Faite (France 1950). Written and directed by André Cayatte, this study of a jury during a murder trial managed to provide entertaining drama while questioning points of law. Cayatte's subsequent films mostly followed a similar pattern, but not so successfully.

Justice, James Robertson (1905–1975). Bearded Scottish actor and personality, former journalist and naturalist.
Fiddlers Three (debut) 44. *Scott of the Antarctic* 48. Christopher Columbus 49. *Whisky Galore* 49. David and Bathsheba 51. The Voice of Merrill 52. *Doctor in the House* 54. Storm over the Nile 55. Land of the Pharaohs 55. Moby Dick 56. Campbell's Kingdom 57. Seven Thunders 57. Doctor at Large 58. A French Mistress 60. *Very Important Person* 61. Das Feuerschiff 62. *The Fast Lady* 62. Crooks Anonymous 62. You Must Be Joking 65. Doctor in Clover 66. Hell is Empty 67. Mayerling 68. Chitty Chitty Bang Bang 68, many others.

Justin, John (1917–). British leading man, on stage from 1933.
The Thief of Baghdad (film debut) 40. The Gentle Sex 43. Journey Together 45. Call of the Blood 47. The Sound Barrier 51. Melba 53. Seagulls over Sorrento 54. The Man Who Loved Redheads 55. The Teckman Mystery 55. Safari 56. Island in the Sun 56. The Spider's Web 61. Candidate For Murder 64. Savage Messiah 72. Valentino 77. The Big Sleep 78. Trenchcoat 83, etc.

Answers

Johnny Who?

1 Henry Silva □ 2 Sterling Hayden □ 3 Dick Powell □ 4 Frank Sinatra □ 5 Tony Curtis □ 6 James Cagney □ 7 George Raft □ 8 Robert Taylor □ 9 Hal Stalmaster □ 10 Peter Finch □

K

Kaczender, George (1933–). Hungarian director.
U-Turn 73. In Praise of Older Women 78. Agency 80. Chanel Solitaire 81. The Finishing Touch 83.

Kadar, Jan (1918–79). Czech director who worked with writer Elmer Klos (1910–).
Kidnap 56. Death Is Called Engelchen 58. The Accused 64. *A Shop on the High Street* (AA) 64. The Angel Levine (US) 70. Adrift 71. Lies My Father Told Me 76. *The Other Side of Hell* (TV) 77. Freedom Road (TV) 80, etc.

Kael, Pauline (–). American critic, most of whose reviews have been collected for publication.

¶ *P.K.:* Movies are so rarely great that if we cannot appreciate great trash we have very little reason to be interested in them.

Kafka, Franz (1883–1924). German/Czech novelist who wrote puzzling tales of guilt and innocence in a glum fantasy world. *The Trial* and *The Castle* have been filmed.

Kagan, Jeremy Paul (1945–). American director.
□Unwed Father (TV) 74. Judge Dee (TV) 75. Katherine (TV) 75. Scott Joplin 76. Heroes 77. The Big Fix 78. The Chosen 82. Sting II 83. The Journey of Natty Gann 85.

Kahn, Gus (1886–1941). German-American lyricist who made a specialty of film scores, and was played by Danny Thomas in *I'll See You in My Dreams*.
The Jazz Singer 27. Whoopee 30. Flying Down to Rio 33. San Francisco 36. Go West 40, many others.

Kahn, Madeline (1942–). American comic actress who tends to overplay her hand; the darling of the Mel Brooks clique.
What's Up Doc? 72. Paper Moon 73. Blazing Saddles 74. Young Frankenstein 74. The Adventure of Sherlock Holmes' Smarter Brother 75. At Long Last Love 75. Won Ton Ton 77. High Anxiety 77. The Cheap Detective 78. The Muppet Movie 79. The First Family 80. Happy Birthday Gemini 80. Simon 80. Wholly Moses 80. History of the World Part One 81. Yellowbeard 83.
City Heat 84. Clue 85.
TV series: Oh Madeline 83.

Kalem. An early American production company founded in 1907, taking its name from the initials of its three principals, George Klein, Sam Long and Frank Marion (K-L-M). Its most famous production is *From the Manger to the Cross* 12.

Kalatozov, Mikhail (1903–1973). Russian director and executive.
Their Kingdom 28. Salt for Svenetia 30. A Nail in a Boot 32. The Conspiracy of the Doomed 50. *The Cranes are Flying* 57. The Unsent Letter 60. I Am Cuba 66. The Red Tent 69.

Kalmar, Bert (1884–1947). American vaudevillian, song-writer (with Harry Ruby) and music executive.
Check and Double Check (& w) 30. The Kid from Spain (& w) 32. *Horse Feathers* (& w) 32. *Duck Soup* (& w) 33. Kentucky Kernels (& w) 34. Everybody Sing 38. Wake Up and Dream 46. Carnival in Costa Rica 48, many others.

Kalmus, Herbert T. (1881–1963). American pioneer photographic expert, later president of Technicolor. His wife *Natalie Kalmus* (1892–1965) was adviser on all Technicolor films from 1933.

Kamen, Michael (–). American composer.
The Dead Zone 83. Brazil 85. Highlander 85. Mona Lisa 85. Lethal Weapon 87, etc.

Kameradschaft (Germany 1931). G. W. Pabst's most acclaimed film shows how a mine disaster in a French town near the German border breaks down the barriers of hatred between the two nations. The original version had a cynical ending. Photographed by Fritz Arno Wagner.

Kaminska, Ida (1899–1980). Polish character actress.
The Shop on High Street 66. The Angel Levine (US) 70, etc.

Kander, John (1927–). American composer, with Fred Ebb, of *Cabaret*.

Kane, Carol (1952–). American leading lady of the late seventies.
Annie Hall 77. The World's Greatest Lover 77. Valentino 77. The Muppet Movie 79. When a Stranger Calls 79. Strong Medicine 81. Norman Loves Rose 82.

Kane, Helen (1904–66) (Helen Schroeder). American singer of the twenties, the 'boop-boop-a-doop' girl. Played by Debbie Reynolds in *Three Little Words* (in which Miss Kane supplied her own voice).
Pointed Heels 29. Dangerous Nan McGrew 29. Heads Up 30, etc.

Kane, Joseph (1894–1975). American director since 1935, mainly of competent but unambitious Republic westerns.
The Man from Music Mountain 38. The Man from Cheyenne 42. Flame of the Barbary Coast 44. The Cheaters 45. The Plainsman and the Lady 46. The Plunderers (& p) 48. California Passage (& p) 50. Hoodlum Empire (& p) 51. Jubilee Trail (& p) 53. Spoilers of the Forest (& p) 57, many others.

Kanin, Garson (1912–). American writer and raconteur who has spent time in Hollywood as director, also as screenwriter, especially in collaboration with his wife Ruth Gordon.
Autobiographical books: *Hollywood* 74, *It Takes a Long Time to Become Young* 76.
□AS DIRECTOR: A Man to Remember 38. Next Time I Marry 38. *The Great Man Votes* 38. *Bachelor Mother* 39. My Favorite Wife 40. They Knew What They Wanted 40. *Tom, Dick and Harry* 41. The True Glory (w co-d) 45. Where It's At (& w) 69. Some Kind of a Nut (& w) 70.
AS WRITER: From This Day Forward 46. A Double Life 48. *Adam's Rib* 49. *Born Yesterday* (oa) 50. The Marrying Kind 52. Pat and Mike 52. It Should Happen to You 53, etc.

Kanin, Michael (1910–). American writer brother of Garson Kanin; often works with his wife Fay.
Anne of Windy Poplars 40. *Woman of the Year* (AA) 42. The Cross of Lorraine 44. Centennial Summer 46. Rhapsody 54. The Opposite Sex 56. Teacher's Pet 58. The Outrage 64, etc.

Kann, Lily (c. 1898–1978). German character actress, long in England.
The Flemish Farm 43. Latin Quarter 45. Mrs Fitzherbert 47. A Tale of Five Cities 51. Betrayed (US) 54. A Kid for Two Farthings 55. No Trees in the Street 59, many others.

Kanner, Alexis (1942–). British character actor.
Reach for Glory 63. Crossplot 69. Connecting Rooms 69. Goodbye Gemini 70. Kings and Desperate Men (w, d, a) 84, etc.

Kanter, Hal (1918–). American writer-director with TV background.
I Married a Woman (d) 55. Loving You (wd) 56. Once Upon a Horse (wd) 58. Pocketful of Miracles (co-w) 61. Move Over Darling (w) 63. Dear Brigitte (w) 65, etc.

Kantor, Mackinlay (1904–77). American writer full of sentiment and patriotism.
The Voice of Bugle Ann 37. Happy Land 43. The Best Years of Our Lives 46. The Romance of Rosy Ridge 47. Follow Me Boys 66.

Kaper, Bronislau (1902–1983). Polish composer who lived in US.
The Chocolate Soldier 41. Two Faced Woman 41. Gaslight 44. Without Love 45. Green Dolphin Street 47. The Forsyte Saga 49. *The Red Badge of Courage* 51. *Lili* (AA) 53. *Them* 54. The Swan 56. The Brothers Karamazov 58. Green Mansions 59. Butterfield 8 61. Mutiny on the Bounty 62. Kisses for My President 64. Lord Jim 64. Tobruk 66. The Way West 67. A Flea in Her Ear 68, etc.

Kaplan, Jonathan (1947–). American director.
Student Teachers 73. Night Call Nurses 74. White Line Fever 75. Mr Billion 77. Over the Edge 79. Heart like a Wheel 83, etc.

Kaplan, Marvin (1924–). Owlish little American comedy actor.
The Reformer and the Redhead 50. I Can Get It for You Wholesale 51. Angels in the

Outfield 51. Behave Yourself 61. Wake Me When It's Over 60. A New Kind of Love 63. It's a Mad Mad Mad Mad World 63. The Great Race 65, etc.
TV series: Chicago Teddybears 71. Alice 81–82.

Kaplan, Nelly (1934–). French woman director.
☐La Fiancée du Pirate/Dirty Mary 69. Papa les Petits Bateaux 71. Néa 76. Le Satéllite de Venus 77. Au Bonheur des Dames 79. Charles et Lucie 79.

Kaplan, Sol (–). American composer.
Tales of Manhattan 42. Port of New York 49. Rawhide 51. Niagara 53. Happy Anniversary 59. The Victors 63. The Spy Who Came in from the Cold 65. Explosion 69. Living Free 72. Lies My Father Told Me 75, etc.

Karas, Anton (1906–85). Viennese composer whose zither music, played by himself, helped to turn *The Third Man* into a classic.

Karina, Anna (1940–) (Hanne Karin Beyer). Danish leading lady, mostly in French films, especially those of Jean-Luc Godard.
She'll Have To Go (GB) 61. *Une Femme Est une Femme* 61. *Vivre Sa Vie* 62. Le Petit Soldat 63. Bande à Part 64. Alphaville 65. Made in USA 66. The Magus 68. Before Winter Comes 68. Laughter in the Dark 69. Justine 69. The Salzburg Connection 72. Bread and Chocolate 73. Chinese Roulette 76. Chausette Surprise 78. Laissez Parler les Adultes 80, etc.

Karlin, Fred (1936–). American composer.
Up the Down Staircase 67. Yours Mine and Ours 68. Lovers and Other Strangers 69. The Little Ark 71. Westworld 73. The Spikes Gang 74. Death Be Not Proud (TV) 75. Futureworld 76. Man From Atlantis (TV) 77. Cloud Dancer 80. Loving Couples 80.

Karlin, Miriam (1925–) (M. Samuels). Rasping-voiced British revue comedienne and character actress.
The Deep Blue Sea 55. The Entertainer 59. On the Fiddle 61. The Small World of Sammy Lee 63. Heavens Above 63. The Bargee 64. Ladies Who Do 64. A Clockwork Orange 71, etc.

Karloff, Boris (1887–1969) (William Henry Pratt). Gaunt British character actor, on stage from 1910, films from 1919, mainly in US. Achieved world fame as the monster in *Frankenstein* 31, and became typed in horrific parts despite his gentle, cultured voice.
Biographies: *Horror Man* (1972) by Peter Underwood. *Karloff, the Man, the Monster, the Movies* (1973) by Denis Gifford. *The Films of Boris Karloff* by Richard Bojarski and Kenneth Beals.
SELECTED SILENTS: His Majesty the American 19. The Last of the Mohicans 20. The Man from Downing Street 22. A Woman Conquers 23. Parisian Nights 25. Never the Twain Shall Meet 25. The Bells 26. Valencia 26. Tarzan and the Golden Lion 27. Two Arabian Knights 27. Vultures of the Sea 28. Phantoms of the North 29, many others.
☐SOUND FILMS: Behind that Curtain 29. King of the Kongo 29. The Unholy Night 29. The Bad One 30. The Sea Bat 30. The Utah Kid 30. Mothers Cry 30. The Criminal Code 30. Cracked Nuts 31. Young Donovan's Kid 31. King of the Wild 31. Smart Money 31. The Public Defender 31. I Like Your Nerve 31. Graft 31. Five Star Final 31. The Mad Genius 31. The Yellow Ticket 31. Guilty Generation 31. *Frankenstein* 31. Tonight or Never 31. Behind the Mask 32. Business and Pleasure 32. Scarface 32. The Cohens and Kellys in Hollywood 32. The Miracle Man 32. Night World 32. *The Old Dark House* 32. *The Mask of Fu Manchu* 32. *The Mummy* 32. The Ghoul 33. The Lost Patrol 34. The House of Rothschild 34. The Black Cat 34. The Gift of Gab 34. *The Bride of Frankenstein* 35. *The Black Room* 35. *The Raven* 35. The Invisible Ray 36. The Walking Dead 36. The Man Who Changed His Mind 36. Juggernaut 36. *Charlie Chan at the Opera* 37. Night Key 37. West of Shanghai 37. The Invisible Menace 37. Mr Wong Detective 38. Son of Frankenstein 39. The Mystery of Mr Wong 39. Mr Wong in Chinatown 39. The Man They Could Not Hang 39. Tower of London 39. The Fatal Hour 40. British Intelligence 40. Black Friday 40. The Man with Nine Lives 40. Devil's Island 40. Doomed to Die 40. Before I Hang 40. The Ape 40. You'll Find Out 40. The Devil Commands 41. The Boogie Man will Get You 42. The Climax 44. *House of Frankenstein* 44. *The Body Snatcher* 45. Isle of the Dead 45. Bedlam 46. The Secret Life of Walter Mitty 47. Lured 47. Unconquered 47. Dick Tracy meets Gruesome 47. Tap Roots 48. Abbott and Costello Meet the Killer 49. The Strange Door 51. The Black Castle 52. Abbott and Costello Meet Dr Jekyll and Mr Hyde 53. Monster of the Island 53. The Hindu 53. Voodoo Island 58. Grip of the Strangler 58. Corridors of Blood 58. Frankenstein 70 58. *The Raven* 63. The

Terror 63. Comedy of Terrors 63. Black Sabbath 64. Bikini Beach 64. Die Monster Die 65. Ghost in the Invisible Bikini 66. The Venetian Affair 67. The Sorcerers 67. *Targets* 68. Curse of the Crimson Altar 68. The Snake People 70. The Incredible Invasion 70. Cauldron of Blood 70. The Fear Chamber 70. House of Evil 70.
TV series: Colonel March of Scotland Yard 53. Thriller 60–61.
❁ For his sinister Englishness, his sepulchral tones and his unfailing eagerness to please. *Bride of Frankenstein.*

¶ When I was nine I played the demon king in Cinderella and it launched me on a long and happy life of being a monster.

Though Karloff fought against being typecast, he later admitted:

> The monster was the best friend I ever had.

How did he get the part? Said producer Carl Laemmle junior:

> His eyes mirrored the suffering we needed.

Director James Whale amplified this:

> His face fascinated me. I made drawings of his head, adding sharp bony ridges where I imagined the skull might have joined.

Karloff however insisted:

> You could heave a brick out of the window and hit ten actors who could play my parts. I just happened to be on the right corner at the right time.

Karlson, Phil (1908–86) (Philip Karlstein). American director, in Hollywood from 1932. Mainly low-budget actioners until he suddenly gained stature in the fifties.
☐A Wave a WAC and a Marine 44. GI Honeymoon 45. There Goes Kelly 45. Shanghai Cobra 45. Swing Parade 46. Live Wires 46. Dark Alibi 46. Behind the Mask 46. Bowery Bombshell 46. The Missing Lady 46. Wife Wanted 46. Black Gold 47. Kilroy was Here 47. Louisiana 47. Rocky 48. Adventures in Silverado 48. Thunderhoof 48. Ladies of the Chorus 49. The Big Cat 49. Down Memory Lane 49. The Iroquois Trail 50. Lorna Doone 51. The Texas Rangers 51. Mask of the Avenger 51. *Scandal Sheet* 52. The Brigand 52. *Kansas City Confidential* 53. 99 River Street 53. They Rode West 54. Tight Spot 55. Hell's Island 55. Five Against the House 55. *The Phenix City Story* 55. The Brothers Rico 57. Gunman's Walk 58. Hell to Eternity 60. Key Witness 60. The Secret Ways 61. The Young Doctors 61. Kid Galahad 62. Rampage 63. *The Silencers* 66. A Time for Killing 67. Wrecking Crew 69. Hornet's Nest 70. Ben 72. Walking Tall 73. Framed 75.

Karno, Fred (1866–1941). English impresario from whose team of slapstick comedians sprang several stars including Stan Laurel and Charles Chaplin.
Biography 1971: *Fred Karno* by J. P. Gallagher.

Karns, Roscoe (1893–1970). American character actor, very active in the thirties, usually in hard-boiled comedy roles.
Beggars of Life 28. *The Front Page* 30. Undercover Man 32. *Night After Night* 32. *Twentieth Century* 34. *It Happened One Night* 34. Thanks for the Memory 38. They Drive by Night 40. *His Girl Friday* 40. His Butler's Sister 43. Will Tomorrow Ever Come? 47. Inside Story 48. Onionhead 58, many others.
TV series: Rocky King Detective 50. Hennessey 59–61.
Famous line (*It Happened One Night*): Shapeley's the name, and that's the way I like 'em.

Karras, Alex (1935–). Heavyweight American character actor, former footballer.
Hardcase (TV) 72. The 500 Pound Jerk (TV) 73. Babe (TV) 75. Mulligan Stew (TV) 77. Blazing Saddles 76. Mad Bull (TV) 77. Centennial (TV) 78. When Time Ran Out 80. Nobody's Perfekt 81. Victor/Victoria 82.
TV series: Webster 83.

Kasdan, Lawrence (–). American writer-director.
Continental Divide (w) 80. The Empire Strikes Back (co-w) 80. Raiders of the Lost Ark (w) 81. *Body Heat* (w, d) 82. *The Big Chill* (w, d) 83.

Kasket, Harold (c. 1916–). British character actor of mixed descent, originally stage impressionist.
Hotel Sahara 51. Moulin Rouge 53. Interpol 57. Sands of the Desert 60. Arabesque 66, etc.

Kastner, Elliott (1930–). American producer, former literary agent.
Bus Riley's Back in Town 65. Harper 66. Kaleidoscope 66. The Night of the Following Day 68. Where Eagles Dare 68. The Walking Stick 69. A Severed Head 70. When Eight Bells Toll 71. Villain 71. Zee and Co. 72. The Nightcomers 72. The Long Goodbye 73.

Harrowhouse 74. Farewell My Lovely 75. The Missouri Breaks 76. The Big Sleep 78. North Sea Hijack 80. Absolution 80. The First Deadly Sin 81. Death Valley 82. Oxford Blues 84. Garbo Talks 85. Angel Heart 87, etc.

Kastner, Erich (1899–1974). German novelist whose *Emil and the Detectives* has been much filmed. He also wrote the original of *The Parent Trap*.

Kastner, Peter (1944–). Canadian actor who made a corner in frustrated adolescents. Nobody Waved Goodbye (Can.) 65. *You're a Big Boy Now* (US) 66. B.S. I Love You 70, etc.
TV series: The Ugliest Girl in Town 68.

Kasznar, Kurt (1913–1979). Chubby Austrian character actor, in US from 1936. The Light Touch (debut) 51. The Happy Time 52. Lili 53. Sombrero 53. My Sister Eileen 55. Anything Goes 56. A Farewell to Arms 58. For the First Time 59. Casino Royale 66. The King's Pirate 67. The Ambushers 67, etc.
TV series: Land of the Giants 68–69.

Katch, Kurt (1896–1958) (Isser Kac). Bald Polish character actor, in Hollywood from 1942.
Ali Baba and the Forty Thieves 43. *The Mask of Dimitrios* 44. Salome Where She Danced 45. The Mummy's Curse 45. Song of Love 47. The Secret of the Incas 54. Abbott and Costello Meet the Mummy 55. Pharaoh's Curse 57, etc.

Katselas, Milton (1933–). American director with Broadway experience.
□Butterflies Are Free 72. Forty Carats 73. Report to the Commissioner 74. When You Comin' Back Red Ryder? 79. Strangers (TV) 79.

Katt, William (1955–). American leading man of the late seventies, son of Bill Williams and Barbara Hale.
Carrie 76. First Love 78. Big Wednesday 79. Butch and Sundance 79. Baby, Secret of the Lost Legend 84. House 85, etc.
TV series: The Greatest American Hero 81–82.

Katzin, Lee H. (1935–). American director. Heaven with a Gun 69. Along Came a Spider (TV) 70. Whatever Happened to Aunt Alice? 70. The Phynx 70. Le Mans 71. The Salzburg Connection 72. The Voyage of the Yes (TV) 72. Savages (TV) 74. The Last Survivors (TV) 75. Sky Heist (TV) 75. Man from Atlantis (TV) 77. The Bastard (TV) 78. Terror Out of the Sky (TV) 78. Samurai (TV) 79, etc.

Katzman, Sam (1901–1973). American producer, chiefly of low-budget co-features including the *Jungle Jim* series, *Rock Around the Clock* 56, many others.

Kaufman, Boris (1906–1980). Polish photographer, in France from 1928, Hollywood from 1942. Brother of Dziga Vertog.
□La Marche des Machines 28. A Propos de Nice (& co-d) 30. Les Halles 30. *Zero de Conduite* 32. Seine 33. *L'Atalante* 34. Pere Lampion 36. Fort Delores 37. Serenade 38. Better Tomorrow 45. Capital Story 45. The Southwest 45. Journey into Medicine 47. The Tanglewood Story 50. The Garden of Eden 54. *On the Waterfront* (AA) 54. Crowded Paradise 56. *Baby Doll* 56. Patterns 56. *Twelve Angry Men* 57. That Kind of Woman 59. The Fugitive Kind 60. Splendor in the Grass 61. Long Day's Journey into Night 62. All the Way Home 63. Gone are the Days 63. *The World of Henry Orient* 64. The Pawnbroker 65. *The Group* 66. *Bye Bye Braverman* 67. Uptight 68. The Brotherhood 68. Tell Me That You Love Me Junie Moon 70.

Kaufman, George S. (1889–1961). American comedy playwright, often in collaboration with Moss Hart (qv). Most of his works were filmed.
Biography 1972: *George S. Kaufman* by Howard Teichman.
Dulcy 23. Beggar on Horseback 25. *Animal Crackers* 30. The Royal Family of Broadway 30. *Once in a Lifetime* 32. Dinner at Eight 33. Stage Door 37. *You Can't Take It With You* 38. *The Man Who Came to Dinner* 41. George Washington Slept Here 42. The Late George Apley 47. The Senator was Indiscreet (wd) 49. The Solid Gold Cadillac 56, etc.

¶ He had great integrity. You never had to watch him when he was dealing.—*Harpo Marx*

He was renowned for marrying very high comedy with very high farce; and with his wit, it came out satire.—*Howard Teichmann*

Kaufman, Millard (1917–). American screenwriter; output sparse and patchy, but interesting.
Gun Crazy 50. Take the High Ground 53. *Bad Day at Black Rock* 55. Raintree County 57. Never So Few 59. Convicts Four (& d)

62. The War Lord 65. Living Free 72. The Klansman 76, etc.

Kaufman, Philip (1936–). American director.
Goldstein (co-d) 63. Fearless Frank 69. The Great Minnesota Raid 72. The White Dawn 73. The Outlaw Josey Wales (co-w only) 75. Invasion of the Body Snatchers 78. The Wanderers 79. Raiders of the Lost Ark (co-w only) 81. *The Right Stuff* (w, d) 83.

Kaufman, Robert (–). American screenwriter.
Dr Goldfoot and the Bikini Machine 65. Getting Straight 70. I Love My Wife (& p) 70. Harry and Walter Go to New York 76. Love at First Bite (& p) 70. How to Beat the High Cost of Living (& p) 80. Split Image (co-w) 82.

Kaufmann, Christine (1944–). German leading lady in international films.
Town without Pity 61. Taras Bulba 62. Wild and Wonderful 64. Tunnel 28 64. Murders in the Rue Morgue 71, etc.

Kaufmann, Maurice (1928–). British supporting actor.
A Shot in the Dark 64. Fanatic 65. Bloomfield 70. The Abominable Dr Phibes 71, etc.

Kautner, Helmut (1908–1980). German director who had an unhappy experience in Hollywood in the fifties.
Kitty and the World Conference 39. Adieu Franciska 41. Romanze in Moll 43. Unter Den Brücken 45. In Jenen Tagen 47. Der Apfel Ist Ab 48. Epilog 50. The Last Brigade 54. Ludwig II 54. The Devil's General 55. Himmel Ohne Sterne 55. The Captain from Koepenick 56. The Wonderful Years (US) 58. Stranger in My Arms (US) 59. The Rest is Silence 59. Der Glas Wasser 60. Die Rote 62, etc.

Kawalerowicz, Jerzy (1922–). Polish director.
Gromada 51. Cien 54. The True End of the Great War 57. *Pociag* (Night Train) 59. *Mother Jeanne of the Angels* (The Devil and the Nun) 60. *The Pharaoh* 64. Maddalena 71. Death of the President 78, etc.

Kaye, Danny (1908/13–87) (David Daniel Kaminsky). Ebullient American star entertainer of stage, screen and TV. After making several unpromising two reelers in the thirties (later compiled as *The Danny Kaye Story*) he was given the big build up by Sam Goldwyn and gained enormous popularity, though his later films were disappointing. Special Academy Award in 1954 'for his unique talents, his service to the industry and the American people'.
Biography 1948: *The Danny Kaye Saga* by Kurt Singer.
Up in Arms 44. *Wonder Man* 45. The Kid from Brooklyn 46. *The Secret Life of Walter Mitty* 47. A Song Is Born 48. The Inspector General 49. On the Riviera 51. *Hans Christian Andersen* 52. *Knock on Wood* 53. White Christmas 54. Assignment Children (UN short) 54. *The Court Jester* 56. Me and the Colonel 57. Merry Andrew 58. The Five Pennies 59. On the Double 62. The Man from the Diners' Club 63. The Madwoman of Chaillot 69. Peter Pan (TV) 75. Pinocchio (TV) 76.
❀ For his perfectionist comedy techniques. *Wonder Man.*

¶ I am a wife-made man.—*D.K.* (His wife Sylvia Fine wrote most of his best lyrics.)

I'm Anatole of Paris,
I shriek with chic;
My 'at of ze week
Caused six divorces, three runaway
'orses . . .
I'm Anatole of Paris, ze 'ats I sell
Make people yell
'Is zat a 'at or a two-room flat?'—*Kaye lyric*

I became an entertainer not because I wanted to but because I was meant to.—*D.K.*

I can't say what Danny Kaye is like in private life. There are too many of them.—*Sylvia Fine*

Kaye, Stubby (1918–). Rotund American comic actor.
Guys and Dolls 55. Lil Abner 59. 40 Pounds of Trouble 62. Cat Ballou 65. Sweet Charity 68, etc.
TV series: Love and Marriage 59. My Sister Eileen 60.

Kazan, Elia (1909–) (Elia Kazanjoglous). Distinguished American stage and screen director of Greek/Turkish descent. Intermittently an actor; with New York's Group Theatre in the thirties.
AS ACTOR: City for Conquest 40. Blues in the Night 41, etc.
AS DIRECTOR: *A Tree Grows in Brooklyn* 45. The Sea of Grass 47. *Boomerang* 47. *Gentleman's Agreement* (AA) 47. Pinky 49. Panic in the Streets 50. A Streetcar Named

Desire 51. *Viva Zapata* 52. Man on a Tightrope 53. *On the Waterfront* (AA) 54. East of Eden 55. Baby Doll 56. *A Face in the Crowd* (& p) 57. Wild River (& p) 60. Splendor in the Grass (& p) 61. America America (& wp) 63. The Arrangement (& wp) 69. The Visitors (& w) 72. The Last Tycoon 76.

Keach, James (–). American actor, brother of Stacy Keach.
Sunburst 75. Death Play 76. Cannonball 76. FM 78. Comes a Horseman 78. Lacy and the Mississippi Queen (TV) 78. Like Normal People (TV) 79. Hurricane 79. *The Long Riders* (as Jesse James) 80. Love Letters 83. The Razor's Edge 84. Wildcats 85, etc.

Keach, Stacy (1941–). American general purpose actor.
□The Heart is a Lonely Hunter 68. End of the Road 68. The Travelling Executioner 69. Brewster McCloud 70. Doc 70. Judge Roy Bean 72. The New Centurions 72. Fat City 72. The Dion Brothers (TV) 74. All the Kind Strangers (TV) 74. Conduct Unbecoming 75. James Michener's Dynasty (TV) 76. Luther 76. Street People 76. The Killer Inside Me 76. The Squeeze 77. Jesus of Nazareth (TV) 77. Slave of the Cannibal God 78. Two Solitudes 78. Gray Lady Down 78. Up in Smoke 78. The Long Riders (as Frank James) 80. The Ninth Configuration 80. Cheech and Chong's Nice Dreams 81. Road Games 81. Butterfly 82. That Championship Season 82. Princess Daisy (TV) 83. Mistral's Daughter (TV) 84.
TV series: Caribe 75. Mike Hammer 83.

Keane, Robert Emmett (1883–1981). Toothbrush-moustached American character actor who played travelling salesmen and fall guys in scores of light comedies and dramas. Men Call It Love 31. Boys' Town 38. We're in the Army Now 40. Tin Pan Alley 41. Jitterbugs 43. When My Baby Smiles at Me 50. When Gangland Strikes 56, etc.

Kearton, Cherry (1871–1940). Pioneer British travel film producer whose success lasted from 1912 to the mid-thirties.

Keating, Larry (1897–1963). American character actor, often as executive or uppity neighbour.
Whirlpool 49. Three Secrets 50. Come Fill the Cup 51. About Face 52. Inferno 53. Daddy Longlegs 55. The Buster Keaton Story 57. Who was that Lady? 60. Boys' Night Out 62, many others.
TV series: *The Burns and Allen Show* 56–58. *Mister Ed* 60–62.

Keaton, Buster (1895–1966) (Joseph Francis Keaton). One of America's great silent clowns, the unsmiling but game little fellow who always came out on top whatever the odds. In two-reelers with Fatty Arbuckle from 1917, but soon began to shape his own material. Special Academy Award 1959 'for his unique talents which brought immortal comedies to the screen'. Trained in vaudeville with family act. Did not easily survive sound, but later came back in featured roles and was gaining a fresh popularity at the time of his death.
Autobiography 1960: *My Wonderful World of Slapstick*. Biographies: *Keaton* (1966) by Rudi Blesh; *Buster Keaton* (1969) by David Robinson. Keaton was played by Donald O'Connor in a 1957 biopic, *The Buster Keaton Story*.
□from 1920: The Saphead 20. *One Week* 20. The High Sign 20. Convict 13 20. The Scarecrow 20. Neighbours 20. The Haunted House 21. The Goat 21. *The Playhouse* 22. *The Boat* 22. *The Paleface* 22. *Cops* 22. My Wife's Relations 22. The Blacksmith 22. The Frozen North 22. The Electric House 22. Daydreams 22. *Balloonatic* 22. The Love Nest 22. The Three Ages 23. *Our Hospitality* 23. *Sherlock Junior* 24. *The Navigator* 24. Seven Chances 25. Go West 25. Battling Butler 26. *The General* 27. College 27. Steamboat Bill Junior 27. *The Cameraman* 28. Spite Marriage 29. Hollywood Revue 29. Free and Easy 30. Doughboys 30. Parlor Bedroom and Bath 31. Sidewalks of New York 32. The Passionate Plumber 32. Speak Easily 32. What No Beer 33. Le Roi des Champs Elysées (Fr.) 34. An Old Spanish Custom (GB) 35. 18 Educational shorts 35–37. Hollywood Cavalcade 39. The Jones Family in Hollywood 39. Quick Millions 39. The Villain Still Pursued Her 40. Lil Abner 40. 8 Columbia shorts 40–41. Forever and a Day 43. *San Diego I Love You* 44. That's the Spirit 45. That Night With You 46. God's Country 46. El Moderno Barba Azul (Mex.) 46. Duel to the Death (Fr.) 48. You're My Everything 49. The Loveable Cheat 50. In the Good Old Summertime 50. Sunset Boulevard 50. Limelight 52. Around the World in Eighty Days 56. Huckleberry Finn 60. Ten Girls Ago 62. It's a Mad Mad Mad Mad World 63. The Triumph of Lester Snapwill 63. *Railrodder* 65. Keaton Rides Again 65. Film 65. Pajama Party 65. Beach Blanket Bingo 65. How to Stuff a Wild Bikini 65. Two Marines and a General (It.) 65. A Funny Thing Happened

on the Way to the Forum 66. The Scribe 66. Sergeant Deadhead 66.

'He passes into the universal folk heritage, as the supreme clown poet.'—*David Robinson, 1968*

❀ For being the funniest and most inventive silent clown of them all. *The General.*

¶ *B.K.:* Only things that one could imagine happening to real people, I guess, remain in a person's memory.

Keaton, Diane (1946–). American leading lady of the seventies and eighties.
□Lovers and Other Strangers 70. The Godfather 72. Play it Again Sam 72. Sleeper 74. Godfather Two 74. Love and Death 75. Harry and Walter Go to New York 76. I Will, I Will . . . For Now 76. *Annie Hall* (AA) 77. Looking for Mr Goodbar 77. Interiors 78. Manhattan 79. Reds 81. Shoot the Moon 82. The Little Drummer Girl 84. Colours of the Heart 86.

Keaton, Joseph (1878–1946). American knockabout comedian who supported his son Buster in several of his best silents.

Keaton, Michael (1951–). American light leading man of the eighties.
Night Shift 82. Mr Mom 83. Johnny Dangerously 84. Gung Ho 85. Touch and Go 86. The Squeeze 87.
TV series: All's Fair 76. Working Stiffs 79.

Keats, Steven (1945–). American general purpose actor.
The Story of Pretty Boy Floyd (TV) 74. The Dream Makers (TV) 75. Promise Him Anything (TV) 75. Black Sunday 76. Seventh Avenue (TV) 77. The Last Dinosaur (TV) 77. The Awakening Land (TV) 78. Zuma Beach (TV) 78. Silent Rage 82. The Executioner's Song (TV) 82.

Kedrova, Lila (1918–). Russian-French character actress, known internationally.
Zorba the Greek (AA) 64. A High Wind in Jamaica 65. Torn Curtain 66. Penelope 67. The Kremlin Letter 69. Soft Beds, Hard Battles 74. The Tenant 76. March or Die 77. Tell Me a Riddle 80. Sunset People 84. Sword of the Valiant 84. The Thrill of Genius 85, etc.

Keel, Howard (1917–) (Harold Keel). Stalwart American leading man and singer whose career faltered when musicals went out of fashion.
□The Small Voice (GB) 48. *Annie Get Your Gun* 50. Pagan Love Song 50. Three Guys Named Mike 51. *Showboat* 51. Texas Carnival 51. Callaway Went Thataway 51. Lovely to Look At 52. Desperate Search 52. Fast Company 53. Ride Vaquero 53. *Calamity Jane* 53. *Kiss Me Kate* 53. Rose Marie 54. *Seven Brides for Seven Brothers* 54. Deep in My Heart 54. Jupiter's Darling 54. Kismet 55. Floods of Fear (GB) 58. The Big Fisherman 59. Armored Command 61. The Day of the Triffids 63. Waco 66. Red Tomahawk 67. The War Wagon 67. Arizona Bushwhackers 68.
TV series: Dallas 81–.

¶ *H.K.:* I was one of God's chosen people, doing what I wanted to do in life.

Keeler, Ruby (1909–) (Ethel Keeler). Petite American singer-dancer who made a small talent go a long way in musicals of the early thirties.
□*42nd Street* 33. Gold Diggers of 1933. Footlight Parade 33. *Dames* 34. Flirtation Walk 35. Go Into Your Dance 35. Shipmates Forever 35. Colleen 36. Ready Willing and Able 37. Mother Carey's Chickens 38. Sweetheart of the Campus 41. The Phynx 70.

Keen, Geoffrey (1916–). Incisive British character actor, son of Malcolm Keen.
His Excellency 50. Genevieve 53. The Long Arm 56. No Love for Johnnie 61. The Spiral Road 62. Live Now Pay Later 63. The Heroes of Telemark 65. Dr Zhivago 65. Born Free 66. Taste the Blood of Dracula 70. Living Free 71. Doomwatch 72. The Spy Who Loved Me 77. Moonraker 79. For Your Eyes Only 81. A View to a Kill 84. The Living Daylights 87, many others.

Keen, Malcolm (1888–1970). British character actor, mostly on stage; father of Geoffrey Keen.
The Manxman 29. Sixty Glorious Years 39. The Great Mr Handel 42. The Mating Season (US) 51. Francis of Assisi 60, etc.

Keene, Ralph (1902–1963). British documentarist, in films from 1934. With Ministry of Information, British Transport, etc.: emphasis on animal studies. *Cyprus Is an Island, Crofters, Journey into Spring, Between the Tides, Winter Quarters, Under Night Streets,* etc.

Keene, Tom (1896–1963) (also known at times as George Duryea and Richard Powers). American western star, mainly in second features of the thirties and forties.
Godless Girl 28. The Dude Wrangler 30. Saddle Buster 32. Our Daily Bread 33. Where the Trails Divide 37. Dynamite Cargo 41. Up in Arms 44. If You Knew Susie 48. Red

Planet Mars 52. Plan 9 from Outer Space 56, many others.

Keighley, William (1899–1984). American director with stage experience: made many highly polished entertainments for Warners. □The Match King 32. Ladies They Talk About 33. Easy to Love 34. Journal of a Crime 34. Dr Monica 34. Kansas City Princess 34. Big Hearted Herbert 34. Babbitt 34. The Right to Live 35. Mary Jane's Pa 35. *G Men* 35. Special Agent 35. Stars over Broadway 35. The Singing Kid 36. Bullets or Ballots 36. *The Green Pastures* 36. God's Country and the Woman 37. The Prince and the Pauper 37. Varsity Show 37. The Adventures of Robin Hood (co-d) 38. Valley of the Giants 38. Secrets of an Actress 38. Brother Rat 38. Yes My Darling Daughter 39. Each Dawn I Die 39. The Fighting 69th 40. Torrid Zone 40. No Time for Comedy 40. Four Mothers 41. The Bride Came COD 41. *The Man Who Came to Dinner* 42. George Washington Slept Here 42. Honeymoon 47. The Street with No Name 48. Rocky Mountain 50. Close to My Heart 51. The Master of Ballantrae 53.

Keir, Andrew (1926–). Scottish character actor, usually in stern roles.
The Lady Craved Excitement 50. The Brave Don't Cry 52. The Maggie 54. Heart of a Child 57. Pirates of Blood River 60. Dracula, Prince of Darkness 65. Daleks Invasion Earth 2500 AD 65. The Viking Queen 67. *Quatermass and the Pit* 67. The Royal Hunt of the Sun 69. Zeppelin 70. Blood from the Mummy's Tomb 71. The 39 Steps 78. Absolution 80. Lion of the Desert 81. Marco Polo (TV) 82. First Among Equals (TV) 86, etc.
TV series: Adam Smith 72. The Outsiders 77.

Keitel, Harvey (1947–). American actor. Mean Streets 73. Alice Doesn't Live Here Any More 74. That's The Way of the World 75. Mother Jugs and Speed 76. Taxi Driver 76. Buffalo Bill and the Indians 76. The Duellists 77. Welcome to L.A. 77. Blue Collar 78. Fingers 78. Deathwatch 79. Eagle's Wing 79. Bad Timing 80. Saturn Three 80. The Border 82. Exposed 83. Order of Death 83. Falling in Love 84. Camorra 85. Off Beat 85. The Men's Club 86. Wise Guys 86, etc.

Keith, Brian (1921–) (Robert Keith Jnr). American actor of easy-going types, understanding fathers and occasional villains. Arrowhead (debut) 52. Alaska Seas 53. The Violent Men 54. Five Against the House 55. Storm Centre 56. Run of the Arrow 57. Sierra Baron 58. The Young Philadelphians 59. The Deadly Companions 61. The Parent Trap 61. Moon Pilot 62. Savage Sam 63. Those Calloways 65. The Hallelujah Trail 65. *Nevada Smith* 66. The Russians Are Coming 66. *Reflections in a Golden Eye* 67. With Six You Get Eggroll 68. Krakatoa 68. Suppose They Gave a War and Nobody Came 69. The Mackenzie Break 70. Scandalous John 71. Something Big 72. The Yakuza 75. *The Wind and the Lion* (as Theodore Roosevelt) 76. The Quest (TV) 76. Nickelodeon 76. Hooper 78. Meteor 79. The Mountain Men 80. Charlie Chan and the Curse of the Dragon Queen 81. Sharkey's Machine 81, etc.
TV series: Crusader 56. The Westerner 60. *Family Affair* 66–70. The Little People 72–73. Archer 75. Hardcastle and McCormick 83. Death before Dishonor 87.

Keith, Ian (1899–1960) (Keith Ross). American actor, latterly in character roles. Manhandled 24. The Divine Lady 27. Abraham Lincoln 31. The Sign of the Cross 32. Queen Christina 33. The Crusades 35. The Three Musketeers (as de Rochefort) 36. The Sea Hawk 40. The Chinese Cat 44. Nightmare Alley 48. The Black Shield of Falworth 54. Prince of Players 55. The Ten Commandments (as Rameses I) 56, many others.

Keith, Penelope (1939–). British character comedienne of haughty mien, familiar from TV's *Kate*, *The Good Life* and *To the Manor Born*.
Every Home Should Have One 71. Penny Gold 72. Ghost Story 73. The Priest of Love 81, etc.

¶ *P.K.:* I was very tall and very plain—I wasn't going to get very far on looks—so I thought I'd better be the funny girl.

Keith, Robert (1896–1966). American character actor with concert and stage experience. Spent some time as a Hollywood writer in the thirties but did not act in films until the late forties.
Boomerang 47. My Foolish Heart 49. Fourteen Hours 51. I Want You 51. *The Wild One* 53. *Young at Heart* 54. Guys and Dolls 55. My Man Godfrey 57. Tempest 58. Cimarron 61, etc.

Kellaway, Cecil (1891–1973). British character actor born in South Africa, who spent many years acting in Australia; came to Hollywood in 1939 and became an endearing exponent of roguish benevolence.

Wuthering Heights 39. Intermezzo 39. *I Married a Witch* 42. My Heart Belongs to Daddy 42. The Good Fellows (leading role) 43. Practically Yours 44. *Frenchman's Creek* 44. Love Letters 45. *Kitty* (as Gainsborough) 45. Monsieur Beaucaire 46. The Postman Always Rings Twice 46. Unconquered 47. Portrait of Jennie 48. *The Luck of the Irish* (as a leprechaun) 48. Joan of Arc 48. *Harvey* 50. The Beast from 20,000 Fathoms 53. The Female on the Beach 55. The Shaggy Dog 59. The Cardinal 63. *Hush Hush, Sweet Charlotte* 64. Spinout 66. Fitzwilly 67. Guess Who's Coming to Dinner 67. Getting Straight 70, many others.
❀ For being content to remain a star supporting actor of unfailing roguish charm. *I Married a Witch*.

Keller, Harry (1913–). American director.
Blonde Bandit 49. Rose of Cimarron 52. The Unguarded Moment 56. The Female Animal 57. Quantez 58. Voice in the Mirror 58. Six Black Horses 61. Tammy and the Doctor 63. Kitten with a Whip 65. In Enemy Country (& p), etc.

Keller, Helen (1881–1968). Blind and deaf American lady whose problems became the subject of *The Miracle Worker* 62. She appeared to tell her story in one film, *Deliverance* 19.

Keller, Marthe (1945–). Swiss leading lady in international films.
Marathon Man 76. Black Sunday 76. Bobby Deerfield 77. Fedora 78. The Formula 80. The Amateur 82.

Kellerman, Annette (1888–1975). Australian dancer and swimming star who pioneered the one-piece bathing suit. Esther Williams played her in a biopic, *Million Dollar Mermaid* 52.
Neptune's Daughter 14. Daughter of the Gods 16. Queen of the Sea 18. What Women Love 20, etc.

Kellerman, Sally (1938–). American leading lady of the seventies.
The Third Day 65. The Boston Strangler 68. The April Fools 69. M*A*S*H 69. Brewster McCloud 70. Last of the Red Hot Lovers 72. Lost Horizon 73. Slither 73. Rafferty and the Gold Dust Twins 75. The Big Bus 76. Welcome to L.A. 77. Magee and the Lady (TV) 77. A Little Romance 79. Foxes 80. Head On 80. Loving Couples 80. Serial 80. Moving Violations 84. Back to School 86. That's Life 86. Meatballs III 87, etc.

Kellett, Bob (1927–). British director.
A Home of Your Own 64. San Ferry Ann 65. Girl Stroke Boy 71. Up the Chastity Belt 71. Up the Front 72. The Garnett Saga 72. Our Miss Fred 72. Spanish Fly 76, etc.

Kelley, Barry (1908–). Tough-looking Irish-American supporting actor, usually in gangster roles.
Boomerang 47. The Asphalt Jungle 50. The Killer That Stalked New York 51. 711 Ocean Drive 52. The Long Wait 54. The Buccaneer 59. The Manchurian Candidate 62, many others.

Kelley, De Forrest (1920–). American general purpose actor.
Fear in the Night (leading role) 47. Duke of Chicago 50. House of Bamboo 55. Gunfight 57. Warlock 59. Johnny Reno 66. Star Trek 79, etc.
TV series: *Star Trek* 66–68.

Kellin, Mike (1922–1983). American actor; much TV.
At War with the Army 52. Lonelyhearts 57. The Great Imposter 60. Invitation to a Gunfighter 63. The Boston Strangler 68. Assignment Danger (TV) 72. Connection (TV) 73. Freebie and the Bean 74. Midnight Express 78. The Jazz Singer 80. FDR: The Last Year (TV) 80. So Fine 81, many others.

Kellino, Pamela (1916–) (Pamela Ostrer). British actress, married first to Roy Kellino and then to James Mason. Now columnist and TV personality.
Jew Süss 34. I Met A Murderer 38. They Were Sisters 45. The Upturned Glass 47. Lady Possessed 51, etc.

Kellino, Roy (1912–1956). British cinematographer and director whose talent never quite displayed itself.
AS CINEMATOGRAPHER: The Phantom Light 37. The Last Adventurers 38. Johnny Frenchman 35, etc.
AS DIRECTOR: Catch as Catch Can 38. *I Met a Murderer* (& ph) 39. Guilt is My Shadow 49. Lady Possessed (US) 51. Charade 53. The Silken Affair 55, etc.

Kellino, Will P. (1873–1958) (William P. Gislingham). British circus clown and acrobat, father of Roy Kellino. Made many early shorts as Pimple and Bumbles, characters from his stage act. Later became a director.

Kelljan, Robert (1930–1982) (Robert Kelljchian). American director.
Little Sister 69. Count Yorga Vampire 69. The Return of Count Yorga 71. Scream Blacula Scream 74. Went on to TV work.

Kelly, Emmett (1895–1979). American character actor, former circus clown.
Autobiography 1968: *Clown.*
The Fat Man 51. The Greatest Show on Earth 52. Wind Across the Everglades 58, etc.

Kelly, Gene (1912–) (Eugene Curran Kelly). Breezy, bouncy American dancer who became one of Hollywood's great star personalities of the forties and fifties, although his acting and singing abilities were minimal and his 'good guy' characterization wore a little thin. When musicals lamentably went out of fashion, he turned to direction. Special Academy Award 1951 'in appreciation of his versatility as an actor, singer, director and dancer, and specially for his brilliant achievements in the art of choreography on film'.
Biography 1974: *Gene Kelly* by Clive Hirschhorn.
□*For Me and My Gal* 42. Pilot Number Five 42. Dubarry was a Lady 43. Thousands Cheer 43. The Cross of Lorraine 43. *Cover Girl* 44. Christmas Holiday 44. Anchors Aweigh 45. Ziegfeld Follies 46. Living in a Big Way 47. *The Pirate* 48. *The Three Musketeers* 48. Words and Music 48. *Take Me Out to the Ball Game* 49. *On the Town* (& co-d) 49. Black Hand 50. Summer Stock 50. It's A Big Country 51. *An American in Paris* 51. *Singin' in the Rain* (& co-d) 52. The Devil Makes Three 52. Love is Better than Ever 52. Brigadoon 54. Seagulls over Sorrento (GB) 54. Deep in My Heart 54. It's Always Fair Weather 55. *Invitation to the Dance* (& d) 56. The Happy Road (& pd) 57. Les Girls 57. Marjorie Morningstar 58. The Tunnel of Love (d only) 58. Inherit the Wind 60. Let's Make Love (cameo) 60. Gigot (d only) 62. What a Way to Go 64. The Young Girls of Rochefort 67. A Guide for the Married Man (d only) 67. Hello Dolly (d only) 69. The Cheyenne Social Club (pd only) 70. Forty Carats 73. That's Entertainment 74. That's Entertainment Two 76. Women of the Year (TV) (d only) 76. Viva Knievel 77. Xanadu 80.
TV series: Going My Way 62.

'His grin could melt stone.'—*New Yorker, 1978*

❀ For terpsichorean delights performed with cheerful proletarian grace. *Singin' in the Rain.*

¶ *G.K.:* The days at MGM were marvellous. Everyone was pitching in. We had real collaboration. It was fun. We didn't think it was work.

G.K.: Fred Astaire represents the aristocracy when he dances. I represent the proletariat.

Famous line (to Nina Foch in *An American in Paris*): That's quite a dress you almost have on.

Kelly, Grace (1928–1982). American leading lady of the fifties: her 'iceberg' beauty quickly made her a top star, but she retired to become Princess of Monaco.
Biography 1976: *Princess Grace* by Gwen Robyns.
□Fourteen Hours 51. High Noon 52. Mogambo 53. Dial M for Murder 54. *Rear Window* 54. *The Country Girl* (AA) 54. Green Fire 54. The Bridges at Toko-Ri 54. To Catch a Thief 55. The Swan 56. *High Society* 56.
†In 1983 Cheryl Ladd appeared in the title role of a TV movie, *Grace Kelly*.

¶ *Pete Martin:* Writing about her is like trying to wrap up 115 pounds of smoke.

Kelly, Jack (1927–). Irish-American actor who usually plays wryly humorous roles; notably in TV series *King's Row* and *Maverick*.
Where Danger Lives 51. Drive a Crooked Road 54. To Hell and Back 56. Hong Kong Affair 58. Love and Kisses 65. Young Billy Young 69, etc.

Kelly, James (1931–78). British director.
□The Beast in the Cellar 70. Night Hair Child 71.

Kelly, Judy (1913–). Australian leading lady, in British films.
Lord Camber's Ladies 32. His Night Out 35. Make Up 37. At the Villa Rose 40. Tomorrow We Live 43. The Butler's Dilemma 43. Dead of Night 45. Warning to Wantons 48, etc.

Kelly, Nancy (1921–). American leading lady, former child model; in films 1938–47, then on Broadway stage.
Submarine Patrol 38. *Tailspin* 38. Jesse James 39. Stanley and Livingstone 39. Parachute Battalion 41. Tornado 43. Show Business 44. Woman in Bondage 45. Betrayal from the East 45. Friendly Enemies 47. *The Bad Seed* 56. Crowded Paradise 56. The Impostor (TV) 73, etc.

Kelly, Patsy (1910–1981). Dumpy American comedienne of the thirties, often a pert wisecracker or a frightened maid.
Going Hollywood 33. The Girl from Missouri 34. Go Into Your Dance 35. Page Miss Glory 35. Kelly the Second 36. Sing Baby Sing 36. Pigskin Parade 36. Wake and Live 37. Merrily We Live 38. The Gorilla 39. Road Show 41. Topper Returns 41. *Broadway Limited* 41. Sing Your Worries Away 42. My Son the Hero 43. Please Don't Eat the Daisies 60. The Naked Kiss 64. The Ghost in the Invisible Bikini 66. Rosemary's Baby 68. Freaky Friday 77. The North Avenue Irregulars 79, etc.
TV series: Valentine's Day 64. The Cop and the Kid 76.

Kelly, Paul (1899–1956). Wiry American leading man of the thirties and forties, almost always in 'B' pictures.
Uncle Sam of Freedom Ridge 20. The New Klondike 26. Slide Kelly Slide 27. The Girl from Calgary 32. Broadway Thro' a Keyhole 33. Side Streets 34. Public Hero Number One 35. The Silk Hat Kid 35. The Accusing Finger 36. Navy Blue and Gold 37. Island in the Sky 38. Within the Law 39. The Roaring Twenties 39. Invisible Stripes 40. Queen of the Mob 40. Mystery Ship 41. Tarzan's New York Adventure 42. Flying Tigers 42. The Man from Music Mountain 43. Dead Man's Eyes 44. China's Little Devils 45. The Cat Creeps 46. Spoilers of the North 47. Fear in the Night 47. *Crossfire* 47. The File on Thelma Jordon 49. The Secret Fury 50. The Painted Hills 51. Springfield Rifle 52. Split Second 53. The High and the Mighty 54. The Square Jungle 55. Storm Center 56. Bail Out at 43,000 57, many others.

Kelly, Paula (1939–). Tall, elegant black American actress and dancer.
Sweet Charity 69. The Andromeda Strain 70. Trouble Man 72. Soylent Green 73. Uptown Saturday Night 74. Drum 76, etc.

Kelly, Tommy (1928–). American child actor of the thirties.
The Adventures of Tom Sawyer 38.

Kelsall, Moultrie (1901–1980). Scottish character actor of stage and screen.
Landfall 49. The Lavender Hill Mob 51. The Master of Ballantrae 53. The Maggie 54. The Man Who Never Was 56. Violent Playground 58. The Battle of the Sexes 60, etc.

Kelsey, Fred (1884–1961). American small part actor, often seen as lugubrious sheriff or cop on the beat.
The Four Horsemen of the Apocalypse 21. The Eleventh Hour 23. The Gorilla 27. The Last Warning 29. Guilty as Hell 32. One Frightened Night 35. The Lone Wolf Keeps a Date 40. The Adventures of Mark Twain 44. Bringing Up Father 46. Hans Christian Andersen 52. Racing Blood 54, many others.

Kelton, Pert (1907–1968). American character comedienne, usually in hard-boiled roles.
Sally 29. *The Bowery* 33. Mary Burns Fugitive 35. Annie Oakley 35. Kelly the Second 36. Cain and Mabel 36. The Hit Parade 37. *The Music Man* 62. Love and Kisses 65. The Comic 69, etc.

Kemp, Jeremy (1934–) (Edmund Walker). British leading man who resigned from TV series *Z Cars* and has had some success in films.
Dr Terror's House of Horrors 65. Operation Crossbow 65. Cast a Giant Shadow 66. The Blue Max 66. Face of a Stranger 66. Assignment K 67. The Strange Affair 68. Darling Lili 70. The Games 70. Eyewitness 70. The Belstone Fox 73. The Seven Per Cent Solution 76. A Bridge Too Far 77. The Rhinemann Exchange (TV) 77. East of Elephant Rock 78. Leopard in the Snow 78. Caravans 78. The Prisoner of Zenda 79. Return of the Soldier 82. The Winds of War (TV) 83. Sadat (TV) 83. George Washington (TV) 84. Top Secret 84. Peter the Great (TV) 86, etc.

Kemper, Victor J. (–). American cinematographer.
Last of the Red Hot Lovers 72. The Candidate 72. Shamus 73. The Gambler 74. The Reincarnation of Peter Proud 75. Dog Day Afternoon 75. The Last Tycoon 76. Slapshot 77. Coma 78. The Jerk 79. The Final Countdown 80. Xanadu 80. Chu Chu and the Philly Flash 81. The Four Seasons 81. Partners 82. Author! Author! 82. Mr Mom 83.

Kemplen, Ralph (1912–). British editor.
The Ghost Train 31. The Ghoul 33. Scrooge 35. Broken Blossoms 36. The Saint Meets the Tiger 41. Carnival 46. Trottie True 49. Pandora and the Flying Dutchman 51. *The African Queen* 52. Moulin Rouge 52. Alexander the Great 56. *Room at the Top* 59. Freud 62. Night of the Iguana 64. A Man for All Seasons 66. Oliver! 68. The Day of the Jackal 73. The Omen 76, many others.
Directed one film: The Spaniard's Curse 52.

Kempson, Rachel (1910–). British actress, widow of Michael Redgrave.
The Captive Heart 46. A Woman's Vengeance (US) 48. Georgy Girl 66. The Jokers 66. Jennie (TV) 76. Out of Africa 85, etc.

Kemp-Welch, Joan (1906–). British character actress who used to play shy girls and spinsters on stage and screen. During the fifties emerged as a TV director of distinction.
Once a Thief 35. The Girl in the Taxi 37. Busman's Honeymoon 40. Pimpernel Smith 41. Jeannie 41 (last film to date), etc.

Kendall, Cyrus Q. (1898–1953). American character actor, a splendid cigar-chewing 'heavy' of the thirties.
The Dancing Pirate 36. Hot Money 36. They Won't Forget 37. The Shadow Strikes 37. Hawaii Calls 38. Stand Up and Fight 38. Angels Wash Their Faces 39. Men without Souls 40. Billy the Kid 41. Johnny Eager 42. The Whistler 44. She Gets Her Man 45, many others.

Kendall, Henry (1897–1962). British entertainer, immaculate star of London revues in the thirties and forties. On stage from 1914; occasional films.
Autobiography 1960: *I Remember Romano's*.
Tilly of Bloomsbury 21. French Leave 30. Rich and Strange 32. King of the Ritz 33. Death at Broadcasting House 34. The Amazing Quest of Ernest Bliss 36. School for Husbands 37. The Butler's Dilemma 43. 29 Acacia Avenue 45. The Voice of Merrill 52. An Alligator Named Daisy 55, etc.

Kendall, Kay (1926–1959) (Justine McCarthy). Vivacious, stylish British leading lady of the fifties.
□Fiddlers Three 44. Dreaming 44. Champagne Charlie 44. Waltz Time 45. *London Town* 46. Dance Hall 50. Night and the City 50. Happy Go Lovely 51. Lady Godiva Rides Again 51. Wings of Danger 52. Curtain Up 52. It Started in Paradise 52. Mantrap 52. Street of Shadows 53. The Square Ring 53. *Genevieve* 53. Meet Mr Lucifer 53. Fast and Loose 54. Abdullah the Great 54. Doctor in the House 54. The Constant Husband 54. *Simon and Laura* 55. Quentin Durward 56. Les Girls 57. *The Reluctant Debutante* 58. Once More with Feeling 59.

Kendall, Suzy (1944–) (Frieda Harrison). British leading lady.
Circus of Fear 67. To Sir With Love 67. Penthouse 67. *Up the Junction* 68. Thirty is a Dangerous Age, Cynthia 68. Fraulein Doktor 68. The Betrayal 69. Darker than Amber (US) 70. The Bird with the Crystal Plumage (It.) 70. Assault 71. Tales that Witness Madness 73. Craze 73. Fear is the Key 73.

Kennaway, James (1928–1968). British novelist and screenwriter.
Violent Playground 58. Tunes of Glory 61. The Mind Benders 63. The Shoes of the Fisherman (co-w) 68. The Battle of Britain (co-w) 69. Country Dance 70, etc.

Kennedy, Arthur (1914–). American leading actor who despite many intelligent performances failed to achieve stardom.
□City for Conquest 40. High Sierra 41. Strange Alibi 41. Knockout 41. Highway West 41. Bad Men of Missouri 41. They Died with Their Boots On 41. Desperate Journey 42. Air Force 43. *Devotion* (as Branwell Brontë) 46. Cheyenne 47. Boomerang 47. Too Late for Tears 49. *Champion* 49. *The Window* 49. The Walking Hills 49. Chicago Deadline 49. *The Glass Menagerie* 50. *Bright Victory* 51. Red Mountain 52. *Rancho Notorious* 52. The Girl in White 52. Bend of the River 52. The Lusty Men 52. Impulse (GB) 54. The Man from Laramie 55. The Naked Dawn 55. Trial 55. The Desperate Hours 55. Crashout 55. The Rawhide Years 56. Peyton Place 57. Twilight for the Gods 58. Some Came Running 58. A Summer Place 59. Elmer Gantry 60. Home is the Hero 61. Claudelle Inglish 61. Murder She Said (GB) 62. Hemingway's Adventures of a Young Man 62. Barabbas 62. *Lawrence of Arabia* 62. Cheyenne Autumn 64. Joy in the Morning 65. Murieta 65. Italiano Brava Gente 65. Fantastic Voyage 66. Nevada Smith 66. Monday's Child (Arg.) 67. The Prodigal Gun 68. Anzio 68. The Day of the Evil Gun 68. Dead or Alive 68. Hail Hero 69. Shark 69. The Movie Murderer (TV) 70. Glory Boy 71. A Death of Innocence (TV) 71. The President's Plane is Missing (TV) 71. Crawlspace (TV) 72. Nakia (TV) 74.
The Living Dead at the Manchester Morgue 74. L'Antricristo 74. The Sentinel 77. Brutal Justice 78. Covert Action 78. The Humanoid 79.

Kennedy, Burt (1923–). American director, originally radio writer (from 1947), later TV writer-director (*Combat* series, etc.).
The Canadians (wd) 61. Mail Order Bride (wd) 63. The Rounders (wd) 64. The Money Trap (d) 65. *Return of the Seven* 66. Welcome to Hard Times (wd) 67. *The War Wagon* 67. Monday's Child ((Arg.) 67. *Support Your Local Sheriff* 69. Young Billy Young 69. The

Good Guys and the Bad Guys 69. The Dubious Patriots 70. Support Your Local Gunfighter 71. The Deserter 71. Hannie Caulder 71. The Train Robbers (& w) 75. The Killer Inside Me 76. Wolf Lake (& w) 79. The Wild Wild West Revisited (TV) 79. The Trouble With Spies 87, etc.

Kennedy, Douglas (1915–1973) (formerly known as Keith Douglas). American leading man of action features, later character actor.
The Way of All Flesh 40. Women without Names 41. Dark Passage 47. Chain Gang 50. I Was an American Spy 51. Ride the Man Down 53. Bomba and the Lion Hunters 54. The Amazing Transparent Man 59, many others.
TV series: Steve Donovan Western Marshal.

Kennedy, Edgar (1890–1948). Bald, explosive American comedian with vaudeville experience. A former Keystone Kop, he continued in demand for supporting roles and also starred in innumerable domestic comedy two-reelers, his exasperated gestures being familiar the world over. His brother Tom Kennedy (1885–1965), also a Keystone Kop, became a professional wrestler, and later played bit parts in movies and TV right up to his death.
Tillie's Punctured Romance 15. The Leather Pushers 22. Midnight Patrol 31. *Duck Soup* 33. King Kelly of the USA 34. Captain Tugboat Annie 46. Unfaithfully Yours 48, scores of others.
❁ For being one of Hollywood's instantly recognizable faces and for never failing to make one laugh. *Duck Soup*.

Kennedy, George (1925–). American character actor, usually seen as menace but graduating to sympathetic roles.
Little Shepherd of Kingdom Come (debut) 60. Lonely Are the Brave 62. The Man from the Diners Club 63. *Charade* 63. Straitjacket 64. Mirage 65. Shenandoah 65. *The Flight of the Phoenix* 65. Hurry Sundown 67. The Dirty Dozen 67. *Cool Hand Luke* (AA) 67. Bandolero 68.The Boston Strangler 68. The Pink Jungle 69. Guns of the Magnificent Seven 69. The Good Guys and the Bad Guys 69. Airport 69. Tick Tick Tick 70. Fool's Parade 71. A Great American Tragedy (TV) 72. Lost Horizon 73. Cahill 73. Airport 75 74. Thunderbolt and Lightfoot 74. Earthquake 74. The Human Factor 75. The Eiger Sanction 75. Airport 77 77. The Double McGuffin 79. The Concorde—Airport 79 79. Death on the Nile 79. Backstairs at the White House (TV) 79. Steel 80. Modern Romance 81. Bolero 84. Rare Breed 84. Delta Force 85. Savage Dawn 85. Radioactive Dreams 86. Creepshow 2 87.
TV series: *Sarge* 71. The Blue Knight 75–76.

Kennedy, Margaret (1896–1967). British best-selling sentimental novelist; *The Constant Nymph* and her play *Escape Me Never* were each filmed more than once.

Kennedy, Merna (1908–1944) (Maude Kahler). American leading lady of the late twenties. Retired to marry Busby Berkeley.
The Circus 28. Broadway 30. Laughter in Hell 32. Arizona to Broadway 33. Police Call 33. I Like It That Way 34, etc.

Kennedy, Tom: see *Kennedy, Edgar*.

Kenney, James (1930–87). British juvenile actor of the late forties, son of vaudeville comedian Horace Kenney.
Circus Boy 47. Captain Horatio Hornblower 50. The Gentle Gunman 52. *Cosh Boy* 53. The Sea Shall Not Have Them 54. The Gelignite Gang 56. Son of a Stranger 58, etc.

Kent, Jean (1921–) (Joan Field). British leading lady of the forties, formerly in the Windmill chorus.
□ The Rocks of Valpre (debut) 35. Hallo Fame 40. It's That Man Again 42. Miss London Ltd 43. Warn That Man 43. Bees in Paradise 43. Fanny by Gaslight 44. 2000 Women 44. Champagne Charlie 44. Madonna of the Seven Moons 44. Soldier Soldier 44. *Waterloo Road* 45. The Rake's Progress 45. Caravan 46. Carnival 46. The Magic Box 46. The Man Within 47. The Loves of Joanna Godden 47. *Good Time Girl* 48. Bond Street 48. Sleeping Car to Trieste 48. *Trottie True* 49. The Reluctant Widow 50. The Woman in Question 50. Her Favourite Husband 50. The Browning Version 51. Before I Wake 54. The Prince and the Showgirl 57. Bonjour Tristesse 58. Grip of the Strangler 58. Beyond This Place 59. Please Turn Over 60. Bluebeard's Ten Honeymoons 60. Shout at the Devil 76.
TV series: *Sir Francis Drake* (as Queen Elizabeth I) 1962–3. *Tycoon* 1978.

Kent, Keneth (1882–1963). British actor and singer, mostly on stage.
House of the Arrow 39. Night Train to Munich 40.

Kenton, Erle C. (1896–1980). American director, from 1914.
Small Town Idol 20. The Leather Pushers 22.

Street of Illusion 25. Father and Son 27. Isle of Lost Souls 32. Remedy for Riches 39. Petticoat Politics 41. North to the Klondike 41. Ghost of Frankenstein 42. Who Done It? 42. Frisco Lil 42. House of Frankenstein 45. *House of Dracula* 45. Should Parents Tell? 49. Killer with a Label 50, etc.

Kenyon, Doris (1897–1979). American silent-screen leading lady who was married to Milton Sills.
The Pawn of Fate 16. A Girl's Folly 17. The Hidden Hand 18. The Ruling Passion 22. Monsieur Beaucaire 24. Blonde Saint 26. The Hawk's Nest 28. Alexander Hamilton 31. Voltaire 33. Counsellor at Law 33. The Man in the Iron Mask 39, etc.
TV series: Tycoon 64.

Kerima (1925–). Algerian actress.
An Outcast of the Islands 51. La Lupa 52. The Quiet American 58, etc.

La Kermesse Héroique (France 1935). Also known as *Carnival in Flanders*, this broad but polished comedy about the occupation by Spanish troops of a 17th-century Flemish town seemed at the time delightfully spontaneous and had world-wide success unprecedented for a French film since sound. Written by Charles Spaak, directed by Jacques Feyder, photographed by Harry Stradling, with Françoise Rosay and Louis Jouvet.

Kern, James V. (1909–1966). American director, former lawyer.
That's Right You're Wrong 39. You'll Find Out 40. *Thank Your Lucky Stars* 43. The Doughgirls (wd) 44. Never Say Goodbye (wd) 46. Stallion Road 47. April Showers 48. Two Tickets to Broadway 52, etc.

Kern, Jerome (1885–1945). Celebrated American songwriter. His Academy Award songs are 'The Way You Look Tonight' and 'The Last Time I Saw Paris'.
Roberta 35. Showboat 35 and 51. Swing Time 36. Cover Girl 44. Can't Help Singing 44. Centennial Summer 46. Till the Clouds Roll By (in which he was played by Robert Walker) 46.

Kerouac, Jack (1922–1969). American novelist of the beat generation, a legend he helped to create before dying of drink. *Heart Beat* was a film about him; there was also an underground film of his autobiographical *On the Road*.

Kerr, Deborah (1921–) (Deborah Kerr-Trimmer). British leading lady usually cast in well-bred roles.
Biography 1977: *Deborah Kerr* by Eric Braun.
□Major Barbara (debut) 40. *Love on the Dole* 41. Penn of Pennsylvania 41. Hatter's Castle 41. The Day Will Dawn 42. *The Life and Death of Colonel Blimp* 43. *Perfect Strangers* 45. *I See a Dark Stranger* 45. *Black Narcissus* 46. The Hucksters 47. If Winter Comes 48. Edward My Son 49. Please Believe Me 49. King Solomon's Mines 50. Quo Vadis 51. Thunder in the East 51. The Prisoner of Zenda 52. Dream Wife 52. Julius Caesar 53. *From Here to Eternity* 53. Young Bess 53. The End of the Affair 55. *The King and I* 56. The Proud and Profane 56. *Tea and Sympathy* 56. Heaven Knows Mr Allison 56. *An Affair to Remember* 57. *Separate Tables* 58. Bonjour Tristesse 58. Count Your Blessings 59. The Journey 59. Beloved Infidel 59. *The Sundowners* 60. The Grass is Greener 61. *The Innocents* 61. The Naked Edge 61. The Chalk Garden 63. *The Night of the Iguana* 64. Marriage on the Rocks 65. Eye of the Devil 66. Casino Royale 67. *Prudence and the Pill* 68. The Gypsy Moths 69. The Arrangement 69. Witness for the Prosecution (TV) 84. Reunion at Fairborough (TV) 85. The Assam Garden 85. A Woman of Substance (TV) 85.

¶ *D.K.:* All the most successful people these days seem to be neurotic. Perhaps we should stop being sorry for them and start being sorry for me—for being so confounded normal.

Kerr, Frederick (1858–1933) (Frederick Keen). British character actor of stage and, latterly, American screen; delightful as slightly doddering old man.
The Honour of the Family 27. Raffles 29. *The Devil to Pay* 30. *Frankenstein* (as the old baron) 31. Waterloo Bridge 31. The Midshipman 32. The Man from Toronto 33, etc.

Kerr, Jean (1923–) (Jean Collins). American humorist and playwright, wife of Walter Kerr the drama critic. Her contributions to film include *Mary Mary* and *Please Don't Eat the Daisies*; *Critic's Choice* was probably based on her.

Kerr, John (1931–). American leading man.
The Cobweb 55. Gaby 56. *Tea and Sympathy* 56. *South Pacific* 58. The Pit and the Pendulum 61. Seven Women from Hell 62, etc.

Kerrigan, J. M. (1885–1964). Irish character actor who went with the Abbey players to Hollywood in 1935, and stayed there.
Little Old New York 23. Song of My Heart 30. The Informer 35. Laughing Irish Eyes 36. Little Orphan Annie 39. Captains of the Clouds 42. Black Beauty 46. The Wild North 52. The Fastest Gun Alive 56, many others.

Kerrigan, J. Warren (1880–1947). American actor of the silent screen.
Samson 13. Landon's Legacy 16. A Man's Man 18. The Covered Wagon 23. Captain Blood 24, etc.

Kerry, Norman (1889–1956) (Arnold Kaiser). American actor of the silent screen.
The Black Butterfly 16. Merry Go Round 23. The Hunchback of Notre Dame 23. Phantom of the Opera 26. The Unknown 28. Air Eagles 31, many others.

Kershner, Irvin (1923–). American director.
□Stakeout on Dope Street 58. The Young Captives 59. The Hoodlum Priest 61. Face in the Rain 63. The Luck of Ginger Coffey 64. A Fine Madness 66. The Flim Flam Man 67. Loving 70. Up The Sandbox 72. S.P.Y.S. 74. The Return of a Man Called Horse 76. Raid on Entebbe (TV) 76. The Eyes of Laura Mars 78. The Empire Strikes Back 80. Never Say Never Again 83.

Kessel, Joseph (1898–1979). German novelist.
Works filmed: The Lion 62. Belle de Jour 67. The Horsemen 75.

The Kettles (Ma and **Pa).** Hillbilly couple played in *The Egg and I* 47, and in a subsequent long-running series of comedy second features, by Marjorie Main and Percy Kilbride. Highly successful in US, less so in Britain.
The films were as follows:
1949: *Ma and Pa Kettle*
1950: *Ma and Pa Kettle Go To Town*
1951: *Ma and Pa Kettle Back on the Farm*
1952: *Ma and Pa Kettle at the Fair*
1953: *Ma and Pa Kettle on Vacation*
1954: *Ma and Pa Kettle at Home*
1955: *Ma and Pa Kettle at Waikiki*
1956: *The Kettles in the Ozarks*
1957 (with Parker Fennelly replacing Percy Kilbride): *The Kettles on Old MacDonald's Farm*

Key Largo (US 1948). Maxwell Anderson's preachy melodrama about gangsters hiding out in a remote Florida hotel was obviously intended to say something about the post-war human condition, and borrowed quite a bit from Sherwood's *The Petrified Forest*. But the film is remembered chiefly as a display of acting pyrotechnics, with Edward G. Robinson as the relentless baddie, Humphrey Bogart as the war veteran who realised that being good is not enough, and Lauren Bacall, Lionel Barrymore and Claire Trevor (AA) as assorted relevant attitudes. John Huston wrote (with Richard Brooks) and directed.

Keyes, Evelyn (1919–). American leading lady of the forties, originally dancer.
Autobiography 1977: *Scarlett O'Hara's Younger Sister*.
The Buccaneer (debut) 38. Gone with the Wind 39. Before I Hang 40. The Face behind the Mask 41. Here Comes Mr Jordan 41. Ladies in Retirement 41. Flight Lieutenant 42. The Adventures of Martin Eden 42. The Desperadoes 43. Nine Girls 44. A Thousand and One Nights 44. *The Jolson Story* 46. Renegades 46. Johnny O'Clock 47. The Mating of Millie 46. Enchantment 48. Mrs Mike 48. House of Settlement 49. The Killer That Stalked New York 50. Smugglers' Island 51. *The Prowler* 51. Rough Shoot (GB) 52. The Seven Year Itch 54. Hell's Half Acre 54. Around the World in Eighty Days 56, etc.

Keys, Anthony Nelson (1913–85). British producer, associated with Hammer horror. Son of actor comedian **Nelson Keys** (1887–1939).
Pirates of Blood River 63. The Gorgon 63. Dracula Prince of Darkness 65. Quatermass and the Pit 68, etc.

The Keystone Kops. A troupe of slapstick comedians led by Ford Sterling who, from 1912–20 under the inspiration of Mack Sennett at Keystone Studios, made innumerable violent comedies full of wild chases and trick effects. *Abbott and Costello Meet the Keystone Kops* 55 was a somewhat poor tribute.

Khambatta, Persis (1950–). Indian leading lady in Hollywood films.
Star Trek 79. Nighthawks 81. Megaforce 82.

Khayyam, Omar (1048–1122) (Gheyas Od-Din Abu al-Fath). Persian poet whose *Rubaiyat*, freely translated in 1859 by Edward Fitzgerald, became a bag of popular clichés and was heavily quoted in the artier Hollywood films, notably those of Albert

Lewin. The film called *Omar Khayyam* was a sword-and-sandal epic having nothing to do with the known facts of Omar's life, which are scant.

Kibbee, Guy (1882–1956). Bald-headed American character comedian, usually in flustered, shifty or genial roles.
Stolen Heaven (debut) 31. City Streets 32. Forty-second Street 33. *Dames* 34. *Babbitt* 34. Captain January 35. Mr Smith Goes to Washington 39. Chad Hanna 41. Scattergood Baines 41. The Power of the Press 43. The Horn Blows at Midnight 45. Gentleman Joe Palooka 47. Fort Apache 48. Three Godfathers 49.

Kibbee, Roland (1914–84). American radio, TV and screen writer.
A Night in Casablanca 45. Angel on My Shoulder 46. *Vera Cruz* 54. Top Secret Affair 57. The Appaloosa 66. Valdez is Coming (& p) 71. The Midnight Man (& co-w, co-d) 75, etc.

Kid Galahad (US 1937). Thought at the time to be one of the best of boxing dramas, this was directed by Michael Curtiz, starred Edward G. Robinson and Bette Davis, and introduced Wayne Morris. It was remade in a disguised form as *The Wagons Roll at Night* 41, with Humphrey Bogart; then it turned up again in 1962 as an Elvis Presley vehicle, directed by Phil Karlson.

Kidd, Michael (1919–) (Milton Greenwald). American dancer and dance director.
Where's Charley? (choreography only) 52. Band Wagon 53. *Seven Brides for Seven Brothers* 54. *It's Always Fair Weather* 54. Guys and Dolls 55. Merry Andrew (& d) 58. Hello Dolly 69. Smile 75. Movie Movie 79, etc.

Kidder, Margot (1948–). Canadian leading lady of the seventies.
Gaily Gaily 69. Quackser Fortune 70. Suddenly Single (TV) 71. The Bounty Man (TV) 72. Sisters 72. The Dion Brothers (TV) 74. Honky Tonk (TV) 74. The Great Waldo Pepper 75. The Reincarnation of Peter Proud 75. 92 in the Shade 77. *Superman* 78. The Amityville Horror 79. Superman II 80. Willie and Phil 80. Some Kind of Hero 82. Heartaches 82. Trenchcoat 83.
TV series: Nichols 71.

kidnapping has been the subject of a great number of films; apart from the various versions of Robert Louis Stevenson's *Kidnapped*, examples include *Nancy Steele is Missing, No Orchids for Miss Blandish, Ransom, The Kidnappers, A Cry in the Night, Cry Terror, Tomorrow at Ten, High and Low, My Name is Julia Ross, Seance on a Wet Afternoon, The Collector, The Happening, Bunny Lake is Missing, Bonnie and Clyde, Big Jake, The Night of the Following Day, The Grissom Gang, Murder on the Orient Express, The Man Who Loved Cat Dancing, Night People, Funeral in Berlin, Sugarland Express, The Wind and the Lion*, and on TV *The Longest Night* and *The Lindbergh Kidnapping Case*.

Kiel, Richard (1939–). American giant (7-foot) actor who came into his own as an adversary for James Bond.
House of the Damned 62. The Magic Sword 62. The Human Duplicators 65. Silver Streak 66. *The Spy Who Loved Me* 77. Force Ten from Navarone 78. Humanoid 78. Moonraker 79. So Fine 81. Hysterical 83. Pale Rider 85.

¶ *R.K.:* My wife is 5′ 4″ and everybody asks me how we do it.

Kieling, Wolfgang (1924–). German character actor.
Maria die Magd (debut) 36. Falstaff in Wien 40. Damsels in Paris 56. Torn Curtain (US) 66. Goya 71. Dollars (US) 72, etc.

Kiepura, Jan (1902–1966). Polish operatic tenor.
Farewell to Love (GB) 30. *My Song for You* (GB) 31. Be Mine Tonight (GB) 32. Give Us This Night (US) 36. Her Wonderful Lie (It.) 50.

Kilbride, Percy (1888–1964). American character actor of wily hayseed roles.
White Woman 33. Soak the Rich 36. George Washington Slept Here 42. Knickerbocker Holiday 44. She Wouldn't Say Yes 45. The Well-Groomed Bride 45. The Egg and I 47. Ma and Pa Kettle (series) 47–59.

Kilburn, Terry (1926–). British boy actor of the thirties; never quite made it as adult.
A Christmas Carol 38. The Boy from Barnardo's 38. Sweethearts 39. Goodbye Mr Chips (as three generations of Colley) 39. The Swiss Family Robinson 40. A Yank at Eton 42. National Velvet 45. Bulldog Drummond at Bay 47. Only the Valiant 51. The Fiend without a Face 58, etc.

Kiley, Richard (1922–). American general purpose actor with stage experience: has

latterly become a Broadway musical star.
The Mob 51. The Sniper 52. Pick Up on South Street 52. The Blackboard Jungle 55. The Phenix City Story 56. Spanish Affair 58. Pendulum 69. AKA Cassius Clay 70. Murder Once Removed (TV) 71. The Little Prince 73. Friendly Persuasion (TV) 75. The Macahans (TV) 76. Looking for Mr Goodbar 77. Endless Love 81. Angel on My Shoulder (TV) 81. Howard the Duck 86.

Kilian, Victor (1897–1979). American character actor, usually as suspicious or downright villainous characters.
The Wiser Sex 32. Air Hawks 35. Seventh Heaven 36. Dr Cyclops 39. Reap the Wild Wind 42. Spellbound 45. Gentleman's Agreement 47. The Flame and the Arrow 50. Tall Target 51, etc.
1976: on TV in *Mary Hartman, Mary Hartman.*

The Killers (US) 1946). A brilliantly intricate and explosive crime melodrama elaborated by writer Anthony Veiller from a Hemingway sketch, photographed by Woody Bredell, and directed with tremendous verve by Robert Siodmak. It introduced Burt Lancaster to the screen and also had an excellent performance by Edmond O'Brien. In 1964 it was remade by Don Siegel in a version originally intended for colour TV had it not proved too violent; the star was Lee Marvin and the film had plenty of fashionable violence but little style.

Killiam, Paul (1916–). American collector of silent movies, clips from which he introduces on TV in various series.

The Killing Fields (GB 1984). A brilliantly made film about Cambodia: everyone admired it, but not too many could stomach its gory detail. Bruce Robinson's script, Roland Joffe's direction and the acting of Sam Waterston and Haing S. Ngor all helped audiences to live the experiences depicted.

Kilpatrick, Lincoln (–). Black American actor.
Cool Breeze 72. Soul Soldier 72. Soylent Green 73. Chosen Survivors 74. Uptown Saturday Night 74, etc.

Kimmins, Anthony (1901–1964). British actor-writer-producer-director, almost entirely of light comedy subjects.
The Golden Cage (a) 33. White Ensign (a) 34. While Parents Sleep (w) 35. Keep Your Seats Please (w) 36. Talk of the Devil (w) 36. *Keep Fit* (wd) 37. The Show Goes On (w) 37. I See Ice (wd) 38. It's In the Air (wd) 38. Trouble Brewing (wd) 39. Under Your Hat (wd) 40. *Mine Own Executioner* (pd) 47. Bonnie Prince Charlie (d) 48. Flesh and Blood (d) 50. Mr Denning Drives North (d) 51. Who Goes There? (d) 52. *The Captain's Paradise* (wpd) 53. Aunt Clara (d) 54. Smiley (pd) 56. *The Amorous Prawn* (wpd) 62, etc.

Kind Hearts and Coronets (GB 1949). Robert Hamer directed this witty comedy of Edwardian bad manners from a script by himself and John Dighton. Despite dull patches it remains supreme of its stylish kind, with Dennis Price as the most elegant of murderers and Alec Guinness as eight aristocratic victims.

A Kind of Loving (GB 1962). The first British film to take a genuinely realistic view of working-class life, without the sophistication of *Look Back in Anger* or the high good humour of *Saturday Night and Sunday Morning.* From a depressingly truthful novel by Stan Barstow, it had Alan Bates and June Ritchie as the young couple driven into a make-do-and-mend marriage; John Schlesinger directed as though it were a documentary.

Kinematograph Renters' Society (K.R.S.). This British organization was founded by film distributors in 1915 for their own protection and collective bargaining power, chiefly against exhibitors.

Kinescope. American term for what the British call a telerecording, i.e. a live or tape show transferred for convenience on to tape. The technical quality is seldom satisfactory, and the process was gradually discontinued in favour of electronic tape conversion from one line standard to another.

Kinetoscope. An early film viewing apparatus (1893) in which a continuous loop of film could be viewed by one person only.

King, Alan (1924–) (Irwin Kniberg). American cabaret comedian who has made a few film appearances.
Hit the Deck 55. Miracle in the Rain 56. The Helen Morgan Story 57. On the Fiddle (GB) 61. Bye Bye Braverman 68. The Anderson Tapes 71. Just Tell Me What You Want 80. Author! Author! 82. I the Jury 82. Lovesick 83. Cat's Eye 84, etc.

King, Allan (1933–). Canadian documentarist.
Skid Row 56. Morocco 58. Rickshaw 60. The Pursuit of Happiness 62. Warrendale 66. The New Woman 68. A Married Couple 69. Who Has Seen the Wind 77. One Night Stand 79. Silence of the North 81.

The King and I: see *Anna and the King of Siam.*

King, Andrea (1915–) (Georgetta Barry). French-American leading lady with experience on the New York stage.
The Very Thought of You 44. Hotel Berlin 45. The Man I Love 46. Shadow of a Woman 46. The Violent Hour 50. The Lemon Drop Kid 51. Red Planet Mars 53. Band of Angels 57. Darby's Rangers 58. Daddy's Gone A-Hunting 69, etc.

King, Anita (1889–1963). American leading lady of the silent screen, who came to fame in *The Virginian* 14.

King Arthur: see *Arthur.*

King, Charles (1889–1944). American song and dance man of the twenties.
Broadway Melody 28. Hollywood Revue 29. Chasing Rainbows 30, etc.

King, Charles (1899–1957). American character actor, usually a western heavy.
Range Law 32. Mystery Ranch 34. O'Malley of the Mounted 36. The Mystery of the Hooded Horsemen 37. Son of the Navy 40. Gunman from Bodie 42. Ghost Rider 43, etc.

King, Dave (1929–). British TV comedian of the sixties; made a few film appearances.
Pirates of Tortuga 61. Go to Blazes 62. Strange Bedfellows 65. Cuba 79. The Long Good Friday 81. Reds 81, etc.

King, Dennis (1897–1971) (Dennis Pratt). British-born opera singer who in the early thirties starred in Hollywood films.
The Vagabond King 30. Fra Diavolo 33.

King, George (1900–1966). British producer-director, mainly of independent quota quickies and melodramas.
Too Many Crooks (d) 31. John Halifax Gentleman (p) 36. The Chinese Bungalow (pd) 39. The Case of the Frightened Lady (pd) 40. The Face at the Window (pd) 40. The First of the Few (p) 42. Tomorrow We Live (pd) 42. Candlelight in Algeria (pd) 44. Gaiety George (pd) 45. The Shop at Sly Corner (pd) 46. Forbidden (pd) 48. Eight O'Clock Walk (p) 54, etc.

King, Henry (1888–1982). Veteran American director with experience in most branches of show business. In Hollywood, he became a skilful exponent of the well-made expensive family entertainment, usually with a sentimental streak.
SELECTED SILENTS: Who Pays? 16. A Sporting Chance 19. *Tol'able David* 21. *The White Sister* 23. Romola 24. *Stella Dallas* 25. The Winning of Barbara Worth 26. The Woman Disputed 28.
□TALKIES: Hell Harbor 30. The Eyes of the World 30. Lightnin' 30. Merely Mary Ann 31. Over the Hill 31. The Woman in Room 13 32. State Fair 33. I Loved You Wednesday 33. Carolina 34. Marie Galante 34. One More Spring 35. Way Down East 35. The Country Doctor 36. Ramona 36. Lloyd's of London 36. Seventh Heaven 37. *In Old Chicago* 38. *Alexander's Ragtime Band* 38. Jesse James 39. *Stanley and Livingstone* 39. Little Old New York 40. *Maryland* 40. *Chad Hanna* 40. A Yank in the RAF 41. Remember the Day 41. *The Black Swan* 42. *The Song of Bernadette* 43. *Wilson* 44. A Bell for Adano 45. *Margie* 46. Captain from Castile 47. Deep Waters 48. Prince of Foxes 49. *Twelve O'Clock High* 49. *The Gunfighter* 50. I'd Climb the Highest Mountain 51. David and Bathsheba 51. Wait Till the Sun Shines Nellie 52. Full House (part) 52. *The Snows of Kilimanjaro* 52. King of the Khyber Rifles 53. Untamed 56. *Love is a Many Splendored Thing* 55. Carousel 56. *The Sun Also Rises* 57. The Bravados 58. This Earth is Mine 59. Beloved Infidel 59. *Tender is the Night* 61.
❀ For his sympathy, professionalism and visual sense. *In Old Chicago.*

King Kong (US 1932–33). The most famous screen monster remains after almost fifty years the most impressive. Willis H. O'Brien's trick photography has not been surpassed, and the film holds together as a splendid adventure for grown-up school-boys; even the acting of Robert Armstrong and Fay Wray is delightfully of its period. Produced and directed by Merian Cooper and Ernest Schoedsack, with suitably throbbing music by Max Steiner. The production team made a further visit to the mysterious island for *Son of Kong* 33, but here the giant gorilla was played for laughs and the trick effects were skimpy. Similar remarks are applicable to 1949's *Mighty Joe Young.* The 1976 remake of the original story was inoffensive but totally lacked the charisma of the 1933 film.

King, Louis (1898–1962). American director in films from 1919; brother of Henry King. Persons in Hiding 38. Typhoon 40. The Way of All Flesh 40. Moon over Burma 41. Thunderhead, Son of Flicka 44. Smoky 46. Bob, Son of Battle 47. Green Grass of Wycoming 48. Mrs Mike 49. The Lion and the Horse 52. Powder River 53. Dangerous Mission 54, etc.

King, Maurice and **Frank** (–) (real name Kozinski). American brothers, independent producers who in the fifties made several fast bucks with such exploitable titles as *The Carnival Story*, *Maya* and *Gorgo*.

King of Comedy (US 1982). A wry piece with Robert de Niro as a comedian who will do anything to get notice, even kidnap the chat show host (Jerry Lewis) who is his idol. Though apparently without a message, the picture underlines several unwelcome aspects of today's media world. Written by Paul D. Zimmermann, directed by Martin Scorsese.

King of Jazz (US 1930). A famous early revue directed by John Murray Anderson, produced by Carl Laemmle Jnr and photographed by Hal Mohr; with Paul Whiteman and his band and guest stars. For its age, an astonishing triumph of style.

King of Kings: see under *Christ*.

King, Perry (1948–). American leading man of the late seventies.
□ The Possession of Joel Delaney 71. Slaughterhouse Five 72. The Lords of Flatbush 74. Mandingo 75. The Wild Party 75. Lipstick 76. Captains and the Kings (TV) 76. Andy Warhol's Bad 77. The Choirboys 77. Aspen (TV) 77. A Different Story 78. The Cracker Factory (TV) 79. Love's Savage Fury (TV) 79. Search and Destroy 81. Striking Back 81. Class of 1984 82.

King Solomon's Mines. Rider Haggard's African adventure novel was less than adequately filmed in Britain in 1937, with Cedric Hardwicke as Allan Quartermain: the director was Robert Stevenson. MGM's 1951 remake with Stewart Granger was an unsatisfactory mishmash in which the plot thread was all but lost and there was so much spare location footage that a semi-remake, *Watusi*, used it up in 1959. Harry Alan Towers' 1975 version, *King Solomon's Treasure*, makes its predecessors look like classics.

King, Stephen (1946–). Best-selling American author of supernatural stories. Works filmed include *Carrie*, *The Shining*, *Salem's Lot*, *Cujo*, *Christine*, *The Dead Zone*. *Creepshow*, *Cat's Eyes*.

¶ *S.K.:* I was sitting one day and thinking about cannibalism, because that's what guys like me do . . . and I thought, suppose a guy was washed up on a rocky island, how much of himself could he eat?

King, Walter Woolf (1899–1984). American actor, Broadway singing star who went to Hollywood and was gradually relegated to villain roles.
A Night at the Opera 35. Call It a Day 37. Swiss Miss 38. Balalaika 39. Marx Brothers Go West 41. Today I Hang 42. Tonight We Sing 53. Kathy O' 58, etc.

kings and queens, of England at least, have been lovingly if not very accurately chronicled in the cinema. We still await an epic of the Norman Conquest, but in 1925 Phyllis Neilson-Terry went still further back to play *Boadicaea*, and in 1969 David Hemmings played *Alfred the Great.* Henry II, played by Peter O'Toole, was protagonist of *Becket* and *The Lion in Winter.* Richard I (Lionheart), also in the latter, was a shadowy figure of do-goodery in scores of films from *Robin Hood* to *King Richard and the Crusaders*; his brother John was just as frequently the villain of the piece, as in *The Adventures of Robin Hood.* Edward IV made an appearance in *Tower of London* and *Richard III*, but only as a pawn in the scheming hands of Richard III (Crookback). Henry IV appeared in *Chimes at Midnight*; *Henry V* was a notable role for Laurence Olivier; Henry VII-to-be was played in *Richard III* by Stanley Baker. Henry VIII was for long personified by Charles Laughton, who played him in 1933, but there have been other contenders: Montagu Love in *The Prince and the Pauper*, Robert Shaw in *A Man for All Seasons*, Richard Burton in *Anne of the Thousand Days*, Keith Michell in *Henry VIII and his Six Wives*, and James Robertson Justice in *The Sword and the Rose.* Similarly Elizabeth I was identified with Bette Davis (*Elizabeth and Essex, The Virgin Queen*) until Glenda Jackson played her on TV and in *Mary Queen of Scots*, though she was also personified by Flora Robson (*Fire over England, The Sea Hawk*), Florence Eldridge (*Mary of Scotland*), Irene Worth (*Seven Seas to Calais*) and others. The unfortunate *Mary of Scotland* was notably played by Katharine Hepburn and Vanessa Redgrave. Young Edward VI was in *The Prince and the Pauper*. The early Stuarts were a dour lot, but Charles I was impersonated by Alec Guinness in *Cromwell*; Charles II, the merry monarch, has been personified by a number of actors including Cedric Hardwicke (*Nell Gwyn*), George Sanders (*Forever Amber*), Vincent Price (*Hudson's Bay*) and Douglas Fairbanks Jnr (*The Exile*). Of the Hanoverians, George I was played by Eric Pohlmann in *Rob Roy* and Peter Bull in *Saraband for Dead Lovers*, George III by Raymond Lovell in *The Young Mr Pitt*, and by Robert Morley in *Beau Brummell*. Prinny, the Prince Regent, later George IV, was undertaken by Cecil Parker in *The First Gentleman* and Peter Ustinov in *Beau Brummell*. Victoria to many people still looks like Anna Neagle, who played her three times; other actresses in the role have included Irene Dunne (*The Mudlark*), Fay Compton (*The Prime Minister*) and Mollie Maureen (*The Private Life of Sherlock Holmes*). James Robertson Justice played Edward VII in *Mayerling*, and Richard Chamberlain Edward VIII in a TV film, *The Woman I Love*. In 1982 two American TV movies about the romance of Prince Charles cast well-known actors as the current royal family; neither was shown in the U.K.

Foreign monarchs who have been notably impersonated include Catherine the Great of Russia (Pola Negri, Elisabeth Bergner, Tallulah Bankhead, Bette Davis, Marlene Dietrich); Russia's last Czar and Czarina, *Nicholas and Alexandra* (Michael Jayston and Janet Suzman); *Peter the Great*; *Ivan the Terrible*; *Queen Christina* of Sweden (Greta Garbo, and Liv Ullmann in *The Abdication*); Louis XI of France (Harry Davenport in *The Hunchback of Notre Dame*, Basil Rathbone in *If I Were King*); Charles VII of France, by Jose Ferrer in *Joan of Arc*; *Marie Antoinette* (Norma Shearer); Louis XIV, by John Barrymore in *Marie Antoinette*; Louis XVI, by Robert Morley in *Marie Antoinette* and by Pierre Renoir in *La Marseillaise*; Louis XVII, by Jean-Pierre Cassel in *The Three Musketeers*; Philip II of Spain (Paul Scofield in *That Lady*, Raymond Massey in *Fire Over England*).

King's Row (US 1942). An unusually adult film to come from Hollywood in the middle of the war, this strong period drama from Henry Bellamann's novel of small-town life was directed with bravura by Sam Wood and acted with relish by Claude Rains, Betty Field, Ann Sheridan, Charles Coburn, and Maria Ouspenskaya, with Ronald Reagan and Robert Cummings making surprisingly interesting heroes. Musical score by Erich Wolfgang Korngold. An undistinguished TV series of 1957 used the title and some of the characters.

Kingsford, Walter (1882–1958). British character actor, in Hollywood from the thirties after long stage experience; usually played kindly professional men. Was Dr Carew in the *Kildare* series.
The Mystery of Edwin Drood 35. Captains Courageous 37. Algiers 38. Kitty Foyle 40. My Favorite Blonde 42. The Velvet Touch 49. Loose in London 53. Merry Andrew 58, many others.

Kingsley, Ben (1944–) (Krishna Banji). Anglo-Indian leading character actor.
Gandhi (AA, BFA) 82. Betrayal 82. Harem 84. Turtle Diary 85. Camille (TV) 85. Testimony 87.

Kingsley, Dorothy (1909–). American scenarist, former radio writer for Bob Hope.
Neptune's Daughter 49. When In Rome 52. Kiss Me Kate 53. Seven Brides For Seven Brothers 54. Pal Joey 57. Can Can 59. Pepe 60. Half a Sixpence 67. Valley of the Dolls 67, etc.

Kingsley, Sidney (1906–) (Sidney Kieschner). American playwright.
Plays filmed include: Men in White 35. Dead End 37. Detective Story 51.

Kinnear, Roy (1934–1988). Bulbous British character comedian whose perspiring bluster is a quickly overplayed hand.
Sparrows Can't Sing 62. Heavens Above 63. French Dressing 65. The Hill 65. Help! 66. A Funny Thing Happened on the Way to the Forum 67. How I Won the War 67. Lock Up Your Daughters 67. Willy Wonka and the Chocolate Factory 71. The Three Musketeers 74. Juggernaut 74. One of Our Dinosaurs is Missing 75. Herbie Goes to Monte Carlo 77. The Last Remake of Beau Geste 77. Hawk the Slayer 80. The Boys in Blue 82. The Zany Adventures of Robin Hood (TV) 84. Pirates 85.

Kinnoch, Ronald (c. 1911–). British producer, former scenarist and production manager.
Escape Route 52. How to Murder a Rich

Uncle 57. The Secret Man (& wd) 58. Village of the Damned 60. Invasion Quartet 61. Cairo 62. The Ipcress File (ap) 65, etc.

Kinoy, Ernest (–). American screenwriter.
Brother John 70. Buck and the Preacher 71. Leadbelly 75.

Kinskey, Leonid (1903–). Lanky Russian character actor, long in US. Was playing intense but not over-bright revolutionaries in 1932 (*Trouble in Paradise*) and still does it on TV.
The Great Waltz 38. Down Argentine Way 40. Can't Help Singing 44. Monsieur Beaucaire 46. The Man with the Golden Arm 55, many others.

Kinski, Klaus (1926–) (Claus Gunther Nakszynski). German character actor of intense roles.
Ludwig II 54. Kali Yug Goddess of Vengeance 63. For a Few Dollars More 65. Dr Zhivago 65. Circus of Fear 67. *Aguirre Wrath of God* 72. The Bloody Hands of the Law 73. *Nosferatu* 78. La Femme-Enfant 80. Android 82. Venom 82. Love and Money 82. Codename Wildgeese 84. The Little Drummer Girl 84. Commando Leopard 85. Crawlspace 86, etc.

¶ *K.K.:* I'm like a wild animal who's behind bars. I need air, I need space.
K.K.: Making movies is better than cleaning toilets.

Kinski, Nastassia (or **Nastassja**) (1959–). German leading lady, daughter of Klaus Kinski.
To the Devil a Daughter 76. Stay as You Are 79. *Tess* 80. Cat People 82. One from the Heart 82. Love and Money 82. Exposed 83. The Moon in the Gutter 83. The Little Drummer Girl 84. Unfaithfully Yours 84. Paris, Texas 84 Maria's Lovers 85. Symphony of Love 85. Harem 85. Revolution 85.

Kinsolving, Lee (1938–1974). American teenage lead of the sixties.
The Dark at the Top of the Stairs 60. All the Young Men 60. The Explosive Generation 61.

Kinugasa, Teinosuke (1896–1982). Japanese director.
Crossways 28. Joyu 47. Gate of Hell 53. The White Heron 58, etc.

Kipling, Rudyard (1865–1936). British novelist who mainly concerned himself with the high days of the British in India. Films from his works include *Gunga Din, Soldiers Three, Elephant Boy, Wee Willie Winkie, Captains Courageous, The Light That Failed, The Jungle Book, Kim, The Man Who Would Be King* (in which he was played by Christopher Plummer).

Kipps. H. G. Wells' comic-sentimental 'story of a simple soul' was first filmed in 1921 (GB) with George K. Arthur as the draper's assistant who comes into money and has an unhappy encounter with high society. In 1941 Carol Reed made a very stylish and satisfying sound version with Michael Redgrave; and 1967 brought the inevitable musical version, *Half a Sixpence*, with Tommy Steele vivacious but somewhat miscast in the lead.

Kirk, Phyllis (1926–) (Phyllis Kirkegaard). American leading lady of the fifties, former model and dancer.
Our Very Own 50. The Iron Mistress 52. House of Wax 53. Canyon Crossroads 55. The Sad Sack 57. That Woman Opposite (GB) 58, etc.
TV series: The Thin Man 57.

Kirk, Tommy (1941–). American juvenile lead, former Disney child actor.
Old Yeller 57. The Shaggy Dog 59. The Swiss Family Robinson 60. The Absent-Minded Professor 60. Babes in Toyland 61. Bon Voyage 62. Son of Flubber 63. The Misadventures of Merlin Jones 63. The Monkey's Uncle 65. How to Stuff a Wild Bikini 65, etc.

Kirkland, Muriel (1903–1971). American stage actress, briefly in films in the thirties.
Fast Workers 33. Hold Your Man 33. The Secret of the Blue Room 33. Nana 34. Little Man What Now? 34, etc.

Kirkop, Oreste (1926–). Maltese operatic tenor whose sole film appearance to date has been in *The Vagabond King* 55.

Kirkwood, James (1883–1963). American silent director.
The House of Discord 13. Classmates 13. Rags 15. Environment 17. Bill Apperson's Boy 19. The Heart of Jennifer 19, many others.
AS ACTOR: A Corner in Wheat 09. The Rocky Road 10. The Great Impersonation 21. Pink Gods 22. Human Wreckage 23. Circe the Enchantress 24. The Reckless Lady 26. The Spoilers 30. Cheaters at Play 32. The Woman They Almost Lynched 53, many others.

Kirkwood, Pat (1921–). British leading lady and entertainer, in variety since her teens.
Come On, George 38. No Leave No Love (US) 42. Once a Sinner 50. After the Ball 56, etc.

Kirsanov, Dmitri (1899–1957). Russian émigré film-maker, at the forefront of France's avant-garde movement of the twenties.
□Autumn Mists 25. *Menilmontant* 26. Rapt 35.

Kismet. Edward Knoblock's rather stolid Arabian Nights play has been filmed five times. In 1920 Louis Gesnier directed Otis Skinner; in 1931 (in Germany) William Dieterle directed Gustav Fröhlich; in 1931 Otis Skinner played in a talkie version directed by John Francis Dillon; in 1944 Dieterle had another crack at it, with Ronald Colman in the lead; and in 1955 the stage version with musical themes by Borodin was filmed by Vincente Minnelli, with Howard Keel.

Kiss Me Deadly (US 1955). A Mickey Spillane thriller directed by Robert Aldrich. Quite incomprehensible and extremely violent but with brilliantly entertaining moments. A phantasmagoria of Hollywood thriller clichés, its arty direction made it a considerable influence on Truffaut and the 'new wave'.

Kiss Me Kate (US 1953). This film of the stage musical based on *The Taming of the Shrew* was probably the best production shot in 3-D; it was, however, released 'flat'. Apart from its Cole Porter score it had lively performances from Howard Keel, Kathryn Grayson and Ann Miller; directed by George Sidney.

Kiss of Death (US 1947). A gangster thriller influential in its violence, despair and incisiveness; also notable for the first appearance of Richard Widmark in the role of a sadistic laughing killer. Written by Ben Hecht and Charles Lederer, photographed by Norbert Brodine, directed by Henry Hathaway. A disguised remake, *The Fiend Who Walked the West*, was issued in 1958 but had nothing to offer except blood-letting.

Kitt, Eartha (1928–). American Creole cabaret singer whose essential vibrance was captured only in her first film.
Autobiography 1956: *Thursday's Child*.
□*New Faces* 54. St Louis Blues 57. Mark of the Hawk 58. Anna Lucasta 58. Saint of Devil's Island 61. Synanon 65. Uncle Tom's Cabin (WG) 65. Up the Chastity Belt (GB) 71. Lt Schuster's Wife (TV) 72. Friday Foster 75. To Kill a Cop (TV) 78. All by Myself 82. The Pink Chiquitas 86. The Serpent Warriors 86.

Kitzmiller, John (1913–1965). Negro character actor, in Italy from 1945 (after army service).
Paisa 46. To Live In Peace 46. Senza Pieta 48. The Naked Earth 57. Doctor No 62. Uncle Tom's Cabin (title role) (Ger.) 65, etc.

Kjellin, Alf (1920–). Swedish actor who went to Hollywood and worked mostly in TV, turning his talents to direction.
Frenzy 44. My Six Convicts 52. The Iron Mistress 53. The Juggler 63. Ship of Fools 65. Assault on a Queen 66. The Midas Run (d) 69. The McMasters (d) 70, etc.

Klein, William (1929–). American director, in Paris.
Far From Vietnam (part) 66. Qui Etes-Vous Polly Magoo? 67. Mr Freedom 68.

Kleiner, Harry (1916–). American screenwriter.
Fallen Angel 46. The Street with No Name 48. Red Skies of Montana 51. Salome 53. Miss Sadie Thompson 53. *Carmen Jones* 54. The Garment Jungle (& p) 56. Ice Palace 60. Fantastic Voyage 66. *Bullitt* 68. Le Mans 71, etc.

Klein-Rogge, Rudolf (1888–1955). German actor who appeared in some of the most famous German films of the twenties.
Der Mude Tod 21. Dr Mabuse 22. Siegfried 24. Metropolis 26. Spione 28. The Testament of Dr Mabuse 33. Between Heaven and Earth 34. The Old and the Young King 35. Intermezzo 36. Madame Bovary 37. Hochzeit auf Barenhof 42, etc.

Kleiser, Randal (1946–). American director.
All Together Now (TV) 75. Dawn: Portrait of a Teenage Runaway (TV) 76. The Boy in the Plastic Bubble (TV) 76. The Gathering (TV) 77. *Grease* 78. The Blue Lagoon 80. Summer Lovers (& w) 82. Grandview USA 84. Flight of the Navigator 86.

Klemperer, Werner (1919–). Bald-pated German-American character actor, often seen as comic or sinister Nazi.
Death of a Scoundrel 56. Five Steps to Danger 56. The Goddess 58. Operation

Eichmann (title role) 61. Judgment at Nuremberg 61. Escape from East Berlin 62. Youngblood Hawke 64. Ship of Fools 65. The Wicked Dreams of Paula Schultz 67. Wake Me When the War Is Over (TV) 69. Assignment Munich (TV) 72. The Rhinemann Exchange (TV) 77. The Return of the Beverly Hillbillies (TV) 81.
TV series: *Hogan's Heroes* 65–70.

Kline, Herbert (1909–). American director, sometimes of documentaries.
Crisis 39. Lights out in Europe 40. The Forgotten Village (& p) 41. My Father's House (& p) 47. The Kid from Cleveland 49. The Fighter (& wp) 52, etc.

Kline, Kevin (1947–). American actor.
Sophie's Choice 82. The Big Chill 83. Silverado 85. Cry Freedom 87.

Kline, Richard (1926–). American cinematographer.
Camelot 67. *The Boston Strangler* 69. A Dream of Kings 69. The Andromeda Strain 70. Kotch 71. Black Gunn 72. The Harrad Experiment 73. Mandingo 75. King Kong 76. The Fury 78. Star Trek 79. The Competition 80. Body Heat 81. Death Wish II 82. Breathless 83. Hard to Hold 84. All of Me 84. The Man With One Red Shoe 85. Howard the Duck 85. Touch and Go 86, etc.

Klinger, Michael (1921–). British producer.
Repulsion 64. Cul de Sac 66. The Yellow Teddy Bears 66. A Study in Terror 67. Baby Love 69. Get Carter 71. Pulp 73. Gold 74. Shout at the Devil 76. Tomorrow Never Comes 78. Heavy Metal 80, etc.

Klos, Elmar: see *Kadar, Jan.*

Kluge, Alexander (1932–). German director.
Abschied von Gestern 66. Artists at the Top of the Big Top 68. Willy Tobler 71. Occasional Work of a Female Slave 74. Strongman Ferdinand 76, etc.

Klugman, Jack (1922–). Lean American actor who can be comically henpecked, tragically weak, or just sinister.
Timetable 56. *Twelve Angry Men* 57. Days of Wine and Roses 62. Act One 63. I Could Go on Singing 63. Yellow Canary 63. The Detective 68. The Split 68. Goodbye Columbus 69. Who Says I Can't Ride a Rainbow? 71. Two Minute Warning 76.
TV series: Harris against the World 64. *The Odd Couple* 70–74. Quincy 76–82.

The Knack (GB 1965). Richard Lester's free-wheeling film version of Ann Jellicoe's sex play was dull only while it stuck to the script; the running gags and visually inventive interludes shot in London streets were almost undiluted joy. Photographed by David Watkin, with a spirited young cast, the film unfortunately encouraged less talented film-makers, and even Lester himself, to think that anything goes providing you keep moving.

Knapp, Evalyn (1908–1981). American leading lady.
Fifty Million Frenchmen 31. Night Mayor 32. Fireman Save My Child 32. Air Hostess 33. The Perils of Pauline (serial) 34. Laughing Irish Eyes 36. The Lone Wolf Takes a Chance 42. Two Weeks to Live 43, etc.

Kneale, Nigel (1922–). Manx writer, best known for BBC TV serials about Professor Quatermass, all three of which were filmed.
Look Back in Anger 59. The Entertainer 60. The First Men in the Moon 64. The Devil's Own 66, etc.

Knef, Hildegard: see *Neff, Hildegard.*

Knight, Castleton (1894–1972). British newsreel producer (Gaumont British).
Directed some films in the thirties, including *Kissing Cup's Race* and *The Flying Scotsman*; also various compilations such as *Theirs Is the Glory* and *Fourteenth Olympiad*, and records of state occasions such as *A Queen Is Crowned.*

Knight, David (1927–) (David Mintz). American leading man, on London stage since 1953.
The Young Lovers (debut) 55. Lost 57. Across the Bridge 57. Battle of the V.1 58. Nightmare 63, etc.

Knight, Eric (1897–1943). British writer whose 1940 juvenile book *Lassie Come Home* started a doggy industry.

Knight, Esmond (1906–). Welsh actor, on stage since 1925, screen since 1931. Partially blinded during World War II.
Autobiography 1943: *Seeking the Bubble.*
The Silver Fleet 42. *Henry V* 44. End of the River 47. Hamlet 47. The Red Shoes 48.

Richard III 56. Sink the Bismarck 60. Where's Jack? 69. Anne of the Thousand Days 70, etc.

Knight, Fuzzy (1901–1976) (J. Forrest Knight). American night club musician who found himself a niche in Hollywood as comic relief in innumerable westerns.
She Done Him Wrong 33. The Trail of the Lonesome Pine 36. Johnny Apollo 40. Trigger Trail 44. Down to the Sea in Ships 50. Topeka 54. These Thousand Hills 59. Waco 66, etc.
TV series: Captain Gallant 55.

Knight, Shirley (1937–). American leading actress, also on stage and TV; latterly known as Shirley Knight Hopkins.
Five Gates to Hell 59. The Dark at the Top of the Stairs 60. Sweet Bird of Youth 62. *The Group* 66. Dutchman 67. *Petulia* 68. The Rain People 69. Secrets 71. Juggernaut 74. Beyond the Poseidon Adventure 79. Endless Love 81. The Sender 82, etc.

Knoblock, Edward (1874–1945). British author of plays *Kismet, Chu Chin Chow, Milestones*, all frequently filmed; in the twenties became a production associate of Douglas Fairbanks Senior.

Knopf, Edwin H. (1899–1981). American producer, sometimes writer and director.
Border Legion (d) 30. Bad Sister (w) 31. The Wedding Night (w) 35. Piccadilly Jim (w) 36. The Trial of Mary Dugan (p) 41. The Cross of Lorraine (p) 44. The Valley of Decision (p) 45. BF's Daughter (p) 48. Edward My Son (p) 49. The Law and the Lady (d) 51. Lili (p) 53. The Vintage (p) 57, many others.

Knotts, Don (1924–). American 'hayseed' comedian, from TV.
Wake Me When It's Over 60. The Last Time I Saw Archie 61. The Incredible Mr Limpet 62. *The Ghost and Mr Chicken* 66. The Reluctant Astronaut 67. The Shakiest Gun in the West 68. The Love God 69. How to Frame a Figg 71. The Apple Dumpling Gang 75. Gus 76. No Deposit No Return 76. Herbie Goes to Monte Carlo 77. The Apple Dumpling Gang Rides Again 79. The Private Eyes 81, etc.
TV series: *The Andy Griffith Show* 60–68. Three's Company 81–.

Knowles, Bernard (1900–). British cinematographer who became a competent director.
AS CINEMATOGRAPHER: Dawn 29. The Good Companions 32. Jew Süss 34. The Thirty-Nine Steps 35. Gaslight 39. Quiet Wedding 40, etc.
□AS DIRECTOR: *A Place of One's Own* 45. The Magic Bow 46. The Man Within 47. The White Unicorn 47. Jassy 47. Easy Money 48. The Lost People 49. The Perfect Woman 49. The Reluctant Widow 50. Park Plaza 605 53. Barbados Quest 54. Frozen Alive 64. Spaceflight IC-1 65. Hell is Empty 68.

Knowles, Patric (1911–) (Reginald Knowles). British light 'second lead' who went to Hollywood in 1936 and stayed.
Irish Hearts (GB) 34. Abdul the Damned (GB) 34. The Guvnor (GB) 35. The Charge of the Light Brigade 36. The Adventures of Robin Hood 38. Storm over Bengal 39. Anne of Windy Poplars 40. How Green Was My Valley 41. The Wolf Man 41. Lady in a Jam 42. Eyes of the Underworld 42. Frankenstein Meets the Wolf Man 43. Always a Bridesmaid 43. Pardon My Rhythm 44. Kitty 45. Of Human Bondage 46. Monsieur Beaucaire 46. Ivy 47. The Big Steal 49. Three Came Home 50. Mutiny 52. Flame of Calcutta 53. Band of Angels 57. Auntie Mame 59. The Devil's Brigade 68. In Enemy Country 68. Chisum 71. Terror in the Wax Museum 73, others.

Knox, Alexander (1907–). Quiet-spoken Canadian actor, on British stage from 1930, films from 1938; also in Hollywood.
The Gaunt Stranger 38. *The Sea Wolf* 40. This Above All 42. None Shall Escape 43. *Wilson* (title role) 44. Over Twenty-One 45. Sister Kenny 46. *The Judge Steps Out* 47. The Sign of the Ram 48. I'd Climb the Highest Mountain 50. Paula 52. The Sleeping Tiger 53. The Divided Heart 54. Reach for the Sky 56. High Tide at Noon 57. The Vikings 58. Operation Amsterdam 59. The Wreck of the Mary Deare 59. The Trials of Oscar Wilde 60. The Damned 61. Crack in the Mirror 62. The Man in the Middle 64. Crack in the World 65. Mister Moses 65. The Psychopath 66. Accident 66. Modesty Blaise 66. Khartoum 66. How I Won the War 67. Villa Rides 68. Shalako 68. Skullduggery 69. Nicholas and Alexandra 71. Puppet on a Chain 71. Meeting at Potsdam (TV) 76. Holocaust 2000 78. Tinker Tailor Soldier Spy (TV) 79. Gorky Park 83, etc.

Knox, Elyse (1917–). American leading lady of the forties.
Lillian Russell 40. The Mummy's Tomb 42.

Hit the Ice 43. Linda be Good 47. There's a Girl in My Heart 49, etc.

Knox, Teddy: see *The Crazy Gang*.

Knudsen, Peggy (1925–1980). American starlet of the forties.
Stolen Life 46. Humoresque 47. Trouble Preferred 48. Copper Canyon 50. Unchained 53. Good Morning Miss Dove 54. Istanbul 57, etc.

Knudtson, Frederic L. (c.1900–64). American editor.
Headline Shooter 33. Gun Law 38. Stage to Chino 40. This Land is Mine 43. The Bachelor and the Bobbysoxer 47. The Window 48. Angel Face 53. Not as a Stranger 55. The Pride and the Passion 57. The Defiant Ones 58. Inherit the Wind 60. Judgment at Nuremberg 61, many others.

Kobayashi, Masaki (1916–). Japanese director.
Ningen No Joken 61. Hara Kiri 63. *Kwaidan* 64. Rebellion 67. Hymn to a Tired Man 68. Inn of Evil 71. Fossils 75. Glowing Autumn 79, etc.

Koch, Howard (1902–). American screenwriter.
The Sea Hawk (co-w) 40. *The Letter* (co-w) 40. *Casablanca* (co-w) (AA) 42. Mission to Moscow (co-w) 43. *Letter from an Unknown Woman* 47. The Thirteenth Letter 51. The War Lover 63. The Fox (co-wp) 68, many others.

Koch, Howard W. (1916–). American executive, from 1965–66 Paramount's vice-president in charge of production. Former producer and director.
Big House USA (d) 54. Beachhead (p) 55. The Black Sleep (p) 56. Frankenstein 70 (d) 58. Sergeants Three (p) 62. The Manchurian Candidate (p) 62. Come Blow Your Horn (p) 63. None But the Brave (p) 65. The Odd Couple (p) 68. On a Clear Day You Can See Forever (p) 70. Badge 373 73. Once Is Not Enough 75. The Other Side of Midnight 77. Heaven Can Wait 78. The Frisco Kid 79. The Idolmaker 80. Some Kind of Hero 82, etc.

Koenekamp, Fred (–). American cinematographer.
Kansas City Bomber 72. Papillon 73. The Towering Inferno 74. Uptown Saturday Night 74. Posse 75. Doc Savage 75. Islands in the Stream 77. Fun with Dick and Jane 77. The Other Side of Midnight 77. The Domino Principle 77. The Amityville Horror 79. The Champ 79. The First Family 80. When Time Ran Out 80. First Monday in October 81. Wrong Is Right 82. Yes Giorgio 82. Two of a Kind 83. The Adventures of Buckaroo Banzai 84, etc.

Kohler, Fred Snr (1889–1938). American character actor often seen as western badman.
Soldiers of Fortune 19. The Stampede 21. Anna Christie 23. Riders of the Purple Sage 25. The Way of All Flesh 27. Chinatown Charlie 28. The Dragnet 28. The Leatherneck 29. Thunderbolt 29. Hell's Heroes 29. Corsair 31. Call Her Savage 32. Wild Horse Mesa 32. Kid Millions 35. Hard Rock Harrigan 35. The Plainsman 36. Daughter of Shanghai 37. Billy the Kid Returns 38, many others.

Kohlmar, Fred (1905–1969). American producer in Hollywood from the early thirties, at first with Goldwyn.
That Night in Rio 41. The Glass Key 42. Kiss of Death 47. When Willie Comes Marching Home 50. It Should Happen to You 53. Picnic 55. Pal Joey 57. The Last Angry Man 59. The Notorious Landlady 62. How To Steal a Million 66. A Flea in Her Ear 68. The Only Game in Town 69, many others.

Kohner, Susan (1936–). American leading lady.
To Hell and Back 55. Imitation of Life 58. All the Fine Young Cannibals 60. Freud 62, etc.

Kolb, Clarence (1874–1964). Veteran character actor, usually of explosive executive types; formerly in vaudeville.
Carefree 38. Nothing but the Truth 41. Hellzapoppin 42. True to Life 43. The Kid from Brooklyn 46. Christmas Eve 47. Adam's Rib 49. The Rose Bowl Story 53. Man of a Thousand Faces 57, many others.

Kolker, Henry (1874–1947). American stage actor who played lawyers and heavy fathers in many films.
The Bigger Man 15. Disraeli 21. West Point 26. The Valiant 29. East Is West 30. Corsair 31. The Devil and the Deep 32. Jewel Robbery 33. Imitation of Life 34. The Ghost Walks 34. The Case of the Curious Bride 34. Diamond Jim 35. Mad Love 35. The Last Days of Pompeii 35. The Black Room 35. Bullets or Ballots 36. Romeo and Juliet (as Friar Laurence) 36. Theodora Goes Wild 36. Conquest 37. Maid of Salem 37. The Cowboy and the Lady 38. *Holiday* 38. Union Pacific 39. The Real Glory 39. Grand Old Opry 40.

A Woman's Face 41. Sarong Girl 43. Bluebeard 44. The Secret Life of Walter Mitty 47, many others.

Komai, Tetsu (1893–1970). Japanese-American character actor.
Daughter of the Dragon 31. Island of Lost Souls 33. Tokyo Joe 49. Japanese War Bride 52. The Night Walker 64, etc.

Konchalovsky, Andrei (–). Russian director in the west.
Maria's Lovers 85. Runaway Train 85. Duet for One 86. Shy People 87.

Konstam, Phyllis (1907–1976). British stage actress who occasionally played film heroines.
Autobiography 1969: *A Mixed Double* (with her husband Bunny Austin).
□Champagne 28. Blackmail 29. Murder 30. Escape 30. Compromising Daphne 30. The Skin Game 31. Tilly of Bloomsbury 31. A Gentleman of Paris 31. The Forgotten Factor 52. Jotham Valley 52. The Crowning Experience 59. Voice of the Hurricane 60.

Kops and Custards, by Kalton C. Lahue and Terry Brewer. A scholarly history of the Keystone Film Company and the apprenticeship of Mack Sennett; published 1968.

Korda, Sir Alexander (1893–1956) (Sandor Corda). Hungarian producer-director who worked in Paris, Berlin and Hollywood before settling in London 1930. More than any other man the saviour of the British film industry. Formed London Films and sealed its success with *The Private Life of Henry VIII* 32; built Denham Studios.
Biographies: *Alexander Korda* (1956) by Paul Tabori; *Alexander Korda* (1975) by Karol Kulik; *Charmed Lives* (1980) by Michael Korda.
□The Duped Journalist (d) 14. Tutyu and Totyo (d) 14. Lea Lyon (d) 15. The Officer's Swordknot (d) 15. Fedora (d) 16. The Grandmother (d) 16. Tales of the Typewriter (d) 16. The Man with Two Hearts (d) 16. The Million Pound Note (d) 16. Cyclamen (d) 16. Struggling Hearts (d) 16. Laughing Saskia (d) 16. Miska the Magnate (d) 16. St Peter's Umbrella (d) 17. The Stork Caliph (d) 17. Magic (d) 17. Harrison and Barrison (d) 17. Faun (d) 18. The Man with the Golden Touch (d) 18. Mary Ann (d) 18. Hail Caesar (d) 19. White Rose (d) 19. Yamata (d) 19. Neither In Nor Out (d) 19. Number 111 (d) 19. The Prince and the Pauper (d) 20. Masters of the Sea (d) 22. A Vanished World (d) 22. Samson and Delilah (d) 22. The Unknown Tomorrow (d) 23. Everybody's Woman (d) 24. Mayerling (d) 24. Dancing Mad (d) 25. Madame Wants No Children (d) 26. A Modern Dubarry (d) 27. (All previous titles in Hungary, France and Germany; now Hollywood.) The Stolen Bride (d) 27. *The Private Life of Helen of Troy* (d) 27. Yellow Lily (d) 28. Night Watch (d) 28. Love and the Devil (d) 29. The Squall (d) 29. Her Private Life (d) 29. Lilies of the Field (d) 30. Women Everywhere (d) 30. The Princess and the Plumber (d) 31. (Now Paris.) Laughter (d) 31. *Marius* (d) 31. (Now London.) Service for Ladies (p, d) 32. Wedding Rehearsal (p, d) 32. That Night in London (p) 33. Strange Evidence (p) 33. Counsel's Opinion (p) 33. Cash (p) 33. Men of Tomorrow (p) 33. *The Private Life of Henry VIII* (p, d) 33. The Girl from Maxim's (p, d) 33. *The Rise of Catherine the Great* (p) 34. The Private Life of Don Juan (p, d) 34. *The Scarlet Pimpernel* (p, some d) 34. *Sanders of the River* (p) 35. *The Ghost Goes West* (p) 35. *Things to Come* (p) 36. Moscow Nights (ep) 36. Men Are Not Gods (p) 36. Forget Me Not (p) 36. *Rembrandt* (p, d) 36. *The Man Who Could Work Miracles* (p) 37. Fire over England (ep) 37. I Claudius (unfinished) (p) 37. Dark Journey (p) 37. Elephant Boy (p) 37. Farewell Again (ep) 37. Storm in a Teacup (ep) 37. Action for Slander (ep) 37. *Knight without Armour* (p) 37. The Squeaker (p) 37. The Return of the Scarlet Pimpernel (ep) 37. Paradise for Two (ep) 37. The Divorce of Lady X (p) 38. The Drum (p) 38. South Riding (ep) 38. The Challenge (ep) 38. Prison without Bars (ep) 38. Q Planes (ep) 39. *The Four Feathers* (p) 39. The Rebel Son (ep) 39. The Spy in Black (ep) 39. The Lion Has Wings (p) 39. Over the Moon (p) 40 (shot 1938). 21 Days (p) 40 (shot 37). Conquest of the Air (p) 40. *The Thief of Baghdad* (p) 40. Old Bill and Son (ep) 41. *That Hamilton Woman* (in US) (p, d) 41. Lydia (in US) (p) 41. *To Be or Not to Be* (in US) (ep) 42. Jungle Book (in US) (p) 42. *Perfect Strangers* (p) 45. The Shop at Sly Corner (ep) 47. A Man about the House (ep) 47. Mine Own Executioner (ep) 47. An Ideal Husband (p, d) 47. Night Beat (ep) 48. *Anna Karenina* (p) 48. The Winslow Boy (ep) 48. The Fallen Idol (ep) 48. Bonnie Prince Charlie (ep) 48. The Small Back Room (ep) 49. That Dangerous Age (ep) 49. The Last Days of Dolwyn (ep) 49. Saints and Sinners (ep) 49. *The Third Man* (ep) 49. The Cure for Love (ep) 50. The Angel with the Trumpet (ep) 50. My Daughter Joy (ep) 50. State Secret (ep)

50. Seven Days to Noon (ep) 50. Gone to Earth (ep) 50. The Elusive Pimpernel (ep) 51. Tales of Hoffman (ep) 51. Lady Godiva Rides Again (ep) 51. The Wonder Kid (ep) 51. Mr Denning Drives North (ep) 52. An Outcast of the Islands (ep) 52. Home at Seven (ep) 52. Who Goes There? (ep) 52. Cry the Beloved Country (ep) 52. *The Sound Barrier* (ep) 52. The Holly and the Ivy (ep) 52. The Ringer (ep) 53. Folly to Be Wise (ep) 53. Twice Upon a Time (ep) 53. The Captain's Paradise (ep) 53. The Story of Gilbert and Sullivan (ep) 53. The Man Between (ep) 53. The Heart of the Matter (ep) 54. Hobson's Choice (ep) 54. The Belles of St Trinian's (ep) 54. The Teckman Mystery (ep) 54. The Man Who Loved Redheads (ep) 55. Three Cases of Murder (ep) 55. The Constant Husband (ep) 55. A Kid for Two Farthings (ep) 55. The Deep Blue Sea (ep) 55. Summer Madness (ep) 55. Storm over the Nile (ep) 55. *Richard III* (ep) 56. Smiley (ep) 56.

†In the above list the abbreviation ep (executive producer) is meant to imply a considerable distancing by Korda from the product, as sponsor, or financier, or head of London Films.

††Other projects announced at various times by Korda include *The Field of the Cloth of Gold*, *Marco Polo*, *Nijinsky*, *Hamlet*, *Zorro*, *Joseph and his Brothers*, *Young Mr Disraeli*, *Marlborough*, *King of the Jews*, *Franz Liszt*, *Lawrence of Arabia*, *Nelson*, *Precious Bane*, *Cyrano de Bergerac*, *Charles II*, *War and Peace*, *Burmese Silver*, *Elizabeth of Austria*, *Pocahontas*, *Manon Lescaut*, *New Wine*, *The Hardy Family in England*, *Greenmantle*, *The Old Wives' Tale*, *Mr Chips' Boys*, *The Pickwick Papers*, *The Wrecker*, *Around the World in Eighty Days*, *Gibraltar*, *The Eternal City*, *The King's General*, *Carmen*, *Salome*, *Faust*, *Arms and the Man*, *Macbeth*, *The Iliad*.

❀ For reviving Britain's flagging film industry and making half-a-dozen imperishable classics. *Rembrandt*.

¶ *A.K.:* The art of film-making is to come to the brink of bankruptcy and stare it in the face.

He represented, and indeed virtually created, the tradition of quality in the British cinema.—*Andrew Sarris*

Korda, Vincent (1896–1979). Hungarian art director who usually worked on the films of his brothers Alexander and Zoltan.
The Private Life of Henry VIII 32. Sanders of the River 35. *Things to Come* 36. The Four Feathers 39. *The Thief of Baghdad* (AA) 40. To Be or Not to Be 42. The Fallen Idol 48. The Third Man 49. The Sound Barrier 52. The Deep Blue Sea 55. Summer Madness 56, etc.

Korda, Zoltan (1895–1961). Hungarian director, brother of Alexander Korda; spent most of his career in Britain and Hollywood.
Cash 32. Sanders of the River 35. The Drum 38. *The Four Feathers* 39. Jungle Book 42. Sahara 43. Counterattack 43. *The Macomber Affair* 47. A Woman's Vengeance 48. Cry the Beloved Country 51, etc.

Korjus, Miliza (1908–1980). Polish operatic soprano who settled in America but did not pursue what looked like being a popular film career.
□*The Great Waltz* 38. Imperial Cavalry (Mexico) 42.

Korman, Harvey (1927–). American character comedian, often as loud-mouthed show-off. On TV with Danny Kaye and Carol Burnett.
Lord Love a Duck 66. Don't Just Stand There 67. The April Fools 68. Blazing Saddles 74. High Anxiety 78. First Family 80. Herbie Goes Bananas 80. History of the World Part One 81. Trail of the Pink Panther 82. The Long Shot 85, etc.

Korngold, Erich Wolfgang (1897–1957). Czech composer-conductor, a child prodigy. To Hollywood in 1935 with Warners.
□Captain Blood 35. *Anthony Adverse* (AA) 36. The Green Pastures 36. A Midsummer Night's Dream 36. The Story of Louis Pasteur 36. Another Dawn 37. The Prince and the Pauper 37. *The Adventures of Robin Hood* (AA) 38. Juarez 39. Elizabeth and Essex 39. *The Sea Hawk* 40. The Sea Wolf 41. *King's Row* 41. The Constant Nymph 43. Between Two Worlds 44. Devotion 44. Deception 46. Of Human Bondage 46. Escape Me Never 47. Magic Fire 56.

❀ For stirring romantic themes of a finer texture than anyone else in Hollywood could accomplish. *King's Row*.

Korris, Harry (1888–1971). British music-hall comedian who became popular on radio and made several slapdash film farces.
Somewhere in England 40. Somewhere in Camp 41. Happidrome 43, etc.

Kortner, Fritz (1892–1970) (Fritz Nathan Kohn). Austrian character actor, in films of many nations, and director.
Autobiography 1959: *The Evening of All Days*.
Police No 1111 (debut) 16. Satanas 20. The

Brothers Karamazov 20. The Hands of Orlac 24. Beethoven 26. Warning Shadows 27. Mata Hari 27. *Pandora's Box* 28. The Murder of Dimitri Karamazov 30. Dreyfus 30. Chu Chin Chow 34. Evensong 34. Abdul the Damned 35. The Crouching Beast 36. The Strange Death of Adolf Hitler 43. The Hitler Gang 44. Somewhere in the Night 46. The Brasher Doubloon 47. Berlin Express 48, many others.
□AS DIRECTOR: Der Brave Suender 31. So Ein Maedel Vergisst Man Nicht 33. Der Ruf 49. Die Stadt ist voller Geheimnisse 55. Sarajero 55. Lysistrata 61.

Korty, John (1941–). American director.
□The Crazy Quilt 65. Funnyman 67. Riverrun 68. The People (TV) 72. Class of 63 (TV) 73. Go Ask Alice (TV) 73. The Autobiography of Miss Jane Pittman (TV) 73. Silence 74. Alex and the Gypsy 76. Farewell to Manzanar (TV) 76. Who Are the De Bolts 77. Forever (TV) 78. Oliver's Story (& w) 78. A Christmas without Snow (TV) 80.

Korvin, Charles (1907–) (Geza Kaiser). Czech-born leading man with varied experience before Hollywood debut.
Enter Arsène Lupin 44. This Love of Ours 45. Temptation 47. The Killer That Stalked New York 50. Lydia Bailey 52. Sangaree 53. Zorro the Avenger 60. Ship of Fools 65. The Man Who Had Power Over Women 70, etc.
TV series: Interpol Calling 59.

Koscina, Sylva (1935–). Jugoslavian leading lady in international films.
Hercules Unchained 60. Jessica 62. Hot Enough for June (GB) 63. Juliet of the Spirits (It.) 65. Three Bites of the Apple (US) 66. Deadlier than the Male (GB) 67. A Lovely Way to Die 68. The Battle for Neretva 70. Hornet's Nest 70, etc.

Kosleck, Martin (1907–) (Nicolai Yoshkin). Russian character actor with experience on the German stage; in America from mid-thirties.
Confessions of a Nazi Spy (as Goebbels) 39. Nurse Edith Cavell 39. A Date with Destiny 40. Foreign Correspondent 40. North Star 43. *The Hitler Gang* (as Goebbels) 44. The Frozen Ghost 44. The Mummy's Curse 45. House of Horrors 46. Hitler (as Goebbels) 61. Something Wild 62. Thirty-Six Hours 64. Morituri 65. The Flesh Eaters 67. Which Way to the Front? 70, etc.

Kosma, Joseph (1905–1969). Hungarian composer, in France from 1933.
La Grande Illusion 37. *La Bête Humaine* 38. *Partie de Campagne* 38. La Règle du Jeu 39. *Les Enfants du Paradis* 44. Les Portes de la Nuit 45. Les Amants de Vérone 48. The Green Glove 52. Huis Clos 54. Calle Mayor 56. The Doctor's Dilemma 59. Lunch on the Grass 59. La Poupée 62. In the French Style 64. The Little Theatre of Jean Renoir 69, etc.

Kossoff, David (1919–). British character actor and stage monologuist.
The Good Beginning 50. The Young Lovers 55. *A Kid for Two Farthings* 56. *The Bespoke Overcoat* 57. The Journey 59. Freud 62. Ring of Spies 64, many others.
TV series: The Larkins. A Little Big Business.

Kostal, Irwin (1911–). American musical supervisor.
West Side Story (AA) 61. Mary Poppins 64. *The Sound of Music* (AA) 65. Half a Sixpence 67.

Koster, Henry (1905–) (Hermann Kosterlitz). German director, in Hollywood from mid-thirties, adept at sentimental comedy.
□Thea Roland (Ger.) 32. Peter (Ger.) 33. Little Mother (Ger.) 33. Peter (Hung.) 35. Marie Bashkirtzeff (Ger.) 36. *Three Smart Girls* 36. *One Hundred Men and a Girl* 37. The Rage of Paris 38. Three Smart Girls Grow Up 38. First Love 39. Spring Parade 40. *It Started with Eve* 41. Between Us Girls 42. Music for Millions 44. Two Sisters from Boston 45. The Unfinished Dance 47. *The Bishop's Wife* 48. The Luck of the Irish 38. Come to the Stable 49. *The Inspector General* 49. Wabash Avenue 50. My Blue Heaven 50. *Harvey* 50. No Highway (GB) 51. Mr Belvedere Rings the Bell 52. Elopement 52. Stars and Stripes Forever 52. My Cousin Rachel 52. *The Robe* 53. Désirée 54. A Man Called Peter 55. The Virgin Queen 55. Good Morning, Miss Dove 55. D-Day the Sixth of June 56. The Power and the Prize 56. My Man Godfrey 57. Fraulein 58. The Naked Maja 59. The Story of Ruth 60. Flower Drum Song 60. Mr Hobbs Takes a Vacation 62. Take Her She's Mine 63. Dear Brigitte 65. The Singing Nun 66.

Kotcheff, Ted (1931–). Canadian director resident in Britain.
□Tiara Tahiti 62. *Life at the Top* 65. Two Gentlemen Sharing 70. Outback 71. Billy Two Hats 73. The Apprenticeship of Duddy Kravitz 74. Fun with Dick and Jane 77.

Someone is Killing the Great Chefs of Europe 78. North Dallas Forty 79. First Blood 82. Split Image 83. Uncommon Valor 83. Joshua Then and Now 85.

Kotto, Yaphet (1937–). Black American actor.
The Thomas Crown Affair 68. The Liberation of L. B. Jones 70. Across 110th Street 72. *Live and Let Die* 73. Truck Turner 74. Report to the Commissioner 74. Drum 76. Monkey Hustle 76. Blue Collar 78. Alien 79. Brubaker 80. The Star Chamber 83. Warning Sign 85. Prettykill 87.

Kovack, Nancy (1935–). American leading lady with stage and TV experience.
Strangers When We Meet 60. Diary of a Madman 62. Jason and the Argonauts 63. The Outlaws Is Coming 65. Frankie and Johnny 66. The Silencers 66. Tarzan and the Valley of Gold 66. Marooned 69, etc.

Kovacs, Ernie (1919–1962). Big, cigar-smoking American comedian and TV personality.
Biography 1976: *Nothing in Moderation* by David G. Walley.
□*Operation Mad Ball* 57. Bell, Book and Candle 58. It Happened to Jane 58. *Our Man in Havana* 59. Wake Me When It's Over 60. Strangers When We Meet 60. North to Alaska 60. Pepe 60. Five Golden Hours 61. Sail a Crooked Ship 62.

Kovacs, Laszlo (1932–). American cinematographer given to experimentation which does not always please the eye.
Targets 68. The Savage Seven 68. Easy Rider 69. Getting Straight 70. Five Easy Pieces 70. Alex in Wonderland 70. The Last Movie 71. Marriage of a Young Stockbroker 71. Pocket Money 72. What's Up Doc? 72. Paper Moon 73. Freebie and the Bean 74. Shampoo 75. At Long Last Love 75. Nickelodeon 76. New York New York 77. Close Encounters of the Third Kind (co-ph) 77. The Last Waltz 78. Butch and Sundance 79. Heartbeat 79. The Legend of the Lone Ranger 81. The Toy 82. Frances 82. Crackers 84. Ghostbusters 84. Mask 85. Legal Eagles 86, etc.

Kowalski, Bernard (1931–). American director, from TV.
Hot Car Girl 58. Attack of the Giant Leeches 58. Night of the Blood Beast 58. Blood and Steel 59. Krakatoa East of Java 69. Stiletto 70. Macho Callahan 70. Sssss 73, etc.

Kozintsev, Grigori (1905–1973). Russian director, in films since 1924.
The Youth of Maxim 35. *Don Quixote* 57. *Hamlet* 64. King Lear 69, etc.

Kramer, Larry (1935–). American screenwriter.
Women in Love (& p) 69. Lost Horizon 72, etc.

Kramer, Stanley (1913–). American producer of clean-cut, well-intentioned films which sometimes fall short on inspiration.
□So Ends our Night 41. *The Moon and Sixpence* 42. So This Is New York 48. Champion 49. Home of the Brave 49. *The Men* 50. Cyrano de Bergerac 50. *Death of a Salesman* 51. *High Noon* 52. The Sniper 52. The Happy Time 52. My Six Convicts 52. The Member of the Wedding 52. Eight Iron Men 52. The Fourposter 53. The Juggler 53. The 5000 Fingers of Dr T 53. The Wild One 54. *The Caine Mutiny* 54. Not as a Stranger (& d) 55. The Pride and the Passion (& d) 57. The Defiant Ones (& d) 58. *On the Beach* (& d) 59. *Inherit the Wind* (& d) 60. Judgment at Nuremberg (& d) 61. Pressure Point 62. A Child is Waiting 62. It's a Mad Mad Mad Mad World (& d) 63. Invitation to a Gunfighter 64. *Ship of Fools* (& d) 65. *Guess Who's Coming to Dinner* (& d) 67. The Secret of Santa Vittoria (& d) 69. R.P.M. (& d) 71. Bless the Beasts and Children (& d) 71. *Oklahoma Crude* (& d) 73. The Domino Principle (& d) 77. The Runner Stumbles (& d) 79.

'He will never be a natural, but time has proved that he is not a fake.'—*Andrew Sarris, 1968*

❀ For trying. *Inherit the Wind.*

¶ *S.K.:* I'm always pursuing the next dream, hunting for the next truth.

Kramer vs Kramer (US 1979). The Academy Awards showered on this small picture (best picture, best director, best actor, best supporting actress, best screenplay) indicated the industry's wish to take the movies back to a period of respectability, but despite the awards in the following two years to *Chariots of Fire* and *Gandhi*, the reversal of trends has not been forthcoming. The film was an old chestnut about the perils of divorce and its effect on a young child; the magic was in the acting by Dustin Hoffman, Meryl Streep and Justin Henry, and the writing and direction by Robert Benton.

Krampf, Gunter (1899–195*). German cinematographer, in Britain from 1931.

The Student of Prague 24. The Hands of Orlac 24. *Pandora's Box* 28. Rome Express 32. Little Friend 34. Latin Quarter 45. Fame is the Spur 46. Portrait of Clare 50. The Franchise Affair 52, many others.

Krasker, Robert (1913–1981). Australian cinematographer, long in Britain.
Dangerous Moonlight 40. *Henry V* 44. Caesar and Cleopatra 45. *Brief Encounter* 46. *Odd Man Out* 47. *The Third Man* (AA) 49. Romeo and Juliet 53. Trapeze 56. The Quiet American 58. The Criminal 60. El Cid 61. Billy Budd 62. The Running Man 63. The Fall of the Roman Empire 64. The Heroes of Telemark 65, many others.

Krasna, Norman (1909–84). American playwright who worked on many films from 1932, including adaptations of his own plays.
Fury 36. *Bachelor Mother* 39. The Flame of New Orleans 41. The Devil and Miss Jones 41. *Princess O'Rourke* (AA) (& d) 43. The Big Hangover (& pd) 50. The Ambassador's Daughter (& d) 56. *Indiscreet* 58. Who Was That Lady? (& d) 60. Let's Make Love 61. Sunday in New York 64, many others.

Krasner, Milton (1901–). American cinematographer.
I Love That Man 33. The Crime of Dr Hallett 36. The House of the Seven Gables 40. *The Woman in the Window* 44. Scarlet Street 45. *The Dark Mirror* 46. The Farmer's Daughter 47. *The Set Up* 49. Rawhide 50. *All About Eve* 50. Monkey Business 51. *Three Coins in the Fountain* (AA) 54. The Rains of Ranchipur 55. Bus Stop 56. An Affair to Remember 57. The Four Horsemen of the Apocalypse 62. Two Weeks in Another Town 62. Love with the Proper Stranger 64. The Sandpiper 65. The Singing Nun 66. Hurry Sundown 67. The Epic of Josie 67. The St Valentine's Day Massacre 68. The Sterile Cuckoo 69. Beneath the Planet of the Apes 70, many others.

Kraushaar, Raoul (1908–). American composer.
Melody Ranch 40. Stardust on the Sage 42. Stork Bites Man 47. Bride of the Gorilla 51. The Blue Gardenia 53. Mohawk 56. Mustang 59, etc.

Krauss, Werner (1884–1959). Distinguished German actor.
ETA Hoffman (debut) 16. *The Cabinet of Dr Caligari* 19. The Brothers Karamazov 20. Othello 22. Nathan the Wise 23. *Waxworks* 24. The Student of Prague 25. A Midsummer Night's Dream 25. Secrets of a Soul 26. Tartuffe 26. Jew Süss 40. John Ohne Heimat 55, etc.

Kress, Harold F. (1913–). American editor.
Bitter Sweet 40. Dr Jekyll and Mr Hyde 41. Mrs Miniver 42. Dragon Seed 44. Command Decision 49. Green Fire 54. The Cobweb 55. Silk Stockings 57. King of Kings 61. How the West Was Won (AA) 63. Alvarez Kelly 66. I Walk the Line 70. The Poseidon Adventure 72. The Towering Inferno (AA) 74. Viva Knievel 77, many others.
□AS DIRECTOR: Purity Squad 45. No Questions Asked 51. The Painted Hills 51. Apache War Smoke 52. Cromwell (2nd unit) 70.

Kreuger, Kurt (1917–). Swiss actor, former ski instructor, who appeared in many Hollywood films as smooth continental heart-throb or menace.
Sahara 43. The Moon Is Down 43. Mademoiselle Fifi 44. Madame Pimpernel 45. Unfaithfully Yours 48. The Enemy Below 58. What Did You Do in the War, Daddy? 66. The St Valentine's Day Massacre 67, etc.

Krige, Alice (1954–). South African leading lady in international films.
Chariots of Fire 81. Ghost Story 81. A Tale of Two Cities (TV) 81. Ellis Island (TV) 84. King David 85. Dream West (TV) 85. Barfly 87.

Krish, John (1923–). British director who began in sponsored documentary field.
□Unearthly Stranger 61. The Wild Affair 65. Decline and Fall 68. The Man Who Had Power Over Women 70.

Kristel, Sylvia (1952–). French leading lady who became famous in the nude.
Emmannuelle 73. Alice or the Last Escapade 76. The Fifth Musketeer 77. The Concorde—Airport 79 79. The Nude Bomb 80. Private Lessons 81. Lady Chatterley's Lover 82.

Kristofferson, Kris (1936–). American leading man of the seventies, former folk singer and musician.
□ The Last Movie 70. Cisco Pike 72. Blume in Love 73. Pat Garrett and Billy the Kid 73. Bring Me the Head of Alfredo Garcia 74. Alice Doesn't Live Here Any More 75. The Sailor who Fell From Grace with the Sea 76. A Star is Born 76. Vigilante Force 76.

Semi-Tough 78. Convoy 78. Heaven's Gate 80. Rollover 81. Flashpoint 84. Songwriter 84. Trouble in Mind 85. Blood and Orchids (TV) 86.

Kruger, Alma (1868–1960). American stage actress who made many films in later life and is specially remembered as the head nurse in the Dr Kildare series.
These Three 36. One Hundred Men and a Girl 37. Marie Antoinette 38. Balalaika 39. Saboteur 42. A Royal Scandal 46. Forever Amber (last film) 47, etc.

Kruger, Hardy (1928–). Blond German leading man who has filmed internationally.
Junge Adler (debut) 43. Insel Ohne Moral 50. Solange 53. Alibi 55. *The One That Got Away* 57. Bachelor of Hearts 58. Blind Date 59. The Rest is Silence 59. Sundays and Cybèle 62. Hatari 62. The Flight of the Phoenix 65. The Defector 66. The Secret of Santa Vittoria 69. The Red Tent 70. Night Hair Child 71. Paper Tiger 75. Barry Lyndon 75. A Bridge Too Far 77. The Wild Geese 78. Blue Fin 79, etc.

Kruger, Otto (1885–1974). Suave American actor with long stage experience.
The Intruder (debut) 32. *Chained* 34. Springtime for Henry 34. Treasure Island 35. *Dracula's Daughter* 36. They Won't Forget 37. *The Housemaster* (GB) 38. Thanks for the Memory 38. Dr Ehrlich's Magic Bullet 40. This Man Reuter 40. The Big Boss 41. *Saboteur* 42. *Murder My Sweet* 44. Escape in the Fog 45. Duel in the Sun 46. Smart Woman 48. Payment on Demand 51. High Noon 52. Magnificent Obsession 54. The Last Command 56. The Wonderful World of the Brothers Grimm 63. Sex and the Single Girl 64, many others.

Kruschen, Jack (1922–). American character comedian of stage and TV.
Red Hot and Blue 49. The Last Voyage 60. The Apartment 60. Lover Come Back 62. The Unsinkable Molly Brown 64. Harlow (TV) (as Louis B. Mayer) 66. Million Dollar Duck 71. Freebie and the Bean 74. Sunburn 79. Under the Rainbow 81. Legend of the Wild 81, etc.

The Ku Klux Klan was sympathetically portrayed in Griffith's *The Birth of a Nation*, a fact which has never ceased to provoke controversy. The villainous actuality has, however, been displayed in *Black Legion* 36, *Legion of Terror* 37, *The Burning Cross* 47, *Storm Warning* 51, *The FBI Story* 59, *The Cardinal* 63 and *The Klansman* 74, among others. See also: *Lynch Law*.

Kubrick, Stanley (1928–). American writer-producer-director, in whose psyche independence seems equated with excess. Biographies: *Stanley Kubrick Directs* (1971) by Alexander Walker; *Kubrick, Inside a Film Artist's Maze* (1982) by T. A. Nelson.
□Fear and Desire (wdph) 53. Killer's Kiss (wd) 55. *The Killing* (wd) 56. *Paths of Glory* (wd) 58. Spartacus (d) 60. Lolita (d) 62. *Dr Strangelove* (wdp) 63. *2001: A Space Odyssey* (wdp) 69. A Clockwork Orange (wdp) 71. Barry Lyndon 75. The Shining 79. Full Metal Jacket 87.

¶ He gives new meaning to the word meticulous.—*Jack Nicholson*

S.K.: Man in the twentieth century has been cast adrift in a rudderless boat on an uncharted sea. The very meaninglessness of life forces man to create his own meaning. If it can be written or thought, it can be filmed.

His tragedy may have been that he was hailed as a great artist before he had become a competent craftsman. However, it is more likely that he has chosen to exploit the giddiness of middlebrow audiences on the satiric level of Mad magazine.—*Andrew Sarris, 1968*

Kulik, Buzz (1923–) (Seymour Kulik). • American director, from TV.
□The Explosive Generation 61. The Yellow Canary 63. Ready for the People 64. Warning Shot (& p) 66. Villa Rides 68. Riot 68. Vanished (TV) 71. Brian's Song (TV) 71. Owen Marshall (TV) 71. To Find a Man 72. Incident in a Dark Street (TV) 72. Shamus 73. Pioneer Woman (TV) 73. Remember When (TV) 74. Bad Ronald (TV) 74. Cage without a Key (TV) 75. Babe (TV) 75. Matt Helm (TV) 75. Feather and Father (TV) 76. The Lindbergh Kidnapping Case (TV) 76. Corey for the People (TV) 77. Kill me if you Can (TV) 77. Ziegfeld: The Man and His Women (TV) 78. From Here to Eternity (TV) 79. The Pursuit of D. B. Cooper 81.

Kulp, Nancy (1921–). American comedy actress, famous for TV portrayals.
The Model and the Marriage Broker 52. Shane 53. Five Gates to Hell 59. The Parent Trap 61. The Patsy 64. The Return of the Beverly Hillbillies (TV) 81, etc.
TV series: *The Beverly Hillbillies* 62–70. The Brian Keith Show 73.

Kurnitz, Harry (1907–1968). American screenwriter, in Hollywood from 1938.

Fast and Furious 38. The Thin Man Goes Home 44. The Web 47. A Kiss in the Dark (& p) 48. Pretty Baby 49. The Inspector General 49. Melba 53. The Man Between 53. Land of the Pharaohs 55. *Witness for the Prosecution* 57. Goodbye Charlie 64. How To Steal a Million 66, many others.

Kurosawa, Akira (1910–). Distinguished Japanese director.
Biography 1974: *Kurosawa* by Michel Mesnil. Autobiography 1982: *Something Like an Autobiography*.
☐Sanshiro Sugata (& w) 43. The Most Beautiful (& w) 44. Sanshiro Sugata II (& w) 44. Tora-no-o (& w) 45. Those Who Make Tomorrow (co-d) 46. No Regrets for Our Youth 46. Wonderful Sunday 47. Drunken Angel 48. A Quiet Duel 49. Stray Dog 49 Scandal 50. *Rashomon* 50. The Idiot 51. *Ikuru* 52. *Seven Samurai* 54. I Live in Fear 55. *Throne of Blood* 56. The Lower Depths 57. *The Hidden Fortress* 58. The Bad Sleep Well 60. Yojimbo 61. Sanjuro 62. High and Low 63. Redbeard 65. Dodeska-den 70. Dersu Uzala 75. *The Shadow Warrior* 81. *Ran* (AAN) 85.

Kwan, Nancy (1938–). Chinese-English leading lady.
The World of Suzie Wong 60. Flower Drum Song 61. Tamahine 63. Fate Is the Hunter 64. The Wild Affair 65. Lt Robin Crusoe 65. Arrivederci Baby 66. Nobody's Perfect 67. The Wrecking Crew 68. The Girl Who Knew Too Much 69. The McMasters 70. Wonder Woman (TV) 73. Project: Kill 76. Night Creature 78, etc.

Kwouk, Burt (1930–). Chinese-English character actor.
Goldfinger 64. You Only Live Twice 68. The Most Dangerous Man in the World 69. Deep End 71. The Return of the Pink Panther 75. The Last Remake of Beau Geste 77. The Fiendish Plot of Dr Fu Manchu 81. Trail of the Pink Panther 82. Plenty 85, etc.

Kydd, Sam (1917–1982). British character comedian whose sharp features were seen in many films from 1945.
The Captive Heart 45. The Small Back Room 48. Treasure Island 50. The Cruel Sea 53. The Quatermass Experiment 55. I'm All Right Jack 59. Follow That Horse 60. Island of Terror 66, etc.

Kyo, Machiko (1924–). Japanese actress.
Rashomon 50. Gate of Hell 52. The Teahouse of the August Moon 56. Ugetsu Monogatari 58, etc.

Kyser, Kay (1897–1985). Mild-mannered American bandleader who made a number of comedy films in the early forties, then retired to become an active Christian Scientist.
☐That's Right You're Wrong 39. You'll Find Out 40. Playmates 41. My Favorite Spy 42. Around the World 43. Swing Fever 44. Carolina Blues 44.

L

La Cava, Gregory (1892–1952). American director, former cartoonist and writer: a delicate talent for comedy usually struggled against unsatisfactory vehicles.
Womanhandled 25. Running Wild 27. Feel My Pulse 28. Laugh and Get Rich 31. Symphony of Six Million 32. The Half-Naked Truth 32. Gabriel over the White House 32. Affairs of Cellini 34. What Every Woman Knows 34. Private Worlds 35. She Married Her Boss 35. *My Man Godfrey* 36. *Stage Door* 37. Fifth Avenue Girl 39. The Primrose Path 40. Unfinished Business 41. Lady in a Jam 42. Living in a Big Way 47, etc.
† La Cava was impersonated by Allen Arbus in *W. C. Fields and Me*.

La Frenais, Ian (c. 1938–). British comedy writer who works in conjunction with Dick Clement (qv).

La Marr, Barbara (1896–1926) (Reatha Watson). American leading lady of silent films from 1920.
The Prisoner of Zenda 22. The Eternal City 23. Thy Name Is Woman 24. The Shooting of Dan McGrew 24. The Girl from Montmartre 26, etc.

La Planche, Rosemary (1923–1979). American leading lady of the forties.
Mad about Music 38. The Falcon in Danger 43. Prairie Chickens 43. Devil Bat's Daughter 46, etc.

La Plante, Laura (1904–). American leading lady of the silent screen.
The Old Swimming Hole 21. Skinner's Dress Suit 24. The Cat and the Canary 27. Smouldering Fires 28. King of Jazz 30. Widow's Might 35. Little Mister Jim 46. Spring Reunion 57, etc.

La Rocque, Rod (1896–1969) (Roderick la Rocque de la Rour). Popular American leading man of the silent screen, in Hollywood from 1917 after circus experience.
Efficiency Edgar's Courtship 17. The Venus Model 18. The Ten Commandments 23. Forbidden Paradise 25. Resurrection 26. Our Modern Maidens 28. Let Us Be Gay 29. One Romantic Night 30. SOS Iceberg 33. Till We Meet Again 36. The Hunchback of Notre Dame 40. Dr Christian Meets the Women 41. Meet John Doe 41, others.

La Rue, Danny (1927–) (Daniel Patrick Carroll). British revue star and female impersonator.
□Our Miss Fred 72.

La Rue, Jack (1903–84) (Gaspare Biondolillo). Grim-faced American actor, typed as gangster from the early thirties.
Lady Killer 34. Captains Courageous 37. Paper Bullets 41. Gentleman from Dixie (a rare sympathetic part) 41. Machine Gun Mama 44. No Orchids for Miss Blandish (GB) (as the maniacal Slim Grisson) 48. Robin Hood of Monterey 49. Ride the Man Down 53. Robin and the Seven Hoods 64. Won Ton Ton 76, many others.

La Shelle, Joseph (1903–). American cinematographer.
Happy Land 43. *Laura* (AA) 44. *Hangover Square* 44. The Foxes of Harrow 47. Come to the Stable 49. Mister 880 50. Les Misérables 52. Marty 55. Storm Fear 55. *The Bachelor Party* 57. I Was a Teenage Werewolf 57. No Down Payment 57 The Naked and the Dead 58. The Apartment 60. Irma La Douce 63. The Fortune Cookie 66. The Chase 66. Barefoot in the Park 67. Kona Coast 68, many others.

Laage, Barbara (1925–) (Claire Colombat). French leading lady of several fifties films.
La Putain Respecteuse 52. L'Esclave Blanche 54. Act of Love 54. Un Homme à Vendre 58. Paris Blues 61. Domicile Conjugale 71. Private Projection 76, etc.

labour relations is too downbeat a subject to be very popular on the screen; but strikes have been treated with seriousness in *Strike, The Crime of Monsieur Lange, Black Fury, How Green Was My Valley, The Agitator, Love on the Dole, Chance of a Lifetime, The*

Whistle at Eaton Falls, and *The Angry Silence*; with humour in *A Nous la Liberté, Modern Times, Carry On at Your Convenience, The Pajama Game,* and *I'm All Right Jack.* The classical comical strike of women against their husbands, led by Lysistrata, was depicted in the French *Love, Soldiers and Women* and Americanized in *The Second Greatest Sex.*

Lacey, Catherine (1904–1979). British stage and screen actress, adept at sympathetic spinsters and eccentric types.
The Lady Vanishes (debut) 38. Cottage to Let 41. I Know Where I'm Going 45. *The October Man* 47. Whisky Galore 49. Rockets Galore 56. Crack in the Mirror 60. The Fighting Prince of Donegal (as Queen Elizabeth I) 66. The Sorcerers 67, etc.

Lacey, Ronald (1935–). Solidly-built British character actor.
The Likely Lads 76. Charleston (TV) 77. Zulu Dawn 79. Raiders of the Lost Ark 80. Firefox 82. Invitation to the Wedding 84. Sword of the Valiant 85. Red Sonja 85, etc.

Lachman, Harry (1886–1975). Anglo-American director, at his best in the thirties.
Weekend Wives 28. Under the Greenwood Tree 29. The Yellow Mask 30. The Outsider 30. The Compulsory Husband 30. Aren't We All 32. Insult 32. Paddy the Next Best Thing 33. Baby Take a Bow 34. *Dante's Inferno* 35. Charlie Chan at the Circus 36. *Our Relations* 36. The Devil is Driving 37. No Time to Marry 38. They Came by Night 40. Dead Men Talk 41. The Loves of Edgar Allan Poe 42, etc.

Lackteen, Frank (1894–1968). American character actor of Russian origin; his sharp features were adaptable to many ethnic roles.
Less Than the Dust 16. The Avenging Arrow 21. The Virgin 24. Hawk of the Hills 27. Hell's Valley 31. Escape from Devil's Island 35. Anthony Adverse 36. Suez 38. Juarez 39. Moon over Burma 40. The Sea Wolf 41. Chetniks 43. Can't Help Singing 44. Frontier Gal 45. Maneater of Kumaon 48. Daughter of the Jungle 49. King of the Khyber Rifles 53. Bengal Brigade 54. Devil Goddess 55. Requiem for a Gunfighter 65, many others.

Ladd, Alan (1913–1964). Unsmiling, pint-sized tough-guy American star who proved to be just the kind of hero the forties wanted.
Biography 1979: *Ladd* by Beverly Linet.
□Once in a Lifetime 32. Pigskin Parade 36. Last Train from Madrid 37. Souls at Sea 37. Born to the West 37. Hold 'em Navy 37. The Goldwyn Follies 38. Come on Leathernecks 38. The Green Hornet 39. Rulers of the Sea 39. Beast of Berlin 39. Light of Western Stars 40. Gangs of Chicago 40. Her First Romance (reissued as The Right Man) 40. In Old Missouri 40. The Howards of Virginia 40. Those were the Days 40. Captain Caution 40. Wildcat Bus 40. Meet the Missus 40. Great Guns 41. Citizen Kane 41. Cadet Girl 41. Petticoat Politics 41. The Black Cat 41. The Reluctant Dragon 41. Paper Bullets 41. Joan of Paris 42. *This Gun for Hire* 42. *The Glass Key* 42. Lucky Jordan 42. Star Spangled Rhythm 42. China 43. And Now Tomorrow 44. Salty O'Rourke 45. Duffy's Tavern 45. *The Blue Dahlia* 46. O.S.S. 46. Two Years Before the Mast 46. Calcutta 47. Variety Girl 47. Wild Harvest 47. Saigon 48. Beyond Glory 48. Whispering Smith 48. *The Great Gatsby* 49. Chicago Deadline 49. Captain Carey USA 50. Branded 51. Appointment with Danger 51. Red Mountain 52. The Iron Mistress 53. Thunder in the East 53. Desert Legion 53. *Shane* 53. Botany Bay 53. The Red Beret (GB) 53. Saskatchewan 54. Hell Below Zero (GB) 54. The Black Knight (GB) 54. Drum Beat 54. The McConnell Story 55. Hell on Frisco Bay 55. Santiago 56. The Big Land 57. Boy on a Dolphin 57. The Deep Six 58. The Proud Rebel 58. The Badlanders 58. The Man in the Net 58. Guns of the Timberland 60. All the Young Men 60. One Foot in Hell 60. Duel of the Champions (It.) 61. 13 West Street 62. *The Carpetbaggers* 64.
Cameo appearance: My Favourite Brunette 47.

¶ A small boy's idea of a tough guy.—*Raymond Chandler*

That man had stature even if he was short.—*Stewart Granger*

He succeeded in reducing murder to an act as casual as crossing the street.—*Richard Schickel*

Nobody ever pretended he could act. He got to the top, therefore, by a combination of determination and luck.—*David Shipman*

A.L.: I have the face of an ageing choirboy and the build of an undernourished featherweight. If you can figure out my success on the screen you're a better man than I.

† Ladd is said to have turned down both the James Dean role in *Giant* and the Spencer Tracy role in *Bad Day at Black Rock.*

Ladd, Cheryl (1951–) (Cheryl Stoppelmoor). American leading lady who became familiar on TV from 1978 as one of *Charlie's Angels.*

Satan's School for Girls 73. Evil in the Deep 76. Now and Forever 82. Grace Kelly (TV) 83. Purple Hearts 84.

Ladd, Diane (1932–) (Diane Ladnier). American character actress.
White Lightning 73. Chinatown 74. *Alice Doesn't Live Here Any More* 75. Thaddeus Rose and Eddie (TV) 78. Willa 79.
Cattle Annie and Little Britches 80. Guyana Tragedy (TV) 80. All Night Long 81. Grace Kelly (TV) 83. Something Wicked This Way Comes 83.

The Lady Eve (US 1941). Written and directed by Preston Sturges, this amusing trifle about a bashful millionaire landed by the daughter of a confidence trickster was a sparkling example of the Sturges penchant for mixing sophisticated romance with pratfall farce. Henry Fonda, Barbara Stanwyck and Charles Coburn were the leads. In 1956 the plot was warmed over as a vehicle for George Gobel, with the assistance of Mitzi Gaynor and David Niven; but *The Birds and the Bees* was merely flat-footed.

Lady for a Day (US 1933). Robert Riskin wrote, and Frank Capra directed, this Runyonesque fantasy about an old flowerseller who is helped by gangster friends to deceive her visiting daughter into thinking she is comfortably placed. Deftly handled, with a vigorous performance from May Robson, it was agreeable Hollywood moonshine. In 1961 Capra remade it as *Pocketful of Miracles*, but it was now dated, and not even Bette Davis and a host of good character actors could save it from tedium, especially as its length was nearly doubled and Capra's direction seemed tired.

The Lady from Shanghai (US 1948). The Orson Welles film which first showed his fatal fault as a solo director: inattention to detail. Even in this Hollywood-produced thriller the lighting is as murky as the plot and most of the dialogue is inaudible, with a dull performance from Welles himself. There are, however, some brilliantly-handled sequences, and the final shoot-up in a hall of mirrors has not been surpassed.

Lady Hamilton: see *That Hamilton Woman*.

Lady in the Dark (US 1944). Moss Hart's now-dated stage play, with songs by Kurt Weill, was about a career girl who was psychologically going to pieces, because she was torn between her work and three different men. The film version by Mitchell Leisen was good to look at but artificial, with dry-ice dream sequences largely replacing the songs. It did however mark the beginning of Hollywood's interest in psychiatry, and its colour photography was coolly superior to any we had seen before.

The Lady in the Lake (US 1946). The suspense and wit of Raymond Chandler's mystery novel were dissipated in this version by the experiment with subjective camera: the entire action was seen as through the hero's eyes, and he did not appear except in mirrors. Robert Montgomery played the role and also directed; but the film was not liked.

Lady Killer (US 1933). Directed by Roy del Ruth, this Warner programmer marks an attempt to spoof gangster movies three years before *A Slight Case of Murder* and a year before the turnaround which put James Cagney on the side of the *G-Men*. Here he plays a cinema usher who turns con-man and gangster, then escapes his pursuers by becoming a Hollywood star. The pace is fast and furious, and the casting of Mae Clarke seems to indicate a direct aping of the *Public Enemy* image.

The Lady Vanishes (GB 1938). Despite model sets and obvious back projection this remains the most likeable and probably the most entertaining of Hitchcock's films, a suspenseful comedy-thriller about a disappearing lady on a train. Scripted by Sidney Gilliat from a novel by Ethel Lina White, it featured Michael Redgrave, Margaret Lockwood, Dame May Whitty, Paul Lukas, Linden Travers, Mary Clare and Cecil Parker, and was notable as the film which introduced Basil Radford and Naunton Wayne as Charters and Caldicott, the Englishmen abroad *par excellence*. The 1979 remake is not even a fair copy.

The Lady with a Little Dog (Russia 1959). This highly pictorial love story, set at Yalta in the nineties, came as a mild revelation to western audiences conditioned for years to Russian films stuffed with propaganda. Full of Chekhovian charm, it was directed by Josif Heifits and photographed by Andrej Moskvine.

The Ladykillers (GB 1955). An odd little black farce in which a fang-toothed Alec Guinness and his sinister gang move in on a little old lady who neatly parries their sinister designs and innocently brings about their doom. With Katie Johnson and many familiar British faces; directed by Alexander Mackendrick from a script by William Rose. Memorable but somehow dislikeable.

Laemmle, Carl (1867–1939). German-American pioneer, in films from 1906; produced *Hiawatha* 09, founded Universal Pictures 1912. A biography by John Drinkwater was published in 1931: *The Life and Adventures of Carl Laemmle.*

¶ Uncle Carl Laemmle
Had a very large faemmle.—*Ogden Nash, satirizing the number of Laemmle relations who were found jobs at Universal Studios*

I hope I didn't make a mistake coming out here.—*C.L., Hollywood, 1915*

The prototype of the slightly mad movie mogul—impulsive, quixotic, intrepid, unorthodox, unpredictable.—*Norman Zierold*

Laemmle, Carl, Jnr (1908–1979). Son of Carl Laemmle; executive producer at Universal for many years. Credited with the success of *Frankenstein, Dracula,* and *All Quiet on the Western Front.*

Laffan, Patricia (1919–). British stage actress.
The Rake's Progress 45. Caravan 46. Quo Vadis (as Poppea) 51. Devil Girl From Mars 54. Twenty-Three Paces to Baker Street 56, etc.

Lahr, Bert (1895–1967) (Irving Lahrheim). Wry-faced American vaudeville comedian who made occasional film appearances.
Biography 1969: *Notes on a Cowardly Lion* by John Lahr (his son).
Faint Heart 31. Flying High 31. Love and Hisses 37. Josette 38. Just Around the Corner 38. Zaza 39. *The Wizard of Oz* 39. Ship Ahoy 42. Meet the People 44. Always Leave Them Laughing 49. Mr Universe 51. Rose Marie 54. The Second Greatest Sex 56. The Night They Raided Minsky's 68, etc.

¶ *B.L.:* After *The Wizard of Oz* I was typecast as a lion, and there aren't all that many parts for lions.

The last and the most marvellous of the American clowns cradled by burlesque. —*Alastair Cooke*

Lahti, Christine (1950–). American character actress.
And Justice For All 79. Whose Life is it Anyway? 81. Ladies and Gentlemen, The Fabulous Stains 81. Swing Shift (AAN) 84. Just Between Friends 85. Season of Dreams 87. Housekeeping 87.

Lai, Francis (1932–). French film composer.
Un Homme et Une Femme (AA) 66. Mayerling 68. House of Cards 68. Rider on the Rain 70. *Love Story* (AA) 71. Le Petit Matin 71. Emmannuelle 75. Seven Suspects for Murder 77. International Velvet 78. Oliver's Story 78. Second Chance 80, etc.

Laine, Frankie (1913–) (Frank Paul Lo Vecchio). American pop singer who made several light musicals in the fifties.
When You're Smiling 50. Make Believe Ballroom 50. The Sunny Side of the Street 51. Rainbow Round My Shoulder 52. Bring Your Smile Along 55. He Laughed Last 56. Viva Las Vegas 56, etc.

Laird, Jenny (1917–). British character actress.
Just William 39. The Lamp Still Burns 43. Black Narcissus 46. *Painted Boats* 47. The Long Dark Hall 51. Conspiracy of Hearts 60, etc.

Lake, Arthur (1905–86) (Arthur Silverlake). Harassed, crumple-faced American light comedy actor, best remembered as Dagwood Bumstead in the Blondie series of 28 films in twelve years.
Jack and the Beanstalk 17. Skinner's Dress Suit 26. The Irresistible Lover 27. *Harold Teen* 28. On with the Show 29. Indiscreet 31. Midshipman Jack 33. Orchids to You 35. Topper 37. *Blondie* (and subsequent series) 38. Three is a Family 44. Sixteen Fathoms Deep 48, many others.
TV series: Blondie 54.

Lake, Florence (1904–1980). American character comedienne best remembered as Edgar Kennedy's bird-brained wife in many of his two-reelers.

Lake, Veronica (1919–1973) (Constance Ockleman). Petite American leading lady who now, with her limited acting ability and her 'peek a boo bang' (long blonde hair obscuring one eye), seems an appropriately artificial image for the Hollywood of the early forties.
Autobiography 1968: *Veronica.*

☐All Women Have Secrets 39. Sorority House 39. Forty Little Mothers 40. *I Wanted Wings* 41. *Sullivan's Travels* 41. *This Gun for Hire* 42. The Glass Key 42. *I Married a Witch* 42. Star Spangled Rhythm 42. So Proudly We Hail 43. The Hour Before the Dawn 44. Bring on the Girls 45. Out of this World 45. Duffy's Tavern 45. Hold that Blonde 45. Miss Susie Slagle's 45. *The Blue Dahlia* 46. Ramrod 47. Variety Girl 47. The Sainted Sisters 48. Saigon 48. Isn't It Romantic? 48. Slattery's Hurricane 49. Stronghold 52. Footsteps in the Snow 66. Flesh Feast 70.

¶ *V.L.:* You could put all the talent I had into your left eye and still not suffer from impaired vision.

Lamarr, Hedy (1913–) (Hedwig Kiesler). Austrian leading lady of the thirties and forties, in Hollywood from 1937 after creating a sensation by appearing nude in the Czech film *Extase* 33. She became a household word for glamour, but lacked the spark of personality.
Autobiography 1966: *Ecstasy and Me.*
☐AMERICAN FILMS: *Algiers* 38. Lady of the Tropics 39. I Take this Woman 40. Boom Town 40. Comrade X 40. Come Live with Me 41. Ziegfeld Girl 41. H.M. Pulham Esq 41. Tortilla Flat 42. Crossroads 42. *White Cargo* (as Tondelayo) 42. The Heavenly Body 43. The Conspirators 44. Experiment Perilous 44. Her Highness and the Bellboy 45. The Strange Woman 46. Dishonoured Lady 47. Let's Live a Little 48. *Samson and Delilah* 49. A Lady without Passport 50. Copper Canyon 50. My Favorite Spy 51. The Face That Launched a Thousand Ships 54. The Story of Mankind 57. The Female Animal 57.

¶ *H.L.:* Any girl can be glamorous: all you have to do is stand still and look stupid.

Lamas, Fernando (1915–1982). Argentinian leading man, in Hollywood from 1950 in routine musicals and comedies.
Rich, Young and Pretty 51. The Law and the Lady 51. The Merry Widow 52. The Girl Who Had Everything 53. Sangaree 53. Rose Marie 54. The Girl Rush 55. The Lost World 60. The Violent Ones (& d) 67. 100 Rifles 69. Powder Keg 71. The Cheap Detective 78, etc.

Lamb, Gil (1906–). Rubber-boned American comic, seen in many forties musicals.
The Fleet's In (debut) 42. Rainbow Island 44. Practically Yours 44. Humphrey Takes a Chance 50. Terror in a Texas Town 58. Blackbeard's Ghost 67, others.

Lambert, Christopher (1958–). Franco-American leading man.
Subway 83. Greystoke 84. Highlander 85.

Lambert, Constant (1905–1951). British conductor whose one film score was *Anna Karenina* 47.

Lambert, Gavin (1924–). British critic and novelist, in Hollywood since 1956. Stories about Hollywood: *The Slide Area.*
AS SCRIPTWRITER: Bitter Victory 57. The Roman Spring of Mrs Stone 61. Inside Daisy Clover 65. I Never Promised You a Rose Garden 77, etc.

Lambert, Jack (1899–1976). Scottish character actor.
The Ghost Goes West 36. Nine Men 43. Hue and Cry 46. Eureka Stockade 47. The Brothers 47. The Lost Hours 50. The Sea Shall Not Have Them 54. Storm over the Nile 56. Reach for the Sky 56. Greyfriars Bobby 60. Modesty Blaise 66, many others.

Lambert, Jack (1920–). American character actor, usually an evil-eyed heavy. The Cross of Lorraine 43. The Killers 46. The Unsuspected 47. The Enforcer 51. Scared Stiff 53. Kiss Me Deadly 55. Machine Gun Kelly 57. The George Raft Story 61. Four for Texas 63, many others.

Lamble, Lloyd (1914–). Australian light actor who has been in many British films as detective, official, or other man.
The Story of Gilbert and Sullivan 53. The Belles of St Trinian's 54. The Man Who Never Was 56. Quatermass II 57. Blue Murder at St Trinian's 58. No Trees in the Street 59. The Trials of Oscar Wilde 60, etc.

Lamont, Charles (1898–). American director, in Hollywood from silent days. With Universal from mid-thirties, making comedies featuring Abbott and Costello, the Kettles, etc.
Love, Honour and Oh Baby 41. The Merry Monahans 44. Bowery to Broadway 44. Frontier Gal 45. The Runaround 46. Slave Girl 47. Baghdad 49. Flame of Araby 51.

Abbott and Costello Meet Dr Jekyll and Mr Hyde 53. Ma and Pa Kettle in Paris 53. Untamed Heiress 54. Abbott and Costello Meet the Mummy 55. Francis in the Haunted House 56. The Kettles in the Ozarks 56, many others.

Lamont, Duncan (1918–). Scottish actor with stage experience, in films since World War II.
The Golden Coach 53. *The Adventures of Quentin Durward* 56. Ben Hur 59. Mutiny on the Bounty 62. Murder at the Gallop 63. The Brigand of Kandahar 65. Arabesque 65. Decline and Fall 68. Pope Joan 72. Escape from the Dark 76, many others.

Lamorisse, Albert (1922–1970). French director known for short fantasy films.
Bim 49. *Crin Blanc* 52. *The Red Balloon* 55. Stowaway in the Sky 61. Fifi La Plume 64, etc.

Lamour, Dorothy (1914–) (Dorothy Kaumeyer). Good-humoured American leading lady of the thirties and forties: became typed in sarong roles, and happily guyed her own image.
□ *The Jungle Princess* 36. Thrill of a Lifetime 37. Swing High Swing Low 37. Last Train from Madrid 37. High Wide and Handsome 37. *The Hurricane* 37. The Big Broadcast of 1938. Her Jungle Love 38. Spawn of the North 38. Tropic Holiday 38. St Louis Blues 39. Man About Town 39. Disputed Passage 39. Johnny Apollo 40. Typhoon 40. *Road to Singapore* 40. Moon Over Burma 40. Chad Hanna 40. Road to Zanzibar 41. Caught in the Draft 41. Aloma of the South Seas 41. The Fleet's In 42. Beyond the Blue Horizon 42. Road to Morocco 42. Star Spangled Rhythm 42. They Got Me Covered 43. Dixie 43. Riding High 43. And the Angels Sing 43. Rainbow Island 44. Road to Utopia 45. A Medal for Benny 45. Duffy's Tavern 45. Masquerade in Mexico 45. My Favorite Brunette 47. Road to Rio 47. Wild Harvest 47. Variety Girl 47. On Our Merry Way 48. Lulu Belle 48. The Girl from Manhattan 48. Slightly French 48. Manhandled 48. The Lucky Stiff 49. Here Comes the Groom 51. The Greatest Show on Earth 52. Road to Bali 52. Road to Hong Kong 62. Donovan's Reef 63. Pajama Party 64. The Phynx 70. Won Ton Ton 75. Death of Love House (TV) 76. Creepshow 2 87.

L'Amour, Louis (1908–). American writer of western novels, including *Hondo* and *How the West Was Won.*

Lampedusa, Giuseppe (1896–1957). Italian novelist, a nobleman whose *The Leopard* was filmed and gave a picture of 19th-century Sicily.

Lampert, Zohra (1936–). American TV actress.
Splendour in the Grass 60. Pay or Die 60. A Fine Madness 66. Opening Night 77. Alphabet City 84. Teachers 84.

Lancaster, Burt (1913–). Athletic American leading man and latterly distinguished actor. Former circus acrobat; acted and danced in soldier shows during World War II.
□*The Killers* 46. Desert Fury 47. I Walk Alone 47. *Brute Force* 47. Variety Girl (cameo) 47. Sorry, Wrong Number 48. Kiss the Blood Off My Hands 48. All My Sons 48. Criss Cross 49. Rope of Sand 49. Mister 880 50. *The Flame and the Arrow* 50. Vengeance Valley 51. Ten Tall Men 51. Jim Thorpe All-American 51. The Crimson Pirate 52. *Come Back Little Sheba* 53. South Sea Woman 53. From Here to Eternity 53. His Majesty O'Keefe 54. Apache 54. *Vera Cruz* 54. The Kentuckian (& d) 55. The Rose Tattoo 55. Trapeze 56. The Rainmaker 57. *Gunfight at the OK Corral* (as Wyatt Earp) 57. Sweet Smell of Success 57. Separate Tables 58. Run Silent Run Deep 58. The Devil's Disciple (GB) 59. The Unforgiven 59. *Elmer Gantry* (AA) 60. The Young Savages 61. Judgment at Nuremberg 61. *Birdman of Alcatraz* 62. A Child is Waiting 62. The Leopard 63. The List of Adrian Messenger 63. Seven Days in May 64. The Train 64. The Hallelujah Trail 65. *The Professionals* 66. *The Swimmer* 67. The Scalphunters 68. Castle Keep 69. The Gypsy Moths 69. Airport 69. Lawman 70. Valdez is Coming 71. Ulzana's Raid 72. Scorpio 73. Executive Action 73. The Midnight Man (& co-p, co-d) 74. Conversation Piece 75. Moses (TV) 75. Buffalo Bill and the Indians 76. *1900* 76. Twilight's Last Gleaming 76. Victory at Entebbe (TV) 76. The Cassandra Crossing 77. The Island of Dr Moreau 77. Go Tell the Spartans 78. Zulu Dawn 79. Atlantic City USA (BFA) 80. Cattle Annie and Little Britches 80. Marco Polo (TV) 81. Local Hero 83. The Osterman Weekend 83. Scandal Sheet (TV) 83. Little Treasure 85. On Wings of Eagles (TV) 85. Tough Guys 86.

❀ For enthusiasm, shrewdness and agility. *The Flame and the Arrow.*

¶ *B.L.:* Life is to be lived within the limits of your knowledge and within the concept of what you would like to see yourself to be.

B.L.: If I'm working with frightened people, I do tend to dominate them. I'm no doll, that's for sure.

Before he can pick up an ashtray he discusses his motivation for a couple of hours. You want to tell him to pick up the ashtray and shut up.—*Jeanne Moreau*

B.L.: Most people seem to think I'm the kind of guy who shaves with a blowtorch. Actually I'm bookish and worrisome.

Lanchester, Elsa (1902–86) (Elizabeth Sullivan). British character actress married to Charles Laughton. On stage and screen in Britain before settling in Hollywood 1940. Autobiography 1938: *Charles Laughton and I.*
Bluebottles 28. *The Private Life of Henry VIII* 32. David Copperfield 35. *The Bride of Frankenstein* 35. The Ghost Goes West 36. *Rembrandt* 37. Vessel of Wrath 38. Ladies in Retirement 41. Tales of Manhattan 42. The Spiral Staircase 45. End of the Rainbow 47. The Inspector-General 49. Androcles and the Lion 53. Bell, Book and Candle 57. *Witness for the Prosecution* 57. Mary Poppins 64. Blackbeard's Ghost 67. Me, Natalie 69. Willard 71. Terror in the Wax Museum 73. *Murder by Death* 76, many others.
TV series: The John Forsythe Show 65.

Landau, David (1878–1935). American character actor, familiar in early talkies as crook or roughneck.
I Take This Woman 31. Street Scene 31. Taxi 32. Polly of the Circus 32. Horse Feathers 32. I Am a Fugitive from a Chain Gang 32. She Done Him Wrong 33. One Man's Journey 33. Wharf Angel 34. Judge Priest 34, etc.

Landau, Ely (1920–). American producer, former distributor.
Long Day's Journey Into Night 62. The Pawnbroker 64, etc; plus all productions of the American Film Theatre 1972–74.

Landau, Martin (1933–). Gaunt American actor often in sinister roles.
North by Northwest 59. The Gazebo 59. Cleopatra 62. The Hallelujah Trail 65. Nevada Smith 66. They Call Me Mr Tibbs 70. Savage (TV) 72. Black Gunn 72. Blazing Magnum 76. Meteor 79. Without Warning 80. Alone in the Dark 82. Sweet Revenge 87, etc.
TV series: Mission Impossible 66–68, Space 1999 75–76.

Landen, Dinsdale (1931–). British stage actor who makes occasional films.
Operation Snatch 62. Rasputin the Mad Monk 66. Every Home Should Have One 70. Digby 71. International Velvet 78, etc.

Landers, Lew (1901–1962) (Lewis Friedlander). American director of 'B' pictures, especially westerns, from silent days.
The Raven 35. The Man Who Found Himself 37. Canal Zone 39. Pacific Liner 39. The Boogie Man Will Get You 42. Return of the Vampire 43. The Enchanted Forest 46. State Penitentiary 49. Man in the Dark (in 3-D) 53. Captain Kidd and the Slave Girl 53. Hot Rod Gang 58. Terrified 62, many others.

Landi, Elissa (1904–1948) (Elizabeth Kuhnelt). Austrian-Italian leading lady, in international films of the thirties.
Underground 29. Children of Chance 30. Always Goodbye 31. The Yellow Ticket 31. Passport to Hell 32. *The Sign of the Cross* 32. The Masquerader 33. The Warrior's Husband 33. By Candlelight 34. Sisters under the Skin 34. *The Count of Monte Cristo* 34. Without Regret 35. Enter Madame 35. The Amateur Gentleman 36. After the Thin Man 36. The Thirteenth Chair 37. Corregidor 43, etc.

Landi, Marla (c. 1937–). Italian leading lady and model, in British films.
Across the Bridge 57. First Man into Space 58. The Hound of the Baskervilles 59. Pirates of Blood River 61. The Murder Game 65, etc.

Landis, Carole (1919–1948) (Frances Ridste). American leading lady, in films from 1937 (as extra).
Man and His Mate (One Million B.C.) 40. *Turnabout* 40. Road Show 41. Topper Returns 41. Hot Spot 41. Orchestra Wives 42. Wintertime 43. Having Wonderful Crime 44. Behind Green Lights 45. It Shouldn't Happen to a Dog 46. A Scandal in Paris 46. Out of the Blue 47. The Brass Monkey (GB) 48. Noose (GB) 48, etc.

Landis, Cullen (1896–1975). American silent screen hero.
Who Is Number One 17. Beware of Blondes

18. Almost a Husband 19. Born Rich 24, many others.

Landis, Jessie Royce (1904–1972) (Jessie Royce Medbury). American character actress of long stage experience; usually in fluttery comedy roles.
Autobiography 1954: *You Won't Be So Pretty*.
□Derelict 30. Mr Belvedere Goes to College 49. It Happens Every Spring 49. My Foolish Heart 49. Mother Didn't Tell Me 50. Meet Me Tonight (GB) 51. *To Catch a Thief* 55. The Swan 56. The Girl He Left Behind 56. My Man Godfrey 57. I Married a Woman 58. *North by Northwest* 59. A Private's Affair 59. Goodbye Again 61. Bon Voyage 62. Boys' Night Out 62. Critic's Choice 63. Gidget Goes To Rome 63. Airport 69. Mr and Mrs Bo Jo Jones (TV) 71.
Famous line (*North by Northwest*): You gentlemen are not really trying to murder my son, are you?

Landis, John (1950–). American director.
□Schlock 76. Kentucky Fried Movie 77. National Lampoon's Animal House 78. The Blues Brothers 80. *An American Werewolf in London* 81. Twilight Zone 83. Trading Places 83. The Muppets Take Manhattan (cameo) 84. Into the Night 85. Spies Like Us 85. Three Amigos 86.

¶ *J.L.:* When *Animal House* turned out the way it did, they all rushed to me with barrels of money begging me to make them rich.

Landon, Michael (1937–) (Eugene Orowitz). American leading man best known as Little Jo in TV series *Bonanza*.
I Was a Teenage Werewolf 57. God's Little Acre 58. The Legend of Tom Dooley 59. Sam's Son (TV) 85.
TV series: Little House on the Prairie 74–82. Highway to Heaven 84–
† A TV movie about Landon's young manhood, *Sam's Son*, was released in 1986.

Landone, Avice (1910–1976). British stage actress, usually in cool, unruffled roles.
My Brother Jonathan 48. The Franchise Affair 51. An Alligator Named Daisy 55. Reach for the Sky 56. Carve Her Name with Pride 58. Operation Cupid 60, etc.

Landres, Paul (1912–). American director, former editor.
Oregon Passage 57. The Miracle of the Hills 58. The Flame Barrier 58. The Vampire 59. The Return of Dracula 58. Son of a Gunfighter 65, etc.

Lane, Allan 'Rocky' (1901–1973) (Harry Albershart). American cowboy star of the thirties, former athlete.
Night Nurse 32. Maid's Night Out 38. The Dancing Masters 44. Trail of Robin Hood 51. The Saga of Hemp Brown 58. Hell Bent for Leather 60, scores of second features.
TV series: Mister Ed (voice) 62–64.

Lane, Burton (1912–) (Burton Levy). American song composer, best known for *Finian's Rainbow* and *On a Clear Day You Can See Forever*.

Lane, Charles (1899–). American character actor seen since early thirties as comedy snoop, salesman or tax inspector; at the age of 80, he was vigorously playing a judge in *Soap*.
Mr Deeds Goes to Town 36. In Old Chicago 38. You Can't Take It With You 38. The Cat and the Canary 39. Hot Spot 41. Arsenic and Old Lace 44. Intrigue 49. The Juggler 53. Teacher's Pet 58. The Gnome-Mobile 67. What's So Bad About Feeling Good? 68. The Little Dragons 80, many others.
TV series: Petticoat Junction 64–69. Karen 75. Soap 80.

Lane, Lupino (1892–1959) (Henry George Lupino). Diminutive, dapper British stage comedian and master of the pratfall, member of a family who had been clowns for generations. His American two-reelers of the twenties were little masterpieces of timing and hair-raising stunts, but he failed to develop a personality for sound.
Biography 1957: *Born to Star* by James Dillon White.
The Reporter 22. Isn't Life Wonderful? 24. The Love Parade 29. Bride of the Regiment 30. The Golden Mask 30. The Deputy Drummer (GB) 35. Me and My Girl (GB) 39, etc.

Lane, Richard (1900–). American supporting player, formerly and latterly sports announcer; frequently seen in the forties as reporter, tough cop, or exasperated executive.
The Outcasts of Poker Flat 37. Union Pacific 39. Hellzapoppin 41. Meet Boston Blackie 41.

What a Blonde 45. Gentleman Joe Palooka 46. Take Me Out to the Ball Game 48. I Can Get It For You Wholesale 51, etc.

The Lane Sisters. American leading ladies, real name Mulligan. Three of the five sisters (all actresses) had sizeable roles in Hollywood films: *Lola* (1909–1981), *Rosemary* (1913–1974) and *Priscilla* (1917–).
TOGETHER: Four Daughters 38. Daughters Courageous 39. Four Wives 39. Four Mothers 40.
OTHER APPEARANCES FOR LOLA: Speakeasy 29. Death from a Distance 35. Marked Woman 37. Zanzibar 40. Why Girls Leave Home 36.
ROSEMARY: Hollywood Hotel 38. The Oklahoma Kid 38. The Return of Dr X 40. Time Out for Rhythm 42. The Fortune Hunter 45.
PRISCILLA: Brother Rat 39. Dust be My Destiny 39. Yes My Darling Daughter 39. The Roaring Twenties 40. Blues in the Night 41. Saboteur 42. Arsenic and Old Lace 44. Fun on a Weekend 46. Bodyguard 48, etc.

Lanfield, Sidney (1900–1972). American director from 1932; former jazz musician.
Hat Check Girl 32. Moulin Rouge 34. Sing Baby Sing 36. *The Hound of the Baskervilles* 39. Swanee River 39. You'll Never Get Rich 41. The Lady Has Plans 41. *My Favorite Blonde* 42. The Meanest Man in the World 42. Let's Face It 43. Standing Room Only 44. Bring on the Girls 45. The Well-Groomed Bride 45. Stations West 47. The Lemon Drop Kid 50. Follow the Sun 51. Skirts Ahoy 52, etc.

Lang, Charles (1902–). Distinguished American cinematographer.
Shopworn Angel 29. *A Farewell to Arms* (AA) 33. Death Takes a Holiday 34. Lives of a Bengal Lancer 35. *Desire* 36. *The Cat and the Canary* 39. Nothing But the Truth 41. Practically Yours 44. The Uninvited 44. The Ghost and Mrs Muir 47. A Foreign Affair 47. *Ace in the Hole* 51. Sudden Fear 52. The Big Heat 53. The Female on the Beach 55. The Man from Laramie 55. Autumn Leaves 56. The Solid Gold Cadillac 56. Gunfight at the OK Corral 57. Some Like It Hot 59. One-Eyed Jacks 59. The Facts of Life 60. The Magnificent Seven 60. Blue Hawaii 61. A Girl Named Tamiko 62. *Charade* 63. Inside Daisy Clover 65. How to Steal a Million 66. Not With My Wife You Don't 66. Hotel 67. The Flim Flam Man 67. Wait Until Dark 67. A Flea in Her Ear 68. Cactus Flower 69. Bob and Carol and Ted and Alice 70. The Love Machine 71, many others.

Lang, Charles (1915–). American writer.
The Magnificent Matador 56. Desire in the Dust 62, etc.

Lang, Fritz (1890–1976). German director of distinguished silent films. Went to Hollywood 1934 and tended thereafter to make commercial though rather heavy-handed thrillers.
Biography 1974: *Fritz Lang* by Lotte Eisner.
□Helbblut 19. Der Herr der Liebe 19. Die Spinnen 19. Hara Kiri 19. Das Wandernde Bild 21. *Destiny* 21. Das Brillanten Schiff 21. Vier um die Frau 20. Der Mude Tod 21. *Dr Mabuse der Spieler* 22. Inferno 22. *Siegfried* 23. Krimhild's Revenge 24. *Metropolis* 26. *The Spy* 27. Frau im Mond 28. *M* 31. The Testament of Dr Mabuse 32. Liliom 33. *Fury* 36. *You Only Live Once* 37. You and Me 38. The Return of Frank James 40. Western Union 41. Man Hunt 41. Confirm or Deny (part) 42. Hangmen Also Die 43. *The Woman in the Window* 44. Ministry of Fear 44. Scarlet Street 45. Cloak and Dagger 46. The Secret Beyond the Door 48. House by the River 49. An American Guerrilla in the Philippines 51. Rancho Notorious 52. Clash by Night 52. The Blue Gardenia 52. *The Big Heat* 53. Human Desire 54. Moonfleet 55. While the City Sleeps 55. Beyond a Reasonable Doubt 56. Der Tiger von Ischnapur (Ger.) 58. Das Indische Grabmal (Ger.) 58. The Thousand Eyes of Dr Mabuse (Ger.) 60. Contempt (a only) 63.

'His cinema is that of the nightmare, the fable, and the philosophical dissertation.'—*Andrew Sarris, 1968*

❀ For spinning out his well-deserved German reputation through an American career of dwindling talent. *Fury*.

Lang, Harold (1923–1970). British actor and drama teacher.
Flood Tide 49. Cairo Road 50. Laughing Anne 53. The Quatermass Experiment 55. Carve Her Name with Pride 58. The Nanny 63, etc.

Lang, June (1915–) (June Vlasek). American leading lady, former dancer.
Chandu the Magician 32. Bonnie Scotland 35.

Ali Baba Goes to Town 38. Redhead 41. Flesh and Fantasy 44. Lighthouse 48, etc.

Lang, Jennings (1915–). American executive, long near the top of MCA TV and latterly executive producer of many Universal films.

Lang, Matheson (1879–1948). Scottish-Canadian stage actor, a London matinée idol of the twenties who made occasional films. Autobiography 1940: *Mr Wu Looks Back*.
Mr Wu 21. Carnival 21 & 31. Dick Turpin's Ride to York 22. The Wandering Jew 23. The Chinese Bungalow 25 & 30. Beyond the Veil 25. Island of Despair 26. The Triumph of the Scarlet Pimpernel 29. Channel Crossing 32. Little Friend 34. Drake of England 35. The Cardinal 36, etc.

Lang, Robert (1934–). British character actor, mainly on stage.
Othello 65. Dance of Death 69. The Mackintosh Man 73. Night Watch 73. Savage Messiah 73. Shout at the Devil 76. The First Great Train Robbery 79, etc.

Lang, Walter (1896–1972). American director of competent but seldom outstanding entertainments.
The Satin Woman 27. The College Hero 27. Brothers 30. Hell Bound 30. Women Go On for Ever 31. No More Orchids 32. The Warrior's Husband 33. Meet the Baron 33. Whom the Gods Destroy 34. The Mighty Barnum 34. Carnival 35. Hooray for Love 35. Love Before Breakfast 36. *Wife, Doctor and Nurse* 37. Second Honeymoon 37. The Baroness and the Butler 38. I'll Give a Million 38. The Little Princess 39. *The Bluebird* 40. Star Dust 40. The Great Profile 40. *Tin Pan Alley* 40. Moon over Miami 41. Weekend in Havana 41. Song of the Islands 42. The Magnificent Dope 42. Coney Island 43. Greenwich Village 44. *State Fair* 45. Sentimental Journey 46. Claudia and David 46. Mother Wore Tights 47. *Sitting Pretty* 48. When My Baby Smiles at Me 48. You're My Everything 49. Cheaper by the Dozen 50. The Jackpot 50. On the Riviera 51. *With a Song in My Heart* 51. *Call Me Madam* 53. There's No Business like Show Business 54. *The King and I* 56. The Desk Set 57. But Not for Me 59. Can Can 60. The Marriage Go Round 61. Snow White and the Three Stooges 61, others.

Langan, Glenn (1917–). American light leading man, in films from the early forties after stage experience.
Four Jills in a Jeep 44. *Margie* 46. Forever Amber 47. The Snake Pit 48. Treasure of Monte Cristo 49. Rapture (Swedish) 50. Hangman's Knot 52. 99 River Street 54. The Amazing Colossal Man 57, etc.

Langdon, Harry (1884–1944). Baby-faced, melancholy American clown who was a great hit in the twenties but could not reconcile his unusual image with sound.
Picking Peaches 23. *Tramp Tramp Tramp* 26. *The Strong Man* 26. *Long Pants* 26. His First Flame 27. Three's a Crowd 27. The Chaser (& d) 28. See America Thirst 30. A Soldier's Plaything 31. Hallelujah I'm a Bum 33. My Weakness 33. There Goes My Heart 38. *Zenobia* 39. Misbehaving Husbands 40. House of Errors 42. Spotlight Scandals 44, etc.

¶ *Mack Sennett:* He was a quaint artist who had no business in business.

Langdon, Sue Ane (1940–). American leading lady and comedienne.
The Outsider 61. The Rounders 65. A Fine Madness 66. A Guide for the Married Man 67. The Cheyenne Social Club 70. Without Warning 80, etc.
TV series: *Arnie* 70–71.

Lange, Arthur (1889–). American composer.
Hollywood Revue 29. Marie Galante 34. Banjo on My Knee 36. This Is My Affair 37. Kidnapped 38. Lady of Burlesque 43. The Woman in the Window 45. Woman on the Run 50. The Mad Magician 54, many others.

Lange, Hope (1931–). American leading lady of the fifties who developed into a mature and pleasing comedienne.
□Bus Stop 56. The True Story of Jesse James 57. Peyton Place 57. The Young Lions 58. In Love and War 58. The Best of Everything 59. Wild in the Country 61. Pocketful of Miracles 61. Love is a Ball 63. Jigsaw (TV) 68. Crowhaven Farm (TV) 70. That Certain Summer (TV) 72. The 500 Pound Jerk (TV) 72. Death Wish 74. I Love You Goodbye (TV) 74. Fer de Lance (TV) 74. The Secret Night Caller (TV) 75. Like Normal People (TV) 79. The Day Christ Died (TV) 80. I Am The Cheese 83. The Prodigal 83. Nightmare on Elm Street II 85. Blue Velvet 86.

TV series: *The Ghost and Mrs Muir* 68. *The New Dick Van Dyke Show* 71.

Lange, Jessica (1949–). American leading lady who developed into an actress.
King Kong 76. All That Jazz 79. How to Beat the High Cost of Living 80. The Postman Always Rings Twice 81. *Frances* 82. Tootsie (AA) 82. Country (AAN) 84. Sweet Dreams (AAN) 85. Crimes of the Heart 86.

Langella, Frank (1940–). American leading man of the seventies.
The Twelve Chairs 70. Diary of a Mad Housewife 70. The Wrath of God 72. The Mark of Zorro (TV) 74. *Dracula* (title role) 79. Those Lips Those Eyes 80. Sphinx 81. The Men's Club 86. Masters of the Universe 87, etc.

Langford, Frances (1914–). American band singer, popular in the forties, mainly in guest spots. Appeared mainly in light musicals.
Every Night at Eight 35. Broadway Melody 36. Hollywood Hotel 37. Too Many Girls 40. Swing It, Soldier 41. The Girl Rush 44. The Bamboo Blonde 45. Beat the Band 46. No Time For Tears 52. The Glenn Miller Story 54, etc.

Langley, Noel (1911–*80). South African playwright and screenwriter, in Britain and Hollywood.
Maytime (co-w) 38. The Wizard of Oz (co-w) 39. They Made Me a Fugitive 47. Tom Brown's Schooldays 51. Scrooge 52. The Pickwick Papers (& d) 53. Our Girl Friday (& d) 53. The Search for Bridey Murphy (& d) 56, others.

Langlois, Henri (1914–1977). Idiosyncratic French archivist, instigator of the Cinematheque Française. His methods annoyed some, but his good intentions were never in question. Received Special Academy Award in 1974.

Langton, Simon (1941–). British director, in TV from 1964. First cinema movie *The Whistle Blower* 86.

Langtry, Lillie (1853–1929) (Emilie Charlotte Le Breton). British light actress who charmed, among others, Judge Roy Bean and Edward VII. Sole film appearance in 1913: *His Neighbour's Wife*.

Lansbury, Angela (1925–). British character actress who has always seemed older than her years. Evacuated to Hollywood during World War II, she played a long succession of unsympathetic parts, but in the sixties became a Broadway musical star.
□Gaslight 44. National Velvet 44. *The Picture of Dorian Gray* 45. The Harvey Girls 46. The Hoodlum Saint 46. The Private Affairs of Bel Ami 47. Till the Clouds Roll By 47. If Winter Comes 47. Tenth Avenue Angel 48. State of the Union 48. The Three Musketeers 48. The Red Danube 49. Samson and Delilah 49. Kind Lady 51. Mutiny 52. Remains to Be Seen 53. A Lawless Street 55. A Life at Stake 55. The Purple Mask 55. Please Murder Me 56. The Court Jester 56. The Reluctant Debutante 58. The Long Hot Summer 58. *The Dark at the Top of the Stairs* 60. A Breath of Scandal 61. Blue Hawaii 61. Summer of the Seventeenth Doll 61. All Fall Down 62. *The Manchurian Candidate* 62. In the Cool of the Day 63. The World of Henry Orient 64. Dear Heart 64. The Greatest Story Ever Told 65. Harlow 65. Moll Flanders 65. Mister Buddwing 66. Something for Everyone 70. *Bedknobs and Broomsticks* 71. Death on the Nile 78. The Lady Vanishes 79. The Mirror Crack'd 80. Little Gloria . . . Happy at Last (TV) 82. The Pirates of Penzance 83. Lace (TV) 84. Company of Wolves 84.
TV series: Murder She Wrote 84– .

Lansing, Joi (1928–1972) (Joyce Wassmansdoff). American leading lady who played a few sharp blondes and left a pleasant impression.
□The Counterfeiters 48. The Girl from Jones Beach 49. Hot Cars 56. The Brave One 56. Hot Shots 56. A Hole in the Head 59. It Started with a Kiss 59. The Atomic Submarine 59. Who Was That Lady? 59. Marriage on the Rocks 65. Bigfoot 71.
TV series: Love That Bob. Klondike.

Lansing, Robert (1929–) (Robert H. Broom). Cold-eyed, virile American leading man of the sixties.
The 4-D Man 59. A Gathering of Eagles 63. Under the Yum Yum Tree 64. The Grissom Gang 71. Wild in the Sky 72. Bittersweet Love 76. Empire of the Ants 77. False Face 77, etc.

TV series: 87th Precinct 61. 12 O'clock High 64. The Man Who Never Was 66.

Lantz, Walter (1900–). American animator, in charge of Universal cartoons since 1928 and the creator of Woody Woodpecker. Special AA 1979 'for bringing joy and laughter to every part of the world'.

Lanza, Mario (1921–1959) (Alfredo Cocozza). American opera singer, popular in MGM musicals until overcome by weight problem.
□That Midnight Kiss 49. The Toast of New Orleans 50. *The Great Caruso* 51. Because You're Mine 52. The Student Prince (voice only) 54. Serenade 56. Seven Hills of Rome 58. For the First Time 58.

¶ *Joseph Ruttenberg:* That idiot Lanza! He had the greatest opportunities in the world, but he just couldn't handle success.
M.L.: Mario, you doll, you sing like a son of a bitch.

Lapotaire, Jane (1944–). Anglo-French stage actress in occasional films.
Crescendo 69. Antony and Cleopatra 72. The Asphyx 72. One of Our Dinosaurs Is Missing 75. Eureka 83.

Lardner, Ring Jnr (1915–). American screenwriter.
Woman of the Year '(AA) 42. The Cross of Lorraine 44. Forever Amber 47. Britannia Mews 48. Cloak and Dagger 48. The Cincinnati Kid 65. *M*A*S*H** (AA) 70. The Greatest 77, etc.

Larsen, Keith (1925–). American secondstring leading man.
Flat Top 52. Hiawatha 52. Arrow in the Dust 54. Wichita 55. Dial Red O 56. Fury River 61. Caxambu 67. The Trap on Cougar Mountain 76, etc.
TV series: The Hunter 54. Brave Eagle 55. Northwest Passage 57. The Aquanaut 60.

LaRue: see *La Rue*.

Lasky, Jesse (1880–1958). American pioneer. Formed his first production company in 1914 and had a big hit with *The Squaw Man*; in 1916 gained control of Famous Players and later Paramount. Later produced for Fox, Warner, RKO.
Autobiography 1958: *I Blow My Own Horn*.
Sergeant York 41. The Adventures of Mark Twain 44. Rhapsody in Blue 45. The Miracle of the Bells 49. The Great Caruso 51, many others.

Lasky, Jesse Jnr (1910–). American screenwriter, son of Jesse Lasky.
Autobiography 1974: *Whatever Happened to Hollywood?*
Union Pacific (co-w) 39. Reap the Wild Wind (co-w) 42. Unconquered (co-w) 48. Samson and Delilah (co-w) 49. The Thief of Venice 50. The Brigand 52. The Ten Commandments (co-w) 56. Seven Women from Hell (co-w) 61, etc.

Lassally, Walter (1926–). German cinematographer, long in Britain.
We Are the Lambeth Boys 58. *A Taste of Honey* 61. The Loneliness of the Long-Distance Runner 62. *Tom Jones* 63. *Zorba the Greek* (AA) 65. The Day the Fish Came Out 67. Oedipus the King 67. Joanna 68. Turnkey 70. Something for Everyone 72. Malachi's Cove 74. Too Far to Go (TV) 77. Gauguin the Savage (TV) 80. Memoirs of a Survivor 82. Heat and Dust 83.

Lasser, Louise (1939–). American TV actress popular in 76 serial *Mary Hartman, Mary Hartman*.
Bananas 71. Such Good Friends 71. Everything You Always Wanted to Know about Sex 72. Coffee, Tea or Me? (TV) 73. Isn't It Shocking? (TV) 73. Slither 73. Just Me and You (TV) 78. In God We Trust 80, etc.

Lassie. The first film featuring this intelligent collie (actually a laddie) was *Lassie Come Home* 42, based on Eric Knight's novel; the dog, born in 1940, was called Pal, and continued his masquerade in several subsequent 'Lassie' adventures, though more recently different dogs have been used. The latest addition is *Lassie's Great Adventure* 62, and there was a long-running TV series from 1955, followed in 1973 by a cartoon series, *Lassie's Rescue Rangers*.

The Last Chance (Switzerland 1945). Almost the only Swiss film of international repute, this story of escape from Italy at the end of the 1943 campaign was directed by Leopold Lindtberg.

The Last Days of Pompeii. Lord Lytton's novel climaxing in the catastrophic eruption of Vesuvius was filmed in Italy in 1912 ('10,000 people, 260 scenes'), 1925 and 1960. In 1935 Cooper and Schoedsack filmed it in Hollywood, with a cast including Basil Rathbone and Preston Foster. The 1960 Italian version is barely worth mentioning. The 1985 TV mini-series is good for a laugh.

The Last Hurrah (US 1958). Edwin O'Connor's amusing novel about the last days of a lovably roguish politician was turned by director John Ford into a sentimental reunion for a number of veteran character actors including Spencer Tracy, Edward Brophy, James Gleason, Basil Rathbone, John Carradine, Pat O'Brien, Donald Crisp, Ricardo Cortez, Wallace Ford, Frank McHugh and Jane Darwell. As a film it was fair, which is more than can be said for the 1976 TV movie version with Carroll O'Connor.

The Last Laugh (Der Letzte Mann) (Germany 1925). A silent drama dispensing entirely with sub-titles. Emil Jannings gave one of his most characteristic and clever performances as the lordly hotel porter degraded to washroom attendant; F. W. Murnau directed from a script by Carl Mayer; photography by Karl Freund.

last lines

? At the end of which films were the following lines spoken, and by whom?

1 This is the end, the absolute end!
2 I always wear a bullet-proof vest around the studio.
3 I knew a feller once . . .
4 Hello, everybody. This is Mrs Norman Maine . . .
5 Marry me, Emily, and I'll never look at any other horse.
6 Ah, Roger, this is silly.
—I know, but I'm sentimental.
7 That's not the northern lights, that's Manderley!
8 Mother of Mercy, is this the end of Rico?
9 Can't nobody wipe us out. Can't nobody lick us. We'll go on forever, pa. We're the people.
10 Louis, I think this is the beginning of a beautiful friendship.

The Last of the Mohicans. Fenimore Cooper's adventure novel of American colonization was filmed in 1920 by Maurice Tourneur, with George Hackathorne; in 1936 by George Seitz, with Randolph Scott, and in 1952, as *The Last of the Redskins*, by George Sherman with Jon Hall. A Canadian TV series in 1956, starred John Hart.

The Last Picture Show (US 1971). The movie which rocketed director Peter Bogdanovich to fame and set him off on a number of flawed nostalgic retrospectives was a potent distillation of small town sexual mores circa 1951: it was itself aped by *American Graffiti* two years later. Cloris Leachman and Ben Johnson distinguished themselves among a generally able cast.

Last Year in Marienbad (France 1961). Written by Alain Robbe-Grillet and directed by Alain Resnais, this curious film was hailed by many critics as a masterpiece, while others suspected a leg-pull. It had only three characters of note, but the problem for audiences was to find out how they were interrelated and what the film was about. Sacha Vierney's photography, in and around a baroque hotel, added its share of mystery.

Lastfogel, Abe (1898–1984). American talent agent, head of the William Morris Organization, which he joined in 1912 as an office boy.

Laszlo, Andrew (1926–). Hungarian-American cinematographer.
You're a Big Boy Now 67. The Night They Raided Minsky's 68. Popi 69. Teacher Teacher 70. The Out of Towners 70. Lovers and other Strangers 71. The Owl and the Pussycat 71. Class of 44 73. The Man without a Country (TV) 74. Countdown at Kusini 76. The Warriors 79. Shogun (TV) 80. Southern Comfort 81. First Blood 82. Thief of Hearts 84. Remo Williams, the Adventure Begins 85. Poltergeist II 86.

Laszlo, Ernest (1905–84). Hungarian-American cinematographer.
The Hitler Gang 44. Two Years Before the Mast 44. The Girl from Manhattan 48. Dead on Arrival 49. The Steel Trap 52. The Star 52. Stalag 17 53. *Vera Cruz* 54. The Big Knife 55. Judgment at Nuremberg 60. *Inherit the Wind* 60. *It's A Mad Mad Mad Mad World* 63. *Ship of Fools* (AA) 65. Fantastic Voyage 66. Star! 68. The First Time 69. Daddy's Gone A-Hunting 69. *Airport* 69. Showdown 73. Logan's Run 76. The Domino Principle (co-ph) 77, many others.

Latham, Louise (–). American actress.
Marnie 64. Firecreek 67. Making It 71. White Lightning 73. The Sugarland Express 74. The Awakening Land (TV) 78, etc.

Lathrop, Philip (1916–). American cinematographer.

The Monster of Piedras Blancas 57. Experiment in Terror 62. *Lonely are the Brave* 62. Days of Wine and Roses 63. The Pink Panther 63. The Americanization of Emily 64. Thirty-Six Hours 65. The Cincinnati Kid 65. What Did You Do in the War Daddy? 66. The Russians are Coming 66. The Happening 67. Point Blank 68. *Finian's Rainbow* 69. The Gypsy Moths 69. The Illustrated Man 69. They Shoot Horses Don't They? 69. Von Richthofen and Brown 71. Airport 77 77. The Driver 78. Little Miss Marker 80. Loving Couples 80. All Night Long 81. Jekyll and Hyde Together Again 82. Hammett 82. National Lampoon's Class Reunion 82, etc.

Latimer, Jonathan (1906–84). American thriller writer.
Topper Returns 41. They Won't Believe Me 47. Alias Nick Beal 49. Plunder of the Sun 51. Botany Bay 54. The Unholy Wife 57, etc.

Latimore, Frank (1925–) (Frank Kline). American leading man with stage experience.
In the Meantime, Darling 44. Three Little Girls in Blue 46. Black Magic 49. Three Forbidden Stories (Italian) 50. John Paul Jones 59. The Sergeant 68. All the President's Men 76, etc.

Lattuada, Alberto (1914–). Italian director.
The Mill on the Po 48. Without Pity 48. Lights of Variety (co-d) 50. Il Capotto 52. The Wolf 53. The Beach 53. Guendalina 56. Tempest 58. The Adolescents 61. La Steppa 62. The Mandrake 65. The Betrayal 68. A Dog's Heart 75. Stay as You Are 78. A Thorn in the Heart 86.

Lauder, Sir Harry (1870–1950). Scottish music-hall entertainer.
Autobiography 1928, *Roamin' in the Gloamin'*.
Huntingtower 27. Auld Lang Syne 33. End of the Road 36.

Laughlin, Tom (1938–). American independent director.
The Young Sinner 65. Born Losers (& ap) 67. Billy Jack (& apw) 71. The Trial of Billy Jack (& apw) 72. The Master Gunfighter (& apw) 75, etc.

Laughton, Charles (1899–1962). Distinguished British character actor, whose plump wry face was one of the most popular on screen in the thirties. His later Hollywood roles showed a regrettable tendency to ham, but he was always worth watching.
Biographies: *Charles Laughton and I* (1938) by his wife Elsa Lanchester; *The Charles Laughton Story* (1952) by Kurt Singer; *Charles Laughton* (1976) by Charles Higham.
□Wolves 27. Bluebottles 28. Daydreams 28. Piccadilly 29. Comets 30. Down River 30. *The Old Dark House* 32. The Devil and the Deep 32. Payment Deferred 32. *The Sign of the Cross* (as Nero) 32. If I Had a Million 32. Island of Lost Souls 32. *The Private Life of Henry VIII* (AA) 33. White Woman 33. *The Barretts of Wimpole Street* 34. *Ruggles of Red Gap* 35. *Les Misérables* 35. *Mutiny on the Bounty* (as Captain Bligh) 35. *Rembrandt* 36. *I Claudius* (unfinished) 37. Vessel of Wrath 37. St Martin's Lane 38. Jamaica Inn 39. *The Hunchback of Notre Dame* 39. They Knew What They Wanted 40. It Started with Eve 41. The Tuttles of Tahiti 42. Tales of Manhattan 42. Stand by for Action 43. Forever and a Day 43. This Land is Mine 43. The Man from Down Under 43. The Canterville Ghost 44. *The Suspect* 44. Captain Kidd 45. Because of Him 46. The Paradine Case 48. The Big Clock 48. Arch of Triumph 48. The Girl from Manhattan 49. The Bribe 49. The Man on the Eiffel Tower (as Maigret) 49. The Blue Veil 51. The Strange Door 51. Full House 52. Abbott and Costello Meet Captain Kidd 52. Salome 53. Young Bess 53. *Hobson's Choice* 54. *Witness for the Prosecution* 57. Under Ten Flags 60. Spartacus 60. *Advise and Consent* 62.
AS DIRECTOR: *Night of the Hunter* 55.
❊For a dozen splendid performances, unassailable by the self-doubt which later turned him into a ham. *Rembrandt*.

¶ They can't censor the gleam in my eye.—*C.L., when told that his performance as Mr Moulton-Barrett must not indicate incestuous love.*

C.L.: I have a face like the behind of an elephant.
Alfred Hitchcock: You can't direct a Laughton picture. The best you can hope for is to referee.
Alexander Korda: With him acting was an act of childbirth. What he needed was not so much a director as a midwife.

Alva Johnson: A great man who only accidentally became an actor.
C.L.: It's got so that every time I walk into a restaurant I get not only soup but an impersonation of Captain Bligh.
Famous line (*Mutiny on the Bounty*): I'll live to see you—all of you—hung from the highest yardarm in the British fleet!

Famous line (*The Private Life of Henry VIII*): Am I a king or a breeding bull?
Famous line (*The Private Life of Henry VIII*): There's no delicacy nowadays. No consideration for others. Refinement's a thing of the past!

Launder, Frank (1907–). British comedy scriptwriter, from 1938 usually in collaboration with Sidney Gilliat (qv); they have produced most of their own films. Biography 1977: *Launder and Gilliat* by Geoff Brown.
Under the Greenwood Tree 29. The W Plan 30. Children of Chance 30. After Office Hours 31. Josser in the Army 31. Facing the Music 33. Those were the Days 34. Emil and the Detectives 35. Seven Sinners 36. Educated Evans 36. *Oh Mr Porter* 38. *The Lady Vanishes* 38. A Girl must Live 39. They Came by Night 40. *Night Train to Munich* 40. Kipps 41. The Young Mr Pitt 42. Millions Like Us (& d) 43. 2000 Women (& d) 43. *I See a Dark Stranger* (& d) 45. Captain Boycott (& d) 47. The Blue Lagoon (& d) 48. *The Happiest Days of Your Life* (& d) 50. Lady Godiva Rides Again (& d) 51. *The Belles of St Trinian's* (& d) 54. Geordie (& d) 55. The Bridal Path (& d) 59. Joey Boy (& d) 65. The Great St Trinian's Train Robbery (& d) 66, etc.

Laura (US 1944). A superior mystery from a novel by Vera Caspary, this was notable for Otto Preminger's spare direction of his small cast, and for Clifton Webb's first star performance as the acidulous Waldo Lydecker. Cinematography: Joseph La Shelle (AA).

Laurel, Stan (1890–1965) (Arthur Stanley Jefferson). British-born comedian, the thin half and gag deviser of the Laurel and Hardy team. Went to USA with Fred Karno's troupe, was in short comedies from 1915, teamed with Hardy 1926. He had director credit on some of their films and virtually directed many others. Special Academy Award 1960 'for his creative pioneering in the field of cinema comedy'. For list of films see *Oliver Hardy*.
❊ For his genius in the invention of comic gags, and for finding his perfect niche in partnership with Oliver Hardy. *Way Out West*.

¶ They were visual comedians, of course. But they successfully transferred to sound by the use of minimum sound, mainly in the form of carefully scattered catch phrases which arose naturally out of their characters as every child's foolish uncles. When disaster struck, as it inevitably did, who could resist the sight of Olly among the debris, gazing reprovingly at the unharmed Stan and saying:

> Here's another nice mess you've gotten me into.

Or:

> Why don't you do something to HELP me?

Or simply:

> I have NOTHING to say.

Such results are Olly's reward for listening to Stan's suggestions earlier on. Stan's meaning is always unclear to begin with, so that Olly has to say:

> Tell me that again.

But he finally gets the drift and agrees:

> That's a *good* idea.

Olly of course was always shy, especially with women. When introduced, he was apt to twiddle his tie and observe:

> A lot of weather we've been having lately.

His great asset was his courtly manner, preserved even when mistaking an open can of milk for the telephone receiver:

> Pardon me for a moment, my ear is full of milk.

Stan, having no catch phrases, relied on lively non sequiturs. When asked:

> You never met my wife, did you?

He would reply:

> Yes, I never did.

His speciality was putting his foot in it, as when he visits Olly in hospital and announces:

> I brought you some hard-boiled eggs and some nuts.

Not surprisingly, he eats them himself, having thoughtfully brought salt and pepper canisters in his pocket. Then there was the time in a bar when they could afford only one beer, ordered by Olly with his usual majesty. Stan did rather ruin the effect by calling after the waiter:

> And two clean straws that haven't been used . . .

But he was capable of saying the right thing, as when Olly prepared a mundane repast of coffee and beans. Stan liked it:

> Boy, you sure know how to plan a meal!

Behind the scenes, Stan was the producer. Olly was ready to admit:

> I have never really worked hard in the creation department.

But he astutely saw the secret of their success:

> Those two fellows we created, they were nice, very nice people. They never get anywhere because they are both so dumb, but they don't know they're dumb. One of the reasons why people like us, I guess, is because they feel superior to us.

That was put another way in the opening title to one of their silent films:

> Neither Mr Laurel nor Mr Hardy had any thoughts of getting married. In fact, they had no thoughts of any kind . . .

And the opening of *Come Clean* summed up their best comedy style very neatly:

> Mr Hardy holds that a man should always tell his wife the whole truth. Mr Laurel is crazy too.

Mr Laurel had his own philosophy:

> We were doing a very simple thing, giving some people some laughs, and that's all we were trying to do.

Lauren, S. K. (1892–1979). American screenwriter who worked on An American Tragedy 32. Blonde Venus 34. Crime and Punishment 35. One Night of Love 36. Mother Carey's Chickens 39. Flight for Freedom 43, etc.

Laurenson, James (1935–). New Zealand actor in British and Australian TV, especially series *Boney*.
The Magic Christian 69. Assault 70. The Monster Club 80. Pink Floyd: The Wall 82. Heartbreakers 84, etc.

Laurents, Arthur (1918–). American playwright.
Caught (original screenplay) 48. Home of the Brave 49. Summertime 55. West Side Story (co-w) 61. The Way We Were (original screenplay) 73. The Turning Point (original screenplay) 77.

Laurie, John (1897–1980). Scottish character actor, often in dour roles. On stage from 1921.
Juno and the Paycock 30. Red Ensign 34. *The Thirty-Nine Steps* 35. Tudor Rose 36. As You Like It 36. Farewell Again 37. Edge of the World 38. Q Planes 39. Sailors Three 40. *The Ghost of St Michael's* 41. Old Mother Riley's Ghosts 41. The Gentle Sex 43. Fanny by Gaslight 43. *The Way Ahead* 44. *Henry V* 44. I Know Where I'm Going 45. Caesar and Cleopatra 45. The Brothers 47. Uncle Silas 47. Bonnie Prince Charlie 48. Hamlet 48. Trio 50. Laughter in Paradise 51. The Fake 53. Hobson's Choice 54. The Black Knight 55. Campbell's Kingdom 57. Kidnapped 60. Siege of the Saxons 63. Mr Ten Per Cent 66. Dad's Army 71. The Prisoner of Zenda 79, etc.

Laurie, Piper (1932–) (Rosetta Jacobs). Pert American leading lady of fifties costume charades; later a notable character actress.
□Louisa 50. The Milkman 50. Francis Goes to the Races 51. The Prince Who Was a Thief 51. No Room for the Groom 52. Has Anybody Seen My Gal 52. Son of Ali Baba 52. Mississippi Gambler 53. The Golden Blade 53. Dangerous Mission 54. Johnny Dark 54. Dawn at Socorro 54. Smoke Signal 55. Ain't Misbehavin' 55. Kelly and Me 57. Until They Sail 59. *The Hustler* 61. *Carrie* 76. Ruby 78. Tim 79. Skag (TV) 80. The Bunker (TV) 81. Mae West (TV) 82. The Thorn Birds (TV) 82. Toughlove (TV) 85. Return to Oz 85. Tender is the Night (TV) 85. Children of a Lesser God 86.

Lauter, Ed (1940–). American general purpose actor.
The Last American Hero 73. Executive Action 73. Lolly Madonna XXX 74. The Longest Yard 75. Last Hours Before Morning (TV) 75. King Kong 76. The Chicken Chronicles 77. Eureka 83. The Big Score 83. Cujo 83. Lassiter 83. Finders Keepers 84. Death Wish 3 85. Youngblood 85. Raw Deal 86, etc.

Lauter, Harry (1920–). American supporting actor.
The Gay Intruders 48. Tucson 49. Whirlwind 51. The Sea Tiger 52. Dragonfly Squadron 54. The Crooked Web 55. Hellcats of the Navy 57. Gunfight at Dodge City 59. Posse from Hell 61. Ambush Bay 66. More Dead than Alive 68, many others.

Laven, Arnold (1922–). American director, former dialogue coach.
Without Warning 52. Down Three Dark Streets 54. The Rack 56. The Monster That Challenged the World 57. Slaughter on Tenth Avenue 58. Anna Lucasta 58. Geronimo (& p) 62. The Glory Guys 66. Rough Night in Jericho 67. Sam Whiskey 68. The Scalphunters (p only) 68, etc.

The Lavender Hill Mob (GB 1950). One of the most affectionately remembered Ealing comedies, a skit on *The Blue Lamp* with Alec Guinness and Stanley Holloway as unlikely gangsters almost getting away with the bullion. Lightly and amusingly scripted by T. E. B. Clarke, directed by Charles Crichton.

lavender print. A high quality, well-contrasted print, sometimes called a 'fine grain', struck from the original negative for the purpose of making duplicates.

Laverick, June (1932–). British leading lady, groomed for stardom by the Rank charm school of the fifties.
Doctor at Large 56. The Gypsy and the Gentleman 57. Son of Robin Hood 58. Follow a Star 59, etc.

Lavery, Emmet (1902–86). American screenwriter.
Hitler's Children 43. Behind the Rising Sun 43. The First Legion (original play) 51. The Magnificent Yankee (original play) 52. The Court Martial of Billy Mitchell 55, etc.

Lavery, Emmet Jnr (1927–). American TV executive producer, mainly with Paramount.
Delancy Street 75. Serpico (and series) 76. Nero Wolfe 77, etc.

Lavi, Daliah (1940–) (D. Levenbuch). Israeli leading lady in international films.
Il Demonio (Italian) 63. Old Shatterhand (WG) 64. Lord Jim 65. Ten Little Indians 65. The Silencers 66. The Spy with a Cold Nose 67. Some Girls Do 67. Nobody Runs Forever 68. Catlow 72, etc.

Law, John Phillip (1937–). American leading man.
The Russians Are Coming, The Russians Are Coming 66. Hurry Sundown 67. Barbarella 68. Skidoo 68. The Sergeant 68. Danger: Diabolik 68. The Hawaiians 70. Von Richthofen and Brown 71. The Love Machine 71. The Last Movie 71. The Golden Voyage of Sinbad 73. Your Heaven, My Hell 76. The Cassandra Crossing 77. Tarzan the Ape Man 81.

Lawford, Peter (1923–84). British light leading man, former child actor, in Hollywood from 1938.
Poor Old Bill 31. The Boy from Barnardo's 38. Mrs Miniver 42. The White Cliffs of Dover 44. Cluny Brown 46. It Happened in Brooklyn 47. Easter Parade 48. Little Women 49. Royal Wedding 52. Exodus 60. Advise and Consent 61. Sylvia 65. Harlow 65. Dead Run (Austria) 67. Salt and Pepper (GB) 68. Buona Sera Mrs Campbell 68. The April Fools 69. One More Time 70. Don't Look Behind You (TV) 71. Phantom of Hollywood (TV) 74. Rosebud 75, etc.
TV series: Dear Phoebe 54. The Thin Man 58.

Lawrance, Jody (1930–) (Josephine Lawrence Goddard). American leading lady.
Mask of the Avenger 51. Son of Dr Jekyll 51. The Brigand 52. Captain John Smith and Pocahontas 53. The Scarlet Hour 55. Stagecoach to Dancer's Rock 62.

Lawrence, Barbara (1928–). American comedy actress, usually seen as wise-cracking friend of the heroine.
Margie 46. You Were Meant for Me 47. Thieves' Highway 49. Two Tickets to Broadway 51. Jesse James Versus the Daltons 54. *Oklahoma* 55. Joe Dakota 57, etc.

Lawrence, D. H. (1885–1930). Introspective British novelist whose novels have been adapted with varying success for the screen.
Lady Chatterley's Lover 58. Sons and Lovers 60. The Fox 68. Women in Love 69. The Virgin and the Gypsy 70, etc.
Lady Chatterley's Lover was filmed again in 1980, and in 1981 Ian McKellen played Lawrence in *Priest of Love*.

Lawrence, Delphi (c. 1927–). Anglo-Hungarian actress, in British films.
Blood Orange 54. Barbados Quest 55. It's Never Too Late 56. Too many Crooks 59. Cone of Silence 60. Farewell Performance 63. Pistolero (US) 67, others.

Lawrence, Florence (1886–1938). American leading lady of the silent screen; one of the industry's chief stars, she was known at first as 'the Biograph Girl'. Retired in the early twenties.
Miss Jones Entertains 09. Resurrection 10. A Singular Cynic 14. The Enfoldment 20, many others.

Lawrence, Gertrude (1898–1952) (Alexandra Dagmar Lawrence-Klasen). Vivacious British revue star of the twenties, especially associated with Noel Coward. Despite sporadic attempts, her quality never came across on the screen. She was impersonated by Julie Andrews in *Star!* 68.
Autobiography 1949: *A Star Danced*.
□The Battle of Paris 29. No Funny Business 32. Aren't We All 32. Lord Camber's Ladies 32. Mimi 35. Rembrandt 36. Men are Not Gods 36. *The Glass Menagerie* 50.

Lawrence, Marc (1910–) (Max Goldsmith). American character actor, former opera singer; usually seen as Italian gangster.
White Woman 33. Dr Socrates 35. Penitentiary 38. The Housekeeper's Daughter

39. Johnny Apollo 40. The Monster and the Girl 41. Hold That Ghost 42. Dillinger 45. I Walk Alone 47. The Asphalt Jungle 50. My Favorite Spy 51. Helen of Troy 55. Kill Her Gently 58. Johnny Cool 64. Nightmare in the Sun (wd only) 64. Savage Pampas 66. Custer of the West 67. Krakatoa East of Java 69. Marathon Man 76. The Big Easy 86, many others.

Lawrence, Marjorie (1902–79). Australian opera star crippled by polio; portrayed in 1955 by Eleanor Parker in *Interrupted Melody*.

Lawrence of Arabia (GB 1962). David Lean's epic account of a finally mysterious character: beautiful, careful, over-long. The supreme example of the modern multi-million-dollar international epic, several years in the making and shot on the actual locations. Peter O'Toole leads an all-star cast; production by Sam Spiegel, script by Robert Bolt. AA best picture, director, score (Maurice Jarre), etc.

Lawrence, Quentin (c. 1920–1980). British director, from TV.
The Trollenberg Terror 55. Cash on Demand 62. The Man Who Finally Died 63. The Secret of Blood Island 65, etc.

Lawrence, T. E. (1888–1935). British adventurer and soldier whose book *Seven Pillars of Wisdom* made him a cult and remotely inspired the film *Lawrence of Arabia*.

Lawrence, Viola (1894–1973). American editor, long with Columbia.
An Alabaster Box 17. Fighting the Flames 21. Bulldog Drummond 29. Man's Castle 33. Craig's Wife 36. Penitentiary 38. Here Comes Mr Jordan 41. My Sister Eileen 42. Cover Girl 44. Hit the Hay 46. The Dark Past 48. Tokyo Joe 49. Sirocco 51. Miss Sadie Thompson 53. Queen Bee 55. Pal Joey 57. Who Was That Lady 60, many others.

Lawson, John Howard (1886–1977). American writer with Marxist affiliations.
Heart of Spain 37. Algiers 38. *Blockade* 38. *Five Came Back* 39. *Sahara* 43. Counter-Attack 43. Smash-Up 47, etc.

Lawson, Leigh (1944–). British light leading man of the seventies.
Ghost Story 74. Percy's Progress 74. Love Among the Ruins (TV) 75. Golden Rendezvous 77. The Devil's Advocate 78. Tess 80. Why Didn't They Ask Evans? (TV) 81. Murder is Easy (TV) 81. Lace (TV) 84. Sword of the Valiant (TV) 85. Queenie (TV) 87, etc.

Lawson, Sarah (1928–). British leading lady of the fifties.
The Browning Version 50. Street Corner 52. Blue Peter 54. It's Never Too Late 55, etc.

Lawson, Wilfrid (1900–66) (Wilfrid Worsnop). British character actor, on stage from 1916; revelled in eccentric parts.
□ East Lynne on the Western Front 31. Strike it Rich 33. Turn of the Tide 35. The Man who made Diamonds 37. Bank Holiday 38. The Terror 38. Yellow Sands 38. The Gaunt Stranger 38. *Pygmalion* 38. Stolen Life 39. Dead Man's Shoes 39. *Pastor Hall* 40. Gentleman of Venture 40. The Man at the Gate 41. Danny Boy 41. Jeannie 41. The Farmer's Wife 41. Tower of Terror 41. *Hard Steel* 42. The Night has Eyes 42. *The Great Mr Handel* 42. Thursday's Child 43. Fanny by Gaslight 44. The Turners of Prospect Road 47. Make me an Offer 55. The Prisoner 55. An Alligator Named Daisy 55. Now and Forever 56. The Naked Truth 57. Hell Drivers 57. Tread Softly Stranger 59. Room at the Top 59. Expresso Bongo 60. The Naked Edge 61. Nothing Barred 61. Over the Odds 61. Go to Blazes 62. Postman's Knock 62. Tom Jones 63. Becket 64. *The Wrong Box* 66. The Viking Queen 66.

Lawton, Charles Jnr (1904–1965). American cinematographer.
My Dear Miss Aldrich 36. Miracles for Sale 39. Gold Rush Maisie 41. Fingers at the Window 42. Abroad with Two Yanks 44. The Thrill of Brazil 46. *The Lady from Shanghai* 48. Shockproof 49. Rogues of Sherwood Forest 50. Mask of the Avenger 51. *The Happy Time* 52. Miss Sadie Thompson 53. Drive a Crooked Road 54. The Long Gray Line 55. Jubal 56. *3.10 to Yuma* 57. The Last Hurrah 58. It Happened to Jane 59. Two Rode Together 61. 13 West Street 62. Spencer's Mountain 63. Youngblood Hawke 64. A Rage to Live 65, many others.

Lawton, Frank (1904–1969). Charming but undynamic British leading man of the thirties, husband of Evelyn Laye; in British and American films.
Young Woodley 28. Birds of Prey 30. The Skin Game 31. The Outsider 31. Michael and Mary 31. After Office Hours 32. Cavalcade 33. Heads We Go 33. Friday the Thirteenth 33. One More River 34. *David Copperfield* (title role) 34. The Invisible Ray 36. The Devil Doll 36. The Mill on the Floss 37. The

Four Just Men 39. Went the Day Well? 42. The Winslow Boy 48. Rough Shoot 52. The Rising of the Moon 57. A Night to Remember 57. Gideon's Day 57, etc.

Lay, Beirne Jnr (1909–1982). American screenwriter.
I Wanted Wings 41. Twelve O'Clock High 49. Above and Beyond 50. Strategic Air Command 54. Toward the Unknown 56, etc.

Laydu, Claude (1927–). Undernourished-looking French leading actor.
Diary of a Country Priest 50. Nous Sommes Tous les Assassins 52. Symphonie d'Amour 55. Le Dialogue des Carmelites 59, etc.

Laye, Evelyn (1900–) (Elsie Evelyn Lay). British musical comedy star of the twenties and thirties; films rare. Married Frank Lawton.
Autobiography 1958: *Boo to My Friends*.
□ Luck of the Navy 27. Queen of Scandal 30. One Heavenly Night (US) 31. Waltz Time 33. Princess Charming 33. *Evensong* 34. The Night is Young 34. I'll Turn to You 46. Make Mine a Million 59. Theatre of Death 66. Say Hello to Yesterday 70. Within and Without (It.) 70. Second Star to the Right 80.

Lazenby, George (1939–). Australian leading man who made the big jump from TV commercials to playing James Bond.
On Her Majesty's Secret Service 69. Universal Soldier 71. The Man from Hong Kong 75. Cover Girls (TV) 77. Evening in Byzantium (TV) 78. Saint Jack 79.

Le Borg, Reginald (1902–). Austrian-born director, in Hollywood from 1937, at first as shorts director. Output mainly routine with occasional flashes of talent.
She's For Me 42. The Mummy's Ghost 44. Calling Dr Death 44. *San Diego I Love You* 45. Joe Palooka, Champ 46. Young Daniel Boone 47. Wyoming Trail 49. Bad Blonde 51. Sins of Jezebel 53. The Black Sleep 56. The Dalton Girls 57. The Flight That Disappeared 61. The Diary of a Madman 62, many others.

Le Breton, Auguste (1915–). French writer.
Razzia sur la Chnouf 54. Rififi 55. Bob le Flambeur 56. Rafles sur la Ville 57, etc.

Le Brock, Kelly (–). American leading lady.
The Woman in Red 84. Weird Science 85.

Le Carré, John (1931–) (David John Moore Cornwell). British spy novelist, whose works have been eagerly filmed, though they centre on the more depressing aspects of espionage.
The Spy Who Came in from the Cold 66. The Deadly Affair (Call for the Dead) 67. The Looking Glass War 70. Tinker Tailor Soldier Spy (TV) 79. Smiley's People 82. The Little Drummer Girl 84. A Perfect Spy (TV) 87.

Le Chanois, Jean-Paul (1909–85) (J.-P. Dreyfus). French director.
l'École Buissonière 48. La Belle Que Voilà 51. Papa, Mama, the Maid and I 54. The Case of Dr Laurent 56. Les Misérables 58. Monsieur 64. Le Jardinier d'Argenteuil 66, etc.

Le Fanu, J. Sheridan (1814–1873). Irish novelist specializing in mystery and the occult. His story *Carmilla*, about lesbian vampires, has been filmed as *Blood and Roses* and *The Vampire Lovers*; *Uncle Silas* was filmed in 1949.

Le Gallienne, Eva (1899–). Distinguished American stage actress.
□Prince of Players 54. The Devil's Disciple 59. Resurrection 80.

Le Mat, Paul (c. 1952–). American leading man.
American Graffiti 73. Firehouse (TV) 74. Aloha Bobby and Rose 75. Citizen's Band 77. More American Graffiti 79. Melvin and Howard 80. Death Valley 81. Jimmy the Kid 82. Strange Invaders 83. The Hanoi Hilton 87. Private Investigations 87.

Le May, Alan (1899–1964). American writer.
Reap the Wild Wind 42. The Adventures of Mark Twain 44. Tap Roots 48. High Lonesome (& d) 50. Thunder in the Dust 51. I Dream of Jeannie 53. The Searchers (oa) 56, etc.

Le Mesurier, John (1912–1983). British character actor. Usually played bewildered professional men; a favourite for cameo roles from 1946.
Autobiography 1983: *A Jobbing Actor*.
Death in the Hand 48. Beautiful Stranger 54. Private's Progress 55. *Happy Is the Bride* 57. I Was Monty's Double 58. *School for Scoundrels* 60. *Only Two Can Play* 61. Invasion Quartet 62. The Pink Panther 63. The Moonspinners 64. Masquerade 65. Where the Spies Are 65. The Wrong Box 66. The Midas Run 69. *The Magic Christian* 70. Dad's Army 71. The Garnett Saga 72. Confessions of a Window Cleaner 75. Stand Up Virgin Soldiers 77. The Spaceman and

King Arthur 79. The Fiendish Plot of Dr Fu Manchu 80. A Married Man (TV) 83, many others.
TV series: *Dad's Army* 67–77.

Le Roy, Mervyn (1900–87). American director, former actor, in Hollywood from 1924.
Autobiography 1975: *Take One*.
Hot Stuff 27. Top Speed 28. Broken Dishes 29. *Little Caesar* 30. Broadminded 31. *Five Star Final* 32. Three on a Match 32. *I Am a Fugitive from a Chain Gang* 32. Two Seconds 32. *Tugboat Annie* 32. Gold Diggers of 1933. Hi Nellie 33. Oil for the Lamps of China 33. Hot to Handle 33. Sweet Adeline 34. Page Miss Glory 34. I Found Stella Parish 35. Anthony Adverse 36. Three Men on a Horse 36. *They Won't Forget* 37. Fools for Scandal 38. Stand Up and Fight (p only) 38. The Wizard of Oz (p only) 39. At the Circus (p only) 39. *Waterloo Bridge* 40. Escape 40. Blossoms in the Dust 41. Unholy Partners 41. Johnny Eager 41. *Random Harvest* 42. Madame Curie 43. Thirty Seconds over Tokyo 44; war service; Without Reservations 47. Homecoming 48. Little Women 49. Any Number Can Play 49. East Side West Side 50. Quo Vadis 51. Lovely To Look At 52. Million Dollar Mermaid 53. Rose Marie 54. Mister Roberts (co-d) 55. Strange Lady in Town (& p) 55. The Bad Seed (& p) 56. Toward the Unknown (& p) 56. No Time for Sergeants (& p) 58. Home Before Dark (& p) 59. The FBI Story (& p) 59. A Majority of One (& p) 60. The Devil at Four O'Clock 61. Gypsy (& p) 62. Mary Mary (& p) 63. Moment to Moment (& p) 65, etc.

Leach, Rosemary (1935–). British character actress, mostly on TV.
Brief Encounter (TV) 74. That'll Be the Day 74. SOS Titanic 79. The Jewel in the Crown (TV) 82. The Bride 84. Turtle Diary 85. A Room with a View 85, etc.

Leachman, Cloris (1926–). American character actress, mostly on TV.
Kiss Me Deadly 54. The Rack 56. The Chapman Report 62. Butch Cassidy and the Sundance Kid 69. WUSA 70. *The Last Picture Show* (AA) 71. Haunts of the Very Rich (TV) 72. Dillinger 73. Charley and the Angel 74. Daisy Miller 74. Hitch Hike (TV) 74. Crazy Mama 75. A Girl Named Sooner (TV) 75. Death Sentence (TV) 75. Young Frankenstein 75. Run Stranger Run 76. High Anxiety 78. SOS Titanic (TV) 79. The North Avenue Irregulars 79. Backstairs at the White House (TV) 79. Willa (TV) 79. Herbie Goes Bananas 80. History of the World Part One 81, Hansel and Gretel 87, etc.
TV series: Lassie (in fifties). The Mary Tyler Moore Show 70–73. *Phyllis* 75–76.

Leacock, Philip (1917–). British director, noted for his way with children; lost to American television.
□*The Brave Don't Cry* 52. Appointment in London 52. *The Kidnappers* 53. Escapade 55. The Spanish Gardener 56. High Tide at Noon 57. Innocent Sinners 58. The Rabbit Trap 58. Let No Man Write My Epitaph 59. Hand in Hand 60. Take a Giant Step 61. Reach for Glory 61. 13 West Street 62. The War Lover 63. Tamahine 63. Adam's Woman 70. The Birdmen (TV) 71. The Great Man's Whiskers (TV) 72. When Michael Calls (TV) 72. Key West (TV) 72. The Daughters of Joshua Cabe (TV) 72. Baffled (TV) 72. Dying Room Only (TV) 73. Killer on Board (TV) 77. Wild and Wooly (TV) 78. The Curse of King Tut's Tomb (TV) 80. Angel City (TV) 80.

Leacock, Richard (1921–). British-born cameraman and director, brother of Philip Leacock. Worked with Flaherty and became associated with the 'cinema vérité' school.
Primary 60. The Chair 62. Quints 63. Chiefs 68, etc.

leader. Length of blank film joined to the beginning of a reel for lacing up in projector. 'Academy' leaders give a numbered countdown to the start of action.

Lean, David (1908–). Distinguished British director, former editor, in films from 1928.
□In Which We Serve (co-d) 42. This Happy Breed 44. *Blithe Spirit* 45. *Brief Encounter* 46. *Great Expectations* 46. *Oliver Twist* 48. The Passionate Friends 48. Madeleine 49. *The Sound Barrier* (& p) 51. *Hobson's Choice* (& p) 54. *Summer Madness* 55. *The Bridge on the River Kwai* (AA) 57. *Lawrence of Arabia* (AA) 62. *Dr Zhivago* 65. *Ryan's Daughter* 70. A Passage to India (AAN d, AAN w, AAN ed) 84.
❀ For his understanding of the art of cinema, despite his final submergence of his sensitive talent in pretentious but empty spectaculars. *Great Expectations*.

¶ *D.L.:* I hope the money men don't find out that I'd pay them to let me do this.
Inside every Lean film there is a fat film screaming to get out.—*Anon*
D.L.: I wouldn't take the advice of a lot of so-called critics on how to shoot a close-up of a teapot.
D.L.: Actors can be a terrible bore on the set, though I enjoy having dinner with them.

Lear, Norman (1926–). American producer.
Divorce American Style 67. The Night They Raided Minsky's 68. Start The Revolution Without Me 69, etc.
TV series: *All in the Family* 71. *Maude* 72, many others.

Learned, Michael (1939–). Motherly American character actress who scored on TV in *The Waltons* (72–81) and briefly in *Nurse* (82).
□Hurricane (TV) 74. It Couldn't Happen to a Nicer Guy (TV) 74. Widow (TV) 76. Little Mo (TV) 78. Touched by Love 80.

Leasor, James (1923–). British thriller writer whose Dr Jason Love was brought to the screen in 1964 in *Where the Spies Are*.

Leaud, Jean-Pierre (1944–). French leading actor who began as a boy star.
Les Quatre Cents Coups 59. Love at Twenty 61. Masculin-Feminin 66. La Chinoise 67. Stolen Kisses 68. Pigsty 69. Last Tango in Paris 72. Day for Night 73. Love on the Run 79. Detective 84. Treasure Island 85. With all Hands 86, etc.

Leaves from Satan's Book (Denmark 1921). A compendium of stories illustrating the work of the devil through the ages; written and directed by Carl Dreyer.

Leavitt, Sam (1917–84). American cinematographer.
The Thief 52. *A Star is Born* 54. Carmen Jones 54. The Man with the Golden Arm 55. *The Defiant Ones* (AA) 58. Anatomy of a Murder 59. Exodus 60. Advise and Consent 62. Two on a Guillotine 64. Major Dundee 65. Brainstorm 65. An American Dream 66. Guess Who's Coming to Dinner 67. The Desperados 68. The Grasshopper 70. Star Spangled Girl 71. The Man in the Glass Booth 75, etc.

Lebedeff, Ivan (1899–1953). Russian character actor, former diplomat, in US from 1925.
The Sorrows of Satan 27. Midnight Mystery 30. Blonde Bombshell 33. China Seas 35. History Is Made at Night 37. Hotel for Women 39. The Shanghai Gesture 41. They Are Guilty 45. The Snows of Kilimanjaro 52, many others.

Leclerc, Ginette (1912–). Sulky-looking French stage and screen actress.
Prison sans Barreaux 38. *La Femme du Boulanger* 38. *Le Corbeau* 43. Le Plaisir 51. Les Amants du Tage 54. Gas-Oil 55. Le Cave Se Rebiffe 61. Goto, Island of Love 68. Tropic of Cancer 69.

Ledebur, Friedrich (*c.*1908–87). Austrian actor of eccentric roles.
Moby Dick 56. Roots of Heaven 58. The Blue Max 66. Alfred the Great 69. Juliet of the Spirits 69, etc.

Lederer, Charles (1906–76). American screenwriter, in Hollywood from 1931.
The Front Page 31. Topaze 33. Comrade X 40. His Girl Friday 40. Ride the Pink Horse 47. *Kiss of Death* 47. The Thing 52. It Started with a Kiss 58. The Spirit of St Louis 58. Can Can 59. Ocean's Eleven 61. Mutiny on the Bounty 62, many others.
□AS DIRECTOR: Fingers at the Window 42. On the Loose 51. Never Steal Anything Small (& w) 58, etc.

Lederer, Francis (1906–). Czech-born leading man, in Hollywood from 1933, after European stage and film experience.
Pandora's Box (Ger.) 28. Atlantic (Ger.) 30. The Bracelet (Ger.) 32. The Pursuit of Happiness 34. It's All Yours 36. The Lone Wolf in Paris 37. Midnight 38. *Confessions of a Nazi Spy* 39. The Man I Married 40. The Bridge of San Luis Rey 44. A Voice in the Wind 45. The Diary of a Chambermaid 45. Million Dollar Weekend 48. Captain Carey USA 49. A Woman of Distinction 50. Stolen Identity 53. Lisbon 56. The Return of Dracula 58. Terror Is a Man 59, etc.

Lederman, D. Ross (1895–1972). American director, former prop man for Mack Sennett.
Man Hunter 30. Riding Tornado 32. Glamour for Sale 40. The Body Disappears 41. Strange Alibi 41. Shadows on the Stairs 43. Key Witness 47, etc.

Lee, Anna (1914–) (Joanna Winnifrith). British leading lady, in US since 1939.
Ebb Tide 32. The Camels Are Coming 36. King Solomon's Mines 37. The Four Just Men 39. My Life with Caroline 41. Summer Storm 44. Fort Apache 48. Whatever Happened to Baby Jane? 62. The Sound of Music 65. Seven Women 65. In Like Flint 67, many others.

Lee, Belinda (1935–1961). Blonde British starlet trained for stardom by Rank but given

poor material: appeared in continental semi-spectaculars and died in car crash.
The Runaway Bus 54. The Belles of St Trinian's 54. Man of the Moment 55. Who Done It? 55. The Feminine Touch 56. The Secret Place 56. The Big Money 56. Miracle in Soho 57. Dangerous Exile 57. Nor the Moon by Night 58. Les Drageurs 59. Nights of Lucretia Borgia 59. Carthage in Flames 61, etc.

Lee, Bernard (1908–1981). British character actor with solid, friendly personality, on stage from 1926. In films, often a sergeant or a superintendent . . . or 'M' in the James Bond films.
The River House Mystery 35. The Terror 37. Spare a Copper 40. Once a Crook 41; war service; The Courtneys of Curzon Street 47. *The Fallen Idol* 48. Quartet 48. *The Third Man* 49. The Blue Lamp 50. Appointment with Venus 51. The Gift Horse 52. The Purple Plain 54. *Father Brown* 54. The Battle of the River Plate 56. Dunkirk 58. Danger Within 59. The Angry Silence 59. The Secret Partner 60. Whistle Down the Wind 61. *Dr No* 62. Two Left Feet 63. From Russia with Love 63. Ring of Spies 63. Goldfinger 64. The Legend of Young Dick Turpin 65. Thunderball 65. The Spy Who Came In from the Cold 65. You Only Live Twice 66. The Raging Moon 70. Dulcima 71. Frankenstein and the Monster from Hell 73. The Man with the Golden Gun 74. Beauty and the Beast 76. The Spy who Loved Me 77. Moonraker 79, many others.

Lee, Billy (1930–). American child star of the thirties.
Wagon Wheels 34. Coconut Grove 38. The Biscuit Eater 40. Hold Back the Dawn 41. Mrs Wiggs of the Cabbage Patch 42, etc.

Lee, Bruce (1940–73) (Lee Yenn Kam). Diminutive Chinese-American leading man and practitioner of the martial arts.
After comparative failure in Hollywood (a bit part in *Marlowe* 69, a supporting role in a TV series *The Green Hornet* 68) he went to Hong Kong and became a sensation in 'chop socky' movies.
Fist of Fury 72. The Big Boss 72. Enter the Dragon 73. The Way of the Dragon 73. Game of Death (posthumously re-edited) 79, etc.

Lee, Canada (1907–1952). (Lionel Canegata). Black American actor.
□Lifeboat 43. Body and Soul 47. Lost Boundaries 49. Cry the Beloved Country 52.

Lee, Christopher (1922–). Gaunt British actor whose personality lends itself best to sinister or horrific parts. Seems to have made more films than any other living actor, and has certainly played most of the known monsters.
Autobiography 1977: *Tall, Dark and Gruesome.*
Corridor of Mirrors 47. Hamlet 48. They Were Not Divided 49. Prelude to Fame 50. Valley of Eagles 51. The Crimson Pirate 52. Moulin Rouge 53. The Dark Avenger 54. Private's Progress 55. Alias John Preston 56. Moby Dick 56. *The Curse of Frankenstein* (as the monster) 56. Ill Met by Moonlight 57. The Traitor 57. A Tale of Two Cities 57. *Dracula* (title role) 58. Corridors of Blood 58. The Hound of the Baskervilles (as Sir Henry) 59. The Man Who Could Cheat Death 59. *The Mummy* (title role) 59. Beat Girl 60. City of the Dead 60. The Hands of Orlac 60. Taste of Fear 61. The Terror of the Tongs 61. The Devil's Daffodil 62. Pirates of Blood River 62. Sherlock Holmes and the Deadly Necklace (Ger.) 62. The Gorgon 63. Dr Terror's House of Horrors 63. She 65. The Face of Fu Manchu 65. The Skull 65. Dracula Prince of Darkness 65. Rasputin the Mad Monk 65. Theatre of Death 66. Night of the Big Heat 67. The Devil Rides Out 68. Curse of the Crimson Altar 68. Julius Caesar 70. I Monster 71. Dracula AD 1972 72. The Wicker Man 73. The Satanic Rites of Dracula 73. The Three Musketeers 74. The Man with the Golden Gun 74. Diagnosis Murder 75. To the Devil a Daughter 75. Killer Force 75. Airport 77 77. Return from Witch Mountain 76. The Silent Flute 78. The Pirate (TV) 78. Starship Invasions 78. The Passage 78. Arabian Adventure 79. Circle of Iron 79. 1941 79. Serial 80. The Salamander 80. An Eye for an Eye 81. Safari 3000 82. The House of Long Shadows 83. The Return of Captain Invincible 83. Howling II 85. The Rosebud Beach Hotel 85. Jocks 86, etc.

Lee, Davey (1925–). American child actor of the early talkies.
The Singing Fool 28. Sonny Boy 29. The Squealer 30, etc.

Lee, Dixie (1911–1952) (Wilma Wyatt). American leading lady, wife of Bing Crosby.
Not for Sale 24. Movietone Follies 29. The Big Party 30. No Limit 31. Manhattan Love Song 34. Love in Bloom 35, etc.

Lee, Dorothy (1911–). American leading lady of the thirties, especially associated with Wheeler and Wolsey.
Syncopation 29. Rio Rita 29. The Cuckoos 30. Half Shot at Sunrise 30. Cracked Nuts 31. Caught Plastered 31. Girl Crazy 32. Take a Chance 33. Hips, Hips Hooray 34. The Rainmakers 35. Silly Billies 36. Twelve Crowded Hours 39, etc.

Lee, Gypsy Rose (1913–1970) (Louise Hovick). American burlesque artiste, on stage from six years old: her early life, glamorized, is recounted in *Gypsy* 62, based on her 1957 book.
□You Can't Have Everything 37. Ali Baba Goes to Town 38. My Lucky Star 39. Belle of the Yukon 44. Babes in Baghdad 52. Screaming Mimi 57. Wind Across the Everglades 58. The Stripper 62. The Trouble with Angels 66.
TV series: The Pruitts of Southampton 66.

¶ *G.R.L.:* Royalties are all very well, but shaking the beads brings in the money quicker.
G.R.L.: God is love, but get it in writing.

Lee, Jack (1913–). British director, originally in documentaries.
Close Quarters 44. Children on Trial 46. The Woman in the Hall 47. *The Wooden Horse* (co-d) 50. Turn the Key Softly 53. *A Town Like Alice* 56. Robbery under Arms 57. The Captain's Table 58. Circle of Deception 61, etc.

Lee, Lila (1902–1973) (Augusta Apple). Demure American leading lady of the twenties.
The Cruise of the Make Believes 18. Male and Female 19. Terror Island 20. Blood and Sand 22. Million Dollar Mystery 25. Queen of the Night Clubs 29, etc.

Lee, Michele (1942–) (Michele Dusiak). American leading lady and singer, with stage experience.
How to Succeed in Business 67. The Love Bug 69. The Comic 69. Dark Victory (TV) 76. Bud and Lou (TV) 78.
TV series: Knots Landing 80.

Lee, Norman (–). British low-budget director.
Streets of London 29. Pride of the Force 32. French Leave 37. Almost a Honeymoon 38. Murder in Soho 39. The Door with Seven Locks 40. The Monkey's Paw 48. The Case of Charles Peace 49. The Girl Who Couldn't Quite 50, etc.

Lee, Peggy (1920–) (Norma Egstrom). American night-club singer, in occasional films.
Mr Music 50. The Jazz Singer 53. Pete Kelly's Blues 55. Lady and the Tramp (voice only) 56, etc.

Lee, Rowland V. (1891–1975). American director, in films from 1918.
Alice Adams 26. Barbed Wire 26. The Mysterious Dr Fu Manchu 29. *Zoo in Budapest* 33. *The Count of Monte Cristo* 34. Cardinal Richelieu 35. The Three Musketeers 35. Service de Luxe 38. *Son of Frankenstein* 39. Tower of London 39. Son of Monte Cristo 41. The Bridge of San Luis Rey 44. Captain Kidd 45. The Big Fisherman (p only) 59, etc.

Lee-Thompson, J. (1914–). British director, former actor and playwright.
□The Middle Watch (w) 36. For Them That Trespass (w) 48. Murder without Crime (wd) 50. *The Yellow Balloon* (wd) 52. The Weak and the Wicked (wd) 53. As Long As They're Happy (d) 54. For Better For Worse (d) 54. An Alligator Named Daisy (d) 55. Yield to the Night (d) 56. The Good Companions (co-pd) 57. No Trees in the Street (d) 58. Woman in a Dressing Gown (d) 59. Tiger Bay (d) 59. Northwest Frontier (d) 59. Ice Cold in Alex (d) 60. I Aim at the Stars (d) (US) 60. *The Guns of Navarone* (d) 61. Cape Fear (d) (US) 61. Taras Bulba (d) (US) 62. Kings of the Sun (d) (US) 63. What a Way To Go (d) (US) 64. John Goldfarb Please Come Home (d) (US) 65. Return from the Ashes (pd) 65. Eye of the Devil (d) 66. Mackenna's Gold (d) (US) 68. Before Winter Comes (d) 68. The Chairman (d) 69. Country Dance (d) 70. Conquest of The Planet of the Apes (d) (US) 72. A Great American Tragedy (TV) 72. Huckleberry Finn (d) (US) 74. The Reincarnation of Peter Proud (d) (US) 74. The Blue Knight (TV) (d) 75. St Ives (d) 75. Widow (TV) (d) 76. The White Buffalo (d) (US) 77. The Greek Tycoon 78. The Passage 78. Cabo Blanco 79. Happy Birthday to Me 81. Ten to Midnight 83. The Ambassador 84. King Solomon's Mines 85. Murphy's Law 86. Firewalker 86.

Leech, Richard (1922–) (Richard McClelland). British character actor, often as army or air force officer.
The Dam Busters 55. A Night to Remember

57. The Good Companions 57. Ice Cold in Alex 59. The Horse's Mouth 59. Tunes of Glory 60. The Wild and the Willing 62. I Thank a Fool 63. The Fighting Prince of Donegal 66. Young Winston 72. Gandhi 82. The Shooting Party 84. A Woman of Substance (TV) 85, etc.

Leeds, Andrea (1914–74) (Antoinette Lees). American leading lady of the late thirties.
Come and Get It 36. *Stage Door* 37. The Goldwyn Follies 39. Letter of Introduction 39. Swanee River 39, etc.

Leeds, Herbert I. (c. 1900–1954) (Herbert I. Levy). American director of second features, former editor.
Mr Moto in Danger Island 38. Island in the Sky 38. The Cisco Kid and the Lady 39. Manila Calling 42. *Time to Kill* 43. It Shouldn't Happen to a Dog 46. Let's Live Again 48. Father's Wild Game 51, etc.

Legends. Over the years a number of Hollywood legends have built up, never proved or disproved. Here is a selection:
George Raft was a protégé of the Mafia.
James Dean is not really dead but on a life support machine.
Walt Disney is cryonically preserved.
Louella Parsons witnessed the murder of Thomas Ince by W. R. Hearst.
Marilyn Monroe was killed by the CIA because of her association with John Kennedy.
Cary Grant and Randolph Scott were lovers.
Ida Lupino is bald.

Legg, Stuart (1910–). British documentarist and administrator. From 1932 with GPO Film Unit and Empire Marketing Board. 1939–45: National Film Board of Canada. 1953 on: director of Film Centre Ltd.

Leggatt, Alison (1904–). British character actress, mainly on stage.
This Happy Breed 44. Marry Me 47. The Card 52. Touch and Go 55. Never Take Sweets from a Stranger 60. Nothing but the Best 64. The Seven Per Cent Solution 76, etc.

Legrand, Michel (1931–). French composer.
Lola 61. Eva 62. Vivre sa Vie 62. La Baie des Anges 63. *The Umbrellas of Cherbourg* 64. Bande à Part 64. Une Femme Mariée 65. Les Demoiselles de Rochefort 67. Ice Station Zebra 68. Peau d'Ane 70. *Summer of 42* (AA) 71. A Time for Loving (& a) 71. One is a Lonely Number 72. Portnoy's Complaint 72. Cops and Robbers 73. The Three Musketeers 74. Ode to Billy Joe 75. The Other Side of Midnight 77. Atlantic City USA 80. Falling in Love Again 80. The Hunter 80. The Mountain Men 80. Best Friends 82. Yentl 83, etc.

Lehman, Ernest (1920–). American screenwriter.
Inside Story 48. Executive Suite 54. Sabrina 54. *The Sweet Smell of Success* 57. *North by Northwest* 59. *The Prize* 63. The Sound of Music 65. Who's Afraid of Virginia Woolf? (& p) 66. Hello Dolly (& p) 69. Portnoy's Complaint (& pd) 72. Family Plot 76. Black Sunday 77, etc.

Lehmann, Beatrix (1898–1979). British character actress, often of withdrawn eccentrics; film appearances few.
The Passing of the Third Floor Back 36. Black Limelight 38. The Rat 38. The Key 58. Psyche 59 64. The Spy who Came in from the Cold 66. Staircase 69, etc.

Lehmann, Carla (1917–). Canadian leading lady, in British films of the forties.
So This Is London 39. Cottage to Let 41. Talk About Jacqueline 42. Candlelight in Algeria 44. 29 Acacia Avenue 45. Fame Is the Spur 47, etc.

Leiber, Fritz (1883–1949). American Shakespearean actor who played many supporting roles in films.
A Tale of Two Cities 35. Anthony Adverse 36. The Hunchback of Notre Dame 40. Phantom of the Opera 43. Humoresque 46. Another Part of the Forest 48, etc.

Leibman, Ron (1937–). American character actor of the seventies.
The Hot Rock 72. Slaughterhouse Five 72. The Super Cops 73. Your Three Minutes Are Up 74. The Art of Crime (TV) 75. Won Ton Ton 76. A Question of Guilt (TV) 78. Norma Rae 79. Up the Academy 80. Rivkin, Bounty Hunter (TV) 81. Zorro the Gay Blade 81, etc.
Romantic Comedy 83. Rhinestone 84, etc.
TV series: *Kaz* 78.

Leigh, Janet (1927–) (Jeanette Morrison). Capable American leading lady of the fifties and sixties; began as a peaches-and-cream heroine but graduated to sharper roles.

□The Romance of Rosy Ridge 47. If Winter Comes 47. Hills of Home 47. Words and Music 48. Act of Violence 48. Little Women 49. *That Forsyte Woman* 49. The Doctor and the Girl 49. The Red Danube 49. Holiday Affair 49. Strictly Dishonourable 51. Angels in the Outfield 51. Two Tickets to Broadway 51. It's a Big Country 51. Just this Once 52. Scaramouche 52. Fearless Fagan 52. The Naked Spur 53. Confidentially Connie 53. *Houdini* 53. Walking My Baby Back Home 54. Prince Valiant 54. Living it Up 54. The Black Shield of Falworth 54. Rogue Cop 54. Pete Kelly's Blues 55. *My Sister Eileen* 55. Safari (GB) 56. Jet Pilot 57. Touch of Evil 58. The Vikings 58. The Perfect Furlough 58. Who was that Lady? 60. *Psycho* 60. Pepe 60. The Manchurian Candidate 62. Bye Bye Birdie 62. Wives and Lovers 63. Three on a Couch 66. Harper 66. Kid Rodelo 66. An American Dream 66. Hello Down There 68. The Spy in the Green Hat 68. Grand Slam 68. Honeymoon with a Stranger (TV) 69. The House on Greenapple Road (TV) 70. The Monk (TV) 70. The Deadly Dream (TV) 71. One is a Lonely Number 72. Night of the Lepus 72. Murdock's Gang (TV) 73. Murder at the World Series (TV) 77. Telethon (TV) 77. Boardwalk 79. The Fog 80. The Thrill of Genius 85.

Leigh, Suzanna (1945–). British leading lady.
Boeing Boeing 66. Paradise Hawaiian Style 66. Deadlier Than the Male 67. Lost Continent 68. Lust for a Vampire 70. The Fiend 71, etc.

Leigh, Vivien (1913–1967) (Vivien Hartley). Distinguished British leading lady whose stage and screen career was limited by delicate health; for many years the wife of Laurence Olivier.
Biographies: *Light of a Star* by Gwen Robyns, 1973; *Vivien Leigh* by Anne Edwards, 1977.
□Things Are Looking Up 34. The Village Squire 35. Gentleman's Agreement 35. Look Up and Laugh 35. Fire Over England 36. *Dark Journey* 37. Storm in a Teacup 37. St Martin's Lane 38. Twenty-One Days 38. *A Yank at Oxford* 38. *Gone with the Wind* (AA: as Scarlett O'Hara) (US) 39. Waterloo Bridge (US) 40. *Lady Hamilton* (US) 41. *Caesar and Cleopatra* 45. Anna Karenina 48. *A Streetcar Named Desire* (AA) (US) 51. The Deep Blue Sea 55. The Roman Spring of Mrs Stone 61. Ship of Fools (US) 65.

❊ For one performance which made each of her later ones an event to be savoured. *Gone with the Wind.*

Leigh-Hunt, Barbara (1935–). British character actress.
Frenzy 72. Henry VIII and his Six Wives 72. A Bequest to the Nation 73. O Heavenly Dog 80, etc.

Leigh-Hunt, Ronald (c. 1920–). Smooth British supporting actor.
Tiger by the Tail 53. Shadow of a Man 55. A Touch of Larceny 59. Sink the Bismarck 60. Piccadilly Third Stop 61. The Truth About Spring 65. Hostile Witness 67. Le Mans 71, many others.
TV series: Sir Lancelot (as King Arthur) 56.

Leighton, Margaret (1922–1976). British leading actress on stage from 1938.
□ Bonnie Prince Charlie 47. *The Winslow Boy* 48. Under Capricorn 49. The Astonished Heart 50. The Elusive Pimpernel 50. Calling Bulldog Drummond 51. Home at Seven 52. The Holly and the Ivy 52. The Good Die Young 54. Carrington VC 54. The Teckman Mystery 54. The Constant Husband 55. The Passionate Stranger 57. The Sound and the Fury 58. The Second Man (TV) 59. The Waltz of the Toreadors 62. The Third Secret 63. The Best Man 64. Seven Women 65. The Loved One 65. The Madwoman of Chaillot 69. The Go-Between 70. Zee and Co 71. Lady Caroline Lamb 72. Bequest to the Nation 73. Frankenstein: the True Story (TV) 73. From Beyond the Grave 73. Galileo 74. Great Expectations 75. Trial by Combat 76.

Leisen, Mitchell (1898–1972). American director, former set designer; his films are mostly romantic trifles, but many have considerable pictorial values.
Biography 1972: *Hollywood Director* by David Chierichetti.
□*Cradle Song* 33. *Death Takes a Holiday* 34. Murder at the Vanities 34. Behold My Wife 35. Four Hours to Kill 35. Hands across the Table 35. Thirteen Hours by Air 36. The Big Broadcast of 1937. Swing High Swing Low 37. *Easy Living* 37. The Big Broadcast of 1938 37. Artists and Models Abroad 38. *Midnight* 39. Remember the Night 40. *Arise My Love* 40. I Wanted Wings 41. *Hold Back the Dawn* 41. The Lady Is Willing 42. Take a Letter Darling 42. No Time for Love (& p) 43. *Lady in the Dark* (also w) 44. *Frenchman's Creek* 44. Practically Yours (& p) 44. *Kitty* 45.

Masquerade in Mexico 45. To Each His Own 46. Suddenly It's Spring 46. Golden Earrings 47. Dream Girl 48. Bride of Vengeance 49. Song of Surrender 49. Captain Carey USA 50. No Man of Her Own (& w) 50. The Mating Season (51). Darling How Could You? 51. Young Man with Ideas 52. Tonight We Sing 53. Bedevilled 55. The Girl Most Likely 57.

'He found himself in the unenviable position of a diamond cutter working with lumpy coal.'—*Andrew Sarris, 1968*

❀ For adding style to comedies and dramas that badly needed it. *Kitty.*

Leiser, Erwin (1923–). Swedish documentarist.
Mein Kampf (Blodige Tiden) 59. Murder by Signature (Eichmann and the Third Reich) 61, etc.

Leister, Frederick (1885–1970). British character actor, on stage from 1906, screen from twenties. Usually played distinguished and kindly professional men.
Dreyfus 30. The Iron Duke 35. Goodbye Mr Chips 39. The Prime Minister 41. *Dear Octopus* 43. *The Hundred Pound Window* 43. The Captive Heart 46. Quartet 48. The End of the Affair 54. Left, Right and Centre 59. A French Mistress 63, many others.

Leith, Virginia (1932–). American leading lady of the fifties.
Black Widow 54. Violent Saturday 55. White Feather 55. A Kiss Before Dying 56. On the Threshold of Space 56. The Beast that Wouldn't Die 63. First Love 77, etc.

Lejeune, C. A. (1897–1973). British film critic, whose work now tends to seem blithe but facetious. A collection of reviews was published in 1947 as *Chestnuts in My Lap.*

Lelouch, Claude (1937–). French director with lush visual style; internationally fashionable in the mid-sixties, but overreached himself.
□Le Propre de l'Homme 60. Une Fille et des Fusils 63. Avec des Si 64. Secret Paris 64. *Un Homme et Une Femme* (AA w, d) 66. *Vivre Pour Vivre* 67. Challenge in the Snow 68. Far from Vietnam 69. A Man I Like 69. Life Love Death 69. Le Rose et le Noir 70. The Crook 71. Smic, Smac, Smoc 71. Adventure is Adventure 72. *La Bonne Année* 73. And Now My Love 75. Seven Suspects for Murder 77. Another Man, Another Chance 77. The Good and The Bad 77. A Nous deux 79. Les Uns et les Autres 80. Edith and Marcel 83.
Long Live Life 84. Departure, Return 85. A Man and a Woman: 20 years later 86.

¶ *C.L.:* Film-making is like spermatozoa: only one in a million makes it.

C.L.: One day I'll make a film for the critics, when I have money to lose.

Lembeck, Harvey (1925–1982). American character actor.
The Frogmen 51. You're In the Navy Now 53. Back at the Front 53. Stalag 17 54. Life after Dark 55. Sail a Crooked Ship 62. Bikini Beach 65. There is No Thirteen 77, etc.
TV series: Bilko. Ensign O'Toole.

Lemmon, Jack (1925–). American light comedy leading actor with Broadway experience: sometimes typed in mildly lecherous or otherwise sex-fraught roles.
Biographies: *Lemmon* by Don Widener, 1975; *The Films of Jack Lemmon* by Joe Baltake, 1977.
□*It Should Happen to You* 53. Three for the Show 53. Phffft 54. My Sister Eileen 55. *Mister Roberts* (AA) 55. You Can't Run Away From It 56. Cowboy 57. Fire Down Below 57. Operation Mad Ball 57. Bell, Book and Candle 58. It Happened to Jane 58. *Some Like It Hot* 59. The Wackiest Ship in the Army 60. *The Apartment* 60. The Notorious Landlady 62. Days of Wine and Roses 62. *Irma La Douce* 63. Under the Yum Yum Tree 64. Good Neighbour Sam 64. How to Murder Your Wife 65. *The Great Race* 65. The Fortune Cookie 66. Luv 67. *The Odd Couple* 68. The April Fools 69. The Out-of-Towners 69. *Kotch* (d only) 71. The War Between Men and Women 72. Avanti 72. Save the Tiger (AA) 73. The Front Page 74. The Prisoner of Second Avenue 75. The Entertainer 75. Alex and the Gypsy 76. Airport 77 77. *The China Syndrome* (BFA) 79. Tribute 80. Buddy Buddy 81. *Missing* 82. Mass Appeal 84. Macaroni 85. That's Life 86.
TV series: Heaven for Betsy 52. Twist of Fate 62.

¶ *J.L.:* The worst part about being me is when people want me to make them laugh.

Famous line (*Mister Roberts*): Now, what's all this crud about no movie tonight?

Lemont, John (1914–). British director.
The Green Buddha 54. And Women Shall Weep (& co-w) 59. The Shakedown (& co-w) 59. Konga 60. Frightened City (& co-w) 61, etc.

Leni, Paul (1885–1929). German director, former set designer; died in Hollywood.
Waxworks 24. *The Cat and the Canary* 27. The Man Who Laughs 28. The Chinese Parrot 28. The Last Warning 29, etc.

Lenica, Jan (1928–). Polish animator.
Dom 58. Monsieur Tete 59. Janko the Musician 60. Rhinosceros 63. A 64, etc.

Lenin (1870–1924) (Vladimir Ilyich Ulyanov). Russian statesman, the power behind the revolution. Little footage of him exists, but he has been played by various actors in such politically-based semi-fictions as *Lenin in October, Lenin in 1918* and *Lenin in Poland*. Michael Bryant played him in *Nicholas and Alexandra*.

Lennart, Isobel (1915–1971). American screenwriter.
Lost Angel 44. Anchors Aweigh 45. East Side West Side 49. Skirts Ahoy 52. Latin Lovers 54. Inn of the Sixth Happiness 58. The Sundowners 60. Period of Adjustment 62. Funny Girl 68, many others.

Lenska, Rula (1947–). Polish born, British leading lady, much on TV.
Soft Beds Hard Battles 73. Alfie Darling 75. The Deadly Females 76, etc.

Lenya, Lotte (1899–1981) (Caroline Blamauer). Austrian character actress; also inimitable singer of her husband Kurt Weill's songs.
Die Dreigroschenoper 31. The Roman Spring of Mrs Stone 61. *From Russia with Love* 63. The Appointment 69. Semi-Tough 77, etc.

Lenz, Kay (1953–). American leading lady of the seventies.
Breezy 73. Lisa Bright and Dark (TV) 73. White Line Fever 75. The Great Scout and Cathouse Thursday 76. Rich Man Poor Man (TV) 76. The Passage 79, etc.

Lenz, Rick (1939–). American actor.
Cactus Flower 70. Where Does It Hurt? 72. The Shootist 76.

Leon, Valerie (–). British leading lady.
Smashing Time 67. Carry On Up the Jungle 70. *Blood from the Mummy's Tomb* 71. Carry On Matron 72. The Spy Who Loved Me 77. Revenge of the Pink Panther 78, etc.

Leonard, Herbert B. (1922–). American independent TV producer; best-known series include *Rin Tin Tin, Circus Boy, Naked City, Route 66*.

Leonard, Murray (1898–1970). American burlesque comedian who played small parts in films, notably with Abbott and Costello, who worked up several of his old routines.
Lost in a Harem 44. A Thousand and One Nights 45. Bring Your Smile Along 55, etc.

Leonard, Robert Z. (1889–1968). American director (former actor), in Hollywood from 1915. Showed care but not much imagination.
The Waning Sex 27. The Demi-Bride 27. Adam and Evil 28. Tea for Three 29. Susan Lenox 31. *Strange Interval* 32. *Dancing Lady* 33. Peg O' My Heart 33. Outcast Lady 34. *The Great Ziegfeld* 36. Piccadilly Jim 37. Escapade 37. *Maytime* 38. The Firefly 38. New Moon (& p) 40. *Pride and Prejudice* 40. Ziegfeld Girl 41. When Ladies Meet (& p) 41. We Were Dancing 42. Stand By for Action 42. The Man from Down Under 43. Marriage Is a Private Affair 44. Weekend at the Waldorf 45. The Secret Heart 46. B.F.'s Daughter 48. The Bride 48. In the Good Old Summertime 49. Nancy Goes to Rio 49. Duchess of Idaho 50. Everything I Have Is Yours 52. The Clown 53. The King's Thief 55. Kelly and Me 56. Beautiful But Dangerous (It.) 56, others.

Leonard, Sheldon (1907–) (Sheldon Bershad). American character actor who played Runyonesque gangsters for years; finally quit to produce TV series.
Another Thin Man 39. Buy Me that Town 41. Street of Chance 42. *Lucky Jordan* 42. To Have and Have Not 44. Zombies on Broadway 45. Somewhere in the Night 46. Violence 47. The Gangster 47. Take One False Step 49. Behave Yourself 51. *Stop You're Killing Me* 52. Money from Home 54. Guys and Dolls 55. Pocketful of Miracles 61. The Brink's Job 78, many others.
TV series: The Duke. Danny Thomas. Big Eddie.

Leone, Sergio (1921–). Italian director who came to the fore internationally via his savage westerns on the American pattern.
The Colossus of Rhodes 61. *A Fistful of Dollars* 64. For a Few Dollars More 65. The Good The Bad and The Ugly 67. Once Upon a Time in the West 69. A Fistful of Dynamite 72. Once Upon a Time in America 84, etc.

Leontovich, Eugenie (1894–). Russian stage actress in occasional American films.

Four Sons 40. The Men in Her Life 41. Anything Can Happen 52. The World in His Arms 53. Homicidal 61, etc.

The Leopard (Italy 1963). An ambitious production based on Lampedusa's complex historical novel about Italian politics and noble life at the time of Garibaldi. Burt Lancaster made a somewhat unconvincing Italian nobleman, and the film in its international version was not popular; but Luchino Visconti's direction and Giuseppe Rotunno's cinematography were praised.

leprechauns have made rare but effective screen appearances in the persons of Cecil Kellaway (*Luck of the Irish*), Jimmy O'Dea (*Darby O'Gill and the Little People*), Don Beddoe (*Jack the Giant Killer*) and Tommy Steele (*Finian's Rainbow*).

Lerner, Alan Jay (1918–86). American lyricist and writer.
An American in Paris (w) (AA) 51. Gigi (score) (AA) 58. My Fair Lady (script and score in collaboration) (AA) 64. Camelot (script and score in collaboration) 67. On a Clear Day You Can See Forever (& p) 70. The Little Prince 74, others.

Lerner, Carl (c. 1905–1975). American editor.
Cry Murder 50. On the Bowery 56. *Twelve Angry Men* 57. The Fugitive Kind 59. Something Wild 61. All the Way Home 63. The Swimmer 68. The Angel Levine 70. Klute 72, etc.
Directed one film: Black Like Me 64.

Lerner, Irving (1909–1976). American director, former cameraman and documentarist.
□Muscle Beach 46. Man Crazy 54. Edge of Fury 58. *Murder by Contract* 58. City of Fear 59. Studs Lonigan 60. Cry of Battle 63. The Royal Hunt of the Sun 69.

Lerner, Michael (–). American character actor.
Alex in Wonderland 70. The Candidate 72. Busting 74. St Ives 76. Outlaw Blues 77. Borderline 80. Coast to Coast 80. The Baltimore Bullet 80. The Postman Always Rings Twice 81. National Lampoon's Class Reunion 82. Strange Invaders 83. Rita Hayworth: The Love Goddess (as Harry Cohn 83. Movers and Shakers 84.

Les Misérables: see under *Misérables, Les*.

lesbianism came fully into its own with the filming of *The Killing of Sister George*; but for many years it was unthinkable as a screen subject. *These Three* in 1936 had to be so changed that it was almost unrecognizable as a version of *The Children's Hour*; and the matter was scarcely broached again until the fifties, when the French brought it up in *Olivia* and *The Girl with the Golden Eyes*. The first Hollywood film to bring the subject to our notice was *A Walk on the Wild Side* 62; since then there have been more or less discreet references in *The Haunting, The Balcony, Lilith, The Silence, Alyse and Chloe, The Vampire Lovers, Beyond the Valley of the Dolls, La Religieuse, The Group, Tony Rome, The Fox, Therese and Isabelle, Baby Love, The Smashing Bird I Used to Know*, and *Once Is Not Enough*; while *The Children's Hour* was filmed again, this time with its full force. In 1982 *Personal Best* again brought the subject into the open.

Lesley, Carole (1935–1974) (Maureen Rippingdale). British leading lady briefly groomed for stardom.
These Dangerous Years 57. Woman in a Dressing-Gown 57. No Trees in the Street 59. Doctor in Love 60. What a Whopper 62. The Pot Carriers 62, etc.

Leslie, Bethel (1930–). American leading actress, mainly on TV.
The Rabbit Trap 58. Captain Newman 63. A Rage to Live 65. The Molly Maguires 69. Old Boyfriends 79, etc.
TV series: The Richard Boone Show 63. The Doctors 66.

Leslie, Joan (1925–) (Joan Brodell). Pert, pretty American leading lady of the forties; in vaudeville from childhood.
Camille (debut) 36. Men with Wings 38. Foreign Correspondent 40. High Sierra 41. *Sergeant York* 41. The Male Animal 42. Yankee Doodle Dandy 42. The Hard Way 42. This Is the Army 43. Thank Your Lucky Stars 43. Hollywood Canteen 44. *Rhapsody in Blue* 45. Where Do We Go From Here? 45. Too Young to Know 45. Cinderella Jones 46. Royal Flush 46. Repeat Performance 47. Northwest Stampede 49. Born To Be Bad 51. The Toughest Man in Arizona 52. The Woman They Almost Lynched 53. Jubilee Trail 54. The Revolt of Mamie Stover 57. The Keegans (TV) 76, etc.

Lesser, Sol (1890–1980). American pioneer exhibitor of silent days, later producer: many Tarzan films.

Thunder Over Mexico 33. Our Town 40. Kontiki 52, etc.

Lester, Bruce (1912–) (Bruce Lister). South African leading man who made some British and American films; now plays support roles.
Death at Broadcasting House 34. Crime over London 37. If I Were King 39. Pride and Prejudice 40. Above Suspicion 43. Golden Earrings 47. King Richard and the Crusaders 54, etc.

Lester, Dick or **Richard** (1932–). American director who found his spurt to fame in Britain doing zany comedies full of fast fragmented action. As soon as commercial backing was available his style went way over the top.
□It's Trad Dad 61. The Mouse on the Moon 63. *A Hard Day's Night* 64. *The Knack* 65. Help 65. A Funny Thing Happened on the Way to the Forum 66. How I Won the War 67. Petulia 68. The Bed Sitting Room 69. The Three Musketeers 73. Juggernaut 74. The Four Musketeers 75. Royal Flash 75. Robin and Marian 76. The Ritz 76. Butch and Sundance: The Early Days 79. Cuba 79. Superman II 80. Superman III 83. Finders Keepers 84.

Lester, Mark (–). American director. Bobbie Jo and the Outlaw 75. Stunts 77. Gold of the Amazon Women 77. Roller Boogie 79. Class of 84 82. Firestarter 84. Commando 85. Armed and Dangerous 86.

Lester, Mark (1958–). Innocent-looking British child star of the sixties.
Allez France 64. Spaceflight IC/1 65. Our Mother's House 67. *Oliver* (title role) 68. Run Wild Run Free 69. Eye Witness 70. Melody 71. Black Beauty 71. Night Hair Child 71. Who Slew Auntie Roo? 72. Scalawag 73. Little Adventurer 75. The Prince and the Pauper 77, etc.

Leterrier, François (1929–). French director.
Les Mauvais Coups 61. Un Roi sans Divertissement 63. La Chasse Royale 68. Projection Privée 73. Goodbye Emmanuelle 77, etc.

Letter from an Unknown Woman (US 1948). Out of Stefan Zweig's romantic novelette Max Ophuls fashioned a finely decorated though studio-bound piece of middle-European nostalgia; elegant, tragic and luxurious. With Joan Fontaine, Louis Jourdan.

letters have provided a starting point or climax for several films. Undelivered ones for *Address Unknown, The Postman Didn't Ring*; misdelivered ones for *Dear Ruth, The Go-Between, A Letter for Evie*; an incriminating one in *Suspicion*; lost ones for *Cause for Alarm, Never Put It In Writing*; indiscreet ones for *A Letter To Three Wives, So Evil My Love, The Last of Mrs Cheyney, The Letter*; posthumous ones for *Letter from an Unknown Woman, Love Letters, The Lost Moment, Mister Roberts*; anonymous ones for *Poison Pen* and *Le Corbeau.*

Lettieri, Al (1927–1975). American actor. The Bobo 68. The Godfather 72. Getaway 73. Mr Majestyk 74. Deadly Trackers 75, etc.

Levant, Oscar (1906–1972). American pianist and master of insult who appeared in several films as his grouchy, neurotic self. Autobiographical books: *A Smattering of Ignorance* 1944. *Memoirs of an Amnesiac* 1965. *The Unimportance of Being Oscar* 68.
□ The Dance of Life 29. In Person 35. Rhythm on the River 40. Kiss the Boys Goodbye 41. *Rhapsody in Blue* 45. Humoresque 46. You Were Meant for Me 47. Romance on the High Seas 48. The Barkleys of Broadway 49. *An American in Paris* 51. *The Band Wagon* 53. The I Don't Care Girl 53. The Cobweb 55.

¶ *O.L.:* In some situations I was difficult, in odd moments impossible, in rare moments loathsome, but at my best unapproachably great.
O.L.: Strip the phoney tinsel off Hollywood and you'll find the real tinsel underneath.
O.L.: I'm a controversial figure. My friends either dislike me or hate me.
I played an unsympathetic part—myself.—*O.L. on his role in Humoresque*
It's not a pretty face, but underneath this flabby exterior is an enormous lack of character.—*O.L. of himself in An American in Paris.*
There is absolutely nothing wrong with Oscar Levant that a miracle can't fix.—*Alexander Woollcott*
O.L.: I hate cold showers. They stimulate me, and then I don't know what to do.
A tortured man who sprayed his loathing on anyone within range.—*Shelley Winters*
Oscar has mellowed – like an old pistol.—*Billy Rose*

I envy people who drink. At least they have something to blame everything on.—*O.L. in Humoresque*.

Leven, Boris (1900–86). Russian-born production designer, long in US.
Alexander's Ragtime Band 38. *The Shanghai Gesture* 41. Mr Peabody and the Mermaid 48. Sudden Fear 52. *Giant* 56. Anatomy of a Murder 59. *West Side Story* (AA) 61. The Sound of Music 65. The Sand Pebbles 67. Star! 68. The Andromeda Strain 70. Jonathan Livingston Seagull 73. Mandingo 75. New York, New York 77, many others.

Levene, Sam (1905–1980). American stage actor, often in Runyonesque film roles.
Three Men on a Horse (debut) 36. Golden Boy 39. The Purple Heart 44. *Crossfire* 47. Boomerang 47. Guilty Bystander 50. Three Sailors and a Girl 53. Sweet Smell of Success 57. Act One 63. A Dream of Kings 69. Such Good Friends 71. Demon 77. Last Embrace 79. And Justice for All 79.

LeVien, Jack (1918–). American documentarist responsible for several distinguished compilation films.
Black Fox 62. The Finest Hours 64. A King's Story 67.
TV series on Churchill: *The Valiant Years* 60.

Levien, Sonya (1888–1960). American writer, former lawyer. Story editor at various times for Fox, MGM, Paramount.
Cavalcade 33. *State Fair* 33. *Berkeley Square* 33. In Old Chicago 38. *The Hunchback of Notre Dame* 40. Ziegfeld Girl 41. Rhapsody in Blue 45. Cass Timberlane 48. Quo Vadis 51. *Interrupted Melody* (AA) 55. *Jeanne Eagels* 58, etc.

Levin, Henry (1909–1980). American director, in Hollywood from 1943 after stage experience.
Cry of the Werewolf 44. I Love a Mystery 45. The Guilt of Janet Ames 47. The Mating of Millie 48. Jolson Sings Again 49. The Petty Girl 50. Convicted 50. Belles on Their Toes 52. The President's Lady 52. Mister Scoutmaster 53. Gambler from Natchez 54. The Lonely Man 57. Bernardine 57. Let's Be Happy (GB) 57. The Remarkable Mr Pennypacker 58. Holidays for Lovers 59. *Journey to the Centre of the Earth* 59. Where the Boys Are 60. The Wonderful World of the Brothers Grimm 62. Come Fly with Me 63. Honeymoon Hotel 64. Genghis Khan 65. Kiss the Girls and Make Them Die 66. Murderers' Row 67. The Desperados 70. That Man Bolt 73. The Thoroughbreds 77, others.

Levin, Ira (1929–). American thriller writer with a sharp edge.
A Kiss Before Dying 56. Rosemary's Baby 68. The Stepford Wives 75.

Levin, Meyer (1905–81). American author, the original writer of *Compulsion*, which was filmed in 1962.

Levine, Joseph E. (1905–87). American production executive and showman, former theatre owner. Formed Embassy Pictures in late fifties, originally to exploit cheap European spectacles; also set up finance for films like *Eight and a Half, Divorce Italian Style, Boccaccio* 70.
AS PRODUCER: The Carpetbaggers 63. Where Love Has Gone 64. Harlow 65. A Bridge Too Far 77. Magic 78, etc.

¶ *J.E.L.:* You can fool all the people all the time if the advice is right and the budget is big enough.

Levinson, Barry (1932–?87). American screenwriter.
Catholics (TV) 73. First Love 77. And Justice for All 80. Inside Moves 81. *Diner* (& d) 82. Best Friends 82. The Natural (d only) 84. Young Sherlock Holmes (d only) 85. Tin Men (w, d) 87.

Levy, Jules (1923–). American independent producer, of Levy-Gardner-Laven. See Arthur Gardner for credits.

Levy, Louis (1893–1957). British musical director and composer, in films from 1916. Scored *Nanook of the North* 20. With Gaumont and Gainsborough 1928/47, supervising all musical productions.
Pygmalion 38. The Citadel 38, many others.

Levy, Ralph (1919–). American director, in TV from 1947.
Bedtime Story 64. Do Not Disturb 65.

Levy, Raoul (1922–66). French producer.
Les Orgueilleux 53. And God Created Woman (& w) 56. Heaven Fell That Night 57. En Cas de Malheur 58. Babette Goes to War (& co-w) 59. Moderato Cantabile 60. The Truth 60. The Defector (& wd) 66, etc.

Lewin, Albert (1895–1968). American writer-producer-director with something of an Omar Khayyam fixation. Production executive 1931/41.
□*The Moon and Sixpence* (wd) 42. *The Picture of Dorian Gray* (wd) 44. The Private Affairs of Bel Ami (wpd) 47. *Pandora and the Flying Dutchman* (wpd) 51. Saadia (wpd) 54. The Living Idol (wpd) 57.

'A most intriguing little man. He completely checked out of his executive office at MGM every year or so when he wanted a year off to make one of his own pictures.'—*James Mason*

'Would that there were more room for accident in his clogged literary narrations and his naive conception of refinement in the cinema.'—*Andrew Sarris, 1968*

Lewis, Albert E. (1884–1978). Polish-American producer and Broadway impresario who was associated with several films.
International House 32. Torch Singer 35. Mutiny on the Bounty 35. Cabin in the Sky 43, etc.

Lewis, Diana (1915–). American leading lady of the late thirties; retired when she married William Powell.
It's a Gift 34. Forty Little Mothers 39. Bitter Sweet 40. Johnny Eager 41. Seven Sweethearts 42. Cry Havoc 43, etc.

Lewis, Fiona (1946–). British leading lady.
The Fearless Vampire Killers 67. Where's Jack? 69. Villain 71. Dracula (TV) 73. Lisztomania 75. The Fury 78. Strange Invaders 83, etc.

Lewis, Gena (1888–1979). American screenwriter.
Sin Town 42. The Climax 44. Cobra Woman 45. Trail Street 49. Lonely Heart Bandits 51, etc.

Lewis, Herschell (1926–). American director of exploitation films.
The Living Venus 61. Goldilocks and the Three Bares 63. Blood Feast 63. Monster a Go Go 65. The Gruesome Twosome 67. A Taste of Blood 67. The Ecstasies of Women 69. The Wizard of Gore 70. Stick it in Your Ear 72, many others.

Lewis, Jay (1914–1969). British producer, in films from 1933.
Morning Departure 50. The Gift Horse 52, etc.
AS DIRECTOR: The Baby and the Battleship 55. Invasion Quartet 61. Live Now Pay Later 62. A Home of Your Own 65, etc.

Lewis, Jerry (1926–) (Joseph Levitch). Goonish American comedian whose style is a mixture of exaggerated mugging and sticky sentiment. Until 1958 he formed a popular partnership with Dean Martin, but his increasingly indulgent solo films since then have gradually reduced his once-fervent band of admirers.
□*My Friend Irma* 49. My Friend Irma Goes West 50. At War with the Army 51. That's My Boy 51. Sailor Beware 52. Jumping Jacks 52. The Stooge 53. Scared Stiff 53. The Caddy 53. Money from Home 54. Living it Up 54. Three Ring Circus 54. You're Never Too Young 54. Artists and Models 55. Pardners 56. Hollywood or Bust 56. The Delicate Delinquent 57. The Sad Sack 58. Rock a Bye Baby 58. The Geisha Boy 58. Don't Give up the Ship 59. Visit to a Small Planet 60. *The Bellboy* 60. Cinderfella 60. Ladies' Man 61. The Errand Boy 61. It's Only Money 62. The Nutty Professor 63. Who's Minding the Store? 64. The Patsy 64. The Disorderly Orderly 64. The Family Jewels 65. Boeing-Boeing 65. Three on a Couch 66. Way Way Out 66. The Big Mouth 67. Don't Raise the Bridge, Lower the River 68. Hook Line and Sinker 69. Which Way to the Front? 70. One More Time (d only) 71. Hardly Working (& d) 79. Slapstick of the Fourth Kind 82. King of Comedy 83. Smorgasbord (& co-w, d) 83.
Gag appearance: It's a Mad Mad Mad Mad World 63.

¶ *J.L.:* When the light goes on in the refrigerator, I do twenty minutes.
At some point he said to himself, I'm extraordinary, like Chaplin. From then on nobody could tell him anything. He knew it all.—*Dean Martin*

Lewis, Joe E. (1901–71) (Joseph Kleevan). American night club comedian, played by Frank Sinatra in *The Joker is Wild* 59.
□ Too Many Husbands 31. Private Buckaroo 42. Lady in Cement 69.

Lewis, Joseph H. (1900–). American director, mainly of second features, some of them well above average.
Two-Fisted Rangers 40. The Mad Doctor of Market Street 41. Bombs over Burma 42. Minstrel Man 44. *My Name Is Julia Ross* 45. *So Dark the Night* 46. *The Jolson Story* (musical numbers only) 46. The Swordsman 47. The Return of October 48. *The Undercover Man* 49. A Lady without Passport 50. Gun Crazy 50. Retreat Hell 52. Cry of the Hunted 53. The Big Combo 55. A Lawless Street 55. Seventh Cavalry 56. The Halliday Brand 56. *Terror in a Texas Town* 58, etc.

Lewis, Michael J. (1939–). British composer.
The Madwoman of Chaillot 69. The Man Who Haunted Himself 70. Unman Wittering and Zigo 72. Theatre of Blood 73. 11 Harrowhouse 74. Russian Roulette 75, etc.

Lewis, Ronald (1928–1982). British leading man, in films from 1953.
The Prisoner 55. Storm over the Nile 55. A Hill in Korea 56. Bachelor of Hearts 59. The Full Treatment 61. Twice Round the Daffodils 62. Mr Sardonicus 62. The Brigand of Kandahar 65. Friends 71. Paul and Michelle 74, etc.

Lewis, Sheldon (1868–1958). American character actor of stage and screen.
The Exploits of Elaine 15. Dr Jekyll and Mr Hyde (title role) 16. Orphans of the Storm 21. The Red Kimono 26. Black Magic 29. The Monster Walks 32. The Cattle Thief (last film) 36, many others.

Lewis, Sinclair (1885–1951). American novelist. Works filmed include Arrowsmith 31. Ann Vickers 33. Babbitt 34. Dodsworth 36. Untamed 40. Cass Timberlane 47. Elmer Gantry 60.

Lewis, Ted (1889–1971) (Theodore Friedman). American bandleader and entertainer ('Me and My Shadow') who appeared in a few movies.
□Is Everybody Happy? 28. Show of Shows 29. Here Comes the Band 35. Manhattan Merry Go Round 37. Hold That Ghost 42. Follow the Boys 44.

Lewton, Val (1904–1951) (Vladimir Leventon). American producer, remembered for a group of low-budget, high quality horror films made for RKO in the forties.
Biography 1973: *The Reality of Terror* by Joel E. Siegel.
□*Cat People* 42. I Walked with a Zombie 43. The Leopard Man 43. The Seventh Victim 43. The Ghost Ship 43. Mademoiselle Fifi 44. Curse of the Cat People 44. Youth Runs Wild 44. *The Body Snatcher* 45. Isle of the Dead 45. Bedlam 46. My Own True Love 49. Please Believe Me 50. Apache Drums 51.
Under the pseudonym Carlos Keith, Lewton contributed to the screenplays of The Body Snatchers and Bedlam.

Lexy, Edward (1897–) (Edward Gerald Little). British character actor in films from 1936, usually as sergeant-major, police inspector or irascible father.
Farewell Again 37. South Riding 38. Laugh It Off 40. Spare a Copper 40. Piccadilly Incident 46. It's Not Cricket 48. Miss Robin Hood 52. Orders Are Orders 55. The Man Who Wouldn't Talk 58, many others.

Leyton, John (1939–). British pop singer who transferred to dramatic roles.
The Great Escape 63. Von Ryan's Express 65. Krakatoa 68. Schizo 77, etc.
TV series: Jericho 66.

L'Herbier, Marcel (1888–1979). French director, an avant-garde leader in silent days.
Autobiography 1979: *La Tête Qui Tourne.*
Rose France 19. Eldorado 22. The Late Mathias Pascal 25. L'Épervier 33. Nuits de Feu 37. La Nuit Fantastique 42. The Last Days of Pompeii 49. Le Père de Mademoiselle 53, etc.

Liberace (1919–87) (Wladziu Valentino Liberace). American pianist-showman of stage, night clubs and TV. Starred in his only major appearance, *Sincerely Yours* 55; also seen as a pianist in *East of Java* 49 and as a coffin salesman in *The Loved One* 65.
Autobiography 1977: *The Things I Love.*

¶ *L.:* You know that bank I used to cry all the way to? I bought it.
L.: Of course, I couldn't go out in the street in clothes like this, I'd get picked up. Come to think of it, it might be fun.
L.: Gee, you've been such a wonderful audience that I don't like to take your money. But I will!

library shot: see *stock shot.*

Licudi, Gabriella (1943–). Italian leading lady in international films.
The Liquidators 65. The Jokers 66. Casino Royale 66. The Last Safari 67. Separate Beds 73, many others.

Liebelei (Austria 1933). A sentimental love story culminating in a duel in which the hero is killed by the husband of an ex-mistress. All the film's merit is in the style of director Max Ophuls and cinematographer Franz Planer.

Lieven, Albert (1906–1971). German actor in films from 1933, including many British productions.
Victoria the Great 37. Night Train to Munich 40. *Jeannie* 40. Yellow Canary 43. *The Seventh Veil* 45. *Beware of Pity* 46. Frieda 47. *Sleeping Car to Trieste* 48. Hotel Sahara 50. Conspiracy of Hearts 60. Foxhole in Cairo 61. The Victors 63. Traitor's Gate 65, many others.

The Life and Death of Colonel Blimp (GB 1943). This amiable and quite ambitiously staged biography of a fictitious military man, whose career ranged from the Boer War to the London blitz, had delightful incidental detail even though it made no very obvious point and had the oddities one was coming to expect from films written, produced and directed by Michael Powell and Emeric Pressburger. Running three hours in its original form, in what then seemed exquisite colour, it had Roger Livesey in the title role, Deborah Kerr as the three women in his life, and Anton Walbrook as a sympathetic German friend.

The Life of Emile Zola (US 1937) (AA best film). This, the only Warner Brothers biographical film to win an award as the best film of its year, was probably the best of them. Stylishly directed by William Dieterle, it also gained Academy Awards for Joseph Schildkraut (as Dreyfus) and for the scenarists Norman Reilly Raine, Heinz Herald and Geza Herczeg. Paul Muni played Zola.

Life Upside Down (La Vie a L'Envers) (France 1964). A simple but curiously haunting little film in the introspective manner of the sixties, about a young man who withdraws from life into the simplicity and solitude of a small white room. Written and directed by Alain Jessua; with Charles Denner.

Lifeboat (US 1944). An Alfred Hitchcock movie notable for confining itself to the smallest acting space of any film ever made: a lifeboat on the open sea. John Steinbeck wrote the script and Tallulah Bankhead and Walter Slezak made the most of the acting chances.

lifts (or elevators) provided a convenient means of murder in *Garment Center, The List of Adrian Messenger* and *House of Wax*, and of unwitting suicide in *Ivy*. Sean Connery in *Diamonds are Forever* had a spectacular fight in a lift. People were trapped in lifts in *Cry Terror, A Night in Casablanca, Love Crazy, Sweet Charity, Towering Inferno* and *Lady in a Cage*, in which last the lift was of the domestic variety used by Katharine Hepburn in *Suddenly Last Summer*. Michael Rennie had more trouble in lifts than any other actor—in *The Power, The Day the Earth Stood Still*, and *Hotel*. Invalid chair-lifts were sported by Ethel Barrymore in *The Farmer's Daughter*, Charles Laughton in *Witness for the Prosecution*, and Eugenie Leontovich in *Homicidal*.

light comedians, the lithe and dapper heroes who can be funny and romantic at the same time, have added a great deal to the mystique and nostalgia of the screen. Linder and Chaplin both partly belong to this debonair tradition, and indeed did much to mould it; but only sound could enable its full realization. Maurice Chevalier had the field pretty well to himself in Hollywood during the early thirties, with strong support from such stalwarts as Roland Young, Edward Everett Horton and Charles Butterworth. Soon Cary Grant entered the lists along with David Niven, William Powell, Louis Hayward, Melvyn Douglas and Ronald Colman when he felt in lighter mood. Britain scored with Jack Buchanan, Jack Hulbert, and the ineffable Aldwych team of Tom Walls and Ralph Lynn; while Leslie Howard scored a major hit in *Pygmalion* and Rex Harrison, who was to play the same role twenty-five years later in *My Fair Lady*, was already demonstrating his talent in less important comedies.

Back in Hollywood *The Philadelphia Story* was a milestone in light comedy and set Katharine Hepburn firmly on the road she later followed in her splendid series with Spencer Tracy. Bette Davis, too, had her moments in this field, and so did Rosalind Russell. Bob Hope and Danny Kaye both clowned around a good deal but still got the girl in the end . . . but Britishers Basil Radford and Naunton Wayne were bachelors born and bred. The more realistic approach of the fifties was stifling the genre, but Dennis Price managed a notable performance in *Kind Hearts and Coronets* before Ian Carmichael cornered the diminishing market. In more recent years actors have had to turn comic or tragic at the drop of a hat: among those best able to manage the light touch are Jack Lemmon, Tony Curtis, Frank Sinatra, Peter O'Toole, Jack Nicholson, Warren Beatey, Shirley Maclaine, Diane Keaton, Jane Fonda and Anne Bancroft.

lighthouses formed dramatic settings for such movies as *Thunder Rock, The Seventh Survivor, The Phantom Light* and *Back Room Boy*, and dominated key scenes of *Portrait of Jennie, A Stolen Life, The Beast from 20,000 Fathoms* and *Pete's Dragon*.

Lightner, Winnie (1901–1971) (Winifred Hanson). American vaudeville comedienne who appeared in several early talkies.
Gold Diggers of Broadway 30. Playgirl 32. Dancing Lady 32. I'll Fix It 34, etc.

Lights of New York (US 1928). The first all-talking film, a backstage gangster drama notable for little except its continuous nasal chatter (still separated by sub-titles). Directed by Bryan Foy from a many-handed script.

Li'l Abner. Al Capp's comic strip about the hillbilly inhabitants of Dogpatch was first filmed, unsuccessfully, in 1940 with Granville Owen; masks were rather oddly used for some characters. In 1957 Panama and Frank made a successful musical version with Peter Palmer, based on the Broadway show. Also, Paramount made a few Li'l Abner cartoons in the late forties.

Liliom. Ferenc Molnar's play about the here and the hereafter was filmed in Hollywood in 1930 by Frank Borzage and in Germany in 1933 by Fritz Lang. In 1956 it turned up again, via a stage musical, as *Carousel*, directed by Henry King. There had also been a 1921 silent under the title *A Trip to Paradise*.

Lillie, Beatrice (1898–) (Constance Sylvia Munston, later Lady Peel). Sharp-faced, mischievous British revue star of the twenties and thirties who graced only a few films with her wit.
Biography 1973: *Every Other Inch a Lady*.
□*Exit Smiling* 26. Show of Shows 29. Are You There? 30. Dr Rhythm 38. *On Approval* 43. Around the World in Eighty Days 56. Thoroughly Modern Millie 67.

Limelight (US 1952). Chaplin's last major film, a sentimental old-fashioned back-stage story which succeeded by its sheer aplomb but overdid the pathos. His theme song, 'Eternally', made it a hit.

Lincoln, Abbey (1930–) (Anna Marie Woolridge). Black American character actress.
For Love of Ivy 68.

Lincoln, Abraham (1809–1865). Sixteenth American president, a familiar screen figure with his stovepipe hat, bushy whiskers, and his assassination during a performance of 'Our American Cousin'. More or less full length screen portraits include *Abraham Lincoln's Clemency* 10; *Lincoln the Lover* 13; Joseph Henabery in *Birth of a Nation* 14; Frank McGlynn in *The Life of Abraham Lincoln* 15; George A. Billings in *Abraham Lincoln* 25; Walter Huston in *Abraham Lincoln* 30; John Carradine in *Of Human Hearts* 38; Henry Fonda in *Young Mr Lincoln* 39; Raymond Massey in *Abe Lincoln in Illinois* 39.

Lincoln, Elmo (1889–1952) (Otto Elmo Linkenhelter). American silent actor who became famous as the first *Tarzan of the Apes* 18, and played small roles up to his death.
Birth of a Nation 14. Elmo the Mighty 19, etc.

Lindblom, Gunnel (1931–). Leading Swedish actress.
The Seventh Seal 56. Wild Strawberries 57. The Virgin Spring 60. Winter Light 62. *The Silence* 63. Rapture 65. Loving Couples 66. Sult 67. Flickorna 68. The Father 69. Brother Can 71, etc.

Linden, Eric (1909–). Swedish-American juvenile lead of the thirties.
Are These Our Children? 32. The Silver Cord 33. Girl of the Limberlost 34. The Voice of Bugle Ann 36. Gone with the Wind 39, etc.

Linden, Hal (1932–) (Harold Lipshitz). American character actor, best known as TV's *Barney Miller*.

Linden, Jennie (1939–). British leading actress.
Nightmare 63. Dr Who and the Daleks 66. *Women in Love* 69. A Severed Head 70. Hedda 75. Valentino 77, etc.
TV series: Lillie 77.

Linder, Cec (1921–). Canadian character actor, long in British films.
Crack in the Mirror 59. Jetstorm 59. Too Young to Love 60. SOS Pacific 60. Goldfinger 64. Explosion 71. A Touch of Class 73. Sunday in the Country 74. Lost and Found 79. Atlantic City 80, many others.

Linder, Max (1883–1925) (Gabriel Leuvielle). Dapper French silent comedian, a likely source for Chaplin. Between 1906 and 1925 he scripted and directed most of his own films, from 1917 in Hollywood.
The Skater's Debut 07. Max Takes a Bath 07. Max and His Mother-in-Law's False Teeth 08. Max's New Landlord 08. Max in a Dilemma 10. Max Is Absent-Minded 10. How Max Went Around the World 11. Max, Victim of Quinquina 11. Max Is Forced to Work 12. Max Teaches the Tango 11. Max Toreador 12. Max Virtuoso 12. Who Killed Max? 13. Max's Hat 14. Max and Jane Make a Dessert 14. Max and the Clutching Hand 15. Max

Comes Across 17. Max Wants a Divorce 17. Max and His Taxi 17. The Little Café 19. Seven Years Bad Luck* 20. Be My Wife* 20. The Three Must-Get-Theres* 22. Help! 24. King of the Circus 25, many others.
*These films formed the basis of a compilation, *Laugh with Max Linder*, which was issued in 1963.

Lindfors, Viveca (1920–). (Elsa Torstendotter). Swedish actress, in films from 1941, Hollywood from 1946.
To the Victor 47. Night Unto Night 48. The New Adventures of Don Juan 48. No Sad Songs for Me 50. Dark City 50. The Flying Missile 51. Four in a Jeep 51. The Raiders 52. Run for Cover 55. Moonfleet 55. I Accuse 57. Tempest 58. King of Kings 61. Sylvia 65. Brainstorm 65. The Way We Were 73. Welcome to L.A. 77. Girlfriends 78. A Wedding 78. Natural Enemies 79. Voices 79. The Hand 82. Creepshow 82, others.

Lindgren, Lars Magnus (1922–). Swedish director.
Do You Believe in Angels? 60. Dear John 64. The Coffin (The Sadist) 66.

Lindley, Audra (–). American character actress.
The Heartbreak Kid 72. Pearl (TV) 79. When You Comin' Back Red Ryder 79. Moviola (TV) 80. Cannery Row 82.
TV series: Bridget Loves Bernie, Three's Company, The Ropers.

Lindo, Olga (1898–1968). Anglo-Norwegian character actress, on British stage and screen.
The Shadow Between 32. The Last Journey 35. *When We Are Married* 42. Bedelia 46. Train of Events 49. *An Inspector Calls* 54. Woman in a Dressing Gown 57. Sapphire 59, etc.

Lindon, Lionel (1905–1971). American cinematographer.
Going My Way 44. A Medal for Benny 45. Road to Utopia 46. *Alias Nick Beal* 49. Destination Moon 50. Conquest of Space 55. *Around the World in Eighty Days* (AA) 56. The Lonely Man 57. The Black Scorpion 57. Too Late Blues 61. *The Manchurian Candidate* 62. The Trouble with Angels 66. Boy Did I Get a Wrong Number 66. *Grand Prix* 66. Generation 69, etc.

Lindsay, Howard (1889–1968). American actor-playwright-stage director. With Russell Crouse wrote *Life with Father* and *State of the Union*, both filmed. Acted in and directed *Dulcy* 21, co-authored *She's My Weakness* 31.

Lindsay, Margaret (1910–1981) (Margaret Kies). American leading lady of the thirties, with stage experience; in Hollywood from 1931.
West of Singapore 32. Lady Killer 34. Bordertown 35. G-Men 35. The Green Light 37. Jezebel 38. The House of Seven Gables 40. There's Magic in Music 41. A Close Call for Ellery Queen 42. No Place for a Lady 43. Crime Doctor 43. Alaska 44. Club Havana 45. Scarlet Street 45. Her Sister's Secret 47. Cass Timberlane 47. Emergency Hospital 56. Jet over the Atlantic 59. Tammy and the Doctor 63, many others.

Lindtberg, Leopold (1902–84). Swiss director.
Marie Louise 44. *The Last Chance* 45. Four Days Leave 48. The Village 52.

The Lion in Winter (GB/US 1968). This curious treatment of the court of Henry II in the vein of *Who's Afraid of Virginia Woolf?* won Oscars for Katharine Hepburn, in her element as the wily Eleanor of Aquitaine, for John Barry's music and for James Goldman's screenplay from his off-Broadway original. Anthony Harvey's direction ensured good clear talk at the expense of cinema; Peter O'Toole was an amusingly rampant Henry.

The Lion's Share, by Bosley Crowther. A lively history of the Metro-Goldwyn-Mayer company, written in 1957 by the critic of the *New York Times*.

Lipman, Jerzy (1922–). Polish cinematographer.
A Generation 54. Kanal 57. The Eighth Day of the Week 58. Lotna 59. Knife in the Water 62. No More Divorces 63. Ashes 65. Zozya 67. Colonel Wolodyjowski 69. Dead Pigeon on Beethoven Street 72. The Martyr 75, etc.

Lippert, Robert L. (1909–76). American exhibitor, latterly head of company making second features for 20th Century-Fox, many of them produced by his son *Robert L. Lippert Jnr* (1928–).

Lipscomb, W. P. (1887–1958). British screenwriter who spent some years in Hollywood.
French Leave 27. The Good Companions 32. I Was a Spy 33. Clive of India (co-w) 34. A Tale of Two Cities 35. The Garden of Allah

36. Pygmalion (co-w) 38. A Town Like Alice 56. Dunkirk (co-w) 58, many others.

Lipstadt, Aaron (–). American director.
Android 82. City Limits 85.

Lisi, Virna (1937–) (Virna Pieralisi). Voluptuous Italian leading lady who after starring in innumerable local spectaculars came on to the international market.
The Black Tulip 63. Eva 63. How to Murder Your Wife (US) 65. Casanova 70 65. Signore e Signori 65. Assault on a Queen (US) 66. Not with My Wife You Don't (US) 66. The Girl and the General 67. The Twenty-fifth Hour 67. Arabella 68. The Secret of Santa Vittoria 69. Un Beau Monstre 70. The Statue 71. The Serpent 72. Bluebeard 72. White Fang 74. Challenge to White Fang 75. Cocktails for Three 78. Ernesto 78, etc.

Listen to Britain (GB 1941). A classic impressionist documentary by Humphrey Jennings, blending the sights and sounds of a country at war.

Lister, Francis (1899–1951). Suave British character actor, mainly on stage.
Comin' Thro' the Rye 24. Atlantic 30. Jack's the Boy 32. Clive of India 35. The Return of the Scarlet Pimpernel 38. Henry V 44. The Wicked Lady 45. Home to Danger 51, etc.

Lister, Moira (1923–). South African leading lady and character actress, in British films.
My Ain Folk 44. Uneasy Terms 48. Another Shore 48. *A Run for Your Money* 49. Grand National Night 53. John and Julie 55. Seven Waves Away 57. The Yellow Rolls Royce 64. Stranger in the House 67, etc.

Litel, John (1895–1972). American character actor, in films since 1929; often seen as judge, lawyer or stern father.
Marked Woman 37. The Life of Emile Zola 37. Virginia City 40. Men Without Souls 40. They Died with Their Boots On 41. Sealed Lips 41. Boss of Big Town 43. Kiss Tomorrow Goodbye 50. Houseboat 58. A Pocketful of Miracles 61. The Sons of Katie Elder 65, many others.
TV series: My Hero 52.

Lithgow, John (1945–). American character actor, a semi-star of the eighties.
Obsession 76. All that Jazz 79. Blow Out 81. The World According to Garp 82. Footloose 83. Twilight Zone: the Movie 83. Terms of Endearment (AAN) 83. Buckaroo Banzai 84. 2010 84. Santa Claus 84. Footloose 84. Mesmerized 84. The Manhattan Project 86. Bigfoot and the Hendersons 87.

Little Caesar (US 1930). The first talking gangster film glorifying the gang wars of the twenties, this powerful melodrama with its famous last line ('. . . is this the end of Rico?') caused a long-lasting controversy but sold a lot of tickets and produced a host of imitators. (The genre wore itself out in the forties but was revived in the late fifties.) Edward G. Robinson was suddenly a star after his performance; Mervyn Le Roy directed.

Little, Cleavon (1939–). Black American comedy actor.
What's So Bad About Feeling Good 68. Cotton Comes to Harlem 70. Vanishing Point 71. *Blazing Saddles* 74. Greased Lightning 77. Scavenger Hunt 79. High Risk 81, etc.
TV series: *Temperatures Rising* 72.

The Little Foxes (US 1941). This admirable adaptation of Lilian Hellman's play about a grasping family after the Civil War was an example of Hollywood at its best, with beautiful photography by Gregg Toland, subtle direction by William Wyler, and a gallery of first-rate performances: Bette Davis, Herbert Marshall, Ray Collins, Charles Dingle, Dan Duryea, Patricia Collinge and others. An unusual kind of sequel, *Another Part of the Forest*, was filmed in 1947: this showed the earlier lives of the Hubbard family.

Little Lord Fauntleroy. The well-known children's novel by Frances Hodgson Burnett, about an American boy who becomes a British earl, was filmed in 1922 as a transvestite vehicle for Mary Pickford; direction appears to have been shared between Alfred E. Green, Jack Pickford and Alfred Werker. In 1936 it was remade by John Cromwell for Selznick, with Freddie Bartholomew in the title role.
In 1980 there was a TV version with Ricky Schroder.

Little Women. Louisa M. Alcott's cosy 19th-century saga of a nice mother's even nicer daughters was a major success when filmed in 1933 by George Cukor, with Katharine Hepburn and Paul Lukas. Remade in 1949 with June Allyson and Rossano

Brazzi, it seemed calculated and coy. A 1978 TV series got nowhere; a sequel, *Little Men*, was filmed in 1940 as a vehicle for Kay Francis.

Littlefield, Lucien (1895–1960). American character actor, in Hollywood from 1913 in supporting roles.
The Sheik 22. Miss Pinkerton 32. Ruggles of Red Gap 34. Rose Marie 36. The Great American Broadcast 40. Scared Stiff 44. Susanna Pass 51. Pop Girl 56, etc.

Littlewood, Joan (1914–). British stage director whose only film to date is *Sparrows Can't Sing* 63. Created London's 'Theatre Workshop'.

Litvak, Anatole (1902–1974). Russian-born director in Germany and France from 1927, Hollywood from 1937.
□Dolly Gets Ahead (Ger.) 31. Nie Wieder Liebe (Ger.) 32. Coeur de Lilas (Fr.) 32. Be Mine Tonight (Ger.) 33. Sleeping Car (GB) 33. Cette Vielle Canaille (Fr.) 35. L'Equipage (Fr.) 36. *Mayerling* (Fr.) 36. *The Woman I Love* 37. Tovarich 38. The Amazing Dr Clitterhouse 38. The Sisters 38. Castle on the Hudson 39. *Confessions of a Nazi Spy* 39. All This and Heaven Too 40. *City for Conquest* 40. Out of the Fog 41. Blues in the Night 41. This Above All 42. The Long Night 47. Sorry Wrong Number 48. *The Snake Pit* 48. Decision Before Dawn 52. Act of Love 53. The Deep Blue Sea 55. Anastasia 56. The Journey 59. Goodbye Again 61. Five Miles to Midnight 63. The Night of the Generals 67. The Lady in the Car 70.

Livesey, Jack (1901–1961). British actor, brother of Roger Livesey.
The Wandering Jew 33. The Passing of the Third Floor Back 35. Old Bill and Son 40. The First Gentleman 47. Paul Temple's Triumph 51, etc.

Livesey, Roger (1906–1976). Husky-voiced, often roguish British character star who divided his time between stage and screen.
□The Old Curiosity Shop 20. Where the Rainbow Ends 21. The Four Feathers 21. Married Love 23. East Lynne on the Western Front 31. A Veteran of Waterloo 33. A Cuckoo in the Nest 33. Blind Justice 34. The Price of Wisdom 35. Lorna Doone 35. Midshipman Easy 35. *Rembrandt* 36. *The Drum* 38. Keep Smiling 38. Spies of the Air 39. The Rebel Son 39. The Girl in the News 40. 49th Parallel 41. *The Life and Death of Colonel Blimp* 43. *I Know Where I'm Going* 45. *A Matter of Life and Death* 46. *Vice Versa* 47. That Dangerous Age 49. Green Grow the Rushes 50. The Master of Ballantrae 53. The Intimate Stranger 56. The League of Gentlemen 59. The Entertainer 60. No My Darling Daughter 61. Of Human Bondage 64. Moll Flanders 65. Oedipus the King 68. Hamlet 69. Futtock's End 70.

Livesey, Sam (1873–1936). British actor, father of Jack and Roger Livesey.
Young Woodley 30. The Flag Lieutenant 32. The Private Life of Henry VIII 32. Jew Süss 34. Turn of the Tide 36. Dark Journey 37, etc.

Living (Ikiru) (Japan 1952). Edited, part-written, and directed by Akira Kurosawa, this step-by-step account of an elderly clerk dying of cancer could hardly have been made in the west at this time; certainly not with so fine and finally uplifting a touch.

The Living Desert (US 1953). The first of Walt Disney's feature-length 'True Life Adventures', an absorbing animal documentary despite the facetious Fitzpatrick-type monotone commentary and many suspect 'dramatic' sequences which must have been either staged or cleverly edited. (By reverse printing, Disney even made scorpions do a square dance.) Outraged scientific critics could not deny the charm and fascination of the piece, nor its popularity; and many of the shots were extremely rare. Disney followed it with *The Vanishing Prairie, The African Lion, Secrets of Life, The Jungle Cat*, and several two-reelers of the same kind: *Seal Island, Beaver Valley, Bear Country, Water Birds, Nature's Half Acre*, etc.

Livingston, Jay (1915–). American songwriter, usually of words and music; often worked with Ray Evans.
To Each His Own 47. Golden Earrings 48. The Paleface (AA for 'Buttons and Bows') 49. Captain Carey USA (AA for 'Mona Lisa') 50. The Man Who Knew Too Much (AA for 'Que Sera Sera') 56. All Hands on Deck 62, many others. Wrote themes for *Bonanza, Mister Ed*, etc.

Livingston, Margaret (1900–1985). American silent screen leading lady.
Within the Cup 18. Lying Lips 21. Divorce 23. Butterfly 24. Havoc 25. A Trip to Chinatown 26. Married Alive 27. Streets of Shanghai 28. The Last Warning 29. Seven Keys to Baldpate 30. Kiki 31. Call Her Savage 32. Social Register 34, many others.

Lizzani, Carlo (1922–). Italian director. Caccia Tragica (co-w only) 47. Bitter Rice (co-w only) 49. Achtung Banditi 51. Ai Margini Della Metropoli 54. The Great Wall 58. Hunchback of Rome 60. The Hills Run Red 66. The Violent Four 68. Crazy Joe 73. The Last Days of Mussolini 74, etc.

Llewellyn, Richard (1906–1983). Welsh best-selling novelist, famous for *How Green Was My Valley*. *Noose* and *None But the Lonely Heart* were also filmed.

Lloyd, Doris (1899–1968). British actress with repertory experience; in Hollywood from the twenties.
Charley's Aunt (as Donna Lucia) 30. Disraeli 30. Tarzan the Ape Man 32. Oliver Twist 33. Clive of India 35. Vigil in the Night 39. Phantom Lady 44. The Secret Life of Walter Mitty 47. A Man Called Peter 55. The Time Machine 60. The Notorious Landlady 62. Rosie 67, etc.

Lloyd, Euan (1923–). British independent producer, former publicist.
Genghis Khan 65. Murderers' Row 66. Shalako 68. Catlow 71. The Man Called Noon 73. Paper Tiger 75. The Wild Geese 78. The Sea Wolves 80. Who Dares Wins 82, etc.

Lloyd, Frank (1887–1960). Scottish-born director, in Hollywood from 1913 after acting experience.
Les Misérables 18. Madame X 20. Oliver Twist 22. The Eternal Flame 23. The Sea Hawk 24. Dark Streets 26. *The Divine Lady* (AA) 29. East Lynne 30. Sin Flood 31. Passport to Hell 32. *Cavalcade* (AA) 33. *Berkeley Square* 33. *Mutiny on the Bounty* 35. Under Two Flags 36. Maid of Salem 37. Wells Fargo 37. If I Were King (& p) 38. Rulers of the Sea 39. The Tree of Liberty (& d) 40. The Lady from Cheyenne (& p) 41. This Woman Is Mine 41. *Blood on the Sun* 45. The Shanghai Story (& p) 54. The Last Command (& p) 55, many others.

Lloyd, Harold (1893–1971). American silent comedian, famous for his timid bespectacled 'nice boy' character and for thrill-comedy situations involving dangerous stunts. In hundreds of two-reelers from 1916.
Autobiography 1928: *An American Comedy*. Biography 1976: *Harold Lloyd* by Richard Schickel.
□A Sailor-Made Man 21. *Grandma's Boy* 22. Dr Jack 22. *Safety Last* 23. Why Worry? 23. Girl Shy 24. Hot Water 24. *The Freshman* 25. For Heaven's Sake 26. *The Kid Brother* 27. Speedy 28. Welcome Danger 29. *Feet First* 30. *Movie Crazy* 32. The Catspaw 34. The Milky Way 36. Professor Beware 38. Mad Wednesday (The Sins of Harold Diddlebock) 47. Later produced two compilations of his comedy highlights: *World of Comedy* and *Funny Side of Life*. Special Academy Award 1952 as 'master comedian and good citizen'.
❁ For skill, daring and ingenuity. *The Kid Brother*.

Lloyd, Norman (1914–). British character actor in Hollywood, usually in mean or weak roles; gave up acting to become TV producer, mainly for Alfred Hitchcock but made an acting comeback in his sixties.
Saboteur (as the villain who fell from the statue of Liberty) 42. The Unseen 45. The Southerner 45. Spellbound 45. The Green Years 46. The Beginning or the End 47. Scene of the Crime 49. The Flame and the Arrow 60. He Ran all the Way 51. Limelight 52. Audrey Rose 77. The Nude Bomb 80, etc.
TV series: St Elsewhere 82.

Lloyd, Russell (1915–). British editor.
The Green Cockatoo 37. Over the Moon 39. School for Secrets 46. Anna Karenina 48. Vice Versa 48. Decameron Nights 52. The Sea Shall Not Have Them 54. Moby Dick 56. Roots of Heaven 58. The Unforgiven 60. Of Human Bondage 64. Reflections in a Golden Eye 67. The Kremlin Letter 70. The Mackintosh Man 73. The Man Who Would Be King 75, many others.

Lloyd, Sue (1939–). British leading lady of the sixties.
The Ipcress File 66. Where's Jack? 68. Percy 71. The Bitch 79.
TV series: *The Baron*.

Lloyd-Pack, Charles (1902–83). British character actor of stage and screen, usually in self-effacing roles; butlers, etc.
High Treason 51. *The Importance of Being Earnest* 52. The Constant Husband 55. Night of the Demon 57. Dracula 58. *Victim* 62. If 68. Song of Norway 70. Madame Sin 72. The Mirror Crack'd 80, etc.

Lo Bianco, Tony (–). American character actor.
The Honeymoon Killers 70. The French Connection 72. The Seven Ups 73. Jesus of Nazareth (TV) 77. Demon 77. Magee and the Lady (TV) 78. Bloodbrothers 78. F.I.S.T. 78. Separate Ways 81, etc.

Loach, Ken (1936–). British director from TV.
Poor Cow 67. *Kes* 69. *Family Life* 72. Days of Hope (TV) 75. Black Jack 79.

location. A shooting site away from the studio, not encouraged in the days of the moguls, but considered essential in the cause of realism as soon as the studio system broke up.

¶ A rock is a rock, a tree is a tree, shoot it in Griffith Park.—*Anon.*

Locke, Sondra (1947–). American leading lady of the tougher type.
The Heart is a Lonely Hunter 68. Willard 71. Reflection of Fear 73. The Outlaw Josey Wales 76. Death Game 76. *The Gauntlet* 77. Wishbone Cutter 78. Every Whicn Way But Loose 78. Any Which Way You Can 80. Bronco Billy 80. Sudden Impact 83. Ratboy (& d) 87.

Lockhart, Calvin (1934–). Black West Indian leading man.
A Dandy in Aspic 68. Joanna 68. Nobody Runs Forever 68. Leo the Last 70. Myra Breckinridge 70. Cotton comes to Harlem 71. Melinda 72. The Beast Must Die 74, etc.

Lockhart, Gene (1891–1957). Canadian character actor at home in genial or shifty parts. Also writer: in films since 1922.
□Smilin' Through 22. The Gay Bride 34. Ah Wilderness 35. I've Been Around 35. Captain Hurricane 35. Star of Midnight 35. Thunder in the Night 35. Storm over the Andes 35. Crime and Punishment 35. Brides Are Like That 35. Times Square Playboy 36. Earthworm Tractors 36. The First Baby 36. Career Woman 36. The Garden Murder Case 36. The Gorgeous Hussy 36. The Devil Is a Sissy 36. Wedding Present 36. Mind Your Own Business 36. Come Closer Folks 36. Mama Steps Out 37. Too Many Wives 37. Make Way for Tomorrow 37. The Sheik Steps Out 37. Something to Sing About 37. Of Human Hearts 38. Listen Darling 38. A Christmas Carol 38. Sweethearts 38. Penrod's Double Trouble 38. Men Are Such Fools 38. Blondie 38. *Algiers* 38. Sinners in Paradise 38. Meet the Girls 38. I'm from Missouri 39. Hotel Imperial 39. Our Leading Citizen 39. Geronimo 39. Tell No Tales 39. Bridal Suite 39. Blackmail 39. The Story of Alexander Graham Bell 39. Edison the Man 40. Dr Kildare Goes Home 40. We Who Are Young 40. South of Pago Pago 40. A Dispatch from Reuters 40. *His Girl Friday* 40. Abe Lincoln in Illinois 40. Billy the Kid 41. Keeping Company 41. Meet John Doe 41. All That Money Can Buy 41. The Sea Wolf 41. One Foot in Heaven 41. Steel Against the Sky 41. International Lady 41. They Died with Their Boots On 41. Juke Girl 42. The Gay Sisters 42. You Can't Escape Forever 42. Forever and a Day 43. Mission to Moscow 43. Hangmen Also Die 43. Find the Blackmailer 43. The Desert Song 43. Madame Curie 43. Northern Pursuit 43. The White Cliffs of Dover 44. *Going My Way* 44. Action in Arabia 44. The Man from Frisco 44. *The House on 92nd Street* 45. Leave Her to Heaven 45. That's the Spirit 45. Meet Me on Broadway 46. A Scandal in Paris 46. She Wolf of London 46. The Strange Woman 46. The Shocking Miss Pilgrim 47. Miracle on 34th Street 47. The Foxes of Harrow 47. Cynthia 47. Honeymoon 47. Her Husband's Affairs 47. Joan of Arc 48. Inside Story 48. That Wonderful Urge 48. Apartment for Peggy 48. I Jane Doe 48. Down to the Sea in Ships 49. Madame Bovary 49. The Red Light 49. The Inspector General 49. Riding High 50. The Big Hangover 50. The Sickle and the Cross 51. I'd Climb the Highest Mountain 51. Rhubarb 51. The Lady from Texas 51. Hoodlum Empire 52. A Girl in Every Port 52. Face to Face 52. Bonzo Goes to College 52. Androcles and the Lion 52. Apache War Smoke 52. Francis Covers the Big Town 53. Down Among the Sheltering Palms 53. Confidentially Connie 53. The Lady Wants Mink 53. World for Ransom 54. The Vanishing American 55. Carousel 56. The Man in the Grey Flannel Suit 56. Jeanne Eagels 57.

Lockhart, June (1925–). American supporting actress, daughter of Gene.
All This and Heaven Too 40. Meet Me in St Louis 44. Keep Your Powder Dry 45. Bury Me Dead 47. Time Limit 47, etc.
TV series: Lassie 55–64. Lost in Space 65–68.

Lockhart, Kathleen (1893–1978). American character actress, widow of Gene Lockhart; known previously as Kathleen Arthur.
The Devil is a Sissy 36. Sweethearts 38. All This and Heaven Too 41. Gentleman's Agreement 47. Plymouth Adventure 52. The Glenn Miller Story 54, many others.

Lockwood, Gary (1937–) (John Gary Yusolfsky). American leading man of the sixties, mostly on TV.
Splendour in the Grass 61. Wild in the Country 61. It Happened at the World's Fair

63. Firecreek 67. 2001: A Space Odyssey 68. The Model Shop 69. RPM 70. Stand Up and Be Counted 72. Bad Georgia Road 77, etc. TV series: *Follow the Sun* 61. *The Lieutenant* 63.

Lockwood, Julia (1941–). British leading lady, daughter of Margaret Lockwood.
My Teenage Daughter 56. Please Turn Over 59. No Kidding 60, etc.

Lockwood, Margaret (1911/1916–) (Margaret Day). Durable, indomitable British leading lady who was an appealing ingénue in the thirties, a rather boring star villainess in the forties, and later a likeable character actress of stage and TV.
Autobiography 1955: *Lucky Star.*
□Lorna Doone 35. The Case of Gabriel Perry 35. Some Day 35. Honours Easy 35. Man of the Moment 35. Midshipman Easy 35. Jury's Evidence 36. The Amateur Gentleman 36. The Beloved Vagabond 36. Irish for Luck 36. The Street Singer 37. Who's Your Lady Friend? 37. Dr Syn 37. Melody and Romance 37. Owd Bob 38. Bank Holiday 38. *The Lady Vanishes* 38. A Girl Must Live 39. The Stars Look Down 39. Susannah of the Mounties (US) 39. Rulers of the Sea (US) 39. *Night Train to Munich* 40. The Girl in the News 40. Quiet Wedding 41. Alibi 42. *The Man in Grey* 43. Dear Octopus 43. Give us the Moon 44. Love Story 44. A Place of One's Own 45. I'll Be Your Sweetheart 45. *The Wicked Lady* 45. Bedelia 46. Hungry Hill 46. Jassy 47. The White Unicorn 47. Look Before You Love 48. Cardboard Cavalier 49. Madness of the Heart 49. Highly Dangerous 50. Trent's Last Case 52. Laughing Anne 53. Trouble in the Glen 54. *Cast a Dark Shadow* 57. The Slipper and the Rose 76.

Loden, Barbara (1932–1980). American general purpose actress.
Wild River 60. Splendor in the Grass 60, etc.
As director: Wanda 72.

Loder, John (1898–) (John Lowe). Handsome British leading man, in international films from 1927 after varied experience.
Autobiography 1977: *Hollywood Hussar.*
The First Born 29. Java Head 34. Lorna Doone 35. Murder Will Out 38. Meet Maxwell Archer 39. How Green Was My Valley 41. *Now Voyager* 42. Gentleman Jim 42. The Gorilla Man 42. Old Acquaintance 43. The Hairy Ape 44. The Brighton Strangler 45. A Game of Death 46. Wife of Monte Cristo 46. Dishonoured Lady 47. Woman and the Hunter 57. Gideon's Day 58, etc.

¶ Why is it that I'm not able
to get the roles they give Clark Gable?
They always say 'You have no name,
But when you have one, come again.'
By that time I'll be old and stiff,
A kind of poor man's Aubrey Smith.—*J. L., 1940s*

Lodge, David (1921–). British character actor, with music-hall and stage experience.
Autobiography 1986: *Up the Ladder to Obscurity.*
Private's Progress 56. Two Way Stretch 60. The Dock Brief 61. Yesterday's Enemy 61. The Long Ships 63. Guns at Batasi 64. Catch Us If You Can 65. Press For Time 66. Corruption 69. Doctors Wear Scarlet 70. The Railway Children 71. Go For a Take 72. The Amazing Mr Blunden 72. The Return of the Pink Panther 74. The Revenge of the Pink Panther 78. Sahara 82, etc. Much on TV.

Lodge, John (1903–85). American leading man of the thirties, mainly European films. Retired to take up politics.
A Woman Accused (debut) 32. Little Women 33. The Scarlet Empress 34. Koenigsmark 35. Sensation 36. The Tenth Man 36. Bulldog Drummond at Bay 37. Bank Holiday 38. L'Esclave Blanche 39.

¶ Mr John Lodge continues to suffer from a kind of lockjaw, an inability to move the tight muscles of his mouth, to do anything but glare with the dumbness and glossiness of an injured seal.—*Graham Greene reviewing The Tenth Man*

The Lodger: see *Jack the Ripper.*

Loeb, Philip (1894–1955). American character actor, usually of smart types.
Room Service 38. A Double Life 48. Molly 51, etc.

Loesser, Frank (1910–1969). American songwriter, in films since 1930. 'Baby It's Cold Outside', 'Jingle Jangle', many others. Scores for *Hans Christian Andersen, Where's Charley?, Guys and Dolls, How to Succeed in Business Without Really Trying,* etc.

Loew, Marcus (1870–1927). Austrian-American exhibitor and distributor, co-founder and controller of MGM, which is still run by Loews Inc.

Loewe, Frederick (1901–). Austrian composer in America, usually of musicals with Alan Jay Lerner.

Gigi, My Fair Lady, Camelot, Paint Your Wagon, etc.

Loft, Arthur (1897–1947). American supporting actor with a slightly bewildered face, often seen as businessman.
Prisoner of Shark Island 36. The Woman in the Window 45. Blood on the Sun 46. Scarlet Street 47, many others.

Lofting, Hugh (1886–1947). English children's author, creator of the Doctor Dolittle stories.

Loftus, Cecilia (1876–1943). British character actress who went to Hollywood with a Shakespearean company in 1895, and stayed.
East Lynne 31. The Old Maid 39. The Bluebird 40. Lucky Partners 40. The Black Cat 41, etc.

Logan, Joshua (1908–). American stage director whose occasional films have tended towards stodginess.
Autobiographies: *Josh, My Up and Down, In and Out Life* (1976); *Movie Stars, Real People and Me* (1978).
□I Met My Love Again 38. *Picnic* 56. *Bus Stop* 56. *Sayonara* 57. South Pacific 58. Tall Story 60. Fanny 61. Ensign Pulver 64. *Camelot* 67. Paint Your Wagon 69.

Logan, Phyllis (1954–). Scottish-born actress.
Another Time Another Place (BFA) 83. 1984 84. The Chain 85.

Logan, Robert F. (–). Brawny hero of American family films.
The Bridge at Remagen 69. The Wilderness Family 75. Across the Great Divide 76. The Wilderness Family Part Two 77. Snowbeast (TV) 77. The Sea Gypsies 78, etc.

Loggia, Robert (1930–). American leading man.
Somebody Up There Likes Me 56. Cop Hater 58. The Nine Lives of Elfego Baca (TV) 59. Cattle King 63. Che! 69. The Moneychangers (TV) 75. First Love 77. The Ninth Configuration 80. S.O.B. 81. An Officer and a Gentleman 82. Trail of the Pink Panther 82. A Woman called Golda (TV) 82. Curse of the Pink Panther 83. Scarface 83. Jagged Edge (AAN) 85. The Believers 87. Over the Top 87, etc.
TV series: *T.H.E. Cat* 66.

Lohr, Marie (1890–1975). Distinguished Australian stage actress, on London stage from 1901; since 1930 in dowager roles.
Aren't We All? (debut) 32. *Pygmalion* 38. *Major Barbara* 40. The Winslow Boy 48. A Town Like Alice 56, many others.

Lola Montes (France/Germany 1955). This last film by Max Ophuls, treating the life of the famous courtesan in a series of complex flashbacks from the circus act in which she later toured, was a bravura piece of cinema in typically tortuous but often stimulating style. Unfortunately it was generally shown in an atrocious dubbed and shortened version with the circus sequences removed and the remainder in roughly chronological order. Photographed in colour by Christian Matras; with Martine Carol, Anton Walbrook and Peter Ustinov.

Lollobrigida, Gina (1927–). Italian glamour girl and international leading lady, in films since 1947.
Pagliacci 47. Fanfan la Tulipe 51. *Belles de Nuit* 52. The Wayward Wife 52. *Bread, Love and Dreams* 53. Beat the Devil 54. Le Grand Jeu 54. Trapeze 56. Where the Hot Wind Blows 58. Solomon and Sheba 59. Come September 61. Woman of Straw 64. Strange Bedfellows 65. Four Kinds of Love (Bambole) 65. Hotel Paradiso 66. Buona Sera, Mrs Campbell 68. Bad Man's River 71. King Queen Knave 72. The Lonely Woman 76, many others.
TV series: Falcon Crest 84.

Lom, Herbert (1917–) (Herbert Charles Angelo Kuchacevich ze Schluderpacheru). Czech actor whose personality adapts itself equally well to villainy or kindliness; in Britain from 1939.
Mein Kampf 40. The Young Mr Pitt (as Napoleon) 41. The Dark Tower 43. Hotel Reserve 44. *The Seventh Veil* 46. Night Boat to Dublin 46. *Dual Alibi* 47. Good Time Girl 48. The Golden Salamander 49. *State Secret* 50. The Black Rose 50. Hell Is Sold Out 51. The Ringer 52. The Net 53. The Love Lottery 54. *The Ladykillers* 55. War and Peace (as Napoleon) 56. Chase a Crooked Shadow 57. Hell Drivers 57. No Trees in the Street 58. Roots of Heaven 58. Northwest Frontier 59. I Aim at the Stars (US) 59. Mysterious Island 61. El Cid 61. Phantom of the Opera (title role) 62. A Shot in the Dark 64. Return from the Ashes 65. Uncle Tom's Cabin (Ger.) 65. Gambit 66. Assignment to Kill 67. Villa Rides 68. Doppelganger 69. The Hot Death (Ger.)

69. Murders in the Rue Morgue 71. Asylum 72. And Now the Screaming Starts 73. The Return of the Pink Panther 74. And Then There Were None 75. The Pink Panther Strikes Again 77. Revenge of the Pink Panther 78. Charleston 78. The Lady Vanishes 79. Hopscotch 80. The Man with Bogart's Face 80. Trail of the Pink Panther 82. Curse of the Pink Panther 83. The Dead Zone 83. Memed My Hawk 84. King Solomon's Mines 85. Whoops Apocalypse 86. Scoop (TV) 87, others.
TV series: *The Human Jungle*.

Lomas, Herbert (1887–1961). Gaunt, hollow-voiced British stage actor.
The Sign of Four 32. Lorna Doone 35. Rembrandt 36. Jamaica Inn 39. Ask a Policeman 39. *The Ghost Train* 41. I Know Where I'm Going 45. Bonnie Prince Charlie 48. The Net 53, etc.

Lombard, Carole (1908–1942) (Jane Peters). American leading lady of the thirties, a fine comedienne with an inimitable rangy style.
Biography 1976: *Screwball* by Larry Swindell.
☐A Perfect Crime 21. Hearts and Spurs 25. Marriage in Transit 25. Me Gangster 28. Power 28. Show Folks 28. Ned McCobb's Daughter 29. High Voltage 29. Big News 29. The Racketeer 29. The Arizona Kid 30. Safety in Numbers 30. Fast and Loose 30. It Pays to Advertise 31. Man of the World 31. Ladies' Man 31. Up Pops the Devil 31. I Take this Woman 31. No One Man 32. Sinners in the Sun 32. Virtue 32. No More Orchids 32. *No Man of Her Own* 32. From Heaven to Hell 33. Supernatural 33. The Eagle and the Hawk 33. Brief Moment 33. White Woman 33. *Bolero* 34. We're Not Dressing 34. *Twentieth Century* 34. Now and Forever 34. Lady by Choice 34. The Gay Bride 34. *Rumba* 34. Hands Across the Table 35. Love Before Breakfast 36. *My Man Godfrey* 36. The Princess Comes Across 36. Swing High Swing Low 37. True Confession 37. *Nothing Sacred* 37. Fools for Scandal 38. Made for Each Other 38. In Name Only 39. Vigil in the Night 40. *They Knew What They Wanted* 40. *Mr and Mrs Smith* 41. *To Be or Not To Be* 42.
❁ For daring to be wacky while glamorous. *Nothing Sacred*.

¶ *C.L.:* I live by a man's code designed to fit a man's world, yet at the same time I never forget that a woman's first job is to choose the right shade of lipstick.

Carole was the first woman I ever met who used four-letter words like a truck driver.—*Radie Harris*

Loncraine, Richard (1946–). British director.
Flame 74. Full Circle 76. Blade on the Feather (TV) 80. Brimstone and Treacle 82. The Missionary 82, etc.
The Missionary 84. Bellman and True 87, etc.

London has provided a background, usually highly inaccurate, for innumerable movies, but few have really explored it, though *The Ipcress File* and *The Pumpkin Eater* found some unusual angles. *London Town* was a half-hearted musical; twenty years later *Three Hats for Lisa* captured the mood better but managed to seem old-fashioned. *Pygmalion* and *My Fair Lady* embodied the spirit of London in some theatrical sets. *Indiscreet* prowled lovingly around the Embankment, and *A Run for Your Money* made good use of the Paddington area as well as suburban Twickenham. The City was the venue of part of *You Must Be Joking*, while *Morgan* used Hampstead to good advantage. The East End, especially the street markets and the railway sidings, were exploited in *Waterloo Road, A Kid for Two Farthings* and *It Always Rains on Sunday*. The docks had *Pool of London* to themselves. Hollywood's idea of London in geography can be pretty weird, as in *Knock on Wood*, when Paramount went to the trouble of having special location material shot with Jon Pertwee doubling for Danny Kaye, but showed the star turning off Marble Arch into Fleet Street two miles away. Similarly in *Twenty-three Paces to Baker Street* the river frontage of the Savoy Hotel could be entered from Portman Square, in actuality another two-mile jaunt. London fog has been a useful cover for many a scrappy set, especially in films presenting the Victorian London associated with Sherlock Holmes. Going further back, *Henry V* presented in model form the London of 1600, and attempts at historical recreation were also made in *Tower of London, Fire over England, Elizabeth and Essex, Nell Gwyn, Forever Amber, Mrs Fitzherbert, The First Gentleman, Victoria the Great, Cromwell* and *The Mudlark*. It was probably Hitchcock who began the fashion of making London a stately background for thrillers, with his East End mission in *The Man Who Knew Too Much*, the music hall in *The Thirty-nine Steps*, the bus journey and the Lord Mayor's Show in *Sabotage*, the fall from Westminster

Cathedral in *Foreign Correspondent*, the theatrical garden party in *Stage Fright*, and Covent Garden in *Frenzy*. Others in this tradition have included *Brannigan, Hennessy, Villain, Robbery*, and innumerable TV series such as *The Sweeney*.
See also: *Swinging London*.

London Films. Production company founded by Alexander Korda and associated with his own major films of the thirties and later with other leading names operating under his banner.

London, Jack (1876–1916). American adventure novelist, whose most-filmed stories include *The Sea Wolf, Adventures of Martin Eden, Call of the Wild* and *White Fang*.

London, Julie (1926–) (Julie Peck). American leading lady and singer.
Jungle Woman 44. The Red House 47. The Fat Man 51. The Great Man 56. Saddle the Wind 58. Man of the West 58. The Third Voice 60. The George Raft Story 62, etc.
TV series: *Emergency* 72–77.

London Town (GB 1946). An attempt by the Rank Organization to make a British musical, often quoted as proof that success in this genre is impossible outside Hollywood (a maxim not disproved till the sixties). Despite an imported American director, Wesley Ruggles, it's all lamentably dull except for Sid Field's sketches, here preserved intact.

The Lone Ranger. This western Robin Hood originally featured in a radio serial, later became a comic strip in 1935; twenty years later Clayton Moore played the hero in a successful TV series and a couple of feature films, with Jay Silverheels as Tonto.
The 1981 attempt to retell the yarn half-seriously, *The Legend of the Lone Ranger*, met with disaster: Klinton Spilsbury was the Lone Ranger, and has not been heard from since.

The Lone Wolf was a gentleman thief created by Louis Joseph Vance. He reached the screen in silent days and was played by H. B. Warner, Jack Holt, and Bert Lytell; in the thirties Melvyn Douglas and Francis Lederer each played him once and then Warren William took over for eight episodes, usually with Eric Blore as his manservant. In 1946 Gerald Mohr played in the first of three episodes, and in 1949 Ron Randell personified Michael Lanyard for the last time on the big screen. In 1954 Louis Hayward played him in a TV series, *The Lone Wolf*, also known as *Streets of Danger*.

Long, Audrey (1924–). American leading lady of the forties.
A Night of Adventure 44. Pan Americana 45. Song of My Heart 47. The Petty Girl 50. Indian Uprising 52, etc.

Long, Richard (1927–1974). American leading man, mainly in second features.
Tomorrow Is Forever 44. The Stranger 45. The Egg and I 47. Criss Cross 49. Saskatchewan 54. Cult of the Cobra 55. Home from the Hills 59. The Tenderfoot 64, etc.
TV series: *77 Sunset Strip* 58–60. *Bourbon Street Beat* 59. *The Big Valley* 65–68. *Nanny and the Professor* 69–71. Thicker Than Water 73.

Long, Shelley (1950–). American leading lady.
Irreconcilable Differences 84. The Money Pit 85. Outrageous Fortune 87.

long shot. One taken from a distance, usually to establish a scene or a situation but sometimes for dramatic effect. Opposite of close-up.

Long, Walter (1879–1952). Burly, evil-faced American character actor of silent days; usually played a bestial Hun in World War I films, and was later a memorable foil for Laurel and Hardy. He also played a Negro in *The Birth of a Nation*.
Intolerance 16. The Little American 17. Scarlet Days 19. Moran of the Lady Letty 22. The Shock Punch 25. Yankee Clipper 27. Moby Dick 30. The Maltese Falcon 31. Pardon Us 31. Six of a Kind 34. Pick a Star 37, etc.

Longden, John (1900–71). British leading man of the early thirties; later graduated to character roles.
Blackmail 30. Atlantic 30. The Ringer 31. Born Lucky 33. French Leave 37. The Gaunt Stranger 38. The Lion Has Wings 39. The Common Touch 41. The Silver Fleet 43. Bonnie Prince Charlie 48. The Man with the Twisted Lip (as Sherlock Homes) 51. Quatermass II 56. An Honourable Murder 60, many others.

Longden, Terence (1922–). British actor, in secondary roles.
Never Look Back 52. Simon and Laura 55. Doctor at Large 57. Carry On Sergeant 58. Ben Hur 59. The Return of Mr Moto 65, etc.

The Longest Day (US 1962). Darryl F. Zanuck master-minded this detailed reconstruction of D-Day 1944. Long and very noisy, it has some brilliantly handled action sequences, and the all-star cast provided box office insurance at the cost of verisimilitude.

Longstreet, Stephen (1907–). American screenwriter.
The Jolson Story 46. The Greatest Show on Earth (co-w) 52. The First Travelling Saleslady 55. The Helen Morgan Story 57, etc.

Lonsdale, Michel (sometimes Michael) (1931–). Chubby French character actor, in some international roles.
La Main Chaude 60. The Trial 62. Behold a Pale Horse 64. The Bride Wore Black 68. Stolen Kisses 68. Souffle au Coeur 71. *The Day of the Jackal* 73. Stavisky 74. Caravan to Vaccares 74. The Phantom of Liberty 74. The Romantic Englishwoman 75. The Pink Telephone 75. Mr Klein 76. The Passage 78. Moonraker 79. Les Jeux de la Comtesse 80. Enigma 82, many others.

Loo, Richard (1903–1983). Hawaiian-Chinese actor who turned to films after business depression. Played hundreds of oriental roles.
Dirigible 31. The Good Earth 37. The Keys of the Kingdom 44. Rogues' Regiment 48. Love is a Many-Splendored Thing 54. The Quiet American 58. The Sand Pebbles 66. One More Time 71, etc.

lookalikes. The old studios would frequently hire less talented performers who looked rather like their main stars, simply to keep the latter in order. Also, if a star with a certain style proved fashionable, a rival might try to repeat the dose. Whatever the reason, Gloria Jean was designed to remind filmgoers of Deanna Durbin; John Carroll of Clark Gable; Anna Sten of Marlene Dietrich; Brian Aherne of Ronald Colman; Patric Knowles of Errol Flynn; Dane Clark of John Garfield; Antonio Moreno and Ricardo Cortez of Rudolph Valentino; Viveca Lindfors of Ingrid Bergman; Roddy McDowall of Freddie Bartholomew; John Gavin of Rock Hudson; Gig Young of Cary Grant; Lizabeth Scott of Lauren Bacall; Mary Beth Hughes of Lana Turner; Yvonne de Carlo of Maria Montez; Mamie Van Doren and Sheree North of Marilyn Monroe; Joel McCrea of Gary Cooper; Tippi Hedren of Grace Kelly. Not too surprisingly, lightning never struck in the same place twice.

Looney Tunes and **Merrie Melodies** are the two umbrella titles under which Warners have long released their cartoon shorts featuring such characters as Bugs Bunny, Daffy Duck, Porky Pig, Pepe le Pew, Sylvester and Tweetie Pie. They have won Academy Awards for *Tweetie Pie* 47, *For Scentimental Reasons* 49, *Speedy Gonzales* 55, *Birds Anonymous* 57, *Knighty Knight Bugs* 58.

Loos, Anita (1891–1981). American humorous writer who spent years in Hollywood studios.
Autobiography 1966: *A Girl Like I.* 1974: *Kiss Hollywood Goodbye.* 1977: *Cast of Thousands*. Also wrote *The Talmadge Girls* (1977).
Intolerance (subtitles) 16. Let's Get a Divorce (w) 18. A Temperamental Wife (oa) 19. Mama's Affair (d) 20. In Search of a Sinner (p) 20. Red Hot Romance (w) 22. Learning to Love (w) 25. Gentlemen Prefer Blondes (oa) 31. Midnight Mary (oa) 33. *San Francisco* (w) 36. Saratoga (w) 37. The Women (w) 39. When Ladies Meet (oa) 41. *Gentlemen Prefer Blondes* (oa) 52, etc.

Lopez, Trini (1937–). American character actor, ex-bandleader.
Marriage on the Rocks 66. The Dirty Dozen 67. Antonio 73, etc.

Lord, Del (1895–). American second feature director who handled most of the Three Stooges shorts.

Lord, Jack (1922–) (John Joseph Ryan). Craggy-faced American leading man who found his greatest success in television.
Cry Murder 51. The Court Martial of Billy Mitchell 55. God's Little Acre 58. Walk Like a Dragon 60. Doctor No 62. The Road to Hangman's Tree 67. The Name of the Game is Kill 68, etc.
TV series: *Stony Burke* 62. *Hawaii Five-O* 68–79.

Lord, Jean-Claude (–). Canadian director.
Eclair au Chocolat 79. Visiting Hours 82. Dreamworld 83.

Lord Jim. Joseph Conrad's saga of a man in search of himself all over the Far East was filmed as a 1925 silent in Hollywood with Percy Marmont. In 1965 Richard Brooks wrote and directed a slap-up international version with Peter O'Toole, but it proved singularly dreary.

Lord, Marjorie (1922–). American leading lady of minor films in the forties, later on TV as Danny Thomas' wife in comedy series.
Forty Naughty Girls 38. Timber 42. Sherlock Holmes in Washington 42. Flesh and Fantasy 44. The Argyle Secrets 48. New Orleans 49. Port of Hell 55. Boy Did I Get a Wrong Number 66, etc.
TV series: Make Room for Daddy 53–57. Make Room for Granddaddy 70.

Lord, Pauline (1890–1950). American stage actress who made only two films.
□Mrs Wiggs of the Cabbage Patch 35. A Feather in Her Hat 36.

Lord, Robert (1900–1976). American writer and producer associated with Warner Brothers throughout the thirties and forties; later joined Humphrey Bogart in Santana Productions.
AS WRITER: The Johnstown Flood 26. A Reno Divorce 27. My Man 28. Five and Ten Cent Annie 28. On with the Show 29. Gold Diggers of Broadway 29. Hold Everything 30. Fireman Save My Child 32. One Way Passage 32. 20,000 Years in Sing Sing 32. The Little Giant 33. Dames 34. Page Miss Glory 35, etc.
AS PRODUCER: Wonder Bar 34. Oil for the Lamps of China 35. Black Legion 37. Tovarich 37. Brother Rat 38. The Dawn Patrol 38. Dodge City 39. Confessions of a Nazi Spy 39. The Letter 40. Dive Bomber 41. High Wall 47. Tokyo Joe 49. In a Lonely Place 50. Sirocco 51, etc.

Loren, Sophia (1934–) (Sophia Scicoloni). Statuesque Italian leading lady, latterly an accomplished international actress. In films from 1950 (as extra).
Biography 1975: *Sophia* by Donald Zec.
Autobiography 1979: *Sophia: Living and Loving* (with A. E. Hotchner).
Aida 53. The Sign of Venus 53. Tempi Nostri 54. Attila 54. The Gold of Naples 54. *Woman of the River* 55. Too Bad She's Bad 55. The Miller's Wife 55. Scandal in Sorrento 55. Lucky To Be a Woman 56. The Pride and the Passion 57. *Boy on a Dolphin* 57. Legend of the Lost 57. Desire under the Elms 58. *The Key* 58. Houseboat 58. Black Orchid 59. That Kind of Woman 59. Heller in Pink Tights 60. A Breath of Scandal 61. *Two Women* (AA, BFA) 61. *The Millionairess* 61. El Cid 61. Boccaccio 70 61. The Condemned of Altona 62. Madame Sans Gêne 62. Five Miles to Midnight 62. Yesterday, Today and Tomorrow 63. The Fall of the Roman Empire 64. Marriage Italian Style 64. Operation Crossbow 65. Judith 65. Arabesque 66. Lady L 66. A Countess from Hong Kong 66. Ghosts Italian Style 68. More than a Miracle 69. Sunflower 70. Man of La Mancha 72. Lady Liberty 74. Brief Encounter (TV) 74. The Voyage 75. The Cassandra Crossing 77. A Special Day 77. Brass Target 78. Firepower 79. Angela 80. Sophia Loren (TV) 80, etc.

¶ *S.L.:* Everything you see, I owe to spaghetti.
S.L.: Sex appeal is fifty per cent what you've got and fifty per cent what people think you've got.
S.L.: I'm not ashamed of my bare-bottomed beginnings.
All the natural mistakes of beauty fall together in her to create a magnificent accident.—*Rex Reed*
S.L.: In a restaurant or at a function I just walk straight in and it's an eternity. When I'm sitting, it's OK, but then I have to start thinking of a short cut out.
Working with her is like being bombed by watermelons.—*Alan Ladd*

Lorentz, Pare (1905–). American documentarist and film critic.
The Plow that Broke the Plains 36. *The River* 37.

Lorne, Marion (1886–1968) (M. L. MacDougal). American character comedienne with long stage experience, latterly seen as eccentric old lady.
Strangers on a Train 51. The Girl Rush 55. The Graduate 68, etc.
TV series: Mr Peepers 52–54. *Bewitched* (as the dotty witch-aunt) 64–67.

Lorre, Peter (1904–1964) (Laszlo Loewenstein). Highly individual Hungarian character actor who filmed in Germany and Britain before settling in Hollywood. His rolling eyes, timid manner and mysterious personality could adapt to either sympathetic or sinister roles; a weight problem restricted his later appearances.
□Frühlings Erwachen 29. Der Weisse Teufel 30. Die Koffer des Herrn O.F. 30. *M* 30. Bomben auf Monte Carlo 31. Funf von der Jazzband 32. Schuss im Morgengrauen 32.

Der Weisse Damon 32. F.P.I. 32. Was Frauen Traumen 33. Unsichtbare Gegner 33. De Haut en Bas 34. *The Man Who Knew Too Much* 34. *Mad Love* 35. *Crime and Punishment* (as Raskolnikov) 35. *The Secret Agent* 36. Crack Up 36. Nancy Steele is Missing 37. Lancer Spy 37. Think Fast Mr Moto 37. Thank You Mr Moto 37. Mr Moto's Gamble 38. I'll Give a Million 38. Mr Moto Takes a Chance 38. Mysterious Mr Moto 38. Mr Moto on Danger Island 39. Mr Moto Takes a Vacation 39. Mr Moto's Last Warning 39. Strange Cargo 40. I Was an Adventuress 40. Island of Doomed Men 40. Stranger on the Third Floor 40. You'll Find Out 40. Mr District Attorney 41. *The Face Behind the Mask* 41. They Met in Bombay 41. *The Maltese Falcon* 41. All through the Night 42. Invisible Agent 42. The Boogie Man Will Get You 42. Casablanca 42. Background to Danger 43. The Cross of Lorraine 43. The Constant Nymph 43. Passage to Marseilles 44. *The Mask of Dimitrios* 44. Arsenic and Old Lace 44. The Conspirators 44. Hollywood Canteen 44. Hotel Berlin 45. Confidential Agent 45. Three Strangers 46. Black Angel 46. The Chase 46. The Verdict 46. *The Beast with Five Fingers* 46. My Favorite Brunette 47. Casbah 48. Rope of Sand 49. Quicksand 50. Double Confession 50. Der Verlorene (& d) 50. Beat the Devil 53. 20,000 Leagues under the Sea 54. *Congo Crossing* 56. Around the World in Eighty Days 56. The Buster Keaton Story 56. Silk Stockings 57. The Story of Mankind (as Nero) 57. Hell Ship Mutiny 57. The Sad Sack 58. The Big Circus 59. Scent of Mystery 59. Voyage to the Bottom of the Sea 61. *Tales of Terror* 62. Five Weeks in a Balloon 62. *The Raven* 63. The Comedy of Terrors 63. The Patsy 64.

❀ For the diffidence of his dark deeds and for his inimitable voice, still enthusiastically parodied by cartoon villains. *The Mask of Dimitrios*.

¶ Those marbly pupils in the pasty spherical face are like the eye pieces of a microscope through which you can see laid flat on the slide the entangled mind of a man: love and lust, nobility and perversity, hatred of itself, and despair jumping up at you from the jelly.—*Graham Greene*

Lorring, Joan (1926–) (Magdalen Ellis). English-Russian actress, evacuated to US in 1939; played some nasty teenagers.
Girls under Twenty-One 41. Song of Russia 44. The Bridge of San Luis Rey 44. The Corn Is Green 45. The Verdict 46. The Lost Moment 47. Good Sam 49. Stranger on the Prowl 53, etc.
TV series: Norby 54.

Los Angeles, being the home of the film studios, was the anonymous background of ninety per cent of Hollywood films from the very beginning. Only more recently, however, has the actual city been explored, usually in a cynical Chandleresque manner as in *The Long Goodbye* and *Marlowe*, or as a vivid sunlit background for police thrillers with their screaming car chases, especially in such TV series as *Police Story, The Blue Knight, Police Woman, The Rookies, Chase, Emergency, The Smith Family* and *Dragnet*. The city's seamy side was shown in *M* and *The Savage Eye,* its future in *The Omega Man,* its sophisticated present in *Divorce American Style*, its sewers in *Them*, and its past in *Chinatown*. Perhaps the most vivid picture of the growing sprawl is to be found as background to the comedies of the Keystone Kops and Laurel and Hardy; and *Earthquake* finally destroyed it.

One positive approach to Tinseltown was expressed in *The Model Shop*: 'How could you find this place ugly? It's pure poetry.'

Losch, Tilly (1901–1975). Austrian exotic dancer, in Hollywood in the thirties and forties.
☐The Garden of Allah 36. The Good Earth 37. Duel in the Sun 46.

Losey, Joseph (1909–84). American director of somewhat pretentious movies, in Britain from 1952 after the communist witch-hunt.
☐The Boy with Green Hair 48. The Lawless 50. *The Prowler* 50. M 51. The Big Night 51. Stranger on the Prowl 53. The Sleeping Tiger 54. The Intimate Stranger 56. Time without Pity 57. The Gypsy and the Gentleman 57. Blind Date 59. The Criminal 60. *The Damned* 61. Eva 62. *The Servant* 63. King and Country 64. Modesty Blaise 66. *Accident* 67. Boom 68. Secret Ceremony 68. Figures in a Landscape 70. The Go-Between 71. The Assassination of Trotsky 72. A Doll's House 73. Galileo 74. The Romantic Englishwoman 75. Mr Klein 76. Don Giovanni 79. The Trout 82. Steaming 84.

¶ *J. L.:* Films can illustrate our existence . . . they can distress, disturb and provoke people into thinking about themselves and certain problems. But NOT give the answers.

Lost Horizon (US 1937). Frank Capra's uneven but attractive film, from the James Hilton novel about a Tibetan Utopia, made Shangri-La a household word. The actors were perfectly cast, with Ronald Colman as Conway, H. B. Warner as Chang and Sam Jaffe as the High Lama. In 1973 Ross Hunter remade the story as a semi-musical, with Peter Finch, John Gielgud and Charles Boyer, and an unhappy result.

The Lost Patrol (US 1934). An unconvincing but savage and relentless melodrama about a British desert patrol picked off one by one by Arabs until rescuers find the one survivor raving mad. Notable for photography by Harold Wendstrom, directed by John Ford (here on the brink of his best period), and heavily overacted but enjoyable performances from Victor McLaglen, Boris Karloff and Reginald Denny. From a novel by Philip MacDonald which later inspired *Sahara* 43, *Bataan* 46 and *Last of the Comanches* 51.

The Lost Weekend (US 1945; AA best picture). Three days in the life of a dipsomaniac, cunningly dramatized by its producer and director, Charles Brackett and Billy Wilder, from a novel by Charles Jackson. Ray Milland (AA) gave the performance of his life, and the film's success gave Hollywood realism a big stride forward.

The Lost World. The 1924 silent version of Arthur Conan Doyle's exciting adventure story was notable for the first efforts of Willis O'Brien in animating prehistoric dinosaurs. The 1960 remake was notable for nothing except doing everything wrong, including the hilarious miscasting of Claude Rains as Professor Challenger.

Lotinga, Ernie (1876–1951). British vaudeville comedian formerly known as Dan Roy. Made a few slapstick comedies which had their followers.
The Raw Recruit 28. PC Josser 31. Josser Joins the Navy 32. Josser in the Army 33. Love Up the Pole 36, etc.

Louise, Anita (1915–1970) (Anita Louise Fremault). American leading lady, usually in gentle roles. Played child parts from 1924.
What a Man 30. A Midsummer Night's Dream 35. The Story of Louis Pasteur 35. Anthony Adverse 36. The Green Light 37. Marie Antoinette 38. The Sisters 39. Phantom Submarine 41. The Fighting Guardsman 45. The Bandit of Sherwood Forest 46. Retreat, Hell! 52.
TV series: *My Friend Flicka* 56.

Louise, Tina (1934–) (Tina Blacker). Statuesque American leading lady of routine films in the sixties.
God's Little Acre 58. Day of the Outlaw 59. Armored Command 61. For Those Who Think Young 64. Wrecking Crew 68. The Good Guys and the Bad Guys 69. How to Commit Marriage 70. The Stepford Wives 75. Mean Dog Blues 78, etc.
TV series: *Gilligan's Island* 64–66.

Lourié, Eugène (1905–). French designer.
Les Bas Fonds 36. *La Grande Illusion* 37. La Règle du Jeu 39. This Land Is Mine (US) 42. *The Southerner* (US) 44. The River 51. What's the Matter with Helen 71. Burnt Offerings 76. Bronco Billy 80, etc.
AS DIRECTOR: The Beast from Twenty Thousand Fathoms 53. The Colossus of New York 58. Gorgo (GB) 60, etc.

love

? Name the lovers in:

1 *Love Affair* (1939)
2 *Love Story*
3 *Love Among the Ruins*
4 *Love Me or Leave Me*
5 *Love Letters*
6 *The Love Parade*
7 *Love Is News*
8 *Love Me Tonight*
9 *Love Is a Many-Splendored Thing*
10 *Love Is a Ball*
11 *Love Under Fire*
12 *Love with the Proper Stranger*

Love, Bessie (1898–1986) (Juanita Horton). Vivacious, petite American leading lady of the twenties. In films from childhood; from the mid-thirties resident in London, playing occasional cameo parts.
Autobiography 1977: *From Hollywood with Love.*
Intolerance 15. The Aryan 16. A Sister of Six 17. The Dawn of Understanding 18. The Purple Dawn 20. The Vermilion Pencil 21. Human Wreckage 23. Dynamite Smith 24. The Lost World 25. Lovey Mary 26. Sally of the Scandals 27. Broadway Melody 28. Chasing Rainbows 30. Morals for Women 31. Conspiracy 32. Atlantic Ferry 42. Journey Together 45. Touch and Go 55. The Wild Affair 64. Isadora 68. Sunday Bloody Sunday 71. Mousey (TV) 74. The Ritz 76, many others.

Love, Montagu (1877–1943). Heavily built British character actor, long in Hollywood, latterly as stern fathers.
Bought and Paid For 16. The Gilded Cage 19. The Case of Becky 21. A Son of the Sahara 24. Son of the Sheik 26. Don Juan 26. King of Kings 27. Jesse James 27. The Haunted House 28. The Divine Lady 29. Bulldog Drummond 29. Outward Bound 30. The Cat Creeps 30. Midnight Lady 32. Clive of India 35. The White Angel 36. The Prince and the Pauper (as Henry VIII) 37. The Adventures of Robin Hood 38. Gunga Din 39. All This and Heaven Too 40. Shining Victory 41. The Constant Nymph 43. Devotion 44, many others.

Love Me Tonight (US 1932). An early sound musical with an apparent 'Lubitsch touch' which actually belongs to director Rouben Mamoulian, who also manages to provide a René Clair view of Paris as a place where everybody sings. Visual and aural experiments jostle the wit and good humour, and memorable songs like 'Mimi' and 'Isn't It Romantic?' complete a masterpiece of light cinema. With Maurice Chevalier, Jeanette MacDonald, Myrna Loy, Charles Butterworth, Charles Ruggles. What plot there is concerns a tailor who makes it in high society.

The Love Parade (US 1930). An early sound comedy by Ernst Lubitsch which set his style, and that of other directors influenced by him, for many years to come. Brittle, sophisticated, finely mounted, with the story told in visual terms, it was written by Ernest Vajda and Guy Bolton, with sets designed by Hans Dreier and music by Victor Schertzinger; and it starred Maurice Chevalier, Jeanette MacDonald, Lupino Lane and Lilian Roth. Its impact cannot now be recaptured.

Love Story (US 1970). A remarkable box office success from the novel by Erich Segal, this very ordinarily made film turned out to be a piece of abject thirties sentimentality dressed up with fashionable four-letter words. About a couple of young marrieds and their parent trouble, it featured a heroine who died of an incurable disease without losing a shred of her beauty. In its wake a flood of similar films was expected, but few materialized and none was successful. Directed by Arthur Hiller, with Ali MacGraw and Ryan O'Neal. An unsuccessful sequel, *Oliver's Story*, appeared in 1979.

The Loved One (US 1965). Advertised as the film with something to offend everybody, this too-free adaptation of Evelyn Waugh's satirical account of the burial customs of southern California got itself tangled up with a number of extraneous matters, including over-eating, film production and military bureaucracy. Despite central miscasting and some pretentious writing, a number of the bravura passages come off amusingly; but the film remains notable for effort rather than achievement. Directed by Tony Richardson, photographed by Haskell Wexler, with John Gielgud, Liberace, Rod Steiger, Milton Berle and others.

Lovejoy, Frank (1912–1962). American actor of tough roles, with stage and radio experience.
Black Bart 48. Home of the Brave 49. In a Lonely Place 50. *The Sound of Fury* 51. I Was a Communist for the FBI 51. Force of Arms 51. The Hitch Hiker 52. Retreat Hell 52. The System 53. House of Wax 53. The Charge at Feather River 54. Beachhead 54. The Americano 55. Top of the World 55. Strategic Air Command 55. The Crooked Web 56. Cole Younger Gunfighter 58, etc.
TV series: Man Against Crime 54. *Meet McGraw* 57–58.

Lovelace, Linda (1952–). American female lead of *Deep Throat* and other porno films.

Lovell, Raymond (1900–1953). Canadian stage actor long in Britain: often in pompous or sinister roles.
Warn London 34. Contraband 40. 49th Parallel 41. *Alibi* 42. Warn That Man 43. The Way Ahead 44. *Caesar and Cleopatra* 45. The Three Weird Sisters 48. Time Gentleman Please 52. The Steel Key 53, etc.

Low, Warren (1905–). American editor.
Dr Socrates 35. Anthony Adverse 36. The Great Garrick 37. The Life of Emile Zola 37. Juarez 39. *The Letter* 40. The Gay Sisters 42. Now Voyager 42. The Searching Wind 46. Sorry Wrong Number 48. September Affair 50. The Stooge 52. About Mrs Leslie 54. The Bad Seed 56. Gunfight at the OK Corral 57. Summer and Smoke 61. Boeing Boeing 65. Will Penny 68. True Grit 69. Willard 71, many others.

Lowe, Arthur (1914–1982). Rotund British character actor who after a career of bit parts achieved star status on TV in a variety of tape shows from *Coronation Street* to *Dad's Army*.

Stormy Crossing 48. Kind Hearts and Coronets 49. This Sporting Life 63. The Rise and Rise of Michael Rimmer 70. *Dad's Army* 71. The Ruling Class 71. Theatre of Blood 73. *O Lucky Man* 73. *No Sex Please, We're British* 73. The Bawdy Adventures of Tom Jones 76. The Lady Vanishes 79. Britannia Hospital 82, etc.

Lowe, Edmund (1890–1971). Suave American leading man of the twenties and thirties who did not manage to age into a character actor.
The Spreading Dawn 17. The Devil 20. Peacock Alley 21. The Silent Command 23. The Fool 25. *What Price Glory?* 26. Is Zat So? 27. Dressed to Kill 28. In Old Arizona 29. The Cockeyed World 29. Scotland Yard 30. Transatlantic 31. *Chandu the Magician* 32. *Dinner at Eight* 33. Gift of Gab 34. Mr Dynamite 35. The Great Impersonation 35. Seven Sinners (GB) 36. The Squeaker (GB) 37. Secrets of a Nurse 38. Our Neighbours the Carters 39. Wolf of New York 40. Call out the Marines 41. Murder in Times Square 43. Dillinger 45. Good Sam 48. Around the World in Eighty Days 56. The Wings of Eagles 57. Heller in Pink Tights 60, etc.
TV series: *Front Page Detective* 52.

Lowe, Rob (1964–). American juvenile lead of the early eighties.
Class 83. Oxford Blues 84. The Hotel New Hampshire 84. St Elmo's Fire 85. Youngblood 85. About Last Night 86. Square Dance 86.

The Lower Depths. Gorki's doss-house study has had two notable filmings. As *Les Bas Fonds*, it provided in 1936 memorable roles for Jean Gabin and Louis Jouvet, with direction by Jean Renoir. In 1958 in Japan, Akira Kurosawa directed Toshiro Mifune in a surprisingly faithful adaptation.

Lowery, Robert (1916–1971) (R. L. Hanks). American leading man of the forties, mainly in routine films.
Wake Up and Live 37. Young Mr Lincoln 39. Lure of the Islands 42. A Scream in the Dark 44. Prison Ship 45. The Mummy's Ghost 46. Death Valley 48. Batman and Robin (serial) (as Batman) 50. Crosswinds 51. Cow Country 53. The Rise and Fall of Legs Diamond 60. Johnny Reno 66, many others.
TV series: Circus Boy 56–57.

Lowry, Morton (c. 1908–). British character actor in Hollywood.
The Hound of the Baskervilles (as Stapleton) 39. How Green Was My Valley 40. The Picture of Dorian Gray 45, etc.

Loy, Myrna (1905–) (Myrna Williams). Likeable American lady of the thirties; began her career in villainous oriental roles but later showed a great flair for sophisticated comedy and warm domestic drama.
SELECTED SILENT FILMS: The Cave Man 26. Don Juan 26. The Climbers 27. Beware of Married Men 28. State Street Sadie 28. The Midnight Taxi 28. Noah's Ark 29, etc.
□SOUND FILMS: The Jazz Singer 27. The Desert Song 29. The Squall 29. Black Watch 29. Hard Boiled Rose 29. Evidence 29. Show of Shows 29. The Great Divide 30. The Jazz Cinderella 30. Cameo Kirby 30. Isle of Escape 30. Under a Texas Moon 30. Cock of the Walk 30. Bride of the Regiment 30. Last of the Duanes 30. The Truth about Youth 30. Renegades 30. Rogue of the Rio Grande 30. The Devil to Pay 30. The Naughty Flirt 31. Body and Soul 31. A Connecticut Yankee 31. Hush Money 31. Transatlantic 31. Rebound 31. Skyline 31. Consolation Marriage 31. Arrowsmith 31. Emma 32. The Wet Parade 32. Vanity Fair 32. The Woman in Room 13 32. New Morals for Old 32. *Love Me Tonight* 32. Thirteen Women 32. *The Mask of Fu Manchu* 32. The Animal Kingdom 32. Topaze 33. The Barbarian 33. The Prizefighter and the Lady 33. *When Ladies Meet* 33. Penthouse 33. Night Flight 33. Men in White 34. Manhattan Melodrama 34. *The Thin Man* 34. Stamboul Quest 34. Evelyn Prentice 34. *Broadway Bill* 34. Wings in the Dark 35. Whipsaw 35. Wife versus Secretary 36. Petticoat Fever 36. The Great Ziegfeld 36. To Mary with Love 36. Libeled Lady 36. After the Thin Man 36. Parnell 37. *Double Wedding* 37. Man Proof 38. Test Pilot 38. Too Hot to Handle 38. Lucky Night 39. *The Rains Came* 39. Third Finger Left Hand 39. Another Thin Man 39. I Love You Again 40. Love Crazy 41. Shadow of the Thin Man 41. The Thin Man Goes Home 44. So Goes My Love 46. *The Best Years of Our Lives* 46. *The Bachelor and the Bobby Soxer* 47. Song of the Thin Man 47. *Mr Blandings Builds His Dream House* 48. The Red Pony 49. That Dangerous Age 49. *Cheaper by the Dozen* 50. Belles on Their Toes 52. The Ambassador's Daughter 56. Lonelyhearts 58. From the Terrace 60. Midnight Lace 60. The April Fools 69. Death Takes a Holiday (TV) 70. Do Not Fold Spindle or Mutilate (TV) 71. The Couple Takes a Wife (TV) 72. Indict and Convict (TV) 73. The Elevator (TV) 73. Airport 75 74. It Happened at Lakewood Manor (TV) 77.

The End 79. Just Tell Me What You Want 80. Summer Solstice (TV) 81.
Gag appearance: The Senator was Indiscreet 49.
❀ For the wit and elegance with which she lived up to her thirties title of 'Queen of Hollywood'. *The Thin Man*.

Loy, Nanni (1925–). Italian director.
Parola di Ladra 56. The Four Days of Naples 62. Made in Italy 65. Head of the Family 67. Why 71. Insieme 79, etc.

Lualdi, Antonella (1931–) (Antoinetta de Pasquale). Italian leading lady of the fifties and sixties.
Three Forbidden Stories 52. Le Rouge et le Noir 54. Wild Love 55. Young Girls Beware 57. Run with the Devil 60. The Mongols 61. My Son the Hero 62. Let's Talk about Women 64. How to Seduce a Playboy 66. Vincent Francois Paul and the Others 75, etc.

Lubin, Arthur (1901–). American director from 1934, mainly of light comedy, and with a penchant for eccentric animals.
□A Successful Failure 34. The Great God Gold 35. Honeymoon Limited 35. Two Sinners 35. Frisco Waterfront 35. The House of a Thousand Candles 36. Yellowstone 37. Mysterious Crossing 37. *California Straight Ahead* 37. I Cover the War 37. Idol of the Crowds 37. Adventure's End 37. Midnight Intruder 38. Beloved Brat 38. Prison Break 38. Secrets of a Nurse 38. Risky Business 38. Big Town Czar 39. Mickey the Kid 39. Call a Messenger 39. The Big Guy 40. *Black Friday* 40. Gangs of Chicago 40. I'm Nobody's Sweetheart Now 40. Meet the Wildcat 40. Who Killed Aunt Maggie? 40. San Francisco Docks 41. Where Did You Get That Girl? 41. *Buck Privates* 41. In the Navy 41. Hold That Ghost 41. Keep 'Em Flying 41. Ride 'Em Cowboy 42. Eagle Squadron 42. White Savage 43. *Phantom of the Opera* 43. Ali Baba and the Forty Thieves 44. Delightfully Dangerous 45. Spider Woman Strikes Back 46. A Night in Paradise 46. New Orleans 47. Impact 49. *Francis* 50. Queen for a Day 51. Francis Goes to the Races 51. *Rhubarb* 51. Francis Goes to West Point 52. It Grows on Trees 52. South Sea Woman 53. Francis Covers Big Town 53. Francis Joins the WACs 54. Francis in the Navy 55. Footsteps in the Fog 55. Lady Godiva 55. Star of India 56. The First Travelling Saleslady 56. Escapade in Japan 57. Thief of Baghdad 61. The Incredible Mr Limpet 64. Hold On 66. Rain for a Dusty Summer 71.
TV series: *Mister Ed* 60–65.

Lubitsch, Ernst (1892–1947). German director, once a comic actor, in a series of silent farces starring him as 'Meyer'. After a variety of subjects he settled for a kind of sophisticated sex comedy that became unmistakably his: the 'Lubitsch touch' was a form of visual innuendo, spicy without ever being vulgar. His greatest period came after 1922, when he settled in Hollywood and became Paramount's leading producer. Early films include many shorts. Awarded special Oscar 1946 'for his distinguished contributions to the art of the motion picture'. A splendid biographical book, *The Lubitsch Touch* (1968), was written by Herman G. Weinberg.
SELECTED EUROPEAN FILMS: Carmen 18. Madame du Barry 19. Sumurun 20. Anne Boleyn 20. Pharaoh's Wife 21. The Flame 21, etc.
□AMERICAN FILMS: Rosita 23. *The Marriage Circle* 24. Three Women 24. *Forbidden Paradise* 24. Kiss Me Again 25. Lady Windermere's Fan 25. So This Is Paris 26. The Student Prince 27. The Patriot 28. Eternal Love 29. *The Love Parade* (first sound film) 29. Paramount on Parade (Chevalier sequences) 30. Monte Carlo 30. The Smiling Lieutenant 31. The Man I Killed 32. *One Hour With You* 32. *Trouble in Paradise* 32. If I Had a Million (Laughton sequence) 32. Design for Living 33. The Merry Widow 34. *Desire* (p only) 36. Angel 37. Bluebeard's Eighth Wife 38. *Ninotchka* 39. *The Shop Around the Corner* 40. That Uncertain Feeling 41. *To Be or Not To Be* 42. *Heaven Can Wait* 43. A Royal Scandal (produced only) 45. Cluny Brown 46. That Lady in Ermine (finished by Otto Preminger) 48.

'He was the last of the genuine continentals let loose on the American continent, and we shall never see his like again because the world he celebrated had died—even before he did—everywhere except in his own memory.'—*Andrew Sarris, 1968*

❀ For extending the period of elegant comedy which is now a part of history. *Trouble in Paradise*.

¶ It's the Lubitsch touch that means so much,

piped the posters.

> He was the only director in Hollywood who had his own signature,

said S. N. Behrman. These were two ways of saying that Lubitsch was a master of cinematic innuendo.

> I let the audience use their imaginations. Can I help it if they misconstrue my suggestions?

he asked archly. In fact he delighted in naughtiness, and carried it off with great delicacy, though he admitted his lapses:

> I sometimes make pictures which are not up to my standard, but then it can only be said of a mediocrity that all his work is up to his standard.

And he gave in finally to the American way:

> I've been to Paris France and I've been to Paris Paramount. Paris Paramount is better.

Some people, Mary Pickford for instance, failed to perceive his talents:

> I parted company with him as soon as I could. I thought him a very uninspired director. He was a director of doors.

Lucan, Arthur (1887–1954) (Arthur Towle). British music hall comedian famous for his impersonation of Old Mother Riley, a comic Irish washerwoman. Made fourteen films featuring her, usually with his wife Kitty McShane (1898–1964) playing his daughter. □Stars on Parade 35. Kathleen Mavourneen 36. Old Mother Riley 37. Old Mother Riley in Paris 38. Old Mother Riley MP 39. Old Mother Riley Joins Up 39. Old Mother Riley in Business 40. Old Mother Riley's Ghosts 41. Old Mother Riley's Circus 41. Old Mother Riley Detective 43. Old Mother Riley Overseas 44. Old Mother Riley at Home 45. Old Mother Riley's New Venture 49. Old Mother Riley Headmistress 50. Old Mother Riley's Jungle Treasure 51. Mother Riley Meets the Vampire 52.

Lucas, George (1945–). American director.
□THX 1138 72. *American Graffiti* (& co-w) 73. *Star Wars* 77. More American Graffiti (p only) 79. The Empire Strikes Back (p only) 80. Raiders of the Lost Ark (p only) 81. Return of the Jedi (p only) 83. Skywalking 83.

¶ He reminded me a little of Walt Disney's version of a mad scientist.—*Steven Spielberg*

Lucas, Leighton (1903–1982). British composer and musical director; former ballet dancer.
Target for Tonight 41. Stage Fright 50. A King in New York 57. Ice Cold in Alex 58. The Millionairess 61, many others.

Lucas, Wilfred (1871–1940). Canadian character actor in Hollywood, best remembered as a foil for Laurel and Hardy. The Barbarian 08. The Spanish Gypsy 11. Cohen's Outing 13. Acquitted 16. The Westerners 18. The Barnstormer 22. The Fatal Mistake 24. Her Sacrifice 26. Just Imagine 30. *Pardon Us* 31. Fra Diavolo 33. The Count of Monte Cristo 34. Modern Times 36. The Baroness and the Butler 38. Zenobia 39. A Chump at Oxford 40. The Sea Wolf 41, many others.

Lucas, William (1926–). British leading man of stage, TV and occasional films.
Timeslip 55. X the Unknown 56. Breakout 59. Sons and Lovers 60. The Devil's Daffodil 61. Calculated Risk 63, etc.

Luchaire, Corinne (1921–1950). French actress who was a big hit in *Prison Without Bars* 38. After World War II was convicted as a collaborator and died in poverty.

Luckinbill, Laurence (1934–). American leading man.
The Boys in the Band 70. Such Good Friends 71. The Delphi Bureau (TV) 72 (and short series). Death Sentence (TV) 74. Panic on the 5.22 (TV) 74. Winner Take All (TV) 75. The Lindbergh Kidnapping Case (TV) 76. Ike (TV) 79. The Promise (TV) 80.

Lucking, Bill (–). Sturdy American supporting actor.
Hell's Babies 69. Wild Rovers 71. Oklahoma Crude 73. The Return of a Man Called Horse 76. Power (TV) 79, etc.
TV series: Big Hawaii 77.

Ludwig, Edward (1899–1982). American director, from 1932.
They Just Had To Get Married 33. Friends of Mr Sweeney 34. *The Man Who Reclaimed His Head* 34. Age of Indiscretion 36. That Certain Age 38. The Last Gangster 39. The Swiss Family Robinson 40. The Man Who Lost Himself 41. They Came To Blow Up America 43. The Fighting Seabees 44. Three's a Family 45. The Fabulous Texan 47. *Wake of the Red Witch* 48. Smuggler's Island 51. Big Jim McLain 52. Sangaree 53. Flame of the Islands 56. The Black Scorpion 57. The Gun Hawk 63, etc.

Ludwig, William (1912–). American writer.
The *Hardy Family* films 38–44. Challenge to Lassie 49. Shadow on the Wall 50. The Great Caruso 51. *Interrupted Melody* (AA) 55. Back Street 61, etc.

Lugosi, Bela (1882–1956) (Bela Ferenc Blasko; known professionally for a time as

Ariztid Olt). Hungarian stage actor of chilling presence and voice; became famous in films as Dracula, but his accent was a handicap for normal roles and he became typecast in inferior horror films.
Biographies: *The Count* (1974) by Arthur Lennig. *Lugosi, the Man behind the Cape* (1976) by Robert Cremer.
The Silent Command 23. The Rejected Woman 24. The Thirteenth Chair 29. Renegades 30. Oh For a Man 30. *Dracula* 30. Broad Minded 31. The Black Camel 31. *The Murders in the Rue Morgue* 31. *White Zombie* 32. *Chandu the Magician* 32. Island of Lost Souls 33. The Death Kiss 33. *The Black Cat* 34. Mysterious Mr Wong 35. The Mystery of the Marie Celeste (GB) 35. Mark of the Vampire 35. The Raven 35. The Invisible Ray 35. Postal Inspector 36. Dark Eyes of London (GB) 38. The Phantom Creeps 39. *Son of Frankenstein* (as Igor) 39. The Saint's Double Trouble 40. Black Friday 40. The Wolf Man 41. Spooks Run Wild 41. Night Monster 42. The Ghost of Frankenstein 42. The Ape Man 43. Frankenstein Meets the Wolf Man (as the monster) 43. The Return of the Vampire 43. One Body Too Many 44. Zombies on Broadway 45. The Body Snatcher 45. Scared to Death 47. *Abbott and Costello Meet Frankenstein* (as Dracula) 48. Bela Lugosi Meets a Brooklyn Gorilla 52. Mother Riley Meets the Vampire (GB) 52. Bride of the Monster 56. Plan 9 from Outer Space 56, etc.
❆ For bringing a touch of European mystery to a succession of rudimentary melodramas. *Son of Frankenstein.*

¶ For some people he was the embodiment of all mysterious forces, a harbinger of evil from the world of shadow. For others he was merely a ham actor appearing in a type of film unsuitable for children and often unfit for adults.—*Arthur Lennig*
Famous line (*Dracula*): Listen to them – children of the night! What music they make!

Lukas, Paul (1887–1971) (Pal Lukacs). Suave Hungarian leading actor, in Hollywood from the late twenties, first as a romantic figure, then as a smooth villain, finally as a kindly old man.
Two Lovers 28. Three Sinners 28. Manhattan Cocktail 28. Half Way to Heaven 29. Slightly Scarlet 30. The Benson Murder Case 30. Slightly Dishonorable 31. City Streets 31. Thunder Below 32. Rockabye 32. The Kiss Before the Mirror 33. The Secret of the Blue Room 33. *Little Women* 33. By Candlelight 33. Affairs of a Gentleman 34. I Give My Love 34. The Fountain 34. The Casino Murder Case 34. The Three Musketeers 35. I Found Stella Parish 35. *Dodsworth* 36. Dinner at the Ritz (GB) 37. *The Lady Vanishes* (GB) 38. The Chinese Bungalow (GB) 38. *Confessions of a Nazi Spy* 39. Strange Cargo 40. The Ghost Breakers 40. They Dare Not Love 41. Lady in Distress 32. *Watch on the Rhine* (AA) 43. Hostages 43. Uncertain Glory 44. *Address Unknown* 44. *Experiment Perilous* 44. Deadline at Dawn 46. Berlin Express 48. Kim 50. 20,000 Leagues Under the Sea 54. Roots of Heaven 58. Tender is the Night 61. 55 Days at Peking 63. Lord Jim 65. Sol Madrid 68, etc.
❆ For being such a gentleman. *The Lady Vanishes.*

Luke, Keye (1904–). Chinese-American actor who was popular in the thirties as Charlie Chan's number two son.
Charlie Chan in Paris 34. Oil for the Lamps of China 35. King of Burlesque 36. Charlie Chan at the Opera 36. Charlie Chan on Broadway 37. International Settlement 38. Mr Moto's Gamble 38. Disputed Passage 39. Bowery Blitzkrieg 41. Invisible Agent 42. Salute to the Marines 43. Three Men in White 44. First Yank into Tokyo 45. Sleep My Love 47. Hell's Half Acre 54. Battle Hell 57. Yangtse Incident (GB) 57. Nobody's Perfect 67. The Chairman (GB) 69. The Amsterdam Kill 78. Gremlins 84. A Fine Mess 86, many others.
TV series: *Anna and the King* 72. *Kung Fu* 72–74.

Lulli, Folco (1912–1970). Italian character actor.
The Bandit 47. Caccia Tragica 48. Without Pity 49. Flight into France 49. No Peace Under the Olives 50. Infidelity 52. *The Wages of Fear* 54. An Eye for an Eye 60. Lafayette 63. Marco the Magnificent 66, many others.

Lulu (1948–) (Marie Lawrie). British pop singer.
□Gonks Go Beat 65. To Sir With Love 68. The Cherry Picker 72.

Lum and Abner: Chester Lauck (1902–1980) and Norris Goff (1906–1978). American comedy actors of hillbilly characters.
Dreaming Out Loud 40. Bashful Bachelors 42, etc.

lumberjacks have figured in comparatively few movies: here are some of them. Conflict 36. Come and Get It 36. God's Country and the Woman 36. The Big Trees 52. Timberjack 55. Guns of the Timberland 60. Freckles 60. Sometimes a Great Notion 71.

Lumet, Sidney (1924–). American director, former child actor and TV producer.
□*Twelve Angry Men* 57. Stage Struck 58. That Kind of Woman 59. The Fugitive Kind 60. A View from the Bridge 61. Long Day's Journey into Night 62. *Fail Safe* 64. *The Pawnbroker* 65. *The Hill* 65. *The Group* 65. The Deadly Affair 66. Bye Bye Braverman 68. The Seagull 68. The Appointment 69. Blood Kin 69. The Anderson Tapes 71. The Offence 72. Child's Play 72. Lovin' Molly 73. Serpico 74. Murder on the Orient Express 74. *Dog Day Afternoon* 75. *Network* 76. Equus 77. The Wiz 78. Just Tell Me What You Want 80. Prince of the City 81. Deathtrap 82. The Verdict 82. Daniel 83. Garbo Talks 84. Power 85. The Morning After 86.

¶ He's the only guy who could double park in front of a whorehouse. He's that fast.—*Paul Newman*

'Those who would be led, Lumet will guide. Those who would lead, Lumet will follow.'—*Andrew Sarris, 1968*

Lumière, Louis (1864–1948). Pioneer French cinematographer, with brother Auguste Lumière (1862–1954). Gave first public demonstration 1895, including *Arrival of Train at Station* and other simple events; later made short comedies.

Lumley, Joanna (1946–). British leading lady.
Some Girls Do 68. On Her Majesty's Secret Service 69. Tam Lin 70. The Breaking of Bumbo 70. Games That Lovers Play 70. Satanic Rites of Dracula 73. Don't Just Lie There, Say Something 73. Trail of the Pink Panther 82. Curse of the Pink Panther 83. Mistral's Daughter (TV) 84.
TV series: *The New Avengers* 76–77. Sapphire and Steel 79.

Lummis, Dayton (1903–). American character actor of stage and radio, latterly in films.
Les Misérables 52. Ruby Gentry 53. The Court Martial of Billy Mitchell 55. The Cobweb 56, etc.

Luna, Barbara (1937–). American actress who usually plays beautiful foreigners.
The Devil at Four O'Clock 60. Five Weeks in a Balloon 62. Synanon 64. Ship of Fools 65. Firecreek 67. Che! 69. The Gatling Gun 73. Woman in the Rain 76. Brenda Starr (TV) 76. Pleasure Cove (TV) 79, etc.

Lund, John (1913–). American leading man with Broadway experience; film roles mainly stodgy.
To Each His Own 46. The Perils of Pauline 47. A Foreign Affair 47. Night Has a Thousand Eyes 48. Miss Tatlock's Millions 48. My Friend Irma 49. Duchess of Idaho 50. Darling, How Could You? 51. Steel Town 52. Bronco Buster 52. The Woman They Almost Lynched 53. Chief Crazy Horse 54. White Feather 55. Battle Stations 56. High Society 56. Affair in Reno 57. The Wackiest Ship in the Army 60, etc.

Lundigan, William (1914–1975). American leading man of routine features, formerly in radio.
Three Smart Girls Grow Up 38. The Old Maid 39. The Sea Hawk 40. Sunday Punch 42. What Next, Corporal Hargrove? 45. Pinky 49. *I'd Climb the Highest Mountain* 51. Down among the Sheltering Palms 52. *Inferno* 53. Serpent of the Nile 53. The White Orchid 54. The Underwater City 61. The Way West 67. Where Angels Go Trouble Follows 68, etc.
TV series: *Men into Space* 59.

Lunghi, Cherie (1954–). Anglo-Italian leading lady.
Excalibur 81. Oliver Twist (TV) 82. Praying Mantis (TV) 82. King David 85. Parker 85. The Mission 85. Harem (TV) 86.

Lunt, Alfred (1892–1977). Distinguished American stage actor, husband of Lynn Fontanne.
□Backbone 23. The Ragged Edge 23. Second Youth 24. Lovers in Quarantine 25. Sally of the Sawdust 26. *The Guardsman* 31. Stage Door Canteen 43.

Lupino, Ida (1914–). British leading lady, daughter of Stanley Lupino, who went to Hollywood and played a variety of mainly fraught roles; later became a director.
□AS ACTRESS: Her First Affaire 33. Money for Speed 33. High Finance 33. The Ghost Camera 33. I Lived with You 34. Prince of Arcadia 34. Search for Beauty 34. Come on Marines 34. Ready for Love 34. Paris in Spring 35. Smart Girl 35. Peter Ibbetson 35. Anything Goes 36. One Rainy Afternoon 36. Yours for the Asking 36. The Gay Desperado 36. Sea Devils 37. Let's Get Married 37. Artists and Models 37. Fight for your Lady 37. The Lone Wolf Spy Hunt 39. The Lady and the Mob 39. The Adventures of Sherlock Holmes 39. The Light that Failed 40. *They Drive by Night* 40. *High Sierra* 41. The Sea Wolf 41. Out of the Fog 41. *Ladies in Retirement* 41. Moontide 42. *The Hard Way*

42. Life Begins at 8.30 42. Forever and a Day 43. Thank your Lucky Stars 43. In Our Time 44. Hollywood Canteen 44. Pillow to Post 45. *Devotion* (as Emily Brontë) 46. The Man I Love 47. Deep Valley 47. Escape Me Never 47. *Roadhouse* 48. Lust for Gold 49. Woman in Hiding 50. On Dangerous Ground 51. Beware My Lovely 52. Jennifer 53. The Bigamist 53. Private Hell 36 54. Women's Prison 55. The Big Knife 55. While the City Sleeps 56. Strange Intruder 56. I Love a Mystery (TV) 67. Backtrack (TV) 69. Deadhead Miles 70. Women in Chains (TV) 71. Female Artillery (TV) 72. Junior Bonner 72. The Letters (TV) 72. The Strangers in 7A (TV) 73. The Devil's Rain 75. The Food of the Gods 76.
TV series: *Mr Adams and Eve* 56.
AS DIRECTOR: Not Wanted (wp only) 49. Outrage (& w) 50. Never Fear 51. Hard, Fast and Beautiful 51. The Hitch Hiker (& w) 53. The Bigamist 53. Private Hell 36 (w only) 54. The Trouble with Angels 66, plus many TV episodes.

¶ Her familiar expression of strained intensity would be less quickly relieved by a merciful death than by Ex-Lax.—*James Agee on Ida Lupino's performance in The Hard Way*

Lupino, Stanley (1893–1942). British comedian on stage from 1900, especially in musical comedy.
Autobiography 1934: *From the Stocks to the Stars*.
□ Love Lies 31. The Love Race 31. *Sleepless Nights* 32. King of the Ritz 33. Facing the Music 33. You Made Me Love You 33. Happy 34. Honeymoon for Three 35. Cheer Up 36. Sporting Love 36. *Over She Goes* 37. Hold My Hand 38. Lucky To Me 39.

Lupu-Pick (1886–1931). German director of silent days.
Die Fremde 17. Der Letzte Augenblick 18. The Wild Duck 22. Gassenhauer 24. Eine Nacht in London 28, etc.

Lustgarten, Edgar (1907–1979). British journalist who introduced the *Scotland Yard* three-reelers of the fifties; also wrote many books on famous crimes and trials.

Lustig, Jan (1901–1978). American screenwriter.
The White Cliffs of Dover 44. Homecoming 47, etc.

Lydon, James (or **Jimmy**) (1923–). American actor familiar in the early forties as gangling adolescent.
Back Door to Heaven 39. *Tom Brown's Schooldays* (title role) 40. Little Men 40. Henry Aldrich for President (and subsequent series of ten) 41. Aerial Gunner 43. The Town Went Wild 45. Life with Father 47. Bad Boy 49. September Affair 51. Island in the Sky 53. Battle Stations 56. I Passed for White 60. The Last Time I Saw Archie 61. Brainstorm 65. Death of a Gunfighter 69. Scandalous John 71. Vigilante Force 76, etc.
TV series: So This Is Hollywood 54. The First Hundred Years 56. Love That Jill 58.

Lye, Len (1901–1980). New Zealander animator, remembered for British GPO and other shorts of the thirties. Went to US and was associated for a while with *The March of Time*.
Tusalava 29. Colour Box 34. Birth of a Robot 36. Rainbow Dance 36. Kaleidoscope 36. Trade Tattoo 37. Swinging the Lambeth Walk 39. Colour Cry 52. Rhythm 53. Free Radicals 58. Particles in Space 66, etc.

Lyel, Viola (1900–1972) (Violet Watson). British character actress, mainly on stage in comedy roles.
Hobson's Choice (leading role) 30. Channel Crossing 32. Quiet Wedding 40. Wanted for Murder 46. No Place for Jennifer 50. Isn't Life Wonderful? 53. See How They Run 56, etc.

Lyles, A. C. (1918–). American producer, former publicist; noted for his second-feature westerns using veteran talent.
Short Cut to Hell 57. Raymie 60. The Young and the Brave 61. Law of the Lawless 64. Stagecoach to Hell 64. Young Fury 65. Black Spurs 65. Town Tamer 65. Apache Uprising 66. Johnny Reno 66. Waco 66. Red Tomahawk 67. Buckskin 68, etc.

Lynch, Alfred (1933–). Raw-boned British actor, often as cockney private.
□On the Fiddle 61. Two and Two Make Six 61. West Eleven 63. 55 Days at Peking 63. The Hill 65. The Taming of the Shrew 67. The Seagull 68.

Lynch, David (1946–). American director.
Eraserhead 78. *The Elephant Man* 80. Dune 85. Blue Velvet 86.

lynch law has been condemned in many outstanding dramatic movies from Hollywood.

Fury 36. They Won't Forget 37. Young Mr Lincoln 39. The Ox-Bow Incident 43. Storm Warning 51. The Sound of Fury 51. The Sun Shines Bright 52. Rough Night in Jericho 68. See also: *Ku Klux Klan*.

Lynch, Richard (1936–). American actor whose scarred skin and haughty mien make him a natural for evil roles.
Scarecrow 73. Steel 80. Vampire (TV) 80. The Formula 80. Alcatraz (TV) 81. The Sword and the Sorcerer 82. The Barbarans 87.

Lynde, Paul (1926–1982). American TV comedian who usually played a flustered character with a funny voice.
New Faces 54. Son of Flubber 62. Bye Bye Birdie 63. Send Me No Flowers 64. The Glass Bottom Boat 66. How Sweet It Is 68. Rabbit Test 78. The Villain 79, etc.
TV series: Stanley 56. Hey Landlord 66. The Pruitts of Southampton 66. *The Paul Lynde Show* 72. Temperatures Rising 73.

Lyndon, Barre (1896–1972) (Alfred Edgar). British playwright, long in Hollywood as scriptwriter.
The Amazing Dr Clitterhouse (oa) 38. Sundown 41. The Lodger 44. The Man in Half Moon Street (oa) 44. The House on 92nd Street 45. Night has a Thousand Eyes 48. The Greatest Show on Earth 51. The War of the Worlds 53. Conquest of Space 54. Sign of the Pagan 55. Omar Khayyam 57. Dark Intruder 65, etc.

Lyne, Adrian (–). British director in America.
Foxes 80. Flashdance 82. 9½ weeks 86. Fatal Attraction 87.

Lynen, Robert (1921–1944). French child actor later executed by Nazis as collaborator.
Poil de Carotte 32. The Little King 33. La Belle Equipe 36. Carnet de Bal 37. Education du Prince 38, etc.

Lynley, Carol (1942–). Talented American leading lady of the sixties.
□The Light in the Forest 58. Holiday for Lovers 59. *Blue Denim* 59. The Hound Dog Man 60. Return to Peyton Place 61. The Last Sunset 61. The Stripper 63. Under the Yum Yum Tree 63. The Cardinal 63. Shock Treatment 64. The Pleasure Seekers 64. *Bunny Lake is Missing* (GB) 65. *Harlow* (TV) 66. The Shuttered Room (GB) 68. Danger Route (GB) 68. The Smugglers (TV) 68. The Maltese Bippy 69. Norwood 69. Once You Kiss a Stranger 70. Weekend of Terror (TV) 70. Crosscurrent (TV) 71. The Night Stalker (TV) 72. The Poseidon Adventure 72. Cotter 73. The Elevator (TV) 74. Death Stalk (TV) 75. Flood (TV) 76. The Four Deuces 76. Out of Control 76. Bad Georgia Road 77. Fantasy Island (TV) 77. Having Babies II (TV) 77. The Cops and Robin (TV) 78. The Beasts Are on the Streets (TV) 78. The Cat and the Canary 78. The Shape of Things to Come (TV) 79. Vigilante 83.

Lynn, Ann (c. 1934–). British actress, mainly on TV; grand-daughter of Ralph Lynn.
Piccadilly Third Stop 60. The Wind of Change 61. Strongroom 61. Flame in the Streets 62. Black Torment 64. Four in the Morning 65. Baby Love 69, etc.

Lynn, Diana (1926–1971) (Dolores Loehr). Pert, witty American leading lady of the forties, former child actress and pianist.
□They Shall Have Music 39. There's Magic in Music 41. Star Spangled Rhythm 42. *The Major and the Minor* 43. Henry Aldrich Gets Glamour 43. *The Miracle of Morgan's Creek* 44. And the Angels Sing 44. Henry Aldrich Plays Cupid 44. *Our Hearts were Young and Gay* 44. Out of this World 45. Duffy's Tavern 45. Our Hearts were Growing Up 46. The Bride Wore Boots 46. Easy Come Easy Go 47. Variety Girl 47. Ruthless 48. Texas Brooklyn and Heaven 48. Every Girl Should Be Married 48. My Friend Irma 49. Paid in Full 50. My Friend Irma Goes West 50. Rogues of Sherwood Forest 50. Peggy 50. Bedtime for Bonzo 51. The People against O'Hara 51. Meet Me at the Fair 52. Plunder of the Sun 53. Track of the Cat 54. An Annapolis Story 55. The Kentuckian 55. You're Never Too Young 55. Company of Killers (TV) 71.

Lynn, Jeffrey (1909–) (Ragnar Lind). American leading man with varied experience, in films from 1938.
Four Daughters 38. Yes, My Darling Daughter 39. Espionage Agent 39. The Roaring Twenties 40. A Child Is Born 40. All This and Heaven Too 40. Four Mothers 40. Million Dollar Baby 41. The Body Disappears 41. Whiplash 47. Black Bart 48. A Letter to Three Wives 49. Up Front 51. Captain China 52. Come Thursday 64. Tony Rome 67, many others.
TV series: My Son Jeep 53.

Lynn, Jonathan (1943–). British writer-director, mainly noted for *Yes, Minister* on TV.

The Internecine Project (w) 74. Clue (w, d) 85.

Lynn, Leni (1925–). American girl singer who after debut in *Babes in Arms* 39 came to England and starred in several low-budget musicals.
Heaven Is Round the Corner 43. Give Me the Stars 44. Spring Song 46, etc.

Lynn, Loretta (1935–). American pop singer and guitarist, phenomenally successful and proud of her hillbilly background which was celebrated in the book and film *Coal Miner's Daughter*.

Lynn, Ralph (1882–1964). Incomparable British comedy actor of the silly ass school; his monocled face, limp hands and mastery of timing were essential ingredients of several films of the Aldwych farces of the thirties.
□*Rookery Nook* 30. Tons of Money 31. Plunder 31. Chance of a Night-Time 31. Mischief 31. A Night like This 32. Thark 32. Just My Luck 33. Summer Lightning 33. Up to the Neck 33. Turkey Time 33. *A Cuckoo in the Nest* 33. A Cup of Kindness 34. Dirty Work 34. Fighting Stock 35. Stormy Weather 35. Foreign Affairs 35. In the Soup 36. Pot Luck 36. All In 36. For Valour 37.
❅ For personifying the Bertie Wooster tradition. *Rookery Nook*.

Lynn, Robert (1918–1982). British director, in films from 1936 as camera assistant. Son of Ralph Lynn.
Postman's Knock 61. Dr Crippen 62. Victim Five 65. Change Partners 66. The Railway Children (p only) 71, etc.

Lynn, Sharon (1910–1963). American leading lady of the thirties.
Sunny Side Up 29. The Big Broadcast 32. Enter Madame 34. *Way Out West* (tickling Stan Laurel) 36. West Point Widow 41, etc.

Lynn, Dame Vera (1917–). British singing star, the 'Forces' Sweetheart' of World War II.
Autobiography 1976: *Vocal Refrain*.
We'll Meet Again 44. One Exciting Night 45, etc.

Lyon, Ben (1901–79). Amiable American leading man of the twenties and thirties; came to Britain with his wife Bebe Daniels and stayed to become popular radio personality; later became casting director for 20th Century-Fox.
Biography 1976: *Bebe and Ben* by Jill Allgood.
Open Your Eyes 19. Potash and Perlmutter 23. So Big 24. Bluebeard's Seven Wives 25. The Prince of Tempters 26. Dance Magic 27. The Air Legion 28. Alias French Gertie 30. *Hell's Angels* 30. The Hot Heiress 31. Her Majesty Love 31. Hat Check Girl 32. I Cover the Waterfront 33. Crimson Romance 34. Dancing Feet 36. I Killed the Count (GB) 38. Hi Gang (GB) 40. Life with the Lyons (GB) 54, etc.

Lyon, Francis D. (1905–). American director, former editor.
□Crazylegs 53. The Bob Mathias Story 54. Cult of the Cobra 55. The Great Locomotive Chase 56. The Oklahoman 56. Bale Out at 43,000 57. Gunsight Ridge 57. South Seas Adventure (co-d) 58. Escort West 59. The Tomboy and the Champ 61. The Young and the Brave 63. Destination Inner Space 66. Castle of Evil 67. The Destructors 68. The Money Jungle 68. The Girl Who Knew Too Much 69.

Lyon, Sue (1946–). American juvenile actress.
Lolita 62. *Night of the Iguana* 64. Seven Women 65. The Flim Flam Man 67. Tony Rome 67. Evel Knievel 72. Crash 77. End of the World 77. The Astral Factor 78. Towing 78, etc.

Lytell, Bert (1888–1954). American leading man of silent films.
To Have and to Hold 17. The Lone Wolf 31. A Message from Mars 23. *Rupert of Hentzau* 23. Lady Windermere's Fan 25. Steele of the Royal Mounted 27. Blood Brothers 30. The Single Sin 31. Stage Door Canteen 43, etc.

Answers

last lines
1 *Lady in the Dark* ☐ Mischa Auer ☐ 2 *Hellzapoppin* ☐ Elisha Cook Jnr ☐ 3 *Destry Rides Again* ☐ James Stewart ☐ 4 *A Star Is Born* ☐ Janet Gaynor or Judy Garland ☐ 5 *A Day at the Races* ☐ Groucho Marx ☐ 6 *North by Northwest* ☐ Eva Marie Saint ☐ Cary Grant ☐ 7 *Rebecca* ☐ Laurence Olivier ☐ 8 *Little Caesar* ☐ Edward G. Robinson ☐ 9 *The Grapes of Wrath* ☐ Jane Darwell ☐ 10 *Casablanca* ☐ Humphrey Bogart ☐

love
1 Charles Boyer ☐ Irene Dunne ☐ 2 Ryan O'Neal ☐ Ali MacGraw ☐ 3 Laurence Olivier ☐ Katharine Hepburn ☐ 4 James Cagney ☐ Doris Day ☐ (Cameron Mitchell can be accepted instead of Cagney) 5 Joseph Cotten ☐ Jennifer Jones ☐ 6 Maurice Chevalier ☐ Jeanette MacDonald ☐ 7 Tyrone Power ☐ Loretta Young ☐ 8 Maurice Chevalier ☐ Jeanette MacDonald ☐ 9 William Holden ☐ Jennifer Jones ☐ 10 Glenn Ford ☐ Hope Lange ☐ 11 Don Ameche ☐ Loretta Young ☐ 12 Steve McQueen ☐ Natalie Wood ☐

M. Fritz Lang was the first, in 1931, to film this story of a child-murderer finally hunted down by the city's organized criminal element, and Peter Lorre had his first great success as the psychopath. In 1950 Joseph Losey directed an almost scene-for-scene American remake starring David Wayne, but it generated no particular atmosphere.

m and e track. A sound track giving music and effects but not dialogue, necessary in dubbing stages.

McAndrew, Marianne (1938–). American leading lady.
Hello Dolly 69. The Seven Minutes 71, etc.

MacArthur, Charles (1895–1956). American playwright and screenwriter, long married to Helen Hayes; often collaborated with Ben Hecht (qv).
Biography 1957: *Charlie* by Ben Hecht.
The Front Page (oaw) 31. The Unholy Garden 31. Rasputin and the Empress 32. 20th Century 34. Crime Without Passion (wpd) 35. Barbary Coast 35. Soak the Rich (wpd) 36. Once in a Blue Moon (wpd) 36. Gunga Din (w) 39. Wuthering Heights (w) 39. His Girl Friday 40. The Senator was Indiscreet (w) 47. Perfect Strangers (oa) 50, etc.

MacArthur, Douglas (1880–1964). American general made famous by the phrase 'I shall return' when he was forced to evacuate the Philippines in 1942. Later a potential president of the U.S., he had been played by Gregory Peck in *MacArthur* and by Laurence Olivier in *Inchon*. Robert Barrat, who looked more like him, played him in both *They Were Expendable* and *An American Guerrilla in the Philippines*.

MacArthur, James (1937–). American leading man, former juvenile; adopted son of Charles MacArthur and Helen Hayes.
The Young Stranger 57. The Light in the Forest 58. The Third Man on the Mountain 59. Kidnapped 60. The Swiss Family Robinson 60. The Interns 62. Spencer's Mountain 63. The Truth about Spring 65. The Bedford Incident 65. Ride Beyond Vengeance 66. The Love-Ins 67. Hang 'Em High 68, etc.
TV series: *Hawaii Five-O* 68–79.

Macauley, Richard (–). American screenwriter.
The Roaring Twenties (co-w) 39. They Drive By Night (co-w) 40. Torrid Zone (co-w) 40. *Across the Pacific* 42, etc.

McAvoy, May (1901–84). American leading lady of the twenties, a casualty of sound.
Hate 17. Mrs Wiggs of the Cabbage Patch 19. Sentimental Tommy 21. Clarence 22. The Enchanted Cottage 24. Ben Hur 26. The Jazz Singer 27. The Lion and the Mouse 28. The Terror 28. No Defense 29, etc.

McBain, Diane (1941–). American leading lady of the sixties.
Ice Palace 60. Claudelle Inglish 61. A Distant Trumpet 64, etc.

McBain, Ed. American novelist, author of the *87th Precinct* crime novels. Actually a pseudonym for Evan Hunter, formerly Salvatore Lombino (1926–).

Macbeth. Among many attempts to film Shakespeare's Scottish tragedy, none of them wholly successful, have been the following: 1. In 1915 John Emerson directed and D. W. Griffith produced a straightforward version starring Sir Herbert Beerbohm Tree and Constance Collier. 2. In 1948 Orson Welles directed and starred in his own adaptation, shot in 21 days for Republic; the would-be Scottish burr in which the cast was drilled completely obscured the poetry, but despite papier-maché sets there were some striking effects. 3. In 1956 Ken Hughes wrote and directed a modernized version, *Joe Macbeth*, in which the kings and princes became rival gangsters; Paul Douglas starred. 4. In 1957 Akira Kurosawa directed *Throne of Blood*, a stylized Japanese version. 5. In 1960 George Schaefer directed an honest G.C.E.-type rendering in colour with Maurice Evans and Judith Anderson; destined for American television, it was released theatrically in Britain. 6. In 1971 Jon Finch and Francesca

Annis starred in a blood-spattered version by Roman Polanski.

McBride, Donald (1894–1957). American character comedian adept at explosive editors, dumb policemen, etc. Made debut in his stage role as the harassed hotel manager in *Room Service* 38.
The Story of Vernon and Irene Castle 39. *Here Comes Mr Jordan* 41. *Topper Returns* 41. Invisible Woman 41. They Got Me Covered 42. The Glass Key 42. Two Yanks in Trinidad 42. Abbott and Costello in Hollywood 45. Good News 48. Bowery Battalion 51. The Seven Year Itch 55, many others.

McCallister, Lon (1923–) (Herbert Alonzo McCallister Jnr). American leading man, usually in callow roles.
Souls at Sea 37. Babes in Arms 39. *Stage Door Canteen* 43. *Home in Indiana* 44. Winged Victory 44. The Red House 47. The Big Cat 50. Letter from Korea 50. Combat Squad 54, etc.

McCallum, David (1933–). Slightly built Scottish juvenile lead of the fifties and sixties; became popular on American television as Ilya Kuriakin in the UNCLE series.
The Secret Place 56. Robbery Under Arms 57. Violent Playground 58. The Long the Short and the Tall 61. Billy Budd 62. Freud 62. *The Great Escape* 63. The Greatest Story Ever Told 65. Around the World Under the Sea 66. Three Bites of the Apple 67. Sol Madrid 68. Mosquito Squadron 69. Frankenstein, The True Story (TV) 73. Diamond Hunters 75. Dogs 76. King Solomon's Treasure 78. The Watcher in the Woods 80. The Return of the Man from UNCLE (TV) 83, etc.
TV series: *The Man from UNCLE* 64–67 (plus eight feature films 'amplified' from TV material for cinema release). *Colditz* 72. *Invisible Man* 75. Sapphire and Steel 79.

McCallum, John (1917–). Australian leading man of stage and screen, in England 1945–55; married Googie Withers.
Joe Goes Back 44. The Root of All Evil 47. The Loves of Joanna Godden 47. The Woman in Question 50. Trent's Last Case 52. Trouble in the Glen 53. Port of Escape 55. The Nickel Queen (d only) 71, etc.

McCallum, Neil (1929–1976). Beefy Canadian actor in British films.
The Inspector 62. The Longest Day 62. The War Lover 63. Witchcraft 64, etc.

McCambridge, Mercedes (1918–). Intense, unpredictable American character actress, often in cynical or hard-bitten roles. She also voiced the demon in *The Exorcist*. Autobiography 1960: *The Two of Us*.
□*All the King's Men* (AA) 50. Lightning Strikes Twice 51. The Scarf 51. Inside Straight 51. Johnny Guitar 54. *Giant* 56. A Farewell to Arms 57. Suddenly Last Summer 59. Cimarron 60. Angel Baby 61. 99 Women 69. The Hot Death (Ger.) 69. The Counterfeit Killer (TV) 70. Killer by Night (TV) 72. Two for the Money (TV) 72. The Girls of Huntington House (TV) 73. The President's Plane Is Missing (TV) 73. The Exorcist (voice only) 73. Who Is the Black Dahlia? (TV) 75. Thieves 77. The Sacketts (TV) 79. Airport 79: The Concorde 79.
TV series: Wire Service 56.

McCarey, Leo (1898–1969). American director with above-average talent and a sentimental streak. Before graduating to features he directed many silent shorts, including Laurel and Hardy as *Two Tars*.
□The Sophomore 29. Red Hot Rhythm 29. Let's Go Native 30. Wild Company 30. Part Time Wife 30. Indiscretion 31. The Kid from Spain 32. *Duck Soup* 33. Six of a Kind 34. Belle of the Nineties 34. *Ruggles of Red Gap* 35. The Milky Way 36. *Make Way for Tomorrow* (& wp) 37. *The Awful Truth* (& w) (AA) 37. *Love Affair* (& w) (AA screenplay) 39. Once Upon a Honeymoon 42. *Going My Way* (AA) (& p) 44. The Bells of St Mary's (& p) 45. Good Sam (& p) 48. My Son John (& wp) 52. An Affair to Remember (& wp) 57. Rally Round the Flag Boys (& wp) 58. Satan Never Sleeps (& wp) 62.

McCarey, Ray (1904–1948). American director of second features, formerly making Hal Roach shorts.
Pack Up Your Troubles 32. Millions in the Air 36. That Other Woman 42. Atlantic City 44. The Falcon's Alibi 46, etc.

McCarthy, Frank (1912–86). American producer.
Decision Before Dawn 51. Sailor of the King 53. A Guide for the Married Man 67. *Patton* 70, etc.

McCarthy, Joseph (1905–1957). American senator who conducted in the early fifties a witch hunt of alleged communists, and was censured by the Senate in 1954. A 1977 television biopic, *Tail Gunner Joe*, starred Peter Boyle.

McCarthy, Kevin (1914–). American leading man and latterly character actor, with stage experience.
Death of a Salesman (debut) 52. Stranger on Horseback 55. *Invasion of the Body Snatchers* 56. The Misfits 61. *The Prize* 63. The Best Man 64. Mirage 65. A Big Hand for the Little Lady 66. Hotel 67. If He Hollers Let Him Go 68. Revenge in El Paso 69. Kansas City Bomber 72. Alien Thunder 73. Buffalo Bill and the Indians 76. Invasion of the Body Snatchers (cameo) 78. Piranha 78. Captain Avenger 79. Those Lips Those Eyes 80. The Howling 81. My Tutor 83. Twilight Zone 83. Innerspace 87, etc.
TV series: The Survivors 69. Flamingo Road 80–81.

McCarthy, Michael (1917–1959). British director, in films from 1934.
Assassin for Hire 51. Mystery Junction 51. Crow Hollow 52. Shadow of a Man 54. It's Never Too Late 56. Smoke Screen 57. The Traitor 57. Operation Amsterdam 58, etc.

McCay, Winsor (1886–1934). American pioneer animator who invented Gertie the dinosaur in 1909.

Macchio, Ralph (1962–). American leading man.
Dangerous Company 82. The Outsiders 83. The Karate Kid 84. Karate Kid 2 85. Crossroads 85.

McClory, Kevin (1926–). Irish production executive, former sound technician. Wrote, produced and directed *The Boy and the Bridge* 59; produced *Thunderball* 65.

McClory, Sean (1923–). Irish actor with Abbey Theatre experience; long in Hollywood.
Beyond Glory 49. Rommel, Desert Fox 51. Les Misérables 52. Ring of Fear 54. Moonfleet 55. Diane 57. Bandolero 68, etc.

McClure, Doug (1935–). American leading man, from TV.
Because They're Young 59. The Unforgiven 60. Shenandoah 65. Beau Geste 66. The King's Pirate 67. Nobody's Perfect 68. The Judge and Jake Wyler (TV) 71. The Land That Time Forgot 75. At The Earth's Core 76. The People That Time Forgot 77. Warlords of Atlantis 77. Rebels (TV) 79. Humanoids from the Deep 80. The House Where Evil Dwells 82. Cannonball Run II 83. 52 Pick-Up 86. Omega 7 86, etc.
TV series: Checkmate 59–61. Overland Trail 60. *The Virginian* 64–69. Search 72. Barbary Coast 76.

McClure, Greg (1918–) (Dale Easton). American leading man who starred in his first film but did little thereafter.
The Great John L 45. Bury Me Dead 47. Lulu Belle 48. Joe Palooka in the Squared Circle 50. Stop That Cab 51, etc.

McCord, Ted (1898–1976). American cinematographer.
So Big 24. We Moderns 25. Irene 26. Valley of the Giants 26. Phantom City 28. The Fighting Legion 30. The Big Stampede 32. The Rainmakers 35. Fugitive in the Sky 36. Secret Service of the Air 39. The Case of the Black Parrot 41. Murder in the Big House 42. Action in the North Atlantic 43. Deep Valley 47. The Treasure of the Sierra Madre 48. *Johnny Belinda* 48. Flamingo Road 49. The Damned Don't Cry 50. Young Man with a Horn 50. The Breaking Point 50. Force of Arms 51. Young at Heart 54. East of Eden 55. The Helen Morgan Story 57. The Proud Rebel 58. The Hanging Tree 59. Two for the Seesaw 62. *The Sound of Music* 65. A Fine Madness 66, many others.

MacCorkindale, Simon (1952–). Budding British leading man of the late seventies.
□ Jesus of Nazareth (TV) 77. Death on the Nile 78. The Riddle of the Sands 79. Quatermass (TV) 79. Cabo Blanco 79. The Manions of America (TV) 80. The Sword and the Sorcerer 82. Jaws 3D 83.
TV series: Manimal 83. Falcon Crest 85–

McCormack, John (1884–1945). Irish tenor.
Song O'My Heart 30. Wings of the Morning 37.

McCormack, Patty (1945–). American juvenile actress who went to Hollywood to repeat her stage role as the evil child of *The Bad Seed* 56.
The Day They Gave Babies Away 57. Kathy O' 58. The Adventures of Huckleberry Finn 60. The Explosive Generation 61. The Young Runaways 68, etc.
TV series: Peck's Bad Girl 59.

McCormick, F. J. (1891–1947) (Peter Judge). Irish character actor, long on the Abbey Theatre stage. Well remembered as Shell in *Odd Man Out* 46.
The Plough and the Stars 37. Hungry Hill 46.

McCormick, Myron (1908–1962). Wry-faced American character actor, with stage experience.
Winterset 37. One Third of a Nation 39. Jigsaw 49. Jolson Sings Again 50. No Time for Sergeants 58. *The Hustler* 61, etc.

McCowan, George (1931–). Canadian TV director who made a Hollywood start with *Frogs* 72.

McCowen, Alec (1925–). Youthful-looking British stage actor, in occasional films.
Time without Pity 57. Town on Trial 57. The Loneliness of the Long Distance Runner 62. In the Cool of the Day 63. The Agony and the Ecstasy 65. The Witches 66. The Hawaiians (US) 70. Frenzy 72. *Travels With My Aunt* 72. Stevie 78. Hanover Street 79. Never Say Never Again 83. The Assam Garden 85. Personal Services 86. Cry Freedom 87, etc.

McCoy, Tim (1891–1978). American cowboy star, in films from 1923 when, an ex-army officer, he went to Hollywood as adviser on *The Covered Wagon*.
War Paint 26. The Indians Are Coming 30. The Fighting Fool 31. Texas Cyclone 32. Whirlwind 33. Hell Bent for Love 34. Square Shooter 35, many others. Later played bit parts: Around the World in Eighty Days 56. Run of the Arrow 57. Requiem for a Gunfighter 65, etc.
TV series: The Tim McCoy Show 52.

McCrea, Joel (1905–). Athletic, good-humoured, dependable American hero of the thirties and forties.
□ The Jazz Age 29. So This is College 29. Dynamite 29. The Silver Horde 29. Lightnin' 30. Once a Sinner 30. Kept Husbands 31. The Common Law 31. Born to Love 31. Girls about Town 31. Business and Pleasure 32. The Lost Squadron 32. *Bird of Paradise* 32. *The Most Dangerous Game* 32. Rockabye 32. The Sport Parade 32. Scandal for Sale 32. Laughter in Hell 33. The Silver Cord 33. Bed of Roses 33. One Man's Journey 33. Chance at Heaven 33. Gambling Lady 34. Half a Sinner 34. The Richest Girl in the World 34. Private Worlds 35. Our Little Girl 35. Woman Wanted 35. Barbary Coast 35. Splendour 35. These Three 36. Two in a Crowd 36. Adventure in Manhattan 36. Come and Get It 36. Banjo on my Knee 36. Internes Can't Take Money 37. Wells Fargo 37. Woman Chases Man 37. *Dead End* 37. Three Blind Mice 38. Youth Takes a Fling 38. Union Pacific 39. They Shall Have Music 39. Espionage Agent 39. He Married His Wife 40. The Primrose Path 40. *Foreign Correspondent* 40. Reaching for the Sun 41. *Sullivan's Travels* 41. The Great Man's Lady 42. *The Palm Beach Story* 42. *The More the Merrier* 43. Buffalo Bill 44. The Great Moment 44. The Unseen 45. The Virginian 46. Ramrod 47. Four Faces West 48. South of St Louis 49. Colorado Territory 49. Stars in My Crown 50. The Outriders 50. Saddle Tramp 50. Frenchie 50. Cattle Drive 51. The San Francisco Story 52. Lone Hand 53. Rough Shoot (GB) 53. Black Horse Canyon 54. Border River 54. Stranger on Horseback 55. Wichita 55. The First Texan 56. The Oklahoman 57. Trooper Hook 57. Gunsight Ridge 57. The Tall Stranger 57. Cattle Empire 58. Fort Massacre 58. Gunfight at Dodge City 59. *Ride the High Country* 62. Cry Blood Apache 71. Mustang Country 76.
TV series: *Wichita Town* 59.
❀ For the amiable generosity of his playing which turned him from a second lead into the undoubted star of several of the most prized films of the early forties. *Sullivan's Travels*.

McCullers, Carson (1917–1967). American novelist, usually on themes pertaining to her homeland, the deep south. *The Member of the Wedding, Reflections in a Golden Eye* and *The Heart is a Lonely Hunter* were filmed.

McCullough, Paul (1884–1936). American farce comedian, with Bobby Clark in two-reelers 1928–35.

McDaniel, Hattie (1895–1952). Black American character actress of cheerful and immense presence; once a radio vocalist.
The Story of Temple Drake 33. Judge Priest 35. *Showboat* 36. Nothing Sacred 37. *Gone with the Wind* (AA) 39. Zenobia 39. *The Great Lie* 41. Thank Your Lucky Stars 43. Margie 46. Song of the South 47. Family Honeymoon 49, many others.
TV series: *Beulah* 52.

McDermott, Hugh (1908–1972). Scottish-born character actor, in British films from mid-thirties, specializing in hearty transatlantic types.

The Wife of General Ling 38. Pimpernel Smith 41. The Seventh Veil 45. No Orchids for Miss Blandish 48. Trent's Last Case 52. A King in New York 57. The First Men in the Moon 64. Captain Apache 71. Chato's Land 72, many others.

McDevitt, Ruth (1895–1976) (Ruth Shoecraft). American character actress.
The Parent Trap 62. The Birds 63. The Out of Towners 69. Change of Habit 72, many others.
TV series: Pistols and Petticoats 66. Kolchak 74.

MacDonald, David (1904–1983). British director who showed promise in the thirties and forties but declined to second features.
Double Alibi 27. It's Never Too Late to Mend 37. Dead Men Tell No Tales 38. A Spot of Bother 38. *This Man is News* 38. This Man in Paris 39. Spies of the Air 39. Law and Disorder 40. Men of the Lightship 40. This England 40. *The Brothers* 47. Good Time Girl 48. Snowbound 48. Christopher Columbus 49. Diamond City 49. The Bad Lord Byron 49. Cairo Road 50. The Adventurers 51. The Lost Hours 52. Tread Softly 53. Devil Girl from Mars 54. Alias John Preston 56. Small Hotel 57. *The Moonraker* 58. Petticoat Pirates 61, etc.

McDonald, Dwight (1906–1982). American film critic of semi-revered status: *On Movies* 69, etc.

McDonald, Frank (1899–1980). American director of second features; former stage actor and author.
The Murder of Dr Harrigan 38. Carolina Moon 40. One Body Too Many 44. My Pal Trigger 46. Father Takes the Air 51. The Treasure of Ruby Hills 55. The Underwater City 61, etc.

McDonald, Grace (1921–). American singing and dancing second lead of many a forties 'B'.

MacDonald, J. Farrell (1875–1952). American minstrel singer who became a familiar Hollywood character actor.
The Maltese Falcon 31. The Thirteenth Guest 32. The Cat's Paw 34. The Irish in Us 36. Topper 37. Little Orphan Annie 39. Meet John Doe 41. My Darling Clementine 46. Mr Belvedere Rings the Bell 51, etc.

MacDonald, Jeanette (1902/3–1965). American concert singer and leading lady of the thirties. Popular on her own account, she made a fondly remembered series of film operettas with Nelson Eddy, and these are noted (E) below.
Biography 1976: *The Jeanette MacDonald Story* by James Robert Parish.
□*The Love Parade* 29. The Vagabond King 30. Monte Carlo 30. Let's Go Native 30. The Lottery Bride 30. Oh For a Man 30. Don't Bet on Women 31. Annabelle's Affairs 31. *One Hour With You* 32. *Love Me Tonight* 32. The Cat and the Fiddle 32. The Merry Widow 34. *Naughty Marietta* (E) 35. *Rose Marie* (E) 36. *San Francisco* 36. Maytime (E) 37. The Firefly 37. The Girl of the Golden West (E) 38. Sweethearts (E) 39. Broadway Serenade 39. New Moon (E) 40. Bitter Sweet (E) 40. Smilin' Through 41. I Married an Angel (E) 42. Cairo 42. Follow the Boys 44. Three Daring Daughters 48. The Sun Comes Up 49.

MacDonald, John D. (1916–86). American detective story writer, author of the Travis McGee novels (For John Ross MacDonald see under *Ross*.)
Mantrap 61. Cape Fear (The Executioners) 62. Darker Than Amber 70. Travis McGee (TV) 82.

MacDonald, Joseph (1906–1968). American cinematographer.
Charlie Chan in Rio 41. Sunday Dinner for a Soldier 44. *Yellow Sky* 48. Panic in the Streets 50. *Viva Zapata* 52. Niagara 53. Titanic 53. How to Marry a Millionaire 53. Broken Lance 54. A Hatful of Rain 57. Ten North Frederick 57. Pepe 60. Kings of the Sun 63. The Carpetbaggers 63. Rio Conchos 64. Invitation to a Gunfighter 64. Mirage 65. Blindfold 65. The Sand Pebbles 66. Mackenna's Gold 68, many others.

McDonald, Marie (1923–1965) (Marie Frye). American leading lady, publicized as 'The Body'; former model.
Pardon My Sarong 42. A Scream in the Dark 44. Getting Gertie's Garter 46. Living in a Big Way 47. Tell It to the Judge 49. Geisha Boy 59. Promises Promises 63, etc.

MacDonald, Philip (1896–). British thriller writer who contributed much material to the screen.
The Lost Patrol 34. The Mystery of Mr X 34. Menace 34. The Hour of Thirteen 52. The List of Adrian Messenger 63, plus scripts for several Chan and Moto films.

McDonald, Ray (1920–1959). American actor-dancer of lightweight forties musicals.
Presenting Lily Mars 43. Good News 47. Till the Clouds Roll By 48, etc.

Macdonald, Richard (–). British production designer.
The Servant 63. Modesty Blaise 66. Boom 68. A Severed Head 71. Jesus Christ Superstar 73. *Day of the Locust* 75. Marathon Man 76. Swashbuckler 76. F.I.S.T. 78. And Justice for All 79. The Rose 79. Cannery Row 82, etc.

MacDonald, Ross (1915–1983) (Kenneth Millar). American detective story writer whose mysteries are much in the vein of Raymond Chandler.
Harper 66. The Drowning Pool 75.
TV series: Archer 75.

McDonell, Fergus (1910–). British director.
The Small Voice 48. Prelude to Fame 50. Private Information 52, etc.

MacDougall, Ranald (1915–1973). American screenwriter.
Objective Burma 45. Possessed 47. The Unsuspected 47. June Bride 48. The Hasty Heart 49. Bright Leaf 50. I'll Never Forget You 51. The Naked Jungle 54. Queen Bee (& d) 55. The Mountain 56. Man on Fire (& d) 57. The World the Flesh and the Devil (& d) 59. Go Naked in the World (& d) 61. The Cockeyed Cowboys of Calico County (& d) 69, etc.

MacDougall, Roger (1910–). British screenwriter and playwright.
This Man is News (w) 38. The Foreman went to France (w) 42. *The Man in the White Suit* (oaw) 51. To Dorothy a Son (oa) 54. *Escapade* (oa) 56. The Mouse that Roared (w) 59. A Touch of Larceny (w) 60, etc.

McDowall, Betty (–). Australian actress who at one time played wives in scores of British films.
The Shiralee 57. Time Lock 57. She Didn't Say No 58. Jack the Ripper 59. Jackpot 60. Spare the Rod 61. Tomorrow at Ten 62. Echo of Diana 63. Ballad in Blue 64. The Liquidator 65. The Omen 76, etc.

McDowall, Roddy (1928–). British child actor of the forties, in Hollywood from 1940. Developed into an unpredictable adult performer, but made a reputation as a photographer.
Murder in the Family 36. Just William 37. This England 40. Man Hunt 41. *How Green Was My Valley* 41. Confirm or Deny 41. The Pied Piper 42. My Friend Flicka 43. Lassie Come Home 43. The White Cliffs of Dover 44. Thunderhead 45. Holiday in Mexico 46. Macbeth 50. Killer Shark 50. The Subterraneans 60. The Longest Day 62. Cleopatra 63. Shock Treatment 64. The Loved One 65. That Darn Cat 65. Lord Love a Duck 66. The Cool Ones 67. It 67. Planet of the Apes 67. Five Card Stud 68. Angel Angel Down You Go 69. Tam Lin (d only) 70. Escape from the Planet of the Apes 71. Bedknobs and Broomsticks 71. Pretty Maids all in a Row 71. Conquest of the Planet of the Apes 72. The Poseidon Adventure 72. The Legend of Hell House 73. Battle for the Planet of the Apes 73. Arnold 74. Funny Lady 75. Mean Johnny Barrows 76. Embryo 77. Rabbit Test 78. The Cat from Outer Space 78. Circle of Iron 79. Scavenger Hunt 79. Evil Under the Sun 82. Class of 1984 82. Dead of Winter 87, etc.
TV series: Planet of the Apes 74. Fantastic Journey 77.

McDowell, Malcolm (1943–). Fashionable British leading actor of the early seventies.
□Poor Cow 67. *If* 69. Figures in a Landscape 70. The Raging Moon 71. *A Clockwork Orange* 71. *O Lucky Man* 73. Royal Flash 75. Voyage of the Damned 76. Aces High 76. The Passage 79. Time after Time 79. Caligula 79. Cat People 82. Britannia Hospital 82. Arthur the King (TV) 83. Blue Thunder 83. Cross Creek 83. Get Crazy 83.

McEachin, James (1931–). Black American actor of the seventies, TV's *Tenafly*.
Play Misty for Me 71. The Alpha Caper (TV) 73. Every Which Way But Loose 79. 2010 84.

McEnery, John (1945–). British light leading man of the seventies.
Romeo and Juliet 68. The Lady in a Car 70. *Bartleby* 71. Nicholas and Alexandra 71. Days of Fury 73. The Land that Time Forgot 74. Little Malcolm 74. The Duellists 78, etc.

McEnery, Peter (1940–). British leading man with TV experience.
Tunes of Glory 60. Victim 62. The Moonspinners 64. The Fighting Prince of Donegal 66. The Game Is Over 66. I Killed Rasputin 68. Negatives 68. Entertaining Mr

Sloane 70. The Adventures of Gerard 70. Tales that Witness Madness 73. The Cat and the Canary 78, etc.

McEveety, Bernard (–). American director, from TV.
Broken Sabre 65. Ride Beyond Vengeance 66. The Brotherhood of Satan 70. Napoleon and Samantha 72. One Little Indian 73. The Bears and I 75, etc.

McEveety, Joseph L. (1926–1976). American producer, long with Disney.

McEveety, Vince or **Vincent** (–). American director.
Firecreek 68. Million Dollar Duck 71. The Strongest Man in the World 74. Gus 76. Herbie Goes to Monte Carlo 77. The Apple Dumpling Gang Rides Again 79. Herbie Goes Bananas 80, etc.

McEwan, Geraldine (1932–). Leading British stage actress.
Escape from the Dark 76. The Bawdy Adventures of Tom Jones 76. Foreign Body 87.

McFadden, Hamilton (1901–). American director of 'B' features.
Harmony at Home 30. Charlie Chan Carries On 31. Second Hand Wife 33. Stand Up and Cheer 34. Elinor Norton 35. The Three Legionnaires 37. Sea Racketeers 39. Inside the Law 42, etc.

McFarland, Spanky (1928–) (George Emmett McFarland). American child actor of the thirties, the fat boy of the 'Our Gang' one-reelers.
Day of Reckoning 33. Kentucky Kernels 35. O'Shaughnessy's Boy 35. Trail of the Lonesome Pine 36. Peck's Bad Boy with the Circus 39. Johnny Doughboy 43, etc.

McGann, William (1895–1977). American director of second features.
I Like Your Nerve 31. Illegal 32. The Case of the Black Cat 36. Penrod and Sam 37. Blackwell's Island 39. The Parson of Panamint 41. Tombstone 42. Frontier Badmen 43, etc.

McGavin, Darren (1922–). American 'character lead' who can play unpleasant villains or tough heroes.
Fear 46. Summer Madness 55. The Court Martial of Billy Mitchell 55. *The Man with the Golden Arm* 56. The Delicate Delinquent 57. Beau James 57. The Case Against Brooklyn 58. Bullet for a Badman 64. The Great Sioux Massacre 65. Mrs Pollifax—Spy 70. Happy Mother's Day Love George 73. The Night Stalker (TV) 74. The Night Strangler (TV) 74. No Deposit No Return 76. Airport 77 77. Hot Lead and Cold Feet 78. Zero to Sixty 78. Ike (TV) 79. Hangar 18 80. From the Hip 87, etc.
TV series: Crime Photographer 53. *Mike Hammer* 58. *Riverboat* 60. The Outsider 68. The Night Stalker 74.

McGee, Fibber (1897–) (James Jordan). American radio comedian, always with his wife 'Molly' (Marion: 1898–1967).
This Way Please 38. Look Who's Laughing 40. Here We Go Again 41. Heavenly Days 44, etc.

McGee, Vonetta (–). Black American actress.
The Lost Man 69. The Kremlin Letter 69. Blacula 72. Shaft in Africa 73. The Eiger Sanction 75. Brothers 77. Superdome (TV) 78.

McGill, Barney (–1941). American cinematographer.
Breezy Jim 19. The Critical Age 23. Casey at the Bat 27. The Terror 28. Show of Shows 29. Doorway to Hell 30. Mammy 30. *Svengali* 31. The Mouthpiece 32. Cabin in the Cotton 32. Twenty Thousand Years in Sing Sing 33. Mayor of Hell 33. *The Bowery* 33. The President Vanishes 34. My Marriage 35. Thank You Jeeves 36. Lancer Spy 37. Sharpshooters 38. The Cisco Kid and the Lady 40, many others.

McGillis, Kelly (1958–). American juvenile actress of the eighties.
Reuben, Reuben 82. Witness 82. Top Gun 85. Made in Heaven 87.

McGinn, Walter (1936–1977). American character actor of the seventies.
The Parallax View 74. Delancy Street (TV) 75.

MacGinnis, Niall (1913–?). Irish-born actor, in films from 1935.
Turn of the Tide 35. Edge of the World 38. 49th Parallel 41. We Dive at Dawn 43. Henry V 44. No Highway 51. *Martin Luther* (title role) 53. The Battle of the River Plate 55. *Night of the Demon* 57. The Nun's Story 58. Billy Budd 62. A Face in the Rain 62. Becket

64. Island of Terror 66. The Torture Garden 67. Sinful Davey 69. The Mackintosh Man 73, etc.

McGiver, John (1913–1975). American character comedian with worried, owl-like features.
Love in the Afternoon 57. *Breakfast at Tiffany's* 61. Mr Hobbs Takes a Vacation 62. The Manchurian Candidate 62. Who's Minding the Store? 63. Man's Favourite Sport? 64. Marriage on the Rocks 65. The Spirit is Willing 67. Fitzwilly 67. Midnight Cowboy 69. Lawman 70. The Great Man's Whiskers (TV) 71. The Apple Dumpling Gang 75, etc.
TV series: *Many Happy Returns* 64. *The James Stewart Show* 71.

McGivern, William P. (1924–1983). American mystery novelist.
The Big Heat 53. Rogue Cop 54. Hell on Frisco Bay 55. Odds Against Tomorrow 59. The Caper of the Golden Bulls 67.

McGlynn, Frank (1867–1951). American character actor, adept at portraying Abraham Lincoln.
Min and Bill 31. Little Miss Marker 34. The Littlest Rebel 35. Trail of the Lonesome Pine 36. Prisoner of Shark Island 37. Wells Fargo 37. Union Pacific 39. Boom Town 40, many others.

McGoohan, Patrick (1928–). American-born leading man with individual characteristics; in British films, after stage experience, from the mid-fifties.
Passage Home 55. Zarak 55. *High Tide at Noon* 56. *Hell Drivers* 57. The Gypsy and the Gentleman 57. Nor the Moon by Night 58. Two Living One Dead 60. All Night Long 61. The Quare Fellow 62. *Life For Ruth* 62. Dr Syn 63. Ice Station Zebra 68. The Moonshine War 70. Mary Queen of Scots 72. Catch My Soul (d only) 73. The Genius (It.) 75. Silver Streak 76. Brass Target 78. Escape From Alcatraz 79. Scanners 81. Jamaica Inn (TV) 83, etc.
TV series: *Danger Man* (Secret Agent) 59–62. *The Prisoner* 67. Rafferty 77.

McGovern, Elizabeth (1961–). American leading lady.
Ordinary People 80. Ragtime 81. Lovesick 83. The Bedroom Window 86.

MacGowan, Kenneth (1888–1963). American film theorist and teacher (at UCLA) who was also a notable producer. Author of several film textbooks.
Little Women 33. Becky Sharp 35. Young Mr Lincoln 39. Man Hunt 41. Lifeboat 43. Jane Eyre 43, etc.

McGowan, Robert A. (1901–). American producer who devised the original 'Our Gang' comedies.

MacGowran, Jack (1916–1973). Irish character actor, usually of mean, sharp-featured fellows. Also on stage and TV.
The Quiet Man 52. The Gentle Gunman 52. The Titfield Thunderbolt 53. The Rising of the Moon 57. Darby O'Gill and the Little People 59. Blind Date 60. Mix Me a Person 61. Lord Jim 65. Cul de Sac 66. The Fearless Vampire Killers 67. How I Won the War 67. Wonderwall 68. The Exorcist 73, etc.
TV series: Sailor of Fortune 56.

McGrath, Frank (1903–1967). Grizzled American stunt-man who appeared in countless westerns but achieved his greatest popularity as the trail cook in TV's *Wagon Train* series.

McGrath, Joe (1930–). Scottish director whose TV style of goonish comedy has adapted less successfully to film.
Casino Royale (part) 67. Thirty is a Dangerous Age Cynthia 68. The Bliss of Mrs Blossom 68. The Magic Christian 70. Digby 73. The Great McGonagall 74, etc.

MacGraw, Ali (1938–) (Alice McGraw). American leading lady.
□A Lovely Way to Die 68. *Goodbye Columbus* 69. *Love Story* 71. Getaway 72. Convoy 79. Players 79. Just Tell Me What You Want 80. The Winds of War (TV) 83. China Girl (TV) 83. The Killer Elite (TV) 85.

McGraw, Charles (1914–1980). American actor, invariably in tough roles.
The Moon Is Down 43. The Killers 46. The Armored Car Robbery 50. *The Narrow Margin* 50. His Kind of Woman 51. The Bridges at Toko-Ri 51. Away All Boats 56. Slaughter on Tenth Avenue 58. The Defiant Ones 58. The Wonderful Country 59. Spartacus 60. Cimarron 61. In Cold Blood 67. Pendulum 69. Johnny Got His Gun 71. Twilight's Last Gleaming 76, etc.
TV series: Casablanca 55. The Smith Family 72.

McGuane, Thomas (1939–). American screenwriter.

Rancho de Luxe 75. 92 in the Shade (& d) 75. The Missouri Breaks 76. Tom Horn 80, etc.

McGuire, Biff (1926–). American character actor.
The Phenix City Story 55. Station Six Sahara 62. The Thomas Crown Affair 68. Serpico 73. Midway 76, etc.
TV series: Gibbsville 76.

McGuire, Don (1919–). American writer-director, former press agent. Then to TV as producer-director of the *Hennessey* series.
Meet Danny Wilson (w) 51. Walking My Baby Back Home (w) 52. Three Ring Circus (w) 54. Bad Day at Black Rock (co-w) 54. Johnny Concho (wd) 56. The Delicate Delinquent (wd) 57.

McGuire, Dorothy (1919–). American leading lady of the forties, latterly playing mothers; always in gentle, sympathetic roles.
☐*Claudia* 43. *A Tree Grows in Brooklyn* 44. The Enchanted Cottage 44. *The Spiral Staircase* 45. Claudia and David 46. Till the End of Time 46. Gentleman's Agreement 47. Mother Didn't Tell Me 50. Mister 880 50. Callaway Went Thataway 50. I Want You 51. Invitation 52. Make Haste to Live 53. *Three Coins in the Fountain* 54. Trial 55. Friendly Persuasion 56. Old Yeller 57. The Remarkable Mr Pennypacker 59. This Earth Is Mine 59. A Summer Place 60. *The Dark at the Top of the Stairs* 60. The Swiss Family Robinson 60. Susan Slade 61. Summer Magic 63. The Greatest Story Ever Told (as the Virgin Mary) 65. Flight of the Doves 71. She Waits (TV) 71. The Runaways (TV) 75. Rich Man Poor Man (TV) 76. Little Women (TV) 78. The Incredible Journey of Dr Meg Laurel (TV) 79. *Ghost Dancing* (TV) 83.

McHattie, Stephen (–). Lean American leading man.
The People Next Door 70. Von Richthofen and Brown 71. Search for the Gods (TV) 75. The Ultimate Warrior 75. Look What Happened to Rosemary's Baby (TV) 76. *James Dean* (TV) (title role) 76. Moving Violation 76. Gray Lady Down 77. Centennial (TV) 77. Roughnecks (TV) 80. Death Valley 82, etc.

Machaty, Gustav (1898–1963). Czech director best remembered for exposing Hedy Lamarr's naked charms in *Extase* 33.
The Kreutzer Sonata 26. Erotikon 29. From Saturday to Sunday 31. Nocturno 35. Within the Law (US) 39. Jealousy (US) 45, etc.

Macht, Stephen (–). Heavy-featured American leading man.
Amelia Earhart (TV) 76. Raid on Entebbe (TV) 77. The Choirboys 77. Loose Change (TV) 78. Ring of Passion (TV) 78. Hunters of the Deep (TV) 78. The Immigrants (TV) 78. Enola Gay (TV) 80. Killjoy (TV) 81. A Caribbean Mystery (TV) 82.

McHugh, Frank (1899–1981). Amiable American character actor with surprised look, frequently in Irish-American roles.
If Men Played Cards as Women Do 28. Dawn Patrol 30. The Mystery of the Wax Museum 33. Footlight Parade 33. Havana Widows 34. A Midsummer Night's Dream 35. Three Men on a Horse 36. Swing Your Lady 38. Going My Way 44. State Fair 45. Mighty Joe Young 49. My Son John 52. There's No Business Like Show Business 54. Career 59. A Tiger Walks 64. Easy Come Easy Go 67, many others.
TV series: *The Bing Crosby Show* 64.

McHugh, Jimmy (1895–1969). American song-writer: 'I Can't Give You Anything But Love, Baby', 'I Feel a Song Comin' On', 'On the Sunny Side of the Street', etc.
You'll Find Out 40. Seven Days Ashore 43. Do You Love Me? 46, etc.

McIntire, John (1907–). Spare, laconic American character actor with radio and stage experience, in Hollywood from the mid-forties, often as sheriff, editor, politician, cop. Married to Jeannette Nolan.
The Asphalt Jungle 50. Lawless Breed 52. A Lion Is in the Streets 53. Apache 54. The Far Country 54. The Kentuckian 55. Backlash 56. The Phoenix City Story 56. The Tin Star 57. Flaming Star 60. Psycho 60. Summer and Smoke 62. Rough Night in Jericho 67. Herbie Rides Again 73. Rooster Cogburn 75. The Jordan Chance (TV) 78. The Fox and the Hound (voice only) 81, etc.
TV series: *Naked City* 59. *Wagon Train* 61–64. *The Virginian* 67–69.

Maciste. A legendary hero of the Italian cinema, a strong man originating in *Cabiria* (14). Such of his adventures as have been dubbed into English usually translate him as Samson.

Mack, Helen (1913–86). American leading lady of the thirties, former child actress.
Zaza 24. Grit 28. The Silent Witness 31. Son of Kong 34. She 35. The Return of Peter Grimm 35. The Milky Way 36. Last Train

from Madrid 37. Gambling Ship 39. His Girl Friday 40. Divorce (last to date) 45, etc.

Mack, Russell (1892–1972). American director of the thirties.
Second Wife 30. Heaven on Earth 31. Once in a Lifetime 32. Private Jones 33. The Band Plays On 34. The Meanest Girl in Town 35, etc.

Mackaill, Dorothy (1903–). British leading lady of the American silent screen, former Ziegfeld chorine.
The Face at the Window (GB) 21. Twenty-one 26. Dancer of Paris 27. Children of the Ritz 29. Once a Sinner 30. Kept Husbands 31. No Man of Her Own 32. Bulldog Drummond at Bay 37, etc.

Mackay, Barry (1906–). British stage leading man and singer.
Evergreen 34. Oh Daddy 35. Forever England 35. Glamorous Night 37. Gangway 37. Sailing Along 38. Smuggled Cargo 40. Pickwick Papers 52. Orders Are Orders 55.

Mackay, Fulton (1922–87). Scottish character actor, best known as the prison guard in TV's comedy *Porridge*.
The Brave Don't Cry 51. Gumshoe 71. Nothing but the Night 73. Porridge 79. Britannia Hospital 82. Local Hero 83. Water 85, etc.

McKellen, Ian (1935–). British stage actor, in occasional films.
Alfred the Great 69. A Touch of Love 69. The Promise 69. The Priest of Love (as D. H. Lawrence) 81. The Scarlet Pimpernel (TV) (as Chauvelin) 82. *Walter* (TV) 82. Walter and June (TV) 83. The Keep 83. Plenty 85, etc.

Mackendrick, Alexander or **Sandy** (1912–). American director, long in Britain; pursued an erratic career with a couple of brilliant spots.
□Midnight Menace (w only) 37. Saraband for Dead Lovers (w only) 48. *Whisky Galore* (& w) 49. Dance Hall (w only) 50. *The Man in the White Suit* (& w) 51. *Mandy* 52. The Maggie 54. The Ladykillers 55. *Sweet Smell of Success* 56. Sammy Going South 62. A High Wind in Jamaica 65. Don't Make Waves 67.

MacKenna, Kenneth (1899–1962) (Leo Mielziner). American general purpose actor (also director).
Miss Bluebeard 25. The Lunatic at Large 27. Crazy that Way 30. Those We Love 32. High Time 60. 13 West Street 62, etc.

McKenna, Siobhan (1923–86). Fiery Irish actress, on stage from 1940, and in very occasional films.
□Hungry Hill 46. Daughter of Darkness 48. The Lost People 49. King of Kings 61. Playboy of the Western World 62. Of Human Bondage 64. Doctor Zhivago 65, etc.

McKenna, T. P. (1929–). Irish general purpose actor.
Ulysses 67. Anne of a Thousand Days 70. The Beast in the Cellar 70. Perfect Friday 70. Villain 71. The Outsider 79, etc.

McKenna, Virginia (1931–). Demure-looking but spirited British leading lady with stage experience; married to Bill Travers.
□The Second Mrs Tanqueray 52. Father's Doing Fine 52. The Oracle 53. *The Cruel Sea* 53. Simba 55. The Ship That Died of Shame 55. *A Town Like Alice* (BFA) 56. The Smallest Show on Earth 57. The Barretts of Wimpole Street 57. *Carve Her Name with Pride* 58. The Passionate Summer 58. The Wreck of the Mary Deare 59. Two Living One Dead 62. *Born Free* 66. Ring of Bright Water 69. An Elephant Called Slowly 70. Waterloo 70. Swallows and Amazons 74. Holocaust 2000 77. The Disappearance 77.

Mackenzie, Sir Compton (1883–1972). Scottish novelist. His *Carnival* was twice filmed, but he became best known for *Whisky Galore*, in which he also played a part.

McKern, Leo (1920–) (Reginald McKern). Australian character actor with wide stage experience and usually explosive personality. On stage from 1942, in England from 1946.
All for Mary 55. X the Unknown 56. *Time without Pity* 57. The Mouse That Roared 59. Mr Topaze 61. The Day the Earth Caught Fire 62. *A Jolly Bad Fellow* 64. King and Country 64. Moll Flanders 65. Help! 65. *A Man for All Seasons* 66. Decline and Fall 68. Ryan's Daughter 71. The Adventure of Sherlock Holmes' Smarter Brother 76. The Omen 76. The House on Garibaldi Street (TV) 79. The Blue Lagoon 80. Rumpole's Return (TV) 80. The French Lieutenant's Woman 81. Ladyhawke 84. The Chain 85. Murder with Mirrors (TV) 85. Monsignor Quixote (TV) 86. Travelling North 86, etc.
TV series: Rumpole of the Bailey 78–80.

Mackie, Philip (1918–85). British playwright whose film scripts included several Edgar Wallace mysteries and his own *The Whole Truth*.

McKinney, Nina Mae (1909–1967). Black American actress.
Hallelujah 29. Sanders of the River 35. Dark Waters 44. Pinky 49, etc.

MacKenzie, John (1932–). British director, ex TV.
□One Brief Summer 69. Unman Wittering and Zigo 71. Made 72. *The Long Good Friday* 80. A Sense of Freedom 81. The Honorary Consul 83.

McLaglen, Andrew V. (1925–). American director, son of Victor McLaglen; has made several big-scale westerns in the manner of John Ford.
□Gun the Man Down 56. *The Abductors* 56. The Man in the Vault 57. Freckles 60. The Little Shepherd of Kingdom Come 61. *McLintock* 63. *Shenandoah* 65. The Rare Breed 66. Monkeys Go Home 67. The Way West 67. The Ballad of Josie 68. The Devil's Brigade 68. Bandolero 68. The Undefeated 69. Hellfighters 69. Chisum 70. One More Train to Rob 71. Something Big (& p) 71. Fool's Parade (& p) 71. The Train Robbers 73. Cahill 73. Stowaway to the Moon (TV) 74. Log of the Black Pearl (TV) 74. Mitchell 76. The Last Hard Men 76. Banjo Hackett (TV) 77. Murder at the World Series (TV) 77. Fantastic Journey (TV pilot) 77. The Wild Geese 78. Breakthrough 78. North Sea Hijack 80. The Sea Wolves 80. Travis McGee (TV) 82.

McLaglen, Victor (1883–1959). Burly, good-humoured star of British silent films; later became popular in Hollywood.
Autobiography 1935: *Express to Hollywood*.
The Call of the Road 20. The Glorious Adventure 21. The Beloved Brute 23. Beau Geste 26. *What Price Glory?* 26. Captain Lash 27. Mother Macree 28. The Cockeyed World 29. *Dishonoured* 30. Wicked 31. Rackety Rax 32. Hot Pepper 33. *Dick Turpin* 33. *The Lost Patrol* 34. *The Informer* (AA) 35. Under Two Flags 36. The Magnificent Brute 37. *Gunga Din* 39. Broadway Limited 41. Call Out the Marines 42. Powder Town 42. The Princess and the Pirate 44. The Michigan Kid 47. Fort Apache 48. *She Wore a Yellow Ribbon* 49. Rio Grande 50. *The Quiet Man* 52. Fair Wind to Java 53. Prince Valiant 54. Lady Godiva 55. Many Rivers to Cross 55. Bengazi 56. The Abductors 57. Sea Fury 58, many others.

Maclaine, Shirley (1934–) (Shirley Maclean Beaty). Impish American leading lady, sister of Warren Beatty. Was signed for films while dancing in a Broadway chorus, and through the seventies was seen in TV musical specials.
Autobiographies: 1970, *Don't Fall Off The Mountain*. 1975, *You Can Get There from Here*. 1983, *Out on a Limb*.
□*The Trouble with Harry* 55. Artists and Models 56. Around the World in Eighty Days 56. Hot Spell 57. *The Matchmaker* 58. Some Came Running 58. The Sheepman 58. *Ask Any Girl* (BFA) 59. Career 59. Can-Can 59. *The Apartment* (BFA) 59. All in a Night's Work 61. Two Loves 61. My Geisha 62. The Children's Hour 62. Two for the Seesaw 63. *Irma La Douce* 63. What a Way To Go 64. The Yellow Rolls Royce 64. John Goldfarb Please Come Home 64. Gambit 66. Woman Times Seven 67. *Sweet Charity* 68. The Bliss of Mrs Blossom (GB) 68. Two Mules for Sister Sara 69. Desperate Characters 71. The Possession of Joel Delaney 72. The Turning Point 77. Being There 79. A Change of Seasons 80. Loving Couples 80. Terms of Endearment (AA) 83. Out on a Limb (TV) 86.
TV series: *Shirley's World* 71.

¶ *S.M.:* I've always felt that I would develop into a really fine actress because I care more about life beyond the camera than the life in front of it.

S.M.: I've played so many hookers they don't pay me in the regular way any more. They leave it on the dresser.

MacLane, Barton (1900–1969). Tough-looking American character actor, often seen as crooked cop, sheriff or gangster. In hundreds of films since 1924 debut.
Tillie and Gus 33. Black Fury 34. Ceiling Zero 36. You Only Live Once 37. Gold Is Where You Find It 38. The Maltese Falcon 41. Bombardier 43. San Quentin 46. The Treasure of the Sierra Madre 47. Kiss Tomorrow Goodbye 51. Captain Scarface (leading role) 53. Backlash 56. Geisha Boy 58. Gunfighters of Abilene 59. Law of the Lawless 63. Town Tamer 65. Buckskin 68, many others.
TV series: Outlaws 60. I Dream of Jeannie 65–69.

McLaren, Norman (1914–87). British-born Canadian animator-director of notable shorts, especially for the National Film Board, mainly with sound as well as picture drawn directly onto the celluloid; occasionally used live action with stop motion, and a variety of other techniques.

Allegro 39. *Dots and Loops* 40. Boogie Doodle 41. Hoppity Pop 46. Fiddle-de-dee 47. *Begone Dull Care* 49. Around is Around 51. *Neighbours* 52. Blinkety Blank 54. Rhythmetic 56. A Chairy Tale 57. Blackbird 58. Parallels 60. *Pas de Deux* 62. Mosaic 65, etc.

McLaughlin, Gibb (1884–1960). British character actor of stage and screen, once a stage monologuist and master of disguise; used his splendidly emaciated features to great advantage.
Carnival 21. Nell Gwyn 24. The Farmer's Wife 27. Kitty 29. Sally in Our Alley 31. The Private Life of Henry VIII 32. No Funny Business 33. The Scarlet Pimpernel 34. Where There's a Will 36. Mr Reeder in Room Thirteen (title role) 40. My Learned Friend 43. Caesar and Cleopatra 45. Oliver Twist 48. The Black Rose 51. The Card 52. Hobson's Choice 54. Sea Wife 57, many others.

MacLean, Alistair (1922–87). Best selling British adventure novelist whose works suddenly became popular as screen fodder.
The Guns of Navarone 61. When Eight Bells Toll 70. Puppet on a Chain 71. Fear is the Key 72. Caravan to Vaccares 75. Breakheart Pass 76. Force Ten from Navarone 78. Bear Island 79, etc.

MacLean, Douglas (1890–1967). American silent screen comedian. Later became writer/producer. Retired 1938.
As Ye Sow 19. Captain Kidd Jnr 19. 23¼ Hours' Leave 21. The Hottentot 22. Never Say Die 24. Introduce Me 25. Seven Keys to Baldpate 25, etc.

McLean, Barbara P. (1909–). American editor.
The Bowery 33. Clive of India 35. Les Misérables 35. Lloyds of London 36. Alexander's Ragtime Band 38. In Old Chicago 38. Jesse James 39. The Rains Came 39. Stanley and Livingstone 39. Tobacco Road 41. The Black Swan 42. The Song of Bernadette 43. *Wilson* (AA) 44. Margie 46. Nightmare Alley 47. All About Eve 50. Twelve O'Clock High 50. Viva Zapata 52. Niagara 53. The Egyptian 54, many others.

McLeod, Catherine (c. 1924–). American leading lady of the forties.
I've Always Loved You 46. Will Tomorrow Ever Come? 47. So Young So Bad 50. The Fortune Hunter 54. Ride the Wild Surf 64, etc.

McLeod, Norman Z. (1898–1964). American director, in Hollywood from the early twenties. Originally an animator; later wrote screenplays (e.g. *Skippy* [31]); then turned to direction.
Monkey Business 31. *Horse Feathers* 32. If I Had a Million (part) 33. Alice in Wonderland 33. *It's a Gift* 34. Pennies from Heaven 36. *Topper* 37. Merrily We Live 38. Panama Hattie 41. The Kid from Brooklyn 46. *The Secret Life of Walter Mitty* 47. *The Paleface* 47. My Favorite Spy 51. Never Wave at a WAC 53. Casanova's Big Night 54. Alias Jesse James 59, etc.

McLerie, Allyn (1926–) (Allyn Ann McLerie; now so known). Canadian-born dancer and leading lady who made films amid stage work.
Words and Music 48. Where's Charley? 52. The Desert Song 53. Phantom of the Rue Morgue 54. Battle Cry 55. The Cowboys 72. Cinderella Liberty 74. All The President's Men 76, etc.
TV series: The Tony Randall Show 76.

MacLiammoir, Micheal (1899–1978) (Alfred Willmore). Irish character actor of the old school; film roles very occasional.
Autobiographical books: *Put Money in Thy Purse* (the story of filming Orson Welles' *Othello*), 1952; *Each Actor on His Ass*, 1961.
Othello 52. Tom Jones (voice) 63. Thirty is a Dangerous Age, Cynthia 68. The Kremlin Letter 70. What's the Matter with Helen? 71, etc.

MacMahon, Aline (1899–). Sad-faced, gentle-mannered American character actress, mostly in films of the thirties.
Five Star Final 31. The Mouthpiece 32. Life Begins 32. Once in a Lifetime 32. *Golddiggers of 1933* 33. Heroes for Sale 33. *Babbitt* 34. Kind Lady 35. I Live My Life 35. Ah Wilderness 35. When You're in Love 37. Back Door to Heaven 39. Out of the Fog 41. The Lady is Willing 42. Dragon Seed 44. Guest in the House 44. The Mighty McGurk 46. The Search 48. Roseanna McCoy 49. The Flame and the Arrow 50. The Eddie Cantor Story 53. The Man from Laramie 55. Cimarron 60. I Could Go on Singing 63. All the Way Home 63, etc.

MacMahon, Horace (1907–1971). American character actor, likely to be best remembered as the older cop in the TV series *Naked City*. In films from 1937, often as cop or gangster.

Navy Blues 37. King of the Newsboys 38. Rose of Washington Square 39. Lady Scarface 41. Lady Gangster 45. Waterfront at Midnight 48. *Detective Story* 51. Man in the Dark 53. Susan Slept Here 54. My Sister Eileen 55. Beau James 57. The Swinger 66. *The Detective* 68, many others.
TV series: Martin Kane 50. The Danny Thomas Show 53. *Naked City* 59–62. Mr Broadway 64.

McMillan, Kenneth (–). Burly American character actor.
The Taking of Pelham 123 74. Oliver's Story 78. Blood Brothers 78. Hide in Plain Sight 80. Carny 80. True Confessions 81. Eyewitness 81. Ragtime 81. Partners 82. Protocol 84. Dune 84. Runaway Train 85, etc.

MacMurray, Fred (1907–). Likeable, durable American leading man of the thirties and forties; found a new lease of life in Walt Disney comedies of the early sixties.
□Friends of Mr Sweeney 34. Grand Old Girl 35. *The Gilded Lily* 35. Car 99 35. Men without Names 35. Alice Adams 35. Hands Across the Table 35. The Bride Comes Home 35. *The Trail of the Lonesome Pine* 36. 13 Hours by Air 36. The Princess Comes Across 36. The Texas Rangers 36. Maid of Salem 37. Champagne Waltz 37. Swing High Swing Low 37. Exclusive 37. True Confession 37. Coconut Grove 38. *Sing You Sinners* 38. Men With Wings 38. Café Society 39. Invitation to Happiness 39. Honeymoon in Bali 39. Little Old New York 40. Remember the Night 40. Too Many Husbands 40. Rangers of Fortune 40. Virginia 41. One Night in Lisbon 41. New York Town 41. Dive Bomber 41. The Lady is Willing 42. Take a Letter Darling 42. The Forest Rangers 42. Star Spangled Rhythm 42. Flight for Freedom 43. Above Suspicion 43. No Time for Love 43. Standing Room Only 44. And the Angels Sing 44. *Double Indemnity* 44. Murder He Says 44. Practically Yours 45. Where Do We Go from Here? 45. Captain Eddie 45. Pardon My Past 46. Smoky 46. Suddenly it's Spring 47. The Egg and I 47. Singapore 47. The Miracle of the Bells 48. On Our Merry Way 48. Don't Trust Your Husband 48. Family Honeymoon 48. Father was a Fullback 48. Borderline 50. Never a Dull Moment 50. A Millionaire for Christy 51. Callaway went Thataway 51. Fair Wind to Java 53. The Moonlighter 53. *The Caine Mutiny* 54. *Pushover* 54. Woman's World 54. The Far Horizons 55. The Rains of Ranchipur 55. At Gunpoint 55. There's Always Tomorrow 56. Gun for a Coward 57. Quantez 57. Day of the Badman 57. Good Day for a Hanging 58. *The Shaggy Dog* 59. Face of a Fugitive 59. The Oregon Trail 59. *The Apartment* 60. *The Absent Minded Professor* 61. Bon Voyage 62. Son of Flubber 63. Kisses for My President 64. Follow Me Boys 66. The Happiest Millionaire 67. Charlie and the Angel 73. The Chadwick Family (TV) 75. Beyond the Bermuda Triangle (TV) 76. The Swarm 78.
TV series: *My Three Sons* 60–71.

McNair, Barbara (1939–). Black American actress and singer.
If He Hollers Let Him Go 69. Stiletto 69. Change of Habit 69. They Call Me Mister Tibbs 70. The Organization 71, etc.

McNally, Stephen (1913–) (Horace McNally). American leading man and sometimes 'heavy', in films from 1942. Former lawyer.
The Man from Down Under 43. The Harvey Girls 45. Johnny Belinda 48. Rogues' Regiment 48. No Way Out 50. Winchester 73 50. The Raging Tide 51. Devil's Canyon 53. Black Castle 53. Make Haste to Live 54. A Bullet Is Waiting 54. Tribute to a Bad Man 56. Hell's Five Hours 58. The Fiend Who Walked the West 58. Hell Bent for Leather 59. Requiem for a Gunfighter 65. Panic in the City 68. Black Gunn 72, etc.
TV series: *Target the Corruptors* 61.

McNamara, Maggie (1928–78). Capable but short-staying American leading lady of the fifties.
□*The Moon is Blue* 53. Three Coins in the Fountain 54. Prince of Players 55. The Cardinal 63.

McNaught, Bob (1915–1976). British director, also associate producer on many films.
Grand National Night 53. Sea Wife 57. A Story of David 61, etc.

McNaughton, Gus (1884–1969) (Augustus Howard). British comedy actor, once a Fred Karno singer.
Murder 30. The Thirty-Nine Steps 35. Keep Your Seats Please 37. The Divorce of Lady X 38. Trouble Brewing 39. Jeannie 41. Much Too Shy 42. Here Comes the Sun 46, etc.

McNear, Howard (1905–1969). American comedy actor, familiar on Burns and Allen's television series as the plumber. Later with Andy Griffith.

The Long Long Trailer 54. Bundle of Joy 56. Voyage to the Bottom of the Sea 61. Follow that Dream 62. Irma La Douce 63. Kiss Me Stupid 64. The Fortune Cookie 66, etc.

MacNee, Patrick (1922–). Smooth British leading man, best-known on TV.
The Life and Death of Colonel Blimp 43. Hamlet 48. Flesh and Blood 51. Three Cases of Murder 55. The Battle of the River Plate 56. Les Girls 58. Mr Jericho (TV) 70. Incense for the Damned 70. King Solomon's Treasure 77. Billion Dollar Threat (TV) 79. The Sea Wolves 80. The Howling 80. Young Doctors in Love 82. For the Term of His Natural Life (TV) 82. The Return of the Man from UNCLE (TV) 83. A View to a Kill 85. Shadey 85, etc.
TV series: *The Avengers* 60–68. *The New Avengers* 76. Gavilan 82. Empire 84.

McNichol, Kristy (1963–). American juvenile actress.
Black Sunday 76. Like Mom, Like Me (TV) 78. The End 79. Summer of My German Soldier (TV) 79. Little Darlings 80. The Night the Lights Went Out in Georgia 81. Only When I Laugh 81. The Pirate Movie 82. Just the Way You Are 84. Dream Lover 85.

Macowan, Norman (1877–1961). Scottish character actor.
Whisky Galore 48. Laxdale Hall 53. X the Unknown 56. Tread Softly Stranger 58. The Boy and the Bridge 59. Kidnapped 60, etc.

MacPhail, Douglas (1910–1944). American singer.
Born to Dance 36. Maytime 37. Sweethearts 38. *Babes in Arms* 39. Little Nellie Kelly 40. Born to Sing 42, etc.

MacPherson, Jeanie (c. 1878–1946). American actress and screenwriter; in the latter capacity, long associated with Cecil B. de Mille.
As actress: The Vaquero's Vow 08. The Death Disc 09. Enoch Arden 10. Carmen 13. Hollywood 23.
As writer: The Affairs of Anatol 21. King of Kings 27. The Buccaneer 37, etc.

McQueen, Butterfly (1911–) (Thelma McQueen). Black American character actress.
Gone with the Wind (as the weeping maid) 39. Cabin in the Sky 43. Flame of the Barbary Coast 45. Mildred Pierce 45. Duel in the Sun 46. The Phynx 70, etc.
Famous line (*Gone with the Wind*): I don't know nothin' about birthin' babies.

McQueen, Steve (1930–1980). Unconventional but fashionable American leading man of the sixties and seventies; usually played tough, sexy and determined. Biography 1974: *Steve McQueen* by Malachy McCoy.
□Somebody Up There Likes Me 56. Never Love a Stranger 58. The Blob 58. Never So Few 59. The Great St Louis Bank Robbery 59. *The Magnificent Seven* 60. The Honeymoon Machine 61. Hell is for Heroes 61. The War Lover 62. *The Great Escape* 63. *Love with the Proper Stranger* 63. Soldier in the Rain 63. Baby the Rain Must Fall 65. *The Cincinnati Kid* 65. Nevada Smith 66. The Sand Pebbles 66. The Thomas Crown Affair 68. *Bullitt* 68. The Reivers 70. Le Mans 71. Junior Bonner 72. Getaway 72. Papillon 73. The Towering Inferno 74. An Enemy of the People 76. Tom Horn 80. The Hunter 80.
TV series: Wanted Dead or Alive 58.

¶ *S.M.:* In my own mind, I'm not sure that acting is something for a grown man to be doing.

'I can honestly say he's the most difficult actor I ever worked with.'—*Norman Jewison*

S.M.: Stardom equals freedom. It's the only equation that matters.

'One thing about Steve, he didn't like the women in his life to have balls.'—*Ali MacGraw*

'You've got to realise that a Steve McQueen performance lends itself to monotony.'—*Robert Mitchum*

Macquitty, William (1905–). British producer who came to feature films via wartime MOI shorts.
The Happy Family 52. The Beachcomber 54. Above Us the Waves 55. A Night to Remember 58. The Informers 64, etc.

Macrae, Duncan (1905–1967). Craggy-faced Scottish stage actor who made some impressive film appearances.
□*The Brothers* 47. Whisky Galore 48. The Woman in Question 50. *The Kidnappers* 53. You're Only Young Twice 53. The Maggie 54. Geordie 55. Rockets Galore 56. The Bridal Path 58. Kidnapped 59. Our Man in Havana 59. Greyfriars Bobby 60. *Tunes of Glory* 60. The Best of Enemies 61. A Jolly Bad Fellow 64. Thirty is a Dangerous Age Cynthia 67. Casino Royale 67.

Macrae, Gordon (1921–86). American actor-singer, a former child performer who broke into films from radio.

□The Big Punch 48. Look for the Silver Lining 49. Backfire 49. The Daughter of Rosie O'Grady 50. Return of the Frontiersman 50. Tea for Two 50. West Point Story 51. On Moonlight Bay 51. Starlift 51. About Face 52. By the Light of the Silvery Moon 53. Three Sailors and a Girl 53. The Desert Song 53. Oklahoma 55. Carousel 56. The Best Things in Life Are Free 56. The Pilot 79.

Macready, George (1909–1973). American character actor, a descendant of Macready the tragedian. A splendid villain, neurotic or weakling, he ran an art gallery before coming to films in 1942.
□The Commandos Strike at Dawn 42. The Seventh Cross 44. Wilson 44. The Story of Dr Wassell 44. The Conspirators 44. Follow the Boys 44. Soul of a Monster 44. The Missing Juror 45. Counterattack 45. Don Juan Quilligan 45. The Fighting Guardsman 45. *I Love a Mystery* 45. The Monster and the Ape 45. A Song to Remember 45. My Name Is Julia Ross 45. *Gilda* 46. The Man Who Dared 46. The Walls Came Tumbling Down 46. The Return of Monte Cristo 46. The Bandit of Sherwood Forest 46. The Swordsman 47. Down to Earth 47. The Big Clock 48. The Black Arrow 48. Coroner Creek 48. Beyond Glory 48. The Gallant Blade 48. *Alias Nick Beal* 49. Knock on Any Door 49. Johnny Allegro 49. The Doolins of Oklahoma 49. The Nevadan 50. A Lady without Passport 50. The Desert Hawk 50. Fortunes of Captain Blood 50. Rogues of Sherwood Forest 50. Tarzan's Peril 51. The Golden Horde 51. *Detective Story* 51. The Desert Fox 51. The Green Glove 52. Treasure of the Golden Condor 53. Julius Caesar 53. The Stranger Wore a Gun 53. The Golden Blade 53. Duffy of San Quentin 54. Vera Cruz 54. A Kiss Before Dying 56. Thunder Over Arizona 56. The Abductors 57. Gunfire at Indian Gap 57. *Paths of Glory* 57. The Alligator People 59. Plunderers of Painted Flats 59. Jet Over the Atlantic 59. Two Weeks in Another Town 62. Taras Bulba 62. *Seven Days in May* 64. Dead Ringer 64. Where Love Has Gone 64. The Great Race 65. The Human Duplicators 65. Fame Is the Name of the Game (TV) 66. The Young Lawyers (TV) 69. Night Gallery (TV) 69. Daughter of the Mind (TV) 69. Tora! Tora! Tora! 70. The Return of Count Yorga 71.
TV series: Peyton Place 66–68.

McShane, Ian (1942–). British general purpose leading man.
The Wild and the Willing 62. The Pleasure Girls 65. Sky West and Crooked 66. The Battle of Britain 68. If It's Tuesday This Must Be Belgium (US) 69. Freelance 70. Pussycat Pussycat I Love You (US) 70. Tam Lin 70. Villain 71. Sitting Target 72. The Last of Sheila 73. Ransom 74. Journey into Fear 75. Jesus of Nazareth (TV) 77. Roots (TV) 77. Dirty Money (TV) 79. Cheaper to Keep Her 80. Grace Kelly (TV) 83. Exposed 83. Too Scared to Scream 84. Ordeal by Innocence 85, etc.
TV series: Disraeli 78.

McTaggart, James (1928–1974). British TV director.
All the Way Up 69.

McWade, Robert (1872–1938). American character actor who after long stage career came to films as an elderly crotch.
Second Youth 24. The Home Towners 28. Sins of the Children 30. Cimarron 31. Grand Hotel 32. Two Seconds 32. Movie Crazy 32. Back Street 32. The Kennel Murder Case 33. The Prizefighter and the Lady 33. College Rhythm 34. The President Vanishes 34. Diamond Jim 35. The Frisco Kid 35. Society Doctor 35. Anything Goes 36. Bunker Bean 36. California Straight Ahead 37. This Is My Affair 37. Of Human Hearts 38, many others.

MacWilliams, Glen (1898–). American cinematographer.
Ever Since Eve 21. Captain January 24. Ankles Preferred 27. Hearts in Dixie 29. The Sea Wolf 30. Hat Check Girl 32. Evergreen (GB) 34. Great Guns 41. He Hired the Boss 43. Lifeboat 44. Wing and a Prayer 44. If I'm Lucky 46, many others.

Macy, Bill (1922–). American character actor.
All Together Now (TV) 75. The Late Show 76. Death at Love House (TV) 76. Stunt Seven (TV) 79.
TV series: Maude 72–77.

Madame De (France/Italy 1952). Elegant adaptation by Max Ophuls of Louise de Vilmorin's novella about a -pair of jewelled ear-rings which are passed back and forth between a husband, a wife and a lover. Photographed by Christian Matras with music by Georges Van Parys and Oscar Straus; star performances from Danielle Darrieux, Charles Boyer and Vittorio de Sica.

Madame du Barry. Lubitsch's German film of 1919, combining realism with spectacle, is probably still the best film made about the 18th century French courtesan. Starring Pola Negri, it was the first post-war German film to find international favour. Other Du Barrys have included Mrs Leslie Carter in *Du Barry* 15; Theda Bara in *Du Barry* 17; Norma Talmadge in *Du Barry, Woman of Passion* 30; Dolores del Rio in *Madame du Barry* 34; Lucille Ball in *Du Barry Was a Lady* 43; and Martine Carol in *Mistress Du Barry* 54.

Madame X. This sentimental tear-jerker about the woman whose son grows up without knowing her, from the play by Alexander Bisson, has been filmed six times. The lead was played by Jane Hading in 1909, Dorothy Donnelly in 1916, Pauline Frederick in 1920, Ruth Chatterton in 1929, Gladys George in 1937, and Lana Turner in 1965.

Madden, Peter (1905–1976). Gaunt British character actor of TV and films.
Counterblast 48. Tom Brown's Schooldays 51. The Battle of the V.1 58. Hell Is a City 60. Saturday Night and Sunday Morning 60. The Loneliness of the Long Distance Runner 62. The Very Edge 63. Doctor Zhivago 66, etc.

Maddern, Victor (1926–). Stocky Cockney character actor, formerly on stage and radio.
Seven Days to Noon (debut) 49. Cockleshell Heroes 55. Private's Progress 56. Blood of the Vampire 58. I'm All Right Jack 59. HMS Defiant 61. Rotten to the Core 65. Circus of Fear 67, many others.
TV series: Fair Exchange (US) 62.

Maddow, Ben (–). American screenwriter.
The Asphalt Jungle (co-w) 50. The Unforgiven 60. The Way West (co-w) 67. The Chairman 69. The Secret of Santa Vittoria (co-w) 69, etc.

Madigan, Amy (–). American leading lady of the eighties.
□ Love Child 82. Love Letters 82. Alamo Bay 84. Places in the Heart 84. Streets of Fire 84. Twice in a Lifetime (AAN) 85.

Madison, Guy (1922–) (Robert Moseley). American leading man, in films since 1944 after naval career.
Since You Went Away (debut) 44. Till the End of Time 46. The Charge at Feather River 53. The Command 54. Five Against the House 55. On the Threshold of Space 55. The Last Frontier 56. Hilda Crane 57. Bullwhip 58. La Schiava di Roma 60. Gunmen of the Rio Grande 65. The Mystery of Thug Island 66. The Last Panzer Battalion 68. Where's Willie 78, etc.
TV series: *Wild Bill Hickok* 51–54.

Madison, Noel (1898–1975) (Nathaniel Moscovitch). American actor of sinister roles, especially gangsters. Formerly known as Nat Madison; son of actor Maurice Moscovitch.
Sinners' Holiday 30. Manhattan Melodrama 34. G-Men 35. The Man Who Made Diamonds 37. Crackerjack (GB) 39. Footsteps in the Dark 41. Jitterbugs 43. Gentleman from Nowhere 49, etc.

Madonna (1961–) (Madonna Louise Veronica Cicone). Punkish American pop singer who became a teen cult in the mid-eighties.
Desperately Seeking Susan 85. Shanghai Surprise 86. Who's That Girl? 87.

Maeterlinck, Maurice (1862–1949). Belgian writer whose fantasy play *The Blue Bird* was filmed several times, never with success.

The Mafia. A Sicilian secret society which emerged spectacularly in the urban Italian sections of the US and is believed to control most organised crime and rackets in that country. Films which have seized on the subject with glee include *The Godfather, The Black Hand, The Don is Dead, Pay or Die, The Sicilian Clan, The Brotherhood, Johnny Cool, New York Confidential, The Brothers Rico, Honor Thy Father, The Valachi Papers* and *Charley Varrick*. In America the Mafia is sometimes known as Cosa Nostra ('our thing' or 'our cause'): the word is an acronym for Morte Alla Francia Italia Anela ('Death to the French is Italy's cry').

Magee, Patrick (1924–1982). British general purpose actor, often in sinister roles.
The Criminal 60. The Servant 63. Zulu 64. Masque of the Red Death 64. The Skull 65. *The Marat/Sade* 67. *The Birthday Party* 68. King Lear 70. You Can't Win 'em All 71. The Fiend 71. A Clockwork Orange 71. Demons of the Mind 72. Asylum 72. Rough Cut 80, etc.

The Magic Box (GB 1951). The British film industry's ambitious but uninspired contribution to the Festival of Britain: a sentimental biography of film pioneer William Friese-Greene, played by Robert Donat. An all-star cast appeared in cameo roles, including Laurence Olivier as the startled policeman who saw the first moving picture. Written by Eric Ambler, photographed by Jack Cardiff, produced by Ronald Neame, directed by John Boulting.

magicians have always had a fascination for film-makers, who on the whole preferred to have their tricks finally discredited, as with Cesar Romero in *Charlie Chan on Treasure Island* and *Two on a Guillotine*, Dante in *A Haunting We Will Go*, Vincent Price in *The Mad Magician*, Jules Berry in *Le Jour Se Lève*, Harold Lloyd in *Movie Crazy* and Tony Curtis in *Houdini*. The most splendidly genuine magician was the sorcerer in *Fantasia*, but Cecil Kellaway was an amiable warlock in *I Married a Witch*, and Edmund Lowe was chilling as *Chandu*. The 1927 version of Somerset Maugham's book *The Magician* contributed a caricature of Aleister Crowley; *The Magician* is also the title of a 1973 TV series starring Bill Bixby. The best 'live' act on film may be Orson Welles sawing Marlene Dietrich in half in *Follow the Boys*.

Magnani, Anna (1907–1973). Volatile Italian star actress (Egyptian-born).
The Blind Woman of Sorrento 34. Tempo Massimo 36. *Open City* 45. Angelina 47. *The Miracle* 50. Volcano 53. The Golden Coach 54. Bellissima 54. *The Rose Tattoo* (AA) 55. Wild is the Wind 57. The Fugitive Kind 59. Mamma Roma 62. Made in Italy 67. The Secret of Santa Vittoria 69, etc.

The Magnificent Ambersons (US 1942). Orson Welles' fascinating but only partially successful follow-up to *Citizen Kane*. Besides directing, he adapted Booth Tarkington's novel about the decline of a mid-Western family in the early years of the century, and the eventual come uppance of its arrogant son. The early scene-setting is brilliant, but the later reels and hurried happy ending seem unbalanced: Welles himself has said that his last three reels were cut by the RKO-Radio chiefs and a final scene tacked on by other hands. Photographed by Stanley Cortez, with impeccable performances from Joseph Cotten, Dolores Costello, Tim Holt, Agnes Moorehead, Anne Baxter and Ray Collins. Welles' end-credits are highly entertaining.

Magnificent Obsession. This tear-jerking novel by Lloyd C. Douglas, about an irresponsible playboy who becomes a surgeon and not only cures but falls in love with the woman he accidentally blinded, was filmed in 1935 by John M. Stahl, with Robert Taylor and Irene Dunne, and again in 1954 by Douglas Sirk, with Rock Hudson and Jane Wyman.

The Magnificent Seven (US 1961). Lively Hollywood remake of the Japanese *Seven Samurai*, transferring the action to a standard Western setting but preserving the essential story of a group of mercenaries who defend a village from plundering by bandits. Yul Brynner leads the goodies with Eli Wallach as a memorably murderous bandit. Directed by John Sturges, photographed by Charles Lang, music by Elmer Bernstein. A 1966 sequel, *Return of the Seven*, proved to be only a routine western, as did *Guns of the Magnificent Seven* 70, and *The Magnificent Seven Ride* 72.

Maharis, George (1928–). Intense-looking American leading man who has been most successful on TV.
□Exodus 60. Sylvia 65. Quick Before it Melts 65. The Satan Bug 65. Covenant with Death 67. The Happening 67. The Land Raiders 69. The Monk (TV) 69. The Desperadoes 69. The Last Day of the War 69. The Victim (TV) 72. Rich Man Poor Man (TV) 76. Look What Happened to Rosemary's Baby (TV) 76. Death Flight (TV) 77. Return to Fantasy Island (TV) 78. Crash (TV) 78. The Sword and the Sorcerer 82.
TV series: *Route 66* 60–63. The Most Deadly Game 70.

Mahin, John Lee (1902–84). American scriptwriter.
Scarface 32. *Red Dust* 32. *Bombshell* 33. Naughty Marietta 35. Captains Courageous 37. Too Hot to Handle 38. Dr Jekyll and Mr Hyde 41. Tortilla Flat 42. Down to the Sea in Ships 49. Quo Vadis? 51. Elephant Walk 54. Heaven Knows Mr Allison 57. The Horse Soldiers (& p) 59. The Spiral Road 62. Moment to Moment 66, many others.

Mahoney, Jock (1919–) (Jacques O'Mahoney). Athletic American leading man who apart from playing Tarzan was confined to routine roles. Former stuntman for Gene Autry and Charles Starrett.
The Doolins of Oklahoma 49. A Day of Fury 55. Away All Boats 56. I've Lived Before 56. A Time to Love and a Time to Die 58. The Land Unknown 58. Tarzan the Magnificent 60. Tarzan Goes to India 62. Tarzan's Three Challenges 64. The Walls of Hell 66. The Bad Bunch 76. The End 78, etc.

TV series: The Range Rider 51–52. Yancey Derringer 58.

Maibaum, Richard (1909–). American scriptwriter.
They Gave Him a Gun 37. Ten Gentlemen from West Point 40. O.S.S. 46. *The Great Gatsby* 49. Cockleshell Heroes 55. Zarak 57. The Day They Robbed the Bank of England 60. *Dr No* 62. From Russia with Love 63. Goldfinger 64. Thunderball 65. On Her Majesty's Secret Service 69. Diamonds Are Forever 71. The Man with the Golden Gun 74. The Spy Who Loved Me 77.

Maigret. The pipe-smoking, thoughtful, sympathetic police inspector from the Paris Sûreté, Jules Maigret, has been played on screen only once in English, by Charles Laughton in *The Man on the Eiffel Tower*. French interpreters have included Harry Baur, Pierre Renoir and, most satisfyingly, Jean Gabin, while Germany's Heinz Ruhmann and Italy's Gino Cervi also had a go. Best of all, perhaps, was Rupert Davies in the British TV series of the early sixties.

Mailer, Norman (1923–). American sensational novelist. Works filmed include *The Naked and the Dead, An American Dream. The Deer Park* was an 'exposé' of Hollywood. He wrote and directed *Beyond the Law* 68, *Wild 90* 69 and *Maidstone* 70; and appeared in *Town Bloody Hall* 70.

Main, Marjorie (1890–1975) (Mary Tomlinson). American character actress, probably best remembered as Ma Kettle in the long-running hillbilly series.
Take a Chance (debut) 33. *Dead End* 37. Stella Dallas 37. Test Pilot 38. Angels Wash Their Faces 39. The Women 39. Turnabout 40. Bad Man of Wyoming 40. A Woman's Face 41. Honky Tonk 41. Jackass Mail 42. Tish 42. Heaven Can Wait 43. Rationing 43. *Meet Me in St Louis* 44. *Murder He Says* 44. The Harvey Girls 45. Bad Bascomb 45. Undercurrent 46. *The Egg and I* 47. The Wistful Widow of Wagon Gap 47. *Ma and Pa Kettle* 49. Ma and Pa Kettle Go to Town 50 (then one Kettle film a year till 1956). Mrs O'Malley and Mr Malone 50. The Belle of New York 52. Rose Marie 54. Friendly Persuasion 56, many others.

Maisie. The hard-boiled (but soft-centred) gold-digging heroine of ten MGM comedy-dramas between 1939 and 1947; played in all of them by Ann Sothern.

Maitland, Marne (1920–). Anglo-Indian actor in British films; adept at sinister orientals.
Cairo Road 50. Father Brown 54. Bhowani Junction 56. The Camp on Blood Island 58. The Stranglers of Bombay 59. Sands of the Desert 60. Nine Hours to Rama 62. Lord Jim 65. The Reptile 65. Khartoum 66. The Pink Panther Strikes Again 76, etc.

Major Barbara (GB 1940). Accomplished screen version of the Bernard Shaw play about a militant young Salvationist. Produced and directed by Gabriel Pascal, who even persuaded Shaw to write additional scenes. Cast includes Wendy Hiller, Rex Harrison, Robert Morley, Robert Newton, Marie Lohr, Emlyn Williams, Sybil Thorndike and Deborah Kerr.

Majors, Lee (1940–) (Harvey Lee Yeary II). American leading man.
□ Will Penny 67. The Ballad of Andy Crocker (TV) 68. The Liberation of L. B. Jones 70. Weekend of Terror (TV) 73. The Six Million Dollar Man (TV) 73. Gary Francis Powers (TV) 76. Just a Little Inconvenience (TV) 78. The Norseman 78. Killer Fish 78. Steel 80. The Naked Sun 80. Agency 80. Sharks 80.
TV series: *The Big Valley* 65–68. The Men from Shiloh 70. Owen Marshall 71–72. *Six Million Dollar Man* 73–78. The Fall Guy 81–86.

Makavejev, Dusan (1932–). Yugoslavian director.
□ The Switchboard Operator 67. Innocence Unprotected 68. WR: My Stories of the Organism 71. Sweet Movie 74. Montenegro 80. The Coca Cola Kid 84.

Makeham, Eliot (1882–1956). British character actor of stage and screen, former accountant. For years played bespectacled little bank clerks who sometimes surprised by standing up for themselves.
Rome Express 32. Orders Is Orders 32. Lorna Doone 35. Dark Journey 37. Farewell Again 37. Saloon Bar 40. *Night Train to Munich* 40. The Common Touch 42. The Halfway House 44. Jassy 47. Trio 50. Scrooge 51. Doctor in the House 53. Sailor Beware 56, etc.

make-up. A general term for the cosmetic application to the body of materials intended to enhance or change the appearance, from glamorization to the creation of monsters.

¶ *Marlene Dietrich:* The relationship between the make-up man and the film actor is that of accomplices in crime.

Mako (–). Japanese-American character actor.
The Sand Pebbles 66. Hawaii 67. The Island at the Top of the World 74. The Big Brawl 80. The Bushido Blade 80. Under the Rainbow 81. Testament 83. Conan the Destroyer 84.

Mala (1906–1952) (Ray Wise). Eskimo actor who was popular in a few American films of the thirties.
Igloo 32. Eskimo 33. Hawk of the Wilderness 35. The Tuttles of Tahiti 42. Red Snow 52, etc.

Malden, Karl (1913–) (Mladen Sekulovich). Respected American stage actor whose film career has been generally disappointing because Hollywood has not seemed to know what to do with him.
□They Knew What They Wanted 40. Winged Victory 44. 13 Rue Madeleine 46. Boomerang 47. Kiss of Death 47. The Gunfighter 50. Where the Sidewalk Ends 50. Halls of Montezuma 50. *A Streetcar Named Desire* (AA) 52. Decision Before Dawn 52. Diplomatic Courier 52. Operation Secret 52. Ruby Gentry 52. I Confess 53. Take the High Ground 53. Phantom of the Rue Morgue 54. *On the Waterfront* 54. *Baby Doll* 56. Fear Strikes Out 57. Time Limit (d only) 57. Bombers B52 57. The Hanging Tree 59. Pollyanna 60. The Great Imposter 60. Parrish 61. One Eyed Jacks 61. All Fall Down 62. Bird Man of Alcatraz 62. Gypsy 62. How the West was Won 63. Come Fly with Me 63. Dead Ringer 64. Cheyenne Autumn 64. The Cincinnati Kid 65. Nevada Smith 66. The Silencers 66. Murderers Row 66. *Hotel* 67. The Adventures of Bullwhip Griffin 67. Billion Dollar Brain 67. Blue 68. Hot Millions 68. Patton 69. Cat O'Nine Tails 69. Wild Rovers 71. Captains Courageous (TV) 78. Meteor 79. Beyond the Poseidon Adventure 79. *Word of Honor* (TV) 81. The Sting II 82. Summertime Killer 82. Twilight Time 83. *Fatal Vision* (TV) 84. Billy Galvin 86.
TV series: *Streets of San Francisco* 72–76. Skag 80.

male impersonation: see *transvestism*.

Malick, Terrence (1945–). American director.
□Pocket Money (w only) 72. *Badlands* (& wp) 73. The Gravy Train (w only) 74. Days of Heaven (& wp) 79.

Malkovich, John (–). American character actor.
The Killing Fields 84. Places in the Heart (AAN) 84. Eleni 85. Empire of the Sun 87.

Malle, Louis (1932–). French 'new wave' director, former assistant to Robert Bresson.
World of Silence (co-d) 56. Lift to the Scaffold 57. *The Lovers* 58. *Zazie dans le Metro* 61. *Le Feu Follet* 63. Viva Maria 65. Le Voleur 67. *Souffle au Coeur* (AA script) 71. Lacombe Lucien 75. Black Moon 75. Pretty Baby 78. Atlantic City (BFA) 80. My Dinner with Andre 81, etc.

¶ *L.M.:* You see the world much better through a camera.

Malleson, Miles (1888–1969). British playwright, screen writer and actor whose credits read like a potted history of the British cinema.
AS WRITER: *Nell Gwyn* 34. Peg of Old Drury 35. Rhodes of Africa 36. *Victoria the Great* 37. The Thief of Baghdad 40. The First of the Few 42. They Flew Alone 43. Mr Emmanuel 44, etc.
AS ACTOR: City of Song 31. The Sign of Four 32. Bitter Sweet 33. Nell Gwyn 34. Tudor Rose 36. Knight without Armour 37. The Thief of Baghdad (as the sultan) 40. Major Barbara 41. They Flew Alone 42. Dead of Night 45. While the Sun Shines 47. Saraband for Dead Lovers 48. *Kind Hearts and Coronets* (as the hangman) 49. The Perfect Woman 49. Stage Fright 50. The Man in the White Suit 51. The Magic Box 51. *The Importance of Being Earnest* (as Canon Chasuble) 52. Folly to Be Wise 52. The Captain's Paradise 53. Private's Progress 56. *Brothers in Law* 57. The Naked Truth 57. *Dracula* 58. The Captain's Table 58. The Hound of the Baskervilles 59. I'm All Right Jack 59. Brides of Dracula 60. The Hellfire Club 61. Heavens Above 63. First Men in the Moon 64. You Must Be Joking 65, many others.

Mallory, Boots (1913–1958) (Patricia Mallory). American leading lady of the thirties; married William Cagney and Herbert Marshall.
Handle with Care 32. Hello Sister 33. Sing Sing Nights 35. Here's Flash Casey 37, etc.

Malo, Gina (1909–1963) (Janet Flynn). Irish-German-American leading lady of the thirties, usually in tempestuous roles. Filmed in Britain; married Romney Brent.
In a Monastery Garden 32. Good Night Vienna 32. Waltz Time 33. The Private Life

of Don Juan 34. Jack of All Trades 36. Over She Goes 38. The Door with Seven Locks 40, etc.

Malone, Dorothy (1925–) (Dorothy Maloney). American leading lady of the fifties, often in sultry roles.
□The Falcon and the Co-Eds 43. One Mysterious Night 44. Show Business 44. Seven Days Ashore 44. Hollywood Canteen 44. Too Young to Know 45. Janie Gets Married 46. *The Big Sleep* 46. Night and Day 48. To the Victor 48. Two Guys from Texas 48. One Sunday Afternoon 48. Flaxy Martin 49. South of St Louis 49. Colorado Territory 49. The Nevadan 50. Convicted 50. Mrs O'Malley and Mr Malone 50. The Killer that Stalked New York 50. Saddle Legion 51. The Bushwhackers 52. Scared Stiff 53. Torpedo Alley 53. Law and Order 54. Jack Slade 54. Loophole 54. Pushover 54. The Fast and Furious 54. Private Hell 36 54. Young at Heart 54. The Lone Gun 54. Five Guns West 55. Battle Cry 55. Tall Man Riding 55. Sincerely Yours 55. Artists and Models 55. At Gunpoint 55. Pillars of the Sky 56. Tension at Table Rock 56. *Written on the Wind* (AA) 56. Quantez 57. *Man of a Thousand Faces* 57. *The Tarnished Angels* 57. Tip on a Dead Jockey 57. *Too Much Too Soon* (as Diana Barrymore) 58. Warlock 59. The Last Voyage 60. The Last Sunset 61. Beach Party 63. Fate is the Hunter 64. The Pigeon (TV) 69. Exzess (WG) 70. The Man Who Would Not Die 75. Rich Man Poor Man (TV) 76. Little Ladies of the Night (TV) 77. Murder in Peyton Place (TV) 77. Katie: Portrait of a Centerfold (TV) 78. Good Luck Miss Wyckoff 79. Winter Kills 79. Condominium (TV) 80. The Being 80. Peyton Place, the Next Generation (TV) 85. TV series: *Peyton Place* 64–68.

Malraux, André (1901–76). French author and politician, finally Minister of Culture; the leading spirit behind the 1937 documentary of the Spanish Civil War, *Days of Hope*.

Maltby, H. F. (1880–1963). British comedy playwright (*The Rotters, The Right Age to Marry*, etc.). Screenwriter (*Over the Garden Wall* 44, etc.) and actor of choleric characters. Autobiography 1950: *Ring Up The Curtain*. Those Were The Days 34. Jack of All Trades 36. Pygmalion 38. Under Your Hat 40. A Canterbury Tale 44. The Trojan Brothers 45, etc.

The Maltese Falcon. Dashiell Hammett's brilliantly written crime story was filmed three times by Warners. In 1931 it starred Bebe Daniels and Ricardo Cortez and was directed by Roy del Ruth; in 1936 it appeared as *Satan Met a Lady*, directed by William Dieterle, with Bette Davis and Warren William. The definitive version, however, did not come till 1941, when John Huston directed it (his first film) from his own script. Humphrey Bogart was the private eye, and the rogues' gallery included Mary Astor, Sydney Greenstreet, Peter Lorre, and Elisha Cook Jnr. It was highly influential on later crime films, and is often claimed as Huston's best film: he spoofed it unsuccessfully in his *Beat the Devil* 54. Another spoof was *The Black Bird* 75.

Maltz, Albert (1908–85). American screenwriter who suffered from the anti-communist witch hunt.
Afraid to Talk 32. This Gun for Hire 42. Destination Tokyo 43. The Man in Half Moon Street 44. Cloak and Dagger 46. *Naked City* 48. Two Mules for Sister Sara 70. Scalawag 73, etc.

Malyon, Eily (1879–1961). English character actress in Hollywood, a familiar supporting face from *His Greatest Gamble* 34 to *The Secret Heart* 46, typically as the acidulous aunt in *On Borrowed Time* 38.

Mamoulian, Rouben (1897–1987). American stage director of Armenian origin. Over the years he made a number of films which vary in quality but at their best show a fluent command of the medium.
□*Applause* 29. *City Streets* 31. *Dr Jekyll and Mr Hyde* 32. *Love Me Tonight* 32. Song of Songs 33. *Queen Christina* 33. We Live Again 34. *Becky Sharp* 35. *The Gay Desperado* 36. High, Wide and Handsome 37. Golden Boy 39. *The Mark of Zorro* 40. Blood and Sand 41. Rings on Her Fingers 42. Summer Holiday 48. Silk Stockings 57. Began work on *Cleopatra* 62 but was replaced.

'His tragedy is that of the innovator who runs out of innovations.'—*Andrew Sarris, 1968*

the man

? Name the actor who played each of the following title roles.

1 *A Man for All Seasons*
2 *The Man* (TV movie)
3 *The Invisible Man* (1933)
4 *The Indestructible Man*
5 *The Man in Grey*
6 *The Man in Half Moon Street*
7 *The Man from Laramie*
8 *The Man from the Alamo*

9 *A Man Alone*
10 *Man About Town*
11 *A Man and a Woman*
12 *The Man I Married*
13 *The Man in the White Suit*
14 *The Man in the Grey Flannel Suit*
15 *Man of a Thousand Faces*
16 *The Flim Flam Man*
17 *The Man without a Star*
18 *The Man without a Country* (TV movie)
19 *The Man Who Cried Wolf*
20 *The Man with the Golden Arm*
21 *The Man Who Broke the Bank at Monte Carlo*
22 *The Man Who Came to Dinner*
23 *The Thin Man* (think twice)
24 *The Man Who Reclaimed His Head*
25 *The Man Who Played God*
26 *A Man to Remember*
27 *The Man Who Could Cheat Death*
28 *The Man Who Understood Women*
29 *The Man Who Loved Cat Dancing*
30 *The Man Who Shot Liberty Valance*

A Man and a Woman: see *Un Homme et une Femme*.

A Man For All Seasons (AA) (GB 1966). A deceptively simple and straightforward piece of film-making by Fred Zinnemann (AA), based on Robert Bolt's play about Sir Thomas More but shedding its stylization in favour of a plain chronological treatment. The result was a triumph of sheer excellence in every department. Paul Scofield (AA) had the role of his life, with effective contributions from Wendy Hiller and Robert Shaw; the cinematography of Ted Moore (AA) was a constant delight. The film also marked an encouraging example of a sober, literate and thoughtful work gaining wide public acceptance.

The Man in Grey (GB 1943). Though fairly flat and unimaginative, this Regency melodrama from Lady Eleanor Smith's novel was so popular that it provoked a rash of similar costume pieces: *Madonna of the Seven Moons* 44, *The Wicked Lady* 45, *Caravan* 46, *Jassy* 47, *Blanche Fury* 47, etc. It also did much for the careers of Margaret Lockwood, James Mason, Phyllis Calvert and Stewart Granger. Leslie Arliss directed.

The Man in the Iron Mask. No one knows what mixture of fact and fiction exists in the famous story of Louis XIV's mysterious prisoner who languished for years in the Bastille, his face always covered (actually with velvet). Some said it was Louis' bastard brother, others an Italian diplomat. Anyway, Dumas wrote an exciting novel on the subject, and it has been twice filmed: in 1929 (as *The Iron Mask*) with Douglas Fairbanks, and in 1939 (by James Whale) with Louis Hayward. A TV movie with Richard Chamberlain was made in 1976 and in the following year *The Fifth Musketeer* trod much the same ground.

The Man in the White Suit (GB 1951). Bubbly Ealing satire, nimbly directed by Alexander Mackendrick, about a scientist who manages to antagonize both management and labour by inventing a fabric which never gets dirty and never wears out. Written by Mackendrick, Roger Macdougall and John Dighton; starring Alec Guinness, Joan Greenwood, Cecil Parker, Ernest Thesiger. A small classic.

Man of Aran (GB 1934). Influential documentarist Robert Flaherty came to Britain and took three years to film this sympathetic account of fisherfolk on a barren island off Ireland's west coast. It encouraged later films like *Edge of the World* 38, and generally opened the way for British film-makers to look more closely at their natural surroundings.

The Man Who Came to Dinner (US 1941). George S. Kaufman and Moss Hart based their hilarious stage success on the real-life figure of Alexander Woollcott, who perfectly fitted the character of the cantankerous, megalomaniac broadcaster who is confined by a broken hip to a normal mid-Western home which he turns into bedlam. Monty Woolley was just right in the film version, and had perfect support from Bette Davis, Reginald Gardiner, Jimmy Durante, Billie Burke and others. William Keighley directed.

The Man Who Knew Too Much. Alfred Hitchcock twice filmed this thriller about a child held hostage by a gang planning to assassinate an international political figure: GB 1934, with Leslie Banks, Edna Best and Peter Lorre; and US 1956, with James Stewart, Doris Day and Bernard Miles. The first version, despite (or perhaps because of) its curious studio sets, made incomparably better entertainment.

The Man with the Golden Arm (US 1956). Otto Preminger produced and directed this film about drug addiction, from Nelson

Algren's novel; at the time it not only flew in the face of the Hollywood production code, but also marked the first time the Rank circuit played an 'X' film since *Detective Story*, after the poor returns of which they had announced that 'X' films were for sensation-seekers and Rank theatres would henceforth play nothing but family entertainment. Frank Sinatra, Eleanor Parker and Kim Novak starred; Elmer Bernstein supplied the music. As a film it was rather a drag.

Mancini, Henry (1924–). American composer.
AS ARRANGER: The Glenn Miller Story 53. The Benny Goodman Story 56, etc.
AS COMPOSER: Touch of Evil 58. High Time 60. *Breakfast at Tiffany's* (AA) 61. Bachelor in Paradise 61. *Hatari* 62. *The Pink Panther* 63. Charade 63. A Shot in the Dark 64. Dear Heart 65. What Did You Do in the War, Daddy? 66. Two for the Road 67. Darling Lili 69. The White Dawn 73. The Return of the Pink Panther 75. Once is Not Enough 76. Silver Streak 76. W. C. Fields and Me 76. House Calls 78. Who is Killing the Great Chefs of Europe? 78 Nightwing 79. Little Miss Marker 80. Back Roads 81. Mommie Dearest 81. Victor/Victoria (AA) 82. Harry and Son 84. Lifeforce 85, others.
Academy Award songs: 'Moon River', 'Days of Wine and Roses'.

Mancunian Films. A small but dauntless little British studio which throughout the forties and early fifties earned its keep locally with a stream of wild farces starring home-grown music hall talent: Frank Randle, Harry Korris, Sandy Powell, Tessie O'Shea, Betty Jumel, Nat Jackley, Josef Locke, Jewel and Warriss, Suzette Tarri and Norman Evans. Neither art nor craft entered into the matter.

Mancuso, Nick (c. 1956–). Heavy-set Canadian leading man.
Dr Scorpion (TV) 78. The House on Garibaldi Street (TV) 79. Torn Between Two Lovers (TV) 80. Nightwing 80. The Kidnapping of the President 80. Scruples (TV) 81. Ticket to Heaven 81. Mother Lode 82. The Legend of Walks Far Woman (TV) 83. Heartbreakers 84. Night Magic 85. Half a Lifetime 86.

Mandel, Johnny (1926–). American composer.
I Want to Live 58. The Third Voice 59. The Americanization of Emily 64. Point Blank 67. M*A*S*H 70. The Last Detail 73. Freaky Friday 76. Agatha 79. Being There 79. The Baltimore Bullet 80. Deathtrap 82. The Verdict 82, etc.

Mandell, Daniel (1895–). American editor.
The Turmoil 24. Showboat 29. Counsellor at Law 33. Diamond Jim 35. Dodsworth 36. Dead End 37. Wuthering Heights 39. The Little Foxes 41. Arsenic and Old Lace 44. Wonder Man 45. The Best Years of Our Lives (AA) 46. My Foolish Heart 49. Valentino 52. Guys and Dolls 55. Witness for the Prosecution 57. The Apartment (AA) 60. Irma la Douce 63. The Fortune Cookie 66, many others.

Mander, Miles (1888–1946) (Lionel Mander). British character actor, a former theatre manager with long experience of all kinds of stage work.
The Pleasure Garden 26. *The First Born* (& wd) 28. Loose Ends (wd only) 30. The Missing Rembrandt (wd only) 31. The Private Life of Henry VIII 32. Loyalties 33. The Morals of Marcus (d only) 35, etc.; then settled in Hollywood as actor. *The Three Musketeers* (as Richelieu) 36. Lloyds of London 37. Slave Ship 37. Suez 38. The Three Musketeers (musical version; as Richelieu again) 39. *Wuthering Heights* 39. Tower of London 39. Lady Hamilton 41. *Five Graves to Cairo* 43. *Farewell My Lovely* 44. The Scarlet Claw 44. Pearl of Death 44. The Bandit of Sherwood Forest 46. The Walls Came Tumbling Down 46, many others.

Mandy (GB 1952). A delicately handled mixture of fiction and documentary about the teaching of a congenitally deaf child. Directed by Alexander Mackendrick from a novel, *The Day Is Ours*, by Hilda Lewis; with Jack Hawkins, Phyllis Calvert and the child actress Mandy Miller.

Mangano, Silvana (1930–). Italian actress, wife of producer Dino de Laurentiis. Former model.
L'Elisir D'Amore 49. Bitter Rice 51. Anna 51. Mambo 53. Ulysses 54. The Wolves 56. The Sea Wall 57. Tempest 59. Five Branded Women 61. Barabbas 62. Theorem 68. The Decameron 70. Death in Venice 71. Ludwig 72. Conversation Piece 76. Dune 84.

Manhunt (US 1941). This then topical, though now dated, adventure melodrama from Geoffrey Household's *Rogue Male* told of a big game hunter's 'stalk' of Hitler and the consequent espionage intrigues. Fritz Lang's directorial style was ponderous, the foggy London settings hilarious; Walter Pidgeon and George Sanders, however, had polish as hero and villain. A TV movie with Peter O'Toole, under the original book title, followed in 1976.

Mankiewicz, Don (1922–). American scriptwriter and novelist, son of Herman Mankiewicz.
Trial 55. House of Numbers 57. I Want to Live 58.

Mankiewicz, Herman (1897–1953). American screenwriter, also journalist and noted wit; brother of Joseph L. Mankiewicz. Biography 1968: *Mank.*
The Road to Mandalay 26. After Office Hours 35. John Meade's Woman 37. *Citizen Kane* (AA) (contribution disputed: some say he wrote most of it) 41. Pride of the Yankees 42. Stand By for Action 43. Christmas Holiday 44. The Enchanted Cottage 44. The Spanish Main 45. A Woman's Secret 48. Pride of St Louis 52, etc.

¶ Will you accept 300 per week to work for Paramount Pictures? All expenses paid. 300 is peanuts. Millions are to be grabbed out here and your only competition is idiots. Don't let this get around.—*H.M.'s wire to Ben Hecht, 1926*
Anon: Tell me, do you know any 75-dollar-a week writers?
H.M.: I know lots of them, but they're all making 1500 dollars a week.
H.M.: In a novel the hero can lay ten girls and marry a virgin for the finish. In a movie this is not allowed. The villain can lay anybody he wants, have as much fun as he wants cheating and stealing, getting rich and whipping the servants. But you have to shoot him in the end. When he falls with a bullet in the forehead, it is advisable that he clutch at the Gobelin tapestry on the wall and bring it down over his head like a symbolic shroud. Also, covered by such a tapestry, the actor does not have to hold his breath while being photographed as a dead man.
H.M.: Barbara Stanwyck is my favourite. My God, I could just sit and dream of being married to her, having a little cottage out in the hills, vines around the door. I'd come home from the office tired and weary, and I'd be met by Barbara, walking through the door holding an apple pie she had cooked herself. And wearing no drawers.
H.M.: I don't know how it is that you start working at something you don't like, and before you know it you're an old man.
Famous line (*Citizen Kane*): If I hadn't been so rich, I might have been a really great man.

Mankiewicz, Joseph L. (1909–). American film creator of many talents. Biography 1977: *Pictures Will Talk* by Kenneth Geist.
AS WRITER: The Mysterious Dr Fu Manchu 29. Million Dollar Legs 32. Forsaking All Others 34. The Keys of the Kingdom 44, etc.
AS PRODUCER: Fury 36. The Bride Wore Red 37. Three Comrades 38. Huckleberry Finn 39. Strange Cargo 40. The Philadelphia Story 40. Woman of the Year 42. The Keys of the Kingdom 44, etc.
□AS WRITER-DIRECTOR: Dragonwyck 46. Somewhere in the Night 46. The Late George Apley 47. The Ghost and Mrs Muir 47. Escape 48. *A Letter for Three Wives* (AA script) 49. House of Strangers (d only) 50. No Way Out 50. *All About Eve* (AA script and direction) 50. People will Talk 51. Five Fingers (d only) 52. Julius Caesar 53. *The Barefoot Contessa* 54. Guys and Dolls 55. The Quiet American (& p) 57. Suddenly Last Summer (d only) 59. Cleopatra 63. The Honey Pot 67. There was a Crooked Man 70. Sleuth (d only) 72.
'A cinema of intelligence rather than inspiration . . . his wit scratches more than it bites.'—*Andrew Sarris, 1968*

¶ *J.L.M.:* I got a job at Metro and went in to see Louis Mayer, who told me he wanted me to be a producer. I said I wanted to write and direct. He said, 'No, you have to produce first, you have to crawl before you can walk.' Which is as good a definition of producing as I ever heard.
J.L.M.: I felt the urge to direct because I couldn't stomach what was being done with what I wrote.
J.L.M.: Every screenwriter worthy of the name has already directed his film when he has written his script.
J.L.M.: There were always financial crises. Someone would come out from the East and announce that the business was in deep trouble, and what would happen was that they'd reduce the number of matzo balls in Louie Mayer's chicken soup from three to two. Then they'd fire a couple of secretaries and feel virtuous.
The toughest three pictures I ever made. It was shot in a state of emergency, shot in confusion, and wound up in blind panic.—*J.L.M. on Cleopatra*

Mankiewicz, Tom (1942–). American screenwriter, son of Joseph L. Mankiewicz.

Live and Let Die 72. The Man with the Golden Gun 73. Mother, Jugs and Speed 76. The Cassandra Crossing 77. The Eagle Has Landed 77.

Mankowitz, Wolf (1924–). British novelist and screenwriter.
A Kid for Two Farthings 56. Expresso Bongo 59. Waltz of the Toreadors 62. The Day the Earth Caught Fire 63. Where the Spies Are 65. Casino Royale 66. Dr Faustus 67. The 25th Hour 67. Bloomfield 71. The Hireling 73.

Mann, Abby (1927–). American playwright and screenwriter.
Judgment at Nuremburg (oaw) 61. A Child is Waiting (w) 63. The Condemned of Altona (w) 63. Ship of Fools (w) 65. The Detective (w) 68. The Marcus Nelson Murders (TV) 73. King (TV) (also d) 80. Skag (TV) 80. The Atlanta Child Murders (TV) (also d) 85, etc.

Mann, Anthony (1906–1967) (Emil Bundesmann). American director, usually of outdoor films; his best work was concerned with the use of violence by thoughtful men.
□Dr Broadway 42. Moonlight in Havana 42. Nobody's Darling 43. My Best Gal 44. Strangers in the Night 44. The Great Flamarion 45. Two O'Clock Courage 45. Sing Your Way Home 45. Strange Impersonation 46. The Bamboo Blonde 46. Desperate 47. Railroaded 47. T-Men 47. Raw Deal 48. The Black Book 49. Border Incident 49. Side Street 49. Devil's Doorway 50. The Furies 50. *Winchester 73* 50. The Tall Target 51. *Bend of the River* 51. The Naked Spur 52. Thunder Bay 53. *The Glenn Miller Story* 54. The Far Country 55. Strategic Air Command 55. *The Man from Laramie* 55. The Last Frontier 56. Serenade 56. Men in War 57. The Tin Star 57. God's Little Acre 58. Man of the West 58. Cimarron 60. El Cid 61. The Fall of the Roman Empire 64. The Heroes of Telemark 65. A Dandy in Aspic (completed by Laurence Harvey) 68.

Mann, Daniel (1912–). American director, ex stage and TV.
□*Come Back Little Sheba* 52. About Mrs Leslie 54. The Rose Tattoo 55. I'll Cry Tomorrow 55. The Teahouse of the August Moon 56. Hot Spell 58. The Last Angry Man 59. The Mountain Road 60. Butterfield 8 60. Ada 61. Who's Got the Action? 62. Five Finger Exercise 62. Who's Been Sleeping in my Bed? 63. Judith 65. Our Man Flint 66. For Love of Ivy 68. A Dream of Kings 69. Willard 71. The Harness (TV) 71. The Revengers 72. Maurie 73. Interval 73. Lost in the Stars 73. Journey into Fear 75. Matilda 78. Playing for Time (TV) 80. The Incredible Mr Chadwick 80. The Day the Loving Stopped (TV) 81.

Mann, Delbert (1920–). American director, ex TV.
□*Marty* (AA) 55. *The Bachelor Party* 57. Desire Under the Elms 58. Separate Tables 58. Middle of the Night 59. *The Dark at the Top of the Stairs* 60. Lover Come Back 61. The Outsider 62. That Touch of Mink 62. A Gathering of Eagles 63. Dear Heart 65. Quick Before it Melts 65. Mister Buddwing 66. Fitzwilly 67. The Pink Jungle 68. Heidi (TV) 68. David Copperfield (TV) 69. She Waits (TV) 71. No Place to Run (TV) 72. Kidnapped 72. Jane Eyre (TV) 72. Man Without a Country (TV) 73. A Girl Named Sooner (TV) 75. Birch Interval 76. Francis Gary Powers (TV) 76. Tell Me My Name (TV) 77. Breaking Up (TV) 78. Love's Dark Ride (TV) 78. Home to Stay (TV) 78. Thou Shalt Not Commit Adultery (TV) 78. Torn Between Two Lovers (TV) 79. All Quiet on the Western Front (TV) 80. To Find My Son (TV) 81. Night Crossing 81. Love Leads the Way (TV) 84. A Death in California (TV) 84.

Mann, Hank (1887–1971) (David Liebermann). Gargantuan American supporting player of silent days, especially with Chaplin; one of the Keystone Kops.
Modern Times 36. Hollywood Cavalcade 39. The Great Dictator 40, etc.

Mann, Heinrich (1871–1950). German novelist. His story 'Professor Unrath', published in 1905, was filmed as *The Blue Angel*. Brother of Thomas Mann.

Mann, Ned (1893–1967). American special-effects director, a one-time professional roller skater who entered films in 1920 as an actor. Best remembered for his long association with Alexander Korda.
Dirigible 30. *The Man Who Could Work Miracles* 35. *The Ghost Goes West* 36. *Things to Come* 36. *The Thief of Baghdad* 40. Anna Karenina 47. Bonnie Prince Charlie 48. Around the World in Eighty Days 56.

Mann, Thomas (1875–1955). German novelist who spent his latter years in California. Brother of Heinrich Mann. *Buddenbrooks* became a TV serial (Germany,

1982), as did *The Confessions of Felix Krull* (Germany, 1981); *Death in Venice* was filmed to general acclaim.

Manners, David (1901–) (Rauff de Ryther Duan Acklom). Canadian leading man of Hollywood films in the thirties; claimed to be descended from William the Conqueror.
□ *Journey's End* 30. He Knew Women 30. Sweet Mama 30. Kismet 30. Mother's Cry 30. The Truth About Youth 30. The Right to Love 30. Dracula 30. The Millionaire 31. *The Last Flight* 31. The Miracle Woman 31. The Ruling Voice 31. The Greeks Had a Word for Them 31. Lady with a Past 32. Beauty and the Boss 32. Stranger in Town 32. Crooner 32. Man Wanted 32. A Bill of Divorcement 32. They Call It Sin 32. The Mummy 32. The Death Kiss 32. From Hell to Heaven 33. The Warrior's Husband 33. The Girl in 419 33. The Devil in Love 33. Torch Singer 33. Roman Scandals 33. The Black Cat 34. The Luck of a Sailor 34. The Great Flirtation 34. The Moonstone 34. The Perfect Clue 35. The Mystery of Edwin Drood 35. Jalna 35. Hearts in Bondage 36. A Woman Rebels 36.

Mannheim, Lucie (1895–1976). German-born character actress, married to Marius Goring.
The Thirty-Nine Steps (as the mysterious victim) 35. The High Command 37. Yellow Canary 43. Hotel Reserve 44. So Little Time 52. Beyond the Curtain 60. Bunny Lake Is Missing 65, etc.

Manni, Ettori (1927–1979). Italian actor.
Girls Marked Danger 52. La Lupa 53. Two Nights with Cleopatra 54. Ulysses 54. Attila the Hun 54. Le Amichi 55. Revolt of the Gladiators 58. Legions of the Nile 59. Revolt of the Slaves 60. Hercules and the Captive Women 61. The Valiant 62. Gold for the Caesars 63. The Battle of the Villa Fiorita 65. The Devil in Love 66. The Battle of El Alamein 69. Street People 76, many others.

Manning, Irene (1917–) (Inez Harvuot). American leading lady of the forties, former café singer.
Two Wise Maids 37. The Big Shot 42. Yankee Doodle Dandy 42. The Desert Song 44. Shine On, Harvest Moon 44. Escape in the Desert 45. Bonnie Prince Charlie (GB) 48, etc.

Mansfield, Jayne (1932–1967) (Vera Jane Palmer). Amply proportioned American leading lady whose superstructure became the butt of many jokes.
Biography 1973: *Jayne Mansfield* by May Mann.
The Female Jungle 55. Illegal 56. Pete Kelly's Blues 56. The Burglar 57. The Girl Can't Help It 57. The Wayward Bus 57. Will Success Spoil Rock Hunter? 57. Kiss Them For Me 57. The Sheriff of Fractured Jaw 59. Too Hot to Handle (GB) 60. The Challenge (GB) 60. It Happened in Athens 62. Panic Button 64. Country Music USA 65. The Fat Spy 66. A Guide for the Married Man 67, etc.

¶ *J.M.:* Men are those creatures with two legs and eight hands.
'Dramatic art in her opinion is knowing how to fill a sweater.'—*Bette Davis*
'Miss United Dairies herself.'—*David Niven*

Mantee, Paul (1936–) (Paul Marianetti). American general purpose actor.
Robinson Crusoe on Mars (leading role) 64. An American Dream 66. They Shoot Horses Don't They 69. W. C. Fields and Me 76. The Day of the Animals 77. The Great Santini 80, etc.

Mantz, Paul (1903–1965). American stunt pilot who died in a crash during the filming of *The Flight of the Phoenix*.
Biography 1967: *Hollywood Pilot* by Don D. Wiggins.

Manvell, Roger (1909–87). British film historian. Director of the British Film Academy from 1947 and author of many books on cinema, the most influential being the Penguin *Film* 44.

Manx, Kate (1930–1964). American leading lady.
□Private Property 60. Hero's Island 62.

Manz, Linda (1961–). American leading lady.
Days of Heaven 78. King of the Gypsies 78. Boardwalk 79. Orphan Train (TV) 80.

Mara, Adele (1923–) (Adelaida Delgado). Spanish-American dancer who played leads in Hollywood co-features of the forties.
Alias Boston Blackie 42. Bells of Rosarita 45. Tiger Woman 46. Diary of a Bride 48. The Sea Hornet 51. Back from Eternity 56. Curse of the Faceless Man 58. The Big Circus 59, etc.

Marais, Jean (1913–) (Jean Marais-Villain). French romantic actor well

remembered in several Cocteau films. Later films less notable; recently in cloak-and-sword epics, also playing 'The Saint', 'Fantomas' and various secret agents.
Autobiography 1975: *Histoires de ma Vie*.
L'Eternel Retour 43. La Belle et la Bête 45. L'Aigle a Deux Têtes 47. Les Parents Terribles 48. Orphée 49, etc.

March, Fredric (1897–1975) (Frederick McIntyre Bickel). One of America's most respected stage and screen actors, who always projected intelligence and integrity and during the thirties and forties was at times an agreeable light comedian. Long married to Florence Eldridge.
□The Dummy 29. The Wild Party 29. The Studio Murder Mystery 29. Paris Bound 29. Jealousy 29. Footlights and Fools 29. The Marriage Playground 29. Sarah and Son 30. Ladies Love Brutes 30. Paramount on Parade 30. True to the Navy 30. Manslaughter 30. Laughter 30. *The Royal Family of Broadway* 30. Honour among Lovers 30. Night Angel 31. My Sin 31. Merrily We Go to Hell 32. *Dr Jekyll and Mr Hyde* (AA) 32. Smiling Through 32. Make me a Star 32. Strangers in Love 32. The Sign of the Cross 33. Tonight Is Ours 33. The Eagle and the Hawk 33. The Affairs of Cellini 34. All of Me 34. Good Dame 34. Design for Living 34. *Death takes a Holiday* 34. The Barretts of Wimpole Street (as Robert Browning) 34. We Live Again 34. *Les Misérables* 35. The Dark Angel 35. Anna Karenina 35. Mary of Scotland 36. Anthony Adverse 36. The Road to Glory 36. *A Star Is Born* 37. *Nothing Sacred* 37. The Buccaneer 38. There Goes My Heart 38. Trade Winds 39. Susan and God 40. Victory 40. So Ends Our Night 41. *One Foot in Heaven* 41. Bedtime Story 42. *I Married a Witch* 42. Tomorrow the World 44. *The Adventures of Mark Twain* 44. *The Best Years of Our Lives* (AA) 46. Another Part of the Forest 48. An Act of Murder 48. Christopher Columbus (GB) 49. It's a Big Country 51. *Death of a Salesman* 52. Man on a Tightrope 53. *Executive Suite* 54. The Bridges at Toko Ri 54. The Desperate Hours 55. Alexander the Great 55. The Man in the Grey Flannel Suit 56. Middle of the Night 59. *Inherit the Wind* 60. The Young Doctors 62. The Condemned of Altona 63. *Seven Days in May* 64. Hombre 67. Tick Tick Tick 70. The Iceman Cometh 73.
Rising Sun 43. Gangway for Tomorrow 44.
❄ For the diligence with which he undertook every role, and for the satisfying success of most of the results. *A Star Is Born*.

¶ 'He was able to do a very emotional scene with tears in his eyes, and pinch my fanny at the same time.'—*Shelley Winters*

March, Hal (1920–1970). American comic actor who never quite made it.
Outrage 50. Yankee Pasha 54. My Sister Eileen 55. *Hear Me Good* 57. Send Me No Flowers 64, etc.

The March of Time. A highly influential series of two-reelers on current affairs, started and financed in 1935 by the founders of *Time* Magazine in association with film-maker Louis de Rochemont. The raucous American commentary by Westbrook van Voorhis marred it for European consumption, but its contents were a first-class in-depth examination of what was happening in the world. It ran with great success until the late forties, when it was gradually replaced by TV series such as *NBC White Paper, CBS Reports*, Granada's *World in Action*, and the BBC's *Panorama*. A book by Raymond Fielding, *The March of Time*, was published in 1977.

Marchand, Corinne (1928–). French leading lady of the sixties.
Cleo de 5 à 7 62. Seven Deadly Sins 63. The Milky Way 69. Rider on the Rain 70. Borsalino 70, etc.

Marchand, Henri (1898–1959). French comedy actor.
À Nous la Liberté 31. Je Vous Aimerai Toujours 33. Volga en Flammes 35. Les Deux Combinards 38. L'Ennemi sans Visage 46. La Sorcière 50. Operation Magali 53. Till Eulenspiegel 56, many others.

Marcus, Lawrence B. (–). American screenwriter.
Petulia 68. Justine 69. Alex and the Gypsy 76. The Stunt Man 80.

Marcuse, Theodore (1920–1967). Shaven-pated American character actor, usually in sinister roles.
The Glass Bottom Boat 65. The Cincinnati Kid 65. Last of the Secret Agents 66. The Wicked Dreams of Paula Schultz 67, etc.

Margetson, Arthur (1897–1951). British stage actor, former stockbroker's clerk, who went to Hollywood in 1940 and played supporting roles.
Other People's Sins 31. His Grace Gives Notice 33. Little Friend 34. Broken Blossoms

36. Juggernaut 37. Action for Slander 38. Return to Yesterday 40. Random Harvest 43. Sherlock Holmes Faces Death 44, etc.

Margo (1918–85) (Maria Marguerita Guadelupe Boldao Castilla y O'Donnell). Mexican actress and dancer, once with Xavier Cugat's band, long married to Eddie Albert, in occasional Hollywood films from 1933.
Crime without Passion 34. Winterset 36. Lost Horizon 37. The Leopard Man 43. Behind the Rising Sun 43. Gangway for Tomorrow 44. Viva Zapata 52. I'll Cry Tomorrow 57. Who's Got the Action? 63, etc.

Margolin, Janet (1943–). American leading lady.
David and Lisa 62. Bus Riley's Back in Town 65. The Greatest Story Ever Told 65. The Saboteur 65. Nevada Smith 66. Enter Laughing 67. Buona Sera Mrs Campbell 68. Take the Money and Run 70. The Last Child (TV) 71. Family Flight (TV) 72. Pray for the Wildcats (TV) 74. Planet Earth (TV) 74. Lanigan's Rabbi (TV) 76. Annie Hall 77. Murder in Peyton Place (TV) 77. The Triangle Factory Fire Scandal (TV) 79. Last Embrace 79, etc.

Margolin, Stuart (c. 1940–). American character actor.
Limbo 72. The Stone Killer 73. Death Wish 74. Lanigan's Rabbi (TV) 76. The Big Bus 76. Futureworld 76. S.O.B. 81, etc.
TV series: Nichols 71. Bret Maverick 81.

Marin, Edwin L. (1901–1951). American director.
The Death Kiss 32. A Study in Scarlet 33. Paris Interlude 34. The Casino Murder Case 35. I'd Give My Life 36. Everybody Sing 38. A Christmas Carol 38. Fast and Loose 39. Maisie 39. Florian 40. A Gentleman After Dark 42. *Show Business* 44. Tall in the Saddle 44. Johnny Angel 45. The Young Widow 46. Nocturne 46. Christmas Eve 47. Race Street 48. Canadian Pacific 49. Fighting Man of the Plains 49. The Cariboo Trail 50. Fort Worth 51, etc.

Marin, Jacques (1919–). French character actor.
The Island at the Top of the World 74. Herbie Goes to Monte Carlo 77.

Marion, Frances (1888–1973) (Frances Marion Owens). American screenwriter. Autobiography 1972: *Off With Their Heads.*
Daughter of the Sea 16. Humoresque 22. Stella Dallas 25. The Winning of Barbara Worth 26. The Scarlet Letter 27. *Love* 27. The Wind 28. *The Big House* (AA) 30. *The Champ* (AA) 32. *Dinner at Eight* 33. Riff Raff 36. *Knight without Armour* 37. Green Hell 40, etc.

Marion-Crawford, Howard (1914–1969). British actor often seen in Watsonian roles or as jovial, beefy, sporting types.
Forever England 32. Freedom Radio 40. The Rake's Progress 45. The Hasty Heart 49. The Man in the White Suit 51. Where's Charley? 52. Reach for the Sky 56. Virgin Island 58. The Brides of Fu Manchu 66, etc.
TV series: Sherlock Holmes 55.

Maris, Mona (1903–) (Maria Capdevielle). Franco-Argentinian 'second lead' in Hollywood films.
Romance of the Rio Grande 29. Secrets 33. Law of the Tropics 41. Tampico 44. Heartbeat 46. The Avengers 50, etc.

Maritza, Sari (1910–) (Patricia Nathan). Anglo-Austrian leading lady, a short-lived sensation of the early thirties.
Monte Carlo Madness 31. Forgotten Commandments 32. Evenings for Sale 32. International House 33. Crimson Romance 34, etc.

Marius (France 1931). The first of a trilogy (the others: *Fanny* 32, *César* 34), written by Marcel Pagnol about characters of the Marseilles waterfront: saloon-owner César; his wayward son Marius; Fanny, the mother of Marius' child; Panisse, an ageing widower who marries Fanny. In 1938 James Whale directed *Port of Seven Seas*, a Hollywood remake with Wallace Beery in Raimu's role; in 1960 Joshua Logan directed another remake, *Fanny*, with Boyer and Chevalier but without the songs which had been used in a Broadway musical version shortly before. The original films were directed respectively by Alexander Korda, Mar Allegret and Pagnol himself.

Marken, Jane (1895–1976) (J. Krab). French character actress with long stage experience.
Fioritures 15. Camille 34. *Partie de Campagne* 37. Hôtel du Nord 38. *Lumière d'Été* 42. Les Enfants du Paradis 44. L'Idiot 46. Clochemerle 47. Une Si Jolie Petite Plage 48. Manèges 49. Ma Pomme 50. Les Compagnes de la Nuit 52. Marie Antoinette 55. And God Created Woman 56. Pot Bouille 57. The Mirror Has Two Faces 58, etc.

Marker, Chris (1921–) (Christian Bouche-Villeneuve). French documentary director. Leader of the modernist 'left bank' school. Olympia 52. Toute la Memoire du Monde 56. Letter from Siberia 58. Description d'un Combat 60. Cuba Si 61. Le Joli Mai 62. La Jetée 63. If I Had Four Dromedaries 66. Le Fond de l'Air est Rouge 77, etc.

Markey, Enid (1890–1981). American character actress. In 1918 she was the first screen Jane, to Elmo Lincoln's Tarzan.

Markey, Gene (1895–1980). American screenwriter.
The Battle of Paris 29. The Florodora Girl 30. As You Desire Me 32. Midnight Mary 33. Fashions 34. A Modern Hero 34. Let's Live Tonight 35. King of Burlesque 36. Private Number 36. *On the Avenue* 37, etc.
AS PRODUCER ONLY: Wee Willie Winkie 37. The Little Princess 39. The Hound of the Baskervilles 39. The Blue Bird 40. Lillian Russell 40. Moss Rose 47.
†Markey's several wives included Joan Bennett, Hedy Lamarr and Myrna Loy.

Markham, Monte (1935–). American leading man, mostly on TV.
Death Takes a Holiday (TV) 71. One is a Lonely Number 72. Midway 76. Airport 77 77, etc.
TV series: The Second Hundred Years 67. Mr Deeds Goes to Town 69. The New Perry Mason 73.

Markle, Fletcher (1921–). Canadian director, briefly in Hollywood.
□Jigsaw 49. Night into Morning 51. The Man with a Cloak 51. The Incredible Journey 63.

Marks, Alfred (1921–). Bald-pated British comedian, in films from 1950 but more usually seen on TV and stage.
Desert Mice 59. There Was a Crooked Man 60. Frightened City 61. Weekend with Lulu 62. She'll Have to Go 63. Scream and Scream Again 70. Our Miss Fred 72. Valentino 77, etc.

Marley, J. Peverell (1899–1964). American cinematographer who worked on de Mille's silent epics.
The Ten Commandments 23. The Volga Boatmen 25. *King of Kings* 27. House of Rothschild 34. Clive of India 35. *Alexander's Ragtime Band* 38. *The Hound of the Baskervilles* 39. Night and Day 46. Life with Father 47. The Greatest Show on Earth 52. House of Wax 53. Serenade 56. The Left-Handed Gun 58. A Fever in the Blood 61, many others.

Marley, John (1907–84). American character actor.
My Six Convicts 52. Timetable 56. I Want to Live 58. America America 65. Cat Ballou 65. Faces 68. *Love Story* 70. A Man Called Sledge 70. The Godfather 72. Blade 73.W. C. Fields and Me 76. The Car 77. The Greatest 77. Hooper 78. Tribute 80, etc.

Marlowe, Hugh (1911–1982) (Hugh Hipple). American actor, former radio announcer, in films from 1937.
Mrs Parkington 44. Meet Me In St Louis 44. *Twelve O'Clock High* 50. *All about Eve* 50. The Day the Earth Stood Still 51. Monkey Business 52. Garden of Evil 54. Earth Versus the Flying Saucers 56. Thirteen Frightened Girls 64. Castle of Evil 66. The Last Shot You Hear 68, etc.
TV series: Ellery Queen 54.

Marlowe, Scott (–). American juvenile actor of the late fifties.
Men in War 57. Young Guns 57. The Subterraneans 60. *A Cold Wind in August* 61.

Marly, Florence (1918–78) (Hana Smekalova). Franco-Czech leading lady, married to Pierre Chenal. Made a few films in Hollywood.
Sealed Verdict 48. Tokyo Joe 49. Tokyo File 212 51. Gobs and Gals 52. The Idol (Chilean) 52. Confession at Dawn (Chilean) 53. Undersea Girl 58. Queen of Blood 65. Games 67. Doctor Death 73, etc.

Marmont, Percy (1883–1977). Veteran British romantic actor of silent era, in films since 1913.
SILENT FILMS: Lord Jim (US) 25. Mantrap (US) 26. The Silver King (GB) 24. Rich and Strange (GB) 27, etc.
SOUND FILMS: The Silver Greyhound 32. Secret Agent 36. Action for Slander 38. I'll Walk Beside You 41. Loyal Heart 45. No Orchids for Miss Blandish 48. Lisbon 56, many others.

Marquand, Christian (1927–). French leading man, who turned director with *Candy* 68.
Lucretia Borgia 53. Senso 54. And God Created Woman 56. Sait-on Jamais? 57. Une Vie 58. Victory at Entebbe (TV) 76. The Other Side of Midnight 77. Je Vous Aime 80, etc.

Marquand, John P. (1893–1960). American novelist who wrote solid popular books about middle-aged men regretting their lost youth; also the Mr Moto series (filmed in the late thirties with Peter Lorre).
H. M. Pulham Esquire 41. The Late George Apley 47. B. F.'s Daughter 49. Top Secret Affair (Melville Goodwin USA) 56. Stopover Tokyo 57, etc.

Marquand, Richard (1938–87). British director.
The Search for the Nile (TV) 75. The Legacy 78. Eye of the Needle 81. Return of the Jedi 83. Until September 84. *Jagged Edge* 85. Hearts of Fire 87.

The Marriage Circle (US 1924). Ernst Lubitsch's famous silent comedy was adapted by Paul Bern from a play by Lothar Schmidt. Basically a very small comedy of adultery, it was impeccably done and gave new screen personas to Monte Blue, Marie Prevost and Adolphe Menjou, as well as bringing forth many imitators anxious to equal Lubitsch's flair for sophisticated sex. In 1932 Lubitsch remade it, equally delightfully, with dialogue, songs, recitative, and characters who frequently addressed the camera, as *One Hour With You*; with Maurice Chevalier, Genevieve Tobin, Jeanette MacDonald and Roland Young.

Marriott, Moore (1885–1949) (George Thomas Moore-Marriott). British character comedian specializing in hoary rustics, chiefly beloved as the ancient but resilient old Harbottle of the Will Hay comedies: *Convict 99* 36, *Oh Mr Porter* 38, *Ask a Policeman* 39, *Where's That Fire?* 40, etc. Also notable with the Crazy Gang in *The Frozen Limits* 39, and *Gasbags* 40. Made over 300 films in all.
Dick Turpin 08. Passion Island 26. The Lyons Mail 31. The Water Gypsies 32. As You Like It 36. Millions Like Us 43. Time Flies 44. Green for Danger 46. The History of Mr Polly 49. High Jinks in Society 49.

Mars, Kenneth (1936–). American character comedian who is usually way over the top.
The Producers 67. Desperate Characters 71. What's Up Doc? 72. Paper Moon 73. The Parallax View 74. Young Frankenstein 74. Night Moves 75. The Apple Dumpling Gang Rides Again 79, etc.

La Marseillaise (France 1938). A revered but patchy and overlong account of the French Revolution, directed and co-written by Jean Renoir, with Pierre Renoir as Louis XVI. It was financed by the French trade unions and popular subscription.

Marsh, Carol (1926–) (Norma Simpson). British leading lady whose career faltered when she outgrew *ingénue* roles.
□*Brighton Rock* 47. Marry Me 49. Helter Skelter 50. Alice in Wonderland (French puppet version) 50. The Romantic Age 50. Scrooge 51. Salute the Toff 51. Private Information 51. Dracula 58. Man Accused 59.

Marsh, Garry (1902–1981) (Leslie March Geraghty). Robust, balding British character actor; in films from 1930, usually as harassed father, perplexed policeman or explosive officer.
Night Birds 30. Dreyfus 30. Number Seventeen 32. The Maid of the Mountains 32. Scrooge 35. When Knights Were Bold 36. Bank Holiday 38. It's in the Air 38. The Four Just Men 39. Hoots Mon 40. I'll Be Your Sweetheart 45. The Rake's Progress 45. Dancing with Crime 46. Just William's Luck 48. Murder at the Windmill 49. Worm's Eye View 51. Mr Drake's Duck 53. Who Done It? 55. Where the Bullets Fly 66, many others.

Marsh, Jean (1935–). British character actress who became internationally known as the maid in *Upstairs Downstairs* and later found Hollywood work in the series *Nine to Five*.
The Eagle Has Landed 77. Master of the Game (TV) 84. Return to Oz 85.

Marsh, Mae (1895–1968) (Mary Warne Marsh). American leading lady of the silent screen; later played small character roles.
Man's Genesis 12. The Birth of a Nation 15. Intolerance 16. Polly of the Circus 17. Spotlight Sadie 18. The Little 'Fraid Lady 20. Flames of Passion 22. The White Rose 23. Daddies 24. The Rat (GB) 25. Tides of Passion 26. Over the Hill 32. Little Man What Now 34. Jane Eyre 43. A Tree Grows in Brooklyn 44. The Robe 53. Sergeant Rutledge 60, many others.

Marsh, Marion (1913–) (Violet Krauth). American leading lady of English, German, French and Irish descent. Began in Hollywood as an extra; chosen by John Barrymore to play Trilby to his *Svengali* 31. The Mad Genius 32. Five Star Final 32. The Eleventh Commandment 33. Love at Second Sight (GB) 34. The Black Room 35. When's Your Birthday? 37. Missing Daughters 40. House of Errors 42, etc.

Marsh, Oliver H. T. (1893–1941). American cinematographer.
The Floor Below 18. Good References 19. Lessons in Love 21. Jazzmania 23. The Dove 27. The Divine Woman 28. Not So Dumb 30. The Sin of Madelon Claudet 31. Arsene Lupin 32. Today We Live 33. The Merry Widow 34. *David Copperfield* 35. *A Tale of Two Cities* 35. The Great Ziegfeld 36. His Brother's Wife 36. After the Thin Man 36. Maytime 37. The Firefly 37. Sweethearts 38. It's a Wonderful World 39. Bitter Sweet 40. Rage in Heaven 41. Lady Be Good 41, many others.

Marshal, Alan (1909–1961). Australian-born actor of light romantic leads: came to films in 1936 after New York stage experience.
The Garden of Allah 36. Night Must Fall 38. The Hunchback of Notre Dame 40. Tom, Dick and Harry 40. *Lydia* 41. The White Cliffs of Dover 43. The Barkleys of Broadway 48. The Opposite Sex 56. The House on Haunted Hill 59, etc.

Marshall, Alan (1938–). British producer involved in all of Alan Parker's films.

Marshall, Brenda (1915–) (Ardis Ankerson Gaines). American leading lady who married William Holden and retired.
Espionage Agent 39. The Sea Hawk 40. Footsteps in the Dark 41. Singapore Woman 41. Background to Danger 43. The Constant Nymph 44. Strange Impersonation 45. Whispering Smith 49. The Tomahawk Trail 50, etc.

Marshall, Connie (1938–). American child actress of the forties.
Sunday Dinner for a Soldier 44. *Sentimental Journey* 45. Dragonwyck 46. Home Sweet Homicide 47. Mother Wore Tights 48. Kill the Umpire 50, etc.

Marshall, E. G. (1910–) (Everett G. Marshall). American character actor with long Broadway experience.
□The House on 92nd Street 45. 13 Rue Madeleine 46. Untamed Fury 47. Call Northside 777 48. The Caine Mutiny 54. Pushover 54. The Bamboo Prison 54. Broken Lance 54. The Silver Chalice 54. The Left Hand of God 55. The Scarlet Hour 56. The Mountain 56. *Twelve Angry Men* 57. *The Bachelor Party* 57. Man on Fire 57. The Buccaneer 58. The Journey 59. Compulsion 59. Cash McCall 59. Town without Pity 61. The Chase 66. Is Paris Burning? 66. The Poppy Is Also a Flower (TV) 66. The Bridge at Remagen 69. A Clear and Present Danger (TV) 70. Tora! Tora! Tora! 70. The Pursuit of Happiness 71. Vanished (TV) 71. The City (TV) 71. Don't Look Behind You (TV) 71. Pursuit (TV) 72. Money to Burn (TV) 73. The Abduction of St Anne (TV) 75. Collision Course (TV) 76. Interiors 78. The Private Files of J. Edgar Hoover 78. The Lazarus Syndrome (TV) 79. Superman II 80. Creepshow 82. Kennedy (TV) (as Joseph Kennedy) 83. Saigon—Year of the Cat (TV) 83. The Winter of our Discontent (TV) 84. Power 85.
TV series: The Defenders 61–64. The Bold Ones 69–71.

Marshall Garry (–). American writer-producer with television success. As film director: Young Doctors in Love 82. The Flamingo Kid 84. Nothing in Common 86.

Marshall, George (1891–1975). American director with over 400 features to his credit. Entered films 1912 as an extra; graduated to feature roles in early serials and comedies; began directing 1917 with a series of Harry Carey westerns.
Pack Up Your Troubles 32. A Message to Garcia 34. The Crime of Dr Forbes 37. In Old Kentucky 38. The Goldwyn Follies 38. You Can't Cheat an Honest Man 39. *Destry Rides Again* 39. *The Ghost Breakers* 40. When the Daltons Rode 40. The Forest Rangers 42. Star Spangled Rhythm 43. And the Angels Sing 43. *Murder He Says* 44. Incendiary Blonde 45. Hold That Blonde 45. The Blue Dahlia 46. The Perils of Pauline 47. Tap Roots 48. *Fancy Pants* 50. The Savage 52. Scared Stiff 53. *Red Garters* 54. The Second Greatest Sex 55. Beyond Mombasa (GB) 56. The Sad Sack 57. The Sheepman 58. Imitation General 58. The Gazebo 59. Cry for Happy 61. How the West Was Won (part) 62. Advance to the Rear 64. Boy, Did I Get a Wrong Number 66. Eight on the Lam 67. Hook Line and Sinker 69.

Marshall, Herbert (1890–1966). Urbane British actor who despite the loss of a leg in World War I invariably played smooth, sometimes diffident but always gentlemanly roles. In Hollywood from early thirties.
□Mumsie 27. The Letter 29. Murder 30. The Calendar 31. Secrets of a Secretary 31. *Michael and Mary* 32. The Faithful Heart 32. Blonde Venus 32. *Trouble in Paradise* 32. Evenings for Sale 32. The Solitaire Man 33. I

Was a Spy 33. Four Frightened People 34. Outcast Lady 34. The Painted Veil 34. Riptide 34. The Good Fairy 35. The Flame Within 35. Accent on Youth 35. *The Dark Angel* 35. If You Could Only Cook 35. The Lady Consents 36. Forgotten Faces 36. Till We Meet Again 36. Girls' Dormitory 36. A Woman Rebels 36. Make Way for a Lady 36. *Angel* 37. Breakfast for Two 37. Mad About Music 38. Always Goodbye 38. Woman against Woman 38. Zaza 39. A Bill of Divorcement 40. *Foreign Correspondent* 40. *The Letter* 40. When Ladies Meet 41. *The Little Foxes* 41. Kathleen 41. Adventure in Washington 41. *The Moon and Sixpence* (as Somerset Maugham) 42. Young Ideas 43. Forever and a Day 43. Flight for Freedom 43. Andy Hardy's Blonde Trouble 44. The Unseen 45. *The Enchanted Cottage* 44. Crack up 46. *The Razor's Edge* (as Somerset Maugham) 46. Duel in the Sun 46. High Wall 47. Ivy 47. The Secret Garden 49. The Underworld Story 50. Anne of the Indies 51. Black Jack 52. Angel Face 53. The Black Shield of Falworth 54. Gog 54. Riders to the Stars 54. The Virgin Queen 55. Wicked as They Come 56. The Weapon 67. *Stage Struck* 57. The Fly 58. A Fever in the Blood 60. Midnight Lace 60. Five Weeks in a Balloon 62. The List of Adrian Messenger 63. The Third Day 65.

❀ For his comforting upper class presence over thirty-five years of talkies. *Trouble in Paradise.*

¶ Fantasy droops before Mr Herbert Marshall, so intractably British in the American scene. He does, I suppose, represent some genuinely national characteristics, if not those one wishes to see exported: a kind of tobacco, a kind of tweed, a kind of pipe; or in terms of dog, something large, sentimental and moulting, something which confirms our preference for cats.—*Graham Greene, reviewing If You Could Only Cook*

Marshall, Herbert (1900–). British documentarist, married to Fredda Brilliant. Associate of John Grierson; worked on English dubbing of Russian films. Produced and directed feature, *Tinker* 49.

Marshall, Penny (1942–). American comedy actress, known from TV's Happy Days and Laverne and Shirley.
How Sweet It Is 68. 1941 79. Movers and Shakers 84. Jumpin' Jack Flash 86.

Marshall, Trudy (1922–). American leading lady of minor films in the forties.
Secret Agent of Japan 42. Girl Trouble 44. Sentimental Journey 46. Disaster 48. Mark of the Gorilla 50. The President's Lady 53, etc.

Marshall, Tully (1864–1943) (William Phillips). American silent screen actor; stage experience from boyhood.
Intolerance 15. Oliver Twist (as Fagin) 16. Joan the Woman 16. The Slim Princess 20. The Hunchback of Notre Dame 23. The Merry Widow 25. The Red Mill 27. The Cat and the Canary 28. Trail of '98 29. Show of Shows 29. The Unholy Garden 31. Scarface 32. Grand Hotel 33. Diamond Jim 35. Souls at Sea 37. A Yank at Oxford 38. Brigham Young 40. Chad Hanna 41. This Gun for Hire 42, many others.

Marshall, William (1924–). Black American character actor.
Lydia Bailey 52. Something of Value 57. The Boston Strangler 68. Blacula 72. Scream Blacula Scream 73, etc.

Marshall, Zena (1926–). British leading lady with French ancestry; stage experience.
Caesar and Cleopatra (debut) 45. Good Time Girl 47. Miranda 48. Sleeping Car to Trieste 48. Marry Me 49. Hell Is Sold Out 51. The Embezzler 54. My Wife's Family 56. The Story of David 61. Dr No 62, etc.

Martelli, Otello (1903–). Italian cinematographer, especially associated with Fellini.
Paisa 46. Bitter Rice 49. La Dolce Vita 50. I Vitelloni 52. La Strada 54. Il Bidone 55. I Tre Volti 63, etc.

Martin, Chris-Pin (1894–1953). Rotund Yaqui Indian actor who provided comic relief in many a western.
Four Frightened People 34. The Gay Desperado 36. The Return of the Cisco Kid 39 (and ensuing series). The Mark of Zorro 41. Weekend in Havana 42. Mexican Hayride 49. Ride the Man Down 53, etc.

Martin, Dean (1917–) (Dino Crocetti). Heavy-lidded, self-spoofing American leading man and singer. Teamed with Jerry Lewis until 1956, then enjoyed spectacular solo success in sixties.
Biography (of Martin and Lewis) 1976: *Everybody Loves Somebody Sometime* by Arthur Marx.
☐My Friend Irma 49. My Friend Irma Goes West 50. At War with the Army 51. That's My Boy 51. Sailor Beware 51. Jumping Jacks

52. The Stooge 52. Scared Stiff 53. The Caddy 53. Money from Home 53. Living It Up 54. Three Ring Circus 54. You're Never Too Young 55. Artists and Models 55. Pardners 56. Hollywood or Bust 56. Ten Thousand Bedrooms 57. *The Young Lions* 58. Some Came Running 58. *Rio Bravo* 59. Career 59. Who was that Lady? 60. Bells are Ringing 60. Ocean's Eleven 60. All in a Night's Work 61. Ada 61. Sergeants Three 62. Who's Got the Action? 62. Toys in the Attic 63. Who's Been Sleeping in my Bed? 63. Four For Texas 64. What a Way to Go 64. Robin and the Seven Hoods 64. *Kiss Me Stupid* 64. The Sons of Katie Elder 65. Marriage on the Rocks 65. *The Silencers* 66. Texas Across the River 66. Murderers' Row 67. Rough Night in Jericho 67. The Ambushers 67. Bandolero 68. How to Save a Marriage 68. Five Card Stud 68. Wrecking Crew 68. Airport 69. Something Big 71. Showdown 73. Mr Ricco 75. Angels in Vegas (TV) 78. The Cannonball Run 80. Cannonball Run II 83.

¶ *D.M.:* I'd hate to be a teetotaller. Imagine getting up in the morning and knowing that's as good as you're going to feel all day.

Martin, Dean Paul (–1987). American actor, son of Dean Martin.
Players 79. Heart Like a Wheel 82. Backfire 87.

Martin, Dewey (1923–). American leading man.
Knock On Any Door (debut) 49. Kansas Raiders 50. The Thing 52. The Big Sky 52. Tennessee Champ 54. Prisoner of War 54. Land of the Pharaohs 55. The Desperate Hours 55. Ten Thousand Bedrooms 57. Wheeler and Murdoch (TV) 72, etc.

Martin, Dick (1923–). See *Rowan, Dan.*

Martin, Edie (1880–1964). The frail, tiny old lady of many British films. On stage from 1886, films from 1932.
□ Farewell Again 37. Under the Red Robe 37. The Demi-Paradise 42. A Place of One's Own 45. Oliver Twist 48. The History of Mr Polly 49. The Lavender Hill Mob 51. *The Man in the White Suit* 51. Time Gentlemen Please 52. The Titfield Thunderbolt 52. The End of the Road 54. Lease of Life 54. As Long as They're Happy 55. The Lady Killers 55. My Teenage Daughter 56. Too Many Crooks 59. Weekend with Lulu 61. Sparrows Can't Sing 63.

Martin, Hugh (1914–). American composer and lyricist, generally in collaboration with Ralph Blane.
Best Foot Forward 41. Meet Me in St Louis 44. Athena 54. The Girl Rush 55, etc.

Martin, Marion (1916–85). American leading lady of 'B' pictures, a statuesque blonde who graduated from the Ziegfeld chorus.
Boom Town 40. Mexican Spitfire at Sea 41. The Big Store 41. They Got Me Covered 42. Abbot and Costello in Hollywood 45. Queen of Burlesque 47. Oh You Beautiful Doll 50. Thunder in the Pines 54, etc.

Martin, Mary (1913–). American musical comedy star; her film career did not seem satisfactory.
Autobiography 1976: *My Heart Belongs*.
□The Great Victor Herbert 39. Rhythm on the River 40. Love Thy Neighbour 40. Kiss the Boys Goodbye 41. New York Town 41. *Birth of the Blues* 41. Star Spangled Rhythm 42. Happy Go Lucky 42. True to Life 43. Night and Day 46. Main Street to Broadway 53. Valentine (TV) 79.

¶ 'She's OK, if you like talent.'—*Ethel Merman*

Martin, Millicent (1934–). British songstress of stage and TV.
The Horsemasters 60. The Girl on the Boat 62. Nothing But the Best 64. Those Magnificent Men in Their Flying Machines 65. Alfie 66. Stop the World I Want To Get Off 66, etc.
TV series: From a Bird's Eye View 69.

Martin, Pamela Sue (1954–). American leading lady who became familiar on TV (1977–78) as Nancy Drew the teenage detective.
To Find a Man 71. The Poseidon Adventure 72. Buster and Billie 73. The Girls of Huntington House (TV) 73. The Gun and the Pulpit (TV) 74. The Lady in Red 79, etc.

Martin, Ross (1920–1981) (Martin Rosenblatt). Polish-American character actor: film appearances sporadic.
Conquest of Space 55. The Colossus of New York 58. Experiment in Terror 62. The Ceremony 64. The Great Race 65. Charlie Chan: Happiness is a Warm Clue (TV: title role) 70.
TV series: *The Wild Wild West* 65–68.

Martin, Steve (1945–). American nightclub comic who turned comic actor and even goes straight occasionally.

☐The Kids Are Alright 78. Sgt Pepper's Lonely Hearts Club Band 78. The Jerk 79. The Muppet Movie 79. Pennies from Heaven 81. Dead Men Don't Wear Plaid 82. The Man with Two Brains 83. The Lonely Guy 83. All of Me 84. Movers and Shakers 84. Three Amigos 86. The Little Shop of Horrors 86. Roxanne 87. Planes, Trains and Automobiles 87.

Martin, Strother (1920–1980). American character actor, often in grizzled western roles.
The Asphalt Jungle 50. Storm over Tibet 52. The Big Knife 55. The Shaggy Dog 59. The Deadly Companions 61. The Man Who Shot Liberty Valance 62. The Sons of Katie Elder 65. Harper 66. *Cool Hand Luke* 67. True Grit 69. Butch Cassidy and the Sundance Kid 69. The Wild Bunch 69. The Ballad of Cable Hogue 70. The Brotherhood of Satan 70. Fool's Parade 71. Pocket Money 72. Sssss 73. Rooster Cogburn 75. Hard Times 75. The Great Scout and Cathouse Thursday 76. Slap Shot 77. The End 78. Up in Smoke 78. The Villain 79, many others.

Famous Line (*Cool Hand Luke*): What we've got here is a failure to communicate.

Martin, Tony (1912–) (Alfred Norris). American cabaret singer and leading man, in Hollywood from 1936 after years of touring with dance bands.
Sing, Baby, Sing 36. Banjo on My Knee 37. Ali Baba Goes to Town 38. Music in My Heart 40. The Big Store 41. Ziegfeld Girl 41. Till the Clouds Roll By 46. Casbah 48. Two Tickets to Broadway 51. Here Come the Girls 53. Deep in My Heart 54. Hit the Deck 55. Let's Be Happy (GB) 57, etc.

Martin Harvey, Sir John (1863–1944). British actor manager of the old school who appeared in a film or two.
Scaramouche 12. A Tale of Two Cities 13. The Cigarette Maker's Romance 13.

Martinelli, Elsa (1933–). Italian leading lady, in films from 1950.
The Indian Fighter (US) 55. Manuela (GB) 57. The Boatmen 60. Hatari (US) 62. The Trial 63. Marco the Magnificent 65. De l'Amour 65. The Tenth Victim 65. Candy 68, etc.

Martini, Nino (1904–76). Italian actor-singer, who made a few English-speaking films.
Here's to Romance (US) 35. The Gay Desperado (US) 36. One Night With You (GB) 48, etc.

Martins, Orlando (1899–1985). West African actor in British films.
Sanders of the River 35. Jericho 37. The Man from Morocco 44. Men of Two Worlds (as the witch doctor) 46. End of the River 47. Where No Vultures Fly 52. Simba 55. Sapphire 59. Mister Moses 65, etc.

Martinson, Leslie H. (–). American director, from TV.
PT 109 62. For Those Who Think Young 64. Batman 66. Fathom 67. Mrs Pollifax—Spy 70, etc.

Marton, Andrew (1904–). Hungarian-born director, in Hollywood from 1923; settled there after return visits to Europe. Co-directed *King Solomon's Mines* 50.
SOS Iceberg 32. The Demon of the Himalayas 34. Wolf's Clothing (GB) 37. Secrets of Stamboul (GB) 37. Gentle Annie 45. The Wild North 52. Prisoner of War 54. Green Fire 55. The Thin Red Line 64. *Crack in the World* 65. Around the World under the Sea 65, etc.
AS SECOND-UNIT DIRECTOR: *The Red Badge of Courage* 51. A Farewell to Arms 57. *Ben Hur* 59. 55 Days at Peking 62. *The Longest Day* 62. Cleopatra 62, etc.

Marty (US 1955) (AA). The film which started Hollywood's TV invasion. From Paddy Chayefsky's small-screen play about a shy butcher who courts an equally shy schoolteacher, its success started an influx of fresh talent from New York. Directed by Delbert Mann (AA), produced by Harold Hecht, with Ernest Borgnine (AA) and Betsy Blair. Chayefsky also won the best screenplay award.

Marvin, Lee (1924–87). Ruthless-looking American actor who latterly switched from unpleasant villains to unsympathetic heroes.
You're in the Navy Now 51. Duel at Silver Creek 52. The Big Heat 53. The Wild One 54. Gorilla at Large 54. The Caine Mutiny 54. Bad Day at Black Rock 54. Violent Saturday 55. Not as a Stranger 55. Pete Kelly's Blues 55. Shack Out on 101 55. I Died a Thousand Times 56. Seven Men from Now 57. *Attack* 57. Raintree County 57. The Missouri Traveller 58. The Comancheros 61. The Man Who Shot Liberty Valance 62. Donovan's

Reef 63. *The Killers* 64. *Cat Ballou* (AA) 65. Ship of Fools 65. The Professionals 66. The Dirty Dozen 67. Point Blank 67. Hell in the Pacific 68. Paint Your Wagon 69. Monte Walsh 70. Prime Cut 72. Emperor of the North Pole 73. The Iceman Cometh 73. The Spikes Gang 75. The Klansman 75. Shout at the Devil 76. The Great Scout and Cathouse Thursday 76. The Big Red One 79. Avalanche Express 79. Death Hunt 81. Gorky Park 83. Dirty Dozen, the Next Mission (TV) 85. Delta Force 85, etc.
TV series: M Squad 57–59. Lawbreaker 63.

The Marx Brothers. A family of Jewish-American comics whose zany humour convulsed minority audiences in its time and influenced later comedy writing to an enormous extent. *Chico* (1886–1961) (Leonard Marx) played the piano eccentrically and spoke with an impossible Italian accent; *Harpo* (1888–1964) (Adolph Marx) was a child-like mute who also played the harp; *Groucho* (1890–1977) (Julius Marx) had a painted moustache, a cigar, a loping walk and the lion's share of the wisecracks. In vaudeville from childhood, they came to films after Broadway success. Originally there were two other brothers: *Gummo* (1893–1977) (Milton Marx), who left the act early on, and *Zeppo* (1901–79) (Herbert Marx), who didn't fit in with the craziness and left them after playing romantic relief in their first five films. These first five films contain much of their best work: later their concentrated anarchy was dissipated by musical and romantic relief. Harpo published his autobiography 1961: *Harpo Speaks!* Among Groucho's semi-autobiographical works are *Groucho and Me* 59, *Memoirs of a Mangy Lover* 64 and *The Groucho Letters* 67. His son Arthur published *Life With Groucho* 52 and *Son of Groucho* 72. In 1974 Richard Anobile and Groucho came up with *The Marx Brothers Scrapbook.* The films are examined in detail in *The Marx Brothers at the Movies* by Paul D. Zimmerman and Burt Goldblatt. In 1978 Charlotte Chandler came up with *Hello, I Must Be Going,* a rather depressing account of Groucho's last years.
□The Cocoanuts 29. *Animal Crackers* 30. *Monkey Business* 31. *Horse Feathers* 32. *Duck Soup* 33. *A Night at the Opera* 35. *A Day at the Races* 37. Room Service 38. *At the Circus* 39. Go West 40. The Big Store 41. *A Night in Casablanca* 46. Love Happy (a curious and unhappy failure) 50. The Story of Mankind (guest appearances) 57.
GROUCHO ALONE: Copacabana 47. Mr Music 50. Double Dynamite 51. A Girl in Every Port 52. Will Success Spoil Rock Hunter? (gag appearance) 57. Skidoo 68. You Bet Your Life (TV series) 56–61.
❁ For shattering all our illusions, and making us love it. *Duck Soup.*

¶ The leader wore a large painted moustache and affected a cigar, and his three henchmen impersonated respectively a mute harpist afflicted with satyriasis, a larcenous Italian, and a jaunty cox-comb, who carried the love interest.—*S. J. Perelman*

Lines written by or for the Marx Brothers would fill a book in themselves. This is a selection of personal favourites, arranged chronologically and attributed to the authors of the films concerned.

1929: *The Cocoanuts* (George S. Kaufman, Morrie Ryskind)

Ah, Mrs Rittenhouse, won't you . . . lie down?

I'll wrestle anybody in the crowd for five dollars.

Be free, my friends. One for all and all for me—me for you and three for five and six for a quarter.

Do you know that this is the biggest development since Sophie Tucker?

Your eyes shine like the pants of my blue serge suit.

1930: *Animal Crackers* (George S. Kaufman and Morrie Ryskind)

You're the most beautiful woman I've ever seen, which doesn't say much for you.

What do you get an hour?
—For playing, we get ten dollars an hour.
What do you get for not playing?
—Twelve dollars an hour. Now for rehearsing, we make a special rate—fifteen dollars an hour.
And what do you get for not rehearsing?
—You couldn't afford it. You see, if we don't rehearse, we don't play. And if we don't play, that runs into money.
How much would you want to run into an open manhole?
—Just the cover charge.
Well, drop in sometime.
—Sewer.
Well, I guess we cleaned that up.

You go Uruguay and I'll go mine.

One morning I shot an elephant in my pajamas. How he got into my pajamas I'll never know.

1931: *Monkey Business* (S. J. Perelman, Will B. Johnstone, Arthur Sheekman)

Do you want your nails trimmed long?
—Oh, about an hour and a half. I got nothing to do.

Look at me: I worked my way up from nothing to a state of extreme poverty.

I want to register a complaint. Do you know who sneaked into my room at three o'clock this morning?
—Who?
Nobody, and that's my complaint.

Do you suppose I could buy back my introduction to you?

Sir, you have the advantage of me.
—Not yet I haven't, but wait till I get you outside.

1932: *Horse Feathers* (Bert Kalmar, Harry Ruby, S. J. Perelman, Will B. Johnstone)

Why don't you bore a hole in yourself and let the sap run out?

There's a man outside with a big black moustache.
—Tell him I've got one.

The dean is furious. He's waxing wroth.
—Is Roth out there too? Tell Roth to wax the dean for a while.

You're a disgrace to our family name of Wagstaff, if such a thing is possible.

You've got the brain of a four-year-old boy, and I bet he was glad to get rid of it.

What a day! Spring in the air!
—Who, me? I should spring in the air and fall in the lake?

1933: *Duck Soup* (Bert Kalmar, Harry Ruby, Arthur Sheekman, Nat Perrin)

Take a card. You can keep it: I've got fifty-one left.

My husband is dead.
—I'll bet he's just using that as an excuse.
I was with him to the end.
—No wonder he passed away.
I held him in my arms and kissed him.
—So it was murder!

This is a gala day for you.
—That's plenty. I don't think I could manage more than one gal a day.

What is it that has four pairs of pants, lives in Philadelphia, and it never rains but it pours?

I could dance with you till the cows come home. On second thoughts I'll dance with the cows and you come home.

Excuse me while I brush the crumbs out of my bed. I'm expecting company.

1935: *A Night at the Opera* (George S. Kaufman, Morrie Ryskind, Al Boasberg)

Do they allow tipping on the boat?
—Yes, sir.
Have you got two fives?
—Oh, yes, sir.
Then you won't need the ten cents I was going to give you.

Let joy be unconfined. Let there be dancing in the streets, drinking in the saloons, and necking in the park.

1937: *A Day at the Races* (George Seaton, Robert Pirosh, George Oppenheimer)

She looks like the healthiest woman I ever met.
—You look like you never met a healthy woman.

Don't point that beard at me, it might go off.

Closer . . . hold me closer . . .
—If I hold you any closer I'll be in back of you!

Marry me and I'll never look at another horse.

Isn't that awfully large for a pill?
—Well, it was too small for a basketball and I didn't know what to do with it.

One dollar and you remember me all your life.
—That's the most nauseating proposition I've ever had.

1939: *At the Circus* (Irving Brecher)

If you hadn't sent for me, I'd be at home now in a comfortable bed with a hot toddy.—That's a drink!

I bet your father spent the first year of your life throwing rocks at the stork.

1945: *A Night in Casablanca* (Joseph Fields, Roland Kibbee, Frank Tashlin)

The first thing we're going to do is change all the numbers on all the doors.
—But sir, think of the confusion . . .
Yeah, but think of the fun.

Hey boss, you got a woman in there?
—If I haven't, I've been wasting thirty minutes of valuable time.

I'm Beatrice Ryner. I stop at the hotel.
—I'm Ronald Kornblow. I stop at nothing.

Groucho himself later proved to be sometimes as funny as his scripts. He wrote to resign from a club:

I don't care to belong to any social organization which would accept me as a member.

And he wrote a threatening letter to *Confidential* magazine:

Dear Sir: If you continue to publish slanderous pieces about me I shall feel compelled to cancel my subscription.

His wit did not fail him with age:

I've been around so long I can remember Doris Day before she was a virgin.

His influence was international; an example of Paris graffiti in 1968 read:

Je suis Marxiste, tendence Groucho.

But life with the Marxes was seldom peaceful. Herman Mankiewicz said:

I never knew what bicarbonate of soda was until I wrote a Marx Brothers picture.

Groucho once removed Greta Garbo's hat and said:

Excuse me, I thought you were a fellow I once knew in Pittsburgh.

George F. Kaufman had soon had enough of them:

Cocoanuts was a comedy; the Marx Brothers are comics; meeting them was a tragedy.

Groucho was perhaps too fearless a critic, as when giving his opinion of *Samson and Delilah*, starring Victor Mature and Hedy Lamarr:

First picture I've seen in which the male lead has bigger tits than the female.

And on the nudist musical *Hair*:

Why should I pay ten dollars for something I can see in the bathroom for nothing?

Harpo could be bitchy too. His appraisal of *Abie's Irish Rose* has lingered down the decades:

No worse than a bad cold.

And he was witty when refusing Alexander Woollcott's invitation to share a holiday on the French riviera:

I can think of forty better places to spend the summer, all of them on Long Island in a hammock.

Groucho even aspired to be a political thinker:

Military intelligence is a contradiction in terms.

Two final thoughts. From Groucho:

If you want to see a comic strip you should see me in a shower.

And from Herman J. Mankiewicz:

I never knew what bicarbonate of soda was until I wrote a Marx Brothers picture.

Well, one more from Groucho for luck:

They say a man is as old as the woman he feels.

Mary Poppins (US 1964). Walt Disney's most successful film for years, a tricksy fantasy from the books by P. L. Travers about a magical nanny who descends on a family in Edwardian London. Over-long, but with pleasant songs and brilliant trick effects. With Julie Andrews (AA), Dick Van Dyke, David Tomlinson, etc.; directed by Robert Stevenson.

M*A*S*H (US 1970). A bitter farce by Richard Hooker and Ring Lardner Jnr, directed by Robert Altman, about high jinks in the face of death at an army hospital in Korea. Highly influential, it spawned in 1972 a toned-down but brilliantly written TV series which ran for ten years and outpaced its inspiration. It also started a run on movies which held nothing sacred, and this trend quickly proved regrettable.

Masina, Giulietta (1921–). Italian gamin-like actress, married to Federico Fellini. In films since 1941.
Senza Pieta 47. *Lights of Variety* 48. *La Strada* 54. Il Bidone 55. *Nights of Cabiria* 57. Juliet of the Spirits 65. The Madwoman of Chaillot 69. Ginger and Fred 85, etc.

mask. A technical device for blocking out part of the image. *Masking* is the black cloth which surrounds the actual cinema screen: these days it has to be electrically adjustable to encompass the various screen sizes.

The Mask of Dimitrios (US 1944). Amusingly entangled and well-staged mystery film about a writer who sets out to uncover the truth about the career of an international crook. It boasted a splendid array of character actors in their best form: Sydney Greenstreet, Peter Lorre, Victor Francen, Steve Geray, Eduardo Cianelli, Kurt Katch, Florence Bates and John Abbott. It was stylishly directed by Jean Negulesco, who subsequently failed to live up to his promise, and introduced actor Zachary Scott, of whom likewise. Frank Gruber wrote the screenplay from Eric Ambler's novel.

Maskell, Virginia (1936–1968). British leading lady with attractively soulful eyes.
□Happy is the Bride 57. Our Virgin Island 58. The Man Upstairs 59. Jet Storm 59. Suspect 60. Doctor in Love 60. The Wild and the Willing 62. *Only Two Can Play* 62. Interlude 68.

Mason, A. E. W. (1865–1948). British novelist whose *The House of the Arrow* and

The Four Feathers have been filmed several times. *Fire Over England* and *At the Villa Rose* also came to the screen.

Mason, Elliott (1897–1949). Scottish character actress with repertory experience. The Ghost Goes West 36. Owd Bob 38. The Ghost of St Michael's 41. The Gentle Sex 43. The Captive Heart 46, etc.

Mason, Herbert (1891–1960). British director.
His Lordship 36. Strange Boarders 38. Back Room Boy 41. Flight from Folly 45, etc.

Mason, James (1909–1984). Leading British and international actor who became a star at home in saturnine roles during World War II, went to Hollywood and initially had a thin time but during the fifties became a respected interpreter of varied and interesting characters.
Autobiography 1982: *Before I Forget.*
□Late Extra 35. Twice Branded 36. Troubled Waters 36. Prison Breaker 36. Blind Man's Bluff 36. The Secret of Stamboul 36. Fire Over England 36. The Mill on the Floss 37. The High Command 37. Catch as Catch Can 37. The Return of the Scarlet Pimpernel 38. *I Met a Murderer* 39. This Man is Dangerous (The Patient Vanishes) 41. Hatter's Castle 42. *The Night Has Eyes* 42. Alibi 42. Secret Mission 42. Thunder Rock 43. The Bells Go Down 43. *The Man in Grey* (a key role as an 18th-century villain) 43. They Met in the Dark 43. Candlelight in Algeria 44. Fanny by Gaslight 44. Hotel Reserve 44. A Place of One's Own 45. They Were Sisters 45. *The Seventh Veil* 45. *The Wicked Lady* 46. *Odd Man Out* 46. The Upturned Glass 47. Caught 49. Madame Bovary 49. The Reckless Moment 49. East Side West Side 49. One Way Street 50. *Pandora and the Flying Dutchman* 51. *The Desert Fox* (as Rommel) 51. Lady Possessed 52. *Five Fingers* 52. The Prisoner of Zenda (as Rupert) 52. Face to Face 52. The Desert Rats 53. *Julius Caesar* (as Brutus) 53. The Story of Three Loves 53. Botany Bay 53. The Man Between 53. Charade 53. Prince Valiant 54. *20,000 Leagues under the Sea* (as Captain Nemo) 54. *A Star is Born* 54. Forever Darling 56. Bigger than Life (& p) 56. Island in the Sun 57. Cry Terror 58. The Decks Ran Red 58. North by Northwest 59. *Journey to the Center of the Earth* 59. A Touch of Larceny 60. The Trials of Oscar Wilde 60. The Marriage Go Round 61. The Land We Love (Hero's Island) 62. Escape from Zahrain 62. Tiara Tahiti 62. *Lolita* (as Humbert) 62. The Fall of the Roman Empire 64. Torpedo Bay 64. *The Pumpkin Eater* 64. Lord Jim 65. The Player Pianos 65. Genghis Khan 65. *The Blue Max* 66. Georgy Girl 66. *The Deadly Affair* 67. Stranger in the House 67. Duffy 68. Mayerling 68. Age of Consent 69. The Seagull 69. Spring and Port Wine 70. Kill! 70. Cold Sweat 70. Bad Man's River 71. A Dangerous Summer 72. Ivanhoe 72. Child's Play 72. The Last of Sheila 73. Frankenstein, the True Story (TV) 73. The Mackintosh Man 73. 11 Harrowhouse 74. The Marseilles Contract 74. Great Expectations (TV) 74. The Tempest 74. Nostro Nero in Casa Nichols 74. Centra di Respetto 75. La Citta Sconvolta 75. Mandingo 75. Autobiography of a Princess 75. Voyage of the Damned 76. Inside Out 76. The Left Hand of the Law 76. Jesus of Nazareth (TV) 77. Cross of Iron 77. The Water Babies 78. Heaven Can Wait 78. The Boys from Brazil 78. *Murder by Decree* (as Dr Watson) 79. The Passage 79. Bloodline 79. North Sea Hijack 80. Evil Under the Sun 82. The Verdict 82. Yellowbeard 83. The Shooting Party 84.

❀ For his incisive professionalism over a long period of gradually declining standards. *A Star is Born.*

Mason, Marsha (1942–). American leading actress, married to Neil Simon.
□Hot Rod Hullaballoo 66. Blume in Love 73. Cinderella Liberty 75. Audrey Rose 77. *The Goodbye Girl* 77. The Cheap Detective 78. Promises in the Dark 79. Chapter Two 79. Only When I Laugh 81. Max Dugan Returns 83. Heartbreak Ridge 86.

Mason, Shirley (1900–1979) (Leona Flugrath). American leading lady of the silent screen, sister of Viola Dana.
Vanity Fair 15. Goodbye Bill 18. Treasure Island 20. Merely Mary Ann 20. Lights of the Desert 22. What Fools Men 25. Don Juan's Three Nights 26. Sally in Our Alley 27. Show of Stars 29, etc.

Massari, Lea (1933–) (Anna Maria Massatani). French-Italian leading lady.
L'Avventura 58. The Colossus of Rhodes 61. Four Days of Naples 62. Made in Italy 65. Les Choses de la Vie 69. Le Souffle au Coeur 71. Impossible Object 73. Violette et Francois 77. Christ Stopped at Eboli 79, etc.

Massen, Osa (1915–). Danish-born actress in Hollywood from the late thirties.
Honeymoon in Bali 39. The Devil Pays Off 41. The Master Race 44. Tokyo Rose 44. Cry

of the Werewolf 44. Deadline at Dawn 47. Rocketship XM 50, etc.

Massey, Anna (1937–). British character actress, daughter of Raymond Massey.
Gideon's Day 58. Bunny Lake is Missing 65. De Sade 69. Frenzy 72. A Doll's House 73. Vault of Horror 73. The Chain 85. Foreign Body 87, etc.
TV series: Rebecca (as Mrs Danvers) 79.

Massey, Daniel (1933–). British actor, son of Raymond Massey, usually seen on stage or TV.
Girls at Sea 57. Upstairs and Downstairs 59. The Queen's Guard 61. Go to Blazes 62. Moll Flanders 65. The Jokers 66. *Star!* (as Noel Coward) 68. Fragment of Fear 70. Mary Queen of Scots 72. Vault of Horror 73. The Incredible Sarah 76. The Cat and the Canary 77. Bad Timing 80, etc.

Massey, Ilona (1912–1974) (Ilona Hajmassy). Hungarian-born leading lady, in Hollywood from the mid-thirties.
□Knox und die Lustigen Vagabunden 35. Der Himmel auf Erden 35. *Rosalie* 37. Balalaika 39. New Wine 41. International Lady 41. Invisible Agent 42. Frankenstein Meets the Wolf Man (as 'Frankenstein') 42. Holiday in Mexico 46. Northwest Outpost 47. The Plunderers 48. Love Happy 50. Jet over the Atlantic 59.

Massey, Raymond (1896–1983). Canadian-born actor, on stage (in Britain) from 1922. In films, has played saturnine, benevolent or darkly villainous, with a penchant for impersonations of Abraham Lincoln.
Autobiographies: *When I Was Young,* 1976; *A Hundred Lives,* 1979.
□The Speckled Band (as Sherlock Holmes) 31. The Face at the Window 31. *The Old Dark House* 32. *The Scarlet Pimpernel* 34. *Things to Come* 36. Fire over England 36. Under the Red Robe 37. *The Prisoner of Zenda* 37. Dreaming Lips 37. The Hurricane 37. The Drum 38. Black Limelight 39. *Abe Lincoln in Illinois* 40. Santa Fe Trail (as John Brown) 40. 49th Parallel 41. Dangerously They Live 41. Desperate Journey 42. Reap the Wild Wind 42. Action in the North Atlantic 43. *Arsenic and Old Lace* 44. The Woman in the Window 44. Hotel Berlin 45. God Is My Co-Pilot 45. A Matter of Life and Death 46. Possessed 47. Mourning Becomes Electra 47. The Fountainhead 48. Roseanna McCoy 49. Chain Lightning 49. Barricade 50. Dallas 50. Sugarfoot 51. Come Fill the Cup 51. David and Bathsheba 51. Carson City 52. The Desert Song 53. Prince of Players 55. Battle Cry 55. *East of Eden* 55. Seven Angry Men 55. Omar Khayyam 57. The Naked and the Dead 58. The Great Impostor 60. The Fiercest Heart 61. The Queen's Guard 61. How the West Was Won 62. Mackenna's Gold 68. All My Darling Daughters (TV) 72. The President's Plane is Missing (TV) 73.
TV series: I Spy 55. Dr Kildare (as Dr Gillespie) 61–66.
❁ For his leathery, reliable and highly intelligent presence during most of the cinema's most interesting years (though in few of its more interesting films). *Things To Come.*

Famous line (*Things to Come*): It is this, or that—all the universe, or nothing. Which shall it be, Passworthy? Which shall it be?

Massie, Paul (1932–). Canadian-born actor, on British stage and screen.
High Tide at Noon 57. *Orders to Kill* 58. Sapphire 59. Libel 60. The Two Faces of Dr Jekyll 60. The Rebel 60. Raising the Wind 61. The Pot Carriers 62, many others.

Massine, Leonid (1896–1979). Russian-born choreographer of international renown, best displayed on film in *The Red Shoes* 48.

Massingham, Richard (1898–1953). British actor-producer-director: a qualified doctor who abandoned his medical career to make numerous short propaganda films for government departments during World War II and after, infusing them with quiet wit and sympathy. Gratefully remembered as the stout party bewildered by government restrictions: bathing in five inches of water, collecting salvage, avoiding colds, preventing rumours, wearing a gas mask, etc.

Masters, Quentin (1946–). Australian director of international films.
□Thumb Tripping (& w) 73. The Stud 78.

Masterson, Bat (1855–1921). American western gunman who reformed; played in films by Albert Dekker in *Woman of the Town*, Randolph Scott in *Trail Street*, George Montgomery in *Masterson of Kansas*, Kenneth Tobey in *Gunfight at the OK Corral*, Joel McCrea in *Gunfight at Dodge City*, and Gene Barry in a long-running TV series.

Mastroianni, Marcello (1923–). Italian leading man, a former clerk who broke into films with a bit part in *I Miserabili* 47. Now

Italy's most respected and sought-after lead. Sunday in August 49. Girls of the Spanish Steps 51. The Bigamist 55. *White Nights* 57. I Soliti Ignoti 58. La Dolce Vita 59. *Il Bell' Antonio* 60. La Notte 61. *Divorce Italian Style* (BFA) 62. Family Diary 62. Eight and a Half 63. *Yesterday, Today and Tomorrow* (BFA) 63. The Organizer 63. Marriage Italian Style 64. Casanova 70 65. The Tenth Victim 65. Shoot Loud, Louder, I Don't Understand 66. The Stranger 67. Diamonds for Breakfast (GB) 68. A Place for Lovers 69. Sunflower 70. What? 72. Blowout 73. The Slightly Pregnant Man 73. Massacre in Rome 74. The Priest's Wife 74. Down the Ancient Stairs 75. The Sunday Woman 76. A Special Day 77. Traffic Jam 78. City of Women 80. Revenge 80. General of the Dead Army 83. Henry IV 84. The Two Lives of Mattia Pascal 85. Big Deal on Madonna Street—20 Years Later 85. Macaroni 85. *Ginger and Fred* 85. The Bee Keeper 86. Black Eyes 87, etc.

¶ *M.M.:* I only really exist when I am working on a film.

Masur, Richard (–). Plump American supporting actor.
W.H.I.F.F.S. 75. Semi Tough 77. Who'll Stop the Rain 78. Hanover Street 79. Scavenger Hunt 79. Walking through the Fire (TV) 79. Heaven's Gate 80. East of Eden (TV) 81. *Fallen Angel* (TV) 81. I'm Dancing as Fast as I Can 82. The Thing 82. Risky Business 83. Under Fire 83. The Mean Season 84. My Science Project 85. Heartburn 86. The Believers 86, etc.
TV series: Empire 84.

Mata Hari. Four films have been made about the French spy executed during World War I: by Friedrich Feher in 1927, with Magda Sonia; by George Fitzmaurice in 1931, with Greta Garbo; by Jean-Louis Richard in 1964, with Jeanne Moreau; by Curtis Harrington in 1984, with Sylvia Kristel. She was also caricatured by Zsa Zsa Gabor in *Up the Front*. Her real name was Margareta Zelle (1876–1917): her pseudonym, in Dutch, means 'eye of the dawn'.

matched pairs

? Who played:

1 *The Baroness and the Butler* in 1937?
2 *Her Highness and the Bellboy* in 1945?
3 *Thunderbolt and Lightfoot* in 1974?
4 *The Feminist and the Fuzz* (TV movie) in 1971?
5 *Tarzan and the Leopard Woman* in 1946?
6 *The Prizefighter and the Lady* in 1933?
7 *Cain and Mabel* in 1936?
8 *The Babbitt and the Bromide* (in *Ziegfeld Follies*) in 1946?
9 *The Cat and the Canary* in 1939?
10 *The Nun and the Sergeant* in 1962?
11 *The Cowboy and the Lady* in 1939?
12 *The Model and the Marriage Broker* in 1952?
13 *Freebie and the Bean* in 1974?
14 *The Cisco Kid and the Lady* in 1940?
15 *The Major and the Minor* in 1942?
16 *The Proud and the Profane* in 1956?
17 *The Gypsy and the Gentleman* in 1957?
18 *Pride and Prejudice* in 1940?
19 *The Prince and the Pauper* in 1937?
20 *The Doctor and the Girl* in 1949?

Maté, Rudolph (1899–1964). Austrian-born cameraman, later in Hollywood.
The Passion of Joan of Arc 28. *Vampyr* 31. Liliom 33. *Dante's Inferno* 35. Dodsworth 36. Love Affair 39. *Foreign Correspondent* 40. To Be or Not To Be 42. Cover Girl 44, etc.
□LATER AS DIRECTOR: It had to Be You (co-d) 47. The Dark Past 49. D.O.A. 50. No Sad Songs for Me 50. *Union Station* 50. Branded 50. The Prince Who Was a Thief 51. When Worlds Collide 51. The Green Glove 52. Paula 52. Sally and Saint Anne 52. Mississippi Gambler 53. Second Chance 53. Forbidden 53. The Siege At Red River 54. *The Black Shield of Falworth* 54. The Violent Men 55. The Far Horizons 55. Miracle in the Rain 56. The Rawhide Years 56. Port Afrique 56. Three Violent People 57. The Deep Six 58. For the First Time 59. The Immaculate Road 60. Revak the Rebel 60. The 300 Spartans 62. Aliki 63. Seven Seas to Calais 64.

Mather, Aubrey (1885–1958). British character actor, on stage from 1905, films from 1931. Settled in Hollywood and became useful member of English contingent, playing butlers and beaming, bald-headed little men.
Young Woodley 31. As You Like It 36. When Knights Were Bold 36. Jane Eyre 44. The Keys of the Kingdom 44. The Forsyte Saga 49. The Importance of Being Earnest 52, many others.

Matheson, Murray (1912–85). Soft-spoken English actor in Hollywood, mostly on TV.
Hurricane Smith 52. Botany Bay 53. Love Is a Many Splendored Thing 55. Assault On a Queen 66. How To Succeed In Business 67, etc.

Matheson, Richard (1926–). American science-fiction novelist and screenwriter.
The Incredible Shrinking Man (oaw) 57. The House of Usher (w) 60. The Pit and the Pendulum (w) 61. The Raven (w) 63. The Comedy of Terrors (w) 63. The Last Man on Earth (oa) 64. The Young Warriors (oaw) 68. The Devil Rides Out (w) 68. De Sade (w) 69. The Omega Man (oa) 71. The Legend of Hell House (w) 73. Dracula (TV) 73. Somewhere in Time 80, etc.

Matheson, Tim (1949–). American leading man, mostly on TV (Bonanza, The Quest).
Yours Mine and Ours 65. Divorce American Style 68. Magnum Force 73. National Lampoon's Animal House 78. The Apple Dumpling Gang Rides Again 79. Dreamer 79. To Be or Not to Be 83. Fletch 84. Impulse 84, etc.

Mathews, Kerwin (1926–). American leading man, former teacher.
Five Against the House 55. The Seventh Voyage of Sinbad 58. Man on a String 60. The Three Worlds of Gulliver 60. Jack the Giant Killer 61. Pirates of Blood River 62. Maniac (GB) 63. Battle Beneath the Earth (GB) 68. Barquero 69. The Boy Who Cried Werewolf 73. Nightmare in Blood 78, etc.

Mathieson, Muir (1911–1975). British musical director, in films from 1931.
Things to Come 36. Dangerous Moonlight 40. In Which We Serve 42. Brief Encounter 46. The Sound Barrier 52. The Swiss Family Robinson 60. Becket 64, many others.

Mathis, June (1892–1927). American screenwriter.
An Eye for an Eye 18. *The Four Horsemen of the Apocalypse* 21. Blood and Sand 22. Three Wise Fools 23. *Greed* 23. *Ben Hur* 27, etc.

Matras, Christian (1903–). French cinematographer, in films from 1928.
La Grande Illusion 37. Boule de Suif 45. Les Jeux Sont Faits 47. La Ronde 50. Madame De 53. *Lola Montes* 55. Les Espions 57. Paris Blues 61. Les Fêtes Galantes 65. The Milky Way 68, many others.

matt or **matte.** A technique (sometimes known as *travelling matt*) for blending actors in the studio with location or trick scenes. The actor is photographed against a non-reflective background (e.g. black velvet) and a high-contrast negative of this image is combined with the desired background. Thus men can move among animated monsters, and ghosts can slowly disappear.

Matt Helm. The laconic hero of a number of self-spoofing secret agent dime novels by Donald Hamilton, personified on screen by a droopy-eyed Dean Martin. Over-sexed and witless, the series represents a rather miserable but commercial sixties blend of high camp, self-indulgence, comic strip and semi-pornography. *The Silencers* 66, *Murderers' Row* 66, *The Ambushers* 67 and *Wrecking Crew* 69 were the titles, and it seemed to be a point of honour with the producer that the title should have no relevance whatever to the movie. In 1975 *Matt Helm* appeared as a TV movie with Tony Franciosa, but the resulting series was brief.

A Matter of Life and Death (GB 1946) (American title: *Stairway to Heaven*). The first film to be selected for the Royal Film Performance. Damned in some quarters and exalted in others, it was a typical product of the Archers (Michael Powell and Emeric Pressburger) and of its time, when war deaths turned the thoughts of many people towards religion. An RAF pilot undergoes a brain operation and dreams the outcome as the result of a trial conducted in heaven: the theme seems curiously unthought through and full of irrelevances, but the production is full of enjoyable lapses of taste as well as flashes of sheer brilliance and incomparable imagination. Décor by Hein Heckroth; acting by David Niven, Roger Livesey, Marius Goring and Raymond Massey; colour and monochrome photography by Jack Cardiff.

Matthau, Walter (1920–) (Walter Matasschanskayasky). American character actor with a penchant for wry comedy; his lugubrious features and sharp talent made him a star in the late sixties.
□The Kentuckian 55. The Indian Fighter 55. Bigger than Life 56. *A Face in the Crowd* 57. Slaughter on Tenth Avenue 57. King Creole 58. Ride a Crooked Trail 58. The Voice in the Mirror 58. Onionhead 58. Strangers when We Meet 60. Gangster Story (& d) 60. Lonely are the Brave 62. Who's Got the Action? 62. Island of Love 63. *Charade* 63. Ensign Pulver 64. Fail Safe 64. Goodbye Charlie 64. *Mirage* 65. *The Fortune Cookie* (AA) 66. *A Guide for the Married Man* 67. *The Odd Couple* 68. The Secret Life of an American Wife 68. Candy 68. *Hello Dolly* 69. Cactus Flower 69. A New Leaf 71. Plaza Suite 71. *Kotch* 71. Pete'n Tillie 72. Charley Varrick 73. The Laughing Policeman 73. Earthquake 74. The Taking of Pelham One Two Three 74. The Front Page 75. The

Sunshine Boys 75. The Bad News Bears 76. Casey's Shadow 77. House Calls 78. California Suite 78. Funny Business (TV) 78. Little Miss Marker 80. *Hopscotch* 80. First Monday in October 81. Buddy Buddy 81. I Ought to Be in Pictures 82. The Survivors 83. Movers and Shakers 84. Pirates 85.
TV series: Tallahassee 7000 59.

¶ Once seen, that antique-mapped face is never forgotten—a bloodhound with a head cold, a man who is simultaneously biting on a bad oyster and caught by the neck in lift-doors, a mad scientist's amalgam of Wallace Beery and Yogi Bear.—*Alan Brien, Sunday Times*

'He's about as likely a candidate for stardom as the neighborhood delicatessen man.'—*Time*

'He looks like a half-melted rubber bulldog.'—*John Simon*

Matthews, A. E. (1869–1960). British actor, on stage from 1886, films from the mid-twenties; in his youth a suave romantic lead, he was later famous for the crotchety cheerfulness of his extreme longevity.
Autobiography 1953: *Matty*.
A Highwayman's Honour 14. The Lackey and the Lady 19. The Iron Duke 35. Men Are Not Gods 36. *Quiet Wedding* 40. The Life and Death of Colonel Blimp 43. Piccadilly Incident 46. Just William's Luck 48. *The Chiltern Hundreds* (in his stage role as Lord Lister) 49. The Galloping Major 51. Made in Heaven 52. The Million Pound Note 54. Three Men in a Boat 56. Inn for Trouble 60, many others.

¶ *A.E.M.:* I always wait for *The Times* each morning. I look at the obituary column, and if I'm not in it, I go to work.

Good God, doesn't he know I haven't got long to live?—*A.E.M., when he thought a long speech was ending, and it wasn't*

'He bumbled through the play like a charming retriever who has buried a bone and can't quite remember where.'—*Noel Coward*

Matthews, Francis (1927–). British leading man with TV and repertory experience.
Bhowani Junction 56. The Revenge of Frankenstein 58. The Lamp in Assassin Mews 62. Dracula, Prince of Darkness 65. That Riviera Touch 66. Just Like a Woman 66. Crossplot 69. The McGuffin (TV) 85. May We Borrow Your Husband? (TV) 86, etc.

Matthews, Jessie (1907–1981). Vivacious British singing and dancing star of light musicals in the thirties; on stage from 1919; later familiar to radio listeners as Mrs Dale in *Mrs Dale's Diary*.
Autobiography 1974: *Over My Shoulder*.
Biography 1974: *Jessie Matthews* by Michael Thornton.
□The Beloved Vagabond 23. Straws in the Wind 24. Out of the Blue 31. There Goes the Bride 32. The Midshipmaid 32. The Man from Toronto 32. *The Good Companions* 32. Friday the Thirteenth 33. Waltzes from Vienna 33. *Evergreen* 34. First a Girl 35. It's Love Again 36. Head over Heels 37. Gangway 37. Sailing Along 38. Climbing High 39. Forever and a Day 43. Candles at Nine 44. Tom Thumb 58. The Hound of the Baskervilles 77. Edward and Mrs Simpson (TV) 79.

Matthews, Lester (1900–75). British stage actor, in Hollywood from 1934.
Creeping Shadows 31. Facing the Music 34. Blossom Time 34. Werewolf of London 35. Thank You, Jeeves 35. The Prince and the Pauper 37. The Adventures of Robin Hood 38. Northwest Passage 40. Man Hunt 41. Between Two Worlds 44. The Invisible Man's Revenge 44. Lorna Doone 51, many others.

Mattsson, Arne (1919–). Swedish director, in films from 1942.
She Only Danced One Summer 51. The Girl in Tails 56. Mannequin in Red 59. The Doll 62, etc.

Mature, Victor (1915–). American leading man of the forties; once known as 'the Hunk', but beneath the brawn lurked some style and a sense of humour.
□The Housekeeper's Daughter 39. One Million BC 40. Captain Caution 40. No No Nanette 40. I Wake Up Screaming 41. The Shanghai Gesture 41. Song of the Islands 42. My Gal Sal 42. Footlight Serenade 42. Seven Days' Leave 42. *My Darling Clementine* (as Doc Holliday) 46. Moss Rose 47. *Kiss of Death* 47. Fury at Furnace Creek 48. Cry of the City 48. Red Hot and Blue 49. Easy Living 49. *Samson and Delilah* 49. Wabash Avenue 50. Stella 50. Gambling House 50. The Las Vegas Story 52. Androcles and the Lion 52. Something for the Birds 52. Million Dollar Mermaid 52. The Glory Brigade 53. Affair with a Stranger 53. *The Robe* 53. Veils of Baghdad 53. Dangerous Mission 54. Demetrius and the Gladiators 54. Betrayed 54. *The Egyptian* 54. Chief Crazy Horse 55. Violent Saturday 55. The Last Frontier 55. Safari (GB) 56. The Sharkfighters 56. Zarak (GB) 57. Interpol (GB) 57. The Long Haul (GB) 57. China Doll 57. No Time to Die

(GB) 58. Escort West 59. The Bandit of Zhobe (GB) 59. The Big Circus 59. Timbuktu 59. Hannibal 60. The Tartars 60. The Mongols 60. *After The Fox* 66. Head 68. Every Little Crook and Nanny 72. Won Ton Ton 76. Firepower 79. Samson and Delilah (TV) 84.

¶ *V.M.:* I'm no actor, and I've 64 pictures to prove it.

'I didn't care for *Samson and Delilah*. No picture can hold my interest when the leading man's bust is bigger than the leading lady's.'—*Groucho Marx*

Mau Mau. The terrorist activities in Kenya during the fifties were the subject of three very savage movies: *Simba* 55, *Safari* 56, *Something of Value* 56.

Mauch, Billy and Bobby (1925–). American twins, boy actors who appeared in several films in the mid-thirties, notably a 'Penrod' series and the Errol Flynn version of *The Prince and the Pauper* 37.

Maugham, Robin (1916–1980). British popular novelist, nephew of Somerset Maugham. *The Servant* and *The Intruder* have been filmed.

Maugham, W. Somerset (1874–1965). Distinguished British novelist, short story writer and playwright whose works have often been filmed.
Smith 17. A Man of Honour 19. The Circle 25 and 30 (as *Strictly Unconventional*). Rain 28 (as *Sadie Thompson*). 32 and 53 (as *Miss Sadie Thompson*). Our Betters 33. The Painted Veil 34 and 57 (as *The Seventh Sin*). Of Human Bondage 34, 46 and 64. Ashenden (as *Secret Agent*) 36. Vessel of Wrath 37 and 54 (as *The Beachcomber*). The Letter 40 (also very freely adapted as *The Unfaithful* 47). The Moon and Sixpence 42. Christmas Holiday 44. The Razor's Edge 46. Theatre (as *Adorable Julia*) 63, etc.

He also introduced three omnibus films of his stories: *Quartet* 48, *Trio* 50 and *Encore* 51; a film of his rather unhappy life is constantly promised.

Maunder, Wayne (1942–). American leading man of the sixties.
The Seven Minutes 71.
TV series: *Custer* 67. Lancer 68–69.

Maureen, Mollie (1904–87) (Elizabeth Mary Campfield). Diminutive British stage actress, in a few films.
□ The Private Life of Sherlock Holmes (as Queen Victoria) 70. The Return of the Pink Panther 75. Jabberwocky 77. The Hound of the Baskervilles 78. The Wicked Lady 83. Little Dorrit 87.

Maurey, Nicole (1925–). French leading lady.
Little Boy Lost (US) 51. The Secret of the Incas (US) 54. The Weapon (GB) 56. Me and the Colonel (US) 58. The House of the Seven Hawks (GB) 59. High Time (US) 60. The Day of the Triffids (GB) 62, etc.

Maxwell, Edwin (1886–1948). Stocky, balding American character actor, frequently cast as shady businessman.
The Jazz Singer 27. The Taming of the Shrew 29. Daddy Longlegs 31. Scarface 32. Cleopatra 34. Fury 36. Young Mr Lincoln 39. His Girl Friday 40. I Live on Danger 42. Holy Matrimony 43. Wilson 44. The Jolson Story 46. The Gangster 47, many others.

Maxwell, Elsa (1883–1963). Dumpy, talkative American columnist and party-giver. Autobiographical books: *My Last Fifty Years* 1943. *I Married the World* 1955. *Celebrity Circus* 1961.
FILM APPEARANCES: Hotel for Women 39. Public Deb Number One 40. Stage Door Canteen 43, etc.

Maxwell, John (1875–1940). Scottish lawyer who turned distributor and became co-founder of Associated British productions and the ABC cinema chain.

Maxwell, Lois (1927–) (Lois Hooker). Canadian leading lady who had a brief Hollywood career (1946–48) before settling in England.
The Decision of Christopher Blake 47. Corridor of Mirrors 48. Women of Twilight 49. Domano E Troppo Tardi (It.) 50. The Woman's Angle 52. Aida (It.) 53. Passport to Treason 55. The High Terrace 56. Kill Me Tomorrow 57. Operation Kid Brother 67, etc.; plays Miss Moneypenny in the James Bond films.

Maxwell, Marilyn (1921–1972) (Marvel Maxwell). Blonde American radio singer and actress, formerly child dancer.
Stand By For Action 42. Swing Fever 42. Thousands Cheer 43. Lost in a Harem 44. Summer Holiday 47. The Lemon Drop Kid 51. Off Limits 53. New York Confidential 55. Rock-a-bye-Baby 58. Critic's Choice 62. Stagecoach to Hell 64, etc.
TV series: Bus Stop 61.

May, Brian (–). Australian composer. Patrick 79. Thirst 79. Mad Max 80. Road Games 81.

May, Elaine (1932–). American cabaret star of the fifties (with Mike Nichols); also screenwriter.
□Luv (a) 67. Enter Laughing (a) 67. A New Leaf (awd) 71. Such Good Friends (w) 72. The Heartbreak Kid (d) 72. Heaven Can Wait (co-w) 78. California Suite (a) 78. Mikey and Nickey (& w) 78.

May, Hans (1891–1959). Viennese composer who settled in Britain in the early thirties. The Stars Look Down 39. Thunder Rock 42. The Wicked Lady 45. Brighton Rock 46. The Gypsy and the Gentleman 57, etc.

May, Joe (1880–1954) (Joseph Mandel). German director of early serials and thrillers. Stuart Webb 15. Veritas Vincit 16. The Hindu Tomb 21, etc. Best German film probably *Asphalt* 29.
IN HOLLYWOOD: Music in the Air 34. The Invisible Man Returns 40. The House of Seven Gables 40. Hit the Road 41. Johnny Doesn't Live Here Any More 44, etc.

Mayehoff, Eddie (1911–). American comic actor, former dance band leader. That's My Boy 51. Off Limits 53. How to Murder Your Wife 65, etc.
TV series: Doc Corkle 52. That's My Boy 54.

Mayer, Arthur L. (1886–1981). American author and commentator, a former cinema exhibitor who displayed his lively wit in *Merely Colossal* (1953) and as co-author of *The Movies*.

Mayer, Carl (1894–1944). German screenwriter.
□ *The Cabinet of Dr Caligari* 19. Genuine 20. Die Hintertreppe 21. Scherben 21. Schloss Vogelod 21. Phantom 22. Vanina 22. Sylvester 23. Die Strasse 23. *The Last Laugh* 24. Tartuff 25. Berlin 27. *Sunrise* 27. Four Devils 28. Ariane 31. Träumende Mund 32. Dreaming Lips 37.

Mayer, Edwin Justus (1896–1960). American screenwriter.
In Gay Madrid 30. Never the Twain Shall Meet 31. Merrily We Go to Hell 32. The Night Is Ours 33. I Am Suzanne 34. Thirty Day Princess 34. The Affairs of Cellini (original play) 34. So Red the Rose 35. Give Us This Night 36. *Desire* 36. Till We Meet Again 36. The Buccaneer 38. Rio 39. They Met in Bombay 41. *To Be or Not to Be* 42. A Royal Scandal 45. Masquerade in Mexico 45, etc.

Mayer, Gerald (1919–). American director.
□Dial 1119 50. Inside Straight 51. The Sellout 52. Holiday for Sinners 52. Bright Road 53. The Marauders 55. Diamond Safari 57.

Mayer, Louis B. (1885–1957). American executive, former production head of MGM. Once a scrap merchant, he became a cinema manager and later switched to distribution. With Sam Goldwyn, formed Metro-Goldwyn-Mayer in 1924, and when Goldwyn bought himself out became one of Hollywood's most flamboyant and powerful tycoons until the fifties when he found himself less in touch and responsible to a board. Special Academy Award 1950 'for distinguished service to the motion picture industry'.
Biographies: *Hollywood Rajah* (1954) by Bosley Crowther. *Mayer and Thalberg* (1975) by Sam Marx.

¶ This 'Hollywood rajah' was perhaps the archetypal movie mogul: sentimental, commonsensical, businesslike, unaesthetic, arrogant, illogical, naïve, amoral, tasteless and physically unappealing. For twenty years he ran MGM splendidly in his own image, and became a legend of autocracy. He did not stint on his surroundings; Sam Goldwyn said of his office:

> You need an automobile to reach the desk.

No detail escaped him. B. P. Schulberg gave him the title:

> Czar of all the rushes.

Though he kept it well hidden, he did have a basic sense of humility:

> You know how I'm smart? I got people around me who know more than I do.

His arguments were often irritatingly unanswerable. Arthur Freed recalls:

> If a writer complained of his work being changed, Mayer always said:
> 'The number one book of the ages was written by a committee, and it was called The Bible.'

To Gottfried Reinhardt, who wanted to make a non-commercial picture, Mayer snapped:

> You want to be an artist, but you want other people to starve for your art.

Mayer's idea of a good commercial movie was simple, homespun, warm, happy . . . in a phrase, the Hardy Family. That series, cheap to make, kept the studio in profit for many a year. Their success did not delude Mayer into thinking they were great movies:

Don't make these pictures any better.
Just keep them the way they are.

This did not mean that he despised the American public, only that he knew what they liked. He even created and acted out for the producer a prayer that the son of the fictional family might speak when his mother was ill:

Dear God, don't let my mom die,
because she's the best mom in the world.

He was similarly quick to correct a plot point:

A boy may hate his father, but he will always respect him.

As early as 1922 his credo in this vein was fully formed:

I will only make pictures that I won't be ashamed to have my children see.

His cry in later years, when permissiveness was creeping in, was:

Don't show the natural functions!

In argument Mayer was a great and exhausting opponent, violent, wheedling and pleading by turns. Robert Taylor remembered going in for more money. When he emerged, a friend asked him:

Did you get the rise?
—No, but I gained a father.

Taylor later remembered Mayer in a respectful light:

He was kind, understanding, fatherly and protective, always there when I had problems.

As did Mayer of himself:

Life without service isn't worth living.

But he saw the dangers of life at the top:

Look out for yourself or they'll pee on your grave.

Herman J. Mankiewicz saw Mayer himself as a danger:

He had the memory of an elephant and the hide of an elephant. The only difference is that elephants are vegetarians and Mayer's diet was his fellow man.

Mayer was very proud of MGM's army of stars and technicians:

We are the only kind of company whose assets all walk out of the gate at night.

He needed their goodwill:

I want to rule by love, not fear.

But when he died, the usual caustic comments were heard:

The only reason so many people attended his funeral was they wanted to make sure he was dead.

He had then been for some years at odds with the MGM hierarchy, an unwilling exile from the boardroom. Said someone at the funeral:

I see MGM got L.B. back at last.
—Yeah, but on its own terms.

For some years people had been heard to remark:

The old grey Mayer he ain't what he used to be.

But Bob Hope, as so often, made the aptest wisecrack:

Louis B. Mayer came out west with twenty-eight dollars, a box camera and an old lion. He built a monument to himself—the Bank of America.

Mayerling (France 1936). A well-remembered tragic-romantic movie about the love of Austrian Archduke Rudolph for Marie Vetsera. The pair were eventually found dead in a hunting lodge, but the suicide alleged by the film is not totally justified by historical facts: it derives from a novel by Claude Anet. The film made international stars of Charles Boyer and Danielle Darrieux, and led to a Hollywood career for director Anatole Litvak, who in 1956 remade it for TV with Mel Ferrer and Audrey Hepburn. Meanwhile in 1949 Jean Delannoy had made another French version under the title *The Secret of Mayerling*. In 1968 Terence Young concocted an expensive European rehash with Omar Sharif and Catherine Deneuve.

Mayes, Wendell (1918–). American screenwriter.
Spirit of St Louis 57. The Enemy Below 58. Anatomy of a Murder 59. Advise and Consent 62. In Harm's Way 64. Hotel 67. The Poseidon Adventure (co-w) 72. Bank Shot 74. Death Wish 74, etc.

Maynard, Bill (1928–). Massive British comic actor familiar on TV 1976–78 as the accident-prone hero of *Oh No, It's Selwyn Froggitt*.
Till Death Us Do Part 69. The Magnificent Six and a Half 69. Carry On Henry 71. The Four Dimensions of Greta 71. Steptoe and Son Ride Again 74. Carry On Dick 74. Confessions of a Pop Performer 75. Robin and Marian 76, etc.

Maynard, Ken (1895–1973). American cowboy star, mainly seen in low-budget features. Once a rodeo rider; broke into films as a stunt man.
Janice Meredith 24. Señor Daredevil 26. The Red Raiders 27. Branded Men 31. Texas Gunfighter 32. Come on, Tarzan 32. Wheels of Destiny 34. Heir to Trouble 34. Wild Horse Stampede 45, many others.

Maynard, Kermit (1898–1971). American action player, brother of Ken Maynard. Once doubled for George O'Brien, Victor McLaglen, Warner Baxter and Edmund Lowe.
The Fighting Trooper 34. Sandy of the Mounted 34. Wild Bill Hickok 38. Golden Girl 51, many others.

Mayne, Ferdy (1916–) (Ferdinand Mayer-Boerckel). German-born actor, long in Britain; often seen as smooth villain.
Meet Sexton Blake 44. You Know What Sailors Are 53. Storm over the Nile 55. Ben Hur 59. Freud 62. Operation Crossbow 65. The Bobo 67. *The Fearless Vampire Killers* 68. Where Eagles Dare 69. When Eight Bells Toll 71. Innocent Bystanders 72. The Eagle Has Landed 76. The Pirate (TV) 78. A Man Called Intrepid (TV) 79. The Black Stallion Returns 83. Conan the Destroyer 84. Howling II 85, many others.

Mayo, Archie (1891–1968). American director of very variable output.
Money Talks 26. The College Widow 27. Beware of Married Men 28. Sonny Boy 29. Is Everybody Happy? 29. The Sacred Flame 29. Doorway to Hell 30. *Svengali* 31. Under Eighteen 31. The Expert 32. Night after Night 32. Mayor of Hell 33. Convention City 33. Desirable 34. *Bordertown* 34. *Go Into Your Dance* 35. The Case of the Lucky Legs 35. *The Petrified Forest* 36. Give Me Your Heart 36. Black Legion 36. Call it a Day 37. It's Love I'm After 37. Youth Takes a Fling 38. They Shall Have Music 39. The House Across the Bay 40. Four Sons 40. The Great American Broadcast 41. Charley's Aunt 41. Confirm or Deny 41. Moontide 42. Orchestra Wives 42. Crash Dive 43. Sweet and Low Down 44. A Night in Casablanca 46. Angel on My Shoulder 46. The Beast of Budapest (p only) 57, etc.

Mayo, Virginia (1920–) (Virginia Jones). American 'peaches and cream' leading lady of the forties; played a few bit parts before being cast as decoration in colour extravaganzas.
The Adventures of Jack London 43. *Up In Arms* 44. *The Princess and the Pirate* 44. Wonder Man 45. The Best Years of Our Lives 46. Out of the Blue 47. *The Secret Life of Walter Mitty* 47. A Song is Born 48. Smart Girls Don't Talk 48. The Girl from Jones Beach 49. White Heat 49. Backfire 50. The Flame and the Arrow 50. Along the Great Divide 51. Captain Horatio Hornblower 51. She's Working Her Way through College 52. South Sea Woman 53. King Richard and the Crusaders 54. Pearl of the South Pacific 55. Congo Crossing 56. The Story of Mankind 57. Fort Dobbs 58. Jet over the Atlantic 59. The Revolt of the Mercenaries (It.) 61. Young Fury 65. Castle of Evil 66. Fort Utah 67. Won Ton Ton 76. French Quarter 78, etc.

Maysles, David (1931–) and **Albert** (1933–). American film-making brothers, semi-professional and semi-underground.
Youth of Poland 57. Kenya 61. Safari Ya Gari 61. *Showman* 63. What's Happening 64. Marlon Brando 65. Truman Capote 66. *Salesman* 69. Gimme Shelter 71. Grey Gardens 75. Running Fence 77, etc.

Mazurki, Mike (1909–) (Mikhail Mazurwski). Immense American character actor of Ukrainian descent; former heavyweight wrestler. Began in Hollywood as an extra.
The Shanghai Gesture (debut) 41. *Farewell My Lovely* 44. The French Key 46. Unconquered 47. Rope of Sand 49. Ten Tall Men 51. My Favorite Spy 52. Blood Alley 55. Davy Crockett 56. Donovan's Reef 63. Cheyenne Autumn 64. Seven Women 66. The Wild McCulloughs 75, many others.
TV series: It's About Time 66. Chicago Teddy Bears 71.

Mazursky, Paul (1930–) (Irwin Mazursky). American writer director.
□I Love you Alice B. Toklas (co-w) 68. *Bob and Carol and Ted and Alice* (co-w, d) 70. Alex in Wonderland (co-w, d) 70. Blume in Love (wd) 73. *Harry and Tonto* (co-w, p, d) 74. Next Stop Greenwich Village (wpd) 76. *An Unmarried Woman* (wd, co-p, a) 78. Willie and Phil 80. Tempest 82. Moscow on the Hudson 84. Down and Out in Beverly Hills 85.
† Mazursky is also an occasional actor: Alex in Wonderland 70. A Star is Born 76. Into the Night 84, etc.

Mc: see under *Mac*.

Meadows, Jayne (1920–) (Jayne Cotter). American actress whose biggest role was in 1947 as the unsympathetic sister in *Enchantment*.

Meara, Anne (1929–). American comedienne who turned straight actress in a 1975 TV series, *Kate McShane*.

Lovers and Other Strangers 69. Kate MacShane (TV) 75. Nasty Habits 76. The Boys from Brazil 78. The Other Woman (TV) 82, etc.

Medak, Peter (–). Hungarian director in Britain.
Negatives 68. *A Day in the Death of Joe Egg* 70. The Ruling Class 71. Third Girl from the Left (TV) 74. Ghost in the Noonday Sun (unreleased) 74. The Odd Job 78. The Changeling 80. Zorro the Gay Blade 81. Mistress of Paradise (TV) 82. The Men's Club 86, etc.

Medford, Don (1917–). American director.
To Trap a Spy 64. Cosa Nostra, Arch Enemy of the FBI (TV) 66. Incident in San Francisco (TV) 71. The Hunting Party 71. The Organization 71, etc.

Medford, Kay (1914–1980). American character actress.
The War Against Mrs Hadley 42. The Rat Race 60. Butterfield 8 60. Bye Bye Birdie 63. Funny Girl 68. But I Don't Want to Get Married (TV) 70. No Place to Run (TV) 72. More Than Friends (TV) 78, etc.

Medina, Patricia (1921–). British-born leading lady of the forties and fifties, in routine international films.
The Day will Dawn 42. They Met in the Dark 42. The First of the Few 42. Don't Take It To Heart 44. Hotel Reserve 44. Waltz Time 45. The Secret Heart 46. Moss Rose 47. The Three Musketeers 48. The Fighting O'Flynn 49. Abbott and Costello in the Foreign Legion 50. The Magic Carpet 51. Lady in the Iron Mask 52. Siren of Baghdad 53. Phantom of the Rue Morgue 54. Pirates of Tripoli 55. Uranium Boom 56. Buckskin Lady 57. Count Your Blessings 59. The Killing of Sister George 68, etc.

medium shot. One taking in the full body of the actor, not so close as a close-up, not so far off as a long shot.

Medwin, Michael (1923–). British light character comedian, usually seen as Cockney.
Piccadilly Incident 46. Boys in Brown 49. Top Secret 52. Above Us the Waves 55. A Hill in Korea 56. I Only Arsked 58. Night Must Fall 63. Rattle of a Simple Man 64. I've Gotta Horse 65. The Sandwich Man 66. Scrooge 70, many others.
AS PRODUCER: Charlie Bubbles 67. If 68. Spring and Port Wine 69. Gumshoe 71. Alpha Beta 73. O Lucky Man 73. Law and Disorder 73.
TV series: *The Army Game* 57–62. Shoestring 79.

Meek, Donald (1880–1946). Scottish-born character actor, long in Hollywood; a bald, worried and timidly respectable little man was his invariable role.
The Hole in the Wall (debut) 28. Mrs Wiggs of the Cabbage Patch 34. Barbary Coast 35. Captain Blood 35. Pennies from Heaven 36. The Adventures of Tom Sawyer 38. *Stagecoach* 39. Tortilla Flat 42. They Got Me Covered 43. State Fair 45. Magic Town 46, many others.

Meeker, Ralph (1920–) (Ralph Rathgeber). American leading man of the Brando type, with Broadway experience.
Teresa (debut) 51. Four in a Jeep 51. Shadow in the Sky 51. Glory Alley 52. The Naked Spur 53. Jeopardy 53. Code Two 53. Big House USA 54. *Kiss Me Deadly* (as Mike Hammer) 55. Desert Sands 56. *Paths of Glory* 58. Ada 61. Something Wild 62. The Dirty Dozen 67. The St Valentine's Day Massacre 67. Gentle Giant 67. The Detective 68. I Walk the Line 70. The Anderson Tapes 71. The Happiness Cage 73. The Food of the Gods 76. Hi-Riders 78. Winter Kills 79. Without Warning 80, etc.

Meerson, Lazare (1900–1938). Russian-born production designer.
Gribiche 25. Carmen 26. An Italian Straw Hat 28. Sous les Toits de Paris 29. *Le Million* 31. À Nous la Liberté 32. *La Kermesse Héroïque* 35. As You Like It 36. *Fire over England* 37. *Knight without Armour* 37. The Citadel 38, etc.

Meet John Doe (US 1941). An interesting Frank Capra film in which pessimism almost won the upper hand: the one sane man nearly had to commit suicide in order to bring the grasping connivers to their senses. Otherwise a typically big, sprawling, superbly proficient Capra production with a newspaper setting, written by Robert Riskin with a cast headed by Barbara Stanwyck and Gary Cooper.

Meet Me in St Louis (US 1944). A somewhat overrated but enjoyable period musical which purveyed charm at a time when it was most needed and can now be seen to have contained much of the best Hollywood talent of the forties. Simply concerned with the ups-and-downs of a middle-class family at the turn of the century, it was directed by Vincente Minnelli from a script by Irving Brecher and Fred Finklehoffe; the songs were by Hugh Martin and Ralph Blane, and included 'The Trolley Song', 'Have Yourself a Merry Little Christmas', and 'The Boy Next Door'. The cast included Judy Garland, Margaret O'Brien, Leon Ames, Mary Astor and Harry Davenport; and the colour at the time seemed rich and luscious.

meetings cute

? Who met who, in what film:

1 On a night train from San Francisco to Los Angeles, when he stole from her purse?
2 In an old mansion when she mistook him for an undertaker?
3 In a blazing hotel when she had no clothes on?
4 On his first trip to Europe, at night on the top deck of the *Queen Mary*?
5 While crossing a street in Paris, on her first night in town?
6 On a street at night, when he got splashed with mud on his way to a furniture warehouse?
7 In a western saloon when he poured water on her?
8 On a Chicago-bound train when he was hunted by police?
9 In her parlour on the afternoon before her wedding, her ex-husband having introduced him as a friend of her absent brother?
10 At a ball when she had heard him say that there was not a young woman in the room he would gladly stand up with?
11 In a Monte Carlo hotel when her older companion had forced an introduction?
12 In a Hollywood diner when he is trying to lose his identity and she has given up being an actress?

Mehboob (1907–1964) (Ramjankhan Mehboobkhan). Prolific Indian director, few of whose films have been seen in the west.
Aan 49. Mother India 56. A Handful of Grain 59, etc.

Meighan, Thomas (1879–1936). American leading man of the silent screen.
The Trail of the Lonesome Pine 16. Male and Female 19. The Miracle Man 19. Conrad in Quest of His Youth 22. Manslaughter 23. The Alaskan 24. Tin Gods 26. The New Klondyke 26. The Racket 27. Young Sinners 31. Peck's Bad Boy 34, etc.

Meillon, John (1934–). Australian character actor, in Britain from 1960.
On the Beach 59. The Sundowners 59. Offbeat 60. The Valiant 61. Billy Budd 62. The Running Man 63. They're a Weird Mob 66. The Cars that Ate Paris 74, etc.

Mekas, Adolfas (1925–). Lithuanian underground film-maker, in US.
Hallelujah the Hills (wd) 63. Guns of the Trees (a) 64. Windflowers (wd) 68, etc.

Mekas, Jonas (1922–). Lithuanian underground film-maker in US, brother of Adolfas Mekas.
The Secret Passions of Salvador Dali 61. The Brig 64. Guns of the Trees 64. Hare Krishna 66. Report from Millbrook 66, etc.

Melcher, Martin (1915–1968). American producer, married to Doris Day and from 1952 the co-producer of all her films.
Calamity Jane 53. Julie 56. Pillow Talk 59. Jumbo 62. Move Over, Darling 63. Send Me No Flowers 64. Where Were You When the Lights Went Out? 68, etc.

Melchior, Ib (1917–). Danish-born writer-director, long in US; former actor and set designer. Son of Lauritz Melchior.
□Angry Red Planet (wd) 59. Reptilicus (wd) 61. The Time Travellers (wd) 64. Robinson Crusoe on Mars (w) 65.

Melchior, Lauritz (1890–1973). Danish operatic tenor, in a few Hollywood films.
□Thrill of a Romance 45. Two Sisters from Boston 46. This Time for Keeps 47. Luxury Liner 48. The Stars Are Singing 53.

Melia, Joe (–). British character comedian.
Oh What a Lovely War 69. Privates on Parade 82.

Méliès, Georges (1861–1938). French film pioneer, an ex-conjuror who produced the cinema's first trick films, most of them ambitious and still effective. Credited with being the first to use the dissolve, double exposure, and fades. After World War I he found his films out of date and his talents unwanted.
Biography 1973: *Méliès Enchanteur* by Madeleine Méliès.
Une Partie de Cartes (debut) 96. The Artist's Dream 98. The Dreyfus Affair 99. Cinderella (1900). Indiarubber Head 01. *Voyage to the*

Moon 02. The Kingdom of the Fairies 03. The Impossible Voyage 04. Twenty Thousand Leagues under the Sea 07. Baron Munchausen 11. The Conquest of the Pole 12, many others.
†In 1952 Georges Franjun made a documentary tribute, *Le Grand Méliès*.
❁ For demonstrating that cinema is a medium of magic; and for devising tricks so effective that eighty years later they are still viewed with delight. *Voyage to the Moon*.

Mell, Marisa (1929–). French leading lady.
French Dressing 64. Anyone Can Play 66. Danger: Diabolik 67. Mahogany 77, etc.

Mellé, Gil (1935–). American composer.
The Andromeda Strain 70. The Organization 71. Frankenstein: The True Story (TV) 73. Dynasty (TV 75. The Sentinel 77. Starship Invasion 78. Borderline 81, etc.

Mellor, William C. (1904–1963). American cinematographer.
Wings in the Dark 35. Disputed Passage 39. The Great McGinty 40. Dixie 43. Abie's Irish Rose 46. Love Happy 49. *A Place in the Sun* (AA) 51. The Naked Spur 52. Give a Girl a Break 53. Bad Day at Black Rock 54. *Giant* 55. The Diary of Anne Frank (AA) 59. State Fair 62, etc.

Melton, James (1904–1961). American operatic tenor, in a few Hollywood films.
Stars over Broadway 35. Sing Me a Love Song 36. Melody for Two 37. Ziegfeld Follies 45.

Melville, Jean-Pierre (1917–1973) (J. P. Grumbach). French director, with stage experience.
Le Silence de la Mer 47. Les Enfants Terribles 48. Quand Tu Liras Cette Lettre 52. Bob le Flambeur 55. *Leon Morin Priest* 61. Second Wind 66. *The Samurai* 67. The Red Circle 70. Dirty Money 72, etc.

Melvin, Murray (1932–). British light character actor with stage experience in Theatre Workshop.
The Criminal (debut) 60. *A Taste of Honey* 61. HMS Defiant 62. Sparrows Can't Sing 63. The Ceremony 64. Alfie 66. A Day in the Death of Joe Egg 70. The Boy Friend 71. Ghost Story 74. Barry Lyndon 75. The Bawdy Adventures of Tom Jones 76. Tales from a Flying Trunk 79. Nutcracker 82, etc.

The Men (US 1950). A typical early Stanley Kramer production, making drama out of an urgent real-life problem, in this case that of paraplegics—war veterans paralysed below the waist. Directed by Fred Zinnemann from a script by Carl Foreman, with Marlon Brando, Teresa Wright, Jack Webb and Everett Sloane.

Mendes, Lothar (1894–1974). Hungarian director, mainly in US.
A Night of Mystery 27. The Four Feathers 29. Payment Deferred 32. Jew Süss (GB) 34. *The Man Who Could Work Miracles* (GB) 36. Moonlight Sonata (GB) 38. International Squadron 41. Flight for Freedom 43. The Walls Came Tumbling Down 46, etc.

Menges, Chris (–). British cinematographer.
Black Beauty 71. Gumshoe 71. Local Hero 83. The Killing Fields (AA) 84, etc.

Menjou, Adolphe (1890–1963). Dapper French-American leading man of the twenties, later a polished, sharp-spoken character actor; had the reputation of being Hollywood's best-dressed man.
Autobiography 1952: *It Took Nine Tailors*.
SELECTED SILENT FILMS: The Kiss 16. The Faith Healer 21. The Three Musketeers 21. Bella Donna 23. *A Woman of Paris* 23. *The Marriage Circle* 24. *Forbidden Paradise* 24. The Swan 25. The Grand Duchess and the Waiter 26. Service for Ladies 27. Serenade 27. His Private Life 28. Marquis Preferred 28.
□SOUND FILMS: Fashions in Love 29. Morocco 30. New Moon 30. Men Call it Love 31. The Easiest Way 31. *The Front Page* 31. The Great Lover 31. Friends and Lovers 31. Prestige 32. Forbidden 32. Two White Arms 32. The Man From Yesterday 32. Bachelor's Affairs 32. Night Club Lady 32. A Farewell to Arms 32. Diamond Cut Diamond 32. The Circus Queen Murder 33. *Morning Glory* 33. The Worst Woman in Paris 33. Convention City 33. Journal of a Crime 34. Easy to Love 34. The Trumpet Blows 34. *Little Miss Marker* 34. Flirtation 34. The Human Side 34. The Mighty Barnum 34. Gold Diggers of 1935. Broadway Gondolier 35. The Milky Way 36. Sing Baby Sing 36. Wives Never Know 36. One in a Million 36. *A Star is Born* 37. Café Metropole 37. *One Hundred Men and a Girl* 37. *Stage Door* 37. The Goldwyn Follies 38. Letter of Introduction 38. Thanks for Everything 38. King of the Turf 39. That's Right You're Wrong 39. Golden Boy 39. *The Housekeeper's Daughter* 39. *A Bill of*

Divorcement 40. Turnabout 41. Road Show 41. Father Takes a Wife 41. *Roxie Hart* 42. Syncopation 42. You Were Never Lovelier 42. Hi Diddle Diddle 43. Sweet Rosie O'Grady 43. *Step Lively* 44. Man Alive 45. Heartbeat 46. The Bachelor's Daughters 46. I'll Be Yours 47. Mr District Attorney 47. The Hucksters 47. *State of the Union* 48. My Dream is Yours 49. Dancing in the Dark 49. To Please a Lady 50. Tall Target 51. Across the Wide Missouri 51. *The Sniper* 52. Man on a Tightrope 53. Timberjack 55. The Ambassador's Daughter 56. Bundle of Joy 56. The Fuzzy Pink Nightgown 57. *Paths of Glory* 57. I Married a Woman 58. Pollyanna 60.
TV series: Target 51. My Favourite Story 53.
❁ For his omnipresent sartorial elegance, and for a surprising number of highly enjoyable performances. *Roxie Hart.*

Menzel, Jiri (1938–). Czech director.
Closely Observed Trains (AA) 66. Capricious Summer 68. Crime at the Nightclub 68. Seclusion Near a Forest 76. The Apple Game 77. Those Wonderful Men with a Crank 79. My Sweet Little Village 85.

Menzies, William Cameron (1896–1957). American art director who did much memorable work, especially with louring, impressionistic skyscapes. Also directed a few rather disappointing low-budget films.
AS ART DIRECTOR: Robin Hood 22. *The Thief of Baghdad* 24. Tempest 27. *The Dove* (AA) 28. Bulldog Drummond 29. Alice in Wonderland 33. *Things to Come* (& co-d) 36. *The Adventures of Tom Sawyer* 38. *Gone with the Wind* 39. *Our Town* 40. *Foreign Correspondent* 40. *King's Row* 41. For Whom the Bell Tolls 43. Ivy 47. Arch of Triumph 48. Around the World in Eighty Days 56, etc.
□AS DIRECTOR: Always Goodbye 31. The Spider 31. Almost Married 32. Chandu the Magician 32. Wharf Angel 34. *Things to Come* 36. The Green Cockatoo 40. Address Unknown 44. Drums in the Deep South 51. The Whip Hand 51. The Maze 53. Invaders from Mars 54.
❁ For styling so many of the cinema's most memorable images. *Things to Come.*

Merande, Doro (c. 1898–1975). American character actress who specialized in acidulous, eccentric and whimsical spinsters.
Our Town 40. Sullivan's Travels 41. Mr Belvedere Rings the Bell 52. The Seven Year Itch 55. The Cardinal 63. Hurry Sundown 67, many others.

Mercer, Beryl (1882–1939). British character actress, of small stature, in Hollywood from 1923; played mothers, maids, landladies.
The Christian 23. Seven Days' Leave 29. *Outward Bound* 30. Merely Mary Ann 31. Supernatural 32. *Cavalcade* 33. Berkeley Square 33. The Little Minister 34. Night Must Fall 37. The Hound of the Baskervilles 39, etc.

Mercer, Johnny (1909–1976). American lyricist and composer, active in Hollywood from the early thirties. Songs include 'Blues in the Night', 'Black Magic', 'Something's Got to Give', 'Accentuate the Positive', etc.
The Harvey Girls (AA) 46. Here Comes the Groom (AA) 51. Seven Brides for Seven Brothers (AA) 54. Lil Abner 59, etc.

Merchant, Ismail (1936–). Indian producer, exclusively associated with films directed by James Ivory (qv).

Merchant, Vivien (1929–1983) (Ada Thompson). British leading actress, mainly on TV: once married to Harold Pinter.
Alfie 66. Accident 67. Under Milk Wood 71. Frenzy 72. The Offence 72. The Homecoming 73. The Man in the Iron Mask (TV) 77, etc.

Mercier, Michele (1939–). French leading lady.
Retour de Manivelle 57. Aimez-vous Brahms? 61. Call of the Wild 72. Jean's Tonic 84.

Mercouri, Melina (1923–). Volatile Greek star actress with flashing smile and dominant personality; married Jules Dassin and appeared in international films.
Autobiography 1971: *I Was Born Greek.*
□*Stella* 54. He Who Must Die 56. The Gypsy and the Gentleman 58. The Law 59. *Never on Sunday* 60. Il Giudizio Universale 61. Phaedra 61. Vive Henri IV 61. The Victors 63. *Topkapi* 64. A Man Could Get Killed 65. The Player Pianos 65. 10.30 pm Summer 66. Gaily Gaily 69. Promise at Dawn 71. Once Is Not Enough 75. Nasty Habits 76. A Dream of Passion 78. Not By Coincidence 83.

Meredith, Burgess (1908–) (George Burgess). American star character actor who was famous on Broadway in the thirties, but never seemed to find the right Hollywood outlet for his enthusiastic, eccentric portrayals.

□*Winterset* 36. There Goes the Groom 37. Spring Madness 38. Idiot's Delight 39. *Of Mice and Men* 39. Castle on the Hudson 40. Second Chorus 40. San Francisco Docks 41. *That Uncertain Feeling* 41. Tom Dick and Harry 41. Street of Chance 42. *The Story of GI Joe* (as Ernie Pyle) 45. The Diary of a Chambermaid 46. Magnificent Doll 46. On Our Merry Way 48. *Mine Own Executioner* (GB) 48. The Man on the Eiffel Tower (& d) 49. The Gay Adventure 53. Joe Butterfly 57. Advise and Consent 62. The Cardinal 63. In Harm's Way 65. A Big Hand for the Little Lady 66. Madame X 66. Batman 66. The Kidnappers (Philipp.) 66. Hurry Sundown 67. The Torture Garden (GB) 67. Mackenna's Gold 68. Stay Away Joe 68. Hard Contract 69. Skidoo 69. There Was a Crooked Man 70. Probe (TV) 71. Such Good Friends 71. Beware the Blob 71. A Fan's Notes 72. Clay Pigeon 72. Golden Needles 74. The Day of the Locust 74. The Hindenberg 76. Burnt Offerings 76. Rocky 77. The Sentinel 77. 92 in the Shade 77. Magic 78. Foul Play 78. The Manitou 78. The Great Georgia Bank Hoax 78. Rocky II 79. Final Assignment 80. When Time Ran Out 80. True Confessions 81. The Last Chase 81. Clash of the Titans 81. Rocky III 82. Santa Claus 85. Broken Rainbow 85. King Lear 87.
TV series: Mr Novak 64. Search 72. That's Incredible 80. Gloria 82.

Meredyth, Bess (1890–1969) (Helen McGlashan). American scriptwriter.
Strangers in the Night 23. Ben Hur 26. A Woman of Affairs 28. Our Blushing Brides 30. Cuban Love Song 31. Strange Interlude 32. The Affairs of Cellini 34. Folies Bergere 35. Under Two Flags 36. The Unsuspected 47, etc.

Merivale, Philip (1886–1946). British stage actor who moved to Hollywood in the late thirties.
The Passing of the Third Floor Back 35. Give Us This Night 36. Rage in Heaven 41. This Above All 42. This Land Is Mine 43. Lost Angel 44. The Stranger 45, etc.

Meriwether, Lee (1935–). Long-legged American leading lady, mostly in 'B's; former beauty queen.
The 4D Man 59. Batman (as Catwoman) 65. Namu the Killer Whale 66. Angel in My Pocket 68. The Undefeated 69. The Brothers O'Toole 73, etc.
TV series: Barnaby Jones 72–80.

Merkel, Una (1903–86). American character actress who started in the thirties as heroine's girlfriend type, later played mothers and aunts.
Abraham Lincoln 30. Daddy Longlegs 31. Whistling in the Dark 33. The Merry Widow 34. Saratoga 37. Destry Rides Again 39. Road to Zanzibar 41. This Is the Army 43. Twin Beds 44. With a Song in My Heart 52. The Kentuckian 55. The Mating Game 59. Summer and Smoke 62. A Tiger Walks 63. Spinout 66, many others.

Merman, Ethel (1908–1984) (Ethel Zimmermann). Brassy, vibrant, much-loved American star entertainer who had an incomparable way with a song that could be belted across. Her style was too outsize for Hollywood.
Autobiography 1955: *Who Could Ask For Anything More?* (UK: *Don't Call Me Madam*). 1978: *Merman.*
□Follow the Leader 30. We're Not Dressing 34. Kid Millions 34. *Anything Goes* 36. The Big Broadcast of 1936. Strike Me Pink 36. Happy Landing 38. *Alexander's Ragtime Band* 38. Straight Place and Show 38. Stage Door Canteen 43. *Call Me Madam* 53. There's No Business Like Show Business 54. It's a Mad Mad Mad Mad World 63. The Art of Love 65. Won Ton Ton 76. Airplane! 80.

¶ *E.M.:* Broadway has been very good to me—but then, I've been very good to Broadway.

Merrall, Mary (1890–1976) (Mary Lloyd). British character actress, on stage from 1907; often in fey or absent-minded roles.
The Duke's Son 20. You Will Remember 39. *Love on the Dole* 41. Squadron Leader X 42. *Dead of Night* 45. Nicholas Nickleby 47. Badger's Green 48. The Late Edwina Black 51. The Pickwick Papers 52. *The Belles of St Trinian's* 54. It's Great To Be Young 56. The Camp on Blood Island 58. Spare the Rod 61. Who Killed the Cat? 66, many others.

Merrick, David (1911–). (David Margulies). American impresario, a Broadway legend who also produced a few films.
Child's Play 72. The Great Gatsby 74. Semi-Tough 77. Rough Cut 80, etc.

Merrie Melodies: see *Looney Tunes.*

Merrill, Dina (1928–) (Nedenia Hutton Rumbough). American leading lady of the sixties, and leading socialite.

The Desk Set 57. The Sundowners 59. The Courtship of Eddie's Father 63. The Pleasure Seekers 64. I'll Take Sweden 65. Running Wild 73. The Greatest 77. A Wedding 78. Just Tell Me What You Want 80, etc.

Merrill, Gary (1914–). Dependable, tough-looking American actor.
Winged Victory 44. Slattery's Hurricane 48. Twelve O'Clock High 49. *All About Eve* 50. Decision Before Dawn 51. Another Man's Poison (GB) 51. Phone Call from a Stranger 53. Night Without Sleep 52. Blueprint for Murder 53. The Human Jungle 54. The Black Dakotas 54. Bermuda Affair 56. The Pleasure of His Company 61. Around the World Under the Sea 66. Destination Inner Space 66. Catacombs (GB) 66. The Power 68. Huckleberry Finn 74. Thieves 77, others.
TV series: The Mash 54. Young Dr Kildare 73. Reporter 74.

Merrill, Robert (1921–) (Henry Lavan). American composer and lyricist whose chief film score has been *Funny Girl*.
Wrote *W. C. Fields and Me*.

Merritt, George (1890–1977). British character actor of solid presence, usually seen as trades unionist, policeman, or gruff north-country type.
Dreyfus 30. The Lodger 32. I Was a Spy 33. Dr Syn 37. Q Planes 39. He Found a Star 41. Hatter's Castle 41. Waterloo Road 45. I'll Be Your Sweetheart 45. I'll Turn to You 46. Nicholas Nickleby 47. Marry Me 49. The Green Scarf 54. Quatermass II 57. Tread Softly Stranger 58. I Monster 70, etc.

Merrow, Jane (1941–). British leading lady.
Don't Bother to Knock 61. The Wild and the Willing 62. The System 63. *The Lion in Winter* 68. Hands of the Ripper 70. Adam's Woman 70. The Horror at 37,000 Feet (TV) 73. Diagnosis Murder 75. The Patricia Neal Story (TV) 81, etc.

The Merry Widow. Franz Lehar's operetta has been filmed at least four times. 1. US 1925; as silent, by Erich Von Stroheim, with John Gilbert, Mae Murray and Roy d'Arcy. 2. US 1934: by Ernst Lubitsch, with Maurice Chevalier and Jeanette MacDonald; added lyrics by Gus Kahn and Lorenz Hart. 3. US 1952: by Curtis Bernhardt, with Fernando Lamas, Lana Turner and Richard Haydn; added lyrics by Paul Francis Webster. 4. Austria 1962: with Karin Huebner and Peter Alexander.

Merton of the Movies. This American comic novel by Harry Leon Wilson, about an innocent in Hollywood in early silent days, has been filmed three times: in 1924 with Glenn Hunter, in 1932 (as *Make Me a Star*) with Stuart Erwin, and in 1947 with Red Skelton.

Merton Park. A small, independent south London studio. Founded in 1930 to make advertising films, it later housed Radio Luxembourg. Training films were made there during the war, and in the fifties it turned to the production of Edgar Lustgarten's *Scotland Yard* shorts, the Edgar Wallace supports, and *Scales of Justice*. It closed in the mid-sixties.

Mervyn, William (1912–1976) (William Pickwood). Portly, plummy-voiced British character actor, much on TV in high comedy roles.
The Blue Lamp 52. The Long Arm 56. Invasion Quartet 61. Murder Ahoy 64. The Jokers 67. The Railway Children 70. The Ruling Class 71. Up The Front 72. The Bawdy Adventures of Tom Jones 76, many others.

Mescall, John (1899–). American cinematographer.
Hold Your Horses 20. So This Is Paris 26. *The Black Cat* 34. *Bride of Frankenstein* 35. *Showboat* 36. The Road Back 37. Josette 38. Kit Carson 40. Dark Waters 44. Bedside Manner 45. The Desperadoes Are In Town 56. Not of This Earth 57, many others.

Messel, Oliver (1904–78). British stage designer who occasionally worked in films. The Scarlet Pimpernel 34. Romeo and Juliet 36. The Thief of Baghdad 40. Caesar and Cleopatra 45. The Queen of Spades 48, etc.

Messemer, Hannes (1924–). German general purpose actor.
Rose Bernd 56. Babette Goes to War 59. The Great Escape 63. Is Paris Burning? 66. Congress Dances 66, etc.

Metalious, Grace (1924–1964). American novelist who hit the best-seller list with *Peyton Place*.

¶ *G.M.*: If I'm a lousy writer, then a lot of people have got lousy taste.

Metaxas, George (1899–1950). Romanian character actor in occasional American films. Swing Time 37. The Mask of Dimitrios 44. Scotland Yard Investigator 48, etc.

Methot, Mayo (1904–1951). American actress who is best remembered for her stormy marriage with Humphrey Bogart.
Corsair 31. The Mind Reader 33. Jimmy the Gent 33. Side Streets 34. Dr Socrates 35. Mr Deeds Goes to Town 36. Marked Woman 37. The Sisters 38. Unexpected Father 39. Brother Rat and a Baby 40, etc.

Metrano, Art (–). Chubby American character actor.
Cheaper to Keep Her 80. How to Beat the High Cost of Living 80. Going Ape 81. Breathless 83.
TV series: Chicago Teddy Bears 71.

Metro-Goldwyn-Mayer. For many years the undoubted leader of the industry, this famous American production company has lately suffered most from the lack of 'front office' control and the proliferation of independent productions: now that it doesn't own the racecourse, it can't seem to pick the winners. The company stems from Loew's Inc., an exhibiting concern which in 1920 bought into Metro Pictures, which then produced two enormous money-spinners, *The Four Horsemen of the Apocalypse* and *The Prisoner of Zenda.* In 1924 Metro was merged with the Goldwyn production company (though Samuel Goldwyn himself promptly opted out and set up independently); and the next year Louis B. Mayer Pictures joined the flourishing group to add further power. Mayer himself became studio head and remained the dominant production force for over twenty-five years. Ideas man and executive producer in the early years was young Irving Thalberg, whose artistic flair provided a necessary corrective to Mayer's proletarian tastes, and who, before his death in 1936, had established a lofty pattern with such successes as *Ben Hur, The Big Parade, Anna Christie, Grand Hotel, The Thin Man, David Copperfield* and *Mutiny on the Bounty*, and stars like Garbo, Gable, Beery, Lionel Barrymore, Joan Crawford, John Gilbert, Lon Chaney, William Powell, Jean Harlow, Spencer Tracy, Lewis Stone, Nelson Eddy, Jeanette MacDonald, Laurel and Hardy and the Marx Brothers. (MGM's motto was in fact 'more stars than there are in heaven . . .') The success story continued through the forties with *Goodbye Mr Chips*, Greer Garson, *The Wizard Of Oz*, Judy Garland, the Hardy Family, Gene Kelly and Esther Williams. Such continuity of product is a thing of the past, but MGM keeps its end up with occasional big guns like *Dr Zhivago, Where Eagles Dare* and *Network*; while reissues of *Gone with the Wind*, which it did not produce, keep the image of Leo the Lion fresh on cinema screens. In the seventies MGM gave up movie-making to concentrate on its huge Las Vegas hotel. A comeback attempt failed, and it was taken over by United Artists and Ted Turner.

¶ *Louis B. Mayer:* Beautiful pictures for beautiful people.
June Allyson: MGM was my mother and father, mentor and guide, my all-powerful and benevolent crutch.
Anon: Mayer's Ganz Mispochen (Mayer's whole family).

Metropolis (Germany 1926). Fritz Lang's futuristic fantasy, from a script by himself and Thea Von Harbou, details the horrors of a mechanized Utopia. The actual story is a dull revamping of the struggle between capital and labour; but the great geometric sets are imaginatively handled. With Brigitte Helm (as a robot) and Rudolph Klein-Rogge; photographed by Karl Freund. In 1983 Giorgio Moroder issued a 'remixed' version with a modern sound track.

Metty, Russell (1906–1978). American cinematographer.
Sylvia Scarlett 35. Bringing Up Baby 38. Music in Manhattan 44. The Story of G.I. Joe 45. *The Stranger* 45. *Ivy* 47. All My Sons 48. We Were Strangers 49. Magnificent Obsession 54. Man without a Star 55. *Miracle in the Rain* 56. Written on the Wind 56. Man with a Thousand Faces 57. A Time to Love and a Time to Die 58. The Misfits 60. *Spartacus* (AA) 61. The Art of Love 65. The War Lord 65. Madame X 66. The Appaloosa 66. The Secret War of Harry Frigg 67. Madigan 68. Eye of the Cat 69. The Omega Man 71. Ben 72, many others.

Metzger, Radley (1930–). American director.
Dark Odyssey 61. The Dirty Girls 64. Carmen Baby 67. Therese and Isabelle 68. Camille 2000 69. The Lickerish Quartet 70. Little Mother 72. Score 73. Naked Came the Stranger 75. The Opening of Misty Beethoven 76. The Cat and the Canary 78, etc.

Metzner, Erno (1892–). Hungarian art director in the silent German cinema.
Sumurun 20. The Loves of Pharaoh 21. Salome 22. Old Heidelberg 23. Secrets of a Soul 26. The White Hell of Pitz Palu 29. Diary of a Lost Girl 29. Westfront 1918 30.

Kameradschaft 31. L'Atlantide 32. Chu Chin Chow (GB) 34. It Happened Tomorrow (US) 44, etc.

Meurisse, Paul (1912–1979). French general purpose actor.
Montemartre sur Seine 41. Marie la Misère 45. Diabolique 54. La Tête contre les Murs 58. Lunch on the Grass 59. La Vérité 60, etc.

Mexican Spitfire. This was the first (1939) of a series of American second-feature comedies which ran till 1943 with such titles as *Mexican Spitfire Sees a Ghost, Mexican Spitfire at Sea.* (The series had virtually begun with a 1938 entry called *The Girl from Mexico.*) Donald Woods was a young businessman with a temperamental wife (Lupe Velez), a scheming Uncle Matt (Leon Errol) and a drunken English client, Lord Epping (also played by Leon Errol). The films were only tolerably well made, but always managed a hectic finale of impersonation and mistaken identity which allowed full play to Mr Errol's jerky convulsions.

Mexico was a late starter in the feature film market, but made a few from about 1920, hampered by competition from Hollywood, which also plundered most of its best actors. The late thirties saw an improvement, with Emilio Fernandez as leading director, and in the forties Buñuel settled there and made some small stylish films. More recent productions have varied between cheap Hollywood-aping hokum and dour politically conscious social dramas.

Meyer, Emile (1903–87). American character actor typically cast as crooked cop or prizefight manager; but sometimes an honest Joe.
The People Against O'Hara 51. Shane 53. The Blackboard Jungle 55. *Riot in Cell Block 11* 55. The Man with the Golden Arm 56. *Sweet Smell of Success* 57. Baby Face Nelson 57. Paths of Glory 58. The Fiend Who Walked the West 59. Young Jesse James 60. Taggart 64. Young Dillinger 65. Hostile Guns 67. More Dead Than Alive 70, etc.

Meyer, Nicholas (1945–). American novelist whose *The Seven Per Cent Solution* became a best-seller and took him from publicity to direction.
The Seven Per Cent Solution (w) 77. Time after Time (w, d) 79. Star Trek: The Wrath of Khan (d) 82. The Day After (d) (TV) 83. Volunteers (d) 85.

Meyer, Russ (1923–). American director of erotic films who broke briefly into the big time.
□The Immoral Mr Teas 59. Eroticon 61. Eve and the Handyman 61. Naked Gals of the Golden West 62. Europe in the Raw 63. Heavenly Bodies 63. Laura 64. Mudhoney 65. Motor Psycho 65. Fanny Hill 65. Faster Pussycat Kill Kill 66. Mondo Topless 66. Good Morning and Goodbye 67. Common Law Cabin 67. Finders Keepers Lovers Weepers 68. *Vixen* 68. Cherry Harry and Raquel 69. Beyond the Valley of the Dolls 70. The Seven Minutes 71. Black Snake 73. The Supervixens 73. *Up* 76. Beyond the Valley of the Ultravixens 79.

¶ *R.M.:* I always had a tremendous interest in big tits.
R.M.: To him, nothing is obscene providing it is done in bad taste.

Meyer, Torben (1884–1975). German-American character actor who played many waiters, music teachers and petty officials, especially memorable in the films of Preston Sturges.
Roberta 35. The Prisoner of Zenda 37. Christmas in July 40. Edge of Darkness 42. The Miracle of Morgans Creek 43. Mad Wednesday 47, many others.

Michael, Gertrude (1911–1964). American actress usually seen in secondary roles.
I'm No Angel 33. The Notorious Sophie Lang (lead) 37. Women in Bondage 44. Caged 50. Women's Prison 55. Twist All Night 62, etc.

Michael, Ralph (1907–) (Ralph Champion Shotter). British character actor of stage and screen, often in stiff-upper-lip roles.
John Halifax Gentleman 38. San Demetrio, London 43. For Those in Peril 44. *Dead of Night* 45. Johnny Frenchman 45. The Captive Heart 46. Eureka Stockade 48. The Astonished Heart 49. The Sound Barrier 52. King's Rhapsody 56. Seven Waves Away 57. A Night to Remember 58. A Jolly Bad Fellow 64. House of Cards 68. Diary of a Mad Old Man 87, others.

Michael Shayne. The American private eye created by Brett Halliday in a string of thirties novels was a lightly shaded character at best, but sufficed for a number of second feature thrillers in the early forties, with Lloyd Nolan as star. (One of them, *Time to Kill*, was actually adapted from Raymond Chandler's *The High Window*, not from a Halliday original.) In 1960 Richard Denning played the lead in a television series.

Michael Strogoff. Jules Verne's historical adventure novel, about espionage in war-torn Russia of 1870, has been a favourite with film makers. Tourjansky made a version with Mosjoukine in 1926. George Nicholls Jnr directed a Hollywood version with Anton Walbrook in 1937. Carmine Gallone made the story again in colour in 1956, with an international cast headed by Curt Jurgens, who continued in 1961 in *The Triumph of Michael Strogoff*. In 1971 John Phillip Law appeared in a new version, *Courier of the Tsar*.

Michaels, Beverly (1927–). American leading lady of sultry dramas in the early fifties.
East Side West Side 49. Pick Up 51. Wicked Woman 53. Crashout 55, etc.

Michaels, Dolores (1930–). American leading lady of the late fifties; retired early.
The Wayward Bus 57. April Love 57. Fraulein 58. Warlock 59. Five Gates to Hell 59. One Foot in Hell 60. The Battle at Bloody Beach 61, etc.

Michelet, Michel (1899–). Russian-born French composer.
Voice in the Wind 44. The Hairy Ape 44. Diary of a Chambermaid 46. Siren of Atlantis 46. Outpost in Morocco 49. Fort Algiers 53. Captain Sinbad 63.

Michell, Keith (1926–). Australian leading man, on British stage and screen from the mid-fifties.
□ True as a Turtle 57. Dangerous Exile 57. The Gypsy and the Gentleman 58. *The Hellfire Club* 61. All Night Long 62. Seven Seas to Calais 63. Prudence and the Pill 68. House of Cards 68. The Executioner 70. *Henry VIII and His Six Wives* 72. Moments 73. The Story of Jacob and Joseph (TV) 74. The Story of David 76. The Day Christ Died (TV) 79. Grendel Grendel Grendel 82. My Brother Tom (TV) 87. The Deceivers 88.

Michener, James A. (1907–). American adventure-epic novelist. Works filmed include: *South Pacific, Return to Paradise, The Bridges at Toko Ri, Sayonara, Hawaii.*

Mickey Mouse. Walt Disney's most famous cartoon character began in the twenties as Mortimer Mouse. By the early thirties his outlines had been simplified and he was perhaps the most certain box office lure in the world. His voice was supplied by Disney himself; his finest hour, perhaps, was in the 'Sorcerer's Apprentice' segment of *Fantasia* 40.

¶ The best known and most popular international figure of his day.—*New York Times 1935*.

Middleton, Charles (1874–1949). American character actor usually in villainous roles; especially remembered as Ming the Merciless in the Flash Gordon serials.
Mystery Ranch 32. Mrs Wiggs of the Cabbage Patch 34. Kentucky 39. The Grapes of Wrath 40. Our Vines Have Tender Grapes 45. The Black Arrow 49, many others.

Middleton, Guy (1906–1973) (Guy Middleton-Powell). Hearty-type British light character actor, in films as amiable idiot or gay Lothario from the early thirties after Stock Exchange career.
A Woman Alone 32. Fame 34. *Keep Fit* 37. *French Without Tears* 39. Dangerous Moonlight 40. The Demi-Paradise 43. Champagne Charlie 44. The Rake's Progress 45. The Captive Heart 46. One Night with You 48. The Happiest Days of Your Life 49. Never Look Back 52. Albert RN 53. The Belles of St Trinian's 54. The Passionate Summer 58. The Waltz of the Toreadors 62. The Magic Christian 70, etc.

Middleton, Noelle (c. 1928–). British leading lady of the fifties.
Carrington V.C. 55. The Iron Petticoat 56.

Middleton, Ray (1908–84). American actor-singer.
Gangs of Chicago 40. Lady For A Night 41. The Girl From Alaska 42. I Dream of Jeannie 52. Jubilee Trail 54. The Road To Denver 55, etc.

Middleton, Robert (1911–77) (Samuel G. Messer). Weighty American character actor usually cast as villain.
The Silver Chalice 55. The Big Combo 55. The Desperate Hours 55. The Court Jester 55. The Friendly Persuasion 56. The Tarnished Angels 58. Career 59. Gold of the Seven Saints 61. For Those Who Think Young 64. Big Hand for a Little Lady 66. Which Way to the Front? 71, many others.

Midler, Bette (1944–). Diminutive but brassy and very vulgar American entertainer. Autobiography 1980: *A View from a Broad*.
Hawaii 65. The Rose 79. Divine Madness (concert) 80. Jinxed 82. Down and Out in Beverly Hills 85. Ruthless People 86. Outrageous Fortune 87.

¶ *B.M.:* I wouldn't say I invented tack, but I definitely brought it to its present high popularity.

B.M.: Underneath all this drag I'm really a librarian, you know.

B.M.: In Hawaii I was the chief chunker in a pineapple canning factory. I used to come home smelling like a compote.

Midnight Cowboy (US 1969). A glossy film about sleazy New York was bound to leave a bad taste in the mouth, which is presumably what director John Schlesinger intended when he adapted this skilful but ultimately pointless film exercise from James Leo Herlihy's novel. Jon Voight and Dustin Hoffman give surprisingly attractive performances as the stud and the bum who sit freezing in a tenement all winter instead of going out to get jobs. On its release the film marked a considerable step forward—or backward—into permissiveness.

Midnight Express (GB 1978). A surprisingly successful account of a young American's incarceration in a Turkish prison on a charge of drug-smuggling. Not an entertainment, but brilliantly scripted by Oliver Stone (AA) and directed by Alan Parker; with Brad Davis, John Hurt.

A Midsummer Night's Dream. Shakespeare's fairy play was filmed in America in 1929 by J. Stuart Blackton, starring Maurice Costello; and there is a Czechoslovakian puppet version by Jiri Trnka. But the best-known version is Max Reinhardt's lavish production for Warners in 1935, directed by Reinhardt and William Dieterle, with a surprising cast including James Cagney as Bottom, Mickey Rooney as Puck, Hugh Herbert, Arthur Treacher, Dick Powell, Anita Louise, Victor Jory and Olivia de Havilland. Peter Hall's 'realistic' version of 1968, aimed primarily at American TV, was generally thought unsuccessful.

Mifune, Toshiro (1920–). Versatile Japanese actor with a ferocious style, seen in many films by Kurosawa and others.
The Drunken Angel 48. The Stray Dog 49. *Rashomon* 50. *Seven Samurai* 54. The Lower Depths 57. *Throne of Blood* 57. The Hidden Fortress 58. The Bad Sleep Well 59. Yojimbo 61. Red Beard 64. The Lost World of Sinbad 64. Grand Prix (US) 66. Rebellion 67. Hell in the Pacific (US) 68. Red Sun 71. Paper Tiger 75. Midway 76. 1941 79. Winter Kills 79. The Bushido Blade 80. Inchon 80. The Challenge 82, etc.
AS DIRECTOR: Legacy of the Five Hundred Thousand 63.

Mike Hammer. The tough, immoral private eye created by Mickey Spillane (qv for list of films).

Miles, Sir Bernard (Lord Miles) (1907–). British actor specializing in slow-speaking countryfolk and other ruminating types. An ex-school master, on stage since 1930. Founder of London's Mermaid Theatre (1959).

Channel Crossing 32. Quiet Wedding 40. *In Which We Serve* 42. Tawny Pipit (& co-w and d) 44. Carnival 46. *Great Expectations* 46. Nicholas Nickleby 47. The Guinea Pig 48. Chance of a Lifetime (& wpd) 49. Never Let Me Go 53. The Man Who Knew Too Much 56. Moby Dick 56. *The Smallest Show on Earth* 57. Tom Thumb 58. Sapphire 59. *Heavens Above* 63. Run Wild Run Free 69, etc.

Miles, Christopher (1939–). British director, brother of Sarah Miles.
□Six-sided Triangle 64. Up Jumped a Swagman 65. *The Virgin and The Gypsy* 70. Time for Loving 71. The Maids 74. That Lucky Touch 75. Alternative 3 (TV) 78. Priest of Love 81.

Miles, Joanna (1949–). American leading lady of the seventies.
Bug 75.

Miles, Peter (1938–) (Gerald Perreau). American child actor of the forties, brother of Gigi Perreau.
Passage to Marseilles 44. The Red Pony 48. Roseanna McCoy 50. Quo Vadis 51, etc.
As Richard Miles, he later became a writer, notably of *That Cold Day in the Park* 68 (based on his own novel).

Miles, Sarah (1941–). Vivacious British leading actress; divorced from Robert Bolt.
□*Term of Trial* 62. The Servant 63. The Ceremony 64. Those Magnificent Men in Their Flying Machines 65. I Was Happy Here 65. Blow Up 66. *Ryan's Daughter* 70. *Lady Caroline Lamb* 72. The Hireling 73. The Man Who Loved Cat Dancing 73. Great Expectations (TV) 75. Dynasty (TV) 76. The Sailor Who Fell from Grace with the Sea 76. The Big Sleep 78. Priest of Love 81. Venom 82. Ordeal by Innocence 84. Steaming 84. Harem (TV) 86. Hope and Glory 87.

Miles, Sylvia (1926–). American character actress.
Parrish 61. Midnight Cowboy 69. *Heat* 72. Farewell My Lovely 75. 92 in the Shade 75. The Great Scout and Cathouse Thursday 76. The Sentinel 77. Zero to Sixty 78. Evil Under the Sun 82. Critical Condition 87, etc.

Miles, Vera (1929–) (Vera Ralston). Dependable American leading lady who came from TV to films.
For Men Only (debut) 52. Charge at Feather River 54. 23 Paces to Baker Street 55. *The Searchers* 56. *The Wrong Man* 57. The FBI Story 59. *Psycho* 60. A Tiger Walks 63. Those Calloways 65. Follow Me, Boys 66. The Spirit is Willing 66. Hell-fighters 68. The Castaway Cowboy 74. One Little Indian 75. Twilight's Last Gleaming 76. The Thoroughbreds 77. Psycho II 83.
Into the Night 84, many others.

Milestone, Lewis (1895–1980) (Levis Milstein). Veteran American director whose later films never quite matched up to his early achievements. Former editor, in Hollywood from 1918.
□Seven Sinners 25. The Cave Man 26. The New Klondike 26. *Two Arabian Knights* (AA) 27. The Garden of Eden 28. The Racket 28. Betrayal 29. New York Nights 29. *All Quiet on the Western Front* (AA) 30. *The Front Page* 31. Rain 32. *Hallelujah I'm a Bum* 33. The Captain Hates the Sea 34. Paris in Spring 35. Anything Goes 36. *The General Died at Dawn* 36. *Of Mice and Men* 39. Night of Nights 40. Lucky Partners 40. My Life with Caroline (& p) 41. Edge of Darkness 43. North Star 43. The Purple Heart 44. The Strange Love of Martha Ivers 46. *A Walk in the Sun* 46. No Minor Vices 47. Arch of Triumph 48. The Red Pony 48. Halls of Montezuma 51. Kangaroo 52. Les Misérables 52. Melba 53. They Who Dare (GB) 54. The Widow (It.) 55. Pork Chop Hill 59. Ocean's Eleven 61. Mutiny on the Bounty 62.
'His professionalism is as unyielding as it is meaningless.'—*Andrew Sarris, 1968*
❀ For a handful of seminal films of the thirties and for devising a fast crabwise tracking shot which was much imitated. *All Quiet on the Western Front.*

Milhollin, James (1920–). Crumple-faced American character comedian, mostly on TV.
No Time For Sergeants 58. Bon Voyage 62, etc.
TV series: *Grindl* 63.

Milian, Thomas (1937–). Cuban leading man in Italian action movies.
The Bounty Killer 66. Face to Face 67. The Big Gundown 67. Run Man Run 68. Django Kill 68. Apache 70. The Companeros 70. The Counsellor 74. La Luna 78. Winter Kills 79. The Day Christ Died (TV) 79, etc.

Milius, John (1944–). American director.
The Devil's Eight (w only) 68. Evel Knievel (w only) 72. Jeremiah Johnson (w only) 72. Judge Roy Bean (w only) 73. Magnum Force (co-w only) 73. *Dillinger* (& w) 73. The Wind and the Lion (& w) 75. Big Wednesday (& w) 78. Apocalypse Now (co-w) 79. Conan the Barbarian (co-w, d) 82. Red Dawn (& co-w) 84.

Miljan, John (1893–1960). American character actor with stage experience; often played the suave villain.
Love Letters 23. The Amateur Gentleman 26. The Painted Lady 29. The Ghost Walks 35. Double Cross 41. The Merry Monahans 44. The Killers 46. Samson and Delilah 50. Pirates of Tripoli 55, etc.

Milland, Ray (1905–86) (Reginald Truscott-Jones). Welsh-born light leading man of ready smile and equable disposition; carved a pleasant niche for himself in Hollywood in the thirties, and later surprised many by becoming an actor and director of some repute before stepping on the inevitable downhill slope.
Autobiography 1976: *Wide-Eyed in Babylon.*
□The Plaything (GB) 29. The Flying Scotsman (GB) 29. The Informer 30. Passion Flower 30. Goodwin Sands 30. Bachelor Father 31. Just a Gigolo 31. Bought 31. Ambassador Bill 31. Blonde Crazy 31. Polly of the Circus 31. The Man Who Played God 32. Payment Deferred 32. This is the Life (GB) 33. Orders is Orders (GB) 33. Bolero 34. We're Not Dressing 34. Many Happy Returns 34. Menace 34. Charlie Chan in London 34. The Gilded Lily 35. One Hour Late 35. Four Hours to Kill 35. The Glass Key 35. Alias Mary Dow 35. Next Time We Love 36. The Return of Sophie Lang 36. The Big Broadcast of 1937. *The Jungle Princess* 36. Three Smart Girls 37. Wings Over Honolulu 37. Easy Living 37. Ebb Tide 37. Wise Girl 37. Bulldog Drummond Escapes 37. Her Jungle Love 38. Tropic Holiday 38. Men with Wings 38. Say It In French 38. Hotel Imperial 39. *Beau Geste* 39. Everything Happens at Night 39. *French Without Tears* (GB) 39. Irene 40. The Doctor Takes a Wife

40. Untamed 40. *Arise My Love* 41. I Wanted Wings 41. Skylark 41. The Lady Has Plans 42. Are Husbands Necessary 42. The Major and the Minor 42. Reap the Wild Wind 42. Star Spangled Rhythm 42. Forever and a Day 43. The Crystal Ball 43. *The Uninvited* 44. Lady in the Dark 44. Till We Meet Again 44. *Ministry of Fear* 44. *The Lost Weekend* (AA) 45. Kitty 45. The Well Groomed Bride 46. California 46. The Imperfect Lady 47. The Trouble with Women 47. Golden Earrings 47. Variety Girl 47. The Big Clock 48. So Evil My Love 48. Sealed Verdict 48. *Alias Nick Beal* 49. It Happens Every Spring 49. A Woman of Distinction 50. A Life of Her Own 50. Copper Canyon 50. Circle of Danger (GB) 51. Night into Morning 51. Rhubarb 52. Close to My Heart 51. Bugles in the Afternoon 52. Something to Live For 52. *The Thief* 52. Jamaica Run 53. Let's Do It Again 53. *Dial M for Murder* 54. A Man Alone (& d) 55. The Girl in the Red Velvet Swing 55. Lisbon (& d) 56. Three Brave Men 57. The River's Edge 57. The Safecracker (& d) (GB) 58. High Flight (GB) 58. The Premature Burial 62. Panic in Year Zero (& d) 62. The Man with X-Ray Eyes 63. The Confession 65. Hostile Witness (& d) (GB) 68. River of Gold (TV) 69. Daughter of the Mind (TV) 69. Love Story 70. Company of Killers (TV) 70. Black Noon (TV) 71. Embassy 72. The Thing with Two Heads 72. Frogs 72. Terror in the Wax Museum 73. The House in Nightmare Park (GB) 73. Gold 74. The Student Connection 74. The Swiss Conspiracy 75. The Dead Don't Die (TV) 75. Look What Happened to Rosemary's Baby (TV) 76. Oil 76. Ellery Queen (TV) 76. Escape to Witch Mountain 76. Rich Man Poor Man (TV) 76. The Last Tycoon 76. Aces High 76. Cruise into Terror (TV) 77. Mayday at 40,000 Feet (TV) 77. Slaves 77. Testimony of Two Men (TV) 77. The Uncanny 77. Blackout 78. The Darker Side of Terror (TV) 79. Oliver's Story 79. Game for Vultures 79. The Attic 79. Cave In (TV) 79. Survival Run 80. Our Family Business (TV) 81. The Royal Romance of Charles and Diana (TV) 82. Starflight One (TV) 82. The Masks of Death (TV) 84.

TV series: Meet Mr McNutley 53. Markham 59.

❄ For his imperturbable cheerfulness, and for briefly demonstrating that with a different start he might have been an actor or director of stature. *Arise My Love.*

Millar, Gavin (1938–). British director and film buff.
Cream in My Coffee (TV) 80. Dreamchild 85. Scoop (TV) 87.

Millar, Stuart (1929–). American producer.
The Young Stranger 57. Stage Struck 58. The Young Doctors 61. I Could Go On Singing 63. The Best Man 64. Paper Lion 68. When the Legends Die (& d) 72. Rooster Cogburn (d only) 75.

Miller, Alice Duer (–1985). American writer who collaborated on several film scripts and whose poem 'The White Cliffs of Dover' was filmed in 1944.

Miller, Ann (1919–) (Lucy Ann Collier). Long-legged American dancer, in films from mid-thirties.
Autobiography 1974: *Miller's High Life*.
New Faces of 1937. *You Can't Take It With You* 38. Go West, Young Lady 41. *Reveille with Beverly* 43. Jam Session 44. Eve Knew Her Apples 45. Easter Parade 48. *On the Town* 49. Two Tickets to Broadway 51. *Kiss Me Kate* 53. The Opposite Sex 56, etc.

¶ 'I have worked like a dog all my life, honey. Dancing, as Fred Astaire said, is next to ditch-digging. You sweat and you slave and the audience doesn't think you have a brain in your head.'—*A.M. in 1979 interview*

Miller, Arthur (1915–). American playwright whose work has been adapted for the cinema.
All My Sons 48. Death of a Salesman 52. The Witches of Salem 57, etc.
Wrote scenes for *Let's Make Love* 60, starring his then wife Marilyn Monroe; also complete screenplay *The Misfits* 61.

Miller, Arthur (1894–1971). Distinguished American cinematographer.
SELECTED SILENT FILMS: At Bay 15. The Iron Heart 17. The Profiteers 19. His House in Order 20. Kick In 22. The Cheat 23. The Coming of Amos 24. The Clinging Vine 26. The Fighting Eagle 28. The Spieler 29, etc. □SOUND FILMS: Oh Yeah 30. Sailor's Holiday 30. Strange Cargo 30. The Lady of Scandal 30. Officer O'Brien 30. The Truth about Youth 30. Behind the Make Up 30. Father's Son 30. Bad Company 31. Panama Flo 32. Big Shot 32. The Young Bride 32. Breach of Promise 32. Me and My Gal 32. Okay America 32. Sailor's Luck 33. Hold Me Tight 33. The Man Who Dared 33. The Last Trail 33. The Mad Game 33. My Weakness 33. Bottoms Up 34. Ever Since Eve 34. Handy Andy 34. Love Time 34. The White

Parade 34. Bright Eyes 34. The Little Colonel 35. It's a Small World 35. Black Sheep 35. Welcome Home 35. Paddy O'Day 35. White Fang 36. 36 Hours to Kill 36. Pigskin Parade 36. Stowaway 36. *Wee Willie Winkie* 37. Heidi 37. The Baroness and the Butler 38. Rebecca of Sunnybrook Farm 38. Little Miss Broadway 38. Submarine Patrol 38. *The Little Princess* 39. Susannah of the Mounties 39. Here I Am a Stranger 39. *The Rains Came* 39. *The Blue Bird* 40. Johnny Apollo 40. On Their Own 40. *The Mark of Zorro* 40. Brigham Young 40. *Tobacco Road* 41. The Men in Her Life 41. Man Hunt 41. *How Green was My Valley* (AA) 41. *This Above All* 42. Iceland 42. The Moon is Down 43. The Immortal Sergeant 43. The Ox Bow Incident 43. *The Song of Bernadette* (AA) 43. The Purple Heart 44. The Keys of the Kingdom 45. A Royal Scandal 45. Dragonwyck 46. *Anna and the King of Siam* 46. The Razor's Edge 46. Gentleman's Agreement 47. The Walls of Jericho 48. A Letter to Three Wives 49. Whirlpool 49. *The Gunfighter* 50. The Prowler 51.

For a long succession of Hollywood's most lustrous black-and-white images. *The Rains Came*.

¶ *A.M.:* The basic principle I have had in making pictures was to make them look like real life, and then emphasise the visuals slightly.

A.M.: I was never a soft focus man—I liked crisp, sharp, solid images.

Miller, Claude (1942–). French director. The Best Way to Walk 76. Tell Him I Love Him 77, etc.

Miller, Colleen (1932–). American leading lady.
The Las Vegas Story 52. The Purple Mask 55. Man with a Shadow 57. Step Down to Terror 59, etc.

Miller, Denny (–). Athletic American actor who had a shot at playing Tarzan.
Tarzan the Ape Man 59. Love in a Goldfish Bowl 61. The Party 68. Buck and the Preacher 72. The Gravy Train 74. The Norsemen 78, etc.

Miller, David (1909–). American director, formerly editor, in Hollywood from 1930.
□Billy the Kid 41. Sunday Punch 42. Flying Tigers 43. Top o' the Morning 49. Love Happy 50. Our Very Own 51. Saturday's Hero 52. *Sudden Fear* 53. Beautiful Stranger 54. Diane 55. The Opposite Sex 56. The Story of Esther Costello 57. Happy Anniversary 59. Midnight Lace 60. Back Street 61. *Lonely Are the Brave* 62. Captain Newman 63. Hammerhead (GB) 68. Hail Hero 69. Executive Action 73. Bittersweet Love 76, etc.

Miller, Dick (1928–). American supporting actor.
Apache Woman 55. The Undead 56. Not of This Earth 57. Thunder over Hawaii 57. A Bucket of Blood 59. The Terror 63. Ski Party 65. The Dirty Dozen 67. The Grissom Gang 71. Ulzana's Raid 72. Big Bad Mama 74. Hustle 75. Cannonball 76. Piranha 78. Used Cars 80. Heartbeeps 81, others.

Miller, George (1945–). Australian director
□ Mad Max 79. Mad Max 2: The Road Warrior 81. Twilight Zone (part) 83. Mad Max Beyond Thunderdome 85.

Miller, George (–). Australian director.
The Man from Snowy River 81. The Aviator 84. Anzacs (TV) 85. Cool Change 86.

Miller, Glenn (1904–1944). American bandleader and composer, whose 'new sound' was immensely popular during World War II. Appeared in *Orchestra Wives* 42. *Sun Valley Serenade* 42. Was impersonated by James Stewart in *The Glenn Miller Story* 53.

Miller, Jason (1939–). American playwright who turned actor.
The Exorcist 74. The Nickel Ride 76. A Home of Our Own (TV) 76. F. Scott Fitzgerald in Hollywood (TV) 76. The Dain Curse (TV) 78. The Devil's Advocate 79. The Ninth Configuration 80. That Championship Season (directing his own play) 82.

Miller, Jonathan (1936–). British satirist, occasionally director.
□ One Way Pendulum (a only) 65. Alice in Wonderland (TV) 67. Take A Girl Like You 70.

Miller, Mandy (1944–). British child star.
The Man in the White Suit 51. *Mandy* 52. Dance Little Lady 54. A Child in the House 56. The Secret 57. The Snorkel 58, etc.

Miller, Marilyn (1898–1936) (Mary Ellen Reynolds). American dancing and singing star of Broadway musicals in the twenties. She was impersonated by June Haver in a biopic,

Look for the Silver Lining 49, and by Judy Garland in *Till the Clouds Roll By* 46.
Sally 30. Sunny 31. Her Majesty Love 32.

Miller, Martin (1899–1969) (Rudolph Muller). Czechoslovakian character actor active in Britain from the late thirties.
Squadron Leader X 40. The Huggetts Abroad 51. Front Page Story 53. Libel 60. 55 Days at Peking 62. Children of the Damned 64. Up Jumped a Swagman 65, many others.

Miller, Marvin (1913–85) (M. Mueller). American tough guy supporting actor who represented menaces of various nations.
Johnny Angel 45. Intrigue 47. The High Window 47. Off Limits 53. The Shanghai Story 54, etc.
TV series: The Millionaire 55–60.

Miller, Max (1895–1963) (Harold Sargent). Ribald British music-hall comedian ('the Cheeky Chappie'). Starred in several vehicles during the thirties but his style and material had to be considerably toned down for the screen.
□*The Good Companions* 32. Channel Crossing 32. Friday the Thirteenth 33. Princess Charming 34. Things Are Looking Up 35. *Educated Evans* 36. Get Off My Foot 36. Take It From Me 37. Don't Get Me Wrong 37. Thank Evans 38. Everything Happens to Me 39. The Good Old Days 39. Hoots Mon 40. Asking for Trouble 43.

Miller, Patsy Ruth (1905–). American leading lady of the silent screen, former juvenile player.
Camille 15. Judgment 18. The Hunchback of Notre Dame 23. Lorraine of the Lions 24. Why Girls Go Back Home 27. The Hottentot 28. Lonely Wives 31. Quebec 51, etc.

Miller, Robert Ellis (1927–). American director, from TV.
□Any Wednesday 66. Sweet November 68. The Heart is a Lonely Hunter 68. The Buttercup Chain 70. The Girl from Petrovka 74. The Baltimore Bullet 80. Reuben, Reuben 83.

Miller, Seton I. (1902–1974). American silent actor (*Brown of Harvard* 26, etc.) who turned into one of Hollywood's most prolific screenwriters.
Dawn Patrol 30. The Criminal Code 32. *Scarface* 32. G-Men 35. *The Adventures of Robin Hood* 38. The Sea Hawk 40. *Here Comes Mr Jordan* (AA) 41. The Black Swan 42. The Ministry of Fear 43. Two Years Before the Mast (& p) 46. Istanbul 57, etc.

Miller, Walter C. (1892–1940). American leading man of the D. W. Griffith company.
The Informer 12. A Beggar Prince of India 14. The Marble Heart 16. Thin Ice 19. The Tie That Binds 23. Manhattan Knights 28. Three Smart Girls 36. Johnny Apollo 40, many others.
†Not to be confused with W. Christie Miller (1843–1922) who played elderly roles for Griffith.

Millhauser, Bertram (1892–1958). American screenwriter mainly engaged on second features, some of them better than average.
The Garden Murder Case 36. Sherlock Holmes in Washington 42 (and others in this series including Pearl of Death 44). The Invisible Man's Revenge 44. Patrick the Great 45. Walk a Crooked Mile 48. Tokyo Joe 48, etc.

Millican, James (1910–1955). American general purpose actor, often in low-budget westerns.
The Remarkable Andrew 42. Bring on the Girls 44. Hazard 47. Rogues' Regiment 48. Carson City 52. The Man from Laramie 55, etc.

Millichip, Roy (1930–). British independent producer.
The Uncle 65. I Was Happy Here 66. A Nice Girl Like Me 69, etc.

Milligan, Spike (1918–). Irish comedian and arch-goon of stage, TV and radio.
The Case of the Mukkinese Battlehorn 56. Watch Your Stern 60. Suspect 60. Invasion Quartet 61. Postman's Knock 62. The Magic Christian 70. Rentadick 72. Alice's Adventures in Wonderland 72. Adolf Hitler, My Part in His Downfall (& oa) 72. Digby, the Biggest Dog in the World 73. The Three Musketeers 74. The Great McGonagall 74. A Man About the House 76. The Last Remake of Beau Geste 77. The Life of Brian 79. Yellowbeard 83, etc.

Le Million (France 1930). Brilliant early sound comedy with music, ranging from slapstick to satire in a zany tale about a search for a lost lottery ticket. Written and directed by René Clair: probably his best film and certainly his most engaging. With René Lefebre, Annabella; photography by Georges Perinal; music by Georges Van Parys, Armand Bernard, Phillipe Pares.

Mills, Donna (1947–). American leading lady, mostly on TV.

The Incident 67. Play Misty for Me 71. Haunts of the Very Rich (TV) 72. Night of Terror (TV) 72. The Bait (TV) 73. Live Again Die Again (TV) 74. Who Is the Black Dahlia? (TV) 75. Smash-Up on Interstate Five (TV) 76. Curse of the Black Widow (TV) 76. The Hunted Lady (TV) 77. Superdome (TV) 78. Bare Essence (TV) 83. He's Not Your Son (TV) 84, etc.

Mills, Hayley (1946–). British actress who shot to fame as a tomboy child; daughter of John Mills.
□*Tiger Bay* 59. *Pollyanna* (US) (special AA as best child actress) 60. *The Parent Trap* (US) 61. Whistle Down the Wind 61. Summer Magic (US) 62. In Search of the Castaways 63. The Chalk Garden 64. The Moonspinners 65. The Truth about Spring 65. That Darn Cat 65. Sky West and Crooked 66. The Trouble with Angels 66. The Family Way 66. Pretty Polly 67. Twisted Nerve 68. Take a Girl Like You 70. Forbush and the Penguins 71. Endless Night 72. Deadly Strangers 75. What Changed Charley Farthing? 75. The Kingfisher Caper 75. The Flame Trees of Thika (TV) 81. Parent Trap II (TV) 86.

Mills, Hugh (c. 1913–1971). British screenwriter.
Blanche Fury 47. Blackmailed (co-w) 50. Knave of Hearts 52. The House by the Lake 54. Prudence and the Pill 68, etc.

Mills, Sir John (1908–). Popular British leading actor with musical comedy experience; overcame short stature to become a useful stiff upper lip type in the forties, and later a character actor of some versatility.
□The Midshipmaid 32. Britannia of Billingsgate 33. The Ghost Camera 33. River Wolves 34. A Political Party 34. *Those Were the Days* 34. The Lash 34. Blind Justice 34. Doctor's Orders 34. Royal Cavalcade 35. Forever England 35. Charing Cross Road 35. Car of Dreams 35. First Offence 36. Tudor Rose 36. OHMS 37. The Green Cockatoo 37. Goodbye Mr Chips 39. Old Bill and Son 40. *Cottage to Let* 41. The Black Sheep of Whitehall 41. The Big Blockade 42. The Young Mr Pitt 42. *In Which We Serve* 42. We Dive at Dawn 43. This Happy Breed 44. *Waterloo Road* 44. *The Way to the Stars* 45. *Great Expectations* 46. So Well Remembered 47. *The October Man* 47. *Scott of the Antarctic* 48. *The History of Mr Polly* (& p) 49. The Rocking Horse Winner 50. Morning Departure 50. Mr Denning Drives North 51. The Gentle Gunman 52. The Long Memory 52. *Hobson's Choice* 54. The Colditz Story 54. The End of the Affair 54. Above Us the Waves 55. Escapade 55. It's Great to be Young 56. The Baby and the Battleship 56. War and Peace 56. Around the World in 80 Days 56. *Town On Trial* 57. Vicious Circle 57. Dunkirk 58. I Was Monty's Double 58. Ice Cold in Alex 58. *Tiger Bay* 59. Summer of the Seventeenth Doll 60. *Tunes of Glory* 60. *The Swiss Family Robinson* (US) 61. Flame in the Streets 61. The Singer Not the Song 61. The Valiant 62. Tiara Tahiti 62. The Chalk Garden 63. The Truth About Spring 64. Operation Crossbow 65. *Sky West and Crooked* (d only) 65. King Rat (US) 66. *The Wrong Box* 66. The Family Way 66. Africa Texas Style (US) 67. Chuka (US) 67. Oh What a Lovely War 69. Run Wild Run Free 69. Emma Hamilton (Ger.) 69. A Black Veil for Lisa 69. *Ryan's Daughter* (AA) 71. Dulcima 71. Young Winston 72. Lady Caroline Lamb 72. Oklahoma Crude 73. The Human Factor 76. Trial by Combat 76. The Devil's Advocate 77. The Big Sleep 78. The 39 Steps 78. Dr Strange (TV) 78. Zulu Dawn 79. Gandhi 82. Sahara 83. Masks of Death (TV) 84. A Woman of Substance (TV) 85. Murder with Mirrors (TV) 85. Who's That Girl? 87.
TV series: Dundee and the Culhane 67. Zoo Gang 73. Quatermass 79. Young at Heart 80–81.
❀ For being so thoroughly reliable. *Great Expectations.*

Mills, Juliet (1941–). British leading lady, daughter of John Mills and sister of Hayley. No My Darling Daughter 61. Twice Round the Daffodils 62. Nurse on Wheels 63. Carry on Jack 64. The Rare Breed (US) 66. Oh What a Lovely War 69. Avanti 72. QB VII (TV) 74, etc.
TV series: *Nanny and the Professor* 69–71.

Milner, Martin (1927–). American general purpose actor.
Life with Father (debut) 47. Our Very Own 50. I Want You 52. Pete Kelly's Blues 55. The Sweet Smell of Success 57. Marjorie Morningstar 58. Thirteen Ghosts 60. Sullivan's County 67. Valley of the Dolls 67, etc.
TV series: The Trouble With Father 53–55. The Life of Riley 56–57. Route 66 60–63. Adam 12 68–75. The Swiss Family Robinson 75.

Milner, Victor (1893–). Distinguished American cinematographer, with Paramount for many years.

Hiawatha 14. The Velvet Hand 18. Haunting Shadows 20. The Cave Girl 22. Thy Name is Woman 24. Lady of the Harem 26. Rolled Stockings 27. Wolf of Wall Street 29. *The Love Parade* 29. Monte Carlo 30. Daughter of the Dragon 31. *Trouble in Paradise* 32. Song of Songs 33. Design for Living 33. *Cleopatra* (AA) 34. The Crusades 35. *The General Died at Dawn* 36. The Plainsman 36. Artists and Models 37. The Buccaneer 39. Union Pacific 39. The Great Victor Herbert 39. Northwest Mounted Police 40. Christmas in July 40. The Lady Eve 41. The Monster and the Girl 41. The Palm Beach Story 42. Hostages 43. The Story of Dr Wassell 44. The Mummy's Curse 44. The Strange Love of Martha Ivers 46. The Other Love 47. Unfaithfully Yours 48. The Furies 50. September Affair 50. *Carrie* 51. Jeopardy 53, many others.

Milton, Billy (1905–). British light actor of the thirties, latterly in small parts. Also singer, pianist and composer.
Autobiography 1976: *Milton's Paradise Mislaid.*
Young Woodley 30. Three Men in a Boat 33. Someone at the Door 36. Aren't Men Beasts? 37. Yes Madam 39. Who Was Maddox 64. Hot Millions 68, etc.

Milton, Ernest (1890–1974). American-born Shakespearean actor with long theatrical history on both sides of the Atlantic. Few film appearances, in small parts.
A Wisp in the Woods 17. The Scarlet Pimpernel 34. Fiddlers Three 44.

Milton, Harry (1900–65). British leading man of thirties stage and screen.
□ The King's Cup 33. To Brighton with Gladys 33. King of the Ritz 33. Adventure Limited 34. Pagliacci 36.

Mimieux, Yvette (1939–). American leading lady signed up for films almost straight from college.
The Time Machine (debut) 60. Where the Boys Are 61. The Four Horsemen of the Apocalypse 62. *The Light in the Piazza* 62. The Wonderful World of the Brothers Grimm 63. Diamondhead 63. Joy in the Morning 65. Monkeys Go Home 66. The Caper of the Golden Bulls 67. Dark of the Sun 67. Three in an Attic 68. Black Noon (TV) 71. Skyjacked 72. The Neptune Factor 73. Hit Lady (& w) (TV) 74. Journey into Fear 75. Jackson County Jail 76. The Black Hole 78. Outside Chance (TV) 78. Berringer's 84, etc.
TV series: The Most Deadly Game 70.

Minciotti, Esther (1883–1962). Italian-American character actress, wife of Silvio Minciotti.
□House of Strangers 49. Shockproof 49. The Undercover Man 50. Strictly Dishonorable 51. *Marty* 55. Full of Life 56. The Wrong Man 57.

Minciotti, Silvio (1883–1961). Italian-American character actor.
House of Strangers 49. Deported 49. The Great Caruso 51. Clash by Night 52. Kiss Me Deadly 54. Marty 55, etc.

mine, all mine

? After the break-up of the big studios many actors formed their own production companies to avoid the middle men getting the profits. Of what actor's involvement is each of the following company names a tip-off?

1 Dena
2 Santana
3 Jalem
4 Batjac
5 Bryna
6 Curtwel
7 Grandon
8 Malpaso
9 Pennebaker
10 Portland
11 Artanis

And which producers own the following companies?

12 Shamley
13 Rastar
14 Arcola

Mine Own Executioner (GB 1947). Hailed as the first 'adult' film to come out of post-war Britain, this interesting melodrama from Nigel Balchin's novel had Burgess Meredith as a lay psychiatrist unsure how to handle a homicidal patient. Directed by Anthony Kimmins.

Mineo, Sal (1939–1976). Diminutive American actor, on Broadway as a child before going to Hollywood.
Six Bridges to Cross (debut) 55. Rebel without a Cause 55. Giant 56. Somebody Up There Likes Me 57. Tonka 58. The Gene Krupa Story 60. Exodus 60. Escape from Zahrain 62. Cheyenne Autumn 64. The Greatest Story Ever Told 65. Who Killed Teddy Bear? 66. Krakatoa 68. Escape from the Planet of the Apes 71, etc.

Miner, Allen H. (–). American director.
Ghost Town 55. The Ride Back 57. Black Patch (& p) 57. Chubasco 67, etc.

Minevitch, Borrah (1904–1955). Russian-American harmonica player who with his Rascals enlivened a few thirties musicals.
One in a Million 36. Love Under Fire 37. Rascals 38. Always in My Heart 42, etc.

miniaturization. Making people small is a theme obviously likely to appeal to the cinema's trick photographers. Characters were reduced by 'scientific' or magic means in *The Devil Doll, Dr Cyclops, The Incredible Shrinking Man,* and *Fantastic Voyage. Land of the Giants* showed the other side of the coin. Laurel and Hardy were miniaturized into their own children in *Brats*; other small humans were in *Darby O'Gill and the Little People, The Adventures of Mark Twain* and *The Bride of Frankenstein.*

Minnelli, Liza (1946–). American singer, daughter of Judy Garland; her gamine looks and vibrant voice made her a fashionable figure of the early seventies.
Biography 1974: *Liza*, by James Robert Parish.
□Charlie Bubbles 67. The Sterile Cuckoo 69. Tell Me that You Love Me Junie Moon 70. *Cabaret* (AA) 72. Lucky Lady 76. A Matter of Time 76. New York New York 77. Arthur 81.

†She first appeared as a baby in her mother's film *In the Good Old Summertime.*

¶ *L.M.:* Reality is something you rise above.

Minnelli, Vincente (1910–86). American director who earned a reputation as a stylist with MGM musicals but whose other output was very variable. Stage experience as art director and producer. The second of Judy Garland's husbands, and the father of Liza Minnelli.

Autobiography 1974: *I Remember It Well.*
□*Cabin in the Sky* 43. I Dood It 43. Ziegfeld Follies 44. *Meet Me in St Louis* 44. *The Clock* 44. Yolanda and the Thief 45. Undercurrent 46. The Pirate 47. Madame Bovary 49. *Father of the Bride* 50. Father's Little Dividend 51. *An American in Paris* 51. The Bad and the Beautiful 52. The Story of Three Loves (part) 52. *The Band Wagon* 53. The Long, Long Trailer 54. Brigadoon 54. Kismet 55. The Cobweb 55. Lust for Life 56. Tea and Sympathy 56. Designing Woman 57. *Gigi* (AA) 58. The Reluctant Debutante 58. Some Came Running 58. Home from the Hill 59. Bells Are Ringing 60. The Four Horsemen of the Apocalypse 62. Two Weeks in Another Town 62. The Courtship of Eddie's Father 63. Goodbye Charlie 65. The Sandpiper 65. On A Clear Day You Can See Forever 70. A Matter of Time 76.

'He believes implicitly in the power of his camera to turn trash into art, and corn into caviar.'—*Andrew Sarris, 1968*

Minney, R. J. (1895–1979). British producer and screenwriter, former journalist, in films since 1934.
AS WRITER: Clive of India 35. Dear Octopus 42. Carve Her Name with Pride 58, many others.
AS PRODUCER: Madonna of the Seven Moons 44. The Wicked Lady 45. The Final Test 53. Carve Her Name with Pride 58, etc.

Minter, George (1911–1966). British producer-distributor, in films from 1938. Made films for his company, Renown.
The Glass Mountain 48. Tom Brown's Schooldays 50. Pickwick Papers 52. The Rough and the Smooth 58, scores of others.

Minter, Mary Miles (1902–84) (Juliet Reilly). American silent screen heroine.
The Nurse 12. Barbara Frietchie 15. Environment 16. Lovely Mary 16. Melissa of the Hills 17. The Ghost of Rosy Taylor 17. Anne of Green Gables 19. Nurse Marjorie 20. Moonlight and Honeysuckle 21. South of Suva 22. The Trail of the Lonesome Pine 23. The Drums of Fate 23, many others.

Miracle in Milan (Italy 1951). Beguiling fantasy about a colony of shantytown poor led by a young idealist whose fervour gives him the power to work miracles and finally flies them all on broomsticks to another, better place. Directed by Vittorio de Sica with a strong element of René Clair; written by Cesare Zavattini and others; with special effects by Ned Mann. By its indirect methods the film managed to make as much protest about post-war conditions as its predecessor *Bicycle Thieves.*

The Miracle of Morgan's Creek (US 1943). An outrageous satirical farce, written and directed in whirlwind style by Preston Sturges, about a small-town girl who gets drunk at an army party, marries a soldier whose name she thinks is Ratskywatsky, can't find him, and has terrible trouble getting someone else to marry her without admitting she's pregnant; finally becomes a heroine by presenting the nation with sextuplets. Funny? Oddly enough, very, and fast enough to stop tastelessness from creeping in. Apart from the usual Sturges repertory company, the film is well served by Betty Hutton and Eddie Bracken, by Diana Lynn as the heroine's sharp young sister, and especially William Demarest as her father, the outraged Officer Kockenlocker. Prudes could console themselves with the thought that the film made quite a comment on the morals of the nation in time of war.

Miracle on 34th Street (US 1947). A charming, endearing piece of whimsy in Hollywood's best style, with Edmund Gwenn (AA) as a benevolent old fellow who may or may not be Santa Claus. Never nauseating in its abundance of goodwill towards men, the film moves smoothly to a hilarious courtroom climax in the Capra manner. Written and directed by George Seaton (AA) against pleasantly observed New York backgrounds.

Miranda (GB 1948). A mild British comedy about a mermaid (played by Glynis Johns) which had sufficient moments of hilarity to call for a sequel (*Mad about Men*) and a Hollywood imitation (*Mr Peabody and the Mermaid*).

Miranda, Carmen (1913–1955) (Maria de Carmo Miranda de Cunha). Portuguese singer, the 'Brazilian Bombshell'; always fantastically over-dressed and harshly made-up, yet emitting a force of personality which was hard to resist.
□Down Argentine Way (debut) 40. That Night in Rio 41. Weekend in Havana 41. Springtime in the Rockies 42. *The Gang's All Here* 43. Four Jills in a Jeep 44. Greenwich Village 44. Something for the Boys 44. Doll Face 46. If I'm Lucky 46. Copacabana 47. A Date with Judy 48. Nancy Goes to Rio 50. Scared Stiff 53.

Miranda, Isa (1905–1982) (Ines Isabella Sanpietro). Italian star actress. Occasional films.
Adventure in Diamonds (US) 38. Hotel Imperial (US) 40. La Ronde (Fr.) 50. Summertime (GB) 55. The Yellow Rolls Royce (GB) 64. The Shoes of the Fisherman 68. The Night Porter 74. Bambina 75.

The Mirisch Brothers: *Harold* (1907–1968), *Marvin* (1918–), *Walter* (1921–). American producers, founders in 1957 of the Mirisch company, one of the most successful independent production groups since the decline of the big studios. Formerly the two elder brothers had been exhibitors, the youngest a producer of cheap second features: the 'Bomba' series, etc.
Man of the West 58. The Magnificent Seven 60. West Side Story 61. Two for the See-Saw 62. The Great Escape 63. Toys in the Attic 63. The Satan Bug 65. The Russians Are Coming, The Russians Are Coming 66. What Did You Do in the War, Daddy? 66. Hawaii 66. The Fortune Cookie 66. In the Heat of the Night 68. The Organization 70. Midway 76. Same Time Next Year 78. Dracula 79. The Prisoner of Zenda 79, etc.
†Walter Mirisch was given the Jean Hersholt Humanitarian Award by the Motion Picture Academy in 1983.

Miroslava (1926–1955) (Miroslava Stern). Czech-born actress who became popular in Mexico.
Blood Wedding 46. The Small House 50. The Brave Bulls (US) 51. Three Happy Wives 52. Dreams of Glory 53. Stranger on Horseback (US) 55.

Mirren, Helen (1945–). British leading actress.
Herostratus 67. A Midsummer Night's Dream (TV) 68. Age of Consent 70. Savage Messiah 72. Miss Julie 73. O Lucky Man 73. Caligula 79. SOS Titanic 79. Hussy 80. The Fiendish Plot of Dr Fu Manchu 80. Excalibur 81. The Long Good Friday 81. Cal 84.

mirrors have a clear psychological fascination, and cameramen have frequently derived dramatic compositions from the use of them. Innumerable characters have talked to their reflections, and *The Man in the Mirror* changed places with his. *Dracula* and his kind cast no reflection; a switch on this was provided in *The Gorgon*, where looking at the monster turned one to stone, but looking at her through a mirror was OK. In *The Lady In the Lake* Robert Montgomery played the lead from the position of the camera lens, so the only time we saw him was when he looked in a mirror. Eric Portman in *Corridor of Mirrors* was surrounded by them: the hero of *The Student of Prague* shot his reflection in one. Then there was the magic mirror in *Snow White and the Seven Dwarfs*, which told the queen all she wanted to hear; and the more evil magic mirror in *Dead of Night*, which had belonged to a murderer and caused Ralph Michael when he looked in it to strangle his wife. Two-way mirrors are now familiar, especially since *From Russia With Love*; but they were used as long ago as 1946 in *The House on 92nd Street*. In *Orphée* a full-length mirror proved liquid to the touch and was the doorway to the other world. *The Lady from Shanghai* had a splendidly confusing finale in a mirror maze which was gradually shot to pieces; *Up Tight* made dramatic use of a distorting mirror arcade. The most-used mirror joke is that in which the glass is broken and a 'double' tries to take the place of the reflection: Max Linder performed it in 1919 in *Seven Years Bad Luck*, and it was superbly reprised by the Marx Brothers in *Duck Soup* 44, and by Abbott and Costello in *The Naughty Nineties* 45.

Les Misérables. Film versions of Victor Hugo's classic novel about escaped convict Jean Valjean were made in 1909 (US), 1913 (France), 1918 (US), 1922 (GB), 1925 (France), 1934 (France), 1935 (US, with Fredric March and Charles Laughton); 1946 (Italy); 1952 (US, with Michael Rennie and Robert Newton) and 1957 (France, with Jean Gabin and Bernard Blier). The recent TV series, *The Fugitive* and *Kung Fu*, acknowledge their indebtedness to the theme.

The Misfits (US 1961). A sad film, over-loaded with talent, notable chiefly for the last appearance of both Clark Gable and Marilyn Monroe, whose then husband Arthur Miller wrote the heavy-going script about cowboys on a savage hunt for wild mustangs. John Huston's direction was lethargic. This kind of pseudo-highbrow non-money-maker would in the old days have been vetoed at script stage by the studio's front office; failures like this are the price of independence.

misnomers

¶ A title has to appeal to the greatest possible number of people. Sometimes it loses its relevance in the progress; sometimes, as in metaphors like *Straw Dogs* and *A Clockwork Orange*, the film-maker is too arrogant to explain it. Here are one or two examples where the irrelevance is still traceable.

The Black Cat. Hardly any of the several films under this title have much to do with Poe's story, and although a black cat may have casually strolled across the scene it has had little bearing on the plot. In Britain the 1934 version was retitled *House of Doom*, which is a little more to the point of the story.

Son of Dracula, like many other horror films, soon proved to have an inapposite label: the protagonist is none other than the old Count himself in disguise. In *Bride of Frankenstein*, the title role is a minor one, played by Valerie Hobson; the real bride is that of the monster. In *Frankenstein Created Woman*, he doesn't: he merely performs some brain-switching. In *Abbott and Costello Meet Frankenstein*, the Baron doesn't appear at all: it's the monster they meet, and he has much less to do with the plot than Dracula or the Wolf Man.

Abbott and Costello were never careful about titles. In *Abbott and Costello Go to Mars*, they go to Venus. And *Abbott and Costello Meet the Killer, Boris Karloff* seems devised purely for equality of billing; it is doubly misleading, for not only is Boris Karloff not a killer, he does not even play a killer in the movie.

The original title *The Thin Man* referred to a minor character in the murder plot. As sequel followed sequel, and continuity had to be maintained, the tag gradually attached itself to the investigator played by William Powell.

The films of W. C. Fields were noted for the studied irrelevance of their titles, the crowning glory being *Never Give a Sucker an Even Break*. Laurel and Hardy were not far behind, as anyone knows who has tried to explain the relevance of *Hog Wild*, *You're Darn Tootin'*, *Be Big*, *Wrong Again*, *Double Whoopee* or *They Go Boom*. Woody Allen is plainly in the great tradition: when asked why he called his movie *Bananas*, he replied, 'because there are no bananas in it'.

The Glass Bottom Boat is seen in the first sequence of the film titled after it, but it is not essential to that sequence and has no relevance at all to the rest of the movie.

It Happened One Night. Which night? The film covers several, and none is central to the plot.

Big Deal at Dodge City is the British title for *Big Hand for a Little Lady*. It is not only less attractive but wildly inaccurate, as the action is clearly denoted as taking place in Laredo! It was the work of a title fiend operating in Warner's London office, who also turned *An American Dream* into the weirdly irrelevant *See You In Hell, Darling*.

Halls of Montezuma is set in the Pacific, and *To the Shores of Tripoli* never leaves a California training camp. All the titles tell you is that the characters are Marines, from whose marching song the labels are taken.

In *Northwest Passage*, the passage is barely

mentioned and never explored. MGM started to film Kenneth Roberts' historical novel in 1939. The script was too long, so they decided to make two films, the first to deal with the training of Rogers' Rangers and the second with their exploits. The second film was never made; the one that exists does have a subtitle, 'Part One: Rogers' Rangers'.

The Silencers, *Murderers Row*, *The Ambushers*. Any reader who can link these Matt Helm titles to their plots deserves a small prize.

Misraki, Paul (1908–). French composer.
Retour à l'Aube 38. Battement de Coeur 39. Manon 48. Confidential Report 55. Les Cousins 59. Alphaville 65. A Murder Is . . . 72, etc.

missionaries have not been popular cinema heroes: the most lauded real-life ones were David Livingstone in *Stanley and Livingstone* and Gladys Aylward in *The Inn of the Sixth Happiness*. Over-zealous ones appeared in *Zulu*, *Hawaii*, *Seven Women*, the various versions of *Rain*, and *The Missionary* itself.

Miss Julie. Strindberg's play about a nobleman's daughter who commits suicide because she loves a valet was filmed in 1912 (Sweden), 1921 (Germany) and 1947 (Argentina). The best-known version was written and directed by Alf Sjoberg in Sweden (1951) with Anita Bjork and Ulf Palme; in 1972 came a draggy British extension directed by Robin Phillips, with Helen Mirren and Donal McCann.

Mission to Moscow (US 1943). A remarkable semi-documentary made by Warners as a modern addendum to their biographical series. Based on US Ambassador Joseph Davies' account of his dealings with the Russians between 1936 and 1941, it was notable for its impersonations of living politicians: Churchill, Stalin, Roosevelt, etc. Walter Huston was ideally cast as Davies, and Michael Curtiz directed with his usual expertise. During the anti-communist era at the end of the forties, Jack Warner had to apologize for making it.

Mr Blandings Builds His Dream House (US 1948). A highly civilized and likeable American domestic comedy from the delightful book by Eric Hodgins; it shows Hollywood in the late forties getting its humour a little nearer to life and away from the studio. H. C. Potter directed with quiet aplomb, and no one would wish for a better husband, wife and friend of the family than Cary Grant, Myrna Loy and Melvyn Douglas as they doggedly build a house in Connecticut.

Mr Deeds Goes to Town (US 1936). The first of the big social comedies of the thirties, directed by Frank Capra (AA), demonstrating the victory of small-town innocence and good intentions over big city sophistication. Gary Cooper was perfectly cast as the naïve hero who refuses to be swindled out of a huge legacy even though he may be a little 'pixillated'. Robert Riskin wrote the script, which today seems slow-moving. In 1969 a TV series starring Monte Markham was based on the original script.

Mr Magoo. Myopic, bumbling cartoon character created by UPA in the early fifties and voiced by Jim Backus. He quickly became a bore, but some of the early shorts were outstandingly funny: *Barefaced Flatfoot, Fuddy Duddy Buddy, Spellbound Hound*, etc.

Mr Moto. A mild-mannered Japanese detective and master of disguise created by novelist John P. Marquand and played in nearly a dozen films by Peter Lorre: from *Think Fast Mr Moto* in 1937 to *Mr Moto Takes a Vacation* in 1939. In 1965 Henry Silva played the role in an unsuccessful second feature.

Mr Smith Goes to Washington (US 1939). Another of Frank Capra's thirties social comedies, a kind of 'Mr Deeds in Politics' with James Stewart as the idealistic young senator from Wisconsin who uproots the evil of Claude Rains. This is a beautifully made picture which judges all its effects exactly and remains consistently entertaining for over two hours. It was the last of its type: World War II made America's country cousins more sophisticated than Capra could have imagined. Among a superb cast were Jean Arthur, Guy Kibbee, Thomas Mitchell, H. B. Warner, Edward Arnold, Harry Carey, Eugene Pallette and William Demarest. Sidney Buchman wrote the script.

Mr T (1952–) (Lawrence Tero). Massive black American performer whose gold chains and Mohawk hairstyle became familiar in the TV series *The A-Team*.
Rocky III 82. D.C. Cab 83. The Toughest Man in the World (TV) 84.

Mr Wong (James Lee Wong, that is) was a Chinese detective thought up in 1938 by Monogram from stories by Hugh Riley, as a counter to Mr Moto who was doing so well for Fox. He was played five times in 1938–39 by the physically unsuitable Boris Karloff, in rather feeble second feature productions: in 1940 Keye Luke took over for *Phantom of Chinatown*.

Mrs Miniver (US 1942). Hollywood's emotional tribute to England's women in wartime was never a good film, but its sentimentality and its never-never picture of the English middle-class scene made it an enormous box office hit even though most people privately jibed at it afterwards and it had absolutely no reissue value. It now seems a quaint curiosity, with Greer Garson tending the roses while Walter Pidgeon dashes off to rescue some chaps from Dunkirk. William Wyler directed fluently in the circumstances; among the many contributors to the script were Arthur Wimperis and James Hilton, who should have known better. However, the film won Academy Awards for Garson, Wyler, the scriptwriters, and the photographer Joe Ruttenberg; it was also named best film. In 1950 a sequel was made showing Mrs Miniver dying of cancer, but not surprisingly *The Miniver Story* flopped.

Mrs Wiggs of the Cabbage Patch. The sentimental shanty-town novel by Alice Hegan Rice was filmed three times: in 1919 with Mary Carr, in 1934 with Pauline Lord, and in 1943 with Fay Bainter.

Mitchell, Cameron (1918–) (Cameron Mizell). American actor, ex-radio commentator and Broadway player.
They Were Expendable 45. Command Decision 48. *Death of a Salesman* 52. How to Marry a Millionaire 53. Love Me or Leave Me 55. Monkey On My Back 57. The Last of the Vikings 61. Unstoppable Man 61. Blood and Black Lace 65. Minnesota Clay (It.) 66. Hombre 67. Monster of the Wax Museum 67. Ride the Whirlwind 68. Buck and the Preacher 71. The Midnight Man 74. Viva Knievel 77. Silent Scream 79. Without Warning 80. Texas Lightning 81. My Favorite Year 82, etc.
TV series: The Beachcomber 60. High Chaparral 67–71. The Swiss Family Robinson 75.

Mitchell, Grant (1874–1957). American character actor, often seen as a worried father, lawyer or small-town politician.
Man to Man 31. Dinner at Eight 33. The Life of Emile Zola 37. New Moon 40. *The Grapes of Wrath* 40. Tobacco Road 41. *The Man Who Came to Dinner* 41. Orchestra Wives 42. Father is a Prince 43. Arsenic and Old Lace 44. Blondie's Anniversary 48, many others.

Mitchell, Guy (1925–) (Al Cernick). Boyish, stocky American singer with a brief career in films.
□Aaron Slick from Punkin Crick 52. Those Redheads from Seattle 53. Red Garters 54.
TV series: Whispering Smith 58.

Mitchell, James (1920–). American dancer and character actor.
Cobra Woman 44. Colorado Territory 49. Stars in My Crown 50. Deep in My Heart 54. Oklahoma 55, etc.

Mitchell, Julien (1884–1954). British stage character actor who made film debut as a crazed train driver in *The Last Journey* 36.
It's in the Air 37. The Drum 38. The Sea Hawk (US) 40. Hotel Reserve 44. Bedelia 46. Bonnie Prince Charlie 48. The Galloping Major 51. Hobson's Choice 54, etc.

Mitchell, Leslie (1905–). British commentator and broadcaster; the voice of British Movietone News from 1938; co-author of a 1946 book *The March of the Movies*.

Mitchell, Margaret (1900–1949). American author of the novel on which Hollywood's most famous film, *Gone with the Wind*, was based.

Mitchell, Millard (1900–1953). Nasal-voiced, rangy American character actor, in films from 1940.
Mr and Mrs Smith 40. Grand Central Murder 42. *A Double Life* 47. *A Foreign Affair* 48. Twelve O'Clock High 49. The Gunfighter 50. My Six Convicts 52. *Singin' in the Rain* 52. The Naked Spur 52. Here Come the Girls 53, etc.

Mitchell, Oswald (c. 1890–1949). British director.
Old Mother Riley 37. Danny Boy 41. The Dummy Talks 43. Loyal Heart 46. Black Memory 47. The Greed of William Hart 47. The Man From Yesterday 49, etc.

Mitchell, Thomas (1892–1962). Irish-American character actor of great versatility; could be tragic or comic, evil or humane.

Former reporter, Broadway star and playwright; in Hollywood from the mid-thirties.
☐Six Cylinder Love 23. Craig's Wife 36. Adventure in Manhattan 36. Theodora Goes Wild 36. Man of the People 37. When You're in Love 37. *Lost Horizon* 37. *The Hurricane* 37. I Promise to Pay 37. Make Way for Tomorrow 37. Love Honor and Behave 38. Trade Winds 38. Only Angels Have Wings 38. *Stagecoach* (AA) 39. Mr Smith Goes to Washington 39. The Hunchback of Notre Dame 39. Gone with the Wind 39. The Swiss Family Robinson 40. Three Cheers for the Irish 40. *Our Town* 40. The Long Voyage Home 40. Angels over Broadway 40. Flight from Destiny 41. Out of the Fog 41. Joan of Paris 42. Song of the Islands 42. This Above All 42. Moontide 42. Tales of Manhattan 42. *The Black Swan* 42. The Immortal Sergeant 43. The Outlaw 43. Bataan 43. *Flesh and Fantasy* 43. *The Sullivans* 44. Wilson 44. Dark Waters 44. Buffalo Bill 44. The Keys of the Kingdom 44. Within These Walls 45. Captain Eddie 45. Adventure 45. It's a Wonderful Life 46. Three Wise Fools 46. The Dark Mirror 46. High Barbaree 47. The Romance of Rosy Ridge 47. Silver River 48. *Alias Nick Beal* 49. The Big Wheel 49. Journey into Light 51. High Noon 52. Tumbleweed 53. The Secret of the Incas 54. Destry 54. Swell Guy 56. While the City Sleeps 56. Handle with Care 58. Too Young for Love (GB) 59. By Love Possessed 61. Pocketful of Miracles 61.
TV series: O. Henry Playhouse 56. Glencannon 58.
❁ For adding solid worth to a number of pictures which without him might not have had it.

Mitchell, Warren (1926–). British comedy character actor, mainly on TV, especially in series *Till Death Us Do Part.*
Tommy the Toreador 60. Postman's Knock 62. Where Has Poor Mickey Gone? 63. The Intelligence Men 65. Arrivederci Baby 66. *Till Death Us Do Part* 68. The Assassination Bureau 68. The Best House in London 69. All the Way Up 70. Innocent Bystanders 72. The Alf Garnett Saga 72. Stand Up Virgin Soldiers 77. The Chain 85. Foreign Body 87, many others.

Mitchell, Yvonne (1925–79) (Yvonne Joseph). British actress and playwright, on stage from 1940.
Autobiography 1957: *Actress.*
The Queen of Spades (film debut) 48. Turn the Key Softly 53. *The Divided Heart* 54. Yield to the Night 56. *Woman in a Dressing Gown* 57. The Passionate Summer 58. Tiger Bay 59. Sapphire 59. The Trials of Oscar Wilde 61. The Main Attraction 63. Genghis Khan 65. The Corpse 70. The Great Waltz 72. The Incredible Sarah 76, etc.

Mitchum, Christopher (–). American minor leading man, son of Robert Mitchum.

Mitchum, James (1938–). American actor, son of Robert Mitchum.
Thunder Road (debut) 58. The Young Guns of Texas 62. The Victors 63. The Tramplers 66. Ambush Bay 67. Moonrunners 75. Trackdown 76, etc.

Mitchum, Robert (1917–). Sleepy-eyed American leading man who has sometimes hidden his considerable talent behind a pretence of carelessness.
Biography 1975: *It Sure Beats Working* by Mike Tomkies.
☐Hoppy Serves a Writ 43. The Leather Burners 43. Border Patrol 43. Follow the Band 43. Colt Comrades 43. The Human Comedy 43. We've Never Been Licked 43. Beyond the Last Frontier 43. Bar 20 43. Doughboys in Ireland 43. Corvette K-225 43. Aerial Gunner 43. The Lone Star Trail 43. False Colors 43. The Dancing Masters 43. Riders of the Deadline 43. Gung Ho 43. Johnny Doesn't Live Here Any More 44. When Strangers Marry 44. The Girl Rush 44. Thirty Seconds Over Tokyo 44. Nevada 44. West of the Pecos 45. *The Story of G.I. Joe* 45. Till the End of Time 46. Undercurrent 46. The Locket 46. *Pursued* 47. *Crossfire* 47. Desire Me 47. *Out of the Past* 47. Rachel and the Stranger 48. Blood on the Moon 48. The Red Pony 49. *The Big Steal* 49. Holiday Affair 49. Where Danger Lives 50. My Forbidden Past 51. His Kind of Woman 51. The Racket 51. Macao 52. One Minute to Zero 52. The Lusty Men 52. Angel Face 53. White Witch Doctor 53. Second Chance 53. She Couldn't Say No 54. River of No Return 54. Track of the Cat 54. Not as a Stranger 55. *Night of the Hunter* 55. The Man with the Gun 55. Foreign Intrigue 56. Bandido 56. Heaven Knows Mr Allison 57. Fire Down Below 57. The Enemy Below 57. Thunder Road 58. The Hunters 58. The Angry Hills 59. The Wonderful Country 59. Home from the Hill 60. A Terrible Beauty 60. The Grass is Greener 60. *The Sundowners* 60. The Last Time I Saw Archie 61. Cape Fear 62. The Longest Day 62. Two for the Seesaw 62. The

List of Adrian Messenger 63. Rampage 63. Man in the Middle 64. What a Way to Go 64. Mr Moses 65. The Way West 67. El Dorado 67. Anzio 68. Villa Rides 68. Five Card Stud 68. Secret Ceremony 68. Young Billy Young 69. The Good Guys and the Bad Guys 69. *Ryan's Daughter* 71. Going Home 71. The Wrath of God 72. The Friends of Eddie Coyle 73. The Yakuza 75. *Farewell My Lovely* 75. Midway 76. The Last Tycoon 76. The Amsterdam Kill 77. The Big Sleep 78. Matilda 78. Breakthrough 78. Nightkill 79. One Shoe Makes It Murder (TV) 82. That Championship Season 82. *The Winds of War* (TV) 83. Killer in the Family (TV) 83. The Ambassador 84. Maria's Lovers 84. Promises to Keep (TV) 85. The Hearst and Davies Affair (TV) 85. Reunion at Fairborough (TV) 85. Thompson's Last Run (TV) 86. War and Remembrance (TV) 87.

❀ For triumphing by sheer force of personality over scores of inferior films; and for enhancing a few good ones. *Farewell My Lovely*.

¶ Robert Mitchum and his sleepy eyes have hypnotized audiences for over thirty years, through bad pictures, bad notices and narcotics cases. Just now and then he has been allowed to prove himself an excellent actor; and he has always been a commanding personality, though his attitude to himself and his career is presumably exemplified by the title of his biography—*It Sure Beats Working*. He claims:

> I've survived because I work cheap and don't take up too much time.

And he adds:

> Movies bore me, especially my own.

He is not even proud of his physique:

> People think I have an interesting walk. Hell, I'm just trying to hold my gut in.

Or his fans:

> You know what the average Robert Mitchum fan is? He's full of warts and dandruff and he's probably got a hernia too, but he sees me up there on the screen and he thinks if that bum can make it, I can be president.

He disclaims ambition:

> I started out to be a sex fiend but I couldn't pass the physical.

He hated his early films:

> I kept the same suit for six years—and the same dialogue. We just changed the title of the picture and the leading lady.

Then he had a stroke of luck:

> I came back from the war and ugly heroes were in.

Even so he thinks films are a joke:

> I gave up being serious about making pictures around the time I made a film with Greer Garson and she took a hundred and twenty-five takes to say no.

He is unashamed of his lapses:

> The only difference between me and my fellow actors is that I've spent more time in jail.

He does have an ambition, to spend every cent he's got:

> When I drop dead and they rush to the drawer, there's going to be nothing in it but a note saying 'Later'.

And when asked why in his mid-sixties he took on the arduous task of starring in an 18-hour mini-series, *The Winds of War*, he answered:

> It promised a year of free lunches.

He is loved by the press, for he doesn't care what they write about him:

> They're all true—booze, brawls, broads, all true. Make up some more if you want to.

And he remains self-deprecating to the last:

> Young actors love me. They think if that big slob can make it, there's a chance for us.

Mitry, Jean (1907–). French director of experimental shorts; also critic.
Pacific 231 49. Images Pour Debussy 51. Symphonie Mecanique 55, etc.

Mix, Tom (1880–1940). A US Marshal (by his own unconfirmed account) who turned actor and starred in over four hundred low-budget westerns.
Biographies: 1972, *The Life and Legend of Tom Mix* by Paul E. Mix. 1957, *The Fabulous Tom Mix* by Olive Stokes.
The Ranch Life in the Great Southwest 10. Child of the Prairie 13. Cupid's Round-Up 18. Tom Mix in Arabia 22. North of Hudson Bay 24. The Last Trail 27. Destry Rides Again 27. Painted Post 28. My Pal the King 32. The Terror Trail 33. The Fourth Horseman 33, etc.

† Mix was noted for wearing his white suit and boots even to fashionable parties.

¶ *Robert Sherwood:* They say he rides like part of the horse, but they don't say what part.

Adela Rogers St John: He was as elegant on a horse as Fred Astaire on a dance floor, and that's the elegantest there is.

Mizoguchi, Kenji (1898–1956). Japanese director, former actor. Directed from 1923, though few of his films were seen in the West. A Paper Doll's Whisper of Spring 25. The Gorge Between Love and Hate 32. The Story of the Last Chrysanthemums 39. Woman of Osaka 40. The Forty-Nine Ronin 42. The Life of O'Haru 52. *Ugetsu Monogatari* 52. Street of Shame 56, many others.

Mobley, Mary Ann (1939–). American leading lady, former 'Miss America'.
Girl Happy 65. Three on a Couch 66. For Singles Only 68, etc.

Moby Dick. Herman Melville's allegorical novel about the pursuit by an obsessed sea captain of a white whale, has been seen on the screen in at least three versions, all American. 1. *The Sea Beast* 26, directed by Millard Webb, with John Barrymore, Dolores Costello and George O'Hara. 2. *Moby Dick* 30, directed by Lloyd Bacon, with John Barrymore, Joan Bennett and Lloyd Hughes. 3. *Moby Dick* 56, directed by John Huston, with Gregory Peck, Richard Basehart and no feminine lead.

Mockridge, Cyril (1896–1979). British-born composer, in America from 1921, films from 1932.
The Littlest Rebel 35. Johnny Apollo 40. Happy Land 43. The Sullivans 44. My Darling Clementine 46. How to Marry a Millionaire 53. Many Rivers to Cross 55. Flaming Star 60. Donovan's Reef 63, many others.

Mocky, Jean-Pierre (1929–) (Jean Mokiejeswki). French director.
Un Couple 60. Snobs 62. Les Vierges 63. La Bourse et la Vie 65. Les Compagnons de la Marguerite 67, etc.

Modern Times (US 1936). The film in which Chaplin's voice was first heard—though only in a gibberish song. Basically this is a dated—almost period—sociological comedy about how to be happy though poor in the machine age. Best to forget the propaganda and see it as a series of gags, impeccably timed and edited. As usual, he wrote (words and music), directed, produced and starred; Paulette Goddard played the waif.

Modine, Matthew (1959–). American juvenile lead of the eighties.
Baby it's You 82. Private School 83. Vision Quest 84. Hotel New Hampshire 84. Birdy 85. Mrs Soffel 85. Full Metal Jacket 87. Orphans 87.

Modley, Albert (1891–1979). British north country comedian who appeared in a few films including the 1951 version of *Up for the Cup*.

Modot, Gaston (1887–1970). French character actor.
Fievre 21. L'Age d'Or 30. Sous Les Toits de Paris 30. La Grande Illusion 37. Pepe le Moko 37. La Regle du Jeu 39. Les Enfants du Paradis 44. French Can Can 55. Le Testament du Docteur Cordelier 59, many others.

Moffatt, Graham (1919–1965). British actor, fondly remembered as the impertinent fat boy of the Will Hay comedies: *Oh Mr Porter* 38. *Ask a Policeman* 39. Where's That Fire 40, etc. Other films include A Cup of Kindness (debut) 34. Dr Syn 38. I Thank You 41. I Know Where I'm Going 45, many others. Retired to keep a pub, but made very occasional appearances: The Second Mate 50. Inn for Trouble 59. Eighty Thousand Suspects 63.

Moffett, Sharyn (1936–). American child actress of the forties.
My Pal Wolf 44. The Body Snatcher 45. Child of Divorce 47. The Judge Steps Out 47. Mr Blandings Builds His Dream House 48. Girls Never Tell 51, etc.

moguls. The name given half-affectionately to the men who ran Hollywood in the golden days of the studios: Mayer, Thalberg, Selznick, Goldwyn, Warner, Zanuck, Zukor, Cohn, etc. The best capsule guide to them is Philip French's *The Movie Moguls* (1970).

¶ They were monsters and pirates and bastards right down to the bottom of their feet but they loved movies. Some of the jerks running the business today don't even have faces.—*Richard Brooks, c. 1970*
I was impressed by the moral potentialities of the screen.—*Adolph Zukor*
Those of us who became film producers hailed from all sorts of occupations – furriers, magicians, butchers, boilermakers—and for this reason highbrows have often poked fun at us. Yet one thing is certain: every man who succeeded was a born showman. And once in the show business he was never happy out of it.—*Adolph Zukor*
There's nothing wrong with Hollywood that six first-class funerals couldn't cure.—*Anon, 1930*
Don't make these pictures any better. Just keep them the way they are.—*Louis B. Mayer on the Hardy Family series*

We should all make a killing in this business. There's so much money in the pot.—*Irving Thalberg*
It's better than being a pimp.—*Harry Cohn*

Moguy, Leonide (1899–1976) (L. Maguilevsky). Russian newsreel producer, later in France and US as director.
Prison Without Bars 38. The Night Is Ending 43. Action in Arabia 44. Whistle Stop 46. Tomorrow Is Too Late 50. Les Enfants de l'Amour 54, etc.

Mohner, Carl (1921–). Austrian actor in films from 1949.
Rififi 55. He Who Must Die 56. The Key 58. Camp on Blood Island 58. The Kitchen 61. Hell is Empty 67. Callan 74, etc.

Mohr, Gerald (1914–1968). Suave American actor, in films from 1941; played the 'Lone Wolf', a gentleman crook, in a mid-forties series.
The Monster and the Girl 41. Ten Tall Men 51. Detective Story 53. The Eddie Cantor Story 53. Angry Red Planet 59. Funny Girl 68, many others.
TV series: Foreign Intrigue 56.

Mohr, Hal (1894–1974). American cinematographer, in Hollywood from 1915.
The Last Night of the Barbary Coast 13. Money 14. The Deceiver 21. Bag and Baggage 23. The Monster 24. The High Hand 26. The Jazz Singer 27. The Last Warning 28. Broadway 29. Big Boy 30. Woman of Experience 31. A Woman Commands 32. State Fair 33. David Harum 34. *A Midsummer Night's Dream* (AA) 35. *Captain Blood* 35. *Green Pastures* 36. The Walking Dead 36. I Met My Love Again 38. Rio 39. *Destry Rides Again* 39. When the Daltons Rode 40. International Lady 41. Twin Beds 42. Phantom of the Opera (AA) 43. Ladies Courageous 44. Salome Where She Danced 45. Because of Him 46. The Lost Moment 47. Another Part of the Forest 48. Johnny Holiday 49. Woman on the Run 50. The Big Night 51. The Fourposter 52. *The Wild One* 54. The Boss 56. Baby Face Nelson 57. The Gun Runners 58. The Last Voyage 60. The Man from the Diner's Club 63. Bamboo Saucer 68, many others.
†Mohr was interviewed in *Behind the Camera*.

Molander, Gustaf (1888–1973). Veteran Swedish director, former actor and writer (including *Sir Arne's Treasure* 19). Directing since 1922, but few of his films have been seen abroad.
Sin 28. Intermezzo 36. A Woman's Face 38. Woman Without a Face 47. Sir Arne's Treasure (remake) 55, many others.

Molinaro, Edouard (1928–). French director.
Evidence in Concrete (Le Dos au Mur) 57. Girls for the Summer 60. A Ravishing Idiot 63. The Gentle Art of Seduction 64. Pain in the A . . . 74. La Cage aux Folles 78. La Cage aux Folles II 80. Sunday Lovers 80, etc.

Molnar, Ferenc (1878–1952). Hungarian dramatist whose comedies were the basis of many Hollywood films including *The Shop Around the Corner, One Two Three, The Guardsman, The Swan, A Breath of Scandal, Double Wedding* and *Liliom*.

Monash, Paul (1917–). American producer, former TV writer.
Peyton Place (TV series) 64–69. Butch Cassidy and the Sundance Kid 69. Slaughterhouse Five 72. The Friends of Eddie Coyle (& w) 74. The Front Page 74. Carrie 76, etc.

Mondo Cane (Italy 1961). The first of many so-called documentaries consisting of a ramshackle collection of true incidents showing humanity at its most ignorant and depraved, mostly involving sex, sadism or paranoia. Director Jacopetti meanwhile found the business very profitable, and after watching his many imitators, produced in 1965 his *Mondo Cane 2*, showing that the field of degradation is far from exhausted.

Mondy, Pierre (1925–) (Pierre Cuq). French actor.
Rendezvous de Juillet 49. Sans Laisser d'Adresse 50. Les Louves 57. Austerlitz (as Napoleon) 60. Bebert et l'Omnibus 63. Retour en Face 80, etc.

Monicelli, Mario (1915–). Italian director.
Cops and Robbers (co-d) 51. Persons Unknown 58. Boccaccio 70 (part) 61. The Organizer 63. Casanova 70 66. Girl With a Pistol 69. Mortadella 71. Romanzo Poplare 75. Caro Michele 76. Travels with Anita 79, etc.

The Monkees sprang to fame in an American TV series of that title 66–67. They were a pop quartet deliberately recruited by Screen Gems to emulate the Beatles in crazy comedy with music; their ensuing popularity surprised not only themselves but their sponsors, and in 1969 they made a movie called *Head*. Individually they were: **Peter Tork** (1942–) (Peter Torkelson); **Mike Nesmith** (1943–); **Micky Dolenz** (1945–), who is the son of George Dolenz and previously starred in the TV series *Circus Boy* 56–57; **Davy Jones** (1944–), the only Britisher in the group.

Monkhouse, Bob (1928–). British comedian of TV, radio and occasional films. Carry On Sergeant 58. Dentist in the Chair 59. Weekend with Lulu 61. She'll Have to Go 61. The Bliss of Mrs Blossom 68, etc.
TV series: Mad Movies.

monks in films have usually been caricatures of the Friar Tuck type; Tuck himself turned up, personified by Eugene Pallette or Alexander Gauge, in most of the versions of Robin Hood (qv). The funny side of monastery life was presented in *Crooks in Cloisters*, while milder humour came from Edward G. Robinson's conversion to the simple life in *Brother Orchid*. Serious crises of the monastic spirit have been treated in two American films, *The Garden of Allah* and *The First Legion*; but on the whole monks have appealed less than priests to film-makers in search of an emotional subject.
See also: *nuns; priests; churches.*

Monogram Pictures: see *Allied Artists.*

Monroe, Marilyn (1926–1962) (Norma Jean Baker or Mortenson). American leading lady, a former model whose classic rags-to-riches story was built on a super-sexy image which quickly tarnished, leaving her a frustrated, neurotic and tragic victim of the Hollywood which created her. The pity was that she had real talent as well as sex appeal. *Marilyn*, a compilation feature, was released after her death. Several biographies have been published. In 1976 Misty Rowe played her in *Goodbye Norma Jean.*
□Dangerous Years 48. Ladies of the Chorus 48. Love Happy 50. A Ticket to Tomahawk 50. *The Asphalt Jungle* 50. All About Eve 50. The Fireball 50. Right Cross 50. Home Town Story 51. As Young as You Feel 51. Love Nest 51. Let's Make It Legal 51. We're Not Married 52. Clash by Night 52. Full House 52. Monkey Business 52. Don't Bother to Knock 52. *Niagara* (here the build-up really started) 52. *Gentlemen Prefer Blondes* 53. *How to Marry a Millionaire* 53. River of No Return 54. There's No Business Like Show Business 54. *The Seven-Year Itch* 55. Bus Stop 56. The Prince and the Showgirl (GB) 57. *Some Like It Hot* 59. Let's Make Love 60. The Misfits 61.
❁ For personifying the Hollywood cliché, the star created and destroyed by the system. *How to Marry a Millionaire.*

¶ A sex symbol becomes a thing. I hate being a thing.

The tragedy of Marilyn Monroe was such that she has inspired more books of reminiscence and analysis than any other star. Her problem was, oddly enough, best expressed in an earlier decade by Clara Bow:

> Being a sex symbol is a heavy load to carry, especially when one is tired, hurt and bewildered.

Monroe knew her own limitations:

> To put it bluntly, I seem to be a whole superstructure with no foundation. But I'm working on the foundation.

What she meant by that was:

> The best way for me to prove myself as a person is to prove myself as an actress.

She was uncertain whether she would ever achieve this aim. She said once:

> I enjoy acting when you really hit it right.

But she seldom felt she did. In her search for meaning she married playwright Arthur Miller, and the headline was:

> EGGHEAD WEDS HOURGLASS

It finally failed to work although he was kind to her with press comments such as:

> Her beauty shines because the spirit is forever showing itself.

Not that she was lacking in moral supporters; even unlikely people such as Edith Sitwell acclaimed her:

> She knows the world, but this knowledge has not lowered her great and benevolent dignity; its darkness has not dimmed her goodness.

She settled for a flip image as expressed in her lively encounters with the press:

> Didn't you have anything on?
> —I had the radio on.
>
> Sex is part of nature, and I go along with nature.
>
> Do you wear falsies?
> —Those who know me better, know better.

The contradictions within herself finally killed her, and the obituaries were many and varied:

> You don't have to hold an inquest to find out who killed Marilyn Monroe. Those bastards in the big executive chairs killed her—*Henry Hathaway*
>
> If she was simple it would have been easy to help her. She could have made it with a little luck.—*Arthur Miller*

A professional amateur.—*Laurence Olivier*
Directing her was like directing Lassie. You needed fourteen takes to get each one of them right.—*Otto Preminger*
Anyone can remember lines, but it takes a real artist to come on the set and not know her lines and give the performance she did.—*Billy Wilder*
I have never met anyone as utterly mean as Marilyn Monroe. Nor as utterly fabulous on the screen, and that includes Garbo.—*Billy Wilder*
She has breasts like granite and a brain like Swiss cheese, full of holes.
Extracting a performance from her is like pulling teeth.—*Billy Wilder*
As near genius as any actress I ever knew.—*Joshua Logan*
She was born afraid. She never got over it. In the end fear killed her.—*Pete Martin*

'There's a broad with her future behind her.'—*Constance Bennett*

'She had curves in places other women don't even have places.'—*Cybill Shepherd*

'She's the girl you'd like to double-cross your wife with.'—*Jean Negulesco*

'An arrogant little tail-twitcher who learned to throw sex in your face.'—*Nunnally Johnson*

'A vacuum with nipples.'—*Otto Preminger*

'Popular opinion, and all that goes to promote it, is a horrible unsteady conveyance for life, and she was exploited beyond anyone's means.'—*Laurence Olivier*

Monroe, Vaughan (1911–1973). American bandleader who unexpectedly appeared as hero of a few westerns.
Meet the People 44. Carnegie Hall 47. Singing Guns 50. The Toughest Man in Arizona 52, etc.

Monsarrat, Nicholas (1910–1979). British adventure novelist whose naval adventures, *The Cruel Sea* and *The Ship That Died of Shame*, were filmed by Ealing.

Monsieur Beaucaire. Booth Tarkington's light novel about a barber who impersonates the King of France was filmed as a straight romantic vehicle for Rudolph Valentino and Bebe Daniels in 1924, directed by Sidney Olcott. In 1946 Bob Hope had his way with it in a version directed by George Marshall.

Monsieur Hulot's Holiday (France 1952). Written and directed by Jacques Tati, this comedy in which he also stars as an accident-prone do-gooder on a seaside holiday will probably be remembered as his best. It has no story, just a collection of tiny incidents: many are hilarious, but some so untidily executed as to make one suspect that Tati would be even more marvellous under someone else's direction.

monster animals. The 1924 version of *The Lost World* set a persisting fashion for giant animals operated by technical ingenuity. The supreme achievement in the genre was of course *King Kong*, who carried on in *Son of Kong* and (more or less) in *Mighty Joe Young*. Dinosaurs and other creatures which once did exist were featured in such films as *Man and His Mate* (in which what we saw were actually magnified lizards), *The Land Unknown, Dinosaurus, The Lost Continent, Gorgo, The Beast from Twenty Thousand Fathoms, Godzilla, Rodan, One Million Years B.C.* and *When Dinosaurs Ruled the Earth*. Other films concentrated on normal species which had been giantized by radiation or some other accident of science: *The Black Scorpion, Them, The Deadly Mantis, The Giant Claw, Tarantula, Mysterious Island, Bug, Night of the Lepus, Squirm, Jaws, Food of the Gods*. More fanciful giant animals were created for *Jason and the Argonauts, Jack the Giant Killer* and *The Seventh Voyage of Sinbad*. The 1976 *King Kong* remake mainly featured a man in a gorilla suit, and the fashion of the late seventies and early eighties was for ordinary animals which turned savage, such as *Alligator*, *Piranha* and *Cujo*.

monsters

? What monster:

1 Gobbled up Cecil Kellaway in a bathysphere?
2 Tickled Fay Wray's tummy?
3 Hanged Dwight Frye?
4 Turned into Matt Dillon?
5 Had Claude Rains for a father?
6 Fell in love with Zita Johann?
7 Abducted Anne Bancroft?
8 Obeyed Roddy Macdowall?
9 Electrocuted Lionel Atwill?
10 Had lunch with Ernest Thesiger?
11 Met his doom in Westminster Abbey?
12 Spelt his name backwards?
13 Shot at his own reflection in a room full of mirrors?
14 Sought a flower called *Mariphasa Lupina*?
15 Was played by Carol Reed's nephew?
16 Lived on Metaluna?
17 Menaced Jane Randolph in a swimming bath?

18 Lost her head to Christopher Lee?
19 Was cured by Onslow Stevens?
20 Caught up with Niall MacGinnis on a railway line?

montage. In the most general sense, the whole art of editing or assembling scenes into the finished film. Specifically, 'a montage' is understood as an impressionistic sequence of short dissolve-shots either bridging a time gap, setting a situation or showing the background to the main story. Classic montages which come to mind are in *The Battleship Potemkin, The Roaring Twenties* and *Citizen Kane*.

Montagu, Ivor (1904–84). British producer, director and film theorist. In films from 1925; was associate of Hitchcock on several of his mid-thirties thrillers; produced *Behind the Spanish Lines* 38, *Spanish ABC* 38, etc.; co-authored many screenplays including *Scott of the Antarctic* 48. Last publication *Film World* 64.
Autobiography 1970: *The Youngest Son*.

Montague, Lee (1927–). British actor, mainly seen on stage and TV.
Savage Innocents 59. The Secret Partner 60. Billy Budd 61. The Horse without a Head 62. You Must Be Joking 65. The Best Pair of Legs in the Business 72. Mahler 74. Jesus of Nazareth (TV) 77. Holocaust (TV) 78. The Legacy 78. The Brass Target 78. Sakharov (TV) 84, etc.

Montalban, Ricardo (1920–). Mexican leading man in Hollywood.
Fiesta 47. The Kissing Bandit 49. Border Incident 49. *Battleground* 50. Right Cross 50. Across the Wide Missouri 51. My Man and I 52. Sombrero 53. Latin Lovers 54. A Life in the Balance 55. *Sayonara* 57. Adventures of a Young Man 62. Love Is a Ball 63. The Money Trap 65. Madame X 66. Sol Madrid 68. Blue 68. *Sweet Charity* 68. Conquest of the Planet of the Apes 72. Desperate Mission (TV) 72. Joe Panther 76. How the West was Won (TV) 77. Joe Panther 78. *Star Trek: The Wrath of Khan* 82, others.
TV series: Fantasy Island 77–.

Montana, Bull (1887–1950) (Luigi Montagna). Italian-American strong man who played ape men and heavies in the twenties.
Brass Buttons 19. Go and Get It 20. Painted People 23. The Lost World 24. Son of the Sheik 26. Good Morning Judge 28. Show of Shows 29. Tiger Rose 29, etc.

Montand, Yves (1921–) (Ivo Levi). French actor-singer in films from the mid-forties; married to Simone Signoret.
Les Portes de la Nuit 46. Lost Property 50. *The Wages of Fear* 53. The Heroes Are Tired 55. The Witches of Salem 56. *Let's Make Love* (US) 60. Sanctuary (US) 61. My Geisha (US) 62. The Sleeping Car Murders 65. The War Is Over 66. Is Paris Burning? 66. Grand Prix 67. Vivre Pour Vivre 67. 'Z' 68. On a Clear Day You Can See Forever 69. L'Aveu 70. The Red Circle 70. The Son 72. Le Sauvage 76. Clair de Femme 79. Garçon! 83, *Jean de Florette* 86. *Manon des Sources* 86, etc.

Montes, Lola (1818–1861) (Maria Dolores Eliza Gilbert). Scottish-Creole dancer who became world-famous as the mistress of King Ludwig I of Bavaria. Max Ophuls made a film about her in 1955, with Martine Carol, and Yvonne de Carlo played her in *Black Bart* 48. There was also a Spanish biopic in 1944 with Conchita Montenegro and Florinda Bolkan played her in *Royal Flash*.

Montez, Maria (1919–1951) (Maria de Santo Silas). Exotic Hollywood leading lady mainly seen in hokum adventures.
The Invisible Woman (debut) 41. South of Tahiti 41. The Mystery of Marie Roget 42. *Arabian Nights* 42. White Savage 43. *Cobra Woman* 44. Ali Baba and the Forty Thieves 44. Gypsy Wildcat 44. Sudan 45. Tangier 46. Pirates of Monterey 47. The Exile 47. Siren of Atlantis 48. The Thief of Venice 51, etc.

¶ *M.M.:* When I see myself on the screen, I am so beautiful I jump for joy.

Montgomery, Belinda (1950–). American leading lady.
The Todd Killings 70. Women in Chains (TV) 72. Letters from Three Lovers (TV) 73. The Other Side of the Mountain 75. Breaking Point 76. Blackout 77. The Other Side of the Mountain Part Two 78, etc.

Montgomery, Bernard (1887–1976). British Field Marshal who through his waspish personality became famous, especially when he commanded the victorious Eighth Army in North Africa in 1942. He has been best played on TV by Ian Richardson, especially in *Ike*. Trevor Reid played him in *The Longest Day* and Michael Bates in *Patton*. An exciting and amusing film of 1958, *I Was Monty's Double*, featured his wartime stand-in Clifton James.

Montgomery, Douglass (1907–1966) (Robert Douglass Montgomery). Canadian leading man with stage experience; once known as *Kent Douglass.*
□Paid 30. Daybreak 31. Five and Ten 31. *Waterloo Bridge* 31. A House Divided 31. *Little Women* 33. Eight Girls in a Boat 34. Little Man What Now 34. Music in the Air 34. The Mystery of Edwin Drood 35. Lady Tubbs 35. Harmony Lane 35. Everything Is Thunder 36. Tropical Trouble 36. Counsel for Crime 37. Life Begins with Love 37. *The Cat and the Canary* 39. *The Way to the Stars* 45. Woman to Woman 46. When in Rome 47. Forbidden 48.

Montgomery, Elizabeth (1933–). Pert American leading lady, daughter of Robert Montgomery; most familiar as the witch-wife of the TV series *Bewitched* 64–71.
The Court Martial of Billy Mitchell 55. Who's Been Sleeping in My Bed? 63. Johnny Cool 63. The Victim (TV) 72. A Case of Rape (TV) 74. The Legend of Lizzie Borden (TV) 75. Dark Victory (TV) 76. A Killing Affair (TV) 77. The Awakening Land (TV) 78. Jennifer: A Woman's Story (TV) 79. Act of Violence (TV) 80. Belle Starr (TV) 81. When the Circus Came to Town (TV) 82. The Rules of Marriage (TV) 83. Second Sight (TV) 85.

Montgomery, George (1916–) (George M. Letz). Genial American leading man, mostly in low-budgeters; former boxer and stunt man who later had ambitions to direct.
The Cisco Kid and the Lady 39. Young People 40. *Roxie Hart* 42. *Ten Gentlemen from West Point* 42. Orchestra Wives 42. Coney Island 43. Bomber's Moon 43. Three Little Girls in Blue 46. The Brasher Doubloon 47. Lulu Belle 48. Dakota Lil 50. Sword of Monte Cristo 51. The Texas Rangers 51. Fort Ti 53. Street of Sinners 55. Huk 56. Black Patch 57. Watusi 59. The Steel Claw (& d) 61. Samar (& d) 62. From Hell to Borneo (& d) 64. Battle of the Bulge 65. Hallucination Generation 66. Huntsville 67, many others.
TV series: Cimarron City 58.

Montgomery, Lee Harcourt (–). American child actor of the seventies.
Million Dollar Duck 71. The Harness (TV) 71. Ben 72. The Savage Is Loose 74. A Cry in the Wilderness (TV) 74. Burnt Offerings 76. Baker's Hawk 76. Dead of Night (TV) 77. True Grit: A Further Adventure (TV) 78, etc.

Montgomery, Robert (1904–1981) (Henry Montgomery). Smooth, smart American leading man of the thirties; later became a director, then forsook show business for politics.
□So This is College 29. Untamed 29. Three Live Ghosts 29. The Single Standard 29. Their Own Desire 29. Free and Easy 30. The Divorcee 30. The Big House 30. Our Blushing Brides 30. Sins of the Children 30. Love in the Rough 30. War Nurse 30. The Easiest Way 31. Strangers May Kiss 31. Inspiration 31. Shipmates 31. The Man in Possession 31. Private Lives 31. Lovers Courageous 31. But the Flesh is Weak 32. Letty Lynton 32. Blondie of the Follies 32. Faithless 32. Hell Below 33. Made on Broadway 33. *When Ladies Meet* 33. Night Flight 33. Another Language 33. Fugitive Lovers 34. Riptide 34. The Mystery of Mr X 34. Hideout 34. Forsaking All Others 35. Vanessa, Her Love Story 35. Biography of a Bachelor Girl 35. No More Ladies 35. Petticoat Fever 36. Trouble for Two 36. Piccadilly Jim 36. The Last of Mrs Cheyney 37. *Night Must Fall* 37. Ever Since Eve 37. Live Love and Learn 37. The First Hundred Years 37. *Yellow Jack* 38. Three Loves has Nancy 38. Fast and Loose 39. The Earl of Chicago 40. *Busman's Honeymoon* (GB) (as Lord Peter Wimsey) 40. Rage in Heaven 41. Mr and Mrs Smith 41. *Here Comes Mr Jordan* 41. Unfinished Business 41. They Were Expendable 45. *The Lady in the Lake* (as Philip Marlowe) (& d) 46. Ride the Pink Horse (& d) 47. The Saxon Charm 48. June Bride 48. Once More My Darling (& d) 49. Your Witness (GB) 50. The Gallant Hours (d only) 60.
TV series: Robert Montgomery Presents 50–56.

¶ *R.M.:* If you are lucky enough to be a success, by all means enjoy the applause and the adulation of the public. But never, never believe it.

Montiel, Sarita (1927–) (Maria Antonia Abad). Spanish leading lady in Mexican and American films.
Vera Cruz 54. Serenade 56. She Gods of Shark Reef 57. Run of the Arrow 57, etc.

Monty Python. An ensemble name for a group of British nonsense comedians who had much influence on television comedy of the sixties and seventies. They include John Cleese, Michael Palin, Terry Gilliam, Eric Idle and Graham Chapman.
□And Now for Something Completely

Different 71. *Monty Python and the Holy Grail* 75. *The Life of Brian* 79. Monty Python's Meaning of Life 83.

Moody, Ron (1924–) (Ronald Moodnick). British character comedian of stage and TV. □Make Mine Mink 59. Follow a Star 59. Five Golden Hours 60. A Pair of Briefs 62. Summer Holiday 63. The Mouse on the Moon 63. Ladies Who Do 63. Murder Most Foul 64. Every Day's a Holiday 64. San Ferry Ann 65. The Sandwich Man 65. *Oliver* (as Fagin) 68. David Copperfield 69. The Twelve Chairs 70. Flight of the Doves 71. Dogpound Shuffle 74. Legend of the Werewolf 75. Dominique 78. The Word (TV) 79. The Spaceman and King Arthur 79. Dial M for Murder (TV) 81. Wrong Is Right 72.
TV series: Nobody's Perfect 79.

The Moon and Sixpence (US 1942). A remarkable first film written and directed by Albert Lewin, whose exotic literary talent later got out of control. From the novel by Somerset Maugham based on the life of Gauguin, it was remarkable in remaining more faithful to its original than most Hollywood films of the period, while still managing to do well at the box office. Herbert Marshall appeared (not for the last time) as Maugham, George Sanders made the most of his meaty role as Strickland, and Steve Geray had his best part as Dirk Stroeve.

The Moon is Blue (US 1953). This straightforward version by Otto Preminger of F. Hugh Herbert's frothy Broadway comedy marked the first breaking-down of the Hollywood Production Code and the Legion of Decency, which Preminger defied by retaining the words 'virgin', 'mistress' and 'seduction' and treating these matters as a great joke. After the film's enormous box office success, Hollywood's mind quickly broadened. The actors involved were David Niven, William Holden and Maggie McNamara.

Moore, Clayton (1908–). Tall American leading man of forties serials such as *The Crimson Ghost, G-Men Never Forget, The Ghost of Zorro*. Later famous on TV as *The Lone Ranger*.

Moore, Cleo (1928–1973). American leading lady who appeared chiefly in Hugo Haas's low-budget emotional melodramas.
This Side of the Law 50. On Dangerous Ground 50. One Girl's Confession 53. Bait 54. Women's Prison 55. Over-Exposed 56, etc.

Moore, Colleen (1900–88) (Kathleen Morrison). American leading lady of the silent screen.
Autobiography 1968: *Silent Star*.
□Bad Boy 17. An Old Fashioned Young Man 17. Hands Up 17. The Savage 18. A Hoosier Romance 18. Little Orphan Annie 18. The Busher 19. Wilderness Trail 19. Man in the Moonlight 19. The Egg Crate Wallop 19. Common Property 19. The Cyclone 20. A Roman Scandal 20. Her Bridal Nightmare 20. The Devil's Claim 20. So Long Letty 20. When Dawn Came 20. Dinty 20. The Sky Pilot 21. The Lotus Eater 21. His Nibs 21. Broken Hearts of Broadway 21. Come on Over 22. The Wallflower 22. Affinities 22. Forsaking All Others 22. Broken Chains 22. The Ninety and Nine 22. Look Your Best 23. Slippy McGee 23. The Nth Commandment 23. April Showers 23. Through the Dark 23. The Huntress 23. Flaming Youth 23. Painted People 24. The Perfect Flapper 24. Flirting with Love 24. *So Big* 24. *Sally* 25. The Desert Flower 25. We Moderns 25. Irene 26. *Ella Cinders* 26. It Must Be Love 26. Twinkletoes 27. Orchids and Ermine 27. Naughty But Nice 27. Her Wild Oat 27. Happiness Ahead 28. Oh Kay! 28. *Lilac Time* 28. Synthetic Sin 28. Why Be Good? 29. Smiling Irish Eyes 29. Footlights and Fools 29. The Power and the Glory 33. Success at Any Price 34. Social Register 34. The Scarlet Letter 34.

Moore, Constance (1919–). American leading lady and singer, mildly popular in the forties; usually in 'sensible' roles.
Prison Break 38. You Can't Cheat an Honest Man 39. La Conga Nights 40. Ma, He's Making Eyes at Me 40. I Wanted Wings 41. Take a Letter, Darling 42. *Show Business* 43. *Atlantic City* 44. Delightfully Dangerous 45. Earl Carroll's Vanities 45. In Old Sacramento 46. Hit Parade of 1947. Hats Off to Rhythm 47, etc.
TV series: Window on Main Street 61.

Moore, Dickie (1925–). American child actor of the thirties, first on screen when one year old.
The Beloved Rogue 26. Passion Flower 30. Blonde Venus 32. Oliver Twist 33. Peter Ibbetson 34. Sergeant York 41. Miss Annie Rooney 42. Dangerous Years 47. Out of the Past (Build My Gallows High) 48. Killer Shark 50. The Member of the Wedding (last to date) 52, etc.

Moore, Dudley (1935–). British cabaret pianist and comedian, often teamed with Peter Cook until Hollywood stardom was surprisingly awarded to him in 1979, and less surprisingly withdrawn in the early eighties. □The Wrong Box 66. Thirty is a Dangerous Age Cynthia 67. Bedazzled 68. Monte Carlo or Bust 69. The Bed Sitting Room 69. Alice's Adventures in Wonderland 72. The Hound of the Baskervilles (as Dr Watson) 77. *Foul Play* 78. '10' 79. Wholly Moses 80. Arthur 81. Six Weeks 82. Lovesick 83. Romantic Comedy 83. Best Defense 84. Unfaithfully Yours 83. Micki and Maude 84. Santa Claus 85. Like Father Like Son 87.

¶ *D.M.:* The ability to enjoy your sex life is central. I don't give a shit about anything else. My obsession is total. What else is there to live for?

D.M.: The confidence I now have is rooted in the discovery that who I am is okay.

'A grubby cherub.'—*Jonathan Miller*

D.M.: I think my own desire to be loved is what makes me sexually attractive.

D.M.: I have a very ribald sense of humour, which is conventionally known as obscene.

Moore, Eva (1870–1955). British stage actress who made a few films in the thirties. Chu Chin Chow 22. Brown Sugar 31. *The Old Dark House* (splendid in her cries of 'No beds! They can't have beds!') (US) 32. I Was a Spy 33. A Cup of Kindness 34. Vintage Wine 35. Old Iron 39. The Bandit of Sherwood Forest (US) 46, etc.

Moore, Grace (1901–1947). American operatic singer who appeared in occasional films; Kathryn Grayson played her in a 1953 biopic, *So This is Love.*
Autobiography 1946: *You're Only Human Once.*
□A Lady's Morals (as Jenny Lind) 30. New Moon 30. *One Night of Love* 34. Love Me Forever 35. The King Steps Out 36. When You're In Love 37. I'll Take Romance 37. Louise 40.

Moore, Ida (1883–1964). American character actress.
The Merry Widow 25. She's a Soldier Too 44. To Each His Own 46. The Egg and I 47. Manhattan Angel 49. Harvey 50. Honeychile 51. Scandal At Scourie 53. The Country Girl 54. Ma and Pa Kettle at Waikiki 55. The Desk Set 57. Rock a Bye Baby 58, etc.

Moore, Juanita (1922–). Black American character actress.
□Lydia Bailey 52. Affair in Trinidad 52. Witness to Murder 54. Women's Prison 55. Ransom 56. The Girl Can't Help It 56. Green Eyed Blonde 57. *Imitation of Life* 59. Tammy Tell Me True 61. A Raisin in the Sun 61. Walk on the Wild Side 62. Papa's Delicate Condition 63. The Singing Nun 66. Rosie 68. Up Tight 68. Fox Style 73. Thomasine and Bushrod 74. Abby 74.

Moore, Kieron (1925–) (Kieron O'Hanrahan). Hangdog Irish leading man with stage experience.
The Voice Within 44. *A Man about the House* 46. *Mine Own Executioner* 47. Anna Karenina 48. Ten Tall Men 51. The Key 58. The Day They Robbed the Bank of England 60. Dr Blood's Coffin 61. The Day of the Triffids 63. The Thin Red Line 64. Crack in the World 65. Arabesque 66. Custer of the West 67, etc.

Moore, Mary Tyler (1936–). Pert American leading lady who has been most successful on TV, and with her then husband Grant Tinker formed her own production company, now known as MTM Productions.
□X15 61. Thoroughly Modern Millie 67. What's So Bad About Feeling Good? 68. Don't Just Stand There 68. Change of Habit 69. Run a Crooked Mile (TV) 69. *First You Cry* (TV) 78. *Ordinary People* 80. Six Weeks 82. Finnegan Begin Again (TV) 84. Just Between Friends 85.
TV series: Steve Canyon 58. Richard Diamond 59–60. *The Dick Van Dyke Show* 61–65. *The Mary Tyler Moore Show* 70–74. Mary 86.

¶ *M.T.M.:* I'm not an actress who can create a character. I play me.

Moore, Matt (1888–1960). American silent actor, youngest of four Irish acting brothers (Tom, Owen and Joe were the others).
Traffic in Souls 13. Pride of the Clan 16. The Bondage of Barbara 19. Fools in the Dark 24. Grounds for Divorce 25. Dry Martini 28. Coquette 29. Spellbound 45, many others.

Moore, Owen (1887–1939). See under *Matt Moore.* (Owen married Mary Pickford.)
The Cricket on the Hearth 09. Battle of the Sexes 13. Mistress Nell 15. Piccadilly Jim 19. Torment 24. The Red Mill 27. What a Widow 30. She Done Him Wrong 33, many others.

Moore, Richard (–). American cinematographer.

The Wild Angels 65. Wild in the Streets 68. Winning 69. The Reivers 69. Myra Breckinridge 70. WUSA 70. Judge Roy Bean 72. The Stone Killer 73. Annie 82, etc.

Moore, Robert (1927–84). American director, from TV.
Murder by Death 76. The Cheap Detective 78. Chapter Two 79, etc.
As actor: Tell Me That You Love Me Junie Moon 70.

Moore, Roger (1928–). British light leading man, most successful on TV; film debut in Hollywood.
☐The Last Time I Saw Paris 54. Interrupted Melody 55. The King's Thief 55. Diane 55. The Miracle 59. The Sins of Rachel Cade 61. Gold of the Seven Saints 61. Rape of the Sabines 61. Crossplot 69. The Man Who Haunted Himself 70. Live and Let Die (as James Bond) 73. The Man with the Golden Gun 74. Gold 74. That Lucky Touch 75. Shout at the Devil 76. Street People 76. The Spy Who Loved Me 77. Sherlock Holmes in New York (TV) 77. The Wild Geese 78. Escape from Athena 79. Moonraker 79. North Sea Hijack 80. Sunday Lovers 80. The Sea Wolves 80. The Cannonball Run 81. For Your Eyes Only 81. Octopussy 83. The Naked Face 84. A View to a Kill 85.

¶ *R.M.:* If I kept all my bad notices, I'd need two houses.
R.M.: My acting range? Left eyebrow raised, right eyebrow raised.
R.M.: You're not a star till they can spell your name in Vladivostok.
TV series: Ivanhoe 57. The Alaskans 59. Maverick 61. *The Saint* 63–68. *The Persuaders* 71.

Moore, Ted (1914–). South African cinematographer, in British films.
The Black Knight 54. Cockleshell Heroes 56. *A Man for All Seasons* (AA) 66. Shalako 68. The Prime of Miss Jean Brodie 69. The Most Dangerous Man in the World 69. Country Dance 70. Diamonds are Forever 71. Live and Let Die 73, etc.

Moore, Terry (1929–) (Helen Koford). American leading lady, former child model, in films from infancy.
The Murder in Thornton Square 43. Mighty Joe Young 50. The Sunny Side of the Street 53. King of the Khyber Rifles 54. Bernardine 57. A Private's Affair 59. Why Must I Die? 60. Town Tamer 65. Death Dimension 78, etc.
TV series: Empire 62.

Moore, Tom (1883–1955). See under *Matt Moore.*
The Atheist 14. The Cinderella Man 17. The Floor Below 18. Harbor Lights 23. Manhandled 25. Good and Naughty 26. Bombay Mail 34. The Fighting O'Flynn 49.

Moore, Victor (1876–1962). Veteran American vaudeville comedian with hesitant, bumbling manner.
☐ Chimmie Fadden 15. Chimmie Fadden Out West 15. Snobs 15. The Clown 16. The Race 16. The Best Man 16. Invited Out 17. Oh! U-Boat 17. Faint Heart and Fair Lady 17. Bungalowing 17. Commuting 17. Flivvering 17. Home Defence 17. The Man Who Found Himself 25. Heads Up 30. Dangerous Nan McGrew 30. Romance in the Rain 34. Gift of Gab 34. *Swing Time* 36. Gold Diggers of 1937 36. We're on the Jury 37. Meet the Missus 37. The Life of the Party 37. She's Got Everything 37. *Make Way for Tomorrow* 37. Radio City Revels 38. This Marriage Business 38. *Louisiana Purchase* 41. *Star Spangled Rhythm* 42. True to Life 43. Riding High 43. The Heat's On 43. Carolina Blues 44. Duffy's Tavern 45. *It's In the Bag* 45. *Ziegfeld Follies* 46. It Happened on Fifth Avenue 47. A Miracle Can Happen 48. A Kiss in the Dark 49. *We're Not Married* 52. The Seven Year Itch 55.
Famous line (*Make Way for Tomorrow*): Two old-fashioneds, for two old-fashioned people.

Moorehead, Agnes (1906–1974). Sharp-featured American character actress, often seen in waspish or neurotic roles.
☐Citizen Kane 41. *The Magnificent Ambersons* 42. Journey into Fear 42. The Big Street 42. The Youngest Profession 43. Government Girl 43. Jane Eyre 43. Since You Went Away 44. Dragon Seed 44. The Seventh Cross 44. Mrs Parkington 44. Tomorrow the World 44. Keep Your Powder Dry 45. Our Vines Have Tender Grapes 45. Her Highness and the Bellboy 45. Dark Passage 47. *The Lost Moment* (as a centenarian) 47. Summer Holiday 48. *The Woman in White* 48. Station West 48. Johnny Belinda 48. The Stratton Story 49. The Great Sinner 49. Without Honor 49. Caged 50. Fourteen Hours 51. Show Boat 51. The Blue Veil 51. The Adventures of Captain Fabian 51. Captain Blackjack 52. The Blazing Forest 52. The Story of Three Loves 53. Scandal at Scourie 53. Main Street to Broadway 53. Those Redheads from Seattle 53. Magnificent Obsession 54. Untamed 55. The Left Hand of God 55. All that Heaven Allows 56. Meet Me in Las Vegas 56. The Conqueror 56. The

Revolt of Mamie Stover 56. The Swan 56. Pardners 56. The Opposite Sex 56. Raintree County 57. The True Story of Jesse James 57. Jeanne Eagels 57. The Story of Mankind 57. Night of the Quarter Moon 59. Tempest 59. *The Bat* 59. Pollyanna 60. Twenty Plus Two 61. Bachelor in Paradise 61. Jessica 62. How the West was Won 63. Who's Minding the Store? 63. Hush Hush Sweet Charlotte 64. The Singing Nun 66. What's the Matter with Helen? 71. Suddenly Single (TV) 71. Rolling Man (TV) 72. Night of Terror (TV) 72. Dear Dead Delilah 72. Frankenstein: the True Story (TV) 73.
TV series: *Bewitched* 64–71.

Mora, Philippe (–). French director.
Mad Dog 76. The Beast Within 81. The Return of Captain Invincible 82. Howling II 85. Death of a Soldier 86, etc.

Morahan, Christopher (c. 1930–). British director with stage and TV experience.
□Diamonds for Breakfast 68. All Neat in Black Stockings 69. The Jewel in the Crown (TV) 83. In the Secret State (TV) 85. Clockwise 86. After Pilkington 87.

Moran, Dolores (1924–1982). American leading lady of the forties.
Old Acquaintance 43. To Have and Have Not 43. The Man I Love 47, etc.

Moran, Peggy (1918–). American leading lady of the forties, with radio experience; married Henry Koster and retired.
Girls' School 39. The Mummy's Hand 40. Horror Island 41. Drums of the Congo 42. Seven Sweethearts 42, etc.

Moran, Polly (1884–1952). American vaudeville comedienne who made some early sound films, notably in partnership with Marie Dressler.
Hollywood Revue 29. Caught Short 29. Reducing 30. Politics 31. The Passionate Plumber 32. Alice in Wonderland 33; later played smaller roles in Two Wise Maids 37. Tom Brown's Schooldays 39. Petticoat Politics 41. Adam's Rib 49, etc.

Moravia, Alberto (1907–). Italian novelist. Among the films based on his work are *The Time of Indifference*, *The Wayward Wife*, *The Woman of Rome* and *The Conformist*.

More, Kenneth (1914–1982). Breezy British leading actor, a recognizable World War II type who later gave compassionate interpretations of middle-aged dreamers; film-makers forsook him after his great fifties success, and he turned to stage and TV.
Autobiographies: *Happy Go Lucky*, 1959; *More or Less*, 1978.
□Look Up and Laugh 35. Windmill Revels 38. Carry on London 38. Scott of the Antarctic 48. Man on the Run 49. Now Barabbas 49. Stop Press Girl 49. Morning Departure 50. Chance of a Lifetime 50. The Clouded Yellow 50. The Franchise Affair 50. No Highway 51. *Appointment With Venus* 51. Brandy for the Parson 52. The Yellow Balloon 52. Never Let Me Go 53. *Genevieve* 53. Our Girl Friday 53. *Doctor In the House* 54. Raising a Riot 54. *The Deep Blue Sea* 55. *Reach For the Sky* (as Douglas Bader) 56. The Admirable Crichton 57. A Night to Remember 58. Next to No Time 58. The Sheriff of Fractured Jaw 58. The 39 Steps 59. Northwest Frontier 59. *Sink The Bismarck* 60. Man in the Moon 60. The Greengage Summer 61. The Longest Day 62. Some People 62. We Joined the Navy 62. The Comedy Man 63. The Mercenaries 67. Oh What a Lovely War 69. Fraulein Doktor 69. Battle of Britain 69. Scrooge 70. Where Time Began 76. The Slipper and the Rose 76. Leopard in the Snow 78. The Spaceman and King Arthur 79. A Tale of Two Cities 81.
TV series: The Forsyte Saga 68. Father Brown 73. An Englishman's Castle 78.
❁ For encapsulating for a nation all the carefree heroes of World War II. *Genevieve*.

More O'Ferrall, George (1907–82). British director who was mainly successful in TV.
AS ASSISTANT DIRECTOR: Midshipman Easy 34 to No Highway 51.
AS DIRECTOR: □ Angels One Five 52. The Holly and the Ivy 53. The Heart of the Matter 53. The Green Scarf 53. A Woman for Joe 55. The March Hare 56. Three Faces of Murder (Lord Mountdrago) 56.

The More the Merrier (US 1943). Perhaps the best of the several farces about overcrowding in Washington hotels during World War II, this amiable movie starred Charles Coburn, Jean Arthur and Joel McCrea, was written by Robert Russell and Frank Ross, and directed by George Stevens. In 1966 it was lethargically remade by Charles Walters, its setting changed to the Tokyo Olympics, as *Walk Don't Run*; Cary Grant took over as ageing Cupid to Samantha Eggar and Jim Hutton.

Moreau, Jeanne (1928–). French actress of stage and screen; the Bette Davis of her time.
The She-Wolves 55. Lift to the Scaffold 57. *The Lovers* 59. Le Dialogue des Carmelites 59. Les Liaisons Dangereuses 60. Moderato Cantabile 60. La Notte 61. *Jules et Jim* 61. Eva 62. The Trial 63. The Victors 63. Le Feu Follet 64. *Diary of a Chambermaid* 64. The Yellow Rolls-Royce 64. The Train 64. Mata Hari 65. *Viva Maria* 65. Mademoiselle 65. Chimes at Midnight 66. Sailor from Gibraltar 66. The Bride Wore Black 67. Great Catherine 68. Le Corps de Diane 68. Monte Walsh 70. Alex in Wonderland 70. Louise 72. Mr Klein 76. The Last Tycoon 76. French Provincial 76. La Lumière (& wd) 76. The Adolescent (w, d only) 79. Plein Sud 80. The Trout 82. Querelle 82. Sauve-toi Lola 86. Le Miracule 87, etc.
❀ For sheer strength of acting. *Louise.*

¶ *J.M.:* When I'm doing a role I'm the part. I'm the person. But when I'm finished, I'm me.

Morecambe, Eric (1926–1984) (Eric Bartholomew) and **Wise, Ernie** (1925–) (Ernest Wiseman). British comedy team with music-hall experience since 1943. In the sixties they became immensely popular on TV, but their films were rather less than satisfactory.
□The Intelligence Men 64. That Riviera Touch 66. The Magnificent Two 67.

Moreland, Mantan (1902–1973). Chubby American Negro actor, long cast as frightened valet.
Frontier Scout 38. Laughing at Danger 40. King of the Zombies 41. The Strange Case of Doctor RX 41. Charlie Chan in the Secret Service (and many others in this series) 44. Murder at Malibu Beach 47. The Feathered Serpent 49. Enter Laughing 68. Watermelon Man 70, etc.

Morell, André (1909–1978) (André Mesritz). Dignified British character actor.
Thirteen Men and a Gun (debut) 38. No Place for Jennifer 49. Seven Days to Noon 50. High Treason 51. Summer Madness 55. The Bridge on the River Kwai 57. Ben Hur 59. The Hound of the Baskervilles 59. Cone of Silence 60. Shadow of the Cat 62. Cash on Demand 64. She 65. Plague of the Zombies 65. The Mummy's Shroud 67. 10 Rillington Place 70. Barry Lyndon 75. The Message 76, etc.

Moreno, Antonio (1886–1967). Romantic Spanish star of Hollywood.
SILENT FILMS: Voice of the Million 12. House of Hate 18. The Trail of the Lonesome Pine 23. The Spanish Dancer 24. Mare Nostrum 25. Beverly of Graustark 26. The Temptress 26. It 27. Synthetic Sin 28, etc.
CHARACTER PARTS: One Mad Kiss 30. Storm over the Andes 35. Rose of the Rio Grande 38. Valley of the Giants 42. The Spanish Main 45. Captain from Castile 47. Thunder Bay 53. The Creature from the Black Lagoon 54. The Searchers 56, many others.

Moreno, Rita (1931–) (Rosita Dolores Alverio). Puerto Rican actress-dancer, in films sporadically since 1950, between stage appearances.
Pagan Love Song 50. Singin' in the Rain 52. Garden of Evil 54. The Vagabond King 55. The King and I 56. The Deerslayer 57. *West Side Story* (AA) 61. The Night of the Following Day 68. Popi 69. Carnal Knowledge 71. *The Ritz* 76. The Boss's Son 78. Happy Birthday Gemini 79. *The Four Seasons* 81, etc.
TV series: Nine to Five 82–83.

Morgan: A Suitable Case for Treatment (GB 1966). A serio-comedy which takes the *Lucky Jim/Look Back in Anger* type of fifties hero to the logical conclusion of madness, wracked by his own selfishness, nihilism and fantasy. David Mercer's script, extended from his own TV play, had very little to say, but there are intermittent enjoyments coupled with uneasy moments of flashy editing and slapstick. (The actual ending is borrowed from Buñuel.) David Warner enjoys himself in the title role; Karel Reisz directs rather uncertainly.

Morgan, Dennis (1910–) (Stanley Morner). American leading man, former opera singer.
Suzy (debut) 36. The Great Ziegfeld 36. Kitty Foyle 40. Captains of the Clouds 42. Thank Your Lucky Stars 43. Two Guys from Texas 46. My Wild Irish Rose 47. Painting the Clouds with Sunshine 51. The Gun That Won the West 55. Uranium Boom 56. Rogues' Gallery 68, etc.
TV series: 21 Beacon Street 59.

Morgan, Frank (1890–1949) (Francis Wupperman). American character actor. In films from 1916, usually playing his endearing if slightly fuddled self, but his real popularity came with sound, when he was an MGM contract player for over twenty years.

□The Suspect 17. The Daring of Diana 17. Light in the Darkness 17. A Modern Cinderella 17. The Girl Philippa 17. Who's Your Neighbour 17. A Child of the Wild 17. Baby Mine 17. Raffles 17. The Knife 18. At the Mercy of Men 18. Gray Towers of Mystery 19. The Golden Shower 19. Manhandled 24. Born Rich 24. The Man Who Found Himself 25. The Crowded Hour 25. The Scarlet Saint 25. Love's Greatest Mistake 27. Queen High 30. Dangerous Dan McGrew 30. Fast and Loose 30. Laughter 30. The Half Naked Truth 32. Secrets of the French Police 32. Luxury Liner 33. *Hallelujah I'm a Bum* 33. Reunion in Vienna 33. The Nuisance 33. When Ladies Meet 33. Broadway to Hollywood 33. *Bombshell* 33. The Best of Enemies 33. Billion Dollar Scandal 33. The Kiss Before the Mirror 33. The Cat and the Fiddle 34. *The Affairs of Cellini* 34. By Your Leave 34. There's Always Tomorrow 34. Success at Any Price 34. Sisters under the Skin 34. A Lost Lady 34. The Good Fairy 35. Naughty Marietta 35. Escapade 35. I Live My Life 35. The Perfect Gentleman 35. Enchanted April 35. The Dancing Pirate 35. *The Great Ziegfeld* 36. *Trouble for Two* 36. *Piccadilly Jim* 36. *Dimples* 36. *The Last of Mrs Cheyney* 37. The Emperor's Candlesticks 37. Saratoga 37. Beg Borrow or Steal 37. Rosalie 37. Paradise for Three 38. Port of Seven Seas 38. The Crowd Roars 38. Sweethearts 38. Broadway Serenade 39. *The Wizard of Oz* 39. Balalaika 39. The Shop Around the Corner 40. Henry Goes to Arizona 40. Broadway Melody of 1940 40. The Ghost Comes Home 40. The Mortal Storm 40. *Boom Town* 40. Hullabaloo 40. Keeping Company 41. Washington Melodrama 41. Wild Man of Borneo 41. Honky Tonk 41. *The Vanishing Virginian* 42. *Tortilla Flat* 42. White Cargo 42. Stranger in Town 43. *The Human Comedy* 43. Thousands Cheer 43. The White Cliffs of Dover 43. Casanova Brown 44. Yolanda and the Thief 45. The Courage of Lassie 45. The Great Morgan 46. The Cockeyed Miracle 46. Lady Luck 46. Green Dolphin Street 47. Summer Holiday 48. The Three Musketeers 48. Any Number Can Play 49. The Great Sinner 49. The Stratton Story 49. Key to the City 50.

Morgan, Harry (1915–) (Harry Bratsburg). Mild-looking American character actor with stage experience.
To the Shores of Tripoli (debut) 42. From This Day Forward 45. The Saxon Charm 49. Moonrise 50. The Well 51. High Noon 52. The Glenn Miller Story 53. Not as a Stranger 55. The Teahouse of the August Moon 56. Inherit the Wind 60. John Goldfarb Please Come Home 64. What Did You Do in the War, Daddy? 66. Support Your Local Sheriff 69. The Barefoot Executive 71. Snowball Express 73. The Apple Dumpling Gang 75. The Apple Dumpling Gang Rides Again 79, many others.
TV series: December Bride 54–58. Pete and Gladys 60–61. The Richard Boone Show 63. Kentucky Jones 64. Dragnet 69. The D.A. 71. M*A*S*H 76–83. Aftermash 83. Black Magic 86. Dragnet 87.

Morgan, Helen (1900–1941). American café singer of the thirties; film appearances few. Biopic 1956 with Ann Blyth: *The Helen Morgan Story*.
Biography 1974: *Helen Morgan, Her Life and Legend* by Gilbert Maxwell.
□*Applause* 29. Roadhouse Nights 30. You Belong to Me 34. Marie Galante 34. Sweet Music 35. Go Into Your Dance 36. *Showboat* 36. Frankie and Johnnie 36.

Morgan, Michele (1920–) (Simone Roussel). French leading lady, in films from mid-thirties.
Orage 36. *Quai des Brumes* 38. Remorques 39. La Loi du Nord 39. La Symphonie Pastorale 40. Joan of Paris (US) 41. Higher and Higher (US) 43. Passage to Marseilles (US) 44. *The Fallen Idol* (GB) 48. Les Orgeuilleux 50. The Seven Deadly Sins 51. Les Grandes Manoeuvres 55. Marguerite de la Nuit 56. The Mirror Has Two Faces 60. Landru 63. Lost Command 66. Benjamin 68. Le Chat et la Souris 75, etc.

Morgan, Ralph (1882–1956) (Ralph Wupperman). American character actor, brother of Frank Morgan. Former lawyer; went on stage, then to films in the twenties. Charlie Chan's Chance 31. Rasputin and the Empress 32. Strange Interlude 32. *The Power and the Glory* 33. Anthony Adverse 36. The Life of Emile Zola 37. Forty Little Mothers 40. Black Market Babies 45. The Monster Maker 45. Sleep My Love 48. Gold Fever 52, many others.

Morgan, Terence (1921–). British leading man.
Hamlet (debut) 48. Mandy 52. Turn the Key Softly 53. They Can't Hang Me 55. The Scamp 56. Shakedown 58. Piccadilly Third Stop 61. The Curse of the Mummy's Tomb 64, others.
TV series: Sir Francis Drake 62.

Moriarty, Michael (1941–). American leading actor of the seventies.

Hickey and Boggs 72. The Last Detail 73. Bang the Drum Slowly 73. Shoot It Black Shoot It Blue 74. Report to the Commissioner 74. *Holocaust* (TV) 77. Who'll Stop the Rain? 78. Too Far to Go (TV) 79. The Winged Serpent 82. Odd Birds 85. Pale Rider 85. The Stuff 85. Troll 85. The Hanoi Hilton 87, etc.

Morison, Patricia (1915–) (Eileen Morison). Slightly sulky-looking American leading lady of the forties; never quite made it but did well later on stage.
□*Persons in Hiding* 39. I'm from Missouri 39. The Magnificent Fraud 39. Untamed 40. Rangers of Fortune 40. One Night in Lisbon 41. Romance of the Rio Grande 41. The Roundup 41. A Night in New Orleans 42. Beyond the Blue Horizon 42. Are Husbands Necessary? 42. Silver Skates 43. Hitler's Madman 43. Calling Dr Death 43. The Fallen Sparrow 43. The Song of Bernadette 43. Where are Your Children? 44. Without Love 45. Lady on a Train 45. Dressed to Kill 46. Danger Woman 46. Queen of the Amazons 47. Tarzan and the Huntress 47. Song of the Thin Man 47. Prince of Thieves 47. Walls of Jericho 48. The Return of Wildfire 48. Sofia 48. Song Without End 60.

Morita, Pat (1930–) (Noriyuki Morita). Japanese-American character actor.
Thoroughly Modern Millie 64. Midway 76. When Time Ran Out 80. *The Karate Kid* (AAN) 84. Karate Kid II 86. Captive Hearts 87.
TV series: Mr T and Tina 76. Ohara 87.

Morlay, Gaby (1897–1964) (Blanche Fumoleau). French character actress.
La Sandale Rouge 13. Les Nouveaux Messieurs 28. Derrière la Façade 38. Le Voile Bleu 42. Gigi 48. Le Plaisir 51. Mitsou 55. Ramuntcho 58, many others.

Morley, Karen (1905–) (Mildred Linton). American leading lady of the thirties.
Inspiration 31. *Scarface* 32. Dinner at Eight 33. Our Daily Bread 34. Beloved Enemy 36. Kentucky 39. Pride and Prejudice 40. Jealousy 45. The Unknown 46. 'M' 51, others.

Morley, Robert (1908–). Portly British character actor (and playwright), on stage from 1929, films from 1938.
Autobiography 1966: *Robert Morley, Responsible Gentleman.*
Marie Antoinette (US) 38. *Major Barbara* 40. *The Young Mr Pitt* 42. I Live in Grosvenor Square 45. An Outcast of the Islands 51. The African Queen 51. *Gilbert and Sullivan* 53. *Beat the Devil* 53. Around the World in Eighty Days 56. The Doctor's Dilemma 59. *Oscar Wilde* 60. The Young Ones 61. Murder at the Gallop 63. Those Magnificent Men in Their Flying Machines 65. The Alphabet Murders 65. Genghis Khan 65. A Study in Terror 65. Hotel Paradiso 66. Way Way Out (US) 66. The Trygon Factor 67. Sinful Davey 69. When Eight Bells Toll 71. Theatre of Blood 73. The Blue Bird 76. *Who is Killing the Great Chefs of Europe?* 78. Scavenger Hunt 79. The Human Factor 79. O Heavenly Dog 80. The Great Muppet Caper 81. High Road to China 82, etc.

¶ *R.M.:* Anyone who works is a fool. I don't work: I merely inflict myself on the public.

R.M.: I believe there are two things necessary for salvation: money and gunpowder.

R.M.: It is a great help for a man to be in love with himself. For an actor it is absolutely essential.

Morning Glory (US 1933). Zoe Akins' play about a maddening but talented young actress in New York was filmed by Lowell Sherman with Katharine Hepburn (who won an Academy Award) and Adolphe Menjou. In 1957 Sidney Lumet remade it as *Stage Struck*, with Susan Strasberg and Henry Fonda.

Morocco (US 1930). The film in which Marlene Dietrich made her American debut, directed by Josef Von Sternberg.
Remembered chiefly for the impudence of the scenes in which Marlene (*a*) dressed in a tuxedo, kisses a young woman on the lips, and (*b*) strides into the Sahara in high heels to follow her departed lover.

Moroder, Giorgio (–). American composer.
Midnight Express (AA) 78. Foxes 80. American Gigolo 80. Cat People 82. Flashdance 83. Superman III 83. Metropolis (new score) 85.

Moross, Jerome (1913–1983). American composer.
When I Grow Up 51. The Sharkfighters 56. The Big Country 58. The Proud Rebel 58. The Jayhawkers 59. The Cardinal 63. The War Lord 65. Rachel Rachel 68, etc.

Morricone, Ennio (1928–). Italian composer and arranger.

A Fistful of Dollars 64. El Greco 64. Fists in the Pockets 65. For a Few Dollars More 65. The Good the Bad and the Ugly 66. The Big Gundown 66. Matchless 67. Theorem 69. Once Upon a Time in the West 69. Investigation of a Citizen 69. Fraulein Doktor 69. The Bird with the Crystal Plumage 70. The Sicilian Clan 70. Two Mules for Sister Sara 70. Cat O'Nine Tails 71. The Red Tent 71. Four Flies in Grey Velvet 71. The Decameron 71. The Burglars 71. The Black Belly of the Tarantula 72. Bluebeard 72. The Serpent 72. A Fistful of Dynamite 72. 1900 76. Exorcist II: The Heretic 77. Orca 77. Days of Heaven 78. Bloodline 79. The Island 80. La Cage aux Folles II 80. So Fine 81. Butterfly 82.

Morris, Chester (1901–1970). Jut-jawed American leading man of the thirties, an agreeable 'B' picture lead who later became a considerable stage and TV actor.
Alibi 29. She Couldn't Say No 30. The Divorcee 30. *The Big House* 30. The Bat Whispers 31. The Miracle Man 32. Red Headed Woman 32. Blondie Johnson 33. The Gift of Gab 34. I've Been Around 35. Society Doctor 35. Moonlight Murder 36. They Met in a Taxi 36. Flight from Glory 37. Law of the Underworld 38. Smashing the Rackets 38. Blind Alibi 39. *Five Came Back* 39. The Marines Fly High 40. No Hands on the Clock 41. Meet Boston Blackie 41 (and subsequent series of 12 films until 1949). I Live on Danger 42. Wrecking Crew 43. Secret Command 44. Double Exposure 45. Unchained 55. The Great White Hope 70, etc.

Morris, Ernest (1915–). British director, mainly of second features for the Danzigers.
The Tell-Tale Heart 60. Echo of Diana 64. The Return of Mr Moto 65, etc.

Morris, Greg (1934–). Black American supporting actor.
The Lively Set 64. The Doomsday Flight (TV) 66. Countdown at Kusini 76, etc.
TV series: Mission Impossible 66–73. Vegas 78–80.

Morris, Howard (1919–). American comedy director.
Boys Night Out (a only) 62. Who's Minding the Mint? 67. With Six You Get Egg Roll 68. Don't Drink the Water 69, etc.

Morris, Lana (1930–). British leading lady of the fifties.
Spring in Park Lane 47. The Weaker Sex 48. Trottie True 49. The Chiltern Hundreds 49. The Woman in Question 50. Trouble in Store 53. Man of the Moment 55. Home and Away 56. I Start Counting 70, others.

Morris, Mary (1895–1970). American stage actress who played her stage role of the evil old lady in *Double Door* 34.

Morris, Mary (1915–). British character actress with dominant personality, on stage from 1925.
Prison without Bars (film debut) 38. The Spy in Black 39. The Thief of Baghdad 40. *Pimpernel Smith* 41. Undercover 43. The Man from Morocco 45. Train of Events 49. High Treason 51, others.

Morris, Oswald (1915–). British cinematographer, in films from 1932.
Green for Danger 46. *Moulin Rouge* 53. Knave of Hearts 53. Beat the Devil 53. Beau Brummell 54. Moby Dick 56. A Farewell to Arms 57. The Key 58. Roots of Heaven 59. Look Back in Anger 59. Our Man in Havana 59. The Entertainer 60. Lolita 62. Of Human Bondage 64. *The Pumpkin Eater* (BFA) 64. The Hill (BFA) 65. Life at the Top 65. The Spy Who Came In from the Cold 65. Stop the World I Want To Get Off 66. *The Taming of the Shrew* 67. Oliver! 68. Goodbye Mr Chips 69. Scrooge 70. Fiddler on the Roof (AA) 71. Lady Caroline Lamb 72. The Mackintosh Man 73. The Odessa File 74. The Man Who Would Be King 75. Equus 77. The Wiz 78. Just Tell Me What You Want 80. The Great Muppet Caper 81, etc.

Morris, Wayne (1914–1959) (Bert de Wayne Morris). Brawny American leading man with stage experience.
China Clipper (debut) 36. *Kid Galahad* 37. Brother Rat and a Baby 39. Bad Men of Missouri 40. The Smiling Ghost 41. Deep Valley 47. The Time of Your Life 47. The Tougher They Come 50. The Master Plan 55. The Crooked Sky 57. Paths of Glory 58, etc.

Morrissey, Paul (1939–). American 'underground' director associated with Andy Warhol.
Flesh 68. Trash 70. *Heat* 72. Women in Revolt 72. Andy Warhol's Frankenstein 73. Andy Warhol's Dracula 74. The Hound of the Baskervilles 77, etc.

Morros, Boris (1891–1963) (Boris Milhailovitch). Russian-born independent producer in America from the late thirties. Later revealed as an American agent via his 1957 book *Ten Years a Counterspy*, filmed in

1960 as *Man on a String*, with Ernest Borgnine as Morros.
The Flying Deuces 39. Second Chorus 41. Tales of Manhattan 42. Carnegie Hall 48, others.

Morrow, Doretta (1925–68) (Doretta Marano). American singing star who appeared in one film, *Because You're Mine* 52.

Morrow, Jeff (1913–). Mature American leading man, former Broadway and TV actor, in Hollywood from 1953.
The Robe 53. Flight to Tangier 53. Siege of Red River 54. Tanganyika 54. Sign of the Pagan 54. *This Island Earth* 55. The Creature Walks Among Us 56. The Giant Claw 57. The Story of Ruth 60. Harbour Lights 63, etc.
TV series: Union Pacific 58.

Morrow, Jo (1940–). American leading lady of the sixties.
Because They're Young 56. Brushfire 57. The Legend of Tom Dooley 59. Our Man in Havana 59. The Three Worlds of Gulliver 60. He Rides Tall 63. Sunday in New York 64. Doctor Death 73, etc.

Morrow, Vic (1932–1982). American actor formerly cast as a muttering juvenile delinquent. Stage experience.
The Blackboard Jungle (film debut) 55. Tribute to a Bad Man 56. Men in War 57. God's Little Acre 58. Cimarron 61. Portrait of a Mobster 61. Sledge (d only) 69. The Glass House (TV) 72. The Take 74. Captains and the Kings (TV) 76. Treasure of Matecumbe 76. The Bad News Bears 76. Roots (TV) 77. Funeral for an Assassin 77. The Hostage Heart (TV) 77. Wild and Wooly (TV) 78. Humanoids from the Deep 80. Twilight Zone 83, etc.
TV series: Combat 62–66. Badcats 80.

Morse, Barry (1919–). British leading man who moved to Canada and became star of stage and TV there.
The Goose Steps Out 42. When We Are Married 42. There's a Future in It 43. Late at Night 46. Daughter of Darkness 48. No Trace 50, then after long gap—Kings of the Sun 63. Justine 69. Asylum 72. Power Play 75. The Shape of Things to Come (TV) 79. The Changeling 80. The Winds of War (TV) 83. Sadat (as Begin) (TV) 83, etc.
TV series: *The Fugitive* (as Lieut. Gerard) 63–66. The Adventurer 72. Zoo Gang 73. Space 1999 75–76.

Morse, Helen (1948–). Australian leading actress.
Jock Petersen 75. *Caddie* 78. Picnic at Hanging Rock 79. Agatha 79. *A Town Like Alice* (TV) 81. Far East 82.

Morse, Robert (1931–). American comedy actor who usually plays the befuddled innocent.
The Matchmaker 58. Honeymoon Hotel 64. Quick Before It Melts 65. *The Loved One* 65. Oh Dad, Poor Dad 66. *How to Succeed in Business without Really Trying* 67. Where Were You When the Lights Went Out? 68. The Boatniks 69. The Emperor's New Clothes 87, etc.
TV series: That's Life 68.

Morse, Terry (1906–84). American second feature director.
□Jane Arden 39. On Trial 39. Waterfront 39. Smashing the Money Ring 39. No Place to Go 39. British Intelligence 40. Tear Gas Squad 40. Fog Island 45. Danny Boy 46. Shadows over Chinatown 46. Dangerous Money 46. Bells of San Fernando 47. Unknown World 51. Godzilla (US version) 56. Taffy and the Jungle Hunter 65. Young Dillinger 65.

morticians: see *undertakers*.

Mortimer, John (1923–). British playwright who has worked in films. Originally scriptwriter for Crown Film Unit. Autobiography 1982: *Clinging to the Wreckage*.
The Innocents 61. Guns of Darkness 63. The Dock Brief 63. The Running Man 63. Bunny Lake Is Missing 65. John and Mary 70. Rumpole of the Bailey (TV) 78–9, Brideshead Revisited 81. Paradise Postponed 86, etc.

Morton, Clive (1904–1975). Straight-faced British character actor on stage from 1926, films from 1932, usually in slightly pompous roles.
The Blarney Stone 32. Dead Men Tell No Tales 39. While the Sun Shines 46. Scott of the Antarctic 48. The Blue Lamp 49. His Excellency 51. Carrington VC 54. Richard III 56. Shake Hands with the Devil 59. Lawrence of Arabia 62. Stranger in the House 67, many others.

M.O.S. Mysterious Hollywood script abbreviation indicating a silent shot. Allegedly it derived from the early thirties, when one of the many immigrant German directors called for a scene 'mit out sound'.

Moscovitch, Maurice (1871–1940) (Morris Maaskoff). American character player, a Russian immigrant who spent many years starring in the Yiddish Theatre. Father of Noel Madison.
□Winterset 36. Make Way for Tomorrow 37. Lancer Spy 37. Gateway 37. Suez 38. Love Affair 39. Susannah of the Mounties 39. In Name Only 39. Rio 39. The Great Commandment 39. Everything Happens at Night 39. South to Karanga 40. The Great Dictator 40. Dance Girl Dance 40.

Mosjoukine, Ivan (1889–1939). Russian actor of the old school, who appeared in many international films.
The Defence of Sebastopol 11. Satan Triumphant 22. Tempest (Fr.) 22. Shadows That Mass (Fr.) 23. Casanova (Fr./It.) 27. Sergeant X (Fr.) 30. Nitchevo (Fr.) 36, etc.

Mosley, Roger E. (–). Black American character actor.
The New Centurions 72. Hit Man 72. Terminal Island 73. Leadbelly (title role) 76. The Greatest 77. Semi-Tough 77. Roots II (TV) 78. The Jericho Mile (TV) 79, etc.

Moss, Arnold (1910–). American character actor often seen in sly or sinister roles.
Temptation 47. The Black Book (as Napoleon) 49. Kim 51. Viva Zapata 52. Casanova's Big Night 54. The Twenty-Seventh Day 57. The Fool Killer 64. Gambit 66. Caper of the Golden Bulls 67, many others.

The Most Dangerous Game (US 1932). Richard Connell's well-known short story concerned a mad sportsman who trapped human beings on a tropical island in order to hunt them and display their heads in his trophy room. This first and best film version was produced by Merian C. Cooper, directed by Ernest Schoedsack and Irving Pichel, photographed by Henry Gazzara; it had a thumping Max Steiner score and starred Leslie Banks. In 1945 it was remade as *A Game of Death*, with Edgar Barrier; in 1948 *Johnny Allegro* borrowed liberally from it, with George Macready shooting arrows at George Raft; *Kill or Be Killed* in 1950 had George Coulouris as the menace; *Run For the Sun* in 1956 made Trevor Howard a refugee Nazi in the Brazilian jungle, pursuing unwary intruders with savage hounds. 1966 found Cornel Wilde on the run from African headhunters in *The Naked Prey*, which used basically the same story; in the same year an exploitation item called *Blood Lust* borrowed the plot once more; in 1973 *To Kill a Clown* proved to be yet another retread, as was the TV movie *Maneater*.

Mostel, Zero (1915–77). Heavyweight American comedian principally seen on Broadway stage.
Panic in the Streets 50. *The Enforcer* 51. A Funny Thing Happened on the Way to the Forum 66. Great Catherine 68. *The Producers* 68. The Great Bank Robbery 69. The Angel Levine 69. The Hot Rock 72. Marco 73. Rhinoceros 73. Journey into Fear 75. The Front 76. Mastermind 76, etc.
Famous line (*The Producers*): Leo, he who hesitates is poor.

mother love has been the driving force of many of the screen's most popular, and therefore most remade, melodramas, such as *Imitation of Life, Madame X, Stella Dallas, Over the Hill, Mrs Wiggs of the Cabbage Patch* and *To Each His Own*. Britain chipped in with *The Woman in the Hall, The White Unicorn*, and *When the Bough Breaks*. Some say that Hitchcock made *Psycho* as the ultimate riposte to this sentimental tendency; but *The Anniversary* came a close second. Nor should mother-motivated gangsters such as those in *White Heat* and *Villain* be forgotten, while Melina Mercouri in *Promise At Dawn* and Rosalind Russell in *Gypsy* were perhaps the most sinister mothers of all.

Motion Picture Association of America. A trade guild in which distributors meet to set tariffs and deal with complaints, also set a censorship code.

motor-cycles, hideous and unbearably noisy machines, have become a badge of aggressive youth, and since *The Wild Angels* in 1966 American drive-in screens have been filled with a host of cheap movies extolling the pleasures of leather-jacketed speed with a bird on the back. All of these appear to have been banned in Britain, as was *The Wild One*, an early example of the genre, in 1954. But we did let through Elvis Presley in *Roustabout*, and Steve McQueen doing his own stunt sequence in *The Great Escape*, and *Easy Rider*, and *Coogan's Bluff*, and *Little Fauss and Big Halsy*, and we even made *The Leather Boys*, about our own ton-up teenagers. As for *Girl on a Motorcycle*, in which the bike becomes the ultimate sex symbol, words fail one. There was a good British film about speedway racing, *Once a*

Jolly Swagman, and one about the fairground called *Wall of Death*. Comedian George Formby went in for the TT races in *No Limit*, and rode a motor-bike also in *It's In the Air*. Groucho Marx used one to comic effect in *Duck Soup*, as did Horst Buchholz in *One, Two, Three*. In American films, the motor-cycle cops are too familiar to warrant individual attention but *Electra Glide in Blue* took one seriously. *Easy Rider*, almost an *hommage* to the machine, is also the most successful film to feature it.

motor racing has been the subject of many a routine melodrama, and always seems to reduce the writer to banalities, even in a spectacular like *Grand Prix*. Some other examples of the genre include *The Crowd Roars, Indianapolis Speedway, Checkpoint, The Green Helmet, The Devil's Hairpin, Red Line 7000, Le Mans*, and *Winning*. The funniest comedy use of the sport was probably in *Ask a Policeman*, when Will Hay accidentally drove a bus on to Brooklands racetrack in the middle of a race.

Moulder Brown, John (1945–). British actor, usually of intense roles.
Deep End 69. Vampire Circus 71. King Queen Knave 72. Ludwig 72. The Confessions of Felix Krull (TV) 82, Rumpelstiltskin 87, etc.

Moulin Rouge. The three films made under this title are unconnected with each other. 1. US 1928: a drama directed by E. A. Dupont, with Eve Grey. 2. US 1933: a romantic comedy directed by Sidney Lanfield, with Constance Bennett and Franchot Tone. 3. GB 1953: a life of Toulouse Lautrec, from Pierre la Mure's novel, directed by John Huston and starring Jose Ferrer; mainly notable for its period atmosphere and Oswald Morris' colour photography.

Mount, Peggy (1916–). British character comedienne with long experience in repertory before starring as the termagant mother-in-law in *Sailor Beware*.
□The Embezzler 54. *Sailor Beware* 56. Dry Rot 57. The Naked Truth 58. Inn for Trouble 59. Ladies Who Do 63. One Way Pendulum 64. Hotel Paradiso 65. Finders Keepers 66. Oliver! 68.
TV series: The Larkins. George and the Dragon. Winning Widows. You're Only Young Twice.

mountains have provided a challenge in innumerable movies including *The Challenge, The White Tower, The Mountain, The White Hell of Pitz Palu, The Gold Rush, Trail of 98, The Eiger Sanction, The Snows of Kilimanjaro, The Abominable Snowman, Lost Horizon* and *Goodbye Mr Chips*.

Movie Parade, by Paul Rotha. An influential and glossy book of stills illustrating the film as an art. First published 1936; revised, with additional work by Roger Manvell, 1950.

The Movies, by Richard Griffith and Arthur Mayer. This witty, large and lavishly illustrated survey has been kept in print, in various editions, since it first appeared around 1960.

movies

¶ The cinema is an art. Movies are . . . well, movies. Are they a good thing?

To Cecil B. de Mille they were:

> The new literature.

To Barbra Streisand, starting to shoot *Funny Girl*:

> This is for posterity. Everything I do will be on film forever.

To Sarah Bernhardt they were:

> My one chance for immortality.

Darryl F. Zanuck called them:

> The greatest political fact in the world today.

Sam Spiegel was careful in his commendation:

> The best motion pictures are those which reach you as entertainment, and by the time you leave have provoked thoughts. A picture that provokes no thoughts is usually not well conceived and does not entertain one anyway.

Warren Beatty gave a verbal shrug:

> Movies are fun, but they're not a cure for cancer.

Ben Hecht took the money and ran:

> Movies are one of the bad habits that have corrupted our century.

and:

> They have slipped into the American mind more misinformation in one evening than the Dark Ages could muster in a decade.

and:

> A movie is never any better than the stupidest man connected with it.

David O. Selznick was thoughtful:

> There might have been good movies if there had been no movie industry.

St John Ervine had little time for them:

American movies are written by the half-educated for the half-witted.

H. L. Mencken similarly called them:

Entertainment for the moron majority.

And added:

The kind of jackass who likes the movies as they are is the kind who keeps them as they are.

And again:

No one ever went broke underestimating the taste of the American public.

Stephen Longstreet knew the root of the trouble:

In the Hollywood studios, the mass attack of a mob of halfwits in sport shirts and fifty dollar shoes stamps any real idea to death before it leaves the studio.

S. J. Perelman summed up his own experiences:

Movie scriptwriting is no worse than playing piano in a call house.

Pare Lorentz was a shade more hopeful:

There's no trick to movies. All the businessman needs to do is to employ a fine playwright, a group of good actors, a skilful cameraman, and put them all under the direction of a man who understands the possibilities of the camera and who has besides a comic gift, charm, and dramatic skill—leave them to work unchecked—and he'll get popular entertainment almost every time.

Ivan Butler despaired:

Whoever has the original idea for a movie, it is soon taken away from him.

E. B. White in 1956 saw a gleam of light:

The movies long ago decided that a wider commercial exploitation could be achieved by a deliberate descent to a lower level, and they walked downhill till they found the cellar. Now they are groping for the light switch, looking for the way out.

Robert E. Sherwood was scathing in 1922:

Who invented hokum? Think how much money he'd have made from the film producers if he'd sold his invention on a royalty basis!

Will Rogers was satirical:

There's only one thing that can kill the movies, and that's education.

Maybe Robert Mitchum has the last word:

What's history going to say about the movies? All those rows of seats facing a blank screen? Crazy!

Meanwhile, a few tips on the making of movies:

You should think of each shot as you make it as the most important one in the film.—*Henry Blanke*

Don't act, think!—*F. W. Murnau*

Making a film is like going down a mine—once you've started you bid a metaphorical goodbye to the daylight and the outside world for the duration.—*John Schlesinger*

In a good movie, the sound could go off and the audience would still have a perfectly clear idea of what was going on.—*Alfred Hitchcock*

If we can make films that are useful as well as entertaining, marvellous. But cinema must reflect the temper of the times. We must choose material not only on the basis of whether we feel deeply, but on whether or not anyone's bloody well going to see it.—*Richard Lester*

Me, if I can't blow up the world in the first ten seconds, the show is a flop.—*Irwin Allen*

You can't overthrow regimes through movies, but it can help.—*J. A. Bardem*

I believe that although the motion picture may not live forever as a work of art, except in a few instances, it will be the most efficient way of showing posterity how we live now.—*Irving Thalberg*

Ninety-five per cent of films are born of frustration, of self-despair, of ambition for survival, for money, for fattening bank accounts. Five per cent, maybe less, are made because a man has an idea, an idea which he must express.—*Samuel Fuller*

The movie is a reflector and not an innovator.—*Jack Valenti*

The cinema is not a slice of life, it's a piece of cake.—*Alfred Hitchcock*

Movies, like detective stories, make it possible to experience without danger all the excitement, passion and desirousness which must be suppressed in a humanitarian ordering of society.—*Carl Jung*

They may cost a lot, but none of the money is wasted. All my pictures can be reissued again and again. They stand up pretty well, and they retain their residual values, both financial and prestige-wise.—*Sam Spiegel*

Messages are for Western Union.—*Sam Goldwyn*

There's too much pretentious nonsense talked about the artistic problems of making pictures. I've never had a goddam artistic problem in my life, never, and I've worked with the best of them.—*John Wayne*

Let me tell you what this business is about. It's cunt and horses!—*Harry Cohn*

Some critics say that people complain about the movies because the movies do not reflect reality. It is this writer's suspicion that more people lament the fact that reality does not reflect the movies.—*Leo Rosten*

I know audiences feed on crap, but I can't believe we are so lacking that we cannot dish it up to them with some trace of originality.—*Darryl F. Zanuck*

The public is never wrong.—*Adolph Zukor*

'It's the kissiest business in the world. You have to keep kissing people.'—*Ava Gardner*

Movies for the Millions, by Gilbert Seldes. A historical account of the American cinema, published in 1937. Also known by the title: *The Movies Come from America.*

The Movies in the Age of Innocence, by Edward Charles Wagenknecht. First published in 1962, this is an enthusiastic account of silent films by a regular filmgoer of those days.

Movita (1915–) (Movita Castenada). Mexican leading lady, briefly in Hollywood.
Mutiny on the Bounty 35. Paradise Isle 36.

Mowbray, Alan (1893–1969). Imperious-mannered British character actor, in America since early 1920s; appeared later in nearly 400 films, often as butler or pompous emissary.
Alexander Hamilton 31. Sherlock Holmes 32. Roman Scandals 33. Becky Sharp 35. Desire 36. *My Man Godfrey* 36. *Topper* 37. Stand In 37. *The Villain Still Pursued Her* 40. Lady Hamilton 41. That Uncertain Feeling 41. A Yank at Eton 42. His Butler's Sister 43. Holy Matrimony 43. Where Do We Go from Here? 45. *Terror by Night* 45. Merton of the Movies 46. *My Darling Clementine* 46. Prince of Thieves 47. The Jackpot 50. Wagonmaster 50. Dick Turpin's Ride 51. Androcles and the Lion 53. The King's Thief 55. The King and I 56, many others.
TV series: Colonel Flack 53. The Mickey Rooney Show 54. Dante 60.

Mower, Patrick (1940–). British leading man, mainly in TV series *Callan, Special Branch, Target.*
The Smashing Bird I Used to Know 69. Cry of the Banshee 70. Black Beauty 70. Catch Me a Spy 71. Carry on England 76. The Devil's Advocate 78. Marco Polo (TV) 81, etc.

Moxey, John (1920–). British TV director who has made occasional films and many TV movies in America (as John Llewellyn Moxey).
City of the Dead 59. The £20,000 Kiss 63. Ricochet 63. Strangler's Web 65. Circus of Fear 67. San Francisco International (TV) 70. The House That Would Not Die (TV) 70. A Taste of Evil (TV) 71. The Night Stalker (TV) 72. The Death of Me Yet (TV) 72. The Bounty Man (TV) 72. The Strange and Deadly Occurrence (TV) 74. Where Have All the People Gone? (TV) 74. Charlie's Angels (TV) 76. Nightmare in Badham County (TV) 77. The President's Mistress (TV) 78. Sanctuary of Fear (TV) 79. The Power Within (TV) 79. The Children of An Lac (TV) 80. No Place to Hide (TV) 81. Killjoy (TV) 81. The Cradle Will Fall (TV) 83.

Mudie, Leonard (1884–1965) (Leonard M. Cheetham). British character actor in Hollywood.
The Mummy 32. The House of Rothschild 34. Clive of India 35. Lancer Spy 37. Dark Victory 39. Berlin Correspondent 42. My Name is Julia Ross 45. Song of My Heart 48. The Magnetic Monster 53. The Big Fisherman 59, many others.

Mueller, Elizabeth (1926–). Swiss-German leading lady who made some Hollywood films.
The Power and the Prize 56. El Hakim 58. Confess Dr Corda 58. The Angry Hills 59, etc.

Muhammed Ali (1942–) (Cassius Clay). Black American prizefighter who became an international personality before the last fight proved too many.
The Greatest 77. Freedom Road (TV) 80.

¶ *M.A.:* I'm young, I'm fast, I'm pretty, and I can't possibly be beat.

M.A.: I have said I am the greatest. Ain't nobody ever heard me say I'm the smartest.

Muhl, Edward E. (1907–). American executive, an ex-accountant who has been in charge of Universal production since 1953.

Muir, Esther (1895–). American character actress usually seen as hard-faced blonde.
A Dangerous Affair 31. So This is Africa 33. The Bowery 33. Fury 36. *A Day at the Races* (in which she suffered memorably at the hands of Groucho Marx) 37. The Law West of Tombstone 38. Stolen Paradise 41. X Marks the Spot 42, etc.

Muir, Gavin (1907–1972). Quiet-spoken American actor with a British accent, usually a smooth villain.
Lloyds of London 36. Wee Willie Winkie 37. Eagle Squadron 41. *Nightmare* 42. The Master Race 44. Salome Where She Danced 45. California 46. Ivy 47. Abbott and Costello Meet the Invisible Man 51. King of the Khyber Rifles 54. The Sea Chase 55. The Abductors 57. Johnny Trouble 59, many others.
TV series: The Betty Hutton Show 59.

Muir, Jean (1911–) (J. M. Fullerton). American leading lady of the thirties.
Female 34. A Midsummer Night's Dream 35. Jane Steps Out (GB) 37. And One Was Beautiful 40. The Lone Wolf Meets a Lady 40. The Constant Nymph 44, etc.

Mulcahy, Russell (–). American director.
Razorback 83. Highlander 85.

Mulcaster, G. H. (1891–1964). British character actor, mainly on stage; played formal types.
The Dummy Talks 43. Bonnie Prince Charlie 47. Spring in Park Lane 48. Under Capricorn 50, etc.

Muldaur, Diana (c. 1943–). Sensitive-looking American leading lady, McCloud's girl friend on TV; adept at nice sophisticated types; also on TV in 1974, played Joy Adamson in *Born Free*.
□The Swimmer 68. Number One 69. The Lawyer 70. The Other 71. One More Train to Rob 72. McQ 73. The Chosen Survivors 74. Charlie's Angels (TV) 76. Pine Canyon Is Burning (TV) 77. Black Beauty (TV) 78. To Kill a Cop (TV) 78. Maneaters Are Loose (TV) 78. The Word (TV) 78.
TV series: The Tony Randall show 76. Fitz and Bones 81.

Mulford, Clarence E. (1895–1970). American western novelist, the creator of Hopalong Cassidy.

Mulhall, Jack (1888–1979). American silent-screen leading man.
Sirens of the Sea 17. Mickey 18. All of a Sudden Peggy 20. Molly O' 21. The Bad Man 23. The Goldfish 24. Friendly Enemies 25. The Poor Nut 27. Just Another Blonde 28. Dark Streets 29, many others; appeared as an 'old-timer' in Hollywood Boulevard 36.

Mulhare, Edward (1923–). Irish leading man who has been on American stage.
Hill Twenty-Four Does Not Answer 55. Signpost to Murder 64. Von Ryan's Express 65. Our Man Flint 65. Eye of the Devil 67. *Caprice* 67. Gidget Grows Up (TV) 72.
TV series: *The Ghost and Mrs Muir* 68–69. Knight Rider 82–.

Mullaney, Jack (1932–1982). Easy-going light American actor.
The Young Stranger 57. Kiss Them for Me 58. The Absent Minded Professor 61. Seven Days in May 64. When the Legends Die 72. Where Does it Hurt? 72.
TV series: The Ann Sothern Show, My Living Doll, Ensign O'Toole, It's About Time.

Mullard, Arthur (1910–). Big, bluff cockney character comedian who became a British television star of the seventies.
The Wrong Arm of the Law 63. The Great St Trinian's Train Robbery 67, many others.

Mullen, Barbara (1914–1979). Irish-American actress, former dancer, who came to films as star of *Jeannie* 42.
Thunder Rock 42. A Place of One's Own 44. The Trojan Brothers 45. Corridor of Mirrors 48. So Little Time 52. The Challenge 60, etc.
TV series: Dr Finlay's Casebook 59-66.

Muller, Renate (1907–1937). German leading lady best known abroad for *Sunshine Susie* 31.
Biography 1944: *Queen of America?* by R. E. Clements.
Liebling der Götter 30. Viktor und Viktoria 34. Allotria 36.

Mulligan, Richard (1932–). Lanky American character actor.
The Group 66. The Undefeated 69. Little Big Man 70. The Big Bus 76. Scavenger Hunt 79. S.O.B. 81. Trail of the Pink Panther 82. Micki and Maude 84. Teachers 84. The Heavenly Kid 85. A Fine Mess 86, etc.
TV series: The Hero 66. *Soap* 77–80.

Mulligan, Robert (1925–). American director, from TV.
□Fear Strikes Out 57. The Rat Race 60. Come September 61. The Great Impostor 61. The Spiral Road 62. *To Kill a Mockingbird* 62. Love with the Proper Stranger 64. Baby the Rain Must Fall 65. Inside Daisy Clover 65. Up the Down Staircase 67. The Stalking Moon 68. The Pursuit of Happiness 70. *Summer of '42* 71. The Other 73. The Nickel Ride 75. Bloodbrothers 78. Same Time Next Year 78. Kiss Me Goodbye 82.

multi-screen techniques are nothing new, but the Montreal Exhibition of 1967 made them fashionable again, so that in such films as *The Boston Strangler, Grand Prix* and *The Thomas Crown Affair* the audience was supposed to look at up to a dozen different images at the same time, which became mighty exhausting. Mercifully, the fashion soon wore off.

multiplane. A word introduced by Walt Disney to explain his new animation process for *The Old Mill* 37. Instead of building up a drawing by laying 'cells' directly on top of each other, a slight illusion of depth was obtained by leaving space between the celluloid images of foreground, background, principal figure, etc. Special Academy Award 1938.

multiple roles. The record for the number of characters played by one actor in a film is held not by Alec Guinness in *Kind Hearts and Coronets* but (probably) by Lupino Lane, who played twenty-four parts in a 1929 comedy called *Only Me*, by Buster Keaton in *The Playhouse*, or by George S. Melies in his 1900 film *The One Man Band.* Others with high scores, apart from Guinness' eight, include Robert Hirsch's dozen in *No Questions on Saturday*, Rod Steiger's seven in *No Way to Treat a Lady*, Paul Muni's seven in *Seven Faces*, Jerry Lewis' seven in *The Family Jewels*, Tony Randall's seven in *The Seven Faces of Dr Lao*, Hugh Herbert's six in *La Conga Nights*, Peter Sellers' six in *Soft Beds, Hard Battles*, Fernandel's six in *The Sheep Has Five Legs*, Anna Neagle's four in *Lilacs in the Spring*, Françoise Rosay's four in *Une Femme Disparait*, Louis Jourdan's and Joan Fontaine's four each in *Decameron Nights*, Rod Steiger's and Claire Bloom's four each in *The Illustrated Man*, Lionel Jeffries' four in *The Secret of My Success*, Alan Young's four in *Gentlemen Prefer Brunettes*, Terry Kilburn's four generations of boy in *Goodbye Mr Chips*, Moira Shearer's three in *The Man Who Loved Redheads*, Deborah Kerr's three in *The Life and Death of Colonel Blimp*, Peter Sellers' three in *The Mouse That Roared* and *Dr Strangelove,* Leon Errol's three in some episodes of the *Mexican Spitfire* series, Joanne Woodward's three in *The Three Faces of Eve* and Eleanor Parker's three in *Lizzie.* One should perhaps also count Danny Kaye's various dream selves in *The Secret Life of Walter Mitty*.

Dual roles have frequently been of the schizophrenic type of which *Dr Jekyll and Mr Hyde* (qv) is the most obvious example. This category includes Henry Hull in *Werewolf of London* and Lon Chaney Jnr in *The Wolf Man*, Phyllis Calvert in *Madonna of the Seven Moons*, Phyllis Thaxter in *Bewitched*, Jerry Lewis in *The Nutty Professor*, and Alec Guinness in *The Captain's Paradise.* Two-character roles include Ronald Colman in *The Masquerader* and *The Prisoner of Zenda*, Lon Chaney in *London After Midnight*, Edward G. Robinson in *The Man with Two Faces*, Laurel and Hardy in *Our Relations*, Allan Jones and Joe Penner in *The Boys from Syracuse*, Chaplin in *The Great Dictator,* Louis Hayward in *The Man in the Iron Mask*, Olivia de Havilland in *The Dark Mirror*, Boris Karloff in *The Black Room*, Herbert Lom in *Dual Alibi*, George M. Cohan in *The Phantom President*, Jack Palance in *House of Numbers*, Peter Whitney in *Murder He Says*, Elisabeth Bergner (and later Bette Davis) in *Stolen Life*, Bette Davis in *Dead Ringer*, Yul Brynner in *The Double Man*, Stanley Baxter in *Very Important Person*, Peter Lawford in *One More Time*, George Arliss in *His Lordship*, Alain Delon in *The Black Tulip*, John McIntire in *The Lawless Breed*, Valentino in *Son of the Sheik*, Jack Mulhall in *Dark Streets* (allegedly the first to use the split-image technique), Larry Parks (playing Jolson *and* himself) in *Jolson Sings Again*, Douglas Fairbanks Jnr in *The Corsican Brothers*, Jessie Matthews in *Evergreen* and Julie Christie in *Fahrenheit 451*.

multiple-story films probably began in 1916 with *Intolerance*, which audiences rejected as too complicated. Later attempts made sure that the stories were clearly woven into a common thread; *The Bridge of San Luis Rey* in 1929, *Grand Hotel* in 1932, *Friday the Thirteenth* and *Dinner at Eight* in 1933, *Un Carnet de Bal* (also known as *Christine*) in 1936, *Tales of Manhattan* in 1942, *Forever and a Day* in 1942, *Flesh and Fantasy* in 1943, *Weekend at the Waldorf* and *Dead of Night* in 1945. In 1948–50 three Somerset Maugham compendiums, introduced by the author, emerged as *Quartet, Trio* and *Encore*; this inspired *O. Henry's Full House* in 1952. In 1963 we had *The VIPs* and in 1964 *The Yellow Rolls-Royce*, the stories in the latter being very casually linked. Meanwhile horror compendiums were becoming popular, 1962's *Tales of Terror* being followed between 1967 and 1972 by *Dr Terror's House of Horrors, The Torture Garden, The House that Dripped Blood, Tales From the Crypt, Asylum*, *Vault of Horror*, *Tales that Witness*

Madness, *From Beyond the Grave*, *The Monster Club*, *Creepshow* and *Cat's Eyes*.

The Mummy. Interest in avenging mummies was aroused during the twenties by the widespread stories of the curse of Tutankhamen whose tomb had recently been discovered and opened. In 1932 Karl Freund directed a rather strange romantic film on the subject with Boris Karloff as a desiccated but active three-thousand-year-old still on the track of his lost love. Despite good box office it was not reprised until 1940, when *The Mummy's Hand*, a pure hokum thriller, appeared with Tom Tyler in the role. Between 1942 and 1944 there were three increasingly foolish sequels starring (if it really *was* him under the bandages) Lon Chaney Jnr: they were *The Mummy's Tomb*, *The Mummy's Ghost* and *The Mummy's Curse*. In 1959 Hammer took over the character and remade *The Mummy* with an English Victorian setting: Christopher Lee was the monster. There have been two poor sequels, *The Curse of the Mummy's Tomb* 64 and *The Mummy's Shroud* 66. *Blood From The Mummy's Tomb* 71 did not feature a monster; it was based on a Bram Stoker story. The lighter side of the subject was viewed by Wheeler and Woolsey in *Mummy's Boys* 35, the Three Stooges in *Mummie's Dummies* 38, and Abbott and Costello in *Meet the Mummy* 54.

Mumy, Billy (–). American child actor of the sixties.
Palm Springs Weekend 63. A Ticklish Affair 63. *Dear Brigitte* 65. Rascal 69. Bless the Beasts and Children 71. Papillon 73, etc.
TV series: Lost in Space 65–68. Sunshine 75.

Mundin, Herbert (1898–1939). British character actor with stage experience, in British films in the twenties, Hollywood from 1930.
The Devil's Lottery 31. Sherlock Holmes 32. Cavalcade 33. *David Copperfield* (as Barkis) 34. Mutiny on the Bounty 35. Another Dawn 37. *The Adventures of Robin Hood* (as Much the Miller) 38. Society Lawyer 39, etc.

Muni, Paul (1896–1967) (Muni Weisenfreund). Distinguished American actor of Austrian parentage. Long stage experience.
Biography 1974: *Actor* by Jerome Lawrence.
□The Valiant (film debut) 28. Seven Faces 29. *Scarface* 32. *I Am a Fugitive from a Chain Gang* 32. The World Changes 33. Hi Nellie 33. Bordertown 34. Black Fury 35. Dr Socrates 35. *The Story of Louis Pasteur* (AA) 36. *The Good Earth* 37. *The Life of Emile Zola* 37. The Woman I Love 38. Juarez 39. We Are Not Alone 39. Hudson's Bay 40. The Commandos Strike at Dawn 42. Stage Door Canteen 43. *A Song to Remember* 44. Counter Attack 45. Angel on My Shoulder 46. Stranger on the Prowl 51. The Last Angry Man 59.
❁ For convincing world audiences of his day that heavy disguise made a great actor; and for his powerful early performances. *Scarface*.

¶ Every time Paul Muni parts his beard and looks down a microscope, this company loses two million dollars.—*Hal B. Wallis, as Warner head of production in the late thirties.*

'His voice is rich and pleasant, his personality is strong and virile, and if he is not pretty, neither is Lon Chaney.'—*Variety 1929*
'He seemed intent on submerging himself so completely that he disappeared.'—*Bette Davis*

Munk, Andrzej (1921–1961). Polish director.
Men of the Blue Cross 55. Eroica 57. Bad Luck 60. The Passenger (incomplete) 61, etc.

Munro, Caroline (1951–). British leading lady.
The Abominable Dr Phibes 71. Captain Kronos 72. The Golden Voyage of Sinbad 73. The Devil Within Her 73. At the Earth's Core 76. The Spy Who Loved Me 77. Maniac 80, etc.

Munro, Janet (1934–1972). Scottish leading lady with brief stage experience before films in both GB and US.
The Trollenberg Terror 57. The Young and the Guilty 57. Darby O'Gill and the Little People 58. Third Man on the Mountain 59. The Swiss Family Robinson 60. The Day the Earth Caught Fire 62. Life for Ruth 62. Bitter Harvest 63. A Jolly Bad Fellow 64. Sebastian 67, etc.

Munsel, Patrice (1925–). American operatic soprano who played the title role in *Melba* 53.

Munshin, Jules (1915–1970). Rubber-limbed American comedian, in occasional films from the mid-forties.
Easter Parade 48. Take Me Out to the Ball Game 48. *On the Town* 49. Ten Thousand

Bedrooms 56. Silk Stockings 57. Wild and Wonderful 64, etc.

Munson, Ona (1906–1955) (Ona Wolcott). American character actress, former dancer. Going Wild 30. Five Star Final 32. Gone with the Wind 39. Drums of the Congo 40. *The Shanghai Gesture* (as Mother Gin Sling) 41. The Cheaters 45. The Red House 47, etc.

murder

? Who played the murderer in the following whodunits?

1 *Green for Danger*
2 *After the Thin Man*
3 *The Maltese Falcon* (of Miles Archer) (1940)
4 *Laura*
5 *The Spiral Staircase*
6 *Crossfire*
7 *The Lady in the Lake*
8 *The List of Adrian Messenger*
9 *The Scarlet Claw*
10 *The Hound of the Baskervilles* (Rathbone 1939 version)
11 *Harper*
12 *And Then There Were None* (1945)
13 *The Ghost Breakers*
14 *Topper Returns*
15 *The Cat and the Canary* (1939)
16 *Charlie Chan at Treasure Island*
17 *The Kennel Murder Case*
18 *Hot Spot/I Wake Up Screaming*
19 *The Greene Murder Case* (1929)
20 *The Naked City*
21 *Witness for the Prosecution*
22 *Dial M for Murder*
23 *The Lodger* (1944)
24 *Stage Fright*
25 *Frenzy*

Murder on the Orient Express (GB 1973). This old-fashioned, twenties-set Agatha Christie thriller came in on a wave of publicity and was decently enough done but proved disappointing and slow in its second half, despite an all-star cast: the set was too restrictive and Albert Finney as Poirot was way over the top. Surprisingly, though the producers continued raiding the Christie canon to slowly diminishing returns (*Death on the Nile*, *The Mirror Crack'd*, *Evil under the Sun*, *Appointment with Death*), other producers were content to spoof the genre (*Murder by Death*, *Clue*). Christie novels however became popular TV movie fodder.

murderers abound in fictional films, but only a handful of real-life cases have been analysed with any seriousness. There have been several 'lives' of Charlie Peace and Landru, and fantasies about the earlier French 'Bluebeard'. More recently a cold clinical eye was applied to Barbara Graham in *I Want to Live* 57, *Dr Crippen* 64, *The Boston Strangler* 68, John Christie in *Ten Rillington Place* 71. Ruth Ellis was said to have inspired *Yield to the Night* 56 and Leopold and Loeb were plainly the subject of *Compulsion* 58 as well as *Rope* 48. More recent years have brought such case histories as *In Cold Blood* 67 and *The Executioner's Song* 82, and TV has done its bit with *Kill Me If You Can* (Caryl Chessman) 77, *The Lindbergh Kidnapping Case* (Bruno Hauptmann) 75 and *Helter Skelter* (Charles Manson) 76.

Murdoch, Richard (1907–). British radio entertainer, long partnered with Arthur Askey and Kenneth Horne.
Band Wagon 39. *The Ghost Train* 41. It Happened in Soho 48. Golden Arrow 52. Not a Hope in Hell 59. Strictly Confidential 61, etc.

Murfin, Jane (1893–1955). American screenwriter.
The Right to Lie 19. Flapper Wives 24. White Fang 25. Meet the Prince 26. Dance Hall 29. Leathernecking 30. Friends and Lovers 31. Our Betters 33. Ann Vickers 33. Spitfire 34. This Man Is Mine 34. Roberta 35. Alice Adams 35. Come and Get It 36. The Shining Hour 38. Stand Up and Fight 39. Pride and Prejudice 40. Andy Hardy's Private Secretary 41. Flight for Freedom 43. Dragon Seed 44, etc.
†Miss Murfin's plays as co-author, usually with Jane Cowl, include *Daybreak* and *Smilin' Through*, both of which were filmed.

Murnau, F. W. (or **Friedrich**) (1889–1931) (F. W. Plumpe). German director in films from 1919; Hollywood from 1927.
Satanas 19. Dr Jekyll and Mr Hyde 20. *Nosferatu* (Dracula) 22. *The Last Laugh* 24. Tartuffe 24. *Faust* 26. *Sunrise* 27. Four Devils 28. Our Daily Bread (City Girl) 30. Tabu (co-d) 31, etc.
❀ For unquestionable brilliance in showing what the camera can do. *The Last Laugh*.

Murphy, Audie (1924–1971). Boyish American leading man of the fifties; came to films on the strength of his war record as America's most decorated soldier, but despite some talent was soon relegated to low-budget westerns.

☐Beyond Glory 48. Texas Brooklyn and Heaven 48. Bad Boy 49. Sierra 50. The Kid from Texas 50. Kansas Raiders 50. *The Red Badge of Courage* 51. The Cimarron Kid 51. The Duel at Silver Creek 52. Gunsmoke 52. Column South 53. Tumbleweed 53. Ride Clear of Diablo 54. Drums Across the River 54. *Destry* 55. *To Hell and Back* (based on his autobiography) 55. The World in My Corner 56. Walk the Proud Land 56. The Guns of Fort Petticoat 57. Joe Butterfly 57. Night Passage 57. *The Quiet American* 58. Ride a Crooked Trail 58. The Gun Runners 58. No Name on the Bullet 59. The Wild and the Innocent 59. Cast a Long Shadow 59. Hell Bent for Leather 60. The Unforgiven 60. Seven Ways from Sundown 60. Posse from Hell 61. The Battle at Bloody Beach 61. Six Black Horses 62. Showdown 63. Gunfight at Comanche Creek 63. The Quick Gun 64. Bullet for a Badman 64. Apache Rifles 64. Arizona Raiders 65. Gunpoint 66. Trunk to Cairo 66. The Texican 66. Forty Guns to Apache Pass 67.
TV series: Whispering Smith 58.

¶ I guess my face is still the same, and so is the dialogue. Only the horses have changed.—*A.M. at 40*

Murphy, Ben (1941–). Athletic American TV hero of *Alias Smith and Jones*, *Griff*, *Gemini Man*, *The Chisholms*, etc.
The Letters (TV) 73. Runaway (TV) 73. Heatwave (TV) 74. This Was the West That Was (TV) 75. Sidecar Racers 75. Bridger (TV) 76. Time Walker 82. The Winds of War (TV) 83, etc.

Murphy, Dudley (1897–). American journalist who was briefly in films as director in the twenties and thirties.
High Speed Lee 23. Alex the Great 28. The Sport Parade 32. *The Emperor Jones* 33. The Night Is Young 35. Don't Gamble with Love 36. One Third of a Nation 39. Main Street Lawyer 39. Alma del Bronce (Mex.) 44, etc.

Murphy, Eddie (1961–). Foul-mouthed black American comedian and actor.
48 Hours 82. Trading Places 83. Best Defense 84. *Beverly Hills Cop* 85. The Golden Child 86. Beverly Hills Cop II 87.

¶ *E.M.:* Wouldn't it be a helluva thing if this was burnt cork and you folk were being tolerant for nothing?

Murphy, George (1902–). Amiable Irish-American actor and dancer, a pleasant light talent who left the screen for politics and became senator for California. Special Academy Award 1951 'for interpreting the film industry to the nation at large'. Autobiography 1970: *Say, Didn't You Use to be George Murphy?*
☐Kid Millions 34, Jealousy 34. Public Menace 35. I'll Love You Always 35. After the Dance 35. Woman Trap 36. Top of the Town 36. London by Night 37. You're a Sweetheart 37. Broadway Melody of 1938. Letter of Introduction 38. Little Miss Broadway 38. Hold that Co-Ed 38. Risky Business 39. Broadway Melody of 1940. *Little Nellie Kelly* 40. Public Deb No. 1 40. A Girl a Guy and a Gob 40. Ringside Maisie 41. *Tom Dick and Harry* 41. Rise and Shine 41. The Mayor of 44th Street 41. For Me and My Gal 41. The Navy Comes Through 42. The Powers Girl 42. Bataan 43. This is the Army 43. Broadway Rhythm 44. *Show Business* 44. *Step Lively* 44. Having Wonderful Crime 44. Up Goes Maisie 46. The Arnelo Affair 47. Cynthia 47. Tenth Avenue Angel 48. Big City 48. Border Incident 49. Battleground 49. No Questions Asked 51. It's a Big Country 51. Walk East on Beacon 52. Talk About a Stranger 52.

Murphy, Mary (1931–). American leading lady.
The Lemon Drop Kid (debut) 51. The Wild One 54. Beachhead 54. Hell's Island 55. The Desperate Hours 55. The Intimate Stranger (GB) 56. Crime and Punishment USA 59. Forty Pounds of Trouble 63. Junior Bonner 72, etc.

Murphy, Michael (1949–). American general purpose actor.
Countdown 67. The Arrangement 69. Brewster McCloud 70. What's Up Doc? 72. The Thief Who Came to Dinner 73. Nashville 75. An Unmarried Woman 77. Manhattan 79. The Year of Living Dangerously 82. Cloak and Dagger 84. Salvador 85, etc.

Murphy, Ralph (1895–1967). American director, in Hollywood from silent days.
The Gay City 41. Hearts in Springtime 41. Mrs Wiggs of the Cabbage Patch 42. Rainbow Island 44. The Man in Half Moon Street 44. Red Stallion in the Rockies 49. Dick Turpin's Ride 51. Captain Blood, Fugitive 52. Desert Rats 53. The Lady in the Iron Mask 53. Three Stripes in the Sun (& w) 55, etc.

Murphy, Richard (1912–). American writer, in Hollywood from 1937.
Boomerang 47. Cry of the City 48. Panic in

the Streets 50. Les Misérables 52. Broken Lance 54. Compulsion 58. The Wackiest Ship in the Army (& d) 60, etc.

Murphy, Rosemary (1925–). American stage actress in occasional films.
□That Night 57. The Young Doctors 61. To Kill a Mockingbird 62. Any Wednesday 66. Ben 72. You'll Like My Mother 72. Walking Tall 73. Forty Carats 73. Ace Eli and Rodger of the Skies 73. Julia (as Dorothy Parker) 77. September 87.

Murray, Barbara (1929–). British leading lady with stage experience.
Anna Karenina 48. Passport to Pimlico 48. Doctor at Large 56. Campbell's Kingdom 58. A Cry from the Streets 58. Girls in Arms 60. A Dandy in Aspic 68. Tales from the Crypt 72, many others.
TV series: The Power Game 66–68. The Bretts 87.

Murray, Bill (1950–). Canadian comic actor of the eighties, fresh from success on TV's *Saturday Night Live*.
Meatballs 79. Caddyshack 80. Stripes 82. Tootsie (uncredited) 82. *Ghostbusters* 84. The Razor's Edge 84. Little Shop of Horrors 86.

Murray, Charlie (1872–1941). American vaudeville comedian long with Mack Sennett. In *Tillie's Punctured Romance* 15, and later played with George Sidney in a long series about the Cohens and Kellys.

Murray, Don (1929–). Ambitious American actor who graduated from innocent to tough roles but does not seem to have received the attention he sought and merited.
□*Bus Stop* 56. *The Bachelor Party* 57. A Hatful of Rain 57. From Hell to Texas 58. These Thousand Hills 59. Shake Hands with the Devil 59. One Foot in Hell 60. *The Hoodlum Priest* (& co-p) 61. *Advise and Consent* 62. Escape from East Berlin 62. One Man's Way 64. Baby the Rain Must Fall 65. Kid Rodelo 66. The Plainsman 66. Sweet Love, Bitter 67. The Viking Queen 67. Tale of the Cock 67. The Borgia Stick (TV) 67. The Intruders (TV) 67. Daughter of the Mind (TV) 69. Childish Things (& wp) 70. Conquest of the Planet of the Apes 72. Happy Birthday Wanda June 72. Cotter 73. A Girl Named Sooner (TV) 74. The Sex Symbol (TV) 74. The Girl on the Late Late Show (TV) 75. Deadly Hero 76. Damien (w, d) 77. Rainbow (TV) 78. Crisis in Mid-air (TV) 79. The Far Turn (TV) 79. Endless Love 81. Peggy Sue Got Married 86. Scorpion 86. Made in Heaven 87.
TV series: The Outcasts 68. Knots Landing 80–81.

Murray, James (1901–1936). American leading man, a former extra who was chosen by King Vidor to play the hero of *The Crowd* 28, but subsequently took to drink and died in obscurity.
The Big City 28. Thunder 29. Bright Lights 30. The Reckoning 32. Heroes for Sale 32. Skull and Crown 35, etc.

Murray, Ken (1903–) (Don Court). American comedy actor, radio and TV entertainer, especially as collector of old 'home movies' of the stars. Collected special Oscar for his 1947 bird fantasy *Bill and Coo*. Autobiography 1960: *Life on a Pogo Stick*.
Half Marriage 29. A Night at Earl Carroll's 41. The Man who shot Liberty Valance 62. Follow Me Boys 66. Power 68.

Murray, Lyn (1909–). American composer.
Son of Paleface 52. The Bridges at Toko Ri 54. To Catch a Thief 55. Escape from Zahrain 61. Promise Her Anything 66. Rosie 67. The Magic Carpet (TV) 71, etc.

Murray, Mae (1889–1965) (Marie Adrienne Koenig). American leading lady of the silent screen; former dancer; usually in flashy roles. Retired to marry.
Biography 1959: *The Self-Enchanted* by Jane Ardmore.
Sweet Kitty Bellairs 17. Her Body in Bond 18. The Mormon Maid 20. Jazz Mania 21. Fashion Row 23. The Merry Widow 25. Circe the Enchantress 27. Peacock Alley 31, etc.

Murray, Stephen (1912–1983). Underused British character actor, on stage from 1933.
Pygmalion 38. *The Prime Minister* 41. *Next of Kin* 42. Undercover 43. *Master of Bankdam* 46. My Brother Jonathan 47. Silent Dust 48. *London Belongs to Me* 48. For Them That Trespass 49. Now Barabbas 50. The Magnet 50. 24 Hours of a Woman's Life 52. Four-Sided Triangle 53. The Stranger's Hand 54. The End of the Affair 55. Guilty 55. The Door in the Wall 56. At the Stroke of Nine 57. A Tale of Two Cities 58. The Nun's Story 59. Master Spy 63, etc.

Murray-Hill, Peter (1908–1957). British leading man of stage and screen; was married to Phyllis Calvert.

A Yank at Oxford 38. The Outsider 39. Jane Steps Out 40. The Ghost Train 41. Madonna of the Seven Moons 44. They Were Sisters (last film) 45, etc.

Murton, Lionel (1915–). Canadian character actor resident in Britain.
Meet the Navy 46. The Long Dark Hall 51. The Runaway Bus 54. The Battle of the River Plate 55. Up the Creek 58. Northwest Frontier 59, many others.

Musante, Tony (1936–). American character actor.
Once a Thief 65. The Detective 68. The Bird with the Crystal Plumage 70. The Grissom Gang 71, The Last Run 71, etc.
TV series: *Toma* 72.

Muse, Clarence (1889–1979). Black American character actor.
Hearts in Dixie 28. Cabin in the Cotton 32. Showboat 36. Tales of Manhattan 42. An Act of Murder 48. So Bright the Flame 52. Car Wash 77. The Black Stallion 79, many others.

musical remakes are becoming thicker on the ground than musical originals. All the following had been filmed at least once before, as straight dramas or comedies with music:
Where's Charley? as *Charley's Aunt*; *Three for the Show* as *My Two Husbands*; *Living It Up* as *Nothing Sacred*; *Carmen Jones* as *Carmen*; *Scrooge* as *A Christmas Carol*; *Step Lively* as *Room Service*; *In the Good Old Summertime* as *The Shop Around The Corner*; *Meet Me After The Show* as *He Married His Wife*; *Annie Get Your Gun* as *Annie Oakley*; *Kismet* as *Kismet*; *The King and I* as *Anna and the King of Siam*; *Carousel* as *Liliom*; *High Society* as *The Philadelphia Story*; *Silk Stockings* as *Ninotchka*; *Gigi* as *Gigi*; *My Fair Lady* as *Pygmalion*; *The Sound of Music* as *The Trapp Family*; *Funny Girl* as *Rose of Washington Square*; *Sweet Charity* as *Nights of Cabiria*; *Camelot* as *Lancelot and Guinevere*; *Oliver!* as *Oliver Twist*; *Hello Dolly* as *The Matchmaker*; *Cabaret* as *I Am a Camera*; *Fiddler on the Roof* as *Tevye the Milkman*; *Mame* as *Auntie Mame*; *Lost Horizon* as *Lost Horizon*; *Goodbye Mr Chips* as *Goodbye Mr Chips*; *A Star Is Born* as *What Price Hollywood?* (and in 1937 as *A Star is Born*).

musicals obviously could not exist before Al Jolson sang 'Mammy', in1927. During the first two or three years of talkies, however, Hollywood produced so many gaudy backstage stories and all-star spectacles that the genre quickly wore out its welcome: *Broadway Melody, The Singing Fool, The Desert Song, Showboat, Chasing Rainbows, Show of Shows, Hollywood Revue, Lights of New York, On with the Show, King of Jazz, Gold Diggers of Broadway, Sunny Side Up* . . . all these before the end of 1930, and there were many poorer imitations. Discipline was needed, and the disciplinarian who emerged was Broadway dance director Busby Berkeley. His kaleidoscopic ensembles first dazzled the eye in Goldwyn-Cantor extravaganzas like *Whoopee* and *Palmy Days*, and came to full flower in the Warner musicals which brought to the fore stars like Joan Blondell, Ruby Keeler and Dick Powell, filling the years from 1933 to 1937 with such shows as *Footlight Parade, Forty-Second Street, Dames, Wonder Bar, Flirtation Walk* and the annual *Gold Digger* comedies. Meanwhile at Paramount Lubitsch had been quietly establishing a quieter style, using recitative, with *The Love Parade* and *One Hour with You*; Mamoulian was equally successful with *Love Me Tonight*; and the Marx Brothers contributed their own brand of musical anarchy. From 1933 to 1939 at RKO Fred Astaire and Ginger Rogers were teamed in an affectionately-remembered series of light comedy-musicals. MGM made sporadic efforts with creaky vehicles like *Cuban Love Song* but did not come into their own until 1935, when they started the Jeanette MacDonald/Nelson Eddy series of operettas; these were followed by a dramatic musical, *The Great Ziegfeld*, by the Eleanor Powell spectaculars like *Rosalie*, by a revived *Broadway Melody* series, and by *The Wizard of Oz* and the early Judy Garland/Mickey Rooney teenage extravaganzas, *Babes in Arms* and *Strike Up the Band*. Fox had Shirley Temple, Sonja Henie and Alice Faye; Goldwyn contributed Cantor and *The Goldwyn Follies*. Paramount concentrated on Maurice Chevalier, Bing Crosby and the all-star *Big Broadcast* series.

The popularity of musicals continued into the war-torn forties, when escapism was *de rigueur*. Universal, whose only major pre-war musical was *Showboat*, continued to build up Deanna Durbin and threw in Donald O'Connor and Gloria Jean for good measure. Warners had *This Is the Army* and several musical biopics: *Yankee Doodle Dandy, Night and Day, Rhapsody in Blue*. RKO had a young man named Sinatra. Fox found goldmines in Carmen Miranda and Betty Grable, but their vehicles were routine;

Columbia did slightly better by Rita Hayworth, and then surprised everyone with *The Jolson Story*, which set the musical back on top just when it was flagging. Paramount was doing very nicely with Bing Crosby and Bob Hope. Everybody did at least one big morale-building musical with all the stars on the payroll blowing kisses to the boys out there: *Star Spangled Rhythm, Thank Your Lucky Stars, Hollywood Canteen, Thousands Cheer* and so on.

Top dog in the forties and fifties was undoubtedly MGM. Specialities like *Ziegfeld Follies, Till the Clouds Roll By* and *Words and Music* came side by side with more routine productions starring Gene Kelly, Judy Garland, and Esther Williams (in aqua-musicals, of course). The decade ended in a blaze of glory with *On the Town*, which led to the even more spectacular heights of *An American in Paris* and *Singin' in the Rain*. By this time Mario Lanza and Howard Keel were needing new vehicles for themselves, *The Great Caruso* and *Seven Brides for Seven Brothers* being outstanding productions in their own right. But by the mid-fifties the demand, or the fashion, for musicals was dying. It lasted longest at Metro, who doggedly remade pictures like *The Belle of New York* and *Rose Marie*, added music to *Ninotchka* and *The Philadelphia Story* and *Gigi*. Warners plugged on until their bright star of 1948, Doris Day, signed with another studio and turned dramatic; Fox had two mammoth tries in *Call Me Madam* and *There's No Business Like Show Business*; Paramount came up with *White Christmas*, the enterprising *Red Garters* and *Funny Face*, and even *Li'l Abner*. But the risk was becoming too great in a chancy market, with expenses growing by the minute; and for the last ten years no original musicals have been written in Hollywood, with the exception of the family-aimed *Mary Poppins, Thoroughly Modern Millie* and the twenty-odd look-alike vehicles of Elvis Presley. Copper-bottomed Broadway hits like *Pal Joey, Oklahoma, Carousel, The Pajama Game, South Pacific, The King and I, West Side Story, Guys and Dolls, Hello Dolly, On a Clear Day You Can See Forever, Fiddler on the Roof, Man of La Mancha, The Sound of Music* and *My Fair Lady* are still filmed, at gargantuan cost, but as cinema they all too often disappoint filmgoers with memories of Berkeley and Kelly and Donen. The most inventive screen musicals have been Bob Fosse's *Sweet Charity* and *Cabaret*.

In Britain, the thirties were a highpoint of the light musical starring such talents as Jack Buchanan, Jessie Matthews, Gracie Fields, George Formby and Anna Neagle; Miss Neagle indeed carried on, dauntless, into the less favourable climate of the fifties. The forties were pretty barren apart from the Rank spectacular *London Town*, which flopped; and it wasn't until the sixties that Elstree struck something like the right note with its energetic though derivative series starring Cliff Richard. In 1968 the old-fashioned though energetic *Oliver!* proved that Britain can handle a really big musical. The seventies brought little but rock operas and one or two curiously old-fashioned stagings of such as *Mame* and *1776*, until John Travolta spurred a new trend with *Saturday Night Fever* and a nostalgic one with *Grease*. *Flashdance* and *Breaking* started new forms, and *A Chorus Line*, long promised, was finally made in 1984, by which time most Broadway musicals had become too expensive to film. Books: *Gotta Sing Gotta Dance* by John Kobal; *The Hollywood Musical* by John Russell Taylor; *All Singing, All Dancing* by John Springer.
See also: *entertainers*.

The Musketeers of Pig Alley (US 1912). A D. W. Griffith melodrama starring Lillian Gish, often quoted as the screen's first step towards social realism; set in the teeming slums of New York.

Mustin, Burt (1884–1977). American comedy character actor who was 67 when he made his first film.
Detective Story 51. The Lusty Men 53. The Desperate Hours 55. The Big Country 57. Huckleberry Finn 61. The Thrill of It All 63. Cat Ballou 65. Speedway 68. Hail Hero 70. The Skin Game 71, etc.
TV series: A Date with the Angels 57. Phyllis 76.

Musuraca, Nicholas (1895–). American cinematographer.
Bride of the Storm 24. Lightning Lanats 25. Tyrant of Red Gulch 27. The Cuckoos 31. Cracked Nuts 33. Long Lost Father 34. Murder on a Bridle Path 36. Blind Alibi 38. Five Came Back 39. Golden Boy 39. The Swiss Family Robinson 40. Tom Brown's Schooldays 40. *Cat People* 42. The Seventh Victim 43. Curse of the Cat People 44. *The Spiral Staircase* 45. The Locket 46. The Bachelor and the Bobbysoxer 47. *Out of the Past* 47. Blood on the Moon 48. Where Danger Lives 51. Clash by Night 52. Devil's Canyon 53. The Story of Mankind 57. Too Much Too Soon 58, many others.

mute print. One with only the picture, no sound track.

Mutiny on the Bounty. Three films have been made of this semi-historical account of how Captain Bligh was cast adrift in an open boat in 1789. 1. US 1935 (AA): directed by Frank Lloyd, with Clark Gable and Charles Laughton. 2. US 1962: directed by Carol Reed (who resigned) and Lewis Milestone, with Marlon Brando and Trevor Howard. The first remains the most impressive despite its technical limitations. 3. Australia 1984. *The Bounty* featured a good performance from Anthony Hopkins as Bligh but was not otherwise acclaimed.

Muybridge, Eadweard (1830–1904) (Edward Muggeridge). British photographer who in 1877, in America, succeeded in analysing motion with a camera by taking a series of pictures of a horse in motion. (He used twenty-four cameras attached to a trip wire.) Later he invented a form of projector which reassembled his pictures into the appearance of moving actuality, and called it the Zoopraxinoscope; in 1877 he published an influential book of his findings, *Animal Locomotion*.

My Darling Clementine (US 1946). A highly atmospheric, semi-literary western based (remotely) on Stuart N. Lake's book *Wyatt Earp Frontier Marshal* which had been previously filmed as *Frontier Marshal* with Randolph Scott in 1939. Excellent performances by Henry Fonda as Earp, Victor Mature as Doc Holliday, and Walter Brennan as the head of the Clantons who get shot up in the OK corral. John Ford directs affectionately. *Gunfight at the OK Corral* 57, with Burt Lancaster and Kirk Douglas, is a partial remake.

My Fair Lady (US 1964) (AA, BFA). A professional but uninspired celluloid version of the fabulous Lerner-Loewe musical play from Shaw's *Pygmalion* (qv). A prodigious expenditure of talent, and to a lesser degree money, is evident, and there is plenty to enjoy; but more might have been packed into the most eagerly anticipated musical of the decade. With Audrey Hepburn, Rex Harrison (AA), Stanley Holloway; directed by George Cukor (AA); designed by Cecil Beaton (AA); photographed by Harry Stradling (AA). A special word is surely due for Marni Nixon, whose singing voice Audrey Hepburn mimes.

My Girl Tisa (US 1947). A charming, neglected, period romance set in New York's immigrant quarter at the turn of the century, with special reference to the political scene and an amusing if unlikely ending with Teddy Roosevelt as *deus ex machina*. Delightfully played by Lilli Palmer, Sam Wanamaker, Alan Hale, Stella Adler and a large cast; written by Allen Boretz, photographed by Ernest Haller, directed by Elliott Nugent.

My Little Chickadee (US 1940). An outlandish comedy-western starring, and written by, W. C. Fields and Mae West, the former as Cuthbert J. Twillie, the latter as Flower Belle Lee. Edward Cline was faced with the task of directing these strange personalities, and didn't quite manage it; the result is one of those engaging Hollywood freaks which no one can afford to have happen any more.

My Man Godfrey. Twice-filmed crazy comedy about a family of bored millionaires brought to heel by a butler they pick up in the gutter. 1936: directed by Gregory La Cava, with William Powell and Carole Lombard. 1957: directed by Henry Koster, with David Niven and June Allyson.

My Sister Eileen. Another twice-filmed comedy, from the book by Ruth McKinney about two sisters on the hunt for fame and men in New York. 1942: directed by Alexander Hall, with Rosalind Russell and Janet Blair. 1955: a semi-musical directed by Richard Quine, with Betty Garrett and Janet Leigh. There has also been a TV series with Elaine Stritch and Shirley Bonne. The men in the case were (1) Brian Aherne, (2) Jack Lemmon, (3) Jack Weston (later replaced by Stubby Kaye).

Mycroft, Walter (1891–1959). British director. Chief scriptwriter and director of productions at Elstree in the thirties.
Spring Meeting 40. My Wife's Family 41. Banana Ridge 41. The Woman's Angle (p only) 52, etc.

Myers, Carmel (1899–1980). American leading lady of the twenties, in the 'vamp' tradition.
Sirens of the Sea 16. Intolerance 16. The Haunted Pyjamas 17. Mad Marriage 21. The Famous Mrs Fair 23. Beau Brummell 24. Ben Hur 25. Sorrell and Son 27. Svengali 31. Lady for a Night 42. Whistle Stop 45, etc.

Myers, Harry (1886–1938). American character actor, in Hollywood from 1908.

Housekeeping 16. *A Connecticut Yankee* 21. The Beautiful and the Damned 26. *City Lights* (as the drunken millionaire) 31. Dangerous Lives 37, etc.

Myers, Stanley (–). American composer.
The Deer Hunter 78. The Watcher in the Woods 80. Lady Chatterley's Lover 81. Moonlighting 82. The Honorary Consul 83.

Myrtil, Odette (1898–1978). French character actress in Hollywood.
Dodsworth 36. Kitty Foyle 40. Yankee Doodle Dandy 42. Forever and a Day 43. Devotion 46. Here Comes the Groom 50. Lady Possessed 52, many others.

mystery has always been a popular element of motion picture entertainment. Always providing scope for sinister goings-on and sudden revelations, mystery films divide themselves into two basic genres: who done it, and how will the hero get out of it? Silent melodramas like *The Perils of Pauline* were full of clutching hands and villainous masterminds, devices adopted by the German post-war cinema for its own purposes: *The Cabinet of Dr Caligari, Dr Mabuse* and *Warning Shadows* are all mysteries, peopled by eccentrics and madmen. American silent who-done-its like *The Cat and the Canary, The Thirteenth Chair* and *One Exciting Night* set a pattern for thrillers which could not come fully into their own until music and sound were added. In the thirties the 'thunderstorm mystery', with its spooky house and mysterious servants (the butler usually did it) quickly became a cliché; but this is not to denigrate the entertainment value of such movies as *The Bat, The Terror, Murder by the Clock, The Gorilla, Seven Keys to Baldpate, Double Door, You'll Find Out, Topper Returns, The House on Haunted Hill*, and the Bob Hope remakes of *The Cat and the Canary* and *The Ghost Breakers.*

The thirties also saw a movement to relegate the puzzle film to the detective series, a genre later taken over eagerly by TV. These films were built around such protagonists as Charlie Chan, Sherlock Holmes, Hercule Poirot, Inspector Hanaud, Ellery Queen, Perry Mason, Inspector Hornleigh, Nero Wolfe, Philo Vance, Nick Carter, The Crime Doctor, The Saint, The Falcon, Bulldog Drummond, Mrs Pym, the 'Thin Man' (the thin man was actually the victim of the first story, but the tag stuck to William Powell), Mr Moto, Michael Shayne, Hildegarde Withers, Mr Wong, Arsène Lupin, Dick Barton, The Baron, The Toff, Gideon, Slim Callaghan, Lemmy Caution and Maigret . . . all soundly spoofed by Groucho Marx as Wolf J. Flywheel in *The Big Store.* The best of these fictional detectives were the creations of Dashiell Hammett (Sam Spade in *The Maltese Falcon*) and Raymond Chandler (Philip Marlowe in *The Big Sleep, Farewell My Lovely* and *The High Window*); and after a twenty-year hiatus the threads were picked up by Ross MacDonald's *Harper*, Craig Stevens as *Gunn*, Frank Sinatra as *Tony Rome*, films of Chandler's *Marlowe* and J. D. MacDonald's *Darker Than Amber*, and Richard Roundtree as *Shaft.* Single who-done-its of great merit were *Gaslight, Laura, Green for Danger* (one ached for a whole series starring Alastair Sim as Inspector Cockrill), *The Spiral Staircase, Crossfire, Boomerang, Bad Day at Black Rock, Les Diaboliques, Charade, Mirage, Taste of Fear, The List of Adrian Messenger*, and the two verisons of *Ten Little Niggers.* Two gentler detectives were provided by Alec Guinness' *Father Brown* and Margaret Rutherford's Miss Marple.

The other type of mystery, with a hero on the run, usually suspected of murder, finally uncovering the real villain after many narrow escapes from death, was developed by Alfred Hitchcock in such films as *The Thirty-Nine Steps, The Lady Vanishes, Saboteur, Spellbound, Strangers on a Train, North by Northwest* and *Torn Curtain.* But stars as various as Alan Ladd, Bob Hope, Danny Kaye, Robert Mitchum, and Paul Newman have also found the device useful.

The recent vogue for tongue-in-cheek spy thrillers is to all intents and purposes a reversion to the Pearl White school, with the hero menaced at every turn but, of course, finally triumphant. Useful books: *The Detective in Film* by William K. Everson; *The Detective in Hollywood* by Jon Tuska.

See also: *spies*; *private eyes.*

The Mystery of the Wax Museum (US 1933). A badly-structured but interesting shocker in two-colour Technicolor, with sets by Anton Grot and direction by Michael Curtiz. Thought for years to be a lost film, it survives as a milestone of its era, with Glenda Farrell and Frank McHugh as wisecracking news hawks, Fay Wray as a frightened lady and Lionel Atwill as a mad sculptor who uses a wax face to disguise his hideously burned features. In 1953 the story was remade in 3-D as *House of Wax*, and in 1966 most of it turned up again in *Chamber of Horrors.*

Answers

the man
1 Paul Scofield ☐ 2 James Earl Jones ☐ 3 Claude Rains ☐ 4 Lon Chaney Jnr ☐ 5 James Mason ☐ 6 Nils Asther ☐ 7 James Stewart ☐ 8 Glenn Ford ☐ 9 Ray Milland ☐ 10 Jack Benny ☐ 11 Jean Louis Trintignant ☐ 12 Francis Lederer ☐ 13 Alec Guinness ☐ 14 Gregory Peck ☐ 15 James Cagney ☐ 16 George C. Scott ☐ 17 Kirk Douglas ☐ 18 Cliff Robertson ☐ 19 Lewis Stone ☐ 20 Frank Sinatra ☐ 21 Ronald Colman ☐ 22 Monty Woolley ☐ 23 In the original film not William Powell, but Edward Ellis ☐ 24 Claude Rains ☐ 25 George Arliss ☐ 26 Edward Ellis ☐ 27 Anton Diffring ☐ 28 Henry Fonda ☐ 29 Burt Reynolds ☐ 30 John Wayne (though Jimmy Stewart thought he did it) ☐

matched pairs
1 Annabella ☐ William Powell ☐ 2 Hedy Lamarr ☐ Robert Walker ☐ 3 Clint Eastwood ☐ Jeff Bridges ☐ 4 Barbara Eden ☐ David Hartman ☐ 5 Johnny Weissmuller ☐ Aquanetta ☐ 6 Max Baer ☐ Myrna Loy ☐ 7 Clark Gable ☐ Marion Davies ☐ 8 Gene Kelly ☐ Fred Astaire ☐ 9 Douglass Montgomery ☐ Paulette Goddard ☐ 10 Anna Sten ☐ Robert Webber ☐ 11 Gary Cooper ☐ Merle Oberon ☐ 12 Jeanne Crain ☐ Thelma Ritter ☐ 13 James Caan ☐ Alan Arkin ☐ 14 Cesar Romero ☐ Marjorie Weaver ☐ 15 Ray Milland ☐ Ginger Rogers ☐ 16 Deborah Kerr ☐ William Holden ☐ 17 Melina Mercouri ☐ Keith Michell ☐ 18 Laurence Olivier ☐ Greer Garson ☐ 19 Billy and Bobby Mauch ☐ ☐ 20 Glenn Ford ☐ Gloria de Haven ☐

meetings cute
1 Veronica Lake ☐ Alan Ladd ☐ *This Gun for Hire* ☐ 2 Gloria Swanson ☐ William Holden ☐ *Sunset Boulevard* ☐ 3 Veronica Lake ☐ Fredric March ☐ *I Married a Witch* ☐ 4 Mary Astor ☐ Walter Huston ☐ *Dodsworth* ☐ 5 Greta Garbo ☐ Melvyn Douglas ☐ *Ninotchka* ☐ 6 Dorothy Comingore ☐ Orson Welles ☐ *Citizen Kane* ☐ 7 Marlene Dietrich ☐ James Stewart ☐ *Destry Rides Again* ☐ 8 Eva Marie Saint ☐ Cary Grant ☐ *North by Northwest* ☐ 9 Katharine Hepburn ☐ James Stewart ☐ *The Philadelphia Story* ☐ 10 Greer Garson ☐ Laurence Olivier ☐ *Pride and Prejudice* ☐ 11 Joan Fontaine ☐ Laurence Olivier ☐ *Rebecca* ☐ 12 Veronica Lake ☐ Joel McCrea ☐ *Sullivan's Travels* ☐

mine, all mine
1 Danny Kaye ☐ 2 Humphrey Bogart ☐ 3 Jack Lemmon ☐ 4 John Wayne ☐ 5 Kirk Douglas (it's his mother's name) ☐ 6 Raquel Welch and her former husband Patric Curtis ☐ 7 Cary Grant ☐ and Stanley Donen ☐ 8 Clint Eastwood ☐ 9 Marlon Brando ☐ 10 James Mason (it's his daughter's name) ☐ 11 Frank Sinatra (spell it backwards) ☐ 12 Alfred Hitchcock ☐ 13 Ray Stark ☐ 14 Aaron Rosenberg ☐

monsters
1 *The Beast from 20,000 Fathoms* (1948) ☐
2 *King Kong* (1933) ☐
3 The monster in *Frankenstein* (1931) ☐
4 *The Thing from Another World* (1952)—who was played by James Arness ☐
5 Lon Chaney Junior as *The Wolf Man* (1940) ☐
6 Boris Karloff as *The Mummy* (1932) ☐
7 The nameless actor who played the *Gorilla at Large* (1954) ☐
8 The Golem in *It* (1957) ☐
9 Lon Chaney Junior as the electric man in *Man Made Monster* (1941) ☐
10 Boris Karloff as the monster in *Bride of Frankenstein* (1935) ☐
11 Richard Wordsworth as the outcome of *The Quatermass Experiment* (1955) ☐
12 Lon Chaney Junior, who in *Son of Dracula* (1942) turned up in America as Count Alucard; or Christopher Lee, who borrowed the trick in *Dracula A.D. 1972* ☐
13 Boris Karloff in *The Raven* (1935) ☐
14 Henry Hill or Warner Oland in *Werewolf of London* (1935) ☐
15 The hero of *Curse of the Werewolf* (1962) (Oliver Reed) ☐
16 The mutant in *This Island Earth* (1955) ☐
17 Simone Simon in her cat form in *Cat People* (1942) ☐
18 *The Gorgon* (1964); he beheaded her ☐
19 Lon Chaney Junior as the wolf man in *House of Dracula* (1945) ☐
20 The demon in *Night of the Demon* (1957) ☐

murder

1 Rosamund John ☐ 2 James Stewart ☐ 3 Mary Astor ☐ 4 Clifton Webb ☐ 5 George Brent ☐ 6 Robert Ryan ☐ 7 Lloyd Nolan ☐ 8 Kirk Douglas ☐ 9 Gerald Hamer ☐ 10 Lowell Gilmore ☐ 11 Arthur Hill ☐ 12 Barry Fitzgerald ☐ 13 Richard Carlson ☐ 14 H. B. Warner ☐ 15 Douglass Montgomery ☐ 16 Cesar Romero ☐ 17 Ralph Morgan ☐ 18 Elisha Cook Jnr ☐ 19 Jean Arthur ☐ 20 Ted De Corsia ☐ 21 Tyrone Power ☐ 22 Nobody actually murders anybody, though Ray Milland hires Anthony Dawson to do one for him. Dawson is killed in self-defence by Grace Kelly ☐ 23 Laird Cregar ☐ 24 Richard Todd ☐ 25 Barry Foster ☐

N

Nabokov, Vladimir (1899–1977). Russian émigré novelist who became fashionable in the mid-fifties. Works filmed include *Lolita*, *Laughter in the Dark*. *King Queen Knave* and *Despair*.

Nader, George (1921–). American leading man who after TV experience starred in many Universal action films of the fifties but has lately been less active.
Monsoon (debut) 52. Four Guns to the Border 54. The Second Greatest Sex 55. Away All Boats 56. Congo Crossing 56. Four Girls in Town 57. Joe Butterfly 57. Nowhere to Go (GB) 58. The Human Duplicators 65. The Million Eyes of Su-Muru 66, etc.
TV series: Ellery Queen 54. The Man and the Challenge 59. Shannon 61.

Nagel, Anne (1912–1966) (Anne Dolan). American supporting actress, the heroine's friend in countless movies of the forties.
Hot Money 36. Black Friday 40. Man Made Monster 41. Women in Bondage 44. Spirit of West Point 47, etc.

Nagel, Conrad (1896–1970). American leading man of the twenties who came to Hollywood after stage experience; latterly ran acting school.
Little Women 19. Fighting Chance 20. Three Weeks 24. The Exquisite Sinner 26. Slightly Used 27. Quality Street 27. One Romantic Night 30. Bad Sister 31. East Lynne 31. Dangerous Corner 34. Navy Spy 37. I Want a Divorce 40. The Woman in Brown 48. All That Heaven Allows 55. Stranger in My Arms 58. The Man Who Understood Women 59, many others.

Naish, J. Carrol (1900–1973). American character actor with stage experience, in films from 1930.
The Hatchet Man 32. Lives of a Bengal Lancer 35. Anthony Adverse 36. King of Alcatraz 38. Persons in Hiding 39. *Beau Geste* 39. Birth of the Blues 41. Blood and Sand 41. The Corsican Brothers 41. The Pied Piper 42. Dr Renault's Secret 42. Batman (serial) 43. Behind the Rising Sun 43. Gung Ho! 44. *A Medal for Benny* 45. House of Frankenstein 45. The Southerner 45. Enter Arsène Lupin 45. The Beast with Five Fingers 46. Joan of Arc 48. Black Hand 49. Annie Get Your Gun 50. Across the Wide Missouri 51. Sitting Bull 54. Violent Saturday 54. New York Confidential 54. The Young Don't Cry 57. The Hanged Man 64. Blood of Frankenstein 70, many others.
TV series: Life With Luigi 52. The New Adventures of Charlie Chan 57. Guestward Ho! 60.

Naismith, Laurence (1908–) (Lawrence Johnson). Amiable British character actor with wide stage experience.
Trouble in the Air 47. A Piece of Cake 48. I Believe in You 51. The Beggar's Opera 52. Mogambo 53. Carrington VC 55. *Richard III* 56. Boy on a Dolphin 57. Tempest 58. A Night to Remember 58. Sink the Bismarck 60. The Singer Not the Song 61. Jason and the Argonauts 63. The Three Lives of Thomasina 63. Sky West and Crooked 65. The Scorpio Letters 67. The Long Duel 67. Fitzwilly 67. *Camelot* 67. The Valley of Gwangi 68. Eye of the Cat 69. Scrooge 70. Diamonds are Forever 71. *The Amazing Mr Blunden* 72.
TV series: *The Persuaders* 71.

Naked City (US 1948). Mark Hellinger's last production was a highly influential police thriller shot on location in New York and using a development of the semi-documentary approach first seen in such films as *The House on 92nd Street* two years earlier. It ended with the famous tag used in all 99 episodes of the TV series which followed twelve years later: 'There are eight million stories in the naked city: this has been one of them.' Barry Fitzgerald played the leading cop and Don Taylor his aide; Jules Dassin directed, enlivening a basically routine story with striking detail; the script was by Albert Maltz and Marvin Wald with photography by William Daniels (AA). Despite hundreds of imitations the 'authentic' crime thriller is still popular.

Naldi, Nita (1899–1961) (Anita Donna Dooley). Italian-American leading lady of the twenties, formerly in the Ziegfeld Follies.
Dr Jekyll and Mr Hyde 20. The Unfair Sex 22. Blood and Sand 22. The Ten Commandments 23. Cobra 25. A Sainted Devil 25. The Marriage Whirl 26. The Lady Who Lied 27, etc.

Namath, Joe (1943–). American professional sportsman who made a few films.
Norwood 69. C. C. and Company 70. Avalanche Express 78. Marriage Is Alive and Well (TV) 80.

Nana. Zola's novel of the Paris demimonde in the 1860s has been seen in four major film versions. 1. Jean Renoir directed a silent French version in 1926, with Catherine Hessling and Werner Krass. 2. Dorothy Arzner directed an American version, sometimes known as *Lady of the Boulevards*, in 1934 with Anna Sten, Lionel Atwill and Phillips Holmes. 3. Christian-Jaque directed a second French version in 1955, this time in colour, with Martine Carol and Charles Boyer. 4. Mac Ahlberg directed a Franco-Swedish 1970 version called *Take Me, Love Me*, with Anna Gael.

Nancy Drew. The teenage heroine of a number of American second features made in 1938–39; all were directed by William Clemens and starred Bonita Granville. The titles included *Nancy Drew Detective, Nancy Drew Reporter, Nancy Drew and the Hidden Staircase, Nancy Drew Trouble Shooter*. A TV series followed in 1977.

Nanook of the North (US 1922). This classic documentary was made by explorer-director Robert Flaherty, who was commissioned by Revillon Frères, a fur company, and spent years in the Arctic among the Eskimos while amassing his material. It is virtually the first significant documentary in the history of the cinema, and even today remains watchable.

Napier, Alan (1903–) (Alan Napier-Clavering). Dignified British character actor, in Hollywood since 1940; usually plays butlers or noble lords.
In a Monastery Garden 31. Loyalties 32. For Valour 37. The Four Just Men 39. The Invisible Man Returns 40. Random Harvest 42. Ministry of Fear 43. Lost Angel 44. *The Uninvited* 44. Forever Amber 47. Tarzan's Magic Fountain 50. Julius Caesar 53. The Court Jester 55. Journey to the Centre of the Earth 59. Marnie 64, scores of others.
TV series: Batman 65–67.

Napier, Diana (1905–82) (Molly Ellis). British leading lady of the thirties; married Richard Tauber.
Wedding Rehearsal 33. Catherine the Great 34. The Private Life of Don Juan 34. Mimi 35. Land Without Music 36. Pagliacci 37, then retired until *I was a Dancer* 48.

Napier, Russell (1910–1975). Australian-born actor, long in Britain. Appeared in numerous small parts, usually as officials; also played the chief inspector in many of the 3-reel 'Scotland Yard' series.

Napoleon, Art (1923–). American director.
Man on the Prowl (& w) 57. Too Much Too Soon 58. Ride the Wild Surf (w only) 64.

Napoleon Bonaparte has been impersonated on screen by Charles Boyer in *Marie Walewska* (*Conquest*), Esmé Percy in *Invitation to the Waltz*, Emile Drain in *Madame sans Gêne* and *Les Perles de la Couronne*, Rollo Lloyd in *Anthony Adverse*, Julien Berthau in *Madame*, Marlon Brando in *Désirée*, Arnold Moss in *The Black Book*, Pierre Mondy in *Austerlitz*, Herbert Lom in several films including *The Young Mr Pitt* and *War and Peace*, Eli Wallach in *The Adventures of Gerard*, and Rod Steiger in *Waterloo*, and Kenneth Haigh in *Eagle in a Cage*.

Abel Gance's 1925 film *Napoleon* (with Albert Dieudonne) is noted for the first use of a triptych screen corresponding very closely to Cinerama, It was revived with international success in 1980, in a version painstakingly reassumbled by Kevin Brownlow, who in 1983 published a book about it.

Nardini, Tom (1945–). Young American character actor.
Cat Ballou 65. Africa Texas Style 67. The Young Animals 68. Siege 82, etc.
TV series: Cowboy in Africa 67.

Nares, Owen (1888–1943) (O. N. Ramsay). British matinée idol and silent screen star.
Autobiography 1925: *Myself and Some Others; Pure Egotism.*
Dandy Donovan 14. The Sorrows of Satan 17. God Bless the Red, White and Blue 18. Indian Love Lyrics 23. Young Lochinvar 23. Milestones 28. The Middle Watch 30. Sunshine Susie 31. The Impassive Footman 32. The Private Life of Don Juan 34. The

Show Goes On 37. The Prime Minister 41, etc.

Narizzano, Silvio (1927–). Canadian director in British TV in the fifties, later making international films.
□Under Ten Flags (co-d) 60. Fanatic 65. *Georgy Girl* 66. Blue (US) 67. Loot 70. Redneck 73. The Sky is Falling 76. *Why Shoot the Teacher* 77. The Class of Miss MacMichael 78. *Staying On* (TV) 80.

narrators are heard at the beginning of many important movies. Well-known actors are normally used, but sometimes take no credit. Here is a selected checklist to silence nagging doubts.
Arizona Bushwhackers: James Cagney.
Barry Lyndon: Michael Hordern.
The Big Knife: Richard Boone.
Casablanca: Lou Marcelle.
The Curse of King Tutankhamun's Tomb: Paul Scofield.
Desert Rats: Michael Rennie.
Dragon Seed: Lionel Barrymore.
Duel in the Sun: Orson Welles.
The Hallelujah Trail: John Dehner.
How Green was my Valley: Irving Pichel.
How the West was Won: Spencer Tracy.
The Human Comedy: Ray Collins.
Kings of the Sun: James Coburn.
An Ideal Husband: Ralph Richardson.
It's a Big Country: Louis Calhern.
Khartoum: Leo Genn.
King of Kings: Orson Welles.
A Letter to 3 Wives: Celeste Holm.
Mackenna's Gold: Victor Jory.
The Master of Ballantrae: Robert Beatty.
Mother Wore Tights: Anne Baxter.
The Mummy's Shroud: Peter Cushing.
The Night They Raided Minsky's: Rudy Vallee.
The Picture of Dorian Gray: Cedric Hardwicke.
Quo Vadis: Walter Pidgeon.
The Red Badge of Courage: James Whitmore.
The Reivers: Burgess Meredith.
Repeat Performance: John Ireland.
Romeo and Juliet (1968): Laurence Olivier.
The Secret Heart: Hume Cronyn.
The Solid Gold Cadillac: George Burns.
The Story of Jacob and Joseph: Alan Bates.
Summer of 42: Robert Mulligan.
The Swiss Family Robinson: Orson Welles.
The Third Man: Wilfrid Thomas.
Those Magnificent Men in Their Flying Machines: James Robertson Justice.
To Hell and Back: John McIntire.
To Kill a Mockingbird: Kim Stanley.
Tom Jones: Micheal MacLiammoir.
The Unseen: Ray Collins.
The Vikings: Orson Welles.
The Wild Heart: Joseph Cotten.
The War of the Worlds: Cedric Hardwicke.
Zulu: Richard Burton.

Nascimbene, Mario (1916–). Italian composer.
OK Nero 51. The Barefoot Contessa 54. Alexander the Great 55. A Farewell to Arms 57. *The Vikings* 58. Room at the Top 58. Solomon and Sheba 59. Sons and Lovers 60. Barabbas 61. Jessica 62. One Million Years BC 66. Dr Faustus 67. When Dinosaurs Ruled the Earth 70, many others.

Nash, Clarence (1904–85). American voice performer, the inimitable sound of Donald Duck for forty years.

Nash, Marilyn (c. 1924–). American leading lady selected by Chaplin to play in *Monsieur Verdoux* 47.

Nash, Mary (1885–1976) (Mary Ryan). American stage actress in occasional films.
□Uncertain Lady 34. College Scandal 35. Come and Get It 36. The King and the Chorus Girl 37. Easy Living 37. Heidi 37. Wells Fargo 37. The Little Princess 39. The Rains Came 39. Charlie Chan in Panama 40. Sailor's Lady 40. Gold Rush Maisie 40. *The Philadelphia Story* 40. Men of Boys Town 41. Calling Dr Gillespie 41. The Human Comedy 43. In the Meantime Darling 44. Cobra Woman 44. The Lady and the Monster 44. Yolanda and the Thief 45. Monsieur Beaucaire 46. Swell Guy 46. Till the Clouds Roll By 46.

Nathan, Robert (1894–1985). American novelist. Works filmed include *Portrait of Jennie* and *The Bishop's Wife*. Also scripted *The Clock* 45.

National Film Archive. A government-financed museum of films of artistic and historical value. Operated by the British Film Institute.

The National Film Board of Canada was set up in 1939, with John Grierson at its head, to show Canada's face to the world. Many excellent documentaries ensued, not to mention the brilliant animation films of Norman McLaren, but by the end of the sixties the Board's fortunes were at a lower ebb and its reputation declined.

The National Film Finance Corporation was founded in 1949 to provide loans for film production, but began to withdraw its facilities in the early seventies, at a time when financial encouragement had never been more needed for British production.

The National Film Theatre on London's South Bank is an extension of the British Film Institute; founded in 1951, it runs a daily repertory in three theatres of films of all nationalities and types.

Natwick, Mildred (1908–). American character actress, at her best in eccentric roles.
□The Long Voyage Home 40. The Enchanted Cottage 45. Yolanda and the Thief 45. The Late George Apley 47. A Woman's Vengeance 47. Three Godfathers 48. The Kissing Bandit 48. She Wore a Yellow Ribbon 49. Cheaper by the Dozen 50. The Quiet Man 52. Against All Flags 52. *The Trouble With Harry* 55. *The Court Jester* 56. Teenage Rebel 56. Tammy and the Bachelor 57. *Barefoot in the Park* 67. If It's Tuesday This Must be Belgium 69. The Maltese Bippy 69. Do Not Fold Spindle or Mutilate (TV) 71. The Snoop Sisters (TV) 72. Daisy Miller 74. At Long Last Love 75. Kiss Me Goodbye 82.

Naughton, Charles: see *The Crazy Gang.*

Naughton, James (1945–). American leading man, mostly on television.
The Paper Chase 74. The Bunker (TV) 80. A Stranger Is Watching 82. The Glass Menagerie 87.
TV series: Faraday and Company 72. Planet of the Apes 74.

naval comedy in British movies usually has a thirties look about it, may well be written by Ian Hay, and almost always concerns the officers; as in *The Middle Watch, Carry on Admiral, The Midshipmaid, The Flag Lieutenant* and *Up the Creek* (though the other ranks had their look in with *The Bulldog Breed, The Baby and the Battleship* and *Jack Ahoy*). In Hollywood movies the focus of interest is set firmly among the other ranks: *Follow the Fleet, Abbott and Costello in the Navy, Anchors Aweigh, Operation Petticoat, Mr Roberts, South Pacific, Ensign Pulver, On the Town, You're in the Navy Now, The Fleet's In, Onion-head, Don't Go near the Water, Don't Give Up the Ship, The Honeymoon Machine.*

The Navigator (US 1924). One of Buster Keaton's classic silent comedies, a succession of brilliant sight gags showing the comedian marooned with a girl at sea on an otherwise empty luxury liner. Written by Clyde Bruckman and Joseph Mitchell; directed by Keaton and Donald Crisp.

Nazarin (Mexico 1959). An arresting and imaginative fantasy about the misadventures of a Roman Catholic priest hounded by the sins of the world. Directed and co-written by Luis Buñuel; with Francisco Rabal.

Nazarro, Ray (1902–86). American director of second features.
The Tougher They Come 50. The Return of the Corsican Brothers 53. Top Gun 55. The Hired Gun 57, etc.; then into TV.

Nazimova, Alla (1879–1945) (Alla Nazimoff). Russian-born stage actress who made a number of films in America.
□War Brides 16. Revelation 18. Toys of Fate 18. An Eye for an Eye 19. The Red Lantern 19. The Brat 19. Stronger than Death 20. Heart of a Child 20. Madame Peacock 20. Billions 20. Camille 21. A Doll's House 22. *Salome* 23. Madonna of the Streets 24. The Redeeming Sin 24. My Son 25. *Escape* 40. Blood and Sand 41. The Bridge of San Luis Rey 44. In Our Time 44. Since You Went Away 45.

Nazzari, Amedeo (1907–1979). Virile Italian leading man, in films from 1935 although few travelled.
The Wolf of Sila 47. The Brigand 51. Nights of Cabiria 57. Labyrinth 59. The Best of Enemies 61. The Valachi Papers 72, etc.

Neagle, Dame Anna (1904–86) (Marjorie Robertson). British leading lady, a former chorus dancer who after her marriage in the thirties to producer Herbert Wilcox built up a formidable film gallery of historical heroines, and when film roles grew hard to find returned successfully to the theatre.
Autobiography 1949: *It's Been Fun*. 1974: *There's Always Tomorrow.*
□The School for Scandal 30. Should a Doctor Tell? 30. The Chinese Bungalow 31. Goodnight Vienna 32. The Flag Lieutenant 32. The Little Damozel 33. *Bitter Sweet* 33. The Queen's Affair 33. *Nell Gwyn* 34. Peg of Old Drury 35. Limelight 36. The Three Maxims 36. London Melody 37. *Victoria the Great* 37. Sixty Glorious Years 38. *Nurse Edith Cavell* 39. Irene (US) 40. No

No Nanette (US) 40. Sunny (US) 41. They Flew Alone (as Amy Johnson) 42. Forever and a Day 43. Yellow Canary 43. I Live in Grosvenor Square 45. *Piccadilly Incident* 46. The Courtneys of Curzon Street 47. *Spring in Park Lane* 48. Elizabeth of Ladymead 49. Maytime in Mayfair 49. *Odette* 50. *The Lady with a Lamp* 51. Derby Day 52. Lilacs in the Spring 55. King's Rhapsody 56. My Teenage Daughter 56. No Time for Tears 57. The Man Who Wouldn't Talk 58. The Lady is a Square 58. In 1958–61 produced three Frankie Vaughan films; returned to stage.
❁ For providing her faithful British admirers with the heroines they wanted her to be; and for her eagerness to please. *Victoria the Great.*

Neal, Patricia (1926–). American leading actress who handled some interesting roles before illness caused her semi-retirement.
□John Loves Mary 49. *The Fountainhead* 49. It's a Great Feeling 49. *The Hasty Heart* (GB) 50. Bright Leaf 50. Three Secrets 50. The Breaking Point 50. Operation Pacific 51. Raton Pass 51. Diplomatic Courier 51. The Day the Earth Stood Still 51. Weekend with Father 51. Washington Story 52. Something for the Birds 52. Stranger from Venus (GB) 54. *A Face in the Crowd* 57. Breakfast at Tiffany's 61. *Hud* (AA, BFA) 63. Psyche 59 (GB) 64. In Harm's Way (BFA) 64. The Subject was Roses 68. The Homecoming (TV) 71. The Night Digger 71. Baxter 72. Happy Mother's Day Love George 73. Run Stranger Run (TV) 74. Things in Their Season (TV) 75. Eric (TV) 77. Tail Gunner Joe (TV) 77. The Bastard (TV) 78. The Passage 79. All Quiet on the Western Front (TV) 80. Ghost Story 81. Glitter (TV) 84. Love Leads the Way (TV) 85.
†A TV movie, *The Patricia Neal Story*, was made in 1981, with Glenda Jackson playing Pat.

Neal, Tom (1914–1972). American leading man, mainly in second features; former athlete.
Out West with the Hardys 39. One Thrilling Night 42. The Racket Man 45. Detour 47. Navy Bound 51. Red Desert 54, etc.

Neame, Ronald (1911–). Outstanding British cinematographer who became a rather disappointing director.
SELECTED FILMS AS CINEMATOGRAPHER: Drake of England 34. The Gaunt Stranger 37. The Crimes of Stephen Hawke 39. Major Barbara 40. In Which We Serve 42. Blithe Spirit 45.
□AS DIRECTOR: Take My Life 47. The Golden Salamander 50. *The Card* (& p) 52. The Million Pound Note 53. The Man Who Never Was 56. The Seventh Sin 57. Windom's Way 58. The Horse's Mouth 59. *Tunes of Glory* 60. Escape from Zahrain 61. I Could Go On Singing 62. The Chalk Garden 64. Mister Moses 65. A Man Could Get Killed (co-d) 66. Gambit 66. The Prime of Miss Jean Brodie 68. Scrooge 70. The Poseidon Adventure 72. The Odessa File 75. Meteor 79. Hopscotch 80. First Monday in October 81. Foreign Body 86.

Nebenzal, Seymour (1899–1961). Distinguished German producer who had a disappointing career after going to Hollywood in the late thirties.
Westfront 30. M 31. Kameradschaft 32. The Testament of Dr Mabuse 33. Mayerling 36. We Who are Young 40. Summer Storm 44. Whistle Stop 46. Heaven Only Knows 47. Siren of Atlantis 48. M (remake) 51, etc.

Nedell, Bernard (1898–1972). American character actor.
The Serpent 16. The Return of the Rat (GB) 29. Shadows (GB) 31. Lazybones (GB) 35. The Man Who could Work Miracles (GB) 36. Mr Moto's Gamble 38. Angels Wash Their Faces 39. Strange Cargo 40. The Desperadoes 43. One Body Too Many 44. Monsieur Verdoux 47. The Loves of Carmen 48. Heller in Pink Tights 60. Hickey and Boggs 72, many others.

Needham, Hal (1931–). American director, former stunt man.
□*Smokey and the Bandit* 77. Hooper 78. The Villain 79. Death Car on the Freeway (TV) 79. Smokey and the Bandit II 80. Stunts (TV) 81. The Cannonball Run 81. Megaforce 82. Stroker Ace 83. Body Slam 87.

Neff, Hildegard (1925–) (Hildegard Knef). German leading lady, former artist and film cartoonist. Briefly on German stage, then to films, and for a time in Hollywood. Autobiography 1971: *The Gift Horse.*
The Murderers are Amongst Us 46. *Film without Title* 47. The Sinner 50. Decision before Dawn 51. *The Snows of Kilimanjaro* 52. Diplomatic Courier 52. Henriette 52. The Man Between 53. The Girl from Hamburg 57. And So to Bed 63. Landru 63. Mozambique 65. The Lost Continent (GB) 68. Fedora 78, etc.

Negri, Pola (1897–1987) (Appolonia Chalupek). Polish-born leading lady with

experience on German stage and screen; went to Hollywood in twenties and was popular until sound came in.
Autobiography 1970: *Memories of a Star.*
Die Bestie 15. Madame du Barry 18. The Flame 20. Bella Donna (US) 23. *Forbidden Paradise* 24. Hotel Imperial 26. Three Sinners 28. A Woman Commands 31. Madame Bovary 35. Hi Diddle Diddle 43. The Moonspinners 64, etc.

Negulesco, Jean (1900–). Rumanian-born director, in US from 1927.
□Kiss and Make Up 34. Singapore Woman 41. *The Mask of Dimitrios* 44. The Conspirators 44. Three Strangers 46. Nobody Lives Forever 46. *Humoresque* 46. Deep Valley 47. *Roadhouse* 48. *Johnny Belinda* 48. Britannia Mews 49. Under My Skin 50. *Three Came Home* 50. *The Mudlark* 51. Take Care of My Little Girl 51. Phone Call from a Stranger 52. Lydia Bailey 52. Lure of the Wilderness 52. Full House (part) 52. Scandal at Scourie 53. Titanic 53. *How to Marry a Millionaire* 53. *Three Coins in the Fountain* 54. *Woman's World* 54. Daddy Longlegs 55. The Rains of Ranchipur 55. Boy on a Dolphin 57. A Certain Smile 58. The Gift of Love 58. Count Your Blessings 59. The Best of Everything 59. Jessica 62. The Pleasure Seekers 65. The Invincible Six 68. Hello Goodbye 70. The Heroes 79.

¶ *James Agee:* A director I had not expected to praise is Jean Negulesco, who has always reminded me of Michael Curtiz on toast. Mr Curtiz, in turn, has always seemed like Franz Murnau under onions.

Neil, Hildegarde (1939–). South African leading lady.
The Man Who Haunted Himself 70. Antony and Cleopatra 71. England Made Me 72. A Touch of Class 73. The Legacy 78. The Mirror Crack'd 80, etc.
TV series: Diamonds 80.

Neilan, Marshall (1891–1958). American director who had meteoric success in the twenties and just as suddenly failed in the mid-thirties. Also acted from 1912; last role *A Face in the Crowd* 57.
The Cycle of Fate 16. Freckles 17. Rebecca of Sunnybrook Farm 17. M'Liss 18. Daddy Longlegs 19. The Lotus Eater 21. Tess of the D'Urbervilles 25. Her Wild Oat 27. Three Ring Marriage 28. The Awful Truth 29. Sweethearts on Parade 30. The Lemon Drop Kid 34. Swing It, Professor 37, many others.

Neill, Roy William (1890–1946) (Roland de Gostrie). Irish-born director, long in Hollywood; never rose above low-budget thrillers but often did them well.
Love Letters 17. Good References 21. Toilers of the Sea 23. The Good Bad Girl 31. The Black Room 34. The Good Old Days (GB) 35. Dr Syn (GB) 37. Eyes of the Underworld 41. *Frankenstein Meets the Wolf Man* 43. Gypsy Wildcat 44. Black Angel 46, etc.; also produced and directed most of the *Sherlock Holmes* series starring Basil Rathbone 42–46.

Neill, Sam (1948–). New Zealand leading actor in international films.
My Brilliant Career 80. Ivanhoe (TV) 82. The Final Conflict 82. From a Far Country 82. The Blood of Others (TV) 84. Robbery Under Arms 85. Plenty 85. For Love Alone 86. The Good Wife 86. Evil Angels 88.
TV series: Reilly Ace of Spies 83.

Neilson, James (1909–1979). American director, former war photographer, who worked mostly for Walt Disney.
□The Blackwell Story (TV) 57. Night Passage 57. The Country Husband (TV) 58. Moon Pilot 62. Bon Voyage 62. Summer Magic 63. Dr Syn 63. The Moon Spinners 63. Return of the Gunfighter (TV) 66. The Adventures of Bullwhip Griffin 67. The Gentle Giant 67. Where Angels Go 68. The First Time 69. Flare Up 69. Tom Sawyer (TV) 75.

Nell Gwyn. Charles II's orange-seller has appeared briefly in many films, but the two devoted to her story were both made in Britain by Herbert Wilcox: in 1927 with Dorothy Gish and in 1934 with Anna Neagle. Both caused censorship problems, the latter because of the lady's cleavage.

Nelligan, Kate (1951–). Canadian actress in Britain.
The Romantic Englishwoman 75. The Count of Monte Cristo (TV) 78. Dracula 79. Eye of the Needle 80. Without a Trace 83. Eleni 85.

Nelson, Barry (1920–) (Robert Neilson). Stocky American leading man who makes films between stage shows.
China Caravan 42. A Guy Named Joe 43. Winged Victory 44. The Beginning of the End 45. The Man with My Face 51. The First Travelling Saleslady 56. Mary Mary 63. The Borgia Stick (TV) 68. Airport 69. Pete 'n Tillie 72, others.
TV series: My Favorite Husband 53–54. Hudson's Bay 59.

Nelson, Craig T. (1946–). Brawny American leading man.
And Justice for All 79. The Formula 80. Private Benjamin 80. Stir Crazy 80. Poltergeist 82. The Chicago Story (TV) 82. The Osterman Weekend 83. Silkwood 83. The Killing Fields 84. Call to Glory (TV) 84. Poltergeist II 86.
TV series: Air Force 84.

Nelson, Ed (1928–). American actor who played gangsters, brothers-in-law and boy friends in innumerable fifties second features, then went into TV and found himself a secure niche as Dr Rossi in *Peyton Place* 64–68, and in *The Silent Force* 70. Midway 76.
Shining Star 77. Police Academy 3 85.

Nelson, Gary (–). American director.
The Girl on the Late Late Show (TV) 74. Medical Story (TV) 75. Panache (TV) 76. *Washington: Behind Closed Doors* (TV) 77. To Kill a Cop (TV) 78. The Black Hole 79. Jimmy the Kid 82. Enigma 82. Allan Quatermain and the Lost City of Gold 86.

Nelson, Gene (1920–) (Leander Berg). American actor-dancer, on stage from 1938, films from mid-forties.
I Wonder Who's Kissing Her Now 47. Gentleman's Agreement 48. The Daughter of Rosie O'Grady 50. Tea for Two 51. Lullaby of Broadway 52. She's Working Her Way through College 52. So This is Paris 55. Oklahoma 55. 20,000 Eyes 62. The Purple Hills 63, etc.
□AS DIRECTOR: Hand of Death 62. Hootenanny Hoot 63. Kissin' Cousins 64. Your Cheatin' Heart 64. Harum Scarum 65. The Cool Ones 67. Wake Me When the War is Over (TV) 69. The Letters (TV) 73.
TV series as director: *Washington Behind Closed Doors* 77.

Nelson, Lord Horatio (1758–1805), the hero of Trafalgar, was portrayed in *Nelson* 19 by Donald Calthrop; in *Nelson* 26 by Cedric Hardwicke; in *The Divine Lady* 29 by Victor Varconi; in *Lady Hamilton* 42 by Laurence Olivier; in *Lady Hamilton* (Ger.) 68 by Richard Johnson; and in *Bequest to the Nation* 73 by Peter Finch.

Nelson, Lori (1933–). American light leading lady of the fifties.
Ma and Pa Kettle at the Fair 52. Bend of the River 52. Walking My Baby Back Home 53. Destry 55. Mohawk 56. Hot Rod Girl 56. The Day the World Ended 56, etc.
TV series: How to Marry a Millionaire 58.

Nelson, Ozzie (1906–1975). American bandleader whose genial, diffident personality became familiar in long-running domestic comedy series on TV.
Sweetheart of the Campus 41. Hi Good Lookin' 44. People are Funny 45. Here Come the Nelsons 52. Love and Kisses (& wpd) 65. The Impossible Years 68, etc.
TV series: *The Adventures of Ozzie and Harriet* 52–65. Ozzie's Girls 73.

Nelson, Ralph (1916–87). American director.
□Requiem for a Heavyweight 62. *Lilies of the Field* 63. Soldier in the Rain 64. Fate is the Hunter 64. Father Goose 64. Once a Thief 65. Duel at Diablo 66. Counterpoint 67. Charly 68. Tick Tick Tick 70. Soldier Blue 70. Flight of the Doves 71. The Wrath of God 72. The Wilby Conspiracy 75. Embryo 76. A Hero Ain't Nothing But a Sandwich 77. Because He's My Friend (Aust.) 78. Lady of the House (TV) 78. You Can't Go Home Again (TV) 79. Christmas Lilies of the Field (TV) 79.

Nelson, Rick (1940–86). American singer and light actor, son of bandleader Ozzie Nelson and his wife Harriet (formerly Harriet Hilliard: qv) with whom he appeared in the long-running TV series *The Adventures of Ozzie and Harriet* 52–65.
Here Come the Nelsons 52. Rio Bravo 59. The Wackiest Ship in the Army 60. Love and Kisses 65. The Over the Hill Gang (TV) 69.

Nelson, Ruth (–). American character actress, usually seen as sympathetic mother.
Abe Lincoln in Illinois 40. Humoresque 46.

Nelson, Willie (1933–). American singer and character actor.
The Electric Horseman 79. Honeysuckle Rose 80. Thief 81. Barbarossa 82. Hells Angels Forever 83. Red Headed Stranger 84. Songwriter 85.

Nemec, Jan (1936–). Czech director.
Diamonds of the Night 64. The Party and the Guests 66. The Martyrs of Love 67, etc.

neo-realism is a term mainly applied to the Italian post-war films which seemed to present a fresh and vivid kind of social realism. The essentials were real locations and at least a proportion of amateur actors. The most famous neo-realist film is *Bicycle Thieves*.

nepotism. Hollywood moguls were at one time well known for promoting within the family. Hence the quip: the son-in-law also rises. Hence the rhyme:

Uncle Carl Laemmle
Has a very large faemmle.

Of an untalented Warner relative, Julius Epstein once commented that he had set the son-in-law business back twenty years. And when another gentleman of similar ilk taunted Oscar Levant with 'Oscar, play us a medley of your hit,' Oscar came back with 'Okay, play us a medley of your father in law.' Of Louis B. Mayer's brother, Irving Brecher remarked: 'Jerry has a very important job and he has to have that big corner office. He's supposed to watch Washington Boulevard and warn everybody to evacuate the studio if icebergs are spotted coming down the street.' Similarly in London, after Alexander Korda's rise to fame and power, it was said that in order to get a job in British films you had to be Hungarian.

Nero, Franco (1942–) (F. Spartanero). Italian leading man in international films.
The Tramplers 66. The Bible 66. *Camelot* 67. The Day of the Owl 68. A Quiet Place in the Country 68. Tristana 70. The Virgin and the Gypsy 70. The Battle of Neretva 70. Pope Joan 72. The Monk 72. White Fang 74. Challenge to White Fang 75. Force Ten from Navarone 78. The Man with Bogart's Face 80. The Salamander 80. Enter the Ninja 81. The Last Days of Pompeii (TV) 84. Ten Days that shook the World 84. Garibaldi 86, etc.

Nervig, Conrad A. (1895–). American editor.
Bardelys the Magnificent 26. The Divine Woman 28. The Guardsman 31. Eskimo (AA) 34. A Tale of Two Cities 36. The Crowd Roars 38. Northwest Passage 40. The Human Comedy 43. High Barbaree 47. Side Street 49. King Solomon's Mines (AA) 50. The Bad and the Beautiful 52. Gypsy Colt 54, many others.

Nervo, Jimmy: see *The Crazy Gang*.

Nesbit, Evelyn (1886–1967). Notorious American beauty involved in a murder case of 1912; portrayed by Joan Collins in *The Girl in the Red Velvet Swing* and by Elizabeth McGivern in *Ragtime*.
□Threads of Destiny 14. Redemption 17. The Hidden Woman 22.

Nesbitt, Cathleen (1888–1982). British character actress, on stage from 1910; very occasional films, but active on stage and television into her nineties.
Autobiography 1973: *A Little Love and Good Companions*.
The Case of the Frightened Lady 32. The Passing of the Third Floor Back 36. Fanny by Gaslight 43. Nicholas Nickleby 47. Three Coins in the Fountain 54. Désirée 54. *An Affair to Remember* 57. Promise Her Anything 66. The Trygon Factor 67. Staircase 69. Villain 71. Family Plot 76. Julia 77, etc.
TV series: *The Farmer's Daughter* 65.

Nesbitt, Derren (c. 1932–). British character actor, usually a smiling villain.
The Man in the Back Seat 60. *Victim* 62. Strongroom 62. *The Naked Runner* 67. Nobody Runs Forever 68. Where Eagles Dare 68. Innocent Bystanders 72. Ooh You are Awful 72. The Amorous Milkman (wd) 74, etc.

Nesbitt, John (1911–1960). American producer of MGM's long-running *Passing Parade* series of informational one-reelers.

Nettleton, John (1929–). British character actor.
A Man for All Seasons 67. Some Will Some Won't 69. And Soon the Darkness 69. Black Beauty 70.

Nettleton, Lois (c. 1929–). American character actress.
□Period of Adjustment 62. Come Fly with Me 63. Mail Order Bride 64. Valley of Mystery 66. Bamboo Saucer 68. The Good Guys and the Bad Guys 69. Dirty Dingus Magee 70. Sidelong Glances of a Pigeon Kicker 71. The Forgotten Man (TV) 71. The Honkers 72. Echoes of a Summer 75. Fear on Trial (TV) 75. Washington: Behind Closed Doors (TV) 77. Centennial (TV) 78. Tourist (TV) 79. Soggy Bottom USA 80. Deadly Blessing 81. Butterfly 82. The Best Little Whorehouse in Texas 82.
TV series: Accidental Family 67.

Network (US 1976). A somewhat hysterical tirade against society in general and television in particular, this vivid but rather tiresome movie won Peter Finch a posthumous Academy Award for his role of the modern messiah; Faye Dunaway won best actress and Beatrice Straight best supporting actress. William Holden also starred; Sidney Lumet directed Paddy Chayefsky's script.

Neumann, Kurt (1908–1958). German director, in Hollywood from 1925.
My Pal the King 32. The Big Cage 33. Rainbow on the River 36. Island of Lost Men 39. Ellery Queen Master Detective 40. The Unknown Guest 43. Tarzan and the Leopard Woman 46. Bad Boy 49. Rocketship XM (& wp) 50. Son of Ali Baba 53. Carnival Story 54. Mohawk 56. Kronos 57. *The Fly* 58. Watusi 58, etc.

Never Give a Sucker an Even Break (US 1941). The wildest of W. C. Fields' comedies, known in GB as *What a Man!*; Fields himself suggested the billing should be shortened to *Fields: Sucker*. The ridiculous plot, reputedly written by Fields on the back of an envelope and sold to Universal for 25,000 dollars, concerns his experiences when, after dropping a bottle of whisky from a plane and diving out after it, he lands on a mountain top where there lives a girl who has never seen a man and promptly falls in love with him, despite the disapproval of her guardian Mrs Haemoglobin. . . . As with all Fields, the humour is a matter of taste.

Never on Sunday (Greece 1960). An inexpensive but highly commercial location comedy made by Jules Dassin, who also played the shy American tourist who 'improves' a vivacious Greek prostitute. The music score by Manos Hadjidakis was as great an asset as Melina Mercouri's performance, and the film as a whole was another significant nail in the coffin of the Hays code, as vice remained triumphant.

Neville, John (1925–). British leading man, primarily on stage.
□ Oscar Wilde 60. Mr Topaze 61. Billy Budd 62. Unearthly Stranger 63. *A Study in Terror* (as Sherlock Holmes) 65. The Adventures of Gerard 70.

new faces

? What stars made their names in the following roles, and in what films?

1 An oriental potentate with many children.
2 A national celebrity who wreaks havoc in the home of Mr and Mrs Stanley.
3 A dramatic critic fired for writing an honest review.
4 A waspish columnist who typed in his bath.
5 A Mr Caspar Gutman, one of several people in pursuit of a *rara avis*.
6 A psychopathic murderer known only by an initial.
7 A scientist named Griffin whose discovery, self administered, gave him megalomania.
8 A frustrated bicycle factory worker who enjoyed his weekends.
9 An Irishman working as a Nazi spy in London during World War II.
10 A night club singer who married a teacher named Immanuel Rath.
11 A radio detective named The Fox.
12 A hired assassin named Raven.

'new wave' or **'nouvelle vague'.** Term given (by themselves?) to a group of new, exploring young French directors towards the end of the fifties: François Truffaut, Jean-Luc Godard, Louis Malle, Alain Resnais, etc. As their talents were widely divergent, the term meant very little. It was coined by Françoise Giroud.

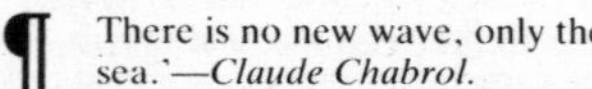
¶ There is no new wave, only the sea.'—*Claude Chabrol.*

New York has provided a vivid backcloth for films of many types, and its skyscrapers allegedly gave Fritz Lang the inspiration for *Metropolis*. Studio re-creations provided the period flavour of *Little Old New York, New York Town, One Sunday Afternoon, A Tree Grows in Brooklyn, Incendiary Blonde, My Girl Tisa*, and *The Bowery*; and it was a studio city which was wrecked by *King Kong*. But the camera has also explored the real article, notably in thrillers like *Saboteur, Naked City, Union Station, The FBI Story* and *North by Northwest*; in realistic comedy dramas like *From This Day Forward, So This is New York, Miracle on 34th Street, Lovers and Lollipops, Marty, It Should Happen to You, Sunday in New York, Breakfast at Tiffany's, The Lost Weekend, The Bachelor Party, A Man Ten Feet Tall, A Fine Madness, Love with the Proper Stranger, The World of Henry Orient, Midnight Cowboy, The Pawnbroker, Barefoot in the Park, Beau James, The French Connection, Cotton Comes to Harlem, Shaft, The Out-of-Towners, Any Wednesday, Serpico, Bye Bye Braverman, Sweet Charity, The Seven-Ups, The Taking of Pelham One Two Three, The Prisoner of Second Avenue, Mean Streets, Taxi Driver, Death Wish* and *Three Days of the Condor*; in hard-hitting social melodramas like *On the Waterfront, Sweet Smell of Success,* and *The Young Savages*; and in musicals like *On the Town* and *West Side Story*. Other films which concern the effect of New York without showing much of the actuality include *Mr Deeds Goes to Town, Bachelor Mother, Lady on a Train, Bell, Book and Candle, Portrait*

of Jennie, Kid Millions, Dead End, The Apartment, Patterns of Power, The Garment Jungle, Mr Blandings Builds His Dream House and *America, America*. Finally Manhattan Island was bought from the Indians by Groucho Marx in *The Story of Mankind, Knickerbocker Holiday* pictured the city in its Dutch colonial days as New Amsterdam and *Godspell* used it as a novel background for its revised version of the Life of Christ.
Television series with authentic New York locations include *Naked City, The Defenders, East Side West Side, N.Y.P.D., Madigan, McCloud, Kojak, Eischied.*

Newall, Guy (1885–1937). British stage actor who became a popular leading man in silent sentimental dramas, especially with his wife Ivy Duke. Also directed most of his films.
Comradeship 18. The Garden of Resurrection 19. The Lure of Crooning Water 20. The Duke's Son 20. Beauty and the Beast 22. Boy Woodburn 22. The Starlit Garden 23. The Ghost Train 27. The Eternal Feminine 30. The Marriage Bond 30. Grand Finale 37, etc.

Newbrook, Peter (1916–). British producer, former cinematographer.
The Yellow Teddy Bears 63. Black Torment 64. Gonks Go Beat 65. The Sandwich Man 66. Press for Time 66. Corruption 69. She'll Follow You Anywhere 70. The Asphyx 72.

Newell, Mike (1942–). British director, from TV.
The Man in the Iron Mask (TV) 77. The Awakening 80. Blood Feud (TV) 83. Dance with a Stranger 85. Amazing Grace and Chuck 87.

Newfeld, Sam (1900–1964). American director of second features.
Reform Girl 33. Big Time or Bust 34. Northern Frontier 35. Timber War 36. Trail of Vengeance 37. Harlem on the Prairie 38. Secrets of a Model 40. Billy the Kid's Fighting Pals 41. The Mad Monster 42. Nabonga 44. Ghost of Hidden Valley 46. The Counterfeiters 48. Motor Patrol 50. Three Desperate Men 51. Thunder Over Sangoland 55. Wolf Dog 58, many others.

Newhart, Bob (1923–). American TV and record comedian who has appeared in a few movies.
Hell is for Heroes 62. Hot Millions 68. On a Clear Day You Can See Forever 70. Catch 22 70. Cold Turkey 70. Thursday's Game (TV) 74. The First Family 80. Little Miss Marker 80. Marathon (TV) 80.
TV series: The Bob Newhart Show 72–77. Newhart 82–86.

Newland, John (c. 1916–). American TV actor (the host of *One Step Beyond*) who also directed a few films.
That Night 57. The Violators 57. The Spy with My Face 65. Hush-a-Bye Murder 70. Played Algy in the Tom Conway Bulldog Drummond films 1948–49.

Newlands, Anthony (1926–). British character actor, mainly on TV; usually plays schemers.
Beyond This Place 59. The Trials of Oscar Wilde 60. Hysteria 64. Theatre of Death 67, etc.

Newley, Anthony (1931–). Versatile but dislikeable British actor, composer, singer, comedian; former child star.
Oliver Twist 48. Vice Versa 48. Those People Next Door 53. *Cockleshell Heroes* 56. X the Unknown 56. High Flight 57. *No Time to Die* 58. Idol on Parade 59. In the Nick 61. The Small World of Sammy Lee 63. Dr Dolittle (US) 67. Sweet November (US) 68. Can Heironymus Merkin Ever Forget Mercy Humpe and Find True Happiness? (& wd) 69. Summertree (d only) 72. Mr Quilp 75. A Good Idea at the Time (Can.) 76. Malibu (TV) 83. The Garbage Pail Kids Movie 87, etc.

Newman, Alfred (1901–1970). American composer, former child pianist; an eminent Hollywood musical director since early sound days, he composed over 250 film scores.
The Devil To Pay 30. Whoopee 31. *Arrowsmith* 31. Cynara 32. *The Bowery* 33. Nana 34. Dodsworth 36. *Dead End* 37. *Alexander's Ragtime Band* (AA) 38. *Gunga Din* 39. *Tin Pan Alley* (AA) 40. *The Grapes of Wrath* 40. Son of Fury 42. The Song of Bernadette (AA) 43. The Razor's Edge 46. *Mother Wore Tights* (AA) 47. Unfaithfully Yours 48. *With a Song in My Heart* (AA) 52. *Call Me Madam* (AA) 53. Love is a Many Splendored Thing (AA) 55. *The King and I* (AA) 56. Flower Drum Song 61. The Counterfeit Traitor 62. How the West was Won 62. Nevada Smith 66, many others.

Newman, Barry (1940–). American leading actor.
□Pretty Boy Floyd 60. *The Lawyer* 69. *Vanishing Point* 71. The Salzburg Connection 72. Fear is the Key 72. City on Fire 79. Fatal Vision (TV) 84.
TV series: Petrocelli 73–74.

Newman, David (1937–). American screenwriter.
WITH ROBERT BENTON: *Bonnie and Clyde* 67. There was a Crooked Man 70. What's Up Doc 72. Bad Company 72. Superman 78.

Newman, Joseph M. (1909–). American director, in films from 1931.
Jungle Patrol 48. 711 Ocean Drive 50. The Outcasts of Poker Flats 52. Red Skies of Montana 52. Pony Soldier 53. The Human Jungle 54. Dangerous Crossing 54. Kiss of Fire 55. *This Island Earth* 55. Flight to Hong Kong (& p) 56. Gunfight at Dodge City 58. The Big Circus 59. Tarzan the Ape Man 59. King of the Roaring Twenties 61. A Thunder of Drums 61. The George Raft Story 61, etc.

Newman, Lionel (1916–). American composer.
The Street with No Name 48. Cheaper by the Dozen 50. Diplomatic Courier 52. Dangerous Crossing 53. Gorilla at Large 54. How to Be Very Very Popular 55. A Kiss Before Dying 56. Mardi Gras 58. Compulsion 59. North to Alaska 60. Move Over Darling 63. Do Not Disturb 65. The Salzburg Connection 72, many others.

Newman, Nanette (1934–). British leading lady, married to Bryan Forbes.
Personal Affair 53. House of Mystery 58. Faces in the Dark 59. The League of Gentlemen 59. Twice Round the Daffodils 62. The Wrong Arm of the Law 63. Of Human Bondage 64. Séance on a Wet Afternoon 64. The Wrong Box 66. The Whisperers 66. The Madwoman of Chaillot 69. *The Raging Moon* 70. The Love Ban 72. Man at the Top 73. The Stepford Wives 75. International Velvet 78, etc.

Newman, Paul (1925–). American leading actor who suffered initially from a similarity to Marlon Brando but later developed a lithe impertinence which served him well in his better films.
Biography 1975: *Paul Newman* by Charles Hamblett.
□The Silver Chalice 54. *Somebody Up There Likes Me* 56. The Rack 56. Until They Sail 57. The Helen Morgan Story 57. *The Long Hot Summer* 58. The Left Handed Gun 58. Rally Round the Flag Boys 58. Cat on a Hot Tin Roof 58. The Young Philadelphians 59. From the Terrace 60. Exodus 60. *The Hustler* (BFA) 61. Paris Blues 61. Sweet Bird of Youth 62. Hemingway's Adventures of a Young Man 62. *Hud* 63. A New Kind of Love 63. *The Prize* 63. What a Way to Go 64. The Outrage 64. Lady L 64. Torn Curtain 66. *Harper* 66. *Hombre* 67. *Cool Hand Luke* 67. The Secret War of Harry Frigg 67. Rachel Rachel (d only) 68. Winning 69. *Butch Cassidy and the Sundance Kid* 69. W.U.S.A. 70. Sometimes a Great Notion (& d) 71. Pocket Money 72. The Effect of Gamma Rays on Man-in-the-Moon Marigolds (d only) 72. *Judge Roy Bean* 72. The Mackintosh Man 73. The Sting 73. The Towering Inferno 74. The Drowning Pool 75. Silent Movie 76. Buffalo Bill and the Indians 76. Slap Shot 77. Quintet 79. Fort Apache the Bronx 80. When Time Ran Out 80. The Shadow Box (d only) 81. Absence of Malice 82. *The Verdict* 82. Harry and Son 84. The Color of Money 86. The Glass Menagerie (d only) 87.

¶ *P.N.:* You don't stop being a citizen just because you have a Screen Actors' Guild card.
P.N.: Acting is a question of absorbing other people's personalities and some of your own experience.
P.N.: Ever since *Slapshot* I've been swearing more. I knew I had a problem one day when I turned to my daughter and said: 'Please pass the fucking salt.'
P.N.: I wasn't driven to acting by an inner compulsion. I was running away from the sporting goods business.

Newman, Walter (1920–). American screenwriter.
Ace in the Hole (co-w) 51. Underwater 55. The Man with the Golden Arm (co-w) 56. Crime and Punishment USA 59. The Interns (co-w) 62. Cat Ballou (co-w) 65. The Champ 79, etc.

Newmar, Julie (1930–) (Julia Newmeyer). Tall American blonde actress.
Seven Brides for Seven Brothers 55. The Marriage Go Round 60. Mackenna's Gold 68. The Maltese Bippy 69, etc.
TV series: My Living Doll 64. Batman 65–67.

newsreels were part of the very earliest cinema programme, and the nine-minute round up of topical events filmed by roving cameramen was a feature of programmes in cinemas throughout the world until the mid-sixties, when it was clear that the newsreel had been replaced by television. Most newsreel companies have looked after their libraries, and the result is a vivid history of the twentieth century, frequently plundered by producers of compilation films.

Newton, Robert (1905–1956). British star character actor with a rolling eye and a voice to match; a ham, but a succulent one.

□Reunion 32. Dark Journey 37. Fire Over England 37. *Farewell Again* 37. The Squeaker 37. The Green Cockatoo 37. Twenty One Days 38. Vessel of Wrath 38. Yellow Sands 38. Dead Men are Dangerous 39. Jamaica Inn 39. Poison Pen 39. Hell's Cargo 39. Bulldog Sees It Through 40. Gaslight 40. Busman's Honeymoon 40. *Major Barbara* 40. *Hatter's Castle* 41. They Flew Alone 42. *This Happy Breed* 44. *Henry V* (as Pistol) 45. Night Boat to Dublin 46. *Odd Man Out* 46. Temptation Harbour 47. Snowbound 48. *Oliver Twist* (as Bill Sikes) 48. Kiss the Blood off My Hands (US) 48. Obsession 49. *Treasure Island* (as Long John) 50. Waterfront 50. *Tom Brown's Schooldays* (as Dr Arnold) 51. Soldiers Three (US) 51. Les Misérables (US) 52. Blackbeard the Pirate (US) 52. *Androcles and the Lion* (US) 53. Desert Rats (US) 53. The High and the Mighty (US) 54. *The Beachcomber* 54. Long John Silver 55. Around the World in Eighty Days (US) 56.
TV series: *Long John Silver* 55.
❀ For being so enjoyably larger than life. *Treasure Island.*

Newton-John, Olivia (1948–). British pop singer.
□Toomorrow 70. *Grease* 78. Xanadu 80. Two of a Kind 83.

Next of Kin (GB 1942). An official wartime film on the dangers of careless talk, treated as a documentary thriller but intended for military audiences, this was successful enough to be sent on general release and proved very popular. It still makes good cinema. Directed by Thorold Dickinson, with Mervyn Johns and Stephen Murray.

Ney, Marie (1895–1981). British stage actress in occasional films.
Escape 30. The Wandering Jew 34. Scrooge 37. Jamaica Inn 39. Seven Days to Noon 50. Simba 54. Yield to the Night 55. Witchcraft 64, etc.

Ney, Richard (1917–). American financier who almost accidentally went into acting but appears only occasionally.
Mrs Miniver 42. The Late George Apley 47. Joan of Arc 48. Babes in Baghdad 52. The Premature Burial 61, etc.

Ngor, Haing S. (–). Vietnamese doctor, a non-professional who won an Academy Award and two BFAs for his supporting role in *The Killing Fields* 84.

Niblo, Fred (1874–1948) (Federico Nobile). American director of silent films; had stage experience.
The Marriage Ring 18. Sex 20. *The Mark of Zorro* 20. *The Three Musketeers* 21. *Blood and Sand* 23. Thy Name is Woman 24. The Temptress 26. *Ben Hur* 27. Camille 27. Redemption 29. The Big Gamble 33. Three Sons o' Guns 41.

Nicholas Brothers, The (c. 1916–) (Fayard and Harold Nicholas). Two black American acrobats who enlivened several musicals of the forties.
□Calling All Stars 37. Tin Pan Alley 41. Down Argentine Way 41. The Great American Broadcast 41. Sun Valley Serenade 42. Orchestra Wives 43. Stormy Weather 43. The Pirate 48.

Nicholas, Paul (*c.*1951–). British light leading man in all media, but especially TV: *Just Good Friends*, *Bust*, etc.
Blind Terror 71. Stardust 74. Tommy 74. Lisztomania 75. Sergeant Pepper's Lonely Hearts Club Band 78. The World is Full of Married Men 79. Yesterday's Hero 79. The Jazz Singer 80. Nutcracker 83. Invitation to a Wedding 84.

Nicholls, Anthony (1902–1977). Distinguished-looking British stage actor, in occasional films.
The Laughing Lady 47. The Guinea Pig 49. The Hasty Heart 49. The Dancing Years 50. The Franchise Affair 50. The Weak and the Wicked 54. Make Me an Offer 55. The Safecracker 58. Victim 62. Mister Ten Per Cent 66, etc.

Nicholls, George (1865–1927). Craggy American character actor.
A Romance of Happy Valley 17. Hearts of the World 18. The Eagle 25. The Wedding March 27, many others.

Nicholls, George Jnr. (1897–1939). American director.
Anne of Green Gables 34. Michael Strogoff 37. Man of Conquest 39, etc.

Nichols, Barbara (1929–76). American comedy actress, former model; adept at portraying not-so-dumb blondes.
Miracle in the Rain 56. The King and Four Queens 57. The Scarface Mob 60. The George Raft Story 61. Where the Boys Are 63. The Disorderly Orderly 64. Dear Heart 65. The Loved One 65. The Swinger 66, etc.

Nichols, Dandy (1907–86). British character comedienne, often seen as nervous maid or cockney char. Became famous on TV as the long-suffering Else in *Till Death Us Do Part* 64–74; appeared in the film version 68.
Hue and Cry 46. Here Come the Huggetts 49. Street Corner 52. The Deep Blue Sea 55. The Vikings 58. Help 65. The Alf Garnett Saga 72. Britannia Hospital 83, many others.

Nichols, Dudley (1895–1960). Distinguished American screenwriter, in Hollywood from 1929.
Born Reckless 30. The Sign of the Cross 32. *The Lost Patrol* 34. Steamboat round the Bend 34. *The Informer* (AA) 35. Mary of Scotland 36. The Hurricane 37. *Bringing Up Baby* 38. *Stagecoach* 39. The Long Voyage Home 40. For Whom the Bell Tolls 43. The Bells of St Mary's 45. *It Happened Tomorrow* 44. *And Then There Were None* 45. Scarlet Street 45. Sister Kenny (& d) 46. Mourning Becomes Electra (& pd) 47. Pinky 49. Prince Valiant 54. The Tin Star 57. The Hangman 59, many others.
❀ For providing the firm basis of a score of outstanding prestige films. *Stagecoach.*

Nichols, Mike (1931–) (Michael Igor Peschkowsky). German-born American cabaret entertainer and latterly film director.
□*Who's Afraid of Virginia Woolf?* 66. *The Graduate* (AA) 67. Catch 22 70. Carnal Knowledge 71. The Day of the Dolphin 73. The Fortune 76. Gilda Live 80. *Silkwood* (AAN) 83. Heartburn 86.

¶ *M.N.:* A movie is like a person. Either you trust it or you don't.

Nicholson, Jack (1937–). American leading actor, a fashionable figure of the early seventies.
□Cry Baby Killer 58. Too Soon to Love 59. Studs Lonigan 61. The Wild Rise 61. The Broken Land 62. The Little Shop of Horrors 62. The Raven 63. The Terror 63. Thunder Island (co-w only) 64. Back Door to Hell 64. Flight to Fury (& w) 65. Ensign Pulver 65. Ride the Whirlwind 66. The Shooting 66. Hell's Angels on Wheels 67. The St Valentine's Day Massacre 67. The Trip (w only) 67. Head (w only) 68. *Easy Rider* 69. On a Clear Day You Can See Forever 70. Five Easy Pieces 70. Drive He Said (d only) 70. Carnal Knowledge 71. A Safe Place 71. The King of Marvin Gardens 72. *The Last Detail* 74. *Chinatown* 74. Tommy 74. The Passenger 74. The Fortune 76. One Flew Over the Cuckoo's Nest (AA) 76. The Missouri Breaks 76. The Last Tycoon 76. Going South (& d) 78. The Shining 80. The Postman Always Rings Twice 81. Reds (BFA) 81. The Border 82. Terms of Endearment (AA) 83. Prizzi's Honor (AAN) 85. Heartburn 86. The Witches of Eastwick 87. Ironweed 87.

¶ *J.N.:* As an actor, I have no desire for anybody to understand my past work. Period.

'He has a fine eye for good paintings and a good ear for fine music. And he's a lovely man to drink with.'—*John Huston*

Nicholson, James H. (1916–1972). American executive, former theatre owner and distributor, who became president of American International Pictures.

Nicholson, Nora (1892–1973). British stage character actress whose film roles have usually been fey or eccentric.
The Blue Lagoon 48. Treat Softly 48. Crow Hollow 52. Raising a Riot 54. A Town Like Alice 56. The Captain's Table 59. Diamonds for Breakfast 69, etc.

Nick Carter. The tough young American detective, the occidental answer to Sexton Blake, was created in 1886 by Ormond G. Smith (1860–1933) and John Russell Coryell (1848–1924) for the *New York Weekly*. Dozens of hack writers later authored the stories under pseudonyms. Four French films starring André Liabel were made in 1912; Thomas Carrigan appeared in some shorts in 1920; Edmund Lowe had a series in 1924; Walter Pidgeon was in three in 1940; Eddie Constantine in two (French) in 1963 and 1965. From 1943 the character was very popular on radio, but television has made one poorish attempt in 1972, *The Adventures of Nick Carter* starring Robert Conrad.

nickelodeon. A humorous term applied to early American cinemas once they had become slightly grander than the converted stores which were used for the purpose at the turn of the century.

nicknames

? For affectionate or other reasons, many stars have had nicknames attached to them by publicists or journalists. How many of these people can you recognize:

1 The Body
2 The It Girl
3 The Oomph Girl
4 The Biograph Girl
5 The Peekaboo Girl
6 The Love Rouser

7 The Fiddle and the Bow
8 America's Sweetheart
9 The Sex Kitten
10 The Threat
11 The Great Profile
12 The Platinum Blonde
13 The Viennese Teardrop
14 The Clothes Horse
15 The Iron Butterfly
16 The Singing Capon
17 King of the Cowboys
18 The Man You Love to Hate
19 The Master
20 The Beard
21 The Man of a Thousand Faces
22 The Magnificent Wildcat
23 The First Lady of the Screen
24 The Empress of Emotion
25 The Duke
26 The World's Greatest Actor
27 The Screen's Master Character Actor
28 The First Gentleman of the Screen
29 The King of Hollywood
30 The Handsomest Man in the World
31 America's Boy Friend
32 The World's Greatest Actress
33 The Dancing Divinity
34 The Anatomic Bomb

Nicol, Alex (1919–). American leading man with stage experience, mainly in Universal action pictures.
The Sleeping City 50. Because of You 52. Law and Order 54. The Man from Laramie 55. Sincerely Yours 55. Under Ten Flags 60. Three Came Back (& pd) 60. Look in Any Window 61. The Savage Guns 62. Ride and Kill 63. Gunfighters of Casa Grande 65. Bloody Mama 69. Point of Terror (d only) 71. The Night God Screamed 75, etc.

Nielsen, Asta (1882–1972). Danish stage actress.
Der Abgrund 10. Enelein 13. Kurfurstendamm 19. Reigen 20. Hamlet 20. Fraulein Julie 21. Vanina Vanini 22. Erdgeist 23. Hedda Gabler 24. Joyless Street 25. Secrets of a Soul 26. Unmogliche Liebe 32, others.

Nielsen, Leslie (1925–). Canadian leading man, former radio disc jockey; much TV work.
The Vagabond King 55. Forbidden Planet 56. Ransom 56. Tammy and the Bachelor 57. Harlow 65. Beau Geste 66. The Poseidon Adventure 72. Project Kill 76. Day of the Animals 77. Little Mo (TV) 78. The Amsterdam Kill 78. Backstairs at the White House (TV) 79. Institute for Revenge (TV) 79. Airplane 80. Prom Night 80. The Creature Wasn't Nice 81, etc.
TV series: The New Breed 61. Bracken's World 68. The Bold Ones 71. Police Squad 82. Soul Man 86. The Patriot 87.

Niesen, Gertrude (1912–1975). American singer-actress of Russian and Swedish ancestry.
Start Cheering 40. Rookies on Parade 42. He's My Guy 44. The Babe Ruth Story 48.

Nigh, Jane (1926–). American leading lady of minor films in the forties and fifties.
Something for the Boys 44. State Fair 45. Dragonwyck 46. Give My Regards to Broadway 48. Red Hot and Blue 49. Fighting Man of the Plains 49. County Fair 50. Blue Blood 51. Fort Osage 53, etc.
TV series: Big Town 52.

Nigh, William (1881–1955). American director.
Marriage Morals 23. Mr Wu 27. The Single Sin 31. Crash Donovan 35. The Ape 40. Corregidor 42. The Right to Live 45. Divorce 45, etc.

A Night at the Opera (US 1935). The Marx Brothers' first film for MGM. Given a big budget, they also had to suffer romantic and musical interludes which made their fans impatient; but the film contained some of their best routines, including the cabin scene, and the final sabotaging of *Il Trovatore* is brilliantly timed. As usual, Margaret Dumont stood the brunt of the insults.

Night Mail (GB 1936). A highly influential two-reel documentary made by Harry Watt and Basil Wright for the GPO Film Unit, building up an exciting pattern of images and sounds as the night mail train steams from London to Scotland. The verse which largely replaces commentary was written by W. H. Auden.

Night Must Fall. Emlyn Williams' macabre play about the homicidal Welsh pageboy who keeps his victim's head in a hatbox was filmed in 1938 by Richard Thorpe for MGM, with Robert Montgomery. When Karel Reisz produced a somewhat modernized version in 1963 with Albert Finney, the critics all yearned for the 1938 film, which they hadn't seen for twenty years. One doubts whether either version really pleased the author.

The Night of the Demon (GB 1957) (US title: *Curse of the Demon*). Charles Bennett adapted M. R. James' story 'Casting the Runes' for this unassuming little thriller which was directed by Jacques Tourneur with a strong Hitchcock flavour. It remains one of the screen's best ventures into the supernatural, though not helped by the colourless playing of the romantic leads. Niall MacGinnis, however, gives a roistering performance as the evil Karswell, and the final train sequence is genuinely exciting.

The Night of the Hunter (US 1955). One of the strangest films to come out of Hollywood, an allegory of good and evil from Davis Grubb's novel about the escape of two children from a psychopathic preacher (Robert Mitchum). Impeccably directed by Charles Laughton so that, although the film does not satisfy as a whole, fragments of it linger in the memory; enhanced by Stanley Cortez' splendid photography.

Nightingale, Florence (1820–1910). English nurse who organized hospitals at the front during the Crimean War, with little official help and under appalling conditions. There have been two biopics of her: *The White Angel* (US) 35, with Kay Francis, and *The Lady with a Lamp* (GB) 51, with Anna Neagle. In *Sixty Glorious Years* she was briefly played by Joyce Bland.

Nights of Cabiria: see under *Cabiria*.

Nilsson, Anna Q. (1889–1974). Swedish-born actress, long in America and popular in silent films from 1919.
The Love Burglar 19. Kingdom of Dreams 20. Soldiers of Fortune 20. Hollywood 22. The Isle of Lost Ships 23. Inez of Hollywood 24. The Masked Woman 25. The Greater Glory 26. Sorrell and Son 27. The World Changes 34. Prison Farm 38. Girls' Town 42. The Farmer's Daughter 47. Sunset Boulevard 50, etc.

Nilsson, Leopold Torre: see *Torre-Nilsson, Leopold.*

Nimmo, Derek (1931–). British character comedian who gets laughs from toe-twiddling and funny voices (especially of the comedy curate kind).
The Millionairess 61. The Amorous Prawn 62. The Bargee 64. Joey Boy 65. The Liquidator 65. Casino Royale 66. Mister Ten Per Cent 66. A Talent for Loving 69. One of Our Dinosaurs is Missing 75, etc.
TV series: All Gas and Gaiters 67. The World of Wooster 68. Oh Brother 70. Oh Father 73. Hell's Bells 85.

Nimoy, Leonard (1931–). Lean-faced American character actor.
Queen for a Day 51. Rhubarb 51. The Balcony 63. Catlow 72. The Alpha Caper (TV) 73. Invasion of the Body Snatchers 78. Star Trek, the Motion Picture 79. Star Trek: The Wrath of Khan 82. A Woman Called Golda (TV) 82. Star Trek 3 (& a) 84. Star Trek 4: The Voyage Home 86, etc.
TV series: *Star Trek* (as Mr Spock) 66–68. Mission Impossible 70–72.

Ninotchka (US 1939). A blithe satire about communism meeting capitalism in Paris, in the shapes of Greta Garbo and Melvyn Douglas. For the most part a felicitous though over-long comedy, with engaging performances from the principals and from Sig Ruman, Alexander Granach and Felix Bressart as the incompetent Russian emissaries. Directed by Ernst Lubitsch from a script by Charles Brackett, Billy Wilder and Walter Reisch. The film in which 'Garbo laughs!'. Remade in 1957 as a musical, *Silk Stockings*, with Cyd Charisse and Fred Astaire.

Nissen, Greta (1906–) (Grethe Rutz-Nissen). Norwegian leading lady in American films.
The Wanderer 25. The Popular Sin 26. Women of All Nations 31. Rackety Rax 32. Melody Cruise 33. Red Wagon 36, etc.

nitrate. Until 1950 film stock had a nitrate base, which helped give a splendid sheen, but was very inflammable. The change was made to safety stock, which burns much more slowly, but black and white films at least never looked so good again.

Nitzche, Jack (–). American composer.
The Exorcist 73. One Flew over the Cuckoo's Nest 76. Cruising 81. Personal Best 82. Cannery Row 82. Without a Trace 83.

Niven, David (1909–1983). Debonair British leading man whose natural enthusiasm found several outlets before he accidentally arrived in Hollywood and was signed up as an extra. His light-hearted approach to life is reflected in his 1972 autobiography *The Moon's a Balloon* and its 1975 sequel *Bring On the Empty Horses*.

Biography 1985 by Sheridan Morley: *The Other Side of the Moon*.
□Barbary Coast 35. Without Regret 35. A Feather in Her Hat 35. Splendor 35. Rose Marie 36. *Thank You Jeeves* 36. Palm Springs 36. The Charge of the Light Brigade 36. *Dodsworth* 36. Beloved Enemy 36. We Have Our Moments 37. Dinner at the Ritz 37. *The Prisoner of Zenda* (as Fritz von Tarlenheim) 37. Four Men and a Prayer 38. Bluebeard's Eighth Wife 38. Three Blind Mice 38. The Dawn Patrol 38. Wuthering Heights 39. *Bachelor Mother* 39. The Real Glory 39. Eternally Yours 39. *Raffles* 40. The First of the Few 41. *The Way Ahead* 44. *A Matter of Life and Death* 46. The Perfect Marriage 46. Magnificent Doll 46. The Other Love 47. The Bishop's Wife 47. Bonnie Prince Charlie 47. Enchantment 48. A Kiss in the Dark 49. A Kiss for Corliss 49. The Elusive Pimpernel 50. The Toast of New Orleans 50. Soldiers Three 51. Happy Go Lovely 51. The Lady Says No 52. Appointment with Venus 52. The Moon is Blue 53. The Love Lottery 54. Happy Ever After 54. The King's Thief 55. *Carrington V.C.* 55. The Birds and the Bees 56. *Around The World in Eighty Days* (as Phineas Fogg) 56. Oh Men Oh Women 57. The Little Hut 57. My Man Godfrey 57. The Silken Affair 57. Bonjour Tristesse 58. *Separate Tables* (AA) 58. Ask Any Girl 59. Happy Anniversary 59. Please Don't Eat the Daisies 60. The Guns of Navarone 61. The Captive City 62. Guns of Darkness 62. The Best of Enemies 62. Road to Hong Kong (gag appearance) 63. 55 Days at Peking 63. The Pink Panther 64. Bedtime Story 64. Where the Spies Are 65. Lady L 66. Casino Royale 67. Eye of the Devil 67. The Extraordinary Seaman 68. Prudence and the Pill 68. The Impossible Years 68. Before Winter Comes 68. The Brain 69. The Statue 70. King Queen Knave 72. Vampira 74. Paper Tiger 75. Murder by Death 76. No Deposit No Return 76. Candleshoe 77. Death on the Nile 78. A Man Called Intrepid (TV) 79. Escape to Athena 79. A Nightingale Sang in Berkeley Square 80. Rough Cut 80. The Sea Wolves 80. Better Late Than Never 82. Trail of the Pink Panther 82. Curse of the Pink Panther 83.
TV series: Four Star Playhouse 56. *The David Niven Show* 59. *The Rogues* 64.
❀ For forty years as a debonair international star. *Around the World in Eighty Days*.

¶ *D.N.:* Can you imagine being wonderfully overpaid for dressing up and playing games?
He's a very, very bad actor, but he absolutely loves doing it.—*D.N. on himself*

D.N.: Actors don't retire, they just get offered fewer roles.

D.N.: I suppose everybody becomes an actor because they want to be liked. I do enjoy being liked, but I don't work hard at it. I try to do the best I can for my age.

D.N.: I have a face that's a cross between two pounds of halibut and an explosion in an old clothes closet. If it isn't mobile, it's dead.

Nixon, Marian (1904–1983). American leading lady.
What Happened to Jones? 26. Rosita 27. General Crack 29. Adios 30. After Tomorrow 32. Rebecca of Sunnybrook Farm 32. Walking Down Broadway 32.

Nixon, Marni (c. 1929–). American singer, former MGM messenger, who has dubbed in high notes for many stars including Margaret O'Brien in *Big City*, Deborah Kerr in *The King and I*, Natalie Wood in *West Side Story* and Audrey Hepburn in *My Fair Lady*. Has made only one film appearance, as a nun in *The Sound of Music* 65.

Noel, Magali (1932–) (M. Guiffrais). French leading lady.
Seul dans Paris 51. Razzia sur la Chnouf 55. Rififi 55. Elena et les Hommes 56. Desire Takes the Men 58. La Dolce Vita 59. The Man Who Understood Women 70. Amarcord 74, etc.

Noel-Noel (1897–) (Lucien Noel). Dapper French character comedian.
Octave 32. A Cage of Nightingales 43. Le Pere Tranquille 46. The Seven Deadly Sins 51. The Diary of Major Thompson 56. Jessica 62, etc.

Noiret, Philippe (1931–). Chubby French character actor in international films.
Zazie dans le Métro 60. Les Copains 62. Cyrano and D'Artagnan 63. Lady L 65. The Night of the Generals 66. Clerambérard 69. *Topaz* 69. Justine 69. Murphy's War 70. A Time for Loving 71. The Serpent 72. La Grande Bouffe 73. The Clockmaker 76. The Old Gun 76. Who is Killing the Great Chefs of Europe? 78. Dear Detective 78. Le Grand Carnaval 83. Fort Saganne 84. Round Midnight 84. The Secret Wife 86, etc.

Nolan, Doris (1916–). American leading lady who married Alexander Knox.
The Man I Married 37. Holiday 38. Irene 40. Moon over Burma 40. Follies Girl 45.

Bindle 66. The Romantic Englishwoman 75, etc.

Nolan, Jeanette (1911–). American character actress, much on TV. Married to John McIntire.
Macbeth (as Lady Macbeth) 48. The Secret of Convict Lake 51. The Happy Time 52. The Big Heat 53. The Guns of Fort Petticoat 57. The Rabbit Trap 58. The Winds of Autumn 76. Lassie: The New Beginning (TV) 78.
TV series: Hotel de Paree 59. The Richard Boone Show 63. The Virginian 67. Dirty Sally 73.

Nolan, Lloyd (1902–85). Dependable American character actor, with stage experience from 1927.
Stolen Harmony (film debut) 34. G Men 35. Ebb Tide 37. Gangs of Chicago 40. Michael Shayne, Private Detective 40. Blues in the Night 41. Buy Me That Town 41. Bataan 43. *A Tree Grows in Brooklyn* 44. *The House on 92nd Street* 45. The Lady in the Lake 46. The Street with No Name 48. The Last Hunt 56. Peyton Place 58. Circus World 64. Never Too Late 65. An American Dream 66. The Double Man (GB) 67. Ice Station Zebra 68. Airport 69. Isn't It Shocking? (TV) 73. Earthquake 74. The Private Files of J. Edgar Hoover 78. Hannah and Her Sisters 85, many others.
TV series: Julia 68–70.

Nolan, Mary (1905–48) (Mary Imogene Robertson). American leading lady, an ex-Ziegfeld girl who made a few films in Germany and Hollywood, then came to grief through drugs.
Sister Veronika 26. Sorrell and Son 27. West of Zanzibar 28. Shanghai Lady 29. Outside the Law 30. X Marks the Spot 31. Midnight Patrol 32, etc.

Nolbandov, Sergei (1895–1971). Russian-born writer-producer, in Britain from 1926.
City of Song (w) 30. Fire over England (w) 36. Ships with Wings (wd) 42. This Modern Age (series) (p) from 1946. The Kidnappers (p) 53. Mix Me a Person (p) 62, many others.

Nolte, Nick (1940–). Virile American leading man of the mid-seventies.
Return to Macon County 75. Death Sentence (TV) 76. The Runaway Barge (TV) 76. *Rich Man Poor Man* (TV) 76. The Deep 77. Who'll Stop the Rain? 78. North Dallas Forty 79. Heart Beat 79. Cannery Row 82. 48 Hours 82. The Ultimate Solution of Grace Quigley 84. Teachers 84. Down and Out in Beverly Hills 85. Extreme Prejudice 87, etc.

¶ *N.N.:* If you feel you have a film that's valid, you stick your ass on the line.

non-theatrical. A descriptive adjective usually applied to film showings at which there is no paid admission on entrance, e.g. schools, clubs, etc. Some distributors apply the term to all 16mm showings.

Noonan, Tommy (1921–1968) (Thomas Noon). Ebullient American comedian.
Starlift 51. Gentlemen Prefer Blondes 53. A Star is Born 54. How to Be Very Very Popular 55. Bundle of Joy 56. *The Ambassador's Daughter* 56. The Rookie (& p) 60, etc.

Norden, Christine (1924–) (Mary Lydia Thornton). British leading lady, a sex symbol of the late forties.
□Night Beat 47. *Mine Own Executioner* 47. Idol of Paris 48. A Yank Comes Back 48. An Ideal Husband 48. Saints and Sinners 49. The Interrupted Journey 49. The Black Widow 50. A Case for PC 49 51. Reluctant Heroes 52. Little Shop of Horrors 87.
TV series: Chance in a Million 87.

Norman, Leslie (1911–). British producer-director, former editor, in films from late twenties.
Where No Vultures Fly (p) 51. The Cruel Sea (p) 54. The Night My Number Came Up (d) 56. X the Unknown (d) 57. The Shiralee (d) 58. Dunkirk (d) 58. The Long, the Short and the Tall (d) 60. Mix Me a Person (d) 61. Summer of the 17th Doll (d) 61, etc.

Normand, Mabel (1894–1930) (Mabel Fortescue). American comedienne, a leading player of Vitagraph and Keystone comedies from 1911, and a Chaplin co-star.
Barney Oldfield's Race for Life 12. Fatty and Mabel Adrift 15. Mickey 17. Sis Hopkins 18. Molly O 21. Suzanna 22. The Extra Girl 24, many others.

Norris, Chuck (1942–) (Carlos Ray). American tough guy hero, former karate champion.
Good Guys Wear Black 79. An Eye for an Eye 81. Forced Vengeance 82. Silent Rage 82. *Missing in Action* 83. Lone Wolf McQuade 83. Missing in Action II 83. Code of Silence 84. Invasion USA 85. Delta Force 85. Firewalker 86, etc.

Norris, Edward (1910–). American leading man of second features; former reporter.
Queen Christina 33. Boys' Town 38. The Man with Two Lives 41. End of the Road 44. Decoy 47. Forbidden Women 49. Inside the Walls of Folsom Prison 51. The Man from the Alamo 53. The Kentuckian (last to date) 55, many others.

Norris, Frank (1870–1902). American novelist, whose *McTeague* was the basis for Von Stroheim's *Greed*.

North, Alex (1910–). American composer.
□*A Streetcar Named Desire* 51. The Thirteenth Letter 51. Death of a Salesman 51. Viva Zapata 52. Les Miserables 52. Pony Soldier 52. The Member of the Wedding 53. Desiree 54. Go Man Go 54. The Racers 55. Unchained 55. The Man with the Gun 55. The Rose Tattoo 55. I'll Cry Tomorrow 56. The Bad Seed 56. The Rainmaker 56. Four Girls in Town 56. The King and Four Queens 56. The Bachelor Party 57. The Long Hot Summer 58. Stage Struck 58. Hot Spell 58. South Seas Adventure 58. The Sound and the Fury 59. The Wonderful Country 59. *Spartacus* 60. The Children's Hour 61. Sanctuary 61. The Misfits 61. All Fall Down 62. Cleopatra 63. The Outrage 64. Cheyenne Autumn 64. The Agony and the Ecstasy 65. Who's Afraid of Virginia Woolf 66. The Devil's Brigade 68. The Shoes of the Fisherman 68. A Dream of Kings 69. Hard Contract 69. Willard 71. Pocket Money 72. Bite the Bullet 75. Rich Man Poor Man (TV) 76. Somebody Killed Her Husband (TV) 78. Wise Blood 79. Carny 80. Dragonslayer 81. Under the Volcano (AAN) 84.

North by Northwest (US 1959). A blithe comedy-thriller, possibly Hitchcock's most likeable film if only because it is an over-size bag of his best old tricks. Cary Grant is irresistibly debonair as the innocent hero chased by spies over the great stone faces of Mount Rushmore and savaged by an aeroplane in a cornfield; Leo G. Carroll and James Mason smoothly represent law and disorder respectively. Written by Ernest Lehman, photographed by Robert Burks, with music by Bernard Herrmann.

North, Edmund H. (1911–). American screenwriter.
One Night of Love 34. I Dream Too Much 35. All the King's Horses 35. Bunker Bean 36. I'm Still Alive 40. Dishonored Lady 47. Young Man with a Horn 50. In a Lonely Place 50. Only the Valiant 51. The Day the Earth Stood Still 51. The Outcasts of Poker Flat 53. The Far Horizons 55. The Proud Ones 56. Cowboy 58. Sink the Bismarck 60. H.M.S. Defiant 62. Patton (co-w) (AA) 70. Meteor 79, etc.

North, Jay (1952–). American juvenile actor, popular as a child on TV in *Dennis the Menace* 59–63 and later *Maya* 67.
Pepe 60. Zebra in the Kitchen 65.

North, Michael (c. 1920–). American leading man of the forties. Formerly known as Ted North; changed and was reintroduced for *The Unsuspected* 48.

North, Sheree (1933–) (Dawn Bethel). Blonde American leading lady, former dancer.
Excuse My Dust 51. *How to Be Very Very Popular* 55. The Best Things in Life are Free 56. The Way to the Gold 57. No Down Payment 57. Mardi Gras 58. Destination Inner Space 66. Madigan 68. The Gypsy Moths 69. Lawman 71. Charley Varrick 73. Breakout 75. The Shootist 76. Telefon 77. *The Night They Took Miss Beautiful* (TV) 78, etc.
TV series: Big Eddie 75. But I'm a Big Girl Now 80.

Northwest Passage (US 1940). Actually this was only part one of Kenneth Roberts' novel, and bore the subtitle 'Rogers' Rangers'; part two unfortunately was never made, and in the film as it stands the northwest passage is never seen and barely talked about. Spencer Tracy gives a splendid performance as the indomitable major exacting retribution from the Indians and nearly killing off his own men in the process. Directed by King Vidor, and beautifully photographed in fairly early Technicolor, it remains one of the screen's most invigorating westerns. A rather tatty TV series of the same title appeared in 1957.

Norton, Jack (1889–1958) (Mortimer J. Naughton). American character actor, invariably seen as an amiable well-dressed drunk with a sour expression; he rarely had a coherent speaking part.
Cockeyed Cavaliers 34. Thanks for the Memory 38. The Ghost Breakers 40. The Bank Dick 40. The Fleet's In 41. The Palm Beach Story 42. Hail the Conquering Hero 44. Hold that Blonde 45. Bringing Up Father 46, many others.

Norwood, Eille (1861–1948) (Anthony Brett). British stage actor who played Sherlock Holmes in a score of twenties two-reelers and a few features.

Nosferatu: see under *Dracula*.

Nosseck, Max (1902–1972) (Alexander Norris). Polish director in Hollywood from 1939; former stage and film actor/director in Europe.
□AMERICAN FILMS: Girls Under Twenty One 40. Gambling Daughters 41. *Dillinger* 45. The Brighton Strangler 45. Black Beauty 46. The Return of Rin Tin Tin 47. Kill or Be Killed 50. Korea Patrol 51. The Hoodlum 51. The Body Beautiful 53. Garden of Eden 57.

Nothing But the Truth. James Montgomery's Broadway comedy about a man who takes a bet to tell the absolute truth for twenty-four hours was filmed in 1920, with Taylor Holmes; in 1929, with Richard Dix; and in 1941, with Bob Hope.

Nothing Sacred (US 1937). One of Hollywood's most successful satirical comedies, perhaps because the bitterness was mixed with slapstick. Carole Lombard plays the girl who thinks she is dying of a rare disease and is propelled by reporter Fredric March to the status of a national heroine; Walter Connolly is a magnificently wrathful editor. Most memorable moment: March finds himself in an unfriendly small town, where the natives are all surly and mutter at him in monosyllables; suddenly a small boy darts out from behind a picket fence and bites him in the leg. Written by Ben Hecht; directed by William Wellman; in Technicolor. Remade 1954, with Jerry Lewis (!) in the Lombard part, as *Living It Up*.

Novak, Eva (1899–). American silent screen leading lady, sister of Jane.
The Lost Trail 21. Society Secrets 21. The Man From Hells River 22. Boston Blackie 23. A Fight for Honor 24. The Forlorn Lover 25. Irene 26. Red Signals 27. Phantom of the Desert 30, etc.

Novak, Jane (1896–). American silent screen leading lady, sister of Eva.
The Barbarian 21. Colleen of the Pines 22. Jealous Husbands 23. The Lullaby 24. Lure of the Wilds 25. Whispering Canyon 26. What Price Love? 27. Free Lips 28. Redskin 29, etc.

Novak, Kim (1933–) (Marilyn Novak). Artificially-groomed American blonde star who never managed to give a natural performance, though she did try.
□The French Line 53. *Pushover* 54. Phffft 54. Five against the House 55. Son of Sinbad 55. *Picnic* 55. The Man with the Golden Arm 56. The Eddy Duchin Story 56. *Jeanne Eagles* 57. Pal Joey 58. Vertigo 58. Bell Book and Candle 58. Middle of the Night 59. Strangers When We Meet 60. Pépé 60. Boys' Night Out 62. The Notorious Landlady 62. Of Human Bondage 64. Kiss Me Stupid 64. The Amorous Adventures of Moll Flanders 65. The Legend of Lylah Clare 68. The Great Bank Robbery 69. Tales That Witness Madness 73. Third Girl from the Left (TV) 74. Satan's Triangle (TV) 75. The White Buffalo 77. Just a Gigolo 79. The Mirror Crack'd 80. Malibu (TV) 83.

Novarro, Ramon (1899–1968) (Ramon Samaniegos). Romantic Mexican leading man of the twenties in Hollywood; later came back as character actor.
The Prisoner of Zenda (as Rupert) 22. Where the Pavement Ends 23. *Scaramouche* 23. The Arab 24. The Midshipman 25. *Ben Hur* 25. The Student Prince 27. Across to Singapore 28. Forbidden Hours 28. The Pagan 29. Call of the Flesh 30. Son of India 31. Mata Hari 31. The Son-Daughter 32. The Barbarian 33. The Cat and the Fiddle 34. The Night is Young 35. The Sheik Steps Out 37. *We Were Strangers* 48. The Big Steal 49. Crisis 50. Heller in Pink Tights 60, etc.

novel into film

? Name the films made from these novels.

1 *Benighted* by J. B. Priestley
2 *The Brick Foxhole* by Richard Brooks
3 *The Off-Islanders* by Nathaniel Benchley
4 *The Wheel Spins* by Ethel Lina White
5 *Some Must Watch* by Ethel Lina White
6 *Your Arkansas Traveller* by Budd Schulberg
7 *Rogue Male* by Geoffrey Household
8 *The Curse of Capistrano* by Johnstone McCulley
9 *The House of Dr Edwardes* by Francis Beeding
10 *The Clansman* by Thomas Dixon
11 *From Among the Dead* by Boileau and Narcejac
12 *Hold Autumn in Your Hand* by George Sessions Perry
13 *The Phantom Crown* by Bertita Harding

14 *A Shilling for Candles* by Josephine Tey
15 *Mute Witness* by Robert L. Pike
16 *Red Alert* by Peter George
17 *Before the Fact* by Francis Iles
18 *The Nutmeg Tree* by Margery Sharp
19 *Mama's Bank Account* by Kathryn Forbes
20 *The Once and Future King* by T. H. White
21 *Glory for Me* by Mackinlay Kantor
22 *The Light of Day* by Eric Ambler
23 *Miami Mayhem* by Marvin H. Albert
24 *A Gun for Sale* by Graham Greene
25 *Man Running* by Selwyn Jepson

Novello, Ivor (1893–1951) (Ivor Davies). Welsh matinée idol with an incredibly successful career in stage musical comedy; also prolific playwright and composer.
Biographies: 1951, *Ivor* by MacQueen Pope. 1951, *Ivor Novello* by Peter Noble. 1974, *Perchance to Dream* by Richard Rose. 1975, *Ivor* by Sandy Wilson.
Carnival 22. The Bohemian Girl 22. The White Rose 23. *The Man without Desire* 23. *The Rat* 25. *The Lodger* 26. The Triumph of the Rat 27. The Constant Nymph 27. Downhill 27. The Vortex 28. Once a Lady 31. The Lodger (remake) 32. Sleeping Car 33. I Lived with You 34. Autumn Crocus 34, etc.

¶ 'Novello looks a little like Conway Tearle, a little like Ramon Novarro and a little like Richard Barthelmess . . . a couple of years under good direction should see him the great idol of the movie fans.'—*Paul Gallico, 1923*

Novello, Jay (1905–1982). Wiry little American actor, familiar in films from Tenth Avenue Kid 38 to Atlantis the Lost Continent 61, usually as scruffy little crook.
TV series: McHale's Navy 65.

Nugent, Elliott (1899–1980). American stage actor, producer and playwright who only dabbled in films but proved a good director of comedies.
Autobiography 1965: *Events Leading Up to the Comedy*.
AS ACTOR: So This is College 29. The Unholy Three 30. Romance 30. The Last Flight 31, etc.
AS DIRECTOR: The Mouthpiece 32. Whistling in the Dark 33. *Three Cornered Moon* 33. She Loves Me Not 34. Love in Bloom 35. And So They Were Married 36. Professor Beware 38. *The Cat and the Canary* 39. Nothing but the Truth 40. The Male Animal (& oa) 42. The Crystal Ball 43. Up in Arms 44. My Favorite Brunette 47. *My Girl Tisa* 48. *The Great Gatsby* 49. My Outlaw Brother 51. Just for You 52, etc.

Nugent, Frank (1908–1966). American screenwriter, former reporter and critic.
Fort Apache 48. *She Wore a Yellow Ribbon* 49. The Quiet Man 52. Trouble in the Glen 53. *The Searchers* 56. The Last Hurrah 58. Donovan's Reef 63, etc.

numbered sequels. This rather offhand practice probably began in 1956 with *Quatermass II*, but did not really become fashionable until the seventies. Among the successes to label their sequels so casually are *The French Connection*, *Jaws**, *The Sting*, *Mad Max*, *Walking Tall*, *Superman**, *Halloween**, *Death Wish*, *Grease*, *That's Entertainment*, *Piranha*, *Friday the 13th**, *La Cage aux Folles*, *The Amityville Horror**, *Porky's*, *Rocky** and *Airplane*. (The starred titles actually ran to a third instalment.)

numbers

? A number is missing from the title of each of the following films, all made before 1950. Supply it.

1 . . . . . . *Strangers*
2 . . . . . . *Came Back*
3 . . . . . . *Men and a Girl*
4 *Over* . . . . . .
5 . . . . . . *Men and a Prayer*
6 . . . . . . *Girls and a Sailor*
7 *Pilot Number* . . . . . .
8 . . . . . . *Sinners*
9 . . . . . . *Graves to Cairo*
10 . . . . . . *Nights*
11 . . . . . . *Seconds*
12 *The Secret* . . . . . .
13 . . . . . . *Sisters from Boston*
14 . . . . . . *Men in White*
15 . . . . . . *Little Girls in Blue*
16 . . . . . . *Smart People*
17 . . . . . . *Hearts for Julia*
18 . . . . . . *Horsemen*
19 . . . . . . *Wives*
20 . . . . . . *Mothers*
21 . . . . . . *Fathers*
22 . . . . . . *Godfathers*
23 . . . . . . *Sons*
24 . . . . . . *Daughters*
25 . . . . . . *Girls*
26 . . . . . . *Years in Sing Sing*
27 . . . . . . *Seconds Over Tokyo*
28 *The* . . . . . . *Steps*
29 *Rendezvous* . . . . . .
30 *Abroad with* . . . . . . *Yanks*

nuns have been popular figures on the screen, though only in *The Nun's Story* and the Polish *The Devil and the Nun* has any real sense of dedication been achieved; the French *Dialogue des Carmélites* tried hard but failed. Sentimentalized nuns were seen in *The Cradle Song, Bonaventure, The White Sister, Conspiracy of Hearts, The Bells of St Mary's, Come to the Stable, Portrait of Jennie, Heaven Knows Mr Allison, Black Narcissus, Lilies of the Field, The Miracle, The Song of Bernadette* and *The Sound of Music*; while nuns who combined modern sophistication with sweetness and light afflicted us in *The Singing Nun* and *The Trouble with Angels*, and in *Two Mules for Sister Sara* Shirley Maclaine played a prostitute disguised as a nun. A nun was raped in *Five Gates to Hell.* The most sinister nun was perhaps Catherine Lacey, with her high heels, in *The Lady Vanishes*, but the nuns in *The Trygon Factor* also count. The most agonized nuns were in *The Devils, La Religieuse*, and *The Awful Story of the Nun of Monza.* The weirdest was TV's *The Flying Nun.*

The Nun's Story (US 1959). Written by Robert Anderson from Kathryn Hulme's book, and directed by Fred Zinnemann, this long and sincere film lapsed into conventional melodrama after a brilliant first half showing the training of a novice. But at least it marked an advance in the kind of subject that can be tackled by a big, expensive movie. Photographed by Franz Planer, with music by Franz Waxman; with Audrey Hepburn in the leading role.

Nureyev, Rudolf (1938–). Russian ballet dancer who ventured into straight acting.
Don Quixote 73. Valentino 77. Exposed 83.

¶ *R.N.:* I love dancing. From the age of six I have not thought of anything else.

nurses have inspired biopics (*Sister Kenny, The White Angel, The Lady with a Lamp, Nurse Edith Cavell*); sentimental low-key studies of the profession (*The Lamp Still Burns, The Feminine Touch, Vigil in the Night, No Time for Tears, White Corridors, Prison Nurse, Private Nurse, Night Nurse*); even comedies (*Carry On Nurse, Twice Round the Daffodils, Nurse on Wheels*). *Green for Danger* is probably still the only thriller in which both victim and murderer were nurses. The best satire has been *The National Health* (or *Nurse Norton's Affair*). There was a popular TV series called *Janet Dean Registered Nurse* 53, and later *The Nurses* 62–64. See also *hospitals*; *doctors*.

Nuyen, France (1939–). Franco-Chinese leading lady, former model, who made some Hollywood films.
In Love and War 57. *South Pacific* 58. Satan Never Sleeps 61. The Last Time I Saw Archie 62. A Girl Named Tamiko 63. Diamondhead 63. The Man in the Middle 64. Dimension Five 66. One More Train to Rob 71. The Horror at 37,000 Feet (TV) 73, etc.

Nyby, Christian (1919–). American director.
□*The Thing* 52. Hell on Devil's Island 57. Six-Gun Law 62. Young Fury 64. Operation CIA 65. First to Fight 66. Emergency! (TV) 71.

Nye, Carrie (–). American actress.
Divorce His, Divorce Hers (TV) 73. The Users (TV) 78. The Seduction of Joe Tynan 79. Creepshow 82.

Nykvist, Sven (1922–). Distinguished Swedish cinematographer.
Sawdust and Tinsel 53. Karin Mansdotter 53. *The Virgin Spring* 60. Winter Light 62. *The Silence* 64. Loving Couples 65. Persona 66. Hour of the Wolf 67. The Shame 69. The Touch 71. The Last Run 71. One Day in the Life of Ivan Denisovitch 71. Cries and Whispers (AA) 73. Scenes From a Marriage 74. Face to Face 76. King of the Gypsies 78. Pretty Baby 78. The Hurricane 79. Starting Over 79. Willie and Phil 80. The Postman Always Rings Twice 81. Cannery Row 82. Fanny and Alexander (AA) 82. Star 80 83.

nymphomaniacs are still fairly rare in normal commercial movies. The fullest studies have been by Suzanne Pleshette in *A Rage to Live*, Françoise Arnoul in *La Rage au Corps*, Claire Bloom in *The Chapman Report*, Merle Oberon in *Of Love and Desire*, Sue Lyon in *Night of the Iguana*, Lee Remick in *The Detective*, Melina Mercouri in *Topkapi*, Maureen Stapleton in *Lonelyhearts*, Jean Seberg in *Road to Corinth*, Elizabeth Taylor in *Butterfield 8*, and Sandra Jullien in *I Am a Nymphomaniac*; but one should not forget Myrna Loy's comic nympho in *Love Me Tonight.*

Answers

new faces

1 Yul Brynner □ *The King and I* □ 2 Monty Woolley □ *The Man Who Came to Dinner* □ 3 Joseph Cotten □ *Citizen Kane* □ 4 Clifton Webb □ *Laura* □ 5 Sidney Greenstreet □ *The Maltese Falcon* □ 6 Peter Lorre □ *M* □ 7 Claude Rains □ *The Invisible Man* □ 8 Albert Finney □ *Saturday Night and Sunday Morning* □ 9 Stephen Boyd □ *The Man Who Never Was* □ 10 Marlene Dietrich □ *The Blue Angel* □ 11 Red Skelton □ *Whistling in the Dark* □ 12 Alan Ladd □ *This Gun for Hire* □

nicknames

1 Marie McDonald □ 2 Clara Bow □ 3 Ann Sheridan □ 4 Florence Lawrence □ 5 Veronica Lake (from her hair-do which covered one eye) □ 6 Buddy Rogers (in 1928) □ 7 Laurel and Hardy □ 8 Mary Pickford □ 9 Brigitte Bardot □ 10 Lizabeth Scott □ 11 John Barrymore □ 12 Jean Harlow □ 13 Luise Rainer □ 14 Joan Crawford □ 15 Jeanette Macdonald □ 16 Nelson Eddy □ 17 Tom Mix □ 18 Erich von Stroheim □ 19 D. W. Griffith, or (more in the theatre) Noël Coward □ 20 Monty Woolley □ 21 Lon Chaney Senior □ 22 Pola Negri □ 23 Norma Shearer □ 24 Elissa Landi □ 25 John Wayne □ 26 John Barrymore (especially for *Don Juan*, 1927) □ 27 Lon Chaney Junior □ 28 George Arliss □ 29 Clark Gable □ 30 Francis X. Bushman □ 31 Charles 'Buddy' Rogers □ 32 Marie Dressler □ 33 Jessie Matthews □ 34 Silvana Pampanini □

novel into film

1 *The Old Dark House* □ 2 *Crossfire* □ 3 *The Russians Are Coming, The Russians Are Coming* □ 4 *The Lady Vanishes* □ 5 *The Spiral Staircase* □ 6 *A Face in the Crowd* □ 7 *Man Hunt* □ 8 *The Mark of Zorro* □ 9 *Spellbound* □ 10 *The Birth of a Nation* □ 11 *Vertigo* □ 12 *The Southerner* □ 13 *Juarez* □ 14 *Young and Innocent (The Girl Was Young)* □ 15 *Bullitt* □ 16 *Dr Strangelove* □ 17 *Suspicion* □ 18 *Julia Misbehaves* □ 19 *I Remember Mama* □ 20 *Camelot* □ 21 *The Best Years of Our Lives* □ 22 *Topkapi* □ 23 *Tony Rome* □ 24 *This Gun for Hire* □ 25 *Stage Fright* □

numbers

1 *Three* □ 2 *Five* □ 3 *One Hundred* □ 4 *Twenty-One* □ 5 *Four* □ 6 *Two* □ 7 *Five* □ 8 *Seven* □ 9 *Five* □ 10 *A Thousand and One* □ 11 *Two* □ 12 *Six* □ 13 *Two* □ 14 *Three* □ 15 *Three* □ 16 *Two* □ 17 *Three* □ 18 *Forty Thousand* □ 19 *Four* □ 20 *Four* □ 21 *Forty-Five* □ 22 *Three* □ 23 *Four* □ 24 *Four* □ 25 *Nine* □ 26 *Twenty Thousand* □ 27 *Thirty* □ 28 *Thirty-Nine* □ 29 *Twenty-Four* □ 30 *Two* □

Oakie, Jack (1903–78) (Lewis D. Offield). Cheerful American comic actor well known for a startled 'double take'; formerly in vaudeville.
Finders Keepers (debut) 27. Paramount on Parade 30. Million Dollar Legs 32. College Humor 33. If I Had a Million 33. Call of the Wild 35. The Texas Rangers 36. The Toast of New York 37. Rise and Shine 39. *The Great Dictator* (a caricature of Mussolini) 40. Tin Pan Alley 40. Footlight Serenade 42. Song of the Islands 42. Something to Shout About 43. Hello Frisco Hello 43. *It Happened Tomorrow* 44. That's the Spirit 44. The Merry Monahans 44. On Stage Everybody 45. When My Baby Smiles at Me 48. Thieves' Highway 49. Last of the Buccaneers 50. The Battle of Powder River 52. Around the World in Eighty Days 56. The Wonderful Country 59. The Rat Race 60. Lover Come Back 62, many others.

Oakland, Simon (1922–1983). American general purpose actor with stage experience.
The Brothers Karamazov 58. I Want to Live 58. Psycho 60. West Side Story 61. Follow That Dream 62. Wall of Noise 63. The Satan Bug 65. The Plainsman 66. The Sand Pebbles 67. Tony Rome 67. Chubasco 68. On a Clear Day You Can See Forever 70. Chato's Land 72. Happy Mother's Day Love George 73. Emperor of the North Pole 73. Evening in Byzantium (TV) 78, etc.
TV series: The Night Stalker 74. Toma Baa Baa Black Sheep

Oakland, Vivian (1895–1958) (V. Anderson). American child star and vaudeville artiste, who later became familiar as wife to the leading comic in many a two-reeler.
Gold Dust Gertie 31. Only Yesterday 32. The Bride Walks Out 36. Way Out West 37. The Man in the Trunk 42. Bunco Squad 51, many others.

Oakley, Annie (1859–1926) (Phoebe Annie Oakley Mozee). American sharpshooter who gained fame in her teens as star of Buffalo Bill's wild west show. Played on screen by Barbara Stanwyck in *Annie Oakley* 35, and by Betty Hutton in *Annie Get Your Gun* 50. A TV series in 1953–57 starred Gail Davis.

Oakman, Wheeler (1890–1949) (Vivian Eichelberger). American silent star, later western supporting actor.
The God of Gold 12. The Spoilers 14. The Black Orchid 16. Mickey 18. The Virgin of Stamboul 20. Outside the Law 21. The Pace That Thrills 25. Lights of New York 28. Roaring Ranch 30. End of the Trail 33. G-Men 35. Mutiny in the Big House 39, etc.

Oates, Warren (1928–1982). American supporting actor who has tended towards psychopathic heavies.
Yellowstone Kelly 59. Private Property 60. Hero's Island 61. Mail Order Bride 64. Major Dundee 65. Return of the Seven 67. In the Heat of the Night 67. The Split 68. Crooks and Coronets (GB) 69. The Wild Bunch 69. There was a Crooked Man 70. Two Lane Blacktop 71. The Hired Hand 71. Tom Sawyer 73. Dillinger (title role) 73. The White Dawn 73. Badlands 73. 92 in the Shade 75. Race with the Devil 75. Drum 76. The Brink's Job 78. True Grit (TV) 78. My Old Man (TV) 79. Baby Comes Home (TV) 80. Stripes 81. Blue Thunder 83.
TV series: Stony Burke 62.

Ober, Philip (1902–1982). American general purpose character actor.
The Secret Fury 50. From Here to Eternity 53. Tammy 56. North by Northwest 59. Let No Man Write My Epitaph 60. The Brass Bottle 64. The Ghost and Mr Chicken 66, etc.

Oberon, Merle (1911–1979) (Estelle O'Brien Merle Thompson). British leading lady. Educated in India; came to Britain 1928, worked as dance hostess until signed up by Korda. Mainly in Hollywood from 1936.
□ A Warm Corner 30. Consolation Marriage 31. Flying High 31. Clara Deane 32. Strange Evidence 32. Service for Ladies 32. Ebb Tide 32. Wedding Rehearsal 32. Men of Tomorrow 32. The Private Life of Henry VIII 33. The Battle 34. The Broken Melody 34. The Private

Life of Don Juan 34. *The Scarlet Pimpernel* 34. Folies Bergère 35. The Dark Angel 35. These Three 36. Beloved Enemy 36. I Claudius (unfinished) 37. Over the Moon 37. *The Divorce of Lady X* 38. The Cowboy and the Lady 38. *Wuthering Heights* 39. The Lion Has Wings 39. 'Til We Meet Again 40. That Uncertain Feeling 41. Affectionately Yours 41. Lydia 41. Forever and a Day 43. Stage Door Canteen 43. First Comes Courage 43. The Lodger 44. Dark Waters 44. *A Song to Remember* 45. This Love of Ours 45. A Night in Paradise 46. Temptation 46. Night Song 47. Berlin Express 48. Pardon My French 51. 24 Hours of a Woman's Life 52. All is Possible in Granada 54. Desiree 54. Deep in My Heart 54. The Price of Fear 56. Of Love and Desire 63. The Oscar 66. Hotel 67. Interval 73.
TV series: Assignment Foreign Legion 56.

Objective Burma (US 1945). The film which brought to a head British resentment about America appearing to have won the war single-handed; in this case it was Errol Flynn who took Burma without any British help. The outcry was so great that the film was withdrawn in Britain. In fact it tells a good yarn efficiently if at too great length, with photography by James Wong Howe and direction by Raoul Walsh. Ranald MacDougall and Lester Cole wrote the script.

Oboler, Arch (1909–87). American writer-producer-director with a long career in radio. Made mainly gimmick films.
□Bewitched 45. Strange Holiday 46. The Arnelo Affair 47. Five 51. Bwana Devil 52. The Twonky 53. One Plus One 61. The Bubble 67.

O'Brian, Hugh (1925–) (Hugh Krampke). Leathery American leading man, former athlete.
Never Fear 50. On the Loose 51. Red Ball Express 52. Seminole 54. There's No Business Like Show Business 54. White Feather 55. The Brass Legend 56. The Fiend Who Walked the West 58. Come Fly with Me 62. In Harm's Way 65. Love Has Many Faces 65. Ten Little Indians 65. Ambush Bay 66. Africa Texas Style 67. Probe (TV) 72. Killer Force 75. The Shootist 76. Murder at the World Series (TV) 77.
TV series: *Wyatt Earp* 56–59. Search 72.

O'Brien, Dave (1912–1969) (David Barclay). American light character actor, in Hollywood from the early thirties. Played supporting roles in innumerable films; most familiar as the hero/victim of the Pete Smith comedy shorts of the forties.
Jennie Gerhardt 33. East Side Kids 39. Son of the Navy 40. 'Neath Brooklyn Bridge 43. Tahiti Nights 44. Phantom of 42nd Street 45. The Desperadoes are in Town 56, etc.

O'Brien, Edmond (1915–85). Anglo-Irish leading man of the forties, latterly character actor; long in Hollywood.
The Hunchback of Notre Dame 39. Parachute Battalion 41. Powder Town 42, etc.; war service; *The Killers* 46. The Web 47. A Double Life 47. Another Part of the Forest 48. An Act of Murder 48. White Heat 49. *D.O.A.* 49. Between Midnight and Dawn 50. Two of a Kind 51. Denver and Rio Grande 52. Julius Caesar 53. The Hitch Hiker 53. Man in the Dark 53. The Bigamist 53. Cow Country 53. *The Barefoot Contessa* (AA) 54. Shield for Murder (& co-d) 54. 1984 (GB) 55. The Girl Can't Help It 57. *The Third Voice* 59. The Last Voyage 60. Mantrap (pd only) 61. The Great Imposter 61. The Man Who Shot Liberty Valance 62. Birdman of Alcatraz 62. *Seven Days in May* 64. Sylvia 65. Fantastic Voyage 66. The Viscount (Fr.) 67. The Wild Bunch 69. The Love God 69. Jigsaw (TV) 72. 99 44/100 Dead 74, etc.
TV series: Johnny Midnight 60. Sam Benedict 62. The Long Hot Summer 65.

O'Brien, George (1900–85). American cowboy star, who entered films as stunt man. The Iron Horse (first starring role) 24. *Sunrise* 27. Noah's Ark 28. Lone Star Ranger 30. Riders of the Purple Sage 31. The Last Trail 33. O'Malley of the Mounted 36. Daniel Boone 36. The Painted Desert 38. Stage to Chino 40. Legion of the Lawless 42. She Wore a Yellow Ribbon 49. Cheyenne Autumn 64, others.

O'Brien, Margaret (1937–) (Angela Maxine O'Brien). Stunningly talented American child actress of the forties; won special Academy Award in 1944. Had no luck with adult comeback.
□Babes on Broadway 41. *Journey for Margaret* 42. Dr Gillespie's Criminal Case 43. Thousands Cheer 43. *Lost Angel* 43. Madame Curie 43. Jane Eyre 43. The Canterville Ghost 44. *Meet Me in St Louis* 44. Music for Millions 45. *Our Vines Have Tender Grapes* 45. Bad Bascomb 46. Three Wise Fools 46. The Unfinished Dance 47. Tenth Avenue Angel 47. Big City 48. *Little Women* 49. The Secret Garden 49. Her First Romance 51. Glory 56. Heller in Pink Tights 60. Split Second to an Epitaph (TV) 68. Testimony of Two Men (TV) 77. Amy 81.
❀ For being so talented up to the age of ten. *Lost Angel*.

¶ When I cry, do you want the tears to run all the way or shall I stop halfway down? *—M.O'B. aged six*
If that child had been born in the middle ages, she'd have been burned as a witch. *—Lionel Barrymore, 1943*

O'Brien, Pat (1899–1983). Easy-going, gentle but tough-looking Irish-American character actor, a popular star of the thirties. Autobiography 1964: *The Wind at My Back.*
The Front Page 31. Honour among Lovers 31. Final Edition 32. Hell's House 32. American Madness 32. Air Mail 32. Bureau of Missing Persons 33. Bombshell 33. Gambling Lady 34. Here Comes the Navy 34. I Sell Anything 34. Devil Dogs of the Air 35. Oil for the Lamps of China 35. Page Miss Glory 35. The Irish in Us 35. Ceiling Zero 35. Public Enemy's Wife 36. China Clipper 36. The Great O'Malley 37. Slim 37. San Quentin 37. *Boy Meets Girl* 38. *Angels with Dirty Faces* 38. Indianapolis Speedway 39. The Fighting 69th 40. Slightly Honorable 40. Castle on the Hudson 40. Torrid Zone 40. Knute Rockne, All American 41. Submarine Zone 41. Broadway 42. The Navy Comes Through 42. Bombardier 43. The Iron Major 43. His Butler's Sister 43. Secret Command 44. Having Wonderful Crime 45. Man Alive 45. Perilous Holiday 46. Riffraff 47. Fighting Father Dunne 48. The Boy with Green Hair 48. A Dangerous Profession 49. Johnny One Eye 50. The People against O'Hara 51. Okinawa 52. Jubilee Trail 54. Inside Detroit 55. Kill Me Tomorrow (GB) 57. The Last Hurrah 58. Some Like It Hot 59. Town Tamer 65. The Phynx 70. The Over the Hill Gang (TV) 69. Welcome Home Johnny Bristol (TV) 72. The Adventures of Nick Carter (TV) 72. Joyride to Nowhere (TV) 73. Kiss Me Kill Me (TV) 76. The End 78. Ragtime 81. Scout's Honor (TV) 81, etc.
TV series: Harrigan and Son 60.

O'Brien, Virginia (1921–). American comedienne, the 'dead pan' singer of the forties.
Hullaballoo 40. *The Big Store* 41. Ship Ahoy 42. Thousands Cheer 43. Dubarry was a Lady 44. The Harvey Girls 45. Till the Clouds Roll By 46. Merton of the Movies 47, etc.

O'Brien, Willis (1886–1962). American specialist in the creation of monster animals for use in stop-motion techniques.
The Ghost of Slumber Mountain 20. *The Lost World* 24. *King Kong* 33. Son of Kong 33. Mighty Joe Young 49. The Animal World 56. The Black Scorpion 58, etc.

O'Brien-Moore, Erin (1902–1979). American stage actress who made a few films.
The Life of Emile Zola 38. Little Men 39. Destination Moon 50. Phantom of the Rue Morgue 53, etc.

O'Casey, Sean (1880–1964). Irish playwright, much preoccupied by 'the troubles'. Works filmed include *Juno and the Paycock* and *The Plough and the Stars*; an alleged biopic, *Young Cassidy*, was made in 1964 with Rod Taylor.

Occupe-Toi d'Amélie (France 1949). High-speed film version of a Feydeau farce, flawlessly and wittily put together by Claude Autant-Lara. Like *Henry V* it begins and ends with a stage performance of the play, but every minute is highly cinematic. Scripted by Jean Aurenche and Pierre Bost, photographed by André Bac; with Danielle Darrieux, Jean Desailly and a nimble cast.

O'Connell, Arthur (1908–1981). American character actor with long Broadway experience; usually mildly bewildered roles.
Law of the Jungle 42. Countess of Monte Cristo 49. The Whistle at Eaton Falls 51. *Picnic* 55. The Solid Gold Cadillac 56. *The Man in the Grey Flannel Suit* 56. Bus Stop 56. Operation Mad Ball 57. Operation Petticoat 59. Anatomy of a Murder 59. Follow That Dream 61. Kissin' Cousins 64. The Monkey's Uncle 65. Your Cheating Heart 65. The Great Race 65. The Silencers 66. Fantastic Voyage 66. The Power 68. There Was a Crooked Man 70. Ben 72. The Poseidon Adventure 72. Huckleberry Finn 74. The Hiding Place 75, etc.
TV series: The Second Hundred Years 67.

O'Connolly, Jim (1926–). British director.
The Traitors (wp only) 62. Smokescreen 63. *The Little Ones* 64. Berserk 67. The Valley of Gwangi 68. Crooks and Coronets 69, etc.

O'Connor, Carroll (1922–). Burly American character actor, often in blustery military roles.
By Love Possessed 61. Lonely are the Brave 62. Cleopatra 63. In Harm's Way 65. What Did You Do in the War Daddy? 65. Waterhole Three 67. Point Blank 67. The Devil's Brigade 68. Marlowe 69. Doctors' Wives 70. Law and Disorder 74, etc.
TV series: Rifleman 58. *All In the Family* (as Archie Bunker) 71–78. Archie Bunker's Place 79–82.

O'Connor, Donald (1925–). Snappy American light comedian, singer and dancer, a teenage star of the forties whose film career suffered with the decline of musicals.
□*Sing You Sinners* 38. Sons of the Legion 38. Men With Wings 38. *Tom Sawyer Detective* 38. Unmarried 39. Death of a Champion 39. Boy Trouble 39. Million Dollar Legs 39. Night Work 39. On Your Toes 39. Beau Geste 39. Private Buckaroo 42. Give Out Sisters 42. Get Hep to Love 42. When Johnny Comes Marching Home 42. Strictly in the Groove 43. It Comes Up Big 43. *Mister Big* 43. Top Man 43. *Chip off the Old Block* 44. This is the Life 44. Follow the Boys 44. The Merry Monahans 44. Bowery to Broadway 44. *Patrick the Great* 45. Something in the Wind 47. Are You With It 48. Feudin' Fussin' and a-Fightin' 48. Yes Sir That's My Baby 49. *Francis* 49. Curtain Call at Cactus Creek 50. The Milkman 50. Double Crossbones 50. Francis Goes to the Races 51. *Singin' In the Rain* 52. Francis Goes to West Point 52. *Call Me Madam* 53. I Love Melvin 53. Francis Covers Big Town 53. Walking My Baby Back Home 53. Francis Joins the WACS 54. There's No Business Like Show Business 54. Francis in the Navy 55. Anything Goes 56. *The Buster Keaton Story* 57. Cry for Happy 61. The Wonders of Aladdin 61. That Funny Feeling 65. That's Entertainment (co-narrator) 74. Ragtime 81. Pandemonium 82.
❀ For his teenage high spirits and talent. *Patrick the Great.*

O'Connor, Glynnis (1956–). Diminutive American leading lady of the seventies. Jeremy 75. Ode to Billy Joe 76. California Dreaming 78. Those Lips Those Eyes 80. Night Crossing 82. Johnny Dangerously 84.

O'Connor, Robert Emmett (1885–1962). American small part player, often as snoop or policeman, on screen from 1909 after circus and vaudeville experience.
Public Enemy 31. A Night at the Opera 35. Tight Shoes 41. Whistling in Brooklyn 44. Boys' Ranch 46, many others.

O'Connor, Tim (c.1927–). Lean American character actor who became known as the long-lost husband in TV's *Peyton Place*. Incident in San Francisco 70. Across 110th Street 72. Manhunter (TV) 74. Murder in Peyton Place (TV) 77. Buck Rogers in the 25th Century 79. The Golden Gate Murders (TV) 79.

O'Connor, Una (1880–1959). Sharp-featured Irish character actress with stage experience before film debut in 1929; in Hollywood from 1932.
□Dark Red Roses 29. To Oblige a Lady 30. Timbuctoo 30. Murder 30. *Cavalcade* 33. Pleasure Cruise 33. *The Invisible Man* 33. Mary Stevens MD 33. The Poor Rich 34. The Barretts of Wimpole Street 34. Orient Express 34. All Men Are Enemies 34. Stingaree 34. Chained 34. David Copperfield 35. *The Informer* 35. Father Brown Detective 35. *The Bride of Frankenstein* 35. Thunder in the Night 35. The Perfect Gentleman 35. Rose Marie 36. Little Lord Fauntleroy 36. Lloyds of London 36. Suzy 36. The Plough and the Stars 36. Call It a Day 37. Personal Property 37. The Return of the Frog 37. *The Adventures of Robin Hood* 38. We Are Not Alone 39. The Sea Hawk 40. Lillian Russell 40. He Stayed for Breakfast 40. It All Came True 40. All Women Have Secrets 40. Kisses for Breakfast 41. How Green Was My Valley 41. The Strawberry Blonde 41. Her First Beau 41. Three Girls about Town 41. Always in My Heart 42. My Favorite Spy 42. Random Harvest 42. This Land Is Mine 43. Forever and a Day 43. Holy Matrimony 43. Government Girl 43. My Pal Wolf 44. The Canterville Ghost 44. The Bells of St Mary's 45. Christmas in Connecticut 45. The Return of Monte Cristo 46. Banjo 46. Child of Divorce 46. Cluny Brown 46. Of Human Bondage 46. Unexpected Guest 46. Lost Honeymoon 47. The Corpse Came COD 47. Ivy 47. Fighting Father Dunne 48. The Adventures of Don Juan 48. *Witness for the Prosecution* 57.

O'Conor, Joseph (c. 1910–). British character actor, mainly on stage and TV. Crooks in Cloisters 63. Oliver! 68. Doomwatch 72. The Black Windmill 74. TV series: The Forsyte Saga (as Old Jolyon) 68.

October (Ten Days that Shook the World) (Russia 1928). Eisenstein's spectacular and exciting reconstruction of the Russian revolution, brilliantly photographed by Tisse. The screen's most persuasive re-creation of fact, and one of its most powerful pieces of propaganda.

Odd Man Out (GB 1947) (BFA). The film which established Carol Reed as a major director; with considerable help from the Abbey Theatre players he created a moving and cinematic impression of the last hours of an IRA gunman on the run. The more theatrical aspects of the picture have not worn well, but it has enough brilliant moments to preserve its reputation. R. C. Sheriff and F. L. Green wrote the script from the latter's novel; photography by Robert Krasker. James Mason played the pathetic central figure, with notable contributions from F. J. McCormick, Robert Newton and many others. The film was more or less remade in 1969 as *The Lost Man*, with Sidney Poitier.

O'Dea, Denis (1905–1978). Irish stage actor who was in occasional films.
The Informer 35. The Plough and the Stars 47. Odd Man Out 47. The Fallen Idol 48. Under Capricorn 49. Treasure Island 50. Niagara 52. Mogambo 53. The Rising of the Moon 57. The Story of Esther Costello 58, etc.

O'Dea, Jimmy (1899–1965). Irish character comedian.
□ Casey's Millions 22. Jimmy Boy 35. Blarney 38. Penny Paradise 38. Cheer Boys Cheer 39. Let's Be Famous 39. The Rising of the Moon 57. Darby O'Gill and the Little People 59. Johnny Nobody 61.

Odets, Clifford (1903–1963). American playwright and occasional scriptwriter.
The General Died at Dawn (w) 36. Golden Boy (oa) 39. None But the Lonely Heart (wd) 44. Deadline at Dawn (w) 46. Humoresque (w) 46. Clash by Night (oa) 52. The Country Girl (oa) 54. The Big Knife (oa) 55. Sweet Smell of Success (w) 57. The Story on Page One (wd) 60, etc.

Odette, Mary (1901–) (Odette Goimbault). French actress in many British silent films from 1915, at first as juvenile.
Cynthia in the Wilderness 15. Dombey and Son 17. The Lady Clare 19. Torn Sails 20. Cherry Ripe 21. The Crimson Circle 22. Eugene Aram 24. She 25. If Youth But Knew 26. Emerald of the East 28, etc.

O'Donnell, Cathy (1923–1970) (Ann Steely). American leading lady with brief stage experience.
□*The Best Years of Our Lives* (debut) 46. Bury Me Dead 47. The Spiritualist 47. *They Live by Night* 48. Side Street 50. The Miniver Story 50. Detective Story 51. Never Trust a Gambler 53. The Woman's Angle (GB) 52. Eight O'Clock Walk (GB) 54. The Face that Launched a Thousand Ships 54. Mad at the World 55. The Man from Laramie 55. The Story of Mankind 58. Ben Hur 59. Terror in the Haunted House 59.

O'Driscoll, Martha (1922–). American leading lady of the forties, mainly in second features.
The Secret of Dr Kildare 40. The Lady Eve 41. My Heart Belongs to Daddy 42. Follow the Boys 44. Ghost Catchers 44. House of Dracula 45. Criminal Court (last to date) 47, etc.

Of Human Bondage. Somerset Maugham's novel has been filmed three times. 1. US 1934, directed by John Cromwell, with Leslie Howard and Bette Davis. 2. US 1946, directed by Edmund Goulding, with Paul Henreid and Eleanor Parker. 3. GB 1964, directed by Ken Hughes and Henry Hathaway, with Laurence Harvey and Kim Novak. None could prevent the hero's tribulations with a tart from seeming mawkishly unlikely, but the first version was the best acted.

Of Mice and Men (US 1939). A curious film to come from comedy producer Hal Roach, this spare little morality about a gentle but homicidal giant who has to be killed by his best friend seemed striking at the time but has dated badly. From John Steinbeck's novel; directed by Lewis Milestone; with Lon Chaney Jnr, Burgess Meredith and Betty Field.

O'Farrell, Bernadette (1926–). British leading lady who married her director, Frank Launder.
Captain Boycott 48. The Happiest Days of Your Life 49. Lady Godiva Rides Again 51. The Story of Gilbert and Sullivan 53, etc.
TV series: Robin Hood 55-59.

O'Ferrall, George More: see *More O'Ferrall, George.*

offices have provided the setting for many a film. *The Crowd* in 1926 and *The Rebel* in 1961 chose pretty much the same way of stressing the dreariness of daily routine; but *Sunshine Susie* in 1931 and *How to Succeed in Business without Really Trying* in 1967 both saw the office as a gay place full of laughter and song. Satyajit Ray in *Company Limited* and Ermanno Olmi in *Il Posto* and *One Fine Day* took a realistic look at office life. Billy Wilder took a jaundiced view of it in *The Apartment*, as did the makers of *Patterns of Power, Executive Suite, Bartleby* and *The Power and the Prize*. Romantic comedies of the thirties like *Wife versus Secretary, After*

Office Hours and *Take a Letter Darling* saw it as ideal for amorous intrigue, and in 1964 *The Wild Affair* took pretty much the same attitude. Orson Welles in *The Trial* made it nightmarish; Preston Sturges in *Christmas in July* made it friendly; *The Desk Set* made it computerized; *The Bachelor Party* made it frustrating. Perhaps the best film office is that of Philip Marlowe in the Raymond Chandler films: there's seldom anyone in it but himself. The most spectacular was that of Alfred Abel in *Metropolis*.

O'Flaherty, Liam (1896–1984). Irish novelist whose *The Informer* was filmed twice under its own title and once as *Up Tight*.

Ogilvy, Ian (1943–). Slightly-built British leading man.
Stranger in the House 67. The Sorcerers 67. Witchfinder General 68. Wuthering Heights 70. And Now the Screaming Starts 72. No Sex Please We're British 73. Menace Unseen (TV) 88, etc.
TV series: *Return of the Saint* 78.

Ogle, Charles (1865–1940). American silent actor, best known for being the first (in 1909) to play the Frankenstein monster.
The Honour of His Family 09. The Ironmaster 14. Joan the Woman 17. Treasure Island 20. The Covered Wagon 23. The Alaskan 24. Contraband 25. The Flaming Forest 26, many others.

Oh Mr Porter (GB 1938). One of the funniest British comedies in the music-hall tradition of the thirties. About an incompetent stationmaster who clears an Irish branch line of gun-runners posing as ghosts, it is superbly written around the talents of Will Hay, with Graham Moffatt (the fat boy) and Moore Marriott (old Harbottle) as foils. Written by Val Guest, Marriott Edgar and J. O. C. Orton, directed by Marcel Varnel.

Oh What a Lovely War (GB 1969). A musical fantasia on World War I, directed with variable wit and imagination by Richard Attenborough, from Joan Littlewood's stage production. Mediocrity and dullness mingled with brilliant sequences such as the final backtrack from war graves; the actors were swamped by the concept. The songs were fine.

O'Hanlon, George (1917–) (George Rice). American comedy actor with stage experience; played Joe McDoakes in the one-reeler 'Behind the Eight Ball' series.
The Great Awakening 41. The Hucksters 47. The Tanks are Coming 51. Battle Stations 55. Bop Girl 57. The Rookie 59. Charley and the Angel 73. Rocky 76, etc.
TV series: The Life of Riley, The Reporter, Nancy Drew.

O'Hara, Gerry (c. 1925–). British director.
That Kind of Girl 61. The Pleasure Girls 64. Maroc 7 67. Amsterdam Affair 68. All the Right Noises (& w) 69. The Spy's Wife, etc.

O'Hara, John (1905–1970). American best-selling novelist who wrote chiefly about sex in suburbia. Works filmed include *Pal Joey, From the Terrace, A Rage to Live, Butterfield 8.* Also co-wrote screenplays. In 1976 a TV series was based on his *Gibbsville* stories.
I was an Adventuress 40. Moontide 42. Strange Journey 46. On Our Merry Way 48. The Best Things in Life are Free 56, etc.

¶ 'He lives in a perpetual state of just having discovered that it's a lousy world.'
—*F. Scott Fitzgerald*

O'Hara, Mary (1885–*) (Mary Alsop). American novelist best known for *My Friend Flicka*, which was filmed in 1943; sequels followed.

O'Hara, Maureen (1920–) (Maureen Fitzsimmons). Striking red-haired Irish leading lady who survived in Hollywood less through acting talent than through pleasing, unassuming personality.
□My Irish Molly 38. Kicking the Moon Around 38. Jamaica Inn 39. *The Hunchback of Notre Dame* 39. A Bill of Divorcement 40. Dance Girl Dance 40. They Met in Argentina 41. How Green Was My Valley 41. To the Shores of Tripoli 42. Ten Gentlemen from West Point 42. *The Black Swan* 42. The Immortal Sergeant 43. This Land is Mine 43. The Fallen Sparrow 43. Buffalo Bill 44. The Spanish Main 45. Sentimental Journey 46. Do You Love Me 46. Sinbad the Sailor 47. The Homestretch 47. Miracle on 34th Street 47. The Foxes of Harrow 47. Sitting Pretty 48. Britannia Mews 49. A Woman's Secret 49. Father was a Fullback 49. Baghdad 49. Comanche Territory 50. Tripoli 50. Rio Grande 50. Flame of Araby 51. At Sword's Point 52. Kangaroo 52. *The Quiet Man* 52. Against All Flags 52. Redhead from Wyoming 52. War Arrow 53. Fire over Africa

54. The Long Gray Line 55. The Magnificent Matador 55. Lady Godiva 55. Lisbon 56. Everything But the Truth 56. The Wings of Eagles 57. Our Man in Havana 59. The Parent Trap 61. The Deadly Companions 61. Mr Hobbs Takes a Vacation 62. Spencer's Mountain 63. McLintock 63. The Battle of the Villa Fiorita 65. The Rare Breed 66. How Do I Love Thee 70. Big Jake 71. The Red Pony (TV) 72.

¶ *Elsa Lanchester:* She looks as though butter wouldn't melt in her mouth—or anywhere else.

'Framed in Technicolor, Miss O'Hara somehow seems more significant than a setting sun.'—*New York Times, 1954*

O'Herlihy, Dan (1919–). Irish character actor and occasional off-beat leading man, with Abbey Theatre and radio experience. *Odd Man Out* (GB) 46. Hungry Hill (GB) 46. Kidnapped 48. Macbeth 48. Actors and Sin 50. Rommel, Desert Fox 51. The Blue Veil 51. The Highwayman 52. *The Adventures of Robinson Crusoe* 52. Bengal Brigade 53. The Black Shield of Falworth 54. The Purple Mask 55. The Virgin Queen 55. That Woman Opposite (GB) 57. Home before Dark 58. Imitation of Life 59. *The Cabinet of Caligari* 61. Fail Safe 64. 100 Rifles 69. Waterloo 69. The Carey Treatment 72. QB VII (TV) 73. The Tamarind Seed 74. MacArthur 77. T. R. Sloane (TV) 79. Halloween III 82, others. TV series: The Travels of Jaimie McPheeters 63. The Long Hot Summer 66. A Man Called Sloane 79. The Last Starfighter 84. The Whoopee Boys 86. The Dead 87.

O'Herlihy, Michael (1929–). Irish director in Hollywood, with TV experience. The Fighting Prince of Donegal 66. The One and Only Genuine Original Family Band 68. Smith! 69.

Ohmart, Carol (1928–). American leading lady with stage experience, whose career in films did not develop. The Scarlet Hour (debut) 55. The House on Haunted Hill 58. Born Reckless 59. The Scavengers 60. Wild Youth 60. One Man's Way 64. Caxambu 67. The Spectre of Edgar Allan Poe 72, etc.

Oil and its procurement from the earth have been the subjects of a number of films including *High Wide and Handsome* 38, *Boom Town* 40, *The Big Gusher* 51, *Tulsa* 49, *Thunder Bay* 53, *Lucy Gallant* 55, *Giant* 56, *The Houston Story* 56, *Maracaibo* 58, *Black Gold* 60, *Hellfighters* 68 and *Oklahoma Crude* 73.

O'Keefe, Dennis (1908–1968) (Edward 'Bud' Flanagan). Cheerful American leading man of the forties; began as an extra after vaudeville experience with his parents. Bad Man of Brimstone 38. That's Right, You're Wrong 39. La Conga Nights 40. You'll Find Out 40. Lady Scarface 41. *Topper Returns* 41. Broadway Limited 41. The Affairs of Jimmy Valentine 42. Good Morning Judge 42. The Leopard Man 43. The Fighting Seabees 43. Up in Mabel's Room 44. Abroad with Two Yanks 44. *The Affairs of Susan* 45. Brewster's Millions 45. Come Back to Me 46. Dishonoured Lady 47. T-Men 47. Mr District Attorney 47. Raw Deal 48. Walk a Crooked Mile 49. Woman on the Run 50. The Company She Keeps 51. Follow the Sun 52. The Fake (GB) 53. The Diamond Wizard (GB) (& d) 54. Angela (& d) 55. Inside Detroit 56. Dragoon Wells Massacre 57. Graft and Corruption 58. All Hands on Deck 61, many others. TV series: The Dennis O'Keefe Show 59.

Oland, Warner (1880–1938). Swedish character actor in Hollywood who oddly enough became the screen's most popular Chinese detective. The Yellow Ticket 18. Witness for the Defense 19. His Children's Children 23. Don Q Son of Zorro 25. Don Juan 26. The Jazz Singer 27. Old San Francisco 27. Chinatown Nights 29. The Mysterious Dr Fu Manchu 29. The Vagabond King 30. *Charlie Chan Carries On* 31 (and 15 other episodes in this series). Shanghai Express 32. The Painted Veil 34. *Werewolf of London* 35. Shanghai 35, many others.

Olcott, Sidney (1873–1949) (John S. Alcott). Irish-Canadian director, in Hollywood from the beginning. Ben Hur (one reel) 07. Florida Crackers 08. Judgement 09. The Miser's Child 10. The O'Neil (Irish) 11. From the Manger to the Cross 12. Madame Butterfly 15. The Innocent Lie 17. Scratch My Back 20. Little Old New York 21. The Humming Bird 23. The Green Goddess 23. Monsieur Beaucaire 24. The Amateur Gentleman 26. The Claw 27, etc.

old age on the screen has seldom been explored, and the commercial reasons for this are obvious. Among the serious studies are *The Whisperers*, with Edith Evans; *Umberto*

D, with Carlo Battisti; *The Shameless Old Lady*, with Sylvie; *Ikuru*, with Takashi Shimura; *The End of the Road*, with Finlay Currie; *I Never Sang for My Father*, with Melvyn Douglas; *Make Way for Tomorrow*, with Beulah Bondi; *Alive and Kicking*, with Sybil Thorndike and Estelle Winwood; *Kotch* with Walter Matthau and *Harry and Tonto* with Art Carney. Sentimentality crept in in *Mr Belvedere Rings the Bell*; and *The Old Man and the Sea* was merely pretentious.

There was an element of black comedy in the attitudes expressed towards the old people in *Grapes of Wrath, Tobacco Road* and *Night of the Iguana*; and more melodramatic caricatures were presented in *The Lost Moment* (Agnes Moorehead), *The Queen of Spades* (Edith Evans), *Little Big Man* (Dustin Hoffman), and *The Old Dark House* (John Dudgeon). Fantasy crept in with *Lost Horizon,* in which the lamas grew incredibly old by natural processes, and *The Man in Half Moon Street*, in which Nils Asther was assisted by science. Other actors who have specialized in geriatric portraits include A. E. Matthews, Edie Martin, Clem Bevans, Andy Clyde, Maria Ouspenskaya, Jessie Ralph, Nancy Price and Adeline de Walt Reynolds, who did not become an actress until she was eighty. Perhaps the Screen's most delightful senior citizens were the capering Harbottle, played by Moore Marriott in Will Hay comedies, and Barry Fitzgerald in *Broth of a Boy*; the most horrific was Cathleen Nesbit in *Staircase*; the most commercially successful were George Burns and Walter Matthau in *The Sunshine Boys.* Katie Johnson became a star at 78 in *The Lady Killers*: Ruth Gordon played capering old dames well into her eighties, and in *Harold and Maude*, when she was 75, played an 80-year-old who had an affair with an immature young boy.

Stars who donned ageing make-up include Hope, Crosby and Lamour in *Road to Utopia*; Barbara Stanwyck in *The Great Man's Lady*; Tyrone Power in *The Long Gray Line*; Anna Neagle in *Victoria the Great*; Madeleine Carroll in *The Fan*; Gable and Shearer in *Strange Interlude*; Rosalind Russell and Alexander Knox in *Sister Kenny*; Joel McCrea in *Buffalo Bill*; Fredric March in *The Adventures of Mark Twain.* The most tasteless treatment of old age was surely that offered in *The Ultimate Solution of Grace Quigley*; the most graceful that of *Going in Style*.

The Old Dark House (US 1932). A connoisseur's horror film, from J. B. Priestley's novel about an assorted group of people marooned in an inhospitable old mansion on a stormy night. Directed by James Whale with a rare sense of the eccentric and bizarre; acted by a splendid cast including Ernest Thesiger ('Have some gin: it's my only weakness'), Eva Moore ('No beds—they can't have beds'), Melvyn Douglas, Charles Laughton, Raymond Massey, Boris Karloff and Brember Wills. The Hammer remake (GB 1963) proved completely unsatisfactory.

Old Mother Riley. The vociferous Irish washerwoman was impersonated by Arthur Lucan for years in the music halls and in a dozen or more films between 1937 and 1952, the last one being *Mother Riley Meets the Vampire.* Daughter Kitty was played by the resistible Kitty McShane. Most of the films were atrociously made but all of them made a sizeable profit from British provincial showings.

Oldfield, Barney (1878–1946) (Berna Eli Oldfield). American racing driver, the first to travel a mile a minute; featured in *Barney Oldfield's Race for Life* 16.

Oldland, Lilian (1905–). British leading lady of the silents, who later changed her name to Mary Newland.
The Secret Kingdom 25. The Flag Lieutenant 26. Troublesome Wives 27. Jealousy 31. Ask Beccles 34. Death at Broadcasting House 34. The Silent Passenger (last to date) 35, etc.

Oldman, Gary (–). British actor of character leads.
Sid and Nancy 86. Prick up your Ears 87.

Oliansky, Joel (1935–). American screenwriter.
The Senator (TV) 71. Masada (TV) 80. The Competition (& d) 81.

Oliver!: see *Oliver Twist.*

Oliver, Anthony (1923–). Welsh general purpose actor, in British films and TV.
Once a Jolly Swagman 48. The Clouded Yellow 50. The Runaway Bus 54. Lost 56. The Fourth Square 61, others.

Oliver, Edna May (1883–1942) (Edna May Cox-Oliver). American character actress, usually of acidulous but often warm-hearted spinsters; on stage from 1912.
Icebound 23. The American Venus 26. Saturday Night Kid 29. Half Shot at Sunrise 31. Cimarron 31. *Fanny Foley Herself* 31. The Penguin Pool Murder 32. Little Women 33. Alice in Wonderland 33. *David Copperfield*

(as Aunt Betsy) 34. A Tale of Two Cities 35. Romeo and Juliet (as the Nurse) 36. Parnell 37. Rosalie 38. Second Fiddle 38. The Story of Vernon and Irene Castle 39. Nurse Edith Cavell 39. *Pride and Prejudice* (as Lady Catherine de Bourgh) 40. Lydia 41, etc.

Oliver, Susan (1937–). American leading TV actress whose film roles have been few. Green-Eyed Blonde 57. The Gene Krupa Story 60. Looking for Love 64. The Disorderly Orderly 65. Your Cheating Heart 66. A Man Called Gannon 68. Change of Mind 69. Ginger in the Morning 75, etc.

Oliver Twist. Dickens' novel was filmed many times in the early silent period: in 1909 by Pathé, in 1910 by Vitagraph, in 1912 by an independent company with Nat C. Goodwin as Fagin. A famous American version of 1916 had Tully Marshall as Fagin and Marie Doro as Oliver; in 1922 the roles were played by Lon Chaney and Jackie Coogan, and in 1933 by Irving Pichel and Dickie Moore. The definitive version to date, however, is the British one directed by David Lean in 1948, with John Howard Davies in the title role. Alec Guinness' brilliant performance as Fagin caused a hold-up in American distribution as it was accused of anti-semitism. Technically a remarkable evocation of the book's melodramatic realism, the film was photographed by Guy Green, designed by John Bryan, with music by Arnold Bax. *Oliver!*, a 1968 musical version, won six Oscars: best film, best director (Carol Reed), best art direction (John Box and Terence Marsh), best score (John Green), best sound (Shepperton Studios), best choreography (Onna White).

Oliver, Vic (1898–1964) (Victor von Samek). Austrian-born comedian, pianist, violinist and conductor, long in Britain. Occasional films.
Autobiography 1954: *Mr Show Business*.
Rhythm in the Air 37. Room for Two 40. He Found a Star 41. Hi Gang 41. Give Us the Moon 44. I'll Be Your Sweetheart 45, etc.

Olivier, Laurence (Lord Olivier) (1907–89). Distinguished British stage actor whose film appearances have been reasonably frequent.
Biographies: 1969, *Cry God for Larry* by Virginia Fairweather. 1975, *Laurence Olivier* by John Cottrell. Autobiography 1982: *Confessions of an Actor*.
□Too Many Crooks 30. The Temporary Widow 30. Potiphar's Wife 30. The Yellow Ticket 31. Friends and Lovers 31. Westward Passage 31. No Funny Business 32. Perfect Understanding (US) 32. Conquest of the Air 35. Moscow Nights 35. As You Like It (as Orlando) 36. Fire over England 36. *The Divorce of Lady X* 38. Twenty-One Days 39. Q Planes 39. *Wuthering Heights* (US) 39. *Rebecca* (US) 40. *Pride and Prejudice* (US) 40. *Lady Hamilton* (US) (as Nelson) 41. 49th Parallel 41. The Demi-Paradise 43. *Henry V* (& p, co-d) (special AA) 44. *Hamlet* (& pd) (AA) 48. The Magic Box (cameo role) 51. *Carrie* (US) 52. The Beggar's Opera (as Macheath) 52. *Richard III* (& pd) 56. The Prince and the Showgirl (& d) 58. The Moon and Sixpence (TV) 59. *The Devil's Disciple* 59. Spartacus (US) 60. *The Entertainer* 60. The Power and the Glory (TV) 61. Term of Trial 62. Uncle Vanya (& d) 63. Bunny Lake is Missing 65. Othello 65. Khartoum 66. The Shoes of the Fisherman 68. Oh What a Lovely War 69. The Dance of Death 69. The Battle of Britain 69. David Copperfield 69. Three Sisters (& d) 70. Nicholas and Alexandra 71. Lady Caroline Lamb 72. *Sleuth* 72. Love Among the Ruins (TV) 74. *Marathon Man* 76. The Seven Per Cent Solution 76. Jesus of Nazareth (TV) 77. The Betsy 77. A Bridge Too Far 77. The Boys from Brazil 78. A Little Romance 78. Dracula 79. Clash of the Titans 81. The Jazz Singer 81. Inchon 81. Brideshead Revisited (TV) 81. A Voyage Round My Father (TV) 82. Wagner 83. A Talent for Murder (TV) 83. Mr Halpern and Mr Johnson (TV) 83. The Last Days of Pompeii (TV) 84. The Bounty 84. The Jigsaw Man 84. Wild Geese II 85. Lost Empires (TV) 86.
Honorary AA 1979 'for the full body of his work, for the unique achievements of his entire career and his lifetime of contribution to the art of film'.
❁ For being consistently the most fascinating actor of his time. *Richard III*.

¶ *L.O.:* Nothing is beneath me if it pays well. I've earned the right to damn well grab whatever I can in the time I've got left.
Famous line (*Wuthering Heights*): I cannot live without my life; I cannot die without my soul.

Olmi, Ermanno (1931–). Italian director noted for gentle realism.
Il Posto (*The Job*) 61. I Fidanzati 62. And There Came a Man 65. One Fine Day 69. Diary of Summer 71. The Circumstance 74. The Tree of Wooden Clogs 77, etc.

O'Loughlin, Gerald S. (1921–). American TV actor, prominent in series *The Rookies* 72–76.
Twilight's Last Gleaming 76. Frances 82.

Olsen, Ole (1892–1965) (John Sigurd Olsen). Norwegian-American comedian, in vaudeville from 1914, almost always with partner Chic Johnson.
Gold Dust Gertie 31. Fifty Million Frenchmen 31. The Country Gentleman 37. *Hellzapoppin* 42. Crazy House 44. Ghost Catchers 44. See My Lawyer 45, etc.

Olsen, Moroni (1889–1954). Heavily-built American character actor, with stage experience.
The Three Musketeers (as Porthos) 36. The Witness Chair 38. The Three Musketeers (as Bailiff) 39. Kentucky 39. The Glass Key 42. Call Northside 777 48. Father of the Bride 50. The Long, Long Trailer 54, many others.

Olson, James (1932–). American general purpose actor.
The Sharkfighters 56. The Strange One 57. Rachel Rachel 67. The Andromeda Strain 70. Moon Zero Two 70. Wild Rovers 71. The Groundstar Conspiracy 72. Ragtime 81. Amityville 2 82. Commando 85, etc.

Olson, Nancy (1928–). American leading lady who came to films from college, retired after a few years and recently reappeared in more mature roles.
Canadian Pacific 49. Union Station 50. *Sunset Boulevard* 50. Submarine Command 51. Force of Arms 52. So Big 52. Battle Cry 55. Pollyanna 60. The Absent-Minded Professor 61. Son of Flubber 63. Smith! 69. Snowball Express 73, etc.

Los Olvidados (Mexico 1950). Luis Buñuel's study of depraved and deprived adolescents in Mexico: the young anti-hero ends up dead on a dung heap. Photographed by Figueroa, it is a comfortless film, but important in the history of social realism.

Olympische Spiele (Germany 1936). Leni Riefenstahl's brilliantly-photographed and edited account of the Olympic Games of 1936, is a hymn to the human body and a superb example of film reporting.

O'Malley, J. Pat (1901–85). Irish character actor in Hollywood.
The Long Hot Summer 58. Blueprint for Robbery 60. The Cabinet of Caligari 62. A House is Not a Home 67. Gunn 67. Hello Dolly 69. Willard 71. Silkwood 83, etc.

O'Malley, John P. (1916–59). Australian character actor.
Kind Lady 51. Julius Caesar 52. Desert Rats 55. The Court Jester 56. The Invisible Boy 57.

O'Malley, Pat (1891–1966). Irish-American character actor in Hollywood.
The Papered Door 11. Happiness 26. The Fall Guy 30. Frisco Jenny 33. Hollywood Boulevard 36. A Little Bit of Heaven 40. Lassie Come Home 43. The Rugged O'Riordans 49. Invasion of the Body Snatchers 56, etc.

O'Malley, Rex (1901–1976). American light actor who was little heard from after a promising start.
Camille 36. *Midnight* 39. Zaza 39. The Thief 52, etc.

O'Mara, Kate (1939–). British leading lady.
Great Catherine 68. The Limbo Line 68. The Desperados 69. Horror of Frankenstein 70. TV series: Dynasty 85– .

On Approval (GB 1944). A curious but very successful one-shot at directing by Clive Brook, who with Googie Withers, Beatrice Lillie and Roland Culver made up the romantic quartet involved in this unexpected version of Frederick Lonsdale's Edwardian comedy. There was a touch of the Marx Brothers about the semi-mocking treatment of the faded material, but it certainly came off even though it had no imitators at the time.

On the Beach (US 1959). Stanley Kramer's bleak film about the end of the world, from Nevil Shute's novel, was about the most downbeat production ever to come from Hollywood. Although interesting it seemed in the long run over-slow and rather pointless, but the last rites of mankind were glossily photographed by Giuseppe Rotunno.

On the Town (US 1949). One of Hollywood's most exhilarating and influential musicals. A tale of three sailors on a day's leave in New York, it had a sextet of principals who lit up the screen with their sheer vivacity and well-nigh perpetual motion: Gene Kelly, Frank Sinatra, Jules Munshin, Betty Garrett, Ann Miller and Vera-Ellen. No one talks in this film when song or dance will do. Direction by Kelly and Stanley

Donen; music by Leonard Bernstein; words by Adolph Green and Betty Comden; photography by Harold Rossen.

On the Waterfront (US 1954). Basically a good location thriller about the docks protection rackets, this film from Budd Schulberg's novel had enough pretensions to win it several Academy Awards: best actor (Marlon Brando), best supporting actress (Eva Marie Saint), best art direction (Richard Day), best picture, best cinematography (Boris Kaufman), best direction (Elia Kazan), best editing (Gene Milford). It wasn't really all that good; but it did bring the method to the masses, mumblings and all.

Ondra, Anny (1903–87) (A. Ondrakova). German-Czech leading lady of British silent films; her accent killed her career when sound came. Returned to Europe and appeared in a few German films.
Chorus Girls 28. The Manxman 29. Blackmail 30. Glorious Youth 31. Schön Muss Mann Sein 50. Die Zuercher Verlorung 57, etc.

Ondricek, Miroslav (1934–). Czech cinematographer in international films.
Diamonds of the Night 64. Peter and Pavla 64. Intimate Lighting 66. The White Bus 67. *If* 67. The Firemen's Ball 68. Taking Off 71. Hair 79. The World According to Garp 82. Silkwood 83. Amadeus (AAN, BFA) 84, etc.

One Flew Over the Cuckoo's Nest (US 1975). Ken Kesey's novel about life in a mental institution was turned into a harrowing comedy-melodrama. It touched the public pulse and won Academy Awards as best picture; for Milos Forman's direction; and for the acting of Jack Nicholson and Louise Fletcher. In 1977 Alan Arkin appeared in a similar but heavier TV movie, *The Other Side of Hell,* directed by Jan Kadar.

One Hour with You: see *The Marriage Circle*.

One Hundred and One Dalmatians (US 1961). Disney's most pleasing post-war full length cartoon, with a strength and delicacy of line which the studio was not able to maintain. Based on an amusing story by Dodie Smith, it makes play with a well-observed London background.

One Million B.C. (US 1939). This curious film, also known as *The Cave Dwellers* and *Man and His Mate*, was produced and directed in 1939 by Hal Roach with assistance from D. W. Griffith, upon whose 1912 *Man's Genesis* it was based. A highly unscientific account of the tribulations of primitive man, it featured Carole Landis and Victor Mature, whose dialogue consisted largely of grunts, and who came up against a remarkable variety of pre-historic monsters which were rather obviously normal reptiles crudely decorated and magnified. In 1966 Hammer remade it in a rather pedestrian colour version with Raquel Welch and John Richardson, directed by Don Chaffey; this time the monsters were plastic animations. 1970 brought a kind of sequel, *When Dinosaurs Ruled the Earth*, directed by Val Guest, and *Creatures the World Forgot* followed in 1971.

One Sunday Afternoon (US 1933). This pleasant romantic comedy-drama, set in Brooklyn in the nineties, was made three times within fifteen years by the same company, Warners. The first version, directed by Stephen Roberts, had Gary Cooper, Neil Hamilton, Fay Wray and Frances Fuller. The second version, made in 1941 under the title *Strawberry Blonde*, was directed by Raoul Walsh and starred James Cagney, Jack Carson, Olivia de Havilland and Rita Hayworth. In 1948 Raoul Walsh again directed under the original title, this time with songs added; the stars were Dennis Morgan, Don Defore, Dorothy Malone and Janis Paige. The scripts stemmed from a play by James Hagan, about a dentist who fell for a glamorous girl but eventually returned to his artless sweetheart.

One, Two, Three (US 1961). Billy Wilder has always liked to take his stories from the newspaper headlines, but this frantic comedy was his most daring, being all about the Berlin Wall at a time when it seemed we were in for a third world war over it. Based on a Molnar play, brought up to date by Wilder and I. A. L. Diamond, it scuttles along with tremendous zip until round about the third act, when the pace flags. James Cagney as an exuberant Coca-Cola salesman makes it practically a one-man show. Photographed by Daniel Fapp.

One Way Passage (US 1932). A popular tear-jerker of its time, about a dying beauty (Kay Francis) and a convicted murderer (William Powell) who meet on an ocean liner and fall in love while keeping their secrets; written and directed by Tay Garnett. In 1940 it was remade by Edmund Goulding as *Till We Meet Again*, with Merle Oberon and George Brent.

O'Neal, Frederick (1905–). Powerful American Negro character actor, mainly on stage.
Pinky 49. No Way Out 50. Something of Value 56. Anna Lucasta 58. Take a Giant Step 59, etc.
TV series: Car 54 Where Are You? 61–62.

O'Neal, Patrick (1927–). American general purpose actor with stage and TV experience.
The Mad Magician 54. From the Terrace 60. The Cardinal 63. In Harm's Way 65. King Rat 65. A Fine Madness 66. Chamber of Horrors 66. Alvarez Kelly 66. *Assignment to Kill* 67. Where Were You When the Lights Went Out? 68. The Secret Life of an American Wife 68. Castle Keep 69. Stiletto 69. The Kremlin Letters 69. Corky 72. The Way We Were 73. Crossfire (TV) 75. The Stepford Wives 75. The Moneychangers (TV) 76. The Deadliest Season (TV) 77. The Last Hurrah (TV) 77. To Kill a Cop (TV) 78. Like Mom Like Me (TV) 78, many others.
TV series: Dick and the Duchess 58. *Kaz* 78.

O'Neal, Ron (1937–). Black American leading man.
Superfly 72. Superfly TNT 73. The Master Gunfighter 75. When a Stranger Calls 79. The Final Countdown 80. St Helens 81, etc.

O'Neal, Ryan (1941–) (Patrick Ryan O'Neal). Bland American leading man of the sixties and seventies after which his career faltered.
□This Rugged Land (TV) 62. The Games 68. The Big Bounce 69. *Love Story* 70. Love Hate Love (TV) 70. Wild Rovers 71. *What's Up Doc* 72. The Thief Who Came to Dinner 73. *Paper Moon* 73. Barry Lyndon 75. Nickelodeon 76. A Bridge Too Far 77. The Driver 78. Oliver's Story 79. The Main Event 79. So Fine 81. Green Ice 81. Partners 82. Irreconcilable Differences 84. Fever Pitch 85. Tough Guys Don't Dance 87.
TV series: Empire 62. *Peyton Place* 64–68.

¶ *R.O.:* I'm as moody and complex and private as anyone I ever knew.
R.O.: The only time I ever had steady employment was in *Peyton Place*. Once I was in control of my own destiny I found it very difficult.

O'Neal, Tatum (1962–). Abrasive child actress of the seventies, daughter of Ryan O'Neal.
□*Paper Moon* (AA) 73. The Bad News Bears 76. Nickelodeon 76. International Velvet 78. Circle of Two 80. Little Darlings 80.

O'Neil, Barbara (1909–1980). American character actress who made a corner in mad wives and other neurotic roles.
□Stella Dallas 37. Love, Honor and Behave 38. The Toy Wife 38. I Am the Law 39. The Sun Never Sets 39. *When Tomorrow Comes* 39. Tower of London 39. Gone with the Wind 39. All This and Heaven Too 40. Shining Victory 41. The Secret Beyond the Door 48. I Remember Mama 48. Whirlpool 49. Angel Face 52. Flame of the Islands 55. The Nun's Story 59.

O'Neil, Nance (1875–1965). American stage actress who starred in a few films.
The Kreuzer Sonata 15. Hedda Gabler 17. The Mad Woman 20. His Glorious Night 29. The Rogue Song 30. Cimarron 31. False Faces 34, etc.

O'Neil, Sally (1910–68) (Virginia Noonan). American leading lady of the twenties.
Sally Irene and Mary 25. Battling Butler 26. Slide Kelly Slide 27. The Lovelorn 27. The Mad Hour 28. Jazz Heaven 29. Hold Everything 30. Salvation Nell 31. Murder by the Clock 31. Sixteen Fathoms Deep 33. Kathleen 37, etc.

O'Neill, Eugene (1888–1953). Irish-American playwright of self-pitying disposition and a tendency in his plays to tragic despair. His gloominess led Hollywood to regard his works as art, which killed many of the film versions stone dead.
Anna Christie (23 with Blanche Sweet, 30 with Garbo). Strange Interlude 32. The Emperor Jones 33. Ah Wilderness 35. The Long Voyage Home 40. The Hairy Ape 44. Summer Holiday 47. Mourning Becomes Electra 48. Desire under the Elms 57. Long Day's Journey into Night 62. The Iceman Cometh 73, etc.
† O'Neill was played by Jack Nicholson in *Reds*.

O'Neill, Henry (1891–1961). American character actor with stage experience, in Hollywood from early thirties. Played scores of judges, guardians, fathers, lawyers, etc.

I Loved a Woman 33. Wonder Bar 34. Black Fury 35. The White Angel 36. First Lady 37. Brother Rat 38. Juarez 39. Billy the Kid 41. White Cargo 43. The Virginian 46. Alias Nick Beal 49. The Milkman 50. Untamed 55. The Wings of Eagles 57, over a hundred others.

O'Neill, James (1847–1920). American stage actor, father of Eugene. Best film part 1913: *The Count of Monte Cristo*.

O'Neill, Jennifer (1947–). American leading lady of the seventies.
Rio Lobo 70. *Summer of 42* 71. Such Good Friends 71. The Carey Treatment 72. Glass Houses 72. Lady Ice 73. The Reincarnation of Peter Proud 75. Whiffs 75. Caravans 78. A Force of One 79. Cloud Dancer 80. Steel 80. Scanners 81, etc.
TV series: Cover Up 83–84.

O'Neill, Maire (1885–1952) (Maire Allgood). Irish character actress, an Abbey player; sister of Sara Allgood.
Juno and the Paycock 30. Sing As We Go 34. Farewell Again 37. Love on the Dole 41. Gaiety George 46. Someone at the Door 50. Treasure Hunt 52, etc.

Onibaba (Japan 1964). A stylish medieval horror comic set entirely within a forest of tall reeds by a river, where two penniless women murder strangers for their clothing, finally coming to grief through lust and jealousy. Its remarkable holding power is attributable to Kaneto Shindo's direction and Kyomi Kuroda's photography.

Ontkean, Michael (1946–). American leading man.
Pickup on 101 71. Necromancy 72. Slap Shot 77. Voices 79. Willie and Phil 80. Making Love 81. The Blood of Others 84.
TV series: The Rookies 73–74.

Opatoshu, David (1918–) (David Opatovsky). American general purpose actor, often seen as villain.
Naked City 48. Exodus 60. Guns of Darkness 63. Torn Curtain 66. The Defector 67. Enter Laughing 67. Death of a Gunfighter 69.
A Walk in the Spring Rain 78. Masada (TV) 81, etc.

Open City (Italy 1945). A semi-documentary record, shot under the noses of the retreating German army by Italian patriots, of what Italy had suffered under the occupation. Occasionally melodramatic but always moving, with a rawness fresh to the western cinema at the time. Also the film which introduced Anna Magnani to a wider audience. Directed by Roberto Rossellini from a script by Sergei Amidei and Federico Fellini; photographed by Uberto Arato.

opening scenes

? What well-known films began with these scenes?

1 A married woman dreams of a deserted and derelict manor-house.
2 Baskul is evacuated.
3 A high wire fence bears a notice: NO TRESPASSING.
4 A fat man listens to a scratchy gramophone in a room in Istanbul.
5 A man in a dark suit walks along a paved highway and stops outside a truckdrivers' cafe.
6 A man tampers with a clock at a lunch wagon counter.
7 A fort full of dead men is found in the Sahara.
8 A dock worker sings to himself as he strolls along just before six a.m.
9 A barrage of shots and miscellaneous noises leads the eye to a sign reading WELCOME TO BOTTLENECK.
10 A Venetian gondolier fills his craft full of garbage and glides away singing a barcarolle.
11 A man walks out on his wife. Following him to the door, she smilingly breaks one of his golf clubs. About to strike her, he thinks better of it and pushes her to the ground.
12 While a private eye waits to be announced, the daughter of the house falls into his arms.
13 At a one-horse desert town, a one-armed stranger gets off the train.
14 An aged actor speaks at an awards dinner.
15 Having driven recklessly through the night streets, a man lets himself into an empty office building and begins to speak into a dictaphone.
16 A gossip columnist interviews stars arriving at a Hollywood premiere many years ago.
17 A train pulls into Vienna's railway station.
18 Three Russians inspect the foyer of an expensive Paris hotel.
19 A diner in a restaurant finds that the lady he invited has been sitting with her back to him at the next table.
20 A gentleman recently deceased descends

to the shades and presents his credentials to His Excellency.
21 An unsuccessful young man visits his father in a nudist camp.
22 A doctor returns to his small town and finds that his friends, acquaintances and patients are not quite themselves.
23 A heavily-bandaged gentleman arrives at an English inn.
24 A ship is torpedoed, and survivors clinging to a life raft relive their recent lives.
25 A film producer, off on a voyage of exploration, picks up the girl who is to be his heroine in a waterfront cafe.

opera has never been a successful commodity on the screen, although many operas have been filmed as from the stalls, and appear to have succeeded with minority audiences. The occasional big opera production such as *Porgy and Bess, Pagliacci* or *Carmen Jones*, however, can expect to meet with only moderate success. Opera does, however, make an excellent background for thrillers (*Charlie Chan at the Opera*), farces (*A Night at the Opera*) and melodramas *(Metropolitan)*. Opera singers who have succeeded as film stars include Grace Moore, Lily Pons, Mario Lanza, Tito Gobbi, Richard Tauber, Lauritz Melchior, Ezio Pinza and Gladys Swarthout. Oddly enough the singer Mary Garden was a big hit in *silent* films.

Ophuls, Marcel (1927–). French director, son of Max Ophuls; mainly associated with elaborate documentaries.
Peau de Banane 63. *The Sorrow and the Pity* 69. A Sense of Loss 73. A Memory of Justice 76.

Ophuls, Max (1902–1957) (Max Oppenheimer). German director of international highly decorated, romantic films.
☐Dann Schon Lieber Lebertran 30. Die Lachenden Erben 31. Die Verliebte Firma 31. Der Verkaufte Braut 32. *Liebelei* 32. Une Histoire d'Amour 33. On a Volé un Homme 34. La Signora Di Tutti 34. Trouble with Money 34. Divine 35. La Tendre Ennemie 36. Yoshimara 37. Werther 38. Sans Lendemain 39. De Mayerling à Sarajevo 40. The Exile 47. *Letter from an Unknown Woman* 48. Caught 48. *The Reckless Moment* 49. *La Ronde* 50. Le Plaisir 51. *Madame De* 53. *Lola Montes* 55.

'If all the dollies and cranes in the world snap to attention when his name is mentioned, it is because he gave camera movement its finest hours in the history of the cinema.'—*Andrew Sarris, 1968*
❀ For elegance of craftsmanship and knowledge of what the camera can do. *Letter from an Unknown Woman.*

¶ 'A shot that does not call for tracks is agony for dear old Max.'—*James Mason*

Oppenheimer, Alan (–). Bald American character actor.
In the Heat of the Night 67. Star! 69. The Groundstar Conspiracy 73. Westworld 73. The Hindenburg 75. Freaky Friday 76. Record City 78, etc.

Oppenheimer, George (1900–1977). American critic and screenwriter who contributed to A Day at the Races 37. Broadway Melody of 1940. Two-Faced Woman 41. The War Against Mrs Hadley 42.

opticals. A general term indicating all the visual tricks such as wipes, dissolves, invisibility, mattes, etc., which involve laboratory work.

Orbach, Jerry (1935–). Loose-limbed American actor and musical comedy star.
The Gang That Couldn't Shoot Straight 72. The Sentinel 79. Underground Aces 81. Prince of the City 81. Street Heat (TV) 84. Brewster's Millions 84. F/X 85. The Imagemaker 85. Dirty Dancing 87.

Orchard, Julian (1930–1979). Lugubrious British revue comedian who enlivened a number of bit parts.
Crooks Anonymous 58. On the Beat 60. Kill or Cure 62. The Spy with a Cold Nose 66. Carry On Doctor 68. Heironymus Merkin 69. Perfect Friday 70. The Slipper and the Rose 76, others.

orchestral conductors have figured as leading men in *Intermezzo, Interlude, Once More with Feeling, Unfaithfully Yours, Song of Russia, Break of Hearts, Prelude to Fame, Counterpoint*; Charles Laughton cut a tragicomic figure in *Tales of Manhattan.* Real conductors who have played dramatic roles in movies include Leopold Stokowski, José Iturbi and many swing and jazz figures such as Paul Whiteman, Tommy Dorsey, Henry Hall, Glenn Miller, Benny Goodman, Xavier Cugat.

Oreste: see *Kirkop, Oreste.*

oriental roles. It never seems a good idea, but occidental actors have often been tempted by the wish to play eastern. Among the less fortunate results are Lee J. Cobb in *Anna and the King of Siam*; John Wayne in *The Conqueror*; Katharine Hepburn in *Dragon Seed*; Alec Guinness in *A Majority of One*; Mickey Rooney in *Breakfast at Tiffany's*; George Raft in *Limehouse Blues*; Edward G. Robinson in *The Hatchet Man*. Those who more or less got away with it include Robert Donat in *Inn of the Sixth Happiness*; Boris Karloff in *The Mask of Fu Manchu*; and Luise Rainer and Paul Muni in *The Good Earth*.

original version. In European countries, this indicates a foreign language film which is sub-titled and not dubbed.

Ornadel, Cyril (1924–). British composer.
Some May Love 67. Die Screaming Marianne 71. Not Now Darling 72. Brief Encounter (TV) 75, etc.
TV series: Edward the Seventh 76.

Ornitz, Arthur J. (1916–85). American cinematographer.
The Goddess 58. Act One 63. The World of Henry Orient 64. Charly 68. Me Natalie 68. The Anderson Tapes 71. Serpico 73. Next Stop Greenwich Village 76. An Unmarried Woman 78. Tattoo 81. Hanky Panky 82. The Chosen 82.

O'Rourke, Brefni (1889–1945). Irish stage actor, an Abbey player, who made some British films, usually as testy types.
The Ghost of St Michael's 41. Hatter's Castle 41. The Lamp Still Burns 43. Don't Take It to Heart 44. I See a Dark Stranger 45, etc.

Orphée (France 1949). A strange poetic fantasy written and directed by Jean Cocteau, based on the myth of Orpheus and Eurydice but with twists of his own. Its real meaning is almost as obscure as that of his 1930 surrealist film *Le Sang d'un Poète*, but there is much pleasure to be gained from watching it purely as a piece of instinctively successful cinema using all the devices of the medium. Photographed by Nicolas Hayer, music by Georges Auric, with Jean Marais as Orpheus and Maria Casares as Death. Cocteau in 1960 made an even stranger sequel, *Le Testament D'Orphée*.

Orry-Kelly (1897–1964). Australian designer, in Hollywood from 1923 after Broadway experience. For many years with Warner, then with Fox. Won Academy Award for costumes of *An American in Paris* 51, *Some Like It Hot* 59.

Orth, Frank (1880–1962). American small part actor who must have played more bartenders than he could count.
Hot Money 36. Serenade 39. The Lost Weekend 45. Father of the Bride 50. Here Come the Girls 54, many others.
TV series: The Brothers 56.

Ortolani, Riz (1925–). Italian composer.
Mondo Cane 63. The Seventh Dawn 64. Woman Times Seven 67. Buona Sera Mrs Campbell 68. The Mackenzie Break 70. Say Hello to Yesterday 71. The Valachi Papers 72. The Fifth Musketeer 77, etc.

Orwell, George (1903–1950) (Eric Blair). British satirist and novelist whose chief bequests to the cinema are *Animal Farm* and *1984*.

Osborn, Andrew (1912–85). British stage and film actor. Latterly BBC TV producer: Maigret series, etc.
Who Goes Next? 38. Idol of Paris 48. Dark Interval 50. Angels One Five 51. The Second Mrs Tanqueray 53, etc.

Osborne, John (1929–). British dramatist.
Plays filmed: *Look Back in Anger* 59. *The Entertainer* 60. *Inadmissible Evidence* 68. Also wrote screenplay for *Tom Jones* 63; acted in *Get Carter* 71, Tomorrow Never Comes 78.

Osborne, Vivienne (1900–1961). American leading lady who left the stage for occasional films but was relegated to supporting roles.
Over the Hill 20. Husband's Holiday 30. Luxury Liner 33. Sailor Be Good 32. Wives Never Know 36. Dragonwyck 46, etc.

'Oscar'. An affectionate name given to the Academy Award statuette; reputedly because when the figure was first struck in 1927 a secretary said: 'It reminds me of my Uncle Oscar.'

Oscar, Henry (1891–1969) (Henry Wale). British character actor, on stage from 1911, films from 1932, usually as meek or scheming fellows.
After Dark (debut) 32. I was a Spy 33. The Man Who Knew Too Much 34. Fire over England 37. *The Return of the Scarlet Pimpernel* (as Robespierre) 39. Hatter's

Castle 41. They Made Me a Fugitive 47. The Greed of William Hart 48. The Black Rose 50. Private's Progress 55. Foxhole in Cairo 60, etc.

Oscarsson, Per (1927–). Swedish leading actor.
The Doll 62. Hunger 66. My Sister My Love 66. Who Saw Him Die? 67. Dr Glas 67. A Dandy in Aspic 68. The Last Valley 71. Secrets 72. *The Emigrants* 72. Endless Night 72. Dream City 76, etc.

O'Shea, Michael (1906–1973). American actor with a 'good guy' personality, who, after circus and vaudeville experience, made several films in the forties and fifties.
Jack London 42. Striptease Lady 43. The Eve of St Mark 44. It's a Pleasure 45. Circumstantial Evidence 45. The Big Wheel 49. The Model and the Marriage Broker 52. It Should Happen to You 55, etc.
TV series: It's a Great Life 54-55.

O'Shea, Milo (1926–). Irish character actor, usually in slightly bumbling comic roles.
Never Put It in Writing 64. *Ulysses* (as Bloom) 67. Romeo and Juliet 68. Barbarella 68. The Adding Machine 69. Loot 70. The Angel Levine 70. Arabian Adventure 79. The Pilot 81. The Verdict 82. The Purple Rose of Cairo 84, etc.

O'Shea, Tessie (1917–). Amply-proportioned British music hall singer.
The Shiralee 58. The Russians are Coming, The Russians are Coming 66. The Best House in London 68. Bedknobs and Broomsticks 71.

Oshima, Nagisa or **Nagashi** (1932–). Japanese director.
Ai No Corrida 77. Empire of Passion 79. Merry Christmas Mr Lawrence 83. Max My Love 86.

Osmond, Cliff (–). Heavyweight American comedy actor.
Kiss Me Stupid 64. The Fortune Cookie 67. The Front Page 74. Sharks Treasure 75. Guardian of the Wilderness 76. The Great Brain 78. The North Avenue Irregulars 80. Hangar 18 81, etc.

O'Steen, Sam (1923–). American editor, later director.
AS EDITOR: Robin and the Seven Hoods 64. Who's Afraid of Virginia Woolf? 66. Cool Hand Luke 67. *The Graduate* 67. Rosemary's Baby 68. Catch 22 70. Carnal Knowledge 71. The Day of the Dolphin 73. Chinatown 74. Hurricane 79. Silkwood 83, etc.
□AS DIRECTOR: A Brand New Life (TV) 73. I Love You Goodbye (TV) 74. Queen of the Stardust Ballroom (TV) 75. High Risk (TV) 76. Look What Happened to Rosemary's Baby (TV) 76. Sparkle 76.

O'Sullivan, Maureen (1911–). Irish leading lady in Hollywood, always in shy, gentle roles. Mother of Mia Farrow.
□Song of My Heart 30. So This is London 30. Just Imagine 30. The Princess and the Plumber 30. A Connecticut Yankee 31. Skyline 31. *Tarzan the Ape Man* 32 (she was his most famous Jane). The Silver Lining 32. Big Shot 32. Information Kid 32. Strange Interlude 32. Skyscraper Souls 32. Payment Deferred 32. The Fast Companions 32. Robbers Roost 33. The Cohens and Kellys in Trouble 33. Tugboat Annie 33. Stage Mother 33. Tarzan and His Mate 34. The Thin Man 34. *The Barretts of Wimpole Street* 34. Hideout 34. West Point of the Air 34. David Copperfield 34. Cardinal Richelieu 35. The Flame Within 35. Anna Karenina 35. Woman Wanted 35. The Bishop Misbehaves 35. Tarzan Escapes 36. The Voice of Bugle Ann 36. The Devil Doll 36. A Day at the Races 37. Between Two Women 37. The Emperor's Candlesticks 37. My Dear Miss Aldrich 37. A Yank at Oxford 38. Hold that Kiss 38. The Crowd Roars 38. Port of Seven Seas 38. Spring Madness 38. Let Us Live 38. Tarzan Finds a Son 39. *Pride and Prejudice* 40. Sporting Blood 40. Maisie was a Lady 41. Tarzan's Secret Treasure 41. Tarzan's New York Adventure 42. The Big Clock 48. Where Danger Lives 50. Bonzo Goes to College 52. All I Desire 53. Mission Over Korea 53. Duffy of San Quentin 54. The Steel Cage 54. The Tall T 57. Wild Heritage 58. *Never Too Late* 65. The Phynx 69. The Crooked Hearts (TV) 72. The Great Houdinis (TV) 76. Hannah and her Sisters 85. Peggy Sue Got Married 86.

O'Sullivan, Richard (1943–). British light leading man, formerly child actor, prominent on TV.
The Stranger's Hand 53. Dangerous Exile 56. A Story of David 60. The Young Ones 61. Wonderful Life 64. Father Dear Father 73. A Man About the House 74, etc.
TV series: *A Man About the House* 73–76. Robin's Nest 77–80. Dick Turpin 78–79.

Oswald, Gerd (1916–). German-American director, son of Richard Oswald.
☐A Kiss before Dying 56. The Brass Legend 57. Crime of Passion 57. Fury at Sundown 57. Valerie 57. Paris Holiday 57. Screaming Mimi 58. Am Tag Als Der Regen Kam 59. Three Moves to Freedom 60. Tempesta Su Ceylon 63. Agent for H.A.R.M. 66. 80 Steps to Jonah 69. Bunny O'Hare 71. To the Bitter End 75.

Oswald, Richard (1880–1963) (R. Ornstein). German director, father of Gerd Oswald.
Pagu 16. Round the World in Eighty Days 19. Victoria and Her Hussar 31. Der Hauptmann von Köpenick 32. I Was a Criminal (US) 41. Isle of Missing Men (US) 42. The Lovable Cheat (US) 49, etc.

O'Toole, Annette (1953–). American leading lady.
The Girl Most Likely To (TV) 73. Smile 75. The Entertainer (TV) 76. One on One 77. The War Between the Tates (TV) 77. King of the Gypsies 78. Foolin' Around 80. Cat People 82. 48 Hours 82.

O'Toole, Peter (1932–). British leading man who after stage and TV experience had fairly meteoric rise to stardom in films.
Biography 1983 by Michael Freedland.
☐Kidnapped (debut) 59. Savage Innocents 59. The Day They Robbed the Bank of England 60. *Lawrence of Arabia* 62. *Becket* 64. Lord Jim 65. What's New Pussycat? 65. How to Steal a Million 66. The Night of the Generals 66. The Bible 66. Casino Royale 66. Great Catherine 67. *The Lion in Winter* 68. *Goodbye Mr Chips* 69. Country Dance 70. Murphy's War 70. Under Milk Wood 71. *The Ruling Class* 71. Man of la Mancha 72. Rosebud 75. Man Friday 75. Foxtrot 75. Rogue Male (TV) 76. Caligula 77. Power Play 78. Zulu Dawn 79. Masada (TV) 80. Strumpet City (TV) 80. *The Stunt Man* 80. *My Favorite Year* 82. Svengali (TV) 82. Superman III 83. Supergirl 84. Buried Alive 84. Kim (TV) 84. Creator 84. Club Paradise 86.

¶ *P.O'T.:* For me, life has been either a wake or a wedding.

P.O'T.: I can't stand light. I hate weather. My idea of heaven is moving from one smoke-filled room to another.

'The very prototype of the ham.'—*Omar Sharif*

Ott, Fred (1860–1936). American laboratory assistant, allegedly the first man ever to act for the cinema when he sneezed in close-up for Edison in 1893.

Ottiano, Rafaela (1894–1942). Italian-born stage actress who went to Hollywood and played sinister housekeepers, etc.
As You Desire Me 32. Grand Hotel 32. She Done Him Wrong 33. Great Expectations 34. Maytime 37. Topper Returns 41, etc.

Ouida (1839–1908) (Marie Louise de la Ramée). Anglo-French novelist. *Under Two Flags* in 1936 was the last of her romances to be filmed, but several were used in silent days.

Oulton, Brian (1908–). British stage and film comedy actor, usually in unctuous or prim roles.
Too Many Husbands 39. Miranda 48. Last Holiday 50. Castle in the Air 52. The Million Pound Note 54. Private's Progress 55. Happy is the Bride 57. The Thirty-Nine Steps 59. A French Mistress 60. Kiss of the Vampire 62. Carry On Cleo 64. The Intelligence Men 64. Carry On Camping 69. On the Buses 71. Ooh You are Awful 72.

Our Daily Bread (US 1933). King Vidor wrote and directed this sequel to his 1928 urban movie *The Crowd*; he now showed his downtrodden hero making good during the depression years by taking to collective farming. Photographed by Robert Planck; with Tom Keene and Karen Morley.

'Our Gang'. A collection of child actors first gathered together in short slapstick comedies by producer Hal Roach in the mid-twenties. They remained popular through the thirties and forties, though the personnel of the team naturally changed. The originals included Mary Kornman, Farina, Joe Cobb, Mickey Daniels and Jackie Condon; a later generation included Spanky Macfarland, Darla Hood and Buckwheat Thomas. Robert McGowan directed most of the films, many of which have been revived on TV. Book 1977: *Our Gang* by Leonard Maltin.

Oury, Gerard (1919–) (Max-Gerard Tannenbaum). Dapper French character actor.
Antoine et Antoinette 46. La Belle Que Voilà 49. Sea Devils (GB) 52. *Father Brown* (GB) 54. House of Secrets (GB) 56. The Journey (US) 58. The Mirror Has Two Faces 59, etc.
NOW DIRECTOR: La Main Chaude 60. *The*

Sucker (*Le Corniaud*) 64. The Big Spree 66. The Brain 69. Adventures of Rabbi Jacob 72. Carapate 78. Le Coup de Parapluie 80, etc.
AS DIRECTOR: The Umbrella Coup 80. Ace of Aces 82. The Vengeance of the Winged Serpent 84. Levy and Goliath 86.

Ouspenskaya, Maria (1876–1949). Distinguished, diminutive Russian character actress who enlivened some Hollywood films after the mid-thirties.
☐Dodsworth 36. Conquest 37. *Love Affair* 39. *The Rains Came* 39. Judge Hardy and Son 39. Dr Ehrlich's Magic Bullet 40. Waterloo Bridge 40. The Mortal Storm 40. The Man I Married 40. Dance Girl Dance 40. Beyond Tomorrow 40. *The Wolf Man* 41. The Shanghai Gesture 41. *King's Row* 42. The Mystery of Marie Roget 42. Frankenstein Meets the Wolf Man 43. Tarzan and the Amazons 45. I've Always Loved You 46. Wyoming 47. A Kiss in the Dark 49.
Famous line (*The Wolf Man*):
Even the man who is pure in heart
And says his prayers by night
May become a wolf when the wolf bane blooms
And the moon is clear and bright.

Out of the Inkwell (US 1920–1924). An influential series of silent cartoons by Max Fleischer, in which the artist's hands and drawing pad were in normal photography and the cartoon characters, superimposed, appeared to animate themselves.

The Outlaw (1943). This notorious censor-baiting western, with its advertising campaign based on Jane Russell's cleavage, has historical interest as an example of how producer-director Howard Hughes managed to fool all of the people all of the time. The movie is neither sensational nor very entertaining, but by withholding it from release for three years and getting into a lot of argument with censor boards, Hughes made the world's press believe it was. Basically a fanciful tale of an encounter between Billy the Kid and Doc Holliday, it needed firmer handling than Hughes was able to supply. The full story of the film's making can be found in the recent biographies of Hughes (qv).

Outward Bound. Sutton Vane's 1923 play concerns a group of people who find themselves travelling on a luxurious but mysterious ship and slowly realize they are dead. It was filmed in 1930 by Robert Milton, with Leslie Howard and Douglas Fairbanks Jnr, and ran into considerable censor trouble. In 1944 an updated and extremely dreary version was directed by Edward A. Blatt under the title *Between Two Worlds*: Paul Henreid and John Garfield had the leads, and Sydney Greenstreet livened up the last half as the heavenly examiner. In 1972 a TV movie called *Haunts of the Very Rich* unofficially brought it up to date.

The Overlanders (GB 1946). Made on location in Australia, this story of an arduous cattle drive seemed to open new horizons for colonial film-making, but they did not develop significantly and the later Australian productions proved disappointing. Even star Chips Rafferty waned in appeal. But this was a good western in a fresh locale, written and directed by Harry Watt and photographed by Osmond Borrodaile.

Overman, Lynne (1887–1943). American character actor with stage experience. Memorable in cynical comedy roles for his relaxed manner and sing-song voice.
☐Midnight 34. Little Miss Marker 34. The Great Flirtation 34. She Loves Me Not 34. You Belong to Me 34. Broadway Bill 34. Enter Madame 34. Rumba 35. Paris in Spring 35. Men without Names 35. Two for Tonight 35. Collegiate 35. Poppy 36. Yours for the Asking 36. Three Married Men 36. The Jungle Princess 36. Blonde Trouble 37. Partners in Crime 37. Nobody's Baby 37. Don't Tell the Wife 37. Murder Goes to College 37. Wild Money 37. Hotel Haywire 37. Night Club Scandal 37. True Confession 37. The Big Broadcast of 1938 38. *Her Jungle Love* 38. Hunted Men 38. Spawn of the North 38. Sons of the Legion 38. Men with Wings 38. Ride a Crooked Mile 38. Persons in Hiding 39. *Death of a Champion* 39. Union Pacific 39. Edison the Man 40. Typhoon 40. Safari 40. Northwest Mounted Police 40. Aloma of the South Seas 41. Caught in the Draft 41. New York Town 41. The Hard Boiled Canary 41. *Roxie Hart* 42. Reap the Wild Wind 42. The Forest Rangers 42. The Silver Queen 42. Star Spangled Rhythm 42. *Dixie* 43. The Desert Song 43.

Owen, Bill (1914–) (Bill Rowbotham). British character comedian, former dance band musician and singer.
The Way to the Stars (debut) 45. When the Bough Breaks 47. The Girl Who Couldn't Quite 49. Trottie True 49. Hotel Sahara 51. The Square Ring 53. The Rainbow Jacket 54.

Davy 57. Carve Her Name with Pride 58. The Hellfire Club 61. The Secret of Blood Island 65. Georgy Girl 66. O Lucky Man 72. In Celebration 74. The Comeback 78, etc.
TV series: Last of the Summer Wine 74–78.

Owen, Cliff (1919–). British director, in films from 1937.
Offbeat 60. A Prize of Arms 62. The Wrong Arm of the Law 63. A Man Could Get Killed 66. That Riviera Touch 66. The Magnificent Two 67. Steptoe and Son 72. Ooh You Are Awful 72. No Sex Please We're British 73. The Bawdy Adventures of Tom Jones 76, etc.

Owen, Reginald (1887–1972). British character actor, on stage from 1905, films (in Hollywood) from 1929.
The Letter (debut) 29. Platinum Blonde 32. Queen Christina 33. Call of the Wild 35. Anna Karenina 35. The Great Ziegfeld 36. A Tale of Two Cities 36. *Trouble for Two* 36. Conquest 37. The Earl of Chicago 39. Florian 40. Charley's Aunt 41. Tarzan's Secret Treasure 41. *Mrs Miniver* 42. Random Harvest 42. White Cargo 42. Madame Curie 43. Lassie Come Home 43. The Canterville Ghost 44. *Kitty* 45. The Diary of a Chambermaid 45. Cluny Brown 46. If Winter Comes 47. The Three Musketeers 48. The Miniver Story 50. Kim 51. Red Garters 54. The Young Invaders 58. Voice of the Hurricane (MRA film) 63. Mary Poppins 64. Rosie 68. Bedknobs and Broomsticks 71, hundreds of others.

Owen, Seena (1894–1966) (Signe Auen). American silent screen leading lady.
Intolerance 16. The Sheriff's Son 19. Victory 19. Shipwrecked 23. Flame of the Yukon 25. The Rush Hour 28. Marriage Playground 29, others.

Owens, Patricia (1925–). Canadian leading lady who made films in Britain and America.
Miss London Ltd 43. While the Sun Shines 46. The Happiest Days of Your Life 49. Mystery Junction 52. The Good Die Young 53. Windfall 55. Island in the Sun 56. Sayonara (US) 57. *No Down Payment* (US) 57. The Fly (US) 58. Five Gates to Hell (US) 59. Hell to Eternity (US) 60. Seven Women from Hell 62. Black Spurs 65, etc.

The Ox-Bow Incident (US 1943). A striking western indictment of lynch law, from the novel by Walter Van Tilburg Clark. A remarkably sombre and atmospheric film to come out of Hollywood in the middle of World War II, it had no popular success. Henry Fonda led an excellent cast; William Wellman directed from a script by Lamar Trotti.

Oxley, David (c. 1929–). British actor.
Ill Met by Moonlight 57. Saint Joan 58. Yesterday's Enemy 58. The Hound of the Baskervilles 59. Life at the Top 64, etc.

Ozep, Fedor (1893–1949). Russian director.
The Crime of Dmitri Karamazov 31. The Living Dead 33. Amok 34. Gibraltar 38. She Who Dares (US) 44. Whispering City (Can.) 48, etc.

Ozu, Yasujiro (1903–1963). Japanese director, since 1927.
Biography 1974: *Ozu* by Donald Ritchie.
A Story of Floating Weeds 34. Late Spring 49. Early Summer 51. Tokyo Story 53. Early Spring 56. Late Autumn 61. Early Autumn 62, etc.

Answers

opening scenes
1 *Rebecca* ☐ 2 *Lost Horizon* ☐ 3 *Citizen Kane* ☐ 4 *Journey into Fear* ☐ 5 *The Grapes of Wrath* ☐ 6 *Little Caesar* ☐ 7 *Beau Geste* ☐ 8 *On the Town* ☐ 9 *Destry Rides Again* ☐ 10 *Trouble in Paradise* ☐ 11 *The Philadelphia Story* ☐ 12 *The Big Sleep* ☐ 13 *Bad Day at Black Rock* ☐ 14 *All About Eve* ☐ 15 *Double Indemnity* ☐ 16 *Singin' in the Rain* ☐ 17 *The Third Man* ☐ 18 *Ninotchka* ☐ 19 *A Night at the Opera* ☐ 20 *Heaven Can Wait* ☐ 21 *I'm All Right Jack* ☐ 22 *Invasion of the Body Snatchers* ☐ 23 *The Invisible Man* ☐ 24 *In Which We Serve* ☐ 25 *King Kong* (1933) ☐

P

Pabst, G. W. (1885–1967) (George Wilhelm). Distinguished German director who usually tackled pessimistic themes.
□Der Schatz 23. Gräfin Donelli 24. *Joyless Street* 25. *Secrets of a Soul* 26. Man Spielt Nicht mit der Liebe 26. *The Love of Jeanne Ney* 27. *Pandora's Box* 28. Abwege 28. *Diary of a Lost Girl* 29. The White Hell of Pitz Palu (co-d) 29.*Westfront 1918* 30. Skandal um Eva 30. *The Threepenny Opera* (*Die Dreigroschenoper*) 31. *Kameradschaft* 31. L'Atlantide 32. Don Quixote 33. A Modern Hero (US) 34. De Haut en Bas 34. Mademoiselle Docteur 37. Le Drama de Shanghai 39. Mädchen in Uniform 39. Komodianten 41. Paracelsus 43. Der Fall Molander 45. Der Prozess 48. Geheimnisvolle Tiefen 49. The Voice of Silence 52. Cose da Pazzi 53. *Ten Days to Die* 54. Das Bekenntnis der Ina Kahr 54. Jackboot Mutiny 55. The Last Act 55. Roses for Bettina 56. Durch die Wälder 56.

Pace, Judy (1946–). Black American leading lady of the seventies.
Three in the Attic 68. Up in the Cellar 70. Cool Breeze 72. Frogs 72, etc.

Pacino, Al (1939–) (Alfredo Pacino). American leading actor of the seventies and eighties of New York/Sicilian descent.
□Me Natalie 68. The Panic in Needle Park 71. *The Godfather* 72. Scarecrow 73. Serpico 73. The Godfather— Part Two 74. *Dog Day Afternoon* 75. Bobby Deerfield 77. And Justice for All 79. Cruising 80. Author! Author! 82. Scarface 83. Revolution 86.

Pack, Charles Lloyd: see *Lloyd Pack, Charles.*

Paderewski, Ignace (1860–1941). Polish prime minister and classical pianist. Appeared in a few films including the British *Moonlight Sonata* 37.

Padovani, Lea (1920–). Italian leading actress, in films from 1945.
Give Us This Day (GB) 49. Three Steps North (US) 51. Tempi Nostri 53. Montparnasse 19 57. The Naked Maja (US) 58, etc.

Page, Anthony (1935–). British director, with stage experience.
□*Inadmissible Evidence* 68. Alpha Beta 73. Pueblo (TV) 73. *The Missiles of October* (TV) 74. Collision Course (TV) 76. F. Scott Fitzgerald in Hollywood (TV) 76. I Never Promised You a Rose Garden 77. The Lady Vanishes 79. The Patricia Neal Story (TV) 81. Grace Kelly (TV) 83. Forbidden (TV) 85. Second Serve (TV) 85.

Page, Gale (1911–1983) (Sally Rutter). American leading lady.
Four Daughters 38. Crime School 38. Daughters Courageous 39. They Drive by Night 40. Four Wives 40. Four Mothers 41. The Time of Your Life 48. About Mrs Leslie 54, etc.

Page, Genevieve (1931–) (G. Bonjean). French leading lady who has made American films.
Foreign Intrigue 56. Trapped in Tangiers 60. Song Without End 60. El Cid 61. L'Honorable Stanislas 63. Youngblood Hawke 64. Les Corsaires 65. Belle de Jour 67. Decline and Fall 68. The Private Life of Sherlock Holmes 70. Beyond Therapy 87, etc.

Page, Geraldine (1924–87). American leading actress, on stage from 1940.
□Taxi 53. Hondo 54. *Summer and Smoke* 61. Sweet Bird of Youth 62. Toys in the Attic 63. *Dear Heart* 65. The Happiest Millionaire 67. You're a Big Boy Now 67. Monday's Child (Arg.) 67. Trilogy (TV) 69. Whatever Happened to Aunt Alice? 69. The Beguiled 71. Pete 'n Tillie 72. J. W. Coop 73. The Day of the Locust 75. Nasty Habits 76. Something for Joey (TV) 77. Interiors (BFA) 78. Honky Tonk Freeway 81. Harry's War 81. I'm Dancing as Fast as I can 82. The Pope of Greenwich Village (AAN) 84. White Nights 85. The Trip to Bountiful (AA) 85. The Bride 85. Nazi Hunter (TV) 86.

Page, Patti (1927–) (Clara Ann Fowler). American TV singer.

□Elmer Gantry 60. Dondi 61. Boys' Night Out 63.

Paget, Debra (1933–) (Debralee Griffin). American leading lady with brief stage experience.
Cry of the City 48. House of Strangers 49. Broken Arrow 50. Les Misérables 52. Prince Valiant 54. Love Me Tender 56. From the Earth to the Moon 58. Tales of Terror 62. The Haunted Palace 64, others.

Pagett, Nicola (1948–). British leading lady of the seventies, much on TV.
Frankenstein, the True Story (TV) 73. Operation Daybreak 76. Oliver's Story 79. Privates on Parade 83. All of You 86. Scoop (TV) 87.

Pagnol, Marcel (1894–1974). French writer-director noted for sprawling comedy dramas which strongly evoke country life without being very cinematic.
Autobiographies: 1960, *The Days Were Too Short*. 1962, *The Time of Secrets*.
Marius (script only) 31. *Fanny* (script only) 32. *César* 34, Joffroi 34. Regain (Harvest) 37. *La Femme du Boulanger* 38. *La Fille du Puisatier* 40. La Belle Meunière 48. Manon des Sources 53. Lettres de Mon Moulin 55, etc.

Paige, Janis (1922–) (Donna Mae Jaden). American leading lady with operatic training.
Hollywood Canteen (debut) 44. Cheyenne 46. Romance on the High Seas 48. Mr Universe 51. Remains to be Seen 53. *Silk Stockings* 57. Please Don't Eat the Daisies 61. The Caretakers 63. Welcome to Hard Times 67. Gibbsville (TV) 75. Lanigan's Rabbi (TV) 76.
TV series: It's Always Jan 56.

Paige, Mabel (1879–1954). American character actress.
My Heart Belongs to Daddy 42. *Lucky Jordan* 43. The Good Fellows 43. *Someone to Remember* (lead role) 43. If You Knew Susie 48. The Sniper 52. Houdini 53.

Paige, Robert (1910–87) (John Arthur) Page). American leading man, former radio announcer, in many films of the forties, little thereafter.
Cain and Mabel 37. Hellzapoppin 41. Shady Lady 42. Son of Dracula 43. Can't Help Singing 44. Red Stallion 47. The Flame 48. Raging Waters 51. Abbott and Costello Go to Mars 53. The Big Payoff 58. The Marriage Go Round 61. Bye Bye Birdie 63, etc.
TV series: Run Buddy Run 66.

Painlevé, Jean (1902–). French documentarist, famous for short scientific naturalist studies of sea horses, sea urchins, shrimps, etc.

painters have frequently had their lives glamorized to provide film-makers with drama to counterpoint art. Among the most notable are Charles Laughton as *Rembrandt*, George Sanders as Gauguin in *The Moon and Sixpence*, José Ferrer as Toulouse Lautrec in *Moulin Rouge*, Anthony Franciosa as Goya in *The Naked Maja*, Kirk Douglas as Van Gogh and Anthony Quinn as Gauguin in *Lust for Life*, Gerard Philipe as Modigliani in *Montparnasse 19,* Cecil Kellaway as Gainsborough in *Kitty*, Charlton Heston as Michelangelo in *The Agony and the Ecstasy*, and Mel Ferrer as *El Greco*.

Paisa (Italy 1946). Episodic story film, a kind of sequel to *Open City*, dramatizing incidents in the German retreat through Italy. Directed by Roberto Rossellini from a script by himself, Fellini, and others. Its success encouraged later short story compendiums such as *Quartet* 48.

Paiva, Nestor (1905–1966). American character actor of assorted foreign peasant types.
Ride a Crooked Mile 38. The Marines Fly High 40. The Falcon in Mexico 44. Fear 46. Road to Rio 46. Five Fingers 52. The Creature from the Black Lagoon 54. The Deep Six 57. The Nine Lives of Elfego Baca 59. The Spirit is Willing 66, many others.

The Pajama Game (US 1957). A wholly successful—and cinematic—version of the stage musical with the unlikely subject of labour unrest in a pajama factory. Stanley Donen's lively direction and Bob Fosse's choreography survive disagreeable colour, and the songs by Richard Adler and Jerry Ross are among the brightest ever written for one show. Book by Richard Bissell and George Abbott; Doris Day, John Raitt and Eddie Foy Jnr head the cast.

Pakula, Alan J. (1928–). American producer who turned director.
□AS PRODUCER: Fear Strikes Out 57. To Kill a Mockingbird 63. Love with the Proper Stranger 63. Baby the Rain Must Fall 65. Inside Daisy Clover 66. Up the Down Staircase 67. The Stalking Moon 68.
□AS PRODUCER-DIRECTOR: The Sterile Cuckoo 69. *Klute* 71. Love, Pain and the

Whole Damn Thing 73. The Parallax View 74. *All The President's Men* 76. Comes A Horseman 78. Starting Over 80. Rollover (d only) 81. Sophie's Choice (w, d only) 82. Dream Lover 85. Orphans 87.

Pal, George (1908–1980). Hungarian puppeteer whose short advertising films enlivened programmes in the late thirties; went to Hollywood 1940 and produced series of 'Puppetoons'; later produced many adventure films involving trick photography. Special Academy Award 1943 'for the development of novel methods and techniques'.
Destination Moon (AA) 50. *When Worlds Collide* (AA) 51. *The War of the Worlds* (AA) 53. The Naked Jungle 55. *Tom Thumb* (AA) (& d) 58. *The Time Machine* (AA) (& d) 60. The Wonderful World of the Brothers Grimm 63. The Power 68.

Palance, Jack (1920–) (Walter Palanuik). Gaunt American leading man with stage experience; started in films playing villains.
Panic in the Streets 50. Halls of Montezuma 51. *Shane* 53. Sign of the Pagan 54. *The Big Knife* 55. I Died a Thousand Times 56. Attack 56. The Man Inside 57. The Lonely Man 57. House of Numbers 57. Ten Seconds to Hell 58. The Mongols 60. Barabbas 62. Warriors Five 62. Le Mépris 63. Once a Thief 65. The Professionals 66. The Torture Garden (GB) 67. Kill a Dragon 67. A Professional Gun 68. Ché! 69. The Desperados 69. They Came to Rob Las Vegas 69. The Companeros 70. Monte Walsh 70. The McMasters 70. The Horsemen 72. Chato's Land 72. Oklahoma Crude 73. Dracula (TV) 73. Craze 73. The Four Deuces 75. God's Gun 77. Mr Scarface 77. One Man Jury 78. The Shape of Things to Come (TV) 79. Hawk the Slayer 80. Without Warning 80. Alone in the Dark 82, etc.
TV series: The Greatest Show on Earth 63. Bronk 75. Believe It or Not 82–.

The Paleface (US 1948). A western romp written by Edmund Hartman and Frank Tashlin, directed by Norman Z. McLeod, this had Bob Hope as a cowardly dentist and Jane Russell as Calamity Jane. In 1952 these stars were joined by Roy Rogers for an even crazier extravaganza called *Son of Paleface*. In 1968 the original was revamped for Don Knotts under the title *The Shakiest Gun in the West*.

Palin, Michael (1943–). British light actor, a member of the Monty Python team who contributed in several ways to all their films before branching out on his own with *The Missionary* in 1982, followed by *A Private Function* 84 and *Brazil* 85.

Pallette, Eugene (1889–1954). Rotund, gravel-voiced American character actor, at his peak as an exasperated father or executive in the thirties and forties.
Intolerance 16. Alias Jimmy Valentine 20. The Three Musketeers 21. To the Last Man 23. Light of the Western Stars 25. Lights of New York 28. The Canary Murder Case 29. The Sea God 30. It Pays to Advertise 31. Shanghai Express 32. The Kennel Murder Case 33. Bordertown 34. Steamboat Round the Bend 35. *The Ghost Goes West* 36. *My Man Godfrey* 36. One Hundred Men and a Girl 37. Topper 37. *The Adventures of Robin Hood* (as Friar Tuck) 38. Mr Smith Goes to Washington 39. The Mark of Zorro 40. The Lady Eve 41. Tales of Manhattan 42. It Ain't Hay 43. Heaven Can Wait 43. Step Lively 44. Lake Placid Serenade 45. In Old Sacramento 46, many others.

Pallos, Stephen (1902–). Hungarian producer who worked with Korda in England from 1942, later as independent.
Call of the Blood 46. The Golden Madonna 48. Jet Storm 59. Foxhole in Cairo 60. A Jolly Bad Fellow 64. Where the Spies Are 65, others.

Palmer, Betsy (1929–) (Patricia Brumek). American light actress and TV panellist.
The Long Gray Line 55. Queen Bee 55. The Tin Star 57. The Last Angry Man 59. It Happened to Jane 59, etc.

Palmer, Ernest (1885–1978). American cinematographer.
Ivanhoe 12. Lothar 17. Ladies Must Live 21. The Wanters 23. The Kiss Barrier 25. The Palace of Pleasure 26. Seventh Heaven 27. The River 29. City Girl 30. A Connecticut Yankee 31. The Painted Woman 32. Cavalcade 33. Berkeley Square 33. Music in the Air 34. Charlie Chan in Paris 35. Banjo on My Knee 36. Slave Ship 37. Four Men and a Prayer 38. News is Made at Night 39. The Great Profile 40. Blood and Sand (AA) 41. Song of the Islands 42. Coney Island 43. Pin Up Girl 44. The Dolly Sisters 45. Centennial Summer 46. I Wonder Who's Kissing Her Now 47. Broken Arrow 50, many others.

Palmer, Gregg (1927–) (Palmer Lee). American 'second lead', former disc jockey.
Son of Ali Baba 51. Veils of Baghdad 53.

Magnificent Obsession 54. The Creature Walks among Us 56. Forty Pounds of Trouble 62. The Undefeated 69. Big Jake 71.

Palmer, Lilli (1911–86) (Lilli Peiser). Austrian leading actress, on stage from childhood, in films from teenage.
Autobiography 1975: *Change Lobsters and Dance.*
Crime Unlimited (GB) 34. Good Morning, Boys (GB) 36. Secret Agent (GB) 36. A Girl Must Live (GB) 38. The Door with Seven Locks (GB) 40. *Thunder Rock* (GB) 42. The Gentle Sex (GB) 43. English without Tears (GB) 44. *The Rake's Progress* (GB) 45. Beware of Pity (GB) 46. Cloak and Dagger (US) 46. *My Girl Tisa* (US) 47. Body and Soul (US) 48. No Minor Vices (US) 48. The Long Dark Hall (GB) 51. The Fourposter (US) 52. Is Anna Anderson Anastasia? (Ger.) 56. La Vie à Deux (Fr.) 58. But Not for Me (US) 58. Conspiracy of Hearts (GB) 60. Rendezvous at Midnight (Fr.) 60. *The Pleasure of His Company* (US) 61. The Counterfeit Traitor (US) 62. Adorable Julia (Ger.) 63. The Flight of the White Stallions (US) 64. Operation Crossbow (GB) 65. Moll Flanders (GB) 65. Sebastian (GB) 67. Oedipus the King (GB) 67. Nobody Runs Forever (GB) 68. The Dance of Death (Swed.) 68. De Sade (US) 69. Hard Contract (US) 69. Murders in the Rue Morgue (GB) 71. Night Hair Child (GB) 71. The Boys from Brazil 78. The Holcroft Covenant 85. Peter the Great (TV) 86, others.
TV series: Lilli Palmer Theatre 54. *Zoo Gang* 73.

Palmer, Maria (1924–1981). Austrian leading lady. Wide stage experience at home, TV and films in America.
Mission to Moscow 42. Lady on a Train 44. Rendezvous 24 46. Slightly Dishonourable 51. Three for Jamie Dawn 56, others.

Palmer, Peter (1931–). American actor-singer who repeated his stage role as *Lil Abner* 59.
TV series: Custer 67.

Paluzzi, Luciana (1939–). Italian leading lady in international films.
Three Coins in the Fountain 54. Sea Fury 58. Thunderball 65. The Venetian Affair 66. Chuka 67. 99 Women 69. The Green Slime 69. Black Gunn 72. War Goddess 74. The Klansman 74. The Greek Tycoon 78, etc.
TV series: Five Fingers 59.

Pampanini, Silvana (1927–). Voluptuous Italian leading lady of such fifties frolics as *Scandal in the Roman Bath.*

pan. A shot in which the camera rotates horizontally. Also used as a verb.

Pan, Hermes (1905–) (H. Panagiotopolous). American dance director.
Top Hat 35. Swing Time 36. Damsel in Distress (AA) 37. Let's Dance 50. Lovely to Look At 52. Silk Stockings 57. Can Can 59. Flower Drum Song 62. Cleopatra 63. My Fair Lady 64. Finian's Rainbow 68. Lost Horizon 73, many others.

Panama, Norman (1914–). Writer-producer-director who has long worked in collaboration with Melvin Frank, (qv) for note on films. Now working solo.
Not with My Wife You Don't (wpd) 66. How to Commit Marriage (d only) 69. The Maltese Bippy (wd) 69. Coffee, Tea or Me? (TV) 73. I Will, I Will . . . For Now (co-w, d) 76. Barnaby and Me 77.

Panavision. A wide-screen system which outdistanced CinemaScope because of its improved anamorphic lens. Super-Panavision and Panavision 70 are 'road show' processes involving projection on wide film: in the first case the film is shot on 65mm, in the second blown up after photography. Great confusion was caused in the seventies by the company insisting on the credit 'filmed with Panavision equipment' even on non-anamorphic films.

Pangborn, Franklin (1894–1958). American character comedian with long stage experience; in scores of films from the twenties, typically as flustered hotel clerk or organizer.
My Friend from India 27. My Man 30. International House 33. My Man Godfrey 36. Stage Door 37. Christmas in July 40. *The Bank Dick* 40. *The Palm Beach Story* 42. The Carter Case 42. Now Voyager 42. *Hail the Conquering Hero* 44. Mad Wednesday 47. Romance on the High Seas 48. The Story of Mankind 57, etc.

Panzer, Paul (1872-1958). American silent screen villain, an extremely hissable specimen.
The Perils of Pauline 14. The Exploits of Elaine 15. The Mystery Mind 19. The Johnstown Flood 26. Under the Red Robe 36. Casablanca 42. The Perils of Pauline 47, many others.

Papas, Irene (1926–) (I. Lelekou). Greek stage actress who has made films at home and abroad. Necripolitia (debut) 51. Theodora Slave Empress 54. Attila the Hun 54. Tribute to a Bad Man (US) 55. The Power and the Prize (US) 56. The Guns of Navarone 61. Electra 62. *Zorba the Greek* 64. Beyond the Mountains 66. The Brotherhood (US) 68. 'Z' 68. A Dream of Kings (US) 69. Anne of the Thousand Days 70. The Trojan Women 71. The Fifth Offensive 73. Moses (TV) 76. The Message 76. Iphigenia 77. Bloodline 79. Into the Night 84. The Assisi Underground 85. High Season 87, etc.

paper prints were made of most films between 1895 and 1912 because the US Copyright Act did not allow for celluloid. This quirk of the law meant the preservation of hundreds of early titles which could otherwise have been lost, and in the sixties they were all copied for the archives of the motion picture academy on to 16mm film.

Paramount Pictures Corporation was basically the creation of Adolph Zukor (qv), a nickelodeon showman who in 1912 founded Famous Players, with the intention of presenting photographed versions of stage successes. In 1914 W. W. Hodkinson's Paramount Pictures took over distribution of Famous Players and Lasky products, and in the complex mergers which resulted, Zukor came out top man. Through the years his studio more than any other gave a family atmosphere, seldom producing films of depth but providing agreeable light entertainment with stars like Valentino, Maurice Chevalier, the Marx Brothers, Mary Pickford, Claudette Colbert, Bob Hope, Bing Crosby, Dorothy Lamour, Alan Ladd, and directors like Lubitsch, De Mille and Wilder. Notable films include *The Sheik, The Covered Wagon, The Ten Commandments* (both versions), *Trouble in Paradise, The Crusades, Union Pacific*, the Road films, *Going My Way, The Greatest Show on Earth*, etc. In recent years, since Zukor's retirement, the company had many difficulties, but was helped by a takeover by Gulf and Western Industries which spurred the commercial instinct, and produced two enormous winners in *Love Story* and *The Godfather*, followed in 1977 by *Saturday Night Fever*, in 1978 by *Grease*, in 1979 by *Star Trek* and in 1981 by *Raiders of the Lost Ark*.

Les Parents Terribles (France 1948). A straight film version by Jean Cocteau of his own claustrophobic play about a family always on the verge of hysteria who come to an emotional crisis when the son announces his intention to marry. With Yvonne de Bray, Jean Marais, Gabrielle Dorziat. Disastrously remade in English by Charles Frank as *Intimate Relations* 53, with Marian Spencer, Russell Enoch and Ruth Dunning.

Paris has usually figured in films as the centre of sophistication, romance and luxury: thus *Ninotchka, I Met Him in Paris, The Last Time I Saw Paris, Innocents in Paris, April in Paris, How to Steal a Million, To Paris With Love, Paris When it Sizzles, A Certain Smile, Funny Face, Paris Holiday, Can Can, Parisienne, Paris Palace Hotel, Two for the Road* and innumerable others. The bohemian aspect is another favourite, as depicted in *An American in Paris, Latin Quarter, Paris Blues, What's New, Pussycat?, Svengali, French Cancan, Moulin Rouge, What a Way to Go, The Moon and Sixpence*, etc. The tourists' Paris has provided a splendid backcloth for films as diverse as *The Great Race, The Man on the Eiffel Tower, Charade, Those Magnificent Men in Their Flying Machines, Zazie dans le Metro, Pig Across Paris, The Red Balloon, Father Brown, Take Her She's Mine, Dear Brigitte, Bon Voyage*, and *Paris Nous Appartient*. French film-makers seem particularly fond of showing the city's seamy side in thrillers about vice, murder and prostitution: *Quai de Grenelle, Quai des Orfvres, Les Compagnes de la Nuit, Le Long des Trottoirs, Rififi*, etc. René Clair has always had his own slightly fantastic view of Paris, from *Paris Qui Dort* through *Sous les Toits de Paris, A Nous la Liberté, Le Million, Le Quatorze Juillet*, and *Porte des Lilas*. Rouben Mamoulian re-created this vision in *Love Me Tonight*, and *The Mad Woman of Chaillot* lived in a city of similar nuances. Historical Paris has been re-created for *The Hunchback of Notre Dame, The Scarlet Pimpernel, The Three Musketeers, Camille, A Tale of Two Cities, Marie Antoinette, So Long at the Fair* and *Les Enfants du Paradis*; while Paris under fire in World War II was depicted in *Is Paris Burning?* As for *Last Tango in Paris*, its emphasis was hardly on the city.

Paris, Jerry (1925–86). American supporting actor: *The Caine Mutiny* 54. *Marty* 55. *Unchained* 55, many others; also played the neighbour in *The Dick Van Dyke Show* 61–66. Turned director: *Never a Dull Moment* 68. *Don't Raise the Bridge Lower the River* 68. *Viva Max* 69. *The Grasshopper* 70. Police Academy 2 84. Police Academy 3 85.

Paris Qui Dort (France 1924). Also known as *The Crazy Ray*, this first film to be written and directed by René Clair is an amusing trifle mostly shot on the Eiffel Tower, about a mad professor whose new invention reduces Paris to silence and sleep.

Parker, Alan (1944–). British director with enough self-assurance to make him an international talking point.
□Melody (w only) 70. Footsteps (& w) 73. Our Cissy (& w) 73. No Hard Feelings 73. The Evacuees (TV) 74. *Bugsy Malone* (& w) 77. *Midnight Express* (BFA) 78. Fame (& w) 79. Shoot the Moon (& w) 82. Pink Floyd: The Wall 82. Birdy 85. Angel Heart 87.

Parker, Barnett (1890–1941). British character actor in Hollywood, one of the perfect butlers of the thirties.
The President's Mystery 36. Espionage 37. Wake Up and Live 37. Listen Darling 38. At the Circus 39. Love Thy Neighbour 40. The Reluctant Dragon 41, etc.

Parker, Cecil (1897–1971) (Cecil Schwabe). British character actor with upper-class personality which could be amiable or chill.
The Silver Spoon (film debut) 33. A Cuckoo in the Nest 33. Storm in a Teacup 37. Dark Journey 37. *The Lady Vanishes* 38. The Citadel 38. *Caesar and Cleopatra* 45. Hungry Hill 46. Captain Boycott 47. *The First Gentleman* (as the Prince Regent) 47. *Quartet* 48. Dear Mr Prohack 49. *The Chiltern Hundreds* 49. Tony Draws a Horse 51. The Man in the White Suit 51. His Excellency 52. I Believe in You 52. Isn't Life Wonderful? 54. *Father Brown* 54. The Constant Husband 55. The Ladykillers 55. *The Court Jester* (US) 55. It's Great to be Young 56. The Admirable Crichton 57. Indiscreet 58. I was Monty's Double 58. Happy is the Bride 58. A Tale of Two Cities 58. The Navy Lark 59. A French Mistress 60. On the Fiddle 61. Petticoat Pirates 62. Heavens Above 63. The Comedy Man 64. Guns at Batasi 64. Moll Flanders 65. A Study in Terror 65. Circus of Fear 67. Oh What a Lovely War 69, others.

Parker, Cecilia (1905–). Canadian leading lady who played many Hollywood roles but is best remembered as Andy's sister in the *Hardy Family* series 37–44.
Young as You Feel 31. The Painted Veil 34. Naughty Marietta 35. A Family Affair (first of the Hardy films) 37. Seven Sweethearts 42. Andy Hardy Comes Home 58, etc.

Parker, Clifton (1905–). British composer.
Yellow Canary 43. Johnny Frenchman 46. Blanche Fury 47. Treasure Island 50. The Gift Horse 52. Hell below Zero 54. Night of the Demon 57. Sea of Sand 59. Sink the Bismarck 60. Taste of Fear 62. The Informers 64, etc.

Parker, Dorothy (1893–1967) American short story writer, reviewer and wit who spent some years in Hollywood as an associate scriptwriter of undistinguished films.
Biography 1971: *You Might as well Live* by John Keats.

¶ 'So odd a blend of Little Nell and Lady Macbeth.'—*Alexander Woollcott*

† DP was played in *F. Scott Fitzgerald in Hollywood* by Dolores Sutton, in *Julia* by Rosemary Harris.

Parker, Eddie (1900–60). American stunt man who doubled for most of Universal's horror stars.

Parker, Eleanor (1922–). American leading lady with brief stage experience before a Hollywood contract; her career followed a typical pattern, with increasingly good leading roles followed by a decline, with a later comeback in character parts.
□They Died with Their Boots On (debut as extra) 41. Buses Roar 42. Mysterious Doctor 43. Mission to Moscow 43. The Very Thought of You 44. Crime by Night 44. Between Two Worlds 44. The Last Ride 44. Pride of the Marines 45. Of Human Bondage (as Mildred) 46. Never Say Goodbye 46. Escape Me Never 47. *The Voice of the Turtle* 47. The Woman in White 48. Chain Lightning 49. Three Secrets 50. *Caged* 50. Valentino 51. A Millionaire for Christy 51. *Detective Story* 51. Scaramouche 52. Above and Beyond 52. Escape from Fort Bravo 53. The Naked Jungle 54. Valley of the Kings 54. Many Rivers to Cross 54. *Interrupted Melody* 55. The Man with the Golden Arm 56. The King and Four Queens 56. Lizzie 57. The Seventh Sin 57. A Hole in the Head 59. Home from the Hill 60. Return to Peyton Place 61. Madison Avenue 62. Panic Button 64. The Sound of Music 65. The Oscar 66. An American Dream 66. Warning Shot 66. The Tiger and the Pussycat 67. How to Steal the World 68. Eye of the Cat 69. Maybe I'll Come Home in the Spring 70. Vanished (TV) 71. Home for the Holidays (TV) 72. The Great American Beauty Contest (TV) 74. *She's Dressed to Kill* (TV) 79. Sunburn 79. Madame X (TV) 81.
TV series: Bracken's World 69.

Parker, Fess (1925–). American leading man with some stage experience.

Untamed Frontier 52. *Davy Crockett* 54 (and two sequels). The Great Locomotive Chase 56. Westward Ho the Wagons 56. Old Yeller 57. The Hangman 59. Hell is for Heroes 62. Smoky 66, etc.
TV series: Mr Smith Goes to Washington 62. Daniel Boone 64–68.

Parker, Jameson (1947–). American leading man.
The Bell Jar 79. A Small Circle of Friends 80. Women at West Point (TV) 80. Anatomy of a Seduction (TV) 80.

Parker, Jean (1912–) (Lois Mae Greene). Once-demure American leading lady, popular in the thirties; latterly playing hard-boiled roles.
Rasputin and the Empress 32. *Little Women* 33. *Sequoia* 34. The Ghost Goes West (GB) 36. Princess O'Hara 37. The Flying Deuces 39. Beyond Tomorrow 40. No Hands on the Clock 42. One Body Too Many 42. Minesweeper 43. Bluebeard 44. Detective Kitty O'Day 44. Lady in the Death House 44. The Gunfighter 50. Those Redheads from Seattle 53. Black Tuesday 54. A Lawless Street 55. Apache Uprising 65, others.

Parker, Suzy (1932–) (Cecelia Parker). Statuesque American leading lady, former model.
Kiss Them for Me (debut) 57. *Ten North Frederick* 58. The Best of Everything 59. Circle of Deception 61. The Interns 62. Chamber of Horrors 66, etc.

Parker, Willard (1912–) (Worster van Eps). Tall American 'second lead', in films from 1938 after stage experience.
A Slight Case of Murder (debut) 38. The Fighting Guardsman 43. You Gotta Stay Happy 48. Sangaree 53. The Great Jesse James Raid 53. The Earth Dies Screaming 64, etc.
TV series: Tales of the Texas Rangers 55–57.

Parkins, Barbara (1942–). Canadian leading lady whose major success was TV.
Valley of the Dolls 67. The Kremlin Letters 69. The Mephisto Waltz 71. Puppet on a Chain 72. Asylum 72. Captains and the Kings (TV) 76. Shout at the Devil 76. Ziegfeld: the Man and his Women (as Anna Held) (TV) 78. The Critical List (TV) 78, etc.
TV series: *Peyton Place* 64–68.

Parks, Gordon (1925–). Black American director, former stills photographer.
The Learning Tree 68. *Shaft* 71. Shaft's Big Score 72. Leadbelly 76, etc.

Parks, Gordon Jnr (1948–1979). American director, son of Gordon Parks.
Superfly 72. Thomasine and Bushrod 74. Three the Hard Way 74. Aaron Loves Angela 75.

Parks, Larry (1914–1975) (Sam Kleusman Lawrence Parks). American light leading man whose career in 'B' pictures was interrupted by his highly successful impersonation of Al Jolson. He subsequently proved difficult to cast, and was forced out of Hollywood after testifying to the Unamerican Activities Committee.
□ You Belong to Me 41. Mystery Ship 41. Harmon of Michigan 41. Blondie Goes to College 42. Harvard Here I Come 42. The Boogie Man Will Get You 42. Atlantic Convoy 42. Canal Zone 42. Three Girls About Town 42. Sing for your Supper 42. Flight Lieutenant 42. Submarine Raiser 42. Honolulu Lu 42. Hello Annapolis 42. You were never Lovelier 42. A Man's World 42. North of the Rockies 42. Alias Boston Blackie 42. They All Kissed the Bride 42. Redhead from Manhattan 43. Is Everybody Happy 43. First Comes Courage 43. Power of the Press 43. The Deerslayer 43. Destroyer 43. Reveille with Beverly 43. She's a Sweetheart 44. The Racket Man 44. The Black Parachute 44. Stars on Parade 44. Hey Rookie 44. Sergeant Mike 44. Counter Attack 45. Jealousy 45. Renegades 46. *The Jolson Story* 46. Her Husband's Affairs 47. Down to Earth 47. The Swordsman 47. Gallant Blade 48. *Jolson Sings Again* 49. Emergency Wedding 50. Love is Better than Ever 52. Tiger by the Tail 55. *Freud* 62.

Parks, Michael (1938–). Brooding American leading man.
Wild Seed 64. Bus Riley's Back in Town 65. The Bible (as Adam) 66. The Idol (GB) 66. The Happening 67. Can Ellen Be Saved (TV) 73. The Last Hard Men 76. Sidewinder One 77. Love and the Midnight Auto Supply 77. The Private Files of J. Edgar Hoover 78. Breakthrough 79. Fast Friends (TV) 79. North Sea Hijack 80. Reward (TV) 81. Savannah Smiles 82, etc.
TV series: Then Came Bronson 69.

Parkyakarkus (1904–1958) (Harry Einstein). American radio comedian formerly known as Harry Parke.
Strike Me Pink 36. Night Spot 38. Glamour Boy 40. Earl Carroll's Vanities 45.

Parkyn, Leslie (–1983). British executive producer, associated with Sergei Nolbandov 1951–57, subsequently with Julian Wintle.
The Kidnappers 53. Tiger Bay 59. The Waltz of the Toreadors 62. Father Came Too 64, many others.

Parlo, Dita (1906–1971) (Gerthe Kornstadt). German star actress of the thirties.
Homecoming 28. Melody of the Heart 30. Secrets of the Orient 31. L'Atalante 34. The Mystic Mountain 36. Mademoiselle Docteur 37. La Grande Illusion 37. Ultimatum 39. Justice est Faite 50. Quand le Soleil Montera 56, etc.

Parnell, Emory (1894–1979). American general purpose character actor: could be villain, prison warden, weakling or kindly father.
King of Alcatraz 39. I Married a Witch 42. Mama Loves Papa 46. Words and Music 48. Call Me Madam 53. Man of the West 58, many others.

parody without satire was never prominent among film genres until the seventies, when the easygoing talents of such as Mel Brooks and Gene Wilder produced films such as *Blazing Saddles, Sherlock Holmes' Smarter Brother, Young Frankenstein, Murder By Death, The Black Bird, The Big Bus, Phantom of the Paradise, High Anxiety* and *The Cheap Detective.* Short films in this vein are headed by *Six-Sided Triangle*, *The Dove* and *Cry Wolf.*

Parrish, Helen (1922–1959). American leading lady, former baby model and child actress.
The Big Trail 31. A Dog of Flanders 34. Mad about Music 38. You'll Find Out 40. They All Kissed the Bride 42. The Mystery of the Thirteenth Guest 44. The Wolf Hunters 50, etc.

Parrish, Robert (1916–). American director, former editor.
Autobiography 1976: *Growing Up in Hollywood.*
□Cry Danger 51. The Mob 51. My Pal Gus 52. The San Francisco Story 52. Rough Shoot (GB) 52. Assignment Paris 52. The Purple Plain 54. Lucy Gallant 55. Fire Down Below 57. Saddle the Wind 58. The Wonderful Country 59. In the French Style (& p) 63. Up from the Beach 65. The Bobo 67. Casino Royale (part) 67. Duffy 68. Journey to the Far Side of the Sun 69. A Town Called Bastard 71. The Marseilles Contract 74.
'His films belong to a director who craves anonymity.'—*Andrew Sarris, 1968*

Parrott, James (1892–1939). American director, mainly of two-reelers featuring Laurel and Hardy (*Blotto, The Music Box, County Hospital*, etc), Charlie Chase and Max Davidson. Features include *Jailbirds* 31, *Sing, Sister, Sing* 35.

Parry, Gordon (1908–1981). British director of mainly secondary films: former actor, production manager, etc.
Bond Street 48. Third Time Lucky 48. Now Barabbas 49. Midnight Episode 50. Innocents in Paris 52. Women of Twilight 52. A Yank in Ermine 55. Sailor Beware 56. Tread Softly Stranger 58. The Navy Lark 60, etc.

Parry, Natasha (1930–). British leading lady who married Peter Brook. Appears occasionally on stage and screen.
Dance Hall 49. The Dark Man 50. Crow Hollow 52. Knave of Hearts 53. Windom's Way 57. The Rough and the Smooth 59. Midnight Lace 60. The Fourth Square 62. The Girl in the Headlines 64. Romeo and Juliet 68. Oh What a Lovely War 69. La Chambre Voisine 80, etc.

Parsons, Estelle (1927–). American character actress with stage background.
Bonnie and Clyde (AA) 67. Rachel Rachel 68. I Never Sang for My Father 69. Don't Drink the Water 69. I Walk the Line 70. Watermelon Man 71. Two People 73. For Pete's Sake 74. Foreplay 75, etc.

Parsons, Harriet (1906–1983). American producer, daughter of Louella Parsons.
I Remember Mama 47. Clash by Night 51. Susan Slept Here 54, etc.

Parsons, Louella (1880–1972) (L. Oettinger). Hollywood columnist whose gossip rivalled in readership that of Hedda Hopper. In occasional films as herself, e.g. *Hollywood Hotel* 37, *Starlift* 51.
Autobiographical books: *The Gay Illiterate* 44. *Tell It to Louella* 62.
Biography 1973: *Hedda and Louella* by George Eels.

¶ Her friends always stand by her. When she prematurely published a claim that an actress was pregnant, the actress' husband hastened to prove her correct.—*Time Magazine*

'Her writings stand out like an asthmatic's gasps.'—*Nunnally Johnson*
'Not a bad old slob.'—*James Mason*

Parsons, Milton (1904–1980). Lugubrious American character actor often seen as undertaker.
The Hidden Hand 42. Margie 44, many others.

Parsons, Nicholas (1928–). British light actor and entertainer.
Master of Bankdam 48. Brothers in Law 57. Too Many Crooks 59. Doctor in Love 62. Don't Raise the Bridge Lower the River 68, etc.

Une Partie de Campagne (France 1936). A rare instance of a film which is unfinished and all the better for it. Based on a Maupassant story, it describes a romantic idyll in the countryside; the spot is revisited fourteen years later by the protagonists, who are of course unable to recapture their original feeling. The film's first and last sequences were filmed by Renoir before production was halted for various reasons. It proved impossible to get the actors together again to film the middle sequence showing how the lives of the characters diverge, and the incomplete film was issued in 1946 to general acclaim. The cast included Sylvie Bataille, Georges Saint-Saens and Jeanne Marken.

parties in movies have often been wild, as for instance in *The Wild Party*, also *The Party's Over, I'll Never Forget Whatshisname, Breakfast at Tiffany's, I Love You Alice B. Toklas, The Impossible Years, Skidoo, Beyond the Valley of the Dolls, Camille 2000, The Pursuit of Happiness, The Party Crashers*, and *The Party* itself, which started out sedately but finished with an elephant in the swimming pool. Some of the more amusing film parties, however, were better behaved, as in *The Apartment, Only Two Can Play, All About Eve* and *Citizen Kane*.

Parton, Dolly (1946–). Voluptuous American country and western singer.
Nine to Five 81. The Best Little Whorehouse in Texas 82. Rhinestone 84.

¶ *D.P.:* I enjoy the way I look, but it's a joke.
D.P.: I'm on a seafood diet—I see food, I eat it.

Pascal, Gabriel (1894–1954). Hungarian producer-director who came to Britain in the thirties, won the esteem of Bernard Shaw, and was entrusted with the filming of several of his plays.
Biography 1971: *The Disciple and his Devil* by Valerie Pascal.
□Pygmalion (p) 38. Major Barbara (pd) 40. Caesar and Cleopatra (pd; a notoriously extravagant production) 45. Androcles and the Lion (p) (US) 53.

Pasco, Richard (1926–). British character actor, mainly on stage and TV.
Room at the Top 59. Yesterday's Enemy 60. The Gorgon 64. Rasputin the Mad Monk 66. The Watcher in the Woods 80, etc.

Pasolini, Pier Paolo (1922–1975). Italian director.
Accattone 61. Mamma Roma 62. The Witches (part) 63. *The Gospel According to St Matthew* 64. Oedipus Rex 67. *Theorem* 68. Pigsty 69. Medea 70. Decameron 70. The Canterbury Tales 71. The Arabian Nights 74. The 120 Days of Sodom 75, etc.

Passer, Ivan (1933–). Czech director, latterly in Hollywood.
A Boring Afternoon 64. Intimate Lighting 66. Born to Win 71. Law and Disorder 74. Silver Bears 78. Ace Up My Sleeve 78. Cutter's Way 81. Creator 85, etc.

The Passing of the Third Floor Back. Jerome K. Jerome's popular novel and play, about a Christ-like stranger who has a benign influence on the down-at-heel inhabitants of a boarding house, was filmed in 1918 with Johnston Forbes-Robertson and in 1935 with Conrad Veidt.

The Passing Parade. A series of one-reel interest films, mostly historical cameos enacted in corners of MGM's great sets, devised and produced by John Nesbitt in the thirties and forties.

La Passion de Jeanne D'Arc (France 1928). A notable silent film directed by Carl Dreyer and photographed by Rudolph Maté. It tells the familiar story as a series of Rembrandtesque tableaux, with stark white décor by Herman Warm. Falconetti gives a remarkable performance in this her only film.

Passport to Pimlico (GB 1948). The first of the 'Ealing comedies', whose special quality was to find humour and wit in the lives of ordinary people who are not music-hall caricatures. This one concerns the discovery that part of London belongs to

France, and is acted by a notable gallery of character players. Directed by Henry Cornelius from a script by T. E. B. Clarke.

Pasternak, Boris (1890–1960). Russian novelist, author of *Dr Zhivago*.

Pasternak, Joe (1901–). Hungarian producer in Hollywood during the golden years; especially identified with cheerful light musicals.
Autobiography 1956: *Easy the Hard Way*.
Three Smart Girls 36. *One Hundred Men and a Girl* 37. Mad About Music 38. *Destry Rides Again* 39. Seven Sinners 40. It Started with Eve 41. Presenting Lily Mars 42. Song of Russia 43. Two Girls and a Sailor 44. Anchors Aweigh 45. Holiday in Mexico 46. The Unfinished Dance 47. On an Island with You 48. In the Good Old Summertime 49. The Duchess of Idaho 50. *The Great Caruso* 51. Skirts Ahoy 52. Latin Lovers 53. The Student Prince 54. Love Me or Leave Me 55. The Opposite Sex 56. Ten Thousand Bedrooms 57. Party Girl 58. Ask Any Girl 59. Please Don't Eat the Daisies 60. The Horizontal Lieutenant 61. Jumbo 62. The Courtship of Eddie's Father 63. Girl Happy 65. Penelope 66. The Sweet Ride 68, many others.

Patch, Wally (1888–1970) (Walter Vinicombe). Burly British Cockney character actor, in films since 1920 after varied show business experience.
Shadows 31. The Good Companions 32. Get Off My Foot 35. Not So Dusty 36. Bank Holiday 38. Quiet Wedding 40. Gasbags 40. The Common Touch 41. Old Mother Riley at Home 45. The Ghosts of Berkeley Square 47. The Guinea Pig 49. Will Any Gentleman? 53. Private's Progress 55. I'm All Right, Jack 59. Sparrows Can't Sing 63, scores of others.

Pate, Michael (1920–). Australian actor in Hollywood in the fifties and sixties, often as Red Indian chief or second-string villain.
The Rugged O'Riordans 49. The Strange Door 51. Five Fingers 52. Houdini 53. The Silver Chalice 54. The Court Jester 56. Congo Crossing 56. The Oklahoman 57. Green Mansions 59. The Canadians 61. McLintock 63. Major Dundee 65, etc.
TV series: Matlock Police 71.

Paterson, Neil (1916–). British screenwriter (and novelist).
The Kidnappers 53. High Tide at Noon 57. *Room at the Top* (AA) 59. The Spiral Road 62. Mister Moses 65.

Paterson, Pat (1911–1978). English leading lady who went to Hollywood but gave up her career to marry Charles Boyer.
□ The Professional Guest 31. The Great Gay Road 31. Night Shadows 31. Murder on the Second Floor 32. Partners Please 32. Here's George 32. Bitter Sweet 33. Love Time 34. Bottoms Up 34. Call it Luck 34. Charlie Chan in Egypt 35. Lottery Lover 35. Spendthrift 36. 52nd Street 37. Idiot's Delight 39.

Pathé, Charles (1863–1957). Pioneer French executive and producer, founder of Pathé Frères and later Pathé Gazette. Also credited with making the first 'long' film: *Les Misérables*. (Made in 1909, it ran four whole reels.)

Pather Panchali (India 1954). The first of a trilogy written and directed by Satyajit Ray (the other titles are *The Unvanquished* 56 and *The World of Apu* 59) showing the hero's development from childhood to manhood against a background of the poverty of modern India. The three films provide the best documentation available on a country whose films have normally been too traditional to interest western audiences.

Paths of Glory (US 1957). A harsh attack on the futility of war in general and in particular the cynical manoeuvrings of World War I. Full of brilliant dialogue and action sequences. Directed by Stanley Kubrick from a script by Calder Willingham and Jim Thompson and a novel by Humphrey Cobb; photographed by George Krause; with Kirk Douglas, Adolphe Menjou and George Macready.

Patrick, Gail (1911–1980) (Margaret Fitzpatrick). American leading lady in Hollywood from early thirties, usually in routine smart woman roles.
The Phantom Broadcast 32. Cradle Song 33. No More Ladies 35. Artists and Models 37. Reno 40. Quiet, Please, Murder 43. Women in Bondage 44. Twice Blessed 45. The Plainsman and the Lady 46. Calendar Girl 47, many others.
Retired from acting and became a TV producer, notably of the successful *Perry Mason* series.

Patrick, John (1905–) (John Patrick Goggan). American playwright. Works filmed include *The Hasty Heart*, *The Teahouse of the August Moon*.
SCREENPLAYS: Educating Father 36. One Mile from Heaven 37. International

Settlement 38. Mr Moto Takes a Chance 38. Enchantment 48. The President's Lady 53. Three Coins in the Fountain 54. Love Is a Many Splendored Thing 55. High Society 56. Les Girls 57. Some Came Running 58. The World of Suzie Wong 61. The Main Attraction 63. The Shoes of the Fisherman 68, etc.

Patrick, Lee (1906–1982). American character actress with stage experience, in Hollywood from 1937, usually as hard-bitten blondes.
Strange Cargo (debut) 29. *The Maltese Falcon* 41. Now Voyager 42. Mother Wore Tights 47. Caged 50. There's No Business Like Show Business 54. Vertigo 58. Summer and Smoke 61. The New Interns 64. *The Black Bird* 75, many others.
TV series: Topper 53–55. Mr Adams and Eve 56–57.

Patrick, Nigel (1913–81) (Nigel Wemyss). Debonair British leading actor, on stage from 1932.
□ Mrs Pym of Scotland Yard 39. Uneasy Terms 48. *Noose* 48. Spring in Park Lane 48. Silent Dust 49. Jack of Diamonds 49. The Perfect Woman 50. *Trio* 50. Morning Departure 50. Pandora and the Flying Dutchman 51. Encore 51. The Browning Version 51. Young Wives' Tale 51. Meet Me Tonight 52. *The Pickwick Papers* (as Mr Jingle) 52. Who Goes There 52. *The Sound Barrier* 52. Grand National Night 53. Forbidden Cargo 54. The Sea Shall Not Have Them 54. All for Mary 55. A Prize of Gold 55. Raintree County 57. How to Murder a Rich Uncle 57. Count Five and Die 58. The Man Inside 58. Sapphire 59. *The League of Gentlemen* 60. The Trials of Oscar Wilde 60. Johnny Nobody (& d) 61. The Informers 63. The Virgin Soldiers 69. The Battle of Britain 69. The Executioner 70. Tales from the Crypt 72. The Great Waltz 72. The Mackintosh Man 73.
TV series: Zero One 62.

Patten, Luana (1938–). American teenage actress of the fifties.
Song of the South 46. So Dear to My Heart 48. Johnny Tremain 57. The Little Shepherd of Kingdom Come 61. A Thunder of Drums 61. Follow Me Boys 66, etc.

Patterson, Elizabeth (1876–1966). American character actress with stage experience; in Hollywood from the late twenties, usually as kindly or shrewish elderly ladies.
Daddy Longlegs 30. A Bill of Divorcement 32. Miss Pinkerton 32. Dinner at Eight 33. So Red the Rose 36. Sing You Sinners 38. *The Cat and the Canary* 39. *Tobacco Road* 41. Hail the Conquering Hero 43. Lady on a Train 45. *Intruder in the Dust* 48. Little Women 49. Bright Leaf 50. Pal Joey 57. The Oregon Trail 59, many others.

Patterson, Lee (1929–). Sturdy Canadian leading man of minor British and American films.
36 Hours 51. The Passing Stranger 54. Above Us the Waves 55. Soho Incident 56. Cat and Mouse 58. Jack the Ripper 60. The Ceremony 63. Valley of Mystery 67. Chato's Land 72, etc.
TV series: Surfside Six 60–61.

Patterson, Neva (1925–). American character actress.
Desk Set 57. Too Much Too Soon 58. The Domino Principle 77, etc.
TV series: The Governor and JJ 69. Nichols 71.

Paul, Robert (1869–1943). Pioneer British movie camera inventor (1895). The following year he invented a projector, which he called a theatrograph. Later turned showman.

Paulvé, André (1898–1982). French producer.
La Comédie du Bonheur 39. Lumière d'Eté 42. L'Eternel Retour 43. Les Visiteurs du Soir 43. La Belle et la Bête 45. Ruy Blas 47. Orphée 49. Manèges 49. Casque d'Or 51, many others.

Pavan, Marisa (1932–) (Marisa Pierangeli). Italian leading lady, sister of Pier Angeli. In Hollywood from 1950.
What Price Glory? (debut) 52. The Rose Tattoo 55. The Man in the Grey Flannel Suit 56. Solomon and Sheba 59. John Paul Jones 59. The Slightly Pregnant Man (Fr.) 73, etc.

Pavarotti, Luciano (1935–). Italian tenor in international opera. Starred in one film in 1982, *Yes Giorgio*.

Pavlow, Muriel (1921–). British leading lady, on stage and screen from 1936; her youthful appearance enabled her to continue in juvenile roles for many years.
A Romance in Flanders (debut) 36. Quiet Wedding 40. Night Boat to Dublin 45. The Shop at Sly Corner 47. Malta Story 53.

Doctor in the House 54. *Reach for the Sky* 56. Tiger in the Smoke 57. Rooney 58. Murder She Said 62, etc.

Pawle, Lennox (1872–1936). British character actor, mainly on stage.
The Admirable Crichton (GB) 18. The Great Adventure (GB) 21. Married in Hollywood (US) 29. The Sin of Madeleine Claudet (US) 32. *David Copperfield* (as Mr Dick) 34. Sylvia Scarlett (US) 35, etc.

The Pawnbroker (US 1964). A somewhat overheated but impressive modern morality with Rod Steiger (BFA) as a Jewish pawnbroker in New York, drained of humanity by his experiences in a Nazi concentration camp. Striking scenes and moments somehow fail to add up to more than a well-meaning melodrama.
Photographed by Boris Kaufman; directed by Sidney Lumet from a script by David Friedkin and Morton Fine.

Paxinou, Katina (1900–1973) (Katina Constantopoulos). Greek actress with international experience; played in some Hollywood films.
For Whom the Bell Tolls (AA) 43. Confidential Agent 44. Uncle Silas (GB) 47. *Mourning Becomes Electra* 47. Confidential Report 55. Rocco and His Brothers 60. Zita 68, etc.

Paxton, John (1911–85). American screenwriter.
□*Murder My Sweet* 44. My Pal Wolf (co-w) 44. Cornered 46. Crack Up (co-w) 46. *Crossfire* 47. So Well Remembered 47. Of Men and Music (co-w) 50. *Fourteen Hours* 51. The Wild One 54. A Prize of Gold (co-w) 55. The Cobweb 55. Interpol 57. How to Murder a Rich Uncle (& p) 59. On the Beach 59. Kotch 71.

Payne, Jack (1899–1969). British bandleader who appeared in two films: *Say it with Music* 32, *Sunshine Ahead* 36.

Payne, John (1912–). General purpose American leading man, mostly of forties musicals and fifties westerns.
Dodsworth 36. Fair Warning 37. Love on Toast 38. Wings of the Navy 39. *Kid Nightingale* 39. Maryland 40. The Great Profile 40. *Tin Pan Alley* 40. *The Great American Broadcast* 41. Weekend in Havana 41. Remember the Day 41. Sun Valley Serenade 41. To the Shores of Tripoli 42. Springtime in the Rockies 42. Hello Frisco Hello 43. The Dolly Sisters 45. Sentimental Journey 46. The Razor's Edge 46. Miracle on 34th Street 47. The Saxon Charm 48. The Crooked Way 49. Captain China 49. Tripoli 50. Crosswinds 51. Caribbean 52. Kansas City Confidential 52. Raiders of the Seven Seas 53. 99 River Street 53. Rails into Laramie 54. Santa Fé Passage 55. Hell's Island 55. Slightly Scarlet 56. *The Boss* 56. Bailout at 43,000 57. Hidden Fear 57. Gift of the Nile 68, etc.
TV series: *The Restless Gun* 58–59.

Payne, Laurence (1919–). British leading man, on stage and (occasionally) screen from 1945.
Train of Events 49. Ill Met by Moonlight 57. Ben Hur 59. The Tell Tale Heart 61. The Court Martial of Major Keller 61. Vampire Circus 72, etc.

Payton, Barbara (1927–1967). American leading lady.
Once More My Darling 49. Dallas 50. Kiss Tomorrow Goodbye 51. Drums in the Deep South 51. Bride of the Gorilla 52. The Great Jesse James Raid 53. Four-Sided Triangle (GB) 54. The Flanagan Boy (GB) 55, etc.

Peach, Mary (1934–). British leading lady, in films from 1957.
Follow That Horse 59. Room at the Top 59. *No Love for Johnnie* 61. A Pair of Briefs 62. A Gathering of Eagles (US) 63. Ballad in Blue 65. The Projected Man 66. Scrooge 70, etc.

Pearce, Alice (1913–1966). American character comedienne, usually in adenoidal roles.
On the Town 49. The Opposite Sex 56. The Disorderly Orderly 64. Dear Brigitte 65. The Glass Bottom Boat 66, etc.
TV series: Bewitched 65–66.

Pearl, Jack (1894–1984). Jewish-American comic known on radio as Baron Munchhausen and famous for his catchphrase. 'Vass you dere, Sharlie?' Film appearance: *Hollywood Party* 34.

Pearson, Beatrice (1920–). American leading lady with a brief career.
□Force of Evil 49. Lost Boundaries 49.

Pearson, George (1875–1973). British writer-producer-director who came to films at the age of 37 after being a schoolmaster. Hundreds of films to his credit.
Autobiography 1957: *Flashback*.

The Fool 12. A Study in Scarlet 14. Ultus the Man from the Dead 15. The Better Ole 18. The Old Curiosity Shop 20. *Squibs* 21. Squibs Wins the Calcutta Sweep 22. Satan's Sister 25. Huntingtower 27. The Silver King 28. Journey's End (p) 30. The Good Companions (p) 32. Four Marked Men 34. The Pointing Finger 38, many others.

Pearson, Lloyd (1897–1966). Portly British character actor, usually of bluff Yorkshire types.
The Challenge 38. Tilly of Bloomsbury 40. Kipps 41. *When We Are Married* 42. Schweik's New Adventures (leading role) 43. My Learned Friend 44. Mr Perrin and Mr Traill 49. Hindle Wakes 52. The Good Companions 57. The Angry Silence 59, etc.

Pearson, Richard (–). British stage character actor in occasional films.
Love Among the Ruins (TV) 75. The Bluebird 77. She Fell Among Thieves (TV) 78. The Mirror Crack'd 80. Water 85. Pirates 86. Whoops Apocalypse 87, etc.

Peary, Harold (1908–85) (Harold Jose Pereira de Faria). American character comedian who for years in the forties played The Great Gildersleeve on radio and in a short-lived film series, also in *Coming Round the Mountain*, *County Fair*, *Clambake*.

Peck, Gregory (1916–). Durable and likeable American leading actor, with stage experience before sudden success in Hollywood.
Autobiography 1978: *An Actor's Life*.
□Days of Glory 43. *The Keys of the Kingdom* 44. The Valley of Decision 44. *Spellbound* 45. The Yearling 46. *Duel in the Sun* 46. *The Macomber Affair* 47. *Gentleman's Agreement* 47. The Paradine Case 47. Yellow Sky 48. The Great Sinner 49. *Twelve O'Clock High* 49. *The Gunfighter* 50. David and Bathsheba 51. Captain Horatio Hornblower (GB) 51. Only the Valiant 52. The World in His Arms 52. The Snows of Kilimanjaro 52. Roman Holiday 53. Night People 54. The Million Pound Note (GB) 54. The Purple Plain (GB) 55. *The Man in the Grey Flannel Suit* 56. Moby Dick 56. Designing Woman 57. The Bravados 58. *The Big Country* 58. Pork Chop Hill 59. Beloved Infidel (as Scott Fitzgerald) 59. On the Beach 59. The Guns of Navarone (GB) 61. Cape Fear 62. How the West was Won 62. *To Kill a Mockingbird* (AA) 63. Captain Newman 63. Behold a Pale Horse 64. Mirage 65. Arabesque 66. Mackenna's Gold 68. The Stalking Moon 68. The Most Dangerous Man in the World 69. Marooned 69. I Walk the Line 70. Shootout 71. Billy Two Hats 73. The Dove (p only) 75. *The Omen* 76. MacArthur 77. The Boys from Brazil 78. The Sea Wolves 80. The Blue and the Gray (TV) (as Lincoln) 82. The Scarlet and the Black (TV) 82. Amazing Grace and Chuck 87.

Peckinpah, Sam (1926–85). American director of tough westerns.
□The Deadly Companions 61. *Ride the High Country* 62. Major Dundee 65. *The Wild Bunch* 69. The Ballad of Cable Hogue 69. Straw Dogs 71. Junior Bonner 72. The Getaway 72. Pat Garrett and Billy the Kid 73. Bring Me the Head of Alfredo Garcia 74. The Killer Elite 76. Cross of Iron 77. Convoy 78. The Osterman Weekend 83.

Peerce, Jan (1904–84). American opera singer who appeared in *Carnegie Hall* and *Something in the Wind*.

Peerce, Larry (c. 1935–). American writer-director, son of opera singer Jan Peerce.
One Potato Two Potato 66. Goodbye Columbus 69. A Separate Peace 73. Ash Wednesday 74. The Other Side of the Mountain 76. Two Minute Warning 76. The Other Side of the Mountain Part Two 78. The Bell Jar 79. Why Would I Lie? 80. Love Child 82.

Peg O' My Heart. This sentimental play by J. Hartley Manners, about an Irish servant girl who stays with her English relatives, was filmed in 1922 by King Vidor with Laurette Taylor, and in 1932 by Robert Z. Leonard, with Marion Davies.

Pelissier, Anthony (1912–). British director with stage experience; son of Fay Compton.
The History of Mr Polly 49. The Rocking Horse Winner 50. Night without Stars 50. Meet Me Tonight 52. Meet Mr Lucifer 54, etc.

Pendleton, Austin (1940–). Slightly built American character actor.
Skidoo 68. What's Up Doc 72. Every Little Crook and Nanny 72. The Thief Who Came to Dinner 73. *The Front Page* 74. The Great Smokey Roadblock 78. Starting Over 79. The First Family 80, etc.

Pendleton, Nat (1895–1967). American character actor, formerly professional

wrestler, usually seen in 'dumb ox' roles. In films from c. 1930.
You Said a Mouthful 32. The Sign of the Cross 32. *The Thin Man* 34. Manhattan Melodrama 34. The Great Ziegfeld 36. The Marx Brothers at the Circus 39. Young Dr Kildare (and series) 39. On Borrowed Time 39. Northwest Passage 40. Top Sergeant Mulligan 42. Rookies Come Home 45. Scared to Death 47. Death Valley 49, many others.

Pene Du Bois, Raoul (1914–85). American set and costume designer, mainly on Broadway but occasionally noticed on Hollywood credits.

Penhaligon, Susan (1950–). British leading lady of the late seventies.
Under Milk Wood 73. No Sex Please We're British 73. The Land that Time Forgot 75. Nasty Habits 77. The Uncanny 77. Leopard in the Snow 78. The Masks of Death (TV) 84.
TV series: Bouquet of Barbed Wire 76.

Penn, Arthur (1922–). American director, from TV.
□The Left Handed Gun 58. The Miracle Worker 62. Mickey One 65. The Chase 66. *Bonnie and Clyde* 67. Alice's Restaurant 69. Little Big Man 70. Night Moves 75. The Missouri Breaks 76. Four Friends 81.
Target 85. Dead of Winter 87.

¶ *A.P.:* There hasn't been that much of a market for what I can do. I'm not into outer space epics or youth pictures.

Penn, Sean (1960–). American pop singer and light actor who makes more headlines off the set than on it.
□ Taps 81. Fast Times at Ridgmont High 82. Bad Boys 83. Racing with the Moon 83. Crackers 84. The Falcon and the Snowman 84. At Close Range 85. Shanghai Surprise 86.

Penner, Joe (1904–1941) (J. Pinter). Hungarian-American radio comedian who made a few films.
College Rhythm 33. Collegiate 36. Go Chase Yourself 38. Glamour Boy 40. The Boys from Syracuse 40, etc.

Pennick, Jack (1895–1964). American small part actor and horse trainer, often in John Ford westerns.
Four Sons 28. Under Two Flags 36. Stagecoach 39. Northwest Mounted Police 40. My Darling Clementine 46. Fort Apache 48. Rio Grande 50. The Alamo 60.

Pennington-Richards, C. M. (1911–). British director, former photographer.
The Oracle 54. Inn for Trouble 60. Double Bunk 62. Ladies Who Do 63. A Challenge for Robin Hood 67, etc.

Penrod. Booth Tarkington's American boy character, in his mid-west small town setting, was for many years a favourite Hollywood subject. Marshall Neilan directed Gordon Griffith in a 1922 version. In 1923 William Beaudine directed Ben Alexander in the role in *Penrod and Sam*, which was remade by Beaudine in 1931 with Leon Janney, and again by William McGann in 1937 with Billy Mauch. Mauch and his twin brother Bobby appeared in two sequels: *Penrod's Double Trouble* 38 directed by Lewis Seiler, and *Penrod and His Twin Brother* 38 directed by McGann. Two Doris Day musicals, *On Moonlight Bay* 51 and *By the Light of the Silvery Moon* 53, were also lightly based on the Tarkington stories: Penrod, unaccountably disguised as 'Wesley', was played by Billy Gray.

People on Sunday (Menschen am Sonntag) (Germany 1930). A rare combination of talents made this attractive comedy-drama showing how Berliners spent their weekends in pre-Hitler days. Written by Robert Siodmak and Billy Wilder, it was directed by Siodmak with assistance from Fred Zinnemann and Edgar G. Ulmer, photographed by Eugene Schufftan.

Pépé le Moko: see *Algiers*.

Peppard, George (1929–). American leading man with Broadway experience; began interestingly, but developed into an acceptable tough lead of hokum adventures.
□*The Strange One* 57. Pork Chop Hill 59. Home from the Hill 60. The Subterraneans 60. *Breakfast at Tiffany's* 61. How the West was Won 62. The Victors 63. *The Carpetbaggers* 64. Operation Crossbow 65. The Third Day 65. *The Blue Max* 66. Tobruk 67. Rough Night in Jericho 67. P.J. 68. What's So Bad about Feeling Good? 68. House of Cards 68. Pendulum 68. The Executioner 69. Cannon for Cordoba 70. One More Train To Rob 70. The Bravos (TV) 71. The Groundstar Conspiracy 72. Newman's Law 74. One of Our Own (TV) 75. Guilty or Innocent: The Sam Sheppard Murder Case

(TV) 75. Damnation Alley 77. Your Ticket is No Longer Valid 79. From Hell To Victory 79. Torn between Two Lovers (TV) 79. Crisis in Mid Air (TV) 79. Battle Beyond the Stars 80. Five Days from Home (& d) 80. Race For the Yankee Zephyr 81.
TV series: *Banacek* 72–73. Doctors' Hospital 75. *The A-Team* 83–86.

Pepper, Barbara (1912–1969). American second-lead actress who usually played tramps.
Our Daily Bread 33. Winterset 36. Lady in the Morgue 38. Brewster's Millions 45. Terror Trail 47. Inferno 53. The D.I. 57. A Child is Waiting 63. Kiss Me Stupid 64, many others.

Percival, Lance (1933–). British light comedian.
Twice Round the Daffodils 62. The VIPs 63. Carry On Cruising 63. The Yellow Rolls-Royce 64. The Big Job 65. Darling Lili 69. Up Pompeii 71. Our Miss Fred 72, etc.

Percy, Esmé (1887–1957). Distinguished British stage actor, especially of Shavian parts. On stage from 1904; occasional films from twenties.
Murder 30. Bitter Sweet 33. *The Frog* 36. Pygmalion 38. Caesar and Cleopatra 45. The Ghosts of Berkeley Square 46. Death in the Hand 48, etc.

Pereira, Hal (1905–83). American art director, supervisor at Paramount from the fifties.
Carrie 52. Ace in the Hole 52. The Greatest Show on Earth 52. Red Garters 54. To Catch a Thief 55. The Ten Commandments 56. Vertigo 58. Hud 63, etc.

Perelman, S. J. (1904–1979). Renowned American humorist whose name appeared on a few films, mostly in collaboration.
Monkey Business 31. Horse Feathers 32. Ambush 39. The Golden Fleecing 40. Around the World in Eighty Days (AA) 56, etc.

Périer, Etienne (1931–). French director.
Bobosse 59. Murder at 45 RPM 60. Bridge to the Sun 61. Swordsman of Siena 63. When Eight Bells Toll 71. Zeppelin 71. Five against Capricorn 72. A Murder is a Murder 72, etc.

Perier, François (1919–) (François Pilu). Sturdy French actor, in films from mid-thirties.
Hotel du Nord 38. Un Revenant 46. Le Silence est d'Or 48. *Orphée* 49. The Bed 53. *Gervaise* 55. Nights of Cabiria 56. Charmants Garçons 57. Weekend at Dunkirk 65. The Samurai 67. The Red Circle 70. Just Before Nightfall 73. La Bar du Téléphone 80, many others.

The Perils of Pauline. Pearl White's famous 1914 serial was directed by Donald Mackenzie, co-starred Crane Wilbur, and concerned the heroine's evasion of attempts on her life by her dastardly guardian. The 1947 film of the same name was a lightly fictionalized biography of Pearl White, with Betty Hutton in the role; George Marshall directed. The 1967 film was vaguely based on the original serial, with Pamela Austin as the heroine, now involved in goings-on zanier than anything Pearl White dreamed of. Direction was by Herbert Leonard and Joshua Shelley.

Perinal, Georges (1897–1965). French cinematographer, in films from 1913.
Les Nouveaux Messieurs 28. Sous les Toits de Paris 30. *Le Sang d'un Poète* 30. *Le Million* 31. *A Nous la Liberté* 32. The Private Life of Henry VIII 32. *Rembrandt* 36. *The Thief of Baghdad* (AA) 40. *The Life and Death of Colonel Blimp* 43. *Nicholas Nickleby* 47. An Ideal Husband 47. *The Fallen Idol* 48. Lady Chatterley's Lover 55. A King in New York 57. Saint Joan 57. Bonjour Tristesse 58. Oscar Wilde 60, many others.

Perkins, Anthony (1932–). Gangly American juvenile lead of the fifties, son of Osgood Perkins. Found mature roles scarce.
□*The Actress* 53. Friendly Persuasion 56. The Lonely Man 57. *Desire Under the Elms* 57. *Fear Strikes Out* 57. The Tin Star 57. *This Angry Age* 58. The Matchmaker 58. Green Mansions 58. On the Beach 59. Tall Story 60. *Psycho* 60. Goodbye Again 61. Phaedra 62. Five Miles to Midnight 62. The Trial 62. Two are Guilty 64. The Fool Killer 64. A Ravishing Idiot 64. Is Paris Burning? 66. The Champagne Murders 68. Pretty Poison 68. Catch 22 70. *WUSA* 70. How Awful About Allan (TV) 70. Ten Days Wonder 71. Someone Behind the Door (Two Minds for Murder) 71. Judge Roy Bean 72. Play It as It Lays 72. Lovin' Molly 73. Murder on the Orient Express 74. Mahogany 75. Remember My Name 78. First You Cry (TV) 78. Winter Kills 79. The Black Hole 79. Double Negative 79. North Sea Hijack 80. Twice a Woman 80. Les Miserables (TV) 80. For the Term of His Natural Life (TV) 82. *Psycho II* 83. Sins of Dorian Gray (TV) 83. Crimes of Passion 85. Psycho III (& d) 86.

Famous line (*Psycho*): A boy's best friend is his mother.

Perkins, Millie (1939–). American leading lady who went to Hollywood from dramatic school.
The Diary of Anne Frank 59. Wild in the Country 61. Wild in the Streets 68. Lady Cocoa 75. Table for Five 83. At Close Range 85. Jake Speed 86. Slam Dance 87, etc.

Perkins, Osgood (1892–1937). American character actor, mainly on stage.
The Cradle Buster 22. Puritan Passions 23. Knockout Reilly 27. Mother's Boy 29. Tarnished Lady 31. Scarface 32. Kansas City Princess 34. I Dream Too Much 35, etc.

Perlberg, William (1899–1969). American producer, often in conjunction with George Seaton; came from agency business, in Hollywood from mid-thirties.
Golden Boy 39. The Song of Bernadette 43. Forever Amber 47. The Country Girl 54. Teacher's Pet 58. The Counterfeit Traitor 62. Thirty-Six Hours 64, many others.

Perreau, Gigi (1941–) (Ghislaine Perreau-Saussine). American child actress of the forties who seems not quite to have managed the transition to adult stardom.
Madame Curie 43. Song of Love 47. My Foolish Heart 49. Has Anybody Seen My Gal? 51. The Man in the Grey Flannel Suit 56. Wild Heritage 58. Look in Any Window 61. Journey to the Center of Time 67, others.
TV series: The Betty Hutton Show 59. Follow the Sun 69.

Perrine, Valerie (1944–). American leading lady of the seventies.
Slaughterhouse Five 72. The Last American Hero 73. Lenny 74. W. C. Fields and Me 76. Mr Billion 77. Ziegfeld: the Man and his Women (TV) 78. Superman 78. The Electric Horseman 79. Can't Stop the Music 80. Superman II 80. Agency 81. The Border 82. Water 85. When your Lover Leaves (TV) 85, etc.

Perrins, Leslie (1902–1962). British character actor, often seen as a smooth crook.
The Sleeping Cardinal 31. The Pointing Finger 34. Tudor Rose 36. Old Iron 39. The Woman's Angle 43. A Run for Your Money 49. Guilty 56, many others.

Perry, Eleanor (1925–81). American screenwriter; wrote all the scripts of her husband Frank Perry's films until their divorce in 1970. Then alone: *Diary of a Mad Housewife*, *The Lady in the Car*, *The Man Who Loved Cat Dancing*.

Perry, Frank (1930–). American director.
□David and Lisa 63. Ladybug, Ladybug 64. The Swimmer 68. Trilogy 68. Last Summer 69. Diary of a Mad Housewife 70. Doc 71. Play It as It Lays 72. Man on a Swing 74. Rancho de Luxe 76. Monsignor 82. Compromising Positions 85.

Perry, Paul P. (1891–1963). Pioneer American cinematographer who experimented with colour.
Rose of the Rancho 14. The Cheat 15. Hidden Pearls 17. The Sea Wolf 21. Rosita 23. Souls for Sables 26, many others.

persistence of vision. The medical explanation for our being able to see moving pictures. Twenty-four ordered still pictures are shown to us successively each second, and our sense of sight is slow enough to merge them into one continuous action. The retina of the eye retains each still picture just long enough for it to be replaced by another only slightly different.

Persoff, Nehemiah (1920–). Israeli actor, long in America; trained at Actors' Studio.
On the Waterfront 54. The Harder They Fall 56. *This Angry Age* 57. The Badlanders 58. Never Steal Anything Small 58. Al Capone 59. Some Like It Hot 59. The Big Show 61. The Comancheros 62. The Hook 63. *Fate is the Hunter* 64. The Greatest Story Ever Told 65. Panic in the City 68. Red Sky at Morning 71. Psychic Killer 75. Voyage of the Damned 76. The Word (TV) 78. Yentl 83, etc.

Persson, Essy (1941–). Swedish leading lady.
I a Woman 67. Thérèse and Isabelle 68. Cry of the Banshee 70, etc.

Pertwee, Jon (1919–). British comic actor, brother of Michael Pertwee, son of Roland.
Murder at the Windmill 48. Mr Drake's Duck 51. Will Any Gentleman? 53. A Yank in Ermine 56. Carry On Cleo 64. Carry On Screaming 66. The House that Dripped Blood 70. One of Our Dinosaurs is Missing 75. Adventures of a Private Eye 77, etc.
TV series: Doctor Who (title role) 70–74. Worzel Gummidge 79.

Pertwee, Michael (1916–). British playwright who has been involved in many screenplays.

Silent Dust (from his play) 48. The Interrupted Journey 49. *Laughter in Paradise* 51. Top Secret 52. Now and Forever 54. *The Naked Truth* 58. In the Doghouse 62. The Mouse on the Moon 62. Ladies Who Do 63. A Funny Thing Happened on the Way to the Forum 66. Finders Keepers 66. The Magnificent Two 67. Salt and Pepper 68. One More Time 70. Digby 73, etc.

Peters, Bernadette (1948–) (B. Lazarro). American leading lady of the seventies.
Ace Eli and Rodger of the Skies 72. The Longest Yard 74. The Jerk 79. Pennies from Heaven 81. Heartbeeps 81. Annie 82, etc.

Peters, Brock (1927–). Black American actor in international films.
To Kill a Mockingbird 62. The L-Shaped Room 62. *Heavens Above* (GB) 63. The Pawnbroker 64. Major Dundee 65. P. J. 67. The McMasters 70. Black Girl 73. Framed 75. Two Minute Warning 76. Star Trek IV: the Voyage Home 76, etc.

Peters, House (1880–1967). American silent screen leading man.
Leah Kleschna 12. The Pride of Jennico 14. The Great Divide 15. Mignon 15. The Storm 22. Held to Answer 23. Raffles 25. Head Winds 25, many others.

Peters, Jean (1926–). Attractive American leading lady of the fifties; retired to marry Howard Hughes.
□Captain from Castile 47. Deep Waters 48. It Happens Every Spring 49. Love That Brute 50. Take Care of My Little Girl 51. As Young as You Feel 51. Anne of the Indies 52. Viva Zapata 52. Wait Till the Sun Shines Nellie 52. Lure of the Wilderness 52. Full House 52. Niagara 53. Pickup on South Street 53. Blueprint for Murder 53. Vicki 53. *Three Coins in the Fountain* 54. Apache 54. Broken Lance 54. *A Man Called Peter* 55. The Moneychangers (TV) 74. Peter and Paul (TV) 81.

Peters, Jon (1947–). American producer, former hairdresser.
A Star Is Born 76. Eyes of Laura Mars 78. The Main Event 79. Die Laughing 80.

¶ *J.P.:* When I was in the hair business I produced huge spectacular shows. Film is just another form of production.

Peters, Susan (1921–1952) (Suzanne Carnahan). American leading lady of the forties; badly injured in an accident, she continued her career from a wheelchair.
Santa Fé Trail 40. *Random Harvest* 42. Assignment in Brittany 43. Song of Russia 44. Keep Your Powder Dry 45. The Sign of the Ram 48, etc.

Peters, Werner (1918–71). German character actor in occasional international films.
L'Affaire Blum 49. Der Untertan 51. The Girl Rosemarie 58. Scotland Yard vs. Dr Mabuse 63. The Corrupt Ones 66. Assignment K 68. Istanbul Express (TV) 68, etc.

Petersen, Colin (1946–). British child actor of the fifties.
Smiley 56. The Scamp 57. A Cry from the Streets 57, etc.

Petersen, Wolfgang (–). German director.
The Consequence 77. One or the Other 78. *The Boat* 81. The Neverending Story 83. Enemy Mine 85.

Peterson, Dorothy (c. 1900–1979). American supporting actress of the thirties, usually in maternal roles.
Cabin in the Cotton 32. I'm No Angel 33. Treasure Island 34. The Country Doctor 36. Dark Victory 39. Lillian Russell 40. The Moon Is Down 43. The Woman in the Window 45. That Hagen Girl 47, many others.

Petit, Pascale (1938–) (Anne-Marie Petit). French leading lady.
The Witches of Salem 57. Les Tricheurs 58. Girls for the Summer 59. L'Affaire d'Une Nuit 60. Demons at Midnight 62, etc.

Petri, Elio (1929–1982). Italian director, a political satirist.
The Assassin 61. The Tenth Victim 65. We Still Kill the Old Way 68. A Quiet Place in the Country 68. Investigation of a Citizen above Suspicion (AA) 69. The Working Class Goes to Heaven 71. Property is No Longer Theft 73. Todo Modo 76, etc.

Petrie, Daniel (1920–). American director with academic background; stage and TV experience.
□The Bramble Bush 59. A Raisin in the Sun 61. The Main Attraction 62. Stolen Hours 63. The Idol 66. The Spy with a Cold Nose 67. Silent Night Lonely Night (TV) 69. The City

(TV) 71. A Howling in the Woods (TV) 71. Moon of the Wolf (TV) 72. Trouble Comes to Town (TV) 72. The Neptune Factor 73. Buster and Billie 74. The Gun and the Pulpit (TV) 74. Eleanor and Franklin (TV) 76. Lifeguard 76. Sybil (TV) 77. The Betsy 78. Resurrection 80. Fort Apache the Bronx 81. Six Pack 82. Bay Boy 84. Square Dance 86.

Petrie, Daniel Jnr (–). American screenwriter who won an AA nomination with *Beverly Hills Cop*.

Petrie, Hay (1895–1948). Scots character actor of stage and screen, specializing in eccentrics.
Suspense 30. The Private Life of Henry VIII 32. Nell Gwyn 34. *The Old Curiosity Shop* (as Quilp) 34. The Ghost Goes West 36. *Twenty-One Days* 38. The Spy in Black 39. Q Planes 39. Jamaica Inn 39. Crimes at the Dark House 40. The Thief of Baghdad 40. One of Our Aircraft is Missing 42. A Canterbury Tale 44. Great Expectations 46. The Red Shoes 48. The Guinea Pig 48, etc.

The Petrified Forest (US 1936). A simple photographed version of Robert Sherwood's talkative play about an idealist, held captive by a gangster in a remote inn, who finally gives his life to save the other hostages. Remarkable chiefly for the opportunities it gave to three talents: Leslie Howard, Humphrey Bogart and Bette Davis. Directed by Archie Mayo.

Petrov, Vladimir (1896–1966). Russian director.
Thunderstorm 34. *Peter the Great* 38, etc.

Petrova, Olga (1886–1977) (Muriel Harding). British-born leading lady of Hollywood silents in which she played *femmes fatales*.
Autobiography 1942: *Butter with My Bread*.
The Tigress 14. The Soul Market 16. The Undying Flame 17. Daughter of Destiny 18. The Panther Woman 18, etc.

Pettet, Joanna (1944–). Anglo-American leading lady.
The Group 65. Night of the Generals 66. Robbery 67. Blue 68. The Weekend Nun (TV) 74. Welcome to Arrow Beach 75. Captains and the Kings (TV) 76. The Evil 78. The Return of Frank Cannon (TV) 80, etc.

Pettingell, Frank (1891–1966). British north-country character actor who dispensed rough good humour on stage from 1910; films from 1931.
Hobson's Choice (as Mossop) 31. Jealousy 31. *The Good Companions* 32. *Sing As We Go* 34. The Last Journey 36. Fame 36. Millions 36. Sailing Along 38. *Gaslight* 39. Busman's Honeymoon 40. The Seventh Survivor 41. This England 41. Kipps 41. Once a Crook 41. *When We are Married* 42. The Young Mr Pitt 42. Get Cracking 44. Gaiety George 46. The Magic Box 51. Meet Me Tonight 52. Value for Money 57. Becket 64, many others.

Pevney, Joseph (1920–). American director, former stage actor.
Shakedown 50. Undercover Girl 50. Iron Man 51. The Strange Door 51. Meet Danny Wilson 51. Just across the Street 52. Because of You 54. Desert Legion 54. The Female on the Beach 55. Three Ring Circus 55. Away All Boats 56. Congo Crossing 56. Tammy 57. *Man of a Thousand Faces* 57. Twilight for the Gods 58. Cash McCall 60. Night of the Grizzly 66, etc.

Peyton Place (US 1957). The film version of Grace Metalious' novel started a fashion for small-town sex exposés on the screen. A well-made film with particularly good colour photography by William Mellor, it was carefully produced by Jerry Wald, directed by Mark Robson and scripted by John Michael Hayes. A sequel, *Return to Peyton Place*, followed in 1961, and in 1964 came a TV serial of two half-hours a week; it proved so popular that from 1965 it was given three half-hours, and lasted until 1969.

Pfeiffer, Michelle (1957–). American actress.
Grease 2 82. Scarface 83. Into the Night 84. Ladyhawke 85. Sweet Liberty 86. The Witches of Eastwick 87.

The Phantom of the Opera. The melodramatic tale of the embittered disfigured composer who haunts the sewers beneath the Paris Opera House and takes a pretty young singer as his protégée has been filmed three times. 1. US 1925; directed by Rupert Julian; with Lon Chaney and Mary Philbin. 2. US 1943; directed by Arthur Lubin; with Claude Rains and Susanna Foster. 3. GB 1962; directed by Terence Fisher; with Herbert Lom and Heather Sears. The first version is without doubt the most interesting; the original story was by Gaston Leroux. In 1977 came a rock version, *Phantom of the Paradise*, and Maximilian Schell turned up in a TV movie in 1982.

The highly successful stage musical, premiered in 1986, will undoubtedly be filmed at some stage.

The Philadelphia Story (US 1940). This glossy cocktail comedy, not without its serious points, stands out as by far the most adult and successful film of its type. Adapted by Donald Ogden Stewart from the play by Philip Barry, it stars Katharine Hepburn in her stage role as Tracy Lord the idle rich heiress with the wrong kind of standards; Cary Grant as C. K. Dexter Haven, her ex-husband; James Stewart (AA) as Macaulay Connor, her would-be next, and in sterling support, Ruth Hussey, Roland Young, John Halliday, Mary Nash, Virginia Weidler and Henry Daniell. George Cukor directed with his accustomed dexterity. In 1956 the script was shortened and devitalized to permit the inclusion of some poor Cole Porter numbers under the title *High Society*. Grace Kelly filled Hepburn's shoes comfortably but Bing Crosby and Frank Sinatra were miscast and the whole thing was a fairly complete disaster; at least for anyone who remembered the original.

Philbin, Mary (1903–). American leading lady of the silent screen.
The Blazing Trail 21. Merry Go Round 23. Phantom of the Opera 25. The Man Who Laughs 28. After the Fog 30, etc.

Philip Marlowe was the weary but incorruptible private eye creation of Raymond Chandler, treading the seamier streets of Los Angeles in a dogged hunt for suspects. On television he was played in a poor series by Phil Carey, on screen by Humphrey Bogart, Robert Montgomery, George Montgomery, Dick Powell, James Garner, Robert Mitchum and (very badly) by Elliott Gould. In 1983 he was portrayed in a British television series, *Chandlertown*, by Powers Boothe.

Philipe, Gérard (1922–1959). France's leading young actor of the fifties, who alternated stage and screen activities.
Biography 1964: *No Longer Than a Sigh* by Anne Philipe.
□La Boite aux Rêves 43. The Children of the Flower Quay 45. Land without Stars 46. *The Idiot* 46. *Le Diable au Corps* 47. La Chartreuse de Parme 47. *Une Si Jolie Petite Plage* 49. All Roads Lead to Rome 49. La Beauté du Diable 50. La Ronde 50. Juliette ou la Clef des Songes 51. *Fanfan la Tulipe* 51. The Seven Deadly Sins 51. *Les Belles de Nuit* 52. Les Orgeuilleux 53. Versailles 53. Knave of Hearts (GB) 54. Villa Borghese 54. The Red and the Black 54. Les Grandes Manoeuvres 55. La Meilleure Part 55. Si Paris Nous Était Conté 55. Till Eulenspiegel 57. Pot Bouille 57. Montparnasse 19 57. La Vie à Deux 58. The Gambler 58. Les Liaisons Dangereuses 59. La Fièvre Monte à El Pao 59.

Philips, Conrad (1930–). British leading man, mostly on TV.
The White Trap 59. Chamber of Horrors 60. The Fourth Square 61. No Love for Johnnie 62. Stopover Forever 64. Who Killed the Cat? 66, etc.
TV series: *William Tell* 58.

Philips, Lee (1927–). American leading man of the late fifties.
Peyton Place 57. The Hunters 58. Middle of the Night 59. Tess of the Storm Country 60. The Lollipop Cover 65, etc.
Became TV director.

Philips, Mary (1900–1975). American stage actress who made very occasional film appearances.
Life Begins 32. A Farewell To Arms 33. That Certain Women 37. Lady in the Dark 44. Leave Her to Heaven 46. Dear Wife 47, etc.

Philips, Robin (1941–). British juvenile lead, later stage director in Canada.
Decline and Fall 68. David Copperfield 69. Two Gentlemen Sharing 70. Tales From the Crypt 72. Miss Julie (d) 73.

Philliber, John (1872–1944). Slightly-built American character actor in a few early forties films; best remembered for *It Happened Tomorrow* 44.

Phillips, Alex (1901–1977). Canadian cinematographer, long in Hollywood.
See My Lawyer 21. The Nervous Wreck 26. Many Mexican films 1930–52. Robinson Crusoe 52. Adam and Eve 57. Last of the Fast Guns 58. Geronimo 62. Then back to Mexico.

Phillips, Frank (–). American cinematographer.
The Island at the Top of the World 74. Escape to Witch Mountain 75. No Deposit No Return 76. The Shaggy D.A. 76. Pete's Dragon 77, etc.

Phillips, Julia (1945–) and **Michael** (1943–). American husband-and-wife producers who hit the big time with *The Sting*, *Taxi Driver* and *Close Encounters of the Third Kind.*

Phillips, Leslie (1924–). British light comedian, former child actor from 1935. The Citadel 38. Train of Events 49. The Sound Barrier 52. Value for Money 57. *Carry On Nurse* 59. Carry On Constable 60. Doctor in Love 60. Watch Your Stern 60. *Very Important Person* 61. Raising the Wind 61. In the Doghouse 62. Crooks Anonymous 62. *The Fast Lady* 62. And Father Came Too 64. Doctor in Clover 66. Maroc 7 (& p) 66. Doctor in Trouble 70. The Magnificent Seven Deadly Sins 71. Not Now Darling 73. Don't Just Lie There Say Something 73. Spanish Fly 75. Not Now Comrade 76, others.

Phillips, MacKenzie (1960–). American second lead of the seventies.
American Graffiti 75. Eleanor and Franklin (TV) 76, etc.

Phillips, Sian (1934–). Dignified British stage actress.
Becket 64. Young Cassidy 64. Laughter in the Dark 69. Goodbye Mr Chips 69. Murphy's War 70. Under Milk Wood 72. I, Claudius (TV) 76. Tinker Tailor Soldier Spy (TV) 79. Nijinksy 80. Clash of the Titans 81. Dune 85. The Doctor and the Devils 85. The Two Mrs Grenvilles (TV) 86.

Philo Vance: see *Van Dine, S. S.*

Philpotts, Ambrosine (1912–1980). British character actress, mainly on stage.
This Man is Mine 46. The Franchise Affair 51. The Captain's Paradise 53. Up in the World 56. Room at the Top 59. Doctor in Love 60. Life at the Top 65, etc.

Phipps, Nicholas (1913–1980). British light comedian often seen in cameo roles. On stage from 1932. Has also scripted or co-scripted many films:
Piccadilly Incident 46. Spring in Park Lane 48. Doctor in the House 53. Doctor in Love 60. The Wild and the Willing 62, many others. He appeared in most of these.

Pialat, Maurice (1925–). French director.
L'Enfance Nue 68. We Will Not Grow Old Together 72. La Guele Ouverte 73, etc.

Piazza, Ben (1934–). Canadian actor who went to Hollywood, but was little heard from.
A Dangerous Age (Can.) 58. The Hanging Tree 59. I Never Promised You a Rose Garden 77, etc.

Piccoli, Michel (1925–). Franco-Italian leading man.
French Cancan 55. The Witches of Salem 56. Le Bal des Espions 60. Le Mépris 63. Diary of a Chambermaid 64. De L'Amour 65. Lady L. 65. La Curée 66. The Young Girls of Rochefort 67. Un Homme de Trop 67. Belle de Jour 67. Dillinger is Dead 68. The Milky Way 69. Topaz 69. Blowout 73. The Infernal Trio 74. Mado 76. The Savage State 78. Le Sucre 78. A City 80. La Chambre Voisine 80. Leap into the Void 81. General of the Dead Army 81. Dangerous Moves 84. Revenge 84. Departure, Return 85. The Nonentity 86. Bad Blood 86, others.

Picerni, Paul (1922–). American leading man, usually in second features.
Saddle Tramp (debut) 50. Maru Maru 52. House of Wax 53. Drive a Crooked Road 54. Hell's Island 55. Omar Khayyam 57. Strangers When We Meet 60. The Scalphunters 68. The Land Raiders 69, etc.
TV series: The Untouchables 59–62.

Pichel, Irving (1891–1954). American actor-director, in Hollywood from 1930.
AS ACTOR: The Right to Love 30. The Miracle Man 31. Oliver Twist (as Fagin) 33. Cleopatra 34. Jezebel 38. Juarez 40. Sante Fé 51, many others.
□AS DIRECTOR: *The Most Dangerous Game* (co-d) 32. Before Dawn 33. *She* (co-d) 35. The Gentleman from Louisiana 36. Beware of Ladies 37. Larceny of the Air 37. The Sheik Steps Out 37. The Duke Comes Back 37. The Great Commandment 39. Earthbound 40. The Man I Married 40. Hudson's Bay 40. Dance Hall 41. Secret Agent of Japan 42. The Pied Piper 42. Life Begins at 8.30 42. *The Moon is Down* 43. *Happy Land* 43. And Now Tomorrow 44. A Medal for Benny 45. Colonel Effingham's Raid 45. Tomorrow is Forever 46. The Bride Wore Boots 46. O.S.S. 46. Temptation 46. They Won't Believe Me 47. Something in the Wind 47. The Miracle of the Bells 48. Mr Peabody and the Mermaid 48. Without Honor 49. The Great Rupert 50. Quicksand 50. Destination Moon 50. Santa Fe 51. Martin Luther 53. Day of Triumph 54.

Pick, Lupu: see *Lupu-Pick.*

Pickens, Slim (1919–83) (Louis Bert Lindley). Slow-talking American character actor, in scores of low-budget westerns from mid-forties, latterly in bigger films. The Sun

Shines Bright 53. The Great Locomotive Chase 56. One-Eyed Jacks 61. Dr Strangelove 63. Major Dundee 65. Rough Night in Jericho 67. The Cowboys 72. Pat Garrett and Billy the Kid 73. Blazing Saddles 74. The Apple Dumpling Gang 75. Whiteline Fever 75. The White Buffalo 77. Mr Billion 77. Wishbone Cutter 78. Beyond the Poseidon Adventure 79. Honeysuckle Rose 80. The Howling 81. Pink Motel 82, etc.
TV series: Outlaws 61. Custer 67.

Pickering, Donald (1933–). British actor who played Holmes in the little seen 1980 TV series *Sherlock Holmes and Dr Watson*.
A Bridge Too Far 76. The 39 Steps 78. Half Moon Street 87, etc.

Pickford, Jack (1896–1933). American light actor, brother of Mary Pickford.
Tom Sawyer 17. Sandy 18. Just Out of College 21. The Goose Woman 25. The Bat 26. Brown of Harvard 26. Exit Smiling 26. Gang War 28, etc.

Pickford, Mary (1893–1979) (Gladys Smith). Canadian actress who in the heyday of silent films was known as 'the world's sweetheart'; became co-founder of United Artists Films and one of America's richest women. Acting on stage from five years old; was brought into films by D. W. Griffith. Autobiography 1955: *Sunshine and Shadow*. Biography 1974: *Sweetheart* by Robert Windeler. Special Academy Award 1976.
Her First Biscuits 09. The Violin Maker of Cremona 10. The Paris Hat 13. Madame Butterfly 15. Less Than the Dust 16. The Little Princess 17. Rebecca of Sunnybrook Farm 17. Stella Maris 18. *Pollyanna* 19. Suds 20. *Little Lord Fauntleroy* 21. The Love Light 21. *Tess of the Storm Country* 22. Rosita 23. Dorothy Vernon of Haddon Hall 24. Little Annie Rooney 25. My Best Girl 27. The Taming of the Shrew 29. Secrets 29. *Coquette* (AA) 29. Kiki 31. Secrets 33, many others.
❀ For entrancing the world, and for knowing when to stop. *Little Lord Fauntleroy*.

¶ The appeal of the world's sweetheart is not well understood in the eighties. Her screen image was ever-childlike, sweet and demure, the antithesis of today's heroines. Alistair Cooke said:

> She was the girl every young man wanted to have—as his sister.

Yet on first encounter D. W. Griffith told her:

> You're too little and too fat, but I might give you a job.

Later, he ruefully recollected:

> She never stopped listening and learning.

She was soon telling Adolph Zukor:

> I can't afford to work for only ten thousand dollars a week.

And Sam Goldwyn reflected:

> It took longer to make one of Mary's contracts than it did to make one of Mary's pictures.

Spoiled by success she may have been, but never blind to her own failings:

> I never liked one of my pictures in its entirety.

By 1929 she was surprisingly intolerant of her screen image:

> I am sick of Cinderella parts, of wearing rags and tatters. I want to wear smart clothes and play the lover.

Richard Griffith and Arthur Mayer thought the secret of her success was that:

> Her sweetness and light were tempered by a certain realism. In spite of her creed, the Glad Girl knew it was no cinch to make everything come out right. Nothing could have been more in tune with an era which combined limitless optimism with a belief that 'git up and git' was necessary to make optimism come true.

But Mabel Normand at a press conference struck a sour note:

> Say anything you like, but don't say I want to work. That sounds like Mary Pickford, that prissy bitch.

Pickles, Vivian (1933–) British character actress.
Play Dirty 68. Nicholas and Alexandra 71. Harold and Maude 71. Sunday Bloody Sunday 72. O Lucky Man 73. Candleshoe 77, etc.

Pickles, Wilfred (1904–1978). British radio personality and latterly character actor; played Yorkshiremen.
Autobiography 1949: *Between You and Me*.
The Gay Dog 53. Billy Liar 63. The Family Way 66. For the Love of Ada 72, etc.

Pickup, Ronald (1940–). British character actor, mainly on stage.
Three Sisters 68. Day of the Jackal 73. Mahler 74. Jennie (TV) (as Randolph Churchill) 75. Joseph Andrews 76. The 39 Steps 78. Zulu Dawn 79. Nijinsky 80. The Letter (TV) 82. Ivanhoe (TV) 82. Never Say Never Again 83. Eleni 85. The Mission 86. Fortunes of War (TV) 87.

Picnic (US 1955). Based on the play by William Inge, this over-heated melodrama of small town American sex life—or rather the lack of it—seemed at the time to be starting an American 'new wave'. It had the new sex symbol Kim Novak; the popular William Holden as the virile young stranger; Rosalind Russell as the repressed schoolmistress; and an insistent theme tune called 'Moonglow' adapted by George Duning from an old jazz standard. Joshua Logan's direction was generally lethargic, but James Wong Howe's colour photography did a lot to compensate.The success of the movie led to a long spate of imitations: *The Long Hot Summer*, *Peyton Place*, *The Bramble Bush*, *A Summer Place*, etc.

Picon, Molly (1898–). American stage actress; films very occasional.
Come Blow Your Horn 63. Fiddler on the Roof 71. For Pete's Sake 74, etc.

Picture, by Lillian Ross. One of the wittiest and indeed most scathing books ever written about the process of Hollywood film-making in the days of the great studios. This journalist was unwisely allowed to sit in on every aspect of the production of *The Red Badge of Courage*, and everybody concerned is allowed to condemn himself by direct quotation. First published 1953.

The Picture of Dorian Gray (US 1944). Albert Lewin adapted and directed Oscar Wilde's macabre fantasy about a man who stays young while his portrait shows his debauchery, and a remarkably successful film it was, like an exotic Victorian hothouse, with Hurd Hatfield suitably impassive in the lead and George Sanders uttering epigrams in the background. The director's obvious passion for Egyptian cats and Omar Khayyam, however, was a signpost to the absurdity of his later films. A German remake in 1969 had little quality.

Pidgeon, Walter (1897–1984).
Good-looking, quiet-spoken Canadian leading man in Hollywood; during the thirties and forties he gave gentlemanly support to several dominant leading ladies.
□Mannequin 25. Old Loves and New 26. The Outsider 26. Miss Nobody 26. Marriage License 26. The Girl from Rio 27. The Heart of Salome 27. The Gorilla 27. The Thirteenth Juror 27. Gateway of the Moon 27. Clothes Make the Woman 28. Woman Wise 28. Turn Back the Hours 28. Melody of Love 28. A Most Immoral Lady 29. Her Private Life 29. Bride of the Regiment 30. Sweet Kitty Bellairs 30. Viennese Nights 30. Kiss Me Again 30. Going Wild 30. The Gorilla 31. The Hot Heiress 31. Rockabye 32. The Kiss Before the Mirror 33. Journal of a Crime 34. Big Brown Eyes 36. Fatal Lady 36. Girl Overboard 37. Saratoga 37. A Girl with Ideas 37. She's Dangerous 37. As Good as Married 37. My Dear Miss Aldrich 37. Man Proof 38. The Girl of the Golden West 38. Shopworn Angel 38. Too Hot to Handle 38. Listen Darling 38. *Society Lawyer* 39. Six Thousand Enemies 39. Stronger than Desire 39. Nick Carter Master Detective 39. The House across the Bay 40. It's a Date 40. Dark Command 40. Phantom Raiders 40. Sky Murder 40. Flight Command 40. *Man Hunt* 41. *Blossoms in the Dust* 41. *How Green was My Valley* 41. Design for Scandal 42. *Mrs Miniver* 42. White Cargo 42. The Youngest Profession 43. *Madame Curie* 43. Mrs Parkington 44. Weekend at the Waldorf 45. Holiday in Mexico 46. The Secret Heart 46. Cass Timberlane 47. If Winter Comes 47. Julia Misbehaves 48. Command Decision 48. *That Forsyte Woman* (as Young Jolyon) 49. The Red Danube 49. The Miniver Story 50. Soldiers Three 51. Calling Bulldog Drummond 51. The Unknown Man 51. The Sellout 52. Million Dollar Mermaid 52. The Bad and the Beautiful 52. Scandal at Scourie 53. Dream Wife 53. *Executive Suite* 54. Men of the Fighting Lady 54. The Last Time I Saw Paris 54. Deep in My Heart 54. Hit the Deck 55. The Glass Slipper 55. *Forbidden Planet* 56. These Wilder Years 56. The Rack 56. Voyage to the Bottom of the Sea 61. *Advise and Consent* 62. The Two Colonels 62. Big Red 62. The Shortest Day 63. Cosa Nostra (TV) 67. Warning Shot 67. Funny Girl (as Ziegfeld) 68. Rascal 69. The Mask of Sheba (TV) 69. The Vatican Affair 69. Skyjacked 72. The Neptune Factor 73. Harry in Your Pocket 73. Yellow Headed Summer 74. Live Again Die Again (TV) 75. You Lie So Deep My Love (TV) 75. The Lindbergh Kidnapping Case (TV) 76. Murder at 40,000 Feet (TV) 76. Two Minute Warning 76. Sextette 77.

Pierce, Jack (1889–1968). American make-up artist who worked at Universal for many years and created the familiar images of Dracula, the Wolf Man, the Mummy and the Frankenstein monster.

Pierlot, Francis (1876–1955). American character actor, usually of mild professorial types.

Night Angel 31. The Captain is a Lady 40. Night Monster 42. The Doughgirls 44. Dragonwyck 46. The Late George Apley 47. That Wonderful Urge 48. My Friend Irma 49. Cyrano de Bergerac 50. The Robe 53, many others.

Pierson, Frank L. (1945–). American director, from TV.
Cat Ballou (co-w) 65. The Looking Glass War 69. The Anderson Tapes (w only) 71. Dog Day Afternoon (AA) (w only) 75. A Star Is Born (d only) 76. King of the Gypsies (w only) 78, etc.
TV series: *Nichols* 71.

Pigott, Tempe (1884–1962). British character actress in Hollywood, usually as garrulous cockney.
Seven Days' Leave 30. Cavalcade 33. One More River 34. Limehouse Blues 35. Becky Sharp 35, etc.

Piggott-Smith, Tim (–). British character actor.
Sweet William 79. Richard's Things (TV) 80. Clash of the Titans 81. Victory 81. *The Jewel in the Crown* (TV) 82. A State of Emergency 86.

Pilbeam, Nova (1919–). British teenage star of the thirties.
Little Friend 34. The Man Who Knew Too Much 34. *Tudor Rose* 35. *Young and Innocent* 37. Spring Meeting 40. Banana Ridge 41. This Man is Mine 46. Counterblast 47. The Three Weird Sisters 48, etc.

pilot: in television terminology, a film which is made as a trial, to see whether a series on the same premise will be ordered.

pin screen animation: a curious and short-lived means of animation by photographing pins pushed through a rubber sheet. The shadows caused by the varying height of the pins gives the single picture. The best example is Alexieff's *Night on Bald Mountain* 33.

Pine, William H. (1896–1955) and **Thomas, William C.** (1892–). An American production executive and an exhibitor-writer who banded together in the early forties to make scores of second features for Paramount. *Power Dive, Wildcat, Midnight Manhunt, They Made Me a Killer, Wrecking Crew, Torpedo Boat, I Cover Big Town*, etc. Continued into the fifties with larger-scale adventures: *Sangaree, Jamaica Run, The Far Horizons*, etc., but never managed a top-notcher. Because of their economy they were known as 'the Dollar Bills'. Thomas was almost always the director of their joint productions.

Pinero, Sir Arthur Wing (1855–1934). British playwright who dealt mainly with the upper middle class. Many films were made of his work in silent days; the most popular later were *The Second Mrs Tanqueray* and *The Enchanted Cottage,* though his farce *The Magistrate* had several incarnations, notably as *Those Were the Days* 34.

Pinewood Studios, seventeen miles northwest of London, was built in 1935 and opened in 1936 by a millionaire named Charles Boot as Britain's reply to Hollywood. It rapidly came under the control of the Rank Organisation, and its fortunes have fluctuated, but on the whole it has been fairly well used.
History published 1976: *Movies from the Mansion* by George Perry.

The Pink Panther (US 1963). An amiable star-studded romp about jewel robbers, this rather patchy comedy by Blake Edwards surprisingly triggered off a cartoon series featuring the Pink Panther (who does not appear in the film except as a title design: the title refers to a jewel) as well as four sequels about the accident-prone detective created by Peter Sellers: *A Shot in the Dark* 64 (with Sellers), *Inspector Clouseau* 68 (with Alan Arkin), *The Return of the Pink Panther* 75 (Sellers), *The Pink Panther Strikes Again* 76 and *The Revenge of the Pink Panther* 78. There were no bouquets for the patchwork jobs made in the eighties, *Trail of the Pink Panther* and *Curse of the Pink Panther.*

Pink, Sidney (1916–). American director.
Journey to the Seventh Planet 61. Reptilicus 62. Finger on the Trigger 65. The Tall Women 66.

Pinky (US 1949). A moderately pioneering Hollywood contribution to race relations, this quiet tale of a negress who 'passed' for white but felt bound to tell the truth about herself was somewhat compromised by the casting of white Jeanne Crain in the role. But the script by Philip Dunne and Dudley Nichols was generally intelligent and thoughtful, and both the photography by Joe MacDonald and the direction by Elia Kazan were more than competent.

Pinsent, Gordon (1933–). Canadian leading actor, much on TV.
The Thomas Crown Affair 68. The Forbin Project 69. Quarantined (TV) 69. The Rowdy Man 72. Newman's Law 74, etc.
TV series: *Quentin Durgens MP* 66.

Pinter, Harold (1930–). British playwright, and juggler of nonsense plotting and obscure motivation. His film scripts have been more straightforward.
□The Servant (w) 63. The Caretaker (oaw) 64. The Pumpkin Eater (w) (BFA) 64. The Quiller Memorandum (w) 67. Accident (w) 67. The Birthday Party (woa) 69. The Go Between (w) 71. The Homecoming (oa) 73. Butley (d) 73. Rogue Male (TV) (a) 76. The Last Tycoon (w) 76. The French Lieutenant's Woman (W) 81. Betrayal (AAN) 83. Turtle Diary 85.

¶ *H.P.:* What concerns me most is shape and structure.

Pintoff, Ernest (1931–). Modernist American cartoon maker: Flebus 57. *The Violinist* 59. *The Interview* 60. *The Critic* 63, etc.
Also wrote and directed live-action features: Harvey Middlemann, Fireman 64. Dynamite Chicken 69. Who Killed Mary What's Her Name 70. Blade 75.

Pinza, Ezio (1893–1957) (Fortunato Pinza). Italian-American opera singer who graced a few films.
□Carnegie Hall 48. Mr Imperium 50. Slightly Dishonorable 51. Tonight We Sing 53.

Pious, Minerva (1909–1979). American radio comedienne of the forties, famous with Fred Allen as Mrs Nussbaum.
It's In the Bag 45. The Ambassador's Daughter 56. Love in the Afternoon 57, etc.

Piper, Frederick (1902–1979). British character actor, mostly on stage: usually played the average man or police inspector.
The Good Companions 32. Jamaica Inn 39. Hue and Cry 46. Passport to Pimlico 48. The Blue Lamp 50. Doctor at Sea 55. Very Important Person 61. One Way Pendulum 64. He Who Rides a Tiger 65, etc.

The Pirate (US 1948). One of the first signs of the new trend in musicals which was to come with *On the Town* and *An American in Paris*, this stage-bound operetta didn't manage as a whole to rise above its conventions, but it did have splendid moments. Judy Garland, Gene Kelly and the Nicholas Brothers were involved, and althcugh Cole Porter's songs were below his best, they were put over with vigour.
Directed by Vincente Minnelli, photographed by Harry Stradling, book by Albert Hackett and Frances Goodrich.

pirates have regularly appeared on the screen. Stories with some claim to historical authenticity, or at least based on the exploits of a pirate who once lived, include *Captain Blood* (and its various sequels), *The Black Swan, Morgan the Pirate, Seven Seas to Calais, Blackbeard the Pirate, Captain Kidd, The Buccaneer*, and *Anne of the Indies* (a rare female pirate: one other was depicted in *The Pirate Queen*). Totally fictitious stories are of course headed by *Treasure Island* (qv) in its various versions; other swashbuckling yarns included *The Sea Hawk, The Black Pirate, The Crimson Pirate, The Golden Hawk, Fair Wind to Java, A High Wind in Jamaica, Pirates of Tortuga, Yankee Buccaneer, The Spanish Main, Pirates of Tripoli, Devil Ship Pirates, Pirates of Blood River, Prince of Pirates*, and *Raiders of the Seven Seas*. The only notable musical pirate was Gene Kelly in *The Pirate*; comic pirates are also rare, but they do include *The Princess and the Pirate, Blackbeard's Ghost, Double Crossbones, The Dancing Pirate* and *Old Mother Riley's Jungle Treasure*. 1983's *Yellowbeard* was a sad spoof of the genre. *Pirates* in 1985 didn't even seem to know whether it was a spoof or not.

Pirosh, Robert (1910–). American writer-director.
The Winning Ticket (oa) 35. A Day at the Races (w) 37. I Married a Witch (w) 42. Rings on Her Fingers (w) 42. Up In Arms (w) 44. *Battleground* (w) (AA) 49. Go for Broke (wd) 51. Washington Story (wd) 52. Valley of the Kings (wd) 54. The Girl Rush (wd) 55. Spring Reunion (wd) 57. Hell is for Heroes (w) 62. A Gathering of Eagles (w) 63. What's so Bad about Feeling Good? (w) 68, etc.

Pisier, Marie-France (1944–). French leading lady of the seventies.
French Provincial 76. Love at Twenty 76. Cousin Cousine 76. The Other Side of Midnight 76. Barocco 77. Sérail 77. Love on the Run 79. French Postcards 79. La Banquière 80.

Pithey, Wensley (1914–). Heavily built British character actor.

Oliver! 68. Oh What a Lovely War 69. One of our Dinosaurs is Missing 74. Ike (TV) (as Churchill) 79, etc.

Pitt, Ingrid (1944–) (Ingrid Petrov). Polish-born leading lady in British films.
Where Eagles Dare 69. The Vampire Lovers 70. The House that Dripped Blood 71. Countess Dracula 71. Nobody Ordered Love 72. The Wicker Man 73. Smiley's People (TV) 82. Who Dares Wins 82. Wild Geese II 86. Parker 86, etc.

Pitts, Zasu (1898–1963). American actress, a heroine of the twenties and a tearful comedienne of the thirties.
The Little Princess 17. Early to Wed 21. *Greed* 23. Twin Beds 27. The Wedding March 28. Seed 30. Bad Sister 31. The Guardsman 32. Back Street 32. Walking Down Broadway 32. many two-reeler comedies with Thelma Todd (32–34), Dames 34. Mrs Wiggs of the Cabbage Patch 34. Ruggles of Red Gap 35. So's Your Aunt Emma 38. Buck Privates 39. Nurse Edith Cavell 40. Niagara Falls 41. Let's Face It 43. Life with Father 47. Francis 50. Francis Joins the WACS 55. This Could be the Night 57. It's a Mad Mad Mad Mad World 63, many others.
TV series: Oh Susanna 56–59.

† Zasu was originally cast as the mother in *All Quiet on the Western Front*. Her scenes were reshot after preview audiences laughed.

Pizer, Larry (–). British cinematographer.
The Party's Over 63. Four in the Morning 65. Morgan 65. Our Mother's House 66. Isadora 68. All Neat in Black Stockings 69. Phantom of the Paradise 74. Grace Quigley 85, etc.

A Place in the Sun (US 1951). Now almost forgotten, this version of Theodore Dreiser's *An American Tragedy* (previously filmed in 1931 with Phillips Holmes) was hailed by some critics at the time of its release as one of the greatest films of all time. It is now difficult to see why. Slowly and pretentiously directed by George Stevens, its story of a young man's efforts to get into high society at any cost even then seemed dated and empty. Montgomery Clift did what he could with an unsympathetic role, and William C. Mellor's photography was luxurious.

The Plainsman (US 1937). Cecil B. de Mille's well-remembered western starred Gary Cooper as Wild Bill Hickok, James Ellison as Buffalo Bill, and Jean Arthur as Calamity Jane. It was poorly remade in 1966 with Don Murray, Guy Stockwell and Abby Dalton.

Planck, Robert (1894–). American cinematographer.
Our Daily Bread 33. *Jane Eyre* 43. Cass Timberlane 47. The Three Musketeers 48. Little Women 49. Rhapsody 54. Moonfleet 55, etc.

Planer, Franz (1894–1963). German cinematographer, in Hollywood from 1937.
Drei von Der Tankstelle 30. *Liebelei* 33. Maskerade 34. The Beloved Vagabond (GB) 36. Holiday 38. The Face Behind the Mask 41. The Adventures of Martin Eden 42. Once Upon a Time 44. The Chase 47. *Letter from an Unknown Woman* 48. Criss Cross 48. The Scarf 51. The Blue Veil 51. *Death of a Salesman* 52. Twenty Thousand Leagues under the Sea 54. Not as a Stranger 55. The Pride and the Passion 57. *The Big Country* 58. *The Nun's Story* 59. The Unforgiven 60. The Children's Hour 62, etc.

Planet of the Apes (US 1967). Adapted by Paul Dehn from a novel by Pierre Boulle and stylishly directed by Franklin Schaffner, this distinctive piece of science fiction had Charlton Heston as an astronaut who, caught in a time warp, finds himself on a planet where the humans have degenerated and the apes rule with wisdom. A last minute twist reveals the planet to be Earth at some time in the future, when war has reduced our present civilizations to ruins. Taken up by the young as a moral parable, the film had great success and spawned four sequels of increasing violence and decreasing interest: *Beneath the Planet of the Apes* 69, *Escape from the Planet of the Apes* 70, *Conquest of the Planet of the Apes* 72, *Battle for the Planet of the Apes* 73. A TV series in 1974 was shortlived. Mention should be made of the splendidly flexible ape make-up by John Chambers.

Pleschkes, Otto (1931–). Austrian producer, in Britain.
Georgy Girl 66. The Bofors Gun 68. The Homecoming 73, etc.

plastic surgery was long a staple of horror films, but improved techniques have made it a subject for 'woman's pictures' such as *Ash Wednesday* and *Once is not Enough*. *Arsenic and Old Lace* made a comedy point of it, and *Seconds* took it seriously. Other examples: *Dark Passage*, *False Faces*, *A Woman's Face*, *Eyes without a Face*.

Platt, Edward (1916–1974). American character actor who usually plays generals, stern fathers and similar types.
The Shrike 55. Rebel Without a Cause 55. Serenade 56. The Great Man 56. Designing Woman 57. The Gift of Love 58. North by Northwest 59. Pollyana 60. A Ticklish Affair 63, many others.
TV series: *Get Smart* 65–69.

Platt, Louise (1914–). American leading lady who retired after a brief career.
Spawn of the North 38. *Stagecoach* 39. Forgotten Girls 40. Captain Caution 40. Street of Chance 41, etc.

Platt, Marc (1913–). American dancer and lightweight actor: few appearances.
Tonight and Every Night 44. Tars and Spars 44. Down to Earth 47. Seven Brides for Seven Brothers 54. Oklahoma 55, etc.

Platt, Polly (–). American production designer.
The Last Picture Show 71. What's Up Doc? 72. Paper Moon 73. The Thief Who Came to Dinner 73. A Star Is Born 76. Pretty Baby 78. Young Doctors in Love 82. Terms of Endearment 83, etc.

Platts-Mills, Barney (1944–). British independent director of low-budget films.
□Bronco Bullfrog 70. Private Road 71.

play into film

? Name the films made from these plays.

1 *Birthday* by Laszlo Bus-Fekete
2 *Heaven Can Wait* by Harry Segall
3 *Matilda Shouted Fire* by Janet Green
4 *Years Ago* by Ruth Gordon
5 *Washington Square* by Henry James
6 *The Merchant of Yonkers* by Thornton Wilder
7 *Diamond Lil* by Mae West
8 *Everybody Comes to Rick's* by Murray Burnett and Joan Alison
9 *Liliom* by Ferenc Molnar
10 *Napoleon of Broadway* by Charles Bruce Milholland
11 *The Time of the Cuckoo* by Arthur Laurents
12 *The Milk Train Doesn't Stop Here Any More* by Tennessee Williams
13 *Amy Jolly* by Benno Vigny
14 *The Silent Voice* by Jules Eckert Goodman
15 *The Tempest* by William Shakespeare
16 *The Sleeping Prince* by Terence Rattigan
17 *Dr Praetorious* by Curt Goetz
18 *Come Primo Mellio de Prima* by Luigi Pirandello
19 *Henry IV, Parts One And Two*, by William Shakespeare
20 *Fragile Fox* by Norman Brooks
21 *Cuisine des Anges* by Albert Husson
22 *A Loss of Roses* by William Inge
23 *Green Grow the Lilacs* by Lynn Riggs
24 *Joan of Lorraine* by Maxwell Anderson

Pleasence, Donald (1919–). Bald, pale-eyed British character actor usually seen in villainous or eccentric roles.
Manuela 57. A Tale of Two Cities 57. The Flesh and the Fiends 59. Hell Is a City 60. No Love for Johnnie 61. Dr Crippen 62. The Great Escape 63. *The Caretaker* 64. The Greatest Story Ever Told 65. The Hallelujah Trail 65. Fantastic Voyage 66. Cul de Sac 66. The Night of the Generals 66. Eye of the Devil 67. Will Penny 67. The Madwoman of Chaillot 69. Soldier Blue 70. Outback 71. The Jerusalem File 72. Henry VIII and His Six Wives 72. Innocent Bystanders 72. Tales That Witness Madness 73. The Mutations 73. The Black Windmill 74. Hearts of the West 75. Trial by Combat 76. The Last Tycoon 76. The Eagle has Landed (as Himmler) 76. Jesus of Nazareth (TV) 77. Oh God 77. Telefon 77. The Passover Plot 77. Hallowe'en 78. Sergeant Pepper's Lonely Hearts Club Band 78. Dracula 79. All Quiet on the Western Front (TV) 80. Escape from New York 81. Halloween II 81. Alone in the Dark 82. The Devonsville Terror 83. Where is Parsifal? 84. Arch of Triumph (TV) 84. The Last Days of Pompeii (TV) 85. Scoop (TV) 87. Ground Zero 87, etc.
TV series: Robin Hood (as Prince John) 55–57.

Pleshette, Suzanne (1937–). Intelligent American leading actress whose roles have been generally disappointing.
□The Geisha Boy 58. Rome Adventure 62. Forty Pounds of Trouble 63. The Birds 63. Wall of Noise 63. A Distant Trumpet 64. Fate is the Hunter 64. Youngblood Hawke 64. A Rage to Live 65. The Ugly Dachshund 66. Nevada Smith 66. Mister Buddwing 66. The Adventures of Bullwhip Griffin 67. Wings of Fire (TV) 67. Blackbeard's Ghost 68. The Power 68. If It's Tuesday This Must Be Belgium 69. Along Came a Spider 69. Suppose They Gave a War and Nobody Came 69. Support Your Local Gunfighter 71. In

Broad Daylight (TV) 71. Beyond the Bermuda Triangle (TV) 75. The Legend of Valentino (TV) 75. Return of the Pink Panther 75. The Shaggy D.A. 76. Kate Bliss and the Tickertape Kid (TV) 78. *Flesh and Blood* (TV) 79. Hot Stuff 79. Oh God Book Two 80.
TV series: The Bob Newhart Show 72. Maggie Briggs 84.

¶ *S.P.:* I don't sit around and wait for great parts. I'm an actress, and I love being one, and I'll probably be doing it till I'm 72, standing around the backlot doing Gunsmokes.

the plot thickens

? Can you recognize these well-known films from the following accurate but rather po-faced descriptions of their plots?

1 A journalist sets out to interview Susan Alexander, followed by Messrs Bernstein, Leland and Raymond, in his search for the truth about a tycoon recently deceased.
2 Mr and Mrs Charles Condomine invite to dinner Dr and Mrs Bradman plus one other guest who inadvertently brings along someone quite unexpected and unwanted.
3 Fred Blythe and Charlie Wilder are among the people who turn up at an old house for the reading of a will by Lawyer Crosby.
4 Johnny Jones is told by his editor to change his name to Huntley Haverstock and head for London.
5 Peter Warne spots a runaway heiress at a bus station.
6 Somewhere in Europe, Miss Froy is among several English people waiting for a train to take them home.
7 As schoolchildren, Randy Monaghan, Parris Mitchell, Cassandra Tower and Drake McHugh form a friendship which in adult life has some tragic repercussions.
8 George Bailey tries to commit suicide but is dissuaded by an angel.
9 In New York's Plaza Hotel, Roger Thornhill is mistaken for someone else.
10 Roger Penderel and Philip Waverton, among others, are stranded at night in the Welsh hills during a storm.
11 Wally Cook is sent by his editor to a Vermont village to cover the story of a dying girl.
12 Marion Crane and her boyfriend enjoy some lunchtime lovemaking, after which events suddenly send her on a fatal drive.
13 A man whose real name is Charles Rainier, but becomes temporarily known as Smitty, escapes from a mental institution in the English Midlands.
14 In San Francisco, a detective named Miles Archer is shot during his first night on what seems to be a simple case.
15 Monte Beragon is murdered in his beach house by one of two women.

Plowright, Joan (1929–). Leading British stage actress, married to Laurence Olivier.
Time Without Pity 58. The Entertainer 60. Equus 77. The Diary of Anne Frank (TV) 81. Britannia Hospital 82. Brimstone and Treacle 82. Wagner 82. Drowning by Numbers 88.

Plummer, Christopher (1927–). Canadian leading man with stage experience including Shakespeare.
□Stage Struck 58. Wind Across the Everglades 58. *The Fall of the Roman Empire* 64. *The Sound of Music* 65. Inside Daisy Clover 65. The Night of the Generals 67. Triple Cross 67. Oedipus the King 67. Nobody Runs Forever 68. Lock Up Your Daughters 69. The Royal Hunt of the Sun 69. The Battle of Britain 69. *Waterloo* (as the Duke of Wellington) 70. The Pyx 73. Conduct Unbecoming 75. The Spiral Staircase 75. The Man Who Would be King 75. The Return of the Pink Panther 75. The Moneychangers (TV) 75. Aces High 76. Jesus of Nazareth (TV) 77. The Day that Shook the World 77. The Assignment 77. The Disappearance 77. The Silent Partner 78. Starcrash 78. International Velvet 78. Murder by Decree 79. Hanover Street 79. Somewhere in Time 80. Highpoint 80. Eyewitness 81. Little Gloria . . . Happy at Last (TV) 82. The Amateur 82. Lily in Love 84. Dreamscape 84. Dragnet 87.

¶ *C.P.:* I'm bored with questions about acting.
C.P.: Unless you can surround yourself with as many beautiful things as you can afford, I don't think life has very much meaning.

Plunkett, Patricia (1928–). British leading lady of the early fifties.
It Always Rains on Sunday 47. Bond Street 48. For Them That Trespass 48. Landfall 50. Murder Without Crime 52. Mandy 53. The Crowded Day 55. Dunkirk 58, etc.

Plunkett, Walter (1902–1982). American costume designer.
Hit the Deck 29. Rio Rita 29. Cimarron 31. *Little Women* 33. *The Gay Divorcee* 34. Of Human Bondage 34. Mary of Scotland 36.

Quality Street 37. *Gone with the Wind* 39. *The Hunchback of Notre Dame* 39. Stagecoach 39. Ladies in Retirement 41. To Be or Not to Be 42. A Song to Remember 45. Duel in the Sun 46. The Three Musketeers 48. That Forsyte Woman 49. *An American in Paris* (AA) 51. *The Prisoner of Zenda* 52. *Kiss Me Kate* 53. Seven Brides for Seven Brothers 54. Lust for Life 56. Pollyanna 60. How the West was Won 63. Seven Women 66, many others.

Podesta, Rossana (1934–). Italian leading lady who has been in international films.
Cops and Robbers 51. La Red 53. Ulysses 54. Helen of Troy 56. Santiago 58. The Golden Arrow 65. Il Prete Sposato 70. The Sensual Man 75, many others.

Poe, Edgar Allan (1809–1849). American poet, story-writer and manic depressive, whose tortured life as well as his strange tales have been eagerly seized upon by film-makers. Griffith made *The Life of Edgar Allan Poe* in 1909, and in 1912 another version was disguised as *The Raven.* In 1915 Charles Brabin made another film called *The Raven* with Henry B. Walthall as Poe; a few months earlier Griffith had released his own alternative version under the title *The Avenging Conscience.* The next film called *The Raven*, in 1935, starred Karloff and Lugosi and had nothing to do with Poe's life, being merely an amalgam of his stories; but in 1942 Fox brought out *The Loves of Edgar Allan Poe* starring Shepperd Strudwick; and in 1951 MGM made a curious melodrama called *Man with a Cloak*, in which the dark stranger who solved the mystery signed himself 'Dupin' and was played by Joseph Cotten in the Poe manner.

Of the stories, *The Mystery of Marie Roget* was filmed by Universal in 1931 and 1942; *The Tell-Tale Heart* was told as an MGM short directed by Jules Dassin in 1942, by a British company with Stanley Baker in 1950, by UPA as a cartoon narrated by James Mason in 1954, by an independent American company in a film known as both *Manfish* and *Calypso* in 1956 (the film also claimed to be partly based on *The Gold Bug*) and by the Danzigers in Britain in 1960. *The Fall of the House of Usher* was filmed in France by Jean Epstein in 1929, in Britain by semi-professionals in 1950, and in Hollywood by Roger Corman in 1960. Universal released films called *The Black Cat* in 1934 and 1941, both claiming to be 'suggested' by Poe's tale; in fact, neither had anything at all to do with it, but the genuine story was told in a German film called *The Living Dead* in 1933, and in Corman's 1962 *Tales of Terror. The Pit and the Pendulum* was filmed in 1913 and 1961, and the central idea has been borrowed by many film makers without credit, most recently by the 'Uncle' boys in *One Spy Too Many. The Premature Burial* was filmed straight in 1962, and around the same time TV's *Thriller* series presented a fairly faithful adaptation; the idea was also used in 1934 in *The Crime of Dr Crespi*, a low-budgeter starring Erich Von Stroheim. *The Murders in the Rue Morgue* was filmed in 1914 and 1932, turned up again in 3-D in 1954 under the title *Phantom of the Rue Morgue*, and was remade under the original title in 1971. Other Poe stories filmed once include *The Bells* 13, *The Facts in the Case of M. Valdemar* (in *Tales of Terror* 62), *The Masque of the Red Death* 64, and *The Tomb of Ligeia* 64.

Poe, James (1918–80). American writer. from radio and TV.
□Without Honor 49. Scandal Sheet (co-w) 52. Paula 52. The Big Knife 55. Around the World in 80 Days (co-w) 56. *Attack!* 56. Hot Spell 58. Cat on a Hot Tin Roof (co-w) 58. Last Train from Gun Hill 59. Sanctuary 61. Summer and Smoke (co-w) 63. Toys in the Attic 63. Lilies of the Field 63. The Bedford Incident 64. They Shoot Horses Don't They? (co-w) 69.

Pogostin, S. Lee (1926–). American writer-director.
Synanon (w) 65. Hard Contract (d) 69. Golden Needles (co-d) 74, etc.

Pohlmann, Eric (1903–1979). Viennese character actor, on British stage and radio from 1948; also a familiar bald, portly villain on screen.
The Constant Husband 55. House of Secrets 56. Expresso Bongo 59. The Kitchen 62. Carry On Spying 64. The Million Dollar Collar (US) 67. The Horsemen 71, many others.
TV series: Colonel March of Scotland Yard 53.

Poil de Carotte (France 1932). Julien Duvivier, who had also directed a silent version of the same story in 1925, made his international reputation with this sensitive, grim story of an unwanted boy being driven to the brink of suicide. It shows a French countryside quite different from Pagnol's: sunlit but bleak and inhospitable. Jules Renard's story and Thirard Monniot's photography enhanced the performances of

Harry Baur as the father and Robert Lynen (who was later killed in the Maquis) as the boy.

Poitier, Sidney (1924–). Handsome black American leading actor; his success in the late sixties helped to break the race barrier.
□*No Way Out* 50. Cry the Beloved Country 52. Red Ball Express 52. Go Man Go 54. *The Blackboard Jungle* 55. Goodbye, My Lady 56. *Edge of the City* 57. Something of Value 57. Band of Angels 58. Mark of the Hawk 58. *The Defiant Ones* 58. *Porgy and Bess* 59. Virgin Islands 60. All the Young Men 60. A Raisin in the Sun 61. Paris Blues 61. Pressure Point 62. *Lilies of the Field* (AA) 63. The Long Ships 64. The Greatest Story Ever Told 65. *The Bedford Incident* (for the first time his colour was not mentioned or relevant) 65. A Patch of Blue 65. The Slender Thread 65. Duel at Diablo 66. *In the Heat of the Night* 67. To Sir with Love 67. *Guess Who's Coming to Dinner* 67. For Love of Ivy 68. The Lost Man 69. They Call Me Mister Tibbs 70. The Organization 71. Brother John 71. Buck and the Preacher (& d) 72. A Warm December (& d) 73. Uptown Saturday Night (& d) 74. The Wilby Conspiracy 75. Let's Do It Again (& d) 76. A Piece of the Action (& d) 77. Stir Crazy (d only) 80. Hanky Panky (d only) 82. Fast Forward (d only) 84.
❁ For being the first black actor to be accepted in a romantic situation with a white girl. *Guess Who's Coming to Dinner.*

Poland had a vigorous cinema school from the earliest days, but subjects were dominated by Russian influence. After World War II Alexander Ford led a new vigorous group of film makers including Wajda and Munk, whose films of post-war problems became world famous. Later directors of note include Polanski, Kawalerowicz, and Skolimowski.

Polanski, Roman (1933–). Polish director, former actor. Gained a reputation with shorts such as *Two Men and a Wardrobe* 58.
Biographies 1982: *Polanski, the Filmmaker as Voyeur* by Barbara Leaming. 1982 *Life and Times of Roman Polanski* by Kiernan.
Autobiography 1984: *Roman.*
□FEATURES: *Knife in the Water* 61. *Repulsion* 65. Cul de Sac 66. The Fearless Vampire Killers 67. *Rosemary's Baby* 68. Macbeth 71. What? 72. *Chinatown* 74. The Tenant 76. Tess 80. Pirates 85.

'His talent is as undeniable as his intentions are dubious.'—*Andrew Sarris, 1968*

¶ *R.P.:* Nothing is too shocking for me. When you tell the story of a man who loses his head, you have to show the head being cut off. Otherwise it's just a dirty joke without a punchline.

R.P.: I know in my heart of hearts that the spirit of laughter has deserted me.

Poledouris, Basil (–). American composer.
Conan the Barbarian 84. Red Dawn 84. Conan the Destroyer 85. Flesh and Blood 85. Robocop 87.

Polglase, Van Nest (1898–1968). American art director, in films from 1919. With RKO 1932–43, then with Columbia.

police in the forties and earlier were offered in British films only for our admiration; in the fifties they began to have human frailties; and in the sixties many of them were shown, truthfully or not, to be corrupt. *The Blue Lamp, The Long Arm,* and *Gideon of Scotland Yard* are only three of many of the first kind, *Violent Playground* one of the second, and *The Strange Affair* a corking example of the last. But the *Z Cars* series on British TV will long uphold the best traditions of the force . . . as will *Maigret* for France.

American cops have always been tougher, but even so a gradual change can be traced through *Naked City, The Big Heat, Detective Story, Shield for Murder, Experiment in Terror, Madigan, The Detective, The French Connection, Fuzz* and *The New Centurions.* TV series which have been influential include *Dragnet* 52–59 and 67–69, *Naked City* 58–62, *87th Precinct* 61, *M Squad* 57–60, *The Detectives* 60–61, *The Line Up* 54–59, *Hawk* 66, *The New Breed* 61, *Adam 12* 68–75, *Hawaii Five O* 68–80, *The Rookies* 72, *Police Story* 73–77, *Police Woman* 74–76, *Starsky and Hutch* 75–78.

Comic policemen go right back to the Keystone Kops. Other examples: Will Hay in *Ask a Policeman*, George Formby in *Spare a Copper*, Norman Wisdom in *On the Beat*, Alastair Sim in *Green for Danger*, Peter Sellers in *The Pink Panther*, Lionel Jeffries in *The Wrong Arm of the Law*, 'Officer Krupke' in *West Side Story*, Donald McBride in *Topper Returns*, Dennis Hoey as Inspector Lestrade in the Sherlock Holmes films, Sidney James and crew in *Carry On Constable*, Laurel and Hardy in *Midnight Patrol*, Buster Keaton's cast in *Cops*, Charles Chaplin in *Easy Street*, the cast of *Police Academy* and on TV, *Car 54 Where are You?*

politics, as any exhibitor will tell you, is the kiss of death to a film as far as box office is concerned. Nevertheless many films with serious political themes have been made. Among those presenting biographies of actual political figures, the American ones include *Young Mr Lincoln, Abe Lincoln in Illinois, Tennessee Johnson, The Man with Thirty Sons* (Oliver Wendell Holmes), *Magnificent Doll* (Dolly Madison and Aaron Burr), *The President's Lady* (Andrew Jackson), *Wilson*, Teddy Roosevelt (in *My Girl Tisa* and others), Franklin Roosevelt (in *Sunrise at Campobello*), *Beau James* (Jimmy Walker) and John Kennedy (*PT 109*), while *All the King's Men* and *A Lion Is in the Streets* are clearly based on Huey Long, and there was a real-life original for the idealistic young senator from Wisconsin in *Mr Smith Goes to Washington.* Fictional presidencies have been involved in *Gabriel over the White House, First Lady, The Tree of Liberty* (*The Howards of Virginia*), *Advise and Consent, The Manchurian Candidate, Seven Days in May, Dr Strangelove, Kisses for My President*, and *Fail Safe.* Among the many films alleging political graft and corruption in the US are *Mr Smith Goes to Washington, Confessions of a Nazi Spy, Louisiana Purchase, Alias Nick Beal, State of the Union, Li'l Abner, The Great McGinty, The Glass Key, Citizen Kane, All the King's Men, Bullets or Ballots, A Lion Is in the Streets, The Last Hurrah, The Best Man, The Senator was Indiscreet* and *The Candidate.* The witch-hunts of 1948 produced a series of right-wing melodramas like *I Was a Communist for the FBI, I Married a Communist* and *My Son John* . . . a striking contrast to 1942, when *Mission to Moscow* could be made. In 1971 TV produced a four-hour thriller called *Vanished* about a president with doubtful motives. The mid-seventies brought a number of TV drama-documentaries about political matters: *Eleanor and Franklin, Collision Course* (Truman and MacArthur), *The Missiles of October, Fear On Trial, Tail Gunner Joe* (McCarthy), *Meeting at Potsdam.*

The British House of Commons and its characters have been involved in many a film with Disraeli (qv) coming out as favourite. Pitt the Younger was impersonated by Robert Donat, and Charles James Fox by Robert Morley, in *The Young Mr Pitt*; Gladstone was played by Ralph Richardson in *Khartoum*, Malcolm Keen in *Sixty Glorious Years* and Stephen Murray in *The Prime Minister*; *Cromwell* by Richard Harris; Canning by John Mills and William Lamb by Jon Finch in *Lady Caroline Lamb*; while Ramsay MacDonald was allegedly pictured in *Fame is the Spur.* MPs were also the leading figures of the fictional *No Love for Johnnie, Three Cases of Murder* and *The Rise and Rise of Michael Rimmer.*

Political films from other countries abound; one might almost say that every Soviet film is political. But politics do not export well, so that for the life of Villa, Zapata, Juarez and Che Guevara we have to turn to glamorized Hollywood versions of the truth; ditto for Parnell, Richelieu and even Hitler. Lenin has been pictured in innumerable Soviet films, and Richard Burton starred in *The Assassination of Trotsky.*

That politics is not entirely a serious matter can be seen from the number of comedies about it. The best of them is the already mentioned *State of the Union*, but one can also instance the *Don Camillo* series, *Old Mother Riley MP, Angelina MP, Dad Rudd MP, Louisiana Purchase, Kisses for My President, The Great Man Votes, Left Right and Centre* and *Vote for Huggett.*

Polito, Gene (–). American cinematographer.
Prime Cut 72. Westworld 73. Five on the Black Hand Side 73. Trackdown 76. The Bad News Bears Go to Japan 78, etc.

Polito, Sol (1892–1960). American cinematographer.
Treason 18. Hard-Boiled Haggerty 27. Five Star Final 31. *I Am a Fugitive from a Chain Gang* 32. *Forty-second Street* 33. *G Men* 35. *The Petrified Forest* 36. *The Charge of the Light Brigade* 36. *The Adventures of Robin Hood* 38. Confessions of a Nazi Spy 39. *The Sea Hawk* 40. The Sea Wolf 41. Now Voyager 42. Arsenic and Old Lace 44. Rhapsody in Blue 45. The Long Night 47. Sorry, Wrong Number 48. Anna Lucasta 48, many others.

Poll, Martin H. (1922–). American producer.
Love is a Ball 62. Sylvia 65. The Lion in Winter 68. Night Watch 73. The Man Who Loved Cat Dancing 73, etc.

Pollack, Sydney (1934–). American director, from TV.
□*The Slender Thread* 65. This Property is Condemned 66. The Scalphunters 68. Castle Keep 69. *They Shoot Horses Don't They?* 69. Jeremiah Johnson 72. The Way We Were 73. The Yakusa 75. *Three Days of the Condor* 76.

Bobby Deerfield 77. The Electric Horseman 79. Absence of Malice 81. Tootsie (& a) 82. Out of Africa (AA) 85.

¶ *S.P.:* I don't value a film I've enjoyed making. If it's good, it's damned hard work.

Pollard, Daphne (1890–1978). Diminutive Australian actress in Hollywood; a famous sharp-tongued wife for Laurel and Hardy. Bright Lights 30. Swing Time 37, etc.

Pollard, Harry (1883–1934). American silent-screen director.
Motherhood 14. The Leather Pushers 22. Oh Doctor 24. California Straight Ahead 25. Uncle Tom's Cabin 27. Showboat (first talkie) 29. The Prodigal 31. Fast Life 32, etc.

Pollard, Michael J. (1939–) (M. J. Pollack). Pint-sized American character actor.
Adventures of a Young Man 62. Summer Magic 62. The Stripper 64. *Bonnie and Clyde* 67. Hannibal Brooks 69. Little Fauss and Big Halsy 70. Dirty Little Billy 72. Sunday in the Country 74. Between the Lines 77, Melvin and Howard 80, etc.

Pollard, Snub (1886–1962) (Harold Fraser). Australian comedian, in America from early silent film days. In many silent slapstick shorts, and later continued to play bit parts, the last being in *A Pocketful of Miracles* 61.

Pollock, Ellen (1903–). British stage actress, in occasional films.
Non Stop New York 37. The Street Singer 37. Sons of the Sea 39. Kiss the Bride Goodbye 44. The Galloping Major 51, etc.

Pollock, George (1907–). British director, former assistant, in films since 1933.
A Stranger in Town 56. Rooney 58. Don't Panic Chaps 60. Murder She Said 63. Murder at the Gallop 63. Murder Most Foul 64. Ten Little Indians 65, etc.

Polonsky, Abraham (1910–). American writer who fell foul of the communist witch-hunt.
Body and Soul 47. *Force of Evil* (& d) 49. I Can Get It for You Wholesale 50. Tell Them Willie Boy is Here (& d) 69. Romance of a Horsethief (d only) 71. Avalanche Express 78. Monsignor (co-w) 82, etc.

Pommer, Erich (1889–1966). German producer since 1915. During the thirties worked briefly in the US and also, with Charles Laughton, formed Mayflower Films in Britain.
The Cabinet of Dr Caligari 19. Dr Mabuse 22. Die Nibelungen 24. *Variety* 25. *Metropolis* 26. *The Blue Angel* 30. Congress Dances 31. Liliom 34. Fire over England 36. Vessel of Wrath 38. Jamaica Inn 39. They Knew What They Wanted 40. Illusion in Moll 52. Kinder, Mutter und Ein General 55, etc.
❀ For his influence over a wide range of European films. *Metropolis.*

Pons, Lily (1904–1976). French-born operatic singer who starred in some Hollywood films.
I Dream Too Much 35. That Girl from Paris 36. Hitting a New High 37. Carnegie Hall 47, etc.

Pontecorvo, Gillo (1919–). Italian director.
Kapo 60. *The Battle of Algiers* 66. The Wide Blue Road 68. Burn! 70, etc.

Ponti, Carlo (1913–). Italian producer, later involved in international productions. Married to Sophia Loren.
I Miserabili 47. Attila the Hun 52. Ulysses 54. War and Peace 56. Black Orchid 58. That Kind of Woman 59. Marriage, Italian Style 65. Operation Crossbow 65. Smashing Time 67. Sunflower 70. Lady Liberty 72. The Passenger 74. Massacre in Rome 74. Brief Encounter (TV) 75. Verdict 75. The Priest's Wife 75. The Cassandra Crossing 77, etc.

Ponting, Herbert G. (1870–1935). British explorer and film-maker, a maker of quality documentaries in the cinema's early days. With Captain Scott R.N. to the South Pole 13, etc.

Pontius Pilate (–). The man who judged Jesus has been played on film as follows: in *King of Kings* 27 by Victor Varconi; in *The Last Days of Pompeii* 35 by Basil Rathbone; in *The Robe* 53 by Richard Boone; in *Ben Hur* 59 by Frank Thring; in *King of Kings* 61 by Hurd Hatfield; in Barabbas 62 by Arthur Kennedy; in *The Greatest Story Ever Told* by Telly Savalas; in *Jesus Christ Superstar* 75 by Barry Dennen.

Popeye. Tough sailorman hero of over 250 cartoon shorts produced by Max Fleischer c. 1933–50. Other characters involved were girl-friend Olive Oyl and tough villain Bluto, against whose wiles Popeye fortified himself with tins of spinach. The films were so popular on TV that a newly-drawn series was produced c. 1959 by King Features—but the old vulgar panache was missing.

In 1980 Robert Altman directed a live-action version, but it was a sad affair.

Popkin, Harry M. (–). American independent producer.
And Then There Were None 45. Impact 48. *D.O.A.* 49. Champagne for Caesar 49. The Thief 52, etc.

Porcasi, Paul (1880–1946). Sicilian character actor in Hollywood films; former opera singer.
The Fall of the Romanoffs 19. Say It Again 26. Broadway 29. The Criminal Code 31. The Passionate Plumber 32. Footlight Parade 32. The Gay Divorcee 34. Maytime 37. Crime School 38. It Started with Eve 41. We Were Dancing 42. Hi Diddle Diddle 43. I'll Remember April 45, many others.

Porten, Henny (1890–1960). German leading lady of the silents.
Lohengrin 07. Anne Boleyn 20. Der Kaufmann von Venedig 23. Kohlhiesel's Tochter 30. Familie Buchholz 40. Das Fraulein Scuderi 55, many others.

Porter, Cole (1893–1964). American songwriter and composer whose lyrics were probably the wittiest ever appended to popular songs. Cary Grant played Porter in a biopic, *Night and Day* 46; other films using Porter scores are: *Anything Goes* 36 and 56. *Rosalie* 38. *Broadway Melody of 1940*. *Something to Shout About* 42. *The Pirate* 48. *Kiss Me Kate* 53. *High Society* 56. *Can Can* 59, etc.
Biography 1967: *The Life That Late He Led* by George Eels.

Porter, Don (1912–). American leading man of second features, latterly character actor.
Top Sergeant 42. Night Monster 43. The Curse of the Allenbys 48. 711 Ocean Drive 50. Because You're Mine 52. The Racket 52. Our Miss Brooks 56. Bachelor in Paradise 61. Youngblood Hawke 64. The Candidate 72. Forty Carats 73. White Line Fever 75, etc.
TV series: Private Secretary. Our Miss Brooks. The Ann Sothern Show.

Porter, Edwin S. (1869–1941). America's first notable director, who later found himself in D. W. Griffith's shadow and left the industry.
The Life of an American Fireman 02. *The Great Train Robbery* 03. The Ex-Convict 05. Rescued from an Eagle's Nest 07. Alice's Adventures in Wonderland 10. The Count of Monte Cristo 12. The Eternal City 15, etc.
†A documentary about Porter, *Before the Nickelodeon*, was released in 1983.

Porter, Eric (1928–). British stage actor who became nationally known as Soames in the TV version of *The Forsyte Saga*.
The Heroes of Telemark 65. Kaleidoscope 66. The Lost Continent 68. Hands of the Ripper 71. Antony and Cleopatra 71. Nicholas and Alexandra 71. The Day of the Jackal 73. The Belstone Fox 73. Callan 74. Hennessy 75. The 39 Steps 78. Why Didn't They Ask Evans? (TV) 80. Little Lord Fauntleroy (TV) 80. The Jewel in the Crown (TV) 83, etc.

Porter, Gene Stratton (1886–1924). American novelist: her sentimental novels of country matters were once ideal film material. *Freckles*, *Laddie* and *Girl of the Limberlost* were among them.

Porter, Katherine Anne (1890–1980). American novelist, author of the allegorical *Ship of Fools* which was filmed in 1963.

Porter, Nyree Dawn (1940–). New Zealand leading lady in British films and TV.
Two Left Feet 63. The Cracksman 63. Jane Eyre 70. The House that Dripped Blood 70. From Beyond the Grave 73, etc.
TV series: *The Forsyte Saga* (as Irene) 67. *The Protectors* 72.

Portman, Eric (1903–1969). Distinguished British stage actor who appeared sporadically in films.
□The Murder in the Red Barn (debut) 35. Abdul the Damned 35. Old Roses 35. Hyde Park Corner 35. The Cardinal 36. Hearts of Humanity 36. The Prince and the Pauper (US) 37. Moonlight Sonata 37. The Crimes of Stephen Hawke 38. *49th Parallel* 41. One of Our Aircraft is Missing 42. Uncensored 42. Squadron Leader X 43. We Dive at Dawn 43. Escape to Danger 43. *Millions Like Us* 43. A Canterbury Tale 44. Great Day 45. Men of Two Worlds 46. *Wanted for Murder* 46. Dear Murderer 47. Daybreak 48. The Mark of Cain 48. Corridor of Mirrors 48. The Blind Goddess 48. The Spider and the Fly 50. The Magic Box 51. Cairo Road 51. His Excellency 51. South of Algiers 52. The Colditz Story 54. *The Deep Blue Sea* 55. Child in the House 56.

The Good Companions 57. The Naked Edge 61. The Man Who Finally Died 62. Freud 62. West Eleven 63. The Bedford Incident 65. The Whisperers 66. The Spy with a Cold Nose 67. Assignment to Kill 67. Deadfall 68.

Portrait of Jennie (US 1948). A pretentious but enjoyable fantasy in Hollywood's lushest manner, about a penniless artist who meets a fey young girl in Central Park and discovers not only that she grows much older every time he sees her but that she actually died many years ago. She finally dies again in a storm off Cape Cod. Not even the author could possibly understand this plot, and even the light relief is of a whimsical nature; but the acting (Joseph Cotten, Jennifer Jones, Ethel Barrymore, David Wayne, Lilian Gish) is so good, the direction (William Dieterle) so accomplished and the photography (Joseph August) so striking that the thing comes off.

The Poseidon Adventure (US 1972). The film which brought the disaster genre back with a bang was directed by Ronald Neame from a story by Paul Gallico about a ship which turns upside down after an explosion, and makes it difficult for survivors to escape. Routine melodramatics were handled by a capable cast. An inferior sequel, *Beyond the Poseidon Adventure*, came out in 1979.

Post, Ted (1925–). American director, from TV.
□The Peacemaker 56. The Legend of Tom Dooley 59. Hang 'Em High 68. Beneath the Planet of the Apes 70. Yuma (TV) 70. Dr Cook's Garden (TV) 70. Night Slaves (TV) 70. The Bravos (TV) 71. Five Desperate Women (TV) 71. Do Not Fold Spindle or Mutilate (TV) 72. The Baby 73. The Harrad Experiment 73. Magnum Force 73. Whiffs 75. Good Guys Wear Black 77. Go Tell the Spartans 78. Nightkill 81.

Posta, Adrienne (1948–) (Adrienne Poster). British juvenile actress specializing in cheeky teenagers.
No Time for Tears 59. To Sir With Love 67. Here We Go Round the Mulberry Bush 67. Up the Junction 68. Some Girls Do 69. Percy 70. Up Pompeii 71. Percy's Progress 74, etc.

Poston, Tom (1927–). American light comedian.
□City That Never Sleeps 53. Zotz! 62. Soldier in the Rain 63. The Old Dark House 63. Cold Turkey 70. The Happy Hooker 75. Rabbit Test 78. Up the Academy 80.
TV series: Newhart 81–.

post-synchronization. Adding sound, by dubbing, to visuals already shot. Sound can only rarely be recorded at the time of shooting because of extraneous noise and requirements of volume, pitch, etc.; actors must usually repeat their lines in accordance with their image on screen.

Potter, H. C. (1904–1977). American director with stage experience, in Hollywood from 1935; an expert at comedy.
□Beloved Enemy 36. Wings Over Honolulu 37. Romance in the Dark 38. Shopworn Angel 38. The Cowboy and the Lady 38. *The Story of Vernon and Irene Castle* 39. Blackmail 39. Congo Maisie 40. Second Chorus 40. *Hellzapoppin* 41. Mr Lucky 43. *The Farmer's Daughter* 47. A Likely Story 47. *Mr Blandings Builds His Dream House* 48. The Time of Your Life 48. You Gotta Stay Happy 48. The Miniver Story 50. Three for the Show 55. Top Secret Affair 57.

Potter, Martin (1944–). British juvenile lead of the early seventies.
Fellini Satyricon 70. Goodbye Gemini 71. Nicholas and Alexandra 71. All Coppers Are 71. Craze 73. The Big Sleep 78, etc.

Potts, Cliff (–). American second lead of seventies action dramas.
Snow Job 72. The Ground Star Conspiracy 72. Face to the Wind 74. Nevada Smith (TV) 75. Once an Eagle (TV) 77, etc.
TV series: Big Hawaii 77.

Poujouly, Georges (1940–). French boy actor of the early fifties.
Jeux Interdits 52. Nous Sommes Tous des Assassins 52. Les Diaboliques 54. Lift to the Scaffold 57. Girls for the Summer 59, etc.

Poulton, Mabel (1905–). British leading lady of the twenties.
The Heart of an Actress 24. Virginia's Husband 25. The Constant Nymph 28. The Return of the Rat 28.

poverty in America and Britain is rare enough now to be little discussed, but in the days when film-makers began to have social conscience a number of films memorably examined the problem in different milieux. American hoboes and shanty town dwellers were revealed in *Sullivan's Travels, Hallelujah I'm a Bum, Man's Castle, My Man Godfrey, One More Spring*; the rural poor were the subject of *Our Daily Bread, The Grapes of Wrath, Tobacco Road*. Hollywood's regretful gaze wandered to China for *The Good Earth* and for *Tortilla Flat* to Mexico, which was more memorably covered by Buñuel in *Los Olvidados*. Poverty in Italy was the subject of *Bicycle Thieves*, and in England of *Love on the Dole, Doss House* and *The Whisperers*.

Powell, Dick (1904–1963). American crooning juvenile of the thirties who later suffered a sea-change and emerged as a likeable tough leading man, a competent director and an ambitious producer, the founder of Four Star Television.
Blessed Event 32. Too Busy to Work 32. The King's Vacation.33 *Forty-Second Street* 33. Gold Diggers of 1933. Footlight Parade 33. College Coach 33. Convention City 33. *Dames* 34. Wonder Bar 34. Twenty Million Sweethearts 34. Happiness Ahead 34. Flirtation Walk 34. Gold Diggers of 1935. Page Miss Glory 35. Broadway Gondolier 35. A Midsummer Night's Dream 35. Shipmates Forever 35. Thanks a Million 35. Colleen 36. Hearts Divided 36. Stage Struck 36. Gold Diggers of 1937. *On the Avenue* 37. The Singing Marine 37. Varsity Show 37. Hollywood Hotel 38. Cowboy from Brooklyn 38. Hard to Get 38. Going Places 38. Naughty but Nice 39. *Christmas in July* 40. I Want a Divorce 40. Model Wife 41. In the Navy 41. Star Spangled Rhythm 42. Happy Go Lucky 42. True to Life 43. Riding High 43. *It Happened Tomorrow* 44. Meet the People 44. *Murder My Sweet* (as Philip Marlowe) 44. Cornered 45. Johnny O'Clock 47. To the Ends of the Earth 48. Pitfall 48. Station West 48. Rogues Regiment 48. Mrs Mike 49. The Reformer and the Redhead 50. Right Cross 50. Callaway Went Thataway 51. Cry Danger 51. The Tall Target 51. You Never Can Tell 51. The Bad and the Beautiful 52. Split Second (d only) 53. Susan Slept Here 54. The Conqueror (pd only) 56. You Can't Run Away From It (d only) 56. The Enemy Below (d only) 57. The Hunters (d only) 58, etc.
TV series: *Dick Powell Theatre* 59–61.

Powell, Dilys (1902–). British film critic, long with the *Sunday Times* and latterly with *Punch*.

Powell, Eleanor (1910–1982). Long-legged American tap dancer whose vitality enhanced a few films.
□George White's Scandals 35. Broadway Melody of 1936. *Born to Dance* 36. Broadway Melody of 1938. *Rosalie* 38. Honolulu 39. Broadway Melody of 1940. Lady Be Good 41. Ship Ahoy 42. I Dood It 43. Thousands Cheer 43. Sensations of 1945 44. The Duchess of Idaho 50.

Powell, Jane (1929–) (Suzanne Burce). Diminutive American singing and dancing leading lady; former child performer.
□Song of the Open Road 44. Delightfully Dangerous 45. Holiday in Mexico 46. Three Daring Daughters 48. A Date with Judy 48. Luxury Liner 48. Nancy Goes to Rio 50. Two Weeks with Love 50. Royal Wedding 51. Rich Young and Pretty 51. Small Town Girl 53. Three Sailors and a Girl 53. *Seven Brides for Seven Brothers* 54. Athena 54. Deep in My Heart 54. Hit the Deck 55. The Girl Most Likely 57. The Female Animal 58. Enchanted Island 58. Wheeler and Murdoch (TV) 70. The Letters (TV) 72. Mayday at 40,000 feet (TV) 78.

Powell, Michael (1905–). Important British writer-producer-director whose highly imaginative work, especially in his collaboration with Emeric Pressburger ('The Archers' 42–57), was sometimes marred by a streak of tastelessness.
Autobiography 1985: *A Life in Movies*.
AS WRITER ONLY: Caste 30. 77 Park Lane 31. The Star Reporter 31. Hotel Splendide 32. The Fire Raisers 33. Night of the Party 34. Lazybones 35. The Phantom Light 35. The Man Behind the Mask 36, many others.
□AS EXECUTIVE wholly or jointly in charge, including work as WRITER-PRODUCER-DIRECTOR: The Edge of the World 37. *The Spy in Black* 38. The Lion Has Wings 39. The Thief of Baghdad 39. Contraband 40. 49th Parallel 41. One of Our Aircraft is Missing 42. *The Life and Death of Colonel Blimp* 43. The Silver Fleet 43. A Canterbury Tale 44. *I Know Where I'm Going* 45. *A Matter of Life and Death* 46. Black Narcissus 46. End of the River 47. *The Red Shoes* 48. The Small Back Room 48. Gone to Earth 50. The Elusive Pimpernel 51. The Tales of Hoffman 51. Oh Rosalinda 55. The Battle of the River Plate 56. Ill Met by Moonlight 57. Peeping Tom 60. Honeymoon 61. The Queen's Guards 61. They're a Weird Mob 66. Sebastian (p only) 67. Age of Consent 69. The Boy Who Turned Yellow 72. Return to the Edge of the World 79.
❀ For being so unpredictable, and at his best so brilliant. *A Matter of Life and Death*.

¶ *M.P.*: Of course all films are surrealist. They are making something that looks like the real world but isn't.

Powell, Robert (1946–). Lithe, pale-eyed British leading man of the seventies.
Walk a Crooked Path 69. The Italian Job 69. Pygmalion (TV) 71. Secrets 71. Running Scared 72. Asylum 72. The Asphyx 73. Mahler 73. Tommy 75. *Jesus of Nazareth* (TV) 77. The Four Feathers (TV) 78. Beyond Good and Evil (It.) 78. The 39 Steps 78. Harlequin 79. Jane Austen in Manhatten 79. The Survivor 80. The Jigsaw Man 83. Secrets of the Phantom Caverns 84. Shaka Zulu (TV) 86, etc.

¶ *R.P. 1975:* I hope Jesus Christ will be the last in my line of sensitive young men for quite a while.

Powell, Sandy (1898–1982) (Albert Powell). British music-hall comedian who made some knockabout films using his radio catch-phrase 'Can you hear me, mother?'
Autobiography 1976: *Can You Hear Me, Mother?*
The Third String 32. Leave It to Me 36. I've Got a Horse 38. Cup Tie Honeymoon 48, etc.

Powell, William (1892–1984). Mature, debonair American leading man of the thirties and forties; a pillar of MGM for many years, he began as a cowboy villain but is probably best remembered as Nick Charles in *The Thin Man*.
Biography 1984: *Gentleman, the William Powell Story*.

SELECTED SILENT FILMS: Sherlock Holmes 22. The Bright Shawl 23. Romola 24. Too Many Kisses 25. Faint Perfume 25. Desert Gold 26. Aloma of the South Seas 26. Beau Geste 26. Señorita 27. Nevada 27. Feel My Pulse 28. The Last Command 28. The Vanishing Pioneer 28, etc.
□SOUND FILMS: Interference 29. *The Canary Murder Case* (as Philo Vance) 29. The Greene Murder Case 29. Charming Sinners 29. The Four Feathers 29. The Benson Murder Case 30. Paramount on Parade 30. Shadow of the Law 30. Pointed Heels 30. Behind the Make-up 30. *Street of Chance* 30. For the Defense 30. Man of the World 31. Ladies' Man 31. The Road to Singapore 31. High Pressure 32. Jewel Robbery 32. *One Way Passage* 32. Lawyer Man 32. Double Harness 33. Private Detective 62 33. The Kennel Murder Case 33. Fashions of 1934. The Key 34. Manhattan Melodrama 34. *The Thin Man* 34. Evelyn Prentice 34. Reckless 35. Star of Midnight 35. Escapade 35. Rendezvous 35. *The Great Ziegfeld* 36. The Ex Mrs Bradford 36. *My Man Godfrey* 36. Libelled Lady 36. After the Thin Man 36. The Last of Mrs Cheyney 37. The Emperor's Candlesticks 37. Double Wedding 37. The Baroness and the Butler 38. Another Thin Man 39. I Love You Again 40. Love Crazy 41. Shadow of the Thin Man 41. Crossroads 42. The Youngest Profession 43. The Heavenly Body 44. The Thin Man Goes Home 44. Ziegfeld Follies 45. The Hoodlum Saint 46. Song of the Thin Man 47. *Life With Father* 47. The Senator was Indiscreet 47. Mr Peabody and the Mermaid 48. Take One False Step 49. Dancing in the Dark 49. Treasure of Lost Canyon 51. It's a Big Country 51. The Girl Who Had Everything 53. How to Marry a Millionaire 53. *Mister Roberts* (as Doc) 55.
❋ For spreading his cheerful suavity over thirties Hollywood; and for being so much at home in a dinner jacket. *The Thin Man*.

Famous line (*Life With Father*): I'm going to be baptized, damn it!

Power, Hartley (1894–1966). Bald-headed American character actor who settled in Britain and was often seen as general, con man or brash agent.
Friday the Thirteenth 33. Evergreen 34. A Window in London 42. The Way to the Stars 45. *Dead of Night* 45. A Girl in a Million 47. Roman Holiday 53. To Dorothy a Son 54. Island in the Sun 56, many others.

Power, Tyrone (1913–1958). American leading man, of theatrical family; in films from 1932, usually deploying smooth gentle personality.
□Tom Brown of Culver 32. Girls' Dormitory 36. Ladies in Love 36. *Lloyds of London* 37. Love is News 37. Café Metropole 37. Thin Ice 37. Second Honeymoon 37. *In Old Chicago* 38. *Alexander's Ragtime Band* 38. Marie Antoinette 38. Suez 38. *Rose of Washington Square* 39. *Jesse James* 39. Second Fiddle 39. The Rains Came 39. Daytime Wife 39. Johnny Apollo 40. Brigham Young 40. *The Mark of Zorro* 40. A Yank in the RAF 41. Blood and Sand 41. This Above All 42. Son of Fury 42. *The Black Swan* 42. Crash Dive 42; war service; The Razor's Edge 46. Captain from Castile 47. Nightmare Alley 47. The Luck of the Irish 48. That Wonderful Urge 48. Prince of Foxes 49. The Black Rose

50. An American Guerilla in the Philippines 51. Rawhide 51. I'll Never Forget You 51. Diplomatic Courier 52. Pony Soldier 52. Mississippi Gambler 53. King of the Khyber Rifles 53. The Long Gray Line 54. Untamed 55. The Eddy Duchin Story 56. Seven Waves Away 57. The Rising of the Moon (narrated only) 57. *The Sun Also Rises* 57. Witness for the Prosecution 57.

Power, Tyrone Snr (1869–1931). American stage actor, father of Tyrone Power: played heavy in a few films.
A Texas Street 15. Where are My Children? 16. Footfalls 21. The Lone Wolf 24. Bride of the Storm 26. The Big Trail 30, etc.

Powers, Mala (1931–) (Mary Ellen Powers). American leading lady, former child actress.
Tough as They Come 41. Outrage 50. Cyrano de Bergerac 50. Rose of Cimarron 52. Rage at Dawn 55. Benghazi 55. The Storm Rider 57. Daddy's Gone A-Hunting 69. Doomsday 72, etc.

Powers, Stefanie (1942–) (Stefania Federkiewicz). American leading lady of the sixties.
Experiment in Terror 62. The Interns 62. Palm Springs Weekend 63. *Fanatic* (GB) 64. Stagecoach 66. Warning Shot 67. Herbie Rides Again 73. Escape to Athena 79. Family Secrets (TV) 84, etc.
TV series: *The Girl from UNCLE* 66. Washington Behind Closed Doors 77. The Feather and Father Gang 78. *Hart to Hart* 79–83.

Powers, Tom (1890–1955). American general purpose supporting actor.
Double Indemnity 44. Two Years Before the Mast 46. Up in Central Park 48. Chicago Deadline 49. Destination Moon 50. Horizons West 52. Julius Caesar 53. The Americano 54, etc.

pratfall. Something in which all silent comedians were skilled: the art of falling on one's fundament without getting hurt.

pre-credits sequence. It has recently become fashionable to start films with an explosive opening scene, sometimes running seven or eight minutes, before the titles appear. This now over-worked device, used by almost all American TV series, is generally traced back to *Rommel, Desert Fox* 51, which had a long pre-credits sequence showing a commando raid; but the titles come quite late in *The Egg and I* 47, and even in *Destry Rides Again* 39 there is nearly a minute of shooting before they appear; while in *The Magnificent Ambersons* 42 they are not seen at all, only spoken at the end of the picture.
More recently, *Cruising* and *Papillon* are among the movies to place all their credits at the end.

Preiss, Wolfgang (–). German character actor in international films.
The Longest Day 62. Von Ryan's Express 65. The Train 65. Hannibal Brooks 68. Raid on Rommel 71. The Salzburg Connection 72. A Bridge too Far 77. The Boys from Brazil 78. The Winds of War (TV) 83. Forget Mozart 85. The Second Victory 86.

Preisser, June (1921–84). Vivacious teenage leading lady of the forties.
Babes in Arms 39. Strike Up the Band 40. The Fleet's In 41. Sweater Girl 41. Babes on Swing Street 44. Sarge Goes to College 47, etc.

Préjean, Albert (1894–1980). French light character actor who was in most of René Clair's early successes.
Le Voyage Imaginaire 25. An Italian Straw Hat 27. Sous les Toits de Paris 30. Die Dreigroschenoper (L'Opéra de Quat'Sous) 31. Jenny 36. Métropolitain 40. L'Etrange Suzy 43. Les Nouveaux Maîtres 49. Les Amants du Tage 54, etc.

Preminger, Ingo (–). Austrian/American producer, brother of Otto.
M*A*S*H 70, etc.

Preminger, Otto (1906–86). Austrian/American director with theatrical background. Always a good craftsman, he latterly applied heavy-handed treatment to potentially interesting subjects.
Biography 1973: *Behind the Scenes of Otto Preminger* by Willi Frischauer.
Autobiography 1977: *Preminger*.
□Die Grosse Liebe (Austrian) 32, then to US: Under Your Spell 36. Danger, Love at Work 37. The Pied Piper (acted only) 42. They Got Me Covered (acted only) 42. Margin for Error (& a) 43. In the Meantime, Darling 44. *Laura* 44. Royal Scandal 45. Where Do We Go from Here 45. Centennial Summer 46. Fallen Angel 46. Forever Amber 47. Daisy Kenyon 47. That Lady in Ermine (part) 48. The Fan 49. Whirlpool 50. Where the Sidewalk Ends 50. The Thirteenth Letter

51. Angel Face 52. *The Moon is Blue* 53. *Stalag 17* (acted only) 53. River of No Return 54. *Carmen Jones* 54. The Court Martial of Billy Mitchell 55. *The Man with the Golden Arm* 56. Bonjour Tristesse 57. Saint Joan (GB) 57. Porgy and Bess 59. *Anatomy of a Murder* 59. Exodus 60. *Advise and Consent* 61. The Cardinal 63. In Harm's Way 65. Bunny Lake is Missing (GB) 65. Hurry Sundown 67. Skidoo 68. Tell Me That You Love Me, Junie Moon 70. Such Good Friends 72. Rosebud 75. The Human Factor 79.

'His enemies have never forgiven him for being a director with the personality of a producer.'—*Andrew Sarris, 1968*

¶ A great showman who has never bothered to learn anything about making a movie . . . no one is more skilled at giving the appearance of dealing with large controversial themes in a bold way, without making the tactical error of doing so.—*Dwight MacDonald*

Otto, let my people go.—*Mort Sahl at the premiere of Exodus*

Prentiss, Paula (1939–) (Paula Ragusa). Tall American leading lady who came almost straight from college to Hollywood.

Where the Boys Are 61. The Honeymoon Machine 62. Bachelor in Paradise 62. The Horizontal Lieutenant 63. *Man's Favorite Sport?* 64. The World of Henry Orient 64. In Harm's Way 65. What's New Pussycat? 65. Catch 22 69. Last of the Red Hot Lovers 72. Crazy Joe 73. The Parallax View 74. The Stepford Wives 75. Having Babies II (TV) 77. The Black Marble 80. Buddy Buddy 81. Saturday the 14th 81, etc.

TV series: *He and She* 67.

prequel. The opposite of a sequel, i.e. a film showing events which happened *before* one already known. The first film prequel may have been *Another Part of the Forest,* which came after *The Little Foxes* but described events before it. The word came into being in the late seventies with the production of *Butch and Sundance: The Early Days.* A game rapidly sprang up in which one had to supply prequel titles for famous films. Among them were *Mr Blandings Applies for Planning Permission; The Boy Who Would Be Prince; Friday Night Slight Temperature; Destry Dismounts;* and *Hello Mr Chips.*

Presle, Micheline (1922–) (Micheline Chassagne). French leading actress with stage experience.

Jeunes Filles en Détresse 38. La Nuit Fantastique 41. Boule de Suif 45. *Le Diable au Corps* 46. Les Jeux Sont Faits 47. Under My Skin (US) 50. The Adventures of Captain Fabian (US) 51. La Dame aux Camélias 52. Villa Borghese 54. The She Wolves 57. Blind Date (GB) 59. The Prize 63. La Religieuse 65. King of Hearts 67. Peau d'Ane 70. The Slightly Pregnant Man 73. Nea: A New Woman 78, etc.

Presley, Elvis (1935–1977). Heavy-lidded American pop singer and guitarist, once known as 'the Pelvis' because of his swivel-hipped style. His popularity with teenagers survived a host of bad movies.

Biography 1977: *Elvis Presley* by W.A. Harbinson.

□Love Me Tender 56. Loving You 57. Jailhouse Rock 57. King Creole 58. G.I. Blues 60. Flaming Star 60. Wild in the Country 61. Blue Hawaii 61. Kid Galahad 62. Girls Girls Girls 62. Follow That Dream 62. Fun in Acapulco 63. It Happened at the World's Fair 63. Kissin' Cousins 64. Viva Las Vegas 64. Roustabout 64. Girl Happy 65. Tickle Me 65. Harem Scarem 65. Frankie and Johnny 66. Paradise Hawaiian Style 66. Spinout 66. Easy Come Easy Go 67. Double Trouble 67. Stay Away Joe 68. Speedway 68. Clambake 68. Live a Little Love a Little 68. Charro 69. Change of Habit 70. The Trouble with Girls 70. Elvis—That's the Way It Is 70. Elvis on Tour 72.

Presnell, Harve (1933–). American light opera singer, in occasional films.

□The Unsinkable Molly Brown 64. The Glory Guys 65. Where the Boys Meet the Girls 66. Paint Your Wagon 69.

Presnell, Robert, Jnr (1914–). American writer.

The Man in the Attic 53. Legend of the Lost 57. Conspiracy of Hearts (GB) 59. Let No Man Write My Epitaph 60. The Third Day 65, etc.

Presnell, Robert, Snr (1894–). American writer, usually in collaboration.

Hi Nellie 32. My Man Godfrey 36. The Real Glory 39. Meet John Doe 41. Second Chance 53. 13 West Street 62, etc.

Pressburger, Arnold (1885–1951). Hungarian producer who worked in Germany, Britain and Hollywood.

City of Song 30. Tell Me Tonight 32. The Return of the Scarlet Pimpernel 38. The Shanghai Gesture 41. Hangmen Also Die 43.

It Happened Tomorrow 44. A Scandal in Paris 46, etc.

Pressburger, Emeric (1902–). Hungarian journalist and scriptwriter in Britain from 1935. Worked on script of *The Challenge* 37 and met Michael Powell, qv for list of their joint films as 'The Archers'.
SOLO: Twice Upon a Time (wpd) 52. Miracle in Soho (wp) 56. Behold a Pale Horse (from his novel) 64. Operation Crossbow (w) (as Richard Imrie) 65. They're a Weird Mob (w) 66. The Boy Who Turned Yellow (w) 72.

Pressman, Edward R. (–). American producer.
The Revolutionary 70. Badlands 73. Phantom of the Paradise 74. Paradise Alley 78. Heart Beat 78. Old Boyfriends 79. You Better Watch Out 80. The Hand 81.

Pressman, Michael (1950–). American director.
The Bad News Bears in Breaking Training 77. Boulevard Nights 79. Those Lips Those Eyes 80.

Preston, Robert (1917–) (Robert Preston Meservey). American leading man who made routine films from 1938, became a theatre star of great vitality in the fifties.
□King of Alcatraz 38. Illegal Traffic 38. Disbarred 38. Union Pacific 39. *Beau Geste* 39. Typhoon 39. Moon over Burma 39. Northwest Mounted Police 40. New York Town 40. The Lady from Cheyenne 40. The Night of January 16th 41. Parachute Battalion 41. Pacific Blackout 41. Reap the Wild Wind 42. *This Gun for Hire* 42. Wake Island 42. Night Plane to Chungking 42; war service; Wild Harvest 47. *The Macomber Affair* 47. Variety Girl 47. Whispering Smith 47. Blood on the Moon 48. Big City 48. The Lady Gambles 48. *Tulsa* 49. The Sundowners 49. Best of the Badmen 51. My Outlaw Brother 51. When I Grow Up 51. Face to Face 52. Cloudburst (GB) 53. The Last Frontier 56. *The Dark at the Top of the Stairs* 60. *The Music Man* (his stage role) 61. Island of Love 63. *All the Way Home* 63. How the West was Won 63. Junior Bonner 72. Child's Play 72. Mame 73. My Father's House (TV) 75. Semi-Tough 77. The Chisholms (TV) 79. S.O.B. 81. *Victor/Victoria* 82.

Prévert, Jacques (1900–1977). French screenwriter whose most memorable work was in conjunction with Marcel Carné.
Drôle de Drame 37. *Quai des Brumes* 38. *Le Jour Se Lève* 39. *Les Visiteurs du Soir* 42. *Les Enfants du Paradis* 44. *Les Portes de la Nuit* 46. Les Amants de Verone 48. Other scripts include L'Affaire est dans le Sac (& a) 32. *Le Crime de Monsieur Lange* 35. *Une Partie de Campagne* 36. *Lumière d'Eté* 42. Notre Dame de Paris 56, etc.

Prévert, Pierre (1906–). French director, brother of Jacques Prévert.
L'Affaire est dans le Sac 32. Adieu Leonard 43. Voyage Surprise 46, etc.

Previn, André (1929–). German composer and arranger, long in Hollywood. Settled in Britain and became orchestral conductor.
Scene of the Crime 49. Three Little Words 51. Bad Day at Black Rock 54. The Fastest Gun Alive 56. Designing Woman 57. Gigi (AA) 58. Porgy and Bess (AA) 59. Elmer Gantry 60. One, Two, Three 62. Irma La Douce (AA) 63. My Fair Lady (AA) 64.

Prévost, Françoise (1929–). French leading lady of international films in the sixties.
Payroll 61. Bon Voyage 63. Paris Nous Appartient 63. The Condemned of Altona 63. Galia 65, etc.

Prévost, Marie (1893–1937) (Marie Bickford Dunn). Anglo-French leading lady of American silent films.
East Lynne with Variations 20. Her Night of Nights 22. The Marriage Circle 24. Red Lights 24. The Loves of Camille 25. Up in Mabel's Room 26. Getting Gertie's Garter 27. Lady of Leisure 28. Side Show 30. Sporting Blood 31. Parole Girl 33. Tango (last film) 36, etc.

Price, Dennis (1915–73) (Dennistoun Franklyn John Rose-Price). British light leading man and latterly equally light character actor; on stage from 1937.
□ No Parking (debut) 37. A Canterbury Tale 43. *A Place of One's Own* 44. The Echo Murders 45. Caravan 46. The Magic Bow 46. Hungry Hill 46. Dear Murderer 47. Jassy 47. *Holiday Camp* 47. Master of Bankdam 47. The White Unicorn 47. Easy Money 47. Snowbound 48. Good Time Girl 48. *The Bad Lord Byron* 48. *Kind Hearts and Coronets* (his best role) 49. The Lost People 49. Helter Skelter 49. The Dancing Years 50. Murder Without Crime 50. The Adventurers 50. The Magic Box 51. Lady Godiva Rides Again 51. The House in the Square 51. Song of Paris 52.

The Tall Headlines 52. The Intruder 53. Noose for a Lady 53. Murder at 3 a.m. 53. Time is my Enemy 54. For Better For Worse 54. Eight Witnesses 54. That Lady 55. Oh Rosalinda 55. *Private's Progress* 55. Charley Moon 56. Port Afrique 56. A Touch of the Sun 56. Fortune is a Woman 57. *The Naked Truth* 57. Danger Within 58. Hello London 58. *I'm All Right Jack* 59. Don't Panic Chaps 59. Dark as the Night (US) 59. School for Scoundrels 60. *Tunes of Glory* 60. Oscar Wilde 60. Piccadilly Third Stop 60. The Millionairess 60. The Pure Hell of St Trinians 60. No Love for Johnnie 61. The Rebel 61. Five Golden Hours 61. Double Bunk 61. Watch it Sailor 61. *Victim* 61. What A Carve Up 61. Go to Blazes 62. Play it Cool 62. Behave Yourself 62. The Pot Carriers 62. The Amorous Prawn 62. Kill or Cure 62. The Wrong Arm of the Law 62. The Cool Mikado 63. The VIPs 63. The Cracksman 63. Doctor in Distress 63. *Tamahine* 63. The Comedy Man 63. A Jolly Bad Fellow 63. The Horror of it All 64. Murder Most Foul 64. The Earth Dies Screaming 64. The Curse of Simba 65. A High Wind in Jamaica 65. Ten Little Indians 65. Just Like A Woman 66. Jules Verne's Rocket to the Moon 67. The Haunted House of Horror 69. The Magic Christian 69. She Will She Won't 70. The Horror of Frankenstein 70. The Rise and Rise of Michael Rimmer 70. Twins of Evil 71. Pulp 72. Alice's Adventures in Wonderland 72. Venus in Furs 72. Go for a Take 72. That's Your Funeral 72. The Adventures of Barry Mackenzie 72. Horror Hospital 73. Theatre of Blood 73.
TV series: *The World of Wooster* (as Jeeves) 1965–8.

¶ *D.P.:* I am a second rate feature actor. I am not a star and never was. I lack the essential spark.

Price, Nancy (1880–1970) (Lillian Maude). Dominant British character actress with long stage experience, especially remembered as Grandma in *Whiteoaks*. Also an indefatigable traveller, naturalist and semi-mystic.
The Stars Look Down 39. Madonna of the Seven Moons 44. I Live in Grosvenor Square 45. The Three Weird Sisters 48. Mandy 52, etc.

Price, Vincent (1911–). Tall, gentle-voiced American character actor, lately typed in horror films. On stage since 1934; also a well-known art expert.
Autobiography 1959: *I Like What I Know*.
Biography 1976: *Vincent Price Unmasked* by J. R. Parish and Steven Whitney.
Service de Luxe (debut) 38. Elizabeth and Essex 39. Green Hell 40. *Tower of London* (as Clarence) 40. Brigham Young 40. The Song of Bernadette 43. The Keys of the Kingdom 44. Laura 44. Wilson 44. Czarina 45. *Dragonwyck* 46. Shock 46. The Long Night 47. The Three Musketeers 49. Champagne for Caesar 49. *His Kind of Woman* 51. *House of Wax* 53. The Mad Magician 54. The Ten Commandments 56. *The Story of Mankind* 57. The Fly 58. The Bat 59. The House on Haunted Hill 60. *The Fall of the House of Usher* 61. The Pit and the Pendulum 61. Tales of Terror 62. *The Raven* 63. A Comedy of Terrors 63. *The Tomb of Ligeia* 64. City under the Sea 65. Dr Goldfoot and the Sex Machine 65. House of a Thousand Dolls 67. The Oblong Box 69. Scream and Scream Again 69. Cry of the Banshee 70. The Abominable Dr Phibes 71. Dr Phibes Rises Again 72. Theatre of Blood 73. Madhouse 73. Journey into Fear 75. Scavenger Hunt 79. The Monster Club 81. The House of Long Shadows 83. Bloodbath at the House of Death 84. The Whales of August 87, etc.
TV series: Time Express 79.

¶ *V.P.:* I sometimes feel that I'm impersonating the dark unconscious of the whole human race. I know this sounds sick, but I love it.
† Price's was the voice on Michael Jackson's phenomenally successful 1983 video 'Thriller'.

Pride and Prejudice (US 1940). A delightful example of Hollywood 'Englishness'. Though Aldous Huxley's script was a simplification of Jane Austen and advanced the period forty years to take advantage of the fuller fashions, this remains a splendid romantic comedy of a more polite age, full of richly satisfying performances: Greer Garson as Elizabeth, Laurence Olivier as Darcy, Edmund Gwenn as Mr Bennet, Edna May Oliver as Lady Catherine, Melville Cooper as Mr Collins. Directed by Robert Z. Leonard in just the right unhurried style.

Priestley, J. B. (1894–1984). Prolific British novelist. There have been film versions of *The Good Companions*, *Benighted* (The Old Dark House), *Let the People Sing*, and also of his plays *Dangerous Corner*, *Laburnum Grove*, *When We Are Married* and *An Inspector Calls*. His autobiographical *Midnight on the Desert* (1937) says much about Hollywood.

Priestley, Jack (–). American cinematographer.

No Way to Treat a Lady 68. Stiletto 69. Where's Poppa 70. The First Deadly Sin 80, etc.

Priestley, Tom (1932–), British editor. Deliverance 72, The Great Gatsby 74, Voyage of the Damned 76. Times Square 80, etc.

priests have been a godsend to film makers. Most male stars have played them occasionally: the combination of masculine attractiveness and non-availability apparently works at the box office. Thus Frank Sinatra in *The Miracle of the Bells*; William Holden and Clifton Webb in *Satan Never Sleeps*; Bing Crosby in *Going My Way, The Bells of St Mary's* and *Say One for Me*; Richard Dix in *The Christian*; Pat O'Brien in a dozen films including *Angels with Dirty Faces, The Fighting 69th* and *Fighting Father Dunne*; ditto Spencer Tracy, in *Boys' Town, San Francisco, The Devil at Four O'Clock*, and others; George Arliss in *Cardinal Richelieu*; Don Murray in *The Hoodlum Priest*; Karl Malden in *On the Waterfront* and *The Great Impostor*; Pierre Fresnay in *Monsieur Vincent*; Claude Laydu in *Diary of a Country Priest*; Jean-Paul Belmondo in *Leon Morin Priest*; John Mills in *The Singer Not the Song*; Tom Tryon in *The Cardinal*; Gregory Peck in *The Keys of the Kingdom*; Geoffrey Bayldon in *Sky West and Crooked*; Richard Burton in *Becket*; David Warner in *The Ballad of Cable Hogue*; Ward Bond in *The Quiet Man*; Mickey Rooney in *The Twinkle in God's Eye*; Montgomery Clift in *I Confess*; Alec Guinness in *Father Brown* and *The Prisoner*; Trevor Howard in *Ryan's Daughter*; Donald Sutherland in *Act of the Heart*; and Marcello Mastroianni in *The Priest's Wife*.

Protestant priests included Anthony Quayle in *Serious Charge*; Richard Burton in *The Sandpiper*; Robert Donat in *Lease of Life*; Wilfred Lawson in *Pastor Hall*; Peter Sellers in *Heavens Above*; Richard Todd in *A Man Called Peter*; Fredric March in *One Foot in Heaven*; David Niven in *The Bishop's Wife*. Actors who have got to play pope include Anthony Quinn and John Gielgud in *The Shoes of the Fisherman*, Rod Steiger in *A Man Called John*, Paolo Stoppa in *Becket* and Rex Harrison in *The Agony and the Ecstasy*.

False priests were Humphrey Bogart in *The Left Hand of God*, Rod Steiger in *No Way to Treat a Lady*, Dennis Price in *Kind Hearts and Coronets*, and Peter Sellers in *After the Fox*; while priestly villains were Ralph Richardson in *The Ghoul*, George Arliss in *Dr Syn* (followed by Peter Cushing in *Captain Clegg*), Keenan Wynn in *Johnny Concho*, Cedric Hardwicke in *The Hunchback of Notre Dame* and Robert Mitchum in *Night of the Hunter*. Classifiable as fallen priests were Henry Fonda in *The Fugitive*, Richard Burton in *Night of the Iguana*, Max Von Sydow in *Hawaii*, Burt Lancaster in *Elmer Gantry*, Lars Hanson in *The Scarlet Letter*, and Pierre Fresnay in *Le Défroqué* and *Dieu a Besoin des Hommes*.

Priests have come into their own again in the recent spate of diabolical thrillers: Max Von Sydow and Jason Miller in *The Exorcist*, Patrick Troughton in *The Omen*, Oliver Reed in *The Devils*. Other troubled priests have included Rod Steiger (and various successors) in *The Amityville Horror* series, Christopher Reeve in *Monsignor*, and the protagonists of *True Confessions*.

Priggen, Norman (1924–). British producer, with Ealing Studios from 1939, later independent.
The Professionals 61. Payroll 61. The Servant 64. Secret Ceremony (co-p) 68. Tales That Witness Madness 73, etc.

Primus, Barry (1938–). American actor.
The Gravy Train 74. Boxcar Bertha 75. New York New York 77. Avalanche 78. The Rose 79. Heartland 80. Absence of Malice 81. Paper Dolls (TV) 82.

The Prince and the Pauper. Mark Twain's medieval story, about a prince and a commoner who change places, was filmed in 1909; in 1915 with Marguerite Clark; in 1923 with Tibi Lubin; in 1937 with the Mauch twins (and Errol Flynn); in 1962 with Sean Scully; and in 1977 with Mark Lester.

Prince, Harold (1924–). American stage producer who dabbles in films.
□Something for Everyone 70. A Little Night Music 77.

Prince, William (1913–). American stage leading man who has been less successful in films.
Destination Tokyo 44. Pillow to Post 46. Dead Reckoning 47. Carnegie Hall 48. Cyrano de Bergerac 51. The Vagabond King 55. Macabre 58. The Stepford Wives 75. Family Plot 76. The Gauntlet 77. Bronco Billy 80. Love and Money 82. Movers and Shakers 84. Spies Like Us 85, etc.

Principal, Victoria (1945–). American leading lady.
The Life and Times of Judge Roy Bean 72. The Naked Ape 73. Earthquake 74. I Will, I

Will, for Now 76. Vigilante Force 76. The Night They Took Miss Beautiful (TV) 77. Fantasy Island (TV) 77.
TV series: Dallas 80–.

Prine, Andrew (1936–). American leading man.
The Miracle Worker 62. Company of Cowards 64. The Devil's Brigade 68. Bandolero 68. A Time for Giving 69. One Little Indian 73. Grizzly 76, etc.
TV series: Wide Country 62.

Pringle, Aileen (1895–) (Aileen Bisbee). American actress of the silent screen, best remembered for her performance in Elinor Glyn's *Three Weeks* 24.
Redhead 19. The Christian 23. Wife of a Centaur 24. Dance Madness 24. Adam and Evil 27. Soldiers and Women 30. Convicted 32. Jane Eyre 33. Piccadilly Jim 36. Nothing Sacred 37. The Girl from Nowhere 39. Happy Land 43, etc.

Pringle, Bryan (1935–). British character actor of stage and TV.
Saturday Night and Sunday Morning 60. The Boy Friend 71, etc.

Printemps, Yvonne (1894-1977) (Yvonne Wigniolle). French musical comedy star in occasional films.
La Dame aux Caméllias. The Paris Waltz. Voyage to America.

Prinz, Le Roy (1895–1983). American choreographer who after adventurous early life came to Hollywood and worked on many Paramount and Warner films.
The Sign of the Cross 32. The 'Road' films 39–42. Yankee Doodle Dandy 42. Night and Day 46. The Ten Commandments 56. South Pacific 58, many others. Directed short subject *A Boy and His Dog* (AA) 48.

prison films have always had an audience, but did not reach their full potential until sound. Then and through the thirties, film-makers took us on a conducted tour of American prisons. *The Big House, The Last Mile, I Was a Fugitive from a Chain Gang, Twenty Thousand Years in Sing Sing, Front Page Woman* (with its gas chamber scene), *Angels with Dirty Faces, San Quentin, Blackwell's Island, Each Dawn I Die, Invisible Stripes, King of Alcatraz, Prison Ship, Prison Doctor, Mutiny in the Big House* and many others. During the war prison films were surpassed in excitement, but they came back with a bang in *Brute Force*, the toughest of them all, and *White Heat*. The fifties brought *Behind the High Wall, Duffy of San Quentin, Riot in Cell Block Eleven, Inside the Walls of Folsom Prison, Black Tuesday, I Want to Live, Cell 2455 Death Row*, and a remake of *The Last Mile*. More recently Burt Lancaster appeared in the factual *Bird Man of Alcatraz*; and in the second half of the sixties the subject became popular again with *The Brig, The Ceremony, Reprieve, Point Blank, The Dirty Dozen, Triple Cross, Riot, There was a Crooked Man, A Clockwork Orange* and *Fortune and Men's Eyes*.

British studios have produced few prison films until the realist wave of the sixties which brought with it *The Criminal, The Pot Carriers*, and the army prison film *The Hill*.

Unusual prisons were shown in *Sullivan's Travels, Devil's Canyon, One Day in the Life of Ivan Denisovich*, and *Nevada Smith*; while among the films poking fun at prison life are *Up the River, Pardon Us* (Laurel and Hardy), *Convict 99* (Will Hay), *Jailhouse Rock* and *Two-Way Stretch*.

Prisons for women crop up quite regularly in such films as *Prison without Bars, Caged* (American), *Caged* (Italian), *Au Royaume des Cieux, Women's Prison, Girls behind Bars, So Evil So Young, The Weak and the Wicked, Yield to the Night* and *The Smashing Bird I Used to Know* and *Women in Chains* (TV).

The Prisoner of Zenda. At least four versions have been made of Anthony Hope's classic Ruritanian romance about a great impersonation, all in Hollywood. 1. 1922: directed by Rex Ingram, with Lewis Stone and Ramon Novarro. 2. 1937: directed by John Cromwell, with Ronald Colman and Douglas Fairbanks Jnr. 3. 1952: directed by Richard Thorpe, with Stewart Granger and James Mason. The 1937 version remains a model of its kind, with a fine cast including C. Aubrey Smith, David Niven, Raymond Massey and Madeleine Carroll; the 1952 version is a mechanical scene-for-scene remake. A parody on the story was included in *The Great Race* 65. *Royal Flash* 75 included another comic variation; and in 1979 Peter Sellers appeared in an unsatisfactory half-humorous version by Dick Clement and Ian La Frenais.

prisoners of war were featured in many films after World War II. The British examples often made the camps seem almost too comfortable, despite the possibility of being shot while attempting to escape; this was perhaps because they were all filled with the same familiar faces. *Albert RN, The Captive Heart, The Colditz Story, The Betrayal, Danger Within, Reach for the Sky* and *The Password is Courage* all found humour in the situation at any rate; whereas the American counterparts, *The Purple Heart, Prisoner of War, Stalag 17* and *The Mackenzie Break* saw the harsher side which doubtless existed. The co-production, *The Bridge on the River Kwai*, gave a mixed picture of a Japanese camp; Britain's Hammer horror studio then produced *The Camp on Blood Island*, a fictitious record of atrocity, followed some years later by *The Secret of Blood Island*. Meanwhile the British in *The One That Got Away* paid tribute to the one German to escape from a British camp; and more recently *The Great Escape* showed the Americans coming some way towards the British idea of how jolly life in a camp can be. The ultimate absurdity was reached by an American TV series, *Hogan's Heroes*, which has a camp almost entirely controlled by the prisoners. The best serious film about prisoners of war remains undoubtedly Renoir's *La Grande Illusion*, made in 1937; though *King Rat* in 1965 made a fair bid to reveal the squalor and futility of the life. Comic adventure stories about the escape of POWs have included *Very Important Person, The Secret War of Harry Frigg, Where Eagles Dare, Hannibal Brooks* and *Situation Hopeless But Not Serious.*

Women's camps were shown in *Two Thousand Women* (GB 1944), *Three Came Home* (US 1950), *A Town Like Alice* (GB 1956) and *Kapo* (It. 1960).

Vietnam has now made a horrifying start to its quota of prisoner-of-war films with *The Deer Hunter*.

private eyes: see *mystery*.

The Private Life of Henry VIII (GB 1932). Credited with being the first British film to win success in the American market, this enjoyable historical romp was directed by Alexander Korda from a script by Lajos Biro and Arthur Wimperis. Charles Laughton (AA) gave one of his richest performances, with memorable assistance from Robert Donat, Elsa Lanchester and Binnie Barnes. Design by Vincent Korda, photography by Georges Perinal. 1972's *Henry VIII and His Six Wives* was a semi-remake.

Private's Progress (GB 1955). The first of the Boulting Brothers' anti-establishment comedies, this took a sound swipe at the army, with Ian Carmichael as the innocent involved in red tape and regulations. Directed by John Boulting, written by himself and Frank Harvey from Alan Hackney's novel. Subsequent Boulting films attacked the unions (*I'm All Right, Jack*) 59, and the Church (*Heavens Above*) 63.

prizefighting: see *boxing*.

Prizmacolour. An early American colour process used for *The Glorious Adventure* 21. Crude in effect, in using orange and turquoise filters, it anticipated Cinecolor.

producer. On the stage this term may be equivalent to 'director', i.e. the man who actually marshals the actors and whose conception of the show is supreme. In the film world it almost always indicates the man in control of the budget, whether an independent or working for a big studio. He controls all personnel including the director, and though the film may originally be his overall conception, he normally delegates his artistic responsiblities, remaining responsible chiefly for the film's ultimate commercial success or failure.

¶ *Jesse L. Lasky:* The producer must be a prophet and a general, a diplomat and a peacemaker, a miser and a spendthrift. He must have vision tempered by hindsight, daring governed by caution, the patience of a saint and the iron of a Cromwell.
Joseph Kennedy: Movie production requires producers, men who can orchestrate the sound and the fury of which pictures are made.
Ben Hecht: The job of turning good writers into movie hacks is the producer's chief task.
Martin Ragaway: A producer is a clever man whose brain starts working the moment he gets up in the morning and doesn't stop until he reaches the studio.
Ben Hecht: Producers are men who will keep their heads in the noisy presence of writers and directors and not be carried away by art in any of its subversive guises. Their task is to guard against the unusual. They are the trusted loyalists of cliché.
Sam Goldwyn: A producer shouldn't get ulcers, he should give them.
David Hemmings: Producing is a thankless task akin to hotel management. Unfortunately there are not too many good hotel managers.

production designer. Technician responsible for the overall 'look' of a film, ranging from actual set design to photographic style.

production manager. The person responsible for administrative details of a production, e.g. salaries, transport, departmental expenditure.

programmer. Trade term for a routine feature of only moderate appeal, likely to form half a bill; similar to 'co-feature'.

Prokoviev, Sergei (1891–1953). Russian composer whose main film scores were *Alexander Nevsky* 39, *Lermontov* 43 and *Ivan the Terrible* 42 and 46.

propaganda: see under *documentary*.

prophecy has interested film-makers only occasionally, but at least two outstanding films have resulted: *Metropolis* and *Things to Come. Just Imagine* painted a light-hearted picture, and *Seven Days in May* was not too frightening about what might be happening politically a few years from now; but one hopes not to take too seriously the predictions in *1984, The Time Machine, Fahrenheit 451, Alphaville, When Worlds Collide, The World, the Flesh and the Devil, The War Game, Dr Strangelove, Punishment Park, Beyond the Time Barrier, No Blade of Grass, Barbarella, A Clockwork Orange, Planet of the Apes, Westworld, Futureworld, Logan's Run, Star Wars, The Final Programme, Death Race 2000, Soylent Green* and *The Ultimate Warrior*.

prostitutes for many years could not be so labelled in Hollywood films, which featured a surprising number of 'café hostesses'. It was however fairly easy to spot the real profession of the various ladies who played Sadie Thompson in *Rain*, of Marlene Dietrich in *Dishonoured* and *Shanghai Express*, of Clara Bow in *Call Her Savage*, of Greta Garbo in *Anna Christie*, of Miriam Hopkins in *Dr Jekyll and Mr Hyde*, of Tallulah Bankhead in *Faithless*, of Bette Davis in *Of Human Bondage*, of Vivien Leigh in *Waterloo Bridge*, and of Joan Bennett in *Man Hunt*, to name but a few. The French, who have always called a spade a spade, flaunted the calling in hundreds of films including *Dedée D'Anvers, La Ronde, Le Plaisir, Boule de Suif, Le Long des Trottoirs, La Bonne Soupe, Adua et sa Compagnie* and *Les Compagnons de la Nuit*; Italy chipped in with *Mamma Roma* and Japan with *Street of Shame*. In the fifties Britain moved into the field with surprising eagerness—every other movie seemed to feature Dora Bryan in a plastic mac—and there were several alleged exposés of Soho corruption under such titles as *The Flesh is Weak, Passport to Shame* and *The World Ten Times Over*. Hollywood half-heartedly followed with some double-talking second features about call girls—*Why Girls Leave Home, Call Girl, Girls in the Night*—and some 'medical case histories' such as *The Three Faces of Eve, Girl of the Night*. Around 1960 the floodgates opened, eased by the sensationally successful Greek comedy *Never on Sunday* (and some continental imitators like *Always on Saturday* and *Every Night of the Week*). Among English-speaking stars who have lately played prostitutes are Shirley Maclaine in *Some Came Running* and *Irma La Douce*, Sophia Loren in *Lady L, Yesterday, Today and Tomorrow, Marriage Italian Style, Boccaccio 70* and *Man of La Mancha*, Anna Karina in *Vivre sa Vie*, Lee Grant in *Divorce American Style* and *The Balcony*, Catherine Deneuve in *Belle de Jour*, Carroll Baker in *Sylvia*, Shirley Jones in *Elmer Gantry*, Nancy Kwan in *The World of Suzie Wong*, Elizabeth Taylor in *Butterfield 8*, Diane Cilento in *Rattle of a Simple Man*, Carol White in *Poor Cow*, Inger Stevens in *Five Card Stud*, Margot Kidder in *Gaily, Gaily*, Kitty Wynn in *Panic in Needle Park*, Jane Fonda in *Klute*. Brothels have been shown in *Lady L, A Walk on the Wild Side, The Revolt of Mamie Stover, A House is not a Home, Ulysses, The Balcony, A Funny Thing Happened on the Way to the Forum, The Assassination Bureau, The Best House in London, Games That Lovers Play, The Reivers, Gaily, Gaily*, and an increasing number of westerns. In *Our Man Flint*, girls were described as 'pleasure units' . . .

See also: *courtesans*.

Prouty, Jed (1879–1956). American character actor with stage experience, in films from the mid-twenties. Best remembered as father of *The Jones Family*; he appeared in over a dozen episodes of this domestic comedy series between 1935 and 1940. Broadway Melody 28. George White's Scandals 35. The Texas Rangers 36. Roar of the Press 41. Mug Town 43. Guilty Bystander 49, many others.

Prouty, Olive Higgins (1882–1974). American novelist, best known to filmgoers for *Now Voyager* and *Stella Dallas*.

Provine, Dorothy (1937–). American leading lady who became well known as night

club entertainer in TV series *The Roaring Twenties*; also in *The Alaskans* 59.
The Bonnie Parker Story 58. Wall of Noise 63. It's a Mad Mad Mad Mad World 63. Good Neighbour Sam 64. That Darn Cat 65. The Great Race 65. One Spy Too Many 66. Kiss the Girls and Make Them Die 66. Who's Minding the Mint? 67, etc.

Prowse, Juliet (1937–). South African leading lady, in Hollywood from 1958, at first as dancer.
Can Can 59. G.I. Blues 60. The Fiercest Heart 61. The Right Approach 61. The Second Time Around 61. Run For Your Wife 66, etc.
TV series: *Meet Mona McCluskey* 65.

Pryce, Jonathan (1947–). Saturnine British leading actor.
Voyage of the Damned 76. Breaking Glass 80. Loophole 80. The Day Christ Died (TV) 80. Praying Mantis (TV) 82. The Ploughman's Lunch 83. Something Wicked This Way Comes 83. Brazil 85. The Doctor and the Devils 86. Haunted Honeymoon 86. Jumping Jack Flash 87, etc.

Pryor, Nicholas (–). American actor who sometimes plays weaklings.
The Way We Live Now 70. Man on a Swing 74. The Happy Hooker 75. Smile 75. Fear on Trial (TV) 75. *Washington: Behind Closed Doors* (TV) 77. The Life and Assassination of the Kingfish (TV) 77. Rainbow (TV) 78. Damien: Omen II 78. The Fish That Saved Pittsburgh 79. The Formula 80. Airplane 80. The Falcon and the Snowman 84. The Believers 86.

Pryor, Richard (1940–). Black American night club comedian.
□ The Busy Body 68. The Green Berets 68. Wild in the Streets 69. The Phynx 70. You've Got to Walk It Like You Talk It or You'll Lose that Beat 71. Dynamite Chicken 72. Lady Sings the Blues 72. Wattstax 73. The Mack 73. Hit 73. Some Call It Loving 73. Blazing Saddles (co-w only) 74. Uptown Saturday Night 74. Adios Amigo 75. The Bingo Long Allstars and Travelling Motor Kings 76. Car Wash 76. Silver Streak 76. Greased Lightning 77. Which Way Is Up 77. Blue Collar 78. The Wiz 78. California Suite 78. Richard Pryor Live in Concert 79. The Muppet Movie 79. In God We Trust 80. Stir Crazy 80. Wholly Moses 81. Bustin' Loose 81. Some Kind of Hero 82. The Toy 82. Superman III 83. Brewster's Millions 85. Jo Jo Dancer, Your Life is Calling 85. Critical Condition 87.

Pryor, Roger (1901–1974). American leading man of minor movies, also stage and radio actor.
Moonlight and Pretzels 33. Belle of the Nineties 34. Ticket to Paradise 36. Money and the Woman 40. She Couldn't Say No 41, etc.

pseudonyms

? Who was also known as:

1 Sleep'n' Eat?
2 William B. Goodrich?
3 Parkyakarkus?
4 Billie Cassin?
5 Diane Belmont?
6 Bryant Fleming?
7 Blade Stanhope Conway?
8 Joseph Walton?
9 Stephen Richards?
10 Bettina Dawes?
11 Robert Rich?
12 Emily Clark, Harriet Brown, Jane Emerson, Gussie Berger, Mary Holmquist, Karin Lund?
13 John Elder, Henry Younger?
14 Mark Canfield?
15 Mahatma Kane Jeeves?

Psycho (US 1960). Alfred Hitchcock's horror comic, which he appears to have made as a joke, in the spirit of seeing whether he could get away with its nastiness. The critics found it revolting at first, but some later came round and admitted that once you were used to the idea of vivid bathtub murders, etc., it was done in Hitchcock's usual accomplished manner. Unfortunately it enabled less talented producers subsequently to indulge in similar shock tactics and is partly responsible for the low ebb of the thriller today with its emphasis on gore. Written by Joseph Stefano from a novel by Robert Bloch which is rather more subtle than the film; photographed by John L. Russell; with Anthony Perkins. Bernard Herrmann's score is perhaps the most frightening thing about it. In 1983 *Psycho II* added more twists, with Norman Bates released from the asylum twenty years later; and the inevitable *Psycho III* followed in 1986.

psychology is featured most prominently in American films—quite naturally since the United States is the home of the psychiatrist.

However, one of the best serious psychological films, *Mine Own Executioner*, did come from Britain and showed the doctor to be more in need of help than the patient; while two other notable British films, *Thunder Rock* and *Dead of Night*, centred on the depiction of psychological states.

Although films about psychology can be firmly traced back to *The Cabinet of Dr Caligari* and *Secrets of a Soul*, the subject took its firmest hold in the middle of World War II, when so many people needed reassurance; the recounting of dreams to an analyst could even take the place of musical numbers in a romantic trifle like *Lady in the Dark*. Soon we were inundated with melodramas like *Spellbound, The Dark Mirror* and *Possessed*, in which the question to be answered was not so much who or how but why; and it wasn't until about 1950, with *Harvey*, that analysts could be laughed at; they were still being analysed in the seventies in such films as *Taking Off*. In the fifties the schizophrenic drama took on a new lease of life (*The Three Faces of Eve, Lizzie, Vertigo*), as did the tendency to guy individual psychiatrists while still claiming to respect the profession (*Oh Men Oh Women, Mirage, A Fine Madness, The Group, What a Way to Go, Marriage of a Young Stockbroker*). Of course, films were still made which took the whole matter with deadly seriousness, as in *The Cobweb, The Mark, Captain Newman MD, The Third Secret* and *Pressure Point*. John Huston's under-rated film on the life of *Freud* may have been unlucky to arrive at a time of change: the fashion is now for case histories in which no solution is offered (*Repulsion, Morgan, Cul-de-Sac*) or psychological horror comics such as *Psycho, Homicidal*, and *The Night Walker*, while in *Promise Her Anything* we were finally shown a psychiatrist (Robert Cummings) who doesn't believe in psychiatry.

See also *dreams; fantasy; amnesia; case histories*.

The Public Enemy (US 1931). One of the most violent of the early sound gangster films; it helped to swell official opinion against them, and James Cagney, who dispensed a lot of sudden death in this one, had to reform in *G-Men* 35, in which he stays on the right side of the law. Directed by William Wellman from a script by Harvey Thew; photographed by Dev Jennings. It still has powerful sequences despite its undeniably dated air.

publicity

¶ No right minded film-maker believes his own publicity . . . but he surely hopes it works. The tag-line devised for a film can have a make-or-break effect on its box-office record. Seldom can such lines be claimed as an honest distillation of truth, and very often they hint at more sensations than can be found in the film to which they are attached. But for sheer ingenuity some are unbeatable, and a few have even passed into the language.

The Twenties:

The dangerous age for women is from three to seventy!—*Adam's Rib* (1922)

A photoplay of tempestuous love between a madcap English beauty and a bronzed Arab chief!—*The Sheik*

A cast of 125,000!—*Ben Hur*

The mightiest dramatic spectacle of all the ages!—*The Ten Commandments* (1923)

The epic of the American doughboy!—*The Big Parade*

A thrill a minute! A laugh a second! A comedy cyclone!—*Feet First*

Love of tender girlhood! Passionate deeds of heroes! A rushing, leaping drama of charm and excitement!—*America*

A thing of beauty is a joy forever . . .—*Street Angel*

The Thirties:

The knockout picture of the year!—*The Champ*

The most startling drama ever produced!—*Strange Interlude*

Mothered by an ape—he knew only the law of the jungle—to seize what he wanted!—*Tarzan of the Apes*

Strange Desires! Loves and hates and secret yearnings . . . hidden in the shadows of a man's mind.—*Dr Jekyll and Mr Hyde*

The picture that will make 1933 famous!—*Gabriel Over the White House*

The dance-mad musical triumph of two continents!—*The Gay Divorcee*

The love affair that shook the world!—*Cleopatra*

The most glorious musical romance of all time!—*One Night of Love*

His love challenged the flames of revolution!—*A Tale of Two Cities*

Love as burning as Sahara's sands!—*Under Two Flags*

The march of time measured by a human heart—a mother's heart!—*Cavalcade*

Romance aflame through dangerous days and nights of terror! In a land where anything can happen—most of all to a beautiful girl alone!—*Gunga Din* (in

which the girl was very dispensable indeed)
The picture made behind locked doors!—*Dr Cyclops*
The strangest love a man has ever known!—*Dracula*
More sensational than her unforgettable father!—*Dracula's Daughter*
A love story that lived for three thousand years!—*The Mummy*
He's just as funny as his old man was fierce!—*Son of Kong*
Three centuries in the making!—*A Midsummer Night's Dream*
He plucked from the gutter a faded rose and made an immortal masterpiece!—*The Life of Emile Zola*
135 women—with men on their minds!—*The Women*
He treated her rough—and she loved it!—*Red Dust*
A story so momentous it required six Academy Award stars and a cast of 1,186 players!—*Juarez*
Only the rainbow can duplicate its brilliance!—*The Adventures of Robin Hood*
Don't pronounce it—see it!—*Ninotchka*
A monster in form but human in his desire for love!—*Bride of Frankenstein*
Boiling passions in the burning sands!—*The Lost Patrol*
Six sticks of dynamite that blasted his way to freedom—and awoke America's conscience!—*I Am a Fugitive from a Chain Gang*

The Forties:
No one is as good as Bette when she's bad!—*In This Our Life*
If she were yours, would you forgive?—*The Unfaithful*
The relentless drama of a woman driven to the depths of emotion by a craving beyond control!—*The Lady Gambles*
The thousands who have read the book will know why WE WILL NOT SELL ANY CHILDREN TICKETS to see this picture!—*The Grapes of Wrath*
Half men, half demons, warriors such as the world has never known—they lived with death and danger for the women who hungered for their love!—*Northwest Passage*
You can't keep a good monster down!—*The Ghost of Frankenstein*
A romantic gentleman by day—a love-mad beast by night!—*Dr Jekyll and Mr Hyde*
The minx in mink with a yen for men!—*Lady in the Dark*
The immortal thriller . . .—*Orpheus*
How'd you like to tussle with Russell?—*The Outlaw*
Gable's back and Garson's got him!—*Adventure*
There never was a woman like . . .—*Gilda*
It tells ALL about those Brontë sisters!—*Devotion*
More thrilling than the deeds of man . . . more beautiful than the love of woman . . . more wonderful than the dreams of children!—*The Jungle Book*
The picture they were born for!—*The Big Sleep*
The picture that helped to win the war!—*Mrs Miniver* (reissue)
He's as fast on the draw as he is in the drawing room!—*The Maltese Falcon*
We're going to see Jennifer Jones AGAIN in . . .—*The Song of Bernadette*
The sum total of all human emotion!—*Leave Her to Heaven*
The truth about the Nazis from the cradle to the battlefront!—*Hitler's Children*
A peek into the other woman's male!—*A Letter to Three Wives*
She knows all about love potions and lovely motions!—*I Married a Witch*
Paramount proudly brings to the screens of America one of the three great love stories of all time!—*To Each His Own* (which were the others?)
'I bought this woman for my own . . . and I'll kill the man who touches her!'—*Unconquered*
A thousand miles of danger with a thousand thrills a mile!—*Santa Fe Trail*
168 minutes of breathless thrills and romance!—*For Whom the Bell Tolls*
The girl of the moment in the wonderful picture of America's hey! hey! day!—*Margie*
The kind of woman most men want—but shouldn't have!—*Mildred Pierce*
They had a date with fate in . . .—*Casablanca*
The flaming drama of a high-born beauty who blindly loved the most icy-hearted big shot gangland ever knew!—*Johnny Eager*
Whisper her name!—*The Strange Love of Martha Ivers*
A mouth like hers is just for kissing . . . not for telling!—*Nora Prentiss*
She insulted her soul!—*Dishonored Lady*
She's got the biggest six-shooters in the west!—*The Beautiful Blonde from Bashful Bend*

The private lady of a public enemy!—*The Damned Don't Cry*
It was the look in her eyes that did it! How could he know it meant murder?—*The Woman in the Window*
A love story every woman would die a thousand deaths to live!—*Jane Eyre*
'The men in her life sometimes lived to regret it!'—*Temptation*

The Fifties:
Greater than IVANHOE!—*Julius Caesar*
First they moved (1895)! Then they talked (1927)! Now they smell!—*Scent of Mystery*
The butler did it! He made every lady in the house oh so very happy!—*My Man Godfrey*
Sing, Judy! Dance, Judy! The world is waiting for your sunshine!—*A Star is Born*
Even in the first wild joy of her arms, he realized that she would be . . . an unfit mother!—*Because of You*
A lion in your lap!—*Bwana Devil* (the first 3-D film)
In making this film, MGM feel privileged to add something of permanent value to the cultural treasure house of mankind . . .—*Quo Vadis*
Ancient Rome is going to the dogs, Robert Taylor is going to the lions, and Peter Ustinov is going crazy!—*Quo Vadis* (revived for TV in the seventies)
You have never really seen Gregory Peck until you see him in CinemaScope!—*Night People*
We didn't say nice people, we said—. *Night People*
Their story is not in the history books. It has never been seen on the screen—until now!—*Désirée*
A hard cop and a soft dame!—*The Big Heat*
A completely new experience between men and women!—*The Men* (about paraplegics)
He faced a decision that someday may be yours to make!—*Ransom* (the hero's son was kidnapped)
The colossus who conquered the world! The most colossal motion picture of all time!—*Alexander the Great*
When the hands point straight up . . . the excitement starts!—*High Noon*
That streetcar man has a new desire!—*The Wild One*
Her treachery stained every stone of the pyramid!—*Land of the Pharaohs*
The supreme screen achievement of our time!—*Salome*
Of what a girl did . . . what a boy did . . . of ecstasy and revenge!—*East of Eden*
If a woman answers . . . hang on for dear life!—*Dial M For Murder*
Body of a boy! Mind of a monster! Soul of an unearthly thing!—*I Was a Teenage Frankenstein*
The story of a family's ugly secret and the stark moment that thrust their private lives into public view!—*Written on the Wind*
'She was too hungry for love to care where she found it!'—*The Female on the Beach*

The Sixties:
If you miss the first five minutes you miss one suicide, two executions, one seduction and the key to the plot!—*The Kremlin Letter*
The motion picture with something to offend everybody!—*The Loved One*
Beware the beat of the cloth-wrapped feet!—*The Mummy's Shroud*
The world's most uncovered undercover agent!—*Fathom*
Don't give away the ending—it's the only one we have!—*Psycho*
The birds is coming!—*The Birds*
Every time a woman turns her face away because she's tired or unwilling, there's someone waiting like me . . .—*The Dark at the Top of the Stairs*
The hot line suspense comedy!—*Dr Strangelove*
A thousand thrills . . . and Hayley Mills!—*In Search of the Castaways*
A picture that goes beyond what men think about—because no man ever thought about it in quite this way!—*Eight and a Half*
You may not believe in ghosts, but you cannot deny terror . . .—*The Haunting*
There are many kinds of love, but are there any without guilt?—*Five Finger Exercise*
You can expect the unexpected!—*Charade*
Now . . . add a motion picture to the wonders of the world!—*Taras Bulba*
One man . . . three women . . . one night!—*The Night of the Iguana*
You'll laugh your pants off!—*Laurel and Hardy's Laughing Twenties*
£10,000 if you die of fright!—*Macabre*
The picture with the fear flasher and the horror horn!—*Chamber of Horrors*
Meet the girls with the thermo-nuclear navels! The most titillating time bombs you've ever been tempted to trigger!—*Dr*

Goldfoot and the Girl Bombs
Keep the children home! And if you're squeamish, stay home with them!—*Witchfinder General*
A side of life you never expected to see on the screen!—*Walk on the Wild Side*
You are cordially invited to George and Martha's for an evening of fun and games!—*Who's Afraid of Virginia Woolf?*
Why the crazy title? If we told you, you'd only laugh!—*The Russians are Coming, The Russians are Coming*
Every father's daughter is a virgin!—*Goodbye Columbus*
They're young . . . they're in love . . . and they kill people.—*Bonnie and Clyde*
'What we've got here is a failure to communicate.'—*Cool Hand Luke*
The big comedy of nineteen-sexty-sex!—*Boeing-Boeing*
He is a shy schoolmaster. She is a music hall star. They marry and immediately have 283 children . . . all boys!—*Goodbye Mr Chips*

The Seventies:
Love means never having to say you're sorry . . .—*Love Story*
Hope never dies for a man with a good dirty mind!—*Hoffman*
The story of a homosexual who married a nymphomaniac!—*The Music Lovers*
Like the act of love, this film must be experienced from beginning to end . . .—*The Sailor Who Fell from Grace with the Sea*
They stand side by side. Young and old. Rich and poor. They gather together for a single purpose. Survival.—*The Seagull*
We don't love—we just make love. And damn little of that!—*The Happy Ending*
She gave away secrets to one side and her heart to the other!—*Darling Lili*
For the price of a movie you'll feel like a million!—*The Sunshine Boys*
The damnedest thing you ever saw.—*Nashville*
1953 was a good year for leaving home.—*Next Stop Greenwich Village*
The epic love story in which everybody has a great role and a big part.—*Joseph Andrews*

NB In 1972 a New York magazine ran a competition, inviting readers to invent way-out and hilarious tag-lines for non-existent movies. The results were indeed hilarious, but not so way-out that one can't imagine them being snapped up and used pretty quickly. Here are some of the winners:

Makes Myra Breckinridge look like Snow White!

It took guts to film. Have you the guts to see it?

There were four men in her life. One to love her. One to marry her. One to take care of her. And one to kill her . . .

They lived a lifetime in 24 crowded hours!

The picture that could change your life—or save it!

If you scoff at the powers of darkness, do not see this film alone!

The book they said could never be written has become the movie they said could never be filmed!

Pudovkin, V. (Vsevolod) (1893–1953). Russian film theorist, writer and actor. Best remembered as director.
Mother 26. *The End of St Petersburg* 27. *Storm over Asia* 28. The Deserter 33. General Suvorov 41, many others which have not travelled.

Puglia, Frank (1892–1975). American character actor with vaudeville experience.
Viva Villa 34. Maisie 39. The Mark of Zorro 40. Jungle Book 42. Phantom of the Opera 43. Blood on the Sun 45. The Desert Hawk 50. The Burning Hills 56. Cry Tough 59. Say Goodbye Maggie Cole (TV) 72. Mr Ricco 75, many others.

Pulver, Lilo or **Liselotte** (1929–). Swiss-German leading lady.
A Time to Live and a Time to Die (US) 59. One, Two, Three (US) 61. A Global Affair (US) 63. La Religieuse (Fr.) 65. Le Jardinier d'Argentueil (Fr.) 66.

The Pumpkin Eater (GB 1964). A flashily-made, kaleidoscopic film by Jack Clayton about an unhappily married well-to-do woman in London; from Penelope Mortimer's novel. Despite the tiresomeness of the character, there are many brilliantly-handled sequences and Anne Bancroft gives a superb performance. The whole film, indeed, has the feel of life about it. With Peter Finch, James Mason; scripted by Harold Pinter (AA); photographed by Oswald Morris; music by Georges Delerue.

Purcell, Dick (1908–1944). American leading man of second features.
Man Hunt 36. Navy Blues 37. Air Devils 38. Nancy Drew, Detective 39. King of the Zombies 41. Phantom Killer 42. The Mystery

of the Thirteenth Guest 43. Timber Queen 44, etc.

Purcell, Noel (1900–85). Tall, usually bearded, Irish character actor and comedian.
Captain Boycott 47. The Blue Lagoon 48. Doctor in the House 53. Moby Dick 56. Watch Your Stern 60. Mutiny on the Bounty 62. Lord Jim 65. Arrivederci Baby 66, many others.
TV series: The Buccaneer 58.

Purdell, Reginald (1896–1953) (R. Grasdorf). British light character actor, mostly on stage and music hall.
Congress Dances 31. Q Planes 38. Many Thanks Mr Atkins 40. Pack Up Your Troubles 40. Variety Jubilee 43. We Dive at Dawn 43. 2000 Women 44. Holiday Camp 47. Captain Boycott 48, etc.

Purdom, Edmund (1924–). British light leading man who in the fifties was given the full Hollywood treatment but failed to emerge as a star.
Titanic 53. *The Student Prince* 54. *The Egyptian* 54. The Prodigal 55. The King's Thief 55. The Cossacks 60. Herod the Great 60. Nights of Rasputin 61. The Comedy Man 63. Suleiman the Conqueror 63. The Beauty Jungle 64. The Yellow Rolls Royce 64. The Man in the Golden Mask 69. The Black Corsair 69. Evil Fingers 72. Mr Scarface 76, etc.
TV series: Sword of Freedom 57.

¶ *E.P.:* One of the symptoms of an approaching nervous breakdown is the belief that one's work is terribly important.

Purl, Linda (1955–). Snub-nosed American leading lady of the late seventies.
W. C. Fields and Me 76. Testimony of Two Men (TV) 77. The Flame is Love (TV) 79. Women at West Point (TV) 80. The Night the City Screamed (TV) 81. Visiting Hours 82, etc.

Purviance, Edna (1894–1958). American leading lady of silent days.
A Night Out 15 (and other early Chaplin films including *Easy Street, The Count, The Cure, The Adventurer, Shoulder Arms*). Sunnyside 19. The Kid 21. The Pilgrim 23. A Woman of Paris 23. The Seagull 26. Limelight 52, many others.

put-downs

¶ Waspish comments about other people always make good reading. Here are a few for starters:

Let's face it, Billy Wilder at work is two people—Mr Hyde and Mr Hyde.—*Harry Kurnitz*
I loved it—particularly the ideas he took from me.—*D. W. Griffith on Citizen Kane*
Jack Lemmon's Hildy Johnson is like a mortuary assistant having a wild fling.—*New Yorker review of The Front Page*
Mae West, playing a ghastly travesty of the travesty of womanhood she once played, has a Mae West face painted on the front of her head and moves to and fro like the Imperial Hotel during the 1923 Tokyo earthquake.—*Joseph Morgenstern reviewing Myra Breckinridge*
As a pompous middle-European intellectual Kenneth Mars mugs and drools in a manner that Jerry Lewis might find excessive.—*Jay Cocks reviewing What's Up Doc?*
To insinuate that Leslie Bricusse's plodding score is merely dreadful would be an act of charity.—*Rex Reed on Goodbye Mr Chips*
Miss Martin, I notice, is playing Jean Arthur, a tendency which even Miss Arthur should learn to curb.—*James Agee on True To Life*
Mr Muni seemed intent on submerging himself so completely in make-up that he disappeared.—*Bette Davis on Juarez*
Which is he playing now?—*W. Somerset Maugham while watching Spencer Tracy on the set of Dr Jekyll and Mr Hyde*
Ryan O'Neal is so stiff and clumsy that he can't even manage a part requiring him to be stiff and clumsy.—*Jay Cocks on What's Up Doc?*
He has a gift for butchering good parts while managing to look intelligent, thus constituting Hollywood's abiding answer to the theatre.—*Wilfred Sheed of Jack Lemmon*
Just how garish her commonplace accent, squeakily shrill voice, and the childish petulance with which she delivers her lines are, my pen is neither scratchy nor leaky enough to convey.—*John Simon of Elizabeth Taylor in The Taming of the Shrew*
George Raft and Gary Cooper once played a scene in front of a cigar store, and it looked like the wooden Indian was overacting.—*George Burns*

Puttnam, David (1941–). British producer and impresario who almost single-handedly raised the level of British film-making in the early eighties and was rewarded by a top

Hollywood job which didn't last.
Melody 71. That'll Be the Day 74. Mahler 74. Lisztomania 75. Bugsy Malone 76. The Duellists 77. Midnight Express 78. Chariots of Fire 80. Local Hero 82. The Killing Fields 84. The Mission 86. Defence of the Realm 86, many others.

¶ *D.P., 1975:* Nothing good will happen while there are still cinemas that are shit heaps and critics who only like popular films when they are thirty years old.

D.P.: I'm not afraid to fail, providing I fail honourably. The only thing I don't want is to end up being an irrelevant 70-year-old egomaniac.

Puzo, Mario (1920–). American novelist whose *The Godfather* in 1969 was a commercial sensation and led to the equally popular film.
He also co-scripted *Earthquake* and the first two *Superman* movies.

Pygmalion (GB 1938). Despite 1964's *My Fair Lady*, this straight version of Shaw's play, directed by Anthony Asquith and Leslie Howard, remains the most satisfying and perfectly cast: Howard as Higgins, Wendy Hiller as Eliza, Scott Sunderland as Pickering and Wilfrid Lawson as Dolittle. Produced by Gabriel Pascal, photographed by Harry Stradling, with music by Arthur Honegger, it remains one of the cinema's most civilized comedies.

Pyle, Denver (1920–). American character actor, mostly in TV and big-screen westerns.
The Man from Colorado 48. To Hell and Back 55. Shenandoah 65. *Bonnie and Clyde* 67. Five Card Stud 68. Something Big 71. Cahill 73. Escape to Witch Mountain 75. Guardian of the Wilderness 77. Welcome to L.A. 77, etc.
TV series: Wyatt Earp 56–59. The Doris Day Show 68–69. The Dukes of Hazzard 79.

Pyriev, Ivan (1901–1968). Russian director.
The Functionary 30. The Party Card 36. Tractor Drivers 39. They Met in Moscow 41. Secretary of the District Committee 42. Song of Siberia 47. Kuban Cossacks 49. Test of Fidelity 54. The Idiot 58. White Nights 60. Our Mutual Friend 61. Light of a Distant Star 65. The Brothers Karamazov 68, etc.

Answers

play into film
1 *Heaven Can Wait* ☐ 2 *Here Comes Mr Jordan* ☐ 3 *Midnight Lace* ☐ 4 *The Actress* ☐ 5 *The Heiress* ☐ 6 *The Matchmaker* or *Hello Dolly* ☐ 7 *She Done Him Wrong* ☐ 8 *Casablanca* ☐ 9 *Liliom* or *Carousel* ☐ 10 *Twentieth Century* ☐ 11 *Summertime/Summer Madness* ☐ 12 *Boom* ☐ 13 *Morocco* ☐ 14 *The Man Who Played God/Sincerely Yours* ☐ 15 *Forbidden Planet* ☐ 16 *The Prince and the Showgirl* ☐ 17 *People Will Talk* ☐ 18 *This Love of Ours/Never Say Goodbye* ☐ 19 *Chimes at Midnight/Falstaff* ☐ 20 *Attack!* ☐ 21 *We're No Angels* ☐ 22 *The Stripper* (GB: *Woman of Summer*) ☐ 23 *Oklahoma!* ☐ 24 *Joan of Arc* ☐

the plot thickens
1 *Citizen Kane* ☐ 2 *Blithe Spirit* ☐ 3 *The Cat and the Canary* ☐ 4 *Foreign Correspondent* ☐ 5 *It Happened One Night* ☐ 6 *The Lady Vanishes* ☐ 7 *King's Row* ☐ 8 *It's a Wonderful Life* ☐ 9 *North by Northwest* ☐ 10 *The Old Dark House* (1932) ☐ 11 *Nothing Sacred* ☐ 12 *Psycho* ☐ 13 *Random Harvest* ☐ 14 *The Maltese Falcon* ☐ 15 *Mildred Pierce* ☐

pseudonyms
1 Willie Best ☐ 2 Fatty Arbuckle, when he attempted a comeback after the scandal which blighted his career ☐ 3 Harry Einstein, a

New York comedian of the thirties ☐ 4 Joan Crawford ☐ 5 Lucille Ball ☐ 6 Gig Young ☐ 7 Robert Cummings, when posing as an Englishman ☐ 8 Joseph Losey, when the McCarthy witch-hunt prevented him from working in England. This is the name under which he directed *The Intimate Stranger* ☐ 9 Mark Stevens ☐ 10 Bette Davis, very briefly when first signed by Warners ☐ 11 Dalton Trumbo, who under this name in 1956 received an Academy Award for the story of *The Brave One* at a time when he was officially blacklisted after the McCarthy witch-hunt ☐ 12 These are all names used by Greta Garbo when travelling 'incognito' ☐ 13 Anthony Hinds and Michael Carreras, when writing scripts for their own Hammer horror films ☐ 14 Darry F. Zanuck when writing screenplays ☐ 15 W. C. Fields when writing screenplays ☐

Quai des Brumes (France 1938). A highly influential study in poetic pessimism, directed by Marcel Carné from Jacques Prévert's script. Romance of the highest order is distilled from a squalid situation in foggy Le Havre, with Jean Gabin as a victim of circumstances on the run from the police, and Michèle Morgan there to comfort him briefly before the inevitable tragic finale. Music by Maurice Jaubert.

Quaid, Dennis (1955–). American actor, brother of Randy Quaid.
Crazy Mama 75. Seniors 77. Breaking Away 78. The Long Riders 80. All Night Long 81. Caveman 81. The Night the Lights Went Out in Georgia 81. Jaws 3D 83. Tough Enough 83. The Right Stuff 83. Dreamscape 84. Enemy Mine 85. The Big Easy 86. Innerspace 87.

Quaid, Randy (1953–). American actor who has been seen in gangling, awkward roles.
□The Last Picture Show 71. What's Up Doc? 72. The Last Detail 73. Lolly Madonna XXX 73. Paper Moon 73. Breakout 75. The Apprenticeship of Duddy Kravitz 75. The Missouri Breaks 76. Bound for Glory 76. The Choirboys 77. Midnight Express 78. The Raid on Coffeyville (TV) 79. Foxes 80. The Long Riders 80. Guyana Tragedy (TV) 80. Heartbeeps 81. National Lampoon's Vacation 83. Fool for Love 85. The Wraith 86.

Qualen, John (1899–1987) (John Oleson). Canadian-born Norwegian character actor, in Hollywood from the thirties playing amiably ineffectual foreign types.
Arrowsmith (debut) 32. Black Fury 35. Seventh Heaven 37. *The Grapes of Wrath* 40. Out of the Fog 41. *All That Money Can Buy* 41. Jungle Book 42. Casablanca 42. Fairy Tale Murder 45. Adventure 46. The Fugitive 48. The Big Steal 49. Hans Christian Andersen 52. The High and the Mighty 54. The Searchers 56. Two Rode Together 60. The Man Who Shot Liberty Valance 62. The Prize 63. The Seven Faces of Dr Lao 64. Cheyenne Autumn 64. The Sons of Katie Elder 65. A Big Hand for the Little Lady 66. Firecreek 67, many others.

Quantrill, Charles Clarke (1837–1865). American guerrilla leader, the scourge of Missouri and a figure in many westerns.

Quarry, Robert (1923–). American character actor who bade fair to be the horror man of the seventies.
A Kiss Before Dying 56. Count Yorga Vampire 69. The Return of Count Yorga 71. Dr Phibes Rises Again 72. The Revenge of Dr Death 73. The Midnight Man 73. Rollercoaster 77, etc.

Quayle, Anna (1937–). British comedienne.
Drop Dead Darling 67. Smashing Time 67. Chitty Chitty Bang Bang 68. Up the Chastity Belt 71, etc.

Quayle, Sir Anthony (1913–). Distinguished British stage actor and director, in occasional films as actor.
□Hamlet 48. Saraband for Dead Lovers 48. Oh Rosalinda 55. The Battle of the River Plate 56. No Time for Tears 57. The Wrong Man (US) 57. Woman in a Dressing-Gown 57. The Man Who Wouldn't Talk 58. *Ice Cold in Alex* 58. Serious Charge 59. Tarzan's Greatest Adventure 59. The Challenge 60. The Guns of Navarone 61. Lawrence of Arabia 62. HMS Defiant 62. The Fall of the Roman Empire 64. East of Sudan 64. Operation Crossbow 64. The Poppy is also a Flower (TV) 64. A Study in Terror 65. Misunderstood 67. Mackenna's Gold 68. Before Winter Comes 69. Anne of the Thousand Days 70. Everything You Always Wanted to Know About Sex 72. A Bequest to the Nation 73. Jarrett (TV) 73. QB VII (TV) 74. The Tamarind Seed 74. Great Expectations (TV) 75. 21 Hours at Munich (TV) 76. Moses (TV) 76. The Eagle has Landed 76. Holocaust 2000 77. Murder by Decree 79. Masada (TV) 80. The Manions of America (TV) 81. Dial M for Murder (TV) 81. The Last Days of Pompeii (TV) 84. Lace (TV)

84. The Key to Rebecca (TV) 85. The Bourne Identity 88.

TV series: Strange Report 68.

Que Viva Mexico (Mexico 1932). Eisenstein's famous epic of Mexican history, based on funds supplied and later withdrawn by Upton Sinclair, was to have been an episodic semi-documentary. It was never completed, but fragments have been bought up and shown as *Thunder Over Mexico* (by Sol Lesser), *Death Day* (by Upton Sinclair) and *Time in the Sun* (by Marie Seton).

Queen Christina (US 1933). This historical romance seemed less a calculated box-office film than an act of homage by its production company (MGM) towards its star (Greta Garbo). Expensively presented, directed with care and craft by Rouben Mamoulian, it makes a flawless example of bespoke tailoring from Hollywood's golden age. The plot, concerning a royal love affair in 16th century Sweden, is fictitious. John Gilbert co-starred at Garbo's own request, but it was his last major role.

Queen Kelly (US 1928). A typical unfinished extravagance written and directed by Erich Von Stroheim, about an ill-fated romance between a young convent girl and the consort of the mad queen of a petty European principality. Further fragments keep on turning up, taking the story into a brothel and to Africa. Gloria Swanson starred, with Walter Byron and Seena Owen.

The Queen of Spades (GB 1948). The Pushkin story has been filmed several times in Russia. This atmospheric version by Rodney Ackland and Arthur Boys, directed by Thorold Dickinson, goes all out to surpass Eisenstein in imagery but despite brilliant moments is finally too slow to have the necessary grip. Edith Evans plays the aged countess who has reputedly sold her soul to the devil in exchange for the secret of winning at faro, Anton Walbrook the soldier desperate to learn the trick.

questions

? Who asked these questions, of whom, in which films?

1 George, didn't you ever want to know what's on the other side of the mountain?
2 How will you eat, through a tube?
3 Would you like a leg or a breast?
4 Do you believe the dead come back to watch the living?
5 Has Michael Finn been in today?
6 Is my aunt Minnie in there?
7 Hey, old man, you home tonight?
8 Where's the rest of me?
9 Why don't you get a divorce and settle down?
10 Got your clock?
11 What other hobbies you got?
12 What seems to be the trouble, Captain?
13 If it be a natural thing, where do it come from? Where do it go?
14 What's the bleeding time?
15 What's the going price on integrity this week?
16 She cut off her nipples with garden shears. You call that normal?
17 Does that mean, sir, that I shall not be able to play for the Old Boys?
18 Why don't you slip out of these wet clothes and into a dry martini?
19 You gentlemen aren't *really* trying to kill my son, are you?
20 Did you ever have the feeling that you wanted to go, and still have the feeling that you wanted to stay?
21 How dare he make love to me and not be a married man?
22 Would you care to come in and see Emma?
23 Look at these breasts, Mike, aren't they beautiful?
24 All I want to know is, is he D and D or is he a canary?
25 What's wrong with Medicine Hat except that it's hot in summer and cold in winter and nothing ever happens there?

Quick, Diana (1946–). British leading lady. Nicholas and Alexandra 71. A Private Enterprise 71. The Odd Job 78. The Duellists 78. The Big Sleep 78. The Three Hostages (TV) 78. *Brideshead Revisited* (TV) 81. Phantom of the Opera (TV) 83. Ordeal by Innocence 85.

The Quiet Man (US 1952). Typically easy-going romantic comedy of John Ford's later period, enjoyably set in a never-never Ireland and concerning an ex-boxer's Petruchio-like courtship of a fiery colleen. John Wayne, Maureen O'Hara, Victor McLaglen and Barry Fitzgerald head a hand-picked cast; music by Victor Young; original story by Maurice Walsh.

Quillan, Eddie (1907–). Bouncy, beaming American comic actor, in Hollywood from 1930.
Big Money 30. *Mutiny on the Bounty* 35. Young Mr Lincoln 39. *The Grapes of Wrath* 40. Dark Streets of Cairo 40. Flying Blind 41. Sideshow 50. Brigadoon 54. The Ghost and Mr Chicken 66; latterly on TV.

Quilley, Dennis (1933–). British leading actor, mostly on stage.
Anne of the Thousand Days 69. The Black Windmill 74. Murder on the Orient Express 74. Clayhanger (TV) 76. Masada (TV) 81. *Evil Under the Sun* 81. *Privates on Parade* 83. Memed My Hawk 84. Foreign Body 87, etc.

Quimby, Fred (1886–1965). American producer, head of MGM's short subjects department 1926–56. Specially known for development of Tom and Jerry cartoons.

Quine, Richard (1920–). American director, former leading man. (*The World Changes* 32 as juvenile also *Babes on Broadway* 40, *My Sister Eileen* 41, *For Me and My Gal* 42, etc.)
The Sunny Side of the Street 51. Drive a Crooked Road 54. Pushover 54. My Sister Eileen 55. *The Solid Gold Cadillac* 56. Operation Mad Ball 58. Bell, Book and Candle 58. The World of Suzie Wong 60. The Notorious Landlady 62. Paris When It Sizzles 64. How to Murder Your Wife 65. Oh Dad, Poor Dad 66. Hotel 67. A Talent for Loving 69. The Moonshine War 70. 'W' 74. The Prisoner of Zenda 79, etc.

Quinlan, Kathleen (1954–). American leading lady of the late seventies.
Can Ellen Be Saved? (TV) 74. Where Have All the People Gone? (TV) 74. The Abduction of St Anne (TV) 75. Little Ladies of the Night (TV) 77. Airport 77 77. I Never Promised You a Rose Garden 77. The Promise 79. The Runner Stumbles 79. Sunday Lovers 80. Hanky Panky 82. Twilight Zone 83. Independence Day 83. Blackout 85. Warning Sign 86.

Quinn, Aidan (1959–). American leading man.
Reckless 84. Desperately Seeking Susan 85. An Early Frost (TV) 85. Stakeout 87.

Quinn, Anthony (1915–). Mexican-born leading actor, in films since 1936, latterly noted for full-blooded performances. Autobiography: *The Original Sin* 72.
Parole 36. The Plainsman 37. Last Train from Madrid 37. Union Pacific 39. Blood and Sand 41. Ghost Breakers 40. The Black Swan 42. The Ox-Bow Incident 43. Buffalo Bill 44. China Sky 45. Tycoon 48. The Brave Bulls 51. *Viva Zapata* (AA) 52. The World in His Arms 52. Ride Vaquero 53. Blowing Wild 54. The Long Wait 54. *La Strada* (It.) 54. Attila the Hun (It.) 54. Ulysses 55. *Lust for Life* (AA) 56. The Man from Del Rio 56. The Hunchback of Notre Dame 56. The River's Edge 57. Hot Spell 58. Black Orchid 58. Last Train from Gun Hill 58. Warlock 59. The Buccaneer (d only) 59. Heller in Pink Tights 60. Savage Innocents 60. The Guns of Navarone 61. Lawrence of Arabia 62. Barabbas 62. Requiem for a Heavyweight 63. The Visit 63. *Zorba the Greek* 64. A High Wind in Jamaica 65. Lost Command 66. The Happening 67. The Twenty-Fifth Hour 67. The Rover 67. *The Shoes of the Fisherman* 68. The Magus 68. The Secret of Santa Vittoria 69. R.P.M. 69. A Walk in the Spring Rain 69. Flap 70. Across 110th Street 72. The Marseilles Contract 74. The Don is Dead 75. Mohammed (The Message) 76. Jesus of Nazareth (TV) 77. Tigers Don't Cry 77. The Inheritance 78. The Children of Sanchez 78. The Greek Tycoon 78. Caravans 78. The Passage 79. Lion of the Desert 80. The Salamander 80. High Risk 81. The Con Artists 81, etc.
TV series: *The Man and the City* 71.

¶ *A.Q.:* They said all I was good for was playing Indians.

'I want to impregnate every woman in the world, he once told me, though I didn't realise until later how literally he meant it.'—*Ruth Warrick*

Quo Vadis? The biblical epic by Henryk Sienkiewicz has been filmed three times: in Italy in 1912 and 1924, and in the US in 1951. The third version, though less impressive as a product of its period than the others, was certainly the most spectacular, with the appropriate cast of thousands and a well-drilled squad of Christian-gorging lions. Robert Taylor and Deborah Kerr suffered under Peter Ustinov's Nero; Mervyn Le Roy directed.

quota. By Act of Parliament renters are obliged to sell, and exhibitors to show, a varying proportion of British-made films. There has not always been enough British talent to fill the necessary number of releases: hence the notorious 'quota quickies' of the twenties and thirties, and much second-feature material more recently, which however bad can invariably get a circuit booking providing it has a British quota ticket. The normal quota which an exhibitor has to fill is 30% for features, 25% for supporting programme. This contrasts markedly with independent television contractors, whose programmes must be 86% British.

Answers

questions

1 Ronald Colman to John Howard in *Lost Horizon* (1937). ☐

2 Groucho Marx to Margaret Dumont in *At the Circus* (1939). She has just been making seating arrangements for dinner: 'You will sit upon my left hand, and you will sit upon my right hand . . .' ☐

3 Grace Kelly to Cary Grant in *To Catch a Thief* (1955). They are picnicking, and she is supposedly offering him chicken, but there are other implications. ☐

4 Judith Anderson to Joan Fontaine in *Rebecca* (1940). Sinister housekeeper Mrs Danvers is provoking the second Mrs de Winter to suicide. ☐

5 W. C. Fields to Shemp Howard in *The Bank Dick* (1941). Mr Howard plays the proprietor of the Black Pussy Cat Café, and Mr Fields is prompting him to prepare a Mickey Finn for his guest. ☐

6 The unidentified actress who pokes her nose into the famous cabin scene in *A Night at the Opera* (1935), and is promptly lost in the mêlée. ☐

7 Paul Newman praying to God in *Cool Hand Luke* (1967) (which has been taken as an allegory of the crucifixion, with Newman as Christ). ☐

8 Ronald Reagan to Ann Sheridan in *King's Row* (1941), on waking to find that his legs have been amputated. ☐

9 Oscar Levant to Joan Crawford in *Humoresque* (1944). Mr Levant, as usual, wrote his own lines. ☐

10 Moore Marriott to Will Hay in *Oh Mr Porter* (1937). Hay as a seedy stationmaster has just arrived at his new post, an Irish hamlet which has lately lost a remarkable number of stationmasters. His aged dogsbody refers to the presentation clock which they all bring from their last assignment; he now has quite a collection. ☐

11 Groucho Marx to Henry Armetta in *The Big Store* (1941). Groucho has been sleeping in the bedding department, and wakes to find himself being looked over by an Italian with a score of children. ☐

12 Mildred Natwick to Edmund Gwenn in *The Trouble with Harry* (1955). As the Captain is tugging a dead body through the bushes, this inquiry perfectly sets a tone for the black comedy which follows. ☐

13 Herbert Lomas to Arthur Askey in *The Ghost Train* (1941). The ghoulish stationmaster has been regaling the stranded passengers with a ghostly yarn. (There were previous versions with other actors.) ☐

14 James Robertson Justice (irascible surgeon) to Dirk Bogarde (callow student) in *Doctor in the House* (1952). The required answer is the time it takes for bleeding to stop, but the student has not been listening and takes the remark for an oath, replying: 'Half-past two, sir . . .' ☐

15 Orson Welles to Oliver Reed in *I'll Never Forget Whatshisname* (1967). ☐

16 Elizabeth Taylor to Marlon Brando, of Julie Harris, in *Reflections in a Golden Eye* (1968). ☐

17 Ivor Novello (schoolboy) to Ben Webster (headmaster) in Alfred Hitchcock's *Downhill* (1926). The boy has just been expelled. (The film being silent, this quotation is a sub-title.) ☐

18 Robert Benchley to Ginger Rogers in *The Major and the Minor* (1942). ☐

19 Jessie Royce Landis to assorted villains in an elevator in *North by Northwest* (1959). ☐

20 The opening of Jimmy Durante's song at the piano to a delighted Monty Woolley in *The Man Who Came to Dinner* (1941). ☐

21 Ingrid Bergman in *Indiscreet*. ☐

22 Henry Fonda offering Barbara Stanwyck an introduction to his pet snake in *The Lady Eve*. Her reply: 'That's a new one, isn't it?' ☐

23 Elizabeth Taylor in *Ash Wednesday*. ☐

24 Lee J. Cobb in *On the Waterfront*. ☐

25 Mary Astor in *Across the Pacific*. ☐

R

Rabier, Jean (1927–). French cinematographer.
Cleo de 5 à 7 61. Ophelia 62. Landru 62. *La Baie des Anges* 63. *Les Parapluies de Cherbourg* 64. Le Bonheur 65. The Champagne Murders 66. Les Biches 68. *Le Boucher* 70, etc.

Rackin, Martin (1918–1976). American screenwriter.
Air Raid Wardens 43. Riff Raff 47. Fighting Father Dunne 48. Three Secrets 50. The Enforcer 51. Sailor Beware 52. The Stooge 53. Santiago (& p) 56. The Helen Morgan Story (p only) 57. The Horse Soldiers (& p) 59. North to Alaska 60. Stagecoach (p only) 66. Rough Night in Jericho (p only) 67. The Revengers (p only) 72, etc.

Radd, Ronald (1924–1976). British character actor, usually in heavy roles. Much on TV.
The Camp on Blood Island 58. The Small World of Sammy Lee 63. Up Jumped a Swagman 65. Where the Spies Are 65. Mr Ten Per Cent 66. The Kremlin Letter 70. The Offence 72. The Spiral Staircase 74, etc.

Rademakers, Fons (1921–). Dutch director, with stage experience.
Doctor in the Village 58. The Knife 61. Max Havelaar 74. Mysteries 76. The Judge's Friend 79, etc.

Radford, Basil (1897–1952). British light character comedian, on stage from 1922, films from 1929 (*Barnum Was Right*). Became popular when he and Naunton Wayne played two imperturbable Englishmen abroad in *The Lady Vanishes* 38.
Just William 38. *Night Train to Munich* 40. *Crooks Tour* 40. Next of Kin 42. Millions Like Us 43. The Way to the Stars 45. *Dead of Night* 45. *The Captive Heart* 46. Girl in a Million 46. It's Not Cricket 48. Passport to Pimlico 48. The Winslow Boy 48. Quartet 48. *Whisky Galore* 48. Chance of a Lifetime 50. The Galloping Major 51, etc.

Radford, Michael (–). British director.
Another Time Another Place 83. 1984 84.

radio, being a competitor, was largely ignored by serious movies in the thirties, but radio stars featured in a number of musicals, especially the *Big Broadcast* series and the British *Radio Parade, Music Hath Charms,* etc.; in the forties, a number of low-budgeters such as *Reveille with Beverly* had a radio background. Popular radio series to be filmed included *Dr Christian, Fibber McGee and Molly, Charlie McCarthy Detective, The Great Gildersleeve, Hi Gang, Band Waggon* and *It's That Man Again.* Mysteries set in radio stations included *Who Done It* and *Death at Broadcasting House*; *Helter Skelter* was a slapstick comedy set at the BBC. In the seventies, *Play Misty for Me* revolved around a disc jockey, as did the TV movie *A Cry for Help*; while *WUSA* was undoubtedly the most serious drama on the subject unless one counts the sharply satirical *A Face in the Crowd.*

Radnitz, Robert B. (1925–). American producer of 'family' films.
A Dog of Flanders 60. Misty 62. Island of the Blue Dolphins 64. And Now Miguel 66. My Side of the Mountain 68. The Little Ark 70. *Sounder* 72. A Hero Ain't Nothing But A Sandwich 77. Cross Creek 83, etc.

Rafelson, Bob (1934–). American director.
Head (co-w, d) 68. Five Easy Pieces 71. The King of Marvin Gardens 72. Stay Hungry 76. The Postman Always Rings Twice 81. Black Widow 87, etc.

Rafferty, Chips (1909–1971) (John Goffage). Rangy Australian character actor with varied experience before coming to films.
Dad Rudd, M.P. 40. Forty Thousand Horsemen 40. The Rats of Tobruk 44. *The Overlanders* 46. The Loves of Joanna Godden (GB) 46. Eureka Stockade 47. Bitter Springs 51. Kangaroo 52. King of the Coral Sea 54. Walk into Paradise 56. *The Sundowners* 60. Mutiny on the Bounty 62. They're a Weird Mob 66. Kona Coast 68. Skullduggery 69. Outback 70, many others.

Rafferty, Frances (1922–). American leading lady.

Seven Sweethearts 42. Dragon Seed 44. Abbott and Costello in Hollywood 45. The Hidden Eye 45. Lady at Midnight 48. Rodeo 52. The Shanghai Story 54, etc.
TV series: December Bride 54–58. Pete and Gladys 61.

Raffil, Stewart (1945–). Anglo-American director.
Napoleon and Samantha 72. Adventures of the Wilderness Family 75. Shipwreck 77. High Risk 81. Ice Pirates 83. The Philadelphia Experiment 84.

Raffin, Deborah (1953–). American leading lady of the late seventies.
Forty Carats 73. Once Is Not Enough 75. Nightmare in Badham County (TV) 76. The Sentinel 77. Demon 77. Ski Lift to Death (TV) 78. How to Pick Up Girls (TV) 78. Willa (TV) 78. Touched by Love 80.
Lace 2 (TV) 85. Death Wish 3 86. Noble House (TV) 87.

Rafkin, Alan (–). American director.
Ski Party 65. The Ghost and Mr Chicken 66. Nobody's Perfect 68. The Shakiest Gun in the West 68, etc.

Raft, George (1895–1980) (George Ranft). Smooth, rather sinister American leading man of the thirties and forties; formerly a professional athlete, gambler, night club dancer and companion of gangsters. In 1961 Ray Danton appeared in the title role of *The George Raft Story*.
Biography 1973: *The George Raft File* by James Robert Parish; 1974: *George Raft* by Lewis Jablonsky.
□Queen of the Night Clubs 29. Quick Millions 31. Hush Money 31. Palmy Days 31. Dancers in the Dark 32. *Scarface* 32. Night World 32. Madame Racketeer 32. Night after Night 32. If I Had a Million 32. Undercover Man 32. Pick Up 33. Midnight Club 33. *The Bowery* 33. All of Me 34. *Bolero* 34. The Trumpet Blows 34. Limehouse Blues 34. *Rumba* 35. Stolen Harmony 35. *The Glass Key* 35. Every Night at Eight 35. She Couldn't Take It 35. It Had to Happen 36. Yours for the Asking 36. *Souls at Sea* 37. You and Me 38. Spawn of the North 38. The Lady's from Kentucky 38. *Each Dawn I Die* 39. I Stole a Million 39. Invisible Stripes 40. The House across the Bay 40. They Drive by Night 40. Manpower 41. Broadway 42. Stage Door Canteen 43. Background to Danger 43. Follow the Boys 44. Nob Hill 45. Johnny Angel 45. Whistle Stop 46. Mr Ace 46. Nocturne 46. Christmas Eve 47. Intrigue 48. Race Street 48. Outpost in Morocco 49. Johnny Allegro 49. A Dangerous Profession 49. The Red Light 50. Lucky Nick Cain 51. Loan Shark 52. The Man from Cairo 53. Rogue Cop 54. Black Widow 54. A Bullet for Joey 55. Around the World in Eighty Days 56. Some Like It Hot 59. Jet over the Atlantic 59. Ocean's Eleven 60. Ladies' Man 64. The Patsy 64. For Those Who Think Young 64. Casino Royale 67. Du Rififi à Paname 67. Five Golden Dragons 67. Skidoo 68. Madigan's Millions 69. Hammersmith is Out 72. Sextette 77.
TV series: I Am the Law 52.

Ragland, Rags (1905–1946). American character comedian, former boxer.
□Ringside Maisie 41. Whistling in the Dark 41. Born to Sing 42. Sunday Punch 42. Maisie Gets Her Man 42. Panama Hattie 42. The War Against Mrs Hadley 42. Somewhere I'll Find You 42. Whistling in Dixie 42. Dubarry Was a Lady 42. Girl Crazy 43. Whistling in Brooklyn 43. Meet the People 44. Three Men in White 44. The Canterville Ghost 44. Her Highness and the Bellboy 45. Anchors Aweigh 45. Abbott and Costello in Hollywood 45. Ziegfeld Follies 46. The Hoodlum Saint 46.

Raiders of the Lost Ark (US 1981). A popular entry in the tradition of the seventies and eighties, of expecting adults to enjoy potted remakes of the Saturday afternoon serials of their youth. This had rather too many unpleasant moments, not to mention longueurs between the action highlights, but on the whole one appreciated that it aimed to please, and did. Producer George Lucas and director Steven Spielberg had now cornered this particular market, but as the sequels kept coming one rather wished they would turn their talent to something more original and adult. Harrison Ford made a stalwart hero, and the picture won Academy Awards for editing, sound, visual effects, art and set direction. *Indiana Jones and the Temple of Doom* followed in 1984.

Railsback, Steve (1948–). American character actor.
The Visitors 71. Cockfighter 74. *Helter Skelter* (TV) 76. The Stunt Man 78. From Here to Eternity (TV) 79. The Golden Seal 83, etc.

railway stations have provided a major setting for some memorable films including *The Ghost Train, Doctor Zhivago, Knight without Armour, I'll Never Forget*

Whatshisname (with its white 'dream' station), *Union Station, 3.10 to Yuma, Last Train from Madrid, Bhowani Junction, Northwest Frontier, 100 Rifles, The Mercenaries, Waterloo Road, Anna Karenina, Grand Central Station, Under the Clock, Brief Encounter, Oh Mr Porter, The Titfield Thunderbolt, High Noon, In the Heat of the Night* and *The Train* . . . while Orson Welles made *The Trial* almost entirely within a deserted station, and de Sica made *Indiscretion* among the crowds of Rome's Stazione Termini.
See also: *trains*.

Raimu (1883–1946) (Jules Muraire). French character actor and comedian with music-hall background.
□L'Homme Nu 12. L'Agence Cacahuete 14. Le Blanc et le Noir 31. Mam'zelle Nitouche 31. *Marius* 31. La Petite Chocolatière 32. Les Gaîtés de l'Escadron 32. *Fanny* 32. Theodore and Company 33. Charlemagne 33. Ces Messieurs de la Santé 34. Tartarin de Tarascon 34. J'ai une Idée 34. Minuit Place Pigalle 35. Faisons un Rêve 35. L'Ecole des Cocottes 35. Gaspard de Besse 35. Le Secret de Polichinelle 36. Le Roi 36. Les Jumeaux de Brighton 36. César 36. Anything to Declare 37. Les Perles de la Couronne 37. La Chaste Suzanne 37. Les Rois du Sport 37. Le Fauteuil 37. *Gribouille* 37. *Un Carnet de Bal* 37. Les Héros de la Marne 38. L'Etrange Monsieur Victor 38. Les Nouveaux Riches 38. *La Femme du Boulanger* 38. Noix de Coco 39. Monsieur Brotonneau 39. Dernière Jeunesse 39. L'Homme Qui Cherche la Verité 39. Untel Père et Fils 40. La Fille du Puisatier 40. Le Duel 40. Parade en Sept Nuits 41. *Les Inconnus dans la Maison* 42. *L'Arlésienne* 42. *Monsieur la Souris* 42. The Benefactor 42. Les Petits Riens 42. Le Colonel Chabert 43. Les Gueux au Paradis 46. L'Homme au Chapeau Rond 46.

'Le plus grand comédien de tous les temps.'—*Arletty*

Rain. Somerset Maugham's story of the conflict between a missionary and a woman of highly doubtful character has been filmed three times in Hollywood: in 1928 with Gloria Swanson and Lionel Barrymore, in 1932 with Joan Crawford and Walter Huston, and in 1957 (as *Miss Sadie Thompson*) with Rita Hayworth and José Ferrer. In each case the Production Code made you guess what the lady's actual profession was.

rain has been put to many uses by film scenarists. It was the direct cause of dramatic situations in *Rebecca* (a shower flattened Joan Fontaine's hair-do just as she arrived at Manderley); in *The Loneliness of the Long Distance Runner* (it revealed evidence which the hero was trying to conceal); in *Floods of Fear* (it permitted the escape of three convicts, one of whom then rescued the heroine); in *The African Queen* (it raised the water level and so released the boat from the reeds which held it captive); in *Desk Set* (it persuaded Spencer Tracy to accept Katharine Hepburn's offer of hospitality); in *Pygmalion* (it caused the meeting of Higgins and Eliza); in *Sands of the Kalahari* (it flooded a pit in which Stuart Whitman was imprisoned and permitted his escape); in *When Tomorrow Comes* (it stranded Charles Boyer and Irene Dunne in a remote church for the night); and in many others. Two splendid symbolic uses were in *Saraband for Dead Lovers* (a raindrop made a stained-glass madonna appear to weep at the ill-fated wedding) and *The Stars Look Down* (as the hero and heroine make love, two raindrops intertwine on the window pane).

Rain has often been used symbolically as a relief from tension and heat, in films as diverse as *Night of the Iguana, Passport to Pimlico, The Long Hot Summer, Key Largo, Twelve Angry Men, Black Narcissus, The Good Earth* and *Rain* itself. It has provided a solemn or ominous background in *Psycho, Term of Trial, Rashomon, It Always Rains on Sunday, Room at the Top, The Robe, Fires on the Plain, The Collector* and many others. It has a particularly depressing effect at a funeral, as was shown in *The Glass Key* and *Our Town*; or at an assassination (*Foreign Correspondent*). But it can also be used for farcical purposes: in *Three Men in a Boat, The Silencers, Fraternally Yours, Oh Mr Porter*, etc. And it can provide a comedy twist, as at the end of *The Lady Vanishes*, when the English travellers so eager to get back to the test match find that rain has stopped play.

It can produce a decorative effect (*Les Parapluies de Cherbourg, Miracle in the Rain, Breakfast at Tiffany's*). It can be spectacular (the climax of *Journey into Fear*, the glistening streets in *The Third Man*, the downpours in *The Rains Came*, and *Pather Panchali*, the battles in the rain in *Tower of London* and *Seven Samurai*). And it can provide a cue for song: 'Isn't it a Lovely Day to be Caught in the Rain' in *Top Hat*, the title songs of *Singin' in the Rain* and *Stormy Weather*, 'The Rain in Spain' in *My Fair Lady*, 'April Showers' in *The Jolson Story*, 'Little April Shower' in Bambi. In fact, it seems to be by far the most versatile of all the film-maker's effects.

Raine, Jack (1895–1979). British light actor, on stage in the twenties and thirties; later in Hollywood.
The Happy Time 52. Julius Caesar 53. Rhapsody 54. My Fair Lady 64. Hello Dolly 69, etc.

Raine, Norman Reilly (1895–1971). American screenwriter.
Tugboat Annie 33. White Woman 33. God's Country and the Woman 36. *The Life of Emile Zola* (AA) 37. The Adventures of Robin Hood 38. Elizabeth and Essex 39. The Fighting 69th 39. Captains of the Clouds 42. Ladies Courageous 44. A Bell for Adano 45. Woman of the North Country 52. Sea of Lost Ships 53, etc.

Rainer, Luise (1909–). Austrian actress on stage from 1930; later in Hollywood films.
Escapade 35. *The Great Ziegfeld* (AA) 36. *The Good Earth* (AA) 37. The Emperor's Candlesticks 37. The Big City 37. The Great Waltz 38. The Toy Wife 38. Dramatic School 38. Hostages 43.

¶ *L.R.:* For my second and third pictures I won Academy Awards. Nothing worse could have happened to me.

Raines, Cristina (1954–). American leading lady of the late seventies.
Sunshine (TV) 74. Nashville 75. The Sentinel 77. The Duellists 77. Touched by Love 80.
TV series: Flamingo Road 80–81.

Raines, Ella (1921–) (Ella Raubes). American leading lady of the forties, with brief stage experience.
Corvette K225 43. Cry Havoc 43. Phantom Lady 43. Hail the Conquering Hero 43. Enter Arsène Lupin 44. Tall in the Saddle 44. Uncle Harry 45. The Suspect 45. The Runaround 46. Time out of Mind 47. Brute Force 47. Mr Ashton was Indiscreet 48. The Walking Hills 48. Impact 48. A Dangerous Profession 49. Ride the Man Down 53. Man in the Road (GB) 54, etc.
TV series: Janet Dean Registered Nurse 57.

Rainger, Ralph (1901–1942) (Ralph Reichenthal). American song composer who usually worked with lyricist Leo Robin. Film scores include *The Big Broadcast of 1932*, *She Done Him Wrong*, *Swing High Swing Low*, *Paris Honeymoon*, *Moon Over Miami*, *Footlight Serenade*, *Coney Island*.

The Rains Came. Louis Bromfield's novel of the high days of British India was filmed in 1939 with Myrna Loy and Tyrone Power, and in 1955 with Lana Turner and Richard Burton. (The title was changed to *The Rains of Ranchipur*.)

Rains, Claude (1889–1967). Suave, incisive British character actor, long resident in America. Wide stage experience.
□*The Invisible Man* 33. *Crime without Passion* 34. The Man Who Reclaimed His Head 34. The Mystery of Edwin Drood 35. The Clairvoyant (GB) 35. The Last Outpost 35. Anthony Adverse 36. Hearts Divided 36. Stolen Holiday 36. The Prince and the Pauper 37. They Won't Forget 37. Gold is Where You Find It 38. *The Adventures of Robin Hood* 38. White Banners 38. Four Daughters 38. They Made Me a Criminal 39. Juarez 39. *Mr Smith Goes to Washington* 39. Four Wives 39. Daughters Courageous 39. Saturday's Children 39. The Sea Hawk 40. Lady with Red Hair (as David Belasco) 40. Four Mothers 40. *Here Comes Mr Jordan* 41. The Wolf Man 41. *King's Row* 41. Moontide 42. Now Voyager 42. *Casablanca* 42. Forever and a Day 43. Phantom of the Opera (title role) 43. Passage to Marseilles 44. *Mr Skeffington* 44. This Love of Ours 45. *Caesar and Cleopatra* (GB) 45. Angel on My Shoulder 46. *Deception* 46. *Notorious* 46. The Unsuspected 47. Strange Holiday 47. *The Passionate Friends* (GB) 47. Rope of Sand 49. Song of Surrender 49. The White Tower 50. Where Danger Lives 50. Sealed Cargo 51. The Man Who Watched Trains Go By (GB) 52. Lisbon 56. This Earth is Mine 59. The Lost World 60. Battle of the Worlds (It.) 61. Lawrence of Arabia 62. Twilight of Honor 63. The Greatest Story Ever Told 65.
❀ For his omnipresent urbanity. *Casablanca.*

¶ 'He was a great influence on me. I don't know what happened to him. I think he failed and went to America.'—*John Gielgud*
Famous line (*The Invisible Man*): We'll start with a few murders. Big men, little men—just to show that we make no distinction.
Famous line (*Casablanca*): I'm only a poor corrupt official.

Raitt, John (1921–). American stage singer whose only film has been *The Pajama Game* 57.

Raki, Laya (1927–). Leading lady of the fifties, from New Zealand.
Up to His Neck 54. The Seekers 55. Quentin Durward 56. The Poppy is Also a Flower (TV) 65, etc.

Rakoff, Alvin (1927–). Canadian TV director resident in Britain.
Passport to Shame 58. Treasure of San Teresa 59. On Friday at Eleven 61. The Comedy Man 64. Hoffman 70. Say Hello to Yesterday 70. Don Quixote (TV) 72. City on Fire 79. Dirty Tricks 80. A Voyage Round My Father (TV) 82. Mr Halpern and Mr Johnson (TV) 83. The First Olympics (TV) 84. Paradise Postponed (TV) 86, etc.

Raksin, David (1912–). American composer, in Hollywood from mid-thirties. Arranged Chaplin's score for *Modern Times* 36.
Laura 44. The Secret Life of Walter Mitty 47. *The Bad and the Beautiful* 52. Separate Tables 58. Too Late Blues 62. Two Weeks in Another Town 62. Invitation to a Gunfighter 65. A Big Hand for the Little Lady 66. Will Penny 67. What's the Matter with Helen? 71, etc.

Ralli, Giovanna (1935–). Italian leading lady.
The Children are Watching Us 43. Lights of Variety 49. La Lupa 53. The Bigamist 56. Il Generale Della Rovere 59. Deadfall 68. Cannon for Cordoba 70. We All Loved Each Other So Much 75, many others.

Ralph, Jessie (1864–1944) (Jessie Ralph Chambers). American character actress who came to Hollywood late in life and played many endearing granny roles.
□Such a Little Queen 21. Elmer the Great 33. Cocktail Hour 33. Child of Manhattan 33. Ann Carver's Profession 33. Coming Out Party 34. One Night of Love 34. Evelyn Prentice 34. Nana 34. We Live Again 34. Murder at the Vanities 34. The Affairs of Cellini 34. *David Copperfield* (as Peggotty) 35. Enchanted April 35. Les Misérables 35. Paris in Spring 35. Vanessa 35. Mark of the Vampire 35. I Live My Life 35. Jalna 35. Metropolitan 35. I Found Stella Parish 35. Captain Blood 35. Bunker Bean 35. The Garden Murder Case 36. The Unguarded Hour 36. *San Francisco* 36. After the Thin Man 36. Camille 36. Little Lord Fauntleroy 36. Yellow Dust 36. Walking on Air 36. The Good Earth 37. Double Wedding 37. The Last of Mrs Cheyney 37. Love Is a Headache 37. Port of Seven Seas 38. Hold That Kiss 38. St Louis Blues 39. Café Society 39. Four Girls in White 39. The Kid from Texas 39. Mickey the Kid 39. Drums Along the Mohawk 39. *The Blue Bird* 40. Star Dust 40. The Girl from Avenue A 40. I Can't Give You Anything But Love Baby 40. *The Bank Dick* 40. I Want a Divorce 40. The Lady from Cheyenne 41. *They Met in Bombay* 41.

Ralston, Esther (1902–). American leading lady of the twenties and thirties.
The Phantom Fortune (serial) 23. Peter Pan 24. A Kiss for Cinderella 25. Lucky Devil 26. Old Ironsides 26. Figures Don't Lie 27. The Sawdust Paradise 28. The Prodigal 31. Sadie McKee 33. Hollywood Boulevard 36. Tin Pan Alley 40, etc.

Ralston, Jobyna (1901–1967). American leading lady of the twenties, especially with Harold Lloyd.
Why Worry 23. Girl Shy 24. The Freshman 24. For Heaven's Sake 26. Wings 27, many others.

Ralston, Vera Hruba (1921–). Czech actress, former skating champion. In US from late thirties, films from 1942. Married Herbert Yates, boss of Republic Studios, and appeared exclusively in his pictures. Now retired.
□Ice Capades 41. Ice Capades Revue 42. The Lady and the Monster 44. Storm Over Lisbon 44. Lake Placid Serenade 44. Dakota 45. Murder in the Music Hall 46. The Plainsman and the Lady 46. The Flame 47. Wyoming 47. I Jane Doe 48. Angel on the Amazon 48. The Fighting Kentuckian 49. Surrender 50. Belle Le Grand 51. The Wild Blue Yonder 51. Hoodlum Empire 52. Fair Wind to Java 53. A Perilous Journey 53. Jubilee Trail 54. Timberjack 55. Accused of Murder 56. Spoilers of the Forest 57. Gunfire at Indian Gap 57. The Notorious Mr Monks 58. The Man Who Died Twice 58.

Rambeau, Marjorie (1889–1970). American character actress.
The Dazzling Miss Davison 16. Her Man 30. Man's Castle 33. The Rains Came 39. Twenty Mule Team 40. Tugboat Annie Sails Again (title role) 41. So Ends Our Night 41. Tobacco Road 41. Broadway 42. Army Wives 45. Abandoned 49. Torch Song 53. The View from Pompey's Head 56. Man of a Thousand Faces 57, others.

Rambo. A character who first appeared in 1982 in *First Blood*. Sylvester Stallone played a former Green Beret who, back in California, set himself against the law. By the time we saw him again in 1985 in *Rambo: First Blood Part Two* he had become a national comic strip hero, blowing up enemies in Vietnam. Though risible, the violence of these films is unwelcome in most countries.

Rambova, Natacha (1897–1966). American dance teacher who had a tempestuous relationship with Rudolph Valentino and directed the last years of his career. In 1926 she starred in *When Love Grows Cold.*

Ramona. Helen Hunt Jackson's novel about an Indian girl was filmed four times: by Griffith in 1910, with Mary Pickford and Henry B. Walthall; by Donald Crisp in 1916, with Adda Gleason and Monroe Salisbury; by Edwin Carewe in 1928, with Dolores del Rio and Warner Baxter; and by Henry King in 1936, with Loretta Young and Don Ameche.

Rampling, Charlotte (1945–). British leading lady.
Rotten to the Core 65. Georgy Girl 66. The Long Duel 67. The Damned 69. Corky 72. The Ski Bum 72. Henry VIII and His Six Wives 72. Asylum 72. Zardoz 73. Caravan to Vaccares 74. The Night Porter 74. Farewell My Lovely 75. Foxtrot 76. Sherlock Holmes in New York (TV) 76. Flesh of the Orchid 76. Orca 77. The Purple Taxi 78. Stardust Memories 80. The Verdict 82. The Viva la Vie 83. He Died with his Eyes Open 84. Sadness and Beauty 85. Max my Love 86. Angel Heart 87. Paris by Night 88, etc.

Rand, Sally (1904–1979) (Helen Gould Beck). American dancer and fan dancer, in a few films.
The Dressmaker from Paris 24. Getting Gertie's Garter 27. King of Kings 27. The Fighting Eagle 28. Bolero 34, etc.

Randall, Tony (1920–) (Leonard Rosenberg). Sardonic American comedy actor, adept at light drunks, depressives and friends of the hero.
□Oh Men Oh Women 57. Will Success Spoil Rock Hunter? 57. No Down Payment 58. The Mating Game 59. *Pillow Talk* 59. The Adventures of Huckleberry Finn 60. Let's Make Love 61. Lover Come Back 61. Boys Night Out 62. Island of Love 63. The Brass Bottle 63. *Send Me No Flowers* 64. *Seven Faces of Dr Lao* 64. Fluffy 65. The Alphabet Murders (hilariously miscast as Hercule Poirot) 66. Our Man in Marrakesh 66. Hello Down There 68. Everything You Always Wanted to Know About Sex 72. Scavenger Hunt 79. Foolin' Around 80. Sidney Shorr: A Girl's Best Friend (TV) 81. King of Comedy 83.
TV series: *Mr Peepers* 52–55. *The Odd Couple* 70–74. Tony Randall Show 76–77. Love, Sidney 81–82.

¶ *T.R.:* Comedy's a serious business. You've got to be true and funny, and not look as though you're trying.

Randell, Ron (1918–). Australian leading man with radio experience; has appeared in films and TV episodes all over the world.
It Had to be You 47. Lorna Doone 50. Kiss Me Kate 53. Bulldog Drummond at Bay 54. I Am a Camera 55. Beyond Mombasa 56. The Story of Esther Costello 58. King of Kings 61. The Longest Day 62. Gold for the Caesars 63. The Seven Minutes 71. Exposed 83, many others.
TV series: O.S.S. 58.

Randle, Frank (1901–1957) (Arthur McEvoy). Lancashire music-hall comedian of immense vulgarity; made his own slapdash but highly popular films in the forties.
Somewhere in England 40. Somewhere in Camp 42. Somewhere in Civvies 43. School for Randle 47. Home Sweet Home 47. Holidays with Pay 48. It's a Grand Life 53, etc.

Randolph, Anders (1876–1930). American character man, usually seen as heavy villain.
The Hero of Submarine D2 16. The Splendid Sinner 18. Dorothy Vernon of Haddon Hall 24. The Black Pirate 28. The Kiss 29, many others.

Randolph, Elsie (1901–82) (Elsie Florence Killick). British revue artiste, often teamed in the thirties with Jack Buchanan.
□Rich and Strange 31. Brother Alfred 32. Life Goes On 32. Rise and Shine 32. Yes, Mr Brown 33. Night of the Garter 33. *That's a Good Girl* 35. *This'll Make You Whistle* 37. Smash and Grab 38. Cheer the Brave 50. Riders of the Sky (Czech) 68. Frenzy 72. Charleston 77.

Randolph, Jane (1919–). American leading lady of the forties.
Highways by Night 42. Cat People 42. In the Meantime, Darling 44. Jealousy 46. T Men 48. Abbott and Costello Meet Frankenstein (last to date) 48, etc.

Randolph, John (1917–). American character actor usually seen as pompous business man.
Naked City 48. *Seconds* 67. Pretty Poison 68. There Was a Crooked Man 70. Little Murders 71. Serpico 73. King Kong 76. Washington Behind Closed Doors (TV) 77. Blind Ambition (TV) 79.
TV series: Lucas Tanner 75. Lucan 77.

Random Harvest (US 1942). Immensely popular in the drab wartime days of its release, this romantic film was taken from a James Hilton novel about a man who marries while suffering from amnesia; he gets his memory back, is restored to his former position in life, and fails to recognize his wife when she comes to work as his secretary. Sheer hokum complete with roses round the door, but persuasively produced in MGM's best manner, carefully directed by Mervyn le Roy, and with irresistible star performances from Ronald Colman and Greer Garson.

Rank, J. Arthur (Lord Rank) (1888–1972). British flour magnate who entered films in the mid-thirties in the hope of promoting interest in religion. Formed or took over so many companies including production, distribution and exhibition that by the mid-forties he was accused of monopolistic tendencies. His influence was generally excellent, and he encouraged independent producers (sometimes unwisely), but his organization generally suffered from a preponderance of accountants unable to understand the ingredients of a good film. Without their financial advice, however, the empire might well have perished altogether. At its height it fostered such production companies as the Archers, Cineguild, Wessex, Individual and Two Cities. In recent years the film side of the organization has proved less important than its hotels, bowling alleys and such developments as Xerox-copying; but it includes Odeon and Gaumont Theatres, Rank Film Distributors, Pinewood Studios, Denham Laboratories, etc. A biography, *Mr Rank* by Alan Wood, was published in 1952.
❀ For doing his best. *Henry V.*

¶ 'Methodist principles may seem a curious guide to the promotion of motion pictures, but at least they gave J. Arthur Rank a considerable start over other film promoters who had no principles at all.'—*Alan Wood*

J.A.R.: If I could recall to you some of my various adventures and experiences in the film world, it would I think be as plain to you as it is to me that I was being led by God.

Ransohoff, Martin (1927–). American writer and executive. Longtime chairman of Filmways, producers of such TV series as *The Beverly Hillbillies* and *The Addams Family*. Has also produced films.
Boys Night Out 62. The Wheeler Dealers 63. The Americanization of Emily 64. Topkapi 64. The Sandpiper 65. The Loved One 65. The Cincinnati Kid 65. Don't Make Waves 67. Ice Station Zebra 68. The Moonshine War 70. The White Dawn 73. Silver Streak 76, etc.

Ransome, Prunella (1943–). British leading lady.
Far from the Madding Crowd 67. Alfred the Great 69. Man in the Wilderness 71. Who Can Kill A Child? (Sp.) 75, etc.

rape was virtually unmentionable in English-speaking films until Warners got away with it in *Johnny Belinda* in 1947. Then it became the centre of attention in *Outrage, Peyton Place, Wicked as They Come, A Streetcar Named Desire, Last Train from Gun Hill, Two Women, To Kill a Mockingbird, Satan Never Sleeps, Shock Corridor, Assault, Trial, Five Gates to Hell, The Chapman Report, The Mark, Anatomy of a Murder, Town without Pity, The Party's Over* (in which the victim proved to be dead), and *The Penthouse.* In *Waterhole Three* James Coburn, accused of the crime, shrugged it off as 'assault with a friendly weapon'. There was much talk of rape in *The Knack* and *Lock Up Your Daughters*, threat of rape in *Experiment in Terror* and *Cape Fear*, and an accusation of rape in *Term of Trial.* Foreign language films on the subject have included *Rashomon, The Virgin Spring, Two Women, Viridiana* and the Greek *Amok.* In seventies films it became too commonplace to be worth mentioning, outstanding fictional instances being *Straw Dogs, A Clockwork Orange, Lipstick*, and *Death Wish*, with *Cry Rape* and *A Case of Rape* adopting a documentary treatment.

Raphael, Frederic (1931–). British writer.
Bachelor of Hearts 58. *Nothing But the Best* 64. *Darling* (AA, BFA) 65. Two for the Road 67. Far from the Madding Crowd 67. A Severed Head 71. Daisy Miller 74. Rogue Male (TV) 76, etc

Raphaelson, Samson (1896–1983). American playwright whose best screenplays were for Lubitsch: he led the saucy, stylish European trends of the thirties.
□The Jazz Singer (& oa) 27. Boudoir Diplomat 30. The Smiling Lieutenant 31. The Magnificent Lie 31. *One Hour with You* 32. Broken Lullaby 32. *Trouble in Paradise* 32. The Merry Widow 34. Caravan 34. Servants' Entrance 34. Ladies Love Danger 35. Dressed to Thrill 35. *Accent on Youth* (& oa) 35. The Last of Mrs Cheyney 37. *The Shop around the Corner* 40. Suspicion 41. Skylark (& oa) 41. *Heaven Can Wait* 43. The Perfect Marriage (& oa) 46. Green Dolphin Street 47. That

Lady in Ermine 48. Bannerline 51. Main Street to Broadway 53. Hilda Crane (oa) 56.

Rappeneau, Jean-Paul (1932–). French director.
La Vie de Chateau 65. Les Mariés de l'An II 70. Le Sauvage 77. Tout Feu, Tout Flamme 82.

Rapper, Irving (1898–). American director with stage experience, long associated with Warner films.
Shining Victory 41. One Foot in Heaven 41. The Gay Sisters 42. *Now Voyager* 42. The Adventures of Mark Twain 44. Rhapsody in Blue 45. The Corn is Green 46. *Deception* 46. *The Voice of the Turtle* 48. The Glass Menagerie 50. Another Man's Poison (GB) 51. Forever Female 52. The Brave One 56. Strange Intruder 57. Marjorie Morningstar 58. The Miracle 59. The Christine Jorgenson Story 70. Born Again 78, others.

Rashomon (In the Woods) (Japan 1951). The film which after many years opened western cinemas to Japanese films; America has even paid it the compliment of remaking it (1964) as *The Outrage.* Concerning the different views of the four people concerned about a moment of violence, it was a stylistic revelation and established Akira Kurosawa as an O.K. name though his subsequent films seldom got beyond the very specialized halls.

Rasp, Fritz (1891–1976). German character actor.
Jugend 22. Warning Shadows 23. Metropolis 27. The Loves of Jeanne Ney 27. Spione 28. Diary of a Lost Girl 29. Die Dreigroschenoper 33. Lina Braake 76, many others.

Rasputin, the mysterious monk who dominated members of the Tsar's family just before the Russian revolution, has been a popular film subject. Conrad Veidt played him in *Rasputin* (Germany 1930); Lionel Barrymore in *Rasputin and the Empress* (US 1932); Harry Baur in *Rasputin* (France 1938); Edmund Purdom in *Nights of Rasputin* (Italy 1960); and Christopher Lee in *Rasputin the Mad Monk* (Britain 1966); while 1968 brought Gert Frobe in the role in *I Killed Rasputin*, and 1971 had Tom Baker as Rasputin in *Nicholas and Alexandra.*

Rasulala, Thalmus (1939–) (Jack Crowder). Black American character actor.
Cool Breeze 71. Blacula 72. Willie Dynamite 73. Mr Ricco 75. Bucktown 75. Adios Amigo 76. Fun with Dick and Jane 77. Bulletproof 87, etc.

Rasumny, Mikhail (1890–1956). Russian character actor with stage experience, long in Hollywood.
Comrade X 40. This Gun for Hire 42. For Whom the Bell Tolls 43. Saigon 47. The Kissing Bandit 49. Hot Blood 55, many others.

Rathbone, Basil (1892–1967). Incisive British actor, on stage since 1911, in America from the mid-twenties.
Autobiography 1962: *In and Out of Character.* Biography 1972: *Basil Rathbone and His Films* by Michael B. Druxman.
□Innocent 21. The Fruitful Vine 21. The School for Scandal 23. Trouping with Ellen 24. The Masked Bride 25. The Great Deception 24. The Last of Mrs Cheyney 29. The Bishop Murder Case 30. A Notorious Affair 30. The Lady of Scandal 30. This Mad World 30. The Flirting Widow 30. A Lady Surrenders 30. Sin Takes a Holiday 30. A Woman Commands 31. One Precious Year 33. After the Ball 33. Loyalties 33. *David Copperfield* (as Murdstone) 35. *Anna Karenina* (as Karenin) 35. The Last Days of Pompeii 35. A Feather in Her Hat 35. A Tale of Two Cities 35. *Captain Blood* 35. Kind Lady 35. Private Number 36. Romeo and Juliet 36. The Garden of Allah 36. Confession 37. Love from a Stranger 37. Make a Wish 37. Tovarich 37. The Adventures of Marco Polo 38. *The Adventures of Robin Hood* (as Gisbourne) 38. If I Were King 38. The Dawn Patrol 38. Son of Frankenstein 39. *The Hound of the Baskervilles* 39. The Sun Never Sets 39. The Adventures of Sherlock Holmes 39. Rio 39. Tower of London 39. Rhythm on the River 40. The Mark of Zorro 40. The Mad Doctor 41. The Black Cat 41. International Lady 41. Paris Calling 41. Fingers at the Window 41. Crossroads 42. Sherlock Holmes and the Voice of Terror 42. Sherlock Holmes and the Secret Weapon 42. Sherlock Holmes in Washington 43. Above Suspicion 43. Sherlock Holmes Faces Death 43. *Spider Woman* 44. The Scarlet Claw 44. Bathing Beauty 44. The Pearl of Death 44. Frenchman's Creek 44. The House of Fear 45. The Woman in Green 45. Pursuit to Algiers 45. Terror by Night 45. *Heartbeat* 46. Dressed to Kill 46. Casanova's Big Night 54. We're No Angels 55. *The Court Jester* 56. The Black Sleep 56. The Last Hurrah 58. The Magic Sword 62. Tales of Terror 62. Two Before Zero 62. The Comedy of Terrors 64. Pontius Pilate 64. Queen of Blood 66. The

Ghost in the Invisible Bikini 66. Voyage to a Prehistoric Planet 67. Autopsy of a Ghost 67. Hillbillies in a Haunted House 67.

† The only time he won a screen duel was in *Romeo and Juliet*: he played Tybalt.

❁ For being everybody's favourite villain and the one and only Sherlock Holmes. *The Hound of the Baskervilles.*

¶ *Dorothy Parker:* Two profiles pasted together.

ratio (screen): see *aspect ratio.*

Ratoff, Gregory (1897–1960). English-fracturing Russian actor and impresario, in Hollywood and Britain from mid-thirties as actor or director.
I'm No Angel (a) 33. Under Two Flags (a) 36. Lancer Spy (d) 37. Rose of Washington Square (d) 39. Intermezzo (d) 39. I Was an Adventuress (d) 40. Adam Had Four Sons (d) 41. The Corsican Brothers (a) 41. The Men in Her Life (d) 42. Song of Russia (d) 44. Where Do We Go from Here? (d) 45. Moss Rose (d) 47. *All about Eve* (a) 50. My Daughter Joy (d) 50. Abdullah the Great (ad) 57. *Oscar Wilde* (d) 60. The Big Gamble (a) 61, many others.

Rattigan, Sir Terence (1912–77). Distinguished British playwright, many of whose successes have been filmed.
Biography 1979 by Michael Darlow and Gillian Hodson: *Terence Rattigan, the Man and his Work*.
French without Tears 39. While the Sun Shines 46. The Winslow Boy 48. The Browning Version 51. The Deep Blue Sea 55. Separate Tables 58, etc.
AS SCREENWRITER: English without Tears 43. The Way to the Stars 45. The Sound Barrier 52. The VIPs 63. The Yellow Rolls-Royce 64. Goodbye Mr Chips 69. Bequest to the Nation 73, others.

Ravetch, Irving (c. 1915–). American writer who with his wife Harriet Frank has frequently worked with director Martin Ritt on scripts that include *Hud* 63. *Hombre* 67. and *Norma Rae* 79. Turned writer-producer with *The Reivers* 69.

Rawi, Ousama (1940–). Iranian cinematographer.
Pulp 73. The Black Windmill 74. Gold 74. Rachel's Man 75. Alfie Darling 75. Sky Riders 76. Power Play 78. Zulu Dawn 79, etc.
Went to Canada to produce commercials. In 1986 directed *Judgment in Stone*.

Rawlins, David (–). American editor.
Bingo Long 76. Saturday Night Fever 77. The Last Remake of Beau Geste 78. The China Syndrome 79. Urban Cowboy 80.

Rawlins, John (1902–). American director, mainly of second features.
State Police 38. Six Lessons from Madame La Zonga 41. Halfway to Shanghai 42. Sherlock Holmes and the Voice of Terror 42. The Great Impersonation 42. Ladies Courageous 44. Sudan 45. Dick Tracy Meets Gruesome 47. Fort Defiance 52. Shark River 53. The Lost Legion 57, etc.

Rawlinson, Herbert (1885–1953). English-born American circus performer, silent star and latterly character actor.
Monte Cristo 12. The Sea Wolf 13. The Black Box (serial) 15. Good Gracious Annabelle 19. Charge It 21. Bullets or Ballots 36. Dark Victory 39. Superman (serial) 48, many others.

Rawnsley, David (1909–). British art director (*49th Parallel, In Which We Serve, The Rake's Progress, I See a Dark Stranger*, etc). Inventor of the Independent Frame system, intended as a production economy; it caused constriction in practice and was quickly abandoned.

Rawsthorne, Alan (1905–1971). British composer.
Burma Victory 45. The Captive Heart 46. Uncle Silas 47. Saraband for Dead Lovers 48, etc.

Ray, Aldo (1926–) (Aldo da Re). Beefy American actor, in local politics before film career.
Saturday's Heroes 51. *The Marrying Kind* 51. Pat and Mike 52. Let's Do It Again 53. Miss Sadie Thompson 54. We're No Angels 55. The Gentle Sergeant 56. Men in War 57. God's Little Acre 58. The Naked and the Dead 58. The Siege of Pinchgut (GB) 58. The Day They Robbed the Bank of England (GB) 60. Johnny Nobody (GB) 61. Nightmare in the Sun 64. Sylvia 65. What Did You Do in the War, Daddy? 66. Dead Heat on a Merry-Go-Round 66. Welcome to Hard Times 67. Riot on Sunset Strip 67. The Power 67. The Green Berets 68. Man Without Mercy 69. And Hope to Die 72. Inside Out 75. The Bad Bunch 76. Haunts 77. Death Dimension 78. The Glove 80, etc.

Ray, Andrew (1939–). British juvenile lead, son of Ted Ray.

The Mudlark (debut) 50. The Yellow Balloon 52. Escapade 55. Woman in a Dressing-Gown 57. Serious Charge 59. Twice Round the Daffodils 62. The System 64. Great Expectations (TV) 75, etc.
TV series: Edward and Mrs Simpson (as George VI) 78.

Ray, Charles (1891–1943). American leading man of the silent screen, often in country boy roles.
SILENT FILMS: Bill Henry 19. The Old Swimming Hole 20. The Barnstormer 22. The Girl I Love 23. Sweet Adeline 23. The Courtship of Miles Standish (& p) 23. Vanity 25. Getting Gertie's Garter 27. The Garden of Eden 28, etc.
SOUND FILMS: Ladies Should Listen 34. By Your Leave 35. Just My Luck 37.

Ray, Johnnie (1927–). American 'crying' singer of the fifties who played a leading role in *There's No Business Like Show Business* 54.

Ray, Man (1890–1976) (Emmanuel Rudnitsky). American photographer, dadaist and surrealist, long resident in France; made a few strange films.
Retour à la Raison (wd) 23. Entr'acte (a) 24. L'Etoile de Mer (wd) 28. The Mystery of the Château of the Dice (wd) 29. Dreams that Money Can Buy (oa) 46, etc.

Ray, Nicholas (1911–1979) (Raymond N. Kienzle). American director, former writer and stage director. Acclaimed for his first film, he later seemed to lack a particular style.
□*They Live by Night* 47. A Woman's Secret 49. Knock on Any Door 49. Born to be Bad 50. *In a Lonely Place* 50. Flying Leathernecks 51. On Dangerous Ground 51. The Lusty Men 52. Johnny Guitar 54. Run for Cover 55. *Rebel without a Cause* 55. Hot Blood 56. Bigger than Life 56. The True Story of Jesse James 57. Bitter Victory 57. Wind Across the Everglades 58. Party Girl 58. Savage Innocents 59. King of Kings 61. 55 Days at Peking 62. Dreams of Thirteen 76. The American Friend (a only) 77.

† In 1980, when he was dying of cancer, he appeared in *Lightning Over Water*, a film about himself.

Ray, René (1912–) (Irene Creese). British actress, on stage from childhood; has often played downtrodden waifs.
Young Woodley 30. *The Passing of the Third Floor Back* 35. Crime over London 36. Farewell Again 37. *The Rat* 38. Bank Holiday 38. The Return of the Frog 39. They Made Me a Fugitive 47. If Winter Comes (US) 47. Women of Twilight 52. The Good Die Young 53. Vicious Circle 57, etc.

Ray, Satyajit (1921–). Indian director, famous for the 'Apu' trilogy of a child growing up in modern India.
Pather Panchali 54. *The Unvanquished* (Aparajito) 56. The Music Room 58. *The World of Apu* 59. The Goddess 60. Kanchenjunga 62. The Adventures of Goopy and Bagha 68. The Adversary 71. Company Limited 72. Distant Thunder 74. The Middle Man 76. The Chess Players 77, etc.

Ray, Ted (1906–1977) (Charles Olden). British music-hall comedian and violinist who was in occasional films.
Autobiography 1952: *Raising The Laughs*. 1963: *My Turn Next*.
Elstree Calling 30. Radio Parade of 1935. A Ray of Sunshine 47. Meet Me Tonight 50. Escape by Night 52. My Wife's Family 54. Carry On, Teacher 59. Please Turn Over 60, etc.

Raye, Carol (1923–) (Kathleen Corkrey). Australian leading lady of British films of the forties.
Strawberry Roan 45. Spring Song 46. While I Live 48, etc.

Raye, Martha (1916–) (Maggie O'Reed). Wide-mouthed American comedienne and vocalist, popular on radio and TV.
Rhythm on the Range (debut) 36. Waikiki Wedding 37. Artists and Models 38. The Boys from Syracuse 40. Keep 'Em Flying 41. *Hellzapoppin* 41. Pin-Up Girl 43. Four Jills in a Jeep 44. *Monsieur Verdoux* 47. Jumbo 62. *Pufnstuf* 70. The Concorde – Airport 79 79, etc.
TV series: The Martha Raye Show 59. The Bugaloos 70–71. McMillan 76.

¶ *M.R.*: I didn't have to work till I was three. But after that, I never stopped.

Raymond, Cyril (c. 1897–1973). British stage and screen actor often seen as the dull husband or professional man.
The Shadow 32. Mixed Doubles 33. The Tunnel 35. Dreaming Lips 37. Come On George 39. Brief Encounter 46. This was a Woman 47. Jack of Diamonds 48. Angels One Five 51. Lease of Life 53. Charley Moon 56, etc.

Raymond, Gary (1935–). British 'second lead'.
The Moonraker 58. *Look Back in Anger* 59. Suddenly Last Summer 59. The Millionairess 61. El Cid 61. Jason and the Argonauts 63. The Greatest Story Ever Told 65. Traitors' Gate 65. The Playboy of the Western World 66, etc.
TV series: The Rat Patrol 65.

Raymond, Gene (1908–) (Raymond Guion). American leading man of the thirties, recently character actor; was married to Jeanette MacDonald. On stage from childhood. Directed one film, *Million Dollar Weekend* (& a) 48.
Personal Maid (debut) 31. *Zoo in Budapest* 33. Flying Down to Rio 33. I Am Suzanne 34. Seven Keys to Baldpate 34. That Girl from Paris 37. Stolen Heaven 38. Mr and Mrs Smith 41. Smilin' Through 41. The Locket 46. Assigned to Danger 49. Hit the Deck 55. The Best Man 64, etc.
TV series: Paris 7000 70.

Raymond, Jack (1892–1953) (John Caines). British producer, mainly lightweight comedy films.
Sorrell and Son 34. Up for the Cup 34. The Frog 36. Splinters 37. The Rat 38. The Mind of Mr Reeder (& d) 39. You Will Remember 41. Worm's Eye View 51. Reluctant Heroes 52, many others.

Raymond, Paula (1923–) (Paula Ramona Wright). American leading lady, former model.
Devil's Doorway 49. Crisis 50. The Tall Target 51. The Beast from Twenty Thousand Fathoms 53. The Human Jungle 54. The Gun that Won the West 55. The Flight That Disappeared 62. Blood of Dracula's Castle 70, etc.

Reagan, Ronald (1911–). American leading man of the forties, former sports reporter. Went into politics and in 1966 was elected Governor of California; in 1976 narrowly missed the Republican presidential nomination; in 1980, elected president. Published autobiography 1965: *Where's the Rest of Me?*
Love is on the Air 37. Accidents Will Happen 38. Dark Victory 39. Hell's Kitchen 39. Brother Rat and a Baby 40. Santa Fé Trail 40. International Squadron 41. Nine Lives are Not Enough 41. *King's Row* 41. Juke Girl 42. *Desperate Journey* 42. This is the Army 43. Stallion Road 47. That Hagen Girl 47. The Voice of the Turtle 47. Night unto Night 48. John Loves Mary 49. The Hasty Heart (GB) 49. Louisa 50. Storm Warning 51. Hong Kong 52. Prisoner of War 54. Law and Order 54. Tennessee's Partner 55. Hellcats of the Navy 57. The Killers 64, etc.
TV series: Death Valley Days 62–64.
Famous line (*King's Row*): Where's the rest of me?
Famous line (*Knute Rockne, All American*): Win one for the Gipper!

Rear Window (US 1954). Alfred Hitchcock here set himself the task of making a thriller in which the action is all confined to one room—and the block of flats opposite at whose inhabitants the peeping-tom hero peers through his binoculars and uncovers a murder. Successful less because of Cornell Woolrich's story than because of John Michael Hayes' witty dialogue; Hitchcock's own talent seemed cramped. Photographed by Robert Burks, with music by Franz Waxman; with James Stewart, Grace Kelly.

Reason, Rex (1928–) (formerly known as **Bart Roberts**). American leading man, mainly in routine films.
Storm over Tibet 52. Salome 53. Yankee Pasha 54. This Island Earth 55. Raw Edge 56. Band of Angels 57. The Rawhide Trail 60, etc.
TV series: Man Without a Gun 58. *The Roaring Twenties* 60.

Reason, Rhodes (1928–). American leading man, mainly in second features. Twin of Rex Reason.
Crime against Joe 56. Jungle Heat 57. Yellowstone Kelly 59. King Kong Escapes (Jap.) 68, etc.
TV series: *White Hunter* 58.

Rebecca (US 1940). A splendid example of the cinema as a popular storyteller. From Daphne du Maurier's smash-hit novel of passion and mystery in a Cornish stately home, Hitchcock fashioned an impeccable film, with the help of a clever screenplay by Robert E. Sherwood and Joan Harrison, and a cast including Laurence Olivier, Joan Fontaine, Judith Anderson, Reginald Denny, George Sanders, Florence Bates, Gladys Cooper, C. Aubrey Smith and Nigel Bruce. Commercial film-making at its best. AA best film, best photography (George Barnes).

Rebecca of Sunnybrook Farm. The American children's classic by Kate Douglas

Wiggin was filmed in 1917 by Marshall Neilan, with Mary Pickford; in 1932 by Alfred Santell, with Marian Nixon; and in 1938 (much changed) by Allan Dwan, with Shirley Temple.

Rebel without a Cause (US 1955). This story of teenage restlessness directed by Nicholas Ray and starring James Dean was felt to be of some significance because for the first time the hoodlums were shown as coming from rich, comfortable homes. Otherwise it was a straightforward star vehicle.

The Red Badge of Courage (US 1951). The story of the making of this film is told in hilarious detail by Lillian Ross in her book *Picture*, and it is a classic example of what happens to artistic intentions when the commercial element of film-making gets its teeth into them. The film as released did not do justice to Stephen Crane's civil war history, or to the box office; director John Huston had tired of the unhappy compromise, and all the viewer could salvage were some stirring battle scenes directed by Andrew Marton, with accomplished photography by Harold Rosson and music by Bronislau Kaper.

The Red Balloon (France 1956). A thirty-six-minute fantasy written and directed by Albert Lamorisse, about a boy's pursuit of a balloon through the streets of Paris. A uniquely charming and happy film which succeeds in a field the cinema should tackle more often.

Red Dust (US 1932). This Cochinese rubber plantation melodrama is remembered for the electric teaming of Clark Gable and Jean Harlow, and for the scene in which Harlow takes a primitive shower. It was remade in 1939 as *Congo Maisie*, with Ann Sothern and John Carroll; and in 1954 Gable himself appeared opposite Ava Gardner in a lavish restyling under the title *Mogambo*.

Red Garters (US 1954). Only a minor musical, but it set out with fair success to stylize the western form, and if the pretty Technicolor sets hadn't got so monotonous it might have had more recognition. Michael Fessier's script was lively and pleasant, George Marshall's direction smooth, and the songs by Jay Livingston and Ray Evans very hummable. With Rosemary Clooney, Gene Barry, Jack Carson, Guy Mitchell.

Red Indians, it is generally thought, were always portrayed as villains on screen until *Broken Arrow* in 1950, when Jeff Chandler played Cochise. But in fact there were many silent films in which Indians were not only on the side of right but the leading figures in the story. In 1911 one finds titles like *An Indian Wife's Devotion, A Squaw's Love, Red-Wing's Gratitude*; *Ramona* (qv) had already been made once and was to survive three remakes; 1913 brought *Heart of an Indian* and *The Squaw Man*. Later there were versions of *In the Days of Buffalo Bill* 21, *The Vanishing American* 25, and *Redskin* 28. It seems to have been sound that made the Indians villainous, and kept them that way for twenty-two years.

After *Broken Arrow* there was a deluge of pro-Indian films. *Devil's Doorway, Across the Wide Missouri, The Savage, Arrowhead, The Big Sky, Apache, Taza—Son of Cochise, Chief Crazy Horse, Sitting Bull, White Feather, Navajo, Hiawatha*, all came within four years. There were even biopics of modern Indians: *The Outsider* (Ira Hayes) and *Jim Thorpe, All American*. In recent years the Indians have been slipping back into villainy: but the sixties brought *Flaming Star, Cheyenne Autumn, Tell them Willie Boy is Here, A Man called Horse, Flap, Little Big Man, The Stalking Moon*; and TV in 1966 boasted a series based on a Red Indian cop in New York (the name is *Hawk*) as well as comic Indians in *F Troop*; and Elvis Presley played a Red Indian hero in *Stay Away Joe*.

Other whites who have played red include Boris Karloff in *Tap Roots*; Victor Mature in *Chief Crazy Horse*; Charlton Heston in *The Savage*; Burt Lancaster in *Apache*; Paul Newman in *Hombre*; Robert Taylor in *Devil's Doorway*; Don Ameche in *Ramona*.

† The Jacarillo tribe financed *A Gunfight* in 1971.

The Red Inn (France 1951). A direction-pointing black comedy which came somewhat ahead of its time. The script by Aurenche and Bost satirizes society, religion and everything else within sight in its nineteenth-century fable of two inn-keepers (Carette and Françoise Rosay) who murder travellers for money. A monk (Fernandel) gets one batch safely away, only to see their carriage topple over a precipice. Claude Autant-Lara directed.

The Red Shoes (GB 1948). Michael Powell and Emeric Pressburger always aimed high in their choice of subject, and here their aim was to give us the feel of the world of ballet: the backstage and private lives of those concerned in it. The detail remains fascinating, the colour evocative, the dancing superb; only the story is rather trite and lumpy. Moira Shearer made a hit as the tragic heroine, Anton Walbrook spat superbly as the impresario; Jack Cardiff's photography was near his best .

Reddy, Helen (1942–). Australian folk singer.
Airport 75 74. Pete's Dragon 77.

Redfield, William (1927–1976). American general purpose actor with long stage experience; former boy actor.
I Married a Woman 58. Fantastic Voyage 66. Duel at Diablo 66. A New Leaf 70. Death Wish 74. For Pete's Sake 74. One Flew Over the Cuckoo's Nest 76, etc.

Redford, Robert (1936–). Blond, athletic American leading actor of the seventies and eighties. Biography 1977: *Robert Redford* by Donald A. Reed.
□War Hunt 61. Situation Hopeless but not Serious 65. Inside Daisy Clover 65. *The Chase* 66. This Property is Condemned 66. Barefoot in the Park 67. Tell Them Willie Boy is Here 69. *Butch Cassidy and the Sundance Kid* 69. Downhill Racer 69. Little Fauss and Big Halsy 70. The Hot Rock 72. Jeremiah Johnson 72. *The Candidate* 72. The Way We Were 73. *The Sting* 73. The Great Gatsby 74. The Great Waldo Pepper 75. Three Days of the Condor 75. *All the President's Men* 76. A Bridge Too Far 77. The Electric Horseman 79. Brubaker 80. Ordinary People (d only) (AA) 80. The Natural 84. Out of Africa 85. Legal Eagles 86.
† Redford is alleged to have turned down the leading roles in *Who's Afraid of Virginia Woolf*, *The Graduate*, *Rosemary's Baby*, *Love Story* and *The Day of the Jackal*.

¶ *R.R.:* Other people have analysis. I have Utah.

R.R.: I often feel I'll just opt out of this rat race and buy another hunk of Utah.

R.R.: A lot of what acting is, is paying attention.

R.R.: All my life I've been dogged by guilt because I feel there is this difference between the way I look and the way I feel inside.

Redgrave, Corin (1939–). British supporting actor, son of Sir Michael Redgrave.
A Man for All Seasons 66. Charge of the Light Brigade 68. Oh What a Lovely War 69. David Copperfield 69. Von Richthofen and Brown 71. Serail 77. Sunday Too Far Away 77, etc.

Redgrave, Lynn (1943–). British actress, daughter of Sir Michael Redgrave; has tended to play gauche comedy roles.
□Tom Jones 63. Girl with Green Eyes 64. *Georgy Girl* 66. The Deadly Affair 67. Smashing Time 67. The Virgin Soldiers 69. Blood Kin 69. Killer from Yuma 71. Every Little Crook and Nanny 72. Everything You Always Wanted to Know about Sex 72. The National Health 73. The Happy Hooker 75. The Big Bus 76. Sunday Lovers 80. Gauguin the Savage (TV) 81. Rehearsal for Murder (TV) 82. The Shooting (TV) 82. Morgan Stewart's Coming Home 87.
TV series: House Calls 80–81. Teachers Only 82.

¶ *L.R.:* Looking up at my horrible ugly bulk on a huge screen was the turning point in my life. (She shed many pounds before making it big in Hollywood and on American TV game shows.)

Redgrave, Sir Michael (1908–85). Tall, distinguished British actor, former schoolmaster, on stage from 1934.
Biography 1956: *Michael Redgrave, Actor* by Richard Findlater. Autobiography 1958: *Mask or Face.*
Autobiography 1983: *In My Mind's Eye.*
□ *The Lady Vanishes* 38. Climbing High 38. A Stolen Life 39. A Window in London 39. *The Stars Look Down* 39. *Kipps* 41. Atlantic Ferry 41. *Jeannie* 41. *Thunder Rock* 42. The Big Blockade 42. The Way to the Stars 45. *Dead of Night* 45. The Captive Heart 46. The Years Between 46. The Man Within 47. *Fame is the Spur* 47. Mourning Becomes Electra (US) 47. The Secret Beyond the Door (US) 48. *The Browning Version* 50. The Magic Box 51. *The Importance of Being Earnest* 52. The Sea Shall Not Have Them 54. The Green Scarf 54. Oh Rosalinda 55. Confidential Report 55. The Night my Number Came Up 55. *The Dam Busters* 55. Nineteen Eighty-Four 56. Time Without Pity 57. *The Quiet American* 58. Law and Disorder 58. Behind the Mask 58. Shake Hands with the Devil 59. No My Darling Daughter 60. The Innocents 61. The Loneliness of the Long Distance Runner 63. Young Cassidy 64. The Hill 65. The Heroes of Telemark 65. Assignment K 67. Oh What a Lovely War 69. Goodbye Mr Chips 69. The Battle of Britain 69. David Copperfield 69.

Connecting Rooms 69. Goodbye Gemini 70. Nicholas and Alexandra 71. The Go-Between 71.

Redgrave, Vanessa (1937–). British leading lady, daughter of Sir Michael Redgrave: as well known for her espousal of causes as for her acting.
□Behind the Mask 58. *Morgan* 66. Red and Blue 66. Sailor from Gibraltar 66. A Man for all Seasons (uncredited) 66. Blow Up 66. *Camelot* 67. The Charge of the Light Brigade 68. *Isadora* 68. A Quiet Place in the Country (It.) 68. Dropout (It.) 69. Vacation (It.) 69. The Seagull 69. Oh What a Lovely War 69. The Trojan Women 71. The Devils 71. *Mary Queen of Scots* 72. Murder on the Orient Express 74. Out of Season 75. The Seven Per Cent Solution 76. Julia (AA) 77. Agatha 79. Yanks 79. Bear Island 79. *Playing for Time* (TV) 81. Wagner 82. My Body My Child (TV) 83. The Bostonians 84. Steaming 85. Wetherby 86. Three Sovereigns for Sarah (TV) 86. Peter the Great (TV) 86. Second Serve (TV) 86. Comrades 86. Prick Up Your Ears 87.

¶ *V.R.:* America is gangsterism for the private profit of the few.

V.R.: I give myself to my parts as to a lover.

V.R.: I have a tremendous use for passionate statement.

V.R.: It's a kinky part of my nature—to meddle.

V.R.: I choose all my roles very carefully so that when my career is finished I will have covered all our recent history of oppression.

Redman, Joyce (1918–). Irish stage actress whose most memorable film role was in the eating scene in *Tom Jones* 63.
Othello 65. Prudence and the Pill 67. Les Miserables (TV) 77.

Redmond, Liam (1913–). Irish character actor, an Abbey player.
I See a Dark Stranger 45. Captain Boycott 48. High Treason 51. The Gentle Gunman 52. The Divided Heart 54. Jacqueline 56. Night of the Demon 57. The Boy and the Bridge 59. The Ghost and Mr Chicken (US) 65. Tobruk (US) 66. The Twenty-Fifth Hour 66. The Last Safari 67, etc.

Redmond, Moira (–). British actress.
Doctor in Love 58. *Nightmare* 62. Jigsaw 62. The Limbo Line 66, etc.

reduction print: one optically reduced from 35mm to 16mm.

Reece, Brian (1913–1962). British light actor whose success was mainly on stage.
A Case for PC 49 51. Fast and Loose 54. Orders are Orders 55. Carry on Admiral 58, etc.

Reed, Alan (1908–1977) (Edward Bergman). Burly American character actor, TV's voice of Fred Flintstone.
Days of Glory 43. Nob Hill 44. Viva Zapata 52. The Desperate Hours 55. Breakfast at Tiffany's 62, etc.

Reed, Sir Carol (1906–1976). Distinguished British director who after a peak in the late forties seemed to lose his way; his infrequent later films, though always civilized, were generally disappointing.
□Midshipman Easy 34. Laburnum Grove 36. Talk of the Devil 36. Who's Your Lady Friend? 37. *Bank Holiday* 38. Penny Paradise 38. Climbing High 38. A Girl Must Live 39. *The Stars Look Down* 39. *Night Train to Munich* 40. The Girl in the News 40. *Kipps* 41. The Young Mr Pitt 42. *The Way Ahead* 44. The True Glory (co-d) 45. *Odd Man Out* 46. *The Fallen Idol* 48. *The Third Man* 49. *An Outcast of the Islands* 51. The Man Between 53. A Kid for Two Farthings 55. Trapeze 56. The Key 58. Our Man in Havana 59. The Running Man 63. The Agony and the Ecstasy 65. *Oliver!* (AA) 68. Flap 70. Follow Me 72.
❀ For the sympathy and expertise which sadly left him after the early fifties. *Kipps*.

¶ 'His career demonstrates that a director who limits himself to solving technical problems quickly lapses into the decadence of the inappropriate effect.'—*Andrew Sarris, 1968.*

Reed, Donna (1921–86) (Donna Mullenger). American leading lady of the forties, later star of long-running TV series *The Donna Reed Show*. Won screen test after a beauty contest while still at college.
The Getaway (debut) 41. Shadow of the Thin Man 42. The Courtship of Andy Hardy 42. Calling Dr Gillespie 42. The Human Comedy 43. See Here, Private Hargrove 44. The Picture of Dorian Gray 44. It's a Wonderful Life 46. Green Dolphin Street 47. Chicago Deadline 49. *From Here to Eternity* (AA) 53. The Last Time I Saw Paris 55. Ransom 56. Backlash 56. The Benny Goodman Story 56. Beyond Mombasa 57. The Best Place to Be (TV) 79. Deadly Lessons (TV) 83, etc.
TV series: Dallas 84.

¶ *D.R.:* Forty pictures I was in, and all I remember is 'What kind of bra will you be wearing today, honey?' That was always the area of big decision—from the neck to the navel.

Reed, George (1867–1952). Black American character actor.
The Birth of a Nation 14. The Green Pastures 36. So Red the Rose 36. Swanee River 39. Tales of Manhattan 42. Home in Indiana 44, many others.

Reed, Maxwell (1920–74). Brooding Irish leading man in British films from 1946, after repertory experience.
The Years Between 46. Daybreak 47. *The Brothers* 48. The Dark Man 49. The Square Ring 53. Before I Wake 56. Notorious Landlady 62. Picture Mommy Dead 66, etc.
TV series: Captain David Grief 56.

Reed, Michael (1929–). British cinematographer.
October Moth 60. Linda 61. The Gorgon 64. Dracula Prince of Darkness 66. On Her Majesty's Secret Service 69. The Mackenzie Break 71. The Groundstar Conspiracy 73. The Hireling 73. Galileo 75. Shout at the Devil 76. Loophole 80, etc.

Reed, Oliver (1938–). Burly British leading man, usually in sullen roles.
The Rebel 60. No Love for Johnnie 61. Curse of the Werewolf 61. Pirates of Blood River 62. *The Damned* 62. Paranoic 63. *The System* 64. The Scarlet Blade 64. The Party's Over 64. The Brigand of Kandahar 65. *The Trap* 66. The Shuttered Room 66. *The Jokers* 66. I'll Never Forget Whatshisname 67. The Assassination Bureau 68. Oliver! 68. Hannibal Brooks 68. *Women in Love* 69. Take a Girl Like You 69. The Lady in the Car 70. The Devils 71. The Hunting Party 71. Z.P.G. 72. Sitting Target 72. Triple Echo 72. Days of Fury 73. The Three Musketeers 73. The Four Musketeers 74. And Then There Were None 74. Royal Flash 74. Tommy 75. The Sellout 75. Great Scout and Cathouse Thursday 76. Burnt Offerings 76. The Prince and the Pauper 77. The Big Sleep 78. Tomorrow Never Comes 78. The Class of Miss MacMichael 78. The Brood 79. Lion of the Desert 81. Dr Heckyl and Mr Hype 81. Condorman 81. Venom 81. The Sting II 82 Masquerade (TV) 82. Second Chance 84. Christopher Columbus (TV) 84. Black Arrow (TV) 85. Castaway 87, etc.

Reed, Philip (1908–). American leading man with long stage experience.
Female 34. Last of the Mohicans 36. Aloma of the South Seas 41. Old Acquaintance 44. I Cover Big Town 47. Unknown Island 50. The Tattered Dress 57. Harem Scarem 67, etc.

Reed, Rex (1938–). American interviewer and showbiz gossip columnist. Collections published include *Valentines and Vitriol*, *Do You Really Sleep in the Nude?*, *Big Screen Little Screen* and *Conversations in the Raw*. Not a great success as an actor when he played the transsexual *Myra Breckinridge*.

reel. A loose term generally taken to mean 1,000 feet of 35mm film, i.e. the amount which would fit on to a reel of the old-fashioned kind, running about ten minutes. Thus short films were spoken of as two-reelers, three-reelers, etc., and charged accordingly. But modern 35mm projector spools will take 2,000 feet and sometimes 3,000 feet, so the term is slowly falling into disuse . . . especially as 16mm projectors have always taken spools of either 400, 800 or 1,600 feet.

Rees, Angharad (1949–). Welsh leading lady.
Hands of the Ripper 72. Under Milk Wood 72. The Love Ban 73. Moments 74. The Curse of King Tut's Tomb (TV) 80, etc.

Reese, Tom (1930–). American character actor, a notable 'heavy'.
Flaming Star 60. Marines Let's Go 61. Forty Pounds of Trouble 62. Murderers' Row 66, etc.

Reeve, Ada (1874–1966). British character actress with long stage career.
Autobiography 1954: *Take It for a Fact.*
They Came to a City 44. When the Bough Breaks 47. Night and the City 50. Eye Witness 56, etc.

Reeve, Christopher (1952–). Strapping American leading man who flew to fame.
□Gray Lady Down 77. *Superman* 78. Superman II 80. Somewhere in Time 80. Death Trap 82. Monsignor 82. Superman III 83. The Aviator 84. The Bostonians 84. Anna Karenina (TV) 84. Street Smart 87. Superman 4 87.

Reeve, Geoffrey (1932–). British director.
Puppet on a Chain 71. Caravan to Vaccares

74. In the eighties turned producer with such projects as *The Far Pavilions*, *The Shooting Party*, *The Whistle Blower*.

Reeves, George (1914–1959) (George Brewer). American leading man.
Gone with the Wind (debut) 39. Strawberry Blonde 41. Blood and Sand 42. Bar 20 44. Jungle Jim 49. Samson and Delilah 50. Sir Galahad (serial) 50. From Here to Eternity 53.
TV series: Superman 52–56

Reeves, Kynaston (1893–1971). British character actor of stage and screen, often seen as academic.
The Lodger 32. The Housemaster 38. The Prime Minister 40. Vice Versa 48. The Guinea Pig 49. The Mudlark 50. Top of the Form 53. Brothers in Law 57. School for Scoundrels 60, many others.

Reeves, Michael (1944–1969). British director whose promising career barely got started.
□Sister of Satan (Revenge of the Blood Beast) (It.) 65. The Sorcerers 67. Witchfinder General 68.

Reeves, Steve (1926–). American actor, formerly 'Mr World' and 'Mr Universe'; found stardom from 1953 in Italian muscleman spectacles.
□Athena 54. The Labours of Hercules 57. Hercules and the Queen of Sheba (Hercules Unchained) 58. The White Warrior 58. Goliath and the Barbarians 59. The Giant of Marathon 59. The White Devil 59. The Last Days of Pompeii 59. Thief of Baghdad 60. Morgan the Pirate 60. The Wooden Horse of Troy 61. Duel of the Titans (Romulus and Remus) 61. Son of Spartacus 62. War of the Trojans 62. Sandokan the Great 63. The Pirates of Malaya 64. A Long Ride from Hell 68.

Reggiani, Serge (1922–). Slightly-built French-Italian actor with stage experience.
Les Portes de la Nuit 46. Manon 48. Les Amants de Vérone 48. La Ronde 50. Secret People (GB) 51. *Casque d'Or* 51. The Wicked Go to Hell 55. Les Misérables 57. Marie Octobre 58. Paris Blues 60. The Leopard 63. The 25th Hour 67. Les Aventuriers 67. Day of the Owl (It.) 68. The Good and the Bad 76. Cat and Mouse 76. L'Empreinte des Géantes 80. Fantastica 80, etc.

La Règle Du Jeu (France 1939). A satire on the decadence of the pre-1939 French aristocracy, directed by Jean Renoir from a script by himself and Carl Koch. Only a butchered version was released after his flight to America, and not until 1958 was the original version pieced together. Not an easy film for any but Frenchmen to understand fully; but well worth the effort if only to appreciate its curious mixture of comedy and farce. Photographed by Claude Renoir; with Marcel Dalio, Nora Gregor and Jean Renoir himself.

Reichenbach, François (1922–). French documentarist with an ironic viewpoint.
L'Amérique Insolite 59. Un Coeur Gros Comme Ça 61. Les Amoureux du France 64. Hollywood through a Keyhole 66. Love of Life (co-d) 68. F for Fake (co-d) 75, etc.

Reicher, Frank (1875–1965). German-born character actor, long in Hollywood.
Her Man O' War 26. Mata Hari 32. *King Kong* 33. Kind Lady 36. Anthony Adverse 36. Lancer Spy 38. They Dare Not Love 41. House of Frankenstein 45. The Mummy's Ghost 46. The Secret Life of Walter Mitty 47. Samson and Delilah 50, many others.
AS DIRECTOR: The Eternal Mother 17. Behind Masks 21. Wise Husbands 21, etc.

Reid, Alastair (1939–). British director. From the mid-seventies on, working in television.
□Baby Love 69. The Night Digger 71. Something to Hide 72.

Reid, Beryl (1918–). British revue comedienne who has latterly weathered a transition to character acting.
The Belles of St Trinian's 54. The Extra Day 56. The Dock Brief 62. Star! 68. Inspector Clouseau 68. The Assassination Bureau 68. *The Killing of Sister George* (her stage role) (US) 68. Entertaining Mr Sloane 70. The Beast in the Cellar 71. Dr Phibes Rises Again 72. Psychomania 72. Father Dear Father 73. No Sex Please We're British 73. Joseph Andrews 76. Smiley's People (TV) 82. Yellowbeard 83. The Doctor and the Devils 85, etc.

Reid, Carl Benton (1894–1973). American character actor with stage career before settling in Hollywood.
The Little Foxes 41. In a Lonely Place 50. Convicted 50. The Great Caruso 51. Lorna

Doone 51. Carbine Williams 52. The Egyptian 54. The Left Hand of God 55. The Gallant Hours 59, etc.
TV series: Amos Burke—Secret Agent 65.

Reid, Elliott (1920–). Giant-sized American comedy actor who often played the dumb son of an executive.
The Story of Dr Wassell 44. Gentlemen Prefer Blondes 53. Woman's World 54. Inherit the Wind 60. Who's Been Sleeping in My Bed 63. The Thrill of It All 63. Some Kind of a Nut 69, etc.

Reid, Kate (1930 –). Canadian actress.
This Property is Condemned 66. The Andromeda Strain 71. Death Among Friends (TV) 75. Equus 77. Atlantic City USA 81.
TV series: The Whiteoaks of Jalna 72.

Reid, Wallace (1890–1923). American leading man of the silent screen.
The Deerslayer 11. The Birth of a Nation 14. The Love Mask 16. House of Silence 18. The Dancing Fool 20. The Affairs of Anatol 21. Forever 21. The Ghost Breaker 22, many others.

reincarnation has seldom been seriously tackled in the cinema: *The Search for Bridey Murphy, I've Lived Before* and *The Reincarnation of Peter Proud* are almost the only examples. Many characters of farce and melodrama have *thought* they were reincarnated, including the hero of *She* and heroine of *The Vengeance of She*. The real thing happened to Oliver Hardy in *The Flying Deuces* (he came back as a horse); to a dog in *You Never Can Tell* (he came back as Dick Powell); and to the luckless heroine of *The Bride and the Beast*, who found that in a former existence she had been a gorilla. Reincarnation was also the basis of *Here Comes Mr Jordan*, and of *The Mummy*. A man came back as Debbie Reynolds in *Goodbye Charlie*, and in *Quest for Love* there were parallel love stories two centuries apart. In 1968 a version was made of Elmer Rice's *The Adding Machine*, with its celestial laundry for souls; and in 1970 there was even a musical on the subject, *On a Clear Day You Can See Forever*.

Reiner, Carl (1922–). Balding, genial American comedy writer and actor.
AS ACTOR: Happy Anniversary 59. The Gazebo 59. Gidget Goes Hawaiian 61. *It's a Mad Mad Mad Mad World* 63. The Art of Love 65. The Russians are Coming, The Russians are Coming 66. A Guide for the Married Man 67. The Comic 69. Heaven Help Us (TV series) 76. The End 78, etc.
AS WRITER: The Thrill of It All 63. The Art of Love 65. Enter Laughing 67. The Comic 69. The Jerk 79. Dead Men Don't Wear Plaid 82. The Man with Two Brains (co-w) 83. Also TV's *The Dick Van Dyke Show* 61–65.
AS DIRECTOR: Enter Laughing 67. The Comic 69. Where's Poppa? 70. Oh God 77. The Jerk 79. Dead Men Don't Wear Plaid 82. The Man with Two Brains 83. Summer School 87, etc.

Reinhardt, Gottfried (1911–). Austrian producer, son of theatrical producer Max Reinhardt. Went to US with his father and became assistant to Walter Wanger. Has since produced and occasionally directed.
The Great Waltz (script) 38. Comrade X (p) 40. Two-Faced Woman (p) 41. Command Decision (p) 48. The Red Badge of Courage (p) 51. Invitation (d) 52. The Story of Three Loves (d) 53. Betrayed (d) 54. The Good Soldier Schweik (p) 59. Town without Pity (pd) 61. Situation Hopeless But Not Serious (pd) 65, etc.

Reinhardt, Max (1873–1943) (Max Goldman). Austrian theatrical producer of great pageants. His only sound screen direction (with William Dieterle) was *A Midsummer Night's Dream* 35, from his stage production. He had made three German silents between 1908 and 1914.

Reiniger, Lotte (1899–1981). German animator, well-known for her silhouette cartoons.
The Adventures of Prince Achmed 26. Dr Dolittle (series) 28. Carmen 33. Papageno 35. The Brave Little Tailor 55, etc.

Reinking, Ann (1949–). American dancer, from Broadway.
□Movie Movie 78. All That Jazz 79. Annie 82.

Reis, Irving (1906–1953). American director, with radio experience.
□One Crowded Night 40. I'm Still Alive 40. Weekend for Three 41. A Date with the Falcon 41. The Gay Falcon 41. The Falcon Takes Over 42. The Big Street 43. Hitler's Children 43. Crack Up 46. *The Bachelor and the Bobby-soxer* 47. *Enchantment* 48. All My Sons 48. Roseanna McCoy 49. Dancing in the Dark 49. Three Husbands 50. New Mexico 51. The Fourposter 52.

Reisch, Walter (1900–1983). Austrian writer who in the thirties came to Britain, then Hollywood.
Men Are Not Gods (& d) 36. Ninotchka 39. Comrade X 40. The Heavenly Body 43. Song of Scheherezade (& d) 46. Titanic (AA) 52. The Girl in the Red Velvet Swing 55. Journey to the Centre of the Earth 59, etc.

Reisner, Allen (–). American director, from TV.
□St Louis Blues 58. All Mine to Give 56. To Die in Paris (TV) (co-d) 68. Your Money or Your Wife (TV) 72.

Reisner, Charles (1887–1962). American director.
The Man in the Box 25. Reducing 32. The Show-Off 34. Sophie Lang Goes West 37. *The Big Store* 41. Meet the People 44. Lost in a Harem 44. The Cobra Strikes 48. The Travelling Saleswoman 50, many others, mainly second features.

Reisz, Karel (1926–). Czech director, in Britain from childhood. Former film critic.
□We are the Lambeth Boys 58. *Saturday Night and Sunday Morning* 60. Night Must Fall 63. This Sporting Life (p only) 63. *Morgan: A Suitable Case for Treatment* 66. Isadora 68. The Gambler 74. Who'll Stop the Rain? 78. The French Lieutenant's Woman 81. Sweet Dreams 86.

Reitherman, Wolfgang (1909–85). American animator, director of Disney cartoon features from the mid-sixties.

Reitman, Ivan (–). Canadian director.
Foxy Lady 71. Cannibal Girls 73. Meatballs 79. Stripes 81. *Ghostbusters* 84. Legal Eagles 86.

rejuvenation is not a theme the cinema has frequently explored. *She* tried it several times with unhappy results, as did Laurel and Hardy in *Dirty Work* (Olly came back as a chimpanzee). *The Man in Half Moon Street* and *Countess Dracula* both kept young on the blood of others; *Dorian Gray* did it by keeping a picture of himself in the attic. Most successful were *Lost Horizon*'s inhabitants of Shangri-La, but once the cold winds of the outside world blew they were done for. Rock Hudson had worse luck in *Seconds*.

religion has inspired film-makers from the beginning—as a commercial trump card. In the early years of the century it was the Italians who produced vast semi-biblical spectacles like *Quo Vadis* and *Cabiria*, but Hollywood was not slow to catch on, and producers soon found that religious shorts gave them extra prestige. There were several versions of *From the Manger to the Cross*; Griffith, in *Judith of Bethulia* and *Intolerance*, contributed his share; *Ben Hur* was the biggest spectacular of all; but it was Cecil B. de Mille in the twenties who brought the Bible to full commercial flower with *The Ten Commandments* and *King of Kings*. (His 1932 *The Sign of the Cross*, 1950 *Samson and Delilah* and 1956 remake of *The Ten Commandments* show that for him at least time continued to stand still.) In 1929, though *Noah's Ark* was spectacle pure and simple, Vidor's *Hallelujah* at least partially transmitted Negro religious fervour. In the thirties Hollywood was seeking fresh ways to combine religion with sentiment or spectacle, in *The Cradle Song, Dante's Inferno, The Garden of Allah, The Green Light* and *Boy's Town*. One result was a new characterization of priests (qv) as jolly good fellows: stars like Spencer Tracy and Pat O'Brien were eager to play them. Yet none had the quiet dignity of Rex Ingram as De Lawd in *Green Pastures*, a Negro version of the Scriptures.

The war naturally brought a religious revival. Every film set in England seemed to end with a service in a bombed church, and religious figures became big time in films like *The Song of Bernadette, Going My Way, The Keys of the Kingdom* and *The Bells of St Mary's*. Savage war films masqueraded under such titles as *God Is My Co-Pilot* and *A Wing and a Prayer*. And heaven was used as a background for lighthearted fantasy films about death and judgement day, such as *Here Comes Mr Jordan, Heaven Can Wait*, and *The Horn Blows at Midnight*. The only film of this period to question religion at all was the British *Major Barbara*. 'What price salvation now?'

In the cynical post-war years religion was at a low ebb. An expensive *Joan of Arc* in 1948 failed disastrously, and an attempt to bring God into our everyday life, *The Next Voice You Hear*, fared no better. A sincere performance by Robert Donat could not bring people to see *Lease of Life*. Indeed, the only religious films to break even at the box office were those with a direct Roman Catholic appeal, such as *Monsieur Vincent* and *The Miracle of Fatima*. True religion, to Hollywood, was out, and the Bible became once more a source book for a string of tawdry commercial epics: *Quo Vadis, Salome, The Prodigal, The Robe*, a remake of *Ben Hur, Barabbas, The Silver Chalice, Sodom and Gomorrah* and many cut-rate dubbed Italian spectacles of a similar kind (most with Hollywood stars). Occasionally a spark of sincerity would flash through, as in the otherwise dull *David and Bathsheba*; while small independent companies could produce interesting films like *The First Legion*. Towards the end of the fifties there were occasional attempts to see religion afresh: *A Man Called Peter, The Nun's Story, Inn of the Sixth Happiness, Whistle Down the Wind.* Otto Preminger, despite a 1957 failure with *Saint Joan,* tried again in 1963 with *The Cardinal.* In 1965 George Stevens unveiled *The Greatest Story Ever Told*, a tepid life of Jesus which found little box office favour, being overtaken in some quarters by Pasolini's *The Gospel According to St Matthew.* 1966 brought the long-promised Italian-American epic known as *The Bible*: in fact it dealt only with the Book of Genesis, and that at such a dull pace and inordinate length that it is doubtful whether sequels will be called for. 1969 offered a drama of modern popes, *The Shoes of the Fisherman*, but it died. The most fashionable film interpretations of religion in the early seventies were the pop operas exemplified by *Godspell* and *Jesus Christ Superstar*; but in 1977 Lew Grade's mammoth six-hour *Jesus of Nazareth*, directed by Franco Zeffirelli, achieved record viewing figures and pointed to a benighted world's requirement to believe in *something.*

Relph, George (1888–1960). British character actor mainly seen on stage. Nicholas Nickleby 47. I Believe in You 52. *The Titfield Thunderbolt* (leading role as the vicar) 53. Doctor at Large 57. Davy 57, etc.

Relph, Michael (1915–). British producer-director, son of George Relph. Former art director and production designer; from 1947 to 1969 he worked almost exclusively with Basil Dearden, usually producing while Dearden directed.
The Captive Heart 46. Frieda 47. Saraband for Dead Lovers 48. *The Blue Lamp* 50. I Believe in You (& co-w) 52. The Rainbow Jacket 54. Davy (d) 57. Rockets Galore (d) 57. Violent Playground 58. Sapphire 59. *The League of Gentlemen* 59. *Victim* 61. Life for Ruth 62. The Mind Benders 63. Woman of Straw 63. Masquerade 65. The Assassination Bureau 68. An Unsuitable Job for a Woman 82, etc.

remake roles

? Each pair of actors played the same key role in different versions of the same story. Give the title(s) and the roles.

1 Pauline Lord, Fay Bainter
2 Basil Rathbone, John Hodiak
3 Maria Ouspenskaya, Cathleen Nesbitt
4 Fay Wray, Phyllis Kirk
5 Ginger Rogers, Debbie Reynolds
6 John Barrymore, Adolphe Menjou
7 Aline McMahon, Ethel Barrymore
8 Leslie Howard, Tyrone Power
9 Leslie Howard, David Niven
10 Bette Davis, Susan Hayward
11 Marlene Dietrich, Brigitte Bardot
12 Rudolph Valentino, Bob Hope
13 Pat O'Brien, Rosalind Russell
14 Carole Lombard, Jerry Lewis
15 Ginger Rogers, Jerry Lewis
16 Charles Laughton, Bob Hope
18 H. B. Warner, John Gielgud
19 Lionel Stander, Jack Carson
20 Paul Muni, Kay Francis
21 Clark Gable, Jack Lemmon
22 Edna Best, Doris Day
23 Sam Jaffe, Sammy Davis Jnr
24 Oliver Hardy, Jack Haley
25 Shirley Booth, Barbra Streisand
26 Charles Coburn, Cary Grant
27 Wendy Hiller, Audrey Hepburn
28 Theda Bara, Claudette Colbert
29 W. C. Fields, Ralph Richardson
30 Edward Van Sloan, Peter Cushing

remakes in disguise. Hollywood studios were famous for squeezing every drop of value from a literary property, even if it meant changing the locale, switching the sexes and generally bamboozling the audience, which hopefully would not get that I-have-been-here-before feeling until they were half-way home. Here are just a few movies which went through a change of title but used up the same old plot:

Sentimental Journey; *The Gift of Love*
Libelled Lady; *Easy to Wed*
Here Comes Mr Jordan; *Heaven Can Wait*
Love Is News; *Sweet Rosie O'Grady*; *That Wonderful Urge*
The Bowery; *Coney Island*; *Wabash Avenue*
The Greeks Had a Word for Them; *Ladies in Love*; *Three Blind Mice*; *Moon over Miami*; *Three Little Girls in Blue*; *How to Marry a Millionaire*; *Three Coins in the Fountain*; *The Pleasure Seekers*
Kentucky; *Down Argentine Way*
Folies Bergere; *That Night in Rio*; *On the Riviera*; *On the Double*

The Front Page; Gunga Din; His Girl Friday; Torrid Zone; Sergeants Three; The Front Page
My Favorite Wife; Move Over Darling
Grand Hotel; Weekend at the Waldorf
It Happened One Night; You Can't Run Away From It
Tiger Shark; Slim; Manpower
House of Strangers; Broken Lance
High Sierra; I Died a Thousand Times
20,000 Years in Sing Sing; Castle on the Hudson
Mystery of the Wax Museum; House of Wax
One Way Passage; Til We Meet Again
Bordertown; They Drive by Night
Dangerous; Singapore Woman
The Petrified Forest; Escape in the Desert
Four Daughters; Young at Heart
Dr Socrates; King of the Underworld
The Butter and Egg Man; The Tenderfoot; Dance Charlie Dance; An Angel from Texas
The Most Dangerous Game; A Game of Death; Run for the Sun
The Kennel Murder Case; Calling Philo Vance
The Letter; The Unfaithful
The Mouthpiece; The Man Who Talked Too Much; Illegal
Oil for the Lamps of China; Law of the Tropics
The Sea Wolf; Wolf Larsen; Barricade; Wolf of the Seven Seas
Kid Galahad; The Wagons Roll at Night; Kid Galahad
Casablanca; Far East
The Man Who Played God; Sincerely Yours
The Millionaire; That Way with Women
The Miracle of Morgan's Creek; Rock-a-bye Baby
Anna and the King of Siam; The King and I
London After Midnight; Mark of the Vampire
Love Affair; An Affair to Remember
Morning Glory; Stage Struck
The Lady Eve; The Birds and the Bees
The Marriage Circle; One Hour with You
Nothing Sacred; Living It Up
Dark Victory; Stolen Hours
One Sunday Afternoon; The Strawberry Blonde
A Slight Case of Murder; Stop! You're Killing Me
The Paleface; The Shakiest Gun in the West
Le Jour se Lève; The Long Night
The Women; The Opposite Sex
The Asphalt Jungle; The Badlanders; Cairo; Cool Breeze
The Four Feathers; Storm Over the Nile
It Started with Eve; I'd Rather Be Rich
Rome Express; Sleeping Car to Trieste
This Gun for Hire; Short Cut to Hell
The Informer; Uptight
Against All Flags; The King's Pirate
Red Dust; Congo Maisie; Mogambo
An American Tragedy; A Place in the Sun
Outward Bound; Between Two Worlds
Ebb Tide; Adventure Island
Ah, Wilderness; Summer Holiday

Remarque, Erich Maria (1898–1970). German novelist.
All Quiet on the Western Front 30. The Road Back 37. Three Comrades 38. So Ends Our Night 41. Arch of Triumph 48. A Time to Love and a Time to Die (& a) 57, etc.

Rembrandt (GB 1937). Perhaps the most satisfying film ever produced about a painter, its hypnotic effect stemming from Charles Laughton's brilliant performance. Script by Carl Zuckmayer, direction by Alexander Korda, design by Vincent Korda, photography by Georges Perinal.

Remick, Lee (1935–). American leading lady with stage and TV experience.
A Face in the Crowd (film debut) 57. The Long Hot Summer 58. *Anatomy of a Murder* 59. Sanctuary 61. Experiment in Terror 62. *Days of Wine and Roses* 63. The Wheeler Dealers 64. Baby the Rain Must Fall 65. The Hallelujah Trail 65. No Way to Treat a Lady 68. A Severed Head 70. Loot 70. Sometimes a Great Notion 72. A Delicate Balance 73. QB VII 74. The Blue Knight (TV) 74. Hennessy 75. *Jennie* (TV) 75. The Omen 76. Telefon 77. The Medusa Touch 77. Ike (TV) 79. The Europeans 79. Torn between Two Lovers (TV) 79. The Competition 80. Tribute 80. The Women's Room (TV) 80.
The Letter (TV) 82. Mistral's Daughter (TV) 84, etc.

¶ *L.R.:* It would be nice to make films for grown-ups again, and when they decide to start filming them, I'll start acting in them.

Renaldo, Duncan (1904–1980) (Renault Renaldo Duncan). American actor and painter with varied experience. In many films from *Trader Horn* 30 to *For Whom the Bell Tolls* 42; later more famous as The Cisco Kid in a series of second feature westerns (1945–50). Directed some films in the twenties.

Rennahan, Ray (1896–). American cinematographer, in Hollywood from 1917; an expert on colour.
Fanny Foley Herself 31. *The Mystery of the Wax Museum* 33. *Becky Sharp* 35. *Wings of*

the Morning 37. *Gone with the Wind* (co-ph) (AA) 39. *The Blue Bird* 40. Down Argentine Way 40. *Blood and Sand* (co-ph) (AA) 42. *For Whom the Bell Tolls* 43. Belle of the Yukon 44. The Perils of Pauline 47. The Paleface 48. A Yankee at King Arthur's Court 49. Arrowhead 53. Terror in a Texas Town 58, many others.

Rennie, James (1890–1965). American hero of the twenties.
Remodelling Her Husband 20. The Dust Flower 22. His Children's Children 23. Clothes Make the Pirate 25. The Girl of the Golden West 30. Illicit 31, etc.

Rennie, Michael (1909–1971). Lean, good-looking British leading man best known as TV's *The Third Man*. Varied experience before going into repertory and film stand-in work.
Secret Agent 36. The Divorce of Lady X 38. Dangerous Moonlight 40. Ships with Wings 41. I'll be Your Sweetheart 45. *The Wicked Lady* 45. The Root of All Evil 47. Idol of Paris 48. The Black Rose 50; Then to US; Five Fingers 52. Les Misérables 52. *The Day the Earth Stood Still* 52. The Robe 53. Désirée 54. The Rains of Ranchipur 55. Island in the Sun 56. Omar Khayyam 57. Third Man on the Mountain 59. *The Lost World* 60. Mary, Mary 63. Ride beyond Vengeance 65. The Power 67. Hotel 67. The Devil's Brigade 68. The Battle of El Alamein (as Montgomery) 68. Subterfuge 69, etc.

Renoir, Claude (1914–). French cinematographer.
Toni 34. *Une Partie de Campagne* 36. La Règle du Jeu 39. Monsieur Vincent 47. *The River* 51. The Green Glove 52. *The Golden Coach* 53. *Eléna et les Hommes* 56. Crime and Punishment 56. The Witches of Salem 56. Les Tricheurs 58. *Blood and Roses* 60. Lafayette 61. Circus World 64. The Game is Over 66. Barbarella 68. The Madwoman of Chaillot (co-ph) 69. The Horsemen 71. Paul and Michelle 74. The Spy Who Loved Me 77, many others.

Renoir, Jean (1894–1979). Distinguished French director, son of painter Auguste Renoir, brother of Pierre Renoir. Stage experience in productions of his own plays. Autobiography 1973: *My Life and My Films*. Biography 1977: *Jean Renoir, The World of His Films* by Len Brandy.
La Fille de L'Eau 24. Nana 26. Charleston 27. The Little Match-Seller 28. *Le Chienne* 31. *Boudu Sauvé des Eaux* 32. Toni 34. Madame Bovary 34. *Le Crime de Monsieur Lange* 35. *Les Bas Fonds* 36. *Une Partie de Campagne* 36. *La Grande Illusion* 37. *La Marseillaise* 38. *La Bête Humaine* 38. *La Règle du Jeu* (& a) 39; To US; Swamp Water 41. This Land Is Mine 43. *The Southerner* 44. Diary of a Chambermaid 45. The Woman on the Beach 47; Back to Europe; The River 51. The Golden Coach 53. French Cancan 55. Eléna et les Hommes 56. Lunch on the Grass 59. The Vanishing Corporal 61. C'est la Revolution 67. Le Petit Theatre de Jean Renoir 69, etc.

'Renoir has a lot of talent, but he isn't one of us.'—*Darryl F. Zanuck*

'Life was not so much the subject as the *stuff* of his movies, spilling over the edges of his frames.'—*Newsweek*

'Only when style is confused with meaningless flourishes does Renoir's economy of expression seem inadequate for textbook critics.'—*Andrew Sarris, 1968*

J.R.: My dream is of a craftsman's cinema in which the author can express himself as directly as the painter in his paintings or the writer in his books.

J.R.: A director makes only one film in his life. Then he breaks it into pieces and makes it again.

J.R.: The saving grace of the cinema is that with patience, and a little love, we may arrive at that wonderfully complex creature which is called man.

Renoir, Pierre (1885–1952). French character actor, brother of Jean Renoir.
Madame Bovary 34. La Marseillaise 38. Les Enfants du Paradis 44. Doctor Knock 50, many others.

Renzi, Eva (1944–). German leading lady in international films.
Funeral in Berlin 66. The Pink Jungle 68. Beiss Mich Liebling 70. La Chambre Voisine 80, etc.

reporters in American films have since the beginning of the sound era been pictured as trench-coated, trilby-hatted, good-looking guys with a smart line in wisecracks. Among the outstanding examples of this tradition are Pat O'Brien in *The Front Page*, Robert Williams in *Platinum Blonde*, Clark Gable in *It Happened One Night* and *Teacher's Pet*, Fredric March in *Nothing Sacred*, Lee Tracy in *Doctor X*, Joel McCrea in *Foreign Correspondent*, David Janssen in *The Green Berets*, James Stewart in *The Philadelphia Story*, Lynne Overman in *Roxie Hart*, Gene Kelly in *Inherit the Wind*; while on the distaff side one can't overlook Glenda Farrell in *The Mystery of the Wax Museum*, Bette Davis in *Front Page Woman*, Jean Arthur in *Mr Deeds Goes to Town*, Rosalind Russell in *His Girl Friday* or Barbara Stanwyck in *Meet John Doe.* Presented somewhat more realistically were William Alland in *Citizen Kane*, James Stewart in *Call Northside 777*, Burgess Meredith as Ernie Pyle in *The Story of G.I. Joe*, Kirk Douglas in *Ace in the Hole*, and Arthur Kennedy in *Lawrence of Arabia.* British films have used their newshawks more flippantly, especially in the case of *This Man Is News* with Barry K. Barnes and *A Run for Your Money* with Alec Guinness. Just as well; for Edward Judd in *The Day the Earth Caught Fire*, Jack Hawkins in *Front Page Story*, Sidney James in *Quatermass II* and Norman Wooland in *All Over the Town* were a pretty dull lot, and Colin Gordon's imitation of the American model in *Escapade* was hardly convincing. Television series, of course, have found the reporter a convenient peg, as in the British *Deadline Midnight* and the American *Saints and Sinners* and *The Reporter.*

Republic Pictures Corporation. A small Hollywood production and distribution company founded in 1935 by a former tobacco executive named Herbert J. Yates (qv) who had spent some years building up a film laboratory. Republic continued as a one-man concern, producing innumerable competently-made second feature westerns and melodramas with such stars as Roy Rogers, Vera Hruba Ralston (Yates' wife), John Carroll, Constance Moore. The studio also churned out the majority of Hollywood's serials. Very occasionally there would be a major production such as *Rio Grande* or *The Quiet Man.* Production stopped in the mid-fifties, when 'bread and butter' pictures were no longer needed, and the company's interests moved into TV.

Repulsion (GB 1965). A curious film setting down in detail the horrifying case history of a homicidal girl repelled by sex. Shot by Roman Polanski almost entirely in a London flat, the film has clever cinematic shock effects but little ear for dialogue. With Catherine Deneuve.

Rescher, Gayne (–). American cinematographer.
Rachel Rachel 68. John and Mary 69. A New Leaf 71. Claudine 74, etc.

Resnais, Alain (1922–). Controversial French director, former editor.
□Statues Also Die 51. Nuit et Brouillard (short) 55. Toute la Memoire du Monde 56. *Hiroshima Mon Amour* 59. *Last Year at Marienbad* 61. Muriel 62. The War is Over 66. Je n'Aime, Je t'Aime 69. Stavisky 74. Providence 77. My American Uncle 80. La Vie est un Roman 83. Love Unto Death 84. Melo 86, etc.

Rettig, Tommy (1941–). American boy actor of the fifties.
Panic in the Streets 50. The Five Thousand Fingers of Dr T 53. The Egyptian 54. The Last Wagon 56. At Gunpoint 57, etc.
TV series: Lassie.

Revel, Harry (1905–1958). British composer in Hollywood, usually in association with Mack Gordon. Scores:
College Rhythm 34. The Gay Divorcee 34. We're Not Dressing 34. Stowaway 36. You Can't Have Everything 37. Are You with It 48, etc.

Revere, Anne (1903–). American character actress, mainly on stage.
Double Door 34. The Devil Commands 41. The Gay Sisters 42. *The Song of Bernadette* 43. The Keys of the Kingdom 44. *National Velvet* (AA) 44. Dragonwyck 46. Body and Soul 47. *Gentleman's Agreement* 48. A Place in the Sun 51. Macho Callahan 70. Birch Interval 76, etc.

Revier, Dorothy (1904–) (Doris Velagra). American leading lady of the silents, usually as a vamp; couldn't cope with sound.
Broadway Madonna 22. The Wild Party 23. The Virgin 24. When Husbands Flirt 25. When the Wife's Away 26. Poor Girls 27. Sinner's Parade 28. The Iron Mask 29. The Dance of Life 29. Call of the West 30. The Black Camel 31. Sally of the Subway 32. By Candlelight 33. Unknown Blonde 34. The Cowboy and the Kid 36, many others.

Revill, Clive (1930–). New Zealander in Britain playing mainly comic character roles.
Bunny Lake is Missing 65. Modesty Blaise 66. Kaleidoscope 66. A Fine Madness (US) 66. The Double Man 67. Fathom 67. Nobody Runs Forever 68. The Shoes of the Fisherman 68. The Private Life of Sherlock Holmes 70. A Severed Head 71. Avanti 72. The Legend of Hell House 73. The Black Windmill 74. Galileo 75. One of Our Dinosaurs Is Missing 75. Matilda 78. T. R. Sloane (TV) 79. Moviola

(as Charlie Chaplin) (TV) 80. Zorro the Gay Blade 81. The Emperor's New Clothes 87. Rumpelstiltskin 87, etc.

Reville, Alma (1900–1982). British screenwriter, married to Alfred Hitchcock; worked on many of his films.
The Ring 27. Rich and Strange 32. The Thirty-Nine Steps 35. Secret Agent 36. Sabotage 37. Young and Innocent 37. The Lady Vanishes 38. Suspicion 41. Shadow of a Doubt 43. The Paradine Case 47. Stage Fright 50, etc.

Rey, Alejandro (1930–87). Argentinian actor in American TV and films.
The Wild Pack 72. The Stepmother 73. Money to Burn 73. Mr Majestyk 74. Breakout 75. High Velocity 76. The Swarm 78. Cuba 79. Sunburn 79. The Ninth Configuration 80. Rita Hayworth the Love Goddess (TV) 83, many others.

Rey, Fernando (1915–) (Fernando Arambillet). Suave Spanish actor in international films, a favourite of Luis Buñuel.
Welcome Mr Marshall 52. Viridiana 61. Villa Rides 68. The Adventurers 70. A Town Called Bastard 71. Tristana 71. *The French Connection* 72. *The Discreet Charm of the Bourgeoisie* 72. French Connection II 75. La Grande Bourgeoise 76. Jesus of Nazareth (TV) 77. *That Obscure Object of Desire* 77. Quintet 79. Monsignor 82. The Hit 84. The Knight of the Dragon 85. Saving Grace 86, many others.

Reynolds, Adeline de Walt (1862–1961). American character actress with long stage experience; for many years Hollywood's oldest bit player.
Come Live with Me (film debut) 41. The Human Comedy 43. Going My Way 44. A Tree Grows in Brooklyn 45. The Girl from Manhattan 48. Lydia Bailey 52. Witness to Murder 54, etc.

Reynolds, Burt (1936–). Lithe, virile American leading man who after years in television became a 'bankable' box office star of the early seventies.
Angel Baby 61. Armored Command 61. Operation CIA 65. Navajo Joe 67. Shark 68. Impasse 68. Skullduggery 69. Sam Whiskey 69. 100 Rifles 69. Fuzz 72. *Deliverance* 72. Shamus 72. White Lightning 73. The Man Who Loved Cat Dancing 73. The Longest Yard 74. WW and the Dixie Dancekings 75. At Long Last Love 75. Hustle 76. Lucky Lady 76. Gator (& d) 76. Nickelodeon 76. *Smokey and the Bandit* 77. Semi-Tough 77. The End (& d) 78. Hooper 78. Starting Over 79. Smokey and the Bandit II 80. Rough Cut 80. The Cannonball Run 81. Sharkey's Machine (also d) 81. The Best Little Whorehouse in Texas 82. Best Friends 82. Stroker Ace 83. The Man Who Loved Women. 83. Cannonball Run II 84. City Heat 84. Stick (& d) 85. Heat 87, etc.
TV series: Riverboat 59–60. Gunsmoke 65–67. Hawk 67. Dan August 70.

¶ *B.R.:* I think the most underrated thing in the world is a good hot bath. With bubbles.

B.R.: My movies were the kind they show in prisons and aeroplanes, because nobody can leave.

Reynolds, Debbie (1932–) (Mary Frances Reynolds). Petite, vivacious American leading lady of fifties musicals; later a pleasing comedienne.
□June Bride 48. The Daughter of Rosie O'Grady 50. Three Little Words 50. Two Weeks with Love 50. Mr Imperium 51. *Singin' in the Rain* 52. Skirts Ahoy 52. I Love Melvin 53. The Affairs of Dobie Gillis 53. Give a Girl a Break 53. *Susan Slept Here* 54. Athena 54. Hit the Deck 55. The Tender Trap 55. The Catered Affair 56. Bundle of Joy 56. Meet Me in Las Vegas 56. Tammy and the Bachelor 57. This Happy Feeling 58. The Mating Game 59. Say One for Me 59. It Started with a Kiss 59. The Gazebo 59. The Rat Race 60. Pépé 60. The Pleasure of His Company 61. The Second Time Around 61. How the West was Won 62. My Six Loves 63. Mary Mary 63. *The Unsinkable Molly Brown* 64. Goodbye Charlie 64. The Singing Nun 66. Divorce American Style 67. How Sweet It Is 68. *What's the Matter with Helen?* 71. Charlotte's Web (voice only) 72.
TV series: *The Debbie Reynolds Show* 69. Aloha Paradise 81.

¶ *D.R.:* I do twenty mintutes every time the refrigerator door opens and the light comes on.

D.R.: I stopped making movies because I don't like taking my clothes off.

Reynolds, Gene (1925–). American boy actor who later became a producer of TV series including *The Ghost and Mrs Muir*, *Anna and the King* and *M*A*S*H*.
Thank You Jeeves 36. In Old Chicago 38. The Blue Bird 40. The Penalty 40. The Tuttles of Tahiti 42. Eagle Squadron 44. The Country Girl 54. Diane 55, many others.

Reynolds, Joyce (1924–). Vivacious American leading lady of the forties, usually in teenage roles.
George Washington Slept Here 42. Janie 44. Always Together 48. Dangerous Inheritance 50, etc.

Reynolds, Marjorie (1921–) (Marjorie Goodspeed). American leading lady of the forties. Former child actress.
Up in the Air 40. Holiday Inn 42. Star Spangled Rhythm 43. Ministry of Fear 43. Dixie 43. Three is a Family 44. Bring on the Girls 45. Meet Me on Broadway 46. Heaven Only Knows 47. Home Town Story 51. The Great Jewel Robber 51. The Silent Witness 54, etc.
TV series: The Life of Riley 53–57. Our Man Higgins 62.

Reynolds, Peter (1926–1975) (Peter Horrocks). British light character actor, given to shifty roles.
The Captive Heart 46. Guilt is My Shadow 49. Smart Alec 50. Four Days 51. The Last Page 52. Devil Girl from Mars 54. You Can't Escape 55. The Delavine Affair 56. Shake Hands with the Devil 59. West Eleven 63. Nobody Runs Forever 68, etc.

Reynolds, Sheldon (1923–). American radio and TV writer who wrote, produced and directed two films.
□Foreign Intrigue 56. Assignment to Kill 68.
TV series: Sherlock Holmes 56. Sherlock Holmes and Dr Watson 81.

Reynolds, William H. (1910–). American editor.
So Ends Our Night 41. Moontide 42. Carnival in Costa Rica 47. Come to the Stable 49. The Day the Earth Stood Still 51. Red Skies of Montana 52. Three Coins in the Fountain 54. Bus Stop 56. South Pacific 58. Compulsion 59. Fanny 61. Kings of the Sun 63. The Sound of Music 65. Star 68. The Great White Hope 70. *The Godfather* 72. *The Sting* (AA) 73. The Great Waldo Pepper 75. The Turning Point 77. A Little Romance 77. Heaven's Gate 80. Nijinsky 80, etc.

Rhoades, Barbara (1947–). American character actress.
The Shakiest Gun in the West 68. There Was a Crooked Man 70. Up the Sandbox 72. Harry and Tonto 74. Conspiracy of Terror (TV) 75. The Choirboys 77, etc.
TV series: Busting Loose 77. Soap 80.

Rhodes, Betty Jane (1921–). American singing second lead of the early forties.
Stage Door 37. Sweater Girl 41. The Fleet's In 42. Salute for Three 43. You Can't Ration Love 44. Practically Yours 44, etc.

Rhodes, Erik (1906–). American comic actor from the musical comedy stage, best remembered as the excitable Italian in two Astaire-Rogers films, *The Gay Divorcee* 34 and *Top Hat* 35. ('Your wife is safe with Tonetti—he prefers spaghetti.')
□*The Gay Divorcee* 34. A Night at the Ritz 35. Charlie Chan in Paris 35. The Nitwits 35. Old Man Rhythm 35. *Top Hat* 35. Another Face 35. Two in the Dark 35. Chatterbox 36. One Rainy Afternoon 36. Special Investigator 36. Second Wife 36. The Smartest Girl in Town 36. Criminal Lawyer 37. Woman Chases Man 37. Music for Madame 37. Fight for Your Lady 37. Beg Borrow or Steal 37. Dramatic School 38. Say It in French 38. Meet the Girls 38. Mysterious Mr Moto 38. On Your Toes 39.

Rhodes, Marjorie (1902–1979). Homely British character actress, on stage from 1920; usually plays warm-hearted mums, nosey neighbours, etc.
Poison Pen (debut) 39. *Love on the Dole* 40. World of Plenty 41. *When We are Married* 43. Uncle Silas 47. *The Cure for Love* 50. Those People Next Door 53. Hell Drivers 58. Watch It, Sailor 62. *The Family Way* 66. Mrs Brown You've Got a Lovely Daughter 68. Hands of the Ripper 71, many others.

Rhue, Madlyn (1934–) (Madeleine Roche). American supporting actress.
Operation Petticoat 59. Escape from Zahrain 62. It's a Mad Mad Mad Mad World 63. He Rides Tall 64. Stand Up and Be Counted 72, etc.
TV series: Bracken's World 69. Executive Suite 76.

Riano, Renie (1899–1971). American comedienne in small film roles, especially the *Jiggs and Maggie* series.
Tovarich 37. Adam Had Four Sons 41. The Time of Your Life 46. Three on a Couch 66, many others.

Rice, Elmer (1892–1967) (Elmer Reizenstern). American playwright. Works filmed include *Street Scene, The Adding Machine, Dream Girl* and *Counsellor at Law.*

Rice, Florence (1907–1974). American leading lady of the late thirties, always in sweet-tempered roles.
The Best Man Wins 34. Sweethearts 39. Miracles for Sale 39. *At the Circus* 39. Fighting Marshal 41. The Ghost and the Guest 43, etc.

Rice, Grantland (1881–1954). American sportscaster who made innumerable one-reelers under the title *Grantland Rice Sportslights*. Father of Florence Rice.

Rice, Jack (1893–1968). American light actor who for many years played Edgar Kennedy's useless brother-in-law in RKO shorts. Last film, *Son of Flubber* 63.

Rice, Joan (1930–) British leading lady, former waitress, briefly popular in the fifties.
Blackmailed 50. One Wild Oat 51. The Story of Robin Hood and His Merrie Men 52. A Day to Remember 54. His Majesty O'Keefe (US) 55. One Good Turn 56. Payroll 61. Horror of Frankenstein 70, etc.

Rich, David Lowell (1923–). American director, from TV.
Senior Prom 58. Hey Boy, Hey Girl 59. Have Rocket Will Travel 59. Madame X 66. The Plainsman 66. Rosie 67. A Lovely Way to Die 68. *Eye of the Cat* 69. The Sex Symbol (TV) 74. The Concorde – Airport 79 79. Thursday's Child (TV) 83, etc.

Rich, Irene (1891–) (Irene Luther). American silent screen heroine, little seen since sound.
Stella Maris 18. Beau Brummell 24. Lady Windermere's Fan 25. So This is Paris 26. *Craig's Wife* 28. Shanghai Rose 29. That Certain Age 38. The Lady in Question 41. New Orleans 47. Joan of Arc 48, etc.

Rich, John (1925–). American director, from TV.
Wives and Lovers 63. The New Interns 64. Boeing Boeing 65. Easy Come Easy Go 67, etc.

Rich, Roy (1909–1970). British producer, director and executive, with widely varied experience including radio and TV.
My Brother's Keeper (d only) 47. It's Not Cricket (d only) 48. Double Profile (d only) 54. Phantom Caravan (d only) 54, etc.

Richard, Cliff (1940–) (Harold Webb). Boyish British pop singer who succeeded by restricting his film appearances.
□Serious Charge 59. Expresso Bongo 60. *The Young Ones* 61. Summer Holiday 62. Wonderful Life 64. Finders Keepers 66. Two a Penny 68. Take Me High 73.

Richard the Lionheart (Richard I of England, 1157–1199) was a king who has gone down into legend rather than history as a nearly wronged idealist. The truth may have been less inspiring. He was played by Wallace Beery in *Robin Hood* (1922), by Henry Wilcoxon in *The Crusades*, by Ian Hunter in *The Adventures of Robin Hood*, by Norman Wooland in *Ivanhoe*, by Patrick Barr in Disney's *Robin Hood*, by George Sanders in *King Richard and the Crusaders*, by Patrick Holt in *Men of Sherwood Forest*, by Anthony Hopkins (as a prince) in *The Lion in Winter*, and by Richard Harris in *Robin and Marian*.

Richard III (GB 1956). Laurence Olivier's third Shakespearean production has a more direct popular appeal than either *Henry V* or *Hamlet*, perhaps because it centres firmly on Olivier's rich caricature of Crookback. It tells its story in a leisurely fashion, production values are economical, and the battle skimped, but Shakespeare and the acting win the day, with an especially fascinating performance from Ralph Richardson as Buckingham. The only other talking version of the story, oddly enough, is Rowland V. Lee's outrageous but amusing *Tower of London* 39, with Basil Rathbone as Richard and Boris Karloff as Mord the Executioner: this was remade in 1963 by Roger Corman, with Vincent Price as Richard. (He played Clarence in the earlier version.)

Richards, Addison (1887–1964). American character actor with long stage experience; in Hollywood from early thirties, usually as professional man; later in TV series.
Riot Squad 34. Colleen 36. Black Legion 37. Boom Town 40. My Favorite Blonde 42. Since You Went Away 44. The Mummy's Curse 46. Indian Scout 50. Illegal 56. The Oregon Trail 59, hundreds of others.
TV series: Fibber McGee 59. Cimarron City 58–60.

Richards, Ann (1918–1982). Australian leading lady.
Tall Timbers 38. The Rudd Family 39, etc. Then to Hollywood: Random Harvest 42. Dr Gillespie's New Assistant 43. An American Romance 44. Love Letters 45. The Searching Wind 46. Sorry, Wrong Number 48. Breakdown 52, etc.

Richards, Beah (–). Black American actress.
The Miracle Worker 62. In the Heat of the Night 67. *Guess Who's Coming to Dinner* 67. Mahogany 76, etc.

Richards, Dick (1936–). American director.
□ The Culpepper Cattle Company 72. *Farewell My Lovely* 75. Rafferty and the Gold Dust Twins 75. March or Die (& w, p) 77. Death Valley 82. Tootsie (co-p only) 82. Man, Woman and Child 83.

Richards, Jeff (1922–) (Richard Mansfield Taylor). American general purpose actor.
Johnny Belinda 48. Kill the Umpire 50. The Strip 51. Above and Beyond 52. Seven Brides for Seven Brothers 55, many others.
TV series: Jefferson Drum 58.

Richards, Paul (1924–1974). American general purpose actor.
The Black Whip 55. Tall Man Riding 56. Battle for the Planet of the Apes 71, etc.
TV series: Breaking Point 63.

Richardson, Ian (1934–). Scottish character actor whose precise playing of many varied roles is an increasing delight.
The Marat/Sade 68. Man of La Mancha 72. The Darwin Adventure 73. *Ike* (TV) (as Bernard Montgomery) 79. The Sign of Four (as Sherlock Holmes) (TV) 84. The Master of Ballantrae (TV) 84. Mistral's Daughter (TV) 84. Mountbatten (TV) 85. Brazil 85. The Fourth Protocol 87. Porterhouse Blue (TV) 87. Cry Freedom 87.

Richardson, John (1936–). British leading man, mainly in fancy dress.
Bachelor of Hearts 58. She 65. One Million Years BC 66. The Vengeance of She 68. The Chastity Belt 68. On a Clear Day You Can See Forever 70. Duck in Orange Sauce (It.) 75, etc.

Richardson, Miranda (–). British actress.
Dance with a Stranger 84. The Innocent 85. Underworld 85. Blackadder (TV) 86. After Pilkington (TV) 87. Empire of the Sun 87.

Richardson, Sir Ralph (1902–1983). Distinguished British stage actor, in occasional films. Despite his splendid theatrical voice and thespian mannerisms, he was at his best playing ordinary chaps, though his gallery included plenty of eccentrics.
□The Ghoul 33. Friday the Thirteenth 33. The Return of Bulldog Drummond 34. Java Head 34. King of Paris 34. *Bulldog Jack* 35. Things to Come 36. The Man who Could Work Miracles 36. Thunder in the City 37. *South Riding* 38. The Divorce of Lady X 38. The Citadel 38. *Q Planes* 39. *The Four Feathers* 39. The Lion has Wings 39. On the Night of the Fire 39. The Day Will Dawn 42. The Silver Fleet 43. The Volunteer 43. School for Secrets 46. *Anna Karenina* 48. *The Fallen Idol* 48. *The Heiress* 49. An Outcast of the Islands 51. Home at Seven (& d) 52. The Sound Barrier 52. The Holly and the Ivy 53. *Richard III* (as Buckingham) 56. Smiley 57. The Passionate Stranger 57. Our Man in Havana 59. *Oscar Wilde* (as Sir Edward Carson) 60. Exodus 61. The 300 Spartans 62. *Long Day's Journey into Night* 62. Woman of Straw 64. Doctor Zhivago 66. *The Wrong Box* 66. Khartoum 67. Oh What a Lovely War 69. The Midas Run 69. The Bed Sitting Room 69. The Battle of Britain 69. The Looking Glass War 69. David Copperfield (as Micawber) 69. Eagle in a Cage 71. Who Slew Auntie Roo? 71. Tales from the Crypt 71. Lady Caroline Lamb 72. Alice's Adventures in Wonderland (as the Caterpillar) 72. A Doll's House 73. O Lucky Man 73. Frankenstein: The True Story (TV) 73. Rollerball 75. Jesus of Nazareth (TV) 77. The Man in the Iron Mask (TV) 77. Time Bandits 80. Dragonslayer 81. Wagner 83. Invitation to a Wedding 83. Greystoke (AAN) 84. Witness for the Prosecution (TV) 84.
❀ For casting his whimsical eye over a surprisingly large range of movies, and invariably walking off with the honours. *Q Planes*.

¶ *R.R.:* I don't like my face at all. It's always been a great drawback to me.

R.R.: The art of acting lies in keeping people from coughing.

Richardson, Tony (1928–) (Cecil Antonio Richardson). British director of stage and screen.
□Momma Don't Allow (short: co-d) 55. Look Back in Anger 58. The Entertainer 60. Sanctuary (US) 61. *A Taste of Honey* 61. The Loneliness of the Long Distance Runner 63. *Tom Jones* (AA) 63. The Loved One (US) 65. Sailor from Gibraltar 66. Mademoiselle 66. Red and Blue 67. The Charge of the Light Brigade 68. Laughter in the Dark 69. Hamlet 69. Ned Kelly 70. A Delicate Balance 73. Dead Cert (& co-w) 74. Joseph Andrews 77. A Death in Canaan (TV) 78. The Border 82. Hotel New Hampshire 84.
'The most prolific and the most prosperous of the *Sight and Sound* crop, and ultimately the least respected.'—*Andrew Sarris, 1968*

Richler, Mordecai (1931–). Canadian novelist on Jewish themes. *Lies My Father Told Me* and *The Apprenticeship of Duddy Kravitz* have been filmed.

Richelieu, Cardinal (1585–1642). Louis XIII's chief minister, doubtless a clever and powerful chap, was used by the movies as a schemer and often a villain, seldom on the hero's side. George Arliss gave the fullest portrait, in *Cardinal Richelieu* in 1935. Others who have played him include Nigel de Brulier in *The Iron Mask*, the 1935 version of *The Three Musketeers* and the 1939 version of *The Man in the Iron Mask*; Osgood Perkins in *Madame Dubarry*; Raymond Massey in *Under the Red Robe*; Miles Mander in the 1939 version of *The Three Musketeers*; Aimé Clairond in *Monsieur Vincent*; Vincent Price in the 1948 version of *The Three Musketeers*; Paul Cavanagh in *Sword of D'Artagnan*; Christopher Logue in *The Devils*; and Charlton Heston in the 1974 versions of *The Three Musketeers* and *The Four Musketeers*.

Richman, Harry (1895–1972) (Harold Reichman). American entertainer, in occasional films.
Autobiography 1966: *A Hell of a Life*.
□Putting on the Ritz 30. The Music Goes Round 36. Kicking the Moon Around 38.

Richman, Mark (1927–). American general purpose actor, much on TV.
Friendly Persuasion 56. The Strange One 57. The Black Orchid 58. The Crime Busters 61. Dark Intruder 65. For Singles Only 68, etc.
TV series: *Cain's Hundred* 61. Longstreet 71.

Richmond, Kane (1906–1973) (Frederick W. Bowditch). American leading man of second features.
The Leather Pushers (serial) 30. Nancy Steele is Missing 36. Hard Guy 41. Action in the North Atlantic 43. Tiger Woman 45. Black Gold 47, many others.

Richmond, Ted (1912–). American producer, former writer.
So Dark the Night 46. The Milkman 50. The Strange Door 51. Desert Legion 53. Forbidden 54. Count Three and Pray 55. Seven Waves Away 57. Solomon and Sheba 59. Advance to the Rear 64. Return of the Seven 66. Villa Rides 68. Papillon 74, others.

Richmond, Tony (1942–). British cinematographer.
Only When I Larf 68. Madame Sin (TV) 72. *Don't Look Now* 73. Vampira 74. The Man Who Fell to Earth 75. The Eagle Has Landed 76. The Greek Tycoon 78. Love and Bullets 79. Bad Timing 80, etc.

Richter, Hans (1888–1976). German dadaist director of animated and surrealist films, most active in twenties.
Prelude and Fugue 20. Film is Rhythm 20. Rhythm 23. Rhythm 25. Film Study 26. Inflation 26. Twopenny Magic 27. Vormittagspuk 28. Everything Revolves 30. Dreams That Money Can Buy 44. 8×8 57, etc.

Richter, W. D. (–). American screenwriter.
□Slither 72. Peeper 75. Nickelodeon 76. Invasion of the Body Snatchers 78. Dracula 79. Brubaker 80. All Night Long 81.

Rickles, Don (1926–). American insult comedian.
Run Silent Run Deep 58. The Rabbit Trap 59. The Rat Race 60. Enter Laughing 67. The Money Jungle 68. Where It's At 69. Kelly's Heroes 70, etc.
TV series: CPO Sharkey 77.

Riddle, Nelson (1921–85). American composer.
A Kiss Before Dying 55. St Louis Blues 58. Ocean's Eleven 60. Lolita 62. Robin and the Seven Hoods 64. Marriage on the Rocks 65. El Dorado 66. Paint Your Wagon 69. The Great Gatsby 74. Harper Valley PTA 78, etc.

Ridgeley, John (1909–1968) (John Huntingdon Rea). American supporting actor generally cast as gangster.
Invisible Menace 38. They Made Me a Fugitive 39. Brother Orchid 40. The Big Shot 42. Destination Tokyo 44. My Reputation 46. The Big Sleep 46. Possessed 47. Command Decision 48. The Blue Veil 52, many others.

Ridges, Stanley (1892–1951). Incisive, heavy-featured British character actor who appeared in many Hollywood films.
□Success 23. Crime without Passion 34. The Scoundrel 35. Winterset 36. Sinner Take All 36. Internes Can't Take Money 37. Yellow Jack 38. The Mad Miss Manton 38. If I Were King 38. There's That Woman Again 38. Let Us Live 39. Confessions of a Nazi Spy 39. I Stole a Million 39. Silver on the Sage 39. Union Pacific 39. Each Dawn I Die 39. Espionage Agent 39. Dust Be My Destiny 39. Nick Carter Master Detective 39. *Black Friday* 40. The Sea Wolf 41. Mr District

Attorney 41. Sergeant York 41. They Died with Their Boots On 41. The Lady Is Willing 42. The Big Shot 42. *To Be or Not to Be* 42. Eagle Squadron 42. Eyes in the Night 42. Tarzan Triumphs 43. Air Force 43. This Is the Army 43. The Master Race 44. The Story of Dr Wassell 44. Wilson 44. *The Suspect* 45. Captain Eddie 45. God Is My Co-Pilot 45. The Phantom Speaks 45. Because of Him 46. Mr Ace 46. Canyon Passage 46. Possessed 47. An Act of Murder 47. You're My Everything 49. Streets of Laredo 49. The File on Thelma Jordon 49. Task Force 49. There's a Song in My Heart 49. Paid in Full 50. No Way Out 50. The Groom Wore Spurs 51.

Riefenstahl, Leni (1902–). German woman director, former dancer, who made brilliant propaganda films for Hitler.
Biography 1976: *Leni Riefenstahl* by Glenn B. Infield.
The White Hell of Pitz Palu (acted) 29. The Blue Light (ad) 32. S.O.S. Iceberg (a) 33. *Triumph of the Will* (the Nuremberg Rally) (d) 34. *Olympische Spiele 1936.* Tiefland 45, etc.

Riegert, Peter (1947–). American character lead, in the George Segal tradition.
National Lampoon's Animal House 78. *Local Hero* 83. Ellis Island (TV) 85.

Riesner, Dean (c. 1930–). American screenwriter.
The Intruders (TV) 67. Stranger on the Run (TV) 69. Coogan's Bluff (co-w) 69. Dirty Harry (co-w) 71. Charlie Varrick (co-w) 73. Rich Man Poor Man (TV) 75, etc.

Rififi (France 1955). The film which re-established Jules Dassin as an international director after years of inactivity following his blacklisting by the Un-American Activities tribunals; also the film which triggered off an unending series of stories about big-scale robberies which come unstuck. Its particular selling-point was that the entire twenty-minute robbery sequence took place in complete silence. Written by René Wheeler and Dassin from a novel by Auguste le Breton; photographed by Philippe Agostini; music by Georges Auric; with Jean Servais, Carl Mohner, Dassin. Several inferior sequels were made by other directors.

Rigby, Edward (1879–1951). British stage character actor in films since 1934; became a familiar figure in endearingly doddery roles.
Lorna Doone 35. Mr Smith Carries On 37. The Proud Valley 39. *Kipps* 41. The Common Touch 41. *Let the People Sing* 42. *Salute John Citizen* 42. Get Cracking 43. *Don't Take It to Heart* 44. Quiet Weekend 47. *Easy Money* 48. It's Hard to be Good 49. *The Happiest Days of Your Life* 49. *The Mudlark* 50, many others.

Rigby, Terence (1937–). British character actor, mostly on stage.
The Little Ones 61. West Eleven 63. Accident 67. Get Carter 71. The Homecoming 73. The Dogs of War 80. The Hound of the Baskervilles (TV) 83. Lace (TV) 84. Lace II (TV) 85.
TV series: Crossroads 86– .

Rigg, Diana (1938–). British leading actress who came to fame in *The Avengers* TV series 65–67.
□The Assassination Bureau 68. A Midsummer Night's Dream 68. On Her Majesty's Secret Service 69. Julius Caesar 70. The Hospital 71. Theatre of Blood 73. In This House of Brede (TV) 75. A Little Night Music 77. Evil Under the Sun 81.
The Great Muppet Caper 81. Witness for the Prosecution (TV) 84.
TV series: The Diana Rigg Show 73.

Rilla, Walter (1895–1980). German actor on stage from 1921; to Britain in mid-thirties.
Der Geiger von Florenz 26. The Scarlet Pimpernel 35. Victoria the Great 37. At the Villa Rose 39. The Adventures of Tartu 43. The Lisbon Story 46. State Secret 50. Behold the Man (pd) 51. Cairo 61. The Thousand Eyes of Dr Mabuse 63. The Face of Fu Manchu 65, etc.

Rilla, Wolf (1920–). British director, son of Walter Rilla.
Noose for a Lady 53. The End of the Road 54. Pacific Destiny 56. The Scamp 57. Bachelor of Hearts 58. Witness in the Dark 50. Piccadilly Third Stop 60. *Village of the Damned* 62. Cairo 63. The World Ten Times Over (& w) 63. Secrets of a Door to Door Salesman 73, etc.

Rimmer, Shane (–). American supporting actor.
S*P*Y*S 74. Twilight's Last Gleaming 77. The People That Time Forgot 77. Silver Bears 79. Arabian Adventure 79. Hanover Street 79. Gandhi 82, etc.

Rin Tin Tin (1916–1932). An ex-German Army dog which became one of the biggest

box office draws of the American silent screen; also in serials.
Where the North Begins 23. The Night Cry 23. The Clash of the Wolves 24. Jaws of Steel 27. The Frozen River 29. A Dog of the Regiment 30, etc.
†A TV series, *Adventures of Rin Tin Tin*, appeared in 1955.

Rinehart, Mary Roberts (1876–1958). American mystery novelist, whose plots usually involve heroines in frightening situations. *The Bat* and *Miss Pinkerton* were each filmed more than once.

Ringwald, Molly (1968–). American teenage actress of the eighties.
Sixteen Candles 84. The Breakfast Club 85. Pretty in Pink 86. The Pick-up Artist 87.

Rio Rita. The operetta by Joseph McCarthy and Henry Tierney became, in 1929, one of the first musicals to be filmed, and Bebe Daniels and John Boles are remembered for their work in what was necessarily a very primitive production. In 1942 the work was retailored for Abbott and Costello, with John Carroll and Kathryn Grayson doing the singing.

Ripley, Arthur (1895–1961). American director whose films are oddly sparse.
□I Met My Love Again 38. Prisoner of Japan 42. *A Voice in the Wind* 44. The Chase 47. Thunder Road 58.

Ripper, Michael (1913–). British character actor, often in comic roles.
Captain Boycott 48. Treasure Hunt 52. The Belles of St Trinian's 54. Richard III 56. Quatermass II 57. The Revenge of Frankenstein 58. Brides of Dracula 60. Captain Clegg 62. The Secret of Blood Island 65. The Reptile 66. The Plague of the Zombies 66. Where the Bullets Fly 66. Scars of Dracula 70, etc.

Riscoe, Arthur (1896–1954). British stage comedian with rare film appearances.
Going Gay 34. Paradise for Two 38. *Kipps* (as Chitterlow) 41, etc.

Risdon, Elizabeth (1887–1958) (E. Evans). British stage actress who in later life went to Hollywood and played many character roles.
Guard That Girl 35. Crime and Punishment 36. The Great Man Votes 39. Lost Angel 44. Grissly's Millions 44. Mama Loves Papa 45. Life with Father 47. Bannerline 51. Scaramouche 52, etc.

Risi, Dino (1916–). Italian director.
The Sign of Venus 55. Poveri ma Belli 56. Il Sorpasso 62. Scent of a Woman 75. How Funny Can Sex Be 76. Viva Italia 78. Primo Amore 78. Caro Papa 79. Sunday Lovers 80, etc.

Riskin, Robert (1897–1955). Distinguished American screenwriter.
Illicit 31. The Miracle Woman 31. *Lady for a Day* 33. *It Happened One Night* (AA) 34. Broadway Bill 34. The Whole Town's Talking 35. *Mr Deeds Goes to Town* 36. *Lost Horizon* 37. *You Can't Take It with You* 38. The Real Glory 39. *Meet John Doe* 41. The Thin Man Goes Home 44. Magic Town 46. Riding High 50. Mister 880 50. The Groom Wore Spurs 51, etc.

Ritchard, Cyril (1896–1977). British dancer and light comedian, mainly on stage; latterly in US.
Piccadilly 29. Blackmail 30. I See Ice 38. Half a Sixpence 67.

Ritchie, June (1939–). British leading lady, mainly in 'realist' films.
A Kind of Loving 61. Live Now Pay Later 63. The Mouse on the Moon 63. The World Ten Times Over 63. This is My Street 64. The Syndicate (GB) 67, etc.

Ritchie, Michael (1939–). American director.
□The Outsider (TV) 67. The Sound of Anger (TV) 69. Downhill Racer 69. Prime Cut 72. *The Candidate* 72. *Smile* 75. The Bad News Bears 76. Semi-Tough 77. An Almost Perfect Affair 79. Divine Madness 80. The Island 80. The Survivors 83. Fletch 84. Wildcats 85. The Golden Child 86.

Ritt, Martin (1919–). American director with stage and TV experience.
□*Edge of the City* 56. *No Down Payment* 57. *The Long Hot Summer* 58. The Sound and the Fury 59. The Black Orchid 59. Five Branded Women 60. Paris Blues 61. Hemingway's Adventures of a Young Man 62. *Hud* 63. The Outrage 64. *The Spy Who Came in from the Cold* 65. Hombre 67. The Brotherhood 68. The Molly Maguires 69. The Great White Hope 71. Sounder 72. Pete 'n Tillie 72. Conrack 74. The Front 76. The End of the Game (a only) 76. Casey's Shadow 77. Norma Rae 79. Cross Creek 83.
Murphy's Romance 85. The Slugger's Wife (a only) 85.

¶ *M.R.:* I don't need final cut. I only cut the thing once. If they're dumb enough to fool aorund with it, let 'em do it.

M.R.: As far as a Martin Ritt Production is concerned, I wouldn't embarrass myself to take that credit. What about the Ravetches? They wrote it. What about the actors who appear in it? If ever I write one, direct it and appear in it, then you can call it a Martin Ritt Production.

Ritter, John (1948–) (Jonathan Ritter). American light actor, son of Tex Ritter, famous on American TV as hero of *Three's Company*.
□The Barefoot Executive 70. The Other 72. Nickelodeon 76. Americathon 79. Hero at Large 80. Wholly Moses 80. They All Laughed 81.

Ritter, Tex (1907–1974) (Woodward Ritter). American singing cowboy star of innumerable second features.
Song of the Gringo 36. Sing, Cowboy, Sing 38. The Old Chisholm Trail 43. Marshal of Gunsmoke 46, etc.

Ritter, Thelma (1905–1969). Wry-faced American character actress and comedienne; she provided a sardonic commentary on the antics of the principals in many fifties comedies.
□Miracle on 34th Street 47. Call Northside 777 48. A Letter to Three Wives 49. City across the River 49. Father was a Fullback 49. Perfect Strangers 50. *All About Eve* 50. I'll Get By 50. The Mating Season 51. As Young as You Feel 51. *The Model and the Marriage Broker* 51. With a Song in My Heart 52. Titanic 53. The Farmer Takes a Wife 53. *Pickup on South Street* 53. Rear Window 54. Daddy Longlegs 55. Lucy Gallant 55. The Proud and Profane 56. A Hole in the Head 59. Pillow Talk 59. The Misfits 61. The Second Time Around 61. Birdman of Alcatraz 62. How the West was Won 62. For Love or Money 63. A New Kind of Love 63. Move Over Darling 63. Boeing Boeing 65. The Incident 67. What's So Bad about Feeling Good? 68.
Famous line (*All About Eve*): What a story. Everything but the bloodhounds snapping at her rear end.
Famous line (*Pillow Talk*): If there's anything worse than a woman living alone, it's a woman saying she likes it.

The Ritz Brothers: Al (1901–1965), **Jim** (1903–85) and **Harry** (the leader) (1906–86). Zany American night club comedians who made many enjoyable appearances in musicals of the thirties. Their real surname was Joachim.
□Hotel Anchovy (short) 34. Sing Baby Sing 36. One in a Million 37. *On the Avenue* 37. You Can't Have Everything 37. Life Begins at College 37. *The Goldwyn Follies* 38. Kentucky Moonshine 38. Straight Place and Show 38. *The Three Musketeers* 39. The Gorilla 39. Pack Up Your Troubles 39. Argentine Nights 40. Behind the Eight Ball 42. Hi Ya Chum 43. Never a Dull Moment 43. Won Ton Ton (guest appearance by Harry and Jim) 76.

Riva, Emmanuele (1932–). French leading actress.
Hiroshima Mon Amour 59. Adua et sa Compagnie (Hungry for Love) 58. Kapo 59. Leon Morin Priest 60. Climats 61. Thérèse Desqueyroux 63. Soledad 66, etc.

The River. There are now three films of this title. 1. US 1938: a documentary by Pare Lorenz, with free-verse commentary, about the Tennessee Valley Authority and its effect on the dwellers in the Mississippi Basin. Words by Thomas Chalmers, music by Virgil Thompson. 2. India 1951: Jean Renoir's colour romance in which the story serves as a slender thread on which to hold the decoration; with Adrienne Corri, Esmond Knight 3. In 1984 Mark Rydell directed a third film under this title.

Rivera, Chita (1933–) (Dolores Conchita Figueroa del Rivero). Dynamic American dancer and singer who in 1969 appeared in the film *Sweet Charity*.

Rivers, Joan (1933–). American cabaret comedienne with a strong line in smut.
Rabbit Test 78.

¶ *J.R.:* I'm Jewish. I don't work out. If God had intended me to bend over he'd have put diamonds on the floor.

Rivette, Jacques (1928–). French director, former critic.
Le Coup du Berger 56. Paris Nous Appartient 60. La Religieuse (& w) 65. L'Amour Fou (& w) 68. Celine and Julie Go Boating 74. La Vengeresse 76. Merry Go Round, etc.

Rix, Brian (1924–). British actor-manager associated with the Whitehall farces.
Autobiography 1977: *My Farce from my Elbow*.

Reluctant Heroes 51. What Every Woman Wants 54. Up to His Neck 54. Dry Rot 55. The Night We Dropped a Clanger 59. And the Same to You 60. Nothing Barred 61. Don't Just Lie There Say Something 73, etc.

RKO Radio Pictures Inc was for many years one of Hollywood's 'big five' production companies, with its own distribution arm. It started in 1921 as a joint enterprise of the Radio Corporation of America and the Keith-Orpheum cinema circuit. Despite severe financial vicissitudes, it struggled on for twenty-seven years, buoyed by a generally decent production standard; stars like Cary Grant, Katharine Hepburn, Wheeler and Woolsey, Leon Errol; individual films such as *Cimarron, King Kong, The Informer, Suspicion, Mr Blandings Builds His Dream House* and *Fort Apache*; and the participation of Goldwyn, Disney and Selznick, all released through RKO at its peak. In 1948 Howard Hughes (qv) acquired a large share of the stock; but after a period of uncertainty RKO ceased production in 1953 and the studio was sold to Desilu TV.

A glossy book by Richard B. Jewell and Vernon Harbin, *The RKO Story*, came out in 1982 and was a valuable research tool.

Roach, Bert (1891–1971). American silent screen actor.
The Millionaire 21. The Rowdy 21. The Flirt 22. Excitement 24. Don't 25. Money Talks 26. The Taxi Dancer 27. The Desert Rider 29. No No Nanette 30. Viennese Nights 30. Hallelujah I'm a Bum 33. San Francisco 36. Algiers 38. Hi Diddle Diddle 43. The Perils of Pauline 47, etc.

Roach, Hal (1892–). American producer chiefly associated with gag comedies. Varied early experience before he teamed with Harold Lloyd 1916; later made films with Our Gang, Laurel and Hardy, etc.
SOUND FILMS: Sons of the Desert 33. *Way Out West* 36. *Topper* 37. *Of Mice and Men* 39. *Turnabout* 40. One Million BC 40. *Topper Returns* 41, many others.
† AA 1983 'in recognition of his distinguished contributions to the motion picture art form'.

¶ 'One of the few producers who knew talent when he saw it, and gave his stars, writers and directors the freedom to create great comedy.'—*Leonard Maltin*

road show. A term which used to mean a travelling show; latterly in cinema terms it indicates the special, prolonged pre-release at advanced prices of a big-screen attraction, e.g. *My Fair Lady* or *The Sound of Music*, which may in this way run for years in a big city before being released to local theatres.

Road to Singapore (US 1940). This modest studio-made romantic comedy happened to star three Paramount contract players: Bing Crosby, Bob Hope and Dorothy Lamour. They worked so well together, with successful ad-libbing and an easy style, that several other 'Road' comedies were made, getting crazier each time and using every kind of gag the writers could think of. The only thing you were sure of in these pictures was that Bob wouldn't get the girl; otherwise anything could happen, from inside gags about Paramount to talking camels. They all date badly. *Road to Zanzibar* 41, *Road to Morocco* 42, *Road to Utopia* 46, *Road to Rio* 47, *Road to Bali* 52, *Road to Hong Kong* 62.

Robards, Jason, Snr (1893–1963). American stage actor, who made character appearances in films.
The Cohens and the Kellys 26. On Trial 28. Abraham Lincoln 30. The Crusades 35. I Stole a Million 39. Isle of the Dead 45. Bedlam 46. Riff Raff 47. Wild in the Country 61, many others.
TV series: Acapulco 61.

Robards, Jason, Jnr (1920–). American stage actor, son of Jason Robards.
The Journey 58. By Love Possessed 59. *Tender is the Night* 61. Long Day's Journey into Night 62. A Thousand Clowns 65. A Big Hand for the Little Lady 66. Any Wednesday 66. Divorce American Style 67. *The Hour of the Gun* 67. The St Valentine's Day Massacre 67. The Night They Raided Minsky's 68. Isadora 68. Once Upon a Time in the West 69. Tora! Tora! Tora! 70. Julius Caesar 70. The Ballad of Cable Hogue 70. Murders in the Rue Morgue 71. Johnny Got His Gun 71. The War Between Men and Women 72. Pat Garrett and Billy the Kid 73. Play It As It Lays 73. All The President's Men (AA) 76. Washington Behind Closed Doors (TV) 77. Julia (as Dashiell Hammett) 77. Comes A Horseman 78. Hurricane 79. Melvin and Howard (as Howard Hughes) 80. Raise the Titanic 80. Caboblanco 81. The Legend of the Lone Ranger 81. Max Dugan Returns 83. The Day After (TV) 83. Something Wicked This Way Comes 83. Sakharov (TV) 84. The Last Frontier (TV) 86. Square Dance 86, etc.

¶ *J.R.:* I've always played disintegrated characters.

Robbe-Grillet, Alain (1922–). French writer, associated with Resnais in *Last Year at Marienbad* 60. Also wrote and directed *L'Immortelle* 62, *Trans-Europe Express* 66.

robberies have been a commonplace of film action fare since *The Great Train Robbery* itself; but of late there has been a fashion for showing the planning and execution of robberies through the eyes of the participants. Perhaps this started in 1950 with *The Asphalt Jungle* (and its two remakes *The Badlanders* and *Cairo*); anyway, some of the films built on this mould are *Rififi, Five against the House, Seven Thieves, The Killing, Payroll, Piccadilly Third Stop, The Day They Robbed the Bank of England, A Prize of Gold, On Friday at Eleven, Once a Thief, He Who Rides a Tiger, Robbery, Charley Varrick, Cops and Robbers, The Taking of Pelham One Two Three, The Getaway, 11 Harrowhouse, The Bank Shot, Gambit, Dog Day Afternoon* and *Inside Out*; while films treating the same subject less seriously included *The Lavender Hill Mob, The Lady Killers, Ocean's Eleven, Persons Unknown, The League of Gentlemen, Topkapi, The Big Job, Assault on a Queen, The Biggest Bundle of Them All, Grand Slam, They Came to Rob Las Vegas, The Italian Job, The Hot Rock* and *The Anderson Tapes*. The biggest attempted robbery of all was probably the raid on Fort Knox in *Goldfinger*. Sometimes one longs for a return to the days of the dapper jewel thieves: Ronald Colman or David Niven in *Raffles*, Herbert Marshall in *Trouble in Paradise*, John Barrymore or even Charles Korvin as Arsène Lupin, Cary Grant in *To Catch a Thief*. The closest we have come to this style for many years, apart from William Wyler's *How to Steal a Million*, is 1973's *The Thief Who Came to Dinner* with Ryan O'Neal. In 1964 TV made a gallant effort with *The Rogues*.

Robbins, Gale (1922–1980). American leading lady and singer.
In the Meantime Darling 44. My Girl Tisa 48. The Barkleys of Broadway 49. Oh You Beautiful Doll 49. Three Little Words 50. Strictly Dishonourable 51. The Belle of New York 52. Calamity Jane 53. Double Jeopardy 55, etc.

Robbins, Harold (1916–) (Francis Kane). American best-selling novelist whose over-sexed tales have been readily transcribed to the screen.
Never Love a Stranger 58. King Creole 58. The Carpetbaggers 64. Where Love Has Gone 64. Nevada Smith 66. Stiletto 69. The Adventurers 69. The Betsy 77. The Pirate (TV) 78. 79 Park Avenue (TV) 79. The Dream Merchants (TV) 80, etc.
TV series: *The Survivors* 69.

¶ I live this way, sometimes.—*H.R.*
Hemingway was a jerk.—*H.R.*

Robbins, Jerome (1918–). American dancer and ballet-master who has choreographed several films.
The King and I 56. *West Side Story* (AA) (& co-d) 61, etc.

The Robe (US 1953). This solemn epic from Lloyd C. Douglas' novel about the aftermath of the Crucifixion is unremarkable except as the first film in CinemaScope (qv). Photographer Leon Shamroy operated under difficulties with a lens as yet imperfect. Victor Mature, who gave the best performance, appeared next year in a sequel, *Demetrius and the Gladiators*.

Rober, Richard (1906–1952). American general purpose actor with stage experience.
Smart Girls Don't Talk 48. Deported 50. The Well 52. The Devil Makes Three 52, etc.

Robert, Yves (1920–). French director, former actor.
The War of the Buttons 61. *Bébert et l'Omnibus* 63. *Copains* 64. *Follow the Guy with One Black Shoe* 72. Pardon Mon Affaire 76. We All Shall Go To Paradise 77, etc.

Roberti, Lyda (1910–1938). German-Polish leading lady, former child café singer, in several Hollywood films of the thirties.
□Million Dollar Legs 32. The Kid from Spain 32. Dancers in the Dark 32. Torch Singers 33. Three-Cornered Moon 33. College Rhythm 34. The Big Broadcast of 1936 35. George White's Scandals 35. Pick a Star 37. Nobody's Baby 37. Wide Open Faces 37.

Roberts, Ben (1916–84) (Benjamin Eisenberg). American writer, almost always with Ivan Goff (qv).

Roberts, Eric (1956–). American leading man of the late seventies.
King of the Gypsies 78. Raggedy Man 81. Star 80 83. The Pope of Greenwich Village 84. The Coca Cola Kid 85. Runaway Train (AAN) 85. Nobody's Fool 86, etc.

Roberts, Ewan (1914–83) (Thomas McEwan Hutchinson). Scottish character actor of stage and screen.

Castle in the Air 52. The Lady Killers 55. Night of the Demon 57. The Day of the Triffids 61. The Traitors 62. Five to One 63. Hostile Witness 67. Bedevilled 71. Endless Night 72, etc.

Roberts, Florence (1860–1940). American character actress best remembered as Granny in the Jones Family series 1936–40.

Roberts, Kenneth (1885–1957). American adventure novelist. The filming of *Northwest Passage* was never completed: the title on King Vidor's film reads *Northwest Passage, Part One: Rogers' Rangers. Lydia Bailey* fared better.

Roberts, Lynne (1922–) (Mary Hart). American leading lady of forties second features.
Dangerous Holiday 37. Winter Wonderland 39. Call of the Klondike 41. Quiet Please Murder 42. The Great Plane Robbery 47. The Blazing Forest 52, many others.

Roberts, Pernell (1930–). American general purpose actor; became famous as one of the brothers in TV's *Bonanza,* but left after four years and never regained the limelight until 1979, when he played the title role in the series *Trapper John MD*.
Ride Lonesome 58. The Silent Gun (TV) 69. The Magic of Lassie 78, etc.

Roberts, Rachel (1927–1980). British stage actress.
Valley of Song 52. The Good Companions 57. Our Man in Havana 59. *Saturday Night and Sunday Morning* (BFA) 60. *This Sporting Life* (BFA) 63. A Flea in Her Ear 68. Doctors' Wives 71. Wild Rovers 71. *O Lucky Man* 73. The Belstone Fox 73. Murder on the Orient Express 74. Great Expectations (TV) 75. Picnic at Hanging Rock 76. Foul Play 78. When a Stranger Calls 79. Yanks (BFA) 79. Charlie Chan and the Curse of the Dragon Queen 81, etc.
TV series: The Tony Randall Show 76.

Roberts, Roy (1900–1975). American character actor who once played cops but graduated to senior executives.
Guadalcanal Diary 43. My Darling Clementine 46. Flaming Fury 49. The Big Trees 52. The Glory Brigade 53. The Boss 56, many others.
TV series: Petticoat Junction 64–68.

Roberts, Stephen (1895–1936). American director.
□Sky Bride 32. Lady and Gent 32. The Night of June 13th 32. If I Had a Million (part) 32. The Story of Temple Drake 33. *One Sunday Afternoon* 33. The Trumpet Blows 34. Romance in Manhattan 34. *Star of Midnight* 35. The Man Who Broke the Bank at Monte Carlo 35. The Lady Consents 36. The Ex Mrs Bradford 36.

Roberts, Theodore (1861–1928). American character actor, the grand old man of the silent screen.
Where the Trail Divides 14. The Trail of the Lonesome Pine 16. Male and Female 19. The Affairs of Anatol 21. Our Leading Citizen 22. *The Ten Commandments* (as Moses) 23. Grumpy 23. Locked Doors 25. Masks of the Devil 28, many others.

Roberts, Tony (1939–). American light leading man.
The Beach Girls and the Monster 70. Star Spangled Girl 71. Play It Again Sam 72. Serpico 73. Le Sauvage 75. Annie Hall 77. Just Tell Me What You Want 80. A Midsummer Night's Sex Comedy 82. Amityville 3D 83. Key Exchange 85. Hannah and her Sisters 85, etc.

Robertshaw, Jerrold (1866–1941). Gaunt British stage actor who made several film appearances.
Dombey and Son 18. She 25. Downhill 27. Kitty 29. Don Quixote (title role) 33, etc.

Robertson, Cliff (1925–). Ambitious American leading man with long stage experience before being spotted for films.
□*Picnic* (debut) 55. Autumn Leaves 56. The Girl Most Likely 57. The Naked and the Dead 58. Gidget 59. Battle of the Coral Sea 59. As the Sea Rages 60. All in a Night's Work 61. The Big Show 61. Underworld USA 61. The Interns 62. My Six Loves 63. *PT 109* (as President Kennedy) 63. Sunday in New York 64. *The Best Man* 64. 633 Squadron 64. Love Has Many Faces 65. Masquerade (GB) 65. Up from the Beach 65. *The Honey Pot* 67. The Devil's Brigade 68. *Charly* (AA) 68. Too Late the Hero 69. The Great Northfield Minnesota Raid 72. J. W. Coop (& pd) 72. Ace Eli and Rodger of the Skies 73. Man on a Swing 74. My Father's House (TV) 75. Out of Season 75. Three Days of the Condor 76. Midway 76. Shoot 76. Obsession 76. *Washington Behind Closed Doors* (TV) 77. Fraternity Row (narrator) 77.

Dominique 78. The Pilot (& w. d) 80. Two of a Kind (TV) 82. Class 83. Brainstorm 83. Star 80 83. The Key to Rebecca (TV) 85. Shaker Run 85.
TV series: Rod Brown of the Rocket Rangers 53.
†In 1979 Robertson's career suffered unfairly when he accused executive David Begelman of having falsely signed a cheque in his name. The incident became a major scandal and is covered in the book *Indecent Exposure* by David McClintock.

¶ *C.R.:* As long as I get phone calls from the Museum of Modern Art, that all the film buffs love it, that's a residual. It isn't a financial residual and it isn't an artistic residual, but it's an ego residual.

Robertson, Dale (1923–). American western star, former schoolteacher.
Fighting Man of the Plains (debut) 49. Two Flags West 50. Lydia Bailey 52. The Silver Whip 53. Sitting Bull 54. A Day of Fury 56. Law of the Lawless 63. Blood on the Arrow 65. Coast of Skeletons 65, etc.
TV series: Tales of Wells Fargo 57–61. The Iron Horse 66. Dynasty 80–81.

Robertson, John S. (1878–1964). Canadian director in Hollywood.
The Money Mill 17. Let's Elope 19. Dr Jekyll and Mr Hyde 20. Sentimental Tommy 21. Tess of the Storm Country 22. The Enchanted Cottage 24. Shore Leave 25. Annie Laurie 27. Shanghai Lady 29. Madonna of the Streets 30. One Man's Journey 33. Wednesday's Child 34. Captain Hurricane 35. Our Little Girl 35, others.

Robertson, Willard (1886–1948). American character actor, often seen as lawyer or prison governor.
Skippy 31. Sky Devils 32. I Am a Fugitive from a Chain Gang 32. Doctor X 32. Tugboat Annie 33. Death on the Diamond 34. Here Comes the Navy 34. Black Fury 35. The Gorgeous Hussy 36. Exclusive 37. Men with Wings 38. Jesse James 39. Each Dawn I Die 39. My Little Chickadee 40. The Monster and the Girl 41. Juke Girl 42. Nine Girls 44. The Virginian 46. To Each His Own 46. Sitting Pretty 48, many others.

Robeson, Paul (1898–1976). Black American actor and singer, on stage including concerts from mid-twenties.
Biographies, all entitled *Paul Robeson*: 1958 by Marie Seton; 1968 by Edwin P. Hoyt; 1974 by Virginia Hamilton.
□Body and Soul 24. The Emperor Jones 33. *Sanders of the River* 35. *Showboat* 36. *Song of Freedom* 37. Jericho 38. Big Fella 38. *King Solomon's Mines* 38. *The Proud Valley* 39. Tales of Manhattan 42. Native Land 42. Il Canto dei Grandi Fiumi 55.

Robey, Sir George (1869–1954) (George Edward Wade). British music-hall comedian, 'the prime minister of mirth'. Appeared in silent farcical comedies, later in character roles.
Autobiography 1933: *Looking Back on Life*.
The Rest Cure 23. Don Quixote (as Sancho Panza) 23 and 33. Her Prehistoric Man 24. Chu Chin Chow 33. Marry Me 33. Birds of a Feather 36. A Girl Must Live 39. Variety Jubilee 40. Salute John Citizen 42. Henry V 44. The Trojan Brothers 45. The Pickwick Papers 52, etc.

Robin, Dany (1927–). French leading lady.
Le Silence est d'Or 46. Histoire d'Amour 52. Act of Love 54. In Six Easy Lessons 60. The Waltz of the Toreadors 62. Topaz 69, etc.

Robin Hood. The legendary outlaw leader of Plantagenet England is one of literature's most oft-filmed characters. There were film versions in 1909 (GB), 1912 (GB), 1912 (US), 1913 (US), and 1913 (GB). Douglas Fairbanks made his big-scale *Robin Hood* in 1922, with Wallace Beery as King Richard. In 1938 came *The Adventures of Robin Hood*, one of Hollywood's most satisfying action adventures, with Errol Flynn as Robin, Claude Rains as Prince John and Basil Rathbone as Guy of Gisbourne; directed by William Keighley and Michael Curtiz, from a script by Norman Reilly Raine and Seton I. Miller. Its exhilaration has not diminished with time. In 1946 (US) Cornel Wilde played Robin's son in *Bandit of Sherwood Forest*; in 1948 (US) Jon Hall was Robin in *Prince of Thieves*; in 1950 (US) John Derek was Robin's son in *Rogues of Sherwood Forest*; Robert Clarke played Robin in an odd concoction called *Tales of Robin Hood* (US 1952). Also in 1952, in Britain, Disney filmed Richard Todd in *The Story of Robin Hood and His Merrie Men*, with only fair success, though the real Sherwood Forest was used for the first time. Robin also appeared briefly (played by Harold Warrender) in *Ivanhoe* 52. *Men of Sherwood Forest* (GB 1956) had Don Taylor as Robin; *Son of Robin Hood* (GB 1959) turned out to be a daughter, played by June Laverick. Most durable Robin is Richard Greene, who played the role not only in 165 half-hour TV films but in a feature,

Sword of Sherwood Forest (GB 1961). In 1967 Barrie Ingham took over in *A Challenge for Robin Hood*, in 1973 the Disney studios produced a cartoon version, and in 1976 came *Robin and Marian*, which traced the sad fortunes of the protagonists twenty years later. A new television series, *Robin of Sherwood*, appeared in 1984.

Robin, Leo (1899–1985). American lyricist. Songs include 'Louise', 'Beyond the Blue Horizon', 'June in January', 'No Love No Nothing'.
Innocents of Paris 29. Monte Carlo 30. One Hour with You 32. Little Miss Marker 34. The Big Broadcast of 1938 (AA for 'Thanks for the Memory'). Gulliver's Travels 39. My Gal Sal 43. Meet Me after the Show 50. My Sister Eileen 55, etc.

Robinson, Andy (–). Baby-faced American character actor who has played a couple of memorable villains.
Dirty Harry 71. Charley Varrick 73. The Drowning Pool 75, etc.

Robinson, Bill (1878–1949). Black American tap-dancer and entertainer, famous for his stairway dance.
The Little Colonel 35. In Old Kentucky 36. Rebecca of Sunnybrook Farm 38. *Stormy Weather* 43, etc.

Robinson, Bruce (–). British screenwriter who in 1984 was AA-nominated for *The Killing Fields*. 1987: *Withnail and I*.

Robinson, Casey (1903–1979). American screenwriter, in Hollywood from 1921.
I Love That Man 33. Captain Blood 35. Call it a Day 37. It's Love I'm After 37. Four's a Crowd 39. *King's Row* 42. Passage to Marseilles 44. Days of Glory 44. *The Macomber Affair* 47. Under My Skin (& p) 50. Two Flags West (& p) 50. Diplomatic Courier (& p) 52. The Snows of Kilimanjaro 52. While the City Sleeps 56. This Earth is Mine (& p) 59, etc.

Robinson Crusoe. There have been many film variations on Defoe's novel. The closest to the original have been Luis Buñuel's *The Adventures of Robinson Crusoe* (Mexico 1953) with Dan O'Herlihy, and oddly enough, Byron Haskin's *Robinson Crusoe on Mars* (US 1964) with Paul Mantee. *Man Friday* (GB 1975) tried to be satirical by showing the situation from Friday's viewpoint.

Robinson, Edward G. (1893–1973) (Emanuel Goldenberg). Dynamic American star actor of Rumanian origin. On stage from 1913; later settled in Hollywood. Special Academy Award 1972.
Autobiography 1973: *All My Yesterdays*.
□The Bright Shawl 23. The Hole in the Wall 29. Night Ride 30. A Lady to Love 30. Outside the Law 30. East is West 30. Widow from Chicago 30. *Little Caesar* (which made him a star) 30. *Five Star Final* 31. Smart Money 31. The Hatchet Man 31. Two Seconds 32. Tiger Shark 32. Silver Dollar 32. The Little Giant 33. I Loved a Woman 33. Dark Hazard 34. The Man with Two Faces 34. *The Whole Town's Talking* 34. Barbary Coast 35. Bullets or Ballots 36. Thunder in the City (GB) 37. Kid Galahad 37. The Last Gangster 38. *A Slight Case of Murder* 38. *The Amazing Dr Clitterhouse* 38. I Am the Law 38. Confessions of a Nazi Spy 39. Blackmail 39. *Dr Ehrlich's Magic Bullet* 40. *Brother Orchid* 40. A Dispatch from Reuters 41. *The Sea Wolf* 41. Manpower 41. Unholy Partners 41. Larceny Inc. 42. Tales of Manhattan 42. Destroyer 43. Flesh and Fantasy 43. Tampico 44. *Double Indemnity* 44. Mr Winkle Goes to War 44. *The Woman in the Window* 44. Our Vines Have Tender Grapes 45. *Scarlet Street* 45. Journey Together (GB) 45. The Stranger 46. The Red House 47. *All My Sons* 48. *Key Largo* 48. Night Has a Thousand Eyes 48. *House of Strangers* 49. My Daughter Joy (GB) 50. Actors and Sin 52. Vice Squad 53. Big Leaguer 53. The Glass Web 53. Black Tuesday 54. The Violent Men 55. Tight Spot 55. A Bullet for Joey 55. Illegal 55. Hell on Frisco Bay 56. Nightmare 56. The Ten Commandments 56. A Hole in the Head 59. Seven Thieves 59. Pépé 60. My Geisha 62. *Two Weeks in Another Town* 62. Sammy Going South (GB) 62. The Prize 63. Good Neighbour Sam 64. Robin and the Seven Hoods 64. Cheyenne Autumn 64. The Outrage 64. *The Cincinnati Kid* 65. Who Has Seen the Wind 65. The Biggest Bundle of Them All 66. Never a Dull Moment 67. Grand Slam 67. Mackenna's Gold 68. It's Your Move 68. Operation St Peter's 68. Blonde from Peking 68. Song of Norway 69. Operation Heartbeat (TV) 69. The Old Man Who Cried Wolf (TV) 71. Soylent Green 73.
❀ For the dynamic personality which turned many a dubious script into dramatic gold. *Double Indemnity*.

¶ *E.G.R.:* Some people have youth, some have beauty—I have menace.

Famous line (*Little Caesar*): Mother of mercy, is this the end of Rico?

Robinson, Frances (1916–1971). American supporting actress, usually in smart roles.
Forbidden Valley 25. The Last Warning 28. Tim Tyler's Luck 35. The Lone Wolf Keeps a Date 37. The Invisible Man Returns 39. Tower of London 39. Smilin' Through 41. Suddenly It's Spring 46. Keeper of the Bees 47. Backfire 50, many others.

Robinson, George (c. 1895–*). American cinematographer.
No Defense 21. Back to God's Country 27. Hell's Heroes 30. Her First Mate 33. The Mystery of Edwin Drood 35. Diamond Jim 35. The Invisible Ray 36. Sutter's Gold 36. Dracula's Daughter 36. The Road Back 37. *Son of Frankenstein* 39. Tower of London 39. Son of Monte Cristo 40. Frankenstein Meets the Wolf Man 43. Son of Dracula 43. *The Scarlet Claw* 44. House of Frankenstein 45. The Naughty Nineties 45. Slave Girl 47. The Creeper 48. Abbott and Costello Meet Dr Jekyll and Mr Hyde 53. Tarantula 55. Joe Dakota 57, many others.

Robinson, Jay (1930–). American stage actor of eccentric roles.
The Robe 53. Demetrius and the Gladiators 54. The Virgin Queen 55. My Man Godfrey 57. Bunny O'Hare 71. Shampoo 75, etc.

Robinson, Joe (1929–). British actor and professional boxer.
Master of Bankdam 48. Daughter of Darkness 49. *A Kid for Two Farthings* 55. The Flesh is Weak 57. The Two Faces of Dr Jekyll 58. Barabbas 62, etc.

Robinson, John (1908–1979). British stage actor, familiar in heavy father or tough executive roles.
The Scarab Murder Case 36. The Lion Has Wings 40. Uneasy Terms 49. Hammer the Toff 51. The Constant Husband 55. Fortune is a Woman 58. The Doctors' Dilemma 59. And the Same to You 61, etc.

Robinson, Madeleine (1916–) (Madeleine Svoboda). French stage and film actress.
Soldats sans Uniformes 43. Douce 43. Une Si Jolie Petite Plage 48. Dieu a Besoin des Hommes 50. Le Garçon Sauvage 51. The She Wolves 57. A Double Tour 59. The Trial 64. A Trap for Cinderella 65. A New World 66. Le Voyage du Père 66. Le Petit Matin 70, etc.

Robison, Arthur (1888–1935). Chicago-born director of German films.
Warning Shadows 24. The Informer (GB) 29. The Student of Prague 35, etc.

Robots have been sparingly used in movies. Brigitte Helm memorably played one in *Metropolis*; so did Patricia Roc in *The Perfect Woman*. Robby the Robot featured sympathetically in *Forbidden Planet* and *Invisible Boy*; then there was *Kronos*, and Gort in *The Day the Earth Stood Still*. *Westworld, Futureworld* and *Star Wars* brought in a whole race of robots, one of whom looked like Yul Brynner; while in TV, *The Avengers* have frequently encountered the Cybernauts and *Dr Who* the Daleks.

Robson, Dame Flora (1902–1984). Distinguished British stage actress.
Biography 1960: *Flora Robson* by Janet Dunbar.
□Dance Pretty Lady 31. One Precious Year 33. Catherine the Great 34. *Fire Over England* 36. Farewell Again 37. Wuthering Heights 39. Poison Pen 39. We Are Not Alone 39. Invisible Stripes 39. The Sea Hawk 40. Banana Passage 41. Saratoga Trunk 43. 2000 Women 44. Great Day 45. Caesar and Cleopatra 45. The Years Between 46. *Black Narcissus* 46. Good Time Girl 47. Frieda 47. Holiday Camp 47. Saraband for Dead Lovers 48. The Tall Headlines 52. The Malta Story 53. Romeo and Juliet 54. *Innocent Sinners* 57. High Tide at Noon 57. No Time for Tears 57. The Gypsy and the Gentleman 58. 55 Days at Peking 62. Murder at the Gallop 63. Guns at Batasi 64. Those Magnificent Men in Their Flying Machines 64. Young Cassidy 65. Seven Women 65. The Shuttered Room 66. A Cry in the Wind 66. Eye of the Devil 67. Fragment of Fear 69. The Beloved 70. The Beast in the Cellar 71. Alice's Adventures in Wonderland 72. Comedy, Tragedy and All That 72. Dominique 78. A Man Called Intrepid (TV) 79. Les Miserables (TV) 80. A Tale of Two Cities (TV) 80. Clash of the Titans 81.

Robson, Mark (1913–78). American director, former editor: began with Lewton and Kramer but progressed to more solidly commercial subjects.
□*The Seventh Victim* 43. The Ghost Ship 43. Youth Runs Wild 44. Isle of the Dead 45. Bedlam 46. *Champion* 49. Home of the Brave 49. Roughshod 49. My Foolish Heart 50. Edge of Doom 50. Bright Victory 51. I Want You 51. Return to Paradise 53. Hell Below Zero (GB) 54. The Bridges at Toko-Ri 54. Phffft 54. A Prize of Gold 55. Trial 55. The

Harder They Fall 56. The Little Hut (& p) 57. Peyton Place 58. The Inn of the Sixth Happiness (GB) 58. From the Terrace (& p) 59. Lisa (The Inspector) (p only) 62. Nine Hours to Rama (GB) (& p) 63. The Prize 63. *Von Ryan's Express* (& p) 65. Lost Command (& p) 66. Valley of the Dolls (& p) 67. Daddy's Gone A-Hunting (& p) 69. Happy Birthday Wanda June 71. Limbo 73. Earthquake 74. Avalanche Express 79.

Robson, May (1858–1942) (Mary Robison). Australian actress, in America from childhood. Long experience on stage tours before coming to Hollywood, where she played domineering but kindly old ladies. □How Molly Made Good 15. Pals in Paris 26. Angel of Broadway 27. Chicago 27. A Harp in Hock 27. King of Kings 27. The Rejuvenation of Aunt Mary 27. Rubber Tires 27. Turkish Delight 27. The Blue Danube 28. Mother's Millions 31. Letty Lynton 32. Strange Interlude 32. Two Against the World 32. Red Headed Woman 32. Little Orphan Annie 32. *If I Had a Million* 32. Reunion in Vienna 33. Dinner at Eight 33. Beauty for Sale 33. Broadway to Hollywood 33. Solitaire Man 33. Dancing Lady 33. *Lady for a Day* 33. One Man's Journey 33. Alice in Wonderland 33. The White Sister 33. Men Must Fight 33. You Can't Buy Everything 34. Straight Is the Way 34. Lady by Choice 34. Vanessa, Her Love Story 35. Reckless 35. Grand Old Girl 35. Age of Indiscretion 35. Anna Karenina 35. Strangers All 35. Mills of the Gods 35. Three Kids and a Queen 36. Wife vs Secretary 36. The Captain's Kid 36. Rainbow on the River 36. Woman in Distress 37. *A Star Is Born* 37. The Perfect Specimen 37. Top of the Town 37. *The Adventures of Tom Sawyer* 38. *Bringing Up Baby* 38. The Texans 38. *Four Daughters* 38. They Made Me a Criminal 39. Yes My Darling Daughter 39. Daughters Courageous 39. Four Wives 39. The Kid from Kokomo 39. Nurse Edith Cavell 39. That's Right You're Wrong 39. Irene 39. The Texas Rangers Ride Again 40. *Granny Get Your Gun* 40. Four Mothers 41. Million Dollar Baby 41. Playmates 42. Joan of Paris 42.

Roc, Patricia (1918–) (Felicia Riese). British leading lady of the forties, signed for films after brief stage experience.
The Rebel Son (Taras Bulba) 38. The Gaunt Stranger 39. The Mind of Mr Reeder 39. Three Silent Men 40. Let the People Sing 42. Millions Like Us 43. 2000 Women 44. Love Story 44. Madonna of the Seven Moons 44. The Wicked Lady 45. Johnny Frenchman 45. Canyon Passage (US) 46. *The Brothers* 47. Jassy 47. When the Bough Breaks 48. One Night with You 48. The Perfect Woman 49. Circle of Danger 50. The Man on the Eiffel Tower 51. Something Money Can't Buy 53. The Hypnotist 55. Bluebeard's Ten Honeymoons 60, etc.

Rocco and His Brothers (Italy 1960). A super-realistic story of a peasant family in the big city, this film by Luchino Visconti was highly acclaimed on its first appearance but seems to have left little mark. Written by Suso Cecchi d'Amico, Vasco Pratolini and Luchino Visconti; photographed by Giuseppe Rotunno.

Roche, Eugene (1928–). American character actor with a slightly bewildered look; much on TV.
They Might Be Giants 71. Newman's Law 74. The Late Show 76. Corvette Summer 78. Foul Play 78. Oh God You Devil 84, etc.

Rock, Joe (1891–1984). American independent producer, in Britain from the mid-thirties.
Krakatoa 33. Everything is Rhythm 36. Edge of the World 38. Cotton Queen 38, etc.

Rocky (US 1976). A minor, vaguely old-fashioned movie about a young boxer's climb to fame was the surprise smash hit of its year, and won Academy Awards for best picture, best direction (John G. Avildsen) and best editing (Richard Halsey). Though pleasant at the time it seems unlikely to endure as a classic, and its new star, Sylvester Stallone, found it difficult to follow up. *Rocky II* came along in 1979, and Rocky III in 1982.

Roddam, Franc (–). British director.
Quadrophenia 79. The Lords of Discipline 82. The Bride 85.

Roddenberry, Gene (1931–). American TV producer of science fiction series *Star Trek* (and of the 1979 film version) and *Galaxy Two*. Wrote and produced *Pretty Maids All in a Row* 70.

Rodgers, Anton (1933–). British comic character actor.
Rotten to the Core 65. Scrooge 70. The Day of the Jackal 73.
TV series: Fresh Fields 83–86.

Rodgers, Richard (1901–1979). American composer who worked variously with lyricists Lorenz Hart and Oscar Hammerstein II.
Love Me Tonight 32. *Hallelujah I'm a Bum*

33. On Your Toes 38. Babes in Arms 39. The Boys from Syracuse 40. *State Fair* 45. *Oklahoma!* 55. *The King and I* 56. *Pal Joey* 57. *South Pacific* 58. *The Sound of Music* 65, many other complete scores and single songs.

Rodrigues, Percy (1924–). Black Canadian character actor.
The Plainsman 67. The Sweet Ride 68. The Heart is a Lonely Hunter 68. Genesis II (TV) 73, etc.

Roeg, Nicolas (1928–). British cinematographer and director.
AS CINEMATOGRAPHER: The System 63. Nothing But the Best 64. The Caretaker 66. Petulia 67. A Funny Thing Happened on the Way to the Forum 68. *Far from the Madding Crowd* 68, etc.
□AS DIRECTOR: Performance (co-d) 72. Walkabout 72. *Don't Look Now* 73. The Man Who Fell to Earth 76. Bad Timing 79. Eureka 83. Insignificance 85. Castaway 87.

Roemheld, Heinz (–1985). German musical director, long in Hollywood.

Rogell, Albert S. (1901–). American director of second features, former cameraman.
Sēnor Daredevil 26. Mamba 30. Riders of Death Valley 32. Argentine Nights 40. Trouble Chaser 40. The Black Cat 41. Tight Shoes 41. In Old Oklahoma 43. Heaven Only Knows 47. Northwest Stampede 48. The Admiral was a Lady (& p) 50. Men against Speed 58, etc.

Rogers, Charles 'Buddy' (1904–). American light leading man of the twenties and thirties; married to Mary Pickford.
Fascinating Youth 26. Wings 27. Abie's Irish Rose 29. Paramount on Parade 30. Varsity 30. Young Eagles 31. This Reckless Age 32. Old Man Rhythm 35. Once in a Million 36. This Way Please 38. Golden Hooves 41. Mexican Spitfire's Baby 43. Don't Trust Your Husband 48, many others.

Rogers, Ginger (1911–) (Virginia McMath). American leading actress, comedienne and dancer, affectionately remembered for her thirties musicals with Fred Astaire. Former band singer; then brief Broadway experience before being taken to Hollywood.
□Young Man of Manhattan 30. Queen High 30. The Sap from Syracuse 30. Follow the Leader 30. Honor among Lovers 31. The Tip Off 31. Suicide Fleet 31. Carnival Boat 32. The Tenderfoot 32. The Thirteenth Guest 32. Hat Check Girl 32. You Said a Mouthful 32. *42nd Street* (as Anytime Annie) 33. Broadway Bad 33. Gold Diggers of 1933 33. Professional Sweetheart 33. A Shriek in the Night 33. Don't Bet on Love 33. Sitting Pretty 33. *Flying Down to Rio* 33. Chance at Heaven 33. Rafter Romance 34. Finishing School 34. Twenty Million Sweethearts 34. Change of Heart 34. Upperworld 34. *The Gay Divorcee* 34. Romance in Manhattan 34. Roberta 35. Star of Midnight 35. *Top Hat* 35. In Person 35. *Follow the Fleet* 36. Swing Time 36. Shall We Dance 36. *Stage Door* 37. Having Wonderful Time 38. Vivacious Lady 38. Carefree 38. The Story of Vernon and Irene Castle 39. *Bachelor Mother* 39. Fifth Avenue Girl 39. The Primrose Path 40. Lucky Partners 40. *Kitty Foyle* (AA) 40. Tom Dick and Harry 41. *Roxie Hart* 42. Tales of Manhattan 42. The Major and the Minor 42. Once Upon a Honeymoon 42. Tender Comrade 43. Lady in the Dark 44. I'll Be Seeing You 44. Weekend at the Waldorf 45. Heartbeat 46. Magnificent Doll 46. It Had to Be You 47. The Barkeleys of Broadway 49. Perfect Strangers 50. Storm Warning 50. The Groom Wore Spurs 51. We're Not Married 52. Monkey Business 52. Dreamboat 52. Forever Female 53. Black Widow 54. Twist of Fate (Beautiful Stranger) 54. Tight Spot 55. The First Travelling Saleslady 56. Teenage Rebel 56. Oh Men Oh Women 57. The Confession 64. Harlow (electronovision) 64.
❀ For being everybody's favourite working girl of the thirties; and for being so unarguably right with Fred Astaire. *The Gay Divorcee.*

¶ He gives her class and she gives him sex.—*Katharine Hepburn of Astaire and Rogers*

G.R. 1983: They're not going to get my money to see the junk that's made today.
Famous line (*Young Man of Manhattan*): Cigarette me, big boy.

Rogers, Jean (1916–) (Eleanor Lovegren). American light leading lady of the thirties.
Eight Girls in a Boat 34. Flash Gordon 36. My Man Godfrey 36. Night Key 37. Flash Gordon's Trip to Mars 38. Hotel for Women 39. Heaven with a Barbed Wire Fence 40. Charlie Chan in Panama 40. Dr Kildare's Victory 42. Whistling in Brooklyn 43. Hot Cargo 46. Backlash 47. The Second Woman 51, etc.

Rogers, Maclean (1899–1962). British director, mainly of low-budget features for

which he often wrote his own unambitious scripts.
The Third Eye 29. Busman's Holiday 36. Old Mother Riley Joins Up 39. Gert and Daisy's Weekend 42. Variety Jubilee 43. The Trojan Brothers 45. Calling Paul Temple 48. The Story of Shirley Yorke 49. Johnny on the Spot 54. Not so Dusty 56. Not Wanted on Voyage 57. Not a Hope in Hell 60, many others.

Rogers, Paul (1917–). British character actor, on stage from 1938, occasional films from 1932.
Beau Brummell 53. Our Man in Havana 59. The Trials of Oscar Wilde 60. No Love for Johnnie 61. Billy Budd 62. Life for Ruth 62. The Prince and the Pauper 62. The Wild and the Willing 63. The Third Secret 64. He Who Rides a Tiger 65. A Midsummer Night's Dream 68. The Looking Glass War 69. Three into Two Won't Go 69. The Reckoning 69. I Want What I Want 72. The Homecoming 73. The Abdication 75. Mr Quilp 75, etc.

Rogers, Peter (1916–). British producer, in films from 1942; wrote and co-produced many comedies during forties and early fifties; conceived and produced the 'Carry On' series (qv)

Rogers, Roy (1912–) (Leonard Slye). American singing cowboy star, usually seen with horse Trigger (1932–65). Varied early experience; formed 'Sons of the Pioneers' singing group; in small film roles from 1935, a star from 1938 till 1953.
Under Western Skies 38. The Carson City Kid 40. Dark Command 40. Robin Hood of the Pecos 42. The Man from Music Mountain 44. Along the Navajo Trail 46. Roll on Texas Moon 47. Night Time in Nevada 49. Trail of Robin Hood 51. Son of Paleface 52. Pals of the Golden West 53. Mackintosh and T.J. 75, etc.
TV series: The Roy Rogers Show 51–56.

¶ When my times comes, just skin me and put me right up there on Trigger, just as though nothing had ever changed.—*R.R.*

Rogers, Wayne (1934–). American light actor, star of TV's M*A*S*H, City of Angels and House Calls.
Once in Paris 78. The Top of the Hill (TV) 80. He's Fired, She's Hired (TV) 84. The Gig 85. The Lady from Yesterday (TV) 85.

Rogers, Will (1879–1935). American rustic comedian, ex-Ziegfeld Follies, whose crackerbarrel philosophy almost moved nations. His home in Los Angeles is the centrepiece of the Will Rogers State Park. Autobiography 1927: *There's Not a Bathing Suit in Russia*. Biography 1953: *Our Will Rogers* by Homer Croy. 1974: *Will Rogers, The Man and His Times* by Richard M. Ketchum. Biopic 1952 (starring his son): *The Story of Will Rogers*.
□Laughing Bill Hyde 18. Almost a Husband 19. Water Water Everywhere 19. *Jubilo* 19. Jes' Call Me Jim 20. The Strange Boarder 20. Scratch My Back 20. A Poor Relation 20. Cupid the Cowpuncher 20. Honest Hutch 20. Guile of Women 21. Boys Will Be Boys 21. An Unwilling Hero 21. Doubling for Romeo 21. One Glorious Day 21. The Headless Horseman 22. The Ropin' Fool 22. One Day in 365 22. Hustling Hank 22. Uncensored Movies 22. Fruits of Faith 22. Just Passing Through 23. Gee Whiz Genevieve 23. Highbrow Stuff 23. Family Fits 23. The Cake Eater 24. Big Moments from Little Pictures 24. Don't Park There 24. The Cowboy Sheik 24. Going to Congress 24. Our Congressman 24. A Truthful Liar 24. Two Wagons 24. A Texas Steer 27. Tiptoes 27. They Had to See Paris 29. Happy Days 30. So This is London 30. Lightnin' 30. A Connecticut Yankee 31. Young as You Feel 31. Ambassador Bill 31. Business and Pleasure 32. Too Busy to Work 32. *State Fair* 33. Doctor Bull 33. Mister Skitch 33. *David Harum* 34. *Handy Andy* 34. *Judge Priest* 34. County Chairman 35. *Life Begins at Forty* 35. Doubting Thomas 35. In Old Kentucky 35. *Steamboat round the Bend* 35.
❀ For establishing the wisdom of the common man. *Judge Priest*.
† When he was killed, Rogers had signed to play Dr Dafoe, who delivered the Dionne Quins, in *The Country Doctor*.

¶ *W.R.:* There's only one thing that can kill the movies, and that's education.
W.R.: When you put down the good things you ought to have done, and leave out the bad things you did do—that's Memoirs.

Rogosin, Lionel (1924–). American documentarist.
On the Bowery 56. *Come Back Africa* 59. Good Times Wonderful Times 66. Black Roots 70. Woodcutters of the Deep South 73, etc.

Rohmer, Eric (1920–) (Jean Maurice Scherer). French director of rarefied conversation pieces.
Le Signe du Lion 59. La Boulangère de Monceau 63. La Carrière de Suzanne 64. La Collectioneuse 67. Ma Nuit chez Maude 69.

Le Genou de Claire 70. Love in the Afternoon 72. The Marquise of O 76. Perceval 78. The Aviator's Wife 81. Pauline at the Beach 83. Full Moon in Paris 84. Summer 86, etc.

Rohmer, Sax (1886–1959) (Arthur Sarsfield Ward). British novelist, the creator of the much filmed Dr Fu Manchu.

Roizman, Owen (–). American cinematographer.
The French Connection 71. Play It Again Sam 72. The Exorcist 73. The Taking of Pelham One Two Three 74. The Stepford Wives 75. Straight Time 78. The Electric Horseman 79. The Black Marble 80. True Confessions 81. Absence of Malice 81. Taps 81. Tootsie 82. Vision Quest 85.

Roland, Gilbert (1905–) (Luis Antonio Damaso De Alonso). Mexican leading man, trained as bullfighter, who gatecrashed Hollywood in the mid-twenties and became immediately popular.
The Plastic Age (debut) 25. Camille 27. Men of the North 29. Call Her Savage 32. *She Done Him Wrong* 33. Last Train from Madrid 37. Juarez 39. The Sea Hawk 40. My Life with Caroline 41. Isle of Missing Men 42. Captain Kidd 45. Pirates of Monterey 47. Riding the California Trail 48. *We Were Strangers* 49. The Furies 50. The Bullfighter and the Lady 51. The Bad and the Beautiful 52. Beyond the Twelve Mile Reef 53. The Racers 54. Treasure of Pancho Villa 56. Guns of the Timberland 58. The Big Circus 59. Cheyenne Autumn 64. The Reward 65. The Poppy is also a Flower (TV) 66. Johnny Hamlet 72. Running Wild 73. Islands in the Stream 77. The Black Pearl 77, many others.

Roland, Ruth (1893–1937). American leading lady, a silent serial queen.
The Red Circle 15. The Neglected Wife 17. Hands Up 18. Tiger's Trail 19, etc.
FEATURES: While Father Telephoned 13. The Masked Woman 26. Reno 30. From Nine to Nine 36, many others.

Rolfe, Guy (1915–). Lean British leading man and character actor, former racing driver and boxer.
Hungry Hill (debut) 46. Nicholas Nickleby 47. Uncle Silas 47. Broken Journey 47. Portrait from Life 49. *The Spider and the Fly* 50. Prelude to Fame 51. Ivanhoe 52. King of the Khyber Rifles 54. It's Never Too Late 56. Snow White and the Three Stooges 62. Taras Bulba 62. Mr Sardonicus 62. The Fall of the Roman Empire 64. The Alphabet Murders 65. The Land Raiders 69. Nicholas and Alexandra 71. And Now the Screaming Starts 73, etc.

Rollins, Howard Jnr (1951–). Black American leading actor.
Ragtime (AAN) 81. A Soldier's Story 84.

Romain, Yvonne (1938–) (Yvonne Warren). British leading lady.
The Baby and the Battleship 56. Seven Thunders 57. Corridors of Blood 58. Chamber of Horrors 60. Curse of the Werewolf 61. Village of Daughters 61. Devil Doll 63. The Brigand of Kandahar 65. The Swinger (US) 66. Double Trouble (US) 67. The Last of Sheila 73, etc.

Roman, Leticia (1939–). American leading lady of the sixties.
Pirates of Tortuga 61. Gold of the Seven Saints 61. The Evil Eye (It.) 62. Fanny Hill 64, etc.

Roman, Ruth (1924–). American actress; leading lady of the fifties, then a plumpish character player.
Ladies Courageous 44. Jungle Queen 45. You Came Along 45. A Night in Casablanca 45. The Big Clock 48. Good Sam 48. *The Window* 49. Champion 49. Barricade 50. Three Secrets 50. Lightning Strikes Twice 51. *Strangers On a Train* 51. Maru Maru 52. Blowing Wild 53. Down Three Dark Streets 54. The Far Country 55. Joe Macbeth 56. Five Steps to Danger 57. Bitter Victory 58. Desert Desperadoes 59. Look in Any Window 61. Love Has Many Faces 65. The Baby 72. Go Ask Alice (TV) 73. Day of the Animals 77, etc.
TV series: *The Long Hot Summer* 65.

Romance, Vivianne (1912–) (Pauline Ortmans). French leading lady of the thirties and forties.
La Belle Equipe 35. Gibraltar 37. The White Slave 38. Blind Venus 39. Box of Dreams 39. Carmen 42. Panique 46. Maya 50. Flesh and Desire 53. Pleasures and Vices 56. Melodie en Sous-Sol 63, etc.

romance I

? Can you name the romantic actors who spoke these lines, and the films in which they did so?

1 I cannot live without my life . . . I cannot love without my soul . . .

2 This Tartar woman is for me—and my blood says 'take her'.
3 Ah me, brown eyes!
4 I'm asking you to marry me, you little fool.
5 Come with me to the Casbah . . .
6 Frankly, my dear, I don't give a damn.
7 Your idea of fidelity is not having more than one man in bed at the same time.
8 It must be a wonderful supper. We may not eat it, but it must be wonderful. And waiter, you see that moon? I want to see that moon in the champagne . . .

And what ladies took the initiative in these terms?

9 The arrangement of the features of your face is not entirely repulsive to me.
10 I wouldn't take you if you were covered in diamonds—upside down!
11 Call me sausage . . .
12 If you want anything, just whistle . . .
13 Oh Jerry, don't let's ask for the moon. We have the stars . . .
14 It's even better when you help.
15 I never dreamed that any mere physical experience could be so stimulating . . .

romance II

? Real instead of assumed names have been used below. Give the stars and the film.

1 Ira Grossel and Ella Geisman were directed by a German in this forgettable piece which also featured Mary Astor.
2 Ruby Stevens and Issur Danielovitch Demsky appeared in this murderous saga which began with the violent end of the heroine's aunt.
3 Maria Magdalena Von Losch meets Reginald Truscott-Jones in a saga of European wanderings.
4 Virginia Katherine McMath and Archibald Leach find fun and romance while eluding the Nazis.
5 Tula Finklea and Frederick Austerlitz in a tale of Russian-American understanding.
6 Jane Peters and Benny Kubelsky in a black comedy about Europe under Nazi rule.
7 Constance Keane and Frederick McIntyre Bickel in a ghost story with the gallic touch.
8 Edythe Marrener was actually the victim of Reginald Carey in this wordy, sometimes witty updating of a seventeenth-century play.
9 Spangler Arlington Brough and Harlean Carpenter in a light comedy about a bailiff in the house.
10 Lucille La Sueur and Jules Garfinkel in a tragic musical romance from a novel by Fannie Hurst.
11 Claire Weinlinger and Marion Michael Morison find romance in the old west.
12 Gladys Greene and Frank Cooper in a story originally called *Opera Hat*.
13 Sarah Jane Fulks and Roy Scherer in a twice-filmed novel by Lloyd C. Douglas.
14 James Stewart and Margarita Carmen Cansino in a story from the Old Testament.

Romanoff, Mike (1890–1972) (Harry Gerguson). Amiable American con man who posed as a Russian prince (but 'renounced' his title in 1958). Best known as proprietor of Hollywood's most famous and expensive restaurant. Played occasional bit parts. Arch of Triumph 48. Do Not Disturb 65. Tony Rome 67, etc.

¶ No one has ever discovered the truth about me—not even myself.—*M.R.*

'A rogue of uncertain nationality.'—*Scotland Yard*

romantic teams who have been popular enough to make several films together are headed by William Powell and Myrna Loy, who made 12 joint appearances. Runners-up include Janet Gaynor and Charles Farrell (11 appearances); Dick Powell and Joan Blondell (10); Fred Astaire and Ginger Rogers (10); Spencer Tracy and Katharine Hepburn (9); Richard Burton and Elizabeth Taylor (9); Judy Garland and Mickey Rooney (8); Clark Gable and Joan Crawford (8); Nelson Eddy and Jeanette Macdonald (8); Greer Garson and Walter Pidgeon (8); Errol Flynn and Olivia de Havilland (8); Bette Davis and George Brent (7); Clark Gable and Jean Harlow (6); James Cagney and Joan Blondell (6). Even though most of these teamings began because both stars happened to be under contract to the same studio, they would not have continued had they not been felicitous. Other teams who struck notable sparks off each other but have fewer films to their credit include Humphrey Bogart and Lauren Bacall; Ronald Colman and Greer Garson; Cary Grant and Irene Dunne; Greta Garbo and John Gilbert; Greta Garbo and Melvyn Douglas; Bob Hope and Paulette Goddard; Danny Kaye and Virginia Mayo; Alan Ladd and Veronica Lake; Donald O'Connor and Peggy Ryan; Marie Dressler and Wallace Beery; Rita Hayworth and Glenn Ford; John Barrymore and Carole Lombard; Charlie Ruggles and Mary Boland; Rock

Hudson and Doris Day; Jack Hulbert and Cicely Courtneidge; John Payne and Betty Grable; James Dunn and Sally Eilers; David Niven and Loretta Young; Van Johnson and June Allyson; Louis Hayward and Patricia Medina; Bob Hope and Dorothy Lamour; John Wayne and Maureen O'Hara.

Romberg, Sigmund (1887–1951). Hungarian composer of light music. Scores include *The Desert Song* 29 and 43, *New Moon* 31 and 40, *Maytime* 37, *Balalaika* 39, *The Student Prince* 54. (Most of these began as stage operettas.) José Ferrer played him in a biopic, *Deep in My Heart* 54.

Rome in its ancient days was reconstructed for *Quo Vadis, The Sign of the Cross, Ben Hur, The Last Days of Pompeii, Androcles and the Lion, The Fall of the Roman Empire, The Robe, I Claudius, Julius Caesar, Cleopatra* and *Spartacus*. The funny side of its life was depicted in *Roman Scandals, Fiddlers Three, Carry On Cleo, Scandal in the Roman Bath* and *A Funny Thing Happened on the Way to the Forum*. Modern Rome has been seen hundreds of times in Italian movies, notably *Bicycle Thieves, Paisà, La Dolce Vita, The Girls of the Spanish Steps, Sunday in August, Rome Eleven o'Clock* and the American co-production *Indiscretion* which was shot entirely within Rome's railway station. American views of Rome include *Three Coins in the Fountain, Seven Hills of Rome, Roman Holiday, Two Weeks in Another Town, The Pigeon That Took Rome* and *The Roman Spring of Mrs Stone;* while the Colosseum was used for the finale of films as various as *House of Cards* and *Twenty Million Miles to Earth*. The Vatican was well shown in *Never Take No for an Answer*, about the small boy who persists in getting an audience with the Pope.

Rome Express. A British train thriller directed by Walter Forde in 1933, starring Conrad Veidt; John Paddy Carstairs remade it in 1948, almost word for word and scene for scene, starring Albert Lieven, as *Sleeping Car to Trieste*. Finlay Currie played the same supporting role in both versions.

Rome, Stewart (1887–1965) (Septimus William Ryott). British stage matinée idol who made several romantic films in the twenties and later appeared in character roles.
The Prodigal Son 25. Sweet Lavender 26. The Gentleman Rider 27. Thou Fool 28. Dark Red Roses 29. The Man Who Changed His Name 30. Designing Women 33. Men of Yesterday 34. Wings of the Morning 37. Banana Ridge 41. The White Unicorn 47. Woman Hater 48, etc.

Romeo and Juliet. Apart from the numerous silent versions of Shakespeare's play, and the ballet adaptations, there have been three major straight versions since sound. In 1936 George Cukor directed Leslie Howard and Norma Shearer in a lavish studio-bound semi-pop version for MGM; in 1953 Renato Castellani came to Britain and made for Rank a more sober, but duller film in colour, with Laurence Harvey and Susan Shentall; and in 1968 came Franco Zeffirelli's version with Leonard Whiting and Olivia Hussey. (This won Oscars for Pasqualina de Santis' cinematography and Danilo Donati's costumes.) In the late 1940s, a French *film noir, Les Amants de Verone*, transposed the story to a modern setting. The musical *West Side Story* 61, is a violent modernization of Shakespeare's tale, and *Romanoff and Juliet* a satirical rendering.

Romero, Cesar (1907–). Handsome Latin-American leading man, former dancer and Broadway actor. Also on TV.
The Thin Man 34. Metropolitan 35. Wee Willie Winkie 37. The Return of the Cisco Kid (and others in this series) 39. The Gay Caballero 40. Weekend in Havana 41. Tales of Manhattan 42. Orchestra Wives 42. Coney Island 43. Carnival in Costa Rica 47. That Lady in Ermine 48. Happy Go Lovely 51. Prisoners of the Casbah 53. Vera Cruz 54. The Racers 55. The Leather Saint 56. Villa 58. Two on a Guillotine 64. Marriage on the Rocks 65. Batman 66. Hot Millions 68. Crooks and Coronets (GB) 69. The Midas Run (GB) 69. A Talent for Loving 69. Now You See Him Now You Don't 72 The Strongest Man in the World 74, etc.
TV series: Passport to Danger 56. *Batman* (as the Joker) 65–67.

Romero, George (1939–). American director of exploitation pictures.
Night of the Living Dead 68. The Crazies 73. Hungry Wives 73. Zombies 78. Martin 79. Knightriders 81. Creepshow 82. Day of the Dead 85, etc.

¶ *G.R.:* Just because I'm showing somebody being disembowelled doesn't mean I have to get heavy and put a message round it.

Romm, Mikhail (1901–1971). Russian director.
Boule de Suif 34. *Lenin in October* 37. Lenin in 1918 39. The Russian Question 48. Nine Days of One Year 61. Ordinary Fascism 64, etc.

Rommel, Field Marshal Erwin (1891–1944). German soldier, a worthy adversary for the Eighth Army in World War II. He killed himself in 1944 after being accused of complicity in the plot against Hitler. In films he was melodramatically impersonated by Erich Von Stroheim in 1943 in *Five Graves to Cairo*, and more soberly in 1951 by James Mason in *The Desert Fox* (also in 1953 in *The Desert Rats*). Other minor portrayals were by Albert Lieven in *Foxhole in Cairo*, by Gregory Gaye in *Hitler*, by Werner Hinz in *The Longest Day*, by Christopher Plummer in *The Night of the Generals*, by Karl Michael Vogler in *Patton*, and by Wolfgang Preiss in *Raid on Rommel*.

Romney, Edana (1919–) (E. Rubenstein). South African-born leading lady, in three British films of the forties.
□East of Piccadilly 41. Alibi 42. Corridor of Mirrors 48.

La Ronde. There had been earlier continental films of Arthur Schnitzler's *Reigen*, a light play about love's merry-go-round; but Max Ophuls' 1950 French version was so piquantly presented by a highly sophisticated cast that it seemed to expand suddenly the possibilities of sex comedy on British and American screens. Previously this sort of thing had always been left to the French, but *La Ronde* was so internationally popular that everyone wanted to get in on the act. Jacques Natanson and Ophuls wrote the screenplay. Christian Matras was photographer, Oscar Straus wrote the music, and the top-flight cast included Anton Walbrook, Jean-Louis Barrault, Danielle Darrieux, Simone Signoret, Daniel Gelin, Simone Simon, Fernand Gravet and Gerard Philipe. Roger Vadim's 1964 remake, with colour but less interesting performers, substituted sensation for subtlety.

Ronet, Maurice (1927–1983). French leading man.
Rendezvous de Juillet 49. La Sorcière 56. He Who Must Die 56. Lift to the Scaffold 47. Carve Her Name with Pride (GB) 58. Plein Soleil 59. Rendezvous de Minuit 61. *Le Feu Follet* 63. Enough Rope 63. The Victors 63. La Ronde 64. Three Weeks in Manhattan 65. Lost Command 66. The Champagne Murders (La Scandale) 67. The Road to Corinth 68. How Sweet It Is (US) 68. L'Infidèle 69. Qui? 73. The Marseilles Contract 74. Bloodline 79. La Balance 83, etc.

Rookery Nook (GB 1930). Although this early talkie was a straight transference of the popular Aldwych farce, directed by Tom Walls as though the camera were in the front row of the stalls, it admirably preserves Ben Travers' very clever dialogue and stage business along with the best performances of a classic team of farceurs: Walls with a perpetually roving eye, Ralph Lynn dropping his monocle at every untoward event, Robertson Hare moaning calamitously and losing his trousers, Mary Brough sniffing suspiciously, and whoever played Poppy Dickey selling flags for the lifeboat in her cami-knickers. No later farce was ever quite so hilariously well-judged.

Rooks, Conrad (–). American experimental director.
□Chappaqua 66. Siddhartha 72.

Room, Abram (1894–1976). Russian director, former journalist, with stage experience.
In Pursuit of Moonshine 24. The Haven of Death 26. Bed and Sofa 27. The Ghost that Never Returns 29. The Five Year Plan 30. Invasion 44. Silver Dust 53, etc.

Room at the Top (GB 1959). This raw version of John Braine's novel about a young man's burning ambition to get to the top in a northern town was significant on several counts. It was franker about sex than any previous British movie. It introduced a new directorial talent in Jack Clayton. And it was the spearhead of a new and successful drive to get British films a wider showing in the US. Simone Signoret was imported from France to put the sex over, and won an Academy Award; so did Neil Paterson who wrote the screenplay. *Room at the Top* was logically followed by an overdose of equally raw films about British provincial life: *Saturday Night and Sunday Morning* 60, *A Taste of Honey* 62, *The Leather Boys* 63, etc.; also by its own sequel *Life at the Top* 65, showing what happened to the same characters ten years after. A later TV series, *Man at the Top*, spawned a third film about the character in 1973.

Room Service (US 1938). This George Abbott farce about a theatrical troupe stranded without cash in a smart hotel made too restricted a vehicle for the Marx Brothers but permitted a splendid comedy performance from Donald McBride as the frantic manager. William Seiter directed. It was remade in 1944 by Tim Whelan as a musical, *Step Lively*, with Frank Sinatra and George Murphy.

Rooney, Mickey (1920–) (Joe Yule Jnr). Diminutive, aggressively talented American performer, on stage from the age of two (in parents' vaudeville act). In films from 1926 (short comedies) as Mickey McGuire, then returned to vaudeville; came back as Mickey Rooney in 1932.
Autobiography 1965: *I.E.*
My Pal the King 32. The Hide-Out 34. *A Midsummer Night's Dream* (as Puck) 35. *Ah Wilderness* 35. Little Lord Fauntleroy (not in title role) 36. Captains Courageous 37. *A Family Affair* (as Andy Hardy) 37. *Judge Hardy's Children* 38. Love Finds Andy Hardy 38. *Boys' Town* (special AA) 38. The Adventures of Huckleberry Finn 39. *Babes in Arms* 39. Young Tom Edison 40. Strike Up the Band 40. Men of Boys' Town 41. Babes on Broadway 41. A Yank at Eton 42. Andy Hardy's Double Life 42. *The Human Comedy* 43. Girl Crazy 43. Andy Hardy's Blonde Trouble 44. National Velvet 44. Love Laughs at Andy Hardy 46. Summer Holiday 47. The Fireball 50. A Slight Case of Larceny 53. *The Bold and the Brave* 56. Andy Hardy Comes Home 58. Baby Face Nelson 58. The Big Operator 59. Breakfast at Tiffany's 61. It's a Mad Mad Mad Mad World 63. Twenty-Four Hours to Kill 65. Ambush Bay 66. The Extraordinary Seaman 68. Skidoo 68. The Comic 69. Pulp 73. The Domino Principle 77. Pete's Dragon 77. The Magic of Lassie 78. Arabian Adventure 79. The Black Stallion 79. *Leave 'Em Laughing* (TV) 80. *Bill* (TV) 81. The Fox and the Hound (voice) 81, others.
TV series: The Mickey Rooney Show (Hey Mulligan) 54. Mickey 64. One of the Boys 81, etc.
†Rooney was given an honorary Academy Award in 1983, for 50 years of versatility in a variety of memorable film performances'.
❀ For never being counted out. *Babes in Arms*.

¶ I was a fourteen-year-old boy for thirty years.—*M.R.*

I've been through four publics. I've been coming back like a rubber ball for years.—*M.R.*

I just want to be a professional. I couldn't live without acting.—*M.R.*

There may be a little snow on the mountain, but there's a lot of fire in the furnace.—*M.R.*

All the muddy waters of my life cleared up when I gave myself to Christ.—*M.R.*

'His favourite exercise is climbing tall people.'—*Phyllis Diller*

Roosevelt, Franklin Delano (1882–1945). American president 1933–45, exponent of the 'New Deal'. He was played by Ralph Bellamy in Dore Schary's play and film of his life, *Sunrise at Campobello* 60, by Capt. Jack Young in *Yankee Doodle Dandy* and by Godfrey Tearle in *The Beginning of the End*. In TV's *Eleanor and Franklin* (1976) he was played by Edward Herrmann, and in *Ike* (1979) by Stephen Roberts.

Roosevelt, Theodore (Teddy) (1858–1919). American president 1901–1909. His extrovert personality and cheerful bullish manners have been captured several times on screen, notably by John Alexander in *Arsenic and Old Lace* (a parody) and *Fancy Pants*, by Wallis Clark in *Yankee Doodle Dandy*, by John Merton in *I Wonder Who's Kissing Her Now*; by Sidney Blackmer in *My Girl Tisa, This is My Affair* and *Buffalo Bill*; and by Brian Keith in *The Wind and the Lion*.
In *The Private Files of J. Edgar Hoover* (1978) it was Howard da Silva's turn; Ralph Bellamy had a revised go in *The Winds of War* (1982), and Edward Herrmann again in *Annie* (1982).

Rope (US 1948). The first film from Transatlantic Pictures, the Alfred Hitchcock-Sidney Bernstein company, showed Hitchcock trying out a new trick: confining the action to one continuous take by using a constantly roving camera and passing something black at reel changes. Patrick Hamilton's suspenseful one-room play about a body in a chest was as suitable for the method as anything ever would be, but the 'ten-minute take' was in fact the negation of cinema and even took away the play's theatrical impact by incessant bewildering movement. It was never tried again. The photographers were Joseph Valentine and William V. Skall.

Roquevert, Noel (1894–1973) (N. Benevent). French character actor, usually as mean-spirited bourgeois.
The Three Must-Get-Theres 22. Cartouche 34. Entrée des Artistes 38. Les Inconnus dans la Maison 42. Le Corbeau 43. Antoine et Antoinette 47. Justice Est Faite 50. Fanfan la Tulipe 52. Les Compagnes de la Nuit 53. The Sheep Has Five Legs 54. Marie Octobre 59. A Monkey in Winter 62, many others.

Rosay, Françoise (1891–1974) (Françoise de Naleche). Distinguished French actress in films from the mid-twenties.
Autobiography 1974: *La Traversée d'une Vie*.
Gribiche 25. *Le Grand Jeu* 33. *La Kermesse Héroïque* 35. Jenny 36. *Un Carnet de Bal* 37. Les Gens du Voyage 38. *Une Femme Disparait* 41. Johnny Frenchman (GB) 45. Macadam 46. September Affair 50. *The Red Inn* 51. The Thirteenth Letter (US) 51. That Lady (GB) 54. The Seventh Sin (US) 57. Le Joueur 58. The Sound and the Fury (US) 58. The Full Treatment (GB) 60. Up from the Beach (US) 65. Le Pietou 72, etc.

Rose, Billy (1899–1966). American nightclub owner and songwriter, husband of Fanny Brice. He was played in *Funny Lady* by James Caan.
Biography 1968: *Manhattan Primitive* by Earl Rogers.

Rose, David (1910–). British-born composer, long in US.
Winged Victory 44. Texas Carnival 51. Jupiter's Darling 54, many others. For TV, composed the *Bonanza* theme.

Rose, David E. (1895–). American producer, in films from 1930, long in charge of United Artists productions. More recently in Britain.
The End of the Affair 55. The Safecracker 58. The House of the Seven Hawks 59, etc.

Rose, George (1920–). British stage and screen character actor.
Pickwick Papers 52. Grand National Night 53. The Sea Shall Not Have Them 54. The Night My Number Came Up 56. Brothers in Law 57. A Night to Remember 58. Jack the Ripper 59. The Devil's Disciple 59. Jet Storm 59. The Flesh and the Fiends 60. Hamlet 64. Hawaii (US) 66. The Pink Jungle 69. A New Leaf 71. Holocaust (TV) 78. The Pirates of Penzance 83, etc.

Rose, Helen (1904–85). American costume designer. With Twentieth Century Fox from 1941, MGM from 1943, Academy Awards: *The Bad and the Beautiful* 53, *I'll Cry Tomorrow* 58.

Rose, Jack; see *Shavelson, Melville*.

Rose Marie. The Rudolph Friml/Oscar Hammerstein operetta about the mounties getting their man was first filmed in 1928 by Lucien Hubbard as a silent: Joan Crawford had the title role. In 1936 W. S. Van Dyke made the well-remembered version with Jeanette MacDonald and Nelson Eddy, and in 1954 Mervyn le Roy directed a remake with Ann Blyth and Howard Keel.

Rose, Reginald (1921–). American writer who has created numerous TV plays, also a series, *The Defenders*.
Crime in the Streets 56. *Twelve Angry Men* 57. The Man in the Net 58. Man of the West 58. The Wild Geese 78. Somebody Killed Her Husband 78. The Sea Wolves 80. Who Dares Wins 82. Wild Geese II 85, etc.

Rose, William (1918–87). American screenwriter who spent some years in Britain.
Once a Jolly Swagman (co-w) 48. The Gift Horse 51. I'll Get You For This 52. *Genevieve* 53. *The Maggie* 54. The Lady Killers 55. Touch and Go 55. Man in the Sky 56. The Smallest Show on Earth 57. *It's a Mad Mad Mad Mad World* 63. The Russians are Coming, The Russians are Coming 66. The Flim Flam Man 67. *Guess Who's Coming to Dinner* (AA) 67. The Secret of Santa Vittoria 69, etc.

Rosen, Phil (1888–1951). Russian-born American director of second features.
The Single Sin 21. The Young Rajah 22. Abraham Lincoln 25. Burning Up Broadway 28. Two-Gun Man 31. Beggars in Ermine 34. Two Wise Maids 37. Double Alibi 40. Forgotten Girls 40. Spooks Run Wild 41. Prison Mutiny 43. Step by Step 46. The Secret of St Ives 49, many others.

Rosenberg, Aaron (1912–1979). American producer, in Hollywood from 1934; working for Universal from 1946.
Johnny Stool Pigeon 47. Winchester 73 50. The Glenn Miller Story 54. To Hell and Back 55. The Great Man 57. Morituri 65. The Reward 65. Tony Rome 67, many others.

Rosenberg, Stuart (1925–). American director with long TV experience.
□Murder Inc. 60. Question 7 61. Fame is the Name of the Game (TV) 66. Asylum for a Spy (TV) 67. *Cool Hand Luke* 67. The April Fools 69. Move 70. W.U.S.A. 70. Pocket Money 72. The Laughing Policeman 73. The Drowning Pool 75. Voyage of the Damned 76. Love and Bullets 78. The Amityville Horror 79. Brubaker 80. The Pope of Greenwich Village 84.

Rosenbloom, 'Slapsie' Maxie (1906–1976). American 'roughneck' comedian, ex-boxer, in occasional comedy films as gangster or punch drunk type.

Mr Broadway 33. Nothing Sacred 37. Louisiana Purchase 41. Hazard 48. Mr Universe 51. Abbott and Costello Meet the Keystone Kops 55. The Beat Generation 59, etc.

Rosenblum, Ralph (1925–). American editor.
Mad Dog Coll 61. *Fail Safe* 64. The Pawnbroker 65. The Group 66. The Night They Raided Minsky's 67. Goodbye Columbus 69. Bananas 71. Sleeper 73. Love and Death 75. *Annie Hall* 77, etc.

Rosenman, Leonard (1924–). American composer.
The Cobweb 55. East of Eden 55. Rebel Without a Cause 55. Lafayette Escadrille 58. The Chapman Report 62. Fantastic Voyage 66. Hellfighters 68. Beneath the Planet of the Apes 71. Phantom of Hollywood (TV) 74. Race with the Devil 75. *Barry Lyndon* (AA as md) 75. Bound for Glory (AA as md) 76. The Car 77. Lord of the Rings 78. Promises in the Dark 79. Hide in Plain Sight 80. Cross Creek (AAN) 83, etc.

Rosenthal, Jack (1931–). British scriptwriter, mainly for television, in which medium he has won many awards. Films include *The Lovers* 72, *The Chain* 85.

Rosher, Charles (1885–1974). Distinguished American cinematographer.
The Clown 16. The Love Night 20. Smilin' Through 22. *Sparrows* 26. *Sunrise* (AA) 27. *Tempest* 28. What Price Hollywood? 32. Our Betters 33. The Affairs of Cellini 34. Little Lord Fauntleroy 36. White Banners 38. A Child Is Born 40. Kismet 44. *The Yearling* (co-ph) (AA) 46. *Show Boat* 51. Scaramouche 52. Kiss Me Kate 53. Young Bess 54, many others.

Rosher, Charles Jnr (–). American cinematographer.
Pretty Maids All in a Row 71. Semi Tough 77. Three Women 77. A Wedding 78. The Muppet Movie 79. The Onion Field 79. Heartbeeps 81.

Rosi, Francesco (1922–). Italian director.
La Sfida 57. Salvatore Giuliano (& w) 61. Hands over the City 63. The Moment of Truth 64. More than a Miracle 68. Three Brothers (& w) 82. Christ Stopped at Eboli 82, etc.

Rosmer, Milton (1881–1971) (Arthur Milton Lunt). British stage actor, in many films from 1913.
General John Regan 21. The Passionate Friends 22. The Phantom Light 35. South Riding 38. Goodbye Mr Chips 39. Atlantic Ferry 41. Fame is the Spur 47. The Monkey's Paw 48. The Small Back Room 49, etc.
AS DIRECTOR: Dreyfus 31. Channel Crossing 32. The Guvnor 36. The Challenge 37.

Ross, Diana (1944–). Black American singer and actress.
□*Lady Sings the Blues* (as Billie Holiday) 72. Mahogany 76. The Wiz 78.

Ross, Frank (1904–). American producer, in Hollywood from early thirties.
Of Mice and Men (associate) 39. The Devil and Miss Jones 41. The Robe 53. The Rains of Ranchipur 55. Kings Go Forth 58. Mister Moses 65. Where It's At 70, others.

Ross, Herbert (1927–). American choreographer.
Doctor Dolittle 67. Funny Girl 69, etc.
□AS DIRECTOR: Goodbye Mr Chips 69. The Owl and the Pussycat 70. T. R. Baskin 71. Play It Again Sam 72. The Last of Sheila (& p) 73. Funny Lady 75. The Sunshine Boys 75. The Seven Per Cent Solution 76. The Turning Point 77. The Goodbye Girl 77. Nijinsky 80. Pennies from Heaven 81. I Ought to Be in Pictures 82. Max Dugan Returns 83. Flashdance 83. Footloose 84. Protocol 84.

Ross, Joe E. (1905–1982). Short, fat American comedian with a frazzled manner, mostly on TV.
TV series: Bilko 56–59. Car 54 Where Are You 61–62. It's About Time 64.

Ross, Katharine (1942–). American leading lady.
□Shenandoah 65. Mr Buddwing 66. The Longest Hundred Miles (TV) 66. The Singing Nun 66. Games 67. *The Graduate* 67. Hellfighters 68. Tell Them Willie Boy is Here 69. Butch Cassidy and the Sundance Kid 69. Fools 70. Get to Know Your Rabbit 72. They Only Kill Their Masters 72. Le Hasard et la Violence 74. The Stepford Wives 75. Voyage of the Damned 76. Wanted, the Sundance Woman (TV) 77. The Legacy 78. The Betsy 78. The Swarm 78. Murder by Natural Causes (TV) 79. The Final Countdown 80. Murder in Texas (TV) 81. Wrong Is Right 82. The Shadow Riders (TV) 82. Travis McGee (TV) 82.

Ross, Lillian (1926–). American journalist who wrote *Picture*, a fascinating account of the production of *The Red Badge of Courage*.

Ross, Shirley (1909–1975) (Bernice Gaunt). American pianist and singer who appeared as leading lady in a few films.
The Age of Indiscretion 35. San Francisco 36. *Thanks for the Memory* 38. Paris Honeymoon 39. Kisses for Breakfast 41. A Song for Miss Julie 45, etc.

Rossellini, Roberto (1906–77). Italian director, in films from 1938. Started as writer; co-scripted his own films.
Open City 45. *Paisa* 46. Germany Year Zero 48. Stromboli 49. Europa 51. General Della Rovere 59. Louis XIV Seizes Power 66. Il Messia 76, others.

Rossellini, Isabella (1952–). Italian actress, daughter of Ingrid Bergman.
White Nights 85. Blue Velvet 86. Tough Guys Don't Dance 87.

Rossen, Robert (1908–1966). American writer-producer-director, in Hollywood from 1936 after stage experience.
□Marked Woman (w) 37. They Won't Forget (w) 37. Racket Busters (w) 38. Dust be My Destiny (w) 39. *The Roaring Twenties* (w) 39. A Child is Born (w) 39. The Sea Wolf (w) 41. Out of the Fog (w) 41. Blues in the Night (w) 41. Edge of Darkness (w) 42. *A Walk in the Sun* (w) 45. The Strange Love of Martha Ivers (w) 46. Desert Fury (w) 47. Johnny O'Clock (wd) 47. *Body and Soul* (d) 47. Treasure of the Sierra Madre (co-w, uncredited) 47. *All the King's Men* (wpd) (AA) 49. The Brave Bulls (pd) 50. Mambo (wd) 54. Alexander the Great (wpd) 56. Island in the Sun (d) 57. They Came to Cordura (wd) 59. *The Hustler* (wpd) 61. Billy Budd (co-w) 62. Lilith (wpd) 64.

'In retrospect, the dreariness of his direction is remarkably consistent.'—*Andrew Sarris, 1968*

Rossi, Franco (1919–). Italian writer-director.
I Falsari 52. Il Seduttore 54. *Amici per la Pelle* (Friends for Life) 55. Morte di un Amico 60. Smog 62, etc.

Rossi-Drago, Eleonora (1925–) (Palmina Omiccioli). Italian leading lady.
Pirates of Capri 48. Persiane Chiuse 50. Three Forbidden Stories 51. The White Slave 53. Le Amiche 55. Maledetto Imbroglio 59. David and Goliath 59. Under Ten Flags 60. Uncle Tom's Cabin (Ger.) 65. Camille 2000 69, etc.

Rossif, Frederic (1922–). French documentarist.
Les Temps du Ghetto 61. Mourir à Madrid 62. The Fall of Berlin 65, etc.

Rossington, Norman (1928–). British character actor of stage, TV and films.
A Night to Remember 58. Carry On Sergeant 58. *Saturday Night and Sunday Morning* 60. Go to Blazes 62. The Comedy Man 63. A Hard Day's Night 64. Tobruk (US) 66. The Charge of the Light Brigade 68. The Adventures of Gerard 70. Deathline 72. Go for a Take 72, etc.

Rossiter, Leonard (1926–84). British comic actor.
Billy Liar 62. King Rat 65. Hotel Paradiso 66. The Wrong Box 66. The Whisperers 67. 2001: A Space Odyssey 68. Oliver 68. Otley 69. Barry Lyndon 75. The Pink Panther Strikes Again 77. Rising Damp 79. Britannia Hospital 82. Trail of the Pink Panther 82, etc.
TV series: Rising Damp 77–80. The Fall and Rise of Reginald Perrin 78–80. Tripper's Day 83.

Rosson, Hal or **Harold** (1895–1960). Distinguished British-born cinematographer.
The Cinema Murder 19. Manhandled 24. Gentlemen Prefer Blondes 28. *Tarzan of the Apes* 32. *The Scarlet Pimpernel* 35. The Ghost Goes West 36. The Garden of Allah (AA) 36. *The Wizard of Oz* 39. Johnny Eager 42. The Hucksters 47. *On the Town* 49. *The Red Badge of Courage* 51. *Singin' in the Rain* 52. The Bad Seed 56. No Time for Sergeants 58, many others.

Rota, Nino (1911–79). Italian composer, responsible for innumerable film scores (including all of Fellini's) as well as operas.
The Popular Train 33. Zaza 43. Open City 46. My Son the Professor 46. Flight into France 48. *The Glass Mountain* 48. To Live in Peace 48. E Primavera 49. Anna 52. I Vitelloni 53. La Strada 54. Amici per la Pelle 56. *War and Peace* 56. Il Bidone 56. Cabiria 58. La Dolce Vita 59. Plein Soleil 60. Rocco and His Brothers 60. Boccaccio 70 62. Eight and a Half 63. Juliet of the Spirits 65. Shoot Loud, Louder, I Don't Understand 66. Romeo and Juliet 68. Satyricon 69. Waterloo 70. *The Godfather* (AA) 72. The Abdication 74. Casanova 77. Death on the Nile 78. Hurricane 79, many others.

Roth, Gene (1903–76) (Gene Stuttenroth). Heavy-set American charactor actor.

Roth, Lillian (1910–1980) (Lillian Rutstein). American leading lady who began her professional career as the baby in the Educational Pictures trademark. After a few films in the early thirties, personal problems caused her retirement. Her story was filmed in 1955 as *I'll Cry Tomorrow*, with Susan Hayward.
She also appeared in *Boardwalk* 79.
The Love Parade 20. The Vagabond King 30. *Madame Satan* 30. Animal Crackers 30. Sea Legs 31. Ladies They Talk About 33. Take a Chance 33, etc.

Roth, Philip (1933–). American novelist, somewhat excessively concerned with Jewish guilt and masturbation. *Portnoy's Complaint* and *Goodbye Columbus* were filmed.

Rotha, Paul (1903–84). British documentarist and film theorist. With GPO Film Unit in thirties, later independent. Author of *The Film till Now, Documentary Film*, etc.
Shipyard 30. Contact 33. The Rising Tide 33. The Face of Britain 34. The Fourth Estate 40. *World of Plenty* 42. Land of Promise 46. The World is Rich 48. No Resting Place 50. World without End (co-d) 52. Cat and Mouse 57. *The Life of Adolf Hitler* 62. The Silent Raid 62, etc.

Rotunno, Giuseppe (1923–). Italian cinematographer.
Scandal in Sorrento 55. White Nights 57. Anna of Brooklyn 58. The Naked Maja 59. On the Beach 59. The Angel Wore Red 60. Rocco and His Brothers 60. The Best of Enemies 61. The Leopard 62. Yesterday, Today and Tomorrow 63. Anzio 68. The Secret of Santa Vittoria 69. Satyricon 69. Sunflower 70. Carnal Knowledge 71. Man of La Mancha 72. Amarcord 74. Casanova 77. The End of the World 78. All That Jazz (BFA) 79. Popeye 81. Five Days One Summer 82, etc.

rough cut. The first assembly of shots in the order in which they will be seen in the finished film, used to show those involved what work still needs to be done.

Roundtree, Richard (1937–). Black American leading man of the seventies.
Shaft 71. Embassy 72. Charley One Eye 72. Shaft's Big Score 72. Earthquake 74. Man Friday 75. Escape to Athena 79. Game for Vultures 79. The Winged Serpent 82. One Down Two to Go 82. The Big Score 83. City Heat 84. Killpoint 84. Opposing Forces 87, etc.
TV series: Shaft 73.

Rounseville, Robert (1914–1974). American opera singer.
□Tales of Hoffman 51. Carousel 56.

Rouquier, Georges (1909–). French documentarist.
Le Tonnelier 42. Farrébique 46. Salt of the Earth 50. Lourdes and Its Miracles 56, etc.

Rourke, Mickey (1950–). Tough, abrasive American actor.
□ 1941 79. Fade to Black 80. Heaven's Gate 80. Body Heat 81. Diner 81. Rumble Fish 83. Eureka 83. The Pope of Greenwich Village 84. *The Year of the Dragon* 85. Angel Heart 87. Barfly 87. A Prayer for the Dying 87.

¶ *M.R.:* I always knew I'd accomplish something very special—like robbing a bank perhaps.

Rouse, Russel (1916–). American director and co-writer, usually in partnership with Clarence Greene (qv).
D.O.A. 50. The Well 51. The Thief 52. New York Confidential 55. The Fastest Gun Alive 56. Thunder in the Sun 59. A House is Not a Home 64. The Oscar 66. Caper of the Golden Bulls 67, etc.

Rowan, Dan (1922–). American comedian, one-half of *Rowan and Martin*, the other being *Dick Martin* (1922–). Belatedly successful on TV with *Laugh In* 68–72, they have not been popular in films.
□Once upon a Horse 57. The Maltese Bippy 69.

Rowland, Roy (1910–). American director, mainly of routine features, in Hollywood from mid-thirties. Many shorts, including *Benchley, Pete Smith, Crime Does Not Pay*.
Lost Angel 44. *Our Vines Have Tender Grapes* 45. Killer McCoy 48. Tenth Avenue Angel 48. Scene of the Crime 49. Two Weeks with Love 50. Bugles in the Afternoon 53. The Moonlighter 53. Rogue Cop 53. The Five Thousand Fingers of Doctor T 53. Affair with a Stranger 53. Many Rivers to Cross 55. Hit the Deck 55. Meet Me in Las Vegas 56. These Wilder Years 56. Gun Glory 57. Seven Hills of Rome 58. The Girl Hunters 64. Gunfighters of Casa Grande 66. They Called Him Gringo 68, others.

Rowlands, Gena (1934–) (Virginia Rowlands). American leading actress, mostly on stage.
The High Cost of Loving 58. A Child is Waiting 62. Lonely are the Brave 62. Tony Rome 67. Faces 68. Minnie and Moskowitz 71. A Woman under the Influence 75. Two Minute Warning 76. Opening Night 77. The Brink's Job 78. Gloria 80. Love Streams 85. Light of Day 87, etc.
TV series: 87th Precinct 61.

Rowlands, Patsy (1934–). British character comedienne.
In the Doghouse 61. Dateline Diamonds 65. Carry on Loving 70. Carry on Girls 73. Joseph Andrews 76, etc.

Roxie Hart (US 1942). Brilliantly scathing, zippy and entertaining satire, now unjustly forgotten, of Chicago in the twenties, with Ginger Rogers as a chorus girl who confesses to a murder for the sake of the publicity. She is splendidly abetted by Adolphe Menjou, Lynne Overman and George Montgomery; script and production are by Nunnally Johnson, music by Alfred Newman, direction by William Wellman.

Roy, Harry (1900–71). British bandleader who made two films: *Everything is Rhythm* 36. *Rhythm Racketeer* 37.

Royal Film Performance. A charity function begun in London in 1946 with *A Matter of Life and Death*. The Queen usually attends, but the film is chosen, usually on the basis of what is least offensive rather than best, by executives of the Cinema Trade Benevolent Organization, for whose financial benefit the evening is staged. Subsequent films have been:
1947: *The Bishop's Wife*
1948: *Scott of the Antarctic*
1949: *That Forsyte Woman*
1950: *The Mudlark*
1951: *Where No Vultures Fly*
1952: *Because You're Mine*
1953: *Rob Roy*
1954: *Beau Brummell*
1955: *To Catch a Thief*
1956: *The Battle of the River Plate*
1957: *Les Girls*
1958: no performance
1959: *The Horse's Mouth*
1960: *The Last Angry Man*
1961: *The Facts of Life*
1962: *West Side Story*
1963: *Sammy Going South*
1964: *Move Over Darling*
1965: *Lord Jim*
1966: *Born Free*
1967: *The Taming of the Shrew*
1968: *Romeo and Juliet*
1969: *The Prime of Miss Jean Brodie*
1970: *Anne of the Thousand Days*
1971: *Love Story*
1972: *Mary Queen of Scots*
1973: *Lost Horizon*
1974: *The Three Musketeers*
1975: *Funny Lady*
1976: *The Slipper and the Rose*
1977: *Silver Streak*
1978: *Close Encounters of the Third Kind*
1979: *California Suite*
1980: *Kramer vs Kramer*
1981: *Chariots of Fire*
1982: *Evil Under the Sun*
1983: *Table for Five*
1984: *The Dresser*
1985: *A Passage to India*
1986: *White Nights*
1987: *84 Charing Cross Road*

Royle, Selena (1904–1983). American character actress.
The Misleading Lady 32. Mrs Parkington 44. The Fighting Sullivans 44. Gallant Journey 47. Cass Timberlane 47. Joan of Arc 48. Branded 50. Robot Monster 53. Murder is My Beat 55, etc.

Rozsa, Miklos (1907–). Hungarian composer, in Hollywood from 1940. Autobiography 1982: *A Double Life*.
Knight without Armour 37. *The Four Feathers* 39. *The Thief of Baghdad* 40. Lady Hamilton 41. Five Graves to Cairo 43. Double Indemnity 44. A Song to Remember 44. The Lost Weekend 45. *Spellbound* (AA) 45. *The Killers* 46. Brute Force 47. *A Double Life* (AA) 47. Naked City 48. Adam's Rib 49. The Asphalt Jungle 50. Quo Vadis 51. Ivanhoe 52. Julius Caesar 53. Moonfleet 55. Lust for Life 56. *Ben Hur* (AA) 59. King of Kings 61. El Cid 61. Sodom and Gomorrah 62. The VIPs 63. The Power 67. The Green Berets 68. The Private Life of Sherlock Holmes 70. Providence 77. Fedora 78. The Private Files of J. Edgar Hoover 78. Time after Time 79. Last Embrace 79. Dead Men Don't Wear Plaid 81, many others.

Rub, Christian (1887–1956). Austrian character actor, long in Hollywood. Was the model and voice for Gepetto the woodcarver in Disney's *Pinocchio*.

The Trial of Vivienne Ware 32. The Kiss behind the Mirror 33. A Dog of Flanders 35. Dracula's Daughter 36. Heidi 37. Mad about Music 38. The Great Waltz 38. The Swiss Family Robinson 40. Tales of Manhattan 42. Fall Guy 48. Something for the Birds 52, many others.

Rubens, Alma (1897–1931) (Alma Smith). American leading lady of the silent screen: her career was prematurely ended by drug addiction.
Intolerance 15. The Firefly of Tough Luck 17. Humoresque 20. Cytherea 24. Fine Clothes 25. Siberia 26. Masks of the Devil 28. Showboat 29, etc.

Rubinstein, Artur (1887–1982). Internationally renowned classical pianist who made guest appearances in occasional films, e.g. *Carnegie Hall.*

Rubinstein, John (1946–). American character actor, and occasional composer.
Getting Straight 70. Zachariah 70. The Wild Pack 72. All Together Now (TV) 75. The Car 77. The Boys from Brazil 78, etc.
TV series: Crazy Like a Fox 84–85.

Ruby, Harry (1895–1974). American songwriter (with Bert Kalmar). See *Kalmar, Bert* for credits.

Ruddy, Albert S. (1934–). American producer.
The Godfather 72. The Longest Yard 74. The McAhans (TV) 76. Matilda 78. Death Hunt 81. The Cannonball Run 81. Megaforce 82, etc.

¶ *A.S.R.:* Show me a relaxed producer and I'll show you a failure.

Rudley, Herbert (1911–). American supporting actor.
Abe Lincoln in Illinois 39. The Seventh Cross 44. *Rhapsody in Blue* (as Ira Gershwin) 45. A Walk in the Sun 46. Joan of Arc 48. The Silver Chalice 55. The Black Sleep 56. Beloved Infidel 59, etc.
TV series: The Californians 57. Michael Shayne 60. Meet Mona McCluskey 65. The Mothers-in-Law 67–68.

Rudolph, Alan (1943–). American screenwriter.
Buffalo Bill and the Indians (co-w) 76. Welcome to L.A. (& d) 77. Remember My Name (& d) 78. Roadie (d only) 80. Endangered Species (& d) 82. Choose Me (& w) 84. Songwriter 84. Trouble in Mind 85. Made in Heaven 87.

Ruggles, Charles (1886–1970). American character comedian, brother of Wesley Ruggles. In films regularly from 1928 after stage experience; quickly became popular for his inimitably diffident manner.
□Peer Gynt 15. The Majesty of the Law 15. The Reform Candidate 15. The Heart Raider 23. Gentlemen of the Press 29. The Lady Lies 29. The Battle of Paris 29. Roadhouse Nights 30. Young Man of Manhattan 30. Queen High 30. Her Wedding Night 30. *Charley's Aunt* 30. Honor Among Lovers 31. The Girl Habit 31. The Smiling Lieutenant 31. Beloved Bachelor 31. Husband's Holiday 31. This Reckless Age 32. One Hour with You 32. This is the Night 32. Make Me a Star 32. *Love Me Tonight* 32. 70,000 Witnesses 32. The Night of June 13th 32. *Trouble in Paradise* 32. Evenings for Sale 32. If I Had a Million 32. Madame Buttlerfly 32. Murders in the Zoo 33. Terror Aboard 33. Melody Cruise 33. Mama Loves Papa 33. Girl without a Room 33. Alice in Wonderland 33. Six of a Kind 34. Goodbye Love 34. Melody in Spring 34. Murder in the Private Car 34. Friends of Mr Sweeney 34. The Pursuit of Happiness 34. *Ruggles of Red Gap* 35. People will Talk 35. No More Ladies 35. The Big Broadcast of 1936 35. Anything Goes 36. *Early to Bed* 36. Hearts Divided 36. Wives Never Know 36. Mind Your Own Business 36. Turn Off the Moon 37. Exclusive 37. *Bringing Up Baby* 38. Breaking the Ice 38. Service De Luxe 38. His Exciting Night 38. Boy Trouble 39. Sudden Money 39. Invitation to Happiness 39. Night Work 39. Balalaika 39. The Farmer's Daughter 40. Opened by Mistake 40. Maryland 40. Public Deb Number One 40. No Time for Comedy 40. Invisible Woman 41. Honeymoon for Three 41. Model Wife 41. The Parson of Panamint 41. Go West Young Lady 41. The Perfect Snob 41. Friendly Enemies 42. Dixie Dugan 43. Our Hearts were Young and Gay 44. The Doughgirls 44. Three is a Family 44. Bedside Manner 45. Incendiary Blonde 45. A Stolen Life 46. Gallant Journey 46. The Perfect Marriage 46. My Brother Talks to Horses 46. *It Happened on Fifth Avenue* 47. Ramrod 47. Give My Regards to Broadway 48. The Loveable Cheat 49. *Look for the Silver Lining* 49. Girl on the Subway (TV) 58. All in a Night's Work 61. *The Pleasure of His Company* 61. The Parent Trap 61. Son of Flubber 63. Papa's Delicate Condition 63. *I'd Rather be*

Rich 64. The Ugly Dachshund 66. Follow Me Boys 66.
TV series: The World of Mr Sweeney 53.
❀ For devoting a lifetime of professional experience to the presentation of dapper optimism, and for helping to cheer up several generations of filmgoers. *Trouble in Paradise.*

Ruggles of Red Gap. This well-known story by Harry Leon Wilson, about a British butler exported to the American mid-west, was filmed with Edward Everett Horton in 1923 and with Charles Laughton in 1935. Bob Hope's *Fancy Pants* in 1950 bore more than a passing resemblance to it.

Ruggles, Wesley (1889–1972). American director, in Hollywood from 1914. One of the original Keystone Kops: brother of Charles Ruggles.
Wild Honey 22. The Plastic Age 26. Silk Stockings 27. Are These Our Children? 30. *Cimarron* 31. No Man of Her Own 32. College Humour 33. *I'm No Angel* 33. Bolero 34. The Gilded Lily 35. Valiant is the Word for Carrie 36. *I Met Him in Paris* 37. True Confession 37. *Sing You Sinners* (& p) 38. Invitation to Happiness 39. My Two Husbands 40. Arizona (& p) 40. Good Morning Doctor 41. Somewhere I'll Find You 42. See Here Private Hargrove 44. London Town (GB) 46, etc.

Ruhmann, Heinz (1902–). German actor whose films have rarely been seen abroad.
Das Deutsche Mutterherz 26. Drei von der Tankstelle 30. Bomben auf Monte Carlo 31. The Man Who Was Sherlock Holmes 37. Die Feuerzangenbowle 44. The Captain from Kopenick 56. Menschen im Hotel 59. The Good Soldier Schweik 59. Das Schwarze Schaf (as Father Brown) 60. *Ship of Fools* (US) 65, etc.

Ruick, Barbara (1932–74). American leading lady of the fifties.
I Love Melvin 51. Invitation 52. Carousel 56. California Split 75, etc.

Rule, Janice (1931–). American leading lady with stage and TV experience.
Goodbye My Fancy 51. Holiday for Sinners 52. Rogues' March 53. Gun for a Coward 57. Bell, Book and Candle 58. The Subterraneans 60. Invitation to a Gunfighter 64. *The Chase* 66. Alvarez Kelly 66. The Ambushers 67. The Swimmer 68. Doctors' Wives 71. Gumshoe 71. Welcome to Hard Times 72. Kid Blue 73. Three Women 77. Missing 82, etc.

Ruman, Sig (or **Siegfried Rumann**) (1884–1967). German character actor, usually of explosive roles, in Hollywood from 1934.
The Wedding Night 35. *A Night at the Opera* 35. *A Day at the Races* 37. *Ninotchka* 39. Bitter Sweet 41. *To Be or Not To Be* 42. The Hitler Gang 44. *A Night in Casablanca* 45. On The Riviera 49. *Stalag 17* 53. The Glenn Miller Story 54. Three-Ring Circus 56. The Wings of Eagles 57. Robin and the Seven Hoods 64. Last of the Secret Agents 66, many others.
Famous line (*To Be or Not To Be*): So they call me Concentration Camp Erhardt!

Runacre, Jenny (1943–). South African character actress in Britain.
Goodbye Mr Chips 69. Dyn Amo 71. The Creeping Flesh 72. The Final Programme 73. The Mackintosh Man 73. Passenger 75. All Creatures Great and Small 75. Joseph Andrews 77. The Duellists 78. Spectre (TV) 78. The Lady Vanishes 79, etc.

running shot. One in which the camera, mounted on wheels, keeps pace with its subject, a moving actor or vehicle.

running speed. In silent days, 35 mm ran through the projector at 16 frames per second or 60 feet per minute. When sound came, this was amended for technical reasons to 24 frames per second or 90 feet per minute. No normal 35 mm projector can now operate at silent speed, which is why silent films look jerky when you see them (unless a special and very expensive laboratory process is adopted). It is said that many films made in the later silent period were in fact intended for showing at about 20 frames per second, and as machines were variable this was easily accomplished: such films now seem unduly slow when projected at 16 frames per second.
See: *slow motion, accelerated motion.*

running time. The length of a film, usually expressed in minutes; if in feet, one must say whether 35mm or 16mm. In European television, for technical reasons, films run faster by one frame in 25, so a 75m film runs only 72m, a 100m film only 96m, etc. Films tended to be shorter and crisper in the thirties, especially when double bills came in; but now nobody seems to have control over self-indulgent directors.

¶ *Alfred Hitchcock:* The length of a film should be directly related to the endurance of the human bladder.

An MGM director: How long should the film be?
Nicholas Schenck: How long is it good?

Runyon, Damon (1884–1946). Inimitable American chronicler of the ways of a never-never New York inhabited by good-hearted and weirdly-named guys and dolls who speak a highly imaginative brand of English. Among the films based on his stories are *Lady for a Day* 33 (and its remake *Pocketful of Miracles* 61), *The Lemon Drop Kid* 34 and 51, *A Slight Case of Murder* 38 (and *Stop You're Killing Me* 52), *The Big Street* 42, and *Guys and Dolls* 55.

Rush, Barbara (1927–). American leading lady who came to Hollywood from college.
The First Legion 51. When Worlds Collide 51. Flaming Feather 52. It Came from Outer Space 53. Magnificent Obsession 54. The Black Shield of Falworth 54. Captain Lightfoot 55. The World in My Corner 56. Bigger Than Life 57. Oh Men! Oh Women! 58. Harry Black 58. The Young Philadelphians (The City Jungle) 59. The Bramble Bush 60. Strangers When We Meet 60. *Come Blow Your Horn* 63. Robin and the Seven Hoods 64. Hombre 67. The Eyes of Charles Sand (TV) 72. Superdad 74. The Last Day (TV) 75. Can't Stop the Music 80. Summer Lovers 80, others.
TV series: Flamingo Road 80–81.

Rush, Richard (1930–). American director.
□Too Soon to Love (w, p) 60. Of Love and Desire 63. The Fickle Finger of Fate 67. Hell's Angels on Wheels 67. Thunder Alley 67. A Man Called Dagger 68. Psych-Out 68. The Savage Seven 68. Getting Straight 70. Freebie and the Bean (& p) 74. The Stunt Man (& p) 80.

rushes. A day's shooting on film when it comes back from the laboratories and is ready for viewing by those involved.

Russell, Gail (1924–1961). American leading lady of the forties; came to Hollywood straight from dramatic training.
Henry Aldrich Gets Glamour (debut) 43. Lady in the Dark 43. *The Uninvited* 44. Our Hearts were Young and Gay 44. Salty O'Rourke 45. Night Has a Thousand Eyes 47. Moonrise 48. Wake of the Red Witch 49. Air Cadet 51. The Tattered Dress 57. The Silent Call 61, etc.

Russell, Harold (1914–). Canadian paratroop sergeant who lost both hands in an explosion during World War II and demonstrated his ability not only to use hooks in their place but to act as well in *The Best Years of Our Lives* 46, for which he won two Oscars. Published autobiography 1949: *Victory in My Hands*. Became a public relations executive. Appeared again 1980 in *Inside Moves*.

Russell, Jane (1921–). American leading lady who came to Hollywood when an agent sent her photo to producer Howard Hughes; he starred her in *The Outlaw* 43 but it was held up for three years by censor trouble. The publicity campaign emphasized the star's physical attributes.
□The Young Widow 47. *The Paleface* 48. Double Dynamite 50. Macao 51. Montana Belle 51. His Kind of Woman 51. Son of Paleface 52. The Las Vegas Story 52. Gentlemen Prefer Blondes 53. The French Line 54. Underwater 55. Gentlemen Marry Brunettes 55. Foxfire 55. Hot Blood 56. The Tall Men 56. The Revolt of Mamie Stover 57. The Fuzzy Pink Nightgown 57. Fate is the Hunter (guest appearance) 64. Waco 66. Johnny Reno 66. Born Losers 67. Darker than Amber 70. The Yellow Rose (TV) 84.

¶ *Howard Hughes:* There are two good reasons why men will go to see her.

Russell, John (1921–). American 'second lead'.
A Bell for Adano 45. The Fat Man 51. The Sun Shines Bright 53. The Last Command 55. Rio Bravo 59. Fort Utah 66. Cannon for Cordoba 70, many others.
TV series: Soldiers of Fortune 55. Lawman 58–60.

Russell, Ken (1927–). British director, a middle-aged *enfant terrible* of the seventies who after a rigorous training in BBC art films turned out to want to shock people, and did so with flair but no subtlety.
□French Dressing 64. Billion Dollar Brain 67. *Women In Love* 69. *The Music Lovers* 70. The Devils 71. The Boy Friend 71. Savage Messiah 72. Mahler 74. Tommy 75. Lisztomania 75. Valentino 77. Clouds of Glory (TV) 78. Altered States 80. Crimes of Passion 84. Gothic 87.

¶ Mr Ken Russell, the film director who now specializes in vulgar travesties of the lives of dead composers . . .—*Nicholas de Jongh, The Guardian*

This is not the age of manners. This is the age of kicking people in the crotch and telling them something and getting a reaction. I want to shock people into awareness. I don't believe there's any virtue in understatement.—*K.R.*

I know my films upset people. I *want* to upset people.—*K.R.*

Life is too short to make destructive films about people one doesn't like. My films are meant to be constructive and illuminating.—*K.R.*

His originality these days seems to consist of disguising the banal behind a barrage of garish, distorted, noisy and fleeting images looted from every juvenile fantasy from Rider Haggard to Superman, with nods to Dali and Bosch, and strong tincture of Kubrick.—*Sunday Times, 1981*

Russell, Kurt (1947–). American boy actor of the sixties, usually in Disney films.
The Absent-Minded Professor 60. Follow Me Boys 66. The Horse in the Grey Flannel Suit 68. Charley and the Angel 73. Superdad 74. *Elvis* (TV) 79. Used Cars 80. Escape from New York 81. The Fox and the Hound (voice) 81. The Thing 82. Silkwood 83, etc.
TV series: The Travels of Jamie McPheeters 63. The New Land 74. The Quest 76.
Swing Shift 84. The Mean Season 84. The Best of Times 85. Big Trouble in Little China 86. Overboard 87.

Russell, Lillian (1861–1922) (Helen Louise Leonard). Statuesque American singer-entertainer, highly popular around the turn of the century. Only one film, *Wildfire* (1914); was played by Alice Faye in a 1940 biopic, by Ruth Gillette in *The Great Ziegfeld*, by Andrea King in *My Wild Irish Rose* and by Binnie Barnes in *Diamond Jim*.

Russell, Rosalind (1908–1976). Dominant American leading lady of the thirties and forties, usually as career women; later attempted character roles, but her choice was sometimes unwise.
Autobiography 1977: *Life is a Banquet*.
□Evelyn Prentice 34. The President Vanishes 34. West Point of the Air 35. The Casino Murder Case 35. Reckless 35. China Seas 35. Rendezvous 35. Forsaking All Others 35. The Night is Young 35. It Had to Happen 36. Under Two Flags 36. Trouble for Two 36. Craig's Wife 36. *Night Must Fall* 37. Live Love and Learn 37. Manproof 38. *The Citadel* 38. Four's a Crowd 38. Fast and Loose 39. *The Women* 39. *His Girl Friday* 40. No Time fo0. No Time for Comedy 40. Hired Wife 40. This Thing Called Love 41. They Met in Bombay 41. The Feminine Touch 41. Design for Scandal 41. Take a Letter Darling 42. *My Sister Eileen* 42. Flight for Freedom 43. What a Woman 43. Roughly Speaking 45. She Wouldn't Say Yes 45. Sister Kenny 46. The Guilt of Janet Ames 47. Mourning Becomes Electra 48. The Velvet Touch 48. Tell it to the Judge 49. A Woman of Distinction 50. Never Wave at a WAC 52. The Girl Rush 55. Picnic 56. Auntie Mame 58. A Majority of One 61. Gypsy 62. Five-Finger Exercise 62. The Trouble with Angels 66. Oh Dad, Poor Dad 67. Where Angels Go Trouble Follows 68. Rosie 68. The Unexpected Mrs Pollifax 70. The Crooked Hearts (TV) 72.

¶ *R.R.:* At MGM there was a first wave of top stars, and a second wave to replace them in case they got difficult. I was in the second line of defence, behind Myrna Loy.

R.R.: Success is a public affair. Failure is a private funeral.

R.R.: Acting is standing up naked and turning around very slowly.

Russell, Theresa (1957–). American leading lady who settled in the UK.
The Last Tycoon 77. Straight Time 78. Bad Timing 80. Eureka 83. The Razor's Edge 84. Insignificance 86. Black Widow 87.

Russell, William D. (1908–1968). American director.
□Our Hearts were Growing Up 46. Ladies' Man 47. *Dear Ruth* 47. The Sainted Sisters 48. The Green Promise 49. Bride for Sale 49. Best of the Badmen 51.

the Russian cinema has been one of the most influential in the world, chiefly owing to a small group of highly talented men. Before the revolution Russian films were old-fashioned and literary; but the Bolsheviks saw the great potential of the film as propaganda and actively encouraged the maturing talents of such men as Eisenstein (*Battleship Potemkin, October, The General Line, Alexander Nevsky, Ivan the Terrible*), Pudovkin (*Mother, The End of St Petersburg, The Deserter, General Suvorov*), Dovzhenko (*Arsenal, Earth*), Turin (*Turksib*) and Petrov (*Peter the Great*). Donskoi in *The Childhood of Maxim Gorki* and its two sequels was allowed to be nostalgic, but this vein only occasionally comes to the surface, most recently in *The Lady with a Little Dog*. The light touch comes hard to Russian film-makers, but Alexandrov achieved it in *Volga Volga*, and recently there have been signs of greater effort in this direction, at least for home consumption. The stolidity of most Russian films since World War II should not blind anyone to the enormous influence which the best Soviet work has had on film-makers the world over, especially in its exploration of the potentialities of camera movement, editing and sound; all these techniques were seen at their best in the mid-sixties in a seven-hour version of *War and Peace*.

Rustichelli, Carlo (1916–). Italian composer.
Gran Premio 43. Gioventu Perduta 47. In the Name of the Law 48. Behind Closed Shutters 50. The Road to Hope 50. Black 13 (GB) 53. Il Ferroviere 55. Maledetto Imbroglio 59. Queen of the Nile 61. Mamma Roma 62. Torpedo Bay 63. Blood and Black Lace 64. The Secret War of Harry Frigg 67. Alfredo, Alfredo 71. The Black Hand 73. Le Gang 76, many others.

Rutherford, Ann (1917–). American leading lady of the forties, former child stage star.
Love Finds Andy Hardy 38. The Hardys Ride High 39. Gone with the Wind 39. Pride and Prejudice 40. Happy Land 43. Two O'Clock Courage 45. *The Secret Life of Walter Mitty* 47. The Adventures of Don Juan 48. They Only Kill Their Masters 72, etc.

Rutherford, Dame Margaret (1892–1972). Inimitable, garrulous, shapeless, endearing British comedy character actress, who usually seemed to be playing somebody's slightly dotty spinster aunt.
Published *An Autobiography* 1972.
□Talk of the Devil 36. Dusty Ermine 38. Beauty and the Barge 38. Catch as Catch Can 38. Missing Believed Married 38. Quiet Wedding 40. Spring Meeting 41. *The Demi Paradise* 43. Yellow Canary 43. English without Tears 44. *Blithe Spirit* (as Madame Arcati) 45. While the Sun Shines 46. Meet Me at Dawn 47. *Miranda* 47. Passport to Pimlico 48. *The Happiest Days of Your Life* 50. Her Favourite Husband 51. The Magic Box 51. Castle in the Air 51. *The Importance of Being Earnest* 52. Curtain Up 52. Miss Robin Hood 53. Innocents in Paris 53. Trouble in Store 53. The Runaway Bus 54. Mad about Men 55. Aunt Clara 55. An Alligator Named Daisy 56. The Smallest Show on Earth 57. I'm All Right Jack 59. Just My Luck 59. On the Double 61. *Murder She Said* (as Miss Marple) 62. Mouse on the Moon 63. Murder at the Gallop 63. *The VIPs* (AA) 63. Murder Most Foul 63. Murder Ahoy 64. The Alphabet Murders 65. Chimes at Midnight 66. A Countess from Hong Kong 67. Arabella 68.

❀ For being her splendidly eccentric self. *Blithe Spirit*.

Ruttenberg, Joseph (1889–1983). Russian cinematographer, in Hollywood from 1915.
Over the Hill 28. Fury 36. *The Great Waltz* (AA) 38. *Dr Jekyll and Mr Hyde* 41. *Mrs Miniver* (AA) 42. Madame Curie 43. Adventure 46. BF's Daughter 48. Side Street 49. The Forsyte Saga 49. The Great Caruso 51. Julius Caesar 53. The Last Time I Saw Paris 54. The Swan 56. *Somebody Up There Likes Me* (AA) 56. *Gigi* (AA) 58. The Reluctant Debutante 58. Butterfield 8 60. Bachelor in Paradise 61. Who's Been Sleeping in My Bed? 63. Sylvia 63. Harlow 65. Love Has Many Faces 65. The Oscar 66. Speedway 68, many others.

Ruttman, Walter (1887–1941). German director most famous for his experimental film *Berlin* 27.
Weekend 30. Mannesmann 37. Deutsche Panzer 40, etc.

Ruysdael, Basil (1888–1960). Authoritative Russian-American character actor, former opera singer.
The Coconuts 29. Come to the Stable 49. Broken Arrow 50. My Forbidden Past 51. Carrie 52. The Blackboard Jungle 56. The Last Hurrah 58. The Story of Ruth 60, many others.

Ryan, Frank (1907–1947). American director.
Hers to Hold 43. Can't Help Singing 44. Patrick the Great 45. A Genius in the Family 46, etc.

Ryan, Irene (1903–1973) (Irene Riordan). Wiry American comedienne, was famous as Granny in TV's *The Beverly Hillbillies*.
Melody for Three 41. San Diego I Love You 44. Diary of a Chambermaid 45. Meet Me after the Show 51. Blackbeard the Pirate 52. Spring Reunion 57, etc.

Ryan, John (1938–). American leading man.
The Tiger Makes Out 65. Five Easy Pieces 70. The King of Marvin Gardens 72. Shamus 72. Dillinger 73. Cops and Robbers 73. It's Alive 75. The Missouri Breaks 76. Futureworld 76. It Lives Again 79. The Cotton Club 84, etc.

Ryan, Kathleen (1922–85). Irish leading lady with stage experience.
Odd Man Out (debut) 47. Captain Boycott

47. Esther Waters 48. Give Us This Day 50. The Yellow Balloon 52. Captain Lightfoot 53. Laxdale Hall 53. *Jacqueline* 56. Sail into Danger 58, etc.

Ryan, Mitchell or **Mitch** (1928–). Stalwart American character actor, mostly on TV.
Flesh and Blood 79. The Chisholms 80. Lethal Weapon 87.
TV series: Chase 74. Executive Suite 76.

Ryan, Peggy (1924–). American teenage comedienne of the early forties, often teamed with Donald O'Connor. In vaudeville from childhood.
Top of the Town 37. Give Out Sisters 42. Top Man 43. The Merry Monahans 44. Bowery to Broadway 44. That's the Spirit 54. On Stage Everybody 45. All Ashore 52, etc.
TV series: Hawaii Five-O 68–80.

Ryan, Robert (1909–1973). Strong-featured American leading actor who never seemed to get the roles he deserved.
□Golden Gloves 40. Queen of the Mob 40. Northwest Mounted Police 40. Texas Rangers Ride Again 41. The Feminine Touch 41. Bombardier 43. *Gangway for Tomorrow* 43. The Sky's the Limit 43. Behind the Rising Sun 43. The Iron Major 43. Tender Comrade 43. The Hitler Gang 44. Marine Raiders 44. The Walls Came Tumbling Down 46. Trail Street 47. The Woman on the Beach 47. *Crossfire* 47. Berlin Express 48. Return of the Badmen 48. The Boy with Green Hair 48. Act of Violence 49. Caught 49. *The Set-Up* 49. The Woman on Pier 13 49. The Secret Fury 50. Born to be Bad 50. Best of the Badmen 51. Flying Leathernecks 51. The Racket 51. On Dangerous Ground 51. Hard Fast and Beautiful 51. *Clash by Night* 52. Beware My Lovely 52. Horizons West 52. City beneath the Sea 53. The Naked Spur 53. Inferno 53. Alaska Seas 54. About Mrs Leslie 54. Her Twelve Men 54. Bad Day at Black Rock 55. Escape to Burma 55. House of Bamboo 55. The Tall Men 55. The Proud Ones 56. Back from Eternity 56. Men in War 57. *God's Little Acre* 58. Lonelyhearts 59. Day of the Outlaw 59. *Odds against Tomorrow* 59. Ice Palace 60. The Canadians 61. King of Kings 61. The Longest Day 62. *Billy Budd* 62. The Crooked Road 65. Battle of the Bulge 65. The Dirty Game 66. The Professionals 66. The Busy Body 67. The Dirty Dozen 67. Hour of the Gun 67. Custer of the West 67. Dead or Alive 67. Anzio 68. Captain Nemo and the Underwater City 68. The Wild Bunch 69. Lawman 71. The Love Machine 71. The Man Without a Country (TV) 72. And Hope to Die 72. The Iceman Cometh 73. Executive Action 73. Lolly Madonna XXX 73. The Outfit 74.

Ryan, Sheila (1921–1975) (Katherine McLaughlin). American light leading lady of the forties.
Something for the Boys 44. The Lone Wolf in London 46. Caged Fury 47. Mask of the Dragon 51. Pack Train 53, etc.

Ryan, Tim (1889–1956). American comedy supporting actor, very adept at drunks, wisecracking reporters, dumb cops, etc.
Brother Orchid 40. The Mystery of the Thirteenth Guest 43. Crazy Knights 45. The Shanghai Chest 48. Sky Dragon 49. Cuban Fireball 51. From Here to Eternity 53. Fighting Trouble 56, etc.

Ryan's Daughter (US 1971). The biggest butterfly ever broken on the wheel of David Lean's talent, a tiny village drama stretched out to the length of *Gone with the Wind*. Directorial style almost keeps the interest, though sadly despite the two years of Irish locations the village is a set and some of the beach scenes were shot in South Africa. Robert Bolt's stuffy dialogue hardly helps, but the playing of Sarah Miles, Trevor Howard and Robert Mitchum does.

Rydell, Bobby (1942–). American pop star who appeared to no great advantage in *Bye Bye Birdie* 63.

Rydell, Mark (1934–). American director.
□The Fox 68. The Reivers 69. The Cowboys (& p) 72. Cinderella Liberty (& p) 74. Harry and Walter Go To New York (& p) 76. The Rose 79. *On Golden Pond* 81. The River 84.
AS ACTOR: Crime in the Streets 56. The Long Goodbye 73, etc.

Ryskind, Morrie (1895–1985). American comedy writer.
Animal Crackers 30. Palmy Days 31. *A Night at the Opera* 35. *My Man Godfrey* 36. Stage Door 37. Room Service 38. Man About Town 39. Penny Serenade 41. Where Do We Go from Here? 45. Heartbeat 46, etc.

Answers

remake roles

1 Mrs Wiggs □ *Mrs Wiggs of the Cabbage Patch* (1934 and 1942) □ 2 The sinister husband □ *Love from a Stranger* (1937 and 1946) □ 3 The grandmother □ *Love Affair* □ *An Affair to Remember* □ 4 The frightened heroine □ *The Mystery of the Wax Museum* □ *House of Wax* □ 5 The heroine □ *Bachelor Mother* □ *Bundle of Joy* □ 6 The father □ *A Bill of Divorcement* (1932 and 1940) □ 7 Title role □ *Kind Lady* (1935 and 1951) □ 8 The hero □ *Berkeley Square* □ *I'll Never Forget You* (GB: *The House in the Square*) □ 9 Sir Percy Blakeney □ *The Scarlet Pimpernel* □ *The Elusive Pimpernel* □ 10 The dying heroine □ *Dark Victory* □ *Stolen Hours* □ 11 The heartless heroine □ *The Devil Is a Woman* (1935 and 1950) □ 12 Title role □ *Monsieur Beaucaire* (1924 and 1946) □ 13 Hildy Johnson □ *The Front Page* □ *His Girl Friday* □ 14 The supposedly ailing heroine/hero □ *Nothing Sacred* □ *Living It Up* □ 15 The adult travelling half fare □ *The Major and the Minor* □ *You're Never Too Young* □ 16 The butler □ *Ruggles of Red Gap* □ *Fancy Pants* □ 17 Charley □ *Charley's Aunt* (1930 and 1941) □ 18 Chang □ *Lost Horizon* (1937 and 1973) □ 19 The publicity man □ *A Star Is Born* (1937 and 1954) □ 20 The doctor □ *Dr Socrates* □ *King of the Underworld* □ 21 The newspaper reporter □ *It Happened One Night* □ *You Can't Run Away From It* □ 22 The frightened wife □ *The Man Who Knew Too Much* (1934 and 1956) □ 23 Title role □ *Gunga Din* □ *Sergeants Three* (corresponding role) □ 24 The Tin Man □ *The Wizard of Oz* (1924 and 1939) □ 25 Dolly □ *The Matchmaker* □ *Hello Dolly* □ 26 The mature boarder □ *The More the Merrier* □ *Walk Don't Run* □ 27 Eliza □ *Pygmalion* □ *My Fair Lady* □ 28 Title role □ *Cleopatra* (1918 and 1934) □ 29 Mr Micawber □ *David Copperfield* (1935 and 1969) □ 30 Van Helsing □ *Dracula* □ (several appearances in thirties and fifties/seventies respectively).

romance I

1 Laurence Olivier as Heathcliff, bemoaning the death of Cathy in *Wuthering Heights* (1939) □ 2 John Wayne of Susan Hayward in *The Conqueror* (1955) □ 3 Eugene Pallette to Margery Wilson in *Intolerance* (1916) (via a sub-title)□4 Laurence Olivier to Joan Fontaine in *Rebecca* (1940) □ 5 Popularly supposed to have been said by Charles Boyer to Hedy Lamarr in *Algiers* (1938), but in fact the line appears nowhere in the film □ 6 Clark Gable to Vivien Leigh in *Gone with the Wind* (1939) □ 7 Dirk Bogarde to Julie Christie in *Darling* (1965) □ 8 Herbert Marshall, escorting Miriam Hopkins in *Trouble in Paradise* (1932) □ 9 Greta Garbo to Melvyn Douglas in *Ninotchka* (1939) □ 10 Joan Crawford to Jeff Chandler in *The Female on the Beach* (1955) □ 11 Joyce Grenfell to Lloyd Lamble in *Blue Murder at St Trinian's* (1952) □ 12 Lauren Bacall to Humphrey Bogart in *To Have and Have Not* (1944) □ 13 Bette Davis to Paul Henreid in *Now Voyager* (1942) □ 14 Again, Bacall to Bogart in *To Have and Have Not* (1944), demonstrating the art of kissing □ 15 Katharine Hepburn to Humphrey Bogart in *The African Queen* (1951)—but in fact she is referring to their descent of the rapids □

romance II

1 Jeff Chandler □ June Allyson □ *A Stranger in My Arms* □ 2 Barbara Stanwyck □ Kirk Douglas □ *The Strange Love of Martha Ivers* □ 3 Marlene Dietrich □ Ray Milland □ *Golden Earrings* □ 4 Ginger Rogers □ Cary Grant □ *Once Upon a Honeymoon* □ 5 Cyd Charisse □ Fred Astaire □ *Silk Stockings* □ 6 Carole Lombard □ Jack Benny □ *To Be or Not to Be* □ 7 Veronica Lake □ Fredric March □ *I Married a Witch* □ 8 Susan Hayward □ Rex Harrison □ *The Honey Pot* □ 9 Robert Taylor □ Jean Harlow □ *Personal Property* □ 10 Joan Crawford □ John Garfield □ *Humoresque* □ 11 Claire Trevor □ John Wayne □ *Stagecoach* □ 12 Jean Arthur □ Gary Cooper □ *Mr Deeds Goes to Town* □ 13 Jane Wyman □ Rock Hudson □ *Magnificent Obsession* □ 14 Stewart Granger □ Rita Hayworth □ *Salome* □

S

Sabatini, Rafael (1875–1950). Anglo-Italian author of swashbuckling historical novels, several of which have been filmed more than once: *The Sea Hawk, Scaramouche, Captain Blood, The Black Swan, Bardelys the Magnificent,* etc.

Sabu (1924–1963) (Sabu Dastagir). Boyish Indian actor, a stable lad in Mysore when he was noticed by director Robert Flaherty and appeared in *Elephant Boy* 37. Came to England, later America.
□The Drum 38. *The Thief of Baghdad* 40. *The Jungle Book* 42. Arabian Nights 42. White Savage 43. Cobra Woman 44. Tangier 46. Black Narcissus 46. *The End of the River* 47. Maneater of Kumaon 48. Song of India 49. Hello, Elephant 52. Jaguar 56. Herrin der Welt (WG) 60. Rampage 63. A Tiger Walks 63.
Famous line (*The Thief of Baghdad*): I'm Abu the thief, son of Abu the thief, grandson of Abu the thief, most unfortunate of ten sons, with a hunger that yearns day and night.

Sackheim, Jerry (–). American screenwriter.
The Night Before the Divorce 42. The Last Crooked Mile 46. The Strange Door 51. Paula 52. The Black Castle 52. Young Jesse James 60, etc.

Sackheim, William (1919–). American writer.
Smart Girls Don't Talk 48. A Yank in Korea 51. Column South 53. Border River 54. The Human Jungle 54, etc.

Sadoul, Georges (1904–1967). French film critic and historian; he published two useful reference works, *Dictionnaire des Films* and *Dictionnaire des Cinéastes*.

safety film took over from nitrate stock in 1950–51. It burns much more slowly and therefore reduces fire risk, but its acetate base also reduces the possibility of gleaming black and white photography, tending instead to a matt look.

Safety Last (US 1923). One of Harold Lloyd's classic gag-and-thrill comedies, probably the best of them, culminating with his climb up a building and many predictable but hilarious mishaps. Directed by Sam Taylor and Fred Newmeyer.

Sagal, Boris (1917–1981). American director, from TV.
□Dime with a Halo 63. Twilight of Honor 64. Girl Happy 65. Made in Paris 66. The Thousand Plane Raid 69. Night Gallery (co-d) (TV) 69. Destiny of a Spy (TV) 69. U.M.C. (TV) 69. The Movie Murderer (TV) 70. Hauser's Memory (TV) 70. Mosquito Squadron 70. The Omega Man 71. Hitched (TV) 71. The Failing of Raymond (TV) 71. Deliver Us from Evil (TV) 73. A Case of Rape (TV) 74. The Greatest Gift (TV) 74. Indict and Convict (TV) 74. The Dream Makers (TV) 75. Man on the Outside (TV) 75. The Runaway Barge (TV) 75. The Oregon Trail (TV) 76. Mallory 76. Three for the Road 76. Ike (TV) (co-d) 78. Masada (TV) 81.
TV series as executive producer: T.H.E. Cat 67.

Sagan, Françoise (1935–) (F. Quoirez). French novelist very popular in the late fifties. Works filmed include *Bonjour Tristesse, A Certain Smile, Aimez-Vous Brahms?* (*Goodbye Again*).

Sagan, Leontine (1899–1974) (Leontine Schlesinger). Austrian lady director.
Maedchen in Uniform 31. Men of Tomorrow 32, etc.

Sahl, Mort (1926–). Sardonic American political comedian fashionable in early sixties. Films untypical.
In Love and War 58. All the Young Men 60. Don't Make Waves 67. Doctor You've Got to be Kidding 68, etc.

¶ *M.S.:* My life needs editing.

sailors of whom screen accounts have been given include Christopher Columbus (1446–

1506), by Fredric March in *Christopher Columbus* 49; Horatio Nelson (qv); Captain Bligh, by Charles Laughton, and later by Trevor Howard, in *Mutiny on the Bounty* (qv); John Paul Jones (1747–92), by Robert Stack in *John Paul Jones* 59; Francis Drake (1540–96), by Matheson Lang in *Drake of England* 35 and by Rod Taylor in *Seven Seas to Calais* 62; Walter Raleigh by Richard Todd in *The Virgin Queen* 55; and Admiral Halsey, by James Cagney in *The Gallant Hours* 61 and by Robert Mitchum in *Midway*.

The Saint. Among the actors who have played Leslie Charteris' 'Robin Hood of crime' in both British and American films since 1937 are Louis Hayward, Hugh Sinclair and George Sanders. One feels that 'the Falcon', a series character played in the forties by George Sanders and later Tom Conway, was heavily indebted to the Saint, who more recently made a strong comeback on television in the person of Roger Moore. In France, a barely recognizable 'Saint' has been played in several films by Jean Marais.

Saint, Eva Marie (1924–). Cool, intelligent American stage actress who played heroine in a variety of films.
□*On the Waterfront* (AA) 54. That Certain Feeling 56. *A Hatful of Rain* 57. Raintree County 57. North by Northwest 59. Exodus 60. All Fall Down 62. 36 Hours 64. The Sandpiper 65. The Russians are Coming, The Russians are Coming 66. Grand Prix 66. The Stalking Moon 68. A Talent for Loving 69. Loving 70. Cancel My Reservation 72. A Christmas to Remember (TV) 78. The Curse of King Tutankhamun's Tomb (TV) 80. The Best Little Girl in the World (TV) 82. Malibu (TV) 83. Jane Doe (TV) 83. Fatal Vision (TV) 84.
TV series: How the West Was Won 76.

St Clair, Malcolm or **Mal** (1897–1952). American director with a reputation for style in the twenties; in the forties however he almost ruined the reputation of Laurel and Hardy.
Find Your Man 24. On Thin Ice 25. A Woman of the World 25. *The Grand Duchess and the Waiter* 26. Breakfast at Sunrise 27. *Gentlemen Prefer Blondes* 28. The Canary Murder Case 29. Dangerous Nan McGrew 30. The Boudoir Diplomat 30. Olsen's Big Moment 33. She Had to Eat 37. A Trip to Paris 38 (and several other Jones Family episodes 36–40). Hollywood Cavalcade 39. Man in the Trunk 42. Over My Dead Body 42. Jitterbugs 43. The Dancing Masters 43. The Big Noise 44. The Bullfighters 45, etc.

St Cyr, Renée (1907–) (Marie-Louise Vittore). French leading lady of the thirties. Les Deux Orphelines 33. Le Dernier Millardaire 34. Les Perles de la Couronne 37. Strange Boarders (UK) 38. La Symphonie Fantastique 42. Pierre et Jean 43. Pamela 45. Le Chevalier de la Nuit 54. Lafayette 71. On Aura Tout Vu 76, etc.

Saint-Exupéry, Antoine de (1900–1944). French aviator and writer. His *The Little Prince* was disappointingly filmed. His *Night Freight* was the basis of *Night Flight* (1933) and also of *Only Angels Have Wings* (1939).

St Jacques, Raymond (1930–) (James Johnson). Black American leading man. Black like Me (debut) 64. Mister Moses 65. Mister Buddwing 66. The Comedians 67. The Green Berets 68. If He Hollers Let Him Go 68. Uptight 68. Change of Mind 70. Cotton Comes to Harlem 70. The Book of Numbers (& pd) 73. Lost in the Stars 73. Born Again 78. The Private Files of J. Edgar Hoover 78. The Evil that Men Do 84, etc.

Saint James, Susan (1946–) (Susan Miller). American leading lady of the seventies, who is mostly seen on TV playing slightly kooky but determined young ladies. PJ 68. Where Angels Go Trouble Follows 68. The Magic Carpet (TV) 72. Love at First Bite 79. How to Beat the High Cost of Living 80, etc.
TV series: *The Name of the Game* 68–71. *McMillan and Wife* 71–75.

St John, Adela Rogers (1893–). Sharp-spoken American journalist who also scripted a few thirties films including *A Free Soul*. Autobiography 1978: *Love, Laughter and Tears*.

St John, Al ('Fuzzy') (1893–1963). American character comedian in many silents from 1913; latterly played comic side-kick in numerous second-feature westerns.
Mabel's Strange Predicament 13. Special Delivery 27. Dance of Life 29. Wanderer of the Wasteland 35. Call of the Yukon 37. Arizona Terrors 42. Frontier Revenge 49, hundreds of others.

St John, Betta (1930–) (Betty Streidler). American leading lady with stage experience.

Dream Wife (debut) 53. The Robe 53. The Student Prince 54. The Naked Dawn 55. High Tide at Noon (GB) 57. Tarzan the Magnificent (GB) 60. City of the Dead (GB) 61, etc.

St John, Howard (1905–1974). American character actor on stage from 1925, films from 1948, usually as father, executive or military commander.
Born Yesterday 50. David Harding, Counterspy 50. Counterspy Meets Scotland Yard 51. The Tender Trap 55. *Lil Abner* 59. Straitjacket 63. Sex and the Single Girl 64. Strange Bedfellows 65. Don't Drink the Water 69, many others.

St John, Jill (1940–) (Jill Oppenheim). American leading lady.
Summer Love 57. The Lost World 60. Come Blow Your Horn 62. Who's Been Sleeping in My Bed? 63. The Liquidator (GB) 65. The Oscar 66. Eight on the Lam 67. Banning 67. Tony Rome 67. Diamonds are Forever 71. Sitting Target 72, etc.

St Trinian's. This school full of little female horrors was originally conceived by cartoonist Ronald Searle. From his formula Frank Launder and Sidney Gilliat made four commercially successful if disappointing farces: *The Belles of St Trinian's* 54, *Blue Murder at St Trinian's* 57, *The Pure Hell of St Trinian's* 60, *The Great St Trinian's Train Robbery* 66. In 1980 Launder alone produced yet another.

Sakall, S. Z. (1884–1955) (Eugene Gero Szakall). Hungarian character actor with vaudeville and stage experience. In films from 1916, Hollywood from 1939; became popular comic support and was nicknamed 'Cuddles'. Autobiography 1953: *The Story of Cuddles.*
It's a Date 40. Ball of Fire 41. Casablanca 42. *Thank Your Lucky Stars* 43. *Wonder Man* 45. Cinderella Jones 46. Whiplash 48. Tea for Two 50. The Student Prince 54, many others.

Sakata, Harold (1920–1982). Korean character actor who in 1963's *Goldfinger* sprang to fame as the villainous Oddjob, but despite wearing the same gear around Hollywood for a number of years never got another substantial role.

Saks, Gene (1921–). American director, from Broadway.
Barefoot in the Park 67. The Odd Couple 67. Cactus Flower 70. Last of the Red Hot Lovers 72. Mame 74. The Prisoner of 2nd Avenue (a only) 74. The One and Only (a) 78. Brighton Beach Memoirs 87.

Sale, Charles (Chic) (1885–1937). American character actor who specialized in grizzled old men.
Star Witness 31. Men of America 32. When a Fellow Needs a Friend 33. *Treasure Island* (as Ben Gunn) 34. Stranger in Town 36, etc.
†Sale was also the author of a best-selling small book called *The Specialist*, compiled from his vaudeville act about a man building an outdoor lavatory.

Sale, Richard (1911–). Prolific American writer of stories and screenplays, none very memorable.
Rendezvous With Annie 46. Spoilers of the North (d only) 47. A Ticket to Tomahawk 49. Meet Me After the Show 51. Half Angel (d only) 51. Let's Make It Legal (d only) 51. My Wife's Best Friend (d only) 52. Suddenly 54. Woman's World 54. Gentlemen Marry Brunettes (& wrote words and music and co-p) 55. Seven Waves Away (& d) 56. The White Buffalo 77, etc.

Sales, Soupy (1926–) (Milton Hines). American entertainer, popular on children's TV. Film debut in *Birds Do It* 66.

Salkind, Alexander (*c.*1915–). Russian producer who moves somewhat mysteriously in international circles.
The Trial 62. The Light at the Edge of the World 71. The Three Musketeers 73. Superman 77. Superman 2 80. Superman 3 82. Supergirl 83. Santa Claus 84.

¶ *A.S.:* I don't want to meet actors, they don't impress me.

Salkow, Sidney (1909–). American director of second features from mid-thirties.
Woman Doctor 39. Café Hostess 40. The Lone Wolf Strikes 40 (and others in this series). The Adventures of Martin Eden 42. Millie's Daughter 46. Bulldog Drummond at Bay 47. Shadow of the Eagle (GB) 50. Sitting Bull 52. The Golden Hawk 52. Jack McCall, Desperado 53. Raiders of the Seven Seas 53. College Confidential 57. Twice Told Tales 63. The Great Sioux Massacre 65, many others.

Sallis, Peter (1921–). Bemused-looking British character actor, often in 'little man' roles.

Anastasia 56. The Doctor's Dilemma 58. Saturday Night and Sunday Morning 60. Charlie Bubbles 67. Inadmissible Evidence 68, many others.
TV series: *Last of the Summer Wine* 74–.

Salmi, Albert (1928–). Chubby American character actor, mainly on stage.
The Brothers Karamazov 58. The Unforgiven 59. Wild River 60. The Ambushers 67. The Deserter 70. Lawman 71. The Take 74. Empire of the Ants 77. Black Oak Conspiracy 77. Viva Knievel 77. Brubaker 80. St Helens 81, etc.
TV series: Daniel Boone 63. Petrocelli 73.

Salt, Jennifer (1944–). American leading lady, daughter of Waldo Salt.
Midnight Cowboy 69. Hi Mom 69. The Revolutionary 70. Brewster McCloud 70. Play It Again Sam 72. Sisters 73. The Great Niagara (TV) 74, etc.
TV series: Soap 78–80.

Salt, Waldo (1914–87). American screenwriter.
The Shopworn Angel 38. Tonight We Raid Calais 43. Mr Winkle Goes to War 44. Rachel and the Stranger 48. The Flame and the Arrow 50. Taras Bulba 62. Flight from Ashiya 64. Midnight Cowboy 68. The Gang That Couldn't Shoot Straight 72. Serpico 73. The Day of the Locust 75. Coming Home 78, etc.

Salter, Hans J. (1896–). German composer in Hollywood.
Call a Messenger 39. It Started with Eve 41. The Mummy's Tomb 42. The Spoilers 42. Frankenstein Meets the Wolf Man 43. Sherlock Holmes Faces Death 44. Scarlet Street 45. The Web 47. The Reckless Moment 49. The Prince Who was a Thief 51. The Far Horizons 55. The Mole People 56. Raw Wind in Eden 58. Come September 61. Hitler 62. Bedtime Story 64. Beau Geste 66, many others.

Saltzman, Harry (1915–). Canadian-born independent producer with TV experience. Very successful in Britain with *Look Back in Anger*, the James Bond films, *The Ipcress File, The Battle of Britain*, etc.

Samoilova, Tatania (1934–). Russian leading actress.
The Cranes are Flying 57. The Letter that was not Sent 60. Anna Karenina 67, etc.

Sampson, Will (1935–87). American (part Indian) character actor.
One Flew Over the Cuckoo's Nest 75. The Outlaw Josey Wales 76. Buffalo Bill and the Indians 76. The White Buffalo 77. Orca 77. Alcatraz: the Whole Shocking Story 78. Insignificance 86.
TV series: Vegas 78.

Samuelson, G. B. (1887–1945). British producer and distributor of silent films. His sons now operate an international production organization.
A Study in Scarlet 14. Little Women 17. Hindle Wakes 18. Quinneys 19. The Last Rose of Summer 21. Should a Doctor Tell? 23. She 25, many others.

San Francisco, replete with cable cars, steep streets, Golden Gate Bridge and Alcatraz out there in the bay, has provided a picturesque location for innumerable movies, outstandingly *Vertigo, What's Up Doc?, The Glenn Miller Story, The Well Groomed Bride, Bullitt, Guess Who's Coming to Dinner, Point Blank, Yours Mine and Ours, The House on Telegraph Hill, Sudden Fear, Experiment in Terror, Flower Drum Song, The Maltese Falcon, The Conversation, Daddy's Gone A-Hunting, Dirty Harry, Pete 'n Tillie, The Laughing Policeman, Dark Passage, Foul Play* and *Petulia*. TV series have also used it ad nauseum: *The Line Up, Sam Benedict, Ironside, McMillan and Wife, Streets of San Francisco, Phyllis*. The Barbary Coast days were well caught in *San Francisco, Nob Hill, Barbary Coast, Flame of the Barbary Coast*, and many other movies.

San Francisco (US 1936). A large-scale Hollywood entertainment of the thirties, its melodramatic story built round a reconstruction of the 1906 earthquake. Typically good performances from Clark Gable, Jeanette MacDonald, Spencer Tracy and Jack Holt; direction by W. S. Van Dyke; special effects, including a still-unsurpassed earthquake sequence, by John Hoffman and others; script by Anita Loos; lavish production values by MGM.

San Juan, Olga (1927–). Vivacious American dancer and comedienne, with radio experience.
Rainbow Island 44. Blue Skies 46. The Beautiful Blonde from Bashful Bend 49. Countess of Monte Cristo 49. The Third Voice 60, etc.

Sand, Paul (1944–) (Paul Sanchez). American light actor.
The Hot Rock 72. The Main Event 79. Can't Stop the Music 80. Wholly Moses 80.

Sanda, Dominique (1948–) (Dominique Varaigne). French leading lady of the seventies.
Une Femme Douce 70. *The Garden of the Finzi-Continis* 71. The Conformist 71. Without Apparent Motive 72. Impossible Object 73. The Mackintosh Man 73. Steppenwolf 74. 1900 76. Damnation Alley 77.

Sande, Walter (1906–1972). American character actor, usually a background heavy.
The Goldwyn Follies 38. Confessions of Boston Blackie 41. To Have and Have Not 44. Wild Harvest 47. Dark City 50. Red Mountain 52. Bad Day at Black Rock 55. The Gallant Hours 60, many others.
TV series: Tugboat Annie 56.

Sanders, Denis (1929–87) and **Terry** (1931–). American producer brothers who for many years promised great things but never quite fulfilled them.
A Time Out of War (short) 54. Crime and Punishment USA 58. War Hunt 61. Shock Treatment 63, etc.

Sanders, George (1906–1972). Suave British actor who played scoundrels, cads and crooks for thirty years. Varied early experience including London revue. Autobiography 1960: *Memoirs of a Professional Cad.*
□Find the Lady 36. Strange Cargo 36. The Man Who Could Work Miracles 36. Dishonour Bright 37. Slave Ship 37. Love is News 37. Lloyds of London 37. *Lancer Spy* 37. The Lady Escapes 37. International Settlement 38. Mr Moto's Last Warning 38. Four Men and a Prayer 38. Allegheny Uprising 39. So this is London 39. The Outsider 39. Nurse Edith Cavell 39. Confessions of a Nazi Spy 39. The House of Seven Gables 40. Green Hell 40. Bitter Sweet 40. Son of Monte Cristo 40. *Rebecca* 40. Foreign Correspondent 40. *The Saint* (series) 40–42. The Falcon (series) 41–43. Rage in Heaven 41. Man Hunt 41. Sundown 41. Her Cardboard Lover 41. Son of Fury 42. *The Moon and Sixpence* 42. The Black Swan 42. Tales of Manhattan 42. Paris After Dark 43. Quiet Please, Murder 43. They Came to Blow Up America 43. This Land is Mine 43. The Lodger 44. Action in Arabia 44. Summer Storm 44. *The Picture of Dorian Gray* 44. Hangover Square 44. Uncle Harry 45. *A Scandal in Paris* 46. The Strange Woman 47. The Ghost and Mrs Muir 47. *Forever Amber* 47. Bel Ami 48. Personal Column 48. *Lady Windermere's Fan* 49. Samson and Delilah 49. *All About Eve* (AA) 50. I Can Get It For You Wholesale 51. The Light Touch 51. Assignment Paris 52. Ivanhoe 52. Voyage in Italy 53. Call Me Madam 53. Witness to Murder 54. King Richard and the Crusaders 54. Jupiter's Darling 54. Moonfleet 55. The King's Thief 55. That Certain Feeling 56. The Scarlet Coat 56. Never Say Goodbye 56. While the City Sleeps 56. Death of a Scoundrel 56. The Whole Truth (GB) 57. The Seventh Sin 57. From the Earth to the Moon 58. Solomon and Sheba 59. That Kind of Woman 59. A Touch of Larceny (GB) 60. The Last Voyage 60. Bluebeard's Ten Honeymoons 60. *Village of the Damned* (GB) 60. A Shot in the Dark 64. The Golden Head 64. Moll Flanders 65. Warning Shot 66. The Quiller Memorandum 66. Trunk to Cairo 67. The Best House in London 68. The Body Stealers 69. The Kremlin Letter 69. The Candy Man 69. Endless Night 72. Doomwatch 72. Psychomania 72.
TV series: George Sanders Mystery Theatre 58.
❀ For being everybody's favourite swine, and for adding a touch of class to some pretty unappetizing movies. *Rebecca.*

¶ *G.S.:* I never really thought I'd make the grade. And let's face it, I haven't.

G.S.: I was beastly but never coarse. A high-class sort of heel.

'I will have had enough of this earth by the time I am 65. After that I shall be having my bottom wiped by nurses and being pushed around in a wheelchair. So I shall commit suicide.'—*G.S. 1937, recalled by David Niven*

'Dear World, I am leaving you because I am bored. I am leaving you with your worries. Good luck.'—*suicide note left by G.S. in 1972*

G.S., 1950s: I am not one of those people who would rather act than eat. Quite the reverse. My own desire as a boy was to retire. That ambition has never changed.

G.S.: I don't ask questions. I just take their money and use it for things that really interest me.

Famous line (*Rebecca*): I say, marriage with Max is not exactly a bed of roses, is it?
Famous line (*All About Eve*): I am Addison de Witt. I am nobody's fool, least of all yours.
Famous line (*The Picture of Dorian Gray*): I apologise for the intelligence of my remarks, Sir Thomas. I had forgotten that you are a member of parliament.

Famous line (*The Picture of Dorian Gray*): If I could get back my youth, I'd do anything in the world except get up early, take exercise or be respectable.

Sandford, Christopher (1939–). Emaciated British character actor.
Half a Sixpence 67. Before Winter Comes 70, etc.

Sandford, Tiny (1894–1961) (Stanley J. Sandford). American character actor who is best remembered as a foil for Laurel and Hardy: traffic cop or other nemesis.
The Immigrant 17. The World's Champion 22. The Circus 28. The Iron Mask 29. Our Relations 36. Modern Times 36, many others.

Sandrich, Mark (1900–1945). American director who came to Hollywood in 1927 as director of Lupino Lane two-reelers; later associated with musicals.
□The Talk of Hollywood 30. Melody Cruise 33. Aggie Appleby, Maker of Men 33. Hips Hips Hooray 34. Cockeyed Cavaliers 34. *The Gay Divorcee* 34. *Top Hat* 35. Follow the Fleet 36. A Woman Rebels 36. Shall we Dance 37. Carefree 38. Man About Town 39. Buck Benny Rides Again 40. Love Thy Neighbour 40. Skylark 41. *Holiday Inn* 42. So Proudly We Hail 43. I Love a Soldier 44. Here Come the Waves 44.

Sands, Diana (1934–1973). Black American actress.
A Raisin in the Sun 61. Ensign Pulver 64. The Landlord 70. Georgia Georgia 72. Willie Dynamite 73, etc.

Sands, Tommy (1937–). American 'teenage rave' singer.
Sing Boy Sing 57. Love in a Goldfish Bowl 59. Babes in Toyland 60. The Longest Day 62. None But the Brave 65, etc.

Sanford, Erskine (1880–1950). American character actor, playing elderly gents in the forties.
Pop Always Pays 40. *Citizen Kane* (as flustered editor) 41. The Magnificent Ambersons 42. Ministry of Fear 44. Possessed 47. Lady from Shanghai 48. Macbeth 50, etc.

Sanford, Ralph (1899–1963). American supporting player, usually in burly 'good guy' roles.
Give Me a Sailor 38. Thunderhead, Son of Flicka 45. Champion 49. Blackjack Ketchum Desperado 56. The Purple Gang 59, many others.

Le Sang d'un Poète (France 1930). Jean Cocteau's first film was short and surrealist, full of nightmare images with a tendency to the erotic, all sandwiched between shots of a chimney falling. Full of interesting pointers to his later work.

Sangster, Jimmy (1924–). British horror screenwriter, long associated with Hammer Films.
The Trollenberg Terror 55. *The Curse of Frankenstein* 56. *Dracula* 58. *The Mummy* 59. Jack the Ripper 59. Brides of Dracula 60. Taste of Fear (& p) 61. Maniac (& p) 63. Hysteria (& p) 65. *The Nanny* (& p) 65. Deadlier than the Male 67. The Anniversary (& p) 68. Horror of Frankenstein (& pd) 70. Lust for a Vampire (& d) 70. Fear in the Night (& pd) 72, etc.

Santell, Alfred (1895–1981). American director, former architect. With Mack Sennett as writer and director in the twenties.
Wildcat Jordan 22. Subway Sadie 26. The Patent Leather Kid 27. The Little Shepherd of Kingdom Come 28. *Daddy Long Legs* 30. The Sea Wolf 30. Tess of the Storm Country 33. A Feather in Her Hat 35. *Winterset* 36. Having Wonderful Time 38. Aloma of the South Seas 41. Beyond the Blue Horizon 42. Jack London 44. The Hairy Ape 44. That Brennan Girl 46, etc.

Santley, Joseph (1889–1971). American director, former child actor and vaudevillian.
The Smartest Girl in Town 32. Spirit of Culver 37. Swing, Sister, Swing 41. Hitting the Headlines 42. Brazil 44. Shadow of a Woman 47. Make Believe Ballroom 49, etc.

Santoni, Reni (1939–). American actor, of French/Spanish ancestry; ex TV writer.
Enter Laughing 67. Anzio 68. Dirty Harry 71. I Never Promised You a Rose Garden 77. They Went Thataway and Thataway 78. Bad Boys 83, etc.

Santschi, Tom (1879–1931). American leading man of the silents.
The Sultan's Power 09. The Spoilers 14. The Garden of Allah 16. Little Orphan Annie 19. Three Bad Men 26. In Old Arizona 29. Ten Nights in a Bar-Room 31, etc.

Sapper. The pen-name of H. C. McNeile (1888–1937), creator of Bulldog Drummond, qv for list of films featuring the character. Only the first made any attempt to convey the essential thuggishness of Drummond.

Sarafian, Richard C. (1925–). American director, of Armenian descent; much TV experience.
□Andy 65. Shadow on the Land (TV) 68. Run Wild Run Free 69. Fragment of Fear 70. *Vanishing Point* 71. Man in the Wilderness 71. The Man Who Loved Cat Dancing 73. Lolly Madonna XXX 73. One of Our Own (TV) 75. The Next Man 76. Sunburn 78. The Bear 84. Eye of the Tiger 86.

Sarandon, Chris (1942–). American character actor.
Dog Day Afternoon 75. Lipstick 76. The Sentinel 77. Cuba 79. The Day Christ Died (TV) (as Jesus) 80. A Tale of Two Cities (TV) 81. The Osterman Weekend 83. Fright Night 85.

Sarandon, Susan (1946–) (Susan Tomaling). American leading lady, ex-wife of Chris Sarandon.
Joe 70. The Front Page 74. The Great Waldo Pepper 75. Dragonfly 77. King of the Gypsies 78. Pretty Baby 78. Atlantic City USA 80. Loving Couples 80. Tempest 82. The Hunger 83. The Buddy System 83. Compromising Positions 85. The Witches of Eastwick 87, etc.
The Buddy System 83. Compromising Positions 85. The Witches of Eastwick 87, etc.

Sargent, Alvin (–). American screenwriter.
□The Stalking Moon 68. The Sterile Cuckoo 69. I Walk the Line 70. Love and Pain and the Whole Damn Thing 72. The Effect of Gamma Rays on Man in the Moon Marigolds 72. Paper Moon 73. Bobby Deerfield 77. Julia (AA, BFA) 77. Straight Time 78. Ordinary People (AA) 80.

Sargent, Dick (1933–). American screen actor who once specialized in gangling youths.
Bernardine 57. Operation Petticoat 59. That Touch of Mink 62. The Ghost and Mr Chicken 66. The Private Navy of Sergeant O'Farrell 68. Rich Man, Poor Man (TV) 76. Hardcore 79, etc.
TV series: One Happy Family 61. Broadside 64.

Sargent, Joseph (1925–) (Giuseppe Sargente). American director.
One Spy Too Many (TV) 65. The Spy in the Green Hat (TV) 66. The Hell with Heroes 68. The Sunshine Patriot (TV) 68. The Immortal (TV) 69. The Forbin Project 69. Tribes (TV) 70. Maybe I'll Come Home in the Spring (TV) 71. White Lightning 73. Sunshine (TV) 74. The Man (TV) 74. The Taking of Pelham One Two Three 74. MacArthur 77. Goldengirl (TV) 79. Coast to Coast 80. Jaws—The Revenge 87, etc.

Sarne, Michael (1939–). British director, former light actor.
AS ACTOR: Sodom and Gomorrah 60. The Guns of Navarone 61. A Place to Go 64. Every Day's a Holiday 65. Two Weeks in September 67, etc.
□AS DIRECTOR: The Road to St Tropez 66. Joanna 68. Myra Breckinridge 69.

Saroyan, William (1908–1981). American writer, mainly of fantasies about gentle people.
The Human Comedy 43. The Time of Your Life 48, etc.

Sarrazin, Michael (1940–). Canadian leading man of the early seventies, usually seen as the young innocent.
□The Doomsday Flight (TV) 66. Gunfight in Abilene 67. *The Flim Flam Man* 67. Journey to Shiloh 67. The Sweet Ride 68. A Man Called Gannon 68. Eye of the Cat 68. They Shoot Horses Don't They? 69. In Search of Gregory 70. The Pursuit of Happiness 71. Believe in Me 71. Sometimes a Great Notion 71. The Groundstar Conspiracy 72. Frankenstein: the True Story (TV) (as the creature) 73. Harry in Your Pocket 74. For Pete's Sake 74. The Reincarnation of Peter Proud 75. The Gumball Rally 76. The Loves and Times of Scaramouche 76. Caravans 78. Double Negative 80. The Seduction 82. Fighting Back 82. Joshua Then and Now 85. Kidnapped 87.

Sartov, Hendrik (–). American portrait photographer who joined Griffith in 1919 and was influential in soft focus close-ups.
Way Down East 20. Orphans of the Storm 21. One Exciting Night 22. America 24. Isn't Life Wonderful 25. The Scarlet Letter 26. Quality Street 27. Under the Black Eagle 28, etc.

Sartre, Jean-Paul (1905–1980). French existentialist writer. Works filmed include: Huis Clos (No Exit) 48. Crime Passionel 51. La Putain Respectueuse 52. Les Jeux Sont Faits 54. The Condemned of Altona 63.

Sasdy, Peter (1934–). Hungarian director in England.
□Taste the Blood of Dracula 69. Countess Dracula 70. Hands of the Ripper 71. Doomwatch 72. Nothing But the Night 72. I Don't Want to Be Born 75. Welcome to Blood City 76. Murder at the Wedding (TV) 79. The Lonely Lady 83. Many television dramas.

Sassard, Jacqueline (1940–). French leading lady.
Accident 67. Les Biches 68.

satire, being defined in theatrical circles as 'what closes Saturday night', has seldom been encouraged by Hollywood, and the few genuinely satirical films have not been commercially successful, from *A Nous la Liberté* through *American Madness, Nothing Sacred* and *Roxie Hart* to *The Loved One*. However, the odd lampoon in the middle of an otherwise straightforward comedy has often brought critical enthusiasm for films as diverse as *Modern Times, Boy Meets Girl, I'm All Right, Jack, The President's Analyst* and *The Groove Tube*; and in future it looks as though one can at least expect that the range of permissible targets will become even wider. The spotty but considerable success in 1976 of *Network*, the screen's most hysterical satire of all, was at least partly due to its sexy scenes and uninhibited language.

Saturday Night and Sunday Morning (GB 1960). Alan Sillitoe's raw, humorous wallow in the sub-life of Nottingham was filmed by Karel Reisz, whose directorial talent has oddly found no satisfactory expression since. The film broadened still further the British attitude to illicit sex and taught us that the subject needn't be treated very seriously. It also introduced a new star in Albert Finney. Photographed by Freddie Francis. BFA for the best British film.

Saturday Night Fever (US 1977). A nothing story of repellent young New Yorkers who get together for Saturday night dancing and fornication, this became a sensational hit because it brought together the music of the Bee Gees and the sinuous movements of John Travolta; but John Badham's direction was also pretty smart.

Saunders, Charles (1904–). British director, former editor.
Tawny Pipit (co-d) 44. Fly Away Peter 47. One Wild Oat 51. Meet Mr Callaghan 54. Kill Her Gently 57. Womaneater 58. Danger by My Side 62, etc.

Saunders, John Monk (1895–1940). American screenwriter with a special interest in aviation.
Wings 27. *Dawn Patrol* 30. *The Last Flight* 31. Devil Dogs of the Air 35. I Found Stella Parish 35.

Sautet, Claude (1924–). French director.
The Big Risk 60. Head First 64. Les Choses de la Vie 69. Vincent, Francois, Paul and the Others 76. Mado 78. Un Mauvais Fils 80. Garçon! 83.

Savage, Ann (1921–) (Bernie Lyon). American leading lady of forties seconds.
Two Señoritas from Chicago 43. Two Man Submarine 44. *Detour* 45. Scared Stiff 45. The Last Crooked Mile 46. Renegade Girl 46. Jungle Flight 47. Satan's Cradle 49. Pygmy Island 50. The Woman They Almost Lynched 53, others.

The Savage Eye (US 1959). One of the first of the exposé pictures which have since flooded the market, this semi-professional job with flashes of brilliance attempts to take the lid off a big American city, with scenes of faith healing, strip-tease and wrestling to show its decadence. The connecting narration by a neurotic woman is unfortunate.
Produced and directed by Ben Maddow and Joseph Strick.

Savage, John (1949–). Babyfaced American leading man who didn't quite become another James Dean.
Bad Company 75. The Killing Kind 65. No Deposit No Return 76. The Deer Hunter 78. Hair 79. The Onion Field 80. Cattle Annie and Little Britches 81. Inside Moves 81. The Amateur 82. Brady's Escape 84. Maria's Lovers 85. Salvador 86. The Beat 87. Hotel Colonial 87, etc.
TV series: Gibbsville 76.

Saval, Dany (1940–) (Danielle Nadine Suzanne Salle). French leading lady.
Les Tricheurs 58. The Mirror Has Two Faces 58. Nathalie 59. Les Parisiennes 61. The Seven Deadly Sins 62. Moon Pilot 62. The Devil and Ten Commandments 62. Web of Fear 64. Boeing Boeing 65. La Vie Parisienne 78, etc.

Savalas, Telly (1924–) (Aristotle Savalas). Bald Greek-American character actor with TV experience; former academic.
The Young Savages 61. Birdman of Alcatraz 62. The Interns 63. Cape Fear 63. The Man from the Diners' Club 63. The New Interns 64. Genghis Khan 65. *The Battle of the Bulge* 65. The Slender Thread 66. Beau Geste 66. The Dirty Dozen 67. *The Scalphunters* 68. Buona Sera Mrs Campbell 68. The Assassination Bureau (GB) 68. Crooks and Coronets (GB) 69. The Land Raiders 69. Mackenna's Gold 69. On Her Majesty's Secret Service 69. Kelly's Heroes 70. A Town Called Bastard 71. Pretty Maids All in a Row 71. Pancho Villa 71. The Marcus Nelson Murders (TV) 73. A Reason to Live a Reason to Die 72. The Killer is on the Phone 72. She Cried Murder (TV) 73. Horror Express 74. The Diamond Mercenaries 75. Inside Out 75. Capricorn One 78. The French Atlantic Affair (TV) 79. Escape to Athena 79. Beyond the Poseidon Adventure 79. The Cartier Affair (TV) 84. Kojak: The Belarus File (TV) 85, etc.
TV series: Acapulco 60. *Kojak* 73–77.

Saville, Victor (1897–1979). British director who after making some outstanding films in the thirties went to Hollywood with very meagre results. Former film salesman and exhibitor.
The Arcadians 27. Roses of Picardy 28. *Woman to Woman* (US) 29. Hindle Wakes 31. Sunshine Susie 31. *The Good Companions* 32. I Was a Spy 33. *Friday the Thirteenth* 33. *Evergreen* 34. The Iron Duke 36. Dark Journey 37. Storm in a Teacup 37. *South Riding* 38. The Citadel (p only) 38. Goodbye Mr Chips (p only) 39. Bitter Sweet (p) 40. Dr Jekyll and Mr Hyde (p) 41. White Cargo (p) 42. Tonight and Every Night (pd) 44. The Green Years (pd) 46. If Winter Comes (d) 47. The Conspirator (d) 47. Kim (p) 51. I the Jury (p) 53. The Long Wait (pd) 54. The Silver Chalice (pd) 55. Kiss Me Deadly (p) 55. The Greengage Summer (p) 61.

Savo, Jimmy (1895–1960). Pint-sized American comedian who failed to repeat his Broadway success on film.
Exclusive Rights 26. Once in a Blue Moon 36. Merry Go Round of 1938, etc.

Sawdust and Tinsel (Sweden 1953). The first of writer-director Ingmar Bergman's films to be internationally noticed, this deftly handled melodrama has Ake Gromberg as the foolish owner of a travelling circus and Harriet Andersson as his repressed wife.

Sawtell, Paul (1906–1971). American composer.
The Gay Falcon 41. Tarzan Triumphs 43. The Scarlet Claw 44. Dick Tracy Meets Gruesome 47. Black Magic 49. Son of Dr Jekyll 51. Inferno 53. Texas Lady 55. Stopover Tokyo 57. The Lost World 60. Five Weeks in a Balloon 62. Island of the Blue Dolphins 64. The Christine Jorgenson Story 70, many others.

Sawyer, Joseph (1901–1982) (Joseph Sauer). American comedy actor usually seen as tough cop or army sergeant.
College Humour 33. The Marines Have Landed 36. Black Legion 37. The Roaring Twenties 40. Sergeant York 41. About Face 42. The McGuerins from Brooklyn 42. Fall In 44. Joe Palooka, Champ 46. Fighting Father Dunne 49. It Came from Outer Space 53. The Killing 56, many others.
TV series: Rin Tin Tin 55.

Saxon, John (1935–) (Carmen Orrico). American leading man, former model.
Running Wild (debut) 55. The Unguarded Moment 56. The Reluctant Debutante 58. Portrait in Black 59. The Unforgiven 59. The Plunderers 60. Posse from Hell 61. War Hunt 62. The Cardinal 63. The Evil Eye (It.) 63. The Appaloosa 66. The Night Caller (GB) 67. Death of a Gunfighter 69. Joe Kidd 72. Enter the Dragon 73. Black Christmas 75. Mitchell 75. The Swiss Conspiracy 75. Blazing Magnum 76. Moonshine County Express 77. The Bees 78. The Electric Horseman 79. Blood Beach 81. The Glove 81. Hardcastle and McCormick (TV) 83. The Big Score 83. A Nightmare on Elm Street 84. Fever Pitch 85.
TV series: The Bold Ones 69.

Sayers, Dorothy L. (1893–1957). British detective novelist, creator of Lord Peter Wimsey, who was personified on film by Peter Haddon in *The Silent Passenger* and Robert Montgomery in *Busman's Honeymoon*. Ian Carmichael had a long run on TV in the seventies.

¶ 'For her warm-hearted admirers she is still the finest detective story writer of the century, to those less enthusiastic her work is long-winded and ludicrously snobbish.'—*Julian Symons*

Sayles, John (1948–). American director.
Return of the Secaucus Seven 80. Baby It's You 82. Lianna 82. The Brother from Another Planet 84.

Sayonara (US 1957). A solemn burying of the hatchet between two countries in the form of a romantic idyll between an American air force officer and a Japanese girl after World War II. Immensely good to look at but extremely long drawn out by director Joshua Logan, with little meat to be had from Paul Osborn's script or James Michener's original novel, and a mumbling Southern-accented performance from Marlon Brando. The armchair travelogue elements come off best, via Ellsworth Fredericks' cinematography. AA best art direction, sound recording, supporting actors Red Buttons and Miyoshi Umeki.

Scacchi, Greta (*c.*1958–). Italian-born leading lady in international films.
Dead on Time 81. Heat and Dust 82. Waterfront (TV) 83. The Ebony Tower (TV) 84. Camille (TV) 85. The Coca Cola Kid 85. Defence of the Realm 86. Good Morning Babylon 87.

Scaife, Ted (1912–). British cinematographer.
Bonnie Prince Charlie 48. An Inspector Calls 54. Sea Wife 57. *Night of the Demon* 57. 633 Squadron 64. *Khartoum* 66. The Dirty Dozen 67. Play Dirty 68. Sinful Davey 69. Forbush and the Penguins 71. Hannie Caulder 71. Sitting Target 72. Catlow 72, many others.

Scala, Gia (1934–1972) (Giovanna Scoglio). Italian leading lady who made a few American films.
The Price of Fear 56. Four Girls in Town 56. Don't Go Near the Water 56. The Garment Jungle 57. The Two-Headed Spy (GB) 58. I Aim at the Stars 59. The Guns of Navarone 61, etc.

Scales, Prunella (*c.*1938–). British leading actress, mainly in comedy and on TV. Films include The Boys from Brazil 78. The Wicked Lady 84.

Scaramouche. Rafael Sabatini's tongue-in-cheek French Revolutionary romance, about a nobleman who, to outwit his enemies, disguises himself as a clown in a travelling theatre, was filmed in 1922 by Rex Ingram, with Ramon Novarro, and in 1952 by George Sidney, with Stewart Granger.

Scarface (US 1932). A highly professional and exciting gangster film based on the career of Al Capone. Written by Seton I. Miller, John Lee Mahin, W. R. Burnett and Ben Hecht, directed by Howard Hawks, it made crime so attractive that the moralists were subsequently able to curb Hollywood's freedom by means of a tougher code. Photography by Lee Garmes and L. W. O'Connell, production by Howard Hughes; cast headed by Paul Muni and George Raft, who have been associated with these roles ever since. The 1983 alleged remake, written by Oliver Stone and directed by Brian de Palma, was a universally condemned orgy of blood-letting.

The Scarlet Empress (US 1934). For its superb visual flair rather than its dramatic sense, this highly romanticized biography of Catherine the Great remains a cinema classic. Fantastically baroque décor, a hypnotic performance from Sam Jaffe as the mad prince, and the mysterious depths of Marlene Dietrich's personality (here suggested but not plumbed) are brought together by Josef Von Sternberg into a fantasy he relishes to the last hysterical note. See also: *Catherine the Great.*

The Scarlet Letter. Nathaniel Hawthorne's story of puritanical eighteenth-century New England was filmed in 1917 with Mary Martin as the adultress and Stuart Holmes as her priest-lover forced to accuse her. In 1926 came Victor Sjostrom's more famous version with Lillian Gish and Lars Hanson. 1934 brought a talkie remake with Colleen Moore and Hardie Albright, and Wim Wenders made a German version in the seventies.

The Scarlet Pimpernel. Baroness Orczy's foppish hero of the French Revolution has been filmed three times since sound. GB 1935: by Harold Young, with Leslie Howard, opposing Raymond Massey as Chauvelin. GB 1938: by Hans Schwarz, with Barry K. Barnes winning out over Francis Lister. GB 1950: by Michael Powell and Emeric Pressburger, with David Niven as Sir Percy. There has also been a TV series starring Marius Goring. Silent versions included one in 1917 starring Dustin Farnum and one in 1929 starring Matheson Lang. The idea was modernized in Leslie Howard's *Pimpernel Smith* 41. In 1982 the original was remade for television with Anthony Andrews, Jane Seymour and Ian McKellen.

Scarlet Street (US 1945). This sombre drama directed by Fritz Lang concerns a cashier (Edward G. Robinson) who is taken in by a tart, finally murders her, and allows her gigolo friend to be executed for the crime. A remake of Renoir's 1931 French film *La Chienne,* it was notable as the first American film in which a character is allowed to commit murder and get away with it—although he is shown to be still tortured by remorse many years later.

Scarwid, Diana (–). American leading lady.
Pretty Baby 78. Inside Moves 80. Mommie Dearest 81. Silkwood 83.

Scattergood Baines, an amiable small-town busybody created by Clarence Buddington Kelland, was personified by Guy Kibbee in six second features (41–42), all directed by Christy Cabanne.

scenario: see *shooting script.*

Schaefer, George (1920–). American director with TV experience.
□Macbeth 61. Pendulum 68. Generation 69. Doctors' Wives 71. A War of Children (TV) 72. A Time for Love (TV) 73. F. Scott Fitzgerald and the Last of the Belles (TV) 74. In This House of Brede (TV) 75. An Enemy of the People 78.

Schafer, Natalie (1912–). American comedienne usually seen as a dizzy rich woman.
Marriage is a Private Affair 43. Wonder Man 45. The Snake Pit 48. Caught 49. Anastasia 56. Oh Men Oh Women 57. Susan Slade 61. Forty Carats 73, etc.
TV series: *Gilligan's Island* 64–66.

Schaffner, Franklin (1920–). Stylish American director, from TV.
□The Stripper 63. *The Best Man* 64. *The War Lord* 65. The Double Man 67. *Planet of the Apes* 68. *Patton* (AA) 69. Nicholas and Alexandra 71. *Papillon* 73. Islands in the Stream 77. The Boys from Brazil 78. Sphinx 81. Yes Giorgio 82.

Schallert, William (1922–). American character actor who played a lot of dull fathers in his day. More recently president of the Screen Actors' Guild.
The Man from Planet X 52. Riot in Cell Block Eleven 55. Written on the Wind 56. Cry Terror 68. Pillow Talk 60. In the Heat of the Night 67. Will Penny 68. Charley Varrick 73, many others.

Scharf, Walter (1910–). American composer.
Chatterbox 43. Dakota 45. The Saxon Charm 48. Deported 50. Hans Christian Andersen 52. Living It Up 54. Hollywood or Bust 56. King Creole 58. A Pocketful of Miracles 61. Where Love Has Gone 64. Pendulum 69. The Cheyenne Social Club 70. Ben 72. Walking Tall 73. Final Chapter, Walking Tall 77. When Every Day was the Fourth of July (TV) 78. This Is Elvis 81, many others.

Schary, Dore (1905–1980). American writer-producer with newspaper and theatrical experience. AA best screenplay *Boys' Town* 38; produced for MGM 1941–45; head of production RKO 1945–48; head of production MGM 1948–56; then independent.
Autobiography 1979: *Heyday*.
Lonelyhearts 59. Sunrise at Campobello 60. Act One (wpd) 63, etc.

¶ A man whose few successes were even more distasteful than his many failures.—*John Simon of D.S.*

Schatzberg, Jerry (1927–). American director, former fashion photographer.
□Puzzle of a Downfall Child 71. The Panic in Needle Park 71. Scarecrow 73. Dandy, the All American Girl 76. The Seduction of Joe Tynan 79. Honeysuckle Rose 80. Misunderstood 83. No Small Affair 84. Street Smart 87.

Schayer, Richard (1882–*). American scriptwriter.
Black Roses 21. The Thrill Chaser 23. Silk Stocking Sal 24. Tell It to the Marines 26. On ze Boulevard 27. The Cameraman 28. Spite Marriage 29. Free and Easy 30. Doughboys 30. Trader Horn 31. The Winning Ticket 35. The Devil Is a Sissy 36. The Black Arrow 48. Lorna Doone 51. Gun Belt 53. Lancelot and Guinevere 63, many others.

Scheider, Roy (1934–). Lean American character actor.
□ The Curse of the Living Corpse 64. Star 68. Stiletto 69. Loving 70. Puzzle of a Downfall Child 70. Klute 71. L'Attentat 72. Assignment Munich (TV) 72. The Outside Man 72. *The French Connection* 72. Sheila Levine is Dead and Living in New York 73. The Seven-Ups 73. *Jaws* 75. Marathon Man 76. Sorcerer 77. Jaws 2 78. Last Embrace 79. *All That Jazz* 79. Prisoner without a Name, Cell without a Number (TV) 80. Still of the Night 82. Blue Thunder 83. 2010 84. Mishima 85. Tiger Town 85. The Men's Club 86. 52 Pick-Up 86.

Schell, Catherine (1946–) (Catherine von Schell). German character actress.
Moon Zero Two 69. Madame Sin (TV) 72. Callan 74. The Black Windmill 74. The Prisoner of Zenda 79, etc.
TV series: Space 1999 75–76.

Schell, Maria (1926–). Austrian leading lady who has been in British and American films.
The Angel with the Trumpet 49. The Magic Box 51. So Little Time 52. The Heart of the Matter 52. Der Traumende Mund 53. The Last Bridge (Aus.) 54. Die Ratten 55. *Gervaise* 56. White Nights (It.) 57. Une Vie (Fr.) 58. The Brothers Karamazov 58. Cimarron 61. The Mark (GB) 61. 99 Women 69. The Odessa File 74. Voyage of the Damned 76. Superman 78. Just a Gigolo 79, etc.

Schell, Maximilian (1930–). Austrian leading man who has been in international films. Brother of Maria Schell.
Kinder, Mütter und ein General 58. The Young Lions 58. *Judgment at Nuremberg* (AA) 61. Five-Finger Exercise 62. The Condemned of Altona 63. The Reluctant Saint 63. Topkapi 64. Return from the Ashes 65. The Deadly Affair 66. Beyond the Mountains 66. Counterpoint 67. The Castle 68. Krakatoa 68. First Love (wpd only) 70. The Pedestrian (p, d) 73. The Odessa File 74. First Love (& d) 75. The Man in the Glass Booth 75. St Ives 76. End of the Game (& d) 76. Julia 77. Cross of Iron 77. Avalanche Express 79. The Black Hole 79. Players 79. The Diary of Anne Frank (TV) 81. The Chosen 81. Man Under Suspicion 84. Marlene (& d) 85. The Assisi Underground 85, etc.

Schenck, Aubrey (1908–). American producer.
Shock 46. Repeat Performance 48. Beachhead 53. Up Periscope 58. Frankenstein 70 59. Robinson Crusoe on Mars 64. Don't Worry We'll Think of a Title 66. The Alpha Caper (TV) 73, etc.

Schenck, Joseph M. (1878–1961). Russian-born executive, in America from 1900, at first as pharmacist, then as fairground showman and owner. By 1924 was chairman of United Artists and creator of its theatre chain. In 1933 he founded Twentieth Century Productions and by 1935 was head of Twentieth Century-Fox. In 1953 he created Magna Productions with Mike Todd. In 1950 he was voted a special Academy Award.

Schenck, Nicholas M. (1881–1969). Russian-born executive, brother of Joseph M. Schenck, with whom after arrival in America in 1900 he ran an amusement park. Later developed theatre chain which emerged as Loew's Consolidated Enterprises; became president of Loew's and thus financial controller of MGM.

Schepisi, Fred (1939–). Australian director.
The Devil's Playground 76. The Chant of Jimmie Blacksmith 78. Iceman 81. Barbarosa 82. Plenty 85. Roxanne 87. A Cry in the Dark 89.

Scherick, Edgar J. (c. 1919–). American independent producer.
For Love of Ivy 68. Sleuth 72. The Heartbreak Kid 72. Gordon's War 74. The Stepford Wives 74. The Taking of Pelham One Two Three 74. I Never Promised You a Rose Garden 77. Little Gloria . . . Happy at Last (TV) 82. Shoot the Moon 82. The Kennedys of Massachusetts (TV) 84. The Dakota (TV) 84. Reckless 84, etc.

Schertzinger, Victor (1880–1941). American director, former concert violinist. Wrote the first film music score, for *Civilisation* 15.
AS DIRECTOR: Forgotten Faces 29. Nothing but the Truth 31. Uptown New York 32. The Cocktail Hour 33. One Night of Love 34. Love Me Forever 35. The Music Goes Round 36. Something to Sing About 36. The Mikado (GB) 39. Road to Singapore 40. Rhythm on the River 41. Road to Zanzibar 41. Kiss the Boys Goodbye 41, etc.

Schiaffino, Rosanna (1939–). Italian leading lady in international films.
Two Weeks in Another Town 62. The Victors 63. El Greco 66. Arrivederci Baby 66. The Man Called Noon 73. The Heroes 75. Cagliostro 76, etc.

Schifrin, Lalo (1932–). Argentinian composer in Hollywood.
Joy House 64. The Cincinnati Kid 64. The Liquidator 66. Cool Hand Luke 67. The Brotherhood 68. Bullitt 68. Kelly's Heroes 70. The Beguiled 71. Dirty Harry 71. Prime Cut 72. The Wrath of God 72. The Four Musketeers 75. Voyage of the Damned 76. Rollercoaster 77. Telefon 77. The Cat from Outer Space 78. The Manitou 78. The Concorde – Airport 79 79. Brubaker 79. The Competition 80. When Time Ran Out 80.

Caveman 81. Buddy Buddy 81. A Stranger Is Watching 82. The Osterman Weekend 83. Sudden Impact 83, many others.

Schildkraut, Joseph (1895–1964). Austrian leading man and character actor, of theatrical family. On American stage from early twenties.
Autobiography 1959: *My Father and I.*
□Schlemiel 14. The Life of Theodore Herzl 18. Orphans of the Storm 22. The Song of Love 24. The Road to Yesterday 25. Shipwrecked 26. Young April 26. Meet the Prince 26. *King of Kings* 27. The Heart Thief 27. His Dog 27. The Forbidden Woman 27. The Blue Danube 28. Tenth Avenue 28. *Showboat* 29. The Mississippi Gambler 29. Cock o' the Walk 30. Night Ride 30. A Lady to Love (German version) 31. Carnival 31. Cleopatra 34. Viva Villa 34. Sisters Under the Skin 34. Blue Danube 34. The Crusades 35. *The Garden of Allah* 36. Slave Ship 37. *The Life of Emile Zola* (AA) (as Dreyfus) 37. Souls at Sea 37. Lancer Spy 37. Lady Behave 37. The Baroness and the Butler 38. Marie Antoinette 38. Suez 38. Idiot's Delight 39. The Three Musketeers 39. *The Man in the Iron Mask* 39. Mr Moto Takes a Vacation 39. Lady of the Tropics 39. *The Rains Came* 39. Barricade 39. Pack Up Your Troubles 39. The Shop Around the Corner 40. Phantom Raiders 40. Rangers of Fortune 40. Meet the Wildcat 40. The Parson of Panamint 41. Flame of the Barbary Coast 45. The Cheaters 45. *Monsieur Beaucaire* 46. The Plainsman and the Lady 46. Northwest Outpost 47. Old Los Angeles 48. Gallant Legion 48. *The Diary of Anne Frank* 59. King of the Roaring Twenties 60. The Greatest Story Ever Told 65.

Schilling, Gus (1908–1957). Wry-faced American comic actor from musical comedy and burlesque.
Citizen Kane (debut; as the waiter) 41. A Thousand and One Nights 44. Lady from Shanghai 47. On Dangerous Ground 52. Glory 56, etc.

Schlesinger, John (1926–). British director, former small-part actor and TV director.
□*Terminus* 60. *A Kind of Loving* 62. *Billy Liar* 63. *Darling* 65. Far from the Madding Crowd 67. *Midnight Cowboy* (US) (AA) 69. *Sunday Bloody Sunday* 72. Visions of Eight 73. The Day of the Locust 75. Marathon Man 76. Yanks 79. Honky Tonk Freeway 81. An Englishman Abroad (TV) 83. The Falcon and the Snowman 85. The Believers 87.

¶ *J.S., 1980:* The days of dealing with one despot are over. Now it's clearly with a whole group of frightened committee people.
J.S.: What I tend to go for, and what interests me, is not the hero but the coward . . . not the success, but the failure.

Schlom, Herman (1904–1983). American producer of forties second features.
The Sheik Steps Out 38. The Brighton Strangler 45. Dick Tracy Meets Gruesome 48. Follow Me Quietly 50, etc.

Schlondorff, Volker (1939–). German director.
Young Torless 66. A Degree of Murder 67. Michael Kohlhaas 69. Baal 70. Summer Lightning 72. The Lost Honour of Katharina Blum 75. Coup de Grace 77. *The Tin Drum* 79. Circle of Deceit 81. Hotel de la Paix 83.

Schmidt, Joseph (1906–1942). Diminutive German opera singer who made two British films: *My Song Goes Round the World* 34. *The Singing Dream* 35.

Schmidt, Richard (1944–). American experimental film maker.
A Man, a Woman and a Killer 75. Showboat 1988—the Remake 78. Emerald Cities 83.

Schnee, Charles (1916–1963). American screenwriter.
I Walk Alone 47. Red River 48. The Furies 50. *The Bad and the Beautiful* (AA) 52. The Next Voice You Hear 53. Butterfield 8 60. The Crowded Sky 61. Two Weeks in another Town 62, etc.

Schneer, Charles (1920–). American producer, mainly of trick films using 'Superdynamation'.
The Seventh Voyage of Sinbad 58. The Three Worlds of Gulliver 60. I Aim at the Stars 61. Mysterious Island 62. *Jason and the Argonauts* 63. The First Men in the Moon 64. You Must Be Joking 65. Half a Sixpence 67. The Executioner 69. Sinbad's Golden Voyage 74. Sinbad and the Eye of the Tiger 77, etc.

Schneider, Bert (1932–) (Berton Schneider). American producer of Hollywood's 'new wave'.
Head 68. Easy Rider 69. Five Easy Pieces 71. The Last Picture Show 71. A Safe Place 72. Drive He Said 72. The King of Marvin Gardens 73.

Schneider, Maria (1952–). German leading actress.
Last Tango in Paris 73. Reigen 74. The Passenger 75. Babysitter 75. A Woman Like Eve 79. Mama Dracula 80, etc.

Schneider, Romy (1938–1982) (Rosemarie Albach-Retty). Austrian leading lady in international films.
Wenn der Weisse Flieder Wieder Blueht 53. Sissi 55. Maedchen in Uniform 58. The Story of Vicki (Ger.) 58. Forever My Love 61. Boccaccio 70. 62. The Cardinal 63. The Trial 63. The Victors 63. Good Neighbour Sam 64. What's New Pussycat 65. 10.30 p.m. Summer 66. Triple Cross 66. Les Choses de la Vie 69. Don't You Cry 70. Bloomfield 70. The Assassination of Trotsky 72. Ludwig 72. Qui? 73. *L'Amour de Pluie* 73. The Infernal Trio 74. Lover on a String 75. The Old Gun 76. Bloodline 79. La Banquière 80, etc.

Schneiderman, George (c. 1890–1964). American cinematographer.
Love is Love 19. Bare Knuckles 21. Boston Blackie 23. *The Iron Horse* 24. The Johnstown Flood 26. Three Bad Men 26. Four Sons 28. Born Reckless 30. Charlie Chan Carries On 31. Young America 32. Doctor Bull 33. *Judge Priest* 34. Steamboat Round the Bend 35. The Devil is a Sissy 36. The Gladiator 38. Michael Shayne Private Detective 40, many others.

Schnitzler, Arthur (1862–1931). Austrian playwright whose chief bequests to the cinema are *Liebelei* and *La Ronde*.

Schoedsack, Ernest B. (1893–1979). American director, former cameraman, who with Merian C. Cooper made the following. *Grass* 26. *Chang* 27. *The Four Feathers* 29. Rango 31. *The Hounds of Zaroff* 32. *King Kong* 33. Son of Kong 34. Long Lost Father 34. Outlaws of the Orient 37. Dr Cyclops 39. Mighty Joe Young 49, etc.

schooldays have often been depicted in films with a thick sentimental veneer, as in *Goodbye Mr Chips, Good Morning Miss Dove* and *Blossoms in the Dust*. But more usually the pupils have serious problems to worry about, as in *Young Woodley, The Guinea Pig, Friends for Life, Tea and Sympathy* and *Tom Brown's Schooldays*; while with at least equal frequency our sympathies are elicited on behalf of the staff: *The Housemaster, Bright Road, The Blackboard Jungle, The Browning Version, Spare the Rod, Edward My Son, The Blue Angel, The Children's Hour, The Corn is Green, Term of Trial, To Sir With Love, Spinster, The Prime of Miss Jean Brodie, Please Sir, Unman Wittering and Zigo*. More light-hearted treatment of the whole business is evident in *The Trouble with Angels* and *Margie*, and in some cases the treatment has undeniably been farcical: *Boys Will Be Boys, The Ghost of St Michael's, Good Morning Boys, A Yank at Eton, Vice Versa, Bottoms Up* and *The Happiest Days of Your Life*; with the St Trinians saga wildest of all. The strangest schools on film are those depicted in *Zéro de Conduite* and its semi-remake *If . . .* while very special schools were seen in *Battement de Coeur* (for pickpockets), *School for Secrets* (for 'boffins'), *Old Bones of the River* (for African tiny tots), *The Goose Steps Out* (for young Nazis), *Orders to Kill, The House on 92nd Street, 13 Rue Madeleine, Carve Her Name with Pride* and *From Russia with Love* (for spies).

Schoonmaker, Thelma (1945–). American editor who won an Academy Award for *Raging Bull*.
Woodstock 70. King of Comedy 83.

Schrader, Paul (1946–). American screenwriter dealing almost obsessively with tough themes.
□The Yakuza (co-w) 75. *Taxi Driver* 76. Obsession 76. Rolling Thunder (co-w) 77. Blue Collar (& d) 78. Old Boyfriends (co-w) 79. Hardcore (& d) 79. American Gigolo (& d) 79. Raging Bull 80. Cat People (& d) 82. Mishima (& d) 85. Light of Day (& d) 87.

Schreck, Max (1879–1936). German actor best known for his eerie portrayal of the vampire count in *Nosferatu* 22.

Schroder, Ricky (1970–). American child actor.
□*The Champ* 79. The Last Flight of Noah's Ark 80. The Earthling 80. Little Lord Fauntleroy (TV) 81.
TV series: Silver Spoons 82–.

Schroeder, Barbet (1941–). Iranian director, long in Paris, at first as director of Eric Rohmer's films.
More 69. The Valley 72. General Idi Amin Dada 74. Maîtress 76. Barfly 87.

Schuck, John (1944–). American character actor familiar as the dumb sergeant in *McMillan and Wife*.

M*A*S*H 70. Blade 73. Thieves Like Us 74. Butch and Sundance: the Early Days 79. Just You and Me Kid 79. Earthbound 81, etc.
TV series: Holmes and Yo Yo 75. Turnabout 79.

Schufftan, Eugene (1893–1977). German cinematographer. Invented the Schufftan process, a variation on the 'glass shot' (qv), by which mirror images are blended with real backgrounds.
People on Sunday 30. L'Atlantide 32. Drôle de Drame 37. *Quai des Brumes* 38. *It Happened Tomorrow* 44. Ulysses 54. Eyes without a Face 59. Something Wild 61. *The Hustler* (AA) 62. Lilith 64, etc.

Schulberg, B. P. (1892–1950). American executive, former publicist; general manager of Paramount (1926–32), then independent producer.

¶ *Advertisement in Variety, 1949:* This is the only industry I know. I am able to work as hard as anybody in it. Sure I have made some mistakes . . . who hasn't? What is the judicial code of the industry? Life imprisonment for a misdemeanour and execution for violating a parking law? Must we always wait until a production pioneer is found dead in a Hollywood hotel room before reflecting on an 'indifferent and forgetful' industry?

Schulberg, Budd (1914–). American novelist whose work has been adapted for the screen. Son of B. P. Schulberg.
Autobiography 1982: *Moving Pictures*.
On the Waterfront (AA) 54. The Harder They Fall 56. A Face in the Crowd 57. Wind Across the Everglades 59. A Question of Honour (TV) 81, etc.

Schultz, Michael (1938–). American director.
Cooley High 75. Car Wash 76. Greased Lightning 77. Which Way Is Up? 77. Sergeant Pepper's Lonely Hearts Club Band 78. Scavenger Hunt 79. Carbon Copy 81. The Last Dragon 84. Krush Grove 85. Disorderlies 87, etc.

Schumacher, Joel (–). American director.
St Elmo's Fire 85. The Lost Boys 87.

Schunzel, Reinhold (1886–1954). German actor and director who came to Hollywood in the thirties.
Around the World in 80 Days 19. Die Dreigroschenoper 31. Viktor und Viktoria 33. Amphitryon 37. Rich Man, Poor Girl (d) 38. Balalaika (d) 39. The Great Awakening (d) 41. Hostages (a) 43. The Man in Half Moon Street (a) 44. Notorious (a) 46. The Woman in Brown (a) 48. Washington Story (a) 52, etc.

Schuster, Harold (1902–86). American director, former editor.
Wings of the Morning 37. Dinner at the Ritz 37. Zanzibar 40. My Friend Flicka 43. The Tender Years 47. So Dear to My Heart 49. Kid Monk Baroni 52. Jack Slade 53. Dragoon Wells Massacre 57. The Courage of Black Beauty 58, etc.

Schwartz, Arthur (1900–84). American producer and composer, former lawyer.
Navy Blues (c) 42. Thank Your Lucky Stars (c) 43. Cover Girl (p) 44. The Band Wagon (c) 53. You're Never Too Young (c) 55, others.

Schwarz, Maurice (1891–1960). American actor famous in the Yiddish theatre; many of his successes, such as *Tevye the Milkman*, were filmed for limited circulation. Appeared in Hollywood's version of *Salome* 53.

Schwarzenegger, Arnold (1947–). American muscleman who took to acting.
Stay Hungry 76. Pumping Iron 77. The Villain 79. The Jayne Mansfield Story (TV) 79. Conan the Barbarian 82. Conan the Destroyer 84. The Terminator 84. Commando 85. Red Sonja 85. Raw Deal 86. Predator 87. The Running Man 87, etc.

¶ 'He has so many muscles that he has to make an appointment to move his fingers.'—*Phyllis Diller*

Schygulla, Hanna (1943–). Polish leading actress, mainly in Fassbinder films.
□ The Bridegroom and the Actress 68. Katzelmacher 69. Beware of a Holy Whore 70. *The Bitter Tears of Petra Von Kant* 72. Effie Briest 74. *The Marriage of Maria Braun* 79. *Berlin Alexanderplatz* 80. Lili Marleen 80. Circle of Deceit 81. La Nuit de Varenne 82. The Story of Piera 83. A Love in Germany 83. The Future is Woman 84. The Delta Force 85. Forever Lulu 87.

science fiction, a term incapable of precise definition, may perhaps be taken as that kind of fantasy which depends not on legend only, like Dracula, but involves the work of man. Thus King Kong and the 'natural' monsters would not qualify, but Frankenstein and the Invisible Man would. Space exploration and prophecy, considered elsewhere, are branches of it, as are all the films about mad doctors and colliding worlds.

scientists have been the subject of many films, though few real-life ones have led sufficiently dramatic lives to warrant filming. Warners led the way in the thirties with *The Story of Louis Pasteur* and *Dr Ehrlich's Magic Bullet.* In 1939 Mickey Rooney played *Young Tom Edison*, followed by Spencer Tracy as *Edison the Man.* Then in 1943, Greer Garson played *Madame Curie.* At this point the movie fan's thirst for scientific knowledge died out, and John Huston's *Freud* in 1962 did not revive it. In the eighties, the lives of Oppenheimer and Sakharov have been filmed.

See also: *inventors.*

Scofield, Paul (1922–). Distinguished British stage actor whose films have been infrequent.
□That Lady 55. Carve Her Name with Pride 58. The Train 64. *A Man For All Seasons* (AA, BFA) 66. King Lear 69. Bartleby 71. Scorpio 73. A Delicate Balance 73. Anna Karenina (TV) 84.

Scola, Ettore (1931–). Italian screen writer and director.
Two Nights with Cleopatra (w) 54. Adua et le Compagne (w) 60. The Visit (w) 63. Made in Italy (w) 65. Let's Talk About Women (w, d) 65. The Devil in Love (w, d) 66. The Pizza Triangle (w, d) 70. We All Loved Each Other So Much (w, d) 75. A Special Day (w, d) 77. Passione d'Amore (w, d) 81.

score. The music composed for a film.

Scorsese, Martin (1942–). American director.
□Who's That Knocking at My Door? 70. Boxcar Bertha 72. *Mean Streets* 73. *Alice Doesn't Live Here Any More* 74. *Taxi Driver* 76. New York, New York 77. The Last Waltz 78. Raging Bull 80. King of Comedy 83. After Hours 85. *The Color of Money* 86.

¶ *M.S.:* Cinema is a matter of what's in the frame and what's out.

Scott, Adrian (1912–1972). American producer.
Murder My Sweet 44. My Pal Wolf 44. Cornered 46. So Well Remembered 47. *Crossfire* 47, etc.

Scott, George C. (1926–). Distinguished but taciturn American actor; usually plays tough or sardonic characters and was the first actor to refuse an Oscar.
□The Hanging Tree 58. *Anatomy of a Murder* 59. *The Hustler* 62. *The List of Adrian Messenger* 63. Dr Strangelove 63. The Yellow Rolls Royce 64. The Bible 66. Not with My Wife You Don't 66. The Flim Flam Man 67. Petulia 69. *Patton* (AA) 70. They Might Be Giants 71. The Last Run 71. *The Hospital* 72. The New Centurions 72. Jane Eyre (TV) 72. Oklahoma Crude 73. The Day of the Dolphin 73. Rage (& d) 73. The Savage is Loose (& d) 74. Bank Shot 75. The Hindenberg 75. This Savage Land (TV) 76. *Fear on Trial* (TV) 76. The Prince and the Pauper 77. Islands in the Stream 77. Beauty and the Beast (TV) 77. Movie Movie 78. Hardcore 79. The Changeling 80. The Formula 80. Taps 81. Oliver Twist (as Fagin) 82. China Girl (TV) 83. Firestarter 84. A Christmas Carol (TV) 84.
TV series: East Side West Side 63.

¶ There is no question you get pumped up by the recognition. Then a self-loathing sets in when you realize you're enjoying it.—*G.C.S.*

Famous line (Dr Strangelove): I don't say we wouldn't get our hair mussed, but I do say no more than ten to twenty million killed, tops—that is, depending on the break.

Scott, Gordon (1927–) (Gordon M. Werschkul). American leading man who after being fireman, cowboy and lifeguard was signed to play Tarzan in *Tarzan's Hidden Jungle* 55; made five further episodes, then went to Italy to make muscleman epics.
□Tarzan's Hidden Jungle 55. Tarzan and the Trappers 55. Tarzan and the Lost Safari 56. Tarzan's Fight for Life 58. Tarzan's Greatest Adventure 59. Tarzan the Magnificent 60. Duel of the Titans 61. Samson and the Seven Miracles 61. Goliath and the Vampires 62. Zorro and the Three Musketeers 62. Battles of the Gladiators 62. A Queen for Caesar 62. The Lion of St Mark 63. Hero of Babylon 63. Hercules Attacks 63. Thunder of Battle 63. Arrow of the Avenger 63. Arm of Fire 64. Buffalo Bill 64. Hercules and the Princess of Troy 65. The Tramplers 66. Top Secret 66. Nest of Spies 67.

Scott, Gordon L. T. (1920–). British producer, former production manager.

Look Back in Anger 58. Petticoat Pirates 61. The Pot Carriers 63. Crooks in Cloisters 64, etc.

Scott, Hazel (1920–). Black American pianist and pop organist.
Something to Shout About 43. The Heat's On 43. I Dood It 43. Broadway Rhythm 44. Rhapsody in Blue 45. The Night Affair (Fr.) 61, etc.

Scott, Janette (1938–). British leading lady, former child star.
Went the Day Well? 42. No Place for Jennifer 49. No Highway 50. The Magic Box 51. As Long As They're Happy 52. Now and Forever 55. The Good Companions 57. The Devil's Disciple 59. The Old Dark House 63. *The Beauty Jungle* 64. Crack in the World 65, etc.

Scott, Ken (1927–86). American action lead of the sixties.
The Three Faces of Eve 57. Woman Obsessed 59. Pirates of Tortuga 61. Desire in the Dust 61. Police Nurse 63. The Murder Game 65. Fantastic Voyage 66, etc.

Scott, Lizabeth (1922–) (Emma Matzo). Sultry American leading lady of the forties, a box office concoction of blonde hair, defiant expression and immobile upper lip.
□*You Came Along* 45. The Strange Love of Martha Ivers 46. Dead Reckoning 47. Desert Fury 47. I Walk Alone 47. Variety Girl 47. Pitfall 48. Too Late for Tears 49. Easy Living 49. Paid in Full 50. Dark City 50. The Racket 51. The Company She Keeps 51. Two of a Kind 51. Red Mountain 51. Stolen Face 52. Scared Stiff 53. Bad for Each Other 54. Silver Lode 54. Loving You 57. The Weapon 57. Pulp 72.

Scott, Margaretta (1912–). British stage (from 1929) and screen (from 1934) actress who usually plays upper-middle-class women.
Dirty Work 34. Things to Come 36. Quiet Wedding 40. Sabotage at Sea 42. Fanny by Gaslight 43. The Man from Morocco 45. Mrs Fitzherbert 47. Idol of Paris 48. Where's Charley? 52. Town on Trial 56. The Last Man to Hang 56. A Woman Possessed 58. An Honourable Murder 60. Crescendo 69. Percy 71, etc.

Scott, Martha (1914–). American actress with stage experience.
Our Town 40. Cheers for Miss Bishop 41. The Howards of Virginia 41. One Foot in Heaven 41. Hi Diddle Diddle 43. In Old Oklahoma 43. So Well Remembered 47. The Desperate Hours 55. The Ten Commandments 56. Ben Hur 59. Airport 75 74. The Turning Point 77. The Word (TV) 78. Charleston (TV) 79. Beulah Land (TV) 80, etc.
TV series: Secrets of Midland Heights 80.

Scott, Peter Graham (1923–). British director, from TV.
Panic in Madame Tussauds 48. Sing Along with Me 52. The Headless Ghost 59. Captain Clegg 62. The Pot Carriers 63. Bitter Harvest 63. Father Came Too 64. Mister Ten Per Cent 67. The Promise 69, etc.

Scott, Pippa (1935–). American actress.
Auntie Mame 58. Petulia 68. Cold Turkey 70, etc.

Scott, Randolph (1898–1987) (Randolph Crane). Rugged American outdoor star, in films from 1931 after stage experience.
Sky Bride 31. Supernatural 32. Home on the Range 33. Roberta 34. *She* 35. So Red the Rose 35. Follow the Fleet 36. Go West Young Man 36. *Last of the Mohicans* 36. High, Wide and Handsome 37. Rebecca of Sunnybrook Farm 38. The Texans 38. Jesse James 39. Virginia City 40. My Favourite Wife 40. When the Daltons Rode 40. Western Union 41. Belle Starr 41. Paris Calling 41. To the Shores of Tripoli 42. The Spoilers 42. Pittsburgh 42. Bombardier 43. Gung Ho 43. The Desperadoes 43. Belle of the Yukon 44. China Sky 44. Captain Kidd 45. Badman's Territory 46. Abilene Town 47. Christmas Eve 47. Fighting Man of the Plains 49. Sugarfoot 51. Santa Fe 51. Hangman's Knot 53. The Stranger Wore a Gun 53. The Bounty Hunter 54. A Lawless Street 55. Seven Men from Now 56. Decision at Sundown 57. Ride Lonesome 58. *Ride the High Country* 62, many others.

Scott, Ridley (1939–). British director.
The Duellists 78. *Alien* 79. Blade Runner 81. Legend 85. Someone to Watch Over Me 87.

¶ *R.S., 1976:* I think it's remarkable that people will give you 10 million dollars to go and get your rocks off.
R.S.: Never let yourself be seen in public unless they pay for it.

Scott, Terry (1927–). Plump British comedy actor, whose *Terry and June* TV series ran through the seventies and into the eighties.

Blue Murder at St Trinian's 58. A Pair of Briefs 62. Carry on Camping 68. Bless This House 72, etc.

Scott, Sir Walter (1771–1832). Scottish novelist, mainly of period adventure stories. His *Ivanhoe, The Talisman* and *Rob Roy* have received most attention from film makers.

Scott, Zachary (1914–1965). American leading man with considerable stage experience.
The Mask of Dimitrios (film debut) 44. *The Southerner* 45. *Mildred Pierce* 46. Stallion Road 47. The Unfaithful 48. Shadow on the Wall 50. Born To Be Bad 51. Let's Make It Legal 53. Appointment in Honduras 53. Bandido 56. The Young One 60. It's Only Money 62, others.

Scotto, Vincente (1876–1952). French composer.
Jofroi 34. Pepe le Moko 36. La Fille du Puisatier 40. Domino 43. L'Ingénue Libertine 50, etc.

Scourby, Alexander (1913–85). American stage character actor.
Affair in Trinidad 52. *The Big Heat* 53. The Silver Chalice 55. Giant 56. Seven Thieves 59. The Big Fisherman 59. Confessions of a Counterspy 60.

screenplay: see *shooting script*.

Scrooge. Dickens' *A Christmas Carol*, the tale of miser Scrooge haunted by his past, has been filmed countless times. Among the best-remembered are the Essanay version of 1908; the Edison version of 1910; the Seymour Hicks versions of 1913 and 1935; the 1916 version with Rupert Julian, who also directed; the MGM 1938 version with Reginald Owen; the 1951 version with Alastair Sim; and the 1970 musical with Albert Finney. In 1984 a quite unnecessary TV film was fashioned for George C. Scott.

The Sea Hawk. Rafael Sabatini's swashbuckling Elizabethan romance about a feuding family was screened with reasonable fidelity in 1924 with Milton Sills. The Errol Flynn pirate yarn of 1940 jettisoned almost everything but the title.

The Sea Wolf. Jack London's stark psychological novel of an obsessed sea captain, Wolf Larsen, has been filmed seven times. In 1913 it starred Hobart Bosworth, in 1920 Noah Beery, in 1925 Ralph Ince, in 1930 Milton Sills, and in 1941 Edward G. Robinson. 1950 brought a disguised western version, *Barricade*, with Raymond Massey, and in 1957 yet another straight version, under the title *Wolf Larsen*, was made with Barry Sullivan. In 1974 Chuck Connors starred in a European version, *Wolf of the Seven Seas*.

Seagull, Barbara (1948–) (formerly and latterly Barbara Hershey) (originally Barbara Herzstein). American leading lady.
With Six You Get Egg Roll 68. Heaven with a Gun 69. *Last Summer* 70. Boxcar Bertha 72. The Crazy World of Julius Vrooder 74. You and Me 75. Diamonds 75. The Stunt Man 78. A Man Called Intrepid (TV) 79. The Entity 82. The Right Stuff 83. The Natural 84. Hannah and her Sisters 85. Hoosiers 86. Shy People 87. Tin Men 87, etc.
TV series: The Monroes 76. From Here to Eternity 79.

Seal, Elizabeth (1935–). British dancer and occasional actress.
Town on Trial 56. Cone of Silence 60. Vampire Circus 72, etc.

seances on the screen have often been shown to be fake, as in *Seance on a Wet Afternoon, Bunco Squad, Palmy Days, The Spiritualist, Houdini,* and *The Medium.* But just occasionally they do result in something being called up from over there: it happened in *Blithe Spirit, The Haunting, The Uninvited, Night of the Demon, Thirteen Ghosts, Hands of the Ripper,* and *The Legend of Hell House.*

Searle, Francis (1909–). British director.
A Girl in a Million 46. Things Happen at Night 48. Cloudburst (& w) 51. Wheel of Fate (& w) 53, many second features.

Searle, Jackie (1920–). American boy actor of the thirties, usually in mean roles.
Tom Sawyer 31. Skippy 31. Peck's Bad Boy 35. Little Lord Fauntleroy 36. That Certain Age 38. Little Tough Guys in Society 39. The Hard Boiled Canary 41. The Paleface 49, many others.

Sears, Fred F. (1913–1957). American director of second features.
Desert Vigilante 49. Raiders of Tomahawk Creek 50. Snake River Desperadoes 51. Last Train from Bombay 52. Ambush at Tomahawk Gap 53. El Alamein 53. The Miami Story 54. Wyoming Renegades 55.

Chicago Syndicate 55. Rock around the Clock 56. Earth versus the Flying Saucers 56. Don't Knock the Rock 56. The Giant Claw 57. The World was His Jury 58, etc.

Sears, Heather (1935–). British actress with repertory experience.
Dry Rot 56. *The Story of Esther Costello* 57. *Room at the Top* 59. Sons and Lovers 60. Phantom of the Opera 62. Saturday Night Out 64. Black Torment 64. Great Expectations (TV) 75, etc.

The Seashell and the Clergyman (France 1928). For many years this surrealist fantasy filled with sexual symbols was justly cited as the cinema's furthest excursion into the avant-garde. Its creator, Germaine Dulac, produced nothing else of equal interest. The film is also notable for provoking a famous remark by the British Board of Film Censors in banning the picture: 'It is so obscure as to have no apparent meaning. If there is a meaning, it is doubtless objectionable.'

seaside resorts have provided lively settings for many British comedies: Douglas in *No Limit*, Brighton in *Bank Holiday*, Blackpool in *Sing As We Go*, and a variety of south coast resorts in *The Punch and Judy Man, French Dressing, All Over the Town, Barnacle Bill.* Sometimes the resort has provided a contrast to more serious goings-on, as in *The Entertainer, Brighton Rock, Room at the Top, The Dark Man, A Taste of Honey, I Was Happy Here, Family Doctor, The System, The Damned.* Hollywood usually comes a cropper when depicting British resorts, either comically as in *The Gay Divorcee* or seriously as in *Separate Tables*; its own resorts have a monotonous look, whether viewed romantically in *Moon Over Miami* and *Fun in Acapulco*, nostalgically in *Some Like It Hot*, trendily in *Beach Party* and its many sequels, or morosely in *Tony Rome.* The French Riviera has never been notably well captured on film since Vigo's *A Propos de Nice*, but among the movies to have a go with the aid of back projection are *On the Riviera, That Riviera Touch* and *Moment to Moment.* Hitchcock got some picture postcard views but little else out of *To Catch a Thief*, while the French had a go for themselves in *St Tropez Blues* and others. A Mediterranean resort was the setting of the climax of *Suddenly Last Summer*; other European watering-places featured memorably in *Une Si Jolie Petite Plage, Sunday in August* and *The Lady with the Little Dog.* The most ingenious use of the seaside for purposes of film fantasy was certainly in *Oh What a Lovely War.*

Seaside settings of the seventies and eighties have included *Out of Season, Atlantic City USA* and *The King of Marvin Gardens.*

Seastrom (or **Sjostrom), Victor** (1879–1960). Distinguished Swedish actor-director with stage experience.
Ingeborg Holm 13. Terje Vigen (ad) 16. Jerusalem (d) 18. *Ordet* (The Word) (a) 21. *The Phantom Carriage* (Thy Soul Shall Bear Witness) (d) 20. The Master of Man (US) (d) 23. He Who Gets Slapped (US) (d) 24. *The Scarlet Letter* (US) (d) 26. Tower of Lies (US) (d) 26. The Divine Woman (US) (d) 28. The Wind (US) (d) 28. Under the Red Robe (GB) (d) 36. Ordet (remake) (a) 43. *Wild Strawberries* (a) 57, many others.

Seaton, George (1911–1979) (George Stenius). American writer-director. Acted and produced on stage; joined MGM writing staff 1933; later independent or working with producer William Perlberg.
A Day at the Races (co-w) 37. *The Song of Bernadette* (w) 43. Diamond Horseshoe (wd) 45. Junior Miss (wd) 45. The Shocking Miss Pilgrim (wd) 47. *Miracle on 34th Street* (wd) (AA) 47. The Big Lift (wd) 51. For Heaven's Sake (wd) 51. Anything Can Happen (wd) 52. Little Boy Lost (wd) 53. *The Country Girl* (wd) (AA) 54. The Proud and Profane (wd) 56. The Tin Star (p) 57. Teacher's Pet (d) 58. The Pleasure of His Company (d) 61. The Counterfeit Traitor (wd) 63. Thirty-Six Hours (wd) 64. What's So Bad About Feeling Good? (wpd) 68. *Airport* (wd) 69. Showdown (wpd) 73, many others.

Seberg, Jean (1938–79). American leading lady who won contest for role of Preminger's *Saint Joan* 57, after which her career faltered but picked up in French films.
Bonjour Tristesse 57. The Mouse That Roared 59. *Breathless* (A Bout de Souffle) 60. Playtime 62. In the French Style 63. Lilith 64. Moment to Moment 65. Estouffade à la Caraïbe 66. The Road to Corinth 68. Pendulum 69. Paint Your Wagon 69. Airport 69. Macho Callahan 71. Mousey (TV) 73. The Wild Duck 76, etc.

Secombe, Sir Harry (1921–). Burly Welsh comedian and singer, who apart from a number of second-feature appearances in the early fifties has filmed only rarely.
Davy 57. Jet Storm 59. *Oliver!* 68. Song of Norway 70. The Magnificent Seven Deadly Sins 71. Sunstruck 73, etc.

second unit director. One who directs not the actors but the spectacular location sequences, stunt men, scenic backgrounds, etc., and is thus sometimes responsible for a film's most striking effects; e.g. Andrew Marton's (and Yakima Canutt's) chariot race sequence in *Ben Hur* 59.

Sedgwick, Edward (1893–1953). American director of mainly routine films.
Live Wires 21. The First Degree 23. Two Fisted Jones 25. Spring Fever 27. *The Cameraman* 28. The Passionate Plumber 32. I'll Tell the World 34. Pick a Star 37. Beware Spooks 39. Ma and Pa Kettle Back on the Farm 50, many others.

Seeley, Blossom (1892–1974). American nightclub entertainer, married to Benny Fields. Played by Betty Hutton in *Somebody Loves Me* 52.
□Broadway Through a Keyhole 33.

Segal, Alex (1915–77). American director, from TV.
□Ransom 56. All the Way Home 63. Joy in the Morning 65. Harlow (electronovision) 66. My Father's House (TV) 73. The Story of David (TV) (co-d) 76.

Segal, Erich (1937–). American university professor who unexpectedly wrote a best-selling sentimental novelette, *Love Story*, which was filmed with equal success. *Oliver's Story* followed rather lamely in both media. He also wrote *Yellow Submarine* 69, *RPM* 70 and *Jennifer on my Mind* 72.

Segal, George (1934–). Leading American actor more at home with thought than with action, which may account for a somewhat fitful career.
□The Young Doctors 61. The Longest Day 62. Act One 62. The New Interns 64. Invitation to a Gunfighter 64. Ship of Fools 65. *King Rat* 65. Lost Command 65. Who's Afraid of Virginia Woolf? 66. The Quiller Memorandum 66. The St Valentine's Day Massacre 67. Bye Bye Braverman 68. No Way to Treat a Lady 68. The Southern Star 69. The Girl who Couldn't Say No 69. The Bridge at Remagen 69. Loving 70. *The Owl and the Pussycat* 70. Where's Poppa? 70. Born to Win 72. The Hot Rock 72. Blume in Love 73. *A Touch of Class* 73. The Terminal Man 74. California Split 75. The Black Bird 75. Russian Roulette 76. The Duchess and the Dirtwater Fox 76. Rollercoaster 77. Fun with Dick and Jane 77. Who is Killing the Great Chefs of Europe? 78. Lost and Found 79. The Last Married Couple in America 80. Carbon Copy 81. The Cold Room 81. Stick 82. Killing 'Em Softly 83. The Zany Adventures of Robin Hood (TV) 84.

¶ *G.S.:* I have a dread of being considered bland, but I've had to reconcile myself to the fact that that's what I am.

Segal, Vivienne (1897–). American Broadway star of the early talkie period.
□ Song of the West 30. Golden Dawn 30. Bride of the Regiment 30. Viennese Nights 30. The Cat and the Fiddle 33.

Segall, Harry (1897–1975). American writer who started the heavenly fantasies of the forties with his play 'Halfway to Heaven'.
Fatal Lady 36. Here Comes Mr Jordan (AA) 41. Angel on My Shoulder 46. For Heaven's Sake 50. Monkey Business 52, etc.

Seiber, Matyas (1905–60). Hungarian composer in London.
Animal Farm 54. The Diamond Wizard 54. A Town Like Alice 56. Chase a Crooked Shadow 58. Robbery Under Arms 58. For Better for Worse 61.

Seidelman, Susan (–). American director.
Smithereens 82. Desperately Seeking Susan 84. Making Mr Right 87.

Seiler, Lewis (1891–1964). American director. Many Tom Mix silents; then *Air Circus* (co-d) 28, second features through thirties.
Dust Be My Destiny 39. It All Came True 40. South of Suez 41. The Big Shot 42. Guadalcanal Diary 43. Molly and Me 44. If I'm Lucky 46. Whiplash 48. The Tanks are Coming 51. The Winning Team 52. The System 53. Women's Prison 55. Battle Stations 56. The True Story of Lynn Stuart 58, many others.

Seiter, William A. (1891–1964). American director, in Hollywood from 1918, then directing shorts.
Boy Crazy 22. The Teaser 25. Skinner's Dress Suit 26. Good Morning Judge 28. The Love Racket 30. Girl Crazy 32. If I Had a Million (part) 33. Diplomaniacs 33. Professional Sweetheart 33. *Sons of the Desert* 33. Roberta 35. *The Moon's Our Home* 36. Dimples 36. *This is My Affair* 37. *Room Service* 38. It's a

Date 40. *Broadway* 42. You Were Never Lovelier 42. Destroyer 43. *The Affairs of Susan* 45. I'll Be Yours 47. One Touch of Venus 48. Dear Brat 51. Make Haste to Live 54, many others.

Seitz, George B. (1888–1944). American director, known as the serial king. A writer-director from 1913, he worked on *The Perils of Pauline*, and directed *The Fatal Ring* 17 and all subsequent Pearl White serials. In the twenties, he acted in his own serials: *Velvet Fingers, The Sky Ranger*, etc. Turning to features, he directed nearly forty between 1927 and 1933, then moved to MGM and kept up an even more rapid output, including episodes of the Hardy Family series.
The Woman in His Life 35. Andy Hardy Meets a Debutante 39. Kit Carson 40. Sky Murder 40. Andy Hardy's Private Secretary 41. China Caravan 42, etc.

Seitz, John F. (1893–1979). American cinematographer, in Hollywood from 1916.
SILENT FILMS: *The Four Horsemen of the Apocalypse* 21. *The Prisoner of Zenda* 22, etc.
SOUND FILMS: East Lynne 30. Over the Hill 30. She Wanted a Millionaire 32. Huckleberry Finn 39. *Sullivan's Travels* 41. The Moon and Sixpence 42. This Gun for Hire 42. The Miracle of Morgan's Creek 43. Hail the Conquering Hero 44. *Double Indemnity* 44. *The Lost Weekend* 45. *Sunset Boulevard* 50. The San Francisco Story 52. Hell on Frisco Bay 55. The Man in the Net 58. Guns of the Timberland 60, etc.

Sekely, Steve (1899–1979) (Istvan Szekely). Hungarian director, in Hollywood from 1938.
Rhapsodie der Liebe 29. Lila Akac 34. Miracle on Main Street 40. Behind Prison Walls 43. Women in Bondage 44. The Scar 48. Stronghold 51. The Blue Camellia 54. The Day of the Triffids 68. Kenner 69. The Girl Who Liked Purple Flowers 73, etc.

Sekka, Johnny (–). West African actor in London.
Flame in the Streets 61. Woman of Straw 64. Khartoum 65. The Last Safari 67. A Warm December 73. Uptown Saturday Night 75, etc.

Selander, Lesley (1900–1979). American director who made low-budget westerns and other action pictures from 1936.
Cattle Pass 37. The Round-Up 41. The Vampire's Ghost 46. Belle Starr's Daughter 48. I Was an American Spy 51. Flight to Mars 51. The Highwayman 52. Tall Man Riding 54. The Lone Ranger and the Lost City of Gold 58. Town Tamer 65. Fort Utah 67, many others.

self-analysis

? What well-known film people spoke of themselves in the following terms? (We're sure that in some cases they didn't mean it.)

1 It's no use asking me to talk about art.
2 For me the best drama is one that deals with a man in danger.
3 My personality is that of the egotistical adventurer.
4 I don't even notice competition. I'm a centre-forward. I don't watch them. Let them watch me.
5 I wouldn't act a role if it was not felt as dominating the whole story.
6 The difference between me and Lubitsch is that he shows you the king on the throne and then he shows you the king in his bedroom. I show you the king in his bedroom first. That way when you see him on the throne you have no illusions about him.
7 I make films that I would like to have seen when I was a young man.
8 I often think my life has been a failure. But whenever I drop into a theatre and hear women laughing at one of my films, I think, well, if I brightened their day before they went home and did the dishes, maybe my life wasn't wasted after all.
9 No one can be exactly like me. Sometimes even I have trouble doing it.
10 I always get an attack of piles on the third week of shooting and my back slips.

Selig, William N. (1864–1948). Pioneer American producer; many serials.
The Count of Monte Cristo 08. The Spoilers 13, etc.

Sellars, Elizabeth (1923–). British leading actress on stage from 1941.
Floodtide (debut) 48. Madeleine 50. Cloudburst 51. The Gentle Gunman 52. The Barefoot Contessa 54. Three Cases of Murder 55. The Shiralee 57. The Day They Robbed the Bank of England 61. The Chalk Garden 64. The Mummy's Shroud 67. The Hireling 73, etc.

Selleck, Tom (1945–). Charismatic American leading man of the eighties, who after much TV experience might just take on the mantle of Gable.

The Movie Murderer (TV) 69. Myra Breckinridge 70. The Seven Minutes 71. Daughters of Satan 72. Terminal Island 73. Returning Home (TV) 75. Most Wanted (TV) 76. Coma 77. The Sacketts (TV) 79. High Road to China 83. Lassiter 84. Gipsy Warriors 87.
TV series: Most Wanted 76. *Magnum* 81–.

Sellers, Peter (1925–1980). British comic actor who became an international star, then faltered. From variety stage and radio's 'Goon Show'.
Biography 1969: *Peter Sellers, The Mask Behind the Mask* by Peter Evans.
□Penny Points to Paradise 51. Down Among the Z Men 52. Orders Are Orders 54. John and Julie 55. The Lady Killers 55. *The Smallest Show on Earth* 57. *The Naked Truth* 58. Tom Thumb 58. Up the Creek 58. Carlton-Browne of the F.O. 58. *The Mouse That Roared* 59. *I'm All Right, Jack* 59. The Battle of the Sexes 60. Two-Way Stretch 60. Never Let Go 61. The Millionairess 61. Mr Topaze (& d) 61. *Only Two Can Play* 62. Lolita 62. Waltz of the Toreadors 62. The Dock Brief 63. Heavens Above 63. The Wrong Arm of the Law 63. *The Pink Panther* 63. *Dr Strangelove* 63. The World of Henry Orient 64. A Shot in the Dark 64. What's New, Pussycat? 65. The Wrong Box 66. After the Fox 66. Casino Royale 67. The Bobo 67. Woman Times Seven 67. The Party 68. *I Love You Alice B. Toklas* 68. The Magic Christian 69. Hoffman 70. There's a Girl in My Soup 70. Where Does it Hurt? 72. Alice's Adventures in Wonderland (as the March Hare) 72. The Optimists of Nine Elms 72. Soft Beds and Hard Battles 73. Ghost in the Noonday Sun 73. The Blockhouse 74. The Great McGonagall (as Queen Victoria) 74. The Return of the Pink Panther 75. Murder by Death 76. The Pink Panther Strikes Again 77. Revenge of the Pink Panther 78. The Prisoner of Zenda 79. Being There 79. The Fiendish Plot of Dr Fu Manchu 79.
†In 1982 offcuts from earlier Panther films were assembled to make a tasteless sequel, *The Trail of the Pink Panther*.
Sellers also had a cameo in *Road to Hong Kong* 61.

¶ The only way to make a film with him is to let him direct, write and produce it as well as star in it.—*Charles Feldman*

Sellers is such an experienced impersonator that one regrets his inability to add to his list of impressions the Peter Sellers that was.—*John Simon of The World of Henry Orient*

'I would squirm with embarrassment at the demeaning lengths he would go to in order to ingratiate himself with the Royal Family.'—*Britt Ekland*

P.S.: There used to be a me behind the mask, but I had it surgically removed.

P.S.: If you ask me to play myself, I will not know what to do. I do not know who or what I am.

P.S.: People will swim through shit if you put a few bob in it.

Selten, Morton (1860–1940) (Morton Stubbs). British stage actor who played distinguished old gentlemen in some thirties films.
Service for Ladies 32. Ten Minute Alibi 35. The Ghost Goes West 36. Fire over England 36. A Yank at Oxford 38. The Divorce of Lady X 38. The Thief of Baghdad 40, etc.

Seltzer, David (–). American screenwriter.
One is a Lonely Number 72. King, Queen, Knave 73. The Other Side of the Mountains 75. *The Omen* 76. Prophecy 79. Six Weeks 82. Table for Five 83, etc.

Seltzer, Walter (1914–). American producer.
One Eyed Jacks 58. The Naked Edge 61. The War Lord 65. Will Penny 67. Darker than Amber 70. Skyjacked 72, etc.

Selwyn, Edgar (1875–1944). American director.
Night Life of New York 25. The Girl in the Show 29. War Nurse 30. The Sin of Madelon Claudet 31. Turn Back the Clock 33. The Mystery of Mr X 34. Pierre of the Plains (wp only) 42.

Selznick, David O. (1902–1965). American independent producer, former writer. Worked for RKO from 1931, MGM from 1933; founded Selznick International Pictures in 1936.
Biographical books: *Selznick* by Bob Thomas, 1970; *Memo From David O. Selznick*, 1972.
□ Roulette 24. Spoilers of the West 27. Wyoming 28. Forgotten Faces 28. Chinatown Nights 29. The Man I Love 29. The Four Feathers 29. The Dance of Life 29. Fast Company 29. Street of Chance 30. Sarah and Son 30. Honey 30. The Texan 30. For the Defense 30. Manslaughter 30. The Lost Squadron 32. Symphony of Six Million 32. State's Attorney 32. Westward Passage 32. What Price Hollywood? 32. Roar of the Dragon 32. Bird of Paradise 32. The Age of Consent 32. A Bill of Divorcement 32. The Conquerors 32. Rockabye 32. The Animal

Kingdom 32. The Half Naked Truth 32. Topaze 33. The Great Jasper 33. Our Betters 33. Christopher Strong 33. Sweepings 33. The Monkey's Paw 33. *Dinner at Eight* 33. Night Flight 33. Meet the Baron 33. Dancing Lady 33. Viva Villa 34. Manhattan Melodrama 34. *David Copperfield* 35. Vanessa 35. Reckless 35. Anna Karenina 35. *A Tale of Two Cities* 35. Little Lord Fauntleroy 36. The Garden of Allah 36. *A Star is Born* 37. *The Prisoner of Zenda* 37. Nothing Sacred 37. The Adventures of Tom Sawyer 38. The Young in Heart 38. Made for Each Other 39. Intermezzo 39. *Gone with the Wind* 39. *Rebecca* 40. Since You Went Away 34. I'll Be Seeing You 44. Spellbound 45. Duel in the Sun 46. The Paradine Case 48. Portrait of Jennie 48. *The Third Man* (co-p) 50. The Wild Heart (co-p) 52. Indiscretion of an American Wife (co-p) 54. A Farewell to Arms 57.

❀ For his integrity; for his memos; and for being a Hollywood monument. *Gone with the Wind*.

¶ Selznick was the mogul who gave up at his peak. He said in retirement:

> Very few people have mastered the art of enjoying their wealth. I have mastered the art, and therefore I spend my time enjoying myself.

This was not unexpected behaviour from the man who once said:

> I don't want to be normal. Who wants to be normal?

Yet his own memorable utterances were few, and on the sad side. He said of Hollywood:

> Once photographed, life here is ended.

And of the house which is so central to *Gone with the Wind*:

> It's somehow symbolic of Hollywood that Tara was just a façade, with no rooms inside.

An unhumorous man, intense and thorough to a fault, he was a hard taskmaster. Nunnally Johnson demurred at working for him:

> I understand that an assignment with you consists of three months' work and six months' recuperation.

His creative impulse surged through his internal memos, the length of which was legendary. Alfred Hitchcock said in 1965:

> When I came to America twenty-five years ago to direct *Rebecca*, David Selznick sent me a memo. (Pause.) I've just finished reading it. (Pause.) I think I may turn it into a motion picture. (Pause.) I plan to call it *The Longest Story Ever Told*.

One memo which has been quoted was to director Charles Vidor, following one of protest from him:

> I don't believe I've ever used such terms with you as idiotic. I may have *thought* your excessive takes and angles were idiotic, but the most I've said was that they were a waste of my personal money.

He certainly interfered:

> The way I see it, my function is to be responsible for everything.

And:

> The difference between me and other producers is that I am interested in the thousands and thousands of details that go into the making of a film. It is the sum total of all these things that either makes a great picture or destroys it.

And, of the making of *A Farewell To Arms*:

> In Mr Huston I asked for a first violinist and got a soloist. When I am the producer, I must produce.

His final claim was to have found a balance between God and Mammon:

> I have never gone after honours instead of dollars. But I have understood the relationship between the two.

'A typical Hollywood combination of oafishness and sophistication.'—*John Houseman*

'He wouldn't hire a secretary who could do less than 200 words per minute dictation. Otherwise it would have interrupted his train of thought.'—*Irene Mayer Selznick*

'The trouble with you, David, is that you did all your reading before you were twelve.'—*Ben Hecht*

Selznick, Lewis J. (1870–1933) (Lewis Zeleznik). Russian-American distributor and impresario, bankrupted in 1923.

Selznick, Myron (1898–1944). American producer and agent, brother of David Selznick and son of Lewis.

Semon, Larry (1889–1928). American silent slapstick comedian, popular in innumerable two-reelers of the twenties; also some features.
The Simple Life 18. The Wizard of Oz 24. The Sawmill 25. Spuds 27, etc.

Semple, Lorenzo Jnr (–). American screenwriter.
Batman 56. Daddy's Gone a Hunting 59. Pretty Poison 68. Marriage of a Young Stockbroker 71. The Sporting Club 71. Papillon (co-w) 73. The Parallax View 74. The Drowning Pool (co-w) 75. Three Days of the Condor (co-w) 75. King Kong 76. Hurricane 79. Flash Gordon 80, etc.

Sennett, Mack (1880–1960) (Michael Sinnott). American 'king of comedy' who in the twenties produced countless slapstick shorts featuring the Keystone Kops, Chester Conklin, Louise Fazenda, Charlie Chaplin, Mack Swain, Billy West, Fred Mace, Heinie Conklin, Slim Summerville and others. By the time sound came, Sennett had exhausted all the possible tricks of his 'fun factory' and found the new methods not to his taste. His output waned almost to nothing, but he was given a special Academy Award in 1937: 'For his lasting contribution to the comedy technique of the screen . . . the Academy presents a Special Award to that master of fun, discoverer of stars, sympathetic, kindly, understanding genius—Mack Sennett.'
A biography, *King of Comedy*, was published in 1955.

¶ As befits the king of slapstick comedy, he was a thoughtful man.

> The joke of life is the fall of dignity,

he once said. And his analysis of custard-pie throwing was perfectly expressed:

> Non-anticipation on the part of the recipient of the pastry is the chief ingredient of the recipe.

He disclaimed originality:

> Anyone who tells you he has invented something new is a fool or a liar or both.

He was firm in matters of taste:

> We never make fun of religion, politics, race or mothers. A mother never gets hit with a custard pie. Mothers-in-law, yes. But mothers, never!

He summed up his comedy technique very simply:

> It's got to move!

And he later admitted:

> I called myself king of comedy, but I was a harassed monarch. I worked most of the time. It was only in the evenings that I laughed.

sensation!

? Each of the following films is notable for a technical advance which was thought worth advertising at the time. Can you say what?

1 *The Big Trail* (1930)
2 *Bwana Devil*
3 *The Glorious Adventure* (1921)
4 *The Robe*
5 *White Christmas*
6 *Fantasia*
7 *Becky Sharp*
8 *The Trail of the Lonesome Pine* (1936)
9 *The Jazz Singer* (1927)
10 *Lights of New York*
11 *Don Juan*
12 *House on Haunted Hill*

Sensurround. A system evolved in 1975 for *Earthquake*, this dispensable gimmick involved the augmentation of violent action on screen by intense waves of high decibel sound, enough almost to crack the ribs. It never caught on except as a big city come-on.

sequels

? Sequels were fairly rare in film business, for the practical reason that it is usually difficult to reassemble casts and/or inspiration. In the seventies however, they came thick and fast. Casting your mind much farther back, to what successful films were the following direct sequels, using at least one continuing cast member in the same character?

1 *By the Light of the Silvery Moon*
2 *I'll Be Yours*
3 *The Road Back*
4 *Belles on Their Toes*
5 *The Return of Frank James*
6 *They Call Me Mister Tibbs*
7 *Where the Bullets Fly*
8 *From Russia with Love*
9 *You're Only Young Once*
10 *Four Wives*
11 *Demetrius and the Gladiators*

sequence: a film paragraph, usually starting and ending with a fade to black.

Serato, Massimo (1917–) (Giuseppe Segato). Italian leading man, usually seen in swashbucklers.
Man of the Sea 41. Outcry 46. La Traviata 47. Sunday in August 49. The Thief of Venice 49. Shadow of the Eagle 50. Lucretia Borgia 53. The Man from Cairo 53. Madame Du Barry 54. The Naked Maja 59. David and Goliath 60. Constantine and the Cross 61. El Cid 61. 55 Days at Peking 63. The Tenth Victim 65. Wild Wild Planet 66. Camille 2000 69. Don't Look Now 73.

Seria, Joel (1944–). French director.
Charlie et ses Deux Nénettes 73. Les Galettes du Pont-Aven 75. Marie-Poupée 76. Comme la Lune 77, etc.

serials demand a book to themselves. They began in the early years of the century and continued until the early fifties, their plethora of adventurous and melodramatic incident being usually divided into fifteen or twenty chapters of about twenty minutes each. They were the domain of mad doctors, space explorers, clutching hands, mysterious strangers, diabolical villains and dewy-eyed heroines. Each chapter ended with a 'cliffhanger' in which the hero or heroine was left in some deadly danger from which it was plain he could not escape; but at the beginning of the next chapter escape he did. A few favourite serials are *Fantomas, The Perils of Pauline, Batman, Flash Gordon's Trip to Mars* and *Captain Marvel*. Almost all of them were American. They were finally killed by the advent of TV and by the increasing length of the double-feature programme.

Books on the subject include *To Be Continued* by Weiss and Goodgold; *Days of Thrills and Adventure* by Alan Barbour; and *The Great Movie Serials* by Harmon and Glut.

series of feature films used to be popular enough, and many are individually noted in this book; in recent years the series concept has been taken over by TV, and in any case low-budget movies featuring cut-to-pattern characters could no longer be made to pay their way in theatres. When one looks back over these old heroes, who flourished chiefly in the thirties and forties, most of them turn out to be sleuths of one kind or another. They included *Sherlock Holmes, The Saint, The Lone Wolf, Father Brown, Nero Wolfe, Duncan McLain, The Crime Doctor, Sexton Blake, Mr Moto, Perry Mason, Bulldog Drummond, Nancy Drew, Mr Wong, Charlie Chan, Ellery Queen, Boston Blackie, The Falcon, Hildegarde Withers, Hercule Poirot, Dick Tracy, Torchy Blane, Michael Shayne, Philip Marlowe* and, more recently, *Inspector Clouseau, Tony Rome, Virgil Tibbs, Coffin Ed Johnson* and *Shaft*. Nor should one forget crime anthologies like *Inner Sanctum* and *The Whistler*. The spy vogue, a recent happening, is naturally headed by *James Bond*: in his wake you may discern *Counterspy, Coplan, Flint, The Tiger, The Man from UNCLE, Harry Palmer*, and *Superdragon*. Among the more muscular outdoor heroes may be counted *Hopalong Cassidy, The Three Mesquiteers, The Lone Ranger, Captain Blood, Zorro, Robin Hood, Tarzan, Jungle Jim, The Cisco Kid, Bomba, The Man with No Name* and the Italian giants who go under such names as *Maciste, Goliath, Hercules* and *Ursus*. The longest surviving series villain is certainly *Fu Manchu*. As for monsters, take your pick from *Frankenstein, Dracula, The Mummy, The Creature from the Black Lagoon, The Invisible Man, The Wolf Man, Dr X*; while if you prefer comedy freaks there are *Topper* and *Francis*. There have been a goodly number of domestic comedies and dramas, including *Squibs, The Jones Family, The Hardy Family, The Cohens and the Kellys, Blondie, Ma and Pa Kettle, Maisie, Henry Aldrich, Scattergood Baines, Lum and Abner, Jeeves, Mr Belvedere, Gidget* and the *Four Daughters* saga. Other comedy series have ranged from the subtleties of *Don Camillo* to the prat-falls of *Old Mother Riley, Mexican Spitfire*, the *Doctor* series, and *Carry On* films. Animals have had series to themselves, as for instance *Rin Tin Tin, Flicka, Lassie, Rusty* and *Flipper*. So have children of various ages: *Our Gang, Gasoline Alley, The Dead End Kids, The East Side Kids, The Bowery Boys*. The best-established musical series were *Broadway Melody* and *The Big Broadcast*. And three cheers for *Dr Kildare, Dr Christian, Dr Defoe, Dr Mabuse* and *Dr Goldfoot* . . . to say nothing of Professor *Quatermass*.

? All the following films are episodes from series featuring a continuing character. Name the series.

1 *Shadows in the Night*
2 *The Bishop Murder Case*
3 *Murder Over New York*
4 *Dig That Uranium*
5 *Blue White and Perfect*
6 *The Ambushers*
7 *Jungle Moon Men*
8 *One Dangerous Night*
9 *Footlight Glamour*
10 *The Hills of Home*
11 *Dark Delusion*
12 *Ride on Vaquero*
13 *A Family Affair*
14 *Pursuit to Algiers*
15 *The Phantom Plainsmen*
16 *Remedy for Riches*
17 *Follow That Camel*
18 *The Fatal Hour*
19 *You Only Live Twice*
20 *13 Lead Soldiers*

Serling, Rod (1924–1975). American TV playwright who contributed scores of scripts to such series as *Twilight Zone* and *Night Gallery* (which he also introduced).

Patterns of Power 56. Saddle the Wind 58. Requiem for a Heavyweight (Blood Money) 63. Yellow Canary 63. *Seven Days in May* 64. Assault on a Queen 66. *Planet of the Apes* 67.

Sernas, Jacques (1925–). Lithuanian-born leading man, in international films.
The Golden Salamander (GB) 50. Jump into Hell (US) 55. Helen of Troy (US/It.) 55. Maddalena (Fr.) 56. The Sign of the Gladiator (It.) 60. Son of Spartacus (It.) 62. Goliath Against the Vampires 67, etc.

Sersen, Fred (1890–1962). American special effects photographer, long with Fox, for whom he produced such spectacles as the fire in *In Old Chicago*, the storm in *The Rains Came*, and the canal-building in *Suez*.

Servais, Jean (1910–1976). French character actor with stage experience.
Criminel 31. La Valse Eternelle 36. La Danse de Mort 47. Une Si Jolie Petite Plage 48. Le Plaisir 51. *Rififi* 55. Les Jeux Dangereux 58. That Man from Rio 64. Lost Command 66. They Came to Rob Las Vegas 69, etc.

servants in movies have provided great pleasure, mainly because the vast majority of the audience has been unlikely to encounter the breed in person. Actors who spent their lives playing stately butlers include Eric Blore, Charles Coleman, Robert Greig, Barnett Parker, Halliwell Hobbes and Arthur Treacher. Louise Beavers and Hattie McDaniel were the leading coloured maids, and many black comedians played frightened valets: Mantan Moreland, Stepin Fetchit, Willie Best. Sinister housekeepers are led by Gale Sondergaard and Judith Anderson. Even more eccentric servants were played by Edward Rigby in *Don't Take it to Heart,* Cantinflas in *Around the World in Eighty Days*, Seymour Hicks in *Busman's Honeymoon*, Edward Brophy in the Falcon series; and downright villainous ones by Dirk Bogarde in *The Servant*, Philip Latham in *Dracula Prince of Darkness*, Boris Karloff in *The Old Dark House* and Bela Lugosi in *The Body Snatcher.* Romantic comedies in which servants have had liaisons with their masters (or mistresses) include *History is Made at Night, When Tomorrow Comes, Common Clay, What Price Hollywood?, The Farmer's Daughter, If You Could Only Cook, Lord Richard in the Pantry* and *Upstairs Downstairs*; while thirties comedies in which Russian exiles and new poor took jobs as servants are exemplified by *Tovarich* and *My Man Godfrey*. One should not forget *The Admirable Crichton* in any of his forms; but other servants less admirable were James Mason in *Five Fingers*, and Glenda Jackson and Susannah York in *The Maids.*

? Who played the housekeeper in:

1 *The Cat and the Canary* (1939)?
2 *Rebecca*?

Who played the butler in:

3 *Sherlock Holmes Faces Death*?
4 *Trouble in Paradise*?
5 *Tovarich*?
6 *The Hound of the Baskervilles* (1939)?
7 *And Then There Were None* (1945)?

Who played the valet in:

8 *Top Hat*?
9 *The Ghost Breakers*?
10 *Thank You Jeeves*?

Who played the maid in:

11 *Mr Blandings Builds His Dream House*?
12 *A Chump At Oxford*?

Sessions, Almira (1888–1974). American character actress, often seen in fluttery or eccentric bit parts.
Little Nellie Kelly 41. The Diary of a Chambermaid 46. The Fountainhead 49. The Boston Strangler 67. Rosemary's Baby 69. Everything You Always Wanted to Know About Sex 72, many others.

Seton, Sir Bruce (1909–1969). British leading man, later character actor; military background.
Blue Smoke 34. Sweeney Todd 36. Love from a Stranger 38. The Curse of the Wraydons 46. Bonnie Prince Charlie 48. Whisky Galore 49. John Paul Jones (US) 59, etc.
TV series: Fabian of the Yard 54.

Seton, Marie (*c.*1900–85). British journalist who met Eisenstein in Russia in the late twenties, wrote a biography of him, and later produced a verison of his Mexican film under the title *Time in the Sun*.

Setton, Maxwell (1909–). British independent producer, former lawyer. Recently held executive posts for Bryanston and Columbia.
The Spider and the Fly 50. So Little Time 52. They Who Dare 54. Footsteps in the Fog 55. Town on Trial 56. I Was Monty's Double 58, etc.

Seven Brides for Seven Brothers (US 1954). A highly successful MGM musical which appeared at the end of the peak period spurred by Gene Kelly, and somehow failed to prolong it. Marred by obvious budget economies, it nevertheless brought tremendous gusto to its western retelling of the story of the rape of the Sabine women. Produced by Jack Cummings, directed by Stanley Donen, with music by Gene de Paul, lyrics by Johnny Mercer, choreography by Michael Kidd; book by Albert Hackett, Frances Goodrich and Dorothy Kingsley. Howard Keel and Jane Powell led a talented cast. An attempt to modernize the story into a TV series was a deserved flop in 1983.

Seven Days in May (US 1964). A fine political melodrama directed by John Frankenheimer and written by Rod Serling from a novel by Fletcher Knebel and Charles W. Bailey II. About a militarist attempt to depose a weak president, it gives first-class opportunities to Fredric March as the president, Burt Lancaster as the ambitious general and Kirk Douglas as his bewildered aide; and apart from an unnecessary sex interest it moves with tremendous pace and attack.

Seven Keys to Baldpate. The famous stage comedy-thriller by Earl Derr Biggers and George M. Cohan has been filmed five times; with Cohan himself in 1917, Douglas Maclean in 1926, Richard Dix in 1929, Gene Raymond in 1935, and Philip Terry in 1947. The most recent version, in 1983, was *House of Long Shadows*.

Seven Samurai (Japan 1954). The film on which *The Magnificent Seven* (qv) was based; a spellbinding piece of oriental savagery which runs nearly three hours even in the abbreviated western version but never allows the eye to wander. Director Akira Kurosawa and actor Toshiro Mifune share the credit. AA best foreign film 1955.

Seventh Heaven. Frank Borzage directed Janet Gaynor (AA) and Charles Farrell in the immensely popular 1927 version of this simple garret love story set in Paris before the 1914 war, from which the hero returns blinded. Henry King remade it in 1937, with Simone Simon and James Stewart. The story has its origins in a play by Austin Strong.

The Seventh Seal (Sweden 1957). Ingmar Bergman's most fascinating and infuriating film, an outpouring of medieval religious images of life and death, pain and joy. Its meaning probably can't be fully analysed, even by Bergman himself, but almost every scene is in some way memorable, and the film stands as a textbook of filmcraft. Photographed by Gunnar Fischer, with music by Eric Nordgren. The cast includes Nils Poppe, Gunnar Bjornstrand, Max Von Sydow, and Bengt Ekerot as Death.

The Seventh Veil (GB 1945). An incredibly successful piece of commercial film-making, one of the first post-war returns to the pre-war novelette school; about a concert pianist undergoing psychiatric treatment because she can't decide which of three men to marry. Expertly concocted by producer Sidney Box, glossily directed by Compton Bennett. With Ann Todd, James Mason, Herbert Lom, Albert Lieven. When the film was televised in Britain over ten years later, cinemas all over the country suffered, and the event helped to toughen the attitude of the film trade to television.

Sewell, George (1924–). British character actor of tough roles, familiar on TV in *Special Branch*.
Sparrows Can't Sing 63. Robbery 67. Get Carter 71, etc.

Sewell, Vernon (1903–). British director, former engineer, photographer, art director and editor.
The Silver Fleet 43. *Latin Quarter* 46. The Ghosts of Berkeley Square 47. Uneasy Terms 48. The Ghost Ship 52. Where There's a Will 55. Battle of the V1 58. House of Mystery 61. Strongroom 62. The Curse of the Crimson Altar 68. Burke and Hare 71, etc.

sewers have figured in several thrillers, most notably *The Third Man* with its exciting final chase; its sewer complex was recently spoofed in *Carry On Spying*. In 1948 in *He Walked by Night* Richard Basehart played a criminal who invariably escaped through the sewers; and our old friend *The Phantom of the Opera* was similarly skilled, as was Lee Marvin in *Point Blank*. As recently as the British thriller *Invasion* a sewer detour was used; while the Frankenstein monster was saved from the burning windmill by falling through to the sewer, where he was found at the beginning of *Bride of Frankenstein*. As for more serious films, sewers are of course featured in the many versions of *Les Misérables*, while the Polish resistance film *Kanal* takes place entirely—and nauseatingly—in the sewers of Warsaw. Fred MacMurray had a comic sewer escape in *Bon Voyage*, and the giant ants of *Them!* were cornered in the sewers of Los Angeles.

sex. This was once called 'romance': the beginnings of corruption set in with de Mille's silent comedies such as *Why Change Your Wife?* and Lubitsch's classics *Forbidden Paradise* and *The Marriage Circle*. These gentlemen carried their sophistication into the early sound period, assisted by such stars as Valentino, Harlow, Dietrich, Clara Bow and Ginger Rogers; and there was considerable help from a film called *The Private Life of Henry VIII*, a lady named Mae West and a director named Josef Von Sternberg; but around 1934 the Hays Code and the Legion of Decency forced innocence upon Hollywood to such an extent that the smart hero and heroine of 1934's *It Happened One Night* just wouldn't dream of sharing a bedroom without a curtain between them. The later thirties, perforce, were the heyday of the boy next door and the *ingénue*: nice people all, personified by such stars as Gary Cooper, Dick Powell, Ray Milland, David Niven, Ruby Keeler, Janet Gaynor, Deanna Durbin and Irene Dunne. Meanwhile a strong reaguard action was being fought by actors like William Powell, Myrna Loy, Melvyn Douglas, Ann Sheridan and Cary Grant, but usually the blue pencil had been wielded so heavily on their scripts that it was difficult to tell what was really being implied. The best way out was found in such comedies as *The Philadelphia Story*, which were basically earthy but gave every appearance of keeping it all in the mind. The war years produced a certain slackening of restrictions; for instance, the pin-up girl became not only permissible but desirable as a way of building up military morale. Preston Sturges brought sex out into the open in *The Palm Beach Story* and *The Miracle of Morgan's Creek*; Spencer Tracy and Katharine Hepburn started (in *Woman of the Year*) a series of films portraying the battle of the sexes in a recognizably human way. The 'love goddesses' became progressively more blatant in their appeal: Jane Russell, Marilyn Monroe, Jayne Mansfield. (But in the fifties it turned out that one of the earthiest of them, Sophia Loren, was also the best actress.) By now the production code had been broken down to the extent of permitting words like 'virgin' and 'mistress' (*The Moon is Blue*), the recognition of adultery and prostitution as human facts (*Wives and Lovers, Kiss Me Stupid*), depiction of the lustfulness of males (*Tom Jones, Alfie*), 'realistic' dramas like *Room at the Top*, erotic romances like *Les Amants*, and the presentation, albeit in a fantasy, of girls as 'pleasure units' (*Our Man Flint*). Indeed, after *Georgy Girl, Night Games* and *Who's Afraid of Virginia Woolf?*, it seemed that public frankness could go very little further; but along came *Blow Up, Midnight Cowboy, Satyricon, Flesh, The Music Lovers, Percy, Last Tango in Paris* and *Deep Throat* to prove the opposite. There even emerged an X-rated cartoon *Fritz the Cat*; and by the mid-seventies pornographic films on view in most cities outnumbered the other kind.

sex changes have not been a profitable line of inquiry for the cinema, though the gimmick thriller *Homicidal* depended on one, as did *Myra Breckinridge*. *The Christine Jorgenson Story* was an account of a genuine case, and *I Want What I Want* presented a fictitious case history. The most amusing film on the subject is certainly *Turnabout*.

Sexton Blake. The lean, ascetic detective hero of several generations of British boys was the creation of Harry Blyth ('Hal Meredith') (1852–98). On screen he was first portrayed in 1914 in *The Clue of the Wax Vesta*. He was played in the twenties by Langhorne Burton, in the thirties by George Curzon, in the forties by David Farrar and in the fifties by Geoffrey Toone; while 1962's *Mix Me a Person* was taken from a Blake story but cast Anne Baxter in the role.

Seyler, Athene (1889–). British comedy actress with long stage career dating from 1908.
This Freedom 22. The Perfect Lady 32. The Citadel 38. *Quiet Wedding* 40. *Dear Octopus* 43. Nicholas Nickleby 47. Queen of Spades 48. Young Wives' Tale 51. *Pickwick Papers* 53. Yield to the Night 56. Campbell's Kingdom 58. The Inn of the Sixth Happiness 58. Make Mine Mink 59. Nurse on Wheels 63, many others.

Seymour, Anne (1909–). American character actress.
All the King's Men 49. Man on Fire 57. Home from the Hill 59. The Subterraneans 60. Sunrise at Campobello 60. Mirage 65. Blindfold 66. Never Never Land 81, etc.
TV series: Empire 62.

Seymour, Dan (1915–1982). Burly American character actor, the scowling menace of countless films.
Casablanca 42. To Have and Have Not 44. Cloak and Dagger 46. Key Largo 48. Rancho Notorious 52. The Big Heat 53. Moonfleet 55. The Sad Sack 57. Watusi 59. Escape to Witch Mountain 75, etc.

Seymour, Jane (1951–) (Joyce Frankenberg). British leading actress in international films.
Oh What a Lovely War 70. Young Winston 72. Live and Let Die 72. Frankenstein: the True Story (TV) 73. The Hanged Man (TV) 74. Sinbad and the Eye of the Tiger 75. Captains and the Kings (TV) 76. Las Vegas Undercover (TV) 77. Seventh Avenue (TV) 77. The Four Feathers (TV) 78. Somewhere in Time 80. *East of Eden* (TV) 81. The Scarlet Pimpernel (TV) 82. Jamaica Inn (TV) 83. The Sun Also Rises (TV) 84. The Dark Mirror (TV) 85. Obsessed with a Married Woman (TV) 85. Crossings (TV) 85. War and Remembrance (TV) 87, etc.

Seyrig, Delphine (1932–). French leading actress.
Pull My Daisy 58. *Last Year in Marienbad* 61. Muriel 63. La Musica 66. Accident (GB) 67. Mr Freedom 68. *Stolen Kisses* 68. Daughters of Darkness 70. Peau d'Ane 70. *The Discreet Charm of the Bourgeoisie* 72. The Day of the Jackal 73. The Black Windmill 74. Aloise 75. Caro Michele 77, etc.

Shadow of a Doubt (US 1943). A very effective, and pleasingly understated, Hitchcock thriller about a small-town family visited by a romantic big-city uncle who turns out to be the Merry Widow Murderer. Hitch's technique has never been more supple, and Thornton Wilder's script is a great asset. Joseph Cotten and Teresa Wright give responsive performances. The film was remade, inadequately, in 1959 as a second feature called *Step Down to Terror*.

Shadows (US 1959). An improvised film shot on 16mm in New York by John Cassavetes with unknown actors. About young people in the big city, its chief interest was in its technique, which influenced the 'cinema vérité' school.

Shaffer, Anthony (1926–). British playwright and screenwriter, twin of Peter Shaffer.
Forbush and the Penguins 71. Sleuth (& oa) 72. Frenzy 73. The Wicker Man 73. Death on the Nile 78. Absolution 80. Evil Under the Sun 82.

Shaffer, Peter (1926–). British playwright, twin of Anthony Shaffer. Works filmed include *Five Finger Exercise*, *The Private Ear and the Public Eye*, *The Royal Hunt of the Sun*, *Equus*, Amadeus (AA) 84.

Shagan, Steve (1927–). American screenwriter.
Save the Tiger 73. Hustle (oa) 75. Voyage of the Damned 76. Nightwing (oa) 78. The Formula 80.

Shakespeare, William (1564–1616). British poet and dramatist whose plays have received plenty of attention from film-makers. *The Taming of the Shrew* was filmed in 1908 by D. W. Griffith; in 1929 with Douglas Fairbanks, Mary Pickford, and the immortal credit line 'additional dialogue by Sam Taylor'; in 1953, more or less, as *Kiss Me Kate*; and in 1966 with Elizabeth Taylor, Richard Burton, and script credits to three writers none of whom is Shakespeare. *As You Like It* was filmed in 1912 with Rose Coghlan and Maurice Costello; the only sound filming was in 1936 by Paul Czinner, with Elisabeth Bergner and Laurence Olivier. *A Midsummer Night's Dream* was tackled in major fashion by Warners in 1935, but the elaborate Max Reinhardt production failed to please at the box-office; in 1968 a 'realistic' version by Peter Hall was equally unsuccessful.

Of the tragedies, *Othello* has been frequently attempted, by Emil Jannings in 1922, Orson Welles in 1952, Sergei Bondartchuk in 1955 and Laurence Olivier in 1966; a 1961 British film called *All Night Long* was a modern up-dating of the plot, and Ronald Colman's Academy Award-winning performance in *A Double Life* 47 had him as an actor who starts playing the Moor in private life, as did Sebastian Shaw in *Men Are Not Gods* 36. *Hamlet* was played by Sir Johnston Forbes Robertson in 1913, Asta Nielsen in 1920, Olivier in 1948, and Innokenti Smoktunovsky in 1964. (Note also a 1972 western called *Johnny Hamlet* and a German modern version of 1959 called *The Rest is Silence*.) *Macbeth* is thought to be an unlucky play; but Sir Herbert Beerbohm Tree appeared in a version for Griffith in 1916; Orson Welles directed himself in the role in 1948, Paul Douglas in 1955 was an updated *Joe Macbeth*, in 1960 Maurice Evans appeared in a version originally intended for TV but shown theatrically, and in 1971 Roman Polanski presented a bloodthirsty version with Jon Finch. One should also mention *The Siberian Lady Macbeth* and the Japanese *Throne of Blood*. In 1969 *King Lear* was filmed with Paul Scofield; there was a one-reel Vitagraph version in 1909 and Frederic Warde starred in a 1916 production. *Romeo and Juliet* was also made in 1916, starring Francis X. Bushman and Beverly

Bayne; this superseded several one-reel versions. In 1936 MGM produced its Leslie Howard/Norma Shearer version directed by George Cukor; in 1954 Renato Castellani directed an unsuccessful colour version with Laurence Harvey and Susan Shentall; in 1961 came the inevitable modernization in *West Side Story*: and 1968 brought another expensive production by Franco Zeffirelli. (There have also been several ballet versions.) There were early potted versions of *Julius Caesar* before the spectacular Italian production of 1914; the play was not filmed again until MGM's excellent 1953 version. The plot was used in a curious British second feature called *An Honourable Murder* 59, with the action moved to a modern executive suite; an all-star version in colour followed in 1970, starring Charlton Heston and finding more action than is normally evident in the play.

Of the histories, most of *Henry IV* has been compressed by Orson Welles into his *Chimes at Midnight, Henry V* was splendidly dealt with by Olivier in 1944, *Richard III* existed in several primitive versions, and John Barrymore recited a speech from it in *Show of Shows* 28; but again it was left to Olivier to do it properly.

The oddest screen fate of a Shakespeare play was surely that of *The Tempest*, which in 1956 yielded its entire plot to that winning bit of science fiction *Forbidden Planet*. Performances of others were put to comedy purpose in *Doubling for Romeo* and *To Be or Not To Be*.

The best book on the subject is 1971's *Shakespeare and the Film* by Roger Manvell.

Shakespeare was impersonated, rather well, by Tim Curry in TV's *Will Shakespeare*; and very badly by Reginald Gardiner in *The Story of Mankind*.

Shamroy, Leon (1901–1974). Distinguished American cinematographer.
Catch as Catch Can 27. Out with the Tide 28. The Women Men Marry 31. Jennie Gerhardt 33. Three Cornered Moon 33. Thirty Day Princess 34. Private Worlds 35. Soak the Rich 36. You Only Live Once 37. *The Young In Heart* 38. The Story of Alexander Graham Bell 39. *The Adventures of Sherlock Holmes* 40. Lillian Russell 40. Tin Pan Alley 40. A Yank in the RAF 41. Roxie Hart 42. *Ten Gentlemen from West Point* 42. *The Black Swan* (AA) 42. *Stormy Weather* 43. Buffalo Bill 44. *Wilson* (AA) 44. *A Tree Grows in Brooklyn* 45. State Fair 45. *Leave Her to Heaven* (AA) 46. Forever Amber 47. That Lady in Ermine 48. Prince of Foxes 49. Twelve O'Clock High 49. Cheaper by the Dozen 50. On the Riviera 51. David and Bathsheba 51. The Snows of Kilimanjaro 53. Call Me Madam 53. *The Robe* 53. The Egyptian 54. Love is a Many Splendored Thing 55. *The King and I* 56. Desk Set 57. South Pacific (co-ph) 58. Porgy and Bess 59. North to Alaska 60. Tender is the Night 61. Cleopatra (AA) 63. The Cardinal 63. The Agony and the Ecstasy 65. The Glass Bottom Boat 66. Caprice (also appeared) 67. *Planet of the Apes* 67. Justine 69, many others.

¶ *L.S.:* God was a great photographer. He'd only gotten one light.

L.S.: Lee Garmes will never see the day that he's as good as I am, and that goes for anybody in the motion picture business.

Shane (US 1953). A serious, atmospheric western about a pioneer family protected by a mysterious stranger; written by A. B. Guthrie Jnr from Jack Schaefer's novel. George Stevens directed it with great feeling and turned it into a classic. Photographed by Loyal Griggs (AA), music by Victor Young; with Alan Ladd, Jean Arthur, Van Heflin. A TV series of 1966 starred David Carradine.

Shane, Maxwell (1905–1983). American writer-director, former publicist.
You Can't Beat Love (co-w) 37. One Body Too Many (w) 43. Fear in the Night (wd) 46 (remade as Nightmare in 1956). City across the River (wdp) 49. The Naked Street (wd) 55, etc.

Shanghai Express (US 1932). This nostalgic melodrama, which even when new seemed to be spoofing itself, has over the years acquired the patina of a Hollywood classic. All about the intertwining of the lives of a Chinese war lord, a high class prostitute, and a stiff-upper-lip British officer on a train beset by rebels, it had suitable performances from Warner Oland, Marlene Dietrich and Clive Brook. Josef Von Sternberg directed from a script by Jules Furthman; Lee Garmes (AA) was cinematographer. There was one direct remake, *Peking Express* 52, but many films borrowed the basic situations: *Half Way to Shanghai, Night Plane from Chungking, The House of Tao Ling,* even *The General Died at Dawn* and *The Lady Vanishes*.

Shannon, Harry (1890–1964). American character actor, often seen as sympathetic father or rustic; musical comedy experience.

Hands Up 31. Young Tom Edison 40. The Eve of St Mark 44. The Gunfighter 50. High Noon 52. Executive Suite 54. Come Next Spring 56. Hell's Crossroads 57, many others.

Shapiro, Stanley (1925–). American writer-producer associated with glossy comedies; long experience in radio and TV.
The Perfect Furlough (w) 58. Pillow Talk (co-w) (AA) 59. Operation Petticoat (co-w) 59. Come September (co-w) 60. That Touch of Mink (co-w) 62. Bedtime Story (wp) 64. How to Save a Marriage (p) 68. For Pete's Sake (co-w, p) 74. Carbon Copy 81, etc.

Sharaff, Irene (c. 1910–). American costume designer, long with Fox.
An American in Paris (AA) 51. The King and I (AA) 56. West Side Story (AA) 61. Cleopatra (AA) 63. Who's Afraid of Virginia Woolf? (AA) 66. The Taming of the Shrew 67. Hello Dolly 69.

Sharif, Omar (1932–) (Michel Shalhouz). Egyptian leading man now in international films.
Autobiography 1977: *The Eternal Male.*
Goha 59. *Lawrence of Arabia* 62. The Fall of the Roman Empire 64. Behold a Pale Horse 64. The Yellow Rolls-Royce 64. Genghis Khan 65. *Dr Zhivago* 65. The Night of the Generals 66. Marco the Magnificent 66. More Than a Miracle 67. Funny Girl 68. Mayerling 68. Mackenna's Gold 68. The Appointment 69. Che! 69. The Last Valley 70. The Horsemen 71. The Burglars 71. The Tamarind Seed 74. Juggernaut 74. The Mysterious Island of Captain Nemo 74. Funny Lady 75. Ace Up My Sleeve 76. Ashanti 78. Bloodline 79. The Baltimore Bullet 80. Oh Heavenly Dog 80, etc.

¶ *O.S.:* I definitely want to do mainly theatre now. Or, two weeks in a film for a remarkable amount of money.
O.S.: Aggressive feminists scare me.

Sharkey, Ray (1952–). American leading man of the eighties.
Trackdown 76. Stunts 77. Paradise Alley 78. Who'll Stop the Rain 78. Heartbeat 80. Willie and Phil 80. The Idolmaker 80. Love and Money 82, etc.

Sharp, Alan (–). Scottish writer in Hollywood.
The Hired Hand 71. The Last Run 71. Ulzana's Raid 72. Billy Two Hats 74. Night Moves 75.

Sharp, Don (1922–). Australian-born director, in British film industry from 1952, at first as writer.
Ha'penny Breeze (w) 52. Robbery Under Arms (w) 56. The Professionals 59. Linda 60. Kiss of the Vampire 62. Devil Ship Pirates 63. *Witchcraft* 64. Those Magnificent Men in Their Flying Machines (second unit) 65. Rasputin the Mad Monk 65. *The Face of Fu Manchu* 65. Our Man in Marrakesh 66. The Million Eyes of Su Muru 66. Rocket to the Moon 67. Psychomania 72. Callan 74. Hennessy 75. The Four Feathers (TV) 78. *The 39 Steps* 78. Bear Island 80. A Woman of Substance (TV) 84. Tusitala (TV) 85. Hold the Dream (TV) 87, etc.

Sharp, Henry (1892–1966). American cinematographer.
Homespun Folks 20. The Hottentot 22. A Girl of the Limberlost 24. Don Q Son of Zorro 25. *The Black Pirate* 26. The Lovelorn 27. *The Crowd* 28. The Iron Mask 29. Lord Byron of Broadway 30. The False Madonna 31. The Devil is Driving 32. Duck Soup 33. Six of a Kind 34. The Glass Key 35. Lady be Careful 36. Hotel Haywire 37. Booloo 38. Geronimo 39. Dr Cyclops (co-ph) 40. Broadway Limited 41. The Hidden Hand 42. Ministry of Fear 44. Jealousy 45. It Happened on Fifth Avenue 47. Perilous Waters 48. Daughter of the West 49. The Young Land (co-ph) 59, many others.

Sharp, Ian (1946–). British director, from TV.
The Music Machine 81. Who Dares Wins 82.

Shatner, William (1931–). Canadian leading actor, seen mostly on TV.
The Brothers Karamazov 58. The Explosive Generation 61. The Intruder (The Stranger) 61. The Outrage 64. Go Ask Alice (TV) 73. The Horror at 37,000 feet (TV) 74. Big Bad Mama 74. Kingdom of the Spiders 77. A Whale of a Tale 77. Land of No Return 78. Star Trek: The Motion Picture 79. The Kidnapping of the President 80. Star Trek: The Wrath of Khan 82. Visiting Hours 82. Star Trek 3: the Search for Spock 84. Star Trek 4: The Voyage Home 87.
TV series: For the People 60. *Star Trek* 66–68. Barbary Coast 75. T. J. Hooker 82–86.

Shaughnessy, Alfred (1916–). British producer.
Brandy for the Parson 51. Cat Girl 57. Heart of a Child 57. Just My Luck (script only) 59. The Impersonator (script and direction only) 61. Lunch Hour 63, etc.

Shaughnessy, Mickey (1920–85). Tough-looking American comic actor with stage experience.
The Last of the Comanches (debut) 52. From Here to Eternity 53. Conquest of Space 55. Jailhouse Rock 57. *Don't Go Near the Water* 57. North to Alaska 60. A Global Affair 63. A House Is Not a Home 64. Never a Dull Moment 68, etc.
TV series: Chicago Teddy Bears 71.

Shavelson, Melville (1917–). American screenwriter, in Hollywood from early forties.
The Princess and the Pirate 44. Always Leave Them Laughing 50. Room for One More 52. The Seven Little Foys (& d) 56. Beau James (& d) 57. Houseboat (& d) 58. The Five Pennies (& d) 59. The Pigeon That Took Rome (& pd) 62. A New Kind of Love (& pd) 63. Cast a Giant Shadow (& pd) 66. The War Between Men and Women (co-wd) 72, many others, usually in collaboration with *Jack Rose* (1911–).
TV: Ike (w, co-d) 79.

Shaw, Artie (1910–) (Arthur Arschawsky). American bandleader and clarinettist.
□Dancing Co-Ed 39. Second Chorus 40.

Shaw, George Bernard (1856–1950). Distinguished Irish playwright who for many years refused to allow film versions of his works: he was reconciled to the idea by Gabriel Pascal. The following versions have been made.
How He Lied to Her Husband 30. Arms and the Man 31. Pygmalion 38. Major Barbara 40. Caesar and Cleopatra 45. Androcles and the Lion 53. Saint Joan 57. The Doctor's Dilemma 58. The Devil's Disciple 59. Helden (Arms and the Man) (WG) 59. The Millionairess 61. My Fair Lady (from Pygmalion) 64. Great Catherine 67.

¶ 'As an iconoclast he is admirable, as an icon somewhat less so.'—*Bertrand Russell*

Shaw, Irwin (1912–1984). American novelist and screenwriter.
Talk of the Town 42. I Want You 51. Fire Down Below 57. The Young Lions (& oa) 58. Tip on a Dead Jockey 58. Two Weeks in Another Town (novel only) 62. *Rich Man Poor Man* (novel only) (TV) 76. Top of the Hill (story) (TV) 79, etc.

Shaw, Martin (*c.*1947–). British leading man who shot to fame in TV's *The Professionals*.
Sinbad's Golden Voyage 72. Operation Daybreak 73. Cream in my Coffee (TV) 80. The Last Place on Earth (TV) 85.

Shaw, Maxwell (–1985). British supporting actor, usually in unsympathetic roles.

Shaw, Reta (1912–1982). Amply proportioned American character actress.
The Pajama Game 57. Pollyanna 60. Mary Poppins 64. Escape to Witch Mountain 74.

Shaw, Robert (1927–1978). British star character actor.
□ The Dam Busters (film debut) 55. Double Cross 55. A Hill in Korea 56. The Birthday Party 58. Libel 59. Sea Fury 59. The Valiant 61. Tomorrow at Ten 62. *From Russia with Love* 63. The Caretaker 63. The Luck of Ginger Coffey 64. The Battle of the Bulge 65. *A Man for All Seasons* (as Henry VIII) 66. Custer of the West 67. The Battle of Britain 69. The Royal Hunt of the Sun 69. Figures in a Landscape 70. A Town Called Bastard 71. Reflection of Fear 72. Young Winston 72. The Hireling 73. The Sting 73. The Taking of Pelham One Two Three 74. Jaws 75. Robin and Marian 75. End of the Game 76. Diamonds 76. Swashbuckler 76. Black Sunday 76. The Deep 77. Force Ten from Navarone 78. Avalanche Express 79.
TV series: The Buccaneers 56.

Shaw, Sebastian (1905–). British leading man of the thirties, latterly character actor. On stage from 1913 (as child).
Caste 30. Taxi to Paradise 33. Men are not Gods 36. The Squeaker 37. The Spy in Black 39. East of Piccadilly 41. The Glass Mountain 48. It Happened Here 64. A Midsummer Night's Dream 68. High Season 87.

Shaw, Susan (1929–1978) (Patsy Sloots). British leading lady groomed by the Rank 'charm school'.
London Town 46. The Upturned Glass 47. Holiday Camp 47. London Belongs to Me 48. The Woman in Question 50. The Intruder 51. The Good Die Young 52. Stock Car 54. Carry On Nurse 59. The Switch 63, etc.

Shaw, Victoria (1935–) (Jeanette Elphick). Australian leading lady in American films.
Cattle Station (Aust.) 55. The Eddy Duchin Story 56. Edge of Eternity 59. The Crimson Kimono 60. Alvarez Kelly 66. Westworld 73, etc.

Shaw, Wini (1899–1982) (Winfred Lei Momi). American singer of Hawaiian descent, used as voice of non-singing stars in many Warner musicals of the thirties. Actually appeared in the following.
Three on a Honeymoon 34. Gold Diggers of 1935 35. In Caliente 35. Melody for Two 37, etc.

Shawlee, Joan (1929–) (formerly Joan Fulton). American character comedienne with night club and stage experience.
Men in Her Diary 45. Cuban Pete 46. I'll Be Yours 47. The Marrying Kind 52. Conquest of Space 54. A Star is Born 54. *Some Like It Hot* 59. The Apartment 60. Irma La Douce 63. The Wild Angels 66. The St Valentine's Day Massacre 67. One More Time 71. Willard 71. Dead Men Tell No Tales (TV) 74. Flash and Firecat 76, etc.
TV series: Aggie 57. The Betty Hutton Show 59. Feather and Father 77.

Shawn, Dick (1928–87) (Richard Schulefand). American comedian, in occasional films.
Wake Me When It's Over 60. It's a Mad Mad Mad Mad World 63. A Very Special Favor 65. What Did You Do in the War, Daddy? 66. Penelope 66. The Producers 68. Looking Up 77. Love at First Bite 79, etc.

Shayne, Robert (c. 1910–) (Robert Shaen Dawe). American general purpose actor.
Keep 'Em Rolling 34. Shine On Harvest Moon 44. The Swordsman 47. The Neanderthal Man (lead role) 53. Spook Chasers 58. Valley of the Redwoods 61, etc.

Shayne, Tamara (1897–1983) (Tamara Nikoulin). Russian-American character actress who played Jolson's mother in *The Jolson Story* and *Jolson Sings Again*. Also: *Ninotchka, Mission to Moscow, Anastasia*, etc.

She. Seven silent versions are said to have been made of Rider Haggard's adventure fantasy about a lost tribe, an ageless queen and a flame of eternal life in darkest Africa. Only the last remains, made in London and Berlin by G. B. Samuelson, with Betty Blythe and Carlyle Blackwell. In 1934 in Hollywood, Merian Cooper and Ernest Schoedsack remade the story in a North Pole setting, with Helen Gahagan and Randolph Scott. In 1965 came a lifeless Hammer version directed by Robert Day, with Ursula Andress and John Richardson; this was followed in 1968 by a sequel, *The Vengeance of She*, that was more than slightly potty.

She Only Danced One Summer (Sweden 1951). This glum romantic tragedy came complete with nude bathing scene and dour puritan priests, amounting to almost a parody of itself. But it was commercial enough to cause a renewal of interest in European films. Arne Matsson directed: Ulla Jacobson and Folke Sundquist were the doomed lovers.

Shean, Al (1868–1949) (Alfred Schoenberg). German-born entertainer, long in American vaudeville; part of the famous 'Mr Gallagher and Mr Shean' act. After his partner's death he played character roles in Hollywood films.
Murder in the Air 35. San Francisco 36. The Great Waltz 38. Ziegfeld Girl 41. Atlantic City 44, etc.

Shear, Barry (1923–1979). American director.
□Wild in the Streets 68. Night Gallery (TV) (co-d) 69. Ellery Queen: Don't Look Behind You (TV) 71. The Todd Killings 71. Short Walk to Daylight (TV) 72. Across 110th Street 72. The Deadly Trackers 73. Jarrett (TV) 73. Punch and Jody (TV) 74. Strike Force (TV) 75. San Pedro Bums (TV) 77.

Shearer, Douglas (1899–1971). American sound engineer, brother of Norma Shearer; at MGM for many years, he won twelve Academy Awards, and developed a new sound head.
The Big House 30. Naughty Marietta 35. San Francisco 36. Strike Up the Band 40. Thirty Seconds Over Tokyo 44. Green Dolphin Street 47. The Great Caruso 51, many others.

Shearer, Moira (1926–) (Moira King). Scottish-born ballet dancer who came to films for the leading role in *The Red Shoes* 48.
□Tales of Hoffman 52. The Story of Three Loves 53. The Man Who Loved Redheads 55. Peeping Tom 59. Black Tights 60.

Shearer, Norma (1900–1983). Canadian actress, in Hollywood from silent days and a big MGM star of the thirties. Widow of Irving Thalberg.
□The Flapper 20. The Restless Sex 20. Way Down East 20. The Stealers 20. The Sign on the Door 20. Torchy's Millions 21. The Leather Pushers 22. The Man Who Paid 22. The Bootleggers 22. Channing of the Northwest 22. A Clouded Name 23. Man and Wife 23. The Devil's Partner 23. Pleasure

Mad 23. The Wanters 23. Lucretia Lombard 23. The Trail of the Law 24. The Wolf Man 24. Blue Water 24. Broadway After Dark 24. Broken Barriers 24. Married Flirts 24. Empty Hands 24. The Snob 24. *He Who Gets Slapped* 24. Excuse Me 25. Lady of the Night 25. Waking Up the Town 25. A Slave of Fashion 25. Pretty Ladies 25. The Tower of Lies 25. His Secretary 25. The Devil's Circus 26. The Waning Sex 26. Upstage 26. The Demi-Bride 27. After Midnight 27. The Student Prince 27. The Latest from Paris 28. The Actress 28. A Lady of Chance 28. *The Trial of Mary Dugan* 29. *The Last of Mrs Cheyney* 29. Hollywood Revue 29. Their Own Desire 29. The Divorcee (AA) 30. Let Us Be Gay 30. Strangers May Kiss 31. *A Free Soul* 31. Private Lives 31. Strange Interlude 32. *Smilin' Through* 32. Riptide 34. *The Barretts of Wimpole Street* 34. Romeo and Juliet 36. Marie Antoinette 38. Idiot's Delight 39. The Women 39. Escape 40. We Were Dancing 41. Her Cardboard Lover 42.

¶ 'A face unclouded by thought.'—*Lillian Hellman*

Sheedy, Ally (–). American leading lady.
Bad Boys 82. War Games 83. St Elmo's Fire 85. Short Circuit 86.

Sheekman, Arthur (1891–1978). American comedy writer, often in collaboration.
Monkey Business 31. Roman Scandals 33. Dimples 36. Wonder Man 45. Welcome Stranger 46. Saigon 47. Young Man with Ideas 52. Bundle of Joy 56. Ada 61, etc.

Sheen, Charlie (–). American actor, son of Martin Sheen.
Wall Street 87.

Sheen, Martin (1940–) (Ramon Estevez). American leading actor of the seventies.
□The Incident 67. The Subject was Roses 68. Catch 22 69. Goodbye Raggedy Ann (TV) 71. No Drums No Bugles 71. Rage 72. Message to My Daughter (TV) 72. Pick-up on 101 72. Pursuit (TV) 73. That Certain Summer (TV) 73. Letters for Three Lovers (TV) 73. Sweet Hostage (TV) 73. *Badlands* 73. Catholics (TV) 74. The Execution of Private Slovik (TV) 74. The Missiles of October (TV) 74. The California Kid (TV) 75. The Legend of Earl Durand 75. The Little Girl Who Lives Down the Lane 76. Sweet Hostage 76. The Cassandra Crossing 77. *Apocalypse Now* 79. Eagle's Wing 79. Loophole 80. The Final Countdown 80. Gandhi 82. That Championship Season 82. Enigma 82. Man, Woman and Child 83. Kennedy (TV) 83. The Dead Zone 83. Broken Rainbow (narrator) 85. The Believers 87. Wall Street 87.

Sheffield, Johnny (1931–). American boy actor of the thirties, especially in the *Tarzan* and later the *Bomba* series.
Babes in Arms 39. Roughly Speaking 45, etc.

Sheffield, Reginald (1901–1957). British actor in Hollywood, father of Johnny Sheffield; formerly a child star.
David Copperfield 23. White Mice 26. The Green Goddess 30. Old English 30. Of Human Bondage 34. Cardinal Richelieu 35. Another Dawn 57. Earthbound 40. Eyes in the Night 42. Wilson 44. Kiss the Blood Off My Hands 48. The Buccaneer 58, etc.

Shefter, Bert (1904–). American composer.
Danger Zone 51. M 51. No Escape 53. Kronos 57. Cattle Empire 58. The Big Circus 59. The Lost World 60. Jack the Giant Killer 62. Curse of the Fly 65. The Last Shot you Hear 69, many others.

The Sheik. Rudolph Valentino first appeared as the romantic Arab in 1922, with Agnes Ayres as his willing co-star, in an adaptation of E. M. Hull's novelette. It was one of his most successful roles, and *Son of the Sheik* came out in 1926 with Vilma Banky partnering him. His death prevented further episodes, but in 1937 Ramon Novarro made fun of the idea in *The Sheik Steps Out*, and in 1962 came an Italian spoof called *The Return of the Son of the Sheik* with Gordon Scott.

Sheldon, Gene (1909–1982). American comedy actor.
A Thousand and One Nights 45. Where Do We Go from Here 45. Golden Girl 52. Three Ring Circus 55. Babes in Toyland 60, etc.

Sheldon, Sidney (1917–). American writer-director.
The Bachelor and the Bobbysoxer (w) (AA) 47. Dream Wife (co-w, d) 53. You're Never Too Young (w) 55. Pardners (w) 56. The Buster Keaton Story (wpd) 57. Jumbo (w) 62. The Other Side of Midnight (oa) 77. Bloodline (oa) 79. Rage of Angels (TV) (oa) 83. Master of the Game (TV) 84, etc.

Shelley, Barbara (1933–). British leading lady who has filmed in Italy; latterly associated with horror films.
Cat Girl 57. Blood of the Vampire 59. Village of the Damned 61. Shadow of the Cat 62. Postman's Knock 62. The Gorgon 64. The Secret of Blood Island 65. Rasputin the Mad Monk 65. Dracula, Prince of Darkness 65. *Quatermass and the Pit* 67. Ghost Story 74, etc.

Shelley, Mary Wollstonecraft (1797–1851). British writer (wife of the poet) who somewhat unexpectedly is remembered as the creator of *Frankenstein*, which she composed to pass the time during a wet summer. She was played in *Bride of Frankenstein* by Elsa Lanchester.

Shelton, John (1917–1972) (John Price). Rather colourless American second lead.
The Smartest Girl in Town 36. Navy Blue and Gold 37. I Take This Woman 40. Blonde Inspiration 41. Whispering Ghosts 42. The Time of Their Lives 46. Siren of Atlantis 48. Sins of Jezebel 51, etc.

Shelton, Joy (1922–). British leading lady.
Millions Like Us 43. Waterloo Road 44. No Room at the Inn 48. A Case for PC 49 51. Impulse 54. No Kidding 60. HMS Defiant 62, etc.

Shenson, Walter (1919–). American producer, former publicist; based in Britain.
Korea Patrol 53. The Mouse That Roared 59. A Matter of Who 61. *A Hard Day's Night* 64. Help! 65. A Talent for Loving 69. Welcome to the Club (d) 70. Digby 73. The Chicken Chronicles 77. Reuben Reuben 83, etc.

Shengeleya, Georgy (–). Russian director, whose *Pirosmani* was widely praised in 1973.

Shentall, Susan (1934–). British leading lady who made a solitary appearance in *Romeo and Juliet* 54.

Shepard, Sam (1943–) (Samuel Shepard Rogers). American leading man.
Renaldo and Clara 78. Days of Heaven 78. Resurrection 80. Raggedy Man 81. Frances 82. The Right Stuff (AAN) 83. Paris Texas (w only) 84. Country 84. Fool for Love (& w) 85. Crimes of the Heart 86.

¶ *S.S.:* I didn't go out of my way to get into this movie stuff. I think of myself as a writer.

Shepherd, Cybill (1949–). American leading lady of the seventies, best known as the protégée of Peter Bogdanovich.
□The Last Picture Show 71. The Heartbreak Kid 72. Daisy Miller 74. At Long Last Love 75. Taxi Driver 76. Special Delivery 76. Silver Bears 77. The Lady Vanishes 79. The Return 80.
TV series: The Yellow Rose 83. Moonlighting 85.

Shepherd, Elizabeth (–). British actress.
The Queen's Guards 61. Blind Corner 63. *The Tomb of Ligeia* 64. Hell Boats 69. Damien: Omen II 78. Double Negative 80.

Shepley, Michael (1907–1961) (Michael Shepley-Smith). British stage actor who usually played amiable buffoons.
Black Coffee 30. Goodbye Mr Chips 39. Quiet Wedding 40. The Demi Paradise 43. Maytime in Mayfair 49. An Alligator Named Daisy 56. Don't Bother to Knock 61, etc.

Shepperd, John (1907–1983) (also known under his real name, Shepperd Strudwick). American leading man and latterly character actor, usually in gentle, understanding roles.
Congo Maisie (debut) 40. *Remember the Day* 41. *The Loves of Edgar Allan Poe* 42. Enchantment 47. Joan of Arc 48. All the King's Men 49. A Place in the Sun 51. Autumn Leaves 56. The Sad Sack 57. The Unkillables 67. Cops and Robbers 73, etc.

Sher, Antony (1949–). British Shakespearian actor.
Yanks 79. Superman II 80. Shadey 84.

Sher, Jack (1913–). American writer-director, former columnist.
My Favorite Spy (w) 51. Off Limits (w) 53. Four Girls in Town (wd) 56. Kathy O' (wd) 58. The Wild and the Innocent (wd) 59. The Three Worlds of Gulliver (wd) 60. Paris Blues (co-w) 61. Critic's Choice (w) 63. Move Over Darling (co-w) 63, etc.

Sheridan, Ann (1915–1967) (Clara Lou Sheridan). American leading lady at her peak in the early forties; a cheerful beauty contest winner who developed a tough style and became known as the 'oomph' girl.
□Search for Beauty 34. Bolero 34. Come on Marines 34. Murder at the Vanities 34. Kiss and Make Up 34. Shoot the Works 34. The Notorious Sophie Lang 34. Ladies Should

Listen 34. Wagon Wheels 34. Mrs Wiggs of the Cabbage Patch 34. College Rhythm 34. You Belong to Me 34. Limehouse Blues 34. Enter Madame 35. Home on the Range 35. Rumba 35. Behold My Wife 35. Car 99 35. Rocky Mountain Mystery 35. Mississippi 35. The Glass Key 35. The Crusades 35. The Red Blood of Courage 35. Fighting Youth 35. Sing Me a Love Song 35. Black Legion 36. The Great O'Malley 37. San Quentin 37. Wine, Women and Horses 37. The Footloose Heiress 37. Alcatraz Island 37. She Loves a Fireman 38. The Patient in Room 18 38. Mystery House 38. Cowboy from Brooklyn 38. Little Miss Thoroughbred 38. Letter of Introduction 38. Broadway Musketeers 38. *Angels with Dirty Faces* 38. They Made Me a Criminal 39. Dodge City 39. Naughty but Nice 39. Winter Carnival 39. Indianapolis Speedway 39. Angels Wash Their Faces 39. Castle on the Hudson 40. It All Came True 40. *Torrid Zone* 40. *They Drive by Night* 40. City for Conquest 40. Honeymoon for Three 41. Navy Blues 41. *Kings' Row* 41. *The Man Who Came to Dinner* 41. Juke Girl 42. Wings for the Eagle 42. George Washington Slept Here 42. Edge of Darkness 43. *Thank Your Lucky Stars* 43. *Shine on Harvest Moon* 44. The Doughgirls 44. One More Tomorrow 46. Nora Prentiss 47. *The Unfaithful* 47. Silver River 48. Good Sam 48. *I Was a Male War Bride* 49. Stella 50. Woman on the Run 50. Steel Town 52. Just Across the Street 52. Take Me to Town 53. Appointment in Honduras 53. *Come Next Spring* 56. The Opposite Sex 56. Woman and the Hunter 57. TV series: Pistols and Petticoats 67.

Sheridan, Dinah (1920–). British leading lady.
Irish and Proud of It 36. Full Speed Ahead 39. Salute John Citizen 42. For You Alone 44. Hills of Donegal 47. Calling Paul Temple 48. The Story of Shirley Yorke 48. Paul Temple's Triumph 50. Where No Vultures Fly 51. *Genevieve* 53. The Railway Children 71. The Mirror Crack'd 80, etc.

Sheriff, Paul (1903–1961) (Paul Schouvaloff). Russian art director in Britain since mid-thirties.
French Without Tears 39. Quiet Wedding 40. The Gentle Sex 43. *Henry V* 44. The Way to the Stars 45. Vice Versa 48. Flesh and Blood 51. Moulin Rouge (AA) 53. Gentlemen Marry Brunettes 55. Interpol 57. The Doctor's Dilemma 58. The Grass is Greener 60, etc.

Sherin, Edwin (1930–). American director.
Valdez is Coming 70. Glory Boy 71, etc.

Sherlock Holmes. Conan Doyle's classic fictional detective, around whom a detailed legend has been created by ardent followers, has a long screen history. There were American one-reel films featuring him in 1903, 1905 and 1908. Also in 1908 there began a series of twelve Danish one-reelers starring Forrest Holger-Madsen. In 1910 there were two German films and in 1912 six French. A second French series began in 1913; also in this year an American two-reel version of *The Sign of Four* featured Harry Benham. British six-reelers were made of *A Study in Scarlet* 14, and *Valley of Fear* 16; also in 1916 the famous stage actor William Gillette put his impersonation of Holmes on film for Essanay. In 1917 came a German version of *The Hound of the Baskervilles*; then nothing till 1922, when John Barrymore played Holmes and Roland Young was Watson in Goldwyn's *Sherlock Holmes*, based on Gillette's stage play. In Britain in the same year Maurice Elvey directed a full-length version of *The Hound of the Baskervilles* and followed it with over 25 two-reelers starring Eille Norwood, remaining faithful to the original stories. In 1929 Carlyle Blackwell played Holmes in a German remake of *The Hound of the Baskervilles*; and in the same year Clive Brook played in a talkie, *The Return of Sherlock Holmes*, with H. Reeves-Smith as Watson. Arthur Wontner, a perfect Holmes, first played the role in *Sherlock Holmes' Final Hour* (GB) 31, later appearing in *The Sign of Four* 32, *The Missing Rembrandt* 33, *The Triumph of Sherlock Holmes* 35, and *The Silver Blaze* 36 (Ian Fleming was Watson). Raymond Massey was Holmes in *The Speckled Band* (GB) 31, with Athole Stewart as Watson; in 1932 Robert Rendel was in *The Hound of the Baskervilles* (GB). Clive Brook again appeared in *Sherlock Holmes* (US) 32, with Reginald Owen as Watson; Owen then played Holmes in *A Study in Scarlet* (US) 33. The Germans made three more Holmes films in the mid-thirties, including yet another remake of *The Hound*, which in 1939 was again tackled by Fox in Hollywood, this time with Basil Rathbone as the detective and Nigel Bruce as Watson. Its success led to a hurried remake of the Gillette play under the title *The Adventures of Sherlock Holmes* 39; two years later the same two actors began a series of twelve films in which the settings were modernized and most of the stories unrecognizable, although the acting and much of the writing were well in character. The titles were *Sherlock Holmes and the Voice of Terror* 41, *Sherlock Holmes and the Secret Weapon* 42, *Sherlock Holmes in Washington* 42, *Sherlock Holmes Faces Death* 43, *Spider Woman* 44, *The Scarlet Claw* 44, *Pearl of Death* 44, *House of Fear* 45, *Woman in Green* 45, *Pursuit to Algiers* 45, *Terror by Night* 46, *Dressed to Kill* (*Sherlock Holmes and the Secret Code*) 46. Then a long silence was broken by Peter Cushing and André Morell in the leads of a British remake of *The Hound of the Baskervilles* 59. In 1962 Christopher Lee and Thorley Walters played Holmes and Watson in a German film, *Sherlock Holmes and the Deadly Necklace*; and in 1965 John Neville and Donald Houston appeared in an original story involving the famous pair with Jack the Ripper: *A Study in Terror*. Also in 1965 a BBC TV series featured Douglas Wilmer and Nigel Stock, with Peter Cushing later taking over as Holmes; the period atmosphere was carefully sought but the stories suffered from being padded out to the standard TV length. (There was also a Franco-American TV series in 1954 with Ronald Howard and Howard Marion-Crawford.) In 1969 Billy Wilder made *The Private Life of Sherlock Holmes* with Robert Stephens, apparently intending a send-up but producing only a further pleasant variation. In 1970 George C. Scott thought he was Sherlock Holmes in *They Might Be Giants*, so did Larry Hagman in a 1976 TV movie, *The Return of the World's Greatest Detective*. Nicol Williamson as Holmes was treated by Sigmund Freud in 1976's *The Seven Per Cent Solution*, and in the same year Gene Wilder tried a spoof, *The Adventure of Sherlock Holmes' Smarter Brother*.

The same year brought a TV movie called *Sherlock Holmes in New York*, with Roger Moore and Patrick MacNee. In 1978 there was a perfectly ghastly, supposedly comic *Hound of the Baskervilles* with Peter Cook and Dudley Moore, while Christopher Plummer starred in a TV half-hour of *Silver Blaze* and a feature called *Murder by Decree*, which again linked Holmes with Jack the Ripper. A stage revival of the William Gillette version was followed by other adaptations.

1979 brought another TV series with Geoffrey Whitehead and Donald Pickering; but *Sherlock Holmes and Doctor Watson* was barely seen outside Poland, where it was shot. In 1983 Sy Weintraub made TV movies of *The Sign of Four* and *The Hound of the Baskervilles*, with Ian Richardson an excellent Holmes; and Tom Baker starred in a BBC serial of *The Hound of the Baskervilles*. In 1984 Granada TV had a 13-hour series starring Jeremy Brett and David Burke, and this continues.

Brett also starred in a full-length 1987 version of *The Sign of Four*.

Sherman, George (1908–). American director who graduated slowly from second feature westerns.

Wild Horse Rodeo 37. Death Valley Outlaws 41. Outside the Law 41. Mantrap 43. Mystery Broadcast 44. The Lady and the Monster 44. *The Bandit of Sherwood Forest* 46. Renegades 46. Last of the Redskins 48. Sword in the Desert 49. Panther's Moon 48. The Golden Horde 51. Against All Flags 52. War Arrow 54. Dawn at Socorro 54. Count Three and Pray 55. Comanche 56. Son of Robin Hood 58. The Enemy General 60. Panic Button 64. Smoky 66. Big Jake 71, many others.

Sherman, Harry (1884–1952). American producer of westerns.

Sherman, Lowell (1885–1934). American leading man with stage experience.

Way Down East 20. Monsieur Beaucaire 24. The Divine Woman 27. Mammy 30. The Greeks Had a Word for Them 32. False Faces 32. She Done Him Wrong (directed only) 33. Morning Glory 33. Broadway Through a Keyhole 33, etc.

Sherman, Richard (1928–) and **Robert** (1925–). American songwriting brothers who have worked mainly for Disney.

Mary Poppins (AA) 64. The Happiest Millionaire 67. The One and Only Genuine Original Family Band 68. Bedknobs and Broomsticks 71. Huckleberry Finn (& w) 74. The Slipper and the Rose (& w) 76, etc.

Sherman, Vincent (1906–) (Abram Orovitz). American director, formerly stage actor.

The Return of Doctor X 39. *All Through the Night* 41. The Hard Way 42. Old Acquaintance 43. In Our Time 44. Mr Skeffington 45. The Unfaithful 47. The New Adventures of Don Juan 48. The Hasty Heart 49. Lone Star 51. Affair in Trinidad 52. The Garment Jungle 57. Naked Earth 57. The Young Philadelphians 59. Ice Palace 60. The Second Time Around 61. Cervantes 66. The Last Hurrah (TV) 77. Women at West Point (TV) 79. Trouble in High Timber Country (TV) 82, etc.

Sherriff, R. C. (1896–1975). Prolific British playwright and screenwriter.
Autobiography 1969: *No Leading Lady.*
AS PLAYWRIGHT: Journey's End 30. Badger's Green 47. Home at Seven 52.
AS SCREENWRITER: *The Invisible Man* 33. *Goodbye Mr Chips* 39. Lady Hamilton 41. *Odd Man Out* 47. *Quartet* 48. No Highway 50. The Dam Busters 55, many others.

Sherrin, Ned (1931–). British ex-barrister who became a BBC producer and performer, then turned to producing movies.
The Virgin Soldiers 69. Every Home Should Have One 70. Girl Stroke Boy 71. Up Pompeii 71. Rentadick 72. Up the Chastity Belt 72. The Alf Garnett Saga 72, etc.

Sherwood, Madeleine (1926–) (Madeleine Thornton). Canadian character actress.
□Cat on a Hot Tin Roof 58. Parrish 61. Sweet Bird of Youth 62. Hurry Sundown 67. Pendulum 69. Wicked Wicked 73, etc.
TV series: The Flying Nun 67–68.

Sherwood, Robert (1896–1955). American dramatist. Plays filmed:
Reunion in Vienna 32. The Petrified Forest 36. Tovarich 38. Idiot's Delight 39. Abe Lincoln in Illinois 39, etc.
OTHER SCRIPTS: Waterloo Bridge 32. The Adventures of Marco Polo 38. *Rebecca* 40. *The Best Years of Our Lives* (AA) 45. The Bishop's Wife 48. Jupiter's Darling (The Road to Rome) 54.

Sheybal, Vladek (1928–). Intense-looking Polish character actor in Britain.
Kanal 56. Women in Love 69. The Music Lovers 70. The Boy Friend 71. QB VII 74. The Wind and the Lion 75, etc.

Shields, Arthur (1895–1970). Irish character actor, an Abbey player, long in Hollywood; brother of Barry Fitzgerald.
The Plough and the Stars 37. *Drums along the Mohawk* 39. *The Long Voyage Home* 40. The Keys of the Kingdom 44. The Corn is Green 45. The River 51. The Quiet Man 52. The King and Four Queens 56. Night of the Quarter Moon 59. The Pigeon That Took Rome 62, etc.

Shields, Brooke (1965–). American juvenile actress of the late seventies.
Alice Sweet Alice 78. King of the Gypsies 78. Pretty Baby 79. Just You and Me Kid 79. Tilt 79. Two of a Kind 79. Wanda Nevada 80. The Blue Lagoon 80. Endless Love 81. Sahara 82. The Muppets Take Manhattan 84.
†When she was only fifteen the press seized on her mother's willingness to have her play too mature roles. Brooke replied: 'What does "good in bed" mean to me? When I'm sick and stay home from school watching TV and my mom brings me soup—that's good in bed.' She went on to make TV commercials for jeans in which she said: 'If my jeans could talk, would I be embarrassed.'

Shigeta, James (1933–). Hawaiian leading man who usually plays Japanese in Hollywood films.
The Crimson Kimono 60. Cry for Happy 60. Walk Like a Dragon 60. Bridge to the Sun 61. Flower Drum Song 61. Paradise Hawaiian Style 66. Nobody's Perfect 68. Lost Horizon 73. Midway 76, etc.

Shilkret, Nathaniel (1895–). American arranger and conductor.
The Plough and the Stars 36. Mary of Scotland 36. The Toast of New York 37. She Went to the Races 45. The Hoodlum Saint 46, many others.

Shimkus, Joanna (1943–). Canadian leading lady in American and European films.
Paris vu Par 66. Les Aventuriers 67. Zita 68. Ho! 68. Boom 68. The Lost Man 69. *The Virgin and the Gypsy* 70. The Marriage of a Young Stockbroker 71. A Time for Loving 71, etc.

Shimoda, Yuki (1924–81). Japanese-American character actor.
Auntie Mame 59. A Majority of One 61. Midway 75. Farewell to Manzanar (TV) 76. MacArthur 77. The Last Flight of Noah's Ark 79, many others.

Shimura, Takashi (1905–1982). Japanese leading actor.
Stray Dog 49. *Rashomon* 50. Seven Samurai 54. Godzilla 56. Throne of Blood 57. The Hidden Fortress 58. Yojimbo 62, etc.

Shindo, Kaneto (1912–). Japanese director.
Children of Hiroshima 53. The Wolf 56. *The Island* 62. Ningen 63. *Onibaba* 64. Kuroneko 67, etc.

Shine, Bill (1911–). Amiable British small part actor often seen as vacuous dandy.
The Scarlet Pimpernel 34. Farewell Again 37. Let George Do It 40. Perfect Strangers 45. Melba 53. Father Brown 54. Jack the Ripper 58, many others.

Shiner, Ronald (1903–1966). British comedy actor, on stage from 1928, films from 1934, at first in bit parts, later as star.
King Arthur Was a Gentleman 42. The Way to the Stars 45. *Worm's Eye View* 50. *Reluctant Heroes* 51. Laughing Anne 53. Top of the Form 54. Up to His Neck 55. Keep It Clean 56. Dry Rot 56. Girls at Sea 58. Operation Bullshine 59. The Night We Got the Bird 60, etc.

Shingleton, Wilfrid (1914–1983). British art director who won an Oscar for *Great Expectations* 46.

Ship of Fools (US 1965). A rather splendid sixties reversion to the star-studded 'Grand Hotel' type of film, with sociological overtones added. The period is 1933, the ship is full of Germans and Jews, and most of the ironies are naïvely and quaintly based on hindsight; but the dramatic situations are well handled, Stanley Kramer's direction of the several stories is well controlled if rather stately, and there is a feast of good acting, notably from Simone Signoret, Oskar Werner, Vivien Leigh and Heinz Ruhmann.

ships, of the modern passenger kind, have provided a useful setting for many films, most recently in *Ship of Fools* (see above). Three notable versions of the Titanic disaster were *Atlantic* 30, *Titanic* 53 and *A Night to Remember* 58; while sinking ships also figured in *We're Not Dressing* 34, *Souls at Sea* 37, *History is Made at Night* 37, *The Blue Lagoon* 48, *Our Girl Friday* 52, *The Admirable Crichton* 57 (and earlier versions), *The Last Voyage* 60 and *The Poseidon Adventure* 72. A sinister time was had on board ship in *Journey into Fear, Across the Pacific, King Kong, My Favorite Blonde, The Ghost Ship, The Mystery of the Marie Celeste, The Sea Wolf, The Hairy Ape, Dangerous Crossing, Ghost Breakers, The Wreck of the Mary Deare, Juggernaut,* and *Voyage of the Damned*; laughter, however, was to the fore in *Monkey Business* 31, *The Lady Eve* 41, *Luxury Liner* 48, *Doctor at Sea* 55, *The Captain's Table* 58, *A Countess from Hong Kong* 66, and *A Night at the Opera* 35 with its famous cabin scene. The romance of a cruise was stressed in *Dodsworth* 36, *The Big Broadcast of 1938, Now Voyager* 42, and the two versions of *Love Affair* 39 (the second being *An Affair to Remember* 56); while in the 'Winter Cruise' section of *Encore* 51, it was almost forced on Kay Walsh. In *Assault on a Queen* 66 the leading characters plan to hi-jack the Queen Mary. The weirdest ship was the ship of the dead in *Outward Bound* 30, and its remake *Between Two Worlds* 44.

Mississippi riverboats have featured in *Mississippi, Rhythm on the River, Mississippi Gambler, The Secret Life of Walter Mitty, The Naughty Nineties, The Adventures of Mark Twain, Four for Texas, Frankie and Johnny,* and the several versions of Showboat; also in the TV series *Riverboat.*

Sailing ships of olden days are too numerous to detail.

Shire, David (1937–). American composer.
One More Train to Rob 71. Drive He Said 71. Showdown 73. The Conversation 74. Farewell My Lovely 75. The Hindenburg 75. All the President's Men 76. Saturday Night Fever 77. Norma Rae 79. Only When I Laugh 81.

Shire, Talia (1947–) (Talia Coppola). American leading lady, sister of Francis Coppola.
The Wild Races 68. The Dunwich Horror 70. Un Homme Est Mort 72. *The Godfather* 72. The Godfather Part Two 74. Rocky 76. Old Boyfriends 79. Rocky II 79. Prophecy 79. Rocky III 82.

Shirley, Anne (1918–) (Dawn Paris). American child star of the twenties (under the name Dawn O'Day) who later graduated to leading lady roles.
So Big 32. *Anne of Green Gables* 35. Stella Dallas 37. Vigil in the Night 39. Anne of Windy Poplars 40. West Point Widow 41. All that Money Can Buy 41. *Farewell My Lovely* 44, etc.

Shoemaker, Ann (1891–1978). American character actress with stage experience.
A Dog of Flanders 35. Alice Adams 35. Stella Dallas 37. Babes in Arms 39. Conflict 45. A Woman's Secret 49. Sunrise at Campobello 60. The Fortune Cookie 66, many others.

Sholem, Lee (c. 1900–). American director.
Tarzan's Magic Fountain 48. Redhead from Wyoming 52. Tobor the Great 53. Emergency Hospital 56. Pharaoh's Curse 56. Sierra Stranger 57, etc.

Shonteff, Lindsay (–). British director, from TV.
The Curse of Simba 63. Devil Doll 64. Licensed to Kill 65. Run with the Wind 66. Sumuru 67. The Yes Girls 71. The Fast Kill 72.

shooting script. This differs from a screenplay, which concentrates on dialogue, in that it includes camera directions and breaks up the script into shots; it is an instruction manual for technicians rather than a work of art.

The Shop around the Corner (US 1939). Written by Samson Raphaelson from a play by Nikolaus Laszlo, produced and directed by Ernst Lubitsch, this was a charming piece of Hollywood schmaltz, though none of the cast really suggested Budapest shop assistants. James Stewart and Margaret Sullavan were the couple who disliked each other by day but fell in love through a lonely hearts bureau; in support were Frank Morgan, Joseph Schildkraut, Felix Bressart. In 1949 Robert Z. Leonard remade it as a musical, *In the Good Old Summertime*, with Judy Garland and Van Johnson.

Shopworn Angel (US 1929). A well-remembered comedy-drama about a hard-boiled Broadway gold-digger (Nancy Carroll) who ultimately gave up her rich provider (Paul Lukas) for a poor doughboy on his way to war (Gary Cooper). This version was directed by Richard Wallace, H. C. Potter remade it in 1938, with Margaret Sullavan, Walter Pidgeon and James Stewart. In 1959 it turned up again as *That Kind of Woman*, with Sidney Lumet directing Sophia Loren, George Sanders and Tab Hunter. It had originally been a silent film of 1919 called *Pettigrew's Girl,* written by Dana Burnett and Ethel Clayton.

Shore, Dinah (1917–) (Frances Rose Shore). American cabaret singer, in very occasional films; latterly running a daily TV chat show for women. As a child singer, was known as Fanny Rose.
□Thank Your Lucky Stars 43. Up in Arms 44. Follow the Boys 44. Belle of the Yukon 45. Till the Clouds Roll By 46. Aaron Slick from Punkin Crick 52. Oh God 77.

shorts are officially any films running less than 3000 feet (about 33 minutes). In the thirties most programmes consisted of a feature and several one-reelers, but the big studios first found shorts uneconomic and then closed down altogether. Shorts fell into the hands of independent producers, who found that the longer they made them the more money they could demand, even if the quality was not high. Double-feature programmes also contributed to their demise.

Shostakovich, Dmitri (1906–1975). Russian composer.
The New Babylon 28. The Youth of Maxim 35. The Fall of Berlin 47. Hamlet 64. War and Peace 64.

Shotter, Winifred (1904–). British leading lady of the thirties, chiefly remembered in the Aldwych farces beginning with *Rookery Nook* 30.

Showalter, Max (1917–) (formerly known as Casey Adams). American supporting actor often seen as reporter, newscaster or good guy friend.
Always Leave Them Laughing 50. With a Song in My Heart 52. Bus Stop 56. The Naked and the Dead 58. Elmer Gantry 60. Bon Voyage 62. Fate is the Hunter 64. The Moonshine War 70. The Anderson Tapes 71, etc.

Showboat. Jerome Kern and Oscar Hammerstein II's operetta from Edna Ferber's novel was filmed by Harry Pollard in 1929 with Laura la Plante and Joseph Schildkraut; by James Whale in 1936 with Irene Dunne, Allan Jones and Paul Robeson; and by George Sidney in 1951 with Kathryn Grayson, Howard Keel and William Warfield.

Shuken, Leo (1906–1976). American orchestrator.
Waikiki Wedding 37. The Flying Deuces 39. *Stagecoach* (AA) 39. The Lady Eve 41. *Sullivan's Travels* 41. The Miracle of Morgan's Creek 44. The Fabulous Dorseys 47. The Greatest Story Ever Told 64, etc.

Shumate, Harold (1893–). American screenwriter.

Shumlin, Herman (1898–1979). American stage producer who directed two films in the forties.
□Watch on the Rhine 43. Confidential Agent 45.

Shurlock, Geoffrey (1895–1976). Film administrator, an Englishman who became the power behind the MPEA Production Code 1954–68.

Shute, Nevil (1899–1960). Australian best-selling novelist.
The Pied Piper 43. No Highway 52. Landfall 54. A Town Like Alice 56. On the Beach 59, etc.

Sidney, George (1878–1945) (Sammy Greenfield). American comedian, once popular in vaudeville.
Potash and Perlmutter 23. Millionaires 26. Clancy's Kosher Wedding 27. The Cohens and Kellys in Paris 28. Manhattan Melodrama 34. Good Old Soak 37, others.

Sidney, George (1911–). American director, former musician and MGM shorts director.
Free and Easy 41. Thousands Cheer 43. Bathing Beauty 44. Anchors Aweigh 45. *The Harvey Girls* 46. Cass Timberlane 47. *The Three Musketeers* 48. The Red Danube 49. Annie Get Your Gun 50. *Showboat* 51. Scaramouche 52. Young Bess 53. *Kiss Me Kate* 53. Jupiter's Darling 54. The Eddy Duchin Story 56. *Jeanne Eagels* 57. Pal Joey 57. Who Was That Lady? 59. Pepe 60. Bye Bye Birdie 62. Viva Las Vegas 63. The Swinger 66. Half a Sixpence 67, etc.

Sidney, Sylvia (1910–) (Sophia Kosow). Fragile, dark-eyed American heroine of the thirties.
□Thru Different Eyes 29. *City Streets* 31. Confessions of a Co-Ed 31. An American Tragedy 31. *Street Scene* 31. Ladies of the Big House 32. The Miracle Man 32. Merrily We Go to Hell 33. Madame Butterfly 33. Pick Up 33. Jennie Gerhardt 33. Good Dame 34. Thirty Day Princess 34. Behold My Wife 34. Accent on Youth 35. Mary Burns Fugitive 35. Trail of the Lonesome Pine 36. Fury 36. Sabotage (GB) 37. *You Only Live Once* 37. Dead End 37. You and Me 37. One Third of a Nation 39. The Wagons Roll at Night 41. Blood on the Sun 45. The Searching Wind 46. Mr Ace 46. Love from a Stranger 47. Les Misérables 53. Violent Saturday 55. Behind the High Wall 56. Do Not Fold Spindle or Mutilate (TV) 71. Summer Wishes Winter Dreams 73. Death at Love House (TV) 76. God Told Me To 76. Raid on Entebbe (TV) 77. I Never Promised You a Rose Garden 77. Siege (TV) 78. Damien: Omen II 79. The Shadow Box (TV) 80. Hammett 82. Corrupt 83. Finnegan Begin Again (TV) 85.

¶ *S.S.:* I'd be the girl of the gangster . . . then the sister who was bringing up the gangster . . . then the mother of the gangster . . . and they always had me ironing somebody's shirt.

S.S.: What did Hitchcock teach me? To be a puppet and not try to be creative.

Siegel, Don (1912–). American director, former editor; an expert at crime thrillers, he has latterly attracted the attention of highbrow critics.
□*Hitler Lives* (short) (AA) 45. Star in the Night (short) (AA) 45. The Verdict 46. Night Unto Night 48. The Big Steal 49. Duel at Silver Creek 52. No Time for Flowers 52. Count the Hours 53. China Venture 54. *Riot in Cell Block 11* 54. Private Hell 36 55. An Annapolis Story 55. *Invasion of the Body Snatchers* 56. Crime in the Streets 57. Spanish Affair 57. *Baby Face Nelson* 57. The Line Up 58. The Gun Runners 58. The Hound Dog Man 59. Edge of Eternity 59. Flaming Star 60. Hell is for Heroes 62. The Killers 64. The Hanged Man 64. Madigan 67. Stranger on the Run (TV) 68. *Coogan's Bluff* 68. Two Mules for Sister Sara 69. Death of a Gunfighter (co-d) 69. The Beguiled 71. Play Misty for Me (acted only) 71. *Dirty Harry* 72. *Charley Varrick* 73. The Black Windmill 74. *The Shootist* 76. Telefon 77. Escape from Alcatraz 79. Rough Cut 80. Jinxed 82. Into the Night (a) 85.

Siegel, Sol C. (1903–1982). American producer, in films from 1929.
Kiss and Tell 44. Blue Skies 46. House of Strangers 49. A Letter to Three Wives 49. I Was a Male War Bride 49. Fourteen Hours 51. Monkey Business 52. Gentlemen Prefer Blondes 52. Call Me Madam 53. Three Coins in the Fountain 54. High Society 56. Les Girls 57. Home from the Hill 59. Walk Don't Run 66. Alvarez Kelly 66. No Way to Treat a Lady 68, etc.

Siegfried (Germany 1924). This, with its sequel *Kriemhilde's Revenge*, is Fritz Lang's version of the Niebelungen saga, full of dragons and national heroes. Heavy-going Teutonic spectacle, but in its day a triumph of filmcraft.

Sienkiewicz, Henryk (1846–1916). Polish novelist, author of the much filmed *Quo Vadis?* (published 1895).

Sierra, Gregory (–). American supporting actor.
The Wrath of God 72. Papillon 72. The Towering Inferno 74. The Prisoner of Zenda 79.
TV series: Sanford and Son, Barney Miller.

Signoret, Simone (1921–85) (Simone Kaminker). Distinguished French leading actress, married to Yves Montand. Autobiography 1976: *Nostalgia Isn't What It Used to Be.*

□Le Prince Charmant 42. Bolero 42. Les Visiteurs du Soir 42. Adieu Leonard 43. Beatrice 43. La Boîte aux Rêves 45. The Ideal Couple 45. Les Démons de l'Aube 45. Macadam 45. Fantomas 47. Against the Wind (GB) 47. *Dédée d'Anvers* 48. L'Impasse des Deux Anges 49. *Manèges* 49. Four Days' Leave 50. *La Ronde* 50. Gunman in the Streets 50. Ombre et Lumière 51. *Casque d'Or* 52. Therese Raquin 53. *Les Diaboliques* 54. Le Mort en ce Jardin 56. The Witches of Salem 57. *Room at the Top* (GB) (AA) 58. Adua and Company 60. Les Mauvais Coups 61. Les Amours Célèbres 61. Term of Trial (GB) 62. The Day and the Hour 63. Dragées au Poivre 63. *Ship of Fools* (US) 65. The Sleeping Car Murders 65. Is Paris Burning? 66. The Deadly Affair (GB) 67. Games (US) 67. The Seagull 68. L'Armée des Ombres 69. The American 69. The Confession 70. Comptes à Rebours 71. *Le Chat* 72. La Veuve Couderc 73. Rude Journée pour la Reine 73. Défense de Savoir 74. The Investigator 74. Flesh of the Orchid 74. Police Python 357 76. Madame Rosa 78. L'Adolescente 79. I Sent a Letter to My Love 81.

silent films began to grow unfashionable during 1927, though for eighteen months or so producers continued to put out so called 'silent versions' of their talkies: these versions were unspeakably bad, as the new talkies used very little camera movement and a great deal of dialogue which had to be given in sub-titles. By 1930 silents had all but disappeared, with exceptions such as Flaherty's *Tabu* 32, Chaplin's *City Lights* 31, and *Modern Times* 36, and an unsuccessful 1952 experiment called *The Thief*, which eschewed dialogue though it did have a music and effects track. In 1976 Mel Brooks produced *Silent Movie*, a comic extravaganza with no dialogue.

¶ There never was a silent film. We'd finish a picture, show it in one of our projection rooms and come out shattered. It would be awful. Then we'd show it in a theatre with a girl pounding away at a piano and there would be all the difference in the world. Without that music there wouldn't have been a movie industry at all.—*Irving Thalberg*

It will never be possible to synchronize the voice with the pictures. Music—fine music—will always be the voice of the silent drama . . . There will never be speaking pictures.—*D. W. Griffith, 1924*

silent films I

? 1 In 1925 John Barrymore appeared in *The Sea Beast*. From what classic novel was this adapted?

2 In 1921 Charles Chaplin discovered and trained a new child star for his film *The Kid*. Who was he?

3 In 1927 Alan Crosland directed the first film with talking sequences. What was it?

4 What film released in 1916 was originally intended to be called *The Mother and the Law*?

5 *The Miracle Man* in 1919 included a part requiring a contortionist rather than an actor. The man who played it rapidly became a star. Who was he?

6 In 1919–20 Cecil B. De Mille made three society dramas (*For Better for Worse*, *Don't Change Your Husband*, *Male and Female*) with the same leading lady. Name her.

7 A big box-office hit of 1925 was *Stella Dallas*, later remade as a talkie with Barbara Stanwyck. Who played the title role in the silent film?

8 Who played 'the chink' in *Broken Blossoms* in 1919?

9 In Britain for about ten years from 1917, big commercial successes were society dramas featuring a husband-and-wife team. She was Ivy Duke. Who was he?

10 Also in Britain, name the music hall comedian who made popular screen comedies in the twenties, including *Prehistoric Man*.

11 Name the Broadway stage actress who in 1918–19 was appearing in such films as *Our Miss McChesney* and *The Divorce*, made only one film in the next twenty-five years, but became a Hollywood star again in old age.

12 Who came to fame as *The Lone Wolf* in 1917?

13 Whose 1922 starring vehicles included *Beyond the Rocks* and *Moran of the Lady Letty*?

14 In 1923 Harold Lloyd made his first skyscraper-climbing comedy. Name it.

15 What celebrated (and lengthy) film of 1923 starred Zasu Pitts, Gibson Gowland and Jean Hersholt?

16 Who directed it?

17 In 1926–27 a famous team came together in films including *Putting Pants on Philip*, *Love 'Em And Weep* and *Do Detectives Think?* Who were they?

18 In what 1924 film did Lon Chaney play a circus clown?

19 In 1913 Cecil B. De Mille made his first film in Hollywood. It is also claimed as

the first film made in Hollywood by anybody. What was it?

20 In 1919 *The Cabinet of Dr Caligari* starred as the somnambulist a German actor who in the thirties and forties became a popular hero/villain of English speaking films. Who was he?

silent films II

1 Who played the title role in Lubitsch's 1919 German film of *Madame Du Barry*? (She later rose to Hollywood fame.)

2 British film-maker George Pearson starred Betty Balfour in a series of twenties comedies about a cockney girl called . . . ?

3 Greta Garbo in 1925 appeared in a German film directed by G. W. Pabst. Name it.

4 Eisenstein's Odessa Steps sequence is a famous piece of film editing. From what 1925 film does it come?

5 In 1927 Walter Ruttmann made a film subtitled 'the symphony of a great city'. The title of the film was the name of the city. Which city?

6 In 1926 Alfred Hitchcock directed Ivor Novello in a film based vaguely on the Jack the Ripper murders, updated from a novel by Mrs Belloc-Lowndes. Title, please.

7 In 1927 Anthony Asquith and A. V. Bramble co-directed a drama set behind the scenes at a film studio. What was it called?

8 In 1928 Luis Bunuel and Salvador Dali made a surrealist film which began with a girl's eye apparently being cut by a razor. Name the film.

9 In 1919 Mauritz Stiller directed a famous story by Selma Lagerlof about three plundering mercenaries of the sixteenth century. Title, please.

10 In 1920 Benjamin Christensen of Sweden made a vivid account of pagan rituals, mixing fiction with instructional documentary. The original title is *Haxan*; by what English title is the film usually known?

11 In 1924 in Germany, F. W. Murnau directed *Der Letzte Mann* or *The Last Laugh*, about a hotel doorman demoted to lavatory attendant. Who played the leading role?

12 In the following year the same actor appeared with Lya de Putti in a 'backstage' drama known by one title in Great Britain and another in America. Give both.

13 Name the 1926 film by Henrik Galeen in which Conrad Veidt played a man haunted by his own mirror-image.

14 In 1926 Brigitte Helm played a robot girl in a futuristic fantasy directed by Fritz Lang. Title, please.

15 Miss Helm also played a blind girl in a 1927 film by G. W. Pabst. What was it?

16 Name the actress who played the title role in Carl Dreyer's 1928 film *The Passion of Joan of Arc*.

17 Twenty-five years in anticipation of Cinerama, Abel Gance in 1927 used a triple screen. For what film?

18 Who wrote *The Cabinet of Dr Caligari* (1919)?

19 In France in 1928 Germaine Dulac made a Freudian film about the sexual repressions of a young priest. Name it.

20 *Paris Qui Dort* (1923) and *Entr'acte* (1924) are among the early comedies of which celebrated French director?

silent films III

1 When Nazimova in 1921 appeared in *Camille*, who was her leading man?

2 In 1923, what son of a famous father made his debut in *Stephen Steps Out*?

3 In 1926 John Barrymore appeared in *Don Juan*, the first film with synchronized music. Who directed it?

4 J. Warren Kerrigan and Lois Wilson starred in 1923 in one of the screen's most historically famous films, a period adventure directed by James Cruze. Name it.

5 In 1921 a fur company named Revillon Frères commissioned Robert J. Flaherty to make a documentary film. Name it.

6 In 1921 *Foolish Wives* established the reputation of director Erich von Stroheim. Name his first feature in similar vein, made two years earlier.

7 In 1921 Harry C. Myers appeared in a Mark Twain story filmed more than once since, including a Bing Crosby version of 1948. What was it?

8 In 1923 Laurette Taylor, the Broadway stage actress, paid her only visit to Hollywood to film her most famous success. Name it.

9 The first part of Fritz Lang's Niebelungen Saga, released in 1923, is known as *Siegfried*. Name the second part.

10 In 1927 D. W. Griffith filmed a novel by Marie Corelli. Name it.

11 Name the 1924 Ernst Lubitsch comedy later remade as *One Hour with You*.

12 Sergei Eisenstein's first film, made in 1924, concerned industrial unrest. Name it.
13 Who played Al Jolson's mother in *The Jazz Singer*?
14 In what 1926 film, remade in 1941 as a Dorothy Lamour vehicle, did Gilda Gray star?
15 In 1923 Charles Chaplin directed but did not appear in his only fully serious film, *A Woman of Paris*. Who played the title role?
16 What dapper actor played opposite her?
17 Which actor, who played five roles in 1903's *The Great Train Robbery*, went on to make over four hundred films as a leading western star?
18 In 1923 a German crew filmed *Dracula* but to avoid payment of literary rights called it . . . what?
19 In 1925, what famous screen cowboy made his last film, *Tumbleweeds*?
20 In 1918, in what D. W. Griffith film did Noël Coward appear?

Silliphant, Sterling (1918–). American writer-producer with much TV experience (*Naked City, Route 66*, etc.). Former advertising executive.
The Joe Louis Story (w) 53. Five Against the House (w, co-p) 55. Nightfall (w) 56. Damn Citizen (w) 57. Village of the Damned 60. The Slender Thread (w) 66. In The Heat of the Night (w) (AA) 67. Charly 68. A Walk in the Spring Rain 69. The Liberation of L. B. Jones 70. The Poseidon Adventure 72. The Towering Inferno 74. The Killer Elite (w) 75. Telefon (co-w) 77. The Swarm (w) 78. Pearl (TV) 79. When Time Ran Out (co-w) 80. Space (TV) 85, etc.

Sillitoe, Alan (1928–). British north-country novelist best known to filmgoers for *Saturday Night and Sunday Morning* and *The Loneliness of the Long Distance Runner*. His less successful novel *The General* was filmed as *Counterpoint*.

Sills, Milton (1882–1930). Stalwart American leading man of the silent screen.
The Rack 15. The Claw 17. Eyes of Youth 19. The Weekend 20. Burning Sands 22. Adam's Rib 23. Madonna of the Streets 24. The Sea Hawk 24. Paradise 26. Valley of the Giants 27. His Captive Woman 29. The Sea Wolf 30, many others.

Silly Symphony. The name given by Walt Disney to all his short cartoon fables of the thirties which did not feature Mickey Mouse, Pluto or Donald Duck.

Silva, Henry (1928–). Pale-eyed American actor of Italian and Basque descent, often seen as sadistic villain or assorted Latin types.
Viva Zapata 52. Crowded Paradise 56. A Hatful of Rain 57. The Bravados 58. Green Mansions 59. Cinderfella 60. *The Manchurian Candidate* 62. *Johnny Cool* (leading role) 63. The Return of Mr Moto 65. The Reward 65. The Plainsman 66. The Hills Ran Red (It.) 66. Never a Dull Moment 68. Five Savage Men 70. The Kidnap of Mary Lou 75. Shoot 76. Cry of a Prostitute 76. Thirst 79. Buck Rogers 79. Alligator 80. Sharkey's Machine 81. Wrong Is Right 82. Allan Quatermain and the Lost City of Gold 86. Bulletproof 87, etc.

Silver, Joan Micklin (1935–). American director.
□Limbo (w) 72. *Hester Street* (& w) 74. Bernice Bobs Her Hair (& w) (TV) 76. Between the Lines 78. Head Over Heels (& w) 79.

Silvera, Frank (1914–1970). American general purpose actor with stage experience.
Viva Zapata 52. Killer's Kiss 55. Crowded Paradise 56. The Mountain Road 60. Mutiny on the Bounty 62. The Appaloosa 66. Che! 69. Valdez is Coming 71, etc.

Silverheels, Jay (1919–1980). Canadian Red Indian actor, mainly in western films.
The Prairie 47. Fury at Furnace Creek 48. Broken Arrow 50. War Arrow 53. The Lone Ranger 55. Indian Paint 65. The Phynx 70. Santee 73, others.
TV series: The Lone Ranger (as Tonto) 52–56.

Silvers, Louis (1889–1954). American composer.
The Jazz Singer 27. Dancing Lady 33. It Happened One Night 34. One Night of Love (AA) 35. Lloyds of London 36. Heidi 37. In Old Chicago (AAN) 38. Suez (AAN) 38. Jesse James 39. Swanee River (AAN) 39. The Powers Girl 42, many others.

Silvers, Phil (1912–85) (Philip Silver). American vaudeville star comedian in occasional films from 1941.
Autobiography 1974: *The Laugh is on Me.*
Tom, Dick and Harry (debut) 41. *You're in the Army Now* 42. Roxie Hart 42. My Gal Sal 42. Coney Island 43. *Cover Girl* 44. A Thousand and One Nights 45. Where Do We

Go from Here? 45. Summer Stock 50. Lucky Me 54. Forty Pounds of Trouble 63. *It's a Mad Mad Mad Mad World* 63. A Funny Thing Happened on the Way to the Forum 66. Follow That Camel (GB) 67. Buona Sera, Mrs Campbell 68. Deadly Tide (TV) 75. Won Ton Ton 76. The Chicken Chronicles 77. The New Love Boat (TV) 77. The Night They Took Miss Beautiful (TV) 78. There Goes the Bride 80, etc.
TV series: *You'll Never Get Rich* (as Bilko) 55–58. *The New Phil Silvers Show* 64.

Silverstein, Elliot (1927–). American director, from TV.
□Belle Sommers (TV) 62. *Cat Ballou* 65. The Happening 67. A Man Called Horse 69. The Car 77.

Silvestri, Alan (–). American composer.
Romancing the Stone 84. Cat's Eye 84. Back to the Future 85. Clan of the Cave Bear 85. Outrageous Fortune 86.

Sim, Alastair (1900–1976). Lugubrious Scottish comedy actor of stage and screen; his diction and gestures were inimitable.
□Riverside Murder 35. The Private Secretary 35. A Fire Has Been Arranged 35. Late Extra 35. The Case of Gabriel Perry 35. Troubled Waters 36. Wedding Group 36. The Big Noise 36. Keep Your Seats Please 36. The Man in the Mirror 36. The Mysterious Mr Davis 36. Strange Experiment 37. Clothes and the Woman 37. Gangway 37. The Squeaker 37. A Romance in Flanders 37. Melody and Romance 37. Sailing Along 38. *The Terror* 38. *Alf's Button Afloat* 38. *This Man is News* 38. Climbing High 38. *Inspector Hornleigh* 39. This Man in Paris 39. Inspector Hornleigh on Holiday 39. Law and Disorder 40. Inspector Hornleigh Goes to It 41. *Cottage to Let* 41. *Let the People Sing* 42. Waterloo Road 44. *Green for Danger* 46. Hue and Cry 47. Captain Boycott 47. *London Belongs to Me* 48. *The Happiest Days of Your Life* 49. Stage Fright 50. *Laughter in Paradise* 51. *Scrooge* 51. Lady Godiva Rides Again 51. Folly to be Wise 52. Innocents in Paris 53. *An Inspector Calls* 54. *The Belles of St Trinian's* 54. Escapade 55. Geordie 55. The Green Man 56. Blue Murder at St Trinian's 57. The Doctor's Dilemma 59. Left, Right and Centre 59. School for Scoundrels 60. The Millionairess 60. The Ruling Class 71. Royal Flash 75. Escape from the Dark 76. Rogue Male (TV) 76.

❀ For marvellous moments of high comedy and for the lasting comic image of his unique physiognomy. *Green for Danger.*

Sim, Gerald (1925–). British supporting actor, often in well bred and slightly prissy roles.
Fame is the Spur 47. The Wrong Arm of the Law 63. The Pumpkin Eater 64. King Rat 64. The Whisperers 66. Oh What a Lovely War 68. Dr Jekyll and Sister Hyde 71. No Sex Please We're British 73. The Slipper and the Rose 76, many others.

Sim, Sheila (1922–). British leading lady, married to Richard Attenborough.
A Canterbury Tale 44. Great Day 45. Dancing with Crime 47. The Guinea Pig 48. Dear Mr Prohack 49. The Magic Box 51. The Night My Number Came Up 55, etc.

Simenon, Georges (1903–). French crime novelist, creator of Inspector Maigret.
Les Inconnus dans la Maison 43. Panique 46. Temptation Harbour (GB) 46. La Marie du Port 50. The Man on the Eiffel Tower (US) 50. Le Fruit Défendu 52. The Brothers Rico (US) 57. Maigret Sets a Trap 58, etc.
TV series: Maigret 63. Thirteen Against Fate 67.

¶ *G.S.:* Can there be a more intimate communication between two beings than copulation?

Simmons, Anthony (c. 1924–). British writer-director, known for short films.
Sunday by the Sea 53. Bow Bells 54. The Gentle Corsican 56. Your Money or Your Wife 59. Four in the Morning 65. The Optimists of Nine Elms 73. Black Joy 78.

Simmons, Jean (1929–). Self-possessed and beautiful British leading lady who married Stewart Granger (later Richard Brooks) and settled in Hollywood to make films which have generally been unworthy of her talents.
□Give Us the Moon 43. Mr Emmanuel 44. Meet Sexton Blake 44. Kiss the Bride Goodbye 44. The Way to the Stars 45. Caesar and Cleopatra 45. Hungry Hill 45. The Woman in the Hall 45. *Great Expectations* 46. *Black Narcissus* 46. Uncle Silas 47. *Hamlet* 48. The Blue Lagoon 48. Adam and Evelyne 49. Trio 50. Cage of Gold 50. So Long at the Fair 50. The Clouded Yellow 50. Angel Face 52. Androcles and the Lion 53. Young Bess 53. Affair with a Stranger 53. The Robe 53. The Actress 53. She Couldn't Say No 54. The

Egyptian 54. A Bullet is Waiting 54. Désirée 54. Footsteps in the Fog 55. Guys and Dolls 56. Hilda Crane 56. This Could Be the Night 57. Until They Sail 57. *The Big Country* 58. Home Before Dark 58. This Earth is Mine 59. *Elmer Gantry* 60. Spartacus 60. *The Grass is Greener* 61. All the Way Home 63. Life at the Top 65. Mister Buddwing 66. Rough Night in Jericho 67. Divorce American Style 67. The Happy Ending 69. Say Hello to Yesterday 71. Mr Sycamore 75. The Dain Curse (TV) 78. Dominique 79. Beggarman Thief (TV) 79. Golden Gate (TV) 80. The Thorn Birds (TV) 82. Midas Valley (TV) 84.

Simms, Ginny (1916–) (Virginia Sims). Glamorous American vocalist, with Kay Kyser's band.
That's Right You're Wrong 39. You'll Find Out 40. Playmates 42. Hit the Ice 43. Broadway Rhythm 44. Shady Lady 45. Night and Day 46, etc.

Simms, Larry (1934–). American boy actor, notably in the *Blondie* series 1938–48. (He was Baby Dumpling.)
The Last Gangster 37. Mr Smith Goes to Washington 39. Madame Bovary 49, etc.

Simon, Melvin (1925–). American independent producer, former shopping plaza developer.
Love at First Bite 79. Scavenger Hunt 79. The Runner Stumbles 79. When a Stranger Calls 79. Cloud Dancer 80. My Bodyguard 80. The Man with Bogart's Face 80. The Stunt Man 80. Porky's 82.

Simon, Michel (1895–1975) (François Simon). Heavyweight French character actor, in films from the twenties after music hall experience.
Feu Mathias Pascal 25. The Passion of Joan of Arc 28. La Chienne 31. *Boudu Sauvé des Eaux* 32. Lac aux Dames 34. *L'Atalante* 34. Jeunes Filles de Paris 36. Drôle de Drame 37. Les Disparus de Saint-Agil 38. Quai des Brumes 38. Fric Frac 39. *La Fin du Jour* 39. Circonstances Attenuantes 39. Vautrin 43. Un Ami Viendra Ce Soir 45. *Panique* 46. Fabiola 48. *La Beauté du Diable* 49. The Strange Desire of Monsieur Bard 53. Saadia 53. La Joyeuse Prison 56. It Happened in Broad Daylight 58. The Head 59. Austerlitz 59. Candide 60. The Devil and Ten Commandments 62. The Train 64. Two Hours to Kill 65. *The Two of Us* 67. La Maison 70. Blanche 71, many others.

Simon, Neil (1927–). American comedy playwright whose Broadway success has been remarkable and his Hollywood follow-up diligent, either as scenarist or as original author with a watching brief.
Come Blow Your Horn 63. After the Fox (oa) 66. Barefoot in the Park 67. The Odd Couple 68. Sweet Charity 68. The Out of Towners 70. Plaza Suite 71. Last of the Red Hot Lovers 72. The Sunshine Boys 75. Murder by Death 76. The Goodbye Girl 78. California Suite 78. Chapter Two 79. I Ought to Be in Pictures 82. Max Dugan Returns 83. The Lonely Guy 84. The Slugger's Wife 85. Brighton Beach Memoirs 87, etc.

Simon, Paul (1942–). American lyricist and singer, long a team element as Simon and Garfunkel. Primarily known to the non-pop public for the music backing *The Graduate*, Simon also appeared in an unsuccessful 1980 movie, *One Trick Pony* and can be glimpsed in *Annie Hall* 77.

Simon, S. Sylvan (1910–1951). American director with radio experience.
A Girl with Ideas 37. Four Girls in White 39. Whistling in the Dark 41. Rio Rita 42. Song of the Open Road 44. Son of Lassie 45. Her Husband's Affairs 47. I Love Trouble 48. The Lust for Gold 49. Born Yesterday (p) 50, etc.

Simon, Simone (1910–). Pert French leading lady with brief stage experience.
Le Chanteur Inconnu (debut) 31. Lac aux Dames 34; to US: Girls' Dormitory 36. *Seventh Heaven* 37. Josette 38. *La Bête Humaine* 38. *All That Money Can Buy* 41. *Cat People* 42. Tahiti Honey 43. Mademoiselle Fifi 44. Temptation Harbour (GB) 47. Donna Senza Nome (It.) 49. La Ronde 50. Olivia 50. Le Plaisir 51. Double Destin 54. The Extra Day (GB) 56, etc.

Simpson, Alan (1929–). British TV and film comedy writer, with *Ray Galton* (qv).

Simpson, Ivan (1875–1951). Scottish character actor in Hollywood.
The Dictator 15. The Green Goddess 23 and 30. The Man Who Played God 32. Phantom of Cresswood 33. David Copperfield 34. Maid of Salem 37. The Hour Before the Dawn 43, many others.

Simpson, O. J. (1947–). Black American actor.

□The Klansman 74. The Towering Inferno 74. The Diamond Mercenaries 75. The Cassandra Crossing 77. Roots (TV) 77. A Killing Affair (TV) 77. Capricorn One 78. Firepower 79. Detour (TV) 79. Goldie and the Boxer (TV) 79. Goldie and the Boxer Go to Hollywood (TV) 80. Hambone and Hillie 84.

Simpson, Russell (1878–1959). American character actor, in Hollywood from silent days.
Billy the Kid 31. Way Down East 36. Ramona 37. Dodge City 39. The Grapes of Wrath 40. Outside the Law 41. They Were Expendable 45. My Darling Clementine 46. The Beautiful Blonde from Bashful Bend 49. Seven Brides for Seven Brothers 54. Friendly Persuasion 56. The Horse Soldiers 59, many others.

Sims, Joan (1930–). British stage, TV and film comedienne, often in cameo roles.
Colonel March Investigates 53. Meet Mr Lucifer 54. The Belles of St Trinian's 54. Dry Rot 56. The Naked Truth 58. Carry On Regardless 60. Twice Round the Daffodils 62. Strictly for the Birds 64. Follow that Camel 67. The Alf Garnett Saga 72. One of Our Dinosaurs is Missing 75, many others.

Sinatra, Frank (1915–). American leading actor and vocalist, former band singer. A teenage rave in the forties, he later became respected as an actor and a powerful producer.
□Las Vegas Nights 41. Ship Ahoy 42. Reveille with Beverly 43. Higher and Higher (acting debut) 43. *Step Lively* 44. *Anchors Aweigh* 45. Till the Clouds Roll By 46. It Happened in Brooklyn 46. The Kissing Bandit 47. The Miracle of the Bells 48. *Take Me Out to the Ball Game* 48. *On the Town* 49. Double Dynamite 50. Meet Danny Wilson 51. *From Here to Eternity* (AA) 53. Suddenly 54. Young at Heart 54. The Tender Trap 55. Not as a Stranger 55. *The Man with the Golden Arm* 56. Johnny Concho 56. The Pride and the Passion 56. Around the World in Eighty Days 56. Guys and Dolls 56. *High Society* 56. *Pal Joey* 57. The Joker is Wild 57. Kings Go Forth 58. Some Came Running 58. A Hole in the Head 59. Can Can 59. Never So Few 59. Pepe 60. Ocean's Eleven 60. The Devil at Four O'Clock 61. Sergeants Three 62. *The Manchurian Candidate* 62. Four for Texas 63. The List of Adrian Messenger 63. Come Blow Your Horn 63. Robin and the Seven Hoods 64. None But the Brave (& d) 65. Von Ryan's Express 65. Marriage on the Rocks 65. Cast a Giant Shadow 66. Assault on a Queen 66. The Naked Runner (GB) 67. Tony Rome 67. *The Detective* 68. Lady in Cement 68. Dirty Dingus Magee 70. Contract on Cherry Street (TV) 77. The First Deadly Sin 80.

¶ He's the kind of guy that, when he dies, he's going up to heaven and give God a bad time for making him bald.—*Marlon Brando*

Don't tell me. Suggest. But don't tell me.—*F.S.*

I detest bad manners. If people are polite, I am. They shouldn't try to get away with not being polite to me.—*F.S.*

'When he dies, they're giving his zipper to the Smithsonian.'—*Dean Martin*

'Make yourself like Frank. Hit somebody.'—*Don Rickles*

'The charm that once made him irresistible was lost in the unpredictable whims of a spoiled child.'—*Roger Vadim*

'I was not impressed by the creeps and Mafia types he kept about him.'—*Prince Charles*

'Age has softened his sinister aura.'—*Newsweek, 1982*

Sinatra, Nancy (1940–). American leading lady and singer, daughter of Frank Sinatra.
For Those Who Think Young 64. The Last of the Secret Agents 66. Speedway 68, etc.

Sinclair, Andrew (1935–). British director.
Before Winter Comes (w only) 69. The Breaking of Bumbo 70. Under Milk Wood 72. Blue Blood 73.

Sinclair, Hugh (1903–1962). British stage leading man, in occasional films.
Our Betters 33. Escape Me Never 35. A Girl Must Live 39. Alibi 42. They Were Sisters 45. Corridor of Mirrors 48. The Rocking Horse Winner 50. The Second Mrs Tanqueray 52, etc.

Sinclair, Robert (1905–1970). American director.
Woman Against Woman 38. Dramatic School 38. Mr and Mrs North 41. Mr District Attorney 46. That Wonderful Urge 48, etc.

Sinden, Donald (1923–). British leading man, on stage from mid-thirties.
The Cruel Sea (film debut) 53. Doctor in the House 54. Simba 55. Eyewitness 57. Doctor at Large 58. Operation Bullshine 59. Twice

Round the Daffodils 62. Decline and Fall 68. Villain 71. Rentadick 72. The National Health 73. The Day of the Jackal 73. The Island at the Top of the World 74. That Lucky Touch 75, etc.
TV series: Our Man at St Mark's 58. Two's Company 77–80. Never the Twain 83–.

Sing As We Go (GB 1934). You can almost smell the tripe and onions in this cheerful Gracie Fields vehicle scripted by J. B. Priestley. As things have happened, it also preserves the most authentic flavour on film of Britain's industrial north in the thirties.

Singer, Alexander (1932–). American director.
☐*A Cold Wind in August* 62. Psyche 59 64. Love Has Many Faces 65. Captain Apache 71. The First 36 Hours of Dr Durant (TV) 75. The Million Dollar Rip-Off (TV) 76.

Singer, Campbell (1909–1976). British character actor, often seen as heavy father, commissionaire, sergeant-major or policeman. Première 37. Take My Life 47. The Ringer 52. Simba 55. The Square Peg 58. The Pot Carriers 63, many others.

The Singing Fool (US 1928). Remembered because Al Jolson sang 'Sonny Boy' in it, this early talkie is otherwise a dismal tear-jerker about a brash entertainer who comes to his senses when his little boy dies. Directed by Lloyd Bacon from a play by Leslie S. Barrows.

Singin' in the Rain (US 1952). One of the most exhilarating and fast-moving comedy-musicals ever to come out of Hollywood, this enjoyably professional piece is also a gentle satire on the movie modes and manners of the twenties. Adolph Green and Betty Comden wrote the script, Arthur Freed and Nacio Herb Brown the words and music, Harold Rosson was cinematographer, and Gene Kelly and Stanley Donen directed. Kelly also starred, along with Donald O'Connor, Debbie Reynolds, Millard Mitchell and Jean Hagen.

Singleton, Penny (1908–). (Mariana McNulty). American leading lady who made her greatest hit as *Blondie* (qv).
Good News 30. After the Thin Man 36. *Swing Your Lady* 38. The Mad Miss Manton 38. *Blondie* 38 (then two films in the series every year, more or less, until 1950). The Best Man 64, etc.

Siodmak, Curt (1902–). German writer-director, in films from 1929, Hollywood from 1937.
People on Sunday (co-w) 29. The Tunnel (co-w) 34. Her Jungle Love (co-w) 38. Frankenstein Meets the Wolf Man (w) 42. Son of Dracula (w) 43. The Beast with Five Fingers (w) 47. Bride of the Gorilla (wd) 51. *The Magnetic Monster* (d) 51. Donovan's Brain (oa) 53. Love Slaves of the Amazon (w, d) 57. Ski Fever (w, d) 66, etc.

Siodmak, Robert (1900–1973). American director with early experience in Germany and France.
People on Sunday 29. The Weaker Sex 32. La Vie Parisienne 35. *Pièges* 39. West Point Widow 41. Son of Dracula 43. *Phantom Lady* 44. *The Suspect* 44. Christmas Holiday 44. *The Spiral Staircase* 45. The Strange Affair of Uncle Harry 45. *The Killers* 46. *The Dark Mirror* 46. Cry of the City 48. Criss Cross 48. The File on Thelma Jordon 49. The Great Sinner 49. Deported 50. The Whistle at Eaton Falls 51. The Crimson Pirate 52. Le Grand Jeu 53. Mein Vater der Schauspieler 56. Jatja 59. The Rough and the Smooth 59. Tunnel 28 (Escape from East Berlin) 62. Custer of the West 67, others.
'He manipulated Hollywood's fantasy apparatus with taste and intelligence.'—*Andrew Sarris, 1968*

Sir Arne's Treasure (Sweden 1919). A famous silent film directed by Mauritz Stiller from the novel by Selma Lagerlöf. It tells a 16th century tale of three Scottish mercenaries in the Swedish army who rob a priest but are prevented from escaping by an icy winter which freezes up their ship; also of the girl Estelle who falls in love with one of them but is killed. The story was remade by Gustav Molander in 1954.

Sirk, Douglas (1900–) (Detlef Sierck). Danish director, with stage experience; in America from early forties.
SELECTED EUROPEAN FILMS: April April 35. Das Hofkonzert 36. La Habanera 37. Home Is Calling 37.
☐AMERICAN FILMS: Hitler's Madman 43. Summer Storm 44. A Scandal in Paris 46. *Lured* 47. *Sleep My Love* 48. Shockproof 49. Slightly French 49. Mystery Submarine 50. The First Legion 51. Thunder on the Hill 51. The Lady Pays Off 51. Weekend with Father 51. No Room for the Groom 52. *Has Anybody Seen My Gal?* 52. Meet Me at the Fair 52. Take Me to Town 53. All I Desire

53. Taza Son of Cochise 54. *Magnificent Obsession* 54. Sign of the Pagan 54. Captain Lightfoot 55. There's Always Tomorrow 56. All That Heaven Allows 56. *Written on the Wind* 57. Battle Hymn 57. Interlude 57. The Tarnished Angels 58. A Time to Love and a Time to Die 58. Imitation of Life 59.

Sitting Bull (1831–1890). Sioux Indian chief, almost always on the warpath. The villain of countless westerns; J. Carrol Naish played him in a 1954 biopic, also in *Annie Get Your Gun* 50.

Sitting Pretty. This title was used for a 1933 comedy directed by Harry Joe Brown, with Jack Oakie and Jack Haley as two songwriters hitch-hiking their way to Hollywood. It is however chiefly associated with the 1947 comedy starring Clifton Webb as Lynn Belvedere, baby-sitter extraordinary. Webb appeared in two sequels, *Mr Belvedere Goes to College* 49 and *Mr Belvedere Rings the Bell* 51.

16mm. A 'sub-standard' gauge to which feature films are reduced for private hire and in many countries for television. Many sponsored documentaries not intended for cinema showing are filmed in 16mm, as are television news and features. The smaller frame and greater magnification do not always lead to unsatisfactory results, but the dangers are obvious.

Sjoberg, Alf (1903–1980). Swedish director, former stage actor and director.
The Road to Heaven 42. *Frenzy* 44. Only a Mother 49. *Miss Julie* 51. Barabbas 53. Karin Mansdotter 54. Wild Birds 55. The Judge 60. The Island 66, others.

Sjoman, Vilgot (1924–). Swedish director, chiefly famous (and notorious) for *'491'* 66. *I Am Curious: Blue* 67, *I Am Curious: Yellow* 67, and *Blushing Charlie* 71.
Also: Troll 73. A Handful of Love 74. The Garage 74. Tabu 77.

Sjostrom, Victor: see *Seastrom, Victor*.

Skala, Lilia (–). German actress in America.
Lilies of the Field 64. Deadly Hero 76. Roseland 77. Heartland 80. The End of August 82. Flashdance 83. House of Games 87, etc.

Skall, William V. (1898–1976). American cinematographer.
Victoria the Great 37. The Mikado 39. Northwest Passage 40. Life with Father 47. *Joan of Arc* (AA) 48. Quo Vadis 51. The Silver Chalice 55, many others.

Skelly, Hal (1891–1934). American character actor from Broadway.
□*The Dance of Life* 29. Woman Trap 29. Behind the Make Up 30. Men Are Like That 30. The Struggle 31. Hotel Variety 31. Shadow Laughs 31.

Skelton, Red (1910–) (Richard Skelton). American comedian of radio and TV; made numerous films in forties, very few since.
□Having Wonderful Time 38. Flight Command 40. The People Versus Dr Kildare 41. Lady Be Good 41. *Whistling in the Dark* 41. Dr Kildare's Wedding Day 41. Ship Ahoy 42. Maisie Gets Her Man 42. Panama Hattie 42. Whistling in Dixie 42. *Dubarry Was a Lady* 43. I Dood It 43. Whistling in Brooklyn 43. Thousands Cheer 43. Bathing Beauty 44. Ziegfeld Follies 46. The Show Off 46. *Merton of the Movies* 47. The Fuller Brush Man 48. A Southern Yankee 48. Neptune's Daughter 49. The Yellow Cab Man 50. The Fuller Brush Girl (gag) 50. Three Little Words 50. Duchess of Idaho (gag) 50. Watch the Birdie 50. Excuse My Dust 51. Texas Carnival 51. Lovely to Look at 52. The Clown 52. Half a Hero 53. The Great Diamond Robbery 53. Susan Slept Here (gag) 54. Around the World in Eighty Days 56. Public Pigeon Number One 57. Ocean's Eleven (gag) 60. Those Magnificent Men in Their Flying Machines 65.

¶ *R.S.:* I'm nuts and I know it. But so long as I make 'em laugh, they ain't going to lock me up.

R.S.: I always believed God puts each one of us here for a purpose . . . and mine is to try to make people happy.

Skerritt, Tom (1933–). American actor.
□War Hunt 62. One Man's Way 64. Those Callaways 65. M*A*S*H 70. Wild Rovers 71. Fuzz 72. Thieves Like Us 74. Big Bad Mama 74. The Devil's Rain 75. The Turning Point 77. Up in Smoke 78. Alien 79. Ice Castles 79. Savage Harvest 81. A Dangerous Summer 81. Silence of the North 81. Fighting Back 82. The Dead Zone 83. Top Gun 86. Wisdom 86. Opposing Force 87.
TV series: Run, Run, Joe 74.

skiing has formed a pleasant background in many romantic comedies including *I Met Him in Paris* and *Two-Faced Woman*; in farces including *The Pink Panther* and *Snowball*

Express; dramas including *Last of the Ski Bums, Ski Fever* and *Downhill Racer*; and in a plethora of spy stories, including *Caprice, The Double Man* and a couple of Bonds. The most musical ski sequence was provided by The Beatles in *Help!*

Skiles, Marlin (1906–). American composer.
The Impatient Years 44. Gilda 46. Dead Reckoning 47. Callaway Went Thataway 51. The Maze 53. Bowery to Baghdad 55. Fort Massacre 58. The Hypnotic Eye 60. The Strangler 64. The Resurrection of Zachary Wheeler 71, many others.

Skinner, Cornelia Otis (1901–1979). American stage actress, daughter of Otis Skinner the tragedian. Toyed with Hollywood occasionally. Her autobiographical book *Our Hearts Were Young and Gay* (co-written with Emily Kimbrough) was filmed with Gail Russell.
The Uninvited 44. The Girl in the Red Velvet Swing 55. The Swimmer 67.

Skinner, Frank (1898–1968). American composer.
Son of Frankenstein 39. Destry Rides Again 39. Hellzapoppin 41. Back Street 41. Saboteur 42. Gung Ho 43. The Suspect 44. The Egg and I 47. Abbott and Costello Meet Frankenstein 48. Francis 49. Harvey 50. The World in His Arms 52. Thunder Bay 53. Battle Hymn 56. Imitation of Life 58. Back Street 61. Shenandoah 65. Madame X 66, many others.

Skinner, Otis (1858–1942). American stage actor who appeared in films only in two versions of *Kismet* 20 & 30. Charles Ruggles played him in *Our Hearts Were Young and Gay* 44.

Skipworth, Alison (1875–1952) (Alison Groom). Chubby British character actress, long in Hollywood; a favourite foil for W. C. Fields.
Raffles 30. Outward Bound 30. Devotion 31. Night After Night 32. *If I Had a Million* 32. Song of Songs 33. *Tillie and Gus* 33. Six of a Kind 34. The Captain Hates the Sea 34. Becky Sharp 35. Shanghai 35. Satan Met a Lady 36. Stolen Holiday 37. Wide Open Faces 38, many others.

Skirball, Jack H. (1896–1985). American independent producer, former salesman.
Miracle on Main Street 38. Lady from Cheyenne 41. Saboteur 42. Shadow of a Doubt 43. It's in the Bag (The Fifth Chair) 45. Guest Wife 46. Payment on Demand 51, etc.

Skolimowski, Jerzy (1938–). Polish director.
The Barrier 66. The Departure 67. Hands Up 67. Dialogue 69. The Adventures of Gerard 70. Deep End 71. King, Queen, Knave 72. The Shout 78. Circle of Deceit (a only) 81. Moonlighting (& w) 82. Success is the Best Revenge 84. The Lightship 85, etc.

Skouras, Spyros (1893–1971). Greek-American executive, former hotelier. President of Twentieth Century-Fox 1943–62; instigator of CinemaScope.

¶ *Billy Wilder:* The only Greek tragedy I know is Spyros Skouras.

slapstick. One of the earliest (1895) Lumière shorts, *L'Arroseur Arrosé*, was a knockabout farce, and in 1966 *A Funny Thing Happened on the Way to the Forum* was keeping the tradition going. Out of simple slapstick developed the great silent clowns, each with his own brand of pathos: Harold Lloyd, Charlie Chaplin, Buster Keaton, Fatty Arbuckle, Harry Langdon, Mabel Normand, Larry Semon, Laurel and Hardy. Pure destructive slapstick without humanity was superbly dispensed by Mack Sennett, especially in his Keystone Kops shorts. France had produced Max Linder; Britain lagged behind, but in the twenties Betty Balfour, Monty Banks and Lupino Lane kept the flag flying. Many of these names survived in some degree when sound came, but cross-talk was an added factor in the success of Wheeler and Woolsey, Charlie Chase, Edgar Kennedy, Leon Errol, Hugh Herbert, Joe E. Brown, W. C. Fields, Eddie Cantor, Abbott and Costello and above all the Marx Brothers. Similarly in Britain there was an influx of stage comics with firm music-hall traditions: George Formby, Will Hay, Max Miller, Gracie Fields, Leslie Fuller, the Crazy Gang, Arthur Askey, Gordon Harker, Sandy Powell, Frank Randle and Old Mother Riley. The forties in Hollywood brought the more sophisticated slapstick of Danny Kaye, writer-director Preston Sturges, and the Bob Hope gag factory, with extreme simplicity keeping its end up via Olsen and Johnson and Jerry Lewis. In the fifties, TV finally brought a female clown, Lucille Ball, to the top; though competition was thin. France since the war has had Fernandel, Louis de Funes, Jacques Tati and Pierre Etaix; Britain Norman Wisdom and Morecambe and Wise; Italy Toto and Walter Chiari. In Hollywood the fashion over the last twenty years has been for epic comedies of violence and destruction, such as *It's a Mad Mad Mad Mad World*, *The Great Race*, *Those Magnificent Men in Their Flying Machines* and *The Blues Brothers*.

Slate, Jeremy (1935–). American general purpose actor.
Wives and Lovers 63. I'll Take Sweden 65. The Sons of Katie Elder 66. The Devil's Brigade 68, etc.

Slater, John (1916–1975). British cockney character actor and comedian of stage and TV, occasionally in films.
Love on the Dole (debut) 40. Went the Day Well? 42. A Canterbury Tale 44. Passport to Pimlico 48. Johnny You're Wanted 54. Violent Playground 58. Three on a Spree 61. A Place to Go 63, many others.

Slaughter, Tod (1885–1956) (N. Carter Slaughter). Barnstorming British actor who toured the provinces with chop-licking revivals of outrageous old melodramas, all of which he filmed after a fashion.
□Maria Marten 35. Sweeney Todd 36. The Crimes of Stephen Hawke 36. Song of the Road 37. Darby and Joan 37. It's Never Too Late to Mend 37. The Ticket of Leave Man 37. Sexton Blake and the Hooded Terror 38. *The Face at the Window* 39. Crimes at the Dark House 40. The Curse of the Wraydons 43. The Greed of William Hart 48. King of the Underworld 52. Murder at Scotland Yard 52.

sleeper: a trade term for a film which suddenly does much better at the box office than was expected.

Slezak, Walter (1902–1983). Austrian character actor, of theatrical family; in America from 1930.
Autobiography 1962: *What Time's the Next Swan?*
Once Upon a Honeymoon (English-speaking debut) 42. *Lifeboat* 44. Step Lively 44. The Spanish Main 45. Cornered 45. Sinbad the Sailor 47. The Pirate 48. *The Inspector General* 49. Call Me Madam 53. White Witch Doctor 54. The Steel Cage 54. Come September 61. Emil and the Detectives 64. Wonderful Life (GB) 64. Twenty-Four Hours to Kill 65. A Very Special Favor 65. Caper of the Golden Bulls 67. Dr Coppelius 68. Black Beauty 71, etc.

slides

¶ A feature of film-going in nickelodeon days were the decorative slides used between the brief entertainments. Here is a nostalgic selection:

Please Read the Titles to Yourself. Loud Reading Annoys Your Neighbours.

Just a Moment Please While the Operator Changes Reels.

If Annoyed When Here Please Tell the Management.

Ladies and Gentlemen May safely visit this Theatre as no Offensive Films are ever Shown Here.

We Aim to Present the Pinnacle of Motion Picture Perfection.

Ladies, We Like your Hats, but Please Remove Them.

You Wouldn't Spit on the Floor at Home, so Please Don't do it Here.

A Slight Case of Murder (US 1938). This black comedy by Damon Runyon, directed by Lloyd Bacon, was Warners' way of eating their cake and having it. In face of mounting official criticism of gangster films, they made one with the highest death-rate of all but turned it into a comedy and left star Edward G. Robinson with clean hands. (A year later, in *Brother Orchid*, they made him see the light and become a monk.) In 1952 the movie was remade as *Stop You're Killing Me*, with Broderick Crawford.

Sloane, Everett (1909–1965). Incisive American character actor, brought to Hollywood by Orson Welles.
□*Citizen Kane* 41. *Journey into Fear* 42. *The Lady from Shanghai* 48. Prince of Foxes 49. *The Men* 50. Bird of Paradise 51. The Enforcer 51. Sirocco 51. The Prince Who Was a Thief 51. The Blue Veil 51. The Desert Fox 51. The Sellout 51. Way of a Gaucho 52. *The Big Knife* 55. *Patterns* 56. *Somebody Up There Likes Me* 56. Lust for Life 56. Marjorie Morningstar 58. The Gun Runners 58. Home from the Hill 60. By Love Possessed 61. Brushfire 62. The Man from the Diners Club 63. The Patsy 64. Ready for the People 64. The Disorderly Orderly 64.
TV series: Official Detective 58.
Famous line (*Citizen Kane*): Old age, Mr Thompson: it's the only disease you don't look forward to being cured of.

Sloane, Olive (1896–1963). British character actress of stage and screen whose best role was in *Seven Days to Noon* 50.

Countless other small roles since film debut in *Soldiers of the King* 33.

Slocombe, Douglas (1913–). British cinematographer, former journalist.
Dead of Night 45. The Captive Heart 46. Hue and Cry 46. The Loves of Joanna Godden 47. *It Always Rains on Sunday* 47. *Saraband for Dead Lovers* 48. Kind Hearts and Coronets 49. Cage of Gold 50. The Lavender Hill Mob 51. Mandy 52. The Man in the White Suit 52. *The Titfield Thunderbolt* 53. Man in the Sky 56. The Smallest Show on Earth 57. Tread Softly Stranger 58. Circus of Horrors 59. The Young Ones 61. The L-Shaped Room 62. *Freud* 63. The Servant 63. Guns at Batasi 64. A High Wind in Jamaica 65. The Blue Max 66. Promise Her Anything 66. The Vampire Killers 67. Fathom 67. Robbery 67. Boom 68. The Lion in Winter 68. The Italian Job 69. *The Music Lovers* 70. Murphy's War 70. The Buttercup Chain 70. Travels with My Aunt 73. The Great Gatsby 74. Love Among the Ruins (TV) 75. Rollerball 75. Hedda 76. Julia 77. Nasty Habits 77. Caravans 78. Lost and Found 79. Julia (BFA) 78. The Lady Vanishes 79. Nijinsky 80. Lost and Found 80. Raiders of the Lost Ark 81. The Pirates of Penzance 83. Never Say Never Again 83. Indiana Jones and the Temple of Doom 84. Lady Jane 85, etc.

slogans

¶ All kinds of claims have been made over the years for all kinds of products. Here are a few of the most memorable.

Famous Players in Famous Plays

is certainly the longest lasting, all the way from 1912. The films hardly lived up to it, any more than it was true that:

Selznick Pictures Create Happy Homes

Or that Warners fooled anybody by linking:

Good Films—Good Citizenship

Or MGM by claiming that their spur was:

Ars Gratia Artis (art for its own sake)

MGM's secondary claim:

More Stars than there are in Heaven

was simply a slight exaggeration. When talkies came in, two favourite lines were:

All Talking, All Singing, All Dancing

And, from Vitaphone:

Pictures that Talk Like Living People!

The whole industry sometimes gets together on a propaganda campaign. In the thirties, it was:

Go to a Motion Picture—and Let Yourself Go!

In the forties, simply:

Let's go to a movie!

In the fifties, in face of the arch-enemy television:

Don't be a Living Room Captive! Go Out and See a Great Movie!

And a few years later:

Movies are Your Best Entertainment!

The one I like best was concocted by the proprietors of CinemaScope in the face of 3-D. Originally it ran:

You see it without the use of glasses!

This not unnaturally brought a few complaints from bespectacled patrons who thought they were being guaranteed a new freedom, so hurriedly and rather lamely it was changed to:

You see it without the use of special glasses!

slow motion. An effect obtained by running the camera faster than usual. When the film passes through the projector at normal speed, each movement appears slower, as it occupies more frames of film. For scientific purposes (e.g. recording the growth of plants) cameras are so arranged that a single frame of film is exposed at regular intervals, thus giving an impression of accelerated growth.

Small, Edward (1891–1977). Veteran American independent producer, former actor and agent, in Hollywood from 1924.
I Cover the Waterfront 35. The Man in the Iron Mask 39. The Corsican Brothers 41. Brewster's Millions 45. Down Three Dark Streets 55. Witness for the Prosecution 57. Jack the Giant Killer 62. I'll Take Sweden 65. Forty Guns to Apache Pass 66, many others; also TV series.

Small, Michael (–). American composer.
Puzzle of a Downfall Child 70. Klute 71. Child's Play 72. The Parallax View 74. Night Moves 75. Marathon Man 76. Comes a Horseman 78. Those Lips Those Eyes 80. The Postman Always Rings Twice 81.

small towns were for many years the staple of the American cinema. Most audiences were small-town folk, and wanted to see slightly idealized versions of themselves. Thus the popularity of the happy families, the Hardys and the Joneses; thus *Our Town, The Human Comedy, Ah Wilderness, The Music Man* and *The Dark at the Top of the Stairs*. The darker side of small-town life was shown in *The Chase, Kings Row, Peyton Place* and *Invasion of the Body Snatchers*. British small towns did not have the same aura; most of the comparable stories were set against industrial backgrounds.

Smart, J. Scott (1903–50). Heavyweight radio actor who took his *Fat Man* character to Hollywood for one 50s film of that name.

Smart, Ralph (1908–). British producer-director, latterly of TV series *The Invisible Man, Danger Man*, etc. Former editor and writer.
DIRECTOR: Bush Christmas 46. A Boy, a Girl and a Bike 48. Bitter Springs 50. Never Take No for an Answer (co-d) 51. Curtain Up 52. Always a Bride 54, etc.

Smedley-Aston, E. M. (1912–). British producer.
The Extra Day 56. Two-Way Stretch 60. Offbeat 61. The Wrong Arm of the Law 63. Ooh You Are Awful 72, etc.

Smight, Jack (1926–). American director, from TV.
□I'd Rather Be Rich 64. The Third Day 65. *Harper* 66. Kaleidoscope 66. The Secret War of Harry Frigg 67. No Way to Treat a Lady 68. The Illustrated Man 69. Strategy of Terror (TV) 69. Rabbit Run (TV) 69. The Travelling Executioner 70. The Screaming Woman (TV) 72. Detour to Nowhere (TV) 72. The Longest Night (TV) 72. Linda (TV) 73. Double Indemnity (TV) 73. Frankenstein: The True Story (TV) 73. Airport 75 74. Midway 76. Damnation Alley 77. Roll of Thunder (TV) 78. Fast Break 78. Loving Couples 80. Number One with a Bullet 87.

Smilin' Through. The popular sentimental stage play by Jane Cowl and Jane Murfin, about a tragedy affecting the romances of two generations, was filmed in 1922 by Sidney Franklin, with Norma Talmadge, Wyndham Standing and Harrison Ford; in 1932, again Sidney Franklin, with Norma Shearer, Leslie Howard and Fredric March. In 1941 Frank Borzage remade it with Jeanette MacDonald, Brian Aherne and Gene Raymond.

Smith, Alexis (1921–) (Gladys Smith). American leading lady of the forties who won an acting contest from Hollywood high school. Married to Craig Stevens.
Lady with Red Hair 41. Dive Bomber 41. The Smiling Ghost 41. Gentleman Jim 42. The Constant Nymph 42. The Doughgirls 44. Conflict 45. Rhapsody in Blue 45. San Antonio 45. Night and Day 46. Of Human Bondage 46. Stallion Road 47. The Woman in White 47. The Decision of Christopher Blake 48. Any Number Can Play 50. Undercover Girl 52. Split Second 53. The Sleeping Tiger (GB) 55. The Eternal Sea 56. The Young Philadelphians (The City Jungle) 59. Once is Not Enough 75. The Little Girl Who Lives Down the Lane 77. Casey's Shadow 78. A Death in California (TV) 85. Tough Guys 86, etc.

¶ *A.S.:* When they tell me one of my old movies is on TV, I don't look at it. Those films weren't very good at the time, and they haven't improved with age.
A.S.: There are so many more interesting things to think about than whether Ida Lupino or Jane Wyman got the roles I should have gotten.

Smith, Art (1899–1973). Bland, avuncular American character actor.
A Tree Grows in Brooklyn 44. Letter from an Unknown Woman 47. Cover Up 50. In a Lonely Place 51, etc.

Smith, Bernard (c. 1905–). American producer, ex publisher and story editor.
Elmer Gantry (AA) 60. How the West Was Won 62. Seven Women 65. Alfred the Great 69.

Smith, Betty (1904–). American novelist. Works filmed include *A Tree Grows in Brooklyn, Joy in the Morning.*

Smith, Sir C. Aubrey (1863–1948). Distinguished British character actor who after a long stage career settled in Hollywood to play crusty, benevolent or authoritarian old gentlemen.
SELECTED SILENT FILMS: The Witching Hour 16. The Bohemian Girl 23. The Rejected Woman 24.
□ SOUND FILMS: Birds of Prey (GB) 30. Such is the Law (GB) 30. Contraband Love (GB) 31. Trader Horn 31. Never the Twain Shall Meet 31. Bachelor Father 31. Daybreak 31. Just a Gigolo 31. Son of India 31. The Man in Possession 31. Phantom of Paris 31. Guilty Hands 31. Surrender 31. Polly of the Circus 31. Tarzan the Ape Man 32. But the Flesh is Weak 32. *Love Me Tonight* 32. Trouble in Paradise 32. No More Orchids 32. They Just Had to Get Married 32. Luxury Liner 33. Secrets 33. The Barbarian 33. Adorable 33. The Monkey's Paw 33. *Morning Glory* 33. Bombshell 33. Queen Christina 33. The House of Rothschild 34. The Scarlet Empress 34. Gambling Lady 34. Curtain at Eight 34. The

Tunnel (GB) 34. Bulldog Drummond Strikes Back 34. Cleopatra 34. Madame du Barry 34. One More River 34. Caravan 34. The Firebird 34. The Right to Live 35. *Lives of a Bengal Lancer* 35. The Florentine Dagger 35. The Gilded Lily 35. Clive of India 35. China Seas 35. Jalna 35. The Crusades 35. Little Lord Fauntleroy 36. Romeo and Juliet 36. The Garden of Allah 36. Lloyds of London 36. Wee Willie Winkie 36. *The Prisoner of Zenda* 37. Thoroughbreds Don't Cry 37. The Hurricane 37. Four Men and a Prayer 38. Kidnapped 38. Sixty Glorious Years (GB) 38. East Side of Heaven 39. Five Came Back 39. *The Four Feathers* (GB) 39. The Sun Never Sets 39. Eternally Yours 39. Another Thin Man 39. The Underpup 39. Balalaika 39. *Rebecca* 40. City of Chance 40. A Bill of Divorcement 40. Waterloo Bridge 40. Beyond Tomorrow 40. A Little Bit of Heaven 40. Free and Easy 41. Maisie was a Lady 41. Dr Jekyll and Mr Hyde 41. Forever and a Day 43. Two Tickets to London 43. Flesh and Fantasy 43. Madame Curie 43. The White Cliffs of Dover 44. The Adventures of Mark Twain 44. Secrets of Scotland Yard 44. Sensations of 1945 44. They Shall Have Faith 44. *And Then There Were None* 45. Scotland Yard Investigator 45. Cluny Brown 46. Rendezvous with Annie 46. High Conquest 47. Unconquered 47. *An Ideal Husband* (GB) 47. Little Women 49.

❀ For relishing and perpetuating the stereotype of the fine old English gentleman. *The Four Feathers*.

Smith, Charles (c. 1920–). American character actor who in the forties played Dizzy in the *Henry Aldrich* series and other amiably doltish roles.
The Shop Around the Corner 40. Tom Brown's Schooldays 40. Three Little Girls in Blue 45. Two Weeks with Love 50. City of Bad Men 53, many others.

Smith, Constance (1929–). British leading lady.
Brighton Rock 47. Don't Say Die 50. The Thirteenth Letter (US) 51. Red Skies of Montana (US) 52. Treasure of the Golden Condor (US) 53. Tiger by the Tail 55, etc.

Smith, Cyril (1892–1963). British character actor of stage and screen, often a henpecked husband but equally likely to be a grocer, dustman or policeman. On stage from 1900, films from 1908, and was in over 500 of the latter.
Friday the Thirteenth 33. School for Secrets 46. It's Hard To Be Good 48. Mother Riley Meets the Vampire 52. John and Julie 54. *Sailor Beware* (his stage role) 56, etc.

Smith, G. A. (1864–1959). British pioneer cinematographer who invented a cine-camera in 1896 and made some trick films.
The Corsican Brothers 97. The Fairy Godmother 98. Faust 98, etc.

Smith, John (1931–) (Robert Van Orden). Boyish American leading man.
The High and the Mighty 54. Ghost Town 56. The Bold and the Brave 57. Circus World 64. Waco 66, etc.
TV series: Cimarron City 58. Laramie 59–62.

Smith, Kate (1909–86). Heavyweight American singer who was popular on radio in the thirties and forties. Made one film in 1933 (*Hello, Everybody*) and another in 1943 (*This is the Army*).

Smith, Kent (1907–85). Smooth, quiet American leading man of the forties; latterly a useful character actor.
Cat People 42. Hitler's Children 43. This Land is Mine 43. *The Spiral Staircase* 46. *Nora Prentiss* 47. The Decision of Christopher Blake 48. The Fountainhead 49. The Damned Don't Cry 50. Paul 52. Comanche 56. Party Girl 58. Strangers When We Meet 60. Moon Pilot 62. A Distant Trumpet 64. The Trouble with Angels 66. Assignment to Kill 68. Death of a Gunfighter 69. Pete'n Tillie 72. Cops and Robbers 73, many others.
TV series: *Peyton Place* 64–67.

Smith, Liz (–). British character actress.
A Private Function (BFA) 84.

Smith, Lois (1930–). American character actress.
Five Easy Pieces 70. Resurrection 80.

Smith, Maggie (1934–). Leading British actress with a taste for eccentric comedy.
□Nowhere to Go 58. Go to Blazes 62. *The VIPs* 63. The Pumpkin Eater 64. Young Cassidy 65. Othello 66. *The Honey Pot* 67. Hot Millions 68. Oh What a Lovely War 69. *The Prime of Miss Jean Brodie* (AA) 69. Love Pain and the Whole Damn Thing 73. Travels with My Aunt 73. Murder by Death 76. California Suite (AA) 78. Death on the Nile 78. Clash of the Titans 81. Quartet 81. Evil Under the Sun 82. Better Late Than Never 82. The Missionary 83. A Private Function (BFA) 84. A Room with a View 85. The Lonely Passion of Judith Hearne 87.

Smith, Paul (–). Towering American character actor who played the guard in *Midnight Express* and Bluto in *Popeye*.

Smith, Paul J. (–). American composer, almost exclusively for Disney. Snow White and the Seven Dwarfs (AAN) 37. Pinocchio (AA) 40. Victory through Air Power (AAN) 43. The Three Caballeros (AAN) 44. Song of the South (AAN) 46. Cinderella (AAN) 50. Twenty Thousand Leagues Under the Sea 54. Perri (AAN) 57. Pollyanna 60. The Parent Trap 61. The Three Lives of Thomasina 64, etc.

Smith, Pete (1892–1979). American producer of punchy one-reel shorts on any and every subject from 1935 to the fifties, all narrated by 'a Smith named Pete'. Former publicist. Special Academy Award 1953 'for his witty and pungent observations on the American scene'.

Smith, Roger (1932–). American leading man.
The Young Rebels 56. Operation Mad Ball 57. Man with a Thousand Faces (as Lon Chaney Jnr) 57. Never Steal Anything Small 59. Auntie Mame 59. Rogues' Gallery 68. The First Time (wp) 70.
TV series: 77 Sunset Strip 58–64. Mr Roberts 65.

Smith, Thorne (1892–1934). American humorous novelist. Works filmed include *Topper, Turnabout, I Married a Witch.*

smoking has served as the springboard of a few plots. *No Smoking* and *Cold Turkey* concerned cures for it, and one also figured in *Taking Off.* In *On a Clear Day You Can See Forever*, Barbra Streisand launched the plot by taking psychiatric advice about it. The most fashionable smoking habit was Paul Henreid's in *Now Voyager*, lighting two cigarettes and passing one to Bette Davis; this was mimicked with eight cigarettes by Bob Hope in *Let's Face It.* The longest cigarette holder was sported by Harpo Marx in *A Night in Casablanca.*

Smoktunovsky, Innokenti (1925–). Leading Russian stage actor, seen in a few films including *Nine Days of One Year* 60. *Hamlet* 64. *Tchaikovsky* 69. Crime and Punishment 75.

Smothers, Tom (1937–). American light leading man and comedian who with his brother Dick (1939–) was popular on American TV in the sixties. Tom himself went on to appear in a few films:
□Get to Know Your Rabbit 74. Silver Bears 78. The Kids Are Alright 78. Serial 80. There Goes the Bride 80. Pandemonium 82.

smugglers of the old-fashioned type are almost entirely a British concern, figuring in *Fury at Smugglers' Bay, Jamaica Inn, The Ghost Train, Oh Mr Porter, Ask a Policeman, I See a Dark Stranger, Moonfleet*, and others. Smuggling in American films has been a much more modern and less picturesque affair.

The Snake Pit (US 1948). Directed by Anatole Litvak from the novel by Mary Jane Ward, this deliberately unsensational study of mental illness did not entirely escape the problem of dramatizing a subject too serious for fiction. But Olivia de Havilland gave a fine performance and the film did much to assist Hollywood's new 'adult' post-war image. Photographed by Leo Tover, with music by Alfred Newman.

sneak preview. An unheralded tryout of a film at a public performance, usually in place of a second feature. Intended to gauge audience reaction, it is often followed by considerable re-editing before the official première.

Snell, David (–). American composer. Madame X 37. Young Dr Kildare 38. Twenty Mule Team 40. Love Crazy 41. Pacific Rendezvous 42. The Man from Down Under 43. Keep your Powder Dry 45. Merton of the Movies 47. The Lady in the Lake 47. Alias a Gentleman 48, etc.

Snodgress, Carrie (1946–). American leading lady of the seventies.
The Forty-Eight Hour Mile (TV) 68. Silent Night Lonely Night (TV) 69. Rabbit Run 71. *Diary of a Mad Housewife* 72. The Fury 78. Homework 82. Trick or Treats 82. A Night in Heaven 83. Pale Rider 85. Murphy's Law 86. etc.

snow, when needed for a movie scene, has been known to consist of a variety of ingredients including bleached cornflakes, soapflakes, chopped feathers, shredded asbestos, balsa chips, sawdust, and a wide range of plastic products.

Snow White and the Seven Dwarfs (US 1937). The first full-length Disney cartoon has remained popular through the years, perhaps because it so admirably suits its creator's Grimm-like imagination. He has certainly never again presented so precisely differentiated a group of comedians as Bashful, Sleepy, Grumpy, Sneezy, Happy, Dopey and Doc.

soap opera. A term used disparagingly of TV domestic drama serials. Originated because such offerings were invariably sponsored by the big soap companies who needed to attract the housewife.

social comedy. Silent romantic comedies were completely unrealistic, though they sometimes found it prudent to pretend satirical intent to cloak their lowbrow commercialism. Social comedy really came in as a substitute for sex comedy when the Hays Office axe fell in 1934. Frank Capra took by far the best advantage of it, with his series of films showing an America filled to bursting point with good guys who only wanted a simple and comfortable home life in some small town where corruption never raised its ugly head. The best of these films were *Mr Deeds Goes to Town, You Can't Take It with You* and *Mr Smith Goes to Washington*; by the time *Meet John Doe* came along in 1941 war had soured the mood again. There was no British equivalent to Capra, unless one counts a few attempts by Priestley (*The Good Companions, Let the People Sing*) and such amusing depictions of the middle class as *Quiet Wedding* and *Dear Octopus*; but in the late forties came the Ealing comedies, delightful and apparently realistic, but presenting a picture of England just as false as Capra's America. In both countries the fifties saw the development of an affluent society in which cynicism was fashionable and few reforms seemed worth urging except in bitterly serious fashion.

social conscience has long been a feature of Hollywood film production. Other countries have presented the odd feature pointing to flaws in their national make-up, but America has seemed particularly keen to wash its own dirty linen on screen, perhaps because this is rather easier than actually cleaning up the abuses.

The evolution of this attitude can be traced back as far as 1912 and Griffith's *The Musketeers of Pig Alley*, showing slum conditions, a theme developed in *Intolerance* 16; and, of course, Chaplin was a master at devising humour and pathos out of the unpleasant realities of poverty, a fact which endeared him to poor people all over the world. But it was not till the late twenties that the flood of socially conscious films began in earnest. Vidor's *The Crowd* investigated the drabness of everyday life for a city clerk. John Baxter's British *Dosshouse* was a lone entry on the lines of *The Lower Depths*. *City Streets* and *One-Third of a Nation* treated slum conditions; Vidor's *Our Daily Bread* concerned a young couple driven out of the city by poverty only to find farming just as precarious. *Little Caesar* and the gangster dramas which followed always assumed a crusading moral tone deploring the lives of vice and crime which they depicted; there was a somewhat more honest ring to *I Was a Fugitive from a Chain Gang*, which showed how circumstance can drive an honest man into anti-social behaviour. Capra sugared his pill with comedy: *American Madness* (the madness was money) and the popular comedies which followed all pitted common-man philosophy against urban sophistication and corruption.

In the mid-thirties there were certainly many abuses worth fighting. *Black Legion* began Hollywood's campaign against the Ku Klux Klan, later followed up in *The Flaming Cross, Storm Warning* and *The Cardinal*. Lynch law, first tackled in *Fury*, was subsequently the subject of *They Won't Forget, The Ox Bow Incident* and *The Sound of Fury*. Juvenile delinquency was probed in *Dead End, Angels with Dirty Faces* and *They Made Me a Criminal*, but the 'Dead End Kids' were later played for comedy. Prison reform was advocated in *Each Dawn I Die, Castle on the Hudson*, and many other melodramas of questionable integrity. *The Good Earth* invited concern for the poor of other nations; *Mr Smith Goes to Washington* and *The Glass Key* were among many dramas showing that politicians are not incorruptible; *Love on the Dole* depicted the poverty of industrial Britain; *The Grapes of Wrath* and *Tobacco Road* pondered the plight of farming people deprived of a living by geographical chance and thoughtless government. In *Sullivan's Travels*, Preston Sturges came to the curious conclusion that the best thing you can do for the poor is make them laugh.

During World War II the nations were too busy removing the abuse of Nazidom to look inward, and indeed much poverty was alleviated by conscription and a fresh national awareness which, together with the increased need for industrial manpower, greatly improved the lot of the lower classes. But with victory came a whole crop of films, led by *The Best Years of Our Lives* and *Till the*

End of Time, about the rehabilitation of war veterans. Concern about mental illness was shown in *The Snake Pit*, about paraplegia in *The Men* and about labour relations in *The Whistle at Eaton Falls*. Alcoholism was treated in *The Lost Weekend* and *Smash-Up*, and the racial issues were thoroughly aired in *Lost Boundaries, Crossfire, Home of the Brave, No Way Out, Gentleman's Agreement* and *Pinky*. A plea was for nations to help and understand each other made in the French *Race for Life*.

With the development in the fifties of the affluent society, the number of reforms worth urging was drastically reduced. Teenage hoodlums figured largely in a score of films of which the best were *The Wild One* and *Rebel without a Cause*. Mentally handicapped children were sympathetically portrayed in *A Child is Waiting*. In recent years, however, it is one world issue which has dominated the film-makers' social consciousness, that of the panic button; and this has manifested itself in films as diverse as *On the Beach, Dr Strangelove, Fail Safe* and *The Bedford Incident*.

Social consciousness was apparent in almost every drama of the seventies, but used as a top dressing, sometimes to permit the exploitation of violence. In films like *A Clockwork Orange* and *O Lucky Man* it is difficult enough to discover what point is being made.

Sofaer, Abraham (1896–). Burmese actor, on British stage since 1921.
Dreyfus (debut) 31. Rembrandt 36. *A Matter of Life and Death* 46. Judgment Deferred 51. *Elephant Walk* (US) 54. The Naked Jungle (US) 54. Bhowani Junction 56. King of Kings 61. Captain Sinbad (US) 63. Head 68. Che! 69, etc.

soft focus. A diffused effect used in photographing ageing leading ladies who can't stand good definition; also frequently used for exotic shots in musical numbers, etc.

Sojin (1884-1954). Japanese actor most memorable in western films as Douglas Fairbanks' antagonist in the 1924 *Thief of Baghdad*. Back in Japan after 1930.

Sokoloff, Vladimir (1889–1962). Russian character actor, in Hollywood from 1936.
The Loves of Jeanne Ney 27. West Front 1918 30. Die Dreigroschenoper 31. L'Atlantide 32. Mayerling 35. The Life of Emile Zola 37. Spawn of the North 38. Juarez 39. Road to Morocco 42. For Whom the Bell Tolls 43. Cloak and Dagger 46. Back to Bataan 46. Istanbul 56. Confessions of a Counterspy 60. Sardonicus 62, many others.

Soldati, Mario (1906–). Italian director.
Scandal in the Roman Bath 51. The Wayward Wife 53. The Stranger's Hand 54. Woman of the River 55, many others.

soldiers depicted at length in films include Alexander the Great (by Richard Burton), Hannibal (by Victor Mature). Genghis Khan (by John Wayne and Omar Sharif), Alexander Nevsky (by Cherkassov), Clive of India (by Ronald Colman), Napoleon (by Charles Boyer, Marlon Brando, Herbert Lom, and others), Bonnie Prince Charlie (by David Niven), Wellington (by George Arliss), General Gordon (by Charlton Heston), Custer (by Errol Flynn and Robert Shaw), La Fayette (by Michel le Royer), Davy Crockett (by Fess Parker and others), Sergeant York (by Gary Cooper), Audie Murphy (by Audie Murphy), Rommel (by Erich von Stroheim and James Mason), Che Guevara (by Omar Sharif), General Patton (by George C. Scott), and General Macarthur (by Gregory Peck).

Solon, Ewen (*c.*1923–85?). New Zealand character actor in Britain, especially on TV in series *Maigret* (as Lucas).
The Sundowners 59. Jack the Ripper 60. The Hound of the Baskervilles 60. The Terror of the Tongs 61. The Wicked Lady 83, etc.

Solzhenitsyn, Alexander (1918–). Russian novelist, expelled from his own country in 1974 for too much free thought. *One Day in the Life of Ivan Denisovitch* was filmed.

Some Like It Hot (US 1959). A fondly remembered but in fact rather overstretched spoof of the gangster era, with Marilyn Monroe at something like her best as a band singer of the Helen Kane type, and Jack Lemmon and Tony Curtis on the run in drag from the St Valentine's Day Massacre. Most of it happens in Florida, where Curtis does a Cary Grant impersonation, Joe E. Brown falls in love with Lemmon, and George Raft makes an appearance as the top gangster. Billy Wilder and I.A.L. Diamond perpetrated it.

Somers, Suzanne (1946–) (S. Mahoney). American leading lady of the late seventies, especially on TV in the series *Three's Company*.

American Graffiti 73. It Happened at Lakewood Manor (TV) 77. Nothing Personal 80, etc.

Somlo, Josef (1885–1973), Hungarian producer with long experience at UFA; in Britain from 1933.
Dark Journey 37. The Mikado 39. Old Bill and Son 40. Uncle Silas 47. The Man Who Loved Redheads 55. Behind the Mask 59, etc.

Sommer, Elke (1940–) (Elke Schletz). German leading lady now in international films.
Don't Bother to Knock (GB) 60. The Victors (GB) 63. *The Prize* (US) 63. A Shot in the Dark (US) 64. The Art of Love (US) 65. Four Kinds of Love (It.) 65. The Money Trap (US) 65. The Oscar (US) 66. Boy, Did I Get a Wrong Number (US) 66. Deadlier than the Male (GB) 66. The Venetian Affair (US) 66. The Corrupt Ones 67. The Wicked Dreams of Paula Schultz (US) 68. Zeppelin (US) 71. Percy (GB) 71. Carry on Behind (GB) 76. Lily in Love 84, etc.

Sommer, Josef (c. 1930–). American character actor.
The Stepford Wives 75. Too Far To Go (TV) 78. Hide in Plain Sight 80. Still of the Night 82. Sophie's Choice 82. Hanky Panky 82. Witness 84.

Sondergaard, Gale (1899–1985) (Edith Sondergaard). Tall, dark American character actress with a sinister smile; career harmed by the anti-communist witch hunt of the early fifties.
□*Anthony Adverse* (AA) 36. Maid of Salem 37. Seventh Heaven 37. The Life of Emile Zola 37. Lord Jeff 38. Dramatic School 38. Never Say Die 38. Juarez 38. *The Cat and the Canary* 39. The Llano Kid 40. *The Bluebird* 40. The Mark of Zorro 40. The Letter 40. The Black Cat 41. Paris Calling 41. My Favourite Blonde 42. Enemy Agent Meets Ellery Queen 42. A Night to Remember 43. Appointment in Berlin 43. Isle of Forgotten Sins 43. The Strange Death of Adolf Hitler 43. *Spider Woman* 44. Follow the Boys 44. Christmas Holiday 44. The Invisible Man's Revenge 44. Gypsy Wildcat 44. The Climax 44. Enter Arsène Lupin 44. Spider Woman Strikes Back 46. A Night in Paradise 46. Anna and the King of Siam 46. The Time of Their Lives 46. *Road to Rio* 47. Pirates of Monterey 47. East Side West Side 49. Slaves 69. The Cat Creature (TV) 74. The Return of A Man Called Horse 76. Pleasantville 76. Echoes 83.

Sondheim, Stephen (1930–). Celebrated American composer and lyricist, usually over the heads of the hoi polloi. His work has penetrated into such films as *Gypsy* (lyrics), *A Funny Thing Happened on the Way to the Forum, West Side Story* (lyrics) and *A Little Night Music*. His film scores include *Stavisky* and *Reds*, and he co-authored *The Last of Sheila*.

The Song of Bernadette (US 1943). An enormous box office success in the middle of World War II, this calculated piece of Hollywood religion turned Franz Werfel's book into sentimental hokum. The miracles of Lourdes have since been more movingly and convincingly treated; Henry King's direction was lethargic; and attempts at acting were smothered by syrupy music and phoney sets. Jennifer Jones' debut as Bernadette was highly successful, but Linda Darnell as the Virgin Mary took some swallowing. The film began a cycle of religious epics, including *Going My Way, The Bells of St Mary's, The Miracle of the Bells*, etc. (See *religion*.)

Song of Ceylon (GB 1934). A documentary written, photographed and directed by Basil Wright for the Ceylon Tea Marketing Board, who must have been very surprised when they saw what they had got: a leisurely 40-minute poetic impression of the island without any direct propaganda. As an 'art house' picture it remains fascinating. Produced by John Grierson, with music by Walter Leigh.

song titles

? A film about a songwriter usually takes as its title one of his most popular songs. Here are some titles: can you identify the composers?

1 *Till the Clouds Roll By*
2 *Night and Day*
3 *Swanee River*
4 *I'll See You in My Dreams*
5 *My Wild Irish Rose*
6 *My Gal Sal*
7 *Yankee Doodle Dandy*
8 *You Will Remember*
9 *Three Little Words*
10 *Deep in my Heart*
11 *I Wonder Who's Kissing Her Now*
12 *The Best Things in Life Are Free*

And here are some song titles associated with performers. Which performers?

13 'Shine on Harvest Moon'
14 'After the Ball'
15 'Champagne Charlie'
16 'Love Me or Leave Me'
17 'Rose of Washington Square'
18 'With a Song in My Heart'
19 'Look for the Silver Lining'
20 'Somebody Loves Me'

Sons and Lovers (GB 1960). A decent and enjoyable film adaptation of D. H. Lawrence's autobiographical novel about growing up in the Nottinghamshire coalfields fifty years ago. Surprisingly produced by Jerry Wald, with Dean Stockwell making a reasonable attempt at the central part and more assured performances coming from Trevor Howard and Wendy Hiller, the film was perhaps most of all enjoyable for the background detail and for Freddie Francis' black-and-white photography. Jack Cardiff directed with care.

Sons of the Desert (Fraternally Yours) (US 1933). The quintessential Laurel and Hardy comedy, in which the boys, hen-pecked as always, devise frantic schemes to get to a weekend convention—and then wish they hadn't. Sociologically, the movie pinpoints its period with total precision.

Soo, Jack (1916-1979) (Goro Suzuki). Japanese character actor in America, best remembered in 1960's *Flower Drum Song* and as one of the gang in TV's *Barney Miller* series.

Sordi, Alberto (1919–). Italian leading man and comic actor.
I Vitelloni 53. The Sign of Venus 55. A Farewell to Arms 57. The Best of Enemies 60. Those Magnificent Men in Their Flying Machines 65. To Bed or Not To Bed 65. Le Streghe 67. Polvere di Stelle 73. Viva Italia 77. Le Temoin 78, many others.

Sorel, Jean (1934–) (Jean de Rochbrune). French-Canadian leading man.
The Four Days of Naples 62. A View from the Bridge 62. Vaghe Stella dell'Orsa 65. Le Bambole 66. Belle de Jour 67, etc.

Sorel, Louise (1944–). French leading lady of occasional films.
The Party's Over 65. B.S. I Love You 70. Plaza Suite 71.

Sorrell and Son. H. B. Warner played Sorrell in both British versions of Warwick Deeping's family novel; in 1927 the son was Nils Asther and the director Herbert Brenon, while in 1933 Hugh Williams replaced Asther and Jack Raymond directed.

Sorvino, Paul (1939–). Chubby American comedy actor.
Where's Poppa 70. Cry Uncle 72. A Touch of Class 72. The Gambler 74. The Day of the Dolphin 75. I Will, I Will . . . For Now 76. Oh God 77. Slow Dancing in the Big City 78. The Brink's Job 78. Bloodbrothers 78. Lost and Found 80. Cruising 80. Reds 81. Turk 182 85, etc.
TV series: Bert D'Angelo 76.

Sothern, Ann (1909–) (Harriette Lake). Pert American comedienne and leading lady with stage experience.
Let's Fall in Love (debut) 34. Kid Millions 35. Trade Winds 38. Hotel for Women 39. *Maisie* 39. Brother Orchid 40. Congo Maisie 40. Gold Rush Maisie 41 (and seven others in series before 1947). Lady Be Good 41. Panama Hattie 42. Cry Havoc 43. The Judge Steps Out 47. *A Letter to Three Wives* 49. Nancy Goes to Rio 50. Lady in a Cage 63. The Best Man 64. Sylvia 65. Chubasco 67. The Great Man's Whiskers (TV) 71. Golden Needles 74. Crazy Mama 75. Captains and the Kings (TV) 76. The Manitou 78. The Whales of August 87, etc.
TV series: *Private Secretary* 52–53. The Ann Sothern Show 58–61.

Soul, David (1943–) (David Solberg). American leading man who made a killing in TV but never found the right movie; nor was singing a wise choice as a second career.
Johnny Got His Gun 71. Magnum Force 73. Dogpound Shuffle 74. The Stick Up 77. Little Ladies of the Night (TV) 77. Salem's Lot (TV) 79. Swan Song (TV) 79. Rage (TV) 80. The Hanoi Hilton 87, etc.
TV series: *Starsky and Hutch* 75–80. The Yellow Rose 83.

sound. The first really successful experiments with synchronized sound had the track on gramophone discs; cylinders were also employed. These systems obviously led to maddening breakdowns, and editing was next to impossible. Fox, using the De Forrest Phonofilm system combined with a German process called Tri-Ergon, contrived in 1926 to record sound directly on to film next to the picture, forming the first sound track. It was this system which by 1930 had superseded the others and is still with us.

The Sound of Music (AA) (US 1965). The huge commercial success of this sentimental Rodgers and Hammerstein musical with its simple story, happy ending and sumptuous Austrian locations seemed to mark a genuine public desire for less sophisticated fare than the sixties had been giving; but producers have been either unwilling or unable to satisfy it. It won Academy Awards for Robert Wise's direction, William Reynolds' editing, Jane Corcoran's sound recording, Irwin Kostal's scoring, and Ted McCord's photography. Julie Andrews played the spunky heroine.
In 1956 and 1958 two non-musical German films were made of the original story: *The Trapp Family* and *The Trapp Family in America* starred Ruth Leuwerik and Hans Holt.

Sous les Toits de Paris (France 1930). This early sound film, a light romantic drama of the Paris garrets, has a well-remembered title and established the fame of writer-director René Clair, but it now seems rather heavier than his usual style, with his accustomed humour breaking through only occasionally. Albert Préjean and Pola Illery had the leading roles.

Sousa, John Philip (1854–1932). American composer, most notably of rousing marches. His 1928 biography, *Marching Along*, was filmed in 1953 as *Stars and Stripes Forever.*

Southern, Terry (1924–). American satirist and black comedy writer.
Hollywood work includes *Candy*, *Dr Strangelove*, *Easy Rider*, *The Loved One*, *Barbarella* and *The Magic Christian*.

The Southerner (US 1945). Jean Renoir's most successful American film, comparable to *The Grapes of Wrath* in its feeling for a poor Texas family scratching a living from cotton-growing. Zachary Scott and Betty Field are man and wife, with Beulah Bondi magnificent as the cantankerous granny and J. Carrol Naish as a suspicious neighbour.
Photographed by Lucien Andriot, with music by Werner Janssen; from a novel, *Hold Autumn in Your Hand*, by George Sessions Perry.

Spaak, Catherine (1945–). Belgian leading lady, daughter of Charles Spaak.
Le Trou 60. The Empty Canvas 64. Weekend at Dunkirk 65. Hotel 67. Libertine 68. Cat O' Nine Tails 71. Take a Hard Ride 75, etc.

Spaak, Charles (1903–1975). Belgian screenwriter associated with many French films.
La Kermesse Héroïque 35. Les Bas-Fonds 36. *La Grande Illusion* 37. *La Fin du Jour* 39. Panique 46. Justice est Faite (co-w) 50. Thérèse Raquin 53. Crime and Punishment 56. Charmants Garçons 57. The Vanishing Corporal 61. Cartouche 62, etc.

Space, Arthur (1908–1983). American character actor, in many film roles and such TV series as *National Velvet* and *Lassie*.
Tortilla Flat 42. Wilson 44. Leave Her to Heaven 45. The Barefoot Mailman 52. Spirit of St Louis 57. The Shakiest Gun in the West 68. On the Nickel 80, etc.

space exploration on screen began in 1899 with Méliès; in the twenties Fritz Lang made *The Woman in the Moon* and in the thirties there was *Buck Rogers in the Twenty-Fifth Century*, but not until 1950 did the subject seem acceptable as anything but fantasy. In that year an adventure of the comic strip type, *Rocketship XM*, competed for box office attention with George Pal's semi-documentary *Destination Moon*, and suddenly the floodgates were opened. During the years that followed we were offered such titles as *Riders to the Stars, Fire Maidens from Outer Space, Satellite in the Sky, From the Earth to the Moon, Conquest of Space, Forbidden Planet, It!, The Terror from Beyond Space, Robinson Crusoe on Mars, The First Men in the Moon, 2001: A Space Odyssey, Saturn Three, Outland* and the *Star Wars* saga. Nor was the traffic all one way: Earth had many strange visitors from other planets, notably in *The Thing From Another World, The Day the Earth Stood Still, Devil Girl from Mars, Stranger from Venus, It Came from Outer Space, Invasion of the Body Snatchers* (the best and subtlest of them all), *The War of the Worlds, The Quatermass Experiment, Quatermass II, Visit to a Small Planet, This Island Earth*, and *The Man Who Fell to Earth*. On television, the most imaginative exploits have been in *Star Trek*, *Space 1999*, *Buck Rogers* and *Galactica*.

Spacek, Sissy (1950–). Tomboyish American leading lady of the seventies.
Prime Cut 71. Ginger in the Morning 72. *Badlands* 73. Katherine (TV) 75. Carrie 76. Three Women 77. Welcome to L.A. 77. Hearthbeat 79. *Coal Miner's Daughter* (AA) 80. Raggedy Man 81. Missing 82. Country 84. The River (AAN) 84. Marie 85. Violets are

Blue 85. 'Night, Mother 86. Crimes of the Heart 86.

spaghetti westerns: a dismissive name for the blood-spattered Italian imitations of American westerns which became popular in the sixties, using such actors as Lee Van Cleef and Clint Eastwood.

Spain produced few distinguished films before the Civil War, Buñuel having settled in France, and afterwards the product was dictated by politics apart from a few pleasing comedies and melodrama by such directors as Berlanga and Bardem. Buñuel made a few visits in the sixties.

The Spanish Civil War featured in a few Hemingway picturizations, notably *For Whom the Bell Tolls* and *The Snows of Kilimanjaro*; in *The Fallen Sparrow, Blockade, The Angel Wore Red, Love Under Fire, Last Train from Madrid, Arise My Love, Confidential Agent* and (remotely) *The Prime of Miss Jean Brodie*. In more documentary style were *L'Espoir, Spanish Earth, Guernica* and *To Die in Madrid*; while British television has produced two extended assemblies of newsreel footage.

Spano, Vincent (1962–). American lead of the mid-eighties.

Spark, Muriel (1918–). British novelist feted by the intelligentsia. Two films of her work, *The Prime of Miss Jean Brodie* and *The Driver's Seat*, have both been unsatisfactory.

Sparks, Ned (1883–1957) (Edward Sparkman). Hard-boiled, cigar-chewing Canadian comic actor often seen in Hollywood films of the thirties as grouchy reporter or agent.
The Big Noise 27. The Miracle Man 30. Forty-Second Street 33. Two's Company (GB) 37. The Star Maker 39. For Beauty's Sake 40. Magic Town 46, etc.

Sparkuhl, Theodor (1894–1945). German cinematographer in Hollywood from the early thirties.
Carmen 18. Manon Lescaut 26. La Chienne 31. Too Much Harmony 33. Enter Madame 35. *Beau Geste* 39. *The Glass Key* 42. Star Spangled Rhythm 43. Blood on the Sun 46. Bachelor Girls 46, many others.

Sparv, Camilla (1943–). Swedish-born leading lady in Hollywood films.
The Trouble with Angels 66. Murderers' Row 66. Dead Heat on a Merry-go-Round 66. Department K 67. Mackenna's Gold 68. Downhill Racer 69. The Italian Job 69, etc.

special effects: a general term covering the many tricks of film-making which cannot be achieved by direct photography: optical wipes, dissolves, sub-titles, invisibility, mattes, etc.

speeches of any length are the antithesis of good film-making, but sometimes a long monologue has been not only an actor's dream but absolutely right, memorable and hypnotic in its context. The record (twenty minutes) is probably held by Edwige Feuillère in *The Eagle Has Two Heads*, but more effective, and somewhat shorter, were Sam Jaffe in *Lost Horizon*, Alec Guinness in *The Mudlark*, Orson Welles in *Compulsion*, Spencer Tracy in *Inherit the Wind*, Anne Baxter in *The Walls of Jericho*, James Stewart in *Mr Smith Goes to Washington*, Paul Muni in *The Life of Emile Zola*, Don Murray in *One Man's Way*, Orson Welles in *Moby Dick*, and Charles Chaplin in *The Great Dictator*.

Spellbound. There are two films of this title. In 1940 John Harlow made a low-budget British attempt to explore spiritualism, with Derek Farr as a distraught young man attempting to get in touch with his dead sweetheart. The years have been unkind to this naïve little movie, but it broke fresh ground at the time. In 1945 Alfred Hitchcock in Hollywood used the title for his glossy adaptation of Francis Beeding's *The House of Dr Edwardes*, with Ingrid Bergman and Gregory Peck, in loving close-up, discovering whether or not Peck, a psychiatrist, is in fact a murderous amnesiac. Full of tricks, but satisfying, the movie had a memorable dream sequence designed by Salvador Dali.

Spencer, Bud (1929–) (Carlo Pedersoli). Italian character actor in many spaghetti westerns.
Blood River 67. Beyond the Law 68. Boot Hill 69. They Call Me Trinity 70. Four Flies on Grey Velvet 71. Watch Out We're Mad 74, etc.

Spencer, Dorothy (1909–). American editor.
The Moon's Our Home 36. Blockade 38. *Stagecoach* 39. *Foreign Correspondent* 40. To Be or Not To Be 42. Heaven Can Wait 43. Lifeboat 43. My Darling Clementine 46. The Snake Pit 48. Three Came Home 50. Fourteen Hours 51. Black Widow 54. The

Man in the Grey Flannel Suit 56. The Young Lions 58. North to Alaska 60. Cleopatra 63. Von Ryan's Express 65. Valley of the Dolls 67. Limbo 71. *Earthquake* 74, many others.

Spencer, Kenneth (1912–64). Black American singer who appeared in a few forties films including *Cabin in the Sky* and *Bataan*, both 43.

Spenser, Jeremy (1937–). British leading man, former child actor, also on stage.
Portrait of Clare 48. *Prelude to Fame* 50. Appointment with Venus 51. Summer Madness 55. The Prince and the Showgirl 57. Wonderful Things 58. Ferry to Hong Kong 58. *The Roman Spring of Mrs Stone* 61. King and Country 64. He Who Rides a Tiger 65. Fahrenheit 451 66, etc.

Sperling, Milton (1912–). American producer.
Cloak and Dagger 46. Three Secrets 50. The Enforcer 51. Blowing Wild 54. The Court Martial of Billy Mitchell (& co-w) 55. The Bramble Bush (& co-w) 59. The Battle of the Bulge 65. Captain Apache (wp) 71, etc.

Spewack, Sam (1899–1971). American playwright who with his wife Bella turned out several scripts for Hollywood.
The Secret Witness 31. Rendezvous 35. *Boy Meets Girl* 38. Three Loves has Nancy 38. My Favorite Wife 40. Weekend at the Waldorf 45. Kiss Me Kate 53. Move Over Darling 63, etc.

Spiegel, Sam (1901–85). Polish-born producer, in Hollywood from 1941. Also known as S. P. Eagle.
Tales of Manhattan 42. *The Stranger* 45. *We Were Strangers* 48. *The African Queen* 51. *On the Waterfront* 54. The Strange One 57. *The Bridge on the River Kwai* 57. *Lawrence of Arabia* 62. The Chase 66. *The Night of the Generals* 66. The Happening 67. The Swimmer 68. Nicholas and Alexandra 71. The Last Tycoon 76. Betrayal 82, etc.

Spielberg, David (–). American character actor.
The Effect of Gamma Rays 72. Newman's Law 74. Hustle 75. The Choirboys 77. The End 78. Stone (TV) 79, etc.
TV series: Bob and Carol and Ted and Alice 73. The Practice 76.

Spielberg, Steven (1946–). American director whose star was high in the heavens during the late seventies and early eighties, largely because of semi-adult treatment of what would once have been considered comic strip material for children.
□ Amblin' (short) 69. Something Evil (TV) 71. Savage (TV) 72. *Duel* (TV) 72. Sugarland Express 73. *Jaws* 75. 1941 75. Close Encounters of the Third Kind 77. Raiders of the Lost Ark 81. Poltergeist (p only) 82. *E.T.* 82. Twilight Zone (co-d) 83. Indiana Jones and the Temple of Doom 84. Gremlins (p) 85. Back to the Future (p) 85. The Goonies (p) 85. The Color Purple 85. An American Tail (p) 86. Innerspace (p) 87. Empire of the Sun (& p) 87.

¶ *S.S.:* I've never been through psychoanalysis. I solve my problems with the pictures I make.

Rosebud will go over my typewriter to remind me that quality in movies comes first.—*S.S. after buying (for 20 thousand dollars) the sled used in Citizen Kane*

S.S.: Stories don't have a middle and an end any more. They usually have a beginning that never stops beginning.

S.S.: I'd rather direct than produce. Any day. And twice on Sunday.

spies are currently enjoying enormous popularity as the heroes of over-sexed, gimmick-ridden melodramas. Real-life spies have been less frequently depicted, the world of James Bond being much livelier than those of Moyzich (*Five Fingers*), Odette Churchill (*Odette V.C.*), *Nurse Edith Cavell*, Violette Szabo (*Carve Her Name with Pride*), *Mata Hari*, or the gangs in *The House on 92nd Street*, *13 Rue Madeleine*, and *Ring of Spies*.

Fictional spy films first became popular during and after World War I: they added a touch of glamour to an otherwise depressing subject, even though the hero often faced the firing squad in the last reel. Right up to 1939 romantic melodramas on this theme were being made: *I Was a Spy*, *The Man Who Knew Too Much*, *The Thirty-Nine Steps*, *Lancer Spy*, *The Spy in Black*, *Dark Journey*, *British Agent*, *Secret Agent*, *The Lady Vanishes*, *Espionage Agent*, *Confessions of a Nazi Spy*. The last-named brought the subject roughly up to date, and with the renewed outbreak of hostilities new possibilities were hastily seized in *Foreign Correspondent*, *Night Train to Munich*, *Casablanca*, *The Conspirators*, *They Came to Blow Up America*, *Berlin Correspondent*, *Across the Pacific*, *Escape to Danger*, *Ministry of Fear*, *Confidential Agent*, *Sherlock Holmes and the Secret Weapon*, *Hotel Reserve*, and innumerable others. (It was fashionable during this period to reveal that the villains of comedy-thrillers and who-done-its were really enemy agents.) During the post-war years two fashions in film spying became evident: the downbeat melodrama showing spies as frightened men and women doing a dangerous job (*Notorious, Cloak and Dagger, Hotel Berlin, Orders to Kill*) and the 'now it can be told' semi-documentary revelation (*O.S.S., Diplomatic Courier, The Man Who Never Was, The Two-Headed Spy, The Counterfeit Traitor, Operation Crossbow*). In the late forties Nazis and Japs were replaced by reds, and we had a spate of melodramas under such titles as *I Married a Communist, I Was a Communist for the FBI, I Was an American Spy, Red Snow* and *The Red Danube*.

There had always been spy comedies. Every comedian made one or two: the Crazy Gang in *Gasbags*, Duggie Wakefield in *Spy for a Day*, Jack Benny in *To Be or Not To Be*, Bob Hope in *They Got Me Covered*, Radford and Wayne in *It's Not Cricket*, George Cole in *Top Secret*, right up to the 'Carry On' Team in *Carry On Spying* and Morecambe and Wise in *The Intelligence Men*. There were also occasional burlesques like *All Through the Night* and sardonic comedies like *Our Man in Havana*. But it was not until the late fifties that the spy reasserted himself as a romantic figure who could be taken lightly; and not until 1962 was the right box-office combination of sex and suspense found in *Dr No*. Since then we have been deluged with pale imitations of James Bond to such an extent that almost every leading man worth his salt has had a go. Cary Grant in *Charade*, David Niven in *Where the Spies Are*, Rod Taylor and Trevor Howard in *The Liquidator*, Dirk Bogarde in *Hot Enough for June*, Michael Caine in *The Ipcress File*, Paul Newman in *Torn Curtain*, James Coburn in *Our Man Flint*, Gregory Peck in *Arabesque*, Yul Brynner in *The Double Man*, George Peppard in *The Executioner*, Stephen Boyd in *Assignment K*, Frank Sinatra in *The Naked Runner*, Anthony Hopkins in *When Eight Bells Toll*, Kirk Douglas in *Catch Me a Spy*, Tom Adams in *Licensed to Kill*. There have also been elaborations such as the extreme sophistication of *The Manchurian Candidate*, the cold realism of *The Spy Who Came in from the Cold*, the op-art spoofing of *Modesty Blaise*, even the canine agent of *The Spy with a Cold Nose* and spies from outer space in *This Island Earth*. And the TV screens of 1970 were filled with such tricky heroes as those in *Danger Man* (Secret Agent), *The Man from U.N.C.L.E., Amos Burke Secret Agent, The Baron, I Spy* and *The Avengers*. The trend of the seventies was towards sour and disenchanted looks at the whole business, such as *Callan, The Killer Elite, Permission to Kill* and *Three Days of the Condor*.

Spillane, Mickey (1918–) (Frank Morrison). Bestselling American crime novelist of the love-'em and kill-'em variety.
I the Jury 53. The Long Wait 54. Kiss Me Deadly 55. *I The Jury* was remade in 1981, with Armand Assante.
AS ACTOR: Ring of Fear 54. The Girl Hunters (as Mike Hammer) (& w) 64.
Darren McGavin played Hammer in a 1960 TV series, as did Stacy Keach in 1983.

Spinetti, Victor (1932–). Italo-Welsh comic actor with stage experience.
A Hard Day's Night 64. The Wild Affair 64. Help! 65. The Taming of the Shrew 66. Hieronymus Merkin 69. The Return of the Pink Panther 76. Voyage of the Damned 76, etc.

The Spiral Staircase (US 1945). Basically a superior 'thunderstorm mystery', this admirably cinematic extension of a suspense novel by Ethel Lina White was notable for Robert Siodmak's direction, Nicholas Musuraca's photography, and the performance of Dorothy McGuire as a mute servant girl terrorized by a maniac in a lonely house. The 1975 remake by Peter Collinson is best forgotten.

The Spoilers. Rex Beach's action novel has been filmed five times, with interest centring on its climactic fight scene between the two male leads, who were as follows. 1914: William Farnum and Tom Santschi. 1922: Milton Sills and Noah Beery. 1930: William Boyd and Gary Cooper. 1942: John Wayne and Randolph Scott. 1956: Jeff Chandler and Rory Calhoun.

Spoliansky, Mischa (1898–1985). Russian composer, in Germany from 1930, Britain from 1934.
Don Juan 34, *Sanders of the River* 35. The Ghost Goes West 36. *King Solomon's Mines* 37. Jeannie 42. Don't Take It To Heart 44. Mr Emmanuel 44. Wanted for Murder 46. *The Happiest Days of Your Life* 50. Trouble in Store 53. Saint Joan 57. Northwest Frontier 59. The Battle of the Villa Fiorita 65. Hitler: The Last Ten Days 73, many others.

sportsmen who have been the subject of biopics include Babe Ruth (William Bendix) in *The Babe Ruth Story*; Grover Cleveland Alexander (Ronald Reagan) in *The Winning Team*; Lou Gehrig (Gary Cooper) in *The Pride of the Yankees*; Monty Stratton (James Stewart) in *The Stratton Story*; Jim Piersall (Anthony Perkins) in *Fear Strikes Out*; Jim Corbett (Errol Flynn) in *Gentleman Jim*; John L. Sullivan (Greg McClure) in *The Great John L.*; Knute Rockne (Pat O'Brien) in *Knute Rockne All-American*; Jim Thorpe (Burt Lancaster) in *Jim Thorpe All-American* (*Man of Bronze*); Ben Hogan (Glenn Ford) in *Follow the Sun*; Annette Kellerman (Esther Williams) in *Million Dollar Mermaid.*

Spring, Howard (1889–1965). British novelist. Works filmed include *Fame is the Spur* and *My Son My Son.*

Spring in Park Lane (GB 1947). An unexpectedly successful light comedy with music, this agreeable but witless affair about a footman who—of course—is really an earl in disguise was dated even when released, but coasted to fame on a blithe teaming of talents. Anna Neagle and Michael Wilding were a popular romantic team, Tom Walls and Nigel Patrick furnished light relief, and the palatial settings were lapped up by the British public after six years of total war. It was directed by Herbert Wilcox from a script by Nicholas Phipps. In the following year the same team attempted a sequel, *Maytime in Mayfair*, but this time the soufflé fell flat.

Springsteen, R. G. (1904–). American director who has been making efficient low-budget westerns since 1930.
Honeychile 48. Hellfire 49. The Enemy Within 49. The Toughest Man in Arizona 53. Track the Man Down 53. Come Next Spring 56. Cole Younger, Gunfighter 58. Battle Flame 59. Black Spurs 64. Taggart 65. Waco 66. Johnny Reno 66. Red Tomahawk 66, many others.

The Spy Who Came in from the Cold (GB 1965). A deliberately dour and chilling look at the spy game, made as a corrective to the James Bond cult. John le Carré's tale provided a splendid series of doublecrosses, and Richard Burton and Oskar Werner extracted plenty of feeling from skeletal parts, but Ossie Morris' photography was perhaps a little too grainy and harsh to be fair. Martin Ritt directed.

The Squaw Man (US 1913). A western generally considered as a milestone in Hollywood's history, being the first major film to be produced there. An enormous success, it starred Dustin Farnum (who later regretted his refusal to take a percentage of the profits instead of salary) and was directed by Cecil B. de Mille for Jesse L. Lasky. A remake starring Jack Holt was made in 1918, and a talkie version starring Warner Baxter appeared in 1931.

Squibs. The cockney flower-seller heroine of George Pearson's silent comedy put in her first successful appearance in 1921. Public acclaim produced three sequels: *Squibs Wins the Calcutta Sweep* 22, *Squibs MP* 23, *Squibs' Honeymoon* 23. Pearson then grew tired of the tomboyish character and cast Betty Balfour in other roles, but she reappeared in a not-too-successful talkie version in 1936, with Gordon Harker and Stanley Holloway.

Squire, Ronald (1886–1958) (Ronald Squirl). Jovial British character actor of stage (from 1909) and screen (from 1934).
Don't Take It to Heart 44. While the Sun Shines 46. Woman Hater 48. The Rocking-Horse Winner 50. Encore 52. My Cousin Rachel (US) 53. The Million Pound Note 54. Now and Forever 55. Count Your Blessings 58, etc.

Stack, Robert (1919–) (Robert Modini). Personable, cold-eyed American leading man of the fifties, later successful in television.
□First Love 39. The Mortal Storm 40. A Little Bit of Heaven 40. *Nice Girl* (in which he gave Deanna Durbin her first screen kiss) 41. Badlands of Dakota 41. To Be or Not To Be 42. Eagle Squadron 42. Men of Texas 42. A Date with Judy 48. Miss Tatlock's Millions 48. Fighter Squadron 48. Mr Music 50. My Outlaw Brother 51. The Bullfighter and the Lady 52. Bwana Devil 53. War Paint 53. Conquest of Cochise 53. Sabre Jet 53. The High and the Mighty 54. The Iron Glove 54. House of Bamboo 55. Good Morning Miss Dove 55. Great Day in the Morning 56. *Written on the Wind* 56. *The Tarnished Angels* 57. The Gift of Love 58. *John Paul Jones* 59. The Last Voyage 60. The Caretakers 63. Is Paris Burning? 66. The Corrupt Ones 67. Le Soleil des Voyous 68. The Story of a Woman 70. The Action Man 70. The Strange and Deadly Occurrence (TV) 75. 1941 75. Adventures of the Queen (TV) 76. Murder on Flight 502 (TV) 76. Airplane 80. Uncommon Valour 83. Big Trouble 84.
TV series: *The Untouchables* 59–62. *The Name of the Game* 68–70. Most Wanted 76. Strike Force 81.

Stafford, Frederick (1928–1979). Austrian leading man who after many he-man roles in European movies imitating James Bond was signed by Alfred Hitchcock to play the lead in *Topaz* 69.

Stagecoach (US 1939). A classic western which cleverly utilizes not only the usual ingredients but the never-failing trick of putting a miscellaneous group of people together in a dangerous situation. (Ernest Haycox's original story 'Stage to Lordsburg' clearly patterned itself after Maupassant's 'Boule de Suif'.) Directed by John Ford from Dudley Nichols' screenplay, with John Wayne, Claire Trevor, Thomas Mitchell, Donald Meek, etc. Remade in 1966 to little effect.

Stahl, John M. (1886–1950). American director, former stage actor; in films from 1914.
Wives of Men 18. Husbands and Lovers 23. The Child Thou Gavest Me 24. The Naughty Duchess 28. Seed 31. *Back Street* 32. *Imitation of Life* 34. *Magnificent Obsession* 35. Parnell 37. Letter of Introduction 38. *When Tomorrow Comes* 39. Our Wife 41. *Holy Matrimony* 43. The Immortal Sergeant 43. The Eve of St Mark 44. *The Keys of the Kingdom* 44. Leave Her to Heaven 45. The Foxes of Harrow 47. The Walls of Jericho 47. Oh You Beautiful Doll 49, many others.

Stainton, Philip (1908–1961). Rotund British actor with surprised expression; often played policemen.
Scott of the Antarctic 47. Passport to Pimlico 48. The Quiet Man 52. Angels One Five 52. Hobson's Choice 54. The Woman for Joe 56, many others.

staircases have provided dramatic backgrounds for many films. Martin Balsam was murdered on one in *Psycho*; the climax of *The Spiral Staircase* took place just there; Vivien Leigh was carried up one by a lustful Clark Gable in *Gone with the Wind*; Jerry Lewis danced down one in *Cinderfella*; Errol Flynn and Basil Rathbone duelled on one in *The Adventures of Robin Hood*; Ann Todd rode a horse up one in *South Riding*; Joan Fontaine in *Rebecca* descended one in delight and ascended it in tears; Raymond Massey ascended a particularly shadowy one in *The Old Dark House*, and later a very sinister character came down it; the entire cast of *Ship of Fools* came down one at the end, like a musical finale; a severed head bumped down one in *Hush Hush Sweet Charlotte*; Gene Tierney threw herself down one in *Leave Her to Heaven*; an old lady was tossed down one in a wheelchair in *Kiss of Death*; Bela Lugosi in *Dracula* passed through the cobwebs on one without breaking them; Laurel and Hardy in *Blockheads* had to descend and ascend innumerable flights of stairs in pursuit of a lost ball; Anna Sten was killed on one in *The Wedding Night*; the lighthouse staircase was a dramatic feature of *Thunder Rock*; James Cagney danced down the White House staircase in *Yankee Doodle Dandy*; and the main feature of *A Matter of Life and Death* was a moving stairway to heaven. In his last film, *Greystoke*, Ralph Richardson slid down a staircase on a tea tray. Universal and Paramount both had very striking and oft-used staircase sets in the forties; the latter was most dramatically used for Kirk Douglas' death in *The Strange Love of Martha Ivers*. Oddly enough in the film called *Staircase* the staircase was not an essential feature.

Stallings, Laurence (1894–1968). American screenwriter.
The Big Parade 25. *What Price Glory?* (co-w) 26. So Red the Rose (co-w) 35. Northwest Passage (co-w) 39. Jungle Book 42. Salome Where She Danced 45. *She Wore a Yellow Ribbon* (co-w) 49. The Sun Shines Bright 52, etc.

Stallone, Sylvester (1946–). Solemn-looking American star who shot to the top in a modest film which he wrote himself.
□A Party at Kitty and Stud's (The Italian Stallion) 70. Bananas 71. The Lords of Flatbush 73. Capone 73. The Prisoner of Second Avenue 75. Death Race 2000 75. Farewell My Lovely 75. Carquake 75. *Rocky* 76. F.I.S.T. (& w) 78. Paradise Alley (& w, d) 78. Rocky II (& w, d) 79. Nighthawks 81. Victory 81. Rocky III 82. First Blood 82. Staying Alive (co-w, co-p, d) 83.
Rhinestone 84. Rambo 85. Rocky IV (& d) 85. Cobra 85. Over the Top 87.

¶ *S.S.:* I'll just go on playing Rambo and Rocky. Both are money-making machines that can't be switched off.

S.S.: I'm not handsome in the classical sense. The eyes droop, the mouth is crooked, the teeth aren't straight, the voice sounds like a Mafioso pallbearer, but somehow it all works.

S.S.: I'd say between 3 p.m. and 8 p.m. I look great. After that it's all downhill. Don't photograph me in the morning or you're gonna get Walter Brennan.

S.S.: I'm not a genetically superior person. I built my body.

S.S.: I'm a very physical person. People don't credit me with much of a brain, so why should I disillusion them?

S.S.: I really am a manifestation of my own fantasy.

S.S.: Once in a man's life, for one mortal moment, he must make a grab for immortality. If not, he has not lived.

Stamp, Terence (1940–). British juvenile lead of the sixties.
Billy Budd 62. Term of Trial 62. The Collector 65. Modesty Blaise 66. Far from the Madding Crowd 67. Poor Cow 67. Blue 68. Theorem (It.) 68. The Mind of Mr Soames 69. Superman 78. Meetings with Remarkable Men 78. The Thief of Bagdad 79. Superman II 81. The Hit 84. Company of Wolves 85. Link 86.

Stamp-Taylor, Enid (1904–1946). British character actress with stage experience.
Feather Your Nest 37. Action for Slander 37. The Lambeth Walk 38. Hatter's Castle 41. The Wicked Lady 45. Caravan 46, etc.

Stander, Lionel (1908–). Gravel-voiced American character actor, on stage and screen from the early thirties. His career was harmed by the communist witch-hunts of the late forties.
The Scoundrel 34. Mr Deeds Goes to Town 36. *A Star is Born* 37. Guadalcanal Diary 42. The Spectre of the Rose 46. Unfaithfully Yours 48. St Benny the Dip 51. *Cul de Sac* (GB) 66. Promise Her Anything (GB) 66. A Dandy in Aspic (GB) 68. The Gang that Couldn't Shoot Straight 72. The Con Men 73. The Black Bird 75. New York New York 77. The Cassandra Crossing 77. Matilda 78, etc.
TV series: Hart to Hart 79.

Standing, Sir Guy (1873–1937). British stage actor, father of Kay Hammond, in some Hollywood films.
□The Story of Temple Drake 33. Midnight Club 33. Hell and High Water 33. The Cradle Song 33. A Bedtime Story 33. The Eagle and the Hawk 33. Death Takes a Holiday 34. Now and Forever 34. The Witching Hour 34. Double Door 34. *The Lives of a Bengal Lancer* 35. Car 99 35. Annapolis Farewell 35. The Big Broadcast of 1936 35. The Return of Sophie Lang 36. Palm Springs 36. I'd Give My Life 36. Lloyds of London 36. Bulldog Drummond Escapes 37.

Standing, John (1934–) (Sir John Leon). British character actor, son of Kay Hammond.
The Wild and the Willing 62. A Pair of Briefs 63. King Rat 65. Walk Don't Run 66. The Psychopath 66. Torture Garden 67. Zee and Co. 71. Rogue Male (TV) 76. The Eagle Has Landed 77. The Elephant Man 80. The Sea Wolves 80, etc.
TV series: Lime Street 86.

Stanley, Kim (1921–) (Patricia Reid). American stage actress.
□The Goddess 58. Seance on a Wet Afternoon 64. Three Sisters 67. Frances 82. The Right Stuff 83.

Stannard, Don (1916–49). British light leading man who played Dick Barton in three serial-like melodramas 1948–49.

Stanton, Harry Dean (1926–). American character actor.
Dragoon Wells Massacre 57. How the West Was Won 62. Cool Hand Luke 67. Cisco Pike 72. Dillinger 73. Cockfighter 74. Farewell My Lovely 75. The Missouri Breaks 76. Alien 79. The Rose 79. Wise Blood 80. The Black Marble 80. Private Benjamin 80. One from the Heart 82. Christine 83. Repo Man 84. Paris Texas 84. Pretty in Pink 86. Fool for Love 86, etc.

Stanwyck, Barbara (1907–) (Ruby Stevens). Durable American star actress, a sultry lady usually playing roles in which she is just as good as a man, if not better.
□Broadway Nights 27. The Locked Door 29. Mexicali Rose 29. Ladies of Leisure 30. Ten Cents a Dance 31. Illicit 31. *Miracle Woman* 31. *Night Nurse* 31. Forbidden 32. Shopworn 32. *So Big* 32. The Purchase Price 32. *The Bitter Tea of General Yen* 33. Ladies They Talk About 33. *Baby Face* 33. Ever in My Heart 33. A Lost Lady 34. Gambling Lady 34. The Secret Bride 35. The Woman in Red 35. Red Salute 35. *Annie Oakley* 35. A Message to Garcia 36. The Bride Walks Out 36. His Brother's Wife 36. Banjo on My Knee 36. The Plough and the Stars 36. Internes Can't Take Money 37. This is My Affair 37. *Stella Dallas* 37. Breakfast for Two 38. The Mad Miss Manton 38. Always Goodbye 38. Union Pacific 39. Golden Boy 39. Remember the Night 40. *The Lady Eve* 41. *Meet John Doe* 41. You Belong to Me 41. *Ball of Fire* 41. The Great Man's Lady 42. The Gay Sisters 42. Lady of Burlesque 42. Flesh and Fantasy 43. *Double Indemnity* 44. Hollywood Canteen 44. Christmas in Connecticut 45. My

Reputation 45. The Bride Wore Boots 46. *The Strange Love of Martha Ivers* 46. California 46. The Other Love 47. The Two Mrs Carrolls 47. Cry Wolf 47. BF's Daughter 48. *Sorry Wrong Number* 48. The Lady Gambles 49. East Side West Side 49. Thelma Jordon 50. No Man of Her Own 50. *The Furies* 50. To Please a Lady 50. Man with a Cloak 51. Clash by Night 52. Jeopardy 53. Titanic 53. All I Desire 53. The Moonlighter 53. Blowing Wild 53. *Executive Suite* 54. Witness to Murder 54. Cattle Queen of Montana 54. The Violent Men 55. Escape to Burma 55. There's Always Tomorrow 56. The Maverick Queen 56. These Wilder Years 56. Crime of Passion 57. Trooper Hook 57. Forty Guns 57. Walk on the Wild Side 62. Roustabout 64. The Night Walker 65. The House That Would Not Die (TV) 70. A Taste of Evil (TV) 71. The Letters (TV) 73. The Thorn Birds (TV) 83.
TV series: *The Big Valley* 65–68.

❀ For holding more than her own in comedy or melodrama, and being a match for any man. *The Lady Eve*.

¶ I want to go on until they have to shoot me.—*B.S.*

Put me in the last fifteen minutes of a picture and I don't care what happened before. I don't even care if I was IN the rest of the damned thing—I'll take it in those fifteen minutes.—*B.S.*

Attention embarrasses me. I don't like to be on display.—*B.S.*

Career is too pompous a word. It was a job, and I have always felt privileged to be paid for doing what I love doing.—*B.S.*

† Honorary AA 1981 'for superlative creativity and a unique contribution to the art of screen acting.'

Stapleton, Jean (1923–) (Jeanne Murray). American actress familiar from TV's *All in the Family*.
Damn Yankees 58. Bells are Ringing 60. Something Wild 61. Up the Down Staircase 67. Cold Turkey 70. Klute 71, etc.

Stapleton, Maureen (1925–). American character actress.
Lonelyhearts 59. The Fugitive Kind 60. A View from the Bridge 62. Bye Bye Birdie 63. Airport 69. Plaza Suite 70. Tell Me Where It Hurts 74. *Queen of the Stardust Ballroom* 75. The Gathering (TV) 77. Lost and Found 80. Reds (AA, BFA) 81. Johnny Dangerously 84. Cocoon 85. The Cosmic Eye 85. The Money Pit 85. Heartburn 86. Sweet Lorraine 87. Made in Heaven 87.

Stapley, Richard: see *Wyler, Richard*.

star is a word coined by some forgotten publicist in the early years of the century who presumably touted his leading actors as twinkling heavenly lights. It came in the thirties to mean any actor who was billed above the title; but nowadays real stars are hard to find, and the word is generally applied only to those thought likely actually to draw patrons to the box office.

¶ Stars may shine so brightly that they dazzle, but the glory of the movie variety is transient. Marie Dressler put it succinctly:

> You're only as good as your last picture.

Myron Selznick expressed the same thought:

> Stars should get as much money as they can, while they can. They don't last long.

On the other hand Bette Davis, taking it easy in the seventies, was able to rely on her past:

> My price for putting my name on that marquee is two hundred thousand dollars and ten per cent of the gross and I won't even talk to anybody for less because when they see me on a screen they're seeing thirty-seven years of sweat.

It didn't work quite as well for Stewart Granger:

> I haven't aged into a character actor. I'm still an old leading man.

And Shirley Temple was disillusioned early:

> I stopped believing in Santa Claus when I was six. Mother took me to see him in a department store and he asked for my autograph.

Paul Mayersburg thought that:

> The star is Hollywood's gift to the twentieth century. Great actors are not the same as stars. A star must depend on some system of reproduction since to become a star you must be available to a large number of people.

Jerry Wald knew that the real trick was to find smart executives:

> There's no shortage of talent. There's only a shortage of talent that can recognize talent.

Robert Redford was suspicious:

> They throw that word 'star' at you loosely, and they take it away equally loosely. You take the responsibility for their crappy movie, that's what that means.

An anonymous wit classically detailed the five stages in a star's life, as seen by a casting director:

> 1 Who is Hugh O'Brian?
> 2 Get me Hugh O'Brian.
> 3 Get me a Hugh O'Brian type.

4 Get me a young Hugh O'Brian.
5 Who is Hugh O'Brian?

While you're at the top, it can be pleasant. Robert Stack says:

If you're a star you go through the front door carrying the roses, instead of through the back door carrying the garbage.

Gloria Swanson:

I have decided that while I am a star I will be every inch and every moment the star. Everyone from the studio gateman to the highest executive will know it.

Dustin Hoffman:

One thing about being successful is that I stopped being afraid of dying. Once you're a star you're dead already. You're embalmed.

Billie Burke:

By the time you get your name up in lights you have worked so hard and so long, and seen so many names go up and down, that all you can think of is: 'How can I keep it here?'

George Sanders was equally cynical:

The important thing for a star is to have an interesting face. He doesn't have to move it very much. Editing and camerawork can always produce the desired illusion that a performance is being given.

Ethel Barrymore took a different view:

To be a success an actress must have the face of Venus, the brain of Minerva, the grace of Terpsichore, the memory of Macaulay, the figure of Juno and the hide of a rhinoceros.

Katharine Hepburn put it more simply:

Show me an actress who isn't a personality and I'll show you a woman who isn't a star.

Jean Arthur found the going tough:

It's a strenuous job every day of your life to live up to the way you look on the screen.

The temptation to try remains great. Director Michael Winner remarked recently:

Hitchcock said actors are cattle, but show me a cow who can earn one million dollars per film.

But as Harry Cohn said:

After a while the stars believe their own publicity. I've never met a grateful performer in the film business.

Likewise Sam Spiegel:

You make a star, you sometimes make a monster.

So in the fifties the top stars gained control over their own careers, setting up their own independent companies. Jack Warner did not like the result:

In the old days you called the actor and made the deal with him. Now, they bring an army.

At the same time, as Vincent Price noted:

One of the deaths of Hollywood is that they tried to make everyone look normal. Some of the actresses who are around today look and sound like my niece in Scarsdale. I love my niece in Scarsdale, but I wouldn't pay to see her act.

People began to realize that they had been deceived by the apparent effortlessness of the old stars, who had lasted so long and given such good service. When Ronald Colman played a bit part in *Around the World in Eighty Days*, he was asked:

Did you really get a Cadillac for one day's work?—No, he replied—for the work of a lifetime.

In the end, as Sam Goldwyn knew from experience of changing fashions, it is not the actors or the moguls who decide who is a star:

Producers don't make stars. God makes stars, and the public recognizes His handiwork.

And Ellen Terry had the simplest definition of star quality:

That little something extra.

Or as Humphrey Bogart said when asked why he was worth two hundred thousand dollars a picture:

Because I can get it.

Or as Barbra Streisand said:

The real, real reason I like to be in movies is because it's an easy place to have my hems done. There's always a seamstress on the set. And if you break a chair, they can fix it—they have people who can do anything. Chair people, hem people.

Or as Louis Armstrong said:

A lotta cats copy the Mona Lisa, but people still line up to see the original.

Or as David Hemmings said:

I quite like being mobbed. After all it is extremely nice to be recognized. That's what acting is all about—being recognized.

Let Humphrey Bogart have the last word:

You're not a star till they can spell your name in Karachi.

Star! (US 1968). A supremely professional if unconvincing account of the life of Gertrude Lawrence, done in the musical style of the thirties and forties and all the better for it. Meticulously directed by Robert Wise on a mammoth budget, with skilled cinematography by Ernest Laszlo. Julie Andrews shows great stamina but her numbers somehow disappoint; Daniel Massey as Noel Coward steals the show.

A Star is Born. This 1937 screenplay by Dorothy Parker, Alan Campbell and Robert Carson has become a Hollywood legend and in some cases a reality: the marriage of two stars goes on the rocks because one of them is on the way up and the other on the way down. It was then tailored for Janet Gaynor and Fredric March with strong support from Adolphe Menjou and Lionel Stander as Hollywood types; William Wellman directed, Howard Greene was photographer, and Max Steiner wrote the music. In 1954 George Cukor directed Judy Garland and James Mason in the star roles, with Charles Bickford and Jack Carson; it was a long and lumpy film but with moments of magic including a couple of show-stopping musical numbers which seemed to distil the essence of Garland. In 1976 it was revamped for Barbra Streisand. The theme is in fact traceable back to a 1930 film called *What Price Hollywood?*

Star Wars (GB 1977). A rather juvenile but high-spirited space fiction romp, much in the manner of the old Flash Gordon serials except that millions were spent on it. It proved to be one of those films that the public just has to see, though not everyone enjoyed it, and the special effects took precedence over the actors. John Dykstra took credit for these, and George Lucas as the presiding genius overall. The movie was much imitated, and in 1980 there appeared a sequel, *The Empire Strikes Back* followed in 1983 by *The Return of the Jedi*.

Stark, Graham (1922–). British comedy actor of films and TV, mostly in cameo roles.
The Millionairess 61. Watch It, Sailor 62. A Shot in the Dark 64. Becket 64. Alfie 66. Finders Keepers 66, etc.

Stark, Ray (c. 1909–). American producer.
The World of Suzie Wong 60. Oh Dad, Poor Dad 66. This Property is Condemned 66. Funny Girl 67. Reflections in a Golden Eye 68. The Way We Were 73. Funny Lady 75. California Suite 78. The Goodbye Girl 78. Chapter Two 79. The Electric Horseman 79. Seems Like Old Times 80. Annie 82, etc.

Starke, Pauline (1901–1977). American silent screen actress.
Intolerance 16. Salvation Nell 19. A Connecticut Yankee 21. Shanghai 24. Twenty Cents a Dance 26, etc.

Starr, Belle (1848–89). American female outlaw of the wild west period. On screen she has been glamorized by Gene Tierney in the film of that name, by Jane Russell in *Montana Belle* and by Isabel Jewell in *Badman's Territory*. Elizabeth Montgomery had an odd view of her in a 1980 TV movie.

Starr, Irving (1906–198). American producer, former agent.
The Crimson Trail 34. Music in My Heart 40. Swing Fever 42. Four Jills in a Jeep 44. Johnny Allegro 47. Slightly French 49, etc.

Starrett, Charles (1904–86). American cowboy star of innumerable second features in the thirties and forties. Inactive after 1952.
The Quarterback (debut) (playing himself, a professional footballer) 26. Fast and Loose 30. Sky Bride 32. Green Eyes 34. So Red the Rose 35. Mysterious Avenger 36. Two Gun Law 37. The Colorado Trail 38. Spoilers of the Range 39. Blazing Six Shooters 40. Thunder Over the Plains 41. Pardon My Gun 42. Fighting Buckaroo 43. Sundown Valley 44. Sagebrush Heroes 45. Gunning for Vengeance 46. Riders of the Lone Star 47. Last Days of Boot Hill 48. The Blazing Trail 49. Texas Dynamo 50. The Kid from Amarillo 51. Rough Tough West 52, many others.

Starrett, Jack (1936–). American director, mainly of low budget action pieces.
Run Angel Run 69. Cry Blood Apache 70. The Strange Vengeance of Rosalie 72. Slaughter 72. Nowhere to Hide (TV) 73. Cleopatra Jones 73. Race with the Devil 75. A Small Town in Texas 76. Final Chapter Walking Tall 77. Big Bob Johnson and His Fantastic Speed Circus (TV) 78. Mr Horn (TV) 79. First Blood (a only) 82.

¶ *J.S., 1975:* I jump in with both feet. I figure if you ain't got balls you're in the wrong business.

State Fair. This agreeable piece of rural Americana was first filmed in 1933 by Henry King, from a script by Sonya Levien and Paul Green. Will Rogers, Lew Ayres, Janet Gaynor and Sally Eilers were the stars. In 1945, with the benefit of added songs by Rodgers and Hammerstein, it was remade by Walter Lang with Charles Winninger, Dick Haymes, Jeanne Craine and Vivian Blaine, and again, with a different score, in 1961 by Jose Ferrer, with Tom Ewell, Pat Boone, Pamela Tiffin and Ann-Margret.

statesmen who have frequently been depicted in films include Disraeli (most often), Gladstone, Melbourne, Ramsay Macdonald (disguised in *Fame is the Spur*), Woodrow Wilson, Churchill, Roosevelt (notably in *Sunrise at Campobello*), Lincoln (qv) and Parnell. Fleeting glimpses of famous leaders were also given in *Mission to Moscow* and some Russian wartime films.

statues have come to life in *Night Life of the Gods*, *Animal Crackers*, *Turnabout* and *One Touch of Venus*. They were central to the plots of *The Light that Failed*, *Latin Quarter*, *Song of Songs* and *Mad Love*, while *A Taste of Honey* involved them in an attractive title sequence. In horror films, they came murderously alive in *Night of the Eagle*, *The Norliss Tapes* (TV) and that grand-daddy of them all, *The Golem*.

Staudte, Wolfgang (1906–84). German director of socially conscious films.
The Murderers are Amongst Us (& w) 46. Der Untertan (& w) 51. Rose Bernd 56. Roses for the Prosecutor 59. Die Dreigroschenoper 63. Herrenpartie 64. Heimlichkeiten 68. Die Herren mit die weissen Weste 70. Wolf of the Seven Seas 73. Zwischengleis (TV) 78, etc.

Steel, Anthony (1920–). Athletic British leading man with slight stage experience.
Saraband for Dead Lovers (film debut) 48. Marry Me 49. *The Wooden Horse* 50. Laughter in Paradise 51. The Malta Story 52. *Albert RN* 53. The Sea Shall Not Have Them 55. Storm over the Nile 56. The Black Tent 56. Checkpoint 56. A Question of Adultery 57. Harry Black 58. Honeymoon 60. The Switch 63. Hell is Empty 67. Anzio 68. Massacre in Rome 74. The World is Full of Married Men 79. The Mirror Crack'd 80. The Monster Club 81, etc.

Steele, Barbara (1938–). British leading lady who has appeared mainly in Italian horror films.
Bachelor of Hearts 58. Sapphire 59. Black Sunday (The Devil's Mask) 60. The Pit and the Pendulum (US) 61. The Terror of Dr Hitchcock 62. Eight and a Half 63. The Spectre 64. Sister of Satan (The Revenge of the Blood Beast) 65, etc.

Steele, Bob (1907–) (Robert Bradbury). American actor on stage from two years old. Since 1920 he has played cowboy roles in over 400 second features, and was one of the 'Three Mesquiteers'. Also played the villainous Canino in *The Big Sleep*.
TV series: F Troop 65–66.

Steele, Tommy (1936–) (Tommy Hicks). Energetic British cockney performer and pop singer.
Kill Me Tomorrow 55. The Tommy Steele Story 57. The Duke Wore Jeans 59. Light Up The Sky 59. Tommy the Toreador 60. It's All Happening 62. *The Happiest Millionaire* (US) 67. *Half a Sixpence* 67. Finian's Rainbow (US) 68. Where's Jack? 69.

Steenburgen, Mary (1953–). American leading actress.
Going South 78. Time after Time 79. Rabbit Test 79. Melvin and Howard (AA) 80. Ragtime 81. A Midsummer Night's Sex Comedy 82. Cross Creek 83. Romantic Comedy 83. One Magic Christmas 85. Dead of Center 87. The Whales of August 87.

Steiger, Rod (1925–). Burly American leading character actor who became known on stage and TV after training at New York's Theatre Workshop.
□Teresa 51. *On the Waterfront* 54. The Big Knife 55. Oklahoma 55. *The Court Martial of Billy Mitchell* 55. The Unholy Wife 56. Jubal 56. *The Harder They Fall* 56. Back from Eternity 57. Run of the Arrow 57. Across the Bridge (GB) 57. *Al Capone* 58. Cry Terror 58. Seven Thieves 59. The Mark 61. 13 West Street 61. On Friday at Eleven 61. The Longest Day 62. Convicts Four 62. Time of Indifference 63. Hands Over the City (It.) 63. *The Pawnbroker* (BFA) 64. A Man Called John 64. The Loved One 65. Doctor Zhivago 65. The Girl and the General 66. *In the Heat of the Night* (AA, BFA) 67. No Way to Treat a Lady 68. The Sergeant 68. The Illustrated Man 69. Three into Two Won't Go 69. Waterloo (as Napoleon) 71. A Fistful of Dynamite 71. The Heroes (Italian) 72. Happy Birthday Wanda June 72. Lolly Madonna XXX 72. Lucky Luciano 73. Hennessy 74. Innocents With Dirty Hands 75. W. C. Fields and Me 76. Jesus of Nazareth (TV) 77. Jimbuck 77. The Last Four Days (as Mussolini) 77. Wolf Lake 78. Love and Bullets 78. F.I.S.T. 78. Breakthrough 79. The Amityville Horror 79. Lucky Star 80. Klondike Fever 80. Lion of the Desert (as Mussolini) 81. Cattle Annie and Little Britches 81. The Chosen 82.

The Magic Mountain 82. The Glory Boys (TV) 84. Hollywood Wives (TV) 84. The Naked Face 84. The Kindred 86. Feel the Heat 87.

Stein, Paul (1891–1952). Austrian director who made films in America and Britain.
Ich Liebe Dich 23. My Official Wife (US) 26. Forbidden Woman (US) 27. Sin Takes a Holiday (US) 30. One Romantic Night 30. Born to Love 31. A Woman Commands (US) 31. Lily Christine (GB) 32. The Outsider (GB) 38. The Saint Meets the Tiger (GB) 41. Talk about Jacqueline (GB) 42. Kiss the Bride Goodbye (GB) 43. Twilight Hour (GB) 44. The Lisbon Story (GB) 46. Counterblast (GB) 48. The Twenty Questions Murder Mystery (GB) 49, etc.

Steinbeck, John (1902–1968). American novelist.
Of Mice and Men 39. The Grapes of Wrath 40. Tortilla Flat 42. The Moon is Down 43. The Red Pony 49. East of Eden 54. The Wayward Bus 57, etc.

Steiner, Max (1888–1971). Austrian composer, in America from 1924; became one of Hollywood's most reliable and prolific writers of film music.
Cimarron 31. A Bill of Divorcement 32. *King Kong* 33. The Lost Patrol 34. *The Informer* (AA) 35. *She* 35. The Charge of the Light Brigade 36. A Star is Born 37. *Gone with the Wind* 39. *The Letter* 40. *The Great Lie* 41. *Now Voyager* (AA) 42. *Casablanca* 42. *Since You Went Away* (AA) 44. Rhapsody in Blue 45. The Big Sleep 46. The Treasure of the Sierra Madre 47. Johnny Belinda 48. The Fountainhead 49. The Glass Menagerie 50. Room for One More 52. The Charge at Feather River 53. The Caine Mutiny 54. Battle Cry 55. Come Next Spring 56. Band of Angels 57. The FBI Story 59. The Dark at the Top of the Stairs 60. Parrish 61. Youngblood Hawke 64, scores of others.

Steinkamp, Fredric (–). American editor.
Two Loves 61. Sunday in New York 64. Grand Prix (co-ed) (AA) 66. Charly 68. A New Leaf 71. Haunts of the Very Rich (TV) 72. Freebie and the Bean 74. Three Days of the Condor 75. Bobby Deerfield 77. Tootsie 82, many others.

Stella Dallas. This weepy novel of frustrated mother-love, written by Olive Higgins Prouty, was filmed by Henry King in 1925, with Belle Bennett and Ronald Colman, and by King Vidor in 1937, with Barbara Stanwyck and John Boles.

Sten, Anna (1908–) (Anjuschka Stenski Sujakevitch). Russian leading actress imported to Hollywood by Goldwyn in 1933 in the hope of rivalling Garbo; but somehow she didn't click.
SELECTED EUROPEAN FILMS: The Yellow Ticket 27. Storm Over Asia 28. The White Eagle 28. The Murder of Dimitri Karamazov 31. Bombs in Monte Carlo 31.
□ENGLISH-SPEAKING FILMS: *Nana* 34. We Live Again 34. The Wedding Night 35. A Woman Alone 36. Exile Express 39. The Man I Married 40. So Ends Our Night 41. Chetniks 43. They Came To Blow Up America 43. Three Russian Girls 43. Let's Live a Little 48. Soldier of Fortune 55. Heaven Knows Mr Allison 57. The Nun and the Sergeant 62.

Stepanek, Karel (1899–1980). Czech character actor, in Britain from 1940. Usually played Nazis or other villains.
They Met in the Dark 43. *The Captive Heart* 46. The Fallen Idol 48. State Secret 50. Cockleshell Heroes 55. *Sink the Bismarck* 60. Operation Crossbow 65. Before Winter Comes 69, many others.

Stephen, Susan (1931–). British leading lady of the fifties.
His Excellency 51. The Red Beret 53. For Better For Worse 54. Golden Ivory 54. The Barretts of Wimpole Street 57. Carry On Nurse 59. Return of a Stranger 61. The Court Martial of Major Keller 63, etc.

Stephens, Ann (1931–). British juvenile actress of the forties.
In Which We Serve 42. Dear Octopus 43. The Upturned Glass 47. The Franchise Affair 51. Intent to Kill 58, others.

Stephens, Martin (1949–). British juvenile player.
The Hellfire Club 61. *Village of the Damned* 62. *The Innocents* 62. Battle of the Villa Fiorita 65. The Witches 66, etc.

Stephens, Robert (1931–). British stage actor, in occasional films.
Circle of Deception 60. Pirates of Tortuga (US) 61. A Taste of Honey 61. The Inspector 62. Cleopatra 62. The Small World of Sammy Lee 63. Morgan 66. Romeo and Juliet 68. The Prime of Miss Jean Brodie 69. *The*

Private Life of Sherlock Holmes 69. The Asphyx 72. Travels with My Aunt 73. Luther 73. QB VII (TV) 73. Holocaust (TV) 78. The Shout 78. Fortunes of War (TV) 87. War and Remembrance (TV) 87. High Season 87. Testimony 87, etc.

Stephenson, Henry (1871–1956) (H. S. Garroway). British stage actor who came to Hollywood films in his sixties and remained to play scores of kindly old men.
□The Spreading Dawn 17. The Black Panther's Cub 21. Men and Women 25. Wild Wild Susan 25. *Cynara* 32. Red Headed Woman 32. Guilty as Hell 32. A Bill of Divorcement 32. The Animal Kingdom 32. Little Women 33. Queen Christina 33. Tomorrow at Seven 33. Double Harness 33. My Lips Betray 33. If I Were Free 33. Blind Adventure 33. Man of Two Worlds 34. The Richest Girl in the World 34. Thirty Day Princess 34. Stingaree 34. The Mystery of Mr X 34. What Every Woman Knows 34. One More River 34. Outcast Lady 34. She Loves Me Not 34. All Men Are Enemies 34. Mutiny on the Bounty 35. Vanessa, Her Love Story 35. Reckless 35. The Flame Within 35. O'Shaughnessy's Boy 35. The Night Is Young 35. Rendezvous 35. The Perfect Gentleman 35. Captain Blood 35. Beloved Enemy 36. Half Angel 36. Hearts Divided 36. Give Me Your Heart 36. Walking on Air 36. Little Lord Fauntleroy 36. *The Charge of the Light Brigade* 36. When You're in Love 37. The Prince and the Pauper 37. The Emperor's Candlesticks 37. Conquest 37. Wise Girl 37. *The Young in Heart* 38. The Baroness and the Butler 38. Suez 38. Marie Antoinette 38. Dramatic School 38. Tarzan Finds a Son 39. The Private Lives of Elizabeth and Essex 39. The Adventures of Sherlock Holmes 39. It's a Date 40. Little Old New York 40. Spring Parade 40. Down Argentine Way 41. The Man Who Lost Himself 41. The Lady from Louisiana 41. This Above All 42. Rings on Her Fingers 42. Half Way to Shanghai 42. Mr Lucky 43. *Mantrap* 43. The Hour Before the Dawn 44. Secrets of Scotland Yard 44. The Reckless Age 44. Two Girls and a Sailor 44. Tarzan and the Amazons 45. The Green Years 46. Her Sister's Secret 46. The Locket 46. Heartbeat 46. Night and Day 46. Of Human Bondage 46. The Return of Monte Cristo 46. Dark Delusion 47. The Homestretch 47. Time Out of Mind 47. Ivy 47. Song of Love 47. Julia Misbehaves 48. Enchantment 48. *Oliver Twist* (as Mr Brownlow) 48. Challenge to Lassie 48.

Stephenson, James (1888–1941). Suave British-born stage actor, in Hollywood from 1938.
When Were You Born? (debut) 38. Boy Meets Girl 38. Confessions of a Nazi Spy 38. Beau Geste 39. Calling Philo Vance 40. The Sea Hawk 40. *The Letter* 40. Shining Victory 41. International Squadron 41, etc.

Stephenson, Pamela (1951–). New Zealand leading lady, who has done a variety of light work on British stage and TV (especially *Not the Nine O'Clock News*).
History of the World Part One 81. Scandalous 83. Superman III 83. Bloodbath at the House of Death 83. Finders Keepers 84.

Steppat, Ilse (1917–1969). German character actress.
Marriage in the Shadow 47. The Bridge 51. The Confessions of Felix Krull 62. On Her Majesty's Secret Service 69, etc.

stereophony: hearing sound from more than one source at the same time, a gimmick used to 'put you in the picture' by surrounding you with loudspeakers when CinemaScope was first introduced.

stereoscopy: viewing in three-dimensions, usually accomplished by watching through polaroid glasses, two films projected one on top of the other after being photographed from slightly different angles corresponding to one's two eyes.

Sterling, Ford (1883–1939) (George F. Stitch). American comic actor, a leading Keystone Kop and slapstick heavy.
Drums of the Desert 26. Gentlemen Prefer Blondes 28. Kismet 30. Alice in Wonderland 33. The Black Sheep 35, etc.

Sterling, Jan (1923–) (Jane Sterling Adriance). Blonde American leading lady with slight stage experience.
Johnny Belinda 48. Rhubarb 51. *Ace in the Hole* 51. Split Second 52. Pony Express 53. Alaska Seas 54. The High and the Mighty 54. Women's Prison 55. The Female on the Beach 55. 1984 56. The Harder They Fall 56. Kathy O 58. Love in a Goldfish Bowl 61. Having Babies (TV) 76. Backstairs at the White House (TV) 79, etc.
Famous line (*Ace in the Hole*): I don't go to church. Kneeling bags my nylons.
Famous line (*Ace in the Hole*): I've met some hard-boiled eggs in my time, but you—you're twenty minutes!

Sterling, Robert (1917–) (William John Hart). American leading man of the forties, mainly in second features.
Only Angels Have Wings 39. I'll Wait for You 41. Somewhere I'll Find You 42. The Secret Heart 46. Bunco Squad 48. Roughshod 50. Thunder in the Dust 51. Column South 53. Return to Peyton Place 61. Voyage to the Bottom of the Sea 62, etc.
TV series: Topper 53–54. Love That Jill 58. Ichabod and Me 61.

Stevens, Andrew (1955–). American leading man of the late seventies.
Las Vegas Lady 76. Vigilante Force 76. The Bastard (TV) 78. The Boys in Company C 78. The Fury 78. Women at West Point (TV) 79. Topper (TV) 80. Miracle on Ice (TV) 81. The Seduction 82. Ten to Midnight 83. Hollywood Wives (TV) 85. Once an Eagle (TV) 86.
TV series: Code Red 81.

Stevens, Connie (1938–) (Concetta Ingolia). American leading lady with mixed Italian, English, Irish and Mohican blood.
Eighteen and Anxious 57. Rockabye Baby 58. Parrish 61. Susan Slade 61. Two on a Guillotine 64. Never Too Late 65. Mr Jericho (TV) 70. The Grissom Gang 71. The Sex Symbol (TV) 73. Scorchy 76. Back to the Beach 87, etc.
TV series: Hawaiian Eye 59–62.

Stevens, Craig (1918–) (Gail Shekles). American leading man, married to Alexis Smith.
Affectionately Yours 41. Since You Went Away 43. The Lady Takes a Sailor 47. The French Line 54. Abbott and Costello Meet Dr Jekyll and Mr Hyde 55. Gunn 66. The Limbo Line 68. The Snoop Sisters (TV) 72. Rich Man Poor Man (TV) 76, etc.
TV series: *Peter Gunn* 58–60. Man of the World 62. Mr Broadway 64.

Stevens, George (1904–1975). American director, in Hollywood from 1923. In the late thirties and early forties he made smooth and lively entertainments, but his infrequent later productions tended towards elephantiasis.
□The Cohens and Kellys in Trouble 33. Bachelor Bait 34. Kentucky Kernels 34. Laddie 34. The Nitwits 34. Alice Adams 34. Annie Oakley 35. Swing Time 36. A Damsel in Distress 37. *Quality Street* 37. Vivacious Lady 38. *Gunga Din* 39. Vigil in the Night 40. Penny Serenade 40. *Woman of the Year* 41. *Talk of the Town* 42. *The More the Merrier* 43. *I Remember Mama* 47. *A Place in the Sun* (AA) 51. Something to Live For 52. *Shane* 53. *Giant* (AA) 56. The Diary of Anne Frank 59. The Greatest Story Ever Told 65. The Only Game in Town 69.

'He was a minor director with major virtues before *A Place in the Sun*, and a major director with minor virtues after.'—*Andrew Sarris, 1968*

Stevens, George Jnr (1932–). American producer, son of George Stevens, who in 1977 became head of the American Film Institute.

Stevens, Inger (1935–1970) (Inger Stensland). Pert and pretty Swedish leading lady, in America from childhood.
Man on Fire (film debut) 57. Cry Terror 58. The World the Flesh and the Devil 58. The Buccaneer 59. The New Interns 64. *A Guide for the Married Man* 67. Firecreek 67. Madigan 68. Five Card Stud 68. Hang 'Em High 68. House of Cards 68. The Borgia Stick (TV) 68. A Dream of Kings 69. Run Simon Run (TV) 70, etc.
TV series: *The Farmer's Daughter* 63–65.

Stevens, K. T. (1919–) (Gloria Wood). American leading lady of a few forties films; daughter of director Sam Wood.
Kitty Foyle 40. The Great Man's Lady 41. Address Unknown 44. Vice Squad 53. Tumbleweed 53. Missile to the Moon 58, etc.

Stevens, Leith (1909–1970). American musical arranger and composer.
The Wild One 52. Julie 56. The Five Pennies 49. A New Kind of Love 63, many others for Fox and Paramount, including TV series.

Stevens, Leslie (1924–). American screenwriter.
The Left-Handed Gun 58. Private Property (& pd) 59. The Marriage-Go-Round (from his play) 60. Hero's Island (& pd) 62, etc.
TV series as creator-producer-director: Stony Burke, The Outer Limits, Battlestar Galactica.

Stevens, Mark (1916–) (also known as Stephen Richards). American leading man with varied early experience; usually in routine roles.
Objective Burma 45. *From This Day Forward* 45. The Dark Corner 46. I Wonder Who's Kissing Her Now 47. The Snake Pit 48. The Street with No Name 48. Sand 49. Mutiny 53. Cry Vengeance (also pd) 54. Timetable (also pd) 55. September Storm 60. Fate is the Hunter 64. Frozen Alive 66. Sunscorched 66.
TV series: Big Town 52–57.

Stevens, Onslow (1902–1977) (Onslow Ford Stevenson). American stage actor occasionally seen in film character roles. Son of Houseley Stevenson.
Heroes of the West (debut) 32. Counsellor at Law 33. The Three Musketeers 36. Under Two Flags 36. When Tomorrow Comes 39. Mystery Sea Raider 40. *House of Dracula* 45. O.S.S. 46. Night Has a Thousand Eyes 48. The Creeper 48. State Penitentiary 50. Them 54. Tarawa Beachhead 58. All the Fine Young Cannibals 60. Geronimo's Revenge 63, etc.

Stevens, Rise (1913–). American opera singer, seen in a few films.
□The Chocolate Soldier 41. Going My Way 44. Carnegie Hall 47.

Stevens, Robert (c. 1925–). American director, from TV.
□The Big Caper 57. Never Love a Stranger 58. I Thank a Fool 62. In the Cool of the Day 63. Change of Mind 69.

Stevens, Ronnie (1925–). British comic actor with stage and TV experience.
Made in Heaven 52. An Alligator Named Daisy 55. I Was Monty's Double 58. I'm All Right, Jack 59. Dentist in the Chair 60. San Ferry Ann 65. Give a Dog a Bone 66. Some Girls Do 68, etc.

Stevens, Stella (1936–) (Estelle Eggleston). American leading lady.
Say One For Me (debut) 58. Lil Abner 59. Too Late Blues 61. The Courtship of Eddie's Father 63. The Nutty Professor 63. Synanon 65. The Secret of My Success 65. The Silencers 66. How to Save a Marriage 67. The Mad Room 69. The Ballad of Cable Hogue 70. A Town Called Bastard 71. Stand Up and be Counted 71. The Poseidon Adventure 72. Arnold 74. Cleopatra Jones and the Casino of Gold 74. Las Vegas Lady 74. Nickelodeon 76. The Manitou 78. The Night They Took Miss Beautiful (TV) 77. Cruise into Terror (TV) 78, etc.
TV series: Ben Casey 65. Flamingo Road 80–81.

Stevens, Warren (1919–). American general purpose actor.
The Frogmen 51. The Barefoot Contessa 54. Forbidden Planet 56. Hot Spell 58. No Name on the Bullet 59. Forty Pounds of Trouble 62. An American Dream 66. Madigan 68, many others.
TV series: 77th Bengal Lancers 56. The Richard Boone Show 64.

Stevenson, Houseley (1879–1953). American character actor, latterly familiar as a gaunt, usually unshaven, old man.
Native Land 42. Somewhere in the Night 46. Dark Passage 47. Casbah 48. Moonrise 49. All the King's Men 49. The Sun Sets at Dawn 51. The Wild North 52, etc.

Stevenson, Robert (1905–86). British director, in Hollywood from 1939.
□Happy Ever After 32. Falling For You 33. Tudor Rose 36. The Man Who Changed His Mind 36. Jack of all Trades 37. *King Solomon's Mines* 37. Non Stop New York 37. Owd Bob 38. The Ware Case 39. Young Man's Fancy 40. *Tom Brown's Schooldays* 40. *Back Street* 41. Joan of Paris 43. Forever and a Day (co-d) 43. *Jane Eyre* 43. Dishonored Lady 47. *To the Ends of the Earth* 48. The Woman on Pier 13 49. Walk Softly Stranger 50. My Forbidden Past 51. The Last Vegas Story 52. Johnny Tremain 57. Old Yeller 57. Darby O'Gill and the Little People 59. Kidnapped 60. The Absent-Minded Professor 61. In Search of the Castaways 62. Son of Flubber 63. The Misadventures of Merlin Jones 64. *Mary Poppins* 64. The Monkey's Uncle 65. That Darn Cat 65. The Gnome-Mobile 67. Blackbeard's Ghost 67. The Love Bug 69. My Dog the Thief 70. Bedknobs and Broomsticks 71. Herbie Rides Again 73. The Island at the Top of the World 74. One of Our Dinosaurs is Missing 75. The Shaggy D.A. 77.

Stevenson, Robert Louis (1850–1894). British novelist and short story writer. Works filmed include *Dr Jekyll and Mr Hyde* (many versions), *Treasure Island* (many versions), *The Body Snatcher, The Suicide Club, Kidnapped, The Master of Ballantrae, Ebb Tide, The Wrong Box*.

Steward, Ernest (–). British cinematographer.
Carry on Camping 71. Callan 74. Hennessy 75, many others.

Stewart, Alexandra (1939–). Canadian leading lady who has filmed mainly in Europe.
Exodus 60. Le Feu Follet 63. Dragees au Poivre 65. Maroc 7 67. The Bride Wore Black 67. The Man Who Had Power Over Women 70. Day for Night 73. Marseilles Contract 74. In Praise of Older Women 78. Phobia 80. Chanel Solitaire 81, etc.

Stewart, Anita (1895–1961) (Anna May Stewart). American silent screen leading lady.

A Million Bid 13. The Goddess 15. Mary Regan 19. Her Kingdom of Dreams 20. Never the Twain Shall Meet 25. Sisters of Eve 28, many others.

Stewart, Athole (1879–1940). British stage character actor.
The Speckled Band 31. The Clairvoyant 34. Dusty Ermine 37. The Spy in Black 39. Tilly of Bloomsbury 40, etc.

Stewart, Donald Ogden (1894–1980). American playwright and screenwriter. Autobiography 1974: *By a Stroke of Luck*.
□Brown of Harvard 26. Laughter 30. Finn and Hattie (oa) 30. Rebound (oa) 31. Tarnished Lady (& oa) 31. Smilin' Through 32. The White Sister 33. Another Language 33. Dinner at Eight 33. The Barretts of Wimpole Street 34. No More Ladies 35. *The Prisoner of Zenda* 37. Holiday 38. Marie Antoinette 38. Love Affair 39. The Night of Nights 39. Kitty Foyle 40. *The Philadelphia Story* (AA) 40. That Uncertain Feeling 41. A Woman's Face 41. Smilin' Through 41. Tales of Manhattan 42. Without Love 45. Life with Father 47. Cass Timberlane 47. Edward My Son 49. Escapade 55. Moment of Danger 60. NB: Some of the above were in collaboration with other writers.

Stewart, Elaine (1929–) (Elsy Steinberg). American leading lady of a few fifties films; former usherette.
Sailor Beware 51. The Bad and the Beautiful 52. Young Bess 53. Brigadoon 54. The Tattered Dress 56. The Adventures of Hajji Baba 57. The Rise and Fall of Legs Diamond 60. The Most Dangerous Man Alive 61, etc.

Stewart, Hugh (1910–). British producer, former editor.
Trottie True 49. The Long Memory 52. Man of the Moment 55 (and all subsequent Norman Wisdom comedies). The Intelligence Men 65, etc.

Stewart, James (1908–). American leading actor of inimitable slow drawl and gangly walk; portrayed slow-speaking, honest heroes for thirty-five years.
□Murder Man 35. Rose Marie 36. Next Time We Love 36. Wife versus Secretary 36. Small Town Girl 36. Speed 36. The Gorgeous Hussy 36. Born to Dance 36. After the Thin Man 36. *Seventh Heaven* 37. The Last Gangster 37. Navy Blue and Gold 37. Of Human Hearts 38. Vivacious Lady 38. Shopworn Angel 38. *You Can't Take It with You* 38. Made for Each Other 38. Ice Follies of 1939. It's a Wonderful World 39. *Mr Smith Goes to Washington* 39. *Destry Rides Again* 39. *The Shop around the Corner* 40. The Mortal Storm 40. No Time for Comedy 40. *The Philadelphia Story* (AA) 40. Come Live with Me 40. Pot O' Gold 41. Ziegfeld Girl 41; war service; *It's a Wonderful Life* 46. Magic Town 46. *Call Northside 777* 47. On Our Merry Way 48. Rope 48. You Gotta Stay Happy 48. The Stratton Story 49. Malaya 49. *Winchester 73* 50. *Broken Arrow* 50. The Jackpot 50. *Harvey* 50. No Highway (GB) 51. The Greatest Show on Earth 51. Bend of the River 52. Carbine Williams 52. The Naked Spur 53. Thunder Bay 53. *The Glenn Miller Story* 53. *Rear Window* 54. The Far Country 54. Strategic Air Command 55. *The Man from Laramie* 55. The Man Who Knew Too Much 56. The Spirit of St Louis 57. Night Passage 57. Vertigo 58. Bell, Book and Candle 58. *Anatomy of a Murder* 59. The FBI Story 59. The Mountain Road 60. Two Rode Together 61. The Man Who Shot Liberty Valance 62. *Mr Hobbs Takes a Vacation* 62. How the West Was Won 62. Take Her She's Mine 63. Cheyenne Autumn 64. Dear Brigitte 65. *Shenandoah* 65. The Flight of the Phoenix 65. The Rare Breed 66. Firecreek 67. Bandolero 68. The Cheyenne Social Club 70. Fool's Parade 71. The Shootist 76. The Big Sleep 77. Airport 77 77. The Magic of Lassie 78. Right of Way (TV) 83. North and South II (TV) 86.
TV series: The Jimmy Stewart Show 71. Hawkins on Murder 73.
❀ For becoming one of everybody's family even when playing a tough westerner. *The Philadelphia Story*.

¶ I don't act. I react.—*J.S.*

He has so many of his pictures being shown on the late show, he keeps more people up than Mexican food.—*Hal Kanter*

I'm the inarticulate man who tries. I don't really have all the answers, but for some reason, somehow, I make it.—*J.S.*

The big studios were an ideal way to make films—because they were a home base for people. When you were under contract, you had a chance to relax.—*J.S.*

If I had my career over again? Maybe I'd say to myself, speed it up a little.—*J.S.*

Famous line (*The Philadelphia Story*): The prettiest sight in this fine pretty world is the privileged class enjoying its privileges.
Famous line (*Harvey*): I wrestled with reality for 35 years, doctor, and I'm happy. I finally won out over it.

Famous line (*It's a Wonderful Life*): Well, you look about the kind of angel I'd get. Sort of a fallen angel, aren't you? What happened to your wings?
† Special AA 1984 'for fifty years of meaningful performances, for his high ideals, both on and off the screen, with the respect and affection of his colleagues'.

Stewart, Paul (1908–86) (P. Sternberg). American character actor, often in clipped, sinister roles.
Citizen Kane 41. Johnny Eager 42. Government Girl 44. *Champion* 49. *The Window* 49. Walk Softly Stranger 50. The Bad and the Beautiful 52. Prisoner of War 54. The Cobweb 55. King Creole 58. A Child is Waiting 62. The Greatest Story Ever Told 65. In Cold Blood 67. The Day of the Locust 75. Bite the Bullet 75. W. C. Fields and Me 76. Opening Night 77. The Dain Curse (TV) 78. The Revenge of the Pink Panther 81. S.O.B. 81, others.

Stewart, Sophie (1909–77). British stage and radio actress, in occasional films.
Maria Marten 35. As You Like It 36. The Return of the Scarlet Pimpernel 38. Nurse Edith Cavell 39. The Lamp Still Burns 43. Uncle Silas 47. Yangtse Incident 56, etc.

Stiers, David Ogden (1942–). Tall, balding American comedy actor.
Drive He Said 70. Charlie's Angels (TV) 76. Oh God 77. The Cheap Detective 78. Magic 78, etc.
TV series: M*A*S*H 77–80.

Stigwood, Robert (1934–). International impresario whose dominance of the pop-music field led him to produce *Saturday Night Fever* and *Grease*.

Stiller, Mauritz (1883–1928) (Mowscha Stiller). Russian-Swedish director who went to Hollywood in the twenties with Garbo, but died shortly after.
Vampyren 12. *Sir Arne's Treasure* 19. Erotikon 20. *The Atonement of Gosta Berling* 24. The Blizzard (US) 26. Hotel Imperial 27. Street of Sin 28, etc.

Sting (1951–) (Gordon Summers).
□ Quadrophenia 78. Radio On 79. The Secret Policeman's Other Ball 81. Brimstone and Treacle 82. Dune 84. The Bride 85. Plenty 85. Bring on the Night 86.

The Sting (US 1973) (AA). A lucky film which brought together the old confidence trickster routines, the happy combination of Robert Redford and Paul Newman, a piano rag music score by Scott Joplin, and a cheerful fadeout after much suspense. The box office reaction was terrific, but attempts to imitate the formula failed apart from a moderate TV series called *Switch*, with Robert Wagner and Eddie Albert. *Sting II*, released in 1983, was a disaster starring Mac Davis and Jackie Gleason.

Stock, Nigel (1919–86). British character actor, former boy performer.
Lancashire Luck 38. Brighton Rock 46. Derby Day 51. The Dam Busters 55. Eye Witness 57. Victim 61. HMS Defiant 62. The Great Escape 63. The Lost Continent 68. The Lion in Winter 68. A Bequest to the Nation 73. Russian Roulette 75. A Man Called Intrepid (TV) (as Winston Churchill) 79, many others.
On TV he played Dr Watson in the 1965 *Sherlock Holmes* series.

stock shot. One not made at the time of filming but hired from a library. It can be either newsreel, specially shot material such as planes landing at an airport, views of a city, etc., or spectacular material lifted from older features. (e.g. *Storm over the Nile* 55 had a large proportion of action footage from the original *Four Feathers* 39, and the same shots have turned up in several other films including *Master of the World* 61 and *East of Sudan* 64.)

Stockfield, Betty (1905–1966). British stage actress, in occasional films.
City of Song 30. The Impassive Footman 32. The Beloved Vagabond 36. Derrière la Façade (Fr.) 40. Flying Fortress 42. Edouard et Caroline (Fr.) 50. The Lovers of Lisbon 55. True As a Turtle 57, etc.

Stockwell, Dean (1938–). American boy actor of the forties, later leading man.
□The Valley of Decision 45. Anchors Aweigh 45. Abbott and Costello in Hollywood 45. *The Green Years* 46. Home Sweet Homicide 46. The Mighty McGurk 47. The Arnelo Affair 47. Song of the Thin Man 47. The Romance of Rosy Ridge 47. Gentleman's Agreement 48. *The Boy with Green Hair* 48. Deep Waters 48. Down to the Sea in Ships 49. The Secret Garden 49. Stars in My Crown 50. The Happy Years 50. Kim 50. Cattle Drive 51. Gun for a Coward 57. The Careless

Years 57. *Compulsion* 59. *Sons and Lovers* 60. Long Day's Journey into Night 62. Rapture 65. Psych-Out 68. The Dunwich Horror 70. Ecstasy 70. The Failing of Raymond (TV) 71. The Last Movie 71. The Loners 72. Another Day at the Races 73. Werewolf of Washington 73. Won Ton Ton 75. Win, Place or Steal 75. Tracks 77. Wrong Is Right 82. Human Highway 82. Paris Texas 84. Dune 84. The Legend of Billie Jean 85. Blue Velvet 86. Gardens of Stone 87.

Stockwell, Guy (1936–). American leading actor.
The War Lord 65. *Blindfold* 65. And Now Miguel 66. *Beau Geste* 66. The Plainsman 66. Tobruk 66. The King's Pirate 67. The Million Dollar Collar 67. In Enemy Country 68. The Gatling Gun 72. Airport 75 74. It's Alive 76, etc.
TV series: Adventures in Paradise 60. The Richard Boone Show 64.

Stoker, Bram (1847–1912). Irish novelist, the creator of *Dracula*. Was also Henry Irving's manager.

Stokowski, Leopold (1882–1977) (Leopold Stokes or Boleslowowicz). British-born orchestral conductor.
□*One Hundred Men and a Girl* 37. The Big Broadcast of 1937 37. *Fantasia* 40. Carnegie Hall 47.

Stoll, George (1905–85). American musical director, with MGM from 1945.
Anchors Aweigh (AA) 45. Neptune's Daughter 49. I Love Melvin 53. The Student Prince 54. Hit the Deck 55. Meet Me in Las Vegas 56, many others.

Stoloff, Morris (1894–1980). American musical director, in Hollywood from 1936.
Lost Horizon 37. You Can't Take It With You 38. Cover Girl (AA) 44. A Song to Remember 45. The Jolson Story (AA) 46. The 5000 Fingers of Dr T 53. Picnic 55, many others.

Stone, Andrew L. (1902–). American producer-director (for a time with his wife Virginia) who made it a rule since the mid-forties not to shoot his melodramas in a studio, always on location, and with real trains, liners, airplanes, etc. Formed Andrew Stone Productions 1943.
The Great Victor Herbert 39. *Stormy Weather* (d only) 42. Hi Diddle Diddle 43. Sensations of 1945. Highway 301 51. The Steel Trap 52. The Night Holds Terror 54. Julie 56. *Cry Terror* 58. The Decks Ran Red 59. The Last Voyage 60. Ring of Fire 61. The Password is Courage 62. Never Put It in Writing 64. The Secret of My Success 65. *Song of Norway* 69. *The Great Waltz* 72, etc.

'If the Stones had made *On The Beach*, none of us would be around now to review it.'—*Andrew Sarris, 1968*

Stone, George E. (1903–1967) (George Stein). Polish-born character actor, who in Hollywood films played oppressed little men; formerly in vaudeville.
The Front Page 30. Little Caesar 30. Cimarron 31. Anthony Adverse 36. *The Housekeeper's Daughter* 38. His Girl Friday 40. The Boston Blackie series. Dancing in the Dark 50. The Robe 53. Guys and Dolls 55. The Man with the Golden Arm 56, many others.

Stone, Harold J. (1911–). American character actor.
The Harder They Fall 56. Garment Center 57. Man Afraid 57. Spartacus 60. The Chapman Report 62. The Man with X-Ray Eyes 63. Which Way to the Front? 70. Mitchell 75, etc.
TV series: My World and Welcome To It 68. Bridget Loves Bernie 74.

Stone, Irving (1903–). American novelist whose *Lust for Life* and *The Agony and the Ecstasy* were filmed.

Stone, Lewis (1879–1953). Distinguished American stage actor, a leading man of silent films and later a respected character actor.
Honour's Altar (debut) 15. *The Prisoner of Zenda* 22. Scaramouche 23. *The Lost World* 24. Madame X 30. The Mask of Fu Manchu 32. Mata Hari 32. Grand Hotel 33. Queen Christina 33. *David Copperfield* 34. *Treasure Island* 35. The Thirteenth Chair 37. *You're Only Young Once* 37. Judge Hardy's Children 38. Love Finds Andy Hardy 38. Out West with the Hardys 39 (and ten further episodes of this series, ending in 1947). Yellow Jack 39. The Bugle Sounds 41. Three Wise Fools 46. The State of the Union 48. Key to the City 50. Scaramouche 52. The Prisoner of Zenda 52. All the Brothers Were Valiant 53, many others.

Stone, Marianne (c. 1920–). British character actress, usually in bit parts. Innumerable appearances.
Angels One Five 51. The Pickwick Papers 54.

The Runaway Bus 54. Yield to the Night 56. Heavens Above 63. Ladies Who Do 65. Here We Go Round the Mulberry Bush 67, many others.

Stone, Milburn (1904–1980). American character actor, in Hollywood from the mid-thirties; was in hundreds of low-budget action features, usually as villain or tough hero; more recently became famous as 'Doc' in the *Gunsmoke* TV series.
Ladies Crave Excitement 35. Port of Missing Girls 37. King of the Turf 39. Enemy Agent 40. The Phantom Cowboy 41. Rubber Racketeers 42. Sherlock Holmes Faces Death 43. Hat Check Honey 44. On Stage Everybody 45. Spider Woman Strikes Back 46. Train to Alcatraz 48. Snow Dog 50. The Sun Shines Bright 53. Black Tuesday 54. Drango 57, many others.

Stone, Oliver (1946–). American screenwriter.
Midnight Express (AA) 78. Scarface 83. The Tear of the Dragon (co-w) 85. Platoon (& d) (AA) 86. Wall Street (& d) 87.

¶ *O.S. (receiving his 1987 award):* I think you are really acknowledging the Vietnam veteran, and for the first time you really understand what happened out there.

O.S.: The film business? I love film, but the film business is shit.

Stone, Peter (1930–). American screenwriter; sometimes uses the name Pierre Marton.
□*Charade* 63. Father Gosse 64. *Mirage* 65. Arabesque 66. The Secret War of Harry Frigg 68. The Mercenaries (as Quentin Werty) 68. Sweet Charity 69. Skin Game 71. 1776 (from his own stage musical) 72. The Taking of Pelham One Two Three 74. Silver Bears 77. Someone Is Killing the Great Chefs of Europe 78.

The Stooges. A trio of American knockabout comics specializing in a peculiarly violent form of slapstick. They originally went from vaudeville to Hollywood with Ted Healy (as Ted Healy and his Stooges) but broke away to become world famous in hundreds of two-reelers throughout the thirties, forties and fifties. The original trio were Larry Fine (1911–1975), Moe Howard (1895–1975) and his brother Jerry (Curly) Howard (1906–1952). In 1947 Curly was replaced by yet another brother, Shemp Howard (Samuel Howard) (1891–1955). On Shemp's death he was replaced by Joe Besser, who in 1959 was replaced by Joe de Rita. Towards the end of their popularity the Stooges appeared in a few features.
Stop Look and Laugh 61. Snow White and the Three Stooges 61. The Three Stooges Meet Hercules 63. The Outlaws is Coming 64. The Three Stooges Go Around the World in a Daze 65, etc.

stop motion. The method by which much trick photography is effected: the film is exposed one frame at a time, allowing time for rearrangement of models, etc., between shots, and thus giving the illusion in the completed film of motion by something normally inanimate. The monsters in *King Kong* 33 are the supreme example of this method.
See: *time-lapse photography*.

Stoppa, Paolo (1906–). Italian character actor, in films from 1932.
La Beauté du Diable 49. Miracle in Milan 50. The Seven Deadly Sins 52. Love Soldiers and Women 55. La Loi 59. The Leopard 63. Becket 64. After the Fox 66. Once Upon a Time in the West 67, etc.

Stoppard, Tom (1937–) (Thomas Strausler). Czechoslovakian playwright in UK. Films include Despair 78. The Human Factor 79. Brazil 85. Empire of the Sun 87.

Storaro, Vittorio (1946–). Italian cinematographer.
The Spiders Stratagem 70. The Conformist 71. Last Tango in Paris 72. 1900 77. Agatha 79. Apocalypse Now (AA) 79. Reds (AA) 81. One from the Heart 82. Ladyhawke 85.

Storch, Larry (1923–). American comic actor.
Captain Newman MD 63. Wild and Wonderful 64. The Monitors 69. The Couple Takes a Wife (TV) 72, etc.
TV series: F Troop.

Storck, Henri (1907–). Belgian documentarist.
Pour Vos Beaux Yeux 29. The Story of the Unknown Soldier 32. Symphonie Paysanne 42. Au Carrefour de la Vie 49. Les Belges de la Mer 54. Les Gestes du Silence 61. La Musée Vivante 65, etc.

Storm, Gale (1922–) (Josephine Cottle). American leading lady of the forties.
Tom Brown's Schooldays 39. Foreign Agent 42. Nearly Eighteen 43. The Right to Live 45.

Sunbonnet Sue 46. It Happened on Fifth Avenue 47. Abandoned 49. Underworld Story 50. The Texas Rangers 51, etc.
TV series: The Gale Storm Show 56–59. My Little Margie 52–54.

Storm over Asia (Russia 1930). Also known as *The Heir to Genghis Khan*, this beautifully-made propagandist melodrama concerned a Mongol fur trapper found in 1918 to be a descendant of Genghis Khan. Tried and half-executed for treason, he is reprieved to become a puppet monarch. Directed by V. I. Pudovkin.

storms of one kind or another have been brilliantly staged in *The Hurricane, The Wizard of Oz, When Tomorrow Comes, Reap the Wild Wind, Typhoon, Lord Jim, A High Wind in Jamaica, The Blue Lagoon, Sunrise, Key Largo, Ryan's Daughter, Portrait of Jennie, Noah's Ark* and *The Bible*, to name but a handful; they have also been essential situation-builders in such films as *Five Came Back, Hatter's Castle, Our Man Flint, The Card, Storm Fear* and *The Blue Lagoon*. A whole genre of films, known as the 'thunderstorm mystery', grew up in the thirties when every screen murder took place in a desolate mansion during a terrifying storm with no means of communication with the outside world; typical of these are *The Black Cat, The Cat and the Canary, The Ghost Breakers, Night Monster, Hold That Ghost, You'll Find Out* and *The Spiral Staircase*. Finally there is nothing like a good electrical storm for breathing life into a monster, as evidenced in a score of films from *Frankenstein* to *The Electric Man* and after.

story into film

? Name the films made from these short stories and magazine articles.

1 *Christ in Concrete* by Pietro di Donato
2 *The Wisdom of Eve* by Mary Orr
3 *Stage to Lordsburg* by Ernest Haycox
4 *Madame La Gimp* by Damon Runyon
5 *Casting the Runes* by M. R. James
6 *Spurs* by Tod Robbins
7 *A Can of Beans* by Charles Brackett and Billy Wilder
8 *Leiningen versus the Ants* by Carl Stephenson
9 *The Short Happy Life of Francis Macomber* by Ernest Hemingway
10 *The Basement Room* by Graham Greene
11 *Night Bus* by Samuel Hopkins Adams
12 *Opera Hat* by Clarence Buddington Kelland
13 *The Killer* by George Scullin
14 *Patrol* by Philip Macdonald
15 *The Killing Frost* by Max Catto
16 *The Six Napoleons* by Sir Arthur Conan Doyle
17 *The Island of Dr Moreau* by H. G. Wells (1932)
18 *The Foghorn* by Ray Bradbury
19 *Who Goes There?* by John W. Campbell Jnr
20 *The Musgrave Ritual* by Sir Arthur Conan Doyle
21 *The Man on the Ledge* by Joel Sayre
22 *Philomel Cottage* by Agatha Christie

The Story of Louis Pasteur (US 1936). The first of Warner Brothers' famous series of historical biographies: later films dealt with Zola, Reuter, Dr Ehrlich, Juarez, etc. In this case popularization managed to make scientific research remarkably exciting. Paul Muni (AA) was Pasteur, William Dieterle directed from a script by Sheridan Gibney and Pierre Collings, and Erich Wolfgang Korngold wrote the music. These films were very successful commercially; but when John Huston revived the form in 1962 with *Freud*, it was a box office disaster.

Stossel, Ludwig (1883–1973). Austrian character actor in Hollywood from the mid-thirties.
Four Sons 39. Man Hunt 41. Woman of the Year 42. Hitler's Madman 43. Cloak and Dagger 46. A Song is Born 48. Call Me Madam 53. Me and the Colonel 58. G.I. Blues 60, many others.

Stothart, Herbert (1885–1949). American composer, long with MGM, and responsible for the scores of many of the studio's most prestigious films.
Madame Satan 30. Rasputin and the Empress 33. Queen Christina 33. David Copperfield 35. Mutiny on the Bounty 35. A Night at the Opera 35. San Francisco 36. Camille 37. The Good Earth 37. Marie Antoinette 38. Idiot's Delight 39. Waterloo Bridge 40. Mrs Miniver 42. Random Harvest 42. Madame Curie 44. The Green Years 46. The Yearling 47. The Three Musketeers 48, many others.

Stout, Archie (1886–?1965). American cinematographer in Hollywood from 1914. Fort Apache 48. Hard Fast and Beautiful 51. *The Quiet Man* (AA) 52. The Sun Shines Bright 53. The High and the Mighty 54.

Stout, Rex (1886–1975). American detective story writer, creator of Nero Wolfe, who appeared in two minor films of the thirties (played by Edward Arnold and Walter Connolly) and in a seventies TV movie (played by Thayer David).

Stowe, Harriet Beecher (1811–1896). American novelist, author of the much-filmed *Uncle Tom's Cabin* (qv).

Stradling, Harry (1907–1970). British-born cinematographer, long in US.
La Kermesse Héroïque 35. *Knight without Armour* 37. *Pygmalion* 38. The Citadel 38. Jamaica Inn 39. Suspicion 41. *The Picture of Dorian Gray* (AA) 44. The Pirate 48. The Barkleys of Broadway 49. *A Streetcar Named Desire* 51. Valentino 51. Hans Christian Andersen 52. Helen of Troy 55. Guys and Dolls 55. The Eddy Duchin Story 56. The Pajama Game 57. A Face in the Crowd 57. The Dark at the Top of the Stairs 60. *My Fair Lady* (AA) 64. How to Murder Your Wife 65. Moment to Moment 65. Walk, Don't Run 66. Funny Girl 68. *Hello Dolly* 69, many others.

Stradling, Harry Jnr (–). American cinematographer, son of Harry Stradling.
Welcome to Hard Times 67. Support Your Local Sheriff 69. The Mad Room 69. Something Big 71. Fools Parade 71. The Way We Were 73. McQ 74. Bite the Bullet 75. Midway 76. The Big Bus 76. Airport 77 77. Damnation Alley 77. Convoy 78. Go Tell the Spartans 78. Prophecy 79. Carny 80, etc.

Stradner, Rose (1913–1958). Austrian actress who made a few Hollywood films.
The Last Gangster 38. Blind Alley 39. The Keys of the Kingdom 44, etc.

Straight, Beatrice (1916–). American character actress.
Network (AA) 76. Bloodline 79. The Promise 79. Poltergeist 82. Two of a Kind 83. Power 85, etc.

Strange, Glenn (1899–1973). Giant-size American character actor, in Hollywood from 1937, mainly in cowboy roles. Also played the monster in *House of Frankenstein* 45, *Abbott and Costello meet Frankenstein* 48, etc.
TV series: Gunsmoke 56–73.

Strange Interlude (US 1932). Eugene O'Neill's sombre romantic drama, with its sense of time and opportunity wasted, was a strange choice for MGM to film at the time, but Norma Shearer and Clark Gable provided powerful box office lure, and the long monologues were overcome by billing the movie as 'the film in which you hear the characters THINK!' Robert Z. Leonard directed unobtrusively.

Strasberg, Lee (1899–1982). American drama teacher, founded the Actors' Studio which in the fifties taught The Method.
□*The Godfather Part Two* 74. The Cassandra Crossing 77. Boardwalk 79. And Justice for All 79. Going in Style 79.

Strasberg, Susan (1938–). American leading lady, daughter of Lee Strasberg, founder of the New York Actors' Studio. Stage and TV experience.
Picnic (film debut) 55. Stage Struck 57. Taste of Fear 59. Kapo 60. Hemingway's Adventures of a Young Man 62. The High Bright Sun 65. Psych-Out 68. The Brotherhood 68. Rollercoaster 77. In Praise of Older Women 78. The Returning 83. The Delta Force 85, etc.
TV series: Toma 73.

Stratton, John (1925–). British general purpose actor.
The Cure for Love 49. Appointment with Venus 52. The Cruel Sea 54. The Long Arm 55, etc.

Straub, Jean-Marie (1933–). French director in German films.
Machorka Muff 63. Nicht Versohnt 65. *The Chronicle of Anna-Magdalena Bach* 67. Othon 72. History Lessons 73, etc.

Strauss, Helen (1909–87). American literary agent (for Michener and others) who became an occasional film producer: *Tom Sawyer*, *Huckleberry Finn*, *The Incredible Sarah*.
Autobiography 1979: *A Talent for Luck*.

Straus, Oscar (1870–1954). Austrian operetta composer who also occasionally provided film music: The Smiling Lieutenant 31. One Hour with You 32. Land Without Music 36. La Ronde 50. Madame De 52, etc.

Strauss, Peter (1942–). American leading man who became well known in *Rich Man Poor Man* (TV) 76.
Soldier Blue 71. The Last Tycoon 76. Young Joe the Forgotten Kennedy (TV) 77. The Jericho Mile (TV) 79. Masada (TV) 80. Spacehunter 83. Tender is the Night (TV) 85, etc.

Strauss, Robert (1913–1975). American comedy actor (occasionally in menacing roles); former salesman.
Sailor Beware 52. *Stalag 17* 53. The Seven Year Itch 54. Attack 56. The Last Time I Saw Archie 61. The Family Jewels 65, etc.

Strayer, Frank (1891–1964). American director of second features.
Rough House Rosie 27. Enemy of Men 30. The Monster Walks 32. The Vampire Bat 33. The Ghost Walks 35. Blondie (and many others in this series) 38. The Daring Young Man 42. Messenger of Peace 50, etc.

Streep, Meryl (1951–) (Mary Louise Streep). American leading lady of the late seventies and star actress of the eightes.
□The Deadliest Season (TV) 77. Julia 77. The Deer Hunter 78. *Holocaust* (TV) 78. Manhattan 79. The Seduction of Joe Tynan 79. *Kramer vs Kramer* (AA) 79. The French Lieutenant's Woman (BFA) 81. Sophie's Choice (AA) 82. Still of the Night 82. Silkwood (AAN) 83. Falling in Love 84. Plenty 85. Heartburn 86. Out of Africa (AAN) 86. Ironweed 87. Evil Angels 88.

¶ *M.S.:* You can't get spoiled if you do your own ironing.

'The danger I'm talking about here is that she tends to sound boring because she's so perfect.'—*Sydney Pollack*

Streeter, Edward (1892–1976). American humorous novelist: *Father of the Bride* and *Mr Hobbs Takes a Vacation* were filmed.

Streisand, Barbra (1942–). American singer and entertainer who made a virtue of her odd looks.
□*Funny Girl* (as Fanny Brice) (AA) 68. Hello Dolly 69. On a Clear Day You Can See Forever 70. The Owl and the Pussycat 70. What's Up Doc? 72. Up the Sandbox 72. The Way We Were 73. For Pete's Sake 74. Funny Lady 75. A Star is Born 76. The Main Event 79. All Night Long 81. Yentl (& co-w, co-p, d) 83. Nuts 87.

¶ This is for posterity. Everything I do will be on film for ever.—*B.S. on Funny Girl*

When I sing, people shut up.—*B.S.*

She really ought to be called Barbra Strident.—*Stanley Kaufmann*

Success to me is having ten honeydew melons and eating only the top half of each one.—*B.S.*

Nobody really knows me: I'm a mixture of self-confidence and insecurity. One thing's for sure—I hate talking about myself.—*B.S.*

'To know her is not necessarily to love her.'—*Rex Reed*

'The most pretentious woman the cinema has ever known.'—*Ryan O'Neal*

'I'd love to work with her again, in something appropriate. Perhaps *Macbeth*.'—*Walter Matthau*

stretch-printing. The reason silent films look jerky is that they were shot at 16 frames a second whereas modern sound projectors operate at 24, making everything move half as fast again as normal. One means of overcoming this jerkiness is stretch-printing in the lab: every second frame is printed twice. This still gives a curious effect, as for every two frames slower than normal sound speed we still get one frame faster.

Strick, Joseph (1923–). American director.
The Savage Eye 59. The Balcony 64. Ulysses 67. Ring of Bright Water (GB) (p only) 69. Tropic of Cancer 69. The Darwin Adventure (p) 71. Janice 73.

Stricklyn, Ray (1930–). American 'second lead' with stage experience.
The Proud and the Profane 56. The Last Wagon 57. Ten North Frederick 58. Young Jesse James 60. Arizona Raiders 65, etc.

Stride, John (1936–). British supporting actor, much on TV.
Bitter Harvest 63. Macbeth 72. Juggernaut 74. Brannigan 75, etc.
TV series: The Main Chance. The Wilde Alliance.

strikes: see *Labour Relations*.

Stritch, Elaine (1926–). Sharp, lanky American character comedienne, mainly on stage; a popular London resident from the mid-seventies.
□The Scarlet Hour 55. Three Violent People 57. A Farewell to Arms 57. The Perfect Furlough 58. Who Killed Teddy Bear? 65. Sidelong Glances of a Pigeon Kicker 70. The Spiral Staircase 75. Providence 77. September 87.
TV series: *My Sister Eileen* 60. The Trials of O'Brien 65. Two's Company 76–78.

Strock, Herbert L. (1918–). American director, former publicist and editor.
The Magnetic Monster 52. Riders to the Stars

54. Battle Taxi 55. Teenage Frankenstein 57. How to Make a Monster 58. Rider on a Dead Horse 62. The Crawling Hand 63, etc.

Strode, Woody or **Woodrow** (1914–). Tall black American actor.
The Lion Hunters 51. The Ten Commandments 56. *Sergeant Rutledge* 60. Spartacus 60. Two Rode Together 62. The Man Who Shot Liberty Valance 62. Genghis Khan 65. *The Professionals* 66. Shalako 68. Che! 69. The Revengers 72. The Gatling Gun 72. Winterhawk 76. Loaded Guns 76. The Black Stallion Returns 83. Vigilante 83.

Stromberg, Hunt (1894–1968). American producer, long with MGM, who went independent in the forties.
Breaking into Society (as d) 24. Fire Patrol (as d) 26. Torrent 27. Our Dancing Daughters 28. Red Dust 32. *The Thin Man* 34. *The Great Ziegfeld* (AA) 36. Maytime 38. Marie Antoinette 38. Idiot's Delight 39. *The Women* 39. Northwest Passage 40. *Pride and Prejudice* 41. Guest in the House 44. Lured 47. Too Late for Tears 49. Betweeen Midnight and Dawn 50. Mask of the Avenger 51, many others.

¶ Boys, I've an idea. Let's fill the screen with tits.—*H.S. on taking over White Shadows in the South Seas in 1928*

Stross, Raymond (1916–). British producer, in films from 1933; married to Anne Heywood.
As Long as They're Happy 52. An Alligator Named Daisy 56. The Flesh is Weak 56. A Question of Adultery 58. A Terrible Beauty 59. The Very Edge 62. The Leather Boys 63. Ninety Degrees in the Shade 65. The Midas Run 69. I Want What I Want 72, etc.

Stroud, Don (1937–). American leading man.
Madigan 68. Games 68. What's So Bad about Feeling Good 68. Coogan's Bluff 69. Bloody Mama 70. Explosion 70. Von Richthofen and Brown 70. Tick Tick Tick 70. Joe Kidd 72. Scalawag 73. The Choirboys 77. The Buddy Holly Story 78. The Amityville Horror 79.

Strudwick, Shepperd: see *Shepperd, John.*

Struss, Karl (1891–1981). American cinematographer.
Ben Hur 26. *Sunrise* (AA) 27. Abraham Lincoln 30. The Sign of the Cross 32. *Dr Jekyll and Mr Hyde* 32. The Great Dictator 40. Bring on the Girls 44. Suspense 46. The Macomber Affair 47. Rocketship XM 50. *Limelight* 52. Tarzan and the She-Devil 53, many others.

Struthers, Sally (1947–). American young character actress, a hit as the daughter in TV's *All in the Family* 71–74.
Five Easy Pieces 70. The Getaway 72. Aloha Means Goodbye (TV) 76.

¶ Acting is cheap group therapy, being a schizo fifty different ways. And we're paid!—*S.S.*

Stuart, Binkie (c. 1932–). British child actress of the thirties.
Moonlight Sonata 37. Little Dolly Daydream 38. My Irish Molly 39, etc.

Stuart, Gloria (1909–83) (Gloria Stuart Finch). American leading lady of the thirties.
The Old Dark House 32. The Invisible Man 33. Roman Scandals 33. Prisoner of Shark Island 36. Rebecca of Sunnybrook Farm 38. The Three Musketeers 39. She Wrote the Book (last to date) 46, etc.

Stuart, John (1898–1979) (John Croall). British leading man of the twenties, character actor of the forties and after.
Autobiography 1971: *Caught in the Act.*
Her Son (debut) 20. We Women 25. The Pleasure Garden 26. Blackmail 29. Elstree Calling 30. Atlantic 30. Number Seventeen 31. Taxi for Two 32. The Pointing Finger 34. Abdul the Damned 35. Old Mother Riley's Ghost 41. The Phantom Shot 46. Mine Own Executioner 47. The Magic Box 51. Quatermass II 57. Blood of the Vampire 58. Sink the Bismarck 60. Superman 78, etc.

Stuart, Leslie (1864–1928) (Thomas Barrett). British songwriter ('Tell Me Pretty Maiden', 'Florodora', etc.) played by Robert Morley in the 1940 biopic *You Will Remember*.

Stuart, Mel (c. 1926–). American director.
If It's Tuesday This Must Be Belgium 69. I Love My Wife 70. Willie Wonka and the Chocolate Factory 71. One is a Lonely Number 72. Mean Dog Blues 78. The Chisholms (TV) 79.

The Student of Prague. The old German legend, about a man who sold his reflection to the devil and bought it back only at the expense of his life, was filmed in 1913 by Stellan Rye, with Paul Wegener; in 1926 by

Henrik Galeen, with Conrad Veidt; and in 1936 by Arthur Robison, with Anton Walbrook.

The Student Prince. The Sigmund Romberg/Dorothy Donnelly operetta about a Ruritanian prince who loves a barmaid was filmed by Lubitsch in 1927 with Ramon Novarro and Norma Shearer. There was no sound version until 1954, when Richard Thorpe directed Ann Blyth and Edmund Purdom (the latter using Mario Lanza's voice).

student protest was a feature of a few films of the late sixties. They were not successful, with the exception of *If*. For the record the other main titles were *Flick*, *The Strawberry Statement*, *Getting Straight*, *R.P.M.* and *The Revolutionary*.

stunt men, who risk their lives doubling for the stars when the action gets too rough, have been featured in remarkably few movies: *Hollywood Stunt Men*, *Lucky Devils*, *The Lost Squadron*, *Sons of Adventure*, *Callaway Went Thataway*, *Singin' in the Rain* and *Hooper*. *Hell's Angels* was said to be the film on which most stunt men were killed; more recently Paul Mantz lost his life while stunt-flying for *The Flight of the Phoenix*, which was subsequently dedicated to him. Most famous stunt men are probably Yakima Canutt, who later became a famous second-unit director; Richard Talmadge, who doubled for Douglas Fairbanks and also directed a few films himself; and Cliff Lyons, who stood in for most of the western stars. Stunt men who became famous in their own right include George O'Brien, Jock Mahoney, Rod Cameron and George Montgomery. In the early eighties a film called *The Stunt Man* took a wry view of the matter and a TV series called *The Fall Guy* was popular for a while.

Sturges, John (1911–). American director of smooth if increasingly pretentious action films, former editor and documentarist.
□The Man Who Dared 46. Shadowed 46. Alias Mr Twilight 47. For the Love of Rusty 47. Keeper of the Bees 48. The Best Man Wins 48. The Sign of the Ram 48. The Walking Hills 49. The Capture 49. Mystery Street 50. The Magnificent Yankee 50. Right Cross 50. Kind Lady 51. The People Against O'Hara 51. It's a Big Country (part) 51. The Girl in White 52. Fast Company 52. Jeopardy 53. Escape from Fort Bravo 53. *Bad Day at Black Rock* 54. Underwater 55. The Scarlet Coat 55. Backlash 56. *Gunfight at the OK Corral* 57. The Law and Jake Wade 58. The Old Man and the Sea 58. Last Train from Gun Hill 58. Never So Few 59. *The Magnificent Seven* 60. By Love Possessed 61. Sergeants Three 62. A Girl Named Tamiko 63. *The Great Escape* 63. The Satan Bug 65. The Hallelujah Trail 65. The Hour of the Gun 67. Ice Station Zebra 68. Marooned 69. Joe Kidd 72. Valdez the Halfbreed (Sp.) 73. McQ 74. The Eagle Has Landed 77.

'It is hard to remember why his career was ever considered meaningful.'—*Andrew Sarris, 1968*

Sturges, Preston (1898–1959) (Edmund P. Biden). American writer-director who in the early forties was Hollywood's wonder boy who never lost the common touch despite his free-wheeling witty style and subject matter. By 1950 his talent had disappeared, and he retired unhappily to France.
AS WRITER: *The Power and the Glory* 33. We Live Again 34. The Good Fairy 35. Diamond Jim 35. Easy Living 37. Port of Seven Seas 38. If I Were King 39. Never Say Die 39. Remember the Night 40, etc.
□AS WRITER-DIRECTOR: *The Great McGinty* (AA) 40. *Christmas in July* 40. *Sullivan's Travels* 41. The Lady Eve 41. *The Palm Beach Story* 42. *The Great Moment* 43. *The Miracle of Morgan's Creek* 43. *Hail the Conquering Hero* 44. Mad Wednesday 46. Unfaithfully Yours 48. The Beautiful Blonde from Bashful Bend 49. The Diary of Major Thompson 56.

'The Breughel of American comedy directors . . . the absurdity of the American success story was matched by the ferocity of the battle of the sexes . . . Lubitsch treated sex as the dessert of a civilized meal of manners. Sturges, more in the American style, served sex with all the courses.'—*Andrew Sarris, 1968*

'Jesus, he was a strange guy. Carried his own hill with him, I tell you.'—*Frank Capra*

'There was a desperate, hectic quality to all his films—an intense desire to believe all the Horatio Alger ideals often associated with America, intermingled with a cynical "European" view of those ideals.'—*James Ursini*

'He has restored to the art of the cinema a certain graphic velocity it has missed since the turmoil of Mack Sennett's zanies.'—*Bosley Crowther*

'Preston is like a man from the Italian Renaissance—he wants to do everything at once.'—*James Agee*

❀ For being the wonder boy of the early forties, with his unique blend of sophisticated comedy and pratfall farce. *Sullivan's Travels*

¶ He was too large for this smelly resort, and the big studios were scared to death of him. A man who was a triple threat kept them awake nights, and I'm positive they were waiting for him to fall on his face so they could pounce and devour this terrible threat to their stingy talents. They pounced, and they got him, good. But he knew the great days when his can glowed like a port light from their kissing it.—*Earl Felton*

When the last dime is gone, I'll sit on the curb outside with a pencil and a ten cent notebook, and start the whole thing over again.—*Preston Sturges, 1957*

Styne, Jule (1905–1981) (Jules Styne). British-born composer, in US from childhood. Former pianist and conductor. Film songs include 'There Goes That Song Again', 'Give Me Five Minutes More', 'It's Magic', 'Three Coins in the Fountain'. Shows filmed include *Gentlemen Prefer Blondes, Bells Are Ringing, Gypsy, Funny Girl.*

submarines have been the setting for so many war action films that only a few can be noted. Pure entertainment was the object of *Submarine Patrol, Submarine Command, Torpedo Run, Destination Tokyo, Run Silent Run Deep, Crash Dive, The Deep Six* and *Ice Station Zebra.* Somewhat deeper thoughts were permitted in *Morning Departure, The Silent Enemy, Les Maudits*, and *We Dive at Dawn.* Submarines became objects of farce in *Jack Ahoy, Let's Face It*, and *Operation Petticoat.*

More unusual submarine vehicles appeared in *Voyage to the Bottom of the Sea, Around the World Under the Sea, Twenty Thousand Leagues Under the Sea, Thunderball, You Only Live Twice, Above Us the Waves* and *The Beast from 20,000 Fathoms.*

Subotsky, Milton (1921–). American independent producer and writer.
Rock Rock Rock 56. The Last Mile 58. City of the Dead (GB) 60. It's Trad Dad (GB) 63. Dr Terror's House of Horrors (GB) 64. Dr Who and the Daleks (GB) 65. The Skull (GB) 66. The Psychopath (GB) 66. Daleks' Invasion Earth 2150 AD (GB) 66. Torture Garden (GB) 67. The House That Dripped Blood (GB) 70. Tales from the Crypt (GB) 71. Asylum (GB) 72. Madhouse (GB) 73. The Land That Time Forgot (GB) 75. At the Earth's Core (GB) 76, etc.

subtitles in silent days came *after* the scene in which the actors mouthed the dialogue. When talkies came the less cumbersome method was evolved of superimposing the dialogue at the foot of the screen, which considerably sharpened up the audience's reading speed.

subways: see *Underground Railways.*

Sucksdorff, Arne (1917–). Swedish documentarist who has normally written and photographed his own films, which vary from six minutes to feature length.
The West Wind 42. Shadows on the Snow 45. *Rhythm of a City* 47. *A Divided World* 48. The Road 48. The Wind and the River 51. *The Great Adventure* 53. The Flute and the Arrow 57. The Boy in the Tree 60. My Home is Copacabana 65. Forbush and the Penguins 71, etc.

suicide became the central subject of two sixties films; *Le Feu Follet* and *The Slender Thread*, in which the motives for it in two particular cases are examined. It has, of course, been part of countless other plots, including factual or legendary ones such as *Cleopatra, Romeo and Juliet* and *Scott of the Antarctic.* Innumerable melodramas have begun with apparent suicides which have been proved by the disbelieving hero to be murder; the least likely of these may be *The Third Secret.* In *An Inspector Calls* a girl's suicide caused guilt complexes in an entire family for different reasons. In *An American Dream* the hero virtually commits suicide by walking into a room full of gangsters out to kill him. In *Leave Her to Heaven* the leading character commits suicide in such a way that her husband will be blamed for her murder. Several Japanese films have been based on the suicide pilots or Kamikaze, and there has also been a graphic account of the principles of *Hara Kiri.* Suicide has often been the way out for villains in mystery pictures: drowning for Herbert Marshall in *Foreign Correspondent*, shooting for Leo G. Carroll in *Spellbound*, poison for Rosamund John in *Green for Danger* and Barry Fitzgerald in *And Then There Were None.* And one could not begin to count the films in which characters have been narrowly saved from suicide, like Ray Milland in *The Lost Weekend.* Attempted suicide was even played for comedy by Laurel and Hardy in *The Flying Deuces*, by Graham Chapman in *The Odd Job*, by Jack Lemmon in *Buddy Buddy* and *Luv*, by Burt Reynolds in *The End*, while in *It's a Wonderful Life* James Stewart was dissuaded from suicide by a friendly angel. In *The Long Goodbye*, Elliott Gould finds a presumed suicide alive, and shoots him.

Sullavan, Margaret (1911–1960) (Margaret Brooke). American leading actress in light films of the thirties and forties; she had a special whimsical quality which was unique. Biography 1977: *Haywire* by Brooke Hayward (her daughter).
□Only Yesterday 33. Little Man What Now? 34. So Red the Rose 35. *The Good Fairy* 35. Next Time We Love 36. The Moon's Our Home 36. *Three Comrades* 38. Shopworn Angel 38. The Shining Hour 39. *The Shop around the Corner* 39. *The Mortal Storm* 40. So Ends Our Night 40. Back Street 41. Appointment for Love 41. Cry Havoc 43. No Sad Songs for Me 50.

Sullivan, Barry (1912–) (Patrick Barry). American leading man with stage experience. *Lady in the Dark* 43. Two Years before the Mast 44. And Now Tomorrow 44. Suspense 46. The Gangster 47. Tension 49. The Great Gatsby 49. The Outriders 50. Three Guys Named Mike 51. *The Bad and the Beautiful* 52. Jeopardy 54. Queen Bee 55. Forty Guns 57. Wolf Larsen 57. Seven Ways from Sundown 60. The Light in the Piazza 62. Stagecoach to Hell 64. My Blood Runs Cold 64. Harlow (electronovision version) 65. An American Dream (See You in Hell, Darling) 66. Intimacy 66. Buckskin 68. Willie Boy 69. Earthquake 74. The Human Factor 75. Oh God 77, etc.
TV series: Harbourmaster 57. The Tall Man 60–61. The Road West 66.

Sullivan, C. Gardner (1885–1965). American screenwriter.
The Battle of Gettysburg 14. The Wrath of the Gods 15. Civilization 16. The Aryan 16. The Zeppelin's Last Raid 17. Carmen of the Klondike 18. Sahara 19. Human Wreckage 23. Sparrows 26. Tempest 27. Sequoia 34. The Buccaneer 38, many others.

Sullivan, Francis L. (1903–56). Heavyweight British character actor, often seen as advocate. On stage from 1921, films from 1933.
The Missing Rembrandt (debut) 33. Chu Chin Chow 33. Great Expectations (US) 35. *The Mystery of Edwin Drood* (US) 35. Sabotage 36. Action for Slander 37. Dinner at the Ritz 37. Twenty-one Days 38. The Citadel 38. The Four Just Men 39. *Pimpernel Smith* 41. *Fiddlers Three* 44. Caesar and Cleopatra 45. *Great Expectations* 46. *Oliver Twist* 48. Night and the City 51. Plunder of the Sun (US) 51. The Prodigal (US) 55. Hell's Island (US) 55, many others.

Sullivan, Pat (1887–1933). Australian newspaper cartoonist who settled in the US and invented Felix the Cat, the most popular character in film cartoons of the twenties.

Sullivan's Travels (US 1941). Perhaps the most meaningful, eccentric and devastating of all Preston Sturges' comedies. About a film director who goes off in search of truth but finally discovers that all people want is to laugh, it is a remarkably sure-footed combination of farce, melodrama and sentiment, and its appeal seems to have increased over the years. Written and directed by Sturges, produced by Paul Jones, photographed by John F. Seitz; with memorable performances by Joel McCrea, Veronica Lake, and the familiar Sturges repertory of supporting players.

Sully, Frank (1910–1975). American small part actor often seen as farmer or dumb crook.
Mary Burns Fugitive 35. The Grapes of Wrath 40. Escape to Glory 41. Thousands Cheer 43. Renegades 46. With a Song in My Heart 52. The Naked Street 56, many others.

Sumac, Yma (1928–) (Emparatriz Chavarri). Peruvian singer with wide octave range.
The Secret of the Incas 54.

Summerfield, Eleanor (1921–). British character comedienne, on stage from 1939. London Belongs to Me (film debut) 47. Scrooge 51. It's Great To Be Young 56. Dentist in the Chair 59. On the Beat 62. Guns of Darkness 63. Some Will Some Won't 70, many others.

Summers, Jeremy (1931–). British director, from TV.
The Punch and Judy Man 62. Crooks in Cloisters 64. Ferry Cross the Mersey 64. House of a Thousand Dolls 67. Vengeance of Fu Manchu 67, etc.

Summers, Walter (1896–1973). British director of the twenties and thirties.
Ypres 25. Mons 26. The Battle of the Coronel and Falkland Islands 31. Deeds Men Do 32. The Return of Bulldog Drummond 33. Mutiny on the Elsinore 36. Music Hath Charms (co-d) 36. At the Villa Rose 38. Dark Eyes of London 38. Traitor Spy 40, etc.

Summertime (Summer Madness) (US 1955). This adaptation of Arthur Laurents' play *The Time of the Cuckoo* successfully balanced its slight emotional story against the exotic background of Venice. Katharine Hepburn gave a brilliant performance as the lonely spinster tourist attracted by a handsome but married Italian (Rossano Brazzi); David Lean's direction was subtle and witty, and Jack Hildyard's colour photography proved a major asset.

Summerville, Slim (1892–1946) (George J. Summerville). Lanky, mournful-looking American character comedian, former gagman and director for Mack Sennett.
The Beloved Rogue 27. *All Quiet on the Western Front* 30. The Front Page 31. Life Begins at Forty 35. White Fang 36. The Road Back 37. Rebecca of Sunnybrook Farm 38. Jesse James 39. *Tobacco Road* 41. Miss Polly 41. Niagara Falls 42. The Hoodlum Saint 46, many others.

Sumner, Geoffrey (1908–). British comic actor of silly ass types.
Helter Skelter 49. The Dark Man 52. A Tale of Five Cities 53. Traveller's Joy 55, etc.

Sundberg, Clinton (1919–). American character actor, former teacher; usually plays flustered clerk or head waiter.
Undercurrent 46. Living in a Big Way 47. Annie Get Your Gun 50. Main Street to Broadway 52. The Caddy 53. The Birds and the Bees 56. The Wonderful World of the Brothers Grimm 63. Hotel 67, many others.

Sunrise (US 1927). An interesting example of the German influence on Hollywood (written by Carl Mayer, directed by F. W. Murnau), this melodrama won a special Academy Award for 'artistic quality of production'. There were awards too for the camerawork (Charles Rosher, Karl Struss) and for Janet Gaynor as the young wife whose life is threatened by her temporarily unbalanced husband (George O'Brien). The story takes place during a journey, and the use of locations to this extent was rare for Hollywood at the time.

Sunset Boulevard (US 1950). A harsh look at Hollywood directed by Billy Wilder from a script by himself, Charles Brackett and D. M. Marsham Jnr. Gloria Swanson enjoys herself as the faded star who makes a tragic comeback, but she, Erich Von Stroheim, Anna Q. Nilsson and Buster Keaton come so close to playing themselves it's macabre. William Holden plays the star's kept man who encourages her false hopes. Photographed by John F. Seitz with music by Franz Waxman.

The Sunshine Boys (US 1975). Only fair as a screen version of Neil Simon's play about the reunion of two elderly vaudevillians, this was notable for bringing George Burns back to the screen and enabling him to win an Academy Award at the age of 80. The other half of the team was one of Walter Matthau's less happy performances, and the treatment was resolutely uncinematic.

superdynamation. A term coined by Ray Harryhausen for his method of animating rubber monsters.

Super-8. Improved 8mm film which can take a sound track, therefore replacing the old 9.5mm.

superimpose: place one image on top of another, usually during a dissolve when one is fading out and the other fading in.

Superman. A comic strip character of the thirties, a being of giant powers from the planet Krypton; until they are needed he masquerades as Clark Kent, a timid newspaperman. Superman has never been out of fashion—1978 brought a multi-million dollar live version to follow the various cartoons and serials which have been popular over the years—and along the way he has inspired Batman, Spiderman, Doc Savage, the Six Million Dollar Man, the Bionic Woman, etc, etc. In 1984, after two further sequels, *Superman* gave way to *Supergirl*.

supervisor. In Hollywood in the early thirties, a studio name for the assigned producer.

supporting players

? These lamentably unsung heroes and heroines all had their moments. Do you remember who, in what films:

1 Offered his guests potatoes, smoked a cigar in a tomb, and said: 'I have a rendezvous with the Duchesse de Guermantes'?
2 Was changed into a black bird, sought the truth about a criminal called Makropolos, and said: 'You will please clasp your hands behind your head'?
3 Impersonated a gorilla, was caught by his wife without his trousers, and said: 'This is the end—the absolute end'?
4 Played billiards with Barry Fitzgerald, preached hellfire in the west, and said: 'The soul—what is that? Can you hear it? Touch it? Smell it? No . . .'?

5 Was fired from a cannon, was lathered and shaved during a medical examination, and said: 'This shall be a gala day'?
6 Ran a hotel in Tahiti, was Danny Kaye's mother-in-law-to-be, and said: 'Tell me, have you been doing anything you shouldn't'?
7 Ran a mental home, played a leprechaun, and sang: 'For tonight we'll merry merry be' from a bottle?
8 Relished a plate of onions, was stabbed by Countess Fosco, and said: 'No, sir, I don't think we can do business along those lines . . .'?
9 Fell off the top of Westminster Cathedral, was prosecuted for impersonating Santa Claus, and said: 'I have a high respect for your nerves. They are my old friends. I have heard you mention them with consideration these twenty years at least'?
10 Served tea at Brighton, assisted Groucho Marx, and said: 'I positively swill in his ale'?
11 Ran a lemonade stall, followed Linda Darnell and, as a bartender, said: 'Sir, you rouse the artist in me'?
12 Was jealous of Maurice Chevalier, got the better of Lewis Stone, and said: 'Peace—it's wonderful!'?
13 Spied on 92nd Street, solved the mystery of Manderley, and said: 'Never thought I'd make it. Getting too old for this kind of work'?
14 Hunted the Frankenstein monster, played a butler in Devonshire, and said: 'I'd get an irrigation ditch so squirmin' full of repented sinners I pretty near drowned half of 'em!'?
15 Murdered Joan Blondell, advised Queen Victoria, and said: 'We rule with moderate strictness, and in return are satisfied with moderate obedience'?
16 Played John Brown twice, Black Michael once, and said: 'All the universe, or nothing: Which shall it be?'

Surtees, Bruce (–). American cinematographer.
The Beguiled 71. Play Misty for Me 71. Dirty Harry 72. The Great Northfield Minnesota Raid 72. Blume in Love 73. High Plains Drifter 73. Lenny 74. Night Moves 75. The Outlaw Josey Wales 76. Movie Movie 78. Big Wednesday 78. Escape from Alcatraz 79. Inchon 81. Firefox 82. Tightrope 84.

Surtees, Robert L. (1906–85). Distinguished American cinematographer, in Hollywood from 1927.
Thirty Seconds over Tokyo 44. Our Vines Have Tender Grapes 45. The Unfinished Dance 47. Act of Violence 48. *Intruder in the Dust* 49. *King Solomon's Mines* (AA) 50. Quo Vadis 51. *The Bad and the Beautiful* (AA) 52. Escape from Fort Bravo 53. Trial 55. *Oklahoma!* 55. The Swan 56. Raintree County 57. Merry Andrew 58. *Ben Hur* (AA) 59. Mutiny on the Bounty 62. The Hallelujah Trail 65. The Collector 65. The Satan Bug 65. Lost Command 66. Doctor Dolittle 67. *The Graduate* 67. *Sweet Charity* 68. The Arrangement 69. Summer of 42 71. The Last Picture Show 71. The Cowboys 72. The Other 72. Oklahoma Crude 73. The Sting 73. The Great Waldo Pepper 75. The Hindenberg 75. A Star Is Born 76. The Turning Point 77. Bloodbrothers 78. Same Time Next Year 78, etc.

Susann, Jacqueline (1921–1974). American best-selling novelist. Films of her books include *Valley of the Dolls, The Love Machine* and *Once is Not Enough*.

Suschitsky, Peter (1941–). British cinematographer.
It Happened Here 65. Privilege 66. Charlie Bubbles 67. A Midsummer Night's Dream 68. Lock Up Your Daughters 68. Leo the Last 70. Lisztomania 76. Valentino 77. The Empire Strikes Back 80. Krull 83, etc.

Suschitsky, Wolfgang (1912–). Austrian cinematographer in Britain.
No Resting Place 51. Cat and Mouse 57. The Small World of Sammy Lee 63. Ulysses 67. Theatre of Blood 73. Something to Hide 74, etc.

Suspicion (US 1941). The film for which Joan Fontaine won an Academy Award was toned down from a novel by Francis Iles: the ending was changed as it was felt that no one would accept Cary Grant as a wife-murderer. Hitchcock directed rather coldly, and the production was only average.

Susskind, David (1920–). American TV and theatre personality and producer who has also produced a few films.
Edge of the City 57. A Raisin in the Sun 61. Requiem for a Heavyweight 62. All the Way Home 63. Lovers and Other Strangers 70. Alice Doesn't Live Here Any More 74.

Buffalo Bill and the Indians 76. Loving Couples 80, etc.

Sutherland, A. Edward (1895–1974). American director, in Hollywood from 1914. Wild Wild Susan 25. Dance of Life 29. Palmy Days 31. Mississippi 35. Diamond Jim 35. Champagne Waltz 37. Every Day's a Holiday 38. The Flying Deuces 39. *The Boys from Syracuse* 40. Beyond Tomorrow 41. Invisible Woman 41. Nine Lives Are Not Enough 42. Dixie 43. Follow the Boys 44. Abie's Irish Rose 46. Having Wonderful Crime 46. Bermuda Affair 56, many others.

Sutherland, Donald (1935–). Gaunt Canadian actor who became very fashionable at the end of the sixties.
□The World Ten Times Over 63. Castle of the Living Dead 64. Dr Terror's House of Horrors 65. Fanatic 65. The Bedford Incident 65. Promise Her Anything 66. The Dirty Dozen 67. Billion Dollar Brain 67. Sebastian 68. Oedipus the King 68. Interlude 68. Joanna 68. The Split 68. Start the Revolution Without Me 69. Act of the Heart 70. *M*A*S*H* 70. Kelly's Heroes 70. Alex in Wonderland 71. Little Murders 70. *Klute* 71. Johnny Got His Gun (as Christ) 71. Steelyard Blues 72. Lady Ice 72. Alien Thunder 73. Don't Look Now 73. S*P*Y*S 74. The Day of the Locust 75. End of the Game 76. 1900 76. Casanova 76. The Eagle Has Landed 77. The Disappearance 77. Blood Relations 78. The Kentucky Fried Movie 78. Invasion of the Body Snatchers 78. National Lampoon's Animal House 78. The First Great Train Robbery 79. Murder by Decree 79. Bear Island 79. A Man, a Woman and a Bank 80. Nothing Personal 80. Ordinary People 80. Eye of the Needle 81. Threshold 81. Gas 81. Max Dugan Returns 83. The Winter of Our Discontent (TV) 84. Crackers 84. Ordeal by Innocence 85. Heaven Help Us 85. Revolution 86. The Wolf at the Door 86.

Sutton, Dudley (1933–). British character actor.
The Leather Boys 63. Rotten to the Core 65. Crossplot 69. The Walking Stick 70. The Devils 71, etc.

Sutton, Grady (1908–). American character comedian usually seen as vacuous country cousin; in Hollywood from 1926. The Story of Temple Drake 32. Alice Adams 35. Stage Door 37. Alexander's Ragtime Band 38. *The Bank Dick* 40. The Great Moment 44. My Wild Irish Rose 48. White Christmas 54. The Birds and the Bees 56. My Fair Lady 64. Paradise Hawaiian Style 66. The Great Bank Robbery 69. Myra Breckinridge 70, many others.
TV series: The Pruitts of Southampton 66.

Sutton, John (1908–1963). British actor with stage experience; in Hollywood from 1937, usually as second lead or smooth swashbuckling villain.
Bulldog Drummond Comes Back 37. The Adventures of Robin Hood 38. The Invisible Man Returns 40. A Yank in the RAF 41. *Ten Gentlemen from West Point* 42. Jane Eyre 43. Claudia and David 46. The Three Musketeers 48. The Golden Hawk 52. East of Sumatra 54. The Bat 59, many others.

Suzman, Janet (1939–). South African stage actress in Britain.
□A Day in the Death of Joe Egg 70. *Nicholas and Alexandra* 72. The Black Windmill 74. Voyage of the Damned 76. The House on Garibaldi Street (TV) 79. Nijinsky 80. The Priest of Love 81. The Draughtsman's Contract 82. And the Ship Sailed On 84. Mountbatten (TV) (as Edwina) 85.

Svengali, the evil genius of George du Maurier's Victorian romance *Trilby*, has been seen at least five times on screen. In 1915 Wilton Lackaye and Clara Kimball Young appeared in a version under the title *Trilby*. There was a British one-reeler in 1922 in the 'Tense Moments with Great Authors' series, and in 1923 James Young directed a second Hollywood version with Arthur Edmund Carewe and Andrée Lafayette. In 1931, under the title *Svengali*, Archie Mayo directed a sound remake with John Barrymore as the hypnotist to Marian Marsh's heroine, and in 1954 Donald Wolfit and Hildegarde Neff appeared in a British version directed by Noel Langley. (Robert Newton had proved incapable of playing the lead.) In 1982 Peter O'Toole and Jodie Foster were in a dismal TV modernization set in New York.

Svenson, Bo (1941–). American action lead of the seventies.
The Great Waldo Pepper 75. Part Two Walking Tall 75. Special Delivery 76. Breaking Point 76. Final Chapter – Walking Tall 77. North Dallas Forty 79. Counterfeit Commandos 81. Heartbreak Ridge 86.

Swain, Mack (1876–1935). American silent actor, a Mack Sennett heavy from 1914; most memorable in *The Gold Rush* 24. Last part, *Midnight Patrol* 32.

swan songs

? Whose final appearances were made in the following films?

1 *Saratoga* (1937)
2 *The Harder They Fall* (1956)
3 *The Inn of the Sixth Happiness* (1958)
4 *The Carpetbaggers* (1963)
5 *Advise and Consent* (1962)
6 *A Funny Thing Happened on the Way to the Forum* (1967)
7 *He Ran All the Way* (1951)
8 *To Be or Not to Be* (1942)
9 *The Story of Mankind* (1957)
10 *The Naked Edge* (1961)
11 *Playmates* (1942)
12 *Ship of Fools* (1965)
13 *The Unholy Three* (1930)
14 *Monkeys Go Home* (1966)
15 *Satan Never Sleeps* (1962)
16 *Guess Who's Coming to Dinner* (1967)
17 *Cuban Rebel Girls* (1959)
18 *Soylent Green* (1973)
19 *Twilight of Honor* (1963)
20 *The Patsy* (1964)
21 *Once More with Feeling* (1960)
22 *Malaya* (1950)
23 *The Defector* (1966)
24 *The Mating Game* (1959)
25 *Night Watch* (1973)

Swanson, Gloria (1897–1983) (G. Svensson). American leading lady of the silent screen who started as a Mack Sennett bathing beauty and made many comebacks.
The Meal Ticket 15. Teddy at the Throttle 17. The Pullman Bride 17. Shifting Sands 18. Don't Change Your Husband 18. *Male and Female* 19. Why Change Your Wife? 19. *The Affairs of Anatol* 21. Adam's Rib 23. Prodigal Daughters 23. Madame Sans Gene 25. Untamed Lady 26. *Sadie Thompson* 28. *Queen Kelly* (unfinished) 28. Indiscreet 31. Perfect Understanding 33. Music in the Air 34. Father Takes a Wife 41. *Sunset Boulevard* 50. Three for Bedroom C 52. Nero's Mistress (It.) 56. Killer Bees (TV) 73. Airport 75 74, many others.

¶ *G.S.:* I acquired my expensive tastes from Mr De Mille.
G.S.: When I die, my epitaph should read: she paid the bills.
G.S.: Dietrich's legs may be longer, but I have seven grandchildren.
Famous line (*Sunset Boulevard*, when told she used to be a big star): I *am* big. It's the pictures that got small.

Swanson, Maureen (1932–). British leading lady who retired to marry after a brief career.
Moulin Rouge 53. A Town Like Alice 56. The Spanish Gardener 56. Robbery under Arms 57. The Malpas Mystery 63, etc.

Swarthout, Gladys (1904–1969). American opera singer who acted in a few films.
Rose of the Rancho 35. Give Us This Night 36. Champagne Waltz 37. Romance in the Dark 38. Ambush 39, etc.

swashbucklers are films of period adventure in which the hero and villain usually settle the issue by a duel to the death. The greatest screen swashbucklers of all are probably Douglas Fairbanks Snr and Errol Flynn, but one should also be grateful for the efforts of Tyrone Power (*The Mark of Zorro*), Douglas Fairbanks Jnr (*Sinbad the Sailor*), Ronald Colman (*The Prisoner of Zenda*), Stewart Granger (*Scaramouche*), Rudolph Valentino (*The Eagle*), Gene Kelly (*The Three Musketeers*), Robert Donat (*The Count of Monte Cristo*), Louis Hayward (*The Man in the Iron Mask*), Cornel Wilde (*The Bandit of Sherwood Forest*), Tony Curtis (*The Purple Mask*) and their numerous imitators. The 1976 attempt to revive (or spoof) the genre in *Swashbuckler* was a sorry failure.

Swayze, Patrick (–). American juvenile lead of the eighties.
□ Skatetown USA 79. The Outsiders 83. Uncommon Valor 83. Grandview USA 84. Red Dawn 84. Youngblood 85. *North and South* (TV) 86. Dirty Dancing 87.

Swedish cinema was at the forefront of world production as early as 1910. Famous directors such as Victor Sjostrom and Mauritz Stiller were well known by 1912, and tended to make films of Swedish legends, which appealed by their very strangeness. *Sir Arne's Treasure* 19, *Thy Soul Shall Bear Witness* 20, *The Atonement of Gosta Berling* 24, are among the best-known titles of the Swedish silent period; but in the mid-twenties all Sweden's best talent—including the newly-discovered Greta Garbo—moved towards Hollywood and the home industry was eclipsed until the late forties saw the appearance of talents like Werner (*Midvinterblot*), Sucksdorff (*Rhythm of a City*) and Sjoberg (*Frenzy*). In the fifties the Swedish vein of romantic pessimism was developed to its ultimate in the semi-mystic but commercial films of Ingmar Bergman, who remains the most significant name in the Scandinavian cinema.

Sweet, Blanche (1895–1986) (Daphne Wayne). American silent heroine.
The Lonedale Operator 11. Judith of Bethulia 13. The Secret Sin 15. The Deadliest Sex 20. In the Palace of the King 23. Anna Christie 23. Tess of the D'Urbervilles 24. Bluebeard's Seven Wives 26. Singed 27. The Woman Racket 30. The Silver Horde 30, etc.

Sweet, Dolph (1921–85). Barrel-chested American character actor.
The Young Doctors 61. The Lost Man 69 Fear Is the Key 72. The Lords of Flatbush 74. Go Tell the Spartans 77, etc.
TV series: *Gimme a Break* 81–.

Sweet Smell of Success (US 1957). An odd, unexpected and harsh attack on Broadway columnists written in venom by Clifford Odets and Ernest Lehman, directed with tremendous polish by Alexander Mackendrick, fresh from Ealing. Not very likeable but highly cinematic, with photography by James Wong Howe, music by Elmer Bernstein, and arresting performances by Burt Lancaster and Tony Curtis.

Swenson, Inga (1932–). American actress.
□Advise and Consent 61. The Miracle Worker 62. Earth II (TV) 71. The Betsy 78.
TV series: Soap 78. Benson 79.

Swerling, Jo (1894–*) (Joseph Swerling). Russian-American writer, long in Hollywood.
Dirigible 31. Platinum Blonde 32. Man's Castle 35. Made for Each Other 38. *The Westerner* 40. Blood and Sand 42. *Lifeboat* 44. Leave Her to Heaven 46. Thunder in the East 52. King of the Roaring Twenties 61, many others.
His son **Jo Swerling Jnr** writes and produces for TV.

Swift, David (1919–). American radio and TV writer-producer-director (TV series include *Mr Peepers*, *Grindl*).
Pollyanna 60. The Parent Trap 61. Love is a Ball 63. The Interns 63. Under the Yum Yum Tree 64. Good Neighbour Sam 64. How to Succeed in Business without Really Trying (wpd) 67. Candleshoe (co-w) 77, etc.

Swift, Jonathan (1667–1745). Irish satirist best known for the much-filmed *Gulliver's Travels*, which is *not* a children's book.

Swinburne, Nora (1902–) (Elinore Johnson). British actress on stage from 1914, screen occasionally from 1921.
Alibi 30. Potiphar's Wife 31. Fanny by Gaslight 43. *Quartet* 48. The River 51. The End of the Affair 55. Conspiracy of Hearts 59. Interlude 68. Up the Chastity Belt 71, many others.

swinging London was a myth, a creation of *Time Magazine* which rebounded through the world's press and lasted for several silly seasons from 1965. It also helped British production finances by persuading American impresarios that London was where the action is, and its influence was felt in scores of trendy and increasingly boring films, including *Georgy Girl, Alfie, The Jokers, Kaleidoscope, Smashing Time, Help!, The Knack, Blow Up, Casino Royale, I'll Never Forget Whatshisname, To Sir With Love, Up the Junction, Bedazzled, Poor Cow, The Strange Affair, Salt and Pepper, Joanna, Darling* and *Otley*.

The Swiss Family Robinson. The classic children's novel by Johann Wyss was filmed in Hollywood in 1940 by Edward Ludwig, with Thomas Mitchell, Edna Best, Freddie Bartholemew and Terry Kilburn. In 1960 Ken Annakin remade it as a Walt Disney spectacular, with John Mills, Dorothy McGuire, James MacArthur and Tommy Kirk as the desert island castaways.

Swit, Loretta (1937–). American comedy actress of the seventies, familiar as Hot Lips Houlihan from TV's *M*A*S*H*.
□Stand Up and Be Counted 72. Shirts/Skins (TV) 73. Freebie and the Bean 74. The Last Day (TV) 75. Race with the Devil 75. The Hostage Heart (TV) 77. The Love Tapes (TV) 79. Cagney and Lacey (TV pilot) 81. S.O.B. 81. The Kid from Nowhere (TV) 82. First Affair (TV) 83. The Execution (TV) 85. Beer 85. Whoops Apocalypse 86.

Switzer, Carl ('Alfalfa') (1926–1959). American boy actor of the thirties, a graduate of 'Our Gang'; later in character roles.
General Spanky 37. The War Against Mrs Hadley 42. State of the Union 48. Track of the Cat 54. The Defiant Ones 58, many others.

Swofford, Ken (–). Burly American character actor.
Father Goose 64. The Lawyer 69. One Little Indian 73. Crisis at Sun Valley (TV) 78, etc.
TV series: Quincy 76–82.

Sydney, Basil (1894–1968) (Basil Nugent). British actor of heavy roles, on stage from 1911.

Romance (film debut) 20. The Midshipmaid 32. The Tunnel 35. Rhodes of Africa 36. The Four Just Men 39. Ships with Wings 41. Went the Day Well? 42. *Caesar and Cleopatra* 45. The Man Within 47. *Hamlet* 48. Treasure Island 50. Ivanhoe 52. Hell Below Zero 54. The Dam Busters 55. The Three Worlds of Gulliver 60, etc.

Sykes, Eric (1923–). British TV comedian. Invasion Quartet 61. Village of Daughters 62. Kill or Cure 63. Heavens Above 63. The Bargee 63. One-Way Pendulum 64. Those Magnificent Men in Their Flying Machines 65. Rotten to the Core 65. The Liquidator 65. The Spy with a Cold Nose 67. The Plank (& d) 67. Shalako 68. Monte Carlo or Bust 69. Rhubarb (& d) 70. Theatre of Blood 73. The Boys in Blue 83.

Sylbert, Richard (1928–). American art director.
Baby Doll 56. Splendor in the Grass 61. Walk on the Wild Side 62. The Manchurian Candidate 62. How to Murder Your Wife 64. Long Day's Journey into Night 64. The Pawnbroker 64. Who's Afraid of Virginia Woolf? 66. The Graduate 67. Rosemary's Baby 68. Catch 22 70. Carnal Knowledge 71. The Day of the Dolphin 73. The Fortune 75. Players 79. Reds 81. Partners 82. Frances 82. The Cotton Club (AAN) 84, etc.

Sylvester. The celebrated cartoon cat with the lisping Bronx accent, always in pursuit of Tweetie Pie but never quite managing to win, appeared from the forties to the sixties in Warner shorts, voiced by the inimitable Mel Blanc.

Sylvester, William (1922–). American leading man, in British films from 1949, later back in U.S.
Give Us This Day 50. The Yellow Balloon 52. Albert RN 53. High Tide at Noon 57. Gorgo 59. Offbeat 60. Ring of Spies 63. Devil Doll 64. Devils of Darkness 65. The Syndicate 67. The Hand of Night 67. 2001: A Space Odyssey 68. Heaven Can Wait 78, many others.
TV series: Gemini Man 76.

Sylvie (1883–1970) (Louise Sylvain). French character actress.
Un Carnet de Bal 37. Le Corbeau 43. Le Diable au Corps 46. Dieu a Besoin des Hommes 51. Nous Sommes Tous des Assassins 56. *The Shameless Old Lady* 64.

Syms, Sylvia (1934–). British leading lady with brief stage and TV experience.
My Teenage Daughter (film debut) 56. Ice Cold in Alex 58. Flame in the Streets 60. Victim 61. The Quare Fellow 62. The World Ten Times Over 63. East of Sudan 64. Operation Crossbow 65. The Big Job 65. Run Wild Run Free 69. Hostile Witness 70. Asylum 72. The Tamarind Seed 74, etc.

synchronization. The arranging of sound and picture to match. Only rarely is this done by shooting them simultaneously; the normal process involves re-recording and much laboratory work to give the optimum results.

Szabo, Istvan (1938–). Hungarian director.
Age of Illusion 65. Father 66. A Film About Love 70. 25 Firemen's Street 74. Tales of Budapest 77. The Hungarians 78. Bizalom 79. *Mephisto* 81. *Colonel Redl* 84, etc.

Szwarc, Jeannot (1936–). French director in America.
□Extreme Close Up 74. Bug 75. Jaws 2 78. Somewhere in Time 80. Enigma 82. Supergirl 84. Santa Claus 85.

Answers

self-analysis
1 John Ford □ 2 Howard Hawks □ 3 Orson Welles □ 4 Nicol Williamson □ 5 Orson Welles □ 6 Erich von Stroheim □ 7 François Truffaut □ 8 Cary Grant □ 9 Tallulah Bankhead □ 10 Richard Burton □

sensation!
1 First film in 70mm □ 2 First colour feature in 3-D □ 3 First British film in colour □ 4 First feature in CinemaScope □ 5 First feature in VistaVision □ 6 First film to use the Multiplane camera (which gives depth to

cartoons) ☐ 7 First feature in three-colour Technicolor ☐ 8 First Technicolor movie filmed outdoors ☐ 9 First film with talking sequences ☐ 10 First all-talking film ☐ 11 First feature with synchronized sound track ☐ 12 First (and last) film in 'Emergo' ☐

sequels
1 *On Moonlight Bay* ☐ 2 *Three Smart Girls Grow Up* (*Three Smart Girls* is OK) ☐ 3 *All Quiet on the Western Front* ☐ 4 *Cheaper by the Dozen* ☐ 5 *Jesse James* ☐ 6 *In the Heat of the Night* ☐ 7 *Licensed to Kill* ☐ 8 *Doctor No* ☐ 9 *A Family Affair* (the Hardy family series) ☐ 10 *Four Daughters* ☐ 11 *The Robe* ☐

series episodes
1 Crime Doctor ☐ 2 Philo Vance ☐ 3 Charlie Chan ☐ 4 The Bowery Boys ☐ 5 Michael Shayne ☐ 6 Matt Helm ☐ 7 Jungle Jim ☐ 8 The Lone Wolf ☐ 9 Blondie ☐ 10 Lassie ☐ 11 Dr Gillespie ☐ 12 The Cisco Kid ☐ 13 The Hardy Family ☐ 14 Sherlock Holmes ☐ 15 The Three Mesquiteers ☐ 16 Dr Christian ☐ 17 Carry on ☐ 18 Mr Wong ☐ 19 James Bond ☐ 20 Bulldog Drummond ☐

servants
1 Gale Sondergaard ☐ 2 Judith Anderson ☐ 3 Halliwell Hobbes ☐ 4 Robert Greig ☐ 5 Charles Boyer ☐ 6 John Carradine ☐ 7 Richard Haydn ☐ 8 Eric Blore ☐ 9 Willie Best ☐ 10 Arthur Treacher ☐ 11 Louise Beavers ☐ 12 Stan Laurel (He really did.) ☐

silent films I
1 *Moby Dick* ☐ 2 Jackie Coogan ☐ 3 *The Jazz Singer* ☐ 4 *Intolerance* ☐ 5 Lon Chaney ☐ 6 Gloria Swanson ☐ 7 Belle Bennett ☐ 8 Richard Barthelmess ☐ 9 Guy Newall ☐ 10 George Robey ☐ 11 Ethel Barrymore ☐ 12 Bert Lytell ☐ 13 Rudolph Valentino ☐ 14 *Safety Last* ☐ 15 *Greed* ☐ 16 Erich Von Stroheim ☐ 17 Laurel and Hardy ☐ 18 *He Who Gets Slapped* ☐ 19 *The Squaw Man* ☐ 20 Conrad Veidt ☐

silent films II
1 Pola Negri ☐ 2 Squibs ☐ 3 *Joyless Street* ☐ 4 *The Battleship Potemkin* ☐ 5 Berlin ☐ 6 *The Lodger* ☐ 7 *Shooting Stars* ☐ 8 *Un Chien Andalou* ☐ 9 *Sir Arne's Treasure* ☐ 10 *Witchcraft Through the Ages* ☐ 11 Emil Jannings ☐ 12 *Variety* or *Vaudeville* ☐ 13 *The Student of Prague* ☐ 14 *Metropolis* ☐ 15 *The Loves of Jeanne Ney* ☐ 16 Falconetti ☐ 17 *Napoleon* ☐ 18 Carl Mayer ☐ and Hans Janowitz ☐ 19 *The Seashell and the Clergyman* ☐ 20 René Clair ☐

silent films III
1 Rudolph Valentino ☐ 2 Douglas Fairbanks Jnr ☐ 3 Alan Crosland ☐ 4 *The Covered Wagon* ☐ 5 *Nanook of the North* ☐ 6 *Blind Husbands* ☐ 7 *A Connecticut Yankee in King Arthur's Court* ☐ 8 *Peg o'My Heart* ☐ 9 *Kriemheld's Revenge* ☐ 10 *The Sorrows of Satan* ☐ 11 *The Marriage Circle* ☐ 12 *Strike* ☐ 13 Eugenie Besserer ☐ 14 *Aloma of the South Seas* ☐ 15 Edna Purviance ☐ 16 Adolphe Menjou ☐ 17 G. M. 'Bronco Billy' Anderson ☐ 18 *Nosferatu* ☐ 19 William S. Hart ☐ 20 *Hearts of the World* ☐

song titles
1 Jerome Kern ☐ 2 Cole Porter ☐ 3 Stephen Foster ☐ 4 Gus Kahn ☐ 5 Chauncey Olcott ☐ 6 Vincent Dresser ☐ 7 George M. Cohan ☐ 8 Leslie Stuart ☐ 9 Bert Kalmar and Harry Ruby ☐ 10 Sigmund Romberg ☐ 11 Joe Howard ☐ 12 Brown, Henderson and de Sylva ☐ 13 Nora Bayes ☐ 14 Vesta Tilley ☐ 15 George Leybourne ☐ 16 Ruth Etting ☐ 17 Fanny Brice ☐ 18 Jane Froman ☐ 19 Marilyn Miller ☐ 20 Blossom Seeley ☐

story into film
1 *Give Us This Day* (US: *Salt to the Devil*) ☐ 2 *All About Eve* ☐ 3 *Stagecoach* ☐ 4 *Lady for a Day* ☐ 5 *Night of the Demon* (US: *Curse of the Demon*) ☐ 6 *Freaks* ☐ 7 *Sunset Boulevard* ☐ 8 *The Naked Jungle* ☐ 9 *The Macomber Affair* ☐ 10 *The Fallen Idol* ☐ 11 *It Happened One Night* ☐ 12 *Mr Deeds Goes to Town* ☐ 13 *Gunfight at the OK Corral* ☐ 14 *The Lost Patrol* ☐ 15 *Trapeze* ☐ 16 *The Pearl of Death* ☐ 17 *Island of Lost Souls* ☐ 18 *The Beast from 20,000 Fathoms* ☐ 19 *The Thing from Another World* ☐ 20 *Sherlock Holmes Faces Death* ☐ 21 *Fourteen Hours* ☐ 22 *Love from a Stranger* ☐

supporting players
1 Ernest Thesiger: *The Old Dark House*, *Bride of Frankenstein*, *Father Brown* ☐ 2 Peter Lorre: *The Raven*, *The Mask of Dimitrios*, *The Maltese Falcon* ☐ 3 Mischa Auer: *My Man Godfrey*, *Destry Rides Again*, *Lady in the Dark* ☐ 4 Walter Huston: *And Then There Were None*, *Duel in the Sun*, *All that Money Can Buy* ☐ 5 Margaret Dumont: *At the Circus*, *A Day at the Races*, *Duck Soup* ☐ 6 Florence Bates: *The Moon and Sixpence*, *The Secret Life of Walter Mitty*, *Rebecca* ☐ 7 Cecil Kellaway: *Harvey*, *The Luck of the Irish*, *I Married a Witch* ☐ 8 Sydney Greenstreet: *They Died with Their Boots On*, *The Woman in White*, *The Maltese Falcon* ☐ 9 Edmund Gwenn: *Foreign Correspondent*, *Miracle on 34th Street*, *Pride and Prejudice* ☐

10 Eric Blore: *The Gay Divorcee*, *Love Happy*, *Sullivan's Travels* ☐ 11 Edgar Kennedy: *Duck Soup*, *Unfaithfully Yours*, *Mad Wednesday* ☐ 12 Roland Young: *One Hour With You*, *David Copperfield*, *The Philadelphia Story* ☐ 13 Leo G. Carroll: *The House on 92nd Street*, *Rebecca*, *North by Northwest* ☐ 14 John Carradine: *Bride of Frankenstein*, *The Hound of the Baskervilles*, *The Grapes of Wrath* ☐ 15 H. B. Warner: *Topper Returns*, *Victoria the Great*, *Lost Horizon* ☐ 16 Raymond Massey: *Santa Fe Trail*, *Seven Angry Men*, *The Prisoner of Zenda*, *Things to Come* ☐

swan songs
1 Jean Harlow ☐ 2 Humphrey Bogart ☐ 3 Robert Donat ☐ 4 Alan Ladd ☐ 5 Charles Laughton ☐ 6 Buster Keaton ☐ 7 John Garfield ☐ 8 Carole Lombard ☐ 9 Ronald Colman ☐ 10 Gary Cooper ☐ 11 John Barrymore ☐ 12 Vivien Leigh ☐ 13 Lon Chaney ☐ 14 Maurice Chevalier ☐ 15 Clifton Webb ☐ 16 Spencer Tracy ☐ 17 Errol Flynn ☐ 18 Edward G. Robinson ☐ 19 Claude Rains ☐ 20 Peter Lorre ☐ 21 Kay Kendall ☐ 22 Sydney Greenstreet ☐ 23 Montgomery Clift ☐ 24 Paul Douglas ☐ 25 Laurence Harvey ☐

T

Tafler, Sidney (1916–1979). British character actor on stage from 1936.
The Little Ballerina (film debut) 46. It Always Rains on Sunday 47. Passport to Pimlico 48. Mystery Junction 51. Venetian Bird 53. The Sea Shall Not Have Them 55. *Carve Her Name with Pride* 58. Sink the Bismarck 60. The Bulldog Breed 61. The Seventh Dawn 64. *The Birthday Party* 69. The Adventurers 71. The Spy Who Loved Me 77, many others.

take. A take is a single recording of a scene during the making of a film. Sometimes one take is enough; but directors have been known to shoot as many as fifty before they are satisfied with the results.

Talbot, Lyle (1904–87) (Lysle Hollywood). Square-built American leading man and sometimes heavy, busy from the early thirties.
Love is a Racket 32. Three on a Match 32. Havana Widows 33. The Dragon Murder Case 34. Red Hot Tyres 35. Trapped by Television 36. Three Legionaires 37. One Wild Night 38. Second Fiddle 39. Parole Fixer 40. Mexican Spitfire's Elephant 42. Up in Arms 44. Champagne for Caesar 50. With a Song in My Heart 52. There's No Business Like Show Business 54. The Great Man 56. Sunrise at Campobello 60, many others.
TV series: The Bob Cummings Show 55–59. Ozzie and Harriet 56–66.

Talbot, Nita (1930–). Smart, wise-cracking American comedienne of the sixties.
Bundle of Joy 56. Once upon a Horse 58. Who's Got the Action? 62. Girl Happy 65. That Funny Feeling 65. *A Very Special Favour* 65. The Cool Ones 67. Buck and the Preacher 71. The Day of the Locust 75. Serial 80. Night Shift 82, etc.
TV series: Joe and Mabel 56. *Hot off the Wire* 60. *Here We Go Again* 71.

A Tale of Two Cities. Apart from three very early one-reel versions, Dickens' novel of the French Revolution was filmed in 1917 with William Farnum, in 1926 with Maurice Costello and (as *The Only Way*) with Martin Harvey, in 1935 with Ronald Colman and in 1958 with Dirk Bogarde.

Tales of Hoffman (GB 1951). An ambitious if rather foolhardy attempt to combine opera and ballet in a popular form. Lacking a modern story, it did not have the box-office value of *The Red Shoes*, made three years earlier by the same team, Michael Powell and Emeric Pressburger. All very Teutonic, with heavy colour, music by Offenbach, décor by Hein Heckroth, choreography by Frederick Ashton, photography by Christopher Challis; and dancing and singing by the best talent money can buy.

Tales of Manhattan (US 1942). Directed by Julien Duvivier, this string of anecdotes linked by the travels of one tail coat can be credited with starting or revivifying the short story compendium form, later developed in such movies as *Flesh and Fantasy, Quartet, Full House, The Story of Three Loves, It's a Great Country* and many others. In itself it was unremarkable apart from Charles Laughton's splendid bit of pathos as a poor conductor; the Negro sequence was incredibly 'Uncle Tom'; and what might have been the best story, starring W. C. Fields, was removed before release because the film was too long. The film's inspiration was Duvivier's own *Un Carnet de Bal*, made in 1937, which gave him his ticket to Hollywood.

Taliaferro, Hal (1895–1980) (Floyd T. Alperson). American stunt man who became a star of silent westerns under the name Wally Wales, then took another name for the years of his decline.

talkies caused the biggest revolution the film industry has known, and provoked critical resentment difficult to understand until one sees a very early talkie and realizes what a raucous and unpleasant experience it must have been until Hollywood caught up with itself. The main steps of development were as follows. In 1923 Lee de Forrest (qv) made primitive shorts. In 1926 Warners created Vitaphone, a disc process, and Fox pioneered sound on film with Movietone. Also in 1926 came *Don Juan*, the first film with synchronized music and effects. The first speaking and singing came in 1927 with Al Jolson in *The Jazz Singer*. In 1928 the first all-talking film, *Lights of New York*, set the seal of popular success on the new medium.

¶ The addition of sound to the movies was ridiculed and frantically opposed; but the industry needed the fresh impetus and at great expense the revolution was achieved.

> No closer approach to resurrection has ever been made by science,

said Professor M. Pupin of the American Institute of Electrical Engineers. But it was years before he could claim perfect reproduction.

> The tinkle of a glass, the shot of a revolver, a footfall on a hardwood floor, and the noise of a pack of cards being shuffled, all sounded about alike,

said Gilbert Seldes in 1929. And Tallulah Bankhead complained:

> They made me sound as if I'd been castrated.

E. V. Lucas complained:

> They are doing away with the greatest boon that has ever been offered to the deaf.

The distinguished documentarist Paul Rotha joined in the dismay:

> A film in which the speech and sound effects are perfectly synchronized and coincide with their visual images on screen is absolutely contrary to the aims of the cinema. It is a degenerate and misguided attempt to destroy the real use of the film.

Nor was the prestige of the industry helped by claims of mathematical impossibility such as:

> 100% talking! 100% singing! 100% dancing!

But the public forgave all: the novelty value was tremendous, even though they missed a number of favourite stars whose voices proved unsuitable. As Jack Warner said:

> Men and women whose names were known throughout the land disappeared as though they had been lost at sea.

And *Variety* summed up:

> Talkies didn't do more to the industry than turn it upside down, shake the entire bag of tricks from its pocket, and advance Warner Brothers from last place to first in the league.

But Ernst Lubitsch took a more cynical view:

> You could name the great stars of the silent screen who were finished; the great directors, gone; the great title writers who were washed up. But remember this, as long as you live: the producers didn't lose a man. They all made the switch. That's where the great talent is.

Talmadge, Constance (1898–1973). American silent heroine and comedienne, sister of Norma Talmadge.
Biography 1978: *The Talmadge Girls* by Anita Loos.
Intolerance 15. Matrimaniac 16. The Honeymoon 17. Happiness à la Mode 19. Lessons in Love 21. Her Primitive Lover 22. The Goldfish 24. Her Sister from Paris 25. Venus 29, many others.

Talmadge, Natalie (1899–1969). American leading lady of a few silent comedies; retired to marry Buster Keaton. Younger sister of Norma and Constance Talmadge.

Talmadge, Norma (1893/7–1957). American silent heroine, sister of Constance Talmadge.
Battle Cry of Peace 14. Going Straight 15. Forbidden City 18. The Sign on the Door 21. Within the Law 23. Secrets 24. The Lady 25. Camille 27. The Dove 28. Dubarry Woman of Passion (last film) 30, many others.

Talmadge, Richard (1896–1981) (Ricardo Metzetti). American stunt man of the twenties, who doubled for Fairbanks, Lloyd, etc., and later became a star of action films such as *The Speed King, Laughing at Danger* and *Fighting Demon*. In the thirties became a director of stunt sequences, and more recently worked on *How the West Was Won, What's New Pussycat?, Hawaii* and *Casino Royale*.

Talman, William (1915–1968). American character actor usually seen as a crook or cop: for seven years was well occupied in TV's *Perry Mason* series as the D.A. who never won a case.
Red Hot and Blue 49. The Armored Car Robbery 50. One Minute to Zero 52. *The Hitch Hiker* 52. City That Never Sleeps 53. This Man Is Armed 56. Two-Gun Lady 59. The Ballad of Josie 67.

Tamba, Tetsuro (c. 1929–). Japanese actor who has appeared in occidental films.
Bridge to the Sun 61. The Seventh Dawn 64. You Only Live Twice 67. The Five Man Army 70. Tange-Sazen 75.

Tamblyn, Russ (1934–). Buoyant American dancer and tumbler, in small film roles from 1949.
Father of the Bride 50. Father's Little Dividend 51. *Seven Brides for Seven Brothers* 54. Hit the Deck 55. Don't Go Near the Water 56. Peyton Place 57. *Tom Thumb* 58. Cimarron 61. *West Side Story* 61. The Wonderful World of the Brothers Grimm 63. The Haunting 63. Son of a Gunfighter 65. Blood of Frankenstein 70. Win, Place or Steal 75. Black Heat 76. Human Highway 82, etc.

Tamiroff, Akim (1899–1972). Russian leading character actor, in America from 1923.
Sadie McKee (film debut) 34. Lives of a Bengal Lancer 35. Naughty Marietta 35. China Seas 36. The Story of Louis Pasteur 36 *The General Died at Dawn* 36. *The Great Gambini* 37. Spawn of the North 38. Union Pacific 39. Geronimo 40. *The Way of All Flesh* 40. The Great McGinty 40. The Corsican Brothers 41. *For Whom the Bell Tolls* 43. The Bridge of San Luis Rey 44. A Scandal in Paris 46. The Gangster 47. My Girl Tisa 48. Outpost in Morocco 50. You Know What Sailors Are (GB) 53. Confidential Report 55. The Black Sleep 56. Me and the Colonel 57. Touch of Evil 58. Romanoff and Juliet 60. Topkapi 64. The Liquidator 65. Alphaville 65. Lord Jim 65. Lieut. Robin Crusoe 66. After the Fox 66. Great Catherine 68. Then Came Bronson (TV) 70, scores of others.

Tandy, Jessica (1909–). British-born actress wife of Hume Cronyn.
The Seventh Cross 44. Dragonwyck 46. The Green Years 46. Forever Amber 48. A Woman's Vengeance 48. Rommel, Desert Fox 51. The Light in the Forest 58. Hemingway's Adventures of a Young Man 62. The Birds 63. Butley 73. The World According to Garp 82. Still of the Night 82. Best Friends 82. The Bostonians 84. Cocoon 85, etc.

Tani, Yoko (1932–). Japanese leading lady, in international films.
The Wind Cannot Read 57. The Quiet American 58. Savage Innocents 59. Piccadilly Third Stop 60. Marco Polo 61. Who's Been Sleeping in My Bed? 63. Invasion 66, etc.

Tanner, Alain (–). Swiss director.
Jonah Who Will Be 25 in the Year 2000 76. Messidor 78. Light Years Away 81. In the White City 82. No Man's Land 85.

Tanner, Peter (1914–). British editor.
Lady from Lisbon 42. Scott of the Antarctic 48. Kind Hearts and Coronets 49. The Blue Lamp 50. Secret People 52. Lease of Life 54. The Night My Number Came Up 55. Man in the Sky 57. Light up the Sky 60. Sodom and Gomorrah 61. A Jolly Bad Fellow 64. Diamonds for Breakfast 68. The House that Dripped Blood 71. Asylum 72. Hedda 75. Nasty Habits 76, many others.

Tanner, Tony (1932–). British light actor and revue artiste.
Strictly for the Birds 64. A Home of Your Own 65. The Pleasure Girls 65. Stop the World I Want to Get Off 66, etc.

Tapley, Colin (1911–). New Zealand character actor who has played a few stalwart types in international pictures.
Search for Beauty 34. The Black Room 35. Samson and Delilah 49. Angels One Five 52. The Dam Busters 56, etc.

Taradash, Daniel (1913–). American screenwriter.
Golden Boy 39. Rancho Notorious 48. *From Here to Eternity* (AA) 53. Désirée 54. Storm Centre (& d) 55. Picnic 55. Bell, Book and Candle 58. Morituri 65. Hawaii 66. Doctors' Wives 71. The Other Side of Midnight (co-w) 77, etc.

Target for Tonight (GB 1941). A feature-length documentary about an RAF bombing raid. Using no actors, it seemed at the time an amazing realistic achievement; but the slang and the understatement have dated it badly, and the aerial photography has since been surpassed. Produced by Ian Dalrymple, written and directed by Harry Watt, with music by Leighton Lucas.

Tarkington, Booth (1869–1946). American novelist. Films of his books include *Alice Adams, Penrod* (qv), *Monsieur Beaucaire* (qv), *The Magnificent Ambersons* (qv).

Tarkovsky, Andrei (1932–86). Russian director.
□There Will Be No Leave Tonight (short) 59. Violin and Roller 61. Ivan's Childhood 62. *Andrei Rublev* 66. *Solaris* 72. *Mirror* 78. Nostalgia 83.

Tarzan. The brawny jungle hero, an English milord lost in Africa as a child and grown up with the apes, was a creation of novelist Edgar Rice Burroughs (1875–1950); the first

Tarzan story was published in 1913. The films quickly followed. *Tarzan of the Apes* 18 starred Elmo Lincoln with Enid Markey as Jane; so did *Romance of Tarzan* 18. *The Return of Tarzan* 20 had Gene Polar and Karla Schramm. *Son of Tarzan* 20 was a serial with Kamuela C. Searle in the title role; Tarzan was P. Dempsey Tabler. Elmo Lincoln returned in another serial, *The Adventures of Tarzan* 21, with Louise Lorraine. *Tarzan and the Golden Lion* 27 starred James Pierce and Dorothy Dunbar. Another serial, *Tarzan the Mighty* 28, had Frank Merrill and no Jane; a runner-up, *Tarzan the Tiger* 30, had the same crew. In 1932 came Johnny Weissmuller in the first of MGM's long line of Tarzan pictures: *Tarzan the Ape Man*, with Maureen O'Sullivan as Jane. There followed *Tarzan and His Mate* 34, *Tarzan Escapes* 36, *Tarzan Finds a Son* 39, *Tarzan's Secret Treasure* 41, and *Tarzan's New York Adventure* 42. Meanwhile in 1935 an independent company had made a serial starring Herman Brix which was later released as two features, *Tarzan and the Green Goddess* and *New Adventures of Tarzan*; and in 1933 producer Sol Lesser had started his Tarzan series with *Tarzan the Fearless*, starring Buster Crabbe; he followed this up with *Tarzan's Revenge* 38 starring Glenn Morris. In 1943 Lesser took over Weissmuller (but not O'Sullivan or any other Jane) for *Tarzan Triumphs*, followed by *Tarzan's Desert Mystery* 44, *Tarzan and the Amazons* (reintroducing Jane in the shape of Brenda Joyce) 45, *Tarzan and the Leopard Woman* 46, *Tarzan and the Huntress* 47, and *Tarzan and the Mermaids* 48. Then Weissmuller was replaced by Lex Barker for *Tarzan's Magic Fountain* 48, *Tarzan and the Slave Girl* 49, *Tarzan's Peril* 50, *Tarzan's Savage Fury* 51, and *Tarzan and the She-Devil* 52. Gordon Scott next undertook the chore in *Tarzan's Hidden Jungle* 55, *Tarzan and the Lost Safari* 57, *Tarzan's Fight for Life* 58, *Tarzan's Greatest Adventure* 59 and *Tarzan the Magnificent* 60. MGM now remade *Tarzan the Ape Man* 60 starring Denny Miller; and, with Jock Mahoney, *Tarzan Goes to India* 62 and National General presented *Tarzan's Three Challenges* 64. There followed *Tarzan and the Valley of Gold* 66, *Tarzan and the Great River* 67, and *Tarzan and the Jungle Boy* 68, all with Mike Henry. A 1982 remake of *Tarzan the Ape Man* had Miles O'Keeffe in the role but concentrated on the charms of Bo Derek as Jane; however, in 1984 *Greystoke* set the record straight by remaining faithful to Burroughs' original legend. A 1966–67 TV series starred Ron Ely.

Tashlin, Frank (1913–1972). American comedy writer-director, former cartoonist.
The Fuller Brush Man (w) 48. *The Paleface* (w) 48. The Good Humour Man (w) 50. Kill the Umpire (w) 51. Susan Slept Here (d) 54. Artists and Models (wd) 55. *The Girl Can't Help It* (wpd) 57. Will Success Spoil Rock Hunter? (wpd) 57. Rockabye Baby (wd) 58. Say One for Me (pd) 59. Cinderfella (wd) 60. It's Only Money (d) 63. The Man from the Diners Club (d) 64. The Alphabet Murders (d) 65. The Glass Bottom Boat (d) 66. Caprice (d) 67. The Private Navy of Sgt O'Farrell (wd) 68, etc.

Tashman, Lilyan (1899–1934). American silent screen sophisticate.
Experience 21. Manhandled 24. Don't Tell the Wife 27. New York Nights 29. Murder by the Clock 31. Scarlet Dawn 32. Frankie and Johnny 33, etc.

A Taste of Honey (GB 1961). A strange and influential little film produced and directed by Tony Richardson from a play by Shelagh Delaney, and lovingly photographed by Walter Lassally. Finding humour and compassion in the depressing background of industrial Lancashire, viewed through the eyes of a gawky adolescent schoolgirl, it paints vivid sketches of her tarty mum and the harmless homosexual who looks after her when a sailor leaves her pregnant. With the help of excellent performances from Rita Tushingham, Dora Bryan (BFA) and Murray Melvin, it succeeds in its determination to wring poetry out of squalor.

Tate, Harry (1872–1940). British music hall comedian famous for 'motoring' sketch. In occasional films.
Motoring 27. Her First Affair 32. Happy 34. Midshipman Easy 35. Hyde Park Corner 35. Keep Your Seats Please 36. Wings of the Morning 37, etc.

Tate, Reginald (1896–1955). British character actor, mainly on stage.
Riverside Murder 35. Dark Journey 37. Next of Kin 42. The Life and Death of Colonel Blimp 43. Uncle Silas 47. Robin Hood 52. King's Rhapsody 55, etc.

Tate, Sharon (1943–1969). American leading lady, victim of a sensational murder.
Eye of the Devil 67. The Fearless Vampire Killers 67. Valley of the Dolls 67. Don't Make Waves 67. Wrecking Crew 69, etc.

Tati, Jacques (1908–1982) (Jacques Tatischeff). French pantomimist and actor who after years in the music halls and in small film roles began to write and direct his own quiet comedies which were really little more than strings of sight gags on a theme.
□*Jour de Fête* 49. *Monsieur Hulot's Holiday* 52. Mon Oncle 58. Playtime 68. Traffic 71. Parade (TV) 74.
† Tati also appeared in several shorts, and played the ghost in *Sylvie et le Fantôme* 47.

Taube, Sven-Bertil (1934–). Swedish leading man.
The Buttercup Chain 70. Puppet on a Chain 70. The Eagle Has Landed 76. Game for Vultures 79, etc.

Tauber, Richard (1892–1948). Austrian operatic tenor, long in Britain where he made a number of artless but likeable musical comedy films.
Biography 1959: *My Heart and I* by Diana Napier Tauber.
Symphony of Love 31. Blossom Time 34. Heart's Desire 35. Land without Music 35. Pagliacci 36. The Lisbon Story 45, etc.

Taurog, Norman (1899–1981). American director, former child actor, in Hollywood from 1917.
Lucky Boy 28. *Skippy* (AA) 31. Huckleberry Finn 33. We're Not Dressing 34. Mrs Wiggs of the Cabbage Patch 35. Strike Me Pink 36. *Mad about Music* 38. The Adventures of Tom Sawyer 38. Boys' Town 38. Broadway Melody of 1940 40. Young Tom Edison 40. A Yank at Eton 42. Girl Crazy 42. The Hoodlum Saint 46. The Bride Goes Wild 48. Please Believe Me 50. Room for One More 52. Living It Up 54. The Birds and the Bees 56. Bundle of Joy 57. Don't Give Up the Ship 59. Palm Springs Weekend 63. Tickle Me 65. Sergeant Deadhead 65. Speedway 67, many others.

Tavernier, Bertrand (1941–). French director.
□*The Watchmaker of St Paul* 74. Que la Fête Commence 75. The Judge and the Assassin 76. Spoiled Children 77. Death Watch 80. Coup de Torchon 82. A Week's Vacation 82. Mississippi Blues 83. *Sunday in the Country* 84. *'Round Midnight* 86.

Taviani, Paolo (1931–) and **Vittorio** (1929–). Italian brother directors who always work together.
□A Man of Bruciare 62. Sovversivi 67. Beneath the Sign of the Scorpion 69. St Michael Had a Rooster 71. Allonsanfan 74. *Padro Padrone* 77. The Field 79. Night of the Shooting Stars 81. Kaos 84. Good Morning Babylon 87.

Tavoularis, Dean (1932–). American production designer.
Bonnie and Clyde 67. Candy 68. Zabriskie Point 70. Little Big Man 70. The Godfather 72. The Conversation 74. The Godfather Part Two 74. Farewell My Lovely 75. The Missouri Breaks 76. Brinks 79. Apocalypse Now 79. Hammett 82. One From the Heart 82. The Outsiders 83. Rumble Fish 83.

Taxi Driver (US 1976). A repellent and ultimately pointless account of the squalor of seventies New York as seen by a cab driver, an ex-Vietnam veteran who eventually goes berserk and kills the pimp of a child prostitute. Several sequences have vigour, but the characterization is unclear and the film eventually compromises its original value, which is that of a probing documentary of our times. Written by Paul Schraeder, directed by Martin Scorsese.

Tayback, Vic (1929–). Tough-looking American supporting actor.
Bullitt 68. With Six You Get Egg Roll 68. Lepke 73. Thunderbolt and Lightfoot 75. No Deposit No Return 76. The Choirboys 77, etc.

Taylor, Alma (1895–1974). British actress of the silent screen.
The Little Milliner and the Thief 09. Oliver Twist 12. Paying the Penalty 13. The Baby on the Barge 15. Annie Laurie 16. The American Heiress 17. Sunken Rocks 19. Alf's Button 20. The Tinted Venus 21. Comin' thro' the Rye 23. The Shadow of Egypt 24. Quinneys 27. Bachelor's Baby 32. Things are Looking Up 35. Lilacs in the Spring 54. Blue Murder at St Trinian's 57, etc.

Taylor, Deems (1886–1966). American journalist and musician whose chief connection with films was to act as narrator for *Fantasia* 40 and to help write *A Pictorial History of the Movies* 48.

Taylor, Don (1920–). American light leading man, with stage experience.
Naked City 48. For the Love of Mary 48. Ambush 49. Father of the Bride 50. Submarine Command 51. The Blue Veil 51. Stalag 17 53. Men of Sherwood Forest 54. I'll Cry Tomorrow 57, etc.

AS DIRECTOR: The Savage Guns 62. Ride the Wild Surf 64. Jack of Diamonds 67. The Five Man Army 70. Escape from the Planet of the Apes 71. Tom Sawyer 73. Echoes of a Summer 75. The Great Scout and Cathouse Thursday 76. The Island of Dr Moreau 77, etc.

Taylor, Elaine (–). British leading lady.
Casino Royale 67. Half a Sixpence 68. Diamonds for Breakfast 68. The Anniversary 68. The Games 69. All the Way Up 70, etc.

Taylor, Elizabeth (1932–). British-born leading lady with a well-publicized private life. Was evacuated to Hollywood during World War II and began as a child star. Scored eight husbands so far, including two helpings of Richard Burton.
Biography 1978: *Who's Afraid of Elizabeth Taylor?* by Brenda Maddox.
□There's One Born Every Minute 42. Lassie Come Home 43. Jane Eyre 43. The White Cliffs of Dover 44. *National Velvet* 44. Courage of Lassie 45. Cynthia 47. Life with Father 47. A Date with Judy 48. Julia Misbehaves 48. *Little Women* 49. Conspirator 49. The Big Hangover 49. *Father of the Bride* 50. Father's Little Dividend 51. Quo Vadis 51. Love is Better Than Ever 51. *A Place in the Sun* 51. The Light Fantastic 51. Ivanhoe 52. The Girl Who Had Everything 53. Rhapsody 54. Elephant Walk 54. Beau Brummell 54. The Last Time I Saw Paris 55. *Giant* 56. *Raintree County* 57. *Cat on a Hot Tin Roof* 58. *Suddenly Last Summer* 59. *Butterfield 8* (AA) 60. Scent of Mystery 60. *Cleopatra* 62. The VIPs 63. The Sandpiper 65. *Who's Afraid of Virginia Woolf?* (AA) 66. The Taming of the Shrew 67. Doctor Faustus 67. The Comedians 67. Reflections in a Golden Eye 67. Boom 68. Secret Ceremony 68. The Only Game in Town 69. Under Milk Wood 71. Zee and Co 71. Hammersmith is Out 72. Divorce His, Divorce Hers (TV) 72. Night Watch 73. Ash Wednesday 73. The Driver's Seat 75. The Blue Bird 76. Victory at Entebbe (TV) 76. A Little Night Music 77. Repeat Performance (TV) 78. The Mirror Crack'd 80. Between Friends (TV) 82. Malice in Wonderland (TV) 84.

¶ I don't pretend to be an ordinary housewife.—*E.T.*

A pharaonic mummy, moving on tiny castors, like a touring replica of the Queen Mother.—*Sunday Times on E.T. in The Mirror Crack'd.*

If someone's dumb enough to offer me a million dollars to make a picture, I'm certainly not dumb enough to turn it down.—*E.T.*

I believe in mind over matter and doing anything you set your mind on.—*E.T.*

'Is she fat? Her favourite food is seconds.'—*Joan Rivers*

'She should get a divorce and settle down.'—*Jack Paar*

'There are three things I never saw Elizabeth Taylor do. Tell a lie; be unkind to anyone; and be on time.'—*Mike Nichols*

Famous line (*Reflections in a Golden Eye*): She cut off her nipples with garden shears. You call that normal?

Taylor, Estelle (1899–1958) (Estelle Boylan). American stage actress who made some silent films.
While New York Sleeps 22. The Ten Commandments 23. Don Juan 26. The Whip Woman 27. When East is East 28, etc.

Taylor, Gilbert (1914–). British cinematographer, in films since 1929.
The Guinea Pig 48. Seven Days to Noon 50. The Yellow Balloon 52. It's Great To Be Young 55. The Good Companions 57. Ice Cold in Alex 58. The Rebel 60. Dr Strangelove 63. Repulsion 65. The Bedford Incident 65. Before Winter Comes 69. Macbeth 71. Frenzy 72. The Omen 76. *Star Wars* 77. Dracula 79. Flash Gordon 80. Green Ice 81, etc.

Taylor, Jud (1940–). American director.
Weekend of Terror (TV) 70. Revenge (TV) 71. Heat of Anger (TV) 72. Say Goodbye Maggie Cole (TV) 72. Hawkins on Murder (TV) 73. Winter Kill (TV) 74. Future Cop (TV) 76. Return to Earth (TV) 76. Tail Gunner Joe (TV) 77. Mary White (TV) 77. Flesh and Blood (TV) 80, etc.

Taylor, Kent (1907–87) (Louis Weiss). Suave American leading man of second features from the early thirties.
Two Kinds of Women 32. I'm No Angel 33. Double Door 34. Two Fisted 35. The Accusing Finger 36. The Jury's Secret 37. I Take this Woman 40. Frisco Lil 42. Bombers Moon 43. The Daltons Ride Again 45. The Crimson Key 47. Payment on Demand 51. Playgirl 54. Slightly Scarlet 56. Ghost Town 56. Harbour Lights 64. The Day Mars Invaded Earth 64. Smashing the Crime Syndicate 73, etc.
TV series: *Boston Blackie* 51–52.

Taylor, Laurette (1884–1946) (Laurette Cooney). American stage leading lady who filmed her great success *Peg O' My Heart* 22 and stayed in Hollywood for a few more silent films: *Happiness, One Night in Rome*, etc.

Taylor, Peter (1922–). British editor. Devil Girl from Mars 54. Summer Madness 55. The Man Who Never Was 55. *The Bridge on the River Kwai* (AA) 57. The Devil's Daffodil 61. Waltz of the Toreadors 62. This Sporting Life 63. Judith 66. The Taming of the Shrew 67. Monte Carlo or Bust 69, many others.

Taylor, Robert (1911–1969) (Spangler Arlington Brugh). Durable American leading man signed by MGM while still a medical student. His boyish good looks turned rather set and grim in middle age, but he remained a star.
□Handy Andy 34. There's Always Tomorrow 36. Wicked Woman 34. Society Doctor 34. West Point of the Air 35. Times Square Lady 35. Murder in the Fleet 35. Broadway Melody of 1936 36. *Magnificent Obsession* 35. Small Town Girl 36. Private Number 36. His Brother's Wife 36. The Gorgeous Hussy 36. *Camille* 36. Personal Property 37. This is My Affair 37. Broadway Melody of 1938 38. *A Yank at Oxford* 38. Three Comrades 38. The Crowd Roars 38. Stand Up and Fight 39. Lucky Night 39. Lady of the Tropics 39. Remember 39. *Waterloo Bridge* 40. Escape 40. Flight Command 40. Billy the Kid 41. When Ladies Meet 41. Johnny Eager 42. Her Cardboard Lover 42. Stand By for Action 43. *Bataan* 43. Song of Russia 44. Undercurrent 46. High Wall 47. The Bribe 49. Ambush 49. Devil's Doorway 50. Conspirator 50. *Quo Vadis* 51. Westward the Women 51. *Ivanhoe* 52. Above and Beyond 52. Ride Vaquero 53. All the Brothers were Valiant 53. *Knights of the Round Table* 53. Valley of the Kings 54. Rogue Cop 54. Many Rivers to Cross 55. Quentin Durward 55. The Last Hunt 56. D Day Sixth of June 56. The Power and the Prize 56. Tip on a Dead Jockey 57. Saddle the Wind 58. The Law and Jake Wade 58. Party Girl 58. The Hangman 59. The House of the Seven Hawks 59. Killers of Kilimanjaro 60. The Miracle of the White Stallions 61. Cattle King 63. A House is Not a Home 64. The Night Walker 65. Savage Pampas 66. The Return of the Gunfighter 66. Johnny Tiger 66. Where Angels Go Trouble Follows 68. The Day the Hot Line Got Hot 68. Devil May Care 68. The Glass Sphinx 68.
TV series: *The Detectives* 59–61.

¶ *R.T.:* I was a punk kid from Nebraska who had an awful lot of the world's good things tossed in his lap.

R.T.: For 17 years it was Mr Mayer who guided me, and I never turned down a picture that he personally asked me to do.

Taylor, Rod (1929–) (Robert Taylor). Australian-born, Hollywood-based leading man with stage experience.
King of the Coral Sea 54. Long John Silver 55. The Catered Affair 56. Giant 56. Raintree County 57. Separate Tables 58. *The Time Machine* 60. *The Birds* 63. *The VIPs* 63. Sunday in New York 63. Fate Is the Hunter 64. *Thirty-Six Hours* 64. Young Cassidy 65. Do Not Disturb 65. The Liquidator 65. The Glass Bottom Boat 66. Hotel 67. Dark of the Sun 67. Chuka 67. Nobody Runs Forever 68. The Hell with Heroes 69. The Man Who Had Power Over Women 70. Darker than Amber 70. The Train Robbers 72. Family Flight (TV) 72. Trader Horn 73. Deadly Trackers 73. Shamus (TV) 73. The Heroes 75. The Picture Show Man 77. An Eye for an Eye 78. On the Run 82. Masquerade (TV) 83, etc.
TV series: Hong Kong 60. Bearcats 71. The Oregon Trail 75.

Taylor, Ronnie (–). British cinematographer who won an Oscar for *Gandhi*. Cry Freedom 87.

Taylor, Sam (1895–1958). American screenwriter of the twenties: *The Freshman, Exit Smiling*, etc. Remembered chiefly for the credit line to the 1928 version of *The Taming of the Shrew*: 'By William Shakespeare, with additional dialogue by Sam Taylor.'

Taylor-Young, Leigh (1944–). American leading lady of the early seventies.
□I Love You Alice B. Toklas 68. The Big Bounce 68. The Adventurers 69. The Buttercup Chain 70. The Horsemen 71. The Gang That Couldn't Shoot Straight 72. Soylent Green 73. Can't Stop the Music 80. Looker 81.

Tazieff, Haroun (1914–). French explorer-photographer, best known for *Rendezvous du Diable* (*Volcano*) 58, *The Forbidden Volcano* 67.

Tcherina, Ludmilla (1925–) (Monique Tchemerzine). French ballerina.
The Red Shoes 48. Tales of Hoffman 50. Sign of the Pagan 54. Oh Rosalinda 55. Honeymoon 59. A Ravishing Idiot 63, etc.

teachers have been notably played by Robert Donat in *Goodbye Mr Chips*; Jennifer Jones in *Good Morning Miss Dove*; Greer

Garson in *Her Twelve Men*; Michael Redgrave in *The Browning Version*; Aline MacMahon in *Back Door to Heaven*; Claudette Colbert in *Remember the Day*; Bette Davis in *The Corn is Green*; Jack Hawkins in *Mandy*; Judy Garland in *A Child is Waiting*; Anne Bancroft in *The Miracle Worker*; Shirley Maclaine in *Spinster*; Glenn Ford in *The Blackboard Jungle*; Sidney Poitier in *To Sir With Love*; Sandy Dennis in *Up the Down Staircase*; Dorothy Dandridge in *Bright Road*; Max Bygraves in *Spare the Rod*; Otto Kruger in *The Housemaster*; Cecil Trouncer in *The Guinea Pig*; Maggie Smith in *The Prime of Miss Jean Brodie*; Joanne Woodward in *Rachel, Rachel*; Robert Mitchum in *Ryan's Daughter*; Laurence Olivier in *Term of Trial*; Richard Todd in *The Love-Ins*; James Whitmore in *The Harrad Experiment*. David Hemmings in *Unman, Wittering and Zigo*; Per Oscarsson in *Who Saw Him Die?*; James Mason in *Child's Play*; Glenda Jackson in *The Class of Miss MacMichael*; Michael Ontkean in *Willie and Phil*.

Comic teachers were to the fore in *Boys Will Be Boys* (Will Hay, the best of them all); the *St Trinian's* films; *Carry On Teacher*; *Old Mother Riley Headmistress*; *Bottoms Up* (Jimmy Edwards); *Fun at St Fanny's* (Fred Emney); *The Happiest Days of Your Lives*; *Please Sir*; and *Vice Versa* (James Robertson Justice). See also: *Schools*.

Teague, Lewis (–). American director, from the Roger Corman stable.
The Lady in Red 78. Alligator 81. Fighting Back 83. Cujo 83. Cat's Eye 84. Jewel of the Nile 87, etc.

Teal, Ray (1902–76). American character actor often seen as sheriff, good or bad. In films from 1938 after stage experience.
The Cherokee Strip 40. A Wing and a Prayer 44. Captain Kidd 45. Joan of Arc 48. The Men 50. *Ace in the Hole* 51. The Lion and the Horse 53. Montana Belle 53. Hangman's Knot 54. Ambush at Tomahawk Gap 54. Run for Cover 55. The Indian Fighter 55. Saddle the Wind 57. One-Eyed Jacks 61. Cattle King 63. Taggart 64. The Liberation of L. B. Jones 71, many others.
TV series: Bonanza 59–71.

teams: see *romantic teams*.

? In the case of each of these well-known films, give the star (easy) and the co-star of the opposite sex (difficult).

1 *Apache*
2 *The Naked Maja*
3 *Don Juan* (1926)
4 *The Singing Fool*
5 *The Scarlet Empress*
6 *Ben Hur* (1926)
7 *Ben Hur* (1959)
8 *The Scarlet Letter* (1927)
9 *Stella Dallas* (1937)
10 *Across the Wide Missouri*
11 *The Sea Hawk* (1940)
12 *It*
13 *The Little Minister*
14 *Big Jim McLain*
15 *The Seventh Cross*
16 *The Big Shot*
17 *Where Love Has Gone*
18 *Mata Hari* (1931)
19 *Raffles* (1940)
20 *The Pride of the Yankees*
21 *My Life with Caroline*
22 *Knock on Wood*
23 *Lost Horizon* (1937)
24 *Yankee Doodle Dandy*
25 *Foreign Correspondent*

Tearle, Conway (1878–1938) (Frederick Levy). American leading actor of silent days; half-brother of Godfrey Tearle.
Stella Maris 18. The Virtuous Vamp 20. Woman of Bronze 23. Bella Donna 25. Gold Diggers of Broadway 29. Vanity Fair 32. Should Ladies Behave? 34. Klondike Annie 36. Romeo and Juliet 36, etc.

Tearle, Sir Godfrey (1884–1953). Distinguished British stage actor, on stage from 1893; occasional films from 1906, when he played Romeo in a one-reeler.
If Youth But Knew 30. The Thirty-Nine Steps 35. *One of Our Aircraft is Missing* 42. The Rake's Progress 45. The Beginning or the End 47. Private Angelo 48. *The Titfield Thunderbolt* 53, etc.

Teasdale, Verree (1904–87). American comedy actress, often as sophisticated friend or suspicious wife.
□Syncopation 29. The Sap from Syracuse 30. Skyscraper Souls 32. Payment Deferred 32. Luxury Liner 33. They Just Had to Get Married 33. Terror Aboard 33. Love Honour and Oh Baby 33. *Roman Scandals* 33. Fashions of 1934 34. Goodbye Love 34. A Modern Hero 34. Madame Du Barry 34. Desirable 34. The Firebird 34. Dr Monica 34. A Midsummer Night's Dream (as Titania) 35. The Milky Way 36. First Lady 37. Topper Takes a Trip 38. Fifth Avenue Girl 39.

Turnabout 40. I Take This Woman 40. Love Thy Neighbour 40. Come Live with Me 41.

teaser. A poster, trailer, or other piece of publicity which whets the appetite for a forthcoming film without giving full details about it, sometimes not even the title. The term was also applied to early pornographic films 1900–05, e.g. *Lovers Interrupted, Making Love in a Hammock*, etc.

Technicolor. Colour process which existed from 1915, though the various improvements virtually amounted to completely new versions. The first had separate red and green films projected simultaneously; the second combined them on panchromatic film; the third used dye transfer. In 1932 came the three-strip process which gave the rich full tones familiar to filmgoers of the forties, but a link with Eastmancolor in 1951 made it difficult to pick out Technicolor from any other process.

Technirama. A process similar to Vistavision for producing extreme clarity of image.

Techniscope. A process saving money by printing two wide images one below the other on the old 4 × 3 frame, then blowing them up to CinemaScope size; the results were awful.

telecine: the machine which enables film to be 'projected' electronically on television. Theoretically it is capable of panning from side to side across the CinemaScope image, picking out the optimum sections of each scene, but the results are usually dire unless the process has been carefully rehearsed.

teleheroes

? A surname is often a sufficient label for a TV series which runs for several seasons, and it usually indicates tough action. Can you name the actors who brought the following he-men into your living-room?

1 Bronco
2 Mannix
3 Maverick (there were three)
4 Cannon
5 Delvecchio
6 Shannon
7 Callan
8 Serpico
9 Hawk
10 Ironside
11 McCloud
12 Banacek
13 Dante
14 Staccato
15 Markham

The following gave their full names. Does that make it easier?

16 Richard Diamond
17 Michael Shayne
18 Philip Marlowe
19 Dan Raven
20 Bat Masterson
21 Peter Gunn
22 China Smith
23 Stoney Burke
24 Joe Forrester

the telephone has been a very useful instrument to film scenarists. The saga of its invention was told in *The Story of Alexander Graham Bell*. It brought sinister, menacing and threatening calls in *Sorry—Wrong Number, The Small World of Sammy Lee, Midnight Lace, I Saw What You Did, Experiment in Terror, Sudden Fear, Strangers on a Train*, and *Dirty Harry. Chicago Calling* and *The Slender Thread* were among the films based entirely on someone trying to contact another character by telephone. *Bells Are Ringing, The Glenn Miller Story* and *Bye Bye Birdie* had musical numbers based on telephones. Shelly Berman, Jeanne de Casalis and Billy de Wolfe are among the revue artists famous for telephone sketches. Single phone calls were of high dramatic significance in *The Spiral Staircase, Little Caesar, Fail Safe, Dr Strangelove, Murder Inc., Dial M for Murder, The Silencers, 2001: A Space Odyssey, No Way to Treat a Lady, Call Northside 777*, and *Phone Call from a Stranger*, while the phone had a special inference in several call girl pictures including *Butterfield 8. Our Man Flint, Indiscreet, Strange Bedfellows, Come Blow Your Horn* and *It's a Mad Mad Mad Mad World* are among the many films deriving comedy from the telephone . . . while the most chilling moment in many a thriller has been the discovery that the phone is disconnected. In *The President's Analyst* the telephone company turned out to be the supreme enemy of civilization.

telephoto lens. One which brings far-off objects apparently very close, but has the disadvantage of distorting and flattening perspective.

television, arch-enemy of the film-makers, was used during the fifties as an object of derision (*The Titfield Thunderbolt, Happy*

Anniversary, It's Always Fair Weather, My Blue Heaven, Simon and Laura, Callaway went Thataway, No Down Payment, Meet Mr Lucifer), or totally ignored. Yet it had featured in films even before World War II: *International House, Television Spy, Murder by Television, Raffles*, and a host of science fiction serials. More recently, television studios have provided a useful background for comedy (*You Must Be Joking, A Hard Day's Night*), for thrillers (*The Glass Web, Arabesque, The Barefoot Executive*) and for melodramas (*Seven Days in May, The Third Secret, The Love Machine*). The only serious movie study of the effects of television is *A Face in the Crowd*; and the funniest scenes about television programmes are probably those in *The Apartment*. Closed circuit TV is extensively used in *The Forbin Project, The Andromeda Strain, Loving* and *The Anderson Tapes*. In *THX 1138* television is used as a mass opiate for the workers of the subterranean world of the future. A wild but fairly barbed satire on television was *The Groove Tube*, and *Network* took a lofty view of it before pitching into hysterical melodrama.

¶ Some definitions, mostly jaundiced:

The bland leading the bland.—*Anon*

Chewing gum for the eyes.—*Frank Lloyd Wright*

The longest amateur night in history.—*Robert Carson*

A medium, so called because it is neither rare nor well done.—*Ernie Kovacs*

A twenty-one-inch prison. I'm delighted with it because it used to be that films were the lowest form of art. Now we have something to look down on.—*Billy Wilder*

Why should people go out and pay money to see bad films when they can stay at home and see bad television for nothing?—*Samuel Goldwyn*

A TV commercial was defined as:

The opening and closing quarter-hours of a half-hour show.

Though Cedric Hardwicke thought the ads were:

The last refuge of optimism in a world of gloom.

Irving Allen had his problems working in the medium:

I've tried to take the lunacy that exists in television and reduce it to a quiet panic.

John Simon was dismissive:

It is inconceivable what trash would be put on film these days if TV had not been invented, and the TV writers were functioning as scenarists.

Fred Allen saw it as:

A triumph of equipment over people. The minds that control it are so small that you could put them in the navel of a flea and still have room for a network vice-president's heart.

Billy Wilder was apprehensive:

A bad play folds and is forgotten, but in pictures we don't bury our dead. When you think it's out of your system your daughter sees it on TV and says: 'My father is an idiot.'

Groucho Marx as usual had a smart answer:

I find television very educational. Every time someone switches it on I go into another room and read a good book.

And it was an anonymous wit who had perhaps the best answer of all:

I prefer television. It's not so far to the bathroom.

Bob Hope as so often had the last word:

The other night I saw a Road picture so cut to make room for forty-five commercials that Bing and I weren't even in it.

television movies became prevalent in the late sixties. For four or five years mediocre movies had failed to get theatrical release and were seen first on television; from this it was a short step to making feature films specifically for television exposure. Aaron Spelling and Universal were the main providers; costs were kept low by assembly line methods, and it soon became just like the old days at the big studios, with stars making fast appearances in superficially glossy vehicles tailored to a specific time requirement. The quality obtained was roughly that of a Universal co-feature of the fifties. Middle-aged or elderly stars who still meant something to the home viewing circle were coaxed back to the studios: Barbara Stanwyck, Susan Hayward, Ray Milland, Bette Davis, Shelley Winters, Broderick Crawford, Myrna Loy, Milton Berle and their peers all starred again in the new forms, some in two-hour slots (97 minutes actual) but most successfully in 90-minute slots (73 minutes actual). By 1972 such films were appearing at the rate of two or three a week, more if one includes long-form series such as *Mystery Movie*, which gave new life to George Peppard, Rock Hudson, Richard Boone, Peter Falk and others. Crime was the most popular element of these films, with a strong flavouring of the supernatural, an occasional western or sob story, and a modicum of comedy. Art was not sought after, but as the touch became more assured, a few films received critical acclaim, notably *Brian's*

Song, Short Walk to Daylight, Duel, and *That Certain Summer*. One such film, *My Sweet Charlie*, was sent on theatrical release after its TV exposure, but the experiment failed. In Britain, several of the films went out on theatrical release before TV exposure, and one of them, *Duel*, received rave reviews. By the mid-seventies the trend in TV movies had turned to drama documentaries (*Eleanor and Franklin. Fear On Trial*) and to character drama, with an unfortunate stress on heroes and heroines dying of leukemia, tumours and similar afflictions. Then the success of two serialized novels (*Rich Man, Poor Man* and *Roots*) started a stampede to climb on this new bandwagon.

A useful guide by Alvin H. Marill was published in 1981 under the title *Movies Made for Television*.

television series based on motion picture originals almost outnumber the other kind. They include *The Thin Man, The Whistler, King's Row, Casablanca, My Friend Flicka, How to Marry a Millionaire, Margie, The Roaring Twenties, I Remember Mama, Blondie, Claudia, Jungle Jim, Hawkeye, The Invisible Man, Hudson's Bay, The Asphalt Jungle, Mr Smith Goes to Washington, Father of the Bride, Life with Father, National Velvet, Bus Stop, No Time for Sergeants, Going My Way, The Greatest Show on Earth, Les Girls, Peyton Place, The Naked City, Rin Tin Tin, Topper, The Virginian, Hopalong Cassidy, The Munsters* (indirectly), *The Wackiest Ship in the Army, Mr Roberts, Gidget, Please Don't Eat the Daisies, Twelve O'Clock High, Dr Kildare, The Farmer's Daughter, The Long Hot Summer, Tarzan, The Rounders, The Saint, Gideon's Way, The Man Who Never Was, Batman, Mr Deeds Goes to Town, The Courtship of Eddie's Father, The Odd Couple, Barefoot in the Park, Anna and the King, Perry Mason, M*A*S*H, Shane, Lassie, Bob and Carol and Ted and Alice, Shaft, Adam's Rib, How the West Was Won, Planet of the Apes, Alice Doesn't Live Here Any More*.

Tellegen, Lou (1881–1934) (Isidor Van Dameler). Dutch matinée idol who made many silent films in Hollywood.
Autobiography 1931: *Women Have Been Kind*.
Queen Elizabeth 12. The Explorer 15. The World and Its Women 19. Single Wives 23. The Redeeming Sin 25, etc.

Tempest, Dame Marie (1864–1942) (Marie Susan Etherington). British stage actress whose very rare films included *Moonlight Sonata* 37, *Yellow Sands* 38.

Temple, Shirley (1928–). American child star of the thirties, performing in short films at three; a genuine prodigy.
□The Red-Haired Alibi 32. To the Last Man 33. Out All Night 33. Carolina 34. Mandalay 34. *Stand Up and Cheer* 34. Now I'll Tell 34. Change of Heart 34. *Little Miss Marker* (her first star vehicle) 34. Baby Take a Bow 34. Now and Forever 34. Bright Eyes 34. The Little Colonel 35. Our Little Girl 35. *Curly Top* 35. The Littlest Rebel 35. Captain January 36. Poor Little Rich Girl 36. *Dimples* 36. Stowaway 36. *Wee Willie Winkie* 37. *Heidi* 37. Rebecca of Sunnybrook Farm 38. Little Miss Broadway 38. Just around the Corner 38. *The Little Princess* 39. Susannah of the Mounties 39. The Blue Bird 40. Young People 40. Kathleen 41. Miss Annie Rooney 42. Since You Went Away 44. I'll Be Seeing You 44. Kiss and Tell 45. Honeymoon 47. The Bachelor and the Bobbysoxer 47. That Hagen Girl 47. Fort Apache 48. Mr Belvedere Goes to College 49. Adventure in Baltimore 49. The Story of Seabiscuit 49. A Kiss for Corliss 49.

Later appeared on TV in *Shirley Temple Storybook*, and in the sixties went into local California politics. Won special Academy Award 1934 'in grateful recognition of her outstanding contribution to screen entertainment'.
❀ For captivating the mass world audience and enabling it to forget the depression. *Curly Top*.

¶ *S.T.*: I stopped believing in Santa Claus at an early age. Mother took me to see him in a department store, and he asked for my autograph.

The Ten Commandments. Cecil B. de Mille made two films under this title. The 1923 version spent only half its length on the biblical story, paralleling this with a modern tale about what happens when the moral laws are broken nowadays. It starred Richard Dix, Rod la Rocque and Estelle Taylor. The 1956 version spent nearly four hours on the Bible story alone, and with less cinematic flair than the silent picture. Charlton Heston was Moses and Yul Brynner Pharaoh.

Tennant, Victoria (1950–). British leading lady.
The Ragman's Daughter 72. Sphinx 80. The Dogs of War 81. Inseminoid 81. *The Winds of*

War (TV) 83. Chiefs (TV) 83. All of Me 84. The Holcroft Covenant 85. Best Seller 87. War and Remembrance (TV) 87.

tennis has accounted for some memorable scenes in the cinema, among them the suspenseful match in *Strangers on a Train* and the hilarious one in *Monsieur Hulot's Holiday*. Professional tennis was the subject of *Hard Fast and Beautiful*. Nor should one forget the championship between Tom and Jerry in *Tennis Chumps*, or the weird game with no ball in *Blow Up*. Other tennis sequences figured in *The System, Nobody Runs Forever*, Come to the Stable, *Pat and Mike*, and *Players*; while there was a TV movie about Little Mo.

Tennyson, Pen (1918–41) (Penrose Tennyson). British director killed in World War II.
□There Ain't No Justice (TV) 39. *The Proud Valley* 39. Convoy 40.

Terhune, Max (1890–1973). American small-time western star, one of the Three Mesquiteers in 30s second features; also appeared in the Range Busters series.

La Terra Trema (Italy 1948). A famous dramatic film written and directed by Luchino Visconti and photographed by G. R. Aldo, about a family of poor Sicilian fishermen and their struggle against exploitation.

Terriss, Ellaline (1871–1971) (Ellen Lewin). British stage actress, widow of Sir Seymour Hicks; in a few films.
Blighty 27. Glamour 31. The Iron Duke 35. The Four Just Men 39, etc.

Terry, Alice (1899–1987) (Alice Taafe). American leading lady of the silent screen.
Not My Sister 16. *The Four Horsemen of the Apocalypse* 21. *The Prisoner of Zenda* 22. Mare Nostrum 27. The Garden of Allah 28, etc.

Terry, Don (1902–) (Donald Locher). American hero of serials and second features in the thirties.
Me Gangster 28. The Valiant 29. Whistlin' Dan 32. Paid to Dance 37. Who Killed Gail Preston? 38 The Secret of Treasure Island (serial) 38. Don Winslow of the Navy (serial) 41. Drums of the Congo 42. White Savage 43. Top Sergeant 43. Don Winslow of the Coastguard (serial) 43, etc.

Terry, Ellen (1848–1928). Distinguished British stage actress whose film appearances were few and ineffective.
□Her Greatest Performance 17. The Invasion of Britain 18. Pillars of Society 18. Potter's Clay 22. The Bohemian Girl 22.

Terry, Paul (1887–1971). American animator, the creator of 'Terry-toons' (starring Mighty Mouse, Heckle and Jeckle, etc.) which filled Fox supporting programmes for over thirty years.

Terry, Philip (1909–). American leading man of the forties, mainly in second features; best remembered for briefly marrying Joan Crawford.
The Parson of Panamint 41. The Monster and the Girl 41. Bataan 43. Music in Manhattan 44. Pan-Americana 45. *The Lost Weekend* 45. Seven Keys to Baldpate 47. Born to Kill 47, etc.

Terry-Thomas (1911–) (Thomas Terry Hoar-Stevens). British comedian with inimitable gap-toothed manner; has recently become Hollywood's favourite idea of the English silly ass. Also on stage and TV.
Private's Progress 56. Blue Murder at St Trinian's 57. The Naked Truth 58. Tom Thumb 58. *Carleton Browne of the FO* 58. *I'm All Right, Jack* 59. School for Scoundrels 60. His and Hers 61. A Matter of Who 62. Bachelor Flat 62. The Wonderful World of the Brothers Grimm 63. Kill or Cure 63. It's a Mad Mad Mad Mad World 63. The Mouse on the Moon 63. *Those Magnificent Men in Their Flying Machines* 65. *How to Murder Your Wife* 65. You Must be Joking 65. Munster Go Home 66. Kiss the Girls and Make Them Die 66. Rocket to the Moon 67. The Perils of Pauline 67. Don't Look Now 68. Where Were You When the Lights Went Out? 68. 2000 Years Later 69. Monte Carlo or Bust 69. The Abominable Dr Phibes 71. Vault of Horror 73. Spanish Fly 75. The Bawdy Adventures of Tom Jones 76. The Last Remake of Beau Geste 77, etc.

Terzieff, Laurent (1935–). French leading man.
Les Tricheurs 58. Le Bois des Amants 59. La Notte Brava 60. Kapo 60. Thou Shalt Not Kill 61. The Seven Deadly Sins 62. Ballade pour un Voyou 64. Le Triangle 65. Le Voyage du Père 66. Two Weeks in September 67. The Milky Way 68. Medea 69. Moses (TV) 75. Couleur Chair 77. Utopia 78, etc.

Teshighara, Hiroshi (1927–). Japanese director.
Pitfall 61. *Woman in the Dunes* 64. The Face of Another 66. The Man Without a Map 68. Out of Work for Years 75, etc.

Tesich, Steve (–). American screenwriter.
Breaking Away (AA) 79. Eyewitness 81. Four Friends 81. The World According to Garp 82.

Tester, Desmond (1919–). British boy actor of the thirties; went to Australia.
Midshipman Easy 35. Tudor Rose 36. Sabotage 37. The Drum 38. The Stars Look Down 39. The Turners of Prospect Road 47. Barry Mackenzie Holds His Own 74, etc.

Tetzel, Joan (1924–77). American leading actress with stage experience, married to Oscar Homolka.
Duel in the Sun 46. The Paradine Case 47. The File on Thelma Jordon 50. Joy in the Morning 65, etc.

Tetzlaff, Ted (1903–). American director, formerly cinematographer.
World Première 41. *Riff Raff* 46. *The Window* 48. Johnny Allegro 48. The White Tower 50. The Treasure of Lost Canyon 52. Time Bomb 53. Son of Sinbad 55. The Young Land 57, etc.

Tewksbury, Peter (1924–). American director, from TV (*Father Knows Best, My Three Sons*, etc.).
□*Sunday in New York* 64. Emil and the Detectives 65. Doctor You've Got to be Kidding 67. Stay Away Joe 68. The Trouble with Girls 69. Second Chance (TV) 71.

Tey, Josephine (1896–1952) (Elizabeth MacKintosh). Scottish writer of plays (as Gordon Daviot) and crime novels. *A Shilling for Candles* was filmed as *Young and Innocent*, and there was also a film of *The Franchise Affair*.

Thackery, Bud (1903–). American cinematographer, especially for Republic, where he photographed innumerable westerns and serials. Moved into TV.

Thalberg, Irving (1899–1936). American producer, MGM's boy wonder of the early thirties, responsible for the literary flavour of films like *The Barretts of Wimpole Street* 34, *Mutiny on the Bounty* 35, *Romeo and Juliet* 36; also for hiring the Marx Brothers. A biography by Bob Thomas, *Thalberg*, was published in 1969. *Mayer and Thalberg* by Samuel Marx followed in 1976. Thalberg was played by Robert Evans in *Man of a Thousand Faces*.

¶ When a man dies young, he is often underestimated. Thalberg has been lucky: the reverse proved true. Head of Universal production at twenty-one and of MGM at twenty-five, his quiet efficiency and stubborn enthusiasm, coupled with his scholarly air, made him a legend even before his untimely death at thirty-seven. As early as 1925 F. L. Collins wrote:

> Wherever Thalberg sits is always the head of the table.

He had apparently high aims:

> I believe that although the motion picture may not live forever as a work of art, except in a few instances, it will be the most efficient way of showing posterity how we live now.

He was modest enough to keep his name off the credits of his films:

> If you are in a position to give credit, you don't need it.

Charles MacArthur said:

> Entertainment is Thalberg's God. He's content to serve Him without billing, like a priest at an altar or a rabbi under the scrolls.

He was a shrewd film-maker:

> Movies aren't made, they're remade.

And he always had an eye for the box office. His idea of a good tag-line was:

> Ladies, have you had a good cry lately? See *Imitation of Life* and cry unashamedly.

And he once said to Cedric Hardwicke:

> We should all make a killing in this business: there's so much money in the pot.

But the screenwriters were suspicious of him:

> He's too good to last. The lamb doesn't lie down with the lion for long.—*Charles MacArthur*
>
> I seriously began to question whether Thalberg ever existed, or whether he might not be a solar myth or a deity concocted by the front office to garner prestige.—*S. J. Perelman*
>
> On a clear day you can see Thalberg.—*George S. Kaufman*

When he died however it was Charles MacArthur who knew the truth:

> Ten years of sixteen-hours-a-day work had tired him. He didn't know how to rest, or play, or even breathe without a script in his hands.

Thank Your Lucky Stars (US 1943). A typical example of the all-star musicals mounted by the big Hollywood studios during World War II—and the best of them. The idea was to gather together all the stars on the payroll doing sketches or numbers joined by a thin story line and ending in a patriotic morale-boost for the boys overseas. In the same year MGM did *Thousands Cheer* and Paramount *Star-Spangled Rhythm*; this Warner job has better songs, a more amusing story, and the bright idea of making most of the stars do things one wouldn't expect from them. Eddie Cantor, Edward Everett Horton and S. Z. Sakall did the linking.

That Hamilton Woman (US 1942) (GB: *Lady Hamilton*). A rather stiff saga of Nelson's famous love affair. This famous film paired Laurence Olivier and Vivien Leigh at their peak, and had the distinction of being Winston Churchill's favourite film. Alexander Korda, directing it in Hollywood, managed to turn it into anti-invasion propaganda.

Thatcher, Heather (1897–198?). Blonde British light actress who filmed also in Hollywood.
Altar Chains 17. The Little House of Peter Wells 20. But the Flesh is Weak 32. Loyalties 33. The 13th Chair 37. Tovarich 37. Beau Geste 39. Man Hunt 41. Gaslight 44. Dear Mr Prohack 50. Will Any Gentleman 55, many others.

Thatcher, Torin (1905–1981). Tough-looking British character actor, on stage from 1923; latterly on stage again after some years in Hollywood.
General John Regan (film debut) 34. Major Barbara 40. The Captive Heart 45. Great Expectations 46. The Crimson Pirate 52. The Robe 53. Love is a Many-Splendored Thing 55. Witness for the Prosecution 57. The Seventh Voyage of Sinbad 58. The Canadians 60. Jack the Giant Killer 62. The Sandpiper 65. Hawaii 66. The King's Pirate 67, many others.

Thaw, John (1942–). Rough-speaking British leading man.
The Loneliness of the Long Distance Runner 62. Dead Man's Chest 65. Praise Marx and Pass the Ammunition 68. The Bofors Gun 68. The Last Grenade 69. Dr Phibes Rides Again 72. Regan (TV) 73. *Sweeney* 76. Sweeney Two 78. Cry Freedom 87. The Sign of Four (TV) 87. Business as Usual 87, etc.
TV series: Redcap 64–66. Sweeney 74–78. Home to Roost 85– . Inspector Morse 86– .

Thaxter, Phyllis (1921–). American leading lady of the forties, recently back in character roles.
Thirty Seconds Over Tokyo (debut) 44. Weekend at the Waldorf 45. Bewitched 45. Tenth Avenue Angel 47. Blood on the Moon 48. Come Fill the Cup 51. Springfield Rifle 53. Women's Prison 54. The World of Henry Orient 64. The Longest Night (TV) 72, etc.

theatres have provided an effective setting for many films apart from the countless putting-on-a-show musicals. Films concerned exclusively with matters theatrical include *The Royal Family of Broadway, Twentieth Century, The Great Profile, The Country Girl, Stage Door, Morning Glory, Queen of Hearts, Heller in Pink Tights, Take the Stage, To Be or Not To Be, Main Street to Broadway, Les Enfants du Paradis, Prince of Players, The Velvet Touch, All About Eve, Curtain Up, Kiss Me Kate, The Producers, The Boyfriend* and *Variety Jubilee*, while a theatre was also the principal setting for *Those Were the Days, Henry V, Occupe-Toi d'Amélie, The Lost People, The High Terrace, Four Hours to Kill, The Phantom of the Opera* and *The Climax*. Thrillers with climaxes in a theatre include *The Thirty-Nine Steps, Torn Curtain, Charlie Chan at the Opera, Cover Girl Killer, The Westerner, Stage Fright, Charade, Scaramouche, The Deadly Affair, No Way to Treat a Lady* and *King Kong*; comedies include *A Night at the Opera, A Haunting We Will Go, Knock On Wood, The Intelligence Men, Trouble in Paradise, The Secret of My Success, My Learned Friend* and *Meet Mr Lucifer*. Less frequent are uses of the theatre as a setting for romance, but it served this purpose in *All This and Heaven Too, The Lady with a Little Dog*, and *Letter from an Unknown Woman*. The scariest theatre was *Theatre of Blood*, with Vincent Price as an actor murdering all the critics who had given him bad notices. See: *cinemas*.

These Three (US 1936). This was a disguised version, directed by William Wyler, of Lillian Hellman's play *The Children's Hour* about a lesbian relationship between two schoolmistresses and the scandal caused by a malicious girl. The affair had to be changed to a more normal one. In 1962 Wyler had another go, censorship being more relaxed, and filmed the original more or less intact, with Audrey Hepburn and Shirley Maclaine.

Thesiger, Ernest (1879–1961). Witty, skeletal-looking British character actor, on stage from 1909.

Autobiography 1927: *Practically True.*
West End Wives 29. *The Old Dark House* 32. The Ghoul 33. Heart Song 34. *The Bride of Frankenstein* 35. The Man Who Could Work Miracles 36. *They Drive By Night* 38. Henry V 44. Caesar and Cleopatra 45. A Place of One's Own 46. The Ghosts of Berkeley Square 47. Quartet 48. Laughter in Paradise 51. *The Man in the White Suit* 52. *Father Brown* 54. Make Me an Offer 55. The Battle of the Sexes 59. The Roman Spring of Mrs Stone 61, many others.
† He also published books on embroidery.
Famous line (*The Old Dark House*): Have some gin. It's my only weakness . . .
Famous line (*The Bride of Frankenstein*): To a new world of gods and monsters!

They Won't Forget (US 1937). Among the first of Hollywood's anti-lynching melodramas, this was a stark and shattering affair to come from Warners in the escapist years. Convincingly set in the deep south, diligently directed by Mervyn le Roy, and not shirking a tragic ending, it was somewhat marred by the miscasting of Claude Rains as a southern senator. Notable for the debut of sweater girl Lana Turner as the murder victim.

The Thief of Baghdad. This Arabian Nights tale was superbly filmed with Douglas Fairbanks in 1924 (US); again in 1940 (GB/US) with Sabu and some remarkable trick photography, directed by Michael Powell, Tim Whelan and Ludwig Berger; and in 1961 (Italy) with Steve Reeves and a much altered plot. A TV movie version followed in 1979.

Thiele, Rolf (1918–). German director.
Nachtwache (p only) 49. Mamitschka (& wp) 55. El Hakim 57. The Girl Rosemarie (& co-w) 58. Venusberg (& w) 63. Tonio Kroger 64, etc.

Thiele, William (1890–1975). German director who went to Hollywood in the thirties but found little work.
His Late Excellency 29. Liebeswalzer 31. *Drei von der Tankstelle* 31. Le Bal 32. The Jungle Princess 36. London by Night 37. Bridal Suite 39. Tarzan Triumphs 43. Tarzan's Desert Mystery 43. The Madonna's Secret 46. The Last Pedestrian 60, etc.

Thiess, Ursula (1929–). German leading lady, in a few American films.
Monsoon 52. The Iron Glove 54. Bengal Brigade 55. The Americano 55, etc.

Thimig, Helene (1889–1974). German character actress, widow of Max Reinhardt, in a few American films.
None But the Lonely Heart 44. Cloak and Dagger 46. The Locket 47, etc.

The Thin Man. In Dashiell Hammett's crime novel of the twenties, the thin man is the murderer's first victim. Oddly enough the tag stuck to William Powell (not all that thin) who played Nick Charles the detective, and he starred in five sequels: *After the Thin Man* 37, *Another Thin Man* 38, *Shadow of the Thin Man* 42, *The Thin Man Goes Home* 44, *Song of the Thin Man* 46. (There was also, later, a TV series with Peter Lawford and Phyllis Kirk.) Myrna Loy played Nora Charles in all the features, and it was said that her domestic scenes with Powell in the original film marked the first time a sophisticated, affectionate marriage had been realistically portrayed on the screen.

The Thing (from Another World) (US 1951). Interesting as one of the first films to combine the old horror with the new science fiction, this was a competent job but disappointingly thin and tame considering its credits. Written by Charles Lederer and photographed by Russell Harlan, it was produced by Howard Hawks (and some say also directed by him despite the credit to Christian Nyby; there are also rumours that Orson Welles had a hand). The gripping early scenes about a USAF base at the North Pole threatened by a temporarily frozen 'intellectual carrot' from a flying saucer weakened when the visitor thawed out and proved to be James Arness in a metallic suit. A 1982 remake by John Carpenter went back to the original story, in which the visitor could transform itself into various guises; but it overdid the horror effects.

Things to Come (GB 1936). This film from H. G. Wells' prophetic tract, though naïve in some of its dialogue scenes, provided not only a tolerably accurate forecast of World War II and the atomic bomb but splendid imaginative spectacle and a musical theme by Sir Arthur Bliss which remains fresh and stirring. William Cameron Menzies directed, and among a cast who refused to be dwarfed were Raymond Massey and Ralph Richardson.

Thinnes, Roy (1938–). Stocky American leading man of some successful television series: *The Long Hot Summer* 64. *The Invaders* 66–67. The Psychiatrist 70.
Journey to the Far Side of the Sun 69.

Charlie One Eye 72. The Horror at 37,000 Feet (TV) 73. The Norliss Tapes (TV) 73. Airport 75 74. The Hindenberg 75. From Here to Eternity (TV) 79, etc.

Thirard, Armand (1899–). French cinematographer.
Remorques 41. Quai des Orfèvres 47. *Manon* 49. *The Wages of Fear* 52. Act of Love 54. Les Diaboliques 54. And God Created Woman 56. The Truth 60, etc.

The Third Man (GB 1949). A lucky combination of talents gave this romantic thriller set in war-torn Vienna an almost poetic quality and an excitement which have kept it vivid. The photogenic ruins provided a suitable background for all four star actors, Joseph Cotten, Valli, Trevor Howard and Orson Welles; Graham Greene wrote a bitter, well-timed script; Robert Krasker photographed lovingly; and Carol Reed directed every scene with the surest of touches except the last one, which was perhaps misjudged. And then there was that insistent zither music by Anton Karas. . . . BFA best British film. (A sixties TV series with Michael Rennie borrowed the title but little else.)

Thiriet, Maurice (1906–72). French composer.
The Woman I Love 37. Les Visiteurs du Soir 37. Les Enfants du Paradis 44. L'Homme au Chapeau Rond 46. Une Si Jolie Petite Plage 48. Fanfan la Tulipe 51. Thérèse Raquin 53. Crime and Punishment 58, etc.

35mm. The standard commercial film gauge or width.

The Thirty-Nine Steps. The first two film versions have little resemblance to John Buchan's lively spy yarn apart from the hero's initial predicament and the Scottish setting for the chase. Hitchcock, however (GB 1935), working from Charles Bennett's pacy script, scattered touches of macabre comedy and romantic banter which hit just the right note; Ralph Thomas (GB 1959) reworked the same ideas stolidly and without flair. And Kenneth More, Taina Elg and Barry Jones were somehow no match for Robert Donat, Madeleine Carroll and Godfrey Tearle. A 1978 version starring Robert Powell restored the original period and some of the plot.

This Gun for Hire (US 1942). This was not only a moderately intelligent though considerably reshaped version of Graham Greene's *A Gun for Sale*: it was also notable for giving Alan Ladd his first starring role as the professional killer, a role which catapulted him into the front rank of box office attractions. Frank Tuttle directed. The story was remade in 1956 as *Short Cut to Hell*, directed by James Cagney: Robert Ivers played the gunman, but both he and the movie passed without comment.

This Modern Age. A series of current affairs two-reelers sponsored in 1946 by Rank as the British answer to *The March of Time*. Although decently produced by Sergei Nolbandov, the monthly issues were not a popular addition to already overlong programmes, and the attempt was given up in 1949.

Thomas, Danny (1914–) (Amos Jacobs). American night club comedian; star of his own seven-year TV series in the sixties and *The Practice* in 1977.
The Unfinished Dance 47. Big City 48. Call Me Mister 51. I'll See You in My Dreams 52. The Jazz Singer 53.

Thomas, Dylan (1914–1953). Welsh poet whose drama *Under Milk Wood* has been filmed. He also worked on the scripts of a number of British films in the late forties, including *The Three Weird Sisters*. He was portrayed by Ronald Lacy in a 1978 BBC film, *Dylan*.

Thomas, Gerald (1920–). British director, former editor, in films from 1946.
Time Lock 57. Vicious Circle 57. The Duke Wore Jeans 58. Carry On Sergeant 58 (and all the subsequent 'Carry Ons'). Watch Your Stern 60. Twice Round the Daffodils 62. The Big Job 65. Don't Lose Your Head 66. Follow that Camel 67. Carry On Loving 70. Carry On Girls 73. Carry On England 76, etc.

Thomas, Henry (–). American child actor of the eighties.
Raggedy Man 81. E.T. 82. Misunderstood 83. Cloak and Dagger 84. The Quest 86.

Thomas, Jameson (1892–1939). British actor who usually played 'the other man'. Went to Hollywood in the early thirties but did not command leading roles.
Blighty 27. A Daughter of Love 28. Piccadilly 29. High Treason 30. Hate Ship 30. Elstree Calling 30. The Phantom President 32. It Happened One Night 34. Lives of a Bengal

Lancer 35. Mr Deeds Goes to Town 36. Death Goes North 38, etc.

Thomas, Lowell (1892–1981). American broadcaster and lecturer who partly controlled Cinerama and appeared as travelling commentator in some of its episodes: *Search for Paradise* 58, etc.

Thomas, Marlo (1943–) (Margaret Thomas). American leading lady, daughter of Danny Thomas.
The Knack 64. Jenny 70. Thieves 77.
TV series: That Girl 66–70.

Thomas, Olive (1898–1920) (Olive Elaine Duffy). American 'Ziegfeld girl' who played a few comedy roles in films.
Beatrice Fairfax 16. Limousine Life 18. The Follies Girl 19. The Glorious Lady 19. Footlights and Shadows 20, etc.

Thomas, Pascal (1945–). French director.
Les Zozos 72. Le Chaud Lapin 74. Un Oursin dans la Poche 77, etc.

Thomas, Ralph (1915–). British director, former trailer maker, who with producer Betty Box has tackled some ambitious subjects in a rather stolid manner.
Helter Skelter 48. Traveller's Joy 49. The Clouded Yellow 51. Appointment with Venus 51. Venetian Bird 53. *Doctor in the House* 54. Above Us the Waves 55. The Iron Petticoat 56. *Campbell's Kingdom* 57. A Tale of Two Cities 57. The Wind Cannot Read 58. The Thirty-Nine Steps 59. No Love for Johnnie 61. The Wild and the Willing 62. Hot Enough for June 64. The High Bright Sun 65. Deadlier than the Male 66. Some Girls Do 68. Percy 71. Quest for Love 71. The Love Ban 73. Percy's Progress 74, etc.

Thomas, Richard (1951–). American juvenile lead of the early seventies.
Winning 69. Last Summer 70. Cactus in the Snow 70. Red Sky at Morning 71. You'll Like My Mother 72. September 30 1955 78. The Silence (TV) 78. Battle Beyond the Stars 80.
TV series: *The Waltons* 72–76.

Thomas, Terry: see *Terry-Thomas*.

Thomas, William C. (1892–1984): see *Pine, William H.*

Thompson, Carlos (1916–) (Juan Carlos Mundanschaffter). Argentinian stage and screen matinée idol who has made some American and German films.
Fort Algiers 53. The Flame and the Flesh 54. Valley of the Kings 54. Magic Fire 56. Stefanie 58. Joaquin Murietta 58. Stefanie in Rio 60, etc.
TV series: Sentimental Agent 66.

Thompson, J. Lee: see *Lee-Thompson, J.*

Thompson, Jack (1940–) (John Pain). Australian leading man.
Outback 70. Libido 73. Petersen 74. Sunday Too Far Away 74. Caddie 76. Mad Dog Morgan 76. The Chant of Jimmie Blacksmith 78. Breaker Morant 79. The Earthling 80. Merry Christmas Mr Lawrence 83. Burke and Wills 85. Flesh and Blood 85. Ground Zero 87.

Thompson, Marshall (1925–) (James Marshall Thompson). American leading man who began by playing quiet juvenile roles.
Reckless Age 44. Gallant Bess 45. The Romance of Rosy Ridge 46. Homecoming 48. Words and Music 48. Battleground 49. The Violent Hour 50. *My Six Convicts* 52. Battle Taxi 55. To Hell and Back 55. Clarence the Cross-Eyed Lion 65. Around the World Under the Sea 66. The Turning Point 77, many others.
TV series: Angel 60. Daktari 66–68.

Thompson, Sada (1929–). Gentle-looking American character actress, usually in maternal roles.
The Pursuit of Happiness 70. Desperate Characters 71, etc.
TV series: *Family* 76–79.

Thomson, Alex (–). British cinematographer.
Here We Go Round the Mulberry Bush 67. The Strange Affair 68. Alfred the Great 69. Excalibur 81. Eureka 83.

Thomson, Fred (1890–1928). American cowboy star of the twenties.
Penrod 22. The Eagle's Talons 23. The Fighting Sap 24. The Wild Bull's Lair 25. Hands Across the Border 26. Arizona Nights 27. Jesse James 27. The Pioneer Scout 28. Kit Carson 28, etc.

Thorburn, June (1931–1967). British leading lady with repertory experience.
The Pickwick Papers (film debut) 53. The Cruel Sea 53. True as a Turtle 56. Tom Thumb 59. The Three Worlds of Gulliver 59. The Scarlet Blade 63, etc.

Thorndike, Andrew (1909–). East German director who with his wife Annelie made the strident anti-Nazi documentary series *The Archives Testify*; also *The German Story, The Russian Miracle*, etc.

Thorndike, Dame Sybil (1882–1976). Distinguished British stage actress who appeared in occasional films.
Biography 1950: *Sybil Thorndike* by Russell Thorndike.
Moths and Rust (debut) 21. Dawn 29. To What Red Hell 30. Hindle Wakes 31. Tudor Rose 36. Major Barbara 40. *Nicholas Nickleby* 47. Stage Fright 50. The Magic Box 51. Melba 53. *Alive and Kicking* 58. Shake Hands with the Devil 59. Hand in Hand 61, etc.

Thornton, Frank (1921–). British comic actor, much on TV.
Crooks and Coronets 68. All the Way Up 70. Our Miss Fred 72. Digby 73. No Sex Please We're British 73. The Three Musketeers 73.

Thornton, Sigrid (1959–). Australian leading lady.
The Getting of Wisdom 80. Snap Shot 81. 1915 (TV) 82. The Man from Snowy River 82. All the Rivers Run (TV) 83. Slate, Wyn and Me 87.

Thorpe, Jerry (1930–). American director from TV.
The Venetian Affair 66. The Day of the Evil Gun (& p) 68, etc.
TV series: *Kung Fu* 72–74.

Thorpe, Jim (1888–1953). American Indian athlete, played by Burt Lancaster in *Jim Thorpe, All-American.* Also small-part actor, in B westerns of the thirties.

Thorpe, Richard (1896–1986) (Rollo Smolt Thorpe). American director, formerly in vaudeville.
The Feminine Touch 28. Forgotten Woman 32. The Last of the Pagans 35. *Night Must Fall* 38. Huckleberry Finn 39. Tarzan Finds a Son 39. Wyoming 40. The Earl of Chicago 40. Tarzan's New York Adventure 42. Above Suspicion 43. Her Highness and the Bellboy 45. Fiesta 47. The Sun Comes Up 48. Malaya 49. *The Great Caruso* 51. The Prisoner of Zenda 52. Ivanhoe 52. The Student Prince 54. Knights of the Round Table 54. The Prodigal 55. *The Adventures of Quentin Durward* 56. Jailhouse Rock 57. The House of the Seven Hawks 59. The Tartars 60. Fun in Acapulco 63. The Golden Head 65. That Funny Feeling 65. The Truth about Spring 65. The Scorpio Letters 67. Pistolero 67, etc.

'His reputation for only needing one take is why we don't remember his films.'—*James Mason*

Those Magnificent Men in Their Flying Machines (GB 1965). This amiable romp about the first London-to-Paris air race was only moderately well written by Jack Davies and directed by Ken Annakin; but it serves as an example of a big budget and a lot of stars on a wide screen being acceptable in the mid-sixties in place of real talent. The primitive airplanes were the real stars. In 1969 a follow-up by the same team, this time about vintage car racing, came off less well: it was known in Britain as *Monte Carlo or Bust* and in the States as *Those Daring Young Men in Their Jaunty Jalopies.*

Three Coins in the Fountain (US 1954). This highly commercial film taught Hollywood the travelogue possibilities of CinemaScope to freshen up a tired story, and encouraged the trek of producers from Hollywood to locations all over the world, thus changing the face of film-making. A simple trio of romantic stories, from John Secondari's novel, the action was deftly directed by Jean Negulesco, who ten years later attempted a disguised remake under the title *The Pleasure Seekers.* But by now there was no novelty left and the picture crept by almost unnoticed.

3-D. Three-dimensional film-making had been tried in 1935 by MGM, as a gimmick involving throwaway paper glasses with one red and one green eyepiece to match the double image on the screen. In 1953, Hollywood really got the idea that this device would save an ailing industry, and a number of cheap exploitation pictures were shot in 3-D before anyone got down to the practical problem of renting out and collecting the necessary polaroid spectacles, which threw cinema managers into fits. *Bwana Devil* was an awful picture; *Man in the Dark* and *Fort Ti* were a shade better, except that the action kept stopping for something to be hurled at the audience; *House of Wax*, a Warner horror remake of *The Mystery of the Wax Museum*, had better production values and seemed to catch on with the public. All the studios began to make 3-D films—*Kiss Me Kate, The Charge at Feather River, Dial M for Murder, Miss Sadie Thompson, Sangaree*—but by the time these were ready, interest had shifted to

Fox's new CinemaScope process, which although it gave no illusion of depth was at least a different shape and didn't need glasses. Nor did it entail such problems as running both projectors at once, with consequent intervals every twenty minutes; or long pauses when the film broke in order to mutilate the second copy in precisely the same way; or one machine running a little slower than the other, with gradual loss of synchronization. The remaining 3-D films were released 'flat', and the industry breathed a sigh of relief. So did the critics, who had wondered whether they would ever again see a film which did not involve frequent violent action. The Russians did claim at the time that they were inventing a 3-D process which would not require the use of glasses, but we are still waiting for that. In 1967 Arch Oboler made *The Bubble* in 3-D and in 1970–71 there was a brief revival of interest in the process as a promotion gimmick for cheap pornographic films. It flared up again in the early eighties as a medium for horror films and such shockers as *Jaws 3-D*, while Hitchcocks's 1954 *Dial M for Murder* was shown for the first time in the process.
A 1983 book, *Amazing 3-D*, was by Hal Morgan and Dan Symmes.

The Three Musketeers. Apart from numerous European versions, Alexandre Dumas' classic swashbuckler has been a Hollywood favourite too. Edison made a version in 1911; so did Edward Laurillard in 1913, C. V. Heinkel in 1914, and Fred Niblo (the Douglas Fairbanks spectacular) in 1921. In the last-named production the musketeers were played by Eugene Pallette, Leon Barry and George Siegmann. Walter Abel was D'Artagnan in a 1935 version for RKO, with Paul Lukas, Moroni Olsen and Onslow Stevens: Rowland V. Lee directed. Don Ameche *sang* in a 1939 musical comedy version (sometimes known as *The Singing Musketeer*) with the Ritz Brothers, no less, as lackeys impersonating the famous trio. Directed by Allan Dwan, it was very, very funny. Gene Kelly made an acrobatic D'Artagnan for MGM in 1948, with Van Heflin, Gig Young and Robert Coote; and 1973 brought an all-star international version directed by Richard Lester, with Michael York, Oliver Reed, Frank Finlay and Richard Chamberlain. A sequel, *The Four Musketeers,* came the following year; but *The Fifth Musketeer,* a rip-roaring multi-national adventure of 1978, told in fact the story of the man in the iron mask.

Three Smart Girls (US 1937). A minor domestic comedy about three teenagers who save Dad from the clutches of a gold digger and restore him to the arms of Mum, this was notable as the first feature appearance, and a highly successful one, of Deanna Durbin. Henry Koster directed this and the 1939 sequel, *Three Smart Girls Grow Up.* In 1943 followed a third film on the adventures of the Durbin character only, *Hers to Hold.*

The Three Stooges: see *The Stooges.*

Thring, Frank (–). Australian actor in occasional films.
A Question of Adultery 58. The Vikings 58. Ben Hur 59. King of Kings 61. El Cid 61. Age of Consent 69. Ned Kelly 70. Mad Max 76. Mad Max Beyond Thunderdome 85.

Thulin, Ingrid (1929–). Swedish leading actress, often in Ingmar Bergman's films.
Foreign Intrigue 55. *Wild Strawberries* 57. So Close to Life 58. The Face 59. The Four Horsemen of the Apocalypse (US) 62. Winter Light 62. *The Silence* 63. Return from the Ashes (US) 65. The War is Over (Fr.) 66. Night Games 66. The Damned 69. The Rite 69. Cries and Whispers 72. Moses 76. The Cassandra Crossing 77, etc.

Thunder Rock (GB 1942). Rather belated in its message, but still one of World War II's most thoughtful films, this intriguing fantasy was about an isolationist in a lighthouse spurred to get back into the world's affairs by the ghosts of passengers drowned near the rock a hundred years before. Memorably acted by Michael Redgrave, Barbara Mullen, Lilli Palmer, Frederick Valk and James Mason: produced and directed by the Boulting brothers from Robert Ardrey's play.

Thurber, James (1894–1961). American humorist whose chief gifts to Hollywood were the original stories of *The Secret Life of Walter Mitty* and *The Male Animal.* TV series based on his cartoons: *My World and Welcome to It* 69.

Thy Soul Shall Bear Witness (Sweden 1920). A fantasy directed by Victor Sjostrom, who also played the leading role of a drunkard whose soul is taken in death's wagon to review the misery he has caused. Remade recently in Sweden, also in France in 1940 by Julien Duvivier, as *La Charrette Fantôme*, with Pierre Fresnay as the drunkard.

Tibbett, Lawrence (1896–1960). American opera star who made some films in the thirties.
□Rogue Song 30. New Moon 30. The Prodigal 31. Cuban Love Song 32. Metropolitan 36. Under your Spell 37.
† Tibbett's first movie appearance was promoted as follows: 'To bring you a new, vital figure for the further glory of your talking screen, MGM has reached into the highest realms of the Metropolitan Opera. From this renowned company of immortal voices has been picked the greatest—your new star, Lawrence Tibbett!' Louella Parsons commented: 'The long-awaited successor to Rudolph Valentino has arrived!'

Tidyman, Ernest (1928–84). American novelist who scripted the *Shaft* films from his own novels.
The French Connection 72. High Plains Drifter 74. Report to the Commissioner (co-w), etc.

Tierney, Gene (1920–). Gentle-featured American leading lady of the forties, typically a smooth socialite.
Autobiography 1979: *Self Portrait.*
□The Return of Frank James 40. Hudson's Bay 40. Tobacco Road 41. *Belle Starr* 41. Sundown 41. The Shanghai Gesture 41. Son of Fury 42. Rings on Her Fingers 42. Thunder Birds 42. China Girl 42. *Heaven Can Wait* 43. *Laura* 44. A Bell for Adano 45. Leave Her to Heaven 45. Dragonwyck 46. *The Razor's Edge* 46. The Ghost and Mrs Muir 47. The Iron Curtain 48. That Wonderful Urge 48. Whirlpool 48. Night and the City 50. Where the Sidewalk Ends 50. The Mating Season 51. On the Riviera 51. The Secret of Convict Lake 51. Close to My Heart 51. Way of a Gaucho 51. The Plymouth Adventure 52. Never Let Me Go (GB) 53. Personal Affair (GB) 53. Black Widow 54. The Egyptian 54. *The Left Hand of God* 54. Advise and Consent 62. Toys in the Attic 63. The Pleasure Seekers 64. Daughter of the Mind (TV) 69.

Tierney, Harry (1890–1965). American songwriter, usually with lyricist Joseph McCarthy. Shows filmed include *Irene, Kid Boots, Rio Rita.*

Tierney, Lawrence (1919–). American 'tough-guy' actor, brother of Scott Brady.
The Ghost Ship 44. *Dillinger* (title role) 45. Step by Step 46. San Quentin 47. The Devil Thumbs a Ride 47. Shakedown 50. The Hoodlum 51. A Child is Waiting 62. Custer of the West 67. Such Good Friends 71. Midnight 82. Prizzi's Honor 85. Silver Bullet 85. Murphy's Law 86. Tough Guys Don't Dance 87, etc.

Tiffin, Pamela (1942–) (Pamela Wonso). American leading lady, former child model.
Summer and Smoke 60. One Two Three 61. State Fair 61. The Hallelujah Trail 65. Viva Max 69, etc.

Tilbury, Zeffie (1863–1950). American character actress.
The Marriage of William Ashe 21. Werewolf of London 35. The Last Days of Pompeii 35. Maid of Salem 37. Balalaika 39. Tobacco Road 41. She Couldn't Say No 45, etc.

Till, Eric (1929–). Canadian director, from TV.
Hot Millions 68. The Walking Stick 69. A Fan's Notes 72. It Shouldn't Happen to a Vet 76. Improper Channels 81. Shock Trauma (TV) 83.

Tiller, Nadja (1929–). Austrian leading lady, in international films.
Rosemary 59. Portrait of a Sinner 61. The World in My Pocket 62. And So to Bed 65. The Upper Hand 67. Lady Hamilton 68, etc.

Tilly, Meg (–). American leading actress.
Fame 80. One Dark Night 82. Tex 82. The Big Chill 83. *Psycho II* 83. Impulse 84. Agnes of God (AAN) 85. Off Beat 85.

tilt. An upward or downward camera movement.

Tilton, Martha (1915–). American singer, in occasional films.
Sunny 41. Swing Hostess 44. Crime Inc 45. The Benny Goodman Story 56, etc.

time-lapse photography. The method by which one can obtain such fascinating results as a flower growing and blooming before one's eyes. The camera is set up and regulated to expose one frame of film at pre-arranged intervals. See also: *stop motion.*

Tingwell, Charles (1923–). Australian actor for a time in British TV and films, especially during the fifties in *Emergency Ward Ten.*
Always Another Dawn 48. Bitter Springs 50. Life in Emergency Ward Ten 58. Cone of Silence 60. Murder She Said 63. The Secret of

Blood Island 65. Dracula—Prince of Darkness 65. Nobody Runs Forever 68, etc. TV series: Homicide 74–75.

Tinling, James (1889–1967). American second-feature director.
Silk Legs 27. Arizona 30. Broadway 33. Charlie Chan in Shanghai 35. Pepper 36. 45 Fathers 37. Mr Moto's Gamble 38. Riders of the Purple Sage 41. Sundown Jim 42. The House of Tao Ling 47. Night Wind 48. Trouble Preferred 49. Tales of Robin Hood 52.

tinting has plainly gone out of fashion now that virtually all films are in colour, but in black-and-white days the use of single colours could lead to interesting effects. In the twenties and earlier it was common practice to tint night scenes blue, sunlit scenes yellow, etc.; I saw one Russian film made in 1917 in which the only scene in black-and-white was that in which the hero hanged himself! When talkies came in these colour effects were forgotten, but towards the mid-thirties when colour was threatening, a tint seemed better than nothing. Films released wholly in sepia included *The Ghost Goes West, Bad Man of Brimstone, The Firefly, Maytime, The Girl of the Golden West, The Oklahoma Kid, Of Mice and Men* and *The Rains Came*: while the 'real' scenes of *The Wizard of Oz* were also sepia, leaving full colour until we landed over the rainbow. *A Midsummer Night's Dream* was released with a blue rinse, as were the water ballet reels of *A Day at the Races*. Other colours have been used for short sequences. Green for *Portrait of Jennie* (the storm), *Luck of the Irish* (the leprechaun forest) and *Lost Continent* (to obscure the poor monster animation). Red for the *Hell's Angels* battle scenes and for the flash at the end of *Spellbound* when the villain turns a gun on himself. Even monochrome has its effectiveness, as shown in *A Matter of Life and Death* and *Bonjour Tristesse*.

Tiomkin, Dmitri or **Dimitri** (1894–1979). Russian-American composer of innumerable film scores.
Autobiography 1959: *Please Don't Hate Me*. Alice in Wonderland 33. *Lost Horizon* 37. The Great Waltz 38. *The Moon and Sixpence* 42. Shadow of a Doubt 43. Duel in the Sun 46. *Portrait of Jennie* 48. The Men 50. *High Noon* (AA) 52. *The High and the Mighty* (AA) 54. Land of the Pharaohs 55. Friendly Persuasion 56. *Giant* 56. Night Passage 57. *Gunfight at the O.K. Corral* 57. The Old Man and the Sea (AA) 58. The Unforgiven 60. The Alamo 60. The Guns of Navarone 61. 55 Days at Peking 62. The Fall of the Roman Empire 64. Tchaikovsky 71, etc.

Tissé, Edouard (1897–1961). Franco-Russian cinematographer who worked closely with Eisenstein.
Strike 24. *The Battleship Potemkin* 25. *The General Line* (The Old and the New) 27. *Que Viva Mexico* 32. Aerograd 36. *Alexander Nevsky* 39. *Ivan the Terrible* 42 and 46. Glinka 54, etc.

title changes. See separate essay, p. 1199.

title quotations
? Many film titles, especially those based on famous books, consist of quotations which may or may not be satisfactorily explained within the film. Can you name the literary source of the following?

1 *The Seventh Seal*
2 *The Root of All Evil*
3 *North by Northwest*
4 *Bullets or Ballots*
5 *The Sun Never Sets*
6 *Ill Met by Moonlight*
7 *The Sound of Music*
8 *The Voice of the Turtle*
9 *Arise My Love*
10 *The Little Foxes*
11 *Our Vines Have Tender Grapes*
12 *From Here to Eternity*
13 *Gone with the Wind*
14 *Behold a Pale Horse*
15 *The Grapes of Wrath*
16 *The Razor's Edge*
17 *The Painted Veil*
18 *Paths of Glory*
19 *Now Voyager*
20 *A Fool There Was*
21 *Deadlier Than the Male*
22 *For Whom the Bell Tolls*
23 *Of Mice and Men*
24 *Room at the Top*
25 *So Red the Rose*
26 *In Harm's Way*

To Be or Not to Be (US 1942). A bitter farce remarkable for the furore it caused on its release because it found humour in the Nazi occupation of Warsaw. Dealing with a troupe of actors who outwit the Nazis, it seems now not only inoffensive but funnier than it was at the time, with a string of running jokes put over as only Ernst Lubitsch knew how. Carole Lombard, whose last film this was, and Jack Benny were perfect comedy leads, and the cast included Sig Ruman, Stanley Ridges, Lionel Atwill, Felix Bressart and Tom Dugan. It was remade rather clumsily in 1984 with Mel Brooks and Anne Bancroft.

To Have and Have Not. Ernest Hemingway's tough, soft-hearted adventure novel has been filmed three times; in 1944 by Howard Hawks, with Bogart, Bacall, and not much left of the plot; in 1951 by Michael Curtiz, as *The Breaking Point*, with John Garfield and Patricia Neal; and in 1958, as *The Gun Runners*, with Audie Murphy.

Tobacco Road (US 1941). Generally regarded as a minor film in the John Ford canon, this adaptation of Erskine Caldwell's savage picture of the southern 'poor whites' was successfully played for laughs and a few tears, and has grown more pleasing with the years. Among the apathetic, even stupid, but delightfully resilient characters, Charley Grapewin's performance as Jeeter stands out as something rare and wholly attractive; there is interesting work, too, by Marjorie Rambeau, Elizabeth Patterson, William Tracy and Slim Summerville.

Toback, James (1943–). American writer-director.
Fingers 78. Love and Money 82. Exposed 83.

Tobey, Kenneth (1919–). American character actor of dependable types.
Kiss Tomorrow Goodbye 49. About Face 51. *The Thing* 52. The Beast from 20,000 Fathoms 55. The Man in the Grey Flannel Suit 56. Terror in the Sky (TV) 72. Billy Jack 73. W. C. Fields and Me 76. MacArthur 77, many others.
TV series: Whirlybirds 54–58.

Tobias, George (1901–1980). American character actor with stage experience.
Saturday's Children (debut) 40. City for Conquest 40. Sergeant York 41. Yankee Doodle Dandy 42. This is the Army 43. Thank Your Lucky Stars 43. Between Two Worlds 44. Objective Burma 45. Mildred Pierce 45. Sinbad the Sailor 47. Rawhide 50. The Glenn Miller Story 53. The Seven Little Foys 55. A New Kind of Love 63. The Glass Bottom Boat 66, many others.
TV series: Hudson's Bay. Adventures in Paradise. Bewitched.

Tobias, Oliver (1947–). Saturnine British leading man.
Jesus of Nazareth (TV) 77.
The Stud 78. Arabian Adventure 79. A Nightingale Sang in Berkeley Square 80. The Wicked Lady 83. Mata Hari 85.

Tobin, Dan (1909–1982). Lightweight American character actor.
The Stadium Murders 38. Woman of the Year 41. Undercurrent 46. The Big Clock 48. The Velvet Touch 49. Dear Wife 52. Wedding Breakfast 56. The Last Angry Man 59. The Love Bug Rides Again 73, etc.
TV series: Perry Mason 57–65.

Tobin, Genevieve (1901–). Vivacious American actress of French parentage. Mainly stage experience; made some films during thirties.
The Lady Surrenders (debut) 31. One Hour With You 32. Easy to Wed 34. The Petrified Forest 36. The Great Gambini 37. Dramatic School 38. Zaza 39, etc.

Toch, Ernst (1887–1964). German composer in Hollywood.
Catherine the Great 34. Little Friend 34. Peter Ibbetson 35. Four Men and a Prayer 38. *The Cat and the Canary* 39. The Ghost Breakers 40. Dr Cyclops 40. Ladies in Retirement 41. Address Unknown 44. The Unseen 45, etc.

Todd, Ann (1909–). Blonde British leading actress, a big star of the forties. Later produced and directed short travel films.
□Keepers of Youth 31. These Charming People 31. The Ghost Train 31. The Water Gypsies 31. The Return of Bulldog Drummond 34. Things to Come 36. The Squeaker 37. Action for Slander 37. *South Riding* 38. Poison Pen 39. Danny Boy 41. Ships with Wings 41. Perfect Strangers 45. *The Seventh Veil* 45. Gaiety George 46. Daybreak 47. So Evil my Love 47. The Paradine Case (US) 48. *The Passionate Friends* 48. Madeleine 49. The Sound Barrier 52. The Green Scarf 54. Time without Pity 57. Taste of Fear 61. Son of Captain Blood 62. Ninety Degrees in the Shade 65. The Fiend 71. The Human Factor 79.

Todd, Ann (1932–) (A. T. Mayfield). American child star of the thirties and forties.
Zaza 39. Blood and Sand 41. King's Row 42. The Jolson Story 46. Bomba and the Lion Hunters 52, etc.

Todd, Bob (1922–). Bald British comic actor, much on TV.
The Intelligence Men 65. Hot Millions 68, etc.

Todd, Mike (1907–1958) (Avrom Goldenborgen). Dynamic American producer of Broadway spectacles. His one personally produced film was in similar vein: *Around the World in Eighty Days* 56. The wide-screen system *Todd-AO* is named after him. A biography, *The Nine Lives of Mike Todd*, by Art Cohn, was published in 1959.

Todd, Richard (1919–). British leading man, in repertory from 1937 until spotted by a film talent scout.
For Them That Trespass (debut) 48. *The Hasty Heart* 49. Stage Fright 50. Lightning Strikes Twice (US) 51. *Robin Hood* 52. Venetian Bird 53. The Sword and the Rose 54. Rob Roy 54. *A Man Called Peter* 55. The Virgin Queen (US) 55. *The Dam Busters* 55. Yangtse Incident 56. Chase a Crooked Shadow 57. Danger Within 58. The Long, the Short and the Tall 59. The Hellions 60. Never Let Go 61. The Longest Day 62. The Boys 62. The Very Edge 63. Operation Crossbow 65. The Battle of the Villa Fiorita 65. Coast of Skeletons 65. Death Drums along the River 66. Last of the Long-haired Boys 68. Subterfuge 69. Dorian Gray 70. Asylum 72. The Big Sleep 78. Home Before Midnight 79. House of the Long Shadows 83, etc.

Todd, Thelma (1905–1935). Perky American leading blonde of the early thirties, heroine of many two-reel comedies. Died in mysterious circumstances.
Fascinating Youth 26. Rubber Heels 27. The Haunted House 28. Her Private Life 29. Aloha 30. The Hot Heiress 31. *Monkey Business* 31. The Maltese Falcon 31. *Horse Feathers* 32. Air Hostess 33. Sitting Pretty 33. Hips Hips Hooray 34. Bottoms Up 34. Two for Tonight 35. The Bohemian Girl 35, many others.

Tognazzi, Ugo (1922–). Italian leading actor.
His Women (Il Mantenuto) (& d) 61. The Fascist (Il Federale) 62. Queen Bee (Ape Regina or The Conjugal Bed) 63. The Magnificent Cuckold 64. An American Wife 65. A Question of Honour 66. Barbarella 68. Property is No Longer a Theft 73. Blowout 73. Duck in Orange Sauce 75. Viva Italia 77. *La Cage aux Folles* 79. La Cage aux Folles II 80. Sunday Lovers 80, etc.

Tokar, Norman (1920–79). American director, from radio; in films, worked almost exclusively for Disney.
□Big Red 62. Savage Sam 63. Sammy the Way Out Seal 63. A Tiger Walks 64. Those Calloways 65. Follow Me Boys 65. The Ugly Dachshund 66. The Happiest Millionaire 67. The Horse in the Grey Flannel Suit 68. Rascal 69. The Boatniks 72. Snowball Express 73. The Apple Dumpling Gang 75. Where the Red Fern Grows 76. No Deposit No Return 77. Candleshoe 78. The Cat from Outer Space 78.

Tokyo Olympiad (Japan 1964). This documentary by Kon Ichikawa and a score of photographers is in its quiet way as remarkable as Leni Riefenstahl's film of the 1936 games. Here the athletes are seen not as gods but as men and women suffering the ultimate in physical stress; the probing cameras achieve many remarkable effects.

Tol'able David. This novel by Joseph Hergesheimer was first, and most successfully, filmed in 1921, with Richard Barthelmess as the gentle youth making good in the tough outdoor life; it was directed by Henry King from a scenario by Edmund Goulding. In 1931 John G. Blystone directed a disappointing sound remake with Richard Cromwell.

Toland, Gregg (1904–1948). Distinguished American cinematographer who worked mainly with Goldwyn.
The Unholy Garden 31. Roman Scandals 33. Tugboat Annie 33. *Nana* 34. *We Live Again* 34. *Mad Love* 35. Les Misérables 35. These Three 36. *Dead End* 37. The Goldwyn Follies 38. Intermezzo 39. *Wuthering Heights* (AA) 39. Raffles 40. *The Grapes of Wrath* 40. The Long Voyage Home 40. *The Westerner* 40. *Citizen Kane* 41. *The Little Foxes* 41; war service; *The Best Years of Our Lives* 46. The Kid from Brooklyn 47. The Bishop's Wife 48. *Enchantment* 48, many others.

Toler, Sidney (1874–1947). Chubby American character actor who in 1938 took over the part of Charlie Chan and played it twenty-two times.
Madame X 29. Is My Face Red? 32. Spitfire 35. Call of the Wild 35. Our Relations 36. Wide Open Faces 38. Charlie Chan in Honolulu 38. Law of the Pampas 39. Charlie Chan at the Wax Museum 40. Castle in the Desert 42. White Savage 43. The Scarlet Clue 45. Dark Alibi 46. The Trap 47, many others.

Tolkien, J. R. R. (1892–1973). Donnish British novelist who created a myth of 'Middle Earth' in his trilogy *The Lord of the*

Rings, which became an instant classic and was filmed in cartoon form.

Tolstoy, Leo (1828–1910). Russian novelist whose *Anna Karenina* and *War and Peace* have been frequently filmed.

Tom and Jerry. Short cartoons featuring the mean-minded, accident-prone cat and his inventive and likeable little adversary were in production at MGM, with a break in the fifties, from 1937, with Fred Quimby (qv) as executive producer until his death. They have been much criticized for their excessive violence, but their humour, coupled with the impossibility of the situations, has won the day. The Academy Award-winning titles are *The Milky Way* 40, *Yankee Doodle Mouse* 43, *Mouse Trouble* 44, *Quiet Please* 45, *Cat Concerto* 46, *The Little Orphan* 48, *The Two Mouseketeers* 51, *Johann Mouse* 52. The original cartoons were drawn by William Hanna and Joe Barbera.

Tom Brown's Schooldays. The two major film versions of this famous Victorian story of life at Rugby School were: 1. US 1939, with Cedric Hardwicke as Dr Arnold and Jimmy Lydon as Tom, directed by Robert Stevenson. 2. GB 1951, with Robert Newton and John Howard Davies, directed by Gordon Parry.

Tom Jones (GB 1963). Bawdy, rollicking, phenomenally popular adaptation of Fielding's eighteenth-century novel about the misfortunes of a foundling. Produced and directed by Tony Richardson, scripted by John Osborne, photographed by Walter Lassally, designed by Ralph Brinton, with a cast led by Albert Finney, Hugh Griffith and Edith Evans. For the most part vivid and hilarious, it runs out of breath before the end; and the colour process sometimes looks like an awful mistake while at other points perfectly capturing the texture of an old print. AA best film, best direction, best music (John Addison); BFA best film. A forgettable rehash, *The Bawdy Adventures of Tom Jones*, followed in 1976.

Tom Sawyer. Mark Twain's boy hero has been played on film by Jack Pickford in 1917 (also in *Huck and Tom* 18), Jackie Coogan in 1920, Tommy Kelly in 1938 (the Selznick production), also in 1938, by Billy Cook in *Tom Sawyer, Detective*, and in 1972 by Johnny Whitaker.

Tomasini, George (1909–1964). American editor.
Wild Harvest 47. Houdini 53. Elephant Walk 54. To Catch a Thief 55. The Wrong Man 57. Vertigo 58. *North By Northwest* 59. Psycho 60. Cape Fear 62. The Birds 63. Marnie 64, etc.

Tombes, Andrew (1889–1976). American supporting actor often seen as cop, undertaker, bartender or harassed official.
Moulin Rouge 33. Charlie Chan at the Olympics 37. Too Busy to Work 39. Phantom Lady 44. Can't Help Singing 44. Oh You Beautiful Doll 49. How To Be Very Very Popular 55, many others.

Tomelty, Joseph (1910–). Irish character actor, in British films since 1945.
Odd Man Out 46. The Sound Barrier 52. Meet Mr Lucifer 54. Simba 55. A Kid for Two Farthings 56. The Black Torment 64, many others.

Tomlin, Lily (1939–). American comedy actress.
□Nashville 75. The Late Show 77. Moment by Moment 78. Nine to Five 80. The Incredible Shrinking Woman 81. All of Me 84.

¶ *L.T.:* The trouble with the rat race is that even if you win, you're still a rat.

Tomlinson, David (1917–). Amiable British leading man and comedian, a latter-day Ralph Lynn.
Quiet Wedding 40. Journey Together 45. The Way to the Stars 45. Master of Bankdam 47. *Miranda* 48. Sleeping Car to Trieste 48. *The Chiltern Hundreds* 49. Hotel Sahara 51. *Three Men in a Boat* 55. Up the Creek 58. Follow That Horse 60. Tom Jones 63. *Mary Poppins* 64. The Truth about Spring 65. City in the Sea 65. The Liquidator 66. The Love Bug 69. Bedknobs and Broomsticks 71. The Water Babies 78. The Fiendish Plot of Fu Manchu 80, many others.

Tone, Franchot (1905–1968) (Stanislas Pascal Franchot Tone). American leading man of stage and screen.
The Wiser Sex (film debut) 32. Gabriel over the White House 33. Moulin Rouge 34. Mutiny on the Bounty 35. Suzy 36. Quality Street 36. *They Gave Him a Gun* 37. Three Comrades 39. The Trail of the Vigilantes 40. Nice Girl 41. The Wife Takes a Flyer 42. *Five Graves to Cairo* 43. His Butler's Sister 43.

Phantom Lady 44. Dark Waters 44. That Night with You 45. Because of Him 46. Her Husband's Affairs 47. I Love Trouble 48. Every Girl Should Be Married 48. The Man on the Eiffel Tower 50. *Advise and Consent* 62. La Bonne Soupe 64. In Harm's Way 65. Nobody Runs Forever 68, etc.

Tonti, Aldo (1910–). Italian cinematographer.
Ossessione 44. Europe 51 50. The Mill on the Po 51. War and Peace 56. Cabiria 57. Reflections in a Golden Eye 67. Ashanti 78, etc.

Toomey, Regis (1902–). American character actor, on screen since 1928, usually as cop or victim in routine crime dramas.
Framed 29. Murder by the Clock 32. G-Men 35. The Big Sleep 46. The Nebraskan 53. Guys and Dolls 55. Man's Favourite Sport? 63. Peter Gunn 67. God Bless Dr Shagetz 77, scores of others.
TV series: Burke's Law.

Top Hat (US 1935). The most delightful and enduring of the Astaire-Rogers musicals of the thirties, with an agreeable wisp of plot and amusing if dated comedy dialogue handled by an expert team of supporting comics: Edward Everett Horton, Eric Blore, Helen Broderick and Erik Rhodes. Irving Berlin's score, one of his best, includes 'The Piccolino', 'Cheek to Cheek' and 'Isn't it a Lovely Day' as well as the title number; and Astaire and Rogers are at their peak. Script by Dwight Taylor and Alan Scott, photography by David Abel, direction by Mark Sandrich, production by Pandro S. Berman.

Topol (1935–) (Chaim Topol). Israeli leading actor who gained fame with London stage run of *Fiddler on the Roof*.
Cast a Giant Shadow 65. Sallah 66. Before Winter Comes 69. *Fiddler on the Roof* 71. Follow Me 72, Galileo 74. The House on Garibaldi Street (TV) 79. Flash Gordon 80. For Your Eyes Only 81. The Winds of War (TV) 83. Queenie (TV) 87. War and Remembrance (TV) 87, etc.

Topper (US 1937). Hal Roach produced this mixture of slapstick, sophistication and the supernatural, from Thorne Smith's novel, and started a new trend in Hollywood comedy. Roland Young was perfectly cast as the henpecked businessman beset by jovial ghosts in the forms of Cary Grant and Constance Bennett; only Norman McLeod's direction tended to lack the necessary lightness of touch. Young also appeared in two sequels, *Topper Takes a Trip* 39 and *Topper Returns* 41. In the fifties *Topper* was personified by Leo G. Carroll in a TV series.

Topper, Burt (1934–). American director.
Diary of a High School Bride 61. The Strangler 64. The Devil's Eight 69. Wild in the Streets (p) 68. The Hard Ride 71. Lovin' Man 72.

Torchy Blane. A series of half a dozen second features, made in 1939–48, starring Glenda Farrell as a wisecracking girl reporter and Barton MacLane as the puzzled policeman who gets the comeback for her zany ideas. Most of the films were directed by William Beaudine.

Toren, Marta (1926–1957). Swedish leading lady signed by Hollywood scout while at dramatic school.
Casbah (debut) 48. Rogues' Regiment 49. One-Way Street 50. Panthers' Moon 51. Sirocco 51. The Man Who Watched the Trains Go By 52. Maddalena 54, etc.

Tormé, Mel (1923–). Amiable American ballad singer who has made occasional films.
Higher and Higher 43. Let's Go Steady 45. Junior Miss 45. Good News 47. Duchess of Idaho 50. The Big Operator 59. Walk like a Dragon 60. The Patsy 64. A Man Called Adam 66, etc.

Torn, Rip (1931–) (Elmore Torn). American general purpose actor, mainly on stage and TV.
Baby Doll 56. Time Limit 57. Cat on a Hot Tin Roof 58. King of Kings 61. Sweet Bird of Youth 62. The Cincinnati Kid 65. You're a Big Boy Now 66. Beach Red 67. The Rain People 69. Tropic of Cancer 69. *Payday* 73. Crazy Joe 73. Birch Interval 76. The Man Who Fell To Earth 76. Nasty Habits 77. The Private Files of J. Edgar Hoover 78. Coma 78. *Blind Ambition* (TV) (as Nixon) 79. The Seduction of Joe Tynan 79. The First Family 80. Heartland 80. One Trick Pony 80. A Stranger Is Watching 82. Cross Creek 83. (AAN) 83. City Heat 84. Songwriter 84. Beer 85. Summer Rental 85. Nadine 87, etc.

Torrence, David (1864–1951). Scottish silent screen actor in Hollywood.
The Inside of the Cup 21. Sherlock Holmes 22. The Abysmal Brute 23. Surging Seas 24. The Reckless Sex 25. Laddie 26. Annie

Laurie 27. The Little Shepherd of Kingdom Come 28. Untamed Justice 29. Raffles 30. Voltaire 33. Mandalay 34. The Dark Angel 35, etc.

Torrence, Ernest (1878–1933). Scottish actor, in American silent films, usually as villain; former opera singer.
Tol'able David 21. The Hunchback of Notre Dame 23. The Trail of the Lonesome Pine 23. *The Covered Wagon* 23. Peter Pan 24. King of Kings 27. The Cossacks 28. The Bridge of San Luis Rey 29. The New Adventures of Get-Rich-Quick Wallingford 31. Cuban Love Song 32. Sherlock Holmes 33, many others.

Torre-Nilsson, Leopoldo (1924–78). Argentinian director, usually of sharp-flavoured melodramas which he also wrote.
The House of the Angel 57. *The Fall* 59. The Hand in the Trap 60. Summer Skin 61. Four Women for One Hero 62. The Roof Garden 63. The Eavesdropper 65. Monday's Child 67. Martin Fierro 68, etc.

Torres, Raquel (1908–87) (Paula Marie Osterman). American leading lady who played fiery sirens in the early thirties.
White Shadows in the South Seas 28. The Bridge of San Luis Rey 29. Under a Texas Moon 30. The Woman I Stole 33. Duck Soup 33. The Red Wagon 36, etc.

Tors, Ivan (1916–1983). Hungarian writer-producer-director, in Hollywood from 1941.
Song of Love (w) 47. The Forsyte Saga (w) 49. Storm over Tibet (wp) 52. The Magnetic Monster (wp) 53. Gog (wp) 54. Riders to the Stars (p) 55. Battle Taxi (p) 56. Flipper (p) 60. Rhino (pd) 64. Zebra in the Kitchen 65. Around the World Under the Sea 65, etc.
TV series as producer include *The Man and the Challenge, Sea Hunt, Flipper, Primus*.

torture has figured in *Arabian Nights, Thief of Baghdad*, and other of this genre; in witchcraft dramas such as *Witchfinder General, The Devils* and *Day of Wrath*; in medieval epics such as *El Cid, Ivanhoe* and *Tower of London*; further back to Roman times, in *The Robe, Barabbas, Spartacus* and *Demetrius and the Gladiators*; in World War II yarns such as *13 Rue Madeleine, OSS, Carve Her Name with Pride, The Seventh Cross* and *633 Squadron*; in cold war melodramas such as *Treason, The Prisoner*, and *The Manchurian Candidate*; in historical mysteries such as *The Man in the Iron Mask* and in documentary adventures such as *A Man Called Horse*.

Tosi, Mario (–). Italian-American cinematographer.
Some Call It Loving 73. Report to the Commissioner 74. Hearts of the West 75. Carrie 76. The Main Event 79. Resurrection 80. The Stunt Man 80. Six Pack 82.

Totheroh, Rollie (1891–1967). American cinematographer who worked notably for Charles Chaplin.
The Pilgrim 23. The Gold Rush 24. City Lights 31. Modern Times 36. The Great Dictator 40. Monsieur Verdoux 47, etc.

Toto (1897–1967) (Antonio Furst de Curtis-Gagliardi). Italian comedian, from music hall and revue.
Fermo con le Mani 36. Toto Le Moko 49. Cops and Robbers 53. Gold of Naples 54. Racconti Romani 55. Persons Unknown 58. Toto of Arabia 63. The Commander 67, many others.

Totter, Audrey (1918–). American leading lady of the 'hard-boiled' type, with stage and radio experience.
Main Street after Dark (debut) 44. Her Highness and the Bellboy 45. The Postman Always Rings Twice 45. *The Lady in the Lake* 46. Tenth Avenue Angel 47. The Unsuspected 48. Alias Nick Beal 49. The Set-Up 49. Tension 51. The Blue Veil 52. Assignment Paris 53. Women's Prison 54. A Bullet for Joey 55. The Carpetbaggers 64. Harlow (electronovision version) 65. Chubasco 68. The Apple Dumpling Gang Rides Again 79, others.
TV series: Cimarron City 58. Our Man Higgins 62. Medical Center 72–76.

Toumanova, Tamara (1917–). Russian ballerina who has made occasional appearances in American films.
Days of Glory 43. Deep in my Heart 54. Torn Curtain 67, etc.

Tourneur, Jacques (1904–77). Franco-American director, son of Maurice Tourneur, with a special flair for the macabre.
Nick Carter, Master Detective 39. *Cat People* 42. *I Walked with a Zombie* 43. *The Leopard Man* 43. Days of Glory 44. *Experiment Perilous* 44. *Out of the Past* 47. Berlin Express 48. Stars in My Crown 50. The Flame and the Arrow 51. Appointment in Honduras 53. Wichita 55. Great Day in the Morning 56. *Night of the Demon* 57. Timbuktu 59. The Giant of Marathon 61. A Comedy of Terrors 63. City under the Sea 65, etc.

Tourneur, Maurice (1876–1961) (Maurice Thomas). French director who made some American films.
Mother 14. Man of the Hour 15. Trilby 15. Poor Little Rich Girl 17. The Bluebird 18. The Last of the Mohicans 20. Treasure Island 20. The Christian (GB) 23. Aloma of the South Seas 26. L'Équipage 27. Mysterious Island 29. Maison de Danses 31. Koenigsmark 35. Volpone 40. The Devil's Hand 42. L'Impasse des Deux Anges 48, etc.

Tover, Leo (1902–1964). American cinematographer in Hollywood from 1918.
Dead Reckoning 47. *The Snake Pit* 48. *The Heiress* 49. The Secret of Convict Lake 51. The President's Lady 53. Soldier of Fortune 55. The Sun Also Rises 57. *Journey to the Centre of the Earth* 59. Follow That Dream 62. Sunday in New York 63. Strange Bedfellows 64. A Very Special Favor 65, many others.

Tower of London (US 1939). A historical melodrama notable chiefly for treating the story of Richard III as a horror yarn: Basil Rathbone and Boris Karloff, who played Richard and his executioner, had just finished *Son of Frankenstein.* Rowland V. Lee directed. Vincent Price, who played Clarence, played Richard in an inferior 1962 remake by Roger Corman.

The Towering Inferno (US 1974). This all-star Irwin Allen extravaganza, with most of the cast dying in flames at the top of a burning skyscraper, was the apex of the seventies disaster cycle and had special effects to match. Dramatically, at nearly three hours, it was far too much. The inevitable TV imitation was *Terror on the Fortieth Floor.*

Towers, Harry Alan (1920–). British executive producer with varied experience in films and TV.
Victim Five (& w) 64. Mozambique (& w) 64. The Face of Fu Manchu 65. Ten Little Indians 65. Our Man in Marrakesh (Bang, Bang, You're Dead) 66. The Brides of Fu Manchu 66. Rocket to the Moon 67. Treasure Island 72. Call of the Wild 73. The Shape of Things to Come 78, etc.

Towne, Gene (1904–79). American screenwriter.
Little Women 33. History is Made at Night 37. The Swiss Family Robinson 40. Joy of Living 41, etc.

Towne, Robert (1936–). American screenwriter.
The Tomb of Ligeia 64. Villa Rides 67. The Last Detail 73. *Chinatown* 74. Shampoo (co-w) 75. The Yakuza (co-w) 75. Personal Best (& d) 81. Greystoke 83, etc.

Toye, Wendy (1917–). British director, former dancer. Drew attention with two ingenious short films, *The Stranger Left No Card* 52 and *On the Twelfth Day* 55.
Features: *Three Cases of Murder* 54. *All for Mary* 55. *True as a Turtle* 56. *We Joined the Navy* 62, etc.

Track of the Cat (US 1954). An interesting but unsuccessful experiment by William Wellman to create a fresh filmic texture and atmosphere by shooting in colour but restricting his subjects to black and white—in this case snowy landscapes and forests—with the very occasional flash of colour. Unfortunately the story in this case, a kind of backwoods *Cold Comfort Farm*, was laborious and unappealing, and the cast led by Robert Mitchum looked understandably glum. William Clothier was the cinematographer.

tracking shot. One taken with a moving camera, usually forwards or backwards, and often on an actual track.

Tracy, Arthur (1903–) (Harry Rosenberg). American singer who made his greatest success in England, especially with his rendering of 'Marta'.
The Big Broadcast 32. Limelight (GB) 36. The Street Singer (GB) 37. Follow Your Star (GB) 38, etc.

Tracy, Lee (1898–1968). American leading actor of stage (from 1919) and screen (sporadically from 1929): had inimitable nasal delivery.
□Big Time 29. Born Reckless 30. Liliom 30. She Got What She Wanted 30. The Strange Love of Molly Louvain 32. Love is a Racket 32. *Doctor X* 32. *Blessed Event* 32. Washington Merry Go Round 32. The Night Mayor 32. *The Half Naked Truth* 32. Clear All Wires 33. Private Jones 33. The Nuisance 33. Dinner at Eight 33. Turn Back the Clock 33. *Bombshell* 33. Advice to the Lovelorn 33. I'll Tell the World 34. You Belong to Me 34. The Lemon Drop Kid 34. Carnival 35. Two Fisted 35. Sutter's Gold 36. Wanted, Jane Turner 36. Criminal Lawyer 37. Behind the Headlines 37. Crashing Hollywood 38. Fixer

Dugan 39. The Spellbinder 39. Millionaires in Prison 40. The Payoff 42. Power of the Press 43. Betrayal from the East 45. I'll Tell the World 45. High Tide 47. *The Best Man* 64. TV series: The Amazing Mr Malone 51. Martin Kane 53.

Tracy, Spencer (1900–1967). Distinguished American actor with stage experience from 1922; exclusively on screen from 1930. His uneven features gained him gangster roles to begin with, then he made a corner in priests and friends of the hero; but his chief mature image was that of a tough, humorous fellow who was also a pillar of integrity.
Biography 1970: *Spencer Tracy* by Larry Swindell. 1973: *Tracy and Hepburn* by Garson Kanin.
□Up the River 30. Quick Millions 31. Six-Cylinder Love 31. Goldie 31. She Wanted a Millionaire 32. Sky Devils 32. Disorderly Conduct 32. Young America 32. Society Girl 32. Painted Woman 32. Me and My Girl 32. *Twenty Thousand Years in Sing Sing* 32. Face in the Sky 33. *The Power and the Glory* 33. Shanghai Madness 33. The Mad Game 33. *A Man's Castle* 33. Looking for Trouble 34. The Show-Off 34. Bottoms Up 34. Now I'll Tell 34. Marie Galante 34. It's a Small World 35. Dante's Inferno 35. The Murder Man 35. Whipsaw 35. Riff Raff 36. *Fury* 36. *San Francisco* 36. *Libeled Lady* 36. *Captains Courageous* (AA) 37. They Gave Him a Gun 37. The Big City 38. Mannequin 38. Test Pilot 38. *Boys' Town* (AA) 38. *Stanley and Livingstone* 39. I Take This Woman 39. *Northwest Passage* 40. *Edison the Man* 40. Boom Town 40. Men of Boys' Town 41. Dr Jekyll and Mr Hyde 41. *Woman of the Year* 42. Tortilla Flat 42. Keeper of the Flame 43. A Guy Named Joe 43. *The Seventh Cross* 44. Thirty Seconds over Tokyo 44. Without Love 45. Sea of Grass 46. Cass Timberlane 47. *State of the Union* 48. Edward My Son (GB) 49. *Adam's Rib* 49. Malaya 49. *Father of the Bride* 50. The People against O'Hara 51. Father's Little Dividend 51. Pat and Mike 52. Plymouth Adventure 52. The Actress 53. Broken Lance 54. *Bad Day at Black Rock* 55. The Mountain 56. The Desk Set 57. The Old Man and the Sea 58. *The Last Hurrah* 58. *Inherit the Wind* 60. The Devil at Four O'Clock 61. *Judgment at Nuremberg* 61. It's a Mad Mad Mad Mad World 63. *Guess Who's Coming to Dinner* (BFA) 67.
❄ For superb performances and for the utter reliability of his on-screen personality, which was so at odds with the insecurity of his private psyche. *Inherit the Wind.*

¶ The guy's good. There's nobody in the business who can touch him, and you're a fool to try. And the bastard knows it, so don't fall for that humble stuff!

This tribute came from Clark Gable, who suffered from co-starring with Tracy in several MGM movies of the thirties. On the other hand, Katharine Hepburn once said:

> I think Spencer always thought that acting was a rather silly way for a man to make a living.

She also caught his essential strength:

> He's like an old oak tree, or the summer, or the wind. He belongs to the era when men were men.

But Hepburn was exposed to his aggressive wit when they met in 1941 to make *Woman of the Year*:

> I'm afraid I'm a little tall for you, Mr Tracy.
> —Don't worry, I'll soon cut you down to my size.

He ranged from supreme self-confidence to abject despair. In 1931 he complained:

> This mug of mine is as plain as a barn door. Why should people pay thirty-five cents to look at it?

He remembered:

> There were times when my pants were so thin, I could sit on a dime and know if it was heads or tails.

Later he wondered at his own success:

> The physical labour actors have to do wouldn't tax an embryo.

Perhaps this puzzlement was responsible for his attitude to the press:

> Write anything you want about me.
> Make up something. Hell, I don't care.

But he did care, and he cared about his work. Perhaps Humphrey Bogart best summed up his appeal:

> Spence is the best we have, because you don't see the mechanism at work.

Tracy, William (1917–1967). American actor who used to play sly or dumb young fellows.
Brother Rat 38. Strike Up the Band 40. Tobacco Road 41. About Face 42. Fall In 44. The Walls of Jericho 49. Mr Walkie Talkie 54. The Wings of Eagles 56, etc.

Trader Horn (US 1930). MGM's safari to darkest Africa to shoot scenes, with actors, for this picture was the first such expedition by a major Hollywood studio. The result, though directed by W. S. Van Dyke, showed that there was much to learn, and the film now seems very naïve. 1973 brought a remake with Rod Taylor, so bad it was barely released.

The Trail of the Lonesome Pine. This backwoods melodrama was first filmed in 1916 with Charlotte Walker and Earle Foxe. In 1923 it was remade with Mary Miles Minter, Antonio Moreno and Ernest Torrence. In 1936 Henry Hathaway made a sound version with Sylvia Sidney, Henry Fonda and Fred MacMurray, and this version was significant as the first outdoor film in the newly-perfected three-colour Technicolor.

trains have above all served film-makers as a splendid background for suspense thrillers. Scores of sequences crowd to mind, all enhanced by the dramatic background of a speeding train: *The Lady Vanishes, North by Northwest, From Russia with Love, The Narrow Margin, The Tall Target, How the West Was Won, 3.10 to Yuma, Lady on a Train, Cat Ballou, Jesse James, Bad Day at Black Rock, Night of the Demon, Time Bomb, Rome Express, Sleeping Car to Trieste, Northwest Frontier, Man without a Star, The Thirty-Nine Steps, Secret Agent, Shanghai Express, Number 17, Last Train from Madrid, Last Train to Bombay, Ministry of Fear, Von Ryan's Express, Across the Bridge, Double Indemnity, Strangers on a Train, The Iron Horse, Union Pacific, Canadian Pacific, Next of Kin, Berlin Express, The Great Locomotive Chase, Terror by Night, Crack-Up, Rampage, Fool's Parade, The Train, Breakheart Pass, Murder on the Orient Express* . . . the list could be almost endless. More serious films using trains include *La Bête Humaine* (and its remake *Human Desire*), *Metropolitan* (and its remake *A Window in London*), *Brief Encounter, The Last Journey, Sullivan's Travels, Indiscretion of an American Wife, Anna Karenina, Terminus, Night Mail, The Manchurian Candidate, The Railway Children, Doctor Zhivago, Boxcar Bertha,* and *Emperor of the North*; while spectacular crashes were featured in *The Greatest Show on Earth, Hatter's Castle, Seven Sinners, The Young in Heart, Mad Love, The Wrong Box, Lawrence of Arabia, Crack in the World, The Ghost Train*, and *King Kong*. Murder was seen from a train in *Metropolitan* and *Lady in a Train* (happening in a second passing train in *Murder She Said),* and *through* a train in *Twelve Angry Men*. The subway, elevated or underground railway was featured in *Practically Yours, On the Town, The Bachelor Party, Boys' Night Out, Union Station, The FBI Story, The Young Savages, Underground, Bulldog Jack, Daleks Invasion Earth 2150 A.D., The French Connection, Beneath the Planet of the Apes*, and *The Liquidator*. The back platforms of American trains have become familiar, especially in political films like *Abe Lincoln in Illinois, Wilson* and *All the King's Men*; but also in *Hail the Conquering Hero, Double Indemnity, The Merry Monahans* and *Mr Deeds Goes to Town*. Comedy train sequences include the Marx Brothers chopping up moving carriages for fuel in *Go West*, the Ale and Quail Club in *The Palm Beach Story*, Buster Keaton's splendidly inventive *Our Hospitality* and *The General, The Great St Trinian's Train Robbery*, Laurel and Hardy going to sleep in the same bunk in *The Big Noise*, Hal Roach's *Broadway Limited*, John Barrymore in *Twentieth Century*, Peter Sellers in *Two-Way Stretch*, the western sequence of *Around the World in Eighty Days*, the pullman car sequence of *Some Like It Hot*, Monty Banks in *Play Safe*, Morecambe and Wise in *The Magnificent Two, The Private Life of Sherlock Holmes*, the whole of *The Titfield Thunderbolt* and *Oh Mr Porter* . . . and many scenes of jaywalking on top of moving carriages, including *Professor Beware, The Merry Monahans* and *Fancy Pants*. Musical sequences with a train motif or setting are found in *A Hard Day's Night, Monte Carlo, Some Like It Hot, The Harvey Girls* ('The Atchison, Topeka and the Santa Fe'), *At the Circus* ('Lydia the Tattooed Lady'), *Sun Valley Serenade* ('Chattanooga Choo Choo'), *Dumbo* ('Casey Junior'), *The Jazz Singer* ('Toot Toot Tootsie, Goodbye'), *Easter Parade* ('When the Midnight Choo Choo Leaves for Alabam'), *Forty-second Street* ('Shuffle off to Buffalo').
TV series involving trains as a regular motif include *Casey Jones, The Wild Wild West, The Iron Horse, Petticoat Junction, Union Pacific* and *Supertrain*.

tramps or hoboes who have figured largely in films include those played by William Powell in *My Man Godfrey*, Joel McCrea in *Sullivan's Travels,* George Arliss in *The Guv'nor*, Jean Gabin in *Archimède le Clochard*, practically the whole cast of *Hallelujah I'm a Bum*, and of course Charlie Chaplin in all his earlier comedies.

transvestism. There have been many films, mostly lightweight ones, making effective use of situations in which men dress up as women. *Charley's Aunt* has proved a perennial, and in silent days Julian Eltinge, a female impersonator, made several popular films: his 1972 successor was Danny la Rue, in *Our Miss Fred*. Well-known actors in female attire have included Wallace Beery as

'Swedy' in a series of silent comedies, Lon Chaney in *The Unholy Tree*, Lionel Barrymore in *The Devil Doll*, William Powell in *Love Crazy*, Cary Grant in *I Was a Male War Bride*, Joe E. Brown as his own grandma in *The Daring Young Man*, Cook and Moore as leaping nuns in *Bedazzled*, Alec Guinness in *The Comedians*, Brian Deacon in *Triple Echo*, Alec Guinness in *Kind Hearts and Coronets*, Peter Sellers in *The Mouse That Roared*, William Bendix and Dennis O'Keefe in *Abroad with Two Yanks*, Jimmy Durante in *You're in the Army Now*, Lee J. Cobb in *In Like Flint*, Ray Walston in *Caprice*, Jerry Lewis in *Three on a Couch*, Stan Laurel in *That's My Wife* and *Jitterbugs*, Bing Crosby in *High Time*, Bob Hope in *Casanova's Big Night*, Tony Curtis and Jack Lemmon in *Some Like It Hot*, Tony Perkins in *Psycho*, Dick Shawn in *What Did You Do in the War, Daddy?*, Phil Silvers and Jack Gilford in *A Funny Thing Happened on the Way to the Forum*, Jerry Lewis in *At War with the Army*, Jack Oakie in *Let's go Native*, Lou Costello in *Lost in a Harem*, Eddie Cantor in *Ali Baba Goes to Town*, Joe E. Brown in *Shut my Big Mouth*, Billy de Wolfe in *Isn't it Romantic?*, William Powell in *Love Crazy*, Melvyn Douglas in *The Amazing Mr Williams*, James Coco in *The Wild Party*, Preston Foster in *Up the River*, Oscar Levant and David Wayne in *The I Don't Care Girl*, Alastair Sim in *The Belles of St Trinian's*, Helmut Berger in *The Damned*, Tim Curry in *The Rocky Horror Movie*, and of course Dustin Hoffman in *Tootsie*; while the device became in the sixties a standard device of spy stories, including *The Kremlin Letter*, *Thunderball*, *Licensed to Kill*, *Where the Bullets Fly*, and *Gunn*. *Myra Breckinridge* also fits in somewhere, as do *Glen or Glenda*, *Dr Jekyll and Sister Hyde*, and the mysterious Divine in *Lust in the Dust*.

Women disguised as men are rarer; but one can instance such notable examples as Katharine Hepburn in *Sylvia Scarlett*, Annabella in *Wings of the Morning*, Signe Hasso in *The House on 92nd Street*, Nita Talbot in *A Very Special Favor*, Marlene Dietrich in *Morocco*, Greta Garbo in *Queen Christina*, Mary Pickford in *Kiki*, Debbie Reynolds in *Goodbye Charlie*, Jessie Matthews in *Gangway*, Miriam Hopkins in *She Loves Me Not*, Marlene Dietrich in *Seven Sinners*, Louise Brooks in *Beggars of Life*, Doris Day in *Calamity Jane*, Frances Farmer in *Badlands of Dakota*, Veronica Lake in *Sullivan's Travels*, Jean Peters in *Anne of the Indies*, Maureen O'Hara in *At Sword's Point*, Merle Oberon in *A Song to Remember*, Lupe Velez in *Honolulu Lu*, and the ambiguous hero-heroine of *Homicidal*. In *Turnabout* a husband and wife exchanged bodies, with dire results

Traubel, Helen (1899–1972). American soprano.
□Deep in My Heart 54. The Ladies' Man 61. Gunn 67.

Trauner, Alexander (1906–). French art director who has worked on international films.
Quai des Brumes 38. Le Jour Se Lève 39. *Les Visiteurs du Soir* 42. *Les Enfants du Paradis* 44. Les Portes de la Nuit 45. Manèges 49. Othello 52. Love in the Afternoon 56. *The Nun's Story* 58. The Apartment 60. One Two Three 61. Irma La Douce 63. Kiss Me Stupid 64. The Night of the Generals 66. *A Flea in Her Ear* 68. The Private Life of Sherlock Holmes 70. Promise at Dawn 71. The Man who would be King 75. Mr Klein 77. The Fiendish Plot of Fu Manchu 79. Don Giovanni 79. La Truite 82, many others.

travelling matte: a masking film overlaid with another in the optical printer so as to produce a trick effect.

Traven, B. (1882–1969). The mysterious author of *The Treasure of the Sierra Madre* was most probably an Austrian called H. A. O. M. Feige. He was a former actor and anarchist, known for a while as Ret Marut. Settling in Mexico, he became a union agitator and was listed as an enemy of the state.

Travers, Ben (1886–1980). Long-lived British playwright responsible for the Tom Walls/Ralph Lynn Aldwych farces which were all filmed in the early thirties.
Autobiographies: *Vale of Laughter* 58. *A-Sitting on a Gate* 79.
Rookery Nook 30. *A Cuckoo in the Nest* 33. A Cup of Kindness 33. Turkey Time 34. Banana Ridge 41, etc.
Also wrote film scripts: Fighting Stock 36. Just My Luck 37. Uncle Silas 47, etc.

Travers, Bill (1922–). Tall British leading man, married to Virginia McKenna; stage experience from 1947.
The Square Ring 54. Geordie 55. Bhowani Junction 56. The Barretts of Wimpole Street 57. *The Smallest Show on Earth* 57. The Seventh Sin (US) 58. The Bridal Path 49. Gorgo 60. Invasion Quartet 61. Two Living, One Dead (Swed.) 62. Born Free 66. Duel at Diablo (US) 66. A Midsummer Night's Dream 68. Ring of Bright Water 69. The Belstone Fox 73. Christian the Lion 77, etc.

Travers, Henry (1874–1965) (Travers Heagerty). British character actor, on stage from 1894, in America from 1901. Came to films in the thirties and usually played benign old gentlemen.
□Reunion in Vienna 32. Another Language 33. My Weakness 33. The Invisible Man 33. The Party's Over 34. Death Takes a Holiday 34. Ready for Love 34. Born to Be Bad 34. Maybe It's Love 35. After Office Hours 35. Escapade 35. Pursuit 35. Captain Hurricane 35. Seven Keys to Baldpate 35. Four Hours to Kill 35. Too Many Parents 36. The Sisters 38. Dark Victory 39. You Can't Get Away with Murder 39. Dodge City 39. On Borrowed Time 39. Remember? 39. Stanley and Livingstone 39. The Rains Came 39. The Primrose Path 40. Anne of Windy Poplars 40. Edison the Man 40. Wyoming 40. *Ball of Fire* 41. High Sierra 41. A Girl, a Guy and a Gob 41. The Bad Man 41. I'll Wait for You 41. *Mrs Miniver* 42. Pierre of the Plains 42. Random Harvest 42. Shadow of a Doubt 42. *The Moon Is Down* 43. Madame Curie 43. Dragon Seed 44. None Shall Escape 44. The Very Thought of You 44. Thrill of a Romance 45. The Naughty Nineties 45. The Bells of St Mary's 45. Gallant Journey 46. *It's a Wonderful Life* 46. The Yearling 46. The Flame 47. Beyond Glory 48. The Girl from Jones Beach 49.

Travers, Linden (1913–) (Florence Lindon-Travers). British leading lady of stage (from 1931), screen shortly after.
Children of the Fog 35. Double Alibi 36. The Lady Vanishes 38. The Terror 39. The Stars Look Down 39. *The Ghost Train* 41. The Missing Million 42. Beware of Pity 46. No Orchids for Miss Blandish 48. *Quartet* 48. Christopher Columbus 49, etc.

Travis, Richard (1913–) (William Justice). American leading man of forties and fifties second features.
The Man Who Came to Dinner 41. The Big Shot 42. Buses Roar 43. Jewels of Brandenberg 44. Alaska Patrol 46. Skyliner 48. Operation Haylift 50. Mask of the Dragon 51. Fingerprints Don't Lie 51. City of Shadows 55, etc.

Travolta, John (1954–). Long-limbed American dancing star of the late seventies.
The Devil's Rain 75. Carrie 76. The Boy in the Plastic Bubble (TV) 77. *Saturday Night Fever* 77. *Grease* 78. Moment by Moment 79. Urban Cowboy 80. Blow Out 81. Staying Alive 83. Two of a Kind 84. Perfect 85.
TV series: Welcome Back Kotter 75–78.

¶ *J.T.:* I'm not an old-fashioned romantic. I believe in love and marriage, but not necessarily with the same person.

J.T.: I would never do anything solely for money. I have to believe in the project.

J.T.: My best quality? The transparency in my eyes. I have only to think a thought and it's seen.

Treacher, Arthur (1894–1975) (A. T. Veary). Tall British character comedian, the perfect butler for 30 years. On stage from twenties, Hollywood from 1933.
David Copperfield 34. A Midsummer Night's Dream 35. *Thank You Jeeves* 36. The Little Princess 39. National Velvet 44. Delightfully Dangerous 45. The Countess of Monte Cristo 48. Love That Brute 50. Mary Poppins 64, many others.

Treasure Island. Robert L. Stevenson's adventure classic for boys was filmed three times by American companies. In 1920 Charles Ogle was Long John and Jim Hawkins was played by a girl—Shirley Mason. Maurice Tourneur directed. In 1935, in a splendid production for MGM, Victor Fleming directed Wallace Beery and Jackie Cooper; in 1950, in Britain for Disney, Byron Haskin directed Robert Newton, who was born to play Long John, and Bobby Driscoll. Newton afterwards played the role in a feature, *Long John Silver* 54, and 26 TV half-hours filmed in Australia. In 1972 Orson Welles starred in a European remake, using such a thick accent that he had to be dubbed; and in 1973 Kirk Douglas appeared in *Scalawag*, which borrowed the plot for a modern story.

The Treasure of the Sierra Madre (US 1948). Written and directed by John Huston from the novel by the mysterious B. Traven, this sombre but gripping saga of thieves falling out over gold, after an arduous search in bandit country, won Academy Awards for Huston on both counts and for his father Walter Huston who played the oldest of the rascals. Humphrey Bogart and Tim Holt were also involved, the photography was by Ted McCord and the music by Max Steiner. The film has not worn too well—it has a studio look—but at the time it was hailed as another stride forward by Hollywood towards productions of adult appeal and integrity.

treatment. The first expansion of a script idea into sequence form, giving some idea of how the story is to be told, i.e. with examples of dialogue, camera angles, etc.

Tree, David (1915–). British comedy actor with stage experience.
Knight Without Armour 37. *Pygmalion* (as Freddy Eynsford-Hill) 38. Q Planes 39. *French Without Tears* 39. Major Barbara 40. Then war service, in which he lost an arm; subsequently retired.

† He made a very brief reappearance as the headmaster in *Don't Look Now* 73.

Treen, Mary (1907–). American comedy actress who usually plays nurses, office girls, or the heroine's plain friend.
Babbitt 35. Colleen 36. First Love 40. I Love a Soldier 44. From This Day Forward 45. Let's Live a Little 48. The Caddy 53. The Birds and the Bees 56. Rockabye Baby 58. Paradise Hawaiian Style 56, many others.

Tremayne, Les (1913–). American small part actor.
The Racket 51. Dream Wife 53. A Man Called Peter 55. The Story of Ruth 60. The Fortune Cookie 66, etc.

Trenchard-Smith, Brian (1946–). British director in Australia.
The World of Kung Fu 74. Man from Hong Kong 75. Deathcheaters 76. Day of the Assassins 80. Turkey Shoot 82. BMX Bandits 83. Jenny Kissed Me 85, etc.

trends

¶ R. D. McCann said that in Hollywood the only familiar, solid, bedrock certainty is sudden change. That goes for the entire industry, which throughout its history has been subject to the whims of fashion and has moved in a gingerly way from one crisis to another. In the midst of such uncertainty the industry's leaders can only comfort themselves with the incontrovertible adage:

> There's nothing wrong with this business that a few good movies can't cure.

The trouble has been to find out what kind of movies, at any given time, are good ones in the eyes of the public. As Adolph Zukor said long ago:

> The public is never wrong.

And Bryan Forbes said:

> Nobody can be a prophet in an industry which is entirely dependent on the public whim.

Walter Wanger knew that:

> Nothing is as cheap as a hit, no matter how much it cost.

Unfortunately the public has not always been in the forefront of good taste. When close-ups were first introduced, many audiences felt cheated and yelled:

> Show us their feet!

But without an advance in technical quality the film could hardly have survived. Billy Bitzer, the famous cameraman, said:

> The fade-out gave us a really dignified touch—we didn't have a five cent movie anymore.

It is true that the moguls have sometimes taken a long time to answer the public's call. Ted Willis said in 1966:

> The film business is like that prehistoric monster the dinosaur, which apparently had two brains, one in its head and one in its rear.

It was not always thus: in the golden years they knew a thing or two. At Warners, for instance, Bette Davis said:

> We had the answer, the sequel and the successor to everything.

But even imitation did not always pay. Darryl Zanuck knew:

> Only the first picture of a cycle really succeeds: all the imitators dwindle.

Cesare Zavattini in 1945 had a similar idea:

> The world is full of people thinking in myths.

Iris Barry in 1926 scorned film clichés:

> Why must all American movie mothers be white-haired and tottery even though their children are mere tots? Does the menopause not operate in the US?

Reality was entirely shunned. Wilson Mizner in the early talkie era commented:

> The public doesn't want to know what goes on behind the scenes. It prefers to believe that a cameraman hung in the clouds, mid-Pacific, the day Barrymore fought the whale.

Samuel Goldwyn is credited with the tersest capsuling of the tradition that audiences wanted to be soothed and not stimulated:

> Messages are for Western Union.

Even Terry Ramsaye, editing a trade journal in 1936, complained:

> If they want to preach a sermon, let them hire a hall.

This was the day of the formula:

> Boy meets girl, boy loses girl, boy gets girl.

The public paid to see it and demanded more of the same. A 1943 exhibitor said:

> You could open a can of sardines and there'd be a line waiting to get in.

Momentary turns of fashion could of course be allowed for, so many movies were being made. When *Variety* headlined:

STICKS NIX HICK PIX

it was a simple matter to discontinue the movies about poor hillbillies to which the midwestern audiences had shown such antipathy. Towards the fifties, however, there were signs of growing unease: no kind of film, and no star, could be absolutely relied on to make money. Hollywood had previously regarded the international market as a pleasant source of extra revenue; now film-making had to be geared to it. Alfred Hitchcock, however, felt that no change of style was necessary:

> When we make films for the United States, we automatically make them for the world, for the United States is full of foreigners.

But Hitch did note a change of emphasis:

> In the old days, villains had moustaches and kicked the dog. Audiences are smarter today. They don't want their villain to be thrown at them with green limelight on his face. They want an ordinary human being with failings.

The studio conveyor belt was outdated: everyone was bitten by the location bug. Rouben Mamoulian said in 1957:

> We have forsaken the magic of the cinema. We have gotten too far away from the cinematic effects achievable by camera angles and creative editing.

There was another increasing danger:

> You have to offer the public something a helluva lot better than they can get for free on TV.

What was offered was 3-D, which failed. As Hitch said:

> A nine-days' wonder—and I came in on the ninth day.

Then came CinemaScope and the other wide-screen processes, but the extra size only rarely contributed towards a better entertainment. Content was what mattered. The only reliable regular audience was for cheap horror films. Said Vincent Price in 1965:

> The cinemas have bred a new race of giant popcorn-eating rats.

At last the English came back into fashion as film-makers, chiefly on the strength of their actors and their 'X' subjects. This success had its drawbacks, according to Tony Garnett:

> To be an Englishman in the film business is to know what it's like to be colonialized.

Sex had come to stay. Said Shelagh Delaney:

> The cinema has become more and more like the theatre: it's all mauling and muttering.

Said Billy Wilder:

> Titism has taken over the country. But Audrey Hepburn singlehanded may make bozooms a thing of the past. The director will not have to invent shots where the girl leans forward for a glass of scotch and soda.

Said Adolphe Menjou:

> The Brando school are grabbers, not lovers. If it wasn't that the script says they get the girl, they wouldn't.

Said Bob Hope in 1960:

> Our big pictures this year have had some intriguing themes: sex, perversion, adultery and cannibalism. We'll get those kids away from their TV sets yet.

Said Bob Hope in 1968:

> Last year Hollywood made the first pictures with dirty words. This year we made the pictures to go with them.

And in 1971:

> The line 'I love you' is no longer a declaration but a demonstration.

In the same year Candice Bergen admitted:

> I may not be a great actress but I've become the greatest at screen orgasms. Ten seconds of heavy breathing, roll your head from side to side, simulate a slight asthma attack and die a little.

And Frank Capra snorted:

> Hollywood film-making of today is stooping to cheap salacious pornography in a crazy bastardization of a great art.

The system had crumbled, the studios were empty, every movie was a new enterprise, usually shot in some far-flung corner of the earth. Bob Hope again, in 1968:

> This year is a good one for Hollywood. Some of the movies nominated for Oscars were even made here.

Hal Wallis had another complaint:

> In the old days we had the time and money to give prospective stars a slow build-up. Today, an actor makes it fast or he just doesn't make it at all.

Orson Welles realized that:

> The trouble with a movie these days is that it's old before it's released. It's no accident that it comes in a can.

And Billy Wilder:

> Today we spend eighty per cent of our time making deals and twenty per cent making pictures.

Otto Preminger remembers when:

> There were giants in the industry. Now it is an era of midgets and conglomerates.

The watchword for the seventies was violence. Hear the producer of *The Strawberry Statement*:

We live in a time when revolution is a very saleable commodity.

Hear Roman Polanski in 1971:

Nothing is too shocking for me. When you tell the story of a man who loses his head, you have to show the head being cut off. Otherwise it's just a dirty joke without a punch line.

Hear Ken Russell, middle-aged enfant terrible of the same year:

This is not the age of manners. This is the age of kicking people in the crotch and telling them something and getting a reaction. I want to shock people into awareness. I don't believe there's any virtue in understatement.

Hear the redoubtable Sam Peckinpah:

You can't make violence real to audiences today without rubbing their noses in it. We've all been anaesthetized by the media.

Hear producer Steve Krantz defending his 'adult cartoon' *Heavy Traffic*:

Mary Poppins is OK, but when did you last date her?

Hear Peter Cook:

I don't like watching rape and violence at the cinema. I get enough of that at home!

And finally:

America's a new country and we have very little history. We have the American Indian and we have Superman. Don't fuck with either.—*R. Donner*

Trenker, Luis (1893–). Italian mountain guide who played leads in several mountain films.
Peaks of Destiny 26. The Fight for the Matterhorn 28. Doomed Battalion (& wd) 31. Der Verlorene Sohn (& wd) 34. The Challenge (& wd) 37. Monte Miracolo (& wd) 43. Duell in den Bergen (& wd) 49. Sein Bester Freund (& wd) 62, others.

Trevelyan, John (1904–85). British executive, secretary of the British Board of Film Censors 1958–1970, responsible for a more liberal policy allowing such controversial films as *Saturday Night and Sunday Morning, Tom Jones, The Servant, The Silence, Repulsion* and *Who's Afraid of Virginia Woolf?* Published memoirs 1973: *What the Censor Saw*.

Trevor, Austin (1897–1978) (A. Schilsky). British character actor with long stage experience.
At the Villa Rose 30. *Alibi* (as Hercule Poirot) 31. Lord Edgware Dies (as Hercule Poirot) 34. Dark Journey 37. Goodbye Mr Chips 39. Champagne Charlie 44. The Red Shoes 48. Father Brown 54. The Horrors of the Black Museum 59, etc.

Trevor, Claire (1909–) (Claire Wemlinger). American character actress on stage from childhood. Made many routine films before gaining critical notice.
Life in the Raw (debut) 33. Hold That Girl 34. Dante's Inferno 35. Career Woman 36. Dead End 37. The Amazing Dr Clitterhouse 38. *Stagecoach* 39. I Stole a Million 39. Dark Command 40. Honky Tonk 41. Crossroads 42. Street of Chance 42. Woman of the Town 43. *Murder My Sweet* 44. Johnny Angel 45. Crack Up 46. Bachelor Girls 47. *Key Largo* (AA) 48. The Lucky Stiff 49. Best of the Badmen 50. Hard, Fast and Beautiful 51. The Stranger Wore a Gun 52. The High and the Mighty 54. The Man without a Star 55. The Mountain 56. Marjorie Morningstar 58. Two Weeks in Another Town 62. How to Murder Your Wife 65. Capetown Affair 67. Kiss Me Goodbye 82, etc.

The Trial (France 1962). Orson Welles' attempt to put Kafka on the screen was mainly filmed in a French railway station and offered some opportunity for bravura direction and photography; but there were obvious technical inadequacies as well as an all-pervading portentousness, so that as a whole it didn't work except as a vehicle for the off-beat talents of Anthony Perkins as the victimized 'K' and Welles himself as a lawyer.

Triesault, Ivan (1898–1980). Eastern European small-part actor in Hollywood.
Mission to Moscow 43. The Hitler Gang 44. Notorious 46. To the Ends of the Earth 48. Five Fingers 52. Fräulein 58. The 300 Spartans 62. Barabbas 62. Von Ryan's Express 65. Batman 66, many others.

Trinder, Tommy (1909–). British cockney music-hall comedian, in occasional films.
Almost a Honeymoon 38. Laugh It Off 40. Sailors Three 41. The Bells Go Down 42. *The Foreman Went to France* 42. Champagne Charlie 44. *Fiddlers Three* 44. Bitter Springs 49. You Lucky People 54. The Beauty Jungle 64, etc.

Trintignant, Jean-Louis (1930–). French leading man.
Race for Life 55. And God Created Woman 56. Austerlitz 59. Château en Suède 63. Mata

Hari 64. Angélique 64. *A Man and a Woman* 66. Trans-Europe Express 66. The Sleeping Car Murders 66. The Libertine 68. Les Biches 68. 'Z' 68. Ma Nuit Chez Maud 69. The American 70. The Conformist 70. Simon the Swiss 71. Aggression 75. Faces of Love 77. The Lifeguard 79. Je Vous Aime 80. La Banquière 80. Vivement Dimanche 83.

triple trouble I

? Name the films described. Each one has the word *Three* in the title.

1 The problems of an irresponsible Brooklyn family.
2 A lady journalist asks her daughters' permission to marry again.
3 Girls in Rome fall in love.
4 Three sisters go to California to find millionaire husbands.
5 After World War II, a Jap-hating sergeant falls in love with a Japanese girl.
6 A sweepstake ticket produces fortune and ill-fortune for its investors.
7 Agnes Newton Keith tries to escape from Borneo during World War II.
8 A naval civil servant is dismissed as a security risk.
9 Daughters break up their father's planned remarriage.
10 Dr Gillespie has new interns.
11 The song-writing career of Bert Kalmar and Harry Ruby.
12 A salesman has a brief affair with a girl who later moves into his home.
13 A greetings card writer picks racetrack winners.
14 A lawman gets an outlaw on the right train despite the menacing presence of his gang.

triple trouble II

? The three stars linked played the same role in different versions of the same story, not always under the same title. Name the films in each case.

1 Mae Clarke, Vivien Leigh, Leslie Caron
2 John Boles, Dennis Morgan, Gordon Macrae
3 Ruth Chatterton, Gladys George, Lana Turner
4 Janet Gaynor, Shirley Temple, Leslie Caron
5 John Gilbert, Fredric March, Kieron Moore
6 Edward G. Robinson, Raymond Massey, Barry Sullivan
7 Theda Bara, Claudette Colbert, Elizabeth Taylor
8 Lewis Stone, Ronald Colman, Stewart Granger
9 Humphrey Bogart, John Garfield, Audie Murphy
10 Maurice Chevalier, Don Ameche, Danny Kaye
11 Lon Chaney, Claude Rains, Herbert Lom
12 Norma Talmadge, Norma Shearer, Jeanette MacDonald
13 Colleen Moore, Barbara Stanwyck, Jane Wyman
14 Richard Dix, Gene Raymond, Philip Terry
15 Mary Pickford, Marian Nixon, Shirley Temple
16 Bette Davis, Eleanor Parker, Kim Novak
17 Glenn Hunter, Stuart Erwin, Red Skelton
18 Warner Baxter, Alan Ladd, Robert Redford
19 Wallace Reid, Bob Hope, Dean Martin
20 Adolphe Menjou, Cary Grant, Walter Matthau
21 Mary Philbin, Susanna Foster, Heather Sears
22 Harry Myers, Will Rogers, Bing Crosby
23 Jack Buchanan, Dennis O'Keefe, Jack Watling
24 Irene Dunne, Margaret Sullavan, Susan Hayward
25 Betty Compson, Marlene Dietrich, Anne Baxter
26 Lionel Barrymore, Walter Huston, Jose Ferrer

Triumph of the Will (Germany 1934). A pictorial record of the sixth Nazi congress at Nuremberg, this controversial film still has a sensational impact and is probably the most powerful propaganda film ever made. Leni Riefenstahl's direction and editing, abetted by Sepp Allgeier's luminous photography, make the Nazis seem more like gods than men; and for this reason the film has been denied a commercial reissue in Britain. The early sequence showing Hitler's plane coming down from the clouds is perhaps the cleverest of all.

Trivas, Victor (1896–1970). Russian writer in America.
War is Hell (d) 31. Song of Russia 44. The Stranger 45, etc.

Trnka, Jiři (1910–1969). Czech animator and puppeteer, many of whose short films have been shown abroad.
The Emperor's Nightingale 49. Song of the Prairie 49. The Good Soldier Schweik 54. Jan Hus 56. A Midsummer Night's Dream 57, etc.

Troell, Jan (1931–). Swedish director.
Here is Your Life 66. Who Saw Him Die 67. *The Emigrants* 72. The New Land 73. Zandy's Bride 74. Hurricane 79, etc.

Tronson, Robert (1924–). British director, from TV.
The Man at the Carlton Tower 62. The Traitors 62. On the Run 63. Ring of Spies 64, etc.

Trotti, Lamar (1900–1952). Prolific American scriptwriter and producer.
Judge Priest (co-w) 34. Steamboat Round the Bend (co-w) 35. Ramona (w) 36. Slave Ship (w) 37. *In Old Chicago* (w) 38. *Young Mr Lincoln* (w) 39. Hudson's Bay (w) 41. *The Ox Bow Incident* (wp) 42. Wilson (AA) (wp) 43. The Razor's Edge (wp) 46. Mother Wore Tights (wp) 47. Yellow Sky (wp) 48. *Cheaper by the Dozen* (wp) 50. I'd Climb the Highest Mountain (wp) 51. Stars and Stripes Forever (wp) 52. With a Song in My Heart (wp) 52, many others.

Trouble in Paradise (US 1932). One feels that Ernst Lubitsch probably enjoyed making this more than any of his other American films: a roguish, pacy tale of cross and double cross among society jewel thieves, it is told with a lively visual wit and has such a gallery of attractive performances as to make it a sophisticated classic. Herbert Marshall, Miriam Hopkins, Kay Francis, C. Aubrey Smith, Charles Ruggles, Edward Everett Horton are all at their best. Written by Samson Raphaelson with sets designed by Hans Dreier.

The Trouble with Harry (US 1956). Alfred Hitchcock's second favourite of his own films is a determinedly gay black comedy which lacks cinematic spontaneity, all its humour coming straight from Jack Trevor Story's original novel about a corpse on the heath which villagers keep burying and digging up again for their own reasons. The autumnal Vermont setting, delightful in itself, is a distraction to a movie which would have worked better in black and white. Mildred Natwick, Edmund Gwenn and Shirley Maclaine make the most of the macabre situations.

Troughton, Patrick (1920–87). British character actor, often in malevolent roles; mainly on TV (Dr Who in the early seventies).
Escape 48. Hamlet 48. Treasure Island 50. The Black Knight 52. Richard III 56. Phantom of the Opera 62.The Gorgon 64. The Omen 76, many others in small roles.

Trouncer, Cecil (1898–1953). British stage character actor with splendidly resonant diction.
Pygmalion 38. While the Sun Shines 46. London Belongs to Me 48. *The Guinea Pig* 49. The Lady with a Lamp 51. Pickwick Papers 52. The Weak and the Wicked 54.

Trowbridge, Charles (1882–1967). American character actor, former architect; usually played professors or kindly fathers.
I Take This Woman 31. The Thirteenth Chair 36. Confessions of a Nazi Spy 39. The Mummy's Hand 40. Mildred Pierce 45. The Wings of Eagles 57, many others.

The True Glory (GB 1945). This brilliantly-made, rather too literary documentary, composed of newsreel material from D-Day to the fall of Berlin, still has that brilliant surface polish which at the time of its release made it by far the best compilation film to have been seen. Directed by Carol Reed and Garson Kanin, with music by William Alwyn.

True-life Adventures: see under *The Living Desert*.

Truex, Ernest (1890–1973). American character actor of 'little man' roles, in films since 1918.
Whistling in the Dark 33. *The Adventures of Marco Polo* 38. Christmas in July 40. His Girl Friday 40. Always Together 48. The Leather Saint 56. Twilight for the Gods 58. Fluffy 65, many others; latterly much on TV.

Truffaut, François (1932–84). French 'new wave' director, former critic.
Autobiography 1982: *Les Films de Ma Vie*. Also wrote *Hitchcock*, a long interview with his idol.
□Les Mistons 58. *Les Quatre Cents Coups* 59. *Shoot the Pianist* 60. *Jules and Jim* 61. Love at Twenty (part) 62. *Silken Skin* 64. Fahrenheit 451 66. The Bride Wore Black 67. Stolen Kisses 68. Mississippi Mermaid 69. L'Enfant Sauvage (& a) 69. Domicile Conjugale 70. Anne and Muriel 72. A Gorgeous Bird Like Me 72. *La Nuit Américaine* 73. The Story of Adele H 75. L'Argent du Poche 76. The Man Who Loved Women 77. Close Encounters of the Third Kind (a only) 77. Love on the Run 79. Le Dernier Métro 80. Vivement Dimanche 83.

¶ I make films that I would like to have seen when I was a young man.—*F.T.*

To make a film is to improve on life, to arrange it to suit oneself, to prolong the games of childhood, to construct something which is at once a new toy and a vase in which one can arrange in a permanent way the ideas one feels in the morning.—*F.T.*

Truman, Michael (1916–74). British director, former editor.
Touch and Go 54. Go to Blazes 62. The Girl in the Headlines 63, etc.

Truman, Ralph (1900–77). British stage character actor who made occasional film appearances.
Henry V 44. Beware of Pity 46. Oliver Twist 48. Quo Vadis 51. The Man Who Knew Too Much 56. El Cid 61. Nicholas and Alexandra 71, many others.

Trumbull, Douglas (1942–). American special effects man.
2001: A Space Odyssey 68. Candy 68. The Andromeda Strain 71. Silent Running (& d) 72. *Close Encounters of the Third Kind* 77. *Star Trek* 79. Brainstorm (& d) 83.

Trumbo, Dalton (1905–1976). American screenwriter, one of the 'Hollywood Ten' who were blacklisted in the forties.
The Remarkable Andrew 42. A Guy Named Joe 43. Our Vines Have Tender Grapes 45. The Prowler (as Hugo Butler) 51. The Brave One (as Robert Rich) 56. Spartacus 60. Exodus 60. The Last Sunset 61. Lonely are the Brave 62. The Sandpiper 65. Hawaii 66. The Fixer 68. Johnny Got His Gun (& d) 71. Executive Action 73. Papillon (co-w, a) 73, many others.

Trundy, Natalie (–). American leading lady in occasional films.
The Careless Years 57. The Monte Carlo Story 58. Mr Hobbs Takes a Vacation 62. Conquest of the Planet of the Apes 71. Huckleberry Finn 73, etc.

Tryon, Tom (1919–). American leading man with stage and TV experience. Later a successful novelist.
The Scarlet Hour (debut) 55. Three Violent People 56. I Married a Monster from Outer Space 57. Moon Pilot 61. Marines Let's Go 61. *The Cardinal* 63. In Harm's Way 65. The Glory Guys 65. The Horsemen 71. Johnny Got His Gun (& pd) 71. The Other (oa only) 72. Fedora (oa only) 78, etc.
TV series: Texas John Slaughter 59.

Tsu, Irene (1943–). Chinese glamour girl in Hollywood.
Caprice 66. The Green Berets 67. Paper Tiger 75. Down and Out in Beverly Hills 85, etc.

Tubbs, William (1909-53). Portly American character actor in Europe.
Paisa 46. Edward and Caroline 50. Three Steps North 50. Quo Vadis 51, etc.

Tuchner, Michael (1934–). British director.
□Villain 71. Fear is the Key 72. Mister Quilp 75. The Likely Lads 76. Summer of My German Soldier (TV) 79. Haywire (TV) 80. The Hunchback of Notre Dame (TV) 81. Trenchcoat 83.

Tuchock, Wanda (1898–1985). American screenwriter at her peak in silent days.
Show People 27. *Hallelujah* 29. Bird of Paradise 32. Hawaii Calls 37. Silver Queen 45. The Foxes of Harrow 47. The Homestretch 49, etc.

Tucker, Forrest (1919–86). Rugged American leading man, mostly in routine action pictures from 1940.
The Westerner (debut) 40. Keeper of the Flame 42. The Yearling 46. The Big Cat 49. Sands of Iwo Jima 50. The Wild Blue Yonder 52. Crosswinds 53. Trouble in the Glen (GB) 54. Break in the Circle (GB) 56. *The Abominable Snowman* (GB) 57. Auntie Mame 58. The Night They Raided Minsky's 68. Cancel My Reservation 72. The Wild McCullochs 75. Final Chapter – Walking Tall 77. Thunder Run 85, many others.
TV series: Crunch and Des 55. F Troop 65–66. Dusty's Trail 73. Ghost Chasers 76. The Rebels 79.

Tucker, George Loane (1881–1921). American silent director.
The Courting of Mary 11. Traffic in Souls 13. Called Back 14. The Prisoner of Zenda 15. Arsene Lupin 16. The Manxman 17. The Miracle Man 19. Ladies Must Live 21, many others.

Tucker, Sophie (1884–1966) (Sophia Abuza or Sonia Kalish). Russian-born, American-oriented popular singer, the heavyweight 'red hot momma' of vaudeville.
□Honky Tonk 29. Gay Love (GB) 34. Gay Time (GB) 34. Broadway Melody of 1937 37. Thoroughbreds Don't Cry 37. Atlantic City 44. Follow the Boys 44. Sensations of 1945 44.

Tufts, Sonny (1911–1970) (Bowen Charleston Tufts). Tall, good-humoured American 'second lead', in Hollywood from the early forties.
□So Proudly We Hail 43. Government Girl 43. In The Meantime Darling 44. I Love a Soldier 44. Here Come the Waves 45. Bring on the Girls 45. Duffy's Tavern 45. Miss Susie Slagle's 45. The Virginian 46. The Well-Groomed Bride 46. Cross My Heart 46. Easy Come Easy Go 47. Blaze Of Noon 47. Variety Girl 47. Swell Guy 47. The Untamed Breed 48. The Crooked Way 49. Easy Living 49. The Gift Horse (GB) 52. No Escape 53. Cat Women of the Moon 53. Run for the Hills 53. Serpent Island 54. The Seven Year Itch 55. Come Next Spring 56. The Parson and the Outlaw 57. Town Tamer 65. Cottonpicking Chickenpicker 67.

Tugboat Annie. This aggressive, middle-aged lady of the waterfront was devised by Norman Reilly Raine and personified in the 1933 film by Marie Dressler. Subsequent films include *Tugboat Annie Sails Again* 40 with Marjorie Rambeau and *Captain Tugboat Annie* 45 with Jane Darwell. A 1956 TV series featured Minerva Urecal.

Tully, Montgomery (1904–). British writer and director.
Murder in Reverse (wd) 45. Spring Song (wd) 47. Boys in Brown (d) 49. A Tale of Five Cities (d) 51. The Glass Cage (d) 55. The Hypnotist (d) 57. Escapement (d) 58. Clash by Night (d) 63. Who Killed the Cat? (wd) 66. Battle Beneath the Earth (d) 68, many other second features and TV episodes.

Tully, Tom (1896–1982). American character actor with stage experience; usually tough-looking but soft-hearted roles.
Destination Tokyo 44. Adventure 45. The Town Went Wild 45. June Bride 48. Where the Sidewalk Ends 50. The Caine Mutiny 54. Ten North Frederick 57. The Wackiest Ship in the Army 61. Coogan's Bluff 68, etc.
TV series: The Line-Up 59.

Tunberg, Karl (1908–). American screenwriter, in Hollywood from 1937.
My Lucky Star 38. Down Argentine Way 40. Orchestra Wives 42. Kitty 45. You Gotta Stay Happy 47. Scandal at Scourie 53. The Scarlet Coat 55. *Ben Hur* 59. Libel 59. Taras Bulba 62. Harlow (electronovision version) 65. Where Were You When the Lights Went Out? 68, many others.

Turkel, Ann (–). American leading lady, wife of Richard Harris.
99 and 44/100 Per Cent Dead 74. Matt Helm (TV) 75. The Cassandra Crossing 77. Golden Rendezvous 78. Humanoids from the Deep 80.

Turman, Laurence (1926–). American producer.
The Young Doctors 61. The Flim Flam Man 66. *The Graduate* 67. Pretty Poison 69. The Great White Hope 70. Marriage of a Young Stockbroker (& d) 71. The Drowning Pool (co-p) 75. First Love (co-p) 77. Walk Proud 79. Tribute 80, etc.

The Turn of the Tide (GB 1935). This small, well-intentioned little drama about family rivalry in a Yorkshire fishing village is said to have persuaded Lord Rank to enter the film industry because it showed that a fiction film could be a teaching instrument. Norman Walker directed: John Garrick and Geraldine Fitzgerald were the leading players.

Turner, Florence (1887–1946). American actress who in 1907 became the first 'movie star' known by name; also as 'the Vitagraph Girl'.
A Dixie Mother 10. Francesca da Rimini 12. The Welsh Singer (GB) 13. My Old Dutch (GB) 15. East is East (GB) 15. The Old Wives' Tale (GB) 21, etc. Went back to Hollywood in roles of diminishing stature; retired in the mid-twenties.

Turner, John (1932–). British leading man with stage experience, also known as TV's 'Knight Errant'.
Behemoth, the Sea Monster 60. Petticoat Pirates 61. Sammy Going South 62. The Black Torment 64, etc.

Turner, Kathleen (1954–). Leading American actress.
Body Heat 82. Romancing the Stone 84. The Man with Two Brains 84. Prizzi's Honor 85. Crimes of Passion 85. Jewel of the Nile 86. *Peggy Sue Got Married* 87. A Breed Apart 87.

Turner, Lana (1920–) (Julia Turner). American leading lady of the forties; began as the 'girl next door' type but became increasingly sophisticated.
Biography 1976: *The Films of Lana Turner* by Lou Valentino.
They Won't Forget (debut) 37. The Great Garrick 37. Four's a Crowd 38. The Adventures of Marco Polo 38. Calling Dr

Kildare 39. *Love Finds Andy Hardy* 39. Rich Man Poor Girl 39. Dramatic School 39. These Glamour Girls 39. Dancing Co-Ed 39. Two Girls on Broadway 40. We Who Are Young 40. Choose Your Partner 40. Ziegfeld Girl 41. Dr Jekyll and Mr Hyde 41. Honky Tonk 41. Johnny Eager 41. *Somewhere I'll Find You* 42. Slightly Dangerous 43. Marriage is a Private Affair 44. Keep Your Powder Dry 44. Weekend at the Waldorf 45. The Postman Always Rings Twice 45. Green Dolphin Street 46. Cass Timberlane 47. Homecoming 48. The Three Musketeers 48. A Life of Her Own 50. Mr Imperium 51. The Merry Widow 52. The Bad and the Beautiful 52. Latin Lovers 53. The Flame and the Flesh 54. Betrayed 55. The Prodigal 55. The Rains of Ranchipur 55. The Sea Chase 55. Diane 56. Another Time Another Place (GB) 57. *Peyton Place* 57. The Lady Takes a Flyer 58. *Imitation of Life* 59. Portrait in Black 60. By Love Possessed 61. Bachelor in Paradise 62. Who's Got the Action? 63. Love Has Many Faces 65. Madame X 66. The Big Cube 69. Persecution 74. Bittersweet Love 76, etc.
TV series: The Survivors 69. Falcon Crest 82.

Turpin, Ben (1874–1940). Cross-eyed American silent comedian, mainly popular in short slapstick skits of the twenties. In films from 1915 after vaudeville experience.
Uncle Tom's Cabin 19. Small Town Idol 21. Show of Shows 29. The Love Parade 30, scores of others.

Turpin, Dick (1706–1739) was a seasoned criminal without too many obvious redeeming characteristics. Film-makers have seized on his ride to York and his affection for his horse as an excuse to view him through rose-tinted glasses. So he was played as a hero by Matheson Lang in 1922, Tom Mix in 1925, Victor McLaglen in 1933, Louis Hayward in 1951, and David Weston (for Walt Disney) in 1965. In the late seventies Richard O'Sullivan appeared in an ITV series, again featuring the highwayman as a kind of Robin Hood.

Turpin, Gerry (c. 1930–). British cinematographer.
The Queen's Guards 61. Seance on a Wet Afternoon 64. The Whisperers 67. Deadfall 68. *Oh What a Lovely War* 69. The Man Who Had Power Over Women 70. I Want What I Want 71. The Last of Sheila 73, etc.

Tushingham, Rita (1940–). British leading character actress with stage experience.
□*A Taste of Honey* 61. The Leather Boys 63. A Place To Go 63. Girl with Green Eyes 64. *The Knack* 65. Dr Zhivago 65. The Trap 66. Smashing Time 67. Diamonds for Breakfast 68. The Guru 69. The Bed-Sitting Room 69. Straight on Till Morning 72. The Human Factor 75. Rachel's Man 75. Mysteries 79. Confessions of Felix Krull (TV) 81. Judgment in Stone 86.

Tutin, Dorothy (1930–). Leading British actress. Occasional films.
□*The Importance of Being Earnest* 52. The Beggar's Opera 53. A Tale of Two Cities 57. Cromwell 69. The Spy's Wife 70. *Savage Messiah* 72. The Shooting Party 85. Murder with Mirrors (TV) 85.

Tuttle, Frank (1892–1963). American director of mainly routine films; in Hollywood from the twenties.
Kid Boots 27. Roman Scandals 33. The Glass Key 35. Waikiki Wedding 37. I Stole a Million 39. *This Gun For Hire* 42. Lucky Jordan 43. Hostages 43. The Hour Before the Dawn 43. A Man Called Sullivan 45. Suspense 46. Swell Guy 47. The Magic Face 51. Gunman in the Streets 51. Hell on Frisco Bay 55. A Cry in the Night 56, etc.

Twain, Mark (1835–1910) (Samuel Langhorne Clemens). Beloved American humorist and travel writer; was played by Fredric March in *The Adventures of Mark Twain* 44. Works filmed include *Tom Sawyer* (qv), *Huckleberry Finn* (qv), *A Connecticut Yankee* (qv), *The Prince and the Pauper* (qv), *The Celebrated Jumping Frog* (as *The Best Man Wins*), *The Million-Pound Banknote.*

Twelve Angry Men (US 1957). One of the most successful results (though not commercially) of the TV invasion of Hollywood: a meticulously detailed reconstruction of Reginald Rose's gripping jury-room TV play, directed by Sidney Lumet. Those present included Henry Fonda, E. G. Marshall, Jack Warden, George Voskovec, Ed Begley, Lee J. Cobb.

Twelve O'Clock High (US 1949). A belated, thoughtful tale of World War II which achieved freshness and realism by concentrating less on the action possibilities of the hazards undergone by American bomber pilots based in Britain than on the strains of command, with Gregory Peck giving a fine performance as the commanding officer who finally cracks up. Written by Sy Bartlett and

Beirne Lay Jnr; photographed by Leon Shamroy; directed by Henry King. A successful TV series was shown in 1964–65.

Twelvetrees, Helen (1908–1958) (Helen Jurgens). American leading lady of the thirties; films fairly unmemorable.
The Ghost Talks 29. Her Man 30. The Painted Desert 31. Is My Face Red? 32. King for a Night 33. Times Square Lady 35. Hollywood Round Up 37, etc.

Twentieth Century-Fox Film Corporation. An American production and distribution company formed in 1935 by a merger of Joseph Schenck's Twentieth Century Pictures with William Fox's Fox Film Corporation. Fox had started in nickelodeon days as a showman, then a distributor. Putting his profits into production, he started the careers of several useful stars including Theda Bara, and pioneered the Movietone sound-on-film process; but in the early thirties, after a series of bad deals, he lost power. The new company had Darryl F. Zanuck as production head from 1935 to 1952; he returned in 1962 as president after the resignation of Spyros Skouras, who had reigned from 1942. These two men are therefore largely responsible for the Fox image, which usually gave the impression of more careful budget-trimming and production-processing than did the films of the rest of the 'big five'. Fox's successful personality stars include Shirley Temple, Alice Faye, Don Ameche, Betty Grable and Marilyn Monroe; its best westerns include *The Big Trail, Drums along the Mohawk, My Darling Clementine* and *The Gunfighter*; in drama it can claim *What Price Glory?, Dante's Inferno, The Grapes of Wrath, How Green Was My Valley, The Ox Bow Incident, The Song of Bernadette, Wilson, The Snake Pit*, and *Gentlemen's Agreement.* In 1953 Spyros Skouras successfully foisted the new screen shape, CinemaScope, on to world markets, but Fox have not used it with greater success than anyone else, their most elaborate 'spectaculars' being *The Robe, There's No Business Like Show Business, The King and I, South Pacific, The Diary of Anne Frank, The Longest Day, Cleopatra, Those Magnificent Men in Their Flying Machines, The Sound of Music, Star!, Hello Dolly*, and *Tora! Tora! Tora!*

¶ 'Leaving Fox was like leaving home at 28; I'd been there since I was sixteen.'—*Linda Darnell*

Twenty Thousand Years in Sing Sing (US 1932). An early exposé of American prison life, from a book by Warden Lewis E. Lawes; its type quickly became too familiar. Spencer Tracy and Bette Davis starred. In 1940 the story was remade as *Castle on the Hudson* with John Garfield and Ann Sheridan.

Twiggy (1946–) (Lesley Hornby). British fashion model of the sixties.
□*The Boy Friend* 71. 'W' 74. There Goes the Bride 80.

Twist, Derek (1905–1979). British director, former editor and associate producer.
The End of the River 47. All over the Town 48. Green Grow the Rushes 51. Police Dog 55. Family Doctor 57, etc.

Twist, John (1895–1976). American screenwriter.
The Toast of New York 36. The Great Man Votes 39. So Big 53. Helen of Troy 55. The FBI Story 56. Esther and the King 60. None But the Brave 64, etc.

Two Cities Films. A British company set up in the early days of World War II by the expatriate Italian Filippo del Giudice. It was responsible for many of Britain's most famous films, including *In Which We Serve, The Way Ahead, Henry V, Blithe Spirit* and *Odd Man Out.*

2001: A Space Odyssey (GB 1968). This bird's-eye-view of the universe past and future made by Stanley Kubrick from a story by Arthur C. Clarke, worked like a huge confidence trick: the special effects (AA, BFA) were so spellbinding that comparatively few patrons complained of the obscure story line and general lack of human feeling. As prophecy it was certainly less optimistic than H. G. Wells' 1936 *Things To Come*. A muddled sequel, *2010*, appeared in 1984 and was quickly forgotten: Roy Scheider starred, Peter Hyams directed.

Tyler, Beverly (1924–). American leading lady of routine forties films.
Best Foot Forward 43. The Green Years 46. The Beginning or the End 47. The Fireball 50. Chicago Confidential 47, etc.

Tyler, Parker (1904–1974). American highbrow film critic. Author of *The Hollywood Hallucination, Magic and Myth of the Movies, The Shadow of an Airplane Climbs the Empire State Building*, etc.

Tyler, Tom (1903–1954) (Vincent Markowsky). American cowboy star of innumerable second features in the thirties: *The Cowboy Cop* 26. *The Sorcerer* 29. *Riding the Lonesome Trail* 34. *Pinto Rustlers* 38. *Roamin' Wild* 39, etc. Also played small roles in such films as *Gone with the Wind* 39. *Stagecoach* 39. *The Mummy's Hand* (as the mummy) 40; and had the title role in *The Adventures of Captain Marvel* (serial) 41.

Tyrrell, Susan (1941–). American leading lady of the late seventies.
Fat City 72. Shootout 72. Catch My Soul 73. The Killer Inside Me 76. I Never Promised You a Rose Garden 77. Islands in the Stream 77. Another Man, Another Chance 77.

Tyson, Cicely (1933–). Black American leading actress.
A Man Called Adam 66. The Comedians 67. The Heart is a Lonely Hunter 68. *Sounder* 72. *The Autobiography of Miss Jane Pittman* (TV) 74. Roots (TV) 77. A Hero Ain't Nothin' But a Sandwich 77. The Concorde—Airport 79 79, etc.
TV series: East Side West Side 63.

Tyzack, Margaret (1933–). British character actress, familiar on TV in *The First Churchills* and *The Forsyte Saga*.
Ring of Spies 64. The Whisperers 67. A Clockwork Orange 71. The Legacy 79, etc.

Tzelniker, Meier (1894–1982). British character actor well known in the Yiddish theatre.
Mr Emmanuel 44. It Always Rains on Sunday 48. Last Holiday 50. The Teckman Mystery 54. Make Me an Offer 54. A Night to Remember 58. *Expresso Bongo* 60. The Sorcerers 67.

Answers

teams

1 Burt Lancaster ☐ Jean Peters ☐ 2 Ava Gardner ☐ Anthony Franciosa ☐ 3 John Barrymore ☐ Mary Astor ☐ 4 Al Jolson ☐ Betty Bronson ☐ 5 Marlene Dietrich ☐ John Lodge ☐ 6 Ramon Novarro ☐ May McAvoy ☐ 7 Charlton Heston ☐ Haya Harareet ☐ 8 Lillian Gish ☐ Lars Hanson ☐ 9 Barbara Stanwyck ☐ John Boles ☐ 10 Clark Gable ☐ Maria Elena Marques ☐ 11 Errol Flynn ☐ Brenda Marshall ☐ 12 Clara Bow ☐ Antonio Moreno ☐ 13 Katharine Hepburn ☐ John Beal ☐ 14 John Wayne ☐ Nancy Olson ☐ 15 Spencer Tracy ☐ Signe Hasso ☐ 16 Humphrey Bogart ☐ Irene Manning ☐ 17 Susan Hayward ☐ Michael Connors ☐ 18 Greta Garbo ☐ Ramon Novarro ☐ 19 David Niven ☐ Olivia de Havilland ☐ 20 Gary Cooper ☐ Teresa Wright ☐ 21 Ronald Colman ☐ Anna Lee ☐ 22 Danny Kaye ☐ Mai Zetterling ☐ 23 Ronald Colman ☐ Jane Wyatt ☐ 24 James Cagney ☐ Joan Leslie ☐ 25 Joel McCrea ☐ Laraine Day ☐

teleheroes

1 Ty Hardin ☐ 2 Mike Connors ☐ 3 James Garner ☐ Jack Kelly ☐ Roger Moore ☐ 4 William Conrad ☐ 5 Rock Hudson ☐ 6 George Nader ☐ 7 Edward Woodward ☐ 8 David Birney ☐ 9 Burt Reynolds ☐ 10 Raymond Burr ☐ 11 Dennis Weaver ☐ 12 George Peppard ☐ 13 Howard Duff ☐ 14 John Cassavetes ☐ 15 Ray Milland ☐ 16 David Janssen ☐ 17 Richard Denning ☐ 18 Phil Carey ☐ 19 Skip Homeier ☐ 20 Gene Barry ☐ 21 Craig Stevens ☐ 22 Dan Duryea ☐ 23 Jack Lord ☐ 24 Lloyd Bridges ☐

title quotations

1 The Bible: Revelation 5:1. ☐
And I saw in the right hand of him that sat on the throne a book . . . sealed with seven seals.

2 The Bible: 1 Timothy 6:10. ☐
For the love of money is the root of all evil.

3 The leading character feigns madness, and the title seems to be a slight misquotation from Shakespeare's *Hamlet*. ☐
I am but mad north-northwest; when the wind is southerly, I know a hawk from a handsaw.

4 Speech by Abraham Lincoln. ☐
The ballot is stronger than the bullet.

5 Speech by Christopher North (1829). ☐
. . .His Majesty's Dominions, on which the sun never sets . . .

6 Shakespeare, *A Midsummer Night's Dream*. ☐
Ill met by moonlight, proud Titania.

7 Shakespeare, *The Merchant of Venice.* □
How sweet the moonlight sleeps upon this bank!
Here will we sit, and let the sounds of music
Creep in our ears . . .

8, 9, 10, 11 The Bible: The Song of Songs. □
. . . the time of the singing of birds is come,
And the voice of the turtle is heard in our land . . .
Arise, my love, my fair one, and come away . . .
Take us the foxes, the little foxes, that spoil the vines . . . for our vines have tender grapes . . .

12 Rudyard Kipling, 'Gentleman Rankers'. □
Gentleman rankers, out on the spree,
Damned from here to eternity.

13 Ernest Dowson, 'Cynara'. □
I have forgot much, Cynara! Gone with the wind,
Flung roses, roses riotously with the throng,
Dancing, to put thy pale, lost lilies out of mind . . .

14 The Bible: Revelation 6:8. □
And I looked, and behold a pale horse: and the name that sat on him was Death.

15 Julia Ward Howe, 'The Battle Hymn of the American Republic'. □
Mine eyes have seen the glory of the coming of the Lord:
He is trampling out the vintage where the grapes of wrath are stored.

16 Oriental proverb. □
The sharp edge of a razor is difficult to pass over; thus the wise say the path to salvation is hard.

17 Percy Bysshe Shelley, 'Sonnet'. □
Lift not the painted veil which those who live
Call life . . .

18 Thomas Gray, 'Elegy in a Country Churchyard', □
The paths of glory lead but to the grave.

19 Walt Whitman, 'Leaves of Grass'. □
Now, voyager, sail thou forth to seek and find.

20 Rudyard Kipling, 'The Vampire'. □
A fool there was, and he made his prayer . . .
To a rag, and a bone, and a hank of hair . . .

21 Rudyard Kipling, 'The Female of the Species'. □
The female of the species is more deadly than the male . . .

22 John Donne, 'Devotions'. □
Any man's death diminishes me, because I am involved in mankind; and therefore never send to know for whom the bell tolls: it tolls for thee.

23 Robert Burns, 'To a Mouse'. □
The best laid plans of mice and men
Gang aft agley . . .

24 Daniel Webster, on entering the overcrowded legal profession: □
There is always room at the top.

25 Edward Fitzgerald, 'The Rubaiyat of Omar Khayyam'. □
I sometimes think that never blows so red
The rose as where some buried Caesar bled . . .

26 John Paul Jones: □
I wish to have no connection with any ship that does not sail fast, for I intend to go in harm's way.

triple trouble I

1 *Three Cornered Moon* □ 2 *Three Daring Daughters* □ 3 *Three Coins in the Fountain* □ 4 *Three Blind Mice* □ 5 *Three Stripes in the Sun* □ 6 *Three Strangers* □ 7 *Three Came Home* □ 8 *Three Brave Men* □ 9 *Three Smart Girls* □ 10 *Three Men in White* □ 11 *Three Little Words* □ 12 *Three into Two Won't Go* □ 13 *Three Men on a Horse* □ 14 *Three-Ten to Yuma* □

triple trouble II

1 *Waterloo Bridge* □ *Waterloo Bridge* □ *Gaby* □ 2 *The Desert Song* □ (all three this title) 3 *Madame X* □ 4 *Daddy Longlegs* □ *Curly Top* □ *Daddy Longlegs* □ 5 *Love* □ *Anna Karenina* □ *Anna Karenina* □ 6 *The Sea Wolf* □ *Barricade* □ *Wolf Larsen* □ 7 *Cleopatra* □ 8 *The Prisoner of Zenda* □ 9 *To Have and Have Not* □ *The Breaking Point* □ *The Gun Runners* □ 10 *Folies Bergere* □ *That Night in Rio* □ *On the Riviera* □ 11 *The Phantom of the Opera* □ 12 *Smilin' Through* □ 13 *So Big* □ 14 *Seven Keys to Baldpate* □ 15 *Rebecca of Sunnybrook Farm* □ 16 *Of Human Bondage* □ 17 *Merton of the Movies* □ *Make Me a Star* □ *Merton of the Movies* □ 18 *The Great Gatsby* □ 19 *The Ghost Breaker* □ *The Ghost Breakers* □ *Scared Stiff* □ 20 *The Front Page* □ *His Girl Friday* □ *The Front Page* □ 21 *The Phantom of the Opera* □ 22 *A Connecticut Yankee in King Arthur's Court* □ 23 *Brewster's Millions* □ *Brewster's Millions* □ *Three on a Spree* □ 24 *Back Street* □ 25 *The Spoilers* □ 26 *Sadie Thomson* □ *Rain* □ *Miss Sadie Thomson* □

U

UFA. Universum Film Aktien Gesellschaft: the main German film production company since 1917, owning its studio and linked in the twenties with Paramount and MGM. In the thirties it was brought under state control and in the forties, with the end of the war, it ceased to exist.

Ugetsu Monogatari (Japan 1953). Rather oddly voted by an international critics' poll in 1958 as one of the ten best films ever made, this genuinely strange and beautiful drama would be unlikely to win such an accolade now. Laid in sixteenth-century Japan, it tells of a potter lured away from home into a castle of ghosts. Slight, charming, impeccably directed by Kenji Mizoguchi. Translated into English the title emerges as *Tales of a Pale and Mysterious Moon after the Rain.*

Uggams, Leslie (1943–). Black American revue actress.
Skyjacked 72. Roots (TV) 77. Backstairs at the White House (TV) 79.

Ullman, Daniel (1918–1979). American scriptwriter.
The Maze 53. Seven Angry Men 54. Wichita 55. Good Day for a Hanging 59. Face of a Fugitive 59. Mysterious Island 61, etc.

Ullmann, Liv (1939–). Norwegian leading actress in international films.
Autobiography 1977: *Changing.*
The Wayward Girl 59. Persona 66. Hour of the Wolf 67. Shame 68. A Passion 70. The Night Visitor 70. Pope Joan 71. Lost Horizon 73. Forty Carats 73. The Abdication 74. Face to Face 76. A Bridge Too Far 77. The Serpent's Egg 77. Leonor 77. *Autumn Sonata* 78. Players 79. Richard's Things (TV) 80. The Wild Duck 82. Bay Boy 84. Dangerous Moves 84. Ingrid 85. Let's Hope It's a Girl 85, etc.

Ulmer, Edgar G. (1900–1972). Austrian-born director long in Hollywood specializing in second features and exploitation subjects. In recent years, somewhat mysteriously revered by French critics.
The Black Cat 34. The Singing Blacksmith 38. Isle of Forgotten Sins 43. Bluebeard 44. The Wife of Monte Cristo 46. Detour 46. Her Sister's Secret 47. Ruthless 48. The Man from Planet X 53. The Naked Dawn 55. Daughter of Dr Jekyll 57. The Amazing Transparent Man 60. Beyond the Time Barrier 61. Atlantis, The Lost Kingdom (L'Atlantide) 62. The Cavern 65, many others.

Ulric, Lenore (1892–1970) (Lenore Ulrich). American stage actress.
Tiger Rose 23. Frozen Justice 29. Camille 36. Temptation 46. Northwest Outpost 47, etc.

Ulysses. The Homerian hero was played by Kirk Douglas in a 1954 Italian production by Dino de Laurentiis: it concentrated on spectacle and the monstrous Cyclops. Joseph Strick's 1967 film of the same title was a very different affair, being based on James Joyce's experimental novel about twenty-four hours in the life of an Irish Jew in Dublin. Although it could hardly do more than present excerpts from the original, it had much charm and imagination, though its faithful retention of Joyce's language caused it to be banned in many areas. Milo O'Shea and Barbara Jefford led the cast.

Umberto D (Italy 1952). Neo-realistic drama in the mould of *Bicycle Thieves* and also directed by Vittorio de Sica from a script by Cesare Zavattini; about a proud but lonely old man who, unable to raise his rent, contemplates suicide. Uses non-professional actors.

The Umbrellas of Cherbourg (Les Parapluies de Cherbourg) (France 1964). Naïve, charming, all-singing love story directed by Jacques Demy with music by Michel Legrand. The tale of starcrossed lovers would be nothing without the musical treatment and the delightful use of colour; as it is, the film has been considered a masterpiece though it failed (luckily) to spark off a cycle of cinematic light operas.

Umeki, Miyoshi (1929–). Japanese leading lady who won an Academy Award for her performance in *Sayonara* 57.

Cry for Happy 61. Flower Drum Song 61. A Girl Named Tamiko 63, etc.
TV series: The Courtship of Eddie's Father 69.

Uncle Tom's Cabin, an anti-slavery novel of excellent intentions and unabashed sentimentality, was written in 1852 by American novelist Harriet Beecher Stowe (1811–1896). It features the dastardly white villain Simon Legree, the cheerful Negro Uncle Tom, and poor Little Eva who is taken to heaven by an angel. The main film versions include a 1903 one-reeler by Edwin S. Porter, a Pathé three-reeler of 1910 and an American three-reeler of 1913. In 1914 came a longer American version with Marie Eline as Little Eva. 1918 brought a full-length version with Marguerite Clark in the dual role of Topsy and Eva. Then in 1927 Harry Pollard directed a full-blown silent spectacle which was frequently revived with sound effects in later years: Virginia Grey was Eva. The subject might have been thought too dated or too touchy for sound treatment, but in 1965 a colour and widescreen European co-production was directed by Geza von Radvanyi and featured Herbert Lom as Simon Legree and Getrud Mittermayer as Eva.

uncredited appearances by well-known stars are usually intended as gags to liven up a film which can do with an extra laugh. Thus the brief cameos of Cary Grant and Jack Benny in *Without Reservations*; Lana Turner in *Du Barry Was a Lady*; Robert Taylor in *I Love Melvin*; Bing Crosby in *My Favourite Blonde, The Princess and the Pirate* and other Bob Hope films; Alan Ladd in *My Favourite Brunette*; Peter Lorre in *Meet Me in Las Vegas*; Myrna Loy in *The Senator was Indiscreet*; Peter Sellers and David Niven in *Road to Hong Kong*; Vincent Price in *Beach Party*; Boris Karloff in *Bikini Beach*; Groucho Marx in *Will Success Spoil Rock Hunter?*; Elizabeth Taylor in *Scent of Mystery, What's New Pussycat?* and *Anne of the Thousand Days*; Richard Burton in *What's New Pussycat?*; Jack Benny and Jerry Lewis in *It's a Mad Mad Mad Mad World*; Robert Vaughn in *The Glass Bottom Boat*; Bob Hope and others in *The Oscar*; Rock Hudson in *Four Girls in Town*; Jack Benny and Jimmy Durante in *Beau James*; Red Skelton in *Susan Slept Here*; Bing Crosby and Bob Hope in *Scared Stiff*; Martin and Lewis, Humphrey Bogart and Jane Russell in *Road to Bali*; Lauren Bacall in *Two Guys from Milwaukee*; Gene Kelly in *Love is Better Than Ever*; Clark Gable and Robert Taylor in *Callaway Went Thataway*; Peter O'Toole in *Casino Royale*; Yul Brynner in *The Magic Christian*; Edward G. Robinson in *Robin and the Seven Hoods*; Humphrey Bogart in *Always Together, Two Guys from Milwaukee* and *The Love Lottery*; Jack Benny in *The Great Lover*; Ray Milland in *Miss Tatlock's Millions*; John Wayne in *I Married a Woman*; Tony Curtis in *Chamber of Horrors*; Sammy Davis Jnr in *A Raisin in the Sun*; Shirley Maclaine in *Ocean's Eleven*; and Margaret Rutherford in *The ABC Murders*.

Sometimes a sequel not featuring the star of the first story will have a brief reminiscence of him with no credit: this happened to Cary Grant in *Topper Takes a Trip* and to Simone Signoret in *Life at the Top*. Then there are deliberate in-jokes like Walter Huston playing bit parts in his son John's movies, Peter Finch playing a messenger in *The First Men in the Moon* because he happened to be there when the hired actor failed to turn up, Joseph Cotten playing a small part in *Touch of Evil* because he dropped in to watch the location shooting and Orson Welles sent a make-up man over for old times' sake, Helen Hayes playing a small role in *Third Man on the Mountain* because her son James MacArthur was in the cast. Occasionally when stars are replaced during production, long shots of them remain in the completed film: thus Vivien Leigh in *Elephant Walk* and George Brent in *Death of a Scoundrel*. The best gag was played by Al Jolson who, determined to get into *The Jolson Story* at all costs, played himself in the theatre runway long shots during 'Swanee'.

There remain a few mysteries. In *The Great Ziegfeld*, 'A Pretty Girl is Like a Melody' was apparently sung by Stanley Morner, soon to become quite famous as Dennis Morgan. He was not credited (perhaps because the voice finally used on the sound track was that of Allan Jones). Nor were the following who had important roles to play and were well-known at the time: Constance Collier in *Anna Karenina*, Marlene Dietrich in *Touch of Evil*, Henry Daniell in *Mutiny on the Bounty*, Audrey Totter in *The Carpetbaggers*, Dorothy Malone and John Hubbard in *Fate is the Hunter*, Wilfrid Lawson in *Tread Softly Stranger*, Ava Gardner in *The Band Wagon*, Edmond O'Brien in *The Greatest Show on Earth*, David Warner in *Straw Dogs*, Henry Daniell in *My Fair Lady*, Edmond O'Brien in *The Greatest Show on Earth*, Mercedes

McCambridge in *Touch of Evil*, Glenda Jackson in *The Boy Friend*, Leo McKern in *The High Commissioner*. And in *Those Magnificent Men in Their Flying Machines*, Cicely Courtneidge and Fred Emney had roughly equal dialogue in their one scene; yet he was credited and she was not. The reasons surely can't have anything to do with modesty. See also: *directors' appearances*.

Under Two Flags. Ouida's romantic melodrama of the Foreign Legion was filmed in 1916 by J. Gordon Edwards, with Theda Bara as Cigarette; in 1922 by Tod Browning, with Priscilla Dean and Jack Kirkwood; and in 1936 by Frank Lloyd with Claudette Colbert and Ronald Colman.

Underdown, Edward (1908–). British actor on stage from 1932; once a jockey. Often cast as a dull Englishman.
The Warren Case 33 (debut). Wings of the Morning 37. They Were Not Divided 50. The Voice of Merrill 52. Beat the Devil 54. The Camp on Blood Island 58. The Day the Earth Caught Fire 62. Khartoum 66. The Hand of Night 67. Running Scared 72, etc.

underground films are generally thought of as those made cheaply to espouse a cause or experimentally at a director's whim, commercial success being a secondary consideration. Underground directors such as Andy Warhol have, however, successfully exploited the audience's desire to be 'with it', even though what they were with probably had no meaning.

underground railways have been used remarkably little in films considering their dramatic possibilities. There were chases through them in *Underground* itself, *Bulldog Jack, Waterloo Road, The French Connection, the Taking of Pelham One Two Three, Death Line* and *Death Wish*; they were also used for a comedy scene in *Rotten to the Core*, a murder in *Man Hunt, Otley*, and *The Liquidator*, and a musical number in *Three Hats for Lisa*. The New York subway was the setting for musical numbers in *Dames* ('I Only Have Eyes for You') and *On the Town* ('Miss Turnstiles' ballet), and it also featured in a romantic comedy (*Practically Yours*) and was the scene of a brutal beating-up in *The Young Savages* and a nasty accidental death in *P.J.*; while the whole of *Dutchman* took place on it, and *Short Walk To Daylight* began with an earthquake trapping passengers in it.

The New York elevated railway, on the other hand, was most dramatically used in *King Kong*, and provided effective backing in *The Lost Weekend, Union Station, The Bachelor Party, The FBI Story, Beneath the Planet of the Apes, Cry of the City* and *The French Connection*.

undertakers, or morticians, have provided comedy relief in many a western, relying on frequent shootings to bring in business: perhaps this theme was first explored in *The Westerner* 39. The comedy elements of the profession were also presented by Vincent Price and Peter Lorre in *A Comedy of Terrors*, by Terry-Thomas in *Strange Bedfellows*, by almost the entire cast of *The Loved One*, by Paul Lynde in *Send Me No Flowers*, and by J. Pat O'Malley in *Willard*. Literature's most famous undertaker is perhaps Mr Sowerberry in *Oliver Twist*, played by Gibb McLaughlin in the 1948 version and by Leonard Rossiter in *Oliver!*

underwater sequences of note were found in *Reap the Wild Wind, The Silent Enemy, The Beast from 20,000 Fathoms, The Golden Mistress, Twenty Thousand Leagues Under the Sea, Around the World Under the Sea, Voyage to the Bottom of the Sea, Thunderball, Shark*, and *Lady in Cement*.

See also: *submarines*.

Underworld (US 1927). Released in Britain as *Paying the Penalty*, this melodrama written by Ben Hecht and directed by Josef Von Sternberg did much to trigger off the gangster cycle. George Bancroft played 'Bull Weed', the anti-hero; Evelyn Brent was 'Feathers McCoy', his moll, and Clive Brook 'Rolls Royce', his side-kick.

unemployment in Britain was the somewhat unpopular subject of *Doss House, Love on the Dole*, and *The Common Touch*; in Europe, *Joyless Street, Little Man What Now?* and *Berliner Ballade*. America has seemed almost to boast about its unemployed, who were featured in *The Crowd, Our Daily Bread, Grapes of Wrath, Hallelujah I'm a Bum, Sullivan's Travels, I Am a Fugitive from a Chain Gang, The Great McGinty, One More Spring, Mr Deeds Goes to Town, Man's Castle, My Man Godfrey* and *Tobacco Road*, among many others.

Unfaithfully Yours (US 1948). Vintage satirical comedy, and the last good one to be written and directed by Preston Sturges. Rex Harrison plays Sir Alfred de Carter (!), a jealous orchestral conductor who suspects his wife of infidelity and plots three revenges during a concert; murder during Rossini, renunciation during Wagner, suicide during Tchaikovsky. 1983 brought a tolerable Dudley Moore remake.

unfinished films. Among the productions which ran out of money halfway, or were terminated for other reasons, are Josef Von Sternberg's *I Claudius*; Errol Flynn's *William Tell*; Orson Welles' *Don Quixote*, *The Other Side of the Moon* and *It's All True*; Eisenstein's *Que Viva Mexico*; Brecht's *Mother Courage*; Zinnemann's *Man's Fate*; David Miller's *The Bells of Hell go Ting-a-ling-a-ling*; Marilyn Monroe in *Something's Got to Give*, and Willis O'Brien's *Creation*. Films which had troubles but were completed in scrappy fashion include Michael Caine in *The Jigsaw Man*, James Caan in *Man Without Mercy*, Natalie Wood in *Brainstorm*, Bela Lugosi in *Plan 9 from Outer Space*, and Bruce Lee in *Game of Death* (in which nearly ninety per cent of his role was played by doubles).

unfinished performances. Here are some cases of actors who began to film roles but then either walked off the set or were let go because of unhappiness, inadequacy or just plain cussedness. Replacements are in brackets.

George Segal in *'10'* (Dudley Moore); John Travolta in *American Gigolo* (Richard Gere); Richard Dreyfuss in *All that Jazz* (Roy Scheider); Marlon Brando in *Child's Play* (Robert Preston); Robert Mitchum in *Rosebud* (Peter O'Toole); Richard Harris in *Flap* (Anthony Quinn); Rip Torn in *Easy Rider* (Jack Nicholson); George C. Scott in *How to Steal a Million* (Eli Wallach); Judy Garland in *Valley of the Dolls* (Susan Hayward); Elvis Presley in *A Star is Born* (Kris Kristofferson); Lana Turner in *Anatomy of a Murder* (Lee Remick); Christopher Plummer in *Dr Dolittle* (Rex Harrison), Judy Garland in *Annie Get Your Gun* (Betty Hutton); Joan Crawford in *Hush Hush Sweet Charlotte* (Olivia de Havilland); Charles Laughton in *David Copperfield* (W. C. Fields); Tyrone Power in *Solomon and Sheba* (he died during filming) (Yul Brynner); Buddy Ebsen in *The Wizard of Oz* (Jack Haley); Bela Lugosi in *Frankenstein* (Boris Karloff).

Performers unavailable to play roles for which they were badly wanted include Cary Grant for *My Fair Lady* (Rex Harrison); Joan Crawford for *From Here to Eternity* (Deborah Kerr); Boris Karloff for *Arsenic and Old Lace* (Raymond Massey); Basil Radford and Naunton Wayne for *I See a Dark Stranger* (Garry Marsh and Tom Macaulay); Gary Cooper and Barbara Stanwyck for *Saboteur* (Robert Cummings and Priscilla Lane); Robert Newton for *The Paradine Case* (Louis Jourdan); Jessie Matthews for *A Damsel in Distress* (Joan Fontaine); Claude Rains for *Bride of Frankenstein* (Ernest Thesiger); Burt Lancaster for *Ben Hur* (Charlton Heston); Lon Chaney for *Dracula* (Bela Lugosi); Robert Donat for *Captain Blood* (Errol Flynn); Frank Sinatra for *Carousel* (Gordon Macrae); Jack Benny for *The Sunshine Boys* (George Burns); Jeff Chandler for *Operation Petticoat* (Cary Grant); Bette Davis and Errol Flynn for *Gone with the Wind* (Vivien Leigh and Clark Gable); W. C. Fields for *The Wizard of Oz* (Frank Morgan); Claude Rains for *The Day the Earth Stood Still* (Michael Rennie); George Raft for *High Sierra* and *The Maltese Falcon* (Humphrey Bogart).

The Uninvited (US 1943). Claimed as Hollywood's first attempt at a serious ghost story, this set-bound adventure now seems rather tame, with its phoney Devon village and cliff-top house in which a girl is driven to desperation by the spirit of her mother but saved by that of her father's mistress. But at least it broadened Hollywood's horizons, and Lewis Allen, directing his first film, led us deftly through the talky script. With Gail Russell, Ray Milland, Donald Crisp, Cornelia Otis Skinner; from a novel, *Uneasy Freehold*, by Dorothy Macardle.

United Artists Corporation was founded in 1919 by Mary Pickford, Douglas Fairbanks, Charlie Chaplin and D. W. Griffith, the object being to make and distribute their own and other people's quality product. Among the company's early successes were *His Majesty the American, Pollyanna* (the first film sold on a percentage basis), *Broken Blossoms, Way Down East*, and *A Woman of Paris*. In the mid-twenties Joe Schenck was brought in to run the company, and he in turn gained Valentino, Goldwyn, Keaton and Swanson; but later all were bought out by various syndicates. Howard Hughes contributed *Hell's Angels* and *Scarface*, but in the thirties the UA product began to thin out, partly because the company was purely a distributor and financer of independent producers, without any studio of its own or any large roster of stars under contract. The hardest times, with only inferior product to sell, were between 1948 and 1953; but after that a new board of directors, through careful choice of product, fought its way back to the top; despite the defection of half its executives to Orion, UA was again riding high with *The Magnificent Seven*, *The Battle of Britain*, *Tom Jones*, *One Flew Over the Cuckoo's Nest*, *Rocky* and the James Bond films. The eighties however brought the 40-million-dollar calamity of *Heaven's Gate* (book, *Final Cut*, by Steven Bach), and as we go to press UA is still recovering, having negotiated a merger with MGM.

¶ The lunatics have taken over the asylum.—*Robert Lord, 1919*

'We maniacs had fun and made good pictures and a lot of money. In the early years United Artists was a private golf club for the four of us.'—*Mary Pickford*

Universal Pictures was founded in 1912 by Carl Laemmle, an exhibitor turned producer. Universal City grew steadily and included among its output many of the most famous titles of Von Stroheim, Valentino and Lon Chaney. In 1930 came *All Quiet on the Western Front*, and soon after *Dracula* and *Frankenstein*, the precursors of a long line of horror pictures. Laemmle lost power in the mid-thirties and the studio settled down to be one of Hollywood's 'little two', producing mainly modest, low-budget co-features without too many intellectual pretensions. The Deanna Durbin series saved it from receivership, and there were occasional notable pictures: *Destry Rides Again, Hellzapoppin, Flesh and Fantasy*. The stars under contract were durable: Boris Karloff, Lon Chaney Jnr, Donald O'Connor, Abbott and Costello, Jeff Chandler, Audie Murphy. More ambition was noted in the fifties, when the era of the bread-and-butter picture was ended by TV. Decca Records gained a large measure of control, but in 1962 a merger gave the ultimate power to the Music Corporation of America, ex-agents and TV producers. The last few years have seen a steady resumption of prestige, with films like *Spartacus*, the Doris Day-Rock Hudson sex comedies, *Charade, The War Lord*, Ross Hunter's soapily sentimental but glossy remakes of Hollywood's choicest weepies, *Thoroughly Modern Millie, The Day of the Jackal, Earthquake, Airport* and *The Seven Per Cent Solution*. The company, now a division of MCA Inc, is currently one of Hollywood's most powerful sources of box-office films and television series, though its venture into 'enlightened' European production was fairly disastrous.

Clive Hirschhorn's splendidly illustrated book *The Universal Story* (1983) is an excellent critical history.

universities have scarcely been studied seriously by movie-makers. Of Britain's most venerable, Cambridge has served as a background for one light comedy, *Bachelor of Hearts*, and Oxford for another, *A Yank at Oxford*, which was subsequently parodied by Laurel and Hardy in *A Chump at Oxford*. *Charley's Aunt* (qv) was also set among dreaming spires. Dramas with Oxford settings include *Accident* and *The Mind Benders*. Provincial universities score one comedy (*Lucky Jim*) and one drama (*The Wild and the Willing*). American campuses used to feature in films of the *Hold That Co-Ed* type, the pleasantest to remember being *The Freshman* and *Horse Feathers*, with *How To Be Very Very Popular* a poor third; but in the late sixties student protest held sway in *The Strawberry Statement, Getting Straight, R.P.M., Drive He Said*, and *The Activist*. Other views of the American higher learning came in *Paper Chase, The Group, The Male Animal, Class of 44,* and *The Magic Garden of Stanley Sweetheart*.

unlikely behaviour

? In what film did:

1 Ralph Richardson play a villainous vicar?
2 Nigel Bruce appear as a strong man?
3 Basil Rathbone sing a music hall song?
4 James Mason play a Chinese?
5 James Stewart turn out to be the murderer?
6 Rex Harrison pretend to be a Gestapo officer?
7 Leslie Howard pretend to be an old lady?
8 Lionel Barrymore pretend to be an old lady?
9 George Sanders disguise himself as a woman?
10 Lon Chaney Jnr as the wolf man get himself cured and romantically attached?
11 John Barrymore become a circus acrobat?
12 Gale Sondergaard turn into a cat?
13 Mickey Rooney play a Japanese?
14 Edmund Gwenn play a professional murderer?
15 Humphrey Bogart play a vampire?
16 Marlene Dietrich make her entrance in a gorilla skin?
17 Anne Bancroft play a murderer?
18 Roland Young play a strangler?
19 Alice Faye get a pie in the face?

20 Reginald Denny turn into a monster?
21 Agnes Moorehead play a centenarian?
22 Mischa Auer impersonate a gorilla?
23 Fredric March sock Carole Lombard on the jaw?
24 Adolphe Menjou take part in a battle of fireworks?
25 Katharine Hepburn fall into a canal?
26 Joel McCrea join the chain gang?
27 Betty Hutton have sextuplets?
28 Dame May Whitty play a spy?
29 Groucho Marx play a historical personage?
30 Buster Keaton drive a bus?

Unsworth, Geoffrey (1914–78). British cinematographer.
The Million Pound Note 53. Hell Drivers 57. *A Night to Remember* 58. Northwest Frontier 59. The 300 Spartans 62. *Becket* (BFA) 64. Genghis Khan 65. Half a Sixpence 67. *2001: A Space Odyssey* 68. The Bliss of Mrs Blossom 68. The Assassination Bureau 68. The Reckoning 69. Three Sisters 70. *Cabaret* (AA) 72. Alice's Adventures in Wonderland 72. Zardoz 73. Murder on the Orient Express 74. Lucky Lady 75. A Matter of Time 76. The Great Train Robbery 78. Superman 78. Tess (AA, BFA) 79, etc.

U.P.A. (United Productions of America) was a cartoon factory which in the early fifties received generous critical plaudits for a hundred or so shorts and even pushed the Disney studio into a more sophisticated style. Its creations included Mr Magoo, Gerald McBoing Boing and Pete Hothead, and it specialized in a stylish economy of line and in an appeal to a much higher intelligence bracket than any cartoon had aspired to in the past.

Urban, Charles (1871–1942). American pioneer of British films. He left Edison to found his own production company in London, and especially developed commercial non-fiction films.

Ure, Mary (1933–1975). British leading actress of stage and (occasionally) screen.
□Storm over the Nile 55. Windom's Way 59. Look Back in Anger 59. *Sons and Lovers* 60. The Mind Benders 63. The Luck of Ginger Coffey 64. Custer of the West 67. Where Eagles Dare 68. Reflection of Fear 71.

Urecal, Minerva (1896–1966). American character actress.
Oh Doctor 37. Boys of the City 40. The Bridge of San Luis Rey 44. Who's Guilty? 47. The Lost Moment 48. Harem Girl 52. Miracle in the Rain 56. The Seven Faces of Dr Lao 64, etc.
TV series: Tugboat Annie.

Urich, Robert (–). American TV actor (*Vegas*) who has made a few films.
Endangered Species 82. The Ice Pirates 83. Turk 182 84.

Urquhart, Robert (1922–). Scottish character actor, in films since 1951 after stage experience.
You're Only Young Twice (debut) 51. Knights of the Round Table 54. You Can't Escape 56. The Curse of Frankenstein 56. Dunkirk 58. 55 Days at Peking 62. Murder at the Gallop 64. Country Dance 70, etc.
TV series: The Pathfinders 72. The Amazing Mr Goodall 74.

Ustinov, Peter (1921–). Garrulous, hirsute, multi-talented British actor-director-playwright-screenwriter-raconteur.
Autobiography 1978: *Dear Me*.
□AS ACTOR: Hullo Fame 40. Mein Kampf 40. The Goose Steps Out 41. One of Our Aircraft is Missing 42. Let the People Sing 42. The Way Ahead 44. *Private Angelo* 49. Odette 50. *Hotel Sahara* 51. The Magic Box 51. *Quo Vadis* (as Nero) 51. *Beau Brummell* (as George IV) 54. The Egyptian 54. We're No Angels 55. Lola Montez 55. The Man Who Wagged His Tail 57. The Spies 57. *The Sundowners* 60. *Spartacus* (AA) 60. *Romanoff and Juliet* 61. Billy Budd 62. Topkapi (AA) 64. John Goldfarb Please Come Home 65. Lady L 65. The Comedians 67. Blackbeard's Ghost 68. Hot Millions 68. Viva Max 69. Hammersmith is Out (&d) 72. One of Our Dinosaurs is Missing 75. Logan's Run 76. Treasure of Matecumbe 76. The Purple Taxi 77. The Last Remake of Beau Geste 77. Jesus of Nazareth (TV) 77. *Death on the Nile* (as Hercule Poirot) 78. Ashanti 78. The Thief of Bagdad (TV) 79. Charlie Chan and the Curse of the Dragon Queen 81. Evil Under the Sun 82. Memed My Hawk (& w, d) 83. Murder with Mirrors (TV) 85. Thirteen at Dinner (TV) 85. Dead Man's Folly (TV) 86.
□ AS DIRECTOR-WRITER: School for Secrets 46. *Vice Versa* 48. *Private Angelo* 49. Romanoff and Juliet 61. Billy Budd 62. Lady L 65.

Uys, Jamie (1921–). South African writer-producer-director.
Rip Van Winkle 60. *Dingaka* 64. The Professor and the Beauty Queen 67. Dirkie 69. Lost in the Desert 70. The Gods Must Be Crazy 81.

Answers

unlikely behaviour

1 *The Ghoul* □ 2 *Rebecca* □ (at a fancy dress ball) 3 *The Adventures of Sherlock Holmes* □ 4 *Genghis Khan* □ 5 *After the Thin Man* □ 6 *Night Train to Munich* □ 7 *The Scarlet Pimpernel* □ 8 *The Devil Doll* □ 9 *The Kremlin Letter* □ 10 *House of Dracula* □ 11 *The Great Profile* □ 12 *The Blue Bird* □ (and vice versa) 13 *Breakfast at Tiffany's* □ 14 *Foreign Correspondent* □ 15 *The Return of Dr X* □ 16 *Blonde Venus* □ 17 *Gorilla at Large* □ 18 *The Great Lover* □ 19 *Hollywood Cavalcade* □ 20 *Abbott and Costello Meet Dr Jekyll and Mr Hyde* □ 21 *The Lost Moment* □ 22 *My Man Godfrey* (1936) □ 23 *Nothing Sacred* □ 24 *The Housekeeper's Daughter* □ 25 *Summertime/ Summer Madness* □ 26 *Sullivan's Travels* □ 27 *The Miracle of Morgan's Creek* □ 28 *The Lady Vanishes* □ 29 *The Story of Mankind* (Peter Minuit) □ 30 *San Diego I Love You* □

V

Vaccaro, Brenda (1939–). American character actress.
Midnight Cowboy 69. Where It's At 69. I Love My Wife 70. Summertree 71. What's a Nice Girl Like You . . . ? (TV) 72. Honor Thy Father 73. Sunshine (TV) 74. Once is Not Enough 76. The House by the Lake 77. Airport 77 77. Capricorn One 78. Fast Charlie the Moonbeam Rider 78. Supergirl 84, etc.
TV series: Sara 76. Dear Detective 79.

Vadim, Roger (1927–) (Roger Vadim Plemiannikow). French writer-director.
Futures Vedettes (w) 54. *And God Created Woman* (wd) 56. Heaven Fell That Night (wd) 57. *Les Liaisons Dangereuses* (wd) 59. Warrior's Rest (wd) 62. Vice and Virtue (wd) 62. La Ronde (wd) 64. Nutty Naughty Château (Château en Suède) 64. The Game is Over (wd) 66. Histoires Extraordinaires (part) 68. Barbarella 68. Pretty Maids All in a Row 71. Don Juan 73. Night Games 79, etc.

The Vagabond King: see *If I Were King*.

Vague, Vera: see *Allen, Barbara Jo*.

Valenti, Jack (1921–). American executive, dynamic president of the Motion Picture Association of America.

Valentine, Joseph (1900–49) (Giuseppe Valentino). Italian-American cinematographer, long in Hollywood.
Curlytop 24. Speakeasy 29. Soup to Nuts 30. Night of Terror 33. Remember Last Night 35. The Moon's Our Home 36. Three Smart Girls 36. One Hundred Men and a Girl 37. Mad About Music 38. That Certain Age 38. First Love 39. My Little Chickadee 40. Spring Parade 40. *The Wolf Man* 41. *Saboteur* 42. *Shadow of a Doubt* 43. Guest Wife 45. Tomorrow Is Forever 46. Magnificent Doll 46. Possessed 47. *Sleep My Love* 48. *Rope* 48. Joan of Arc (AA) 48. Bride for Sale 49, etc.

Valentine, Karen (1948–). American light actress who has had most success on television.
Gidget Grows Up (TV) 69. The Daughters of Joshua Cabe (TV) 72. Coffee, Tea or Me? (TV) 73. The Girl Who Came Gift Wrapped (TV) 74. Having Babies (TV) 76. Murder at the World Series (TV) 77. Go West Young Girl (TV) 78. The North Avenue Irregulars 78, etc.
TV series: *Room 222* 69–72. Karen 75.

Valentino, Rudolph (1895–1926) (Rodolpho d'Antonguolla). Italian-American leading man, the great romantic idol of the twenties; his personality still shows. His sudden death caused several suicides and his funeral was a national event. Among the published biographies of him are his wife Natacha Rambova's *Rudy* 1926, George S. Ullman's *The Real Valentino* 1927, Alan Arnold's *Valentino* 1952, Robert Oberfirst's *Rudolph Valentino, The Man Behind the Myth* 1962, and Irving Shulman's *Valentino* 1967.
□My Official Wife 14. Patria 16. Alimony 18. A Society Sensation 18. All Night 18. The Delicious Little Devil 19. A Rogue's Romance 19. The Homebreaker 19. Virtuous Sinners 19. The Big Little Person 19. Out of Luck 19. Eyes of Youth 19. The Married Virgin 20. An Adventuress 20. The Cheater 20. Passion's Playground 20. Once to Every Woman 20. Stolen Moments 20. The Wonderful Chance 20. *The Four Horsemen of the Apocalypse* (the part that made him a super-star) 21. Unchained Seas 21. Camille 21. The Conquering Power 21. *The Sheik* 21. Moran of the Lady Letty 21. Beyond the Rocks 22. The Young Rajah 22. *Blood and Sand* 22. *Monsieur Beaucaire* 24. A Sainted Devil 24. Cobra 24. *The Eagle* 25. *Son of the Sheik* 26.
❀ For turning animal magnetism into at least the semblance of talent. *The Eagle*.
† There have been two films called *Valentino*. Anthony Dexter played him in 1951, Rudolf Nureyev in 1977. A TV movie, *The Legend of Valentino*, appeared in 1975 with Franco Nero.

¶ His acting is largely confined to protruding his large, almost occult eyes until the vast areas of white are visible, drawing back the lips of his wide, sensuous mouth to bare his gleaming teeth, and flaring his nostrils.

Thus Adolph Zukor's famous put-down; but Valentino's simple technique was very effective on female audiences the world over. Yet in the year of his death, 1926, he wrote:

A man should control his life. Mine is controlling me.

And H. L. Mencken summed him up:

He was essentially a highly respectable young man; his predicament touched me. Here was one who was catnip to women . . . he had youth and fame . . . and yet he was very unhappy.

Valk, Frederick (1901–1956). Heavyweight Czech stage actor, in Britain from 1939.
Gasbags 40. *Thunder Rock* 42. *Dead of Night* 45. Latin Quarter 46. An Outcast of the Islands 51. Top Secret 52. The Colditz Story 53. Zarak 55, etc.

Vallee, Rudy (1901–86) (Hubert Vallee). American character comedian, the former crooning idol of the late twenties; in the early forties Preston Sturges gave him a new lease of life.
Autobiography 1976: *Let the Chips Fall.*
The Vagabond Lover 29. Sweet Music 34. Gold Diggers in Paris 38. Second Fiddle 39. Too Many Blondes 41. *The Palm Beach Story* 42. Happy Go Lucky 43. It's in the Bag 45. *The Bachelor and the Bobbysoxer* 47. Unfaithfully Yours 48. The Beautiful Blonde from Bashful Bend 49. Ricochet Romance 54. Gentlemen Marry Brunettes 55. The Helen Morgan Story 57. *How to Succeed in Business Without Really Trying* (his stage role) 67. Live a Little, Love a Little 68. Won Ton Ton 76, etc.

¶ People called me the guy with the cock in his voice. Maybe that's why in 84 years of life I've been with over 145 women and girls.—*R.V. in The RKO Story*
Famous line (*The Palm Beach Story*): That's one of the tragedies of life—that the men most in need of a beating-up are always enormous.

Valley of the Dolls (US 1967). A workaday film version of a notorious novel by Jacqueline Susann about the effect of drugs on Hollywood actresses. Directed by Mark Robson, it proved a little tame for sensation seekers. An apparent 1970 sequel, *Beyond the Valley of the Dolls*, had nothing in common with the original, being a fairly outlandish sexploitation epic by porn director Russ Meyer.

Valli, Alida (1921–) (Alida Maria Altenburger). Beautiful Italian actress.
I Due Sergenti 36. Manon Lescaut 39. Piccolo Mondo Antico 41. Eugénie Grandet 46. The Paradine Case (US) 47. The Miracle of the Bells 48. *The Third Man* 49. Walk Softly Stranger 49. The White Tower 50. The Lovers of Toledo 52. *Senso* 53. The Stranger's Hand 53. Heaven Fell That Night 57. The Sea Wall (This Angry Age) 57. Le Dialogue des Carmélites 59. Ophelia 61. Une Aussi Longue Absence 61. The Spider's Stratagem 71. 1900 76. The Cassandra Crossing 77. Suspiria 77. Aspern 82, etc.

Valli, Virginia (1898–1968) (Virginia McSweeney). American silent screen heroine who retired in 1932 to marry Charles Farrell.
Efficiency Edgar's Courtship 17. The Storm 22. A Lady of Quality 23. Paid to Love 27. Isle of Lost Ships 32, etc.

Vallone, Raf (1916–). Italian leading man, former journalist.
Bitter Rice 48. Vendetta 49. Il Cristo Proibito 50. Anna 51. Thérèse Raquin 53. The Beach 53. The Sign of Venus 55. El Cid 61. *A View from the Bridge* (US) 61. Phaedra 62. The Cardinal 63. Harlow 65. Beyond the Mountains 66. The Italian Job 69. Cannon for Cordoba 70. A Gunfight 71. Rosebud 75. The Human Factor 75. The Other Side of Midnight 77. The Greek Tycoon 78. An Almost Perfect Affair 79. A Time to Die 79. Lion of the Desert 80. The Scarlet and the Black (TV) 83. Power of Evil 85, etc.

Vampyr (France 1931). Also called *The Strange Adventure of David Gray*, this chic and mystical horror film by Carl Dreyer, with misty photography by Rudolf Maté, is slow, unsatisfying and mystifying to sit through. Its fame rests on a number of effective moments, notably the hero's dream of death and the villain's end in a flour mill (buried in white flour), which have been much copied.

Van, Bobby (1930–1980) (Robert Stein King). American song-and-dance man who went out of fashion with musicals but found a new audience in his forties and became a TV personality.
□Because You're Mine 52. Small Town Girl 52. Kiss Me Kate 53. The Navy Versus the Night Monsters 66. *Lost Horizon* 73. Lost Flight (TV) 73.

Van Cleef, Lee (1925–). American character actor who after years as a sneaky western villain found fame and fortune as the hero of tough Italian westerns.
High Noon 52. Arena 53. Yellow Tomahawk

54. A Man Alone 55. Joe Dakota 57. Guns Girls and Gangsters 58. The Man Who Shot Liberty Valance 62. *For a Few Dollars More* 65. Day of Anger 66. *The Good the Bad and the Ugly* 67. Death Rides a Horse 67. Sabata 69. Barquero 70. El Condor 70. Captain Apache 71. Bad Man's River 71. The Magnificent Seven Ride 72. Take a Hard Ride 75. Vendetta 76. God's Gun 77. Kid Vengeance 77. The Octagon 80. Escape from New York 81. The Squeeze 82, etc.

Van Devere, Trish (1943–). American leading lady of the seventies.
Where's Poppa? 70. The Last Run 71. One is a Lonely Number 72. The Day of the Dolphins 73. Beauty and the Beast (TV) 76. Movie Movie 78. The Hearse 80. The Changeling 80, etc.

¶ Barely more than a smiling hole in the air.—*Sunday Times*

Van Dine, S. S. (1888–1939) (Willard Huntingdon Wright). American author who created the wealthy man-about-town detective Philo Vance, personified on screen by several actors. William Powell played him in *The Canary Murder Case* 29, *The Greene Murder Case* 29, *The Benson Murder Case* 30, and *The Kennel Murder Case* 33. Basil Rathbone had one attempt, *The Bishop Murder Case* 30. Warren William took over for *The Dragon Murder Case* 34 and *The Gracie Allen Murder Case* 39. Meanwhile there were Paul Lukas in *The Casino Murder Case* 35, Edmund Lowe in *The Garden Murder Case* 36, and Grant Richards in *Night of Mystery* 37. 1940 brought James Stephenson in *Calling Philo Vance*; in 1947 there was William Wright in *Philo Vance Returns*; and Alan Curtis in 1948 appeared in two poor attempts, *Philo Vance's Gamble* and *Philo Vance's Secret Mission.*

Van Doren, Mamie (1933–) (Joan Lucille Olander). American leading lady, the blonde bombshell of the second feature, in Hollywood from 1954.
Forbidden (debut) 54. Yankee Pasha 54. The Second Greatest Sex 55. Running Wild 55. The Girl in Black Stockings 56. Teacher's Pet 58. The Navy Versus the Night Monsters 66, etc.

Van Druten, John (1901–1957). British dramatist who latterly lived in America.
Plays filmed include *Young Woodley, I Am a Camera, Old Acquaintance, The Voice of the Turtle, I Remember Mama.*

Van Dyke, Dick (1925–). Lanky American TV comedian who never quite made it in movies.
□Bye Bye Birdie 63. What a Way to Go 64. *Mary Poppins* 64. The Art of Love 65. Lt Robin Crusoe 65. Never a Dull Moment 67. Divorce American Style 67. Fitzwilly 67. Chitty Chitty Bang Bang 68. *The Comic* 69. Some Kind of a Nut 70. Cold Turkey 71. The Morning After (TV) 74. The Runner Stumbles 79. Dropout Father (TV) 82. Found Money (TV) 84. The Wrong Way Kid (TV) 84. Strong Medicine (TV) 86.
TV series: *The Dick Van Dyke Show* 61–66. The New Dick Van Dyke Show 71–72.

Van Dyke, W. S. (1889–1943). Competent, adaptable American director, at his peak in the thirties.
□Men of the Desert 18. Gift of Gab 18. Land of Long Shadows 18. Open Spaces 18. Lady of the Dugout 19. Our Little Nell 20. According to Hoyle 22. Boss of Camp 4 22. Forget Me Not 22. Little Girl Next Door 23. Miracle Makers 23. Loving Lies 23. You Are In Danger 23. The Destroying Angel 23. The Battling Fool 24. Winner Take All 24. Barriers Burned Away 24. Half Dollar Bill 24. The Beautiful Sinner 25. Gold Heels 25. Hearts and Spurs 25. The Trail Rider 25. Ranger of the Big Pines 25. The Timber Wolf 25. The Desert's Price 25. The Gentle Cyclone 26. War Paint 26. Winners of the Wilderness 27. Heart of the Yukon 27. Eyes of the Totem 27. Foreign Devils 27. California 27. Spoilers of the West 27. Wyoming 28. Under the Black Eagle 28. *White Shadows in the South Seas* 28. The Pagan 29. *Trader Horn* 30. Never the Twain Shall Meet 31. Guilty Hands 31. Cuban Love Song 32. *Tarzan the Ape Man* 32. Night World 32. Penthouse 33. Eskimo 33. The Prizefighter and the Lady 33. Laughing Boy 34. Hideout 34. *Manhattan Melodrama* 34. *The Thin Man* 34. Forsaking all Others 35. Naughty Marietta 35. I Live My Life 35. Rose Marie 36. *San Francisco* 36. His Brother's Wife 36. The Devil is a Sissy 36. Love on the Run 36. After the Thin Man 36. Personal Property 37. They Gave Him a Gun 37. Rosalie 37. Marie Antionette 38. *Sweethearts* 38. Stand Up and Fight 39. It's a Wonderful World 39. Andy Hardy Gets Spring Fever 39. Another Thin Man 39. I Take This Woman 40. I Love You Again 40. Bitter Sweet 40. Rage in Heaven 41. The Feminine Touch 41. Shadow of the Thin Man 41. Dr Kildare's Victory 41. I Married an Angel 42. Cairo 42. Journey for Margaret 42.

Van Enger, Charles (1890–). American cinematographer.
Treasure Island 20. A Doll's House 22. The Famous Mrs Fair 23. The Marriage Circle 24. Forbidden Paradise 24. *Phantom of the Opera* 25. Kiss Me Again 25. Puppets 26. Easy Pickings 27. Port of Missing Girls 28. Fox Movietone Follies 29. High Society Blues 30. Mad Parade 31. I Was a Spy 33. The Case of Gabriel Perry 34. Seven Sinners 36. Wife Doctor and Nurse 37. Miracle on Main Street 40. Never Give a Sucker an Even Break 41. Night Monster 42. Sherlock Holmes Faces Death 43. The Merry Monahans 44. That Night with You 45. The Time of Their Lives 46. The Wistful Widow 47. Abbott and Costello Meet Frankenstein 48. Africa Screams 49. Ma and Pa Kettle Back on the Farm 51. The Magnetic Monster 53. Sitting Bull 54. Time Table 56. Gun Fever 58, many others.

Van Eyck, Peter (1911–1969). Blond German actor, in America from mid-thirties, later international.
The Moon is Down 42. Five Graves to Cairo 43. Rommel, Desert Fox 51. *The Wages of Fear* 53. Retour de Manivelle 57. The Girl Rosemarie 58. The Snorkel 58. Foxhole in Cairo 60. Station Six Sahara 63. The Spy Who Came in from the Cold 65. Million Dollar Man 67. Shalako 68. Assignment to Kill 69, many others.

Van Eyssen, John (1925–). South African actor who appeared in a number of British films before turning agent.
Quatermass II 56. Dracula 57. I'm All Right Jack 59. The Criminal 60. Exodus 60, etc.
1969–73: chief production executive in Britain for Columbia.

Van Fleet, Jo (1919–). American character actress who usually plays older than her real age.
□*East of Eden* (AA) 55. The Rose Tattoo 55. I'll Cry Tomorrow 55. The King and Four Queens 56. Gunfight at the OK Corral 57. This Angry Age 58. *Wild River* 60. Cool Hand Luke 67. I Love You Alice B. Toklas 67. 80 Steps to Jonah 69. The Gang that Couldn't Shoot Straight 72. The Tenant 76.

Van Heusen, Jimmy (1919–). American songwriter, usually with lyrics by Johnny Burke. 'Swinging on a Star' (AA 1944), 'Sunday, Monday or Always', 'Sunshine Cake', many others; films include *Road to Rio* 47. *A Yankee in King Arthur's Court* 49. *Road to Bali* 53. *Little Boy Lost* 53, etc.

Van Pallandt, Nina (1932–). Danish actress, formerly singer.
The Long Goodbye 73. Guilty or Innocent (TV) 75. Quintet 78. A Wedding 79. American Gigolo 80. Cloud Dancer 80.

Van Parys, Georges (1902–1971). French composer.
Le Million 31. Jeunesse 34. Café de Paris 38. Le Silence est d'Or 46. Fanfan La Tulipe 51. Adorables Créatures 52. Les Diaboliques 55. French Cancan 55. Charmants Garçons 57, many others.

Van Patten, Dick (1928–). Chubby American character actor usually in comedy roles; husband of Joyce Van Patten.
Joe Kidd 72. Westworld 73. The Strongest Man in the World 75. Gus 76. Freaky Friday 77. High Anxiety 77, etc.
TV series: *Eight is Enough* 77–83.

Van Patten, Joyce (1934–). American leading lady of the seventies. Wife of Dick Van Patten.
The Goddess 58. I Love You Alice B. Toklas 68. Something Big 71. The Bravos (TV) 72. Thumb Tripping 72. The Manchu Eagle Murder Caper Mystery 75, etc.

Van Peebles, Melvin (1932–). Black American director. The Story of a Three-Day Pass 67. Watermelon Man 69. Sweet Sweetback's 71, etc.

Van Rooten, Luis (1906–1973). Mexican-born American character actor.
The Hitler Gang (as Himmler) 44. Two Years Before the Mast 44. To the Ends of the Earth 48. Champion 49. Detective Story 51. The Sea Chase 55, etc.

Van Sloan, Edward (1882–1964). American character actor with stage experience; often seen as elderly professors.
Dracula 30. *Frankenstein* 31. The Mummy 33. Death Takes a Holiday 34. The Last Days of Pompeii 35. *Dracula's Daughter* 36. The Phantom Creeps 39. The Doctor Takes a Wife 40. The Conspirators 44. The Mask of Dijon 47. A Foreign Affair 47, etc.

Van Upp, Virginia (1912–1970). American executive producer, at Columbia in the late forties. Former writer.
Young and Willing 40. The Crystal Ball 42. Cover Girl 44. The Impatient Years (& p) 44. Together Again (& p) 45, etc.

Van Vorhees, Westbrook (1904–1968). American commentator whose familiar stentorian voice as narrator of *The March of Time* was widely imitated.

Van Zandt, Philip (1904–1958). Dutch character actor, in Hollywood films.
Citizen Kane 41. House of Frankenstein 45. April Showers 48. Viva Zapata 52. Knock on Wood 54. The Pride and the Passion 57, etc.

Vanbrugh, Irene (1872–1949) (Irene Barnes). Distinguished British stage actress. Films rare.
Autobiography 1978: *To Tell My Story*.
The Gay Lord Quex 27. Moonlight Sonata 37.

Vance, Vivian (1911–1979). Cheerful American character comedienne, long a partner of Lucille Ball in various TV series.
The Secret Fury 50. The Blue Veil 51. The Great Race 65, etc.

Vanel, Charles (1892–). French character actor, with stage experience.
Les Misérables 33. Le Grand Jeu 34. La Belle Equipe 36. Légion d'Honneur 38. Carrefour 39. *La Ferme du Pendu* 45. In Nome della Legge 49. *The Wages of Fear* 53. Maddalena 54. *Les Diaboliques* 55. Rafles sur la Ville 57. Le Dialogue des Carmélites 59. La Vérité 60. Un Homme de Trop 67. La Puce et le Privé 79, many others.

Vangelis (–) (Vangelis Papathanassiou). British composer.
Chariots of Fire (AA) 81. Missing 82. Blade Runner 82. The Bounty 84.

Varconi, Victor (1896–1976) (Mihaly Varkonyi). Hungarian actor long in Hollywood.
Autobiography 1976: *It's Not Enough to be Hungarian*.
The Volga Boatmen 26. King of Kings 27. The Divine Lady (as Nelson) 29. The Doomed Battalion 31. Roberta 34. The Plainsman 36. Disputed Passage 39. Reap the Wild Wind 42. For Whom the Bell Tolls 43. Samson and Delilah 49, etc.

Varda, Agnes (1928–). French writer-director of the 'left bank' school.
La Pointe Courte 56. Cléo de 5 à 7 62. Le Bonheur 65. Les Créatures 66. Lions Love 69, etc.

Varden, Evelyn (1895–1958). American stage character actress who made several films.
Pinky 49. Cheaper by the Dozen 50. Phone Call from a Stranger 52. The Student Prince 54. Night of the Hunter 55. The Bad Seed 56, etc.

Varden, Norma (c. 1898–). British character actress, usually as haughty aristocrat in comedies; went to Hollywood in the forties.
A Night Like This 32. The Iron Duke 35. Foreign Affairs 36. Shipyard Sally 39. Random Harvest 42. The Green Years 46. Strangers on a Train 51. Gentlemen Prefer Blondes 53. Witness for the Prosecution 58. The Sound of Music 65. Doctor Dolittle 67, many others.

variable area and **variable density.** Types of sound track. Variable area appears as a spiky symmetrical line (like a long folded ink blot). Variable density is the same width throughout but with horizontal bars of varying light and shade.

Variety (Germany 1925). Also known as *Vaudeville*, this trapeze melodrama had a plot very similar to the later *Three Maxims* and *Trapeze*. Solemnly but sylishly directed by E. A Dupont, with Emil Jannings, Warwick Ward and Lya de Putti.

Varley, Beatrice (1896–1969). British character actress who played worried little elderly ladies for thirty years.
Hatter's Castle 41. So Well Remembered 47. No Room at the Inn 49. Hindle Wakes 53. The Feminine Touch 55, scores of others.

Varnel, Marcel (1894–1947). French-born director, in Hollywood from 1924; came to England in the thirties and made some of the best comedies of Will Hay and the Crazy Gang.
The Silent Witness 32. Chandu the Magician 32. Girls will be Boys 34. No Monkey Business 35. Good Morning Boys 36. OK for Sound 37. *Oh Mr Porter* 38. Convict 99 38. *Alf's Button Afloat* 38. *Old Bones of the River* 38. *Ask a Policeman* 39. *The Frozen Limits* 39. Where's that Fire? 39. Let George Do It 40. Gasbags 40. I Thank You 41. Hi Gang 41. *The Ghost of St Michaels* 41. Much Too Shy 42. King Arthur was a Gentleman 42. Get Cracking 43. He Snoops to Conquer 44. I

Didn't Do It 45. George in Civvy Street 46. This Man is Mine 46. The First Gentleman 47, etc.

¶ 'The only pure comedy director we've ever had in this country.'—*Basil Wright*

Varnel, Max (1925–). British second feature director, son of Marcel Varnel.
A Woman Possessed 58. The Great Van Robbery 49. A Taste of Money 60. Return of a Stranger 61. Enter Inspector Duval 62. The Silent Invasion 63, etc.

Varney, Reg (1922–). Chirpy British comedian who after years of availability found fame in the sixties in TV series *The Rag Trade* and *On the Buses*.
The Great St Trinian's Train Robbery 66. On the Buses 71. Mutiny on the Buses 72. Go for a Take 72. The Best Pair of Legs in the Business 72. Holiday on the Buses 73, etc.

Varsi, Diane (1938–). Slightly-built American leading lady who had a brief career in the fifties, with sporadic appearances later.
□*Peyton Place* 57. *Ten North Frederick* 58. From Hell to Texas 59. Compulsion 59. Sweet Love, Bitter 66. Wild in the Streets 68. Killers Three 69. Bloody Mama 70. Johnny Got His Gun 71. I Never Promised You a Rose Garden 77.

vaudeville is the American equivalent of the British *music hall.* Eight or ten variety acts, booked separately, formed a two-hour bill for the family. Burlesque was different, being for adults only.

Vaughan, Frankie (1928–) (Frank Abelsohn). Flamboyant British song and dance man who never really made it in movies despite a sojourn in Hollywood.
□Ramsbottom Rides Again 56. *These Dangerous Years* 57. The Lady is a Square 58. Wonderful Things 58. Heart of a Man 59. Let's Make Love 61. The Right Approach 62. It's All Over Town 64.

Vaughan, Peter (1923–) (Peter Ohm). British character actor of solid presence, good or evil.
Sapphire 59. Village of the Damned 60. The Punch and Judy Man 63. Fanatic 65. The Naked Runner 67. Hammerhead 68. The Bofors Gun 68. Alfred the Great 69. Eye Witness 70. Straw Dogs 71. The Pied Piper 72. 11 Harrowhouse 74. Zulu Dawn 79. Fox (TV) 80. Time Bandits 81. The French Lieutenant's Woman 81. Jamaica Inn (TV) 83. The Razor's Edge 84. Brazil 85. Haunted Honeymoon 86. Monte Carlo (TV) 86. War and Remembrance (TV) 87. The Bourne Identity 88.

Vaughn, Robert (1932–). Slight, intense American actor who didn't quite make the front rank.
Teenage Caveman 58. No Time to be Young 58. The Young Philadelphians 59. *The Magnificent Seven* 60. The Big Show 61. The Caretakers 63. One Spy Too Many 66. The Venetian Affair 67. The Helicopter Spies 68. Bullitt 68. The Mind of Mr Soames 69. The Bridge at Remagen 69. The Statue 71. The Towering Inferno 74. *Washington Behind Closed Doors* (TV) 76. Brass Target 78. Good Luck Miss Wyckoff 79. Battle Beyond the Stars 80. Inside the Third Reich (TV) 82. The Return of the Man from UNCLE (TV) 83. Superman III 83. Private Sessions (TV) 85. International Airport (TV) 85. The Delta Force 85. Hour of the Assassin 87, etc.
TV series: The Lieutenant 63. *The Man from UNCLE* 64–67. The Protectors 72.

Védrès, Nicole (1911–1965). French director, mainly of probing documentaries.
Paris 1900 47. *La Vie Commence Demain* 50. Aux Frontières de l'Homme 53, etc.

Veidt, Conrad (1893–1943). Distinguished German character actor who also filmed in Britain and Hollywood.
The Cabinet of Dr Caligari 19. *Waxworks* 24. Lucrezia Borgia 25. *The Student of Prague* 26. *The Hands of Orlac* 26. The Beloved Rogue (US) 27. The Man Who Laughs 27. Rasputin 30. *Congress Dances* 31. *Rome Express* (GB) 32. I Was a Spy (GB) 33. F.P.I. 33. The Wandering Jew (GB) 33. Jew Süss (GB) 34. Bella Donna (GB) 34. *The Passing of the Third Floor Back* (GB) 35. King of the Damned (GB) 35. *Under the Red Robe* (GB) 36. *Dark Journey* (GB) 37. *The Spy in Black* (GB) 39. Contraband (GB) 40. *The Thief of Baghdad* (GB) 40. Escape (US) 40. A Woman's Face (US) 41. Whistling in the Dark (US) 41. All Through the Night (US) 41. The Men in Her Life (US) 42. Nazi Agent (US) 42. Casablanca (US) 42. Above Suspicion (US) 43, etc.
❀ For his almost liquid villainy, and for a score of authentic star performances. *The Thief of Baghdad.*

¶ Women fight for Conrad Veidt!—*thirties publicity*

No matter what roles I play, I can't get Caligari out of my system.—*C.V.*

Veiller, Anthony (1903–1965). American scriptwriter, in Hollywood from 1930.
Her Cardboard Lover 42. The Killers 46. Along the Great Divide 51. Moulin Rouge 53. Red Planet Mars (& p) 53. Safari 56. The List of Adrian Messenger 63, many others.

Velez, Lupe (1908–1944) (Guadeloupe Velez de Villalobos). Temperamental Mexican leading lady of the thirties; best remembered with Leon Errol in the Mexican Spitfire series.
The Gaucho 27. Wolf Song 29. East is West 30. The Squaw Man 31. Kongo 32. Hot Pepper 33. Palooka 34. The Morals of Marcus (GB) 36. Gypsy Melody (GB) 37. *The Girl from Mexico* 39. *Mexican Spitfire* 39. Six Lessons from Madame La Zonga 41. Playmates 42. Mexican Spitfire's Elephant 42. Mexican Spitfire's Blessed Event 43, many others.

¶ *L.V.:* The first time you buy a house you think how pretty it is and sign the cheque. The second time you look to see if the basement has termites. It's the same with men.

Venable, Evelyn (1913–). American leading lady of the thirties, usually in demure roles.
Cradle Song 33. Mrs Wiggs of the Cabbage Patch 34. Alice Adams 35. The Frontiersman 38. He Hired the Boss (last to date) 43, etc.

Veness, Amy (1876–1960). British character actress who latterly played cheerful old souls.
My Wife's Family 31. Hobson's Choice 31. Lorna Doone 35. Aren't Men Beasts? 37. Yellow Sands 39. The Man in Grey 43. This Happy Breed 44. Here Come the Huggetts 49. Doctor in the House 54, etc.

Venice has been most persuasively caught by the movie camera in *Summertime, Venetian Bird*, and (for the depressed view) *Death in Venice* and *Don't Look Now*.

Ventham, Wanda (1938–). British leading lady.
My Teenage Daughter 56. The Navy Lark 59. Solo for Sparrow 62. The Cracksman 63. The Big Job 65. The Knack 65. The Spy with a Cold Nose 67. Carry On Up the Khyber 68. Captain Kronos 73. Lost Empires (TV) 86, etc.

ventriloquists rarely stray from music hall to cinema, but Michael Redgrave played a demented one in *Dead of Night,* and very similar themes were explored in 1929's *The Great Gabbo*, in 1964's *Devil Doll* and in 1978's *Magic.* A vent's dummy was used for comedy in *Knock on Wood*, for satire in *How I Won the War*, and for mystery in *The Dummy Talks* and *The Thirty-Nine Steps* (1959 version). The most movie-exposed performing ventriloquist is certainly Edgar Bergen, who with his dummies Charlie McCarthy and Mortimer Snerd appeared in a dozen or more films between 1937 and 1944.

Ventura, Lino (1920–87) (Angelino Borrini). Italian leading man, former boxer.
Touchez Pas au Grisbi 53. Marie Octobre 57. Crooks in Clover 63. Les Aventuriers 67. The Valachi Papers 72. Wild Horses (US) 72. La Bonne Année 73. The Pink Telephone 75. Le Silencieux 76. Sunday Lovers 80. Les Misérables 82, others.

Vera-Ellen (1920–1981) (Vera-Ellen Westmeyr Rohe). Diminutive American dancer and songstress of forties musicals.
□*Wonder Man* 45. The Kid from Brooklyn 46. Three Little Girls in Blue 46. Carnival in Costa Rica 47. Words and Music 48. Love Happy 49. *On the Town* 49. Three Little Words 50. Happy Go Lovely (GB) 51. The Belle of New York 52. *Call Me Madam* 53. The Big Leaguer 53. White Christmas 54. Let's Be Happy (GB) 56.

Verdon, Gwen (1925–). Vivacious American dancer and singer, once married to Bob Fosse.
□On the Riviera 51. Meet Me After the Show 51. David and Bathsheba 51. The Merry Widow 52. The I Don't Care Girl 53. The Farmer Takes a Wife 53. *Damn Yankees* 58. Legs (TV) 83. The Cotton Club 84. Cocoon 85. Nadine 87.

Verdugo, Elena (1926–). Spanish-American leading lady.
Down Argentine Way 40. The Moon and Sixpence 42. House of Frankenstein 45. Song of Scheherazade 47. Cyrano de Bergerac 50. Thief of Damascus 52. How Sweet It Is 68, etc.
TV series: Meet Millie 52. The New Phil Silvers Show 63. *Marcus Welby M.D.* 69–75.

Vereen, Ben (1946–). Black American dancer.
Funny Lady 75. *Roots* (TV) 77. All That Jazz 79.
TV series: Tenspeed and Brown Shoe 80.

Vermilyea, Harold (1889–1958). Russian-American character actor, former operatic singer.
O.S.S. 46. The Big Clock 48. Edge of Doom 50. Born to be Bad 51, etc.

Verne, Jules (1828–1905). French adventure novelist whose inventive science-fiction themes have latterly endeared him to Hollywood. Films of his works since 1954 include *Twenty Thousand Leagues Under the Sea, Around the World in Eighty Days, From Earth to the Moon, Journey to the Centre of the Earth, Five Weeks in a Balloon, Master of the World, The Children of Captain Grant (In Search of the Castaways), Rocket to the Moon, The Light at the Edge of the World, The Southern Star* and *Michael Strogoff.*

Verne, Karen (1915–67) (Ingabor Katrine Klinckerfuss). German leading lady who made a number of Hollywood films.
Ten Days in Paris (GB) 39. All Through the Night 41. King's Row 42. The Seventh Cross 44. A Bullet for Joey 55. Ship of Fools 65. Torn Curtain 67, etc.

Verneuil, Henri (1920–). French director, former journalist.
La Table aux Crevés 50. Forbidden Fruit 52. Public Enemy Number One 53. Paris Palace Hotel 56. The Cow and I 59. L'Affaire d'une Nuit 61. The Big Snatch (Mélodie en Sous-Sol) 63. Guns for San Sebastian 68. The Burglars 71. The Serpent 72. The Night Caller 72, many others.

Verno, Jerry (1895–1975). British cockney character actor.
His Lordship 32. The Thirty-Nine Steps 35. Farewell Again 37. Old Mother Riley in Paris 38. The Common Touch 41. The Red Shoes 48. The Belles of St Trinian's 54. After the Ball 57, many others.

Vernon, Anne (1925–) (Edith Vignaud). Vivacious French leading lady who has also filmed in Britain and Hollywood.
Le Mannequin Assassiné 48. Warning to Wantons (GB) 48. Shakedown (US) 49. *Edward and Caroline* 50. Rue de l'Estrapade 52. The Love Lottery (GB) 54. Time Bomb (GB) 54. Le Long des Trottoirs 56. Les Lavandières de Portugal 57. *The Umbrellas of Cherbourg* 64. Patate 64. La Démoniaque 67. Therese and Isabelle 68, etc.

Vernon, Bobby (1896–1939). Boyish American star comedian of the silents, usually in shorts.

Vernon, John (1935–). Canadian character actor.
Point Blank 67. Topaz 69. Dirty Harry 71. One More Train to Rob 71. The Black Windmill 74. The Outlaw Josey Wales 76. A Special Day 76. National Lampoon's Animal House 78. Herbie Goes Bananas 80, etc.

Vernon, Richard (1925–). British character actor of stage and TV, usually in soft-spoken aristocratic roles.
Accidental Death 63. A Hard Day's Night 64. Goldfinger 64. The Secret of My Success 65. The Satanic Rites of Dracula 73. The Pink Panther Strikes Again 76. The Human Factor 79. O Heavenly Dog 80. Evil Under the Sun 82. Gandhi 82, many others.

Vernon, Wally (1904–1970). American eccentric comedian.
Mountain Music 37. Alexander's Ragtime Band 38. The Gorilla 39. Tahiti Honey 43. Always Leave Them Laughing 49. What Price Glory? 52. What a Way to Go 64, many others.

verse and worse

? Can you name the films in which the following snatches of poetry, verse or song were of significance?

1 So stand by, your glasses steady.
The world is a world of lies.
Here's to the dead already—
Hurrah for the next man who dies!

2 You remind me of a man.
—What man?
Man with a power.
—What power?
The power of voodoo.
—Who do?
You do.
—Do what?
Remind me of a man.
—What man?
Man with a power . . .

3 They're either too young or too old.
They're either too grey or too grassy green.
The pickings are poor and the crop is lean.
There isn't any gravy: the gravy's in the navy . . .

4 The pellet with the poison's in the chalice from the palace.
The flagon with the dragon has the brew that is true.

5 Do not despair
For Johnny Head-in-Air.
He sleeps as sound
As Johnny Underground.

Fetch out no shroud
For Johnny in-the-Cloud.
Best save your tears
For him in after years.
Better by far
For Johnny the bright star
To keep your head
And see his children fed.

6 Every night when the moon is bright
The miller's ghost is seen.
The mill wheel turns though the night is still . . .
He haunts the station, he haunts the mill
And the land that lies between . . .

7 I build my house of stones;
I build my house of bricks.
I have no chance to sing and dance
For work and play don't mix.

8 Some men goes for women,
And some men goes for boys;
But my love's warm and beautiful,
And makes a baa-ing noise . . .

9 When stars are bright
On a frosty night,
Beware thy bane
On the rocky lane . . .

10 When the tide runs low in the smugglers' cove
And the headless horseman rides above,
He drives along with his wild hallo,
And that's the time when smugglers go in their little boats to the schooner and bring back the kegs of brandy and rum and put them all in the Devil's Cove below.

11 If you ain't eatin' Wham
You ain't eatin' ham.

12 Your wife is safe with Tonetti—
He prefers spaghetti.

13 Find the number beneath the vine
The sparkling gems will then be thine.
Oh love, what number rhymes with mine?

14 I found a bow and arrow and learned to shoot.
I found a little horn and learned to toot.
Now I can shoot and toot. Ain't that cute?

15 I'd like to get in, get on with it, get it over with, and get out. Get it?
—Got it.
—Good.

16 When the house is filled with dread,
Place the beds at head to head.

17 Oh, he flew through the air with the greatest of ease,
And the daring young man owes me twenty rupees.

Versois, Odile (1930–1980) (Militza de Poliakoff-Baidarov). French leading lady, sister of Marina Vlady.
Les Dernières Vacances 46. Into the Blue (GB) 48. Bel Amour 51. A Day to Remember (GB) 53. *The Young Lovers* (Chance Meeting) (GB) 55. To Paris with Love (GB) 55. Passport to Shame (GB) 58. Cartouche (Swords of Blood) 62. Benjamin 68, etc.

Vertov, Dziga (1896–1954) (Dennis Kaufman). Russian director and film theorist. Many documentaries.
One-Sixth of the World 27. The Man with the Movie Camera 28. Three Songs of Lenin 34. In the Line of Fire 41, etc.

Vetri, Victoria (1944–) (Angela Dorian). Australian leading lady.
Chuka 67. Rosemary's Baby 68. When Dinosaurs Ruled the Earth 69, etc.

Vicas, Victor (1918–85). Franco-Russian director.
No Way Back 53. Double Destiny 54. Back to Kandara 57. The Wayward Bus 57. Count Five and Die (GB) 58. Les Disparus 60, etc.
Later in French TV.

Vickers, Martha (1925–1971) (M. MacVicar). American leading lady of the forties.
The Falcon in Mexico 44. *The Big Sleep* 46. Love and Learn 47. Ruthless 48. Bad Boy 49. Daughter of the West 51. The Burglar 57. Four Fast Guns 60, etc.

Victim (GB 1962). This first British film to tackle homosexuality did so under cover of a detective story. Whether or not this invalidates it as social comment, it was an exciting film. Written by Janet Green and John McCormack, produced and directed by Michael Relph and Basil Dearden, photographed by Otto Heller; with Dirk Bogarde doing well in the difficult, ambiguous central role.

Victor, Charles (1896–1965). British character actor with long stage experience; in films from 1938, usually in cockney roles.
While the Sun Shines 46. The Calendar 48. The Ringer 52. Those People Next Door 53. The Embezzler 55. Now and Forever 57, scores of others.

Victor, Henry (1898–1945). British character actor, a silent screen star who went

to Hollywood in the thirties and played villainous bit roles.
She 25. The Guns of Loos 28. The Fourth Commandment 28. The Mummy 33. Our Fighting Navy 37. Confessions of a Nazi Spy 39. Zanzibar 40. King of the Zombies 41, etc.

Victoria, Queen of England 1837–1901, was born in 1819. Her full-length screen portraits were by Anna Neagle in *Victoria the Great* and *Sixty Glorious Years*, and by Irene Dunne, who failed rather badly, in *The Mudlark*. She was also played by Fay Compton in *The Prime Minister*, by Helena Pickard in *The Lady with the Lamp*, by Muriel Aked in *The Story of Gilbert and Sullivan*, by Sybil Thorndike in *Melba*, and by Mollie Maureen in *The Private Life of Sherlock Holmes*.

Victoria the Great (GB 1937). A phenomenally successful British film which, rather daringly at the time, told the domestic story of a recent monarch. Anna Neagle starred under Herbert Wilcox's direction and in the following year a colour sequel, *Sixty Glorious Years*, was equally successful.

The Victors (GB 1963). By devising the anti-war film to end them all, writer-producer-director Carl Foreman pushed bits of this World War II compendium into absurdity: there simply wasn't a decent character around. But it does have moving and horrifying sequences, also some which impress as pure cinema. Photographed by Christopher Challis, with a generally effective American-international cast.

Vidal, Henri (1919–1959). Tough-looking French leading man, in films from 1940.
Les Maudits 46. Quai de Grenelle 50. Port du Désir 54. The Wicked Go to Hell 55. Porte des Lilas 56. Come Dance with Me 59, etc.

video cassettes can provide programmes on the home television set. They are played in through special equipment and can accommodate feature films or any other kind of entertainment or instruction.

During the seventies, video cassettes were much talked about, but the opinion was that new documentary programmes would have to be made for them as nobody would want to buy or rent old movies. How wrong they were. By the mid-1980s Britain soared at the top of the world markets, largely because cassettes could be rented for a pound a night from local shops. There was a great deal of fuss about porn and video nasties, but the great surge was from people who simply wanted to see newish movies without going to the trouble and expense of a cinema visit. Other countries were slower to follow suit, but there was no doubt that video was one more nail in the coffin of an industry which had lasted ninety years, especially since the domestic machines also allowed owners to record whatever films and other programmes they liked from their television sets.

See also *cassettes*.

video discs operate similarly to video cassettes, but instead of being stored on tape the information is mounted on a circular disc similar to a gramophone record.

Vidor, Charles (1900–1959). Hungarian-American director, in Hollywood from 1932.
Double Door 34. Sensation Hunters 34. The Great Gambini 37. *Blind Alley* 39. My Son My Son 40. The Lady in Question 40. Ladies in Retirement 41. The Tuttles of Tahiti 42. The Desperadoes 43. *Cover Girl* 44. Together Again 44. A Song to Remember 45. Over 21 45. *Gilda* 46. The Guilt of Janet Ames 48. Hans Christian Andersen 52. Love Me or Leave Me 55. The Swan 56. The Joker is Wild 57. A Farewell to Arms 58. Song without End (part) 59, many others.

Vidor, Florence (1895–1977) (Florence Arto). American leading lady of the silent screen.
Lying Lips 21. Barbara Frietchie 24. The Grand Duchess and the Waiter 26. Are Parents People? 26. The Patriot 28. Chinatown Nights 29, etc.

Vidor, King (1894–1982). American director, formerly journalist; high style alternates with disappointing banality. Special AA 1979 'for his incomparable achievements as a cinematic creator and innovator'.
Autobiography 1953: *A Tree is a Tree.*
□The Turn in the Road 18. Better Times 19. The Other Half 19. Poor Relations 19. The Jack Knife Man 19. The Family Honour 20. The Sky Pilot 21. Love Never Dies 21. Conquering the Woman 21. Woman Wake Up 21. The Real Adventure 22. Dusk to Dawn 22. Alice Adams 22. Peg O' My Heart 23. The Woman of Bronze 23. Three Wise Fools 23. Wild Oranges 23. Happiness 23. Wine of Youth 24. His Hour 24. Wife of the Centaur 24. Proud Flesh 25. *The Big Parade* 25. La Bohème 25. Bardelys the Magnificent 26. *The Crowd* 28. *Show People* 28.

Hallelujah 29. Not So Dumb 30. *Billy the Kid* 30. *Street Scene* 31. *The Champ* 31. Bird of Paradise 32. Cynara 32. The Stranger's Return 33. *Our Daily Bread* 34. The Wedding Night 34. So Red the Rose 35. The Texas Rangers 36. Stella Dallas 37. The Citadel (GB) 38. *Northwest Passage* 39. Comrade X 40. H.M. Pulham Esq 41. An American Romance 44. Duel in the Sun 46. On Our Merry Way 47. *The Fountainhead* 49. Beyond the Forest 49. Lightning Strikes Twice 51. Japanese War Bride 52. Ruby Gentry 52. The Man without a Star 55. *War and Peace* 56. Solomon and Sheba 59.
† In the last year of his life he acted a role in *Love and Money*.

Vienna was frequently pictured in pre-war films such as *The Great Waltz, Bitter Sweet* and *Vienna Waltzes*, but the myths were always perpetuated on a studio backlot. The post war reality was caught vividly in *Four in a Jeep* and *The Third Man.*

Vierny, Sacha (1919–). French cinematographer.
Hiroshima Mon Amour 58. *Last Year in Marienbad* 61. Muriel 63. Do You Like Women? 64. *Belle de Jour* 67, etc.

Viertel, Berthold (1885–1953). Austrian director who moved to Britain and Hollywood in the early thirties.
The Wise Sex 31. The Man from Yesterday 32. Little Friend 34. The Passing of the Third Floor Back 35. Rhodes of Africa 36, etc.

The Vietnam War stunned America to such an extent that few films were made about it until long after its end. An exception was John Wayne's gung-ho *The Green Berets* 68. *Go Tell the Spartans* followed in 1978, rapidly followed by *The Deer Hunter* and *Apocalypse Now. Coming Home* (1982) covered the effect on veterans. In 1987 there was a deluge: *Hamburger Hill*, *Platoon*, and *Full Metal Jacket.*

vigilantes were originally groups of honest citizens who formed together to rid San Francisco's Barbary Coast of some of its villains. In the early seventies it became fashionable to make films about citizens who took the law of our violent cities into their own hands, notably in *Death Wish, Walking Tall* and *Law and Disorder.*

Vigo, Jean (1905–1934) (Jean Almereyda). Influential French director on the strength of three semi-experimental, dream-like films.
□*A Propos de Nice* 30. *Zéro de Conduite* 32. *L'Atalante* 34.

Vigoda, Abe (1921–). American character actor, popular on TV in *Barney Miller* and *Fish*.
The Godfather 71. The Don Is Dead 73. Newman's Law 74. Having Babies (TV) 76. The Cheap Detective 78. The Comedy Company (TV) 78, etc.

Villa-Lobos, Heitor (1887–1959). Brazilian composer who worked in Hollywood on *Green Mansions* 59.

Villard, Frank (1917–1980) (François Drouineau). French leading man, often in shifty roles.
Le Dernier des Six 41. Gigi 48. Manèges (The Wanton) 49. L'Ingénue Libertine 50. Le Garçon Sauvage 51. Huis Clos 54. Crime Passionel 55. Mystères de Paris 57. Le Cave se Rebiffe 61. Gigot 62. Mata Hari 64, etc.

Villechaize, Herve (1943–). French dwarf actor in international films.
The Man with the Golden Gun 73. The One and Only 78, etc.
TV series: Fantasy Island 77–82.

Villiers, James (1933–). British actor, usually in snooty or villainous roles.
The Entertainer 60. The Damned 64. King and Country 64. The Nanny 65. Half a Sixpence 67. Some Girls Do 68. Otley 68. A Nice Girl Like Me 69. Blood from the Mummy's Tomb 70. The Ruling Class 71. Saint Jack 79. The Scarlet Pimpernel (TV) 82. Under the Volcano 84. Fortunes of War (TV) 87, etc.

Villon, François (1431–c. 1470) (François de Loges). French poet who led the life of a Robin Hood and was romanticized in *If I Were King* (in which he was played by Ronald Colman) and its musical version *The Vagabond King* (Dennis King, Oreste Kirkop).

Vincent, Jan-Michael (1944–). American leading man of the seventies.
The Undefeated 68. Tribes (TV) 70. The Mechanic 72. The World's Greatest Athlete 73. Buster and Billie 74. Bite the Bullet 74. White Line Fever 75. Baby Blue Marine 76. Damnation Alley 77. Hooper 78. Big Wednesday 78. Defiance 80. Hard Country 81. The Winds of War (TV) 83. Last Plane Out 83, etc.

Vincent, June (1919–). Blonde American leading lady of some forties 'B's.
Ladies Courageous 44. The Climax 44. Can't Help Singing 44. Here Come the Co-eds 45. That's the Spirit 45. Black Angel 46. Shed No Tears 48, etc.

Vincze, Ernest (1942–). British cinematographer.
Jane Austen in Manhattan 81. A Woman of Substance (TV) 84. Biggles 85. Shanghai Surprise 85. Escape from Sobibor (TV) 86, etc.

Vinson, Helen (1907–) (Helen Rulfs). Cool, aristocratic leading lady of Hollywood films of the thirties and forties.
Jewel Robbery 31. I Am a Fugitive from a Chain Gang 32. The Power and the Glory 33. The Tunnel (GB) 35. Vogues of 1938. In Name Only 39. Torrid Zone 40. Nothing But the Truth 41. They Are Guilty 44. The Lady and the Doctor (last to date) 46, etc.

violence caused little concern until the fifties. Even the makers of the horror and gangster films of the thirties were comparatively subtle in their approach: they delighted in machine guns and clutching hands, but would not have dreamed of showing fist connect against flesh or suggesting the sight of actual blood. The rot began to set in in 1952 with films like *The Wild One*, which still showed little but pointed out that imitable forms of violence were on the streets of our cities; location shooting was inviting greater realism than had been necessary in the studio. In 1956, when Hammer began to remake the great horror stories, a new ghoulishness was found to have set in, especially in the versions prepared for the Far East. Still the censor held sway until the late sixties, when he gave up the ghost. *Witchfinder General* was a sadistic piece of Grand Guignol, *The Wild Bunch* a blood-spattered western, *Get Carter* and *Villain* new-fashioned gangster films in which the killing was merciless and explicit. *Soldier Blue* has as its high point a mutilation scene which its director seemed to claim as a protest against Vietnam; *Straw Dogs* featured an irrelevant but thoroughly detailed rape. As for *A Clockwork Orange* and *The Devils*, our eyes were spared no conceivable atrocity. According to one's point of view, the cinema had either come of age or ventured beyond the pale. By the eighties, much more violence was being accepted in a family film like *Raiders of the Lost Ark* than would have been passed twenty years earlier for adults only; but the excesses of Brian de Palma's remake of *Scarface* caused most critical hands to be thrown up in horror.

The Virginian. Owen Wister's western novel was filmed in 1914 with Dustin Farnum, in 1930 with Gary Cooper, and in 1945 with Joel McCrea; in 1964 it turned up as a long-running TV series with James Drury. *Spawn of the North* 38 borrowed the basic plot, and in its turn was remade as *Alaska Seas* 54.

Viridiana (Spain 1961). Luis Buñuel's startlingly allusive allegory of good and evil, with the latter winning in the end, is a ramshackle but absorbing film rounding up all the diverse moods of his earlier career: poetic, sacrilegious, melodramatic, enigmatic, hilarious and often moving.

Visconti, Luchino (1906–1976) (L. V. de Modrone). Italian writer-director, former art director.
Biography 1982 by Gaia Servadio: *Luchino Visconti.*
Ossessione 42. *La Terra Trema* 48. Bellissima 51. Siamo Donne (part) 52. *Senso* 53. White Nights 57. *Rocco and His Brothers* 60. Boccaccio 70 62. *The Leopard* 63. *The Damned* 69. Death in Venice 70. Conversation Piece 76, etc.

Les Visiteurs du Soir (France 1942). A medieval fantasy written by Jacques Prévert and directed by Marcel Carné; remarkable in that, though made under the German occupation, it contrived to point an allegory of the resistance. (The devil turns the lovers to stone; but their hearts still beat no matter how hard he whips them.) As a film slow-moving, though full of elegant visuals, it has excellent performances from Jules Berry as the devil and Arletty as his agent. Music by Maurice Thiriet, décor by Wakhevitch.

VistaVision. In 1953, when some companies were reluctant to follow Fox's lead and adopt CinemaScope, Paramount introduced VistaVision, a non-anamorphic, deep focus process retaining the old frame ratio of 4 × 3. The chief innovation was that none of the essential action took place at the top or bottom of the picture, so that exhibitors with appropriate lens and apperture plates could choose their own screen ratio (from 4 × 3 to 2 × 1). At 2 × 1 on a big screen, VistaVision did not look very different from CinemaScope.

Vitagraph. An early American production company which had great success but was taken over in the twenties by Warners.

Vitaphone. The sound-on-disc process introduced in 1926 by Warners.

Vitale, Milly (1928–). Italian leading lady in American films.
The Juggler 53. The Seven Little Foys 55. A Breath of Scandal 60.

Vitti, Monica (1933–) (Monica Luisa Ceciarelli). Italian leading lady in international demand in the sixties.
L'Avventura 59. La Notte 60. *L'Eclisse* 62. Dragées au Poivre 63. Nutty Naughty Château 64. *The Red Desert* 64. Modesty Blaise (GB) 65. The Chastity Belt 67. Girl with a Pistol 69. The Pacifist 71. Duck in Orange Sauce 75. An Almost Perfect Affair 79, etc.

Vlad, Roman (1919–). Romanian composer.
La Beauté du Diable 49. Sunday in August 50. Three Steps North 51. Romeo and Juliet 54. Knave of Hearts 54. The Law 60. The Mighty Ursus 62, etc.

Vlady, Marina (1938–) (Marina de Poliakoff-Baidarov). French leading lady, sister of Odile Versois.
Orage d'Eté 49. Avant le Déluge 53. The Wicked Go to Hell 55. Crime and Punishment 56. Toi le Venin 59. La Steppa 61. Climats 62. Enough Rope 63. Dragées au Poivre 63. Queen Bee 64. Chimes at Midnight 66. Sapho 70. Les Jeux de la Comtesse 80, etc.

Vogel, Paul C. (1899–1975). American cinematographer.
The Lady in the Lake 46. Black Hand 49. *Battleground* (AA) 49. Rose Marie 54. High Society 56. The Wings of Eagles 56. The Time Machine 60. The Rounders 64, etc.

Vogel, Virgil (–). American director, from TV.
The Mole People 56. Terror in the Midnight Sun 58. Son of Ali Baba 64. The Return of Joe Forrester (TV) 75. Law of the Land (TV) 76. Centennial (part) (TV) 78. Beulah Land (TV) 80, etc.

Vogler, Karl Michael (1928–). German stage actor who has appeared in a few international films.
Those Magnificent Men in Their Flying Machines 65. The Blue Max 67. How I Won the War 67. Patton 69. Downhill Racer 69, etc.

Voight, Jon (1938–). American leading actor of the seventies.
□The Hour of the Gun 67. Fearless Frank 68. Out of It 69. *Midnight Cowboy* 69. The Revolutionary 70. The All American Boy 70. Catch 22 70. *Deliverance* 72. Conrack 74. The Odessa File 74. End of the Game 75. Coming Home (AA) 78. The Champ 79. Lookin' to Get Out 82. Table for Five 83. Desert Bloom 85. Runaway Train (AAN) 85.
Famous line (*Midnight Cowboy*): I'll tell you the truth now. I ain't a real cowboy, but I am one hell of a stud.

volcanoes in the late thirties seemed to belong mostly to Paramount, which used them as the climax of most of Dorothy Lamour's jungle pictures and of odd adventures like *Cobra Woman* and *Mysterious Island*. They more recently turned up in *The Devil at Four O'Clock*, and in *Journey to the Centre of the Earth* in which the way was down an extinct Icelandic crater and back on a fountain of lava up the inside of Etna. The famous eruption of Vesuvius was staged for the various versions of *The Last Days of Pompeii* (and for *Up Pompeii*), and *Krakatoa, East of Java* featured another historical disaster. An extinct volcano formed a lair for giant monsters in *The Black Scorpion*. A volcano was also the climax of Hal Roach's *Man and His Mate* and of its recent remake *One Million Years B.C.*; but the most spectacular pictures were obtained for the documentary compilation simply called *Volcano*.

Volonte, Gian Maria (1930–). Italian leading man of the sixties.
A Fistful of Dollars 64. For a Few Dollars More 65. We Still Kill the Old Way 68. *Investigation of a Citizen above Suspicion* 69. Sacco and Vanzetti 71. The Working Class Go To Heaven 72. Lucky Luciano 73. Christ Stopped at Eboli 82, etc.

Von Harbou, Thea (1888–1954). German screenwriter, mainly associated with Fritz Lang's silent films.
Der Müde Tod 21. *Dr Mabuse* 22. *Nibelungen Saga* 24. Chronicles of the Grey House 25. *Metropolis* 26. The Spy 28. The Woman in the Moon 29. *The Testament of Dr Mabuse* 32. The Old and the Young King 35. Annélie 41. Fahrt ins Gluck 45. The Affairs of Dr Holl 51, others.

Von Seyffertitz, Gustav (1863–1943). Dignified German character actor in Hollywood films; during World War I was known as G. Butler Clonblough.
Old Wives for New 18. Moriarty (title role) 22. Sparrows 26. The Wizard 27. Docks of New York 28. The Bat Whispers 30. Shanghai Express 32. Queen Christiana 33. She 35. In Old Chicago 38. Nurse Edith Cavell 39, many others.

Von Sternberg, Josef (1894–1969) (Jonas Sternberg). Austrian-American director, a great pictorial stylist and the creator of Marlene Dietrich's American image. Autobiography 1965: *Fun in a Chinese Laundry*. A critical study by Herman G. Weinberg was published in 1967.
□*The Salvation Hunters* 25. The Seagull (unreleased) 26. *Underworld* 27. The Last Command 28. The Dragnet 28. *Docks of New York* 28. The Case of Lena Smith 29. Thunderbolt 29. *The Blue Angel* (Ger.) 30. *Morocco* 30. Dishonoured 31. An American Tragedy 31. *Shanghai Express* 32. Blonde Venus 32. *The Scarlet Empress* 34. *The Devil is a Woman* 35. The King Steps Out 36. Crime and Punishment 36. I Claudius (unfinished) 37. Sergeant Madden 39. *The Shanghai Gesture* 41. Jet Pilot 50. Macao 51. The Saga of Anatahan (Jap.) 53.

'A lyricist of light and shadow rather than a master of montage.'—*Andrew Sarris, 1968*

❁ For being the kind of director who, if he didn't exist, publicists would have to invent. *The Scarlet Empress*.

¶ I care nothing about the story, only how it is photographed and presented.—*J.V.S.*

The only way to succeed is to make people hate you. That way they remember you.—*J.V.S.*

¶ 'He brought to the screen new horizons in the art of lighting, to the photography of shadowed and broken rays . . . His scenes seem almost always to be seen through streamers and feathers, through loose gauze, through slatted shutters or an intricate lattice wall.'—*Ivan Butler*

Von Stroheim, Erich (1885–1957) (Hans Erich Maria Stroheim Von Nordenwall). Austrian actor and director whose ruthless extravagance in Hollywood in the twenties harmed his later career. Usually played despotic villains or stiff-necked Prussians. Biographies: 1954, *Hollywood Scapegoat* by Peter Noble. 1972, *Erich Von Stroheim* by Tom Curtis.
AS ACTOR: The Heart of Humanity 18. Blind Husbands 19. *Foolish Wives* 21. The Wedding March 27. The Great Gabbo 29. Three Faces East 30. Friends and Lovers 30. The Lost Squadron 32. As You Desire Me 32. Walking Down Broadway 32. Crimson Romance 35. The Crime of Dr Crespi 35. *La Grande Illusion* 37. Mademoiselle Docteur 37. Alibi 38. Boys' School 39. I Was an Adventuress 40. Thunder Over Parièges 40. So Ends Our Night 41. *Five Graves to Cairo* (as Rommel) 43. North Star 43. The Lady and the Monster 44. Storm Over Lisbon 44. 32 Rue de Montmartre 44. The Great Flamarion 45. La Danse de Mort 47. *Sunset Boulevard* 50. La Maison du Crime 52. Napoleon 54. L'Homme aux Cents Visages 56, etc.
□AS DIRECTOR: *Blind Husbands* 19. *The Devil's Passkey* 19. *Foolish Wives* 21. Merry Go Round 22. *Greed* 23. The Merry Widow 25. *The Wedding March* 27. *Queen Kelly* 28.

❁ For taking Hollywood on and winning—for a while. *Greed*.

¶ The difference between me and Lubitsch is that he shows you the king on the throne and then he shows you the king in his bedroom. I show you the king in his bedroom first. Then when you see him on the throne you have no illusions about him.—*E.V.S.*

When I first saw Von Stroheim at the wardrobe tests, I clicked my heels and said, 'Isn't it ridiculous, little me directing you, when you were always ten years ahead of your time?' And he replied, 'Twenty.'—*Billy Wilder, 1942*

'As to directing his own performance, Von always had an assistant to give him an opinion of his acting. Whether he listened to it or not was another matter.'—*William Daniels*

'One of the cinema's great enigmas . . . he conjured up a world very much in its infancy psychologically. It was a grotesque and brutal world, and the bleakness and callousness of his characters' lives were revealed with a meticulous realism.'—*Claire Johnston*

'He was a short man, almost squat, with a vulpine smirk that told you, as soon as his image flashed on to the screen, that no wife or bankroll must be left unguarded.'—*S. J. Perelman*

Von Sydow, Max (1929–) (Carl Adolf Von Sydow). Swedish actor, a member of Ingmar Bergman's company.
Miss Julie 51. *The Seventh Seal* 56. Wild Strawberries 57. So Close to Life 58. *The Face* 59. The Virgin Spring 60. *Through a Glass Darkly* 61. Winter Light 62. The

Mistress 62. *The Greatest Story Ever Told* (as Jesus) (US) 65. The Reward (US) 65. *Hawaii* (US) 66. The Quiller Memorandum (GB) 66. *Hour of the Wolf* 67. The Shame 68. The Kremlin Letter (US) 69. The Touch 71. Embassy 72. *The Emigrants* 72. The Exorcist (US) 73. The New Land 75. Foxtrot 76. Three Days of the Condor (US) 76. Voyage of the Damned 76. Exorcist II: The Heretic 77. March or Die 77. Brass Target 78. Hurricane 79. Flash Gordon 80. Victory 81. Never Say Never Again 83. Kojak: The Belarus File (TV) 85. Christopher Columbus (TV) 85. Hannah and her Sisters 85. The Wolf at the Door 85. The Second Victory 86. Duet for One 86, etc.

Von Trotta, Margarethe (1942–). German director who married Volker Schlöndorff.
The Lost Honour of Katerina Blum (co-d) 75. The Second Awakening of Krista Clarges 77. Sisters 79. The German Sisters 81. Friends and Husbands 83. Rosa Luxemburg 85, etc.

Vorhaus, Bernard (c. 1898–). German director, mostly in Britain and Hollywood.
Money for Speed (GB) 33. Broken Melody (GB) 35. Cotton Queen (GB) 37. Three Faces West (US) 40. Lady from Louisiana (US) 41. Bury Me Dead (US) 47. So Young So Bad (US) 50. The Lady from Boston (US) 51, etc.

Vorkapitch, Slavko (1892–1976). Yugoslavian writer who came to Hollywood in 1922, did a little screenwriting, tried direction in 1931 (*I Take This Woman*), then settled as a montage expert.
Viva Villa 34. *Crime without Passion* 34. San Francisco 36. Maytime 37. The Last Gangster 38. Shopworn Angel 38. Mr Smith Goes to Washington 39, etc.

Voskovec, George (1905–81) (Jiri Voskovec). Czech stage actor, long in US.
Anything Can Happen 52. *Twelve Angry Men* 57. The Bravados 58. Butterfield 8 60. The Spy Who Came in from the Cold 65. Mister Buddwing 66. The Boston Strangler 68. Skag (TV) 80. Somewhere in Time 80. Barbarossa 82, etc.

Vosper, Frank (1899–1937). British stage actor and playwright who appeared in a few films.
Blinkeyes 26. The Last Post 27. Rome Express 32. Waltzes from Vienna 33. The Man Who Knew Too Much 34. Jew Süss 34. Open All Night 34. Heart's Desire 35.

Vye, Murvyn (1913–1976). Burly American character actor who usually played heavies.
Golden Earrings 48. A Connecticut Yankee at King Arthur's Court 49. Pick-Up 51. Road to Bali 52. Green Fire 54. Pearl of the South Pacific 55. Al Capone 58. Pay or Die 60. Andy 64, etc.

Answers

verse and worse

1 The toast in *The Dawn Patrol.* ☐

2 Juvenile doggerel used by Cary Grant in *The Bachelor and the Bobbysoxer* when he has to play up to Shirley Temple's crush on him. ☐

3 Sung by Bette Davis in *Thank Your Lucky Stars*, ☐ and attacked at the time as against the best interests of wartime propaganda. The star's delivery naturally added to the disenchanted effect. One more couplet from the song:
Tomorrow I'll go hiking with that Eagle
 Scout unless
I get a call from Grandpa for a snappy
 game of chess . . .

4 The basis of a hilarious sequence in *The Court Jester*. ☐ Danny Kaye has to joust against a large and vicious opponent, and Mildred Natwick spikes one of the drinking cups. Unfortunately repetition of the couplet gets everyone confused.

5 John Pudney's famous poem written for *The Way to the Stars* in which it has been written by a squadron leader who is killed; his friend reads it to his widow. ☐

6 For British comedy specialists! The old Irish legend in *Oh Mr Porter*, recited by the toothless Harbottle. ☐

7 Sung by the third of Disney's *Three Little Pigs*. ☐
8 Sung by the public house drunks in *Straw Dogs*. ☐
9 For film buffs only! The family curse of the Hammonds in *The Undying Monster* (1942). ☐
10 Another Will Hay comedy, *Ask a Policeman* (1939). ☐ This insane piece of doggerel, remembered by aged Moore Marriott's even more aged father, provides a clue to and a cover for the activities of the criminals.
11 The slogan which eluded ad man Cary Grant all through *Mr Blanding Builds His Dream House* finally dropped casually from the lips of his black cook. ☐
12 Erik Rhodes as the professional co-respondent in *The Gay Divorcee*. ☐
13 *The Cat and the Canary*. ☐ The treasure should not be difficult to find.
14 Danny Kaye in *The Court Jester*. ☐
15 Ditto and likewise; he who says 'got it' is Basil Rathbone. ☐
16 Emma Dunn as the housekeeper in *Son of Frankenstein*. ☐
17 Franchot Tone to Gary Cooper in *Lives of a Bengal Lancer*. ☐

Waddington, Patrick (1900–87). Elegant British character actor, mostly on stage.
Journey Together 45. School for Secrets 46. The Wooden Horse 51. A Night to Remember 56, etc.

Wadsworth, Henry (1902–1974). American juvenile of the twenties and thirties.
Applause 29. Luxury Liner 33. The Thin Man 34. Ceiling Zero 35. Dr Rhythm 38, many others.

Wager, Anthony (1933–). British juvenile actor who played Young Pip in the 1946 *Great Expectations* and later turned up on Australian television.

The Wages of Fear (France 1953). A long, solid shocker with serious undertones about four drivers with a cargo of nitroglycerine. It showed that France could make a big commercial thriller as well as anybody, and very nearly forced acceptance of continental movies in British cinemas (it was given a full circuit release, sub-titles and all, but not enough others in a similar category came along to make foreign films a habit, and dubbing finally won the day). Written and directed by Henri-Georges Clouzot from a novel by Georges Arnaud; photographed by Armand Thirard with music by Georges Auric. With Yves Montand, Charles Vanel, Peter Van Eyck. BFA (best film). William Friedkin's 1977 remake *Sorcerer* was an artistic and commercial disaster.

Waggner, George (1894–1984). American director, mainly of routine low-budgeters, in Hollywood from 1920.
The Wolf Man 41. The Climax (& p) 44. Cobra Woman (& p) 45. The Fighting Kentuckian (& w) 49. Operation Pacific (& w) 51. Bitter Creek 54. Destination 60,000 (& w) 57. Pale Arrow 58, many others.

Wagner, Fritz Arno (1889–1958). German cinematographer.
Nosferatu 23. *The Loves of Jeanne Ney* 27. The Spy 28. Westfront 1918 30. *Die Dreigroschenoper* 31. Kameradschaft 31. Amphitryon 35. Ohm Krüger 41. Hotel Adlon 55, many others.

Wagner, Lindsay (1949–). American leading lady of the seventies.
The Paper Chase 73. Two People 74. The Incredible Journey of Meg Laurel (TV) 79. Scruples (TV) 81. The Two Worlds of Jennie Logan (TV) 81. Callie and Company (TV) 82. Princess Daisy (TV) 83.
TV series: *Bionic Woman* 76–77. Jessie 84.

Wagner, Robert (1930–). American leading man spotted by talent scout while still at college.
Halls of Montezuma (debut) 50. With a Song in My Heart 52. Titanic 53. Prince Valiant 54. Broken Lance 54. White Feather 55. The Mountain 56. A Kiss Before Dying 56. The Hunters 57. Say One for Me 58. All the Fine Young Cannibals 59. The Longest Day 62. The Condemned of Altona 63. Harper 66. The Biggest Bundle of Them All 66. Don't Just Stand There 68. Winning 69. The Streets of San Francisco (TV) 71. City Beneath the Sea (TV) 71. The Affair (TV) 73. The Towering Inferno 74. Death at Love House (TV) 76. Midway 76. The Concorde—Airport 79 79. Curse of the Pink Panther 83. I Am the Cheese 83, etc.
TV series: It Takes a Thief 65–69. Colditz 72–73. Switch 75–76. Hart to Hart 79–83. Lime Street 85.

Wahl, Ken (1957–). Giant-sized American leading man.
□ The Buddy Holly Story 78. Every Which Way But Loose 79. The Champ 79. The Wanderers 79. Running Scared 79. Fort Apache—The Bronx 81. Race for the Yankee Zephyr 81. Jinxed! 82. Code Name The Soldier 82. Purple Heart 84.

Wainwright, James (–). American general purpose actor.
The President's Plane Is Missing (TV) 71. Joe Kidd 72. Killdozer (TV) 74. The Private Files of J. Edgar Hoover 77. Mean Dog Blues 78. My Undercover Years with the Ku Klux Klan (TV) 78, etc.
TV series: Jigsaw 72. Beyond Westworld 79.

Waite, Ralph (1928–). Reliable-looking American general purpose actor.
Cool Hand Luke 67. Last Summer 69. Five Easy Pieces 70. The Grissom Gang 71. Kid Blue 72. The Stone Killer 73. On the Nickel (p, d, w only) 80. OHMS (TV) 80. Angel City (TV) 81, etc.
TV series: The Waltons 72–78.

Wajda, Andrzej (1926–). Polish director.
A Generation 54. *Kanal* 55. *Ashes and Diamonds* 58. Innocent Sorcerers 60. The Siberian Lady Macbeth 61. Love at Twenty (part only) 62. Ashes 64. Everything for Sale 67. Gates to Paradise 67. The Birch Wood 71. Landscape after a Battle 72. The Wedding 72. Promised Land 74. Shadow Line 76. *Man of Marble* 77. Without Anesthetic 79. *Man of Iron* 80. Danton 82, etc.

Wakefield, Duggie (1899–1951). British music-hall comedian, in character as a simpleton who always triumphed. Films include *Look Up and Laugh* 35, *Spy for a Day* 39, etc.

Wakefield, Hugh (1888–1971). British character actor on stage from childhood. Usually seen in monocled roles.
City of Song 30. The Sport of Kings 31. The Man Who Knew Too Much 34. The Crimson Circle 36. The Street Singer 37. Blithe Spirit 45. One Night with You 48. Love's a Luxury 52. The Million Pound Note 54, etc.

Wakeford, Kent L. (–). American cinematographer.
Black Belt Jones 74. Alice Doesn't Live Here Anymore 75.

Wakhevitch, Georges (1907–84). Russian art director in international films.
Madame Bovary 34. La Grande Illusion 37. Prison without Bars 38. Les Visiteurs du Soir 42. L'Eternel Retour 43. L'Homme au Chapeau Rond 46. Dédée 48. The Medium 51. The Beggar's Opera 53. Don Juan 56. Marie-Octobre 59. Black Tights 60. King of Kings 61. Diary of a Chambermaid 64. Tendre Voyou 66. Mayerling 68. King Lear 70.

Walbrook, Anton (1900–1967) (Adolf Wohlbruck). Distinguished Austrian actor who came to Britain in the mid-thirties.
Maskerade 34. The Student of Prague 35. *Michael Strogoff* (US) 37. *Victoria the Great* 37. The Rat 37. Sixty Glorious Years 38. *Gaslight* 39. Dangerous Moonlight 40. 49th Parallel 41. *The Life and Death of Colonel Blimp* 43. The Man from Morocco 44. *The Red Shoes* 48. The Queen of Spades 48. *La Ronde* 50. Vienna Waltzes 51. Oh Rosalinda 55. Lola Montes 55. Saint Joan 57. I Accuse 57, etc.

Walburn, Raymond (1887–1969). American comedy actor with an inimitable bumbling pomposity; on stage from 1912, films from early thirties.
The Count of Monte Cristo 34. The Great Ziegfeld 36. *Mr Deeds Goes to Town* 36. Born to Dance 37. Professor Beware 38. Eternally Yours 40. Christmas in July 41. Dixie 43. *Hail the Conquering Hero* 43. The Man in the Trunk 43. The Cheaters 45. Henry the Rainmaker 48. State of the Union 48. Riding High 49. Father Takes the Air 51. Beautiful but Dangerous 53. The Spoilers 55, etc.

Wald, Jerry (1911–1962). Live-wire American writer-producer, said to be the original of Budd Schulberg's novel 'What Makes Sammy Run?' Former journalist, in Hollywood from early thirties.
Stars over Broadway (w) 35. Hollywood Hotel (w) 38. George Washington Slept Here (p) 42. *Mildred Pierce* 45. *Johnny Belinda* (p) 48. The Glass Menagerie (p) 50. Clash by Night (p) 52. Queen Bee (p) 55. Peyton Place (p) 57. The Sound and the Fury (p) 58. Sons and Lovers (p) 60. The Stripper (p) 63, many others.

Waldron, Charles D. (1874–1946). American stage actor who made a few films.
Mary Burns Fugitive 35. The Garden of Allah 36. Kentucky 38. On Borrowed Time 39. The Devil and Miss Jones 41. The Song of Bernadette 43. The Black Parachute 44. The Big Sleep 46, etc.
Famous line (*The Big Sleep*): You may smoke, sir. I can still enjoy the smell of it. Nice state of affairs, when a man has to indulge his vices by proxy.

Walken, Christopher (1943–). American young actor of the late seventies.
□The Anderson Tapes 71. The Happiness Cage 72. Next Stop Greenwich Village 76. The Sentinel 77. Annie Hall 77. Roseland 77. The Deer Hunter (AA) 78. Last Embrace 79. Heaven's Gate 80. The Dogs of War 81. Pennies from Heaven 81. Brainstorm 83. The Dead Zone 83. A View to a Kill 85. At Close Range 86. Deadline 87.

Walker, Charlotte (1878–1958). American leading lady with stage experience, in silent films. Mother of Sara Haden.
Kindling 15. Trail of the Lonesome Pine 16. Eve in Exile 19. Classmates 24. The Manicure Girl 25. Paris Bound 29. Scarlet Pages 30. Millie 31, etc.

Walker, Clint (1927–). Giant-size American leading man from TV. No acting training.
Fort Dobbs 57. Yellowstone Kelly 60. Gold of the Seven Saints 61. Send Me No Flowers 64. Night of the Grizzly 66. The Dirty Dozen 67. Sam Whiskey 68. The Great Bank Robbery 69. Yuma (TV) 70. The Bounty Man (TV) 72. Baker's Hawk 76. The White Buffalo 77. Hysterical 83. Serpent Warriors 86, etc.
TV series: Cheyenne 55–62. Kodiak 75.

Walker, H. M. ('Beanie') (1887–1937). American dialogue writer who provided most of Laurel and Hardy's classic exchanges in the early thirties, though these were usually based on Stan Laurel's gags.

Walker, Hal (1896–1972). American director, mainly of routine films; stage experience.
□Out of this World 45. Duffy's Tavern 45. The Stork Club 45. *Road to Utopia* 45. My Friend Irma Goes West 50. At War with the Army 50. That's My Boy 51. Sailor Beware 51. Road to Bali 52.

Walker, Helen (1921–1968). American leading lady of the forties.
Lucky Jordan 42. Abroad with Two Yanks 44. Murder He Says 45. Cluny Brown 46. The Homestretch 47. Nightmare Alley 47. Impact 49. My True Story 51. Problem Girls 52. The Big Combo (last role) 55, etc.

Walker, Joseph (1892–1985). American cinematographer.
Danger 23. Flaming Fury 26. Virgin Lips 29. Dirigible 30. The Miracle Woman 31. American Madness 32. Lady for a Day 33. It Happened One Night 34. Broadway Bill 34. Mr Deeds Goes to Town 36. *Lost Horizon* 37. You Can't Take it With You 38. Mr Smith Goes to Washington 39. His Girl Friday 40. Here Comes Mr Jordan 41. *It's a Wonderful Life* 46. *The Jolson Story* 46. Born Yesterday 51, many others.
†On his retirement, Walker invented the zoom lens.

Walker, Nancy (1921–) (Ann Swoyer Barto). Pint-sized American character comedienne.
Best Foot Forward 43. The World's Greatest Athlete 73. Forty Carats 73. Murder By Death 76, etc.
TV series: McMillan and Wife 71–75. The Nancy Walker Show 76. Mrs Blansky's Beauties 77. Can't Stop the Music (d only) 80.

Walker, Nella (1886–1971). American character actress, usually placid mother or socialite.
Seven Keys to Baldpate 29. Trouble in Paradise 32. Humanity 33. Four Frightened People 34. Three Smart Girls 36. The Rage of Paris 38. No Time for Comedy 40. Kitty Foyle 40. Hellzapoppin 41. Wintertime 43. In Society 44. The Locket 46. That Hagen Girl 47. Sabrina 54, many others.

Walker, Norman (1892–1963). British director.
Tommy Atkins 27. The Middle Watch 31. Turn of the Tide 35. The Man at the Gate 40. Hard Steel 41. They Knew Mr Knight 45, etc.

Walker, Pete (1935–). British producer-director of exploitation films.
I Like Birds 67. School for Sex 68. Cool it Carol 70. Die Screaming Marianne 71. Four Dimensions of Greta 72. Tiffany Jones 73. House of Whipcord 74. Frightmare 75. The House of Mortal Sin 76. Schizo 76. The Comeback 77. Home Before Midnight 79. House of the Long Shadows 83, etc.

Walker, Robert (1914–1951). Slight, modest-looking American leading man of the forties.
□Winter Carnival 39. These Glamour Girls 39. Dancing Co-Ed 39. Bataan 43. Madame Curie 43. *See Here Private Hargrove* 43. *Since You Went Away* 44. Thirty Seconds Over Tokyo 44. *The Clock* 45. Her Highness and the Bellboy 45. What Next Corporal Hargrove? 45. The Sailor Takes a Wife 45. *Till the Clouds Roll By* (as Jerome Kern) 46. The Sea of Grass 47. The Beginning or the End 47. Song of Love 47. One Touch of Venus 48. Please Believe Me 50. The Skipper Surprised His Wife 50. Vengeance Valley 51. *Strangers on a Train* 51. My Son John 52.

Walker, Robert Jnr (1941–). American second lead of the sixties.
The Hook 63. Ensign Pulver 64. The Ceremony 64. The Happening 67. The War Wagon 67. Easy Rider 69. Road to Salina 70.

The Spectre of Edgar Allan Poe 72. God Bless Dr Shagetz 77. A Touch of Sin 83, etc.

Walker, Stuart (1887–1941). American director, former stage producer.
□The Secret Call 31. The False Madonna 32. The Misleading Lady 32. Evenings for Sale 32. Tonight is Ours 33. *The Eagle and the Hawk* 33. White Woman 33. Romance in the Rain 34. Great Expectations 34. The Mystery of Edwin Drood 35. Werewolf of London 35. Manhattan Moon 35. Bulldog Drummond's Bride 39. Emergency Squad 40.

Walker, Syd (1887–1945). British comic actor and monologuist.
Over She Goes 37. Oh Boy 38. Hold My Hand 39. What Would You Do, Chums? (his catchphrase) 39, etc.

Walker, Zena (1934–). British leading actress of the sixties, mostly on TV.
The Hellions 61. The Traitors 63. One of Those Things 69. The Dresser 83, etc.

Wallace, Dee (–). American leading lady.
E.T. 82. Cujo 83.

Wallace, Edgar (1875–1932). Prolific British crime story writer. Films of his books include: *The Case of the Frightened Lady* 30 and 40. *The Calendar* 32 and 48. *The Crimson Circle* 30, 37 and 61. *The Terror* 28 and 39. *Kate Plus Ten* 38. Sanders of the River 35. The Squeaker 37. The Four Just Men 39. The Mind of Mr Reeder 39 (and series). *The Ringer* 32 and 52, and many episodes of a second feature series made at Merton Park in the sixties.

Wallace, Irving (1916–) (Irving Wallechinsky). American writer who with his son David and daughter Amy writes encyclopaedias (*The Book of Lists*) but on his own account is a best-selling novelist. *The Chapman Report*, *The Prize*, *The Man* and *The Seven Minutes* have all been filmed.

Wallace, Jean (1923–) (Jean Wallasek). American leading lady, married to Cornel Wilde.
You Can't Ration Love 44. Jigsaw 48. The Good Humour Man 50. Song of India 50. Storm Fear 55. The Big Combo 55. Maracaibo 58. Lancelot and Guinevere 63. Beach Red 67. No Blade of Grass 71, etc.

Wallace, Lew (1827–1905). American novelist who in 1880 published the much filmed *Ben Hur*.

Wallace, Richard (1894–1951). American director, former cutter for Mack Sennett. MacFadden's Flats 27. Innocents of Paris 30. Seven Days' Leave 31. The Road to Reno 32. Shopworn Angel 33. The Little Minister 35. *The Young in Heart* 39. Captain Caution 40. The Navy Steps Out 41. She Knew All the Answers 41. The Fallen Sparrow 43. Bride by Mistake 44. *It's in the Bag* 45. Sinbad the Sailor 46. Tycoon 47. Let's Live a Little 48. A Kiss for Corliss 50, many others.

Wallach, Eli (1915–). American stage actor (from 1940) who has latterly concentrated on films, often in villainous roles which he spices with 'the method'.
□*Baby Doll* (debut) 56. The Line Up 58. Seven Thieves 59. The Magnificent Seven 60. The Misfits 61. Hemingway's Adventures of a Young Man 62. How the West Was Won 62. The Victors 63. Act One 63. The Moonspinners 64. Kisses for My President 64. Lord Jim 65. Genghis Khan 65. How to Steal a Million 66. The Good the Bad and the Ugly (It.) 67. *The Tiger Makes Out* 67. How to Save a Marriage 68. Mackenna's Gold 68. A Lovely Way to Die 68. Revenge in El Paso (It.) 68. Ace High 69. The Brain 69. Zigzag 70. The People Next Door 70. The Angel Levine 70. The Adventures of Gerard 70. Romance of a Horsethief 71. A Cold Night's Death (TV) 72. Crazy Joe 73. Last Chance 73. Don't Turn the Other Cheek 73. Cinderalla Liberty 74. Samurai 74. Indict and Convict (TV) 74. The Deep 77. Nasty Habits 77. The Sentinel 77. The Domino Principle 77. Seventh Avenue (TV) 77. Girl Friends 78. The Pirate (TV) 78. Movie Movie 78. Firepower 79. Winter Kills 79. Circle of Iron 79. The Pride of Jesse Hallam (TV) 80. The Salamander 80. The Hunter 81. The Executioner's Song (TV) 82. Anatomy of an Illness (TV) 84. Christopher Columbus (TV) 85. Sam's Son (TV) 85. Tough Guys 86.

Waller, Fats (1904–1943). Black American jazz pianist and composer.
□Hooray for Love 35. King of Burlesque 36. Stormy Weather 43.

Waller, Fred (1886–1954). American research technician who invented Cinerama and saw it open successfully only two years before his death.

Wallis, Hal B. (1898–1986). American producer, latterly independent, responsible for a long line of solidly commercial films. In films from 1922.
Little Caesar 30. *The Story of Louis Pasteur* 36. Jezebel 38. *King's Row* 42. *Casablanca* 42. The Strange Love of Martha Ivers 46. My Friend Irma 49. *Gunfight at the OK Corral* 57. G.I. Blues 60. Becket 64. Boeing-Boeing 65. The Sons of Katie Elder 65. Five Card Stud 68. True Grit 69. Anne of the Thousand Days 70. Mary Queen of Scots 72. Bequest to the Nation 73. Rooster Cogburn 75, scores of others (often as executive producer for major studios).

Wallis, Shani (1938–). British cabaret singer.
□ The Extra Day 56. Ramsbottom Rides Again 56. A King in New York 67. Oliver! 68. Terror in the Wax Museum 73. Arnold 73.

Walls, Tom (1883–1949). British actor and director, on stage from 1905 after experience as policeman, busker, jockey, etc. Associated from mid-twenties with the Aldwych farces, which he produced and later transferred to the screen, as well as playing amiable philanderers in them. Subsequently in character roles.
□*Rookery Nook* 30. On Approval 30. Canaries Sometimes Sing 30. Tons of Money 31. *Plunder* 31. A Night Like This 32. *Thark* 32. Leap Year 32. The Blarney Stone 32. Just Smith 33. Turkey Time 33. A Cuckoo in the Nest 34. A Cup of Kindness 34. Lady in Danger 34. Dirty Work 34. Fighting Stock 35. Me and Marlborough 35. Stormy Weather 35. Foreign Affaires 36. Pot Luck 36. Dishonour Bright 36. For Valour 37. Second Best Bed 38. Old Iron 38. *Strange Boarders* 38. Crackerjack 38. Undercover 43. They Met in the Dark 43. Halfway House 43. Love Story 44. Johnny Frenchman 45. This Man is Mine 46. *Master of Bankdam* 47. While I Live 47. *Spring in Park Lane* 47. Maytime in Mayfair 48. Derby Day 49. The Interrupted Journey 49.

Walpole, Sir Hugh (1884–1941). British novelist who has been oddly neglected by the cinema but did some scripting in thirties Hollywood and appeared as the vicar in *David Copperfield* 34.

Walsh, Bill (1918–1976). American producer for the Walt Disney Organization.

Walsh, David M. (–). American cinematographer.
I Walk the Line 70. The Other Side of the Mountain 75. The Silver Streak 76. Rollercoaster 77. House Calls 78. Movie Movie 78. Goldengirl 78. Seems Like Old Times 80. Only When I Laugh 81. Max Dugan Returns 83. Romantic Comedy 83, etc.

Walsh, Dermot (1924–). British leading man, usually in second features.
My Sister and I 49. The Frightened Man 52. The Floating Dutchman 53. The Night of the Full Moon 56. Woman of Mystery 57. Crash Drive 59. The Trunk 61. The Cool Mikado 63, many others.
TV series: Richard the Lionheart 62.

Walsh, Kay (1914–). British character actress, former leading lady. Trained in West End revue.
Get Your Man (debut) 34. I See Ice 38. In Which We Serve 42. This Happy Breed 44. *The October Man* 47. Vice Versa 48. Oliver Twist 48. Stage Fright 50. Last Holiday 50. *Encore* 51. Meet Me Tonight 52. Lease of Life 54. Cast a Dark Shadow 55. The Horse's Mouth 59. *Tunes of Glory* 60. Eighty Thousand Suspects 63. The Beauty Jungle 64. A Study in Terror 65. The Witches 66. Connecting Rooms 69. The Ruling Class 71, many others.
TV series: Sherlock Holmes and Dr Watson 80.

Walsh, Raoul (1887–1981). Veteran American director of many commercial and several distinguished pictures. In films from 1912; former actor and assistant to D. W. Griffith.
Autobiography 1974: *Each Man in His Time*. Carmen 15. *The Thief of Baghdad* 24. *What Price Glory?* 26. *Sadie Thompson* 28. In Old Arizona 29. *The Big Trail* 30. *The Bowery* 33 Every Night at Eight 35. Artists and Models 38. St Louis Blues 39. *They Drive by Night* 40. *High Sierra* 41. They Died with Their Boots On 41. Strawberry Blonde 41. Manpower 41. Desperate Journey 42. Gentleman Jim 43. Northern Pursuit 44. Uncertain Glory 44. The Horn Blows at Midnight 45. *Objective Burma* 45. The Man I Love 46. Pursued 47. Silver River 48. *White Heat* 49. Colorado Territory 49. Along the Great Divide 49. Captain Horatio Hornblower 50. Distant Drums 51. The World in His Arms 52. Glory Alley 52. Blackbeard the Pirate 53. A Lion is in the Streets 54. Saskatchewan 54. Battle Cry 55.

The Tall Men 55. The Revolt of Mamie Stover 57. The King and Four Queens 57. Band of Angels 57. The Naked and the Dead 58. The Sheriff of Fractured Jaw (GB) 58. Esther and the King 60. Marines Let's Go 61. A Distant Trumpet 64, many others.
❁For vigorous treatment of action subjects. *White Heat.*

¶ 'To Raoul Walsh, a tender love scene is burning down a whorehouse.'—*Jack L. Warner*

Walston, Ray (1917–). American character comedian with stage experience.
□Kiss Them for Me 57. South Pacific 58. *Damn Yankees* 58. Say One for Me 59. The Apartment 60. Tall Story 60. Portrait in Black 60. Convicts Four 62. Wives and Lovers 63. Who's Minding the Store? 64. *Kiss Me Stupid* 64. Caprice 67. Paint Your Wagon 69. Viva Max 69. The Sting 73. Silver Streak 76. The Happy Hooker Goes to Washington 77. Popeye 81. Galaxy of Terror 81. Fast Times at Ridgmont High 82. O'Hara's Wife 82. Private School 83. Johnny Dangerously 84. O.C. and Stiggs 87.
TV series: My Favorite Martian 63–65.

Walter, Jessica (1944–). American leading lady of the sixties.
□Lilith 64. *The Group* 66. Grand Prix 67. Bye Bye Braverman 68. Number One 69. Play Misty for Me 71. Women in Chains (TV) 71. Home for the Holidays (TV) 72. Amy Prentiss (TV) 76. Victory at Entebbe (TV) 76. Secrets of Three Hungry Wives (TV) 78. She's Dressed to Kill (TV) 79. Spring Fever 83.

Walters, Charles (1911–1982). American director specializing in musicals. Former stage dancer and director of musical sequences in films.
Presenting Lily Mars (seq) 43. Meet Me in St Louis (seq) 44. Good News 47. *Easter Parade* 48. Summer Stock 50. Easy to Love 53. *Lili* 53. The Glass Slipper 55. The Tender Trap 55. High Society 56. Don't Go Near the Water 57. Ask Any Girl 59. Please Don't Eat the Daisies 60. Jumbo 62. The Unsinkable Molly Brown 64. Walk, Don't Run 66, etc.

Walters, Julie (1950–). British character actress, often in tarty roles.
Educating Rita (AAN) 83. She'll Be Wearing Pink Pajamas 84. Car Trouble 86. Prick Up Your Ears 87. Personal Services 87.

¶ *J.W.:* When I think of the future I think of doing my washing so I've something to wear tomorrow.

Walters, Thorley (1913–). British comedy actor on stage and screen from 1934. Film parts usually cameos, as incompetent officers, etc.
They Were Sisters 45. Private's Progress 56. Carleton Browne of the FO 58. Two-Way Stretch 60. Murder She Said 62. Ring of Spies 64. Joey Boy 65. *Rotten to the Core* 65. *Dracula, Prince of Darkness* 65. The Wrong Box 66. Frankenstein Must Be Destroyed 69. Vampire Circus 72. The Adventure of Sherlock Holmes' Smarter Brother 75. The People That Time Forgot 78. The Wildcats of St Trinian's 80. The Sign of Four (TV) 83, The Little Drummer Girl 84, etc.

Walthall, Henry B. (1878–1936). American leading man of the silent screen, in films from 1909.
In Old Kentucky 09. A Convict's Sacrifice 10. The Birth of a Nation 14. The Raven 15. Ghosts 15. His Robe of Honour 18. Single Wives 23. The Scarlet Letter 25. The Barrier 26. Abraham Lincoln 31. Police Court 32. Laughing at Life 33. Viva Villa 34. Dante's Inferno 35. A Tale of Two Cities 35. China Clipper 36, many others.

Walton, Tony (1934–). British production designer.
Mary Poppins 64. Fahrenheit 451 66. A Funny Thing Happened on the Way to the Forum 66. The Seagull 68. Boy Friend 71. Murder on the Orient Express 74. The Wiz 78. All That Jazz 79. Just Tell Me What You Want 80. Prince of the City 81. Deathtrap 82.

Walton, Sir William (1902–1983). British composer whose film scores include *Henry V* 44. *Hamlet* 48. *Richard III* 56.

Wambaugh, Joseph (1937–). American novelist, an ex-policeman who capitalized on his experience and tends to rub his readers' noses in the gutter. Films resulting include *The New Centurions*, *The Onion Field*, *The Black Marble*, *The Choirboys*.

W.A.M.P.A.S. (Western Association of Motion Picture Advertisers). A group of publicity executives who, from 1922 to 1934, gave annual certificates of merit to promising female starlets, known as 'Wampas baby stars'. Among those who succeeded were Bessie Love (nominated 1922), Laura la Plante 23, Clara Bow 24, Mary Astor 26, Joan Crawford 26, Dolores del Rio 26, Janet Gaynor 26, Lupe Velez 28, Jean Arthur 29, Loretta Young 29, Joan Blondell 31, Anita Louise 31, Ginger Rogers 32.

Wanamaker, Sam (1919–). American stage actor and director who has also appeared in films; now resident in Britain.
My Girl Tisa 48. Give Us This Day 50. Mr Denning Drives North 51. The Secret 55. The Criminal 60. Taras Bulba 62. The Man in the Middle 64. Those Magnificent Men in Their Flying Machines 65. The Spy Who Came in from the Cold 65. Warning Shot 66. The Day the Fish Came Out 67. File of the Golden Goose (d only) 69. The Executioner (d only) 69. Catlow (d only) 72. Mousey (TV) 73. The Sell Out 75. Voyage of the Damned 76. Sinbad and the Eye of the Tiger (d only) 77. Holocaust (TV) 78. Death on the Nile 78. Private Benjamin 80. The Competition 80. The Aviator 84. Irreconcilable Differences 84. Raw Deal 86. Superman IV 87, etc.

Wang Yu, Jimmy (–). Chinese leading man and Kung Fu expert.
The Legend of Seven Golden Vampires 74. The Man from Hong Kong 75, etc.

Wanger, Walter (1894–1968) (W. Feuchtwanger). American independent producer who during a long career held at various times senior executive posts with major studios.
Queen Christina 33. The President Vanishes 35. Private Worlds 35. Mary Burns Fugitive 35. The Trail of the Lonesome Pine 36. *You Only Live Once* 37. History is Made at Night 37. 52nd Street 38. Stand In 38. *Blockade* 38. Trade Winds 38. Algiers 38. *Stagecoach* 39. *Foreign Correspondent* 40. The Long Voyage Home 40. *Scarlet Street* 45. The Lost Moment 47. Tap Roots 48. Joan of Arc 48. Riot in Cell Block Eleven 54. *Invasion of the Body Snatchers* 55. I Want to Live 58. Cleopatra 62.

¶ He always wanted to be European.—*James Mason*
Nothing is as cheap as a hit, no matter how much it costs.—*W.W.*

War and Peace. The main film versions of Tolstoy's epic novel were a Russian one of 1916; King Vidor's of 1955 with Henry Fonda and Audrey Hepburn, photographed by Jack Cardiff and Aldo Tonti; and Sergei Bondartchuk's seven-hour colossus of 1964, photographed by Anatole Petrinsky.

war heroes who have become the subject of biopics include Eddie Rickenbacker (Fred MacMurray, *Captain Eddie*); Audie Murphy (himself, *To Hell and Back*); Guy Gabaldon (Jeffrey Hunter, *Hell to Eternity*); Alvin York (Gary Cooper, *Sergeant York*); Douglas Bader (Kenneth More, *Reach for the Sky*); Guy Gibson (Richard Todd, *The Dam Busters*); Ernie Pyle (Burgess Meredith, *The Story of G.I. Joe*); John Hoskins (Sterling Hayden, *The Eternal Sea*).

The War of the Worlds (US 1953). This George Pal version (AA special effects) of the H. G. Wells fantasy about a Martian invasion was by no means as imaginative as it might have been, but was notable for introducing a streak of viciousness into science fiction: neither side showed much mercy, and the noise was deafening.

Ward, Burt (1945–) (Herbert Jervis). American juvenile of the sixties who played Robin in TV's *Batman* series, then disappeared from view.

Ward, Edward (–). American composer.
Kismet 31. Great Expectations 34. The Mystery of Edwin Drood 35. Navy Blue and Gold 37. Stablemates 38. Thunder Afloat 39. Mr and Mrs Smith 41. Phantom of the Opera 43. The Climax 44. Salome Where She Danced 45. Copacabana 47. The Babe Ruth Story 48, etc.

Ward, Fannie (1865–1952). American stage actress, a famous beauty of her time who in middle age began a Hollywood film career playing parts too young for her, and was the inspiration of novel and film *Mr Skeffington*.
The Marriage of Kitty 15. The Cheat 15. The Years of the Locust 16. The Yellow Ticket 18. Innocent 18. A Japanese Nightingale 18. Common Clay 19, etc.

Ward, Fred (–). American leading man
Escape from Alcatraz 82. The Right Stuff 83. Silkwood 83. Remo Williams 85.

Ward, Michael (1915–). British comic actor usually seen as nervous photographer or twee shopwalker.
An Ideal Husband 47. Sleeping Car to Trieste 48. Street Corner 53. Private's Progress 55. I'm All Right, Jack 59. Carry On Screaming 66, etc.

Ward, Polly (1908–) (Byno Poluski). British-born leading lady of several thirties comedies.
Shooting Stars 28. His Lordship 32. The Old Curiosity Shop 34. Feather Your Nest 37. Thank Evans 38. It's in the Air 38. Bulldog

Drummond Sees It Through 40. Women Aren't Angels 42, etc.

Ward, Rachel (1957–). British-born leading lady, in America at first as a model.
Sharky's Machine 81. Dead Men Don't Wear Plaid 82. The Thorn Birds (TV) 83. The Good Wife 86. Hotel Colonial 87.

Ward, Simon (1941–). British leading actor of the seventies.
□ Frankenstein Must Be Destroyed 69. Quest for Love 70. I Start Counting 71. *Young Winston* 72. Hitler – the Last Ten Days 73. Dracula (TV) 73. The Three Musketeers 74. The Four Musketeers 75. Deadly Strangers 75. All Creatures Great and Small 75. Aces High 76. Holocaust 2000 77. Children of Rage 77. Battle Flag 77. Dominique 78. Zulu Dawn 79. La Sabina 79. The Monster Club 80. Supergirl 84. The Corsican Brothers (TV) 85.

Warden, Jack (1920–). Burly American character actor, also on stage and TV.
From Here to Eternity 53. *Twelve Angry Men* 57. Edge of the City 57. *The Bachelor Party* 57. Escape from Zahrain 62. Mirage 65. Blindfold 65. Welcome to the Club 70. Who is Harry Kellerman . . . ? 71. Billy Two Hats 73. The Apprenticeship of Duddy Kravitz 74. Shampoo 75. All the President's Men 76. Voyage of the Damned 76. The White Buffalo 77. Death on the Nile 78. The Champ 79. And Justice for All 79. Used Cars 80. So Fine 81. A Private Battle (TV) 81. The Verdict 82. Hobson's Choice (TV) 83. The Aviator 84. Crackers 84. September 87, etc.
TV series: Mr Peepers 53–55. The Asphalt Jungle 60. The Wackiest Ship in the Army 65. N.Y.P.D. 67–68. The Bad News Bears 79. *Crazy Like a Fox* 84–85.

Warhol, Andy (1926–1987). American 'underground' film-maker of the sixties: his works usually run for several hours and are totally boring except to the initiated.
Sleep 63. Blow Job 64. Harlot 65. The Chelsea Girls (shown on two screens side by side, with different images) 66. F**k, or Blue Movie 69. Trash (p only) 70. Flesh (p only) 71. Bad 76, etc.

¶ Sex is the biggest nothing of all time.—*A.W.*

Warner Brothers Pictures Inc. is a family affair started in 1923 by four American exhibitor brothers. After a very shaky start it soared to pre-eminence through their gamble on talking pictures in the shape of *The Jazz Singer* and *The Singing Fool*. Through the thirties and forties the company kept its popularity through tough gangster films starring James Cagney, Edward G. Robinson and Humphrey Bogart, and musicals with Dick Powell and Ruby Keeler; and its prestige by exposés like *Confessions of a Nazi Spy* and *Mission to Moscow* and biographies of Zola, Pasteur, Ehrlich and Reuter. Other Warner stars included Bette Davis and Errol Flynn, both enormously popular with all classes. Warner films were not usually over-budgeted but contrived to look immaculate through solid production values and star performances. Since 1950 the company's product has been more variable, as deals have had to be done with independent producers, and there has been a patchy flirtation with TV; yet on the serious side directors like Kazan have been encouraged, popular taste is taken care of by spectaculars like *My Fair Lady* and *The Great Race*, and the company took a calculated risk (which paid off in spades) with *Who's Afraid of Virginia Woolf?* In the mid-sixties came a merger with Seven Arts, and in 1969 the company was taken over by a conglomerate. In the eighties the famous production company seemed to be kept solvent by Clint Eastwood toughies. Various books were published about its glory days, including a 1986 collection of memos: *Inside Warner Brothers 1935–51* by Rudy Behlmer.

¶ Working for Warner Brothers is like fucking a porcupine. It's a hundred pricks against one.—*Wilson Mizner*

I would rather take a fifty-mile hike than crawl through a book. I prefer to skip the long ones and get a synopsis from the story department.—*Jack Warner*

'This studio has more suspensions than the Golden Gate Bridge.'—*Humphrey Bogart*

Warner, David (1941–). Lanky British stage actor who has made film appearances.
□Tom Jones (as Blifil) 63. The Deadly Affair 66. *Morgan* 66. Work is a Four-Letter Word 68. A Midsummer Night's Dream 68. *The Bofors Gun* 68. The Fixer 68. The Seagull 68. Michael Kohlhaas 69. The Ballad of Cable Hogue 70. Perfect Friday 70. The Engagement 70. The French Lieutenant's Woman 71. Straw Dogs 71. A Doll's House 73. Mr Quilp 75. Little Malcolm 75. The Omen 76. Victory at Entebbe (TV) 76. Age of Innocence 77. The Disappearance 77. Cross of Iron 77. Providence 77. The 39 Steps 78. *Holocaust* (TV) (as Heydrich) 78. Silver Bears 78. The

Concorde—Airport 79 79. Time after Time (as Jack the Ripper) 79. Nightwing 79. The Islands 80. Time Bandits 81. Iron 82. The Man with Two Brains 83. Company of Wolves 84. A Christmas Carol (TV) 84. Hansel and Gretel 87.

Warner, H. B. (1876–1958) (Henry Byron Warner-Lickford). Distinguished British actor, on stage from 1883; in Hollywood as film actor from around 1917.
The Beggar of Cawnpore 15. The Man White 19. One Hour Before Dawn 20. Zaza 23. *King of Kings* (as Jesus) 27. Sorrell and Son 27. The Divine Lady 28. The Trial of Mary Dugan 29. Five Star Final 31. *Mr Deeds Goes to Town* 36. *Lost Horizon* 37. *Victoria the Great* 37. You Can't Take It With You 38. Bulldog Drummond Strikes Back 39. The Rains Came 39. All That Money Can Buy 41. Topper Returns 41. The Corsican Brothers 41. It's a Wonderful Life 46. Prince of Thieves 48. Sunset Boulevard 50. Savage Drums 51. The Ten Commandments 56, many others.
❁ For bringing dignity to a wildly disparate collection of films. *Lost Horizon*.

Warner, Jack (1894–1981) (Jack Waters). Genial British character actor, former music-hall comedian; TV's 'Dixon of Dock Green'. Autobiography 1975: *Jack of all Trades*.
The Dummy Talks (debut) 43. *The Captive Heart* 46. Hue and Cry 46. It Always Rains on Sunday 47. Holiday Camp 47. *Here Come the Huggetts* 48. The Huggetts Abroad 49. *The Blue Lamp* 50. Valley of Eagles 51. Scrooge 51. The Quatermass Experiment 55. Home and Away 56. Carve Her Name with Pride 58. *Jigsaw* 62, many others.

Warner, Jack L. (1892–1978). American executive producer, last member of the four Warner Brothers who started up a small production company in the twenties and pioneered sound pictures with *The Jazz Singer* 27. The other brothers: Albert, Harry M., and Sam.
Jack has published his autobiography (1965): *My First Hundred Years in Hollywood*. See also *Warner Brothers*.
RECENT PRODUCTIONS: *My Fair Lady* 64. *Camelot* 67. *'1776'* 72. Dirty Little Billy 73.
❁ For running a studio with the discipline of a prison, and living to see the results endure. *A Midsummer Night's Dream*.

¶ 'He was a generous host, a big gambler at work and at play, and with superb confidence he put his money where his mouth was.'—*David Niven*

'He bore no grudge against those he had wronged.'—*Simone Signoret*

'I can't see what J.W. can do with an Oscar. It can't say yes.'—*Al Jolson*

'He existed behind a self-made wall. Besides a lot of him wasn't that nice to know. At times he gloried in being a no-good sonofabitch.'—*Jack Warner Jnr*

'A man who would rather tell a bad joke than make a good movie.'—*Jack Benny*

'I have a theory of relatives too. Don't hire 'em.'—*J.W. to Einstein*

'If his brothers hadn't hired him, he'd have been out of work.'—*Jack Warner Jnr*

(In retirement in Palm Springs): You're nothing if you don't have a studio. Now I'm just another millionaire, and there are a lot of 'em around.—*J.W.*

Warnercolor. Actually Eastmancolor, though it always looked as though it had had a blue rinse.

Warning Shadows (Germany 1922). Directed by Arthur Robison, this structurally interesting but very Teutonic fantasy concerns a shadow-man who forces the inhabitants of an unhappy household to see themselves in a shadowy play. Full of weird effects largely achieved by expressionist use of light and shadow.

Warren, C. Denier (1889–1971). Chubby American character comedian, in British films; vaudeville experience.
Counsel's Opinion 33. Kentucky Minstrels 34. A Fire Has Been Arranged 35. Cotton Queen 37. Trouble Brewing 39. Kiss the Bride Goodbye 44. Old Mother Riley, Headmistress 50. Bluebeard's Ten Honeymoons 60, etc.

Warren, Charles Marquis (1912–). American writer-director. Moved into TV and became creator and executive producer of *Gunsmoke, Rawhide, The Virginian*, etc.
Little Big Horn 51. Hellgate 52. Arrowhead 53. Flight to Tangier 54. Seven Angry Men 55. The Black Whip 56. Charro (pd) 69, etc.

Warren, Harry (1893–1981) (Salvatore Guaragno). American songwriter, mainly with Al Dubin; busy on many Warner musicals of the early thirties, they made a personal appearance in *42nd Street*.

Warren, Jennifer (1941–). American general purpose actress.
Night Moves 75. Slap Shot 77. Another Man Another Chance 77. Ice Castles 78, etc.

Warren, Lesley Ann (1946–). American leading lady.
The Happiest Millionaire 67. Seven in Darkness (TV) 69. Assignment Munich (TV) 72. 79 Park Avenue (TV) 77. Beulah Land (TV) 80. Victor/Victoria 82. A Night in Heaven 83. Evergreen (TV) 84. Choose Me 84. Songwriter 84. Clue 85.

Warren, Robert Penn (1905–). American novelist.
All the King's Men 49. Band of Angels 57.

Warrender, Harold (1903–1953). British stage and screen actor.
Friday the Thirteenth 33. Contraband 40. Sailors Three 41. Scott of the Antarctic 49. Pandora and the Flying Dutchman 51. Where No Vultures Fly 51. Intimate Relations 53, etc.

Warrick, Ruth (1915–). American leading lady of the forties. Former radio singer.
Citizen Kane (debut) 41. The Corsican Brothers 41. Journey into Fear 42. Forever and a Day 43. Mr Winkle Goes to War 44. Guest in the House 44. China Sky 45. Swell Guy 47. Arch of Triumph 48. Three Husbands 50. Killer with a Label 50. Let's Dance 52. Ride Beyond Vengeance 65. How to Steal the World 68. The Great Bank Robbery 69. The Returning 83, etc.
TV series: Father of the Bride 61. Peyton Place 65.

Warwick, John (1905–1972) (John McIntosh Beattie). Australian leading man, later character actor, in British films, including many of the 'Scotland Yard' series as police inspector.
Down on the Farm 35. Lucky Jade 37. The Face at the Window 39. Danny Boy 40. The Missing Million 42. Dancing with Crime 48. Street Corner 53. Up to His Neck 54. Just My Luck 57. Horrors of the Black Museum 59.

Warwick, Robert (1878–1965) (Robert Taylor Bien). American character actor, adept at executives and heavy fathers. A star of such silent films as *A Modern Othello, The Mad Lover, Thou Art the Man.*
So Big 32. Night Life of the Gods 35. A Tale of Two Cities 35. The Life of Emile Zola 37. The Adventures of Robin Hood 38. Sullivan's Travels 41. The Palm Beach Story 42. I Married a Witch 43. Gentleman's Agreement 47. Francis 49. Sugarfoot 51. Mississippi Gambler 53. Lady Godiva of Coventry 55. Night of the Quarter Moon 59, many others.

Washbourne, Mona (1903–). British stage character actress.
Wide Boy 48. Child's Play 53. Doctor in the House 54. The Good Companions 57. Brides of Dracula 60. *Billy Liar* 63. *Night Must Fall* 63. One Way Pendulum 64. *My Fair Lady* (US) 64. The Third Day (US) 65. Mrs Brown You've Got a Lovely Daughter 68. Fragment of Fear 70. What Became of Jack and Jill? 71. O Lucky Man 73, etc.

Washburn, Bryant (1889–1963). American romantic hero of the silent screen.
The Blindness of Virtue 15. Venus in the East 18. The Parasite 25. Swing High 30. Sutter's Gold 36, many others.

Washington, George (1732–1799). The first American president, the lad who could not tell a lie, has been impersonated in many films, including *Alexander Hamilton* (Alan Mowbray, who also had the role in *The Phantom President* and *Where Do We Go from Here?*); *America* (Arthur Dewey); *The Howards of Virginia* (George Houston); *The Remarkable Andrew* (Montagu Love); *Unconquered* (Richard Gaines); *John Paul Jones* (John Crawford); *Lafayette* (Howard St John).

Washington, Ned (1901–76). American composer with wide show business experience.
Show of Shows 29. Illegal 32. A Night at the Opera 35. Romance in the Dark 38. Pinocchio 40. Dumbo 41. For Whom the Bell Tolls 43. Passage to Marseilles 44. The Uninvited 44. Green Dolphin Street 47. My Foolish Heart 50. Miss Sadie Thompson 53. The High and the Mighty 54. The Man from Laramie 55. Fire Down Below 57. Gunfight at the OK Corral 57. The Unforgiven 60. The Last Sunset 61. The Fall of the Roman Empire 64. Ship of Fools 65. Five Card Stud 68, many others.

Wasson, Craig (1954–). American general purpose actor.
The Boys in Company C 77. Rollercoaster 77. Go Tell the Spartans 78. The Outsider 80. Schizoid 80. Four Friends 81. Ghost Story 81. Body Double 84. The Men's Club 86, etc.

water, in inconvenient quantity, played a dramatic part in *Way Down East*; *Noah's Ark*; *The Rains Came* and its remake *The Rains of Ranchipur*; *The Bible*; *Floods of Fear*; *The Hurricane*; *Campbell's Kingdom*; *When Worlds Collide*; *Rain*; *Whistling in*

Dixie; *Foreign Correspondent*; *Who Was That Lady?*; and no doubt a hundred others.
See also: *Rain*.

waterfront films have turned up frequently. Among the more seriously-intended are *On the Waterfront, Anna Christie, Waterfront*, and *Slaughter on Tenth Avenue*; melodramas include *The Mob*, the *Tugboat Annie* films, and *I Cover the Waterfront*. Laurel and Hardy worked the milieu in *The Live Ghost*. TV series include yet another *Waterfront*.

Waterhouse, Keith (1929–). British light journalist and novelist. His *Billy Liar* was successful also as play and film. With Willis Hall he wrote screenplays including *Whistle Down the Wind*, *A Kind of Loving*, *Pretty Polly*.

Waterloo Bridge. Robert E. Sherwood's sentimental romance, about a ballet dancer who turns prostitute when her rich lover is reported killed at the war and commits suicide when he returns, was filmed in 1930 by James Whale, with Kent Douglass and Mae Clarke; in 1940 by Mervyn le Roy, with Robert Taylor and Vivien Leigh; and in 1956 (as *Gaby*) by Curtis Bernhardt, with John Kerr, Leslie Caron and a happy ending.

Waterloo Road (GB 1944). A small and now dated melodrama about a soldier who takes French leave to beat up his wife's seducer, this film can now be seen as the beginning of the British realist movement which eventually led to *Saturday Night and Sunday Morning*. Getting out of the studio into South London slums, it gave at the time a fresh and vivid sensation now impossible to recapture. Written and directed by Sidney Gilliat; photographed by Arthur Crabtree; with John Mills, Joy Shelton, Stewart Granger and Alastair Sim.

Waterman, Dennis (1948–). British juvenile of the sixties, tough TV hero of the seventies.
Pirates of Blood River 61. *Up the Junction* 67. My Lover My Son 69. A Smashing Bird I Used to Know 69. Scars of Dracula 70. Fright 70. Man in the Wilderness 71. The Belstone Fox 73. The Sweeney 77. Sweeney Two 78, etc.
TV series: Fair Exchange 62. *The Sweeney* 74–78. Minder 79–.

Waters, Ethel (1896–1977). Distinguished black American actress and singer.
Autobiography 1953: *His Eye is on the Sparrow*.
On with the Show 29. Tales of Manhattan 42. *Cabin in the Sky* 43. *Pinky* 49. *Member of the Wedding* 52. The Sound and the Fury 59, etc.
TV series: Beulah 50–53.

Waters, Russell (1908–82). British character actor usually in meek and mild parts. The 'hero' of many of Richard Massingham's short and light-hearted instructional films.
The Woman in the Hall 47. The Happiest Days of Your Life 50. The Maggie 54. Left, Right and Centre 59, many others.

Waterston, Sam (1940–). American general purpose actor.
A Time for Giving 69. Savages 72. A Delicate Balance 73. *The Great Gatsby* 74. Rancho de Luxe 75. Capricorn One 78. Interiors 78. Eagle's Wing 79. Sweet William 79. Heaven's Gate 80. Hopscotch 80. Oppenheimer (TV) 81. Q.E.D. (TV) 81. Finnegan Begin Again (TV) 84. The Killing Fields (AAN) 84. September 87, etc.

Watkin, David (1925–). British cinematographer.
The Knack 64. Help 65. The Marat/Sade 66. How I Won the War 67. The Charge of the Light Brigade 67. The Bed Sitting Room 69. Catch 22 70. The Devils 71. The Boy Friend 71. A Delicate Balance 73. The Three Musketeers 74. Robin and Marian 76. Chariots of Fire 81. Yentl 83. Out of Africa (AAN) 85, etc.

Watkin, Pierre (1889–1960). American character actor often seen as lawyer, doctor or kindly father.
Dangerous 35. Pride of the Yankees 41. Whistling in Dixie 43. Shanghai Chest 46. Knock On Any Door 59. The Dark Page 51. Johnny Dark 54, many others.

Watkins, Peter (1937–). British director from TV (*Culloden, The War Game*).
□Privilege 67. Punishment Park 71. Edvard Munch 75.

Watling, Jack (1923–). Boyish British character actor.
Sixty Glorious Years 38. Journey Together 45. The Courtneys of Curzon Street 47. Quartet 48. The Winslow Boy 48. Meet Mr Lucifer 54. The Sea Shall Not Have Them 55. The Admirable Crichton 57. A Night to Remember 58. Mary Had a Little 61. 11 Harrowhouse 74, many others.

Watson, Bobs (1931–). American boy actor of the thirties and forties; noted for his ability to weep at the drop of a hat.
In Old Chicago 38. Kentucky 39. *On Borrowed Time* 39. Dr Kildare's Crisis 41. Men of Boys' Town 41. The Bold and the Brave 56. First to Fight 67, etc.
TV series: The Jim Backus Show 60.

Watson, Jack (1921–). Tough-looking British general purpose actor.
Konga 61. This Sporting Life 62. The Hill 65. Tobruk 67. *The Strange Affair* 67. Every Home Should Have One 70. The Mackenzie Break 71. Kidnapped 72. Juggernaut 76. Schizo 77. The Wild Geese 79. The Sea Wolves 80, etc.

Watson, Lucile (1879–1962). Canadian character actress with stage experience; usually in imperious roles.
□What Every Woman Knows 34. The Bishop Misbehaves 35. A Woman Rebels 36. The Garden of Allah 36. Three Smart Girls 36. The Young in Heart 38. Sweethearts 38. Made for Each Other 39. The Women 39. Florian 40. *Waterloo Bridge* 40. Mr and Mrs Smith 41. Rage in Heaven 41. Footsteps in the Dark 41. The Great Lie 41. Model Wife 41. *Watch on the Rhine* 43. Till We Meet Again 44. The Thin Man Goes Home 44. Uncertain Glory 44. My Reputation 46. Tomorrow Is Forever 46. Never Say Goodbye 46. *The Razor's Edge* 46. Song of the South 46. Ivy 47. The Emperor Waltz 48. Julia Misbehaves 48. That Wonderful Urge 48. Little Women 49. Everybody Does It 49. Harriet Craig 50. Let's Dance 50. My Forbidden Past 51.

Watson, Minor (1889–1965). American character actor who often played lawyers or kindly fathers.
Our Betters 33. Babbitt 34. When's Your Birthday? 37. Boys' Town 38. Moon over Miami 41. The Big Shot 42. The Virginian 46. The File on Thelma Jordon 49. Mister 880 50. My Son John 51. Trapeze 56, etc.

Watson, Moray (*c.*1927–). British light actor.
The Grass is Greener 60. Every Home should Have One 70. Operation Crossbow 65. The Sea Wolves 80. Crazy Like a Fox (TV) 87, etc.

Watson, Robert (1888–1965). American character actor who became famous for his resemblance to Hitler; played the lead in *The Hitler Gang* 43, and other films of this type. Moonlight and Melody 33. Mary of Scotland 36. The Devil with Hitler 42. Nazty Nuisance 43. The Big Clock 48. Red Hot and Blue 49. Singin' in the Rain 52. The Story of Mankind 57, etc.

Watson, Wylie (1889–1966) (John Wylie Robertson). British character actor, usually in 'little man' roles; formerly in music hall.
□For the Love of Mike 32. Leave It to Me 33. Hawleys of the High Street 33. *The 39 Steps* (as Mr Memory) 35. Black Mask 35. Radio Lover 36. Please Teacher 37. Why Pick on Me? 37. Paradise for Two 37. Queer Cargo 38. Yes Madam 38. Jamaica Inn 39. She Couldn't Say No 39. Pack Up Your Troubles 40. Bulldog Sees It Through 40. Danny Boy 41. My Wife's Family 41. The Saint Meets the Tiger 41. The Flemish Farm 43. The Lamp Still Burns 43. Tawny Pipit 44. Kiss the Bride Goodbye 44. Don't Take It to Heart 44. Waterloo Road 45. The World Owes Me a Living 45. Strawberry Roan 45. Don Chicago 45. Waltz Time 45. Murder in Reverse 45. The Trojan Brothers 46. The Years Between 46. Girl in a Million 46. Temptation Harbour 47. Fame Is the Spur 47. Brighton Rock 47. My Brother Jonathan 48. *London Belongs to Me* 48. No Room at the Inn 48. Things Happen at Night 48. The History of Mr Polly 49. *Whisky Galore* 49. Train of Events 49. Your Witness 50. Morning Departure 50. Shadow of the Past 50. The Magnet 50. Happy Go Lovely 51. *The Sundowners* 61.

Watt, Harry (1906–87). British director with varied early experience before joining GPO Film Unit as assistant in 1931.
Autobiography 1974: *Don't Look at the Camera.*
Night Mail 36. North Sea 38. Squadron 992 40. Target for Tonight 41. *Nine Men* (& w) 44. Fiddlers Three 44. The Overlanders 46. Eureka Stockade 48. Where No Vultures Fly 51. West of Zanzibar 53. The Siege of Pinchgut 59, etc.

Wattis, Richard (1912–1975). Bespectacled British character comedian with stage experience.
The Happiest Days of Your Life 49. The Clouded Yellow 51. Hobson's Choice 54. I am a Camera 55. Simon and Laura 55. The Prince and the Showgirl 58. The VIPs 63. Moll Flanders 65. Up Jumped a Swagman 65. Wonderwall 68. Games That Lovers Play 69. That's Your Funeral 73. Diamonds on Wheels 73. Hot Property 73, many others.
TV series: Dick and the Duchess 59. Sykes (through sixties).

Waxman, Franz (1906–1967) (Franz Wachsmann). German composer, in America from 1934.
Bride of Frankenstein 35. Sutter's Gold 36. Fury 36. Captains Courageous 38. The Young in Heart 38. *Rebecca* 40. *The Philadelphia Story* 40. Dr Jekyll and Mr Hyde 41. Woman of the Year 42. Air Force 42. Mr Skeffington 44. Objective Burma 45. Humoresque 46. The Paradine Case 48. *Alias Nick Beal* 49. *Sunset Boulevard* (AA) 50. *A Place in the Sun* (AA) 51. My Cousin Rachel 53. Rear Window 54. Mister Roberts 56. Sayonara 57. The Nun's Story 59. Cimarron 60. Taras Bulba 62. Lost Command 66, etc.

Waxman, Harry (1912–84). British cinematographer.
Brighton Rock 46. They Were Not Divided 48. Valley of Eagles 51. The Baby and the Battleship 56. *Innocent Sinners* 57. The Secret Partner 60. The Roman Spring of Mrs Stone 61. *The Day the Earth Caught Fire* 62. Lancelot and Guinevere 63. Crooks in Cloisters 64. The Nanny 65. *Khartoum* (2nd unit) 66. The Family Way 66. The Trygon Factor 67. The Anniversary 67. Wonderwall 68. Twisted Nerve 68. There's a Girl in My Soup 70. Flight of the Doves 71. Endless Night 72. Digby 73. Blue Blood 73. Vampira 74. Journey into Fear 75. The Pink Panther Strikes Again 76, etc.

waxworks have featured from time to time in horror films and other thrillers, notably *The Mystery of the Wax Museum, House of Wax, Nightmare in Wax, Terror in the Wax Museum, The Florentine Dagger, Charlie Chan in the Wax Museum, Midnight at Madame Tussaud's* and the original German *Waxworks*.

The Way Ahead (GB 1944). World War II's best film tribute to the British Army, as seen through the eyes of a group of very unwilling conscripts. The film survives chiefly by virtue of the good comedy writing of its first half; the final baptism of fire is more routine. Directed by Carol Reed from a script by Eric Ambler and Peter Ustinov (originally intended as a short army propaganda film); photographed by Guy Green; music by William Alwyn. With David Niven, Stanley Holloway, Raymond Huntley, Jimmy Hanley, William Hartnell, Peter Ustinov, etc.

Way Down East (US 1920). D. W. Griffith's sentimental melodrama is remembered now for its brilliantly and hazardously filmed ice-floe sequence. Written by Griffith from a play by Lottie Blair Parker; photographed by Hendrik Sartov and Billy Bitzer. With Lillian Gish, Richard Barthelmess. Remade as a talkie in 1936 with Rochelle Hudson and Henry Fonda.

The Way to the Stars (GB 1945). A gentle, satisfying film about the RAF in World War II. Hardly a plane is seen, as the action takes place mainly in a small hotel near the airfield. Both writer Terence Rattigan and director Anthony Asquith are in their best and most typical forms, and a distinguished cast includes Michael Redgrave, John Mills, Rosamund John, Douglass Montgomery, Stanley Holloway, Renée Asherson and Joyce Carey. Mention should also be made of Nicholas Brodszky's music and John Pudney's poems.

Wayne, David (1914–) (Wayne McKeekan). Wiry American character actor, in films since late forties, also stage star.
Portrait of Jennie 48. *Adam's Rib* 49. My Blue Heaven 50. Up Front 51. With a Song in My Heart 52. *Wait till the Sun Shines Nellie* 52. The I Don't Care Girl 53. Tonight We Sing 53. How to Marry a Millionaire 53. The Tender Trap 55. The Three Faces of Eve 57. The Last Angry Man 59. The Big Gamble 60. The Andromeda Strain 70. Huckleberry Finn 74. The Front Page 74. The Apple Dumpling Gang 75. Lassie: the New Beginning 79. House Calls 80, etc.
TV series: Norby 51. The Good Life 71. Ellery Queen 74. Dallas 78. House Calls 80.

Wayne, John (1907–79) (Marion Michael Morrison). Tough, genial, generally inimitable American leading man of action films, who after a slow start became one of the best known and most successful actors in Hollywood.
Biography 1974: *Shooting Star* by Maurice Zolotow.
□Hangman's House 28. Mother Machree 28. Salute 29. Men Without Women 30. Rough Romance 30. Cheer Up and Smile 30. *The Big Trail* 30. Girls Demand Excitement 31. Three Girls Lost 31. Men are Like That 31. Range Feud 31. Hurricane Express (serial) 31. Shadow of the Eagle (serial) 32. Maker of Men 32. Two Fisted Law 32. Texas Cyclone 32. Lady and Gent 32. Ride Him Cowboy 32. The Big Stampede 32. The Three Mesquiteers (serial) 33. Haunted Gold 33. Telegraph Trail 33. His Private Secretary 33. Central Airport 33. Baby Face Harrington 33. The Sagebrush Trail 33. Somewhere in Sonora 33. The Life

of Jimmy Dolan 33. Baby Face 33. The Man from Monterey 33. Riders of Destiny 33. College Coach 33. West of the Divide 34. Blue Steel 34. Lucky Texan 34. The Man from Utah 34. Randy Rides Alone 34. The Star Packer 34. The Trail Beyond 34. Neath Arizona Skies 34. Texas Terror 35. The Lawless Frontier 35. New Frontier 35. Lawless Range 35. Rainbow Valley 35. Paradise Canyon 35. The Dawn Rider 35. Westward Ho 35. Desert Trail 35. The Lawless Nineties 36. King of the Pecos 36. The Oregon Trail 36. Winds of the Wasteland 36. The Sea Spoilers 36. The Lonely Trail 36. Conflict 36. California Straight Ahead 37. Cover the War 37. Idol of the Crowds 37. Adventure's End 37. Born to the West 37. Pals of the Saddle 37. Overland Stage Raiders 38. Santa Fe Stampede 38. Red River Range 38. *Stagecoach* 39. Night Riders 39. Three Texas Steers 39. Wyoming Outlaw 39. New Frontier 39. Allegheny Uprising 39. Dark Command 40. Three Faces West 40. *The Long Voyage Home* 40. *Seven Sinners* 40. A Man Betrayed 40. The Lady from Louisiana 41. The Shepherd of the Hills 41. Lady for a Night 41. Reap the Wild Wind 42. The Spoilers 42. In Old California 42. Flying Tigers 42. Reunion in France 42. Pittsburgh 42. A Lady Takes a Chance 43. In Old Oklahoma 43. The Fighting Seabees 44. Tall in the Saddle 44. Back to Bataan 44. Flame of the Barbary Coast 44. Dakota 45. They Were Expendable 45. Without Reservations 46. Angel and the Badman 47. Tycoon 47. Fort Apache 48. *Red River* 48. Three Godfathers 48. Wake of the Red Witch 48. The Fighting Kentuckian 49. *She Wore a Yellow Ribbon* 49. *Sands of Iwo Jima* 49. Rio Grande 50. Operation Pacific 51. Flying Leathernecks 51. Big Jim McLain 52. *The Quiet Man* 52. Trouble Along the Way 53. Island in the Sky 53. Hondo 53. *The High and the Mighty* 54. The Sea Chase 55. Blood Alley 55. The Conqueror 55. I Married a Woman (gag appearance) 55. *The Searchers* 56. The Wings of Eagles 57. Jet Pilot 57. The Barbarian and the Geisha 58. *Rio Bravo* 59. The Horse Soldiers 59. North to Alaska 60. *The Alamo* (& p d) 60. The Comancheros 61. The Man Who Shot Liberty Valance 62. Hatari 62. The Longest Day 62. How the West Was Won 63. Donovan's Reef 63. McLintock 63. Circus World 64. The Greatest Story Ever Told 65. In Harm's Way 65. The Sons of Katie Elder 65. Cast a Giant Shadow 66. El Dorado 67. The War Wagon 67. The Green Berets (& d) 68. Hellfighters 68. The Undefeated 69. *True Grit* (AA) 69. Rio Lobo 70. Chisum 70. Big Jake 71. The Cowboys 72. The Train Robbers 73. Cahill 73. McQ 74. Brannigan 75. Rooster Cogburn 75. *The Shootist* 76.

❀ For appearing in more films than any other star, and for winning respect after a lifetime of larger-than-life roles. *The Quiet Man*.

† Wayne was known as Duke because as a child he had a dog of that name. They were Big Duke and Little Duke; Wayne was Little Duke.

†† In 1971 he was named by the Marine Corps League as 'the man who best exemplifies the word American'.

¶ I play John Wayne in every picture regardless of the character, and I've been doing all right, haven't I?—*J. W.*

I never had a goddam artistic problem in my life, never, and I've worked with the best of them. John Ford isn't exactly a bum, is he? Yet he never gave me any manure about art.—*J. W.*

'He has an endless face and he can go on forever.'—*L. B. Mayer*

Westerns are closer to art than anything else in the motion picture business.—*J. W.*

Famous line (*True Grit*): Come and see a fat old man sometime!

Famous line (*Hondo*): A man oughta do what he thinks is right.

? In what film did John Wayne:

1 Consult a doctor played by James Stewart?
2 Play Captain Nathan Brittles?
3 Have Oliver Hardy as a follower?
4 Antagonize Red Will Danaher?
5 Co-star with Lauren Bacall?
6 Play Genghis Khan?
7 Fall for a Russian aviatrix?
8 Build a railroad in the Andes?
9 Succumb to a giant squid?
10 Play a centurion?
11 Have Earl Holliman and Michael Anderson for brothers?
12 Romance Elsa Martinelli?
13 Lead a party of settlers to Oregon?
14 Have the berth below Claudette Colbert?
15 Chase communists in Hawaii?
16 Get stranded in Labrador?

Wayne, Michael (1934–). American producer, son of John Wayne.
McLintock 63. The Green Berets 67. Cahill 73, etc.

Wayne, Naunton (1901–1970) (Naunton Davies). Mild-mannered British light comedy actor, on stage from 1920, films from 1931;

became well known with Basil Radford in many films as Englishmen abroad.
The First Mrs Fraser (debut) 31. Going Gay 33. For Love of You 34. *The Lady Vanishes* 38. *Night Train to Munich* 40. *Crooks' Tour* 41. Next of Kin 42. Millions Like Us 43. *Dead of Night* 45. The Calendar 47. *It's Not Cricket* 48. Quartet 48. Passport to Pimlico 48. Obsession 49. Highly Dangerous 50. *The Titfield Thunderbolt* 53. You Know What Sailors Are 53. Nothing Barred 61. Double Bunk 64, others.

Wayne, Patrick (1939–). American leading man, son of John Wayne.
The Searchers 56. The Alamo 60. The Comancheros 62. McLintock 63. The Bears and I 74. The People that Time Forgot 77. Sinbad and the Eye of the Tiger 77, etc.
TV series: The Rounders 66. Shirley 78. The Monte Carlo Show 81.

Wead, Frank 'Spig' (1895–1947). American screenwriter of the thirties, a former navy flier whose early life was played by John Wayne in *The Wings of Eagles* (1957).

Weathers, Carl (–). Black American actor.
Bucktown 75. Friday Foster 75. *Rocky* 76. Close Encounters of the Third Kind 77. Semi-Tough 77. Force Ten from Navarone 78. Rocky II 79. Death Hunt 81. Rocky III 82. Rocky IV 86. Predator 87.

Weaver, Dennis (1924–). American character actor and TV star.
The Raiders 52. War Arrow 54. Seven Angry Men 55. Touch of Evil 58. The Gallant Hours 60. Duel at Diablo 66. The Great Man's Whiskers (TV) 71. What's the Matter with Helen 71. Duel (TV) 71. The Forgotten Man (TV) 71. Rollin' Man (TV) 72. The Islander (TV) 78. Centennial (TV) 78. Pearl (TV) 78. Ishi: the last of His Tribe (TV) 78. The Ordeal of Patty Hearst (TV) 79. The Ordeal of Dr Mudd (TV) 80, etc.
TV series: Gunsmoke (as Chester) 55–63. Kentucky Jones 65. McCloud 70–76. Stone 79. Navy 83.

Weaver, Doodles (1911–1983) (Winstead Sheffield Weaver). American character comedian, once a member of Spike Jones' band. Starred in TV's *The Doodles Weaver Show* in 1951.
Topper 37. The Pied Piper 43. Since You Went Away 43. San Antonio 45. Gentlemen Prefer Blondes 52. Pocketful of Miracles 60. The Birds 63. Rosie 67, etc.

Weaver, Fritz (1926–). American stage actor.
Fail Safe 64. The Borgia Stick (TV) 68. The Maltese Bippy 69. A Walk in the Spring Rain 70. The Day of the Dolphin 73. Marathon Man 76. Demon Seed 77. Black Sunday 77. The Big Fix 78. *Holocaust* (TV) 78.
Jaws of Satan 79. Creepshow 82. Power 85, etc.

Weaver, Marjorie (1913–). American leading lady, mainly of second features.
China Clipper 36. Three Blind Mice 38. Young Mr Lincoln 39. Maryland 40. The Mad Martindales 42. We're Not Married 52, others.

Weaver, Sigourney (1949–). American leading lady, niece of Doodles Weaver.
Alien 79. Eyewitness 81. The Year of Living Danerously 83. Deal of the Century 83. Ghostbusters 84. Half Moon Street 87. Aliens 87.

¶ *S.W.:* I think I get sent the roles Meryl's not doing.

Webb, Alan (1906–1982). Lean British character actor, mainly on stage.
Lease of Life 54. The Pumpkin Eater 64. Chimes at Midnight 66. The Taming of the Shrew 67. Entertaining Mr Sloane 69. Women in Love 69. Nicholas and Alexandra 71.
The First Great Train Robbery 78. Rough Cut 80, etc.

Webb, Clifton (1893–1966) (Webb Parmelee Hollenbeck). American leading character actor, former dancer and stage star. In films, became in middle age well-known in waspish roles.
□Polly with a Past 20. Let No Man Put Asunder 24. New Toys 25. The Heart of a Siren 25. The Still Alarm 26. *Laura* 44. The Dark Corner 46. *The Razor's Edge* 46. *Sitting Pretty* 48. Mr Belvedere Goes to College 49. *Cheaper by the Dozen* 50. For Heaven's Sake 50. Mr Belvedere Rings the Bell 51. Elopement 51. Dreamboat 52. Stars and Stripes Forever 52. Titanic 53. Mister Scoutmaster 53. *Three Coins in the Fountain* 54. Woman's World 54. *The Man Who Never Was* 55. Boy on a Dolphin 57. The Remarkable Mr Pennypacker 58. Holiday for Lovers 59. Satan Never Sleeps 62.
Famous line (*The Dark Corner*): I detest the dawn. The grass always looks as though it's been out all night.
Famous line (*The Razor's Edge*): The enjoyment of art is the only remaining ecstasy that's neither immoral nor illegal.

Famous line (*The Razor's Edge*): If I live to be a hundred I shall never understand how any young man can come to Paris without evening clothes.

Webb, Jack (1920–1982). American TV star and executive: starred and directed in *Dragnet* and other series: was briefly head of Warner TV.
AS ACTOR: The Men 50. Sunset Boulevard 50. You're in the Navy Now 52. Dragnet (& pd) 54. Pete Kelly's Blues (& pd) 55. The D.I. (& pd) 57. The Last Time I Saw Archie (& pd) 62, others.

Webb, James R. (1910–1974). American screenwriter.
The Charge at Feather River 53. Phantom of the Rue Morgue (co-w) 54. Trapeze 56. The Big Country (co-w) 58. Pork Chop Hill 59. How the West Was Won (AA) 63. Guns for San Sebastian 67. Alfred the Great (co-w) 69, many others.

Webb, Robert D. (1903–). American director, former cameraman.
White Feather 55. On the Threshold of Space 55. The Proud Ones 56. Love Me Tender 56. The Way to the Gold 57. Seven Women from Hell 61. The Agony and the Ecstasy (second unit) 65. Capetown Affair 67, etc.

Webb, Roy (1888–1982). American composer.
Alice Adams 35. Quality Street 37. Room Service 38. Kitty Foyle 40. Cat People 42. Journey into Fear 42. Experiment Perilous 44. The Body Snatcher 45. Murder My Sweet 45. Notorious 46. The Spiral Staircase 46. Blood on the Moon 48. Mighty Joe Young 49. Flying Leathernecks 51. Houdini 53. Blood Alley 55. Top Secret Affair 57. Teacher's Pet 58, many others.

Webber, Robert (1928–). American leading man with stage and TV experience.
Highway 301 51. *Twelve Angry Men* 57. The Stripper 63. Hysteria (GB) 64. The Sandpiper 65. The Third Day 65. No Tears for a Killer (It.) 65. Harper 66. The Silencers 67. The Dirty Dozen 67. Dollars 72. Bring Me the Head of Alfredo Garcia 74. Midway 76. The Choirboys 77. Casey's Shadow 78. Revenge of the Pink Panther 78. '10' 79. Private Benjamin 80. S.O.B. 81. Wrong Is Right 82. Wild Geese II 84, etc.

Webster, Ben (1864–1947). British stage character actor of the old school, married to May Whitty.
The House of Temperley 13. Enoch Arden 14. The Vicar of Wakefield 16. Because 18. The Call of Youth 20. The Only Way 25. Downhill 27. The Lyons Mail 31. The Old Curiosity Shop 34. Drake of England 35, etc.

Webster, Ferris (1916–). American editor.
The Picture of Dorian Gray 45. If Winter Comes 47. Father of the Bride 50. Lone Star 52. Lili 53. The Blackboard Jungle 55. Forbidden Planet 56. Cat on a Hot Tin Roof 58. The Magnificent Seven 60. *The Manchurian Candidate* 62. The Great Escape 63. Seven Days in May 64. Seconds 66. Ice Station Zebra 68. Zigzag 70. High Plains Drifter 73. The Enforcer 76. The Gauntlet 77. Every Which Way But Loose 78. Escape from Alcatraz 79. Bronco Billy 80, many others.

Webster, Paul Francis (1907–84). American lyricist. Various Shirley Temple songs in the thirties; later *Love is a Many Splendored Thing* (AA) 54. *Friendly Persuasion* 56. *The Sandpiper* (AA) 65, etc.

weddings have formed a happy ending for innumerable films, and an unhappy start for others, but some are more memorable than the rest. Weddings on a lavish scale were seen in *Camelot, Royal Wedding, The Scarlet Empress, Ivan the Terrible (Part One), The Private Life of Henry VIII*. More domestic occasions were in *Quiet Wedding, The Member of the Wedding. The Catered Affair, Father of the Bride, June Bride, A Kind of Loving, Lovers and Other Strangers, Brigadoon*. Weddings were interrupted in *The Philadelphia Story, The Bride Wasn't Willing, I Married a Witch, The Runaround, You Gotta Stay Happy, The Bride Went Wild, The Lion in Winter, The Graduate* and *I Love You Alice B. Toklas*. Macabre weddings were found in *The Night Walker, The Bride Wore Black, The Bride of Frankenstein, the Bride and the Beast, Chamber of Horrors*. The wedding night was the centre of interest in *The Man in Grey, The Wicked Lady, Wedding Night, The Family Way* and *My Little Chickadee*. And the funniest wedding still remains that in *Our Wife*, when cross-eyed justice of the peace Ben Turpin married Mr Hardy to his best man Mr Laurel.

Weeks, Stephen (1948–). British director.
☐I Monster 70. Sir Gawain and the Green Knight 72. Ghost Story 74. Sword of the Valiant 84.

Wegener, Paul (1874–1948). Distinguished German actor-writer-director.

The Student of Prague (a) 13. The Golem (ad) 14 and 20. Vanina (a) 22. Svengali (awd) 27. Lucrezia Borgia (a) 27. Ein Mann Will Nach Deutschland (d) 34. Der Grosse König (a) 41. Der Grosse Mandarin (a) 48, many others.

Weidler, Virginia (1927–1968). American child actress who usually played a little horror.
Surrender 31. Mrs Wiggs of the Cabbage Patch 34. Souls at Sea 37. The Women 39. *The Philadelphia Story* 40. Born to Sing 42. The Youngest Profession 43. Best Foot Forward 43, etc.

Weill, Claudia (1947–). American director.
□Joyce at 34 72. The Other Half of the Sky 75. Girl Friends 78. It's My Turn 80.

Weill, Kurt (1900–1950). German composer whose scores include *Die Dreigroschenoper, One Touch of Venus* and *Knickerbocker Holiday*, all filmed.

Weingarten, Laurence (1898–1975). American producer, in films from around 1917.
Broadway Melody 28. A Day at the Races 37. Escape 40. Adam's Rib 49. The Tender Trap 54. Cat on a Hot Tin Roof 58. The Unsinkable Molly Brown 64, scores of others.

Weir, Peter (1944–). Australian director.
□ Homesdale 71. The Cars That Ate Paris 71. *Picnic at Hanging Rock* 75. *The Last Wave* 77. The Plumber (TV) 78. Gallipoli 81. The Year of Living Dangerously 82. *Witness* (AAN) 85. The Mosquito Coast 86.

Weis, Don (1922–). American director; came to Hollywood from college as trainee.
Bannerline 51. I Love Melvin 53. A Slight Case of Larceny 53. Ride the High Iron 57. Critics' Choice 63. Pajama Party 63. Looking for Love 64. Billie 65. Pajama Party in a Haunted House 66. The King's Pirate 66, etc.

Weisbart, David (1915–1967). American producer, former editor; in Hollywood from 1935.
Mara Maru 52. Rebel Without a Cause 55. Love Me Tender 56. Holiday for Lovers 59. Kid Galahad 63. Rio Conchos 64. Goodbye Charlie 65. Valley of the Dolls 67, many others.

Weissmuller, Johnny (1904–1984) (Peter John Weissmuller). American leading man, former Olympic athlete who from 1932 played Tarzan (qv) more often than anyone else. In late forties and early fifties appeared in 'Jungle Jim' second features, also on TV. Only 'straight' role: *Swamp Fire* 46.
Guest appearances: Glorifying the American Girl 29. Stage Door Canteen 43. The Phynx 70. Won Ton Ton 76. That's Entertainment Two 76.

Welch, Elisabeth (1904–). Black singing star, born in New York but working mostly in Britain.
Song of Freedom 36. Big Fella 37. Alibi 42. Fiddlers Three 44. Dead of Night 45. Girl Stroke Boy 71, etc.

Welch, Joseph N. (1891–1960). Real-life American judge who became famous during the army-McCarthy hearings in 1954 and was later persuaded to play the judge in *Anatomy of a Murder* 59.

Welch, Raquel (1940–) (Raquel Tejada). Dynamic, curvaceous American sex symbol of the late sixties.
□Roustabout 64. A House is Not a Home 64. A Swinging Summer 65. Fantastic Voyage 66. One Million Years BC 66. The Biggest Bundle of Them All 66. Shoot Loud, Louder I Don't Understand 66. The Queens 67. Fathom 67. Bandolero 68. The Oldest Profession 68. Bedazzled 68. The Beloved 68. Lady in Cement 68. 100 Rifles 68. Myra Breckinridge 70. Flare Up 70. The Magic Christian 70. Hannie Caulder 71. Kansas City Bomber 72. Fuzz 72. Bluebeard 72. The Last of Sheila 73. The Three Musketeers 73. The Four Musketeers 74. The Wild Party 75. Mother Jugs and Speed 76. The Prince and the Pauper 77. The Legend of Walks Far Woman (TV) 84.

¶ *R.W.:* Being a sex symbol was rather like being a convict.
R.W.: If you have physical attractiveness you don't have to act.

Weld, Tuesday (1943–) (Susan Ker Weld). American leading actress, a model from childhood.
Rock Rock Rock 56. Rally Round the Flag Boys 57. The Five Pennies 59. Return to Peyton Place 61. Wild in the Country 62. Bachelor Flat 63. I'll Take Sweden 65. *The Cincinnati Kid* 65. Lord Love a Duck 66. *Pretty Poison* 68. I Walk the Line 70. A Safe Place 71. Play It as It Lays 73. Looking for Mr Goodbar 77. Who'll Stop the Rain? 78.

A Question of Guilt (TV) 78. Serial 80. Thief 81. Author! Author! 82. Once Upon a Time in America 84, etc.

Welden, Ben (1901–). British character actor who moved to Hollywood.
The Missing Rembrandt 32. The Triumph of Sherlock Holmes 34. Marked Woman 37. Crime Ring 38. Hollywood Cavalcade 39. Angel on My Shoulder 45. The Lemon Drop Kid 51, many others.

Welland, Colin (1934–). British actor-writer, mostly for television.
AS ACTOR: Kes 69. Villain 71. Straw Dogs 71. Sweeney 77, etc.
AS WRITER: Yanks 79. Chariots of Fire (AA) 81. Twice in a Lifetime 86.

Welles, Orson (1915–85). Ebullient American actor-writer-producer-director with stage and radio experience (in 1938 he panicked the whole of America with a vivid radio version of *The War of the Worlds*). His extravagance and unconventionality in Hollywood forced him to Europe, where his projects continued interesting and ambitious but generally undisciplined; he never again achieved the standard of his first two films. AA 1970 'for supreme artistry and versatility in the creation of motion pictures'.
Biographies: *The Fabulous Orson Welles* (1956) by Peter Noble. *Orson Welles* (1973) by Peter Bogdanovich. *A Ribbon of Dreams* (1973) by Peter Cowie.
□This list of Welles' films assumes his presence as actor unless otherwise stated: *Citizen Kane* (& d) (AA script, co-w with Herman J. Mankiewicz) 41. *The Magnificent Ambersons* (wd only) 42. *Journey into Fear* 42. *It's All True* (unreleased) (wd only) 42. Jane Eyre 43. Follow the Boys 44. Tomorrow is Forever 44. *The Stranger* (& d) 45. *The Lady from Shanghai* (& d) 47. Black Magic 47. Macbeth (& d) 48. Prince of Foxes 49. *The Third Man* 49. The Black Rose 50. Othello (& d) 51. Trent's Last Case 53. Trouble in the Glen 53. Si Versailles M'Etait Conté 53. Man Beast and Virtue 53. Napoleon 54. Three Cases of Murder 55. Confidential Report (& d) 55. Moby Dick 56. Man in the Shadow 57. Touch of Evil (& d) 58. The Long Hot Summer 58. Roots of Heaven 58. Ferry to Hong Kong 58. David and Goliath 59. Compulsion 59. Crack in the Mirror 60. The Mongols 60. The Tartars 60. Lafayette 61. *The Trial* (& d) 62. The VIPs 63. Chimes at Midnight (& d) 66. Is Paris Burning? 66. A Man For All Seasons 66. Marco the Magnificent 66. I'll Never Forget Whatshisname 67. Casino Royale 67. Sailor from Gibraltar 67. Oedipus the King 67. House of Cards 68. The Immortal Story (& d) 68. Start the Revolution without Me 69. The Southern Star 69. The Kremlin Letter 70. The Battle of Neretva 70. Waterloo 70. Catch 22 70. Safe Place 71. Malpertuis 72. Necromancy 72. Rogopag 72. Treasure Island (as Long John) 72. Ten Days Wonder 72. Get to Know Your Rabbit 72. F for Fake 73. The Other Side of the Wind 76 (unfinished). Voyage of the Damned 76. The Muppet Movie 79. It Happened One Christmas (TV) 79. The Man who Saw Tomorrow 81. Genocide 81. History of the World Part I 82. Butterfly 82. Almonds and Raisins 83. In Our Hands 83. Where is Parsifal? Transformers 86. Someone to Love 87.
❀For starting as big as could be, and not minding about the inevitable tailing-off (and even encouraging it). *Citizen Kane.*

¶ There, but for the grace of God, goes God.

So snapped Herman Mankiewicz during the making of *Citizen Kane*. There must have been something infuriatingly godlike about Orson the young Messiah from New York, brought out with his troupe to play with what he called:

> The biggest toy train set any boy ever had.

Unfortunately, as he later admitted,

> I started at the top and worked down.

It was indeed the only way to go: he could not, either by temperament or ability, make the films Hollywood wanted. The end of his reign came when:

> They let the studio janitor cut *The Magnificent Ambersons* in my absence.

The years that followed saw an amassment of unfinished projects and haphazard wanderings over Europe, with flashes of acting genius in between. Paul Holt called him:

> The oldest enfant terrible in the world.

Jean Cocteau saw him as:

> An active loafer, a wise madman.

Ken Tynan called him:

> A superb bravura director, a fair bravura producer, and a limited bravura writer; but an incomparable bravura personality.

John Simon opined:

> The sad thing is that he has consistently put his very real talents to the task of glorifying his imaginary genius.

Charles Higham adds a reason:

> His genius fed on Hollywood's marvellous machinery.

Pauline Kael was revolted:

> By the sixties he was encased in make-up

and his own fat, like a huge operatic version of W. C. Fields.

Perhaps he best summed up his own career:

Everybody denies I am a genius—but nobody ever called me one!

By 1982 the *Sunday Times* would state:

His talents now seem as deeply buried as a sixpence in a Christmas pudding.

Gluttony is not a secret vice.—*O. W.*

There is nothing about him to convince us that he has ever felt humility or love anywhere but in front of a mirror.—*John Simon*

I'm not bitter about Hollywood's treatment of me, but over its treatment of Griffith, Von Sternberg, Von Stroheim, Buster Keaton and a hundred others.—*O. W.*

When you're down and out, something always turns up—usually the noses of your friends.—*O. W.*

Famous line (*Citizen Kane*): I run a couple of newspapers. What do you do?

Famous line (*The Third Man*): In Italy for thirty years under the Borgias they had warfare, terror, murder, bloodshed—they produced Michelangelo, Leonardo da Vinci and the Renaissance. In Switzerland they had brotherly love, five hundred years of democracy and peace, and what did that produce? The cuckoo clock.

Wellman, William (1896–1975). American director, former pilot, actor and Foreign Legionary; in Hollywood from 1921.
Autobiography 1977: *A Short Time for Insanity*.
The Man Who Won 23. You Never Know Women 26. *Wings* 27. Beggars of Life 28. *Public Enemy* 31. The Conquerors 32. Central Airport 33. Looking for Trouble 34. Small Town Girl 35. Call of the Wild 35. Robin Hood of Eldorado 36. *Nothing Sacred* 37. *A Star is Born* (AA as writer) 37. Men with Wings (& p) 38. Beau Geste 39. The Light that Failed 39. The Great Man's Lady 42. *The Ox Bow Incident* 42. *Roxie Hart* 42. Buffalo Bill 43. *The Story of G.I. Joe* 45. Magic Town 46. Yellow Sky 48. The Iron Curtain 48. Battleground 49. The Next Voice You Hear 50. Westward the Women 50. Across the Wide Missouri 51. My Man and I 52. *The High and the Mighty* 54. *Track of the Cat* 54. Blood Alley 55. Darby's Rangers 57. Lafayette Escadrille 58, others.

¶ *James Mason:* He was a tough little bastard but I liked him . . . he shot real bullets and stuff.

Andrew Sarris, 1968: What is at issue is not the number of bad films he has made, but a fundamental deficiency in his direction of good projects.

Wells, George (1909–). American writer, with MGM since 1944.
Take Me Out to the Ball Game (Everybody's Cheering) 48. Three Little Words 50. Everything I Have is Yours (& p) 52. Jupiter's Darling (p only) 55. Designing Woman (AA) 57. Ask Any Girl 59. The Honeymoon Machine 62. The Horizontal Lieutenant 63. Penelope 66. The Impossible Years 68, etc.

Wells, H. G. (1866–1946). Distinguished British author, several of whose novels have been filmed.
The Island of Dr Moreau (Island of Lost Souls) 32. The Invisible Man 33. The Man Who Could Work Miracles 35. Things To Come 36. Kipps 41. The History of Mr Polly 49. The War of the Worlds 53. The Time Machine 60. The Island of Dr Moreau 77, etc.

Welsh, John (1904–85). Lean British character actor adept at professors, fathers, scientists, barristers etc.

Wenders, Wim (1945–). German director.
The Goalie's Anxiety of the Penalty Kick 71. The Scarlet Letter 72. *Alice in the Cities* 74. Wrong Movement 75. Kings of the Road 76. The American Friend 77. Lightning Over Water 80. Hammett 82. The State of Things 83. Tokyo-Ga 84. Aus der Familie der Panzereschen 84. Paris Texas (BFA) 84.

Wendkos, Paul (1922–). American director.
The Burglar 57. Tarawa Beachhead 58. Gidget 59. Face of a Fugitive 59. Because They're Young 60. *Angel Baby* 60. Gidget Goes to Rome 63. 52 Miles to Terror 66. Guns of the Magnificent Seven 69. Cannon for Cordoba 70. The Mephisto Waltz 71. *Haunts of the Very Rich* (TV) 72. Honor Thy Father (TV) 73. Special Delivery 76. The Death of Richie (TV) 77. Good Against Evil (TV) 77. 79 Park Avenue (TV) 78. A Woman Called Moses (TV) 78. The Ordeal of Patty Hearst (TV) 79. A Cry for Love (TV) 80, etc.

Wengraf, John (1897–1974) (Johann Wenngraft). Lean Austrian actor, mainly in Hollywood; played a lot of Nazis in his time.
Homo Sum 22. Night Train To Munich 39. Mission To Moscow 43. Sahara 43. The Seventh Cross 44. Weekend at the Waldorf 45. T Men 47. Five Fingers 51. Call Me Madam 53. The Pride and The Passion 57. The Return of Dracula 58. Judgment at Nuremberg 60. The Prize 63, etc.

Werker, Alfred (1896–). American director, in Hollywood from 1917.
Little Lord Fauntleroy 21. Nobody's Children 28. Bachelor's Affairs 32. *The House of Rothschild* 34. Kidnapped 38. *The Adventures of Sherlock Holmes* 39. Moon over Her Shoulder 41. The Mad Martindales 42. Whispering Ghosts 42. A Haunting We Will Go 42. Shock 45. Lost Boundaries 46. Repeat Performance 47. Pirates of Monterey 48. Sealed Cargo 51. Walk East on Beacon 52. Devil's Canyon 53. Canyon Crossroads 55. At Gunpoint 58, many others.

Werner, Gosta (1908–). Swedish director, mainly of shorts.
Midvinterblot 46. *The Train* 48. The Street 49. Meeting Life 50. To Kill a Child 52. Matrimonial Announcement 55. The Forgotten Melody 57. A Glass of Wine 60. Human Landscape 65. When People Meet 66, others.

Werner, Oskar (1922–84) (Josef Schliessmayer). Austrian leading actor with international stage and screen credits.
□Eroica 49. Angel with a Trumpet 49. The Wonder Kid (GB) 50. Ruf aus dem Aether (Aus.) 51. Ein Laecheln in Sturm (Aus.) 51. Das Gestohlene Jahr (WG) 51. *Decision before Dawn* 51. The Last Act (WG) 55. Lola Montes 55. Spionage (Aus.) 55. Der Letzte Akt (Aus.) 55. The Life of Mozart 56. *Jules et Jim* 61. *Ship of Fools* 65. The Spy Who Came in from the Cold 65. *Fahrenheit 451* 66. Interlude 68. The Shoes of the Fisherman 68. Voyage of the Damned 76.

Wertmuller, Lina (1928–) (Angela Wertmuller von Elg). Italian director, whose favourite theme is the little man.
The Lizards 63. Rita la Zanzarra 66. Mimi the Metalworker 72. Swept Away 74. *Seven Beauties* 76. The End of the World 77, etc.

Wessel, Dick (1910–1965). American supporting actor, usually in comedy roles.
Arson Racket Squad 38. They Made Me a Criminal 39. Action in the North Atlantic 42. Slattery's Hurricane 48. Texas Carnival 51. Calamity Jane 53. The Gazebo 60. The Ugly Dachshund 65, many others.
TV series: Riverboat 59–61.

Wessely, Paula (1908–). Austrian leading actress.
Maskerade 34. Julika 36. Spiegel des Lebens 38. Die Kluge Marianne 43. Maria Theresa 51. The Third Sex 57. Die Unvollkommene Ehe 59, many others.

Wesson, Dick (1922–1979). American character actor.
Destination Moon 49. Breakthrough 50. Inside the Walls of Folsom Prison 51. About Face 52. The Desert Song 53. Calamity Jane 54, etc.
TV series: The People's Choice 60. The Bob Cummings Show 62. Friends and Lovers 78.

West, Adam (1929–) (William Anderson). American light leading man.
The Young Philadelphians 59. Geronimo 62. Robinson Crusoe on Mars 64. Mara of the Wilderness 65. Batman 66. The Girl Who Knew Too Much 68. Marriage of a Young Stockbroker 71. The Specialist 75. Partisan 75. Hooper 78, etc.
TV series: The Detectives 59–61. *Batman* 65–68.

West, Billy (1893–1975) (Roy B. Weissberg). American silent screen comedian, a successful imitator of Charlie Chaplin; later a Hollywood restaurateur.

West, Mae (1892–1980). American leading lady of the thirties, the archetypal sex symbol, splendidly vulgar, mocking, overdressed and endearing. Wrote most of her own stage plays and film scripts, which bulge with double meanings.
Autobiographies 1959: *Goodness Had Nothing To Do With It.* 1975: *Life, Sex and ESP.*
□Night After Night 32. *She Done Him Wrong* 33. *I'm No Angel* 33. Going to Town 34. Belle of the Nineties 34. Klondike Annie 36. Go West Young Man 37. Every Day's a Holiday 37. My Little Chickadee 39. The Heat's On 43. *Myra Breckinridge* 70. Sextet 77.
❀ For enjoying the sensations she caused in the thirties, and for having the talent to exploit them to the full. *She Done Him Wrong.*

¶ Whole books of Mae West's wit have been published. A much cleverer woman than she was usually given credit for being, she seemed to talk in epigrams. In her seventies on TV, when someone gushed:

> Oh, Miss West, I've heard so much about you

the reply was:

> Yeah, but you can't prove a thing.

When a life jacket was named after her during World War II, her reaction had the appearance of spontaneity:

> I've been in *Who's Who* and I know what's what, but it's the first time I ever made the dictionary.

However, she never did say:

Come up and see me sometime . . .

At least, not quite, and not in the film she was supposed to. She did however say:

Beulah, peel me a grape.

which for some reason has passed into the language. Her first screen appearance is also legendary:

Goodness, what beautiful diamonds!
—Goodness had nothing to with it, dearie.

For the rest, one can only list a few sparklers:

She's one of the finest women who ever walked the streets.

It's not the men in my life, it's the life in my men that counts.

I wouldn't let him touch me with a ten foot pole.

How tall are you son?
—Ma'am, I'm six feet seven inches.
Let's forget the six feet and talk about the seven inches.

(On arriving at her office and being greeted by a score of virile young men)

I'm feeling a little tired today. One of those fellows'll have to go home.

(In a Broadway costume play, when the romantic lead got his sword so tangled in his braid that it stuck up at an unfortunate angle)

Is that your sword, or are you just pleased to see me?

I wouldn't even lift my veil for that guy.

When I'm good I'm very good, but when I'm bad I'm better.

It isn't what I do, but how I do it. It isn't what I say, but how I say it. And how I look when I do it and say it.

(On the mirrored ceiling over her bed)

I like to know what I'm doing.

Whenever I'm caught between two evils, I take the one I've never tried.

Small wonder that her first co-star, George Raft, remarked of her debut:

She stole everything but the cameras.

In a non-permissive age, she made remarkable inroads against the taboos of her day, and did so without even lowering her neckline. Indeed, her most effective moment may have been in a scene in which she drove a funfair crowd wild with a dance that did nothing but tease. As she disappears into the tent, she wraps up years of experience, enjoyment and disapproval of the sex war into one word:

Suckers!

West, Morris (1916–). Australian best-selling novelist, internationally popular; usually on religious themes. Films include *The Devil's Advocate*, *The Shoes of the Fisherman*.

West, Nathanael (1904–1940) (Nathan Weinstein). American novelist. Works filmed include *Lonelyhearts*, but he also drew a scathing picture of Hollywood in *The Day of the Locust* which was filmed in 1975.

West, Roland (1887–1952). American director of the late silent period.
□De Luxe Annie 18. The Silver Lining 21. Nobody 22. The Unknown Purple 23. The Monster 25. *The Bat* 26. The Dove 27. Alibi 29. *The Bat Whispers* 31. Corsair 31.

West Side Story (AA) (US 1961). A film version by Robert Wise and Jerome Robbins (both AA) of the stage musical re-telling the Romeo and Juliet story in a New York slum setting. A downbeat book (Ernest Lehman) is lifted by good art direction (Boris Leven: AA) and Leonard Bernstein's music. Natalie Wood, Richard Beymer and Russ Tamblyn head the cast. George Chakiris won AA for supporting actor and Rita Moreno for supporting actress.

West, Timothy (1934–). British character actor who became famous as TV's *Edward the Seventh*.
Twisted Nerve 68. Nicholas and Alexandra 71. The Day of the Jackal 74. Hedda 76. Agatha 78. The 39 Steps 78. Churchill and the Generals (TV) 80. Rough Cut 80. Murder Is Easy (TV) 82. Oliver Twist (as Bumble) (TV) 82. Tender is the Night (TV) 84, etc.

Westcott, Gordon (1903–1935). American support actor of the thirties, almost always for Warners and usually the other man.
Love Me Tonight 32. The Working Man 33. Heroes for Sale 33. Footlight Parade 33. Fog Over Frisco 34. Registered Nurse 34. Go into Your Dance 35. Bright Lights 35. Two Fisted 35, etc.

Westcott, Helen (1929–) (Myrthas Helen Hickman). American leading lady, former child actress.
A Midsummer Night's Dream 35. The New Adventures of Don Juan 48. The Gunfighter 50. With a Song in My Heart 52. The Charge at Feather River 53. Hot Blood 55. The Last Hurrah 58. I Love My Wife 71.

Westerby, Robert (1909–1968). British screenwriter, in films from 1947.
Broken Journey 48. The Spider and the Fly 50. They Who Dare 54. War and Peace (co-w) 56. Town on Trial 56. Cone of Silence 60. Greyfriars Bobby 60. The Three Lives of Thomasina 64, etc.

Westerfield, James 1912–1971).
Heavyweight American character actor.
Undercurrent 46. The Whistle at Eaton Falls 51. On the Waterfront 54. Chief Crazy Horse 55. Three Brave Men 57. The Shaggy Dog 59. Wild River 60. Birdman of Alcatraz 62. Blue 68. True Grit 69, many others.

westerns have been with us almost as long as the cinema itself; and although Britain supplied *Carry On Cowboy* and a number of continental countries are now making passable horse operas of their own, it is natural enough that almost all westerns should have come from America.

The Great Train Robbery was a western, and two of the most popular stars of the early silent period, Bronco Billy Anderson and William S. Hart, played western heroes, establishing the conventions and the legends still associated with the opening of America's west—Hollywood style. The attractions of western stories included natural settings, cheapness of production, readymade plots capable of infinite variation, and a general air of tough simplicity which was saleable the world over. Many of Hollywood's most memorable films of the teens and twenties were westerns: *The Squaw Man, The Spoilers, The Vanishing American, The Covered Wagon, The Iron Horse, The Virginian, In Old Arizona, The Cisco Kid, Cimarron.* The western adapted itself to sound with remarkable ease, and throughout the thirties provided many entertainments of truly epic stature: *Wells Fargo, Arizona, The Texas Rangers, Union Pacific, The Plainsman, Drums Along the Mohawk, Jesse James, The Westerner, Destry Rides Again, Stagecoach.* By now the major directorial talents in the field were established: they included John Ford, William Wyler, Howard Hawks, King Vidor, Victor Fleming, Michael Curtiz, Henry King, Frank Lloyd. And each year brought in the wake of epics scores of cheap but entertaining second features, usually running in familiar series with such stars as Buck Jones, Tom Mix, Tim McCoy, John Wayne, Bob Steele, William Boyd ('Hopalong Cassidy'), Ken Maynard, Tom Tyler, Gene Autry, and the Three Mesquiteers. The singing cowboy familiarized by Autry led to the arrival of other practitioners in the forties: Roy Rogers, Eddie Dean, Lee 'Lasses' White. The forties also based westerns more firmly on historical events, telling such stories as *Brigham Young, Northwest Passage, My Darling Clementine, Santa Fe Trail, They Died with Their Boots On.* But by the end of the decade this genre had worn itself out except in the case of Ford, whose films became increasingly stylish and personal. Elsewhere westerns deteriorated into routine action adventures starring actors a little past their best: Gary Cooper, Errol Flynn, Dennis Morgan, Alan Ladd. Howard Hawks' *Red River* was a useful move towards realism, and was followed in the early fifties by films like *The Gunfighter* and *Shane*, intent on proving how unpleasant a place the real West must have been. Side by side with realism came the 'message' western, given its impetus by *Broken Arrow* 50, the first western since silent days to sympathize with the Indians. It was followed by western allegories like *High Noon* and *3.10 to Yuma*, in which the action elements were restricted or replaced by suspense in taut stories of good versus evil. In these ways the western became a highly respectable form, attracting actors of the calibre of James Stewart, Marlon Brando, Glenn Ford, Henry Fonda, Burt Lancaster, Richard Widmark and Kirk Douglas, all of whom tended to play half-cynical heroes who preserved their sense of right by indulging in violent action in the last reel. The later fifties brought many spectacular western productions including *Gunfight at the OK Corral, Last Train from Gun Hill, One-Eyed Jacks, Warlock* and *The Magnificent Seven*; but no new ground was broken. Second features continued to prosper in the capable hands of Randolph Scott, Joel McCrea and Audie Murphy. Comedy westerns were seldom successful, though exceptions include *Go West* (Keaton and Marx versions), Laurel and Hardy's *Way Out West*, and *Blazing Saddles.*

The galloping success of TV made potted westerns so familiar that even the biggest epics made for the cinema found it hard to attract a paying audience. Ford persevered with *The Man Who Shot Liberty Valance* and *Cheyenne Autumn*, both rehashes of earlier and better work; Cinerama made a patchy spectacle called *How the West Was Won*; novelty westerns have tried violence, horror and sentimentality as gimmicks. However hard the times, one can't imagine westerns ever dying out altogether, though the violent

Italian imitations ('spaghetti westerns') of the sixties came close to killing them as an art form while stimulating their box office potential, and Hollywood is still, at the time of writing, trying clumsily to rival the Italian imitations of its own product, with occasional 'realistic' experiments such as *The Shootist*.

¶ 'An adult western is where the hero still kisses his horse at the end, only now he worries about it.'—*Milton Berle*

Westlake, Donald E. (1933–). Very variable American novelist who also writes as Richard Stark. Works filmed include *The Bank Shot*, *The Hot Rock*.

Westley, Helen (1879–1942) (Henrietta Conroy). American character actress of stage and screen; usually played crotchety but kind-hearted dowagers.
Death Takes a Holiday 34. The House of Rothschild 34. Moulin Rouge 34. Anne of Green Gables 34. Roberta 35. Showboat 36. *Dimples* 36. Banjo on My Knee 36. Stowaway 36. Heidi 37. Rebecca of Sunnybrook Farm 38. Zaza 39. Lady with Red Hair 40. Lillian Russell 40. Adam Had Four Sons 41. Sunny 41. My Favorite Spy 42, etc.

Westman, Nydia (1902–1970). American character comedienne, usually in fluttery, nervous roles.
King of the Jungle 33. The Invisible Ray 36. *The Cat and the Canary* 39. When Tomorrow Comes 40. The Late George Apley 47. The Velvet Touch 49. The Ghost and Mr Chicken 66, many others.

Westmore. The famous family of Hollywood make-up artists was headed by George Westmore (1879–1931), English by birth but a west coast success from the moment he changed Valentino's hair style. The sons all worked for different studios, and most had health and emotional problems. They were Mont (1902–1940), Perc (1904–1970), Ern (1904–1968), Wally (1906–1973), Bud (1918–1973) and Frank (1923–85) who, in 1976, wrote a book about the family, *The Westmores of Hollywood*.

Weston, David (1938–). British actor of TV and films.
Doctor in Distress 63. Becket 64. The Legend of Young Dick Turpin 65. The Red Baron 70. Go for a Take 73. The Incredible Sarah 75. A Man Called Intrepid (TV) 79, etc.

Weston, Jack (1926–). American roly-poly character actor, often an incompetent minor villain.
Stage Struck 58. It's Only Money 62. *Mirage* 65. *Wait Until Dark* 67. The Thomas Crown Affair 68. The April Fools 69. Fuzz 72. A New Leaf 72. Marco 73. Gator 76. The Ritz 77. Cuba 79. Can't Stop the Music 80. The Four Seasons 81. High Road to China 83, many others.
TV series: The Hathaways 61.

Wexler, Haskell (1926–). American cinematographer.
The Savage Eye 59. Angel Baby 60. The Hoodlum Priest 61. A Face in the Rain 62. America America 63. *The Best Man* 64. The Loved One (co-ph) 65. Who's Afraid of Virginia Woolf? (AA) 66. *In the Heat of the Night* 67. *The Thomas Crown Affair* 68. Medium Cool (& d) 69. The Conversation 73. American Graffiti 73. One Flew Over The Cuckoo's Nest 75. Coming Home 78. Days of Heaven 78. No Nukes 80. Second Hand Hearts 80. The Man Who Loved Women 83, etc.

Whale, James (1886–1957). British stage director of somewhat mysterious personality; went to Hollywood 1930 to film his stage production of *Journey's End* and stayed to make other movies.
□Waterloo Bridge 30. *Frankenstein* 31. The Impatient Maiden 32. *The Old Dark House* 32. The Kiss before the Mirror 33. *The Invisible Man* 33. By Candlelight 33. One More River 34. *Bride of Frankenstein* 35. *Remember Last Night* 35. *Showboat* 36. The Road Back 37. The Great Garrick 37. Sinners in Paradise 37. Wives under Suspicion 38. Port of Seven Seas 38. *The Man in the Iron Mask* 39. Green Hell 40. They Dare Not Love 40. Hello Out There 49.
❀ For contriving to make four classics of the macabre before his enthusiasm ran out. *Bride of Frankenstein*.

Whalen, Michael (1899–1974) (Joseph Kenneth Shovlin). American leading man of the thirties.
Country Doctor 36. Time Out for Murder 38. Sign of the Wolf 41. Tahiti Honey 43. Gas House Kids in Hollywood 48. Mark of the Dragon 51. The Phantom from Ten Thousand Leagues 56, many others.

Whatham, Claude (–). British director.
□That'll Be the Day 72. Swallows and Amazons 74. The Captain's Doll (TV) 82.

Wheatley, Alan (1907–). Suave British character actor best known as the Sheriff of Nottingham in TV's *Robin Hood*.
Inn for Trouble 60. Shadow of the Cat 61. Tomorrow at Ten 63. A Jolly Bad Fellow 64, etc.

wheelchairs have usually had sinister connotations in the cinema. The Spanish film *The Wheelchair* was a very black comedy indeed, and villains who have operated from wheelchairs include Lionel Atwill in *The Mystery of the Wax Museum*, Vincent Price in *House of Wax*, Ralph Morgan in *Night Monster*, and Francis L. Sullivan in *Hell's Island*. General 'heavies' confined to wheelchairs include Eleanor Parker in *The Man with the Golden Arm* and *Eye of the Cat*, cantankerous Dame May Whitty (and later Mona Washbourne) in *Night Must Fall*, and crusty old Lionel Barrymore in the Dr Kildare series and every other film he made after 1939 (he was confined to a chair after twice breaking his hip). Wheelchair victims included Estelle Winwood in *Notorious Landlady*, careering away over the countryside, and the old lady who was pushed downstairs in a wheelchair in *Kiss of Death*. Perhaps the most fearsome wheelchair occupant was Monty Woolley, of the barbed tongue, in *The Man Who Came to Dinner*. Electric staircase chairs were used by 'invalids' Ethel Barrymore in *The Farmer's Daughter*, Eugenie Leontovitch in *Homicidal* and Charles Laughton in *Witness for the Prosecution*.

Wheeler, Bert (1895–1968). American comedian who teamed as double act with Robert Woolsey (qv).
Rio Rita 29. Half Shot at Sunrise 30. Hook Line and Sinker 30. Cracked Nuts 30. Caught Plastered 32. Hold 'Em Jail 32. Diplomaniacs 33. Hips Hips Hooray 34. The Nitwits 35. The Rainmakers 35. Mummy's Boys 37. High Flyers 37. On Again Off Again 37. The Gay City (solo) 41.
TV series: Brave Eagle 55.

Wheeler, Charles F. (–). American cinematographer.
Tora! Tora! Tora! 70. Cold Turkey 70. The Cat from Outer Space 78. Condorman 81, etc.

Wheeler, Lyle (1905–). American art director.
The Prisoner of Zenda 37. *Tom Sawyer* 38. *Gone with the Wind* (AA) 39. *Rebecca* 40. *Laura* 44. *Anna and the King of Siam* (AA) 46. Fourteen Hours 51. *The Robe* (AA) 53. Love is a Many-Splendored Thing 55. Daddy Longlegs 55. *The Diary of Anne Frank* (AA) 59. *Journey to the Centre of the Earth* 59. The Cardinal 63, many others.

Whelan, Arleen (1916–). American leading lady of the forties.
Kidnapped 38. Young Mr Lincoln 39. Charley's American Aunt 42. Ramrod 47. The Sun Shines Bright 52. The Badge of Marshal Brennan 57, etc.

Whelan, Tim (1893–1957). American director who often filmed in Britain.
Safety Last 23. It's a Boy (GB) 33. Murder Man 35. The Mill on the Floss (GB) 36. *Farewell Again* (GB) 37. The Divorce of Lady X (GB) 37. *St Martin's Lane* (GB) 38. *Q Planes* (GB) 39. Ten Days in Paris (GB) 39. *The Thief of Baghdad* (GB) (co-d) 40. A Date with Destiny 40. International Lady 41. Twin Beds 42. Nightmare 42. Seven Days' Leave 42. Higher and Higher 42. Step Lively 44. Badman's Territory 46. This Was a Woman (GB) 47. Texas Lady 55. Rage at Dawn 55, etc.

Whiley, Manning (1915–). British actor, usually in sinister roles.
Consider Your Verdict 38. The Trunk Crime 39. The Ghost of St Michael's 41. The Seventh Veil 45. Teheran 47. The Shop at Sly Corner 50. Little Big Shot (last to date) 52, etc.

Whipper, Leigh (1877–1975). Black American character actor.
Of Mice and Men 39. The Ox Bow Incident 42. Mission to Moscow 43, etc.

Whisky Galore (GB 1948). One of the most successful of regional comedies, this lively romp from Ealing Studios was taken from Compton Mackenzie's novel about a boatload of whisky wrecked on a remote Scottish island. Brilliantly directed by Alexander Mackendrick and photographed by Gerald Gibbs, with a first-rate cast of character actors: Basil Radford, Duncan Macrae, Joan Greenwood, Jean Cadell, Wylie Watson, Gordon Jackson, etc.

The Whisperers (GB 1967). The film that won a BFA for Edith Evans is in itself an often likeable but often unduly melodramatic little mood piece, chiefly commendable for daring to tackle the unfashionable and therefore uncommercial problems of old age. Bryan Forbes wrote and directed with considerable intelligence but failed to sort out various elementary confusions of character and verisimilitude.

The Whistler. Based on a popular American radio show, this crime anthology ran as a film series from 1944 to 1947, with Richard Dix playing the hero of each. The only other connection was the whistled theme tune at the beginning. The first story was the old chestnut about the man who hires someone to kill him and then changes his mind. In the late fifties there was a TV series using the same title.

Whistling in the Dark. This crime comedy play by Lavinia Cross and Edward Carpenter was first filmed in 1933 by Elliott Nugent, with Ernest Truex as the little man who beats the crooks in the end. In 1940 it was revamped as a vehicle for Red Skelton, directed by S. Sylvan Simon, who also handled two sequels, *Whistling in Dixie* 42 and *Whistling in Brooklyn* 43.

White, Alice (1907–1983). American leading lady of 'B' features who played flappers and gangsters' molls from the twenties to the forties.
The Thief of Bagdad 23. Hot Stuff 27. The Sea Wolf 30. Gentlemen Prefer Blondes 31. The Picture Snatcher 33. Big City 38. Annabel Takes a Tour 39. Flamingo Road 48, many others.

White, Barbara (1924–). British leading lady of the forties.
It Happened One Sunday 44. The Voice Within 45. Quiet Weekend 46. While the Sun Shines 46. Mine Own Executioner 47. This Was a Woman 48, etc.

White Cargo. This much-caricatured play was based on a book by Vera Simonton called *Hell's Playground*: it dealt with the difficulties of acclimatization for Malayan rubber planters, and in particular with a shapely native distraction called Tondelayo. It was filmed in Britain by J. B. Williams in 1929, with Leslie Faber and Gypsy Rhouma, and in Hollywood in 1942 with Walter Pidgeon and Hedy Lamarr.

White, Carol (1941–). British leading lady.
Linda 60. Slave Girls 66. *Poor Cow* 67. I'll Never Forget Whatshisname 68. Daddy's Gone A-Hunting 69. The Man Who Had Power Over Women 70. Dulcima 71. Something Big 71. Made 72. The Squeeze 77, etc.

White, Chrissie (1894–?1979). British leading lady of the silent screen, especially popular when teamed with her husband Henry Edwards (qv). Films include *Broken Threads*, *David Garrick*, *Barnaby Rudge*, *Sweet Lavender*, *Trelawny of the Wells*, *The City of Beautiful Nonsense*, *Possession*; last appearance in *General John Regan* 34.

White Heat (US 1949). This bid to revive gangster movies ten years after the last gangster was jailed succeeded brilliantly as tough entertainment but its new violence left a nasty taste in the mouth. James Cagney is splendidly maniacal, Raoul Walsh's direction swift: the script by Ivan Goff and Ben Roberts is full of tension.

White, Jesse (1918–) (Jesse Wiedenfeld). American comic character actor, usually seen as nervous cigar-chewing crook. Wide stage experience.
Harvey (debut) 50. Death of a Salesman 52. Not as a Stranger 55. Designing Woman 57. The Rise and Fall of Legs Diamond 59. It's Only Money 62. A House is Not a Home 64. Dear Brigitte 65. The Reluctant Astronaut 67. The Brothers O'Toole 73. The Cat from Outer Space 78, many others.
TV series: *Make Room for Daddy* 53–57.

White, Jules (1900–85). American (originally Hungarian) shorts director in charge of the Three Stooges from 1945 to 1957.

White, Merrill (c. 1895–1959). American editor.
The Love Parade 29. *Love Me Tonight* 32. Nell Gwyn 34. The Frog 37. Victoria the Great 37. The Red House 47. Blaze of Glory 50. One Girl's Confession 53. Carnival Story 54. The Fly 58. Crime and Punishment USA 59, many others.

White, Onna (–). American choreographer.
The Music Man 62. Bye Bye Birdie 63. *Oliver* (AA) 68. 1776 72. The Great Waltz 72. Mame 73, etc.

White, Pearl (1889–1938). American leading lady, 'queen of the silent serials'. On stage from six years old. At first a stunt woman, then in such serials as *The Perils of Pauline* 14

and *The Exploits of Elaine* 15, involving circus-like thrills. Later in features: *The White Moll* 20. *Know Your Men* 21. *A Virgin Paradise* 21, etc.; retired 1921. A pseudo-biography, *The Perils of Pauline*, was filmed with Betty Hutton in 1947.
Autobiography 1919: *Just Me*.

White, Ruth (1914–1969). American character actress.
To Kill a Mockingbird 63. Up the Down Staircase 67. The Tiger is Out 68. Charly 69. Midnight Cowboy 69, etc.

White Shadows in the South Seas (US 1928). Robert Flaherty had a hand in scripting and photographing this South Seas melodrama, and also co-directed with W. S. Van Dyke. The story dealt with an alcoholic doctor who finds contentment with a native girl on a remote island.

White, Valerie (1916–1975). British character actress.
Halfway House 43. My Learned Friend 44. Hue and Cry 46. Travels with My Aunt 73, etc.

Whitehead, Geoffrey (1939–). British light actor who in 1980 played Holmes in the Anglo-Polish TV series *Sherlock Holmes and Dr Watson*.
Inside the Third Reich (TV) 82. Peter the Great (TV) 85. War and Remembrance (TV) 87.

Whitelaw, Billie (1932–). British leading actress of stage and TV, also in occasional films.
The Fake 54. Make Mine Mink 59. Bobbikins 59. Hell is a City 60. *No Love for Johnnie* 61. Payroll 61. The Comedy Man 63. *Charlie Bubbles* (BFA) 68. Twisted Nerve 68. The Adding Machine 69. Gumshoe 71. Eagle in a Cage 71. Frenzy 72. Night Watch 73. *The Omen* 76. The Water Babies 78. An Unsuitable Job for a Woman 82. Jamaica Inn (TV) 83. Camille (TV) 84. The Chain 86. Shadey 86. Maurice 87, etc.

Whiteley, Jon (1945–). British boy actor.
Hunted 52. *The Kidnappers* (special AA) 53. Moonfleet 55. The Weapon 56. The Spanish Gardener 56. Capetown Affair 67, etc.

Whiteman, Paul (1890–1967). Tall, portly American bandleader who made several film appearances.
King of Jazz 30. Thanks a Million 35. Strike Up the Band 40. Atlantic City 44. Rhapsody in Blue 45. The Fabulous Dorseys 47, etc.

Whiting, Leonard (1950–). British juvenile lead.
The Legend of Young Dick Turpin 66. *Romeo and Juliet* (as Romeo) 68. The Royal Hunt of the Sun 69. Young Casanova 70. Say Hello to Yesterday 71. Frankenstein: The True Story 73 (TV), etc.

Whitlock, Albert (1915–). British special effects technician.
The Birds 63. Marnie 64. Torn Curtain 66. Diamonds Are Forever 70. Frenzy 73. The Sting 73. *Earthquake* (AA) 74. *The Hindenburg* (AA) 75. Family Plot 75. The Car 77. High Anxiety 77. Dracula 79. Heartbeeps 81. History of the World Part One 81. Missing 82. Dune 84.

Whitman, Ernest (–). Black American character actor of sizeable presence.
Prisoner of Shark Island 36. The Green Pastures 36. Nothing Sacred 37. Gone with the Wind 39. Congo Maisie 40. Road to Zanzibar 41. Cabin in the Sky 43. *Stormy Weather* 43. The Sun Shines Bright 53, many others.

Whitman, Stuart (1926–). American leading man, former boxer and stage and TV actor.
When Worlds Collide 52. Rhapsody 54. Darby's Rangers 57. *Ten North Frederick* 58. The Decks Ran Red 58. The Story of Ruth 60. Murder Inc. 61. *The Mark* 62. The Comancheros 62. Reprieve 63. Shock Treatment 64. Signpost to Murder 64. Rio Conchos 64. Those Magnificent Men in Their Flying Machines 65. Sands of the Kalahari 65. An American Dream 66. The Invincible Six 68. The Only Way Out is Dead 70. Captain Apache 71. City Beneath the Sea (TV) 71. Night of the Lepus 73. Mean Johnny Barrows 76. Strange Shadows in an Empty Room 77. Eaten Alive 77. The White Buffalo 77. Run for the Roses 78. Guyana 80. Sweet Dirty Tony 81. Butterfly 82, etc.
TV series: Cimarron Strip 67. The Men from Shiloh 70.

Whitmore, James (1921–). Craggy American character actor.
Undercover Man 49. The Asphalt Jungle 50. Across the Wide Missouri 51. Kiss Me Kate 53. *Them* 54. Battle Cry 55. Oklahoma 55. The Eddy Duchin Story 56. Who Was That

Lady? 60. Black Like Me 64. Chuka 67. Planet of the Apes 68. Madigan 68. The Split 68. Guns of the Magnificent Seven 69. Tora! Tora! Tora! 70. Chato's Land 71. If Tomorrow Comes (TV) 71. The Harrad Experiment 73. Give 'Em Hell Harry 75. Where the Red Fern Grows 75. The Serpent's Egg 77. The Word (TV) 78, etc.
TV series: *The Law and Mr Jones* 60–61.

Whitney, Peter (1916–1972) (Peter King Engle). Portly American character player.
Reunion in France 42. *Murder He Says* (as twins) 45. Hotel Berlin 45. The Iron Curtain 48. The Big Heat 53. Great Day in the Morning 56. Sword of Ali Baba 65. Chubasco 67. The Ballad of Cable Hogue 70, etc.

Whitrow, Benjamin (1939–). British light actor, mostly on stage and radio.
Quadrophenia 78. Brimstone and Treacle 82. Clockwise 85. Personal Services 86.

Whitsun-Jones, Paul (1923–1974). Rotund British character actor, usually in comedy.
The Constant Husband 55. *The Moonraker* 57. Room at the Top 59. Tunes of Glory 60, etc.

Whittingham, Jack (1910–1972). British screenwriter.
Q Planes 39. Kiss the Bride Goodbye 44. Twilight Hour 45. I Believe in You 51. Hunted 52. The Divided Heart 54. The Birthday Present (& p) 57, etc.

Whitty, Dame May (1865–1948). Distinguished character actress, on stage from 1881. Settled in Hollywood in the mid-thirties and played dozens of indomitable but kindly old ladies.
Biography 1969 by her daughter: *The Same Only Different.*
□ Enoch Arden 14. The Little Minister 15. Colonel Newcombe 20. The Thirteenth Chair 37. *Night Must Fall* 37. Conquest 37. I Met My Love Again 37. *The Lady Vanishes* (GB) 38. Return to Yesterday (GB) 40. Raffles 40. A Bill of Divorcement 40. One Night in Lisbon 41. Suspicion 41. Mrs Miniver 42. Thunder Birds 42. Slightly Dangerous 42. Forever and a Day 43. Crash Dive 43. The Constant Nymph 43. Lassie Come Home 43. Flesh and Fantasy 43. Madame Curie 43. Stage Door Canteen 43. The White Cliffs of Dover 44. Gaslight 44. *My Name is Julia Ross* 45. Devotion 46. This Time for Keeps 47. Green Dolphin Street 47. If Winter Comes 47. The Sign of the Ram 48. The Return of October 48.

¶ *M.W.:* So long as I can do my bit, I'll keep right on doing it.

Who said that?

? Most film buffs will have heard the following lines. But who said them, in what circumstances? In films, or in reality?

1 Bring on the empty horses!
2 So they call me Concentration Camp Erhardt?
3 I'm not happy. I'm not happy at all.
4 Life's never quite interesting enough, somehow. You people who come to the movies know that.
5 I'm terrified of policemen.
6 Oh, Victor, please don't go to the underground meeting tonight . . .
7 The trouble is that you are only interested in art, and I am only interested in money.
8 Yonda is the castle of my fodda . . .
9 No mean Machiavelli is smiling, cynical Sidney Kidd.
10 It's the only disease you don't look forward to being cured of.
11 Move those ten thousand horses a little to the right.
12 I have lived in the theatre as a trappist monk lives in his faith.
13 Paint it!
14 *L'oiseau chante avec ses doigts . . .*
15 There can only be one winner, folks, but isn't that the American way?
16 Hush up, telephone—I's a-comin', I's a-comin'!
17 I know he's a good man—you know he's a good man. My bad days are when he knows he's a good man.
18 If you can't sleep at night, it isn't the coffee, it's the bunk!
19 Massa Benny, we don't do that no more . . .
20 I hate the dawn. The grass always looks as though it's been left out all night.
21 Out of the cradle, endlessly rocking . . .
22 You have no idea what a long-legged gal can do without doing anything.
23 The last man who said that to me was Archie Leach a week before he cut his throat.
24 Sometimes they get into the machinery.
25 For one who has not lived even a single lifetime, you are a wise man, Van Helsing.
26 They tell me everything isn't black and white. Well, I say why the hell not?
27 Our new one-piece foundation garment—zips up the back and no bones . . .
28 Give him an evasive answer. Tell him to go fuck himself.

29 Nothing wrong with shooting as long as the right people get shot.
30 Do you, Ernest Sidney Gubbins, take Esther Blodgett . . . ?
31 You go through Warm Springs, along Paradise Valley, to Climax.
32 Fight, fight, fight. That's all you think of, Dick Plantagenet!
33 Reading a fan magazine is similar to eating a banana under water.
34 I've got your happy ending. We'll let the Germans win the war.
35 Did you read it all the way through? —I read part of it all the way through.
36 You don't belong to any man now—you belong to Broadway!
37 Drink Pike's Pale—the ale that won for Yale!
38 Yer beautiful in yer wrath . . .
39 The most positive thing in the motion picture business is the negative.
40 It's one of the tragedies of life that the people most in need of a good thrashing are usually enormous.
41 It is a great picture without political significance. We are not for or against anybody.
42 'Taint a fit night out for man nor beast!
43 It would be a terrific innovation if you could get your mind to stretch a little further than the next wisecrack.
44 Feets, do your stuff!

Whoopee (US 1930). A Broadway musical which became an early talkie starring Eddie Cantor, with dances directed by Busby Berkeley. 35mm colour prints have survived. It was remade in 1944 as *Up In Arms*, with Danny Kaye.

Whorf, Richard (1906–1966). Sullen-looking American actor-director.
AS ACTOR: Midnight 34. *Blues in the Night* 41. Yankee Doodle Dandy 42. Keeper of the Flame 43. Christmas Holiday 44. Chain Lightning 50, etc.
AS DIRECTOR: The Hidden Eye 45. Till the Clouds Roll By 46. It Happened in Brooklyn 47. Love from a Stranger 47. Luxury Liner 48. Champagne for Caesar 50. Lots of TV half-hours and hours, especially *Rawhide* and *The Beverly Hillbillies*.

Who's Afraid of Virginia Woolf? (US 1966). This somewhat misguidedly opened-out film version of Edward Albee's electrifying domestic comedy-drama was rather dingily photographed by Haskell Wexler and sometimes dully directed by Mike Nichols, but its basic force and entertainment value could not be totally disguised, particularly in view of a brilliant performance by Richard Burton and excellent ones by Elizabeth Taylor, George Segal and Sandy Dennis. But its chief interest for historians will be that it further extended the bounds of what is permissible on public screens, its unbridled treatment of matters sexual being decorated by 'blue' jokes and expletives.

Why We Fight. A brilliant series of World War II documentaries using all the resources of the cinema, compiled by Frank Capra and the U.S. Signal Corps Film Unit from material shot by Allied cameramen and from pre-war newsreel material. Each lasted just over an hour, and was kept absorbingly entertaining as well as instructive by the use of music, diagrams and optical work. Titles were *Prelude to War, The Nazis Strike, Divide and Conquer, The Battle of Britain, The Battle of Russia, The Battle of China.*

Wickes, Mary (1916–) (Mary Wickenhauser). American character comedienne.
The Man Who Came to Dinner (as the nurse) 41. Higher and Higher 43. June Bride 48. Young Man with Ideas 52. The Actress 54. Good Morning, Miss Dove 56. It Happened to Jane 59. The Trouble with Angels 66. Where Angels Go Trouble Follows 68. Snowball Express 73, many others.
TV series: Halls of Ivy 54. Doc 75.
Famous line (*The Man Who Came to Dinner*): If Florence Nightingale had ever married you, Mr Whiteside, she would have married Jack the Ripper instead of founding the Red Cross!

Wicki, Bernhard (1919–). Swiss actor-director.
AS ACTOR: Der Fallende Stern 50. The Last Bridge 54. Kinder, Mütter und ein General 54. Jackboot Mutiny 55. The Face of the Cat 57. La Notte 61, etc.
AS DIRECTOR: The Bridge 59. The Miracle of Malachias 61. The Longest Day (co-d) 62. The Visit (US) 63. The Saboteur 65. Karpfs Karriere 72, etc.

Widdoes, Kathleen (1939–). American actress with stage experience.
The Group 66. Petulia 68. The Seagull 68. The Mephisto Waltz 71, etc.

wide screen. Strictly speaking this does not mean anamorphic processes such as CinemaScope, which requires a wide, *wide* screen, but the now-standard 1:1.65 ratio which was achieved by projecting the old

1.3:1 image, cutting the top and bottom from it, and magnifying the result.

Widerberg, Bo (1930–). Swedish writer-director.
Raven's End 63. Karlek 63. Thirty Times Your Money 66. *Elvira Madigan* 67. Adalen 31 69. The Ballad of Joe Hill 69. The Man on the Roof 75. Victoria 79, etc.

Widmark, Richard (1914–). American leading actor; once typed as cold-eyed killer, he fought successfully for more varied roles.
□*Kiss of Death* 47. Road House 48. The Street with No Name 48. Yellow Sky 49. Down to the Sea in Ships 49. Slattery's Hurricane 49. Night and the City 50. Panic in the Streets 50. No Way Out 50. Halls of Montezuma 50. The Frogmen 51. Full House 52. Don't Bother to Knock 52. Red Skies of Montana 52. My Pal Gus 52. Destination Gobi 53. Pickup on South Street 53. Take the High Ground 53. Hell and High Water 54. Garden of Evil 54. Broken Lance 54. The Cobweb 55. A Prize of Gold 55. Backlash 56. Run for the Sun 56. The Last Wagon 56. Saint Joan 57. Time Limit 57. The Law and Jake Wade 58. The Tunnel of Love 58. The Trap 59. Warlock 59. The Alamo 60. The Secret Ways 61. Two Rode Together 61. Judgment at Nuremberg 61. How the West Was Won 63. Flight from Ashiya 64. The Long Ships 64. Cheyenne Autumn 64. *The Bedford Incident* 65. Alvarez Kelly 66. The Way West 67. *Madigan* 68. Death of a Gunfighter 69. A Talent for Loving 69. The Moonshine War 70. Brock's Last Case (TV) 71. Vanished (TV) 71. When the Legends Die 72. Murder on the Orient Express 74. To the Devil a Daughter 75. The Sellout 76. Twilight's Last Gleaming 76. Rollercoaster 77. The Domino Principle 77. Mr Horn (TV) 78. Coma 78. The Swarm 78. Bear Island 79. All God's Children (TV) 80. A Whale for the Killing (TV) 81. Who Dares Wins 82. Hanky Panky 82. National Lampoon's Movie Madness 82. The Final Option 82. Against all Odds 83. Blackout 83.
TV series: *Madigan* 72.

¶ 'It is clear that murder is one of the kindest things he is capable of.'—*James Agee*

Wieck, Dorothea (1908–86). German character actress.
Maedchen in Uniform 31. Cradle Song (US) 33. The Student of Prague 35. Der Vierte Kommt Nicht 39, etc.

Wiene, Robert (1881–1938). German director of expressionist films.
The Cabinet of Dr Caligari 19. Genuine 20. Raskolnikov 23. The Hands of Orlac 24, etc.

The Wiere Brothers. German eccentric comedians, long in America: *Harry* (1908–), *Herbert* (1909–), *Sylvester* (1910–1970). Films very occasional.
The Great American Broadcast 41. Swing Shift Maisie 44. *Road to Rio* 47. Double Trouble 68, etc.
TV series: *Oh Those Bells* 62.

Wiest, Dianne (–). American character actress.
Footloose 84. Falling in Love 84. The Purple Rose of Cairo 85. *Hannah and her Sisters* 86. Radio Days 87. September 87. The Lost Boys 87.

Wilbur, Crane (1887–1973). American writer-director.
Canon City 48. The Story of Molly X 49. Outside the Wall 49. Inside the Walls of Folsom Prison 50. House of Wax (script only) 53. The Bat 59. Solomon and Sheba (script only) 59, etc.

Wilcox, Frank (1907–1974). Tall American character actor, a bit player who was always seen in Warner films of the forties—sometimes in two parts in the same film.
The Fighting 69th 39. River's End 40. Highway West 41. Across the Pacific 42. Juke Girl 43. The Adventures of Mark Twain 44. Conflict 45. Gentleman's Agreement 47. Samson and Delilah 49. Those Redheads from Seattle 53. Dance with Me Henry 56. A Majority of One 61, many others.

Wilcox, Fred M. (1905–64). American director, former publicist; films mainly routine.
Lassie Come Home 43. Blue Sierra 46. Courage of Lassie 46. Hills of Home 48. Three Daring Daughters 48. The Secret Garden 49. Shadow in the Sky 50. Code Two 53. Tennessee Champ 54. *Forbidden Planet* 56. I Passed for White 60.

Wilcox, Herbert (1890–1977). British independent producer-director in films from 1919 (as salesman); married to Anna Neagle.
The Wonderful Story 20. The Dawn of the World 21. Chu Chin Chow 23. *Nell Gwyn* 24. *Dawn* 26. Wolves 28. Rookery Nook 30. Good Night Vienna 32. Carnival 32. *Bitter*

Sweet 33. *Nell Gwyn* 34. Peg of Old Drury 35. Limelight 36. The Three Maxims 36. The Frog 37. *Victoria the Great* 37. Sixty Glorious Years 38. Our Fighting Navy 38. *Nurse Edith Cavell* (US) 39. Sunny (US) 39. *No No Nanette* (US) 40. Irene (US) 40. They Flew Alone 42. Yellow Canary 43. I Live in Grosvenor Square 45. *Piccadilly Incident* 46. The Courtneys of Curzon Street 47. *Spring in Park Lane* 48. Elizabeth of Ladymead 49. Maytime in Mayfair 49. *Odette* 50. The Lady with a Lamp 51. Trent's Last Case 52. Laughing Anne 53. Lilacs in the Spring 55. King's Rhapsody 56. Yangtse Incident 56. My Teenage Daughter 56. Those Dangerous Years 57. The Lady is a Square 58. Heart of a Man 59. To See Such Fun (exec. p only) 77, etc.

¶ Mr Herbert Wilcox proceeds on his appointed course. As slow and ponderous and well protected as a steamroller, he irons out opposition. We get from his films almost everything except life, character, truth.—*Graham Greene reviewing Nurse Edith Cavell*

Wilcox, Jack (or John) (1905–84). British cinematographer.
Mr Topaz 61. Where's Jack? 68. The Chairman 68. The Last Valley 70. Legend of the Werewolf 75, etc.

Wilcoxon, Henry (1905–84). British leading man with stage experience, in Hollywood from early thirties, latterly as executive for Cecil B. de Mille.
The Perfect Lady 31. The Flying Squad 32. Cleopatra 34. The Crusades 35. The Last of the Mohicans 36. Mrs Miniver 42. Samson and Delilah 49. Scaramouche 52. The Greatest Show on Earth 53. The Ten Commandments (& co-p) 56. The Buccaneer (& p) 59. The Private Navy of Sergeant O'Farrell 69. Man in the Wilderness 71. Against a Crooked Sky 75. Pony Express Rider 76. F.I.S.T. 78. Caddyshack 80. Sweet Sixteen 81, etc.

Wild, Jack (1952–). British juvenile, popular around 1970.
Oliver 68. Melody 70. Flight of the Doves 71. The Pied Piper 72. The Fourteen 73, etc.
TV series: *H. R. Pufnstuf* 69.

The Wild One (US 1954). A Stanley Kramer production written by John Paxton and directed by Laslo Benedek, about a gang of motor-cycle hooligans who terrorize a small western town. Photographed by Hal Mohr, with music by Leith Stevens, it starred Marlon Brando in a typical role, with Mary Murphy and Lee Marvin. Banned by the British Board of Film Censors, it was shown at only one English cinema (then managed by the author of this book), with local watch committee approval. It was finally given a certificate in 1967.

Wild Strawberries (Sweden 1957). Ingmar Bergman's quietly showmanlike film about old age, superbly written (by himself), photographed (by Gunnar Fischer) and acted (by Victor Sjostrom). Its movement from past to present and back is particularly well achieved, and for once Bergman manages to make almost all his points explicit.

wild track: one recorded *in situ*, not prepared in the studio.

Wilde, Cornel (1915–). American leading man of the forties; later produced and directed some interesting films, but never equalled his 1944 impact as Chopin.
□Lady with Red Hair 40. Kisses for Breakfast 41. High Sierra 41. Right to the Heart 41. The Perfect Snob 42. Life Begins at 8.30 42. Manila Calling 42. Wintertime 43. *A Song to Remember* 45. A Thousand and One Nights 45. Leave Her to Heaven 45. *The Bandit of Sherwood Forest* 46. Centennial Summer 46. The Homestretch 46. Forever Amber 47. It Had to be You 47. Roadhouse 48. The Walls of Jericho 48. Shockproof 49. Four Days' Leave 50. Two Flags West 50. At Sword's Point 52. Operation Secret 52. The Greatest Show on Earth 52. California Conquest 52. Treasure of the Golden Condor 53. Main Street to Broadway 53. Saadia 53. Passion 54. *Woman's World* 54. The Scarlet Coat 55. Storm Fear (& d) 55. The Big Combo 55. Star of India 55. Hot Blood 56. The Devil's Hairpin (& w) 57. Omar Khayyam 57. Beyond Mombasa 57. Maracaibo (& d) 58. Edge of Eternity 59. Constantine and the Cross 60. Sword of Lancelot (& d) 63. *The Naked Prey* (& d) 66. Beach Red (& d) 67. The Comic 69. No Blade of Grass (& d) 71. Gargoyles (TV) 72. Shark's Treasure (& d) 75. The Fifth Musketeer 78. The Norseman 78.

Wilde, Hagar (1904–1971). American screenwriter.
Bringing Up Baby 38. Carefree 39. Fired Wife 43. Guest in the House 44. The Unseen 45. I Was a Male War Bride 49. This is My Love 54, etc.

Wilde, Marty (1939–) (Reginald Smith). British pop singer who appeared in a film or two.
Jetstorm 59. The Hellions 61. What a Crazy World 63. Stardust 74, etc.

Wilde, Oscar (1854–1900). British playwright, poet and wit, the subject in 1960 of two film biographies: *Oscar Wilde* starring Robert Morley and *The Trials of Oscar Wilde* starring Peter Finch. The former was directed by Gregory Ratoff from a script by Jo Eisinger, and had Ralph Richardson as Carson, John Neville as Lord Alfred, and Edward Chapman as the Marquis of Queensbury. The latter, written and directed by Ken Hughes, had James Mason, John Fraser and Lionel Jeffries respectively in these roles. Films have been made of several of Wilde's works including *The Importance of Being Earnest, An Ideal Husband, Lady Windermere's Fan, The Picture of Dorian Gray, Lord Arthur Savile's Crime* (in *Flesh and Fantasy*) and *The Canterville Ghost.*

Wilder, Billy (1906–) (Samuel Wilder). Austro-Hungarian writer-director, in Hollywood from 1934. A specialist for years in bitter comedy and drama torn from the world's headlines, he has lately concentrated on rather heavy-going bawdy farce.
Biography 1970: *The Brighter Side of Billy Wilder, Primarily* by Tom Wood; 1976: *Billy Wilder in Hollywood* by Maurice Zolotow.
□AS WRITER: People on Sunday 30. (Followed by ten other German films.) Adorable (French) 34. Music in the Air (co-w) 34. Lottery Lover (co-w) 35. Bluebeard's Eighth Wife (co-w) 38. *Midnight* (co-w) 39. What a Life (co-w) 39. *Ninotchka* (co-w) 39. *Arise My Love* (co-w) 40. Ball of Fire (co-w) 41. Hold Back the Dawn (co-w) 41.
□AS WRITER-DIRECTOR (script always in collaboration): Mauvaise Graine (French) 33. *The Major and the Minor* 42. *Five Graves to Cairo* 43. *Double Indemnity* 44. *The Lost Weekend* (AA) 45. The Emperor Waltz 47. *A Foreign Affair* 48. *Sunset Boulevard* 50. *Ace in the Hole* 51. *Stalag 17* 53. Sabrina 54. *The Seven Year Itch* 55. The Spirit of St. Louis 57. Love in the Afternoon 57. *Witness for the Prosecution* 58. *Some Like It Hot* 59. *The Apartment* (AA) 60. *One Two Three* 61. Irma La Douce 63. Kiss Me Stupid 64. The Fortune Cookie 66. *The Private Life of Sherlock Holmes* 70. Avanti 72. The Front Page 74. Fedora 78. Buddy Buddy 81.

For being Hollywood's most mischievous immigrant. *Sunset Boulevard.*

¶ The pixie wit of this Hollywood Viennese has sporadically brightened the film scene for more than thirty years. Nor does he save all his wit for his scripts: he is the most quotable of film-makers:

> I have ten commandments. The first nine are, thou shalt not bore. The tenth is, thou shalt have right of final cut.

On critical prejudice:

> What critics call dirty in our movies, they call lusty in foreign films.

On fashion:

> You watch, the new wave will discover the slow dissolve in ten years or so.

On messages:

> In certain pictures I do hope they will leave the cinema a little enriched, but I don't make them pay a buck and a half and then ram a lecture down their throats.

On direction:

> The best director is the one you don't see.

On technique:

> The close-up is such a valuable thing—like a trump at bridge.

A man with such waspish wit naturally invites retaliation, even from his wife:

> Long before Billy Wilder was Billy Wilder, he thought he was Billy Wilder.

That may have been in response to a cable he sent her from Paris just after the war. She had requested him to buy and send a bidet. After a vain search he sent the message:

> Unable obtain bidet. Suggest handstand in shower.

Wilder is the kind of man who can scarcely observe anything without being funny about it. For instance:

> France is a country where the money falls apart in your hands and you can't tear the toilet paper.

But he could be just as ornery as anybody else. As Harry Kurnitz said:

> Billy Wilder at work is two people: Mr Hyde and Mr Hyde.

Andrew Sarris summed up accurately:

> Wilder is a curdled Lubitsch, romanticism gone sour, 78rpm played at 45, an old-worldling from Vienna perpetually sneering at Hollywood as it engulfs him.

Wilder wouldn't be listening—too busy constructing scenarios:

> An actor enters through a door, you've got nothing. But if he enters through a window, you've got a situation.

Wilder, Gene (1934–) (Jerry Silberman). American comic actor.
Bonnie and Clyde 67. *The Producers* 68. Start

the Revolution Without Me 69. Quackser Fortune has a Cousin in the Bronx 70. Willy Wonka and the Chocolate Factory 71. Everything You Always Wanted to Know About Sex 72. Rhinoceros 73. The Little Prince 73. Blazing Saddles 74. Young Frankenstein 74. The Adventure of Sherlock Holmes' Smarter Brother (& pd) 75. Silver Streak 76. The World's Greatest Lover (& wpd) 77. The Frisco Kid 79. Stir Crazy 80. Sunday Lovers 80. Hanky Panky 82. The Woman in Red (& d) 84. Haunted Honeymoon (& d) 86, etc.

Wilder, Robert (1901–1974). American novelist and screenwriter.
Flamingo Road (& oa) 48. *Written on the Wind* (& oa) 56. The Big Country 58. Sol Madrid 66, etc.

Wilder, Thornton (1897–1975). American playwright and novelist. Works filmed include *Our Town, The Bridge of San Luis Rey* (several times), *The Matchmaker*; also wrote screenplay of Hitchcock's *Shadow of a Doubt.*

Wilder, W. Lee (1904–). Austro-Hungarian producer in America, brother of Billy Wilder. Films mainly low-budget oddities.
The Great Flamarion 44. Phantom from Space 53. The Snow Creature 54. Bluebeard's Ten Honeymoons 60, etc.

Wilding, Michael (1912–79). British leading man of the forties.
Posthumous autobiography 1982: *Apple Sauce*.
Wedding Group 35. Tilly of Bloomsbury 40. *Sailors Three* 40. Kipps 41. Cottage To Let 41. *In Which We Serve* 42. Dear Octopus 43. *English Without Tears* 44. Carnival 46. *Piccadilly Incident* 46. The Courtneys of Curzon Street 47. An Ideal Husband 47. *Spring in Park Lane* 48. Maytime in Mayfair 50. Under Capricorn 50. Stage Fright 50. Into the Blue 51. The Law and the Lady (US) 52. Derby Day 52. Trent's Last Case 53. The Egyptian 54. The Glass Slipper 55. Zarak 56. Danger Within 57. The World of Suzie Wong 60. The Naked Edge 61. The Best of Enemies 61. A Girl Named Tamiko 63. The Sweet Ride 68. Waterloo 69. Lady Caroline Lamb 72. Frankenstein: The True Story (TV) 73, etc.

¶ *M.W.:* I was the worst actor I ever came across.

Wilke, Robert J. (1911–). American character actor, usually in mean, shifty or villainous roles.
San Francisco 36. Sheriff of Sundown 44. The Last Days of Boot Hill 47. Kill the Umpire 50. Twenty Thousand Leagues under the Sea 54. Night Passage 57. The Gun Hawk 63. The Hallelujah Trail 65. Tony Rome 67. A Gunfight 71, etc.

William. The argumentative small boy created in over thirty novels by Richmal Crompton had several British film incarnations, none very satisfactory, in the thirties and forties.

William, Warren (1895–1948) (Warren Krech). Suave American leading man with stage experience.
The Perils of Pauline 14. The Woman from Monte Carlo 32. The Mouthpiece 33. *Lady for a Day* 33. *Imitation of Life* 34. Cleopatra (as Julius Caesar) 34. The Case of the Lucky Legs 35. Satan Met a Lady 36. The Firefly 37. *The Lone Wolf's Spy Hunt* 39 (and others in this series). The Man in the Iron Mask 39. Lillian Russell 40. The Wolf Man 41. Counter Espionage 42. One Dangerous Night 43. Fear 46. Bel Ami 47, etc.

Williams, Adam (1929–). American 'second lead'.
Queen for a Day 50. Without Warning 52. Crashout 55. Garment Centre 57. Darby's Rangers 58. North by Northwest 59. The Last Sunset 61. The Glory Guys 67, etc.

Williams, Bill (1916–) (William Katt). American leading man, an innocent-type hero of the forties. Former professional swimmer and singer.
Murder in the Blue Room (debut) 44. Those Endearing Young Charms 45. Till the End of Time 46. Deadline at Dawn 47. The Great Missouri Raid 51. The Outlaw's Daughter 53. Wiretapper 56. A Dog's Best Friend 61. Tickle Me 65, etc.
TV series: Kit Carson 52–54. Assignment Underwater 61.

Williams, Billy (1929–). British cinematographer.
Just Like a Woman 66. Billion Dollar Brain 67. *Women in Love* 69. Two Gentlemen Sharing 70. Tam Lin 70. *Sunday Bloody Sunday* 72. Night Watch 73. The Wind and the Lion 75. Eagle's Wing 79. Saturn Three 80. *On Golden Pond* 81. *Gandhi* (AA) 82. Monsignor 82. The Survivors 83. Dreamchild 85. Eleni 85, etc.

Williams, Billy Dee (1937–). Black American leading man.

Brian's Song (TV) 71. Lady Sings the Blues 72. Hit 73. The Take 74. Mahogany 75. Bingo Long and the Travelling All Stars 76. *Scott Joplin* 78. The Empire Strikes Back 80. Nighthawks 81. Marvin and Tige 83. Number One with Buller 87.

Williams, Bransby (1870–1961).
Distinguished British stage actor who made an early talkie appearance in an experimental Lee de Forest Phonofilm. Later appeared in The Cold Cure 25. Jungle Woman 26. Troublesome Wives 28. Song of the Road 37, etc.

Williams, Cara (1925–) (Bernice Kamiat). American TV and radio comedienne.
Happy Land 43. Don Juan Quilligan 45. Sitting Pretty 48. The Girl Next Door 53. The Defiant Ones 58. The Man from the Diners Club 63. The White Buffalo 77.
TV series: Pete and Gladys 60–61. The Cara Williams Show 64.

Williams, Cindy (1948–). American leading lady.
Drive He Said 71. American Graffiti 73. Travels with My Aunt 73. The Conversation 74. Mr Ricco 75. More American Graffiti 79. The Creature Wasn't Nice 81.

Williams, Elmo (1913–). American editor and producer. Produced, edited and directed *The Cowboy* 54; worked as editor on several major productions; became head of 20th Century-Fox British productions.

Williams, Emlyn (1905–87). Welsh actor and playwright, on stage from 1927. Autobiographies: *George* 1972. *Emlyn* 1974.
The Case of the Frightened Lady (film debut) 32. Men of Tomorrow 33. Friday the Thirteenth 33. Sally Bishop 33. Broken Blossoms 36. *The Citadel* 38. The Stars Look Down 39. Major Barbara 40. You Will Remember 40. *Hatter's Castle* 41. *The Last Days of Dolwyn* (& wd) 48. *Three Husbands* 50. Ivanhoe 52. *The Deep Blue Sea* 56. I Accuse 57. Beyond This Place 59. The L-Shaped Room 62. Eye of the Devil 66. The Walking Stick 69. David Copperfield 69, others.
Plays filmed: *Night Must Fall, The Corn is Green.*

Williams, Esther (1923–). Aquatic American leading lady, former swimming champion.
□Andy Hardy's Double Life (debut) 42. A Guy Named Joe 43. *Bathing Beauty* 44. Ziegfeld Follies 44. Thrill of a Romance 45. Easy to Wed 45. This Time for Keeps 46. Till the Clouds Roll By 46. Fiesta 47. On an Island with You 48. *Take Me Out to the Ball Game* 48. Neptune's Daughter 49. Pagan Love Song 50. Duchess of Idaho 51. Callaway Went Thataway 51. Texas Carnival 52. Skirts Ahoy 52. Million Dollar Mermaid 52. *Dangerous When Wet* 53. Easy to Love 54. Jupiter's Darling 54. The Unguarded Moment 56. Raw Wind in Eden 57. The Big Show 61. The Magic Fountain (Sp.) 61.

¶ Wet she was a star.—*Joe Pasternak*
All they ever did for me at MGM was change my leading men and the water in my pool.—*E.W.*

Williams, Grant (1930–85). American leading man who never quite made the bigtime.
Written on the Wind 56. *The Incredible Shrinking Man* 57. The Monolith Monsters 58. PT 109 63. Doomsday 72, etc.
TV series: Hawaiian Eye 59–63.

Williams, Guinn 'Big Boy' (1900–1962). American character actor, usually in amiably tough roles. In Hollywood 1919 as an extra.
Noah's Ark 29. Dodge City 39. Mr Wise Guy 42. The Desperadoes 43. Thirty Seconds Over Tokyo 44. Bad Men of Tombstone 49. Hangman's Knot 53. The Outlaw's Daughter 55. The Comancheros 62, scores of others.
TV series: Circus Boy 56–57.

Williams, Guy (1924–). American leading man, the 'Zorro' of Walt Disney's TV series and films.
The Prince and the Pauper 62. Captain Sinbad 63, etc.
TV series: Lost in Space 65–68.

Williams, Harcourt (1880–1957). Distinguished British stage actor.
Henry V 44. *Brighton Rock* 47. Hamlet 48. Third Time Lucky 48. *The Late Edwina Black* 51. Roman Holiday 53. Around the World in Eighty Days 56.

Williams, Hugh (1904–1969) (Brian Williams). British leading man and playwright on stage from 1921.
Charley's Aunt (film debut) 30. In a Monastery Garden 31. Rome Express 33. Sorrell and Son 34. *David Copperfield* (US) 34. The Amateur Gentleman 36. Dark Eyes of London 38. Wuthering Heights (US) 39. A Girl in a Million 46. *An Ideal Husband* 47. Take My Life 47. The Blind Goddess 48.

Elizabeth of Ladymead 49. The Gift Horse 52. The Fake 53. Twice Upon a Time 53. Khartoum 66, etc.

Williams, Jobeth (1953–). American leading lady.
Kramer vs Kramer 79. The Dogs of War 80. Stir Crazy 80. Poltergeist 82. Endangered Species 82. The Big Chill 83. American Dreamer 84. Teachers 84. Desert Bloom 85. Poltergeist II 86.

Williams, John (1903–1983). Suave British stage actor who has appeared in films, usually in polished comedy roles.
Emil and the Detectives 35. Next of Kin 42. A Woman's Vengeance 48. Dick Turpin's Ride 51. *Dial M for Murder* 54. Sabrina Fair 54. To Catch a Thief 55. *The Solid Gold Cadillac* 56. Island in the Sun 56. Witness for the Prosecution 57. Visit to a Small Planet 60. Last of the Secret Agents 66. The Secret War of Harry Frigg 67. A Flea in Her Ear 68. The Hound of the Baskervilles (TV) 72. No Deposit No Return 76. Hot Lead and Cold Feet 78, etc.

Williams, John (1932–). American composer.
The Secret Ways 61. Diamond Head 62. None But the Brave 65. How to Steal a Million 66. Valley of the Dolls 67. The Cowboys 71. The Poseidon Adventure 72. Tom Sawyer 73. Earthquake 74. The Towering Inferno 74. *Jaws* (AA) 75. The Eiger Sanction 75. *Star Wars* (AA) 77. Close Encounters of the Third Kind 77. Jaws 2 78. Superman 78. The Fury 78. 1941 79. Dracula 79. Superman II 80. The Empire Strikes Back (BFA) 80. Raiders of the Lost Ark 81. E.T. (AA, BFA) 82. Return of the Jedi (AAN) 83. Monsignor 83. Indiana Jones and the Temple of Doom (AAN) 84. The River (AAN) 84. Spacecamp 85. The Witches of Eastwick 87. Empire of the Sun 87, etc.

Williams, Kathlyn (1888–1960). American leading lady of silent films: one of the first serial queens.
Witch of the Everglades 11. Driftwood 12. The Adventures of Kathlyn 13. Sweet Alyssum 15. The Highway of Hope 17. Just a Wife 20. Morals 23. The Enemy Sex 24. Our Dancing Daughters 28. Blood Money 33, many others.

Williams, Kenneth (1926–88). British comic actor adept at 'small boy' character and a variety of outrageous voices. Also on stage, radio and TV.
The Beggar's Opera 52. The Seekers 54. *Carry On Sergeant* 58 (and most other 'Carry Ons'). Raising the Wind 61. Twice Round the Daffodils 62. Don't Lose Your Head 67. Follow That Camel 68. Carry On Dick 74, etc.

Williams, Paul (1940–). Diminutive American singer, composer and actor.
The Chase (a) 65. Phantom of the Paradise (a, m) 74. Bugsy Malone (m) 76. Smokey and the Bandit (a) 77. The End (m) 78. The Muppet Movie (a) 79. The Wild Wild West Revisited (TV) (a) 79. Rooster (TV) (a) 82, etc.

Williams, Rhys (1892–1969). Welsh character actor, long in Hollywood; former technical adviser.
How Green Was My Valley 40. The Spiral Staircase 45. Scandal at Scourie 53. There's No Business Like Show Business 54. The Kentuckian 55. The Fastest Gun Alive 56. The Sons of Katie Elder 65. Skullduggery 69, many others.

Williams, Richard (1933–). Canadian animator in England.
The Little Island 58. *The Charge of the Light Brigade* (titles) 67. *A Christmas Carol* 73, etc. Designed title sequences for *What's New Pussycat*, *The Liquidator*, *Casino Royale*, *Sebastian*, etc.

Williams, Robert (1897–1932). Slow-speaking American leading man of the early thirties.
The Common Law 31. Rebound 31. Devotion 31. *Platinum Blonde* 31, etc.

Williams, Robin (1951–). Eccentric American night club comedian who became a TV star as Mork from Ork in *Mork and Mindy*.
Popeye 80. The World According to Garp 82. The Survivors 83. Moscow on the Hudson 84. The Best of Times 85. Club Paradise 86. Good Morning Vietnam 87.

¶ *R.W.:* Cocaine is God's way of saying you're making too much money.
R.W.: You're only given a little madness. You mustn't lose it.

Williams, Simon (1946–). British light leading man, son of Hugh Williams, who became a TV star in *Upstairs Downstairs*.
The Incredible Sarah 75. Jabberwocky 76. The Odd Job 77. The Prisoner of Zenda 79. The Fiendish Plot of Fu Manchu 80. The Return of the Man from UNCLE (TV) 83.

Williams, Tennessee (1911–1983) (Thomas Lanier Williams). American playwright whose sleazy characters have proved popular screen fodder.
Published 1976: *Memoirs*.
□*The Glass Menagerie* 50. *A Streetcar Named Desire* 52. The Rose Tattoo 56. Baby Doll 56. Cat on a Hot Tin Roof 58. Suddenly Last Summer 59. The Fugitive Kind 60. Summer and Smoke 61. Period of Adjustment 62. Sweet Bird of Youth 63. *The Night of the Iguana* 64. This Property is Condemned 66. Boom 68. Blood Kin 70.

¶ Why did I write? Because I found life unsatisfactory.—*T.W.*

Williams, Treat (1952–) (Richard Williams). American leading actor of heavy presence; from Broadway.
The Ritz 76. The Eagle Has Landed 77. *Hair* 79. 1941 79. Why Would I Lie? 80. The Pursuit of D. B. Cooper 81. Prince of the City 81. Flashpoint 84. Once Upoon a Time in America 84. Dempsey (TV) 85. Smooth Talk 85. The Men's Club 86.

Williamson, Fred (1938–). Black American action hero.
M*A*S*H 70. The Legend of Nigger Charley 72. Hammer 72. Black Caesar 72. Crazy Joe 73. That Man Bolt 74. Boss Nigger 75. Darktown 75. Take a Hard Ride 75. Mr Mean (& pd) 77. Fist of Fear, Touch of Death 80. Vigilante 83. The Big Score (& d) 83, etc.

Williamson, James A. (1855–1933). British production pioneer.
The Big Swallow 01. Fire! 01, etc.

Williamson, Lambert (1907–). British composer.
Edge of the World 38. End of the River 48. One Night With You 48.

Williamson, Nicol (1938–). British leading actor of stage and screen; tends to play bulls in china shops.
□Six Sided Triangle 64. *Inadmissible Evidence* 67. *The Bofors Gun* 68. Laughter in the Dark 68. *The Reckoning* 69. Hamlet 69. The Jerusalem File 72. The Wilby Conspiracy 75. Robin and Marian 76. The Seven Per Cent Solution 76. The Word (TV) 78. The Cheap Detective 78. The Human Factor 79. Venom 81. Excalibur 81. I'm Dancing as Fast as I Can 82. Sakharov (TV) 85. Return to Oz 85.

¶ I don't even notice competition. I'm a centre-forward. I don't watch them. Let them watch me.—*N.W.*

I can understand people's pain, passion, fear, hurt, and I can mirror it and set it up for them to look at.—*N.W.*

Willis, Bruce (–). American leading man.
Blind Date 87.

Willis, Gordon (–). American cinematographer.
□Loving 70. The Landlord 70. The People Next Door 70. Klute 71. Little Murders 71. Bad Company 72. *The Godfather* 72. Up the Sandbox 72. The Paper Chase 73. The Godfather Part Two 74. The Parallax View 74. The Drowning Pool 75. All the President's Men 76. Annie Hall 77. Comes a Horseman 78. Manhattan 79. Stardust Memories 80. Windows 80. Pennies from Heaven 81. A Midsummer Night's Sex Comedy 82. Zelig (AAN) 83. Broadway Danny Rose 84. The Purple Rose of Cairo 85.

Willis, Ted (1918–) (Lord Willis). Influential British writer who set the scene for television's preoccupation with low life via such items as *Dixon of Dock Green* and *Woman in a Dressing Gown*. Dixon was derived from his film script *The Blue Lamp*; *Hot Summer Night* was later filmed as *Flame in the Streets*.

Willman, Noel (1918–). British actor and stage director whose film roles have often been coldly villainous.
Pickwick Papers 52. The Net 53. Beau Brummell 54. Cone of Silence 60. The Girl on the Boat 62. *Kiss of the Vampire* 63. The Reptile 65. Doctor Zhivago 65. The Vengeance of She 68, etc.

Willock, Dave (1909–). American light actor, usually the hero's friend.
Legion of Lost Flyers 39. Let's Face It 43. Pin Up Girl 44. The Runaround 46. Chicago Deadline 49. Call Me Mister 51. It Came from Outer Space 53. The Buster Keaton Story 57. Wives and Lovers 63. Send Me No Flowers 64, many others.
TV series: Boots and Saddles 57. Margie 61.

Wills, Brember (1883–1948). Slightly built British character actor best remembered for playing the mad arsonist Saul Femm in *The Old Dark House* (1932).

Wills, Chill (1903–78). Gravel-voiced American character actor, in films from 1938, mainly low-budget westerns. Also the voice of

the talking mule in the 'Francis' series.
Boom Town 40. Best Foot Forward 43. The Harvey Girls 46. Raw Deal 48. High Lonesome 50. Bronco Buster 52. City That Never Sleeps 53. Timberjack 55. Giant 56. The Alamo 60. The Deadly Companions 62. The Cardinal 63. The Over the Hill Gang Rides Again (TV) 71. Mr Billion 77, etc.
TV series: Frontier Circus 61. The Rounders 67.

Willson, Meredith (1902–84) (Robert Meredith Reiniger). American song composer and lyricist whose chief bequests to the cinema are *The Music Man* and *The Unsinkable Molly Brown*.

Wilmer, Douglas (1920–). British character actor of stage, screen and TV.
Richard III 56. An Honourable Murder 60. El Cid 61. Cleopatra 62. The Fall of the Roman Empire 64. One Way Pendulum 65. Brides of Fu Manchu 66. Unman Wittering and Zigo 71. The Golden Voyage of Sinbad 73. The Adventure of Sherlock Holmes' Smarter Brother 75. Sarah 76. The Revenge of the Pink Panther 78. Rough Cut 80. Octopussy 83, others.

Wilson, Dooley (1894–1953). Black American character actor.
Casablanca (as Sam, who played it again) 42. Stormy Weather 43. Come to the Stable 49. Passage West 51, etc.
† It is alleged that Elliott Carpenter played the piano for Wilson in *Casablanca* . . . and some say Wilson didn't sing either.

Wilson, Flip (1933–) (Clerow Wilson). Black American actor and entertainer.
Uptown Saturday Night 74. Pinocchio (TV) 76. Skatetown USA 79.

Wilson, Harry Leon (1867–1939). American comedy novelist: chief works filmed are *Ruggles of Red Gap* and *Merton of the Movies*.

Wilson, Lois (1895–1983). American leading lady of the silent screen.
The Dumb Girl of Potici 16. Why Smith Left Home 19. The Covered Wagon 23. Miss Lulu Bett 24. Monsieur Beaucaire 24. What Every Woman Knows 24. Icebound 24. The Show Off 26. Seed 28. Manslaughter 28. The Crash 32. Laughing at Life 33. Bright Eyes 34. The Girl from Jones Beach 49, etc.

Wilson, Marie (1916–1972) (Katherine Elizabeth White). American leading lady often seen as 'dumb blonde'.
Satan Met a Lady 36. Fools for Scandal 38. *Boy Meets Girl* 40. Broadway 42. The Young Widow 47. Linda Be Good 48. *Mr Friend Irma* (title role) 49. A Girl in Every Port 51. Marry Me Again 54. Mr Hobbs Takes a Vacation 62, etc.
TV series: My Friend Irma 52.

Wilson, Michael (1914–78). American screenwriter whose career was interrupted by the communist witch hunt of the late forties.
The Men in Her Life 42. It's a Wonderful Life (co-w) 46. Salt of the Earth 51. Five Fingers 52. *A Place in the Sun* (AA) 52. Friendly Persuasion (uncredited) 56. *The Bridge on the River Kwai* (uncredited) 57. Lawrence of Arabia 62. The Sandpiper 65. *Planet of the Apes* 67. Che! 69, etc.

Wilson, Richard (1915–). American producer and director, former radio actor.
The Golden Blade (p) 54. Man with a Gun (pdw) 55. Raw Wind in Eden (d) 58. Al Capone (d) 59. Pay or Die (pd) 60. Invitation to a Gunfighter (pd) 64. Three in an Attic (pd) 68, etc.

Wilson, Sandy (1924–). British songwriter and lyricist whose best show, *The Boy Friend*, reached the screen in mangled form through the intervention of Ken Russell.

Wilson, Scott (1942–). American general purpose actor, usually in tough roles.
In Cold Blood 67. The Grissom Gang 71. The New Centurions 72. Lolly Madonna XXX 73. The Great Gatsby 74. The Passover Plot 77. The Ninth Configuration 80.

Wilson, Whip (1915–1964) (Charles Meyer). American cowboy actor who appeared in a great number of second features in the thirties and forties.

Wimperis, Arthur (1874–1953). British librettist and screenwriter, usually in collaboration.
The Private Life of Henry VIII 32. Sanders of the River 35. The Four Feathers 39. Mrs Miniver (AA) 42. Random Harvest 43. The Red Danube 48. Calling Bulldog Drummond 51. Young Bess 53, others.

Winchell, Walter (1897–1972). American columnist and commentator with a keen eye for crime and show business. Appeared in a few thirties movies such as *Love and Hisses* 37; wrote *Broadway Thro' a Keyhole* 33; narrated TV series *The Untouchables* 59–63.

Windom, William (1923–). American leading man, usually in minor film roles.
To Kill a Mockingbird 62. For Love or Money 63. One Man's Way 64. The Americanization of Emily 64. The Detective 68. Brewster McCloud 70. Fool's Parade 71. Now You See Him Now You Don't 72. Echoes of a Summer 75. Mean Dog Blues 78. Grandview USA 84, etc.
TV series: The Farmer's Daughter 63–66. My World and Welcome To It 69.

Windsor, Barbara (1937–) (Barbara Deeks). British cockney actress specializing in dumb blondes.
Lost 55. Too Hot to Handle 59. Sparrows Can't Sing 64. Carry On Spying 64. Crooks in Cloisters 64. The Boy Friend 71. Carry On Abroad 72. Carry On Girls 73, etc.

Windsor, Claire (1898–1972) (Olga Cronk). American leading lady of the silent screen.
To Please a Woman 20. Rich Men's Wives 22. Nellie the Beautiful Cloak Model 24. Money Talks 26. Captain Lash 29, etc.

Windsor, Marie (1923–) (Emily Marie Bertelson). American leading lady with stage and radio experience; films mainly routine.
All American Co-Ed 41. Song of the Thin Man 47. Force of Evil 48. Outpost in Morocco 49. Dakota Lil 50. *The Narrow Margin* 51. The Tall Texan 53. City That Never Sleeps 53. Abbott and Costello Meet the Mummy 55. *The Killing* 56. The Unholy Wife 57. Bedtime Story 64. Chamber of Horrors 66. The Good Guys and the Bad Guys 69. Support Your Local Gunfighter 71. Cahill 73. Hearts of the West 75, many others.

Windust, Bretaigne (1906–1960). American director, from the New York stage.
Winter Meeting 47. June Bride 48. Pretty Baby 50. *The Enforcer* 51. Face to Face 52. The Pied Piper of Hamelin 59, etc.

Winfield, Paul (1941–). Black American leading actor.
The Lost Man 69. RPM 70. Brother John 71. *Sounder* 72. Gordon's War 73. Conrack 74. Hustle 75. Damnation Alley 77. Twilight's Last Gleaming 77. The Greatest 77. Backstairs at the White House (TV) 79. King (TV) 80. Angel City (TV) 81. Star Trek II: The Wrath of Khan 82. On the Run 82. Mike's Murder 82. Star Trek II 82. Go Tell it on the Mountain 84. The Terminator 84. Blue City 85, etc.

Winfrey, Oprah (–). American actress.
The Color Purple (AAN) 85.

Winger, Debra (1955–). American leading lady of the early eighties, in increasingly strong roles.
Thank God It's Friday 78. French Postcards 79. Urban Cowboy 80. Cannery Row 82. An Officer and a Gentleman 82. Terms of Endearment (AAN) 83. Mike's Murder 84. Legal Eagles 85. Black Widow 87. Made in Heaven 87.

Wings (US 1927) (AA). The last of the silent spectaculars and the first film to win an Oscar. A field day of stunt flying with a World War I background, directed by William Wellman, with Charles Rogers, Clara Bow and Richard Arlen.

Winkler, Henry (1946–). Extrovert American actor best known as Fonz in TV's *Happy Days* 74–83.
The Lords of Flatbush 72. Heroes 77. The One and Only 78, etc.

Winkler, Irwin (–). American producer.
The Split 68. They Shoot Horses Don't They? 69. The Strawberry Statement 70. The Mechanic 72. Up the Sandbox 72. Peeper 75. The Gambler 75. Nickelodeon 76. Rocky 76. New York New York 77. Comes a Horseman 78. Rocky II 79. Raging Bull 81. True Confessions 81.

Winn, Godfrey (1908–1971). British journalist who made rare film appearances.
Blighty 27. Very Important Person 62, etc.

Winner, Michael (1935–). Ebullient British director who never shoots in a studio. His own best publicist.
□Climb Up the Wall 57. The Clock Strikes Eight 57. Man with a Gun 58. Shoot to Kill 59. Some Like It Cool 61. Haunted England 61. Play It Cool 62. The Cool Mikado 63. West Eleven 63. *The System* 64. You Must be Joking 65. *The Jokers* 66. *I'll Never Forget Whatshisname* 67. Hannibal Brooks 69. The Games 69. *Lawman* 70. The Night Comers 71. Chato's Land 72. The Mechanic 72. Scorpio 72. The Stone Killer 73. *Death Wish* 74. Won Ton Ton 76. The Sentinel 77. The Big Sleep 78. Firepower 79. Death Wish II

81. The Wicked Lady 83. Scream for Help 84. Death Wish 3 85. Appointment with Death 87.

¶ In a time when diffidence is fashionable, it is refreshing to find a youngish British director who seems deliberately to court comparison with Erich Von Stroheim:

A team effort is a lot of people doing what I say.

Original? It seems so. It is also true; and unlike Von Stroheim Mr Winner does get his films out on time and below budget, facts which tend to atone for his arrogance. He knows that:

In this business, disaster is always just around the corner.

He remembers the days when:

You could make a film for £100,000 and get your money back from people sheltering from the rain.

He won't make the mistake of imagining that those days are still here. He enjoys the big money:

Success has gone to my stomach.

And he finds that:

The hardest part of directing is staying awake for nine weeks at a stretch.

He has no qualms about what he purveys:

There's no moralistic side to *Death Wish*: it's a pleasant romp.

And he is proud of his prowess:

Being in the movie business is like being a tennis player. You have to keep your total concentraiton and your mind on the ball. The minute you fall in love with Tatum O'Neal or get flabby, you've had it.

Winninger, Charles (1884–1969) (Karl Winninger). Chubby, lovable American character actor, in films from 1916 as vaudeville appearances permitted. His catchphrase: '*Happ*-y new year . . .'
□Pied Piper Malone 24. The Canadian 24. Summer Bachelors 26. Soup to Nuts 30. Bad Sister 31. Night Nurse 31. Flying High 31. God's Gift to Women 31. Fighting Caravans 31. Gun Smoke 31. Children of Dreams 31. The Sin of Madelon Claudet 31. Husband's Holiday 31. Social Register 34. *Show Boat* (as Captain Andy) 36. White Fang 36. *Three Smart Girls* 36. You're a Sweetheart 37. Woman Chases Man 37. *Nothing Sacred* 37. Café Metropole 37. You Can't Have Everything 37. The Go-Getter 37. Every Day's a Holiday 37. Goodbye Broadway 38. Hard to Get 38. Three Smart Girls Grow Up 39. *Destry Rides Again* 39. *Babes in Arms* 39. Barricade 39. If I Had My Way 40. My Love Came Back 40. Beyond Tomorrow 40. Little Nellie Kelly 40. When Ladies Meet 41. *Ziegfeld Girl* 41. The Getaway 41. My Life with Caroline 41. Pot o' Gold 41. Friendly Enemies 42. Coney Island 43. A Lady Takes a Chance 43. Flesh and Fantasy 43. Hers to Hold 43. Broadway Rhythm 44. Belle of the Yukon 44. Sunday Dinner for a Soldier 44. She Wouldn't Say Yes 45. *State Fair* 45. Lover Come Back 46. Living in a Big Way 47. Something in the Wind 47. The Inside Story 48. *Give My Regards to Broadway* 48. Father Is a Bachelor 50. *The Sun Shines Bright* 53. Torpedo Alley 53. A Perilous Journey 53. Champ for a Day 53. Las Vegas Shakedown 55. Raymie 60.
TV series: The Charlie Farrell Show 56.

Winslow, George (1946–) (George Wenzlaff). American boy actor whose throaty voice earned him the nickname 'Foghorn'.
Room for One More 52. My Pal Gus 52. Mr Scoutmaster 53. Artists and Models 55. Wild Heritage 58, etc.

Winter, Donovan (–). British director of eccentric low-budgeters.
The Trunk 60. A Penny for Your Thoughts 65. Promenade 68. Come Back Peter 69. Give Us Tomorrow 77, etc.

Winter, Vincent (1947–). British child actor, in films since *The Kidnappers* 53 (special AA).
The Dark Avenger 55. Time Lock 56. Beyond This Place 59. Gorgo 60. Greyfriars Bobby 61. Almost Angels 63. The Three Lives of Thomasina 63. The Horse Without a Head 64, etc.

Winters, Jonathan (1925–). American comedian with TV and night-club experience.
It's a Mad Mad Mad Mad World 63. *The Loved One* 65. The Russians are Coming, The Russians are Coming 66. Penelope 66. Oh Dad Poor Dad 67. Viva Max 69. The Fish That Saved Pittsburgh 79, etc.
TV series: Mork and Mindy 81.

Winters, Roland (1904–). Heavily-built American character actor with stage and radio experience, in Hollywood from 1946; played Charlie Chan in six Monogram features 1948–52.
13 Rue Madeleine 46. Inside Straight 52. So Big 53. Loving 70, etc.
TV series: Meet Millie 52–55. The Smothers Brothers Show 65.

Winters, Shelley (1922–) (Shirley Schrift). American leading character actress with vaudeville and stage experience, in Hollywood from 1943.

Autobiography 1980: *Shelley*.
□What a Woman 43. Sailor's Holiday 44. The Racket Man 44. Two Man Submarine 44. She's a Soldier Too 44. Nine Girls 44. Cover Girl 44. Knickerbocker Holiday 44. 1001 Nights 45. Tonight and Every Night 45. Living in a Big Way 47. The Gangster 48. Red River 48. Larceny 48. *A Double Life* 48. Cry of the City 48. Take One False Step 49. Johnny Stool Pigeon 49. The Great Gatsby 49. Winchester 73 50. East of Java 51. He Ran All The Way 51. Frenchie 51. Behave Yourself 51. The Raging Tide 51. A Place in the Sun 51. My Man and I 52. Phone Call from a Stranger 52. Meet Danny Wilson 52. Untamed Frontier 52. Tennessee Champ 54. Saskatchewan 54. Playgirl 54. Executive Suite 54. To Dorothy a Son 54. *The Big Knife* 55. *The Night of the Hunter* 55. Mambo 55. I Am a Camera 55. I Died a Thousand Times 56. Treasure of Pancho Villa 56. Odds Against Tomorrow 58. *The Diary of Anne Frank* (AA) 59. Let No Man Write My Epitaph 60. The Young Savages 61. Lolita 62. Wives and Lovers 63. The Chapman Report 63. The Balcony 63. A House is Not a Home 64. Time of Indifference 64. The Greatest Story Ever Told 65. *A Patch of Blue* (AA) 65. Alfie (GB) 66. Harper 66. Enter Laughing 67. The Scalp Hunters 67. Wild in the Streets 68. Buona Sera Mrs Campbell 68. The Mad Room 69. Arthur! Arthur! 69. Flap 70. Bloody Mama 70. How Do I Love Thee 70. What's the Matter with Helen 70. Who Slew Auntie Roo? 71. Revenge! (TV) 71. The Poseidon Adventure 72. Something to Hide 72. The Devil's Daughter (TV) 72. Blume in Love 73. Cleopatra Jones 73. Big Rose (TV) 74. Diamonds 75. That Lucky Touch 75. Journey Into Fear 75. Next Stop Greenwich Village 76. The Tenant 76. Pete's Dragon 77. Tentacles 77. Black Journey 77. King of the Gypsies 78. City on Fire 79. The Magician of Lublin 79. Redneck County Rape 79. The Visitor 79. Elvis (TV) 79. Over the Brooklyn Bridge 83. S.O.B. 81. Deja Vu 84. Delta Force 85.

¶ *S.W.:* I did a picture in England one winter and it was so cold I almost got married.

Wintle, Julian (1913–1980). British producer, former editor, in films from 1934. Co-founder of Independent Artists 1958.
Hunted 51. High Tide at Noon 57. Tiger Bay 59. Very Important Person 61. This Sporting Life 63. And Father Came Too 64, many others.

Winwood, Estelle (1882–1984) (Estelle Goodwin). British stage character actress who played in many American films, usually as eccentric ladylike flutterers.
The House of Trent 34. Quality Street 37. The Glass Slipper 55. *The Swan* 56. Twenty-three Paces to Baker Street 56. *Alive and Kicking* (GB) 58. Darby O'Gill and the Little People 59. Notorious Landlady 62. Dead Ringer 64. Camelot 67. Games 67. The Producers 68. Murder by Death 76, etc.

wipe. A wipe is an optical device used for quick changes of scene: a line appears at one edge or corner of the screen and 'wipes' across, bringing the new picture with it. Wipes can also be devised in complex patterns or as expanding images, etc.

Wisbar, Frank (1899–1967). German director in America; made one memorable low-budgeter, *Strangler of the Swamp* 46.

Wisberg, Aubrey (1909–). British-born writer-producer of Hollywood films, mainly second features.
So Dark the Night (w) 41. The Man from Planet X (wp) 51. The Neanderthal Man (wp) 53. Captain Kidd and the Slave Girl (wp) 54. Son of Sinbad (w) 55, many others.

Wisdom, Norman (1918–). British slapstick comedian, also on stage and TV.
□*Trouble in Store* (film debut) 53. One Good Turn 54. Man of the Moment 55. Up in the World 56. Just My Luck 58. The Square Peg 58. Follow a Star 59. There Was a Crooked Man 60. The Bulldog Breed 61. The Girl on the Boat 61. On the Beat 62. A Stitch in Time 63. The Early Bird 65. Press for Time 66. The Sandwich Man 66. The Night They Raided Minsky's (US) 68. What's Good for the Goose 69, etc.

Wise, Ernie: see *Morecambe, Eric*.

Wise, Robert (1914–). American director, former editor (worked on *Citizen Kane, All That Money Can Buy, The Magnificent Ambersons*).
□Mademoiselle Fifi 44. Curse of the Cat People 44. *The Body Snatcher* 45. A Game of Death 46. Criminal Court 46. Born to Kill 47. Mystery in Mexico 47. Blood on the Moon 48. *The Set-Up* 49. Three Secrets 50. Two Flags West 50. The House on Telegraph Hill 51. *The Day the Earth Stood Still* 51. Captive City 52. Destination Gobi 52. Something for the Birds 52. Desert Rats 52. So Big 53. *Executive Suite* 54. Helen of Troy 55. Tribute to a Bad Man 56. Somebody Up There Likes Me 56. Until They Sail 57. This Could Be the

Night 57. Run Silent Run Deep 58. I Want to Live 58. Odds Against Tomorrow 59. *West Side Story* (AA) 61. Two for the Seesaw 62. The Haunting (GB) 63. *The Sound of Music* (AA) 65. The Sand Pebbles 66. Star! 68. The Andromeda Strain 70. Two People 73. The Hindenberg 75. Audrey Rose 77. Star Trek 79.

Wiseman, Frederick (1930–). American documentarist, former law professor.
Titicut Follies 67. High School 68. Law and Order 69. Hospital 70. Basic Training 71. Essene 72, etc.

Wiseman, Joseph (1918–). American stage actor who has made several film appearances.
Detective Story 51. Viva Zapata 52. Les Misérables 52. The Prodigal 55. The Garment Jungle 57. The Unforgiven 60. *Dr No* (title role) 62. *The Night They Raided Minsky's* 68. Bye Bye Braverman 68. Stiletto 69. The Valachi Papers 72. The Apprenticeship of Duddy Kravitz 74. Buck Rogers 79. Rage of Angels (TV) 83, etc.

Wister, Owen (1860–1938). American western novelist whose *The Virginian*, published in 1902, was the basis of several films and a television series.

witchcraft has not been frequently tackled by film-makers, usually for censorship reasons, and *Witchcraft through the Ages* (qv) remains the most comprehensive cinematic treatise on the subject. Dreyer's *Day of Wrath* took it seriously, as did *The Witches of Salem, Maid of Salem, Witchfinder General, The Dunwich Horror, The Devils* and *Il Demonio*, but all were chiefly concerned with the morals of witch-hunting. Witch doctors are familiar figures from African adventure films like *King Solomon's Mines* and *Men of Two Worlds*; more lightheartedly, witches featured in *The Wizard of Oz, I Married a Witch* and *Bell Book and Candle*, as well as in TV's *Bewitched* and all the films featuring Merlin. A nasty cannibalistic coven was seen in Gosta Werner's *Midvinterblot* and several recent thrillers (*Night of the Demon, City of the Dead, Night of the Eagle, Witchcraft, The Witches, Rosemary's Baby, Satan's Skin, Cry of the Banshee, The Illustrated Man, The Mephisto Waltz, The Brotherhood of Satan, The Sentinel*) purported to believe in the effects of witchcraft. Angela Lansbury in *Bedknobs and Broomsticks* played a kindly witch.
See also: *the devil*.

Witchcraft through the Ages (Häxan) (Sweden 1921). A unique and still horrifying film by Benjamin Christensen: a semi-documentary with fictional elements, reconstructing pagan ritual with such care as to make it a handbook of diabolism.

Withers, Googie (1917–) (Georgette Withers). British leading lady of stage and screen, married to John McCallum with whom she moved some years ago to Australia.
Biography 1979: *Life with Googie* by John McCallum.
Girl in the Crowd 34. Accused 36. Strange Boarders 37. The Lady Vanishes 38. Trouble Brewing 39. Back Room Boy 41. *One of Our Aircraft is Missing* 42. *On Approval* 44. They Came to a City 44. Dead of Night 45. The Loves of Joanna Godden 46. Pink String and Sealing Wax 46. *It Always Rains on Sunday* 47. Miranda 48. Once Upon a Dream 49. Traveller's Joy 50. Night and the City 50. *White Corridors* 51. Derby Day 52. Devil on Horseback 54. Port of Escape 55. The Nickel Queen 70, etc.

Withers, Grant (1904–1959). American general purpose actor in films since the twenties.
Tiger Rose 29. Sinner's Holiday 30. Red-Haired Alibi 32. Society Fever 35. Men of Steel 37. Mr Wong, Detective 39. Mexican Spitfire Out West 41. The Apache Trail 43. My Darling Clementine 46. Tripoli 50. Run for Cover 55. The White Squaw 58, many others.

Withers, Jane (1926–). American child star of the thirties, more mischievous and less pretty than Shirley Temple.
Bright Eyes 34. Ginger 35. The Farmer Takes a Wife 35. The Mad Martindales 42. North Star 43. Faces in the Fog 44. Affairs of Geraldine 46. Giant 56. The Right Approach 62. Captain Newman 63, etc.

Witherspoon, Cora (1890–1957). American character comedienne often seen as shrewish wife; on stage from 1910.
Libeled Lady 36. Madame X 38. The Bank Dick 40. This Love of Ours 45. The Mating Season 50. The First Time 52, etc.

Witness for the Prosecution (US 1957). One of the most successful adaptations of an Agatha Christie original, the courtroom melodrama benefited from a witty script by Billy Wilder, who also directed.

Witney, William (1910–). American director, mainly of routine westerns for Republic.
Roll On Texas Moon 46. Night Time in Nevada 49. The Fortune Hunter 52. City of Shadows 54. Stranger at My Door 56. The Bonnie Parker Story 58. Paratroop Command 59. Master of the World 61. Girls on the Beach 65. Arizona Raiders 66. I Escaped from Devil's Island 73, many others.

Wixted, Michael James (–). American child actor of the seventies.
Lost in the Stars 74. Where Have All the People Gone? (TV) 74. Islands in the Stream 77, etc.
TV series: The Smith Family 71. The Swiss Family Robinson 75.

Wizan, Joe (1935–). American producer.
Jeremiah Johnson 72. Junior Bonner 72. Prime Cut 72. The Last American Hero 73. Audrey Rose 77. And Justice for All 79. Voices 79.

The Wizard of Oz (US 1939). Despite décor which now seems vulgar, this well-loved film survives as Hollywood's best retelling of a fairy story, mainly because of the delightful score by Harold Arlen and E. Y. Harburg, and because Judy Garland, who, though actually too old for Dorothy, successfully portrayed the essential innocence and wonder which make such stories live. An excellent supporting cast included Ray Bolger as the Scarecrow, Jack Haley as the Tin Man, Bert Lahr as the Cowardly Lion, Margaret Hamilton as the Wicked Witch and Frank Morgan as the Wizard. Mervyn le Roy produced, Victor Fleming directed, Harold Rosson was cameraman; the Technicolor which added so much at the time now seems garish. There had been two silent versions of Frank Baum's book, in 1910 and 1924.
Book published 1977: *The Making of the Wizard of Oz* by Aljean Harmetz.

Wodehouse, Sir P. G. (1881–1975). British comic novelist whose sagas of upper class twits and manservants in the the twenties have been oddly neglected by the screen, though they were much imitated and two films about the perfect manservant Jeeves were made in the thirties.

The Wolf Man. The werewolf or lycanthrope, a man who turns into a ravaging beast at full moon, is a fairly ancient Central European mythological figure. Hollywood did not develop the idea until *Werewolf of London* 34, a one-shot in which Henry Hull, a victim of his own well-intentioned research, was firmly despatched before the end. Not until 1941 was the possibility of a series character envisaged. *The Wolf Man* had a splendid cast: Claude Rains, Warren William, Patric Knowles, Bela Lugosi, Maria Ouspenskaya, and Lon Chaney Jnr as Lawrence Talbot, heir to a stately English home but unlucky enough to be bitten by a werewolf and thus condemned to monstrous immortality until despatched by a silver bullet. In this film he was battered to apparent death by Claude Rains, but arose from the family crypt for *Frankenstein Meets the Wolf Man* 43, which ended with him and the Frankenstein monster being swept away in a flood. In *House of Frankenstein* he was discovered in a block of ice and promptly thawed out, only to be shot with the requisite silver bullet by a gipsy girl. The producers, however, played so unfair as to revive him for *House of Dracula* 45, in which he lived to be the only movie monster with a happy ending: brain surgery cured him and he even got the girl. Years later, however, in *Abbott and Costello Meet Frankenstein* 48, it seemed that his affliction was again tormenting him; this time we last saw him falling into a rocky and turbulent sea. Mr Chaney had by now done with the character apart from a cod appearance in an episode of TV's *Route 66*. But Hammer Films revived the basic plot in *Curse of the Werewolf* 61, with Oliver Reed as the mangy hero. To date this has provoked no sequels. One should also mention *The Werewolf* 56, *I Was a Teenage Werewolf* 57, *La Casa del Terror* (Mexican) 59, *Werewolf in a Girl's Dormitory* (with its theme song 'The Ghoul in School') 61 and *Legend of the Werewolf* 74, but the less said about these the better.
There was a werewolf in *Dr Terror's House of Horrors* 65, and in *The Beast Must Die* 74, while the eighties brought a whole slew of hairy monsters in *Wolfen*, *An American Werewolf in London*, *Werewolf of Washington*, *Teen Wolf* and *The Howling*.

Wolfe, Ian (1896–). American character actor who usually plays worried, grasping or officious roles.
The Barretts of Wimpole Street 33. Clive of India 35. Hudson's Bay 40. The Moon is Down 43. The Invisible Man's Revenge 44. Mr Blandings Builds His Dream House 48. The Great Caruso 50. Gaby 56. The Lost World 60. Games 67. The Fortune 74. Jinxed 82, many others.
TV series: Soap 78–80.

Wolff, Lothar (1909–). German producer-director, former editor; with 'The March of Time' for many years, and still associated with Louis de Rochemont.
Lost Boundaries (p) 45. Martin Luther (co-wp) 53. Windjammer (p) 57. Question Seven (pd) 61. Fortress of Peace (p) 63, etc.

Wolfit, Sir Donald (1902–1968). Distinguished British thespian who, having brought Shakespeare to the provinces, gave some enjoyably hammy performances in films.
Autobiography 1954: *First Interval.*
Biography 1971: *The Knight Has Been Unruly* by Ronald Harwood.
□ Death at Broadcasting House 34. Drake of England 35. The Silent Passenger 35. Sexton Blake and the Bearded Doctor 35. Checkmate 35. Late Extra 35. Hyde Park Corner 35. Calling the Tune 36. *The Ringer* 52. Pickwick Papers 53. Isn't Life Wonderful? 53. Svengali 54. A Prize of Gold 55. Guilty 56. The Man in the Road 56. The Man on the Beach 56. Satellite in the Sky 56. The Traitor 57. I Accuse 57. Blood of the Vampire 58. *Room at the Top* 59. The House of Seven Hawks 59. The Angry Hills 59. The Rough and the Smooth 59. The Hands of Orlac 60. The Mark 61. Lawrence of Arabia 62. Dr Crippen 63. Becket 64. Ninety Degrees in the Shade 65. Life at the Top 65. The Sandwich Man 66. *Decline and Fall* 68. The Charge of the Light Brigade 68.

Wolfson, P. J. (1903–79). American screenwriter.
Madison Square Garden 31. The Picture Snatcher 33. Mad Love 35. Public Enemy's Wife 37. Shall We Dance? (co-w) 37. Vivacious Lady (co-w) 38. Allegheny Uprising (& p) 39. They All Kissed the Bride (co-w) 42. Saigon (co-w & p) 48, many others.

Wolheim, Louis (1880–1931). German-born character actor, often of semi-brutish roles, with American stage experience; in Hollywood from 1919.
Dr Jekyll and Mr Hyde 20. Little Old New York 22. America 24. *Two Arabian Knights* 27. The Racket 28. Tempest 28. Frozen Justice 29. *All Quiet on the Western Front* 31. Sin Ship (& d) 31, etc.

Wolper, David (1928–). American documentarist who turned feature film producer and TV executive.
If It's Tuesday This Must Be Belgium 69. The Bridge at Remagen 69. The Hellstrom Chronicle 71. Roots (TV) 77, etc.

A Woman of Paris (US 1923). Charlie Chaplin wrote and directed but appeared only in a minute role in this society melodrama, with Edna Purviance as the distraught heroine and Adolphe Menjou as a smooth philanderer. Chaplin kept it under cover for fifty years but it contains moments of still-effective cinema.

Woman of the Dunes (Suna no Onna) (Japan 1964). A strange erotic fable about an entomologist on a remote beach who is trapped into living with a nubile woman in a deep sandpit. Overlong, but an exciting piece of pure cinema, written by Kobo Abe, directed by Hiroshi Teshigahara, with Eiji Okada and Kyoko Kishida.

Woman to Woman. This tearjerking play by Michael Morton, about a doomed love affair between a British officer and a French dancer, was first filmed by Graham Cutts in 1923, and achieved some renown as one of the better examples of British silent cinema. Clive Brook and Betty Compson had the leads, and Miss Compson appeared with Georges Barraud in the talkie remake of 1929, directed by Victor Saville. In 1946 Maclean Rogers directed an updated version with Douglass Montgomery and Joyce Howard.

women!

? Who played each of the following women?

1 *Woman Chases Man*
2 *The Woman in White*
3 *Woman of the River*
4 *Woman of the Year* (1942)
5 *The Woman on the Beach*
6 *Marked Woman*
7 *The Woman in the Window*
8 *Woman on the Run*
9 *Woman in Hiding*
10 *Singapore Woman*
11 *White Woman*
12 *Woman in a Dressing Gown*
13 *Invisible Woman*
14 *Spider Woman*
15 *The Miracle Woman*
16 *Red Headed Woman*
17 *A Woman Alone*
18 *The Woman I Love*
19 *The Woman in Question (Five Angles on Murder)*
20 *A Woman's Face*

The Women. Clare Boothe Luce's venomous comedy was filmed twice by MGM; in 1939 with an all-woman cast headed by Norma Shearer, Rosalind Russell, Paulette Goddard and Joan Crawford. In 1956 it became a semi-musical called *The Opposite Sex*, with June Allyson and Ann Sheridan.

Wong, Anna May (1907–1961) (Wong Liu Tsong). Chinese-American actress popular in the thirties.
Red Lantern 19. The Thief of Baghdad 24. *Piccadilly* (GB) 29. On the Spot 30. Shanghai Express 32. *Chu Chin Chow* (GB) 33. *Java Head* (GB) 34. Limehouse Blues 36. Bombs Over Burma 42. Impact 49. Portrait in Black 60, etc.

Wontner, Arthur (1875–1960). Gaunt British character actor of stage and screen; a splendid, if elderly, Sherlock Holmes.
Frailty 16. Bonnie Prince Charlie 23. Eugene Aram 24. The Infamous Lady 28. The Sleeping Cardinal 31. *The Sign of Four* 32. *The Triumph of Sherlock Holmes* 35. Dishonour Bright 36. Silver Blaze 36. Storm in a Teacup 37. Kate Plus Ten 38. The Terror 38. The Life and Death of Colonel Blimp 43. Blanche Fury 47. Brandy for the Parson 52. *Genevieve* 53, etc.

Wood, Charles (1932–). British playwright with a penchant for military matters.
Help 65. The Knack 65. How I Won the War 67. The Charge of the Light Brigade 68. The Long Day's Dying 68. The Bed Sitting Room 69. Cuba 79. The Red Monarch (TV) 83. Wagner 83.

Wood, Edward D. Jnr (1922–78). Inept American director of grade 'Z' movies.

Wood, Mrs Henry (1814–1887). British Victorian novelist whose *East Lynne* has been filmed several times.

Wood, John (1937–). British stage actor usually seen in intellectual roles.
The Rebel 60. Nicholas and Alexandra 72. Slaughterhouse Five 72. Somebody Killed Her Husband 77. War Games 83. Ladyhawke 85.

Wood, Natalie (1938–1981) (Natasha Gurdin). Former American child actress, who became a top star of the sixties.
Happy Land 43. Tomorrow is Forever 45. The Bride Wore Boots 46. Miracle on 34th Street 47. No Sad Songs for Me 50. The Blue Veil 52. Rebel Without a Cause 55. A Cry in the Night 56. The Searchers 56. *Marjorie Morningstar* 58. Kings Go Forth 59. Cash McCall 60. *Splendor in the Grass* 61. *West Side Story* 61. Gypsy 62. *Love with the Proper Stranger* 64. Sex and the Single Girl 64. *The Great Race* 65. Inside Daisy Clover 66. This Property is Condemned 66. Penelope 66. *Bob and Carol and Ted and Alice* 69. The Affair (TV) 73. Peeper 74. *From Here to Eternity* (TV) 79. Meteor 79. Brainstorm 83 (release), etc.
TV series: Pride of the Family 53.

Wood, Peggy (1894–1978). American character actress, former opera singer.
Almost a Husband 19. Handy Andy 34. The Housekeeper's Daughter 39. The Story of Ruth 60. *The Sound of Music* 65, etc.
TV series: Mama 49–56.

Wood, Sam (1883–1949). American director, in business before becoming assistant to Cecil B. de Mille c. 1915; directing from 1920.
The Beloved Villain 20. Under the Lash 22. Bluebeard's Eighth Wife 23. One Minute to Play 26. The Latest from Paris 28. Within the Law 30. Stamboul Quest 32. The Late Christopher Bean 33. Get-Rich-Quick Wallingford 34. *A Night at the Opera* 35. The Unguarded Hour 36. *A Day at the Races* 37. Madame X 37. Lord Jeff 38. *Goodbye Mr Chips* 39. Raffles 39. *Our Town* 40. Kitty Foyle 40. *The Devil and Miss Jones* 41. The Pride of the Yankees 42. *Kings Row* 42. Saratoga Trunk 43 (released 46). *For Whom the Bell Tolls* (& p) 43. Casanova Brown 44. Guest Wife 45. Heartbeat 46. Ivy 47. Command Decision 48. Ambush 49, etc.

Woodard, Alfre (1953–). Black American actress.
Health 79. Remember My Name 80. Cross Creek (AAN) 83. Go Tell it on the Mountain 84.

Woodbridge, George (1907–1973). Portly British character actor, often seen as tavernkeeper or jovial policeman.
Tower of Terror 42. Green for Danger 46. Bonnie Prince Charlie 48. The Story of Gilbert and Sullivan 53. The Constant Husband 55. Dracula 58. Two-Way Stretch 60. Dracula Prince of Darkness 65, many others.

Woodbury, Joan (1915–). American leading lady of forties second features.
Without Children 35. Forty Naughty Girls 38. The Mystery of the White Room 39. The

Desperadoes 43. Flame of the West 46. Here Comes Trouble 49. The Ten Commandments 56, many others.

Woods, Arthur B. (1904–1942). British director.
On Secret Service 34. Radio Parade 35. Drake of England 35. The Dark Stairway 37. The Return of Carol Deane 38. *They Drive by Night* 38. The Nursemaid Who Disappeared 39. Busman's Honeymoon 40, etc.

Woods, Aubrey (1928–). British character actor.
Nicholas Nickleby 47. Queen of Spades 48. Father Brown 54. School for Scoundrels 59. Spare the Rod 61. Just Like a Woman 66. The Abominable Dr Phibes 71. The Darwin Adventure 72. That Lucky Touch 75, etc.

Woods, Donald (1904–) (Ralph L. Zink). American leading man of the thirties and forties.
Sweet Adeline 33. *A Tale of Two Cities* 35. *Anthony Adverse* 36. Forgotten Girls 40. Love, Honour and Oh Baby 41. I Was a Prisoner on Devil's Island 41. Watch on the Rhine 43. Roughly Speaking 45. Wonder Man 45. Barbary Pirate 49. Undercover Agent 54. Thirteen Ghosts 60. Kissing Cousins 64. Moment to Moment 65, many others.
TV series: Craig Kennedy Criminologist 53. Tammy 65.

Woods, Eddie (–). American leading man of the early thirties: he seems to have lost heart after swapping roles with Cagney for *The Public Enemy* (he was originally cast for the top role and elected to take the less interesting role of the brother).

Woods, James (1947–). Lean American actor, in roles of increasing stature.
The Way We Were 72. Alex and the Gypsy 76. The Choirboys 78. The Onion Field 79. The Black Marble 80. Eyewitness 80. Split Image 82. Videodrome 83. Against All Odds 83. Once Upon a Time in America 84. Cat's Eye 84. *Salvador* 85. Joshua Then and Now 87. Best Seller 87.

Woodward, Edward (–). British stage actor who achieved popularity on TV as *Callan* 67–73.
Where There's a Will 54. Becket 64. The File of the Golden Goose 69. Sitting Target 72. The Wicker Man 73. Young Winston 73. Callan 74. Stand Up Virgin Soldiers 77. Breaker Morant 79. Winston Churchill, the Wilderness Years (TV) 81. Who Dares Wins 82. A Christmas Carol (TV) 84. King David 85.
TV series: The Equalizer 86–.

Woodward, Joanne (1930–). Tomboyish American leading actress, married to Paul Newman.
□Count Three and Pray 55. A Kiss Before Dying 56. *The Three Faces of Eve* (AA) 57. *No Down Payment* 57. The Long Hot Summer 58. Rally Round the Flag Boys 58. The Sound and the Fury 59. The Fugitive Kind 59. From the Terrace 60. Paris Blues 61. The Stripper 63. A New Kind of Love 63. Signpost to Murder 64. *A Big Hand for the Little Lady* 66. A Fine Madness 66. *Rachel Rachel* 68. Winning 69. W.U.S.A. 70. They Might Be Giants 71. The Effect of Gamma Rays on Man-in-the-Moon Marigolds 72. Summer Wishes Winter Dreams 73. The Drowning Pool 75. Sybil (TV) 77. The End 78. See How She Runs (TV) 78. A Christmas to Remember (TV) 78. The Shadow Box (TV) 80. Harry and Son 84.

Woody Woodpecker. A cartoon character with an infectious laugh, created in the thirties by Walter Lantz for Universal, and still going strong in 1973 via a new TV incarnation.

Wooland, Norman (1905–). British actor, former radio announcer.
Hamlet (film debut) 48. All Over the Town 48. Escape 49. Romeo and Juliet 53. The Master Plan 55. Richard III 56. Guilty 56. The Rough and the Smooth 59. The Fall of the Roman Empire 64. Saul and David 65. The Projected Man 66, etc.

Woolf, James (1919–1966). British producer. With brother **Sir John Woolf** (1913–) founded Romulus Films 1949. Both are sons of leading producer-distributor C. M. Woolf, who died in 1942.
Pandora and the Flying Dutchman 51. The African Queen 52. Moulin Rouge 53. Three Men in a Boat 56. Room at the Top 59, etc.
JAMES ONLY: The L-Shaped Room 62. The Pumpkin Eater 64. Life at the Top 65. King Rat 65.
JOHN ONLY: Oliver! (AA) 68. Day of the Jackal 73. No Sex Please We're British 73. The Odessa File 74.

Woolf, Virginia (1882–1941). British novelist whose introspection and sensitivity, rather than her themes, were used as symbols in the title *Who's Afraid of Virginia Woolf?*

Woolfe, H. Bruce (1880–1965). British producer, best known for his war reconstructions of the twenties (*Armageddon, Ypres, The Battle of the Somme,* etc.) and for the *Secrets of Nature* series begun in 1919. Head of British Instructional Films from 1926; later in charge of production for children.

Woollcott, Alexander (1887–1943). Waspish American columnist and critic, the original inspiration for Kaufman and Hart's *The Man Who Came to Dinner*.
Biography 1976: *Smart Aleck* by Howard Teichmann.
□Gift of Gab 34. *The Scoundrel* 35. Babes on Broadway 41.

Woolley, Monty (1888–1963) (Edgar Montillion Woolley). American comedy character actor of ebullient personality, a former Yale professor who came to movie stardom via a big hit as Alexander Woollcott on the Broadway stage.
Live, Love and Learn 37. Nothing Sacred 37. Arsène Lupin Returns 38. Girl of the Golden West 38. Everybody Sing 38. Three Comrades 38. Lord Jeff 38. Artists and Models Abroad 38. Young Dr Kildare 38. Vacation from Love 48. Never Say Die 39. Midnight 39. Zaza 39. Man About Town 39. Dancing Co-Ed 39. *The Man Who Came to Dinner* 41. The Pied Piper 42. Life Begins at 8.30 42. *Holy Matrimony* 43. Since You Went Away 44. Irish Eyes are Smiling 44. Molly and Me 45. *Night and Day* 46. The Bishop's Wife 47. *Miss Tatlock's Millions* 48. As Young as You Feel 51. Kismet 55, etc.

Famous line (*The Man Who Came to Dinner*): Gentlemen, will you all now leave quietly, or must I ask Miss Cutler to pass among you with a baseball bat?
Famous line (*The Man Who Came to Dinner*) (to his nurse who has reproved him for eating chocolates): My great aunt Elizabeth ate a box of chocolates every day of her life. She lived to be a hundred and two, and when she had been dead three days, she looked healthier than you do now.

Woolrich, Cornell (1903–68). American mystery writer also known as William Irish. A recluse, he handed some interesting ideas to Hollywood, but most were ineptly handled.
Street of Chance (from The Black Curtain) 42. The Leopard Man (from Black Alibi) 43. Phantom Lady 44. Deadline at Dawn 46. Black Angel 46. Fear in the Night 47. Night Has a Thousand Eyes 48. The Window 49. No Man of Her Own 50. Rear Window 54. The Bride Wore Black 67, etc.

Woolsey, Ralph (–). American cinematographer.
The Culpeper Cattle Company 72. The New Centurions 72. The Mack 73. The Iceman Cometh 73. Black Eye 74. 99 44/100 Per Cent Dead 74. Rafferty and the Gold Dust Twins 75. Mother, Jugs and Speed 76. The Promise 79. The Great Santini 80, etc.

Woolsey, Robert (1889–1938). American comedian; see *Wheeler, Bert.*

Worden, Hank (1901–) (Norton Earl Worden). American western character actor.
The Plainsman 36. Northwest Passage 40. The Bullfighters 45. The Secret Life of Walter Mitty 47. Yellow Sky 48. Fort Apache 48. Red River 48. Wagon Master 50. The Searchers 56. McLintock 63, many others.

work print: the same as cutting copy, the first edited print from which, when it is satisfactory, the negative will be cut accordingly.

World of Plenty (GB 1943). A feature-length survey of the global food problem, notable as the first documentary to get a full circuit release in Britain. Directed by Paul Rotha from a script by himself and Eric Knight, it showed advanced use of newsreel material, specially-staged scenes, and Adprint diagrams, and confidently adapted the technique invented by 'The March of Time'.

World War I (1914–18), now a remote and comparatively concentrated event, was seen by film-makers of the next four decades chiefly as an opportunity for pacifist propaganda arising from horror and disillusion. This is the kind of attitude struck in *Civilisation, War Brides, The Battle Cry of Peace, All Quiet on the Western Front* (and its sequel *The Road Back*), *Westfront 1918, J'Accuse, The Man Who Reclaimed His Head, Journey's End, La Grande Illusion, The Man I Killed, The Road to Glory, They Gave Me a Gun, Sergeant York*, and *Paths of Glory. Oh What a Lovely War* made the same points by use of bitter comedy. The romantic aspect of war was however not neglected by *The White Sister, A Farewell to Arms, Hearts of the World, The Four Horsemen of the Apocalypse, The Big Parade, Lilac Time, Hell's Angels, Seventh Heaven, The Dark*

Angel, Waterloo Bridge, Lawrence of Arabia, and many others. *What Price Glory?* was pure cynicism, *The Fighting 69th* pure jingoism. The spy element was to the fore in *I Was a Spy, Dark Journey, The Spy in Black, Mata Hari, Nurse Edith Cavell* and *Darling Lili*; aviation in *Hell's Angels, Wings, The Red Baron* and *The Blue Max*. Comedy aspects of the war were depicted in *Shoulder Arms, Spy for a Day, Pack Up Your Troubles, We're in the Army Now, Half Shot at Sunrise* and *Up the Front*. Rehabilitation problems were dealt with in *The Sun Also Rises, The Last Flight, Isn't Life Wonderful?, The Lost Squadron, The Roaring Twenties* and the 'Forgotten Man' number in *Gold Diggers of 1933*.

World War II

? 1 Name the film in which Margaret O'Brien began her meteoric child star career as a London blitz orphan adopted by an American newspaperman.

2 Who played the title role in *A Guy Named Joe*?

3 Samuel Goldwyn in 1943 made a propaganda piece about a Russian village invaded by Nazis. When the cold war began it was an embarrassment and he sold off the rights; it later resurfaced, heavily cut, as *Armored Attack*. What was the original title?

4 Irene Dunne in 1944 made a film in which she married a landed Englishman, lost him in World War I and their son in World War II. Give the title.

5 The above film was based on a long narrative poem. By whom?

6 In 1944 MGM brought *The Good Earth* up to date by filming Pearl Buck's *Dragon Seed*, about Chinese villagers at war. Who played Jade, the heroine?

7 In 1943 an eminent Broadway cast (including Ruth Gordon, Judith Anderson, Walter Huston and Morris Carnovsky) went to Hollywood and made a picture called *Edge of Darkness*, about Norwegian villagers resisting the Nazis. Who was the leading male star?

8 Cary Grant played the captain of a submarine in what 1943 adventure film? (The answer is NOT *Operation Petticoat*.)

9 Name the book by Jan Struther which was turned into Hollywood's most persuasive (if artificial) account of the British at war.

10 In 1941 Tyrone Power was *A Yank in the RAF*. Who was his leading lady?

11 Jules Dassin's first directorial chore, in 1942, concerned a loyal German American whose twin brother forced him to aid the Nazis. Who played the dual role? What was the film?

12 In 1943 Howard Hawks made a film about the crew of a Flying Fortress called Mary Ann. Name it.

13 A book named *Education for Death*, by Gregor Ziemer, was the basis in 1943 of a surprisingly successful movie starring Bonita Granville and Kent Smith. Name it.

14 Jack L. Warner was later very sorry that in 1943 he produced a picture called *Mission to Moscow*, from Ambassador Joseph E. Davies' book promoting goodwill between Russia and America. Who played the ambassador?

15 Claudette Colbert, Paulette Goddard and Veronica Lake starred in 1943 as nurses trapped with the army on Corregidor. Name the picture.

16 Name also the very similar movie of the same year in which Margaret Sullavan, Joan Blondell and Ann Sothern played nurses caught on Bataan.

17 In *Four Jills in a Jeep*, an account of an actual USO tour by four stars, three of them were Carole Landis, Martha Raye and Mitzi Mayfair. Name the fourth.

18 Who played Colonel James Dolittle in *Thirty Seconds Over Tokyo*?

19 In 1945 Errol Flynn appeared in a war movie which was banned in Britain because it ignored the British contribution in that particular theatre. Name it.

20 John Garfield played a blinded Marine named Al Schmid in a 1945 movie which began on Guadalcanal but became more of a documentary on help for returning veterans. Title, please.

Worlock, Frederick (1886–1973). British character actor in Hollywood after long stage career.
Miracles for Sale 39. The Sea Hawk 40. Rage in Heaven 41. The Black Swan 43. Sherlock Holmes Faces Death 44. Terror by Night 46. Joan of Arc 48. Notorious Landlady 62. Spinout 66, etc.

Worsley, Wallace (1880–1944). American director of the twenties.
Honor's Cross 18. The Little Shepherd of Kingdom Come 19. *The Penalty* 20. A Blind Bargain 21. Rags to Riches 22. *The Hunchback of Notre Dame* 23. The Man Who Fights Alone 24. The Shadow of Law 26. The Power of Silence 28, etc.

Worth, Brian (1914–1978). British light leading man.
The Lion Has Wings 39. One Night with You 48. Hindle Wakes 52. An Inspector Calls 54. Ill Met by Moonlight 57. Peeping Tom 60. On Her Majesty's Secret Service 69, etc.

Worth, Irene (1916–). American leading actress, in recent years mainly on British stage.
□ One Night with You 48. Another Shore 48. Secret People 51. *Orders to Kill* (BFA) 58. The Scapegoat 59. Seven Seas to Calais (as Elizabeth I) 63. King Lear 69. Nicholas and Alexandra 71. Rich Kids 79. Deathtrap 82.

Wouk, Herman (1915–). American best-selling novelist.
The Caine Mutiny 54. Marjorie Morningstar 58. Youngblood Hawke 64. The Winds of War (TV) 83.

Wray, Fay (1907–). American leading lady of the thirties, a great screamer.
Street of Sin 28. The Wedding March 28. The Four Feathers 29. The Texan 30. Dirigible 30. Doctor X 31. *The Most Dangerous Game* 32. The Vampire Bat 33. The Mystery of the Wax Museum 33. *King Kong* 33. The Bowery 33. Madame Spy 34. The Affairs of Cellini 34. The Clairvoyant 35. They Met in a Taxi 36. Murder in Greenwich Village 37. The Jury's Secret 38. Adam Had Four Sons 41. Small Town Girl 53. Queen Bee 55. Crime of Passion 56. Tammy and the Bachelor 57. Gideon's Trumpet (TV) 80, etc.
TV series: Pride of the Family 53.

¶ *F.W.:* At the premiere of *King Kong* I wasn't too impressed. I thought there was too much screaming . . . I didn't realise then that King Kong and I were going to be together for the rest of our lives, and longer . . .

Wray, John (1890–1940) (John Malloy). American general purpose actor.
All Quiet on the Western Front 30. Doctor X 32. I Am a Fugitive from a Chain Gang 32. The Defence Rests 34. The Whole Town's Talking 35. Valiant is the Word for Carrie 36. You Only Live Once 37. The Cat and the Canary 39. The Man from Dakota 40, etc.

Wrede, Caspar (1929–). Finnish director, in British TV.
□The Barber of Stamford Hill 62. Private Potter 64. One Day in the Life of Ivan Denisovitch 71. Ransom 74.

Wren, P. C. (1885–1941) (Percival Christopher Wren). British adventure novelist who after a military life wrote the much filmed *Beau Geste*, followed by *Beau Sabreur* and *Beau Ideal*.

Wright, Basil (1907–). British producer-director. In films from 1929: worked with John Grierson in creation of 'documentary'. Historical book 1975: *The Long View*.
Windmill in Barbados (d) 30. Song of Ceylon (pd) 34. Night Mail (co-d) 36. Waters of Time (pd) 51. World Without End (d) 53. The Immortal Land (pd) 58. A Place for Gold (pd) 61, etc.

Wright, Teresa (1918–). American leading actress with stage experience.
□ *The Little Foxes* (film debut) 41. *Mrs Miniver* (AA) 42. The Pride of the Yankees 42. *Shadow of a Doubt* 43. Casanova Brown 44. *The Best Years of Our Lives* 46. Pursued 47. The Imperfect Lady 47. The Trouble with Women 47. Enchantment 48. *The Men* 50. The Captive 50. The Steel Trap 52. Something to Live For 52. Count the Hours 53. The Actress 53. Track of the Cat 54. *The Search for Bridey Murphy* 56. Escapade in Japan 57. The Wonderful Years 58. Hail Hero 69. The Happy Ending 69. Crawlspace (TV) 71. The Elevator (TV) 73. Flood (TV) 76. *Roseland* 77. Somewhere in Time 80.

Wright, Tony (1925–86). British light leading man, with stage experience.
The Flanagan Boy (film debut) 51. Jumping for Joy 54. Jacqueline 56. Seven Thunders 57. Faces in the Dark 60. Journey to Nowhere 62. All Coppers Are 72, etc.

Wright, Will (1894–1962). Lugubrious American character actor.
China Clipper 36. World Première 41. Bewitched 45. *The Blue Dahlia* (his best role, as the murderer) 46. Adam's Rib 49. Excuse My Dust 51. The Wild One 52. The Deadly Companions 62, many others.

writers depicted in films include the following: Rod Taylor as Sean O'Casey in *Young Cassidy*, John Shepperd as Edgar Allan Poe in *The Loves of Edgar Allan Poe*, Beau Bridges as Ben Hecht in *Gaily Gaily*, James Mason as Gustave Flaubert in *Madame Bovary*, Herbert Marshall as Somerset Maugham in *The Moon and Sixpence* and *The Razor's Edge*, Reginald Gardiner as Shakespeare in *The Story of Mankind*, Turhan Bey as Aesop in *A Night in Paradise*,

Michael O'Shea as Jack London in *Jack London*, Dean Stockwell as Eugene O'Neill in *Long Day's Journey into Night*, Daniel Massey as Noel Coward in *Star!*, Frederick Jaeger as Henrik Ibsen in *Song of Norway*, Danny Kaye as *Hans Christian Andersen*, Paul Muni in *The Life of Emile Zola*, Gregory Peck as F. Scott Fitzgerald in *Beloved Infidel*, Burgess Meredith as Ernie Pyle in *The Story of G.I. Joe*, Michael Redgrave as W. B. Yeats in *Young Cassidy*, Laurence Harvey and Karl Boehm in *The Wonderful World of the Brothers Grimm*, Dennis Price in *The Bad Lord Byron*, Richard Chamberlain as Byron in *Lady Caroline Lamb*, Fredric March (later Bill Travers) as Robert Browning in *The Barretts of Wimpole Street*, Olivia de Havilland, Nancy Coleman and Ida Lupino as the Brontë Sisters in *Devotion*, Arthur Kennedy as Branwell Brontë in *Devotion*, Sydney Greenstreet as Thackeray in *Devotion*, Robert Morley in *Oscar Wilde*, Peter Finch in *The Trials of Oscar Wilde*, Cornel Wilde in *Omar Khayyam*, Fredric March in *The Adventures of Mark Twain*, Ian McKellen as D. H. Lawrence in *Priest of Love*.

¶ Despite the greater reputations of stars and directors, no Hollywood film could begin to be made without a writer, and it is often the dialogue which lingers most effectively in the mind, bringing life even to corny old yarns which were anonymously satirized as follows:

> Arizona. Indians thronging.
> Arrows pinging. Pistols ponging.
> Something smelly—old and hoary.
> Not to worry: it's the story.

A bad story can be salvaged by a good director, just as vice versa. Richard Corliss remarked:

> While these two functions can be distinguished for research purposes, they are really the inseparable halves of a work of art.

What happens, of course, isn't always art; Mr Corliss was referring to *Citizen Kane*. And some writers give up trying soon after they get to Hollywood with its compromises. As William Holden remarked in *Sunset Boulevard*,

> Audiences don't know anybody writes a picture. They think the actors just make it up as they go along.

Other cynics have claimed that there are only six basic plots. As Mr Holden said in another film, *Paris When It Sizzles*,

> *Frankenstein* and *My Fair Lady* are really the same story.

He was right. But of all the arts, the screen is most capable of transforming old sows' ears into shining new silk purses. It can be tremendously subtle in its effects, as Dudley Nichols knew:

> The stage is a medium of action, but the screen is a medium of reaction.

Leading those who made screencraft their own was Preston Sturges.

> Among the handful of screenwriters whose influence was critical to the craft, Sturges deserves at least two fingers and a thumb.

That's the view of Richard Corliss, who also admires Samson Raphaelson:

> Style may be said to comprise his theme: the way people embody it, employ it.

Wrixon, Maris (1917–). American light leading lady of the thirties.
Broadway Musketeers 38. The Ape 41. The Man Who Talked Too Much 42. Bullets for O'Hara 43. As You Were 51, etc.

Wuthering Heights (US 1939). A good example of the superior pre-war Hollywood film. Emily Brontë's brooding novel of the Yorkshire moors was shortened in incident, shot in America, scripted by Charles MacArthur and Ben Hecht, directed by William Wyler; yet it emerged truer to its original in mood than any of the earlier British silent attempts. Laurence Olivier as Heathcliff dominated the film; Merle Oberon, David Niven and Geraldine Fitzgerald gave sound performances; Gregg Toland's photography was first-rate. A subsequent Mexican version of the story by Luis Buñuel, *Abismos de Pasion* 50, has not been widely seen. There was also a 1970 remake, directed by Robert Fuest, starring Timothy Dalton and Anna Calder-Marshall.
† It is said that Goldwyn's original casting preferences for Heathcliff were Ronald Colman, Douglas Fairbanks Jnr. and Robert Newton.

Wyatt, Jane (1912–). Pleasing American leading lady of the thirties and forties, with stage experience.
One More River 34. The Luckiest Girl in the World 36. *Lost Horizon* 37. Kisses for Breakfast 41. The Kansan 42. The Iron Road 43. None But the Lonely Heart 44. Boomerang 47. Gentleman's Agreement 47. Pitfall 48. Bad Boy 49. Task Force 49. Our Very Own 50. The Man Who Cheated Himself 51. Never Too Late 65. Tom Sawyer

(TV) 73. Treasure of Matecumbe 76. Star Trek IV 86, many others.
TV series: Father Knows Best 54–59 (reunion show 1977).

Wycherly, Margaret (1881–1956). British-born character actress with American stage experience.
The Thirteenth Chair 29. Sergeant York 41. Keeper of the Flame 43. The Yearling 46. *White Heat* 49. Man with a Cloak 51. That Man from Tangier 53, others.

Wyler, Richard (1934–) (also known as Richard Stapley). American leading man of the fifties.
The Three Musketeers 48. The Strange Door 51. King of the Khyber Rifles 53. Target Zero 55. The Ugly Ones 68, etc.
TV series: Man from Interpol 60.

Wyler, William (1902–1981). Distinguished German-American director, former film publicist, in Hollywood from 1920. Director from 1925, starting with low-budget silent westerns.
□TALKIES: Hell's Heroes 30. The Storm 30. A House Divided 31. Tom Brown of Culver 32. Her First Mate 33. Counsellor at Law 33. Glamour 34. *The Good Fairy* 35. The Gay Deception 35. These Three 36. Come and Get It (co-d) 36. *Dodsworth* 36. *Dead End* 37. *Jezebel* 38. *Wuthering Heights* 39. *The Letter* 40. *The Westerner* 40. *The Little Foxes* 41. *Mrs Miniver* (AA) 42. The Memphis Belle (documentary) 44. The Fighting Lady (documentary) 44. *The Best Years of Our Lives* (AA) 46. *The Heiress* 49. *Detective Story* 51. Carrie 52. Roman Holiday 53. The Desperate Hours 55. The Friendly Persuasion 56. *The Big Country* 58. *Ben Hur* (AA) 59. The Children's Hour 62. The Collector 65. How to Steal a Million 66. Funny Girl 68. The Liberation of L. B. Jones 70.
¶ *Charlton Heston:* Doing a picture with Willie is like getting the works at a Turkish bath. You damn near drown, but you come out smelling like a rose.

Wyman, Jane (1914–) (Sarah Jane Faulks). American leading lady of the forties, at first in dumb blonde roles, later as serious actress.
My Man Godfrey 36. Brother Rat 38. Flight Angels 40. Bad Men of Missouri 41. The Body Disappears 41. You're in the Army Now 41. My Favourite Spy 42. Princess O'Rourke 43. Crime by Night 44. The Doughgirls 44. Make Your Own Bed 44. *The Lost Weekend* 45. Night and Day 46. Magic Town 46. The Yearling 46. *Johnny Belinda* (AA) 48. Three Guys Named Mike 49. Here Comes the Groom 51. The Blue Veil 52. Just For You 53. So Big 53. *Magnificent Obsession* 54. All That Heaven Allows 55. Miracle in the Rain 56. Pollyanna 60. Bon Voyage 63. How To Commit Marriage 69. The Failing of Raymond (TV) 71. The Incredible Journey of Dr Meg Laurel (TV) 79, etc.
TV series: The Jane Wyman Theater 56–60. Falcon Crest 81–.
† When asked why she divorced Ronald Reagan, she said: He talked too much.

Wymark, Patrick (1920–70) (Patrick Cheesman). British TV actor, in occasional films. The voice of Churchill in *The Finest Hours* 64, *A King's Story* 65.
The Criminal 60. Repulsion 65. The Secret of Blood Island 65. The Psychopath 66. Where Eagles Dare 68. Cromwell 69. Satan's Skin 70, etc.

Wymore, Patrice (1926–). American leading lady.
Tea for Two 50. Rocky Mountain 50. The Big Trees 52. She's Working Her Way Through College 52. She's Back on Broadway 53. Chamber of Horrors 66, etc.

Wyndham, John (1903–1969). British science fiction novelist. Works filmed include *Village of the Damned* (The Midwich Cuckoos) and *The Day of the Triffids*.

Wynn, Ed (1886–1966) (Isaiah Edwin Leopold). American vaudeville, radio and TV comic who after initial film failure returned to Hollywood in the fifties as a character actor of fey old gentlemen.
□Rubber Heels 27. Follow the Leader 30. Manhattan Mary 30. The Chief 33. Stage Door Canteen 43. *The Great Man* 56. Marjorie Morningstar 58. *The Diary of Anne Frank* 59. The Absent Minded Professor 60. Cinderfella 60. Babes in Toyland 61. Son of Flubber 63. Those Calloways 64. *Mary Poppins* 64. That Darn Cat 65. Dear Brigitte 65. The Greatest Story Ever Told 65. The Gnome-Mobile 67.
TV series: The Ed Wynn Show 58.

Wynn, Keenan (1916–66). American character actor, son of Ed Wynn. In Hollywood from early forties after stage experience.
Autobiography 1960: *Ed Wynn's Son.*
See Here Private Hargrove 44. Under the Clock 45. Weekend at the Waldorf 45. The

Hucksters 47. Annie Get Your Gun 50. Kiss Me Kate 53. The Glass Slipper 55. The Great Man 57. A Hole in the Head 59. The Absent-Minded Professor 60. Man in the Middle 63. Dr Strangelove 63. The Americanization of Emily 65. The Great Race 65. The War Wagon 67. Mackenna's Gold 68. Smith 69. Once Upon a Time in the West 69. Five Savage Men 70. Pretty Maids all in a Row 71. Herbie Rides Again 73. Hit Lady (TV) 75. Nashville 75. The Devil's Rain 76. Orca 77. High Velocity 77. Coach 78. Piranha 78. Sunburn 79. Just Tell Me What You Want 80. The Glove 81. Best Friends 82, many others.
TV series: The Trouble Shooters 59.

¶ He's the fellow who, when Esther Williams jumps into the pool, gets splashed.—*Ed Wynn of Keenan Wynn*

Wynn, May (1931–) (Donna Lee Hickey). American leading lady of the fifties.
□3The Caine Mutiny 54. The Violent Men 54. They Rode West 55. Hong Kong Affair 59.

Wynn, Tracy Keenan (1945–). American screenwriter, son of Keenan Wynn.
The Glass House (TV) 70. Tribes (TV) 71. *The Autobiography of Miss Jane Pittman* (TV) 73. The Longest Yard 74. The Drowning Pool (co-w) 75. The Deep (co-w) 77, etc.

Wynter, Dana (c. 1930–) (Dagmar Wynter). British leading lady.
White Corridors 51. Colonel March Investigates 53. *Invasion of the Body Snatchers* (US) 56. D Day Sixth of June 56. Value 57. Shake Hands with the Devil 59. *Sink the Bismarck* 60. The List of Adrian Messenger 63. If He Hollers Let Him Go 68. Airport 69. Santee 73. Backstairs at the White House (TV) 79. The Royal Romance of Charles and Diana (TV) 82. The People from Another Star 86, etc.
TV series: The Man Who Never Was 66.

Wynyard, Diana (1906–1964) (Dorothy Isobel Cox). Distinguished British stage actress.
□Rasputin and the Empress 32. *Cavalcade* 33. Men Must Fight 33. Reunion in Vienna 33. Where Sinners Meet 34. Let's Try Again 34. One More River 34. On the Night of the Fire 39. Freedom Radio 40. *Gaslight* 40. The Prime Minister 40. *Kipps* 41. An Ideal Husband 47. Tom Brown's Schooldays 51. The Feminine Touch 56. Island in the Sun 57.

Answers

John Wayne

1 *The Shootist* □ 2 *She Wore a Yellow Ribbon* □ 3 *The Fighting Kentuckian* □ 4 *The Quiet Man* □ 5 *Blood Alley* □ 6 *The Conqueror* □ 7 *Jet Pilot* □ 8 *Tycoon* □ 9 *Reap the Wild Wind* □ 10 *The Greatest Story Ever Told* □ 11 *The Sons of Katie Elder* □ 12 *Hatari* □ 13 *The Big Trail* (1930) □ 14 *Without Reservations* □ 15 *Big Jim McLain* □ 16 *Island in the Sky* □

Who said that?

1 Director Michael Curtiz, whose command of English was somewhat haphazard, is alleged to have issued this instruction during the location filming of *The Charge of the Light Brigade* (1936). □
2 An oft-repeated line (by Sig Ruman and Jack Benny) in Lubitsch's *To Be or Not To Be* (1942). □
3 Walter Abel as the harassed editor in Wilder's *Arise, My Love* (1940). □ The line became something of a catchphrase in the forties.
4 Shirley Booth's introduction to *The Matchmaker* (1957). □
5 Alfred Hitchcock, invariably, when asked what, if anything, scares him. □
6 Ingrid Bergman to Paul Henreid in *Casablanca* (1942). □
7 Bernard Shaw, allegedly, to Samuel Goldwyn when they were trying to negotiate terms for the filming of Shaw's plays. □
8 Tony Curtis in *The Black Shield of Falworth* (1954). □ His Brooklyn accent was derided: he was playing an English nobleman.
9 Cary Grant to James Stewart (speaking about Henry Daniell) in *The Philadelphia Story* (1940). □
10 Everett Sloane speaking of old age in *Citizen Kane* (1941). □
11 An instruction from D. W. Griffith during the filming of *The Birth of a Nation* (1915). □

12 George Sanders as Addison de Witt in *All About Eve* (1950).
13 Howard Hughes' only instruction to the staff of RKO Studios which he had just acquired. ☐
14 The wireless message from the other world in *Orphée* (1949). ☐
15 Gig Young as MC of the marathon dance contest in *They Shoot Horses, Don't They?* (1970). ☐
16 Hattie McDaniel as the black mammy in *The Great Lie* (1941). ☐
17 Katharine Hepburn of Spencer Tracy in *The State of the Union*. ☐
18 The slogan that won the all-important competition in *Christmas in July*. ☐
19 Eddie 'Rochester' Anderson on a 1970 TV show, when asked once again to play Jack Benny's manservant. ☐
20 Clifton Webb in *The Dark Corner*. ☐
21 A sub-title repeated ubiquitously throughout the four hours of *Intolerance*. ☐
22 Claudette Colbert in *The Palm Beach Story*. ☐
23 An irrelevant line tossed away by Cary Grant in *His Girl Friday*. ☐ The point of the joke is that Archie Leach is Mr Grant's real name.
24 Gale Sondergaard says this of her spirits in *The Cat and the Canary*. ☐
25 Bela Lugosi playing the title role in *Dracula*. ☐
26 John Wayne when reproved for taking such a positive stand on Vietnam. ☐
27 An announcement oft repeated during the opening fashion salon scene of *The Women*. ☐
28 Who else but W. C. Fields? ☐ A reputed remark which needless to say did not appear on film.
29 Clint Eastwood in *Magnum Force*. ☐
30 The justice of the peace in the 1937 version of *A Star Is Born*. ☐ These were the 'real names' of Fredric March and Janet Gaynor.
31 Instructions given to Dean Martin in *Kiss Me Stupid*. ☐
32 Memorable indeed. Virginia Mayo to George Sanders in *King Richard and the Crusaders*. ☐
33 Ezra Goodman in his book *The Fifty Year Decline and Fall of Hollywood*. ☐
34 Lewis Milestone's wry joke to his Universal bosses when they insisted on a happy ending for *All Quiet on the Western Front*. ☐
35 A famous answer given by Jack Warner to a producer anxious to film a book which Warner had airily dismissed. ☐
36 Adolphe Menjou to Katharine Hepburn in *Morning Glory*. ☐
37 The slogan of the ale that has made Henry Fonda rich in *The Lady Eve*. ☐
38 John Wayne as Genghis Khan to Susan Hayward in *The Conqueror*. ☐
39 Attributed to Steve Broidy, once president of Monogram.
40 Rudy Vallee in *The Palm Beach Story*. ☐
41 Adolph Zukor drumbeating his own production *For Whom the Bell Tolls*. ☐
42 W. C. Fields in *The Fatal Glass of Beer*. ☐
43 Katharine Hepburn to Eve Arden in *Stage Door*. ☐
44 The catchphrase of Mantan Moreland, Hollywood's archetypal frightened Negro. ☐

women!

1 Miriam Hopkins ☐ 2 Eleanor Parker ☐ 3 Sophia Loren ☐ 4 Katharine Hepburn ☐ 5 Joan Bennett ☐ 6 Bette Davis ☐ 7 Joan Bennett ☐ 8 Ann Sheridan ☐ 9 Ida Lupino ☐ 10 Brenda Marshall ☐ 11 Carole Lombard ☐ 12 Yvonne Mitchell ☐ 13 Virginia Bruce ☐ 14 Gale Sondergaard ☐ 15 Barbara Stanwyck ☐ 16 Jean Harlow ☐ 17 Anna Sten ☐ 18 Miriam Hopkins ☐ 19 Jean Kent ☐ 20 Joan Crawford ☐

World War II

1 *Journey for Margaret* ☐ 2 Nobody. The script had it that 'in the Army Air Force, any fellow who is a right fellow is called Joe' ☐ 3 *North Star* ☐ 4 *The White Cliffs of Dover* ☐ 5 Alice Duer Miller ☐ 6 Katharine Hepburn ☐ 7 Errol Flynn ☐ 8 *Destination Tokyo* ☐ 9 *Mrs Miniver* ☐ 10 Betty Grable ☐ 11 Conrad Veidt ☐ *Nazi Agent* ☐ 12 *Air Force* ☐ 13 *Hitler's Children* ☐ 14 Walter Huston ☐ 15 *So Proudly We Hail* ☐ 16 *Cry Havoc* ☐ 17 Kay Francis ☐ 18 Spencer Tracy ☐ 19 *Objective Burma* ☐ 20 *The Pride of the Marines* ☐

Yablans, Frank (1935–). American independent producer.
The Other Side of Midnight 77. The Silver Streak 77. The Fury 78. North Dallas Forty (& w) 80. Mommie Dearest 81.

Yablans, Irwin (1934–). American independent producer.
Badge 373 73. Halloween 78. Roller Boogie 79. Fade to Black 80. The Seduction 82.

A Yank at Oxford (GB 1938). The first major production of MGM-British under Michael Balcon, a significant precedent and a happy blend of talent from both countries. It was a simple enough romantic comedy-drama, but packed with appeal. Robert Taylor was the stranger to English academic routine, Lionel Barrymore his father, Vivien Leigh and Maureen O'Sullivan his girl friends. Jack Conway directed. Imitations included *A Chump at Oxford* 40, with Laurel and Hardy, and *A Yank at Eton* 42 with Mickey Rooney.

Yankee Doodle Dandy (US 1942). Biopic about George M. Cohan, famous American playwright-entertainer; held together by the immense zest of James Cagney (AA), with Walter Huston and Joan Leslie in tow. Tuneful songs helped; so did the skilled direction of Michael Curtiz.

Yanne, Jean (1933–) (J. Gouye). Heavy-set French actor.
Life Upside Down 65. Weekend 67. *Le Boucher* 69. Cobra 73. The Accuser 75. The Pink Telephone 76.

Yarbrough, Jean (1900–). American director of second features, former prop man.
Devil Bat 41. Lure of the Islands 42. Good Morning Judge 43. In Society 44. The Naughty Nineties 45. The Brute Man 46. Curse of the Allenbys 47. The Creeper 48. Abbott and Costello Lost in Alaska 52. Jack and the Beanstalk 52. Women of Pitcairn Island 57. Saintly Sinners 61. Hillbillies in a Haunted House 67, many others.

Yates, Herbert (1880–1966). American executive, ex-president of Republic Pictures, where his word was law in the forties and many of his productions starred his wife, Vera Hruba Ralston.

Yates, Peter (1929–). British director.
Summer Holiday 62. One Way Pendulum 64. *Robbery* 67. *Bullitt* (US) 68. John and Mary (US) 69. Murphy's War 70. The Hot Rock (US) 72. The Friends of Eddie Coyle 73. For Pete's Sake 74. Mother Jugs and Speed 76. The Deep 77. Breaking Away 79. Eyewitness 81. Krull 83. The Dresser (& p) 83. Eleni 85. Suspect 87, etc.

Yordan, Philip (1913–). Prolific American writer-producer.
SCREENPLAYS: Syncopation 42. Dillinger 45. House of Strangers 49. Detective Story 51. Johnny Guitar 54. El Cid 61. 55 Days at Peking 62. The Fall of the Roman Empire 64, many others.
WROTE AND PRODUCED: The Harder They Fall 56. Men in War 57. God's Little Acre 58. Day of the Outlaw 59. Studs Lonigan 60. The Day of the Triffids 62. The Thin Red Line 64. The Battle of the Bulge 65. Captain Apache 71, etc.

York, Dick (1928–). American actor.
My Sister Eileen 55. Operation Mad Ball 57. They Came to Cordura 58. Inherit the Wind 60, etc.
TV series: Going My Way. Bewitched.

York, Michael (1942–). British leading man with stage experience.
☐The Taming of the Shrew 67. *Accident* 67. Red and Blue 67. Smashing Time 67. Romeo and Juliet 68. The Strange Affair 68. The Guru 69. Alfred the Great 69. Justine 69. Something for Everyone 70. Zeppelin 71. *Cabaret* 72. England Made Me 72. *Lost Horizon* 73. The Three Musketeers 73. The Four Musketeers 74. Murder on the Orient Express 74. Conduct Unbecoming 75. Great Expectations 75. Logan's Run 76. *Jesus of Nazareth* (TV) 77. The Last Remake of Beau Geste 77. Seven Nights in Japan 77. The Island of Dr Moreau 77. Fedora 78. The Riddle of the Sands 79. A Man Called

Intrepid (TV) 79. The White Lions 80. Final Arrangement 80. Phantom of the Opera (TV) 82. The Master of Ballantrae (TV) 83. Success is the Best Revenge 84. Space (TV) 85. The Dawn 85. The Far Country (TV) 86. Sword of Gideon (TV) 86.

York, Susannah (1941–) (Susannah Yolande Fletcher). British leading lady of stage and screen.
□*Tunes of Glory* (debut) 60. There Was a Crooked Man 60. *The Greengage Summer* 61. Freud 62. Tom Jones 63. The Seventh Dawn 64. Scene Nun Take One 64. Scruggs 64. Sands of the Kalahari 65. Kaleidoscope 66. A Man For All Seasons 66. Sebastian 67. The Killing of Sister George 68. Duffy 68. Oh What a Lovely War 69. The Battle of Britain 69. Lock Up Your Daughters 69. *They Shoot Horses Don't They?* (US) 69. Country Dance 70. Jane Eyre 70. Zee and Co. 71. Happy Birthday Wanda June (US) 71. *Images* 72. The Maids 73. Gold 74. Conduct Unbecoming 75. That Lucky Touch 75. Sky Riders 76. Eliza Frazer 76. Superman 78. The Golden Gate Murders (TV) 79. The Silent Partner 79. The Shout 79. Falling in Love Again 80. Superman II 80. The Awakening 80. Loophole 81. Yellowbeard 83. A Christmas Carol (TV) 84. Prettykill 87.
TV series: Second Chance 80. We'll Meet Again 81.

Yorkin, Bud (1926–) (Alan Yorkin). American director, from TV.
Come Blow Your Horn 63. Never Too Late 65. Divorce American Style 67. Inspector Clouseau 68. Start the Revolution Without Me 69. The Thief Who Came To Dinner 73, etc.

You Can't Take It With You (US 1938) (AA best picture). Vintage crazy comedy from the stage play by George S. Kaufman and Moss Hart about a family of New Yorkers who do exactly what they want to in life and even convert a stuffy tycoon whose son falls for their daughter. Directed by Frank Capra (AA); played with all the stops out by Lionel Barrymore, Jean Arthur, James Stewart, Spring Byington, Edward Arnold, Mischa Auer, Ann Miller, Samuel S. Hinds, Donald Meek, H. B. Warner and Halliwell Hobbes.

Youmans, Vincent (1898–1946). American song composer of the twenties. Shows filmed include *No No Nanette* and *Hit the Deck*.

Young, Alan (1919–) (Angus Young). British-born comic actor, in Canada since childhood.
Margie (debut) 46. Mr Belvedere Goes to College 49. Aaron Slick from Punkin Crick 52. *Androcles and the Lion* 53. Gentlemen Marry Brunettes 55. Tom Thumb 58. The Time Machine 60. The Cat from Outer Space 78, etc.
TV series: Mister Ed 60–65.

Young, Arthur (1898–1959). Portly British stage actor; film appearances usually in self-important roles.
No Limit 35. Victoria the Great 37. My Brother Jonathan 48. The Lady with a Lamp 51. An Inspector Calls 54. The Gelignite Gang 56, etc.

Young, Burt (1940–). American support actor.
The Gambler 74. The Killer Elite 75. Rocky 76. The Choirboys 77. Twilight's Last Gleaming 77. Convoy 78. Rocky II 79. Murder Can Hurt You (TV) 79. All the Marbles 81. Blood Beach 81. Once Upon a Time in America 84. Rocky III 85.

Young, Carleton (1906–1971). American character actor, from radio; father of Tony Young.
The Glory Brigade 53. The Court Martial of Billy Mitchell 55. The Horse Soldiers 59. Sergeant Rutledge 60, many others.

Young, Clara Kimball (1890–1960). Popular American heroine of the silent screen.
Cardinal Wolsey (debut) 12. Beau Brummell 13. Goodness Gracious 16. Eyes of Youth 19. Cheating Cheaters 19. Forbidden Woman 20. Hush 21. Charge It 21. Lying Wives 25. Kept Husbands 31. Love Bound 33. Romance in the Rain 34. The Frontiersman 39. Mr Celebrity 42, etc.

Young, Collier (1908–1980). American writer-producer.
The Hitch-Hiker 53. The Bigamist 54. Mad at the World 55. Huk 56, etc.
TV series: One Step Beyond. Ironside, etc.

Young, Frederick (1902–). Distinguished British cinematographer.
Bitter Sweet 33. Nell Gwyn 34. When Knights Were Bold 36. Victoria the Great 37. Sixty Glorious Years 38. Goodbye Mr Chips 39. The Young Mr Pitt 41. 49th Parallel 41; war service; Bedelia 46. So Well Remembered 47.

Edward My Son 40. Treasure Island 50. Ivanhoe 52. *Lust for Life* 56. *Invitation to the Dance* 56. Bhowani Junction 56. Island in the Sun 56. *Lawrence of Arabia* (AA) 62. The Seventh Dawn 64. Lord Jim 65. Rotten to the Core 65. *Doctor Zhivago* (AA) 65. The Deadly Affair 67. You Only Live Twice 67. The Battle of Britain 69. *Ryan's Daughter* (AA) 70. Nicholas and Alexandra 71. The Tamarind Seed 74. The Blue Bird 76. Seven Nights in Japan 77. Stevie 78. Bloodline 79. Rough Cut 80, etc.

† At the age of 82 he directed his first film, *Arthur's Hallowed Ground*, in 1985.

Young, Gig (1913–78) (Byron Barr: also known as Bryant Fleming). American light comedy leading man with a pleasantly bemused air.

Misbehaving Husbands 40. They Died With Their Boots On 41. Dive Bomber 41. The Gay Sisters (in which he played a character called Gig Young and thereafter used the name) 41. Old Acquaintance 43. Air Force 43; war service; Escape Me Never 46. The Woman in White 47. Wake of the Red Witch 48. The Three Musketeers 49. *Come Fill the Cup* 51. City That Never Sleeps 54. Young at Heart 55. Desk Set 57. The Story on Page One 59. Ask Any Girl 59. *That Touch of Mink* 62. For Love or Money 63. Strange Bedfellows 65. The Shuttered Room 67. *They Shoot Horses Don't They?* (AA) 69. *Lovers and Other Strangers* 70. The Neon Ceiling (TV) 71. A Son-in-Law for Charlie McReady 73. Bring Me the Head of Alfredo Garcia 74. The Hindenberg 75. The Killer Elite 75. Sherlock Holmes in New York (TV) 77. Spectre (TV) 78.

TV series: *The Rogues* 64. *Gibbsville* 76.

Famous line (*They Shoot Horses, Don't They?*): There can only be one winner, folks, but isn't that the American way?

Young, Harold (1897–1970). American director who made distinguished British films for Korda but was little heard from on his return to Hollywood.

The Scarlet Pimpernel 35. 52nd Street 38. Code of the Streets 39. Juke Box Jenny 42. The Frozen Ghost 43. I'll Remember April 44, etc.

Young, Loretta (1913–) (Gretchen Young). American leading lady whose career in films began when she accidentally, at 15, answered a studio call meant for her elder sister, Polly Ann Young.

Autobiography 1962: *The Things I Had To Learn.*

Laugh Clown Laugh (debut) 28. Loose Ankles 29. The Squall 30. Kismet 30. I Like Your Nerve 31. *The Devil to Pay* 30. Platinum Blonde 32. The Hatchet Man 32. Big Business Girl 32. Life Begins 32. Zoo in Budapest 33. *Man's Castle* 33. The House of Rothschild 34. Midnight Mary 35. The Crusaders 35. Clive of India 35. Call of the Wild 35. Shanghai 36. *Ramona* 36. Ladies in Love 37. Wife, Doctor and Nurse 37. Second Honeymoon 38. Four Men and a Prayer 38. Suez 38. Kentucky 38. Three Blind Mice 38. The Story of Alexander Graham Bell 39. The Doctor Takes a Wife 39. He Stayed for Breakfast 40. Lady from Cheyenne 41. The Men in Her Life 41. *A Night to Remember* 42. China 43. Ladies Courageous 44. And Now Tomorrow 44. The Stranger 45. Along Came Jones 46. The Perfect Marriage 46. *The Farmer's Daughter* (AA) 47. The Bishop's Wife 48. Rachel and the Stranger 48. Come to the Stable 49. Cause for Alarm 51. Half Angel 51. Paula 52. Because of You 52. It Happens Every Thursday 53. Christmas Eve (TV) 86, others.

TV show of anthology dramas 53–60.

Young Mr Lincoln (US 1939). Biopic directed by John Ford, picturing Abraham Lincoln before he became a political figure. Written by Lamar Trotti, with a first-class performance by Henry Fonda and an all-pervading genuine feeling for American pioneer life.

The Young Ones (GB 1961). Derivative but zestful British musical determined to sell teenage music not only to other kids but to adults. Cliff Richard and his gang proved so endearing that two agreeable but overlong sequels were made: *Summer Holiday* 63, *Wonderful Life* 64. Sidney Furie's direction was undisciplined but full of bright ideas.

Young, Otis (1932–). American black actor.

The Last Detail 73.

TV series: The Outcasts 68.

Young, Robert (1907–). American leading man invariably cast in amiable, dependable roles. A former clerk, with stage experience.

□The Sin of Madelon Claudet (debut) 31. Strange Interlude 31. The Kid from Spain 32. Hell Below 32. Tugboat Annie 33. Lazy River 34. The House of Rothschild 34. Spitfire 34. Whom the Gods Destroy 35. West Point of the Air 35. It's Love Again (GB) 36. *Secret Agent* (GB) 36. Stowaway 36. The Emperor's

Candlesticks 37. I Met Him in Paris 37. The Bride Wore Red 37. Josette 38. Frou Frou 38. Three Comrades 39. Rich Man, Poor Girl 39. Honolulu 39. Miracles for Sale 39. Maisie 39. Northwest Passage 40. The Mortal Storm 40. Florian 40. Western Union 41. The Trial of Mary Dugan 41. Lady Be Good 41. *H. M. Pulham Esq.* 41. Joe Smith American 42. Cairo 42. Journey for Margaret 42. Sweet Rosie O'Grady 43. *Claudia* 43. The Canterville Ghost 44. The Enchanted Cottage 44. Those Endearing Young Charms 45. Lady Luck 46. Claudia and David 46. The Searching Wind 46. They Won't Believe Me 47. *Crossfire* 47. Sitting Pretty 48. The Forsyte Woman 49. And Baby Makes Three 50. The Second Woman 51. Goodbye My Fancy 51. The Half-Breed 52. The Secret of the Incas 54. Vanished (TV) 71. All My Darling Daughters (TV) 72. My Darling Daughters' Anniversary (TV) 73.
TV series: Father Knows Best 54–60. Window on Main Street 61. Marcus Welby M.D. 69–75.

Young, Robert M. (1924–). American director.
Short Eyes 77. Rich Kids 79. One Trick Pony 80. The Ballad of Gregorio Cortez 83. Extremities 86. Saving Grace 86.

Young, Roland (1887–1953). British character actor with stage experience; made a screen career in Hollywood and is affectionately remembered for a gallery of whimsical or ineffectual types.
Sherlock Holmes (debut) 22. Moriarty 22. The Unholy Night 29. Madame Satan 30. New Moon 30. *One Hour With You* 32. Wedding Rehearsal (GB) 32. The Guardsman 32. His Double Life 33. *David Copperfield* (as Uriah Heep) 34. Ruggles of Red Gap 34. One Rainy Afternoon 36. *The Man Who Could Work Miracles* (GB) 36. Call It a Day 37. King Solomon's Mines (GB) 37. *Topper* (title role) 37. Ali Baba Goes to Town 38. Sailing Along (GB) 38. *The Young in Heart* 39. Topper Takes a Trip 39. No No Nanette 40. *The Philadelphia Story* 40. Flame of New Orleans 41. Topper Returns 41. The Lady Has Plans 42. They All Kissed the Bride 42. Tales of Manhattan 42. Forever and a Day 43. Standing Room Only 44. And Then There Were None 45. Bond Street (GB) 47. The Great Lover 49. Let's Dance 50. St Benny the Dip 51. That Man from Tangier 53, others.
❀ For his inimitable diffidence; and for becoming quite a character actor whenever he shaved off his moustache. *The Young in Heart.*
Famous line (*The Philadelphia Story*): Oh, this is one of those days that the pages of history teach us are best spent lying in bed.

Young, Sean (–). American actor young in the eighties.
Dune 84. Baby, Secret of the Lost Legend 85.

Young, Stephen (c. 1931–) (Stephen Levy). Canadian leading man, former extra.
TV series: Seaway 64. Judd for the Defence 66–68.

Young, Terence (1915–). British screenwriter who became a successful director.
AS WRITER: On the Night of the Fire 39. Dangerous Moonlight 40, etc.
□AS DIRECTOR: Corridor of Mirrors 48. One Night with You 48. Woman Hater 49. They Were Not Divided 50. Valley of Eagles 51. The Tall Headlines 52. The Red Beret 53. That Lady 55. Storm Over the Nile (co-d) 55. Safari 56. Zarak 56. Action of the Tiger 57. No Time to Die 57. Serious Charge 59. Too Hot to Handle 60. Black Tights 60. *Doctor No* 62. *From Russia With Love* 63. The Amorous Adventures of Moll Flanders 65. Thunderball 65. The Poppy is Also a Flower 66. Secret War 66. Triple Cross 66. The Rover (It.) 66. *Wait Until Dark* 67. Mayerling 68. The Christmas Tree 69. Cold Sweat 70. Red Sun 71. The Valachi Papers 72. War Goddess 73. The Klansman 74. Bloodline 79. Inchon 80. The Jigsaw Man 83. Sweet Revenge 86.

Young, Tony (c. 1932–). American leading man, from TV series *Gunslinger.*
He Rides Tall 63. Taggart 64. Charro 69. The Outfit 73.

Young, Victor (1900–1956). American composer with over 300 film scores to his credit.
Fatal Lady 36. Wells Fargo 37. Golden Boy 39. Raffles 40. The Way of All Flesh 40. Caught in the Draft 41. The Outlaw 41. Reap the Wild Wind 42. Beyond the Blue Horizon 42. The Glass Key 42. The Palm Beach Story 42. For Whom the Bell Tolls 43. Frenchman's Creek 44. Ministry of Fear 44. *The Uninvited* 44. Love Letters 45. The Blue Dahlia 46. To Each His Own 47. Unconquered 47. Golden Earrings 47. The Big Clock 48. The Paleface 48. My Foolish Heart 49. Samson and Delilah 49. Our Very Own 50. September Affair 50. My Favorite Spy 51. The Greatest Show on

Earth 52. The Quiet Man 52. *Shane* 53. The Country Girl 54. Knock on Wood 54. Strategic Air Command 55. *Around the World in Eighty Days* (AA) 56. Omar Khayyam 57, many others.

Youngson, Robert (1917–1974). American producer specializing in compilation films. Started as writer-director of short films, including *World of Kids* (AA) 50, *This Mechanical Age* (AA) 51. Later released omnibus editions of silent comedy snippets. *The Golden Age of Comedy* 58. *When Comedy Was King* 59. Days of Thrills and Laughter 60. Thirty Years of Fun 62, etc.

Yulin, Harris (1937–). American general purpose actor.
Doc 71. The Midnight Man 74. Night Moves 75. The Last Ride of the Dalton Gang (TV) 79. Steel 80. Scarface 83. The Believers 87, etc.

Yung, Sen (also known as **Victor Sen Yung**) (1915–80). Chinese-American character actor familiar 1938–48 as Charlie Chan's number one son.
The Letter 40. *Across the Pacific* 42. The Breaking Point 50. The Left Hand of God 55. Flower Drum Song 61. A Flea in Her Ear 68, etc.
TV series: Bonanza 59–72. Bachelor Father 61.

Yurka, Blanche (1887–1974). Czech-American character actress.
Autobiography 1970: *Bohemian Girl.*
□*A Tale of Two Cities* 36. *Queen of the Mob* 40. Escape 40. City for Conquest 40. Ellery Queen and the Murder Ring 41. Lady for a Night 42. Pacific Rendezvous 42. A Night to Remember 42. Keeper of the Flame 43. Tonight We Raid Calais 43. Hitler's Madman 43. The Bridge of San Luis Rey 44. Cry of the Werewolf 44. One Body Too Many 44. The Southerner 45. 13 Rue Madeleine 46. The Flame 47. The Furies 50. At Sword's Point 51. Taxi 53. Thunder in the Sun 57.

Z

'Z' (France/Italy 1968). Political thrillers are rare; this one mirrored recent events in Greece and so became a *cause célèbre.* Directed in vivid hit-or-miss fashion by Costa-Gavras, it developed into a suspense situation in which the official police were eventually persuaded to investigate a murder they had been prepared to write off as an accident.

Zadora, Pia (1956–). American 'sexpot' star of *Butterfly* (1981) and *The Lonely Lady* (1983).

Zampa, Luigi (1905–). Italian director, formerly scriptwriter. Films, all on neo-realist lines, include *To Live in Peace* 46. *City on Trial* 52. *The Woman of Rome* 54.

Zampi, Mario (1903–1963). Italian director, long in Britain, mainly involved in semi-crazy comedies which he usually wrote and produced.
The Fatal Night 48. *Laughter in Paradise* 50. Top Secret 52. Happy Ever After 54. The Naked Truth 56. Too Many Crooks 58. Five Golden Hours 61, etc.

Zanuck, Darryl F. (1902–1979). American production executive. Started career in twenties, writing stories for Rin Tin Tin. Production chief for Warners 1931. Co-founder 20th-Century Productions 1933; merged with Fox 1935. Vice-president in charge of production for 20th Century-Fox 1935–52, then independent; returned in 1962 as executive president.
Clive of India 35. Lloyds of London 37. *In Old Chicago* 38. Drums along the Mohawk 40. *The Grapes of Wrath* 40. *How Green Was My Valley* 42. Wilson 45. *Gentleman's Agreement* 47. *All About Eve* 50. Twelve O'Clock High 51. Viva Zapata 52. Island in the Sun 57. Roots of Heaven 58. *The Longest Day* (& d scenes) 62. Under the name Mark Canfield wrote the screenplay of *Crack in the Mirror* 60.
❀ For being Hollywood's most efficient mogul, and for making very good films. *The Grapes of Wrath*.

¶ Don't say yes until I finish talking!—*D.F.Z.* (It is also the title of his biography by Mel Gussow.)

I decided to become a genius.—*D.F.Z.*

From Poland to Polo in one generation.—*Arthur Mayer on D.F.Z.*

The hardiest and longest-lived of the moguls of Hollywood's golden age was somehow the most disappointing in terms of colour and personality. His most personal trait was his allegedly avid sexual appetite, though he himself said:

> Any of my indiscretions were with people, not actresses.

He was a tough employer:

> There was only one boss I believed in, and that was me.

As his biographer Mel Gussow said:

> He couldn't stand stubbornness in anybody but himself.

He spent thirty-five years, more or less, as boss of Twentieth Century Fox, and before that for ten years was production head of Warners. His ideas for remakes were legendary:

> I want to do *Air Force* in a submarine.

Another of his credos is now outdated:

> When you get a sex story in biblical garb, you can open your own mint.

He produced many worthy films, perhaps for rather stodgy reasons:

> We are in the business primarily to provide entertainment, but in doing so we do not dodge the issue if we can also provide enlightenment.

Or, more pithily:

> I know audiences feed on crap, but I cannot believe we are so lacking that we cannot dish it up to them with some trace of originality.

On another occasion however he was optimistic:

> Public taste is an ascending spiral.

But his final production philosophy was:

> Take a chance and spend a million dollars and hope you're right.

Time summed him up in 1950:

> He is richly endowed with tough-mindness, talent, an outsized ego, and a glutton's craving for hard work.

And his son has the last word:

> He had guts. He was willing to take the responsibility and the blame. He would say yes or no. They would ask is it any

good, and if he thought it was, that was enough to put it into production.

Zanuck, Richard (1934–). American producer who started career as assistant to his father, Darryl F. Zanuck. Solo ventures: *Compulsion* 59. *Sanctuary* 61. *The Chapman Report* 62, etc. Was vice-president in charge of production for 20th Century-Fox; moved to Warner 1971, then independent producer for Universal. Produced The Sting 73. Jaws 75. MacArthur 77. The Island 80.

Zanussi, Krzystof (1939–). Polish director. Illumination 73. The Spiral 78. Night Paths 79. The Constant Factor 80. Imperative 82. The Year of the Quiet Sun 84. Power of Evil 85.

Zavattini, Cesare (1902–). Italian scriptwriter and film theorist.
Shoeshine 46. *Bicycle Thieves* 48. *Miracle in Milan* 51. First Communion 51. Umberto D 52. Gold of Naples 55. The Roof 56. Two Women 61. Marriage Italian Style 64. A Brief Vacation 75, etc.

Zazie dans le Métro (France 1960). Breakneck comedy, an up-to-date French *Hellzapoppin*, about a demoniac ten-year-old girl on the loose in Paris. A non-stop stream of cinematic trickery directed with great glee by Louis Malle.

Zecca, Ferdinand (1864–1947). French pioneer producer.
The Prodigy 01. Catastrophe in Martinique 04. Vendetta 05. Whence Does He Come? 06. Mutiny in Odessa 07. The Dreyfus Affair 08. The Dissolute Woman 10, etc.

Zeffirelli, Franco (1922–). Italian stage director turning to films.
□The Taming of the Shrew 66. Romeo and Juliet 68. Brother Sun and Sister Moon 73. Jesus of Nazareth (TV) 77. The Champ 79. Endless Love 81. *La Traviata* 82. Otello 86.

Zelnik, Fred (1885–1950). Rumanian director of English films in the thirties.
Happy 32. Mr Cinders 34. The Lilac Domino 37. I Killed the Count 39. Give Me the Stars (p only) 44. The Glass Mountain (p only) 49, etc.

Zeman, Karel (1910–). Czech producer-director of trick and fantasy films of which the best known internationally are *Journey to Primeval Times* 55 and *Baron Münchhausen* 61.

Zemeckis, Robert (1952–). American director, one of the brightest of the movie brats.
□ I Wanna Hold Your Hand 78. Used Cars 80. Romancing the Stone 84. *Back to the Future* 85.

¶ *R.Z.*: When I showed Twentieth Century Fox the finished cut of *Romancing the Stone*, they fired me from *Cocoon*. It's the great mystery of my career.

Zerbe, Anthony (–). American character actor.
Will Penny 67. The Liberation of L. B. Jones 69. The Omega Man 71. The Life and Times of Judge Roy Bean 72. The Laughing Policeman 73. Farewell My Lovely 75. The Turning Point 77. The First Deadly Sin 80. The Dead Zone 83. North and South (TV) 86, etc.
TV series: Harry O 73–76.

Zéro de Conduite (France 1933). A nightmarish fantasy of schoolboy life, directed in surrealist vein by Jean Vigo. Music by Maurice Jaubert, photographed by Boris Kaufmann.

Zetterling, Mai (1925–). Capable Swedish leading lady in Britain.
□ *Frenzy* 44. Frieda 47. The Bad Lord Byron 48. Portrait from Life 48. *Quartet* 48. The Romantic Age 49. Blackmailed 50. Hell is Sold Out 51. The Tall Headlines 51. The Ringer 52. Desperate Moment 53. Dance Little Lady 54. Knock on Wood 54. A Prize of Gold 55. Seven Waves Away 56. The Truth about Women 58. Jetstorm 59. Faces in the Dark 60. Piccadilly Third Stop 60. Offbeat 61. The Man Who Finally Died 62. *Only Two Can Play* 62. The Main Attraction 62. The Bay of St Michel 63.
□AS DIRECTOR: The War Game 62. Loving Couples 64. Night Games 66. Doctor Glas 68. Visions of Eight (part) 73. Scrubbers 83.

Zieff, Howard (1943–). American director.
□Hearts of the West 75. Slither 76. House Calls 78. The Main Event 79. Private Benjamin 80. Unfaithfully Yours 83.

Ziegfeld, Florenz (1867–1932). American Broadway impresario who had three films named after him (*The Great Ziegfeld, Ziegfeld Girl, Ziegfeld Follies*). He was impersonated in two of them by William Powell and in *Funny Girl* by Walter Pidgeon. He also 'supervised' 1929's *Glorifying the American Girl*.
Biography 1973: *Ziegfeld* by Charles Higham.

Ziegfeld Follies (US 1944; released 1946). Spectacular plotless musical revue 'inspired' by the great showman Florenz Ziegfeld (glimpsed in Heaven in the person of William Powell). Several MGM performers are seen at or near their best: Fred Astaire in two numbers with Lucille Bremer and a comedy dance routine with Gene Kelly, Judy Garland burlesquing a star's press interview, Lena Horne singing 'Love', etc. Mostly directed by Vincente Minnelli.

Ziegler, William (–1978). American editor.
The Housekeeper's Daughter 39. No Hands on the Clock 41. Minesweeper 43. Abie's Irish Rose 46. Rope 49. *Strangers on a Train* 51. The Desert Song 53. Rebel Without a Cause 55. Auntie Mame 58. Ice Palace 60. *The Music Man* 62. My Fair Lady 64. A Fine Madness 66. Firecreek 68. Topaz 69. The Omega Man 71, many others.

Ziemann, Sonja (1926–). German leading actress.
Ein Windstoss 42. Girl of the Black Forest 50. Made in Heaven (GB) 52. My Sister and I 54. Menschen im Hotel 59. A Matter of Who 62. The Bridge at Remagen 69. De Sade 70, etc.

Zimbalist, Efrem Jnr (1918–). American leading man with stage experience; plays characters who inspire confidence.
House of Strangers 49. Band of Angels 57. Too Much Too Soon 58. By Love Possessed 61. A Fever in the Blood 61. The Chapman Report 62. The Reward 65. Wait Until Dark 67. Airport 75 74. A Family Upside Down (TV) 78, etc.
TV series: 77 Sunset Strip 58–63. The F.B.I. 65–73.

Zimbalist, Sam (1904–1958). American producer.
The Crowd Roars 38. Boom Town 40. King Solomon's Mines 50. Quo Vadis 51. Mogambo 53. Beau Brummell 54. Ben Hur 59 (died during production).

Zinnemann, Fred (1907–). Austrian-born director, with varied experience before coming to Hollywood in 1929. Was an extra (in *All Quiet on the Western Front*), script clerk, and director of shorts (*That Others Might Live* (AA) 38, several episodes of *Crime Does Not Pay*, etc.).
□Kid Glove Killer 42. Eyes in the Night 42. *The Seventh Cross* 44. Little Mister Jim 46. My Brother Talks to Horses 47. The Search 48. *Act of Violence* 49. *The Men* 50. Teresa 51. *High Noon* 52. The Member of the Wedding 53. *From Here to Eternity* (AA) 53. Oklahoma 55. A Hatful of Rain 57. *The Nun's Story* 58. *The Sundowners* 60. Behold a Pale Horse 64. *A Man For All Seasons* (AA) 66. The Day of the Jackal 73. Julia 77. Five Days One Summer 82.

¶ *F.Z.:* I'm not in pictures to promote my private personality. I'm in it for the joy of it.

Zola, Emile (1840–1902). Prolific French novelist of the seamy side. Works filmed include *Nana, La Bête Humaine* and *Thérèse Raquin*. A 1937 biopic, *The Life of Emile Zola*, starred Paul Muni and centred on Zola's participation in the Dreyfus case.

zombies originate from Haitian legend, and are generally held to be dead people brought back to life by voodoo. In movies they invariably shamble along with sightless eyes, looking pretty awful but doing no real damage. They were most convincingly displayed in Victor Halperin's 1932 *White Zombie*; other examples of the species turned up in *Revolt of the Zombies, The Zombies of Mora Tau, I Walked With a Zombie, King of the Zombies, The Ghost Breakers* (and its remake *Scared Stiff*), and *Dr Terror's House of Horrors*. The species gave its name to a strong rum punch, and one treasured memory is a movie in which the Ritz Brothers walked up to a bar and said: 'Three zombies.' 'I can see that,' said the barman, 'but what'll you have to drink?' In the seventies George Romero adopted the theme in such repellent films as *Night of the Living Dead* and *Dawn of the Dead*; but the most fearsome undead of all appeared in the dream scene of Hammer's 1965 *Plague of the Zombies*.

zoom. A lens of variable focal length, normally used for swiftly magnifying a distant object or moving rapidly away from a close one.

Zorba the Greek (Greece 1964). A zestful, uncontrolled, open-air film, written and directed by Michael Cacoyannis from a novel by Nikos Kazantzakis about a huge peasant who persuades a timid Englishman to share his joy in life even when surrounded by disaster. Marred by over-indulgent writing and an unnecessary sub-plot about a widow who is stoned to death by Cretan peasants, the film remains a pleasure to watch by virtue of Walter Lassally's photography, Mikos Theodorakis' music, and the performances of Anthony Quinn, Alan Bates and (in moderation) Lila Kedrova.

Zorina, Vera (1917–) (Eva Brigitta Hartwig). Norwegian ballet dancer and actress in American films. Now retired.
The Goldwyn Follies 39. On Your Toes 39. *I Was an Adventuress* 40. Star Spangled Rhythm 43. Follow the Boys 44.

Zorro (Don Diego de Vega). The black-garbed Robin Hood of Spanish California originated as the hero of a 1919 strip cartoon by Johnston McCulley. (Zorro, incidentally, is Spanish for fox.) Films featuring the devil-may-care righter of wrongs include *The Mark of Zorro* 20 with Douglas Fairbanks, and its 1925 sequel *Don Q, Son of Zorro*; *The Bold Caballero* 37 with Robert Livingston; *Zorro Rides Again* 37, a serial with John Carroll; *Zorro's Fighting Legion* 39, a serial with Reed Hadley; Mamoulian's splendid remake of *The Mark of Zorro* 40, with Tyrone Power; *The Ghost of Zorro* 49, a serial with Clayton Moore; Walter Chiari in *The Sign of Zorro* 52; *Zorro the Avenger* 60 and other Disney TV films with Guy Williams; Sean Flynn in *The Sign of Zorro* 62; Frank Latimore in *Shadow of Zorro* 62; Pierre Brice in *Zorro versus Maciste* 63; George Ardisson in *Zorro at the Court of Spain* 63; Gordon Scott in *Zorro and the Three Musketeers* 63; and Alain Delon in *Zorro* 75. Almost inevitably the eighties brought a spoof version, *Zorro the Gay Blade* 82, featuring a limp-wristed avenger.

Zsigmond, Vilmos (1930–). Hungarian cinematographer.
Deliverance 72. Images 72. The Long Goodbye 73. Scarecrow 73. Cinderella Liberty 73. The Sugarland Express 64. The Girl from Petrovka 74. Obsession 76. Close Encounters of the Third Kind 77. The Deer Hunter (AAN) 78. Flesh and Blood (TV) 79. Winter Kills 79. The Rose 79. Heaven's Gate 80. Blow Out 81. Jinxed 82. Table for Five 83. The River (AAN) 84, etc.

Zucco, George (1886–1960). Sepulchral-toned British stage actor, long in Hollywood and typecast in horror films in which he admirably exuded upper-bracket malignancy.
Autumn Crocus 30. Dreyfus 31. The Good Companions 32. The Man Who Could Work Miracles 35. Marie Antoinette 38. *The Cat and the Canary* 39. The Hunchback of Notre Dame 39. Arise My Love 40. *The Mummy's Hand* 40. *The Adventures of Sherlock Holmes* (as Moriarty) 40. Sherlock Holmes in Washington 42. The Black Swan 42. Dead Men Walk 43. The Black Raven 43. The Mad Ghoul 43. House of Frankenstein 45. Fog Island 45. Dr Renault's Secret 46. The Pirate 47. Joan of Arc 48. Madame Bovary 49. Let's Dance 50. David and Bathsheba 51. The First Legion 51, many others.

Zuckmayer, Carl (1896–1977). German playwright whose *The Captain from Koepenick* has been much filmed. His screenplays include:
The Blue Angel 30. Escape Me Never 35. *Rembrandt* 36. Mayerling 40. I Was a Criminal 41.

Zugsmith, Albert (1910–). American producer-director with a taste for exploitation subjects.
Written on the Wind (p) 57. The Tattered Dress (p) 57. The Incredible Shrinking Man (p) 58. Touch of Evil (p) 58. High School Confidential (d) 60. Teacher was a Sexpot (d) 60. The Private Life of Adam and Eve (d) 61. Confessions of an Opium Eater (d) 63. Fanny Hill (p) 64. Movie Star American Style (or LSD I Hate You) (d) 66. The Incredible Sex Revolution (d) 67, etc.

Zukor, Adolph (1873–1976). Hungarian-born film pioneer. Emigrated to America, became film salesman, nickelodeon owner, and independent producer (in 1913), by persuading New York stage stars James O'Neill, James K. Hackett and Minnie Maddern Fiske to appear in productions of, respectively, *The Count of Monte Cristo, The Prisoner of Zenda* and *Tess of the D'Urbervilles*. This was the start of 'Famous Players', which in 1916 merged with Jesse Lasky's production interests and later became Paramount Pictures. He remained board chairman of the latter from 1935. His autobiography, *The Public is Never Wrong*, was published in 1945. Special Academy Award 1948 'for his services to the industry over a period of forty years'.
❁ For being the industry's first centenarian. *The Covered Wagon.*

¶ Fish stinks from the head.—*A.Z.*

If I'd known I was going to live this long, I'd have taken better care of myself.—*A.Z.*

Zweig, Stephen (1881–1942). Austrian novelist. Films of his books include *Beware of Pity, Twenty Four Hours of a Woman's Life, Letter from an Unknown Woman.*

Graduation Quiz

Answers appear on p. 1228

1 What is the obvious link between these three films of the early fifties: *Those Redheads from Seattle*, *Gun Fury*, *Sangaree*?

2 Who played Puck in the 1935 version of *A Midsummer Night's Dream*?

3 Name the novel by Jerome Weidman on which was based the 1951 film now known variously as *Only the Best* (American TV) and *This Is My Affair* (GB).

4 In which film did Faye Dunaway and Steve McQueen play chess?

5 And in which film did Boris Karloff and Bela Lugosi play chess?

6 And in which film did Nigel Green and Richard Johnson play chess with outsize pieces?

7 Finally on this topic, in what film did the floor-stones of the hall of an old mansion, when viewed as a chessboard, help towards finding long lost treasure?

8 The same title was used for a film made in 1942 with Brian Donlevy, a quite different film in 1956 with Edward G. Robinson, and in 1956 a Hammer horror mystery with Moira Redmond. What was the title?

9 What Harold Lloyd film is in danger of being confused with one by Luis Buñuel?

10 What came between *In the Heat of the Night* and *The Organization*?

11 Bette Davis was *Jezebel* but what female star in 1953 appeared in *Sins of Jezebel*?

12 The three dancing male leads of *It's Always Fair Weather* were Gene Kelly, Dan Dailey and . . . ?

13 John Carradine in 1943 and Anton Diffring in 1976 played the same real-life role. Whom did they portray, and name the two films.

14 What Edgar Wallace play was filmed by Paramount in 1938 as *Dangerous to Know*, starring Akim Tamiroff and Anna May Wong?

15 What book by J. Edgar Hoover provided the substance for four Paramount second features in 1938–40, vaguely based on real public enemies of the thirties?

16 Name the four films.

17 Claude Rains was *The Invisible Man* but who played the lead in *The Invisible Man Returns*?

18 And who was the villain of that film?

19 In *Four Daughters* in 1938 Claude Rains played the father. Who did so in the 1955 remake called *Young at Heart*?

20 Name the two direct sequels to *Four Daughters*.

21 Name also the semi-sequel made in 1939 with virtually the same cast playing different characters in very much the same atmosphere.

22 Name the 1939 film about lady pilots, starring Alice Faye, Constance Bennett and Nancy Kelly.

23 The Massachusetts witch trials of 1692, treated famously in *Les Sorcières de Salem*, were also the subject of a surprisingly serious Paramount film of 1937. Name it and its two stars.

24 A Warren Beatty film, made as *The Presbyterian Church Wager*, had its title changed to . . .

25 An American writer-director whose career suffered from the McCarthy witch hunt is perhaps best known for a 1948 film about the numbers racket. Name him, the film and its star.

26 Can you name the original novel and author?

27 A three-hour TV movie made in 1976 treated the 1954 court case in which a Cleveland osteopath was accused of murdering his wife. Name film and star.

28 An even longer TV movie in 1974 dramatized Leon Uris' book *QB VII*. Name the two male leads.

29 Who played the judge?

30 Who in the 1971 TV movie *Goodbye Raggedy Ann* played a Hollywood starlet driven to the brink of suicide?

31 A 1972 TV movie called *Haunts of the Very Rich* was a partial and unofficial remake of a 1924 play by Sutton Vane which was filmed in 1931 with Leslie Howard. Name it.

32 The 1944 remake starring Paul Henreid and Eleanor Parker had a different title. What was it?

33 Who played the Examiner?

34 The gorilla was a fairly innocent party in 1954's *Gorilla at Large*. So whodunit?
35 Who played Saladin in the 1953 *King Richard and the Crusaders*?
36 *Human Desire* (1950) was an American remake (more or less) of what 1938 French film?
37 Who compered in the 1950 version of *La Ronde*?
38 Who directed it?
39 What 1934 period piece now appears on American TV as *Forbidden Alliance*?
40 Why?
41 For the same reason the 1934 version of *The Merry Widow* is shown on TV as . . . ?
42 Who were the co-stars of the 1952 version?
43 John Gregory Dunne wrote a book called *The Studio*. What studio?
44 Give the title and author of the famous book about the making of *The Red Badge of Courage*.
45 What was remarkable about Claude Rains' film debut?
46 What classic film makes heroes of the Ku Klux Klan?
47 What did Arthur Housman and Jack Norton have in common?
48 For what contemporary historical role, which he played many times, was Robert Watson famous?
49 One might ask the same of Martin Kosleck.
50 What British leading man more or less forsook acting to be Cecil B. De Mille's right hand and associate producer?
51 What part did he play in *Mrs Miniver*?
52 What elderly British gentleman was the leading character, though not the top-billed star, of *Mister 880* and *Apartment for Peggy*?
53 What famous star of the fifties was seen briefly as a soda jerk in *Has Anybody Seen My Gal*?
54 What novel by Hervey Allen was filmed in 1936 and helped Gale Sondergaard win an Academy Award as best supporting actress?
55 What star of the forties is to be glimpsed as a pipesmoking reporter towards the end of *Citizen Kane*?
56 What has *The King and the Chorus Girl* to do with *Double Dynamite*?
57 Novelist Hugh Walpole played what role in what Hollywood film in 1935?
58 In what film did Humphrey Bogart play a murderer, hounded into giving himself away by Sydney Greenstreet's clever ruses?
59 Under what name did Arthur Stanley Jefferson, of Ulverston, Lancashire, England, become famous when he went to Hollywood?
60 In what film did Colonel Strasser and Captain Renault appear, and who played them?
61 In what semi-horror film did Elspeth Dudgeon play a gentleman?
62 What distinction was given in the fifties to Adeline de Walt Reynolds?
63 Who held the same distinction in 1976, and in what film of that year did she co-star?
64 Who thought he could imitate the cry of a loon in *Bringing Up Baby*?
65 What continuing star role was played by a fellow named Pal?
66 Who played Soames Forsyte in *That Forsyte Woman*?
67 What is the connection between Melville Crossman and Mark Canfield?
68 What famous studio has a motto meaning 'art for art's sake'?
69 In what film did James Mason, uncredited, play an Arab beggar?
70 Why was Anthony Quinn a fairly natural choice to direct De Mille's last film *The Buccaneer* when C.B. wasn't up to it?
71 In what film did Will Hay play a magistrate and John Mills his son?
72 In *Sorrowful Jones* (1949) Mary Jane Saunders played an orphan girl involved with racetrack gangsters and Bob Hope. The 1934 version of the same story starred Shirley Temple and was called . . . ?
73 In what film did Shirley Temple co-star with Carole Lombard and Gary Cooper?
74 Who directed it?
75 Laird Cregar is said to have died from losing weight to play the lead in what film?
76 In what film did he play a character called Stephen Spettigue, and who played the title role?
77 In what 1973 TV movie did Tom Courtenay play a young priest dying in a remote Canadian village?
78 *The Moon and Sixpence* (1942) was based on a novel by . . . ?
79 On the life of what famous artist is it said to be based?
80 Who played the artist whose wife George Sanders steals?
81 And who played the wife?
82 Name the *Mr Belvedere* sequels to the 1948 *Sitting Pretty*.

83 In what film did Lena Horne and Eddie Anderson sing 'Consequence'?

84 What film made Walter Huston's rendering of 'September Song' popular?

85 In what film did Ray Bolger sing 'Once in Love with Amy'?

86 Of what film did the British Board of Film Censors say many years ago: 'It has no apparent meaning. If there is a meaning it is doubtless objectionable.'

87 In *Mr Blandings Builds His Dream House*, who played the helpful but bewildered architect Mr Simms?

88 Who played Frollo in the Charles Laughton version of *The Hunchback of Notre Dame*?

89 Who directed it?

90 With what TV project do you connect Nick Nolte and Peter Strauss?

91 Who played Dracula in *The Return of Dracula*?

92 Name the 1933 comedy about a slightly pixillated family; it was said to mark the beginning of the crazy comedy cycle, and starred Claudette Colbert and Mary Boland.

93 A 1968 comedy based on a novel by Charles Webb was a great commercial success. Name it.

94 Who played Mr Jordan in *Here Comes Mr Jordan*?

95 A 1974 TV film called *In Tandem* led to a two-season series called . . . ?

96 Name the two stars.

97 Who played the American who tried to educate a Greek prostitute in *Never on Sunday*?

98 Will Hay, comedy star of *Oh Mr Porter* and *Ask a Policeman*, had two regular stooges. Name them.

99 In 1941 they appeared in a revamping of *Oh Mr Porter* called *Back Room Boy*. Who was the star?

100 Who in 1932 directed *Love Me Tonight*?

101 What director made *The Cool Mikado*, *Lawman* and *Won Ton Ton, The Dog Who Saved Hollywood*?

102 Of what *Mystery Movie* TV segments were these the pilots? a) *Once Upon a Dead Man* b) *Ransom for a Dead Man* c) *Say Hello to a Dead Man* d) *The Big Rip-Off* e) *Who Killed Miss USA*? f) *Detour to Nowhere*

103 Name the comedy which put Cary Grant and Tony Curtis in a submarine.

104 And the comedy which put Cary Grant and Ann Sheridan on a motor bike.

105 In which musical did we hear the songs 'Steam Heat', 'I'm Not at All in Love' and 'Hernando's Hideaway'?

106 Name the leading man.

107 What much-filmed best seller was written by Grace Metalious?

108 And what earlier small-town saga, also filmed and later made the basis of a TV series, was written by Henry Bellamann?

109 In what film did George Sanders wear women's clothes?

110 Who was the common star of *The Phantom Creeps* (1939) and *The Ape Man* (1943)?

111 Name the 1944 film in which Cary Grant promoted a dancing caterpillar.

112 Who played the boy owner of the caterpillar?

113 Name the lady who in 1932 was billed above Jean Harlow in *Platinum Blonde*.

114 The hero of *Platinum Blonde* gave an excellent performance but died soon after it was finished. Name him.

115 Who directed the 1967 film *Planet of the Apes*?

116 What 1930 Cecil B. De Mille film has for its climax a disaster in an airship?

117 What episodic 1942 film was linked by a tail-coat?

118 And which 1943 ditto by the ramblings of a club bore?

119 The last two films had the same director. Name him.

120 What musical was based on a Richard Bissell novel called *7½ Cents*?

121 What actor played Dr Watson to the Sherlock Holmes of Arthur Wontner?

122 What actor played Inspector Lestrade in six of the films in which Basil Rathbone played Sherlock Holmes?

123 Name the Rathbone/Holmes film based on the original Conan Doyle story *The Six Napoleons*.

124 Who played Moriarty in *The Adventures of Sherlock Holmes*?

125 And who in *The Woman in Green*?

126 Who played in the 1931 versions of both *Frankenstein* and *Dracula*, in the former as Frankenstein's elderly mentor and in the latter as Van Helsing?

127 Name also the actor who played the hunchback assistant in *Frankenstein* and Jonathan Harker in *Dracula*.

128 What was the 1932 horror movie of circus life made by Tod Browning, which MGM disowned after seeing it?

129 Who played Katharine Hepburn's sister in *The Philadelphia Story*?

130 Who in 1942 played *The Young Mr Pitt*?

131 In the same film, who played Charles James Fox?

132 In 1938, who played opposite Joan Crawford in *Mannequin*?
133 Who was the director of *Les Enfants du Paradis*?
134 With what branch of cinema art do you associate Joseph H. August?
135 And Constantin Bakaleinikoff?
136 Name the unseen zither player in *The Third Man*.
137 What famous comedy-thriller was filmed three times, starring Guy Newall, Jack Hulbert, and Arthur Askey?
138 Name the Martin and Lewis remake of *The Ghost Breakers*.
139 Who should have played the Raymond Massey part in *Arsenic and Old Lace*?
140 In what film were Lamberto Maggiorani and Enzo Staiola the leading players?
141 A 1932 Warren William film called *The Mouthpiece* was twice remade, once with George Brent and once with Edward G. Robinson. Name the two films.
142 Who played Judas in the 1927 *King of Kings*?
143 Who played Hamlet in the 1964 Russian version?
144 A 1936 Al Jolson film was known in Great Britain as *Casino de Paree*. Give the American title and say who co-starred.
145 *The Spoilers* has been filmed five times. Who wrote the novel?
146 Who took over in 1955 Marlene Dietrich's role of the saloon entertainer Cherry Malotte?
147 Name the Roman epic which Alexander Korda began in 1937 but never finished.
148 What continuing role did Tom Conway take over from George Sanders?
149 Who provided the voices for cartoon characters Speedy Gonzales, Bugs Bunny and Sylvester (among others)?
150 In the films of the same names, what are the Blue Gardenia, the Blue Angel and the Blue Dahlia?
151 Who played Poppea in *The Sign of the Cross*?
152 In what liquid did she allegedly take her bath?
153 Who played Androcles in *Androcles and the Lion*?
154 And who played Petronius in the 1951 *Quo Vadis?*
155 What does 'Quo Vadis?' mean?
156 What does *Hatari* mean?
157 What singing star, whose story was filmed in 1955, appeared in *Roman Scandals* with Eddie Cantor?
158 Name the 1955 film.
159 How many stories were there in *The Naked City* (1948), according to the closing voice-over? (It will be more now.)
160 Who are The Archers? What was their function?
161 In 1950 David Lean directed a period crime story about a famous unsolved case. Whose case, and who played the title role?
162 Margaret Lockwood and James Mason provided the villainous element in *The Man in Grey*. Who completed the stellar quartet?
163 What horror film produced—and some say directed—by Howard Hawks took place north of the Arctic Circle?
164 Who played Citizen Kane's second wife?
165 And who played his butler?
166 What was the name of his castle?
167 In *Journey into Fear* Orson Welles played the head of the Turkish police. Name him.
168 Who played Esmeralda to Lon Chaney's Hunchback of Notre Dame?
169 And to Charles Laughton's?
170 And to Anthony Quinn's?
171 In *The Wizard of Oz*, who played the Witch of the East?
172 What is the connection between that film and one by John Boorman?
173 Name the film from a novel by John O'Hara in which Suzanne Pleshette played a nymphomaniac.
174 *Storm Over the Nile* was a 1956 remake of what famous story filmed in 1929 and 1939?
175 Who wrote the novel?
176 Who played Pa Joad in *The Grapes of Wrath*?
177 Which studio made it?
178 To what film was this tagline applied? 'He's just as funny as his old man was fierce.'
179 Who played Ferrari the black marketeer of *Casablanca*?
180 Who played Ugarte?
181 In what film did James Mason play the evil Sir Brack?
182 Who co-starred with Robert Donat in *The Count of Monte Cristo*?
183 In 1951 Donat appeared as a cinema pioneer in a biopic called *The Magic Box*. Who was the pioneer?
184 Who played the policeman brought off the street to see the first moving pictures?
185 Who is Eddie Egan?
186 Who was Van Nest Polglase?

187 Who was Edith Head?
188 What did Lawrence Tierney have in common with Warren Oates?
189 Who directed *The King and I*, *Can Can* and *Snow White and The Three Stooges*?
190 To what producer-director, who died in 1963, was Maureen O'Sullivan married?
191 In what film did she play Jane Bennet?
192 What in 1914 did Phyllis Haver, Marie Prevost and Ruth Taylor have in common?
193 Who was the female star of *Rosalie* and *I Dood It*?
194 Name the 1939 film in which John Barrymore was directed by Garson Kanin.
195 Which famous director, early in his career, made *Laburnum Grove*, *Midshipman Easy* and *A Girl Must Live*?
196 Who played Lady Catherine de Bourgh in *Pride and Prejudice*?
197 Who played the monster in *The Ghost of Frankenstein*?
198 And in *House of Frankenstein*?
199 In the above picture, who played Dracula?
200 Who played Nurse Peggotty in *David Copperfield* (1935)?
201 She married Barkis the coachman, played by whom?
202 Who played Jack Holt's mother in *San Francisco*?
203 Who played Carlotta Vance in *Dinner at Eight*?
204 Who were the stars of *Half Shot at Sunrise*, *Mummy's Boys* and *Cracked Nuts*?
205 Who played Granny in *Granny Get Your Gun*?
206 What was curious about the script of this film?
207 Which silent film directed by Erich von Stroheim had its climax in Death Valley?
208 Name the two male leads.
209 Name the little-seen film starring Rod Steiger, Susannah York, Don Murray and George Grizzard.
210 What famous star was seen as a dancer in the 1935 *Dante's Inferno*?
211 In what city was *What's Up Doc* shot?
212 Of what film was a character named Charlie Allnutt the hero?
213 In what film did Bob Hope perform with a penguin?
214 In what film was a director asked to make *Ants in Your Pants of 1941?* (He preferred to make *O Brother Where Art Thou*.)
215 Who said, in what film, 'Your wife is safe with Tonetti; he prefers spaghetti'?
216 In what film did H. B. Warner play Chang?
217 In what film was Private Ratskywatsky much talked of though he never appeared?
218 Who played Cardinal Richelieu in Richard Lester's *The Three Musketeers*?
219 And in the Ritz Brothers version of 1939?
220 Who directed the 1945 version of *And Then There Were None*?
221 Who directed Humphrey Bogart in *Sahara*?
222 Who played Watson in the 1922 *Sherlock Holmes*?
223 Philip Barry wrote the play *The Philadelphia Story*. Who wrote the film script?
224 What have Charles Ruggles, Arthur Askey, Jack Benny and Ray Bolger in common (apart from all being very funny fellows)?
225 Of what film was *Weekend at the Waldorf* (1945) a revised remake?
226 In *The Bullfighters* Laurel and Hardy did a breaking eggs routine, first performed by them and Lupe Velez in what film?
227 In what film did Grusinskaya appear, played by whom?
228 In what film did Cary Grant take a shower fully clothed?
229 In 1948 the first 'cold war' film was the story of Igor Gouzenko. It was called . . . ?
230 Who in 1971 directed *The Garden of the Finzi-Continis*?
231 With whom did Laurel and Hardy have their tit-for-tat wrecking war in *Big Business*?
232 And in *Bacon Grabbers*?
233 And in *Tit for Tat*?
234 Who played Dr Christian in the series put out by RKO between 1938 and 1941?
235 Who was the director of *Docks of New York*, *Thunderbolt* and *Sergeant Madden*?
236 What three famous old-timers starred in a 1972 TV movie called *The Crooked Hearts*?
237 What did Maurice Chevalier originate that Don Ameche and Danny Kaye took over?

238 Who directed the 1921 version of *The Four Horsemen of the Apocalypse*?

239 Who played the would-be suicide in *Fourteen Hours* (1951)?

240 In what film did Marlene Dietrich co-star with Charles Boyer?

241 Who said this? 'I don't care if he is a walrus. I like him. I like him.'

242 What famous film was adapted from a book called *Personal History* by Vincent Shehan?

243 Who played Jolson's mentor, later partner and manager in *The Jolson Story*?

244 Name the actress who played mother in the Hardy family series.

245 What actor *first* played Judge Hardy?

246 Liza Minnelli played Sally Bowles in *Cabaret*; but what actress, discovered by Otto Preminger for *Exodus*, first played the role on Broadway?

247 Who played uncredited bit parts in *The Maltese Falcon* and *In This Our Life*?

248 Who were Flagg and Quirt in the original silent *What Price Glory*?

249 Who starred in *The Scoundrel*, written and directed in 1935 by Ben Hecht and Charles MacArthur?

250 Who played Hildy Johnson in the 1930 version of *The Front Page*?

251 How many times has *Jane Eyre* been filmed since sound?

252 Name the actresses who played the title role in these versions.

253 What connection can you make between Mary Kornmann, Joe Cobb, Mickey Daniels and Jackie Condon?

254 One of Andy Hardy's girl-friends turned up again in 1972 in *They Only Kill Their Masters*. Who was she?

255 Who was Anton Grot?

256 Who played the monster in the immensely long TV movie of 1972: *Frankenstein: The True Story*?

257 The Thing from Another World became the star of what long-running TV series?

258 Peter Falk is Columbo and Dennis Weaver is McCloud; but who played Faraday of *Faraday and Company*?

259 And who were *The Snoop Sisters*?

260 What famous Hollywood star of the forties played the victim in their first episode?

261 Who played the hero of the 1922 version of *The Prisoner of Zenda* and the Cardinal in the 1952 version?

262 Who played Rupert of Hentzau in 1922; 1937; and 1952?

263 In which film did Groucho make the following reply to the remark: 'This shall be a gala day for you': 'Well, a gal a day is enough for me. I don't think I could manage any more.'

264 In which film did W. C. Fields play Egbert Souse, pronounced sue-say?

265 Is it true that Sig Ruman suffered at Groucho Marx's hands in *A Day at the Races*, *A Night in Casablanca* and *The Big Store*?

266 In which film did James Stewart play Wyatt Earp?

267 For what film was the song 'Isn't It Romantic' written?

268 Who directed *High Noon*?

269 Messrs Allen, Flanagan, Knox, Gold, Naughton and Nervo were collectively known as what?

270 Can you name any of their films?

271 Who played Douglas Bader in what film?

272 What 1924 film starred Wallace Beery and had monsters created by Willis O'Brien?

273 What had Mary Gordon to do with the Basil Rathbone/Sherlock Holmes films?

274 Who had the last line in *Some Like It Hot*? (The 1959 film.)

275 Who played Uncle Matt and Lord Epping, in what series?

276 What was the name of Popeye's girl-friend?

277 What producer-director was responsible for *Homicidal*, *The House on Haunted Hill* and *The Tingler*?

278 What famous film was based on a novel called *Glory for Me* by Mackinlay Kantor?

279 Who was the common star of *The Mummy's Tomb*, *Bowery to Broadway*, *The Climax* and *The Mad Ghoul*?

280 Who was Hans Dreier?

Last Words

¶ A few favourite unclassifiable moments.
Bette Davis, on having pointed out to her a starlet who had allegedly slept her way to the top:

> I see—she's the original good time that was had by all.

Billy Wilder to his cinematographer during the filming of *Sunset Boulevard*:

> Johnny, keep it out of focus. I want to win the foreign picture award.

An anonymous wartime crack:

> In case of an air raid, go directly to RKO: they haven't had a hit in years.

Will Rogers, philosophizing:

> What's the salvation of the movies? I say, run 'em backwards. It can't hurt, and it's worth a trial.

King Vidor, evaluating one of his own movies:

> The picture was so bad they had to do retakes before they could put it on the shelf.

Carole Lombard, refusing a role in an Orson Welles film:

> I can't win working with Welles. If the picture's a hit he will get the credit, and if it's a flop, I'll be blamed.

John Grierson, evaluating the decline of Josef von Sternberg:

> When a director dies, he becomes a photographer.

Sir Cedric Hardwicke on judgment by sneak preview:

> On Hollywood's theory that the audience knows best, the schoolboy's 'lousy' becomes the last word in dramatic criticism.

Jean Renoir, leaving Hollywood after an enforced wartime sojourn:

> Goodbye, Mr Zanuck: it certainly has been a pleasure working at 16th Century Fox.

Howard Hawks, commenting on his penchant for remaking films with similar characters and situations:

> When you find out a thing goes pretty well, you might as well do it again.

Victor Mature, when Rita Hayworth deserted him for Orson Welles, with whom she had been working in a charity magic act:

> Apparently the way to a girl's heart is to saw her in half.

Walter Wanger on Hollywood gossip columnists:

> This is the only industry that finances its own blackmail.

Robert Lord on the film city:

> It's such nonsense, this immorality of Hollywood. We're all too tired.

Robert Benchley after viewing an arty film:

> There's less in this than meets the eye.

And Spencer Tracy, on finding himself working for a director with 'artistic' ideas who tried to turn every gesture into a symbol:

> I'm too tired and old and rich for all this, so let's do the scene.

A final thought from Auguste Lumière, pioneer of cinematography, in 1895:

> Young man, you can be grateful that my invention is not for sale, for it would undoubtedly ruin you. It can be exploited for a certain time as a scientific curiosity, but apart from that it has no commercial value whatsoever.

Alphabetical List of Films

This is a note of all the films given individual mention in the body of the book. I should try to explain this spotlight treatment. A glance will show that these are not necessarily the best films ever made. They include films which were significant to the industry, in that they started trends; films which were popular enought to be frequently remade; films which began series; films which were notable milestones in the history of censorship, or which uniquely held up a mirror to reality; and some films which are simply excellent of their kind.

In a way, therefore, it is a list of films which have had impact of one kind or another: impact on the art, the industry, the audience.

The entries are necessarily short, and the credits and comment given are restricted to establishing the reason for the film's inclusion. The student who has found a reason to look up the film will know many ways of extending his knowledge; my aim is simply to provide a toehold.

Blood and Sand
Blow Up
The Blue Angel
The Blue Lamp
The Bluebird
The Body Snatcher
Bonnie and Clyde
Boomerang
Born Free
Boudu Sauvé des Eaux
Boule de Suif
The Bowery
Boys' Town
Breathless
Brewster's Millions
The Bride of Frankenstein
The Bridge of San Luis Rey
The Bridge on the River Kwai
A Bridge Too Far
Brief Encounter
Brighton Rock
Bringing Up Baby
Broadway Bill
Broadway Melody
Broken Arrow
Broken Blossoms
Brother Orchid
Brother Rat
The Brothers Karamazov
Brute Force
The Burmese Harp
Butch Cassidy and the Sundance Kid

Cabaret
Cabin in the Sky
The Cabinet of Dr Caligari
Cabiria
Caesar and Cleopatra
The Caine Mutiny
Calamity Jane
Camelot
Camille
Captain Blood
Carmen
Un Carnet de Bal
The Carpetbaggers
Carrie
Casablanca
Casino Royale
Casque d'Or
The Cat and the Canary
Cat Ballou
Cat People
Cavalcade
The Champ
Chang
The Charge of the Light Brigade
Chariots of Fire
Charley's Aunt
Charlie Bubbles
Cheaper by the Dozen
The Cheat
La Chienne
A Child is Waiting
The Childhood of Maxim Gorky
Children of Hiroshima
The China Syndrome
The Chinese Bungalow
Cimarron
The Citadel
Citizen Kane
City Lights
Civilisation
Claudia
Cléo de 5 à 7
Cleopatra
Close Encounters of the Third Kind
Closely Observed Trains
Coming Thru the Rye
Confessions of a Nazi Spy
Congress Dances
A Connecticut Yankee . . .
The Constant Nymph
The Corsican Brothers
The Count of Monte Cristo
The Covered Wagon
The Cranes are Flying
The Creature from the Black Lagoon
The Crime of Monsieur Lange
Crime Without Passion
Crossfire
The Crowd
The Crowd Roars
Cyrano de Bergerac

Daddy Longlegs
Damaged Goods
Les Dames du Bois de Boulogne
The Damned
Dangerous Moonlight
The Dark Angel
Dark Victory
Darling
David Copperfield
The Dawn Patrol
Day for Night
Day of Wrath
Dead End
Dead of Night
Dear Ruth
Death of a Salesman
Death Wish
The Deer Hunter
Deliverance
The Desert Song
Destry Rides Again
Le Diable au Corps
Les Diaboliques
A Diary for Timothy
Diary of a Chambermaid
The Discreet Charm of the Bourgeoisie
Docks of New York
Dr Cyclops
Dr Ehrlich's Magic Bullet
Doctor in the House
Dr Jekyll and Mr Hyde
Dr Strangelove
Dr Syn
Doctor Zhivago
Dodsworth
La Dolce Vita
Don Juan
Don Quixote
Double Indemnity
A Double Life
Dracula
Drifters
Drôle de Drame
Duck Soup
Duel in the Sun

E.T.
Earth
Earthquake
East Lynne
East of Eden
Easy Rider
Easy Street
Edouard et Caroline
Eight and a Half
El
Elephant Boy
Elmer Gantry
Elvira Madigan
Emil and the Detectives
Les Enfants du Paradis
L'Equipage
Erotikon
Escape
Escape Me Never
L'Eternel Retour
Evergreen
Executive Suite
Exodus
The Exorcist
Extase
The Exterminating Angel

A Face in the Crowd
Fahrenheit 451
The Fall of the House of Usher
The Fallen Idol
Fanny
Fantasia

Fantomas
A Farewell to Arms
The Farmer's Daughter
Farrebique
Father Brown
Father of the Bride
La Femme du Boulanger
La Fin du Jour
Fire over England
Fires Were Started
The First of the Few
A Fistful of Dollars
Five Fingers
Five Graves to Cairo
Five Star Final
The Flag Lieutenant
Flesh and Fantasy
The Fly
Flying Down to Rio
Folies Bergère
Foolish Wives
For Whom the Bell Tolls
Forbidden Paradise
Forbidden Planet
Force of Evil
Foreign Correspondent
Forever and a Day
Forty-Ninth Parallel
42nd Street
Four Daughters
The Four Feathers
The Four Horsemen of the Apocalypse
The Four Hundred Blows
Four Steps in the Clouds
Fourteen Hours
Frankenstein
Freaks
The French Connection
Freud
Fritz the Cat
From Here to Eternity
From This Day Forward
The Front Page
The Fugitive
Fury

G Men
Gandhi
The Garden of Allah
Gaslight
Gate of Hell
The General
The General Died at Dawn
The General Line
A Generation
Genevieve
Gentleman's Agreement
Gentlemen Prefer Blondes
Georgy Girl
Gerald McBoing Boing
Gervaise
The Ghost Breaker
The Ghost Goes West
The Ghost Train
Gigi
Gilda
The Glenn Miller Story
The Glorious Adventure
The Godfather
Going My Way
The Gold Diggers
The Gold Rush
The Golem
Gone with the Wind
The Good Companions
Goodbye Mr Chips
The Graduate
Grand Hotel
Le Grand Jeu
Grand Prix
La Grande Illusion
The Grapes of Wrath
Grass
The Great Caruso
The Great Dictator
Great Expectations
The Great Gatsby
The Great Impersonation
The Great Race
The Great Train Robbery
The Great Ziegfeld
The Greatest Story Ever Told
Greed
Green Pastures
Gregory's Girl
Greyfriars Bobby
The Group
Guess Who's Coming to Dinner
Gulliver's Travels
Gunfight at the OK Corral
Gunga Din
The Guns of Navarone
Hallelujah
Hamlet
The Hands of Orlac
Harvey
Heaven Can Wait
Heavens Above
The Heiress
Hell's Angels
Hellzapoppin
Henry V
Here Comes Mr Jordan
High Noon
High Sierra
The Hill
Hindle Wakes
Hiroshima Mon Amour
Hobson's Choice
Holiday
Un Homme et une Femme
House of Wax
The House on 92nd Street
How Green was My Valley
How the West was Won
How to Marry a Millionaire
Hud
Hue and Cry
The Hunchback of Notre Dame
The Hustler

I Am a Fugitive from a Chain Gang
I, Claudius
I Love a Mystery
I Married a Witch
Idiot's Delight
If . . .
If I Had a Million
If I Were King
If Winter Comes
I'm All Right Jack
Imitation of Life
In the Heat of the Night
In Which We Serve
The Informer
Inherit the Wind
The Inn of the Sixth Happiness
Intermezzo
Intolerance
Invasion of the Body Snatchers
The Invisible Man
Invitation to the Dance
The Ipcress File
It Always Rains on Sunday
It Happened Here
It Happened One Night
An Italian Straw Hat
It's a Mad Mad Mad Mad World
It's a Wonderful Life
Ivan the Terrible

Jane Eyre
Jaws
The Jazz Singer
Les Jeux Interdits
Jew Süss
Jour de Fête
Le Jour se Lève
Journal d'un Curé de Campagne
Journey into Fear
Journey to the Center of the Earth
Journey's End

Joyless Street
Judex
Judge Priest
Jules et Jim
Jungle Jim
The Jungle Princess
Justice est Faite

Kameradschaft
La Kermesse Héroïque
Key Largo
Kid Galahad
The Killers
The Killing Fields
Kind Hearts and Coronets
A Kind of Loving
King Kong
King of Comedy
King of Jazz
King of Kings
King Solomon's Mines
Kings Row
Kipps
Kismet
Kiss Me Deadly
Kiss Me Kate
Kiss of Death
The Knack
Kramer vs Kramer

The Lady Eve
Lady for a Day
The Lady from Shanghai
Lady in the Dark
The Lady in the Lake
Lady Killer
The Lady Vanishes
The Lady with a Little Dog
The Ladykillers
The Last Chance
The Last Days of Pompeii
The Last Hurrah
The Last Laugh
The Last of the Mohicans
The Last Picture Show
Last Year in Marienbad
Laura
The Lavender Hill Mob
Lawrence of Arabia
Leaves from Satan's Book
The Leopard
The Letter
Letter from an Unknown Woman
Liebelei
The Life and Death of Colonel Blimp
The Life of Emile Zola
Life Upside Down
Lifeboat
Lights of New York
Li'l Abner
Liliom
Limelight
The Lion in Winter
Listen to Britain
Little Caesar
The Little Foxes
Little Lord Fauntleroy
Little Women
Living
The Living Desert
Lola Montez
London Town
The Longest Day
Lord Jim
Lost Horizon
The Lost Patrol
The Lost Weekend
The Lost World
Love Me Tonight
The Love Parade
Love Story
The Loved One
The Lower Depths

M
Macbeth
Madame De
Madame du Barry
Madame X
The Magic Box
The Magnificent Ambersons
Magnificent Obsession
The Magnificent Seven
Major Barbara
The Maltese Falcon
A Man For All Seasons
The Man in Grey
The Man in the Iron Mask
The Man in the White Suit
Man of Aran
The Man Who Came to Dinne
The Man Who Knew Too Muc
The Man with the Golden Arm
Mandy
Manhunt
Marius
The Marriage Circle
La Marseillaise
Marty
Mary Poppins
M*A*S*H
The Mask of Dimitrios
Mata Hari
Matt Helm
A Matter of Life and Death
Mayerling
Meet John Doe
Meet Me in St Louis
The Men
The Merry Widow
Merton of the Movies
Metropolis
Michael Strogoff
Midnight Cowboy
A Midsummer Night's Dream
Le Million
Mine Own Executioner
Miracle in Milan
The Miracle of Morgan's Creek
Miracle on 34th Street
Miranda
Les Misérables
The Misfits
Miss Julie
Mission to Moscow
Mr Blandings Builds His Dream House
Mr Deeds Goes to Town
Mr Smith Goes to Washington
Mrs Miniver
Mrs Wiggs of the Cabbage Patch
Moby Dick
Modern Times
Mondo Cane
Monsieur Beaucaire
Monsieur Hulot's Holiday
The Moon and Sixpence
The Moon is Blue
The More the Merrier
Morgan: A Suitable Case for Treatment
Morning Glory
Morocco
The Most Dangerous Game
Moulin Rouge
Murder on the Orient Express
The Musketeers of Pig Alley
Mutiny on the Bounty
My Darling Clementine
My Fair Lady
My Girl Tisa
My Little Chickadee
My Man Godfrey
My Sister Eileen
The Mystery of the Wax Museum

Naked City
Nana
Nanook of the North
The Navigator
Nell Gwyn
Network
Never Give a Sucker an Even Break
Never on Sunday
Next of Kin
A Night at the Opera
Night Mail

Night Must Fall
The Night of the Demon
The Night of the Hunter
Ninotchka
North by Northwest
Northwest Passage
Nothing But the Truth
Nothing Sacred
The Nun's Story

Objective Burma
Occupe-Toi d'Amélie
October
Odd Man Out
Of Human Bondage
Of Mice and Men
Oh Mr Porter
Oh What a Lovely War
The Old Dark House
Oliver Twist
Los Olvidados
Olympische Spiele
On Approval
On the Beach
On the Town
On the Waterfront
One Flew Over the Cuckoo's Nest
One Hundred and One Dalmatians
One Million BC
One Sunday Afternoon
One Two Three
One Way Passage
Onibaba
Open City
Orphée
Our Daily Bread
The Outlaw
Outward Bound
The Overlanders
The Ox Bow Incident

Paisa
The Pajama Game
The Paleface
Les Parents Terribles
Paris Qui Dort
Une Partie de Campagne
The Passing of the Third Floor Back
Le Passion de Jeanne D'Arc
Passport to Pimlico
Pather Panchali
Paths of Glory
The Pawnbroker
Peg O'My Heart
People on Sunday
The Perils of Pauline
The Petrified Forest
Peyton Place
The Phantom of the Opera
The Philadelphia Story
Picnic
The Picture of Dorian Gray
The Pink Panther
Pinky
The Pirate
A Place in the Sun
The Plainsman
Planet of the Apes
Poil de Carotte
Portrait of Jennie
The Poseidon Adventure
Pride and Prejudice
The Prince and the Pauper
The Prisoner of Zenda
The Private Life of Henry VIII
Private's Progress
Psycho
Public Enemy
The Pumpkin Eater
Pygmalion

Quai des Brumes
Que Viva Mexico
Queen Christina
Queen Kelly
The Queen of Spades
The Quiet Man
Quo Vadis

Raiders of the Lost Ark
Rain
The Rains Came
Ramona
Random Harvest
Rashomon
Rear Window
Rebecca
Rebecca of Sunnybrook Farm
Rebel without a Cause
The Red Badge of Courage
The Red Balloon
Red Dust
Red Garters
The Red Inn
The Red Shoes
La Règle du Jeu
Rembrandt
Repulsion
Richard III
Rififi
Rio Rita
The River
Road to Singapore
The Robe
Robinson Crusoe
Rocco and His Brothers
Rocky
Rome Express
Romeo and Juliet
La Ronde
Rookery Nook
Room at the Top
Room Service
Rope
Rose Marie
Roxie Hart
Ruggles of Red Gap
Ryan's Daughter

Safety Last
San Francisco
Le Sang d'Un Poète
Saturday Night and Sunday Morning
Saturday Night Fever
The Savage Eye
Sawdust and Tinsel
Sayonara
Scaramouche
Scarface
The Scarlet Empress
The Scarlet Letter
The Scarlet Pimpernel
Scarlet Street
Scrooge
The Sea Hawk
The Sea Wolf
The Seashell and the Clergyman
Seven Brides for Seven Brothers
Seven Days in May
Seven Keys to Baldpate
Seven Samurai
Seventh Heaven
The Seventh Seal
The Seventh Veil
Shadow of a Doubt
Shadows
Shane
Shanghai Express
She
She Only Danced One Summer
The Sheik
Ship of Fools
The Shop around the Corner
Shopworn Angel
Showboat
Siegfried
Sing As We Go
The Singing Fool
Singin' in the Rain
Sir Arne's Treasure
Sitting Pretty
A Slight Case of Murder
Smilin' Through
The Snake Pit
Snow White and the Seven Dwarfs

Some Like It Hot
The Song of Bernadette
Song of Ceylon
Sons and Lovers
Sons of the Desert
Sorrell and Son
The Sound of Music
Sous les Toits de Paris
The Southerner
Spellbound
The Spiral Staircase
The Spoilers
Spring in Park Lane
The Spy Who Came in from the Cold
The Squaw Man
Squibs
Stagecoach
Star!
A Star is Born
Star Wars
State Fair
Stella Dallas
The Sting
Storm Over Asia
The Story of Louis Pasteur
Strange Interlude
The Student of Prague
The Student Prince
Sullivan's Travels
Summertime
Sunrise
Sunset Boulevard
The Sunshine Boys
Suspicion
Svengali
Sweet Smell of Success
The Swiss Family Robinson

A Tale of Two Cities
Tales of Hoffman
Tales of Manhattan
Target for Tonight
A Taste of Honey
Taxi Driver
The Ten Commandments
La Terra Trema
Thank Your Lucky Stars
That Hamilton Woman
These Three
They Won't Forget
The Thief of Baghdad
The Thin Man
The Thing from Another World
Things to Come
The Third Man
The Thirty-Nine Steps
This Gun for Hire
Those Magnificent Men in Their Flying Machines
Three Coins in the Fountain
The Three Musketeers
Three Smart Girls
Thunder Rock
Thy Soul Shall Bear Witness
To Be or Not to Be
To Have and Have Not
Tobacco Road
Tokyo Olympiad
Tol'able David
Tom Brown's Schooldays
Tom Jones
Top Hat
Topper
Tower of London
The Towering Inferno
Track of the Cat
Trader Horn
The Trail of the Lonesome Pine
Treasure Island
The Treasure of the Sierra Madre
The Trial
Triumph of the Will
Trouble in Paradise
The Trouble with Harry
The True Glory
The Turn of the Tide
Twelve Angry Men
Twelve O'Clock High
Twenty Thousand Years in Sing Sing
2001: A Space Odyssey

Ugetsu Monogatari
Ulysses
Umberto D
The Umbrellas of Cherbourg
Uncle Tom's Cabin
Under Two Flags
Underworld
Unfaithfully Yours
The Uninvited

Valley of the Dolls
Vampyr
Variety
Victim
Victoria the Great
The Victors
The Virginian
Viridiana
Les Visiteurs du Soir

The Wages of Fear
War and Peace
The War of the Worlds
Warning Shadows
Waterloo Bridge
Waterloo Road
The Way Ahead
Way Down East
The Way to the Stars
West Side Story
Whisky Galore
The Whisperers
Whistling in the Dark
White Cargo
White Heat
White Shadows in the South Seas
Whoopee
Who's Afraid of Virginia Woolf?
The Wild One
Wild Strawberries
Wings
Witchcraft through the Ages
Witness for the Prosecution
The Wizard of Oz
A Woman of Paris
Woman of the Dunes
Woman to Woman
The Women
World of Plenty
Wuthering Heights

A Yank at Oxford
Yankee Doodle Dandy
You Can't Take It with You
Young Mr Lincoln
The Young Ones

'Z'
Zazie dans le Métro
Zéro de Conduite
Ziegfeld Follies
Zorba the Greek

Alphabetical List of Fictional Screen Characters and Series

The following are noted in the main text:

Ali Baba
Arsène Lupin
Arthur
Betty Boop
Black Beauty
Blondie
Bomba the Jungle Boy
Bonzo
Boston Blackie
The Bowery Boys
Bugs Bunny
Bulldog Drummond
Carry On
Casper the Friendly Ghost
Charlie Chan
The Cohens and the Kellys
The Cisco Kid
The Creature from the Black Lagoon
The Crime Doctor
Crime Does Not Pay
Dead End Kids
Dick Tracy
Dr Kildare
Dr Mabuse
Donald Duck
Dracula
Ellery Queen
The Falcon
Fantomas
Flash Gordon
The Fly
Francis
Frankenstein
Fu Manchu
Gerald McBoing Boing
Gertie the Dinosaur
Gidget
Godzilla
Gold Diggers
The Hardy Family
Henry Aldrich
Hopalong Cassidy
Huckleberry Finn
I Love a Mystery
Inner Sanctum
The Invisible Man
Jack the Ripper
James Bond
Joe Palooka
The Jones Family
Jungle Jim
The Kettles
The Keystone Kops
Lassie
The Lone Ranger
The Lone Wolf
Looney Tunes
Maciste
Maigret
Maisie
The March of Time
Matt Helm
Mexican Spitfire
Michael Shayne
Mike Hammer
Mr Magoo
Mr Moto
Mr Wong
The Mummy
Nancy Drew
Nick Carter
Old Mother Riley
Our Gang
Passing Parade
Penrod
Philip Marlowe
Philo Vance
Popeye
Rin Tin Tin
Robin Hood
Robinson Crusoe
The Saint
St Trinian's
Scattergood Baines
Sexton Blake
Sherlock Holmes
Squibs
Superman
Sylvester
Tarzan
The Thin Man
This Modern Age
Tom and Jerry
Tom Sawyer
Torchy Blane
Tugboat Annie
The Whistler
Why We Fight
William
The Wolf Man
Woody Woodpecker
Zorro

Alphabetical List of Themes Explored

Please check these headings in the text for notes on the use of the subjects listed in films past and present, with examples

Abortion
Actor-directors
Actors
Adaptations
Addresses
Advertising
Air balloons
Airplanes
Airships
The Alamo
Alcoholics
All star films
American Revolution
Amnesia
Anachronisms
Ancient Egypt
Angels
Animals
Anti-Semitism
Arabian Nights
Army comedies
Assassination
Authors as actors
Automobiles
Babies
Backstage
Bad language
Ballet
Baseball
Bathtubs
Berlin
The Bible
Big business
Bigamists
Birds
Black comedy
Blacks in films
Blindness
Boffins
Boo-boos
Boxing
The British Empire
Brothels
Bullfights
Burlesque
Buses
Business
Butlers
Cable cars
Cannibalism
Case histories
Casting
The chase
Child stars
Christ
Christmas
Churches
Cinemas
Circuses
Clairvoyance
Coal mines
The Cold War
Colour
Colour sequences
Comedy teams
Comic strips
Communism
Compilation films
Composers
Computers
Concentration camps
Concerts
Confidence tricksters
Courtesans
Courtroom scenes
Crazy comedy
Criminals
Custard pies
Dance bands
Deaf mutes
Death
Dentists
Department stores
Desert islands
Deserts
The Devil
Devil's Island
Directors' appearances
Disguise
Doctors
Documentary
Dreams
Drug addiction
Drunk scenes
Dubbing
Duels
The electric chair
Elephants
The end of the world
Enoch Arden
Entertainers
Epidemics
Episodic films
Eskimos
Excerpts
Explorers
The FBI
Falling
The family
Fans
Fantasy
Farce
Fashions
Films à clef
Fire
Firing squads
Flashbacks
Fog
The Foreign Legion
Forest fires
Funerals
Funfairs
Gambling
Gangsters
Giants
Gigolos
Gimmicks
Governesses
The guillotine
Gypsies
Hands
Helicopters
Hell
Hillbillies
Hollywood on film
Homosexuality
Horror
Horses
Hospitals
Hotels
Houses
Hypnosis
Impresarios
Incest
India
In-jokes
Insanity
Insects
Inventors
Ireland

Jazz
Jewel thieves
Jews
Kidnapping
Kings and Queens
Ku Klux Klan
Labour relations
Leprechauns
Lesbianism
Letters
Lifts (elevators)
Light comedians
Lighthouses
London
Lookalikes
Los Angeles
Lynch law
Mafia
Magicians
Mau Mau
Media
Miniaturization
Mirrors
Missionaries
Monks
Monster animals
Mother love
Motor cycles
Motor racing
Mountains
Multiple roles
Multiple-story films
Murders
Musical remakes
Musicals
Mystery
Narrators
Naval comedy
New York
Numbered sequels
Nuns
Nurses
Nymphomaniacs
Offices
Old age
Opera
Orchestral conductors
Oriental roles
Painters
Paris
Parody
Parties

Pirates
Plastic surgery
Police
Politics
Poverty
Pre-credits sequences
Priests
Prison
Prisoners of war
Private eyes
Prophecy
Prostitutes
Psychology

Radio
Railway stations
Rain
Rape
Red Indians
Reincarnation
Rejuvenation
Religion
Remakes in disguise
Reporters
Robberies
Robots
Romantic teams
Rome

Sailors
San Francisco
Satire
Schooldays
Science fiction
Scientists
Seances
Seaside resorts
Serials
Series
Servants
Sewers
Sex
Sex changes
Ships
Skiing
Slapstick
Small towns
Smoking
Smugglers
Social comedy
Social conscience
Soldiers
Space exploration

Spanish Civil War
Spies
Sportsmen
Staircases
Statesmen
Statues
Storms
Strikes
Student protest
Stunt men
Submarines
Suicide
Swashbucklers
Swinging London
Teachers
Telephones
Television
Television movies
Television series
Tennis
Theatres
3-D
Tinting
Title changes
Torture
Trains
Tramps (hoboes)
Transvestism
Uncredited appearances
Underground railways
Undertakers (morticians)
Underwater scenes
Unemployment
Universities

Venice
Ventriloquists
Vienna
Vietnam War
Vigilantes
Violence
Volcanoes
War heroes
Water
Waxworks
Weddings
Westerns
Wheelchairs
Witchcraft
World War I
Writers
Zombies

Title Changes

The reason for changing any title is to make it more attractive at the box office. Even a famous play or novel may not be the right bait for film fans; so *The Private Ear and the Public Eye* became *The Pad and How to Use It*, *Orpheus Descending* turned into *The Fugitive Kind*, and *The Clansman* emerged as *The Birth of a Nation*. Even when a film has been well publicized during production, the title can be changed at the whim of the producer whenever he feels that what he has on his hands is by no means a one-hundred-per-cent copper-bottomed winner. Some very well-known films were rechristened at the very last moment. *Seven Brides for Seven Brothers* was made as *Sobbin' Women*, and *Three Coins in the Fountain* as *We Believe in Love. The Bad and the Beautiful* was almost released as *Tribute to a Bad Man*, a title which was later used for a different movie. And *I Love Louisa*, which has never in fact been used, was the working title for no fewer than three well-known movies: *Dancing in the Dark, The Band Wagon* and *What a Way to Go*.

Sometimes the new title seems weaker than the original, but decisions of this kind are far from easy, being usually taken at fraught moments. *Dr Goldfoot and the Sex Machine*, for instance, had to be changed because a real Dr Goldfoot protested; so it became *Dr G and the Bikini Machine*. For years British producers had been toying with a rustic love story called *Bats with Baby Faces*, but during production it was finally decided that people would take the film for a horror story, so it became, ill-advisedly, *Sky West and Crooked*; and after a fairly calamitous British release it was changed again for world markets into *Gypsy Girl*. A popular black comedy started production as *My Last Duchess*; this was felt to be too subtle to convey the theme of light-hearted wife murder, so the title became successively, in descending order of wit, *Arrivederci Baby*, *You Just Kill Me*, and *You're Dead Right*; but before release it reverted to *Arrivederci Baby* in most of the world and *See You Later Baby* for the apparently ignorant British. Then at the last minute it was shown to Londoners as *Drop Dead Darling*. Perhaps the most desperate last-minute change happened to *Morituri*, a title which had had world-wide publicity up to and including press shows. Suddenly the chill word came from New York: patrons were staying away from the movie like flies, ninety-nine per cent of them being unable to understand the title, and the few who could considering it less than entertaining to be reminded of their own mortality. So Fox changed the title, in one of the most drastic and expensive publicity actions of recent years; but so as to retain any goodwill they had accumulated for the old title, they incorporated it, with one of the clumsiest results ever perpetrated on the public: *The Saboteur, Code Name Morituri*.

Some other examples of re-thinking during production:

A modernization of *Volpone* began, unpromisingly, as *The Tale of a Fox*, brightened somewhat into *Anyone for Venice?*, and was released as *The Honey Pot*; but after poor business it was shown in the States as *It Comes Up Murder*. The film of Tennessee Williams' *The Milk Train Doesn't Stop Here Any More* was announced at first as *Boom*, then *Goforth*, then *Sunburst*, before *Boom* was finally revived and given the accolade. *A Suitable Case for Treatment*, a title utterly unappealing except to the handful of TV cognoscenti, was personalized into *Morgan*, the name of the leading character – with the old title in small print underneath, presumably for luck.

When AIP began to film H. P. Lovecraft's *The House at the End of the World*, and publicized it under this title, it seemed that we might for once get a fairly subtle horror film. Alas, the treatment was more fitted to the titles under which the film was released: in Britain *Monster of Terror*, in America *Die, Monster, Die*. Then there was a film announced in Britain as *Jules Verne's Rocket to the Moon*, and in the US as *P. T. Barnum's Rocket to the Moon*. Owing to poor business the American title was abandoned and became *Those*

Fantastic Flying Fools; this too was unsuccessful and the distributor finally settled on *Blast-Off*.

Incidentally, the notion of attaching author or director to a film title becomes popular occasionally, as in *Billy Rose's Jumbo*, *Sidney Sheldon's Bloodline*, and *Jacqueline Susann's Once is Not Enough*. They say it lost favour after Joshua Logan tried to have his new film released as *Joshua Logan's Fanny*.

When the Rank Organisation decided some years ago to film Rumer Godden's novel *An Episode of Sparrows*, about children who steal from church to feed starving animals, they made a most pleasing job of it. But John Davis as distributor had not much faith in John Davis as producer, and the film was released under the title *Innocent Sinners*, with a highly dubious publicity campaign which left no doubt that the sin involved was sexual. It is almost pleasing to record that the film failed at the box-office, whereas under its original title, with a tasteful campaign, it would certainly have had reasonable if limited success.

A 1969 ad in *Variety* spoofed this kind of indecision about titling a film; it purported to be a dialogue between Rowan and Martin of *Laugh-In*:

R: Guess what, Dick! MGM have taken a super survey to find a title for our new flick.

M: Well, ring my chimes! I thought it was called *The Strange Case of the* @%!£&?

R: No, dum-dum. That was last week's title. Only 9,673 people favoured it.

M: My aunt loves *Who Killed Cock Robin?*

R: 11,089 people voted for that, but we think your aunt stuffed the ballot box again.

M: My favourite is *The Farquahar Case*. Look that up in your Funk and Wagnalls.

R: It pulled very strong in the mid-west, with 18,909 votes.

M: I'll drink to that. So it's our new title?

R: No. And it's not *One of Our Bippies is Missing* either, even though it got 27,000½ votes.

M: ½? Sounds like one of our producers voted for it. Anyway, what *is* the new title? *The Monster Who Ate Beautiful Downtown Burbank*?

R: The new title is *The Maltese Bippy*. Leo the Lion roared his approval of it . . . and when he roars, you listen!

M: You bet your sweet bippy!

(And what, you may ask, happened to *The Maltese Bippy*? It was so poor that both theatrical and television buyers turned it down.)

Sometimes a film is hauled back and retitled after its first release, as a last trump card when nothing else will save the situation. John Huston's enterprising but ill-fated *Freud* was touted as *The Secret Passion*, or in some cases, even more meaninglessly, as *Freud – The Secret Passion*. (In no guise did it take money.) Billy Wilder's mordant *Ace in the Hole* reached the sticks as *The Big Carnival*. Danny Kaye's stolid-sounding *The Inspector General* was later corrected to *Happy Times* (the title of one of its songs). In America *Mr Topaze* became *I Like Money*, and *The Sea Wall* was shown as *This Angry Age* (a title justified by nothing in the movie). When William Dieterle's superb *All That Money Can Buy* failed to please the multitude, it was variously tried out as *The Devil and Daniel Webster* and *Daniel and the Devil*. A British drama called *The Tall Headlines* was about the effect on a family when its eldest son is hanged for murder. The title was commercially a non-starter, so the film was withdrawn and later revived under the utterly cheating tag *The Frightened Bride*. And a more recent ragbag of sensations which failed as *Our Incredible World* quickly re-emerged as *The Mystery and the Pleasure*.

Novels keep their original titles fairly seldom, being designed to attract a much more specialized public than the film version must command. But there may be other reasons. One presumes that Launder and Gilliat might have kept *That Uncertain Feeling* as the title of their adaptation from Kingsley Amis' book, had it not been for the constant reissues of an old Lubitsch film of the same name and for the more recent releases of similar-sounding films such as *That Certain Feeling* and *This Happy Feeling*. So they thought up a new joke and called it *Only Two Can Play*. A unique reason for not filming one novel under its original title was that the censor forbade it: so notorious in 1932 was William Faulkner's *Sanctuary* that it had to be filmed as *The Story of Temple Drake*. (Thirty years later it was remade under the original title.)

Very often a wily distributor with reissues to sell will alter the titles in the hope of persuading exhibitors that he is offering something new. A classic reissue bill of a few years back, presented as an all-action war show, consisted of two seriously-intentioned films with hardly a battle scene between them: *The Men*, which dealt with the hospital problems of paralysed veterans, became *Battle Stripe*, and *North Star*, Goldwyn's propaganda tribute to the Russian peasants in World War II, was carefully re-edited to avoid any suspicion of communist leanings and emerged as *Armoured Attack*. Another shining example of a publicist having an eye to the main chance dates from 1942, when President Roosevelt was asked to name the base from which US planes had bombed Tokyo. The President, who knew his movies, smiled and said: 'Shangri-La'. Columbia Pictures promptly put out a film called *The Lost Horizon at Shangri-La*, an edited version of their five-year-old classic *Lost Horizon*.

One British purveyor of Continental 'X' attractions hit upon the bright idea of reviving them under their original foreign titles if an English title was previously used – and sometimes vice versa. The advantage of this is that any patron complaining of having paid to see *Le Repos du Guerrier* and getting a second helping of *Warrior's Rest* has only his own ignorance to blame. (The distributors, incidentally, had hoped to issue this particular film under the title *Love on a Pillow*, but the censor wasn't having any.)

Retitling reissues is acknowledged in the trade to be a bit naughty, but Hollywood thinks remakes are fair game. Of course, the title of a really big film is still a strong drawing card when it is remade ten or twenty years later, so presumably *Cimarron* and *Stagecoach* and *The Four Horsemen of the Apocalypse* and *The Prisoner of Zenda* can go on being remade indefinitely under the same titles, but with a change of cast for each generation. It is different with medium-budget pictures which are likely to be forgotten within a year or two: if the plot has a clever twist, why waste it? Brush up the characters, vary the location, think of a fresh title and you have an original movie . . . more or less. Well-known though it is, the basic plot of *The Asphalt Jungle* has been re-used three times by Metro since the original came out in 1950: in *The Badlanders* it had a Western setting, and in *Cairo* an Eastern, while in *Cool Breeze* the orientation was black. *The More the Merrier*, a 1943 comedy, reappeared in 1966 as *Walk, Don't Run*, with Cary Grant replacing Charles Coburn. The first picture to exploit the situation in which a group of assorted people are marooned among savages after a plane crash was (probably) *Five Came Back* in 1939; it was remade as *Back from Eternity* in 1955, and ten years later *Sands of the Kalahari* trod very similar ground except that the savages had become baboons; while *The Flight of the Phoenix* was pretty similar, too, despite its emphasis on rebuilding the plane, and several TV movies including *Lost Flight* and *Valley of Mystery* have got in on the same act. The version of *The Maltese Falcon* which everyone remembers was made in 1941 by John Huston, but Warners had also made talkies of the story in 1932 and 1936, the latter disguised as *Satan Met a Lady*; and Huston himself spoofed the plot in *Beat the Devil* (1954). Warners, in fact, are way ahead in this particular field. The plot of *Kid Galahad*, a successful boxing picture, was remade four years later as *The Wagons Roll at Night*, with the sport changed to lion-taming; *Tiger Shark* was recast and became *Manpower*; while a 1932 gangster movie called *The Mouthpiece* turned up in 1940 as *The Man Who Talked Too Much* and in 1955 as *Illegal*. Raymond Chandler's detective stories *Farewell My Lovely* and *The High Window* (American titles: *Murder My Sweet* and *The Brasher Doubloon*) were filmed straight in the mid-40s, but each had in fact appeared twice before on celluloid, disguised as adventures of The Falcon and Michael Shayne. Four famous films remade as Westerns were *The Sea Wolf, The Petrified Forest, Kiss of Death* and *House of Strangers*; they became *Barricade, Escape in the Desert, The Fiend Who Walked the West* and *Broken Lance*.

It seems fair enough for a famous film to get a new title when music is added: *Pygmalion* can change to *My Fair Lady*, *The Women* to *The Opposite Sex*, *Anna and the King of Siam* to *The King and I*. But was it quite proper to remake *Love Affair* and call it *An Affair To Remember*, *Vessel of Wrath* and call it *The Beachcomber*, *My Favourite Wife* and call it *Move Over Darling*?

If the borrowing is admitted in the credits of the remake, it doesn't seem so much like cheating; but two fairly recent examples are inexcusable. One of Hitchcock's most celebrated thrillers, *Shadow of a Doubt*, was quietly remade by Universal as a second feature known in the US as *Step Down to Terror* and in Britain as *The Silent Stranger*; while anyone watching a Warner second called *Law versus Gangster* might recognize not only the storyline of *White Heat* (49) but most of the action sequences from the original, including long shots of Jimmy Cagney.

The most remade, and disguised, film, is probably the 1932 Cooper-Schoedsack thriller *The Most Dangerous Game*, released in Britain as *The Hounds of Zaroff*. It was remade in 1944 as *Johnny Allegro* (*Hounded* in Britain), and in 1946 as *A Game of Death*. In 1956 it was modernized as *Run for the Sun*; while in the seventies Alan Alda appeared in *To Kill a Clown* and Richard Basehart (for TV) in *Maneater*, both of which were disguised remakes.

There are, of course, cases where a change of title is logical, to avoid having two films of the same name in release. *Gaslight*, Thorold Dickinson's highly-acclaimed Victorian thriller, was released in Britain in 1940. Metro subsequently bought up the negative and released their remake in 1943, as *Gaslight* in the US, but in Britain, to avoid confusion, as *The Murder in Thornton Square*. Later some copies of the original were released in the US under the inexplicable title *Angel Street*. Similarly, the British farce *Sailor Beware* was released in the US as *Panic in the Parlor* to avoid confusion with a Martin and Lewis comedy. Universal's 1964 version of *The Killers* was first intended to be known as *Johnny North*, but the original title was adopted at the last minute; so when the 1947 version was released to TV, it had to be called *A Man Afraid*. And the Marilyn Monroe *Bus Stop* was shown on TV as *The Wrong Kind of Girl* because a TV series was thought to have worn out the welcome of the original title.

The case of *The Children's Hour* is complicated but instructive. When William Wyler first, in 1936, came to film this play about lesbians, the code compelled him to emasculate it, so rather than promise what he couldn't give he changed the title to *These Three*. In 1962 he remade it with full force and kept the original title; but in Britain, where the play was not widely known, *The Children's Hour* was felt not to accord with the film's 'X' certificate, and the picture was released as *The Loudest Whisper*.

The industry has long had its favourite title words, though most of them have no more justification in fact than superstitions. A producer is still encouraged by front office to call his film *The Big* this or *The Great* that, despite the fact that hundreds of others have done so before him and that even these trusted crowd-pulling epithets are subject to the law of diminishing returns. During the 30s, *Murder* and *Death* were surprisingly well thought of, and later we had epidemics of *Naked, Man, Woman, Girl, Lady, Violent, High, Long, Night, Song, Teenage, Party, Thunder, Beach* and *Spy*. (The most evocative Christian name, it seems, is *Johnny*, which during the last twenty years or so has been the word preceding such diverse title epithets as *Allegro, Angel, Belinda, O'Clock, Cool, Concho, Dark, Frenchman, Guitar, Holiday, In the Clouds, One-Eye, Rocco, Stool Pigeon, Tremain*, and *Trouble*.)

During the fifties and sixties the industry apparently found *Operation* to be a most useful ingredient of a title, almost a cure-all. You could tack it on to almost anything and come up with something appealing to the masses, as in *Operation Murder*, *Operation Bikini, Operation Eichmann, Operation Snatch, Operation Mad Ball, Operation Pacific, Operation Amsterdam, Operation Petticoat*. At the height of Sean Connery's sudden world-wide popularity, an old British service comedy called *On the Fiddle*, in which he appeared as a gormless private, was dusted off for the American market as *Operation SNAFU* and did big business. (SNAFU is an American army term which can be bowdlerized as 'situation normal, all fouled up'.) And when Cary Grant's comedy *Father Goose* did less than was expected at the box-office, the posters were redesigned to make the title look like *Operation Father Goose*. So imagine the shock MGM had when its all-star spy thriller *Operation Crossbow* failed to reach the box-office heights, and market research insisted that the title was to blame. 'It sounds like Robin Hood' was the cry from the Mid-West. A change was obviously in order, and what did the picture end up as? *The Great Spy Mission*. You can't beat subtlety.

There are unfavourite words too. Wherever films are bought and sold it has long been whispered that there can be no hope of box-office success when the title contains the word *Miracle*. Instances cited include *The Miracle of Morgan's Creek, The Modern Miracle, The Miracle Worker, Miracle in Milan, The Miracle of Fatima, The Miracle of the Bells, Miracle in the Rain,* and *The Miracle* itself. It isn't surprising that such films are sometimes retitled, but the odd thing is that the alternatives are so unappealing. The delightful *Miracle on 34th Street*, for instance, went out dolefully to Britishers as *The Big Heart, A Miracle Can Happen* became *On Our Merry Way, Miracle of the White Stallions* changed to *Flight of the White Stallions* (but still did no business).

Another highly suspect word in Britain is *Experiment*, despite the success of Quatermass; indeed there seems little reason for this phobia, but *Experiment in Terror* was changed to *The Grip of Fear* on account of it, and it is true that little trade was drummed up by *Experiment Perilous*, *Experiment Alcatraz* or *Experiment in Evil*.

Titles are often used again to cover plots quite different from the original. Since 1942, for instance, there have been three films and two TV movies called *Nightmare*, none of them in any way connected; indeed, one was a remake of another film called *Fear in the Night*, while a second owed more than a little of its plot to *The Thirty-nine Steps*. When *Monkey Business* appeared in 1951, it was a Cary Grant comedy about rejuvenation, not a remake of the Marx Brothers extravaganza released in 1931; but the latter movie, then being revived, was withdrawn by arrangement between the two renters concerned so that it should not harm the business of the new arrival.

By far the majority of title switches are in fact sea changes. When the title has to be translated into another language, it can be affected by anything from local idioms to national characteristics, and the often weird results are beyond the comfortable scope of these notes. But simple transatlantic changes, in the same language, between Great Britain and the US, are a study in themselves, and can offer a surprising amount of insight into national psychology (the list following this essay is pretty comprehensive).

Taking the eastward direction first, it is accepted that Hollywood gained its early stranglehold on British audiences because the audiences liked what they saw and clamoured for more. Yet to this day there are many facets of the American way of life which British renters think their customers won't stomach. Obviously, the names of American politicians, sportsmen and less familiar entertainers will be the first to go, with such transitions as *Tennessee Johnson* to *The Man on America's Conscience*, *Jim Thorpe, All-American* to *Man of Bronze*, *Abe Lincoln in Illinois* to *Spirit of the People*, and *The Bob Mathias Story* to *The Flaming Torch*.

Even the devil has a different nickname in the US, so *Alias Nick Beal* had to become *The Contact Man* (and the film lost some of its point).

Of course there are hundreds of American phrases and allusions incomprehensible to British ears. Some of the changes occasioned by that particular difficulty were *Buck Privates* to *Rookies*, *The Petty Girl* (in northern Britain a 'petty' is a lavatory) to *Girl of the Year*, *Hallelujah I'm a Bum* ('bum' in Britain is a vulgarism for backside) to *Hallelujah I'm a Tramp*, *A Girl, a Guy and a Gob* to *The Navy Steps Out*, and *Eight on the Lam* to *Eight on the Run*.

In 1951 a film called *The Enforcer* (which has no British equivalent) was translated as *Murder Inc*. This caused some confusion when a second film called *Murder Inc* came along a few years later, and even more when Clint Eastwood appeared in *The Enforcer* with a different plot.

Even American place-names are thought by British renters to be off-putting – despite the success of films like *Arizona, Texas, Union Pacific, In Old Oklahoma*, and hundreds of others. Anyway, a few examples: *The Doolins of Oklahoma* changed to *The Great Manhunt*, *Chicago Masquerade* to *Little Egypt*, *Kansas City Confidential* to *The Secret Four*, and *The Hawaiians* to *Master of the Islands*.

Even folksy humour as evidenced by *Aaron Slick from Punkin Creek*, or by *Curtain Call at Cactus Crick*, is thought to be impermissible. These two films came through, respectively, as *Marshmallow Moon* and *Take the Stage*.

The British are also very dubious of propaganda, or anything that smacks of old-fashioned Yankee jingoism. It just has to be put down, as follows: *America, America* to *The Anatolian Smile* (the thought processes involved here are beyond guesswork), *First Yank into Tokyo* to *Hidden Secret/Mask of Fury*, *The Magnificent Yankee* to *The Man with Thirty Sons* (the joke couldn't be intentional, one supposes), and *An American Dream* to *See You in Hell, Darling*.

How Britishers ever let *Yankee Doodle Dandy* through, I just don't know. But quotations from American patriotic songs are obviously OK as the British won't know the context: the fact that such titles as *Halls of Montezuma*, *To the Shores of Tripoli* and *So Proudly We Hail* are meaningless to them is apparently of no importance.

Sometimes there are censorship reasons, obvious or not, why an American title just won't do in Britain. Take *BF's Daughter*, for instance; although the title of a John Marquand novel, it had to become *Polly Fulton* in Britain, where a BF is a bloody fool. The monarchy must be protected, so *The Royal Bed* became *The Queen's Husband* and *Royal Wedding* turned into *Wedding Bells*. *A Royal Scandal* was obviously unthinkable: it turned up as *Czarina*. Religion sets similar problems: *The Man Who Played God*, in case anyone got the same idea, became *The Silent Voice*. *Damn Yankees*, being both offensive *and* over-American, was changed to *What Lola Wants*, and quickly sank without trace.

Suggestions of sex must obviously be toned down for strait-laced Britishers, in the golden age, at least, which saw such changes as *Vice Squad* to *The Girl in Room 17*, *I Was a Male War Bride* to *You Can't Sleep Here*, and *Professional Sweetheart* to *Imaginary Sweetheart*. Yet by the sixties *Any Wednesday* could show as *Bachelor Girl Apartment*.

Excess of any kind seems to scare British renters. When the gangster films of the early 30s were causing a press storm, the obvious solution was to tone down not the films but the titles. Who could object to *Public Enemy* when it became *Enemies of the Public*? This devious change technically made the public, not the gangster, into the hero. *The Hatchet Man* became *The Honourable Mr Wong*, *I am a Fugitive from a Chain Gang* lost its last four words, *Scarface* was subtitled *The Shame of a Nation*. Weirdest of all (it must have had a very adaptable plot-line), *Public Enemy's Wife* became *G-Man's Wife*.

Much later, *Confessions of an Opium Eater* became *Evils of Chinatown*, *Son of Slade* (a very violent Western) became *Texas Rose*, *The Bottom of the Bottle* became *Beyond the River*, *The Violent Men* became *Rough Company*, and *Scandal Sheet* became *The Dark Page*. Even *The Killer That Stalked New York*, in which the killer was smallpox, became *Frightened City*; and a moving little drama called *The Judge Steps Out* was shown as *Indian Summer* (a British judge 'stepping out' was apparently unthinkable).

At least on one occasion the British were less sensitive than their American cousins. Agatha Christie's murder puzzle *Ten Little Niggers* was filmed by René Clair in 1945 – in America, where the title could not be used. The nursery rhyme was rewritten, and the picture became *Ten Little Indians*. This brought more protests from the minority groups, so it was released as *And Then There Were None*. But Britons staunchly saw it under the original title, despite the fact that the china figures were plainly Indians, and only Indians were mentioned in the dialogue. The sixties remake settled firmly on Indians all round, which made it less puzzling.

When two versions of a film exist, and both are sold to TV, the earlier one is sometimes given a different title. Thus you may come across something called *Forbidden Alliance* which turns out to be the Laughton version of *The Barretts of Wimpole Street*; similarly *Flight Commander* is the 1930 *Dawn Patrol*, *Tops is the Limit* is the Bing Crosby *Anything Goes*, and *Oriental Dream* is the Ronald Colman *Kismet*.

British renters seem convinced that no audience can see a joke in a title. This often deprives we Britishers of a choice morsel of wit. Not, I grant you, in *Who Killed Doc Robbin?* (shown as *Sinister House*) or *Callaway Went Thataway* (shown as *The Star Said No*). But surely we might have kept *State of the Union* rather than *The World and His Wife*, *The Desk Set* instead of *His Other Woman*, *Advance to the Rear* instead of *Company of Cowards*, *Take a Letter Darling* and not *Green-Eyed Woman*? I might have gone to see something called *The Bar Sinister*, but not *It's a Dog's Life*. And how dull for *I Can Get It For You Wholesale* (now on TV as *Only the Best*!) to be shown as *This Is My Affair* – especially as the latter is the rejected American title of a Robert Taylor movie shown in Britain as *His Affair*. (Got that?)

Indeed, when all allowances have been made, some title changes must remain inexplicable. It isn't surprising that Universal, having filmed J. M. Barrie's *Alice Sit by the Fire*, should feel like changing the title. But why, for America, did they settle on *Darling How Could You*, and for Britain, *Rendezvous*? One agrees with the British distributor that *Requiem for a Heavyweight* won't break any box-office records. But then, nor will *Blood Money*. Why did the concise *Edge of the City* revert in Britain to the title of its original story, *A Man Is Ten Feet Tall*? And at a time when Alan Ladd and others were doing very nicely with one-word titles like *Saigon*, *Calcutta*, *China* and *Santiago*, why was *Malaya* shown in Britain as *East of the Rising Sun* (which is geographically inaccurate of Malaya anyway)?

In particular, since horror films always keep their market, which is based on an appetite for excess, why the following attempts to tone down the bogeymen? *Frankenstein Versus the Space Monster* became *Duel of the Space Monsters*; *Blood of Dracula* became *Blood is My Heritage*, *The Astounding She-Monster* became *Mysterious Invader*, and *The Corpse Vanishes* became *The Case of the Missing Brides*.

It is rare for British renters deliberately to toughen up American titles. But it happened to *A Woman's Devotion* which became *War Shock*, to *Dino* (*Killer Dino*), and to *No Place To Land* (*Man Mad*). There were also two occasions when Hollywood chose British adventure themes but did them so badly that they had to be disguised: *Royal African Rifles* became *Storm Over Africa*, and *El Alamein* was released as *Desert Patrol*. The prize for falsification should probably go to the witch-hunting *I Married a Communist*, which RKO played in Britain as *The Woman on Pier 13* – a title 'justified' by an incident at the very end of the picture.

The westward traffic to America seems to keep relatively few British titles intact, the reasons for change being usually to stress the concrete rather than the allusive and action rather than subtlety, in other words to suggest excitements of the kind not provided by the picture. Consider the following examples in which sex has been made to rear its head: *Summer of the Seventeenth Doll* became *Season of Passion*, *The Romantic Age* became *Naughty Arlette*, *Who Goes There?* became *The Passionate Sentry*, *Love Story* became *A Lady Surrenders*, and *The Weak and the Wicked* became *Young and Willing*.

A general toughening process is evident in such changes as: *The Informers* (formerly *The Snout*) to *Underworld Informers*, *HMS Defiant* to *Damn the Defiant*, *Time Bomb* to *Terror on a Train*, *Serious Charge* to *A Touch of Hell*, and *The Late Edwina Black* to *Obsessed*.

More particularly, observe from the following changes how unacceptable are quotations and allusions, which are invariably replaced by something unmistakably personal, full of the promise of action: *Dangerous Moonlight* to *Suicide Squadron*, *Ill Met By Moonlight* to *Night*

Ambush, *A Terrible Beauty* to *Night Fighters*, *Cry the Beloved Country* to *African Fury*, and *The First of the Few* to *Spitfire*.

It appears that America does not take to any title formed by a character's name: not, at least, if it's a British character, so *Father Brown* changed to *The Detective* and *Albert RN* to *Break for Freedom*. It seems too that when the British go in for horror they are a shade too reticent about it, which accounts for *The Quatermass Experiment* being changed to *The Creeping Unknown*, *City of the Dead* to *Horror Hotel* and *Fanatic* to *Die, Die, My Darling*.

Fashion has a lot to do with title changes. The spy vogue, for instance, produced such amendments as *The Intelligence Men* to *Spylarks* and *Licensed to Kill* to *The Second Best Secret Agent in the Whole Wide World*. But then it seems spies were just as popular way back in 1939, when a Rex Harrison comedy called *Ten Days in Paris* turned up in the US as *Spy in the Pantry*.

Sometimes American distributors of British films have the excuse of unintelligibility for their title changes. It was reasonable enough that *The Chiltern Hundreds* (pretty unintelligible to most Britons, too) should become *The Amazing Mr Beecham*, and that *The Card* should be translated as *The Promoter*. Similarly *The Guinea Pig* means less to an American audience than *The Outsider*. *The Battle of the River Plate* is how we remember the famous naval action of 1939; but to an American audience *Pursuit of the Graf Spee* pinpoints it better as well as being more actionful. And *I Live in Grosvenor Square* just might perplex mid-westerners, who can immediately grasp *A Yank in London*.

There are some words which the American code will not, or would not, allow. *Fanny by Gaslight*, having possibilities of *double entendre*, must change to *Man of Evil*; *The Rake's Progress*, Hogarth or not, emerges as *Notorious Gentleman*, and *The Passionate Friends* as *One Woman's Story*. The celebrated stand of the Hays Office to the effect that the word 'behind' is impermissible unless immediately followed by a noun, does not alas appear to have affected any British titles. (Under this ruling, a certain well-known poem would have to begin: 'If winter comes, can spring be far in back of?')

Ealing's group of Scottish comedies survived the Atlantic crossing quite pleasingly: *Whisky Galore* changed to *Tight Little Island*, *Rockets Galore* to *Mad Little Island*, and *The Maggie* to *High and Dry*. But it would be interesting to hear, in view of the honourable box-office history of Stevenson's schizophrenic doctor, why *The Two Faces of Dr Jekyll* was changed to *House of Fright*. Even less understandable is the change of the British *Give Us This Day*, taken from a story called *Christ in Concrete*. One can sympathize with the distributor's reluctance to use either of these alternatives, but what he finally hit on, *Salt to the Devil*, is equally unlikely to have sold any tickets. And why did *I Was Happy Here* become *Time Lost and Time Remembered*?

A curious thing happened when the sombre historical romance *Saraband for Dead Lovers* crossed the water. One might reasonably have expected something more punchy, less downbeat; instead it was simply shortened to *Saraband*. Oddlier and oddlier, *Tomorrow We Live* was released in the States as *At Dawn We Die*.

Let me conclude with three personal favourites. Whoever rechristened the story of deaf little *Mandy* as *The Crash of Silence* surely deserves some kind of prize. The runner-up, perhaps, is the gentleman who discarded *The Woman with No Name* in favour of *Her Panelled Door*. And a special award for topicality. That mild theatrical comedy *The Amorous Prawn* would not normally have expected much American exposure. But its plot line made it possible to play it very profitably in the States, just after a certain well-reported British scandal of the sixties, as *The Playgirl and the War Minister*.

[Reprinted from the fourth edition]

British/American Alternative Titles (extended 1983)

This list is in two parts: the first gives alphabetically those American titles which have been changed in Britain, with the changed title opposite; the second list shows British titles which were changed in America. The reasons for many changes should be sufficiently obvious to provide some amusement.

American to British

Aaron Slick from Punkin Crick	Marshmallow Moon
Abbott and Costello Meet Frankenstein	Abbott and Costello Meet the Ghosts
Abe Lincoln in Illinois	Spirit of the People
Advance to the Rear	Company of Cowards
Adventure in Baltimore	Bachelor Bait
Adventure in Washington	Female Correspondent
Adventures of Don Juan	The New Adventures of Don Juan
Alias Nick Beal	The Contact Man
All American	The Winning Way
Alleghany Uprising	The First Rebel
All Mine to Give	The Day They Gave Babies Away
The Alpha Caper (TV)	Inside Job
America	Love and Sacrifice
America, America	The Anatolian Smile
An American Dream	See You in Hell, Darling
American Empire	My Son Alone
An American Guerrilla in the Philippines	I Shall Return
And Then There Were None	Ten Little Niggers
Angels in the Outfield	Angels and the Pirates
The Animal Kingdom	The Woman in His House
An Annapolis Story	The Blue and the Gold
Any Wednesday	Bachelor Girl Apartment
Anzio	The Battle for Anzio
The Ape Man	Lock Your Doors
The Appaloosa	Southwest to Sonora
Appointment with a Shadow	The Big Story
Artists and Models Abroad	Stranded in Paris
The Astounding She-Monster	Mysterious Invader
At Sword's Point	Sons of the Musketeers
Attack of the Giant Leeches	Demons of the Swamp
The Bachelor and the Bobbysoxer	Bachelor Knight
The Bachelor's Daughters	Bachelor Girls
The Bad Man	Two Gun Cupid
Badman's Country	Badman's Territory
The Bank Dick	The Bank Detective
The Bar Sinister	It's a Dog's Life
Battle at Bloody Beach	Battle on the Beach
Bela Lugosi Meets a Brooklyn Gorilla	The Monster Meets the Gorilla
Bend of the River	Where the River Bends
Bengal Brigade	Bengal Rifles
BF's Daughter	Polly Fulton
The Big Boodle	Night in Havana
Big Hand for a Little Lady	Big Deal at Dodge City
The Big Land	Stampeded
The Birdmen (TV)	Escape of the Birdmen

The Black Book	Reign of Terror
The Black Cat (1934)	House of Doom
Blonde Crazy	Larceny Lane
Blood of Dracula	Blood is My Heritage
Blue Denim	Blue Jeans
The Bob Matthias Story	The Flaming Torch
Bombers B-52	No Sleep till Dawn
Born to Kill	Lady of Deceit
The Bottom of the Bottle	Beyond the River
The Brasher Doubloon	The High Window
Bright Victory	Lights Out
Broadway Bill	Strictly Confidential
Broadway Limited	The Baby Vanishes
Buck Privates	Rookies
Buck Privates Come Home	Rookies Come Home
Buckskin Frontier	The Iron Road
Cactus in the Snow	You Can't Have Everything
Callaway Went Thataway	The Star Said No
Cannonball	Carquake
Caper of the Golden Bulls	Carnival of Thieves
Captain Carey USA	After Midnight
Captain John Smith and Pocahontas	Burning Arrows
Captain Pirate	Captain Blood, Fugitive
The Caretakers	Borderlines
Castle on the Hudson	Years without Days
The Catered Affair	Wedding Breakfast
Cattle King	Guns of Wyoming
The Chairman	The Most Dangerous Man in the World
Chief Crazy Horse	Valley of Fury
The Children's Hour	The Loudest Whisper
Christmas in Connecticut	Indiscretion
Circus World	The Magnificent Showman
City Beneath the Sea	One Hour to Doomsday
Claudelle Inglish	Young and Eager
The Clock	Under the Clock
The Cockeyed Miracle	Mr Griggs Returns
Colonel Effingham's Raid	Man of the Hour
The Concorde: Airport '79	Airport '80: The Concorde
Confessions of an Opium Eater	Evils of Chinatown
A Connecticut Yankee in King Arthur's Court	A Yankee in King Arthur's Court
Conquest	Marie Walewska
Convicts Four	Reprieve
The Corpse Vanishes	The Case of the Missing Brides
The Corrupt Ones	The Peking Medallion
Corvette K225	The Nelson Touch
Corvette Summer	The Hot One
Count the Hours	Every Minute Counts
The Court Martial of Billy Mitchell	One Man Mutiny
Crime Wave	The City is Dark
Cry Uncle	Super Dick
Curtain Call at Cactus Crick	Take the Stage
Cynthia	The Rich Full Life
Damn Yankees	What Lola Wants
Dawn of the Dead	Zombies
Dancing Co-Ed	Every Other Inch a Lady
Darby's Rangers	The Young Invaders
Dark Delusion	Cynthia's Secret
Darling How Could You?	Rendezvous

Dead Ringer	Dead Image
Deadline USA	Deadline
Dementia 13	The Haunted and the Hunted
The Desert Fox	Rommel – Desert Fox
Desk Set	His Other Woman
Dial 1119	The Violent Hour
Dino	Killer Dino
A Dispatch from Reuters	This Man Reuter
Doll Face	Come Back to Me
Dollars ($)	The Heist
The Domino Principle	The Domino Killings
The Doolins of Oklahoma	The Great Manhunt
Dracula vs Frankenstein	Blood of Frankenstein
Dragstrip Riot	The Reckless Age
Dressed to Kill	Sherlock Holmes and the Secret Code
Duck, You Sucker	A Fistful of Dynamite
Eaten Alive	Death Trap
Edge of Doom	Stronger than Fear
Edge of the City	A Man is Ten Feet Tall
Eight on the Lam	Eight on the Run
El Alamein	Desert Patrol
The Enforcer	Murder Inc.
Experiment in Terror	The Grip of Fear
Eye Witness (1981)	The Janitor
The Falcon Takes Over	The Gay Falcon
The Fan	Lady Windermere's Fan
Fer de Lance (TV)	Death Dive
The Fearless Vampire Killers	Dance of the Vampires
Fighting Back (1982)	Death Vengeance
Fire Over Africa	Malaga
The First Time	You Don't Need Pajamas at Rosie's
First Yank into Tokyo	Hidden Secret/Mask of Fury
Five and Ten	Daughter of Luxury
Flap	The Last Warrior
Flat Top	Eagles of the Fleet
The Flim Flam Man	One Born Every Minute
Fool's Parade	Dynamite Man from Glory Jail
The Fortune Cookie	Meet Whiplash Willie
Four Faces West	They Passed This Way
Framed	Paula
Frankenstein Meets the Space Monsters	Duel of the Space Monsters
The Freshman	College Days
From Hell to Texas	Man Hunt
From the Mixed-Up Files of Mrs Basil E. Frankweiler	The Hideaways
Frontier Gal	The Bride Wasn't Willing
The Fuller Brush Girl	The Affairs of Sally
The Fuller Brush Man	The Mad Mr Jones
Gaily, Gaily	Chicago, Chicago
The Gang's All Here	The Girls He Left Behind
Gaslight	The Murder in Thornton Square
The Gene Krupa Story	Drum Crazy
Generation	A Time for Giving
The George Raft Story	Spin of a Coin
Ghosts on the Loose	Ghosts in the Night
A Girl, a Guy and a Gob	The Navy Steps Out
The Girl from Missouri	One Hundred Per Cent Pure

The Girl in White	So Bright the Flame
Girls in the Night	Life After Dark
Glory Boy	My Old Man's Place
Gobs and Gals	Cruising Casanovas
Go into Your Dance	Casino de Paree
Great Guy	Pluck of the Irish
The Great John L	A Man Called Sullivan
The Great McGinty	Down Went McGinty
The Green Promise	Raging Waters
Griffin and Phoenix (TV)	Today Is Forever (theatrical)
Gunfighters	The Assassin
Hallelujah I'm a Bum	Hallelujah I'm a Tramp
Hard Times	The Streetfighter
The Hard-Boiled Canary	Hearts in Springtime
Hardcore	The Hardcore Life
Harem Scarem	Harem Holiday
Harper	The Moving Target
The Hatchet Man	The Honourable Mr Wong
The Hawaiians	Master of the Islands
Hearts of the West	Hollywood Cowboy
The Heat's On	Tropicana
The Helen Morgan Story	Both Ends of the Candle
The Hideous Sun Demon	Blood on His Lips
The Hills of Home	Master of Lassie
Hold That Co-Ed	Hold That Gal
Honeymoon	Two Men and a Girl
The Hot Rock	How to Steal a Diamond in Four Uneasy Lessons
Hot Rod Gang	Fury Unleashed
House of Horrors	Joan Medford Is Missing
The House of Usher	The Fall of the House of Usher
The Howards of Virginia	The Tree of Liberty
I Am a Fugitive from a Chain Gang	I Am a Fugitive
I Can Get It for You Wholesale	This Is My Affair
I Dood It	By Hook or by Crook
I Jane Doe	Diary of a Bride
I Married a Communist	The Woman on Pier 13
I, Mobster	The Mobster
I Wake Up Screaming	Hot Spot
I Was a Male War Bride	You Can't Sleep Here
Icecapades Revue	Rhythm Hits the Ice
Iceland	Katina
I'll Never Forget You	The House on the Square
The Imperfect Lady	Mrs Loring's Secret
Indianapolis Speedway	Devils on Wheels
Indiscretion of an American Wife	Indiscretion
Intermezzo	Escape to Happiness
Internes Can't Take Money	You Can't Take Money
It Ain't Hay	Money from Home
It's In the Bag	The Fifth Chair
I've Always Loved You	Concerto
Jim Thorpe, All-American	Man of Bronze
Joan of the Ozarks	The Queen of Spies
Joe Smith – American	Highway to Freedom
Johnny Come Lately	Johnny Vagabond
The Judge Steps Out	Indian Summer
Kansas City Confidential	The Secret Four

The Killer That Stalked New York	Frightened City
King of the Roaring Twenties	The Big Bankroll
Kiss the Blood off My Hands	Blood on My Hands
The Lady and the Bandit	Dick Turpin's Ride
Lady from Boston	Pardon My French
Lady of Burlesque	Striptease Lady
Lafayette Escadrille	Hell Bent for Glory
The Land We Love	Hero's Island
The Last Challenge	Pistolero of Red River
Last of the Comanches	The Sabre and the Arrow
The Laughing Policeman	An Investigation of Murder
The Lawless	The Dividing Line
Leathernecking	Present Arms
Let 'Em Have It	False Faces
Lilac Time	Love Never Dies
Little Big Horn	The Fighting Seventh
Little Egypt	Chicago Masquerade
The Little Giant	On the Carpet
The Little Horse Thieves	Escape from the Dark
London after Midnight	The Hypnotist
The Longest Yard	The Mean Machine
Lord Jeff	The Boy from Barnardo's
Love from a Stranger (1946)	A Stranger Walked In
Love Is a Ball	All This and Money Too
Love Is Better Than Ever	The Light Fantastic
A Lovely Way to Die	A Lovely Way to Go
Lured	Personal Column
The McConnell Story	Tiger in the Sky
The Mad Doctor	A Date with Destiny
Mad Love	The Hands of Orlac
The Magnificent Matador	The Brave and the Beautiful
The Magnificent Yankee	The Man with Thirty Sons
Mail Order Bride	West of Montana
Malaya	East of the Rising Sun
Man in the Shadow	Pay the Devil
Man Made Monster	The Electric Man
Man on a String	Confessions of a Counterspy
The Man Who Played God	The Silent Voice
The Man with Nine Lives	Behind the Door
The Man with the Gun	The Trouble Shooter
Manfish	Calypso
Meet Me in Las Vegas	Viva Las Vegas
Midas Run	A Run on Gold
The Midnight Story	Appointment with a Shadow
Midway	Battle of Midway
Million Dollar Mermaid	The One Piece Bathing Suit
Miracle of the White Stallions	Flight of the White Stallions
Miracle on 34th Street	The Big Heart
Miss Grant Takes Richmond	Innocence Is Bliss
Mission over Korea	Eyes of the Skies
Mister Buddwing	Woman without a Face
Mr Imperium	You Belong to My Heart
Mr Winkle Goes to War	Arms and the Woman
The Mob	Remember that Face
Models Inc.	That Kind of Girl
The Most Dangerous Game	The Hounds of Zaroff
Mother Is a Freshman	Mother Knows Best
Murder My Sweet	Farewell My Lovely

Navy Wife	Mother, Sir
Never Give a Sucker an Even Break	What a Man
Never Wave at a WAC	The Private Wore Skirts
The New Centurions	Precinct 45 – Los Angeles Police
A Nice Little Bank That Should Be Robbed	How to Rob a Bank
Night Monster	House of Mystery
The Night They Raided Minsky's	The Night They Invented Striptease
No Man Is an Island	Island Rescue
No Place to Land	Man Mad
The North Avenue Irregulars	Hill's Angels
Northwest Outpost	End of the Rainbow
Off Limits	Military Policemen
Okay America	Penalty of Fame
One Million Years BC	Man and His Mate
Only When I Laugh	It Hurts Only When I Laugh
The Other Side of the Mountain	Window in the Sky
Our Daily Bread	The Miracle of Life
Out of the Past	Build My Gallows High
The Outcast	The Fortune Hunter
Pardon Us	Jailbirds
Paris After Dark	The Night Is Ending
Paris Underground	Madame Pimpernel
Part Two: Walking Tall	Legend of the Lawman
Paula	The Silent Voice
The Perfect Furlough	Strictly for Pleasure
Perfect Strangers	Too Dangerous to Love
Personal Property	The Man in Possession
The Petty Girl	Girl of the Year
Pick-Up on 101	Echoes of the Road
Pillars of the Sky	The Tomahawk and the Cross
PJ	New Face in Hell
Platinum High School	Rich, Young and Deadly
Pony Soldier	MacDonald of the Canadian Mounties
The Poppy Is Also a Flower	Danger Grows Wild
Pot O'Gold	The Golden Hour
The Powers Girl	Hello Beautiful
The President Vanishes	The Strange Conspiracy
Pride of the Marines	Forever in Love
Private Number	Secret Interlude
Professional Sweetheart	Imaginary Sweetheart
Public Enemy	Enemies of the Public
Public Enemy's Wife	G-Man's Wife
Purple Heart Diary	No Time for Tears
The Racers	Such Men Are Dangerous
Raton Pass	Canyon Pass
Report to the Commissioner	Operation Undercover
Requiem for a Heavyweight	Blood Money
The Return of Dracula	The Fantastic Disappearing Man
Return of Monte Cristo	Monte Cristo's Revenge
Return to Macon County	Highway Girl
Revenge of the Colossal Man	The Terror Strikes
Revenge of the Zombies	The Corpse Vanished
Riding High (1943)	Melody Inn
Roger Touhy Gangster	The Last Gangster
Romance on the High Seas	It's Magic
Royal African Rifles	Storm Over Africa
The Royal Bed	The Queen's Husband

A Royal Scandal	Czarina
Royal Wedding	Wedding Bells
Saskatchewan	O'Rourke of the Royal Mounted
Satan Never Sleeps	The Devil Never Sleeps
Saturday's Hero	Idols in the Dust
Savage Wilderness	The Last Frontier
Scandal Sheet	The Dark Page
Scudda Hoo Scudda Hay	Summer Lightning
The Sea Gypsies	Shipwreck
The Second Woman	Ellen
The Senator Was Indiscreet	Mr Ashton Was Indiscreet
She Couldn't Say No	Beautiful but Dangerous
She Wolf of London	The Curse of the Allenbys
Silver City	High Vermilion
Smash-Up	A Woman Destroyed
S.N.A.F.U.	Welcome Home
So Goes My Love	A Genius in the Family
So This Is Love	The Grace Moore Story
Sob Sister	The Blonde Reporter
Sol Madrid	The Heroin Gang
Something for Everyone	Black Flowers for the Bride
Sometimes a Great Notion	Never Give an Inch
Sons of the Desert	Fraternally Yours
Sorcerer	Wages of Fear
Sorority Girl	The Bad One
Sorority House	The Girl from College
South of Tahiti	White Savage
South Sea Sinner	East of Java
A Southern Yankee	My Hero
Southwest Passage	Camels West
Spinout	California Holiday
Stage to Tucson	Lost Stage Valley
Stars and Stripes Forever	Marching Along
State of the Union	The World and His Wife
Step down to Terror	The Silent Stranger
The Sterile Cuckoo	Pookie
The Story of Seabiscuit	Pride of Kentucky
The Story of Alexander Graham Bell	The Modern Miracle
Strange Interlude	Strange Interval
The Strange One	End as a Man
The Stripper	Woman of Summer
Summer Stock	If You Feel Like Singing
Summertime	Summer Madness
The Sundowners (1950)	Thunder in the Dust
Susan and God	The Gay Mrs Trexel
Swamp Water	The Man Who Came Back
Swashbuckler	The Scarlet Buccaneer
Swing Shift Maisie	The Girl in Overalls
Symphony of Six Million	Melody of Life
Synanon	Get off My Back
Take a Letter, Darling	Green Eyed Woman
Take Me Out to the Ball Game	Everybody's Cheering
Tammy and the Bachelor	Tammy
Tank Commandos	Tank Commando
Tarzan's Peril	Tarzan and the Jungle Queen
Teenage Caveman	Out of the Darkness
Teenagers from Outer Space	The Gargon Terror
Tennessee Johnson	The Man on America's Conscience

Terror from the Year 5000	Cage of Doom
Texas Rose	The Return of Jack Slade
That Forsyte Woman	The Forsyte Saga
That Hamilton Woman	Lady Hamilton
That Hunter Girl	Bride by Mistake
That's My Man	Will Tomorrow Ever Come?
They Shall Have Music	Melody of Youth
Thin Ice	Lovely to Look At
– 30 –	Deadline Midnight
This Is My Affair	His Affair
This Thing Called Love	Married but Single
Those Daring Young Men in Their Jaunty Jalopies	Monte Carlo or Bust
Three Daring Daughters	The Birds and the Bees
Three Stripes in the Sun	The Gentle Sergeant
Three Weeks	Romance of a Queen
Thunder in the Valley	Bob, Son of Battle
Thundercloud	Colt 45
Thunder on the Hill	Bonaventure
A Time for Killing	The Long Ride Home
Tip on a Dead Jockey	Time for Action
Tomahawk	Battle of Powder River
Too Many Husbands	My Two Husbands
Top Secret Affair	Their Secret Affair
The Torch	Bandit General
Toward the Unknown	Brink of Hell
T. R. Baskin	A Date with a Lonely Girl
The Trap	The Baited Trap
Trapped (TV)	Doberman Patrol (theatrical)
Tribes (TV)	The Soldier Who Declared Peace (theatrical)
Trouble for Two	The Suicide Club
The True Story of Jesse James	The James Brothers
Try and Get Me	The Sound of Fury
Twenty Plus Two	It Started in Tokyo
Twilight of Honor	The Charge is Murder
Two Girls on Broadway	Choose Your Partner
Two Guys from Milwaukee	Royal Flush
Two Guys from Texas	Two Texas Knights
Two Loves	Spinster
Underworld (1927)	Paying the Penalty
The Undying Monster	The Hammond Mystery
Vice Squad	The Girl in Room 17
The View from Pompey's Head	Secret Interlude
The Violent Men	Rough Company
Von Richthofen and Brown	The Red Baron
The WAC from Walla Walla	Army Capers
Waco (1952)	The Outlaw and the Lady
Walk East on Beacon	The Crime of the Century
War of the Colossal Beast	The Terror Strikes
Washington Story	Target for Scandal
Welcome to Hard Times	Killer on a Horse
West Point Story	Fine and Dandy
What a Woman	The Beautiful Cheat
The Wheeler Dealers	Separate Beds
When You're in Love	For You Alone
The Whistle at Eaton Falls	Richer than the Earth
White Savage	White Captive
Who Is Killing the Great Chefs of Europe?	Too Many Chefs

Who Killed Doc Robbin?	Sinister House
The Whole Town's Talking	Passport to Fame
Who'll Stop the Rain?	Dog Soldiers
The Wife Takes a Flyer	A Yank in Dutch
The Wild Blue Yonder	Thunder in the Pacific
Wild Seed	Fargo
Will Success Spoil Rock Hunter?	Oh! For a Man
Wings of the Eagle	The Wings of Eagles
A Woman's Devotion	War Hunt
Wrong Is Right	The Man with the Deadly Lens
A Yank in Indo China	Hidden Secret
You Never Can Tell	You Never Know
Young Man with a Horn	Young Man of Music
The Young Philadelphians	The City Jungle
Zenobia	Elephants Never Forget
Zig Zag	False Witness
Zombies of Mora-Tau	The Dead That Walk
Zombies on Broadway	Loonies on Broadway

British to American

The Admirable Crichton	Paradise Lagoon
The Adventurers	Fortune in Diamonds
Albert R.N.	Break for Freedom
The Amazing Quest of Ernest Bliss	Romance and Riches
The Amorous Prawn	The Playgirl and the War Minister
Appointment with Venus	Island Rescue
Atlantic Ferry	Sons of the Sea
Background	Edge of Divorce
Ballad in Blue	Blues for Lovers
Bank Holiday	Three on a Weekend
Barnacle Bill	All at Sea
The Battle of the River Plate	Pursuit of the Graf Spee
Battle of the V.1	Missiles from Hell
Beat Girl	Wild for Kicks
Beautiful Stranger	Twist of Fate
The Beauty Jungle	Contest Girl
Before I Wake	Shadow of Fear
Bequest to the Nation	The Nelson Affair
Beyond This Place	Web of Evidence/P.O. Box 303
Blind Date	Chance Meeting
Blind Terror	See No Evil
Bloomfield	The Hero
Blossom Time	April Romance
Brighton Rock	Young Scarface
Britannia Mews	The Forbidden Street
Bulldog Jack	Alias Bulldog Drummond
Busman's Honeymoon	Haunted Honeymoon
Captain Clegg	Night Creatures
The Card	The Promoter
The Caretaker	The Guest
Carleton Browne of the F.O.	Man in a Cocked Hat
Carrington V.C.	Court Martial
Carry On Admiral	The Ship Was Loaded
Carry On Jack	Carry On Venus
Catch Us if You Can	Having a Wild Weekend

The Chiltern Hundreds	The Amazing Mr Beecham
Circus of Fear	Psycho Circus
City of the Dead	Horror Hotel
City Under the Sea	War Gods of the Deep
Cone of Silence	Trouble in the Sky
Confidential Report	Mr Arkadin
Conflict of Wings	Fuss over Feathers
Contraband	Blackout
Cosh Boy	The Slasher
Cottage to Let	Bombsight Stolen
Country Dance	Brotherly Love
The Courtneys of Curzon St	The Courtney Affair
The Criminal	The Concrete Jungle
Crooks and Coronets	Sophie's Place
Curse of the Crimson Altar	The Crimson Cult
Cry the Beloved Country	African Fury
The Damned	These Are the Damned
Danger Within	Breakout
Dangerous Moonlight	Suicide Squadron
The Dark Avenger	The Warriors
Dark Eyes of London	The Human Monster
The Day will Dawn	The Avengers
Dear Octopus	The Randolph Family
Death Line	Raw Meat
The Demi-Paradise	Adventure for Two
Derby Day	Four Against Fate
The Devil Rides Out	The Devil's Bride
The Devil's Men	Land of the Minotaur
The Dock Brief	Trial and Error
Downhill	When Boys Leave Home
Dracula (1958)	Horror of Dracula
Drake of England	Drake the Pirate
The Drum	Drums
Dusty Ermine	Hideout in the Alps
The Elusive Pimpernel	The Fighting Pimpernel
Emergency Call	Hundred Hour Hunt
English without Tears	Her Man Gilbey
An Englishman's Home	Madmen of Europe
Escape Route	I'll Get You
Escapement	The Electronic Monster
Every Home Should Have One	Think Dirty
Eye Witness (1970)	Sudden Terror
Family Doctor	RX Murder
Family Life	Wednesday's Child
Fanatic	Die Die My Darling
Fanny by Gaslight	Man of Evil
Farewell Again	Troopship
Father Brown	The Detective
The Final Programme	The Last Days of Man on Earth
The First Gentleman	Affairs of a Rogue
The First Great Train Robbery	The Great Train Robbery
The First of the Few	Spitfire
The Flesh and the Fiends	Mania
Follow Me	The Public Eye
The Foreman Went to France	Somewhere in France
49th Parallel	The Invaders
Fortune is a Woman	She Played with Fire

The Four Just Men	The Secret Four
Freedom Radio	A Voice in the Night
The Full Treatment	Stop Me Before I Kill
Gaiety George	Showtime
Gaslight	Angel Street
The Gaunt Stranger	The Phantom Strikes
Geordie	Wee Geordie
Gideon's Day	Gideon of Scotland Yard
The Gift Horse	Glory at Sea
The Girl in the Headlines	The Model Murder Case
Give Us This Day	Salt to the Devil
Golden Arrow	The Gay Adventure
Gone to Earth	The Wild Heart
Grand National Night	Wicked Wife
The Greengage Summer	Loss of Innocence
Grip of the Strangler	The Haunted Strangler
The Guinea Pig	The Outsider
The Guvnor	Mister Hobo
The Hands of Orlac	Hands of a Strangler
Happy Ever After	Tonight's the Night
The Happy Family	Mr Lord Says No
Her Favourite Husband	The Taming of Dorothy
The High Bright Sun	McGuire Go Home
Highly Dangerous	Time Running Out
A Hill in Korea	Hell in Korea
His Lordship	Man of Affairs
HMS Defiant	Damn the Defiant
Holocaust 2000	The Chosen
Home at Seven	Murder on Monday
Hot Enough for June	Agent 8¾
The House in Nightmare Park	Crazy House
House of Secrets	Triple Deception
Hunted	The Stranger in Between
I Don't Want to Be Born	The Devil within Her
I Killed the Count	Who Is Guilty
I Live in Grosvenor Square	A Yank in London
I See a Dark Stranger	The Adventuress
I Was Happy Here	Time Lost and Time Remembered
Ice Cold in Alex	Desert Attack
I'll Get You for This	Lucky Nick Cain
Ill Met by Moonlight	Night Ambush
The Informers	Underworld Informers
The Inspector	Lisa
Inspector Hornleigh Goes to It	Mail Train
The Intelligence Men	Spylarks
Interpol	Pickup Alley
The Intimate Stranger	Finger of Guilt
Into the Blue	Man in the Dinghy
The Iron Maiden	The Swingin' Maiden
Isadora	The Loves of Isadora
Jericho	Dark Sands
Jew Suss	Power
A Jolly Bad Fellow	They All Died Laughing
Jump for Glory	When Thief Meets Thief
Kate Plus Ten	Queen of Crime

The Kidnappers	The Little Kidnappers
Kiss of the Vampire	Kiss of Evil
Knave of Hearts	Lover Boy
Lady Godiva Rides Again	Beauty Queen
Lancelot and Guinevere	Sword of Lancelot
The Last Days of Dolwyn	Woman of Dolwyn
The Last Page	Manbait
The Late Edwina Black	Obsessed
Latin Quarter	Frenzy
Laxdale Hall	Scotch on the Rocks
Licensed to Kill	The Second Best Secret Agent in the Whole Wide World
Life for Ruth	Walk in the Shadow
Light up the Sky	Skywatch
Lilacs in the Spring	Let's Make Up
The Lodger (1933)	The Phantom Fiend
London Belongs to Me	Dulcimer Street
The London Connection	The Omega Connection
London Town	My Heart Goes Crazy
The Long Arm	The Third Key
The Long, the Short and the Tall	Jungle Fighters
Lost	Tears for Simon
Love Story	A Lady Surrenders
The Maggie	High and Dry
The Man in the Sky	Decision Against Time
The Man Who Watched Trains Go By	Paris Express
The Man Within	The Smugglers
Mandy	The Crash of Silence
Manuela	Stowaway Girl
The Marseilles Contract	The Destructors
A Matter of Life and Death	Stairway to Heaven
Men of Two Worlds	Witch Doctor
The Mercenaries	Dark of the Sun
Midshipman Easy	Men of the Sea
The Million Pound Note	Man with a Million
Mr Topaze	I Like Money
Moment of Danger	Malaga
Monster of Terror	Die Monster Die
Morning Departure	Operation Disaster
Moscow Nights	I Stand Condemned
The Mountain Eagle	Fear of God
Mumsy, Nanny, Sonny and Girly	Girly
My Daughter Joy	Operation X
My Teenage Daughter	Teenage Bad Girl
The Naked Truth	Your Past is Showing
The Net	Project M7
The Night Has Eyes	Terror House
Night of the Demon	Curse of the Demon
Night of the Eagle	Burn Witch Burn
No Kidding	Beware of Children
No Time to Die	Tank Force
Nobody Lives Forever	The High Commissioner
Nor the Moon by Night	Elephant Gun
Northwest Frontier	Flame over India
O.H.M.S.	You're in the Army Now
Obsession	The Hidden Room
Odd Man Out	Gang War

On the Fiddle	Operation SNAFU
Once a Jolly Swagman	Maniacs on Wheels
Ooh You Are Awful	Get Charlie Tully
Our Fighting Navy	Torpedoed
Our Girl Friday	The Adventures of Sadie
Our Man in Marrakesh	Bang Bang You're Dead
Owd Bob	To the Victor
The Passionate Friends	One Woman's Story
The Passionate Stranger	A Novel Affair
Penn of Pennsylvania	The Courageous Mr Penn
Percy's Progress	It's Not the Size That Counts
Perfect Strangers	Vacation from Marriage
Persecution	The Terror of Sheba
Pimpernel Smith	Mister V
The Planter's Wife	Outpost in Malaya
Portrait from Life	The Girl in the Painting
Portrait of Alison	Postmark for Danger
Pretty Polly	A Matter of Innocence
Q Planes	Clouds over Europe
Quatermass and the Pit	Five Million Years to Earth
The Quatermass Experiment	The Creeping Unknown
Quatermass II	Enemy from Space
A Question of Adultery	The Case of Mrs Loring
The Raging Moon	Long Ago Tomorrow
The Rake's Progress	Notorious Gentleman
Ransom	The Terrorists
The Rebel	Call Me Genius
The Red Beret	Paratrooper
Rich and Strange	East of Shanghai
Ring of Spies	Ring of Treason
Rocket to the Moon	Those Fantastic Flying Fools
Rockets Galore	Mad Little Island
The Romantic Age	Naughty Arlette
Rookery Nook	One Embarrassing Night
The Rough and the Smooth	Portrait of a Sinner
Rough Shoot	Shoot First
Sabotage	A Woman Alone
Sailor Beware	Panic in the Parlor
Sailors Three	Three Cockeyed Sailors
St Martin's Lane	Sidewalks of London
The Saint's Return	The Saint's Girl Friday
Sammy Going South	A Boy Ten Feet Tall
Saraband for Dead Lovers	Saraband
The Satanic Rites of Dracula	Count Dracula and His Vampire Bride
Saturday Island	Island of Desire
The Scamp	Strange Affection
The Scarlet Blade	The Crimson Blade
Sea of Sand	Desert Patrol
Seagulls over Sorrento	Crest of the Wave
The Seekers	Land of Fury
Serious Charge	A Touch of Hell
Seven Sinners	Doomed Cargo
Seven Thunders	The Beasts of Marseilles
Seven Waves Away	Abandon Ship
The Ship That Died of Shame	P. T. Raiders

The Shop at Sly Corner	The Code of Scotland Yard
The Siege of Pinchgut	Four Desperate Men
Silver Blaze	Murder at the Baskervilles
Singlehanded	Sailor of the King
Sixty Glorious Years	Queen of Destiny
Sky West and Crooked	Gypsy Girl
The Small Back Room	Hour of Glory
The Smallest Show on Earth	Big Time Operators
The Small Voice	Hideout
Smash and Grab	Larceny Street
Soft Beds, Hard Battles	Undercover Hero
Soho Incident	Spin a Dark Web
The Sound Barrier	Breaking the Sound Barrier
South of Algiers	The Golden Mask
Spellbound (1940)	The Spell of Amy Nugent
The Spy in Black	U-Boat 29
The Squeaker	Murder on Diamond Row
State Secret	The Great Manhunt
The Story of Esther Costello	The Golden Virgin
Strange World of Planet X	Cosmic Monsters
The Stranger Came Home	The Unholy Four
Stranger in the House	Cop-Out
Street Corner	Both Sides of the Law
A Study in Terror	Fog
Summer of the Seventeenth Doll	Season of Passion
Sunshine Susie	Office Girl
Suspect	The Risk
The System	The Girl-Getters
A Tale of Five Cities	A Tale of Five Women
The Tall Headlines	The Frightened Bride
Taste of Fear	Scream of Fear
Teheran	The Plot to Kill Roosevelt
Tell England	The Battle of Gallipoli
Ten Days in Paris	Spy in the Pantry
A Terrible Beauty	Night Fighters
That Dangerous Age	If This Be Sin
That Woman Opposite	City After Midnight
There is Another Sun	Wall of Death
These Dangerous Years	Dangerous Youth
They Flew Alone	Wings and the Woman
They Made Me a Fugitive	I Became a Criminal
36 Hours	Terror Street
Till Death Us Do Part	Alf 'n' Family
Time Bomb	Terror on a Train
Timeslip	The Atomic Man
To Dorothy a Son	Cash on Delivery
Tom Brown's Schooldays	Adventures at Rugby
The Tommy Steele Story	Rock around the World
Tomorrow We Live	At Dawn We Die
Top Secret	Mr Potts Goes to Moscow
Tower of Evil	Horror on Snape Island
A Town Like Alice	The Rape of Malaya
Trial by Combat	Dirty Knights' Work
The Trials of Oscar Wilde	The Man with the Green Carnation
The Trollenberg Terror	The Crawling Eye
Trottie True	The Gay Lady
Tudor Rose	Nine Days a Queen
The Tunnel	Transatlantic Tunnel
Twenty Four Hours in a Woman's Life	Affair in Monte Carlo

Twenty One Days	Twenty One Days Together
Twinky	Lola
The Two Faces of Dr Jekyll	House of Fright
Uncle Silas	The Inheritance
Vampira	Old Dracula
Venetian Bird	The Assassin
Vengeance	The Brain
Very Important Person	A Coming Out Party
Vessel of Wrath	The Beachcomber
The Vicious Circle	The Circle
Visa to Canton	Passport to China
The Voice of Merrill	Murder Will Out
Walk into Paradise	Walk into Hell
Waterfront	Waterfront Women
The Way Ahead	Immortal Battalion
The Way to the Stars	Johnny in the Clouds
The Weak and the Wicked	Young and Willing
Went the Day Well?	48 Hours
What a Carve Up	No Place Like Homicide
Where No Vultures Fly	Ivory Hunter
Whisky Galore	Tight Little Island
White Cradle Inn	High Fury
The White Unicorn	Bad Sister
Who Goes There?	The Passionate Sentry
The Wild and the Willing	Young and Willing
A Window in London	Lady in Distress
Witchfinder General	The Conqueror Worm
Wolves	Wanted Men
The Woman in Question	Five Angles on Murder
The Woman with No Name	Her Panelled Door
Women of Twilight	Twilight Women
The World Ten Times Over	Pussycat Alley
Yangtse Incident	Battle Hell
Yield to the Night	Blonde Sinner
Young and Innocent	The Girl Was Young
The Young Lovers	Chance Meeting
Your Witness	Eye Witness
Zee and Co	X, Y and Zee

List of Recommended Books

This is given because it has been requested; but it is given with some diffidence. The best books for you will depend on your particular angle of interest. Personally I have little patience with the kind of book which sees the director's hand in every moment of celluloid and builds up volumes of signs and meaning of which all concerned in the production were totally unaware. Hitchcock in particular has had cause to chuckle at this type of interpretation, and I can only counsel the young reader to beware of pretentious treatises on something which after all is an industry as much as it is an art. When the art does break through, it is the joint work of fifty or more creative people, and enjoyment of a particular film may well be attributable more to the writer or the editor than the director.

This then is a basic list of books which I have found informative, entertaining and stimulating. I have starred my own particular favourites, books which seem to me to encapsulate a whole feeling towards movies, wider than their own particular subject.

I have given the barest detail of each book. Many will be out of print, but many specialist bookshops are springing up which can (at some cost) produce second-hand copies. Many standard cinema books are now being reprinted by university publishers in America. Information can be had from the British Film Institute in London or the American Film Institute in New York; the best shops I know are the Cinema Bookshop in London's Great Russell Street and the Larry Edmunds Bookshop on Los Angeles' Hollywood Boulevard.

Reference

A Technological History of Motion Pictures: Raymond Fielding
The Focal Encyclopaedia of Film Techniques
International Motion Picture Almanac (current edition)
The British Film and TV Yearbook: Peter Noble (current edition)
The American Movies Reference Book: Paul Michael
Screen World: Daniel Blum (every year)
Winchester's Screen Encyclopaedia (1933)
World Film Encyclopaedia (1947)
*TV Movies: Leonard Maltin (current edition)
The American Film Institute Catalogue
The Cinema Today: Spencer and Waley
International Encyclopedia of Film: Roger Manvell
Halliwell's Film Guide: Leslie Halliwell
The British Film Catalogue: Denis Gifford

Histories: General

*The Movies: Raymond Griffith and Arthur Mayer
*The Liveliest Art: Arthur Knight
A Picture History of the Cinema: Ernest Lindgren
*A Pictorial History of the Silent Screen: Daniel Blum
*A Pictorial History of the Talkies: Daniel Blum
A Million and One Nights: Terry Ramsaye
The Film Till Now: Paul Rotha
The Silent Cinema: Liam O'Leary
Hollywood in the Twenties: David Robinson
Hollywood in the Thirties: John Baxter
Hollywood in the Forties: Charles Higham and Joel Greenberg
Hollywood in the Fifties: Charles Higham and Joel Greenberg
Where We Came In: Charles Oakley
The Rise of the American Film: Lewis Jacobs
Movie Parade: Paul Rotha
The American Cinema: Andrew Sarris
The History of the British Film: Rachel Low (several volumes to date)
A Competitive Cinema: Norton and Perry
Early American Cinema: Anthony Slide
Archaeology of the Cinema: C W Ceram
The Contemporary Cinema: Penelope Gilliatt
Twenty Years of British Films: Michael Balcon
Spellbound in Darkness: George C Pratt

Social Effects

The Factual Film: P E P
Sociology of Film: J P Mayer
British Cinemas and Their Audiences: J P Mayer
*America at the Movies: Margaret Farrand Thorpe
Hollywood the Dream Factory: Hortense Powdermaker
Red Roses Every Night: Guy Morgan
The Best Remaining Seats: Ben Hall
Parade of Pleasure: Geoffrey Wagner
*The Face on the Cutting Room Floor: Murray Schumach
Movies by the Millions: Gilbert Seldes
The Film Answers Back: E M and W W Robson
The Decline of the Cinema: John Spraos
The British Film Industry: P E P

Those Great Movie Ads: Joe Morella, Edward Z Epstein, Eleanor Clark

Periodicals

*The Monthly Film Bulletin 1935 to date
*Films in Review 1950 to date
Sight and Sound 1935 to date
Screen Facts 1967 to date
Penguin Film Review 1946-9
British National Film Catalogue 1963 to date

Theory

A Discovery of Cinema: Thorold Dickinson
Grierson on Documentary
Films Beget Films: Jay Leyda
The Art of the Film: Ernest Lindgren
Footnotes to the Film: Charles Davy
The Immediate Experience: Robert Warshow
The Technique of Film Editing: Karel Reisz
Film as Art: Arnheim
*Film: Roger Manvell
Let's Go to the Pictures: Iris Barry
Film Form and the Film Sense: Sergei Eisenstein
Introduction to the Art of the Movies: Lewis Jacobs
A Grammar of Film: Raymond Spottiswoode
Behind the Screen: Kenneth Macgowan
Pudovkin on Film Technique
Rotha on Film
Documentary Film: Paul Rotha
Celluloid: Paul Rotha

Hollywood and the Studios

*Picture: Lillian Ross
*The Studio: John Gregory Dunne
This Was Hollywood: Beth Day
*Hollywood the Haunted House: Paul Mayersburg
Hollywood Babylon: Kenneth Anger
The Story of 'The Misfits': John Goode
Who Killed Marilyn Monroe: Charles Hamblett
Hollywood at Sunset: Charles Baxter
In Hollywood Tonight: Peter Duncan
*My Life with Cleopatra: Walter Wanger
The Lion's Share: Bosley Crowther
The Citizen Kane Book: Pauline Kael
*Hello Hollywood: Rivkin and Kerr
*Hollywood: Garson Kanin
*The Hollywood Exiles: Charles Higham
Mountain of Dreams: Leslie Halliwell
*The MGM Story: Douglas Eames
*The Warner Bros Story: Clive Hirschorn
*Growing Up in Hollywood: Robert Parrish
*The War, the West and the Wilderness: Kevin Brownlow

Critics

*Chestnuts in Her Lap: C A Lejeune
Garbo and the Night Watchmen: ed Alistair Cooke
Around Cinemas: James Agate
Shots in the Dark: ed Edgar Anstey
*Agee on Film (first volume)
On Movies: Dwight Macdonald
I Lost It at the Movies: Pauline Kael
Kiss Kiss Bang Bang: Pauline Kael
The New York Times Film Reviews
*The Pleasure Dome: Graham Greene
The Private Eye, the Cowboy and the Very Naked Girl: Judith Crist
Film 67/68 (and succeeding years): American National Society of Film Critics
Cinema: C A Lejeune
*Movies into Film: John Simon
*The Film Criticism of Otis Ferguson

Performers

Mr Laurel and Mr Hardy: John McCabe
Ecstasy and Me: Hedy Lamarr
The Lonely Life: Bette Davis
*Mother Goddam: Bette Davis and Whitney Stine
A Portrait of Joan: Joan Crawford
Steps in Time: Fred Astaire
Garbo: Norman Zierold
*The Movies, Mr Griffith, and Me: Lillian Gish
My Wicked Wicked Ways: Errol Flynn
Too Much too Soon: Diana Barrymore
Good Night Sweet Prince (John Barrymore): Gene Fowler
Valentino: Irving Shulman
Harlow: Irving Shulman
Goodness Had Nothing To Do With It: Mae West
Charles Laughton: Charles Higham
Harold Lloyd's World of Slapstick: William Cahn
My Wonderful World of Comedy: Buster Keaton
*The Parade's Gone By: Kevin Brownlow
I E, An Autobiography: Mickey Rooney
The Marx Brothers at the Movies: Zimmermann and Goldblatt
*The Marx Brothers Scrapbook: Richard J Anobile
*Whatever Became Of . . .? (6 volumes): Richard Lamparski
This Is On Me: Bob Hope
Movie Comedy Teams: Leonard Maltin
Sunshine and Shadow: Mary Pickford
The Stars: Richard Shickel
*The Great Movie Stars: David Shipman (two volumes)
W C Fields, His Follies and Fortunes: Robert Lewis Taylor
A Life on Film: Mary Astor
*The Moon's a Balloon: David Niven
Bring on the Empty Horses: David Niven
Picture books (various publishers) are available on the films of:
Spencer Tracy
Gary Cooper
Laurel and Hardy
James Stewart
Humphrey Bogart
Greta Garbo
Judy Garland
Marilyn Monroe

Charles Chaplin
Ronald Colman
W C Fields
Marlene Dietrich
Joan Crawford
The Fondas
Dirk Bogarde
John Wayne
Norma Shearer
Boris Karloff
Frank Sinatra
Cary Grant

and many other stars. Those by James Robert Parish are among the best documented: see especially The Paramount Pretties, The Fox Girls, The RKO Gals, The MGM Stock Company, Hollywood's Great Love Teams, The Swashbucklers, Hollywood Character Actors.

Producers, Directors, Writers, Cinematographers

The Hollywood Tycoons: Norman Zierold
*The Movie Moguls: Philip French
Mr Rank: Alan Wood
*King Cohn: Bob Thomas
Thalberg: Bob Thomas
Selznick: Bob Thomas
A Lifetime of Films: Michael Balcon
Twenty Five Thousand Sunsets: Herbert Wilcox
Flashback: George Pearson
Came the Dawn: Cecil Hepworth
Hollywood Rajah (Louis B Mayer): Bosley Crowther
Alexander Korda: Paul Tabori
Howard Hughes: John Keats
My First Hundred Years in Hollywood: Jack Warner
The Director's Event: Sherman and Rubin
Hitchcock: François Truffaut
There's Always Tomorrow: Anna Neagle
*Hollywood Cameramen: Charles Higham
Hollywood Scapegoat (Eric Von Stroheim): Peter Noble
Fun in a Chinese Laundry: Josef Von Sternberg
The Lubitsch Touch: Herman G Weinberg
Autobiography: Cecil B de Mille
My Autobiography: Charles Chaplin
My Life in Pictures: Charles Chaplin
Charlie Chaplin: Theodore Huff
The Filmgoer's Book of Quotes: Leslie Halliwell
Sergei Eisenstein: Autobiography
With Eisenstein in Hollywood: Ivor Montagu
The Celluloid Mistress: Rodney Ackland
No Leading Lady: R C Sherriff
*The Westmores of Hollywood: Frank Westmore
Art and Design in the British Film: Edward Carrick
The Public is Never Wrong: Adolph Zukor
The Great Goldwyn: Alva Johnson
Carl Laemmle: John Drinkwater
The Name above the Title: Frank Capra
The Hollywood Screenwriters: Richard Corliss
*Memo from David O Selznick: Rudy Behlmer
The Disney Version: Richard Shickel
Upton Sinclair Presents William Fox
King of Comedy: Mack Sennett
I Blow My Own Horn: Jesse Lasky
Film Makers on Film Making: Harry M Geduld
The World of Entertainment (Arthur Freed at MGM): Hugh Fordin

Screenplays

Twenty Best Film Plays: ed John Gassner
Best Film Plays 1940-45: ed John Gassner
and most others which have been published, certainly including:
The Third Man
Les Enfants Du Paradis
A Matter of Life and Death
Four Bergman Films
Citizen Kane (The Citizen Kane Book by Pauline Kael)
North by Northwest
Adam's Rib
*The Classics Film Library: Richard J Anobile (shot-by-shot picture analyses of Dr Jekyll and Mr Hyde, Frankenstein, The Maltese Falcon, Ninotchka, Casablanca, etc.)
The 'Masterworks of the Cinema' series

National Cinema

The Japanese Movie: Donald Ritchie
Eastern Europe: Nina Hibbin
Kino: Jay Leyda
French Film: Roy Armes
The Haunted Screen: Lotte Eisner
From Caligari to Hitler: Siegfried Kracauer

Types of Film

*Horror Movies: Carlos Clarens
Gotta Sing! Gotta Dance!: John Kobal
The Western: Fenin and Everson
Suspense in the Cinema: Gordon Gow
Movie Monsters: Denis Gifford
Religion in the Cinema: Ivan Butler
The Bad Guys: William K Everson
The Celluloid Sacrifice: Alexander Walker
*The Great Movie Series: James Robert Parish
*The Great Movie Shorts: Leonard Maltin
All Singing! All Talking! All Dancing!: John Springer
The Detective in Film: William K. Everson
*A Pictorial History of Horror Movies: Denis Gifford
*'B' Movies: Don Miller
Kings of the B's: McCarthy and Flynn

Fiction

The Last Tycoon: Scott Fitzgerald
The Little Sister: Raymond Chandler
The Slide Area: Gavin Lambert
The Producer: Richard Brooks
The Day of the Locust: Nathanael West
The Carpetbaggers: Harold Robbins

The Dream Merchants: *Harold Robbins*
A Voyage to Purilia: Elmer Rice
Prater Violet: Christopher Isherwood
Nobody Ordered Wolves: Jeffrey Dell

Gossip

Scratch an Actor: Sheilah Graham
Tell It to Louella: Louella Parsons
From Under My Hat: Hedda Hopper
The Celebrity Circus: Elsa Maxwell
*The 50-Year Decline and Fall of Hollywood: Ezra Goodman

…nswers to A Preliminary Canter

1 Paris ☐ 2 John Ford ☐ 3 *Conquest* (GB: *Marie Walewska*) ☐ 4 *The Covered Wagon* ☐ 5 *Broken Blossoms* ☐ 6 Alfred Hitchcock ☐ 7 Alexander Korda ☐ 8 Herman J. Mankiewicz ☐ 9 Jack Oakie ☐ 10 *Fantasia* ☐ 11 *The Pride of the Yankees* ☐ 12 David Lean ☐ 13 *Utopia* ☐ 14 *Miracle in Milan* ☐ 15 Sidney Howard ☐ was credited, though many others contributed, including the producer, David O. Selznick 16 *The Mummy* ☐, *Mad Love* ☐ 17 Sergei Eisenstein ☐ 18 Boris Karloff ☐ 19 *The Music Box* ☐ 20 Werner Krauss ☐ 21 Abbott and Costello ☐ 22 *Smiles of a Summer Night* ☐ 23 Leslie Banks ☐ 24 Humphrey Jennings ☐ 25 *The Road Back* ☐ 26 Anton Walbrook ☐ 27 Noël Coward ☐ 28 Horace Horsecollar ☐ 29 *Forbidden Paradise* ☐ 30 John Wayne ☐ 31 Grumpy ☐ Doc ☐ 32 Stanley Cortez ☐ 33 *Monsieur Verdoux* ☐ 34 *Un Carnet de Bal* ☐ 35 *Lydia* ☐ Merle Oberon ☐ 36 *Kind Hearts and Coronets* ☐ 37 *Jour de Fête* ☐ 38 *Carry on Sergeant* ☐ 39 *Room Service* ☐ 40 *Step Lively* ☐ 41 William S. Hart ☐ 42 Milos Forman ☐ 43 *It Happened One Night* ☐ 44 *Scarface* ☐ 45 Mickey Rooney ☐ 46 Andre Morell ☐ 47 Anton Walbrook ☐ 48 Howard Hawks ☐ 49 Anna Neagle ☐ 50 Irving Berlin ☐ 51 Nelson Eddy ☐ Jeanette MacDonald ☐ 52 *Silk Stockings*, a musical reprise of *Ninotchka* ☐ 53 *Fury* ☐ 54 United Productions of America, or UPA ☐ 55 Alexander Knox ☐ 56 *Monkey Business* ☐ 57 *Drifters* ☐ 58 René Clair ☐ 59 *The Eagle* ☐ 60 Compton Mackenzie ☐ 61 David Niven ☐ 62 *The Small Back Room* ☐ 63 *Shadow of a Doubt* ☐ 64 Ealing ☐ 65 Will Rogers ☐ 66 *Judge Priest* ☐ 67 *Boomerang* ☐ 68 *Return to Glennascaul* ☐ 69 *Trouble in Paradise* ☐ 70 *Dames* ☐ 71 Norman MacLaren ☐ 72 *On the Town* ☐ 73 Frank Capra ☐ 74 It was the first CinemaScope cartoon ☐ 75 Richard Tauber ☐ 76 Charles Laughton ☐ 77 Robert Flaherty ☐ 78 Charles Bickford ☐ 79 Raymond Massey ☐ 80 Leslie Banks ☐ 81 *Alf's Button Afloat* ☐ 82 Arthur Knight ☐ 83 Jean Vigo ☐ 84 Walter Wanger ☐ 85 'He couldn't speak words, he went boing-boing instead.' ☐ 86 Cartooning ☐ 87 G. W. Pabst ☐ 88 Will Hay ☐ 89 French director Marcel Carné ☐ 90 Lumière ☐ 91 Harold Lloyd ☐ 92 Paramount ☐ 93 Clark Gable ☐ 94 Laurel and Hardy ☐ 95 *Star Spangled Rhythm* ☐ 96 Paramount ☐ 97 *Back Street* ☐ 98 *Red Dust* ☐ 99 Trick films ☐ 100 Erich Wolfgang Korngold ☐ 101 Paul Muni ☐ 102 Agnes Ayres ☐ 103 Victor Mature ☐ 104 Thomas Mitchell ☐ 105 *Batman* ☐ 106 Wrong: *Red Harvest* remains unfilmed ☐ 107 Lee Majors ☐ Steve Austin ☐ 108 *Triumph of the Will* ☐ Leni Riefenstahl ☐ 109 George Stevens ☐ 110 Victor Sjostrom ☐ 111 *The Palm Beach Story* ☐ 112 Gloria Swanson ☐ 113 Tim Holt, playing young George ☐ 114 *Devotion* ☐ 115 Adolph Zukor ☐ 116 Gregg Toland ☐ 117 Buddy Swan ☐ Sonny Bupp ☐ 118 Anti-semitism ☐ 119 Josef von Sternberg ☐ 120 *Sons of the Desert* (GB: *Fraternally Yours*) ☐ 121 Charlie Chase ☐ 122 It was the first Royal Performance Film ☐ 123 George Arliss ☐ 124 W. C. Fields and Mae West ☐ 125 Elmo Lincoln ☐ 126 George Lazenby ☐ 127 *Intermezzo* ☐ 128 Billy Bitzer ☐ 129 *One Million BC/Man and His Mate* ☐ 130 *The Thing from Another World* ☐ 131 *Monsieur Beaucaire* ☐ 132 From the initials of its founders Spoor and Anderson, S 'n' A ☐ 133 *The Great Race* ☐ 134 Henri-Georges Clouzot ☐ 135 *The Best Years of Our Lives* ☐ a handless ex-serviceman, which he was ☐ 136 Lynn Belvedere ☐ 137 Betty Grable ☐ Dan Dailey ☐ 138 Sam Levene ☐ 139 *Ziegfeld Girl* ☐ 140 Charles Winninger ☐ 141 *National Velvet* ☐ 142 *Claudia and David* ☐ 143 *Meet Me in St Louis* ☐ 144 Mary Astor ☐ Leon Ames ☐ 145 Nigel Bruce ☐ 146 Wilfred Lawson ☐ 147 Lon Chaney Jnr ☐ 148 Pepe Le Moko ☐ 149 Billie Burke ☐ 150 Theodore Roberts ☐ 151 Maria Ouspenskaya ☐ 152 Rupert Julian ☐ 153 John Gilbert ☐ 154 King Vidor ☐ 155 Gary Cooper ☐ 156 Emil Jannings ☐ 157 Alan Crosland ☐ 158 William Randolph Hearst ☐ 159 Walt Disney: they are Silly Symphonies of the thirties ☐ 160 *Gone with the Wind* ☐ 161 Warner ☐ 162 Universal ☐ 163 *Anchors Aweigh* ☐ 164 *Dangerous When Wet* ☐ 165 Gene Tierney ☐ 166 Richard Crenna ☐ Samantha Eggar ☐ 167 *Up in Arms* ☐ 168 *The Man Who Came to Dinner* ☐ 169 May Robson ☐ 170 *Pocketful of Miracles* ☐ 171 *King Kong* ☐ 172 W. C. Fields ☐ 173 *Secrets* ☐ 174 *The Moon's a Balloon* ☐ 175 *Bring on the Empty Horses* ☐ 176 *Fancy Pants* ☐ 177 *Blackmail* ☐ 178 *The Blue Angel* ☐ 179 Harry Langdon ☐ 180 Jean Renoir ☐ 181 Naunton Wayne ☐ Basil Radford ☐ 182 *Spellbound* ☐ 183 Mary Pickford ☐ D. W. Griffith ☐ 184 Max Fleischer ☐ 185 Anna Neagle ☐ 186 René Clair ☐ 187 Luis Buñuel

☐ 188 Rondo Hatton ☐ 189 Ludwig Donath ☐ 190 *Ninotchka* ☐ 191 *The Miracle of Morgan's Creek* ☐ 192 *I Married a Witch* ☐ 193 *The Beast from 20,000 Fathoms* ☐ 194 Charles Lang Jnr ☐ 195 *The Cure* ☐ 196 Charles Winninger ☐ 197 Joe E. Brown ☐ 198 *The Green Pastures* ☐ 199 Rex Ingram ☐ 200 Mischa Auer ☐ 201 Rosalind Russell ☐ 202 *Escape in the Desert* ☐ 203 George Cukor ☐ 204 Evelyn Keyes ☐ 205 Boxing and its attendant corruptions ☐ 206 John Barrymore ☐ 207 Alice Brady ☐ *In Old Chicago* ☐ 208 *Wings* ☐ 209 *Watch on the Rhine* ☐ 210 *Living It Up* ☐ Jerry Lewis ☐ 211 The old lady in *Night Must Fall* ☐ 212 Tommy Kelly ☐ 213 Fritz Lang ☐ 214 Robert Wiene ☐ 215 Robert Cummings ☐ 216 Tallulah Bankhead ☐ 217 Cecil B. De Mille ☐ 218 A prologue showing American airmen over Rome ☐ 219 *Steamboat Willie* ☐ 220 James Whale ☐ 221 *Morocco* ☐ 222 Eileen Herlie ☐ 223 *The Barkleys of Broadway* ☐ 224 Henry Daniell ☐ 225 A leopard ☐ 226 Kay Kendall—or the clever ones may say Eddie Calvert on the sound track ☐ 227 Leo McCarey ☐ 228 Walter Huston ☐ 229 Ernest Thesiger ☐ 230 Mischa Auer ☐ 231 Lilli Palmer ☐ 232 Theodore Roosevelt ☐ Sidney Blackmer ☐ 233 A dog owned by Laurel and Hardy ☐ 234 *Green for Danger* ☐ Alastair Sim ☐ 235 General Sternwood ☐ 236 Finlay Currie ☐ 237 Eddie Cantor ☐ 238 Gertrude Lawrence ☐ Elsa Lanchester ☐ 239 Thumper ☐ 240 Felix Salten ☐ 241 Ponchielli's 'Dance of the Hours' ☐ 242 Lewis Milestone ☐ 243 The Nicholas Brothers ☐ 244 Al ☐ Jim ☐ Harry ☐ 245 Patty ☐ Maxine ☐ La Verne ☐ 246 *The Carpetbaggers* ☐ 247 Ralph Richardson ☐ 248 Ryan O'Neal ☐ 249 Ralph Richardson ☐ 250 Barbara O'Neil ☐ 251 *To Be or Not to Be* ☐ 252 Dana Wynter ☐ Kevin McCarthy ☐

swers to Graduation Quiz

1 They were all in 3-D □ 2 Mickey Rooney □ 3 *I Can Get It for You Wholesale* □ 4 *The Thomas Crown Affair* □ 5 *The Black Cat* □ 6 *Deadlier Than the Male* □ 7 *Sherlock Holmes Faces Death* □ 8 *Nightmare* □ 9 *The Milky Way* □ 10 *They Call Me Mr Tibbs* □ 11 Paulette Goddard □ 12 Michael Kidd □ 13 Heydrich □ *Hitler's Madman* □ *Operation Daybreak* □ 14 *On the Spot* □ 15 *Persons in Hiding* □ 16 *Persons in Hiding* □ *Undercover Doctor* □ *Parole Fixer* □ *Queen of the Mob* □ 17 Vincent Price □ 18 Cedric Hardwicke □ 19 Robert Keith □ 20 *Four Wives* □ *Four Mothers* □ 21 *Daughters Courageous* □ 22 *Tailspin* □ 23 *Maid of Salem* □ Fred MacMurray □ Claudette Colbert □ 24 *McCabe and Mrs Miller* □ 25 Abraham Polonsky □ *Force of Evil* □ John Garfield □ 26 *Tucker's People* □ Ira Wolfert □ 27 *Guilty or Innocent: The Sam Sheppard Case* □ George Peppard □ 28 Ben Gazzara □ Anthony Hopkins □ 29 Jack Hawkins □ 30 Mia Farrow □ 31 *Outward Bound* □ 32 *Between Two Worlds* □ 33 Sydney Greenstreet □ 34 Anne Bancroft □ 35 Rex Harrison □ 36 *La Bête Humaine* □ 37 Anton Walbrook □ 38 Max Ophuls □ 39 *The Barretts of Wimpole Street* □ 40 To avoid confusion with the colour remake □ 41 *The Lady Dances* □ 42 Lana Turner □ Fernando Lamas □ 43 Twentieth Century Fox □ 44 *Picture* □ Lillian Ross □ 45 He played the invisible man, and became a star on the basis of his voice only □ 46 *The Birth of a Nation* □ 47 They were Hollywood's most famous small-part drunks of the thirties □ 48 Adolf Hitler □ 49 Josef Goebbels □ 50 Henry Wilcoxon □ 51 The vicar □ 52 Edmund Gwenn □ 53 James Dean □ 54 Anthony Adverse □ 55 Alan Ladd □ 56 Groucho Marx co-authored the first and appeared in the second □ 57 The vicar □ *David Copperfield* □ 58 *Conflict* □ 59 Stan Laurel □ 60 *Casablanca* □ Conrad Veidt □ Claude Rains □ 61 *The Old Dark House*: she played the centenarian head of the Femm family, and was credited as John Dudgeon □ 62 She was Hollywood's oldest working actress □ 63 Estelle Winwood □ *Murder by Death* □ 64 Charles Ruggles □ 65 Lassie □ 66 Errol Flynn □ 67 They are both pseudonyms of Darryl F. Zanuck □ 68 Metro Goldwyn Mayer □ 69 *Escape from Zahrain* □ 70 He was De Mille's son-in-law □ 71 *Those Were the Days* □ 72 *Little Miss Marker* □ 73 *Now and Forever* □ 74 Henry Hathaway □ 75 *Hangover Square* □ 76 *Charley's Aunt* □ Kay Francis □ 77 *I Heard the Owl Call My Name* □ 78 W. Somerset Maugham □ 79 Paul Gauguin □ 80 Steve Geray □ 81 Doris Dudley □ 82 *Mr Belvedere Goes to College* □ *Mr Belvedere Rings the Bell* □ 83 *Cabin in the Sky* □ 84 *September Affair*; which was made after his death □ 85 *Where's Charley* □ 86 *The Seashell and the Clergyman* □ 87 Reginald Denny □ 88 Cedric Hardwicke □ 89 William Dieterle □ 90 *Rich Man Poor Man*; they played the leads □ 91 Francis Lederer □ 92 *Three Cornered Moon* □ 93 *The Graduate* □ 94 Claude Rains □ 95 *Movin' On* □ 96 Claude Akins □ Frank Converse □ 97 Jules Dassin □ 98 Graham Moffatt □ Moore Marriott □ 99 Arthur Askey □ 100 Rouben Mamoulian □ 101 Michael Winner □ 102 a. *Macmillan and Wife* □ b. *Columbo* □ c. *Faraday and Company* □ d. *McCoy* □ e. *McCloud* □ f. *Banacek* □ 103 *Operation Petticoat* □ 104 *I Was a Male War Bride* □ 105 *The Pajama Game* □ 106 John Raitt □ 107 *Peyton Place* □ 108 *King's Row* □ 109 *The Kremlin Letter* □ 110 Bela Lugosi □ 111 *Once Upon a Time* □ 112 Ted Donaldson □ 113 Loretta Young □ 114 Robert Williams □ 115 Franklin Schaffner □ 116 *Madame Satan* □ 117 *Tales of Manhattan* □ 118 *Flesh and Fantasy* □ 119 Julien Duvivier □ 120 *The Pajama Game* □ 121 Ian Fleming □ 122 Dennis Hoey □ 123 *The Pearl of Death* □ 124 George Zucco □ 125 Henry Daniell □ 126 Edward Van Sloan □ 127 Dwight Frye □ 128 *Freaks* □ 129 Virginia Weidler □ 130 Robert Donat □ 131 Robert Morley □ 132 Spencer Tracy □ 133 Marcel Carne □ 134 Cinematography □ 135 Musical scoring □ 136 Anton Karas □ 137 *The Ghost Story* □ 138 *Scared Stiff* □ 139 Boris Karloff: he could not be released from his stage contract □ 140 *Bicycle Thieves* □ 141 *The Man Who Talked Too Much* □ *Illegal* □ 142 Joseph Schildkraut □ 143 Innokenti Smoktunovsky □ 144 *Go into Your Dance* □ Ruby Keeler □ 145 Rex Beach □ 146 Anne Baxter □ 147 *I Claudius* □ 148 The Falcon □ 149 Mel Blanc □ 150 Night clubs □ 151 Claudette Colbert □ 152 Asses' milk □ 153 Alan Young □ 154 Leo Genn □ 155 Whither goest thou? □ 156 Danger □ 157 Ruth Etting □ 158 *Love Me or Leave Me* □ 159 Eight million □ 160 Michael Powell □ and Emeric Pressburger □; they wrote,

produced and directed their films ☐ 161 Madeleine Smith ☐ Ann Todd ☐ 162 Phyllis Calvert ☐ Stewart Granger ☐ 163 *The Thing from Another World* ☐ 164 Dorothy Comingore ☐ 165 Paul Stewart ☐ 166 Xanadu ☐ 167 Colonel Haki ☐ 168 Patsy Ruth Miller ☐ 169 Maureen O'Hara ☐ 170 Gina Lollobrigida ☐ 171 Billie Burke ☐ 172 The God in *Zardoz* was named after the Wizard of Oz ☐ 173 *A Rage to Live* ☐ 174 *The Four Feathers* ☐ 175 A. E. W. Mason ☐ 176 Russell Simpson ☐ 177 Twentieth Century Fox ☐ 178 *Son of Kong* ☐ 179 Sydney Greenstreet ☐ 180 Peter Lorre ☐ 181 *Prince Valiant* ☐ 182 Elissa Landi ☐ 183 William Friese-Greene ☐ 184 Laurence Olivier ☐ 185 A New York cop, original hero of the exploits portrayed in *The French Connection* ☐ 186 A famous Hollywood art director ☐ 187 A Hollywood dress designer ☐ 188 They both played Dillinger in films of that name ☐ 189 Walter Lang ☐ 190 John Farrow ☐ 191 *Pride and Prejudice* ☐ 192 They were all Mack Sennett Bathing Beauties ☐ 193 Eleanor Powell ☐ 194 *The Great Man Votes* ☐ 195 Carol Reed ☐ 196 Edna May Oliver ☐ 197 Lon Chaney Jnr ☐ 198 Glenn Strange ☐ 199 John Carradine ☐ 200 Jessie Ralph ☐ 201 Herbert Mundin ☐ 202 Jessie Ralph ☐ 203 Marie Dressler ☐ 204 Wheeler and Woolsey ☐ 205 May Robson ☐ 206 It was written as a Perry Mason adventure by Erle Stanley Gardner ☐ 207 *Greed* ☐ 208 Jean Hersholt ☐ Gibson Gowland ☐ 209 *Happy Birthday Wanda June* ☐ 210 Rita Hayworth ☐ 211 San Francisco ☐ 212 *The African Queen* ☐ 213 *My Favorite Blonde* ☐ 214 *Sullivan's Travels* ☐ 215 Erik Rhodes ☐ *The Gay Divorcee* ☐ 216 *Lost Horizon* ☐ 217 *The Miracle of Morgan's Creek* ☐ 218 Charlton Heston ☐ 219 Miles Mander ☐ 220 René Clair ☐ 221 Zoltan Korda ☐ 222 Roland Young ☐ 223 Donald Ogden Stewart ☐ 224 They have all played the lead in *Charley's Aunt* or variations on it ☐ 225 *Grand Hotel* ☐ 226 *Hollywood Party* ☐ 227 *Grand Hotel* ☐ Greta Garbo ☐ 228 *Charade* ☐ 229 *The Iron Curtain* ☐ 230 Vittorio de Sica ☐ 231 James Finlayson ☐ 232 Edgar Kennedy ☐ 233 Charles Hall ☐ 234 Jean Hersholt ☐ 235 Josef Von Sternberg ☐ 236 Rosalind Russell ☐ Douglas Fairbanks Jnr ☐ Maureen O'Sullivan ☐ 237 The role in *Folies Bergere* which was rewritten for *That Night in Rio* and *On the Riviera* ☐ 238 Rex Ingram ☐ 239 Richard Basehart ☐ 240 *The Garden of Allah* ☐ 241 Mr Magoo in *Fuddy Duddy Buddy* ☐ 242 *Foreign Correspondent* ☐ 243 William Demarest ☐ 244 Fay Holden ☐ 245 Lionel Barrymore ☐ 246 Jill Haworth ☐ 247 Walter Huston ☐ 248 Victor McLaglen ☐ Edmund Lowe ☐ 249 Noel Coward ☐ 250 Pat O'Brien ☐ 251 Three ☐ 252 Virginia Bruce ☐ Joan Fontaine ☐ Susannah York ☐ 253 They were all members of the original *Our Gang* ☐ 254 Ann Rutherford ☐ 255 Warner's great art director of the thirties ☐ 256 Michael Sarrazin ☐ 257 *Gunsmoke*: he was James Arness ☐ 258 Dan Daily ☐ 259 Helen Hayes ☐ Mildred Natwick ☐ 260 Paulette Goddard ☐ 261 Lewis Stone ☐ 262 Ramon Novarro ☐ Douglas Fairbanks Jnr ☐ James Mason ☐ 263 *Duck Soup* ☐ 264 *The Bank Dick* ☐ 265 No: he was not in *The Big Store* ☐ 266 *Cheyenne Autumn* ☐ 267 *Love Me Tonight* ☐ 268 Fred Zinnemann ☐ 269 The Crazy Gang ☐ 270 *OK For Sound* ☐ *Alf's Button Afloat* ☐ *Gasbags* ☐ *The Frozen Limits* ☐ *Life Is a Circus* ☐ 271 Kenneth More ☐ *Reach for the Sky* ☐ 272 *The Lost World* ☐ 273 She played their landlady ☐ 274 Joe E. Brown ☐ 275 Leon Errol ☐ *Mexican Spitfire* ☐ 276 Olive Oyl ☐ 277 William Castle ☐ 278 *The Best Years of Our Lives* ☐ 279 Turhan Bey ☐ 280 Paramount's famous art director of the thirties ☐